Quantitative Magnetic Resonance Imaging

Quantitative Magnetic Resonance Imaging

Lead Editors

Nicole Seiberlich

Department of Radiology, University of Michigan, Ann Arbor, MI, United States

Vikas Gulani

Department of Radiology, University of Michigan, Ann Arbor, MI, United States

Section Editors

Fernando Calamante

Sydney Imaging Core Research Facility and School of Biomedical Engineering, The University of Sydney, Sydney, Australia

Adrienne Campbell-Washburn

MRI Technology Program, Cardiovascular Branch, Division of Intramural Research, National Heart, Lung, and Blood Institute, National Institutes of Health, Bethesda, MD, United States

Mariya Doneva

Philips Research, Hamburg, Germany

Houchun Harry Hu

Department of Radiology, Nationwide Children's Hospital, Columbus, Ohio, United States

Steven Sourbron

Department of Imaging, Infection, Immunity and Cardiovascular Disease, University of Sheffield, Sheffield, United Kingdom

Academic Press is an imprint of Elsevier
125 London Wall, London EC2Y 5AS, United Kingdom
525 B Street, Suite 1650, San Diego, CA 92101, United States
50 Hampshire Street, 5th Floor, Cambridge, MA 02139, United States
The Boulevard, Langford Lane, Kidlington, Oxford OX5 1GB, United Kingdom

Notices

Knowledge and best practice in this field are constantly changing. As new research and experience broaden our understanding, changes in research methods, professional practices, or medical treatment may become necessary.

Practitioners and researchers must always rely on their own experience and knowledge in evaluating and using any information, methods, compounds, or experiments described herein. In using such information or methods they should be mindful of their own safety and the safety of others, including parties for whom they have a professional responsibility.

To the fullest extent of the law, neither the Publisher nor the authors, contributors, or editors, assume any liability for any injury and/or damage to persons or property as a matter of products liability, negligence or otherwise, or from any use or operation of any methods, products, instructions, or ideas contained in the material herein.

Library of Congress Cataloging-in-Publication Data
A catalog record for this book is available from the Library of Congress

British Library Cataloguing-in-Publication Data
A catalogue record for this book is available from the British Library

ISBN: **978-0-12-817057-1**
ISSN: **2666-9099**

For information on all Academic Press publications visit our website at https://www.elsevier.com/books-and-journals

Publisher: Mara Conner
Acquisitions Editor: Tim Pitts
Editorial Project Manager: Emily Thomson
Production Project Manager: Poulouse Joseph
Cover Designer: Matthew Limbert

Typeset by SPi Global, India

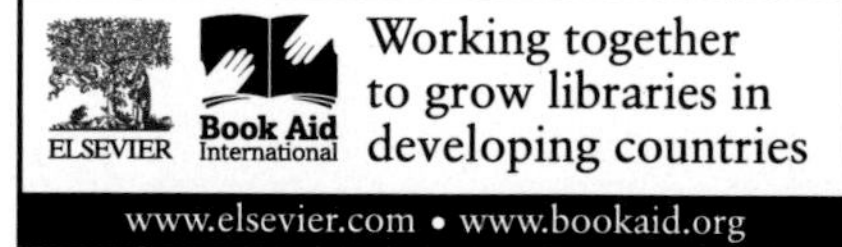

Cover Credit: Designed by Danielle Dobbs and Sarah Abate, University of Michigan

To our families, and our teachers and colleagues of past and present who have instilled in us the love of science.

Advances in Magnetic Resonance Technology and Applications Series

Series Editors

Titles published:

Volume 1 – Quantitative Magnetic Resonance Imaging – Edited by Nicole Seiberlich and Vikas Gulani

Visit the Series webpage at https://www.elsevier.com/catalog/all/all/all/advances-in-magnetic-resonance-technology-and-applications

Contents

Contributors

Ganesh Adluru
Utah Center for Advanced Imaging Research (UCAIR), Department of Radiology and Imaging Sciences; Department of Biomedical Engineering, University of Utah, Salt Lake City, Utah, United States

Shalini Amukotuwa
Department of Imaging, Faculty of Medicine, Nursing and Health Sciences, Monash University, Melbourne, VIC, Australia

Tess Armstrong
Department of Radiological Sciences, David Geffen School of Medicine, University of California Los Angeles, Los Angeles, CA, United States

Andrew W. Barritt
Hurstwood Park Neurosciences Centre, Haywards Heath, West Sussex; Clinical Imaging Sciences Centre, Brighton and Sussex Medical School, Brighton, United Kingdom

Laura C. Bell
Neuroimaging Innovation Center, Barrow Neurological Institute, Phoenix, AZ, United States

Noam Ben-Eliezer
Department of Biomedical Engineering; Sagol School of Neuroscience, Tel Aviv University, Tel Aviv, Israel; Center for Advanced Imaging Innovation and Research (CAI2R), New York University Langone Medical Center, New York, NY, United States

Atle Bjørnerud
Department of Diagnostic Physics; Computational Radiology & Artificial Intelligence (CRAI), Division of Radiology and Nuclear Medicine, Oslo University Hospital, Oslo, Norway

Matthew Blackledge
Division of Radiotherapy and Imaging, Institute of Cancer Research, Sutton, United Kingdom

René M. Botnar
King's College London, School of Biomedical Engineering and Imaging Sciences, London, United Kingdom; Pontificia Universidad Católica de Chile, Escuela de Ingeniería, Santiago, Chile

Mathieu Boudreau
Montreal Heart Institute, Université de Montréal; NeuroPoly Lab, Institute of Biomedical Engineering, Polytechnique Montréal, Montréal, Canada

Marco Bozzali
Department of Neuroscience, Brighton and Sussex Medical School, University of Sussex, Brighton; Hurstwood Park Neurosciences Centre, Haywards Heath, West Sussex, United Kingdom; Neuroimaging Laboratory, Santa Lucia Foundation IRCCS, Rome, Italy

Fernando Calamante
Florey Department of Neuroscience and Mental Health, University of Melbourne, Melbourne, VIC; The University of Sydney, Sydney Imaging; The University of Sydney, School of Biomedical Engineering, Sydney, NSW, Australia

Yong Chen
Department of Radiology, Case Western Reserve University, Cleveland, OH, United States

Daan Christiaens
Centre for the Developing Brain; Department of Biomedical Engineering, School of Biomedical Engineering & Imaging Sciences, King's College London, London, United Kingdom; Department of Electrical Engineering, ESAT/PSI, KU Leuven, Leuven, Belgium

Alan Connelly
Florey Institute of Neuroscience and Mental Health; Florey Department of Neuroscience and Mental Health; Department of Medicine, Austin Health and Northern Health, University of Melbourne, Melbourne, VIC, Australia

Stig P. Cramer
Functional Imaging Unit, Department of Clinical Physiology, Nuclear Medicine and PET, Rigshospitalet, Copenhagen, Denmark

Gastão Cruz
King's College London, School of Biomedical Engineering and Imaging Sciences, London, United Kingdom

Erica Dall'Armellina
Leeds Institute of Cardiovascular and Metabolic Medicine, Department of Biomedical Imaging Sciences, University of Leeds, Leeds, United Kingdom

Arka Das
Leeds Institute of Cardiovascular and Metabolic Medicine, Department of Biomedical Imaging Sciences, University of Leeds, Leeds, United Kingdom

Sean Deoni
Maternal, Newborn, and Child Health Discovery & Tools, Bill & Melinda Gates Foundation, Seattle, WA; Advanced Baby Imaging Lab, Rhode Island Hospital; Department of Pediatrics, Warren Alpert Medical School at Brown University, Providence, RI, United States

Jonathan R. Dillman
Department of Radiology, Cincinnati Children's Hospital Medical Center; Department of Radiology, University of Cincinnati College of Medicine, Cincinnati, OH, United States

Ricardo Donners
Department of Imaging, University Hospital of Basel, Basel, Switzerland

Richard D. Dortch
Division of Neuroimaging Research; Barrow Neuroimaging Innovation Center, Barrow Neurological Institute, Phoenix, AZ, United States

Philipp Ehses
German Center for Neurodegenerative Diseases (DZNE), Bonn, Germany

Noam Ben-Eliezer
Department of Biomedical Engineering; Sagol School of Neuroscience, Tel Aviv University, Tel Aviv, Israel; Center for Advanced Imaging Innovation and Research (CAI2R), New York University Langone Medical Center, New York, NY, United States

Kyrre Eeg Emblem
Department of Diagnostic Physics, Division of Radiology and Nuclear Medicine, Oslo University Hospital, Oslo, Norway

Thomas R. Eykyn
School of Biomedical Engineering and Imaging Sciences, King's College London, St Thomas' Hospital, London, United Kingdom

Susan Francis
Sir Peter Mansfield Imaging Centre, University of Nottingham, Nottingham, United Kingdom

Endre Grøvik
Department of Diagnostic Physics, Division of Radiology and Nuclear Medicine, Oslo University Hospital, Oslo, Norway

Rahel Heule
Max Planck Institute for Biological Cybernetics, Tübingen, Germany

Claudia M. Hillenbrand
Research Imaging NSW, University of New South Wales, Sydney, NSW, Australia

Neil Peter Jerome
Department of Circulation and Medical Imaging, Norwegian University of Science and Technology, Trondheim, Norway

Florian Joly
Laboratory of Imaging Biomarkers, INSERM U1149, Centre for Research on Inflammation, Paris, France

Hermien E. Kan
C.J. Gorter Center for High Field MRI, Department of Radiology, Leiden University Medical Center, Leiden, The Netherlands

Dimitrios C. Karampinos
Department of Diagnostic and Interventional Radiology, School of Medicine, Technical University of Munich, Munich, Germany

Ulrich Katscher
Philips Research Hamburg, Hamburg, Germany

Kathryn E. Keenan
Physical Measurement Laboratory, National Institute of Standards and Technology, Boulder, Colorado

Dow-Mu Koh
Department of Radiology, Royal Marsden Hospital, Sutton, United Kingdom

Sebastian Kozerke
Department of Information Technology and Electrical Engineering, ETH Zürich, Zurich, Switzerland

Christopher D. Kroenke
Advanced Imaging Research Center, Oregon Health & Science University, Portland, OR, United States

Janet L. Kwiatkowski
Division of Hematology, The Children's Hospital of Philadelphia; Department of Pediatrics, Perelman School of Medicine of the University of Pennsylvania, Philadelphia, PA, United States

Henrik B.W. Larsson
Functional Imaging Unit, Department of Clinical Physiology, Nuclear Medicine and PET, Rigshospitalet; Department of Clinical Medicine, Faculty of Health and Medical Science, Copenhagen University, Copenhagen, Denmark

Cornelia Laule
Department of Radiology; Department of Physics & Astronomy; Department of Pathology & Laboratory Medicine; International Collaboration on Repair Discoveries, University of British Columbia, Vancouver, BC, Canada

Xiaojuan Li
Department of Biomedical Engineering, Lerner Research Institute; Department of Diagnostic Radiology, Imaging Institute, Cleveland; Program of Advanced Musculoskeletal, Imaging (PAMI), Cleveland Clinic, Cleveland, OH, United States

Ulrich Lindberg
Functional Imaging Unit, Department of Clinical Physiology, Nuclear Medicine and PET, Rigshospitalet, Copenhagen, Denmark

Ralf B. Loeffler
Research Imaging NSW, University of New South Wales, Sydney, NSW, Australia

Jacob A. Macdonald
Department of Radiology, University of Michigan, Ann Arbor, MI, United States

Jürgen Machann
Institute for Diabetes Research and Metabolic Diseases, Helmholtz Center Munich at the University of Tübingen; German Center for Diabetes Research; Section on Experimental Radiology, Department of Diagnostic and Interventional Radiology, University Hospital Tübingen, Tübingen, Germany

Alex L. MacKay
Department of Radiology; Department of Physics & Astronomy, University of British Columbia, Vancouver, BC, Canada

Bruno Madore
Brigham and Women's Hospital, Harvard Medical School, Advanced Lab for MRI and Acoustics (ALMA), Boston, MA, United States

Shaihan J. Malik
School of Imaging Sciences and Biomedical Engineering, King's College London, London, United Kingdom

Yogesh K. Mariappan
Philips Healthcare, Bangalore, India

Jennifer A. McNab
Department of Radiology, Stanford University, Stanford, CA, United States

Christina Messiou
Department of Radiology, Royal Marsden Hospital, Sutton, United Kingdom

Prashant P. Nair
Manipal Academy of Higher Education, Manipal; Philips Healthcare, Bangalore, India

Muhummad Sohaib Nazir
Biomedical Engineering and Imaging Sciences, Kings College London, London, United Kingdom

Matthew Orton
Division of Radiotherapy and Imaging, Institute of Cancer Research, Sutton, United Kingdom

Hansel J. Otero
Department of Radiology, The Children's Hospital of Philadelphia; Department of Pediatrics, Perelman School of Medicine of the University of Pennsylvania, Philadelphia, PA, United States

Shivani Pahwa
Department of Radiology, Case Western Reserve University; Department of Radiology, University Hospitals Cleveland Medical Center, Cleveland, OH, United States

Sven Plein
Leeds Institute of Cardiovascular and Metabolic Medicine, University of Leeds, Leeds, United Kingdom

Claudia Prieto
King's College London, School of Biomedical Engineering and Imaging Sciences, London, United Kingdom; Pontificia Universidad Católica de Chile, Escuela de Ingeniería, Santiago, Chile

Mihaela Rata
Department of Radiology, Royal Marsden Hospital, Sutton, United Kingdom

Maxime Ronot
Department of Radiology, APHP, University Hospitals Paris Nord Val de Seine, Beaujon, Clichy; University of Paris; Laboratory of Imaging Biomarkers, INSERM U1149, Centre for Research on Inflammation, Paris, France

Sébastien Roujol
King's College London, School of Biomedical Engineering and Imaging Sciences, London, United Kingdom

Suraj D. Serai
Department of Radiology, The Children's Hospital of Philadelphia; Department of Pediatrics, Perelman School of Medicine of the University of Pennsylvania, Philadelphia, PA, United States

Laura Serra
Neuroimaging Laboratory, Santa Lucia Foundation IRCCS, Rome, Italy

Samir D. Sharma
Canon Medical Research USA, Inc., Mayfield, Village, OH, United States

Noam Shemesh
Champalimaud Research, Champalimaud Centre for the Unknown, Lisbon, Portugal

Karin Shmueli
Department of Medical Physics and Biomedical Engineering, University College London, London, United Kingdom

Robert Elton Smith
Florey Institute of Neuroscience and Mental Health; Florey Department of Neuroscience and Mental Health, University of Melbourne, Melbourne, VIC, Australia

Nikola Stikov
Montreal Heart Institute, Université de Montréal; NeuroPoly Lab, Institute of Biomedical Engineering, Polytechnique Montréal, Montréal, Canada

Shigeki Sugii
Institute of Bioengineering and Nanotechnology (IBN), A*STAR; Cardiovascular and Metabolic Disorders Program, Duke-NUS Medical School, Singapore, Singapore

Phillip Zhe Sun
Yerkes Imaging Center, Yerkes National Primate Research Center, Emory University; Department of Radiology and Imaging Sciences, Emory University School of Medicine, Atlanta, GA, United States

David L. Thomas
Leonard Wolfson Experimental Neurology Centre, University College London, London, United Kingdom

Ye Tian
Utah Center for Advanced Imaging Research (UCAIR), Department of Radiology and Imaging Sciences; Department of Physics and Astronomy, University of Utah, Salt Lake City, Utah, United States

Jean A. Tkach
Department of Radiology, Cincinnati Children's Hospital Medical Center; Department of Radiology, University of Cincinnati College of Medicine, Cincinnati, OH, United States

J. Donald Tournier
Centre for the Developing Brain; Department of Biomedical Engineering, School of Biomedical Engineering & Imaging Sciences, King's College London, London, United Kingdom

Andrew T. Trout
Department of Radiology, Cincinnati Children's Hospital Medical Center; Department of Radiology, University of Cincinnati College of Medicine, Cincinnati, OH, United States

Bernard E. Van Beers
Department of Radiology, APHP, University Hospitals Paris Nord Val de Seine, Beaujon, Clichy; University of Paris; Laboratory of Imaging Biomarkers, INSERM U1149, Centre for Research on Inflammation, Paris, France

Moriel Vandsburger
Department of Bioengineering, University of California, Berkeley, CA, United States

S. Sendhil Velan
Metabolic Imaging Group (MIG), Singapore Bioimaging Consortium (SBIC) & Singapore Institute for Clinical Sciences (SICS), A*STAR, Singapore, Singapore

Mark B. Vestergaard
Functional Imaging Unit, Department of Clinical Physiology, Nuclear Medicine and PET, Rigshospitalet, Copenhagen, Denmark

Oliver Wieben
Departments of Medical Physics and Radiology, University of Wisconsin-Madison, Madison, WI, United States

Carl S. Winalski
Department of Biomedical Engineering, Lerner Research Institute; Department of Diagnostic Radiology, Imaging Institute; Program of Advanced Musculoskeletal, Imaging (PAMI), Cleveland Clinic, Cleveland, OH, United States

Tobias C. Wood
Department of Neuroimaging, King's College London, London, United Kingdom

Holden H. Wu
Department of Radiological Sciences, David Geffen School of Medicine, University of California Los Angeles, Los Angeles, CA, United States

Grant Yang
Department of Radiology, Stanford University, Stanford, CA, United States

Zhongliang Zu
Institute of Imaging Science; Department of Radiology, Vanderbilt University Medical Center, Nashville, TN, United States

SECTION

Introduction

Quantitative MRI: Rationale and Challenges

Vikas Gulani and Nicole Seiberlich
Department of Radiology, University of Michigan, Ann Arbor, MI, United States

1 The goal of radiological imaging

The goal of radiological imaging is to diagnose, monitor, and treat human disease using non- or minimally invasive technologies. From its beginning in the late 19th century with the discovery of X-rays by Wilhelm Roentgen, the radiology workflow has remained largely unchanged: images are acquired, the radiologist identifies an abnormality, and a diagnosis is made or the patient is treated. This same paradigm persists despite a multitude of technological advances and the advent of numerous new imaging modalities since that time, including Magnetic Resonance Imaging (MRI) and computed tomography (CT), which have famously been called the most important innovations in medicine [1]. Anatomical structures are identified based on their contrast differences or enhancement patterns, and on the basis of these differences, normal and abnormal tissues may be distinguished from one another. Presently, MRI image interpretation is largely qualitative—the quantitative measurements most commonly used in clinical practice are the size/volume of an object or region and the distance between structures of interest [2].

From the outset, many scientists and physicians had a more quantitative future in mind for MRI, due to the fact that MRI can theoretically be used to measure almost any physical, chemical, or physiological property. However, the inherent speed limitations of MRI precluded widespread clinical adoption of quantitative tissue property measurements. Since at least two (and ideally more) images are needed to quantitatively map most tissue properties, and each image can potentially take minutes to acquire, it was rarely practical in the early history of MRI to collect quantitative information in a clinical setting. A second barrier to the early clinical adoption of quantitative MR was a lack of reproducibility, a challenge which still plagues the quantitative MRI community, and which is discussed in detail later in this chapter.

Thus an approach was adopted which sought to maximize the contrast differences between two tissues on a single image, making use of differences in the relaxation times or other properties of the two tissues. These qualitative images include the well-known T_1-weighted or T_2-weighted contrasts, where the images are weighted predominantly by one tissue property in a way that is tailored to the imaging application at hand. While weighted imaging may not always be ideal, qualitative MRI provides such important anatomical information, with a stunning variety of contrasts, that many of the inherent limitations of this approach have been easily dismissed. The result of this history is the widespread acceptance of qualitative imaging today, even when MRI could potentially offer so much more information.

The largely structural and contrast-weighting-based interpretation of qualitative MRI images does enable important anatomical analysis and communication between physicians. In many instances, the anatomical information derived from qualitative MRI images is sufficient for diagnosis. The identification of actionable pathologies such as vessel stenoses, duct strictures, ischemic tissues, and diseases that have a characteristic imaging appearance is sufficient to drive clinical care in the appropriate direction without the need for quantitative tissue measurements. Such anatomical information is most useful to a subset of physicians who are anatomically oriented themselves, such as surgeons and gastroenterologists. However, this qualitative imaging-only approach leaves a large amount of MRI-accessible information on the table.

The contrast-weighted approach starts to partially break down when multiple contrast mechanisms are involved (for example proton density and T_1 or T_2 weighting), or when there are more than two tissue types in the image, where the weighting may separate the appearance of some tissues and not others [3]. Moreover, images weighted by the same contrast mechanism can appear dramatically different. For instance, Fig. 1 shows a common bile duct stone in two different T_2-weighted turbo spin echo (TSE) images. Fig. 1A was generated with a single shot technique with an echo time of 60 ms, and Fig. 1B shows a single partition from a three-dimensional magnetic resonance cholangiopancreatography (3D MRCP) acquisition with an echo time of 673 ms. While both images are "T_2-weighted," they differ vastly in appearance due to the different echo times used. In Fig. 1A, significant soft tissue contrast is present, and thus fine details of the liver parenchyma, bile ducts, vessels, fat, and bowel can be appreciated. In Fig. 1B, all structures that do not have very long T_2 values are invisible, and only structures containing simple fluid are seen. Thus, the only sources of image contrast are filling defects within fluid-filled structures, and their boundaries. Note that in Fig. 1B, there is no way to recover contrast in tissues for which signal has been attenuated, and in Fig. 1A, structures with long but different T_2 values may not be distinguishable. Thus, while contrast-weighted qualitative imaging is powerful, the appearance of different structures can be dramatically different depending on the specific protocol used and the degree of weighting applied.

Moreover, given the myriad contrasts and user-controllable settings, these weighted MR images are difficult to reproduce from scanner to scanner even at the same site, let alone at different locations, with scanners from multiple vendors and software versions. See, for example, Fig. 2, showing two different 3D fat-suppressed T_1-weighted gradient echo images from the same patient who was scanned twice (10 months apart) on two different 3 tesla (3 T) scanners from different vendors (each a major manufacturer of MR equipment). These images were collected with the same nominal slice thickness, using the vendor recommended settings, at the same stages of enhancement. Although standard protocols were used, the liver parenchyma and cyst walls have quite different appearances on these images. Similar differences can be seen in other parts of the body, and in pathology. Fig. 3 shows a right anterior transition zone prostate cancer on T_2-weighted images in a biopsy-naïve man (one of the images is just prior to biopsy), imaged less than 1 month apart on MRI scanners from two major vendors, with near-identical protocols, at the same institution. Note differences in contrast between tumor and adjacent transition zone, and inflammation and adjacent peripheral zone. This lack of reproducibility in image appearance is marked when examining images collected on MRI scanners from different vendors but is also observed when using slightly different protocol setups or post-processing algorithms, each of which may be modified easily at the console (or behind the scenes by the vendor) and not necessarily obvious to the reporting radiologist.

The qualitative nature of image contrasts and variability in MR images leads to ambiguity in image interpretation which is apparent in radiology reports. While not the sole determinant, image variability does contribute to the myriad uncertainties in the interpretation of images that give radiologists the reputation of hedging rather than being definitive. Indeed, the propensity to equivocate even after

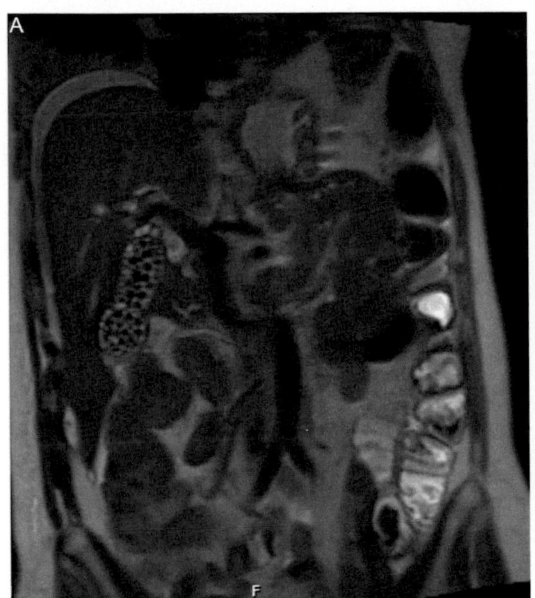

FIG. 1

T_2-weighted images generated via (A) single-shot turbo spin echo (TSE) with TE=60ms and (B) three-dimensional (3D) TSE with TE=673ms. While in this case, the pathology of a common bile duct stone can be seen in both images, the tissue contrast obtained is markedly different, with only fluid versus nonfluid contrast remaining in (B), and significant soft-tissue contrast and fat signal in (A).

expensive imaging remains a common problem in radiology that dates back to the earliest days of medical imaging [4]. However, the inability to be definitive is sometimes due to the fact that the answer is also not unequivocally available in the images, or due to equivocal interpretive criteria. Often the best a radiologist can offer is a subjective interpretation, including the best attempt at an ordered list of everything that could be wrong given the location and qualitative appearance of the abnormality. There may be confounding changes in the same anatomical region, adding to the difficulty in image interpretation.

Besides the myriad of jokes made by clinicians about hedging radiologists, this uncertainty has real consequences for patients. Because images typically cannot be used to definitively diagnose abnormal tissue, the gold standard of diagnostics remains histopathological tissue diagnosis, requiring a biopsy. Diagnosis based on biopsy has a built-in disadvantage—the tissue is collected in a hyperlocalized fashion, and thus provides the pathologist only a very small sample of a much larger organ or lesion and further, a small portion of the sample is reviewed. Further treatment is based on this very limited sample. Moreover, and more importantly to patients, biopsies are invasive and come with a nonnegligible risk of complications. ***If the goal of imaging is diagnosis without invasive interrogation, then every biopsy is an imaging failure.*** Unfortunately, in this respect, imaging fails often in 2020. It is hard to imagine that this current reality will be tolerated 30 or 50 years from now. A movement towards definitive and objective interpretation or quantification of uncertainty is needed.

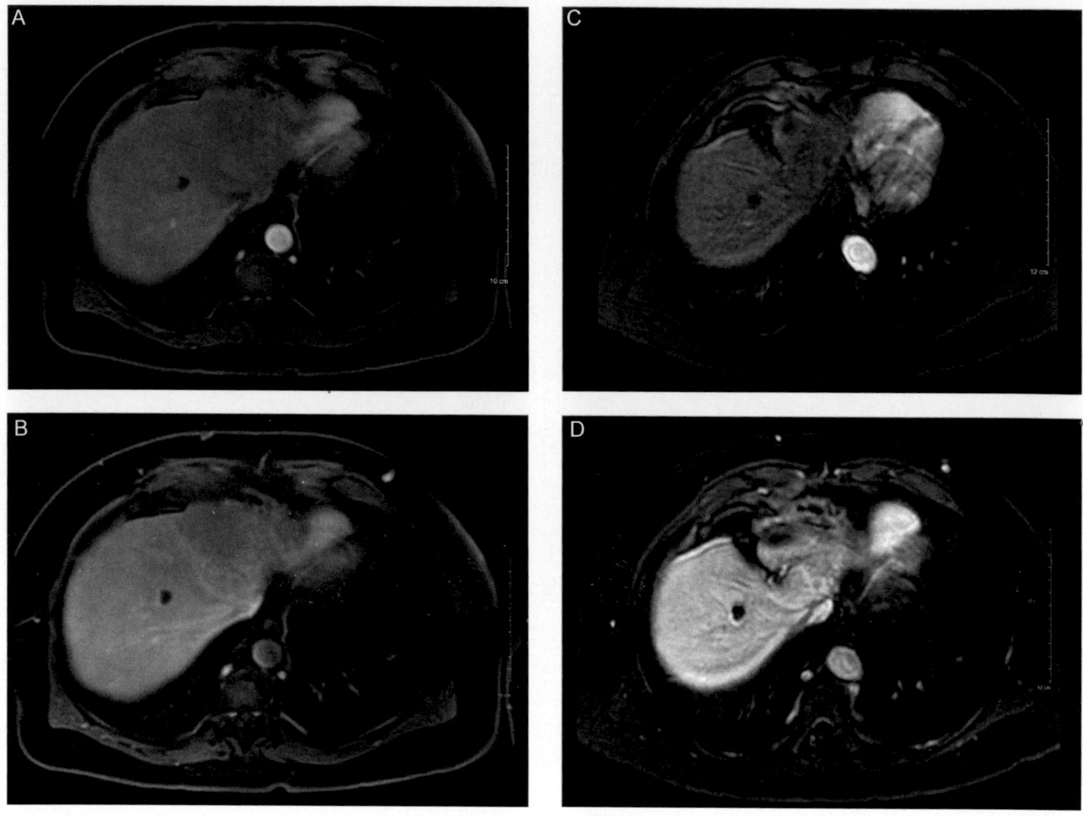

FIG. 2

Lack of standardization in current qualitative imaging, seen in images collected on MRI scanners from different vendors. Fat-suppressed T_1-weighted three-dimensional (3D) gradient echo images through a cyst at the dome of the liver for Vendor A in the (A) arterial and (B) interstitial phases of contrast enhancement; and Vendor B in the (C) arterial and (D) interstitial phases. Note the marked difference in the appearance of the liver parenchyma, cyst walls, and aorta.

The qualitative paradigm in MR is different from many other forms of testing in modern medicine. For example, lab testing, often with panels of cheap fluid- or tissue-based tests, is definitive and reproducible across sites, with well-understood measurement errors and quantitative cutoffs and overlaps in disease states. Even in radiology, many imaging modalities yield definite measurements, which can be used to determine tissue composition. Simple density measurement in CT is critical for characterization of structures as fluid- or fat-filled, and for objective assessment of enhancement. Both ultrasound, which can be used to measure flow and velocity, and nuclear medicine provide quantitative information about targeted questions. Thus, assessment of entities such as cysts in abdominal organs, fat-containing lesions, and flow in carotid stenosis is quantitative, objective, and definitive. When the collection of such quantitative information is possible, objective criteria can be used for diagnosis, and the radiologist is correspondingly less likely to hedge.

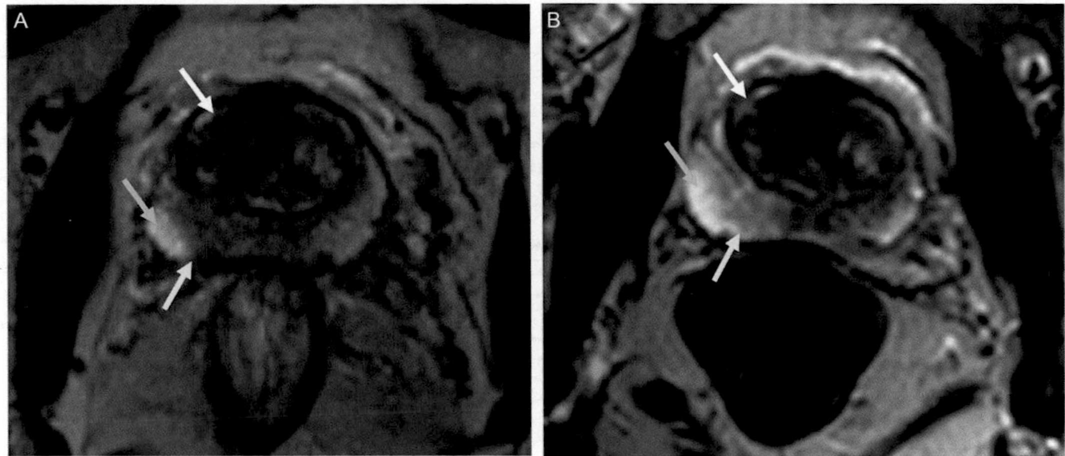

FIG. 3

Lack of standardization in current qualitative imaging, seen in pathology. The same patient with right anterior transition zone biopsy-proven prostate cancer, imaged with a T_2-weighted fast spin echo protocol at 3 T on MRI scanners from Vendor A and Vendor B. Besides the blurring, note the differences in contrast between the tumor *(white arrows)* and adjacent tissue, and also the bright peripheral zone *(orange arrows)* and areas of inflammation *(yellow arrows)*.

The current state of MRI is also in direct contradiction to the direction of change in modern medicine. Patients and physicians are increasingly looking for a move towards precision medicine, with patient-tailored evaluation and treatment planning. Such personalized medicine must involve consolidation of data about the specific patient from multiple streams—including lab pathology, genomics, proteomics, clinical data, etc., and the more objective the information, the better. Imaging is an important data stream, but one that is difficult to incorporate into this thinking due to the qualitative nature of the exams and interpretations. Although radiomics approaches have tried to overcome some of these limitations [5], these analyses usually require harmonization of the images in some form [6], and there is always a possibility of normalizing away important information contained within the images. Moreover, radiomics cannot extract information that is simply not present in the images. For instance, radiomic analyses are not helpful in cases where a lesion is apparent only when using a specific contrast mechanism (i.e., diffusion-weighted imaging), which was not collected.

2 Using quantitative MRI to meet the goals of medical imaging

While MR images are typically assessed in a qualitative way, MRI can be deployed to collect quantitative information about tissue properties which can be used to characterize tissue. The range of properties that have been accessed with MRI includes the nuclear magnetic resonance (NMR) relaxation times T_1 and T_2, $T_2{}^*$, diffusion, perfusion, fat and water fractions, iron fraction, elastic properties of tissue, temperature, chemical composition, and chemical exchange, to name but a few. By using the sensitivity of MRI to these tissue properties, it is possible to generate quantitative maps instead of qualitative anatomical images, where the intensity of each pixel corresponds to a measurement of one specific physical or physiological property. In fact, attempts to measure and map relaxation properties [2–5] and diffusion [6–8] go back to the very early history of MRI, but were not deployed commonly in the clinic with a few important exceptions. Examples include diffusion mapping, with an increasingly quantitative approach in applications such as prostate imaging [7–10]; fat fraction mapping finding application in the follow-up of liver disease [11–18]; and follow-up of iron deposition in multiple organs and disease states [19–24]. Many more established and emerging quantitative MRI techniques have been deployed in research settings, with broad applications such as diffusion tensor imaging and fiber tracking, MR thermometry, etc. However, despite the massive research effort aimed at moving MRI from a primarily qualitative imaging method to a system of pixel-wise quantitative measurements of tissue properties, most of these approaches have not been clinically adopted.

While challenging, the benefits of transitioning to all-quantitative MRI protocols could be immense, enabling complete tissue characterization using this noninvasive modality. In an ideal world, radiologists would measure values of relevant tissue properties to assess the overall health of the organ or system. In cases where there is an abnormality in the tissue, probability maps could be constructed for various diseases, pulling in both imaging and nonimaging information from the medical record to construct the maps. Serial measurements in a single patient could be compared to ascertain if an intervention is working. Quantitative measurements may be helpful not only for identifying anatomical abnormalities but also for identifying loss of function to assist function-driven specialties such as endocrinology or nephrology, which are currently less aided by radiological imaging than anatomy-driven surgical or procedural specialties.

Moreover, if these measurements could be consistent from scanner to scanner, and institution to institution, maps from a variety of patients with different diseases could be pooled for machine learning analyses, which require large and consistent datasets. Radiomic analyses may be improved with quantitative maps as inputs, due to the reduction in confounding factors from weighted imaging. With computing-based data analytics that is also now being enabled, such complex datasets could be coupled with input from other modalities such as positron emission tomography (PET) or CT, and quantitative input from nonimaging diagnostics in genetics, pathology, etc., to provide a true movement towards precision medicine.

There is reason to believe that comprehensive quantitative measurements could enable MRI to improve on the goal of noninvasive diagnosis. Unhealthy tissues should have characteristics that can be used to distinguish them from healthy tissues. If these characteristics manifest in some physical or physiological property to which the MRI signal can be sensitized, they should be measurable via MRI, and identifiable on a quantitative map of said property. Ideally, future MRI scans would measure such information to provide definitive, quantitative, and reproducible tissue property or even disease maps, with a measurable and reliable probability of correctly identifying the health state of a tissue. In such a world, there would be less of a need for histopathological diagnosis, as noninvasive imaging would more often yield accurate and actionable information about the individual patient.

3 Why tackle quantitative MRI now?

The past two decades in MRI have brought significant hardware and computing advancements to the field. The acceleration of data collection using parallel imaging [25] and sparsity-based or constrained reconstruction approaches [26] have lifted many traditional barriers imposed by imaging speed.

Moreover, advances in computing power and storage capacity have enabled the interrogation and analysis of data from complex physiological systems in a way that was previously unimaginable. The computing power provided by tools such as modern graphics processing units (GPUs) and cloud and edge computing dwarf the capabilities of prior hardware generations. Plug-and-play toolboxes facilitated by advances in computing technology, such as those for image reconstruction, iterative numerical analysis, and machine learning, have now made many previously impractical complex analyses feasible. These important enabling technologies make it possible to merge alternative MR acquisition and reconstruction methods for rapid imaging and mapping. By combining new ways of thinking about MRI signals, the imaging process, optimization tools, and high-end computing, we have entered an era where technology will soon make quantitative MRI a practically achievable reality in all settings. Even now it is possible to obtain rapid quantitative measurements of numerous physiologically relevant tissue properties—diffusion, perfusion, fat content, iron content, tissue elasticity, T_1, T_2, temperature, etc.—and each property has found scientific and clinical utility in various applications.

It is also becoming clear that no one tissue property or measurement technique is likely to be sufficient alone to answer most complex research/clinical questions, and many of these tissue properties will need to be used together to reach our goals of comprehensive tissue assessments that provide actionable information. This situation is parallel to standard clinical practice, where MRI protocols are comprised of scans weighted by multiple tissue properties which are all used together by the radiologist for the overall impression. For example, a standard liver exam may make use of T_1-weighted and T_2-weighted images, fat suppression, and Dixon imaging for the assessment of fat, diffusion-weighted imaging to assess cellularity, elastography images to assess stiffness, and dynamic post-contrast imaging to assess vascularity. While in the conventional examination, much of this information is collected indirectly in a qualitative fashion, it is currently possible to instead measure the relevant tissue properties in an all quantitative counterpart exam, comprised of T_1, T_2, fat fraction, diffusion, elastography, and perfusion mapping. Given that these exams are now available, even if not currently deployed clinically, it is possible to envision a completely quantitative approach to MRI in the not-so-distant future.

4 Open needs in quantitative MRI

Before quantitative MRI can routinely take the place of conventional qualitative imaging, many open needs must be addressed. As discussed by Hockings et al. in the next chapter, entitled of "MRI Biomarkers," six stages of technology assessment have been formally defined [27–31] and summarized in Table 1. It is evident from examining these stages that much of MRI research, including quantitative MRI, focuses on Stage 1. However, for new MR techniques in general, and quantitative MR techniques in particular, to make a jump to widespread clinical use, there is a need to consider the remaining stages of diagnostic tool assessment. If the eventual goal of developing a quantitative technology is to generate an imaging biomarker, then we must pay attention to the stages of biomarker development. These issues are clearly spelled out in the next chapter of this book, an important read for researchers seeking to move quantitative MRI beyond the current state, which generally hovers between Stages 1 and 2. This section describes what is required of our field to make this jump.

Table 1 Stages of technology assessment.

Stage	Title	Goals
1	Technical efficacy	Assess factors such as harm, technique function, or image aesthetics
2	Diagnostic accuracy or clinical efficacy	Evaluate function of a technique in a diagnostic setting
3	Diagnostic thinking	Comparison to existing standards or changes in diagnostic thinking of the clinicians using the technique
4	Therapeutic efficacy	Assess whether the technique is able to predict some response to treatment
5	Clinical utility	Assess whether the technique results in improvements in patient care, in outcomes such as improved morbidity or mortality
6	Cost effectiveness	Evaluate cost for each quality-adjusted life year added by the technology, and how does this compare to gold standards

4.1 Technical needs

In order to develop robust quantitative MRI technologies for clinical deployment, a number of factors must be considered. First and foremost, although this may seem obvious when considering the subject of ***quantitative*** MRI, publishing maps with clear measurement values/colorbars along with tables reporting key values is necessary so that different groups may view and compare data. Explicit comparison to published literature is needed, and differences between the measured values should be noted and explained if possible. A reluctance to share measured values is unfortunately common in the community, most likely driven by a concern that the values will change as the measurement technique is refined, or perhaps by fear of known inaccuracy or imprecision. This reticence does the field no service. If quantitative measurements are not sufficiently trustworthy to publish for direct comparison, why bother with the measurements at all? This is a critical need in the field.

The demonstration of reproducibility and repeatability of measurements [32–38] is also needed to overcome some of the problems that are seen in both qualitative and quantitative imaging; these issues are even more important in the latter since the core goal is objective comparison between states or patient groups. Scanning the same subject at different institutions over time is not always feasible, and biological variability can overshadow the evaluation of technical variability, and thus these data must be collected in other ways. Testing the accuracy, reproducibility, and repeatability of quantitative MRI techniques using widely accepted phantoms is extremely helpful [32,37,38]. The involvement of agencies such as the National Institute of Standards and Technology (NIST) in the generation of these phantoms [39–41] is expected to add rigor to the field. In cases where motion is a concern, testing in digital phantoms may be a consideration [42], or even physically moving a phantom within the MRI scanner may be the best solution. Quantitative measurements published without explicit validation in (at least) phantoms are harmful to the field; not only do they provide little ability to compare measurements, but they unfortunately make future, better-performed studies more difficult to publish as there is a tendency to believe that the work has already been done.

However, while phantom testing is essential to ensure rigor, it is not enough—there must also be a demonstration of the quantitative technique in humans to assess both accuracy/reproducibility and practicality [33–36,43]. Human tissue has properties that are challenging to mimic in a phantom; these include heterogeneity of tissue composition, flow/perfusion, and of course motion, to name a few.

Moreover, even if a measurement scheme results in perfectly reproducible measurements, there is normal physiological variation, which, in addition to measurement error, helps define the measurement effect size that can be studied with a technology. Thus, measurements in healthy subjects are immensely valuable not only to ensure that the measured values are consistent with those measured in phantoms (or the inconsistencies are understood) but also to better understand the variation that can be expected due to physiological differences.

Reproducibility should ideally include standardization across vendors [32,35,36,43], to ensure that a measurement on any MRI scanner can be understood in the context of a measurement on any other MRI scanner. For example, it is widely recognized that relaxation time measurements in the heart vary from scanner to scanner and institution to institution; indeed, the generation of normative data sets on individual MRI scanners is a suggested practice [44–46]. The practical consequence of the variation in these measurements is that each institution is obliged to perform normative and repeatability/reproducibly studies, and also possible initial pathology studies, before a technology can be deployed to its full capacity clinically. This lack of robustness would leave a technology only applicable in research-oriented tertiary care settings and is a major barrier to widespread use. Moreover, if each institution has measurements that can only be understood in the context of other measurements at the same institution, it becomes impossible to pool data to form larger datasets. Without these large and consistent datasets, analyses for small effect sizes or trends become challenging, and the use of machine learning greatly hindered. In such situations, equipment vendor interests may be orthogonal to societal or scientific interests; vendors seek to distinguish their products from those of competitors, and standardization may be at odds with gaining a marketing advantage. Harmonization of quantitative measurements will certainly necessitate industry cooperation in a manner that has not been required over the past several decades of MRI. Thus, standardization across vendors may need to be enforced through the involvement of government agencies such as NIST and the Centers for Medicare and Medicaid Services (CMS) via mechanisms such as Clinical Laboratory Improvement Amendments (CLIA), working with dedicated quantitative imaging groups promoting harmonization, such as Quantitative Imaging Biomarkers Alliance (QIBA).

4.2 Clinical needs

Even when an MRI technology has been validated, unexpected and simple barriers can arise when scanning patients. For example, for use in clinical practice, quantitative MRI techniques must be made rapid and robust enough for push-button use with immediate image availability. Patients can not be asked to lie still for hours for idealized data collection, nor can the information generation wait for specialized and slow off-scanner reconstructions. Thus, testing quantitative MRI techniques in the clinical setting may offer important insights into the practicality of the technology.

Another major challenge is that while significant differences in measured values may be shown between groups or cohorts of patients, or a disease-free and diseased regions, there need to be cut-off values that can be applied in individuals for the information to be actionable clinically [47–51]. While these cut-off values can sometimes be inferred by using nonoverlapping measurements between two groups, these can become less useful in real practice if the overlap between two groups of patients is great or if there are difficulties with standardization of cutoffs [10,51]. Thus, attention to generating important and actionable cutoffs for clinical practice is an important consideration. The inability to identify practical cutoffs could indicate that the measurement of a single tissue property alone is insufficient to separate healthy tissue from pathology. In such cases, a combination of MR-based measurements, or such measurements in conjunction with other streams of data beyond MR, may be required. These streams could be other imaging technologies such as CT or PET, or data from non-imaging sources such as laboratory testing, circulating biomarkers, genomics, or even natural language processing of the clinical record.

In addition to the challenges outlined above, a basic need is to tie MR measurements to pathological changes. In order to be clinically useful, a measured fat fraction or stiffness in the liver, for example, must be predictive of pathologic changes such as liver disease due to non-alcoholic steatohepatosis (NASH) [15]. These studies are painfully complex but are critical if technology is to progress along the pathway to imaging biomarker development. Moreover, as discussed above, there may be limitations when attempting to use a property to assess disease.

Finally, radiology orthodoxy has long maintained that, "a radiologist with a ruler is a radiologist in trouble" [2,52]. In other words, a focus on quantitative measurements may distract the radiologist from making the qualitative and clinically important judgments that are possible from the images. Thus, in order to avoid moving backward while working towards comprehensive quantitative protocols, we must acknowledge that we cannot "give up" the existing power of qualitative exams. Especially in the initial stages of technology development, when quantitative maps may have weaknesses such as lower resolution than weighted images, the latter may be needed (perhaps temporarily) for important parts of interpretation. As an example, qualitative images may be preferable for lesion detection, but quantitative measurements are needed for lesion characterization [53–55]. A recognition of these limitations and appropriate and cautious combination of qualitative and quantitative imaging is essential to avoid losing the current strengths of imaging.

4.3 The translational gap

A significant amount of time and energy has been invested in developing new quantitative MRI techniques. Unfortunately, much of this research is limited because it is inherently wedded to the perspective of the MR developer, who often focuses on improving imaging speed, resolution, or signal-to-noise ratio (SNR), as these are features of an image or map which can readily be measured and optimized (and there are well-recognized tradeoffs in the improvement of these factors).

While these aspects of imaging are important, this focus leaves out critical stakeholders in the technology—namely, the physicians who will use the technology, and the patients whose wellness will be assessed with the technology. To these latter groups, physiological questions such as disease characterization and aggression, and biochemical response to therapy are the key issues. Resolution, speed, and SNR are either irrelevant or only tangentially relevant in that they may affect the ability to visualize the structures of interest, or may pertain to comfort. Further society level questions such as cost effectiveness of a technology are also generally excluded from the discussion.

Much of this practical translational work is not as exciting in proposals as a new sequence or technique for measuring a quantity of interest. The latter appears innovative, while demonstrating reproducibility and reproducibility or cross-vendor standardization, or further steps such as the painstaking demonstration of ties of quantitative markers to pathology, appear comparatively boring and mundane, and on-scanner implementation of previously specialized off-scanner code even more so. Proposals that focus on the important Stage 3 (and beyond) work are often rejected, if they are even written at all, due to "lack of innovation." The comparative dearth of support for translation has been well documented, and the difficulty of bridging basic research to clinical utilization has been described as the "Valley of Death" [56,57]. For quantitative MRI technology to find wider use, we as a community must shift our expectations definitions of innovation and creativity, and mindfully enable efforts for translational work.

A subtle contribution to the translational gap may also come from the aforementioned misalignment of interest between industry vendors and the scientific/medical community regarding standardization. Since most imaging is carried out on commercial hardware, vendors are the ultimate route to clinical adoption of quantitative imaging, and could well become final barriers to adoption. When appropriately harmonized, quantitative mapping may lead to all maps "looking" the same, removing any real or perceived advantage of working with one vendor over another. This barrier will remain until vendors focus not on distinguishing their products based on unique image appearance (Fig. 2), but instead distinguishing themselves by the precision, reproducibility, and clinical utility of their measurements. The demand for this shift will need to come from the clinical and scientific communities.

5 Organization of the book

This book is meant to serve as a link between basic and clinical researchers in MRI in order to facilitate our goal of moving the translation of quantitative MRI forward by opening a dialogue between these groups. We aim to provide an introduction to the myriad aspects that are relevant to the field of quantitative MRI, including:

- The physiological meaning of tissue properties,
- Approaches for sensitizing MRI signals to measure these properties,
- Specialized image reconstruction techniques for improved imaging and mapping,
- The extraction of relevant tissue properties from MRI data,
- Scientific and/or clinical applications for tissue property measurements.

The book starts with an introduction to the idea of quantitative imaging biomarkers ("MRI Biomarkers" chapter), describing what is required for a measurement to be used as a biomarker in research and clinical work, important steps that must be taken to meet these requirements, and a real-life example of the process of a measurement becoming a biomarker. This chapter is meant to set the stage for the book as a whole, providing both context for the desire to map tissue properties quantitatively, as well as a warning about the complexities and potential challenges to converting single-site observations to true universally accepted quantitative measurements.

Following this introduction are five sections, each addressing a broad area of quantitative imaging:

- Relaxometry (Section Editor, Dr. Mariya Doneva)
- Perfusion and Permeability (Section Editor, Dr. Steven Sourbron)
- Diffusion (Section Editor, Dr. Fernando Calamante)
- Fat and Iron Mapping (Section Editor, Dr. Houchun Harry Hu)
- Quantification of Other MRI-Accessible Tissue Properties (Section Editor, Dr. Adrienne Campbell-Washburn)

This last section covers important fields such as electromagnetic property mapping, exchange mapping, pH and temperature, elastography, and flow, but is by no means comprehensive with respect to all the property measurements that could be made via MR. The chapters in each section are meant as an overview of the subject, to provide the reader as a starting point for digging more deeply into the literature. The sections are organized such that the physiological aspects of the tissue properties discussed in the section are introduced first. Following this chapter, basic measurement approaches, including the pulse sequences and post-processing required to encode and extract quantitative tissue property information from the data, are described. Current limitations to these approaches and potential solutions are also included. Following these technical details are chapters describing how this quantitative information is currently used in clinical and research settings. Depending on the tissue property, these application chapters are divided to cover different organ systems with different physiological features and thus different data collection and mapping requirements. The exception to this organizational structure is the last section, Quantification of Other MRI-Accessible Tissue Properties, where the same information is provided in a condensed version within each chapter in the section.

The astute reader will note that many of the technologies presented in this book do not yet meet the requirements for clinical adoption discussed above. For instance, while we endeavored to provide quantitative maps with colorbars and clear units in each section, this was not always possible, either because these measurements were not available or because researchers may have found it politically inexpedient to include them in publications. Moreover, some of the maps that are presented do not show consistent values; in some cases, measurement accuracy or biases have not been assessed, and the confounding influences of one tissue property on the measurement of another may not have been taken into account. Testing in phantoms has not necessarily been performed, normative values may not be available, and the physiological spread in healthy subjects unknown. Links between measured values and physiological changes are not always clear. Please do note that this aside is not meant as a criticism of the techniques that are presented, but instead a comment on the current state of research in quantitative MRI. It is our hope that by explicitly pointing out the present limitations, future researchers will better understand the need to work together to develop robust, accurate, reproducible, cost-effective, and clinically useful measurement technologies.

As with any broad topic such as this, it is impossible to be definitive in covering all aspects of the work. We do hope this book will provide a grounding in the general approaches to solving the issues encountered in quantitative MR, and serve as an inspiration to basic, translational, and clinical imaging scientists working in this important field of MRI research.

Acknowledgments

The authors are grateful to Drs. Christopher Hess (UCSF), Doug Noll (University of Michigan), and William Masch (University of Michigan) for their helpful comments and detailed reviews of this chapter, which greatly improved the manuscript.

References

[1] Fuchs VR, Sox Jr HC. Physicians' views of the relative importance of thirty medical innovations. Health Aff (Millwood) 2001;20(5):30–42.

[2] Abramson RG, Su PF, Shyr Y. Quantitative metrics in clinical radiology reporting: a snapshot perspective from a single mixed academic-community practice. Magn Reson Imaging 2012;30(9):1357–66.

[3] Yokoo T, et al. A quantitative approach to sequence and image weighting. J Comput Assist Tomogr 2010;34(3):317–31.
[4] Enfield CD. The scope of the roentgenologist's report. J Am Med Assoc 1923;80:999–1001.
[5] Larue RTHM, et al. Quantitative radiomics studies for tissue characterization: a review of technology and methodological procedures. Br J Radiol 2017;90(1070):20160665. https://doi.org/10.1259/bjr.20160665.
[6] Scalco E, et al. T2w-MRI signal normalization affects radiomics features reproducibility. Med Phys 2020;47(4):1680–91.
[7] Kim CK, et al. Diffusion-weighted imaging of the prostate at 3 T for differentiation of malignant and benign tissue in transition and peripheral zones: preliminary results. J Comput Assist Tomogr 2007;31(3):449–54.
[8] Gibbs P, et al. Correlation of ADC and T2 measurements with cell density in prostate cancer at 3.0 Tesla. Investig Radiol 2009;44(9):572–6.
[9] Hambrock T, et al. Relationship between apparent diffusion coefficients at 3.0-T MR imaging and Gleason grade in peripheral zone prostate cancer. Radiology 2011;259(2):453–61.
[10] Nagel KN, et al. Differentiation of prostatitis and prostate cancer by using diffusion-weighted MR imaging and MR-guided biopsy at 3 T. Radiology 2013;267(1):164–72.
[11] Reeder SB, et al. Quantitative assessment of liver fat with magnetic resonance imaging and spectroscopy. J Magn Reson Imaging 2011;34(4):729–49.
[12] Bashir MR, et al. Quantification of hepatic steatosis with a multistep adaptive fitting MRI approach: prospective validation against MR spectroscopy. Am J Roentgenol 2015;204(2):297–306.
[13] Eskreis-Winkler S, et al. IDEAL-IQ in an oncologic population: meeting the challenge of concomitant liver fat and liver iron. Cancer Imaging 2018;18:51.
[14] Henninger B, et al. 3D multiecho dixon for the evaluation of hepatic iron and fat in a clinical setting. J Magn Reson Imaging 2017;46(3):793–800.
[15] Jayakumar S, et al. Longitudinal correlations between MRE, MRI-PDFF, and liver histology in patients with non-alcoholic steatohepatitis: analysis of data from a phase II trial of selonsertib. J Hepatol 2019; 70(1):133–41.
[16] Loomba R, et al. The ASK1 inhibitor selonsertib in patients with nonalcoholic steatohepatitis: a randomized, phase 2 trial. Hepatology 2018;67(2):549–59.
[17] Loomba R, et al. Ezetimibe for the treatment of nonalcoholic steatohepatitis: assessment by novel magnetic resonance imaging and magnetic resonance elastography in a randomized trial (MOZART trial). Hepatology 2015;61(4):1239–50.
[18] Middleton MS, et al. Cross-sectional and longitudinal agreement of magnetic resonance imaging proton density fat fraction with pathologist grading of hepatic steatosis in adults with nonalcoholic steatohepatitis in a multi-center trial. Hepatology 2015;62:1255a.
[19] Acosta-Cabronero J, et al. In vivo quantitative susceptibility mapping (QSM) in Alzheimer's disease. PLoS One 2013;8(11):e81093.
[20] Zivadinov R, et al. Brain iron at quantitative MRI is associated with disability in multiple sclerosis. Radiology 2018;289(2):487–96.
[21] Wood JC, Noetzli L. Cardiovascular MRI in thalassemia major. Ann N Y Acad Sci 2010;1202:173–9.
[22] Wood JC. Cardiac iron across different transfusion-dependent diseases. Blood Rev 2008;22(Suppl 2):S14–21.
[23] Schwenzer NF, et al. T2* relaxometry in liver, pancreas, and spleen in a healthy cohort of one hundred twenty-nine subjects-correlation with age, gender, and serum ferritin. Investig Radiol 2008;43(12):854–60.
[24] Wood JC. Use of magnetic resonance imaging to monitor iron overload. Hematol Oncol Clin North Am 2014;28(4):747–64, vii.
[25] Deshmane A, et al. Parallel MR imaging. J Magn Reson Imaging 2012;36(1):55–72.
[26] Yang AC, et al. Sparse reconstruction techniques in magnetic resonance imaging: methods, applications, and challenges to clinical adoption. Investig Radiol 2016;51(6):349–64.
[27] Fryback DG, Thornbury JR. The efficacy of diagnostic imaging. Med Decis Mak 1991;11(2):88–94.

[28] Bossuyt PM, et al. STARD 2015: an updated list of essential items for reporting diagnostic accuracy studies. Radiology 2015;277(3):826–32.

[29] Schweitzer M. Stages of technical efficacy: Journal of Magnetic Resonance Imaging style. J Magn Reson Imaging 2016;44(4):781–2.

[30] Van den Bruel A, et al. The evaluation of diagnostic tests: evidence on technical and diagnostic accuracy, impact on patient outcome and cost-effectiveness is needed. J Clin Epidemiol 2007;60(11):1116–22.

[31] Gazelle GS, et al. A framework for assessing the value of diagnostic imaging in the era of comparative effectiveness research. Radiology 2011;261(3):692–8.

[32] Hernando D, et al. Multisite, multivendor validation of the accuracy and reproducibility of proton-density fat-fraction quantification at 1.5T and 3T using a fat-water phantom. Magn Reson Med 2017;77(4):1516–24.

[33] Panda A, et al. Repeatability and reproducibility of 3D MR fingerprinting relaxometry measurements in normal breast tissue. J Magn Reson Imaging 2019;50(4):1133–43.

[34] Wright KL, et al. Simultaneous magnetic resonance angiography and perfusion (MRAP) measurement: initial application in lower extremity skeletal muscle. J Magn Reson Imaging 2013;38(5):1237–44.

[35] Serai SD, et al. Repeatability of MR elastography of liver: a meta-analysis. Radiology 2017;285(1):92–100.

[36] Serai SD, et al. Cross-vendor validation of liver magnetic resonance elastography. Abdom Imaging 2015;40(4):789–94.

[37] Jiang Y, et al. Repeatability of magnetic resonance fingerprinting T1 and T2 estimates assessed using the ISMRM/NIST MRI system phantom. Magn Reson Med 2017;78(4):1452–7.

[38] Captur G, et al. T1 mapping performance and measurement repeatability: results from the multi-national T1 mapping standardization phantom program (T1MES). J Cardiovasc Magn Reson 2020;22(1):31.

[39] Keenan KE, et al. Quantitative magnetic resonance imaging phantoms: a review and the need for a system phantom. Magn Reson Med 2018;79(1):48–61.

[40] Keenan KE, et al. Recommendations towards standards for quantitative MRI (qMRI) and outstanding needs. J Magn Reson Imaging 2019;49(7):e26–39.

[41] Keenan KE, et al. Design of a breast phantom for quantitative MRI. J Magn Reson Imaging 2016; 44(3):610–9.

[42] Lo WC, et al. Realistic 4D MRI abdominal phantom for the evaluation and comparison of acquisition and reconstruction techniques. Magn Reson Med 2019;81(3):1863–75.

[43] Bachtiar V, et al. Repeatability and reproducibility of multiparametric magnetic resonance imaging of the liver. PLoS One 2019;14(4):e0214921.

[44] Messroghli DR, et al. Clinical recommendations for cardiovascular magnetic resonance mapping of T1, T2, T2* and extracellular volume: a consensus statement by the Society for Cardiovascular Magnetic Resonance (SCMR) endorsed by the European Association for Cardiovascular Imaging (EACVI). J Cardiovasc Magn Reson 2017;19(1):75.

[45] Messroghli DR, et al. Correction to: Clinical recommendations for cardiovascular magnetic resonance mapping of T1, T2, T2* and extracellular volume: a consensus statement by the Society for Cardiovascular Magnetic Resonance (SCMR) endorsed by the European Association for Cardiovascular Imaging (EACVI). J Cardiovasc Magn Reson 2018;20(1):9.

[46] Moon JC, et al. Myocardial T1 mapping and extracellular volume quantification: a Society for Cardiovascular Magnetic Resonance (SCMR) and CMR Working Group of the European Society of Cardiology consensus statement. J Cardiovasc Magn Reson 2013;15:92.

[47] Kim D, et al. Advanced fibrosis in nonalcoholic fatty liver disease: noninvasive assessment with MR elastography. Radiology 2013;268(2):411–9.

[48] Bensamoun SF, et al. Cutoff values for alcoholic liver fibrosis using magnetic resonance elastography technique. Alcohol Clin Exp Res 2013;37(5):811–7.

[49] Nasr P, et al. Using a 3% proton density fat fraction as a cut-off value increases sensitivity of detection of hepatic steatosis, based on results from histopathology analysis. Gastroenterology 2017;153(1):53–5, e7.

[50] Shin HJ, et al. Normal range of hepatic fat fraction on dual- and triple-echo fat quantification MR in children. PLoS One 2015;10(2):e0117480.
[51] van Dijken BRJ, et al. Perfusion MRI in treatment evaluation of glioblastomas: clinical relevance of current and future techniques. J Magn Reson Imaging 2019;49(1):11–22.
[52] Miller GM. A radiologist with a ruler. AJNR Am J Neuroradiol 2003;24(4):556.
[53] Yu AC, et al. Development of a combined MR fingerprinting and diffusion examination for prostate cancer. Radiology 2017;283(3):729–38.
[54] Panda A, et al. MR fingerprinting and ADC mapping for characterization of lesions in the transition zone of the prostate gland. Radiology 2019;292(3):685–94.
[55] Panda A, et al. Targeted biopsy validation of peripheral zone prostate cancer characterization with magnetic resonance fingerprinting and diffusion mapping. Investig Radiol 2019;54(8):485–93.
[56] Butler D. Translational research: crossing the valley of death. Nature 2008;453(7197):840–2.
[57] Jain MK. Advancing the mission. J Clin Invest 2015;125(9):3308–15.

MRI Biomarkers☆

Paul Hockings[a], Nadeem Saeed[b], Roslyn Simms[f], Nadia Smith[c], Matt G. Hall[c], John C. Waterton[d,e], and Steven Sourbron[f]

[a]*Antaros Medical, Mölndal, Sweden* [b]*Bioclinica, London, United Kingdom* [c]*National Physical Laboratory, Teddington, United Kingdom* [d]*Centre for Imaging Sciences, Division of Informatics Imaging & Data Sciences, School of Health Sciences, Faculty of Biology Medicine & Health, University of Manchester, Manchester Academic Health Sciences Centre, Manchester, United Kingdom* [e]*Bioxydyn Ltd, Manchester, United Kingdom* [f]*Department of Imaging, Infection, Immunity and Cardiovascular Disease, University of Sheffield, Sheffield, United Kingdom*

1 Introduction

An imaging biomarker is an objective characteristic derived from an in vivo image which can be used as an indicator of normal biological processes, pathogenic processes, or a response to a therapeutic intervention. If an imaging biomarker is measured on a ratio scale (meaning that the ratio of two values can be meaningfully interpreted) or interval scale, then it is referred to as a *quantitative* imaging biomarker or QIB [1].

The range of biological tissue properties that can be interrogated with QIBs in Magnetic Resonance Imaging (MRI) is vast and includes tissue microstructure (e.g., from diffusion-weighted imaging or quantitative susceptibility mapping), metabolism (e.g., from MR spectroscopy or hyperpolarized MRI), tissue composition (e.g., fat and iron mapping), function (e.g., perfusion, brain activation, renal filtration), and gross morphology (e.g., organ or lesion volumes). Quantitative MRI has been a very active and dynamic field of research since the birth of MRI in the 1970s [2], an invention partially driven by the idea that nuclear magnetic relaxation times could be used as a biomarker for malignant tissues [3]. The field of quantitative MRI relies on a spectrum of specialties such as sequence development, image reconstruction, postprocessing and optimization, computational modeling as well as applications in biology and physiology, drug development, and patient management [1].

Considering the interest that MRI-based QIBs have generated in the research community over almost 50 years, it is surprising how few QIBs have been adopted for routine use in clinical practice. In a recent consensus statement, O'Connor et al. [4] reviewed the imaging biomarkers for cancer studies, a major application area of MRI. From their list of imaging biomarkers that have been adopted for the care of cancer patients, only five do (or could) use MR. Although each of these has some quantitative component, they are mainly simple *extensive* variables: morphological measures based on dimensions of lesions or anatomical structures. Only one, the Magnetic Resonance Imaging for Breast Screening (MARIBS) score [5], involves *intensive* MR variables constructed

☆In memory of Prof. Edward Jackson, past chair of the RSNA's Quantitative Imaging Biomarkers Alliance and the ISMRM's ad-hoc committee on standards for quantitative MR.

from voxel-level QIBs.[a] However, even the MARIBS score uses only descriptive parameters that are intrinsically dependent on the measurement approach. None of the QIBs listed uses the physical tissue properties that make up the bulk of the research activity in quantitative MRI.

The significant gap between research and clinical application reflects a skewed distribution of activity in MRI-based QIB research. *There is a clear concentration of activity at the earlier, discovery stages of QIB development, recognized and rewarded as "innovation," but a marked failure-to-translate after the proof-of-concept has been delivered.* Yet demonstrating feasibility is only the very beginning of the QIB translation process, and the subsequent stages are considerably more expensive, laborious, time-consuming, and risky. These stages are often of lower interest to funders, are perceived as less novel, and face significant nonscientific issues such as vendor business interests, clinical culture, weak intellectual property, and poorly aligned incentives. Successful clinical translation of QIBs requires a level of international, industry, and academic research coordination that is typically absent in discovery work, which is generally single-centered and thrives on competition rather than collaboration. The cost of QIB translation, and the breath of expertise required, is generally beyond the capacity of individual stakeholders such as academic centers, pharmaceutical companies, or scanner manufacturers.

There is thus a major role for the international research community in driving the formation of collaborative private/public partnerships to identify promising QIBs and assays and feed them through a systematic translational process. The chapter will outline the steps that are needed to translate novel ideas into clinical impact, with the ultimate aim of encouraging a shift in quantitative MRI research activity with more emphasis on translational work.

2 Fundamentals of imaging biomarkers

2.1 What is a biomarker?

The term "biomarker" was introduced in the 1970s in the context of blood-born analytes [6], although the concept is much older. The formal 2016 BEST definition of a biomarker is a "defined characteristic that is measured as an indicator of normal biological processes, pathogenic processes, or responses to an exposure or intervention, including therapeutic interventions" [7]. Historically the concept of a biomarker refers to analytes measured in biospecimens such as blood, urine, or tissues (see Appendix A for a classic example). In 1999, an NIH/FDA consensus recognized and exemplified imaging biomarkers as formally equivalent to biospecimen biomarkers[b]: "molecular, histologic, radiographic, or physiologic characteristics are examples of biomarkers." The BEST term "assay" is also increasingly used to refer to the methods used to measure an imaging biomarker. An imaging assay typically includes patient preparation, scan technique, image reconstruction, modeling, image processing, and reporting. Any given biomarker can usually be measured with different assays, each with different trade-offs in accuracy, precision, practicality, and cost.

[a]The MARIBS score classifies lesions as malignant, suspicious or benign based on a total score determined by morphological features and visual assessment of contrast agent uptake patterns, but also by semiquantitative measures such as % maximum focal enhancement after contrast agent injection, and maximum intensity over time.

[b]This consensus was updated with the BEST resource in 2016.

Despite the recognized role of imaging as a source of biomarkers, the idea that an MRI measurement can also be seen as a biomarker may still be unfamiliar to many working with more traditional "biospecimen" biomarkers; conversely, many of the concepts and terminologies used to describe biomarkers may be unfamiliar to MRI scientists. In particular, many of the basic assumptions about technical and clinical validation that are routinely accepted by those working with biospecimen biomarkers appear absurd when translated to the context of imaging. For instance, the Crystal City VI workshop report [8], states that a definitive quantitative assay should include a reference material that represents an exact copy of the endogenous material. If one applies this to, for instance, MRI measurement of cerebral blood flow, this translates to a requirement to have a perfused brain with known cerebral blood flow values in the scanner with each patient.

Separate treatment is needed for QIBs. In this first section, we introduce the basic properties and expectations of an imaging biomarker, before moving on in the next sections to describe how new quantitative MRI measurements can be translated to clinically useful biomarkers, the so-called roadmap.

2.2 What is an imaging biomarker?

In 2014, the metrology working group of the Quantitative Imaging Biomarkers Alliance (QIBA) published a series of papers offering a terminology for metrology concepts, algorithm comparisons, and technical performance of an imaging assay [9]. The working group adopted the general National Institutes of Health and the Food and Drug Administration (FDA-NIH) definition of biomarker but also defined a subgroup of QIBs that are measured on an interval or ratio scale (i.e., a scale that includes a zero and where ratios of values can be meaningfully interpreted). With this definition, radiological scoring systems such as Prostate Imaging-Reporting and Data System (PI-RADS) [10] that are measured on an ordered or nominal scale (*ordered categorical* variables) are imaging biomarkers but do not qualify as QIBs. QIBs are further subdivided into *intensive* variables (typically voxel-wise quantities that can be represented as a color-coded map) or *extensive* variables (typically volumes, dimensions, or other properties of larger structures). Table 1 presents some examples of imaging biomarkers in each of these categories. Fig. 1 illustrates an MRI-based QIB that is already available in clinical practice, an estimate of liver iron concentration (LIC) derived from liver T_2 values.

With these definitions, it would appear that any quantitative MRI parameter is an imaging biomarker. This is not the case—exceptions are, for instance, quantitative MRI parameters that are measured for quality assurance or technical characterization of methods, such as the signal-to-noise ratio [11], slice profiles, or the B_1 field strength in tissue. While these are objectively measurable and reproducible numerical quantities, they are not measured as indicators of biological processes and, therefore, are not classed as biomarkers. The term imaging biomarker in that sense merely signals an intended use of the quantitative MRI measurement. Magnetic susceptibility, for instance, is not a biomarker when it is measured purely as a means of correcting artifacts in other scans. The same physical quantity becomes a QIB when it is measured for its sensitivity to tissue type and intended to be used clinically [12]. The implications of labeling it as a QIB are that it will have to go through an appropriate program of validation and perhaps qualification depending on its intended use.

Table 1 Classification of imaging biomarkers in metrological terms, including examples.

Type	Statistical definition	Examples in MRI	Notes
Extensive variable	A quantity whose magnitude is additive for subsystems	Hippocampus volume; Articular cartilage denuded area; Cartilage thickness; % stenosis; Several enhancing lesions	"how big" Typically in 3, 2, 1, or 0 spatial dimensions; Typically a property of an RoI; Maybe a QIB
Intensive variable	A quantity whose magnitude is independent of the extent of the system	K^{trans}; T_2; tCho/Cr; Any quantity that can be mapped	"how hot"; Can be an average or some other summary parameter within an RoI; Maybe a QIB
Ordered categorical	A characteristic with ordered labeled categories	RAMRIS synovitis score; TNM stage; PIRADS2 score	"how ugly"; Typically a radiologist's score; Not a QIB

2.3 Where are imaging biomarkers used?

The BEST resource [7] defines seven categories of biomarkers based on their context of use (CoU) in clinical trials or clinical practice (see Table 2). Each can be used in three different settings: in basic science and exploratory drug development; as regulatory endpoints in clinical trials of new therapies such as drugs or devices; or in directing patients down the best care pathway in routine clinical practice.

2.3.1 Imaging biomarkers in research or internal decision making

Biomarkers can be used in basic science to help improve our understanding of normal biological processes, disease progression, or the effect of the intervention. The CoU is the testing of hypotheses of interest to the biomedical scientific community (including drug developers), and only of tangential interest to regulators or healthcare practitioners [13]. Validation is required only to the extent necessary for the needs of the investigator and others who may use the research findings.

An added value of imaging biomarkers in research is the opportunity to observe features that are not easily accessible by other means, such as the spatial heterogeneity of the disease, organ interactions, or dynamic information. An example is the use of MRI biomarkers of cardiac function to monitor changes over time in regenerating neonatal mouse hearts [14]. Without the use of MRI, such properties can only be characterized by destructive methods that do not allow for longitudinal observations in the same animals. In this context, MRI biomarkers avoid confounding effects of between-subject differences and can contribute to the reduction of animals in research.

Where animal models provide insufficient insight into the human disease, research must be performed in human participants [15]. This further reduces the ability to rely on invasive observations and, therefore, increases the importance of imaging biomarkers and other noninvasive assessments. The observations made in human studies can then also be replicated in animals to guide the development of improved disease models, a concept known as back-translation [13].

FerriScan®

Liver Iron Concentration Report

Report No:	10000001_S12	Scan Date:	19 May 2019
Birth Date:	10 Aug 2003	Analysis Date:	20 May 2019
Patient Name:	PATIENT, Patient		
Patient ID:	ABC-12345678		
Referrer:	Dr Doctor		
MRI Centre:	MRI Centre Name		

Average Liver Iron Concentration	**6.8 mg/g dry tissue**	(NR: 0.17-1.8)
	121 mmol/kg dry tissue	(NR: 3-33)

Normal range (NR) is taken from Bassett et al., Hepatology 1986; 6: 24-29

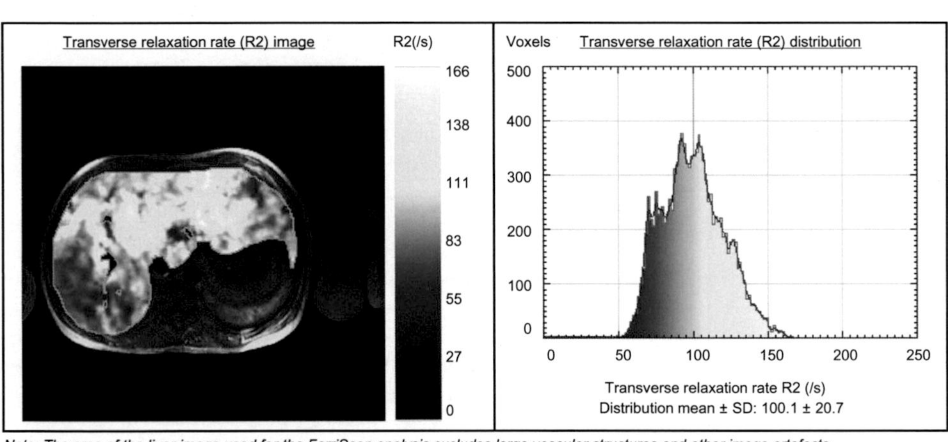

Note: The area of the liver image used for the FerriScan analysis excludes large vascular structures and other image artefacts.

Table showing liver iron concentration thresholds in transfusional iron overload only

Extract from Olivieri et al, Blood 1997; 89, 739-61

LIC range	Clinical relevance
0.17–1.8 mg Fe/g dw	Normal range in nondisease patients in healthy population
3.2–7.0 mg Fe/g dw	Suggested optimal range of LIC for chelation therapy in transfusional iron loading
7.0–15.0 mg Fe/g dw	Increased risk of complications
≥15.0 mg Fe/g dw	Greatly increased risk of cardiac disease and early death in patients with transfusional iron overload

A follow-up FerriScan may be required every 6 – 12 months.

Authorised by: Service Centre Manager

Resonance Health Analysis Services Pty Ltd www.resonancehealth.com

CE 0805 **CONFIDENTIAL** **ARTG: 116071** **510(k): K043271**

FIG. 1

See figure legend on next page.

Response assessment with imaging biomarkers is especially useful to support internal decision-making by drug developers. Conclusive clinical trials are expensive [16] and it can take several years (10–15 years) for a drug to come to the market from the initial concept. An early Go/No-Go decision [17] on an investigational new drug can save significant cost and time, and improve the drug development pipeline, as cost savings from early No-Go decisions can be channeled to other programs. Imaging biomarkers can also be used by drug developers in Phase 1/2 pharmacokinetic/pharmacodynamic studies for proof-of-mechanism, proof-of-principle, and dose setting. This approach has been taken for instance in the development of antiangiogenics in oncology where pharmacodynamic Dynamic Contrast-Enhanced (DCE)-MRI biomarkers such as K^{trans} were used [18,19] to examine the

Table 2 Seven categories of biomarkers based on their context of use in clinical trials or clinical practice, as defined by the BEST resource [6].

Category	Context of use
Susceptibility/risk biomarker	A biomarker that indicates the potential for developing a disease or medical condition in an individual who does not currently have a clinically apparent disease or the medical condition.
Diagnostic biomarker	A biomarker used to detect or confirm the presence of a disease or condition of interest or to identify individuals with a subtype of the disease.
Monitoring biomarker	A biomarker measured serially for assessing the status of a disease or medical condition or for evidence of exposure to (or effect of) a medical product or an environmental agent.
Prognostic biomarker	A biomarker used to identify the likelihood of a clinical event, disease recurrence, or progression in patients who have the disease or medical condition of interest.
Predictive biomarker	A biomarker used to identify individuals who are more likely than similar individuals without the biomarker to experience a favorable or unfavorable effect from exposure to a medical product or an environmental agent.
Pharmaco-dynamic/ response biomarker	A biomarker used to show that a biological response has occurred in an individual who has been exposed to a medical product or an environmental agent.
Safety biomarker	A biomarker measured before or after an exposure to a medical product or an environmental agent to indicate the likelihood, presence, or extent of toxicity as an adverse effect.

FIG. 1

An example of an MRI-based QIB currently available for clinical use, kindly provided by ResonanceHealth. The QIB shown is a measurement of liver iron concentration (LIC) based on liver R_2 ($=1/T_2$) values. The assay, FerriScan, was regulatory cleared by the FDA for the measurement of LIC in 2005. In January 2013, FerriScan gained an additional clearance from the FDA as a companion diagnostic to aid in the identification and monitoring of nontransfusion-dependent thalassemia patients receiving therapy with deferasirox. The figure shows a typical report returned to a referring physician by the central Service Center where the quality of the data is verified and the images are processed. The main result is a measurement of LIC in units of mg/g, in this particular case showing an elevated level of iron (6.8 mg/g) compared to the normal range (NR) of 0.17–1.8 mg/g. As the color-coding shows *(bottom of figure)*, this value is within an optimal range of 3.2–7.0 mg/g for chelation therapy in transfusional iron loading. An R_2 map is included in the report to show the heterogeneity across the liver. For more detail please see Ferriscan.com.

relationship between dose/plasma concentration of investigational new drugs and tumor pathophysiology. Additionally, imaging biomarkers can provide a mechanistic understanding of a drug's mode of action that can contribute to a regulatory submission even if included as exploratory endpoints instead of primary or secondary endpoints [20].

2.3.2 Imaging biomarkers in drug or device development

The role of imaging biomarkers in drug/device development has been increasing over the years. Indeed, imaging biomarkers of tumor size or cartilage loss were first introduced in the 1950s, when molecular biology was in its infancy. Their use became more prominent in 2004 when the FDA produced the Clinical Research Initiative [21] that encouraged the inclusion of technology such as imaging in clinical trials to establish the safety and efficacy of investigational new drugs. In this case, the CoU is in establishing the evidence base which regulators can use to determine the risks and benefits to the public health of approving a new drug. To be considered MRI biomarkers in this context, regulators have stringent requirements for validation.

Imaging biomarkers are used across all of the seven categories (Table 2):

- As safety biomarkers, to assess the possible harms associated with an intervention. An example would be the use of MR biomarkers of edema and effusion associated with investigational therapies for Alzheimer's Disease [22].
- A susceptibility, diagnostic, or prognostic biomarker, to establish subject eligibility in a clinical trial (See Appendix B for a detailed case study). For example, in oncology, tumor, node, metastasis (TNM) stage (an ordered categorical biomarker obtained mainly by imaging) is often used to exclude patients with early disease (who are unlikely to progress during the trial) and/or patients with very advanced disease (who are likely to progress or die irrespective of treatment). Often the regulator will approve the treatment only for those groups included in the trial, with the implication that the drug must be assumed to have no benefit in groups in which it has not been tested.
- As a response biomarker, to show the efficacy of an intervention. For example, a reduction in MRI spleen volume from baseline showed the efficacy of taliglucerase alfas in Gaucher's disease [23] to the satisfaction of a regulatory agency.[c] MRI, in particular, is beneficial here as it does not involve radiation and can, therefore, be undertaken more frequently. The effect of the drug can be detected at an earlier stage than clinical outcomes, hence reducing the size or duration of the trial.
- A predictive biomarker, to identify which patients will benefit from the drug. An example is liver T_2 using the "Ferriscan" assay [24] as a companion diagnostic to determine eligibility for deferasirox[d] (see also Fig. 1).

Phase III ("pivotal") trials may involve large numbers of subjects (hundreds or thousands). They aim to satisfy the regulator that the investigational drug or device will improve how a patient feels, functions, or survives: biomarkers are, therefore, of secondary importance. For example, an oncology drug that has a spectacular effect on imaging biomarkers, but no effect on survival, is unlikely to be approved.

[c] https://www.accessdata.fda.gov/drugsatfda_docs/label/2012/022458lbl.pdf.

[d] http://www.accessdata.fda.gov/cdrh_docs/reviews/K124065.pdf.

However, in certain circumstances, regulators may use biomarkers, including imaging biomarkers, as surrogate endpoints, with a concomitant reduction in subject numbers and/or study duration resulting in significant cost savings. Of the 197 new drugs approved by FDA between 2010 and 2014,[e] 84 (43%) were approved based on surrogate rather than clinical endpoints and in 30 of those cases (36%), the surrogate endpoint was an imaging biomarker.

2.3.3 Imaging biomarkers in clinical practice

Biomarkers are used in clinical practice to inform decisions on patient management, but the CoU is fundamentally different than in clinical trials. In medical product development, the treatment is the hypothesis and the primary question is whether patients will have an improved outcome after treatment. In clinical practice, the question is which (if any) of multiple available treatments (including doing nothing) will lead to the best improvement in outcome. In the practice of medicine, this decision may be made using the collective judgment of the clinical team including the radiologist, without any quantitation at all. The advantage of using a properly measured biomarker to inform clinical decision-making is the (often large) evidence base in the literature for the relationship between exact biomarker value and clinical outcome.

In theory, the same seven categories of biomarkers identified for clinical trials (Table 2) exist in clinical practice. However, susceptibility/risk, diagnostic, and prognostic biomarkers add little value unless they redirect patients down alternative care pathways with different treatment options. Hence in practice, these will effectively act as predictive biomarkers to select the right treatment for the right patient. For example, bicalutamide[f] is indicated for patients with locally advanced, nonmetastatic prostate cancer (where MRI is often a major component of the TNM score—another biomarker) [25,26]. Patients with localized disease (T_1–T_2, N_0/N_x, M_0), or metastatic patients (any T, any N, M_1) do not benefit from bicalutamide and should receive alternative therapies.

A risk, diagnostic, or prognostic biomarker employed in drug development may *become* a predictive biomarker if the drug is approved. For example, MRI cortical thinning predicts the onset of Alzheimer's disease in cognitively normal adults [27]. In a clinical trial of a new drug expected to postpone the onset of Alzheimer's disease, it can, therefore, be used as a risk biomarker to identify subjects that are most likely to develop the disease in the absence of treatment. If the drug ends up being approved for clinical use, the same biomarker can then be used as a predictive to help determine whether a given patient is likely to benefit from the intervention.

2.4 Regulatory aspects of biomarkers

Depending on their (intended) use, biomarkers (and the assays used to measure them) are subject to different regulatory requirements [28] (Fig. 2).

2.4.1 Approval for use in research or internal decision making

When a biomarker is used in human research, the study must be approved by the institutional review board (IRB) and the risks from the assay need to be acceptable. There is no regulatory requirement for them to be effective, though funders or IRBs may well choose to reject studies that rely on biomarkers

[e]https://www.fda.gov/downloads/NewsEvents/Testimony/UCM445375.pdf.
[f]Bicalutamide 150 mg, UK PL 17901/0006, revision of 3rd December 2015.

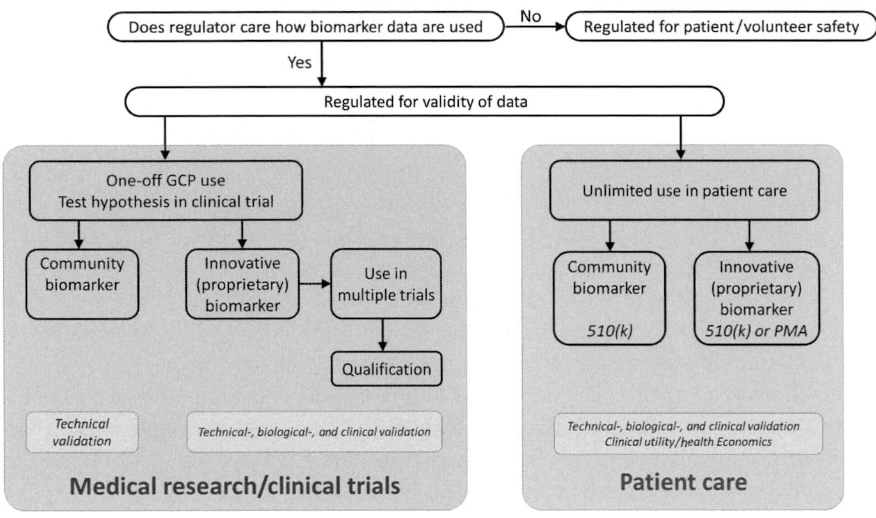

FIG. 2

Regulatory pathways for biomarkers and their assays. On the left *(blue box)* the use in clinical trials is shown, on the right, the use in clinical routine *(green box)* is shown.

without strong evidence of utility for the proposed use. The same conclusions hold for biomarkers that are used to guide internal decision making by drug developers in the early phases of clinical drug development (e.g., Phase II trials). Whether privately or publicly funded, the emphasis is on good and ethical science supported by convincing data. Pharmaceutical companies use imaging biomarkers to reduce the risks of late-stage drug failure and they will, therefore, typically collect enough evidence to ensure that the benefits of deploying a new imaging biomarker outweigh the risks.

2.4.2 Qualification for use in drug or device development

When a biomarker is used in drug development as an endpoint in a late phase clinical trial, and this trial is reviewed by regulators to ensure the new drug is safe and effective, then the biomarker needs to be *qualified* (i.e., deemed acceptable for its intended context of use by the regulators). Biomarkers applied in animal studies also need to be qualified if the data are part of a regulatory submission for a new drug—for instance, to demonstrate the safety of the drug. Biomarkers considered for qualification must be conceptually independent of the assays used to measure them, and qualification of the biomarker does not indicate endorsement or specification of any specific device for measuring the biomarker. However, preanalytical considerations and the technical performance of the test or assay used to measure the biomarker are considered as part of the qualification process.

Biomarker qualification may be done as part of a single new drug application where the sponsor generates enough data to justify the use of the new biomarkers only in that one setting. However, regulators have also created biomarker qualification programs that allow a single qualification to be used in multiple trials. For the FDA this is part of the Drug Development Tools (DDT) Qualification Program [29]. The qualification of a new DDT requires a higher initial investment compared to qualifying the biomarker for a single trial. However, multiple interested parties (stakeholders) can pool their resources and data to decrease cost, expedite drug development, and facilitate a regulatory review. This is a typical arena for large public-private partnerships involving industry, academia, small-and-medium enterprises, and other stakeholders.

The FDA biomarker qualification is a three-step process [30]. The submission of a letter of intent (LOI) launches the application and should clarify what the biomarker will be used for and how it will be measured. If the LOI is acceptable to the FDA, a qualification plan (QP) can be submitted which details a development plan for the biomarker, including existing data that support the context of use and areas that need further investigation. If the QP is acceptable to the FDA, a full qualification package (FQP) can be submitted, including comprehensive data and supporting evidence. If the FDA is satisfied after a comprehensive review of the FQP then it will issue a qualification recommendation for the proposed context of use. The European Medicines Agency (EMA) has a similar process for biomarker qualification [31] and publishes qualification opinions on its website [32].

At the time of writing (April 2020) only eight biomarkers have been qualified by the FDA, including one imaging biomarker [33], namely, Total Kidney Volume (TKV) as a prognostic biomarker for autosomal dominant polycystic kidney disease (see Appendix B). However, 24 LOIs, including seven for imaging biomarkers (23%), have been accepted between July 2017 and April 2020 [34], showing the clear upwards trajectory of imaging biomarkers in drug development.

2.4.3 Approval for use in clinical practice

Many commonly-used imaging biomarkers involve long-established community-developed assays, for example, Left Ventricular Ejection Fraction, LVEF [35]. While the device used to measure LVEF is regulated as a medical device, the assay itself (i.e., the method established and published by expert groups in professional societies) can be used in clinical practice without further regulatory review. However, a *new* biomarker assay cannot be marketed before it has been reviewed by regulators and *cleared* or *approved* for use in patients.

Approval is a separate process from qualification (Fig. 2): a biomarker can be used in clinical practice without having been qualified, and a biomarker can be qualified for use in clinical trials even when it is measured with devices that are not approved for clinical use. Generally, approval will require sufficient evidence that the assay is safe and that it is effective, i.e., that the technical performance is sufficient to reliably characterize the effect sizes in the intended context of use. Approval of assays also requires robust quality assurance—not only of the assays themselves but also of the manufacturing or software development processes used to produce them.

For biomarker assays on the market, by far the most common pathway to regulatory approval is by demonstrating *substantial equivalence* to a device that is already approved (the predicate). This pathway, in the United States, referred to as section 510(k), requires evidence that the new device has the same intended use and is at least as safe and effective as the predicate for that use. If no predicate is available, then an independent demonstration of safety and effectiveness is needed [36], either through a de novo 510(k) if the risk is moderate, or premarket approval (PMA) if the device is riskier.

Substantial equivalence is a popular route to approval because the burden of proof is lower and definition is fairly general. Different indications of use, such as the population for which a device is intended or the disease it is intended to treat, are allowed as long as these differences can not affect the safety and/or effectiveness of the device. Similarly, the new device can be significantly different in terms of design, materials, or other technological features, as long as these differences do not raise different safety issues. An example in the context of MRI biomarkers is the recent clearance of

IschemaView RAPID (510(k) number K182130, December 27, 2018)—an image viewing and processing software that produces predictive QIBs for mechanical thrombectomy. Tracing back the chain of predicates,[g] we find that this recent assay is "substantially equivalent" to a 30-year old teleradiology system.

2.4.4 Approval for in-house clinical use

Assays that are developed in-house by a single institute and clinically used within the institute ("in-house manufacturing") are subject to weaker regulations than those that are on the market. However, the gap is increasingly narrowing with new regulations. The EU is currently in transition from the Medical Devices Directive (MDD) to the Medical Device Regulations (MDR), which comes into effect in May 2020. Under the MDD, devices (including software) that were developed and used within a single institution were considered out of scope and the legislation did not apply. Under MDR, this is no longer the case. A "health institution exemption" can be applied for which softens some of the requirements, but the baseline requirements are still substantial [37]. In-house manufacturers will need an appropriate quality management system and must meet the general safety and performance requirements as a minimum. This will effectively scale down much in-house software development and implementation, especially in smaller hospitals.

2.5 Metrology of imaging biomarkers

The concept of biomarker changes greatly from field to field, and prospective QIBs vary greatly in their reliability and sensitivity. However, one concept unifies them all: QIBs are a form of measurement. They are numbers derived from an experimental process that estimates the amount of a quantity of interest. In that sense, we can approach QIBs from a metrological perspective. Note that ordered categorical biomarkers, which are not QIBs, often lack rigorous metrology and carry very different risks as a consequence. In this section, we introduce several concepts from formal metrology. Specific internationally standard definitions can be found in the International Vocabulary of Metrology.[h]

2.5.1 Reproducibility and traceability

Metrology encompasses many subfields and a wealth of analytical techniques, but a metrologically rigorous measurement has two key criteria: reproducibility and traceability. A great deal has been written about reproducibility and the importance that a measurement can be verified independently by a different investigator with a quantifiable bias and precision. This tenet is central to good scientific practice. As measurement processes and analysis methodologies become more complicated,

[g]The predicate of K182130 was a previous version of IschemaView RAPID that was identical except for the intended use in thrombectomy (K172477, April 19, 2018). The latter was itself approved by substantial equivalence to an older version of IschemaView RAPID (K121447, October 4, 2013). The chain continues via OLEA MEDICAL's Olea Sphere (K120196, April 19, 2012), Nordic Image Control and Evaluation (nordicICE) software (K090546, June 8, 2009), two older nordicICE softwares (K082441, November 21, 2008; K063539, January 17, 2007), eFILM Workstation with Modules (Merge eMED, K020995, April 12, 2002), eFilm Workstation (eFilm Medical, K012211, July 4, 2001), Radworks Medical Imaging Software with Quality Control Module (Applicare Medical Imaging, K982862, October 21, 1998), Radworks Medical Imaging Software (K962699, July 5, 1996), and ICON Teleradiology System (ICON Medical Systems, K911752, 31 July, 1991).

[h]https://www.bipm.org/en/publications/guides/vim.html.

reproducibility becomes more challenging to demonstrate, and experimental design becomes more involved, but the central concept is familiar to every scientist.

Traceability is perhaps less familiar but is nevertheless a key metrological concept. It refers to the idea that a particular measurement is related to a primary standard through an unbroken chain of calibrations, each contributing to the measurement uncertainty, i.e., to an agreed-upon reference that allows consistency between measurements undertaken in different places, by different individuals, using different measurement equipment. Temperature is a good example—the temperature is measurable by many different methods, but these can all be calibrated against the same primary standard. Traceability underpins reproducibility and enables different measurements to be directly compared. In any laboratory in the world, a meter is always a meter, a kilogram is always a kilogram, at least to within stated uncertainties.[i]

If we think about these concepts in the context of biomarkers, the importance of both is clear. Biomarkers are measurements that indicate the presence or progress of some biomedical object of inquiry. To be useful, biomarkers too must be reproducible so that clinicians and researchers can be confident that their trials are based on relevant data. Similarly, for clinicians and researchers to be confident that biomarkers are reliable and deployable in different contexts, the measurement processes must be traceable to an agreed-upon reference. For QIBs the ideal of traceability may not be accomplished exactly due to the difficulty of building reference objects with sufficiently realistic tissue properties (fractional anisotropy, T_2^*, and so on). In imaging, therefore, simpler test objects must be used which can offer necessary, but perhaps not sufficient, criteria for an assay to be traceable.

2.5.2 Reference standards for imaging biomarkers

The imaging community has been very active in developing QIBs, but few of them have been rigorously evaluated for their technical and clinical performance. This is possibly due to the inconsistent use of terminology and methods related to the evaluation of the technical performance of these markers [38]. Standardization and metrology can play an important role to improve this issue by helping scientists describe accurately and consistently what physical phenomenon is being measured, its relation to disease progress or outcome, and the measurement uncertainty associated with it.

One important method for validating measurements and providing traceability is through the use of well-characterized test objects, or phantoms. Measurement Institutes, such as the National Physical Laboratory (NPL) in the United Kingdom and the National Institute of Standards and Technology (NIST) in the United States, are already working on aspects of validation with the development and testing of numerical and physical imaging phantoms (test objects). A phantom provides traceable, verifiable ground-truth values against which quantitative measurements can be compared. Phantoms can also be used to validate image processing pipelines, resulting in a better understanding of the bias, precision, and overall uncertainty in a measurement, or even whether a particular measurement process may result in values that mimic pathological changes or disease states.

The physical characteristics of a phantom are often dictated by the nature of the biomarker. For image-based biomarkers, phantoms often need to contain structures of a certain size and with specified absorption or response characteristics that dictate the selection of material and manufacturing process.

[i]Strictly speaking, in order to be traceable, any measurement must be accompanied by its associated measurement uncertainty. This is rarely available for the outputs of clinical imaging systems.

It is these choices that allow both traceability and uncertainty quantification. Manufacturing tolerances allow a base uncertainty to be established, and traceability in the manufacturing process allows the phantom to be related to a primary standard. For example, a phantom may contain an MRI contrast agent made up of a manganese salt in water at a specified concentration and verifiable via an alternative measurement process, such as mass spectrometry.[j]

2.5.3 Standardization as a driver for innovation

Once established, QIBs have the potential for high levels of standardization and reproducibility. Unlike qualitative imaging which has been designed for visual assessment, quantification means that images can be treated as measurements, where the measurement uncertainty can be evaluated, and traceability confirmed. This allows standards to be written which specify desired bias and precision properties without reference to individual measurement approaches or component designs.

It is important to emphasize that it is not the assays themselves that are standardized, but the metrics and associated methods used to determine their bias and precision.[k] This allows manufacturers and regulatory bodies to produce devices and procedures to meet the required standard without preventing innovation or being overly prescriptive of methodology. Standardization in this sense *promotes* competition, as vendors will now have universally accepted and independent criteria to demonstrate the quality and cost/benefit ratio of their assays, and any advances over competing assays.

Quantification and standardization also support metaanalyses and data reuse since they allow the results of different studies to be quantitatively compared while minimizing intersite variability. This property is important when attempting to scale up the evidence level of clinical trials by combing data from multiple smaller studies. It is also useful when exploring machine learning, radiomics, and other advanced inference approaches, where the requirements for large datasets mean that intersite variability is a serious confounding effect.

3 Imaging biomarker translation

A newly devised MRI metric is merely a laboratory curiosity: it requires *validation* to become a biomarker useful for medical research or healthcare. An important lesson that MRI scientists can learn from successful biospecimen biomarkers such as HbA1c (Appendix A) is the significant time and effort required for clinical translation of a new metric. Despite the compelling rationale, it took close to 40 years from the discovery of HbA1c to universal clinical adoption as a monitoring biomarker, and ongoing challenges over the subsequent 20 years to resolve differences between standards that allowed it to be used as a diagnostic biomarker. For imaging biomarkers, where the link to the biological mechanism and the technology itself is more complex, and clinical studies at the epidemiological scale are almost prohibitively expensive, the time scale from discovery to clinical adoption risks being significantly longer.

[j] See https://www.eurachem.org/index.php/publications/guides/trc for more information on chemical traceability and reference standards.

[k] In clinical trials with novel QIBs it is not always feasible to standardize QIBs up to this level, and in those circumstances it is often preferable to standardize the assay itself. In multi-center clinical trials, the central imaging lab will generally aim to use identical imaging sequences, even when scanners from different vendors are used.

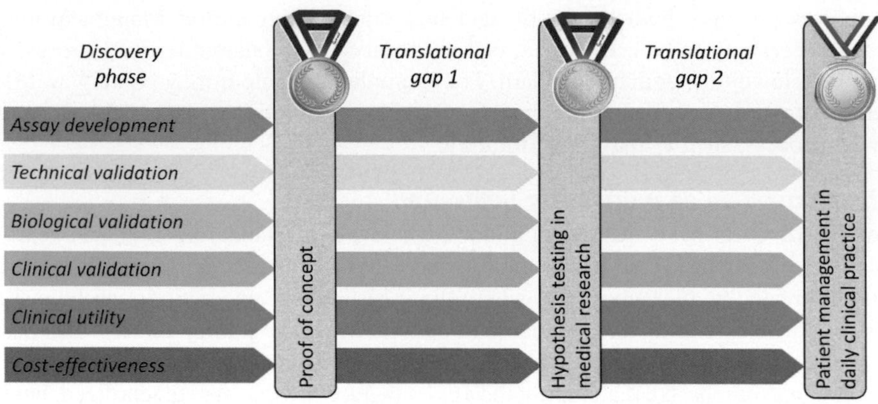

FIG. 3

Imaging biomarker development roadmap, showing the two translational gaps that need to be crossed, as well as the spectrum of research and development activities that need to be performed in parallel to cross the gaps.

This highlights the need for a well-planned and coordinated process that is initiated early on in the lifecycle of the biomarker. Following a generally efficient sequence of validation activities, or a *roadmap* can help to speed up translation by identifying problems at an early stage and avoiding unnecessary iterations and late-stage failures. In recent years the roadmap illustrated in Fig. 3 has emerged as a template for imaging biomarker development [4]. In this section, we present the basic concepts and the evidence that is required to traverse it effectively. Appendix B presents a case study in more detail.

3.1 The imaging biomarker roadmap

The imaging biomarker roadmap (Fig. 3) recognizes two *translational gaps* [39,40] separating domains with different scientific cultures. For MR biomarkers [41], the first gap lies between the initial discovery and proof-of-concept in MR research, and the availability of an MR tool to test hypotheses in medical research. The second gap takes the MR biomarker into routine daily use to help direct patients down different care pathways. In the discovery phase, the MR physicist or radiologist is interested in the measurement itself. In medical research, the investigator must be confident that the MR biomarker provides a valid test of the hypothesis. In healthcare, the MR biomarker must cost-effectively improve patient outcomes and public health.

A spectrum of *research and development activities* is needed to cross each translational gap (horizontal tracks in Fig. 3, defined in Table 3). Imaging biomarkers are unusual in that these tracks are usually best conducted in parallel, in contrast to conventional biospecimen biomarkers, where they occur largely in series [4].

The exact type and level of evidence required to cross each translational gap depend on the context of use, and it is, therefore, critical to determining this upfront. This also implies that the roadmap needs to be traveled again when an existing clinical biomarker is repurposed for a different context of use. For instance, when a monitoring biomarker is repurposed as a diagnostic (Appendix A), not

Table 3 Research and development activities needed to cross the translational gaps defined by the roadmap in Fig. 3.

R&D activity	Description
Assay development	An ongoing process of increasing refinement and upscaling of the assays to move from single-center studies through to multicenter studies and ultimately deployment on a population level.
Technical validation	(Also known as "analytical" or "assay" validation) ensures that the measurement can be made reproducibly, robustly, ethically, and legally anywhere it is requested. Technical validation is not concerned with the biological meaning or clinical utility of the biomarker.
Biological validation	Assembles an evidence base linking the biomarker to the underlying biology it purports to measure. Biological validation is not concerned with the clinical implications of that biology. It is, therefore, not always recognized as a necessary activity [7], as clinical validation is sufficient for a biomarker to be useful. However, for QIBs where the link to biology is complex, a separate biological validation is often useful to justify investment in clinical validation.
Clinical validation	Assembles an evidence base linking the biomarker to a relevant clinical outcome: how a patient feels, functions, or survives. The choice of the outcome depends on the particular context of use.
Clinical utility	Involves demonstrating that *using* the biomarker to inform patient management improves patient outcomes. Collecting evidence of clinical utility requires a case-control trial where a group of patients is treated using a management strategy that involves the biomarker, and a control group that is treated without the biomarker.
Cost-effectiveness	Involves demonstrating that biomarker cost-effectively improves outcomes. This step depends quite strongly on the local healthcare system and is thus separate from the clinical utility.

only is a new clinical validation required, but additional requirements on measurement bias or cost-effectiveness may also be needed. This, in turn, may require additional assay development and technical validation.

The *discovery phase* is generally regarded as a less structured process leading to a proof-of-concept that is sufficient to justify further development. Nevertheless, it useful to assess the different validation tracks at the discovery phase as well and collect preliminary evidence across all tracks. While the level of evidence will not be decisive at this stage, comprehensive coverage of different validation types can act as a screening process to help decide which biomarkers to take forward and identify the context of use to be prioritized.

As an illustration of these concepts in MRI, consider the example of the apparent diffusion coefficient (ADC) as a biomarker of kidney fibrosis, where the context of use is to reduce the number of biopsies needed to predict disease progression. This is an emerging QIB that has not yet fully crossed the first translational gap. Assay development includes optimization of diffusion sequences with sufficient specificity for cortico-medullary differentiation [42]. Technical validation involves demonstrating that ADC values can be measured reliably in the kidney; biological validation involves demonstrating a correlation between kidney ADC and kidney fibrosis as measured on pathology [43]; clinical validation involves demonstrating that kidney ADC can predict disease progression [44]; clinical utility involves demonstrating that ADC can be used to predict disease progression at least as well as biopsy, so that (some) biopsies can be replaced by ADC measurements without adversely effecting outcome; cost-effectiveness involves demonstrating that this management strategy reduces cost or that it is a worthwhile investment.

3.2 Crossing the first translational gap: MR biomarkers used in medical research

3.2.1 Assay development

For an MRI biomarker to be applicable in medical research it must be acquired ethically, and in a manner acceptable to the relevant patients. Long scan times, uncomfortable patient positioning, high power deposition, or invasive aspects (e.g., the use of endoscopic coils) may be unacceptable. A contrast agent or other administered substance must have regulatory approval, either as a licensed drug used off-label or as an investigational new drug, in the jurisdiction(s) where the research is to be performed. Assays must be standardized across vendors to minimize differences between results obtained in different sites. Robust quality assurance procedures must be developed to verify compliance with the prescribed standards.

3.2.2 Technical validation

Medical research usually requires sample size calculations and significance testing, and thus assessments of repeatability (same subject, same scanner) are essential. Reproducibility (same subject, different scanner) is important for multicenter studies. For a response biomarker (the most common use of MR biomarkers in medical research), the repeatability error should be as small as possible compared to the effect size (i.e., expected change in the biomarker value after treatment). If the MRI biomarker is a primary endpoint and, therefore, forms the basis of the power calculation, smaller uncertainties are beneficial as they allow the detection of given effect size with a smaller trial.

3.2.3 Biological validation

Identifying the relationship with biology is critical in crossing the first translational gap. In a study to test a hypothesis in medical research, the observations can be linked to pathophysiology. Observing, for instance, that T_2^* values in the liver are different between patients and healthy volunteers is not very informative unless there is hard evidence from biological validation studies that T_2^* in these patients is a marker of, for instance, iron content. In drug development, such as in studies testing the effect of an investigational drug in a Phase 2 trial, investigators must be highly confident that a change in the imaging biomarker reflects a true change in the underlying biology (sensitivity), and perhaps more importantly that a lack of change in the MR biomarker means that the relevant biology remains unchanged (specificity).

3.2.4 Clinical validation

A separate clinical validation is not always necessary. For instance, if biological validation has demonstrated that a novel QIB is strongly sensitive and specific to hypoxia, then this novel QIB can be used to test whether hypoxia is a driver for disease progression. Or, in situations where hypoxia is known to correlate with outcome, the new QIB can be used in clinical research to substitute for invasive measurements of hypoxia. In practice, such strong links are not often available, in which case a separate clinical validation study is necessary before the QIB can be used in medical research.

Clinical validation can be evidenced with a single well-powered clinical study, but the evidence is stronger when it comes from multiple independent sources. The strongest evidence comes from prospective studies that are specifically designed and powered to assess how the biomarker relates to the outcome and can be linked to clinically meaningful changes in how the subject feels, functions, or survives.

This level of validation will almost certainly be necessary to support biomarker qualification submissions to regulatory authorities. In some cases, clinical validation can be performed using data from studies conducted for other purposes, or QIB validation can be added as a secondary aim in studies performed for other reasons. An example is an evidence from cross-sectional, epidemiological studies that can be used to link the imaging biomarker to the severity of the disease. For example, hepatic triglyceride content was measured with MR spectroscopy in 2349 participants in the Dallas Heart Study (DHS) [45], and the data were used to calculate the upper limit of normal of hepatic triglyceride content and the prevalence of hepatic steatosis in the population.

3.2.5 Clinical utility

Hard evidence of clinical utility is not necessary for hypothesis testing in medical research. Nevertheless, it may be useful to make some preliminary assessments of future use when designing the research. Ultimately, a biomarker is incorporated into a research study because it is assumed to provide important information about the disease or the intervention that is not available by other means. If the trial is positive, the way the biomarker has been used in the trial may well end up defining how it is ultimately used in clinical practice [46]. Conversely, there is little point in demonstrating that a treatment is effective in a certain specific patient population if patient selection requires a biomarker that is not scalable to clinical practice.

3.2.6 Cost-effectiveness

In publicly funded medical research, the cost is an important consideration and can be a limiting factor. In that case, it may be worth considering whether trade-offs can be made in the assay design that reduces the cost without a major impact on efficacy. In drug trials, a very high cost may be acceptable if the hypothesis is important. Nevertheless, even in drug development, there is a risk that any benefit of using the biomarker is minor and not offset by the cost of measuring it. Especially for novel imaging biomarkers that are associated with significant setup and management costs, this is an important consideration.

3.3 Crossing the second translational gap: MR biomarkers used in healthcare

3.3.1 Assay development

Significantly more technical development is needed to cross the second gap: the MR biomarker must be robustly measurable on a wide range of MRI scanners (including makes and models not yet conceived) and yield comparable results. Metrology becomes increasingly important, ensuring traceability to a reference standard that does not reference specific assay designs. Depending on the type and nature of the QIB, this may require the development and commercialization of phantoms and a network of certified reference laboratories that are qualified to measure a high standard [4]. Regulatory approval of devices, contrast agents, and analysis software is needed in each jurisdiction. The assay must be embedded in a commercial infrastructure that can support large-scale deployment.

3.3.2 Technical validation

Validating a clinical assay requires extensive reproducibility studies under real-world conditions (different scanner, comparable patients). In addition to the assay itself, the quality assurance and manufacturing processes (hardware but also software development) must be tested and validated as well.

The demands on measurement accuracy are not necessarily more stringent than in clinical trials, but the measurement uncertainty now affects the specificity and sensitivity of the test rather than the statistical power of the trial.

3.3.3 Biological and clinical validation

The link to biology and relevant clinical outcomes should be largely proven after crossing the first translational gap and, therefore, plays less of a role in crossing the second gap. An argument for revisiting these aspects could potentially exist if correlations with biology and outcome are weak and technical validation studies demonstrated that the clinical assay is less accurate/precise than the prototypes used in medical research.

3.3.4 Clinical utility

Evidence of utility is essential to make a case for clinical application. An improved patient management strategy must be proposed using the biomarker, and a clinical trial must be performed to demonstrate that this new strategy improves outcome compared to standard of care. The major additional complication here is that the biomarker is now used to *modify* the treatment of patients in the intervention arm, and thus also carries the risk of negatively impacting on the outcome. Due to the need to demonstrate a difference between two strategies, the trials tend to be larger and last longer than those for clinical validation and are often beyond the reach of individual companies. Clinical utility studies, if positive, would normally be sufficiently strong to prompt guidelines from international advisory bodies such as the World Health Organization (WHO), or national bodies such as the National Institute for Health and Care Excellence (NICE) in the United Kingdom.

3.3.5 Cost-effectiveness

Cost-effectiveness for clinical practice involves assembling an evidence base to show that the cost of employing the MR biomarker test is outweighed by the improved health resulting from a better choice of treatment. This is a critical issue in the routine clinical use of QIBs. A routine blood-based biomarker such as hemoglobin or hematocrit may cost as little as a few euros. An MRI biomarker may carry a cost closer to a thousand euros, a difference of as much as two orders of magnitude. This means that the clinical benefit of the MRI biomarker must also be significantly higher for the trade-off to be cost-effective for healthcare systems. Cost-effectiveness studies should ultimately support reimbursement of the QIB by healthcare providers, which is necessary to enable to QIB to be used at scale.

4 Specific challenges in the development of MRI-based QIBs

The development of MRI-based imaging biomarkers poses specific challenges as compared to other types of biomarkers, including those derived from other imaging modalities such as nuclear medicine or computed tomography. Besides, there are important distinctions to be made between morphological (extensive) MRI biomarkers such as volumes or distances, or more functional (intensive) MRI biomarkers that can be measured for individual pixels and which are the focus of this book (relaxation times, fat fraction, perfusion, diffusion, and so on).

4.1 Technical validation

4.1.1 Specific challenges in technical validation of MRI-based QIBs

Achieving accurate, precise, and reproducible measurements of QIBs, and providing evidence of the accuracy, raises several particular challenges:

Complex (bio)physics: The complexity of the technology makes it difficult to understand, let alone quantify and control, all the different contributions to measurement error. This situation is different than for instance HbA1c (Appendix A), where the sources of error for the reference assays can be reliably modeled and propagated into the final result. Other biospecimen assays such as immunohistochemistry are also difficult to validate [47] but the physical basis of MRI in electromagnetic tissue properties is very different. This is also much more of an issue for intensive voxel-based biomarkers than for instance for lesion volume.

Realistic test objects: For most MRI QIBs, reliable reference methods do not exist. Hence verification of bias often has to rely on measurements in reference objects (phantoms) which represent highly idealized versions of reality that may significantly underestimate the actual bias. For blood-based biomarkers such as HbA1c (Appendix A), it is much more straightforward to build solutions with known concentrations that can be used to calibrate the assays.

Measuring with imaging devices: Assays for MRI QIBs in patients require data collection on devices (MRI scanners) that are designed to generate images with good visual quality, rather than perform accurate measurements. Since the history of MRI was built on qualitative analyses (unlike computed tomography), the equipment tolerances and quality checks are built on qualitative assessments as well. Building MRI scanners dedicated to quantification would require a redesign and possible compromises in image quality to obtain a transparent architecture where sources of error can be more easily understood, modeled, and propagated.

Controlling experimental conditions: The quality of a QIB measurement is largely determined by the site where the MR images are acquired. This makes quality assurance significantly more challenging compared to fluid-based biomarkers, where all of the critical processing is done in specialized labs under well-controlled conditions. In the case of QIBs, image processing can be performed centrally but this only controls for a small part of the overall uncertainty.

Traceability: QIB assays are more difficult to trace back to generally accepted standards. For blood-based biomarkers, it is sufficient to collect some extra blood, send it to a central reference laboratory, and compare the results with a local analysis. The equivalent experiment for a QIB would require the actual patient to travel to the reference laboratory, which is not only difficult to realize in practice but also leads to a risk of actual physiological changes taking place between the two measurements.

4.1.2 Specific solutions for technical validation of MRI QIBs

The specific challenges in technical validation of MRI-based QIBs often require a combination of experimental designs, each of which are insufficiently conclusive in isolation but when combined can add up to a compelling case if the evidence is aligned.

In vivo studies (human, stand-alone): Repeatability and reproducibility studies using volunteers *and* patients are essential for the validation of MRI-based QIBs. These studies involve assessing the variability of the measurement over repeated applications of the protocol on the same subjects on the same device (repeatability) and different devices, vendors, locations, and observers (reproducibility). These studies have the advantage that they are done on real subjects but they are also time-consuming, logistically challenging, and costly (especially reproducibility). Moreover, they only measure certain contributions to the measurement error, in particular, they do not capture bias. Finally, they are likely to overestimate the pure measurement error as actual physiological changes in QIBs are difficult to avoid when patients need to travel between sites for reproducibility assessment.

In vivo studies (human, integrated with clinical validation): Technical validation of QIBs in patients can sometimes be integrated into clinical validation studies by including a pilot phase with a repeatability arm. This setup may be preferred over a separate repeatability study when the results may not translate from healthy volunteers or between different patient populations. For instance, in renal MRI, biomarkers that involve cortical regions of interest are likely to be significantly more repeatable in healthy volunteers or early-stage patients than in more advanced disease due to the loss of cortico-medullary differentiation. From the analysis of the clinical results, this approach also has the advantage of providing measurement uncertainties under the exact conditions of the study. For multisite studies, reproducibility data should ideally be collected as well, though traveling patient data may be hard to obtain.

In vivo studies (animals): Animal experiments are generally less useful for the technical validation of human assays. When using dedicated small animal scanners, the assays are different from those deployed in humans, so the measurement uncertainty is not representative. In principle, animal experiments can be performed on clinical scanners, but even when larger animals are used the uncertainty may not translate well to humans. Animals need to be sedated for instance, but also the different anatomy and physiology can have an impact on the measurement error.

In vitro studies: Measurements on a test object with known ground truth values can be used to assess bias. On the downside, phantoms suffer from a lack of realism which may lead to a significant underestimation of the actual bias. For instance, a T_1 mapping sequence developed for the liver may yield highly accurate and precise measurements in a phantom, but these results may not hold up in a living and breathing subject. The opposite can also happen; for instance, breathing-compensated sequences involving a navigator signal may work well in vivo but poorly in a static phantom.

In silico studies: Computational modeling of subjects and/or measurement devices can involve digital reference objects (DROs) that range from simple analytical structures to complex microstructure simulations and digital anthropomorphic human phantoms. The simulation of the measurement process can involve full Monte-Carlo models that calculate the behavior of individual protons or some level of analytical modeling to reduce the computational demand. The advantage of in silico work is that a more complete range of the parameter space can be explored, and biases can be investigated in detail. On the downside, simulations tend to be highly simplified representations of the subject and assay that may not capture all relevant sources of error.

4.2 Biological validation

Biological validation creates the evidence base to show that a change in an MR biomarker faithfully reflects a change in the relevant biology (sensitivity), or that no change faithfully reflects no change in the relevant biology (specificity).

4.2.1 Specific challenges in biological validation of MRI-based QIBs

Biological validation of MRI-based QIBs is often challenging due to the significant conceptual distance to the biological phenomena of interest. The relationship between biological properties and those that can be measured with MRI crosses multiple scales and involves physical phenomena as diverse as biochemistry, biology, physiology, biomechanics, fluid dynamics, and electromagnetism. Gold-standard measurements or reference methods that could allow a purely experimental validation, are not often available or are equally limited.

A detailed mechanistic understanding of the relationships between MRI parameters and underlying biology is often lacking, and in general, multiple biological factors will affect the QIB. T_1 and T_2 relaxation times are classic examples. While they are known to be sensitive to changes in tissue caused by disease, they are generally unspecific in the sense that many different types of changes can cause an effect. The magnitude of the effects may be variable and will depend on organ and disease status, making them challenging to model in detail.

Formally biological validation may be unnecessary for regulatory or clinical acceptance, and it may be sufficient to provide clinical validation. However, without a proper understanding of QIB changes in biological terms, it may be difficult to put forward credible hypotheses for how a QIB will respond to treatment, change with disease progression, or differ between patients. And without credible hypotheses, it may be difficult to justify the significant investment required for clinical validation.

4.2.2 Specific solutions for biological validation of MRI QIBs

Biological validation is similar to technical validation in that it usually requires scientific judgment based on a portfolio of disparate evidence, none of which is definitive in isolation. Biological validation relies heavily on imaging-pathology correlations, which are often impractical in human subjects. Hence in this field, there is a major role for well-designed animal MR studies.

Bradford Hill's criteria for causation provide a useful framework for assembling and assessing an evidence base [4,48,49]. As an example, consider dynamic gadoxetate-enhanced MRI biomarkers of flux from the hepatocyte into bile canaliculi through dedicated transporters, relevant to drug-induced liver injury [50]. Bradford Hill's criteria could be used in the following way to assemble a biological validation evidence base:

I. *Coherence*: Is there a relationship between the MR biomarker and the supposed underlying biochemical or pathologic correlate? In our example, there are known transporter polymorphisms with functional consequences. When humans with functionally different transporter genotypes were imaged, the expected rank differences in imaging biomarker values were seen [51].

II. *Experiment (intervention)*: When drug intervention changes the MR biomarker, does the corresponding biochemical or pathologic measurement change likewise? For the drug developer, this is often an animal experiment, particularly for novel pharmaceuticals were, by definition, no human data are describing the response of the MR biomarker to the drug at the outset. Examples of this type of evidence are the change of the MR biomarker observed in response to known inhibitors such as estradiol-17β-D-glucuronide [52] or rifampicin [53], or response to an investigational agent with known hepatotoxicity [50].

III. *Biological gradient (dose-response)*: Is there a dose-response for the drug-induced changes in the MR biomarker, and does the corresponding biochemical or pathologic measurement follow the same dose-response? Here again animal studies can be compelling, as in a rat study where increasing doses of investigational drug-induced increasing changes in the imaging biomarker with concomitant dose-dependent effects on other biomarkers [50].

IV. *Specificity*: Is the MR biomarker negative where the underlying biology is missing? In our example, specificity evidence is provided by the delayed efflux of gadoxetate in rats that lack the specific transporters [54].

V. *Consistency*: Can the findings be replicated by different investigators, in different labs, perhaps with different animal models or clinical cohorts? In our example, transporter inhibition by rifampicin was found to be quantitatively similar in different laboratories providing evidence that the biomarker is generalizable [53].

Such an assessment of the biological validity of an MR biomarker in the Bradford Hill style is usually instructive and can highlight critical gaps in the evidence base.

4.3 Assay development

4.3.1 MRI biomarker assays for medical research

An assay for a QIB in clinical trials involves more than a scan protocol and some processing software, and also includes several processes that are essential to ensure the quality of the output. Site setup, image analysis, and quality assurance of QIBs in medical research are often performed by an independent central MRI facility or core lab. Depending on the size and geographical location of the trial, an imaging protocol must be developed and validated to deploy it at several sites and globally in mind.

The main activity of the central imaging facility is to set up the sites where the data are collected, verify that they produce data conform with the required standard (*site qualification*), and provide ongoing support and quality assurance during the trial. Table 4 lists some key steps that are typically performed by the central lab for the setup and qualification of sites.

A second key activity of the central imaging facility is to perform central image processing and interpretation. While technically speaking this can be performed by training local analysts on-site, in trials, it is often desirable (and required by regulators) to perform these activities centrally. Since the central imaging facility has no other involvement in the trial, this will ensure that there is no bias and/or external influence in the assessment of the images and interpretation of the results. Besides, image analysis and quality control are not likely to be automated at this stage, and a centralized reading provides more control over the quality of the outputs. Table 5 list the processes for image interpretation that are typically implemented in the central imaging facility.

The imaging charter [56] is a formal document that details the image acquisition, analysis methodology, reader paradigm, roles, and responsibility of the various parties in the trial, and so on. The charter is developed in conjunction with the sponsor and typically covers the following sections:

- *Image acquisition and collection*: Basic information on modality, anatomical coverage, a summary of views acquired, and time-point details, concerning the imaging manual containing comprehensive information on acquisition parameters.
- *Receipt, tracking, and quality control of imaging data*: Data submission procedure, tracking of data, query generation, quality control.

Table 4 Key steps in the setup and qualification of sites for multicenter clinical trials.

Activity	Description
Imaging hardware assessment	The magnet, software (and version), gradients, and coils need to be reviewed to ensure that all sites can deliver data with between-site reproducibility adequate for the trial. It is also important to ensure that in the unfortunate event that the magnet or other critical hardware (such as the coils) must be replaced in the course of the clinical trial, any effects on quantitation can be corrected.
MRI scanner setup	The MRI acquisition protocol has to be robust and fairly easy to implement without compromising the objectives and endpoints of the trial. In global clinical trials, language translation requirements also have to be taken into account. For more complex protocols, specialists from the central MRI facility may need to travel to the sites to assist in setting up the protocol on the scanner and performing essential testing.
Site personnel experience	The site personnel conducting the MRI must be assessed to make sure they have the relevant qualifications and experience to perform the imaging for the trial.
Training of MRI personnel	Training can be accomplished through self-training on the web or an instructor-led remote training of the clinical sites by the central imaging facility. In certain cases, face-to-face training may be needed. The training may need to be held in conjunction with a language translator when working with sites where the language is different from that of the sponsor.
Image storage and archiving	Clinical sites must have secure storage and image archiving facility, as the original data needs to be stored at the sites per the requirements of the regulatory authority (FDA, EMA, etc.).
Image submission	It is preferred that clinical sites submit the data to the central MRI facility through the web, as this saves time and cost. Courier submission of disks or data on external drives is also acceptable. In all cases, the transmission protocol must strip the personally identifiable information from the images [55] before the submission of data to the central facility.
Imaging manual production	The central MRI facility must provide an imaging manual to all the clinical sites in the trial. This document must include detailed information about the image acquisition protocol (e.g., list of MRI sequences, parameters, etc.) for the clinical trial.
Site qualification	In general, sites are asked to submit test data to the independent central MRI facility for assessment before scanning the first patient at the site. This is to make sure that the site is acquiring images to the specifications stipulated in the trial. If the test data pass the quality control step, then the site is considered qualified to start scanning real subjects in the trial. The test data can be from a healthy volunteer using the MRI sequence stipulated in the imaging manual for the trial.
Ongoing quality assurance	In studies involving the collection of QIBs, it is often necessary that regular testing is performed at the sites with standardized phantoms, and the resulting images sent to the central MRI facility for review.

- *Design and methodology of independent review*: Analysis procedure, reader roles, including adjudication; reader training process and validation; intra- and interreader variability assessment.
- *Data management*: Database setup and maintenance, data transfer procedure to sponsor and/or third parties, data storage, and backup, image transfer to third parties.

Table 5 Processes implemented in the central imaging facility of a multicenter trial.

Process	Description
Reading system rollout	The central reading (or image processing) system is configured to the needs of the clinical trial and goes through a thorough testing and validation procedure, and changes are documented through a change management process. In general, scoring criteria are built into the reading system.
Reader experience	Experienced readers or image analysts in the particular disease area of the trial (e.g., osteoarthritis in musculoskeletal imaging, multiple sclerosis in neuroimaging, etc.) are employed in the trial.
Reader training	The readers go through extensive training on test cases; the training is monitored and a record kept of the training date. On training completion, this is signed-off by each reader and the trainer
Reader variability assessment	During the trial, readers' performance (intra- and interreader) is monitored on a routine basis and can also involve 2 + 1 reader paradigm: i.e., 2 primary readers and an adjudicator. Where significant reader deviations are noted, retraining of readers is conducted. Throughout the clinical trial, an audit trail is maintained of the reader activity.
Data management	The results of the image analyses are collated, formatted per the specifications agreed with the sponsor, and then transferred to the sponsor of the clinical trial as a cumulative or incremental transfer and on a frequency (e.g., monthly, quarterly, final transfers) agreed with the sponsor. At the end of the study, the database is locked and archived per the regulatory requirements.
Quality assurance	Data acquired at the clinical sites need to be submitted in a timely fashion so they can be quality controlled. If needed, corrective action can then be taken swiftly, especially when the baseline acquisition against which change is computed is a critical time point that needs to be monitored closely. Sites need to be provided with prompt feedback on the quality of scans, and if there is a quality failure the site may be asked to repeat the scan over a certain limited time window.

4.3.2 MRI biomarker assays for clinical practice

It is not uncommon that novel QIBs are first rolled out within individual clinical institutions through in-house development. Often this takes place in institutes that were involved in clinical validation or clinical utility studies or served as a central imaging facility in a trial. The situation is comparable to the use of physician-modified surgical devices [57], or generally the introduction of novel surgical techniques [58]. However, in the long run, successful clinical deployment of QIBs requires a commercialization strategy that can support a roll-out on a global, population-level scale. Usually, this will require some redesign of the assay as it is used in clinical trials, which is usually highly centralized and, therefore, may not scale well to clinical practice.

The inventor of a new imaging diagnostic needs to decide at an early stage on the business model for commercializing the new imaging biomarker, as this dictates the design of the assay and, therefore, setup of the validation studies. Different models are possible, ranging from a fully centralized service model similar to clinical trials where a licensed provider installs the scanner, performs QA, analyses the data centrally and returns a report; to a minimally centralized model where local sites purchase software and training materials to measure the QIBs locally as part of the image acquisition process. The developer must also consider whether the product can be sold or licensed to an imaging equipment vendor or a vendor-neutral diagnostic company. The optimal model depends on considerations such as the sensitivity of the measurements to common variations such as scanner drift or observer effects, the practical feasibility of central/local analysis, the need for dedicated hardware such as calibration devices, or reliance on custom-made MRI sequences.

IP protection is a separate consideration in the choice of business model. The validation of new biomarkers is an expensive and time-consuming process. If the work is being conducted by a company, that company may want to protect the commercial value of its investment by delaying the use of the new biomarker by competitors. However, in Europe and the United States diagnostic methods are not eligible for patenting. Instead, IP can potentially be protected by patenting certain technical aspects of the invention, keeping parts of the technique private, or ownership of a database of images or results with which new images can be compared to establish a diagnosis (for example, using machine learning approaches). Another option is that the biomarker can be made openly available and protected by maintaining know-how so that potential competitors find it difficult to enter the field.

5 Summary

The starting point of this chapter was the significant gap that continues to exist between the discovery of novel QIBs and assays and their use in clinical decision making. This problem is also recognized in other types of biomarkers. Sullivan et al. [38] cite a commentary by Poste in 2011 [59] calling for "a coordinated 'big science' approach" to replace the "dismal patchwork of fragmented research on disease-associated biomarkers." Poste was referring to biomarkers in body tissues and fluids, and supported his case with a frightening statistic: "technologies such as proteomics and DNA microarrays have contributed a voluminous literature of more than 150,000 papers documenting thousands of claimed biomarkers, but fewer than 100 have been validated for routine clinical practice." This constitutes 1500 papers, or the equivalent of >4 years of *Magnetic Resonance in Medicine* publications, for each biomarker in clinical use.

These are statistics that should concern researchers working in MRI-based QIBs. While there are too few QIBs in widespread use to make a meaningful comparison, it is clear that translating MRI QIBs is significantly more challenging than translating biomarkers derived from blood or urine. MRI-based QIBs are expensive to develop and measure and, therefore, the impact on patient outcomes must be proportionally higher to achieve a cost-effective trade-off. They are difficult to validate clinically due to the complex relationship between the biomarker and the underlying biology. Moreover, they are hard to validate technically because of the complexity of the acquisition/postprocessing methods, the lack of reference measurements, and the fact that accuracy and quality need to be controlled on-site with equipment and facilities that are not designed for quantitative measurement.

Despite these challenges, it is clear that MRI-based QIBs have significant potential to impact patient management. Like all QIBs, they have the massive advantage of being able to characterize disease or treatment effects in the tissue itself, noninvasively and in high spatial detail across the entire organ or body area investigated. MRI in particular is unique among all other modalities in the rich spectrum of soft tissue properties that can be characterized. To realize this potential, MRI researchers must be conscious of the long road that remains to be traveled after the initial discovery of the new contrast mechanism, or the development of the new acquisition sequence, modeling approach, or image analysis method. *Translating these exciting discoveries into clinical impact will require a long-term collaborative mindset where the proof-of-concept study is seen as the start, rather than the endpoint, of an intensive program of translational research.*

Acknowledgments

The authors would like to thank Dr. Jonathan Taylor (sheffield3dlab.com) for helpful input on the approval of in-house methods for local clinical use.

Appendix A: A case study in biospecimen biomarker translation

It is insightful for researchers in quantitative MRI to study examples of more traditional biochemical markers. They define much of the language and processes of biomarker development and often set the standard for other types of biomarkers. Many are in routine clinical practice, producing a rich body of experience on the challenges faced in biomarker translation. In this section, we will discuss as an example of the development of HbA1c or glycated hemoglobin. HbA1c was discovered in the 1950s [60] and today is routinely used in the diagnosis and management of diabetes mellitus [61].

Development of HbA1c involved all levels of validation, though like many other biospecimen biomarkers this has not progressed along the stages of the imaging biomarker roadmap (Fig. 3). Nevertheless, the example is useful for those working in imaging biomarkers, as it covers the full roadmap from discovery to widespread clinical use, and involves the setup of an international network of reference laboratories.

A.1 Biological validation

In the late 1970s it was demonstrated that HbA1c was produced by the binding of glucose to Hb and that this binding was an *irreversible* and *slow* process [62]. This implies that the concentration of HbA1c in the blood is indicative of average glucose (AG) levels over the 120-day life span of the red blood cell (RBC). Independent clinical evidence for this link derives from observations in the late 1960s that HbA1c is elevated in patients with diabetes [63,64] and clinical studies in the 1970s demonstrating a close relationship between glucose control and HbA1c levels [65,66].

The precise quantitative relationship between HbA1c levels and AG is more difficult to pin down, an issue which illustrates that biological validation is a continuous process of refinement. A key problem is the effect of variations in the RBC life span, which can alter HbA1c values independent of AG [67,68]. Empirical conversions to an estimated AG [69] are, therefore, not currently recommended [70] and AG measurement remains an active area of research.

A.2 Clinical validation

A measure of AG is clinically useful because many of the long-term complications in diabetes are caused by elevated AG. HbA1c assays, therefore, became clinically available in the late 1970s, but the biomarker was not universally adopted in the 1980s [71] due to issues with the early assays, difficulties in relating the data to known measurements of glucose control, and absence of clear benchmarks to inform management. These problems were overcome in the 1990s, after the first large-scale studies in Type 1 [72] and Type 2 Diabetes [73] demonstrated a clear link between HbA1c levels and long-term complications.

As a result, HbA1c was firmly established in the management of patients with diabetes mellitus by the late 1990s. The evidence of these two studies also led to the acceptance of HbA1c as a surrogate endpoint for clinical trials [7], which means that regulators can approve drugs based on evidence that they lower HbA1c. As a result, there is no need to evidence an impact on long-term hard outcomes, which can dramatically reduce the cost of drug development and lead to increased treatment options for patients.

A.3 Technical validation

A wide range of assays has been developed to measure the amount of HbA1c in the blood [74]. By the end of the 1990s, various assays had become established, generating results that were not comparable between labs, or between countries with different national standards [75]. While such systematic differences were less of an issue when HbA1c was used for monitoring individual patients over time, they formed a hard barrier to the adoption of HbA1c as a diagnostic or screening tool, which relies on a single measurement.

In 1998, the International Federation of Clinical Chemistry and Laboratory Medicine (IFCC) developed a new reference method that was adopted as an international standard in 2002 [76]. However, implementing the new standard was challenging due to the risk that new numerical values might lead to inappropriate management decisions. A consensus meeting in 2007 [77], therefore, recommended that HbA1c should be reported for both the IFCC assay as for the widely used alternative NGSP assay, using different units to avoid any possible risk of confusion (millimole/milliliter and percentage, respectively). Because both are very strongly correlated by a known linear conversion, only one must be measured [78].

A.4 Clinical utility as a diagnostic

As a result of the efforts in developing a global standard, the World Health Organization (WHO) recommended in 2011 "that HbA1c can be used as a diagnostic test for diabetes, provided that stringent quality assurance tests are in place and assays are standardized to criteria aligned to the international reference values,. . ." Specifically, an HbA1c of 48 mmol/mol (6.5%) is recommended as the cut-off point for diagnosing diabetes [79]. As a result of these and other endorsements, the first diagnostic HbA1c laboratory assays were approved by the FDA in 2013, and the first point-of-care diagnostics for patients at risk of developing diabetes in 2018. Over 60 years after its original discovery, HbA1c is today becoming a cornerstone in the diagnosis and management of diabetes [60].

Appendix B: A case study in imaging biomarker translation

Total Kidney Volume (TKV) is an extensive variable and was the first imaging biomarker to be formally qualified by the FDA, and thus far still the only one. It is categorized as a prognostic biomarker (with a specific context of use described in the following section) and was approved by the EMA in November 2015 [32] and the Food and Drug Administration [80,81] in September 2016.

The qualification of TKV is a success story in imaging biomarker development and evidences the impact that can be achieved if all stakeholders join forces and coordinate their efforts. TKV development has broadly followed the stages of the imaging biomarker roadmap (Fig. 3), though the second translational gap is not yet fully crossed.

B.1 Discovery and proof of concept

Autosomal dominant polycystic kidney disease (ADPKD) is the most common inherited kidney disease and the fourth leading cause of kidney failure worldwide [82]. It is characterized by the progressive development and growth of renal cysts over decades which leads to increased TKV and ultimately kidney failure in 50% of patients by their fifth decade [83]. Similar to other chronic kidney diseases, clinically progression of ADPKD is monitored by kidney blood tests (estimated glomerular filtration (eGFR)) despite their limitations [83,84]. However, in ADPKD, normal (preserved) eGFR falsely implies initial disease stability [85], because the kidneys compensate by glomerular hyperfiltration [83], despite the insidious disease progression indicated by the simultaneous increase in TKV [86]. Indeed, kidney blood tests have been shown to remain near normal in ADPKD until kidneys grow to approximately five times normal size [87].

There is longstanding evidence of the clinical relevance of increased TKV [88] and its inverse correlation with kidney function since first described in 43 patients using computed tomography (CT) in 1981 [89]. Different imaging modalities (ultrasound, CT, and MRI) for measuring TKV have been reported. In 2000, two small (9–10 patients) longitudinal studies (5–8 years) used CT to measure TKV (including assessing accuracy and reproducibility) as a surrogate measure of progression in ADPKD [90,91]. They identified that TKV increased annually in ADPKD, and the rate of increase correlated with the rate of decline in kidney function (eGFR). Furthermore, in 2001–02, two large (182 and 229 patients) longitudinal (8 and 20 years) studies using ultrasound identified that the rate of increase in TKV was exponential, correlated with hypertension [92], and confirmed the association with reduced eGFR [93].

B.2 Crossing the first translational gap

In the early 2000s, the PKD community was prompted to collaboratively work together to establish TKV as a prognostic biomarker in clinical trials. New treatments were too slow to be approved because (a) blood tests are insufficient to identify the patients that are rapidly progressing and, therefore, can benefit from more aggressive management, and (b) trials that require hard endpoints can take decades in early-stage patients.

In 2003, the NIH sponsored the Consortium for Radiologic Imaging Studies of Polycystic Kidney Disease (CRISP) to accurately and reliably measure TKV, detect small changes in TKV over time (annual MRI for 3 years), and identify if an increase in TKV was associated with a decline in measured GFR. This was a large (241 young patients with early kidney disease) multicenter [4] study and included reproducibility studies using phantoms and patients on 1.5 T scanners from different models or manufacturers [94]. Key findings reported in 2006 were that TKV measurement was 99.9% reliable, increased at a rate of 5.3% per year, increased with age and hypertension, and correlated with declining measured GFR [87].

This collective evidence supported the first meeting between the PKD Foundation (PKDF) and the FDA in 2007 to discuss the process of validating kidney growth (TKV) as an endpoint for PKD clinical trials. In 2008, it was recommended that a PKD clinical database be established to combine data and evidence from different registries and trials and used to simulate the design of clinical trials to detect progression [86]. To enable evidence collected in various formats to be interpreted and analyzed, a formal Clinical Data Interchange Standards Consortium (CDISC) data standards for PKD had to be created [86]; this was undertaken between 2009 and 2013. The result was a combined dataset of 2355 patients with ADPKD who have at least one TKV measurement.

In 2010, PKD Outcomes Consortium (PKDOC) was established to continue to generate evidence and facilitate the qualification of TKV as a prognostic biomarker for use in clinical trials in ADPKD. PKDOC was a collaboration of the PKDF, FDA, Critical Path Institute (C-Path), Clinical Data Interchange Standards Consortium (CDISC), PKD expert clinicians and scientists, pharmaceutical companies, and patients. In 2011, discussions focused on the "context of use" for TKV to propose in the LOI. In January 2012, following support from the FDA to proceed, PKDOC submitted the LOI to qualify TKV as a prognostic biomarker for patient selection for clinical trials. The context of use was for baseline TKV to be a prognostic biomarker, in combination with age and eGFR, to predict patients at high risk of progression and enrich clinical trial populations with patients who may demonstrate a response to a novel treatment.

The LOI was accepted by the FDA and they requested a qualification plan/briefing document describing ADPKD and the need for a biomarker and detailing the clinical evidence (submitted September 2012). Further discussions and revisions in 2013 led to the final submission to the FDA in September 2013. While the outcome of the FDA was awaited, using their experience, the PKDOC submitted a similar LOI to the EMA and following acceptance, a qualification plan/briefing document in April 2013. Queries from the EMA were addressed in June and the final submission made in July 2013. Final approval of TKV as a prognostic imaging biomarker by the EMA was in November 2015 and the FDA in September 2016.

Although a considerable volume of evidence, multidisciplinary collaboration, and negotiation with regulatory agencies were required for over 15 years to achieve the qualification of TKV, this success will benefit patients by facilitating the process of identifying effective evidence-based therapies to delay disease progression.

B.3 Crossing the second translational gap

The qualification of TKV by FDA and EMA has proven to be a major driver for use in clinical practice. The efforts to qualify TKV coincided with the introduction of a new treatment, tolvaptan, which slows the progression of the disease but is also associated with common adverse events [95]. A Phase III trial on the efficacy of tolvaptan, TEMPO 3:4, selected participants based on their TKV and also used TKV change as a primary endpoint [96]. The trial demonstrated that tolvaptan slowed the increase of TKV and the decline in kidney function, and was the basis for formal guidance and reimbursement of tolvaptan to patients with evidence of rapidly progressing disease [97].

Due to potential issues of access to MRI, the guidance stopped short of recommending MRI-based TKV as the means of determining whether the disease was rapidly progressing. Nevertheless, the result has sparked an effort the develop simpler and automated means to determine TKV from MRI images [98,99]. Today some specialized healthcare institutions offer TKV in local clinical practice [100,101], but a widely available commercial service is still lacking.

References

[1] Kessler LG, Barnhart HX, Buckler AJ, Choudhury KR, Kondratovich MV, Toledano A, et al. The emerging science of quantitative imaging biomarkers terminology and definitions for scientific studies and regulatory submissions. Stat Methods Med Res 2015;24(1):9–26.

[2] Lauterbur PC. Image formation by induced local interactions: examples employing nuclear magnetic resonance. Nature 1973;242(5394):190–1.

[3] Weisman ID, Bennett LH, Maxwell LR, Woods MW, Burk D. Recognition of cancer in vivo by nuclear magnetic resonance. Science 1972;178(4067):1288–90.

[4] O'Connor JPB, Aboagye EO, Adams JE, Aerts HJWL, Barrington SF, Beer AJ, et al. Imaging biomarker roadmap for cancer studies. Nat Rev Clin Oncol 2017;14(3):169–86.

[5] Leach MO. Screening with magnetic resonance imaging and mammography of a UK population at high familial risk of breast cancer: a prospective multicentre cohort study (MARIBS). Lancet 2005; 365(9473):1769–78.

[6] Carini C, Seyhan AA, Fidock MD, van Gool AJ. Definitions and conceptual framework of biomarkers in precision medicine. In: Handbook of biomarkers and precision medicine. 2019. p. 2–7.

[7] Amur S, Becker RL, Chakravarty AG, Cho DS, Faris O, Fitzpatrick S, et al. BEST (Biomarkers, EndpointS, and other Tools) resource, Silver Spring, MD/Bethesda, MD: Food and Drug Administration (US)/National Institutes of Health (US); 2016. Available from: https://www.ncbi.nlm.nih.gov/books/NBK338449/.

[8] Arnold ME, Booth B, King L, Ray C. Workshop report: crystal city VI—bioanalytical method validation for biomarkers. AAPS J 2016;18(6):1366–72.

[9] QIBA metrology papers, [cited 2 March 2020]; Available from:https://www.rsna.org/en/research/quantitative-imaging-biomarkers-alliance/metrology-papers; 2014.

[10] Barentsz JO, Richenberg J, Clements R, Choyke P, Verma S, Villeirs G, et al. ESUR prostate MR guidelines 2012. Eur Radiol 2012;22(4):746–57.

[11] Dietrich O, Raya JG, Reeder SB, Reiser MF, Schoenberg SO. Measurement of signal-to-noise ratios in MR images: influence of multichannel coils, parallel imaging, and reconstruction filters. J Magn Reson Imaging 2007;26(2):375–85.

[12] Wang Y, Liu T. Quantitative susceptibility mapping (QSM): decoding MRI data for a tissue magnetic biomarker. Magn Reson Med 2015;73(1):82–101.

[13] Parent MJ, Zimmer ER, Shin M, Kang MS, Fonov VS, Mathieu A, et al. Multimodal imaging in rat model recapitulates Alzheimer's disease biomarkers abnormalities. J Neurosci 2017;37(50):12263–71.

[14] Gunadasa-Rohling M, Masters M, Maguire ML, Smart SC, Schneider JE, Riley PR. Magnetic resonance imaging of the regenerating neonatal mouse heart. Circulation 2018;138(21):2439–41.

[15] Gooding KM, Lienczewski C, Papale M, Koivuviita N, Maziarz M, Andersson A-MD, et al. Prognostic imaging biomarkers for diabetic kidney Disease (iBEAt): study protocol, medRxiv 2020. https://doi.org/10.1101/2020.01.13.20017228v1. Available from: https://www.medrxiv.org/content/10.1101/2020.01.13.20017228v1.

[16] DiMasi JA, Grabowski HG, Hansen RW. Innovation in the pharmaceutical industry: new estimates of R&D costs. J Health Econ 2016;47:20–33.

[17] Murphy PS, TJ MC, ASK D-J. The role of clinical imaging in oncological drug development. Br J Radiol 2008;81:685–92.

[18] Drevs J, Siegert P, Medinger M, Mross K, Strecker R, Zirrgiebel U, et al. Phase I clinical study of AZD2171, an oral vascular endothelial growth factor signaling inhibitor, in patients with advanced solid tumors. J Clin Oncol 2007;25(21):3045–54.

[19] Evelhoch JL. In vivo MR in the drug pipeline. J Magn Reson 2018;292:117–28.

[20] Bolinder J, Ljunggren Ö, Kullberg J, Johansson L, Wilding J, Langkilde AM, et al. Effects of dapagliflozin on body weight, total fat mass, and regional adipose tissue distribution in patients with type 2 diabetes mellitus with inadequate glycemic control on metformin. J Clin Endocrinol Metab 2012;97(3):1020–31.

[21] FDA. Innovation or stagnation: Challenge and opportunity on the critical path to new medical products. Available from: http://wayback.archive-it.org/7993/20180125035500/https://www.fda.gov/downloads/ScienceResearch/SpecialTopics/CriticalPathInitiative/CriticalPathOpportunitiesReports/UCM113411.pdf; 2004.

[22] Barkhof F, Daams M, Scheltens P, Brashear HR, Arrighi HM, Bechten A, et al. An MRI rating scale for amyloid-related imaging abnormalities with edema or effusion. Am J Neuroradiol 2013;1550–5.

[23] Zimran A, Wajnrajch M, Hernandez B, Pastores GM. Taliglucerase alfa: safety and efficacy across 6 clinical studies in adults and children with Gaucher disease. Orphanet J Rare Dis 2018;13.

[24] St. Pierre TG, Clark PR, Chua-Anusorn W, Fleming AJ, Jeffrey GP, Olynyk JK, et al. Noninvasive measurement and imaging of liver iron concentrations using proton magnetic resonance. Blood 2005;105(2):855–61.

[25] Waterton JC. Incorporating predictive imaging biomarkers in clinical trials for personalised healthcare. In: Handbook of biomarkers and precision medicine. 2019.

[26] Iversen P, McLeod DG, See WA, Morris T, Armstrong J, Wirth MP. Antiandrogen monotherapy in patients with localized or locally advanced prostate cancer: final results from the bicalutamide early prostate cancer programme at a median follow-up of 9.7 years. BJU Int 2010;105(8):1074–81.

[27] Dickerson BC, Stoub TR, Shah RC, Sperling RA, Killiany RJ, Albert MS, et al. Alzheimer-signature MRI biomarker predicts AD dementia in cognitively normal adults. Neurology 2011;76(16):1395–402.

[28] Buckler AJ, Bresolin L, Dunnick NR, Sullivan DC. Quantitative imaging test approval and biomarker qualification: interrelated but distinct activities. Radiology 2011;259(3):875–84.

[29] Food and Drug Administration. Drug Development Tool (DDT) Qualification Programs, [cited 27 February 2020]; Available from: https://www.fda.gov/drugs/development-approval-process-drugs/drug-development-tool-ddt-qualification-programs; 2020.

[30] FDA. CDER biomarker qualification program, [cited 28 February 2020]; Available from: https://www.fda.gov/drugs/developmentapprovalprocess/drugdevelopmenttoolsqualificationprogram/biomarkerqualificationprogram/default.htm; 2018.

[31] EMA. Qualification of novel methodologies for medicine development, [cited 28 February 2020]; Available from: https://www.ema.europa.eu/en/human-regulatory/research-development/scientific-advice-protocol-assistance/qualification-novel-methodologies-medicine-development; 2018.

[32] EMA. Qualification opinion Total Kidney Volume (TKV) as a prognostic biomarker for use in clinical trials evaluating patients with Autosomal Dominant Polycystic Kidney Disease (ADPKD), Available from: https://www.ema.europa.eu/en/documents/regulatory-procedural-guideline/qualification-opinion-total-kidney-volume-tkv-prognostic-biomarker-use-clinical-trials-evaluating_en.pdf; 2015.

[33] CDER-Biomarker Qualification Program. List of qualified biomarkers, [cited 6 August 2019]; Available from: https://www.fda.gov/drugs/cder-biomarker-qualification-program/list-qualified-biomarkers; 2019.

[34] FDA. Biomarker qualification submissions, [cited 17 March 2020]; Available from: https://www.fda.gov/drugs/cder-biomarker-qualification-program/biomarker-qualification-submissions.

[35] Lang RM, Badano LP, Mor-Avi V, Afilalo J, Armstrong A, Ernande L, et al. Recommendations for cardiac chamber quantification by echocardiography in adults: an update from the American society of echocardiography and the European association of cardiovascular imaging. Eur Heart J Cardiovasc Imaging 2015;16(3):233–71.

[36] FDA. The 510(k) program: Evaluating substantial equivalence in premarket notifications [510(k)], Available from: https://www.fda.gov/media/82395/download; 2014.

[37] Health Facilities Scotland. Health institution exemption, [cited 17 March 2020]; Available from: http://www.hfs.scot.nhs.uk/services/incident-reporting-and-investigation-centre-iric/health-institution-exemption/; 2020.

[38] Sullivan DC, Obuchowski NA, Kessler LG, Raunig DL, Gatsonis C, Huang EP, et al. Metrology standards for quantitative imaging biomarkers. Radiology 2015;277(3):813–25.

[39] Sung NS, Crowley WF, Genel M, Salber P, Sandy L, Sherwood LM, et al. Central challenges facing the national clinical research enterprise. J Am Med Assoc 2003;289:1278–87.

[40] Cooksey D. A review of UK health research funding, Available from: https://www.gov.uk/government/publications/a-review-of-uk-health-research-funding; 2006.

[41] Waterton JC. Translational magnetic resonance imaging and spectroscopy: opportunities and challenges, In: New applications of NMR in drug discovery and development. The Royal Society of Chemistry; 2013. p. 336–60. Available from: https://doi.org/10.1039/9781849737661-00333.

[42] Friedli I, Crowe LA, Viallon M, Porter DA, Martin PY, de Seigneux S, et al. Improvement of renal diffusion-weighted magnetic resonance imaging with readout-segmented echo-planar imaging at 3T. Magn Reson Imaging 2015;33(6):701–8.
[43] Berchtold L, Friedli I, Crowe LA, Martinez C, Moll S, Hadaya K, et al. Validation of the corticomedullary difference in magnetic resonance imaging-derived apparent diffusion coefficient for kidney fibrosis detection: a cross-sectional study. Nephrol Dial Transplant 2020;35(6):937–45.
[44] Berchtold L, Crowe LA, Friedli I, Legouis D, Moll S, de Perrot T, et al. Diffusion magnetic resonance imaging detects an increase in interstitial fibrosis earlier than the decline of renal function. Nephrol Dial Transplant 2020. Available from: https://doi.org/10.1093/ndt/gfaa007.
[45] Szczepaniak LS, Nurenberg P, Leonard D, Browning JD, Reingold JS, Grundy S, et al. Magnetic resonance spectroscopy to measure hepatic triglyceride content: prevalence of hepatic steatosis in the general population. Am J Physiol Endocrinol Metab 2005;288:E462–8.
[46] Powers WJ, Rabinstein AA, Ackerson T, Adeoye OM, Bambakidis NC, Becker K, et al. Guidelines for the early management of patients with acute ischemic stroke: 2019 update to the 2018 guidelines for the early management of acute ischemic stroke a guideline for healthcare professionals from the American Heart Association/American Stroke A. Stroke 2019;50:E344–418.
[47] Fitzgibbons PL, Linda AB, Lisa AF, Alsabeh R, Regan SF, Jeffrey DG, et al. Principles of analytic validation of immunohistochemical assays: guideline from the College of American Pathologists Pathology and Laboratory Quality Center. Arch Pathol Lab Med 2014;138(11):1432–43.
[48] Hill AB. The environment and disease: association or causation? Proc R Soc Med 1965;58(5):295–300. Available from: https://pubmed.ncbi.nlm.nih.gov/14283879.
[49] Chetty RK, Ozer JS, Lanevschi A, Schuppe-Koistinen I, McHale D, Pears JS, et al. A systematic approach to preclinical and clinical safety biomarker qualification incorporating Bradford hill's principles of causality association. Clin Pharmacol Ther 2010;88:260–2.
[50] Ulloa JL, Stahl S, Yates J, Woodhouse N, Kenna JG, Jones HB, et al. Assessment of gadoxetate DCE-MRI as a biomarker of hepatobiliary transporter inhibition. NMR Biomed 2013;26(10):1258–70.
[51] Nassif A, Jia J, Keiser M, Oswald S, Modess C, Nagel S, et al. Visualization of hepatic uptake transporter function in healthy subjects by using gadoxetic acid-enhanced MR imaging. Radiology 2012; 264(3):741–50.
[52] Ulloa J, Stahl S, Liess C, Bright J, McDermott A, Woodhouse N, et al. Effects of a single intravenous dose of Estradiol-17B D-glucuronide on biliary excretion: assessment with gadoxetate DCEMRI. In: Proceedings 18th scientific meeting, international society for magnetic resonance in medicine; 2010. p. 2593.
[53] Karageorgis A, Lenhard SC, Yerby B, Forsgren MF, Liachenko S, Johansson E, et al. A multi-center preclinical study of gadoxetate DCE-MRI in rats as a biomarker of drug induced inhibition of liver transporter function. PLoS ONE 2018;13(5).
[54] Saito S, Obata A, Kashiwagi Y, Abe K, Murase K. Dynamic contrast-enhanced MRI of the liver in mrp2-deficient rats using the hepatobiliary contrast agent Gd-EOB-DTPA. Investig Radiol 2013;48:548–53.
[55] Freymann JB, Kirby JS, Perry JH, Clunie DA, Jaffe CC. Image data sharing for biomedical research—meeting HIPAA requirements for de-identification. J Digit Imaging 2012;25(1):14–24.
[56] FDA. Clinical trial imaging endpoint process standards guidance for industry. Available from: https://www.fda.gov/media/81172/download; 2018.
[57] Starnes BW. A surgeon's perspective regarding the regulatory, compliance, and legal issues involved with physician-modified devices. J Vasc Surg 2013;57(3):829–31.
[58] Strong VE, Forde KA, MacFadyen BV, Mellinger JD, Crookes PF, Sillin LF, et al. Ethical considerations regarding the implementation of new technologies and techniques in surgery. Surg Endosc 2014;28:2272–6.
[59] Poste G. Bring on the biomarkers. Nature 2011;469:156–7.
[60] Allen DW, Schroeder WA, Balog J. Observations on the chromatographic heterogeneity of normal adult and fetal human hemoglobin: a study of the effects of crystallization and chromatography on the heterogeneity and isoleucine content. J Am Chem Soc 1958;80(7):1628–34.

[61] Gillery P. A history of HbA 1c through clinical chemistry and laboratory medicine. Clin Chem Lab Med 2013;51:65–74.
[62] Dolhofer R, Wieland OH. In vitro glycosylation of hemoglobins by different sugars and sugar phosphates. FEBS Lett 1978;85(1):86–90.
[63] Rahbar S. An abnormal hemoglobin in red cells of diabetics. Clin Chim Acta 1968;22(2):296–8.
[64] Trivelli LA, Ranney HM, Lai HT. Hemoglobin components in patients with diabetes mellitus. N Engl J Med 1971;284(7):353–7.
[65] Koenig RJ, Peterson CM, Jones RL, Saudek C, Lehrman M, Cerami A. Correlation of glucose regulation and hemoglobin AIc in diabetes mellitus. N Engl J Med 1976;295(8):417–20.
[66] Gabbay KH, Hasty K, Breslow JL, Curtis Ellison R, Franklin Bunn H, Gallop PM. Glycosylated hemoglobins and long-term blood glucose control in diabetes mellitus. J Clin Endocrinol Metab 1977; 44(5):859–64.
[67] Cohen RM, Franco RS, Khera PK, Smith EP, Lindsell CJ, Ciraolo PJ, et al. Red cell life span heterogeneity in hematologically normal people is sufficient to alter HbA1c. Blood 2008;112(10):4284–91.
[68] Beck RW, Connor CG, Mullen DM, Wesley DM, Bergenstal RM. The fallacy of average: how using hba1c alone to assess glycemic control can be misleading. Diabetes Care 2017;40(8):994–9.
[69] Nathan DM, Kuenen J, Borg R, Zheng H, Schoenfeld D, Heine RJ. Translating the A1C assay into estimated average glucose values. Diabetes Care 2008;31(8):1473–8.
[70] Hanas R, John G. 2010 consensus statement on the worldwide standardization of the hemoglobin A1C measurement. Diabetes Care 2010;27:1903–4.
[71] Goldstein DE. Is glycosylated hemoglobin clinically useful? N Engl J Med 1984;310:384–5.
[72] Shamoon H, et al. The effect of intensive treatment of diabetes on the development and progression of long-term complications in insulin-dependent diabetes mellitus. N Engl J Med 1993;329(14):977–86.
[73] Turner R. Intensive blood-glucose control with sulphonylureas or insulin compared with conventional treatment and risk of complications in patients with type 2 diabetes (UKPDS 33). Lancet 1998; 352(9131):837–53.
[74] Little RR, Sacks DB. HbA1c: how do we measure it and what does it mean? Curr Opin Endocrinol Diabetes Obes 2009;16:113–8.
[75] Berg AH, Sacks DB. Haemoglobin A1c analysis in the management of patients with diabetes: from chaos to harmony. J Clin Pathol 2008;61:983–7.
[76] Jeppsson JO, Kobold U, Barr J, Finke A, Hoelzel W, Hoshino T, et al. Approved IFCC reference method for the measurement of HbA1c in human blood. Clin Chem Lab Med 2002;40(1):78–89.
[77] Kahn R, Hicks J, Muller M, Panteghini M, John G, Deeb L, et al. Consensus statement on the worldwide standardization of the hemoglobin A1C measurement: the American diabetes association, European association for the study of diabetes, international federation of clinical chemistry and laboratory medicine, and the international diabetes federation. Diabetes Care 2007;2399–400.
[78] NGSP. IFCC Standardization of HbA1c, [cited 5 March 2020]; Available from: http://www.ngsp.org/ifccngsp.asp; 2010.
[79] Diabetes UK. Diagnostic criteria for diabetes, [cited 5 March 2020]; Available from: https://www.diabetes.org.uk/professionals/position-statements-reports/diagnosis-ongoing-management-monitoring/new_diagnostic_criteria_for_diabetes.
[80] Thompson A. Clinical review of PKD outcomes consortium biomarker qualification submission. Available from: https://www.fda.gov/media/93159/download; 2015.
[81] FDA. Qualification of biomarker—Total kidney volume in studies for treatment of autosomal dominant polycystic kidney disease. Available from: https://www.fda.gov/media/93105/download; 2018.
[82] Grantham JJ. Autosomal dominant polycystic kidney disease. N Engl J Med 2008;359(14):1477–85.
[83] Chapman AB, Devuyst O, Eckardt KU, Gansevoort RT, Harris T, Horie S, et al. Autosomal-dominant polycystic kidney disease (ADPKD): executive summary from a kidney disease: improving global outcomes (KDIGO) controversies conference. Kidney Int 2015;88(1):17–27.

[84] Levey AS, Inker LA, Matsushita K, Greene T, Willis K, Lewis E, et al. GFR decline as an end point for clinical trials in CKD: a scientific workshop sponsored by the national kidney foundation and the US food and drug administration. Am J Kidney Dis 2014;64(6):821–35.
[85] Grantham JJ, Mulamalla S, Swenson-Fields KI. Why kidneys fail in autosomal dominant polycystic kidney disease. Nat Rev Nephrol 2011;7:556–66.
[86] Perrone RD, Neville J, Chapman AB, Gitomer BY, Miskulin DC, Torres VE, et al. Therapeutic area data standards for autosomal dominant polycystic kidney disease: a report from the polycystic kidney disease outcomes consortium (PKDOC). Am J Kidney Dis 2015;66(4):583–90.
[87] Grantham JJ, Torres VE, Chapman AB, Guay-Woodford LM, Bae KT, King BF, et al. Volume progression in polycystic kidney disease. N Engl J Med 2006;354(20):2122–30.
[88] Grantham JJ, Torres VE. The importance of total kidney volume in evaluating progression of polycystic kidney disease. Nat Rev Nephrol 2016;12:667–77.
[89] Thomsen HS, Madsen JK, Thaysen JH, Damgaard-Petersen K. Volume of polycystic kidneys during reduction of renal function. Urol Radiol 1981;3(2):85–9.
[90] King BF, Reed JE, Bergstralh EJ, Sheedy PF, Torres VE. Quantification and longitudinal trends of kidney, renal cyst, and renal parenchyma volumes in autosomal dominant polycystic kidney disease. J Am Soc Nephrol 2000;11(8):1505–11.
[91] Sise C, Kusaka M, Wetzel LH, Winklhofer F, Cowley BD, Cook LT, et al. Volumetric determination of progression in autosomal dominant polycystic kidney disease by computed tomography. Kidney Int 2000;58(6):2492–501.
[92] Fick-Brosnahan GM, Vu Tran Z, Johnson AM, Strain JD, Gabow PA. Progression of autosomal-dominant polycystic kidney disease in children. Kidney Int 2001;59(5):1654–62.
[93] Fick-Brosnahan GM, Belz MM, McFann KK, Johnson AM, Schrier RW. Relationship between renal volume growth and renal function in autosomal dominant polycystic kidney disease: a longitudinal study. Am J Kidney Dis 2002;39(6):1127–34.
[94] Chapman AB, Guay-Woodford LM, Grantham JJ, Torres VE, Bae KT, Baumgarten DA, et al. Renal structure in early autosomal-dominant polycystic kidney disease (ADPKD): the consortium for radiologic imaging studies of polycystic kidney disease (CRISP) cohort. Kidney Int 2003;64(3):1035–45.
[95] Higashihara E, Torres VE, Chapman AB, Grantham JJ, Bae K, Watnick TJ, et al. Tolvaptan in autosomal dominant polycystic kidney disease: three years' experience. Clin J Am Soc Nephrol 2011;6(10):2499–507.
[96] Torres VE, Chapman AB, Devuyst O, Gansevoort RT, Grantham JJ, Higashihara E, et al. Tolvaptan in patients with autosomal dominant polycystic kidney disease. N Engl J Med 2012;367(25):2407–18.
[97] NICE. Tolvaptan for treating autosomal dominant polycystic kidney disease. Available from: https://www.nice.org.uk/guidance/ta358/resources/tolvaptan-for-treating-autosomal-dominant-polycystic-kidney-disease-pdf-82602675026629; 2015.
[98] Sharma K, Caroli A, Van Quach L, Petzold K, Bozzetto M, Serra AL, et al. Kidney volume measurement methods for clinical studies on autosomal dominant polycystic kidney disease. PLoS ONE 2017;12(5).
[99] van Gastel MDA, Edwards ME, Torres VE, Erickson BJ, Gansevoort RT, Kline TL. Automatic measurement of kidney and liver volumes from MR images of patients affected by autosomal dominant polycystic kidney disease. J Am Soc Nephrol 2019;30(8):1514–22.
[100] Sheffield Teaching Hospitals. Sheffield 3D lab, [cited 21 March 2020]; Available from: http://sheffield3dlab.com/services/#3d-lab; 2020.
[101] Mayo Clinic. Imaging core (Mayo Clinic pirnie translational polycystic kidney disease center), [cited 21 March 2020]. Available from: https://www.mayo.edu/research/centers-programs/imaging-core/services/image-analysis; 2020.

SECTION 1

Relaxometry

CHAPTER

Biophysical and Physiological Principles of T_1 and T_2

1

Sean Deoni

Maternal, Newborn, and Child Health Discovery & Tools, Bill & Melinda Gates Foundation, Seattle, WA, United States

Advanced Baby Imaging Lab, Rhode Island Hospital, Providence, RI, United States

Department of Pediatrics, Warren Alpert Medical School at Brown University, Providence, RI, United States

1.1 Introduction

To be of diagnostic, clinical, or research value, a radiological image must contain sufficient contrast to allow discrimination within or between differing tissues. For example, radiologists may seek to differentiate central nervous system white and gray matter, healthy brain and tumor, or healthy brain and ischemic penumbra in neurological applications; morphological changes, and subtleties within cartilage in musculoskeletal applications; and areas of infarction and fibrosis in cardiac applications. Unlike X-ray, computed tomography (CT), or ultrasound (US), in which tissue contrast is essentially fixed (omitting the use of exogenous contrast agents), Magnetic Resonance Imaging (MRI) is unique, in that tissue contrast may be altered at the discretion of the operator through the choice of imaging pulse sequence and the user-defined sequence parameters and timings.

Acquisition of a T_1- and/or T_2-weighted image lies at the heart of almost every MRI exam. The most basic MRI sequence, a saturation recovery or spin echo sequence, results in a signal that is described by

$$SI_{SR}(TE, TR) = \Phi\left(1 - e^{-TR/T_1}\right)e^{-TE/T_2} \tag{1.1}$$

where the echo time (TE) is the time between the excitation and the middle of the acquired echo, the repetition time (TR) is the time between each successive excitation, and T_1 and T_2 denote the longitudinal and transverse relaxation constants, respectively. The Φ term is a factor proportional to the equilibrium magnetization, or proton density (M_0), but also includes extraneous factors such as the receive coil sensitivity and signal amplifier gains.

By varying the acquisition parameter values (TE and TR), the resultant signal intensity can be preferentially made sensitive, or *weighted,* to differences in tissue T_2 values ($TR >> T_1$, $TE \approx T_2$), T_1 values ($TR \approx T_1$, $TE << T_2$), or proton density ($TR >> T_1$, $TE << T_2$) (Fig. 1.1). As will be described throughout subsequent chapters, variations from the basic spin echo sequence, such as gradient echoes, i.e., gradient echo sequence; smaller flip angle radio frequency excitation pulses, e.g., spoiled gradient recalled echo (SPGR) or balanced steady-state sequences; or the use of additional "preparation" excitation pulses, e.g., inversion-prepared (IR)-SPGR, allow the sensitivity to different relaxation properties to be changed and exploited to improve tissue contrast and pathological or physiological visibility.

Advances in Magnetic Resonance Technology and Applications. Volume 1. ISSN 2666-9099. https://doi.org/10.1016/B978-0-12-817057-1.00003-2

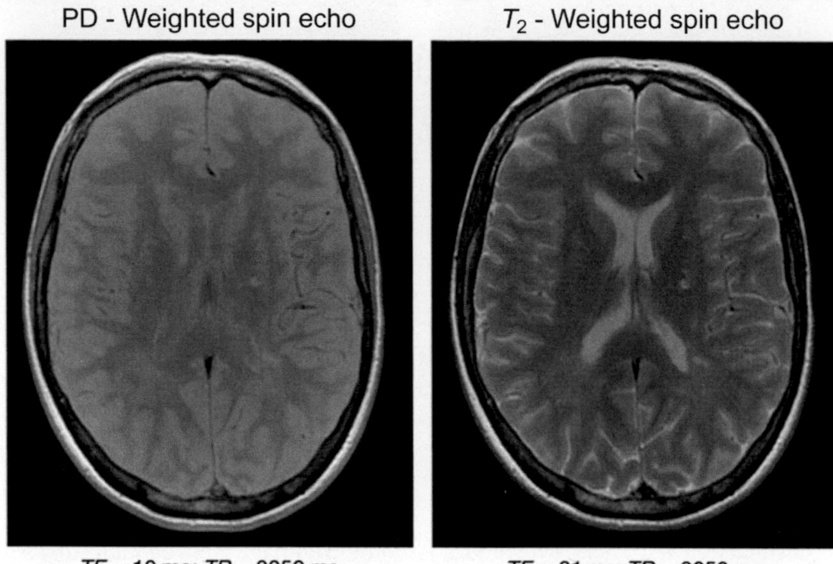

FIG. 1.1

Example of varying tissue contrast of a spin echo image by varying the echo time, TE, from short (proton density, or PD-weighted) to long (T_2-weighted).

The one constant across these imaging techniques, however, is their dependence on using the tissue relaxation properties to generate contrast. But what governs these relaxation properties? And what physiological processes underlie them?

In this chapter, we will explore the basic physical properties of relaxation, including the mechanisms by which they arise, why they may differ between tissues, and how they may be exploited to generate tissue contrast, visualize tissue microstructure, and investigate biological phenomena such as blood flow and functional activity.

1.2 The biophysical basis of relaxation

Before delving into the underlying mechanisms of relaxation, it is useful to review and define some general terminology. For the sake of this chapter, individual MR-visible nuclei are termed spins, a collection of spins that behave similarly are termed an isochromat, and collection of isochromats is termed a spin system. Under general conditions, individual spins within a spin system assume random orientations so that the net magnetization of the system is zero. However, when placed in an external magnetic field, B_0, spins align either parallel or antiparallel to B_0, with slightly more spins aligning in the lower energy parallel orientation, leading to a small but measurable net magnetization, M_0. The application of an excitation pulse, B_1, both tips M_0 away from its equilibrium orientation parallel to B_0 (conventionally denoted the z-axis) into the transverse (x–y) plane and aligns the orientation of the individual spins (i.e., they become phase-coherent) (Fig. 1.2). Over time, the magnetization recovers back to equilibrium, with the individual spins returning to their parallel or

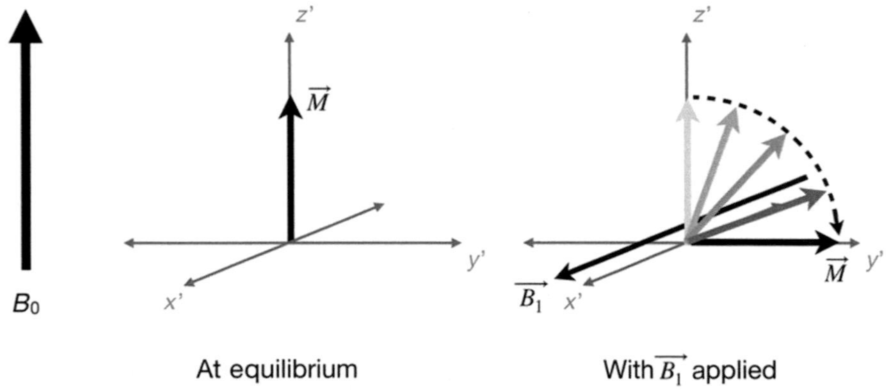

FIG. 1.2

The application of an RF pulse (B_1 field) tips the equilibrium magnetization away from its equilibrium orientation parallel to B_0 and into the transverse x–y plane. Once the RF is removed, the system begins to relax back to its equilibrium.

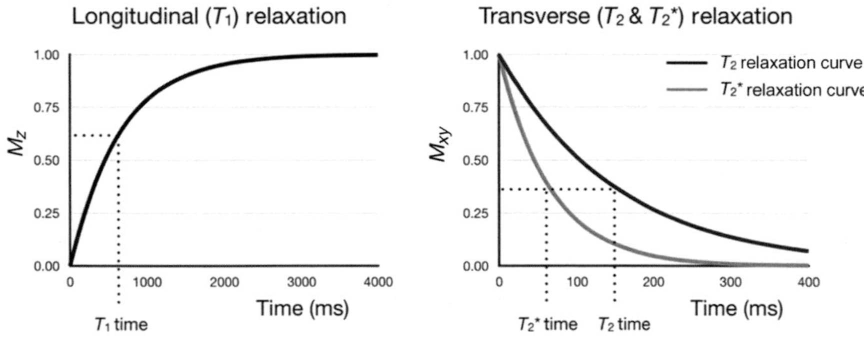

FIG. 1.3

After an RF pulse, the spin system begins to relax back to equilibrium in both the longitudinal (z) axis and transverse (x–y) planes. The longitudinal magnetization recovers via T_1 relaxation, and the transverse relaxation decays via T_2 (and T_2*) relaxation.

antiparallel orientation and losing their phase coherence. M_Z reforms along the z-axis, parallel with B_0, and with a magnitude of M_0; M_{XY} returns to its equilibrium value of 0. The return of M_Z and M_{XY} to equilibrium is characterized by two orthogonal processes: longitudinal (T_1) and transverse (T_2) relaxation, governed by the T_1 and T_2 relaxation time constants (Fig. 1.3).

T_1 relaxation describes the recovery of magnetization along the longitudinal (z) direction (with the T_1 time corresponding to the recovery of 63% of the equilibrium value), while T_2 characterizes the loss of phase coherence in the transverse plane (with the T_2 time corresponding to the loss of 63% of the initial value). Assuming a 90° excitation pulse, the relaxation processes can be described by exponential functions, with M_Z returning to its equilibrium value, M_0, by

$$M_Z(t) = M_0\left(1 - e^{-t/T_1}\right) \tag{1.2}$$

and M_{XY} decaying to 0 as

$$M_{XY}(t) = M_0 e^{-t/T_2} \tag{1.3}$$

Intrinsically, the T_1 and T_2 relaxation processes are the result of molecular motion, interaction, and energy exchange, and arise due to fluctuations in the local magnetic field experienced by each proton spin. In particular, T_1 relaxation involves an exchange of energy between water protons and protons attached to other surrounding lipids, proteins, and macromolecules (collectively termed the "lattice"). To acknowledge these interactions, T_1 relaxation is also commonly referred to as spin-lattice relaxation. In contrast, T_2 relaxation results from interactions between the water protons themselves and, accordingly, is also termed spin-spin relaxation. An important distinction between the T_1 and T_2 processes that arise from these interactions is that while T_1 is an energy-loss process (with the energy transferred from the water protons to the bulk lattice), T_2 is an energy-conserving process, resulting solely from the dephasing of the individual spin magnetic moments in an ensemble. The first theoretical description that related the relaxation processes to the molecular motion was presented by Bloembergen, Purcell, and Pound (BPP) in 1948 [1].

1.2.1 T_2 relaxation

Once the magnetization is in the x–y plane, the magnetization vector M_{XY} precesses around B_0 at the Larmor frequency ($\omega = \gamma B_0$) (Fig. 1.4). This effect can be conceptionally thought of like a lighthouse, with the magnetization sweeping past an observer like a beam in the same way the beam of light rotates about the lighthouse.

Under the ideal case where every spin experiences the same magnetic field, all spins within the system would continue to process at the same Larmor frequency and, thus, their phase coherence would last indefinitely. In reality, however, spins precess at slightly different frequencies throughout the system, and over time their phase coherence decays and is lost. On a macroscopic level, these differences in precessional frequencies are caused by imperfections in the magnetic field, the presence of paramagnetic materials (e.g., iron), or other sources of perturbation. However, even if these field variations were

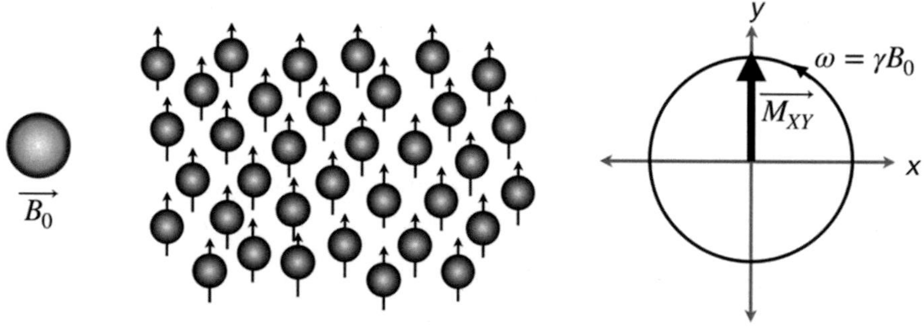

FIG. 1.4

Looking down on the rotating transverse magnetization following an RF pulse. All the individual spins have the same orientation and precessional Larmor frequency, ω, providing a well-defined net transverse magnetization, M_{XY}.

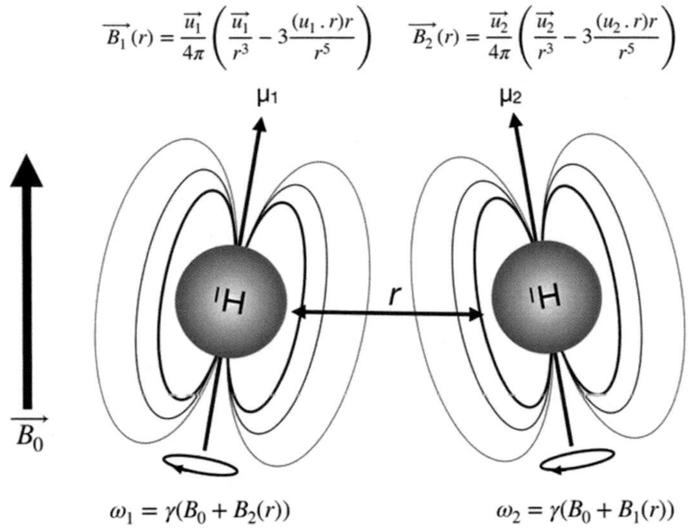

FIG. 1.5

Each proton spin creates a small magnetic field that subtly affects the magnetic field experienced by surrounding spins and, consequently, their precessional frequency. As spins move, their precessional frequencies vary, resulting in a slow but progressive loss of phase coherence with other spins. This basic concept lies at the heart of the T_1 and T_2 relaxation processes.

eliminated through perfect shimming and in a homogeneous substance, subtle differences in the magnetic field experienced by each spin will persist since, on the spin level, each spin itself is a field perturber with its own small magnetic moment which alters the magnetic field experienced by neighboring protons (Fig. 1.5).

As individual spins freely move and diffuse throughout their environment over the course of an imaging experiment, they experience a subtle but rapidly varying magnetic field environment that causes small variations in their precessional frequencies. Since no two spins are likely to experience the same field variation over time (the so-called "field history"), a collection of initially phase-coherent spins will slowly lose their coherence. This is the fundamental basis of T_2 relaxation, and it results solely from the motion and interaction of spins as they move about through their environment (Fig. 1.6). Examined over time, the transverse magnetization, M_{XY}, slowly decays as the individual spins dephase. The envelope of this exponentially decaying magnetization is defined by the time constant, T_2.

1.2.2 T_1 relaxation

T_1 relaxation is also driven by magnetic field fluctuations, though in a less direct and intuitive manner. In the simple case of two spins oscillating back and forth next to each other, each will create a sinusoidally varying magnetic field that is experienced by the other (Fig. 1.7). This is analogous to the varying B_1 field produced by a radiofrequency (RF) pulse and, if the frequency of oscillation is equal to the Larmor frequency, this will induce rotation in the spin's magnetic moment.

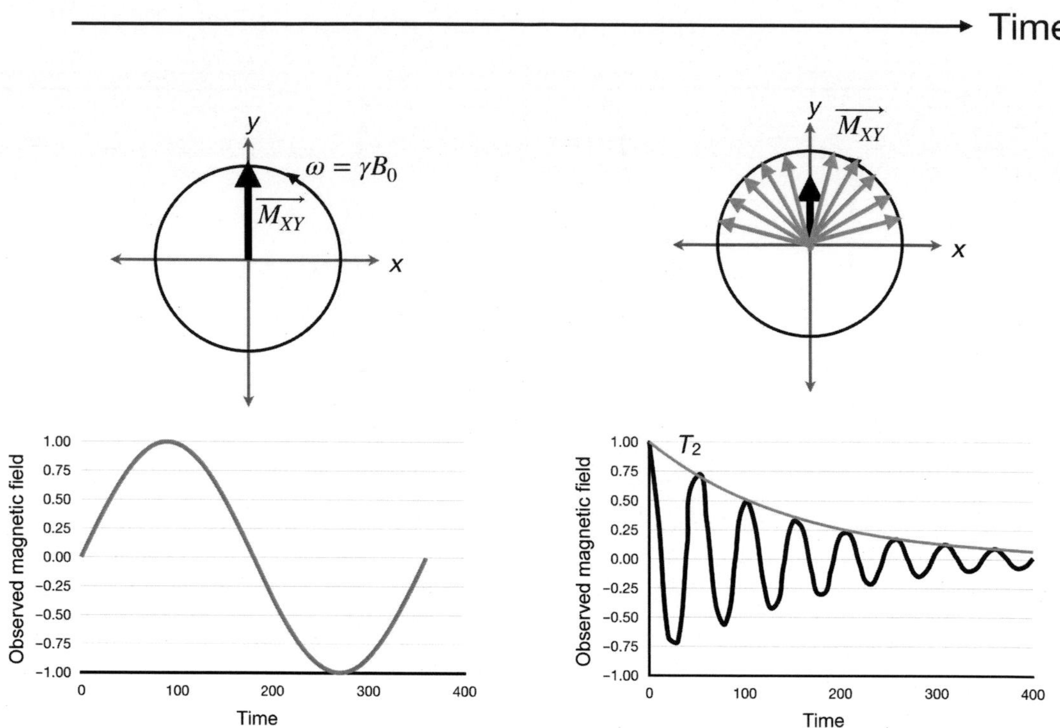

FIG. 1.6

Top: Following an RF pulse, differences in the magnetic fields experienced by each spin cause them to precess at slightly different frequencies and "fan out" about the transverse plane. The result of the dephasing spins (shown as long *gray arrows* at the *right*) is that the net M_{XY} magnetization (*black arrows* both *left and right*) decays away with a time constant of T_2. *Bottom left*: The signal that would be observed in the case of no dephasing, where the changes in intensity are solely due to precession. *Bottom right*: When considering T_2 and T_2* decay, the signal reflects both the precession of the spins and the loss of phase coherence which follows an exponential decay.

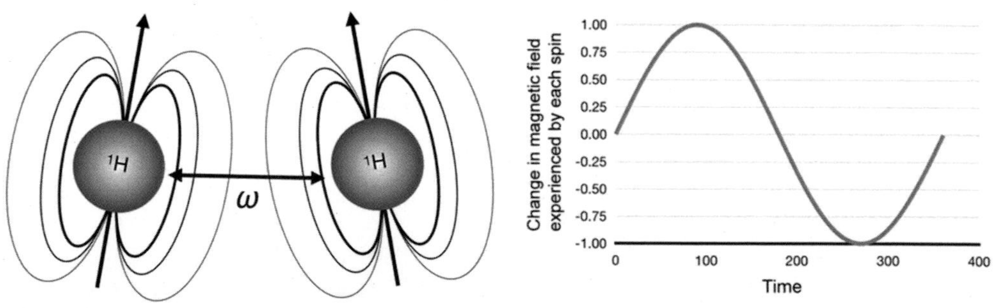

FIG. 1.7

A simple 1D *(right-left)* oscillation of two neighboring spins causes each to experience a sinusoidally varying magnetic field. If the frequency of oscillation is the same as the Larmor frequency of the spin, this will cause rotation of the magnetic moment, similar to the effect of an RF pulse.

While true three-dimensional (3D) molecular motion in tissue is far more complicated than this simple oscillation example, it nevertheless serves as an illustration of how the varying field due to motion can act as an RF pulse to rotate a magnetic moment. As spins move, collide, rotate, and interact with other water and lattice spins, they experience a time-varying magnetic field. If a component of that variation is at the Larmor frequency, it will induce a rotation analogous to an RF pulse.

1.2.3 Mathematical formulation of relaxation

Distilling these concepts and effects into mathematical formulas, Bloembergen, Purcell, and Pound derived the following expressions for T_1 and T_2 relaxation in a homogeneous aqueous solution that relates the effects of molecular motion (denoted by the correlation time, τ_C), Larmor frequency (ω), and interaction strength (κ), to the relaxation times as

$$\frac{1}{T_1} = \kappa\left(\frac{\tau_C}{1+\omega^2\tau_C^2} + \frac{4\tau_C}{1+4\omega^2\tau_C^2}\right) \tag{1.4}$$

and

$$\frac{1}{T_2} = \kappa\left(\frac{3}{2}\tau_C + \frac{5/2\tau_C}{1+\omega^2\tau_C^2} + \frac{\tau_C}{1+4\omega^2\tau_C^2}\right) \tag{1.5}$$

The correlation time can be interpreted as a measure of molecular motion and tumbling. Short correlation times are associated with rapid motion and long correlation times with slower molecular motions. T_1 and T_2 values in solutions characterized by different correlation times can be assessed using Eqs. (1.4), (1.5) and seen in Fig. 1.8, and this relationship can be used to infer the relaxation time behavior in different biophysical environments. Tissues with fast molecular motion are most associated with aqueous environments, such as the cerebral spinal fluid (CSF), blood, or areas of inflammation or edema, and have long T_1 and T_2 relaxation values. Soft tissues, such as brain gray and white matter, fat, and muscle, which correspond to intermediate motion, have shorter T_1 and T_2 values. Rigid structures, such as bone and teeth, have long correlation times and long T_1 but very short T_2 values that often renders them invisible in conventional MRI.

While these expressions were derived for homogenous solutions, they nevertheless provide important intuition on how different factors may affect T_1 and T_2 differently. For example, though both T_1 and T_2 are sensitive to motion at the Larmor frequency, and the additional τ_C term in the T_2 expression accurately describes the sensitivity of T_2 to slow molecular motions, such as in rigid structures, including bone and teeth. The enhanced sensitivity of T_1 to motion at the Larmor frequency, however, results in a strong field dependence of T_1 relaxation, unlike T_2, which is relatively independent of field strength. This helps explain the prolongation of T_1 for tissues (other than CSF) at higher field strengths, with T_1 varying with field strength as

$$T_1 = \Gamma B_0^k \tag{1.6}$$

where Γ is a proportionality constant and the exponent k varies from 0.3 to 0.5 depending on the tissue [2].

In the preceding BPP analyses, a homogeneous solution and homogeneous magnetic field (apart from the subtle variations caused by the individual spins themselves) was assumed. In practice, however, a perfectly homogeneous B_0 field is not possible, and macroscopic inhomogeneities in the

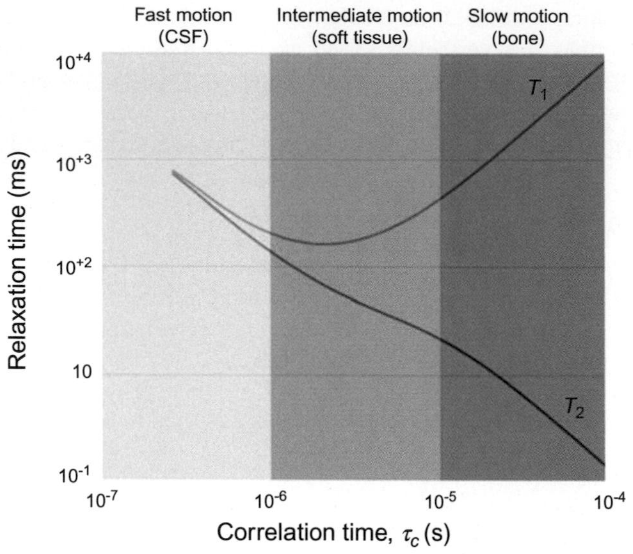

FIG. 1.8

Theoretically predicted relaxation times calculated from the BPP theory. While these plots do not directly correspond to in vivo cases they provide useful insight into expected differences between different tissues and offer intuition as to why certain tissues and structures (e.g., bone or teeth) may be "invisible" with conventional MRI methods.

external field, the presence of large paramagnetic molecules, differing magnetic susceptibilities in bordering or adjacent tissues, or even paramagnetic materials such as iron can cause large scale field variations. In their presence, spins experience an accelerated dephasing that can be characterized by an additional T_2 term, denoted T_2', leading to the net decay constant T_2^*:

$$\frac{1}{T_2^*} = \frac{1}{T_2} + \frac{1}{T_2'}, \tag{1.7}$$

with the transverse magnetization decay described by

$$M_{XY}(t) = M_0 e^{-t/T_2^*}. \tag{1.8}$$

The temporal behavior of the transverse and longitudinal magnetization is illustrated in Fig. 1.3. Under normal conditions, $T_2^* < T_2 < T_1$.

1.3 Biophysical factors that influence relaxation

As T_1 and T_2 (and T_2^*) result from molecular motion, they are directly influenced by the local tissue structure and biochemical environment. Micro- and macrostructural characteristics, such as tissue density (water content and mobility), macromolecule, protein, and lipid composition, and paramagnetic atom (e.g., iron) concentration all influence the relaxation properties and, therefore, tissue signal and contrast. As a result, changes in relaxation times can be indicative of disease or pathology, reflective of biological processes such as neurodevelopment, and indicative of physiological phenomena including function and blood and fluid flow.

Though it seems obvious now that the microstructural differences between tissues would lead to measurable T_1 and/or T_2 differences, it was not until 1971, more than 33 years after the discovery of the nuclear magnetic resonance (NMR) phenomenon in solids [2a,2b] and the first detailed theory of NMR relaxation [1] that T_1 and T_2 values were shown to vary in different tissues [2c] (e.g., Fig. 1.9). It was even later still that they were shown to change with pathology [2d]. Since these initial demonstrations, however, novel pulse sequences have been designed to capitalize upon and exploit these relaxation differences to provide novel contrasts and better characterize tissue microstructure, pathology, and physiology.

While the BPP theory provides insight into the expected relaxation behavior within homogeneous, or single compartment, solutions, it does not fully account for the in vivo complexities introduced by intra voxel differences in the tissue microstructure, chemical composition, architecture, and organization. Each of these aspects can act as additional field perturbers that alter the relaxation times beyond theoretical predictions. Over the following sections, we briefly examine some of these additional effects and their overall influence on relaxation.

1.3.1 Multicomponent relaxometry

Within a typical imaging voxel (typically a 1 mm × 1 mm × 1 mm cube), tissue such as brain parenchyma is highly structured and water is tightly compartmentalized into anatomical subdomains with unique biophysical and biochemical properties. These differing characteristics result in each domain having different T_1, T_2, and T_2^* relaxation properties. Thus, each anatomical compartment has a distinct MR signal signature and the overall measured signal is a powder average of these individual contributions [3]. Further, if the boundaries between these compartments are permeable, water may readily exchange between them. The net result of this complexity and exchange is that relaxation within a voxel is seldom adequately described by a single T_1, T_2, and/or T_2^* relaxation rate.

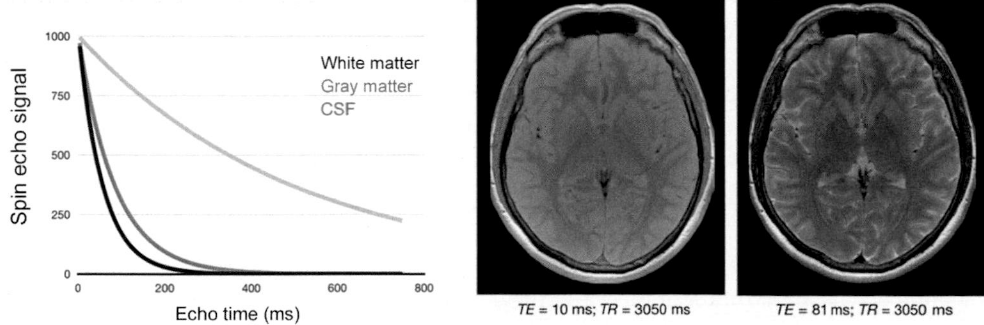

FIG. 1.9

Left: Differences in the T_2 signal decay following a 90° saturation pulse for *white and gray matter* and cerebral spinal fluid. *Right*: Representative images acquired with short (low T_2 weighting) and long (high T_2 weighting) echo times generating differential contrast and tissue visibility.

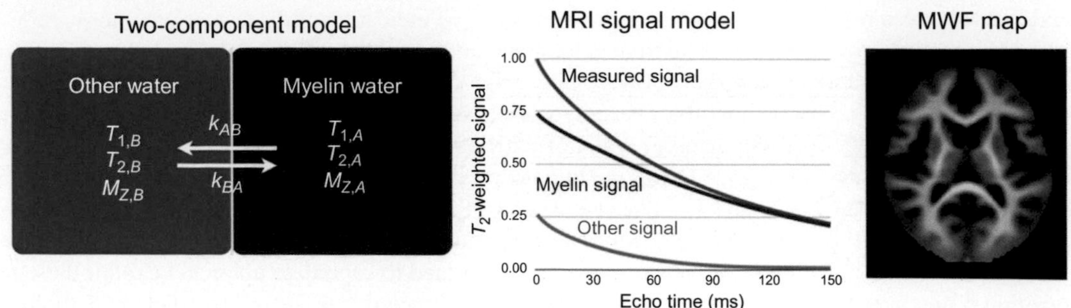

FIG. 1.10

On the voxel scale, brain and other tissue microstructures are often comprised of multiple water compartments with unique biophysical and biochemical characteristics. These differing characteristics mean each also has unique relaxation properties and, therefore, differing signal signatures that may sum to yield the overall measured signal. MCR analysis aims to decompose these individual signal sources in order to quantify the individual compartments.

This complexity, however, does offer the potential of examining this microstructure via relaxation measurements. Multicomponent relaxometry (MCR) analysis (Fig. 1.10) aims to decompose the measured signal into the independent signal contributions [4] to investigate the subvoxel tissue microstructure. For example, within the brain and spinal cord, MCR analysis of T_2 and, more recently T_1 and $T_2{}^*$, relaxation data has yielded two distinct and reproducible water environments: one that has been broadly attributed to the less-restricted intra and extracellular water, and the other to water trapped within the lipid bilayers of the myelin sheath [5, 6]. To apply MCR analysis, imaging data is acquired that allows these individual signals to be distinguished and quantified, providing estimates of each compartment's relaxation properties and volume fractions. Quantitative estimates of the myelin water volume fraction (MWF) has seen increasing utility in the study of MS and other demyelinating disorders [7–10].

In the most direct multiecho approach to MCR, the exchange between the water compartments is ignored because it is assumed that the timescale of exchange is much greater than T_2. In other words, the transverse magnetization within each compartment has fully dephased prior to proton spins exchanging to other compartments. This scenario is termed the "slow exchange" regime and the use of this approximation simplifies the analysis since the total signal can be modeled as the simple sum of the individual compartments:

$$S(TE) = M_0\left(f_A e^{-TE/T_{2,A}} + f_B e^{-TE/T_{2,B}} + \ldots\right) \tag{1.9}$$

where f_A and f_B are the relative volume fractions of each component, and $T_{2,A}$ and $T_{2,B}$ are the corresponding relaxation times. In this case, the apparent T_2 can be calculated as

$$\frac{1}{T_{2,app}} = R_{2,app} = f_A \cdot R_{2,A} + f_B \cdot R_{2,B} \tag{1.10}$$

where R_2 is the reciprocal of T_2. An important consideration in this analysis is that the MRI signal is fully recovered during acquisition ($TR >> T_1$). Unlike T_2, T_1 is long compared to the exchange time

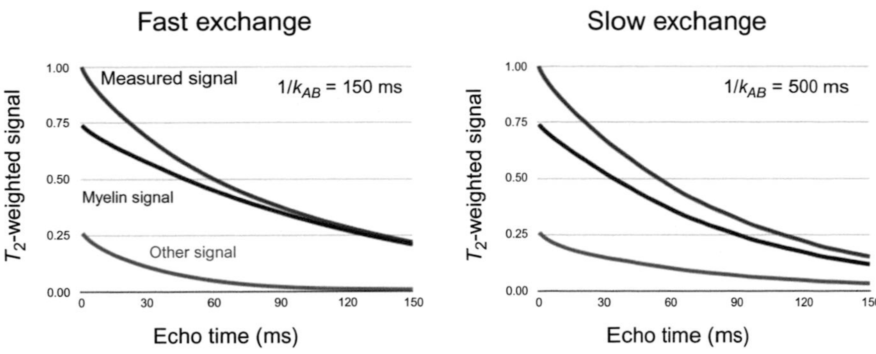

FIG. 1.11

In a multicomponent system with exchange, the rate of exchange relative to the T_1 and T_2 relaxation times can result in different signal characteristics. In the fast exchange limit, the system is a well-mixed container and it is difficult to isolate the individual components; in the slow exchange limit, each compartment can be considered independent and multicomponent relaxation is easily observed. In most in vivo applications, T_2 is often considered to be in slow exchange while T_1 is in fast exchange.

and, as a result, the magnetization is able to exchange between compartments prior to fully returning to equilibrium [11]. In this case, T_1 is said to be in the "fast exchange" regime [3, 12] (Fig. 1.11). In the extreme case where exchange is very fast relative to T_1 (i.e., a well-mixed container), both compartments will have the same powder averaged apparent $T_{1,apparent}$ that depends on the relative volume fractions, relaxation characteristics, and exchange dynamics. Under these conditions, it is difficult to distinguish the T_1-weighted signal from each compartment. For this reason, multicomponent relaxation is commonly observed with respect to T_2, but seldom with respect to T_1.

More recent MCR methods, including mcDESPOT [13] and Magnetic Resonance Fingerprinting approaches [14], make use of rapid sequences without full T_1 recovery. In these cases, the simplistic signal model in Eq. (1.9) is no longer appropriate, and more complex and complete signal modeling is required to accurately disentangle the multiple compartments.

Though seemingly straightforward, it should be noted that meaningful multicomponent analysis is possible only with high quality and robustly sampled data and only when appreciable differences exist between the compartment relaxometry characteristics.

1.3.2 Microstructural orientation and magnetic susceptibility

The magnetic susceptibility of tissue describes its degree of magnetization in response to an applied magnetic field; this effect is described in detail in Chapter 31. Perhaps surprisingly, different tissue types and pathologies have different magnetic susceptibility values [15]. Consequently, this property provides a potential source of contrast that can be used to distinguish certain tissues/pathologies from the background. Prominent examples include deoxyhemoglobin in veins, hemorrhage, iron-rich tissue (e.g., various gray matter structures like the caudate nucleus, red nucleus, substantia nigra, etc.), and calcium depositions in pathologic tissue. As a result of their susceptibility differences, the magnetic field experienced by these tissues and structures differs ever so slightly from the applied field value.

Consequently, spins within them have subtle precessional frequency differences relative to other tissues. Over long echo times, these small frequency differences manifest as measurable differences in the phase of net transverse magnetization and can be thought of as an enhanced $T_2{}^*$ decay.

Interestingly, these susceptibility effects are strongly dependent on the orientation of the tissue with respect to the main magnetic field. The $T_2{}^*$ values measured in highly ordered structures, such as the peripheral and brain vasculature, muscle and cardiac fibers, cartilage, and neuronal axons, differ depending on the orientation of these structures within the MRI magnet [16–20]. While this effect can confound comparison of measures across individuals or time, it also presents an opportunity to assess tissue architecture and aspects of fiber orientation and cohesion.

1.3.2.1 Neuronal activity, hemodynamics, and T_2

Among the many notable achievements in MRI has been the development of functional (*f*) MRI, which allows noninvasive investigations of neuronal activity without the need for exogenous contrast agents. The basis of fMRI lies in the relationship between relaxation and chemical composition. Hemoglobin, the protein responsible for oxygen transport in humans and other vertebrates, consists of four subunits, each consisting of an iron atom bound to a heme group. Of importance to MRI, hemoglobin can be either paramagnetic or diamagnetic, depending on whether or not an oxygen atom is attached to the iron group within the subunits. Deoxygenated hemoglobin is paramagnetic, while oxyhemoglobin is diamagnetic [21].

In the event of sustained neuronal activity, such as in a task fMRI experiment, the local tissue oxygen requirements increase, resulting in a temporary local increase in deoxyhemoglobin concentration [22]. In response, blood flow to the area is increased in excess of need, resulting in an increase in local oxyhemoglobin concentration. The initial increase in paramagnetic deoxyhemoglobin results in a local increase in T_2 relaxation rate (i.e., a decrease in the T_2 and $T_2{}^*$ relaxation times) and reduced T_2- and $T_2{}^*$-weighted signal. At the same time, the subsequent increase in diamagnetic oxyhemoglobin results in increased T_2 and $T_2{}^*$ relaxation times, and increased T_2- and $T_2{}^*$-weighted signal. By monitoring signal changes in response to various stimuli, tremendous insight has been gained into brain systems and circuits underlying particular neurofunctions, as well as differences in function across neurological, psychiatric, and intellectual disorders.

1.3.2.2 Blood flow and exchange

Within the context of multicomponent relaxometry, exchange of water protons between subvoxel water compartments with differing relaxation properties provides the basis for discriminating between the individual compartments. An additional source of magnetization exchange is the introduction of proton spins from the blood into the surrounding tissue which, depending on the circumstances, can result in either increased or decreased T_1 and T_2 [23].

In the first case, blood from outside of the imaging region (e.g., the neck) enters the imaging volume (e.g., brain) between the RF pulse and signal acquisition. Here, the protons in the blood are at equilibrium (Fig. 1.2) and have no phase coherence ($M_{XY}=0$), and are preferentially oriented along B_0 ($M_Z=M$). As this blood moves into the imaging volume and exchanges into the tissue, it acts to reduce the phase-coherence of the tissue spins (decreasing the apparent T_2 relaxation time), and increase the proportion of B_0-aligned spins (decreasing the apparent T_1 relaxation time).

In the second case, blood from outside of the imaging region (e.g., the neck) also enters the imaging volume (e.g., brain) between the RF pulse and signal acquisition. In this case, the blood's magnetization has been "prepared" by applying an inversion pulse to the blood in the neck as it flows into the brain. Now, the protons in the blood are in phase-coherence and are aligned antiparallel to B_0. As this blood moves into the imaging volume and exchanges into the tissue, it acts to increase the phase-coherence of the tissue spins (increasing the apparent T_2 relaxation time), and decrease the proportion of B_0-aligned spins (increasing the apparent T_1 relaxation time). The latter case is termed "spin labeling," and the acquisition of images with and without the blood labeling inversion prepulse is the basis of arterial spin labeling. This technique will be described in greater detail in Chapter 12.

1.3.2.3 Magnetization transfer

Throughout this chapter, we have considered only the MR signal arising from protons associated with free water. In contrast to this simplified picture, it is important to note that all protons contribute to the MR signal. The signal from some protons, however, decays too rapidly to be detected using conventional imaging strategies. Recalling the relationship between T_2 and molecular movement (Fig. 1.8 and Eq. 1.5), as proton motion becomes more restricted the T_2 decreases rapidly. This effect underlies the difficultly in imaging rigid structures, such as bone or teeth using MRI, and is why they appear invisible in conventional MR images. In addition to the physical restriction of water molecules due to extracellular matrices, the motion of protons bound to large molecules, including protons within cell walls and protein structures, may also be restricted, with the result that these protons also have short T_2 values that render them undetectable ($<20\,\mu s$). However, the influence of these protons on the MRI signal can be detected indirectly by exploiting the transfer of magnetization between them and the more mobile free water protons.

Magnetization transfer (MT), as the name suggests, refers to the transfer of magnetization from tightly bound protons into the free water where it becomes MR visible. Traditionally, these bound protons are excited through the application of a strong off-resonance RF pulse (i.e., a pulse with a frequency much lower or higher than the water proton Larmor frequency); this pulse does not excite the free water molecules. Following this pulse, bound protons exchange with the free water protons, and a conventional imaging sequence is used to image the free water. Although the bound protons do not produce visible MR signal, they will still have disrupted the longitudinal magnetization of the free water, typically resulting in a decreased T_1 time of the free water. Tissues with significant macromolecule content (such as white and gray matter) will display greater signal difference following an MT pulse than tissues without (such as CSF). MT effects, and their influence on quantitative measurements in MRI, are covered in detail in Chapter 32.

1.4 Summary

T_1, T_2, and T_2^* relaxation provide the basis for much of the contrast possible with MRI. Understanding the biophysical underpinnings of these processes, as well as the biomechanical, biochemical, and physiological factors that influence them, allows us to design and optimize novel imaging sequences, maximize image contrast, and investigate detailed aspects of tissue microstructure, composition, and function. Fundamentally, as processes of molecular motion, relaxation is intimately and intricately linked to tissue structure and composition though, as we have seen, nonspecifically. As it is sensitive to processes of exchange, relaxation is also linked to microstructure and physiology, though again, nonspecifically. The continued question in MRI is how to better understand the structure-function-relaxation linkages so as to further improve the diagnostic content of MR images.

References

[1] Bloembergen N, Purcell E, Pound R. Relaxation effects in nuclear magnetic resonance absorption. Phys Rev 1948;73(7):679–712.

[2] Bottomley PA, Foster TH, Argersinger RE, Pfeifer LM. A review of normal tissue hydrogen NMR relaxation times and relaxation mechanisms from 1-100 MHz: dependence on tissue type, NMR frequency, temperature, species, excision, and age. Med Phys 1984;11(4):425–48.

[2a] Bloch F. Nuclear induction. Phys Rev 1946;70(7–8):460–74. https://doi.org/10.1103/PhysRev.70.460.

[2b] Purcell EM, Torrey HC, Pound RV. Resonance absorption by nuclear magnetic moments in a solid. Phys Rev 1946;69(1–2):37–8. https://doi.org/10.1103/PhysRev.69.37.

[2c] Damadian R. Tumor detection by nuclear magnetic resonance. Science 1971;171(3976):1151–3.

[2d] Bottomley PA, Hardy CJ, Argersinger RE, Allen-Moore G. A review of ^{1}H nuclear magnetic resonance relaxation in pathology: are T_1 and T_2 diagnostic? Med Phys 1987;14(1):1–37.

[3] MacKay A, Laule C, Vavasour I, Bjarnason T, Kolind S, Mädler B. Insights into brain microstructure from the T2 distribution. Magn Reson Imaging 2006;24(4):515–25.

[4] MacKay A, Whittall K, Adler J, Li D, Paty D, Graeb D. In vivo visualization of myelin water in brain by magnetic resonance. Magn Reson Med 1994;31(6):673–7.

[5] Laule C, Leung E, Lis DKB, Traboulsee AL, Paty DW, Mackay AL, et al. Myelin water imaging in multiple sclerosis: quantitative correlations with histopathology. Mult Scler 2006;12(6):747–53.

[6] Whittall KP, Mackay AL, Graeb DA, Nugent RA, Li DK, Paty DW. In vivo measurement of T2 distributions and water contents in normal human brain. Magn Reson Med 1997;37(1):34–43.

[7] Kolind S, Seddigh A, Combes A, Russell-Schulz B. Brain and cord myelin water imaging: a progressive multiple sclerosis biomarker. Neuroimage Clin 2015;9:574–80.

[8] Kolind S, Sharma R, Knight S, Johansen-Berg H, Talbot K, Turner MR. Myelin imaging in amyotrophic and primary lateral sclerosis. Amyotroph Lateral Scler Frontotemporal Degener 2013;14(7-8):562–73.

[9] Laule C, Vavasour IM, Leung E, Li DKB, Kozlowski P, Traboulsee AL, et al. Pathological basis of diffusely abnormal white matter: insights from magnetic resonance imaging and histology. Mult Scler 2011; 17(2):144–50.

[10] Mackay AL, Vavasour IM, Rauscher A, Kolind SH, Mädler B, Moore GRW, et al. MR relaxation in multiple sclerosis. Neuroimaging Clin N Am 2009;19(1):1–26.

[11] Quirk JD, Bretthorst GL, Duong TQ, Snyder AZ, Springer CS, Ackerman JJH, et al. Equilibrium water exchange between the intra- and extracellular spaces of mammalian brain. Magn Reson Med 2003;50(3):493–9.

[12] Deoni SCL, Rutt BK, Jones DK. Investigating the effect of exchange and multicomponent T1 relaxation on the short repetition time spoiled steady-state signal and the DESPOT1 T1 quantification method. J Magn Reson Imaging 2007;25(3):570–8.

[13] Deoni S, Rutt BK, Arun T. Gleaning multicomponent T1 and T2 information from steady-state imaging data. Magn Reson Med 2008;60(6):1372–87.

[14] Chen Y, Chen M-H, Baluyot KR, Potts TM, Jimenez J, Lin W, et al. MR fingerprinting enables quantitative measures of brain tissue relaxation times and myelin water fraction in the first five years of life. NeuroImage 2019;186:782–93.

[15] Acosta-Cabronero J, Milovic C, Mattern H, Tejos C, Speck O, Callaghan MF. A robust multi-scale approach to quantitative susceptibility mapping. NeuroImage 2018;183:7–24.

[16] Dibb R, Xie L, Wei H, Liu C. Magnetic susceptibility anisotropy outside the central nervous system. Liu C, Bowtell R, Schenck J, editors. NMR Biomed 2017;30(4):e3544.

[17] Duyn JH, Schenck J. Contributions to magnetic susceptibility of brain tissue. Liu C, Bowtell R, Schenck J, editors. NMR Biomed 2017;30(4):e3546.

[18] Kor D, Birkl C, Ropele S, Doucette J, Xu T, Wiggermann V, et al. The role of iron and myelin in orientation dependent R2* of white matter. NMR Biomed 2019;32(7):e4092.

[19] Weber AM, Zhang Y, Kames C, Rauscher A. Myelin water imaging and R2* mapping in neonates: investigating R2* dependence on myelin and fibre orientation in whole brain white matter. NMR Biomed 2020;33(3):e4222.
[20] Wei H, Gibbs E, Zhao P, Wang N, Cofer GP, Zhang Y, et al. Susceptibility tensor imaging and tractography of collagen fibrils in the articular cartilage. Magn Reson Med 2017;78(5):1683–90.
[21] Buxton RB. The physics of functional magnetic resonance imaging (fMRI). Rep Prog Phys 2013;76(9), 096601.
[22] Buxton RB. Dynamic models of BOLD contrast. NeuroImage 2012;62(2):953–61.
[23] Buxton RB. Quantifying CBF with arterial spin labeling. J Magn Reson Imaging 2005;22(6):723–6.

CHAPTER

Quantitative T_1 and $T_{1\rho}$ Mapping

2

Mathieu Boudreau[a,b], Kathryn E. Keenan[c], and Nikola Stikov[a,b]

[a]*Montreal Heart Institute, Université de Montréal, Montréal, Canada* [b]*NeuroPoly Lab, Institute of Biomedical Engineering, Polytechnique Montréal, Montréal, Canada* [c]*Physical Measurement Laboratory, National Institute of Standards and Technology, Boulder, Colorado*

2.1 Introduction

The longitudinal (or spin-lattice) relaxation time (T_1) is one of the fundamental parameters in Magnetic Resonance Imaging (MRI). It characterizes the rate ($R_1 = 1/T_1$) at which longitudinal magnetization recovers to its equilibrium state, which for most tissues can be described by an exponential growth curve [1]. Knowledge of this value is of the utmost importance for many MRI applications, such as pulse sequence design (e.g., optimized signal-to-noise ratio), imaging protocol planning (e.g., improved contrast between tissues), and calibration of other quantitative measurements (e.g., quantitative dynamic contrast enhancement, quantitative magnetization transfer imaging). T_1 is a field-dependent property [2], and also has a temperature dependence [3]. Moreover, it is well-known that many tissue pathologies can be inferred from abnormal T_1 values (e.g., multiple sclerosis lesions, tumors) [4–8].

T_1 mapping has mostly been limited to research applications and is not widely used in clinical imaging protocols. One reason for this is that early T_1 mapping implementations were either very slow (e.g., inversion recovery) or required additional calibration measurements (e.g., variable flip angle, which depends on transmit radiofrequency amplitude maps (B_1^+)). Lack of standardization has also led to a wide range of reported T_1 values when using different methods or scanning at different sites [9]. Recently, however, MRI manufacturers have started adopting rapid techniques such as MP2RAGE (Magnetization Prepared 2 Rapid Acquisition Gradient Echoes) [10] as standard sequences for their scanners, leading to growing interest in adding T_1 maps to clinically-oriented protocols.

This chapter[a] covers three T_1 mapping techniques (inversion recovery, variable flip angle, MP2RAGE) that represent the fundamental types of methods currently in use (signal recovery, steady-state, dictionary-based). Most other T_1 mapping approaches are variants of these techniques, some of which will also be briefly discussed. Only monoexponential T_1 mapping is covered; although some biexponential longitudinal relaxation behavior has been observed in tissues [11], multiexponential T_1 mapping has not garnered the same level of interest as multiexponential mapping of the

[a]Sections 2.2–2.5 in this book chapter have been previously published under a creative commons license on the qMRLab blog. Visit the original blog posts for interactive versions of the figures: https://qmrlab.org/jekyll/2018/10/23/T1-mapping-inversion-recovery.html.https://qmrlab.org/jekyll/2018/12/11/T1-mapping-variable-flip-angle.html.https://qmrlab.org/2019/04/08/T1-mapping-mp2rage.html.https://qmrlab.org/2019/04/09/T1-mapping-t1rho.html.

Advances in Magnetic Resonance Technology and Applications. Volume 1. ISSN 2666-9099. https://doi.org/10.1016/B978-0-12-817057-1.00004-4

transverse relaxation component (T_2). Lastly, quantitative mapping of the spin-locked relaxation ($T_{1\rho}$) will be discussed. $T_{1\rho}$ is closely related to both T_1 and T_2 but sensitive to different properties of the tissue, and has therefore garnered interest in specialized applications (e.g., cartilage imaging).

2.2 Inversion recovery

Widely considered the gold-standard for T_1 mapping on an MRI system, the inversion recovery technique estimates T_1 values by fitting the signal recovery curve acquired at different delays after an inversion pulse (180°). In a typical inversion recovery experiment (Fig. 2.1), the magnetization at thermal equilibrium is inverted using a 180° RF pulse. After the longitudinal magnetization recovers through spin-lattice relaxation for a predetermined delay ("inversion time," TI), a 90° excitation pulse is applied, followed by a readout imaging sequence (typically a spin echo or gradient echo readout) to create a snapshot of the longitudinal magnetization state at that TI.

Inversion recovery was first developed for nuclear magnetic resonance (NMR) in the 1940s [12,13], and the first T_1 map was acquired using a saturation recovery technique (90° as a preparation pulse instead of 180°) [14]. NMR systems have higher signal-to-noise ratio, have precise phase data, and the measurement errors are more easily understood [15]; for this reason, NMR inversion recovery is more accurate than MRI measurements. Some distinct advantages of inversion recovery are its large dynamic range of signal change and an insensitivity to pulse sequence parameter imperfections [9]. Despite its proven robustness at measuring T_1, inversion recovery is scarcely used in practice, because conventional implementations require repetition times (TRs) on the order of 2–5 times the longest T_1 value in the system [16], making it challenging to acquire whole-organ T_1 maps in a clinically feasible time. Nonetheless, it is continuously used as a reference measurement during the development of new techniques, or when comparing different T_1 mapping techniques. Moreover, several variations of the inversion recovery technique have been developed, making it practical for some applications [17,18].

2.2.1 Signal modeling

The steady-state longitudinal magnetization of an inversion recovery experiment can be derived from the Bloch equations for the pulse sequence $\{\theta_{180}\text{-TI-}\theta_{90}\text{-(TR-TI)}\}$, and is given by:

$$M_z(\mathrm{TI}) = M_0 \frac{1-\cos(\theta_{180})e^{-\frac{\mathrm{TR}}{T_1}} - [1-\cos(\theta_{180})]e^{-\frac{\mathrm{TI}}{T_1}}}{1-\cos(\theta_{180})\cos(\theta_{90})e^{-\frac{\mathrm{TR}}{T_1}}} \tag{2.1}$$

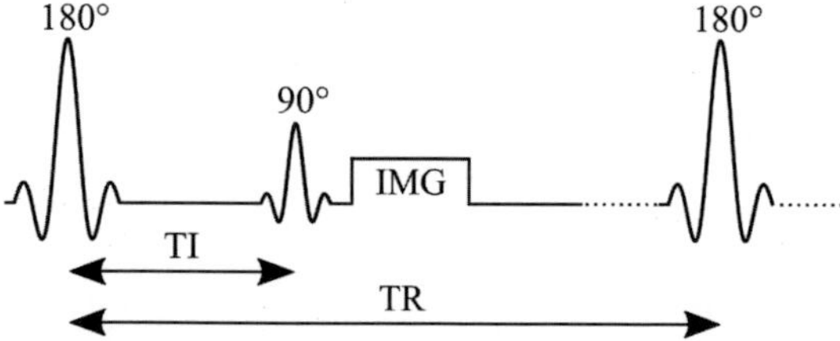

FIG. 2.1

Simplified pulse sequence diagram of an inversion recovery pulse sequence with a gradient echo readout. *TR*, repetition time; *TI*, inversion time; *IMG*, image acquisition window (*k*-space readout).

where M_z is the longitudinal magnetization prior to the θ_{90} pulse, and (θ_{90}, θ_{180}) are the actual flip angles generated by the nominal 90° and 180° pulses. If the in-phase real signal is desired, it can be calculated by multiplying Eq. (2.1) by $k\sin(\theta_{90})\exp(-\mathrm{TE}/T_2)$, where k is a constant. This general equation can be simplified by grouping together the constants for each measurement regardless of their values (i.e., at each TI, the same TE and θ_{90} are used) and assuming an ideal inversion pulse:

$$M_z(\mathrm{TI}) = C\left(1 - 2e^{-\frac{\mathrm{TI}}{T_1}} + e^{-\frac{\mathrm{TR}}{T_1}}\right) \tag{2.2}$$

where M_0 and the denominator of Eq. (2.1) have been grouped together into the constant C (the denominator can be assumed to be constant for each TI, as θ_{90} and TR do not change in inversion recovery protocols). If the experiment is designed such that TR is long enough to allow for full relaxation of the magnetization ($\mathrm{TR} > 5T_1$), an additional approximation can be made by dropping the last term in Eq. (2.2):

$$M_z(\mathrm{TI}) = C\left(1 - 2e^{-\frac{\mathrm{TI}}{T_1}}\right) \tag{2.3}$$

Note that this approximation is only accurate if TR is also much longer than the longest TI, otherwise there will be a small but nonnegligible bias of the model for long TI values. The simplicity of the signal model described by Eq. (2.3), both in its equation and experimental implementation, has made it the most widely used equation to describe the signal evolution in an inversion recovery T_1 mapping experiment. The magnetization curves are plotted in Fig. 2.2 for approximate T_1 values of three different tissues in the brain. Note that in many practical implementations, magnitude-only images are acquired, so the signal measured would be proportional to the absolute value of Eq. (2.3).[b]

Practically, Eq. (2.1) is the better choice for simulating the signal of an inversion recovery experiment, as the TRs are often chosen to be greater than $5T_1$ of the tissue-of-interest, which rarely coincides with the longest T_1 present (e.g., TR may be sufficiently long for white matter, but not for cerebral spinal fluid which could also be present in the volume). Eq. (2.3) also assumes ideal inversion pulses, which is rarely the case due to slice profile effects. Fig. 2.3 shows the inversion recovery signal magnitude (complete relaxation normalized to 1) of an experiment with $\mathrm{TR} = 5$ s and $T_1 = 2.5$ s, calculated using both equations.[b]

2.2.2 Data fitting

Several factors impact the choice of the inversion recovery fitting algorithm. If only magnitude images are available, then polarity-inversion is often implemented to restore the nonexponential magnitude curves (Fig. 2.3) into the exponential form (Fig. 2.2). This process is sensitive to noise due to the Rician distribution [19] which creates a nonzero noise floor at the signal null. If phase data are also available, then a phase term must be added to the fitting equation [20]. Strictly speaking, Eq. (2.3) should only be used to fit data for the long TR regime ($\mathrm{TR} > 5T_1$), which in practice is rarely satisfied for all tissues.

Early implementations of inversion recovery fitting algorithms were designed around the computational power available at the time. These included the "null method" [21], assuming that each T_1 value has unique zero-crossings (see Fig. 2.2), and linear fitting of a rearranged version of Eq. (2.3) on a semi-log plot [22]. Now, a nonlinear least-squares fitting algorithm (e.g., Levenberg-Marquardt)

[b]Interactive figure available at https://qmrlab.org/jekyll/2018/10/23/T1-mapping-inversion-recovery.html.

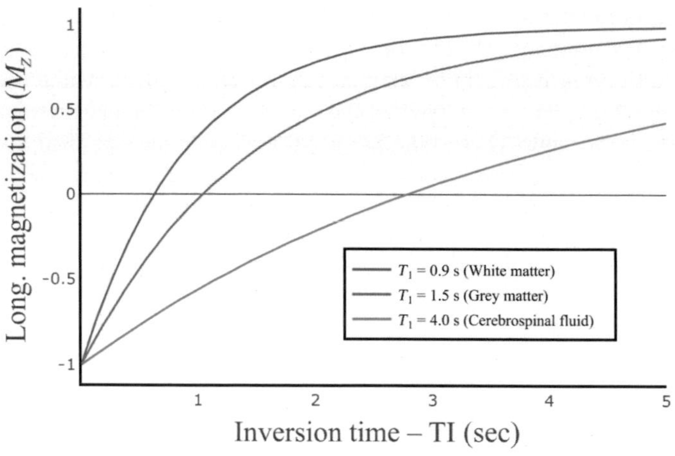

FIG. 2.2

Inversion recovery curves (Eq. 2.3) for three different T_1 values, representing the main types of tissue in the brain.

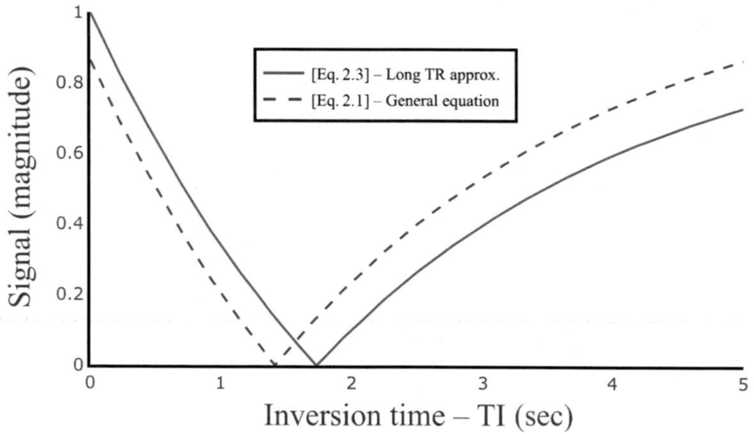

FIG. 2.3

Signal recovery curves simulated using Eq. (2.3) *(solid)* and Eq. (2.1) *(dotted)* with a TR=5s for T_1=2.5s.

is more appropriate and can be applied to either approximate or general forms of the signal model (Eq. 2.3 or Eq. 2.1). More recent work [20] demonstrated that T_1 maps can also be fitted much faster and without a precision penalty by using a reduced-dimension nonlinear least squares (RD-NLS) algorithm (up to 75 times faster compared to Levenberg-Marquardt to fit Eq. 2.1). It was demonstrated that the following simplified five-parameter equation is sufficient for accurate T_1 mapping:

$$S(\mathrm{TI}) = a + be^{-\frac{\mathrm{TI}}{T_1}} \tag{2.4}$$

where a and b are complex values. If magnitude-only data are available, a three-parameter model can be sufficient if the absolute value of Eq. (2.4) is used. While the RD-NLS algorithms are too complex to be presented here (the reader is referred to the paper [20]), the code for these algorithms was released open-source along with the original publication (http://www-mrsrl.stanford.edu/~jbarral/t1map.html), and is also available as a qMRLab T_1 mapping model (http://github.com/qMRLab/qMRlab). One important thing to note about Eq. (2.4) is that it is general—no assumption is made about the TR—and is thus as robust as Eq. (2.1) as long as all pulse sequence parameters (other than TI) are kept constant between each measurement. Fig. 2.4 compares simulated data (Eq. 2.1) using a range of TR values ($1.5T_1$ to $5T_1$) fitted using either RD-NLS and Eq. (2.4) or a Levenberg-Marquardt fit of Eq. (2.3). As seen in this example, fitting data simulated with Eq. (2.3) using the Levenberg-Marquardt approach fails to find a good fit for short TRs ($\text{TR} \sim T_1$) because Eq. (2.3) assumes complete signal recovery at the end of each TR ($\text{TR} > 5T_1$). On the other hand, Eq. (2.4), fitted using the RD-NLS algorithm, results in a good fit, because it is not limited by this assumption (full recovery to the equilibrium magnetization state).[b]

Fig. 2.5 shows an example brain dataset from an inversion recovery experiment, along with the T_1 map fitted using the RD-NLS technique.[b]

2.2.3 Benefits and pitfalls

The conventional inversion recovery experiment is considered the gold-standard T_1 mapping technique for several reasons. A typical protocol has a long TR value and a sufficient number of inversion times for stable fitting (typically five or more) covering the range [0, TR]. It offers a wide dynamic range of signals (up to [-kM_0, kM_0], where k is a signal constant), allowing a number of inversion times where high SNR is available to sample the signal recovery curve [22]. T_1 maps produced by inversion

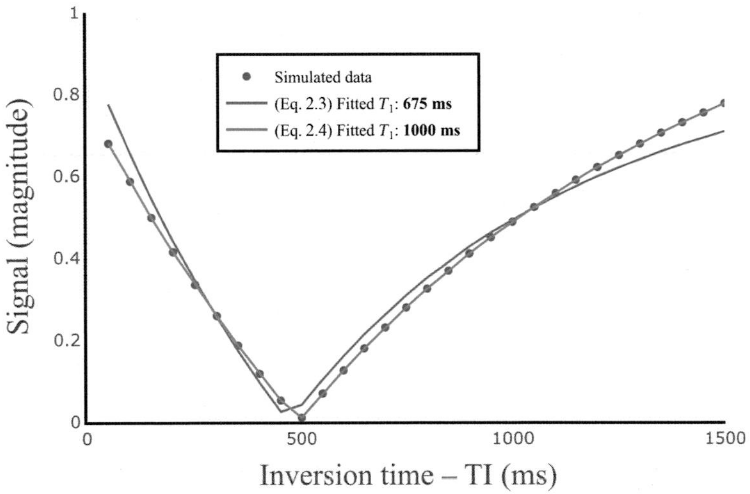

FIG. 2.4

Fitting comparison of simulated data (*blue* markers) with $T_1 = 1$ s and $\text{TR} = 1.5$s, using RD-NLS & Eq. (2.4) *(green)* and Levenberg-Marquardt & Eq. (2.3) (*orange*, long TR approximation). The T_1 value measured when using Eq. (2.3) is 675 ms, significantly shorter than the actual T_1 value of 1000ms, which is generated when using Eq. (2.4).

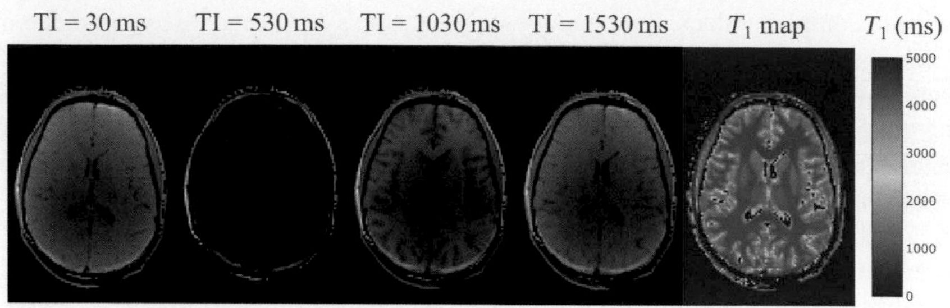

FIG. 2.5

Example inversion recovery images from a healthy adult brain. Inversion times used to acquire this magnitude image dataset were 30 ms, 530 ms, 1030 ms, and 1530 ms, and the TR used was 1550 ms. The T_1 map was fitted using a RD-NLS algorithm.

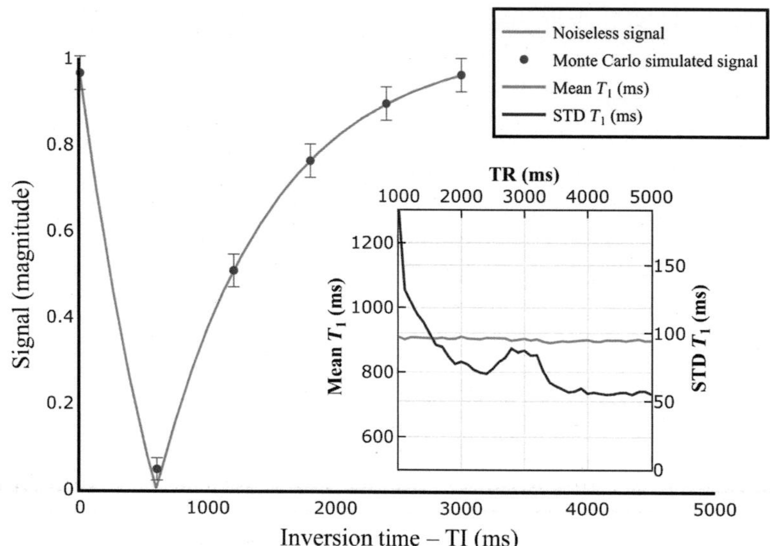

FIG. 2.6

Monte Carlo simulated signals generated for a T_1 value of 900 ms and TR = 3000 ms, with five TI values linearly spaced across the TR (mean and standard deviation (STD), *blue* markers). The inset figure shows fitted T_1 values from Monte Carlo simulations using $T_1 = 900$ ms and a range of TR values (mean and STD, *green* and *red* respectively); note that the chosen TI values are a function of the TR value. The Monte Carlo simulations consisted of 1000 signal simulations at a signal-to-noise ratio (SNR) of 25. A bump in the standard deviation (STD) of the measured T_1 value occurs near TR = 3000 ms, which coincides with the TR where the second TI is located near a null point for this T_1 value.

recovery are largely insensitive to inaccuracies in excitation flip angles and imperfect spoiling [9], as all parameters except TI are constant for each measurement and only a single acquisition is performed (at TI) during each TR. One important pulse sequence design consideration is to avoid acquiring data at inversion times where the signal for T_1 values of the tissue-of-interest is nulled, as the magnitude images at this TI time will be dominated by Rician noise that can negatively impact the fit under low SNR circumstances (Fig. 2.6). Inversion recovery data can also often be acquired using standard pulse sequences available on most MRI scanners by setting up a customized acquisition protocol, and does not require any additional calibration measurements.[b]

Despite its widely acknowledged robustness and accuracy, inversion recovery is not often used for in vivo studies. An important drawback of this technique is the need for long TR values, typically on the order of a few times the T_1 value for general models (e.g., Eqs. 2.1, 2.4), and up to $5T_1$ for long TR approximated models (Eq. 2.3). It takes about 5–20 min to acquire a single-slice T_1 map using the inversion recovery technique, as only one TI is acquired per TR (2–5 s) and the use of conventional Cartesian readouts enables only one phase encode line to be collected per excitation. As an example, using a TR of 5 s to collect images with a resolution of 1 mm in-plane over a field-of-view of 25 cm, an inversion recovery experiment would require an acquisition time of 20.8 min to measure a single TI (250 phase encoding lines $\times$ 5 s). The long acquisition time makes it challenging to acquire whole-organ T_1 maps in clinically feasible protocol times. Nonetheless, the inversion recovery approach is indispensable as a reference measurement for comparisons against other T_1 mapping methods, or to acquire a single-slice T_1 map of a tissue to get T_1 measurements for optimization of other pulse sequences.

2.2.4 Other saturation recovery T_1 mapping techniques

Several variations of the inversion recovery pulse sequence were developed to overcome the challenges specified above. Among them, the Look-Locker technique [23] stands out as one of the most widely used in practice. Instead of applying a single 90° pulse followed by one acquisition per TR, a periodic train of small excitation pulses θ are applied after the inversion pulse, $\{\theta_{180}$ - τ - θ - τ - θ - . . .$\}$, where images are acquired following each θ and $\tau = \text{TR}/n$ and n is the number of sampling acquisitions. This pulse sequence samples the inversion time relaxation curve much more efficiently than conventional inversion recovery, but at a cost of lower SNR. However, because the magnetization state of each TI measurement depends on the previous series of θ excitations, this approach exhibits a higher sensitivity to B_1 inhomogeneities and imperfect spoiling compared to inversion recovery [9,24]. Nonetheless, Look-Locker is widely used for rapid T_1 mapping applications, and variants like MOLLI (Modified Look-Locker Inversion recovery) and ShMOLLI (Shortened MOLLI) are instrumental for cardiac T_1 mapping [17,18].

Another inversion recovery variant that is worth mentioning is saturation recovery, in which the inversion pulse is replaced with a saturation pulse: $\{\theta_{90}\text{-TI-}\theta_{90}\}$. This technique was used to acquire the very first T_1 map [14]. Unlike inversion recovery, this pulse sequence does not need a long TR to allow the magnetization to recover to its initial state; every saturation θ_{90} pulse resets the longitudinal magnetization to the same initial state ($M_z = 0$). However, to properly sample the recovery curve, the TI values still need to be on the order of T_1. Two additional problems with the saturation recovery approach is that the dynamic range of the signal is cut in half ([0, kM_0]), and the short TIs do not allow the magnetization to fully recover to its initial value, resulting in maps with lower SNR.

2.3 Variable flip angle

Variable flip angle (VFA) T_1 mapping [25–27], also known as driven equilibrium single pulse observation of T_1 (DESPOT1) [28,29], is a rapid quantitative T_1 measurement technique that is widely used to acquire 3D T_1 maps (e.g., whole-brain) in a clinically feasible time. VFA is used to estimate T_1 values

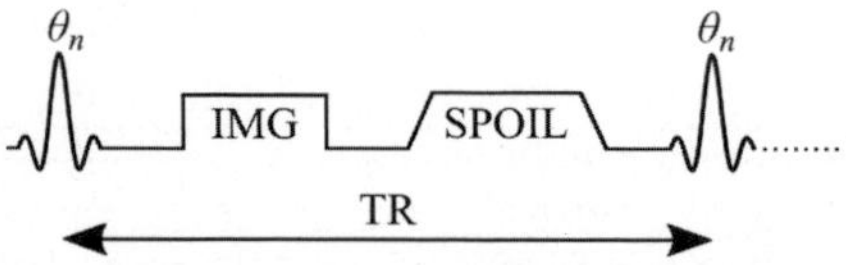

FIG. 2.7

Simplified pulse sequence diagram of a variable flip angle (VFA) pulse sequence with a gradient echo readout. *TR*, repetition time; θ_n, excitation flip angle for the nth measurement; *IMG*, image acquisition (*k*-space readout); *SPOIL*, spoiler gradient.

by acquiring multiple spoiled gradient echo acquisitions, each with different excitation flip angles (θ_n for $n=1, 2, \ldots,$ N and $\theta_i \neq \theta_j$). This pulse sequence (Fig. 2.7) uses very short TRs (on the order of 10ms) and is sensitive to T_1 values for a wide range of flip angles.

VFA is a technique that originates from the NMR field, and was adopted because of its time efficiency and the ability to acquire accurate T_1 values simultaneously for a wide range of values [25,27]. For imaging applications, VFA also benefits from an increase in SNR because it can be acquired using a 3D acquisition instead of a multislice measurement, which also helps to reduce slice profile effects (although this technique may still be susceptible to slice-to-slice variations due to effects like the slab profile and Gibbs ringing). One important drawback of VFA for T_1 mapping is that the signal is very sensitive to inaccuracies in the flip angle value, thus potentially reducing the accuracy of T_1 estimates. In practice, the nominal flip angle (i.e., the value set at the scanner) is different than the actual flip angle experienced by the spins (e.g., at 3.0T, variations of up to $\pm 30\%$ are observed [30]), an issue that worsens with field strength. VFA typically requires the acquisition of another quantitative map, the transmit RF amplitude (B_1^+, or B_1 for short), to calibrate the nominal flip angle to its actual value because of the B_1 inhomogeneities that occur in most loaded MRI coils [31]. The need to acquire an additional B_1 map reduces the time savings offered by VFA over saturation recovery techniques, and inaccuracies/imprecisions of the B_1 map are also propagated into the VFA T_1 map [30,32].

2.3.1 Signal modeling

The steady-state longitudinal magnetization of an ideal variable flip angle experiment can be analytically solved from the Bloch equations for the spoiled gradient echo pulse sequence $\{\theta_n\text{-TR}\}$:

$$M_z(\theta_n) = M_0 \frac{1 - e^{-\frac{TR}{T_1}}}{1 - \cos(\theta_n)} \sin(\theta_n) \tag{2.5}$$

where M_z is the longitudinal magnetization, M_0 is the magnetization at thermal equilibrium, TR is the pulse sequence repetition time (Fig. 2.7), and θ_n is the excitation flip angle. The M_z curves of different T_1 values for a range of θ_n and TR values are shown in Fig. 2.8.[c]

[c]Interactive figure available at https://qmrlab.org/jekyll/2018/12/11/T1-mapping-variable-flip-angle.html.

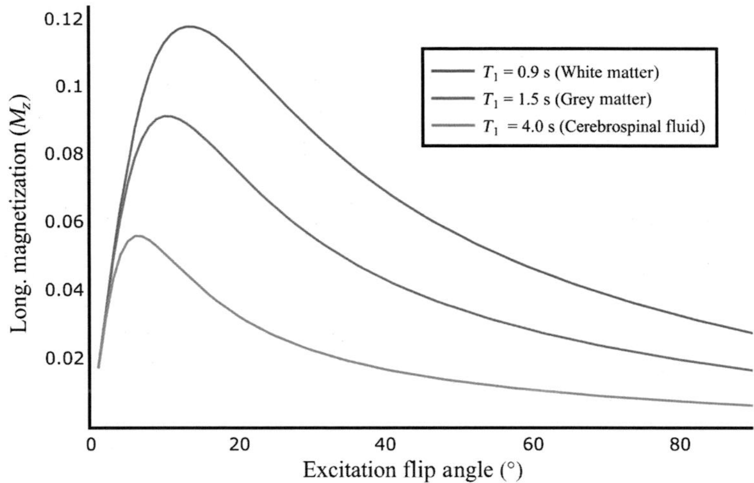

FIG. 2.8

Variable flip angle technique signal curves (Eq. 2.5) for three different T_1 values, representing the main types of tissue in the brain at 3T.

From Fig. 2.8, it can be clearly appreciated that the flip angle at which the steady-state signal is maximized is dependent on the T_1 and TR values. This flip angle is a well-known quantity, called the Ernst angle [33], which can be solved analytically from Eq. (2.5):

$$\theta_{Ernst} = \arccos\left(e^{-\frac{TR}{T_1}}\right) \tag{2.6}$$

The closed-form solution of Eq. (2.5) makes several assumptions, which in practice may not always hold true if care is not taken. Mainly, it is assumed that the longitudinal magnetization has reached a steady-state after a large number of TRs, and that the transverse magnetization is perfectly spoiled at the end of each TR. Bloch equation simulations—a numerical approach to solve the Bloch equations for an ensemble of spins at each time point—provide a more realistic estimate of the signal if the number of repetition times is small (i.e., steady-state is not achieved). As can be seen from Fig. 2.9, the number of repetitions required to reach steady-state not only depends on T_1, but also on the flip angle; more TRs are required to reach steady-state if flip angles near the Ernst angle are used. Preparation pulses or an outward-in k-space acquisition pattern is typically sufficient to allow the magnetization to reach a steady-state by the time that the center of k-space is acquired, which is where most of the image contrast resides.[c]

The degree of spoiling is also a parameter that must be tailored in a VFA experiment. A combination of both gradient spoiling and RF phase spoiling [34,35] is typically recommended (Fig. 2.10). It has also been shown that the use of very strong gradients may introduce diffusion-induced spoiling into the images (not considered in Fig. 2.10), further improving the spoiling efficacy in the VFA pulse sequence [36].[c]

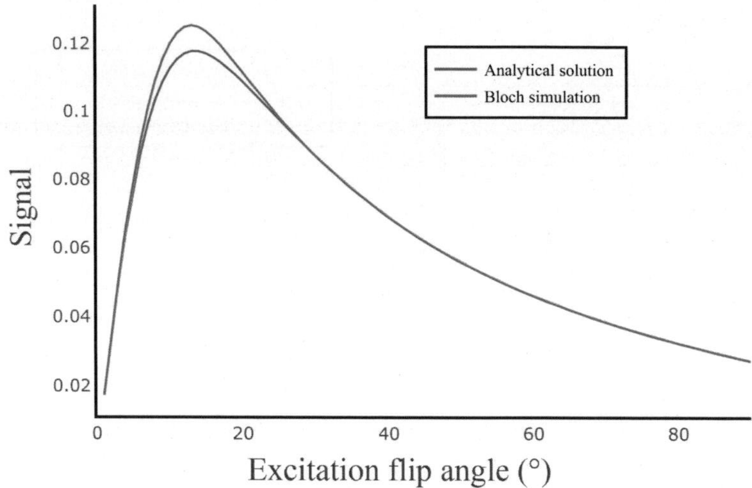

FIG. 2.9

Signal curves generated using Bloch equation simulations *(orange)* for a total of 50 TR repetitions, plotted against the ideal case (Eq. 2.5—*blue*). Simulation details: TR = 25 ms, T_1 = 900 ms, 100 spins, ideal RF pulses (instantaneous). Ideal spoiling was used for this set of Bloch equation simulations (transverse magnetization was set to 0 at the end of each TR).

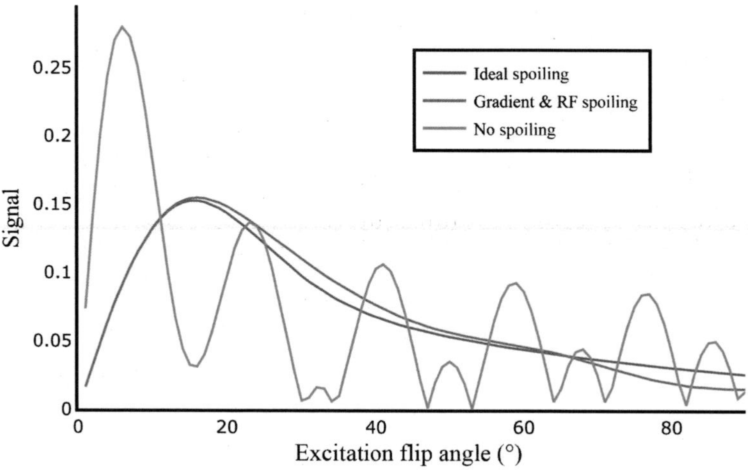

FIG. 2.10

Signal curves estimated using Bloch equation simulations for three categories of signal spoiling: (1) ideal spoiling *(blue)*, gradient and RF spoiling *(orange)*, and no spoiling *(green)*. Simulation details: TR = 25 ms, T_1 = 900 ms, T_2 = 100 ms, TE = 5 ms, 100 spins, 20 TR repetitions. For the ideal spoiling case, the transverse magnetization is set to zero at the end of each TR. For the gradient and RF spoiling case, each spin is rotated by different increments of phase (2π / # of spins) to simulate complete decoherence from gradient spoiling, and the RF phase of the excitation pulse is $\phi_n = \phi_{n-1} + n\phi_0 = ½\ \phi_0(n^2 + n + 2)$ [34] with $\Phi_0 = 117°$ [35] after each TR.

2.3.2 Data fitting

At first glance, one could be tempted to fit VFA data using Eq. (2.5), which typically only has two free fitting variables (T_1 and M_0), and a nonlinear least squares fitting algorithm such as Levenberg-Marquardt. Although this is a valid way of estimating T_1 from VFA data, it is rarely done in practice because a simple refactoring of Eq. (2.5) allows T_1 values to be estimated with a linear least squares fitting algorithm, which substantially reduces the processing time. Without any approximations, Eq. (2.5) can be rearranged into the form $\mathbf{y} = \mathrm{m}\mathbf{x} + \mathrm{b}$ [27]:

$$\frac{S_n}{\sin(\theta_n)} = e^{-\frac{TR}{T_1}} \frac{S_n}{\tan(\theta_n)} + C\left(1 - e^{-\frac{TR}{T_1}}\right) \tag{2.7}$$

The third term does not change between measurements (it is constant for each θ_n), and it can be grouped into a constant for a simpler representation:

$$\frac{S_n}{\sin(\theta_n)} = e^{-\frac{TR}{T_1}} \frac{S_n}{\tan(\theta_n)} + C \tag{2.8}$$

With this rearranged form of Eq. (2.5), T_1 can be simply estimated from the slope of a linear regression calculated from $S_n/\sin(\theta_n)$ and $S_n/\tan(\theta_n)$ values:

$$T_1 = -\frac{\mathrm{TR}}{\ln(slope)} \tag{2.9}$$

If data are acquired using only two flip angles—a very common VFA acquisition protocol [28,37–39]—then the slope can be calculated using the elementary slope equation. Fig. 2.11 displays both Eqs. (2.5), (2.8) plotted for a noisy dataset.[c]

There are two important imaging protocol design considerations that should be taken into account when planning to use VFA: (1) how many and which flip angles to use when acquiring VFA data, and (2) how to correct for inaccurate flip angles due to transmit RF field inhomogeneity. Most VFA experiments use the minimum number of required flip angles (two) to minimize acquisition time. When using only two flip angles, it has been shown that the flip angle choice resulting in the best precision for VFA T_1 estimates for a sample with a single T_1 value (i.e., single tissue) are the two flip angles that result in 71% of the maximum possible steady-state signal (i.e., at the Ernst angle) [28,38].

Time allowing, additional flip angles are often acquired at higher values and in between the two angles specified by the Ernst equation, because the signal differences between tissue T_1 values are greater in those regions (e.g., Fig. 2.8). If more than two flip angles are acquired, then Eqs. (2.5), (2.8) do not have the same noise weighting for each fitting point, which may bias linear least-square T_1 estimates at lower SNRs. Thus, it has been recommended that low SNR data should be fitted with either Eq. (2.5) using nonlinear least-squares (more computational time required) or with a weighted linear least-squares form of Eq. (2.8) [40].

Accurate knowledge of the flip angle values is very important for producing accurate T_1 maps. Because of how the RF field interacts with matter [31], the excitation RF field (B_1^+, or B_1 for short) of a loaded RF coil results in spatial variations in intensity/amplitude, unless RF shimming is available to counteract this effect (not common on clinical systems). For quantitative measurements like VFA,

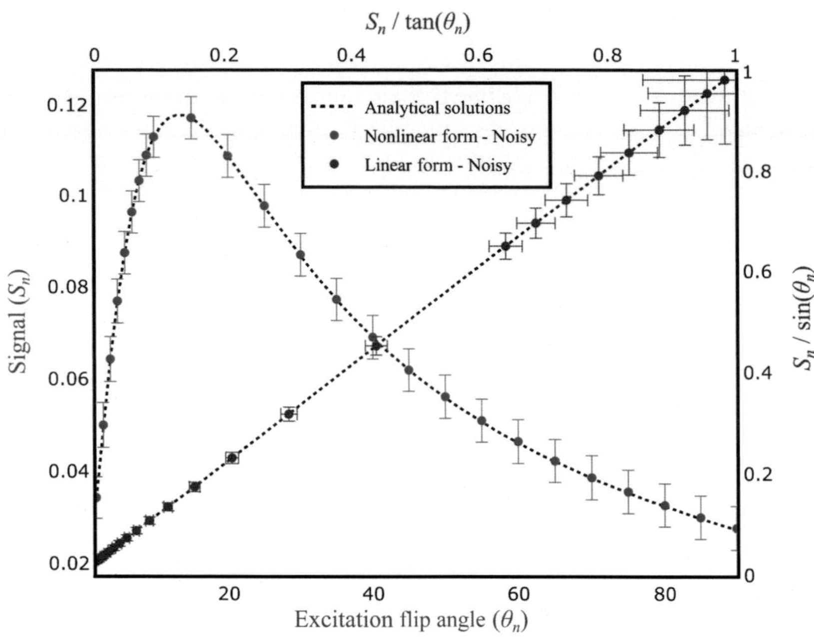

FIG. 2.11

Mean and standard deviation of the VFA signal plotted using the nonlinear form (Eq. 2.5—*blue*) and linear form (Eq. 2.8—*red*). Monte Carlo simulation details: SNR=25, N=1000. VFA simulation details: TR=25 ms, T_1=900 ms.

which are sensitive to this parameter, the flip angle can be corrected (voxelwise) relative to the nominal value by multiplying it with a scaling factor (B_1) from a B_1 map that is acquired during the same session:

$$\theta_{corrected} = B_1 \theta_{nominal} \tag{2.10}$$

B_1 in this context is normalized, meaning that it is unitless and has a value of 1 in voxels where the RF field has the expected amplitude (i.e., where the nominal flip angle is the actual flip angle). Fig. 2.12 displays the VFA T_1 values from a Monte Carlo dataset simulated using biased flip angle values, and fitted without/with B_1 correction.[c]

Fig. 2.13 shows an example VFA dataset and a B_1 map in a healthy brain, along with the T_1 map estimated using a linear fit (Eqs. 2.8, 2.9).[c]

2.3.3 Benefits and pitfalls

It has been widely reported in recent years that the accuracy of VFA T_1 estimates is very sensitive to pulse sequence implementations [9,41,42], and as such is less robust than the gold-standard inversion recovery technique. In particular, the signal bias resulting from insufficient spoiling can result in

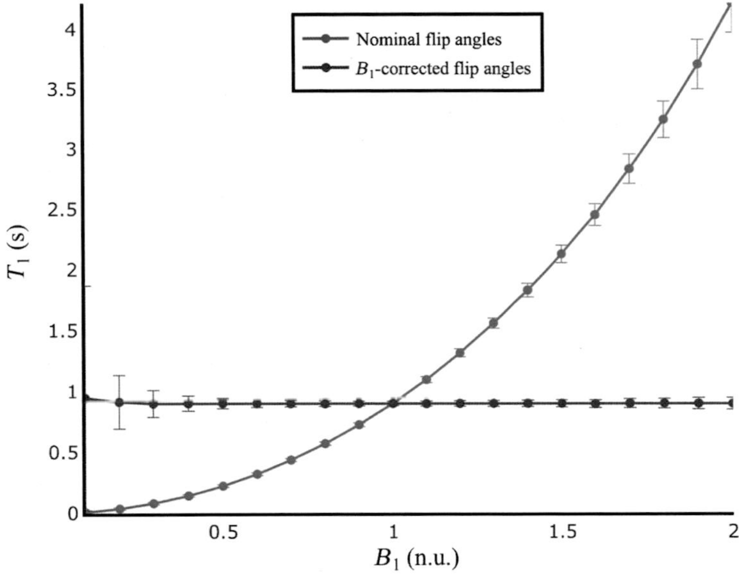

FIG. 2.12

Mean and standard deviations of VFA T_1 values for a set of Monte Carlo simulations (SNR = 100, N = 1000), simulated using a wide range of biased flip angles and fitted without *(blue)* or with *(red)* B_1 correction. Simulation parameters: TR = 25 ms, T_1 = 900 ms, $\theta_{nominal}$ = 6 and 32° (optimized values for this TR/T_1 combination). Notice how even after B_1 correction, fitted T_1 values at B_1 values far from the nominal case ($B_1 = 1$) exhibit larger variance, as the actual flip angles of the simulated signal deviate from the optimal values for this TR/T_1 [28]. Note that the range of typical B_1 variations in the brain at 3 T is between 0.7 and 1.3 [30].

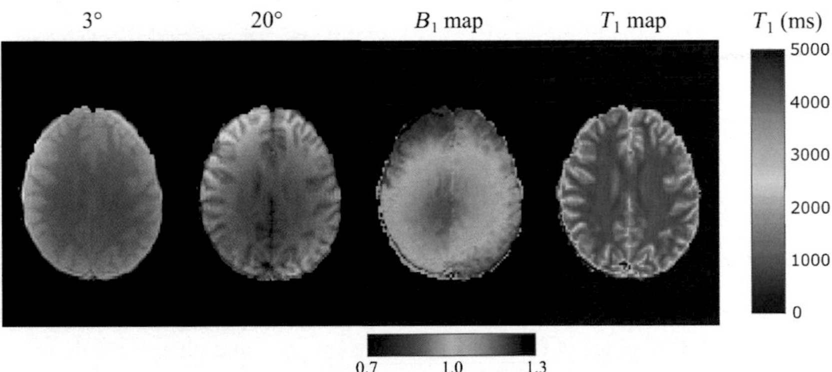

FIG. 2.13

Example variable flip angle dataset and B_1 map (normalized units [n.u.]) of a healthy adult brain along with the fitted T_1 map. The relevant VFA protocol parameters used were: TR = 15 ms, $\theta_{nominal}$ = 3 and 20°. The T_1 map was fitted using a linear regression (Eqs. 2.8, 2.9).

inaccurate T_1 estimates of up to 30% relative to inversion recovery estimated values [9]. VFA T_1 map accuracy and precision are also strongly dependent on the quality of the measured B_1 map [32], which can vary substantially between implementations [30]. Modern, rapid B_1 mapping pulse sequences are not as widely available as the VFA pulse sequence, and thus some groups attempt alternative ways of removing the bias from the T_1 maps (for example, generating an artificial B_1 map through the use of image processing techniques [43] or even omitting B_1 correction altogether). The latter is not recommended, because most MRI scanners have default pulse sequences that, with careful protocol settings, can rapidly provide B_1 maps of sufficient quality [30,44,45], and omitting B_1 maps altogether can results in large T_1 inaccuracies (e.g., Liberman et al. reported a mean absolute difference in T_1 of 235 ms in the brain at 3 T if B_1 was omitted [43]).

Despite some drawbacks, VFA is still one of the most widely used T_1 mapping methods in research. Its rapid acquisition time, short image processing time, and widespread availability makes it easy to use within other quantitative imaging acquisition protocols like quantitative magnetization transfer imaging [46,47] and dynamic contrast-enhanced imaging [48,49].

2.4 MP2RAGE

Dictionary-based MRI techniques capable of generating T_1 maps are increasing in popularity, due to their growing availability on clinical scanners, rapid scan times, and fast post-processing computation time, thus making quantitative T_1 mapping accessible for clinical applications. Generally speaking, dictionary-based quantitative MRI techniques use numerical dictionaries—databases of pre-calculated signal values simulated for a wide range of tissue and protocol combinations—during the image reconstruction or post-processing stages. Popular examples of dictionary-based techniques that have been applied to T_1 mapping are MR Fingerprinting (MRF) [50], certain flavors of compressed sensing (CS) [51,52], and Magnetization Prepared 2 Rapid Acquisition Gradient Echoes (MP2RAGE) [10]. Dictionary-based techniques can usually be classified into one of two categories: techniques that use information redundancy from parametric data to assist in accelerated imaging (e.g., CS, MRF), or those that use dictionaries to estimate quantitative maps using the MR images after reconstruction. Because MP2RAGE is a technique implemented primarily for T_1 mapping, and it is becoming increasingly available as a standard pulse sequence on many MRI systems, the remainder of this section will focus solely on this technique. However, many concepts discussed are shared by other dictionary-based techniques.

MP2RAGE is an extension of the conventional MPRAGE pulse sequence widely used in clinical studies [53,54]. A simplified version of the MP2RAGE pulse sequence is shown in Fig. 2.14. MP2RAGE can be seen as a hybrid between the inversion recovery and VFA pulse sequences: a 180° inversion pulse is used to prepare the magnetization with T_1 sensitivity at the beginning of each $TR_{MP2RAGE}$, and then two images are acquired at different inversion times using gradient recalled echo (GRE) imaging blocks with low flip angles and short repetition times (TR). During a given GRE imaging block, each excitation pulse is followed by a constant in-plane phase encode weighting (varied for each $TR_{MP2RAGE}$), but with different 3D phase encoding gradients (changed after each TR). The center of k-space for the 3D phase encoding direction is acquired at the TI time for each GRE imaging block. The main motivation for developing the MP2RAGE pulse sequence was to provide a metric similar to MPRAGE, but with self-bias correction of the static (B_0) and receive (B_1^-) magnetic fields, and a first order correction of the transmit magnetic field (B_1^+). However, because two

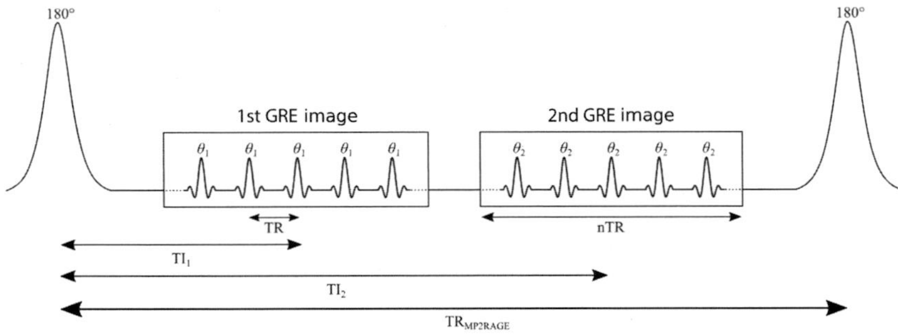

FIG. 2.14

Simplified diagram of an MP2RAGE pulse sequence. *TR*, repetition time between successive gradient echo readouts; $TR_{MP2RAGE}$, repetition time between successive adiabatic 180° inversion pulses; TI_1 *and* TI_2, inversion times; θ_1 *and* θ_2, excitation flip angles. The imaging readout events occur within each TR using a constant in-plane phase encode gradient set for each $TR_{MP2RAGE}$, but varying 3D phase encode gradients between each successive TR.

images at different TI times are acquired (unlike MPRAGE, which only acquires data at a single TI), information about the T_1 values can also be inferred, thus making it possible to generate quantitative T_1 maps using this data.

2.4.1 Signal modeling

Prior to considering the full signal equations, we will first introduce the equation for the MP2RAGE parameter ($S_{MP2RAGE}$) that is calculated in addition to the T_1 map. For complex data (magnitude and phase, or real and imaginary), the MP2RAGE signal ($S_{MP2RAGE}$) is calculated from the images acquired at two TIs ($S_{GRE,TI1}$ and $S_{GRE,TI2}$) using the following expression [10]:

$$S_{MP2RAGE} = \mathrm{Re}\left(\frac{S_{GRE_{TI_1}}{}^{*} S_{GRE_{TI_2}}}{\left|S_{GRE_{TI_1}}\right|^2 + \left|S_{GRE_{TI_2}}\right|^2}\right) \tag{2.11}$$

This value is bounded between [-0.5, 0.5], and helps reduce some B_0 inhomogeneity effects by using the phase data. For real data, or magnitude data with polarity restoration, this metric is instead calculated as:

$$S_{MP2RAGE} = \frac{S_{GRE_{TI_1}} S_{GRE_{TI_2}}}{S^2_{GRE_{TI_1}} + S^2_{GRE_{TI_2}}} \tag{2.12}$$

Because MP2RAGE is a hybrid of pulse sequences used for inversion recovery and VFA, the resulting signal equations are more complex. Typically, steady-state is not achieved during the short train of GRE imaging blocks, so the signal at the center of *k*-space for each readout (which defines the contrast weighting) will depend on the number of phase-encoding steps. For simplicity, the equations presented here assume that the 3D phase-encoding dimension is fully sampled (no partial Fourier or parallel imaging acceleration). For this case (see appendix of [10] for derivation details), the signal equations are:

$$S_{\mathrm{GRE}_{\mathrm{TI}_1}} = B_1^{-} M_0 \sin(\theta_1) \times \left[\left(\frac{-\mathrm{eff}\cdot m_{z,ss}}{M_0}\mathrm{EA} + (1-\mathrm{EA})\right)(\cos(\theta_1)\mathrm{ER})^{n/2-1} + (1-\mathrm{ER})\frac{1-(\cos(\theta_1)\mathrm{ER})^{n/2-1}}{1-\cos(\theta_1)\mathrm{ER}}\right] \tag{2.13}$$

$$S_{\mathrm{GRE}_{\mathrm{TI}_2}} = B_1^{-} e^{-\frac{\mathrm{TE}}{T_2^*}} M_0 \sin(\theta_2) \times \left[\frac{\frac{m_{z,ss}}{M_0} - (1-\mathrm{EC})}{\mathrm{EC}(\cos(\theta_2)\mathrm{ER})^{n/2}} - (1-\mathrm{ER})\frac{(\cos(\theta_2)\mathrm{ER})^{-n/2} - 1}{1-\cos(\theta_2)\mathrm{ER}}\right] \tag{2.14}$$

where B_1^- is the receive field sensitivity, "eff" is the adiabatic inversion pulse efficiency, ER = exp(-TR/T_1), EA = exp(-TA/T_1), EB = exp(-TB/T_1), EC = exp(-TC/T_1). The variables TA, TB, and TC are the three different delay times (TA: time between inversion pulse and beginning of the GRE_1 block, TB: time between the end of GRE_1 and beginning of GRE_2, TC: time between the end of GRE_2 and the end of the TR). If no *k*-space acceleration is used (e.g., no partial Fourier or parallel imaging acceleration), then these values are TA = TI_1 - (n/2)TR, TB = TI_2 - TI_1 + (n/2)TR, and TC = $\mathrm{TR}_{\mathrm{MP2RAGE}}$ - TI_2 + (n/2)TR, where n is the number of voxels acquired in the 3D phase encode direction varied within each GRE block. The value $m_{z,ss}$ is the steady-state longitudinal magnetization prior to the inversion pulse, and is given by:

$$m_{z,ss} = \frac{M_0\left[\beta(\cos(\theta_2)\mathrm{ER})^n + (1-\mathrm{ER})\frac{1-(\cos(\theta_2)\mathrm{ER})^n}{1-\cos(\theta_2)\mathrm{ER}}\right]\mathrm{EC} + (1-\mathrm{EC})}{1 + \mathrm{eff}[\cos(\theta_1)\cos(\theta_2)]^n e^{-\frac{\mathrm{TR}_{\mathrm{MP2RAGE}}}{T_1}}} \tag{2.15}$$

$$\beta = \left[(1-\mathrm{EA})(\cos(\theta_1)\mathrm{ER})^n + (1-\mathrm{ER})\frac{1-(\cos(\theta_1)\mathrm{ER})^n}{1-\cos(\theta_1)\mathrm{ER}}\right]\mathrm{EB} + (1-\mathrm{EB}) \tag{2.16}$$

From Eqs. (2.13)–(2.16), it is evident that the MP2RAGE parameter S_{MP2RAGE} (Eqs. 2.11, 2.12) cancels out the effects of receive field sensitivity, T_2^*, and M_0. The signal sensitivity related to the transmit field (B_1^+), hidden in Eqs. (2.13)–(2.16) within the flip angle values θ_1 and θ_2, can also be reduced by careful pulse sequence protocol design [10], but not entirely eliminated [55].

2.4.2 Data fitting

Dictionary-based techniques such as MP2RAGE do not typically use conventional minimization algorithms (e.g., Levenberg-Marquardt) to fit signal equations to observed data. Instead, the MP2RAGE technique uses pre-calculated signal values for a wide range of parameter values (e.g., T_1), and then interpolation is done within this dictionary of values to estimate the T_1 value that matches the observed signal. This approach results in short post-processing times because the dictionaries can be simulated/generated prior to scanning and interpolating between these values is much faster than most fitting algorithms. This means that the quantitative image can be produced and displayed directly on the MRI scanner console rather than needing to be fitted offline.

To produce T_1 maps with high accuracy and precision using dictionary-based interpolation methods, it is important that the signal curves are unique for each parameter value. MP2RAGE can produce good T_1 maps by using a dictionary with only two dimensions (T_1, S_{MP2RAGE}), since S_{MP2RAGE} is unique for each T_1 value for a given protocol [10]. However, as was noted above, S_{MP2RAGE} is also sensitive to B_1 because of θ_1 and θ_2 in Eqs. (2.13)–(2.16). The B_1^- sensitivity can be reduced substantially with careful MP2RAGE protocol optimization [10], and further improved by including B_1 as one of the dictionary dimensions [T_1, B_1, S_{MP2RAGE}] (Fig. 2.15). This requires an additional acquisition of a B_1 map [55], which lengthens the scan time.

Example images collected using MP2RAGE sequence, and the corresponding T_1 map, are shown in Fig. 2.16. The MP2RAGE pulse sequence is increasingly being distributed by MRI vendors, thus typically a data fitting package is also available to reconstruct the T_1 maps online. Alternatively, several open source packages to create T_1 maps from MP2RAGE data are available online [56,57], and for new users these are recommended—as opposed to programming one from scratch—as there are many potential pitfalls (e.g., adjusting the equations to handle partial Fourier or parallel imaging acceleration).

2.4.3 Benefits and pitfalls

The widespread availability and turnkey acquisition/fitting procedures of MP2RAGE are main contributing factors to the growing interest for including quantitative T_1 maps in clinical and neuroscience studies. T_1 values measured using MP2RAGE show high levels of reproducibility for the brains of two subjects in an inter- and intra-site study at eight sites (same MRI hardware/software and at 7T) [58]. Not only does MP2RAGE have one of the fastest acquisition and post-processing times among quantitative T_1 mapping techniques, it can also be used to acquire very high resolution T_1 maps (1 mm isotropic at 3T and submillimeter at 7T, both in under 10min [59]), opening the doors to cortical studies which greatly benefit from the smaller voxel size [60–62].

Despite these benefits, MP2RAGE and similar dictionary-based techniques have certain limitations that are important to consider before deciding to incorporate them in a study. Good reproducibility of the quantitative T_1 map is dependent on using one pre-calculated dictionary. If two different

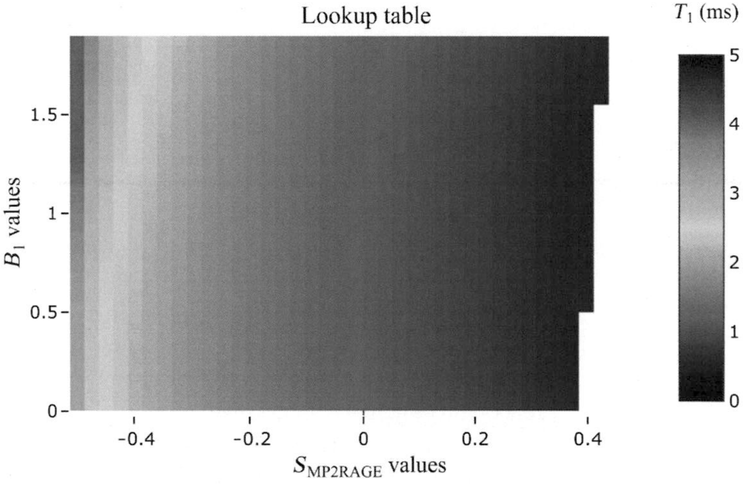

FIG. 2.15

T_1 lookup table as a function of B_1 and S_{MP2RAGE} value. Inversion times used to acquire this magnitude image dataset were 800ms and 2700ms, the flip angles were 4° and 5° (respectively), $\mathrm{TR}_{\mathrm{MP2RAGE}}=6000$ms, and TR = 6.7 ms. The code that was used was open-sourced by the authors of the original MP2RAGE paper (https://github.com/JosePMarques/MP2RAGE-related-scripts).

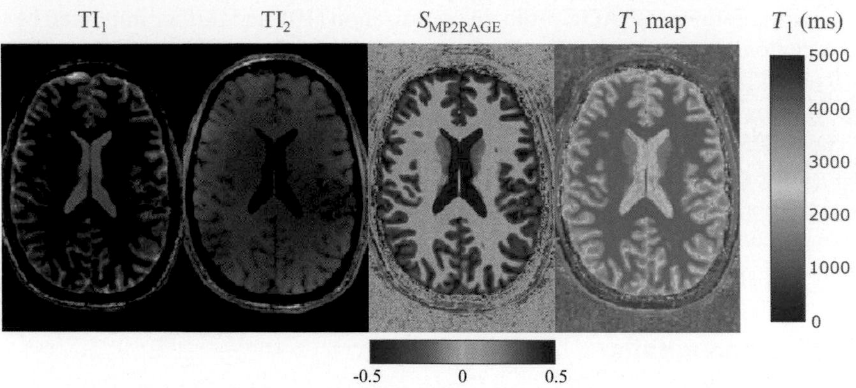

FIG. 2.16

Example MP2RAGE dataset of a healthy adult brain at 7T and T_1 map. Inversion times used to acquire this magnitude image dataset were 800ms and 2700ms, the flip angles were 4° and 5°, $TR_{MP2RAGE}=6000$ms, and TR=6.7ms. The dataset and code that was used were open-sourced by the authors of the original MP2RAGE paper (https://github.com/JosePMarques/MP2RAGE-related-scripts).

dictionaries are used (e.g., cross-site with different MRI vendors), the differences in the dictionary interpolations will likely result in minor differences in T_1 estimates for the same data. Also, although the B_1-sensitivity of the MP2RAGE T_1 maps can be reduced with proper protocol optimization, it can be substantial enough that further correction using a measured B_1 map should be done [55,61]. However B_1 mapping brings an additional potential source of error, so carefully selecting a B_1 mapping technique and accompanying post-processing methods (e.g., filtering) should be done before integrating it in a T_1 mapping protocol [30]. Lastly, the MP2RAGE equations (and thus, dictionaries) assume monoexponential longitudinal relaxation, and this has been shown to result in suboptimal estimates of the long T_1 component for a biexponential relaxation model [11], an effect that becomes more important at higher fields.

2.5 $T_{1\rho}$ mapping

T_1 relaxation time at clinical fields (1.5 T or 3T) probes the molecular motional processes in the MHz range (e.g., 64 or 128MHz). To measure such processes in the kHz range, while still performing the experiment at clinical fields, $T_{1\rho}$ relaxation can be used [63]. In a $T_{1\rho}$ relaxation experiment, a spin-lock RF pulse with amplitude B_1 is applied in the rotating frame, parallel to the transverse magnetization [64]. The result is that the spins rotate around the spin-lock pulse in the rotating frame at a frequency $\omega_1=\gamma B_1$, and will relax toward B_1, similar to T_1 relaxation (where the spins rotate around and relax toward B_0). Owing to that similarity to the T_1 relaxation experiment, $T_{1\rho}$ is known as the spin-lattice relaxation time in the rotating frame [64]. $T_{1\rho}$ has previously been used with $\omega_1=1$ to 20kHz to acquire information about T_1 relaxation times at lower field strengths using a clinical system operating at 0.15T [65], which had more available signal than imaging at 0.001T as had previously been done [66].

The $T_{1\rho}$ experiment is also similar to the T_2 experiment; the typical implementation is to precede a T_2 mapping experiment with a $T_{1\rho}$ preparation. The applied spin-lock pulse suspends any relaxation mechanisms that occur at or below the specific spin-lock pulse frequency, and once the spin-lock pulse is removed, these relaxation mechanisms will proceed [67]. T_2 relaxation is sensitive to water molecule diffusion, dipole–dipole interaction and local field inhomogeneities. $T_{1\rho}$ relaxation is sensitive to the same processes as T_2 relaxation, along with chemical exchange processes and slow rotational motions of protons associated with large macromolecules [68–70]. The spin-lock pulses can be used, for example, to suppress the effect of dipolar interaction, and as a result, the $T_{1\rho}$ relaxation times are longer than T_2 relaxation times [71]. In this example, the difference between the $T_{1\rho}$ and T_2 relaxation times is driven by the amount of water-macromolecule interaction [69].

$T_{1\rho}$ has been applied to many clinical applications including the breast [65,72], heart [73–76], liver [77], brain [78–81], and musculoskeletal systems [82–84]. A particularly interesting application of $T_{1\rho}$ mapping is the examination of $T_{1\rho}$ dispersion, where the spin-lock frequency is systematically varied to probe different mechanisms of relaxation in tissue. The information acquired is comparable to T_1 dispersion studies; however, because only B_1 is varied, the data can be acquired using any MRI system. The major challenge preventing adoption of $T_{1\rho}$ methods is that the spin-lock pulse frequencies are limited by the specific absorption rate (SAR) [85].

2.5.1 Signal modeling

In the $T_{1\rho}$ experiment (Fig. 2.17), a spin-lock pulse is applied at a frequency ω_1, which will affect some relaxation processes. The spins precess around the spin-lock axis in the rotating frame (Fig. 2.18A), and when the spin-lock pulse is removed, the spins return to their original orientation. The spin-lock pulse will sensitize measurements to processes at or around the time scale $1/\omega_1$. $T_{1\rho}$ relaxation can then be characterized at a single spin-lock frequency by:

$$S(\mathrm{TSL}) = M_0 e^{-\frac{\mathrm{TSL}}{T_{1\rho}}} \tag{2.17}$$

where TSL is the time of the spin-lock pulse and M_0 is a constant, which is independent of TSL. The TSL varies from ~2 ms to 100 ms, depending on the tissue of interest, and it is recommended that a minimum of four TSL values be used. At clinical field strengths, spin-lock frequencies in the range from 100 to 500 Hz are typically used.

In a simple $T_{1\rho}$ preparation, a 90° RF pulse is applied to tip the magnetization into the M_{xy} plane. The spin-lock pulse is then applied parallel to the magnetization for duration TSL, and then another 90° RF pulse is applied to flip the magnetization back to the longitudinal direction. A crusher is used to dephase any residual signal in the transverse plane, and the signal is read-out using an imaging module, which can be a spin echo method (Fig. 2.17).

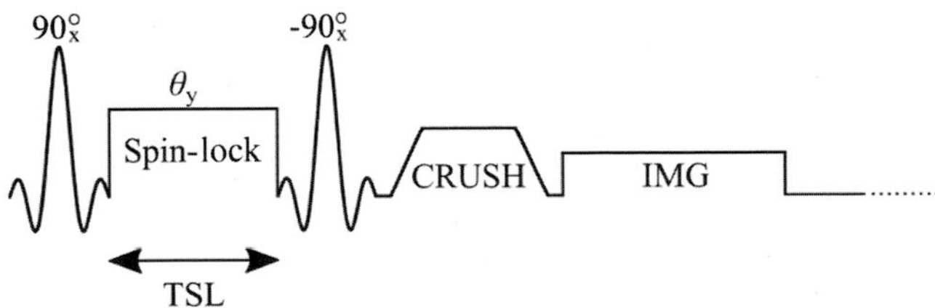

FIG. 2.17

Simplified diagram of a $T_{1\rho}$ spin-lock pulse sequence illustrating the tip-down RF pulse, spin-lock pulse (θ_y), the tip-up RF pulse and the crusher to dephase residual signal in the transverse plane. The IMG pulse rotates the signal back into the transverse plane for acquisition.

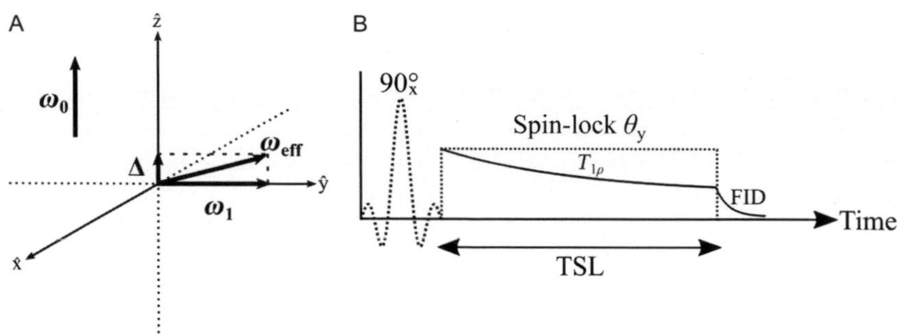

FIG. 2.18

(A) Rotating frame representation of the $T_{1\rho}$ experiment. In the rotating frame of reference, the spins experience an effective RF field, ω_{eff}. Typically, the spin-lock pulse is applied on-resonance, and the spins experience $\omega_{eff} = \omega_1 = \gamma B_1$. If an off-resonance pulse is used, the spins experience $\omega_{eff} = \Delta + \omega_1$, where Δ is the off-resonance component. (B) The timing diagram of a simplified $T_{1\rho}$ experiment illustrating the suspension of some relaxation processes during the application of the spin-lock pulse, θ_y. After the spin-lock pulse is removed, the magnetization relaxes as a free induction decay, FID.

Several potential artifacts can result from this simple sequence. A complete signal model of this sequence results in the following expression:

$$S(\text{TSL}) = M_0\left(\sin^2(\theta_{90})e^{-\frac{\text{TSL}}{T_{1\rho}}} + \cos(\theta_y)\cos^2(\theta_{90})e^{-\frac{\text{TSL}}{T_{2\rho}}}\right) \tag{2.18}$$

where θ_{90} is the actual tip-up/tip-down RF pulse flip angle, $\theta_y = \gamma B_1 \text{TSL}$ is the total flip angle accrued during spin-locking (proportional to TSL), and $T_{2\rho}$ is the magnetization decay rate in the plane perpendicular to the spin-locking RF pulse. $T_{2\rho}$ is not regularly studied and is beyond the scope of this discussion.

It is well documented that with this pulse sequence, B_0 and B_1inhomogeneities can cause oscillations in the relaxation decay curve [86,87]. Simply reversing the amplitude or phase of the second half of the spin-locking pulse to create a rotary echo [88] is insufficient to address the B_1inhomogeneities [89,90]. A solution is to use phase cycling to address B_1 inhomogeneities, and one method works by acquiring two data sets with opposite phase of the tip-up RF pulse, which are then subtracted from each other [86]. The resulting longitudinal magnetization is:

$$S(\text{TSL}) = 2M_0\sin^2(\theta_{90})e^{-\frac{\text{TSL}}{T_{1\rho}}} \tag{2.19}$$

As a result, the monoexponential decay model (Eq. 2.17) can be used. It should be noted that because the method requires two data sets, the scan time is doubled. However, there is no scan time penalty to incorporate this method in the 3D sequence designed by Li et al. [91]. Finally, to address the effect of B_0 and B_1 inhomogeneities simultaneously, it is possible to combine a composite RF pulse [73] with the phase cycling method [86] or use the method proposed by Witschey et al. [87] that uses four different pulse clusters: a conventional spin-lock, a B_1 insensitive spin-lock [89,90], a ΔB_0 insensitive spin-lock [92], and finally a ΔB_0 and B_1 insensitive spin-lock, which aligns the final magnetization along the z-axis.

2.5.2 Data fitting

$T_{1\rho}$ relaxation is typically modeled and fitted using a monoexponential function, Eq. (2.17), similar to T_2 relaxation, and a linear least squares fitting algorithm can be used. However, depending on the sequence, the signal model may need to be modified to account for the effect of $T_{2\rho}$ relaxation, as in Eq. (2.18) [89]. The model used can also be modified to account for chemical exchange [93,94]. An example $T_{1\rho}$ relaxation map of cartilage in the knee is shown in Fig. 2.19.

The linear least squares fit is appropriate when the SNR is sufficiently high. In the case of low SNR, large bias can appear with both the linear and nonlinear fit to Eq. (2.17). Several approaches have been developed to fit T_2 values from low SNR data, which can also be applied to low SNR $T_{1\rho}$ data [95–97].

In the $T_{1\rho}$ dispersion experiment, the $T_{1\rho}$ experiment is repeated with different spin-lock pulse frequencies, and $T_{1\rho}$ relaxation is plotted against the spin-lock frequency to generate the $T_{1\rho}$ dispersion curve. An example set of $T_{1\rho}$ relaxation dispersion curves in the cartilage of veal patella is shown in Fig. 2.20. In tissues, $T_{1\rho}$ relaxation times increase with increasing spin-lock frequencies [98]. The dispersion curve shape will depend on the tissue components [98,99], and the fit to the curve can be used to characterize the tissue. For example, Koskinen et al. used a small range of spin-lock frequencies and fit the slope of $1/T_{1\rho}$ over the spin-lock frequency to characterize various rat organs [99,100], whereas $1/T_{1\rho}$ in cartilage, examined over a large range of spin-lock frequencies, was fitted using a bi-Lorentzian model [98].

2.5.3 Benefits and pitfalls

$T_{1\rho}$ can be used to probe small changes in the macromolecular content using clinically available equipment. By manipulating ω_1 in the spin-lock pulse, it is possible to measure, for example, exchange-dependent pH changes [101]. $T_{1\rho}$ has been used extensively to study the musculoskeletal system, including cartilage, meniscus and interverterbral discs and is covered in Chapter 8. $T_{1\rho}$ relaxation may be able to distinguish tumor, healthy, and adipose tissues in the breast [65]; improve delineation of myocardial borders [73] and detect acute myocardial injuries [75]; and aid in detection and assessment of liver cirrhosis [77]. Spin-lock sequences have specifically been developed for accelerated 3D

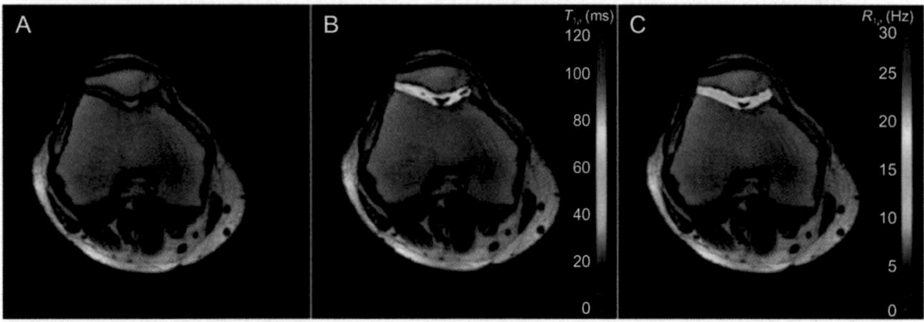

FIG. 2.19

An example of (A) a spin-lock image, (B) $T_{1\rho}$ relaxation map and (C) an $R_{1\rho}$ map of cartilage in the knee, using a spin-lock frequency of 350 Hz, five TSLs linearly spaced from 2 to 82 ms, and TR/TE 3300 ms/10 ms.

(Reproduced with permission from Wang P, Block J, Gore JC. Chemical exchange in knee cartilage assessed by R1ρ (1/T1ρ) dispersion at 3T. Magn Reson Imaging 2015;33(1):38–42.)

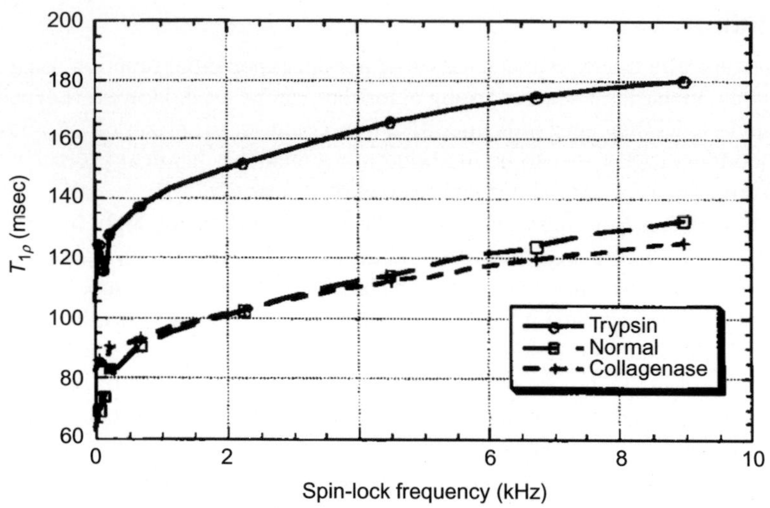

FIG. 2.20

An example set of $T_{1\rho}$ dispersion curves for normal, proteoglycan-degraded and collagen-degraded samples of veal patella. Note that at zero spin-lock frequency, the $T_{1\rho}$ value is the measured T_2 value.

(Reproduced with permission from Duvvuri U, et al. T1ρ-relaxation in articular cartilage: effects of enzymatic degradation. Magn Reson Med 1997;38(6):863–67.)

acquisition in the heart [74]. In the brain, $T_{1\rho}$ relaxation was used at low field (0.1 T) with contrast to identify gliomas [78] and at higher fields (4 T) to study macromolecules [81]. These macromolecular changes detected by $T_{1\rho}$ in the brain (in this case at 1.5 T), may be indicative of neurodegenerative diseases such as Alzheimer's and Parkinson's disease [79,80].

The major challenge preventing $T_{1\rho}$ from being adopted clinically is that the power deposition required by spin-locking pulses approaches the clinical SAR limits. $T_{1\rho}$ dispersion, in particular, has limited clinical application because of power limitations from SAR concerns. There have been pulse sequence developments to overcome these challenges through the use of parallel transmit [102], partial k-space application of the spin-lock pulse [85], or the use of off-resonance pulses [103], though off resonance $T_{1\rho}$ is beyond the scope of this discussion. However, there are benefits of even very low frequency (0 to 400 Hz) spin-lock pulses, which are within clinical limits, to detect residual dipolar interactions in structured tissues such as oriented collagen fibers or myelinated axons [87].

2.6 Concluding remarks

T_1 mapping dates back to the earliest NMR experiments, and it is still a vibrant and relevant field. With advances in hardware and the growing availability of post-processing tools, it is becoming easier and faster to obtain accurate T_1 and $T_{1\rho}$ maps in clinically feasible times. This chapter reviews the three basic types of T_1 mapping techniques, exemplified by inversion recovery, variable flip angle, and MP2RAGE, although there are many other variants in the literature. The mechanisms of and techniques for $T_{1\rho}$ mapping are also described. Subsequent chapters will delve more deeply into the clinical uses of T_1 and $T_{1\rho}$ mapping.

References

[1] Bloch F. Nuclear induction. Phys Rev 1946;70(7):460–74.

[2] Dieringer MA, et al. Rapid parametric mapping of the longitudinal relaxation time T1 using two-dimensional variable flip angle magnetic resonance imaging at 1.5 tesla, 3 tesla, and 7 tesla. PLoS One 2014;9(3), e91318.

[3] Nelson TR, Tung SM. Temperature dependence of proton relaxation times in vitro. Magn Reson Imaging 1987;5(3):189–99.

[4] Bitsch A, et al. A longitudinal MRI study of histopathologically defined hypointense multiple sclerosis lesions. Ann Neurol 2001;49(6):793–6.

[5] Cheng H-LM, et al. Practical medical applications of quantitative MR relaxometry. J Magn Reson Imaging 2012;36(4):805–24.

[6] Englund E, et al. Relaxation times in relation to grade of malignancy and tissue necrosis in astrocytic gliomas. Magn Reson Imaging 1986;4(5):425–9.

[7] Müller A, et al. Quantitative T1-mapping detects cloudy-enhancing tumor compartments predicting outcome of patients with glioblastoma. Cancer Med 2017;6(1):89–99.

[8] Vrenken H, et al. Whole-brain T1 mapping in multiple sclerosis: global changes of normal-appearing gray and white matter. Radiology 2006;240(3):811–20.

[9] Stikov N, et al. On the accuracy of T1 mapping: searching for common ground. Magn Reson Med 2015;73(2):514–22.

[10] Marques JP, et al. MP2RAGE, a self bias-field corrected sequence for improved segmentation and T1-mapping at high field. Neuroimage 2010;49(2):1271–81.

[11] Rioux JA, Levesque IR, Rutt BK. Biexponential longitudinal relaxation in white matter: characterization and impact on T1 mapping with IR-FSE and MP2RAGE. Magn Reson Med 2016;75(6):2265–77.

[12] Drain LE. A direct method of measuring nuclear spin-lattice relaxation times. Proc Phys Soc Sect A 1949;62(5):301–6.

[13] Hahn EL. An accurate nuclear magnetic resonance method for measuring spin-lattice relaxation times. Phys Rev 1949;76(1):145–6.

[14] Pykett IL, Mansfield P. A line scan image study of a tumorous rat leg by NMR. Phys Med Biol 1978;23(5):961–7.

[15] Boss MA, et al. Magnetic resonance imaging biomarker calibration service: proton spin relaxation times, Available at: https://www.nist.gov/publications/magnetic-resonance-imaging-biomarker-calibration-service-proton-spin-relaxation-times; 2018. Accessed 19 March 2019.

[16] Steen RG, et al. Precise and accurate measurement of proton T1 in human brain in vivo: validation and preliminary clinical application. J Magn Reson Imaging 1994;4(5):681–91.

[17] Messroghli DR, et al. Modified look-locker inversion recovery (MOLLI) for high-resolution T1 mapping of the heart. Magn Reson Med 2004;52(1):141–6.

[18] Piechnik SK, et al. Shortened Modified Look-Locker Inversion recovery (ShMOLLI) for clinical myocardial T1-mapping at 1.5 and 3 T within a 9 heartbeat breathhold. J Cardiovasc Magn Reson 2010;12:69.

[19] Gudbjartsson H, Patz S. The Rician distribution of noisy MRI data. Magn Reson Med 1995;34(6):910–4.

[20] Barral JK, et al. A robust methodology for in vivo T1 mapping. Magn Reson Med 2010;64(4):1057–67.

[21] Pykett IL, et al. Measurement of spin-lattice relaxation times in nuclear magnetic resonance imaging. Phys Med Biol 1983;28(6):723–9.

[22] Fukushima E, Roeder S. Experimental pulse NMR. A nuts and bolts approach. Reading, Massachusetts: Addison-Wesley Publ. Comp. Inc; 1981.

[23] Look DC, Locker DR. Time saving in measurement of NMR and EPR relaxation times. Rev Sci Instrum 1970;41(2):250–1.

[24] Gai ND, et al. Modified look-locker T1 evaluation using Bloch simulations: human and phantom validation. Magn Reson Med 2013;69(2):329–36.

[25] Christensen KA, et al. Optimal determination of relaxation times of fourier transform nuclear magnetic resonance. Determination of spin-lattice relaxation times in chemically polarized species. J Phys Chem 1974;78(19):1971–7.

[26] Fram EK, et al. Rapid calculation of T1 using variable flip angle gradient refocused imaging. Magn Reson Imaging 1987;5(3):201–8.

[27] Gupta RK. A new look at the method of variable nutation angle for the measurement of spin-lattice relaxation times using fourier transform NMR. J Magn Reson 1977;25(1):231–5.

[28] Deoni SCL, Rutt BK, Peters TM. Rapid combined T1 and T2 mapping using gradient recalled acquisition in the steady state. Magn Reson Med 2003;49(3):515–26.

[29] Homer J, Beevers MS. Driven-equilibrium single-pulse observation of T1 relaxation. A reevaluation of a rapid "new" method for determining NMR spin-lattice relaxation times. J Magn Reson 1985;63(2):287–97.

[30] Boudreau M, et al. B1 mapping for bias-correction in quantitative T1 imaging of the brain at 3T using standard pulse sequences. J Magn Reson Imaging 2017;46(6):1673–82.

[31] Sled JG, Pike GB. Standing-wave and RF penetration artifacts caused by elliptic geometry: an electrodynamic analysis of MRI. IEEE Trans Med Imaging 1998;17(4):653–62.

[32] Lee Y, Callaghan MF, Nagy Z. Analysis of the precision of variable flip angle T1 mapping with emphasis on the noise propagated from RF transmit field maps. Front Neurosci 2017;11:106.

[33] Ernst RR, Anderson WA. Application of fourier transform spectroscopy to magnetic resonance. Rev Sci Instrum 1966;37(1):93–102.

[34] Bernstein M, King K, Zhou X. Handbook of MRI pulse sequences. Elsevier; 2004.

[35] Zur Y, Wood ML, Neuringer LJ. Spoiling of transverse magnetization in steady-state sequences. Magn Reson Med 1991;21(2):251–63.

[36] Yarnykh VL. Optimal radiofrequency and gradient spoiling for improved accuracy of T1 and B1 measurements using fast steady-state techniques. Magn Reson Med 2010;63(6):1610–26.

[37] Deoni SCL, Peters TM, Rutt BK. Determination of optimal angles for variable nutation proton magnetic spin-lattice, T1, and spin-spin, T2, relaxation times measurement. Magn Reson Med 2004;51(1):194–9.

[38] Schabel MC, Morrell GR. Uncertainty in T(1) mapping using the variable flip angle method with two flip angles. Phys Med Biol 2009;54(1):N1–8.

[39] Wang HZ, Riederer SJ, Lee JN. Optimizing the precision in T1 relaxation estimation using limited flip angles. Magn Reson Med 1987;5(5):399–416.

[40] Chang L-C, et al. Linear least-squares method for unbiased estimation of T1 from SPGR signals. Magn Reson Med 2008;60(2):496–501.

[41] Baudrexel S, et al. T1 mapping with the variable flip angle technique: a simple correction for insufficient spoiling of transverse magnetization. Magn Reson Med 2018;79(6):3082–92.

[42] Lutti A, Weiskopf N. Optimizing the accuracy of T1 mapping accounting for RF non-linearities and spoiling characteristics in FLASH imaging, In: Proceedings of the 21st annual meeting of ISMRM, Salt Lake City, Utah, USA; 2013. p. 2478.

[43] Liberman G, Louzoun Y, Ben Bashat D. T1 mapping using variable flip angle SPGR data with flip angle correction. J Magn Reson Imaging 2014;40(1):171–80.

[44] Samson RS, et al. A simple correction for B1 field errors in magnetization transfer ratio measurements. Magn Reson Imaging 2006;24(3):255–63.

[45] Wang J, Qiu M, Constable RT. In vivo method for correcting transmit/receive nonuniformities with phased array coils. Magn Reson Med 2005;53(3):666–74.

[46] Cercignani M, et al. Three-dimensional quantitative magnetisation transfer imaging of the human brain. Neuroimage 2005;27(2):436–41.

[47] Yarnykh VL. Pulsed Z-spectroscopic imaging of cross-relaxation parameters in tissues for human MRI: theory and clinical applications. Magn Reson Med 2002;47(5):929–39.

[48] Li ZF, et al. A simple B 1 correction method for dynamic contrast-enhanced MRI. Phys Med Biol 2018;63(16):16NT01.

[49] Sung K, Daniel BL, Hargreaves BA. Transmit B1+ field inhomogeneity and T1 estimation errors in breast DCE-MRI at 3 tesla. J Magn Reson Imaging 2013;38(2):454–9.

[50] Ma D, et al. Magnetic resonance fingerprinting. Nature 2013;495(7440):187–92.

[51] Doneva M, et al. Compressed sensing reconstruction for magnetic resonance parameter mapping. Magn Reson Med 2010;64(4):1114–20.

[52] Li W, Griswold M, Yu X. Fast cardiac T1 mapping in mice using a model-based compressed sensing method. Magn Reson Med 2012;68(4):1127–34.

[53] Haase A, et al. Inversion recovery snapshot FLASH MR imaging. J Comput Assist Tomogr 1989;13(6): 1036–1040.

[54] Mugler 3rd JP, Brookeman JR. Three-dimensional magnetization-prepared rapid gradient-echo imaging (3D MP RAGE). Magn Reson Med 1990;15(1):152–7.

[55] Marques JP, Gruetter R. New developments and applications of the MP2RAGE sequence focusing the contrast and high spatial resolution R1 mapping. PLoS One 2013;8(7):e69294.

[56] de Hollander G. PyMP2RAGE, Available at: https://github.com/Gilles86/pymp2rage; 2017. Accessed 2 January 2019.

[57] Marques J. MP2RAGE related scripts, Available at: https://github.com/JosePMarques/MP2RAGE-related-scripts; 2017. Accessed 2 January 2019.

[58] Voelker MN, et al. The traveling heads: multicenter brain imaging at 7 tesla. MAGMA 2016;29(3):399–415.

[59] Fujimoto K, et al. Quantitative comparison of cortical surface reconstructions from MP2RAGE and multi-echo MPRAGE data at 3 and 7 T. Neuroimage 2014;90:60–73.

[60] Beck ES, et al. Improved visualization of cortical lesions in multiple sclerosis using 7T MP2RAGE. Am J Neuroradiol 2018;39(3):459–66. https://doi.org/10.3174/ajnr.A5534.

[61] Haast RAM, Ivanov D, Uludağ K. The impact of B1+ correction on MP2RAGE cortical T1 and apparent cortical thickness at 7T. Hum Brain Mapp 2018;39(6):2412–25.

[62] Waehnert MD, et al. Anatomically motivated modeling of cortical laminae. Neuroimage 2014;93 (Pt 2):210–20.

[63] Redfield AG. Nuclear magnetic resonance saturation and rotary saturation in solids. Phys Rev 1955;98(6):1787–809.

[64] Jones GP. Spin-lattice relaxation in the rotating frame: weak-collision case. Phys Rev 1966;148(1):332–5.

[65] Santyr GE, Henkelman RM, Bronskill MJ. Spin locking for magnetic resonance imaging with application to human breast. Magn Reson Med 1989;12(1):25–37.

[66] Koenig SH, Brown RD, 3rd. Determinants of proton relaxation rates in tissue. Magn Reson Med 1984;1(4):437–49.

[67] Borthakur A, et al. Sodium and T1rho MRI for molecular and diagnostic imaging of articular cartilage. NMR Biomed 2006;19(7):781–821.

[68] Akella SVS, et al. Proteoglycan-induced changes inT1ρ-relaxation of articular cartilage at 4T. Magn Reson Med 2001;46(3):419–23.

[69] Duvvuri U, et al. T1ρ-relaxation in articular cartilage: effects of enzymatic degradation. Magn Reson Med 1997;38(6):863–7.

[70] Mlynárik V, et al. Transverse relaxation mechanisms in articular cartilage. J Magn Reson 2004;169(2):300–7.

[71] Regatte RR, Schweitzer ME. Novel contrast mechanisms at 3 tesla and 7 tesla. Semin Musculoskelet Radiol 2008;12(3):266–80.

[72] Fairbanks EJ, Santyr GE, Sorenson JA. One-shot measurement of spin-lattice relaxation times in the off-resonance rotating frame using MR imaging, with application to breast. J Magn Reson B 1995;106(3): 279–283.

[73] Dixon WT, et al. Myocardial suppression in vivo by spin locking with composite pulses. Magn Reson Med 1996;36(1):90–4.
[74] Kamesh Iyer S, et al. Accelerated free-breathing 3D T1ρ cardiovascular magnetic resonance using multicoil compressed sensing. J Cardiovasc Magn Reson 2019;21(1):5.
[75] Muthupillai R, et al. Acute myocardial infarction: tissue characterization with T1rho-weighted MR imaging—initial experience. Radiology 2004;232(2):606–10.
[76] Witschey WRT, et al. In vivo chronic myocardial infarction characterization by spin locked cardiovascular magnetic resonance. J Cardiovasc Magn Reson 2012;14:37.
[77] Allkemper T, et al. Evaluation of fibrotic liver disease with whole-liver T1ρ MR imaging: a feasibility study at 1.5 T. Radiology 2014;271(2):408–15.
[78] Aronen HJ, et al. 3D spin-lock imaging of human gliomas. Magn Reson Imaging 1999;17(7):1001–10.
[79] Borthakur A, et al. T1rho MRI of Alzheimer's disease. Neuroimage 2008;41(4):1199–205.
[80] Haris M, et al. T1rho (T1ρ) MR imaging in Alzheimer's disease and Parkinson's disease with and without dementia. J Neurol 2011;258(3):380–5.
[81] Michaeli S, et al. T1rho MRI contrast in the human brain: modulation of the longitudinal rotating frame relaxation shutter-speed during an adiabatic RF pulse. J Magn Reson 2006;181(1):135–47.
[82] Johannessen W, et al. Assessment of human disc degeneration and proteoglycan content using T1rho-weighted magnetic resonance imaging. Spine 2006;31(11):1253–7.
[83] Keenan KE, et al. T1ρ dispersion in articular cartilage: relationship to material properties and macromolecular content. Cartilage 2015;6(2):113–22.
[84] Li X, et al. In vivo T(1rho) and T(2) mapping of articular cartilage in osteoarthritis of the knee using 3 T MRI. Osteoarthr Cartil 2007;15(7):789–97.
[85] Wheaton AJ, et al. Method for reduced SAR T1rho-weighted MRI. Magn Reson Med 2004;51(6):1096–102.
[86] Chen W, Takahashi A, Han E. Quantitative T(1)(ρ) imaging using phase cycling for B0 and B1 field inhomogeneity compensation. Magn Reson Imaging 2011;29(5):608–19.
[87] Witschey 2nd WRT, et al. Artifacts in T1 rho-weighted imaging: compensation for B(1) and B(0) field imperfections. J Magn Reson 2007;186(1):75–85.
[88] Solomon I. Rotary spin echoes. Phys Rev Lett 1959;2(7):301–2.
[89] Charagundla SR, et al. Artifacts in T(1rho)-weighted imaging: correction with a self-compensating spin-locking pulse. J Magn Reson 2003;162(1):113–21.
[90] Chen W. Errors in quantitative T1rho imaging and the correction methods. Quant Imaging Med Surg 2015;5(4):583–91.
[91] Li X, et al. In vivo T(1rho) mapping in cartilage using 3D magnetization-prepared angle-modulated partitioned k-space spoiled gradient echo snapshots (3D MAPSS). Magn Reson Med 2008;59(2):298–307.
[92] Zeng H, et al. A composite spin-lock pulse for deltaB0 + B1 insensitive T1rho measurement, In: Proceedings of the 14th annual meeting of ISMRM, Seattle, Washington, USA; 2006. p. 2356.
[93] Chopra S, McClung RED, Jordan RB. Rotating-frame relaxation rates of solvent molecules in solutions of paramagnetic ions undergoing solvent exchange. J Magn Reson 1984;59(3):361–72.
[94] Cobb JG, et al. Exchange-mediated contrast in CEST and spin-lock imaging. Magn Reson Imaging 2014;32(1):28–40.
[95] Bonny JM, et al. T2 maximum likelihood estimation from multiple spin-echo magnitude images. Magn Reson Med 1996;36(2):287–93.
[96] Hardy PA, Andersen AH. Calculating T2 in images from a phased array receiver. Magn Reson Med 2009;61(4):962–9.
[97] Raya JG, et al. T2 measurement in articular cartilage: impact of the fitting method on accuracy and precision at low SNR. Magn Reson Med 2010;63(1):181–93.
[98] Duvvuri U, et al. Water magnetic relaxation dispersion in biological systems: the contribution of proton exchange and implications for the noninvasive detection of cartilage degradation. Proc Natl Acad Sci U S A, 2001;98(22):12479–84.

[99] Koskinen SK, et al. T1rho Dispersion profile of rat tissues in vitro at very low locking fields. Magn Reson Imaging 2006;24(3):295–9.
[100] Koskinen SK, et al. T1ρ dispersion of rat tissues in vitro. Magn Reson Imaging 1999;17(7):1043–7.
[101] Cobb JG, et al. Exchange-mediated contrast agents for spin-lock imaging. Magn Reson Med 2012;67(5):1427–33.
[102] Chen W, Chan Q, Wáng Y-XJ. Breath-hold black blood quantitative T1rho imaging of liver using single shot fast spin echo acquisition. Quant Imaging Med Surg 2016;6(2):168–77.
[103] Santyr GE, et al. Off-resonance spin locking for MR imaging. Magn Reson Med 1994;32(1):43–51.

CHAPTER

Quantitative T_2 and T_2^* Mapping

3

Richard D. Dortch[a,b]

[a]*Division of Neuroimaging Research, Barrow Neurological Institute, Phoenix, AZ, United States* [b]*Barrow Neuroimaging Innovation Center, Barrow Neurological Institute, Phoenix, AZ, United States*

3.1 Introduction

As described in Chapter 1, numerous biophysical and physiological mechanisms contribute to a loss of signal coherence following excitation. The resulting exponential signal decay can be characterized by the spin-spin relaxation time constant (T_2) for spin-echo-based acquisitions. For gradient echo (and asymmetric spin echo) based acquisitions, a shorter effective spin-spin relaxation time constant (T_2^*) is observed due to the additional influence of static magnetic field gradients. In either case, the transverse relaxation time (T_2 and T_2^*) provides a measure that is sensitive to a number of microanatomical tissue features (e.g., myelination [1], iron content [2]). Because many of these features are altered in diseased tissues, transverse relaxation time mapping has long been investigated with the goal of developing imaging biomarkers.

Unfortunately, while relaxation parameters are exquisitely sensitive, they are not necessarily specific to a given feature. As an example, consider white matter lesions in multiple sclerosis where numerous pathological features that affect transverse relaxation (e.g., inflammation/edema, de/remyelination, iron accumulation [3]) present concurrently. In such cases, it becomes difficult to relate observed T_2 or T_2^* changes to a particular pathological process, which limits the potential clinical impact of these measurements. To address this apparent lack of specificity, researchers have proposed multiparametric methods, which combine complementary information from transverse relaxation and the other quantitative Magnetic Resonance Imaging (MRI) methods outlined in this book. In addition, multicompartment models, which isolate signals from specific cellular compartments (e.g., water between myelin bilayers) based upon multiexponential transverse relaxation, have shown promise as a means to improve specificity. For more information on the topic of multicompartment tissue modeling, the reader is referred to [1,4,5].

Given this promise, researchers have increasingly focused on developing rapid and robust methods for mapping transverse relaxation times in tissues. Beyond this research potential, transverse relaxation measurements provide essential information for sequence and contrast optimization, which is a primary goal of most clinical MRI protocols. Thus, in both clinical and research settings, there is a significant need for sequences that provide accurate and precise measures of T_2 or T_2^* within reasonable scan times.

In this chapter, MRI methods for mapping both T_2 and T_2^* are detailed, with an emphasis on practical implementation within the time constraints of clinical imaging, as well as the presence of

Advances in Magnetic Resonance Technology and Applications. Volume 1. ISSN 2666-9099. https://doi.org/10.1016/B978-0-12-817057-1.00005-6

main magnetic field (B_0) and transmit radiofrequency field (B_1) variations. More specifically, spin-echo-based acquisitions for T_2 mapping will be discussed followed by both gradient- and asymmetric spin-echo-based acquisitions for T_2^* mapping. For T_2 mapping applications, water diffusion through microscopic field gradients and chemical exchange mechanisms can result in T_2 estimates that vary with echo spacing [6]. The impact of these mechanisms, as well as methods to mitigate them, will also be outlined. In addition, the sampling requirements (e.g., number of echoes, echo spacing, *TR*) for single and multicompartment models will be discussed, as the latter generally requires more echoes and a higher signal-to-noise ratio (SNR). Finally, combined spin- and gradient echo methods for simultaneous estimation of T_2 and T_2^* will be presented. Following a detailed discussion of acquisition methods, numerical methods to covert the measured signal into parameter maps will also be outlined. Additional information on emerging signal analysis methods related to this topic can be found in this chapter. Note that methods that combine transverse and spin-lattice relaxation (T_1) measurements (e.g., MR fingerprinting [7]) will not be discussed, as they are the subject of later chapters. Furthermore, tissue-specific applications (Chapters 7–10) will be described elsewhere in this book. Finally, additional technical information on transverse relaxation mapping can be found in two recent review articles [4,5].

3.2 Spin-spin relaxation (T_2) measurement sequences

3.2.1 Single spin echo sequences

In this section, we assume a single compartment tissue model, where T_2 is uniform within a given voxel. Relevant discussions on the methods for mapping multiexponential T_2 relaxation are covered in subsequent sections.

The most straightforward method for mapping T_2 is to acquire serial images with a single spin echo sequence (shown in Fig. 3.1) at two or more different echo times (*TE*). The resulting decay of transverse magnetization $M_\perp$ (or M_{xy}) can be expressed from the transverse component of the Bloch equations

$$M_\perp(TE) = M_z(0^-)\exp(-TE/T_2) \tag{3.1}$$

where $M_z(0^-)$ is the longitudinal magnetization immediately prior to each 90° excitation pulse. Assuming that the observed signal is proportional to the resulting transverse magnetization, one can estimate T_2 and $M_z(0^-)$ by fitting signals acquired at two or more *TE*s with Eq. (3.1) provided that $M_z(0^-)$ is constant as a function of *TE* (for additional details see Section 3.5).

This constraint is met when the repetition time (*TR*) is much longer than T_1, or the signal is at thermal equilibrium prior to the 90° excitation pulse (i.e., $TR \gtrsim 5T_1$). In this case, $M_z(0^-)$ can be defined by the proton density (M_0). Note that because M_0 is scaled by numerous experimental factors (e.g., receiver gain, transmit RF amplitude), this method can only provide relative estimates of M_0 that are of limited biological relevance. For information on methods to quantify absolute M_0 values, which may provide biologically relevant information on water and macromolecular content, the reader is referred to [8].

Shorter *TR*s ($TR < 5T_1$) are often desired to obtain estimates of T_2 within clinically feasible scan times. For the short-TR case, $M_z(0^-)$ can be determined from the longitudinal component of the Bloch equations, resulting in the following expression

$$M_\perp(TE, TR) = M_0\{1 - 2\exp[-(TR - TE/2)/T_1] + \exp(-TR/T_1)\}\exp(-TE/T_2) \tag{3.2}$$

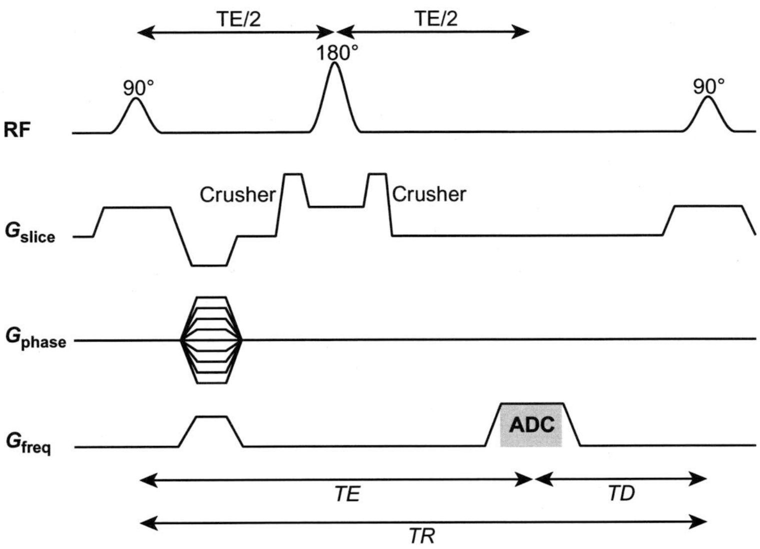

FIG. 3.1

Single spin echo imaging pulse sequence. A 180° refocusing pulse is applied after a delay *TE*/2, forming a spin echo at *TE*. Crusher gradients are applied on each side of the refocusing pulse to ensure that the acquired signal arises from spins excited by the excitation pulse. The gray ADC box represents the point at which the signal is sampled by the analog-to-digital converter (ADC). To estimate T_2, the sequence is repeated at different *TE*s and a constant *TD* (or *TR* in some scenarios as discussed in the text).

Unfortunately, it can be seen that the $M_z(0^-)$ term in Eq. (3.2) is no longer a constant with respect to *TE*; therefore, one cannot estimate T_2 by acquiring images at multiple *TE*s and a fixed *TR* using this expression. Fortunately, there are two conditions under which Eq. (3.2) can be simplified. For the first, if we assume that $TR \gg TE$, Eq. (3.2) can be approximated as

$$M_{\perp}(TE, TR) \approx M_0\{1 - \exp(\text{-}TR/T_1)\}\exp(\text{-}TE/T_2) \tag{3.3}$$

where $M_z(0^-)=M_0\{1\text{-}\exp(\text{-}TR/T_1)\}$ can be defined as the apparent relative proton density, which is simply the relative proton density weighted by the recovery of longitudinal magnetization during *TR*. In Eq. (3.3), it can be seen that the $M_z(0^-)$ term is independent of *TE*; thus, T_2 can be accurately mapped from spin echo sequences acquired at different *TE*s and a constant *TR* when $TR \gg TE$. For the second condition, one can assume that the longitudinal magnetization is ≈ 0 at *TE* because the refocusing pulse in the spin echo sequence inverts any growth of longitudinal magnetization between the excitation and refocusing pulses. Solving the longitudinal component of the Bloch equations based upon this assumption yields

$$M_{\perp}(TE, TD) \approx M_0\{1 - \exp(\text{-}TD/T_1)\}\exp(\text{-}TE/T_2) \tag{3.4}$$

where $TD = TR\text{-}TE$ is the predelay time, or the time from the center of the spin echo to the next excitation pulse as shown in Fig. 3.1. Once again, it can be seen that the $M_z(0^-)$ term is independent of *TE* in Eq. (3.4), and T_2 can be accurately mapped from spin echo sequences acquired at different *TE*s and a constant *TD*. This is a particularly attractive approach for mapping T_2 with short-*TR* spin echo sequences, as it does not require any assumptions about the relative size of TE, TR, and T_1, although it does require the user to manually adjust $TR=TD+TE$ for each TE to maintain a constant TD across acquisitions.

Although these signal models afford the user flexibility in selecting a TD (or TR), the specific value should be chosen carefully given the competing needs for SNR and scan time. For example, while choosing a long TD ($\gtrsim 5T_1$) maximizes SNR, it also results in prohibitively long scan times. In contrast, short TDs yield short acquisitions, but with limited SNR that may affect the precision of the resulting T_2 estimates. Generally, one would like to choose the TD that balances these two needs, or that maximizes the SNR for a given scan time. This optimal TD can be determined by first assuming that the total number of acquisitions (N_{acq}=number of shots to fill k-space × number of signal averages) per unit-time is inversely proportional to TD. Under this assumption, it can be shown that the observed signal magnitude is proportional to $N_{acq}\{1 - \exp(-TD/T_1)\} \propto \{1 - \exp(-TD/T_1)\}/TD$, while the noise standard deviation is proportional to the square-root of $N_{acq} \propto 1/TD$. The resulting SNR per unit acquisition time, or SNR efficiency, can then be expressed as

$$SNR_{eff} \propto \frac{1-\exp(-TD/T_1)}{\sqrt{TD}} \tag{3.5}$$

As shown in Fig. 3.2, SNR_{eff} is optimized for a specific T_1 when $TD \approx 1.26T_1$. For applications in the body, however, a large range of T_1 values is expected rather than a specific value. In this case,

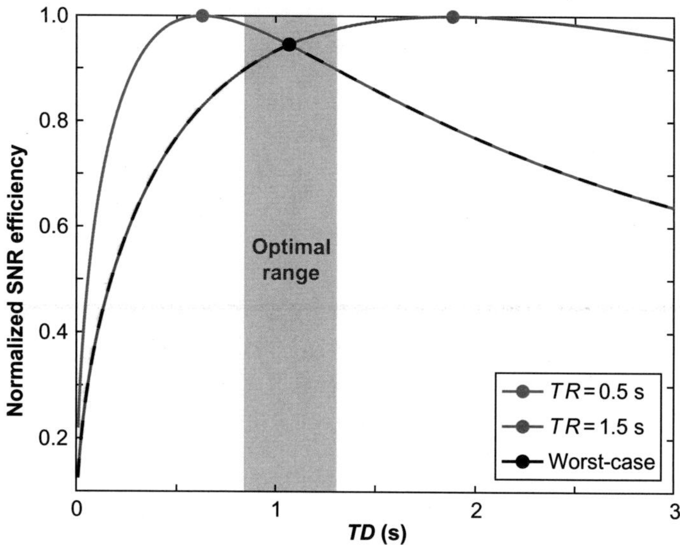

FIG. 3.2

SNR efficiency as a function of TD. The SNR efficiency was normalized to the maximum value for each T_1, which is indicated via the blue ($T_1 = 0.5$s) and orange circles ($T_1 = 1.5$s). In both the cases, SNR efficiency is maximized at $TD \approx 1.26T_1$. The worst-case SNR efficiency across the different T_1 values is shown with the black dashed line overlaid on the blue and orange curves, and the corresponding optimal $TD = 1067$ms is indicated with the black circle. Finally, the range of TD values that yield SNR efficiencies >90% the maximum achievable value is shown in the gray box.

maximizing the "worst-case" SNR_{eff} across the expected range of T_1 values yields near optimal results for all tissues. As an example, consider the case where we expect to observe $T_1 = 500$–1500 ms. It can be shown that selecting a $TD = 1067$ ms maximizes the "worst-case" scenario with respect to SNR efficiency across this range of T_1 values. Furthermore, selecting a TD in the range of approximately 850–1300 ms yields SNR efficiencies >90% the maximum achievable value for all T_1 values, which affords the user some flexibility in cases where a specific scan time is desired.

The precision of T_2 estimates also depends on the chosen TE values. Cramér-Rao Lower Bound (CRLB) theory sets a lower limit on the uncertainty of parameter estimates and has been used to determine optimal TE values for T_2 mapping applications [9]. For the simplest case where images at two different TEs are desired, the optimal sampling scheme involves acquiring one acquisition at the minimum achievable TE (ideally $TE = 0$ ms) and the other at $1.11T_2$. Extending this approach to an arbitrary number of TEs, the recommendation is to acquire 22% of the acquisitions at the minimum TE and the remaining acquisitions at $1.28T_2$. The main issue with this approach is that it only yields suitable results for a narrow range of T_2 values and is, therefore, not practical across healthy and diseased tissues, where a large range of T_2 values is expected. As a result, the general recommendation is to acquire images over a large range of logarithmically spaced TEs [10,11], although this approach may result in scan times that are too long for most clinical applications when single spin echo acquisitions are used. In addition, when multiple T_2 values are expected within a voxel (i.e., multicompartment systems), single spin echo approaches are challenging to optimize and the methods in the following section are preferred.

Single spin echo acquisitions are also susceptible to a variety of confounding factors that can decrease their accuracy for T_2 mapping. For example, water diffusion through susceptibility-induced magnetic field gradients (e.g., from deoxygenated hemoglobin [6]) results in an additional exponential signal decay with TE, resulting in a reduced apparent T_2 value when these effects are ignored. Chemical exchange between frequency-shifted environments or tissue compartments results in a similar effect. In tissues where these effects are significant (e.g., blood [6]), measuring T_2 using single spin echo acquisitions is, therefore, not recommended and the methods described in the following section are required.

3.2.2 Multiecho spin echo sequences

Multiecho spin echo sequences generally involve the application of an excitation pulse followed by a series of refocusing pulses. When refocusing pulses are applied at odd integers of a given delay, and signals are collected at even integers of the same delay, a series of spin echoes are formed that decay exponentially. This allows one to fully sample the exponential decay following a single excitation, which has advantages over single-echo approaches in terms of both precision and speed. Furthermore, unlike single-echo mapping approaches, diffusion and chemical exchange effects can be reduced in multiecho sequences by employing a constant echo spacing at the minimum achievable value (within hardware and safety limitations). In addition, multiecho sequences are recommended for multiexponential T_2 mapping applications, which generally require a large number of echoes to precisely estimate model parameters.

The primary drawback of multiecho methods is their use of multiple refocusing pulses, which results in signal contributions from non-spin-echo pathways (i.e., stimulated echoes) that can contaminate the signal decay and bias T_2 estimates, even in the presence of relatively minor B_0 and B_1

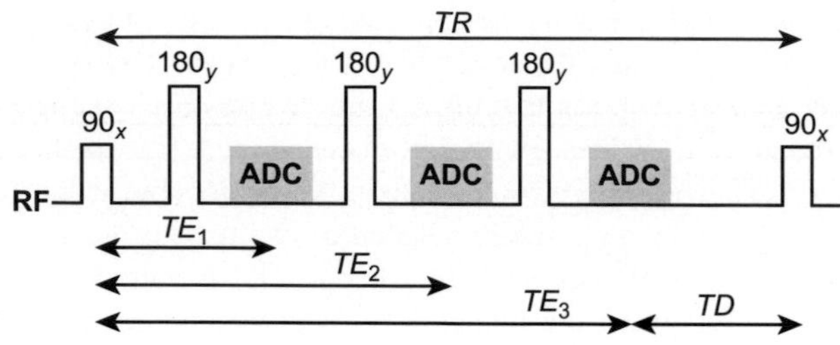

FIG. 3.3

CPMG pulse sequence for nonlocalized measurement of T_2. The relative phase of each RF pulse is indicated via its subscript (e.g., 90_x indicates a pulse with a 90° nominal flip angle applied along the *x*-axis in the transverse plane). The relative phase of the excitation (90_x) and refocusing (180_y) pulses is designed to reduce sensitivity to B_0 and B_1 inhomogeneities. Only the first three spin echoes are shown; however, one typically acquires thousands of echoes following each excitation to estimate T_2.

imperfections. For spectroscopic applications, the Carr-Purcell-Meiboom Gill (CPMG) sequence [12,13] shown in Fig. 3.3 is often chosen because the relative phase of the excitation and refocusing pulses minimizes this effect. Unfortunately, extrapolating the CPMG phase cycling approach to an imaging sequence typically yields biased T_2 estimates when an exponential decay model is used. This is due the effect of slice-selective refocusing pulses and/or the large B_0 and B_1 variations observed in the body, both of which result in large amplitude stimulated echo pathways. As a result, researchers have developed two broad strategies for T_2 mapping applications with multiecho spin echo sequences: (*i*) eliminate non-spin-echo pathways using non-CPMG approaches or (*ii*) alter the standard exponential decay model to account for all pathways present in the signal decay.

The first solution that was widely adopted involved broadband composite refocusing pulses (e.g., $90_x180_y90_x$ [14], Version S [15]) applied between pairs of optimized crusher gradients [16,17]. The broadband composite pulses serve to correct refocusing flip angle errors due to B_1 and/or B_0 variations, while the arrangement of crusher gradients is optimized to dephase any remaining signal from nonspin-echo pathways. Following this development, a single-slice version of this sequence (typically with 32 evenly spaced echoes at 10 ms increments) was developed and served as the standard method for multiexponential T_2 mapping in humans for many years [18]. An example of this sequence is shown in Fig. 3.4. The primary impediments to the widespread adoption of this method are the limited coverage (single slice) and long scan times, which are typically >20 min. Although efficient multislice approaches are available, they typically yield inaccurate T_2 estimates due to the presence of stimulated echoes (i.e., from incomplete spoiling by the crusher gradients) and off-resonance magnetization transfer effects from the slice-selective refocusing pulses of adjacent slices [19]. As a result, three-dimensional versions of the multiple spin echo sequence are generally required when larger volumetric coverage is desired; however, this results in acquisition times that are often unsuitable for clinical imaging.

Several methods have been proposed to reduce scan times for 3D multiecho methods. As discussed in Section 3.2.1, *TR* can be shortened to increase SNR efficiency. Previous work [20] has shown that this reduction does not significantly bias estimates from multiexponential models provided that the T_1 values of each compartment are not significantly different. In addition, multiple lines of *k*-space can be acquired around each spin echo via a so-called gradient and spin echo (GRASE) acquisition [21],

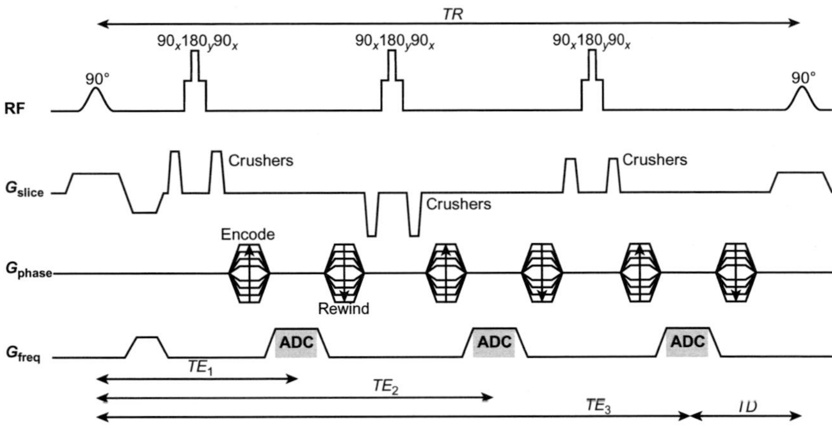

FIG. 3.4

Multiecho spin echo imaging pulse sequence for measuring T_2. The combination of broadband composite refocusing pulses ($90_x180_y90_x$) and crusher gradients placed around each refocusing pulse in an alternating and descending fashion serve to eliminate signal from unwanted coherence pathways (e.g., stimulated echoes). Typically, phase encoding is applied for each spin echo ("Encode" in G_{phase}) then rewound ("Rewind" in G_{phase}) so that all signal pathways are identically encoded (i.e., overlap in the final image). Only the first three echoes are shown; however, typically 32 echoes or more are acquired per excitation to estimate T_2.

although this may result in an increased echo spacing and reduced SNR. In cases where SNR is adequate and reduced scan times are essential, parallel imaging and/or Partial Fourier reconstructions may also be used to reduce the total number of shots required to fill *k*-space. In addition, compressed sensing techniques, which exploit the ability to sparsely represent T_2 decay data following an appropriate transform, have been proposed to further accelerate T_2 mapping methods [22].

More recently, signal models that account for non-spin-echo pathways have been developed (e.g., the extended phase graph [23] and Bloch equation simulations [24]). These approaches alleviate the need for broadband composite refocusing pulses and complicated gradient crusher schemes, which allows for reduced echo spacings and/or increased number of echoes per *TR*. Recent work has focused on refining these models to account for imperfect slice profiles [25] and optimally account for B_1 variations [26]. By combining these models with the aforementioned methods to reduce 3D scan times, researchers have demonstrated that whole-brain multiexponential T_2 mapping can be robustly performed within 15 min [21].

3.2.3 T_2-prepared sequences

Another method for increasing volumetric coverage is the use of T_2-prepared multislice sequences, an example of which is shown in Fig. 3.5. In this approach, the T_2 preparation consists of an excitation pulse followed by a variable number of B_1-insensitive refocusing pulses (e.g., MLEV [27], adiabatic [28]) applied at a constant refocusing rate, which minimizes the impact of diffusion and/or chemical exchange effects as discussed previously, and a "flip-back" pulse to store the resulting T_2-weighted magnetization on the longitudinal axis. The T_2-weighted signal is then read out via an efficient,

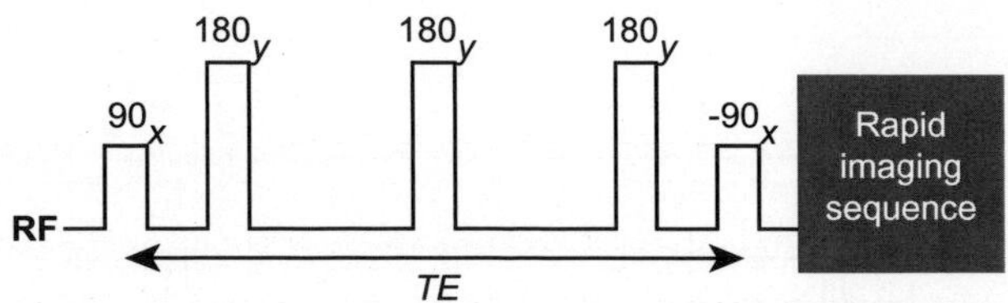

FIG. 3.5

T_2-prepared imaging pulse sequence. The nonspatially selective T_2-preparation module consists of an excitation pulse, a series of B_0- and B_1-insensitive refocusing pulses, and a flip-back pulse at *TE* to store the T_2 contrast on the longitudinal axis. The T_2-prepared magnetization is then excited and spatially encoded via a rapid, multislice imaging readout (e.g., EPI, spiral), and this process is repeated with different duration preparation periods, or *TE*s, to estimate T_2. In general, the spacing between refocusing pulses is set to the minimum possible value (within hardware and safety limitations) to mitigate the effect of diffusion and/or chemical exchange, and different *TE*s are acquired by varying the number of refocusing pulses in the preparation module.

multislice readout, and T_2 can be mapped by acquiring images serially with different T_2-preparation durations (or effective *TE*s). As an example, Oh et al. [27] proposed using a T_2 preparation period followed by a multislice spiral readout as a means to rapidly acquire volumetric T_2 data. In addition to increased readout flexibility, this approach also allows one to optimally sample the T_2 decay curve using a logarithmic echo spacing [10,11]. Even with optimal sampling strategies, these approaches often employ low-flip angle readouts, which improve efficiency at the cost of reduced SNR. Therefore, although T_2-prepared methods remain promising for applications that require shorter scan times, additional work is required to demonstrate their effect on precision and accuracy.

3.2.4 Unspoiled gradient echo sequences

As described in Section 3.3, spoiled gradient echo sequences are commonly used for T_2* mapping applications. In addition, these sequences can be acquired with a short *TR* and a range of flip angles for T_1 mapping applications (see Chapter 2). Although less common, the unspoiled (or coherent) gradient echo sequence with balanced gradients (see Fig. 3.6) generates a combined T_1 and T_2 contrast that varies with flip angle. As a result, this method has been proposed for single component T_2 mapping applications (e.g., DESPOT2 [29]). This approach is particularly attractive for rapid clinical applications, as 3D gradient echo sequences are efficient in terms of SNR and can be accelerated using low flip angles and short *TR*s. One drawback of this method is its sensitivity to banding artifacts from B_0 inhomogeneities [30]. In addition, independent estimates of both T_1 (e.g., via spoiled gradient echoes at different flip angles) and B_1 are required to invert the model. Finally, although multicompartment models have been proposed for these sequences (e.g., mcDESPOT [31]), the resulting parameter estimates lack precision [32] and may be biased in the presence of magnetization transfer effects [33].

3.2.5 Model-based reconstructions

As described in Section 3.2.1, one method for mapping T_2 is to acquire serial acquisitions at different *TE*s. One common method to accelerate these acquisitions is to incorporate fast-imaging

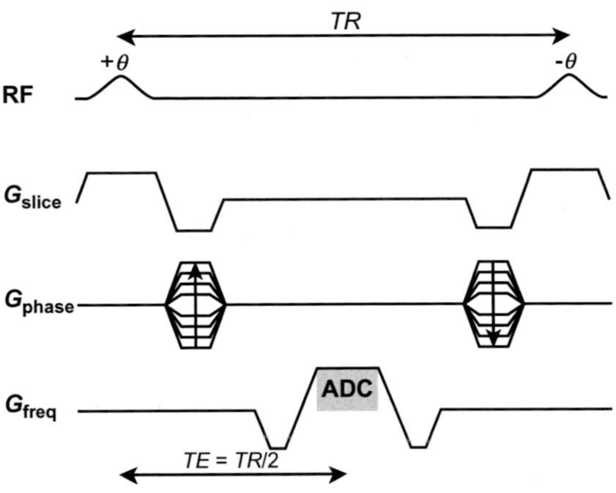

FIG. 3.6

Unspoiled balanced gradient echo imaging pulse sequence. This sequence requires all gradient dephasing moments to be zero (or balanced) before the next excitation pulse is applied. The alternating phase of each consecutive RF pulse ($\pm\theta$) ensures that the passband for the steady-state magnetization is on-resonance. This sequence generates an echo at $TE = TR/2$ whose magnitude is a complex function of both T_1 and T_2.
In DESPOT2, the sequence is repeated over a range of flip angles θ, while holding TR and TE constant. This approach also requires independent estimates of B_1 and T_1, the latter of which can be obtained by acquiring data from the spoiled gradient sequence shown in Fig. 3.7 over a range of θ (and the same TR and TE).

readouts (e.g., echo-planar imaging, EPI; or fast spin echo, FSE), which acquire multiple lines of k-space per shot. In this scenario, the same k-space trajectory (e.g., center-out, linear) is used for each acquisition, and different TEs are sampled by varying the delay between the excitation pulse and the beginning of the fast-imaging readout. One drawback of this method is that short TEs can be difficult to achieve for certain trajectories (e.g., linear). In addition, this method does not make use of all of the available signal for longer TEs because of the required delay between excitation and readout. An alternate method is to use the minimum possible delay between excitation and readout and alter the k-space trajectory for each acquisition to sample different effective TEs. Unfortunately, the point-spread function changes as a function of k-space trajectory (or effective TE) in this scenario. This results in a TE-dependent blurring of each image when conventional Fourier-based reconstruction methods are used, which lead to artifacts in the corresponding T_2 maps.

Model-based reconstructions overcome this limitation by adding a T_2 decay term the conventional Fourier k-space model. In this approach, images and T_2 maps are jointly estimated from highly undersampled Cartesian [34,35] or non-Cartesian [36] data using iterative reconstruction methods and prior knowledge (e.g., similarity between neighboring voxels). More recently, these models have been expanded to account for non-spin-echo pathways in the signal decay [37]. The primary advantage of these methods is that they enable data to be efficiently collected with large undersampling factors, although the resulting inverse problem is more computationally expensive than conventional T_2 mapping methods and convergence to the global minimum is not always guaranteed.

3.3 Effective spin-spin relaxation (T_2*) measurement sequences

3.3.1 Single and multiecho spoiled gradient echo sequences

While both single (Fig. 3.7) and multiecho spoiled gradient echo sequences (Fig. 3.8) can be used to quantify T_2*, the latter is generally preferred in practical applications where a wide range of T_2* values are likely to be observed. One attractive feature of T_2* mapping is that the sequences do not require multiple RF pulses and, therefore, are readily amenable to multislice imaging. As a result, multiecho spoiled gradient echo sequences allow one to collect whole-brain T_2* maps within clinically feasible scan times when optimized (with respect to *TE* and *TR*) using the same approaches described above for T_2. In addition, the methods used for single component T_2* mapping are generally translatable to multiexponential mapping, although higher SNR and more echoes may be required for the latter.

Where T_2* differs from T_2 mapping is in the practical issues that arise, specifically the sensitivity of the spoiled gradient echo signal to macroscopic magnetic field gradients that arise due to susceptibility variations between tissues. In the presence of these magnetic field gradients, an additional fractional signal loss is observed that is a function of the magnitude of the gradients relative to the voxel dimensions. Thus, to accurately estimate T_2* in the presence of susceptibility-induced field gradients, these effects must either be corrected for prospectively and/or accounted for retrospectively. For multislice sequences where the slice thickness is typically much larger than the in-plane voxel dimensions, in-plane contributions are often neglected because of the voxel dimension dependence of this effect.

3.3.2 Prospective correction of susceptibility-induced field gradients

Shimming should always be the first method used to minimize susceptibility-induced field gradients. Most clinical scanners have an array of automated methods for optimizing shims [38], and advances in

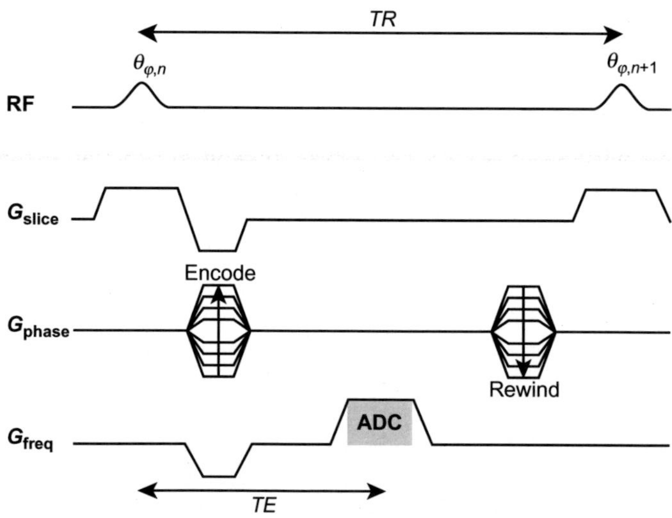

FIG. 3.7

Spoiled gradient echo imaging pulse sequence. A gradient echo is acquired following an excitation flip angle of θ and phase of subscript *n*. The phase encode rewind gradients ensures that the phase accrual is the same for each *TR* period. This allows one to perform RF spoiling by incrementing the phase of each consecutive RF phase. To estimate T_2*, the sequence is repeated at different *TE*s and constant a *TR*.

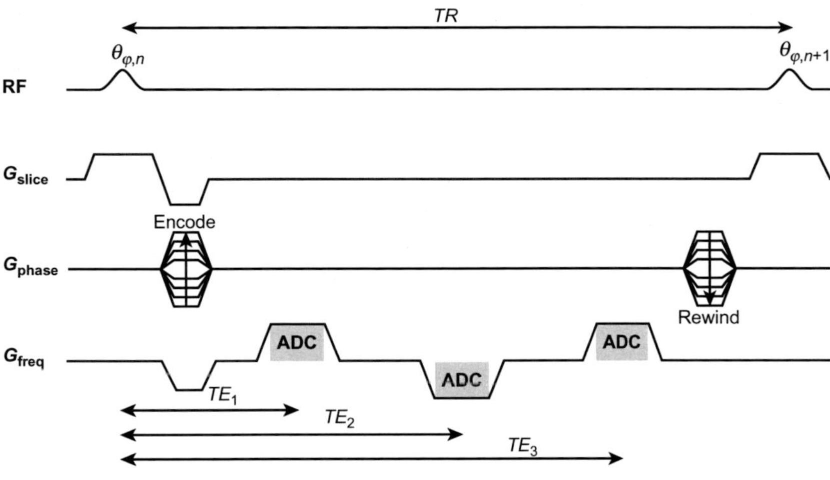

FIG. 3.8

Multiecho gradient echo imaging pulse sequence for measuring T_2*. Multiple gradient echoes are acquired following a single excitation by alternating the polarity of the read gradient, resulting in a signal that decays according to T_2*. Only the first three echoes are shown; however, many more echoes can be acquired per excitation to estimate T_2*.

dynamic shimming [39] offer further improvement by updating shims on a slice-by-slice basis. Despite these advances, complete removal of these magnetic field gradients is not possible in many cases (e.g., higher magnetic fields) due to their nonlinear nature. As such, additional techniques are often required to accurately quantify T_2* in tissue.

One method for minimizing through-slice signal loss uses tailored excitation pulses, which are designed with phase profiles that are the inverse of the profile generated from a given gradient amplitude [40]. Note that these RF pulses can only be tailored for a single *TE* and gradient amplitude, making it difficult to implement for T_2* mapping in the presence of spatially varying susceptibility-induced field gradients. Another method employs modulated slice refocusing gradient amplitudes (or "z-shimming", see Fig. 3.9) [41]. Unfortunately, the correction factor for this "z-shim" once again varies both spatially and temporally, requiring a number of images with different slice refocusing amplitudes to be collected. Alternatively, 3D sequences typically have much smaller through-plane dimensions than 2D sequences, which can substantially minimize the signal loss due to magnetic field gradients. An obvious tradeoff is the decreased SNR associated with the decreased voxel dimension; however, SNR can be recovered by averaging the magnitude of adjacent voxels in the reconstructed image volume.

3.3.3 Retrospective correction of susceptibility-induced field gradients

When possible, it is recommended to prospectively reduce susceptibility-induced field gradients using one or more of the methods described above (e.g., shimming, 3D sequences). However, additional corrections can be made retrospectively using one of two methods. The first method involves estimation of the main magnetic field offset, which can be determined from two gradient echo phase images acquired at different *TE*s [42]. The gradient of the estimated main magnetic field offset can then be determined numerically (e.g., center differencing), which can be used to estimate the phase accrual

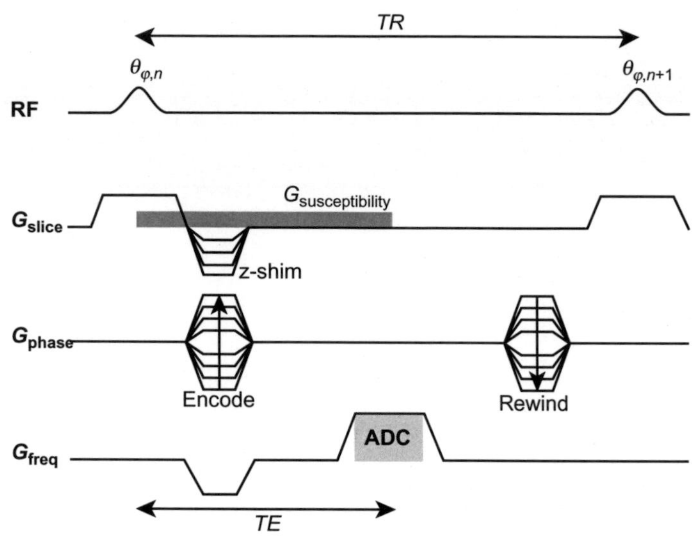

FIG. 3.9

z-Shimming pulse sequence. The slice refocusing gradient is modulated (or z-shimmed) to experimentally correct for the effect of a susceptibility-induced field gradient (see gray box in slice-select direction) at *TE*. When used for T_2* mapping, numerous modulations are required to correct for all susceptibility-induced gradient amplitudes at all *TE*s.

at *TE* and the corresponding fractional signal loss using the appropriate signal model [43]. Alternatively, one can simply include the fractional signal loss from susceptibility-induced field gradients as additional free parameter in the signal model, although this may require additional model constraints to obtain a unique solution [44,45].

3.3.4 Asymmetric spin echo sequences

Multiecho asymmetric spin echo pulse sequences [46] (Fig. 3.10) are an alternate method for measurement of T_2* that may have applications in cardiac imaging [43]. This pulse sequence is similar to a multiecho gradient echo pulse sequence with the addition of a single refocusing pulse prior to the first echo, making it a spin echo. All subsequent asymmetric spin echoes decay according to T_2* when referenced relative to the spin echo. The primary advantage of this approach is that the first spin echo nulls blood flow, resulting in a "black blood" image. In other words, this approach removes unwanted signals from blood, and in some cases corresponding flow artifacts, potentially yielding more precise estimates of T_2* in myocardial tissue.

3.4 Simultaneous T_2 and T_2^* measurement sequences

Combined spin and gradient echo (SAGE) methods [47] are also available for applications where one wishes to simultaneously measure T_2 and T_2*. This approach is particularly attractive in dynamic

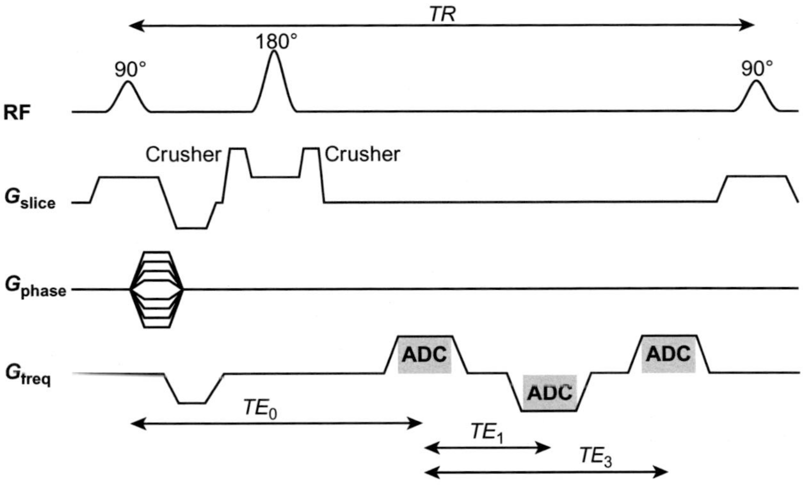

FIG. 3.10

Multiple asymmetric-echo imaging pulse sequence for measuring T_2*. A spin echo is acquired at TE_0 followed by a series of asymmetric echoes, resulting in a signal that decays according to T_2* relative to the spin echo. Only the first three echoes are shown; however, many more echoes can be acquired by alternating the polarity of the read gradient to estimate T_2*.

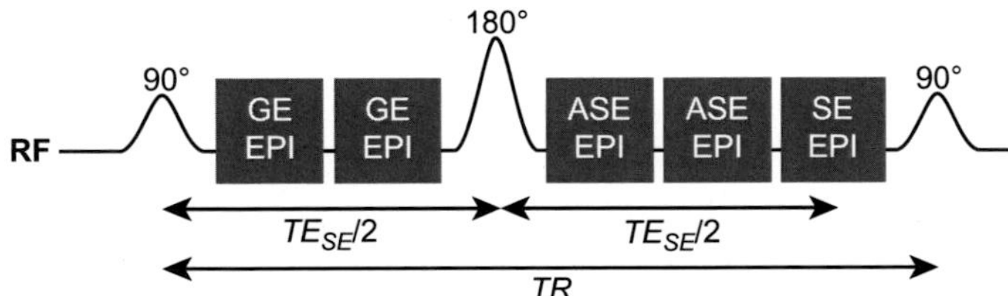

FIG. 3.11

Combined spin- and gradient echo (SAGE) sequence for simultaneously measuring T_2 and T_2*. A series of five EPI-accelerated echoes are acquired, including two gradient echo (GE) before the refocusing pulses, two asymmetric spin echoes (ASE) after the refocusing pulse, and a spin echo (SE) at $TE = TE_{SE}$. Together, information from these five echoes can be used to dynamically estimate both T_2 and T_2*.

susceptibility contrast MRI, where dynamic measurements can be used to estimate various parameters related to hemodynamic status and tissue perfusion. The SAGE sequence in Fig. 3.11 is comprised of a series of echoes acquired using an EPI readout, starting with two spoiled gradient echoes, followed by a refocusing pulse, two asymmetric spin echoes, and finally a spin echo. By analyzing the signal decay from all different echoes simultaneously, rapid and simultaneous estimates of T_2 and T_2* can be obtained. Note that this approach is similar to the so-called gradient echo sampling of the free induction decay and echo (GESFIDE [48]) method, although the standard GESFIDE technique does not employ single-shot readouts and is, therefore, not generally used for dynamic studies.

3.5 Approaches for estimating T_2 and T_2*

Once transverse relaxation data are acquired, the measured data need to be fit with the appropriate model to estimate relevant parameters (e.g., T_2, T_2*, relative apparent proton density). In the following sections, numerical strategies to estimate these parameters are outlined for both single- and multi-exponential T_2 models. Note that similar strategies can be applied to T_2*, assuming the influence of susceptibility-induced field gradients is minimized or the model is amended to account for this effect.

3.5.1 Single-exponential models

In this section, it is assumed that signal from a voxel can be described by a single T_2 component due to *similar* intrinsic T_2 values within all tissue compartments (e.g., intra/extracellular water) and/or *fast* inter-compartmental exchange. In addition, it is assumed that perfect refocusing has been achieved and/or that signal from non-spin-echo pathways has been removed by spoiling. In this case, the observed signal S can be expressed from Eq. (3.1) as

$$S_i = S_0 \exp(-TE_i/T_2) + v_i \tag{3.6}$$

where the subscript i indexes measurements acquired at different TE values, v is additive noise drawn from a Gaussian distribution, and S_0 is the apparent relative proton density.

Given an appropriate set of noisy observations, it can be shown that both T_2 and S_0 can be estimated by fitting these observations with the model in Eq. (3.6) using nonlinear least-squares methods, as shown in Fig. 3.12. Alternatively, Eq. (3.6) can be linearized via log-transformation and T_2 and S_0 can be estimated using linear least-squares methods. Although this eliminates the need to provide initial parameter guesses and reduces computation complexity, this approach produces biased parameter estimates because Gaussian noise is no longer additive following log-transformation. As a result, nonlinear least-squares regression approaches are generally recommended because they yield maximum likelihood parameter estimates in the presence of Gaussian noise.

Unfortunately, biased estimates can still result when using magnitude MRI data because noise in governed by a Rician instead of Gaussian distribution in these images [50]. For signals acquired at

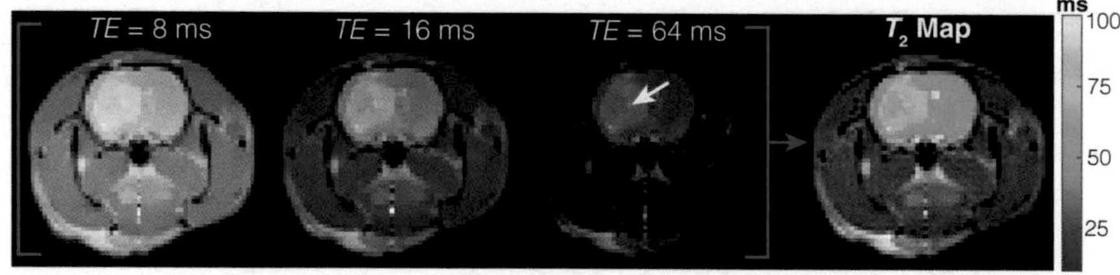

FIG. 3.12

Example multiecho spin echo data and T_2 map in a rat glioblastoma model [49]. Data are shown for three of 32 echoes in the blue brackets. These data are fit with the model in Eq. (3.6) using nonlinear regression methods (represented by the blue arrow) to generate the T_2 map in the right panel. Note the elevated T_2 in the tumor (white arrow) relative to the surrounding normal appearing brain tissue. This same general procedure is followed for all of the T_2 and T_2* mapping procedures in this chapter, although the details of the acquisition method and signal model must be tailored to the specific application as outlined in the text.

shorter *TE*s, this effect is minor because Rician noise can be approximated as Gaussian noise when SNR $>\approx 10$. At longer *TE*s, however, this effect results in an artificial increase in the baseline that biases T_2 estimates toward longer values. One simple method to eliminate this bias is to truncate the signal decay at longer *TE*s (i.e., when the SNR < 10), although this may affect the precision of the resulting parameter estimates. Alternatively, an additional baseline offset term can be added to Eq. (3.6); however, this approach is empirical and often yields biased estimates. Given these limitations, a more appropriate approach in many instances (e.g., when SNR < 10 at longer TE values) is to correct for Rician-induced bias via maximum likelihood estimators [51].

As previously discussed, imperfect refocusing and/or spoiling in multiecho sequences can result in a signal decay that deviates from the exponential signal model in Eq. (3.6). This error results in an oscillation between odd and even echoes that decreases with *TE* [52]. A simple method to minimize these errors is to discard certain echoes (e.g., the first, even or odd echoes) during the fitting procedure [50]. However, this approach does not make use of all the data, which negatively impacts precision for shorter T_2 values. An alternative approach is to amend the signal model to fully account for all signal pathways [23,24], which results in a model that is additionally sensitive to T_1 and B_1. Fortunately, the signal dependence on T_1 is relatively small, allowing one to assume a reasonable value without impacting estimates of the other model parameters. In addition, methods have been developed to optimally account for B_1 variations by either (*i*) including B_1 as a free parameter in the model or (*ii*) independently estimating B_1 using field mapping approaches [26].

3.5.2 Multiexponential models

In this section, it is assumed that signal from a voxel are described by multiple T_2 components due to *different* intrinsic T_2 values within each tissue compartment (e.g., intra/extracellular water) and *slow* inter-compartmental exchange. Assuming perfect refocusing and spoiling, the resulting signal equation can be expressed by expanding Eq. (3.6) to account for N decaying exponentials:

$$S_i = \sum_{j=1}^{N} S_{0,j} \exp\left(-TE_i/T_{2,j}\right) + v_i \tag{3.7}$$

where j indexes each exponential signal component. Although this model can be inverted using the same nonlinear regression methods described for single-exponential models, estimating the resulting parameters becomes highly dependent on the initial guesses, even for systems with only two (biexponential) or three (triexponential) signal components. Furthermore, the number of decaying exponentials is often unknown, especially in pathological tissue.

An alternative approach is to rewrite Eq. (3.7) into a linear system that spans all possible T_2 values

$$\mathbf{s} = \mathbf{A}\mathbf{d} + \mathbf{v} \tag{3.8}$$

where $\mathbf{s}$ is a vector of observed signal intensities, $\mathbf{v}$ is a corresponding vector of additive noise, $\mathbf{A}$ is a matrix of *known* decaying exponentials, and $\mathbf{d}$ is a vector of *unknown* relative apparent proton densities for each decaying exponential (often referred to as a "T_2 spectrum"). Although this model can be inverted using conventional linear least-squares methods, $\mathbf{A}$ is rank-deficient, and the resulting estimates of $\mathbf{d}$ are very sensitive to noise. As a result, the nonnegative least square (NNLS) algorithm [53], which enforces positive proton densities for each component, and regularization methods [54–56] are commonly employed. This results in smooth spectra that are often easier to interpret and potentially more representative of heterogenous tissue. In addition, these methods reduce sensitivity to noise, although a relatively high SNR (typically >100) is generally required to robustly invert the model. Note that similar methods can be applied when imperfect refocusing and/or spoiling is observed. In this case, the multiexponential signal model in Eqs. (3.7), (3.8) can be amended to account for non-spin-echo pathways using the same methods described for single-exponential models.

3.6 Summary

Over the past several decades, researchers have developed a wide array of methods for mapping T_2 and T_2* values in tissue. The choice of the particular method depends on numerous factors, including the signal model (single- versus multi-compartment), required scan time, available SNR, and the tissue of interest (e.g., asymmetric spin echoes for T_2* mapping in the heart). In all cases, care must be taken to (*i*) optimize sequence parameters (*TE*, *TR*, *TD*) for the given application and (*ii*) minimize the impact of diffusion or B_0 and B_1 variations on parameter estimates. Moving forward, it is likely that more efficient and robust methods for estimating T_2 and T_2* in tissue will continue to be developed, especially as multicompartment models continue to illustrate their ability to quantify microstructural features of interest (e.g., myelin content).

References

[1] Laule C, et al. Magnetic resonance imaging of myelin. Neurotherapeutics 2007;4(3):460–84.
[2] Haacke EM, et al. Imaging iron stores in the brain using magnetic resonance imaging. Magn Reson Imaging 2005;23(1):1–25.
[3] Filippi M, et al. Association between pathological and MRI findings in multiple sclerosis. Lancet Neurol 2012;11(4):349–60.
[4] Does MD. Inferring brain tissue composition and microstructure via MR relaxometry. Neuroimage 2018;182(1):136–48.
[5] Alonso-Ortiz E, Levesque IR, Pike GB. MRI-based myelin water imaging: a technical review. Magn Reson Med 2015;73(1):70–81.
[6] Gardener AG, Francis ST, Prior M, Peters A, Gowland PA. Dependence of blood R_2 relaxivity on CPMGecho-spacing at 2.35 and 7 T. Magn Reson Med 2010;64(4):967–74.
[7] Bipin Mehta B, et al. Magnetic resonance fingerprinting: a technical review. Magn Reson Med 2019;81(1):25–46.
[8] Shah NJ, Ermer V, Oros-Peusquens AM. Measuring the absolute water content of the brain using quantitative MRI. Methods Mol Biol 2011;711:29–64.
[9] Jones JA, Hodgkinson P, Barker AL, Hore PJ. Optimal sampling strategies for the measurement of spin-spin relaxation times. J Magn Reson 1996;113(1):25–34.
[10] Shrager R, Weiss G, Spencer R. Optimal time spacings for T_2 measurements: monoexponential and biexponential systems. NMR Biomed 1998;11(6):297–305.
[11] Does MD, Gore JC. Complications of nonlinear echo time spacing for measurement of T_2. NMR Biomed 2000;13(1):1–7.
[12] Carr HY, Purcell EM. Effects of diffusion on free precession in nuclear magnetic resonance experiments. Phys Rev 1954;94(3):630–8.
[13] Meiboom S, Gill D. Modified spin-echo method for measuring nuclear relaxation times. Rev Sci Instrum 2009;29(8):688–91.

[14] Levitt MH, Freeman R. Compensation for pulse imperfections in NMR spin-echo experiments. J Magn Reson 1981;43(1):65–80.

[15] Poon CS, Henkelman RM. 180° refocusing pulses which are insensitive to static and radiofrequency field inhomogeneity. J Magn Reson 1992;99(1):45–55.

[16] Crawley A, Henkelman R. Errors in T_2 estimation using multislice multiple-echo imaging. Magn Reson Med 1987;4(1):34–47.

[17] Poon CS, Henkelman RM. Practical T_2 quantification for clinical applications. J Magn Reson Imaging 1992;2(5):541–53.

[18] Mackay A, Whittall K, Adler J, Li D, Paty D, Graeb D. In vivo visualization of myelin water in brain by magnetic resonance. Magn Reson Med 1994;31(6):673–7.

[19] Maier CF, Tan SG, Hariharan H, Potter HG. T_2 quantitation of articular cartilage at 1.5 T. J Magn Reson Imaging 2003;17(3):358–64.

[20] Laule C, Kolind SH, Bjarnason TA, Li DKB, MacKay AL. In vivo multiecho T_2 relaxation measurements using variable TR to decrease scan time. Magn Reson Imaging 2007;25(6):834–9.

[21] Prasloski T, et al. Rapid whole cerebrum myelin water imaging using a 3D GRASE sequence. Neuroimage 2012;63(1):533–9.

[22] Doneva M, Bornert P, Eggers H, Stehning C, Senegas J, Mertins A. Compressed sensing reconstruction for magnetic resonance parametermapping. Magn Reson Med 2010;64(4):1114–20.

[23] Prasloski T, Mädler B, Xiang QS, MacKay A, Jones C. Applications of stimulated echo correction to multicomponent T_2 analysis. Magn Reson Med 2012;67(6):1803–14.

[24] Ben-Eliezer N, Sodickson DK, Block KT. Rapid and accurate T_2 mapping from multi-spin-echo data using Bloch-simulation-based reconstruction. Magn Reson Med 2015;73(2):809–17.

[25] McPhee KC, Wilman AH. Transverse relaxation and flip angle mapping: evaluation of simultaneous and independent methods using multiple spin echoes. Magn Reson Med 2017;77(5):2057–65.

[26] Lankford CL, Does MD. Propagation of error from parameter constraints in quantitative MRI: Example application of multiple spin echo T_2 mapping. Magn Reson Med 2018;79(2):673–82.

[27] Oh J, Han E, Pelletier D, Nelson S. Measurement of in vivo multi-component T_2 relaxation times for brain tissue using multi-slice T_2 prep at 1.5 and 3 T. Magn Reson Imaging 2006;24(1):33–43.

[28] Nguyen TD, et al. Feasibility and reproducibility of whole brain myelin water mapping in 4 minutes using fast acquisition with spiral trajectory and adiabatic T_2prep (FAST-T_2) at 3T. Magn Reson Med 2016;76(2): 456–65.

[29] Deoni SCL, Rutt BK, Peters TM. Rapid combined T_1 and T_2 mapping using gradient recalled acquisition in the steady state. Magn Reson Med 2003;49(3):515–26.

[30] Miller KL, Tijssen RHN, Stikov N, Okell TW. Steady-state MRI: methods for neuroimaging. Imaging Med 2011;3(1):93–105.

[31] Deoni SCL, Rutt BK, Arun T, Pierpaoli C, Jones DK. Gleaning multicomponent T_1 and T_2 information from steady-state imaging data. Magn Reson Med 2008;60(6):1372–87.

[32] Lankford CL, Does MD. On the inherent precision of mcDESPOT. Magn Reson Med 2013;69(1):127–36.

[33] Gloor M, Scheffler K, Bieri O. Quantitative magnetization transfer imaging using balanced SSFP. Magn Reson Med 2008;60(3):691–700.

[34] Sumpf TJ, Uecker M, Boretius S, Frahm J. Model-based nonlinear inverse recostruction for T_2 mapping using using highly undersampled spin-echo MRI. J Magn Res Imaging 2011;34(2):420–8.

[35] Lankford CL, Dortch RD, Does MD. Fast T_2 mapping with multiple echo, Caesar cipher acquisition and model-based reconstruction. Magn Reson Med 2015;73(3):1065–74.

[36] Block KT, Uecker M, Frahm J. Model-based iterative reconstruction for radial fast spin-echo MRI. IEEE Trans Med Imaging 2009;28(11):1759–69.

[37] Sumpf TJ, Petrovic A, Uecker M, Knoll F, Frahm J. Fast T_2mapping with improved accuracy using undersampled spin-echo MRI and model-based reconstructions with a generating function. IEEE Trans Med Imaging 2014;33(12):2213–22.

[38] Stockmann JP, Wald LL. In vivo B_0 field shimming methods for MRI at 7 T. Neuroimage 2018; 168(3):71–87.

[39] Sengupta S, et al. Dynamic B_0 shimming at 7 T. Magn Reson Imaging 2011;29(4):483–96.

[40] Chen N, Wyrwicz AM. Removal of intravoxel dephasing artifact in gradient-echo images using a field-map based RF refocusing technique. Magn Reson Med 1999;42(4):807–12.

[41] Yang QX, Williams GD, Demeure RJ, Mosher TJ, Smith MB. Removal of local field gradient artifacts in T_2*-weighted images at high fields by gradient-echo slice excitation profile imaging. Magn Reson Med 1998;39(3):402–9.

[42] Irarrazabal P, Meyer CH, Nishimura DG, Macovski A. Inhomogeneity correction using an estimated linear field map. Magn Reson Med 1996;35(2):278–82.

[43] Dortch RD, Does MD. Temporal ΔB_0 and relaxation in the rat heart. Magn Reson Med 2007;58(5):939–46.

[44] Fernandez-Seara MA, Wehrli FW. Postprocessing technique to correct for background gradients in image-based R_2* measurements. Magn Reson Med 2000;44(3):358–66.

[45] Alonso-Ortiz E, Levesque IR, Paquin R, Pike GB. Field inhomogeneity correction for gradient echo gradient echo myelin water fraction imaging. Magn Reson Med 2017;78(1):49–57.

[46] Stables LA, Kennan RP, Gore JC. Asymmetric spin-echo imaging of magnetically inhomogeneous systems: theory, experiment, and numerical studies. Magn Reson Med 1998;40(3):432–42.

[47] Stokes AM, Skinner JT, Quarles CC. Assessment of a combined spin- and gradient-echo (SAGE) DSC-MRI method for preclinical neuroimaging. Magn Reson Imaging 2014;32(10):1181–90.

[48] Ma J, Wehrli FW. Method for image-based measurement of the reversible and irreversible contribution to the transverse relaxation rate. J Magn Reson 1996;111(1):61–9.

[49] Dortch RD, Yankeelov TE, Yue Z, Quarles CC, Gore JC, Does MD. Evidence of multiexponential T_2 in rat glioblastoma. NMR Biomed 2009;22(6):609–18.

[50] Gudbjartsson H, Patz S. The Rician distribution of noisy MRI data. Magn Reson Med 1995;34(6):910–4.

[51] Bonny JM, Zanca M, Boire JY, Veyre A. T_2 maximum likelihood estimation from multiple spin-echo magnitude images. Magn Reson Med 1996;36(2):287–93.

[52] Milford D, Rosbach N, Bendszus M, Heiland S. Monoexponential fitting in T_2 relaxometry: relevance of offset and first echo. PLoS One 2015;10(12):e0145255.

[53] Lawson CL, Hanson RJ. Solving least squares problems. Englewood Cliffs, NJ: Prentice-Hall; 1974.

[54] Whittall KP, Mackay AL. Quantitative interpretation of NMR relaxation data. J Magn Reson 1989; 84(1):134–52.

[55] Graham SJ, Stanchev PL, Bronskill MJ. Criteria for analysis of multicomponent tissue T_2 relaxation dat. Magn Reson Med 1996;35(3):370–8.

[56] Golub GH, Heath M, Wahba G. Generalized cross-validation as a method for choosing a good ridge parameter. Dent Tech 1979;21(2):215–23.

CHAPTER

Multiproperty Mapping Methods

4

Philipp Ehses[a] and Rahel Heule[b]

[a]German Center for Neurodegenerative Diseases (DZNE), Bonn, Germany [b]Max Planck Institute for Biological Cybernetics, Tübingen, Germany

4.1 Simultaneous quantification of multiple relaxometry parameters

This chapter presents an overview of techniques for the joint quantification of multiple relaxometry parameters from a single experiment. The joint approach has several advantages over the sequential quantification of multiple parameters. First, it guarantees that the two (or more) parameter maps are registered to each other, that is, they are in a similar motion state with similar amount of physiological motion induced blur. For this reason, simultaneous quantification is especially beneficial in a contrast-enhanced acquisition. In addition, chemical shift and distortion artifacts are also automatically matched. Furthermore, a single multiproperty technique experiment can sometimes be more efficient than running separate experiments for each parameter of interest. And finally, the correlation between parameters within one voxel can be of interest, for example, the dependency of T_1 on T_2^* and vice versa, which is something that only (some) multiproperty techniques can provide.

4.2 Simultaneous quantification of T_1 and T_2

T_1 and T_2 are important parameters for tissue; the quantitative measurement of these properties can aid diagnosis and evaluation of disease progression. Another interesting use of T_1 and T_2 maps is the synthetic generation of T_1- and T_2-weighted images that are otherwise acquired in separate time-consuming scans [1–3].

Most imaging sequences are sensitive to T_1 (provided that the TR is sufficiently short and depending on the flip angle), and thus many different types of experiments can be designed that make use of this sensitivity to quantify T_1. It can also be helpful to prepare the magnetization with a saturation or inversion module and then monitor the signal evolution toward the steady-state. For simultaneous mapping of T_1 and T_2, it is necessary to additionally introduce T_2 sensitivity to the imaging sequence. A common way of achieving this is by using a balanced steady-state free precession (bSSFP) readout [4, 5] that shows T_2/T_1 weighting, or by acquiring specific spin echo configurations with a nonbalanced SSFP sequence. The following sections will describe several pulse sequences with sensitivity to T_1 and T_2 which can be deployed to simultaneously measure both of these relaxometry values.

Advances in Magnetic Resonance Technology and Applications. Volume 1. ISSN 2666-9099. https://doi.org/10.1016/B978-0-12-817057-1.00006-8

4.2.1 Inversion recovery-bSSFP (IR-bSSFP, IR TrueFISP)

The IR-bSSFP sequence [6] was first introduced for T_1 mapping as an alternative to a gradient-echo-based Look-Locker (LL) [7, 8] acquisition. Later, Schmitt et al. [9] showed that it enables quantification of T_2 as well. This sequence consists of an inversion pulse followed by the acquisition of several bSSFP images as the signal time course approaches the steady-state, as illustrated in Figs. 4.1 and 4.2. The T_1 and T_2 maps can then be obtained from a mono-exponential fit of the signal to the following equation (for the nth TR after inversion):

$$S(t=n\,\mathrm{TR}) = S_{\mathrm{bSSFP}} - (S_0 + S_{\mathrm{bSSFP}})\cdot \exp(-t/T_1{}^*) \tag{4.1}$$

where S_{bSSFP} is the bSSFP steady-state signal, S_0 is the transient signal extrapolated to $t=0$, and $T_1{}^*$ is the apparent relaxation time. For full inversion, the signal at the beginning of the IR-bSSFP experiment can be described in good approximation by

$$S_0 = M_0 \sin \alpha/2 \tag{4.2}$$

Using this equation and with knowledge of the excitation flip angle α, the relative spin density M_0 can be directly obtained from the fit parameter S_0. In order to obtain T_1 and T_2, it is necessary to identify their relationships with the other two fit parameters. For TR $\ll T_{1,2}$, the bSSFP signal equation for the steady-state can be written as

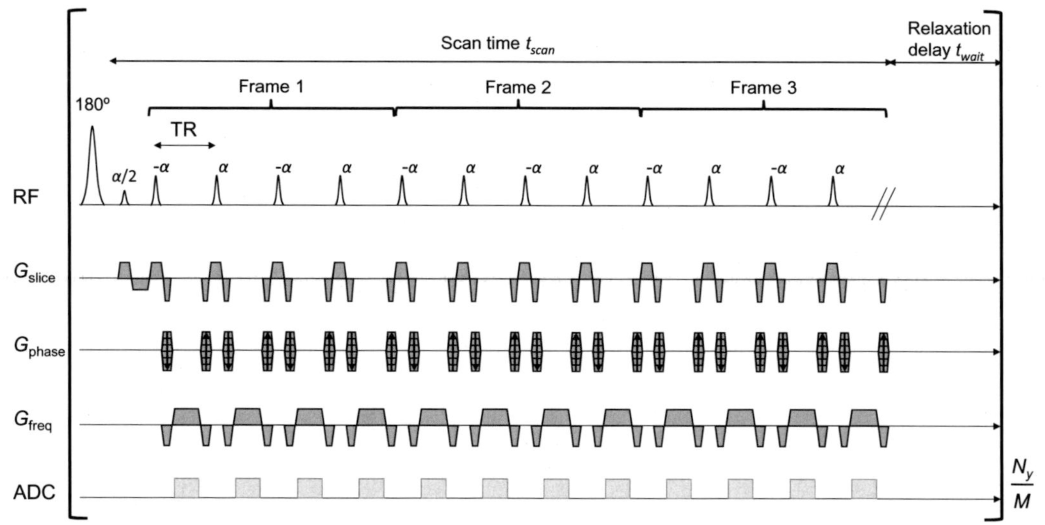

FIG. 4.1

2D IR-bSSFP sequence diagram: Inversion is followed by a bSSFP preparation module (in this case a conventional $\alpha/2$ preparation). Then, M segments of a sequence of bSSFP images are acquired in order to follow the signal evolution toward the steady-state ($M=4$ in this example). In the case where M is equal to the number of phase-encoding steps N_y, the sequence is run with a single inversion pulse in a single shot. Otherwise, N_y/M repetitions of the inversion experiment are necessary in order to fully cover k-space. In this case, the next inversion pulse is played out after allowing for relaxation during a waiting period t_{wait}.

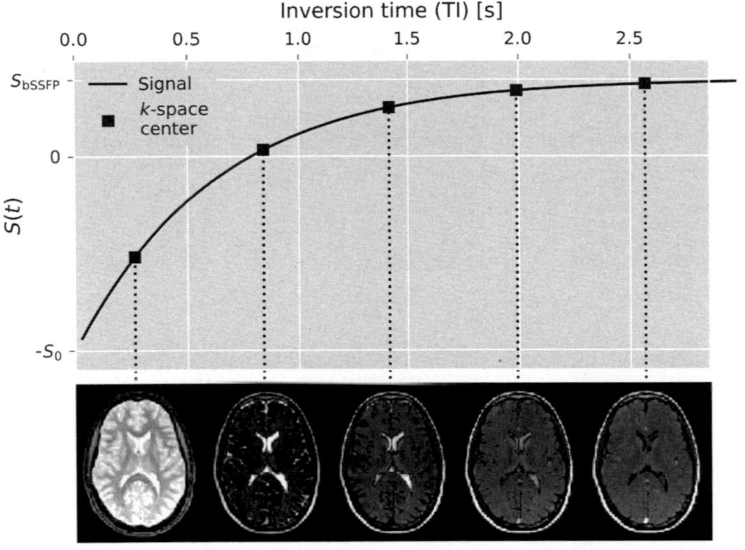

FIG. 4.2

Top: Signal evolution in an IR-bSSFP experiment. Following inversion, the signal follows an exponential approach toward the steady-state during a continuous run of bSSFP acquisitions. *Bottom*: Example magnitude images for different inversion times. The approximate acquisition position of the center of *k*-space is shown on the relaxation curve for each image (indicated by *squares* and *dotted lines).*

$$S_{\text{bSSFP}} = \frac{M_0 \sin\alpha}{\left(\frac{T_1}{T_2}+1\right) - \cos\alpha\left(\frac{T_1}{T_2}\text{-}1\right)} \tag{4.3}$$

The exponential decay with time constant $T_1{}^*$ is a weighted average of T_1 and T_2 relaxation, with the flip angle α determining the weighting [6, 9]:

$$T_1{}^* \overset{\text{TR}\ll T_{1,2}}{=} \left(\frac{1}{T_1}\cos^2\alpha/2 + \frac{1}{T_2}\sin^2\alpha/2\right)^{-1} \tag{4.4}$$

Using Eqs. (4.2)–(4.4), it is possible to derive expressions for T_1, T_2, and M_0 from the three fit parameters, and generate maps of these tissue properties, as shown in Fig. 4.3:

$$T_1 = T_1{}^* \frac{S_0}{S_{\text{bSSFP}}} \cos\alpha/2 \tag{4.5}$$

$$T_2 = T_1{}^* \sin^2\alpha/2 \left(1 - \frac{S_{\text{bSSFP}}}{S_0}\cos\alpha/2\right)^{-1} \tag{4.6}$$

$$M_0 = \frac{S_0}{\sin\alpha/2} \tag{4.7}$$

In a multishot acquisition with finite relaxation delay t_{wait} in between inversion pulses, the measured M_0 is in reality a reduced effective M_0^{eff} due to incomplete relaxation before the application of the next

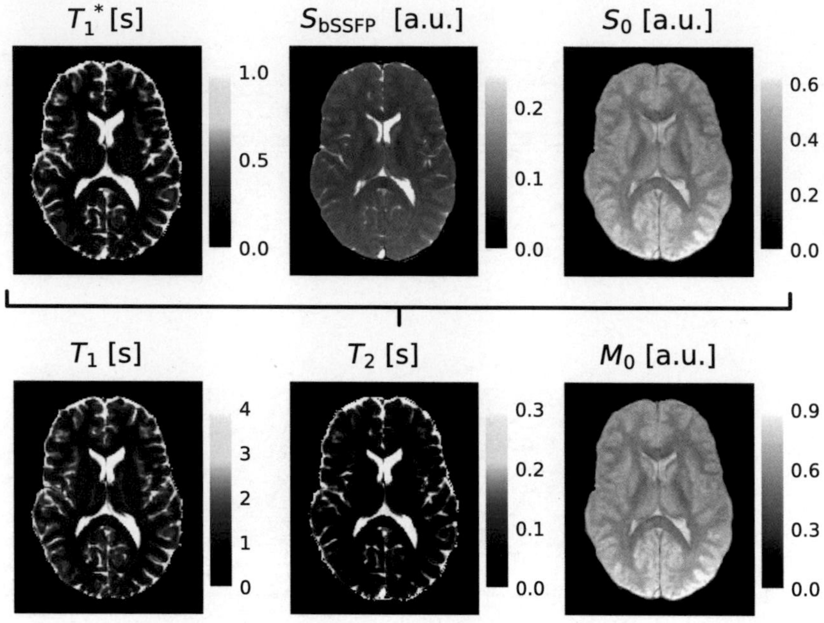

FIG. 4.3

Maps for the three IR-bSSFP fit parameters $T_1{}^*$, S_{bSSFP}, and S_0 are displayed on *top*. T_1, T_2, and M_0 maps shown at the *bottom* can be obtained from these parameters according to Eqs. (4.5)–(4.7).

inversion pulse. This underestimation of M_0 also has implications for T_1 and T_2 quantification. The following correction [1] helps to reduce the impact of a short relaxation delay:

$$M_0 = \frac{M_0^{eff} - S_{bSSFP} \cdot \left[1 - (1 + \frac{S_0}{S_{bSSFP}}) \cdot \exp(-\frac{t_{scan}}{T_1{}^*})\right] \cot(\alpha/2) \exp(-\frac{t_{wait}}{T_1})}{1 - \exp(-t_{wait} T_1)}$$

where t_{scan} is the duration of the bSSFP readout train (compare Fig. 4.1).

The transient bSSFP signal shows signal oscillations for spins that are not on-resonance. These signal oscillations can be reduced by using a suitable preparation scheme, such as a linearly increasing flip angle ramp. In addition to these oscillations, the relaxation curve deviates from the ideal case for off-resonant spins, leading to quantification errors in an IR-bSSFP experiment. For off-resonance spins that are not too close to a bSSFP banding artifact and when deploying low to medium flip angles, the errors in T_1 quantification are relatively low (compare Fig. 4.4). However, even relatively small off-resonances can lead to large T_2 quantification errors. In principle, these quantification errors can be corrected if the field offset is known.

At higher magnetic field strengths, constructive and destructive interference of the RF field at higher Larmor frequencies can lead to deviations of the actual from the nominal flip angle. For the inversion, this problem can be avoided by employing an adiabatic inversion pulse. To account for deviations of the excitation flip angle, it can be necessary to acquire a flip angle map, so that the actual flip angle can be used to obtain the relaxometry maps from the fit parameters.

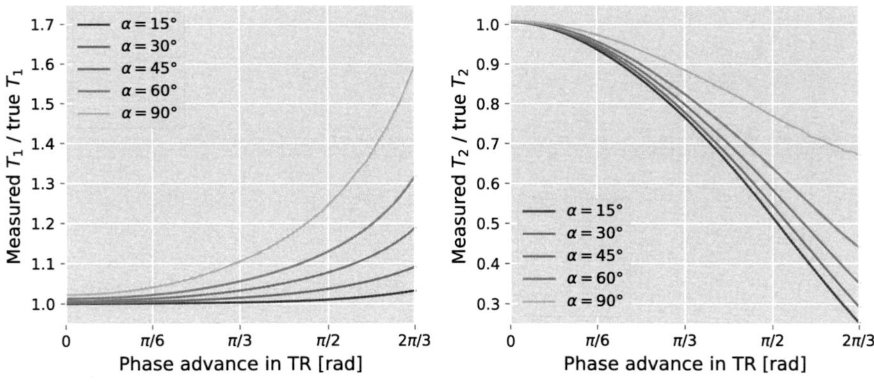

FIG. 4.4

IR-bSSFP is sensitive to off-resonance effects. For small to medium flip angles, T_1 quantification is remarkably stable: Even two-thirds along the way to a bSSFP banding artifact, T_1 is overestimated by only about 3% and 9% for flip angles of 15° and 30°, respectively. In contrast, even small off-resonances can lead to a severe T_2 underestimation. The following parameters were used in the Bloch equation simulation: $T_1 = 1$ s, $T_2 = 0.1$ s, TR = 5 ms.

A similar problem arises due to the fact that the excited slice profile is not perfectly rectangular. This problem can be completely avoided in a 3D acquisition, with the small caveat that the flip angle may slightly drop off in the outer slices in case of selective excitation. For the case that 2D imaging is absolutely necessary, several slice profile correction techniques have been proposed [10–12].

Furthermore, it has been shown that magnetization transfer can lead to a significant reduction of the bSSFP steady-state signal [13], especially in macromolecule-rich tissues such as brain white matter and muscle. In an IR-bSSFP experiment, MT additionally leads to a reduction of the apparent relaxation time [10]. For T_1 quantification, the shorter T_1^* and smaller S_{bSSFP} counteract each other, but overall the effect of S_{bSSFP} on quantification dominates, resulting in an overestimation of T_1. However, the effect of MT on T_2 quantification is amplified by the fact that both shorter T_1^* and smaller S_{bSSFP} result in a T_2 underestimation. MT-related quantification errors can be minimized by reducing the RF power of the excitation pulse [14].

The original IR-bSSFP implementation employed a segmented Cartesian sequence acquired in multiple shots with relaxation delays in between, leading to a relatively long scan time (~2 min/slice). More recently, IR-bSSFP was combined with a radial trajectory with golden-ratio-based profile order and a radial view-sharing technique [10]. This combination allows the acquisition of a full set of T_1, T_2, and M_0 maps for a single slice in under 6 s, albeit with some view-sharing related blurring in the M_0 and T_2 maps (T_1 is less affected). Technically speaking, view-sharing reconstructions rely on the expectation that the signal evolution is smooth, which may not be the case for rapidly relaxing spin species. Quantification can be improved further if more information about the expected signal evolution is included in the reconstruction. Magnetic resonance fingerprinting (MRF) is a technique that employs matching with a model-based dictionary of signal evolutions that can be obtained from a Bloch equation simulation for a range of expected combinations of the parameters of interest. As described in the next section, a spiral implementation of IR-bSSFP with a variable readout flip angle was used for T_1 and T_2 quantification in the first demonstration of the MRF concept [15]. Recently, T_2 shuffling [16] has been proposed which uses calibration information in the form of a principal component analysis of training data to reconstruct highly undersampled multiecho spin echo data for T_2 quantification. This technique has also been applied to IR-bSSFP [17].

4.2.2 Magnetic resonance fingerprinting

MRF [15] relies on an MRI sequence that generates unique signal evolutions that can be matched to a dictionary of theoretical signal evolutions or "fingerprints" in order to yield the underlying quantitative information. One of the advantages of the MRF approach is that it removes the need for a highly controlled signal readout that provides a smooth (e.g., exponential) signal evolution that fits into a signal equation and instead allows for the optimization of the signal acquisition to provide the most quantitative information per unit time. Furthermore, this concept provides a straightforward way to include additional parameters in the multiparameter quantification process by extending the signal dictionary accordingly. However, a necessary prerequisite is that the MRI sequence that is used to acquire the data is sufficiently sensitive to the parameters of interest.

In its original implementation, MRF uses the data from an interleaved spiral IR bSSFP sequence with variable readout flip angle. The highly undersampled data from each spiral interleave are then matched to a signal dictionary that includes T_1, T_2, and off-resonance (B_0 offset) in order to yield the corresponding parameter maps. Thus due to its similar acquisition, the original MRF implementation shares many of the advantages and disadvantages of the IR bSSFP sequence that is described in the previous section. However, since off-resonance effects are already included in the signal model, MRF quantification is relatively insensitive to magnetic field inhomogeneities and does not require an additional fieldmap-based off-resonance correction step. Similarly, other parameters such as magnetization transfer (MT) could also be included in the dictionary in order to remove an error source and/or to provide additional quantitative information about the underlying tissue. However, please note that the extension of the signal dictionary will in most cases require more data (i.e., a longer scan) and adjustment of the MRI sequence in order to provide sufficient information about the additional parameter.

For more information on MRF, refer to Chapters 5 and 6.

4.2.3 Magnetization-prepared dual echo steady-state

The magnetization-prepared dual echo steady-state (MP-DESS) approach [18] is similar to IR-bSSFP as it is also based on a combination of an LL-type inversion recovery acquisition that provides high sensitivity to T_1 with a steady-state free precession (SSFP) module whose main purpose is to provide T_2 sensitivity. As the name implies, a double-echo steady-state (DESS) readout [19] is used in this case. In DESS, two contrasts are acquired in each TR, namely, the F_0 configuration (the free induction decay, FID) and the F_{-1} echo (the "spin echo"), where the latter is being highly sensitive to T_2.

In MP-DESS, every $(N + 1)$th excitation pulse is replaced by an inversion pulse. The echo train of length N is divided into segments of size M that encode the same image, that is, N/M different images are acquired for F_0 and F_{-1}. The echo train has to be repeated N_yN_z/M times in a 3D acquisition with $N_y \cdot N_z$ phase-encoding steps. The MP-DESS signal evolution can be calculated using the extended phase graph (EPG) formalism [20], as illustrated in Fig. 4.5, which allows for efficient generation of a precomputed dictionary of signal evolutions that is used for fitting. An advantage of this approach is that relaxation delays between inversions are not necessary as the incomplete relaxation between shots can be easily included in the model via the EPG calculation.

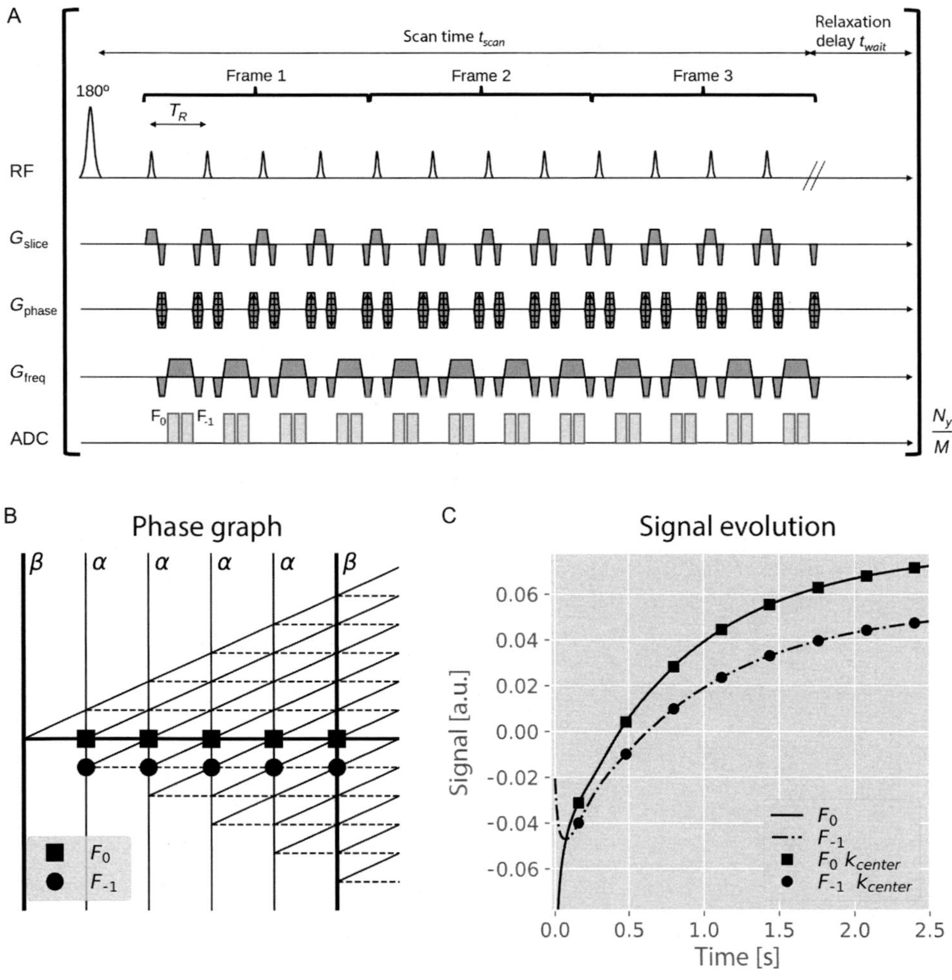

FIG. 4.5

(A) The MP-DESS sequence diagram is similar to IR-bSSFP (compare Fig. 4.1) except that a DESS readout module is used to acquire the F_0 and F_1 signal configurations in each TR. (B) Phase graph for the first MP-DESS inversion cycle. Every $(N+1)$th excitation pulse α is replaced by an inversion pulse with flip angle β, indicated by *thin and thick vertical lines*, respectively. The F_0 and F_{-1} configurations that are of interest in a DESS experiment are marked by *black squares and circles*, respectively. (C) Signal evolution in MP-DESS obtained from an extended phase graph (EPG) simulation for the two configurations. The *black squares and circles* indicate the position at which the center of *k*-space for each image is sampled during the evolution.

The lack of relaxation delays makes a whole-brain 3D approach with nonselective RF pulses feasible, which completely avoids the problem of slice profile effects. B_1^+ inhomogeneity is mapped in a prescan, so that it can be included in the signal model. Furthermore, in contrast to IR-bSSFP, MP-DESS is mostly insensitive to off-resonance effects and the optimal excitation flip angle is rather low (approximately 10°), so that magnetization transfer effects are reduced. However, DESS is more sensitive to motion and flow than bSSFP or RF-spoiled gradient echo sequences.

4.2.4 Triple-echo steady-state

Multiecho SSFP imaging with nonbalanced gradient schemes enables the acquisition of multiple SSFP configurations including higher-order echoes within each TR, by extending and expanding the gradients along the frequency encoding axis [21, 22]. Since the produced steady-state signal amplitudes exhibit varying mixed T_1 and T_2 dependencies, this class of multiecho SSFP sequences offers imaging of different contrasts based on a single MR scan in combination with multiparametric tissue characterization.

Three-dimensional double-echo steady-state (DESS) acquisitions are a well-established technique for the combined morphological and quantitative assessment of rigid targets, for example, cartilage in the knee joint [23]. However, without magnetization preparation (see previous section), quantification is restricted to a single parameter, that is, T_2, and subject to a residual T_1 bias for the low flip angles that are commonly used [24]. To resolve the T_1 bias in DESS-based T_2 mapping and to offer simultaneous estimation of the T_1 and T_2 relaxation times, a triple-echo steady-state (TESS) relaxometry approach has recently been introduced [25]. While DESS imaging allows the acquisition of the lowest order SSFP-FID (F_0) and the lowest order SSFP-Echo (F_{-1}), TESS additionally acquires a higher order SSFP-FID (F_1), compare Fig. 4.6.

The TESS sequence can be implemented by sampling the three echoes F_1, F_0, and F_{-1} either within a single TR (cf. Fig. 4.6A) or within separate TRs (i.e., each echo within one TR, cf. Fig. 4.6B). The first variant has the advantage that the overall acquisition time is shorter; on the other hand, the second approach allows the use of shorter repetition times. Short TRs are especially beneficial in the prospect

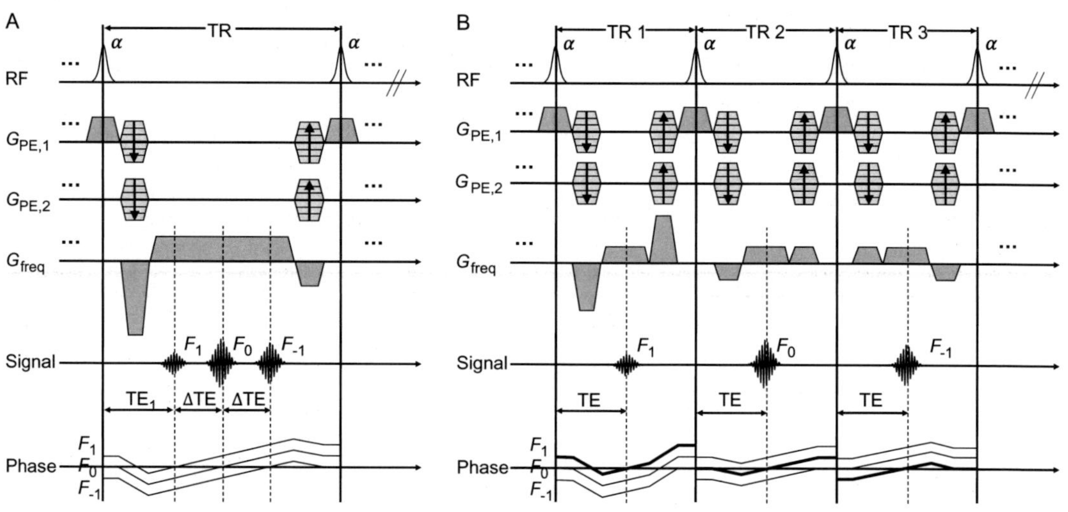

FIG. 4.6

Triple-echo steady-state (TESS) sequence schemes with nonbalanced gradient waveforms along the frequency-encoding axis, which induce a net dephasing of 2π in each voxel. The resulting phase evolutions of the acquired SSFP configurations F_1, F_0, and F_{-1} are depicted in the *last row*. The three echoes can be sampled either within a single TR (A) or within separate TRs (B). In (A), the F_0 mode in the center is flanked by F_1 to the left and by F_{-1} to the right, with TEs of TE_1, $TE_0 = TE_1 + \Delta TE$, $TE_{-1} = TE_1 + 2\Delta TE$ for F_1, F_0, and F_{-1}, respectively. In (B), the three SSFP modes are acquired at the same TE.

of high- to ultrahigh-field imaging (≥3 T) as they reduce susceptibility sensitivity, which becomes pronounced for higher-order SSFP configurations [26] (in case of TESS for the F_1 contrast) and at high-field strength where B_0 imperfections as well as susceptibility effects lead to strong local magnetic field variations. The nonbalanced gradient waveforms needed to acquire the desired SSFP signals can be applied along any gradient axis; that is, along the frequency encoding (as depicted in Fig. 4.6), the phase encoding, or the partition encoding axis.

TESS-based T_1 and T_2 quantification makes use of an analytical description for the F_1, F_0, and F_{-1} modes. General analytical expressions for the SSFP configurations F_n under ideal conditions (no motion, no magnetization transfer/chemical exchange, no diffusion, quasiinstantaneous RF pulses, rectangular slice/slab profiles) are reported, for example, in Ref. [27]. Accordingly, the steady-state signal amplitudes of the two lowest order SSFP modes immediately after the excitation pulse for the relative spin density M_0 and flip angle α are given by

$$F_0(T_1,T_2) = M_0 \tan(\alpha/2)\cdot[1-(E_1-\cos\alpha)\cdot r] \tag{4.8}$$

$$F_{-1}(T_1,T_2) = -M_0 \tan(\alpha/2)\cdot[1-(1-E_1\cos\alpha)\cdot r]/E_2 \tag{4.9}$$

with

$$\begin{aligned} E_{1,2} &:= e^{-TR/T_{1,2}} \\ r &:= \frac{1-E_2^2}{\sqrt{p^2-q^2}} \\ p &:= 1-E_1\cos\alpha - E_2^2(E_1-\cos\alpha) \\ q &:= E_2(1-E_1)(1+\cos\alpha). \end{aligned}$$

From these lowest order configurations, higher-order modes are directly derived as

$$F_n(T_1,T_2) = \begin{cases} (u_1/u_0)^n \cdot F_0 & \text{for } n \geq 0 \\ (u_1/u_0)^{|n|-1} \cdot F_{-1} & \text{for } n < 0 \end{cases} \tag{4.10}$$

with $u_0 := p(p^2-q^2)^{-1/2}$ and $u_1 := p(u_0 - 1)/q$.

Using Eq. (4.10), the F_1 mode can be expressed as

$$F_1(T_1,T_2) = M_0 \cdot \frac{p-\sqrt{p^2-q^2}}{q} \cdot \tan(\alpha/2)\cdot[1-(E_1-\cos\alpha)\cdot r] \tag{4.11}$$

Considering the echo time (TE > 0), the measured magnitude of the SSFP configurations F_n is described by

$$|F_n|_{\text{meas}} = |F_n(T_1,T_2)| \cdot e^{-\text{TE}_n/T_2} \tag{4.12}$$

In Eq. (4.12), a T_2 weighting is assumed and the influence of main magnetic field inhomogeneities leading to T_2^* decay is neglected. This approximation is justified for sufficiently short repetition and echo times of the order of $\text{TE}_n < TR \lesssim 20$ ms at clinical field strengths (i.e., 1–3 T), cf., for example, Bruder et al. [19].

As can be seen from Eqs. (4.8) to (4.12), the three SSFP configurations acquired with TESS depend on the proportionality factor M_0 and the two tissue-specific variables T_1 and T_2. The sequence-specific parameters (i.e., TR, TE, and the nominal flip angle α_{nom}) can be retrieved from the MR protocol.

In the original TESS relaxometry work [25], it was suggested that two independent signal ratios (s_1 and s_2) be considered; both with a mixed dependence on T_1 and T_2, however, one with a predominant dependency on T_1:

$$s_1(T_1,T_2) := \frac{|F_1|_{\text{meas}}}{|F_0|_{\text{meas}}} \tag{4.13}$$

and one with a predominant dependency on T_2:

$$s_2(T_1,T_2) := \frac{|F_{-1}|_{\text{meas}}}{|F_0|_{\text{meas}} - |F_1|_{\text{meas}}} \tag{4.14}$$

in which the proportionality factor M_0 cancels out. Based on Eqs. (4.13), (4.14), estimates for T_1 and T_2 can be obtained using dedicated numerical minimization algorithms, for example, by a rapid one-dimensional golden section search algorithm [28] to derive T_1 based on Eq. (4.13) and T_2 based on Eq. (4.14) in an iterative procedure.

TESS T_2 estimation is virtually unaffected by RF transmit (B_1^+) field inhomogeneities, whereas T_1 quantification retains the typical sensitivity to B_1^+ variations as inherent to most steady-state-based methods, cf. Fig. 4.7. Therefore, for accurate T_1 mapping, the actual flip angle $\alpha_{act} = c_{B_1^+} \cdot \alpha_{nom}$ has to be used for the calculation of the F_1, F_0, and F_{-1} signal amplitudes (cf. Eqs. 4.8, 4.9, 4.11). The B_1^+ scaling factor $c_{B_1^+}$ can be derived for each voxel based on an external flip angle mapping scan. To obtain reliable T_1 values with residual B_1^+-related errors $\leq 5\%$, a high accuracy in the employed flip angle map with deviations $\leq 2\%–3\%$ from the actual flip angle is required (cf. Fig. 4.7).

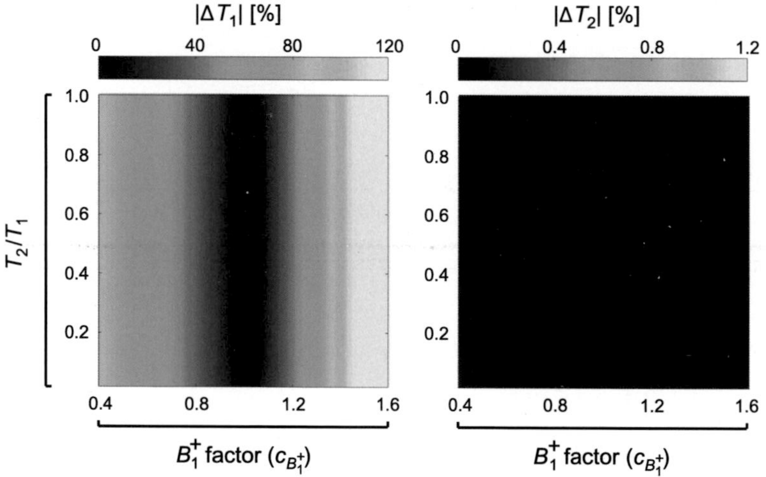

FIG. 4.7

Sensitivity of TESS T_1 and T_2 estimation to B_1^+ inhomogeneities, simulated versus the T_2/T_1 ratio and the B_1^+ scaling factor ($c_{B_1^+}$). The error in T_1 and T_2 arising from flip angle miscalibrations due to B_1^+ is modeled as the relative deviation $\Delta T_{1,2} = [(T_{1,2} - T_{1,2\ TESS})/T_{1,2}] \times 100\%$ ($T_{1,2}$: true relaxation times, $T_{1,2\ TESS}$: relaxation times calculated with TESS). Note the different scaling used for T_2, which is, in contrast to T_1, virtually insensitive to B_1^+. Accurate T_1 estimation requires B_1^+ correction. Simulation parameters: TR/TE = 5 ms/2.5 ms, nominal flip angle $\alpha_{nom} = 15°$. The T_2/T_1 ratio is calculated for a fixed T_1 of 1000 ms and a T_2 ranging from 20 to 1000 ms.

When using 3D TESS to generate T_1 and T_2 maps, optimal flip angles in terms of SNR in the derived maps are reported to lie between 10° and 20° [25]. Nonrectangular slice profiles lead to slightly increased optimal flip angles in the range of 20° and 25° for 2D imaging. The effect of diffusion, which modulates the F_1, F_0, and F_{-1} signal amplitudes, negligibly affects the quantification accuracy of TESS for tissues with short T_2 but introduces a substantial bias for targets with long T_2 and high diffusion coefficients such as CSF in the brain [29]. Generally, the diffusion sensitivity of TESS, specifically the diffusion-related signal attenuation of the SSFP-Echo mode (F_{-1}), can be reduced by increasing the excitation flip angle. If the apparent diffusion coefficient (ADC) is known a priori, as derived from a separate ADC mapping scan, the effect of diffusion can be incorporated into the calculation of the SSFP signal amplitudes [29], for example, by using an analytical solution for the magnetization of spins diffusing in a uniform gradient [30] or based on the EPG formalism [31, 32].

Three-dimensional TESS is suited to imaging of the musculoskeletal system, for example, the knee joint as illustrated in Fig. 4.8. Spectral-spatial excitation is beneficial for musculoskeletal imaging to suppress the fat (cf. Fig. 4.8, first row), which is often seen adjacent to or interspersed with the target tissues. A drawback of spectral-spatial pulses is their susceptibility to flip angle calibration

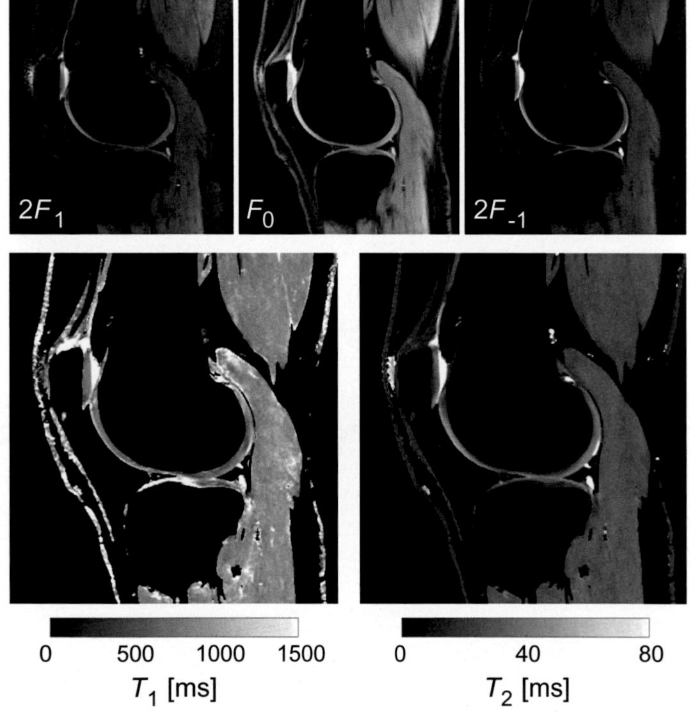

FIG. 4.8

Representative T_1 and T_2 maps generated using TESS for sagittal acquisitions of the knee joint at 3 T with water-selective pulses. The acquired base contrasts (F_1, F_0, and F_{-1}) are shown in the *top row*. For improved visualization, the F_1 and F_{-1} mode have been multiplied by a factor of 2. The T_1 and T_2 maps are derived from the three measured SSFP configurations according to Eqs. (4.8)–(4.14) with correction for RF transmit field inhomogeneities, which is crucial to ensure a homogeneous T_1 contrast.

errors in the presence of B_0 inhomogeneities. As TESS T_2 measurements are virtually B_1^+-insensitive, accurate values can be obtained in combination with spectral-spatial excitation even at ultrahigh magnetic field strengths; however, the accuracy of T_1 may be impaired. Without fat suppression, periodic signal modulations as a function of the echo time can occur, for example, in articular cartilage or bone marrow, due to the presence of intravoxel off-resonance compartments [33].

The application of nonbalanced gradients within each TR mitigates the B_0 sensitivity seen with balanced techniques, but at the cost of increased sensitivity to motion and flow. In the human brain, 3D nonbalanced SSFP imaging is subject to motion artifacts arising from CSF pulsations. It has been shown that averaging several rapidly acquired 2D TESS scans leads to a reduction in motion artifacts in comparison to 3D imaging, and this approach can be applied to quantify T_1 and T_2 of human brain tissues [34, 35]. The 2D scans can be accelerated by simultaneous multislice techniques. If TESS images are acquired in 2D mode, the effect of the nonrectangular slice profile must be incorporated into the signal model for the F_1, F_0, and F_{-1} configurations to ensure accurate relaxometry. Proposed slice profile correction schemes consist of a summation over the slice profile for in-plane spoiling (i.e., for dephasing gradients along frequency or phase encoding axis) [34] and additional consideration of configuration state mixing for through-plane spoiling (i.e., for dephasing gradients along slice selection axis) [36].

The B_1^+ insensitivity of the derived T_2 values and the low optimal flip angles make TESS particularly interesting for T_2 quantification at ultrahigh fields where the transmitted RF field becomes considerably inhomogeneous and spin echo techniques are restricted due to SAR constraints. Ultrahigh-field 2D TESS T_2 mapping in the human brain at 9.4 T is illustrated in Fig. 4.9.

4.2.5 Phase-cycled bSSFP

The signal produced by a bSSFP sequence shows a characteristic sensitivity to off-resonance effects, which can lead to signal voids appearing as dark bands in the acquired images [37]. The response of the bSSFP signal to a frequency offset Δf is equivalent to an RF phase cycling with linear increment $\phi = 2\pi\Delta f \cdot TR$. Consequently, the bSSFP frequency response can be sampled by acquiring a series of N

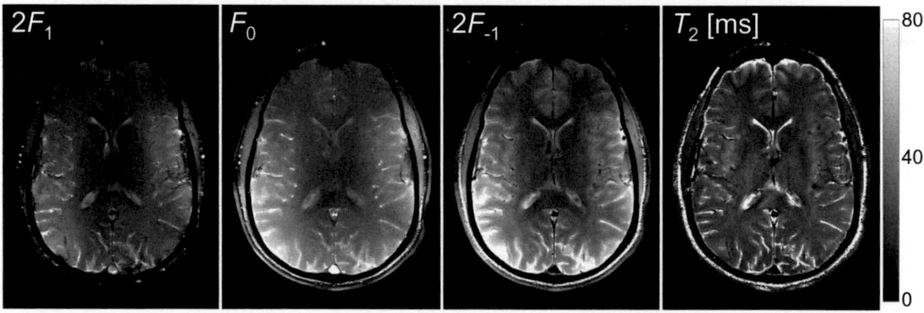

FIG. 4.9

Ultrahigh-field TESS T_2 mapping benefits from the unique insensitivity of TESS to variations in B_1^+, as illustrated here for 2D TESS acquisitions in the human brain at 9.4 T. The obtained T_2 map (on the *right*) has a homogeneous contrast without any visible degradations from B_1^+ inhomogeneity. In the base images (F_1, F_0, and F_{-1}) susceptibility sensitivity is visible at the edges of the brain, for example, in the frontal lobe, which is particularly apparent for the F_1 contrast, but this inhomogeneity is not seen in the T_2 map. The F_1 and F_{-1} contrasts have been multiplied by a factor of 2 relative to F_0.

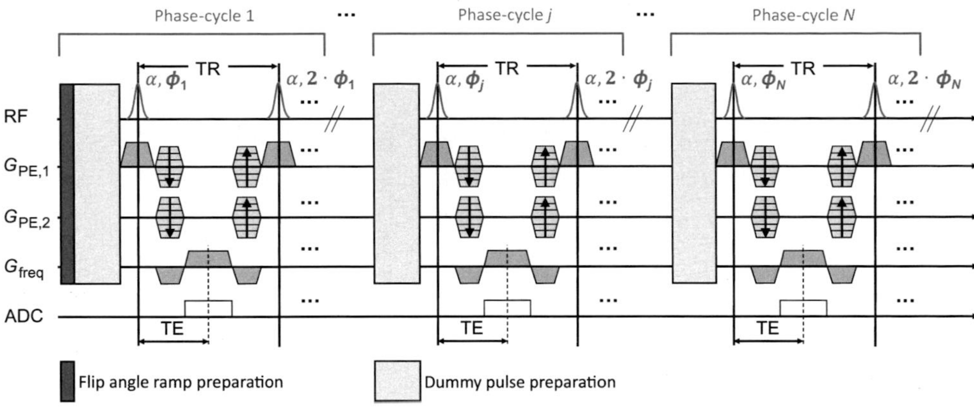

FIG. 4.10

Phase-cycled bSSFP imaging employed by MIRACLE [40] or PLANET [41] consists of a series of N phase-cycled bSSFP scans. During the jth scan, the phase of the RF pulses is linearly increased by the increment $\phi_j = 2\pi(j - 1)/N$. A dummy pulse preparation module without data acquisition typically precedes each phase-cycle measurement to ensure steady-state conditions. For the first measurement ($j = 1$), a catalyzation scheme can be used additionally prior to the dummy cycle period to stabilize the transient phase such as a linear or Kaiser-windowed flip angle ramp.

phase-cycled bSSFP datasets with varying RF phase increments $\phi_j = 2\pi(j - 1)/N$ where j enumerates the scan. The increment ϕ_j is constant during the jth scan and then increased by $2\pi/N$ for the subsequent scan ($\phi_{j+1} = \phi_j + 2\pi/N$). Typically, the measurement of each phase-cycled dataset is preceded by a dummy pulse preparation period without data acquisition to ensure that steady-state conditions are met, as sketched in Fig. 4.10. The first measurement ($j = 1$) can additionally be initiated by a flip angle ramp preparation scheme, for example, using a linear [38] or a Kaiser-windowed [39] flip angle ramp to stabilize the transition to steady-state.

As simulated in Fig. 4.11A, the frequency response profile obtained from phase-cycled bSSFP is sensitive to T_1 and T_2. Two different methods have been proposed in the literature which exploit the relaxation time dependence of the bSSFP frequency profile for combined T_1 and T_2 quantification: motion-insensitive rapid configuration relaxometry (MIRACLE [40]) and an ellipse fitting approach (PLANET [41]).

T_1 and T_2 mapping based on MIRACLE is closely related to TESS but makes use of a balanced instead of a nonbalanced gradient scheme to mitigate motion sensitivity. The SSFP configurations F_1, F_0, and F_{-1} are indirectly retrieved from a series of N bSSFP scans with different phase cycling applied. The bSSFP signal can be described as the coherent sum over all SSFP configurations of orders F_n. For an off-resonance-related phase accumulation during TR of ψ and a given RF phase increment ϕ, this leads to the following expression for the complex steady-state magnetization at time t following the RF pulse [42, 43]:

$$M_+(t,\phi) = M_0 \cdot e^{-t/T_2} \cdot e^{i\psi t/TR} \cdot \sum_{n=-\infty}^{+\infty} F_n \cdot e^{in(\psi-\phi)} \tag{4.15}$$

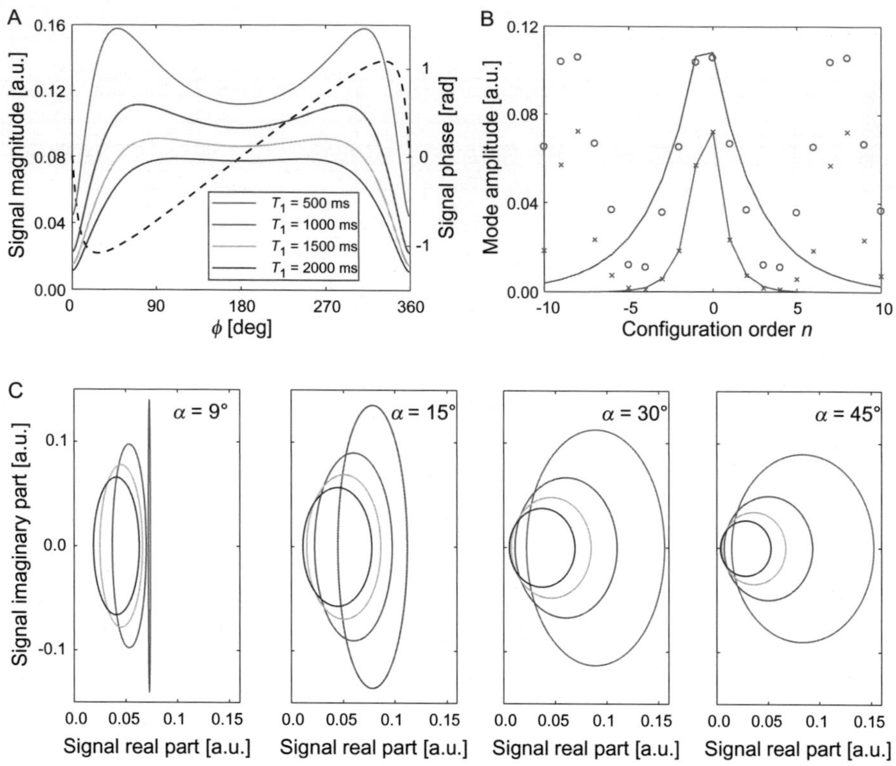

FIG. 4.11

(A) Balanced SSFP frequency response profile calculated as a function of the RF phase increment ϕ for TR/TE = 6 ms/3 ms, $\alpha = 15°$, a fixed T_2 of 50 ms, and four different T_1 values as specified in the *inset*. The *solid lines* represent the signal magnitude, the *dashed line* the signal phase. (B) SSFP configurations F_n derived from an N-point Fourier transform of N bSSFP datasets acquired with varying phase increments ϕ_j. *Blue*: tissue-like relaxation times ($T_1/T_2 = 1000$ ms/50 ms); *red*: fluid-like relaxation times ($T_1/T_2 = 4000$ ms/2000 ms); *cross/circle*: N=8; *solid line*: continuous ϕ, where the mode amplitudes are connected for improved visualization; other simulation parameters as defined in (A). (C) For RF phase increments ϕ covering 2π, the bSSFP steady-state magnetization traces out an ellipse in the complex plane as simulated here for the parameters specified in (A), including the same color coding but using four different flip angles (α = [9°, 15°, 30°, 45°], from left to right). It can be noted that the ellipse can collapse to a line for lower flip angles depending on the relaxation times.

As is apparent from Eq. (4.15), the effect of the RF phase increment ϕ is to shift the phase of the nth echo by $n\phi$. The SSFP modes F_n can then be isolated by performing an N-point discrete Fourier transform of N bSSFP data sets acquired by applying the RF phase increment $\phi_j = 2\pi(j - 1)/N$ during the jth scan (cf. Fig. 4.10).

Generally, aliasing will occur in the isolated modes F_n as visible in Fig. 4.11B, since an infinite number of echoes contributes to the bSSFP signal (cf. Eq. 4.15), which cannot be extracted based on a finite number of measurements. In Refs. [40, 43], it was demonstrated that for the isolation of the lowest order SSFP configurations (n = -1, 0, 1), at least $N = 8$ phase-cycled bSSFP scans are required to prevent aliasing and accurately describe the true SSFP mode amplitudes (cf. Eqs. 4.8–4.12) for tissues.

At lower T_1/T_2 ratios (as for fluids) aliasing becomes more pronounced (cf. Fig. 4.11B), demanding an increased number of scans. For conventional MIRACLE measurements with a rather low number of acquired phase-cycles ($N = 8$–16), the retrieved SSFP modes of fluids might thus be biased.

After the isolation of the F_1, F_0, and F_{-1} configurations from N bSSFP scans with varying RF phase increments, T_1 and T_2 can be estimated following the TESS relaxometry principle (cf. Eqs. 4.13, 4.14). As MIRACLE relies on a balanced acquisition scheme, it is less sensitive to motion in comparison to TESS and suited for 3D relaxometry of human brain tissues at optimal flip angles of ~15° similar to TESS.

PLANET [41] is a variant of MIRACLE, which makes use of the same acquisition scheme for relaxometry, that is, a series of bSSFP measurements with varying RF phase increments ϕ, but employs different postprocessing steps. In this approach, the RF phase-cycled balanced steady-state signal is described by an elliptical model [44]. Directly after the RF pulse, this model yields for the complex bSSFP signal [45]:

$$I(\theta) = M\frac{1 - ae^{i\theta}}{1 - b\cos\theta} \tag{4.16}$$

with $\theta := \psi$ - ϕ. The parameters M, a, and b are independent from θ and defined by

$$M := M_0\frac{(1-E_1)\sin\alpha}{1 - E_1\cos\alpha - E_2^2(E_1 - \cos\alpha)}$$

$$a := E_2$$

$$b := \frac{E_2(1-E_1)(1+\cos\alpha)}{1 - E_1\cos\alpha - E_2^2(E_1 - \cos\alpha)}.$$

Varying the phase-cycle ϕ by 2π, for example, from 0 to 2π, the signal $I(\theta)$ described by the parametric equation (4.16) defines an ellipse in the complex plane (cf. Fig. 4.11C). To quantify T_1 and T_2, direct linear least squares ellipse fitting of the acquired complex-valued phase-cycled bSSFP data is performed in a first step. Then, by investigating the geometric characteristics of the ellipse, solutions for the parameters a and b can be obtained, from which T_1 and T_2 can be calculated analytically according to Shcherbakova et al. [41].

$$T_1 = -\frac{\mathrm{TR}}{\ln\frac{a(1+\cos\alpha - ab\cos\alpha) - b}{a(1+\cos\alpha - ab) - b\cos\alpha}} \tag{4.17}$$

$$T_2 = -\frac{\mathrm{TR}}{\ln a} \tag{4.18}$$

It has to be noted that choosing a flip angle which is equal to the Ernst angle (i.e., $\alpha = \cos^{-1}E_1$) effects a collapse of the ellipse to a line (cf. Fig. 4.11C) and results in fitting failure. A proper choice of the flip angle should be based on $\alpha > \cos^{-1}[\exp(-\mathrm{TR}/T_{1,\mathrm{shortest}})]$ [41]. Similar to MIRACLE, reliable relaxometry with reasonable SNR can be achieved from at least eight phase-cycled bSSFP scans.

As observed with TESS, the T_2 derived with MIRACLE and PLANET exhibits a low B_1^+-sensitivity. The T_1 quantification, on the other hand, requires highly accurate actual flip angle maps to effectively correct for B_1^+ inhomogeneities (similar to TESS, cf. Fig. 4.7). Phase-cycled bSSFP T_1 and T_2 mapping is illustrated in Fig. 4.12 using MIRACLE. The T_1 estimates obtained from MIRACLE and PLANET are reported to be considerably underestimated, in particular in white matter structures (by about 30%–40%), even after B_1^+ correction [40, 41]. This bias is likely linked to an asymmetric

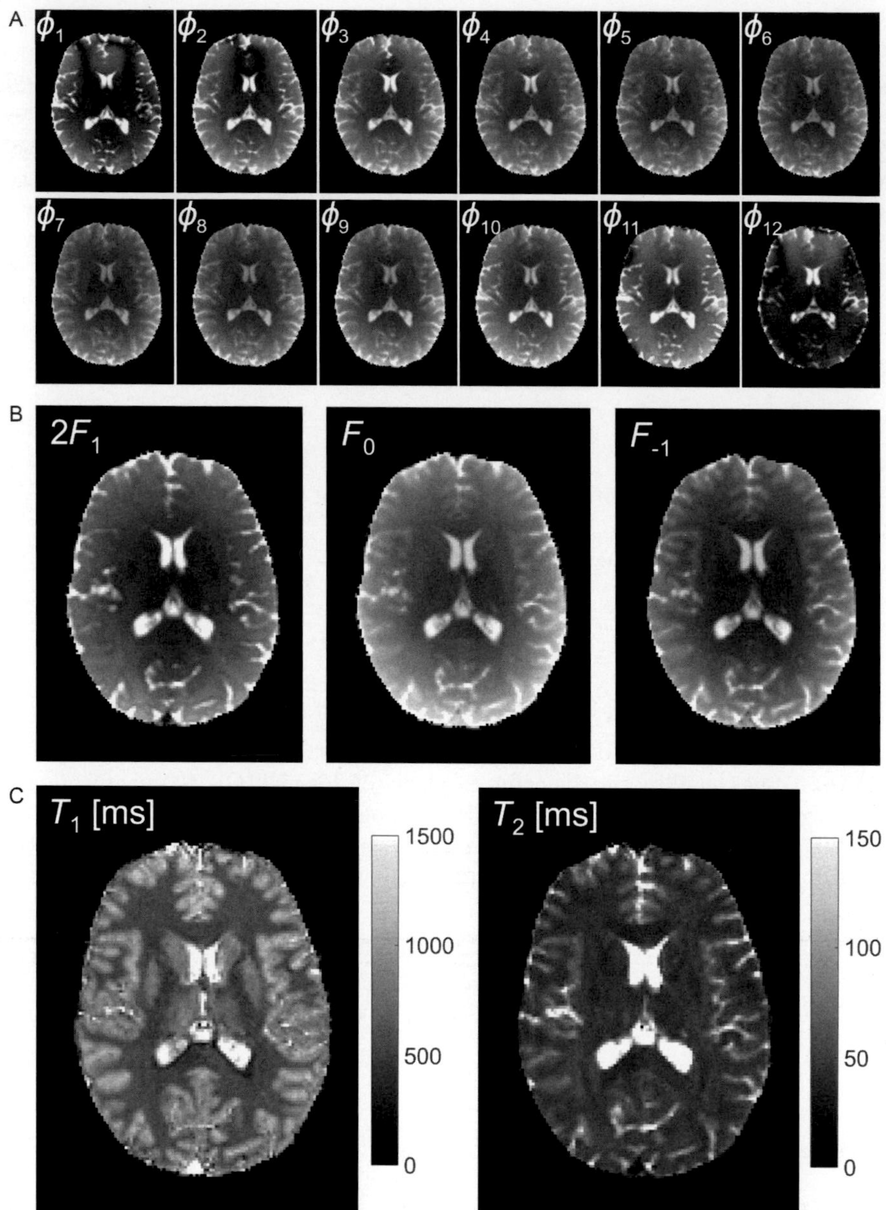

FIG. 4.12

Three-dimensional phase-cycled bSSFP relaxometry in the human brain at 3 T based on MIRACLE. A 12-point phase-cycling scheme is used with RF phase increments ϕ_j ($j = 1, \ldots, 12$) distributed evenly in the range from 0° to 360° as illustrated in (A) for an axial slice. The corresponding three lowest order SSFP configuration modes are shown in (B) (note that F_1 is differently scaled), from which T_1 and T_2 maps can be calculated following the TESS relaxometry principle (C).

intravoxel frequency content in combination with multicomponent relaxation, for example, due to a second brain tissue component reflecting myelin. This leads to an asymmetric bSSFP frequency profile [46, 47], which is not incorporated into the signal models used by MIRACLE and PLANET. The sensitivity of these methods to the frequency distribution in a voxel and thus to the tissue microstructure may be explored, for example, for myelin assessment in the human brain.

4.3 Simultaneous quantification of T_1 and T_2^*

T_1 and T_2^* relaxation times are not only both important tissue parameters for optimization and understanding of the biophysical origin of image contrast, but it has also been shown that their interrelation can provide additional insight into brain composition (specifically myelin and iron content) [48]. Furthermore, in combination with O_2-enhanced MRI, T_1 and T_2^* quantification allows the assessment of tumor oxygenation and to differentiate between the blood oxygen level dependent (BOLD) and the tissue oxygen level dependent (TOLD) effect [49].

4.3.1 Absolute quantification

A straightforward approach for simultaneous T_1 and T_2^* quantification is the combination of a fast LL-based T_1 quantification [7, 8] with a multigradient echo acquisition to form a multiecho LL sequence. T_1 and T_2^* can then be obtained from two independent exponential fits. The QRAPTEST technique [50] uses as similar approach, where the inversion pulse is replaced by a saturation pulse in order to allow for a fast 3D acquisition without the need for relaxation delays in between encoding shots. In addition, it is possible to obtain a flip angle map from this technique by including the flip angle of the saturation pulse in the fit.

Another variation of the LL approach is the MP2RAGE sequence [51]. In this case, two gradient-echo blocks are acquired after adiabatic inversion at inversion times TI_1 and TI_2 with free relaxation periods before and in between. Optimization of the flip angles α_1 and α_2 in the two blocks allows for T_1 quantification that is relatively insensitive to B_1^+ variations. Recently, a modification has been proposed that—in addition to T_1—allows for T_2^* and susceptibility mapping from multiple gradient echoes that are acquired in each TR [52], as illustrated in Fig. 4.13.

4.3.2 Quantification relative to baseline

The steady-state signal of an RF-spoiled gradient echo sequence is dependent on T_1 as well as T_2^* which can be exploited for relaxometry. While it is straightforward to obtain T_2^* from a single multigradient echo experiment, the quantification of T_1 usually requires multiple experiments with variable TR and/or flip angle. However, if only the change from baseline is of interest (e.g., after respiratory challenge with oxygen or bolus injection with a contrast agent), a multigradient echo sequence can offer simultaneous quantification of both parameters in a single experiment (relative to baseline). Since this acquisition can be performed very quickly (on the order of seconds), this relative quantification technique is well suited to monitor dynamic relaxation time changes.

For time-dependent relaxation times $T_1(t)$ and $T_2^*(t)$, the signal of an RF-spoiled gradient echo sequence at time t is given by

$$S(t,\mathrm{TE}) = M_0 \cdot \sin\alpha \frac{1-E_1(t)}{1-E_1(t)\cos\alpha} \exp(\text{-TE}/T_2^*(t)) \tag{4.19}$$

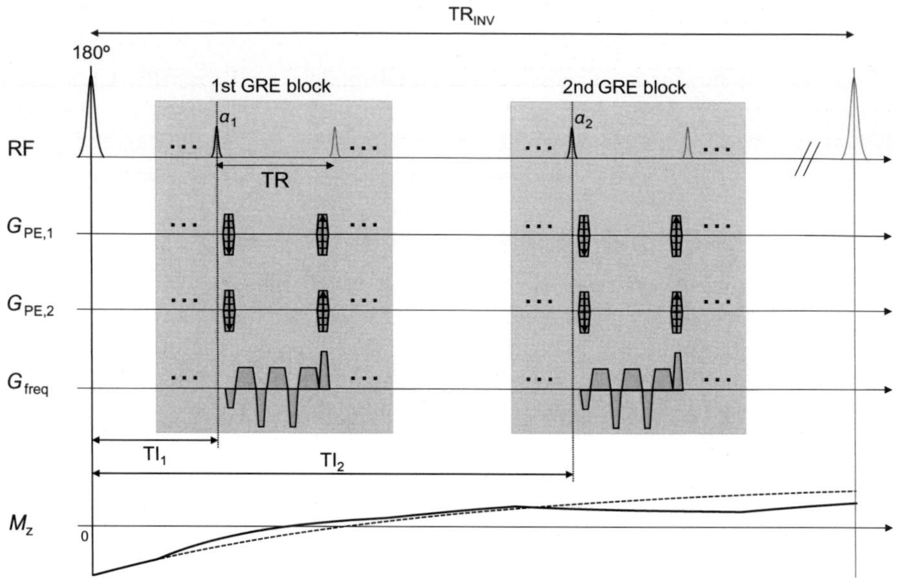

FIG. 4.13

Diagram of the multiecho MP2RAGE sequence. After inversion, two gradient echo (GRE) readout blocks are acquired with excitation flip angles α_1 and α_2. The same number of *k*-space lines is acquired in each block, and the *k*-space center is acquired in the center of the block at times TI_1 and TI_2. The inversion loop is repeated after TR_{INV} until all *k*-space lines are acquired. The *bottom row* shows the evolution of the *z*-magnetization. Outside of the GRE blocks, the magnetization (*solid line*) follows the free relaxation curve (*dashed line*). Inside the blocks, the effective relaxation time T_1^* is reduced by the application of the excitation pulses. Compared to a conventional MP2RAGE sequence, the only modification is the acquisition of data at multiple echo times in each TR, which enables T_2^* fitting and susceptibility mapping.

with $E_1(t) = \exp(\text{-TR}/T_1(t))$. $T_2^*(t)$ can simply be determined from an exponential fit of the multiecho data. Alternatively, the change from baseline $\Delta T_2^*(t)$ can be determined from the ratio of the decay curve to baseline which has the advantage that large-scale field gradients have no impact on quantification [49]. For T_1 quantification it is useful to perform a weighted average over all measured echo times, so that the TE-dependent exponential in the signal equation can be ignored. Alternatively, only the shortest echo time an be employed in order to minimize the influence of T_2^* changes. If the baseline $T_1(0)$ value is known, $T_1(t)$ can then be determined from the baseline signal level $S(0)$ and the signal at time t according to [49, 53]:

$$T_1(t) = \text{-TR}/\ln\left(\frac{S(0)\cdot(1-E_1(0)\cos\alpha)+S(t)\cdot(E_1(0)-1)}{S(0)\cdot(1-E_1(0)\cos\alpha)+S(t)\cdot(E_1(0)-1)\cos\alpha}\right)$$

4.4 Simultaneous quantification of T_2 and T_2^*

T_2 and T_2^* are both important parameters for tissue characterization as well as for contrast optimization between tissues. In addition, measuring both parameters before and after application of a superparamagnetic iron-oxide particle (SPIO) contrast agent allows for the determination of the mean vessel size and the blood volume within a voxel [54] (see also Chapter 14, which describes Dynamic Susceptibility Contrast MRI). Therefore, and due to the fast washout of the contrast agent, techniques that allow for simultaneous and rapid T_2 and T_2^* quantification are of high interest.

Simultaneous T_2 and T_2^* mapping can be performed by combining a spin echo sequence with a multigradient echo sequence. To this end, several related techniques have been proposed, based on sampling of the FID and the ascending (rephasing) part of the spin echo (GESFIDE [55]), sampling of both sides of the spin echo (GESSE [56]), and a combination of the two that additionally acquires multiple (usually two) spin echoes (MGEMSE [54]). Sequence diagrams for these three techniques are shown side by side in Fig. 4.14.

In the following, the term relaxation rate is used instead of relaxation time (i.e., the inverse of the relaxation times: $R_2 = 1/T_2$, $R_2^* = 1/T_2^*$). The reason for this is that relaxation rates are additive for

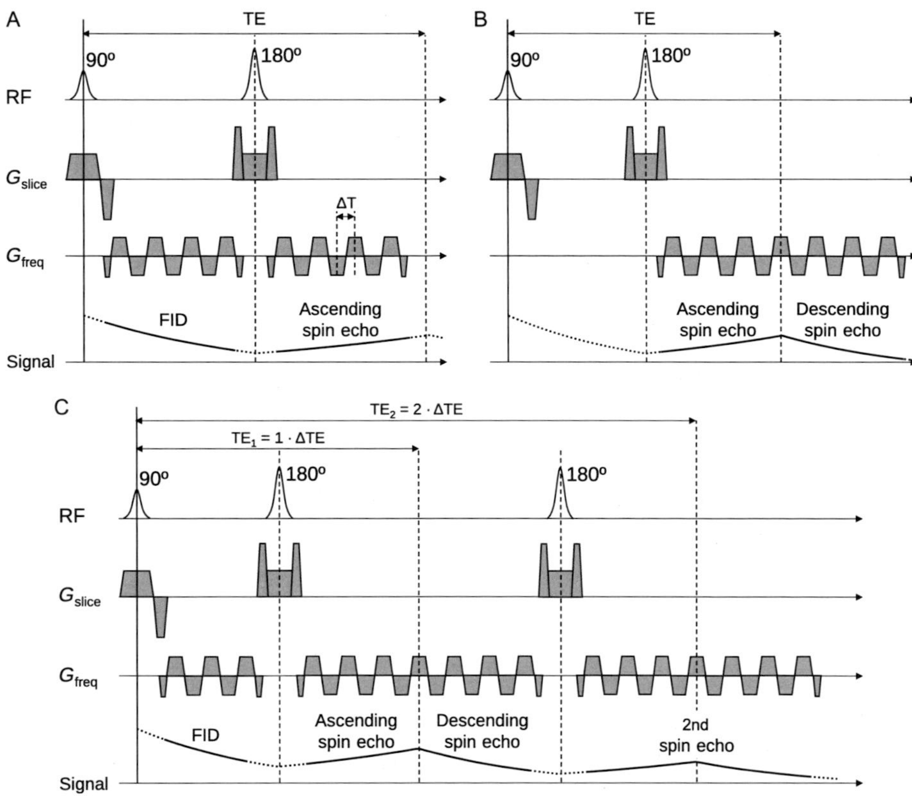

FIG. 4.14

Sequence diagrams for three closely related combined T_2 and T_2^* quantification techniques (in their historical order): (A) Gradient echo sampling of FID and echo (GESFIDE) [55], (B) gradient echo sampling of the spin echo (GESSE) [56], (C) multigradient echo multispin echo (MGEMSE) [54]. Consecutive gradient echoes are spaced in time by ΔT. The observed signal is illustrated at the bottom of the diagrams by a *solid line.* Intervals during which the signal evolution is not observed are indicated by a *dotted line.*

different relaxation processes, which simplifies many expressions such as the relation between $R_2{}^*$ and R_2:

$$R_2{}^* = R_2 + R_2'$$

$R_2{}^*$ is the sum of the irreversible relaxation rate R_2 and a reversible relaxation component R_2' that is a result of magnetic field inhomogeneities. R_2' decay can be reversed using a refocusing pulse which results in the formation of a spin echo. The evolution of the FID that follows signal excitation and the ascending and descending part of multiple consecutive spin echoes can be described by the following signal equation (assuming perfect 180° refocusing):

$$S(t) = M_0 \cdot \begin{cases} \exp(-(R_2 + R_2')t) & \text{FID} \\ \exp(-R_2 t + R_2'(t\text{-TE}_i)) & i\text{th ascending spin echo} \\ \exp(-R_2 t - R_2'(t\text{-TE}_i)) & i\text{th descending spin echo} \end{cases} \tag{4.20}$$

where TE_i denotes the echo time of the ith spin echo (only a single spin echo is acquired in case of GESSE and GESFIDE). The descending half of the spin echo decays with $R_2 + R_2' = R_2{}^*$, the same as the FID. Thus both FID and descending spin echo can be used to fit $R_2{}^*$.

In GESFIDE, R_2 is obtained from the FID and the ascending spin echo according to the following relationship:

$$R_2 = \frac{\ln\left(\frac{S(\mathrm{TE}/2 - \tau)}{S(\mathrm{TE}/2 + \tau)}\right)}{2\tau}$$

where the center of the refocusing pulse is placed at time TE/2, and τ is the time interval between the pulse and the acquired gradient echoes.

A disadvantage of the GESFIDE approach is its sensitivity to flip angle variations from slice profile imperfections and B_1^+ inhomogeneity, since the spin echo signal exhibits an additional decrease relative to the FID for a refocusing flip angle that is different from 180°. In contrast, R_2 quantification in GESSE relies on the two halves of the spin echo which are affected by incomplete refocusing in the same way. Thus flip angle variations only lead to an SNR reduction but not to systematic quantification errors. This advantage comes at the cost of an overall lower signal-to-noise ratio compared to GESFIDE.

In GESSE, R_2 can be obtained from the signal ratio of the gradient echoes at time τ before and after the spin echo (at TE) according to:

$$R_2 = \frac{\ln\left(\frac{S(\mathrm{TE} - \tau)}{S(\mathrm{TE} + \tau)}\right)}{2\tau}$$

Finally, R_2 quantification in the MGEMSE technique includes the FID and the full spin echo as well as one or more additional spin echoes (compare Fig. 4.14). As a result, this approach is again sensitive to flip angle variations. However, if only the change of R_2 is of interest, for example, after contrast agent application, quantification errors from static effects (such as B_1^+) can be avoided by directly fitting for ΔR_2 using the signal ratio before and after bolus injection. Compared to GESSE, the main advantages of this approach lie in its higher signal-to-noise ratio as well as a more accurate $R_2{}^*$ quantification.

4.5 Common challenges in simultaneous relaxation time measurements

Although longitudinal and transverse relaxation times are fundamental NMR properties and the most extensively investigated parameters in quantitative MRI, there is a wide range of reported values for given in vivo targets. While multiproperty methods enable the quantification of multiple relaxation parameters simultaneously in reduced acquisition times as compared to sequential approaches, they generally rely on more complex signal evolution patterns with increased sensitivity to instrumental factors such as transmit or static field inhomogeneities, imperfect slice profiles, diffusion, or magnetization transfer. Reproducibility and standardization across imaging sites is hence a major challenge to make these fast quantitative relaxometry techniques suited for clinical practice.

The relaxometry methods presented in this chapter are all based on the assumption that the acquired MR signal is governed by single-component relaxation, that is, that only a single T_1 and a single T_2 component contribute to the signal from each imaging voxel. However, many biological tissues are not well characterized by a single T_1, T_2, and resonance frequency, but rather by multicomponent relaxation and a distribution of frequencies since their biochemical composition and microstructure is heterogeneous within a voxel. White matter, for example, has been observed to exhibit biexponential relaxation, which is believed to be caused by a second fast-relaxing brain tissue component associated with myelin [57]. In the presence of more than one T_1 and T_2 species, the T_1 and T_2 values calculated with single-component relaxometry techniques are thus rather apparent than true relaxation times.

4.6 Summary

As outlined in this chapter, many different strategies have been suggested in the past few years to address the long-standing goal in MR relaxometry to extract relaxation parameters simultaneously from the same fast acquisition scheme.

The proposed joint T_1 and T_2 quantification techniques can be classified into three basic groups; transient phase imaging using SSFP readouts after magnetization preparation, MR fingerprinting acquisitions, and multicontrast steady-state sequences. Magnetization-prepared techniques such as IR-bSSFP or MP-DESS are based on sampling the signal recovery time course after an inversion pulse, which provides high T_1 sensitivity, while using rapid SSFP modules for readout to introduce T_2 sensitivity. MRF sequences are frequently as well initialized by an inversion recovery pulse to increase the signal level in the transverse plane but utilize a pseudo-random variation of sequence parameters during data collection to produce signal evolution patterns with distinct T_1 and T_2 sensitivity. Whereas MRF generates several hundreds of highly undersampled images at different time points, typically using spiral *k*-space trajectories, SSFP techniques approach the goal of multiparametric relaxometry from a different angle, acquiring only a few but often fully sampled contrasts. Multipathway nonbalanced SSFP imaging such as TESS offers the acquisition of several steady-state configurations including higher-order modes in a single scan. A series of phase-cycled balanced SSFP scans allows sampling the characteristic tissue-specific frequency profile. These SSFP contrasts exhibit an intrinsic mixed sensitivity to both T_1 and T_2, which is suited for combined mapping.

Simultaneous quantification of T_1 and T_2^* can be achieved by modifying an LL or MP2RAGE sequence for the acquisition of multiple gradient echoes within each TR. The QRAPTEST method is similar but makes use of a saturation instead of an inversion pulse. If absolute quantification of T_1 is not needed but mainly the change relative to a baseline is of interest, for example, after oxygen breathing challenge or bolus contrast agent injection, the combined mapping of both T_1 and T_2^* relative to the baseline is feasible based on a single multiecho gradient echo acquisition. Joint T_2 and T_2^* estimation is provided by various techniques, which are related to each other and based on a combination of a spin-echo sequence with a multiecho gradient echo acquisition in order to sample the FID and/or ascending and descending spin echoes. In GESFIDE, the FID and ascending part of the spin echo are utilized to quantify T_2 and T_2^* simultaneously. The GESSE sequence samples both sides of the spin echo while the MGEMSE technique includes both the FID and the full spin echo as well as additional spin echoes.

Table 4.1 Overview of relative strengths and weaknesses of techniques for simultaneous mapping of T_1 and T_2 (top), T_1 and T_2^* (middle), and T_2 and T_2^* (bottom).

	T_1 mapping sensitivity to				T_2 mapping sensitivity to			
Method	B_0	B_1^+	**Motion**	**MT/ myelin**	B_0	B_1^+	**Motion**	**MT/ myelin**
IR-bSSFP	Medium	Low	Medium	High	High	High	Medium	Very high
MRF	Low	Low	Medium	Medium	Low	High	Medium	High
MP-DESS	Low	High	High	Medium	Low	Medium	High	Medium
TESS	Low	High	High	Medium	Low	Very low	High	Low
MIRACLE	Low	High	Medium	High	Low	Very low	Medium	High
PLANET	Low	High	Medium	High	Low	Very low	Medium	High

	T_1 mapping		T_2^* mapping	Overall
Method	**Accuracy**	B_1^+ **Sensitivity**	**Accuracy**	**SNR**
Multiecho LL	Medium	Medium	Adjustable (TEs)	Medium
QRAPTEST	Medium	Low	Adjustable (TEs)	Medium
ME-MP2RAGE	Low	Medium	Adjustable (TEs)	High

	T_2 mapping		T_2^* mapping	Overall
Method	**Accuracy**	B_1^+**sensitivity**	**Accuracy**	**SNR**
GESFIDE	Medium	High	High	High
GESSE	High	Low	Low	Medium
MGEMSE	Medium (ΔT_2: high)	High (ΔT_2: low)	High	High

Notes: *A 3D acquisition is assumed in all cases which removes slice profile-related issues and generally provides higher motion stability. Please note that possible correction strategies were not considered and that the comparison also depends on the chosen sequence parameters and spatial encoding strategy. For these and other reasons, the comparison remains necessarily subjective. In case of MRF, the original implementation [15] is assumed which is based on an IR-bSSFP with variable flip angles.*

All multiproperty relaxometry methods discussed in this chapter come along with their own advantages and drawbacks. Common benefits are their acquisition speed and the simultaneous generation of intrinsically coregistered quantitative maps. However, their sensitivity to hardware-related factors, for example, B_0 and B_1^+ field inhomogeneities, or tissue characteristics, for example, magnetization transfer, differs, making them beneficial in different targets and at different field strengths. These properties are summarized in a simplified fashion in Table 4.1 to facilitate the selection of a specific multiparametric relaxometry technique and to point out potential pitfalls that need to be considered after the selection has been made.

References

[1] Gulani V, Schmitt P, Griswold MA, Webb AG, Jakob PM. Towards a single sequence neurologic magnetic resonance imaging examination: multiple-contrast images from an IR TrueFISP experiment. Invest Radiol 2004;39:767.

[2] Riederer SJ, Lee JN, Farzaneh F, Wang HZ, Wright RC. Magnetic resonance image synthesis. Clinical implementation. Acta Radiol Suppl 1986;369:466–8.

[3] Warntjes JBM, Leinhard OD, West J, Lundberg P. Rapid magnetic resonance quantification on the brain: optimization for clinical usage. Magn Reson Med 2008;60:320–9. https://doi.org/10.1002/mrm.21635.

[4] Carr HY. Steady-state free precession in nuclear magnetic resonance. Phys Rev 1958;112:1693–701. https://doi.org/10.1103/PhysRev.112.1693.

[5] Oppelt A, Graumann R, Barfuss H, Fischer H, Hartl W, Schajor W. FISP, a novel, fast pulse sequence for nuclear magnetic resonance imaging. Electromedica 1986;54:15–8.

[6] Scheffler K, Hennig J. T1 quantification with inversion recovery TrueFISP. Magn Reson Med 2001;45:720–3. https://doi.org/10.1002/mrm.1097.

[7] Deichmann R, Haase A. Quantification of T1 values by SNAPSHOT-FLASH NMR imaging. J Magn Reson 1992;96:608–12. https://doi.org/10.1016/0022-2364(92)90347-A.

[8] Look DC, Locker DR. Time saving in measurement of NMR and EPR relaxation times. Rev Sci Instrum 1970;41:250–1. https://doi.org/10.1063/1.1684482.

[9] Schmitt P, Griswold MA, Jakob PM, Kotas M, Gulani V, Flentje M, et al. Inversion recovery TrueFISP: quantification of T1, T2, and spin density. Magn Reson Med 2004;51:661–7. https://doi.org/10.1002/mrm.20058.

[10] Ehses P, Seiberlich N, Ma D, Breuer FA, Jakob PM, Griswold MA, et al. IR TrueFISP with a golden-ratio-based radial readout: fast quantification of T1, T2, and proton density. Magn Reson Med 2013;69:71–81. https://doi.org/10.1002/mrm.24225.

[11] McRobbie DW, Lerski RA, Straughan K. Slice profile effects and their calibration and correction in quantitative NMR imaging. Phys Med Biol 1987;32:971. https://doi.org/10.1088/0031-9155/32/8/002.

[12] Santini F, Kawel-Boehm N, Greiser A, Bremerich J, Bieri O. Simultaneous T1 and T2 quantification of the myocardium using cardiac balanced-SSFP inversion recovery with interleaved sampling acquisition (CABIRIA). Magn Reson Med 2015;74:365–71. https://doi.org/10.1002/mrm.25402.

[13] Bieri O, Scheffler K. On the origin of apparent low tissue signals in balanced SSFP. Magn Reson Med 2006;56:1067–74. https://doi.org/10.1002/mrm.21056.

[14] Bieri O, Scheffler K. Optimized balanced steady-state free precession magnetization transfer imaging. Magn Reson Med 2007;58:511–8. https://doi.org/10.1002/mrm.21326.

[15] Ma D, Gulani V, Seiberlich N, Liu K, Sunshine JL, Duerk JL, et al. Magnetic resonance fingerprinting. Nature 2013;495:187–92. https://doi.org/10.1038/nature11971.

[16] Tamir JI, Uecker M, Chen W, Lai P, Alley MT, Vasanawala SS, et al. T2 shuffling: sharp, multicontrast, volumetric fast spin-echo imaging. Magn Reson Med 2017;77:180–95. https://doi.org/10.1002/mrm.26102.

[17] Pfister J, Blaimer M, Jakob PM, Breuer FA. Simultaneous T1/T2 measurements in combination with PCA-SENSE reconstruction (T1* shuffling) and multicomponent analysis. Proc Int Soc Mag Reson Med 2017;25:452.

[18] Stöcker T, Keil F, Vahedipour K, Brenner D, Pracht E, Shah NJ. MR parameter quantification with magnetization-prepared double echo steady-state (MP-DESS). Magn Reson Med 2014;72:103–11. https://doi.org/10.1002/mrm.24901.

[19] Bruder H, Fischer H, Graumann R, Deimling M. A new steady-state imaging sequence for simultaneous acquisition of two MR images with clearly different contrasts. Magn Reson Med 1988;7:35–42. https://doi.org/10.1002/mrm.1910070105.

[20] Hennig J. Echoes—how to generate, recognize, use or avoid them in MR-imaging sequences. Part I: fundamental and not so fundamental properties of spin echoes. Concepts Magn Reson 1991;3:125–43. https://doi.org/10.1002/cmr.1820030302.

[21] Mizumoto CT, Yoshitome E. Multiple echo SSFP sequences. Magn Reson Med 1991;18:244–50. https://doi.org/10.1002/mrm.1910180126.

[22] Scheffler K. A pictorial description of steady-states in rapid magnetic resonance imaging. Concepts Magn Reson 1999;11:291–304. https://doi.org/10.1002/(SICI)1099-0534(1999)11:5%3C291::AID-CMR2%3E3.0.CO;2-J.

[23] Welsch GH, Scheffler K, Mamisch TC, Hughes T, Millington S, Deimling M, et al. Rapid estimation of cartilage T2 based on double echo at steady state (DESS) with 3 Tesla. Magn Reson Med 2009;62:544–9. https://doi.org/10.1002/mrm.22036.

[24] Heule R, Ganter C, Bieri O. Rapid estimation of cartilage T2 with reduced T1 sensitivity using double echo steady state imaging. Magn Reson Med 2014;71:1137–43. https://doi.org/10.1002/mrm.24748.

[25] Heule R, Ganter C, Bieri O. Triple echo steady-state (TESS) relaxometry. Magn Reson Med 2014;71:230–7. https://doi.org/10.1002/mrm.24659.

[26] Ganter C. Static susceptibility effects in balanced SSFP sequences. Magn Reson Med 2006;56:687–91. https://doi.org/10.1002/mrm.20986.

[27] Hänicke W, Vogel HU. An analytical solution for the SSFP signal in MRI. Magn Reson Med 2003;49:771–5. https://doi.org/10.1002/mrm.10410.

[28] Press WH, Teukolsky SA, Vetterling WT, Flannery BP. Numerical recipes: the art of scientific computing. Cambridge: Cambridge University Press; 2007.

[29] Qiao Y, Zou C, Cheng C, Wan Q, Tie C, Liang D, et al. Diffusion effect on T2 relaxometry in triple-echo steady state free precession sequence. J Magn Reson 2018;292:25–35. https://doi.org/10.1016/j.jmr.2018.04.018.

[30] Freed DE, Scheven UM, Zielinski LJ, Sen PN, Hürlimann MD. Steady-state free precession experiments and exact treatment of diffusion in a uniform gradient. J Chem Phys 2001;115:4249–58. https://doi.org/10.1063/1.1389859.

[31] Weigel M. Extended phase graphs: dephasing, RF pulses, and echoes—pure and simple. J Magn Reson Imaging 2015;41:266–95. https://doi.org/10.1002/jmri.24619.

[32] Weigel M, Schwenk S, Kiselev VG, Scheffler K, Hennig J. Extended phase graphs with anisotropic diffusion. J Magn Reson 2010;205:276–85. https://doi.org/10.1016/j.jmr.2010.05.011.

[33] Liu D, Steingoetter A, Curcic J, Kozerke S. Exploiting multicompartment effects in triple-echo steady-state T2 mapping for fat fraction quantification. Magn Reson Med 2018;79:423–9. https://doi.org/10.1002/mrm.26680.

[34] Heule R, Bär P, Mirkes C, Scheffler K, Trattnig S, Bieri O. Triple-echo steady-state T2 relaxometry of the human brain at high to ultra-high fields. NMR Biomed 2014;27:1037–45. https://doi.org/10.1002/nbm.3152.

[35] Heule R, Celicanin Z, Kozerke S, Bieri O. Simultaneous multislice triple-echo steady-state (SMS-TESS) T1, T2, PD, and off-resonance mapping in the human brain. Magn Reson Med 2018;80:1088–100. https://doi.org/10.1002/mrm.27126.

[36] Günthner C, Amthor T, Kozerke S, Doneva M. Fast multi-parametric mapping competition: MR fingerprinting vs. triple-echo steady state. In: Proceedings of the International Society for Magnetic Resonance in Medicine, vol. 27. p. 761.

[37] Bieri O, Scheffler K. Fundamentals of balanced steady state free precession MRI. J Magn Reson Imaging 2013;38:2–1511. https://doi.org/10.1002/jmri.24163.

[38] Deshpande VS, Chung YC, Zhang Q, Shea SM, Li D. Reduction of transient signal oscillations in true-FISP using a linear flip angle series magnetization preparation. Magn Reson Med 2003;49:151–7. https://doi.org/10.1002/mrm.10337.

[39] Le Roux P. Simplified model and stabilization of SSFP sequences. J Magn Reson 2003;163:23–37. https://doi.org/10.1016/S1090-7807(03)001150.

[40] Nguyen D, Bieri O. Motion-insensitive rapid configuration relaxometry. Magn Reson Med 2017;78:518–26. https://doi.org/10.1002/mrm.26384.

[41] Shcherbakova Y, van den Berg CAT, Moonen CTW, Bartels LW. PLANET: an ellipse fitting approach for simultaneous T1 and T2 mapping using phase-cycled balanced steady-state free precession. Magn Reson Med 2018;79:711–22. https://doi.org/10.1002/mrm.26717.

[42] Ganter C. Steady state of gradient echo sequences with radiofrequency phase cycling: analytical solution, contrast enhancement with partial spoiling. Magn Reson Med 2006;55:98–4107. https://doi.org/10.1002/mrm.20736.

[43] Zur Y, Wood ML, Neuringer LJ. Motion-insensitive, steady-state free precession imaging. Magn Reson Med 1990;16:444–59. https://doi.org/10.1002/mrm.1910160311.

[44] Lauzon ML, Frayne R. Analytical characterization of RF phase-cycled balanced steady-state free precession. Concepts Magn Reson Part A 2009;34A:133–43. https://doi.org/10.1002/cmr.a.20138.

[45] Xiang Q-S, Hoff MN. Banding artifact removal for bSSFP imaging with an elliptical signal model. Magn Reson Med 2014;71:927–33. https://doi.org/10.1002/mrm.25098.

[46] Miller KL. Asymmetries of the balanced SSFP profile. Part I: theory and observation. Magn Reson Med 2010;63:385–95. https://doi.org/10.1002/mrm.22212.

[47] Miller KL, Smith SM, Jezzard P. Asymmetries of the balanced SSFP profile. Part II: white matter. Magn Reson Med 2010;63:396–406. https://doi.org/10.1002/mrm.22249.

[48] Stüber C, Morawski M, Schäfer A, Labadie C, Wähnert M, Leuze C, et al. Myelin and iron concentration in the human brain: a quantitative study of MRI contrast. NeuroImage 2014;93(Pt 1):95–1106. https://doi.org/10.1016/j.neuroimage.2014.02.026.

[49] Remmele S, Sprinkart AM, Müller A, Träber F, von Lehe M, Gieseke J, et al. Dynamic and simultaneous MR measurement of R1 and R2* changes during respiratory challenges for the assessment of blood and tissue oxygenation. Magn Reson Med 2013;70:136–46. https://doi.org/10.1002/mrm.24458.

[50] Warntjes JBM, Dahlqvist O, Lundberg P. Novel method for rapid, simultaneous T1, T*2, and proton density quantification. Magn Reson Med 2007;57:528–37. https://doi.org/10.1002/mrm.21165.

[51] Marques JP, Kober T, Krueger G, van der Zwaag W, Van de Moortele P-F. Gruetter R. MP2RAGE, a self bias-field corrected sequence for improved segmentation and T1-mapping at high field. NeuroImage 2010;49:1271–81. https://doi.org/10.1016/j.neuroimage.2009.10.002.

[52] Metere R, Kober T, Möller HE, Schäfer A. Simultaneous quantitative MRI mapping of T1, T2* and magnetic susceptibility with multi-echo MP2RAGE. PLoS ONE 2017;12. https://doi.org/10.1371/journal.pone.0169265.

[53] Ishimori Y, Kimura H, Uematsu H, Matsuda T, Itoh H. Dynamic T1 estimation of brain tumors using double-echo dynamic MR imaging. J Magn Reson Imaging 2003;18:113–20. https://doi.org/10.1002/jmri.10331.

[54] Remmele S, Ring J, Sénégas J, Heindel W, Mesters RM, Bremer C, et al. Concurrent MR blood volume and vessel size estimation in tumors by robust and simultaneous ΔR2 and ΔR2* quantification. Magn Reson Med 2011;66:144–53. https://doi.org/10.1002/mrm.22810.

[55] Ma J, Wehrli FW. Method for image-based measurement of the reversible and irreversible contribution to the transverse-relaxation rate. J Magn Reson B 1996;111:61–9. https://doi.org/10.1006/jmrb.1996.0060.

[56] Yablonskiy DA, Haacke EM. An MRI method for measuring T2 in the presence of static and RF magnetic field inhomogeneities. Magn Reson Med 1997;37:872–6. https://doi.org/10.1002/mrm.1910370611.

[57] Deoni SC, Rutt BK, Arun T, Pierpaoli C, Jones DK. Gleaning multicomponent T1 and T2 information from steady-state imaging data. Magn Reson Med 2008;60:1372–87. https://doi.org/10.1002/mrm.21704.

CHAPTER

Specialized Mapping Methods in the Heart

5

Gastão Cruz[a], Sébastien Roujol[a], René M. Botnar[a,b], and Claudia Prieto[a,b]

[a]*King's College London, School of Biomedical Engineering and Imaging Sciences, London, United Kingdom* [b]*Pontificia Universidad Católica de Chile, Escuela de Ingeniería, Santiago, Chile*

5.1 Introduction

Cardiac Magnetic Resonance Imaging (MRI) has been established as a clinically important technique for the assessment of cardiac morphology, function, perfusion, and viability, and is currently used to diagnose congenital, ischemic and valvular heart disease, pericardial lesions, cardiac tumors and cardiomyopathies. Recently, T_1, T_2, T_2^*, and extracellular volume (ECV) mapping techniques have emerged, providing quantitative tissue characterization and objective assessment of myocardial tissue properties. MR relaxation parameter mapping offers the potential for early disease detection and monitoring over time, shifting the MR paradigm from visualization to quantification. Myocardial T_1 mapping may be performed before (native T_1 map) and also after contrast media injection (post-contrast T_1 map), enabling quantification of ECV. Clinical studies have shown the utility of native T_1 and ECV mapping in a wide range of cardiac pathologies, including acute and chronic myocardial infarction, myocarditis, cardiac amyloidosis, cardiac involvement in systemic disease, and other conditions characterized by diffuse myocardial fibrosis [1]. T_2 mapping techniques have demonstrated utility for evaluation of a variety of cardiac pathologies including acute myocardial infarction, myocarditis, Takotsubo cardiomyopathy, iron overload, and heart transplant rejection [2]. T_2^* is primarily used to detect myocardial iron overload in diseases like thalassemia major [3].

The signal measured with MRI depends on a multitude of different parameters such as the proton spin density, the longitudinal T_1 relaxation time, and the transverse T_2 relaxation time. These parameters, together with other sequence-specific parameters (such as echo time, repetition time, and flip angle) and preparation pulses (such as inversion recovery (IR) and T_2 preparation pulses) are exploited in MRI to generate different contrasts between tissues in the images. The conventional approach for T_1 mapping is to acquire data at multiple points along the T_1 signal recovery curve (longitudinal magnetization). Similarly, the conventional approach for T_2 (or T_2^*) mapping is to acquire data at multiple points along the T_2 (or T_2^*) signal decay curve (transverse magnetization) with multiple spin echo (or gradient echo) images. However, in cardiac parametric mapping, these strategies must be modified to avoid artefacts due to physiological cardiac and respiratory motion. In this chapter, specialized methods for myocardial T_1, T_2, and T_2^* mapping are discussed.

Advances in Magnetic Resonance Technology and Applications. Volume 1. ISSN 2666-9099. https://doi.org/10.1016/B978-0-12-817057-1.00008-1

5.2 Cardiac T_1 and extracellular volume mapping

Sampling of the T_1 exponential recovery is a common strategy for T_1 mapping. One of the first approaches, the Look-Locker method [4], relies on continuous sampling of the signal recovery after a 180° inversion pulse. However, in cardiac parametric mapping, this strategy can be problematic due to cardiac (and respiratory) motion. In the presence of motion, the temporal T_1 recovery signal can be corrupted due to misalignment between images, leading to errors in the estimated T_1 values. Consequently, pixel-wise Look-Locker-derived T_1 maps can have considerable errors. To overcome this limitation, the modified Look-Locker inversion recovery technique (MOLLI) [5] was developed, where data are acquired in the same cardiac phase over several heartbeats. MOLLI has enabled the collection of 2D cardiac T_1 maps in a breath-hold, and inspired further improvements [6,7] to reduce breath-hold duration, such as shortened MOLLI (ShMOLLI) [8]. However, the T_1 values measured using MOLLI are heart-rate-dependent and consistently underestimated due to confounding factors such as T_2 dependence, sensitivity to magnetization transfer (MT) effects, and field in homogeneities, among others [7,9–11]. One strategy to deal with some of these issues is to erase the magnetization history before sampling the T_1 recovery via a 90° saturation pulse. This is the general approach used in short acquisition period T_1 (SAP-T_1) [12] and two-dimensional (2D) saturation recovery single-shot acquisition (SASHA) [13] T_1 mapping. While the saturation pulse removes many confounding factors, it also reduces the dynamic range of the T_1-weighted signal. Consequently, saturation-based T_1 mapping techniques exhibit a higher accuracy, but lower precision compared to MOLLI [7,11]. The following sections will cover some of the most common cardiac T_1 mapping techniques divided in three groups: inversion-based, saturation-based, and hybrid inversion/saturation-based approaches.

5.2.1 Inversion recovery-based T_1 mapping

A generalized diagram of an inversion recovery (IR)-based myocardial T_1 mapping sequence such as MOLLI is shown in Fig. 5.1. 2D MOLLI uses a 180° inversion pulse and single-shot acquisitions over several heartbeats, followed by a recovery period of several heartbeats where no radio frequency (RF) pulses are applied. The number of heartbeats in which data are collected following the inversion pulse and recovery heartbeats depends on the MOLLI variant. Cardiac motion is minimized by acquiring data at the same cardiac phase (typically a mid-diastolic acquisition window of ~100–200 ms) over multiple cardiac cycles, using the electrocardiogram (ECG) to trigger the scan. A trigger delay (TD) is manually prescribed for each patient, defining the time between the RR wave and the diastolic period. Respiratory motion is minimized by performing the acquisition under breath-hold, and therefore the acquisition needs to be limited to 20 heartbeats (ideally less), leading to scan durations of 10–20 s. Every time an inversion pulse is applied, the inversion time (TI) delay between the inversion pulse and image acquisition is changed such that different points along the T_1 recovery curve are sampled, while the cardiac phase is fixed. The recovery period allows for (almost) full T_1 recovery, therefore M_z has (almost) always the same value when another inversion pulse is applied. A shorthand notation is commonly used to denote the number of acquisition heartbeats (numbers) and recovery heartbeats (numbers in parenthesis), where inversion pulses are applied before each group of acquisition heartbeats. The original MOLLI sequence structure is described as "3(3)3(3)5", meaning that an inversion

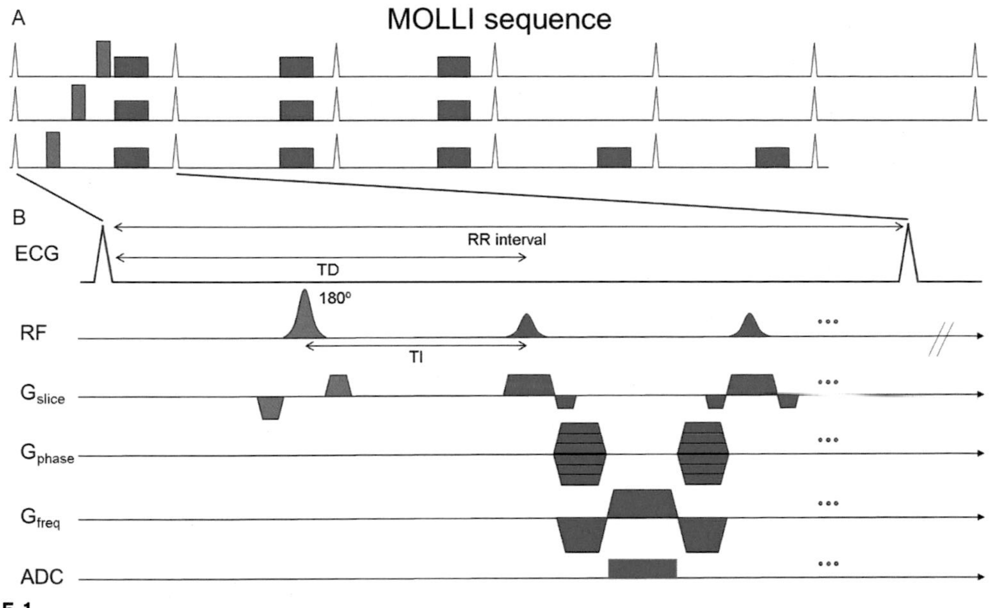

FIG. 5.1

(A) Modified Look-Locker inversion recovery (MOLLI) sequence diagram for variant 3(3)3(3)5. ECG triggering is used to synchronize data acquisition with mid-diastolic period, setting a subject-specific trigger delay (TD) after the R wave. Three inversion recovery pulses with varying inversion times (TI) provide T_1 encoding and recovery heartbeats are used to sample additional points along the T_1 recovery curve. Inversion pulses are shown in *green*, whereas data acquisition modules are shown in *blue*. (B) Sequence diagram for a specific heartbeat. Inversion pulse is applied TI ms before the data acquisition (only the first readout is shown).

pulse is applied before three acquisition heartbeats, followed by three recovery heartbeats, followed by another inversion pulse plus three acquisition and three recovery heartbeats, and finally an inversion pulse plus five acquisition heartbeats.

MOLLI typically achieves high precision, but has limited accuracy [7,11]. There are several reasons for this behavior. Within each cardiac acquisition window, several RF imaging pulses are applied that disturb the otherwise natural T_1 recovery: $M_z(t) = M_0[1 - 2\,exp\,(-t/T_1)]$. This effect introduces an underestimation bias in the measured T_1^*, which is modeled by $M_z(TI) = A - Bexp(-TI/T_1^*)$. Under the assumption of small flip angles ($\alpha < 10°$) and continuous (non-triggered) RF-spoiled (FLASH) readouts (i.e., negligible T_2 weighting), the true T_1 value may be approximated as $T_1 = T_1^*(B/A - 1)$ [14]. While this is not exactly the case for the triggered, medium flip angle, balanced steady-state free precession (bSSFP) readouts commonly used in MOLLI, this three-parameter fit and correction factor have often been used in inversion-based T_1 mapping methods. The signal-to-noise ratio (SNR) is improved when employing a bSSFP readout instead of FLASH; however a T_2 dependency is also introduced [15]. Errors in the B_0 and B_1 fields also produce deviations in the bSSFP signal from the ideal case, and consequently can lead to errors in the estimated T_1 values [7,16]. Similarly, there can be modeling errors associated with the inversion pulse. Errors in the transmit B_1 field will result in a pulse which deviates from the ideal 180°. Even if B_1 errors are negligible, T_2 relaxation occurring during the (usually long adiabatic) inversion pulse will lead to an incomplete inversion [17], particularly in tissues with short T_2 values (myocardial $T_2 \sim 50$ ms at 1.5 T would have an expected inversion efficiency of ~95%). One of the main sources of variability in MOLLI measurements comes from the dependency of this technique on the heart rate [18]. The heart rate not only determines which points along the inversion recovery are sampled following an inversion pulse, but can also affect the length of the recovery period when defined as a function of the heartbeat number. The variable lengths of recovery periods violate the assumption of a constant, almost fully relaxed M_z whenever an inversion pulse is applied. Consequently, T_1 is increasingly underestimated with increasing heart rate and T_1 value [8]. One work-around is to define the recovery period as a fixed duration of time (e.g., a minimum of 3 s), reducing the heart rate dependence [7]. Residual cardiac and respiratory motion in MOLLI acquisitions can also introduce errors in the estimated T_1 values [19,20]. Moreover, MOLLI is sensitive to magnetization transfer effects from both the inversion pulse and the RF readouts, causing further underestimation of T_1 [10]. Despite these limitations, MOLLI achieves good reproducibility [11,21] and has shown high sensitivity to most cardiomyopathies, which makes MOLLI the preferred T_1 mapping technique in the clinic [22].

Encouraging results from MOLLI T_1 mapping [5] have inspired a series of developments focused on further optimization of this technique, minimizing its limitations and reducing the associated breath-hold duration. Initial studies optimized the acquisition parameters for MOLLI, suggesting the use of a flip angle of 35°, minimum TI of 100 ms with 80 ms increments, and three recovery heartbeats [23]. To address the dependency on heart rate, the accuracy and precision of several sampling schemes have been studied, such as "5(3)3" or "4(1)3(1)2" [7,24]. Reduction of the number of heartbeats is possible without significantly affecting T_1 estimates, and acquiring most of the data after the first inversion pulse (as in the "5(3)3" scheme) has been shown to improve accuracy. However, these accelerated acquisition strategies do incur a penalty on precision.

One of the fastest protocol in the group of IR-based methods is the Shortened MOLLI (ShMOLLI) technique, featuring a breath-hold duration of only nine heartbeats via a "5(1)1(1)1" scheme [8], as illustrated in Fig. 5.2. Reducing the number of recovery heartbeats from three to one leads to incomplete T_1 recovery of high T_1 values by the time the second inversion pulse is applied, violating assumptions of the fitting model. This issue is addressed in ShMOLLI with a conditional fitting approach, where different T_1 values are fit with different IR data. Generally, the heartbeats used to fit each T_1 range are as follows: 1–5 heartbeats for long T_1 values ($T_1 > T_{RR}$), 1–7 heartbeats for short T_1values ($0.4T_{RR} < T_1 < T_{RR}$) and all [1–9] heartbeats for very short T_1 values ($T_1 < 0.4T_{RR}$), where T_{RR} corresponds to heartbeat duration. Long T_1 values only use data from the first inversion, reducing the underestimation bias observed in MOLLI for high T_1 values and heart rates. Data acquired with a long TI (e.g., heartbeats 4 and 5) are less useful for mapping short T_1 values and this is addressed with the inclusion of extra inversion pulses. ShMOLLI is also an efficient protocol for post-contrast T_1 mapping as myocardial T_1values drop to ~300–500 ms and most samples can be used in the fit. Conversely, the ShMOLLI approach may have a lower accuracy at 3.0 T field strength than at 1.5 T, as T_1 increases with increasing field strength. ShMOLLI has reduced precision compared to MOLLI as fewer data are acquired in ShMOLLI; however, ShMOLLI achieves comparable accuracy to MOLLI with a considerable reduction in breath-hold duration [8,24]. The reduced scan time also leads to fewer respiratory motion artefacts which are a common occurrence during incomplete breath-holds [13,25].

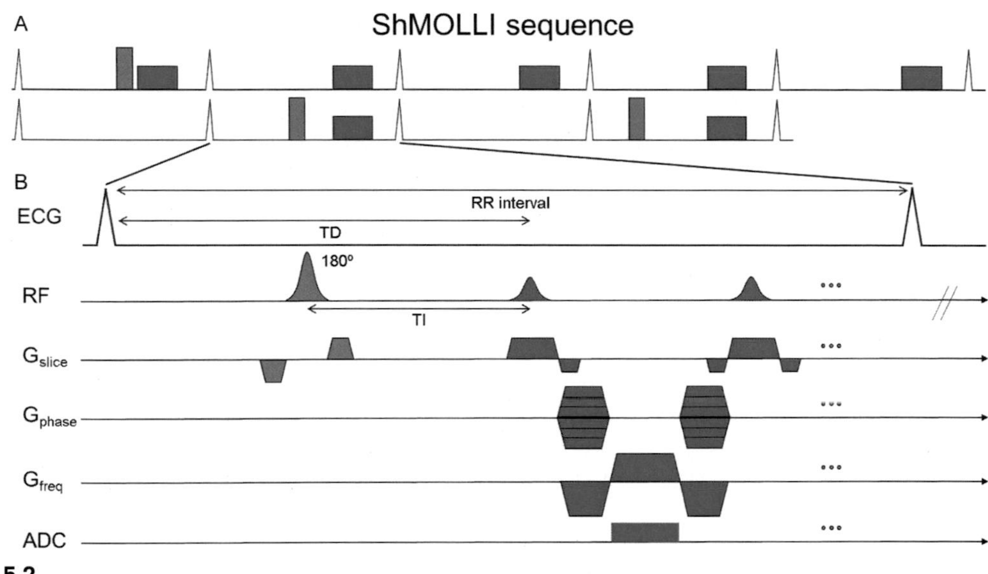

FIG. 5.2

(A) Shortened modified Look-Locker inversion recovery (ShMOLLI) sequence diagram. A similar acquisition strategy to MOLLI is used, where varying inversion times (TI) are used to sample the T_1 recovery. Only one recovery heartbeat is employed and a conditional fit is used. Consequently the data used for the fit depends on the T_1: 1-5 heartbeats for long T_1 values, 1-7 heartbeats for short T_1 values and 1-9 heartbeats for very short T_1 values. Inversion pulses are shown in *green*, whereas data acquisition modules are shown in *blue*. (B) Sequence diagram for a specific heartbeat. Inversion pulse is applied TI ms before the data acquisition (only the first readout is shown).

5.2.2 Saturation recovery-based T_1 mapping

2D SASHA is the most common deployed technique in the group of saturation recovery (*SR*)-based methods [12,13]. Instead of using a 180° pulse to invert the magnetization, a 90° pulse is used to saturate it instead. Although the dynamic range of T_1 weighting is reduced (from [- 1.1] to [0,1]), the saturation erases any existing magnetization history, significantly increasing the robustness and accuracy of T_1 estimation. SASHA acquires one non-saturated image ($M_z = 1$), followed by a set of 10 images with different saturation weightings in subsequent heartbeats, as illustrated in Fig. 5.3. At each heartbeat, the saturation time (TS) delay between the saturation pulse and the acquisition of the central line of *k*-space is changed such that a different point along the saturation curve is measured. Only one image is acquired per saturation pulse, significantly reducing the influence of the readout on the T_1 recovery, which also enables the usage of higher flip angles. SASHA further includes the effect of the bSSFP readout on T_1 recovery within each heartbeat (i.e., until the center of *k*-space is sampled), which can be modeled as $M_z(TS) = A[1 - Bexp(-TS/T_1)]$. The fitting parameters A and B absorb errors due to saturation efficiency, T_2, the bSSFP readout, and other sequence parameters. There are no recovery heartbeats in SASHA (unless $TS > T_{RR}$) and since every acquisition is preceded by a saturation pulse, the heart rate dependency is reduced. Moreover, this method has reduced sensitivity to T_2 and

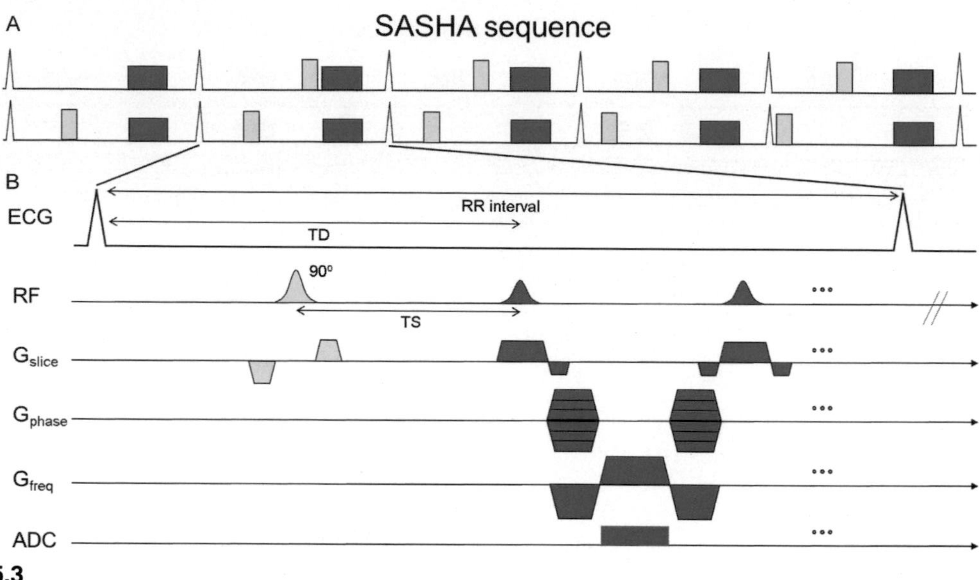

FIG. 5.3

(A) Saturation recovery single shot acquisition (SASHA) sequence diagram. An initial non-saturated image is acquired, followed by images acquired with varying saturation times (TS) to provide T_1 encoding. Saturation recovery modules are shown in *yellow*, whereas data acquisition modules are shown in *blue*. (B) Sequence diagram for a specific heartbeat. Saturation pulse is applied TS ms before the data acquisition (only the first readout is shown).

magnetization transfer effects, as magnetization transfer is reduced when using saturation compared with inversion pulses [10]. These key properties resolve several of the limitations of MOLLI, leading to substantially improved accuracy.

However, the reduced dynamic range, in conjunction with a three-parameter fit model, leads to a loss in precision for SASHA. This loss can be mitigated by employing a two-parameter fit model: $M_z(TS) = A[1 - exp(-TS/T_1)]$, but nevertheless a bias is introduced since errors from saturation efficiency and readout are not taken into account. Precision may be further improved with a variable flip angle (VFA) SASHA approach [26], which uses a slow sinusoidal ramping of the flip angle. This strategy leads to improved SNR, reduced transient state artefacts and reduced errors as compared to the standard approach. Together with a two-parameter model, VFA SASHA achieves a considerable improvement in precision when compared to the original SASHA. Another limitation of SASHA is related to some heart rate dependency. A saturation pulse is applied in every heartbeat and a (typically) mid-diastolic acquisition window is used to suppress cardiac motion. Thus, for high heart rates, it becomes difficult to acquire long SR-weighted images, limiting the amount of T_1 encoding available. One way around this limitation is to introduce recovery heartbeats between the SR and the readout in order to sample T_1 information otherwise unavailable. This is indeed what is proposed with the saturation method using adaptive recovery times for cardiac T_1 mapping (SMART1) [27,28], where a non-saturated image is acquired followed an SR acquisition with a "3(2)1(4)1" sampling scheme. Such a strategy leads to improved reproducibility, but may impact precision [29]. Additional research on optimal sampling strategies has been explored for saturation-based methods [29,30]. When looking at a given T_1 value, precision may be improved by collecting data at three points: low TS (~150 ms), high TS (~T_1 ms) and infinite TS (i.e., non-saturated image) [30]. However, this sampling strategy is expected to incur in precision penalties in other regions of the T_1 spectrum.

5.2.3 Combined inversion recovery and saturation recovery-based T_1 mapping

More recent developments have led to combined methods using both IR and SR pulses, with the aim of achieving simultaneously the precision of MOLLI and accuracy of SASHA. One such approach is the saturation pulse prepared heart-rate independent inversion recovery (SAPPHIRE) method [31], illustrated in Fig. 5.4. In 2D SAPPHIRE, one initial non-saturated image is collected, as in SASHA. In the following eight heartbeats, a saturation pulse is applied immediately after the RR wave, followed by an inversion pulse applied *TS* - *TI* ms before data acquisition. The timing of the inversion pulse is changed for every data acquisition block, including $TI > T_{RR}$, to sample long inversion times (i.e., inversion pulse in one heartbeat and readout in the following heartbeat, similar to MOLLI). After data collection, the T_1 map is calculated using a two-parameter fit: $M_z(t) = M_0\{1 - [2 - exp\,(-(TS - TI)/T_1)\,\exp(-t/T_1)]\}$. The saturation pulse clears the magnetization history such that M_z is known when the inversion pulse is applied, and thus the residual magnetization does not depend on the heart rate. In addition, the lack of recovery heartbeats (similar to SASHA) makes SAPPHIRE an efficient acquisition strategy. The saturation plus inversion combination also enables full control of the sampling points along the T_1 recovery curve, which leads

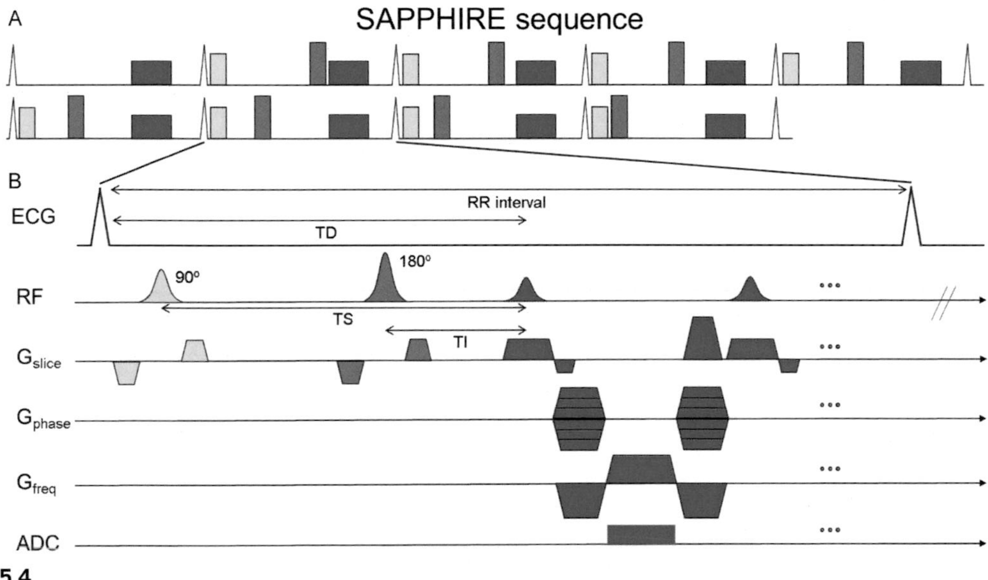

FIG. 5.4

(A) Saturation pulse prepared heart-rate independent inversion recovery (SAPPHIRE) sequence diagram. An initial non-saturated image is acquired. In the following heartbeats a saturation pulse erases the spin history and a subsequent inversion pulse provides additional T_1 encoding. Inversion pulses are shown in *green*, saturation modules are shown in *yellow* and data acquisition modules are shown in *blue.* (B) Sequence diagram for a specific heartbeat. A saturation pulse is applied, followed by an inversion pulse (TS-TI) ms later, followed by data acquisition TI ms later (only first readout is shown).

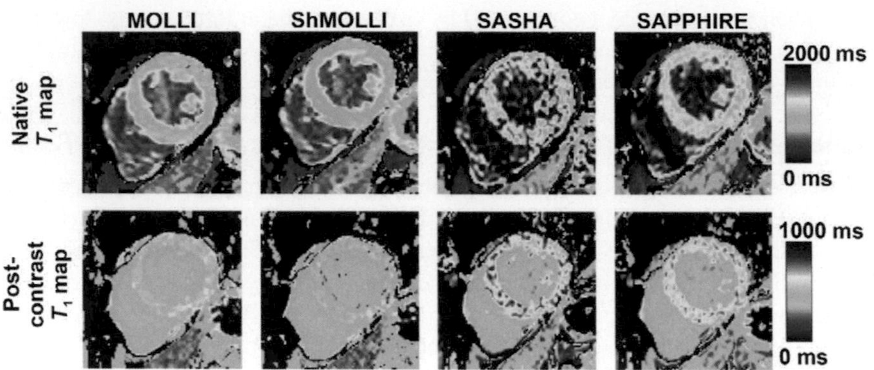

FIG. 5.5

2D T_1 maps acquired at 1.5 T with MOLLI, ShMOLLI, SASHA and SAPPHIRE T_1 mapping sequences *(top row)* before and *(bottom row)* after administration of contrast material. Myocardial T_1 values over the left ventricle obtained with MOLLI (native, 1012 ± 60 ms; post-contrast, 527 ± 30 ms) and ShMOLLI (native, 924 ± 70 ms; post-contrast, 501 ± 33 ms) were underestimated in comparison to those obtained with SASHA (native, 1254 ± 191 ms; post-contrast, 659 ± 81 ms) and SAPPHIRE (native, 1160 ± 95 ms; post-contrast, 625 ± 55 ms). MOLLI and ShMOLLI provided improved pre-contrast and post-contrast map quality with less variability (better precision).

(Reproduced with permission from Roujol S, Weingärtner S, Foppa M, et al. Accuracy, precision, and reproducibility of four T1 mapping sequences: a head-to-head comparison of MOLLI, ShMOLLI, SASHA, and SAPPHIRE. Radiology 2014;272:683–689 doi:10.1148/radiol.14140296.)

to a better condition of the exponential fit. This flexibility in T_1 sampling further makes SAPPHIRE a candidate for both pre-contrast and post-contrast T_1 mapping.

Despite individual limitations, MOLLI, ShMOLLI, SASHA, and SAPPHIRE have all proved to be viable methods for cardiac T_1 mapping. Studies have been developed to further evaluate the merits of different approaches [7,11,32]. Cardiac T_1 maps for these methods obtained under similar conditions for the same patient are shown in Fig. 5.5. Higher precision can be observed for MOLLI, followed by ShMOLLI, SAPPHIRE, and finally SASHA. On the other hand, higher accuracy is obtained for SASHA and SAPPHIRE, with reduced accuracy for MOLLI and more so for ShMOLLI. The underestimation bias of the IR-based methods is more prominent with increasing T_1 and decreasing T_2. All sequences have shown good reproducibility (<50 ms), with IR methods being slightly better (<35 ms) in this regard.

5.2.4 Cardiac extracellular volume mapping

Qualitative late gadolinium enhancement (LGE) imaging is a gold standard for characterization of myocardial infarct and other focal diseases. However it is not as sensitive to diffuse diseases where potentially the entire myocardium is affected, which can be confused with homogenously healthy tissue. A quantitative alternative is to measure the ECV [33], which is correlated with collagen volume fraction (an indication of fibrosis) [34]. Following (commonly gadolinium-based) contrast administration, the agent perfuses into the available extracellular space and the myocardial T_1 value is reduced in proportion to the local concentration of contrast agent. The ratio of T_1 change (before/after contrast) between myocardium and blood can be used to estimate the ECV. Formally put:

$$ECV = (1 - H)\frac{\Delta R_1^m}{\Delta R_1^b}$$

where H is the hematocrit (volume fraction of red blood cells), $\Delta R_1^m = R_{1(pc)}^m$ - $R_{1(n)}^m$ is the change in relaxation rate ($R_1 = T_1^{-1}$), m (or b) denote myocardium (or blood), pc and n denote post-contrast and native, respectively. Note that ECV measurement requires two T_1 measurements (before and after contrast), which can be obtained with one of the methods previously described (e.g., MOLLI). Inversion-based methods have shown higher ECV values than saturation-based methods (~0.26 vs. ~0.19), but all ECV measurements have showed high repeatability (ΔECV between scans <0.02) [11]. Post-contrast T_1 maps should be acquired at least 10 min after administration and the hematocrit (ideally from a blood sample) should be obtained within 24 h of scanning. Pre and post-contrast images are acquired in separate breath-holds, often resulting in mis-registration between pre- and post-contrast T_1 maps, leading to errors in the ECV maps. Respiratory motion correction is recommended as it significantly reduces the variability of the measurements [20]; however, residual errors are still possible due to through plane motion or different cardiac phases between the two scans. Moreover, common sources of error in T_1 mapping (e.g., partial volume or incorrect inversion efficiency) can propagate into errors in ECV. Despite these challenges, ECV is generally well-reproduced, making it a valuable and recommended biomarker for myocardial tissue characterization [2].

5.2.5 Novel developments in cardiac T_1 mapping

The methods discussed so far have resolution and coverage limitations, as they are 2D acquisitions performed within a breath-hold. Recent work has enabled T_1 mapping in 2–5 heartbeats with novel fitting models [35] or coverage of multiple slices via slice-selective inversion pulses [36] within a breath-hold. More recently, model-based reconstructions have enabled high-resolution inversion-based T_1 mapping in 4 s [37]. Breath-holding can itself be a problem for some patients, which means that T_1 mapping simply cannot be performed with these methods in these patients. Partial volume and motion also affect these methods in clinical practice. 3D free-breathing extensions of saturation-based methods have been developed, such as 3D SASHA [38,39], using diaphragmatic navigators to compensate for respiratory motion. 3D SASHA has been shown to exhibit superior SNR, leading to increased precision relative to 2D SASHA, while maintaining the accuracy expected from a saturation-based method (Fig. 5.6). Similar extensions for inversion-based methods have also been developed, combining ECG and respiratory triggering [40]. This approach enables a six-slice coverage acquired under free-breathing in 5–10 min, depending on the subject's breathing pattern. Recent developments on inversion-based methods have further combined a 3D acquisition with highly accelerated stack-of-spirals to achieve 3D coverage in a breath-hold duration [41].

Respiratory motion (due to incomplete breath-hold or diaphragmatic drift) is a significant challenge in cardiac-triggered T_1 mapping methods, limiting scan time to a breath-hold duration. However, with a combination of navigator gating and image registration, free-breathing 2D SASHA can alleviate this problem [42]. Combining respiratory navigators with saturation-based T_1 mapping has also enabled 3D free-breathing T_1 mapping [43]. Residual cardiac motion can also be present despite triggering and introduce errors. Motion between different heartbeats may be estimated and used to co-register

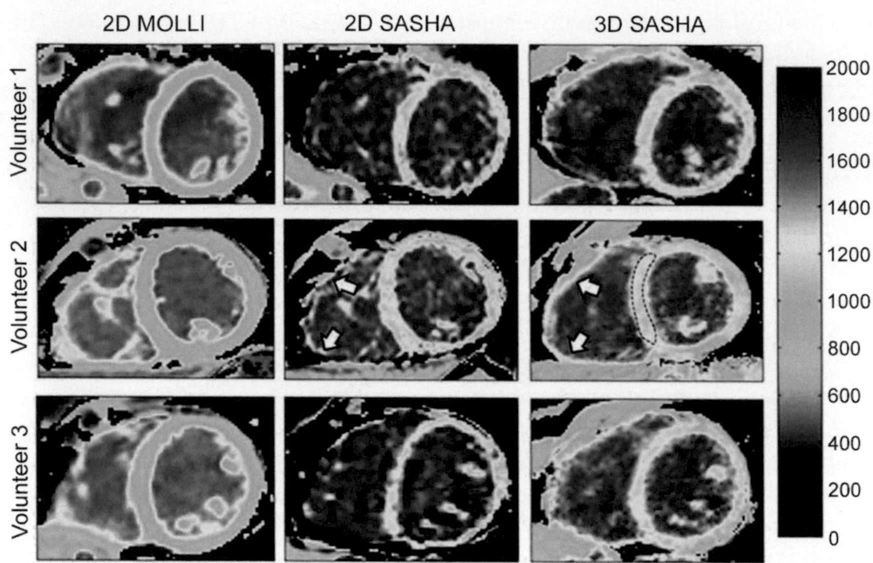

FIG. 5.6

Mid-ventricular myocardial T_1 maps of three healthy subjects using the sequences 2D MOLLI, 2D SASHA, and 3D SASHA collected at 1.5 T. The higher resolution of the 3D SASHA technique allows better delineation of the right ventricle *(white arrows)*.

(Reproduced with permission from Nordio G, Henningsson M, Chiribiri A, Villa ADM, Schneider T, Botnar RM. 3D myocardial T1 mapping using saturation recovery. J Magn Reson Imaging 2017;46:218–27. doi: 10.1002/jmri.25575.)

the acquired T_1-weighted images, although the varying contrast is a challenge. Accurate motion estimation has been achieved using synthesized T_1 contrasts [20] or by incorporating the contrast evolution into the motion estimation model with adaptive registration of varying contrast-weighted images for improved tissue characterization (ARCTIC) [19]. These developments have enabled applications like fully automated motion-corrected ECV measurements [44,45] or free breathing, multi-slice T_1 mapping with slice-interleaved T_1 (STONE) using in-plane and through-plane motion correction [46] (Fig. 5.7). 3D free-breathing and free-running T_1 mapping has also been achieved with self-navigated 3D radial trajectories, translation correction, and low rank reconstructions [47].

Cardiac T_1 mapping has been achieved with a variety of methods, several of which have become routine in the clinic. As such, T_1 mapping is recommended for the characterization of many cardiac diseases, like amyloid or infarction [2]. Limitations such as susceptibility to motion artefacts, low resolution, and limited coverage have been partially answered, and continued research efforts are producing faster and more reliable methods. One of the main remaining challenges is reproducibility, particularly between different MR scanners (and vendors). An absolute, accurate, system-independent, clinically applicable T_1 method remains the key research goal.

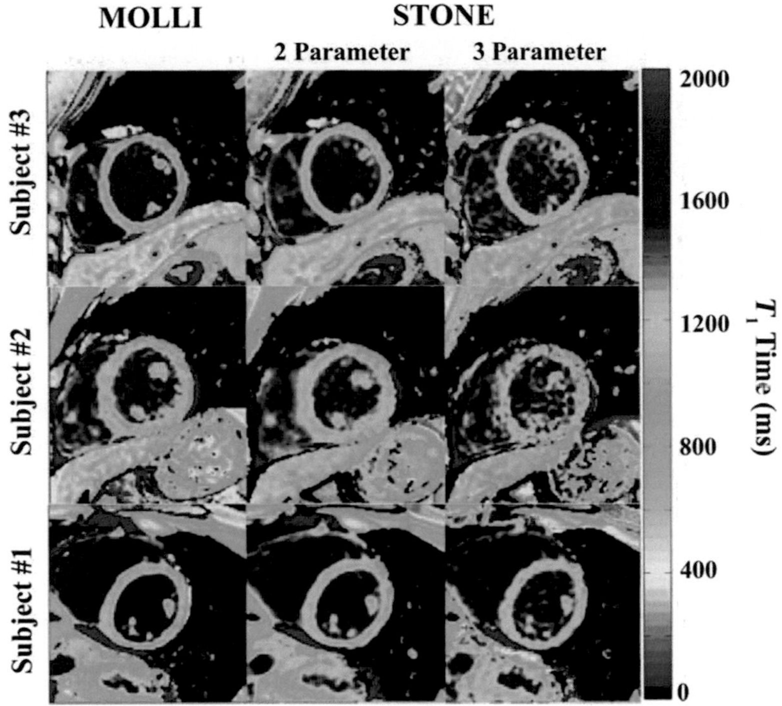

FIG. 5.7

Native 2D T_1 maps collected in three healthy subjects at 1.5 T using the MOLLI and STONE sequences with two- and three-parameter fit model. Visually improved T_1 map quality can be seen with MOLLI and STONE with a two-parameter fit model, compared with a three-parameter fit model fit.

(Reproduced with permission from Weingärtner S, Roujol S, Akçakaya M, Basha TA, Nezafat R. Free-breathing multislice native myocardial T1 mapping using the slice-interleaved T1 (STONE) sequence. Magn Reson Med 2015;74:115–24. doi: 10.1002/mrm.25387.)

5.3 Cardiac T_2 and T_2* mapping

Analogous to T_1 mapping, T_2 mapping is achieved by acquiring several images along the natural T_2 decay. In this case, the set of images is fit to the T_2 decay model: $M_{xy}(TE) = M_0 \exp(-TE/T_2)$, where M_0 corresponds to the proton density. Conventional T_2 mapping can be performed with a multi-echo spin echo (MESE) sequence to sample the T_2 decay curve. However, long TE/TR values are needed to achieve the required T_2 encoding, making the sequence sensitive to motion. MESE methods are associated with long acquisition times, imposing some limitations in clinical practice. Consequently, alternative approaches have been explored for cardiac T_2 mapping. Myocardial T_2 mapping may be performed with as few as three T_2-weighted images. These images may be obtained by increasing the echo time, but also via spin and stimulated echoes, or with T_2-preparation pulses (T_2-prep) [48].

The main approaches for cardiac T_2 mapping involve T_2-prepared with bSSFP (or FLASH) readout [49,50] and T_2 Gradient and SE (GraSE) sequences [51,52].

5.3.1 T_2-prepared T_2 mapping

The breath-hold acquisition for 2D T_2-prepared with bSSFP readout is depicted in Fig. 5.8: three T_2-prepared single-shot images are acquired with at least two (ideally three or four) recovery heartbeats between them. Longitudinal magnetization recovery occurs during these heartbeats and reduces the potential bias from T_1. The use of a single-shot acquisition minimizes respiratory and cardiac motion, but residual misregistration may exist between different T_2-weighted images. The T_2 preparation (T_2-prep) is a composite pulse that induces T_2 contrast prior to image acquisition and is achieved with a sequence of excitation and refocusing pulses: 90°_{x+} - 180°_{y+} - 180°_{y-} - 90°_{x-} (Fig. 5.8). The first pulse (90°_{x+}) excites magnetizationinto the transverse plane, where it undergoes T_2 decay. Refocusing pulses (e.g., 180°_{y+} - 180°_{y-}) are employed during this time to reduce T_2* and flow effects. The final pulse (90°_{x-}) returns the (now T_2-weighted) magnetization to the longitudinal orientation, ready for subsequent image acquisition (a gradient spoiler is included to destroy any residual transverse magnetization). Three different T_2-preps are typically deployed, with $TE_{T2\text{-prep}}$ of 0 ms (no T_2-preparation), 24 ms and 55 ms. This set of echo times produces three relevant contrasts for the myocardium ($T_2 \sim 50$ ms at 1.5 T);

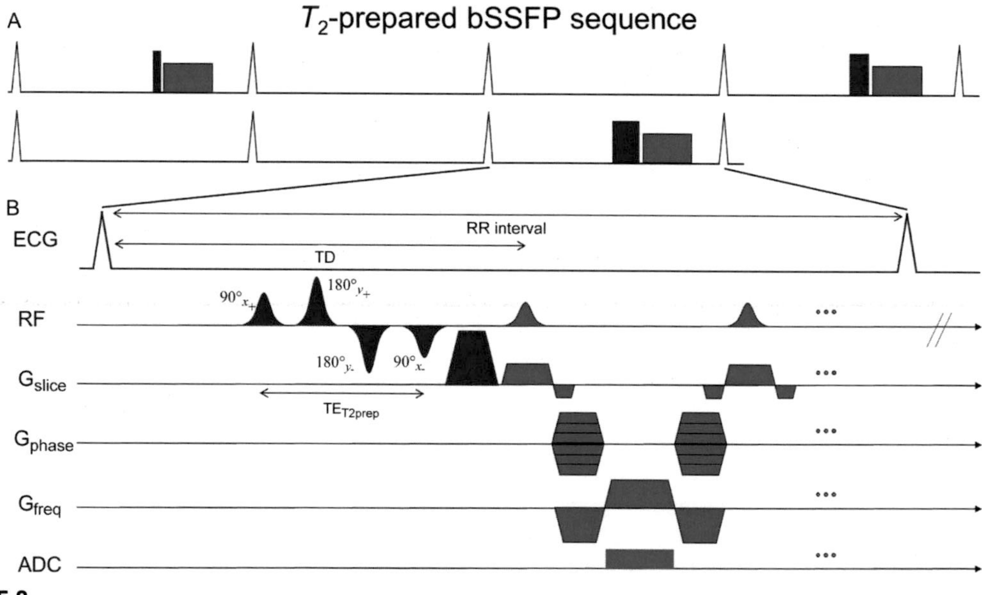

FIG. 5.8

(A) T_2-prepared bSSFP sequence diagram. T_2-preparation pulses with varying echo times ($TE_{T2\text{-prep}}$) are used to provide the T_2 encoding. Recovery heartbeats are introduced to reduce the dependency on T_1. The T_2-preparation module is shown in *red,* whereas data acquisition is shown in *blue.* (B) Sequence diagram for a specific heartbeat. A T_2 preparation pulse is applied with a duration of $TE_{T2\text{-prep}}$ ms that determines the amount of T_2 weighting before the data acquisition (only the first readout is shown).

longer echo times introduce more T_2 weighting, but are avoided due to SNR constraints which may lead to T_2 overestimation [53]. Both bSSFP and FLASH readouts are commonly employed in this method. The bSSFP readout improves the SNR relative to FLASH (at the expense of increased B_0 sensitivity) and carries its own T_2/T_1 signal dependency, although the latter has minimal impact on this approach [50]. bSSFP has generally the most robust readout to flow artefacts, however it is also more sensitive to imperfect slice profiles and excitations occurring out of slice [54]. FLASH acquisitions, on the other hand, are more robust to field errors (B_0 and B_1) that can produce confounding factors in the resulting parametric maps. An acquisition immediately following the T_2-preparation module is desirable to maximize T_2 contrast and model consistency. This weighting can be achieved with a centric k-space sampling trajectory; however, acquisition of low frequency data in the bSSFP transient state can introduce artefacts [49]. This issue can be addressed with steady-state catalysers (e.g., transient state stabilization (STAB)) or with a linear k-space sampling trajectory. In both cases a time gap is introduced between the T_2-prep module and the acquisition of the center of k-space, in addition to several RF pulses, all of which are not accounted for by the fitting model. T_1 recovery that occurs during this time gap is generally the dominant source of error in this case, leading to a T_2 overestimation bias [49] (particularly for low T_1 values). Residual T_1 bias may also be present due to the use of a small number of recovery heartbeats, leading to a trade-off between accuracy and scan time (and potentially residual respiratory motion artefacts). The use of T_2-preparation modules to generate T_2 contrast, in conjunction with the need for recovery heartbeats and breath-hold limitations on scan time, typically leads to a small number of images acquired along the T_2 decay curve. This can impact the precision and accuracy of the T_2fit and limit the usage of higher parameter fitting models to account for model errors (e.g., three-parameter fit). Residual motion can also affect T_2 mapping, although prospective respiratory navigators [50] and non-rigid registration [55,56] can minimize these problems. In addition, the T_2-preparation composite pulse is sensitive to both B_0 and B_1 errors, although some of these errors may be reduced with adiabatic T_2 preparation modules [57].

5.3.2 Gradient and spin echo T_2 mapping

One of the main limitations of T_2-prepared bSSFP/FLASH for myocardial T_2 mapping is the small number of T_2-weighted images that are acquired. T_2GraSE is an alternative mapping approach that bypasses this limitation and is illustrated in Fig. 5.9. Instead of using a T_2-prep module, T_2 contrast is generated naturally via spin echoes. Between each spin echo, a set of k-space lines is acquired with echo planar imaging (EPI) readouts [51,52]. The entirety of k-space is covered in one GraSE block (with large k-space gaps) and the T_2 contrast of that block is determined by the k-space line closest to the centre, in the middle of the block. The number of spin echoes determines the number of T_2-weighted images that are acquired, enabling $\sim$9 images to be acquired in a segmented fashion. This sequence is often combined with a double inversion recovery (DIR) black blood preparation to avoid issues with partial volume from bright blood [58]. The DIR preparation is composed of two inversion pulses: the first is (spatially) non-selective, whereas the second is slice selective. In this way, the magnetization of all tissues outside of the imaging slice (including flowing blood) is inverted, leaving the imaging slice unaffected. The inversion time delay between the DIR and image acquisition is chosen such that the longitudinal magnetization of the blood (which flows into the imaging slice) is nulled, achieving the so-called "black blood" contrast. The scan duration of T_2GraSE is overall comparable to T_2-prepared bSSFP/FLASH T_2 mapping, while acquiring more points along the T_2 recovery.

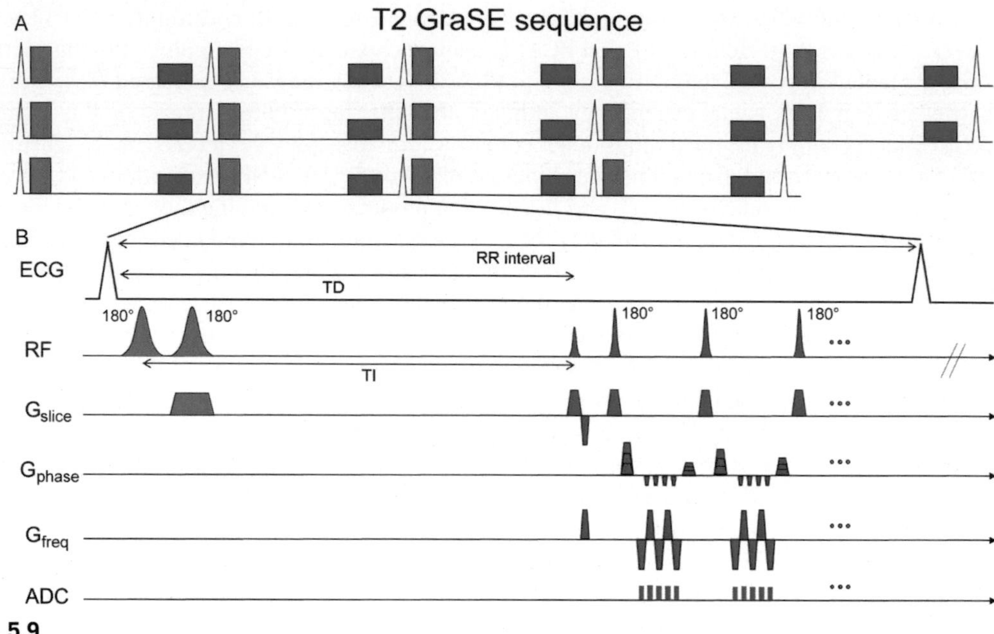

FIG. 5.9

(A) T_2 gradient- and spin echo (GraSE) sequence diagram. An (optional) double inversion recovery (DIR) pulse is applied after R wave detection to suppress signal from flowing blood. T_2 encoding is achieved with spin echoes (as in multi-echo spin echo), and echo planar imaging (EPI) is leveraged to reduce the scan time. DIR pulses are shown in *orange*, data acquisition is shown in *blue*. (B) Sequence diagram for a specific heartbeat. A DIR pulse is applied TI ms before data acquisition.

However, the acquisition of more T_2-weighted images can lead to longer GraSE blocks, making it more susceptible to motion artefacts [51,52]. Furthermore, both the DIR preparation pulse commonly used and the GraSE block (due to spin echoes) are both sensitive to motion which may introduce errors in the resulting T_2 maps. The EPI component of GraSE enables considerable scan time reduction, but is sensitive to fat chemical shifts, $T_2{}^*$ decay and SNR loss, off-resonance, and image distortions. T_2GraSE is also sensitive to errors in the 180° refocusing pulses as they may generate additional stimulated echoes and can introduce unwanted T_1weighting in the acquired signal.

5.3.3 Comparison of T_2 mapping techniques

T_2 mapping techniques are affected by several confounding factors and as such it is useful to compare the performance of various approaches. Cardiac T_2 maps collected using T_2-prepared bSSFP, T_2GraSE, T_2GraSE with fat suppression, and MESE are shown in Fig. 5.10, at 1.5 T and 3.0 T field strength [58]. Except for the T_2-prepared bSSFP (flow resistant), all other spin-echo-based acquisitions used a black blood preparation pulse. Results suggested a slight overestimation of T_2 when using GraSE and slight underestimation of T_2 when using T_2-prepared bSSFP relative to the reference MESE, at both 1.5 T and 3 T. In this example, only two refocusing pulses are used for the T_2-prep, leading to $T_2{}^*$ contamination

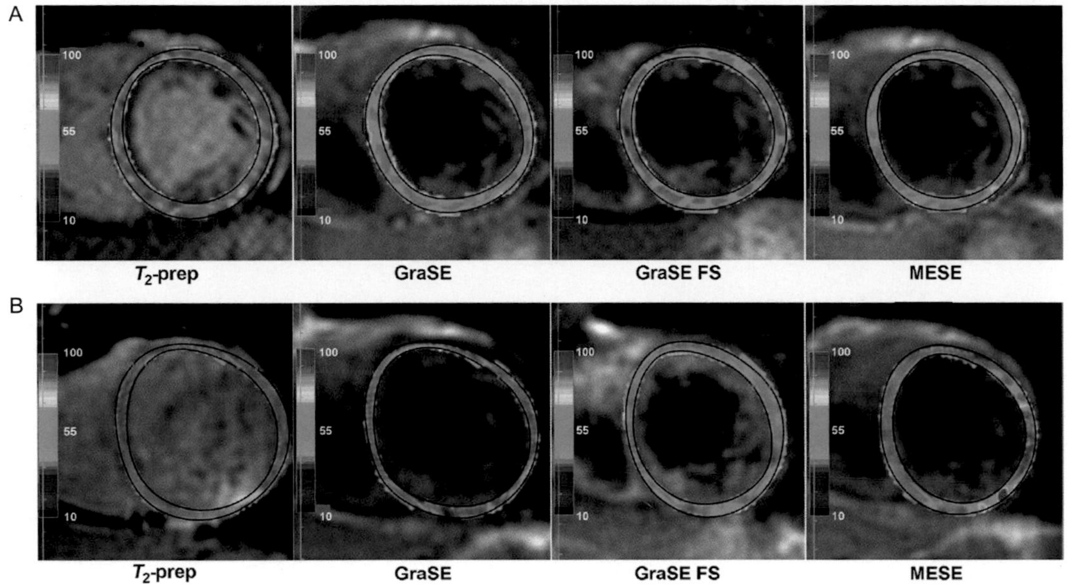

FIG. 5.10

2D T_2 maps in a mid-ventricular slice for a healthy subject, acquired with T_2-prepared bSSFP, GraSE, GraSE with fat suppression (GraSE FS) and MESE at 1.5 T (A) and 3 T (B). Similar values are obtained between T_2-prep bSSFP and MESE at 1.5 T, while both GraSE variants led to slightly higher T_2 values. Similar values were obtained for all methods at 3 T, except for T_2-prepared bSSFP, which estimated lower T_2 values.

(Reproduced with permission from Baeßler B, Schaarschmidt F, Stehning C, Schnackenburg B, Maintz D, Bunck AC. A systematic evaluation of three different cardiac T2-mapping sequences at 1.5 and 3T in healthy volunteers. Eur J Radiol 2015;84:2161–70. doi: 10.1016/j.ejrad.2015.08.002.)

at 3 T (in addition to increased B_0 errors at the higher field strength). On the other hand, GraSE and MESE with black-blood preparation pulses are generally sensitive to bright blood or flow artefacts. In contrast to T_1, T_2 decreases slightly with field strength. GraSE without fat suppression estimates slightly higher T_2 values than GraSE with fat suppression due to fat partial volume, an issue also present in T_1 mapping. Artefacts in the T_2-weighted images can propagate into errors in the T_2 maps. In this regard, T_2-prepared bSSFP has the potential to be more robust at 1.5 T, but performance may decrease at 3.0 T (where FLASH readouts may be preferable). Higher order fitting models have been studied for T_2-prepared bSSFP approaches [59] using a large number of T_2-weighted images [27], including one saturated image to represent a very large T_2-prep duration ($TE = \infty$), and a 6 s recovery between acquisitions (to minimize potential bias from T_1). Scan times are increased beyond the breath hold duration with this approach; however, respiratory navigators can enable free-breathing scans. For this case, a new fitting model may be considered: $M_{xy}(TE) = A \exp(-TE/T_2) + B$, where A and B capture errors originating from T_1 relaxation within the T_2-prep and sequence parameters (k-space ordering, flip angle, start-up pulses, TR) that determine the effect of the bSSFP readout on the magnetization before the center of k-space is sampled. The $TE = \infty$ saturated anchor point is key to fitting B.

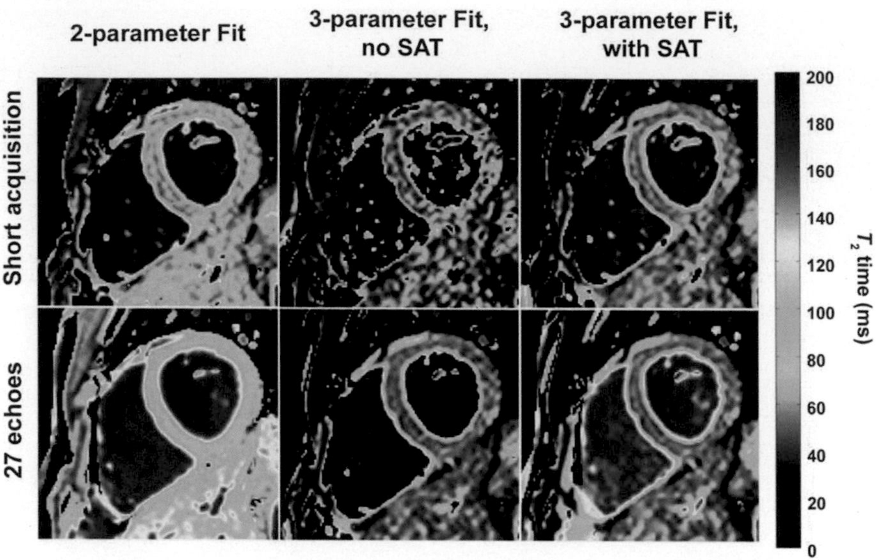

FIG. 5.11

2D T_2 maps from a healthy subject using various T_2-prepared-bSSFP-type acquisitions. In addition to multiple T_2-preparation echo times (including no T_2-prep), a saturated image can be acquired to approximate the effect of a very long T_2-prep. T_2 maps are generated using two-parameter fitting *(left column)*, three-parameter fitting without a saturation image *(middle column)* and a three-parameter fitting with a saturation image *(right column)*. The *top row* shows T_2 maps obtained with three T_2-prep echo times whereas the *bottom row* shows the maps obtained using 27 T_2-prep echo times. The myocardial T_2 value increases when going from three to 27 T_2-weighted images using the two-parameter fit. For the short acquisition (three echoes), the T_2 map generated using the three-parameter fit without saturation image has more variation in the septum compared with that generated using the three-parameter fit with a saturation image. When using all 27 T_2-weighted images, the three-parameter fits with and without a saturation image leads to similar quality in the myocardium.

(Reproduced with permission from Akçakaya M, Basha TA, Weingärtner S, Roujol S, Berg S, Nezafat R. Improved quantitative myocardial T2 mapping: impact of the fitting model. Magn Reson Med 2015;74:93–105. doi: 10.1002/mrm.25377.)

The $TE = 0$ image is acquired after a set of +90° and -90° RF pulses such that this image too is equally biased by field inhomogeneities that affect the T_2-prep module. This study revealed that a 4-point T_2-prep bSSFP (16 s) acquisition with TE = [0, 25, 50, ∞] can achieve similar quality to a 27-point (3 min) acquisition, as seen in Fig. 5.11.

5.3.4 Cardiac T_2* mapping

T_2* is a measure of the combined signal decay from spin-spin interactions and local field inhomogeneities. As such, this property is primarily used to detect myocardial iron overload in diseases like thalassemia major or hemochromatosis [2]. Multi-echo gradient echo (MEGE) sequences are commonly used to sensitize the acquisition to local field inhomogeneities, with data acquired along different echo times [60,61] and fit to the model: $M_{xy}(TE) = M_0 \exp(-TE/T_2^*)$. T_2* mapping is commonly performed

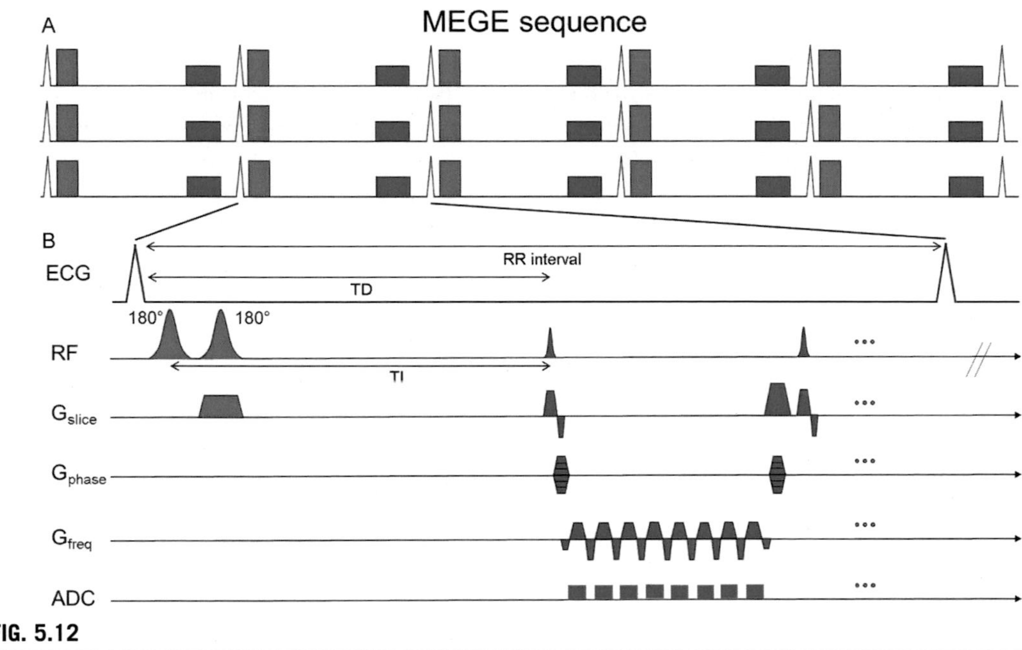

FIG. 5.12

(A) Multi-echo gradient echo (MEGE) sequence diagram. An (optional) double inversion recovery (DIR) pulse is applied after R-wave detection to suppress signal from flowing blood. T_2* encoding is achieved with successive gradient echos. DIR pulses are shown in *orange*, data acquisition is shown in *blue*. (B) Sequence diagram for a specific heartbeat. A DIR pulse is applied TI ms before data acquisition.

[62] in a ECG triggered, breath-held scan using at least eight echoes spanning the range of 2-20 ms, as illustrated in Fig. 5.12. T_2*-weighted images are acquired in a segmented fashion, over several cardiac cycles, which can lead to cardiac motion artefacts. The high signal of flowing blood can also create artefacts and partial volume errors, and thus DIR preparation pulses are also recommended with this technique [63,64]. T_2* measurements are sensitive to susceptibility artefacts that occur at tissue boundaries (e.g., between the lung and the heart or between deoxygenated blood and surrounding tissue) and additional sources of intravoxel dephasing (e.g., diffusion, B_0 errors), making this technique more challenging at 3 T [65,66]. For tissues with low T_2* values (<10 ms, i.e., severe iron overload) parameterization of the exponential decay can be challenging due to a positive noise bias. Magnitude T_2* fitting is commonly used and the underlying Rician noise distribution at low magnitude values introduces this bias; however, the error can be reduced by truncating low SNR measurements before performing the fit [67,68]. The presence of fat can also bias results, but combining T_2* estimation with water-fat separation can reduce these errors [69]. Finally, breath-holds can be challenging in some patient populations, resulting in motion artefacts. Recent works have demonstrated the use of motion correction methods to enable free-breathing T_2* mapping [70]. Free-breathing, non-rigid respiratory-motion-corrected imaging using single shot echo-planar imaging (no segmented readouts) has also enabled T_2* mapping in patients that cannot hold their breath [71]. T_2* values show good reproducibility at 1.5 T [64] and this tissue property has been suggested as a biomarker to detect iron overload [2].

5.3.5 Novel developments in cardiac T_2 mapping

B_0 inhomogeneities can affect the T_2-prep module and lead to an overestimation of T_2 [53], particularly at off-resonance frequencies greater than 100 Hz. Low SNR can also introduce an overestimation bias in T_2, which will limit the use of long T_2-preparation modules. Similar to T_1 mapping, myocardial T_2 techniques are sensitive to motion [56]. This is an issue even in short scans, as some patients are unable to maintain even a short breath-hold. A combination of respiratory navigation (for through-plane motion) with in-plane registration-based motion correction permits free-breathing T_2 mapping, improving robustness to poor breath-holds and enabling longer acquisitions, as shown in Fig. 5.13.

Removing the breath-hold restriction also allows larger numbers of T_2-weighted images to be acquired, which improves precision and reproducibility of myocardial T_2 measurements. Additionally, 3D whole-heart acquisitions become possible [72–75]. In [72], 3D free-breathing motion-corrected (3D-FB-MoCo) T_2 mapping is achieved with adiabatic T_2 preparations and GRE readouts. A navigator is used to guide a 3D affine motion correction model. Another technique is 3D T_2-prep SPGR using saturation pulses and FLASH readouts [73]. This method is similar to T_2-prepared bSSFP/FLASH, but uses additional saturation pulses in the beginning of each heartbeat, as in SAPPHIRE. Image acquisition is segmented, interleaved and respiratory navigated, reducing motion artefacts and potential mis-registrations. The sensitivity of the method to field inhomogeneities is reduced (due to the use of the SPGR readout), T_1 recovery heartbeats are not needed, heart rate dependence is reduced (due to the saturation pulse), and through-plane motion and partial volume errors are removed (due to the 3D nature of the scan). In [75], 3D motion-corrected undersampled signal matched (MUST) is performed with a combination of saturation and T_2 preparation pulses, enabling data acquisition every heartbeat. Low-resolution image navigators [76] enable beat-to-beat translation correction

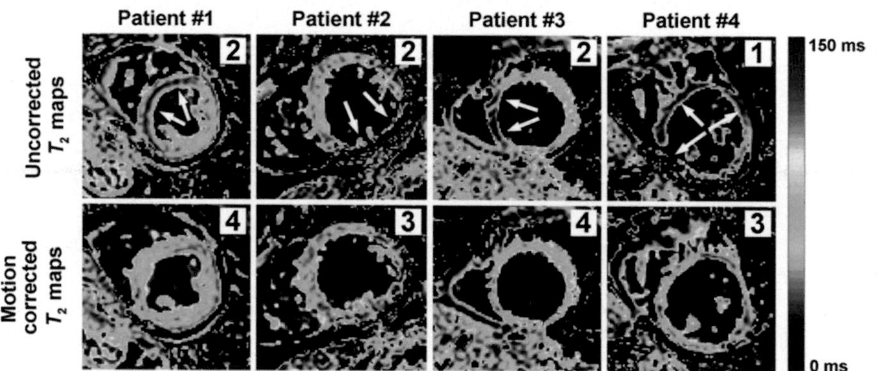

FIG. 5.13

Uncorrected and ARCTIC motion corrected 2D T_2 maps obtained in patients at 1.5 T. Subjective T_2 map quality scores are shown for each map *(right upper corner)* (m). Motion among T_2-weighted images resulted in large regional variations/artefacts in myocardial T_2 estimates in the uncorrected maps *(white arrows)* which were substantially reduced using the ARCTIC motion correction.

(Reproduced with permission from Roujol S, Foppa M, Weingärtner S, Manning WJ, Nezafat R. Adaptive registration of varying contrast-weighted images for improved tissue characterization (ARCTIC): application to T1 mapping. Magn Reson Med 2015;73:1469–82. doi: 10.1002/mrm.25270.)

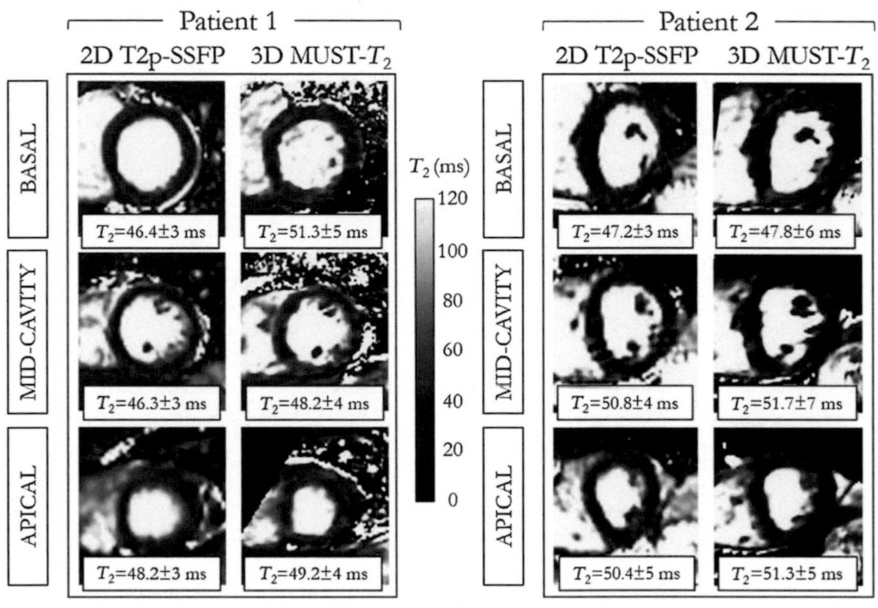

FIG. 5.14

Short axis T_2 maps at basal, mid and apical level for two patients acquired with 3D MUST-T_2 and 2D T_2-prepared bSSFP.

(Reproduced with permission from Bustin A, Milotta G, Ismail TF, Neji R, Botnar RM, Prieto C. Accelerated free-breathing whole-heart 3D T2 mapping with high isotropic resolution. Magn Reson Med 2019:988–1002. doi: 10.1002/mrm.27989.)

and a patch-based low rank reconstruction is employed to reduce artefacts [77]. Representative maps in two patients are compared with 2D T_2-prepared bSSFP in Fig. 5.14.

Cardiac T_2 mapping has demonstrated high reproducibility [78,79] and is recommended for the assessment of acute infarction, inflammation, and other diseases [2]. Similar to cardiac T_1 mapping, research efforts target further improving coverage, resolution, and motion insensitivity, as well as reproducibility across different scanners. Recent developments have also focused on efficient acquisition strategies to acquire more than one parameter in a single scan.

5.4 Beyond single parameter mapping in the heart

Both T_1 and T_2 mapping have clinical value in cardiac MRI. T_1 is commonly used to study fibrosis and infarction; T_2 is typically used to evaluate inflammation and edema. The acquisition of both T_1 and T_2 maps provides complementary information: for example, T_1 can identify myocardial infarction and T_2 can help distinguish between acute and chronic. In addition, having both maps can help with visualization and characterization of myocardial tissue with greater confidence [80,81]. This has driven recent research focus toward multi-parametric mapping (i.e., the quantification of several parameters in a single scan) in order to further improve myocardial tissue characterization. Multi-parametric mapping has several advantages compared to sequential single-parameter mapping. For the patient it means fewer breath-holds and a more comfortable experience; for the radiographer, it means less scan planning and higher patient throughput; and for the cardiologist, it means joint and co-registered quantitative maps for facilitated analysis.

5.4.1 Joint T_1-T_2 mapping of the heart

Several recent research efforts have focused on developing protocols capable of mapping both T_1 and T_2, from a single scan, in a clinically acceptable time. Simultaneous T_1 and T_2 cardiac maps in 2D have been obtained with a combination of elements from MOLLI and T_2-prepared bSSFP/FLASH [82]. By interleaving heartbeats with (varying) inversion pulses, heartbeats for recovery and heartbeats with (varying) T_2 preparation it is possible to achieve the necessary T_1 and T_2 encoding to produce co-registered parametric maps (Fig 5.15A). A similar strategy has been studied for 3D quantification

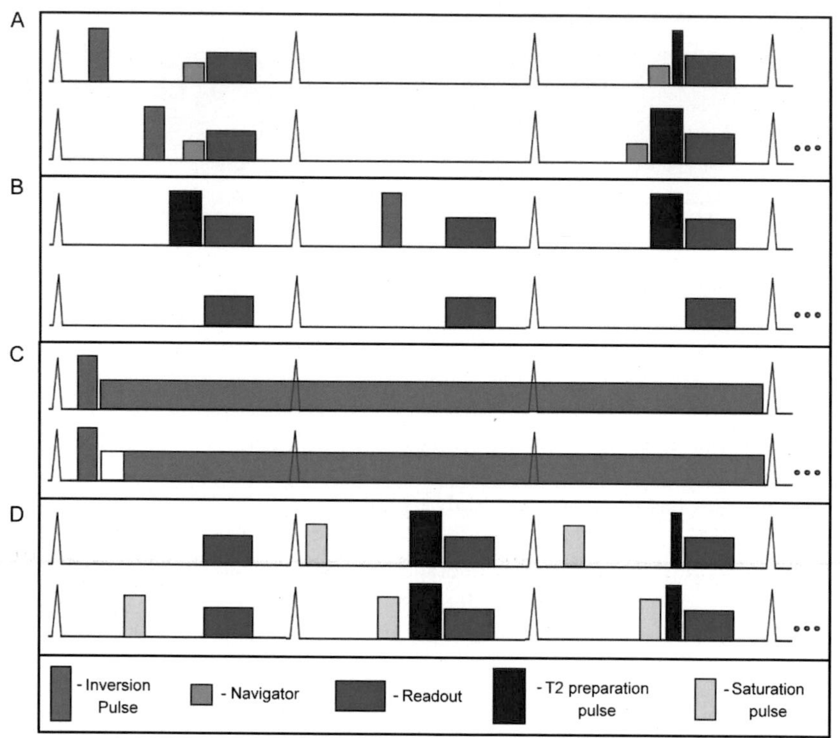

FIG. 5.15

Sequence diagrams for four different simultaneous T_1/T_2 mapping approaches. (A) Interleaved T_1 and T_2 proposed by Blume et al. alternates between inversion pulses and T_2-prepation pulses to provide the necessary T_1 and T_2 encoding; navigators are used to compensate for respiratory motion. (B) QALAS proposed by Kvnerby et al. is based on a block of five heartbeats with different preparation pulses: T_2-prep pulse, IR pulse, followed by three heartbeats with no preparations. (C) CABIRIA proposed by Santini et al. acquires data continuously (non-triggered) relying on the bSSFP sequence to provide T_2 encoding while inversion pulses regularly interrupt the acquisition to provide additional T_1 encoding. (D) Joint T_1 and T_2 proposed by Akçakaya et al. uses saturation pulses and T_2-preparation pulses for T_1 and T_2 encoding, respectively; varying the corresponding TS and $TE_{T2\text{-prep}}$ in different heartbeats is used to sample the T_1 and T_2 exponential evolutions.

using an interleaved Look-Locker acquisition sequence with T_2 preparation pulse (3D-QALAS) (Fig. 5.15B) [83]. This approach separates T_1 and T_2 encoding: a T_2 prepared heartbeat is acquired, followed by an inversion pulse and three additional acquisition heartbeats for continued sampling of T_1 recovery. This block is repeated several times to encode a full 3D volume. Whole-heart T_1/T_2 mapping has also been proposed with free-breathing, free-running, self-navigated 3D radial acquisitions interrupted by inversion pulses and T_2-preparation pulses [84]. In this approach, data are retrospectively sorted, translationally motion corrected, and reconstructed with low rank prior to enable high acceleration factors. Simultaneous parametric mapping has also been achieved without T_2-preparation modules, using a 2D cardiac balanced-SSFP inversion recovery with interleaved sampling acquisition (CABIRIA) (Fig. 5.15C) [85]. Unlike the previous examples, CABIRIA employs a continuous (non-ECG triggered) acquisition after an inversion pulse. T_2 encoding is provided by the bSSFP readout and motion is reduced via image registration. This acquisition block is followed by a recovery heartbeat and then repeated using a different TI. Diastolic images are retrospectively triggered and registered to minimize cardiac motion. Joint T_1 and T_2 mapping has also been achieved with a combination of saturation pulses and T_2-preparation modules, in a similar fashion to SAPPHIRE [86]. An initial (non-saturated) 2D image is acquired; in the subsequent 12 heartbeats, saturation pulses with varying timings and T_2-preparation modules with different durations are acquired, as illustrated in Fig. 5.15D. In a single breath-hold, both T_1 and T_2 maps can be collected, with comparable quality to T_1 mapping and T_2-prep-based T_2 mapping, as seen in Fig. 5.16. Multi-parametric acquisitions generally have more complex fitting models; in this case a simultaneous estimation of T_1 and T_2 is obtained with a four parameter fit: $M(TE, TS) = A[1 - exp\,(-TS/T_1)]\,exp\,(-TE/T_2) + B$.

5.4.2 Cardiac magnetic resonance fingerprinting

The methods discussed so far focus on sampling a few selected points along the recovery/decay curves, fitting these measurements to approximated exponential models. Recent works have shown that a theoretically higher parameter encoding efficiency can be achieved by exploiting transient information [87,88]. Magnetic resonance fingerprinting (MRF) is a novel multi-parametric mapping technique that continuously samples the transient state magnetization, matching it to the signal predicted by the Bloch equations [89]. Sequence parameters are continuously varied throughout the acquisition, leading the magnetization through various T_1 and T_2 encoding states. Instead of sampling a small number of points ($\sim$10) along T_1/T_2 exponential evolutions, MRF densely samples the transient state evolution with a large number of points ($\sim$1000). The magnetization evolution of relevant tissues is computed beforehand via the Bloch equations, for a particular MRF sequence, generating a dictionary of signal evolutions. After the acquisition, template matching is performed to match the signal evolution from each pixel to a dictionary entry, immediately revealing the tissue's characteristics (e.g., T_1, T_2, etc.). 2D cardiac MRF has been developed using an interleaved encoding strategy, similar to previous T_1/T_2 approaches [90,91]. An acquisition block of four ECG-triggered heartbeats is performed: inversion heartbeat, no preparation pulse heartbeat, short T_2-prep heartbeat and long T_2-prep heartbeat, as shown in Fig. 5.17. This block can be further repeated using different inversion delay times for the heartbeat with the inversion preparation. Within each heartbeat, flip angles, and repetition times are continuously varied to further aid in T_1 and T_2 encoding. Cardiac MRF with 16 heartbeats is shown in Fig. 5.18, achieving T_1 and T_2 maps which are comparable to those collected using MOLLI and T_2-prepared bSSFP/FLASH. The approach is flexible and has produced simultaneous, co-registered T_1/T_2 maps with as

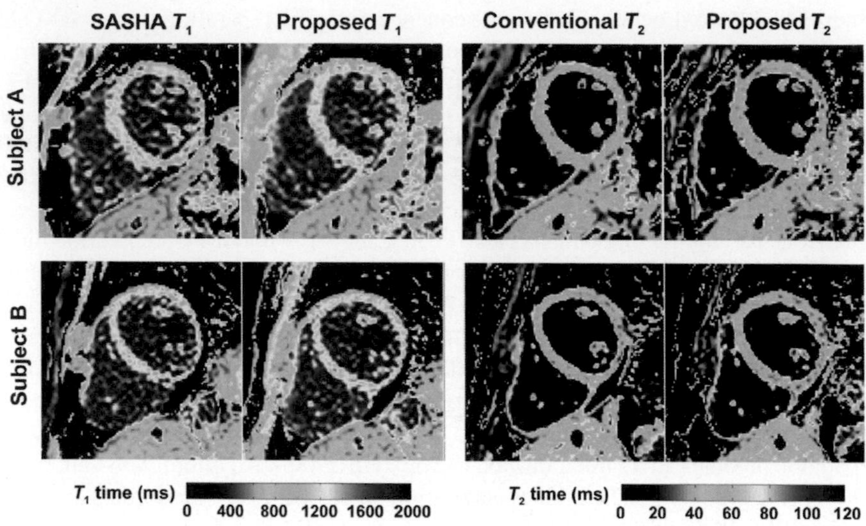

FIG. 5.16

In vivo 2D T_1 and T_2 maps from two healthy subjects using the method proposed in [73] in comparison to conventional SASHA T_1 and T_2-prepared bSSFP mapping. The maps show similar quality and good agreement of the myocardial T_1 and T_2 values was obtained (Subject A: 1211 ± 82 ms versus 1210 ± 92 ms for SASHA and simultaneous approach for T_1, respectively; 49.0 ± 5.8 ms and 47.3 ± 6.5 ms for conventional and simultaneous approach for T_2, respectively. Subject B: 1217 ± 90 ms versus 1210 ± 96 ms for SASHA and simultaneous approach for T_1; 47.8 ± 7.0 ms and 45.6 ± 7.3 ms for conventional and simultaneous approach for T_2).

(Reproduced with permission from Akçakaya M, Weingärtner S, Basha TA, Roujol S, Bellm S, Nezafat R. Joint myocardial T1 and T2 mapping using a combination of saturation recovery and T2-preparation. Magn Reson Med 2016;76:888–96. doi: 10.1002/mrm.25975.)

few as four heartbeats. In cardiac MRF, a dictionary is generated after every scan, as the magnetization evolution depends on the heart rate of the subject. This also means that cardiac MRF may be more robust to variable heart rates, since a subject specific model (dictionary) is constructed for every scan. Confounding factors, such as MT, B_0, and B_1 inhomogeneities may be incorporated into the Bloch simulations (or extended phase graphs) to improve accuracy and precision. Furthermore, additional parameters such as diffusion, T_2^* or $T_{1\rho}$ may also be incorporated into the model, allowing for a truly multi-parametric scan. These extensions are an open area of research, however they can be challenging since a patient specific MRF dictionary is required and the computational time increases considerably with the number of parameters. The initial cardiac MRF features an acquisition of approximately 16 heartbeats with a cardiac window of ~250 ms. In patients, such breath-holds can be challenging and long cardiac acquisition windows may capture cardiac motion as heart rates are often elevated; clinical validation is now warranted to characterize the accuracy, precision and reproducibility of cardiac MRF. Respiratory and cardiac motion can still affect cardiac MRF, introducing artefacts (in-plane motion) or potentially bias (through-plane motion). Ideally, motion could be resolved, producing additional functional information in the process.

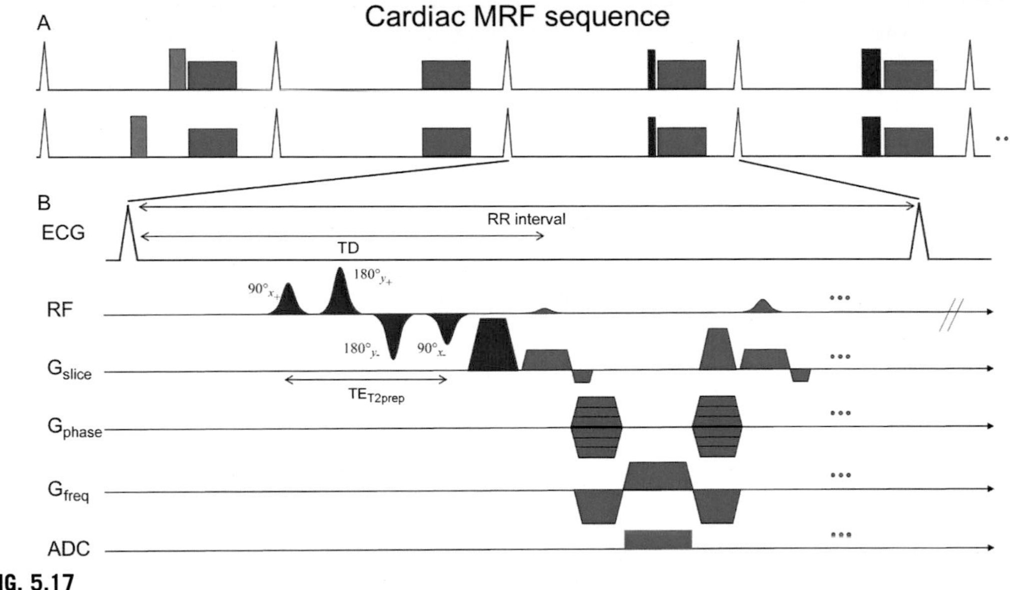

FIG. 5.17

(A) Cardiac MR Fingerprinting sequence diagram. Each heartbeat features a different preparation pulse, similar to some of the approaches depicted in Fig. 5.15. Here the flip angle and repetition time are varied throughout the scan to provide additional parametric encoding. Inversions pulses are shown in green, T_2-preparation modules are depicted in *red*, and data acquisition is shown in *blue*. (B) Sequence diagram for a specific heartbeat. A T_2 preparation pulse is applied with a duration of $TE_{T2\text{-prep}}$ms that determines the amount of T_2 weighting, before the data acquisition (only the first readout is shown).

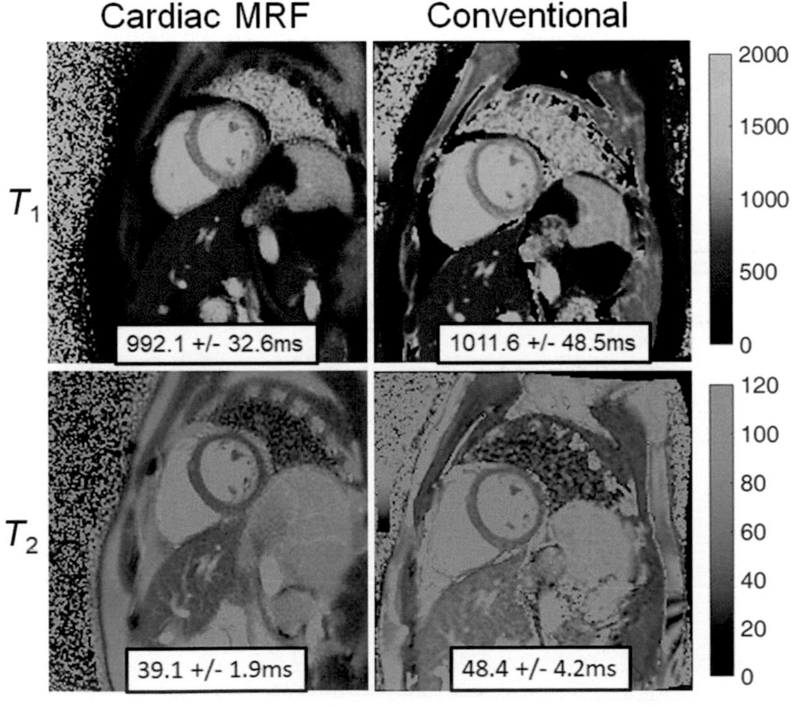

FIG. 5.18

2D triggered T_1, T_2, and M_0 parametric maps in a healthy subject acquired with cardiac MR fingerprinting *(left, top and bottom)*, MOLLI *(top right)*, and a T_2-prepared bSSFP *(bottom right)*.

5.4.3 Cardiac Multitasking

Simultaneous T_1, T_2, and functional assessment has been demonstrated with the recently introduced Multitasking approach [92]. Simultaneous T_1/T_2 multitasking can be used to acquire data continuously without ECG-triggering, similar to CABIRIA and TOPAZ [93] (a cardiac-resolved T_1 mapping method). A T_2IR preparation pulse is introduced to produce the necessary T_1/T_2 encoding; this pulse block is similar to the T_2-preparation pulse, except the last pulse is $90^\circ_{x_+}$ (instead of 90°_{x}), consequently inverting the longitudinal magnetization with a T_2 weighting. Each T_2IR is followed by a continuous FLASH readout, and repeated every 2.5 s with varying echo time for the T_2-prep component of the T_2IR, as depicted in Fig. 5.19. The entire acquisition is performed under free-breathing without ECG-triggering over the course of 60 s, which would generally produce strong motion artefacts. The novel solution introduced in Multitasking is to frame all the acquired data as a large tensor and exploit the low rank property of this tensor in the reconstruction process. In this case, Multitasking considers a tensor with four dimensions that share redundant information between them: cardiac motion, respiratory motion, T_1 recovery and T_2 decay. This approach produces simultaneous T_1/T_2 maps in every cardiac and respiratory dimension, adding functional information to the scan. Multitasking has been shown to produce T_1 and T_2 maps which are comparable to MOLLI and T_2-prepared bSSFP, respectively. Multitasking has also been validated for pre- and post-contrast T_1 mapping and perfusion T_1 mapping. It is currently limited to 2D; however, a 3D extension would be desirable to achieve whole-heart coverage. This could potentially

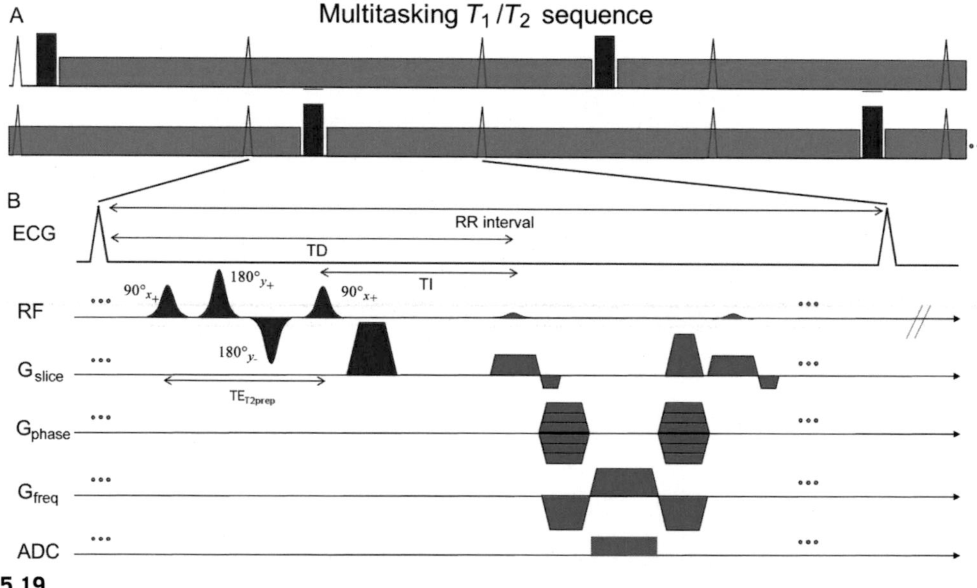

FIG. 5.19

(A) Native T_1/T_2 Multitasking sequence diagram. Data are continuously acquired (no ECG triggering nor respiratory gating) with a FLASH readout *(blue)* and routinely interrupted by a T_2IR preparation pulse *(in purple)* for T_1 and T_2 encoding. Respiratory and cardiac motion are estimated via self-navigation and resolved with a novel low-rank tensor reconstruction. (B) Sequence diagram for a specific heartbeat. A T_2IR preparation pulse is applied with a duration of $TE_{T2\text{-}prep}$ ms that determines the amount of T_2 weighting, TI ms before the data acquisition (only the first readout is shown).

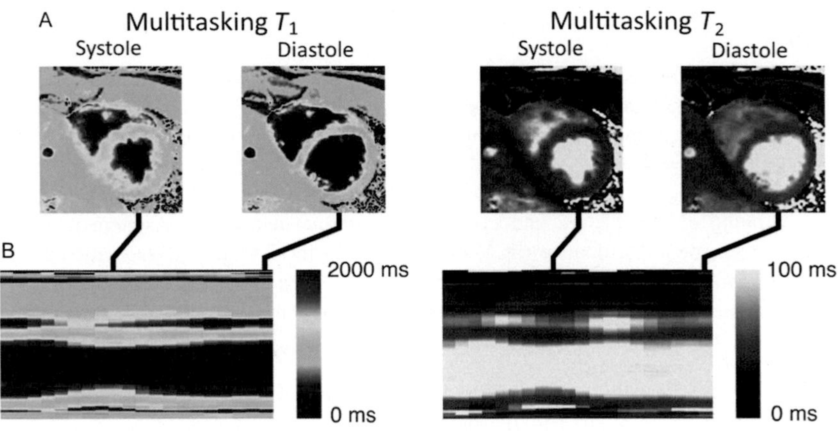

FIG. 5.20

(A) Multitasking T_1 and T_2 maps at systole and diastole, two of several cardiac phases resolved with this method. (B) 1D + time profiles of the T_1 and T_2 maps characterizing the cardiac function.

be an obstacle to clinical deployment since it is based on computationally demanding tensor reconstructions. Nevertheless, Multitasking has produced encouraging advances toward simultaneous T_1, T_2, and functional assessment, and in-depth patient studies are expected in the near future. Representative parametric maps generated with Multitasking are shown in Fig. 5.20.

5.5 Concluding remarks

Significant progress has been made toward cardiac parametric mapping over the last 15 years using dedicated approaches which can contend with the limitations posed by cardiac and respiratory motion. These efforts have resulted in mature methods that are now used in clinical practice, such as MOLLI and SASHA for T_1 mapping, or T_2-prepared bSSFP/FLASH and T_2GraSE for T_2 mapping. However, these methods have varying limitations in terms of accuracy, precision, robustness, or reproducibility. Confounding factors originating from field inhomogeneities, magnetization transfer, diffusion, partial volume, and motion, among others, have affected the performance of cardiac parametric mapping. In addition, 3D coverage and/or high resolution would be desirable to characterize many diseases. However quantitative imaging requires longer scans than qualitative imaging, imposing further obstacles on clinical translation. The majority of methods developed remain sensitive to system and protocol characteristics, creating a major obstacle in the way of standardized parametric measurements and inter-site reproducibility. Progress has been made toward this goal by considering MR physics models with higher detail, supported by improved sequence design and advances in reconstruction algorithms. The most recent developments have considered extended parametric models, including e.g. diffusion, magnetization transfer or fat imaging, which could not only help improve T_1 and T_2 measurements, but also provide clinically complementary information on their own. In the future of cardiac parametric mapping we can expect simultaneous, multi-parametric, whole-heart, high resolution quantitative imaging with accuracy, precision, and reproducibility required for clinical assessment.

References

[1] Moon JC, Messroghli DR, Kellman P, et al. Myocardial T1 mapping and extracellular volume quantification: a Society for Cardiovascular Magnetic Resonance (SCMR) and CMR Working Group of the European Society of cardiology consensus statement. J Cardiovasc Magn Reson 2013;15:1–12. https://doi.org/10.1186/1532-429X-15-92.

[2] Messroghli DR, Moon JC, Ferreira VM, et al. Clinical recommendations for cardiovascular magnetic resonance mapping of T1, T2, T2 and extracellular volume: a consensus statement by the Society for Cardiovascular Magnetic Resonance (SCMR) endorsed by the European Association for Cardiovascular Imagin. J Cardiovasc Magn Reson 2017;19:1–24. https://doi.org/10.1186/s12968-017-0389-8.

[3] Pennell DJ, Udelson JE, Arai AE, et al. Cardiovascular function and treatment in β-thalassemia major: a consensus statement from the american heart association. Circulation 2013;128:281–308. https://doi.org/10.1161/CIR.0b013e31829b2be6.

[4] Look DC, Locker DR. Time saving in measurement of NMR and EPR relaxation times. Rev Sci Instrum 1970;41:250–1. https://doi.org/10.1063/1.1684482.

[5] Messroghli DR, Radjenovic A, Kozerke S, Higgins DM, Sivananthan MU, Ridgway JP. Modified look-locker inversion recovery (MOLLI) for high-resolution T1 mapping of the heart. Magn Reson Med 2004;52:141–6. https://doi.org/10.1002/mrm.20110.

[6] Salerno M, Janardhanan R, Jiji RS, et al. Comparison of methods for determining the partition coefficient of gadolinium in the myocardium using T1 mapping. J Magn Reson Imaging 2013;38:217–24. https://doi.org/10.1002/jmri.23875.

[7] Kellman P, Hansen MS. T1-mapping in the heart: accuracy and precision. J Cardiovasc Magn Reson 2014;16:1–20. https://doi.org/10.1186/1532-429X-16-2.

[8] Piechnik S, Ferreira V, Dall'Armellina E, et al. Shortened Modified Look-Locker Inversion recovery (ShMOLLI) for clinical myocardial T1-mapping at 1.5 and 3T within a 9 heartbeat breathhold. J Cardiovasc Magn Reson 2010;12:1–69.

[9] Messroghli DR, Walters K, Plein S, et al. Myocardial T1 mapping: application to patients with acute and chronic myocardial infarction. Magn Reson Med 2007;58:34–40. https://doi.org/10.1002/mrm.21272.

[10] Robson MD, Piechnik SK, Tunnicliffe EM, Neubauer S. T1 measurements in the human myocardium: the effects of magnetization transfer on the SASHA and MOLLI sequences. Magn Reson Med 2013;70:664–70. https://doi.org/10.1002/mrm.24867.

[11] Roujol S, Weingärtner S, Foppa M, et al. Accuracy, precision, and reproducibility of four T1 mapping sequences: a head-to-head comparison of MOLLI, ShMOLLI, SASHA, and SAPPHIRE. Radiology 2014;272:683–9. https://doi.org/10.1148/radiol.14140296.

[12] Higgins DM, Ridgway JP, Radjenovic A, Sivananthan UM, Smith MA. T1 measurement using a short acquisition period for quantitative cardiac applications. Med Phys 2005;32:1738–46. https://doi.org/10.1118/1.1921668.

[13] Chow K, Flewitt JA, Green JD, Pagano JJ, Friedrich MG, Thompson RB. Saturation recovery single-shot acquisition (SASHA) for myocardial T1 mapping. Magn Reson Med 2014;71:2082–95. https://doi.org/10.1002/mrm.24878.

[14] Deichmann R, Haase A. Quantification of T1 values by snapshot-flash NMR imaging. J Magn Reson 1992;96:608–12. https://doi.org/10.1016/0022-2364(92)90347-A.

[15] Gai ND, Stehning C, Nacif M, Bluemke DA. Modified look-locker T1 evaluation using Bloch simulations: human and phantom validation. Magn Reson Med 2013;69:329–36. https://doi.org/10.1002/mrm.24251.

[16] Kellman P, Herzka DA, Arai AE, Hansen MS. Influence of off-resonance in myocardial T1-mapping using SSFP based MOLLI method. J Cardiovasc Magn Reson 2013;15:1–8. https://doi.org/10.1186/1532-429X-15-63.

[17] Kellman P, Herzka DA, Hansen MS. Adiabatic inversion pulses for myocardial T1-mapping. Magn Reson Med 2014;71:1428–34. https://doi.org/10.1002/mrm.24793.Adiabatic.

[18] Amano Y, Omori Y, Yanagisawa F, Ando C. Relationship between measurement errors in myocardial T1 mapping and heart rate. Magn Reson Med Sci 2020. https://doi.org/10.2463/mrms.mp.2019-0166.

[19] Roujol S, Foppa M, Weingärtner S, Manning WJ, Nezafat R. Adaptive registration of varying contrast-weighted images for improved tissue characterization (ARCTIC): application to T1 mapping. Magn Reson Med 2015;73:1469–82. https://doi.org/10.1002/mrm.25270.

[20] Xue H, Shah S, Greiser A, et al. Motion correction for myocardial T1 mapping using image registration with synthetic image estimation. Magn Reson Med 2012;67:1644–55. https://doi.org/10.1002/mrm.23153.

[21] Messroghli DR, Plein S, Higgins DM, et al. Human myocardium: single-breath-hold MR T1 mapping with high spatial resolution—reproducibility study. Radiology 2006;238:1004–12. https://doi.org/10.1148/radiol.2382041903.

[22] Radenkovic D, Weingärtner S, Ricketts L, Moon JC, Captur G. T1 mapping in cardiac MRI. Heart Fail Rev 2017;22:415–30. https://doi.org/10.1007/s10741-017-9627-2.

[23] Messroghli DR, Greiser A, Fröhlich M, Dietz R, Schulz-Menger J. Optimization and validation of a fully-integrated pulse sequence for modified look-locker inversion-recovery (MOLLI) T1 mapping of the heart. J Magn Reson Imaging 2007;26:1081–6. https://doi.org/10.1002/jmri.21119.

[24] Kellman P, Arai AE, Xue H. T1 and extracellular volume mapping in the heart: estimation of error maps and the influence of noise on precision. J Cardiovasc Magn Reson 2013;15:1. https://doi.org/10.1186/1532-429X-15-56.

[25] Messroghli DR, Plein S, Higgins DM, et al. Human myocardium: single-breath-hold MR T1 mapping with high spatial resolution—reproducibility study. Radiology 2006;238:1004–12. https://doi.org/10.1148/radiol.2382041903.

[26] Chow K, Spottiswoode BS, Pagano JJ, Thompson RB. Improved precision in SASHA T1 mapping with a variable flip angle readout. J Cardiovasc Magn Reson 2014;16:M9. https://doi.org/10.1186/1532-429X-16-S1-M9.

[27] Stainsby JA, Slavin GS. Comparing the accuracy and precision of SMART1Map, SASHA and MOLLI. J Cardiovasc Magn Reson 2014;16:P11. https://doi.org/10.1186/1532-429X-16-S1-P11.

[28] Slavin GS, Stainsby JA. True T1 mapping with SMART1Map: a comparison with MOLLI. Proc Intl Soc Mag Reson Med 2013;21:1416.

[29] Kellman P, Xue H, Chow K, Spottiswoode BS, Arai AE, Thompson RB. Optimized saturation recovery protocols for T1-mapping in the heart: influence of sampling strategies on precision. J Cardiovasc Magn Reson 2014;16:1–15. https://doi.org/10.1186/s12968-014-0055-3.

[30] Akçakaya M, Weingärtner S, Roujol S, Nezafat R. On the selection of sampling points for myocardial T1 mapping. Magn Reson Med 2015;73:1741–53. https://doi.org/10.1002/mrm.25285.

[31] Weingärtner S, Akçakaya M, Basha T, et al. Combined saturation/inversion recovery sequences for improved evaluation of scar and diffuse fibrosis in patients with arrhythmia or heart rate variability. Magn Reson Med 2014;71:1024–34. https://doi.org/10.1002/mrm.24761.

[32] Weingärtner S, Meßner NM, Budjan J, et al. Myocardial T1-mapping at 3T using saturation-recovery: reference values, precision and comparison with MOLLI. J Cardiovasc Magn Reson 2016;18:1–9. https://doi.org/10.1186/s12968-016-0302-x.

[33] Arheden H, Saeed M, Higgins CB, et al. Measurement of the distribution volume of gadopentetate dimeglumine at echo-planar MR imaging to quantify myocardial infarction: comparison with 99mTc-DTPA autoradiography in rats. Radiology 1999;211:698–708. https://doi.org/10.1148/radiology.211.3.r99jn41698.

[34] Flett AS, Hayward MP, Ashworth MT, et al. Equilibrium contrast cardiovascular magnetic resonance for the measurement of diffuse myocardial fibrosis: preliminary validation in humans. Circulation 2010;122:138–44. https://doi.org/10.1161/CIRCULATIONAHA.109.930636.

[35] Huang L, Neji R, Nazir MS, et al. Fast myocardial T1 mapping using shortened inversion recovery based schemes. J Magn Reson Imaging 2019;50:641–54. https://doi.org/10.1002/jmri.26649.

[36] Huang L, Neji R, Nazir MS, et al. FASt single-breathhold 2D multislice myocardial T1 mapping (FAST1) at 1.5T for full left ventricular coverage in three breathholds. J Magn Reson Imaging 2019;51(2):492–504. https://doi.org/10.1002/jmri.26869.

[37] Wang X, Kohler F, Unterberg-Buchwald C, Lotz J, Frahm J, Uecker M. Model-based myocardial T1 mapping with sparsity constraints using single-shot inversion-recovery radial FLASH cardiovascular magnetic resonance. J Cardiovasc Magn Reson 2019;21:1–11. https://doi.org/10.1186/s12968-019-0570-3.

[38] Nordio G, Henningsson M, Chiribiri A, Villa ADM, Schneider T, Botnar RM. 3D myocardial T1 mapping using saturation recovery. J Magn Reson Imaging 2017;46:218–27. https://doi.org/10.1002/jmri.25575.

[39] Henningsson M, Botnar R, Voigt T. 3D saturation recovery imaging for free breathing myocardial T1 mapping. J Cardiovasc Magn Reson 2013;15:P44. https://doi.org/10.1186/1532-429X-15-S1-P44.

[40] Coniglio A, Di Renzi P, Vilches Freixas G, et al. Multiple 3D inversion recovery imaging for volume T_1 mapping of the heart. Magn Reson Med 2013;69:163–70. https://doi.org/10.1002/mrm.24248.

[41] Chen Y, Lo WC, Hamilton JI, et al. Single breath-hold 3D cardiac T1 mapping using through-time spiral GRAPPA. NMR Biomed 2018;31:1–13. https://doi.org/10.1002/nbm.3923.

[42] Chow K, Yang Y, Shaw P, Kramer CM, Salerno M. Robust free-breathing SASHA T1 mapping with high-contrast image registration. J Cardiovasc Magn Reson 2016;18:1–14. https://doi.org/10.1186/s12968-016-0267-9.

[43] Guo R, Chen Z, Wang Y, Herzka DA, Luo J, Ding H. Three-dimensional free breathing whole heart cardiovascular magnetic resonance T1 mapping at 3T. J Cardiovasc Magn Reson 2018;20:1–15. https://doi.org/10.1186/s12968-018-0487-2.

[44] Kellman P, Wilson JR, Xue H, Ugander M, Arai AE. Extracellular volume fraction mapping in the myocardium, part 1: evaluation of an automated method. J Cardiovasc Magn Reson 2012;14:1. https://doi.org/10.1186/1532-429X-14-63.

[45] Kellman P, Wilson JR, Xue H, et al. Extracellular volume fraction mapping in the myocardium, part 2: initial clinical experience. J Cardiovasc Magn Reson 2012;14:1–8. https://doi.org/10.1186/1532-429X-14-64.

[46] Weingärtner S, Roujol S, Akçakaya M, Basha TA, Nezafat R. Free-breathing multislice native myocardial T1 mapping using the slice-interleaved T1 (STONE) sequence. Magn Reson Med 2015;74:115–24. https://doi.org/10.1002/mrm.25387.

[47] Qi H, Jaubert O, Bustin A, et al. Free-running 3D whole heart myocardial T1 mapping with isotropic spatial resolution. Magn Reson Med 2019;1331–42. https://doi.org/10.1002/mrm.27811.

[48] Brittain JH, Hu BS, Wright GA, Meyer CH, Macovski A, Nishimura DG. Coronary angiography with magnetization-prepared T2 contrast. Magn Reson Med 1995;33:689–96. https://doi.org/10.1002/mrm.1910330515.

[49] Giri S, Chung YC, Merchant A, et al. T2 quantification for improved detection of myocardial edema. J Cardiovasc Magn Reson 2009;11:1–13. https://doi.org/10.1186/1532-429X-11-56.

[50] Huang TY, Liu YJ, Stemmer A, Poncelet BP. T2 measurement of the human myocardium using a T2-prepared transient-state true FISP sequence. Magn Reson Med 2007;57:960–6. https://doi.org/10.1002/mrm.21208.

[51] Baeßler B, Schaarschmidt F, Stehning C, Schnackenburg B, Maintz D, Bunck AC. Cardiac T2-mapping using a fast gradient echo spin echo sequence – first in vitro and in vivo experience. J Cardiovasc Magn Reson 2015;17:1–8. https://doi.org/10.1186/s12968-015-0177-2.

[52] Sprinkart AM, Luetkens JA, Träber F, et al. Gradient spin Echo (Gra SE) imaging for fast myocardial T2 mapping. J Cardiovasc Magn Reson 2015;17:1–9. https://doi.org/10.1186/s12968-015-0127-z.

[53] Bano W, Feliciano H, Coristine AJ, Stuber M, van Heeswijk RB. On the accuracy and precision of cardiac magnetic resonance T2 mapping: a high-resolution radial study using adiabatic T2 preparation at 3 T. Magn Reson Med 2017;77:159–69. https://doi.org/10.1002/mrm.26107.

[54] Markl M, Alley MT, Elkins CJ, Pelc NJ. Flow effects in balanced steady state free precession imaging. Magn Reson Med 2003;50:892–903. https://doi.org/10.1002/mrm.10631.

[55] Giri S, Shah S, Xue H, et al. Myocardial T2 mapping with respiratory navigator and automatic nonrigid motion correction. Magn Reson Med 2012;68:1570–8. https://doi.org/10.1002/mrm.24139.

[56] Roujol S, Basha TA, Weingärtner S, et al. Impact of motion correction on reproducibility and spatial variability of quantitative myocardial T2mapping. J Cardiovasc Magn Reson 2015;17:1–11. https://doi.org/10.1186/s12968-015-0141-1.

[57] Jenista ER, Rehwald WG, Chen EL, et al. Motion and flow insensitive adiabatic T2-preparation module for cardiac MR imaging at 3 tesla. Magn Reson Med 2013;70:1360–8. https://doi.org/10.1002/mrm.24564.

[58] Baeßler B, Schaarschmidt F, Stehning C, Schnackenburg B, Maintz D, Bunck AC. A systematic evaluation of three different cardiac T2-mapping sequences at 1.5 and 3T in healthy volunteers. Eur J Radiol 2015;84:2161–70. https://doi.org/10.1016/j.ejrad.2015.08.002.

[59] Akçakaya M, Basha TA, Weingärtner S, Roujol S, Berg S, Nezafat R. Improved quantitative myocardial T2 mapping: impact of the fitting model. Magn Reson Med 2015;74:93–105. https://doi.org/10.1002/mrm.25377.

[60] Anderson LJ, Holden S, Davis B, et al. Cardiovascular T2-star (T2*) magnetic resonance for the early diagnosis of myocardial iron overload. Eur Heart J 2001;22:2171–9. https://doi.org/10.1053/euhj.2001.2822.

[61] Westwood M, Anderson LJ, Firmin DN, et al. A single breath-hold multiecho T2 * cardiovascular magnetic resonance technique for diagnosis of myocardial iron overload. J Magn Reson Imaging 2003;39:33–9. https://doi.org/10.1002/jmri.10332.

[62] Triadyaksa P, Oudkerk M, Sijens PE. Cardiac T2 * mapping: techniques and clinical applications. J Magn Reson Imaging 2019. https://doi.org/10.1002/jmri.27023.

[63] He T, Gatehouse PD, Kirk P, et al. Black-blood T2* technique for myocardial iron measurement in thalassemia. J Magn Reson Imaging 2007;25:1205–9. https://doi.org/10.1002/jmri.20929.

[64] Kirk P, He T, Anderson LJ, et al. International reproducibility of single breathhold T2* MR for cardiac and liver iron assessment among five thalassemia centers. J Magn Reson Imaging 2010;32:315–9. https://doi.org/10.1002/jmri.22245.

[65] Meloni A, Positano V, Keilberg P, et al. Feasibility, reproducibility, and reliability for the T2* iron evaluation at 3 T in comparison with 1.5 T. Magn Reson Med 2012;68:543–51. https://doi.org/10.1002/mrm.23236.

[66] Reeder SB, Faranesh AZ, Boxerman JL, McVeigh ER. In vivo measurement of T2(*) and field inhomogeneity maps in the human heart at 1.5 T. Magn Reson Med 1998;39:988–98. https://doi.org/10.1002/mrm.1910390617.

[67] He T, Gatehouse PD, Smith GC, Mohiaddin RH, Pennell DJ, Firmin DN. Myocardial T*2 measurements in iron-overloaded thalassemia: an in vivo study to investigate optimal methods of quantification. Magn Reson Med 2008;60:1082–9. https://doi.org/10.1002/mrm.21744.

[68] Sandino CM, Kellman P, Arai AE, Hansen MS, Xue H. Myocardial T2* mapping: influence of noise on accuracy and precision. J Cardiovasc Magn Reson 2015;17:1–9. https://doi.org/10.1186/s12968-015-0115-3.

[69] Yu H, Shimakawa A, McKenzie CA, Brodsky E, Brittain JH, Reeder SB. Multiecho water-fat separation and simultaneous R*2 estimation with multifrequency fat spectrum modeling. Magn Reson Med 2008;60:1122–34. https://doi.org/10.1002/mrm.21737.

[70] Kellman P, Xue H, Spottiswoode BS, et al. Free-breathing T2* mapping using respiratory motion corrected averaging. J Cardiovasc Magn Reson 2015;17:1–8. https://doi.org/10.1186/s12968-014-0106-9.

[71] Jin N, Da Silveira JS, Jolly MP, et al. Free-breathing myocardial T2 mapping using GRE-EPI and automatic non-rigid motion correction. J Cardiovasc Magn Reson 2015;17:1–12. https://doi.org/10.1186/s12968-015-0216-z.

[72] Yang HJ, Sharif B, Pang J, et al. Free-breathing, motion-corrected, highly efficient whole heart T2 mapping at 3T with hybrid radial-Cartesian trajectory. Magn Reson Med 2016;75:126–36. https://doi.org/10.1002/mrm.25576.

[73] Ding H, Fernandez-De-Manuel L, Schär M, et al. Three-dimensional whole-heart T2 mapping at 3T. Magn Reson Med 2015;74:803–16. https://doi.org/10.1002/mrm.25458.
[74] Van Heeswijk RB, Piccini D, Feliciano H, Hullin R, Schwitter J, Stuber M. Self-navigated isotropic three-dimensional cardiac T2 mapping. Magn Reson Med 2015;73:1549–54. https://doi.org/10.1002/mrm.25258.
[75] Bustin A, Milotta G, Ismail TF, Neji R, Botnar RM, Prieto C. Accelerated free-breathing whole-heart 3D T2 mapping with high isotropic resolution. Magn Reson Med 2019;988–1002. https://doi.org/10.1002/mrm.27989.
[76] Henningsson M, Koken P, Stehning C, Razavi R, Prieto C, Botnar RM. Whole-heart coronary MR angiography with 2D self-navigated image reconstruction. Magn Reson Med 2012;67:437–45. https://doi.org/10.1002/mrm.23027.
[77] Bustin A, Cruz G, Jaubert O, Lopez K, Botnar RM, Prieto C. High-dimensionality under sampled patch-based reconstruction (HD-PROST) for accelerated multi-contrast MRI. Magn Reson Med 2019;3705–19. https://doi.org/10.1002/mrm.27694.
[78] Langhans B, Nadjiri J, Jähnichen C, Kastrati A, Martinoff S, Hadamitzky M. Reproducibility of area at risk assessment in acute myocardial infarction by T1- and T2-mapping sequences in cardiac magnetic resonance imaging in comparison to Tc99m-sestamibi SPECT. Int J Cardiovasc Imaging 2014;30:1357–63. https://doi.org/10.1007/s10554-014-0467-z.
[79] Baeßler B, Schaarschmidt F, Stehning C, et al. Reproducibility of three different cardiac T2-mapping sequences at 1.5T. J Magn Reson Imaging 2016;44:1168–78. https://doi.org/10.1002/jmri.25258.
[80] Tahir E, Sinn M, Bohnen S, et al. Acute versus chronic myocardial infarction: diagnostic accuracy of quantitative native T1 and T2 mapping versus assessment of edema on standard T2-weighted cardiovascular MR images for differentiation. Radiology 2017;285:83–91. https://doi.org/10.1148/radiol.2017162338.
[81] Lurz P, Luecke C, Eitel I, et al. Comprehensive cardiac magnetic resonance imaging in patients with suspected myocarditis: the MyoRacer-trial. J Am Coll Cardiol 2016;67:1800–11. https://doi.org/10.1016/j.jacc.2016.02.013.
[82] Blume U, Lockie T, Stehning C, et al. Interleaved T1and T2 relaxation time mapping for cardiac applications. J Magn Reson Imaging 2009;29:480–7. https://doi.org/10.1002/jmri.21652.
[83] Kvernby S, Warntjes M, Haraldsson H, Carlhall C-J, Engvall J, Ebbers T. Simultaneous three-dimensional myocardial T1 and T2 mapping in one breath hold with 3D-QALAS. J Cardiovasc Magn Reson 2014;16:102. https://doi.org/10.1002/mrm.21272.
[84] Qi H, Bustin A, Cruz G, et al. Free-running simultaneous myocardial T1/T2 mapping and cine imaging with 3D whole-heart coverage and isotropic spatial resolution. Magn Reson Imaging 2019;63:159–69. https://doi.org/10.1016/j.mri.2019.08.008.
[85] Santini F, Kawel-Boehm N, Greiser A, Bremerich J, Bieri O. Simultaneous T1 and T2 quantification of the myocardium using cardiac balanced-SSFP inversion recovery with interleaved sampling acquisition (CABIRIA). Magn Reson Med 2015;74:365–71. https://doi.org/10.1002/mrm.25402.
[86] Akçakaya M, Weingärtner S, Basha TA, Roujol S, Bellm S, Nezafat R. Joint myocardial T1and T2mapping using a combination of saturation recovery and T2-preparation. Magn Reson Med 2016;76:888–96. https://doi.org/10.1002/mrm.25975.
[87] Asslander J, Novikov DS, Lattanzi R, Sodickson DK, Cloos MA. Hybrid-state free precession in nuclear magnetic resonance. Commun Phys 2019;2:1–73. https://doi.org/10.1103/PhysRev.112.1693.
[88] Zhao B, Haldar JP, Member S, et al. Optimal experiment design for magnetic resonance fingerprinting: cram meets spin dynamics. IEEE Trans Med Imaging 2018;1. https://doi.org/10.1109/TMI.2018.2873704.
[89] Ma D, Gulani V, Seiberlich N, et al. Magnetic resonance fingerprinting. Nature 2013;495:187–92. https://doi.org/10.1038/nature11971.
[90] Hamilton JI, Jiang Y, Chen Y, et al. MR fingerprinting for rapid quantification of myocardial T_1, T_2, and proton spin density. Magn Reson Med 2017;77:1446–58. https://doi.org/10.1002/mrm.26216.

[91] Jaubert O, Cruz G, Bustin A, et al. Water–fat dixon cardiac magnetic resonance fingerprinting. Magn Reson Med 2019, mrm.28070. https://doi.org/10.1002/mrm.28070.

[92] Christodoulou AG, Shaw JL, Nguyen C, et al. Magnetic resonance multitasking for motion-resolved quantitative cardiovascular imaging. Nat Biomed Eng 2018;2:215–26. https://doi.org/10.1038/s41551-018-0217-y.

[93] Weingärtner S, Shenoy C, Rieger B, Schad LR, Schulz-Menger J, Akçakaya M. Temporally resolved parametric assessment of Z-magnetization recovery (TOPAZ): dynamic myocardial T1 mapping using a cine steady-state look-locker approach. Magn Reson Med 2018;79:2087–100. https://doi.org/10.1002/mrm.26887.

CHAPTER

Advances in Signal Processing for Relaxometry

6

Noam Ben-Eliezer

Department of Biomedical Engineering, Tel Aviv University, Tel Aviv, Israel

Sagol School of Neuroscience, Tel Aviv University, Tel Aviv, Israel

Center for Advanced Imaging Innovation and Research (CAI2R), New York University Langone Medical Center, New York, NY, United States

6.1 Introduction

Relaxation is one of the fundamental mechanisms governing MRI signals. Although it is an essentially molecular mechanism, operating at nanometer length-scales, measuring macroscopic, voxel-averaged, relaxation values provides valuable information regarding the tissue state. MRI T_1, T_2, and $T_2{}^*$ relaxation times reflect intrinsic properties of the tissue, such as microarchitecture, exchange rates, biochemical state, as well as its viability and pathological state. These parameters are thus utilized ubiquitously for generating contrast, and contribute to almost every clinical MRI image. The field of MRI is gradually moving from the traditional contrast-weighted imaging approach toward a more quantitative approach, where the actual values of the relaxation parameters are measured. Quantitative MRI (qMRI) offers three potential advantages:

- **Sensitivity**: quantitative measurements are potentially more sensitive to tissue changes, for example, a few percent change in relaxation time might not be visually apparent, albeit, easily detectable on a qMRI parametric map.
- **Scalability**: the ability to accurately measure actual physical values reproducibly across scanners and scan-settings has the potential to facilitate the use of quantitative maps in multicenter and longitudinal studies.
- **Flexibility**: the availability of quantitative values will allow one to produce contrast-weighted (*qualitative*) images, with arbitrary contrast.

qMRI thus transforms MR scanners to a scientific measurement device while retaining the diverse anatomic imaging capabilities of the modality. These capabilities, however, have an inherent downside, which is the need to collect more data than standard scans, and resultant longer scan times. As a result, significant effort is being invested in ensuring that qMRI acquisitions are rapid enough that they can be included in clinical practice. These efforts include developing both advanced acquisition and postprocessing techniques, which generally interconnect as advances in one area are often dependent on advances in the other. Three different concepts for rapid and robust qMRI can be identified in this context:

Advances in Magnetic Resonance Technology and Applications. Volume 1. ISSN 2666-9099. https://doi.org/10.1016/B978-0-12-817057-1.00007-X

(1) New signal models based on a deeper understanding and more comprehensive modeling of spin dynamics.
(2) Advanced reconstruction algorithms for postprocessing undersampled datasets.
(3) Identification of **new signal motifs**, including the development of new encoding heuristics, or the incorporation of tissue microstructural features into the reconstruction algorithm.

The continuing increase in computation power has played a salient role in the development of new techniques, opening the door to more comprehensive signal models, and the ability to jointly fit multiple parameters. This chapter reviews some of the advanced techniques introduced in recent years, building on the discussion of conventional relaxation mapping such as classic multiecho spin echo (MESE) for T_2, multigradient echo (GRE) for T_2*, or Inversion Recovery [1,2], Look-Locker [3], and variable flip angle (VFA) [4,5] for T_1.

6.2 Advanced signal models

MRI signals depend on a wide range of parameters. These include physical mechanisms such as proton density, relaxation, diffusion, magnetization transfer (MT), and tissue electric properties; hardware settings including main field (B_0) inhomogeneities, and transmit (B_1^+) /receive (B_1^-) coil profiles; pulse-sequence design, for example, the timing diagram, RF pulse shapes, and crusher/spoiler gradient scheme; and lastly, tissue properties covering macro- and micro-architecture, local susceptibility, and compartmentation. In addition, in vivo scans are subjected to physiological effects such as motion or flow, further complicating the interpretation of the MRI signal.

The construction of new signals models entails identifying the subset of parameters that are relevant to a certain MRI acquisition, and incorporating them into a model-based reconstruction process. This procedure exploits a priori knowledge regarding the parameters in question, as well as their interrelations, to reconstruct quantitative maps. The acquisition process is in many cases accelerated—i.e., data are undersampled—in order to reduce scan time to acceptable clinical levels. Herein a few analytic and numerical signal models are reviewed, and their advantages, as well as potentially confounding factors, are discussed.

6.2.1 T_2 mapping using the slice-resolved Extended Phase Graph formalism

Classically, T_2 relaxation times are measured using a spin echo protocol, in which signal is acquired at different TEs to produce an exponential decay curve $S(t) = S_0 \exp(-TE/T_2)$. Due to the long scan times of single spin echo protocols, fast MESE (a.k.a. CPMG) protocols are the preferred method of choice for measuring T_2 in vivo. MESE data, however, are inherently contaminated by stimulated indirect echoes due to nonrectangular slice profiles and transmit field imperfections. The Extended Phase Graph (EPG) formalism was designed by Jürgen Hennig in 1988 with the purpose of analyzing the MESE class of sequences, where a train of refocusing pulses with arbitrary flip angles are applied following a single excitation pulse [6]. This formalism outputs the overall intensity of each echo in the train, by summing over entire set of stimulated and indirect echoes that contribute to the signal at any specific time point. This method is derived based on "quantizing" the level of dephasing and rephasing of all coherence pathways, and tracking their re-distribution, following (a) the application of a refocusing pulse, and (b) under the influence of magnetic field gradients. Once all pathways are mapped, one can integrate over the subset of pathways that are in-phase at a given TE to produce its corresponding intensity. Implementations of the basic algorithm can be found in [7,8].

The slice-resolved EPG (SEPG) algorithm [9] provides an important extension of the basic EPG algorithm to account for the range of refocusing pulse angles (effectively 0–180°), which appear along an imaging slice profile. Assuming a constant echo-spacing TE, the magnetization M at every z-location along the slice profile can be described using the SEPG algorithm as follows:

$$M_i(z) = M_{EXC}(z) \cdot \text{EPG}\left[T_1, T_2, i \cdot TE, B_1^+(x, y) \cdot \alpha(z)\right] \quad (6.1)$$

where M_{EXC} (z) is the initial transverse magnetization immediately after the excitation RF, $B_1{}^+(x,y)$ is a unitless parameter denoting the in-plane transmit field inhomogeneity (with unity marking a completely homogeneous field), and α is the local flip angle, varying across the slice profile. The spatially dependent refocusing flip angle $\alpha(z)$ can be estimated by calculating the frequency response of the refocusing RF. Calculating the frequency response by taking the Discrete Fourier Transform of the RF pulse shape for this purpose, however, is only accurate at small flip angles. A more exact profile can be calculated via precise Bloch equation simulations of the RF pulse on a numeric one dimensional sample a procedure requiring very little computation time. The final echo amplitude at each echo time TE can be then calculated by integrating over the magnetization components at each point along the slice profile:

$$S_i = \int M_i(z')dz', \; 1 \leq i \leq ETL \quad (6.2)$$

The number of points that must be "sampled" along the slice profile can be determined experimentally; 50–80 points have been found to be generally sufficient for standard Gaussian or SINC shaped profiles [9]. Fig. 6.1 illustrates the efficiency of SEPG for predicting MESE signal profile. In Fig. 6.1A, the effect of non-180° refocusing pulse angle can be seen: a very wide refocusing slice thickness ($\Delta z_{REF} = 5 \times \Delta z_{EXC}$ of the excited slice) offers uniform 180° refocusing across the slice, and results in a theoretical exponential decay (black lines). This is naturally not practical for volumetric imaging, where multislice acquisitions are used with minimal slice gap. Matching the refocusing and excitation slice thicknesses ($\Delta z_{REF} = \Delta z_{EXC}$) causes a significant stimulated echoes effect (gray lines). In both cases the SEPG algorithm is able to accurately predict the experimental decay curve (solid lines). Fig. 6.1B illustrates SEPG sensitivity to transmit field inhomogeneities, in comparison to simple exponential fit. As can be seen, an error 1%–5% is achieved for practical range of $B_1{}^+$ scaling = 0.7–1.3. This is very similar to the variability of exponentially fitted T_2 values (upper three curves), although it is clear that these latter values are highly overestimated due to not accounting for stimulated and indirect echoes. Residual $B_1{}^+$ dependent error of SEPG values can result from several factors including inaccurate simulation of the slice profile, $B_1{}^+$ field inhomogeneities, or T_1 relaxation. Fig. 6.1C gives an in vivo example comparing SEPG T_2 maps acquired using a very wide refocusing slice $\Delta z_{REF} = 5 \times \Delta z_{EXC}$ (left), producing a simple exponential decay, vis-à-vis the use of equal slice thicknesses $\Delta z_{REF} = \Delta z_{EXC}$ (right). Similar T_2 values are obtained in both cases attesting to the effectiveness of the SEPG algorithm in vivo.

The introduction of the SEPG extension has facilitated the use of the EPG formalism, making it the basis for many advanced acquisition schemes, signal-processing algorithms [10,11], as well as specific applications like fat/water separation [12]. A potential limitation of the SEPG algorithm is the modeling of RF pulses as instantaneous events, i.e., having infinitely short duration. This means that relaxation is modeled before or after the pulse, but not *during* the RF pulses. Considering a typical refocusing RF duration of 3 ms embedded in inter-echo duration of 10 ms, this assumption might lead to a systematic error such as the one reported in [13] for the fitted T_2 and flip angle maps. This limitation can be avoided by splitting the RF pulse into short time intervals to include relaxation when computing the slice profile, which can improve the accuracy of this approach at the expense of computation time.

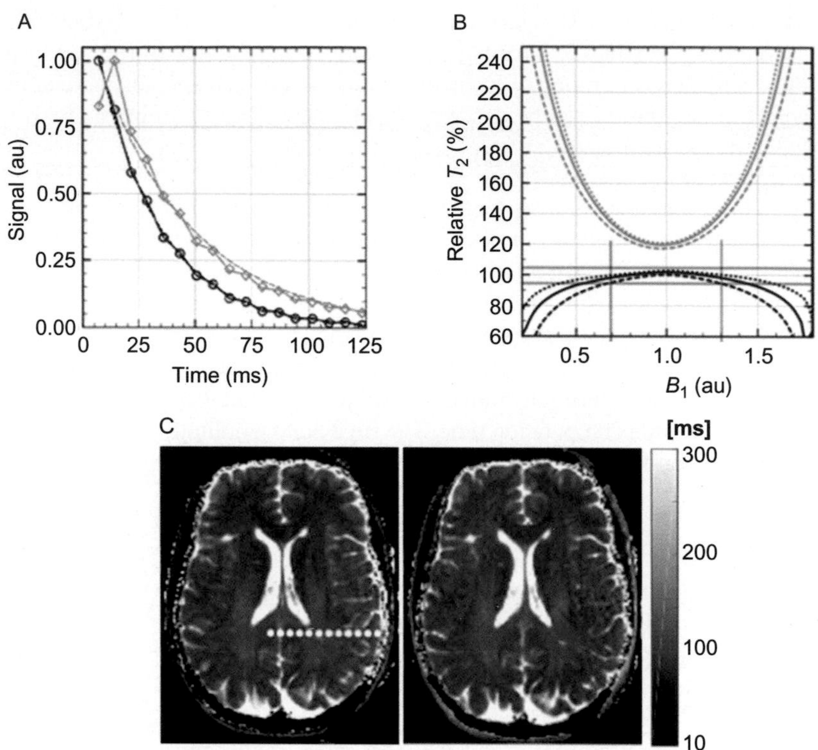

FIG. 6.1

(A) Experimental signal decay and simulated fits from a 0.30 mM manganese phantom. Black curves: a near-ideal measurement, achieved using refocusing slice-thickness Δz_{REF} equal to $\times 5$ the excitation value Δz_{EXC} and homogeneous $B_1{}^+$ scale *(open circles)*, its exponential fit *(dashed line)*, and SEPG fit *(solid line)*. Gray curves: a nonideal acquisition with $\Delta z_{REF}=\Delta z_{EXC}$ and $B_1{}^+$ scale of 0.67 *(open diamonds)*, its exponential fit *(dashed line)*, and SEPG fit *(solid line)*. (B) Simulated accuracy of the exponential fit *(upper three curves, gray)* and SEPG fit *(lower three curves, black)* as a function of $B_1{}^+$. Three T_1/T_2 ratios are shown: 5 *(dashed lines)*, 10 *(solid lines)*, and 20 *(dotted lines)*. (C) In vivo T_2 maps with $\Delta z_{REF}=5\times\Delta z_{EXC}$ (left) and maps with $\Delta z_{REF}=\Delta z_{EXC}$ (right). Intensity scale is from 10 to 300 ms.

Adapted from Lebel RM, Wilman AH. Transverse relaxometry with stimulated echo compensation. Magn Reson Med, 2010. 64(4): p. 1005–14.

6.2.2 Bloch equation simulation-based signal models

Many of the techniques for modeling the signal evolution in MESE protocols rely on analytic analysis, or mathematical representation of the theoretical spin dynamics [14,15]. An approach that avoids the challenge of formulating a mathematical model altogether is to simulate the response of the spin system using the time-dependent Bloch equations. One such technique is the echo-modulation curve (EMC) algorithm [16] designed to extract T_2 and PD values from MESE data. Contrary to simulating the theoretical MESE pulse-sequence scheme, this technique imports the specific sequence implementation into its reconstruction model, allowing it to overcome one of the main causes of instabilities in qMRI, namely, the implementation differences between vendors and software versions. By including the exact RF pulse shapes and gradient events, a more faithful representation of the signal is achieved, leading to more accurate parameter mapping.

Notwithstanding the benefits of Bloch-based approaches, simulating an entire volumetric pulse sequence can become computationally intractable considering that 10^3–10^4 spins need to be tracked through the ~10^4–10^5 time points, and across a three-dimensional space of approximately 100^3 voxels. Reducing MESE simulations to computationally feasible runtimes is possible because the bias from stimulated and indirect echoes is confined to imperfections along the slice dimension. Hence, instead of covering the full (x,y,z,t) space, simulations can be performed along the (z,t) domain, significantly reducing computation time. The EMC algorithm involves precalculation of a dictionary of signal decay curves expected to arise from the experimental acquisition protocol, while following the exact pulse sequence timing diagram executed on the MRI scanner (code is available at [17]). The temporal resolution of these simulations is matched to that used in the actual MESE scan. The internal spatial resolution is, in turn, set high enough to accurately account for intra-voxel dephasing (10–100 μm for data acquired on standard clinical scanners). Each run of the simulation generates a single echo-modulation curve, predicting the intensity of consecutive echoes along the MESE echo train and for a given parameter set. The fully dictionary of simulated EMCs is thus constructed by repeating the simulations for a range of $T_2 = 1$–1000 ms, and transmit field (B_1^+) inhomogeneity scales of 70% and 130%, where a value of 100% corresponds to a perfectly homogeneous B_1^+ field. An example of an EMC dictionary is shown in Fig. 6.2A.

Quantitative T_2 values are calculated using voxel-by-voxel matching of the experimental EMCs to the calculated dictionary of simulated EMCs. Following this procedure, a unique pair of $[T_2, B_1^+]$ values is assigned to each voxel, yielding the T_2 parametric map. Finally, PD maps are calculated by extrapolating the intensity of each voxel in the image from the first TE image to time $t=0$ using the fitted T_2 map, while assuming pure exponential decay occurred between the excitation and the first acquisition event.

While theoretical formalisms exist for most physical mechanisms that affect MRI signals, it is not always trivial to integrate these into the simulations, particularly due to the additional computational time that is required. A few examples are MT, the existence of multiple T_2 compartments, or diffusion. This being said, by isolating the main mechanisms that affect MESE protocols, namely stimulated echoes, the EMC or similar techniques such as Magnetic Resonance Fingerprinting (MRF) [18] are able to produce highly accurate qMRI values. A distinctive advantage of using full Bloch equation simulations is the incorporation of relaxation during the RF pulses. This is particularly important when the RF pulse duration is not negligible compared to TE, which might explain the higher relative error reported for EPG values vis-à-vis a Bloch-based approach [13]. Lastly, tailoring the signal model to the vendor-specific protocol implementation is an essential part of qMRI. This improves the data reproducibility by removing any scanner or parameter-dependent variability, and facilitates the use of qMRI in longitudinal and multicenter studies [19].

6.2.3 Multi-GRE-based relaxation mapping

A more comprehensive family of relaxation-mapping techniques is based on GRE sequence schemes, whose signals depend not only on T_2, but also on T_1 and, in some cases, T_2^*. These employ short TR, low flip angle GRE sequences, such as the spoiled gradient echo (SPGR) used by DESPOT1 [20] and synthetic MR [21], or a balanced steady-state free precession (bSSFP) employed in IR-bSSFP and in

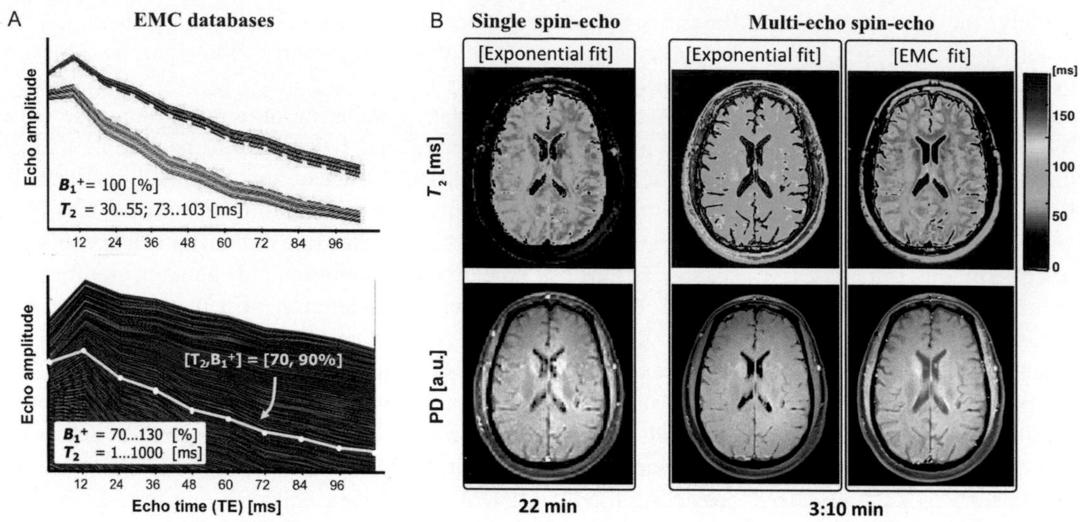

FIG. 6.2

(A) Examples of simulated echo-modulation curve (EMC) databases for a MESE protocol. Top: simplified database containing two ranges of consecutive T_2 values and $B_1{}^+ = 100\%$. Bottom: database spanning T_2 range of 1 to 1000 ms and $B_1{}^+$ inhomogeneity scales of 70%–130%. (B) In vivo T_2 and PD maps of a human brain. Left: Reference maps derived from a single-SE dataset and fitted to an exponential decay curve. Middle: exponential fitting of MESE data produces erroneously overestimated T_2 values. Right: EMC reconstruction produces corrected T_2 values and at clinically feasible scan times.

Adapted from Ben-Eliezer N, Sodickson DK, Block KT. Rapid and accurate T2 mapping from multi-spin-echo data using Bloch-simulation-based reconstruction. Magn Reson Med 2015;73(2):809–17.

DESPOT2 [20,22–24]. Another central relaxation time relevant to many of these reconstruction techniques is the *apparent* longitudinal relaxation time $T_1{}^*$, described formally by Kay and Henkelman [3]. Essentially, $T_1{}^*$ denotes the longitudinal relaxation during the application of repetitive series of small flip angle RF pulses, which can be applied separately, or following an inversion pulse. For brevity, we omit a full description of the above acquisition schemes and refer the reader to Chapter 4 for an elaborate analysis of the corresponding signal models.

6.2.4 Confounding factors

Accurate quantification of relaxation times requires accounting for each and every spin interaction that affects the acquired signal, while inaccurate or incomplete signal models will bias any parametric estimation. This can result from intentional omission of mechanisms that are too challenging to model, or due to the lack of a complete theoretical description. This section describes two common factors known to confound the quantification of relaxation times: MT and partial volume. Other confounding factors include flow and motion, which have a relatively small effect on relaxation times unless specifically encoded during signal acquisition, and magic angle effects. Interestingly, this latter mechanism can change the actual (physical) T_2 or T_1 value of a tissue as a function of its angle with the external B_0 magnetic field and its internal order [25,26]. This complex effect, however, arises only in tissues with high internal order and hydrophilic surface area, like collagen fibers in cartilage and tendons, or in highly ordered nerve bundles. Full analysis of this mechanism in the context of biological tissues may reveal highly pertinent information on the tissue microstructure [27,28].

6.2.4.1 Magnetization transfer (MT)

An important factor that can bias the measurement of relaxation times is spurious transfer of magnetization between the macromolecular pool and the free water pool (this effect is also discussed in detail in Chapter 32). The incidental saturation of the macromolecular pool and subsequent MT can be instigated by the large number of refocusing RF pulses employed in MESE protocols [29,30] or by the large number of RF pulses in steady-state sequences [24,31]. MT saturation effects (MT_{SAT}) can occur due to cross-relaxation or chemical exchange between the water molecules and the macromolecular pool, and are particularly apparent when shifting to multislice acquisitions owing to the increase in the number of RF pulses. Due to its low mobility, the macromolecular pool has a very broad spectral line shape, causing it to be indirectly excited by RF pulses that are targeted at other slices, outside the slice of interest. The protons in the macromolecular pool then interact with the observable water, causing attenuation of its signal [32]. Another, somewhat complementary effect, is the direct attenuation of the water that does not fully recover between consecutive TRs, or due to partial excitation from neighboring slices as a result of imperfect slice profile. Remarkably, these effects cannot be distinguished from macromolecular pool-related MT, and are thus also classified under the same phenomenon, and denoted as direct MT (MT_{DIR}) [33].

Although MT occurs ubiquitously in MRI, MT-related signal bias will have a varying effect on the estimated relaxation times, depending on the specific pulse sequence being used. Thus different protocol schemes will have different sensitivity to MT as exemplified by the significantly different T_1 values obtained using the modified Look-Locker sequence (MOLLI) and saturation recovery (SASHA) sequences [34–36]. Hafyane et al. further showed a T_1 baseline bias of +30 to +60 ms versus -100 to -150 ms using SASHA and MOLLI, respectively, as well as their different dependence on local magnetization transfer ratio (MTR) [37].

Fig. 6.3 illustrates the complex effect of MT in a phantom with varying concentrations of urea and for in vivo human brain. Fig. 6.3A compares T_2 values measured with SE and MESE, showing that while at very low urea concentration single SE T_2 values are lower due to diffusion-related attenuation, MT attenuation dominates the signal at most assayed concentrations, leading to underestimation of MESE T_2 values as concentrations increase. When examining the MT ratio between single and multislice acquisitions, an expected positive correlation emerges between MTR and the number of slices, with a smaller effect occurring in the urea phantom due to its lower macromolecular content compared to tissues. In contrast to this elevation in *signal* MTR, a negligible and incongruent change is seen in the corresponding T_2 values (Fig. 6.3D and E) implying that the MT signal attenuation occurs similarly for all echoes in the train.

The extent of MT-related bias of relaxation measurements remains an open question. Correcting for such biases requires either additional MT-weighted scans, or the construction of more comprehensive signal models [38]. One strategy for alleviating MT bias is the use of longer RF pulses with lower B_1^+ power, causing less off-resonance saturation of the macromolecular pool [24]. This approach, however, should be employed while bearing in mind that many signal models assume RF pulses to operate instantaneously (having zero duration), thereby neglecting relaxation effects that occur during the RF pulse. Using longer RF pulses to minimize MT effects (e.g., $T_{RF} > 0.2 \times$ TR in an SSFP scan, or $T_{RF} > 0.2 \times$ TE in an MESE scan) may thus increase the inaccuracy of the signal model, resulting in a different source of error in the estimated relaxation values [31].

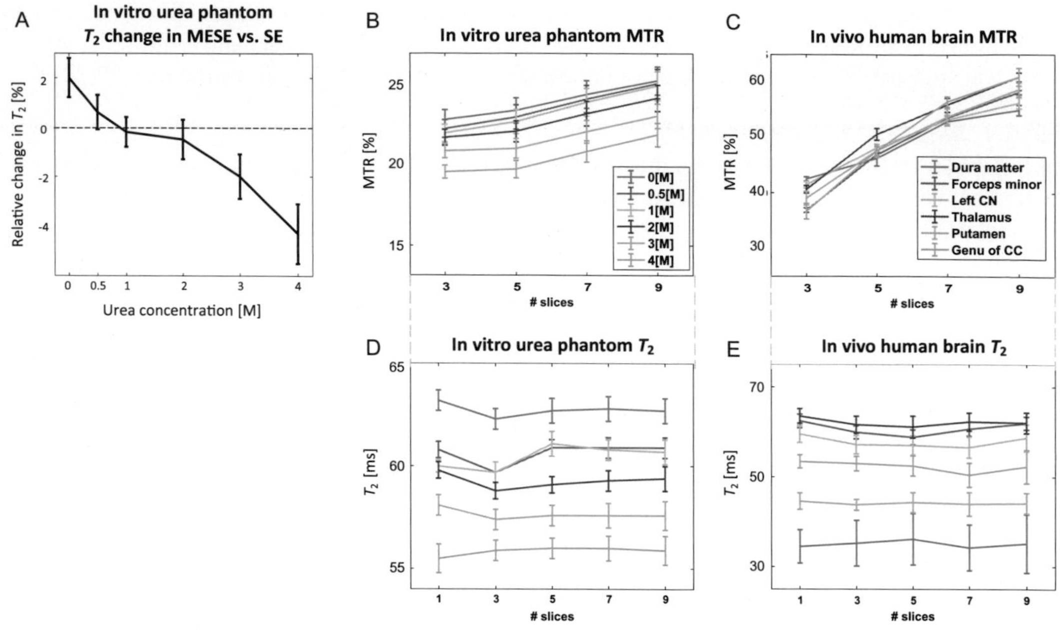

FIG. 6.3

The effect of MT on quantitative T_2 values. (A) Comparison of T_2 values between single spin echo (SE) and multiecho spin echo (MESE) protocols for a series of test tubes containing urea at increasing molar concentrations (% change calculated as $100 \times (T_2^{MESE} - T_2^{SSE})/T_2^{SSE}$. SE T_2values measured via SE are lower at low urea concentrations due to diffusion-related signal attenuation. As the urea concentration increases, MT attenuation dominates the signal, resulting in lower T_2 values for the MESE protocol. (B and C) MT ratio (MTR) as a function of the number of slices in the urea phantom and for six brain regions [CN: caudate nucleus; CC: corpus callosum]. The multislice MESE MTR exhibits direct positive correlation with the number of slices, and furthermore with the higher macromolecular content that characterizes the physiological tissues (MTR calculated as the ratio between the signal in the single-slice acquisition and the middle slice in a multislice series). Average MTR values for the group of urea concentrations and for a set of brain regions displayed a growth of 2.8% in vitro, and 18.9% in vivo when increasing the number of slices. MTR dependence on the number of slices, however, does not translate to the corresponding T_2 values (D and E). These vary between urea concentration due to natural increase in dipolar coupling but lack correlation with the number of slices, suggesting that MT attenuation is constant across the MESE echo train.

Adapted from Radunsky D, Ben-Eliezer N. Analysis of magnetization transfer (MT) effect on Bloch-simulation based T2 mapping accuracy, demonstrated on in vitro urea phantom. Paris: Intr. Soc. Magn. Reson. Med.; 2018.

6.2.4.2 Subvoxel compartmentation

Perhaps the most challenging aspect of quantifying relaxation values is the existence of different microstructural compartments within the same voxel (also described in Chapter 1). The acquired signal thus reflects a spatial average of several physiological environments, each having specific relaxation values and moreover affected differently by diffusion, flow, and MT interactions [39].

Similar to partial volume effects, multicomponent signals can arise in many tissues, for example, the brain white matter which consists of three water pools—intra-axonal water, water trapped between myelin sheaths, and extra-axonal pool. Another example are tissues that contain water and fat within the same pixel such as liver, intramyocardial fat, or diseased muscle [39–41]. Having very different relaxation times than water, the presence of fat will bias any estimate of the water relaxation times.

The bias due to multiple microscopic compartments cannot be circumvented, but it presents an opportunity to extract additional relevant information on the tissue given the correct signal model. Further discussion of such multicompartment techniques is given in Section 6.4.2.

6.3 Advanced reconstruction of undersampled datasets

Quantifying relaxation values requires the collection of large amounts of data compared to standard relaxation-weighted images. The most common way to meet this requirement is to employ undersampling either in the spatial or temporal domain. This section reviews a few advanced approaches for employing and reconstructing undersampled data.

6.3.1 Non-Cartesian data sampling

Sampling of k-space along non-Cartesian trajectories has many advantages for qMRI. The use of a radial trajectory, or "spokes," was first introduced by Lauterbur in his original paper on MRI [43], and subsequently deployed by Glover and Pauli in 1992 [44]. Radial spokes are essentially the analog of readout lines in Cartesian sampling, yet follow a trajectory that starts at a point in the periphery of k-space, traverses through its center, and end at the opposite k-space location. The lack of phase encoding in this sampling scheme endows it with two unique advantages, exemplified in Fig. 6.4: (1) reduction in sensitivity to motion-related and other off-resonance artifacts; (2) lack of folding artifact, allowing imaging of arbitrarily small FOVs, which saves valuable scan time when only part of the anatomy needs to be imaged. Contrary to Cartesian sampling where some lines reside at the center and some at the periphery of the k-space, radial spokes all sample both the periphery and the center of k-space. Thus every spoke contains the same amount of high- and low-resolution information, and thus can act as a navigator for effective motion correction [45]. The use of spiral trajectories is also becoming more frequent in qMRI due to advances in gradient hardware. Spirals can be designed to cover large areas of k-space efficiently, and also have the potential to be used in a self-navigating fashion [46].

The reconstruction of non-Cartesian data constitutes the main drawback of these sampling schemes, because straightforward (uniform) Fourier Transform cannot be directly performed. Two popular approaches for processing radial data are complex back-projection [47], or interpolation onto a Cartesian grid prior to Fourier Transform [48,49], although the latter in the form of the NUFFT is preferred as it can be applied to any non-Cartesian trajectory. Another essential aspect of any reconstruction algorithm is the need to compensate for the nonuniform sampling density when using non-Cartesian trajectories. This is done by applying a "roll off" filter that convolves the final image with the Fourier Transform of the k-space density profile [50]. More complex reconstruction algorithms based on iterative model-based reconstructions are discussed in the next sections.

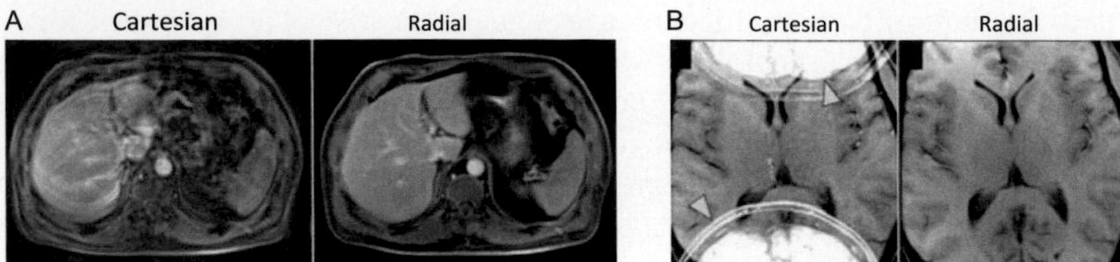

FIG. 6.4

(A) Free-breathing abdominal exam using conventional Cartesian sampling (left) and radial sampling (right), and otherwise identical sequence parameters and acquisition time. While the Cartesian scan suffers from strong "ghosting" artifacts, the radial acquisition provides diagnostic image quality. (B) Scan with reduced FOV using Cartesian sampling (left) and radial sampling (right). The large object size causes aliasing to occur along the phase-encoding direction with Cartesian sampling, while no aliasing appears with radial sampling because readout oversampling can be applied in both directions.

Adapted from Block KT, Chandarana H, Milla S, Bruno M, Mulholland T, Fatterpekar G, Hagiwara M, Grimm R, Geppert C, Kiefer B, Sodickson DK. Towards routine clinical use of radial stack-of-stars 3D gradient-echo sequences for reducing motion sensitivity. J Korean Soc Magn Reson Med 2014; 18(2):87.

6.3.2 Model-based reconstruction of undersampled relaxation mapping

To achieve feasible in vivo scan times, quantitative relaxation mapping generally requires undersampling the signal either in the spatial domain, the parametric domain, or both. One of the emerging ways to cope with these undersampled datasets is to identify and incorporate the set MR mechanisms affecting a given protocol into a single comprehensive signal model, which will cover both the spatial and parametric domains alongside hardware settings such as transmit/receive coil profiles. The reconstruction process then consists of estimating the most probable parametric values by solving a complex inverse problem, which becomes much less ill-conditioned owing to the incorporation of the entire spatio-parametric data into one comprehensive model.

Model-based reconstruction is typically done iteratively, and includes a data-fidelity term (i.e., keeping the current estimate of the parametric maps consistent with the measured data) alongside regularization terms that help compensate for the missing data. These are combined into a cost function, which penalizes differences between the signal model and the measured data, such that the optimal solution can be identified by minimizing the value of this function. Because experimental MRI data are typically contaminated by Gaussian noise, cost functions employ the L2 norm for data fidelity, and have the following general form:

$$\Phi\left[\rho\left(\vec{r}\right), p\left(\vec{r}\right)\right] = \sum_{c}\sum_{TE}\sum_{j}\left\|\vec{F}(\rho, p, TE, j, c) - \vec{S}(TE, j, c)\right\|_2^2 \tag{6.3}$$

where ρ denotes the proton density, p represents relaxation weighting, c loops over the different receiver coil profiles, TE is the readout echo time, and j is an index into the series of k-space points of a single readout event. The forward operator F contains the actual signal model, incorporating the type of scan protocol and the k-space sampling scheme. Taking, for example, a T_2 mapping CPMG protocol, F will assume the following form [51]:

$$F_{TE,c,j}(\rho, T_2) = \mathbf{U}\sum_{r\in FOV}\rho\left(\vec{r}\right)\cdot\mathbf{R}(B_1{}^{+}, T_2, TE)\cdot C_c\left(\vec{r}\right)\cdot e^{-ik_j\vec{r}} \tag{6.4}$$

Here, $\boldsymbol{U}$ is the *k-t* undersampling operator, $\mathbf{R}$ is a T_2 relaxation operator, accounting for stimulated echoes and transmit field inhomogeneity, and C_c is the cth coil profile. Notably, the relaxation term $\mathbf{R}$ can follow any of the advanced MESE signal models presented in Section 6.2.1 or 6.2.2. The reconstruction procedure can now be formalized as an optimization problem:

$$(\rho, T_2) = \underset{\rho, T_2}{\arg\min} \left\{ \Phi\left[\rho\left(\vec{r}\right), p\left(\vec{r}\right)\right] + \text{regularization terms} \right\} \tag{6.5}$$

Regularization: Notwithstanding the accuracy of the model being employed, the optimization problem in Eq. (6.3) can be highly ill-conditioned (i.e., having a large number of degenerate solutions) due to the signal undersampling. Additional confounding factors can result from phase inconsistencies relating to irregular patient or physiological motion, partial volume effects, or simple thermal noise. To stabilize and improve the convergence of the reconstruction process, regularization terms are added to the cost function. These include prior knowledge about the spatial or k space data, the field distributions, or the relaxation pattern. Common strategies include Tikhonov regularization of the proton-density and $B_1{}^+$ transmit field, total variation (TV) of the raw data to limit improbable *k*-space irregularities, and smoothness constraint on the coil profiles. Another common strategy, described in the next section, is to enforce data sparsity by using of compressed sensing L1 regularization.

Gradient descent approaches: A very effective way for solving the minimization problem in Eq. (6.3) is to use a gradient descent algorithm [52,53]. Common to this family of techniques is the need to calculate the gradient of the cost function with respect to all of the fit parameters (e.g., $\rho, T_1, T_2, B_1{}^+$). The success and speed of the optimization algorithm strongly depends on the accuracy of these calculations and specifically on relative scaling of the cost function partial derivatives with respect to each component. Because the fitting is done for multiple parameters, each having a very different dynamic range, prescaling the parameter values to equalize the relative magnitude of the partial derivatives and ensure similar convergence rates is a necessary preparatory step.

Readers are encouraged to refer to [50,53–56] for further insight on customized regularization terms, partial derivative calculations, and other general strategies for stabilizing nonlinear iterative model-based reconstructions. Examples of three model-based T_2 and T_1 mapping reconstructions are given in Figs. 6.5–6.7. Fig. 6.5 shows PD and T_2 maps of the brain using Cartesian model-based reconstruction of MESE data, producing accurate parametric maps even at five-fold acceleration [56]. Fig. 6.6 presents PD and T_2 maps of the spinal cord generated using model-based reconstruction of a radially undersampled dataset, demonstrating the two unique features of this sampling strategy: less susceptibility to motion caused by breathing and cardiac pulsations, and the ability to acquire arbitrarily small FOVs [51]. Fig. 6.7 shows quantitative PD and T_1 maps of a human brain, reconstructed from IR FLASH data, using an iteratively regularized Gauss-Newton model-based algorithm [57]. As can be seen, faithful reconstruction of both PD and T_1 maps is achieved at very short scan time of 4 s, avoiding the need for the long standard 5-min IR protocol.

6.3.3 Compressed sensing (CS) and sparsity-driven reconstruction

The previous section discussed the use of regularization to improve the convergence and stability of iterative model-based reconstructions. One of the most effective data-driven priors is compressed sensing (CS), exploiting the fact that MR images, as well as parametric maps, are sparse in some domain. The existence of a sparse representation allows the reconstruction of full parametric maps from *k*-space

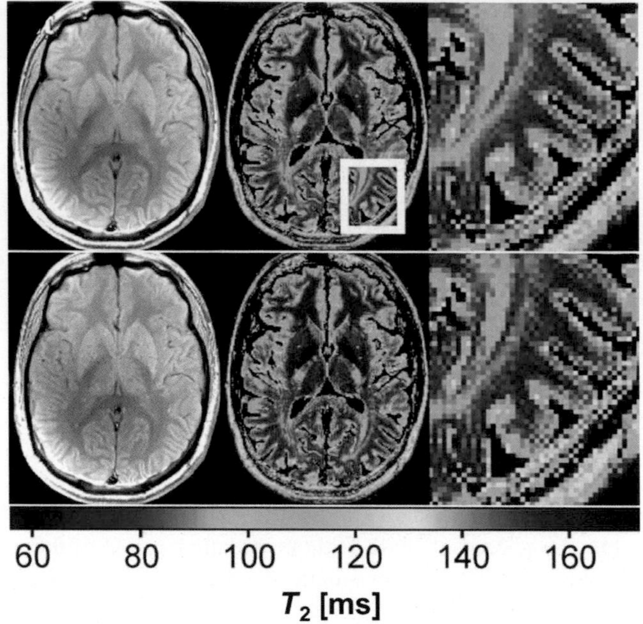

FIG. 6.5

Top: Standard, fully-sampled fitting and bottom: model-based reconstructions of (left) PD and (middle, right) T_2 maps of the human brain. Data were acquired using a 32-element coil and ×5 undersampling factor, reducing scan time from 8 min to 1:36 min.

Adapted from Sumpf TJ, Uecker M, Boretius S, Frahm J. Model-based nonlinear inverse reconstruction for T_2 mapping using highly undersampled spin-echo MRI. J Magn Reson Imaging 2011;34(2):420–8.

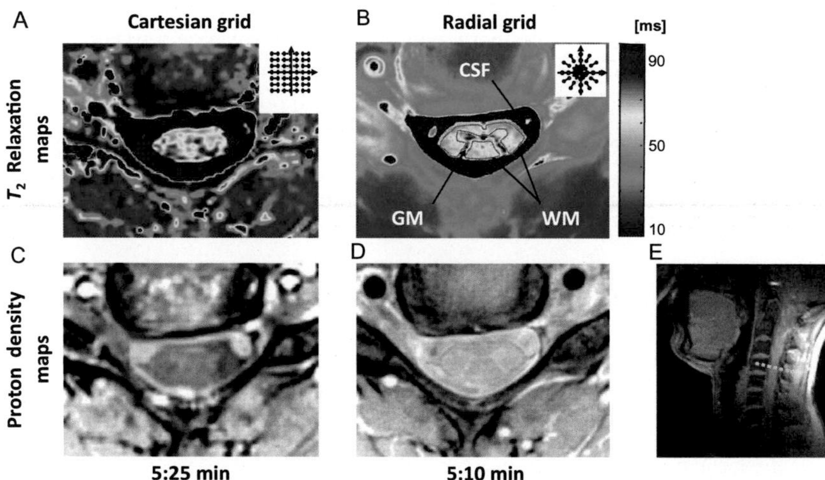

FIG. 6.6

A comparison of Cartesian and radial sampling schemes for parametric mapping of the human spinal cord in vivo. (A and B) T_2 relaxation maps and (C and D) proton density maps for the axial slice shown in (E). Radial sampling offers significantly higher immunity to motion as well as improved spatial resolution which enables differentiation of white/gray matter structures of the cord.

Adapted from Ben-Eliezer N, Sodickson DK, Shepherd T, Wiggins GC, Block KT. Accelerated and motion-robust in vivo T_2 mapping from radially undersampled data using bloch-simulation-based iterative reconstruction. Magn Reson Med 2016;75(3):1346–54.

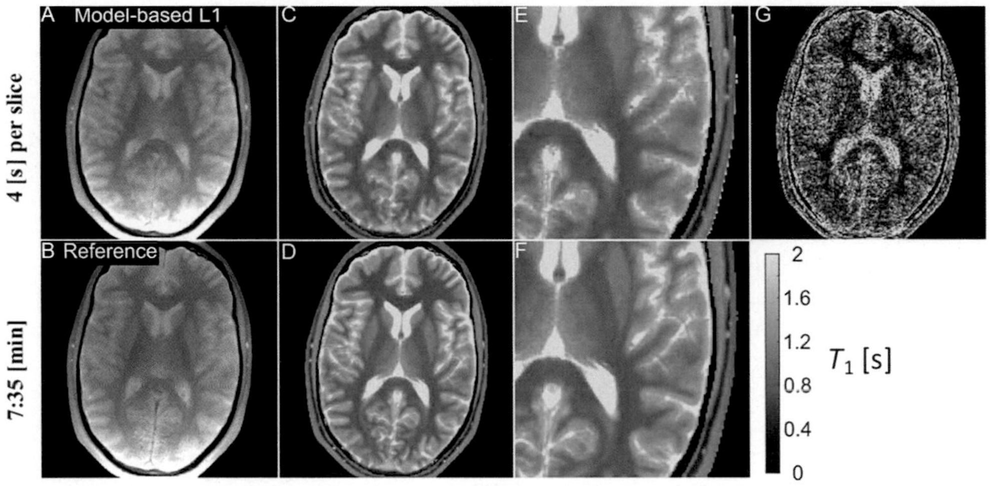

FIG. 6.7

Example of a model-based reconstruction of IR-FLASH data. (A and B) Estimated PD maps, (C and D) T_1 maps with magnified regions (E and F), (G) T_1 difference map between radially undersampled (top row) and fully sampled Cartesian reference (bottom row) of the human brain. Undersampled data were reconstructed using a model-based algorithm with L1 regularization of the parameter wavelet domain (sparse constraint), and an L2 smoothness constraint for the $\overline{B_1}$ coil profiles, reducing scan time to approximately 4 s per frame.

Adapted from Wang X, Roeloffs V, Klosowski J, Tan Z, Voit D, Uecker M, Frahm J. Model-based T1 mapping with sparsity constraints using single-shot inversion-recovery radial FLASH. Magn Reson Med 2018;79(2):730–40.

data that are sampled below the Shannon-Nyquist criterion. The ability of CS to shorten the scan time has been demonstrated in many MRI applications [58,59], and this approach can be adapted to accelerate relaxometry scans, where both the spatial and parametric domains can be undersampled. The minimization problem is formulated as a combination of an L2-norm data fidelity term, which ensures consistency of the solution with respect to the acquired k-space data, and an L1-norm CS term, which penalizes nonsparse solutions [60,61]:

$$\text{minimize } \|\boldsymbol{\Psi}\mathbf{x}\|_1, \text{ subject to } \|\mathbf{y}-\boldsymbol{\Phi}\mathbf{x}\|_2 \le \boldsymbol{\varepsilon} \tag{6.6}$$

Here $\boldsymbol{\Psi}$ is a sparsifying transform of the unknown image or parametric map $\mathbf{x}$, $\mathbf{y}$ is the acquired k-space data, and $\boldsymbol{\Phi}$ denotes the acquisition operator. The use of the L1 norm to promote sparsity constitutes the basis of CS and can be integrated into any model-based reconstruction by incorporating a regularization term of the form $\|\boldsymbol{\Psi}(\bullet)\|_1$ with $(\bullet)$ representing any of the fitted parameters, for example, the proton density, T_2 or $B_1{}^+$. Huang et al. [62] employed this strategy, in combination with principle component analysis (PCA), to construct a MESE time series $\mathbf{M}_j$ from undersampled data using the following optimization problem

$$\arg\min_{\mathbf{M}}\left\{\sum_{j=1}^{N}\left\|\mathrm{FT}_j(\mathbf{MB}_j)-\vec{\mathbf{K}}_j\right\|^2+\sum_i \lambda_i P_i(\mathbf{M})\right\} \tag{6.7}$$

Here **K** denotes the k-space data, j is an echo-time index, FT is the Fourier Transform from image to k-space domain, and $\mathbf{MB}_j$ is a PCA representation of the fully reconstructed T_2-weighted image series. Similar to Eq. (6.6), the left term employs L2 minimization to enforce consistency with the sampled data, while sparsity is enforced in both the space and parametric domains. First, sparsity of the temporal relaxation curve is imposed by limiting the number of PC coefficients in the **M** and **B** matrices. While a full relaxation curve consists of echo-train-length (ETL) number of points ranging between 10 and 20, the same curve can be accurately approximated using only 2–4 principal components, for example, for the exponentially decaying signal model used in [62], or 4–6 principal components for more complex signal models such as the EMC [16]. Secondly, spatial sparsity is enforced using conventional CS regularization, in this case L1-norm penalization of the wavelet transform of the principal components as well as their total variation transform. Fig. 6.8 demonstrates the potential of using the model in Eq. (6.7) to highly accelerate the acquisition of quantitative T_2 maps (acceleration factor $=13$). This particular example also benefits from the use of radial sampling, which provides a very efficient coverage of k-space even for a small number of spokes. Fig. 6.9 exemplifies another feature of the spatial sparsity constraint, namely, to remove Gaussian noise in the image. While the image features are sparse in the transform domain, random noise exhibits nonsparse distribution under any transformation, and is thereby suppressed by sparsity-promoting regularization terms.

Most sparsifying transforms employ blind orthonormal transforms such as FT or PCA. An extension of this idea was presented by Doneva et al. to include a data-adapted dictionary transform for mapping T_1 and T_2 relaxation times [61]. In this case, an overcomplete dictionary of learned signal prototypes (atoms) is used to represent the data. By matching the dictionary to the specific protocol scheme and signal model, a sparser representation can be achieved compared to arbitrary orthonormal basis-sets. The minimization problem then assumes the following form:

$$\text{minimize } \Phi = \|x - D\mathbf{s}\|_2 \quad s.t. \quad \|\mathbf{s}\|_0 \leq K \tag{6.8}$$

with D denoting the dictionary and **s** representing a vector of weights, mixing several dictionary atoms to generate the estimated signal x. The dictionary is generated offline in a two-stage procedure. First, a large number of atoms is generated using a theoretical relaxation-weighted model of the form

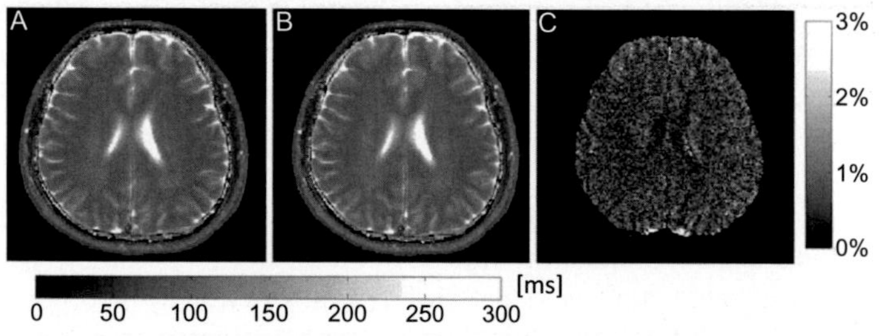

FIG. 6.8

(A) T_2 map calculated from 16 fully-sampled TE images using conventional least-squares fitting (scan time $=$ 17:20 min). (B) T_2 map generated from highly undersampled data (scan time $=$ 1:20 min), reconstructed using the signal model in Eq. (6.7). (C) Percent error of T_2 map in (B) taking (A) as the gold standard.

Adapted from Huang C, Graff CG, Clarkson EW, Bilgin A, Altbach MI. T_2 mapping from highly undersampled data by reconstruction of principal component coefficient maps using compressed sensing. Magn Reson Med 2012;67(5):1355–66.

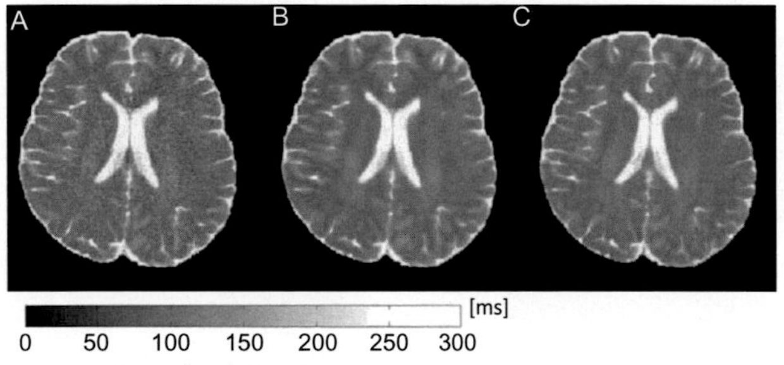

FIG. 6.9

Denoising effects of spatial sparsity priors. (A) T_2 map reconstructed using the REPCOM algorithm [62] from radial fast spin echo (FSE) data acquired with ETL=16 and 16 radial lines per TE. (B) Spatial penalties added to the T_2 map in (A) provide an effective denoising filter with no visible tradeoff on anatomical detail. (C) Corresponding gold standard T_2 map reconstructed from radial FSE acquired in a separate scan with ETL=16 and 256 radial lines per TE. Data were acquired with a preparatory time=35.2 ms between the 90° excitation pulse and the train of 180° refocusing pulses to intentionally increase noise levels.

Adapted from Huang C, Graff CG, Clarkson EW, Bilgin A, Altbach MI. T_2 mapping from highly undersampled data by reconstruction of principal component coefficient maps using compressed sensing. Magn Reson Med 2012;67(5):1355–66.

$S(t,T_{1,2}) = \alpha + \beta\cdot\exp(-t/T_{1,2})$. Atoms are generated for the range of α, β, T_1, and T_2 values that are expected to appear in the scanned object, or that can be produced by the scanning protocol. For example, an MESE protocol with ETL= 10 and echo spacing of 10 ms will practically be limited to mapping T_2 relaxation times in the range of 10–150 ms. The second step uses the K-SVD algorithm [63] to update and compress the dictionary. This stage improves the dictionary's compatibility with prospectively acquired data, while also enforcing sparsity in the dictionary representation, by limiting K—the number of atoms needed to approximate the training data. For a typical MRI relaxation curve, the value of K is in the order of 3–5, and will be determined by the K-SVD algorithm to be as small as possible whilst keeping the approximation error in the learned dictionary below a given threshold, for example, 10^{-5}.

The minimization problem in Eq. (6.8) can be solved using the algorithm described in [61] consisting of an iterative process, which alternates between data consistency and dictionary update stages. The former is performed by substituting the undersampled experimental data into the k-space representation of the current estimate, while the latter is done in the time domain by "projecting" the current estimate onto the dictionary space. Using $\mathbf{x}_n$ to denote the relaxation curve at voxel 'n', the projection procedure translates to calculating $\mathbf{x}_n^{(i)} = \mathbf{D}\mathbf{s}_n^{(i)}$ $s.\ t.$ $\|\mathbf{s}_n^{(i)}\|_0 = \mathrm{K}$, using an orthogonal matching pursuit (OMP) procedure that is limited to a fixed number of K atoms. One common alternative for solving this minimization problem is based on nonlinear gradient-descent approach. One, however, should take into account that numerical gradient calculations will be needed in this case owing to the nonanalytic representation of the dictionary $\mathbf{D}$, and hence of the cost function.

The sparsity promoted by limiting the number of atoms during the dictionary update stage can be complemented by exploiting sparsity in the image domain. This is done by expanding the iterative procedure to include an intermediate stage where the wavelet transform $\boldsymbol{\Psi}$ of each image $\mathbf{x}_l$ is calculated, and applying soft thresholding to produce an updated sparse estimate: $\mathbf{x}_l = \boldsymbol{\Psi}^{-1}\mathrm{SoftThreshold}(\boldsymbol{\Psi}\ \mathbf{x}_l)$.

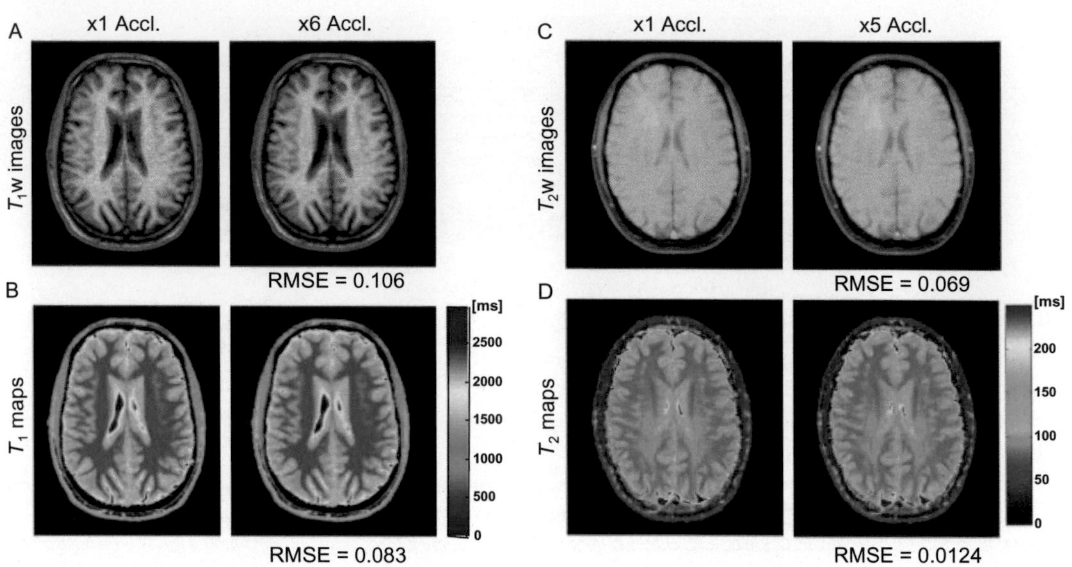

FIG. 6.10

Compressed sensing reconstruction of quantitative T_1 and T_2 maps using a dictionary-adapted model-based optimization. (A) T_1-weighted images (TI = 1.65 s) for (left) fully sampled and (right) ×6 accelerated Look-Locker Inversion Recovery protocol. Slight denoising is observed in the CS-reconstructed image. (B) Model-based reconstructed T_1 maps, with total scan time reduction from 120 to 20 s. (C) T_2-weighted image for TE = 20 ms (left) fully sampled and (right) ×5 accelerated multiecho spin echo data. (D) Model-based reconstructed T_2 maps, with total scan time reduction from 256 to 51 s. Accelerated maps show minimal differences compared with the reference maps. The normalized root mean squared error (NRMSE) with respect to the fully sampled reference is given below each image/map.

Adapted from Doneva M, Börnert P, Eggers H, Stehning C, Senegas J, Mertins A. Compressed sensing reconstruction for magnetic resonance parameter mapping. Magn Reson Med 2010;64(4):1114–20.

The final algorithm is thus embedded with twofold sparsity, allowing it to produce maps from highly undersampled datasets. This can be seen in Fig. 6.10 showing T_1 maps acquired using an ×8 accelerated IR protocol, and T_2 map acquired using an ×6 accelerated MESE protocol. Faithful reconstruction of quantitative maps is achieved in this case at clinically feasible scan times of 20 s and 51 s, respectively.

6.4 Identification of new signal motifs

The evolution of signal models has improved the quantification of relaxation times based on better understanding and more faithful representation of the spin dynamics. A somewhat complementary aspect of this advancement is the identification of heuristic signal motifs. These include specific properties of the *k*-space signal (e.g., its compressibility), characteristics of undersampled signals, or specific macro- and microscopic tissue properties. This section provides two such examples, one relating to pixel-based macroscopic analysis and one relating to analysis of subvoxel features.

6.4.1 Magnetic Resonance Fingerprinting

MRF is a model-based technique offering a conceptually different approach to data acquisition and reconstruction. Although based on an analytic signal model, this technique relies on a unique property of MR signals whereby a pseudorandomized acquisition of sufficiently large number of data points will cause signals from different materials or tissues to have a distinct signal evolution pattern [18,64].

MRF can be based on various data sampling schemes. One of the first implementations was based on IR-bSSFP acquisition of a highly undersampled image each TR using a variable density spiral trajectory. Although each single acquisition produces a highly aliased image (see Fig. 6.11A), acquiring a large series of such images while constantly varying the acquisition parameters—for examplethe flip angle and phase of RF pulses, TR, TE, and sampling patterns—will produce a unique time-dependent fingerprint per voxel. This pseudorandomized acquisition pattern is advantageous as it "sensitizes" the signal to a wide range of tissue properties, allowing the use of comprehensive signal models which incorporate not only tissue-related parameters, but also account for hardware imperfections such as inhomogeneities of the main magnetic field (B_0) and the transmit/receive profiles ($B_1{}^+$ and $B_1{}^-$) [65,66].

The uniqueness of MRF signal "fingerprints" is reflected by their one-to-one correspondence with a set of encoded tissue property values. Through the use of a pattern recognition algorithm, each fingerprint can then be matched to a multiparametric dictionary of predicted signal curves, translating the fingerprints into quantitative parametric maps. This is somewhat analogous to matching a person's fingerprint to a database, enabling the extraction of additional information about the person, such as their name, address and phone number, once a match is made. Dictionary atoms are calculated offline by simulating the MRF pulse-sequence protocol for a range of parameter values, for example, T_1, T_2, and B_0. One should, however, remember that only parameters that are encoded by the pulse sequence can be practically extracted from an MRF reconstruction. Simulating, for example, an SSFP protocol for a range of diffusion values will lead to a degenerate dictionary in the diffusion dimension, as this protocol is not sensitive to variation in the tissue diffusion coefficient.

Similar to other qMRI techniques, the main advantage of MRF is its ability to reconstruct full parametric maps from highly undersampled data. The fingerprint matching process acts, in this case, as a filter which differentiates the coherent signal patterns, i.e., the parameters of interest, from the incoherent patterns associated with undersampling artifacts. Fig. 6.11 illustrates the effectiveness of the MRF technique in reconstructing quantitative parametric maps. The high undersampling factor ($\times 48$) used in this case results in an extremely low quality image at each TR. The pattern matching process (shown in Fig. 6.11B for a single voxel) is able to "see through" the undersampling artifacts and identify the correct a theoretical curve. The encoding protocol was based on the IR-bSSFP sequence, which can be used to reconstruct both T_1 and T_2 relaxation maps, along with the underlying proton density. The maps are undistorted by main field inhomogeneities as these were incorporated into the signal model, producing a fourth B_0 map shown in Fig. 6.11D.

The importance of quantifying multiple parameters simultaneously is discussed in Chapter 4. This capability can be extrapolated beyond basic physical MR parameters to direct identification of a different materials, tissues or pathologies based on a combination of MR parameters (e.g., T_1, T_2 and self-diffusion tensor). Such combinations become readily available using multiparametric methods such as MRF, as these can be performed in clinically feasible timescales, avoid misregistration errors, and, moreover, tailored to encode the subset of physiological properties relating to a specific pathology.

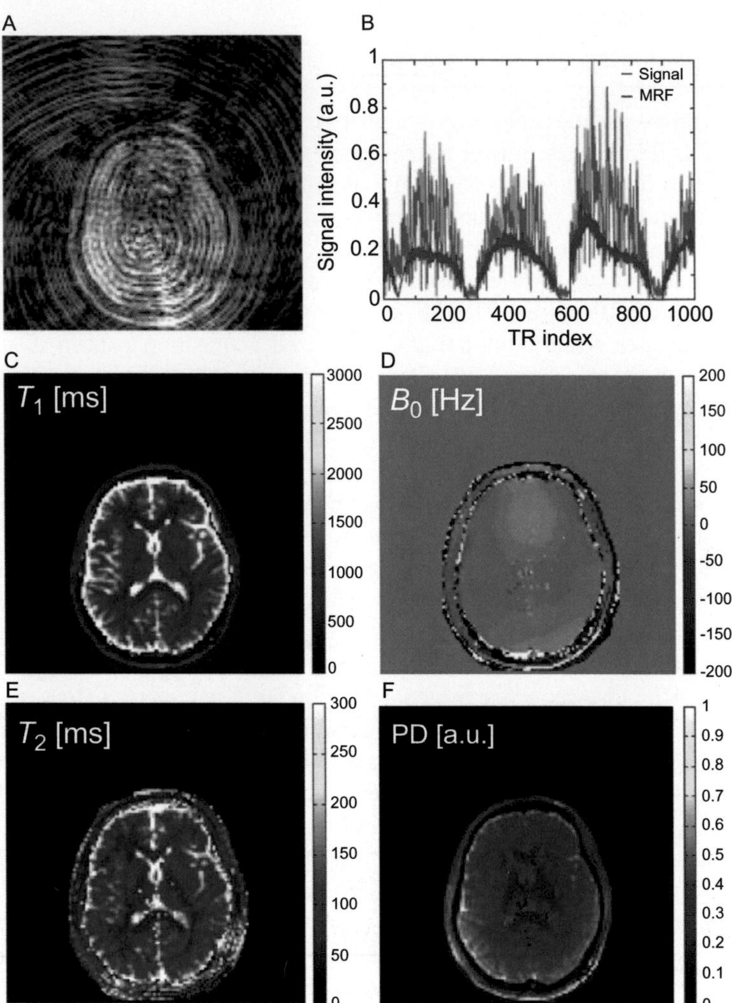

FIG. 6.11

MRF results from highly undersampled data. (A) An image at the 5th repetition time out of 1000 was reconstructed from only one spiral readout, demonstrating the significant errors from undersampling. (B) One example of an acquired signal evolution and its match to the dictionary. Note the significant interference resulting from the undersampling. a.u., arbitrary units. (C–F) Reconstructed quantitative parameter maps showing a near complete rejection of these errors based solely on the incoherence between the underlying MRF signals and the undersampling errors; (C) T_1 map; (D) main field (B_0) off-resonance frequency map; (E) T_2 map; and (F) proton density (PD) map (normalized color scale). Total scan time for all parameter maps was 12.3 s.

Adapted from Ma D, Gulani V, Seiberlich N, Liu K, Sunshine JL, Duerk JL, Griswold MA. Magnetic resonance fingerprinting. Nature 2013;495(7440):187–92.

6.4.2 Subvoxel multicompartment relaxometry

The physical length scale of biological processes spans several orders of magnitude, with molecular interactions occurring at nanometer length-scales, cellular processes taking place at a mesoscopic micrometer range, and macroscopic processes extending across millimeters. MRI, however, is still limited to sampling only the latter of these regimes, with microscopic effects being typically averaged out across voxels. This being said, intermediate mesoscopic information can still be extracted using MRI by incorporating the subvoxel morphology into comprehensive signal-tissue models [67]. A simple two-component example is the coexistence of water and fat within the same voxel, for example, in fatty liver, dystrophic muscle, or hematopoietic bone marrow [12,68]. Another highly studied example is illustrated in Fig. 6.12, showing the division of myelinated axons into three main compartments: intracellular, extracellular, and water trapped between myelin sheaths. The intricate tissue complexity leads to the lack of a gold-standard technique for modeling the different compartments, each having different relaxation properties, interacting through active/passive exchange, and affected by temperature, molecular diffusion, MT, and chemical exchange.

This section reviews a representative multicompartment relaxation mapping technique based on the EPG model described in Section 6.2.1. Readers interested in the particular case of axonal architecture are encouraged to refer to the comprehensive review by Alonso-Ortiz et al. [67].

One of the key parameters for studying subvoxel compartmentation is the T_2 relaxation time. This is due to the intrinsically high variability of T_2 values at the cellular level, and owing to the high contrast-to-noise (CNR) of T_2-weighted protocols. Most techniques for multi-T_2-component analysis rely on rapid MESE acquisitions, in conjugation with multiexponential signal decomposition of the form [66,68–70].

$$S(x,y,t)=\sum_{i=1}^{M} PD^{(i)}(x,y)\cdot e^{-t/T_2^{(i)}(x,y)} \tag{6.9}$$

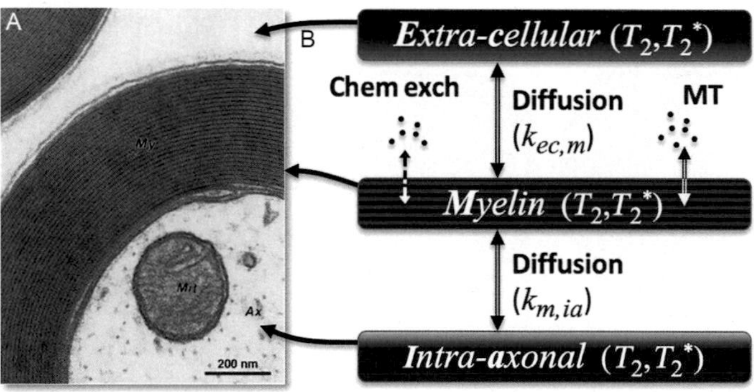

FIG. 6.12

Model of the different tissue compartments in myelinated axons. (A) Electron micrograph showing three compartments: extracellular space (ec), layers of myelin sheaths (m), and intra-axonal space (ia). (B) The mechanisms affecting the MRI signal include compartment-specific relaxation times, molecular diffusion, magnetization transfer (MT), and chemical exchange.

Here, M denotes the number of subvoxel components, and $PD^{(i)}$ is the proton density of the ith component at each location $[x,y]$. Solving Eq. (6.9) is not trivial as it involves computation of an inverse Laplace transform—a numerically ill-conditioned problem. Further to that, as detailed in Section 6.2.1, this model breaks down for clinically relevant multiecho protocols, or in the presence of B_1^+ inhomogeneities. An alternative model was suggested by Prasloski et al. [11] using a simplified EPG model, where the effects of stimulated echoes are circumvented through the use of slab-selective refocusing pulses in conjugation with 3D spin echo acquisitions. The resulting signal model resembles the one in Eq. (6.9), with the EPG replacing the exponential decay

$$S(x,y,z,TE_j) = \sum_{i=1}^{M} PD^{(i)}(x,y) \cdot EPG\left[T_1^{(i)}, T_2^{(i)}, TE_j, B_1^+(x,y) \cdot \alpha(z)\right] \tag{6.10}$$

The modified signal decay curve reflects a superposition of several subvoxel EPG components, each having a different relaxation time, while sharing the same macroscopic slice profile $\alpha(z)$ and field distribution B_1^+. Separation into the different components is achieved using a multiparametric nonlinear least square (NNSL) fitting, producing the relative intensity of each component, and their corresponding T_2 values [72]. Fig. 6.13 gives an example of using the model in Eq. (6.10) to extract intra-voxel T_2 distributions and corresponding myelin water fraction maps, where short T_2 content is assumed to reflect the myelin water compartment. To reduce the number of fitted parameters and computation time, T_1 was set in this example to a fixed value of 1 s—an appropriate assumption owing to the low sensitivity of MESE protocols to changes in T_1. The use of a 3D protocol—although limiting time-wise—also plays an important role as it increases the signal SNR and CNR, while removing any contamination from stimulated echoes, which are still the major source of error and instability of myelin water fraction mapping techniques.

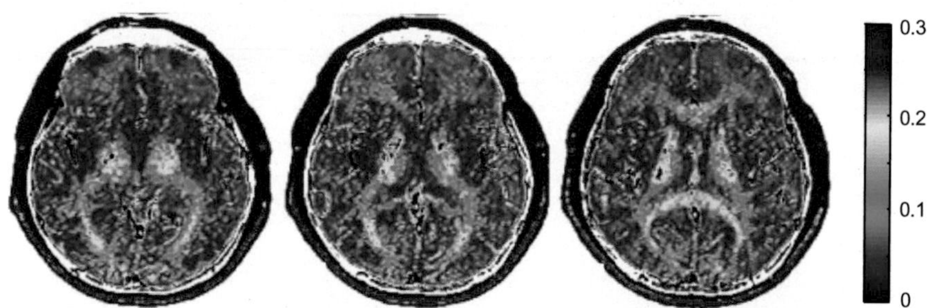

FIG. 6.13

Myelin/water fraction (MWF) maps generated for three consecutive slices in a 3D multi spin echo dataset. MWF was calculated using multicomponent EPG analysis, yielding values of 0.14 ± 0.025 and 0.10 ± 0.025 in the splenium and genu of corpus callosum, and 0.16 ± 0.025 in the right internal capsule. Analysis was done using the multi-T_2-component in (10), producing a "T_2 spectrum" at each voxel, which was then used to estimate the relative fraction of the myelin water (15–40 ms) and intra/extra cellular water component (40–200 ms).

Adapted from Prasloski T, Madler B, Xiang QS, MacKay A, Jones C. Applications of stimulated echo correction to multicomponent T2 analysis. Magn Reson Med 2012;67(6):1803–14.

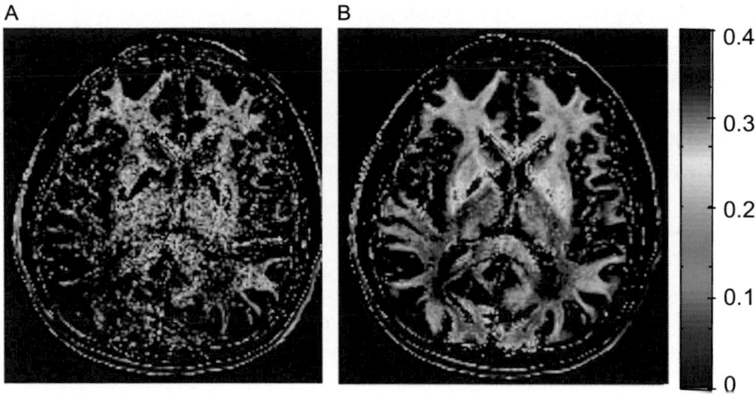

FIG. 6.14

Qualitative example demonstrating the benefit of incorporating a priori information regarding the tissue T_2 distribution into multicompartment reconstruction of myelin water fraction (MWF) maps. Data were acquired using MESE protocol, while T_2 relaxation was modeled using the EPG algorithm [9]. (A) Nonlinear least squares (NNLS) decomposition of the MESE signal into its different contributions results in relatively noisy parametric map. (B) Modeling the T_2 distribution patterns using a mixture of Wald distribution yields higher quality maps with lower apparent reconstruction noise.

Adapted from Akhondi-Asl A, Afacan O, Mulkern RV, Warfield SK. T(2)-relaxometry for myelin water fraction extraction using wald distribution and extended phase graph. Med Image Comput Comput Assist Interv 2014;17(Pt. 3):145–52.

Generalizations of the above approach have been reported, where a priori knowledge on the expected T_2 distribution patterns is incorporated into the model. Two instructional examples are given by Akhondi-Asl et al. who suggested the use of Wald distributions to describe the T_2 spectrum in conjugation with EPG-based relaxation model [73], and by McGivney et al. who deployed Gamma distributions in conjugation with an MRF signal model [74]. The incorporation of a predefined distribution of T_2 values within a voxel removes the need to estimate the contribution of each and every T_2 value, and thereby significantly reduces the number of unknown parameters. This simplification helps to overcome the ill-posed nature of these inverse problems and deliver cleaner parametric maps with lower reconstruction noise (Fig. 6.14). One, however, should keep in mind that these approaches are still simplified models, constituting some kind of a "transfer function" from the microscopic to macroscopic length scale, and thus do not necessarily depict the actual tissue microanatomy and physiology. This consists of a multitude of mechanisms including a range of inter-compartmental exchange rates, complex diffusion patterns, MT, and chemical exchange, all of which are part of a biological complexity that is still out of the reach of current MRI techniques.

6.5 Concluding remarks

Quantitative relaxation mapping constitutes the forefront of qMRI with numerous new techniques being constantly introduced. In this chapter advanced, yet more generic signal models were described, which can provide the building-blocks for handling the various challenges of parametric mapping. Readers are encouraged to overview some of the other techniques, referenced herein. These include the incorporation of specific T_1-to-T_2 parameter relationships to classify cortical areas [75]; stabilization of multicomponent analysis by spreading T_1 and T_2 relaxation values along a joint two-dimensional parametric map [76]; synthesizing arbitrary T_2 contrast while altogether avoiding classical quantitative mapping, through the use of low-rank reconstruction of randomly undersampled k-space [77]; the use of spiral k-space sampling trajectories [77–80]; or employing sparsity-promoting smoothness regularization in the parametric (rather than image) domain to achieve the acceleration needed for effectively sampling the spatio-relaxation domain [82].

References

[1] Crawley AP, Henkelman RM. A comparison of one-shot and recovery methods in T1 imaging. Magn Reson Med 1988;7(1):23–34.

[2] Paul T. Quantitative MRI of the brain: measuring changes caused by disease. John Wiley & Sons, Ltd; 2004.

[3] Kay I, Henkelman RM. Practical implementation and optimization of one-shot T1 imaging. Magn Reson Med 1991;22(2):414–24.

[4] Fram EK, Herfkens RJ, Johnson GA, Glover GH, Karis JP, Shimakawa A, Perkins TG, Pelc NJ. Rapid calculation of T1 using variable flip angle gradient refocused imaging. Magn Reson Imaging 1987;5(3):201–8.

[5] Gupta RK. A new look at the method of variable nutation angle for the measurement of spin-lattice relaxation times using fourier transform NMR. J Magn Reson (1969) 1977;25(1):231–5.

[6] Hennig J. Multiecho imaging sequences with low refocusing flip angles. J Magn Reson 1988;78:397–407.

[7] Hennig J. Echoes—how to generate, recognize, use or avoid them in MR-imaging sequences. Part II. Echoes in imaging sequences. Concepts Magn Reson 1991;3:125–43.

[8] Busse RF, Hariharan H, Vu A, Brittain JH. Fast spin echo sequences with very long echo trains: design of variable refocusing flip angle schedules and generation of clinical T2 contrast. Magn Reson Med 2006;55(5):1030–7.

[9] Lebel RM, Wilman AH. Transverse relaxometry with stimulated echo compensation. Magn Reson Med 2010;64(4):1005–14.

[10] Huang C, Bilgin A, Barr T, Altbach MI. T2 relaxometry with indirect echo compensation from highly undersampled data. Magn Reson Med 2013;70(4):1026–37.

[11] Prasloski T, Madler B, Xiang QS, MacKay A, Jones C. Applications of stimulated echo correction to multicomponent T2 analysis. Magn Reson Med 2012;67(6):1803–14.

[12] Marty B, Baudin PY, Reyngoudt H, Azzabou N, Araujo EC, Carlier PG, de Sousa PL. Simultaneous muscle water T2 and fat fraction mapping using transverse relaxometry with stimulated echo compensation. NMR Biomed 2016;29(4):431–43.

[13] McPhee KC, Wilman AH. Transverse relaxation and flip angle mapping: evaluation of simultaneous and independent methods using multiple spin echoes. Magn Reson Med 2016;77(5):2057–65.

[14] Bernstein M, King K, Zhou X. Handbook of MRI pulse sequences. Elsevier Academic Press; 2004.

[15] Zur Y. An algorithm to calculate the NMR signal of a multi spin-echo sequence with relaxation and spin-diffusion. J Magn Reson 2004;171(1):97–106.

[16] Ben-Eliezer N, Sodickson DK, Block KT. Rapid and accurate T2 mapping from multi-spin-echo data using Bloch-simulation-based reconstruction. Magn Reson Med 2015;73(2):809–17.

[17] EMC package, Available from: http://tam-son3.eng.tau.ac.il/~noambe/?page_id=309.

[18] Ma D, Gulani V, Seiberlich N, Liu K, Sunshine JL, Duerk JL, Griswold MA. Magnetic resonance fingerprinting. Nature 2013;495(7440):187–92.

[19] Shepherd TM, Kirov I, Charlson E, Bruno M, Babb J, Sodickson DK, Ben-Eliezer N. New rapid, accurate T2 quantification detects pathology in normal-appearing brain regions of relapsing-remitting MS patients. Neuroimage Clin 2017;14:363–70.

[20] Deoni SC, Rutt BK, Peters TM. Rapid combined T1 and T2 mapping using gradient recalled acquisition in the steady state. Magn Reson Med 2003;49(3):515–26.

[21] Warntjes JB, Dahlqvist O, Lundberg P. Novel method for rapid, simultaneous T1, T2*, and proton density quantification. Magn Reson Med 2007;57(3):528–37.

[22] Scheffler K, Hennig J. T(1) quantification with inversion recovery TrueFISP. Magn Reson Med 2001;45(4):720–3.

[23] Schmitt P, Griswold MA, Jakob PM, Kotas M, Gulani V, Flentje M, Haase A. Inversion recovery TrueFISP: quantification of T(1), T(2), and spin density. Magn Reson Med 2004;51(4):661–7.

[24] Ehses P, Seiberlich N, Ma D, Breuer FA, Jakob PM, Griswold MA, Gulani V. IR TrueFISP with a golden-ratio-based radial readout: fast quantification of T1, T2, and proton density. Magn Reson Med 2013;69(1):71–81.

[25] Xia Y, Moody JB, Alhadlaq H. Orientational dependence of T2 relaxation in articular cartilage: a microscopic MRI (microMRI) study. Magn Reson Med 2002;48(3):460–9.

[26] Fullerton GD, Rahal A. Collagen structure: the molecular source of the tendon magic angle effect. J Magn Reson Imaging 2007;25(2):345–61.

[27] Furman GB, Meerovich VM, Sokolovsky VL. Correlation of transverse relaxation time with structure of biological tissue. J Magn Reson 2016;270:7–11.

[28] Schyboll F, Jaekel U, Weber B, Neeb H. The impact of fibre orientation on T1-relaxation and apparent tissue water content in white matter. MAGMA 2018;31(4):501–10.

[29] Constable RT, Anderson AW, Zhong J, Gore JC. Factors influencing contrast in fast spin-echo MR imaging. Magn Reson Imaging 1992;10(4):497–511.

[30] MacKay A, Laule C, Vavasour I, Bjarnason T, Kolind S, Madler B. Insights into brain microstructure from the T2 distribution. Magn Reson Imaging 2006;24(4):515–25.

[31] Zhang J, Kolind SH, Laule C, MacKay AL. How does magnetization transfer influence mcDESPOT results? Magn Reson Med 2015;74(5):1327–35.

[32] van Zijl PC, Yadav NN. Chemical exchange saturation transfer (CEST): what is in a name and what isn't? Magn Reson Med 2011;65(4):927–48.

[33] Radunsky D, Ben-Eliezer N. Analysis of magnetization transfer (MT) effect on Bloch-simulation based T2 mapping accuracy, demonstrated on in vitro urea phantom. Paris: Intr. Soc. Magn. Reson. Med.; 2018.

[34] Messroghli DR, Radjenovic A, Kozerke S, Higgins DM, Sivananthan MU, Ridgway JP. Modified Look-Locker inversion recovery (MOLLI) for high-resolution T1 mapping of the heart. Magn Reson Med 2004;52(1):141–6.

[35] Chow K, Flewitt JA, Green JD, Pagano JJ, Friedrich MG, Thompson RB. Saturation recovery single-shot acquisition (SASHA) for myocardial T(1) mapping. Magn Reson Med 2014;71(6):2082–95.

[36] Roujol S, Weingartner S, Foppa M, Chow K, Kawaji K, Ngo LH, Kellman P, Manning WJ, Thompson RB, Nezafat R. Accuracy, precision, and reproducibility of four T1 mapping sequences: a head-to-head comparison of MOLLI, ShMOLLI, SASHA, and SAPPHIRE. Radiology 2014;272(3):683–9.

[37] Hafyane T, Karakuzu A, Duquette C, Mongeon FP, Cohen Adad J, Jerosch Herold M, Friedrich MG, Stikov N. Let's talk about cardiac T1 mapping. Cold Spring Harbor Laboratory; 2018, bioRxiv.

[38] Bieri O, Scheffler K. On the origin of apparent low tissue signals in balanced SSFP. Magn Reson Med 2006;56(5):1067–74.

[39] Vavasour IM, Whittall KP, Li DK, MacKay AL. Different magnetization transfer effects exhibited by the short and long T(2) components in human brain. Magn Reson Med 2000;44(6):860–6.

[40] Leporq B, Ratiney H, Pilleul F, Beuf O. Liver fat volume fraction quantification with fat and water T1 and T2* estimation and accounting for NMR multiple components in patients with chronic liver disease at 1.5 and 3.0 T. Eur Radiol 2013;23(8):2175–86.

[41] Kellman P, Bandettini WP, Mancini C, Hammer-Hansen S, Hansen MS, Arai AE. Characterization of myocardial T1-mapping bias caused by intramyocardial fat in inversion recovery and saturation recovery techniques. J Cardiovasc Magn Reson 2015;17:33.

[42] Bertram HC, Karlsson AH, Rasmussen M, Pedersen OD, Donstrup S, Andersen HJ. Origin of multiexponential T(2) relaxation in muscle myowater. J Agric Food Chem 2001;49(6):3092–100.
[43] Lauterbur PC. Image formation by induced local interactions: examples employing nuclear magnetic resonance. Nature 1973;242(5394):190–1.
[44] Glover GHP, J.M. Projection reconstruction techniques for reduction of motion effects in MRI. Magn Reson Med 1992;28:275–89.
[45] Feng L, Coppo S, Piccini D, Yerly J, Lim RP, Masci PG, Stuber M, Sodickson DK, Otazo R. 5D whole-heart sparse MRI. Magn Reson Med 2018;79(2):826–38.
[46] Zhou R, Yang Y, Mathew RC, Mugler 3rd JP, Weller DS, Kramer CM, Ahmed AH, Jacob M, Salerno M. Free-breathing cine imaging with motion-corrected reconstruction at 3T using SPiral Acquisition with Respiratory correction and Cardiac Self-gating (SPARCS). Magn Reson Med 2019;82(2):706–20.
[47] Rosenfeld A, Kak AC. Digital picture processing. New York: Academic Press; 1982.
[48] O'Sullivan JD. A fast sinc function gridding algorithm for fourier inversion in computer tomography. IEEE Trans Med Imaging 1985;4(4):200–7.
[49] Fessler JA, Sutton BP. Nonuniform fast fourier transforms using min-max interpolation. IEEE Trans Signal Process 2003;51(2):560–74.
[50] Beatty PJ, Nishimura DG, Pauly JM. Rapid gridding reconstruction with a minimal oversampling ratio. IEEE Trans Med Imaging 2005;24(6):799–808.
[51] Ben-Eliezer N, Sodickson DK, Shepherd T, Wiggins GC, Block KT. Accelerated and motion-robust in vivo T2 mapping from radially undersampled data using bloch-simulation-based iterative reconstruction. Magn Reson Med 2016;75(3):1346–54.
[52] Hager WW, Zhang H. A new conjugate gradient method with guaranteed descent and an efficient line search. SIAM J Optim 2005;16(1):170–92.
[53] Bakushinsky AB, Yu KM. Iterative methods for approximate solution of inverse problems. In: Mathematics and its applications. Dordrecht, The Netherlands: Springer; 2004.
[54] Engl HW, Neubauer A, Hanke-Bourgeois M. Regularization of inverse problems. vol. 375. Netherlands: Springer; 2000.
[55] Block KT, Uecker M, Frahm J. Model-based iterative reconstruction for radial fast spin-echo MRI. IEEE Trans Med Imaging 2009;28(11):1759–69.
[56] Sumpf TJ, Uecker M, Boretius S, Frahm J. Model-based nonlinear inverse reconstruction for T2 mapping using highly undersampled spin-echo MRI. J Magn Reson Imaging 2011;34(2):420–8.
[57] Wang X, Roeloffs V, Klosowski J, Tan Z, Voit D, Uecker M, Frahm J. Model-based T1 mapping with sparsity constraints using single-shot inversion-recovery radial FLASH. Magn Reson Med 2018;79(2):730–40.
[58] Yang AC, Kretzler M, Sudarski S, Gulani V, Seiberlich N. Sparse reconstruction techniques in magnetic resonance imaging: methods, applications, and challenges to clinical adoption. Invest Radiol 2016; 51(6):349–64.
[59] Feng L, Benkert T, Block KT, Sodickson DK, Otazo R, Chandarana H. Compressed sensing for body MRI. J Magn Reson Imaging 2017;45(4):966–87.
[60] Lustig M, Donoho D, Pauly JM. Sparse MRI: the application of compressed sensing for rapid MR imaging. Magn Reson Med 2007;58(6):1182–95.
[61] Doneva M, Börnert P, Eggers H, Stehning C, Senegas J, Mertins A. Compressed sensing reconstruction for magnetic resonance parameter mapping. Magn Reson Med 2010;64(4):1114–20.
[62] Huang C, Graff CG, Clarkson EW, Bilgin A, Altbach MI. T2 mapping from highly undersampled data by reconstruction of principal component coefficient maps using compressed sensing. Magn Reson Med 2012;67(5):1355–66.
[63] Aharon M, Elad M, Bruckstein A. $rm K$-SVD: an algorithm for designing overcomplete dictionaries for sparse representation. IEEE Trans Signal Process 2006;54(11):4311–22.
[64] Doneva M, Amthor T, Koken P, Sommer K, Börnert P. Matrix completion-based reconstruction for undersampled magnetic resonance fingerprinting data. Magn Reson Imaging 2017;41:41–52.

[65] Cloos MA, Knoll F, Zhao T, Block KT, Bruno M, Wiggins GC, Sodickson DK. Multiparametric imaging with heterogeneous radiofrequency fields. Nat Commun 2016;7:12445.

[66] Hamilton JI, Jiang Y, Ma D, Lo WC, Gulani V, Griswold M, Seiberlich N. Investigating and reducing the effects of confounding factors for robust T1 and T2 mapping with cardiac MR fingerprinting. Magn Reson Imaging 2018;53:40–51.

[67] Alonso-Ortiz E, Levesque IR, Pike GB. MRI-based myelin water imaging: a technical review. Magn Reson Med 2015;73(1):70–81.

[68] Machanna J, Stefan N, Schick F. 1H MR spectroscopy of skeletal muscle, liver and bone marrow. Eur J Radiol 2008;67:275–84.

[69] Laule C, Vavasour IM, Moore GR, Oger J, Li DK, Paty DW, MacKay AL. Water content and myelin water fraction in multiple sclerosis. A T2 relaxation study. J Neurol 2004;251(3):284–93.

[70] Meyers SM, Laule C, Vavasour IM, Kolind SH, Madler B, Tam R, Traboulsee AL, Lee J, Li DK, MacKay AL. Reproducibility of myelin water fraction analysis: a comparison of region of interest and voxel-based analysis methods. Magn Reson Imaging 2009;27(8):1096–103.

[71] Bjork M, Zachariah D, Kullberg J, Stoica P. A multicomponent T2 relaxometry algorithm for myelin water imaging of the brain. Magn Reson Med 2016;75(1):390–402.

[72] Whittall K, MacKay A. Quantitative interpretation of NMR relaxation data. J Magn Reson 1989;84:134–52.

[73] Akhondi-Asl A, Afacan O, Mulkern RV, Warfield SK. T(2)-relaxometry for myelin water fraction extraction using wald distribution and extended phase graph. Med Image Comput Comput Assist Interv 2014; 17(Pt. 3):145–52.

[74] McGivney D, Deshmane A, Jiang Y, Ma D, Badve C, Sloan A, Gulani V, Griswold M. Bayesian estimation of multicomponent relaxation parameters in magnetic resonance fingerprinting. Magn Reson Med 2018;80(1):159–70.

[75] Glasser MF, Van Essen DC. Mapping human cortical areas in vivo based on myelin content as revealed by T1- and T2-weighted MRI. J Neurosci 2011;31(32):11597–616.

[76] Celik H, Bouhrara M, Reiter DA, Fishbein KW, Spencer RG. Stabilization of the inverse Laplace transform of multiexponential decay through introduction of a second dimension. J Magn Reson 2013;236:134–9.

[77] Tamir JI, Uecker M, Chen W, Lai P, Alley MT, Vasanawala SS, Lustig M. T2 shuffling: Sharp, multicontrast, volumetric fast spin-echo imaging. Magn Reson Med 2017;77(1):180–95.

[78] Chen Y, Lo WC, Hamilton JI, Barkauskas K, Saybasili H, Wright KL, Batesole J, Griswold MA, Gulani V, Seiberlich N. Single breath-hold 3D cardiac T1 mapping using through-time spiral GRAPPA. NMR Biomed 2018;31(6):e3923.

[79] Claeser R, Zimmermann M, Shah NJ. Sub-millimeter T1 mapping of rapidly relaxing compartments with gradient delay corrected spiral TAPIR and compressed sensing at 3T. Magn Reson Med 2019; 82(4):1288–300.

[80] Foltz WD, Al-Kwifi O, Sussman MS, Stainsby JA, Wright GA. Optimized spiral imaging for measurement of myocardial T2 relaxation. Magn Reson Med 2003;49(6):1089–97.

[81] Nolte T, Gross-Weege N, Doneva M, Koken P, Elevelt A, Truhn D, Kuhl C, Schulz V. Spiral blurring correction with water-fat separation for magnetic resonance fingerprinting in the breast. Magn Reson Med 2019.

[82] Velikina JV, Alexander AL, Samsonov A. Accelerating MR parameter mapping using sparsity-promoting regularization in parametric dimension. Magn Reson Med 2013;70(5):1263–73.

CHAPTER

Relaxometry: Applications in the Brain

7

Alex L. MacKay[a,b] and Cornelia Laule[a,b,c,d]

[a]*Department of Radiology, University of British Columbia, Vancouver, BC, Canada* [b]*Department of Physics & Astronomy, University of British Columbia, Vancouver, BC, Canada* [c]*Department of Pathology & Laboratory Medicine, University of British Columbia, Vancouver, BC, Canada* [d]*International Collaboration on Repair Discoveries, University of British Columbia, Vancouver, BC, Canada*

7.1 Introduction

This goal of this chapter is to briefly discuss how best to obtain accurate brain T_1 and T_2 estimates, review the current understanding about what determines T_1 and T_2 in the brain, and summarize human clinical studies using relaxation time measurements. Applications of $T_{1\rho}$ and $T_2{}^*$ will also be summarized. The most promising potential clinical applications of brain relaxation measurements will be highlighted and challenges facing clinical integration will be noted.

7.2 Overview of the brain

To interpret magnetic resonance (MR) relaxation in the human brain, a brief overview of the tissue being probed may be helpful. The adult brain is $\sim$1.5 kg and mainly made up of glia and neurons. Glial cells include oligodendrocytes, astrocytes, ependymal cells, and microglia, which together perform key functions including maintaining structural and metabolic support of neurons, insulating neurons from each other, guiding development, destroying pathogens, and clearing debris. Neurons are electrically excitable cells that communicate with other cells, and consist of dendrites, a cell body, and an axon. Axons are typically wrapped in myelin, a lipid-protein bilayer that acts as an insulator and facilitates signal transmission between neurons. The brain can be divided into grey matter and white matter. The grey matter is largely made up of the cell bodies of the neurons, as well as glial cells, while white matter mainly consists of myelinated portions of the tissue—the high lipid content gives the tissue a whiteish appearance, hence the name "white matter." While the lipid, protein, and nucleic acid components of brain have complex and dynamic structures, the majority of the mass of our brains is actually water ($\sim$70% for white matter, $\sim$82% for grey matter). The interactions of brain water with the normally MR invisible nonaqueous molecules determine T_1 and T_2 relaxation measures.

Advances in Magnetic Resonance Technology and Applications. Volume 1. ISSN 2666-9099. https://doi.org/10.1016/B978-0-12-817057-1.00009-3

7.3 T_1 in brain

7.3.1 Measuring T_1 in brain

T_1 measurement techniques that work well in other body regions generally also work well in brain; for example, inversion recovery (IR), Look-Locker or a steady-state technique (e.g., SPGR). Quantitative T_1 measures are normally presented as an image or "map" where the voxel intensities are the computed T_1 times. Generally, T_1 mapping studies of normal brain tissue from different research sites are in approximate agreement and reproducibility studies of variable flip angle, IR and MP2RAGE T_1 measurements at 3T have reported coefficients of variation of less than 5% in brain tissue [1–4]. The creation of normative T_1 parametric atlases will enable single subject clinical studies [5]. For quantitative T_1 results, it is important that the analysis technique take into account changes in signal due to B_1^+ inhomogeneity [6–8]. It is also important to be aware that for brain the T_1 times extracted may depend upon the measurement technique. For example, Stikov et al. found that, compared to the IR spin echo technique, the Look-Locker method underestimates T_1 and the variable flip angle approach overestimates T_1 (Fig. 7.1) [9].

7.3.2 Physiological influences of T_1 in brain

Much effort has been exerted to find out what determines longitudinal relaxation in brain tissue. Brain T_1 times are strongly dependent upon magnetic field strength, and between 0.2T and 7T, T_1 values range from <400ms to >1200ms for white matter, and <500 ms to >1700ms for grey matter (Fig. 7.2) [10]. Many studies have shown a relationship between brain T_1 and tissue water content (Fig. 7.3) [10–22]. T_1 in brain has been modeled by assuming rapid exchange between "bound" water molecules restricted by proximity to macromolecules and "free" water molecules [23]. This application of a fast exchange, two-site model in normal brain tissue yields a linear relationship between $1/T_1$ and 1/(water content), providing theoretical support for attributing changes in T_1 to changes in water content [11]. Other factors influencing T_1 include myelin [24–28], fiber orientation [29], and iron (Fig. 7.4) [19,27].

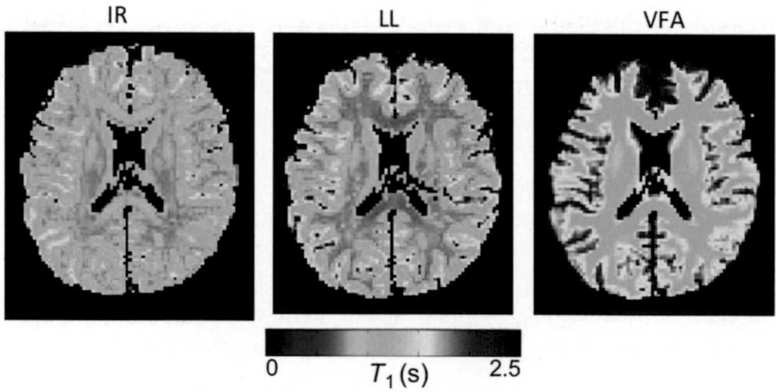

FIG. 7.1

Representative single-slice T_1 maps generated using the inversion recovery (IR), Look-Locker (LL), and variable flip angle (VFA) techniques in vivo.

Stikov N, et al. On the accuracy of T_1 mapping: searching for common ground. Magn Reson Med, 2015;73(2):514–22.

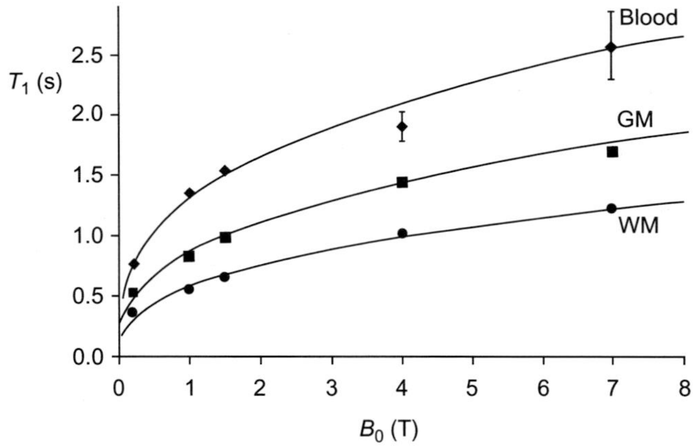

FIG. 7.2

B_0-dependence of the mean grey matter (GM) and white matter (WM) ^1H_2O T_1 values. The squares, circles, and diamonds represent group-averaged T_1 data obtained from putamen, frontal WM, and sagittal sinus ROIs, respectively. The error bars represent 1 SD of the group mean T_1 values. The error bars are about the same size as the symbols, for most data points. The solid curves represent the best fittings of the empirical function $T_1 = C(\gamma B_0)^\beta$. See text for details.

Rooney WD, et al. Magnetic field and tissue dependencies of human brain longitudinal ^1H_2O relaxation in vivo. Magn Reson Med 2007;57(2):308–18.

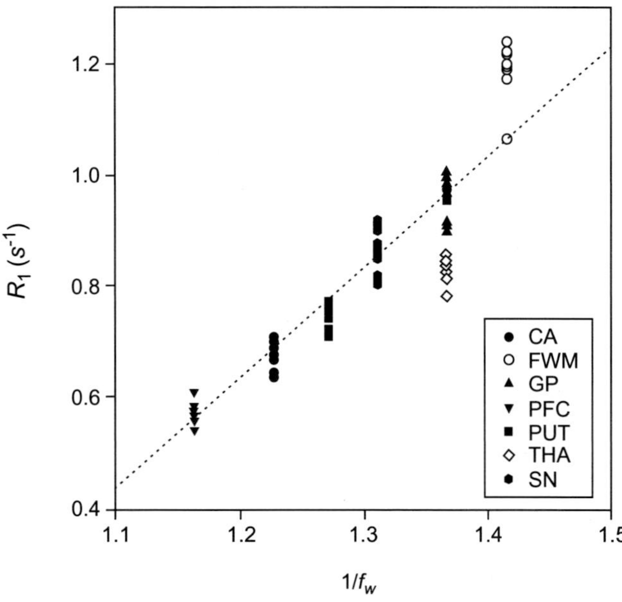

FIG. 7.3

Plot of regional R_1 values versus estimates of $1/f_w$ (f_w = water content) for globus pallidus (GP), substantia nigra (SN), putamen (PUT), caudate head (CA), prefrontal cortex (PFC), thalamus (THA), and frontal white matter (FWM). Regional values of f_w were obtained as described in the Methods section. A linear regression *(dotted line)* was applied to the data from all regions excluding THA and FWM.

Gelman N, et al. Interregional variation of longitudinal relaxation rates in human brain at 3.0 T: relation to estimated iron and water contents. Magn Reson Med 2001;45(1):71–9.

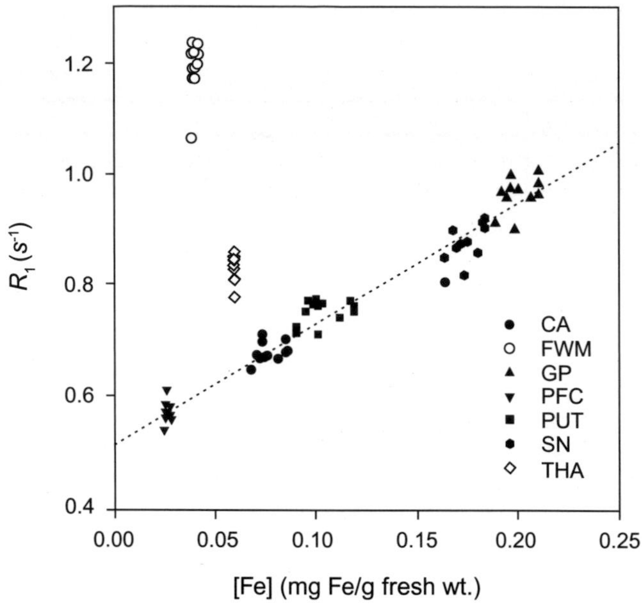

FIG. 7.4

Plot of regional R_1 values versus estimates of nonheme iron levels ([Fe]) for globus pallidus (GP), substantia nigra (SN), putamen (PUT), caudate head (CA), thalamus (THA), prefrontal cortex (PFC), and frontal white matter (FWM). Regional estimates of [Fe] were obtained from the work of Hallgren and Sourander. A linear regression *(dotted line)* was applied to the data from all regions, excluding THA and FWM.

Gelman N, et al. Interregional variation of longitudinal relaxation rates in human brain at 3.0 T: relation to estimated iron and water contents. Magn Reson Med 2001;45(1):71–9.

7.3.3 Single or multiple T_1 components?

Most of the literature on T_1 values in brain has assumed single exponential relaxation, but several groups have reported multicomponent T_1 relaxation from IR curves with many TI times [30–35]. Some of these studies attributed a small, short T_1 component to magnetization exchange between nonaqueous protons and water; Gochberg and colleagues used this effect to estimate the nonaqueous proton pool size ratio in brain [30,31,36,37]. Labadie et al. used a Look-Locker IR sequence with 64 TIs to demonstrate an intermediate T_1 component which they attributed to water in myelin bilayers [33]. This concept was used by Oh et al to create "myelin water images" by using a double IR measurement called Visualization of Short Transverse relaxation time component (ViSTa) which suppresses signal from longer T_1 components [38]. Finally, an ex vivo NMR study of bovine brain fitted four T_1 components in the MR signal from white matter [34]. Two components with T_1 values of less than 100 ms were related to magnetization exchange between water and myelin protons and between water and glial cell protons, a third component with T_1 of ~200 ms was related to myelin water exchanging with intra- and extra-cellular water, and the dominant component with T_1 close to 1 s was related to the remaining water in brain. Owing to magnetization exchange between compartments, the relative proportions of the four T_1 components were not expected to be equal to the relative populations of protons in the four reservoirs.

7.3.4 Interpreting T_1 in the brain

In summary, although not all researchers agree, the literature is consistent with an interpretation where water content is a primary determinant of T_1 in most brain tissue. It is also important to keep in mind that the various contributors to T_1 do not necessarily work independently. While myelin appears to influence T_1, the interpretation of T_1 being a direct myelin measure may be confounded by the fact that changes in myelin content are accompanied by changes in water content. For example, grey matter has ~12% greater water content than white matter, and while grey/white matter T_1 contrast disappears when myelin is removed from normal brain, this may reflect changes in relative water content resulting from myelin removal [28]. Furthermore, changes in iron content are also accompanied by changes in water content [19]. Also, the above mentioned linear relationship between $1/T_1$ and 1/(water content) is not necessarily reliable in the presence of iron, contrast agents or in complex pathology like tumors which may exhibit multifarious changes in iron, manganese, melanin, calcium, or methemoglobin [39]. More accurate techniques for measuring water content in brain are available and recommended [39–41].

Using T_1 to assess cortical myelin is a growing trend. Recently, many grey matter studies have used T_1-weighted images, T_1 mapping, or the ratio of T_1-weighted images to T_2-weighted images to map cortical myelin [26,42–47]. While this approach has been presented as a qualitative measure of cortical myelin and there is a good correspondence between T_1 and fMRI activations in the visual cortex [48], it has not yet been validated by histology and may not hold in the presence of pathology [49]. The T_1-myelin relationship does not hold for white matter; several studies found that T_1/T_2-weighted images were not correlated with T_2-derived and histologically validated myelin water fraction (MWF) in white matter [50–52]. However, the myelin water imaging techniques discussed in the following section do not work well in grey matter due to signal to noise problems. Hence, T_1 contrast is currently the best MR technique available for mapping cortical myelin.

7.4 Clinical applications of T_1 relaxation

7.4.1 Development and aging

Conventional T_1-weighted imaging is often used to assess brain maturation in infants [53], but there is also substantial research on changes in T_1 values in normal brain over the lifespan. Whole brain T_1 histograms at 1.5 T before the age of 1 year contain a single peak centered around 1200-1500 ms (Fig. 7.5) [54]. By age 2 years, a peak at ~750 ms begins to grow. Between 2 and 50 years the histogram continues to exhibit two peaks at ~600 ms and ~1100 ms, and with further aging, the T_1 histogram returns to a single peak at ~700 ms. The two peaks in the histogram are identified as white matter and grey matter and the shifting of the histograms over the lifespan represent development of white matter tracts in young children and breakdown of brain cells during senescence. Yeatman et al. measured T_1 values in white matter tracts of 102 healthy subjects between 7 and 85 years old [20]. For all tracts investigated, R_1 (= $1/T_1$) increased until ~40-50 years, and then decreased with age in a continuous curve. Several other studies, including an MR fingerprinting based approach, support the findings by Yeatman of decreasing T_1 with age in younger individuals [55–59]. However, cross-sectional studies can only provide an inference about true longitudinal changes in individuals. Gracien et al. investigated the change in brain T_1 over 7 years for healthy subjects aged 51-77 years

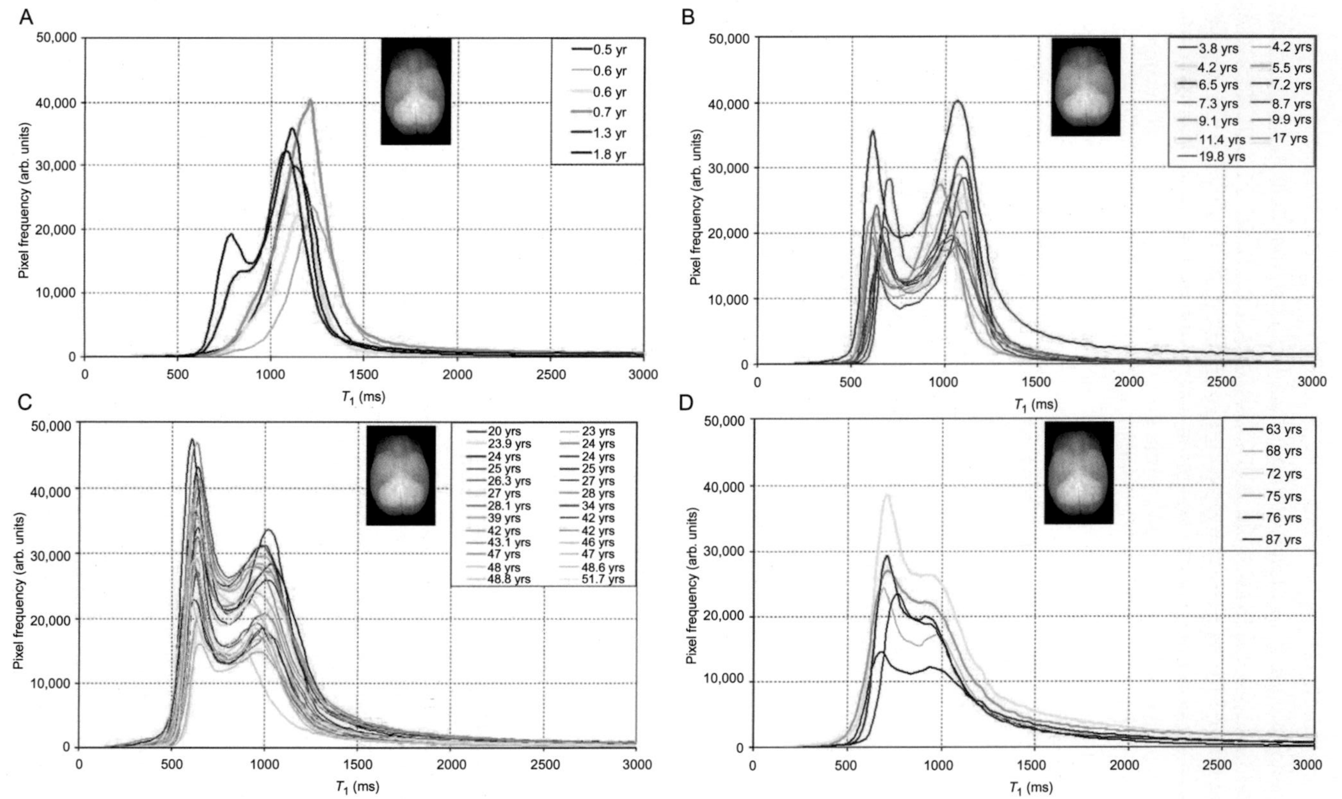

FIG. 7.5

T_1 histograms for all subjects divided into four groups by shape and position of histograms: (A) 0–2 years old (maturation period), (B) 2–20 years old (development period), (C) 20–60 years old (adulthood period) and (D) $\geq$60 years (senescence period). The shorter T_1 peak represents the white matter (WM), and the longer one represents the grey matter (GM). The histograms' transition from monomodal to bimodal between 0.7 and 1.3 years of age is noted (A) and the prominent increase of the WM components with age is demonstrated in the development period (B). The adulthood period is characterized by the relative histogram stability (C). The WM peaks shift in the direction of longer T_1, leading to a gradual loss of histogram bimodality in the senescence period (D).

Saito N, et al. Relaxo-volumetric multispectral quantitative magnetic resonance imaging of the brain over the human lifespan: global and regional aging patterns. Magn Reson Imaging 2009;27(7):895–906.

at baseline [60]. While white matter T_1 was relatively constant, substantial decreases in T_1 occurred in lateral, frontal, and temporal cortex, in contrast to the findings by Yeatman et al. These changes, which were much larger in older subjects, were attributed to decreases in water content and increases in iron.

7.4.2 Multiple sclerosis

The largest clinical application of quantitative T_1 (and T_2) relaxation methods has been in multiple sclerosis (MS), a demyelinating disease of the central nervous system. While two studies demonstrated a reduction of ViSTa-derived myelin signal in both lesions and normal appearing white matter (NAWM) (Fig. 7.6) [38,61], the overwhelming majority of MS T_1 studies have focused on measurement of T_1 relaxation time values. Beyond lesion-focused studies which report increased T_1 values in enhancing and black hole lesions [62,63], there is a fairly extensive literature investigating MS NAWM and normal appearing grey matter (NAGM). For example, Vrenken et al. examined T_1 maps from healthy control normal white matter (NWM) and NAWM in patients with primary progressive MS (PPMS), relapsing remitting MS (RRMS) and secondary progressive MS (SPMS) and found that T_1 values showed the following relationship: NWM T_1 < PPMS NAWM T_1, <RRMS NAWN T_1, <SPMS NAWM T_1 (Fig. 7.7) [64–66]. Similar changes were found in NAGM. This work highlights the message that MS NAWM is different from NWM in controls and the various phenotypes of MS are associated with measurable NAWM differences. This work is supported by Parry et al. who found that NAWM T_1 histogram height was negatively correlated with disease duration in RRMS and SPMS, indicating increased T_1 inhomogeneity with longer disease duration [67]. Manfredfonia et al. reported that in PPMS increased NAWM T_1 values at baseline predicted disability 2 years later, as measured with the MS functional composite score [68]. The increased T_1 in MS NAWM is most likely due to increases in water content, presumably from inflammation or edema.

Longitudinal studies can provide insight into the timescale of T_1 abnormality evolution. Liang et al found no change in RRMS NAWM T_1 over 6 months [69]. Longer studies with 19.5 months to 5 years follow-up time also showed stability of T_1 measures in NAWM [67,70–72]. Since the aforementioned T_1 versus water content relationship is generally valid in MS brain, one may conclude that while the water content of RRMS NAWM is elevated relative to normal brain and differs between subjects, it changes very slowly over time.

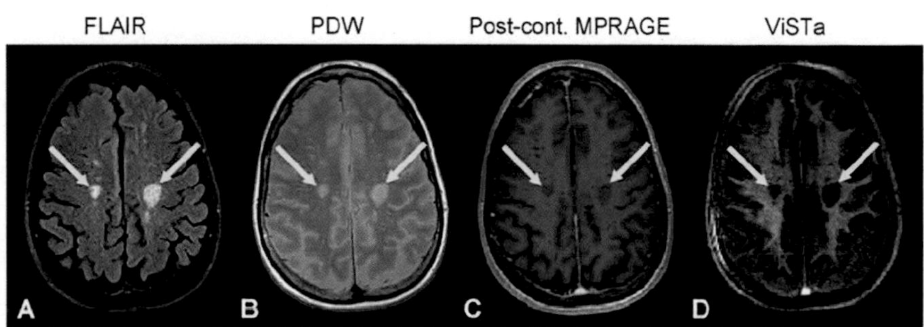

FIG. 7.6

FLAIR (A), PDW (B), postcontrast MPRAGE (C), and single-echo ViSTa (D) images from an MS patient. Chronic lesions (arrows) show significant signal reduction in the ViSTa image.

Oh SH, et al. Direct visualization of short transverse relaxation time component (ViSTa). Neuroimage 2013;83:485–92.

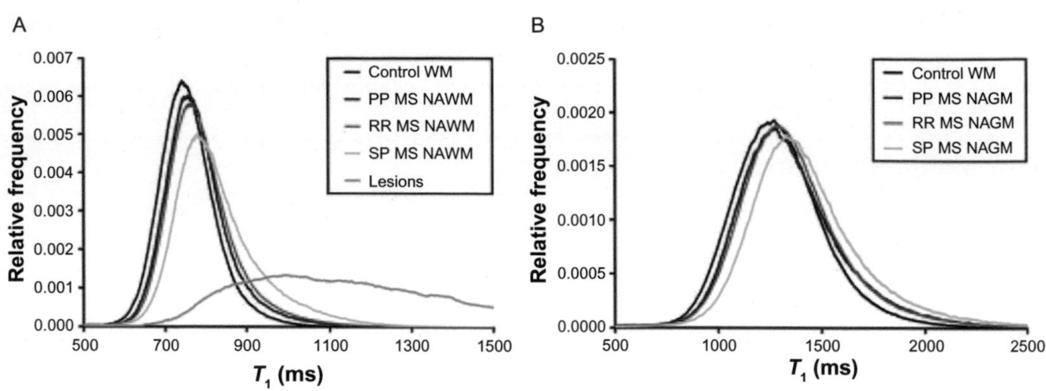

FIG. 7.7

Group mean T_1 histograms for (A) normal-appearing white matter (NAWM) and (B) normal-appearing grey matter (NAGM). Both horizontal and vertical scales differ between the two figures. In (A), the mean T_1 histogram of MS lesions, averaged over all patients, is shown for comparison. This histogram has a peak position around 1000 ms and is much wider than the histograms for normal-appearing WM. In both NAWM and NAGM, there is a shift of T_1 histograms toward higher T_1 values in patients with MS, which is most severe for the group with SPMS.

Vrenken H, et al. Whole-brain T_1 mapping in multiple sclerosis: global changes of normal-appearing gray and white matter. Radiology 2006;240(3):811–20.

7.4.3 Parkinson's disease

Parkinson's disease (PD) is a long-term degenerative disorder of the central nervous system mainly affecting the motor system. Deep grey matter regions are one of the earliest areas to be affected, an observation supported by Baudrexel et al. who found the substantia nigra on the side contralateral to the more severely affected limbs had a shorter T_1 [73]. A 6.5-year longitudinal study found the average decrease in T_1 across widespread regions of cortex was more than three times larger in PD subjects than controls [74]. Given that cortical thinning could not differentiate between PD and controls, T_1 may be a new imaging biomarker to provide information about cortical changes in PD.

7.4.4 Brain cancer and radiation

Tumor subtype differentiation may be possible with T_1, where, for example, MR fingerprinting can identify quantitative T_1 differences between peritumoral regions of low-grade **gliomas** versus glioblastomas [75]. **Glioblastoma** patient management is hampered by a lack of robust techniques for monitoring tumor progression. Longitudinal T_1 mapping has the potential to provide more quantitative feedback on tumor changes, in particular tumor enhancement. Comparing quantitative T_1 with gadolinium enhancement, Hattingen et al. found that regions with $T_1 > 2051$ ms at 3 T predicted contrast-enhancing brain tissue [76]. T_1 mapping can also be used to detect tumor enhancement earlier, and more extensively, than conventional contrast-enhanced T_1-weighted images [77,78].

Another potential application of quantitative T_1 mapping is for differentiation between tumor recurrence and **radiation necrosis**, a common challenge in gamma knife radiosurgery. T_1 mapping was performed 5 min and 60 min after contrast injection in subjects with brain metastases and subsequent biopsy [79]. The study found that the best differential diagnosis parameter was the difference in T_1 values between 5 min and 60 min after contrast injection, opening the possibility for eventual clinical utility of this approach for differentiating tumor from radiation-induced brain changes. A second study also used T_1, in addition to other quantitative MR methods, to differentiate areas of radiation necrosis following stereotactic radiosurgery for an arteriovenous malformation [80].

7.4.5 Other applications

There are several other interesting reports in the literature applying T_1 relaxation in a clinical context. Patients with **sickle cell disease** demonstrated an abnormal trajectory of brain maturation from birth to 4 years; infant patients (<2 years) had grey and white matter T_1 values higher than normal, but these T_1 values declined rapidly and by age 4 patient T_1 values were lower than normal [81]. Treatment monitoring with T_1 mapping in children is also possible. Along with other quantitative MR methods, T_1 mapping was used to monitor brain repair in a Phase 1 study of early-onset severe **Pelizaeus-Merzbacher disease**, treated with human central nervous system stem cell transplantation therapy, where posttreatment reduction in T_1 was observed in focal areas of transplant [82].

Adult applications include work showing that welders exposed to **manganese toxicity** for over a decade had shorter T_1 values than controls in the globus pallidus, substantia nigra, caudate nucleus, and the anterior prefrontal lobe. The T_1 metrics were associated with lower neuropsychological test performance, most strikingly in verbal domains, suggesting that verbal function may be one of the first areas affected by brain manganese deposition [83]. Reduced globus pallidus T_1 is also observed in individuals with repeated **gadobutrol** exposure [84], and through the white and grey matter of women with **anorexia nervosa** [85]. Elevated T_1 is reported in psychiatric diseases including **schizophrenia, affective disorder, psychosis** [86–90], as well as **mild traumatic brain injury, HIV,** and **dementia** [91–93] and ViSTa-derived myelin signal is reduced in **neuromyelitis optica spectrum disorder** and **moderate-to-severe diffuse traumatic brain injury** [94,95], highlighting the diverse potential for use of T_1 to learn about disease processes and monitor therapy.

7.5 T_2 in brain

7.5.1 Measuring multicomponent T_2 in brain

In brain, accurately measuring T_2 is more challenging than accurately measuring T_1 because T_2 decay curves cannot be accurately fitted with a single exponential component. While many investigators continue to carry out T_2 studies in brain from analysis of data collected at two echo times, it is not possible to accurately characterize T_2 relaxation in brain using two-echo datasets. T_2 values extracted from these data not only vary substantially based on the echo times chosen, due to the multicomponent nature of T_2, but also are influenced by B_1^+ inhomogeneity without the possibility for correction which exists when multiple TEs are acquired. In healthy control white matter, spin-spin relaxation exhibits at least two components: one with T_2 of ~10–20 ms assigned to water trapped within the myelin bilayers ("myelin water") and one with T_2 of ~60–80 ms assigned to water in the intra/extra-cellular spaces [96–98]. Human MR systems cannot distinguish intra from extra-cellular water, with the possible exception of the corticospinal tract [99]. It should be noted that in pathological brain, there can be more than two T_2 peaks in the T_2 distribution from white matter [100–102].

The most common approach for in vivo brain T_2 acquisitions is 3D multiple spin echo or multiple spin and gradient echo sequences [103–107], although 2D multislice approaches have also been proposed [108,109]. The range of echo times should span from ~10 ms or less to 320 ms or more for accurate T_2 measurements, preferably with equal echo spacings. Brain T_2 analysis is nontrivial and a number of different approaches exist [110–121]. For extracting exponential components from T_2 decay curves, the most common approach is the regularized nonnegative least squares (NNLS) algorithm [110,111] which has the advantage of not requiring a priori knowledge about the number of tissue components. NNLS provides a T_2 distribution, which is a plot of amplitude versus T_2 value. The usual outputs from a T_2 study are the myelin water fraction (MWF, fractional signal with $T_2 < 40$ ms) and the geometric mean T_2 time (mean T_2 on a log scale 40-200 ms) of the intra/extra-cellular water T_2 peak (Fig. 7.8). It is possible to estimate an average T_2 value from the entire T_2 distribution, but for mapping purposes most researchers present images of the MWF and, perhaps, also images of the geometric mean of the intra/extra-cellular T_2 time. This approach has led to the concept of *myelin water imaging* [111,122,123]. The assignment of the short T_2 component to myelin water is supported by histological validation measurements in both animal models and human tissue (Fig. 7.9) [124–131]. A number of studies have investigated the precision and accuracy of multiecho T_2 relaxation-based MWF estimations [132–135]. Published coefficients of variation for MWF in small ROIs vary from >20% to <10% using data from a single slice method at 1.5 T and ~4% for averages across white matter at 3 T. Inter-MR vendor reproducibility studies are now emerging with promising results [136] and, as for T_1 relaxation studies, the creation of normative T_2 parametric atlases will enable single subject clinical studies [5,137,138].

An alternate approach to myelin water imaging uses multicomponent-driven equilibrium single pulse observation of T_1/T_2 (mcDESPOT) [139]. The mcDESPOT approach is fundamentally different from myelin water imaging techniques derived from T_2 decay curves and, instead, makes use of

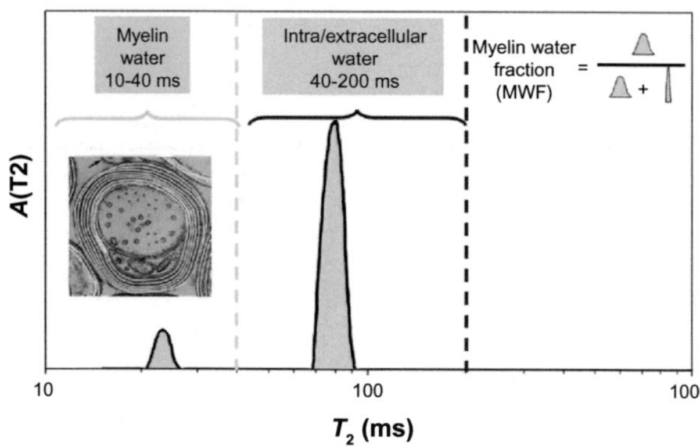

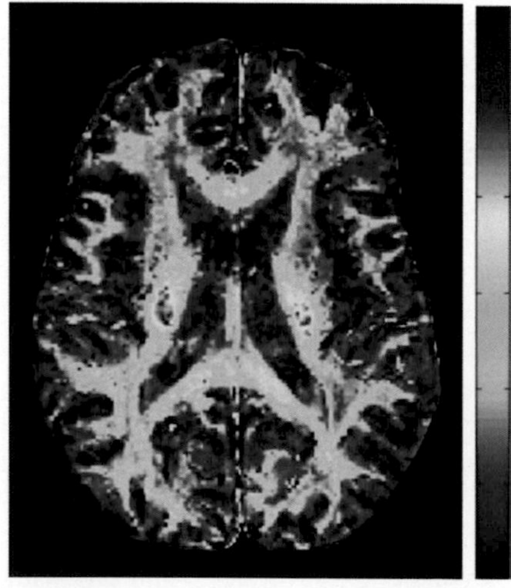

FIG. 7.8

(Left) A T_2 distribution arising from normal human white matter. (Right) A myelin water fraction (MWF) map from normal human brain.

MacKay AL, Laule C. Magnetic resonance of myelin water: an in vivo marker for myelin. Brain Plast 2016;2(1):71–91.

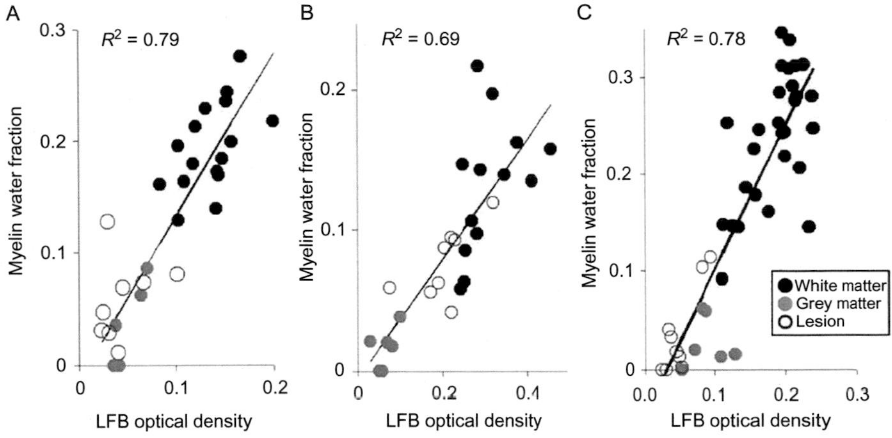

FIG. 7.9

Examples of the quantitative correlation between myelin water fraction (MWF) and Luxol fast blue optical density (LFB) for normal appearing white matter, grey matter and lesion for three different MS cases (A–C). LFB stains phospholipid molecules and is used as a marker for myelin.

Laule C, et al. Myelin water imaging in multiple sclerosis: quantitative correlations with histopathology. Mult Scler 2006;12(6):747–53.

T_1-weighted and steady-state gradient echo acquisitions to estimate T_1 and T_2 times of the tissue components in brain. The most common analysis for mcDESPOT has been the stochastic regional contraction method [140]. mcDESPOT can provide volume fraction of myelin (VFM) values in brain [141] and advantages of this approach include high spatial resolution and relatively short scan time. However, it should be noted that the spatial distributions of MWF and VFM are quite different, and only one third of the variance in one measure can be accounted for in the other [142]. Also, several studies have questioned the overall accuracy of VFM [143–146], so a multimodal complementary approach of using both multiecho and mcDESPOT techniques may be appropriate in some research settings [142].

7.5.2 Physiological influences of T_2 in brain

As with T_1 relaxation, much effort has also been exerted to identify what determines T_2 relaxation in brain. Brain T_2 times decrease with field strength [147,148]. T_2 relaxation is influenced by changes in water content [149–152]; increases in water content due to edema and inflammation will be reflected by a lengthening of the mean T_2 time of the intermediate T_2 component [153] and/or the appearance of longer T_2 components [100–102]. Although swelling of myelin-associated water spaces may occur due to intra-myelinic edema, which would in theory lengthen myelin water T_2 time, with current human scanner technology it is not possible to accurately measure the T_2 time of the myelin water component. The role of metals such as iron and manganese on T_2 is conflicting, with some studies suggesting no impact on T_2 [147,154], while others report a shortening of relaxation time with the presence of iron [49,155]. Changes in pH also influence T_2 relaxation time [156,157], which may be particularly relevant when studying tumors.

Beyond the aforementioned validated link between MWF and histological staining for myelin, several other confounding factors should be considered as possible influencers of the MWF metric.

Given that MWF is the fraction of myelin water relative to total water, increases in total water will lead to reductions in MWF, which could be interpreted as loss of myelin. However, large increases in water are required to account for the degree of MWF reductions reported in the majority of disease studies. For example, for the 16% global reduction in MWF observed in MS brain NAWM to arise from global edema or cellular infiltrates alone, the required increase in water content would lead to the physiologically unrealistic scenario of a 14.5%–18.9% increase in brain volume [158]. Nevertheless, large increases in water will influence MWF, and studies which report small reductions in MWF should interpret their findings with the role of edema/inflammation in mind. It is also possible to determine the myelin water *content*, using internal or external standards and corrections for temperature, as well as T_1 and T_2 relaxation [159,160].

The potential influence of magnetization exchange on MWF cannot be ignored. Studies of rodent spine [161,162] suggest water can move from myelin water to the intra/extra-cellular spaces during the T_2 measurement causing the measured MWF to be artificially low. This phenomenon has also been characterized using a four-pool model of white matter [163]. However, other animal studies involving bovine brain and optic nerve suggest exchange plays only a small role in MWF measurements [164,165]. Water exchange in human brain has not yet been accurately characterized; however, it seems likely that measured MWF are underestimates of the true MWF [166].

MWF cannot distinguish between intact myelin and myelin debris. Damage to myelin from an acute event (i.e., trauma) or a chronic condition (i.e., MS) results in myelin debris. Eventually macrophages will clear debris away from the injury site, but until that occurs, the myelin debris will compartmentalize water that is indistinguishable from water in intact myelin. Using a rat sciatic nerve cut/crush injury model it was shown that myelin water imaging was unable to distinguish between intact myelin, degenerating myelin and myelin debris [124]. In a longitudinal study of rat spinal cord injury via dorsal column transection, MWF *increased* 3 weeks post injury due to reduced extracellular space filled with myelin debris [131]. Finally, a lysolecithin induced injury in mouse spinal cord found that demyelination shown by MWF lagged behind histological evidence of demyelination by 1 week [127]. These observations suggest that myelin debris would impact MWF measurement of recent demyelination in humans in vivo.

7.5.3 Interpreting T_2 in the brain

In summary, multiecho T_2 relaxation-based MWF is a histologically validated measure for myelin. Small changes in MWF should be interpreted with the role of edema or inflammation in mind, while myelin water *content* can provide an absolute measure of myelin water in g/mL. Confounding factors for MWF measurement include the presence of myelin debris and exchange. Lengthening of T_2 can be interpreted as increased water in the intra/extracellular spaces, typically from edema, inflammation, or axonal swelling.

7.6 Clinical applications of T_2 relaxation

7.6.1 Development and aging

Many studies have examined T_2 relaxation over the lifespan. T_2 is longer in early preterm infants compared to late preterm ones [167,168], and a very rapid decrease in T_2 occurs over the first year of life which can be fit to a single exponential [169], double exponential [170], or logarithmic [59] relationship of T_2 versus age. This trend of T_2 reducing with age continues into adolescence and adulthood, with T_2 times varying with development for different brain structures, highlighting the need to correct for age-related effects in some studies [171–173].

Variations with age are also documented using MWF. Deoni et al. measured mcDESPOT-derived MWF in 153 healthy children between 3 and 60months old [174,175]. They found that MWF versus age data was well fitted by a Gompertz function with slow growth at early and late times—this model may be useful for identifying developmental abnormalities, and was later replicated using an MR fingerprinting approach for determining MWF [59]. Recent work suggests that Cesarean delivery influences infant MWF brain development, although the impact may be transient as sustained effects were not observed in older children [176], and prenatal stress is associated with lower corpus callosum MWF in adulthood [177]. EEG markers of sleep activity in young children predicts brain white matter MWF 3.5years later [178], distinct boy/girl developmental patterns are observed [179], and there is evidence for a relationship between MWF and cognition measures in children using both mcDESPOT and multiecho T_2-derived MWF [179,180]. MWF increases are reported during late childhood and adolescence [181], and continue well into adulthood, but the trajectory of adult MWF changes is still an active area of investigation. Arshad et al. examined controls aged 18-84years, and fit multiecho T_2-based MWF versus age curves with a quadratic function (Fig. 7.10) [182], these findings are in line with work by Papadaki et al. who examined a similar age range and also reported a quadratic relationship [183]. Flynn et al reports a linear increase in frontal lobe and global white matter multiecho T_2-based MWF with age [184] for controls aged 19-55years, a finding in contrast to multiecho T_2-based MWF work by Faizy et al. in normal subjects aged 18-79years which reports linear decreases in frontal white matter, genu and splenium MWF across the entire age range sampled [185]. All four studies, and many other multiecho and mcDESPOT investigations, show regional variation in adult white matter MWF, which is thought to correspond to regional differences in myelin content [186].

In the largest known multiecho MWF study to date, Ocklenburg et al. examined 246 healthy controls to probe the effects of genetic variation in PLP1, a gene linked to encoding the predominant protein in myelin. Significant asymmetries in MWF were associated with genetic variation in PLP1, supporting the assumption that this gene affects white matter myelination in the healthy human brain [187]. Adult male-female MWF differences have also been reported [188], MWF correlates with IQ [189], physical activity level [190] and, for several brain regions, MWF depends not only on age, but also upon years of education [184,189]; all of these factors complicate the task of finding an appropriate control group for T_2 studies of disease populations.

7.6.2 Developmental and genetic disorders

Autism is a common developmental disorder that impacts communication and behavior. Several studies report prolonged T_2 in both white and grey matter in individuals with autism [191,192], and mcDESPOT MWF studies show widespread MWF differences compared to controls, with worse social interaction skills being related to reduced MWF [193]. No differences in brain MWF were found in children with **prenatal alcohol exposure** and matched controls, but this study did report correlations between frontal white matter tract MWF and age [194].

Quantitative T_2 has also been used to study a number of myelin-related genetic diseases. **Phenylketonuria** (PKU) is a metabolic disorder whereby people lack the ability to metabolize the amino acid phenylalanine, leading to damage in the brain. Several studies have shown focal and diffuse

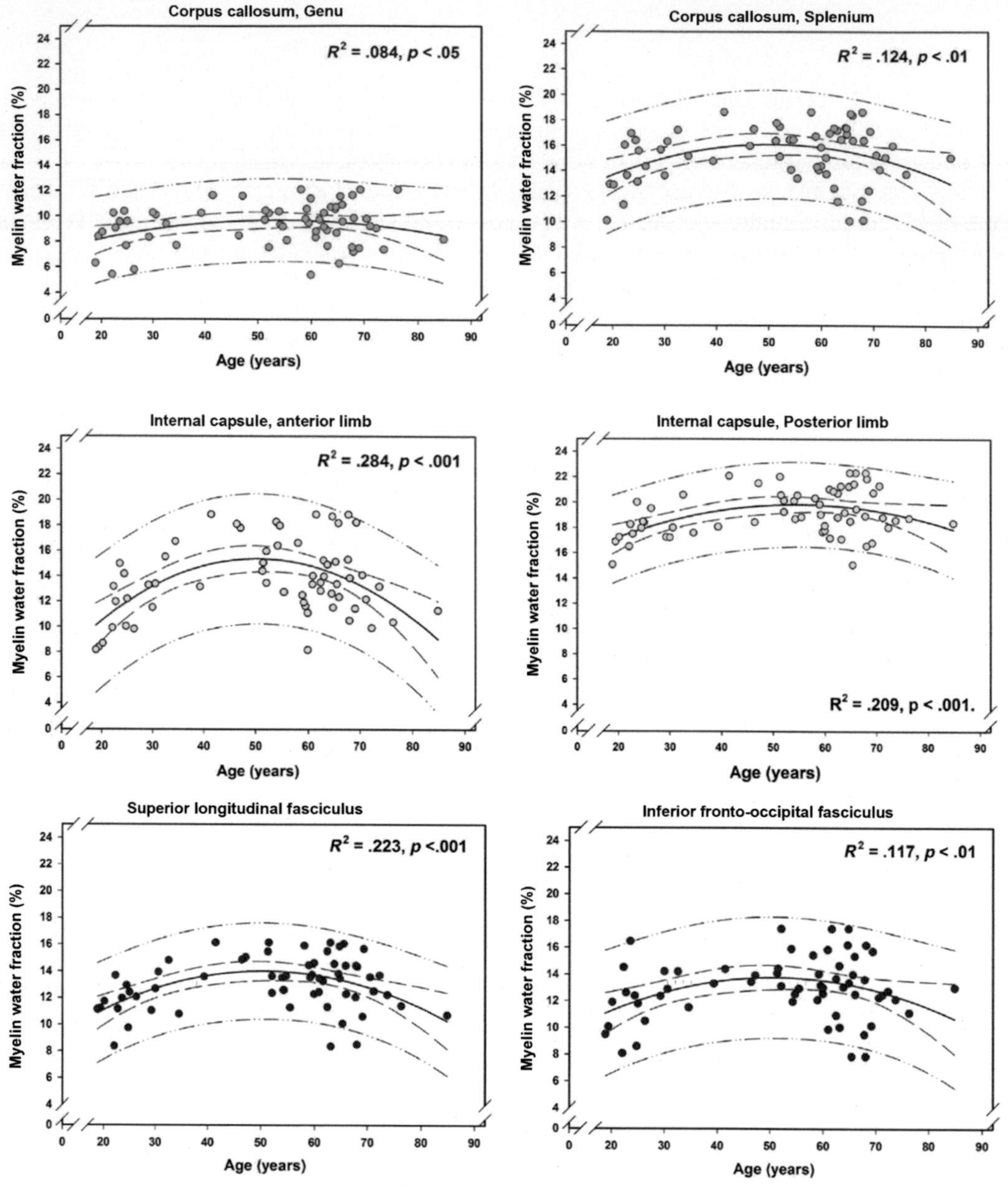

FIG. 7.10

Associations between MWF and age for different ROIs. 95% confidence limits *(dashed line)* and prediction limits *(dot-dot-dash line)* are drawn around the regression line. Plotted on the same scale, the regional differences in myelin content are apparent.

Arshad M, Stanley JA, Raz N. Adult age differences in subcortical myelin content are consistent with protracted myelination and unrelated to diffusion tensor imaging indices. Neuroimage 2016;143:26–39.

reduction of MWF and elevated T_2 in PKU, as well as an additional long T_2 component, possibly attributed to vacuoles in myelin [100,195,196]. Prolonged T_2 is also observed in **Pelizaeus-Merzbacher disease**, and treatment with stem cell transplantation appears to ameliorate this effect [82,197]. **Niemann-Pick disease** is a rare progressive lipid storage disorder characterized by an inability of the body to metabolize cholesterol and other lipids inside of cells. MWF is regionally reduced and may be linked to clinical severity [198]. While animal models show diffusely elevated T_2 throughout the white matter [199], only a small number of human Niemann-Pick patients have been studied and further research is required to draw conclusion about clinical significance. **Krabbe disease** is rare lysosomal storage disorder resulting from a deficiency in galactocerebrosidase, an enzyme required for making myelin. Brain abnormalities include prolonged T_2 [197], and hematopoietic stem cell transplantation is a new promising treatment option [200–202]. A single case report followed an extremely rare adult-onset patient posttransplant for 7.5 years clinically and 4 years with advanced MRI. MWF was stable posttransplant, supporting this approach as effective treatment strategy for stopping progression associated with Krabbe disease [203].

7.6.3 Multiple sclerosis

Quantitative T_2 mapping has been used most frequently to study MS. The literature for myelin water studies is expanding at a rapid rate, and the hallmark myelin loss found in MS makes this disease an ideal application. Perhaps not surprisingly, T_2 is increased and MWF is decreased in MS lesions [103,122,158,204–212]. On average, MWF is reduced by 50%; however, MS lesion myelin loss varies drastically, with some lesions having no myelin, and others having normal, or near normal levels. In patients with clinically isolated syndrome, T_2-based lesion MWF can provide a risk estimate of the conversion to clinically definite MS [213]. MWF is also able to differentiate black holes, contrast enhancing lesions and T_2 lesion subtypes based on myelin content [160,210], and compared to magnetization transfer ratio, fractional anisotropy, and radial diffusivity, MWF was the most sensitive when differentiating T_2 lesions from NAWM [211]. In addition, using discriminant function analysis, Vavasour et al. found that MWF was most important in separating lesions based on their age, clearly delineating lesions <1 year old from lesions >1 year [160]. Diffusely abnormal white matter and NAWM also shows widespread reductions in MWF, as well as global increases in GMT_2 values and water content [103,134,153,158,206,210,214–216], further supporting the preposition that nonlesional white matter in MS patients is not normal. Deep learning approaches are beginning to probe spatial features using NAWM MWF to potentially improve the detection of MS pathology at early stage [217].

Longitudinal T_2 mapping studies can determine the temporal evolution of pathological changes in MS. New lesions demonstrate reductions and subsequent increases in MWF as lesions develop and resolve over the time scale of months [134,208,218]. In RRMS NAWM mean MWF and GMT_2 values do not change significantly over 6 months or 24 months, but over 3-5 years there is an 8% mean drop in MWF [69,71,72] (Fig. 7.11). Based on relaxation measures, one can deduce that for RRMS patients not on therapy, the main pathological change in NAWM is gradual loss of myelin on a 5-year timescale. Longitudinal changes in MWF have also been reported in the cervical spinal cord of PPMS patients, where MWF decreased at a rate of 10% over 2 years [219]. T_2-based myelin mapping techniques, in particular MWF mapping, may be valuable for the assessment of new treatments designed to

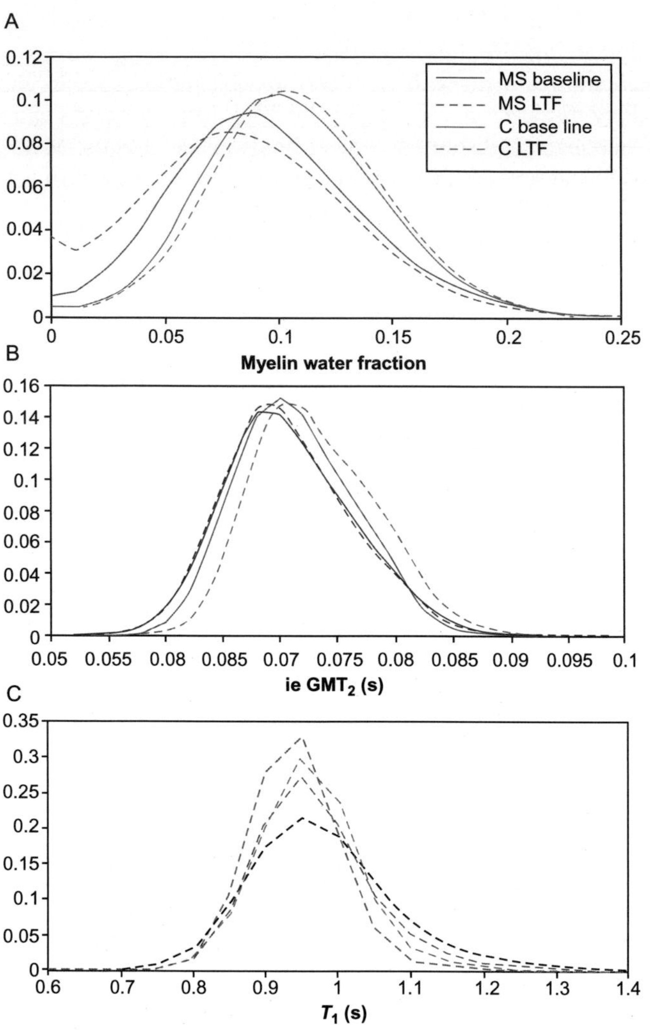

FIG. 7.11

Average normal-appearing white matter (NAWM) and normal white matter (NWM) histograms for MS subjects and controls (C in legend) at baseline and long-term follow-up (LTF) for (A) myelin water fraction, (B) intra/extracellular geometric mean T_2, and (C) T_1.

Vavasour IM, et al. Global loss of myelin water over 5 years in multiple sclerosis normal-appearing white matter. Mult Scler 2018;24(12):1557–68.

promote remyelination. For example, in an exercise intervention study, MWF was associated with change in functional mobility following slope walking training, suggesting that this MRI method may identify potential responders to interventions targeting functional impairments in MS [220]. In another study, MWF increased in healthy young adults who completed repeated visuomotor skill training [221], providing evidence of MWF's ability to measure training associated brain changes.

7.6.4 Alzheimer's disease

One common challenge in Alzheimer's disease (AD) and related dementias is the lack of objective measures for quantifying disease severity. A number of studies have used quantitative T_2 mapping in AD to address this challenge. For example, studies compared mono-exponential T_2 estimations in healthy controls, and subjects with mild cognitive impairment (MCI) and AD and found that in specific white matter regions [222], and the medial temporal lobe [223], T_2 values could be used to distinguish between the three subject groups. MWF can also be used to differentiate subject groups, where, compared to older controls, MWF was lower in MCI and lower still in AD and vascular dementia [224]. Age-related MWF loss in MCI and AD is also associated with memory impairment and symptoms of depression in an anatomically specific manner [225].

7.6.5 Epilepsy

Temporal lobe epilepsy (TLE) is the most common form of focal epilepsy; ~2/3 of surgery-requiring epilepsy cases have TLE. Approximately 15% of these patients do not have detectable hippocampal atrophy; however, hippocampal T_2 mapping provides evidence of damage in the hippocampus [226]. A total of 70% of TLE subjects, and 33% of TLE subjects with normal hippocampal volumes, have increased white matter T_2 values relative to controls, and the white matter T_2 values can provide a correct lateralization of the seizure focus [227]. Voxel-based mapping approaches may be superior to ROI-based T_2 measurement methods as they can provide spatial variation information [228]. A small study used mcDESPOT MWF to examine children with febrile seizures; findings suggest lower MWF may indicate a pathological condition that could lead to nonfebrile epilepsy, but a larger study is needed to confirm these preliminary observations [229].

7.6.6 Cancer

There have been many attempts to characterize brain tumors using T_2. Early work showed that meningiomas have a shorter T_2 than astrocytomas [230] and gliomas [15,231], and that glioblastomas show a single T_2 component if they consist mainly of solid tissue [15] but two T_2 components if they are a solid/necrotic mixture [15,232]. A fairly recent, small case report of three different human brain tumors (glioblastoma, oligodendroglioma, meningioma) using a more comprehensive data collection and analysis scheme showed that each tumor had a distinct T_2 distribution profile (Fig. 7.12) [233]. Quantitative assessment of T_2 relaxation in brain cancer may be useful in evaluating grades of brain tumors and monitoring therapy. Further study with a larger sample size and varying grades of tumors is warranted.

Neurofibromatosis-1 can cause tumors within the nervous system, and often has brain unidentified bright objects (UBOs) associated with it. MWF measurements show no significant abnormalities, suggesting myelin is likely not affected in UBOs, but there is a prolongation of the intra/extracellular water T_2 value [234] which may arise from altered microstructural compartmentalization, and an increase in "extracellular-like" intracellular water, possibly due to intramyelinic edema.

7.6.7 Other diseases

The rapid expansion of quantitative T_2 measurement, in particular myelin water imaging, over the last decade has led to many new clinical applications in neuroinflammatory and neurodegenerative diseases. **Neuromyelitis optica**, often considered similar to MS, is a unique and rare relapsing

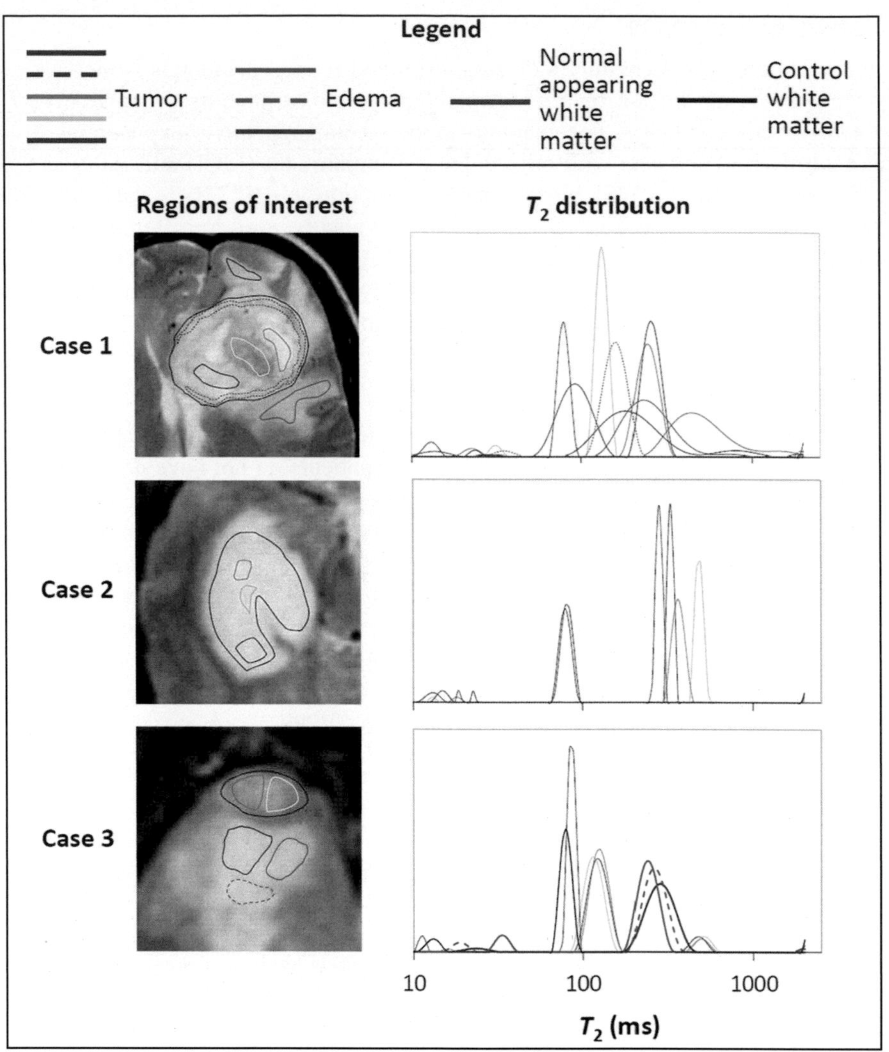

FIG. 7.12

T_2 distributions from various ROIs within the tumor and surrounding periphery for Case 1 (Glioblastoma), Case 2 (Oligodendroglioma), and Case 3 (Meningioma). Each tumor showed unique T_2 profiles. Vertical axis on T_2 distribution plots is intensity in arbitrary units.

Laule C, et al. Characterization of brain tumors with spin-spin relaxation: pilot case study reveals unique T_2 distribution profiles of glioblastoma, oligodendroglioma and meningioma. J Neurol 2017;264(11):2205–14.

autoimmune disorder that causes damage to the optic nerve and spinal cord. MWF measurements show different extents and longitudinal evolution patterns of myelin damage between NMO and MS, and T_2 is diffusely elevated in NAWM from patients with 20+ year disease duration, but normal in patients with a shorter disease duration [209,235–237]. **Progressive solitary sclerosis** is another demyelinating disease with a unifocal etiology that has recently been proposed as a possible MS variant; MWF demonstrates diffuse myelin reductions far beyond the focal lesion and through NAWM [238]. Several studies report elevated T_2 in **amyotrophic lateral sclerosis** (ALS) brain [239–241], a finding also observed in ALS muscle [242]. A single study has examined differences between ALS and **primary lateral sclerosis** (PLS) using mcDESPOT MWF. ALS showed a significant increase in mean T_2 values of intra/extra-cellular water compared to PLS, and PLS showed more active cerebral pathological processes than the rate of clinical deterioration suggested, offering the possibility that this method may have the potential to distinguish these two forms of the disease [241]. Studies of T_2 in **concussion** and **traumatic brain injury** (TBI) are also emerging [243]. For example, varsity hockey players show reduced MWF 2 weeks post mild TBI followed by recovery to preseason values by 2 months postinjury, suggestive of a transient myelin disruption with subsequent remyelination of affected neurons [244,245]. Examining veterans using mcDESPOT-derived MWF found more clusters of low MWF in those veterans with a history of TBI (on average 6 years prior) and an association of lower MWF with worse performance on a speeded attention tasks [246]. Psychiatric disease applications include schizophrenia and first episode psychosis. Increased T_2 relaxation times and reduced MWF provide evidence of **schizophrenia** white matter abnormalities [87,184,247–251]. Unlike healthy controls, people with schizophrenia show no relationship between white matter MWF and age or years of education (Fig. 7.13) [184], but cognitive deficits are correlated with MWF [248,251]. People with **first episodes of psychosis** also show altered patterns of association between MWF and age, and years of education, suggesting there may be subtle disturbances in myelination present early in disease [252].

Quantitative assessment of T_2 shows promise for studying diseases which have a significant clinical impact on older individuals. **Ischemic stroke** shows elevated T_2 and reduced MWF in whole-cerebrum white matter, as well as the ipsilesional and contralesional posterior limb of the internal capsule [253]. Asymmetric myelination in motor-specific brain regions is a predictor of upper-extremity impairment and function in individuals with chronic stroke, suggesting that myelination may be utilized as a more specific marker of the neurobiological changes that predict long term impairment and recovery [254]. T_2 has also been used in combination with other MR-derived physiological measurements to characterize irregular, scattered, or heterogeneous ischemic regions [255]. A potential future application in the acute stroke setting may be using T_2 to estimate stroke onset based on relaxation signal characteristics and extent [256]. In **PD** MWF was linked to distinct clinical subtypes [257] and measures of disease severity, daily levodopa equivalent dose, and disease duration, were related with myelin content in diffuse brain regions [258]. T_2 relaxation of the subthalamic nucleus can also predict which patients are most likely to benefit from deep brain stimulation, but further studies are needed to evaluate clinical prognostic and predictive value [259].

7.7 $T_{1\rho}$ in brain

7.7.1 Measuring $T_{1\rho}$ in brain

Sequences used for probing $T_{1\rho}$ values in the brain have elements of both T_1 and T_2 weighting. After the magnetization is tipped into the transverse plane, a long pulse is applied parallel to the tipped magnetization, which "locks" the magnetization into the transverse plane. During this pulse, the loss

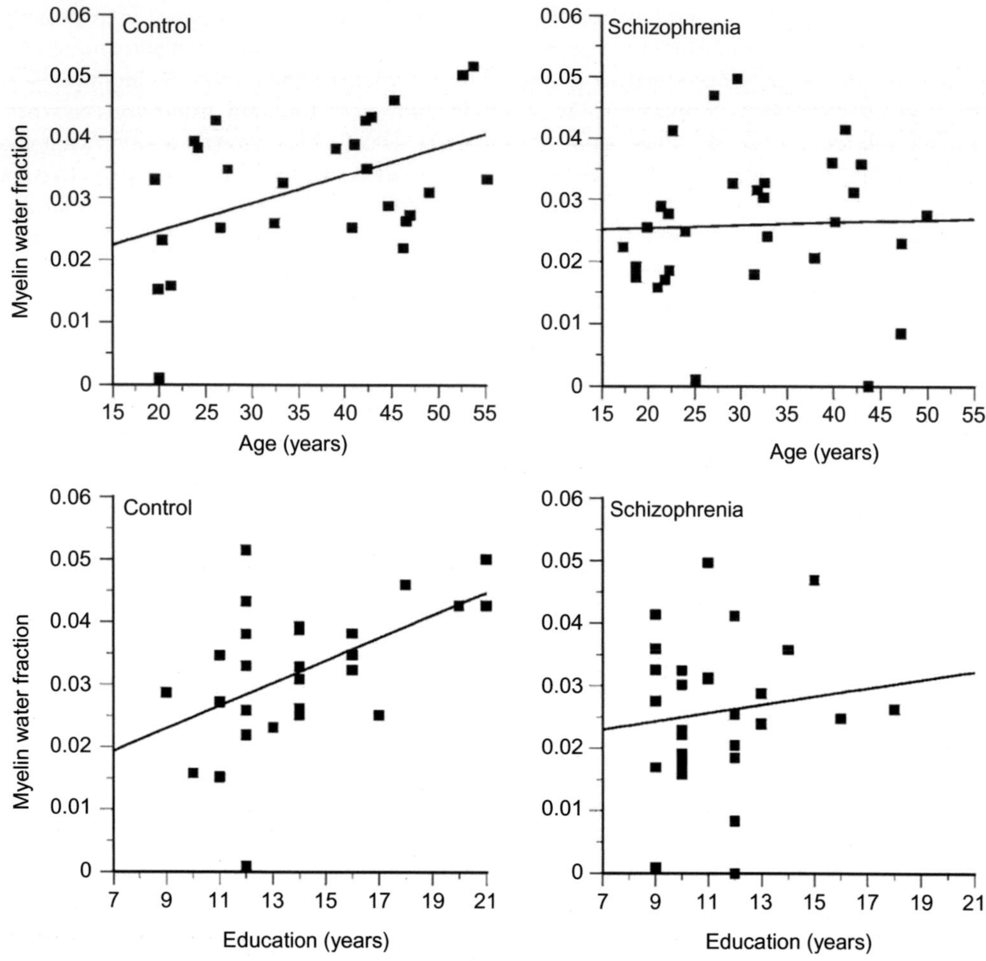

FIG. 7.13

Plots of frontal myelin water fraction in relation to age and to education in healthy comparison subjects (control) and patients with schizophrenia. While statistically significant relations between frontal myelin water fraction and both age ($P = 0.01$) and education ($P = 0.006$) were observed in healthy subjects, no statistically significant relations were seen in people with schizophrenia.

Flynn SW, et al. Abnormalities of myelination in schizophrenia detected in vivo with MRI, and post-mortem with analysis of oligodendrocyte proteins. Mol Psychiatr 2003;8(9):811–20.

of phase coherence due to T_2 relaxation does not occur. The characteristic frequency for $T_{1\rho}$ relaxation is the Larmor frequency corresponding to the B_1 of the long pulse, hence $T_{1\rho}$ is sensitive to slow motions (e.g., slow motions in the lattice such as proteins) [260] and falls between T_2 and T_1. By changing the amplitude of the spin-locking pulse, the $T_{1\rho}$ sensitive frequency can be varied.

7.7.2 Interpreting $T_{1\rho}$ in brain and clinical applications

$T_{1\rho}$ may be useful for studying low-frequency motional processes and chemical exchange, but the mechanisms of $T_{1\rho}$ relaxation time in biological tissues are not yet fully understood, and the literature on $T_{1\rho}$ in human brain is relatively small. $T_{1\rho}$ imaging of the normal human brain demonstrates regional heterogeneity with significant differences between structurally distinct regions, for example, $T_{1\rho}$ is higher in the basal ganglia compared to grey matter and higher in grey matter compared to white matter [261,262]. The reproducibility coefficient-of-variation of $T_{1\rho}$ mapping is $<2\%$ [262] and cross-sectional analysis of controls 18-76 years old shows that $T_{1\rho}$ decreases linearly with age in grey matter [263] (mirroring T_1 and T_2 relaxation findings), but increases in white matter (opposite to T_1 and T_2 literature [60,171]). Several clinical studies show promising results, but findings need confirmation. For example, $T_{1\rho}$ measurements may provide estimates of ischemic time in cerebral **stroke** [264], differentiate between vasogenic edema from intracranial **metastases** and infiltrative edema associated with lower grade **glioma** or **glioblastoma** [265], assess histologic grade and gene mutation status of gliomas [266], as well as provide enhanced **MS** lesion contrast compared with T_2 [267]. The substantia nigra in **PD** has a higher $T_{1\rho}$ value than controls, and shows a significant correlation between asymmetric clinical motor features and asymmetry based on $T_{1\rho}$ [268]. Attempts to differentiate PD with and without dementia from **AD** using $T_{1\rho}$ of the hippocampus have been successful, although no correlation with the mini-mental status exam was observed [269]. $T_{1\rho}$ is elevated in MCI and further still in Alzheimer's, in both global white and grey matter, as well as the hippocampus [270–272]. Further $T_{1\rho}$ brain research is warranted to expand upon the aforementioned interesting studies.

7.8 T_2^* in brain

7.8.1 Measuring T_2^* in brain

The measurement of T_2^* in brain is relatively straight forward and not different from T_2^* measurements elsewhere in the body. The most efficient approach is a multiecho gradient echo sequence [273]. However, the analysis of T_2^* can be more complex due to the concomitant influences of B_0 inhomogeneity, T_2 (exponential components from myelin water and intra/extra-cellular water) and magnetic susceptibility (orientation-dependent frequency shifts) [274,275]. Magnetic field inhomogeneities also complicate T_2^* analysis, but these can be corrected via postprocessing [276] and by z-shimming [277].

7.8.2 Interpreting T_2^* in brain and clinical applications

Much of the early work on T_2^* mapping in the brain has focused on using T_2^* as an iron marker. Langkammer et al. reported a strong correlation between $1/T_2^*$ and iron concentration in postmortem brain [278]. A rodent study showed that T_2^* changes after **intracranial hemorrhage** are indicative of iron overload [279] and Akhlaghpoor et al. used T_2^* measurements for evaluation of brain iron overload in **β thalassemia major** patients [280]. Khalil et al. found that T_2^* values in the basal ganglia was correlated with age and **MS** disease duration, suggesting that iron accumulation in the basal ganglia might be associated with MS morbidity [281].

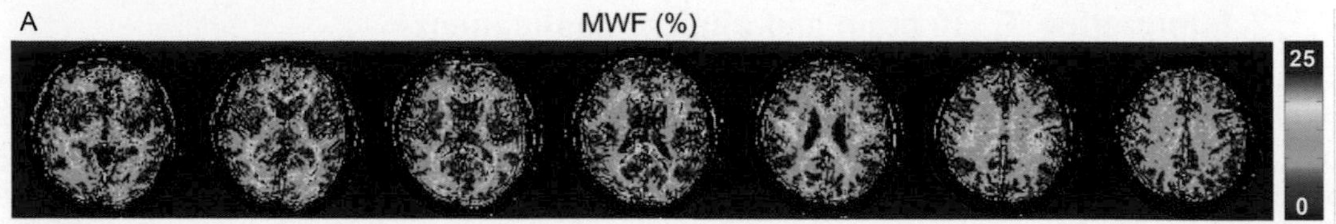

FIG. 7.14

Seven representative MWF maps from a healthy volunteer (three-pool complex model fitted to complex data).

Nam Y, et al. Improved estimation of myelin water fraction using complex model fitting. Neuroimage 2015;116:214–21.

Earlier work on $T_2{}^*$ in the brain also involved fitting $T_2{}^*$ decay curves to exponential components to produce myelin water maps from postmortem [282] and in vivo human brain [283]. Van Gelderen et al. fitted $T_2{}^*$ decay curves from brain with a discrete model of two (at 3 T) and three (at 7 T) exponential components with frequency shifts related to magnetic susceptibility [284]. Alonso-Ortiz et al. subsequently showed that myelin maps at 3 T were more accurate when fitted by a three-component model without frequency shifts [285]. By fitting the three pool model to complex data, Nam et al. showed robust myelin water mapping was possible (Fig. 7.14) [286,287], although $T_2{}^*$ MWF values are slightly larger than those from T_2 measurements, possibly due to exchange effects [288]. One application of this model demonstrates $T_2{}^*$ MWF microstructural parameter variations across the corpus callosum [289]. While $T_2{}^*$-based myelin water mapping is progressing and new sequence and postprocessing methods are emerging [290], there have been few clinical studies to date. As research efforts continue in $T_2{}^*$ mapping [291–293], further clinical utility of this approach may emerge.

7.9 Challenges with clinical application of relaxation

Beyond the technical challenges of multisite/multivendor implementation and standardization, as well as clinically feasible data analysis pipelines, the application of relaxation mapping methods to clinical problems may present challenges in the interpretation of the data. When a disease state involves more than one type of pathology, for example, demyelination and inflammation, then a single parameter like T_1 or T_2 is incapable of providing accurate data about both pathologies. For example, changes in blood O_2 concentration can affect measured T_1 times in the brain. Hyperoxia up to a partial pressure of 500 mm/Hg has a negligible effect on the T_1 values of white or grey matter in normal brain, but does result in decreased T_1 for CSF [294]. Thus, care should be taken to distinguish actual parenchymal tissue T_1 changes from those which may be related to partial volume effect with CSF or regions with increased fluid content such as edema. Factors such as water content, metals, and pH will all contribute to relaxation measures and need to be kept in mind when interpreting clinical findings.

7.10 Concluding remarks

Modern MR scanners are capable of accurate and precise relaxation time measurements in brain. However, a single relaxation time provides limited pathological information and there are currently few circumstances where knowing relaxation times can provide more clinical value to the neuroradiologist than what is obtained with largely qualitative relaxation time-weighted images (the commonly acquired T_1-weighted or T_2-weighted images). For example, T_1 is influenced by many different factors, including age, water content, iron, etc. In the case of T_2, the existence of multiple components decreases the accuracy of measuring the T_2 values of individual components. Potentially, the most promising metric available from relaxation measurements is the myelin water fraction, which is purported to be specific for myelin (albeit with some limitations with regard to myelin debris and exchange effects) and should be reliable, even in the presence of other pathologies such as edema, inflammation and axonal loss. More research is required to refine the measurement technique and to explore clinical applications that require accurate measurements of myelin. The creation of normative atlases for quantitative relaxation metrics like myelin water fraction will enable clinical use on an individual patient level.

Acknowledgments

Research by ALM is supported by a Program Discovery Grant from the Natural Sciences and Engineering and Research Council (NSERC) of Canada. CL is supported by operating grants from the Multiple Sclerosis Society of Canada and by a Program Discovery Grant from NSERC. The authors would like to acknowledge the collaborations of our colleagues at the University of British Columbia (UBC) MRI Research Centre, the UBC MS/MRI Research Group, the UBC Hospital MS Clinic and the International Collaboration on Repair Discoveries (ICORD).

References

[1] Weiskopf N, et al. Quantitative multi-parameter mapping of R1, PD(*), MT, and R2(*) at 3T: a multi-center validation. Front Neurosci 2013;7:95.

[2] Marques JP, et al. MP2RAGE, a self bias-field corrected sequence for improved segmentation and T1-mapping at high field. Neuroimage 2010;49(2):1271–81.

[3] Vavasour IM, et al. Multicenter measurements of T1 relaxation and diffusion tensor imaging: intra and intersite reproducibility. J Neuroimaging 2019;29(1):42–51.

[4] Schwartz DL, et al. Multisite reliability and repeatability of an advanced brain MRI protocol. J Magn Reson Imaging 2019.

[5] Bonnier G, et al. Personalized pathology maps to quantify diffuse and focal brain damage. Neuroimage Clin 2019;21:101607.

[6] Deoni SC. High-resolution T1 mapping of the brain at 3T with driven equilibrium single pulse observation of T1 with high-speed incorporation of RF field inhomogeneities (DESPOT1-HIFI). J Magn Reson Imaging 2007;26(4):1106–11.

[7] Castro MA, et al. Template-based B(1) inhomogeneity correction in 3T MRI brain studies. IEEE Trans Med Imaging 2010;29(11):1927–41.

[8] Weiskopf N, et al. Unified segmentation based correction of R1 brain maps for RF transmit field inhomogeneities (UNICORT). Neuroimage 2011;54(3):2116–24.

[9] Stikov N, et al. On the accuracy of T1 mapping: searching for common ground. Magn Reson Med 2015;73(2):514–22.

[10] Rooney WD, et al. Magnetic field and tissue dependencies of human brain longitudinal $1H_2O$ relaxation in vivo. Magn Reson Med 2007;57(2):308–18.

[11] Kamman RL, et al. Nuclear magnetic resonance relaxation in experimental brain edema: effects of water concentration, protein concentration, and temperature. Magn Reson Med 1988;6(3):265–74.

[12] Kamman RL, et al. Changes of relaxation times T1 and T2 in rat tissues after biopsy and fixation. Magn Reson Imaging 1985;3(3):245–50.

[13] MacDonald HL, et al. Correlation of human NMR T1 values measured in vivo and brain water content. Br J Radiol 1986;59(700):355–7.

[14] Naruse S, et al. Proton nuclear magnetic resonance studies on brain edema. J Neurosurg 1982;56(6):747–52.

[15] Naruse S, et al. Signifcance of proton relaxation time measurement in brain oedema, cerebral infarction and brain tumors. Magn Reson Med 1986;4:293–304.

[16] Fatouros PP, Marmarou A. Use of magnetic resonance imaging for in vivo measurements of water content in human brain: method and normal values. J Neurosurg 1999;90(1):109–15.

[17] Fatouros PP, et al. In vivo brain water determination by T1 measurements: effect of total water content, hydration fraction, and field strength. Magn Reson Med 1991;17(2):402–13.

[18] Fatouros PP, Marmarou A. Experimental studies for use of magnetic resonance in brain water measurements. Acta Neurochir Suppl 1990;51:37–8.

[19] Gelman N, et al. Interregional variation of longitudinal relaxation rates in human brain at 3.0 T: relation to estimated iron and water contents. Magn Reson Med 2001;45(1):71–9.

[20] Yeatman JD, Wandell BA, Mezer AA. Lifespan maturation and degeneration of human brain white matter. Nat Commun 2014;5:4932.

[21] Bell BA, et al. Brain water measured by magnetic resonance imaging. Correlation with direct estimation and changes after mannitol and dexamethasone. Lancet 1987;1(8524):66–9.

[22] Abbas Z, et al. Analysis of proton-density bias corrections based on T1 measurement for robust quantification of water content in the brain at 3 tesla. Magn Reson Med 2014;72(6):1735–45.

[23] Fullerton GD, Potter JL, Dornbluth NC. NMR relaxation of protons in tissues and other macromolecular water solutions. Magn Reson Imaging 1982;1(4):209–26.

[24] Koenig SH, et al. Relaxometry of brain: why white matter appears bright in MRI. Magn Reson Med 1990;14(3):482–95.

[25] Mottershead JP, et al. High field MRI correlates of myelin content and axonal density in multiple sclerosis—a post-mortem study of the spinal cord. J Neurol 2003;250(11):1293–301.

[26] Bock NA, et al. Optimizing T1-weighted imaging of cortical myelin content at 3.0 T. Neuroimage 2013;65:1–12.

[27] Stüber C, et al. Myelin and iron concentration in the human brain: a quantitative study of MRI contrast. Neuroimage 2014;93(Pt 1):95–106.

[28] Leuze C, et al. The separate effects of lipids and proteins on brain MRI contrast revealed through tissue clearing. Neuroimage 2017;156:412–22.

[29] Schyboll F, et al. The impact of fibre orientation on T1-relaxation and apparent tissue water content in white matter. MAGMA 2018;31(4):501–10.

[30] Gochberg DF, Gore JC. Quantitative imaging of magnetization transfer using an inversion recovery sequence. Magn Reson Med 2003;49(3):501–5.

[31] Gochberg DF, Gore JC. Quantitative magnetization transfer imaging via selective inversion recovery with short repetition times. Magn Reson Med 2007;57(2):437–41.

[32] Prantner AM, et al. Magnetization transfer induced biexponential longitudinal relaxation. Magn Reson Med 2008;60(3):555–63.

[33] Labadie C, et al. Myelin water mapping by spatially regularized longitudinal relaxographic imaging at high magnetic fields. Magn Reson Med 2014;71(1):375–87.
[34] Barta R, et al. Modeling T(1) and T(2) relaxation in bovine white matter. J Magn Reson 2015;259:56–67.
[35] Pfister J, et al. Simultaneous T1 and T2 measurements using inversion recovery TrueFISP with principle component-based reconstruction, off-resonance correction, and multicomponent analysis. Magn Reson Med 2019;81(6):3488–502.
[36] Ou X, et al. Quantitative magnetization transfer measured pool-size ratio reflects optic nerve myelin content in ex vivo mice. Magn Reson Med 2009;61(2):364–71.
[37] Xu J, et al. Quantitative magnetization transfer imaging of rodent glioma using selective inversion recovery. NMR Biomed 2014;27(3):253–60.
[38] Oh SH, et al. Direct visualization of short transverse relaxation time component (ViSTa). Neuroimage 2013;83:485–92.
[39] Volz S, et al. Quantitative proton density mapping: correcting the receiver sensitivity bias via pseudo proton densities. Neuroimage 2012;63(1):540–52.
[40] Abbas Z, et al. Quantitative water content mapping at clinically relevant field strengths: a comparative study at 1.5 T and 3 T. Neuroimage 2015;106:404–13.
[41] Meyers SM, Kolind SH, MacKay AL. Simultaneous measurement of total water content and myelin water fraction in brain at 3T using a T2 relaxation based method. Magn Reson Imaging 2017;37:187–94.
[42] Glasser MF, Van Essen DC. Mapping human cortical areas in vivo based on myelin content as revealed by T1- and T2-weighted MRI. J Neurosci 2011;31(32):11597–616.
[43] Glasser MF, et al. Trends and properties of human cerebral cortex: correlations with cortical myelin content. Neuroimage 2014;93(Pt 2):165–75.
[44] Ganzetti M, Wenderoth N, Mantini D. Whole brain myelin mapping using T1- and T2-weighted MR imaging data. Front Hum Neurosci 2014;8:671.
[45] Lutti A, et al. Using high-resolution quantitative mapping of R1 as an index of cortical myelination. Neuroimage 2014;93(Pt 2):176–88.
[46] Shafee R, Buckner RL, Fischl B. Gray matter myelination of 1555 human brains using partial volume corrected MRI images. Neuroimage 2015;105:473–85.
[47] Lebenberg J, et al. Mapping the asynchrony of cortical maturation in the infant brain: a MRI multi-parametric clustering approach. Neuroimage 2019;185:641–53.
[48] Sereno MI, et al. Mapping the human cortical surface by combining quantitative T(1) with retinotopy. Cereb Cortex 2013;23(9):2261–8.
[49] Desmond KL, et al. Differences in iron and manganese concentration may confound the measurement of myelin from R1 and R2 relaxation rates in studies of dysmyelination. NMR Biomed 2016;29(7):985–98.
[50] Arshad M, Stanley JA, Raz N. Test-retest reliability and concurrent validity of in vivo myelin content indices: myelin water fraction and calibrated T1 w/T2 w image ratio. Hum Brain Mapp 2017;38(4):1780–90.
[51] Uddin MN, et al. Can T1 w/T2 w ratio be used as a myelin-specific measure in subcortical structures? Comparisons between FSE-based T1 w/T2 w ratios, GRASE-based T1 w/T2 w ratios and multi-echo GRASE-based myelin water fractions. NMR Biomed 2018;31(3).
[52] Uddin MN, et al. Comparisons between multi-component myelin water fraction, T1w/T2w ratio, and diffusion tensor imaging measures in healthy human brain structures. Sci Rep 2019;9(1):2500.
[53] Dubois J, et al. The early development of brain white matter: a review of imaging studies in fetuses, newborns and infants. Neuroscience 2014;276:48–71.
[54] Saito N, et al. Relaxo-volumetric multispectral quantitative magnetic resonance imaging of the brain over the human lifespan: global and regional aging patterns. Magn Reson Imaging 2009;27(7):895–906.
[55] Cafiero R, et al. The concurrence of cortical surface area expansion and white matter myelination in human brain development. Cereb Cortex 2019;29(2):827–37.

[56] Schneider J, et al. Evolution of T1 relaxation, ADC, and fractional anisotropy during early brain maturation: a serial imaging study on preterm infants. AJNR Am J Neuroradiol 2016;37(1):155–62.
[57] Eminian S, et al. Rapid high resolution T1 mapping as a marker of brain development: normative ranges in key regions of interest. PLoS One 2018;13(6):e0198250.
[58] Steen RG, et al. Age-related changes in the pediatric brain: quantitative MR evidence of maturational changes during adolescence. AJNR Am J Neuroradiol 1997;18(5):819–28.
[59] Chen Y, et al. MR fingerprinting enables quantitative measures of brain tissue relaxation times and myelin water fraction in the first five years of life. Neuroimage 2019;186:782–93.
[60] Gracien RM, et al. Evaluation of brain ageing: a quantitative longitudinal MRI study over 7 years. Eur Radiol 2017;27(4):1568–76.
[61] Choi JY, et al. Evaluation of Normal-appearing white matter in multiple sclerosis using direct visualization of short transverse relaxation time component (ViSTa) myelin water imaging and gradient Echo and Spin Echo (GRASE) myelin water imaging. J Magn Reson Imaging 2019;49(4):1091–8.
[62] Parry A, et al. White matter and lesion T1 relaxation times increase in parallel and correlate with disability in multiple sclerosis. J Neurol 2002;249(9):1279–86.
[63] Thaler C, et al. T1 recovery is predominantly found in black holes and is associated with clinical improvement in patients with multiple sclerosis. AJNR Am J Neuroradiol 2017;38(2):264–9.
[64] Vrenken H, et al. Normal-appearing white matter changes vary with distance to lesions in multiple sclerosis. AJNR Am J Neuroradiol 2006;27(9):2005–11.
[65] Vrenken H, et al. Whole-brain T1 mapping in multiple sclerosis: global changes of normal-appearing gray and white matter. Radiology 2006;240(3):811–20.
[66] Vrenken H, et al. Voxel-based analysis of quantitative T1 maps demonstrates that multiple sclerosis acts throughout the normal-appearing white matter. AJNR Am J Neuroradiol 2006;27(4):868–74.
[67] Parry A, et al. MRI brain T1 relaxation time changes in MS patients increase over time in both the white matter and the cortex. J Neuroimaging 2003;13(3):234–9.
[68] Manfredonia F, et al. Normal-appearing brain T1 relaxation time predicts disability in early primary progressive multiple sclerosis. Arch Neurol 2007;64(3):411–5.
[69] Liang AL, et al. Short-term stability of T1 and T2 relaxation measures in multiple sclerosis normal appearing white matter. J Neurol 2012;259(6):1151–8.
[70] Davies GR, et al. Normal-appearing grey and white matter T1 abnormality in early relapsing-remitting multiple sclerosis: a longitudinal study. Mult Scler 2007;13(2):169–77.
[71] Vavasour IM, et al. Global loss of myelin water over 5 years in multiple sclerosis normal-appearing white matter. Mult Scler 2018;24(12):1557–68.
[72] Vavasour IM, et al. A 24-month advanced magnetic resonance imaging study of multiple sclerosis patients treated with alemtuzumab. Mult Scler 2019;25(6):811–8.
[73] Baudrexel S, et al. Quantitative mapping of T1 and T2* discloses nigral and brainstem pathology in early Parkinson's disease. Neuroimage 2010;51(2):512–20.
[74] Nurnberger L, et al. Longitudinal changes of cortical microstructure in Parkinson's disease assessed with T1 relaxometry. Neuroimage Clin 2017;13:405–14.
[75] Badve C, et al. MR fingerprinting of adult brain Tumors: initial experience. AJNR Am J Neuroradiol 2017;38(3):492–9.
[76] Hattingen E, et al. Value of quantitative magnetic resonance imaging T1-relaxometry in predicting contrast-enhancement in glioblastoma patients. Oncotarget 2017;8(32):53542–51.
[77] Lescher S, et al. Quantitative T1 and T2 mapping in recurrent glioblastomas under bevacizumab: earlier detection of tumor progression compared to conventional MRI. Neuroradiology 2015;57(1):11–20.
[78] Muller A, et al. Quantitative T1-mapping detects cloudy-enhancing tumor compartments predicting outcome of patients with glioblastoma. Cancer Med 2017;6(1):89–99.

[79] Wang B, et al. Postcontrast T1 mapping for differential diagnosis of recurrence and radionecrosis after gamma knife radiosurgery for brain metastasis. AJNR Am J Neuroradiol 2018;39(6):1025–31.

[80] Wiggermann V, et al. Longitudinal advanced MRI case report of white matter radiation necrosis. Ann Clin Transl Neurol 2019;6(2):379–85.

[81] Steen RG, et al. Brain T1 in young children with sickle cell disease: evidence of early abnormalities in brain development. Magn Reson Imaging 2004;22(3):299–306.

[82] Gupta N, et al. Neural stem cell engraftment and myelination in the human brain. Sci Transl Med 2012;4(155):[155ra137].

[83] Bowler RM, et al. Association of MRI T1 relaxation time with neuropsychological test performance in manganese-exposed welders. Neurotoxicology 2018;64:19–29.

[84] Saake M, et al. MRI brain signal intensity and relaxation times in individuals with prior exposure to Gadobutrol. Radiology 2019;290(3):659–68.

[85] Boto J, et al. Cerebral Gray and white matter involvement in anorexia nervosa evaluated by T1, T2, and T2* mapping. J Neuroimaging 2019;29(5):548–604.

[86] Besson JA, et al. Nuclear magnetic resonance brain imaging in chronic schizophrenia. Br J Psychiatry 1987;150:161–3.

[87] Andreasen NC, et al. T1 and T2 relaxation times in schizophrenia as measured with magnetic resonance imaging. Schizophr Res 1991;5(3):223–32.

[88] Spaniel F, et al. Magnetic resonance relaxometry in monozygotic twins discordant and concordant for schizophrenia. Eur Psychiatry 2005;20(1):41–4.

[89] Dolan RJ, et al. Altered magnetic resonance white-matter T1 values in patients with affective disorder. Br J Psychiatry 1990;157:107–10.

[90] Drakesmith M, et al. Volumetric, relaxometric and diffusometric correlates of psychotic experiences in a non-clinical sample of young adults. Neuroimage Clin 2016;12:550–8.

[91] Aribisala BS, et al. A histogram-based similarity measure for quantitative magnetic resonance imaging: application in acute mild traumatic brain injury. J Comput Assist Tomogr 2014;38(6):915–23.

[92] Wilkinson ID, et al. Cerebral magnetic resonance relaxometry in HIV infection. Magn Reson Imaging 1996;14(4):365–72.

[93] Besson JA, et al. Magnetic resonance imaging in Alzheimer's disease, multi-infarct dementia, alcoholic dementia and Korsakoff's psychosis. Acta Psychiatr Scand 1989;80(5):451–8.

[94] Jeong IH, et al. Normal-appearing white matter demyelination in neuromyelitis optica spectrum disorder. Eur J Neurol 2017;24(4):652–8.

[95] Choi JY, et al. Myelin water imaging of moderate to severe diffuse traumatic brain injury. Neuroimage Clin 2019;22:101785.

[96] Menon RS, Allen PS. Application of continuous relaxation time distributions to the fitting of data from model systems and excised tissue. Magn Reson Med 1991;20(2):214–27.

[97] Menon RS, Rusinko MS, Allen PS. Proton relaxation studies of water compartmentalization in a model neurological system. Magn Reson Med 1992;28(2):264–74.

[98] Stewart WA, et al. Spin-spin relaxation in experimental allergic encephalomyelitis. Analysis of CPMG data using a non-linear least squares method and linear inverse theory. Magn Reson Med 1993;29(6): 767–75.

[99] Russell-Schulz B, et al. What causes the hyperintense T2-weighting and increased short T2 signal in the corticospinal tract? Magn Reson Imaging 2013;31(3):329–35.

[100] Sirrs SM, et al. Normal appearing white matter in subjects with phenylketonuria: water content, myelin water fraction, and metabolite concentrations. Radiology 2007;242(1):236–43.

[101] Laule C, et al. MR evidence of long T(2) water in pathological white matter. J Magn Reson Imaging 2007;26(4):1117–21.

[102] Laule C, et al. Long T2 water in multiple sclerosis: what else can we learn from multi-echo T2 relaxation? J Neurol 2007;254(11):1579–87.
[103] Oh J, et al. Multislice brain myelin water fractions at 3T in multiple sclerosis. J Neuroimaging 2007;17(2):156–63.
[104] Oh J, et al. Measurement of in vivo multi-component T2 relaxation times for brain tissue using multi-slice T2 prep at 1.5 and 3 T. Magn Reson Imaging 2006;24(1):33–43. [Epub 2005 Dec 19].
[105] Nguyen TD, et al. T(2) prep three-dimensional spiral imaging with efficient whole brain coverage for myelin water quantification at 1.5 tesla. Magn Reson Med 2012;67(3):614–21.
[106] Nguyen TD, et al. Feasibility and reproducibility of whole brain myelin water mapping in 4 minutes using fast acquisition with spiral trajectory and adiabatic T2prep (FAST-T2) at 3T. Magn Reson Med 2015;76(2):456–65.
[107] Prasloski T, et al. Rapid whole cerebrum myelin water imaging using a 3D GRASE sequence. Neuroimage 2012;63(1):533–9.
[108] Drenthen GS, et al. Applicability and reproducibility of 2D multi-slice GRASE myelin water fraction with varying acquisition acceleration. Neuroimage 2019;195:333–9.
[109] Akhondi-Asl A, et al. Fast myelin water fraction estimation using 2D multislice CPMG. Magn Reson Med 2016;76(4):1301–13.
[110] Whittall KP, MacKay AL. Quantitative interpretation of NMR relaxation data. J Magn Reson 1989;84:134–52.
[111] Whittall KP, et al. In vivo measurement of T2 distributions and water contents in normal human brain. Magn Reson Med 1997;37(1):34–43.
[112] Stanisz GJ, Henkelman RM. Diffusional anisotropy of T2 components in bovine optic nerve. Magn Reson Med 1998;40(3):405–10.
[113] Raj A, et al. Multi-compartment T2 relaxometry using a spatially constrained multi-Gaussian model. PLoS One 2014;9(6):e98391.
[114] Kumar D, et al. Bayesian algorithm using spatial priors for multiexponential T(2) relaxometry from multi-echo spin echo MRI. Magn Reson Med 2012;68(5):1536–43.
[115] Shen X, et al. Robust myelin quantitative imaging from multi-echo T2 MRI using edge preserving spatial priors. Med Image Comput Comput Assist Interv 2013;16(Pt 1):622–30.
[116] Akhondi-Asl A, et al. T(2)-relaxometry for myelin water fraction extraction using wald distribution and extended phase graph. Med Image Comput Comput Assist Interv 2014;17(Pt 3):145–52.
[117] Guo J, Ji Q, Reddick WE. Multi-slice myelin water imaging for practical clinical applications at 3.0 T. Magn Reson Med 2013;70(3):813–22.
[118] Zimmermann M, et al. Multi-exponential relaxometry using l1-regularized iterative NNLS (MERLIN) with application to myelin water fraction imaging: supplementary material. IEEE Trans Med Imaging 2019.
[119] Drenthen GS, et al. A new analysis approach for T2 relaxometry myelin water quantification: orthogonal matching pursuit. Magn Reson Med 2019;81(5):3292–303.
[120] Bouhrara M, et al. Use of the NESMA filter to improve myelin water fraction mapping with brain MRI. J Neuroimaging 2018;28(6):640–9.
[121] Kumar D, et al. Using 3D spatial correlations to improve the noise robustness of multi component analysis of 3D multi echo quantitative T2 relaxometry data. Neuroimage 2018;178:583–601.
[122] MacKay A, et al. In vivo visualization of myelin water in brain by magnetic resonance. Magn Reson Med 1994;31(6):673–7.
[123] Alonso-Ortiz E, Levesque IR, Pike GB. MRI-based myelin water imaging: a technical review. Magn Reson Med 2014.
[124] Webb S, et al. Is multicomponent T2 a good measure of myelin content in peripheral nerve? Magn Reson Med 2003;49(4):638–45.

[125] Moore GRW, et al. A pathology-MRI study of the short-T2 component in formalin-fixed multiple sclerosis brain. Neurology 2000;55(10):1506–10.
[126] Gareau PJ, et al. Magnetization transfer and multicomponent T2 relaxation measurements with histopathologic correlation in an experimental model of MS. J Magn Reson Imaging 2000;11(6):586–95.
[127] McCreary CR, et al. Multiexponential T2 and magnetization transfer MRI of demyelination and remyelination in murine spinal cord. Neuroimage 2009;45(4):1173–82.
[128] Laule C, et al. Myelin water imaging in multiple sclerosis: quantitative correlations with histopathology. Mult Scler 2006;12(6):747–53.
[129] Laule C, et al. Myelin water imaging of multiple sclerosis at 7 T: correlations with histopathology. Neuroimage 2008;40:1575–80.
[130] Laule C, et al. High-resolution myelin water imaging in post-mortem multiple sclerosis spinal cord: a case report. Mult Scler 2016;22(11):1485–9.
[131] Kozlowski P, et al. Characterizing white matter damage in rat spinal cord with quantitative MRI and histology. J Neurotrauma 2008;25(6):653–76.
[132] Vavasour IM, et al. Reproducibility and reliability of MR measurements in white matter: clinical implications. Neuroimage 2006;32(2):637–42.
[133] Meyers SM, et al. Reproducibility of myelin water fraction analysis: a comparison of region of interest and voxel-based analysis methods. Magn Reson Imaging 2009;27(8):1096–103.
[134] Levesque IR, et al. Quantitative magnetization transfer and myelin water imaging of the evolution of acute multiple sclerosis lesions. Magn Reson Med 2010;63(3):633–40.
[135] Meyers SM, et al. Multicenter measurements of myelin water fraction and geometric mean T2: intra- and intersite reproducibility. J Magn Reson Imaging 2013;38(6):1445–53.
[136] Lee LE, et al. Inter-vendor reproducibility of myelin water imaging using a 3D gradient and spin Echo sequence. Front Neurosci 2018;12:854.
[137] Neeb H, Schenk J, Weber B. Multicentre absolute myelin water content mapping: development of a whole brain atlas and application to low-grade multiple sclerosis. Neuroimage Clin 2012;1(1):121–30.
[138] Liu H, et al. Myelin water atlas: a template for myelin distribution in the brain. J Neuroimaging 2019; 29(6):699–706.
[139] Deoni SC, et al. Gleaning multicomponent T1 and T2 information from steady-state imaging data. Magn Reson Med 2008;60(6):1372–87.
[140] Deoni SC, Kolind SH. Investigating the stability of mcDESPOT myelin water fraction values derived using a stochastic region contraction approach. Magn Reson Med 2015;73(1):161–9.
[141] Kolind S, et al. Brain and cord myelin water imaging: a progressive multiple sclerosis biomarker. Neuroimage Clin 2015;9:574–80.
[142] O'Muircheartaigh J, et al. Quantitative neuroimaging measures of myelin in the healthy brain and in multiple sclerosis. Hum Brain Mapp 2019;40(7):2104–16.
[143] Lankford CL, Does MD. On the inherent precision of mcDESPOT. Magn Reson Med 2012.
[144] Zhang J, et al. Comparison of myelin water fraction from multiecho T2 decay curve and steady-state methods. Magn Reson Med 2015;73(1):223–32.
[145] Zhang J, et al. How does magnetization transfer influence mcDESPOT results? Magn Reson Med 2015;74(5):1327–35.
[146] West DJ, et al. Inherent and unpredictable bias in multi-component DESPOT myelin water fraction estimation. Neuroimage 2019;195:78–88.
[147] Hocq A, et al. Effect of magnetic field and iron content on NMR proton relaxation of liver, spleen and brain tissues. Contrast Media Mol Imaging 2015;10(2):144–52.
[148] Brooks RA, et al. Comparison of T2 relaxation in blood, brain, and ferritin. J Magn Reson Imaging 1995;5(4):446–50.

[149] Kato H, et al. Correlations between proton nuclear magnetic resonance imaging and retrospective histochemical images in experimental cerebral infarction. J Cereb Blood Flow Metab 1985;5(2):267–74.
[150] Kamman RL, et al. Nuclear magnetic resonance relaxation in experimental brain edema: effects of water concentration, protein concentration, and temperature. Magn Reson Med 1988;6(3):265–74.
[151] Bederson JB, et al. Nuclear magnetic resonance imaging and spectroscopy in experimental brain edema in a rat model. J Neurosurg 1986;64(5):795–802.
[152] Kiricuta Jr IC, Simplaceanu V. Tissue water content and nuclear magnetic resonance in normal and tumor tissues. Cancer Res 1975;35(5):1164–7.
[153] Whittall KP, et al. Normal-appearing white matter in multiple sclerosis has heterogeneous, diffusely prolonged T(2). Magn Reson Med 2002;47(2):403–8.
[154] Chen JC, et al. T2 values in the human brain: comparison with quantitative assays of iron and ferritin. Radiology 1989;173(2):521–6.
[155] Hardy PA, et al. Correlation of R2 with total iron concentration in the brains of rhesus monkeys. J Magn Reson Imaging 2005;21(2):118–27.
[156] Schilling AM, et al. Intracerebral pH affects the T2 relaxation time of brain tissue. Neuroradiology 2002;44(12):968–72.
[157] Kucharczyk W, et al. Relaxivity and magnetization transfer of white matter lipids at MR imaging: importance of cerebrosides and pH. Radiology 1994;192(2):521–9.
[158] Laule C, et al. Water content and myelin water fraction in multiple sclerosis: a T2 relaxation study. J Neurol 2004;251(3):284–93.
[159] Nguyen TD, et al. Rapid whole brain myelin water content mapping without an external water standard at 1.5T. Magn Reson Imaging 2017;39:82–8.
[160] Vavasour IM, et al. Multi-parametric MR assessment of T(1) black holes in multiple sclerosis: evidence that myelin loss is not greater in hypointense versus isointense T(1) lesions. J Neurol 2007;254(12):1653–9.
[161] Dula AN, et al. Multiexponential T2, magnetization transfer, and quantitative histology in white matter tracts of rat spinal cord. Magn Reson Med 2010;63(4):902–9.
[162] Harkins KD, Dula AN, Does MD. Effect of intercompartmental water exchange on the apparent myelin water fraction in multiexponential T2 measurements of rat spinal cord. Magn Reson Med 2011. https://doi.org/10.1002/mrm.23053.
[163] Levesque IR, Pike GB. Characterizing healthy and diseased white matter using quantitative magnetization transfer and multicomponent T(2) relaxometry: a unified view via a four-pool model. Magn Reson Med 2009;62(6):1487–96.
[164] Stanisz GJ, et al. Characterizing white matter with magnetization transfer and T(2). Magn Reson Med 1999;42(6):1128–36.
[165] Bjarnason T, et al. Characterization of the NMR behaviour of white matter in bovine brain. Magn Reson Med 2005;54:1072–81.
[166] Kalantari S, et al. Insight into in vivo magnetization exchange in human white matter regions. Magn Reson Med 2011.
[167] Knight MJ, et al. Cerebral white matter maturation patterns in preterm infants: an MRI T2 relaxation anisotropy and diffusion tensor imaging study. J Neuroimaging 2018;28(1):86–94.
[168] Melbourne A, et al. Longitudinal development in the preterm thalamus and posterior white matter: MRI correlations between diffusion weighted imaging and T2 relaxometry. Hum Brain Mapp 2016;37(7):2479–92.
[169] Leppert IR, et al. T(2) relaxometry of normal pediatric brain development. J Magn Reson Imaging 2009;29(2):258–67.
[170] Ding XQ, et al. Clinical applications of quantitative T2 determination: a complementary MRI tool for routine diagnosis of suspected myelination disorders. Eur J Paediatr Neurol 2008;12(4):298–308.

[171] Kumar R, et al. Development of T2-relaxation values in regional brain sites during adolescence. Magn Reson Imaging 2011;29(2):185–93.

[172] Bultmann E, et al. Measuring in vivo cerebral maturation using age-related T2 relaxation times at 3T. Brain Dev 2018;40(2):85–93.

[173] Hasan KM, Walimuni IS, Frye RE. Global cerebral and regional multimodal neuroimaging markers of the neurobiology of autism: development and cognition. J Child Neurol 2013;28(7):874–85.

[174] Dean 3rd DC, et al. Modeling healthy male white matter and myelin development: 3 through 60 months of age. Neuroimage 2014;84:742–52.

[175] Deoni SC, et al. Investigating white matter development in infancy and early childhood using myelin water faction and relaxation time mapping. Neuroimage 2012;63(3):1038–53.

[176] Deoni SC, et al. Cesarean delivery impacts infant brain development. AJNR Am J Neuroradiol 2019;40(1):169–77.

[177] Jensen SKG, et al. Associations between prenatal, childhood, and adolescent stress and variations in white-matter properties in young men. Neuroimage 2018;182:389–97.

[178] LeBourgeois MK, et al. A simple sleep EEG marker in childhood predicts brain myelin 3.5 years later. Neuroimage 2019;199:342–50.

[179] Dean 3rd DC, et al. Characterizing longitudinal white matter development during early childhood. Brain Struct Funct 2015;220(4):1921–33.

[180] Whitaker KJ, et al. Quantifying development: investigating highly myelinated voxels in preadolescent corpus callosum. Neuroimage 2008.

[181] Geeraert BL, Lebel RM, Lebel C. A multiparametric analysis of white matter maturation during late childhood and adolescence. Hum Brain Mapp 2019.

[182] Arshad M, Stanley JA, Raz N. Adult age differences in subcortical myelin content are consistent with protracted myelination and unrelated to diffusion tensor imaging indices. Neuroimage 2016;143:26–39.

[183] Papadaki E, et al. Age-related deep white matter changes in myelin and water content: a T2 relaxometry study. J Magn Reson Imaging 2019.

[184] Flynn SW, et al. Abnormalities of myelination in schizophrenia detected in vivo with MRI, and post-mortem with analysis of oligodendrocyte proteins. Mol Psychiatry 2003;8(9):811–20.

[185] Faizy TD, et al. Age-related measurements of the myelin water fraction derived from 3D multi-echo GRASE reflect myelin content of the cerebral white matter. Sci Rep 2018;8(1):14991.

[186] Bjornholm L, et al. Structural properties of the human corpus callosum: multimodal assessment and sex differences. Neuroimage 2017;152:108–18.

[187] Ocklenburg S, et al. Myelin water fraction imaging reveals hemispheric asymmetries in human white matter that are associated with genetic variation in PLP1. Mol Neurobiol 2018.

[188] Liu F, et al. Sex differences in the human corpus callosum microstructure: a combined T2 myelin-water and diffusion tensor magnetic resonance imaging study. Brain Res 2010;1343:37–45.

[189] Lang DJ, et al. 48 echo T2 myelin imaging of white matter in first-episode schizophrenia: evidence for aberrant myelination. Neuroimage Clin 2014;6:408–14.

[190] Bracht T, et al. Myelination of the right parahippocampal cingulum is associated with physical activity in young healthy adults. Brain Struct Funct 2016;221(9):4537–48.

[191] Hendry J, et al. White matter abnormalities in autism detected through transverse relaxation time imaging. Neuroimage 2006;29(4):1049–57.

[192] Petropoulos H, et al. Gray matter abnormalities in autism spectrum disorder revealed by T2 relaxation. Neurology 2006;67(4):632–6.

[193] Deoni SC, et al. White-matter relaxation time and myelin water fraction differences in young adults with autism. Psychol Med 2015;45(4):795–805.

[194] McLachlan K, et al. Myelin water fraction imaging of the brain in children with prenatal alcohol exposure. Alcohol Clin Exp Res 2019.
[195] Vermathen P, et al. Characterization of white matter alterations in phenylketonuria by magnetic resonance relaxometry and diffusion tensor imaging. Magn Reson Med 2007;58(6):1145–56.
[196] Bick U, et al. White matter abnormalities in patients with treated hyperphenylalaninaemia: magnetic resonance relaxometry and proton spectroscopy findings. Eur J Pediatr 1993;152(12):1012–20.
[197] Ono J, et al. Evaluation of myelination by means of the T2 value on magnetic resonance imaging. Brain Dev 1993;15(6):433–8.
[198] Davies-Thompson J, et al. Reduced myelin water in the white matter tracts of patients with Niemann-pick disease type C. AJNR Am J Neuroradiol 2016;37(8):1487–9.
[199] Totenhagen JW, et al. In vivo assessment of neurodegeneration in Niemann-pick type C mice by quantitative T2 mapping and diffusion tensor imaging. J Magn Reson Imaging 2012;35(3):528–36.
[200] Sharp ME, et al. Stem cell transplantation for adult-onset krabbe disease: report of a case. J Inherit Metab Dis Reports 2013;10:57–9.
[201] Langan TJ, et al. Evidence for improved survival in postsymptomatic stem cell-transplanted patients with Krabbe's disease. J Neurosci Res 2016;94(11):1189–94.
[202] Allewelt H, et al. Long-term functional outcomes after hematopoietic stem cell transplant for early infantile Krabbe disease. Biol Blood Marrow Transplant 2018;24(11):2233–8.
[203] Laule C, et al. Hematopoietic stem cell transplantation in late-onset Krabbe disease: no evidence of worsening demyelination and axonal loss 4 years post-allograft. J Neuroimaging 2018;28(3):252–5.
[204] Vavasour IM, et al. A comparison between magnetization transfer ratios and myelin water percentages in normals and multiple sclerosis patients. Magn Reson Med 1998;40(5):763–8.
[205] Tozer DJ, et al. Correlation of apparent myelin measures obtained in multiple sclerosis patients and controls from magnetization transfer and multicompartmental T2 analysis. Magn Reson Med 2005;53(6): 1415–22.
[206] Kolind S, et al. Myelin water imaging reflects clinical variability in multiple sclerosis. Neuroimage 2012;60(1):263–70.
[207] Llufriu S, et al. Magnetic resonance spectroscopy markers of disease progression in multiple sclerosis. JAMA Neurol 2014;71(7):840–7.
[208] Vargas WS, et al. Measuring longitudinal myelin water fraction in new multiple sclerosis lesions. Neuroimage Clin 2015;9:369–75.
[209] Jeong IH, et al. Comparison of myelin water fraction values in periventricular white matter lesions between multiple sclerosis and neuromyelitis optica spectrum disorder. Mult Scler 2016;22(12):1616–20.
[210] Faizy TD, et al. Heterogeneity of multiple sclerosis lesions in multislice myelin water imaging. PLoS One 2016;11(3):e0151496.
[211] Lipp I, et al. Comparing MRI metrics to quantify white matter microstructural damage in multiple sclerosis. Hum Brain Mapp 2019.
[212] Shepherd TM, et al. New rapid, accurate T2 quantification detects pathology in normal-appearing brain regions of relapsing-remitting MS patients. Neuroimage Clin 2017;14:363–70.
[213] Kitzler HH, et al. Multi-component relaxation in clinically isolated syndrome: lesion myelination may predict multiple sclerosis conversion. Neuroimage Clin 2018;20:61–70.
[214] Seewann A, et al. Diffusely abnormal white matter in chronic multiple sclerosis: imaging and histopathologic analysis. Arch Neurol 2009;66(5):601–9.
[215] Laule C, et al. Pathological basis of diffusely abnormal white matter: insights from magnetic resonance imaging and histology. Mult Scler 2011;17(2):144–50.
[216] Baranovicova E, et al. Quantitative evaluation of cerebral white matter in patients with multiple sclerosis using multicomponent T2 mapping. Neurol Res 2016;38(5):389–96.

[217] Yoo Y, et al. Deep learning of joint myelin and T1w MRI features in normal-appearing brain tissue to distinguish between multiple sclerosis patients and healthy controls. Neuroimage Clin 2018;17:169–78.

[218] Vavasour IM, et al. Longitudinal changes in myelin water fraction in two MS patients with active disease. J Neurol Sci 2009;276(1-2):49–53.

[219] Laule C, et al. Two-year study of cervical cord volume and myelin water in primary progressive multiple sclerosis. Mult Scler 2010;16(6):670–7.

[220] King EM, et al. Myelin status is associated with change in functional mobility following slope walking in people with multiple sclerosis. Mult Scler J Exp Transl Clin 2018;4(2), 2055217318773540.

[221] Lakhani B, et al. Motor skill acquisition promotes human brain myelin plasticity. Neural Plast 2016;2016: 7526135.

[222] Knight MJ, et al. Quantitative T2 mapping of white matter: applications for ageing and cognitive decline. Phys Med Biol 2016;61(15):5587–605.

[223] Arfanakis K, et al. Investigating the medial temporal lobe in Alzheimer's disease and mild cognitive impairment, with turboprop diffusion tensor imaging, MRI-volumetry, and T2-relaxometry. Brain Imaging Behav 2007;1:11–21.

[224] Bouhrara M, et al. Evidence of demyelination in mild cognitive impairment and dementia using a direct and specific magnetic resonance imaging measure of myelin content. Alzheimers Dement 2018;14(8): 998–1004.

[225] Kavroulakis E, et al. Myelin content changes in probable Alzheimer's disease and mild cognitive impairment: associations with age and severity of neuropsychiatric impairment. J Magn Reson Imaging 2018;47(5):1359–72.

[226] Bernasconi A, et al. T2 relaxometry can lateralize mesial temporal lobe epilepsy in patients with normal MRI. Neuroimage 2000;12(6):739–46.

[227] Townsend TN, et al. Quantitative analysis of temporal lobe white matter T2 relaxation time in temporal lobe epilepsy. Neuroimage 2004;23(1):318–24.

[228] Pell GS, et al. Voxel-based relaxometry: a new approach for analysis of T2 relaxometry changes in epilepsy. Neuroimage 2004;21(2):707–13.

[229] Moldovan K, et al. Myelin water fraction changes in febrile seizures. Clin Neurol Neurosurg 2018;175: 61–7.

[230] Kjaer L, et al. Tissue characterization of intracranial tumors by MR imaging. In vivo evaluation of T1- and T2-relaxation behavior at 1.5 T. Acta Radiol 1991;32(6):498–504.

[231] Oh J, et al. Quantitative apparent diffusion coefficients and T2 relaxation times in characterizing contrast enhancing brain tumors and regions of peritumoral edema. J Magn Reson Imaging 2005;21(6):701–8.

[232] Martin-Landrove M, et al. A quasi-analytical method for relaxation rate distribution determination of T2-weighted MRI in brain. Conf Proc IEEE Eng Med Biol Soc 2007;2007:1318–21.

[233] Laule C, et al. Characterization of brain tumours with spin-spin relaxation: pilot case study reveals unique T2 distribution profiles of glioblastoma, oligodendroglioma and meningioma. J Neurol 2017;264(11): 2205–14.

[234] Billiet T, et al. Characterizing the microstructural basis of "unidentified bright objects" in neurofibromatosis type 1: a combined in vivo multicomponent T2 relaxation and multi-shell diffusion MRI analysis. Neuroimage Clin 2014;4:649–58.

[235] Manogaran P, et al. Corticospinal tract integrity measured using transcranial magnetic stimulation and magnetic resonance imaging in neuromyelitis optica and multiple sclerosis. Mult Scler 2016;22(1):43–50.

[236] Combes AJE, et al. Cervical cord myelin water imaging shows degenerative changes over one year in multiple sclerosis but not neuromyelitis optica spectrum disorder. Neuroimage Clin 2017;16:17–22.

[237] Aradi M, et al. Quantitative MRI analysis of the brain after twenty-two years of neuromyelitis optica indicates focal tissue damage. Eur Neurol 2013;69(4):221–5.

[238] Lee LE, et al. Advanced imaging findings in progressive solitary sclerosis: a single lesion or a global disease? Mult Scler J Exp Transl Clin 2019;5(1), 2055217318824612.

[239] Keller J, et al. Quantitative brain MR imaging in amyotrophic lateral sclerosis. MAGMA 2011;24(2):67–76.

[240] Ding XQ, et al. Value of quantitative analysis of routine clinical MRI sequences in ALS. Amyotroph Lateral Scler 2011;12(6):406–13.

[241] Kolind S, et al. Myelin imaging in amyotrophic and primary lateral sclerosis. Amyotroph Lateral Scler Frontotemporal Degener 2013;14(7-8):562–73.

[242] Bryan WW, et al. Magnetic resonance imaging of muscle in amyotrophic lateral sclerosis. Neurology 1998;51(1):110–3.

[243] Weber AM, Torres C, Rauscher A. Imaging the role of myelin in concussion. Neuroimaging Clin N Am 2018;28(1):83–90.

[244] Wright AD, et al. Myelin water fraction is transiently reduced after a single mild traumatic brain injury—a prospective cohort study in collegiate hockey players. PLoS One 2016;11(2):e0150215.

[245] Weber AM, et al. Pathological insights from quantitative susceptibility mapping and diffusion tensor imaging in ice hockey players pre and post-concussion. Front Neurol 2018;9:575.

[246] Jurick SM, et al. Pilot investigation of a novel white matter imaging technique in veterans with and without history of mild traumatic brain injury. Brain Inj 2018;32(10):1256–65.

[247] Williamson P, et al. Frontal, temporal, and striatal proton relaxation times in schizophrenic patients and normal comparison subjects. Am J Psychiatry 1992;149(4):549–51.

[248] Vanes LD, et al. White matter changes in treatment refractory schizophrenia: does cognitive control and myelination matter? Neuroimage Clin 2018;18:186–91.

[249] Buckley P, et al. Basal ganglia T2 relaxation times in schizophrenia: a quantitative magnetic resonance imaging study in relation to tardive dyskinesia. Psychiatry Res 1995;61(2):95–102.

[250] Pfefferbaum A, et al. Brain gray and white matter transverse relaxation time in schizophrenia. Psychiatry Res 1999;91(2):93–100.

[251] Vanes LD, et al. Cognitive correlates of abnormal myelination in psychosis. Sci Rep 2019;9(1):5162.

[252] Lang DJ, et al. 48 echo T(2) myelin imaging of white matter in first-episode schizophrenia: evidence for aberrant myelination. Neuroimage Clin 2014;6:408–14.

[253] Borich MR, et al. Evaluation of white matter myelin water fraction in chronic stroke. Neuroimage Clin 2013;2:569–80.

[254] Lakhani B, Hayward KS, Boyd LA. Hemispheric asymmetry in myelin after stroke is related to motor impairment and function. Neuroimage Clin 2017;14:344–53.

[255] Bernarding J, et al. Histogram-based characterization of healthy and ischemic brain tissues using multiparametric MR imaging including apparent diffusion coefficient maps and relaxometry. Magn Reson Med 2000;43(1):52–61.

[256] Rogers HJ, et al. Timing the ischaemic stroke by 1H-MRI: improved accuracy using absolute relaxation times over signal intensities. Neuroreport 2014;25(15):1180–5.

[257] Baumeister TR, et al. White matter myelin profiles linked to clinical subtypes of Parkinson's disease. J Magn Reson Imaging 2018.

[258] Dean 3rd DC, et al. Alterations of myelin content in Parkinson's disease: a cross-sectional neuroimaging study. PLoS One 2016;11(10):e0163774.

[259] Lonnfors-Weitzel T, et al. T2-relaxometry predicts outcome of DBS in idiopathic Parkinson's disease. Neuroimage Clin 2016;12:832–7.

[260] Wang YX, et al. T1rho magnetic resonance: basic physics principles and applications in knee and intervertebral disc imaging. Quant Imaging Med Surg 2015;5(6):858–85.

[261] Ali SO, et al. Evaluation of the sensitivity of R1rho MRI to pH and macromolecular density. Magn Reson Imaging 2019;58:156–61.

[262] Borthakur A, et al. In vivo measurement of T1rho dispersion in the human brain at 1.5 tesla. J Magn Reson Imaging 2004;19(4):403–9.
[263] Watts R, et al. In vivo whole-brain T1-rho mapping across adulthood: normative values and age dependence. J Magn Reson Imaging 2014;40(2):376–82.
[264] Tan Y, et al. Use of T1 relaxation time in rotating frame (T1 rho) and apparent diffusion coefficient to estimate cerebral stroke evolution. J Magn Reson Imaging 2018;48(5):1247–54.
[265] Villanueva-Meyer JE, et al. Differentiation of brain tumor-related edema based on 3D T1rho imaging. Eur J Radiol 2017;91:88–92.
[266] Cao M, et al. Brain T1rho mapping for grading and IDH1 gene mutation detection of gliomas: a preliminary study. J Neurooncol 2019;141(1):245–52.
[267] Gonyea JV, et al. In vivo quantitative whole-brain T1 rho MRI of multiple sclerosis. J Magn Reson Imaging 2015;42(6):1623–30.
[268] Nestrasil I, et al. T1rho and T2rho MRI in the evaluation of Parkinson's disease. J Neurol 2010;257(6):964–8.
[269] Haris M, et al. T1rho (T1rho) MR imaging in Alzheimer's disease and Parkinson's disease with and without dementia. J Neurol 2011;258(3):380–5.
[270] Haris M, et al. T(1rho) MRI in Alzheimer's disease: detection of pathological changes in medial temporal lobe. J Neuroimaging 2011;21(2):e86–90.
[271] Haris M, et al. Early marker for Alzheimer's disease: hippocampus T1rho (T(1rho)) estimation. J Magn Reson Imaging 2009;29(5):1008–12.
[272] Borthakur A, et al. T1rho MRI of Alzheimer's disease. Neuroimage 2008;41(4):1199–205.
[273] Denk C, Rauscher A. Susceptibility weighted imaging with multiple echoes. J Magn Reson Imaging 2010;31(1):185–91.
[274] Wharton S, Bowtell R. Fiber orientation-dependent white matter contrast in gradient echo MRI. Proc Natl Acad Sci U S A 2012;109(45):18559–64.
[275] Sati P, et al. Micro-compartment specific T2* relaxation in the brain. Neuroimage 2013;77:268–78.
[276] Alonso-Ortiz E, et al. Field inhomogeneity correction for gradient echo myelin water fraction imaging. Magn Reson Med 2017;78(1):49–57.
[277] Lee D, et al. Single-scan z-shim method for reducing susceptibility artifacts in gradient echo myelin water imaging. Magn Reson Med 2018;80(3):1101–9.
[278] Langkammer C, et al. Quantitative MR imaging of brain iron: a postmortem validation study. Radiology 2010;257(2):455–62.
[279] Wu G, et al. T2* magnetic resonance imaging sequences reflect brain tissue iron deposition following intracerebral hemorrhage. Transl Stroke Res 2010;1(1):31–4.
[280] Akhlaghpoor S, et al. Quantitative T2* magnetic resonance imaging for evaluation of iron deposition in the brain of beta-thalassemia patients. Clin Neuroradiol 2012;22(3):211–7.
[281] Khalil M, et al. Quantitative assessment of brain iron by R(2)* relaxometry in patients with clinically isolated syndrome and relapsing-remitting multiple sclerosis. Mult Scler 2009;15(9):1048–54.
[282] Du YP, et al. Fast multislice mapping of the myelin water fraction using multicompartment analysis of T2* decay at 3T: a preliminary postmortem study. Magn Reson Med 2007;58(5):865–70.
[283] Hwang D, Kim DH, Du YP. In vivo multi-slice mapping of myelin water content using T2* decay. Neuroimage 2010;52(1):198–204.
[284] van Gelderen P, et al. Nonexponential T(2) decay in white matter. Magn Reson Med 2012;67(1):110–7.
[285] Alonso-Ortiz E, Levesque IR, Pike GB. Impact of magnetic susceptibility anisotropy at 3 T and 7 T on T2*-based myelin water fraction imaging. Neuroimage 2018;182:370–8.
[286] Nam Y, et al. Improved estimation of myelin water fraction using complex model fitting. Neuroimage 2015;116:214–21.

[287] Lee H, Nam Y, Kim DH. Echo time-range effects on gradient-echo based myelin water fraction mapping at 3T. Magn Reson Med 2019;81(4):2799–807.

[288] Alonso-Ortiz E, Levesque IR, Pike GB. Multi-gradient-echo myelin water fraction imaging: comparison to the multi-echo-spin-echo technique. Magn Reson Med 2018;79(3):1439–46.

[289] Thapaliya K, et al. Assessment of microstructural signal compartments across the corpus callosum using multi-echo gradient recalled echo at 7 T. Neuroimage 2018;182:407–16.

[290] Shin HG, et al. Advances in gradient echo myelin water imaging at 3T and 7T. Neuroimage 2019;188:835–44.

[291] Thapaliya K, et al. 7T GRE-MRI signal compartments are sensitive to dysplastic tissue in focal epilepsy. Magn Reson Imaging 2019;61:1–8.

[292] Caan MWA, et al. MP2RAGEME: T1 , T2 (*) , and QSM mapping in one sequence at 7 tesla. Hum Brain Mapp 2019;40(6):1786–98.

[293] Dusek P, et al. The choice of embedding media affects image quality, tissue R2 (*) , and susceptibility behaviors in post-mortem brain MR microscopy at 7.0T. Magn Reson Med 2019;81(4):2688–701.

[294] Bhogal AA, et al. Quantitative T1 mapping under precisely controlled graded hyperoxia at 7T. J Cereb Blood Flow Metab 2017;37(4):1461–9.

CHAPTER

Relaxometry: Applications in Musculoskeletal Systems

Xiaojuan Li[a,b,c] and Carl S. Winalski[a,b,c]

[a]*Department of Biomedical Engineering, Lerner Research Institute, Cleveland, OH, United States* [b]*Department of Diagnostic Radiology, Imaging Institute, Cleveland, OH, United States* [c]*Program of Advanced Musculoskeletal Imaging (PAMI), Cleveland Clinic, Cleveland, OH, United States*

8.1 Introduction

Musculoskeletal (MSK) disorders, including arthritis (osteoarthritis [OA], rheumatoid arthritis, and other types of inflammatory arthritis), lower back pain, osteoporosis, sarcopenia, and sports injuries, constitute major health and economic burdens, as these conditions have a very high prevalence in the United States and worldwide (http://www.boneandjointburden.org) [1]. Without effective treatment, patients with MSK disorders will suffer from impaired quality of life. As such, reliable techniques are needed to provide early diagnoses and to assess early responses after interventions and treatments. Quantitative Magnetic Resonance Imaging (MRI) relaxometry is one such technique that may help to achieve these goals. Important advances have been made over the past two decades in the use of quantitative MRI techniques to noninvasively evaluate MSK tissues and pathologies. In this chapter, we will firstly review the use of MRI relaxometry to assess cartilage in the context of OA, followed by a discussion of the use of MRI relaxometry to assess muscle, menisci, ligaments, tendons, and vertebral discs. The chapter includes a description of the technical basics of MRI relaxometry, results of validation studies, clinical applications and advantages and limitations of these techniques, and potential future uses for MRI relaxometry in MSK applications.

8.2 MRI relaxometry of cartilage

8.2.1 Cartilage biochemistry and degeneration

Articulating ends of diarthrodial joints are covered by hyaline cartilage, which serves as a load-bearing elastic material responsible for resistance to compressive forces, distribution of load, and together with the synovial fluid, frictionless movement of the joint [2]. Fig. 8.1 illustrates the knee joint anatomy as an example. Hyaline articular cartilage consists primarily of a low density of chondrocytes embedded within a large extracellular matrix (ECM). The ECM is composed primarily of water and a mixture of solid components, proteoglycans (PGs, predominantly aggrecans in cartilage), and collagen fibers (mainly type II) (Table 8.1), which interact with each other electrostatically to form

Advances in Magnetic Resonance Technology and Applications. Volume 1. ISSN 2666-9099. https://doi.org/10.1016/B978-0-12-817057-1.00010-X

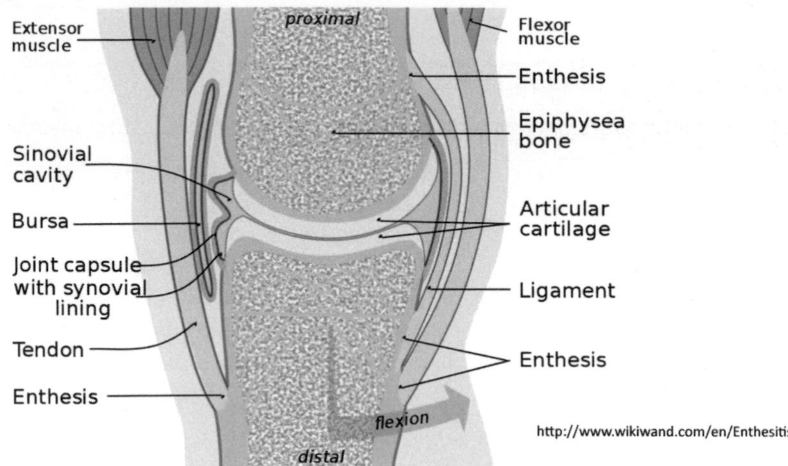

FIG. 8.1

Knee joint anatomy.

Table 8.1 Composition of extracellular matrix of selected musculoskeletal tissues.

	Hyaline Cartilage [3]	Menisci [4]	Tendon [5]	Ligament [5]	Vertebral disk (NP) [6]	Vertebral disk (AF) [6]
Water (%)	65–80	~70	66–75	~75	~80	~65
Collagen (% dry weight) (primary type)	~60 (type II)	60–70 (type I)	65–87 (type I)	79–80 (type I)	25 (type II)	67 (type I)
PG (% dry weight)	25–35 (or 5%–15% wet weight)	2–8	0.2–5	4.6–9.9	50	3–8

a cross-linked matrix. The glycosaminoglycans (GAGs) on aggrecans are highly negatively charged, which provides a stable environment of high fixed-charge density (FCD) and retains water in the tissue via high osmotic swelling pressure. Biomechanically, the collagen network provides tensile stiffness to the tissue and the PG provides compressive stiffness. The distribution and orientation of collagen in cartilage vary depending on the anatomical zone [7] (Fig. 8.2); the collagen fibers are oriented parallel to the articular surface in the superficial zone, arcade-like in the transitional zone, and perpendicular in the radial zone. The water concentration differs slightly between zones, ranging from 82% in the superficial zone to 76% in the radial zone, and the superficial zone has a lower PG concentration than the other zones [3]. Degeneration of cartilage is characterized by progressive degradation of the components of the cartilage ECM, resulting from an imbalance between anabolic and catabolic processes that are predominately controlled by the chondrocytes. Loss of proteoglycan and alteration of collagen structure and contents occur before cartilage thinning and tissue loss, which is the stage that quantitative MRI techniques aim to detect.

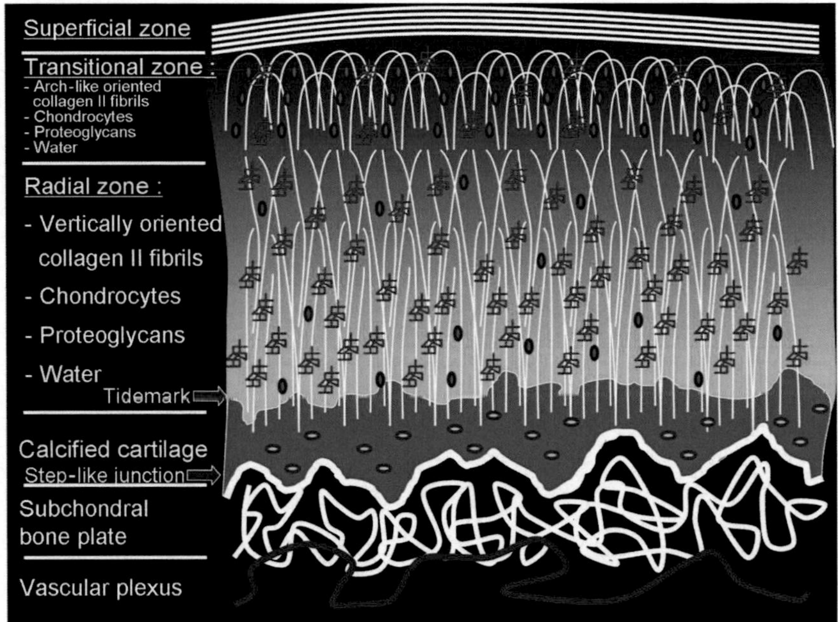

FIG. 8.2

Structure and biochemistry of articular cartilage. Hyaline cartilage consists of a multilayered structure with chondrocytes and a large extracellular matrix, composed primarily of water with electrolytes, collagen II fibrils, and highly negatively charged aggregates of proteoglycans.

(Image with permission from Verstraete KL, Almqvist F, Verdonk P, Vanderschueren G, Huysse W, Verdonk R, et al. Magnetic resonance imaging of cartilage and cartilage repair. Clin Radiol 2004;59(8):674–89. PubMed PMID: 15262541.)

8.2.2 Post-contrast T_1 relaxation time mapping with delayed gadolinium-enhanced MRI of cartilage

Delayed gadolinium-enhanced MRI of cartilage (dGEMRIC) measures cartilage FCD, equivalent to GAG content, by quantifying cartilage T_1 equilibrated with an ionic gadolinium-chelate contrast agent [8]. Non-enhanced cartilage T_1 is insensitive to matrix changes because T_1 reflects much faster relaxation correlation times than the slow, restricted proton motion of cartilage water. However, since T_1 is sensitive to paramagnetic contrast agents and the equilibrium distribution of an anionic contrast agent in cartilage is inversely proportional to the local GAG concentration (FCD), cartilage T_1 measurements (dGEMRIC) can be used to determine the spatial distribution of cartilage FCD. Based on Donnan equilibrium theory and known $Gd(DTPA)^{2-}$ relaxivity, cartilage GAG concentration can be calculated from cartilage T_1 change after Gd(DTPA) injection and tissue equilibration using equations outlined elsewhere [9,10].

T_1 mapping options include 2D and 3D inversion recovery and saturation recovery techniques, and fast methods including variable flip angle, and Look-Locker techniques. Regarding the fast methods, 3D Look-Locker methods have reportedly better reproducibility than variable flip angle methods (root-mean-square coefficients of variation [RMS-CV]=5.8%–8.4% vs. 9.3%–15.2%, respectively) [11].

Ex vivo dGEMRIC cartilage GAG concentration values have been validated by biochemical and histologic measurements [9,12], and experimentally correlated with cartilage biomechanical properties [13,14]. Potential limitations of dGEMRIC include variations in contrast agent relaxivity with cartilage tissue degeneration [15] and incomplete/uneven tissue equilibrium due to slow and/or variable cartilage contrast agent diffusion rates [16]. Besides, Gd-chelate contrast agents hold risks for potential nephrogenic systematic fibrosis in patients with renal insufficiency, and the implications of Gd deposition in the brain and other tissues are still poorly understood [17,18].

For in vivo/clinical dGEMRIC, an ionic contrast agent, most commonly $Gd(DTPA)^{2-}$, is injected intravenously (IV) or intra-articularly and allowed to naturally diffuse into the cartilage. Following intra-articular injection, diffusion occurs solely from the articular surface. The IV technique uses a double or triple clinical dose for optimal differentiation of healthy tissue from GAG-depleted cartilage [19]. After IV injection, contrast crosses the synovium into the fluid [20] within all joints and then diffuses into cartilage, primarily from the articular surface. While the importance of diffusion from subchondral bone vessels is debated, cartilage enhancement occurs more quickly following IV compared to intra-articular injection [16,21]. Immediately following injection, the joint to be imaged is moved through a range of motion to promote uniform, optimal joint fluid enhancement [20,22]. The "equilibration time" required for contrast agent diffusion into cartilage depends on cartilage thickness. For thin hip cartilage, a 15–30 min delay prior to imaging is recommended [22]. Two hour equilibration is suggested to enhance all knee cartilage compared to 45 min for measurement limited to the thinner femoral cartilage [22].

Clinical/in vivo cartilage GAG calculation from dGEMRIC is challenging because several experimental factors are unmeasurable or unknown, including variable blood and joint fluid concentrations that may affect $Gd(DTPA)^{2-}$ equilibration [8,22,23]. Most investigators obtain only post-contrast T_1 measurements (the "dGEMRIC index") since including pre- and post-contrast T_1 measurements require a long imaging session. The dGEMRIC index does not account for spatial variations of non-enhanced cartilage T_1 that have been considered "probably insignificant" for native cartilage [15,22], but may be important following cartilage repair surgery [24] (Fig. 8.3). Unlike ex vivo experiments, in vivo vascular, joint fluid, and cartilage contrast concentrations change over time, and thus no true equilibrium state is reached, and only a "dynamic" cartilage contrast equilibrium is achieved.

Longitudinal studies have demonstrated baseline dGEMRIC indices may predict radiographic knee and hip OA [25,26]. Lower knee dGEMRIC index, indicating cartilage GAG loss, occurs with early cartilage degeneration [27] and radiographically narrowed joint compartments [28]. Decreased dGEMRIC index develops following anterior cruciate ligament injuries [29,30], meniscectomy [23], and in hips with femoroacetabular impingement [31], suggesting potential for OA development. dGEMRIC indices of patients with hip dysplasia, a developmental deformity associated with early OA, correlate with hip pain and severity of dysplasia [32] and were the best preoperative predictor of failed periacetabular osteotomy, better than patient age, radiographic arthritis severity, and dysplasia severity [33]. Following surgical cartilage repair, the dGEMRIC index of the repaired tissue correlated with KOOS, IKDC, or Lysholm clinical outcome scores [34].

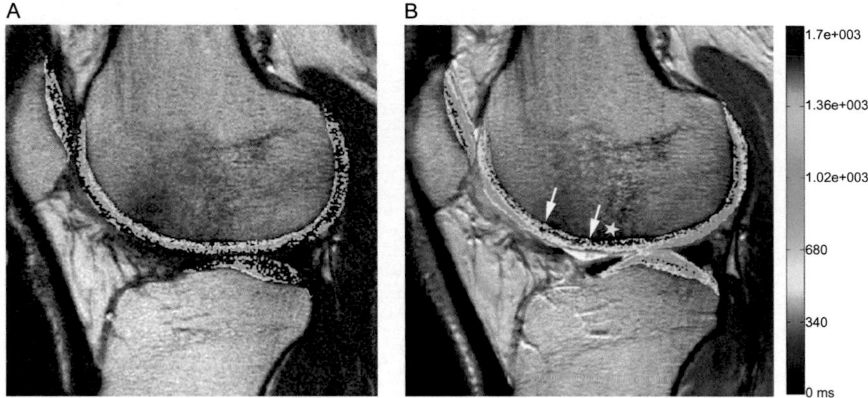

FIG. 8.3

Sagittal T_1 maps of the lateral knee compartment 4 years following microfracture of the anterior lateral femoral condyle (*arrows*, B). (A) Pre-contrast T_1 map of the segmented cartilage shows little difference between articular regions. (B) Post-contrast dGEMRIC T_1 map demonstrates lower T_1 values in the region of the cartilage repair *(arrows)* and degeneration in a region of non-operated cartilage *(star)* posterior to the microfracture.

8.2.3 T_2 and T_2* relaxation time mapping in cartilage

Compared to T_1, which is sensitive to molecular motions in the MHz frequency range, T_2 has increased sensitivity to slower molecular motions, as described in Chapter 1. In normal cartilage, T_2 relaxation is dominated by the anisotropic motion of water molecules in a fibrous collagen network. The collagen-PG matrix restricts the motion of water protons, leading to shorter T_2 values. T_2 relaxation times may increase as cartilage degenerates because of damage to the collagen-PG matrix, allowing greater water mobility, as well as an overall increase in water content.

Studies using high-field microscopic MRI have demonstrated that T_2 spatial variation is dominated by the ultrastructure of collagen fibrils; thus, the angular dependency of T_2 with respect to the external magnetic field B_0 can provide specific information about the collagen structure [35,36] (Fig. 8.4). T_2 variations have also been correlated with histology using polarized light microscopy [37]. This angular dependency of T_2 also results in the "magic angle" effect and commonly leads to a laminar appearance in cartilage imaging. Multiexponential T_2 relaxation components have been identified using ex vivo samples, offering the potential to improve the specificity of evaluating cartilage matrix by including these metrics as potential biomarkers [38]. More recently, research has shown that the number of T_2 (and $T_{1\rho}$, as discussed later) relaxation components depend on multiple experimental parameters including pulse sequences, bath solution (which affects proton exchange of the samples), image resolution (or spectral voxel size), and specimen orientation [39].

T_2 mapping using a multiecho spin echo (MESE) sequence was included in the OA initiative (OAI) protocol, as this approach showed an RMS-CV $<5\%$ for longitudinal reproducibility in phantoms over 3 years at three of the four imaging sites [40]. Variations in T_2 quantification were observed using different sequences, potentially because of the different sensitivity of each sequence to system

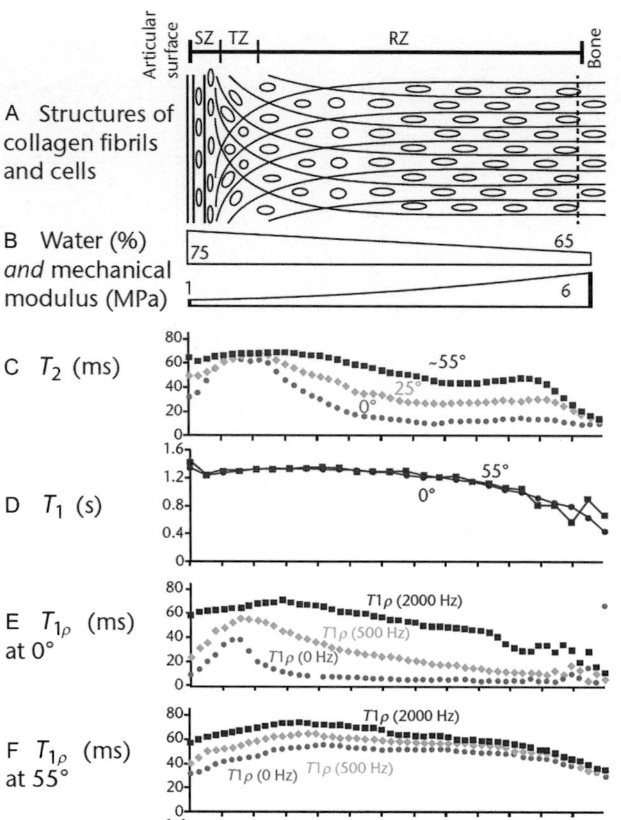

FIG. 8.4

The depth-dependent structures and properties of canine humeral articular cartilage by high-resolution MRI. (A) Schematic diagram of cartilage showing the orientation of the collagen fibrils *(the short lines)* in different histological zones and the orientation of the chondrocytes *(the circles and ovals)* (not to scale). (B) Approximate water concentration and depth-dependent compressive modulus in cartilage. (C)–(F) Depth-dependent profiles of T_2, T_1, $T_{1\rho}$ values at different specimen orientations (and at different spin-lock frequencies for $T_{1\rho}$). An orientation of 0° indicates a positioning where the articular surface is perpendicular to the magnetic field direction.

(Image modified with permission from Xia Y. MRI of articular cartilage at microscopic resolution. Bone Joint Res 2013;2(1):9–17. doi:10.1302/2046-3758.21.2000135. PubMed PMID: 23610697.)

imperfections (e.g., stimulated echoes, off-resonance signal, and eddy current issues). Different fitting methods also introduce variations in T_2 quantification, especially in the setting of low SNR [41]. These factors must be considered when comparing results from different studies and when designing multicenter studies. Other techniques for T_2 quantification in cartilage include using a single scan based on a double-echo in steady-state (DESS) [42] or a triple-echo steady-state (TESS) [43] approach, and multicomponent-driven equilibrium single-shot observation of T_1 and T_2 methods [44].

Cartilage T_2 values correlate with age [45] and body mass index [46]. Decreased T_2 was observed in patients after running [47] and acute loading [48], suggesting a loss of water content and alteration to cartilage matrix structure under loading. Elevated cartilage T_2 relaxation times have been reported in knees with OA [49], while studies have also demonstrated that once cartilage shows more severe degeneration, T_2 values may decrease again, raising concern that T_2 measurements may be less suited for more advanced disease stages [50]. The addition of T_2 mapping to a routine MR protocol at 3 T has been reported to significantly improve sensitivity for the detection of cartilage lesions [51]. Elevated and more heterogeneous cartilage T_2 values have been observed in patients with risk factors for OA compared to healthy controls within the OAI cohort, whereas these groups showed no significant difference in the prevalence of MRI morphologic abnormalities [52]. Further, cartilage T_2 and its heterogeneity have been shown to predict the development of cartilage morphologic lesions and radiographic OA [53,54], and predicted symptom development and patient outcomes [55]. Cartilage T_2 values have been correlated with physical activity [56] and weight loss [57] both cross-sectionally and longitudinally, suggesting that cartilage T_2 can serve as a potential marker for evaluating outcomes of these important interventions for OA management.

T_2^* mapping has also been used to evaluate cartilage health. As described in Chapter 3, T_2^* is sensitive to change in T_2 as well as global and local inhomogeneity, with the latter reflecting tissue structure at a microscopic level. Compared to T_2 mapping, T_2^* mapping has the advantage of faster acquisition given its use of gradient echoes with small flip angles rather than spin echoes. This allows for 3D acquisitions and higher resolution within a clinically relevant acquisition time. However, the higher sensitivity to susceptibility artifacts and other causes of local field inhomogeneity may affect its repeatability and limit its clinical acceptance. Studies in the literature reported both elevated [58] and decreased [59] T_2^* in degenerated cartilage. Such discrepancy, caused by either different imaging protocols used or the real differences in matrix changes associated with the specific specimens/cohorts studied, present challenges when interpreting these measurements in cartilage T_2^* mapping. Cartilage T_2/T_2^* relaxation times decrease from the superficial zone to the deep zone, and values can be 10 ms or less near the calcified cartilage zone. Ultrashort TE (UTE, discussed more in Section 8.4) relaxation quantification including T_2^*, T_1, T_2, and $T_{1\rho}$ enables more accurate evaluation of the deep layer of hyaline cartilage and the bone-cartilage interface [60] and may serve as a promising biomarker for OA, as changes within these regions play an important role in OA pathophysiology.

8.2.4 $T_{1\rho}$ relaxation time mapping of cartilage

As discussed in Chapter 2, the $T_{1\rho}$ relaxation time describes spin-lattice relaxation in the rotating frame and is normally measured using a spin-lock sequence. $T_{1\rho}$ can be described as follows:

$$R_{1\rho} = \frac{1}{T_{1\rho}} = A\left[\frac{3\tau_c}{1+4\omega_1^2\tau_c^2} + \frac{5\tau_c}{1+\omega_0^2\tau_c^2} + \frac{2\tau_c}{1+4\omega_0^2\tau_c^2}\right] \tag{8.1}$$

where ω_1 is the spin-lock field strength and τ_c is the correlation time (see Chapter 2 for more details). $T_{1\rho}$ increases as the spin-lock field strength increases, a phenomenon termed $T_{1\rho}$ dispersion. When the nutation frequency of the spin-lock pulse ω_1 is equal to 0, $T_{1\rho}$ is identical to T_2. $T_{1\rho}$ relaxation phenomena are sensitive to physicochemical processes with inverse correlation times on the order of ω_1, which normally ranges from a few hundred to a few thousand hertz. In cartilage, the degradation of the PG-collagen matrix normally results in elevated $T_{1\rho}$ values. However, the mechanism of $T_{1\rho}$

relaxation time in cartilage is not yet fully understood, and the various contributions of different potential mechanisms at different field strengths are still being debated.

Chemical exchange between protons on the protein side-chain groups of GAG and bulk water has been suggested to contribute to $T_{1\rho}$ relaxation and dominate low-frequency (0–1.5 kHz) $T_{1\rho}$ dispersion [61,62]. Evidence of this chemical exchange contribution to $T_{1\rho}$ includes the pH dependency of $T_{1\rho}$ values and significant $T_{1\rho}$ dispersion with spin-lock frequencies ranging from 0 to 3 kHz [39,61–64]. The exchange rate of this chemical exchange can be evaluated by taking the second derivative of the $R_{1\rho}$ ($1/T_{1\rho}$) dispersion curve according to the Chopra two-site exchange model [64]. The feasibility of applying this model in human knees has been demonstrated, resulting in exchange rates in cartilage estimated to range from 1 to 3 kHz at 3 T [65]. However, other studies suggested that the dominant relaxation mechanism in the rotating frame in the cartilage at $B_0 \leq 3$T is dipolar interaction, and the contribution of scalar relaxation caused by proton exchange is relevant only at high fields such as 7T [66]. In the study of reference [66], different $T_{1\rho}$ sequences were used at 3 T and 7 T, which may have led to an underestimation of the $T_{1\rho}$ increase from 3 T to 7 T, thus leading to an underestimation of the contribution of chemical exchange to $T_{1\rho}$. Additional factors that may have contributed to varied results of these $T_{1\rho}$ studies include differences in sample types and bath solutions, sample orientation, acquisition techniques and parameters, and post-processing methods.

In vitro studies have demonstrated that $T_{1\rho}$ relaxation time increases with PG depletion and is correlated with GAG concentration and histologic evaluation [67–69], whereas other studies have demonstrated an inconsistent correlation between $T_{1\rho}$ and GAG concentration [70]. Studies have shown that $T_{1\rho}$ is more sensitive (larger increase) than T_2 in detecting trypsin-induced tissue degradation (a treatment that cleaves PG but relatively spares intact collagen), with a 63% change in $T_{1\rho}$ at 2 kHz vs. 30% change for T_2 [39]; and a 21.6% change for $T_{1\rho}$ at 1 kHz vs. 14.5% for T_2 [70]. Both T_2 and $T_{1\rho}$ measures have been correlated with cartilage biomechanical properties [14,71–73].

The anisotropy or orientation dependency to collagen of cartilage $T_{1\rho}$ mapping depends on the spin-lock frequency. When the spin-lock frequency is equal to 0, $T_{1\rho}$ is identical to T_2 and shows the same anisotropy patterns like that seen via T_2. With increased spin-lock frequency, $T_{1\rho}$ demonstrates less anisotropy compared to T_2 due to reduced dipolar interactions. The anisotropy is minimized at SL = 2 kHz [74] or 1 kHz [39]. With very high (extreme) spin-lock frequency, $T_{1\rho}$ values approach T_1 (with an isotropic pattern in cartilage) in the laboratory frame. Fig. 8.5 shows the transition of anisotropic patterns of $T_{1\rho}$ mapping from T_2 to T_1 with increased spin-lock frequencies [75]. Interestingly, the number of relaxation components of $T_{1\rho}$ has also been shown to be dependent on the spin-lock frequency and orientation. At low spin-lock frequencies (<500 Hz), cartilage $T_{1\rho}$ measurements indicate the presence of multiple relaxation components; however, only one component is present at the magic angle regardless of spin-lock frequency or at frequencies of less than 1 kHz regardless of orientation [39]. This transition from multiple components to a single component implies that there are sufficient exchange processes in the tissue system that can mask the difference between different pools of water molecules when the dipolar interaction is minimized (at the magic angle or with sufficiently high spin-lock frequency).

With clinical imaging, the spin-lock frequency is normally limited to 500 Hz because of constraints on radiofrequency power deposition to the tissue, i.e., the allowable specific absorption rate (SAR), and hardware limitations. Therefore, clinical cartilage $T_{1\rho}$ mapping is still subject to the influence of dipolar interaction and orientation dependency. Changes in $T_{1\rho}$ values are related to a combination of changes in hydration and the collagen-PG matrix. $T_{1\rho}$ dispersion

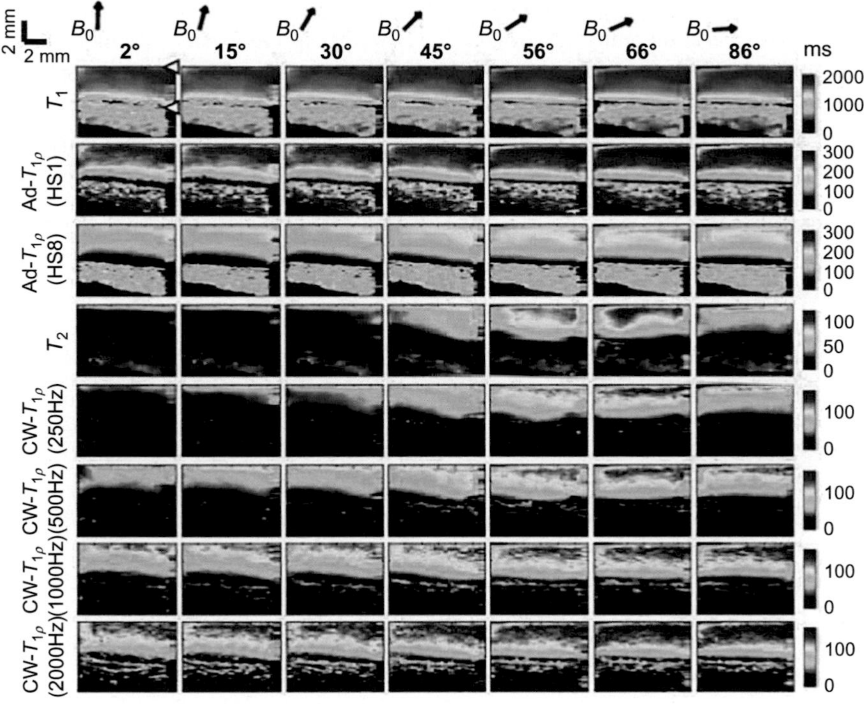

FIG. 8.5

Relaxation parameter maps for one representative sample at different angles with respect to B_0 (*arrows* mentioned previously). Orientation anisotropy is seen for T_2 and continuous wave (CW)-$T_{1\rho}$ values with low spin-lock frequency, as well as the transition from T_2-like to T_1-like appearance with increasing spin-lock frequency. Articular surface and cartilage-bone interface are marked with arrowheads. Adiabatic $T_{1\rho}$ maps (using pulses from the hyperbolic secant HSn family, HS1, and HS8) show less anisotropy compared to CW- $T_{1\rho}$ maps.

(Figure modified with permission from Hanninen N, Rautiainen J, Rieppo L, Saarakkala S, Nissi MJ. Orientation anisotropy of quantitative MRI relaxation parameters in ordered tissue. Sci Rep 2017;7(1):9606. doi:10.1038/s41598-017-10053-2. PubMed PMID: 28852032.)

experiments with multiple spin-lock frequencies may provide more specific information regarding the chemical exchange and GAG concentration [65].

In vivo $T_{1\rho}$ mapping sequences provide $T_{1\rho}$ weighting using a spin-lock pulse cluster, followed by 2D or 3D data acquisition. Methods using transient signals immediately after $T_{1\rho}$ preparation and multiple TRs after each preparation [76,77] are more SNR efficient and less SAR intensive compared to those using steady-state signals and one TR after each preparation. RF cycling and variable flip angle trains have been applied to eliminate the adverse effect of longitudinal relaxation and *k*-space filtering caused by transient signal evolution on quantitative accuracy (sequence termed "MAPSS") [77]. Self-compensation phase-cycling for spin-lock pulses, inserting a 180° refocusing pulse in the middle of the rotary echo, and the deployment of composite pulses for tip-down and tip-up have been used to improve the robustness to B_0 and B_1 inhomogeneity [78,79]. $T_{1\rho}$ mapping using adiabatic spin-lock pulses with varying amplitude and frequency show less orientation dependency than continuous wave $T_{1\rho}$ mapping [80,81]. Fast $T_{1\rho}$ mapping has been implemented using parallel imaging and compressed sensing techniques [82,83].

Excellent in vivo reproducibility of cartilage $T_{1\rho}$ and T_2 mapping has been reported, with test/retest intra-class correlation values typically greater than 0.8 and coefficient-of-variation (CV) values less than 10% [84]. Several multicenter single vendor studies reported the inter-site variation of $T_{1\rho}$ and T_2 values to be comparable or slightly higher than single-site reproducibility (CVs in phantoms ranged 2.8%–6.9%) [40,85]. The MAPSS $T_{1\rho}$ and T_2 mapping approach have been implemented on three major vendors and the mean inter-vendor CVs were reported to be 8.1% and 10.1% for $T_{1\rho}$ and T_2 values in human knee cartilage, respectively [86].

Recent systematic reviews demonstrated that $T_{1\rho}$ and T_2 relaxometry values can be significant discriminators between healthy subjects and patients with mild and established OA [84], and for patients at risk for knee OA [87] (Fig. 8.6) [88]; among dGEMRIC, $T_{1\rho}$ and T_2, $T_{1\rho}$ was suggested to be the best discriminator for both mild OA and OA [84]. Baseline $T_{1\rho}$ and T_2 values were shown to predict OA-related lesion development at 2 years [89]. Significantly elevated knee cartilage $T_{1\rho}$ and T_2 values were also observed after acute ACL injury and reconstruction (ACLR) [90–92]. Elevated cartilage $T_{1\rho}$ values after ACL injury have been correlated with worse patient outcomes after ACLR [93,94]. Voxel-based relaxometry analysis and principle component analysis have been applied to knee $T_{1\rho}$ and T_2 maps after ACLR and indicate that these patients show different degeneration patterns as compared to those with primary OA [95]. In addition to knees, $T_{1\rho}$ mapping has been applied to other joints, such as a hip [96,97], ankle [98], shoulder [99,100], and hand/wrist [101,102].

These results suggest that $T_{1\rho}$ and T_2 measurements provide valuable information which can be used to detect early cartilage degeneration in OA and can serve as useful outcome markers for developing novel intervention/treatment strategies to slow disease progression. $T_{1\rho}$ and T_2 quantification require no contrast agent injection and no special hardware. However, at the time of writing, commercially available pulse sequences of $T_{1\rho}$ mapping are still under development. The technical challenges of $T_{1\rho}$ quantification include the high energy deposited to tissue (high SAR), especially with high spin-lock frequency and at high and ultra-high main field strengths. Although T_2 mapping based on MESE acquisition is available as product sequences on most MR systems, T_2 values derived from this sequence is prone to variations introduced by stimulated echoes and magnetization transfer effect [103], and significant differences in T_2 values between vendors were reported, with inter-vendor mean T_2 differences ranged 5.4 to 10.0 ms (10%–25%) [104].

8.3 MRI relaxometry to assess skeletal muscle

The skeletal muscular system, which is the set of organs that controls movement and posture, constitutes approximately one-third of the total human body weight [105]. Muscle tissue is composed of individual fibers that are bundled together into a muscle spindle. A single muscle fiber is composed mostly of actin and myosin fibers covered by a cell membrane (sarcolemma). There are two major types of skeletal muscle: type I (slow oxidative) and type II (fast-twitch). The functions of different muscle groups vary dramatically, with differences in contraction speed and length dependent on the makeup of each skeletal muscle [106].

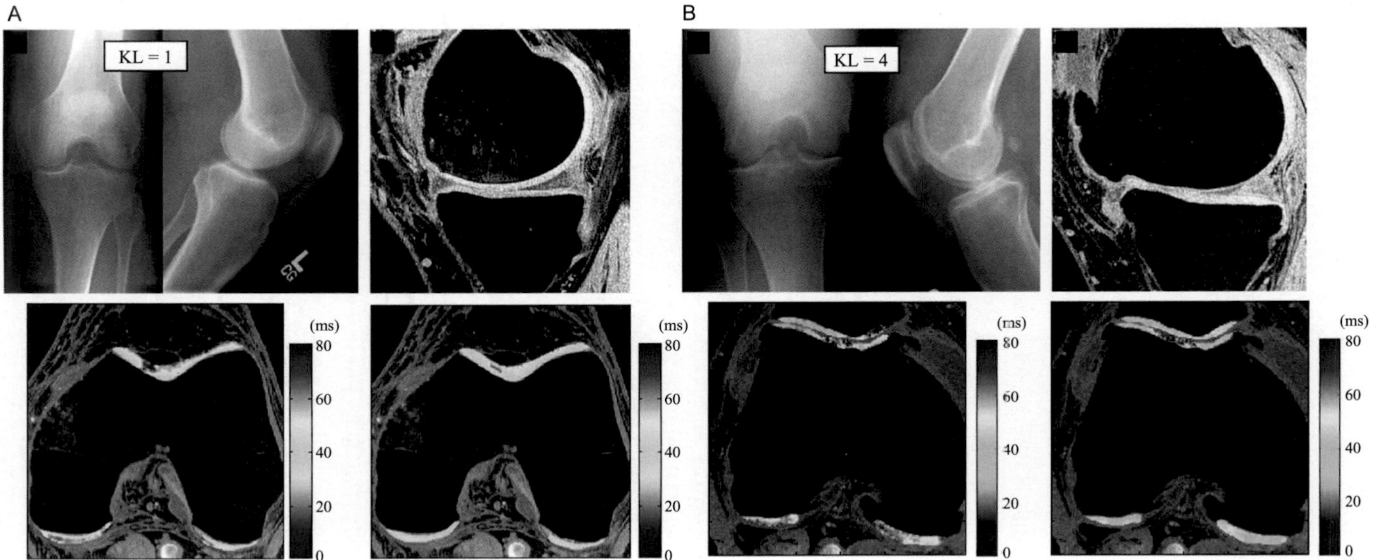

FIG. 8.6

A radiograph *(left top)*, T_1-weighted SPGR images *(right-top)*, $T_{1\rho}$ *(left bottom)* and T_2 *(right bottom)* maps of subjects with Kellgren Lawrence (KL) Grade = 1 (A, male, 66 years old) and KL Grade = 4 (B, male, 46 years old), respectively. Elevations of $T_{1\rho}$ and T_2 values were observed in trochlea cartilage in subject A, indicating early cartilage degeneration. The mean cartilage $T_{1\rho}$ and T_2 values were 45.5 ± 14.5 ms and 35.0 ± 10.9 ms, respectively. Subject B had significantly elevated cartilage $T_{1\rho}$ and T_2 values in trochlear and femoral condyle cartilage, where the mean cartilage $T_{1\rho}$ and T_2 values were 55.4 ± 26.0 ms and 43.8 ± 11.1 ms, respectively.

(Figure modified with permission from Li X, Ma C, Link T, Castillo D, Blumenkrantz G, Lozano J, et al. In vivo T1rho and T2 mapping of articular cartilage in osteoarthritis of the knee using 3 Tesla MRI. Osteoarthr Cartil 2007;15(7):789–97.)

Myopathies, including muscular dystrophy (MD), idiopathic inflammatory myopathies, sarcopenia, and acute injuries, share a common set of complex pathologies that include inflammation, compromised membrane integrity, fat deposition, and fibrosis. Clinically established biomarkers for muscle injury and disease include serum intramyocellular enzymes, muscle biopsy, and muscle force measurement. Imaging-based biomarkers can potentially provide complementary, noninvasive and more specific markers of disease with spatial information in cases when there is regional disease presentation [107,108]. The most commonly used imaging measures for muscle include morphology (areas and volume), fatty infiltration, and T_2 relaxation times to assess muscle composition and functions.

In ex vivo muscle samples, multiple T_2 relaxation time components have been observed, including water in macromolecular hydration shells ($T_2 \sim 10$ ms; not observable in typical MRI studies), intracellular water that is free to diffuse within the cell ($T_2 \sim 35$ ms; ~90% of total tissue-free water signal), and interstitial water ($T_2 \sim 100$–150 ms; ~10% of total tissue-free water signal) [107]. However, observations of muscle T_2 in human and animal in vivo studies have been inconsistent, with many studies reporting a single relaxing component (suggesting relatively fast exchange between different proton pools) [109] and other studies reporting multiple components [110,111].

In vivo muscle single component T_2 measurements have been reported to be highly reproducible, with CVs ranging from 1.3% to 5.9% [112]. However, as when making measurements in cartilage, accurate muscle T_2 measurements have proven challenging as the values measured depend on the MR sequence used [113]. Elevation of muscle T_2 values has been observed in human patients with skeletal muscle disorders such as MD [114] and idiopathic inflammatory myopathies [115]. Mildly but significantly lower T_2 values have also been reported in patients with limb-girdle muscular dystrophies, potentially due to significant fibrosis at advanced stages of the disease [116]. In patients with Duchenne muscular dystrophy (DMD), muscle T_2 values correlate with clinically meaningful measures of ambulatory functions [117]. Furthermore, elevated muscle T_2 values have been reported to be normalized with successful therapy in patients with steroid treatment [118].

While these studies suggest that muscle T_2 is a promising biomarker for evaluating and monitoring muscle disorders, the elevation of muscle T_2 values is a nonspecific event that can be caused by many mechanisms including edema, inflammation, membrane damage, dystrophy, and denervation. Since fat has a longer T_2 than muscle, fatty infiltration of muscles may also contribute to the elevation of muscle T_2, and the fat percentage has been reported to be significantly correlated with muscle T_2 [119]. This suggests on one hand that T_2 can be used as an indicator of an overall pathologic process that includes fatty infiltration, but on the other hand, the degree of muscle damage may be confounded by the amount of fatty infiltration [107] (Fig. 8.7). For this reason, it has been suggested that muscle water T_2 should be assessed rather than global T_2 measurements of fatty infiltrated muscles [108]. To this end, fat suppression or fat-water imaging, MR spectroscopy, and multiple-exponential fitting techniques have been used to remove (or separate) the signal from fat to enable the measurement of muscle water T_2 values [107,108,120].

Muscle T_2 has been correlated with measurements of muscle force and isometric strength [121]. Muscle T_2 increases with exercise [109], and "muscle functional MRI (mfMRI)" has been proposed using a comparison of muscle T_2 values before and after exercise [122]. Such measurements may also indicate the extent to which a specific muscle has been activated during a particular exercise. Higher osmotic and pH changes within the loaded muscle unit, the physiological processes indicating higher metabolic muscle activity, lead to an increased T_2 elevation [123]. In a study of soccer players with and without a history of hamstring injuries, mfMRI indicated that an increase in the T_2 of the biceps

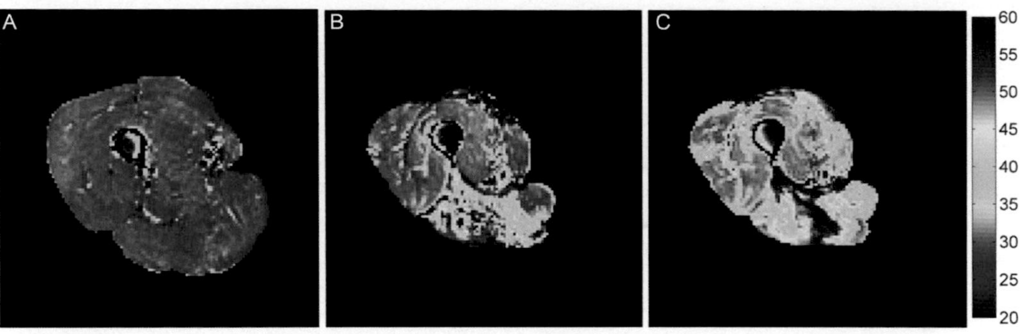

FIG. 8.7

Quantitative T_2 maps from a healthy control (A) and polymyositis patients (B and C). In (A) and (B), fat signal-suppressed T_2 values are illustrated; in panel (C), the fat signal has not been suppressed and so the T_2 values reflect both muscle and fat tissue values. The color scale at right indicates the T_2 in ms.

(Figure with permission from Damon BM, Li K, Bryant ND. Magnetic resonance imaging of skeletal muscle disease. Handb Clin Neurol 2016;136:827–42. doi:10.1016/B978-0-444-53486-6.00041-7. PubMed PMID: 27430444.)

femoris, as well as the relative activity between the biceps femoris and semitendinosus as measured by T_2 increase, may serve as biomarkers for the prediction of a first-time hamstring injury [123].

The feasibility of muscle $T_{1\rho}$ mapping has been demonstrated. Muscle $T_{1\rho}$ values are higher in females than in males, increase with age [124], and increase in patients with myositis [125], suggesting that $T_{1\rho}$ mapping and $T_{1\rho}$ dispersion, although only in early development, maybe promising biomarkers for muscle evaluation.

8.4 MRI relaxometry of menisci, tendons, and ligaments

Menisci, tendons, and ligaments are important connective tissues in joints [4,5]. The knee menisci are semilunar, fibrocartilaginous structures situated between the femoral condyles, and tibial plateaus, and are vital for proper knee function and protection of the articular cartilage. Tendons and ligaments are soft, fibrous tissues; tendons connect muscle to bone, ligaments connect bone to bone and help stabilize the joint, and entheses are regions in which tendons, ligaments, or joint capsules are connected to bone. Fig. 8.1 illustrates these tissues using the knee joint as an example. Compared to tendons, ligaments are more metabolically active and have slightly less total collagen and more GAG [5]. Compared with the makeup of hyaline cartilage, the matrix of menisci, tendons, and ligaments are primarily composed of denser collagen (primarily type I), a lower concentration of PG, and less water (Table 8.1), resulting in shorter MR T_2/T_2^* relaxation times.

Meniscal degeneration is an important feature in OA pathology; meniscal damage/tear is also one of the most common knee injuries and is a risk factor for post-traumatic OA development [126]. Elevated meniscal T_2 and $T_{1\rho}$ values have been reported in patients with OA [127] and with meniscal tears [128]. After acute ACL injures, meniscal $T_{1\rho}$ and T_2 values of the injured knees are significantly higher than uninjured contralateral knees [129–131]. Interestingly, intact menisci (no tears or signal changes were observed in morphologic MRI) within ACL-injured knees also had significantly higher $T_{1\rho}$ and T_2

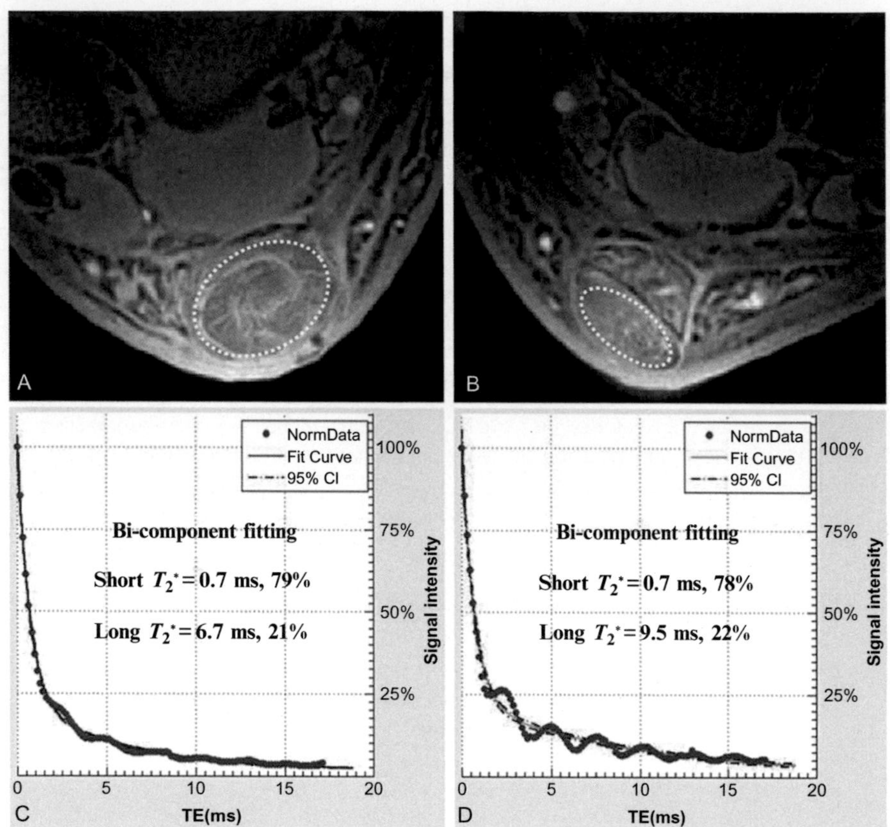

FIG. 8.8

A 60-year-old man several years after successful right Achilles tendon repair. Axial UTE MR images of the repaired right Achilles tendon (A) compared with the same patient's asymptomatic left Achilles tendon (B). UTE-based T_2* bicomponent analysis performed in the tendons *(dashed ovals)* show that the short T_2* value and fraction of the repaired right tendon (C) has approached the asymptomatic left side (D), confirming adequate collagen remodeling.

(Figure with permission from Chang EY, Du J, Chung CB. UTE imaging in the musculoskeletal system. J Magn Reson Imaging 2015;41(4):870–83. doi:10.1002/jmri.24713. PubMed PMID: 25045018.)

values compared to menisci of uninjured knees, suggesting that $T_{1\rho}$ and T_2 measures are more sensitive than morphologic MRI in detecting subtle damage [131]. Elevations in meniscal $T_{1\rho}$ and T_2 values have also been correlated with adjacent cartilage $T_{1\rho}$ and T_2 elevations [129,132], suggesting a close relationship between damage and degeneration in these two tissues.

Despite the excellent reproducibility of meniscal $T_{1\rho}$ and T_2 measurements (CV ~ 5%) [129] using conventional methods, these techniques may underestimate the short T_2/T_2* components and overestimate the overall $T_{1\rho}$ and T_2 values. To address this problem, UTE has been used to quantify the relaxation time in short T_2 tissues including the menisci, tendons, and ligaments [133,134] (Fig. 8.8).

Multiecho UTE acquisitions with multiple TEs can be used for T_2^* measurement. Decreases in meniscal UTE-based T_2^* values over 2 years following ACLR was observed in subjects without meniscal tears, suggesting potential healing, while elevated UTE-based T_2^* values were still evident after 2 years in subjects with meniscal tears at the time of injury [135].

Tendon and enthesis UTE-based T_2^* measurements are promising markers for improved diagnosis of tendinopathy. Significant elevations of Achilles tendon and enthesis T_2^* values have been reported in patients with psoriatic arthritis [136] and those with symptomatic Achilles tendinosis [137]. With biexponential analysis, significantly greater short T_2^* components and lower short T_2^* components have been observed in patients with patellar tendinopathy as compared with healthy controls [138].

In addition to T_2^*, other relaxation times have been quantified using UTE techniques. T_1 values have been measured in tendons using UTE with saturation recovery [139] and in cortical bones [140]. $T_{1\rho}$ values have been quantified in tendons, menisci, and other tissues in the knee [141,142], and $T_{1\rho}$ dispersion has been observed in tendons and menisci [141]. 3D radial UTE readouts have also been incorporated into DESS for T_2 quantification in tendons and ligaments [143].

8.5 MRI relaxometry of intervertebral discs

Lower back pain (LBP) is a leading cause of disability worldwide [144]. The pathophysiology of LBP is complex and may involve injury or degeneration of multiple components of the spine and/or paraspinal muscles, and most commonly intervertebral disc degeneration. The intervertebral disc is composed of the nucleus pulposus (NP), a hydrated gel with a high concentration of PGs and water that is embedded in a loose collagen network (primarily type II); and an outer fibrous ring, the annulus fibrosus (AF), which has a high concentration of collagen (primary type I), organized into concentric lamellae with a low concentration of PGs [6] (Table 8.1). Early signs of disc degeneration are manifested by biochemical changes (PG loss, dehydration, and collagen degradation) that eventually lead to morphologic degradation in the vertebral bodies (loss of disc height, disc herniation, annual tears, radial bulging), vertebral endplates, and the separate facet joints.

MR relaxation time mapping techniques have been applied to intervertebral disc evaluation to detect and follow early disc degeneration. Spatial variations of T_1, T_2 and $T_{1\rho}$ relaxation times have been reported in discs, with longer values reported in the NP than in the AF (Table 8.2), primarily reflecting the higher water content in the NP [159]. Inconsistent results have been found for disc T_1 measurements, with lower T_1 values in degenerated and herniated discs reported by some [160], while others found no correlation between disc T_1 values and disc degeneration grade [145]. T_1 mapping following intravenous ionic Gd-chelate administration, i.e., "dGEMRIC for discs," has reported being clinically feasible and of potential value for orthopedic patients [161,162], although one study showed its potential limitation in detecting early disc degeneration [163].

T_2 [148,160] and $T_{1\rho}$ [155,164,165] relaxation times have been reported to decrease in degenerated or herniated discs (Fig. 8.9), and also to decrease with increased age [157]. One study comparing disc $T_{1\rho}$ and T_2 values observed that, in NP, both $T_{1\rho}$ and T_2 decreased quadratically with increased disc degeneration grades, with no significant difference in trend between $T_{1\rho}$ and T_2. However, in AF, $T_{1\rho}$ and T_2 decreased linearly with increased disc degeneration grades with different slopes (-4.56 vs. -1.84) (Fig. 8.10) [166]. In another study using caprine models, $T_{1\rho}$ values correlated

Table 8.2 MR relaxation times (in ms) of selected musculoskeletal tissues.

	B_0	Cartilage	Muscle	Menisci	Patellar tendon	Achilles tendon	ACL	PCL	Bone marrow	Synovial fluid	Vertebral disk (NP)	Vertebral disk (AF)	References
T_2	1.5 T	26–39	31–35						47–165	535–1210	91.4–155	31.1–42.4	[145–147]
	3 T	30–67	29–32	11–13					51–133	653–767	119–120	40–70	[45,46,48,51,132,148–150]
	7 T	27–86	23						46.7	324.5			[150–153]
T_2^*	1.5 T		40	5–8	6–10	0.3–1.2	6–10	6–10	30–40				[133]
	3 T	10–28		4–8	1–2	0.8–3.4					79	30–34	[134,135,139,151,154]
	7 T	16–20											[151]
$T_{1\rho}$	1.5 T	40–57	35.4								100–150		[101,155,156]
	3 T	39–58	43.2	14–19	9.7	3.06	34.9	21.6			100–183	72–74	[84,85,124,127,130,141, 142,149,157]
	7 T	38–42											[152,158]
T_1	1.5 T	770–1060	500–1130		350–450		350–450	350–450	250–350	1470–2850	1179	887	[145,146]
	3 T	1016–1240	1256–4120			600–675			371–381	2564–3620			[139,150,153]
	7 T	1093–1760	1553						549	4813			[150,153]

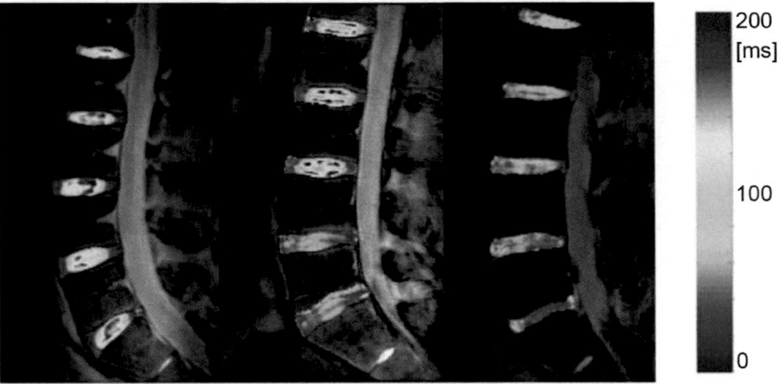

FIG. 8.9

Representative $T_{1\rho}$ maps from (left) a 24-year-old subject with nondegenerated discs (Pfirrmann grades L5/S1 = 1, L4/L5 = 1, L3/L4 = 1, L2/L3 = 1, L1/L2 = 2), an Oswestry Disability Index (ODI) score of 0, and an SF-36 Physical Health score of 57.9; (middle) a 32-year-old subject with mildly degenerated discs (Pfirrmann grades L5/S1 = 3, L4/L5 = 3, L3/L4 = 2, L2/L3 = 2, L1/L2 = 2), an O.D.I. score of 12, and an SF- 36 Physical Health score of 48.8; and (right) a 65-year-old subject with mild and severely degenerated discs (Pfirrmann grades L5/S1 = 5, L4/L5 = 4, L3/L4 = 3, L2/L3 = 3, L1/L2 = 3), an ODI score of 20, and an SF-36 Physical Health score of 44.4. The $T_{1\rho}$ values in the healthy discs are greater than those in the degenerative discs.

(Figure with permission from Blumenkrantz G, Zuo J, Li X, Kornak J, Link TM, Majumdar S. In vivo 3.0-tesla magnetic resonance T1rho and T2 relaxation mapping in subjects with intervertebral disc degeneration and clinical symptoms. Magn Reson Med 2010;63(5):1193–200. doi:10.1002/mrm.22362. PubMed PMID: 20432290.)

more strongly with the biomechanics, histology, and PG contents of the degenerated discs than did T_2 or MR-based diffusion coefficient measurements [167]. These results suggest that $T_{1\rho}$ may be a more sensitive and reliable biomarker than T_2 for evaluating disc degeneration. Texture analysis of disc $T_{1\rho}$ and T_2 maps have demonstrated significant differences between normal and degenerated discs [168]. Standard deviation and texture measurements of these values showed sharper and more significant changes during early degeneration than during more advanced degenerative states [165].

Despite these promising results, challenges remain for researchers attempting to correlate quantitative imaging metrics with clinical symptoms and to noninvasively identify the specific source of pain in LBP [169]. In one study, $T_{1\rho}$ (but not T_2 or Pfirrmann grading) was correlated with clinical symptoms as measured by the SF-36 and Oswestry Disability Index [149]. Combining $T_{1\rho}$ mapping with disc height analysis may hold promise in determining which discs are painful without the need for provocative discography [170]. Alternatively, in vivo MR spectroscopy may provide more sensitive imaging biomarkers than $T_{1\rho}$ mapping to distinguish between discs with positive and negative discography results [171]. More studies are needed before imaging biomarkers are adequate for the direction of clinical management of the primary pain source for individual patients with this highly prevalent disease.

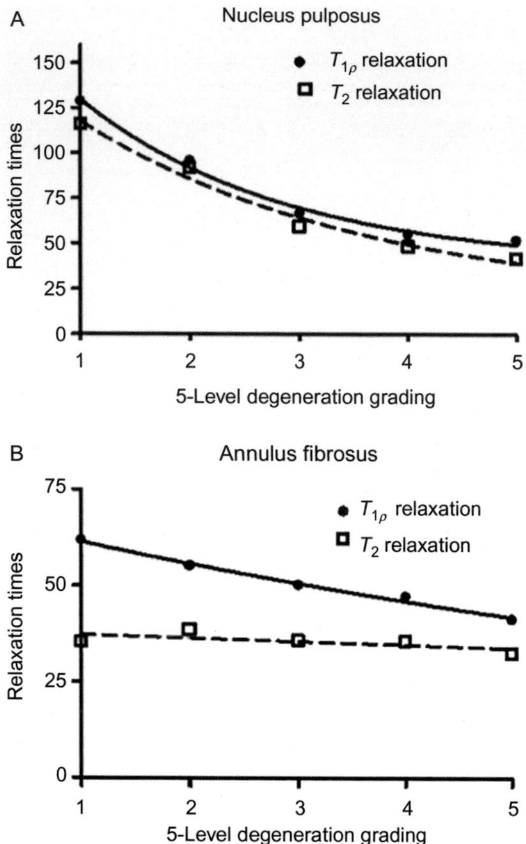

FIG. 8.10

Thirty-eight subjects (mean age: 48years; range, 23–71years) scanned at a 3 T scanner. (A) For nucleus pulposus (NP), $T_{1\rho}$ and T_2 values decreased following disc degeneration and had a similar trend (P=.67). (B) For annulus fibrosus (AF), $T_{1\rho}$ values decreased following disc degeneration and had a slope of -4.33 for 5-level gradings; the slopes for T_2 values were-1.53, and thus significantly flatter (P=.002) as compared to those of $T_{1\rho}$.

(Figure modified with permission from Wang YX, Zhang Q, Li X, Chen W, Ahuja A, Yuan J. T1rho magnetic resonance: basic physics principles and applications in knee and intervertebral disc imaging. Quant Imaging Med Surg 2015;5(6):858–85. doi:10.3978/j.issn.2223-4292.2015.12.06. PubMed PMID: 26807369.)

8.6 Outlook and Conclusion

This chapter discussed the applications of MR relaxometry in major MSK tissues including articular cartilage, muscle, menisci, tendons, ligaments, and vertebral discs and the potential of these quantitative techniques as clinically useful biomarkers of early disease. The relaxation times of these tissues at different field strengths are summarized in Table 8.2. With regulatory approval for clinical use of 7 T MRI for neuro and extremity applications in the United States and Europe in 2017, more studies are expected to take advantage of the higher SNR for further development and applications of MR relaxometry to improve diagnosis and prognosis for MSK disorders [172]. MR relaxometry has also been proposed for other tissues/lesions such as synovial fluid and synovitis [173], bone [174–177] and bone marrow [178]. The clinical application of MSK relaxometry remains challenging since most MSK diseases affect multiple joint tissues as a whole organ, and normal joint tissues have a large range of relaxation times (e.g., synovial fluid and synovitis have very long T_1 and T_2 values; while cartilage, menisci, ligaments, tendons, and bone have short to very short T_2 values). Thus, the optimization of conventional MR relaxometry sequences (such as the TE selection for T_2 quantification) must be optimized for specific tissues if the mapping is to be performed within a clinically feasible acquisition time. MR fingerprinting (MRF) is an emerging technology that enables fast imaging and quantification of multiple tissue parameters simultaneously [179] and shows promising results in neural, body and cardiac applications. However, at the time of this writing, the application of MRF to MSK imaging has been limited, but certainly warrants further investigation. Another emerging area of fast mapping includes machine learning-based reconstructions [180,181]; the application of these techniques to quantitative mapping is still in its very early stages.

In conclusion, MR relaxometry has been widely applied in MSK tissues and has played an important role in identifying novel imaging markers to improve diagnosis and prognosis for MSK disorders by isolating contributions from individual MR contrast mechanisms (T_1, T_2, T_2*). However, these techniques are currently used primarily in research applications and are not available for routine clinical use in MSK disorders. Several hurdles must be overcome before these techniques become widely available in the clinical setting, including the following: (a) the establishment of repeatability and reproducibility including standardization across different vendors and platforms; (b) the development of standardized and fully automated analysis techniques; (c) the establishment of normative values; (d) the development of cut-off values for normal and abnormal tissue, and (e) the implementation these biomarkers in risk scores to predict disease progression [182]. These goals require synergized efforts from researchers, healthcare professionals, and industry professionals to advance quantitative tissue property mapping and the use of imaging biomarkers in clinical trials and clinical practice for eventually improving patient care of MSK disorders.

Acknowledgments

The authors would like to thank helpful discussion with Dr. Yang Xia and Dr. Ronald Midura, Figure preparation by Dr. Ceylan Colak and Dr. Mei Li, Table preparation by Jeehun Kim, and scientific editing by Megan Griffiths.

References

[1] Murray CJ, Vos T, Lozano R, Naghavi M, Flaxman AD, Michaud C, et al. Disability-adjusted life years (DALYs) for 291 diseases and injuries in 21 regions, 1990-2010: a systematic analysis for the global burden of disease study 2010, Lancet 2012;380(9859):2197–223. https://doi.org/10.1016/S0140-6736(12)61689-4. 23245608.

[2] Huber M, Trattnig S, Lintner F. Anatomy, biochemistry, and physiology of articular cartilage, Invest Radiol 2000;35(10):573–80. 11041151.

[3] Sophia Fox AJ, Bedi A, Rodeo SA. The basic science of articular cartilage: structure, composition, and function, Sports Health 2009;1(6):461–8. https://doi.org/10.1177/1941738109350438. 23015907.

[4] McDevitt CA, Webber RJ. The ultrastructure and biochemistry of meniscal cartilage, Clin Orthop Relat Res 1990;252:8–18. 2406077.
[5] Riley G. Tendon and ligament biochemistry and pathology. In: Bea H, editor. Soft tissue rheumatology. Oxford: Oxford University Press; 2004. p. 20–53.
[6] Eyre DR. Biochemistry of the intervertebral disc, Int Rev Connect Tissue Res 1979;8:227–91. 389859.
[7] Verstraete KL, Almqvist F, Verdonk P, Vanderschueren G, Huysse W, Verdonk R, et al. Magnetic resonance imaging of cartilage and cartilage repair, Clin Radiol 2004;59(8):674–89. 15262541.
[8] Gray ML, Burstein D, Kim YJ, Maroudas A. 2007 Elizabeth Winston Lanier award winner. Magnetic resonance imaging of cartilage glycosaminoglycan: basic principles, imaging technique, and clinical applications, J Orthop Res 2008;26(3):281–91. https://doi.org/10.1002/jor.20482. 17876836.
[9] Bashir A, Gray ML, Burstein D. Gd-DTPA2-as a measure of cartilage degradation, Magn Reson Med 1996;36(5):665–73. 8916016.
[10] Zheng S, Xia Y. The impact of the relaxivity definition on the quantitative measurement of glycosaminoglycans in cartilage by the MRI dGEMRIC method, Magn Reson Med 2010;63(1):25–32. https://doi.org/10.1002/mrm.22169. 19918900.
[11] Siversson C, Tiderius CJ, Neuman P, Dahlberg L, Svensson J. Repeatability of T1-quantification in dGEMRIC for three different acquisition techniques: two-dimensional inversion recovery, three-dimensional look locker, and three-dimensional variable flip angle, J Magn Reson Imaging 2010;31(5):1203–9. https://doi.org/10.1002/jmri.22159. 20432357.
[12] Trattnig S, Mlynarik V, Breitenseher M, Huber M, Zembsch A, Rand T, et al. MRI visualization of proteoglycan depletion in articular cartilage via intravenous administration of Gd-DTPA, Magn Reson Imaging 1999;17(4):577–83. 10231184.
[13] Samosky JT, Burstein D, Eric Grimson W, Howe R, Martin S, Gray ML. Spatially-localized correlation of dGEMRIC-measured GAG distribution and mechanical stiffness in the human tibial plateau, J Orthop Res 2005;23(1):93–101. https://doi.org/10.1016/j.orthres.2004.05.008. 15607880.
[14] Lammentausta E, Kiviranta P, Nissi MJ, Laasanen MS, Kiviranta I, Nieminen MT, et al. T2 relaxation time and delayed gadolinium-enhanced MRI of cartilage (dGEMRIC) of human patellar cartilage at 1.5 T and 9.4 T: relationships with tissue mechanical properties, J Orthop Res 2006;24(3):366–74. https://doi.org/10.1002/jor.20041. 16479569.
[15] Gillis A, Gray M, Burstein D. Relaxivity and diffusion of gadolinium agents in cartilage, Magn Reson Med 2002;48(6):1068–71. https://doi.org/10.1002/mrm.10327. 12465119.
[16] Kulmala KA, Korhonen RK, Julkunen P, Jurvelin JS, Quinn TM, Kroger H, et al. Diffusion coefficients of articular cartilage for different CT and MRI contrast agents, Med Eng Phys 2010;32(8):878–82. https://doi.org/10.1016/j.medengphy.2010.06.002. 20594900.
[17] Forghani R. Adverse effects of gadolinium-based contrast agents: changes in practice patterns, Top Magn Reson Imaging 2016;25(4):163–9. https://doi.org/10.1097/RMR.0000000000000095. 27367314.
[18] Levine D, McDonald RJ, Kressel HY. Gadolinium retention after contrast-enhanced MRI, JAMA 2018;320(18):1853–4. https://doi.org/10.1001/jama.2018.13362. 30208489.
[19] Tiderius CJ, Olsson LE, de Verdier H, Leander P, Ekberg O, Dahlberg L. Gd-DTPA2-enhanced MRI of femoral knee cartilage: a dose-response study in healthy volunteers, Magn Reson Med 2001;46(6):1067–71. 11746570.
[20] Winalski CS, Aliabadi P, Wright RJ, Shortkroff S, Sledge CB, Weissman BN. Enhancement of joint fluid with intravenously administered gadopentetate dimeglumine: technique, rationale, and implications, Radiology 1993;187(1):179–85. https://doi.org/10.1148/radiology.187.1.8451409. 8451409.
[21] Bashir A, Gray ML, Boutin RD, Burstein D. Glycosaminoglycan in articular cartilage: in vivo assessment with delayed Gd DTPA 2-enhanced MR imaging. Radiology 1997;205(2):551–8.

[22] Burstein D, Velyvis J, Scott KT, Stock KW, Kim YJ, Jaramillo D, et al. Protocol issues for delayed Gd(DTPA)(2-)-enhanced MRI (dGEMRIC) for clinical evaluation of articular cartilage, Magn Reson Med 2001;45(1):36–41. https://doi.org/10.1002/1522-2594(200101)45:1<36::AID-MRM1006>3.0.CO;2-W. 11146483.

[23] Ericsson YB, Tjornstrand J, Tiderius CJ, Dahlberg LE. Relationship between cartilage glycosaminoglycan content (assessed with dGEMRIC) and OA risk factors in meniscectomized patients, Osteoarthr Cartil 2009;17(5):565–70. https://doi.org/10.1016/j.joca.2008.10.009. 19058980.

[24] Watanabe A, Wada Y, Obata T, Ueda T, Tamura M, Ikehira H, et al. Delayed gadolinium-enhanced MR to determine glycosaminoglycan concentration in reparative cartilage after autologous chondrocyte implantation: preliminary results, Radiology 2006;239(1):201–8. https://doi.org/10.1148/radiol.2383050173. 16484349.

[25] Owman H, Tiderius CJ, Neuman P, Nyquist F, Dahlberg LE. Association between findings on delayed gadolinium-enhanced magnetic resonance imaging of cartilage and future knee osteoarthritis, Arthritis Rhcum 2008;58(6):1727–30. https://doi.org/10.1002/art.23459. 18512778.

[26] Palmer A, Fernquest S, Rombach I, Park D, Pollard T, Broomfield J, et al. Diagnostic and prognostic value of delayed gadolinium enhanced magnetic resonance imaging of cartilage (dGEMRIC) in early osteoarthritis of the hip, Osteoarthr Cartil 2017;25(9):1468–77. https://doi.org/10.1016/j.joca.2017.05.004. 28506842.

[27] Tiderius CJ, Olsson LE, Leander P, Ekberg O, Dahlberg L. Delayed gadolinium-enhanced MRI of cartilage (dGEMRIC) in early knee osteoarthritis, Magn Reson Med 2003;49(3):488–92. 12594751.

[28] Williams A, Sharma L, McKenzie CA, Prasad PV, Burstein D. Delayed gadolinium-enhanced magnetic resonance imaging of cartilage in knee osteoarthritis: findings at different radiographic stages of disease and relationship to malalignment, Arthritis Rheum 2005;52(11):3528–35. https://doi.org/10.1002/art.21388. 16255024.

[29] Tiderius CJ, Olsson LE, Nyquist F, Dahlberg L. Cartilage glycosaminoglycan loss in the acute phase after an anterior cruciate ligament injury: delayed gadolinium-enhanced magnetic resonance imaging of cartilage and synovial fluid analysis, Arthritis Rheum 2005;52(1):120–7. 15641092.

[30] Neuman P, Tjornstrand J, Svensson J, Ragnarsson C, Roos H, Englund M, et al. Longitudinal assessment of femoral knee cartilage quality using contrast enhanced MRI (dGEMRIC) in patients with anterior cruciate ligament injury—comparison with asymptomatic volunteers, Osteoarthr Cartil 2011;19(8):977–83. https://doi.org/10.1016/j.joca.2011.05.002. 21621622.

[31] Mamisch TC, Kain MS, Bittersohl B, Apprich S, Werlen S, Beck M, et al. Delayed gadolinium-enhanced magnetic resonance imaging of cartilage (dGEMRIC) in Femoacetabular impingement, J Orthop Res 2011;29(9):1305–11. https://doi.org/10.1002/jor.21371. 21437964.

[32] Kim YJ, Jaramillo D, Millis MB, Gray ML, Burstein D. Assessment of early osteoarthritis in hip dysplasia with delayed gadolinium-enhanced magnetic resonance imaging of cartilage, J Bone Joint Surg Am 2003;85-A(10):1987–92. 14563809.

[33] Cunningham T, Jessel R, Zurakowski D, Millis MB, Kim YJ. Delayed gadolinium-enhanced magnetic resonance imaging of cartilage to predict early failure of Bernese periacetabular osteotomy for hip dysplasia, J Bone Joint Surg Am 2006;88(7):1540–8. https://doi.org/10.2106/JBJS.E.00572. 16818980.

[34] Hayashi D, Li X, Murakami AM, Roemer FW, Trattnig S, Guermazi A. Understanding magnetic resonance imaging of knee cartilage repair: a focus on clinical relevance, Cartilage 2018;9(3):223–36. https://doi.org/10.1177/1947603517710309. 28580842.

[35] Xia Y. Relaxation anisotropy in cartilage by NMR microscopy (muMRI) at 14-microm resolution, Magn Reson Med 1998;39(6):941–9. 9621918.

[36] Xia Y. MRI of articular cartilage at microscopic resolution, Bone Joint Res 2013;2(1):9–17. https://doi.org/10.1302/2046-3758.21.2000135. 23610697.

[37] Nieminen MT, Rieppo J, Toyras J, Hakumaki JM, Silvennoinen J, Hyttinen MM, et al. T2 relaxation reveals spatial collagen architecture in articular cartilage: a comparative quantitative MRI and polarized light microscopic study, Magn Reson Med 2001;46(3):487–93. https://doi.org/10.1002/mrm.1218. 11550240.
[38] Reiter DA, Roque RA, Lin PC, Doty SB, Pleshko N, Spencer RG. Improved specificity of cartilage matrix evaluation using multiexponential transverse relaxation analysis applied to pathomimetically degraded cartilage, NMR Biomed 2011;24(10):1286–94. https://doi.org/10.1002/nbm.1690. 21465593.
[39] Wang N, Xia Y. Experimental issues in the measurement of multi-component relaxation times in articular cartilage by microscopic MRI, J Magn Reson 2013;235:15–25. https://doi.org/10.1016/j.jmr.2013.07.001. 23916991.
[40] Schneider E, NessAiver M, White D, Purdy D, Martin L, Fanella L, et al. The osteoarthritis initiative (OAI) magnetic resonance imaging quality assurance methods and results, Osteoarthr Cartil 2008;16(9):994–1004. https://doi.org/10.1016/j.joca.2008.02.010. 18424108.
[41] Raya JG, Dietrich O, Horng A, Weber J, Reiser MF, Glaser C. T2 measurement in articular cartilage: impact of the fitting method on accuracy and precision at low SNR, Magn Reson Med 2010;63(1):181–93. https://doi.org/10.1002/mrm.22178. 19859960.
[42] Sveinsson B, Chaudhari AS, Gold GE, Hargreaves BA. A simple analytic method for estimating T2 in the knee from DESS, Magn Reson Imaging 2017;38:63–70. https://doi.org/10.1016/j.mri.2016.12.018. 28017730.
[43] Heule R, Ganter C, Bieri O. Triple echo steady-state (TESS) relaxometry, Magn Reson Med 2014;71(1):230–7. https://doi.org/10.1002/mrm.24659. 23553949.
[44] Liu F, Choi KW, Samsonov A, Spencer RG, Wilson JJ, Block WF, et al. Articular cartilage of the human knee joint: in vivo multicomponent T2 analysis at 3.0 T, Radiology 2015;142201. https://doi.org/10.1148/radiol.2015142201 26024307.
[45] Mosher T, Liu Y, Yang Q, Yao J, Smith R, Dardzinski B, et al. Age dependency of cartilage magnetic resonance imaging T2 relaxation times in asymptomatic women. Arthritis Rheum 2004;50(9):2820–8.
[46] Joseph GB, McCulloch CE, Nevitt MC, Heilmeier U, Nardo L, Lynch JA, et al. A reference database of cartilage 3 T MRI T2 values in knees without diagnostic evidence of cartilage degeneration: data from the osteoarthritis initiative, Osteoarthr Cartil 2015;23(6):897–905. https://doi.org/10.1016/j.joca.2015.02.006. 25680652.
[47] Mosher TJ, Liu Y, Torok CM. Functional cartilage MRI T2 mapping: evaluating the effect of age and training on knee cartilage response to running, Osteoarthr Cartil 2010;18(3):358–64. https://doi.org/10.1016/j.joca.2009.11.011. 19948266.
[48] Nishii T, Kuroda K, Matsuoka Y, Sahara T, Yoshikawa H. Change in knee cartilage T2 in response to mechanical loading, J Magn Reson Imaging 2008;28(1):175–80. https://doi.org/10.1002/jmri.21418. 18581338.
[49] Mosher T, Dardzinski B. Cartilage MRI T2 relaxation time mapping: overview and applications. Semin Musculoskelet Radiol 2004;8(4):355–68.
[50] Jungmann PM, Kraus MS, Nardo L, Liebl H, Alizai H, Joseph GB, et al. T(2) relaxation time measurements are limited in monitoring progression, once advanced cartilage defects at the knee occur: longitudinal data from the osteoarthritis initiative, J Magn Reson Imaging 2013;38(6):1415–24. https://doi.org/10.1002/jmri.24137. 24038491.
[51] Kijowski R, Blankenbaker DG, Munoz Del Rio A, Baer GS, Graf BK. Evaluation of the articular cartilage of the knee joint: value of adding a T2 mapping sequence to a routine MR imaging protocol, Radiology 2013;267(2):503–13. https://doi.org/10.1148/radiol.12121413. 23297335.
[52] Joseph GB, Baum T, Carballido-Gamio J, Nardo L, Virayavanich W, Alizai H, et al. Texture analysis of cartilage T2 maps: individuals with risk factors for OA have higher and more heterogeneous knee cartilage MR T2 compared to normal controls—data from the osteoarthritis initiative, Arthritis Res Ther 2011;13(5):R153. https://doi.org/10.1186/ar3469. 21933394.

[53] Joseph GB, Baum T, Alizai H, Carballido-Gamio J, Nardo L, Virayavanich W, et al. Baseline mean and heterogeneity of MR cartilage T2 are associated with morphologic degeneration of cartilage, meniscus, and bone marrow over 3 years—data from the osteoarthritis initiative, Osteoarthr Cartil 2012;20(7):727–35. https://doi.org/10.1016/j.joca.2012.04.003. 22503812.

[54] Liebl H, Joseph G, Nevitt MC, Singh N, Heilmeier U, Subburaj K, et al. Early T2 changes predict onset of radiographic knee osteoarthritis: data from the osteoarthritis initiative, Ann Rheum Dis 2015;74(7):1353–9. https://doi.org/10.1136/annrheumdis-2013-204157. 24615539.

[55] Ashinsky BG, Bouhrara M, Coletta CE, Lehallier B, Urish KL, Lin PC, et al. Predicting early symptomatic osteoarthritis in the human knee using machine learning classification of magnetic resonance images from the osteoarthritis initiative, J Orthop Res 2017;35(10):2243–50. https://doi.org/10.1002/jor.23519. 28084653.

[56] Lin W, Alizai H, Joseph GB, Srikhum W, Nevitt MC, Lynch JA, et al. Physical activity in relation to knee cartilage T2 progression measured with 3 T MRI over a period of 4 years: data from the Osteoarthritis Initiative, Osteoarthr Cartil 2013;21(10):1558–66. https://doi.org/10.1016/j.joca.2013.06.022. 23831632.

[57] Gersing AS, Solka M, Joseph GB, Schwaiger BJ, Heilmeier U, Feuerriegel G, et al. Progression of cartilage degeneration and clinical symptoms in obese and overweight individuals is dependent on the amount of weight loss: 48-month data from the Osteoarthritis Initiative, Osteoarthr Cartil 2016;24(7):1126–34. https://doi.org/10.1016/j.joca.2016.01.984. 26828356.

[58] Tsai PH, Wong CC, Chan WP, Lu TW. The value of MR T2* measurements in normal and osteoarthritic knee cartilage: effects of age, sex, and location, Eur Radiol 2019;29(8):4514–22. https://doi.org/10.1007/s00330-018-5826-z. 30617477.

[59] Ellermann J, Ziegler C, Nissi MJ, Goebel R, Hughes J, Benson M, et al. Acetabular cartilage assessment in patients with femoroacetabular impingement by using T2* mapping with arthroscopic verification, Radiology 2014;271(2):512–23. https://doi.org/10.1148/radiol.13131837. 24520945.

[60] Mahar R, Batool S, Badar F, Xia Y. Quantitative measurement of T2, T1rho and T1 relaxation times in articular cartilage and cartilage-bone interface by SE and UTE imaging at microscopic resolution, J Magn Reson 2018;297:76–85. https://doi.org/10.1016/j.jmr.2018.10.008. 30366222.

[61] Makela HI, Grohn OH, Kettunen MI, Kauppinen RA. Proton exchange as a relaxation mechanism for T1 in the rotating frame in native and immobilized protein solutions, Biochem Biophys Res Commun 2001;289(4):813–8. 11735118.

[62] Duvvuri U, Goldberg AD, Kranz JK, Hoang L, Reddy R, Wehrli FW, et al. Water magnetic relaxation dispersion in biological systems: the contribution of proton exchange and implications for the noninvasive detection of cartilage degradation, Proc Natl Acad Sci U S A 2001;98(22):12479–84. 11606754.

[63] Kettunen M, Gröhn O, Silvennoinen M, Penttonen M, Kauppinen R. Effects of intracellular pH, blood, and tissue oxygen tension on T1rho relaxation in rat brain. Magn Reson Med 2002;48(3):470–7.

[64] Cobb JG, Xie J, Gore JC. Contributions of chemical exchange to T1rho dispersion in a tissue model, Magn Reson Med 2011;66(6):1563–71. https://doi.org/10.1002/mrm.22947. 21590720.

[65] Wang P, Block J, Gore JC. Chemical exchange in knee cartilage assessed by R1rho (1/T1rho) dispersion at 3T, Magn Reson Imaging 2015;33(1):38–42. https://doi.org/10.1016/j.mri.2014.07.008. 25093631.

[66] Mlynarik V, Szomolanyi P, Toffanin R, Vittur F, Trattnig S. Transverse relaxation mechanisms in articular cartilage, J Magn Reson 2004;169(2):300–7. 15261626.

[67] Regatte R, Akella S, Lonner J, Kneeland J, Reddy R. T1rho relaxation mapping in human osteoarthritis (OA) cartilage: comparison of T1rho with T2. J Magn Reson Imaging 2006;23(4):547–53.

[68] Li X, Cheng J, Lin K, Saadat E, Bolbos RI, Jobke B, et al. Quantitative MRI using T1rho and T2 in human osteoarthritic cartilage specimens: correlation with biochemical measurements and histology, Magn Reson Imaging 2011;29(3):324–34. https://doi.org/10.1016/j.mri.2010.09.004. 21130590.

[69] Keenan KE, Besier TF, Pauly JM, Han E, Rosenberg J, Smith RL, et al. Prediction of glycosaminoglycan content in human cartilage by age, T1rho and T2 MRI, Osteoarthr Cartil 2011;19(2):171–9. https://doi.org/10.1016/j.joca.2010.11.009. 21112409.

[70] Menezes NM, Gray ML, Hartke JR, Burstein D. T2 and T1rho MRI in articular cartilage systems, Magn Reson Med 2004;51(3):503–9. 15004791.

[71] Wheaton A, Dodge G, Elliott D, Nicoll S, Reddy R. Quantification of cartilage biomechanical and biochemical properties via T1rho magnetic resonance imaging. Magn Reson Med 2005;54(5):1087–93.

[72] Tang SY, Souza RB, Ries M, Hansma PK, Alliston T, Li X. Local tissue properties of human osteoarthritic cartilage correlate with magnetic resonance T(1) rho relaxation times, J Orthop Res 2011;29(9):1312–9. https://doi.org/10.1002/jor.21381. 21445940.

[73] Keenan KE, Besier TF, Pauly JM, Smith RL, Delp SL, Beaupre GS, et al. T1rho dispersion in articular cartilage: relationship to material properties and macromolecular content, Cartilage 2015;6(2):113–22. https://doi.org/10.1177/1947603515569529. 26069714.

[74] Akella SV, Regatte RR, Wheaton AJ, Borthakur A, Reddy R. Reduction of residual dipolar interaction in cartilage by spin-lock technique, Magn Reson Med 2004;52(5):1103–9. 15508163.

[75] Hanninen N, Rautiainen J, Rieppo L, Saarakkala S, Nissi MJ. Orientation anisotropy of quantitative MRI relaxation parameters in ordered tissue, Sci Rep 2017;7(1):9606. https://doi.org/10.1038/s41598-017-10053-2. 28852032.

[76] Witschey W, Borthakur A, Elliott M, Fenty M, Sochor M, Wang C, et al. T1rho-prepared balanced gradient echo for rapid 3D T1rho MRI. J Magn Reson Imaging 2008;28(3):744–54.

[77] Li X, Han E, Busse R, Majumdar S. In vivo T1rho mapping in cartilage using 3D magnetization-prepared angle-modulated partitioned k-space spoiled gradient echo snapshots (3D MAPSS). Magn Reson Med 2008;59(2):298–307.

[78] Chen W. Errors in quantitative $T_{1\rho}$ imaging and the correction methods. Quant Imaging Med Surg 2015;5(4):583–91.

[79] Mitrea BG, Krafft AJ, Song R, Loeffler RB, Hillenbrand CM. Paired self-compensated spin-lock preparation for improved $T_{1\rho}$ quantification. J Magn Reson 2016;268:49–57.

[80] Michaeli S, Sorce DJ, Idiyatullin D, Ugurbil K, Garwood M. Transverse relaxation in the rotating frame induced by chemical exchange, J Magn Reson 2004;169(2):293–9. https://doi.org/10.1016/j.jmr.2004.05.010. 15261625.

[81] Nissi MJ, Salo EN, Tiitu V, Liimatainen T, Michaeli S, Mangia S, et al. Multi-parametric MRI characterization of enzymatically degraded articular cartilage, J Orthop Res 2016;34(7):1111–20. https://doi.org/10.1002/jor.23127. 26662555.

[82] Pakin S, Schweitzer M, Regatte R. Rapid 3D-T1rho mapping of the knee joint at 3.0T with parallel imaging. Magn Reson Med 2006;56(3):563–71.

[83] Zhou Y, Pandit P, Pedoia V, Rivoire J, Wang Y, Liang D, et al. Accelerating T1rho cartilage imaging using compressed sensing with iterative locally adapted support detection and JSENSE, Magn Reson Med 2016;75(4):1617–29. https://doi.org/10.1002/mrm.25773. 26010735.

[84] MacKay JW, Low SBL, Smith TO, Toms AP, AW MC, Gilbert FJ. Systematic review and meta-analysis of the reliability and discriminative validity of cartilage compositional MRI in knee osteoarthritis, Osteoarthr Cartil 2018. https://doi.org/10.1016/j.joca.2017.11.01829550400.

[85] Li X, Pedoia V, Kumar D, Rivoire J, Wyatt C, Lansdown D, et al. Cartilage T1rho and T2 relaxation times: longitudinal reproducibility and variations using different coils, MR systems and sites, Osteoarthr Cartil 2015;23(12):2214–23. https://doi.org/10.1016/j.joca.2015.07.006. 26187574.

[86] Kim J, Mamoto K, Lartey R, et al. Multi-vendor multi-site $T_{1\rho}$ and T_2 quantification of knee cartilage. Osteoarthr Cartil 2020;S1063-4584(20):31085–92. https://doi.org/10.1016/j.joca.2020.07.005 [published online ahead of print, 2020 Jul 30].

[87] Atkinson HF, Birmingham TB, Moyer RF, Yacoub D, Kanko LE, Bryant DM, et al. MRI T2 and T1rho relaxation in patients at risk for knee osteoarthritis: a systematic review and meta-analysis, BMC Musculoskelet Disord 2019;20(1):182. https://doi.org/10.1186/s12891-019-2547-7. 31039785.

[88] Li X, Ma C, Link T, Castillo D, Blumenkrantz G, Lozano J, et al. In vivo T1rho and T2 mapping of articular cartilage in osteoarthritis of the knee using 3 Tesla MRI. Osteoarthr Cartil 2007;15(7):789–97.

[89] Prasad AP, Nardo L, Schooler J, Joseph GB, Link TM. T(1)rho and T(2) relaxation times predict progression of knee osteoarthritis, Osteoarthr Cartil 2013;21(1):69–76. https://doi.org/10.1016/j.joca.2012.09.011. 23059757.

[90] Li X, Kuo D, Theologis A, Carballido-Gamio J, Stehling C, Link TM, et al. Cartilage in anterior cruciate ligament-reconstructed knees: MR imaging T1{rho} and T2--initial experience with 1-year follow-up, Radiology 2011;258(2):505–14. https://doi.org/10.1148/radiol.10101006. 21177392.

[91] Potter HG, Jain SK, Ma Y, Black BR, Fung S, Lyman S. Cartilage injury after acute, isolated anterior cruciate ligament tear: immediate and longitudinal effect with clinical/MRI follow-up, Am J Sports Med 2012;40(2):276–85. https://doi.org/10.1177/0363546511423380. 21952715.

[92] Monu UD, Jordan CD, Samuelson BL, Hargreaves BA, Gold GE, McWalter EJ. Cluster analysis of quantitative MRI T2 and T1rho relaxation times of cartilage identifies differences between healthy and ACL-injured individuals at 3T, Osteoarthr Cartil 2017;25(4):513–20. https://doi.org/10.1016/j.joca.2016.09.015. 27720806.

[93] Su F, Pedoia V, Teng HL, Kretzschmar M, Lau BC, McCulloch CE, et al. The association between MR T1rho and T2 of cartilage and patient-reported outcomes after ACL injury and reconstruction, Osteoarthr Cartil 2016;24(7):1180–9. https://doi.org/10.1016/j.joca.2016.01.985. 26850823.

[94] Pietrosimone B, Nissman D, Padua DA, Blackburn JT, Harkey MS, Creighton RA, et al. Associations between cartilage proteoglycan density and patient outcomes 12months following anterior cruciate ligament reconstruction, Knee 2018;25(1):118–29. https://doi.org/10.1016/j.knee.2017.10.005. 29329888.

[95] Pedoia V, Russell C, Randolph A, Li X, Majumdar S, Consortium A-A. Principal component analysis-T-1rho voxel based relaxometry of the articular cartilage: a comparison of biochemical patterns in osteoarthritis and anterior cruciate ligament subjects, Quant Imaging Med Surg 2016;6(6):623–33. https://doi.org/10.21037/qims.2016.11.03. 28090441.

[96] Beaule PE, Speirs AD, Anwander H, Melkus G, Rakhra K, Frei H, et al. Surgical correction of cam deformity in association with Femoroacetabular impingement and its impact on the degenerative process within the hip joint, J Bone Joint Surg Am 2017;99(16):1373–81. https://doi.org/10.2106/JBJS.16.00415. 28816897.

[97] Grace T, Samaan MA, Souza RB, Link TM, Majumdar S, Zhang AL. Correlation of patient symptoms with labral and articular cartilage damage in femoroacetabular impingement, Orthop J Sports Med 2018;6(6), 2325967118778785. https://doi.org/10.1177/23259671187787852997942.

[98] Wikstrom EA, Song K, Tennant JN, Dederer KM, Paranjape C, Pietrosimone B. T1rho MRI of the talar articular cartilage is increased in those with chronic ankle instability, Osteoarthr Cartil 2019;27(4):646–9. https://doi.org/10.1016/j.joca.2018.12.019. 30634032.

[99] Saxena V, D'Aquilla K, Marcoon S, Krishnamoorthy G, Gordon JA, Carey JL, et al. T1rho magnetic resonance imaging to assess cartilage damage after primary shoulder dislocation, Am J Sports Med 2016;44(11):2800–6. https://doi.org/10.1177/0363546516655338. 27466221.

[100] Nardo L, Carballido-Gamio J, Tang S, Lai A, Krug R. Quantitative assessment of morphology, T1rho, and T2 of shoulder cartilage using MRI, Eur Radiol 2016;26(12):4656–63. https://doi.org/10.1007/s00330-016-4322-6. 26993651.

[101] Akella SV, Regatte RR, Borthakur A, Kneeland JB, Leigh JS, Reddy R. T1rho MR imaging of the human wrist in vivo, Acad Radiol 2003;10(6):614–9. 12809414.

[102] Ku E, Pedoia V, Tanaka M, Imboden J, Graf J, Link T, et al., Radiocarpal cartilage matrix changes 3-months after anti-TNF treatment for Rheumatoid Arthritis – a feasibility study using MR T1ρ imaging. The annual meeting of American College of Rheumatology (ACR); 2015 November 7–11; San Francisco, USA; 2015.

[103] Maier CF, Tan SG, Hariharan H, Potter HG. T2 quantitation of articular cartilage at 1.5 T, J Magn Reson Imaging 2003;17(3):358–64. https://doi.org/10.1002/jmri.10263. 12594727.

[104] Balamoody S, Williams TG, Wolstenholme C, Waterton JC, Bowes M, Hodgson R, et al. Magnetic resonance transverse relaxation time T2 of knee cartilage in osteoarthritis at 3-T: a cross-sectional multicentre, multivendor reproducibility study, Skeletal Radiol 2013;42(4):511–20. https://doi.org/10.1007/s00256-012-1511-5. 23053200.

[105] Janssen I, Heymsfield SB, Wang ZM, Ross R. Skeletal muscle mass and distribution in 468 men and women aged 18–88 yr, J Appl Physiol (1985) 2000;89(1):81–8. https://doi.org/10.1152/jappl.2000.89.1.81. 10904038.

[106] Frontera WR, Ochala J. Skeletal muscle: a brief review of structure and function, Calcif Tissue Int 2015;96(3):183–95. https://doi.org/10.1007/s00223-014-9915-y. 25294644.

[107] Damon BM, Li K, Bryant ND. Magnetic resonance imaging of skeletal muscle disease, Handb Clin Neurol 2016;136:827–42. https://doi.org/10.1016/B978-0-444-53486-6.00041-7. 27430444.

[108] Carlier PG, Marty B, Scheidegger O, Loureiro de Sousa P, Baudin PY, Snezhko E, et al. Skeletal muscle quantitative nuclear magnetic resonance imaging and spectroscopy as an outcome measure for clinical trials, J Neuromuscul Dis 2016;3(1):1–28. https://doi.org/10.3233/JND-160145. 27854210.

[109] Ploutz-Snyder LL, Nyren S, Cooper TG, Potchen EJ, Meyer RA. Different effects of exercise and edema on T2 relaxation in skeletal muscle, Magn Reson Med 1997;37(5):676–82. 9126941.

[110] Saab G, Thompson RT, Marsh GD. Multicomponent T2 relaxation of in vivo skeletal muscle, Magn Reson Med 1999;42(1):150–7. 10398961.

[111] Sharafi A, Chang G, Regatte RR. Bi-component T1rho and T2 relaxation mapping of skeletal muscle in-vivo, Sci Rep 2017;7(1):14115. https://doi.org/10.1038/s41598-017-14581-9. 29074883.

[112] Forbes SC, Walter GA, Rooney WD, Wang DJ, DeVos S, Pollaro J, et al. Skeletal muscles of ambulant children with Duchenne muscular dystrophy: validation of multicenter study of evaluation with MR imaging and MR spectroscopy, Radiology 2013;269(1):198–207. https://doi.org/10.1148/radiol.13121948. 23696684.

[113] Klupp E, Weidlich D, Schlaeger S, Baum T, Cervantes B, Deschauer M, et al. B1-insensitive T2 mapping of healthy thigh muscles using a T2-prepared 3D TSE sequence, PLoS One 2017;12(2):e0171337. https://doi.org/10.1371/journal.pone.017133728196133.

[114] Huang Y, Majumdar S, Genant HK, Chan WP, Sharma KR, Yu P, et al. Quantitative MR relaxometry study of muscle composition and function in Duchenne muscular dystrophy, J Magn Reson Imaging 1994;4(1):59–64. 8148557.

[115] Yao L, Gai N. Fat-corrected T2 measurement as a marker of active muscle disease in inflammatory myopathy, AJR Am J Roentgenol 2012;198(5):W475–81. https://doi.org/10.2214/AJR.11.7113. 22528929.

[116] Arrigoni F, De Luca A, Velardo D, Magri F, Gandossini S, Russo A, et al. Multiparametric quantitative MRI assessment of thigh muscles in limb-girdle muscular dystrophy 2A and 2B, Muscle Nerve 2018;58(4):550–8. https://doi.org/10.1002/mus.26189. 30028523.

[117] Kim HK, Laor T, Horn PS, Racadio JM, Wong B, Dardzinski BJ. T2 mapping in Duchenne muscular dystrophy: distribution of disease activity and correlation with clinical assessments, Radiology 2010;255(3):899–908. https://doi.org/10.1148/radiol.10091547. 20501727.

[118] Arpan I, Willcocks RJ, Forbes SC, Finkel RS, Lott DJ, Rooney WD, et al. Examination of effects of corticosteroids on skeletal muscles of boys with DMD using MRI and MRS, Neurology 2014;83(11):974–80. https://doi.org/10.1212/WNL.0000000000000775. 25098537.

[119] Azzabou N, Loureiro de Sousa P, Caldas E, Carlier PG. Validation of a generic approach to muscle water T2 determination at 3T in fat-infiltrated skeletal muscle, J Magn Reson Imaging 2015;41(3):645–53. https://doi.org/10.1002/jmri.24613. 24590466.

[120] Friedman SD, Poliachik SL, Carter GT, Budech CB, Bird TD, Shaw DW. The magnetic resonance imaging spectrum of facioscapulohumeral muscular dystrophy, Muscle Nerve 2012;45(4):500–6. https://doi.org/10.1002/mus.22342. 22431082.

[121] Bryan WW, Reisch JS, McDonald G, Herbelin LL, Barohn RJ, Fleckenstein JL. Magnetic resonance imaging of muscle in amyotrophic lateral sclerosis, Neurology 1998;51(1):110–3. 9674787.

[122] Cagnie B, Elliott JM, O'Leary S, D'Hooge R, Dickx N, Danneels LA. Muscle functional MRI as an imaging tool to evaluate muscle activity, J Orthop Sports Phys Ther 2011;41(11):896–903. https://doi.org/10.2519/jospt.2011.3586. 21891877.

[123] Schuermans J, Van Tiggelen D, Danneels L, Witvrouw E. Biceps femoris and semitendinosus—teammates or competitors? New insights into hamstring injury mechanisms in male football players: a muscle functional MRI study, Br J Sports Med 2014;48(22):1599–606. https://doi.org/10.1136/bjsports-2014-094017. 25388959.

[124] Peng XG, Wang Y, Zhang S, Bai Y, Mao H, Teng GJ, et al. Noninvasive assessment of age, gender, and exercise effects on skeletal muscle: initial experience with T1 rho MRI of calf muscle, J Magn Reson Imaging 2017;46(1):61–70. https://doi.org/10.1002/jmri.25546. 27862560.

[125] Virta A, Komu M, Lundbom N, Jaaskelainen S, Kalimo H, Airio A, et al. Low field T1rho imaging of myositis, Magn Reson Imaging 1998;16(4):385–91. 9665549.

[126] Lohmander L, Englund P, Dahl L, Roos E. The long-term consequence of anterior cruciate ligament and meniscus injuries: osteoarthritis. Am J Sports Med 2007;35(10):1756–69.

[127] Rauscher I, Stahl R, Cheng J, Li X, Huber MB, Luke A, et al. Meniscal measurements of T1rho and T2 at MR imaging in healthy subjects and patients with osteoarthritis, Radiology 2008;249(2):591–600. https://doi.org/10.1148/radiol.2492071870. 18936315.

[128] Kajabi AW, Casula V, Nissi MJ, Peuna A, Podlipska J, Lammentausta E, et al. Assessment of meniscus with adiabatic T1rho and T2rho relaxation time in asymptomatic subjects and patients with mild osteoarthritis: a feasibility study, Osteoarthr Cartil 2018;26(4):580–7. https://doi.org/10.1016/j.joca.2017.12.006. 29269326.

[129] Bolbos RI, Link TM, Ma CB, Majumdar S, Li X. T1rho relaxation time of the meniscus and its relationship with T1rho of adjacent cartilage in knees with acute ACL injuries at 3 T, Osteoarthr Cartil 2009;17(1):12–8. https://doi.org/10.1016/j.joca.2008.05.016. 18602280.

[130] Wang L, Chang G, Bencardino J, Babb JS, Rokito A, Jazrawi L, et al. T1rho MRI at 3T of menisci in patients with acute anterior cruciate ligament (ACL) injury, J Magn Reson Imaging 2015;41(2):544–9. https://doi.org/10.1002/jmri.24594. 24616029.

[131] Wang A, Pedoia V, Su F, Abramson E, Kretzschmar M, Nardo L, et al. MR T1rho and T2 of meniscus after acute anterior cruciate ligament injuries, Osteoarthr Cartil 2016;24(4):631–9. https://doi.org/10.1016/j.joca.2015.11.012. 26620091.

[132] Knox J, Pedoia V, Wang A, Tanaka M, Joseph GB, Neumann J, et al. Longitudinal changes in MR T1rho/T2 signal of meniscus and its association with cartilage T1p/T2 in ACL-injured patients, Osteoarthr Cartil 2018;26(5):689–96. https://doi.org/10.1016/j.joca.2018.02.001. 29438746.

[133] Robson MD, Gatehouse PD, Bydder M, Bydder GM. Magnetic resonance: an introduction to ultrashort TE (UTE) imaging, J Comput Assist Tomogr 2003;27(6):825–46. 14600447.

[134] Chang EY, Du J, Chung CB. UTE imaging in the musculoskeletal system, J Magn Reson Imaging 2015;41(4):870–83. https://doi.org/10.1002/jmri.24713. 25045018.

[135] Chu CR, Williams AA, West RV, Qian Y, Fu FH, Do BH, et al. Quantitative magnetic resonance imaging UTE-T2* mapping of cartilage and meniscus healing after anatomic anterior cruciate ligament reconstruction, Am J Sports Med 2014;42(8):1847–56. https://doi.org/10.1177/0363546514532227. 24812196.

[136] Chen B, Zhao Y, Cheng X, Ma Y, Chang EY, Kavanaugh A, et al. Three-dimensional ultrashort echo time cones (3D UTE-cones) magnetic resonance imaging of entheses and tendons, Magn Reson Imaging 2018;49:4–9. https://doi.org/10.1016/j.mri.2017.12.034. 29309823.

[137] Qiao Y, Tao HY, Ma K, Wu ZY, Qu JX, Chen S. UTE-T2* analysis of diseased and healthy achilles tendons and correlation with clinical score: an in vivo preliminary study, Biomed Res Int 2017;2017:, 2729807. https://doi.org/10.1155/2017/272980728154823.

[138] Kijowski R, Wilson JJ, Liu F. Bicomponent ultrashort echo time T2* analysis for assessment of patients with patellar tendinopathy, J Magn Reson Imaging 2017;46(5):1441–7. https://doi.org/10.1002/jmri.25689. 28263448.

[139] Filho GH, Du J, Pak BC, Statum S, Znamorowski R, Haghighi P, et al. Quantitative characterization of the Achilles tendon in cadaveric specimens: T1 and T2* measurements using ultrashort-TE MRI at 3 T, AJR Am J Roentgenol 2009;192(3):W117–24. https://doi.org/10.2214/AJR.07.3990. 19234239.

[140] Ma YJ, Lu X, Carl M, Zhu Y, Szeverenyi NM, Bydder GM, et al. Accurate T1 mapping of short T2 tissues using a three-dimensional ultrashort echo time cones actual flip angle imaging-variable repetition time (3D UTE-Cones AFI-VTR) method, Magn Reson Med 2018;80(2):598–608. https://doi.org/10.1002/mrm.27066. 29314235.

[141] Du J, Carl M, Diaz E, Takahashi A, Han E, Szeverenyi NM, et al. Ultrashort TE T1rho (UTE T1rho) imaging of the Achilles tendon and meniscus, Magn Reson Med 2010;64(3):834–42. https://doi.org/10.1002/mrm.22474. 20535810.

[142] Ma YJ, Carl M, Searleman A, Lu X, Chang EY, Du J. 3D adiabatic T1rho prepared ultrashort echo time cones sequence for whole knee imaging, Magn Reson Med 2018;80(4):1429–39. https://doi.org/10.1002/mrm.27131. 29493004.

[143] Chaudhari AS, Sveinsson B, Moran CJ, McWalter EJ, Johnson EM, Zhang T, et al. Imaging and T2 relaxometry of short-T2 connective tissues in the knee using ultrashort echo-time double-echo steady-state (UTEDESS), Magn Reson Med 2017;78(6):2136–48. https://doi.org/10.1002/mrm.26577. 28074498.

[144] Hoy D, March L, Brooks P, Blyth F, Woolf A, Bain C, et al. The global burden of low back pain: estimates from the global burden of disease 2010 study, Ann Rheum Dis 2014;73(6):968–74. https://doi.org/10.1136/annrheumdis-2013-204428. 24665116.

[145] Chiu EJ, Newitt DC, Segal MR, Hu SS, Lotz JC, Majumdar S. Magnetic resonance imaging measurement of relaxation and water diffusion in the human lumbar intervertebral disc under compression in vitro, Spine (Phila Pa 1976) 2001;26(19):E437–44. 11698903.

[146] Duewell SH, Ceckler TL, Ong K, Wen H, Jaffer FA, Chesnick SA, et al. Musculoskeletal MR imaging at 4 T and at 1.5 T: comparison of relaxation times and image contrast, Radiology 1995;196(2):551–5. https://doi.org/10.1148/radiology.196.2.7617876. 7617876.

[147] Hannila I, Raina SS, Tervonen O, Ojala R, Nieminen MT. Topographical variation of T2 relaxation time in the young adult knee cartilage at 1.5 T, Osteoarthr Cartil 2009;17(12):1570–5. https://doi.org/10.1016/j.joca.2009.05.011. 19501682.

[148] Stelzeneder D, Welsch GH, Kovacs BK, Goed S, Paternostro-Sluga T, Vlychou M, et al. Quantitative T2 evaluation at 3.0T compared to morphological grading of the lumbar intervertebral disc: a standardized evaluation approach in patients with low back pain, Eur J Radiol 2012;81(2):324–30. https://doi.org/10.1016/j.ejrad.2010.12.093. 21315527.

[149] Blumenkrantz G, Zuo J, Li X, Kornak J, Link TM, Majumdar S. In vivo 3.0-tesla magnetic resonance T1rho and T2 relaxation mapping in subjects with intervertebral disc degeneration and clinical symptoms, Magn Reson Med 2010;63(5):1193–200. https://doi.org/10.1002/mrm.22362. 20432290.

[150] Jordan CD, Saranathan M, Bangerter NK, Hargreaves BA, Gold GE. Musculoskeletal MRI at 3.0 T and 7.0 T: a comparison of relaxation times and image contrast, Eur J Radiol 2013;82(5):734–9. https://doi.org/10.1016/j.ejrad.2011.09.021. 22172536.

[151] Welsch GH, Apprich S, Zbyn S, Mamisch TC, Mlynarik V, Scheffler K, et al. Biochemical (T2, T2* and magnetisation transfer ratio) MRI of knee cartilage: feasibility at ultra-high field (7T) compared with high field (3T) strength, Eur Radiol 2011;21(6):1136–43. https://doi.org/10.1007/s00330-010-2029-7. 21153551.

[152] Wyatt C, Guha A, Venkatachari A, Li X, Krug R, Kelley DE, et al. Improved differentiation between knees with cartilage lesions and controls using 7T relaxation time mapping, J Orthop Translat 2015;3(4): 197–204. https://doi.org/10.1016/j.jot.2015.05.003. 30035058.

[153] Regatte RR, Schweitzer ME. Ultra-high-field MRI of the musculoskeletal system at 7.0T, J Magn Reson Imaging 2007;25(2):262–9. https://doi.org/10.1002/jmri.20814. 17260399.

[154] Han Z, Gao L, Shi Q, Chen L, Chen C. Quantitative magnetic resonance imaging for diagnosis of intervertebral disc degeneration of the cervico-thoracic junction: a pilot study, Am J Transl Res 2018;10(3):925–35. 29636882.

[155] Auerbach JD, Johannessen W, Borthakur A, Wheaton AJ, Dolinskas CA, Balderston RA, et al. In vivo quantification of human lumbar disc degeneration using T(1rho)-weighted magnetic resonance imaging, Eur Spine J 2006;15(Suppl 3):S338–44. https://doi.org/10.1007/s00586-006-0083-2. 16552534.

[156] Duvvuri U, Charagundla SR, Kudchodkar SB, Kaufman JH, Kneeland JB, Rizi R, et al. Human knee: in vivo T1(rho)-weighted MR imaging at 1.5 T—preliminary experience, Radiology 2001;220(3):822–6. 11526288.

[157] Wang YX, Griffith JF, Leung JC, Yuan J. Age related reduction of T1rho and T2 magnetic resonance relaxation times of lumbar intervertebral disc, Quant Imaging Med Surg 2014;4(4):259–64. https://doi.org/10.3978/j.issn.2223-4292.2014.07.14. 25202661.

[158] Singh A, Haris M, Cai K, Kogan F, Hariharan H, Reddy R. High resolution T1rho mapping of in vivo human knee cartilage at 7T, PLoS One 2014;9(5), e97486. https://doi.org/10.1371/journal.pone.009748624830386.

[159] Chatani K, Kusaka Y, Mifune T, Nishikawa H. Topographic differences of 1H-NMR relaxation times (T1, T2) in the normal intervertebral disc and its relationship to water content, Spine (Phila Pa 1976) 1993;18(15):2271–5. 8278845.

[160] Boos N, Dreier D, Hilfiker E, Schade V, Kreis R, Hora J, et al. Tissue characterization of symptomatic and asymptomatic disc herniations by quantitative magnetic resonance imaging, J Orthop Res 1997; 15(1):141–9. https://doi.org/10.1002/jor.1100150121. 9066539.

[161] Niinimaki JL, Parviainen O, Ruohonen J, Ojala RO, Kurunlahti M, Karppinen J, et al. In vivo quantification of delayed gadolinium enhancement in the nucleus pulposus of human intervertebral disc, J Magn Reson Imaging 2006;24(4):796–800. https://doi.org/10.1002/jmri.20693. 16929532.

[162] Bostelmann R, Bostelmann T, Nasaca A, Steiger HJ, Zaucke F, Schleich C. Biochemical validity of imaging techniques (X-ray, MRI, and dGEMRIC) in degenerative disc disease of the human cervical spine-an in vivo study, Spine J 2017;17(2):196–202. https://doi.org/10.1016/j.spinee.2016.08.031. 27568543.

[163] Tibiletti M, Galbusera F, Ciavarro C, Brayda-Bruno M. Is the transport of a gadolinium-based contrast agent decreased in a degenerated or aged disc? A post contrast MRI study, PLoS One 2013;8(10):e76697. https://doi.org/10.1371/journal.pone.0076697. 24146913.

[164] Blumenkrantz G, Li X, Han ET, Newitt DC, Crane JC, Link TM, et al. A feasibility study of in vivo T1rho imaging of the intervertebral disc, Magn Reson Imaging 2006;24(8):1001–7. https://doi.org/10.1016/j.mri.2006.04.013. 16997069.

[165] Pandit P, Talbott JF, Pedoia V, Dillon W, Majumdar S. T1rho and T2 -based characterization of regional variations in intervertebral discs to detect early degenerative changes, J Orthop Res 2016;34(8):1373–81. https://doi.org/10.1002/jor.23311. 27227485.

[166] Wang YX, Zhang Q, Li X, Chen W, Ahuja A, Yuan J. T1rho magnetic resonance: basic physics principles and applications in knee and intervertebral disc imaging, Quant Imaging Med Surg 2015;5(6):858–85. https://doi.org/10.3978/j.issn.2223-4292.2015.12.06. 26807369.

[167] Paul CPL, Smit TH, de Graaf M, Holewijn RM, Bisschop A, van de Ven PM, et al. Quantitative MRI in early intervertebral disc degeneration: T1rho correlates better than T2 and ADC with biomechanics, histology and matrix content, PLoS One 2018;13(1):e0191442. https://doi.org/10.1371/journal.pone.019144229381716.

[168] Mayerhoefer ME, Stelzeneder D, Bachbauer W, Welsch GH, Mamisch TC, Szczypinski P, et al. Quantitative analysis of lumbar intervertebral disc abnormalities at 3.0 Tesla: value of T(2) texture features and geometric parameters, NMR Biomed 2012;25(6):866–72. https://doi.org/10.1002/nbm.1803. 22161807.

[169] Brayda-Bruno M, Tibiletti M, Ito K, Fairbank J, Galbusera F, Zerbi A, et al. Advances in the diagnosis of degenerated lumbar discs and their possible clinical application, Eur Spine J 2014;23(Suppl 3): S315–23. https://doi.org/10.1007/s00586-013-2960-9. 23978994.

[170] Fenty M, Crescenzi R, Fry B, Squillante D, Turk D, Maurer PM, et al. Novel imaging of the intervertebral disk and pain, Global Spine J 2013;3(3):127–32. https://doi.org/10.1055/s-0033-1347930. 24436863.

[171] Zuo J, Joseph GB, Li X, Link TM, Hu SS, Berven SH, et al. In-vivo intervertebral disc characterization using magnetic resonance spectroscopy and t1rho imaging: association with discography and oswestry disability index and SF-36, Spine (Phila Pa 1976) 2011https://doi.org/10.1097/BRS.0b013e3182294a6321697767.

[172] Juras V, Mlynarik V, Szomolanyi P, Valkovic L, Trattnig S. Magnetic resonance imaging of the musculoskeletal system at 7T: morphological imaging and beyond, Top Magn Reson Imaging 2019;28(3):125–35. https://doi.org/10.1097/RMR.0000000000000205. 30951006.

[173] Burnett C, Wright P, Keenan AM, Redmond A, Ridgway J. Magnetic resonance imaging of synovitis in knees of patients with osteoarthritis without injected contrast agents using T1 quantification, Radiography (Lond) 2018;24(4):283–8. https://doi.org/10.1016/j.radi.2018.04.009. 30292495.

[174] Link TM, Majumdar S. Current diagnostic techniques in the evaluation of bone architecture, Curr Osteoporos Rep 2004;2(2):47–52. 16036082.

[175] Wehrli FW, Song HK, Saha PK, Wright AC. Quantitative MRI for the assessment of bone structure and function, NMR Biomed 2006;19(7):731–64. https://doi.org/10.1002/nbm.1066. 17075953.

[176] Du J, Bydder GM. Qualitative and quantitative ultrashort-TE MRI of cortical bone, NMR Biomed 2013;26(5):489–506. https://doi.org/10.1002/nbm.2906. 23280581.

[177] Chang G, Boone S, Martel D, Rajapakse CS, Hallyburton RS, Valko M, et al. MRI assessment of bone structure and microarchitecture, J Magn Reson Imaging 2017;46(2):323–37. https://doi.org/10.1002/jmri.25647. 28165650.

[178] Le Ster C, Gambarota G, Lasbleiz J, Guillin R, Decaux O, Saint-Jalmes H. Breath-hold MR measurements of fat fraction, T1, and T2 * of water and fat in vertebral bone marrow, J Magn Reson Imaging 2016;44(3):549–55. https://doi.org/10.1002/jmri.25205. 26918280.

[179] Ma D, Gulani V, Seiberlich N, Liu K, Sunshine JL, Duerk JL, et al. Magnetic resonance fingerprinting, Nature 2013;495(7440):187–92. https://doi.org/10.1038/nature11971. 23486058.

[180] Hammernik K, Klatzer T, Kobler E, Recht MP, Sodickson DK, Pock T, et al. Learning a variational network for reconstruction of accelerated MRI data, Magn Reson Med 2018;79(6):3055–71. https://doi.org/10.1002/mrm.26977. 29115689.

[181] Hyun CM, Kim HP, Lee SM, Lee S, Seo JK. Deep learning for undersampled MRI reconstruction, Phys Med Biol 2018;63(13):135007. https://doi.org/10.1088/1361-6560/aac71a. 29787383.

[182] Link TM, Li X. Establishing compositional MRI of cartilage as a biomarker for clinical practice, Osteoarthr Cartil 2018;26(9):1137–9. https://doi.org/10.1016/j.joca.2018.02.902. 29550402.

CHAPTER

Relaxometry: Applications in the Body

9

Jonathan R. Dillman[a,b], Andrew T. Trout[a,b], and Jean A. Tkach[a,b]

[a]*Department of Radiology, Cincinnati Children's Hospital Medical Center, Cincinnati, OH, United States*
[b]*Department of Radiology, University of Cincinnati College of Medicine, Cincinnati, OH, United States*

9.1 Introduction

Magnetic Resonance Imaging (MRI) relaxometry, or the measurement of the intrinsic magnetic resonance relaxation properties of tissue (e.g., T_2, T_2^*, T_1, and $T_{1\rho}$), is increasingly used to discriminate normal from abnormal tissue in the human body as well as to quantify and follow disease processes. In simplistic terms, relaxometry involves the repeated acquisition of MRI data; usually each acquisition being identical except for the value of a specific acquisition parameter (e.g., echo time [TE] for T_2 or spin-lock time for $T_{1\rho}$ relaxometry) that is successively incremented over a predefined range (optimized for the specific application). A signal relaxation curve can then be generated on a pixel by pixel basis from the data collected allowing determination of the relaxation parameter of interest, typically by curve fitting. The calculated relaxation properties are commonly displayed in the form of parametric maps, the values of which can then be interrogated through the placement of regions of interest (ROIs).

In the abdomen and pelvis, relaxometry (also referred to as "mapping") has been described for the assessment of diseases affecting the liver, spleen, kidneys, pancreas, and prostate gland. A few studies also have described the use of relaxometry in the evaluation of the breasts. T_2, T_2^*, T_1, and $T_{1\rho}$ relaxometry have been described in the literature, with some accepted as clinical or near-clinical and others currently preclinical or used strictly for research. In this chapter, we will review the use of MRI relaxometry in the abdomen and pelvis, presenting both clinical and emerging applications.

9.2 Liver

The liver is the organ in the abdomen and pelvis for which the use of relaxometry has been most extensively described. Uses for relaxometry in the liver include detection and quantification of iron deposition (T_2 and T_2^*) and detection of inflammation and fibrosis (T_2, T_1, and $T_{1\rho}$).

T_2 relaxometry of the liver is most commonly used to detect and measure the effect of tissue iron (also covered in Chapter 29). This imaging method is usually performed clinically in patients with known or suspected whole body iron overload. For example in patients who have a predilection for iron deposition because they have undergone repeated blood transfusions due to chronic anemia (e.g., sickle cell disease or thalassemia major) or cancer [1]. Liver iron concentration (LIC) based on measurement of T_2 has been shown to correlate with whole-body iron stores as well as important

Advances in Magnetic Resonance Technology and Applications. Volume 1. ISSN 2666-9099. https://doi.org/10.1016/B978-0-12-817057-1.00012-3

complications related to iron overload, including cardiac and endocrine dysfunction [2–4]. T_2-derived estimates of liver iron can be used to indicate the need for therapy (e.g., chelation or phlebotomy) as well as assess response to therapy [5].

T_2 relaxometry allows the creation of parametric maps of liver T_2 based on transverse or spin-spin relaxation. FerriScan (Resonance Health; Ltd., Claremont WA, Australia) is a commercial United Stated Food and Drug Administration-approved (as of 2005) T_2 relaxometry-based method whereby MRI spin-echo images are acquired at varying echo times with a reference standard included in the field of view for quality control. Images are acquired free-breathing, require approximately 10 min, and are transmitted via a secure internet portal for post-processing (Fig. 9.1). Measurements of T_2 relaxation have been shown to be accurate over a wide range of liver iron concentrations and reproducible across MRI scanner platforms, although patients with extremely high LIC may still be a challenge to accurately assess. T_2 relaxation is commonly presented as R_2 (Hz, or sec^{-1}), equivalent to $1/T_2$, with increasing R_2 values associated with increasing LIC. LIC in milligrams of iron per gram of dry liver then can be estimated from T_2 (R_2).

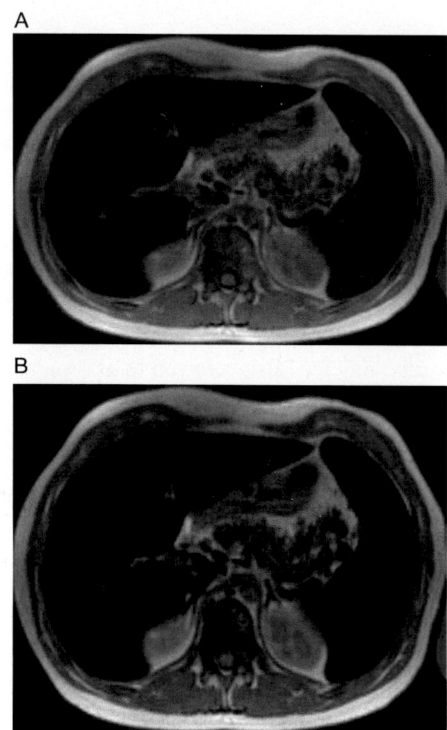

FIG. 9.1

21-year-old woman with Diamond-Blackfan anemia. (A) Axial spin echo image with an echo time of 6 msec shows abnormal hepatic, splenic, and pancreatic signal hypointensity. (B) Another axial spin echo image with longer echo time (18 msec) shows even darker appearance of the liver, spleen, and pancreas. (C) FerriScan report indicates a liver iron concentration greater than 43 mg/g of dry tissue. Liver T_2* in this case was measured to be 0.75 msec based on only two echo times acquired by conventional T_2* relaxometry (non-UTE), with an estimated liver iron concentration of 34 mg/g of dry tissue. Imaging was performed at 1.5 T.

Liver Iron Concentration Report

Average Liver Iron Concentration	> 43.0 mg/g dry tissue	(NR: 0.17-1.8)
	> 770 mmol/kg dry tissue	(NR: 3-33)

Normal range (NR) is taken from Bassett et. al., Hepatology 1986; 6: 24-29

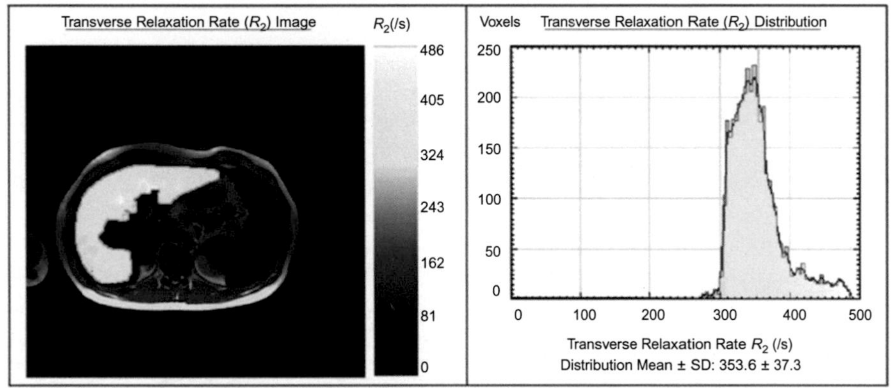

Note: The area of the liver image used for the FemScan analysis exciucies large vascular structure and other imge artefacts

Authorised by: Service Centre Manager

Resonance Health Analysis Services Pty Ltd www.resonancehealth.com

CE 0805 ARTG: 116071 510(k): K043271

FIG. 9.1—Cont'd

Pirasteh et al. recently demonstrated that biexponential T_2 relaxometry for determination of LIC is reproducible between proprietary (i.e., FerriScan) and nonproprietary analysis methods (e.g., nonlinear least squares), with excellent measurement agreement and no significant bias between methods [6].

T_2 relaxometry also has been used to detect and measure liver fibrosis and inflammation in the absence of iron deposition. Increasing parenchymal fibrosis is associated with greater extracellular water, and thus there is an accompanying increase in measured T_2. In a study by Guimaraes et al. using T_2 mapping and monoexponential curve fitting to assess 123 patients with known or suspected chronic liver disease, T_2 measurements were demonstrated to monotonically increase with increasing histopathologic fibrosis stage based on liver biopsy performed within 6 months of MRI (Fig. 9.2) [7].

A

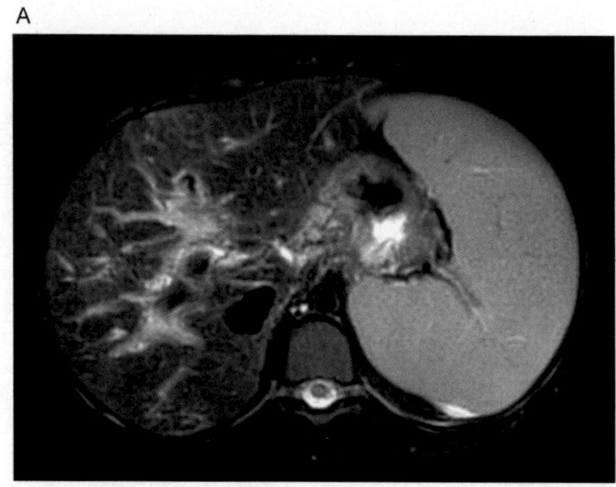

B

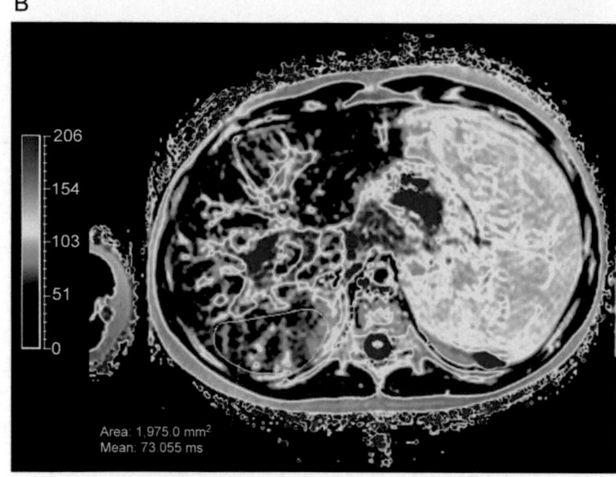

FIG. 9.2

21-year-old woman with long-standing autoimmune liver disease. (A) Axial T_2-weighted fat-suppressed image shows patchy reticular hepatic T_2-weighted signal hyperintensity related to fibrosis. The spleen is enlarged due to portal hypertension. (B) T_2 map shows increased liver T_2 values in the posterior right lobe, measuring 73 msec at 1.5 T (18 echo times, ranging from 24 to 240 msec).

However, the authors noted that T_2 relaxometry is probably impacted by both tissue fibrosis and inflammation and thus is a confounded measure of histopathologic fibrosis. Fihlo et al. performed T_2 relaxometry in 105 patients diagnosed with nonalcoholic steatohepatitis that had also undergone a recent liver biopsy (within 6 months). These authors used a more complex curve fitting model and concluded that T_2 data could be used to measure both liver fibrosis and inflammation, with fibrosis increasing the hepatic extracellular space and inflammation lowering extracellular R_2 values relative to intracellular R_2 values [8]. Additional research is needed to confirm these authors' findings and to implement T_2 relaxometry into clinical practice for assessment of liver fibrosis and inflammation.

Like T_2 relaxometry, T_2^* relaxometry is used to assess whole-body iron stores in patients with suspected iron overload [9]. Like T_2 measurements, T_2^* measurements (or R_2^* [Hz, or sec^{-1}], which is $1/T_2^*$) can be used to estimate LIC. With this technique, a multiecho gradient recalled echo pulse sequence is used to assess accelerated signal decay due to iron-related magnetic field inhomogeneity (Fig. 9.3). The measured T_2^* can then be used to calculate LIC based on one of several relational formulas available in the literature [9–11]. Mean liver T_2^* values in a cohort of 129 healthy subjects was 28.1 ± 7.1 msec at a field strength of 1.5 T [12]. LIC as determined by both T_2^* and T_2 relaxometry have been shown by Serai et al. to be highly correlated, with most discrepancies occurring in patients with marked iron overload (>20 mg iron per gram of dry liver) (Fig. 9.1) [13]. Woods et al. concluded that while T_2 and T_2^* relaxometry are not necessarily interchangeable, both methods are similarly effective for evaluating response to iron chelation therapy over time [14].

A key advantage of T_2^* relaxometry compared to T_2 relaxometry in the evaluation of liver iron is that it can be performed in a single breath-hold (less than 1 min) as opposed to requiring ~10 min of scan time [15]. The primary disadvantage of T_2^* relaxometry is that when LIC is very high, there may be little or no signal at even the shortest echo times, thus preventing the measurement of T_2^*. This effect is even more exaggerated at higher field strengths (3 T vs. 1.5 T). Fortunately, ultrashort echo time (UTE) pulse sequences that allow acquisition of images at extremely short echo times (e.g., 0.1 msec) are becoming increasingly available, thereby permitting T_2^* measurement in the setting of extreme iron overload [16–18] (Fig. 9.4). UTE-based methods of T_2^* relaxometry also allow unbiased measurement of T_2^* at a field strength of 3 T across a wide range of LIC, something that was not previously possible [17].

T_2^* relaxometry has historically been acquired as a dedicated series of images with increasing echo times and subsequent curve fitting. A recent study by Serai et al. at 1.5 T has shown that reliable liver T_2^* measurements also can be obtained from a multiecho Dixon pulse sequence designed primarily to measure hepatic proton density fat fraction (PDFF) [19]. While not marketed for iron quantification, the data collected allow for T_2^* to be determined which is then used to correct for T_2^* signal decay in the calculation of the PDFF and is presented as a T_2^* or R_2^* (depending on the vendor) parametric map.

Patients who accumulate iron in their livers are disposed to accumulating iron in other organs, such as the pancreas and heart, which are typically completely or partially included in the field of view used to perform liver T_2^* relaxometry. Serai et al. showed that both liver and cardiac T_2^* often can be accurately ascertained from a single breath-hold acquisition that covers portions of both organs [20]. Pancreas T_2^* (discussed later in this chapter) is commonly performed as a separate acquisition to allow for thinner/more closely spaced images, although this may not be necessary.

T_1 relaxometry is increasingly used to assess chronic liver diseases, as it is impacted by changes in extracellular water and increasing tissue fibrosis, both of which cause increases in T_1. With this form of relaxometry, quantitative images and measurements of liver T_1 are based on longitudinal or spin-lattice relaxation. Native (noncontrast) liver T_1 measurements, which are based on a simple monoexponential signal recovery curve, typically range from ~500 to ~1200 msec at 1.5 T and vary based on whether or

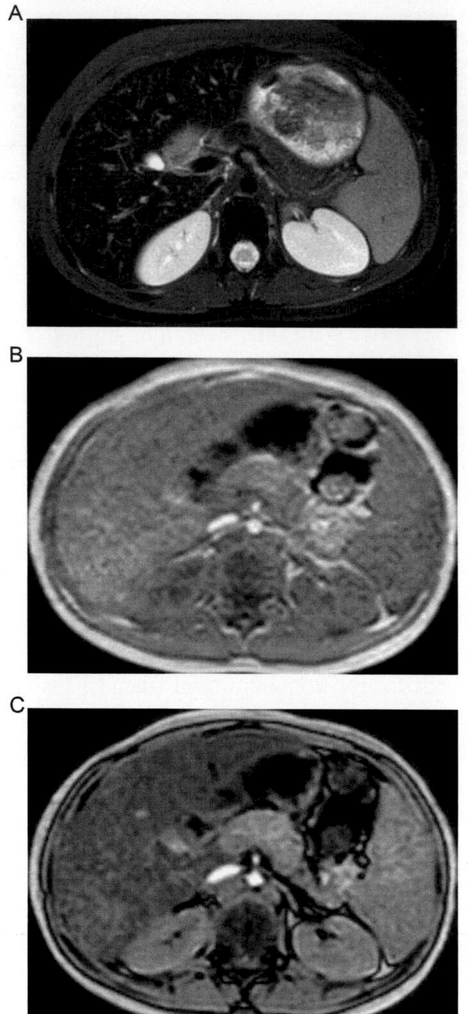

FIG. 9.3

12-year-old girl with beta-thalassemia. (A) Axial T_2-weighted fat-suppressed image shows abnormally low hepatic and splenic signal intensity, consistent with iron overload. (B)–(E) Representative axial gradient recalled echo images from a 1.5 T scanner show decreasing liver and spleen signal intensity with increasing echo time (four of eight images shown, with echo times of ~0.7, 4.0, 7.2, and 10.5 ms respectively). (F) Right lobe T_2* measurement confirmed moderate-severe iron deposition in the liver (T_2*=3.8 ms).

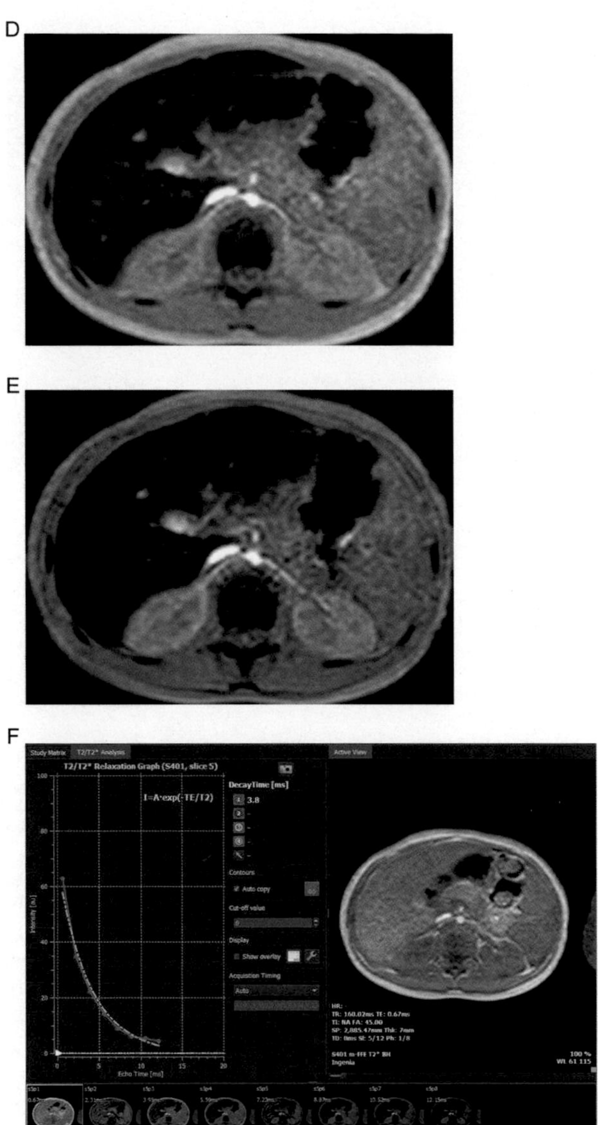

FIG. 9.3—Cont'd

not iron correction methods are employed [21]. Liver T_1 is most often measured in clinical settings using a modified Look-Locker (MOLLI) or shortened MOLLI (shMOLLI) pulse sequence, with one anatomic level imaged during a single breath-hold [22]. However, other techniques are available, including a volumetric method for T_1 measurement that uses a spiral *k*-space trajectory to cover the entire liver in a single breath-hold [23].

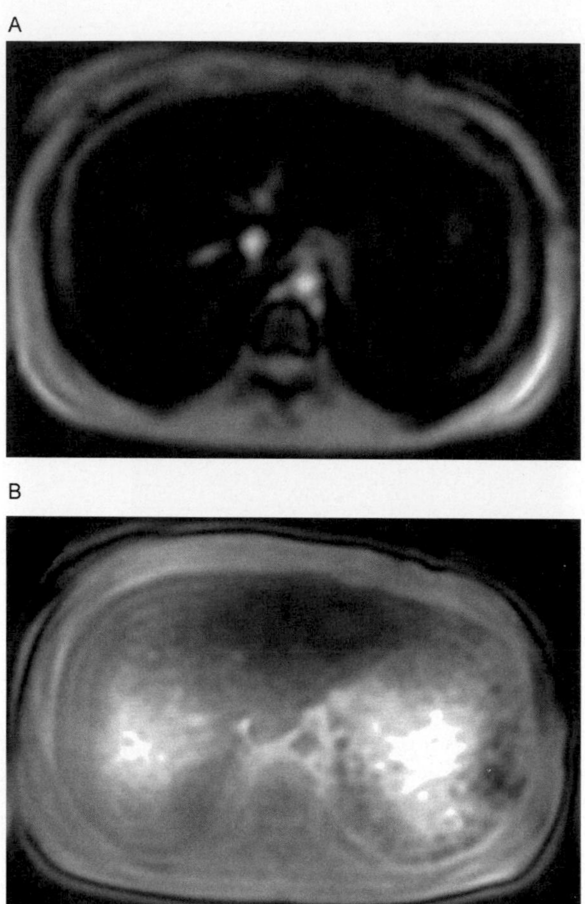

FIG. 9.4

23-year-old woman with transfusion-dependent sickle cell disease. (A) Axial gradient echo image with an echo time of 0.7 msec shows no measurable liver signal, and thus $T_2{}^*$ is not quantifiable. (B) Axial ultrashort echo (UTE) image with an echo time of 0.19 msec acquired using a radial *k*-space trajectory shows measurable liver signal. $T_2{}^*$ was able to be quantified (pixel-wise fit) using the following echo times: 0.19, 0.23, 0.35, 0.60, 0.85, 1.2, and 2.0 msec. Images were acquired at a field strength of 3 T.

(Image courtesy of John C. Wood, MD, PhD, Children's Hospital Los Angeles.)

Preclinical data suggest that liver T_1 may be a viable biomarker for both detecting and quantifying liver injury as well as assessing changes over time. Banerjee et al. showed that liver T_1, when corrected for the presence of iron (iron-corrected T_1, or cT_1), was positively associated with increasing histologic fibrosis in 79 unselected patients that underwent both liver MRI and biopsy [21]. These authors showed a receiver operating characteristic (ROC) area under the curve of 0.94 ($P < .0001$) for discriminating healthy volunteers and patients with no liver fibrosis from patients with any degree of liver fibrosis. A recent study by Mojtahed et al. established normal cT_1 values in a very large adult patient population with presumably healthy livers (PDFF less than 5% and body mass index less than 25 kg/m^2) [24].

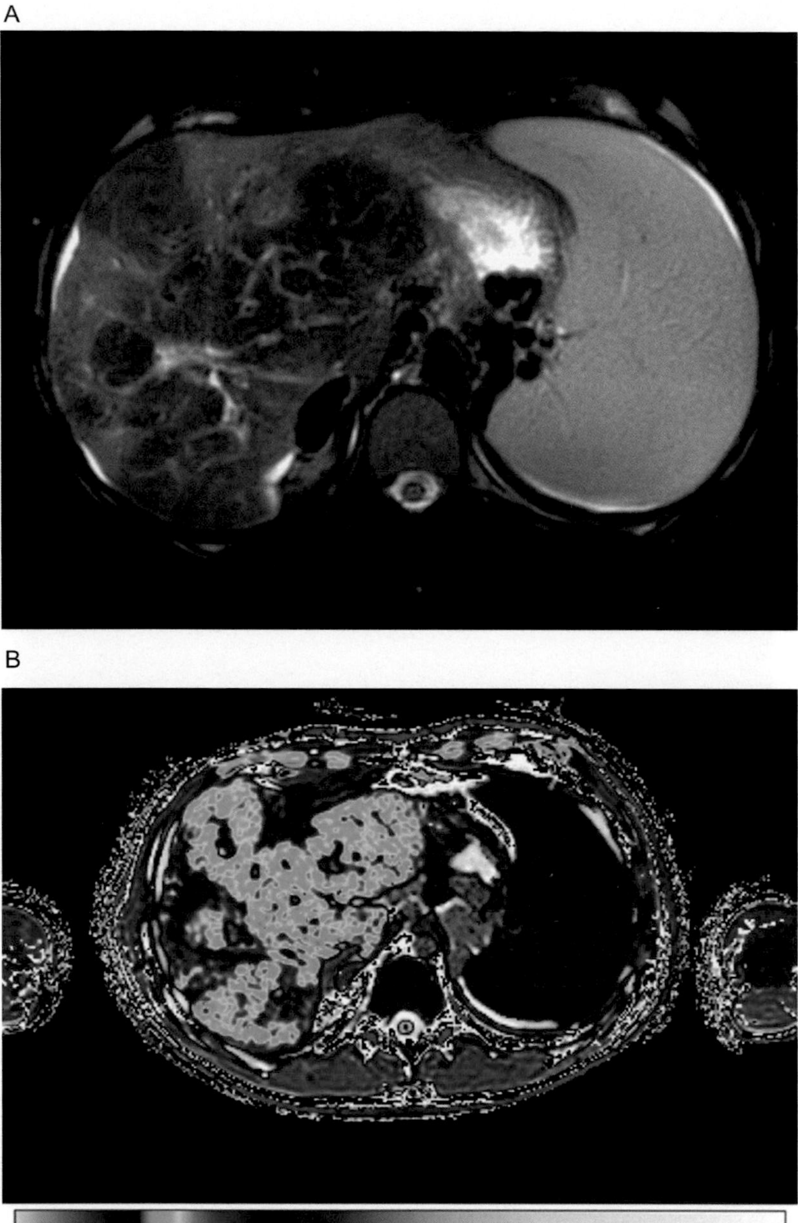

FIG. 9.5

(A) 22-year-old man with autoimmune liver disease. Axial T_2-weighted fat-suppressed image shows areas of peripheral patchy signal hyperintensity associated with capsular retraction due to fibrosis. (B) Iron-corrected

(Continued)

C

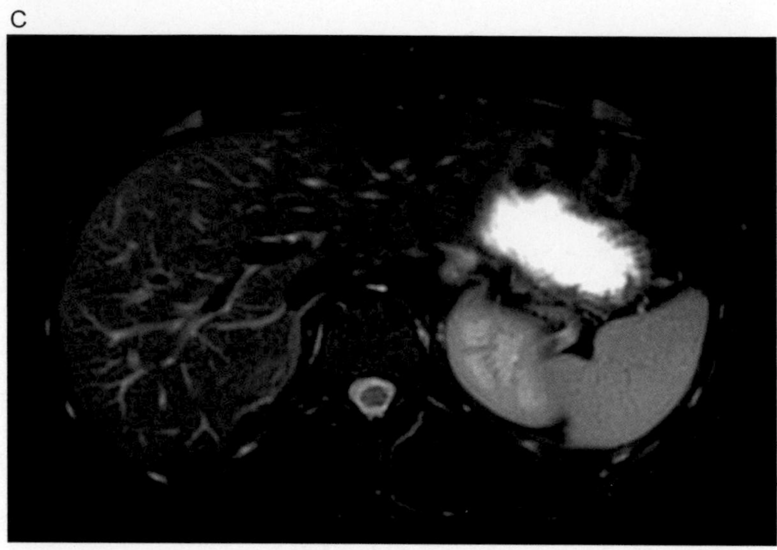

D

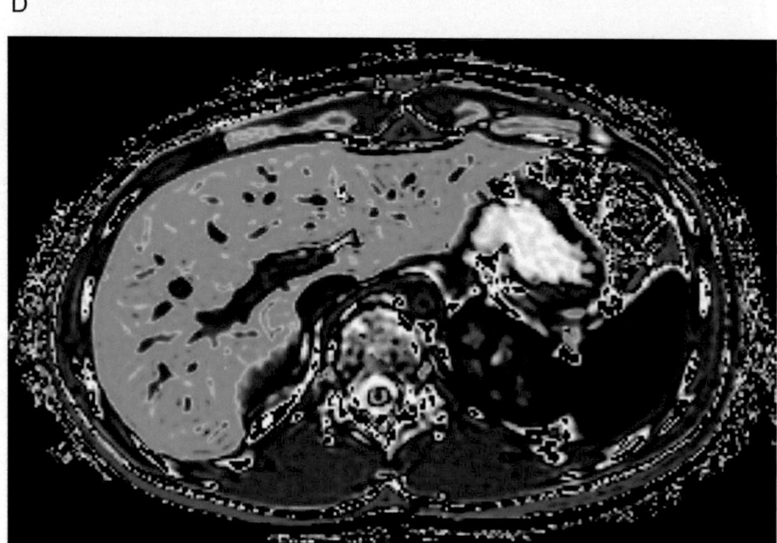

FIG. 9.5—Cont'd

T_1 map (Perspectum Diagnostics; Oxford, UK; map in units of msec) demonstrates heterogeneous appearance of the liver with areas of visible fibrosis showing markedly increased cT_1 values (appearing redder on the color scale). Overall mean liver cT_1 (mean cT_1 of four axial images through the mid liver = 1018 msec) is considerably elevated when compared to the United Kingdom Biobank population. (C) A 20-year-old man with autoimmune liver disease. Axial T_2-weighted fat-suppressed image shows normal appearance of the liver. (D) Iron-corrected T_1 map (Perspectum Diagnostics; Oxford, UK) demonstrates homogeneous appearance of the liver with an overall mean cT_1 = 853 msec, which is mildly elevated when compared to the United Kingdom Biobank population. Both exams were performed at 1.5 T.

In that population, derived from the United Kingdom Biobank, the median iron-corrected T_1 was 666 msec, with an interquartile range of 643 to 694 msec (Fig. 9.5). They also demonstrated in this adult population that iron-correction was necessary for 36.5% of individuals. It is also worth noting that T_1 relaxometry can be performed without iron correction (although it may be confounded by the presence of iron) as well as following the intravenous administration of gadolinium-based contrast material. Postcontrast T_1 values have been shown to be associated with liver function (Child-Pugh score) and complications of portal hypertension [25].

$T_{1\rho}$ mapping is an MRI relaxometry method that has been used in the preclinical and research settings to detect and measure liver fibrosis. Also known as "spin-lattice relaxation time in the rotating frame", this imaging technique measures relaxation in the presence of an on-resonant continuous wave radiofrequency pulse that "locks" magnetization in the transverse plane [26]. $T_{1\rho}$ describes the decay of this "locked" magnetization and is influenced by the interactions between water and large macromolecules, such as collagen and proteoglycans. It has been hypothesized that $T_{1\rho}$ measurements should increase with increasing liver fibrosis (Fig. 9.6).

In a small study by Rauscher et al., $T_{1\rho}$ measurements were measured in healthy volunteers and patients with liver cirrhosis [27]. These authors concluded that liver $T_{1\rho}$ values are significantly higher in patients with liver cirrhosis when compared to healthy individuals (57.4 msec vs. 47.8 msec; $P = .0007$). Another small study by Singh et al. that performed $T_{1\rho}$ relaxometry in patients with varying degrees of liver fibrosis also confirmed that $T_{1\rho}$ measurements increase with increasing histologic fibrosis [28].

9.3 Spleen

Similar to the liver, T_2 and $T_2{}^*$ relaxometry of the spleen can be performed to detect excess iron deposition. Schwenzer et al. determined the mean splenic $T_2{}^*$ to be 43.9 ± 20.6 msec at a field strength of 1.5 T in 129 healthy adult subjects [12]. $T_2{}^*$ measurements, of course, would be shorter at 3 T. Brewer et al. assessed both splenic $R_2{}^*$ and R_2 and showed that for spleen and liver tissue with the same $R_2{}^*$ value, R_2 in the spleen was significantly lower than R_2 in the liver. These authors also concluded that splenic iron measurements "have little predictive value" for estimating cardiac, pancreatic, and renal iron [29]. Interestingly, in a study of T_2 relaxometry in patients with beta-thalassemia major, not all patients with evidence of hepatic iron overload showed evidence of excess splenic iron deposition, thus showing a pattern resembling primary hemochromatosis [1]. Other than for confirming the presence of splenic iron (e.g., to distinguish secondary hemochromatosis from primary hemochromatosis), which at anything but the lowest pathologic levels is rarely an open question, there is a little clinical role for T_2 and $T_2{}^*$ relaxometry of the spleen at this time.

There is a paucity of literature describing the use of T_1 relaxometry for assessment of the spleen. However, Liu et al. performed native splenic T_1 relaxometry using a shMOLLI pulse sequence during perfusion cardiovascular MRI to predict the adequacy of adenosine stress [30]. Specifically, rest and postadenosine splenic T_1 measurements were acquired, with T_1 values significantly decreasing during stress. This finding was highly correlated with the visual "splenic switch-off" sign, or loss of splenic signal during contrast-enhanced imaging secondary to stress-related decreased perfusion but does not require the use of gadolinium-based contrast material.

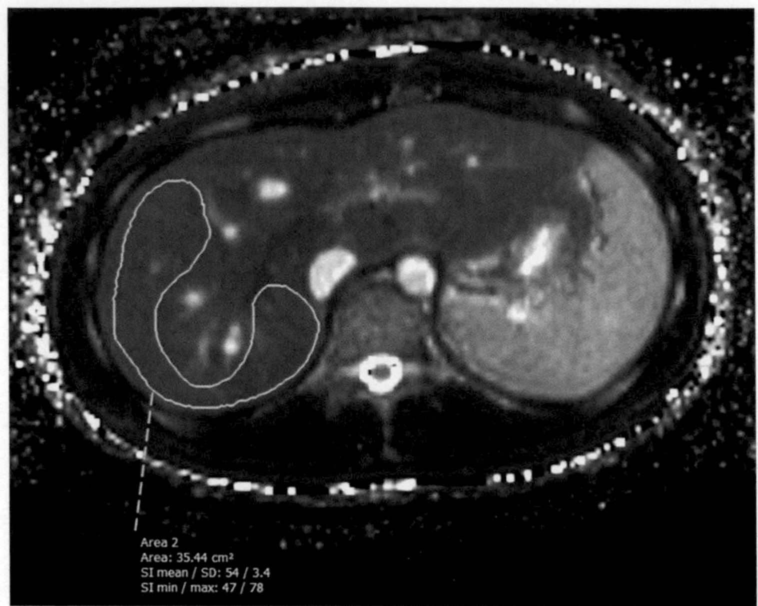

A

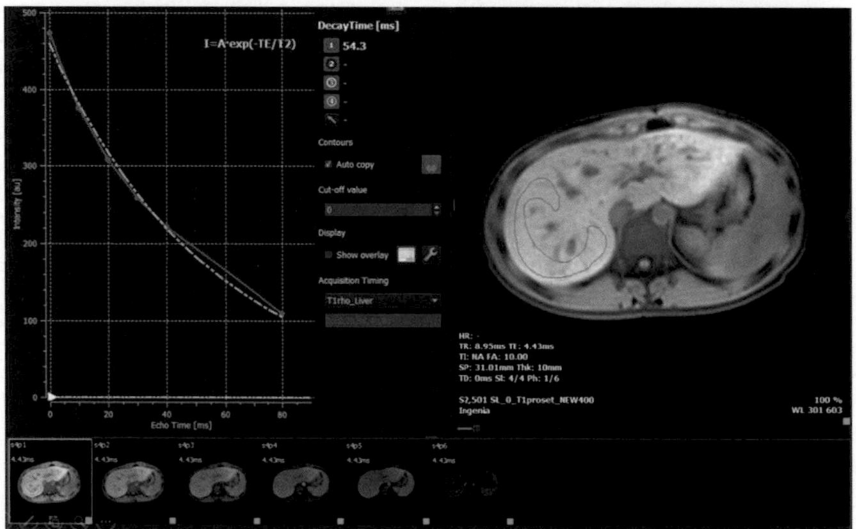

B

FIG. 9.6

18-year-old man with autoimmune liver disease. $T_{1\rho}$ mapping was performed using a spin-lock frequency of 400 Hz and spin-lock times of 0, 10, 20, 30, 40, and 80 msec. (A) $T_{1\rho}$ map shows a mean right hepatic lobe measurement of 54 msec. (B) $T_{1\rho}$ analysis performed using conventional monoexponential curve fitting yields similar results to the parametric map shown in (A) ($T_{1\rho}$ = 54 msec).

9.4 Kidneys

Currently, MRI relaxometry of the kidneys is primarily used for preclinical and research purposes. A systematic review performed by the European Cooperation in Science and Technology Action Magnetic Resonance Imaging Biomarkers for Chronic Kidney Disease that focused on potential clinical applications of T_1 and T_2 MRI relaxometry in nontumor renal disease concluded that there is currently a lack of standardization in patient preparation and acquisition protocols as well as a paucity of widely accepted reference values for renal T_1 and T_2 [31]. Their review also suggested that renal relaxometry measurements are impacted by multiple factors, including renal perfusion, oxygenation/ischemia, tissue edema and fibrosis, state of hydration, and co-morbidities, thus bringing the specificity of these techniques into question.

Despite these limitations, there is a small but increasing body of research assessing renal relaxometry techniques. Peperhove et al. performed native T_1 mapping using a MOLLI pulse sequence to evaluate the kidneys in the setting of solid organ transplantation [32]. They demonstrated that renal cortical T_1 values are, on average, increased in this setting and increase with increasing renal impairment, thus suggesting that T_1 relaxometry may be a useful biomarker in the setting of acute kidney injury. A feasibility study by Cox et al. also showed that renal cortex and medulla T_1 values were significantly higher in patients with chronic kidney disease compared to healthy individuals [33]. These same authors established normal renal cortical and medullary T_1 values using a MOLLI pulse sequence (mean renal cortex $T_1 = 1053 \pm 72$ msec; mean renal medulla $T_1 = 1318 \pm 98$ msec at 1.5 T). Further research is needed to establish the diagnostic performance of renal T_1 (and T_2) relaxometry for assessing various disease states (Fig. 9.7).

When compared to T_1 and T_2 relaxometry, there is a greater body of literature related to T_2* relaxometry of the kidneys. Grassedonio et al. established that a mean renal T_2* value less than 31 msec is

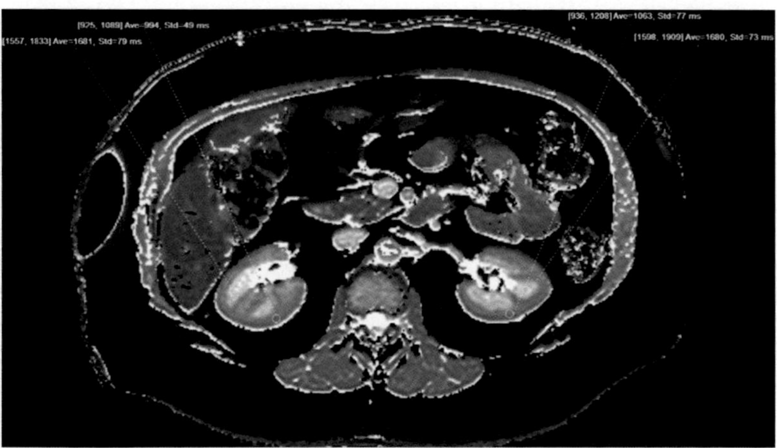

FIG. 9.7

50-year-old female volunteer subject with normal kidney function. T_1 map obtained using a modified Look-Locker (MOLLI) pulse sequence at 1.5 T shows presumably normal renal cortical (994 and 1063 msec) and medullary (1680 and 1681 msec) T_1 measurements. Renal corticomedullary differentiation is preserved.

abnormal based on the imaging of 20 consecutive healthy adult patients. Further, the authors demonstrated no relationship between kidney T_2* measurements and age or sex [34]. In clinical practice, T_2* relaxometry can be used to confirm the presence of iron in the kidneys, but there is no current indication for quantifying renal iron. Renal iron deposition is most often observed in the setting of chronic intravascular hemolysis (typically sickle cell disease) and resides in the cortex (proximal and distal convoluted tubules) (Fig. 9.8) [15]. This pattern of deposition results in cortical T_1 prolongation and T_2 shortening, giving the renal cortex a strikingly hypointense appearance compared to the spared renal medulla and a reversed signal intensity pattern of corticomedullary differentiation on T_1-weighted images. In a study by Schein et al. that included both sickle cell disease and thalassemia major patients as well as healthy control subjects, mean renal R_2* in sickle cell disease patients was significantly higher than R_2* measured in thalassemia patients and healthy control subjects; there was no difference in measured R_2* between the other two groups [35]. These authors concluded that intravascular hemolysis and not chronic blood transfusions are responsible for renal iron deposition. In the setting of sickle cell disease, renal iron concentration is independent of both LIC and cardiac T_2*, and the effect of iron deposition on renal function remains unknown [15,35]. Limited research also suggests that kidney T_2* may be associated with local renal tissue oxygen levels, although much more research is needed, in part to determine the impact of likely numerous confounders [36,37].

9.5 Pancreas

Assessment of tissue iron deposition is currently the most common clinical application for MRI relaxometry of the pancreas. While T_2 relaxometry has been described for this specific indication, T_2* relaxometry methods are more commonly employed [1]. In 129 healthy adult subjects, Schwenzer et al. determined the normal mean pancreatic T_2* to be 41.5 ± 7.4 msec at 1.5 T [12]. While T_2* imaging can be used to evaluate patients with both the neonatal and primary (hereditary) forms of hemochromatosis, the pancreas is most commonly assessed in patients with secondary hemochromatosis [38]. Excess pancreas iron has been shown to be a strong predictor of cardiac iron overload in thalassemia major [39]. Specifically, a pancreatic R_2* greater than 100 Hz had a positive predictive value of greater than 60%. These authors concluded that pancreatic R_2* measurements can be used to identify physiologic conditions suitable for future cardiac deposition and may be used to guide the need for radiologic cardiac iron assessment (Fig. 9.9). A study by Noetzli et al. assessed pancreatic iron load in both sickle cell disease and thalassemia major patients [40]. Their results showed that pancreatic R_2* was significantly lower in patients with sickle cell disease (52 vs. 253 Hz; $P < .0001$), despite LIC being similar in both groups. Interestingly, pancreatic R_2* has been shown to predict diabetes mellitus in thalassemia patients, a relatively common endocrine complication [41].

The amount of fat interspersed within the pancreas gland may increase with age and/or obesity. The presence of pancreatic fat leads to exaggerated signal loss during out of phase echo times when performing T_2* relaxometry (Fig. 9.9). One possible solution is to acquire a relatively large number of echo times (e.g., 16 or 32) and exclude out of phase data. Based on work by Meloni et al., accurate pancreatic T_2* measurements can be acquired using fat saturation and discarding data from certain echo times until the fitting error (the normalized root mean square error between the decay curve and the optimal model expressed as a percentage) is less than 5% [42].

A

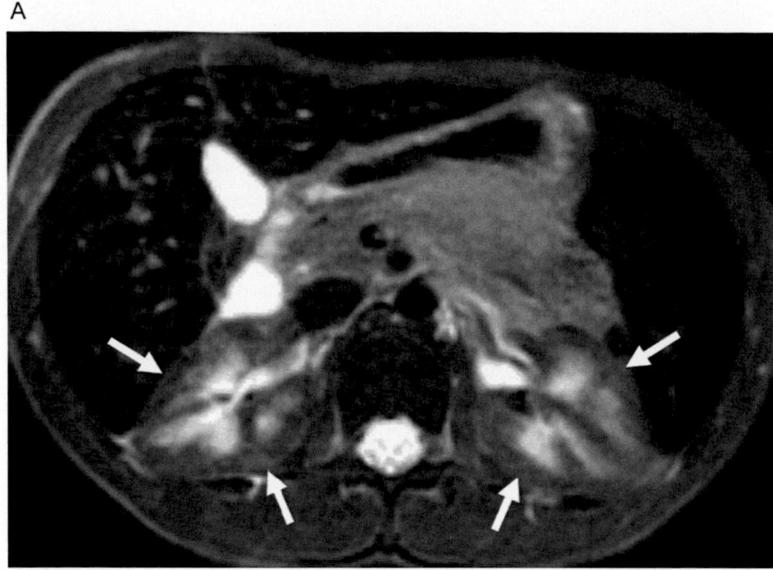

B

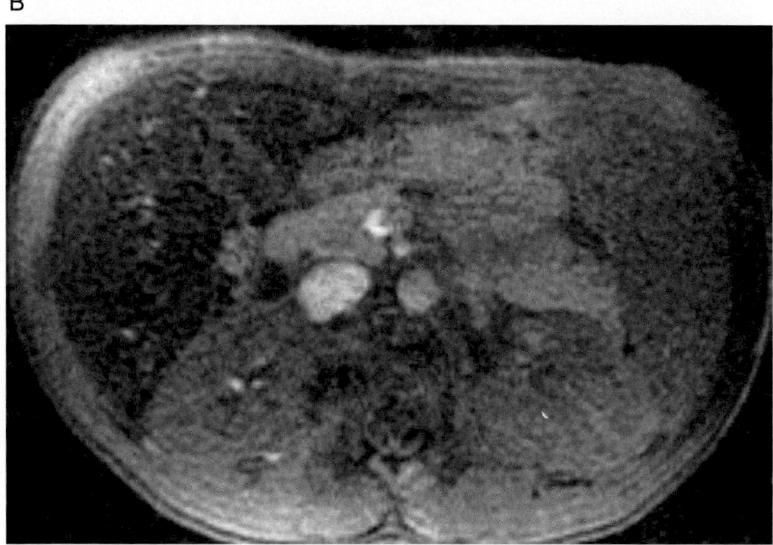

FIG. 9.8

21-year-old woman with sickle cell disease. (A) Axial T_2-weighted fat-suppressed image shows abnormally hypointense appearance of the liver, spleen, and bone marrow due to iron overload. The pancreas is spared. There is marked renal cortical signal hypointensity *(arrows)* and exaggerated corticomedullary differentiation, consistent with kidney iron deposition from intravascular hemolysis. (B) Axial gradient recalled echo image with an echo time of 1.68 msec shows normal appearance of the kidneys. The liver is abnormally hypointense due to iron overload. (C) Another axial gradient recalled echo image with an echo time of 7.2 msec shows marked loss of renal cortical signal as well as abnormal hepatic, splenic, and bone marrow signal hypointensity. Kidney signal loss is confirmatory for the presence of iron. Renal T_2^* can be measured, although it does not correlate well with whole body or cardiac iron stores based on the literature. (D) T_2^* map from a multiecho gradient recalled echo Dixon acquisition in another sickle cell disease patient confirms the presence of renal and hepatic iron (renal cortical $T_2^* = 5$ msec). Images were acquired at 1.5 T.

(Continued)

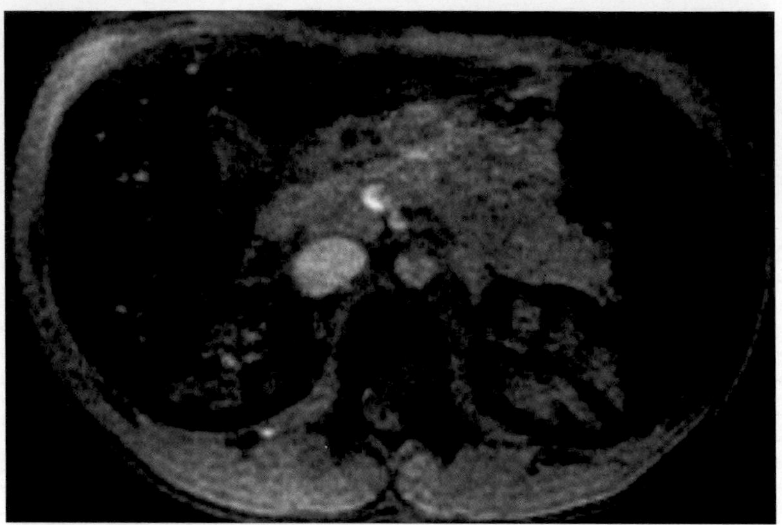

C

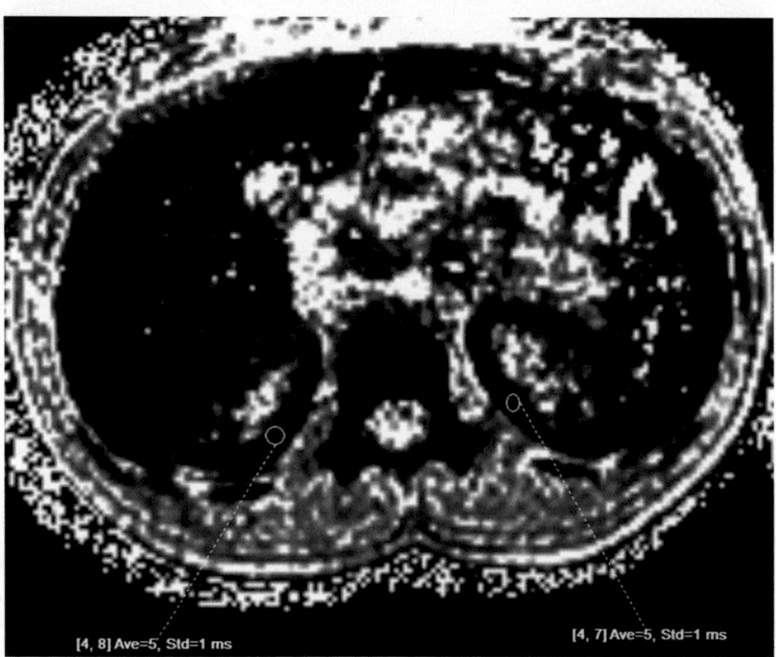

D

FIG. 9.8—Cont'd

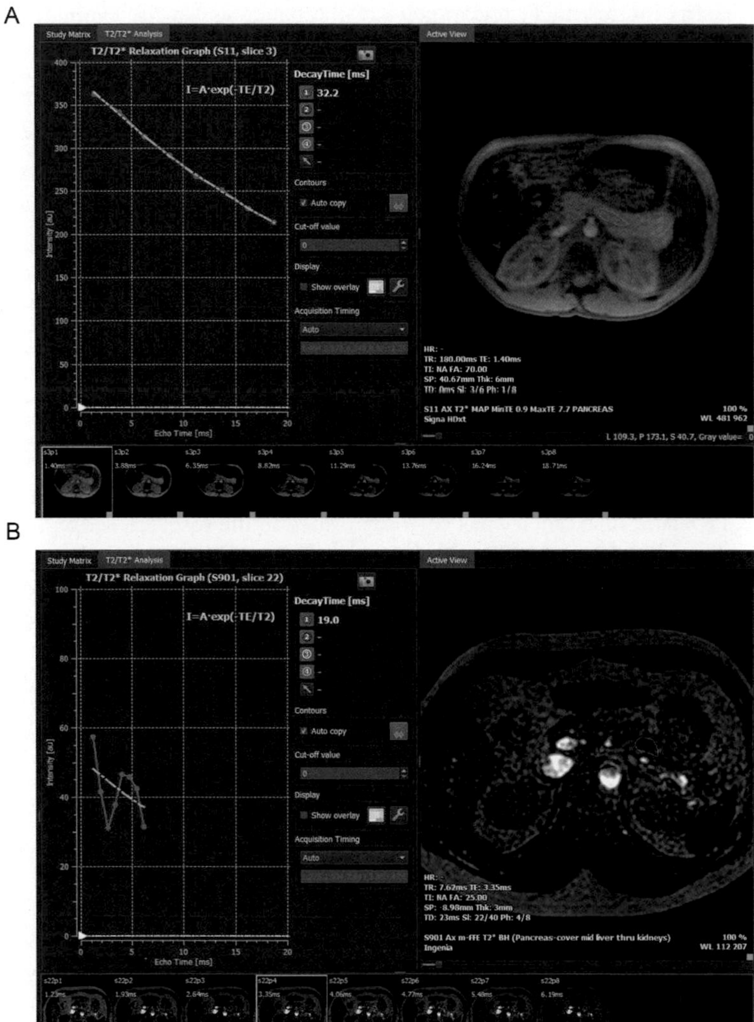

FIG. 9.9

Pancreas T_2* relaxometry in two different patients with transfusion-dependent chronic anemia. (A) In the first patient, T_2* relaxometry shows mild loss of pancreatic signal intensity with increasing echo time, with a normal mean T_2* measurement of 36.4 msec. (B) In the second patient, T_2* relaxometry shows much more rapid pancreatic signal loss with increasing echo time, with a borderline abnormal mean T_2* measurement of 21.0 msec. “Saw tooth” appearance of the T_2* curve suggests the presence of fat within the pancreas, which can make curve fitting challenging. Images were acquired at 1.5 T.

There is increasing interest in T_1 relaxometry of the pancreas for the evaluation of patients with recurrent and chronic pancreatitis. Some authors have suggested that T_1 can be used to detect chronic pancreatitis earlier and to follow disease progression. Tirkes et al. found that mean pancreas T_1 measurements at 3 T were significantly higher in patients with mild chronic pancreatitis compared to normal patients (1099 vs. 797 msec; $P < .0001$) [43]. Another study by Wang et al. used T_1 mapping to attempt to identify different stages of chronic pancreatitis based on the Cambridge classification [44]. These authors found increasing mean pancreas T_1 values for control, mild chronic pancreatitis, and moderate/severe chronic pancreatitis patient groups at 3 T (865 vs. 1075 vs. 1350 msec; $P < .0001$). Pancreas T_1 relaxometry had a ROC area under the curve of 0.91 for diagnosing moderate/severe chronic pancreatitis. While primarily preclinical, this technique is likely close to clinical implementation in the recurrent and chronic pancreatitis population (Figs. 9.10 and 9.11).

9.6 Prostate

MRI relaxometry methods are not presently used to evaluate the prostate gland or prostate cancer in clinical practice. Prostatic relaxometry has been performed in the research setting, however, with several studies investigating T_2 mapping of the prostate. Gilani et al. described a protocol with echo times optimized for prostate imaging and that allows biexponential curve fitting [45]. These authors found similar results to Storas et al. who concluded that prostatic T_2 signal decay was, in general, biexponential [46]. Using *k*-space undersampling, Liu et al. showed that T_2 mapping could be performed in an accelerated manner yielding results similar to conventional imaging [47]. These authors also showed that the T_2 values of histologically proven cancers were significantly lower than either (1) suspicious but ultimately nonmalignant lesions or (2) normal prostate tissue. Wu et al. used $T_2{}^*$ relaxometry to characterize prostate cancer aggressiveness and showed that cancerous areas of the prostate had significantly lower mean $T_2{}^*$ values than areas of normal prostate tissue (42.5 vs. 74.9 msec; $P < .001$) [48]. Lower $T_2{}^*$ values also were associated with higher histopathologic Gleason scores.

Yu et al. analyzed 109 prostate gland lesions and showed that a multiparametric approach using a combination of T_1 values, T_2 values, and diffusion-weighted imaging apparent diffusion coefficients (ADCs) was able to distinguish normal-appearing peripheral zone from prostate cancer with an area under the ROC curve of 0.99 [49]. Specifically, T_1, T_2, and ADC values were lower in patients with prostate cancer compared to normal-appearing peripheral zone tissue (T_1: 1628 msec vs. 2247 msec, T_2: 73 msec vs. 169 msec, and 0.773×10^{-3} mm^2/s vs. 1.711×10^{-3} mm^2/s) (all P values $< .0001$). In their same study, ADC and T_2 values together produced the highest ROC area under the curve for distinguishing high-/intermediate-grade from low-grade cancers. Further studies are needed to confirm these results and ultimately to determine if MRI relaxometry can improve the diagnostic performance of prostate MRI.

9.7 Breast

There is a small but increasing amount of preclinical published literature using MRI relaxometry to evaluate the breasts. Panda et al. showed using coefficients of variation that the T_1 and T_2 values of normal fibroglandular tissue at 3 T show only mild variability both within and between subjects,

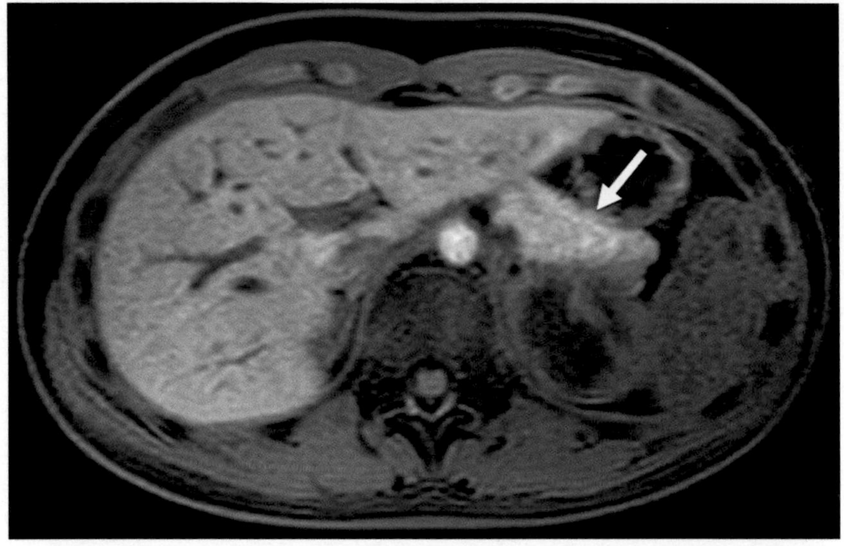

A

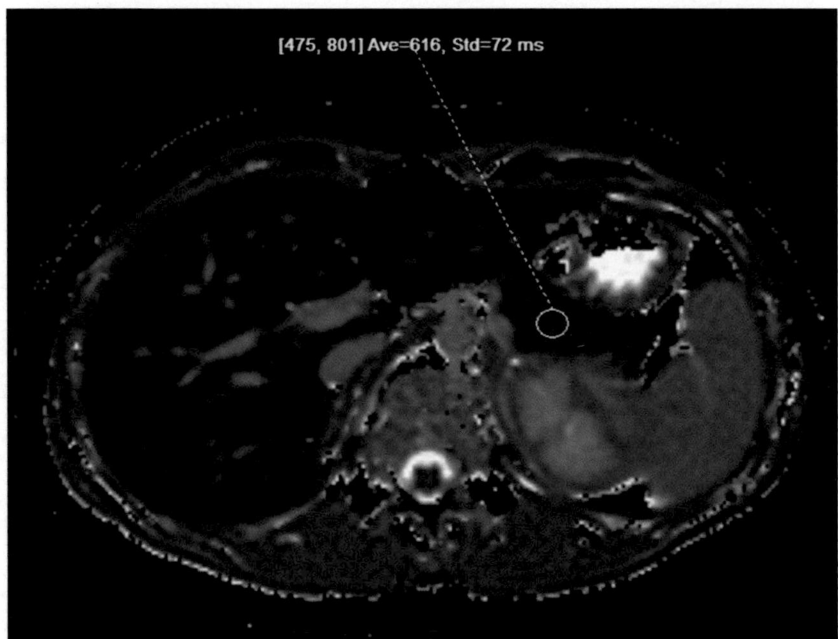

B

FIG. 9.10

12-year-old girl with persistent abdominal pain, genetic mutation associated with recurrent pancreatitis, and sister with chronic pancreatitis. MRI was performed to evaluate for evidence of chronic pancreatitis using a 1.5T scanner. (A) Axial T_1-weighted gradient echo Dixon water image shows normal pancreatic bulk and preserved signal hyperintensity *(arrow)*. (B) T_1 map through the pancreas obtained using a modified Look-Locker (MOLLI) sequence shows a normal mean T_1 value of 616 msec at the junction of the pancreatic body and tail.

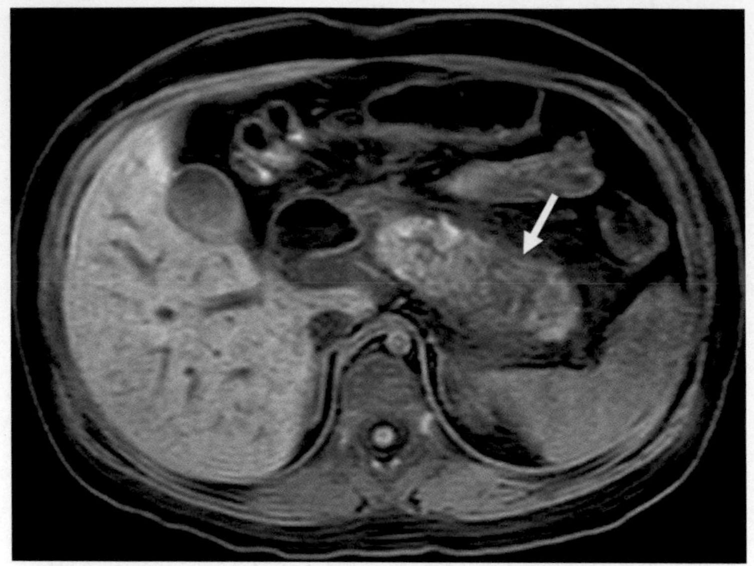

A

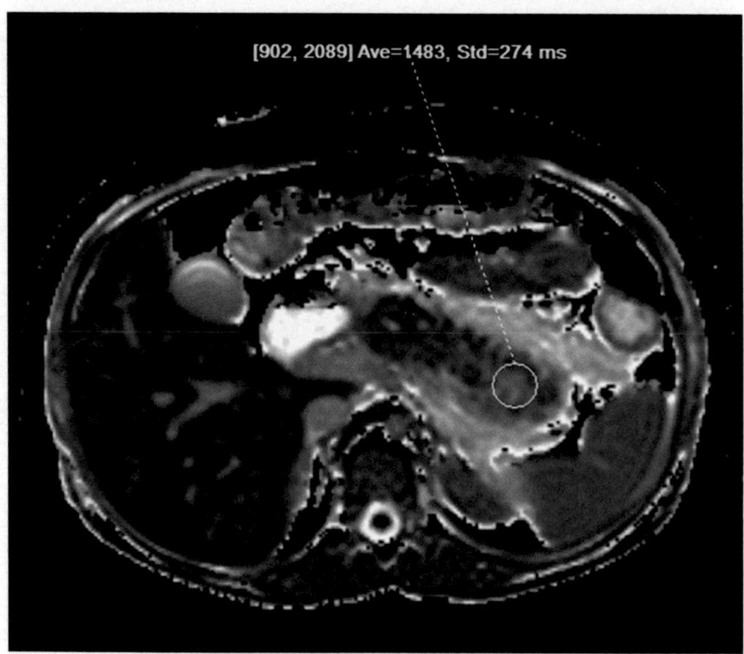

B

FIG. 9.11

5-year-old girl with acute pancreatitis. (A) Axial T_1-weighted gradient echo Dixon water image shows findings of acute pancreatitis, include pancreatic enlargement, peripancreatic inflammation, and abnormally low signal in the pancreatic body and tail *(arrow)*. (B) T_1 map through the pancreas obtained using a modified Look-Locker (MOLLI) sequence shows an abnormally increased mean T_1 value of 1483 msec in the pancreatic tail. Images were acquired at 1.5 T.

and that these values are reproducible between scanners [50]. In 26 women with breast cancers undergoing neoadjuvant therapy prior to surgery, Liu et al. showed that lesion T_2 measurements significantly decreased after treatment compared to baseline (1.34 ± 13.68 ms vs. 64.50 ± 8.71 ms; $P < .001$), and that responders to neoadjuvant therapy had significantly shorter T_2 relaxation times on follow-up [51]. As with the prostate, further studies are needed to establish whether MRI relaxometry can improve the diagnostic performance of breast MRI, including prediction of therapy response, tumor biology, and prediction of meaningful clinical outcomes.

9.8 Challenges

While MRI relaxometry is currently used to image select patients in clinical practice, there are challenges that prevent more widespread adoption. First, normal values for the various techniques and organs mentioned above are lacking. This is true in both the pediatric and adult populations. Normal values also need to be established for both 1.5 T and 3 T, as MRI relaxometry is field strength dependent. Second, cut-off values for normal versus abnormal need to be established for numerous disease states in both children and adults. Third, measurement strategies need to be devised to avoid sampling error. There is generally a paucity of literature assessing whether making relaxometry measurements using a single region of interest, multiple regions of interest, or segmentation of an entire organ performs better for detecting and characterizing tissue abnormalities. Finally, conventional MRI relaxometry methods are dependent to some degree on curve fitting, and can be challenging in certain disease states (e.g., extreme iron overload which causes very rapid signal decay or when attempting to quantify liver iron in the presence of steatosis). This is particularly true in the settings of very short and very long T_1 and T_2 values, although the latter is less often clinically relevant. Also, further research is needed to determine if more complex modeling of relaxation curves (e.g., monoexponential vs. biexponential) can improve the diagnostic performance of these quantitative MRI methods.

References

[1] Papakonstantinou O, et al. Assessment of iron distribution between liver, spleen, pancreas, bone marrow, and myocardium by means of R2 relaxometry with MRI in patients with beta-thalassemia major. J Magn Reson Imaging 2009;29(4):853–9.

[2] Wood JC, et al. Liver MRI is more precise than liver biopsy for assessing total body iron balance: a comparison of MRI relaxometry with simulated liver biopsy results. Magn Reson Imaging 2015;33(6):761–7.

[3] Noetzli LJ, et al. Pituitary iron and volume predict hypogonadism in transfusional iron overload. Am J Hematol 2012;87(2):167–71.

[4] Wood JC, et al. Predicting pituitary iron and endocrine dysfunction. Ann N Y Acad Sci 2010;1202:123–8.

[5] Stanley HM, et al. Transfusional Iron overload in a cohort of children with sickle cell disease: impact of magnetic resonance imaging, transfusion method, and chelation. Pediatr Blood Cancer 2016;63(8):1414–8.

[6] Pirasteh A, et al. Inter-method reproducibility of biexponential R2 MR relaxometry for estimation of liver iron concentration. Magn Reson Med 2018;80(6):2691–701.

[7] Guimaraes AR, et al. T2 relaxation time is related to liver fibrosis severity. Quant Imaging Med Surg 2016;6(2):103–14.

[8] Filho HML, et al. Novel mapping of fibrosis and hepatic inflammation in NASH patients with dual R2 MRI relaxometry, in European Association for the study of the liver. J Hepatol 2017;S243–4.

[9] Hankins JS, et al. R2* magnetic resonance imaging of the liver in patients with iron overload. Blood 2009;113(20):4853–5.

[10] St Pierre TG, et al. Noninvasive measurement and imaging of liver iron concentrations using proton magnetic resonance. Blood 2005;105(2):855–61.

[11] Wood JC, et al. MRI R2 and R2* mapping accurately estimates hepatic iron concentration in transfusion-dependent thalassemia and sickle cell disease patients. Blood 2005;106(4):1460–5.

[12] Schwenzer NF, et al. T2* relaxometry in liver, pancreas, and spleen in a healthy cohort of one hundred twenty-nine subjects-correlation with age, gender, and serum ferritin. Invest Radiol 2008;43(12):854–60.

[13] Serai SD, et al. Retrospective comparison of gradient recalled echo R2* and spin-echo R2 magnetic resonance analysis methods for estimating liver iron content in children and adolescents. Pediatr Radiol 2015;45(11):1629–34.

[14] Wood JC, et al. R2 and R2* are equally effective in evaluating chronic response to iron chelation. Am J Hematol 2014;89(5):505–8.

[15] Wood JC. Use of magnetic resonance imaging to monitor iron overload. Hematol Oncol Clin North Am 2014;28(4):747–64 [vii].

[16] Krafft AJ, et al. Quantitative ultrashort echo time imaging for assessment of massive iron overload at 1.5 and 3 tesla. Magn Reson Med 2017;78(5):1839–51.

[17] Doyle EK, et al. Ultra-short echo time images quantify high liver iron. Magn Reson Med 2018; 79(3):1579–85.

[18] Tipirneni-Sajja A, et al. Radial ultrashort TE imaging removes the need for breath-holding in hepatic iron overload quantification by R2* MRI. AJR Am J Roentgenol 2017;209(1):187–94.

[19] Serai SD, et al. Agreement between manual relaxometry and semi-automated scanner-based multi-echo Dixon technique for measuring liver T2* in a pediatric and young adult population. Pediatr Radiol 2018;48(1):94–100.

[20] Serai SD, et al. Measuring liver T2* and cardiac T2* in a single acquisition. Abdom Radiol (NY) 2018; 43(9):2303–8.

[21] Banerjee R, et al. Multiparametric magnetic resonance for the non-invasive diagnosis of liver disease. J Hepatol 2014;60(1):69–77.

[22] Roujol S, et al. Accuracy, precision, and reproducibility of four T1 mapping sequences: a head-to-head comparison of MOLLI, ShMOLLI, SASHA, and SAPPHIRE. Radiology 2014;272(3):683–9.

[23] Chen Y, et al. Rapid volumetric T1 mapping of the abdomen using three-dimensional through-time spiral GRAPPA. Magn Reson Med 2016;75(4):1457–65.

[24] Mojtahed A, et al. Reference range of liver corrected T1 values in a population at low risk for fatty liver disease-a UK biobank sub-study, with an appendix of interesting cases. Abdom Radiol (NY) 2019; 44(1):72–84.

[25] Yoon JH, et al. Quantitative assessment of hepatic function: modified look-locker inversion recovery (MOLLI) sequence for T1 mapping on Gd-EOB-DTPA-enhanced liver MR imaging. Eur Radiol 2016; 26(6):1775–82.

[26] Wang L, Regatte RR. T(1)rho MRI of human musculoskeletal system. J Magn Reson Imaging 2015; 41(3):586–600.

[27] Rauscher I, et al. Evaluation of T1rho as a potential MR biomarker for liver cirrhosis: comparison of healthy control subjects and patients with liver cirrhosis. Eur J Radiol 2014;83(6):900–4.

[28] Singh A, et al. T1rho MRI of healthy and fibrotic human livers at 1.5 T. J Transl Med 2015;13:292.

[29] Brewer CJ, Coates TD, Wood JC. Spleen R2 and R2* in iron-overloaded patients with sickle cell disease and thalassemia major. J Magn Reson Imaging 2009;29(2):357–64.

[30] Liu A, et al. Splenic T1-mapping: a novel quantitative method for assessing adenosine stress adequacy for cardiovascular magnetic resonance. J Cardiovasc Magn Reson 2017;19(1):1.

[31] Wolf M, et al. Magnetic resonance imaging T1- and T2-mapping to assess renal structure and function: a systematic review and statement paper. Nephrol Dial Transplant 2018;33(Suppl 2):ii41–50.

[32] Peperhove M, et al. Assessment of acute kidney injury with T1 mapping MRI following solid organ transplantation. Eur Radiol 2018;28(1):44–50.
[33] Cox EF, et al. Multiparametric renal magnetic resonance imaging: validation, interventions, and alterations in chronic kidney disease. Front Physiol 2017;8:696.
[34] Grassedonio E, et al. Quantitative T2* magnetic resonance imaging for renal iron overload assessment: normal values by age and sex. Abdom Imaging 2015;40(6):1700–4.
[35] Schein A, et al. Magnetic resonance detection of kidney iron deposition in sickle cell disease: a marker of chronic hemolysis. J Magn Reson Imaging 2008;28(3):698–704.
[36] Ding J, et al. Evaluation of renal oxygenation level changes after water loading using susceptibility-weighted imaging and T2* mapping. Korean J Radiol 2015;16(4):827–34.
[37] Pohlmann A, et al. Detailing the relation between renal T2* and renal tissue pO2 using an integrated approach of parametric magnetic resonance imaging and invasive physiological measurements. Invest Radiol 2014;49(8):547–60.
[38] Henninger B, et al. R2*-relaxometry of the pancreas in patients with human hemochromatosis protein associated hereditary hemochromatosis. Eur J Radiol 2017;89:149–55.
[39] Noetzli LJ, et al. Pancreatic iron loading predicts cardiac iron loading in thalassemia major. Blood 2009;114(19):4021–6.
[40] Noetzli LJ, Coates TD, Wood JC. Pancreatic iron loading in chronically transfused sickle cell disease is lower than in thalassaemia major. Br J Haematol 2011;152(2):229–33.
[41] de Assis RA, et al. Pancreatic iron stores assessed by magnetic resonance imaging (MRI) in beta thalassemic patients. Eur J Radiol 2012;81(7):1465–70.
[42] Meloni A, et al. Accurate estimate of pancreatic T2* values: how to deal with fat infiltration. Abdom Imaging 2015;40(8):3129–36.
[43] Tirkes T, et al. T1 mapping for diagnosis of mild chronic pancreatitis. J Magn Reson Imaging 2017; 45(4):1171–6.
[44] Wang M, et al. Magnetic resonance elastography and T1 mapping for early diagnosis and classification of chronic pancreatitis. J Magn Reson Imaging 2018;48:837–45.
[45] Gilani N, et al. Minimization of errors in biexponential T2 measurements of the prostate. J Magn Reson Imaging 2015;42(4):1072–7.
[46] Storas TH, et al. Prostate magnetic resonance imaging: multiexponential T2 decay in prostate tissue. J Magn Reson Imaging 2008;28(5):1166–72.
[47] Liu W, et al. Accelerated T2 mapping for characterization of prostate cancer. Magn Reson Med 2011;65(5):1400–6.
[48] Wu LM, et al. Feasibility and preliminary experience of quantitative T2* mapping at 3.0 T for detection and assessment of aggressiveness of prostate cancer. Acad Radiol 2014;21(8):1020–6.
[49] Yu AC, et al. Development of a combined MR fingerprinting and diffusion examination for prostate Cancer. Radiology 2017;283(3):729–38.
[50] Panda A, et al. Repeatability and reproducibility of 3D MR fingerprinting relaxometry measurements in normal breast tissue. J Magn Reson Imaging 2019.
[51] Liu L, et al. Changes of T2 relaxation time from neoadjuvant chemotherapy in breast cancer lesions. Iran J Radiol 2016;13(3):e24014.

CHAPTER

Relaxometry: Applications in the Heart

10

Erica Dall'Armellina and Arka Das

Leeds Institute of Cardiovascular and Metabolic Medicine, Department of Biomedical Imaging Sciences, University of Leeds, Leeds, United Kingdom

10.1 Introduction

One of the major advantages of cardiac Magnetic Resonance Imaging (CMR) is the ability to characterize tissue composition. Assessment via late gadolinium imaging (LGE) [1] has played a key role in establishing CMR as the clinical gold-standard noninvasive imaging technique to assess the presence of myocardial fibrosis and enabling the differentiation between ischemic and nonischemic cardiomyopathy. Novel mapping techniques (T_1, T_2, and T_2*) have advanced the field, making it possible to overcome the limitation of arbitrary signal intensity-based assessment by providing quantitative voxel-wise tissue quantification which can provide the information above and beyond that offered by LGE. Changes in mapping parameters (T_1, T_2, T_2*) can be linked to a variety of disease processes. Abnormal T_1 values can indicate intracellular (for example, iron overload or glycosphingolipid accumulation in Anderson-Fabry disease [AFD]) or extracellular changes (accumulation of collagen or deposition of amyloid proteins). An increase in native T_1 values can be influenced by excess water content due to edema [2,3] or by deposition of proteins (such as amyloid) [4]. Lipids and iron accumulation in case of hemorrhage or siderosis can cause a decrease in T_1 values [5] (Fig. 10.1). Elevated T_2 values are usually found in cases of edema or inflammation [6]. T_2* values decrease in the presence of iron (hemosiderosis and hemorrhage) [7].

Mapping techniques have also generated new imaging biomarkers beyond the quantitative T_1 and T_2 values such as the "extracellular volume," (ECV). ECV maps are derived from non-contrast T_1 maps (otherwise known as "native" T_1 maps) and post-contrast T_1 maps by performing the following voxel-wise calculation:

$$\text{myocardial ECV} = (1 - \text{hematocrit}) \times \left(\Delta R_{1,\text{myocardium}} / \Delta R_{1,\text{blood}}\right)$$

where $R_1 = 1/T_1$, and ΔR_1 is the difference between the native and post-contrast T_1 maps [8]. This new metric enables the assessment of diffuse myocardial disease previously not easily detectable by standard CMR techniques, including LGE. ECV assessed by contrast-enhanced T_1 mapping represents a robust measure of collagen deposition and myocardial fibrosis [9], and shows excellent agreement with standard LGE techniques for assessment of scarred tissue [10]. Normal ECV values have been established to be on the order of $25.3\% \pm 3.5\%$ at 1.5 T [11].

Advances in Magnetic Resonance Technology and Applications. Volume 1. ISSN 2666-9099. https://doi.org/10.1016/B978-0-12-817057-1.00011-1

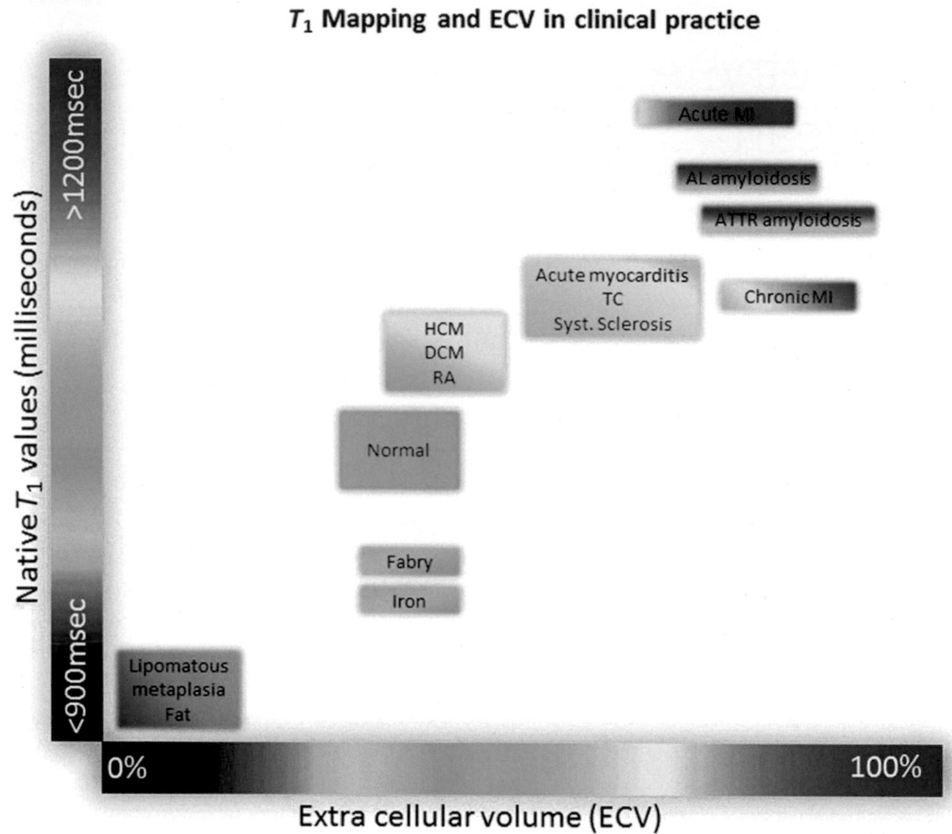

FIG. 10.1

Alterations of T_1 and ECV in different myocardial diseases. T_1 values refer to MOLLI-based techniques at 1.5 T. *(Reproduced with permission from Haaf P, Garg P, Messroghli DR, Broadbent DA, Greenwood JP, Plein S. Cardiac T1 Mapping and Extracellular Volume (ECV) in clinical practice: a comprehensive review. J Cardiovasc Magn Reson 2016;18:89.)*

While the clinical utility of multiparametric mapping in the heart is being increasingly explored, the clinical application requires specific hardware, software, data acquisition, and evaluation procedures, which are not completely standardized. For example, different T_1 values are expected when different T_1 mapping methods such as MOLLI and SASHA are used due to differences in the assumptions that these methods make about the MRI signals. Moreover, different variants of mapping techniques, including MOLLI and shMOLLI, also yield different T_1 values [12]. These variations occur because the collection of these tissue parameter maps is challenging for multiple reasons, most specifically the need to avoid cardiac and respiratory motion. Leading experts in the field of quantitative cardiac imaging agree the differences in conventional quantitative measurements between different institutions, or even on two scanners at the same institution, are so large that normative data must be collected for each institution and each scanner at that institution [13]. This requirement dramatically reduces the power of quantitative imaging for tissue characterization, as no globally applicable database of disease-specific quantitative values can be established with the current mapping techniques.

Thus, the possibility for multicenter trials is currently limited, and this challenge contributes to the sometimes conflicting data presented concerning the clinical utility of these mapping approaches in the heart.

Another weakness of parametric mapping is that one particular value can potentially represent several cardiomyopathies (high sensitivity but low specificity), as depicted in Fig. 10.1. Hence, these measurements should be used in conjunction with other CMR techniques in a multiparametric approach, rather than as a single diagnostic or prognostic biomarker.

However, despite these challenges, there are a wide variety of applications where cardiac T_1, T_2, T_2*, and ECV mapping have been shown to provide additional clinical value. These applications, along with the reported changes seen in parametric maps, are detailed in the following section.

10.2 Acute chest pain syndromes

In situations other than ST-elevation myocardial infarction (STEMI), patients presenting with acute chest pain can pose a diagnostic challenge. CMR mapping can inform the clinical decision-making process by enabling the differentiation between myocarditis and Takotsubo [14], and myocardial infarction with nonobstructive coronary arteries (MINOCA) and acute coronary syndrome/myocardial infarction. Recent data demonstrate the additional prognostic value of CMR imaging in these patients [15].

10.2.1 Myocarditis

Viral myocarditis causes the damage of the myocardium due to an inflammatory process which can lead to long-term scarring, mostly in the sub-epicardium and intramural regions [16]. Thanks to the unique ability of CMR to depict inflammatory changes and myocardial fibrosis [17], the use of CMR imaging diagnostic criteria (also known as Lake Louise Criteria [LLC]) is recommended in patients with clinically suspected myocarditis [18,19]. Evidence continues to emerge to support the clinical utility of multiparametric mapping in patients with suspected myocarditis [20] (see Fig. 10.2). Recently published recommendations by an expert consensus panel updated the CMR criteria for the diagnosis of myocarditis to include the use of mapping techniques. The consensus states that CMR may provide strong evidence for active myocardial inflammation based on at least one T_2-based criterion (either an increase in signal intensity T_2-weighted images as measured via increased global signal intensity ratio, normalized against reference regions in skeletal muscle >2 or increased T_2 mapping values above normal reference values) with at least one T_1-based criterion (i.e., elevated T_1 or ECV values or presence of LGE) [21].

T_1 mapping is emerging as a potential novel diagnostic criterion for myocarditis with superior sensitivity to T_2-weighted and LGE imaging. By more accurately detecting diffuse patterns of edema/inflammation as well as necrosis/fibrosis, native T_1 mapping enables the detection of additional areas of myocardial involvement and outperforms conventional methods which often fail to identify abnormalities [22–24]. When compared to endomyocardial biopsy, it has been shown that in patients with acute symptoms and suspected myocarditis, native T_1 yields the best diagnostic performance with an area under the curve (AUC) of receiver-operating curves of 0.82, followed by T_2 (0.81), ECV (0.75), and LLC (0.56) [24]. In patients with chronic symptoms, only T_2 mapping yields an acceptable AUC (0.77). The additional clinical utility of multiparametric mapping compared to LGE and T_2-weighted imaging is that T_1 mapping can be used for longitudinal monitoring of disease activity [25] and thus enables the quantification of the gradual reduction of native T_1 values between the acute and chronic healing stages of myocarditis.

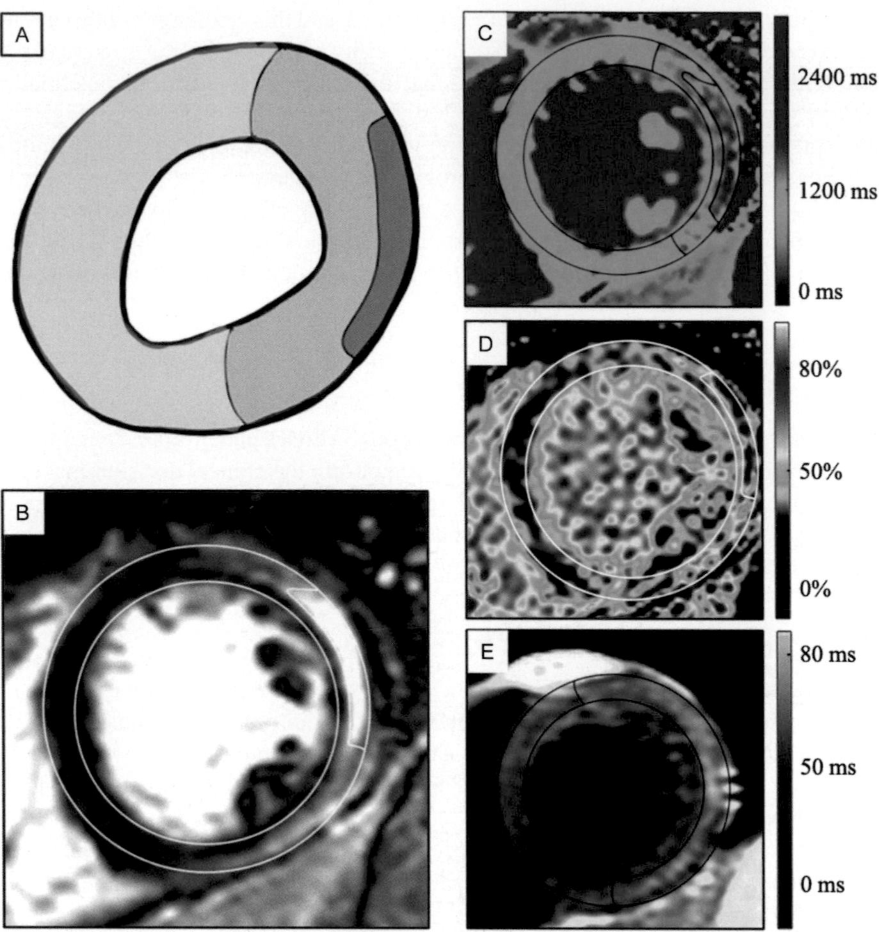

FIG. 10.2

Multiparametric mapping to assess myocarditis. (A) A representation of a case of myocarditis. The subepicardial scar in the lateral wall *(red)* is surrounded by edema *(orange)*, whilst the remote segments are shown in green. (B) The corresponding LGE acquisition. On the lateral wall, there is an area of subepicardial enhancement with focal brighter intensity (shown *red* in the representation in (A)) and surrounding hazier signal. (C) Native T_1 mapping acquisition showing high T_1 values in the lateral wall indicating active inflammation. (D) An ECV map showing increased ECV in the lateral wall. (E) A T_2 mapping acquisition with high T_2 values in the lateral wall.

In patients with severe subacute myocarditis, post-contrast T_1 mapping for ECV quantification has also shown to provide highest diagnostic accuracy compared to other standalone CMR parameters; ECV also improved the diagnostic accuracy of CMR imaging compared with standard LLC [26]. The accuracy of this method in patients with different degrees of severity is, however, unknown. Further investigations are needed to establish whether the use of ECV imaging alone could potentially simplify CMR protocols in myocarditis by replacing the current standard which requires the assessment of several different tissue properties.

T_2 mapping for the detection of myocardial edema in myocarditis is superior not only to standard CMR techniques (such as T_2-weighted edema imaging and LGE) [27] but also to global myocardial T_1 and ECV fraction values for assessing the level of activity of myocarditis [28]. In the largest study to date involving patients with confirmed myocardial edema on endomyocardial biopsies [29], the diagnostic accuracy of T_2 mapping was superior to ECV and the LLC and was only inferior to native T_1 mapping at the acute stage of myocarditis. At the chronic stage, T_2 mapping was the only method that yielded an acceptable diagnostic performance.

Despite these advancements, there is significant heterogeneity in the published evidence due mostly to a lack of standardization of different quantitative mapping techniques and a consequent lack of established normal values and thresholds [13].

The clinical meaning of prolonged T_1 values is also not fully clarified, as high T_1 values are seen in both acute and chronic pathologies. T_2 mapping is considered a more specific method for the detection of inflammation. Hence, a multiparametric approach is still recommended with consequent prolongation of the imaging protocol [30]. Furthermore, two recently published meta-analyses [20,31] comparing the diagnostic performance of mapping versus LLC have shown different results: while Kotanidis et al. showed that native T_1 mapping is superior to all other techniques (mapping and standard) and LLC [31], Salerno et al. have shown that native T_1 had significantly better sensitivity than LLC in diagnosing acute myocarditis but that otherwise native T_1, T_2, and ECV mapping were comparable to LLC [20].

10.2.2 Takostubo

Takotsubo, or stress-induced cardiomyopathy, is characterized by acute transient left ventricular (LV) dysfunction due to mid and apical left ventricular segment akinesia with ballooning and compensatory hyperkinesia of basal segments [32]. CMR imaging features include diffuse or transmural myocardial edema by T_2-weighted imaging, in both apical and mid regions, with no coronary distribution and typically matching the dysfunctional ventricular contraction area [14].

Both native T_1 and T_2 mapping techniques have shown to have potentially higher diagnostic performance than standard T_2-weighted imaging techniques in depicting myocardial edema [28,33]. Besides, these approaches are superior in detecting persistent myocardial fibrotic changes as increased T_1 and T_2 values above normal values leading to heart failure several months after the acute event [34,35]. The prognostic value of mapping techniques in Takostubo patients is yet to be fully determined and further larger studies will be needed to confirm the additional diagnostic and clinical value of multiparametric mapping.

10.2.3 Ischemic chest pain and nonobstructive coronary artery disease

Patients with angina and nonobstructive coronary disease remain a diagnostic and treatment challenge. These patients have a "normal" angiogram, persistent symptoms, recurrent hospitalizations, a poor functional status, and adverse cardiovascular outcomes, without a clear diagnosis [36]. Recent pilot data in a small group of patients show that native T_1 mapping values at rest could be significantly increased in patients with microvascular dysfunction and inversely correlated with the vasodilatory reserve [37]. The mechanisms underpinning such findings are unclear and could potentially include increased diffuse fibrosis or increased myocardial water content; further evidence on larger studies will be needed.

10.3 Acute myocardial infarction

10.3.1 ST-elevation myocardial infarction

In recent decades, the availability worldwide of primary percutaneous coronary intervention (PCI) to treat myocardial infarction (MI) has led to a decrease in mortality rates [38–40] but an increase in the incidence of heart failure due to long-term remodeling of the left ventricle [41,42]. Although LV ejection fraction (EF) assessment is widely used as a marker for clinical decision-making and treatment on patients following MI, limitations of LVEF measurements are known [43]. By providing tissue characterization in addition to EF quantification, the role of quantitative CMR for stratification has emerged in recent years. Quantitative mapping techniques are a novel tool with recognized superior accuracy in detecting changes in tissue composition and potential incremental prognostic values as described in detail in the paragraphs in the following section.

Changes in native T_1 values are influenced by tissue water content, the degree of binding with macromolecules (water mobility), and cell content [2,3]. An ischemic insult leads to a significant increase in myocardial edema [44], reflected by an increase in native T_1 values [45]. It has been shown that post-ischemia-reperfusion, native T_1 mapping enables accurate assessment of the edematous area downstream from the culprit vessel [46–48], also when compared to more standard imaging techniques such as SPECT measurements [49]. Compared to standard CMR techniques (such as T_2-weighted imaging), quantitative mapping techniques enable the anatomical extent of the area at risk to be measured and also allow an assessment of the severity of the injury within that area on a continuous scale (Fig. 10.3). By determining the degree of damage, native T_1 mapping following acute MI could potentially differentiate reversible versus irreversible injury; areas with higher acute T_1 values are more likely to develop scar long-term [50] and will not recover functionally at 6 months [5]. Native T_1 mapping shows persistently high T_1 values in areas of chronically scarred tissue, and thus this technique could potentially become a valid alternative to contrast-based techniques for detection of chronic scar [51].

In reperfused acute MI patients, microvascular obstruction (MVO) is a common occurrence [52] and a known poor prognostic factor [53,54] as depicted by standard late gadolinium enhancement (LGE) CMR techniques. T_1 mapping can assist in detecting the infarct core, which appears as an area with lower T_1 values relative to the surrounding myocardium [5]. This effect is most likely due to the presence of degradation products of the hemoglobin in the context of myocardial hemorrhage [55,56]. Native T_1 values (ms) within the hypointense infarct core have been shown to have a prognostic value similar to that of MVO by LGE [57].

In the context of acute ischemic myocardial injury, the involvement of the remote myocardium as a contributing factor to long term remodeling has been debated, with evidence showing remote myocardial dysfunction [58–60]. The prognostic significance of such findings is uncertain. More recently, data have demonstrated a systemic inflammatory reaction following an acute ischemic event involving the myocardium globally [61–63]. Using mapping techniques, an increase in T_1 values has been shown in remote myocardium in reperfused MI patients [64–66]. The increase in remote T_1 values was shown to be associated with adverse remodeling of the left ventricle and poor prognosis [65,66].

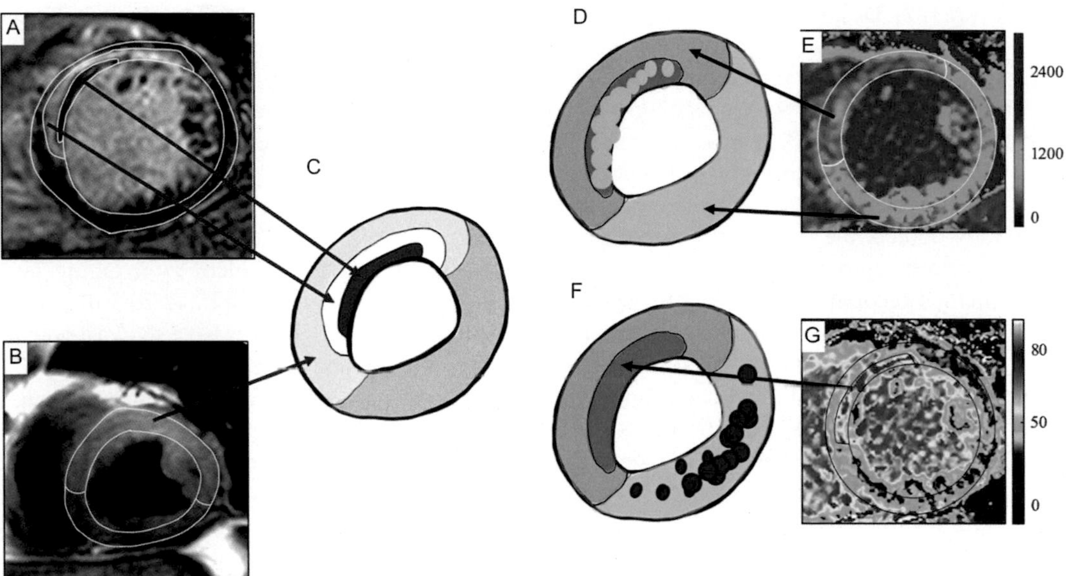

FIG. 10.3

Acute myocardial infarction: standard versus novel mapping techniques. (A) A LGE image of a case of anterior myocardial infarction with a core of microvascular obstruction. (B) A T_2-weighted image showing extensive myocardial edema in the anterior myocardium (same location positive on LGE image). (C) A schematic drawing of the heart: the *yellow area* is the edematous region, the *white area* corresponds to the scar with the *black core* of microvascular obstruction. (D) A representation of a map with normal values in the remote myocardium *(green),* high native T_1 values in the injured area shown in *orange* with a core of normalized T_1 values indicating the presence of microvascular obstruction. (E) A native T_1 map with increased values in the anterior wall in keeping with myocardial edema. T_1 values are green in keeping with lower/normalized values due to microvascular obstruction. (F) A representation of an ECV map with normal values in the remote myocardium *(blue),* high ECV in the injured area and the core (shown in *red*). (G) An ECV map showing normal ECV values remotely and high ECV in the anterior wall, indicating increased interstitial volume post-ischemic injury with higher values in the core.

Following acute ischemic injury, ECV expands due to the development of significant interstitial edema and changes in the vasculature [67,68]. Post-acute MI, ECV depicts the area of necrosis with similar accuracy to standard LGE [69–71], and initial data suggest that ECV could represent a novel imaging biomarker, more accurate than LGE, in predicting functional recovery long-term [70,72,73].

Post-contrast T_1 and ECV changes have been identified in the remote myocardium in the early stages post-acute infarction [72–75] suggesting that adverse cardiac remodeling may commence at the time of infarction rather than being a long-term consequence. The acute expansion of the ECV in the remote myocardium has potentially predictive relevance for long-term functional recovery [75] and LV remodeling [72], independent of other biomarkers such as the presence of MVO or infarct core [72]. Despite the appealing perspective of shortening the scan time in acutely ill patients by assessing myocardial salvage using T_1 mapping techniques only, further studies will be needed to support this change in the standard protocol [76].

The accumulation of water, leading to myocardial edema, in ischemically injured myocardium leads to an increase in T_2 relaxation times. The area-at-risk has been traditionally measured using signal intensity-based T_2-weighted imaging techniques, which can be used to visualize the extent of edematous myocardium. Preclinical microsphere experiments have demonstrated that T_2 mapping accurately depicts the edematous myocardium downstream from the culprit coronary lesion [77], and is a more reproducible method than T_2-weighted imaging [78]. As such, T_2 mapping is the CMR method recommended by CMR experts to measure myocardial edema [45,47,79,80].

Following the use of mapping techniques in the early hour's post-MI, studies have shown a potential highly dynamic course after reperfusion [79,81–83]. Not only the time course but also the complexity of the pathophysiology of the tissue changes in the early hours post MI has raised questions about the optimal imaging timing. Expert consensus recommends 5–7 days post-MI as the optimal imaging time.

The effects of hemorrhage on T_2 values are well-known and complex, with paramagnetic effects dominating between 1 and 7 days after reperfusion [84]. As such, for an accurate assessment of the extent and severity of the myocardial injury post-ischemia, [85–87] multiparametric mapping including both T_2 and T_2* mapping is essential (see paragraph below on T_2* mapping for further details).

While the persistence of edema within the infarcted tissue over time has been previously reported [88–90], it has remained a controversial subject, most likely due to the small numbers of patients in these studies and the use of different T_2-weighted CMR techniques. By using T_2 mapping, it has been possible to demonstrate not only prolonged T_2 relaxation times up to 6 months after the acute event but most importantly the association with long term remodeling and outcomes [83].

Post-ischemia-reperfusion, MVO as well as hemorrhage can characterize the core of the infarcted tissue [55,91,92]. MVO, as depicted by LGE, is a well-recognized poor prognostic factor and marker of adverse LV remodeling [53,93]. Compared to T_2-weighted edema imaging techniques, T_2* mapping techniques allow for more accurate characterization of the infarct core, and depiction of hemorrhage [85,94–97], which would otherwise go undetected, thereby potentially underestimating the area at risk by up to 50% [85]. T_2* values of less than 20 ms indicate hemorrhage [96,98] (Fig. 10.4), and by performing pixel-wise mapping and counting these pixels, longitudinal changes in the size of the hemorrhage can be assessed. Recent studies using T_2* measurements in this manner have shown that hemorrhage reaches maximal extent at 3 days post-MI and then decreases progressively at 10 days and 7 months [87].

A growing body of evidence recognizes the prognostic value of acute hemorrhage [99–102] and supports the notion that hemorrhagic MIs are associated with prolonged inflammation, well after the formation of scar tissue [103,104]. The presence of residual iron deposits within the scar up to 6 months after the acute event might represent a suitable target for prevention of adverse remodeling and persistent inflammation [103,105].

10.3.2 Non-ST elevation myocardial infarction (NSTEMI)

NSTEMI is a heterogeneous condition which leads to a certain diagnostic and treatment variability [106]. NSTEMI patients usually present with smaller myocardial injury, often limited to ischemic insult causing edema rather than necrosis, due to multiple vessel disease, often nonobstructive. Standard T_2-weighted techniques (both black or bright blood), are known to have limitations, including

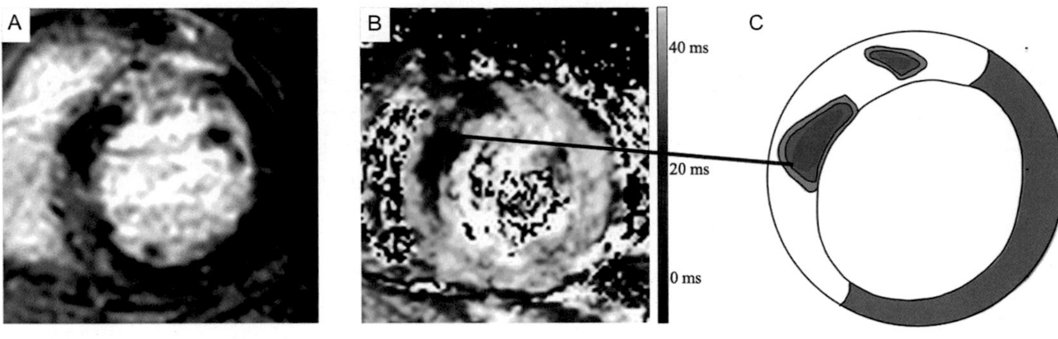

FIG. 10.4

T_2* mapping for assessment of myocardial hemorrhage. (A) An LGE image of a case of acute septal myocardlal infarction with a dark core representative of microvascular obstruction. (B) The corresponding T_2* map which depicts hemorrhage localized in two different areas shown in purple (see *arrow*). (C) A representation showing the scarred myocardium in white and two corresponding areas of hemorrhage as detected by T_2* mapping.

signal drop-out, bright signals adjacent to the subendocardium due to slow-flowing blood, image quality impairment in tachyarrhythmias, and long breath-holds [107]. Several studies have demonstrated that mapping techniques are far more robust in detecting small areas of myocardial edema following ischemic injury in NSTEMI patients [5,108,109]. Recent evidence shows that in a non-negligible percentage of NSTEMI patients, T_1 and T_2 mapping can be used to detect myocardial edema in the absence of significant coronary stenosis [110]. While mapping techniques have additional diagnostic value, further studies are needed to assess the clinical prognostic value of these techniques in NSTEMi patients; evidence shows that in up to 25% of acute NSTEMI cases with obstructive coronary artery disease (CAD), mapping techniques depicted no edema [110].

10.4 Chronic stable coronary artery disease

Risk stratification in patients with CAD is crucial to determine the appropriate therapy. A range of imaging techniques are available; CMR imaging is increasingly recommended in international guidelines as a frontline test for workup of patients with ischemic heart disease. Several clinical studies have demonstrated the superior diagnostic accuracy [111,112] and prognostic value of CMR perfusion imaging compared to SPECT [113]. However, CMR perfusion uses contrast and might not be suitable for patients with contraindications.

Preliminary results using native mapping techniques demonstrate their potential to enable detection of perfusion defects without thc need for intravascular contrast [114]. During stress testing in patients with coronary stenosis, the increase in capillary recruitment and myocardial blood volume (MBV) following coronary vasodilatation [115,116] leads to prolonged T_1, enabling detection of microvascular and MBV changes during ischemia. Specifically, initial evidence using adenosine stress and rest T_1 mapping together suggest the potential to detect changes in MBV and enable differentiation between normal, infarcted, and ischemic myocardium [114]. However, these results have not yet been reproduced and further evidence is needed to consider this a clinically applicable and validated method.

Mapping techniques have not only been shown to have a diagnostic role, but data may also support the prognostic relevance of T_1 mapping. Specifically, the characterization of non-infarcted myocardium by native T_1 could be an important predictor of outcome in CAD patients [117].

10.5 Cardiomyopathy

10.5.1 Hypertrophic cardiomyopathy

Hypertrophic cardiomyopathy (HCM) is an autosomal dominant condition involving the sarcomeric genes, leading to myocyte disarray, fibrosis, and asymmetric left ventricular hypertrophy, most commonly affecting the septum. In addition to providing an accurate assessment of wall thickness and LV mass, CMR LGE depicts the presence of focal fibrosis. Histology, however, indicates the presence of diffuse fibrosis which is often undetected by LGE imaging [118].

The potential incremental diagnostic role of native T_1 mapping in HCM has been recently demonstrated [119] (Fig. 10.5). As healthy tissue is replaced by fibrotic tissue, native T_1 values become

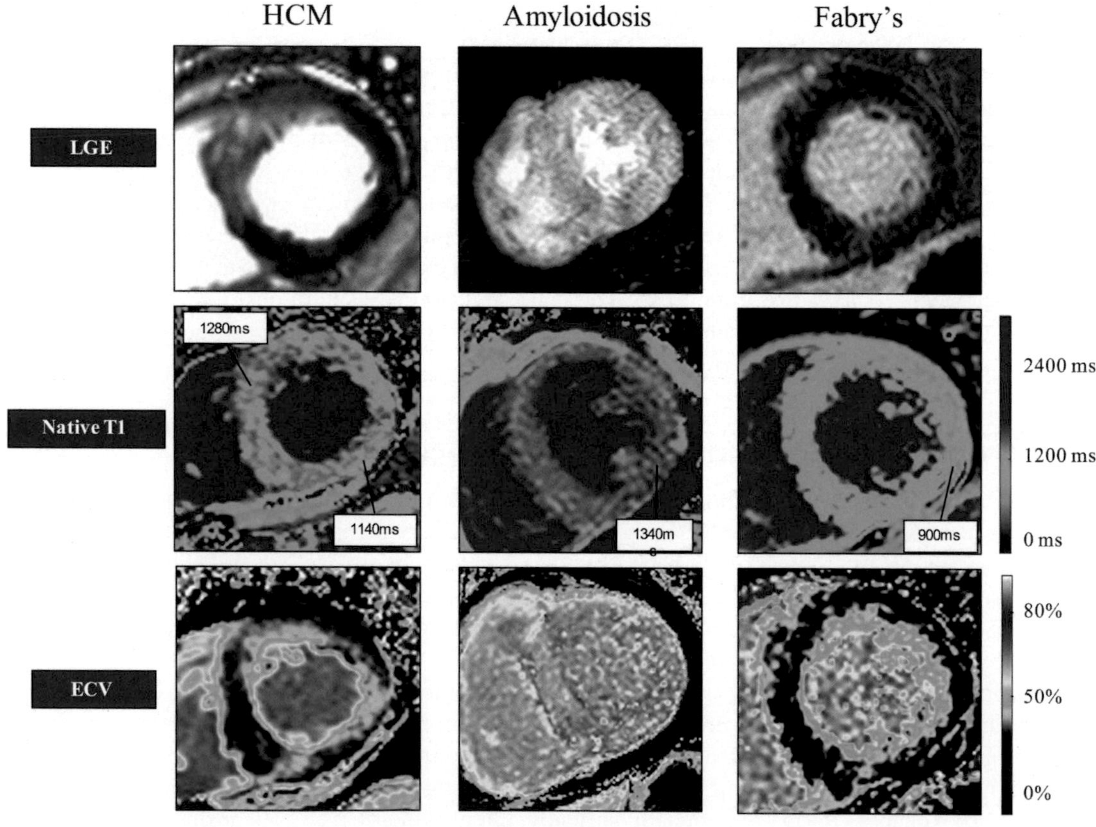

FIG. 10.5

Multiparametric mapping in cardiomyopathy. LGE, native T_1 mapping, and post-contrast T_1 mapping for assessment of ECV are acquired in HCM, amyloidosis, and Fabry disease. Whilst native T_1 values are increased in both HCM and amyloidosis, these are reduced in Fabry disease.

prolonged in HCM [120,121]. Importantly, in patients with HCM, the impairment of contractile function is predominantly associated with the degree of hypertrophy and the native T_1 value [122]. T_1 mapping may also play a diagnostic role in discriminating patients with LV hypertrophy due to HCM from those with hypertrophy secondary to arterial hypertension [114].

Using ECV for assessment of diffuse fibrosis has provided clinically useful information beyond the standard LGE [123]. In HCM patients, post-contrast T_1 values are lowered compared with healthy myocardium, resulting in elevated ECV values even outside areas of LGE. Not only is ECV increased in patients with typical HCM phenotype, but also asymptomatic relatives without clinical findings but with the positive phenotype [124]. The prognostic value of such early findings of increased ECV in this cohort is unknown.

Furthermore, evidence would suggest that ECV could have incremental diagnostic value in differentiating between HCM and athletic remodeling of the heart. Initial data show that while ECV increases with increasing LV hypertrophy in HCM (due to extracellular matrix expansion from myocardial disarray), ECV is reduced in athletes with an increased wall thickness (due to an increase in healthy myocardium via cellular hypertrophy) [125].

Longitudinal studies regarding the prognostic value of T_1 and ECV mapping are currently lacking, as well as an exploration of the potential use of T_1 values for therapy guidance.

10.5.2 Amyloidosis

Amyloidosis is a systemic, infiltrative disorder caused by plasma cell dyscrasia, which results in the deposition of abnormal protein light chains in various tissues, causing multiorgan damage. Myocardial amyloid deposition causes myocyte death, leading to reactive fibrosis and expansion of interstitial space. While CMR LGE can show typical features such as subendocardial "zebra/tramline" enhancement; still there is significant heterogeneity amongst patients. There are also limitations to adopting post-contrast methods due to the often poor renal function of amyloidosis patients.

Native T_1 mapping is emerging clearly as a robust diagnostic non-contrast tool in this population (Fig. 10.4). Native T_1 values are significantly increased throughout the myocardium, reflecting the diffuse fibrotic process in cardiac amyloidosis. Clinical studies to date have demonstrated that native T_1 maps have higher diagnostic accuracy for detecting cardiac amyloid than LGE [4,126] and can help reliably differentiate amyloidosis from HCM, a common differential diagnosis [127]. However, in early disease, the prolongation of T_1 values is aspecific and as such clinically useful only with high test probability [45].

Cardiac amyloid is associated with a higher ECV than any other cardiomyopathy due to the widespread and extensive extracellular infiltration. In a study involving 100 patients with systemic amyloid light-chain amyloidosis, Banypersad et al. [128] demonstrated both native T_1 and ECV to be reliable biomarkers for predicting mortality. Patients with higher ECV values (>0.45) had a three- to a four-fold increased likelihood of death at 23 months compared to patients with lower ECV values. Finally, ECV could potentially be used also to monitor the effects of therapy [129].

10.5.3 Anderson-Fabry disease

In Anderson-Fabry disease (AFD), mutations of the α-galactosidase gene result in intracellular lipid accumulation in various organs including the heart, kidneys, and skin. Cardiac involvement manifests clinically as LV hypertrophy, heart failure, and arrhythmias. Focal fibrosis can be depicted by LGE imaging, typically displaying mid-wall enhancement of the inferolateral wall. However much like other diffuse infiltrative conditions, such patterns only become evident at a late stage in the disease progression.

Due to the increased fat content of affected myocardium, native T_1 values become *reduced* even at initial stages of the disease, for instance before developing LV hypertrophy, serving as an early surrogate biomarker and a potential tool for screening family members of AFD patients. In all other common causes of LV hypertrophy (HCM, amyloidosis, aortic stenosis, hypertension), native T_1 increases, meaning low T_1 values can distinguish AFD from other causes with no overlap [130] (Fig. 10.4).

However, as the disease progresses, damaged myocardium is replaced by fibrotic tissue (most commonly in the basal inferolateral wall), causing a pseudo-normalization or even increased native T_1 values in these areas. This highlights the four-step pathological progression from normal, to low, to pseudonormalized, to high T_1 values. Values should ideally be measured in the septum, which seems to be relatively spared of this phenomenon even late on in the disease process [131]. ECV on the other hand typically remains normal as AFD is an *intra*cellular (lysosomal) storage disorder [132].

10.5.4 Dilated cardiomyopathy

Dilated cardiomyopathy (DCM) is characterized by the development of diffuse myocardial fibrosis with dilatation and impaired systolic function of one or both ventricles without any detectable cause. Evidence of a circumferential mid-wall ring of enhancement in LGE CMR images is associated with poorer outcomes, and to potentially guide risk stratification for implantation of cardiac defibrillators (ICD) [133]. However, in the majority of cases, there is a lack of any detectable LGE [118].

Native T_1 values are prolonged in DCM [121] allowing for accurate discrimination between healthy and diseased myocardium [120]. High native myocardial T_1 is associated with an increased risk for cardiovascular events and heart failure [134,135] and the only independent predictor of appropriate ICD therapies [136]. ECV values in DCM have shown to be in a similar range to HCM; however, given that DCM and HCM have such distinct ventricular appearances, this overlap in values is not clinically important [118]. Wong et al. [135] demonstrated that DCM patients with higher ECV values (>28.5%) had more hospital admissions relating to heart failure and higher mortality rates.

10.5.5 Iron overload cardiomyopathy

Iron overload cardiomyopathy results from the accumulation of iron caused by repeated blood transfusions (e.g., in cases of anemia due to thalassemia major), or increased iron absorption (e.g., hereditary hemochromatosis) or administration (i.e., diet) [137]. Iron overload cardiomyopathy is the leading cause of death in patients receiving chronic blood transfusion therapy [138]. Noninvasive CMR T_2* mapping is recognized by international guidelines [139] as an accurate method to quantify cardiac iron load [140], stratify patients at risk for heart failure or arrhythmia [141], monitor disease progression, and guide therapy [142]. Further investigations are needed to determine the diagnostic power of native T_1 and ECV mapping in iron-overload cardiomyopathy [143,144].

10.6 Systemic inflammatory diseases

Cardiac involvement in systematic inflammatory diseases (such as rheumatoid arthritis, lupus erythematosus, systemic sclerosis, pheochromocytoma, human immunodeficiency virus infection, and cardiac sarcoidosis) can lead to poor prognosis [145,146]. Although the presence of LGE is a powerful predictor of risk in patients with sarcoidosis, it may not identify patients who have earlier stages of cardiac sarcoidosis before the development of myocardial scar or overt inflammation.

Native T_1 and T_2 mapping techniques might have an emerging role in the early identification of patients at risk of severe cardiac involvement [137–141,147–149]. Specifically, patients with the connective disease have diffusely increased native T_1 and T_2 values and increased ECV with recognized superior diagnostic performance of native T_1 mapping in discriminating healthy from diseased myocardium [147,150]. However, in patients with cardiac involvement, while inflammation and diffuse fibrosis can be depicted, it is often not possible to define a pathognomonic pattern or range of values diagnostic for a specific disease.

Further larger studies are needed to demonstrate the added value of quantitative mapping techniques for diagnosis and prognosis of patients with systemic inflammatory diseases.

10.7 Valve disease

In patients with either stenotic or regurgitant valve disease, the heart progressively remodels due to the pressure or volume overload. The remodeling of the left ventricle involves diffuse myocardial fibrosis, which can be detected by mapping techniques, both native and post-contrast, with excellent reproducibility [151]. The increase in ECV not only has been shown to correlate with histologically determined diffuse fibrosis [152] but also associated with reduced myocardial deformation and diastolic dysfunction [153–155]. Future T_1 and ECV mapping studies are required to investigate whether the finding of myocardial fibrosis in patients with left-sided valvular heart disease mandates early surgical intervention to prevent progressive and irreversible myocardial fibrosis.

10.7.1 Aortic stenosis

In patients with severe aortic stenosis, both native T_1 and ECV values increase, and these values correlate with the degree of biopsy-quantified fibrosis [156–159]. However, the underpinning mechanism for the lengthening of native T_1 values is not known. While ECV reflects fibrosis in the extracellular volumes, the tissue assessed via native T_1 mapping also includes the cellular compartment [160] and as such T_1 mapping is subject to other confounders such as the presence of edema or increased vascular space [161].

Furthermore, the discriminatory power of native T_1 mapping in patients with aortic stenosis is still uncertain. While some published data show that T_1 values in asymptomatic patients with aortic stenosis might not be longer than values in matched controls [151], several studies in aortic stenosis patients have shown that T_1 values and ECV correlate with disease progression, with ECV being a strong predictor of cardiovascular complications [157,158]. However, further studies are needed to understand fully the clinical value of native T_1 mapping as a biomarker for risk stratification of patients in need of aortic valve replacement and an as a tool to optimize the timing of the intervention before significant diffuse myocardial fibrosis develops [162,163].

10.7.2 Mitral regurgitation

Mitral regurgitation is the most common valve disease in the current era. In asymptomatic patients with severe regurgitation, conservative management is the treatment of choice; there are no randomized data on alternative management options such as early intervention [164]. To address management, there is a need for novel imaging biomarkers with predictive relevance enabling early patient stratification. In light of the likely association between increasing myocardial fibrosis due to overload and LV dysfunction, mapping techniques for assessment of ECV are emerging as a potentially valuable tool for early assessment [153]. Increased ECV and diffuse fibrosis have been found in patients with asymptomatic moderate to severe mitral valve regurgitation [153,154]. Myocardial fibrosis was also shown to be associated with reduced myocardial deformation and reduced exercise capacity in these patients [153].

10.8 Heart failure with preserved ejection fraction

Heart failure with preserved ejection fraction (HFpEF) presents a major challenge in modern cardiology. Despite the increasing prevalence and unfavorable outcomes, treatment trials have failed to establish effective therapies. In HFpEF, comorbidities promote a systemic inflammatory state, leading to cellular stiffening and the occurrence of reactive interstitial fibrosis, eventually leading to diastolic dysfunction [165]. ECV determined through post-contrast T_1 mapping is significantly elevated in HFpEF patients compared with controls but significantly lower compared with heart failure with reduced ejection fraction (HFrEF) patients [166]. ECV was suggested not only to be predictive of increased myocardial stiffness but also to potentially enable the identification of alternative mechanisms of diastolic dysfunction [167].

10.9 Heart transplant

Survival after cardiac transplantation is linked to the occurrence of complications, especially the risk of acute rejection during the first year [168]. Following a heart transplant, patients are closely monitored using an endomyocardial biopsy, which is limited by cost and invasiveness, and echocardiography, which is limited regarding detailed structural and functional evaluation. CMR mapping for tissue characterization is emerging as a promising technique for early detection of inflammatory and fibrotic changes, which may decrease overall graft rejection.

Both native T_1 and T_2 values are prolonged posttransplant [169–171] in patients with both acute cardiac allograft rejection (ACAR) or cardiac allograft vasculopathy (CAV) compared to controls [170]. Despite the reported findings of native T_1 and T_2 changes [169,171], there is contrasting evidence regarding the diagnostic accuracy of each mapping technique for the diagnosis of acute rejection, in some cases indicating higher diagnostic accuracy of T_2 mapping [169,171]. Sade et al. demonstrated that native T_1 values can help to identify patients with significant ACAR requiring treatment [172]. These results are in disagreement with Miller et al. [169], who showed the inability of CMR mapping to identify significant rejection [173]. In patients 6 months post heart transplant, there is an association between increased ECV and diffuse fibrosis on histology, in keeping with myocardial hypertrophy and associated with graft rejection [174]. Evidence of diffuse fibrosis has been shown even in children 1 year after heart transplant [175,176]. ECV could emerge as a marker of tissue remodeling in patients post heart transplant.

10.10 Conclusions

CMR mapping techniques are becoming more widely available and hold great promise in a variety of clinical applications [21,45]. Current evidence indicates that there is additional value in the information provided by T_1, T_2, and ECV mapping; however, there are objective difficulties related to a lack of standardization and different methods available [177]. At the moment, major efforts are underway to overcome these challenges (see Chapters 5 and 6). In the future, mapping techniques could become the CMR method of choice for tissue characterization and patient stratification, radically changing current clinical practice.

References

[1] Kim RJ, Wu E, Rafael A, Chen EL, Parker MA, Simonetti O, Klocke FJ, Bonow RO, Judd RM. The use of contrast-enhanced magnetic resonance imaging to identify reversible myocardial dysfunction. N Engl J Med 2000;343(20):1445–53.

[2] Mathur-De Vre R. Biomedical implications of the relaxation behaviour of water related to NMR imaging. Br J Radiol 1984;57(683):955–76.

[3] Cameron IL, Ord VA, Fullerton GD. Characterization of proton NMR relaxation times in normal and pathological tissues by correlation with other tissue parameters. Magn Reson Imaging 1984;2(2):97–106.

[4] Karamitsos TD, Piechnik SK, Banypersad S, Fontana M, Ntusi N, Ferreira VM, Whelan C, Myerson SG, Robson MD, Hawkins P, Neubauer S, Moon J. Non-contrast T1 mapping for the diagnosis of cardiac amyloidosis. JACC Cardiovasc Imaging 2012;6:488–97. https://doi.org/10.1016/j.jcmg.2012.11.013.

[5] Dall'armellina E, Piechnik SK, Ferreira VM, Le Si Q, Robson MD, Francis JM, Cuculi F, Kharbanda RK, Banning AP, Choudhury RP, Karamitsos TD, Neubauer S. Cardiovascular magnetic resonance by non contrast T1 mapping allows assessment of severity of injury in acute myocardial infarction. J Cardiovasc Magn Reson 2012;14(1):15.

[6] Salerno M, Kramer CM. Advances in parametric mapping with cardiac magnetic resonance imaging. J Am Coll Cardiol Img 2013;6(7):806–22.

[7] O'Regan DP, Ahmed R, Karunanithy N, Neuwirth C, Tan Y, Durighel G, Hajnal JV, Nadra I, Corbett SJ, Cook SA. Reperfusion hemorrhage following acute myocardial infarction: assessment with T2* mapping and effect on measuring the area at risk1. Radiology 2009;250(3):916–22.

[8] White SK, Sado DM, Fontana M, Banypersad SM, Maestrini V, Flett AS, Piechnik SK, Robson MD, Hausenloy DJ, Sheikh AM, Hawkins PN, Moon JC. T1 mapping for myocardial extracellular volume measurement by CMR: bolus only versus primed infusion technique. JACC Cardiovasc Imaging 2013; 6(9):955–62.

[9] Miller CA, Naish JH, Bishop P, Coutts G, Clark D, Zhao S, Ray SG, Yonan N, Williams SG, Flett AS, Moon JC, Greiser A, Parker GJM, Schmitt M. Comprehensive validation of cardiovascular magnetic resonance techniques for the assessment of myocardial extracellular volume. Circ Cardiovasc Imaging 2013;6(3):373–83.

[10] Varga-Szemes A, van der Geest RJ, Spottiswoode BS, Suranyi P, Ruzsics B, De Cecco CN, Muscogiuri G, Cannao PM, Fox MA, Wichmann JL, Vliegenthart R, Schoepf UJ. Myocardial late gadolinium enhancement: accuracy of T1 mapping-based synthetic inversion-recovery imaging. Radiology 2016;278(2):374–82.

[11] Sado DM, Flett AS, Banypersad SM, White SK, Maestrini V, Quarta G, Lachmann RH, Murphy E, Mehta A, Hughes DA, McKenna WJ, Taylor AM, Hausenloy DJ, Hawkins PN, Elliott PM, Moon JC. Cardiovascular magnetic resonance measurement of myocardial extracellular volume in health and disease. Heart 2012; 98(19):1436–41.

[12] Raman FS, Kawel-Boehm N, Gai N, Freed M, Han J, Liu C-Y, Lima JAC, Bluemke DA, Liu S. Modified look-locker inversion recovery T1 mapping indices: assessment of accuracy and reproducibility between magnetic resonance scanners. J Cardiovasc Magn Reson 2013;15(1):64.

[13] Moon JC, Messroghli DR, Kellman P, Piechnik SK, Robson MD, Ugander M, Gatehouse PD, Arai AE, Friedrich MG, Neubauer S, Schulz-Menger J, Schelbert EB, Society for Cardiovascular Magnetic Resonance Imaging, and Cardiovascular Magnetic Resonance Working Group of the European Society of Cardiology. Myocardial T1 mapping and extracellular volume quantification: a society for cardiovascular magnetic resonance (SCMR) and CMR working group of the European society of cardiology consensus statement. J Cardiovasc Magn Reson 2013;15:92.

[14] Eitel I, Lucke C, Grothoff M, Sareban M, Schuler G, Thiele H, Gutberlet M. Inflammation in takotsubo cardiomyopathy: insights from cardiovascular magnetic resonance imaging. Eur Radiol 2010;20(2):422–31.

[15] Dastidar AG, Baritussio A, De Garate E, Drobni Z, Biglino G, Singhal P, Milano EG, Angelini GD, Dorman S, Strange J, Johnson T, Bucciarelli-Ducci C. Prognostic role of CMR and conventional risk factors in myocardial infarction with nonobstructed coronary arteries. JACC Cardiovasc Imaging 2019;12(10):1973.

[16] Mahrholdt H, Goedecke C, Wagner A, Meinhardt G, Athanasiadis A, Vogelsberg H, Fritz P, Klingel K, Kandolf R, Sechtem U. Cardiovascular magnetic resonance assessment of human myocarditis: a comparison to histology and molecular pathology. Circulation 2004;109(10):1250–8.

[17] Lurz P, Eitel I, Adam J, Steiner J, Grothoff M, Desch S, Fuernau G, de Waha S, Sareban M, Luecke C, Klingel K, Kandolf R, Schuler G, Gutberlet M, Thiele H. Diagnostic performance of CMR imaging compared with EMB in patients with suspected myocarditis. JACC Cardiovasc Imaging 2012;5(5):513–24.

[18] Friedrich MG, Sechtem U, Schulz-Menger J, Holmvang G, Alakija P, Cooper LT, White JA, Abdel-Aty H, Gutberlet M, Prasad S, Aletras A, Laissy JP, Paterson I, Filipchuk NG, Kumar A, Pauschinger M, Liu P, International Consensus Group on Cardiovascular Magnetic Resonance in Myocarditis. Cardiovascular magnetic resonance in myocarditis: a JACC White paper. J Am Coll Cardiol 2009;53(17):1475–87.

[19] Caforio AL, Pankuweit S, Arbustini E, Basso C, Gimeno-Blanes J, Felix SB, Fu M, Helio T, Heymans S, Jahns R, Klingel K, Linhart A, Maisch B, McKenna W, Mogensen J, Pinto YM, Ristic A, Schultheiss HP, Seggewiss H, Tavazzi L, Thiene G, Yilmaz A, Charron P, Elliott PM, European Society of Cardiology Working Group on M, Pericardial D. Current state of knowledge on aetiology, diagnosis, management, and therapy of myocarditis: a position statement of the European Society of Cardiology Working Group on Myocardial and Pericardial Diseases. Eur Heart J 2013;34(33):2636–48. 48a-48d.

[20] Pan JA, Lee YJ, Salerno M. Diagnostic performance of extracellular volume, native T1, and T2 mapping versus Lake Louise criteria by cardiac magnetic resonance for detection of acute myocarditis: a meta-analysis. Circ Cardiovasc Imaging 2018;11(7):e007598.

[21] Ferreira VM, Schulz-Menger J, Holmvang G, Kramer CM, Carbone I, Sechtem U, Kindermann I, Gutberlet M, Cooper LT, Liu P, Friedrich MG. Cardiovascular magnetic resonance in nonischemic myocardial inflammation: expert recommendations. J Am Coll Cardiol 2018;72(24):3158–76.

[22] Ferreira VM, Piechnik SK, Dall'Armellina E, Karamitsos TD, Francis JM, Ntusi N, Holloway C, Choudhury RP, Kardos A, Robson MD, Friedrich MG, Neubauer S. Native T1-mapping detects the location, extent and patterns of acute myocarditis without the need for gadolinium contrast agents. J Cardiovasc Magn Reson 2014;16:36.

[23] Luetkens JA, Doerner J, Thomas DK, Dabir D, Gieseke J, Sprinkart AM, Fimmers R, Stehning C, Homsi R, Schwab JO, Schild H, Naehle CP. Acute myocarditis: multiparametric cardiac MR imaging. Radiology 2014;273(2):383–92.

[24] Lurz P, Luecke C, Eitel I, Föhrenbach F, Frank C, Grothoff M, de Waha S, Rommel K-P, Lurz JA, Klingel K, Kandolf R, Schuler G, Thiele H, Gutberlet M. Comprehensive cardiac magnetic resonance imaging in patients with suspected myocarditis: the myoracer-trial. J Am Coll Cardiol 2016;67(15):1800–11.

[25] Baydes RH, Ucar EA, Foote L, Dabir D, Mahmoud I, Jackson T, Higgins DM, Schaeffter T, Nagel E, Puntmann V. Native T1 values in discrimination between in acute and chronic myocarditis. J Cardiovasc Magn Reson 2014;16(1):O62.

[26] Radunski UK, Lund GK, Stehning C, Schnackenburg B, Bohnen S, Adam G, Blankenberg S, Muellerleile K. CMR in patients with severe myocarditis: diagnostic value of quantitative tissue markers including extracellular volume imaging. JACC Cardiovasc Imaging 2014;7(7):667–75.

[27] Bohnen S, Radunski UK, Lund GK, Kandolf R, Stehning C, Schnackenburg B, Adam G, Blankenberg S, Muellerleile K. Performance of t1 and t2 mapping cardiovascular magnetic resonance to detect active myocarditis in patients with recent-onset heart failure. Circ Cardiovasc Imaging 2015;8(6):e003073.

[28] Thavendiranathan P, Walls M, Giri S, Verhaert D, Rajagopalan S, Moore S, Simonetti OP, Raman SV. Improved detection of myocardial involvement in acute inflammatory cardiomyopathies using T2 mapping. Circ Cardiovasc Imaging 2012;5(1):102–10.

[29] Lurz P, Luecke C, Eitel I, Fohrenbach F, Frank C, Grothoff M, de Waha S, Rommel KP, Lurz JA, Klingel K, Kandolf R, Schuler G, Thiele H, Gutberlet M. Comprehensive cardiac magnetic resonance imaging in patients with suspected myocarditis: the MyoRacer-trial. J Am Coll Cardiol 2016;67(15):1800–11.

[30] Friedrich MG. Cardiovascular magnetic resonance for myocardial inflammation. Circ Cardiovasc Imaging 2018;11(7):e008010.

[31] Kotanidis CP, Bazmpani MA, Haidich AB, Karvounis C, Antoniades C, Karamitsos TD. Diagnostic accuracy of cardiovascular magnetic resonance in acute myocarditis: a systematic review and meta-analysis. JACC Cardiovasc Imaging 2018;11(11):1583–90.

[32] Prasad A, Lerman A, Rihal CS. Apical ballooning syndrome (Tako-Tsubo or stress cardiomyopathy): a mimic of acute myocardial infarction. Am Heart J 2008;155(3):408–17.

[33] Ferreira VM, Piechnik SK, Dall'armellina E, Karamitsos TD, Francis JM, Choudhury RP, Friedrich MG, Robson MD, Neubauer SM. Non-contrast T1-mapping detects acute myocardial edema with high diagnostic accuracy: a comparison to T2-weighted cardiovascular magnetic resonance. J Cardiovasc Magn Reson 2012;14(1):42.

[34] Scally C, Rudd A, Mezincescu A, Wilson H, Srivanasan J, Horgan G, Broadhurst P, Newby DE, Henning A, Dawson DK. Persistent long-term structural, functional, and metabolic changes after stress-induced (Takotsubo) cardiomyopathy. Circulation 2018;137(10):1039–48.

[35] Schwarz K, Ahearn T, Srinivasan J, Neil CJ, Scally C, Rudd A, Jagpal B, Frenneaux MP, Pislaru C, Horowitz JD, Dawson DK. Alterations in cardiac deformation, timing of contraction and relaxation, and early myocardial fibrosis accompany the apparent recovery of acute stress-induced (Takotsubo) cardiomyopathy: an end to the concept of transience. J Am Soc Echocardiogr 2017;30(8):745–55.

[36] Lee BK, Lim HS, Fearon WF, Yong AS, Yamada R, Tanaka S, Lee DP, Yeung AC, Tremmel JA. Invasive evaluation of patients with angina in the absence of obstructive coronary artery disease. Circulation 2015;131(12):1054–60.

[37] Shaw JL, Nelson MD, Wei J, Motwani M, Landes S, Mehta PK, Thomson LEJ, Berman DS, Li D, Bairey Merz CN, Sharif B. Inverse association of MRI-derived native myocardial T1 and perfusion reserve index in women with evidence of ischemia and no obstructive CAD: a pilot study. Int J Cardiol 2018;270:48–53.

[38] Fox KA, Steg P, Eagle KA, et al. Decline in rates of death and heart failure in acute coronary syndromes, 1999–2006. JAMA 2007;297(17):1892–900.

[39] McManus DD, Gore J, Yarzebski J, Spencer F, Lessard D, Goldberg RJ. Recent trends in the incidence, treatment, and outcomes of patients with ST and non-ST-segment acute myocardial infarction. Am J Med 2011;124(1):40–7.

[40] Jernberg T, Johanson P, Held C, et al. Association between adoption of evidence-based treatment and survival for patients with st-elevation myocardial infarction. JAMA 2011;305(16):1677–84.

[41] Gerber Y, Weston SA, Enriquez-Sarano M, Berardi C, Chamberlain AM, Manemann SM, Jiang R, Dunlay SM, Roger VL. Mortality associated with heart failure after myocardial infarction: a contemporary community perspective. Circ Heart Fail 2016;9(1):e002460.

[42] Ezekowitz JA, Kaul P, Bakal JA, Armstrong PW, Welsh RC, McAlister FA. Declining in-hospital mortality and increasing heart failure incidence in elderly patients with first myocardial infarction. J Am Coll Cardiol 2009;53(1):13–20.

[43] Task Force on the management of STseamiotESoC, Steg PG, James SK, Atar D, Badano LP, Blomstrom-Lundqvist C, Borger MA, Di Mario C, Dickstein K, Ducrocq G, Fernandez-Aviles F, Gershlick AH, Giannuzzi P, Halvorsen S, Huber K, Juni P, Kastrati A, Knuuti J, Lenzen MJ, Mahaffey KW, Valgimigli M, Van't Hof A, Widimsky P, Zahger D. ESC Guidelines for the management of acute myocardial infarction in patients presenting with ST-segment elevation. Eur Heart J 2012;33(20):2569–619.

[44] Reimer KA, Jennings RB, Tatum AH. Pathobiology of acute myocardial ischemia: metabolic, functional and ultrastructural studies. Am J Cardiol 1983;52(2):72A–81A.

[45] Messroghli DR, Moon JC, Ferreira VM, Grosse-Wortmann L, He T, Kellman P, Mascherbauer J, Nezafat R, Salerno M, Schelbert EB, Taylor AJ, Thompson R, Ugander M, Van Heeswijk RB, Friedrich MG. Clinical recommendations for cardiovascular magnetic resonance mapping of T1, T2, T2* and extracellular volume: a consensus statement by the Society for Cardiovascular Magnetic Resonance (SCMR) endorsed by the European Association for Cardiovascular Imaging (EACVI). J Cardiovasc Magn Reson 2017;19(1):75.

[46] Dall'Armellina E, Piechnik SK, Ferreira VM, Si QL, Robson MD, Francis JM, Cuculi F, Kharbanda RK, Banning AP, Choudhury RP, Karamitsos TD, Neubauer S. Cardiovascular magnetic resonance by non contrast T1-mapping allows assessment of severity of injury in acute myocardial infarction. J Cardiovasc Magn Reson 2012;14:15.

[47] Bulluck H, White SK, Rosmini S, Bhuva A, Treibel TA, Fontana M, Abdel-Gadir A, Herrey A, Manisty C, Wan SMY, Groves A, Menezes L, Moon JC, Hausenloy DJ. T1 mapping and T2 mapping at 3T for quantifying the area-at-risk in reperfused STEMI patients. J Cardiovasc Magn Reson 2015;17(1):73.

[48] Ugander M, Bagi PS, Oki AJ, Chen B, Hsu L-Y, Aletras AH, Shah S, Greiser A, Kellman P, Arai AE. Myocardial edema as detected by pre-contrast T1 and T2 CMR delineates area at risk associated with acute myocardial infarction. JACC Cardiovasc Imaging 2012;5:596–603.

[49] Langhans B, Nadjiri J, Jahnichen C, Kastrati A, Martinoff S, Hadamitzky M. Reproducibility of area at risk assessment in acute myocardial infarction by T1- and T2-mapping sequences in cardiac magnetic resonance imaging in comparison to Tc99m-sestamibi SPECT. Int J Cardiovasc Imaging 2014;30(7):1357–63.

[50] Liu D, Borlotti A, Viliani D, Jerosch-Herold M, Alkhalil M, De Maria GL, Fahrni G, Dawkins S, Wijesurendra R, Francis J, Ferreira V, Piechnik S, Robson MD, Banning A, Choudhury R, Neubauer S, Channon K, Kharbanda R, Dall'Armellina E. CMR native T1 mapping allows differentiation of reversible versus irreversible myocardial damage in ST-segment-elevation myocardial infarction: an OxAMI study (Oxford Acute Myocardial Infarction). Circ Cardiovasc Imaging 2017;10(8)):e005986.

[51] Kali A, Choi EY, Sharif B, Kim YJ, Bi X, Spottiswoode B, Cokic I, Yang HJ, Tighiouart M, Conte AH, Li D, Berman DS, Choi BW, Chang HJ, Dharmakumar R. Native T1 mapping by 3-T CMR imaging for characterization of chronic myocardial infarctions. JACC Cardiovasc Imaging 2015;8(9):1019–30.

[52] Rochitte CE, Lima JA, Bluemke DA, Reeder SB, McVeigh ER, Furuta T, Becker LC, Melin JA. Magnitude and time course of microvascular obstruction and tissue injury after acute myocardial infarction. Circulation 1998;98(10):1006–14.

[53] van Kranenburg M, Magro M, Thiele H, de Waha S, Eitel I, Cochet A, Cottin Y, Atar D, Buser P, Wu E, Lee D, Bodi V, Klug G, Metzler B, Delewi R, Bernhardt P, Rottbauer W, Boersma E, Zijlstra F, van Geuns RJ. Prognostic value of microvascular obstruction and infarct size, as measured by CMR in STEMI patients. JACC Cardiovasc Imaging 2014;7(9):930–9.

[54] Fearon WF, Low AF, Yong AS, McGeoch R, Berry C, Shah MG, Ho MY, Kim HS, Loh JP, Oldroyd KG. Prognostic value of the index of microcirculatory resistance measured after primary percutaneous coronary intervention. Circulation 2013;127(24):2436–41.

[55] Robbers LF, Eerenberg ES, Teunissen PF, Jansen MF, Hollander MR, Horrevoets AJ, Knaapen P, Nijveldt R, Heymans MW, Levi MM, van Rossum AC, Niessen HW, Marcu CB, Beek AM, van Royen N. Magnetic resonance imaging-defined areas of microvascular obstruction after acute myocardial infarction represent microvascular destruction and haemorrhage. Eur Heart J 2013;34(30):2346–53.

[56] Robbers LFHJ, Nijveldt R, Beek AM, Teunissen PFA, Hollander MR, Biesbroek PS, Everaars H, van de Ven PM, Hofman MBM, van Royen N, van Rossum AC. The influence of microvascular injury on native T1 and T2* relaxation values after acute myocardial infarction: implications for non-contrast-enhanced infarct assessment. Eur Radiol 2018;28(2):824–32.

[57] Carrick D, Haig C, Rauhalammi S, Ahmed N, Mordi I, McEntegart M, Petrie MC, Eteiba H, Hood S, Watkins S, Lindsay M, Mahrous A, Ford I, Tzemos N, Sattar N, Welsh P, Radjenovic A, Oldroyd KG, Berry C. Prognostic significance of infarct core pathology revealed by quantitative non-contrast in comparison with contrast cardiac magnetic resonance imaging in reperfused ST-elevation myocardial infarction survivors. Eur Heart J 2016;37(13):1044–59.

[58] Bogaert J, Bosmans H, Maes A, Suetens P, Marchal G, Rademakers FE. Remote myocardial dysfunction after acute anterior myocardial infarction: impact of left ventricular shape on regional function: a magnetic resonance myocardial tagging study. J Am Coll Cardiol 2000;35(6):1525–34.

[59] Götte MJW, van Rossum AC, Twisk JWR, Kuijer JPA, Marcus JT, Visser CA. Quantification of regional contractile function after infarction: strain analysis superior to wall thickening analysis in discriminating infarct from remote myocardium. J Am Coll Cardiol 2001;37(3):808–17.

[60] Kramer CM, Rogers WJ, Theobald TM, Power TP, Petruolo S, Reichek N. Remote noninfarcted region dysfunction soon after first anterior myocardial infarction. A magnetic resonance tagging study. Circulation 1996;94(4):660–6.

[61] Libby P, Nahrendorf M, Swirski FK. Leukocytes link local and systemic inflammation in ischemic cardiovascular disease: an expanded "cardiovascular continuum". J Am Coll Cardiol 2016;67(9):1091–103.

[62] Lee WW, Marinelli B, van der Laan AM, Sena BF, Gorbatov R, Leuschner F, Dutta P, Iwamoto Y, Ueno T, Begieneman MPV, Niessen HWM, Piek JJ, Vinegoni C, Pittet MJ, Swirski FK, Tawakol A, Di Carli M, Weissleder R, Nahrendorf M. PET/MRI of inflammation in myocardial infarction. J Am Coll Cardiol 2012;59(2):153–63.

[63] Ruparelia N, Godec J, Lee R, Chai JT, Dall' Armellina E, McAndrew D, Digby JE, Forfar JC, Prendergast BD, Kharbanda RK, Banning AP, Neubauer S, Lygate CA, Channon KM, Nicholas Haining W, Choudhury RP. Acute myocardial infarction activates distinct inflammation and proliferation pathways in circulating monocytes, prior to recruitment, and identified through conserved transcriptional responses in mice and humans. Eur Heart J 2015;36(29):1923–34. https://doi.org/10.1093/eurheartj/ehv195.

[64] Biesbroek PS, Amier RP, Teunissen PFA, Hofman MBM, Robbers LFHJ, van de Ven PM, Beek AM, van Rossum AC, van Royen N, Nijveldt R. Changes in remote myocardial tissue after acute myocardial infarction and its relation to cardiac remodeling: a CMR T1 mapping study. PLOS One 2017;12(6):e0180115.

[65] Carrick D, Haig C, Rauhalammi S, Ahmed N, Mordi I, McEntegart M, Petrie MC, Eteiba H, Lindsay M, Watkins S, Hood S, Davie A, Mahrous A, Sattar N, Welsh P, Tzemos N, Radjenovic A, Ford I, Oldroyd KG, Berry C. Pathophysiology of LV remodeling in survivors of STEMI: inflammation, remote myocardium, and prognosis. JACC Cardiovasc Imaging 2015;8(7):779–89.

[66] Reinstadler SJ, Stiermaier T, Liebetrau J, Fuernau G, Eitel C, de Waha S, Desch S, Reil JC, Poss J, Metzler B, Lucke C, Gutberlet M, Schuler G, Thiele H, Eitel I. Prognostic significance of remote myocardium alterations assessed by quantitative noncontrast T1 mapping in ST-segment elevation myocardial infarction. JACC Cardiovasc Imaging 2018;11(3):411–9.

[67] Hammer-Hansen S, Bandettini WP, Hsu LY, Leung SW, Shanbhag S, Mancini C, Greve AM, Kober L, Thune JJ, Kellman P, Arai AE. Mechanisms for overestimating acute myocardial infarct size with gadolinium-enhanced cardiovascular magnetic resonance imaging in humans: a quantitative and kinetic study. Eur Heart J Cardiovasc Imaging 2016;17(1):76–84.

[68] Jablonowski R, Engblom H, Kanski M, Nordlund D, Koul S, van der Pals J, Englund E, Heiberg E, Erlinge D, Carlsson M, Arheden H. Contrast-enhanced CMR overestimates early myocardial infarct size: mechanistic insights using ECV measurements on day 1 and day 7. JACC Cardiovasc Imaging 2015;8(12):1379–89.

[69] Bulluck H, Hammond-Haley M, Fontana M, Knight DS, Sirker A, Herrey AS, Manisty C, Kellman P, Moon JC, Hausenloy DJ. Quantification of both the area-at-risk and acute myocardial infarct size in ST-segment elevation myocardial infarction using T1-mapping. J Cardiovasc Magn Reson 2017;19(1):57.

[70] Kidambi A, Motwani M, Uddin A, Ripley DP, McDiarmid AK, Swoboda PP, Broadbent DA, Musa TA, Erhayiem B, Leader J, Croisille P, Clarysse P, Greenwood JP, Plein S. Myocardial extracellular volume estimation by CMR predicts functional recovery following acute MI. JACC Cardiovasc Imaging 2017;10(9):989–99.

[71] Garg P, Broadbent DA, Swoboda PP, Foley JRJ, Fent GJ, Musa TA, Ripley DP, Erhayiem B, Dobson LE, McDiarmid AK, Haaf P, Kidambi A, van der Geest RJ, Greenwood JP, Plein S. Acute infarct extracellular volume mapping to quantify myocardial area at risk and chronic infarct size on cardiovascular magnetic resonance imaging. Circ Cardiovasc Imaging 2017;10(7):e006182.

[72] Bulluck H, Rosmini S, Abdel-Gadir A, White SK, Bhuva AN, Treibel TA, Fontana M, Gonzalez-Lopez E, Reant P, Ramlall M, Hamarneh A, Sirker A, Herrey AS, Manisty C, Yellon DM, Kellman P, Moon JC, Hausenloy DJ. Automated extracellular volume fraction mapping provides insights into the pathophysiology of left ventricular remodeling post-reperfused ST-elevation myocardial infarction. J Am Heart Assoc 2016;5(7):e003555.

[73] Carberry J, Carrick D, Haig C, Rauhalammi SM, Ahmed N, Mordi I, McEntegart M, Petrie MC, Eteiba H, Hood S, Watkins S, Lindsay M, Davie A, Mahrous A, Ford I, Sattar N, Welsh P, Radjenovic A, Oldroyd KG, Berry C. Remote zone extracellular volume and left ventricular remodeling in survivors of ST-elevation myocardial infarction. Hypertension 2016;68(2):385–91.

[74] Chan W, Duffy SJ, White DA, Gao X-M, Du X-J, Ellims AH, Dart AM, Taylor AJ. Acute left ventricular remodeling following myocardial infarction: coupling of regional healing with remote extracellular matrix expansion. JACC Cardiovasc Imaging 2012;5(9):884–93.

[75] Garg P, Broadbent DA, Swoboda PP, Foley JRJ, Fent GJ, Musa TA, Ripley DP, Erhayiem B, Dobson LE, McDiarmid AK, Haaf P, Kidambi A, Crandon S, Chew PG, van der Geest RJ, Greenwood JP, Plein S. Extra-cellular expansion in the normal, non-infarcted myocardium is associated with worsening of regional myocardial function after acute myocardial infarction. J Cardiovasc Magn Reson 2017;19:73.

[76] Bulluck H, Hausenloy DJ. Mapping myocardial salvage index by extracellular volume fraction. Circ Cardiovasc Imaging 2017;10(7). https://doi.org/10.1161/CIRCIMAGING.117.006680.

[77] Ugander M, Bagi P, Oki A. Myocardial edema as detected by pre-contrast T1 and T2 MRI delineates area at risk associated with acute myocardial infarction. JACC Cardiovasc Imaging 2012;5(6):596–603.

[78] McAlindon EJ, Pufulete M, Harris JM, Lawton CB, Moon JC, Manghat N, Hamilton MCK, Weale PJ, Bucciarelli-Ducci C. Measurement of myocardium at risk with cardiovascular MR: comparison of techniques for edema imaging. Radiology 2014;275(1):61–70.

[79] Masci P-G, Pavon AG, Muller O, Iglesias J-F, Vincenti G, Monney P, Harbaoui B, Eeckhout E, Schwitter J. Relationship between CMR-derived parameters of ischemia/reperfusion injury and the timing of CMR after reperfused ST-segment elevation myocardial infarction. J Cardiovasc Magn Reson 2018;20:50.

[80] Ibanez B, Aletras AH, Arai AE, Arheden H, Bax J, Berry C, Bucciarelli-Ducci C, Croisille P, Dall'Armellina E, Dharmakumar R, Eitel I, Fernández-Jiménez R, Friedrich MG, García-Dorado D, Hausenloy DJ, Kim RJ, Kozerke S, Kramer CM, Salerno M, Sánchez-González J, Sanz J, Fuster V. Cardiac MRI endpoints in myocardial infarction experimental and clinical trials: JACC Scientific Expert Panel. J Am Coll Cardiol 2019;74(2):238–56.

[81] Fernández-Jiménez R, Barreiro-Pérez M, Martin-García A, Sánchez-González J, Agüero J, Galán-Arriola C, García-Prieto J, Díaz-Pelaez E, Vara P, Martinez I, Zamarro I, Garde B, Sanz J, Fuster V, Sánchez PL, Ibanez B. Dynamic edematous response of the human heart to myocardial infarction. Circulation 2017;136(14):1288. https://doi.org/10.1161/CIRCULATIONAHA.116.025582.

[82] Fernandez-Jimenez R, Galan-Arriola C, Sanchez-Gonzalez J, Aguero J, Lopez-Martin G, Gomez-Talavera S, Garcia-Prieto J, Benn A, de Molina A, Barreiro-Perez M, Martin-Garcia A, Garcia-Lunar I, Pizarro G, Sanz J, Sanchez P, Fuster V, Ibanez B. Effect of ischemia duration and protective interventions on the temporal dynamics of tissue composition after myocardial infarction. Circ Res 2017; 121(4):439–50.

[83] Carberry J, Carrick D, Haig C, Ahmed N, Mordi I, McEntegart M, Petrie MC, Eteiba H, Hood S, Watkins S, Lindsay M, Davie A, Mahrous A, Ford I, Sattar N, Welsh P, Radjenovic A, Oldroyd KG, Berry C. Persistence of infarct zone T2 hyperintensity at 6 months after acute ST-segment–elevation myocardial infarction: incidence, pathophysiology, and prognostic implications. Circ Cardiovasc Imaging 2017;10(12):e006586-e.

[84] Lotan CS, Miller SK, Cranney GB, Pohost GM, Elgavish GA. The effect of postinfarction intramyocardial hemorrhage on transverse relaxation time. Magn Reson Med 1992;23(2):346–55.

[85] O'Regan DP, Ahmed R, Karunanithy N, Neuwirth C, Tan Y, Durighel G, Hajnal JV, Nadra I, Corbett SJ, Cook SA. Reperfusion hemorrhage following acute myocardial infarction: assessment with T2* mapping and effect on measuring the area at risk. Radiology 2009;250(3):916–22.

[86] Berry C, Carrick D, Haig C, Oldroyd KG. "Waves of Edema" seem implausible. J Am Coll Cardiol 2016;67(15):1868–9.

[87] Carrick D, Haig C, Ahmed N, Rauhalammi S, Clerfond G, Carberry J, Mordi I, McEntegart M, Petrie MC, Eteiba H, Hood S, Watkins S, Lindsay MM, Mahrous A, Welsh P, Sattar N, Ford I, Oldroyd KG, Radjenovic A, Berry C. Temporal evolution of myocardial hemorrhage and edema in patients after acute ST-segment elevation myocardial infarction: pathophysiological insights and clinical implications. J Am Heart Assoc 2016;5(2):e002834.

[88] Ripa RS, Nilsson JC, Wang Y, Søndergaard L, Jørgensen E, Kastrup J. Short- and long-term changes in myocardial function, morphology, edema, and infarct mass after ST-segment elevation myocardial infarction evaluated by serial magnetic resonance imaging. Am Heart J 2007;154(5):929–36. https://doi.org/10.1016/j.ahj.2007.06.038.

[89] Nilsson JC, Nielsen G, Groenning BA, Fritz-Hansen T, Sondergaard L, Jensen GB, Larsson HB. Sustained postinfarction myocardial oedema in humans visualised by magnetic resonance imaging. Heart 2001; 85(6):639–42.

[90] Dall'Armellina E, Karia N, Lindsay AC, Karamitsos TD, Ferreira V, Robson MD, Kellman P, Francis JM, Forfar C, Prendergast B, Banning AP, Channon KM, Kharbanda RK, Neubauer S, Choudhury RP. Dynamic changes of Edema and late gadolinium enhancement after acute myocardial infarction and their relationship to functional recovery and salvage index. Circ Cardiovasc Imaging 2011;4(3):228–36.

[91] Lima JAC, Judd RM, Bazille A, Schulman SP, Atalar E, Zerhouni EA. Regional heterogeneity of human myocardial infarcts demonstrated by contrast-enhanced MRI: potential mechanisms. Circulation 1995; 92(5):1117–25.

[92] Cannan C, Eitel I, Hare J, Kumar A, Friedrich M. Hemorrhage in the myocardium following infarction. JACC Cardiovasc Imaging 2010;3(6):665–8.

[93] Wu KC, Zerhouni EA, Judd RM, Lugo-Olivieri CH, Barouch LA, Schulman SP, Blumenthal RS, Lima JAC. Prognostic significance of microvascular obstruction by magnetic resonance imaging in patients with acute myocardial infarction. Circulation 1998;97(8):765–72.

[94] Ghugre NR, Ramanan V, Pop M, Yang Y, Barry J, Qiang B, Connelly KA, Dick AJ, Wright GA. Quantitative tracking of edema, hemorrhage, and microvascular obstruction in subacute myocardial infarction in a porcine model by MRI. Magn Reson Med 2011;66(4):1129–41.

[95] Kumar A, Green JD, Sykes JM, Ephrat P, Carson JJ, Mitchell AJ, Wisenberg G, Friedrich MG. Detection and quantification of myocardial reperfusion hemorrhage using T2*-weighted CMR. JACC Cardiovasc Imaging 2011;4(12):1274–83.

[96] Kandler D, Lücke C, Grothoff M, Andres C, Lehmkuhl L, Nitzsche S, Riese F, Mende M, de Waha S, Desch S, Lurz P, Eitel I, Gutberlet M. The relation between hypointense core, microvascular obstruction and intramyocardial haemorrhage in acute reperfused myocardial infarction assessed by cardiac magnetic resonance imaging. Eur Radiol 2014;24(12):3277–88.

[97] Kali A, Tang RL, Kumar A, Min JK, Dharmakumar R. Detection of acute reperfusion myocardial hemorrhage with cardiac MR imaging: T2 versus T2. Radiology 2013;269(2):387–95.

[98] O'Regan DP, Ariff B, Neuwirth C, Tan Y, Durighel G, Cook SA. Assessment of severe reperfusion injury with T2* cardiac MRI in patients with acute myocardial infarction. Heart 2010;96(23):1885–91.

[99] Carrick D, Haig C, Ahmed N, McEntegart M, Petrie MC, Eteiba H, Hood S, Watkins S, Lindsay MM, Davie A, Mahrous A, Mordi I, Rauhalammi S, Sattar N, Welsh P, Radjenovic A, Ford I, Oldroyd KG, Berry C. Myocardial hemorrhage after acute reperfused ST-segment–elevation myocardial infarction: relation to microvascular obstruction and prognostic significance. Circ Cardiovasc Imaging 2016;9(1):e004148.

[100] Ganame J, Messalli G, Dymarkowski S, Rademakers FE, Desmet W, Van de Werf F, Bogaert J. Impact of myocardial haemorrhage on left ventricular function and remodelling in patients with reperfused acute myocardial infarction. Eur Heart J 2009;30(12):1440–9.

[101] Eitel I, Kubusch K, Strohm O, Desch S, Mikami Y, de Waha S, Gutberlet M, Schuler G, Friedrich MG, Thiele H. Prognostic value and determinants of a hypointense infarct core in T2-weighted cardiac magnetic resonance in acute reperfused ST-elevation, myocardial infarction/clinical perspective. Circ Cardiovasc Imaging 2011;4(4):354–62.

[102] Cokic I, Kali A, Wang X, Yang HJ, Tang RL, Thajudeen A, Shehata M, Amorn AM, Liu E, Stewart B, Bennett N, Harlev D, Tsaftaris SA, Jackman WM, Chugh SS, Dharmakumar R. Iron deposition following chronic myocardial infarction as a substrate for cardiac electrical anomalies: initial findings in a canine model. PLoS One 2013;8(9):e73193.

[103] Bulluck H, Rosmini S, Abdel-Gadir A, White SK, Bhuva AN, Treibel TA, Fontana M, Ramlall M, Hamarneh A, Sirker A, Herrey AS, Manisty C, Yellon DM, Kellman P, Moon JC, Hausenloy DJ. Residual myocardial iron following intramyocardial hemorrhage during the convalescent phase of reperfused ST-segment–elevation myocardial infarction and adverse left ventricular remodeling. Circ Cardiovasc Imaging 2016;9(10). https://doi.org/10.1161/CIRCIMAGING.116.004940.

[104] Kali A, Cokic I, Tang R, Dohnalkova A, Kovarik L, Yang HJ, Kumar A, Prato FS, Wood JC, Underhill D, Marban E, Dharmakumar R. Persistent microvascular obstruction after myocardial infarction culminates in the confluence of ferric iron oxide crystals, proinflammatory burden, and adverse remodeling. Circ Cardiovasc Imaging 2016;9(11):e004996.

[105] Wang G, Yang H-J, Kali A, Cokic I, Tang R, Xie G, Yang Q, Francis J, Li S, Dharmakumar R. Influence of myocardial hemorrhage on staging of reperfused myocardial infarctions with T2 cardiac magnetic resonance imaging: insights into the dependence on infarction type with ex vivo validation. JACC Cardiovasc Imaging 2019;12(4):693–703.

[106] Carrick D, Behan M, Foo F, Christie J, Hillis WS, Norrie J, Oldroyd KG, Berry C. Usefulness of fractional flow reserve to improve diagnostic efficiency in patients with non-ST elevation myocardial infarction. Am J Cardiol 2013;111(1):45–50.

[107] Kellman P, Aletras AH, Mancini C, McVeigh ER, Arai AE. T2-prepared SSFP improves diagnostic confidence in edema imaging in acute myocardial infarction compared to turbo spin echo. Magn Reson Med 2007;57(5):891–7.

[108] Layland J, Rauhalammi S, Lee MM, Ahmed N, Carberry J, Teng Yue May V, Watkins S, McComb C, Mangion K, McClure JD, Carrick D, O'Donnell A, Sood A, McEntegart M, Oldroyd KG, Radjenovic A, Berry C. Diagnostic accuracy of 3.0-T magnetic resonance T1 and T2 mapping and T2-weighted dark-blood imaging for the infarct-related coronary artery in non-ST-segment elevation myocardial infarction. J Am Heart Assoc 2017;6(4):e004759.

[109] Verhaert D, Thavendiranathan P, Giri S, Mihai G, Rajagopalan S, Simonetti OP, Raman SV. Direct T2 quantification of myocardial edema in acute ischemic injury. JACC Cardiovasc Imaging 2011; 4(3):269–78.

[110] Tessa C, Del Meglio J, Lilli A, Diciotti S, Salvatori L, Giannelli M, Greiser A, Vignali C, Casolo G. T1 and T2 mapping in the identification of acute myocardial injury in patients with NSTEMI. Radiol Med 2018;123(12):926–34.

[111] Greenwood JP, Maredia N, Younger JF, Brown JM, Nixon J, Everett CC, Bijsterveld P, Ridgway JP, Radjenovic A, Dickinson CJ, Ball SG, Plein S. Cardiovascular magnetic resonance and single-photon emission computed tomography for diagnosis of coronary heart disease (CE-MARC): a prospective trial. Lancet 2012;379(9814):453–60.

[112] Schwitter J, Wacker CM, Wilke N, Al-Saadi N, Sauer E, Huettle K, Schonberg SO, Debl K, Strohm O, Ahlstrom H, Dill T, Hoebel N, Simor T, Investigators M-I. Superior diagnostic performance of perfusion-cardiovascular magnetic resonance versus SPECT to detect coronary artery disease: the secondary endpoints of the multicenter multivendor MR-IMPACT II (magnetic resonance imaging for myocardial perfusion assessment in coronary artery disease trial). J Cardiovasc Magn Reson 2012;14:61.

[113] Greenwood JP, Herzog BA, Brown JM, Everett CC, Nixon J, Bijsterveld P, Maredia N, Motwani M, Dickinson CJ, Ball SG, Plein S. Prognostic value of cardiovascular magnetic resonance and single-photon emission computed tomography in suspected coronary heart disease: long-term follow-up of a prospective, Diagnostic Accuracy Cohort Study. Ann Intern Med 2016;165(1):1–9.

[114] Liu A, Wijesurendra RS, Francis JM, Robson MD, Neubauer S, Piechnik SK, Ferreira VM. Adenosine stress and rest T1 mapping can differentiate between ischemic, infarcted, remote, and normal myocardium without the need for gadolinium contrast agents. JACC Cardiovasc Imaging 2016;9(1):27–36.

[115] McCommis KS, Goldstein TA, Abendschein DR, Misselwitz B, Pilgram T, Gropler RJ, Zheng J. Roles of myocardial blood volume and flow in coronary artery disease: an experimental MRI study at rest and during hyperemia. Eur Radiol 2010;20(8):2005–12.

[116] McCommis KS, Goldstein TA, Zhang H, Misselwitz B, Gropler RJ, Zheng J. Quantification of myocardial blood volume during dipyridamole and dobutamine stress: a perfusion CMR study. J Cardiovasc Magn Reson 2007;9(5):785–92.

[117] Puntmann VO, Carr-White G, Jabbour A, Yu C-Y, Gebker R, Kelle S, Rolf A, Zitzmann S, Peker E, D'Angelo T, Pathan F, Elen, Valbuena S, Hinojar R, Arendt C, Narula J, Herrmann E, Zeiher AM, Nagel E. Native T1 and ECV of noninfarcted myocardium and outcome in patients with coronary artery disease. J Am Coll Cardiol 2018;71(7):766–78.

[118] Haaf P, Garg P, Messroghli DR, Broadbent DA, Greenwood JP, Plein S. Cardiac T1 mapping and extracellular volume (ECV) in clinical practice: a comprehensive review. J Cardiovasc Magn Reson 2016;18(1):89.

[119] Hinojar R, Varma N, Child N, Goodman B, Jabbour A, Yu CY, Gebker R, Doltra A, Kelle S, Khan S, Rogers T, Arroyo Ucar E, Cummins C, Carr-White G, Nagel E, Puntmann VO. T1 mapping in discrimination of hypertrophic phenotypes: hypertensive heart disease and hypertrophic cardiomyopathy: findings from the international T1 multicenter cardiovascular magnetic resonance study. Circ Cardiovasc Imaging 2015;8(12):e003285.

[120] Puntmann VO, Voigt T, Chen Z, Mayr M, Karim R, Rhode K, Pastor A, Carr-White G, Razavi R, Schaeffter T, Nagel E. Native T1 mapping in differentiation of normal myocardium from diffuse disease in hypertrophic and dilated cardiomyopathy. JACC Cardiovasc Imaging 2013;6(4):475–84.

[121] Dass S, Suttie JJ, Piechnik SK, Ferreira VM, Holloway CJ, Banerjee R, Mahmod M, Cochlin L, Karamitsos TD, Robson MD, Watkins H, Neubauer S. Myocardial tissue characterization using magnetic resonance noncontrast T1 mapping in hypertrophic and dilated cardiomyopathy. Circ Cardiovasc Imaging 2012;5(6):726–33.

[122] Swoboda PP, McDiarmid AK, Erhayiem B, Law GR, Garg P, Broadbent DA, Ripley DP, Musa TA, Dobson LE, Foley JR, Fent GJ, Page SP, Greenwood JP, Plein S. Effect of cellular and extracellular pathology assessed by T1 mapping on regional contractile function in hypertrophic cardiomyopathy. J Cardiovasc Magn Reson 2017;19(1):16.

[123] Treibel TA, Zemrak F, Sado DM, Banypersad SM, White SK, Maestrini V, Barison A, Patel V, Herrey AS, Davies C, Caulfield MJ, Petersen SE, Moon JC. Extracellular volume quantification in isolated hypertension – changes at the detectable limits? J Cardiovasc Magn Reson 2015;17(1):74.

[124] Ho CY, Abbasi SA, Neilan TG, Shah RV, Chen Y, Heydari B, Cirino AL, Lakdawala NK, Orav EJ, Gonzalez A, Lopez B, Diez J, Jerosch-Herold M, Kwong RY. T1 measurements identify extracellular volume expansion in hypertrophic cardiomyopathy sarcomere mutation carriers with and without left ventricular hypertrophy. Circ Cardiovasc Imaging 2013;6(3):415–22.

[125] Swoboda PP, McDiarmid AK, Erhayiem B, Broadbent DA, Dobson LE, Garg P, Ferguson C, Page SP, Greenwood JP, Plein S. Assessing myocardial extracellular volume by T1 mapping to distinguish hypertrophic cardiomyopathy from Athlete's heart. J Am Coll Cardiol 2016;67(18):2189–90.

[126] Fontana M, Banypersad SM, Treibel TA, Maestrini V, Sado DM, White SK, Pica S, Castelletti S, Piechnik SK, Robson MD, Gilbertson JA, Rowczenio D, Hutt DF, Lachmann HJ, Wechalekar AD, Whelan CJ, Gillmore JD, Hawkins PN, Moon JC. Native T1 mapping in transthyretin amyloidosis. JACC Cardiovasc Imaging 2014;7(2):157–65.

[127] Ruberg FL. T1 mapping in cardiac amyloidosis: can we get there from here? JACC Cardiovasc Imaging 2013;6(4):498–500.

[128] Banypersad SM, Fontana M, Maestrini V, Sado DM, Captur G, Petrie A, Piechnik SK, Whelan CJ, Herrey AS, Gillmore JD, Lachmann HJ, Wechalekar AD, Hawkins PN, Moon JC. T1 mapping and survival in systemic light-chain amyloidosis. Eur Heart J 2015;36(4):244–51.

[129] Richards DB, Cookson LM, Berges AC, Barton SV, Lane T, Ritter JM, Fontana M, Moon JC, Pinzani M, Gillmore JD, Hawkins PN, Pepys MB. Therapeutic clearance of amyloid by antibodies to serum amyloid P component. N Engl J Med 2015;373(12):1106–14.

[130] Sado DM, White SK, Piechnik SK, Banypersad SM, Treibel T, Captur G, Fontana M, Maestrini V, Flett AS, Robson MD, Lachmann RH, Murphy E, Mehta A, Hughes D, Neubauer S, Elliott PM, Moon JC. Identification and assessment of Anderson-Fabry disease by cardiovascular magnetic resonance noncontrast myocardial T1 mapping. Circ Cardiovasc Imaging 2013;6(3):392–8.

[131] Maestrini V, Treibel TA, White SK, Fontana M, Moon JC. T1 mapping for characterization of intracellular and extracellular myocardial diseases in heart failure. Curr Cardiovasc Imaging Rep 2014;7:9287.

[132] Thompson RB, Chow K, Khan A, Chan A, Shanks M, Paterson I, Oudit GY. T(1) mapping with cardiovascular MRI is highly sensitive for Fabry disease independent of hypertrophy and sex. Circ Cardiovasc Imaging 2013;6(5):637–45.

[133] Brown PF, Miller C, Di Marco A, Schmitt M. Towards cardiac MRI based risk stratification in idiopathic dilated cardiomyopathy. Heart 2018;105(4). https://doi.org/10.1136/heartjnl-2018-313767.

[134] Puntmann VO, Carr-White G, Jabbour A, Yu C-Y, Gebker R, Kelle S, Hinojar R, Doltra A, Varma N, Child N, Rogers T, Suna G, Arroyo Ucar E, Goodman B, Khan S, Dabir D, Herrmann E, Zeiher AM, Nagel E. T1-mapping and outcome in nonischemic cardiomyopathy: all-cause mortality and heart failure. JACC Cardiovasc Imaging 2016;9(1):40–50.

[135] Wong TC, Piehler K, Meier CG, Testa SM, Klock AM, Aneizi AA, Shakesprere J, Kellman P, Shroff SG, Schwartzman DS, Mulukutla SR, Simon MA, Schelbert EB. Association between extracellular matrix expansion quantified by cardiovascular magnetic resonance and short-term mortality. Circulation 2012; 126(10):1206–16.

[136] Chen Z, Sohal M, Voigt T, Sammut E, Tobon-Gomez C, Child N, Jackson T, Shetty A, Bostock J, Cooklin M, O'Neill M, Wright M, Murgatroyd F, Gill J, Carr-White G, Chiribiri A, Schaeffter T,

Razavi R, Rinaldi CA. Myocardial tissue characterization by cardiac magnetic resonance imaging using T1 mapping predicts ventricular arrhythmia in ischemic and non-ischemic cardiomyopathy patients with implantable cardioverter-defibrillators. Heart Rhythm 2015;12(4):792–801.

[137] Gujja P, Rosing DR, Tripodi DJ, Shizukuda Y. Iron overload cardiomyopathy: better understanding of an increasing disorder. J Am Coll Cardiol 2010;56(13):1001–12.

[138] Olivieri NF, Nathan DG, MacMillan JH, Wayne AS, Liu PP, McGee A, Martin M, Koren G, Cohen AR. Survival in medically treated patients with homozygous beta-thalassemia. N Engl J Med 1994;331(9):574–8.

[139] Pennell DJ, Udelson JE, Arai AE, Bozkurt B, Cohen AR, Galanello R, Hoffman TM, Kiernan MS, Lerakis S, Piga A, Porter JB, Walker JM, Wood J, American Heart Association Committee on Heart Failure, Transplantation of the Council on Clinical Cardiology and Council on cardiovascular Radiology and Imaging. Cardiovascular function and treatment in beta-thalassemia major: a consensus statement from the American Heart Association. Circulation 2013;128(3):281–308.

[140] Anderson LJ, Holden S, Davis B, Prescott E, Charrier CC, Bunce NH, Firmin DN, Wonke B, Porter J, Walker JM, Pennell DJ. Cardiovascular T2-star (T2*) magnetic resonance for the early diagnosis of myocardial iron overload. Eur Heart J 2001;22(23):2171–9.

[141] Kirk P, Roughton M, Porter JB, Walker JM, Tanner MA, Patel J, Wu D, Taylor J, Westwood MA, Anderson LJ, Pennell DJ. Cardiac T2* magnetic resonance for prediction of cardiac complications in thalassemia major. Circulation 2009;120(20):1961–8.

[142] Pennell DJ, Porter JB, Piga A, Lai YR, El-Beshlawy A, Elalfy M, Yesilipek A, Kilinc Y, Habr D, Musallam KM, Shen J, Aydinok Y, CORDELIA study investigators. Sustained improvements in myocardial T2* over 2 years in severely iron-overloaded patients with beta thalassemia major treated with deferasirox or deferoxamine. Am J Hematol 2015;90(2):91–6.

[143] Sado DM, Maestrini V, Piechnik SK, Banypersad SM, White SK, Flett AS, Robson MD, Neubauer S, Ariti C, Arai A, Kellman P, Yamamura J, Schoennagel BP, Shah F, Davis B, Trompeter S, Walker M, Porter J, Moon JC. Noncontrast myocardial T1 mapping using cardiovascular magnetic resonance for iron overload. J Magn Reson Imaging 2015;41(6):1505–11.

[144] Hanneman K, Nguyen ET, Thavendiranathan P, Ward R, Greiser A, Jolly MP, Butany J, Yang IY, Sussman MS, Wintersperger BJ. Quantification of myocardial extracellular volume fraction with cardiac MR imaging in thalassemia major. Radiology 2016;279(3):720–30.

[145] Murtagh G, Laffin LJ, Beshai JF, Maffessanti F, Bonham CA, Patel AV, Yu Z, Addetia K, Mor-Avi V, Moss JD, Hogarth DK, Sweiss NJ, Lang RM, Patel AR. Prognosis of myocardial damage in Sarcoidosis patients with preserved left ventricular ejection fraction: risk stratification using cardiovascular magnetic resonance. Circ Cardiovasc Imaging 2016;9(1):e003738.

[146] Coleman GC, Shaw PW, Balfour Jr PC, Gonzalez JA, Kramer CM, Patel AR, Salerno M. Prognostic value of myocardial scarring on CMR in patients with cardiac sarcoidosis. JACC Cardiovasc Imaging 2017;10(4):411–20.

[147] Puntmann VO, Isted A, Hinojar R, Foote L, Carr-White G, Nagel E. T1 and T2 mapping in recognition of early cardiac involvement in systemic sarcoidosis. Radiology 2017;285(1):63–72.

[148] Crouser ED, Ono C, Tran T, He X, Raman SV. Improved detection of cardiac sarcoidosis using magnetic resonance with myocardial T2 mapping. Am J Respir Crit Care Med 2014;189(1):109–12.

[149] Greulich S, Kitterer D, Latus J, Aguor E, Steubing H, Kaesemann P, Patrascu A, Greiser A, Groeninger S, Mayr A, Braun N, Alscher MD, Sechtem U, Mahrholdt H. Comprehensive cardiovascular magnetic resonance assessment in patients with sarcoidosis and preserved left ventricular ejection fraction. Circ Cardiovasc Imaging 2016;9(11):e005022.

[150] Puntmann VO, D'Cruz D, Smith Z, Pastor A, Choong P, Voigt T, Carr-White G, Sangle S, Schaeffter T, Nagel E. Native myocardial T1 mapping by cardiovascular magnetic resonance imaging in subclinical cardiomyopathy in patients with systemic lupus erythematosus. Circ Cardiovasc Imaging 2013;6(2):295–301.

[151] Singh A, Horsfield MA, Bekele S, Khan JN, Greiser A, McCann GP. Myocardial T1 and extracellular volume fraction measurement in asymptomatic patients with aortic stenosis: reproducibility and comparison with age-matched controls. Eur Heart J Cardiovasc Imaging 2015;16(7):763–70.

[152] de Meester de Ravenstein C, Bouzin C, Lazam S, Boulif J, Amzulescu M, Melchior J, Pasquet A, Vancraeynest D, Pouleur A-C, Vanoverschelde J-LJ, Gerber BL. Histological Validation of measurement of diffuse interstitial myocardial fibrosis by myocardial extravascular volume fraction from Modified Look-Locker imaging (MOLLI) T1 mapping at 3T. J Cardiovasc Magn Reson 2015;17(1):48.

[153] Edwards NC, Moody WE, Yuan M, Weale P, Neal D, Townend JN, Steeds RP. Quantification of left ventricular interstitial fibrosis in asymptomatic chronic primary degenerative mitral regurgitation. Circ Cardiovasc Imaging 2014;7(6):946–53.

[154] Sparrow P, Messroghli DR, Reid S, Ridgway JP, Bainbridge G, Sivananthan MU. Myocardial T1 mapping for detection of left ventricular myocardial fibrosis in chronic aortic regurgitation: pilot study. AJR Am J Roentgenol 2006;187(6):W630-5.

[155] Shah ASV, Chin CWL, Vassiliou V, Cowell SJ, Doris M, Kwok TC, Semple S, Zamvar V, White AC, McKillop G, Boon NA, Prasad SK, Mills NL, Newby DE, Dweck MR. Left ventricular hypertrophy with strain and aortic stenosis. Circulation 2014;130(18):1607–16.

[156] Bull S, White SK, Piechnik SK, Flett AS, Ferreira VM, Loudon M, Francis JM, Karamitsos TD, Prendergast BD, Robson MD, Neubauer S, Moon JC, Myerson SG. Human non-contrast T1 values and correlation with histology in diffuse fibrosis. Heart 2013;99(13):932–7.

[157] Lee H, Park J-B, Yoon YE, Park E-A, Kim H-K, Lee W, Kim Y-J, Cho G-Y, Sohn D-W, Greiser A, Lee S-P. Noncontrast myocardial T1 mapping by cardiac magnetic resonance predicts outcome in patients with aortic stenosis. JACC Cardiovasc Imaging 2018;11(7):974–83.

[158] Chin CWL, Everett RJ, Kwiecinski J, Vesey AT, Yeung E, Esson G, Jenkins W, Koo M, Mirsadraee S, White AC, Japp AG, Prasad SK, Semple S, Newby DE, Dweck MR. Myocardial fibrosis and cardiac decompensation in aortic stenosis. JACC Cardiovasc Imaging 2017;10(11):1320–33.

[159] Flett AS, Sado DM, Quarta G, Mirabel M, Pellerin D, Herrey AS, Hausenloy DJ, Ariti C, Yap J, Kolvekar S, Taylor AM, Moon JC. Diffuse myocardial fibrosis in severe aortic stenosis: an equilibrium contrast cardiovascular magnetic resonance study. Eur Heart J Cardiovasc Imaging 2012;13(10):819–26.

[160] Schelbert EB, Moon JC. Exploiting differences in myocardial compartments with native T1 and extracellular volume fraction for the diagnosis of hypertrophic cardiomyopathy. Circ Cardiovasc Imaging 2015; 8(12):e004232.

[161] Mahmod M, Piechnik SK, Levelt E, Ferreira VM, Francis JM, Lewis A, Pal N, Dass S, Ashrafian H, Neubauer S, Karamitsos TD. Adenosine stress native T1 mapping in severe aortic stenosis: evidence for a role of the intravascular compartment on myocardial T1 values. J Cardiovasc Magn Reson 2014;16:92.

[162] Dweck MR, Joshi S, Murigu T, Alpendurada F, Jabbour A, Melina G, Banya W, Gulati A, Roussin I, Raza S, Prasad NA, Wage R, Quarto C, Angeloni E, Refice S, Sheppard M, Cook SA, Kilner PJ, Pennell DJ, Newby DE, Mohiaddin RH, Pepper J, Prasad SK. Midwall fibrosis is an independent predictor of mortality in patients with aortic stenosis. J Am Coll Cardiol 2011;58(12):1271–9.

[163] Kvernby S, Rönnerfalk M, Warntjes M, Carlhäll C-J, Nylander E, Engvall J, Tamás É, Ebbers T. Longitudinal changes in myocardial T1 and T2 relaxation times related to diffuse myocardial fibrosis in aortic stenosis; before and after aortic valve replacement. J Magn Reson Imaging 2018;48(3):799–807.

[164] Baumgartner H, Falk V, Bax JJ, De Bonis M, Hamm C, Holm PJ, Iung B, Lancellotti P, Lansac E, Rodriguez Munoz D, Rosenhek R, Sjogren J, Tornos Mas P, Vahanian A, Walther T, Wendler O, Windecker S, Zamorano JL, Group ESCSD. 2017 ESC/EACTS guidelines for the management of valvular heart disease. Eur Heart J 2017;38(36):2739–91.

[165] Paulus WJ, Tschöpe C. A novel paradigm for heart failure with preserved ejection fraction: comorbidities drive myocardial dysfunction and remodeling through coronary microvascular endothelial inflammation. J Am Coll Cardiol 2013;62(4):263–71.

[166] Su M-YM, Lin L-Y, Tseng Y-HE, Chang C-C, Wu C-K, Lin J-L, Tseng W-YI. CMR-verified diffuse myocardial fibrosis is associated with diastolic dysfunction in HFpEF. JACC Cardiovasc Imaging 2014;7(10):991–7.

[167] Rommel KP, Lucke C, Lurz P. Diagnostic and prognostic value of CMR T1-mapping in patients with heart failure and preserved ejection fraction. Rev Esp Cardiol 2017;70(10):848–55.

[168] Chambers DC. The registry of the International Society for Heart and Lung Transplantation: thirty-fourth adult lung and heart-lung transplantation report-2017; focus theme: allograft ischemic time. J Heart Lung Transplant 2017;36:1047–59.

[169] Miller C. Multiparametric cardiovascular magnetic resonance surveillance of acute cardiac allograft rejection and characterization of transplantation-associated myocardial injury: a pilot study. J Cardiovasc Magn Reson 2014;16(1):52.

[170] Dolan RS, Rahsepar AA, Blaisdell J, Lin K, Suwa K, Ghafourian K, Wilcox JE, Khan SS, Vorovich EE, Rich JD, Anderson AS, Yancy CW, Collins JD, Markl M, Carr JC. Cardiac structure–function mri in patients after heart transplantation. J Magn Reson Imaging 2018;49(3):678–87.

[171] Vermes E, Pantaléon C, Auvet A, Cazeneuve N, Machet MC, Delhommais A, Bourguignon T, Aupart M, Brunereau L. Cardiovascular magnetic resonance in heart transplant patients: diagnostic value of quantitative tissue markers: T2 mapping and extracellular volume fraction, for acute rejection diagnosis. J Cardiovasc Magn Reson 2018;20(1):59.

[172] Sade LE, Hazirolan T, Kozan H, Ozdemir H, Hayran M, Eroglu S, Pirat B, Sezgin A, Muderrisoglu H. T1 mapping by cardiac magnetic resonance and multidimensional speckle-tracking strain by echocardiography for the detection of acute cellular rejection in cardiac allograft recipients. JACC Cardiovasc Imaging 2018;12(8 Pt 2):1601–14.

[173] Wong TC, McNamara DM. Imaging-based surveillance for graft rejection following heart transplantation: ready for prime time? JACC Cardiovasc Imaging 2018;12(8 Pt 2):1615–7.

[174] Coelho-Filho OR, Shah R, Lavagnoli CFR, Barros JC, Neilan TG, Murthy VL, de Oliveira PPM, Souza JRM, de Oliveira Severino ESB, de Souza Vilarinho KA, da Mota Silveira Filho L, Garcia J, Semigran MJ, Coelho OR, Jerosch-Herold M, Petrucci O. Myocardial tissue remodeling after orthotopic heart transplantation: a pilot cardiac magnetic resonance study. Int J Cardiovasc Imaging 2018;34(1):15–24.

[175] Riesenkampff E, Chen CK, Kantor PF, Greenway S, Chaturvedi RR, Yoo SJ, Greiser A, Dipchand AI, Grosse-Wortmann L. Diffuse myocardial fibrosis in children after heart transplantations: a magnetic resonance T1 mapping study. Transplantation 2015;99(12):2656–62.

[176] Ide S, Riesenkampff E, Chiasson DA, Dipchand AI, Kantor PF, Chaturvedi RR, Yoo S-J, Grosse-Wortmann L. Histological validation of cardiovascular magnetic resonance T1 mapping markers of myocardial fibrosis in paediatric heart transplant recipients. J Cardiovasc Magn Reson 2017;19:10.

[177] Higgins DM, Keeble C, Juli C, Dawson DK, Waterton JC. Reference range determination for imaging biomarkers: myocardial T1. J Magn Reson Imaging 2019;50(3):771–8.

SECTION

2

Perfusion and Permeability

CHAPTER

Physical and Physiological Principles of Perfusion and Permeability 11

Stig P. Cramer[a], Mark B. Vestergaard[a], Ulrich Lindberg[a], and Henrik B.W. Larsson[a,b]

[a]*Functional Imaging Unit, Department of Clinical Physiology, Nuclear Medicine and PET, Rigshospitalet, Copenhagen, Denmark* [b]*Department of Clinical Medicine, Faculty of Health and Medical Science, Copenhagen University, Copenhagen, Denmark*

11.1 Introduction to perfusion and permeability

Perfusion describes the microcirculation and passage of fluid through tissue and organs. Most commonly, perfusion refers to the passage of blood through the densely distributed network of capillaries throughout the tissue. The capillaries are the smallest blood vessels in the body and typically measure 5–10 μm in diameter. The main function of blood perfusion is to deliver nutrients, most importantly oxygen, to the tissue and remove waste products.

Blood perfusion is highly regulated. If the metabolic demand is increased, the tissue requires more nutrients and oxygen, which can lead to an up-regulation of the blood perfusion. For example, perfusion in skeleton muscle can increase by 20-fold during exercise, whereas the brain maintains a constant perfusion level. Perfusion pressure can be controlled at a local level to maintain stable perfusion via autoregulation. Particularly, in critical organs such as the brain, heart, and kidneys, the regulation of perfusion is highly reactive and pressure changes can occur within seconds [1–3]. Blood perfusion is regulated at both systemic and local levels. Systemic regulation is primarily controlled by the heart rate and cardiac output, whereas local regulation occurs via constriction and dilation of arteries and arterioles controlled by smooth muscle cells. This system allows tight regulation of perfusion to individual tissues. Microcirculation in the capillaries can be further regulated by pericytes, cells that wrap the endothelial cell layer, which are capable of constricting the capillary. The intimate regulation of the constriction and dilation of arteries and capillaries is not completely understood but is extensively researched and likely works on several different levels. Long-term regulation of perfusion is primarily accomplished through increased vascularization by angiogenesis.

The permeability of capillaries describes the rate at which substances in the blood can cross the endothelial wall and enter into the tissue. The passage occurs by either diffusion, bulk fluid flow, or active specific transport. The wall of the capillary is composed of a single layer of endothelial cells surrounded by a basal membrane. The ability of a specific substance to move from the capillaries and into the tissue largely depends on the size and solubility of the molecule. Small or lipid-soluble molecules, for example, oxygen or steroid hormones, diffuse from the intravascular space through the endothelial layer to the extracellular space. Likewise, CO_2 molecules diffuse freely from cells into the blood and are removed from the tissue. Larger and lipid-insoluble molecules cannot cross the endothelial layer but can permeate by bulk flow of fluid through intercellular junctions of the

Advances in Magnetic Resonance Technology and Applications. Volume 1. ISSN 2666-9099. https://doi.org/10.1016/B978-0-12-817057-1.00013-5

endothelium layer. This fluid exchange is primarily driven by capillary hydrostatic pressure, which drives the flow of fluid from the intravascular space into interstitial space at the arterial end of the capillary (~1 kPa). Reabsorption of fluid back into the capillaries at the venous end is driven by the colloid osmotic pressure. The lymph capillaries and the lymphatic system remove excess fluid that is not reabsorbed by blood capillaries. Capillary permeability depends on the density and tightness of the junctions in the endothelial wall, which varies among tissue types. Note that the capillary permeability is not constant and is dynamically altered by cell signaling mediators often as part of immune system regulation.

With the use of MRI-based techniques, perfusion and permeability of various organs and tissue types can be measured quantitatively. Perfusion is typically expressed as the flow of blood in mL/min divided by the weight (or volume) of the examined tissue or organ (mL/100 g/min or mL/100 mL/min). Permeability is often expressed as the permeability-surface area (PS) product, defined as the product of the permeability of the capillaries and the capillary surface area, also expressed in units mL/100 g/min.

11.2 Perfusion and vascular anatomy in different tissues and organs

11.2.1 The brain

The brain is the organ in the human body with the highest energy demand; the resting brain accounts for 20% of the body's total oxygen consumption. Blood is delivered to the brain by the carotid and vertebral arteries converging into the Circle of Willis securing collateral blood supply. Arterial supply is derived from recurrent branches of arteries penetrating into the Virchow Robin spaces. Brain microcirculation encompasses vessels with a diameter below 200 μm, which includes arterioles, capillaries, and postcapillary venules [4]. Their main function is the delivery of blood, transportation of oxygen and nutrients, as well as removal of waste products and toxins from the tissue. Capillary density is about threefold higher in cerebral gray matter compared to white matter. In contrast to other organs, both large arteries and small arterioles (<100 μm diameter) contribute significantly to vascular resistance, which is a protective measure preventing vasogenic edema in case of suddenly elevated blood pressure.

The brain also has an extraordinary level of functional capillaries compared to other organs, with about 90% of cortical capillaries being functional at rest. This organization ensures a tight regulation of blood flow to individual tissue areas paramount for optimal delivery and extraction of oxygen. In the brain, this control is executed primarily by the pericytes, which are specialized cells which ensheathe the blood vessels in the brain [5]. It has been shown that a homogenous distribution of blood perfusion to the tissue results in the most optimal delivery of oxygen and nutrients. If this tight regulation is disturbed, for example, as a result of disease, a situation with more heterogeneous perfusion will arise. Such heterogeneous perfusion may perturb homeostasis in an undesirable way, rendering certain areas hypoxic while at the same time delivering a surplus of oxygen to other areas which cannot be extracted from the vessels into the tissue [6].

Brain perfusion is also unique in that the capillaries in the brain have a very low permeability due to the blood-brain barrier (BBB), which prevents transfer of most molecules into the brain tissue. The function of the BBB is to protect the brain from toxic substances and pathogens in the blood. The BBB is constructed from tight junctions between the endothelial cells supported by astrocyte endfeet, which cover the outer surface of the endothelium wall. This highly impermeable barrier only allows passive transport of gases, water, and small lipid-soluble molecules; selective transportation of target molecules occurs through highly specific transfer protein structures [7].

11.2.2 The heart

Normally two coronary arteries supply blood to the heart, namely the right coronary artery and the left coronary artery, which bifurcates into the left anterior descending and the left circumflex arteries. However, the coronary arteries are highly variable in anatomical origin, course, and branching, and other coronary variants are common. Circulation is distinguished from other vascular systems by its phasic flow pattern, related to the contraction of the heart muscle. The main coronary arterial flow occurs in the diastole, whereas during the systole the arterial flow decreases or even reverses, while the venous flow increases. Heart capillaries are relatively resistant to the powerful compression occurring during the systole compared to pre- and postcapillary microvessels, which is beneficial for myocardial oxygen delivery throughout the cardiac cycle. A high perfusion pressure and a long diastole also compensates for the cyclic contraction, ensuring homogenous perfusion over the myocardium. Even at normal heart rate, the oxygen extraction is high, about 80%. Thus, during exercise, more oxygen can only be provided by increasing perfusion.

11.2.3 The liver

The liver has a unique dual blood supply, with approximately 25% of blood originating from the hepatic artery and the remaining 75% from the portal vein. Around 50% of oxygen is provided by the portal venous blood. Intrahepatic branches of the portal vein and the hepatic artery run in parallel and terminate in the portal venules and hepatic arterioles. They supply blood to the fenestrated sinusoids that are oriented radially within the functional units of the liver, the hepatic lobules. The fenestrae in the liver sinusoids are large perforations that result in a very high permeability. The blood is evacuated from the sinusoids through the central veins that originate from the center of each lobule and join together in hepatic veins.

11.2.4 The kidneys

The kidneys are most commonly supplied with blood from single hilar arteries originating from the abdominal aorta. However, in 25%–30% of individuals, accessory renal arteries are present, commonly supplying the inferior pole of the kidney. The main renal artery divides into anterior and posterior presegments, which subsequently subdivide into four or more segmental branches, with no collateral blood supply between the segments. Afferent arterioles supply unfiltered blood to the glomeruli, which filter up to 1 L of blood per minute, around 20% of the total cardiac output. The filtered blood is passed to the renal tubuli which ultimately produce urine. However, most of the filtered blood (99%) is reabsorbed again into a second capillary network, the peritubular capillaries that are wrapped around the renal tubuli. Filtered and unfiltered blood is collected into the interlobular veins and evacuated through the kidney vein. Thus, a specialized feature of kidney circulation is the dual capillary bed in the renal glomeruli and surrounding the tubules, which allows efficient control of the process of filtration, secretion, and reabsorption of minerals.

11.2.5 Perfusion and permeability in disease

In many disease processes, abnormal tissue perfusion and solute permeability is part of the pathology, and perfusion quantification can thus provide important clinical information. A direct clinical application of MRI-based perfusion measurement techniques is to assess patients for disturbed perfusion patterns, particularly in the brain and in the heart, but also in other organs as the liver and the kidneys [8–10]. Another useful clinical application of MRI perfusion and permeability quantification is in oncology for evaluation of tumor physiology. A crucial part of malignant tumor physiology is increased vascularization by angiogenesis to accommodate the increased metabolic demand. The degree of tumor growth and risk of metastasis has been shown to depend on the level on angiogenesis, and thus quantification of perfusion has high clinical relevance in the evaluation of disease severity and prognosis [11].

As described earlier, the healthy brain is a special case for perfusion quantification due to the uniquely low permeability of the BBB. If the BBB is disrupted, harmful toxic substances can enter the brain tissue. For instance, in multiple sclerosis, the BBB is disrupted presumably as a result of the autoimmune inflammatory disease process. Perfusion measurements with MRI using exogenous contrast agents have been used to establish an association between BBB leakage, disease activity, and treatment efficacy in patients with MS [12–15]. The permeability of the BBB has been proposed to be disrupted in inflammatory diseases such as meningitis and encephalitis. Breakdown of the BBB may also play a part in the neurodegenerative process seen in dementia [16], where increased leakage may cause higher accumulation of beta-amyloid in brain tissue [17].

11.3 MRI signal and tracer agents

Perfusion and permeability can be quantified in multiple ways using MRI, but the most common methods involve the tracking of an MRI-visible tracer in the bloodstream that is assumed to reflect perfusion properties. The most common tracers are magnetically labeled water in the blood or MR contrast agents with magnetic properties that are injected into the bloodstream. By following the effects of the tracer on the MRI signal, the concentration of the tracer at different points in time at different locations in the body can be derived. Once the kinetics of the tracer are understood, spatially-resolved tissue perfusion maps can be derived.

MRI techniques that use magnetically labeled (arterial) blood as the tracer are referred to arterial spin labeling (ASL). Techniques that use exogenous MRI contrast agents are referred to as either Dynamic Contrast-Enhanced MRI (DCE-MRI) if they use dynamic T_1-weighted sequences to measure contrast agent concentration or Dynamic Susceptibility Contrast MRI (DSC-MRI) if they use dynamic T_2*- or T_2-weighted sequences. Dynamic multiecho techniques that allow a simultaneous measurement of T_1 and T_2* or T_2 also have been proposed but do not have a generally recognized acronym. Depending on context they are referred to as multiecho DCE-MRI, multiecho DSC-MRI, or combined DSC/DCE-MRI.

11.3.1 Safety of MR contrast agents

Different contrast agents exist, but typically the Gadolinium molecule is used as the magnetic component. Gadolinium-based contrast agents are used in daily clinical routine to amplify and correctly differentiate pathology from healthy tissue. In many cases imaging with Gadolinium is by far the most sensitive method to distinguish between tissues, that is, tumor necrosis and tumor recurrence. The risks associated with the use of Gadolinium-based contrast agents include allergic and adverse reactions (which are infrequent but can be serious) and nephrogenic systemic fibrosis (NSF) in patients with renal impairment. Clinical practice is therefore aimed at reducing the incidence of NSF development by using low-risk contrast agent types (e.g., macrocyclic over linear forms) as well as screening subjects for renal impairment before gadolinium exposure [18, 19].

Recently it has been discovered that contrast agent accumulates in the kidneys, bones, and deep nuclei of the brain, especially in the globus pallidum and in the dentate nucleus of the cerebellum, based on in vivo human [20] and animal studies [21] as well as post mortem studies [22]. Evidence indicates that the chelates of Gadolinium might play a role in the extent of deposition, with the macrocyclic chelates accumulating to a lesser extent than the linear chelates [23, 24]. No clinical manifestations or symptoms have been related to this accumulation [25–28]. However, until further evidence on the potential toxicity associated with this deposition of contrast agent can be established, the MRI community recommends adopting a cautious approach which involves careful evaluation of the benefits and the risks in each individual case [18, 29].

11.3.2 Relaxivity of contrast agents

The concentration of contrast agents can be assessed with MRI, as the presence of contrast agents alters the relaxation times of the protons which generate the MRI signal [30]. Gadolinium-based contrast agents shorten T_1 relaxation times of the protons in water molecules when these water molecules interact with the paramagnetic core of the contrast agent. The theoretical foundation of this interaction is called the inner-sphere relaxation and can be described by the Solomon-Bloembergen-Morgan equation. An additional but smaller T_1 shortening effect is caused by the so-called outer-sphere interaction of translational diffusion of water molecules past the contrast agent molecules. Inner-sphere and outer-sphere relaxation are short-range effects that are the main source of signal changes detected in DCE-MRI.

Gadolinium-based contrast agents can also affect the transverse relaxation time $T_2{}^*$, but this effect is long-range compared to the effect on T_1. The effect is strongest when the contrast agent is compartmentalized in a tissue compartment such as the intravascular space. The agent then increases the magnetic susceptibility of that compartment, inducing microscopic gradients that increase dephasing and thereby reduce $T_2{}^*$. It is these effects that form the basis of signal changes detected in DSC-MRI.

To a good approximation, the change in relaxation rate $1/T_1$ is directly proportional to the contrast agent concentration C at clinical doses. The proportionality constant is the relaxivity r_1 of the tracer measured in units of $\mathrm{mM}^{-1}\,\mathrm{s}^{-1}$:

$$\frac{1}{T_1}=\frac{1}{T_{1,0}}+r_1C \tag{11.1}$$

where $T_{1,0}$ is the relaxation time in the absence of tracer and T_1 is the relaxation time in the presence of a concentration C of the tracer. Except for agents with strong protein-binding characteristics, the relaxivity r_1 is relatively independent of tissue type and therefore can be treated as a known constant and measured in vitro.

An additional important assumption in Eq. (11.1) is that the tissue can always be characterized by mono-exponential relaxation with a single T_1 value, even if the contrast agent has different concentrations in plasma, interstitial or intracellular spaces. Since most MRI contrast agents act primarily by changing the T_1 values of adjacent water protons in the first hydration layer, this condition is fulfilled if water exchange between compartments is sufficiently fast to mitigate any local T_1 variation caused by differences in concentration. Within this fast-exchange limit, the precise location of contrast agent molecules within the tissue is not relevant to the overall T_1 value measured. Thus, a contrast agent that accumulates at high concentration in a small tissue compartment can have a strong effect on T_1 of all other tissue compartments. If, however, the contrast agent molecules become confined in a compartment with a lower degree of water exchange between that compartment and adjacent contrast-free compartments, then the contrast agent will mainly affect the T_1 of the water within the contrast-containing compartment. The relaxation then becomes biexponential and the signal can no longer be described with a single T_1 value. In that scenario, multiexponential relaxation models, incorporating also the water exchange rate between compartments, must be used to determine the relationship between signal and concentrations [31].

A similar relationship to Eq. (11.1) can be assumed for T_2^* in the presence of tracer, defining $T_{2,0}^*$ as the relaxation time in the absence of tracer:

$$\frac{1}{T_2^*} = \frac{1}{T_{2,0}^*} + r_2^* C \tag{11.2}$$

In contrast to Eq. (11.1), the linear approximation in Eq. (11.2) is generally less accurate at clinical doses, and the relaxivity r_2^* is more tissue-dependent than r_1. It is also dependent on the tissue compartment that contains the tracer, for example, the r_2^* relaxivity of intravascular tracer is generally different from interstitial tracer. This also means that r_2^* can change over time, for instance when the agent leaks out of the intravascular space due to extravasation. If the compartmentalization is reduced and r_2^* becomes small, then the T_1 effects may start playing a more significant role, leading to ambiguous signal behavior in DSC-MRI—the so-called leakage effect.

In general, the transverse relaxivity r_2^* is about an order of magnitude higher than the longitudinal relaxivity r_1. This means that, at the same concentration C, the change in relaxation rate (and therefore also signal and contrast-to-noise) is many times higher in DSC-MRI than in DCE-MRI. For this reason, DSC-MRI is generally preferred in situations where the maximum tracer concentration is limited, for instance, because the contrast agent is compartmentalized in small tissue compartments. The typical example is perfusion measurement in the brain, which has a very small blood volume fraction (2%–4% in normal tissue) and therefore benefits from the sensitivity of DSC-MRI to small concentrations. The benefit is lost when the agent is not compartmentalized, for example, in very leaky tissues such as brain tissue with a defective BBB, or when the tissue compartments are sufficiently large to allow higher concentrations. In those conditions DCE-MRI may be preferred because the r_1 relaxivity is relatively constant and the competing T_2^* effects are easier to suppress in a T_1-weighted sequence than vice versa. In the kidney, for instance, while DSC-MRI was originally proposed for perfusion or filtration measurement, it has since been completely replaced by DCE-MRI as the method of choice. For myocardial perfusion quantification, DCE-MRI is preferred for similar reasons. Furthermore, brain surgery has recently been shown to render DSC-MRI impractical because of huge susceptibility artifacts caused by surgery-related deposition of very small metal particles.

11.3.3 Measuring contrast agent concentration

Eqs. (11.1), (11.2) show that the contrast agent concentration can be calculated from a measurement of the T_1 or T_2^* relaxation times, and prior knowledge of the relaxivities. Hence the problem of measuring contrast agent concentration becomes one of measuring relaxation times dynamically, rapidly, and accurately, as a function of time.

In DCE-MRI, a series of T_1-weighted images are collected after the administration of a gadolinium-based contrast agent. Often a T_1-weighted saturation recovery gradient echo sequence is used to acquire this series of images, from which the changes in T_1 relaxation time due to the contrast agent can be obtained [32]. When using a sufficiently short echo time (TE) and centric phase encoding, the signal from the saturation recovery gradient echo sequence can then be related to tracer concentration:

$$S(t) = S_0\left(1 - e^{-SRT\left(\frac{1}{T_{1,0}} + r_1 C(t)\right)}\right) \tag{11.3}$$

where SRT is the saturation recovery time. Due to the short TE, the $T_2{}^*$ effects of the tracer can be assumed negligible, in which case S_0 is a constant that only depends on voxel location. Under those conditions, S_0 can be determined from $T_{1,0}$ and $S(t=0)$, before contrast agent injection when $C(t)=0$. Assuming $T_{1,0}$ has been measured before the introduction of the contrast agent, the contrast agent concentration $C(t)$ can then be derived from the signal $S(t)$.

In DSC-MRI, the contrast agent concentration is assessed by following changes in the $T_2{}^*$ (or T_2) relaxation time, typically acquired by a gradient echo or spin echo sequence. In this case the relationship between signal and concentration has the following form:

$$S(t) = S_0' e^{-TE\, r_2{}^* C(t)} \tag{11.4}$$

The sequence is deployed with a longer repetition time (TR) so that T_1 effects can be considered negligible, in which $S_0{}'$ is constant in time and equal to $S(t=0)$, before contrast agent injection when $C(t)=0$. Assuming $r_2{}^*$ is a known constant, the contrast agent concentration $C(t)$ can then again be derived from the signal $S(t)$.

Exogenous contrast agents not only affect the relaxation times but also alter the phase information of the acquired MRI signal due to their magnetic susceptibility. This feature has been leveraged to quantify contrast agent concentrations in large blood vessels. If a large vessel containing contrast agent is modeled as a long tube in a stationary B_0 magnetic field, the contrast agent concentration can be related linearly to the phase rotation $\phi(t)$ in a gradient echo sequence:

$$\phi(t) = \pi \cdot \chi_{CA} \cdot C(t) \cdot TE \cdot \gamma \cdot B_0 \cdot \left(3\cos^2\theta - 1\right) \tag{11.5}$$

where γ is the gyromagnetic ratio, θ is the angle between the vessel and the B_0 field, and χ_{CA} is the molar susceptibility of the contrast agent. This relationship enables measurement of concentrations in blood vessels by way of phase images.

11.4 Basic tracer kinetics

After the contrast agent concentration has been quantified according to the specific technique and sequence, tracer kinetic modeling can be used to extract the relevant physiological parameters. In general two separate concentration-time curves are required to fully characterize the tissue: a tissue concentration as a function of time in the tissue of interest, $C_T(t)$; and an arterial concentration as a function of time in the blood of an artery feeding the tissue, $C_A(t)$. The latter is commonly known as the arterial input function (AIF). An example of a measured AIF curve is shown in Fig. 11.1.

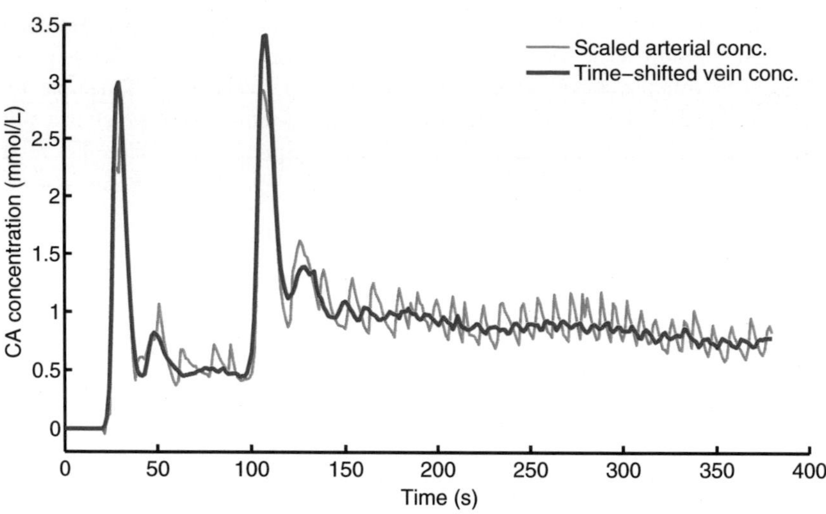

FIG. 11.1

The arterial input function (AIF, *gray*) obtained from the internal carotid artery; the venous signal curve *(purple)* obtained from the sagittal sinus. The arterial curve often suffers from partial volume effects, which can be reduced by fitting it to the venous curve obtained in the sagittal sinus. Matching of these two curves is performed by scaling the AIF and time-shifting the venous curve as shown here. Note that in this case, two separate bolus injections, each consisting of half a clinical dose, were administered, giving rise to two separate bolus peaks. Also note that the AIF often suffers from what is believed to be inflow effects (oscillations that are particularly visible in the tail of the *gray curve*) which are less prominent in the venous curve.

11.4.1 Linear and stationary tissues

The fundamental tracer kinetic equation [33] describes the relationship between tissue concentration and AIF in terms of the perfusion f and the residue function of the tissue $R(t)$:

$$C_T(t) = \int_0^t C_A(\tau) \cdot f \cdot R(t-\tau)\mathrm{d}\tau \tag{11.6}$$

The residue function $R(t)$ is defined as the fraction of the contrast agent remaining in the tissue at time t after an instantaneous bolus is injected into the tissue at time zero. This concept was originally used in residue detection of a radioactive tracer by a scintillation detector over the organ of interest. $R(t)$ is dimensionless and nonincreasing, and satisfies $R(0)=1$ because the entire bolus by definition is injected at time zero. $R(t)$ is constant at a value of one until the minimum transit time when tracer molecules start leaving the tissue of interest.

Eq. (11.6) can be derived by considering a given time t, and adding up the residues of injections at all earlier times $\tau < t$. First, note that $f\mathrm{d}\tau$ is the amount of blood flowing into the tissue in any time interval $\mathrm{d}\tau$, so $f\mathrm{d}\tau C_A(\tau)$ is the amount of contrast agent entering the tissue in an interval $[\tau, \tau+\mathrm{d}\tau]$. By definition a fraction $R(t\text{-}\tau)$ of this amount is still in the tissue at a later time $t > \tau$. Adding up the contributions $f\mathrm{d}\tau C_A(\tau)R(t\text{-}\tau)$ of all $\tau < t$ by integration then produces Eq. (11.6). The latter step implicitly assumes that no contrast agent is produced inside the tissue. If f is a constant, and $R(t)$ itself does not depend on the injected dose (linearity) or on the time of injection (stationarity or time-invariance), then the integral in Eq. (11.6) can be expressed as a convolution product:

$$C_T(t) = C_A(t) \otimes f \cdot R(t) \tag{11.7}$$

This is the basic kinetic equation for linear and stationary tissues, which is a good approximation in the majority of cases. Fig. 11.2 shows an example of the convolution operation, and the filtering effect that the residue function has on the contrast concentration as it moves from the arteries into the tissue.

When $C_T(t)$ and $C_A(t)$ are measured, the impulse response function $I(t) = fR(t)$ can be derived by deconvolution, either using a model-based (Section 11.5) or a model-free approach (Section 11.6). Since $R(t)$ is a nonincreasing function with $R(0) = 1$, the perfusion and residue function can be determined as $f = \max(I)$, and $R(t) = I(t)/\max(I)$.

11.4.2 The transit time distribution

Apart from the residue function, another useful concept is the probability distribution of transit times through the tissue, denoted as $h(t)$. Explicitly, of all contrast agent molecules that enter the tissue at $t = 0$, a fraction $h(t)\mathrm{d}t$ leaves the tissue in the time interval $[t, t + \mathrm{d}t]$. Since the molecules remaining at time t are exactly those that leave the tissue at times greater than t, we find a direct relation between $h(t)$ and $R(t)$:

$$R(t) = \int_t^\infty h(\tau)\mathrm{d}\tau = 1 - \int_0^t h(\tau)\mathrm{d}\tau \tag{11.8}$$

Here we used the fact that $h(t)$ is a probability distribution and therefore has unit area. By taking the derivative of both sides, we find $h = -\mathrm{d}R/\mathrm{d}t$. The expectation value of $h(t)$ is the mean transit time (MTT), which also equals the time-integral of $R(t)$:

$$\mathrm{MTT} = \int_0^\infty t\,h(t)\mathrm{d}t = \int_0^\infty R(t)\mathrm{d}t \tag{11.9}$$

The result can be shown by using $h = -\mathrm{d}R/\mathrm{d}t$ and partial integration. Thus, the MTT can either be estimated from $h(t)$ or from $R(t)$. In Fig. 11.3, several different forms of $h(t)$ are shown, including a gamma variate function, as well as the corresponding $R(t)$ and $1 - R(t)$ plots.

Is the probability distribution $h(t)$ interesting from a clinical perspective? In 1992, Kuschinsky and Paulson suggested that the heterogeneity of capillary perfusion has a significant impact on capillary diffusion capacity. With increasing homogeneity of the perfusion pattern, the capillary diffusion capacity is also increased, a response elicited by neurovascular stimulation [6]. This has recently been theoretically substantiated in relation to brain oxygen extraction [34]. In this context, the variance of the distribution $h(t)$ can be used as a measure of capillary heterogeneity. Thus, by modeling $h(t)$ as a gamma-variate function, and relating this function to the $R(t)$ by integration using either a numerical or analytical approach, the distribution of capillary transit times can be assessed. It should be mentioned that this modeling necessitates the collection of images with a high temporal resolution, preferably at a rate of one frame every 3 s or faster.

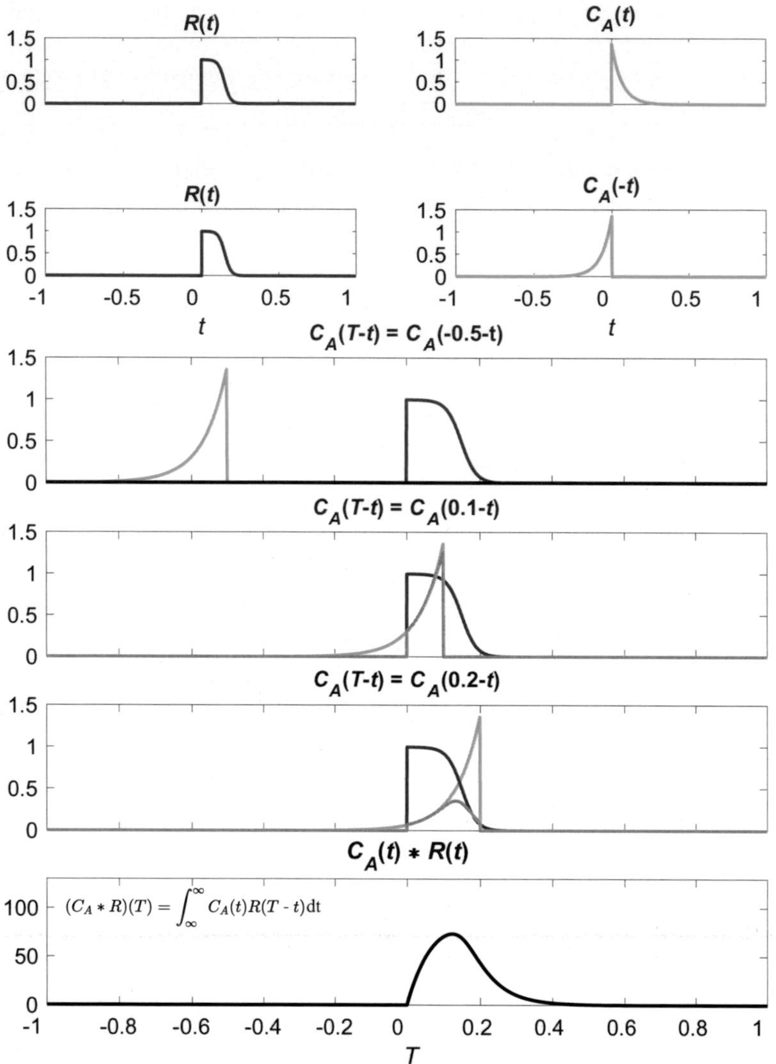

FIG. 11.2

The concentration of contrast agent in the tissue $C_T(t)$ can be expressed as the convolution of the residue function $R(t)$ *(top left)* and the arterial input function $C_A(t)$ *(top right)*; the order of the functions is interchangeable. The convolution is calculated by reflecting $C_A(t)$, that is, by changing the sign of the argument, $C_A(-t)$, as shown in the second row. Intuitively, this can be understood as the contrast bolus flowing into the tissue. The function $C_A(T-t)$ is created, where T determines the position of this function; three examples where T is equal to -0.5, 0.1, and 0.2 are shown. At $T=-0.5$, the contrast bolus has not yet reached the tissue, at $T=0$ the contrast bolus arrives (not shown), and at $T=0.1$, the contrast bolus has begun to flow into the tissue. For each value of T, the function $C_A(T-t)$ is multiplied with $R(t)$ for all values of t, yielding the *gray curves*. The result of the convolution between $C_A(t)$ and $R(t)$ is found by calculating the area of the *gray curves* at each timepoint T, shown as the *black curve* in the *bottom panel*. In this example, the *black curve* is the measured tissue concentration $C_T(T)$ in a specific voxel. Note how the bolus shown as $C_A(t)$ is tempered by the residue function, which leads to the gradual increase and then decrease of contrast agent in the tissue. The scaling factor f is omitted for clarity.

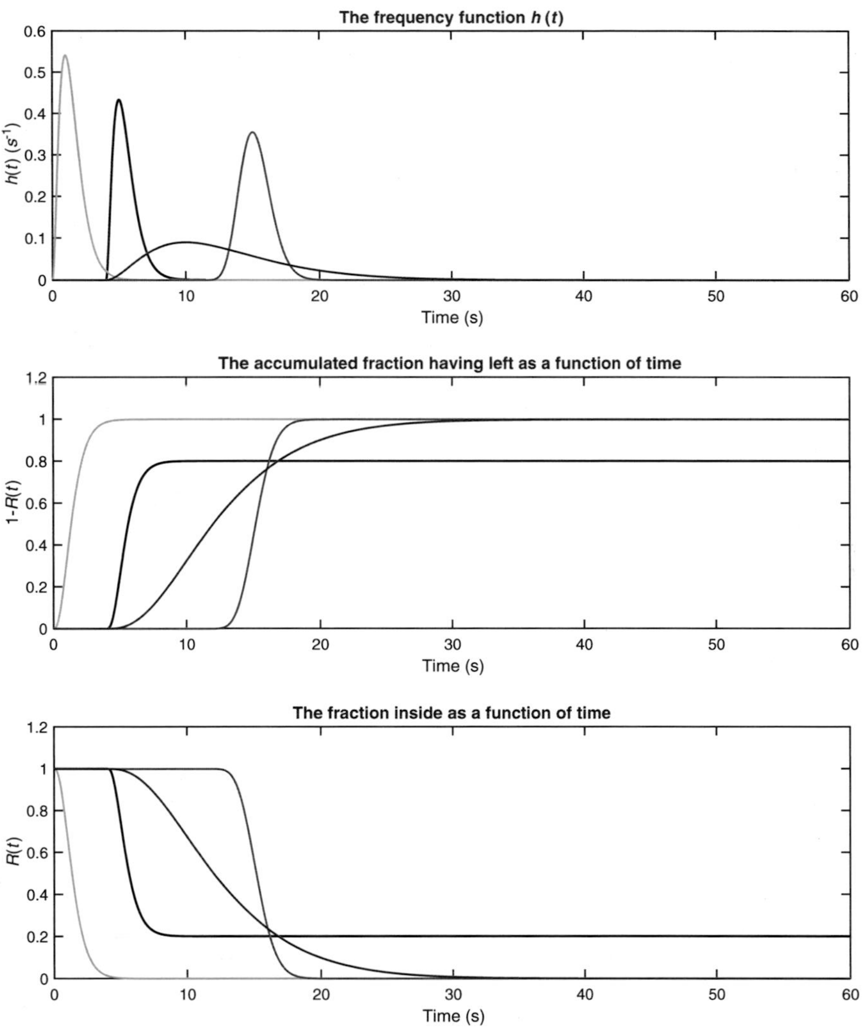

FIG. 11.3

Top: Examples of the probability distribution functions of the transit times, $h(t)$, modeled as gamma variate functions. The *green curve* depicts a tissue with a short transit time, while the magenta function shows a long transit time. The *blue curve* is an example of a tissue with a wide range of different transit times. Note that the area under $h(t)$ is equal to one for all curves except for the $h(t)$ shown in *black*. In this case, 20% of the injected contrast agent bolus is irreversibly trapped in the tissue, and thus the area is 0.8. Middle: Integration of $h(t)$ gives the accumulated fraction which has left the tissue as a function of time, $1 - R(t)$. *Bottom*: $R(t)$ is the residue function, the fraction remaining in the tissue as a function of time. As expected, the *green curve* shows that the contrast agent rapidly leaves the tissue; the *magenta curve* shows that the contrast agent washes out rapidly at a later time, and the *blue curve* indicates that contrast agent exits slowly over a longer period of time. Note that at the peak of $h(t)$, $\frac{\partial h(t)}{\partial t} = -\frac{\partial^2 R(t)}{\partial t^2} = 0$, corresponding to a turning point for $R(t)$. Also note that the *black* $R(t)$ curve ends at 20%, corresponding to the situation where 20% of the contrast agent is irreversibly trapped in the tissue.

11.4.3 The central volume theorem

The contrast agent volume of distribution (V_D) in a tissue is defined as $V_D = Q_T/C_{ref}$, where Q_T is the number of contrast agent molecules in a volume of tissue and C_{ref} is the concentration of a reference solution of the contrast agent, for example, plasma concentration. V_D is defined in a situation where equilibration between the tissue and the reference solution has been established. In other words, V_D describes the volume of the reference solution, which contains an amount of contrast agent equivalent to the amount in the tissue. If we normalize with respect to the mass or volume of the tissue (V_T), we get the partition coefficient:

$$\lambda = \frac{V_D}{V_T} = \frac{Q_T}{V_T C_{ref}} = \frac{C_T}{C_{ref}} \text{ (mL/mL)} \tag{11.10}$$

Note that the tissue concentration is defined as $C_T = Q_T/V_T$. If we use the arterial concentration as a reference concentration, the partition coefficient becomes $\lambda = C_T/C_A$ with concentrations measured in steady-state. We could also choose the capillary concentration at the venous outlet as a reference.

In systems that satisfy Eq. (11.7), the partition coefficient with an arterial reference concentration can be calculated by considering an (hypothetical) experiment with a constant arterial concentration $C_A(t) = C_A$. A steady-state is then reached as $t \to \infty$, in which case Eq. (11.9) can be used to rewrite Eq. (11.7) as:

$$\lambda = \frac{C_T(\infty)}{C_A} = f\,\text{MTT} \tag{11.11}$$

This relation between the partition coefficient, perfusion and MTT is also known as the "central volume theorem" [33]. Considering now a more realistic experiment with a time-varying $C_A(t)$, we can integrate both sides of Eq. (11.7) and use Eq. (11.11) to conclude that the partition coefficient can be determined directly from the data:

$$\lambda = \frac{\int_0^\infty dt\, C_T(t)}{\int_0^\infty dt\, C_A(t)} \tag{11.12}$$

The partition coefficient is determined by various compartment volumes, including the plasma (V_P) or the full blood volume (V_B), the extravascular extracellular volume (V_E), and the extravascular intracellular tissue volume (V_C). In this notation, $V_B + V_E + V_C = V_T$, and $V_B/V_T + V_E/V_T + V_C/V_T = v_B + v_E + v_C = 1$, where volume is either a fractional volume or has the dimension mL/100 mL or mL/100 g. The relationship between V_B and V_P is given by $V_P = V_B(1 - Hct_{SV})$, where Hct_{SV} is the small vessel hematocrit. In a situation where contrast agent is confined to the vascular space, and C_A is measured in arterial blood, λ represents the blood volume V_B (e.g., in the brain λ will represent the cerebral blood volume, CBV). If contrast agent leakage occurs across the capillary membrane, without entering the cells, then λ will be equal to $V_B + V_E/(1 - Hct_{SV})$.

11.5 Compartment models

The section above models the concentrations in terms of the partition coefficient (λ), perfusion (f), and MTT, but does not show how other parameters such as compartmental volumes or exchange rates between compartments affect the concentrations. To estimate these physiological "free" parameters, we need to find an analytical model that relates them to the shape of the residue function.

The most commonly applied models are the compartment models, which describe the various physical locations in which the contrast agent may reside and the exchange between these compartments. The model assumes that the agent is instantaneously and uniformly distributed within each compartment (well-mixed). Compartment models are used to model biological systems, but are also applied in many other fields, for example, epidemiology or engineering. Apart from the assumption of uniform distribution, compartment models assume mass conservation, which states that the rate of change in the amount Q of a substance in a compartment is the difference between ingoing and outgoing fluxes:

$$\frac{dQ}{dt} = \sum_m J^m_{influx} - \sum_n J^n_{outflux} \tag{11.13}$$

11.5.1 One-compartment model

In some cases, a single-compartment model is adequate for describing the fate of the contrast agent in tissue. In such a model, contrast agent enters the biological tissue from the blood and, if not trapped in the tissue, will subsequently be "washed out" of the tissue again.

A schematic representation of the one-compartment model is shown in Fig. 11.4A. The plasma flow in and out of the compartment is described by F, and the concentration of contrast agent in arterial plasma is $C_A(t)$. The influx can then be written as $FC_A(t)$, that is, the plasma flow times the tracer concentration in the plasma entering the tissue. The amount of contrast agent in the tissue is $Q_T = V_T C_T(t)$, and since the plasma compartment is well-mixed, the concentration at the outlet is proportional to $C_T(t)$. So we can write the outflux as $FC_T(t)/\lambda$ and mass conservation then becomes:

$$\frac{dC_T(t)}{dt} = fC_A(t) - \frac{f}{\lambda} C_T(t) \tag{11.14}$$

where $f = F/V_T$ is the perfusion, that is, the blood flow per tissue mass in the examined voxel. For the initial condition where no contrast agent is present in the tissue $C_T(0) = 0$, Eq. (11.14) can be solved as Eq. (11.7) with:

$$R(t) = e^{\left(-\frac{f}{\lambda} t\right)} \tag{11.15}$$

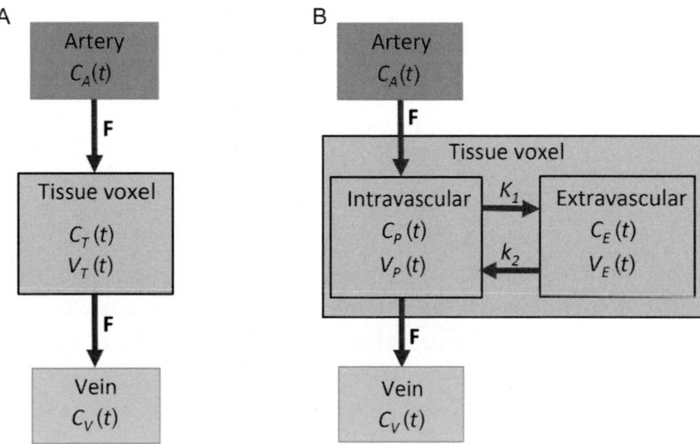

FIG. 11.4

Schematic representation of a one-compartment model (A) and a two-compartment model (B).

Hence the residue function $R(t)$ for the one-compartment model is a simple mono-exponential function, with MTT equal to λ/F (Eq. 11.9). Eq. (11.12) shows that λ is indeed the partition coefficient. The physiological parameters f and λ can be estimated by fitting a mono-exponential function convolved with the AIF to the measured tracer concentration time series. This equation was first applied by Kety and Schmidt when using a freely diffusible inert gas in the brain [35].

The single-compartment model described above assumes that the tracer is uniformly distributed over a single tissue compartment, for instance in the case of free diffusion of the tracer from intravascular to extravascular space. This is often not the case. For example, in the brain, the permeability of the tracer from intravascular to extravascular space though the BBB is very close to zero, so that the tracer is largely confined to the vascular space and any concentration in the extravascular space will be significantly smaller. If the BBB is intact the tissue may still be modeled with a single (intravascular) compartment, but in the presence of (subtle) BBB leakage one may end up with two compartments at very different concentrations.

11.5.2 Two-compartment exchange model

The theoretical assumptions for the single-compartment model are fulfilled in a situation with a freely diffusible tracer. In many situations, this is not the case and the passage of tracer from intravascular to extravascular space is more limited. In such a case the model can be extended to include two compartments: one for the intravascular space (the plasma compartment) and one for the extravascular space. The schematic representation of this two-compartment model is shown in Fig. 11.4B. The tracer concentration (C_P and C_E) in each compartment can be described by a set of differential equations:

$$\frac{\mathrm{d}V_P C_P(t)}{\mathrm{d}t} = F C_A(t) - (F + K_i) C_P(t) + K_i C_E(t) \tag{11.16}$$

$$\frac{\mathrm{d}V_E C_E(t)}{\mathrm{d}t} = K_i C_P(t) - K_i C_E(t) \tag{11.17}$$

The solution for $C_P(t)$ and $C_E(t)$ can be derived by solving the equations in the Laplace domain, giving:

$$R(t) = \frac{1}{\alpha_+ - \alpha_-}\left(\left(\alpha_+ - \frac{K_i}{V_E} - \frac{K_i}{V_P}\right)e^{-\alpha_+ t} + \left(\frac{K_i}{V_E} + \frac{K_i}{V_P} - \alpha_-\right)e^{-\alpha_- t}\right) \tag{11.18a}$$

where the constants α_+ and α_- are defined as follows:

$$\alpha_\pm = \frac{1}{2}\left(\frac{K_i}{V_E} + \frac{F + K_i}{V_P} \pm \sqrt{\left(\frac{K_i}{V_E} + \frac{F + K_i}{V_P}\right)^2 - 4\frac{F K_i}{V_E V_P}}\right) \tag{11.18b}$$

The residue function of the two-compartment model is a biexponential function with four free parameters: perfusion f, permeability between the vascular space and extracellular space (the unidirectional influx constant K_i), and the plasma and extracellular volumes V_P and V_E. This model has been used to examine changes in the permeability of the BBB.

The differences between the assumptions in the above-described compartment models underscore the importance of using a compartment model that correctly describes the underlying physiology, in terms of both the number of compartments and permeability between them. The selection of the residue function (Fig. 11.5) and the complexity of the model (Figs. 11.6 and 11.7) will dramatically affect the resulting fit values. The use of an inappropriate model will lead to perfusion measurements which are at best unstable and at worst inaccurate.

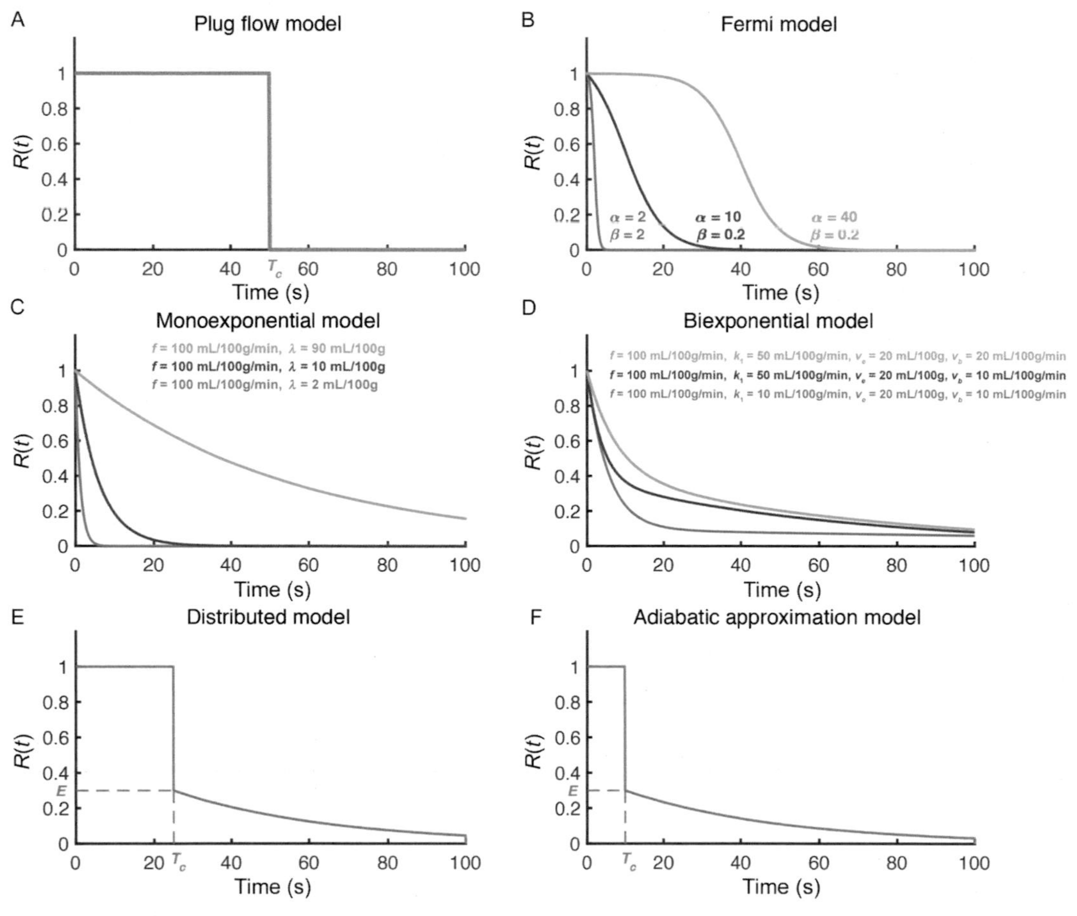

FIG. 11.5

Examples of different models for the residue impulse response function $R(t)$. (A) A simple model based on the assumption that all contrast agent molecules leave the tissue simultaneously at time T_C. (B) A Fermi function, where the curve is shown for three different sets of values; note the flexibility of the configuration. (C) A mono-exponential $R(t)$, compatible with a one-compartment model; note how the distribution volume λ influences the timing of the curve. (D) A bi-exponential $R(t)$ compatible with a two-compartment model. Note how k_1 influences the slow component. (E) and (F) $R(t)$ models that take into account the fact that a contrast agent concentration can be a function of both time and position in a capillary. Essentially, the functions consist of a vascular phase, where a fraction of the contrast agent moves through the tissue like a plug flow and leave the tissue simultaneously, while another fraction leaks into the extravascular space, and gradually leaves the tissue afterward (f=perfusion; k_1=permeability of the blood-brain barrier; v_b=blood volume, v_e=extravascular space).

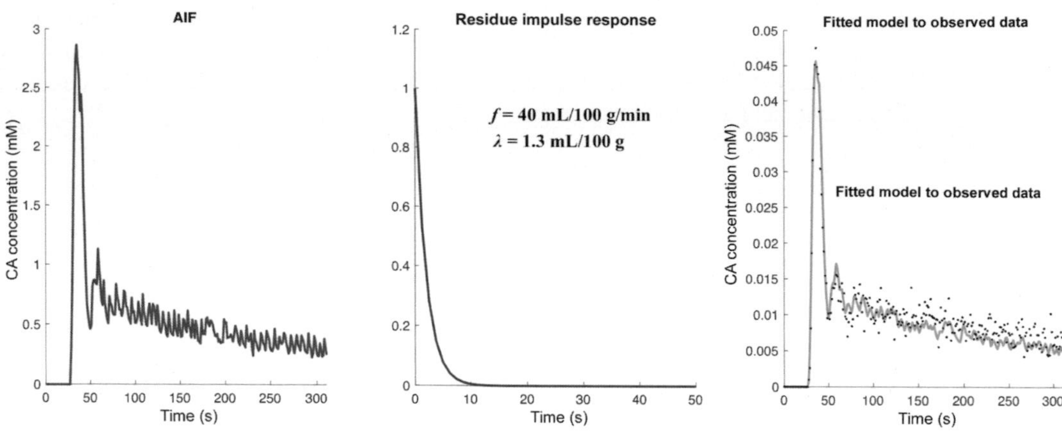

FIG. 11.6

Tissue concentration enhancement curves from a DCE-MRI experiment. *Left*: The arterial input function (AIF, *magenta color*), obtained from the internal carotid artery. *Right*: Observed data obtained from an ROI placed in brain cortical gray matter *(black points)*. The *green curve* is a one-compartment model fitted to the data, where the AIF *(magenta curve)* is convolved with the residue impulse function, $R(t)$ *(blue curve)* of a one-compartment system. The optimal fit values for the two free parameters, perfusion (f) and distribution volume (λ), are shown. Because the contrast agent is nearly confined to the vascular space due to the blood-brain barrier, the distribution volume (λ) becomes a measure of the cerebral blood volume in the ROI.

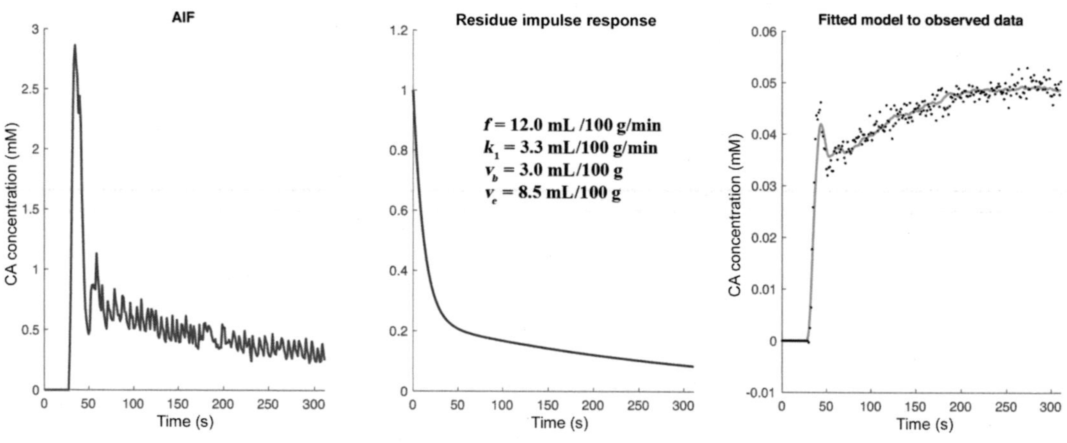

FIG. 11.7

Tissue concentration enhancement curves from a DCE-MRI experiment in a brain tumor patient. *Left*: The arterial input function (AIF, *magenta color*). *Right*: Observed data *(black dots)* are the tissue concentration enhancement timepoints obtained from an ROI placed in a brain tumor. Note the initial pronounced "vascular" peak followed by a steadier enhancement due to deficiency of the BBB. The *green curve* shows a two-compartment model fit to the data, where the AIF *(magenta curve)* is convolved with the residue impulse function ($R(t)$, *blue curve*) of a two-compartment system. The optimal fit values for the four free parameters are shown (f=perfusion; k_1=permeability of the blood-brain barrier; v_b=blood volume, v_e=extravascular space).

11.5.3 The Patlak model

The Patlak analysis belongs to a family of multi-time-point graphical analysis methods that has the advantage of being computationally very fast. The Patlak method represents a simplified version of the general two tissue compartment model which relies on the assumption that the tracer becomes irreversibly trapped in the extravascular compartment [36]. Furthermore, the model assumes that the concentration of tracer in arterial and tissue plasma is in equilibrium: $C_A(t) = C_P(t)$. When these conditions are fulfilled, the solution to the Patlak model can be written in linear form where the slope represents the influx of tracer, K_i and the intercept on the y-axis the plasma volume V_P.

The concentration in the extravascular compartment of the Patlak model can be derived from Eq. (11.17) by setting the outflux to zero:

$$\frac{\mathrm{d}V_E C_E(t)}{\mathrm{d}t} = K_i C_P(t) \tag{11.19}$$

The total tissue concentration in the examined voxel $C_T(t)$ can be expressed as:

$$V_T C_T(t) = V_P C_P(t) + V_E C_E(t) \tag{11.20}$$

Inserting the solution of Eq. (11.19) into Eq. (11.20) we find the solution of the Patlak model (note $C_P(t) = C_A(t)$ is the AIF). In terms of $v_P = V_P/V_T$ and $k_i = K_i/V_T$:

$$C_T(t) = v_P C_P(t) + k_i \int_0^t C_P(\tau) d\tau \tag{11.21}$$

The classical linearized Patlak model is then created by rearranging Eq. (11.21):

$$\frac{C_T(t)}{C_P(t)} = k_i \frac{\int_0^t C_P(\tau) d\tau}{C_P(t)} + v_P \tag{11.22}$$

By defining $x(t) = \int_0^t C_P(\tau) d\tau / C_P(t)$ and $y(t) = C_T(t)/C_P(t)$ a plot of $y(t)$ against $x(t)$ should approximately form a straight line with slope k_i, and intercept v_P (Fig. 11.8).

When applied to real data, a linear trend is typically observed after an initial vascular phase occurring during the first bolus passage.

11.6 Model-free perfusion quantification

So far the approaches described for estimating perfusion or permeability necessitate building a model based on some specific assumptions of how the tissue "processes" the contrast agent. Any model will have strengths and limitations, which will influence the results in a way that is specific to the given model. It is often very difficult to provide evidence that one model is more accurate when compared to another model, and even microsphere injection or radioactive water ($^{15}H_2O$) in conjunction with PET, normally considered as a gold standard, have their limitations [37]. However, if a given model provides meaningful clinical results, then accuracy might be secondary.

To circumvent the problem of specifying a model, model-free solutions have been proposed. These approaches rely on the fact that a convolution (Eq. 11.7) can be written in discrete form, which can be structured as a matrix equation:

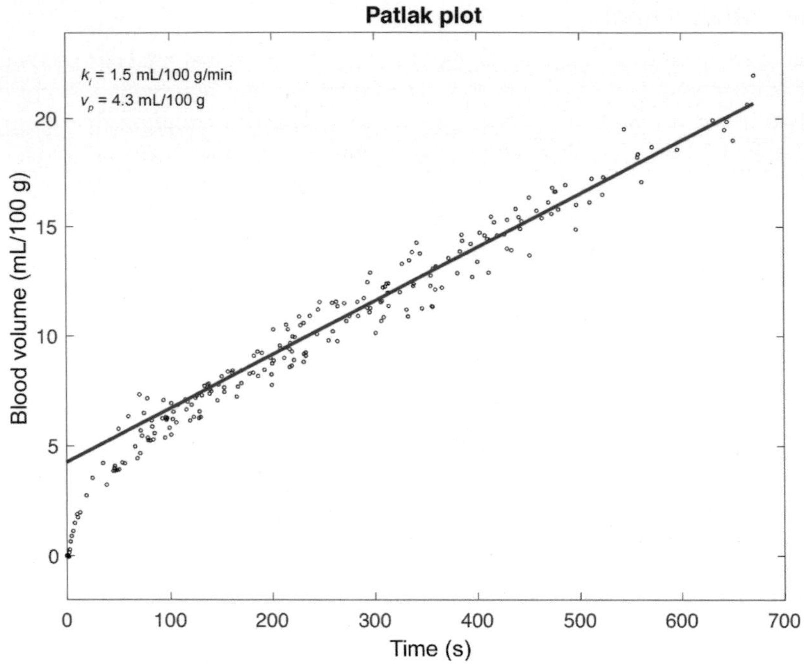

FIG. 11.8

An example of a Patlak plot. The slope of the regression line corresponds to k_i, while the intercept corresponds to the blood plasma volume fraction $v_P = V_p/V_T$. The shown data were obtained from a brain tumor patient with a leaky blood-brain barrier; the measured permeability (k_i) and blood volume (V_p) values are shown in the top left corner.

$$\vec{y} = f \Delta t \mathbf{A} \vec{x} \tag{11.23}$$

Here $\vec{y}$ is a column vector representation of C_T, $\mathbf{A}$ is a matrix depending on C_A and $\vec{x}$ is a column vector representation of $R(t)$. Eq. (11.23) can be specifically written by defining the single elements of the matrix equation:

$$\begin{bmatrix} C_T(1) \\ C_T(2) \\ C_T(3) \\ \vdots \\ C_T(N) \end{bmatrix} = f\Delta t \begin{bmatrix} C_A(1) & 0 & 0 & \cdots & 0 \\ C_A(2) & C_A(1) & 0 & \cdots & 0 \\ C_A(3) & C_A(2) & C_A(1) & \cdots & 0 \\ \vdots & \vdots & \vdots & \ddots & \vdots \\ C_A(N) & C_A(N\text{-}1) & C_A(N\text{-}2) & \cdots & C_A(1) \end{bmatrix} \begin{bmatrix} R(1) \\ R(2) \\ R(3) \\ \vdots \\ R(N) \end{bmatrix} \tag{11.24}$$

Note that the equation is discretized with a total of N samples and a time resolution of Δt. Since deconvolution is an ill-posed problem, Eq. (11.24) cannot be solved by inverting the matrix $\mathbf{A}$. Fortunately, a least-squares solution can always be found, using the singular value decomposition (SVD) method to obtain the pseudo-inverse matrix $\mathbf{A}^{-1}$:

$$f\vec{x} = \Delta t^{-1} \mathbf{A}^{-1} \vec{y} \tag{11.25}$$

This solution can be shown to also minimize the residuals, that is, the distance between the observed tissue concentration and calculated tissue concentration. Leif Østergaard was the first to introduce this technique in the MR community focusing on perfusion measurements using exogenous contrast agents and tracer kinetic theory [38]. An example showing the use of the SVD method to estimate perfusion in the brain can be seen in Fig. 11.9; note that the selection of the number of singular values to be included has a major impact on the measured perfusion values and thus must be considered carefully.

The use of the pseudo-inverse matrix does have vulnerabilities: the method is extremely noise sensitive, often resulting in aphysiological oscillations of the residue function $fR(t)$, which are a manifestation of this noise sensitivity. To suppress these undesirable oscillations, an empirical threshold (i.e., 20%) can be adopted below which all eigenvalues are set to zero, but this approach will result

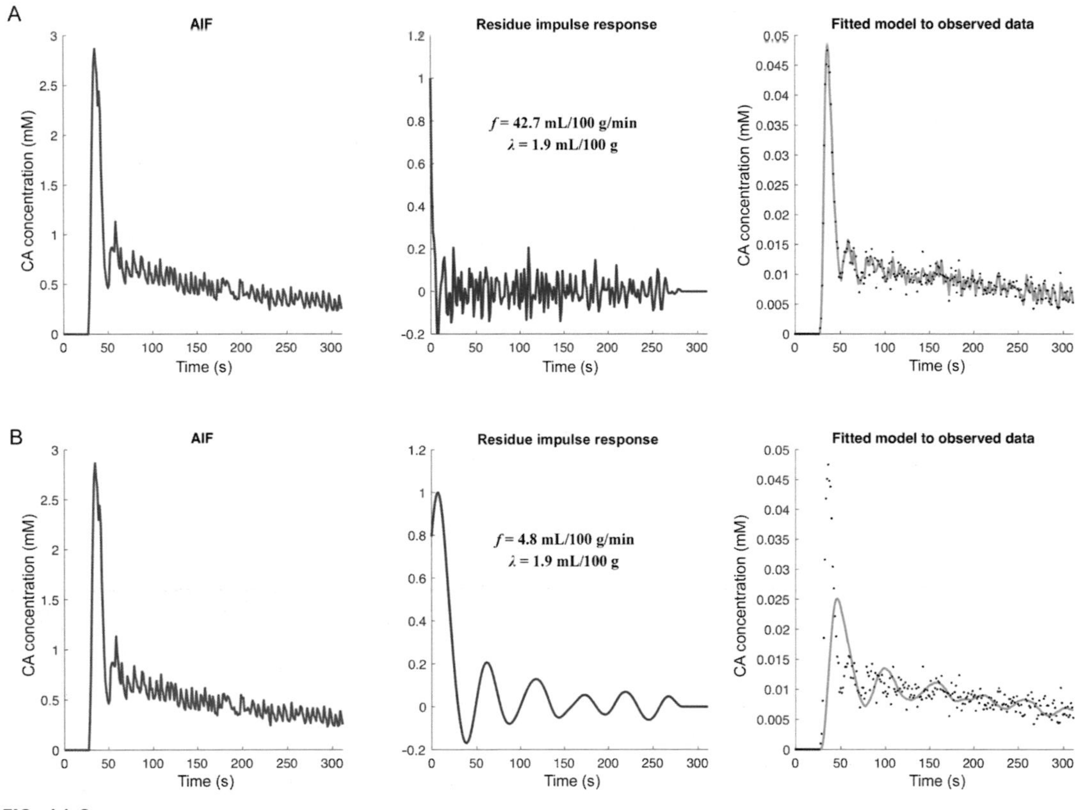

FIG. 11.9

Example of the use of the singular value decomposition (SVD) for the determination of perfusion parameters. The AIF and observed data are the same as in Fig. 11.6. Note that the perfusion (f) and distribution volume (λ) were measured to be 40 mL/100 g/min and 1.3 mL/100 g in these data when using a single-compartment model. (A) The use of the SVD, keeping nearly all eigenvalues (no regularization), results in a noisy residue impulse response function and a tendency to over-fitting of the data. (B) Keeping only those eigenvalues which are >20% of the first (largest) eigenvalue results in a smoother residue impulse response function, although this curve suffers from spurious oscillations and a considerable underestimation of brain perfusion f.

in underestimation of the perfusion. Thus, the optimal threshold setting will become a tradeoff between spurious aphysiological oscillations with consequent distortions of $fR(t)$ and overfitting on one hand, and a blunted $fR(t)$ and underestimation of perfusion f on the other hand.

Yet another possibility is to directly incorporate theoretical knowledge about the residual function $R(t)$, namely that it is a smooth function. The "generalized singular value decomposition" (GSVD) [39, 40], seeks to find a solution through the minimization of the following cost function:

$$\min\left\{\left\|\mathbf{A}\vec{x}-\vec{y}^{obs}\right\|^2+\mu^2\left\|L\left(\vec{x}\right)\right\|^2\right\} \tag{11.26}$$

where L is an operator (typically one or the first derivative operator) and μ is the degree of regularization. If μ is set to zero, the solution is not regularized, and noise-related oscillations will become evident. Conversely, if μ is set to a very high value, the solution will become very smooth without oscillations.

One approach to estimate the optimal value of the regularization parameter, μ, is to use the curvature of the so-called L-curve, a heuristic approach that attempts to balance the tradeoff between obtaining a smooth $R(t)$ and match $\mathbf{A}\vec{x}$ and $\vec{y}$ [41]. This procedure can be implemented as an automatic procedure on a voxel-wise level, with a practical implementation given by Larsson et al. [32]. However, this approach of GSVD with regularization, which tends to eliminate abrupt changes of the $R(t)$, does appear to underestimate perfusion under some circumstances [42]. Examples of brain perfusion estimation by use of GSVD can be seen in Figs. 11.10 and 11.11. An example of voxel-wise calculation of CBF and permeability using GSVD in a patient with a brain tumor can be seen in Figs. 11.12 and 11.13, respectively.

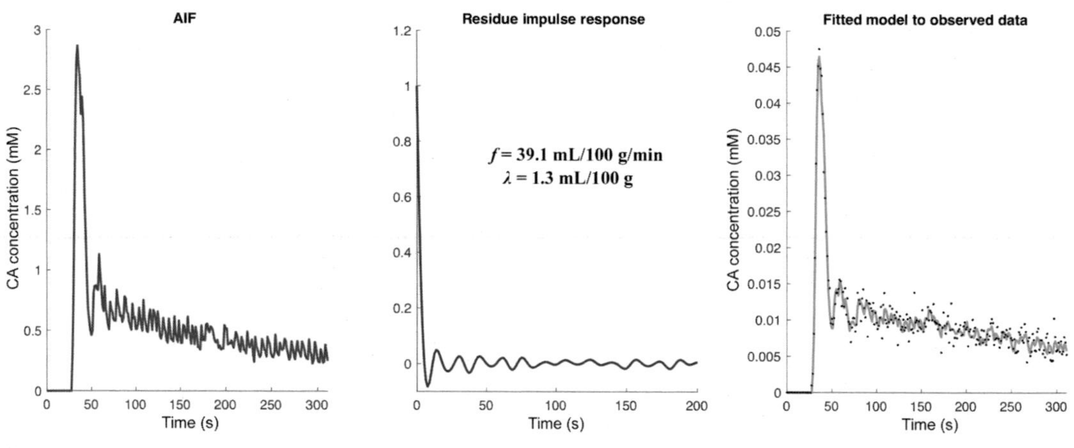

FIG. 11.10

Example of the use of the generalized singular value decomposition (GSVD) with regularization using the L-curve method (see text). AIF and data are the same as in Figs. 11.6 and 11.9. Recall that the perfusion (f) and distribution volume (λ) were measured to be 40 mL/100 g/min and 1.3 mL/100 g in these data when using a single-compartment model. Note the reduction in the oscillations of the residue impulse response function when using GSVD, which fit the data with no obvious underestimation of perfusion.

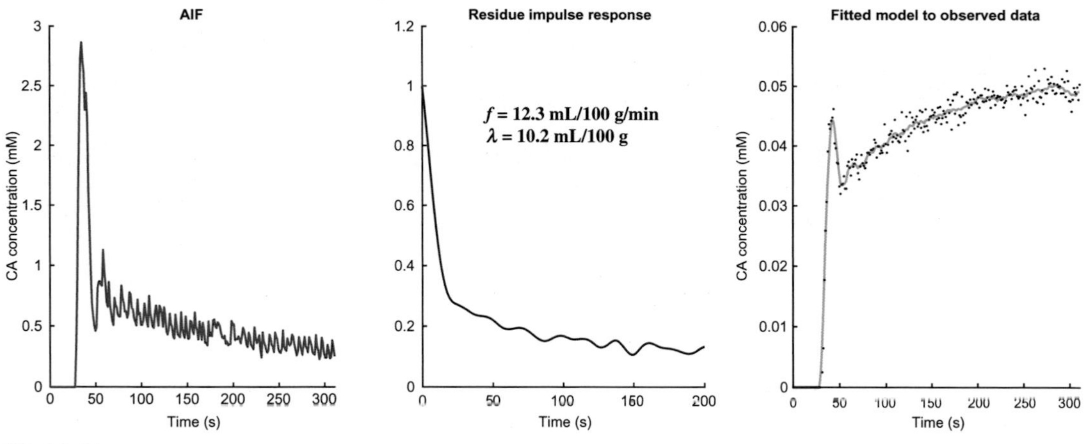

FIG. 11.11

Example of the use of the generalized singular value decomposition (GSVD) with regularization using the L-curve method (see text). AIF and data are the same as in Fig. 11.7. In this example, λ should be interpreted as the volume of distribution, and corresponds approximately to the sum of v_b and v_e in Fig. 11.7.

Eq. (11.24) is derived by the lowest-order step-wise integration of Eq. (11.7). If $C_A(i)$ or $R(j)$ are characterized by a pronounced change from sample to sample, then this discrete calculation will overestimate or underestimate the area compared to a convolution performed by a real continuous integration. This will introduce a bias of the estimated perfusion. To ameliorate this problem, one can either interpolate data to a finer temporal grid, for example, by a factor of 2–10, or one can use the trapezoid rule and Eq. (11.24) will be given as follows [43]:

$$\begin{bmatrix} C_T(1) \\ C_T(2) \\ C_T(3) \\ \vdots \\ C_T(N) \end{bmatrix} = f\Delta t \begin{bmatrix} \frac{C_A(1)}{2} & 0 & 0 & \cdots & 0 \\ \frac{C_A(2)}{2} & \frac{C_A(1)}{2} & 0 & \cdots & 0 \\ \frac{C_A(3)}{2} & C_A(2) & \frac{C_A(1)}{2} & \cdots & 0 \\ \vdots & \vdots & \vdots & \ddots & \vdots \\ \frac{C_A(N)}{2} & C_A(N\text{-}1) & C_A(N\text{-}2) & \cdots & \frac{C_A(1)}{2} \end{bmatrix} \begin{bmatrix} R(1) \\ R(2) \\ R(3) \\ \vdots \\ R(N) \end{bmatrix} \tag{11.27}$$

In short, it is possible to find a solution to the general tracer kinetic equation (Eq. 11.7), without the inherent assumptions of a specifying model. This approach is highly noise sensitive but it is possible to alleviate this sensitivity by regularization of the solution by thresholding eigenvalues or by incorporating a smoothing operator, with a possible impact on the shape of $R(t)$ and potential underestimation of f.

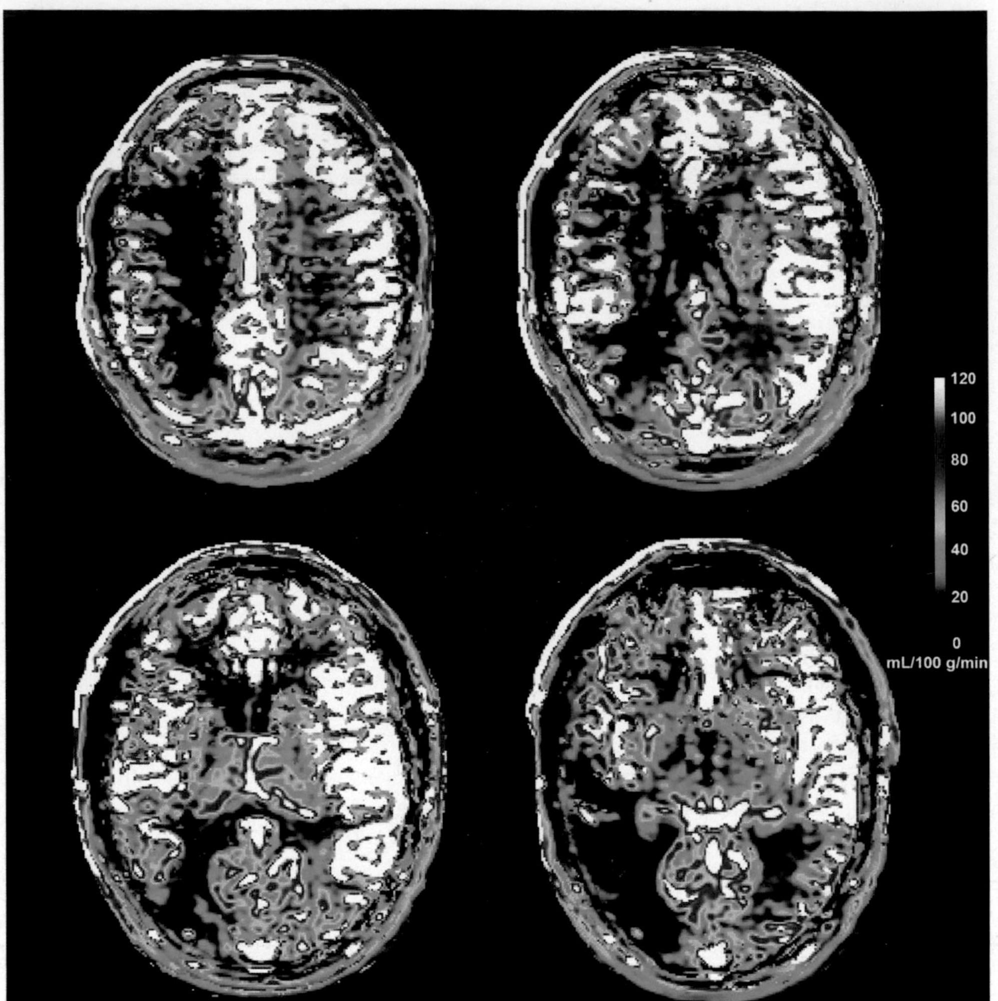

FIG. 11.12

Perfusion (f) maps derived from dynamic contrast-enhanced T_1-weighted MRI imaging at 3 T, using a saturation fast field echo MR sequence with a temporal resolution of about 1 s per frame. f is calculated pixelwise in each of the slice locations using the generalized singular value decomposition with L-curve regularization. The subject suffers from a stenosis of the right internal carotid artery, resulting in decreased perfusion in the area supplied by the right middle cerebral artery.

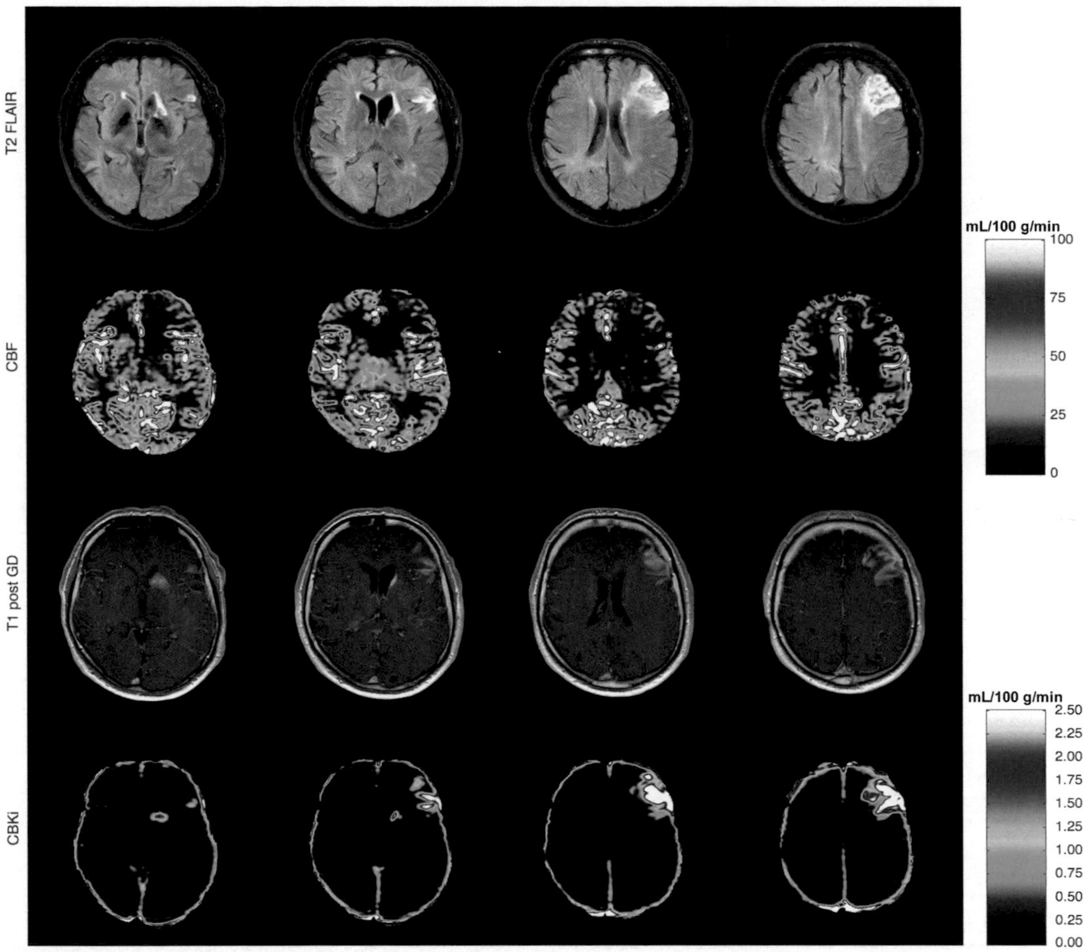

FIG. 11.13

Example data from a subject with a contrast-enhancing brain tumor in the left frontal lobe. Shown are the T_2 FLAIR images, cerebral perfusion maps (f), T_1-weighted post-contrast imaging, and permeability (k_i) maps from dynamic contrast-enhanced T_1-weighted MRI at 3T, using a saturation fast field echo MR sequence with a temporal resolution of about one frame per second. Pixelwise perfusion maps are calculated using generalized singular value decomposition with L-curve regularization and permeability is calculated using the Patlak method. The brain tumor in the left frontoparietal area shows pronounced leakage across the blood-brain-barrier in the permeability maps and reduced perfusion when compared to the surrounding healthy tissue.

11.7 Conclusion

Quantitative perfusion MRI has the ability to provide important physiologic information about the human body. Recent improvements in both hardware stability and sequence development enable reliable, yet sufficiently fast acquisitions for dynamic sampling of a multitude of pharmacokinetic variables such as perfusion, blood volume, and capillary permeability as well as capillary transit time heterogeneity. By modeling these data using appropriate physiologically-based assumptions, accurate measurements of basic physiological processes in the healthy human body can be made. These measurements also provide value in a clinical context for characterization of pathological processes, disease etiology, prognostics, as well as treatment efficacy.

References

[1] Paulson OB, Strandgaard S, Edvinsson L. Cerebral autoregulation. Cerebrovasc Brain Metab Rev 1990;2:161–92.
[2] Carlström M, Wilcox CS, Arendshorst J. Renal autoregulation in health and disease. Physiol Rev 2015;95:405–511.
[3] Dole WP. Autoregulation of the coronary circulation. Prog Cardiovasc Dis 1987;29:293–323.
[4] Engelhardt B, Sorokin L. The blood-brain and the blood-cerebrospinal fluid barriers: function and dysfunction. Semin Immunopathol 2009;31:497–511.
[5] Hill J, Rom S, Ramirez SH, Persidsky Y. Emerging roles of pericytes in the regulation of the neurovascular unit in health and disease. J NeuroImmune Pharmacol 2014. https://doi.org/10.1007/s11481-014-9557-x.
[6] Kuschinsky W, Paulson OB. Capillary circulation in the brain. Cerebrovasc Brain Metab Rev 1992;4:261–86.
[7] Weiss N, Miller F, Cazaubon S, Couraud PO. The blood-brain barrier in brain homeostasis and neurological diseases. Biochim Biophys Acta Biomembr 2009;1788:842–57.
[8] Copen WA, Schaefer PW, Wu O. MR perfusion imaging in acute ischemic stroke. Neuroimaging Clin N Am 2011;21:259–83.
[9] Thng CH, Koh TS, Collins DJ, Koh DM. Perfusion magnetic resonance imaging of the liver. World J Gastroenterol 2010;16:1598–609.
[10] Nielsen G, Fritz-Hansen T, Dirks CG, Jensen GB, Larsson HBW. Evaluation of heart perfusion in patients with acute myocardial infarction using dynamic contrast-enhanced magnetic resonance imaging. J Magn Reson Imaging 2004;20:403–10.
[11] Nishida N, Yano H, Nishida T, Kamura T, Kojiro M. Angiogenesis in cancer. Vasc Health Risk Manag 2006;2:213–9.
[12] Cramer SP, Simonsen H, Frederiksen JL, Rostrup E, Larsson HBW. Abnormal blood-brain barrier permeability in normal appearing white matter in multiple sclerosis investigated by MRI. Neuroimage Clin 2014;4:182–9.
[13] Cramer SP, Modvig S, Simonsen HJ, Frederiksen JL, Larsson HBW. Permeability of the blood-brain barrier predicts conversion from optic neuritis to multiple sclerosis. Brain 2015;138:2571–83.
[14] Cramer SP, Simonsen HJ, Varatharaj A, Galea I, Frederiksen JL, Larsson HBW. Permeability of the blood-brain barrier predicts no evidence of disease activity at 2 years after natalizumab or fingolimod treatment in relapsing-remitting multiple sclerosis. Ann Neurol 2018. https://doi.org/10.1002/ana.25219.
[15] Varatharaj A, Liljeroth M, Darekar A, Larsson HBW, Galea I, Cramer SP. Blood-brain barrier permeability measured using dynamic contrast-enhanced magnetic resonance imaging: a validation study. J Physiol 2018;1–11.

[16] Montagne A, Barnes SR, Law M, et al. Blood-brain barrier breakdown in the aging human report blood-brain barrier breakdown in the aging human hippocampus. Neuron 2015;85:296–302.

[17] Zipser BD, Johanson CE, Gonzalez L, et al. Microvascular injury and blood-brain barrier leakage in Alzheimer's disease. Neurobiol Aging 2007;28:977–86.

[18] Gulani V, Calamante F, Shellock FG, Kanal E, Reeder SB. Gadolinium deposition in the brain: summary of evidence and recommendations. Lancet Neurol 2017;16:564–70.

[19] Pasquini L, Napolitano A, Visconti E, et al. Gadolinium-based contrast agent-related toxicities. CNS Drugs 2018;32:229–40.

[20] Kanda T, Ishii K, Kawaguchi H, Kitajima K, Takenaka D. High signal intensity in the dentate nucleus and globus pallidus on unenhanced T1-weighted MR images: relationship with increasing cumulative dose of a gadolinium-based contrast material. Radiology 2014;270:834–41.

[21] Smith APL, Marino M, Roberts J, et al. Clearance of gadolinium from the brain with no pathologic effect after repeated administration of gadodiamide in healthy rats: an analytical and histologic study. Radiology 2017;282:743–51.

[22] Kanda T, Fukusato T, Matsuda M, et al. Gadolinium-based contrast agent accumulates in the brain even in subjects without severe renal dysfunction: evaluation of autopsy brain specimens with inductively coupled plasma mass spectroscopy. Radiology 2015;276:228–32.

[23] Radbruch A, Weberling LD, Kieslich PJ, et al. Gadolinium retention in the dentate nucleus and globus pallidus is dependent on the class of contrast agent. Radiology 2015;275:783–91.

[24] Murata N, Gonzalez-Cuyar LF, Murata K, et al. Macrocyclic and other non–group 1 gadolinium contrast agents deposit low levels of gadolinium in brain and bone tissue. Investig Radiol 2016;51:447–53.

[25] Robert P, Lehericy S, Grand S, et al. T1-weighted hypersignal in the deep cerebellar nuclei after repeated administrations of gadolinium-based contrast agents in healthy rats: difference between linear and macrocyclic agents. Investig Radiol 2015;50:473–80.

[26] Welk B, McArthur E, Morrow SA, et al. Association between gadolinium contrast exposure and the risk of parkinsonism. JAMA 2016;316:96.

[27] Perrotta G, Metens T, Absil J, Lemort M, Manto M. Absence of clinical cerebellar syndrome after serial injections of more than 20 doses of gadoterate, a macrocyclic GBCA: a monocenter retrospective study. J Neurol 2017;264:2277–83.

[28] Bussi S, Penard L, Bonafè R, et al. Non-clinical assessment of safety and gadolinium deposition after cumulative administration of gadobenate dimeglumine (MultiHance®) to neonatal and juvenile rats. Regul Toxicol Pharmacol 2018;92:268–77.

[29] European Medicine Agency. EMA's final opinion confirms restrictions on use of linear gadolinium agents in body scans, http://www.ema.europa.eu/docs/en_GB/document_library/Referrals_document/gadolinium_contrast_agents_31/European_Commission_final_decision/WC500240575.pdf; 2017.

[30] Lauffer RB. Paramagnetic metal complexes as water proton relaxation agents for NMR imaging: theory and design. Chem Rev 1987;87:901–27.

[31] Larsson HB, Rosenbaum S, Fritz-Hansen T. Quantification of the effect of water exchange in dynamic contrast MRI perfusion measurements in the brain and heart. Magn Reson Med 2001;46:272–81.

[32] Larsson HBW, Hansen AE, Berg HK, Rostrup E, Haraldseth O. Dynamic contrast-enhanced quantitative perfusion measurement of the brain using T1-weighted MRI at 3T. J Magn Reson Imaging 2008;27:754–62.

[33] Meier P, Zierler KL. On the theory of the indicator-dilution method for measurement of blood flow and volume. J Appl Physiol 1954;6:731–44.

[34] Jespersen SN, Østergaard L. The roles of cerebral blood flow, capillary transit time heterogeneity, and oxygen tension in brain oxygenation and metabolism. J Cereb Blood Flow Metab 2012;32:264–77.

[35] Kety SS, Schmidt CF. The determination of cerebral blood flow in man by the use of nitrous oxide in low concentrations. Am J Phys 1945;143:53–66.

[36] Patlak CS, Blasberg RG. Graphical evaluation of blood-to-brain transfer constants from multiple-time uptake data. Generalizations. J Cereb Blood Flow Metab 1985;5:584–90.

[37] Bassingthwaighte JB, Malone MA, Moffett TC, et al. Validity of microsphere depositions for regional myocardial flows. Am J Phys 1987;253:H184–93.

[38] Østergaard L, Weisskoff R, Chesler D, Gyldensted C, Rosen BR. High resolution measurement of cerebral blood flow using intravascular tracer bolus passages. Part I: mathematical approach and statistical analysis. Magn Reson Med 1996;36:715–25.

[39] Tikhonov AN, Arsenin V. John F, editor. Solutions of ill-posed problems. Washington, DC: V.H. Winston; 1977.

[40] Tikhonov AN. Ill-posed problems in natural sciences, In: Leonov AS, editor. Proceedings of international conference, Moscow; 1991.

[41] Fritz-Hansen T, Rostrup E, Larsson HB, Søndergaard L, Ring P, Henriksen O. Measurement of the arterial concentration of Gd-DTPA using MRI: a step toward quantitative perfusion imaging. Magn Reson Med 1996;36:225–31.

[42] Larsson HBW, Courivaud F, Rostrup E, Hansen AE. Measurement of brain perfusion, blood volume, and blood-brain barrier permeability, using dynamic contrast-enhanced T1-weighted MRI at 3 tesla. Magn Reson Med 2009;62:1270–81.

[43] Koh TS, Tan CKM, Cheong LHD, Lim CCT. Cerebral perfusion mapping using a robust and efficient method for deconvolution analysis of dynamic contrast-enhanced images. NeuroImage 2006;32:643–53.

CHAPTER

Arterial Spin Labeling MRI: Basic Physics, Pulse Sequences, and Modeling

12

Susan Francis

Sir Peter Mansfield Imaging Centre, University of Nottingham, Nottingham, United Kingdom

12.1 Introduction

Arterial spin labeling (ASL) is a noninvasive Magnetic Resonance Imaging (MRI) technique that uses endogenous arterial blood water as a kinetic tracer to quantify tissue perfusion of an organ [1–3]. Perfusion describes the amount of arterial blood water that is delivered to and exchanges in the capillary bed of a given volume of tissue in an organ and is measured in units of mL/100 g/min. ASL is most commonly applied in the human brain, where cerebral perfusion is of the order of 70 mL/100 g/min for gray matter and 20 mL/100 g/min for white matter. Due to its noninvasive nature, ASL is now being more widely applied to other organs including the kidney [4, 5], liver [6–9], peripheral muscle [10–12], pancreas [13, 14], and heart [15–19]. Since ASL requires no exogenous contrast agent, it is safe to repeat over time and can, therefore, be used to track changes in perfusion due to disease progression or drug therapy.

12.2 Basic physics

The basis of any ASL technique is the acquisition of two images, a "label" and a "control" image. The label image is acquired following magnetic labeling (inverting) of the blood spins flowing into the tissue of interest, whereas the control image is collected without manipulating the magnetization of the inflowing blood (fully relaxed). When collecting the label/control images, a short period (termed the inversion time [TI] or postlabel delay [PLD]) is allowed between labeling the inflowing blood and acquiring an image, such that the labeled blood spins can travel into the imaging plane and traverse the capillaries in the transit time Δt before exchanging with tissue water. By subtracting the label image from the control image, a perfusion-weighted difference image is generated, as illustrated in Fig. 12.1. The ASL signal change is typically expressed as a fractional ratio between the perfusion-weighted difference image ΔM and the equilibrium magnetization M_0 and converted to a percentage signal change before quantification in units of mL/100 g/min.

The percentage signal change in ASL is dependent on many parameters, not just the tissue perfusion. Other factors including the magnetic field strength (B_0), which alters the longitudinal (T_1) relaxation time of both blood and tissue, and the ASL scheme used to label the blood influence the signal level. By including these influences into a signal model, the perfusion-weighted difference image can be quantified to yield a perfusion map in units of mL/100 g/min.

Advances in Magnetic Resonance Technology and Applications. Volume 1. ISSN 2666-9099. https://doi.org/10.1016/B978-0-12-817057-1.00014-7

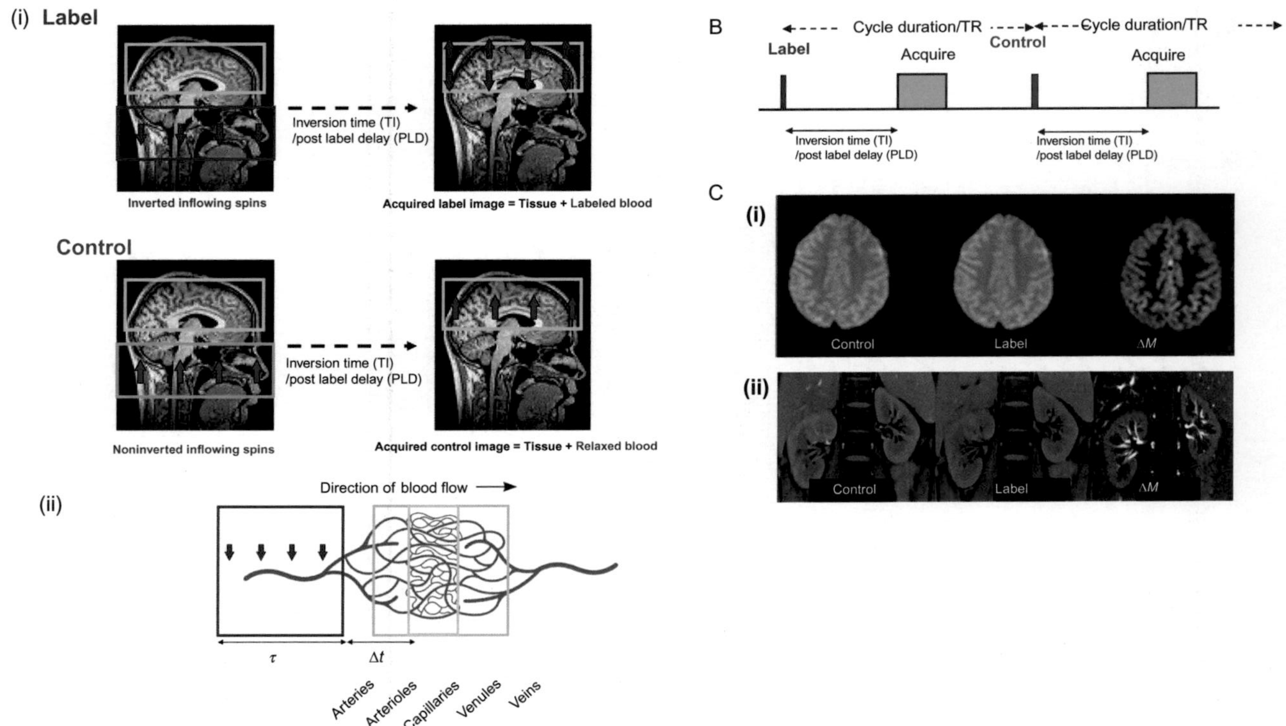

FIG. 12.1

Schematic of arterial spin labeling illustrated for brain ASL showing (A) (i) the different magnetic states of the inflowing blood in the label condition (*red box* with inverted spins denoted by the *red arrows*) and control condition (*blue box* with noninverted spins denoted by the *blue arrows*). The inflowing blood arrives at the tissue in the imaging plane *(green box)* after a short period (termed the inversion time [TI] or postlabel delay [PLD]); (ii) Illustration of the labeled arterial blood water *(red)* delivered to a network of cerebral arteries and arterioles. The labeled arterial blood will arrive at the imaging plane *(green box)* and traverse the arteriolar network to the capillary bed in a transit time Δt at which point labeled spins exchange with the tissue. Note: The inverted labeled blood will recover with the longitudinal relaxation time of blood (T_{1b}) during its transit time through the vasculature, while upon exchange with the fully recovered tissue water it will subsequently recover with the T_1 of the tissue (T_{1t}). (B) Simplified pulse sequence diagram illustrating the alternation between a label and control condition in each cycle duration (or TR) period, with each followed by the image acquisition (Acquire). (C) Label and control images collected at a given TI/PLD and resultant perfusion-weighted difference image, ΔM, which is proportional to tissue perfusion, for the (i) brain and (ii) kidney.

For all ASL labeling schemes, it is important to consider the magnetization transfer (MT) effects of the labeling pulse in the imaging region; if this effect is not accounted for, the difference image may contain signal not related to perfusion. Since the label condition inverts blood distal to the imaging region, protons in bound water in the imaging region (such as macromolecules) may be on- or near-resonance and will thus be perturbed by the labeling pulse. As magnetization exchanges between the free and bound proton pools, free water signal in the image region can falsely appear to be signal from inflowing blood. To ensure such MT effects are not reflected in the perfusion-weighted difference image, a control condition with MT effects that match the label image should be collected.

12.3 ASL labeling schemes

ASL labeling schemes can be separated into three main categories: pulsed arterial spin labeling (PASL) [20–22], continuous arterial spin labeling (CASL) [3], and pseudo-continuous ASL (PCASL) [23].

12.3.1 Pulsed ASL

PASL schemes use adiabatic radio frequency (RF) pulses to invert spins across a large volume. Adiabatic inversion pulses can achieve a relatively consistent high inversion efficiency of ~98% across a large labeling region. Many PASL labeling schemes have been proposed with several associated acronyms; Fig. 12.2 illustrates three commonly used schemes and the location of their labeling slabs when used for brain ASL. FAIR (Flow Alternating Inversion Recovery) [21] is one of the most commonly used PASL approaches and is widely used outside of the brain due to its ease of planning [24–26]. In PASL, selective and nonselective inversion slabs are used for the control and label conditions, respectively. In STAR (Signal Targeting with Alternating Radiofrequency) [20], an inversion slab is applied below the imaging slice to label the inflowing blood. In the control condition, two 180° pulses are applied below the imaging plane resulting in fully recovered inflowing blood and matched MT effects. In PICORE (Proximal Inversion Controlling for Off Resonance Effects) [27] the label is similar to that for STAR, while the control condition uses an off-resonance pulse in the absence of a slice gradient.

For FAIR-based schemes, the nonselective slab is on the order of 30 cm, while the selective slab is typically 10–20 mm wider than the imaging volume. For non-FAIR-based schemes, the labeling slab typically has a thickness of 15–20 cm with a gap (transition zone) to the imaging volume of 1–2 cm such that labeling pulse does not significantly perturb the magnetization in the imaging volume.

12.3.2 Continuous ASL

CASL was the original implementation of ASL [3]. CASL uses flow-driven adiabatic inversion to invert the arterial magnetization as it flows through a narrow labeling plane. In the brain, this labeling plane is positioned through the carotids in the neck as shown in Fig. 12.3. A gradient field with constant amplitude is applied along the direction of flow at the same time as a long continuous amplitude low power RF pulse. The effective field that the flowing spin experiences as it moves through the labeling plane cause the spin to become inverted. CASL has higher SNR compared to PASL schemes, but the long inversion pulse results in large deposition of RF energy within the tissue, increasing the specific

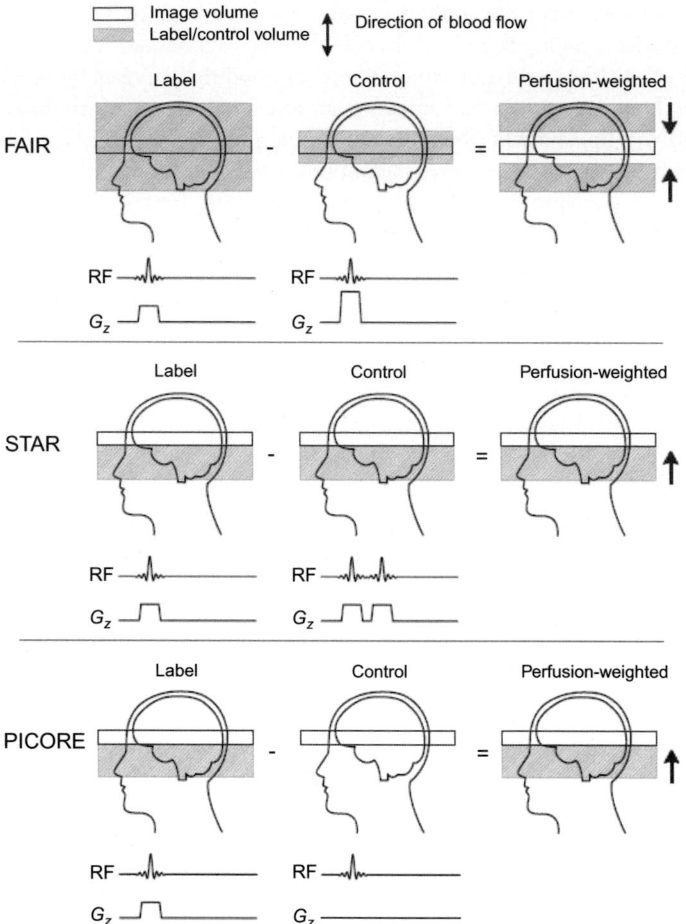

FIG. 12.2

Illustration of three common PASL labeling schemes for brain ASL: FAIR, STAR, and PICORE. The schematic shows the placement of the label and control volume for each scheme in *gray* and the imaging volume in *red*. Below each schematic is the associated pulse sequence diagram showing the RF pulse(s) and slice gradient(s) used for the label/control conditions. The final image indicates with *arrows* the directionality of inflowing blood contributing to the perfusion-weighted difference image. For the FAIR scheme, a nonselective and selective inversion slab is used for the control and label conditions respectively, resulting in the perfusion-weighted difference image being sensitive to bidirectional blood flow. In the STAR scheme, the label and control are applied below the imaging slice, with the control condition of fully-relaxed inflowing blood being generated from two sequential 180° pulses, resulting in unidirectional blood flow contributing to the perfusion-weighted difference image. For the PICORE scheme the inversion slab is applied below the imaging slice and the control pulse is off-resonance, resulting in unidirectional blood flow contributing to the perfusion-weighted difference image.

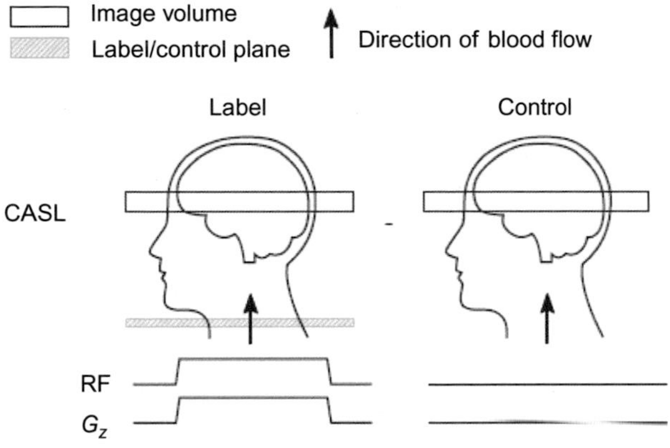

FIG. 12.3

Illustration of the continuous ASL (CASL) scheme for brain ASL. The schematic shows the placement of the label plane in *gray* and the imaging volume in *red*. The directionality of inflowing blood contributing to the perfusion-weighted difference image is shown by the *red arrow*. Below each schematic is the associated pulse sequence diagram showing the RF pulse(s) and slices selective gradient(s) used for the label/control conditions. Note the RF power is not matched between label and control conditions, leading to error-inducing MT effects.

absorption rate (SAR) and MT effects. Standard CASL uses a control condition of a labeling plane placed above the head to match MT effects, but MT is only matched for the single slice equidistant to the label and control plane. To overcome this potential source of error, a cosine-modulated RF pulse can be placed proximal to the brain for the control condition. This pulse un-inverts the labeled blood while matching the MT effects at the labeling plane. Alternatively, a small dedicated neck labeling coil can be used, which results in a negligible B_1 field in the imaging volume, removing MT effects and the need for a control condition. However, dedicated hardware is necessary for such local labeling, and the RF amplifiers on clinical scanners are often unable to produce long continuous RF B_1 fields.

12.3.3 Pseudo-continuous ASL

PCASL was introduced to exploit the high SNR of CASL while overcoming its high SAR and MT effects [28]. PCASL is the recommended ASL scheme of choice for brain studies by the ISMRM Perfusion Study Group and the European ASL in Dementia consortium [29]. PCASL mimics the flow-driven adiabatic inversion of blood spins as they pass through a selected plane. Rather than applying a long continuous RF pulse, PCASL applies a long train of short duration, evenly-spaced selective RF pulses in combination with a switching slice-selection gradient, as shown in Fig. 12.4. The recommended PCASL scheme for use in the brain employs 900 Hanning-shaped 20° RF pulses with an average B_1 amplitude (B_{1ave}) of 1.5 μT, each lasting 0.5 ms and applied every 1 ms over a 1.8 s labeling duration. Using such RF pulses, PCASL results in lower SAR, and RF-amplifier duty cycle

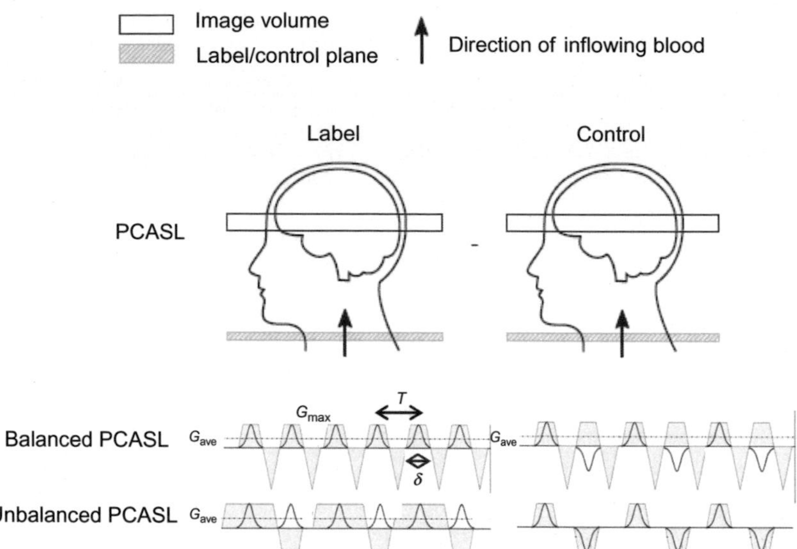

FIG. 12.4

Illustration of the pseudo-continuous (PCASL) scheme for brain ASL. The schematic shows the placement of the label and control planes in *gray* and the imaging volume in *red*. The directionality of inflowing blood contributing to the perfusion-weighted difference image is shown by the *red arrows*. Below each schematic is a segment of the pulse sequence for the balanced and unbalanced PCASL schemes, with the Hanning-shaped RF pulses shown in *black* and the and slice selective gradients shown in *gray*, where δ is the RF pulse duration, T is the RF pulse spacing, G_{max} is the amplitude of the slice selection gradient, and G_{ave} represents the net average gradient. For the label condition, the average B_1 (B_{1ave}) is nonzero, while for the control condition, the alternating polarity leads to a zero B_{1ave} such that the magnetization of the inflowing blood spins is noninverted. The RF power is matched between label and control conditions to ensure similar MT effects. Note the different gradient scheme between balanced and unbalanced PCASL.

requirements than CASL. The PCASL inversion can be considered as a steady-state free-precession (SSFP) pulse sequence. Ignoring relaxation effects, the steady-state longitudinal magnetization (M_z) of the repeated Hanning-shaped RF pulses in the PCASL scheme is described by:

$$M_z = \frac{\pm M_0 \sin\alpha \sin\frac{\varphi}{2}}{\sqrt{(1\text{-}\cos\alpha)^2 + \sin^2\alpha \sin^2\frac{\varphi}{2}}} \tag{12.1}$$

where α is the flip angle and φ is the phase shift experienced between the RF pulses in the PCASL pulse train. As shown in Fig. 12.4, in the gaps between successive RF pulses in the PCASL train, the slice selective gradient (G_{max}) is only partially rephased, resulting in a net average gradient (G_{ave}) being applied throughout the labeling duration. This average gradient acts to increase the phase of successive RF pulses in the PCASL train by $\varphi = \gamma G_{ave} TZ$, where γ is the gyromagnetic ratio, T is the RF pulse spacing, and Z is the position of the labeling plane with respect to the gradient isocenter. By setting the appropriate parameters in the PCASL labeling scheme, the inflowing blood is inverted as it flows through the labeling plane (typically a plane through the carotids for brain ASL). The control condition is achieved by alternating the phase of the RF pulses in the PCASL train by π radians, yielding a zero average B_1 while matching the MT effects to those of the label condition.

Two variants of PCASL exist, namely, balanced and unbalanced schemes [30] which differ in their gradient waveforms (shown in Fig. 12.4). In the balanced scheme, the net area under the gradients for both label and control conditions is equal to zero. This condition results in matched eddy current effects but increases sensitivity to off-resonance effects which can affect the inversion efficiency of the label, thereby decreasing the ASL perfusion-weighted difference signal. However, a balanced scheme facilitates vascular territory imaging in which individual vessels are selectively labeled [31, 32]. In the unbalanced scheme, the mean gradient for the label condition has a nonzero net area but is zero for the control condition. This provides greater robustness to off-resonance effects [33]; however, since different (unbalanced) gradients are used for the label and control condition, each condition experiences different eddy currents. An unbalanced PCASL is now recommended as the preferred scheme due to its robustness to off-resonance effects.

The recommended label duration for use in PCASL is 1.8 s, based on a trade-off between ASL signal (which increases with label duration determined by the T_1 relaxation time of the label) and diminishing returns for label durations longer than the T_1 of blood (increasing the repetition time [TR] and power deposition). The PCASL labeling plane should be positioned perpendicular to a relatively straight section of the feeding arteries. Position planning can be accomplished using an angiogram or anatomical landmarks. For the brain, the labeling plane is often placed 85 mm inferior to the AC-PC line, while for body ASL the labeling plane is placed through the aorta. It should be noted that off-resonance effects are likely to be more of an issue for PCASL in the abdomen, due to the proximity of the lungs and vertebral column. Similarly, off-resonance effects can be problematic at ultra-high field, where magnetic field variations are likely to be more pronounced; the minimization of such effects is an active area of research [34].

12.3.4 Velocity selective ASL

Velocity selective ASL (VSASL) [35] is an alternative strategy in which arterial blood water is labeled based on its velocity rather than its spatial position. Using velocity selective pulses, a velocity cutoff, V_c, is imposed with the resulting perfusion-weighted image theoretically containing only the spins whose velocity meets the labeling condition. Assuming that the velocities in the arterial tree are monotonically decreasing, the ASL signal is given by $f \cdot TI$, where f denotes the amount of perfusion and TI the labeling delay for that voxel.

12.4 Sampling strategies

To quantify perfusion, the ASL signal overtime must be sampled at a given delay(s) after labeling (see Section 12.8). Note that the terminology to describe this delay differs for PASL and CASL/PCASL schemes. For PASL, this time is characterized by the delay following the labeling RF pulse, termed the TI. For CASL/PCASL the timing is defined by both the PCASL labeling duration and the PLD, the time between the end of the PCASL labeling train and image acquisition. Several sampling schemes have been reported in the literature to collect ASL perfusion-weighted difference images to quantify perfusion; these are outlined in the following section.

12.4.1 Single-TI and multi-TI sampling

One approach to capture the dynamic ASL signal curve is to collect ASL data at a single TI or PLD, with the greatest ASL signal change seen at 1.5–2 s. After applying the label, a time TI/PLD is waited before the image is collected, and then a period termed the cycle duration (or TR) is allowed for complete washout of the labeled blood before repeating this process for the control condition (see Fig. 12.1). This collection of label/control images is repeated at the TI/PLD (typically with 20–30 averages) to provide sufficient SNR in the ASL perfusion-weighted difference image. In multi-TI sampling, this whole process is repeated across several different TIs/PLDs, but this can result in a long acquisition time if a large number of TIs/PLDs are collected. Example FAIR data collected at four TIs is shown in Fig. 12.5.

12.4.2 Multiphase or Look-Locker (LL) sampling strategy

There is a large amount of unused time between applying the label and the image readout when collecting data with a single TI/PLD at the peak of the ASL signal curve. A more efficient approach is to collect multiple image readouts at several different TIs/PLDs [36–39] following each labeling pulse within the cycle duration (TR) period, Fig. 12.5. This approach is termed multiphase ASL and is similar to the method developed by Look and Locker for T_1 mapping [40]. Since the blood label and tissue signal is modulated by each readout, the image acquisition uses low flip angles with each readout spaced to increase the steady-state longitudinal magnetization and thus ASL perfusion signal. A single-phase acquisition has higher SNR per shot compared to multiphase sampling, but the SNR per unit time is higher for multiphase sampling. Multiphase sampling allows a whole dataset to be acquired within 5 min with a temporal resolution between samples of $\sim$300 ms. However, quantification of perfusion using data collected using multiphase sampling requires detailed modeling to account for the complex effect on the labeled blood and tissue signal (See Section 12.9.3).

12.4.3 Time-encoded multi-PLD

For PCASL, an alternative to acquiring images at separate PLDs is time-encoded PCASL (te-PCASL), where the PLDs are encoded into the PCASL preparation [41]. In time-encoded PCASL the labeling duration is divided into multiple blocks during which the PCASL condition switches between label and control. Each acquired image thus has a varying contribution of a labeled signal accumulation from each block. The signal from each of the individual blocks can be extracted by the addition and subtraction of the acquired images according to the encoding pattern. Several variants of time-encoded PCASL exist including Hadamard encoding scheme, the "free-lunch" method,

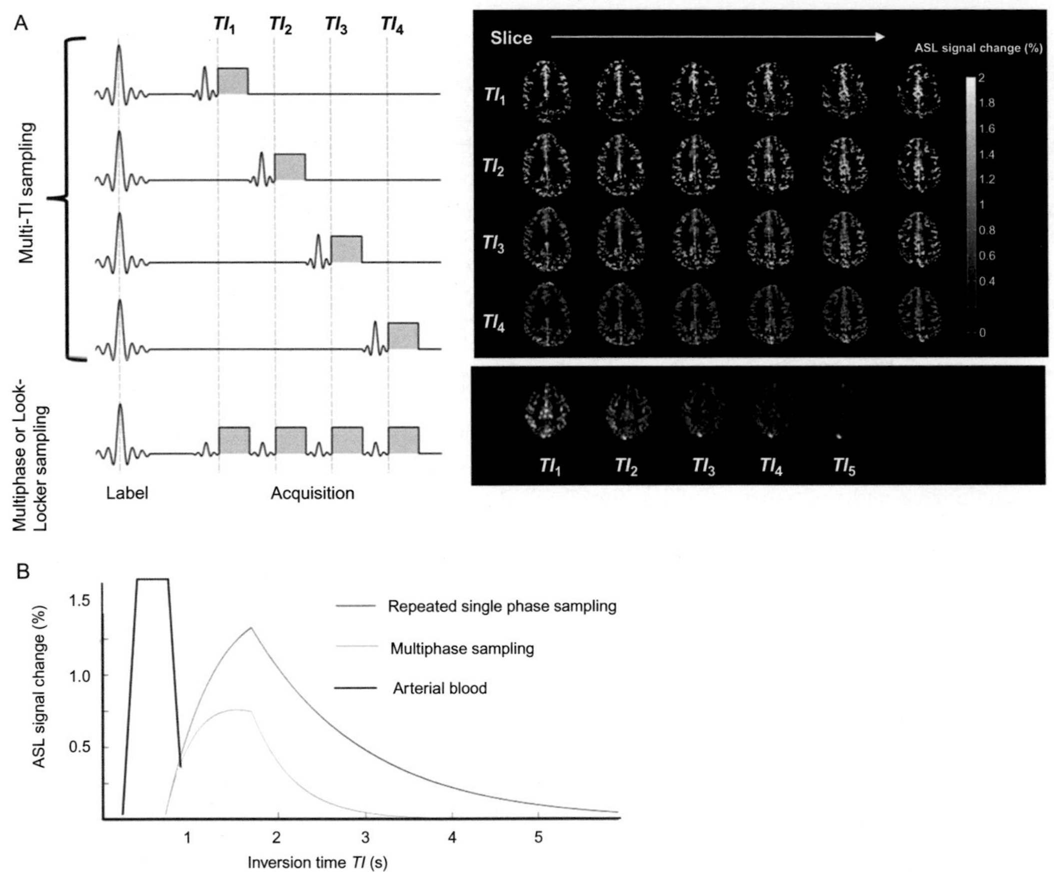

FIG. 12.5

Schematic showing multi-TI and multiphase or Look-Locker (LL) sampling for a PASL scheme. (A) Multi-TI sampling collecting single-TI data in sequential runs at several TIs. Multiphase or LL sampling collects all data time points (TI_1, TI_2, TI_3, TI_4, …) after a single labeling pulse. ASL images are shown with no vascular crushing. (B) The ASL signal change from the tissue for repeated single-TI sampling *(blue)* and multiphase or LL sampling *(green)*. Also shown is the arterial blood signal *(red)*. Note that multiphase or LL sampling ASL signal is lower than that measured with multi-TI sampling, but multiphase sampling results in higher SNR per unit time than repeated multi-TI sampling.

and "T_1-adjusted" designs, which are reviewed in van Osch et al. [42]. Time-encoded PCASL is more sensitive to motion than standard PCASL because it requires multiple label/control repeats to decode any of the images. Time-encoded PCASL has recently been combined with a multiphase readout to provide high temporal resolution ASL MRI with whole-brain coverage [43].

12.5 Readout scheme

The image readout schemes used for ASL experiments must be rapid to sample a complete image volume in a single shot at discrete times across the ASL signal curve. The most common single-shot acquisitions are 2D Echo-Planar Imaging (2D-EPI) and 3D-Gradient and Spin Echo (3D-GRASE) [44]. However, collecting multiple 2D acquisitions can lead to a variation in the actual TIs/PLD across each of the slices in the imaging volume, and longitudinal relaxation can result in a poor sampling of the ASL signal and poor background suppression in the later acquired slices of the imaging volume (see Section 12.6.2). Fig. 12.6 compares a 2D-EPI and 3D-EPI acquisition scheme to illustrate this effect. Multiband or Simultaneous MultiSlice (SMS) excitation can be used to accelerate the acquisition of 2D multislice readouts and thus decrease the variability in the TIs/PLDs and background suppression across slices [45–47]. For brain ASL, the ISMRM/EU ASL perfusion consensus paper [29] recommends the use of Cartesian or stack-of-spirals 3D readouts due to their superior SNR, uniform PLD across the entire volume, and compatibility with background suppression techniques. For abdominal ASL applications, such as in the kidney, SE-EPI is the preferred readout scheme for 2D single-slice and multislice imaging, with bSSFP and single-shot RARE considered adequate 2D single-slice alternatives, particularly for high spatial resolution acquisitions.

In general, large voxel sizes (3–4 mm in-plane and 4–8 mm through-plane) are used for ASL to improve the SNR of the technique; however, the use of large voxels can cause significant partial volume effects impacting the measured tissue perfusion. It is possible to reduce this type of error in postprocessing by correcting the ASL signal for partial volume effects (see Section 12.7.4).

Importantly, the perfusion-weighted difference image alone cannot be used for perfusion quantification; additional information must be collected in the same session using the same readout scheme. The perfusion-weighted image must be normalized to that of the equilibrium magnetization of blood ($M_{b,0}$). This correction can be performed by acquiring a proton density image from which the tissue magnetization, $M_{t,0}$, can be converted to arterial blood magnetization by accounting for the relative density of protons in tissue and blood, a value termed the partition coefficient λ (taken to be 0.9 mL/g for brain tissue and 0.8 mL/g for renal tissue). Further, blood and tissue T_1 values are used in the perfusion quantification, and these values should be based on the field strength at which the data are acquired. Alternatively, T_1 mapping can be performed as an additional sequence at the time of ASL data acquisition. Measurement of T_1 is especially important in cases when T_1 values are inhomogeneous due to pathology such as in tumors in the brain or in diseases where whole organ tissue T_1 values may change, such as the increased T_1 which occurs in kidney disease due to fibrosis.

12.6 Improving the signal-to-noise ratio of ASL data

ASL measurements typically suffer from low SNR, and different methods have been suggested to improve the SNR of perfusion measurements.

12.6.1 Pre- and postsaturation schemes

Saturation of the imaging volume just before and/or after the label and control pulses is recommended to minimize any residual label/control differences from MT and/or slice profile effects. This procedure is also useful as an initial step in the background suppression process, as described in the following section.

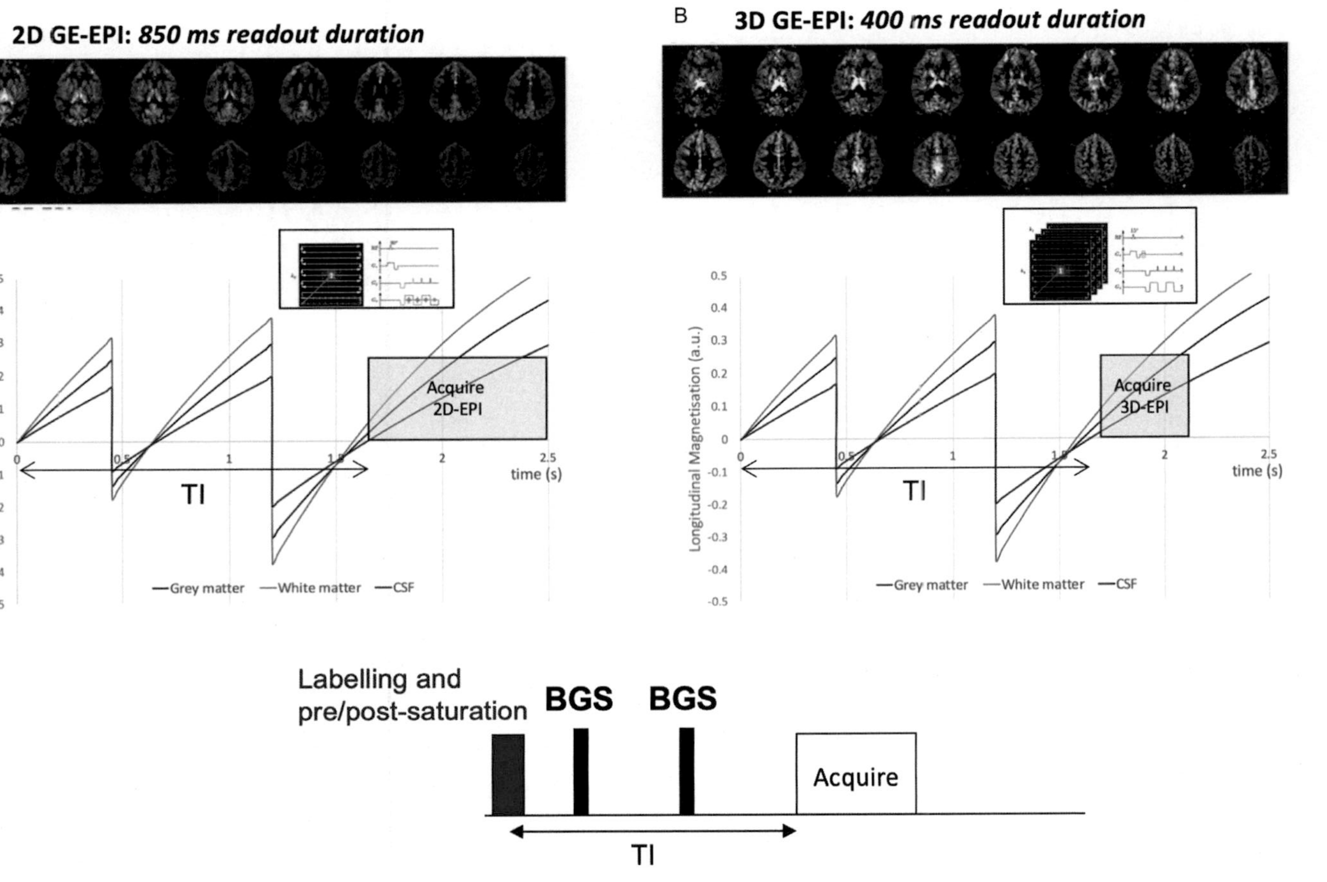

FIG. 12.6

Comparison of 2D-EPI and 3D-EPI acquisitions collected at 7T with a FAIR labeling scheme with a TI of 1700ms. (A) The 16 slice 2D-EPI acquisition has a readout duration of 850 ms, which results in considerable variation in the ASL signal across the slices of the imaging volume. Further, the simulation of the static tissue signal in the presence of pre-/postsaturation and two background suppression (BGS) pulses at 500 and 1200ms shows there will be considerably reduced background suppression of the later slices in the imaging volume. (B) In contrast, the 3D-EPI acquisition has a 400ms readout duration (with acceleration in two directions), and due to its 3D nature has a constant ASL signal across the slices and constant background suppression.

12.6.2 Background suppression

Ye et al. [48] suggested the use of background suppression inversion pulses to reduce static signal contamination not related to perfusion, and demonstrated that the use of background suppression substantially reduces the variance in the measured perfusion signal. Background suppression is accomplished by applying one or more inversion pulses to null the static signal in the acquired images (see Fig. 12.6) since only blood that has perfused into the tissue in the imaging slice is of interest. The timing of the background suppression pulses is dependent on the T_1 of the tissue of interest [49] and must be optimized for a given organ of interest and field strength. Fig. 12.7 shows the application of background suppression to the acquisition of kidney ASL data.

12.6.3 Vascular crushing

The desired outcome of ASL experiments is a measurement of tissue perfusion. However, the tissue perfusion signal can be contaminated by arterial blood, particularly at short TI/PLD times. The simplest approach to suppress arterial blood is to collect data at long TIs/PLD times such that the labeled water protons have moved from the blood into the tissue compartment. However, for transit time mapping, and more accurate perfusion quantification, "vascular crushing" or "flow sensitization" is required. The basic concept of vascular crushing is to eliminate the blood in the arterial compartment which travels faster than perfusing blood in the tissue compartment. This can be achieved by applying bipolar gradients with two lobes of equal duration and magnitude but opposite polarity before the image

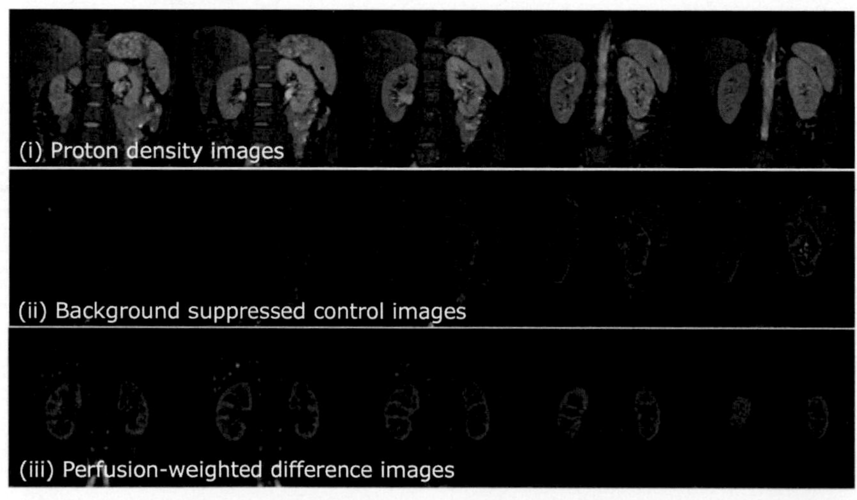

FIG. 12.7

Example of background suppression applied to kidney ASL data at 3T. Five coronal oblique slices through the kidneys shown to illustrate: (i) proton density images, (ii) background suppressed images using two background suppression pulses to null the static control and label signal (note recovery across the five slices), (iii) perfusion-weighted difference images.

readout. For spins moving at a constant velocity, these gradients induce a phase shift which is linearly proportional to velocity. By setting a cutoff velocity v_{enc} above which the spins will be dephased, only spins traveling slower than this velocity will be visible in the perfusion-weighted image. The v_{enc} is given by

$$v_{enc} = \frac{\pi}{\gamma G \delta \Delta}$$

where γ is the gyromagnetic ratio, δ is the duration of a gradient lobe, G is the strength of the gradient, and Δ is the distance between the center of the gradient lobes. A typical v_{enc} is 50 mm/s, which eliminates moving signals from arteries and arterioles while retaining signal from tissue (Fig. 12.8). It must be noted that the addition of the vascular crushing bipolar gradients increases the echo time of an EPI readout and is not possible for all readout schemes.

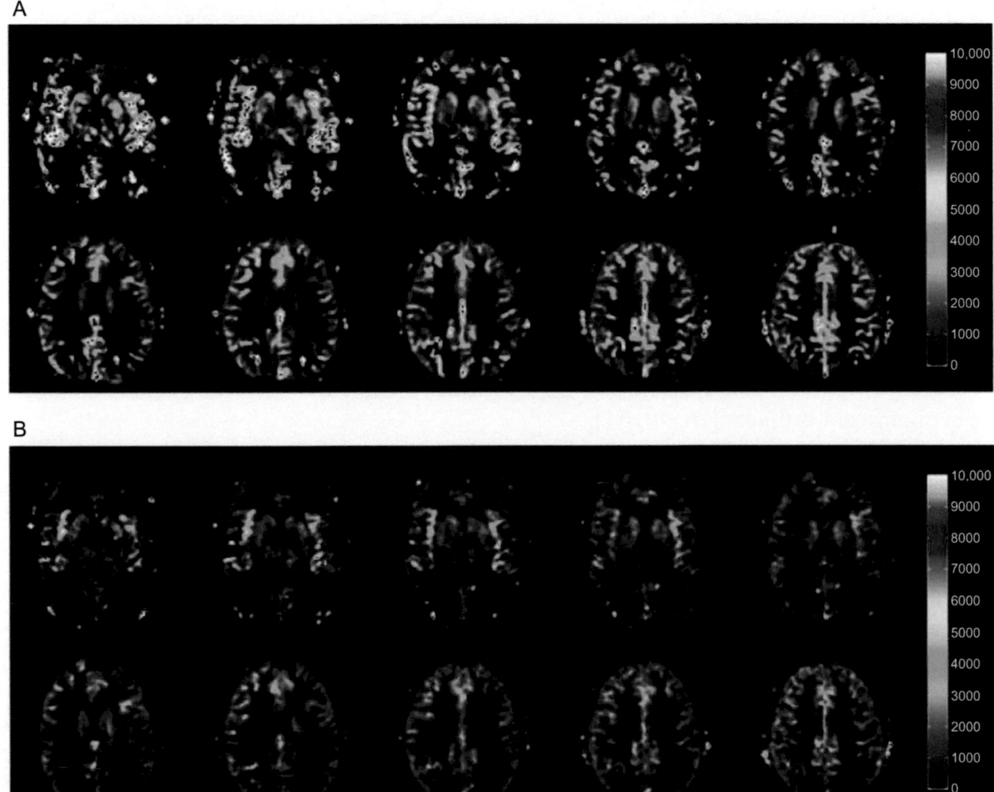

FIG. 12.8

Axial brain perfusion-weighted difference images collected using a FAIR ASL scheme with a 2D-EPI readout at an inversion time of 800 ms. Images are acquired (A) with no vascular crushing and thus show a large arterial blood contribution, and (B) with vascular crushing (v_{enc}) of 50 mm/s to suppress the arterial contribution.

12.7 Preprocessing ASL data

Once ASL data have been acquired, a perfusion-weighted image can be estimated using a simplistic analysis of computing the difference between the label and control images. However, it is common to practice to clean the data before perfusion quantification. This preprocessing may include alternative subtraction methods, motion correction, outlier detection, and partial volume correction, as described in the following section.

12.7.1 Subtraction methods

A typical ASL sequence collects several label and control images in an interleaved manner (Fig. 12.1). Perfusion-weighted images are generated from their pairwise subtraction and averaged to generate a single perfusion-weighted difference image. For studies in which the dynamic change in perfusion is of interest, for example, when using ASL to study brain function, either a running subtraction or "nearest neighbor" subtraction can be used. Running subtraction is susceptible to accompanying BOLD (blood oxygenation level-dependent) signal changes during a dynamic time course, while "nearest neighbor" or surround subtraction attempts to suppress BOLD weighting and noise variations by averaging the two labels surrounding the control image [29].

12.7.2 Motion correction

As ASL is a subtraction technique, any movement between the control and label image will lead to poor quality data. Typically motion artifacts appear as bright and dark edges where imperfect subtraction occurs, which can lead to focal or diffuse areas of false hypo- or hyper-perfusion. Pre-/postsaturation and background suppression methods can help to reduce artifacts due to motion. However, to ensure accurate perfusion estimates, motion correction to realign label-control repeats can be performed (Fig. 12.9). This is especially important in patient groups susceptible to involuntary head motion, such as Parkinson's or Huntington's disease, or for abdominal ASL where respiratory-induced motion can result in significant artifacts [26, 50, 51].

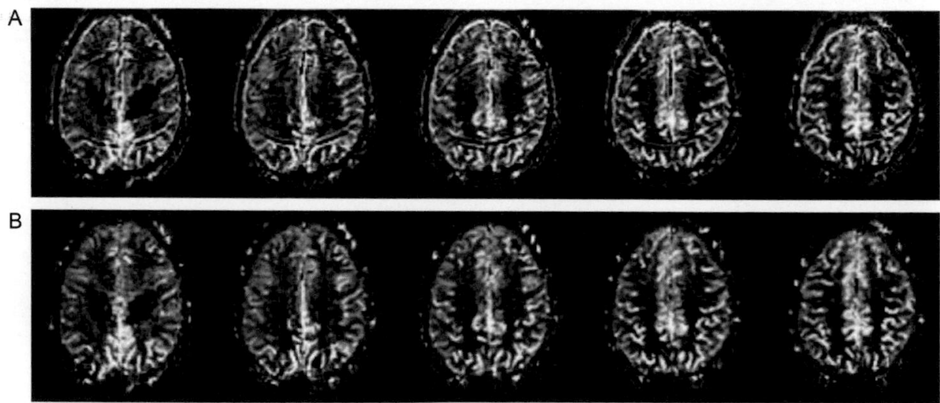

FIG. 12.9

ASL perfusion-weighted images (A) displaying head motion between label and control, where imperfect subtractions cause bright and dark edges and enhanced fat artifacts and (B) after motion correction.

12.7.3 Outlier detection

Since the ASL signal is low, an outlying label-control pair can significantly alter the sample mean and produce inaccurate perfusion estimates. Outliers are common artifacts arising from subtraction errors due to motion. One approach is to manually discard entire label-control pairs from the dataset [52]. Alternatively, outliers can be suppressed using a robust mean [53] by identifying outlying label-control pairs from the mean and standard deviation of the perfusion-weighted images. Alternatively, outliers can be removed from the ASL dataset using the Huber M-estimator [53] to suppress the effects of statistically abnormal values.

12.7.4 Partial volume effects

A perfusion map will often contain information arising from various tissue types due to partial volume effects. To estimate the perfusion of a given tissue type, an additional structural image is required to determine the fractional volume of each tissue type. For example, in the brain, both gray matter and white matter may contribute to the perfusion signal detected within a single voxel. Various methods have been proposed to separate the perfusion signals from the two tissues, but notable is the linear regression method of Asllani et al. [54]. This algorithm quantifies the perfusion-weighted by the fractional tissue volumes of the white matter/gray matter distribution in the voxel.

12.8 Modeling the ASL signal

To convert perfusion-weighted difference images (ΔM) into a quantitative perfusion map, a physiological model for ASL that combines perfusion kinetics and longitudinal relaxation is needed. The relationship between ΔM and tissue perfusion depends on the proton density of the tissue, the longitudinal relaxation time (T_1) of tissue and blood, the transit time between the label plane and the image volume of interest (Δt), and the duration of the labeled bolus (τ). There are two main approaches to model the ASL signal: compartmental models and tracer kinetics models. Compartmental models measure the concentration of labeled spins in the tissue of the difference image. These models use the modified Bloch equation to form a set of differential equations describing the rate of change of the labeled spins inside the tissue compartment due to both relaxation and exchange processes (see Section 12.8.1). Tracer kinetics models provide a mathematical description of the fraction of the original concentration of the labeled blood bolus that is still in the voxel at the time of the measurement (see Section 12.8.2).

12.8.1 Single compartment model using the modified Bloch equations

The first and simplest model to quantify perfusion was proposed for PASL. This model made several assumptions: (1) a single well-mixed compartment, termed the tissue compartment, (2) immediate arrival of the labeled blood into the tissue (and so zero transit time to the capillary bed Δt), (3) the idea that labeled water is a diffusible tracer that passes into the tissue as soon it arrives, and (4) equal tissue and arterial blood T_1 values [3, 55].

This approach was updated with more accurate modeling using the modified Bloch equation which includes flow-dependent delivery and clearance terms:

$$\frac{dM_t(t)}{dt} = \frac{M_{t,0} - M_t(t)}{T_{1t}} + f\left(M_b(t) - \frac{M_t(t)}{\lambda}\right)$$

where $M_{t,0}$ is the equilibrium tissue magnetization, $M_t(t)$ and $M_b(t)$ are the time-dependent tissue and arterial longitudinal magnetization, respectively, and T_1 is the longitudinal relaxation rate of the tissue.

λ is the tissue-blood partition coefficient, defined as the grams of water per gram of tissue divided by the grams of water per milliliter of blood, and is assumed to take a value of 0.9 mL/g. This modified Bloch equation can be solved for the three time periods: the time before the arrival of arterial blood: $0<t<\Delta t$; the time after the arrival of arterial blood but before end of label bolus: $\Delta t<t<\tau+\Delta t$; the time after the end of the labeled bolus: $t>\tau+\Delta t$, resulting in the solutions mentioned in the following section.

$$\Delta M_t(t)=0 \quad \text{for } t<\Delta t$$

$$\Delta M_t(t)=2\alpha M_{t,0}\frac{f}{\lambda\left(\frac{1}{T_{1app}}-\frac{1}{T_{1b}}\right)}e^{\frac{-\Delta t}{T_{1b}}}\left(e^{\frac{-(t-\Delta t)}{T_{1b}}}-e^{\frac{-(t-\Delta t)}{T_{1app}}}\right) \quad \text{for } \Delta t\leq t\leq \tau+\Delta t$$

$$\Delta M_t(t)=2\alpha M_{t,0}\frac{f}{\lambda\left(\frac{1}{T_{1app}}-\frac{1}{T_{1b}}\right)}e^{\frac{-\Delta t}{T_{1b}}}\left(e^{\frac{-\tau}{T_{1b}}}-e^{\frac{-\tau}{T_{1app}}}\right)e^{\frac{-(t-\Delta t-\tau)}{T_{1app}}} \quad \text{for } t>\tau+\Delta t$$

where α is the labeling efficiency (taken to be 1 for ideal inversion) and $\frac{1}{T_{1app}}=\frac{1}{T_{1\text{tissue}}}+\frac{f}{\lambda}$. This model generates the ASL signal curve shown in Fig. 12.10. By fitting each voxel of the normalized average perfusion-weighted image ($\Delta M_t(t)$) to this curve, maps of perfusion f, arterial transit time Δt, and label bolus τ can be generated using assumed values of α, λ, T_{1b}, and measured values from additional scans for T_{1t} and $M_{t,0}$ (see Section 12.5).

12.8.2 General kinetic model

Alternatively, it is possible to calculate perfusion using a tracer kinetics model, such as the general kinetic model as proposed by Buxton et al. [56], in which a bolus of labeled spins traveling through the vasculature is assumed. The difference in magnetization between the label and control images (ΔM) is described by the convolution integral:

$$\Delta M(t)=2M_{b,0}\cdot f\cdot \int_0^t c(\tau)\cdot r(t-\tau)\cdot m(t-\tau)d\tau$$

where $M_{b,0}$ is the magnetization at equilibrium in an arterial blood voxel, $c(\tau)$ is the normalized arterial input function (AIF) describing the arterial magnetization arriving at the voxel, $r(t\text{-}\tau)$ is the residual function describing the fraction of the labeled protons in the voxel, and $m(t\text{-}\tau)$ is the magnetization relaxation function describing the effect of longitudinal relaxation. The label bolus takes time Δt to reach the voxel, which it passes through for a duration of τ (Fig. 12.11).

The general kinetic model can be solved for a PASL scheme using:

$$c(t)=\begin{cases}0 & t<\Delta t\\ \alpha e^{-\frac{t}{T_{1b}}} & \Delta t\leq t\leq \tau+\Delta t\\ 0 & t>\tau+\Delta t\end{cases}$$

$$r(t)=e^{-\frac{f}{\lambda}t}$$

$$m(t)=e^{-\frac{t}{T_1}}$$

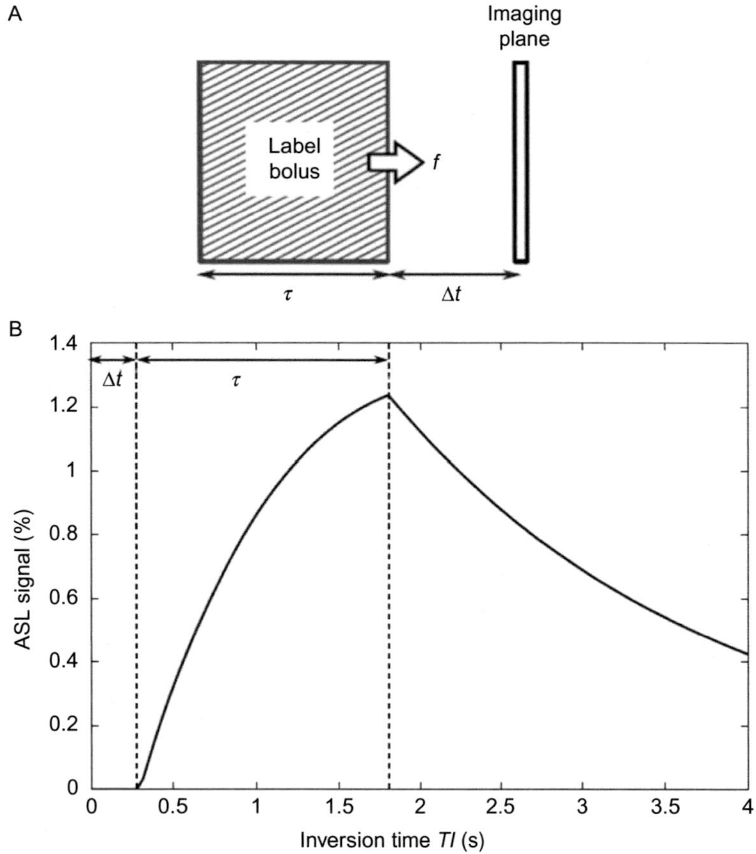

FIG. 12.10

(A) Illustration for a PASL scheme of labeled blood perfusing into the imaging plane after an arterial transit time Δt with the label bolus duration of τ. (B) Simulation of the resulting PASL signal assuming tissue perfusion of the gray matter of 60 mL/100 g/min, tissue T_1 of 1.65 s, blood T_1 of 1.45 s, arterial arrival time $\Delta t = 0.3$ s, and label bolus duration $\tau = 1.5$ s. Note the ASL signal change is expressed here as a percentage change.

Solving the convolution integral yields

$$\Delta M(t) = \begin{cases} 0 & t < \Delta t \\ -\dfrac{2\alpha M_{b,0}}{\delta R} f e^{-R_{1b}t}\left(1 - e^{\delta R(t-\Delta t)}\right) & \Delta t \le t \le \tau + \Delta t \\ -\dfrac{2\alpha M_{b,0}}{\delta R} f e^{-R_{1b}t} e^{\delta R(t-\Delta t)}\left(e^{-\delta R\tau} - 1\right) & t > \tau + \Delta t \end{cases}$$

for which

$$R_{1t} = \frac{1}{T_{1t}};\ R_{1b} = \frac{1}{T_{1b}};\ R_{1app} = \frac{1}{T_{1app}} = R_{1t} + \frac{f}{\lambda};\ \delta R = R_{1b} - R_{1app}$$

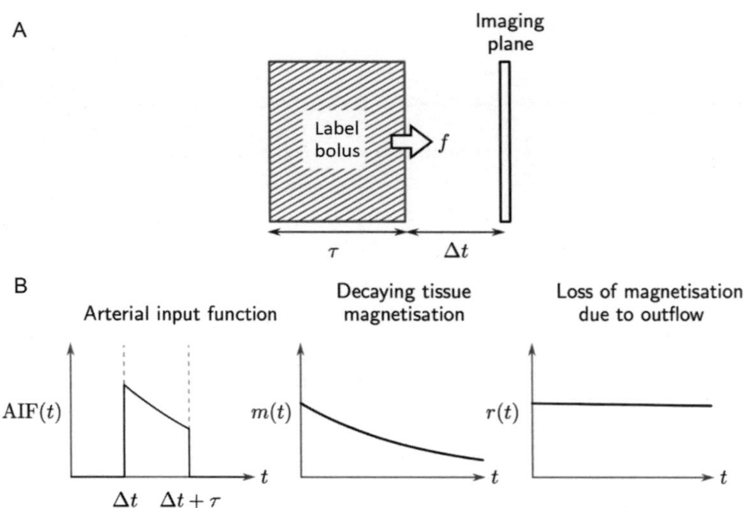

FIG. 12.11

A schematic of the general kinetic model proposed by Buxton et al. for an (A) PASL scheme with labeled blood perfusing into the imaging plane after an arterial transit time Δt for a label bolus duration of τ, and (B) showing the resultant arterial input function, decaying tissue magnetization and loss of magnetization due to outflow.

This solution is equivalent to that of solving the differential equations of the single-compartment model (Section 12.8.1) and results in the ASL signal curve shown in Fig. 12.10. Again, by fitting each voxel of the normalized average PASL perfusion-weighted image ($\Delta M_t(t)$) to this PASL signal curve, maps of perfusion f, arterial transit time Δt, and label bolus τ can be generated using assumed values of α, λ, T_{1b}, and measured values from additional scans for T_{1t}, and $M_{b,0}$ in the fit (see Section 12.5).

The general kinetic model for a PCASL scheme can be expressed using:

$$c(t) = \begin{cases} 0 & t < \Delta t \\ \alpha e^{-\frac{\Delta t}{T_{1b}}} & \Delta t \leq t \leq \tau + \Delta t \\ 0 & t > \tau + \Delta t \end{cases}$$

$$r(t) = e^{-\frac{f}{\lambda}t}$$

$$m(t) = e^{-\frac{t}{T_1}}$$

Solving the convolution integral yields the following solution of the PCASL signal curve.

$$\Delta M(t) = \begin{cases} 0 & t < \Delta t \\ \dfrac{2\alpha M_{b,0}}{R_{1app}} f e^{-R_{1b}\Delta t}\left(1 - e^{-R_{1app}(t-\Delta t)}\right) & \Delta t \leq t \leq \tau + \Delta t \\ \dfrac{2\alpha M_{b,0}}{R_{1app}} f e^{-R_{1b}\Delta t} e^{-R_{1app}(t-(\Delta t+\tau))}\left(1 - e^{-R_{1app}\tau}\right) & t > \tau + \Delta t \end{cases}$$

12.9 Perfusion quantification

12.9.1 Perfusion quantification using data collected at a single TI/PLD

The simplest method to compute a perfusion map is to collect a perfusion-weighted image at only a single TI/PLD time [29], allowing many averages to be acquired within a short scan time.

However, if the TI/PLD is shorter than $\tau+\Delta t$, perfusion can be severely underestimated. It should be noted that the use of longer TI/PLDs reduces the risk of such errors, but this must be balanced against the loss of label through T_1 decay and increased noise because fewer averages are collected in given scan time.

To obtain a quantitative value of perfusion using a single TI acquisition, the time duration of the labeled bolus must be known. PASL creates a bolus of labeled spins of unknown and relatively short temporal width, which can lead to errors in the perfusion measurement. Another single-time point approach for use in combination with PASL schemes is QUIPSS-II (quantitative imaging of perfusion using a single subtraction version II) [57]. This approach involves the application of a slab selective saturation pulse to cutoff the labeled bolus a certain period, removing the tail end of the labeled bolus. An alternative is to use the Q2TIPS scheme (QUIPSS II with Thin-slice TI1 Periodic Saturation [58]), in which saturation pulses are applied at time TI_1 after the inversion pulse to destroy the tail end of the labeled bolus, thus effectively setting the bolus duration to be equal to TI_1.

If the single measurement is made following the complete entry of the labeled bolus into the tissue voxel (i.e., when $t>\tau+\Delta t$ in Fig. 12.10), then the signal is no longer dependent on arrival time and perfusion f can be estimated from

$$f=\frac{6000\cdot\lambda\cdot\Delta M_t\cdot e^{\frac{TI}{T_{1b}}}}{2\cdot\alpha\cdot TI\cdot M_{t,0}}$$

To scale the signal intensity of the subtracted ASL images (ΔM_t) to absolute perfusion units, the signal intensity of fully relaxed blood spins is needed. This is computed by scaling a separately acquired proton density image ($M_{t,0}$) on a voxel-by-voxel basis by λ (the signal intensity of tissue to that of blood), while an assumed T_1 value of blood (T_{1b}) is used. The factor α is the labeling efficiency, and the factor of 6000 converts the units from mL/g/s to mL/100 g/min.

12.9.2 Perfusion quantification using multi-TI/PLD data

If multiple ASL images are collected serially at a range of TIs/PLDs values, these ASL images (ΔM_t) at each TI/PLD can be used in the least-squares model fit to the modified Bloch equations (see Section 12.8.1) or general kinetic model (see Section 12.8.2). Multi TI/PLD data allows the estimation of both perfusion f and transit time Δt, which itself may reflect important aspects of the underlying physiology. Further, as the bolus duration τ can also be a free parameter in such a model, problems associated with variable bolus duration time can be alleviated. Alternatively, Bayesian inference methods can be used for kinetic-model inversion such as BASIL (Bayesian Inference for Arterial Spin Labeling MRI) in the FMRIB Software Library (FSL) [59]. Fig. 12.12 shows example perfusion maps generated from a multi-TI scheme in healthy subjects and Alzheimer's disease patients, for whom perfusion is reduced and transit time is increased.

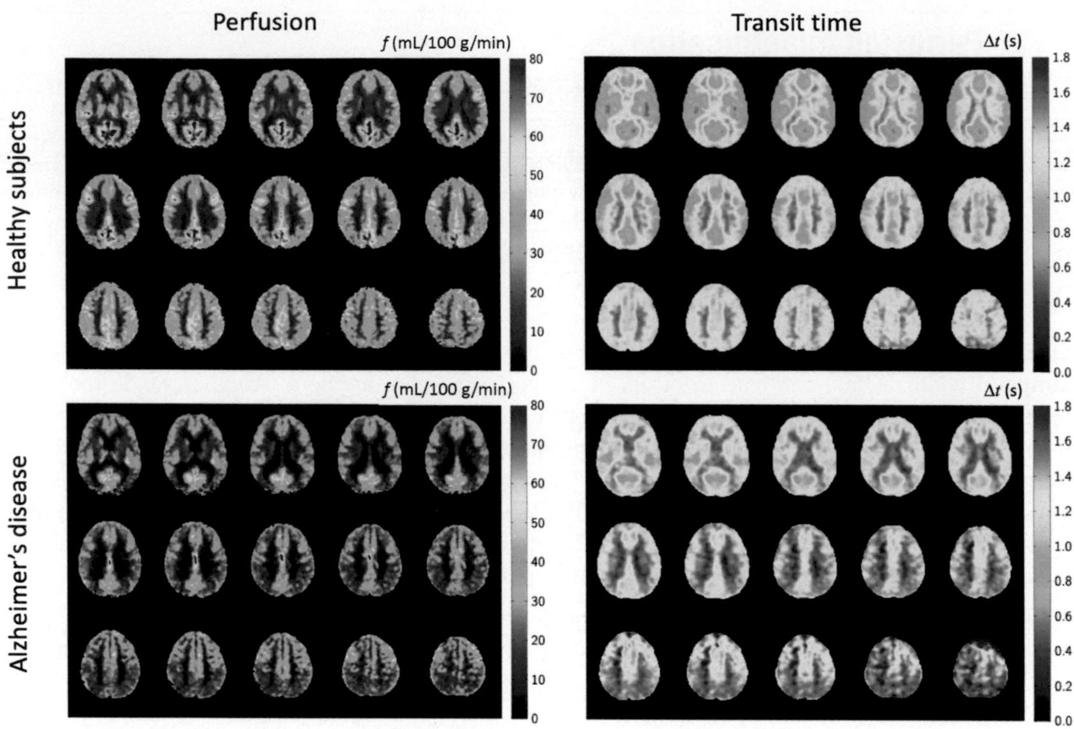

FIG. 12.12

Example perfusion f and transit time Δt maps in Alzheimer's disease patients (67 ± 6 years) and age-matched healthy subjects (64 ± 8 years) collected at 7T using a multi-TI (400, 700, 1000, 1300, 1700, and 2000 ms) FAIR acquisition with 3 mm isotropic 2D GE-EPI readout with vascular crushing. Regional variation in f and Δt can be seen across the brain, reflecting the different pathways that the labeled bolus follows. Note reduced perfusion and increased transit time in the AD patients.

The use of multiple TIs/PLDs constitutes an experimental design problem to find the optimal TIs/PLDs, and several studies have attempted to address this [60, 61]. If flow suppression is not applied to the multi-TI/PLD data, there will be a significant signal from labeled arterial blood in the region of major vessels at short TIs/PLDs (<1 s). This can be accounted for by adding a second arterial component in the analysis, allowing the arterial cerebral blood volume (aCBV) to be computed.

12.9.3 Perfusion quantification using multiphase or Look-Locker sampling

In the case where a multiphase sampling scheme is used to collect several TI/PLD data points in a given cycle duration/TR (see Fig. 12.5), a more intricate three-compartment modeling approach can be used (Fig. 12.13). Such a model includes compartment 1—arterial blood located outside of the imaging volume; compartment 2—arterial blood inside the imaging volume; compartment 3—blood in the capillary bed in exchange with the tissue. This three-compartment model [37] allows step-wise temporal analysis of the evolution of the arterial blood and tissue magnetization. The time it takes for

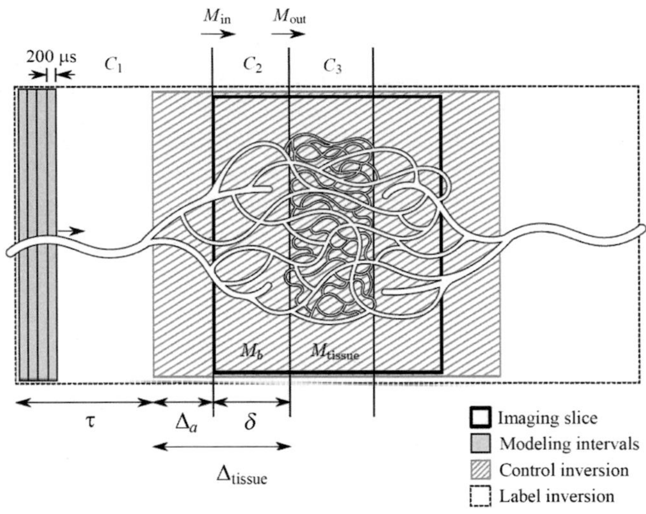

FIG. 12.13

A three-compartment model used to quantify perfusion in multiphase FAIR ASL data. Compartment 1 (C_1)—arterial blood located outside of the imaging volume, the leading edge of which has an arrival time to the imaging slice (transit time) of Δ_a; Compartment 2 (C_2)—arterial blood inside the imaging volume traversing the arterioles in time δ; Compartment 3 (C_3)—blood which arrives at the capillary bed after a transit time Δ_{tissue} and then exchanges with the tissue.

the labeled blood to reach the imaging slice, the effect of the readout pulses on both the arteriolar blood and the tissue magnetization, and spin history effects of incomplete recovery of blood and tissue magnetization at short repetition times can all be considered to yield more accurate voxel-wise measurements of tissue perfusion by fitting the perfusion-weighted images at each time point of this model.

12.9.4 Comparison of methods of perfusion quantification

The use of a single-TI acquisition for perfusion quantification has the advantage of a short scan duration but has some limitations. Single-TI quantification accounts for the unknown transit time Δt by sufficiently delaying the acquisition time point, but the reduced sensitivity to Δt can be compromised whenever transit times are unexpectedly long (for instance in many pathological conditions). Besides, the long TI/PLD required to account for prolonged transit times Δt can also significantly limit the SNR of perfusion-weighted difference images.

Multi-TI acquisitions measure the ASL signal difference time course, solving the problem of single-TI methods described earlier. However, these data are more time-consuming to collect and must be fit to a model for perfusion quantification. The two ASL models described earlier in Section 12.8 allow estimation of perfusion f, transit time Δt, and bolus duration τ. In both ASL signal models, sudden and simultaneous arrival of labeled blood into the imaged region is assumed (uniform plug flow), where the leading and the trailing edge of the labeled blood bolus takes the form of a sharp-edge step function. However, using the general kinetic model, it is possible to generate a more realistic arrival of the label by replacing $c(\tau)$ with a smoother input function that accounts for the distributed nature of the arrival time as the labeled blood traverses pathways of varying lengths and at different speeds.

Multiphase data provides an alternative to the multi-TI method to sample the ASL signal curve and has the advantage that it can be collected in a short time, making it compatible with clinical workflow. However, multiphase perfusion quantification has an extra level of complexity due to the need to model multiple compartments and how the readout excitation in the LL acquisition alters the signal evolution.

12.10 Applications of ASL

ASL has been applied mostly in the field of neuroscience and has begun to be used for clinical brain imaging, as outlined in [62]. Wolf and Detre [63] highlighted the benefit of perfusion mapping with ASL in conditions such as stroke, vascular malformations, tumors of the central nervous system, epilepsy, and in the study of degenerative diseases such as Alzheimer's disease, as shown in Fig. 12.12. Rather than form a single perfusion map, it is also possible to study brain activation by analyzing the ASL perfusion time course during a task to directly assess the variations in perfusion that accompany neuronal activation [64].

ASL is now being more widely deployed outside the brain, with a large number of studies applying ASL in the kidney, as shown in Fig. 12.14, an organ in which measuring perfusion is desirable due to the need to limit gadolinium-based contrast agents in subjects with renal impairment. Given recent technical developments, it is now possible to apply ASL to a wide range of other applications, including a perfusion of organs with low perfusions, such as the prostate [65], pancreas [14, 66, 67], as well as the liver [6–9], and peripheral muscle [10–12].

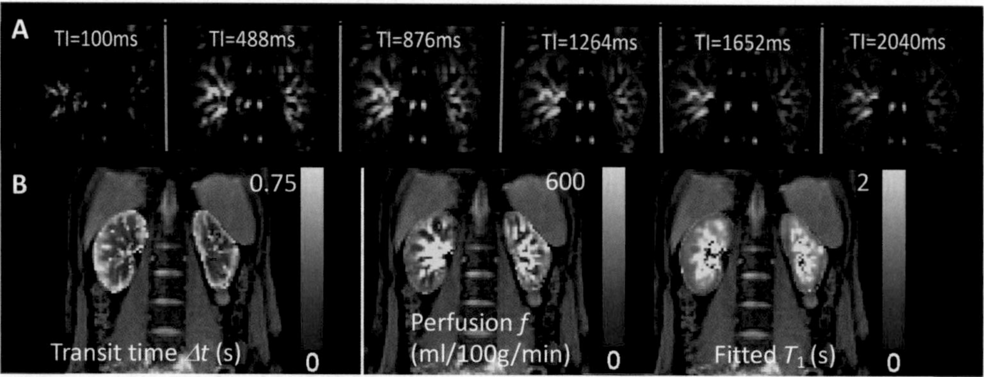

FIG. 12.14

(A) Example multiphase images collected using FAIR ASL in the kidney. (B) Resultant transit time and perfusion maps generated from the perfusion-weighted difference images and T_1 maps derived from the control images.

12.11 Summary

In summary, ASL is a noninvasive method to quantitatively map tissue perfusion. There exist several ASL labeling methods and associated acronyms, and this chapter includes an overview of the most common methods, sampling strategies, and image readouts. The steps involved in the quantification of perfusion maps from ASL data, including preprocessing methods and kinetic modeling are introduced. This chapter provides an outline for the reader to make a more informed choice in terms of acquisition and analysis when performing ASL studies in their organ of choice.

References

[1] Alsop DC, Detre JA. Multisection cerebral blood flow MR imaging with continuous arterial spin labeling. Radiology 1998;208:410–6.

[2] Detre JA, Alsop DC, Vives LR, et al. Noninvasive MRI evaluation of cerebral blood flow in cerebrovascular disease. Neurology 1998;50:633–41.

[3] Williams DS, Detre JA, Leigh JS, et al. Magnetic resonance imaging of perfusion using spin inversion of arterial water. Proc Natl Acad Sci U S A 1992;89:212–6.

[4] Selby NM, Blankestijn PJ, Boor P, et al. Magnetic resonance imaging biomarkers for chronic kidney disease: a position paper from the European Cooperation in Science and Technology Action PARENCHIMA. Nephrol Dial Transplant 2018;33:ii4–ii14.

[5] Odudu A, Nery F, Harteveld AA, et al. Arterial spin labelling MRI to measure renal perfusion: a systematic review and statement paper. Nephrol Dial Transplant 2018;33:ii15–21.

[6] Schalkx HJ, Petersen ET, Peters NH, et al. Arterial and portal venous liver perfusion using selective spin labelling MRI. Eur Radiol 2015;25:1529–40.

[7] Ramasawmy R, Campbell-Washburn AE, Wells JA, et al. Hepatic arterial spin labelling MRI: an initial evaluation in mice. NMR Biomed 2015;28:272–80.

[8] Palaniyappan N, Cox E, Bradley C, et al. Non-invasive assessment of portal hypertension using quantitative magnetic resonance imaging. J Hepatol 2016;65:1131–9.

[9] Bradley CR, Cox EF, Scott RA, et al. Multi-organ assessment of compensated cirrhosis patients using quantitative magnetic resonance imaging. J Hepatol 2018;69:1015–24.

[10] Schewzow K, Fiedler GB, Meyerspeer M, et al. Dynamic ASL and T2-weighted MRI in exercising calf muscle at 7 T: a feasibility study. Magn Reson Med 2015;73:1190–5.

[11] Fulford J, Vanhatalo A. Reliability of arterial spin labelling measurements of perfusion within the quadriceps during steady-state exercise. Eur J Sport Sci 2016;16:80–7.

[12] Decorte N, Buehler T, Caldas de Almeida Araujo E, et al. Noninvasive estimation of oxygen consumption in human calf muscle through combined NMR measurements of ASL perfusion and T(2) oxymetry. J Vasc Res 2014;51:360–8.

[13] Hirshberg B, Qiu M, Cali AM, et al. Pancreatic perfusion of healthy individuals and type 1 diabetic patients as assessed by magnetic resonance perfusion imaging. Diabetologia 2009;52:1561–5.

[14] Cox EF, Smith JK, Chowdhury AH, et al. Temporal assessment of pancreatic blood flow and perfusion following secretin stimulation using noninvasive MRI. J Magn Reson Imaging 2015;42:1233–40.

[15] Yoon AJ, Do HP, Cen S, et al. Assessment of segmental myocardial blood flow and myocardial perfusion reserve by adenosine-stress myocardial arterial spin labeling perfusion imaging. J Magn Reson Imaging 2017;46:413–20.

[16] Kober F, Jao T, Troalen T, et al. Myocardial arterial spin labeling. J Cardiovasc Magn Reson 2016;18:22.

[17] Jao TR, Nayak KS. Demonstration of velocity selective myocardial arterial spin labeling perfusion imaging in humans. Magn Reson Med 2018;80:272–8.

[18] Dongworth RK, Campbell-Washburn AE, Cabrera-Fuentes HA, et al. Quantifying the area-at-risk of myocardial infarction in-vivo using arterial spin labeling cardiac magnetic resonance. Sci Rep 2017;7:2271.

[19] Buchanan C, Mohammed A, Cox E, et al. Intradialytic cardiac magnetic resonance imaging to assess cardiovascular responses in a short-term trial of hemodiafiltration and hemodialysis. J Am Soc Nephrol 2017;28:1269–77.

[20] Edelman RR, Siewert B, Darby DG, et al. Qualitative mapping of cerebral blood flow and functional localization with echo-planar MR imaging and signal targeting with alternating radio frequency. Radiology 1994;192:513–20.

[21] Kim SG. Quantification of relative cerebral blood flow change by flow-sensitive alternating inversion recovery (FAIR) technique: application to functional mapping. Magn Reson Med 1995;34:293–301.

[22] Kwong KK, Chesler DA, Weisskoff RM, et al. MR perfusion studies with T1-weighted echo planar imaging. Magn Reson Med 1995;34:878–87.

[23] Wu WC, Jiang SF, Yang SC, et al. Pseudocontinuous arterial spin labeling perfusion magnetic resonance imaging—a normative study of reproducibility in the human brain. NeuroImage 2011;56:1244–50.

[24] Buchanan CE, Cox EF, Francis ST. Evaluation of 2D imaging schemes for pulsed arterial spin labeling of the human kidney cortex. Diagnostics (Basel) 2018;8:43.

[25] Gutjahr FT, Gunster SM, Kampf T, et al. MRI-based quantification of renal perfusion in mice: improving sensitivity and stability in FAIR ASL. Z Med Phys 2017;27:334–9.

[26] Nery F, De Vita E, Clark CA, et al. Robust kidney perfusion mapping in pediatric chronic kidney disease using single-shot 3D-GRASE ASL with optimized retrospective motion correction. Magn Reson Med 2019;81:2972–84.

[27] Wong EC, Buxton RB, Frank LR. Implementation of quantitative perfusion imaging techniques for functional brain mapping using pulsed arterial spin labeling. NMR Biomed 1997;10:237–49.

[28] Dai W, Garcia D, de Bazelaire C, et al. Continuous flow-driven inversion for arterial spin labeling using pulsed radio frequency and gradient fields. Magn Reson Med 2008;60:1488–97.

[29] Alsop DC, Detre JA, Golay X, et al. Recommended implementation of arterial spin-labeled perfusion MRI for clinical applications: a consensus of the ISMRM perfusion study group and the European consortium for ASL in dementia. Magn Reson Med 2015;73:102–16.

[30] Wu WC, Fernandez-Seara M, Detre JA, et al. A theoretical and experimental investigation of the tagging efficiency of pseudocontinuous arterial spin labeling. Magn Reson Med 2007;58:1020–7.

[31] Berry ESK, Jezzard P, Okell TW. Off-resonance correction for pseudo-continuous arterial spin labeling using the optimized encoding scheme. NeuroImage 2019;199:304–12.

[32] Helle M, Norris DG, Rufer S, et al. Superselective pseudocontinuous arterial spin labeling. Magn Reson Med 2010;64:777–86.

[33] Zhao L, Vidorreta M, Soman S, et al. Improving the robustness of pseudo-continuous arterial spin labeling to off-resonance and pulsatile flow velocity. Magn Reson Med 2017;78:1342–51.

[34] Gardener AG, Gowland PA, Francis ST. Implementation of quantitative perfusion imaging using pulsed arterial spin labeling at ultra-high field. Magn Reson Med 2009;61:874–82.

[35] Wong EC, Cronin M, Wu WC, et al. Velocity-selective arterial spin labeling. Magn Reson Med 2006;55:1334–41.

[36] Brookes MJ, Morris PG, Gowland PA, et al. Noninvasive measurement of arterial cerebral blood volume using look-locker EPI and arterial spin labeling. Magn Reson Med 2007;58:41–54.

[37] Francis ST, Bowtell R, Gowland PA. Modeling and optimization of look-locker spin labeling for measuring perfusion and transit time changes in activation studies taking into account arterial blood volume. Magn Reson Med 2008;59:316–25.

[38] Francis ST, Pears JA, Butterworth S, et al. Measuring the change in CBV upon cortical activation with high temporal resolution using look-locker EPI and Gd-DTPA. Magn Reson Med 2003;50:483–92.

[39] Gunther M, Bock M, Schad LR. Arterial spin labeling in combination with a look-locker sampling strategy: inflow turbo-sampling EPI-FAIR (ITS-FAIR). Magn Reson Med 2001;46:974–84.

[40] Look DC, DR. L. Time saving in measurement of NMR and EPR relaxation times. Rev Sci Instrum 1970;41:250–1.

[41] Teeuwisse WM, Schmid S, Ghariq E, et al. Time-encoded pseudocontinuous arterial spin labeling: basic properties and timing strategies for human applications. Magn Reson Med 2014;72:1712–22.

[42] van Osch MJ, Teeuwisse WM, Chen Z, et al. Advances in arterial spin labelling MRI methods for measuring perfusion and collateral flow. J Cereb Blood Flow Metab 2018;38:1461–80.

[43] van der Plas MCE, Teeuwisse WM, Schmid S, et al. High temporal resolution arterial spin labeling MRI with whole-brain coverage by combining time-encoding with look-locker and simultaneous multi-slice imaging. Magn Reson Med 2019;81:3734–44.

[44] Fernandez-Seara MA, Wang Z, Wang J, et al. Continuous arterial spin labeling perfusion measurements using single shot 3D GRASE at 3 T. Magn Reson Med 2005;54:1241–7.

[45] Feinberg DA, Beckett A, Chen L. Arterial spin labeling with simultaneous multi-slice echo planar imaging. Magn Reson Med 2013;70:1500–6.

[46] Kim T, Shin W, Zhao T, et al. Whole brain perfusion measurements using arterial spin labeling with multiband acquisition. Magn Reson Med 2013;70:1653–61.

[47] Lee Y, Kim T. Assessment of hypertensive cerebrovascular alterations with multiband look-locker arterial spin labeling. J Magn Reson Imaging 2018;47:663–72.

[48] Ye FQ, Frank JA, Weinberger DR, et al. Noise reduction in 3D perfusion imaging by attenuating the static signal in arterial spin tagging (ASSIST). Magn Reson Med 2000;44:92–100.

[49] Garcia DM, Duhamel G, Alsop DC. Efficiency of inversion pulses for background suppressed arterial spin labeling. Magn Reson Med 2005;54:366–72.

[50] Bones IK, Harteveld AA, Franklin SL, et al. Enabling free-breathing background suppressed renal pCASL using fat imaging and retrospective motion correction. Magn Reson Med 2019;82:276–88.

[51] Taso M, Guidon A, Alsop DC. Influence of background suppression and retrospective realignment on free-breathing renal perfusion measurement using pseudo-continuous ASL. Magn Reson Med 2019;81:2439–49.

[52] Tan H, Maldjian JA, Pollock JM, et al. A fast, effective filtering method for improving clinical pulsed arterial spin labeling MRI. J Magn Reson Imaging 2009;29:1134–9.

[53] Maumet C, Maurel P, Ferre JC, et al. Robust estimation of the cerebral blood flow in arterial spin labelling. Magn Reson Imaging 2014;32:497–504.

[54] Asllani I, Borogovac A, Brown TR. Regression algorithm correcting for partial volume effects in arterial spin labeling MRI. Magn Reson Med 2008;60:1362–71.

[55] Detre JA, Leigh JS, Williams DS, et al. Perfusion imaging. Magn Reson Med 1992;23:37–45.

[56] Buxton RB, Frank LR, Wong EC, et al. A general kinetic model for quantitative perfusion imaging with arterial spin labeling. Magn Reson Med 1998;40:383–96.

[57] Wong EC, Buxton RB, Frank LR. Quantitative imaging of perfusion using a single subtraction (QUIPSS and QUIPSS II). Magn Reson Med 1998;39:702–8.

[58] Luh WM, Wong EC, Bandettini PA, et al. QUIPSS II with thin-slice TI1 periodic saturation: a method for improving accuracy of quantitative perfusion imaging using pulsed arterial spin labeling. Magn Reson Med 1999;41:1246–54.

[59] Chappell MA, Groves AR, Whitcher B, et al. Variational Bayesian inference for a nonlinear forward model. IEEE Trans Signal Process 2009;57:223–36.

[60] Xie J, Gallichan D, Gunn RN, et al. Optimal design of pulsed arterial spin labeling MRI experiments. Magn Reson Med 2008;59:826–34.

[61] Kramme J, Gregori J, Diehl V, et al. Improving perfusion quantification in arterial spin labeling for delayed arrival times by using optimized acquisition schemes. Z Med Phys 2015;25:221–9.
[62] Detre JA, Rao H, Wang DJ, et al. Applications of arterial spin labeled MRI in the brain. J Magn Reson Imaging 2012;35:1026–37.
[63] Wolf R, Detre JA. Clinical neuroimaging using arterial spin-labeled perfusion MRI. Neurotherapeutics 2007;4:346–59.
[64] Raoult H, Gauvrit JY, Petr J, et al. Innovations in functional MR imaging of the brain: arterial spin labeling and diffusion. J Radiol 2011;92:878–88.
[65] Li X, Metzger GJ. Feasibility of measuring prostate perfusion with arterial spin labeling. NMR Biomed 2013;26:51–7.
[66] Taso M, Guidon A, Zhao L, et al. Pancreatic perfusion and arterial-transit-time quantification using pseudocontinuous arterial spin labeling at 3T. Magn Reson Med 2019;81:542–50.
[67] Taso M, Papadopoulou F, Smith MP, et al. Pancreatic perfusion modulation following glucose stimulation assessed by noninvasive arterial spin labeling (ASL) MRI. J Magn Reson Imaging 2019.

CHAPTER

Dynamic Contrast-Enhanced MRI: Basic Physics, Pulse Sequences, and Modeling

13

Ye Tian[a,b] and Ganesh Adluru[a,c]

[a]*Utah Center for Advanced Imaging Research (UCAIR), Department of Radiology and Imaging Sciences, University of Utah, Salt Lake City, Utah, United States* [b]*Department of Physics and Astronomy, University of Utah, Salt Lake City, Utah, United States* [c]*Department of Biomedical Engineering, University of Utah, Salt Lake City, Utah, United States*

13.1 Introduction

Dynamic contrast-enhanced Magnetic Resonance Imaging (DCE-MRI) is a promising tool to study the physiological properties of tissue. T_1-weighted images are acquired before, during, and after injection of a contrast agent which shortens the tissue T_1 relaxation time by interacting with surrounding water molecules. Since the T_1 shortening is related to the contrast agent concentration, the measured signal intensity changes in the dynamic images can be used to quantify the contrast agent concentration over time. By modeling the concentration-time profiles, clinically relevant parameters that characterize biophysical and biochemical processes can be quantified.

DCE-MRI has been applied to several organs in the body. It is used to quantify blood flow in the myocardium, allowing the detection of regions of perfusion deficit or ischemia [1,2]. In the kidney, renal blood flow, glomerular filtration rate, and cortical and medullary blood flow can be determined to assess renal function [3]. As a tumor grows to a few millimeters in size, new vasculature must be developed to support its growth, and DCE-MRI can be used to detect the leakiness in tumor vessels [4]. DCE-MRI has also been applied to the liver [5], prostate [6], breast [7]. Figs. 13.1–13.4 show examples of DCE-MRI scans in different organs.

Several aspects must be carefully considered when performing DCE-MRI, including data acquisition, image reconstruction, and postprocessing. This chapter will review the options available and identify the issues that need to be considered when setting up a protocol and interpreting the data.

13.2 Contrast agent mechanism

The most widely used types of contrast agents in DCE-MRI include a gadolinium (Gd) atom, which is strongly paramagnetic at room temperature. As free gadolinium is highly toxic, it is chelated with a carrier molecule to shield it from the environment, making it safer to use as an intravenous contrast agent. In chelated gadolinium-based contrast agents such as gadopentetic acid (Gd-DTPA), the gadolinium is in the form of a Gd^{+3} ion which creates a strong local magnetic field in the presence of an external magnetic field. This induced field provides additional relaxation pathways for the surrounding protons through either inner-sphere relaxation (direct interaction by water molecules near the Gd^{+3})

Advances in Magnetic Resonance Technology and Applications. Volume 1. ISSN 2666-9099. https://doi.org/10.1016/B978-0-12-817057-1.00015-9

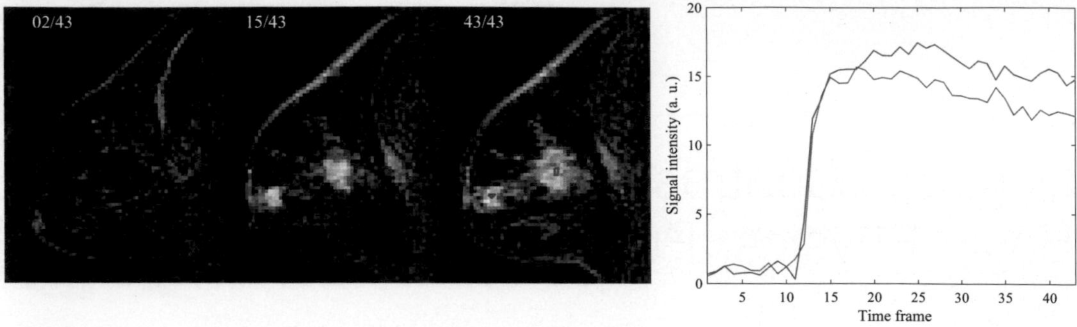

FIG. 13.1

DCE-MRI of the breast. The left figure shows three time frames at different stages of enhancement. The time frame number is indicated in the upper left corner. The three frames correspond to the baseline (frame 2), the peak enhancement (frame 15), and the washout (frame 43). The averaged precontrast/baseline image has been subtracted from subsequent images to remove the residual signal from stationary tissue and better illustrate the contrast enhancement. The tumors can be seen on the enhanced frames and are denoted with the *red and blue marks* in the washout phase. The right image shows mean signal intensity time curves for these two ROIs that are likely to be malignant.

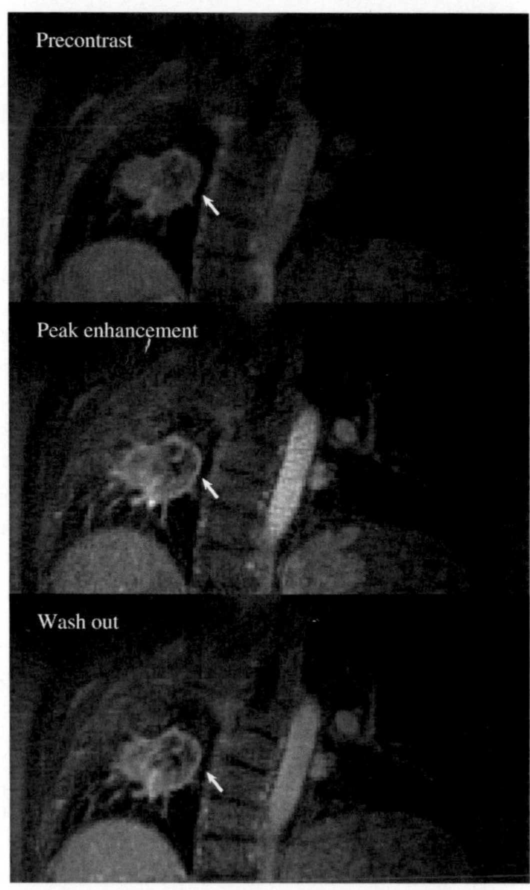

FIG. 13.2

Three different contrast phases of DCE-MRI of the lung. A tumor in the right lung is denoted by an *arrow* [8].

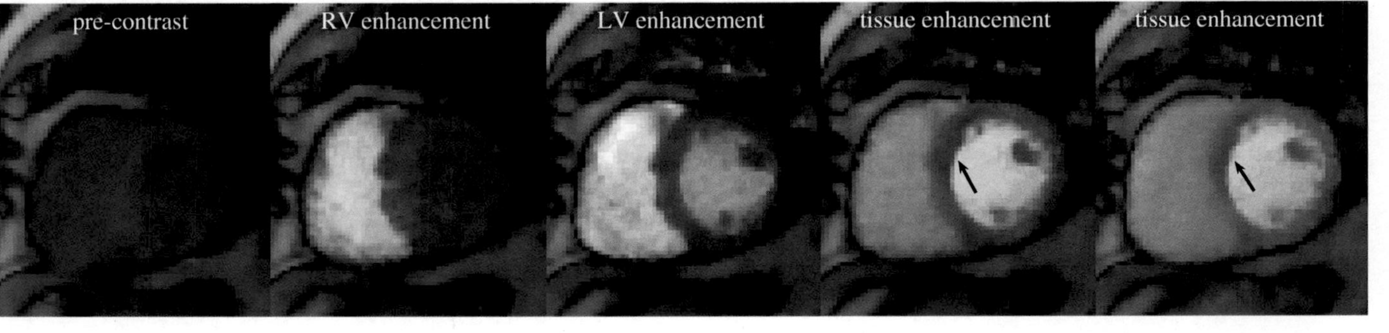

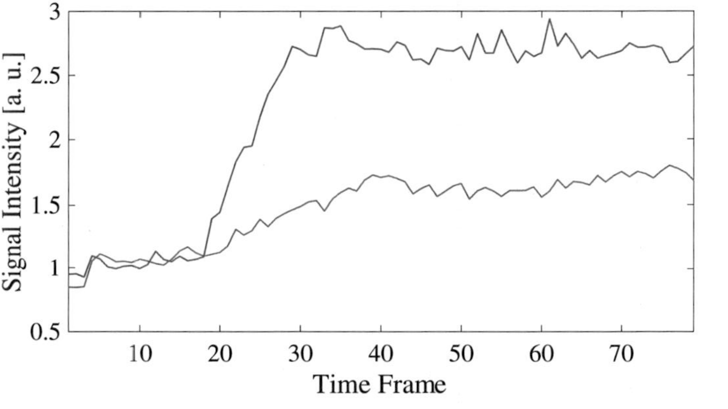

FIG. 13.3

DCE-MRI of the heart. The top image shows precontrast, right ventricle (RV) enhancement, left ventricle (LV) enhancement, and two myocardial enhancement frames. The *arrows* point to an infarcted area, which does not take up as much contrast agent as normal tissue. The bottom left image shows signal intensity time curves of infarcted *(blue)* and normal tissue *(red)*.

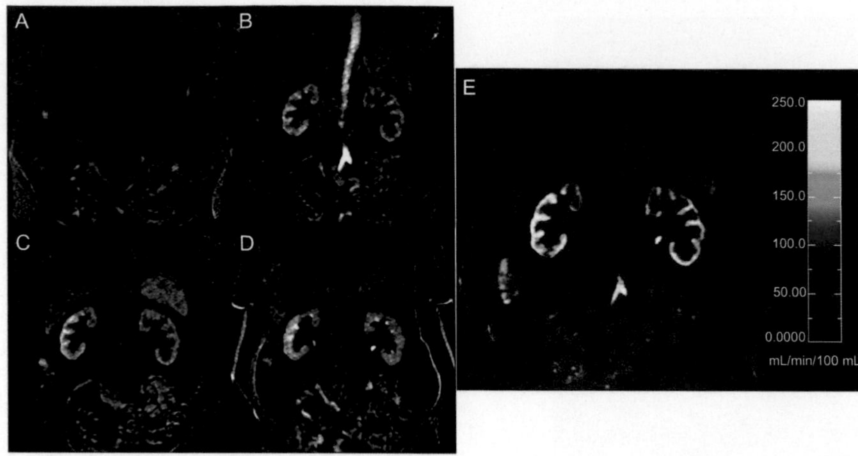

FIG. 13.4

DCE-MRI of the kidney. (A–D) Selected contrast phases, including (A) precontrast, (B) first-pass, (C) peak-enhancement, and (D) excretion phases of kidney DCE-MRI. (E) The perfusion map estimated from these dynamic images. The images were obtained from the iBEAt study [9].

or outer-sphere relaxation (via interaction with the chelate). The Solomon-Bloembergen-Morgan equations describe the inner-sphere relaxation, which depends on factors such as the residence lifetime of inner-sphere water molecules and the rotational tumbling time. The outer-sphere relaxation contributes a relatively small amount compared to the inner-sphere relaxation and is affected by the closest approach of outer-sphere water molecules and the diffusional correlation time. Interested readers are referred to Refs. [10–13] for more detailed discussions on gadolinium-based contrast agents.

Despite the complexity of the detailed interactions between water protons and contrast agent molecules, the effect of contrast agents on relaxation times can in practice be described by a simple model. With the relatively low concentrations in body tissue after injection of a standard clinical dose (0.1 mmol/kg), the change in relaxation rate $1/T_1$ is directly proportional to the contrast agent concentration:

$$\frac{1}{T_1}=\frac{1}{T_{1,0}}+r_1\times[\mathrm{CA}] \tag{13.1}$$

Here $1/T_1$ is the observed relaxation rate in the presence of contrast agent, $1/T_{1,0}$ is the relaxation rate in the absence of contrast agent, r_1 is the relaxivity of the contrast agent ($s^{-1}\times mM^{-1}$) and [CA] is the contrast agent concentration (mM or mmol/L). The contrast agent also shortens the transverse (T_2 and $T_2{}^*$) relaxation times of protons in body tissue but in DCE-MRI signals this effect is minimized by using a short echo time. The T_1 shortening, therefore, dominates the DCE-MRI signal changes.

Eq. (13.1) holds for tissues where the exchange of water is sufficiently fast so that the relaxation can be characterized by single relaxation time. This relationship is mostly valid for unenhanced tissues, but it may become a poor approximation when the contrast agent is present, and different tissue compartments contain very different concentrations. An example is during the first pass of the contrast agent when high concentrations are present in blood and very small concentrations in the extravascular space. Another example is several minutes after bolus injection when the contrast has extravasated and strong concentration differences exist between intra- and extracellular spaces. In those circumstances, the rapid exchange of water between the compartments may no longer be sufficient to counteract the large differences in T_1 values between the compartments, and the relaxation becomes multiexponential. The combined observed relaxation time will then in general be a nonlinear function of the relaxation times in the individual compartments, their relative volume fractions, and the exchange rate of water molecules between them. The situation can be modeled by generalizing Eq. (13.1) to also include the exchange of magnetization between neighboring compartments.

13.3 Data acquisition in DCE-MRI

A standard protocol for quantitative DCE-MRI starts by localizing the organ and prescribing the slices (or a slab) to be scanned. Then, an injection of contrast agent is performed using a power injector at a rate of 2–4 mL/s followed by a 20–30 mL saline flush at the same rate, to create a sharp bolus. The gadolinium-based contrast agent dose is typically around 0.1 mmol/kg. The DCE-MRI pulse sequence should start a few seconds before the injection, to capture a few baseline/precontrast images, and run for a few minutes after the injection of the contrast agent to capture the contrast agent's first-pass as well as few postcontrast images. Depending on the DCE-MRI protocol, calibration sequences that measure the B_1 field, the baseline T_1 values, or the proton density-weighted images may be performed before the actual DCE acquisition [14,15].

13.3.1 Requirements of DCE-MRI data

Sequence optimization often requires carefully choosing an organ-specific or application-specific trade-off between temporal resolution, spatial resolution, and slice coverage. For example, in myocardial DCE-MRI, the volume that can be covered per time frame is limited because data can only be collected during part of the cardiac cycle to avoid motion artifacts. Typically three slices are acquired per heartbeat (0.5–1 s) with an in-plane resolution of $2 \times 2\ \text{mm}^2$ to cover the left ventricular myocardium. In DCE-MRI of the brain, temporal resolution is typically lower (5 s), but these acquisitions aim for complete coverage of the brain (e.g., 30 slices with 4 mm slice thickness). When DCE-MRI is performed to characterize small tumors, the temporal resolution is typically lower to achieve a high spatial resolution.

The different requirements of qualitative and quantitative analyses must also be considered when selecting appropriate sequence settings. For example, breast DCE-MRI studies designed for reporting curve-types, a qualitative analysis, use only a limited number of time frames to enable a very high spatial resolution and volume coverage [16,17]. Quantitative analysis, on the other hand, requires high temporal resolution to capture the very rapid contrast agent concentration changes. As a result, compromises have to be made in terms of organ coverage and/or spatial resolution.

There are several considerations in pulse sequence design for DCE-MRI. Since the aim is to capture the changes in contrast agent concentration in the ROI, signal intensities between baseline and peak enhancement should be well distinguishable. Moreover, in quantitative studies, to be able to convert signal intensities into contrast agent concentration, a linear relationship between the contrast agent concentration and signal intensity is preferred within the expected range of concentrations. Each pulse sequence provides a unique relationship between contrast concentration and signal intensity. The Bloch equations can be used to simulate signal intensities as a function of concentration for a specific sequence, producing calibration curves, or look-up tables that can be used to design pulse sequences and derive concentrations from measured signals.

The dose of contrast agent should be chosen carefully to balance the image signal-to-noise ratio (SNR) and signal linearity. At high contrast agent concentration, the relationship between signal intensity and concentration is no longer linear, increasing the uncertainty in measurements of concentration as illustrated in Fig. 13.5 for a saturation recovery sequence. Using the curve showing a saturation recovery time (SRT) = 100 ms as an example, at the linear part of the curve ([CA] < 2 mmol/L), a 0.02 uncertainty

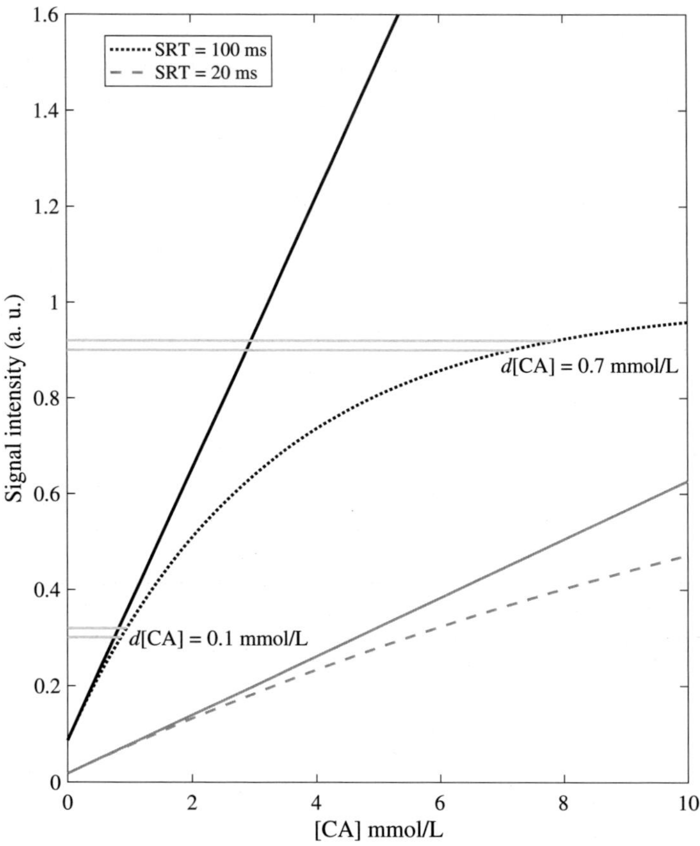

FIG. 13.5

Simulation of signal intensities at different contrast agent concentrations and saturation recovery times which show how nonlinearity can affect perfusion quantification. A saturation recovery spoiled gradient echo (SPGR) sequence was used in the simulation. Contrast agent was assumed to be GD-DTPA, which has relaxivity of 3.1 mmol $\times$ L^{-1} at 3 T, and baseline T_1 was assumed to be 1100 ms. Signal intensities at different contrast agent concentrations were simulated, and two different SRTs are shown. The *solid line* along with each *dotted line* shows a linear relationship between signal intensity and concentration; as the concentration of contrast agent increases, the assumption of a linear relationship between signal intensity and concentration is invalid.

in the signal intensity (which could be a result of noise in the image, T_2^* effect, B_0 inhomogeneity, etc.) will lead to an [CA] uncertainty of 0.1; however, in the nonlinear part of the curve ([CA] > 6 mmol/L), the same signal uncertainty can lead to 0.7 [CA] uncertainty. When CA concentration cannot be further reduced, it is often possible to maximize linearity by sequence optimization, though this may come at a cost of reduced SNR.

13.3.2 DCE-MRI pulse sequences

The steady-state spoiled gradient echo sequence [18,19] is the most commonly used pulse sequence for acquiring T_1-weighted DCE-MRI images. Variants including spoiled gradient-recalled echo (SPGR), fast low-angle shot (FLASH), and fast field echo (T_1-FFE) belong to this category. A 2D Cartesian FLASH pulse sequence uses a train of low flip angle slice-selective RF pulses to acquire k-space data. Each RF excitation is followed by the collection of a line of k-space with a gradient echo. Spoiling is applied after each gradient echo to remove the magnetization history on the x-y plane [20]. After a short number of pulses, the signal intensity (SI) will reach a steady-state which is determined by the repetition time (TR) between pulses and the flip angle α:

$$\mathrm{SI} = ke^{-\mathrm{TE}/T_2^*} \sin\alpha \frac{1 - e^{-\mathrm{TR}/T_1}}{1 - \cos\alpha e^{-\mathrm{TR}/T_1}} \tag{13.2a}$$

where k is a scaling factor that includes proton density weighting and any system scaling. To acquire T_1-weighted images, the echo time (TE) and the TR should be short. By using a small flip angle (e.g., 2°), the FLASH sequence can also be used to acquire proton density-weighted images, which may be useful to correct for the coil inhomogeneities and improve quantification. The FLASH sequence can be performed very rapidly with an extremely short TR (e.g., TR = 2.3 ms) and is thus favorable for DCE-MRI, which requires rapid sampling. This sequence can be implemented for both 2D and 3D acquisitions, with Cartesian or non-Cartesian (radial or stack-of-stars) sampling.

A variation of the standard FLASH sequence in DCE-MRI employs a nonselective saturation pulse before reading out k-space data and is known as a saturation recovery (SR) sequence. The main aim of the preparation pulse is to reduce the signal difference between blood flowing into the readout slab (which is in equilibrium without preparation) and tissue in the readout slab (which is in steady-state without preparation). If the FLASH sequence has a center-encoded readout, then the signal model has the following form:

$$\mathrm{SI} = ke^{-\mathrm{TE}/T_2^*} \sin\alpha\left(1 - e^{-\mathrm{SRT}/T_1}\right) \tag{13.2b}$$

where SRT is the saturation recovery time or the time between saturation pulse and collection of the k-space center. Fig. 13.6 shows the signal curves of an SR-prepared sequence and a sequence without magnetization preparation. The figure shows that the same steady-state is reached with or without an SR pulse, but SR-prepared sequences can be used to collect signals before it reaches a steady-state, and the acquired signal can be converted to contrast concentration with proper modeling. Inversion prepulses are usually not applied in DCE-MRI because perfect inversion is more difficult to achieve than perfect saturation and because the signal at any given time point then becomes dependent on its history.

For SR sequences, the SRT is an important parameter that has a significant impact on image contrast. After a saturation pulse is applied, the longitudinal magnetization is zero and starts to recover to equilibrium. Tissues with different T_1 values return to equilibrium at different rates, which leads to different

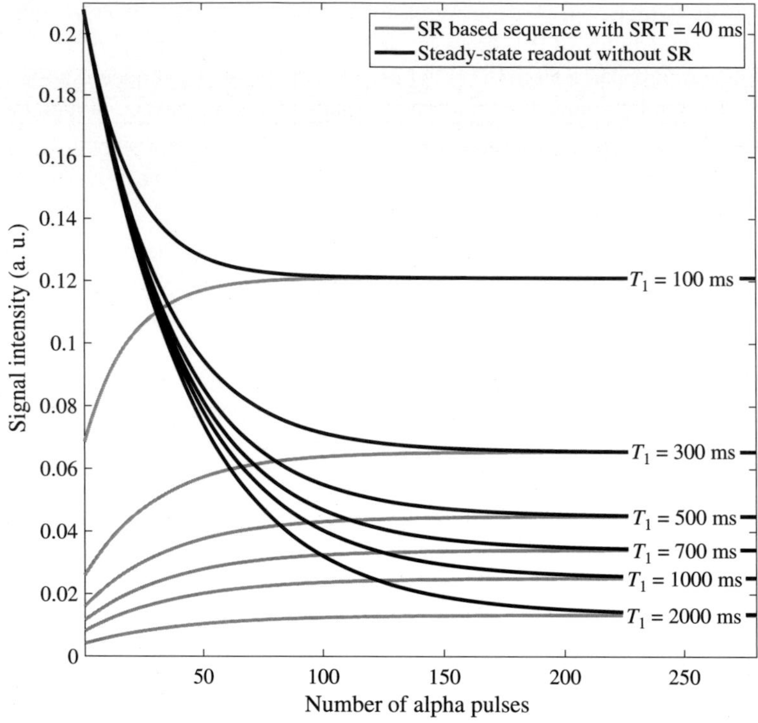

FIG. 13.6

Signal intensities for two different sequences, SR-SPGR and SPGR with no magnetization preparation. The SR-prepared sequence was simulated with SRT=40ms. Both sequences used TR=3ms and a flip angle of 12°. Note that while both sequences eventually reach the steady-state, the SR-prepared sequences do so much faster, enabling data collection after a smaller number of dummy scans.

signal intensities. Fig. 13.7 shows a plot of signal intensities of several tissues with different T_1 values at different SRTs. Using a short SRT can preserve contrast agent concentration linearity, but the image SNR is low. A short SRT can also help avoid the effects of water exchange and associated errors during quantification with a model that assumes a fast exchange of water [21]. Using a long SRT results in high SNR but poor contrast, as tissues with different T_1 values will all have experienced a nearly full recovery.

When DCE-MRI data are collected for quantitative perfusion mapping, a baseline T_1 measurement is required to convert the acquired SI curves into contrast concentration curves according to Eq. (13.1). Whichever sequence is used, since the effects of T_2^*-related changes are assumed to be negligible, the dynamic DCE-MRI signal model will always have the form $S(T_{1,t})=k{\cdot}f(T_{1,t})$, where $f(T_{1,t})$ is a known function derived from the sequence and k is a scaling factor which may depend on pixel location. Eqs. (13.2a), (13.2b) are examples of the $f(T_{1,t})$ functions. Given a measurement of precontrast $T_{1,0}$, k can be determined for every pixel from the precontrast signal as $k=S(T_{1,0})/f(T_{1,0})$. Subsequently, $T_{1,t}$ can be measured for each time point as $T_{1,t}f^{-1}{\cdot}[S(T_{1,t})/k]$. The precontrast $T_{1,0}$ measurement can be performed in a variety of ways, for instance, using a variable flip angle (VFA) method [22,23].

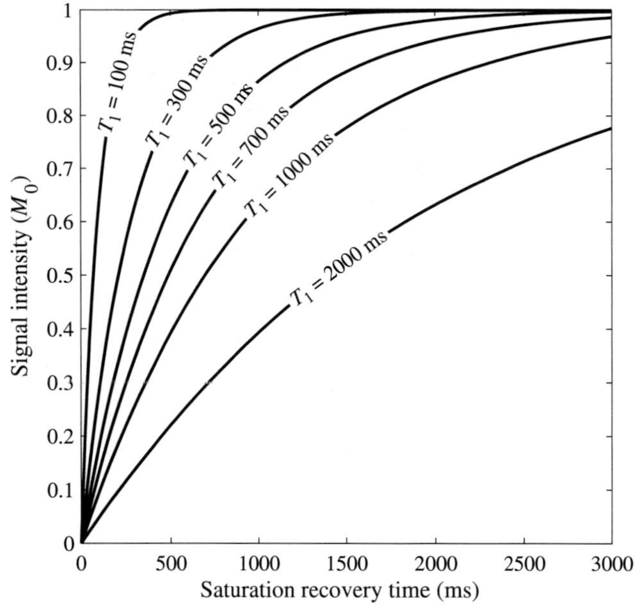

FIG. 13.7

Signal intensity at different recovery times for tissues with different T_1 values.

13.3.3 Sampling trajectories

Cartesian sampling is the most commonly used sampling trajectory for MRI. In Cartesian sampling, *k*-space is acquired line-by-line. Images can be reconstructed from *k*-space sampled along a Cartesian trajectory by the application of the discrete Fourier transform (or the optimized Fast Fourier Transform (FFT)). However, Cartesian sampling is easily affected by intra-scan motion and can lead to dark rim artifacts in myocardial perfusion imaging, especially at lower spatial resolutions.

Non-Cartesian *k*-space trajectories are also used in DCE-MRI, and the selection of the optimal trajectory is an active area of research, especially for undersampled acquisitions. For 2D, the radial and spiral sampling schemes are commonly used. The radial trajectory goes through the *k*-space center at every line. This trajectory is less efficient than Cartesian sampling, but the sampling redundancy at the *k*-space center can reduce motion artifacts. The spiral trajectory can be efficient in filling *k*-space, but this requires long readouts and can lead to off-resonance artifacts at high field strengths. For 3D imaging, the stack-of-stars and stack-of-spirals are commonly used non-Cartesian trajectories. Reconstruction of images from non-Cartesian trajectories can be performed with a nonuniform FFT (NUFFT) or gridding algorithms in which the acquired *k*-space samples are convolved with an interpolation kernel (e.g., Kaiser-Bassel kernel), followed by the application of the discrete Fourier transform and apodization [24]. The NUFFT is slower compared to the FFT for the same image size, and the NUFFT is not invertible, which makes non-Cartesian reconstructions more complex and time-consuming. Methods to avoid the interpolation steps in NUFFT during iterations [25–28] and non-Cartesian GRAPPA [29–32] have been studied to perform fast reconstructions.

Simultaneous multislice (SMS) techniques can also be used to accelerate 2D acquisitions [33]. Instead of exciting and acquiring a single slice, multiple parallel slices are excited and acquired simultaneously in SMS. Since the acquired *k*-space is a summation of the data from all slices, the different slices have to be separated during reconstruction. By using slice-GRAPPA [34] or a SENSE-based approach, the slices can be separated in *k*-space and image space, respectively. For non-Cartesian SMS, SENSE-based iterative reconstructions are commonly used to reconstruct the slices jointly. A phase modulation strategy known as controlled aliasing in parallel imaging results in higher acceleration (CAIPIRINHA) is also useful to deploy in SMS acquisitions [35]. By shifting the FOV of different slices for Cartesian acquisitions, the slices can be better separated. Simultaneously excited slices overlap on top of each other in a staggered fashion, which is easier to resolve via a parallel imaging reconstruction than when slices fold directly on top of one another. For non-Cartesian acquisitions such as radial or spiral sampling, the CAIPIRINHA scheme produces a more noise-like slice aliasing pattern [36]. Cartesian, as well as non-Cartesian SMS techniques, have been applied in the context of perfusion imaging, where speed is most critical [37–40].

13.3.4 Arterial input function

The arterial input function (AIF) describes the contrast agent concentration changes over time in the main artery that is close to the examined region of interest. Measurement of the AIF is required for quantification of tissue-specific properties and should ideally be acquired for each patient to account for interindividual differences. Using a population-averaged AIF has been proposed as an alternative to patient-specific measurements, and this can be the best solution in scenarios where the measurement error in the AIF is expected to be larger than any differences between individuals.

AIF measurement can be affected by various sources of uncertainties [41,42], such as flow effects, partial volume, or T_2^* decay. Another challenge for accurate measurement of the AIF is to maintain the linear relationship between signal and contrast agent concentration, particularly at the typically high concentrations observed during the first pass in an arterial voxel. Different strategies have been proposed to ensure this linearity. For example, in myocardial perfusion MRI, a dual sequence method has been proposed that uses different sequence parameters to assess the AIF and the (lower) tissue concentrations [43,44]. Typically, the AIF slice is acquired with a short SRT, and the low SNR is mitigated by using a lower spatial resolution, which is sufficient to estimate AIF from the large left ventricular cavity. The AIF can also be measured using a dual bolus technique [45], which involves the injection of two separate doses of contrast agent. The first injection is performed at a low dose, usually 1/10 or 1/20 that of the second injection. Images from the lower contrast agent dose are only used to estimate the AIF since at low concentration the signal linearity is preserved. The AIF estimated form the first injection is multiplied by the dose ratio between the two injections and is used as the final AIF for quantification.

13.4 Image reconstruction in DCE-MRI

13.4.1 Parallel imaging

Considering the crucial role of high temporal resolution, all current quantitative DCE-MRI approaches achieve the high required sampling speed by undersampling the *k*-space data and reconstructing unaliased images using a dedicated mathematical technique. One such technique is parallel imaging, a standard data acceleration strategy that is available on all commercial scanners. By using a multicoil array to acquire k-space data, images can be reconstructed from fewer samples by exploiting the coil sensitivity variations between different coils. The two main parallel imaging reconstruction techniques are SENSE and GRAPPA. SENSE requires a sensitivity map estimation of each coil, which can be acquired separately or estimated from the acquired data [46]. Note that DCE-MRI acquisitions do not require a separate calibration scan because all measured data can be combined to estimate coil sensitivities. GRAPPA works by estimating a reconstruction matrix that can be used to synthesize missing k-space samples from their neighbors [47]. The estimation requires the fully-sampled k-space center for calibration. It inherently exploits the smoothness of the coil sensitivity variations but is performed in k-space. With accurate coil sensitivity maps, SENSE reconstructions can result in higher SNR images than GRAPPA; however, it may not always possible to obtain accurate sensitivity maps and the GRAPPA approach can be more robust [48]. When combined with non-Cartesian data collection trajectories, parallel imaging can enable data collection for perfusion modeling at very high acceleration rates; for example, full liver coverage can be achieved with a spatial resolution of $1.9 \times 1.9 \times 3\,\text{mm}^3$ and frame rates of $<2\,\text{s}$ when combining stack-of-spirals trajectory with GRAPPA [49]. This high spatiotemporal resolution allows pixel-wise quantitative liver perfusion mapping, as shown in Fig. 13.8.

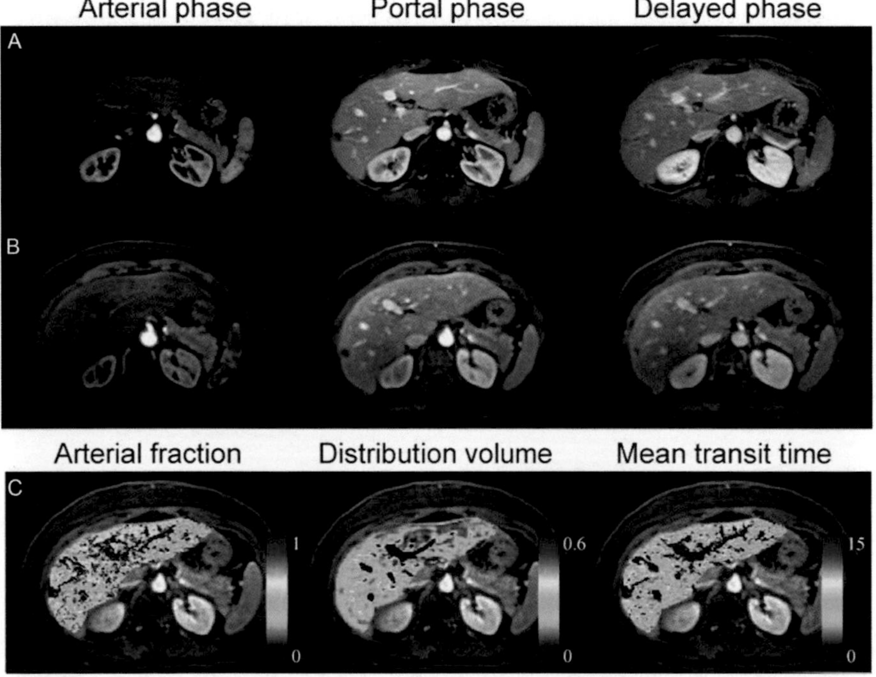

FIG. 13.8

DCE-MRI images and perfusion maps in the liver. (A) Clinical standard images acquired during a breath-hold and Cartesian readout at 18 s per image volume. (B) Images acquired with a free-breathing stack-of-spirals sequence at 1.9 s per volume. (C) Perfusion maps generated from the high temporal resolution stack-of-spirals readout images [49].

13.4.2 Constrained reconstruction

Constrained reconstruction is a rich and active research area, both in perfusion mapping and beyond. The basic principle of constrained reconstruction approaches is that the images to be reconstructed are assumed to have certain properties, i.e., the images are piecewise smooth, the data have a low-rank structure, or the signal follows certain physical models. These assumptions can then be used to constrain the reconstruction and reduce the data dependence of the acquisition. These approaches are of particular interest in DCE-MRI, where the need for rapid temporal sampling imposes a fundamental limitation on the amount of data that can be collected. In practice constrained reconstruction can be performed by including the constraints along with a data fidelity term in a combined cost function and solving the corresponding optimization problem. The cost function for constrained reconstruction often has the following form:

$$m = \arg\min_{m} \frac{1}{2} \|Am - d\|_2^2 + \lambda \|Tm\|_1 \tag{13.3}$$

The first term is the data fidelity term and the second term is the regularization term which encodes the constraints. The fidelity term is written as the square of the l_2 norm, which compares the estimated image m with measured data d, and $A = D\mathcal{F}S$ is the sampling matrix that simulates the data sampling process including a Fourier transform $\mathcal{F}$, a sensitivity map S (if a multicoil array is used), and an undersampling mask D. The regularization term is written as the l_1 norm of a sparse transform of the image, where T is the transform operator and λ the regularization weight. The cost function can include multiple regularization terms to constrain the image in different aspects (i.e., along the spatial direction, temporal direction, and so on).

Compressed sensing (CS) is one particular type of constrained reconstruction that has been proposed for DCE-MRI [50,51]. In DCE-MRI, the same slice positions are sampled frequently over time, providing redundancy in the information along the temporal dimension. By exploiting this redundancy, a single time frame can be highly undersampled but still reconstructed faithfully; thus in DCE-MRI, regularization in the temporal dimension of the images is commonly applied. Some popular reconstruction methods include temporal total variation (TV) [52], *k-t* principal component analysis (PCA) [53], low-rank [54], and L+S approach [55]. The temporal TV method assumes piece-wise smoothness of the time curves in dynamic images, and the reconstruction is performed by minimizing the following cost function:

$$m = \operatorname{argmin}_{m} \frac{1}{2} \|Am\text{-}d\|_2^2 + \lambda \left\| \sqrt{(\nabla_t m)^2 + \epsilon} \right\|_1 \tag{13.4}$$

where in this case the sparsifying transform is the temporal finite-difference of the images. Fig. 13.9 shows an example of reconstruction using the temporal total variation (TV) as the sparsifying transform. In *k-t* PCA, an FFT is applied along the temporal dimension followed by a principal component analysis (PCA), and smaller principal components are penalized. The low-rank method works by performing a singular value decomposition (SVD) along the time dimension and penalizing the rank of the dynamic images. The L+S method decomposes the dynamic images into a low-rank, L, component, and a sparse, S, component, and applies different regularizations on these components.

An emerging technique known as GRASP [56] combines golden-angle radial sampling, parallel imaging, and compressed sensing, and has been applied to DCE-MRI. The golden-angle radial

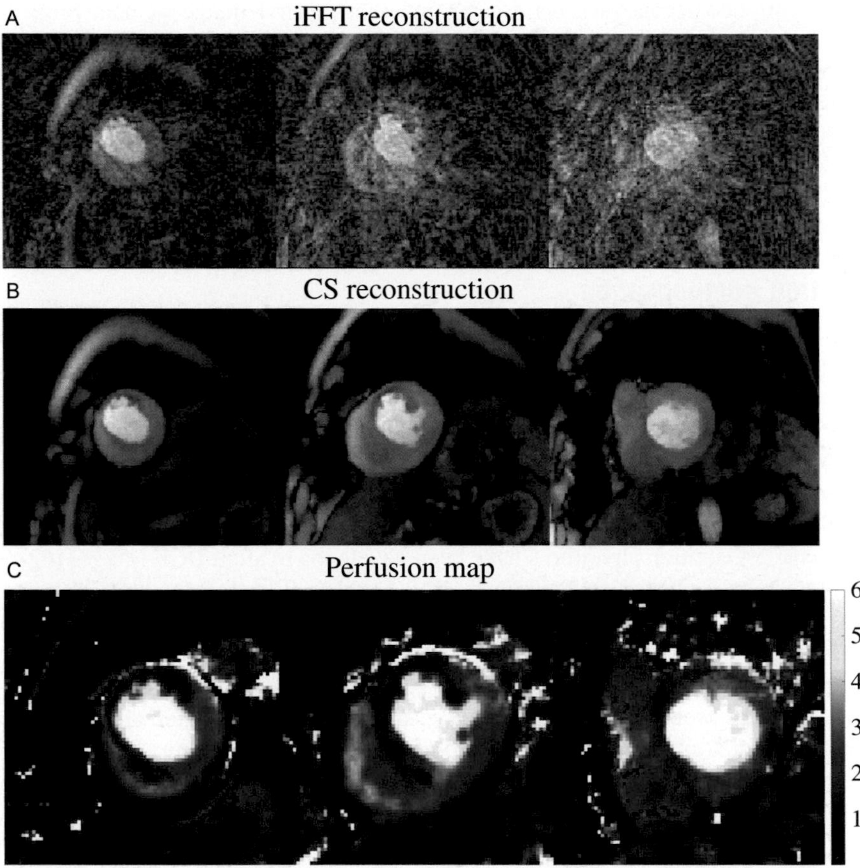

FIG. 13.9

Compressed sensing (CS) reconstruction of DCE-MRI images and perfusion maps. (A) Accelerated undersampled cardiac DCE-MRI images and (B) the CS reconstructions of the same time frames. The images were acquired with a saturation-prepared FLASH sequence using a golden-angle radial sampling with CAIPIRINHA phase modulation to acquire three slices simultaneously. The CS reconstruction used a motion-compensated spatial/temporal constrained reconstruction to remove the artifacts due to aliasing which can be seen in the top images [40]. (C) The CS reconstructions allowed perfusion maps to be estimated in units of mL/min/g, where perfusion deficits are seen on multiple slices.

sampling provides incoherent undersampling artifacts across time and mitigates motion effects. Incorporating advanced CS reconstruction techniques with a high undersampling allows a high spatiotemporal resolution. Typically, a spatial resolution of $1 \times 1\ \text{mm}^2$, slice thickness of 2–3 mm and a temporal resolution of 2–7 s per frame is feasible for volumetric DCE-MRI. An additional advantage of the golden-angle sampling approach is that the temporal resolution can be chosen in the reconstruction, and does not need to be fixed when the data are acquired.

The aforementioned reconstructions assume inherent general image or data properties such as smoothness. Another category of constrained reconstruction methods uses the physiological model to solve for parameter maps directly from *k*-space data. The advantage of this category is that the parameter maps are directly reconstructed instead of the dynamic images, thus the inverse problem may be less ill-posed. In DCE-MRI, tracer kinetic models are used in the reconstruction to obtain pixel-wise parameter maps directly from measured *k*-space data [57–61].

13.5 Postprocessing for DCE-based perfusion mapping

13.5.1 Motion compensation

Motion across DCE images can be caused by breathing or unwanted movement of the patient during the contrast agent injection. Motion across time frames can cause unwanted signal changes on top of the contrast-enhanced dynamics that can lead to errors in the model parameters; thus correcting for motion between time frames in the dynamic images is an important first postprocessing step for visual interpretation as well as for further model-based analysis. Fig. 13.10 shows an example of the effect of breathing motion on signal intensity time curves in a myocardial perfusion dataset. The time curve varies smoothly after image registration.

Several image registration algorithms have been developed to align DCE images [62–68] using either rigid or deformable registration techniques. Deformable registration methods are computationally more expensive than rigid registration techniques but can suppress complex motion in the data that can arise from the deformation of tissue. The main challenge for compensating motion in DCE images is that the image contrast changes over time and this can cause errors when registering time frames. One way of addressing this problem is by using a model-based image registration approach [64,65]. In this approach, a two-compartment model is used to fit each pixel to the concentration-time curves, and the model fit is then used to generate static reference images that have similar contrast as the original

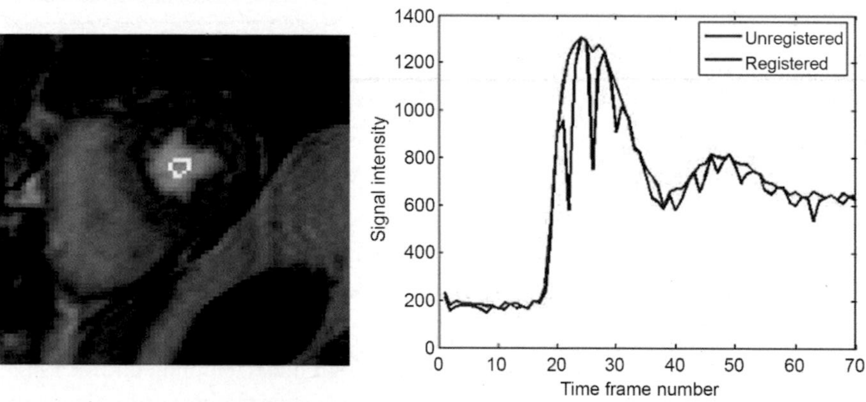

FIG. 13.10

The effects of breathing motion on the signal intensity time curves in a myocardial perfusion DCE dataset. A region of interest is drawn on a single time frame in the left ventricular blood pool. Corresponding mean signal intensity time curves before and after registration are shown in the plot on the right-hand side.

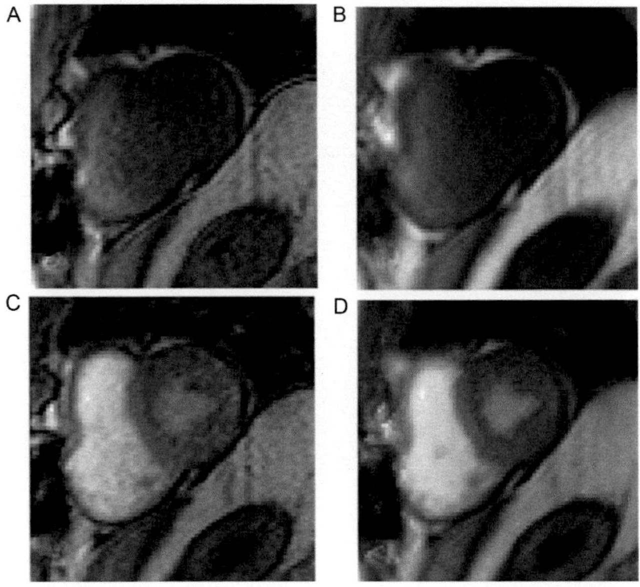

FIG. 13.11

Illustration of model reference images. (A,C) Two different time frames in a myocardial perfusion DCE sequence. (B,D) Corresponding model reference images obtained by fitting a two-compartment model [64].

images. Fig. 13.11 shows an example of modeled reference images and the corresponding original images for myocardial perfusion data. Pair-wise image registration can then be performed between the original image and the corresponding model image [64], and the process is iterated if needed. A similar approach has also been applied to DCE tumor imaging [65].

Image registration methods can also help to improve the underlying image quality of undersampled DCE images by incorporating motion information into the reconstruction [8,69,70]. For example, temporal regularization constraints used in CS-based reconstructions are not effective when there is irregular motion across images. Sudden temporal variations lead to reduced temporal sparsity in the transform domain. Incorporating motion information can suppress these variations and improve the temporal regularization leading to fewer artifacts in the reconstructed images. Motion information can be obtained from a preliminary reconstruction [71] or the acquired *k*-space data directly in the form of self-gating [8]. Fig. 13.12 shows examples from DCE tumor imaging [8] where the incorporation of motion into the reconstruction leads to improved image quality.

13.5.2 ROI-based and pixel-based methods

Perfusion parameter estimation can be performed on an ROI basis or a pixel basis. In ROI-based analysis, a single signal intensity time curve is extracted by averaging the signals of all pixels over an ROI, and a single set of quantitative parameters is derived by fitting the time curve to a suitable model. In a pixel-based analysis, each pixel is treated as a small ROI and quantitative parameters are derived for each pixel, producing perfusion maps (see Figs. 13.8 and 13.12, for example).

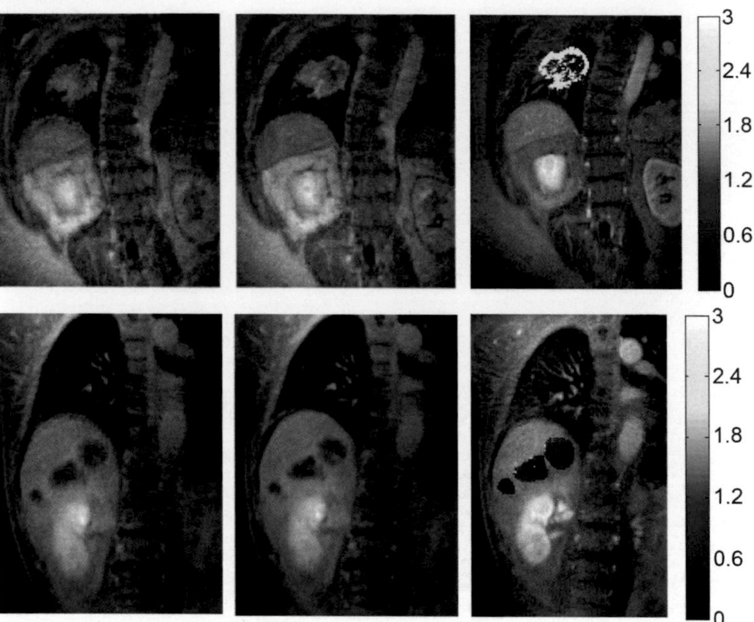

FIG. 13.12

Illustration of image quality improvement after incorporating motion information into reconstruction. Images on the left were reconstructed without incorporating motion information. Images in the middle correspond to reconstructions where motion information has been incorporated. K^{trans} maps (min^{-1}) are shown at the right for the corresponding motion-corrected datasets. Images in the first and second rows depict tumors in the lung and liver, respectively [8].

In a biomarker study, an ROI can then be defined afterward and averages over the ROI can be reported. However, the pixel-based analysis also provides information on the heterogeneity and spatial structure of perfusion, and may also aid in defining suitable ROIs or distinguishing tissue types [72]. On the other hand, pixel-wise approaches can be more sensitive to noise than ROI-based methods. In both cases, errors in selecting these ROIs can lead to incorrect estimates of the clinically relevant parameters [73].

ROI analysis can also serve other purposes beyond reporting averages or other summary parameters. Segmentation of an ROI is needed to obtain the AIF in a nearby artery that feeds the tissue of interest. For example, in cardiac DCE a region of interest in the left ventricular blood pool cavity is typically used to determine the AIF, as shown in Fig. 13.13. Segmenting the tissue into ROIs can help to provide a meaningful interpretation of the underlying disease. For example, in coronary artery disease, the culprit artery can be identified by segmenting the myocardium according to the AHA model. Fig. 13.13 shows the segmentation of the myocardium in a mid-ventricular short-axis slice into six regions, along with their corresponding mean signal intensity time curves and myocardial blood flow estimations. In other areas such as oncology, segmentation of tumor areas is important for instance in radiotherapy planning or prognosis evaluation.

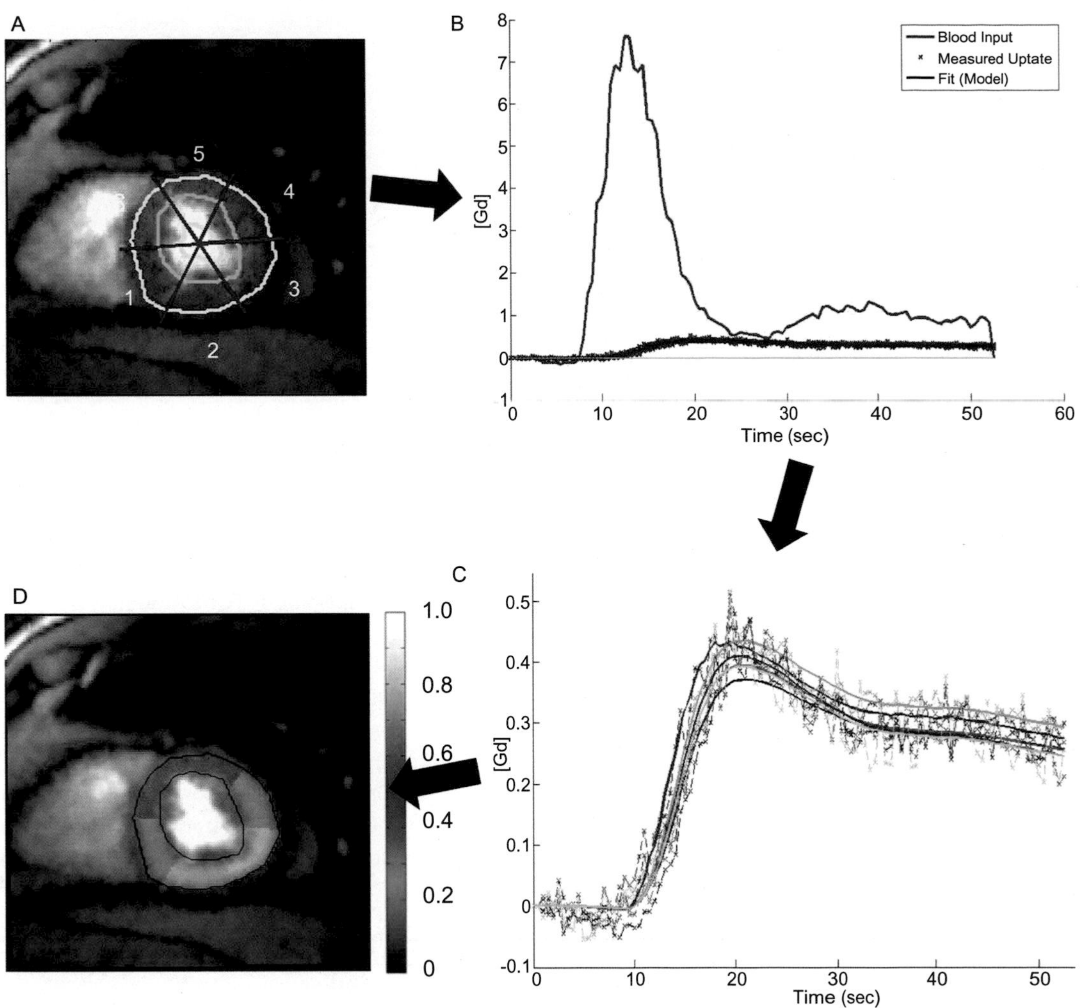

FIG. 13.13

Illustration of segmentation-based quantification in a DCE myocardial perfusion dataset. ROI for the AIF is obtained from the left ventricular blood pool. (A) The myocardial wall is segmented in six equiangular regions. The AIF (blood input, shown prominently in B) and signal intensity time curves for the six regions after subtraction of the baseline (C) are shown as a function of time. (D) Myocardial blood flow estimations in units of mL/min/g for the six regions [74].

Segmentation of motion-corrected DCE images is often done manually by drawing an ROI on a selected time frame and using the same ROI across all time frames. Semiautomatic and automatic segmentation methods exist [75–77] that can take in "seeds" as input and use region-growing methods to give the fully segmented ROIs as outputs. Methods that perform joint segmentation and registration have also been proposed [78,79].

13.5.3 Modeling

After extracting the signal intensity time curves for the AIF and tissue in the DCE images, contrast agent concentration curves are estimated by converting the signal intensities at each time point to T_1 values, as described in Section 13.3. Care should be taken during the conversion to correct for any nonlinearity in the AIF due to high concentrations of gadolinium, as described in Section 13.3. B_1 correction for errors in the flip angle may increase the estimation accuracy. Correcting for $T_2{}^*$ effects in the AIF is also important to avoid artificially high flow values [80,81]. After the raw image signal is converted to concentration, pharmacokinetic models can be applied to relate the concentrations to physiological parameters. The appropriate model depends on the organ being assessed, and the characteristics of the contrast agent administered.

The fundamental kinetic equation for DCE-MRI analysis models the tissue concentration of any linear and stationary tissue as:

$$C_T(t) = C_A(t) \otimes f \cdot R(t) \tag{13.5}$$

where $C_T(t)$ is the contrast agent concentration in the tissue of interest at time t; $C_A(t)$ is the AIF or the contrast agent concentration in arterial blood at time t; $\otimes$ represents the convolution operator; f is the blood flow; and $R(t)$ is the residue function of the system [82]. $R(t)$ is typically parametrized using a physiologically meaningful model which describes the organ in question in terms of several tissue compartments and their interactions [83,84]. For example in the one-compartment Tofts model [83], $fR(t)$ is represented as $K^{\text{trans}}e^{-k_{ep}t}$. Here K^{trans} is the contrast agent uptake rate into the extravascular, extracellular space, and k_{ep} is the efflux rate constant of contrast agent from extravascular extracellular space to the vasculature. Model-free approaches that do not require the parameterization of $fR(t)$ but perform a model-free deconvolution with regularization constraints have also been proposed [85–87]. For a more complete description, see Chapter 11, and for a comparison of multiple approaches see [88].

Deconvolution methods involve optimization of a cost function such that the curves estimated with the forward model (Eq. 13.5) match closely with the acquired tissue curves. Iterative optimization techniques like Levenberg-Marquardt are commonly used to estimate the parameters of the residue function. This approach can be time-consuming, especially if pixel-wise quantitative analyses are performed. Alternatively, the model can be rewritten in a linear form to speed up the estimation of the parameters and increase the robustness of the estimated parameters, as a globally optimal fit is guaranteed without dependence on the choice of initial estimates [89,90].

Quantitative analysis using pharmacokinetic modeling aids in improving the accuracy of clinical diagnosis, as perfusion maps can indicate regions of unusual perfusion that may not be obvious when examining raw DCE images. Quantitative analysis can also help to remove image artifacts. It was recently shown that quantitative analysis of myocardial perfusion images can help separate the dark rim artifact from a true perfusion deficit [91]. As mentioned before, modeling can also help in removing undersampling artifacts in accelerated DCE acquisitions, as these artifacts are not well-represented using the models [57-59,92]. While parallel imaging or CS-type approaches can be deployed to remove artifacts from the individual accelerated DCE images, model-based reconstruction approaches allow for more specific constraints to be employed for DCE data. These constraints may enable the direct estimation of quantitative parametric maps from undersampled k-space data [57,58,60].

13.6 Summary

Dynamic contrast-enhanced (DCE)-MRI is a promising tool to study the physiological properties of tissue and has found applications in virtually all organs including the brain, heart, lungs, liver, kidney, breast, pancreas, spleen, male and female pelvis, and muscle. Each body area comes with particular challenges and demands, but in all areas, several issues need to be carefully considered when performing DCE-MRI. These including choice and optimization of data acquisition strategies, image reconstruction, and postprocessing approaches.

For perfusion assessment, data acquisition should be performed at a high temporal resolution to track the rapid changes of contrast agent in the first pass through the vasculature. This is often in conflict with the concurrent need for a high spatial resolution to reveal detailed substructures in small areas of pathology. The acquisition parameters should be carefully selected to ensure that the signal intensities are sensitive to changes of contrast agent concentration at all relevant concentrations. The contrast agent dose should be chosen to be low enough so that signal intensity is essentially linear in the contrast agent concentration, but also high enough to ensure that poorly perfused tissues can be distinguished. Another important consideration is motion robustness. Some natural motion, such as respiration and cardiac pulsation, is unavoidable, and bulk motion can arise if the patient moves throughout the scan.

To fulfill the requirements of high temporal and high spatial resolution, and freeze the motion during acquisition, data undersampling with advanced reconstructions can be used. The use of multicoil arrays with parallel imaging reconstructions can be used to accelerate data acquisition. Advanced reconstruction methods like compressed sensing (CS) or machine learning (ML) can push the data acceleration even further. These techniques essentially reduce the dependence on data by using prior information about the images. As a result, individual time frames in a dynamic sequence can be reconstructed with less data, allowing faster sampling rates.

Postprocessing of reconstructed images is important for reliable clinical interpretation. Image registration is typically done to align the dynamic set of images acquired at different phases of contrast agent passage. Image segmentation may be performed to select an ROI to perform quantitative analysis; pixel-wise analysis providing high-resolution perfusion maps is also becoming possible with emerging acquisition and reconstruction approaches Both registration and segmentation require the knowledge of the tissue properties and anatomy. Finally, mathematical models of contrast agent kinetics in tissue are fit to the image signal intensities to extract the physiological properties of the tissue. One of the key difficulties in DCE-MRI quantification is that such models require an accurate measurement of the arterial input function. A particular problem is the high contrast agent concentration in the artery, which means that the assumption of signal linearity may be broken in the AIF with standard doses of contrast agent.

Beyond these general considerations, several organ-specific properties must be taken into account when optimizing a method, such as the low baseline signal intensity in the lungs, the rapid motion in the heart, the dual blood supply in the liver, the water reabsorption in the kidney, or the blood-brain-barrier in the brain. These considerations are discussed in further chapters dedicated to these organs.

References

[1] Shehata ML, Basha TA, Hayeri MR, Hartung D, Teytelboym OM, Vogel-Claussen J. MR myocardial perfusion imaging: insights on techniques, analysis, interpretation, and findings. Radiographics 2014;34(6):1636–57.

[2] Coelho-Filho OR, Rickers C, Kwong RY, Jerosch-Herold M. MR myocardial perfusion imaging. Radiology 2013;266(3):701–15.

[3] Bokacheva L, Rusinek H, Zhang JL, Lee VS. Assessment of renal function with dynamic contrast-enhanced MR imaging. Magn Reson Imaging Clin N Am 2008;16(4). 597–611, viii.

[4] Yankeelov TE, Gore JC. Dynamic contrast enhanced magnetic resonance imaging in oncology: theory, data acquisition, analysis, and examples. Curr Med Imaging Rev 2009;3(2):91–107.

[5] Do RK, Rusinek H, Taouli B. Dynamic contrast-enhanced MR imaging of the liver: current status and future directions. Magn Reson Imaging Clin N Am 2009;17(2):339–49.

[6] Franiel T, Hamm B, Hricak H. Dynamic contrast-enhanced magnetic resonance imaging and pharmacokinetic models in prostate cancer. Eur Radiol 2011;21(3):616–26.

[7] El Khouli RH, Macura KJ, Jacobs MA, Khalil TH, Kamel IR, Dwyer A, et al. Dynamic contrast-enhanced MRI of the breast: quantitative method for kinetic curve type assessment. Am J Roentgenol 2009;193(4):W295–300.

[8] Lin W, Guo J, Rosen MA, Song HK. Respiratory motion-compensated radial dynamic contrast-enhanced (DCE)-MRI of chest and abdominal lesions. Magn Reson Med 2008;60(5):1135–46.

[9] Gooding KM, Lienczewski C, Papale M, Koivuviita N, Maziarz M, Dutius Andersson A-M, et al. Prognostic imaging biomarkers for diabetic kidney disease (iBEAt): study protocol. medRxiv. 2020:2020.01.13.20017228.

[10] Lauffer RB. Paramagnetic metal-complexes as water proton relaxation agents for NMR imaging—theory and design. Chem Rev 1987;87(5):901–27.

[11] Strijkers GJ, Mulder WJ, van Tilborg GA, Nicolay K. MRI contrast agents: current status and future perspectives. Anti Cancer Agents Med Chem 2007;7(3):291–305.

[12] Que EL, Chang CJ. Responsive magnetic resonance imaging contrast agents as chemical sensors for metals in biology and medicine. Chem Soc Rev 2010;39(1):51–60.

[13] De Leon-Rodriguez LM, Martins AF, Pinho MC, Rofsky NM, Sherry AD. Basic MR relaxation mechanisms and contrast agent design. J Magn Reson Imaging 2015;42(3):545–65.

[14] Schabel MC, Parker DL. Uncertainty and bias in contrast concentration measurements using spoiled gradient echo pulse sequences. Phys Med Biol 2008;53(9):2345–73.

[15] Jerosch-Herold M. Quantification of myocardial perfusion by cardiovascular magnetic resonance. J Cardiovasc Magn Reson 2010;12:57.

[16] Orel SG, Schnall MD, LiVolsi VA, Troupin RH. Suspicious breast lesions: MR imaging with radiologic-pathologic correlation. Radiology 1994;190(2):485–93.

[17] Nunes LW, Schnall MD, Orel SG, Hochman MG, Langlotz CP, Reynolds CA, et al. Breast MR imaging: interpretation model. Radiology 1997;202(3):833–41.

[18] Chavhan GB, Babyn PS, Jankharia BG, Cheng HL, Shroff MM. Steady-state MR imaging sequences: physics, classification, and clinical applications. Radiographics 2008;28(4):1147–60.

[19] Hargreaves BA. Rapid gradient-echo imaging. J Magn Reson Imaging 2012;36(6):1300–13.

[20] Epstein FH, Mugler JP, Brookeman JR. Spoiling of transverse magnetization in gradient-echo (GRE) imaging during the approach to steady state. Magn Reson Med 1996;35(2):237–45.

[21] Larsson HB, Rosenbaum S, Fritz-Hansen T. Quantification of the effect of water exchange in dynamic contrast MRI perfusion measurements in the brain and heart. Magn Reson Med 2001;46(2):272–81.

[22] Cheng HL, Wright GA. Rapid high-resolution T(1) mapping by variable flip angles: accurate and precise measurements in the presence of radiofrequency field inhomogeneity. Magn Reson Med 2006;55(3): 566–74.

[23] Baudrexel S, Nöth U, Schüre JR, Deichmann R. T1 mapping with the variable flip angle technique: a simple correction for insufficient spoiling of transverse magnetization. Magn Reson Med 2018;79(6):3082–92.

[24] Fessler JA, Sutton BP. Nonuniform fast Fourier transforms using min-max interpolation. IEEE Trans Signal Process 2003;51(2):560–74.

[25] Fessler JA, Sangwoo L, Olafsson VT, Shi HR, Noll DC. Toeplitz-based iterative image reconstruction for MRI with correction for magnetic field inhomogeneity. IEEE Trans Signal Process 2005;53(9):3393–402.

[26] Benkert T, Tian Y, Huang C, DiBella EVR, Chandarana H, Feng L. Optimization and validation of accelerated golden-angle radial sparse MRI reconstruction with self-calibrating GRAPPA operator gridding. Magn Reson Med 2018;80(1):286–93.

[27] Tian Y, Erb KC, Adluru G, Likhite D, Pedgaonkar A, Blatt M, et al. Technical note: evaluation of pre-reconstruction interpolation methods for iterative reconstruction of radial k-space data. Med Phys 2017;44(8):4025–34.

[28] Baron CA, Dwork N, Pauly JM, Nishimura DG. Rapid compressed sensing reconstruction of 3D non-Cartesian MRI. Magn Reson Med 2018;79(5):2685–92.

[29] Seiberlich N, Breuer F, Heidemann R, Blaimer M, Griswold M, Jakob P. Reconstruction of undersampled non-Cartesian data sets using pseudo-Cartesian GRAPPA in conjunction with GROG. Magn Reson Med 2008;59(5):1127–37.

[30] Seiberlich N, Breuer F, Blaimer M, Jakob P, Griswold M. Self-calibrating GRAPPA operator gridding for radial and spiral trajectories. Magn Reson Med 2008;59(4):930–5.

[31] Seiberlich N, Ehses P, Duerk J, Gilkeson R, Griswold M. Improved radial GRAPPA calibration for real-time free-breathing cardiac imaging. Magn Reson Med 2011;65(2):492–505.

[32] Seiberlich N, Lee G, Ehses P, Duerk JL, Gilkeson R, Griswold M. Improved temporal resolution in cardiac imaging using through-time spiral GRAPPA. Magn Reson Med 2011;66(6):1682–8.

[33] Barth M, Breuer F, Koopmans PJ, Norris DG, Poser BA. Simultaneous multislice (SMS) imaging techniques. Magn Reson Med 2016;75(1):63–81.

[34] Setsompop K, Gagoski BA, Polimeni JR, Witzel T, Wedeen VJ, Wald LL. Blipped-controlled aliasing in parallel imaging for simultaneous multislice echo planar imaging with reduced g-factor penalty. Magn Reson Med 2012;67(5):1210–24.

[35] Breuer FA, Blaimer M, Heidemann RM, Mueller MF, Griswold MA, Jakob PM. Controlled aliasing in parallel imaging results in higher acceleration (CAIPIRINHA) for multi-slice imaging. Magn Reson Med 2005;53(3):684–91.

[36] Yutzy SR, Seiberlich N, Duerk JL, Griswold MA. Improvements in multislice parallel imaging using radial CAIPIRINHA. Magn Reson Med 2011;65(6):1630–7.

[37] Wang H, Adluru G, Chen L, Kholmovski EG, Bangerter NK, DiBella EV. Radial simultaneous multi-slice CAIPI for ungated myocardial perfusion. Magn Reson Imaging 2016;34(9):1329–36.

[38] Yang Y, Meyer CH, Epstein FH, Kramer CM, Salerno M. Whole-heart spiral simultaneous multi-slice first-pass myocardial perfusion imaging. Magn Reson Med 2018;81(2):852–62.

[39] Stab D, Wech T, Breuer FA, Weng AM, Ritter CO, Hahn D, et al. High resolution myocardial first-pass perfusion imaging with extended anatomic coverage. J Magn Reson Imaging 2014;39(6):1575–87.

[40] Tian Y, Mendes J, Pedgaonkar A, Ibrahim M, Jensen L, Schroeder JD, et al. Feasibility of multiple-view myocardial perfusion MRI using radial simultaneous multi-slice acquisitions. Plos One 2019;14(2), e0211738.

[41] Kim H. Variability in quantitative DCE-MRI: sources and solutions. J Nat Sci 2018;4(1), e484.

[42] JM EDB, Ibrahim M, Tian Y, Wilson B, Adluru G, editors. Multiple sets of simultaneous multi-slice (SMS) for improved short and long axis coverage of myocardial DCE perfusion. Proceedings of the 26th annual meeting of ISMRM, Paris, France; 2018.
[43] Kellman P, Hansen MS, Nielles-Vallespin S, Nickander J, Themudo R, Ugander M, et al. Myocardial perfusion cardiovascular magnetic resonance: optimized dual sequence and reconstruction for quantification. J Cardiovasc Magn Reson 2017;19(1):43.
[44] Gatehouse PD, Elkington AG, Ablitt NA, Yang GZ, Pennell DJ, Firmin DN. Accurate assessment of the arterial input function during high-dose myocardial perfusion cardiovascular magnetic resonance. J Magn Reson Imaging 2004;20(1):39–45.
[45] Christian TF, Aletras AH, Arai AE. Estimation of absolute myocardial blood flow during first-pass MR perfusion imaging using a dual-bolus injection technique: comparison to single-bolus injection method. J Magn Reson Imaging 2008;27(6):1271–7.
[46] Pruessmann KP, Weiger M, Scheidegger MB, Boesiger P. SENSE: sensitivity encoding for fast MRI. Magn Reson Med 1999;42(5):952–62.
[47] Griswold MA, Jakob PM, Heidemann RM, Nittka M, Jellus V, Wang J, et al. Generalized autocalibrating partially parallel acquisitions (GRAPPA). Magn Reson Med 2002;47(6):1202–10.
[48] Blaimer M, Breuer F, Mueller M, Heidemann RM, Griswold MA, Jakob PM. SMASH, SENSE, PILS, GRAPPA: how to choose the optimal method. Top Magn Reson Imaging 2004;15(4):223–36.
[49] Chen Y, Lee GR, Wright KL, Badve C, Nakamoto D, Yu A, et al. Free-breathing liver perfusion imaging using 3-dimensional through-time spiral generalized autocalibrating partially parallel acquisition acceleration. Investig Radiol 2015;50(6):367–75.
[50] Lustig M, Donoho DL, Santos JM, Pauly JM. Compressed sensing MRI. IEEE Signal Process Mag 2008;25(2):72–82.
[51] Lustig M, Donoho D, Pauly JM. Sparse MRI: the application of compressed sensing for rapid MR imaging. Magn Reson Med 2007;58(6):1182–95.
[52] Adluru G, McGann C, Speier P, Kholmovski EG, Shaaban A, Dibella EV. Acquisition and reconstruction of undersampled radial data for myocardial perfusion magnetic resonance imaging. J Magn Reson Imaging 2009;29(2):466–73.
[53] Pedersen H, Kozerke S, Ringgaard S, Nehrke K, Kim WY. k-t PCA: temporally constrained k-t BLAST reconstruction using principal component analysis. Magn Reson Med 2009;62(3):706–16.
[54] Lingala SG, Hu Y, DiBella E, Jacob M. Accelerated dynamic MRI exploiting sparsity and low-rank structure: k-t SLR. IEEE Trans Med Imaging 2011;30(5):1042–54.
[55] Otazo R, Candes E, Sodickson DK. Low-rank plus sparse matrix decomposition for accelerated dynamic MRI with separation of background and dynamic components. Magn Reson Med 2015;73(3):1125–36.
[56] Feng L, Grimm R, Block KT, Chandarana H, Kim S, Xu J, et al. Golden-angle radial sparse parallel MRI: combination of compressed sensing, parallel imaging, and golden-angle radial sampling for fast and flexible dynamic volumetric MRI. Magn Reson Med 2014;72(3):707–17.
[57] Guo Y, Lingala SG, Bliesener Y, Lebel RM, Zhu Y, Nayak KS. Joint arterial input function and tracer kinetic parameter estimation from undersampled dynamic contrast-enhanced MRI using a model consistency constraint. Magn Reson Med 2018;79(5):2804–15.
[58] Guo Y, Lingala SG, Zhu Y, Lebel RM, Nayak KS. Direct estimation of tracer-kinetic parameter maps from highly undersampled brain dynamic contrast enhanced MRI. Magn Reson Med 2017;78(4):1566–78.
[59] Awate SP, DiBella EV, Tasdizen T, Whitaker RT. Model-based image reconstruction for dynamic cardiac perfusion MRI from sparse data, In: Conference proceedings: annual international conference of the IEEE Engineering in Medicine and Biology Society IEEE Engineering in Medicine and Biology Society annual conference, vol. 1; 2006. p. 936–41.

[60] Dikaios N, Arridge S, Hamy V, Punwani S, Atkinson D. Direct parametric reconstruction from undersampled (k, t)-space data in dynamic contrast enhanced MRI. Med Image Anal 2014;18(7):989–1001.
[61] Felsted B, Whitaker R, Schabel M, EV DB. Model-based reconstruction for undersampled dynamic contrast enhanced MRI. Lake Buena Vista (Orlando Area), FL, USA: SPIE; 2009.
[62] Bidaut LM, Vallee JP. Automated registration of dynamic MR images for the quantification of myocardial perfusion. J Magn Reson Imaging 2001;13(4):648–55.
[63] Dornier C, Ivancevic MK, Thevenaz P, Vallee JP. Improvement in the quantification of myocardial perfusion using an automatic spline-based registration algorithm. J Magn Reson Imaging 2003;18(2):160–8.
[64] Adluru G, DiBella EVR, Schabel MC. Model-based registration for dynamic cardiac perfusion MRI. J Magn Reson Imaging 2006;24(5):1062–70.
[65] Buonaccorsi GA, O'Connor JP, Caunce A, Roberts C, Cheung S, Watson Y, et al. Tracer kinetic model-driven registration for dynamic contrast-enhanced MRI time-series data. Magn Reson Med 2007;58(5): 1010–1019.
[66] Hamy V, Dikaios N, Punwani S, Melbourne A, Latifoltojar A, Makanyanga J, et al. Respiratory motion correction in dynamic MRI using robust data decomposition registration—application to DCE-MRI. Med Image Anal 2014;18(2):301–13.
[67] Feng Q, Zhou Y, Li X, Mei Y, Lu Z, Zhang Y, et al. Liver DCE-MRI registration in manifold space based on robust principal component analysis. Sci Rep 2016;6:34461.
[68] Benovoy M, Jacobs M, Cheriet F, Dahdah N, Arai AE, Hsu L-Y. Robust universal nonrigid motion correction framework for first-pass cardiac MR perfusion imaging. J Magn Reson Imaging 2017;46(4):1060–72.
[69] Reconstruction with diffeomorphic motion compensation for undersampled dynamic MRI. Adluru G, EV DB, editors. SPIE optical engineering + applications. San Diego, CA, USA: SPIE; 2013.
[70] Lingala SG, DiBella E, Jacob M. Deformation corrected compressed sensing (DC-CS): a novel framework for accelerated dynamic MRI. IEEE Trans Med Imaging 2015;34(1):72–85.
[71] DiBella EVR, Chen L, Schabel MC, Adluru G, McGann CJ. Myocardial perfusion acquisition without magnetization preparation or gating. Magn Reson Med 2012;67(3):609–13.
[72] He D, Zamora M, Oto A, Karczmar GS, Fan X. Comparison of region-of-interest-averaged and pixel-averaged analysis of DCE-MRI data based on simulations and pre-clinical experiments. Phys Med Biol 2017;62(18):N445–59.
[73] Biglands J, Magee D, Boyle R, Larghat A, Plein S, Radjenovic A. Evaluation of the effect of myocardial segmentation errors on myocardial blood flow estimates from DCE-MRI. Phys Med Biol 2011;56(8): 2423–2443.
[74] Likhite D, Adluru G, Hu N, McGann C, DiBella E. Quantification of myocardial perfusion with self-gated cardiovascular magnetic resonance. J Cardiovasc Magn Reson 2015;17:14.
[75] Yang X, Le Minh H, Tim Cheng KT, Sung KH, Liu W. Renal compartment segmentation in DCE-MRI images. Med Image Anal 2016;32:269–80.
[76] Irving B, Cifor A, Papiez BW, Franklin J, Anderson EM, Brady SM, et al. Automated colorectal tumour segmentation in DCE-MRI using supervoxel neighbourhood contrast characteristics, In: Medical image computing and computer-assisted intervention: MICCAI international conference on medical image computing and computer-assisted intervention, vol. 17(Pt 1); 2014. p. 609–16.
[77] Adluru G, DiBella EVR, Whitaker RT, editors. Automatic segmentation of cardiac short axis slices in perfusion. Biomedical imaging: nano to macro, 2006 3rd IEEE international symposium on; 2006 6–9 April; 2006.
[78] Zujun H, Yue W, Choon Hua T, Quan-Sing N, Vicky G, Tong SK. Automatic region-of-interest segmentation and registration of dynamic contrast-enhanced images of colorectal tumors. Phys Med Biol 2014; 59(23):7361.

[79] Hodneland E, Hanson EA, Lundervold A, Modersitzki J, Eikefjord E, Munthe-Kaas AZ. Segmentation-driven image registration-application to 4D DCE-MRI recordings of the moving kidneys. IEEE Trans Image Process 2014;23(5):2392–404.
[80] Zhang J, Freed M, Winters K, Kim SG. Effect of T2* correction on contrast kinetic model analysis using a reference tissue arterial input function at 7 T. Magma 2015;28(6):555–63.
[81] Kleppesto M, Larsson C, Groote I, Salo R, Vardal J, Courivaud F, et al. T2*-correction in dynamic contrast-enhanced MRI from double-echo acquisitions. J Magn Reson Imaging 2014;39(5):1314–9.
[82] Kl Z. Theoretical basis of indicator-dilution methods for measuring flow and volume. Circ Res 1962;10:393.
[83] Tofts PS, Brix G, Buckley DL, Evelhoch JL, Henderson E, Knopp MV, et al. Estimating kinetic parameters from dynamic contrast-enhanced t1-weighted MRI of a diffusable tracer: standardized quantities and symbols. J Magn Reson Imaging 1999;10(3):223–32.
[84] Jerosch-Herold M, Wilke N, Stillman AE. Magnetic resonance quantification of the myocardial perfusion reserve with a Fermi function model for constrained deconvolution. Med Phys 1998;25:73–84.
[85] Pack NA, DiBella EVR, Rust TC, Kadrmas DJ, McGann CJ, Butterfield R, et al. Estimating myocardial perfusion from dynamic contrast-enhanced CMR with a model-independent deconvolution method. J Cardiovasc Magn Reson 2008;10(1):52.
[86] Sourbron S, Dujardin M, Makkat S, Luypaert R. Pixel-by-pixel deconvolution of bolus-tracking data: optimization and implementation. Phys Med Biol 2007;52(2):429.
[87] Jerosch-Herold M, Swingen C, Seethamraju RT. Myocardial blood flow quantification with MRI by model-independent deconvolution. Med Phys 2002;29:886–97.
[88] Pack NA, DiBella EV. Comparison of myocardial perfusion estimates from dynamic contrast-enhanced magnetic resonance imaging with four quantitative analysis methods. Magn Reson Med 2010;64:125–37.
[89] Murase K. Efficient method for calculating kinetic parameters using T1-weighted dynamic contrast-enhanced magnetic resonance imaging. Magn Reson Med 2004;51(4):858–62.
[90] Flouri D, Lesnic D, Sourbron SP. Fitting the two-compartment model in DCE-MRI by linear inversion. Magn Reson Med 2016;76(3):998–1006.
[91] Ta AD, Hsu L-Y, Conn HM, Winkler S, Greve AM, Shanbhag SM, et al. Fully quantitative pixel-wise analysis of cardiovascular magnetic resonance perfusion improves discrimination of dark rim artifact from perfusion defects associated with epicardial coronary stenosis. J Cardiovasc Magn Reson 2018;20(1):16.
[92] Goud Lingala S, Guo Y, Lebel RM, Zhu Y, Bliesener Y, Law M, et al. Tracer kinetic models as temporal constraints during DCE-MRI reconstruction, ArXiv e-prints [Internet] 2017;(July 01):2017. Available from:https://ui.adsabs.harvard.edu/#abs/2017arXiv170707569G.

CHAPTER

Dynamic Susceptibility Contrast MRI: Basic Physics, Pulse Sequences, and Modeling

14

Endre Grøvik[a], Atle Bjørnerud[a,b], and Kyrre Eeg Emblem[a]

[a]*Department of Diagnostic Physics, Division of Radiology and Nuclear Medicine, Oslo University Hospital, Oslo, Norway* [b]*Computational Radiology & Artificial Intelligence (CRAI), Division of Radiology and Nuclear Medicine, Oslo University Hospital, Oslo, Norway*

14.1 Introduction

Perfusion Magnetic Resonance Imaging (MRI) is a powerful tool to characterize tissue hemodynamic properties. In this setting, perfusion MRI involves the dynamic acquisition of MR images in combination with intravenous administration of a contrast-enhancing agent, usually a gadolinium-based contrast agent (GBCA). A range of diseases is inherently associated with perfusion through impaired, irregular, or abnormal vascularization. These include vascular diseases such as ischemic stroke, cancer, infectious, or inflammatory diseases, as well as neurodegenerative diseases of the central nervous system (CNS). Monitoring perfusion in vivo is therefore an essential target in clinical settings with the potential for an early and accurate diagnosis. Although "perfusion MRI" is commonly used to collectively describe both dynamic contrast-enhanced (DCE)-MRI, dynamic susceptibility contrast (DSC)-MRI, and arterial spin labeling (ASL), this chapter will focus on DSC-MRI and detail various aspects related to basic principles, pulse sequences, and pharmacokinetic modeling.

Whereas DCE-MRI is sensitive to the T_1-shortening effect caused by contrast agent extravasation, the contrast in DSC-MRI is generated by susceptibility effects caused by the rapid passage of contrast agent through the capillary bed following a bolus injection [1]. Because the susceptibility effect of GBCA is strongly dependent on compartmentalization of the agent in tissue, DSC-MRI is particularly useful in CNS applications [2,3]. GBCA typically cannot cross the intact blood-brain barrier (BBB), and this compartmentalization gives rise to large intra-to-extravascular susceptibility gradients during the contrast agent bolus passage. The resulting transient signal loss due to the shortening of transverse relaxation times reflects local microvascular status and enables estimation of perfusion-related metrics.

The standard signal models used to derive perfusion-related metrics from DSC-MRI acquisitions explicitly presume that the contrast agent remains in the intravascular compartment during the entire measurement period. However, this presumption, combined with the reduced susceptibility effect in "leaky" tissues, has challenged the application of DSC-MRI outside the brain. Similarly, within the CNS, disruption of the BBB and consequent extravasation of GBCA is a confounding factor in DSC-MRI. Nevertheless, several studies have shown the feasibility and potential of using DSC-MRI to assess perfusion-impaired pathology in other organs [4–8].

Advances in Magnetic Resonance Technology and Applications. Volume 1. ISSN 2666-9099. https://doi.org/10.1016/B978-0-12-817057-1.00016-0

14.2 Biophysical foundations

14.2.1 Dose-response in DSC-MRI

Gadolinium is a paramagnetic metal, and when compartmentalized to a small fraction of the tissue volume (e.g., the intravascular fraction) as a blood-borne tracer, GBCA will induce large local variations in the magnetic field, significantly reducing T_2^+ (transversal) relaxation times. Here, T_2^+ refers jointly to both T_2 and T_2^* relaxation, where T_2 is the transverse relaxation time due to direct dipole-dipole interactions, and T_2^* is the "effective" transverse relaxation time, reflecting the combined effect of T_2 and additional relaxation due to macroscopic magnetic field inhomogeneities. Contrast agent-induced T_2^+ relaxation affects not only voxels in the compartment where the contrast agent is present, but also gives rise to a so-called "blooming effect," with corresponding signal loss outside the tissue volume of origin. In fact, most of the observed signal change in brain DSC-MRI is due to extravascular relaxation [9]. DSC-sequences are thus heavily T_2^+-weighted for optimal sensitivity to susceptibility-induced relaxation and relative insensitivity to the concurrent T_1 relaxivity of the GBCA.

The DSC-MRI formalism requires knowledge of contrast agent concentrations both in blood and tissues, and conversion from MR signal intensity to contrast agent concentration is essentially a two-step process:

$$\Delta S(t) \rightarrow \Delta R_2{}^+(t) \rightarrow \Delta C(t) \tag{14.1}$$

where $\Delta S(t)$ is the measured change in signal during contrast agent passage, $\Delta R_2^+(t)$ is corresponding changes in transverse relaxation rate $(=1/T_2{}^+)$ and $\Delta C(t)$ is the contrast agent concentration.

In DSC-MRI, echo-planar imaging (EPI) sequences are almost exclusively used; either the gradient echo (GRE) signal (GRE-EPI) is directly read out, or a refocusing pulse is added to generate a spin echo (SE) signal (SE-EPI). Assuming a monoexponential $T_2{}^+$-induced signal decay, the resulting MR signal measured by EPI sequences can be approximated by the expression [10]:

$$S = S_0 E_1(R_1, \mathrm{TR}, \alpha) \cdot \exp\left(\text{-TE} \cdot R_2^+\right) \tag{14.2}$$

where TE is the echo time, TR is the repetition time, α is the flip angle, E_1 is a factor reflecting the T_1-dependent signal contribution, and S_0 is a constant that generally depends on voxel location. The effect of a contrast agent bolus in tissue can then be assessed by normalizing the signal during bolus passage, $S(t)$ to the prebolus signal, $S(0)$:

$$\frac{S(t)}{S(0)} = \frac{E_1(R_1(t), \mathrm{TR}, \alpha)}{E_1(R_1(0), \mathrm{TR}, \alpha)} \exp\left[\text{-TE}\left(R_2^+(t) - R_2^+(0)\right)\right] \tag{14.3}$$

Assuming $\Delta R_2{}^+(t) = \text{-}R_2{}^+(t)\text{-}R_2{}^+(0)$ and rearranging gives

$$\Delta R_2^+(t) = \frac{1}{\mathrm{TE}}\left\{ \ln\left(\frac{S(0)}{S(t)}\right) - \ln\left(\frac{E_1(0)}{E_1(t)}\right)\right\} \approx \frac{1}{\mathrm{TE}} \ln\left(\frac{S(0)}{S(t)}\right) \tag{14.4}$$

In the presence of significant T_1-shortening effects, $E_1(t) \gg E_1(0)$ and $\Delta R_2{}^+(t)$ is underestimated by a factor given by $\ln[E_1(t)/E_1(0)]/\mathrm{TE}$, when calculated from the log ratio of $S(0)/S(t)$. Note that the T_1-dependent signal contribution can be dramatically increased in the case of contrast agent extravasation [11].

The second step of Eq. (14.1) involves converting the change in T_2^+ to a change in contrast agent concentration. For this conversion, a linear relationship is usually assumed for simplicity:

$$\Delta R_2'(t) = C(t) \cdot r_2{}^+ \tag{14.5}$$

where $C(t)$ is the concentration (in millimolar, mM) of contrast agent in tissue and r_2^+ is the in vivo T_2^+ *relaxivity* of the agent (in units of $mM^{-1}s^{-1}$). The measured $\Delta R_2^+(t)$ can thus be directly converted to contrast agent concentration if r_2^+ is known or can be estimated. It should, however, be stressed that the assumption $\Delta R_2^+(t) = C(t) \cdot r_2^+$ (with r_2^+ equal for all tissue types and pure blood) is a gross simplification. While this relationship is almost exclusively applied in clinical DSC-MRI, in reality, $\Delta R_2^+(t)$ is composed of a sum of multiple relaxation rates where the magnitude of each component has a different dependency on $C(t)$ as a function of both image readout (i.e., SE- versus GRE-EPI) and tissue microstructure.

14.2.2 Transverse relaxivity of contrast agents in vivo

The MR signal behavior in magnetically inhomogeneous tissue structures has been extensively investigated using both analytical and simulation approaches. Yablonskiy and Haacke [12] and later Kiselev and Posse [13], through their pioneering work in the 1990s, established the theoretical framework describing transverse relaxation effects in magnetically inhomogeneous media. In parallel, models based on Monte Carlo simulations were developed, providing estimates of relaxation effects across a wider range of relaxation regimes [14–17].

From this comprehensive research (see Ref. [9] for an in-depth review) it can be concluded that effective transverse relaxivity in vivo is dependent on multiple MR system, tissue, and contrast-agent specific parameters including

- Size and geometry of contrast-agent-containing tissue compartments giving rise to susceptibility variations.
- Tissue water diffusivity.
- Magnitude of susceptibility variations: i.e., contrast agent dose, injection regime, and MR field strength.
- Dominant MR sequence contrast weighting: i.e., SE-type versus GRE-type sequence.
- Time-scale of MR measurement: echo time, TE.

The efficacy of a magnetic perturber (e.g., capillaries containing GBCA) can be expressed in terms of its characteristic shift in the Larmor frequency, $\Delta\omega$. The resulting transverse relaxation effect is divided into different relaxation regimes, depending on the magnitude of $\Delta\omega$ relative to the size of the perturbers (effective radius) and water diffusivity. The "static dephasing regime" refers to the condition where water diffusion effects are insignificant, and protons experience different but essentially time-invariant magnetic fields between the MR excitation pulse and the corresponding signal readout (during one TE). Signal dephasing can then be rephased with RF-refocusing pulses in SE-based sequences. The resulting transverse relaxation change is therefore much less in SE-based (T_2-weighted) sequences than in GRE-based (T_2*-weighted) sequences where spin rephasing cannot be achieved even in a static regime. The condition for the assumptions of the static dephasing regime to be valid can then be expressed in terms of $\Delta\omega$, the perturber radius, R, and diffusion constant, D, according to

$$\Delta\omega^{-1} \ll R^2/D \quad \text{and} \quad \sqrt{D \cdot \mathrm{TE}} \ll R \tag{14.6}$$

The other end of the relaxation spectrum refers to the *diffusion narrowing regime* where the diffusion length of the protons during the echo time TE is comparable to or greater than the temporal field variations these protons will experience. Consequently, significant diffusion averaging will occur and both SE- and GRE-signals are attenuated.

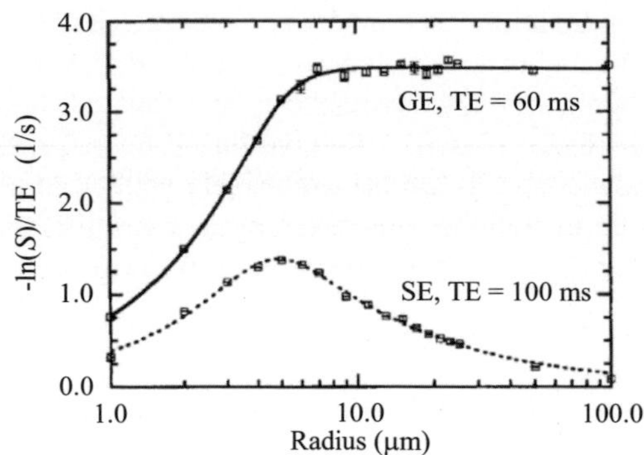

FIG. 14.1

Monte Carlo simulations of transverse relaxation rate dependence on vessel radius in spin echo (SE) and gradient echo (GE) sequences. See the text for details.

Reprinted with permission from Boxerman JL, et al. MR contrast due to intravascular magnetic susceptibility perturbations, Magn Reson Med 1995;34(4):555–66. https://doi.org/10.1002/mrm.1910340412.

Fig. 14.1 shows a simulation of T_2 and T_2* relaxation rates as a function of vessel radius for intravascular contrast agent distribution. These results were obtained using Monte Carlo simulations, assuming clinically relevant GBCA concentrations, TE, and tissue blood volume fractions [14]. This differential T_2- versus T_2*-relaxivity dependency on vessel caliber has been described and confirmed in numerous other studies [13,16]. Here, the shift from the diffusion narrowing regime to the static dephasing regime happens at peak SE relaxivity equal to a perturber radius of a few μm (the capillary diameter range) [16]. For smaller radii, proton diffusion is so fast that the SE refocusing pulse is basically ineffective. In contrast, for larger radii, the SE refocusing pulse will modulate the protons with rapidly decreasing relaxivity, while correspondingly the GRE-based signal is dominated by intravoxel dephasing and diffusion effects become insignificant. Consequently, for larger perturber radius, the GRE- and SE-signals are weakly correlated.

The important take-home message from these results is that contrast agent relaxivity in DSC-MRI is strongly dependent on MR sequence type and microvascular tissue properties. Although this complex relaxation behavior poses challenges for obtaining absolute quantitative perfusion measures from DSC-MRI, it also opens intriguing new opportunities to probe microvascular structure and function.

14.3 DSC-MRI data acquisition

14.3.1 Current recommendations

Optimized and standardized DSC-MRI data acquisition and postprocessing protocols are essential for clinical use and data compatibility between studies and sites [18]. Efforts to provide much-needed consensus guidelines for clinical imaging are ongoing by the Quantitative Imaging Biomarker Alliance (QIBA), and recent guidelines have been established by the clinical practice committee of the American Society for Functional Neuroradiology (ASFNR). Table 14.1 summarizes the current recommendations of the ASFNR for DSC-MRI of the brain [19].

Table 14.1 Overview of key imaging parameters and recommendations for DSC-MRI.

Parameter	Recommendation
Sequence	GRE-EPI or SE-EPI
TR	$\leq$1.5 s or "as short as possible"
TE	40–45 ms at 1.5 T; 25–35 ms at 3 T.
Flip angle	60°–70°
Temporal coverage	90–120 time points (2–3 min)
Acquisition matrix[a]	128 × 128 (range, 64 × 64 to 256 × 256)
FOV[a]	20 × 20 cm (range, 16 × 16 to 24 × 24 cm)
In-plane resolution[a]	Approximately 1.5 mm (range, 1.5 to 2.0 mm)
Slice thickness	3–5 mm
Number of dynamic frames	90–120 (2–3 min)
Number of slices	15–25
CA dose	0.1 mmol/kg body weight
Number of baseline (precontrast) images	30–50

EPI, *echo planar imaging;* FOV, *field-of-view;* GRE, *gradient echo;* SE, *spin echo;* TE, *echo time;* TR, *repetition time.*
[a]*General recommendation given applies for CNS imaging. Parameter selection may vary depending on the body part being scanned (see range).*

Commonly, a DSC-MRI exam is conducted using a two-dimensional GRE- or SE-EPI readout with a repetition time of ~1.5 s, resulting in a total imaging time of a few minutes with over 100 time points. The recommended dose of GBCA administered during this time is 0.1 mmol/kg of body weight. For CNS imaging, a minimum injection rate of 3 mL/s (range, 3–5 mL/s) is recommended to provide a well-defined first-pass bolus in the tissue of interest. Contrast agent injection should be directly followed by a 25 mL (range, 10–30 mL) saline flush at the same injection rate. In the case of CNS-imaging, an additional administration of a small preload dose (approx. 25% of total GBCA dose) 5–10 min prior to the DSC-MRI acquisition is recommended, especially if a high flip angle (toward 90°) is used. The presence of this contrast agent saturates the tissue signal by suppressing confounding T_1-shortening effects caused by contrast agent extravasation [20,21]. The aim of preload dose is to obtain more accurate DSC-based perfusion estimates in permeable tissues [22,23], and it has the attractive side benefit that the predose can be used for complementary DCE-MRI. However, because the high sensitivity of the perfusion estimates to the predose, the true added value of this approach has also been questioned [24]. Alternatively, minimizing T_1 weighting in EPI sequences can be achieved using a combination of lower flip angle, longer TR, and longer TE, i.e., the values given in Table 14.1 [11].

The choice of acquisition parameters is ultimately dictated by image signal-to-noise ratio (SNR) considerations, temporal resolution requirements, and the presence of excessive susceptibility effects at very long TEs [25]. The optimal settings for DSC-based perfusion mapping are contingent on disease- and tissue-specific properties. For instance, a shorter TE is advised for CNS glioma characterization, as well as for quantification of arterial inflow [26].

Although DSC-MRI can be adequately performed on all modern $\geq$1.5 T MR systems, the susceptibility effect increases linearly with increasing field strength [27]. Consequently, at 3 T or even at the ultrahigh fields of 7 T and beyond [28], equivalent contrast agent effect (in terms of SNR) to that of lower magnetic field strengths can be achieved at a lower contrast agent dose or at shorter TEs, potentially enabling a higher temporal resolution and/or improved brain coverage.

Both 2D and 3D EPI sequences may be used for DSC-MRI [29], but 2D GRE-EPI sequences are most common due to high temporal resolution and acceptable level of through-plane blurring [19]. While both SE- and GRE-based EPI sequences are in use, GRE-EPI tends to be preferred in clinical routine due to higher contrast agent sensitivity and consequently higher SNR in the resulting parametric maps. Fig. 14.2 shows sample cases of dose-response curves and resulting parametric maps for SE- versus GRE-EPI sequences (generated from a double echo SE/GRE EPI-acquisition).

14.3.2 Susceptibility artifacts

Due to the need for high spatiotemporal resolution and wide spatial coverage, DSC-MRI is challenged by certain limitations. One major hurdle with EPI sequences is that they are sensitive to all susceptibility differences, both from the contrast agent and also those associated with the inherent and concurrent susceptibility effects in the body. These can give rise to signal loss and geometric/intensity distortions, which can complicate perfusion quantification [30,31]. These artifacts are most severe in regions with large variations in magnetic susceptibility; namely interfaces between tissue and bone or air. Moreover, rapid magnetic field variations over short distances (relative to the voxel size) result in intra-voxel dephasing, and consequent (TE-dependent) signal loss. Intravoxel dephasing is less dominant in SE-EPI than that in GRE-EPI because static dephasing effects can be partly rephased. Fig. 14.3 illustrates the difference in signal loss between SE- and GRE-EPI sequences from intravoxel dephasing in a postoperative patient with metastasis to the brain.

In addition to intravoxel dephasing, the collective bulk susceptibility effects can cause image voxel misregistration if the voxel bandwidth is low relative to the bulk offset in the magnetic field:

$$\Delta x = \pm\gamma\Delta B(x)/BW_x \tag{14.7}$$

where Δx is the artificial shift in image voxel position, BW_x is the pixel bandwidth along the x-direction, and $\Delta B(x)$ is the bulk shift in B_0. The pixel BW in the frequency encoding direction is inversely proportional to the readout time of a single k-space line. Since the readout time is very short in EPI sequences, the resulting BW is high (of the order of 1000–3000 Hz/pixel) and the resulting geometric distortion is thus usually minor in the frequency encoding direction. In the phase encoding direction, however, the effective pixel bandwidth, BW_y, is given by the inverse of the total readout time per slice. Hence, for a single-shot EPI sequence, it follows $BW_y = BW_x/N_y$, where N_y equals the number of phase encoding k-space lines. The resulting low BW_y (typically 10–50 Hz/pixel) makes EPI imaging very sensitive to geometric distortions in the phase encoding direction, and the pixel shift can be several centimeters, resulting in severe geometric distortions [32].

To reduce spatial distortions in EPI sequences, several correction techniques have been proposed; the most promising being the "reverse gradient polarity" approach [33–35]. Here, one or more additional EPI volumes are acquired where the polarity (i.e., the direction of the k-space trajectory along the phase encoding axis) of the phase encoding gradient is reversed relative to that of the reference series. The polarity of the phase encoding gradient determines the "direction" of the susceptibility induced voxel shift and it can be shown that a spatially correct undistorted image can be determined directly from the EPI magnitude images acquired with the opposite phase encoding polarity as the "midway" between two images. Although this approach has thus far mainly been applied to diffusion-weighted SE-EPI scans, it has also shown utility in DSC-MRI [32]. The main advantage of the reversed polarity approach is that it

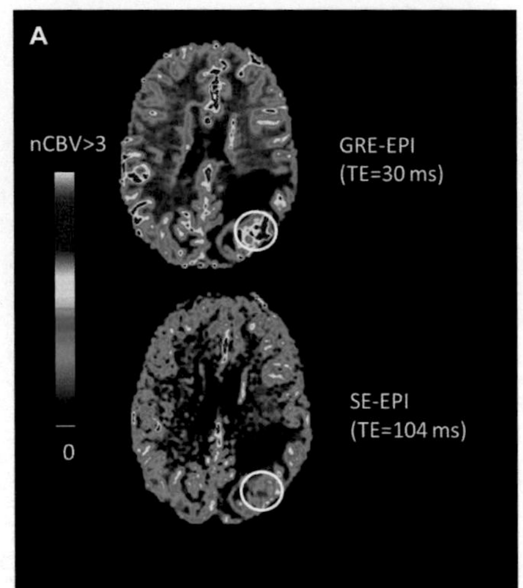

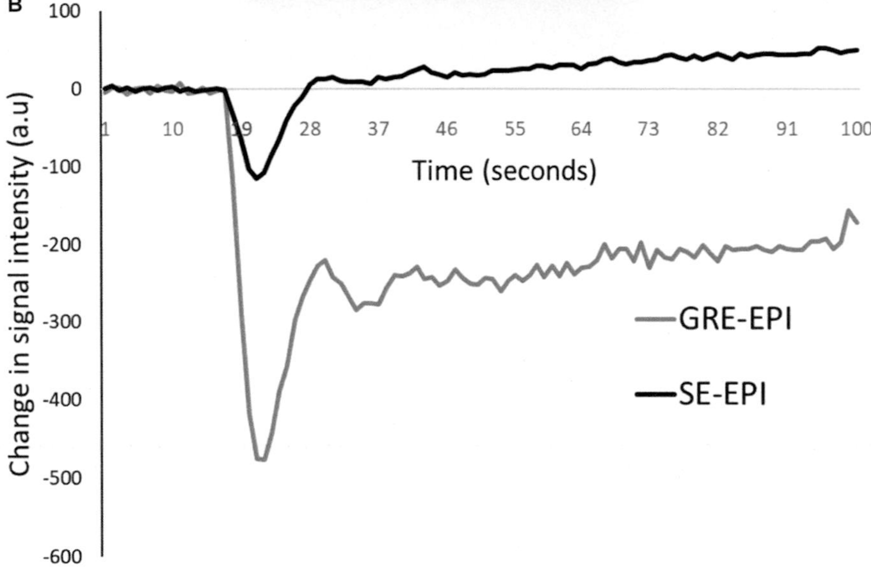

FIG. 14.2

(A) Normalized CBV maps (nCBV) collected using GRE-EPI and SE-EPI, respectively. (B) The corresponding signal time course for the tumor in the ROI shown in the white circles. The larger magnitude of the first-pass response in the GRE-EPI sequence is evident despite a much shorter TE, resulting in higher quality blood volume maps compared to SE-EPI. The shorter TE in GRE-EPI also enables the acquisition of more slices for a given TR. Note the tumor ROI signal "overshoot" in the SE-EPI series reflecting T_1-dominant extravasation effects, whereas the leakage induces T_2*-dominant extravasation effects in the GRE-EPI series. Finally, the appearance of macroscopic vessels in the GRE-EPI derived blood volume map is more prominent, reflecting the higher sensitivity of GRE-EPI to larger vessels.

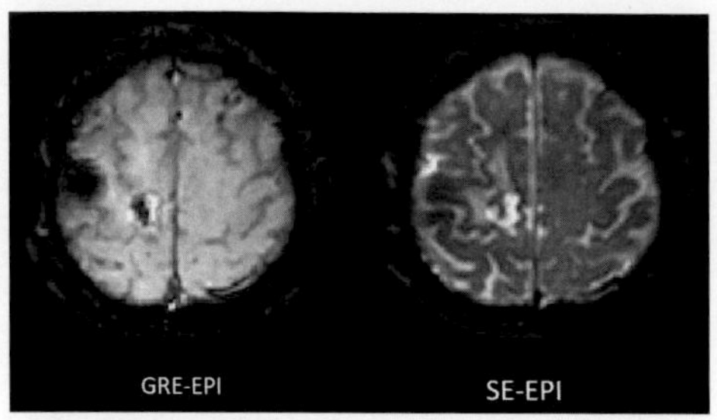

FIG. 14.3

Difference in signal loss between SE- and GRE-EPI sequences from intravoxel dephasing in a postoperative patient with a metastasis to the brain. Note the large areas of total signal loss in the GRE-EPI series compared to the SE-EPI series regardless of shorter echo time (30 versus 104ms).

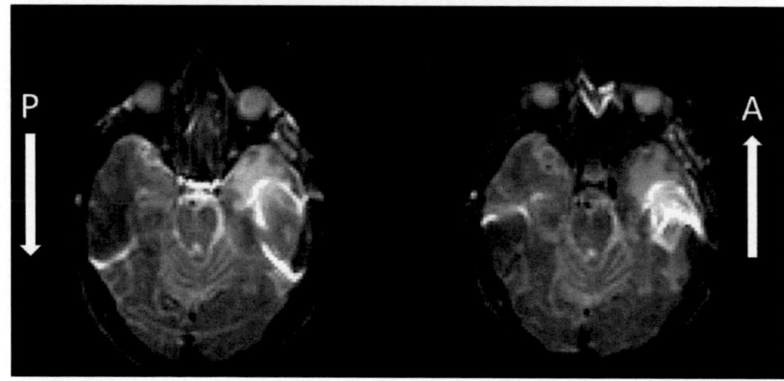

FIG. 14.4

EPI images are very sensitive to geometric distortions in the phase encoding direction. An illustrative example of a patient with an intra-axial glioma and two parallel EPI readouts with opposite phase encoding in the posterior (P) and anterior (A) directions, respectively. The apparent geometric distortions from phase encoding gradient polarity on the observed (apparent) tumor location and shape are clearly evident.

only requires one extra EPI series, taking only a few seconds to acquire. The method is probably most easily applicable to SE-EPI scans, while GRE-based acquisitions may also require alternative and more time-consuming approaches based on the generation of additional phase maps [36]. Fig. 14.4 shows the effect of reversing the phase encoding gradient polarity in SE-EPI DSC of a glioma patient.

14.3.3 Non-GBCA tracers

In recent years, non-GBCA tracers have increasingly been recognized for their potential in DSC-MRI. Even though manganese-based contrast agents were first introduced in the late 1970s [37], the benefits of these agents over GBCA were not widely appreciated, and the only Food and Drug Administration (FDA)-approved manganese-based contrast agent mangafodipir (Teslascan) was withdrawn from the market in 2012 [38]. However, in light of the association between GBCA and the development of nephrogenic systemic fibrosis and the recent reports of gadolinium accumulation in the central nervous system, manganese-based contrast agents may again be taken up as an alternative to GBCAs [39]. Furthermore, submicron superparamagnetic iron-oxide particles (SPIOs/USPIOs) are highly potent MR contrast agents [40]. In particular, ferumoxytol, an agent originally marketed for treating anemia in adult patients [41], is increasingly being used off-label owing to its inherent T_1- and T_2-shortening effect and long blood pool residence time [42]. Given that iron is a naturally occurring element in the body, ferumoxytol-enhanced imaging is feasible in adult patients as well as children with impaired renal function [43]. The use of ferumoxytol as a substitute for GBCAs in MR angiography was demonstrated early after its introduction [44,45], and more recently its potential to yield similar perfusion maps when used for DSC-MRI of the brain has also been demonstrated [46,47].

14.4 DSC-MRI data analysis for perfusion mapping

14.4.1 Forward models

The concept of deriving functional information from dynamic contrast-based MRI data is based on the *tracer kinetic modeling* presented in Chapter 13, applied to the specific context of intravascular tracers in the brain. In DSC-MRI of the brain, the arterial input function (AIF) is typically defined in arterial blood (as opposed to plasma) and the *central volume principle* is expressed for intravascular tracers as [48]:

$$MTT = \frac{CBV}{CBF} \tag{14.8}$$

where CBV is the cerebral blood volume (the volume of blood per unit mass of tissue in units of mL/g), CBF is the cerebral blood flow (the net blood flow per mass of tissue in units of mL/g/min), and MTT is the mean transit time of blood through the capillary bed (the mean time required for the tracer to pass through the tissue from the arterial input to the venous output in units of seconds).

The equation for determining CBV directly from the concentration-time curves takes the following form in DSC-MRI:

$$CBV = \frac{k_h}{\rho}\frac{\int_0^\infty C_T(t)dt}{\int_0^\infty C_A(t)dt} = \frac{k_h}{\rho}\psi\frac{\int_0^\infty \Delta R_{2,T}^+(t)dt}{\int_0^\infty \Delta R_{2,A}^+(t)dt} \tag{14.9}$$

where ΔR_{2T} and ΔR_{2A} are the dynamic change in $R_2{}^+$ in the tissue of interest and the supplying artery, respectively; C_T and C_A are the corresponding concentration-time curves in the tissue of interest and the supplying artery; ψ is the ratio of the transverse relaxivity of the contrast agent ($r_2{}^+$) in blood versus tissue, with $r_2{}^+$ in units of $mM^{-1}s^{-1}$ so that $\Delta R_2{}^+(t) = r_2{}^+ C(t)$; k_h is a constant reflecting hematocrit (Hct) differences between large vessels and capillaries [49], and is conventionally inserted in DSC-MRI; and ρ is the density of tissue (g/mL), which is needed to derive CBV in the units of mL/g as is conventional in DSC-MRI. Typically, a fixed value of $\rho = 1.04$ g/mL is used.

In theory, Eq. (14.9) requires integration over the entire time axis (or until concentrations return to zero) to avoid errors due to data truncation. Because DSC-MRI data are usually measured over a relatively short time this is not practically feasible and therefore the integrations are sometimes restricted to the first pass of the contrast agent. In DSC-MRI, it is unfortunately not trivial to extract the first pass from the total measurement duration of $C_T(t)$. One approach is to fit $C_T(t)$ to a gamma-variate function [50], but such curve fitting is generally noise sensitive. For brain applications, the ASFNR recommend not to apply curve fitting to the raw data but instead integrate over the entire range of input data [19].

Whereas CBV can be estimated directly from the concentration-time curves, determination of CBF and MTT requires a deconvolution of the basic kinetic equation for linear and stationary systems. For DSC-MRI this deconvolution takes the following form [51,52]:

$$C_T(t) = f\,C_A(t) \otimes R(t) \tag{14.10}$$

where f is flow (in units of 1/time) and $R(t)$ is referred to as the *tissue residue function,* reflecting the relative proportion of the contrast agent tracer present in the tissue at time t so that $R(0) \equiv 1$. $R(t)$ can then be estimated by mathematical deconvolution of Eq. (14.10) from measurements of $C_A(t)$ and $C_T(t)$, and f is then obtained at $t=0$ since $R(0) \equiv 1$. Tissue perfusion, CBF, is then given by

$$\text{CBF} = \left(\frac{k_h}{\rho}\right) f \tag{14.11}$$

and is usually given in units of mL/100 g/min. CBV can be determined using two different approaches; either from the time-integral of $f{\cdot}R(t)$ or from the integral ratio (Eq. 14.9). Fig. 14.5 is a conceptual illustration that summarizes the different relationships in the kinetic model.

Note that in the above expressions, a linear relationship between contrast agent concentration and $\Delta R_2^{\,+}$ is assumed, both for the calculation of CBV and CBF. As discussed in Section 14.2.2, the dose-response of GBCAs is a complex function of tissue structure and DSC-MRI sequence used. Studies have shown that the linear assumption is invalid in the blood [53]. Further, even in tissue with a linear dose-response, the value of r_2^+ is tissue-dependent [15]. In practical analysis, a linear and equal dose-response is usually assumed in tissue and blood (=1 in Eq. 14.9), since the actual relaxivity values are typically not known for a given tissue and these approximations will introduce systematic errors in quantitative DSC-MRI analysis.

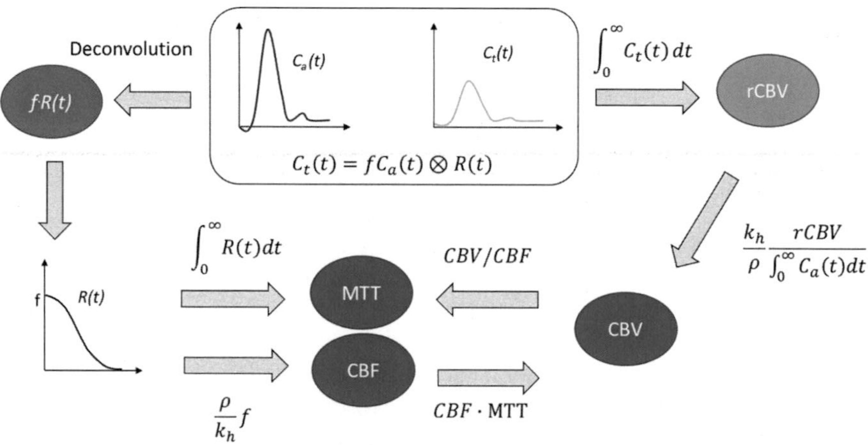

FIG. 14.5

Summary of the different relationships in the tracer kinetic model used to derive perfusion (*CBF*), blood volume (*CBV*), and mean transit time (*MTT*). $C_a(t)$ is the measured arterial input function, $C_t(t)$ is the measured tissue response, *rCBV* is the relative blood volume, $R(t)$ is the tissue residue function, and f is the measured peak height of $R(t)$, which is proportional to perfusion. See the text for further details.

14.4.2 Deconvolution

Different approaches exist for determining $f\ R(t)$ and hence CBF. In *model-dependent* methods, a priori knowledge or assumptions about the functional form of $R(t)$ is assumed (e.g., a single exponential function) and Eq. (14.10) can then be solved by nonlinear least squares methods [52]. *Model-independent* approaches are more commonly used, in which no assumptions are made about the functional form of $R(t)$, beyond it being monotonically decreasing with time. The main rationale for using model-independent techniques is that $R(t)$ is highly dependent on local microvascular structure and function, and any given functional form of $R(t)$ is unlikely to be valid across all tissues, especially in the case of vascular pathology [54]. The main challenge of using model-free approaches is to obtain stable solutions, given a large number of free parameters in $R(t)$, effectively equal to the number of datapoints in the DSC series.

The most common model-independent deconvolution approach in DSC-MRI is to reformulate the deconvolution as a matrix inversion problem $\boldsymbol{Ar}=\boldsymbol{b}$, where $\boldsymbol{A}$ is a matrix reflecting the convolution operation on the measured AIF values, $\boldsymbol{b}$ is the vector of the tissue response, and $\boldsymbol{r}$ is the vector containing discrete values of $R(t)$, scaled by f (Eq. 14.10). f can be obtained from the maximum value of $\boldsymbol{r}=\boldsymbol{A}^{+}\boldsymbol{b}$. Here, $\boldsymbol{A}^{+}$ is the regularized pseudoinverse of $\boldsymbol{A}$. Many different methods have been proposed for efficient and stable inversion of $\boldsymbol{A}$, the most established being truncated *singular value decomposition* (SVD) [52]. The SVD formalism works by decomposing $\boldsymbol{A}$ into three matrices according to

$$\boldsymbol{A}=\boldsymbol{U}\boldsymbol{\Sigma}\boldsymbol{V}^{T}=\sum_{i=1}^{N}u_i\sigma_i v_i^{T} \tag{14.12}$$

where $\boldsymbol{U}$ and $\boldsymbol{V}$ are orthonormal matrices and $\boldsymbol{\Sigma}$ is a diagonal matrix made up of the *singular values* (σ_i) of $\boldsymbol{A}$ in decreasing order. For an invertible matrix $\boldsymbol{A}$ the solution for $\boldsymbol{r}$ is given by

$$\boldsymbol{r}=\boldsymbol{V}\boldsymbol{\Sigma}^{-1}\boldsymbol{U}^{T}\boldsymbol{b}=\sum_{i=1}^{N}\frac{u_i^{T}\boldsymbol{b}}{\sigma_i}v_i \tag{14.13}$$

It can be challenging to obtain a stable and "meaningful" solution in the presence of noise, where the singular values σ_i become arbitrarily small, resulting in nonphysiological and highly oscillating values of $R(t)$ [55]. Hence, the solution needs to be regularized to ensure stable behavior:

$$\boldsymbol{r}_{\text{reg}}=\sum_{i=1}^{N}\lambda_i\frac{u_i^{T}\boldsymbol{b}}{\sigma_i}v_i \tag{14.14}$$

where λ is a regularization function, which in its simplest form is just a binary function so that $\lambda_i=1$; $i<n$ and $\lambda_i=0$; $i\geq n$ with $n<N$. This approach is referred to as truncated SVD and the actual cutoff value beyond which λ_i is set to zero is determined according to $\sigma_n\leq c\ \sigma_{\max}$; where c is a predefined cutoff value (typically 0.2) and $\sigma_{\max}$ is the largest singular value [52,56]. Fig. 14.6 shows the effect on $R(t)$ and the resulting CBF maps of using different singular value cutoffs for truncated SVD, going from $\sigma_n=0.8\ \sigma_{\max}$ to $\sigma_n=0.02\ \sigma_{\max}$. The optimal range of singular values is dependent on the SNR in the temporal signal and is therefore not constant across all image voxels. In more advanced approaches, therefore, the regularization function is varied voxel-wise according to the local noise profile of each voxel [11,55].

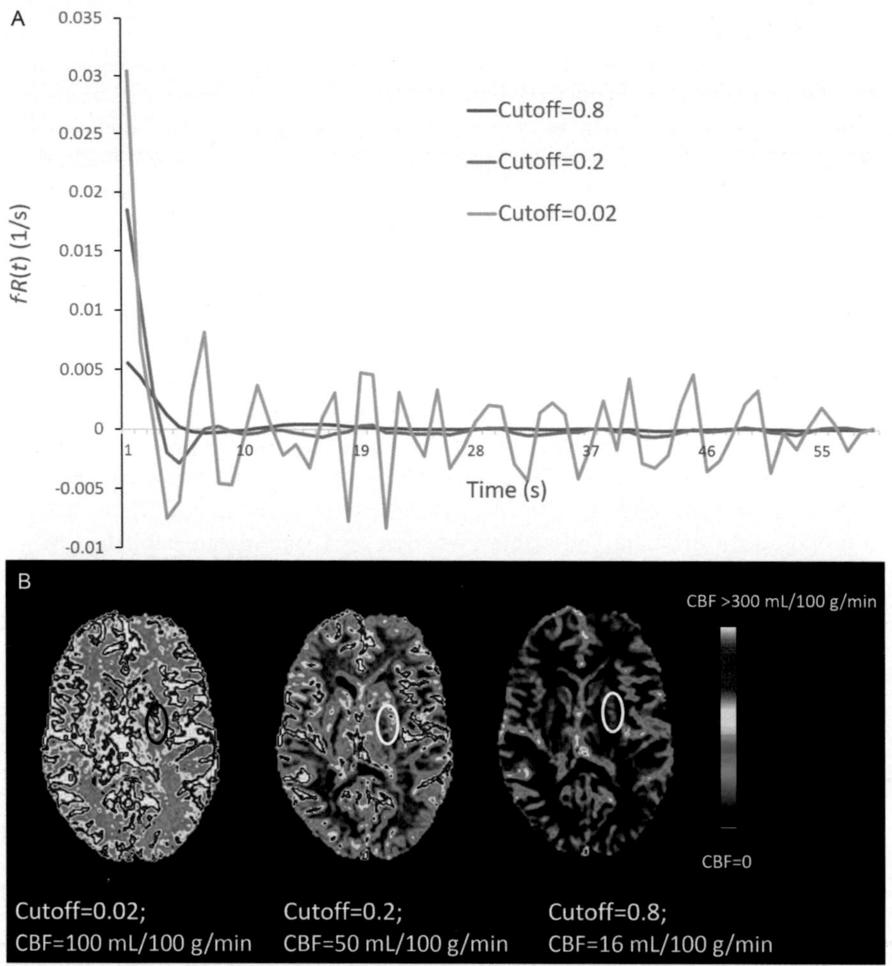

FIG. 14.6

The selection of the singular value cutoff in truncated singular value decomposition (SVD) will heavily influence the resulting DSC parameters. In this example, the corresponding regularization of the frequency function $I(t) = f\,R(t)$ is shown for cutoffs of 0.02, 0.2, and 0.8, respectively (A), and also illustrating the resulting dependency on cerebral blood flow (CBF) (B). A cutoff of 0.2 refers to a value at 20% of the maximum singular value.

14.4.3 Delay effects

One typical challenge of traditional SVD deconvolution is the sensitivity of the method to delays between the AIF and the tissue response. If the measured tissue response onset is delayed relative to the AIF signal onset [57], the peak value of $fR(t)$ (Eq. 14.10) will no longer occur at $t=0$ but at $t=T_{\text{delay}}$, where T_{delay} is the time-delay between the bolus arrival in the artery (C_A) and the tissue (C_T). $fR(t)$ will thus be a step function at $t=T_{\text{delay}}$, going from 0 to f. The step contains infinitely high frequencies and the required regularization will remove the higher frequencies, smoothing $R(t)$ and thereby underestimating f. The measured CBF then becomes a complex function of delay and regularization correction methods.

The AIF is typically measured in a major artery some distance from the area of interest, and these effects are more significant in patients (or hemispheres) with vascular abnormalities (i.e., stenosis or occlusion) that increase the delay [57] but may also be present in healthy subjects [58]. Moreover, if for any reason the AIF onset occurs *after* the tissue concentration onset, the deconvolution will fail completely and give inconclusive results. Although the scenario of the contrast agent arriving in the tissue before the feeding arteries is a nonphysiological situation, it may still occur in real data if the AIF is measured distal to stenosis and part of the tissue is supplied by an adjacent nonoccluded artery.

One way of limiting this source of uncertainty is by measuring the AIF locally, i.e., closer to the tissue of interest [59,60]. However, this approach can be prone to other sources of error, such as partial volume effects. Different extensions to linear SVD methods have also been proposed to address this issue [61,62]. The method of Wu et al., avoids the delay sensitivity be reformulating the $\boldsymbol{A}$ matrix in Eq. (14.11) to a so-called "block circular" matrix, which can be shown to be insensitive to both positive and negative delays. When analyzed correctly, the measured T_{delay} (also referred to as T^{max}) is a useful marker for voxel-wise assessment of vascular pathology, as delayed contrast agent arrival can signify pathology, i.e., acute stroke [63].

14.4.4 Contrast agent extravasation considerations

One of the main advantages of DSC-MRI in CNS applications is that the intravascular properties of GBCA in the brain, combined with the very potent T_2*-effect of gadolinium when compartmentalized in small vascular volume fractions, can lead to a number of descriptive parameter maps that accurately reflect tissue perfusion. However, in the case of contrast agent extravasation from pathologic BBB disruption, the blood volume obtained by Eq. (14.9) no longer reflects the intravascular volume but a combination of intravascular and extravascular extracellular space (EES) volumes according to the distribution volume of the tracer in tissue. This scenario instead becomes equivalent to the kinetic regime assumed in permeability analysis by DCE-MRI, aiming at quantification of contrast agent transfer constants and EES volume [64], and covered in-depth in Chapter 13.

The challenges associated with contrast agent extravasation in DSC-MRI are further complicated by the complex dose-response of GBCAs in the EES. $T_2{}^+$-dominant relaxation is dependent on contrast agent compartmentalization, and once the agent extravasates into the EES, it becomes more homogeneously distributed over a larger fraction of the total tissue volume. This can lead to a reduction in $T_2{}^+$ relaxation and a dramatic increase in T_1 relaxation [11]. The concept of contrast agent extravasation in DSC-MRI, therefore, requires considerations related to both modified dose-responses and kinetic modeling. While reducing T_1 contamination from extravasation in the dose-response includes measures such as administration of a predose load and modifications of the image acquisition, the adapted kinetic analysis also involves different correction schemes.

The influence of cerebral contrast agent extravasation on DSC-MRI was addressed in the early 1990s. Weisskoff et al., in 1994 suggested a correction method based on automatic identification of a reference first-pass response curve in healthy-appearing tissue (i.e., not affected by contrast agent extravasation) and applying voxel-wise corrections according to the deviation from this reference curve [65]. This model dovetails with the "Patlak model" used in DCE-MRI [66], but uses a tissue response curve as reference rather than an AIF. The observed tissue response in the presence of contrast agent extravasation can then be expressed as:

$$\Delta R_2^+(t) = K_1\overline{\Delta R_2^+(t)} - K_2\int_0^t \overline{\Delta R_2^+(t')}dt' \tag{14.15}$$

where $\overline{\Delta R_2^+(t)}$ is the average change in R_2^+ from a mask of reference (nonextravasating) image voxels, K_1 is the fractional blood volume and K_2 is a permeability constant. K_1 and K_2 can be determined by standard linear regression and the extravasation-corrected relative CBV is given by

$$r\text{CBV}_{\text{corr}} = r\text{CBV}_{\text{uncorr}} + K_2\int_0^\infty dt\int_0^t \overline{\Delta R_2^+(t')}dt' \tag{14.16}$$

This approach has become a reference correction method and shown to improve DSC-MRI in glioma characterization, among other applications [22]. It should be noted here that the extravasation term K_2 in Eq. (14.15) is subtracted from the nonextravasation term. This concept of a "negative" permeability constant stems from the assumption that the T_1-shortening effects are the dominant relaxation mechanism of GBCA extravasation. T_1-dominant extravasation manifests itself as an "overshoot" in the resulting $\Delta R_2^+(t)$ curve. However, depending on the image sequence parameters, pathology, contrast agent type, and dose, T_2^+-dominant extravasation may instead become the dominant relaxation mechanism. The result is contrasted by a ΔR_2^+ (t) "undershoot" with K_2 of the opposite sign. The correction method of Eq. (14.16) is therefore usually implemented so that K_2 may represent both positive and negative values in order to reflect T_1- and T_2^+-dominant relaxation effects, respectively [11]. Fig. 14.7 shows examples of tumors with T_1- and T_2^+-dominant extravasation in a CNS tumor patient, resulting in undershoot and overshoot of the $\Delta R_2^+(t)$ curves, respectively.

The kinetic model described by Eq. (14.15) relies on two important simplifying assumptions; (1) that the contrast agent extravasation is unidirectional (flow from the intravascular space to the EES) during the observation period and (2) that the intravascular MTT is constant across all voxels and equal to the MTT of the reference curve. Assumption (1) is reasonable because of the relatively short observation time of a clinical DSC-MRI (about 2 min). Assumption (2) however, is more problematic, especially in CNS tumors where MTT may deviate significantly from the MTT of unaffected tissue [67]. Methods to overcome limitation (2) have been proposed, whereby AIF deconvolution is performed, enabling estimation of both perfusion metrics and contrast agent extravasation directly from the residue function and independent of any potential MTT variations [11,67].

14.4.5 Arterial input function determination

Because deconvolution with an AIF is required to derive perfusion metrics by DSC-MRI, accurate determination of the AIF is essential to obtain reliable quantitative perfusion estimates [68]. In addition to the nonlinear dose-response in the blood [10,69,70], AIF determination is challenged by limited spatial image resolution and coverage, as well as susceptibility-induced geometric and intensity distortions from blood vessels [33,35]. Manual identification of AIFs from DSC-MRI is challenging and time-consuming due to lack of proper anatomical references and because minor variations in the relatively few image voxels selected can dramatically change the shape and magnitude of the resulting AIF [71].

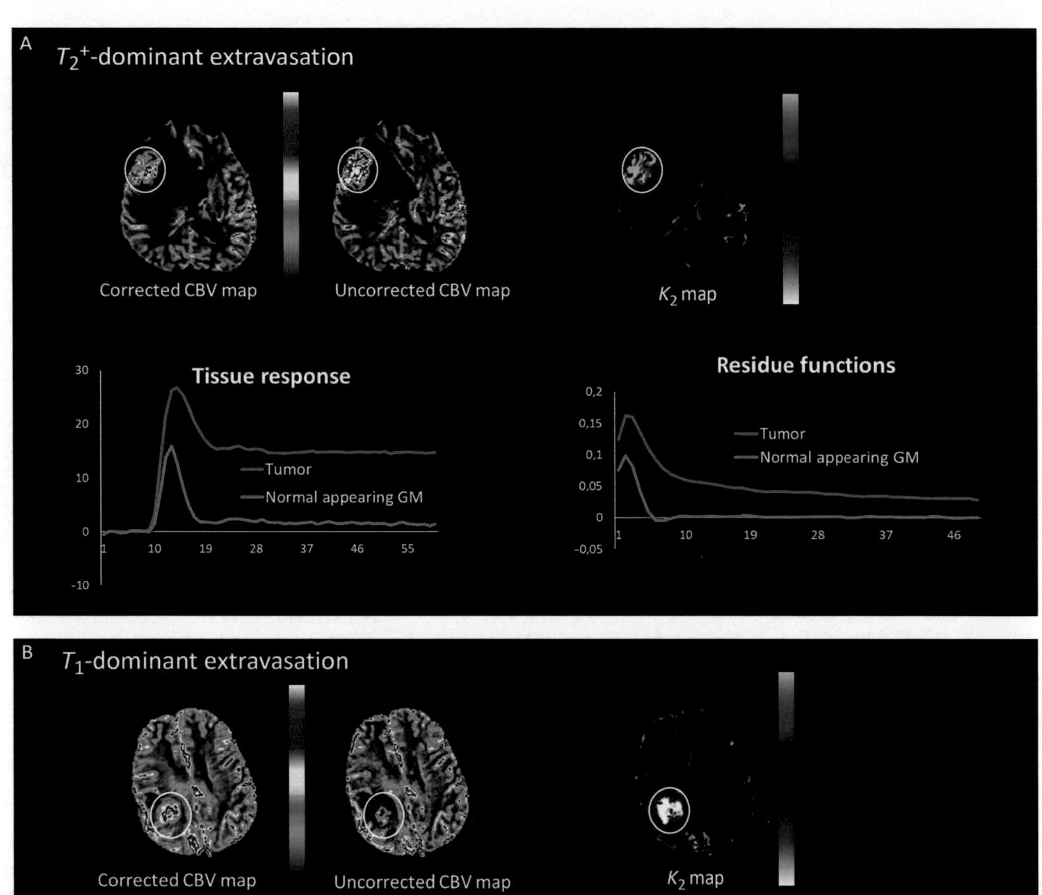

FIG. 14.7

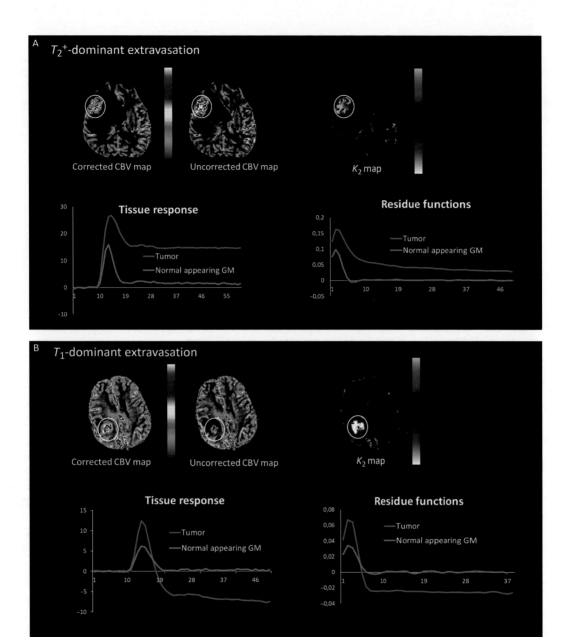

Examples of tumor cases with T_2*-dominant leakage (A) and T_1-dominant leakage (B). Note the resulting overshoot and undershoot in the resulting tissue residue functions from the resulting tumor ROIs. The K_2 maps represent the resulting apparent leakage constant obtained from the leakage correction model (see Eqs. 14.15 and 14.16 in the main text), where *blue colors* indicate T_2*-dominant leakage and *red colors* indicate T_1-dominant leakage.

The challenges of manual AIF determination have spurred efforts into developing automated AIF detection methods [72–74]. These methods typically aim at identifying AIF voxels from a region-based or exhaustive search of predefined properties of the contrast agent first-pass, including early-onset time, a large and narrow peak, and low first momentum. The final AIF is obtained using classifying algorithms, such as fuzzy or *k*-means clustering, to identify the cluster representing the image voxels with the most correct combination of assumed AIF properties.

14.5 Advanced DSC-MRI methods

In recent years, several advanced DSC-MRI sequences have emerged, partly to address some of the shortcomings of standard DSC imaging, but also to explore the underlying physiological information yet to be utilized in clinical settings.

An intriguing concept specific to DSC-MRI is *vessel caliber imaging*, or vessel size MRI [75–77]. The highly susceptibility-sensitive GRE signal is influenced by blood vessels of all calibers, whereas SE is predominantly sensitive to microscopic vessels or capillaries (radius $< 10\ \mu m$) [78]. By collecting both types of signals in a combined SE/GRE approach, parametric measures of the mean vessel diameter and vessel density can be computed by taking the ratio of GRE to SE signal, and vice versa, respectively [79]. An apparent measure of the vessel size index may also be estimated by accounting for levels of water diffusion and the blood volume fraction [77].

Another interesting observation of the combined SE and GRE DSC-MRI readout is the hysteresis effect. Depending on the underlying tissue type, the SE and GRE readouts have different selective sensitivity to the susceptibility effect. This difference creates a hysteresis effect, observed as a relative shift in the shape and peak position of the contrast agent-induced signal curves. Shown in a parametric plot, the pairwise data points form a loop that reveals information on the vascular efficiency through the voxel-wise arteriovenous relationship [76,80–82].

Traditionally, DSC-MRI in clinical practice has been limited by the desire to obtain full brain coverage while maintaining an acceptable and sufficient temporal resolution. However, recent advances in scanner hardware and MRI acquisition techniques dramatically push the limits of conventional DSC-MRI. Multiple image echo readouts have long been available for clinical MRI [83], but are now combined using *accelerated* or *parallel* imaging methods [84].

Several approaches are currently in clinical review, of which simultaneous multislice (SMS) EPI has received much attention [85]. In SMS-EPI, multiple slices are excited simultaneously to gain higher spatial and temporal image resolution and coverage [86]. An additional potential feature of these time-accelerated imaging methods is rapid and reliable estimates of R_2 and $R_2{}^*$, that in turn may improve the estimates of tissue perfusion and permeability [87]. Moreover, the use of multiple GRE readouts (or potentially SE) may further improve the selection of the AIF [88], or even help eliminate the need for an AIF altogether in certain clinical scenarios [89].

With increased computational power, another application of DSC-MRI with high potential is the combination of image observations with vascular model systems. In methods including *vascular fingerprinting*, advanced computer models are used to describe microvascular networks and vessel architectures in a range of disease scenarios, and subsequently applied to extract quantitative information from the corresponding MRI images [90–93]. With time, this approach may also potentially be expanded to include features of tissue cytoarchitecture to derive unique signatures of disease [94].

14.6 DSC-MRI beyond the brain

In the late 1990s, Kuhl et al. [6] and Kvistad et al. [8] demonstrated the value of DSC-MRI in the assessment of breast cancer. These studies showed that the assessment of signal loss in T_2*-weighted first-pass DSC-MRI may improve the differential diagnosis of breast lesions. However, both studies only assessed the qualitative change in T_2* without applying more advanced kinetic modeling accounting for contrast agent extravasation. Somewhat similar to the scenario of BBB disruption, applying DSC-MRI techniques in organs other than the brain renders the fundamental assumption that the contrast agent remains intravascular incorrect. Consequently, DSC-MRI beyond the brain necessitates the use of dedicated acquisition strategies and correction techniques.

One approach to obtain better differentiation between the T_1- and T_2*-dependent signal fractions is to acquire multiple echoes in a dynamic-contrast based MRI acquisition. The dynamic change in R_2* can then be estimated by assuming a monoexponential signal decay as a function of TE:

$$S(t,\mathrm{TE}_n) = S_{PD}(t)e^{-\mathrm{TE}_n \cdot R_2^*(t)} \tag{14.17}$$

where the subscript $n = 1,\ldots,N$ labels the echo number, and $S_{PD}(t)$ is the peak SI in the absence of T_2*-effects (TE = 0). From Eq. (14.16), $\Delta R_2^*(t)$ can readily be obtained by linear or nonlinear curve fitting. The advantage of this approach is that it provides both a quantitative $\Delta R_2^*(t)$ signal as well as a "pure" T_1-weighted signal, $S_{PD}(t)$,unaffected by T_2* contamination. This opens up an opportunity for a dual DCE/DSC-based analysis.

Recently, the dual-echo approach has been applied in the assessment of breast cancer, enabling simultaneous acquisition of DCE- and DSC-MRI with a single contrast agent administration [4,95,96]. These studies showed that adding DSC-MRI to the more conventional DCE-MRI improved the differential diagnosis of breast cancer. Moreover, a multiecho approach has also been proven valuable in assessing rectal cancer patients [5]. Similar to breast cancer, combining DCE- and DSC-MRI was shown to improve the staging of rectal cancer and aid for the reliable detection of metastatic lymph nodes. Evaluation of perfusion imaging has also been demonstrated in human skeletal muscle [84], and for measuring perfusion changes during hyperemia [97].

14.7 Conclusion

Due to the many sources of uncertainties in the assessment of perfusion via DSC-MRI, validation and standardization of imaging endpoints across multiple institutions are essential for widespread clinical acceptance [18]. For example, one practical implication that may reduce the accuracy of DSC-MRI perfusion quantification is violation of the fundamental assumptions in tracer kinetic modeling stating that the dynamic change in R_2* is linearly proportional to contrast agent concentration [98]. This linear assumption breaks down under conditions with high contrast agent concentrations such as in bulk blood [69], resulting in systematic errors for parameter quantification. Further, quantitative perfusion metric estimations in DSC-MRI will be strongly dependent on the choice of AIF as well as the deconvolution method used, as discussed above.

Hence, studies and initiatives addressing the reliability and repeatability of DSC-MRI are becoming increasingly important as the technique continues to move toward clinical utility [99]. In addition to protocol and acquisition standardization, there is a strong need for better standardization of image processing and analysis tools. Jafari-Khouzani et al. have evaluated the repeatability of different post-processing techniques and concluded that DSC-MRI is highly repeatable in high-grade glioma patients [100]. Similar results were reported by Essock-Burns, providing histopathological support for both nonparametric and nonlinear techniques [101]. Finally, as DSC-MRI protocols are now deployed in areas beyond the brain, validation studies are needed to test their reliability and robustness [102].

Acknowledgment

Funding Sources: This work was supported by the European Research Council under the European Union's Horizon 2020 Program (ERC Grant Agreement No. 758657-ImPRESS), South-Eastern Norway Regional Health Authority (grant 2017073 and 2013069); and The Research Council of Norway FRIPRO (Grant 261984).

References

[1] Shiroishi MS, et al. Principles of T2 *-weighted dynamic susceptibility contrast MRI technique in brain tumor imaging. J Magn Reson Imaging 2015;41(2):296–313. https://doi.org/10.1002/jmri.24648.

[2] Barbier EL, Lamalle L, Décorps M. Methodology of brain perfusion imaging. J Magn Reson Imaging 2001;13(4):496–520. https://doi.org/10.1002/jmri.1073.

[3] Zaharchuk G. Theoretical basis of hemodynamic MR imaging techniques to measure cerebral blood volume, cerebral blood flow, and permeability, AJNR Am J Neuroradiol 2007;28(10):1850–8. pii:28/10/1850. https://doi.org/10.3174/ajnr.A0831.

[4] Grøvik E, et al. Single bolus split dynamic MRI: is the combination of high spatial and dual-echo high temporal resolution interleaved sequences useful in the differential diagnosis of breast masses? J Magn Reson Imaging 2015;42(1):180–7. https://doi.org/10.1002/jmri.24753.

[5] Grøvik E, et al. Dynamic multi-echo DCE- and DSC-MRI in rectal cancer: low primary tumor K^{trans} and $\Delta R2^*$ peak are significantly associated with lymph node metastasis. J Magn Reson Imaging 2017;46(1): 194–206. https://doi.org/10.1002/jmri.25566.

[6] Kuhl CK, et al. Breast neoplasms: T2* susceptibility-contrast, first-pass perfusion MR imaging. Radiology 1997;202(1):87–95. https://doi.org/10.1148/radiology.202.1.8988196.

[7] Kuhl CK, et al. Do T2-weighted pulse sequences help with the differential diagnosis of enhancing lesions in dynamic breast MRI? J Magn Reson Imaging 1999;9(2):187–96. https://doi.org/10.1002/(SICI)1522-2586(199902)9:2<187::AID-JMRI6>3.0.CO;2-2.

[8] Kvistad KA, et al. Differentiating benign and malignant breast lesions with T2*-weighted first pass perfusion imaging. Acta Radiol 1999;40(1):45–51. https://doi.org/10.1080/02841859909174402.

[9] Kiselev VG, Novikov DS. Transverse NMR relaxation in biological tissues. NeuroImage 2018;(May):1–20. https://doi.org/10.1016/j.neuroimage.2018.06.002.

[10] Calamante F, Vonken EPA, van Osch MJP. Contrast agent concentration measurements affecting quantification of bolus-tracking perfusion MRI. Magn Reson Med 2007;58(3):544–53. https://doi.org/10.1002/mrm.21362.

[11] Bjornerud A, et al. T1- and T2*-dominant extravasation correction in DSC-MRI: part I—theoretical considerations and implications for assessment of tumor hemodynamic properties. J Cereb Blood Flow Metab 2011;31(10):2041–53. https://doi.org/10.1038/jcbfm.2011.52.

[12] Yablonskiy DA, Haacke EM. Theory of NMR signal behavior in magnetically inhomogeneous tissues: the static dephasing regime. *Magn Reson* Med 1994;32(6):749–63. https://doi.org/10.1002/mrm.1910320610.

[13] Kiselev VG, Posse S. Analytical model of susceptibility-induced MR signal dephasing: effect of diffusion in a microvascular network. Magn Reson Med 1999;499–509. https://doi.org/10.1002/(SICI)1522-2594(199903)41:3<499::AID-MRM12>3.0.CO;2-O.

[14] Boxerman JL, et al. The intravascular contribution to fMRI signal change: Monte Carlo modeling and diffusion-weighted studies in vivo. Magn Reson Med 1995;4–10. https://doi.org/10.1002/mrm.1910340103.

[15] Kjølby BF, Østergaard L, Kiselev VG. Theoretical model of intravascular paramagnetic tracers effect on tissue relaxation. Magn Reson Med 2006;56(1):187–97. https://doi.org/10.1002/mrm.20920.

[16] Weisskoff R, et al. Microscopic susceptibility variation and transverse relaxation: theory and experiment. Magn Reson Med 1994;601–10. https://doi.org/10.1002/mrm.1910310605.

[17] Ye FQ, Allen PS. Relaxation enhancement of the transverse magnetization of water protons in paramagnetic suspensions of red blood cells. Magn Reson Med 1995;713–20. https://doi.org/10.1002/mrm.1910340510.

[18] Anzalone N, et al. Brain gliomas: multicenter standardized assessment of dynamic contrast-enhanced and dynamic susceptibility contrast MR images. Radiology 2018;287(3):933–43. https://doi.org/10.1148/radiol.2017170362.

[19] Welker K, et al. ASFNR recommendations for clinical performance of MR dynamic susceptibility contrast perfusion imaging of the brain. AJNR Am J Neuroradiol 2015;E41–51. https://doi.org/10.3174/ajnr.A4341.

[20] Leu K, Boxerman JL, Ellingson BM. Effects of MRI protocol parameters, preload injection dose, fractionation strategies, and leakage correction algorithms on the Fidelity of dynamic-susceptibility contrast MRI estimates of relative cerebral blood volume in gliomas, AJNR Am J Neuroradiol 2017;38(3):478–84. pii:ajnr.A5027. https://doi.org/10.3174/ajnr.A5027.

[21] Schmainda KM, et al. Multisite concordance of DSC-MRI analysis for brain tumors: results of a National Cancer Institute quantitative imaging network collaborative project. AJNR Am J Neuroradiol 2018;1008–16. https://doi.org/10.3174/ajnr.A5675.

[22] Boxerman JL, Schmainda KM, Weisskoff RM. Relative cerebral blood volume maps corrected for contrast agent extravasation significantly correlate with glioma tumor grade, whereas uncorrected maps do not, Am J Neuroradiol 2006;27(4):859–67.16611779.

[23] Paulson ES, Schmainda KM. Comparison of dynamic susceptibility-weighted contrast-enhanced MR methods: recommendations for measuring relative cerebral blood volume in brain tumors. Radiology 2008;249(2):601–13. https://doi.org/10.1148/radiol.2492071659.

[24] Bell LC, et al. Characterizing the influence of preload dosing on percent signal recovery (PSR) and cerebral blood volume (CBV) measurements in a patient population with high-grade glioma using dynamic susceptibility contrast MRI. Tomography 2017;3(2):89–95. https://doi.org/10.18383/j.tom.2017.00004.

[25] Boxerman JL, Rosen BR, Weisskoff RM. Signal-to-noise analysis of cerebral blood volume maps from dynamic NMR imaging studies. J Magn Reson Imaging 1997;7(3):528–37. https://doi.org/10.1002/jmri.1880070313.

[26] Bell LC, et al. Optimization of DSC MRI echo times for CBV measurements using error analysis in a pilot study of high-grade gliomas. Am J Neuroradiol 2017;1710–5. https://doi.org/10.3174/ajnr.A5295.

[27] Kennan RP, Zhong J, Gore JC. Intravascular susceptibility contrast mechanisms in tissues. Magn Reson Med 1994;9–21. https://doi.org/10.1002/mrm.1910310103.

[28] Knutsson L, et al. Dynamic susceptibility contrast MRI at 7 T: tail-scaling analysis and inferences about field strength dependence. Tomography 2017;3(2):74–8. https://doi.org/10.18383/j.tom.2017.00001.

[29] Jahng GH, et al. Perfusion magnetic resonance imaging: a comprehensive update on principles and techniques. Korean J Radiol 2014;554–77. https://doi.org/10.3348/kjr.2014.15.5.554.

[30] Bernstein MA, et al. Handbook of MRI pulse sequences. Burlington, MA: Elsevier; 2004.

[31] Haacke EM, et al. Magnetic resonance imaging: physical principles and sequence design. John Wiley and Sons. Wiley-Liss; 1999. https://doi.org/10.1063/1.3554697.

[32] Vardal J, et al. Correction of b0-distortions in echo-planar-imaging-based perfusion-weighted mri. J Magn Reson Imaging 2014;39(3):722–8. https://doi.org/10.1002/jmri.24213.

[33] Andersson JLR, Skare S, Ashburner J. How to correct susceptibility distortions in spin-echo echo-planar images: application to diffusion tensor imaging. NeuroImage 2003;20(2):870–88. https://doi.org/10.1016/S1053-8119(03)00336-7.

[34] Chang H, Fitzpatrick JM. A technique for accurate magnetic resonance imaging in the presence of field Inhomogeneities. IEEE Trans Med Imaging 1992. https://doi.org/10.1109/42.158935.

[35] Holland D, Kuperman JM, Dale AM. Efficient correction of inhomogeneous static magnetic field-induced distortion in echo planar imaging. NeuroImage 2010;175–83. https://doi.org/10.1016/j.neuroimage.2009.11.044.

[36] Jezzard P, Clare S. Sources of distortion in functional MRI data. Hum Brain Mapp 1999;80–5. https://doi.org/10.1002/(SICI)1097-0193(1999)8:2/3<80::AID-HBM2>3.0.CO;2-C.

[37] Lauffer RB. Paramagnetic metal complexes as water proton relaxation agents for NMR imaging: theory and design. Chem Rev 1987;901–27. https://doi.org/10.1021/cr00081a003.

[38] Pierre VC, Allen MJ, Caravan P. Contrast agents for MRI: 30+ years and where are we going? J Biol Inorg Chem 2014;127–31. https://doi.org/10.1007/s00775-013-1074-5.

[39] Pan D, et al. Manganese-based MRI contrast agents: past, present, and future. Tetrahedron 2011;8431–44. https://doi.org/10.1016/j.tet.2011.07.076.

[40] Wang YXJ, Hussain SM, Krestin GP. Superparamagnetic iron oxide contrast agents: physicochemical characteristics and applications in MR imaging. Eur Radiol 2001;2319–31. https://doi.org/10.1007/s003300100908.

[41] Kowalczyk M, Banach M, Rysz J. Ferumoxytol: a new era of iron deficiency anemia treatment for patients with chronic kidney disease. J Nephrol 2011;24(6):717–22. https://doi.org/10.5301/jn.5000025.

[42] Toth GB, et al. Current and potential imaging applications of ferumoxytol for magnetic resonance imaging. Kidney Int 2017;92(1):47–66. https://doi.org/10.1016/J.KINT.2016.12.037.

[43] Vasanawala SS, et al. Safety and technique of ferumoxytol administration for MRI. Magn Reson Med 2016;2107–11. https://doi.org/10.1002/mrm.26151.

[44] Li W, et al. First-pass contrast-enhanced magnetic resonance angiography in humans using ferumoxytol, a novel ultrasmall superparamagnetic iron oxide (USPIO)-based blood pool agent. J Magn Reson Imaging 2005;46–52. https://doi.org/10.1002/jmri.20235.

[45] Prince MR, et al. A pilot investigation of new superparamagnetic iron oxide (ferumoxytol) as a contrast agent for cardiovascular MRI. J Xray Sci Technol 2003;231–40. pii:22388293.

[46] Gahramanov S, et al. Pseudoprogression of glioblastoma after chemo- and radiation therapy: diagnosis by using dynamic susceptibility-weighted contrast-enhanced perfusion MR imaging with ferumoxytol versus gadoteridol and correlation with survival. Radiology 2013;842–52. https://doi.org/10.1148/radiol.12111472.

[47] Varallyay CG, et al. Cerebral blood volume mapping with ferumoxytol in dynamic susceptibility contrast perfusion MRI: comparison to standard of care. J Magn Reson Imaging 2018;48(2):441–8. https://doi.org/10.1002/jmri.25943.

[48] Meier P, Zierler KL. On the theory of the indicator-dilution method for measurement of blood flow and volume. J Appl Physiol 1954;6(12):731–44. https://doi.org/10.1152/jappl.1954.6.12.731.

[49] Rempp KA, et al. Quantification of regional cerebral blood flow and volume with dynamic susceptibility contrast-enhanced MR imaging. Radiology 1994;193(3):637–41. https://doi.org/10.1148/radiology.193.3.7972800.

[50] Gall P, Mader I, Kiselev VG. Extraction of the first bolus passage in dynamic susceptibility contrast perfusion measurements. MAGMA 2009;22(4):241–9. https://doi.org/10.1007/s10334-009-0170-6.

[51] Calamante F, et al. Measuring cerebral blood flow using magnetic resonance imaging techniques. J Cereb Blood Flow Metab 1999;19(7):701–35. https://doi.org/10.1097/00004647-199907000-00001.

[52] Østergaard L, et al. High resolution measurement of cerebral blood flow using intravascular tracer bolus passages. Part I: mathematical approach and statistical analysis. Magn Reson Med 1996;36:715–25. https://doi.org/10.1002/mrm.1910360510.

[53] van Osch MJ, et al. Measuring the arterial input function with gradient echo sequences. Magn Reson Med 2003;49(6):1067–76. https://doi.org/10.1002/mrm.10461.

[54] Eskildsen SF, et al. Increased cortical capillary transit time heterogeneity in Alzheimer's disease: a DSC-MRI perfusion study. Neurobiol Aging 2017;107–18. https://doi.org/10.1016/j.neurobiolaging.2016.11.004.

[55] Liu HL, et al. Cerebral blood flow measurement by dynamic contrast MRI using singular value decomposition with an adaptive threshold. Magn Reson Med 1999;42(1):167–72. https://doi.org/10.1002/(sici)1522-2594(199907)42:1<167::aid-mrm22>3.0.co;2-q.
[56] Calamante F, Gadian DG, Connelly A. Quantification of bolus-tracking MRI: improved characterization of the tissue residue function using Tikhonov regularization. Magn Reson Med 2003;1237–47. https://doi.org/10.1002/mrm.10643.
[57] Calamante F, et al. Bolus delay and dispersion in perfusion MRI: implications for tissue predictor models in stroke. Magn Reson Med 2006;1180–5. https://doi.org/10.1002/mrm.20873.
[58] Ostergaard L, et al. Cerebral blood flow measurements by magnetic resonance imaging bolus tracking: comparison with [(15)O]H2O positron emission tomography in humans. J Cereb Blood Flow Metab 1998;18(9):935–40. https://doi.org/10.1097/00004647-199809000-00002.
[59] Calamante F, Mørup M, Hansen LK. Defining a local arterial input function for perfusion MRI using independent component analysis. Magn Reson Med 2004;789–97. https://doi.org/10.1002/mrm.20227.
[60] Willats L, et al. Validating a local arterial input function method for improved perfusion quantification in stroke. J Cereb Blood Flow Metab 2011;2189–98. https://doi.org/10.1038/jcbfm.2011.78.
[61] Smith MR, et al. Removing the effect of SVD algorithmic artifacts present in quantitative MR perfusion studies. Magn Reson Med 2004;51(3):631–4. https://doi.org/10.1002/mrm.20006.
[62] Wu O, et al. Effects of tracer arrival time on flow estimates in MR perfusion-weighted imaging. Magn Reson Med 2003;856–64. https://doi.org/10.1002/mrm.10610.
[63] Christensen S, et al. Comparison of 10 perfusion MRI parameters in 97 Sub-6-hour stroke patients using voxel-based receiver operating characteristics analysis. Stroke 2009;2055–61. https://doi.org/10.1161/STROKEAHA.108.546069.
[64] Sourbron SP, Buckley DL. Tracer kinetic modelling in MRI: estimating perfusion and capillary permeability. Phys Med Biol 2011;57(2):R1–R33. https://doi.org/10.1088/0031-9155/57/2/R1.
[65] Weisskoff RM, et al. Simultaneous blood volume and permeability mapping using a single Gd-based contrast injection, In: Proceedings of the ISMRM; 1997.
[66] Patlak CS, Blasberg RG, Fenstermacher JD. Graphical evaluation of blood-to-brain transfer constants from multiple-time uptake data. J Cereb Blood Flow Metab 1983;1–7. https://doi.org/10.1038/jcbfm.1983.1.
[67] Quarles CC, Ward BD, Schmainda KM. Improving the reliability of obtaining tumor hemodynamic parameters in the presence of contrast agent extravasation. Magn Reson Med 2005;53(6):1307–16. https://doi.org/10.1002/mrm.20497.
[68] Calamante F. Arterial input function in perfusion MRI: a comprehensive review. Prog Nucl Magn Reson Spectrosc 2013;1–32. https://doi.org/10.1016/j.pnmrs.2013.04.002.
[69] Calamante F, Connelly A, Van Osch MJP. Nonlinear $\Delta R2^*$effects in perfusion quantification using bolus-tracking MRI. Magn Reson Med 2009;486–92. https://doi.org/10.1002/mrm.21839.
[70] Hadizadeh DR, et al. Effects of arterial input function selection on kinetic parameters in brain dynamic contrast-enhanced MRI. Magn Reson Imaging 2017;40:83–90. https://doi.org/10.1016/j.mri.2017.04.006.
[71] Bleeker EJW, van Buchem MA, van Osch MJP. Optimal location for arterial input function measurements near the middle cerebral artery in first-pass perfusion {MRI}. J Cereb Blood Flow Metab 2009;29(4):840–52. https://doi.org/10.1038/jcbfm.2008.155.
[72] Mouridsen K, et al. Automatic selection of arterial input function using cluster analysis. Magn Reson Med 2006;524–31. https://doi.org/10.1002/mrm.20759.
[73] Murase K, et al. Determination of arterial input function using fuzzy clustering for quantification of cerebral blood flow with dynamic susceptibility contrast-enhanced MR imaging. J Magn Reson Imaging 2001;13(5):797–806. https://doi.org/10.1002/jmri.1111.
[74] Peruzzo D, et al. Automatic selection of arterial input function on dynamic contrast-enhanced MR images. Comput Methods Prog Biomed 2011;148–57. https://doi.org/10.1016/j.cmpb.2011.02.012.

[75] Donahue KM, et al. Utility of simultaneously acquired gradient-echo and spin-echo cerebral blood volume and morphology maps in brain tumor patients. Magn Reson Med 2000;845–53. https://doi.org/10.1002/1522-2594(200006)43:6<845::AID-MRM10>3.0.CO;2-J.

[76] Kiselev VG, et al. Vessel size imaging in humans. Magn Reson Med 2005;53(3):553–63. https://doi.org/10.1002/mrm.20383.

[77] Troprès I, et al. Vessel size imaging. Magn Reson Med 2001;397–408. https://doi.org/10.1002/1522-2594(200103)45:3<397::AID-MRM1052>3.0.CO;2-3.

[78] Boxerman JL, et al. MR contrast due to intravascular magnetic susceptibility perturbations. Magn Reson Med 1995;34(4):555–66. https://doi.org/10.1002/mrm.1910340412.

[79] Jensen JH, Chandra R. MR imaging of microvasculature. Magn Reson Med 2000;44(2):224–30. https://doi.org/10.1002/1522-2594(200008)44:2<224::AID-MRM9>3.0.CO;2-M.

[80] Emblem KE, et al. Vessel architectural imaging identifies cancer patient responders to anti-angiogenic therapy. Nat Med 2013;19(9):1178–83. https://doi.org/10.1038/nm.3289.

[81] Stadlbauer A, et al. Vascular hysteresis loops and vascular architecture mapping in patients with glioblastoma treated with antiangiogenic therapy. Sci Rep 2017;8508. https://doi.org/10.1038/s41598-017-09048-w.

[82] Xu C, et al. Dynamic hysteresis between gradient echo and spin echo attenuations in dynamic susceptibility contrast imaging. Magn Reson Med 2013;981–91. https://doi.org/10.1002/mrm.24326.

[83] Schmainda KM, et al. Characterization of a first-pass gradient-echo spin-echo method to predict brain tumor grade and angiogenesis. Am J Neuroradiol 2004;1524–32. pii:25/9/1524.

[84] Skinner JT, et al. Evaluation of a multiple spin- and gradient-echo (SAGE) EPI acquisition with SENSE acceleration: applications for perfusion imaging in and outside the brain. Magn Reson Imaging 2014;1171–80. https://doi.org/10.1016/j.mri.2014.08.032.

[85] Eichner C, et al. Slice accelerated gradient-echo spin-echo dynamic susceptibility contrast imaging with blipped CAIPI for increased slice coverage. Magn Reson Med 2014;770–8. https://doi.org/10.1002/mrm.24960.

[86] Chakhoyan A, et al. Improved spatiotemporal resolution of dynamic susceptibility contrast perfusion MRI in brain tumors using simultaneous multi-slice echo-planar imaging, AJNR Am J Neuroradiol 2018;39(1):43–5. pii:ajnr.A5433. https://doi.org/10.3174/ajnr.A5433.

[87] Stokes AM, et al. Assessment of a simplified spin and gradient echo (sSAGE) approach for human brain tumor perfusion imaging. Magn Reson Imaging 2016;1248–55. https://doi.org/10.1016/j.mri.2016.07.004.

[88] Newton AT, et al. Improving perfusion measurement in DSC-MR imaging with multiecho information for arterial input function determination, AJNR Am J Neuroradiol 2016;37(7):1237–43. pii:ajnr.A4700. https://doi.org/10.3174/ajnr.A4700.

[89] Nasel C, et al. Normalised time-to-peak-distribution curves correlate with cerebral white matter hyperintensities—could this improve early diagnosis? J Cereb Blood Flow Metab 2016;444–55. https://doi.org/10.1177/0271678X16629485.

[90] Christen T, et al. MR vascular fingerprinting: a new approach to compute cerebral blood volume, mean vessel radius, and oxygenation maps in the human brain. NeuroImage 2013;262–70. https://doi.org/10.1016/j.neuroimage.2013.11.052. pii:S1053-8119(13)01201-9.

[91] Digernes I, et al. A theoretical framework for determining cerebral vascular function and heterogeneity from dynamic susceptibility contrast MRI. J Cereb Blood Flow Metab 2017;2237–48. https://doi.org/10.1177/0271678X17694187.

[92] Hernández-Torres E, et al. Anisotropic cerebral vascular architecture causes orientation dependency in cerebral blood flow and volume measured with dynamic susceptibility contrast magnetic resonance imaging. J Cereb Blood Flow Metab 2017;37(3):1108–19. https://doi.org/10.1177/0271678X16653134.

[93] Lemasson B, et al. MR vascular fingerprinting in stroke and brain tumors models, Sci Rep 2016;6:37071. pii:srep37071. https://doi.org/10.1038/srep37071.

[94] Semmineh NB, et al. Assessing tumor cytoarchitecture using multiecho DSC-MRI derived measures of the transverse relaxivity at tracer equilibrium (TRATE). Magn Reson Med 2015;772–84. https://doi.org/10.1002/mrm.25435.

[95] Grøvik E, et al. Split dynamic MRI: single bolus high spatial-temporal resolution and multi contrast evaluation of breast lesions. J Magn Reson Imaging 2014;39:673–82. https://doi.org/10.1002/jmri.24206.

[96] Wang S, et al. Differentiation of breast cancer from fibroadenoma with dual-echo dynamic contrast-enhanced MRI. PLoS One 2013;8(7), e67731. https://doi.org/10.1371/journal.pone.0067731.

[97] Englund EK, et al. Combined measurement of perfusion, venous oxygen saturation, and skeletal muscle T2* during reactive hyperemia in the leg. J Cardiovasc Magn Reson 2013;15:70. https://doi.org/10.1186/1532-429X-15-70.

[98] Kiselev VG. On the theoretical basis of perfusion measurements by dynamic susceptibility contrast MRI. Magn Reson Med 2001;46(6):1113–22. https://doi.org/10.1002/mrm.1307.

[99] Ellingson BM, et al. Consensus recommendations for a standardized brain tumor imaging protocol in clinical trials. Neuro-Oncology 2015;1188–98. https://doi.org/10.1093/neuonc/nov095.

[100] Jafari-Khouzani K, et al. Repeatability of cerebral perfusion using dynamic susceptibility contrast MRI in glioblastoma patients. Transl Oncol 2015;8(3):137–46. https://doi.org/10.1016/j.tranon.2015.03.002.

[101] Essock-Burns E, et al. Comparison of DSC-MRI post-processing techniques in predicting microvascular histopathology in patients newly diagnosed with GBM. J Magn Reson Imaging 2013;38(2):388–400. https://doi.org/10.1002/jmri.23982.

[102] Grøvik E. Multimodal dynamic MRI for structural and functional assessment of cancer. 1501-7710 University of Oslo; 2017.

CHAPTER

Applications of Quantitative Perfusion and Permeability in the Brain

15

Shalini Amukotuwa[a], Laura C. Bell[b], and David L. Thomas[c]

[a]*Department of Imaging, Faculty of Medicine, Nursing and Health Sciences, Monash University, Melbourne, VIC, Australia* [b]*Neuroimaging Innovation Center, Barrow Neurological Institute, Phoenix, AZ, United States* [c]*Leonard Wolfson Experimental Neurology Centre, University College London, London, United Kingdom*

15.1 Introduction

The brain is arguably the most common application area of perfusion Magnetic Resonance Imaging (MRI), and all main techniques (arterial spin labeling (ASL), dynamic contrast-enhanced (DCE), and dynamic susceptibility contrast (DSC)) have been proposed for clinical application. Brain perfusion is unique due to the existence of the blood-brain barrier (BBB), which causes contrast agents to remain intravascular in normal conditions, and the typically low blood volume fraction of healthy brain tissue (2%–4%). With an intact BBB, this means that contrast agents have a very small distribution space and therefore do not generate much signal change on DCE sequences due to the low T_1 relaxivity. Hence, DSC, which relies on $T_2{}^*$ and benefits from the much higher contrast agent relaxivities, is the most commonly used contrast-agent-based perfusion measurement technique under those conditions. When the BBB is ruptured, the distribution space increases, leading to larger perfusion-based signal in DCE-MRI; at the same time, the DSC signal becomes ambiguous due to competition between T_1 and $T_2{}^*$ effects of the contrast agent. For this reason, in applications that aim to measure BBB permeability, DCE is the more commonly used contrast-agent based method. ASL used labeled arterial blood water as an endogenous tracer, which crosses the BBB almost freely and thus is not affected by the state of the BBB. ASL is therefore applicable in all clinical application areas but is not generally suitable for measurement of BBB permeability.

This chapter will discuss the most common clinical application areas of perfusion MRI in the brain: cerebrovascular disease, brain cancer, and dementia.

- *Cerebrovascular diseases* are a heterogeneous group of disorders that affect the blood vessels of the brain. These are subdivided into ischemic and hemorrhagic. Since they affect the blood vessels of the brain, it stands to reason that perfusion mapping may be valuable in the diagnosis and treatment of cerebrovascular disease. This chapter will describe the role of MR perfusion in the diagnosis and management of acute ischemic stroke and chronic cerebrovascular ischemia.
- *Gliomas*, specifically glioblastomas (GBMs), are the most common type of brain cancer in adults, with a median survival rate of 15–16 months [1]. In the last 50 years, the survival rate of GBMs has improved slowly compared to other types of cancer due to the aggressive and difficult-to-treat nature of these tumors [2]. Recent research advances have led to the development of promising

Advances in Magnetic Resonance Technology and Applications. Volume 1. ISSN 2666-9099. https://doi.org/10.1016/B978-0-12-817057-1.00017-2

targeted drug therapies. Quantitative perfusion MRI parameters may serve as important imaging biomarkers for the evaluation of these new drugs as well as improving the current standard of care.
- The term "*dementia*" covers a range of progressive, chronic neurodegenerative diseases, including Alzheimer's disease (AD), frontotemporal dementia (FTD), vascular dementia, and dementia with Lewy bodies (DLB) [3]. While the precise mechanisms of neurodegeneration caused by the accumulation of these neurotoxic proteins are not well understood, it is well known that these increases are accompanied by associated decreases in metabolism. These changes in metabolism are mirrored by local changes in cerebral perfusion, which can be measured by DSC or ASL, and which may act as a surrogate for metabolic change or potentially an early predictor.

15.2 Applications of perfusion MRI in ischemic cerebrovascular disease

15.2.1 Acute ischemic stroke

15.2.1.1 Background

Acute stroke is defined as the rapid development of a neurological deficit lasting more than 24h resulting from a focal injury to the brain by a vascular cause [4–6]. The vast majority (approximately 85%) of strokes are *ischemic*, caused by obstruction of a blood vessel either within the brain or the neck [7] by thrombus or embolus [4]. Such an obstruction disrupts blood flow to the downstream brain tissue, depriving it of oxygen and nutrients [8,9]. Neurons are exquisitely metabolically sensitive. Reduction of blood flow below a certain "ischemic" threshold, shown in primate studies with physiological monitoring to be 10–20mL/100g per minute, causes reversible cessation of electrical activity [8,10,11]. Further reduction to less than 10mL/100mg per minute has been shown to cause irreversible cellular depolarization (infarction) [8,10,11]. This irreversibly damaged tissue represents the "infarct core" while tissue that is electrically silent but remains viable is the "ischemic penumbra" [12].

Studies in humans and animals have shown that the infarct core enlarges and expands into the ischemic penumbra over time if blood flow is not restored [8,13,14]. This evolution of penumbra into infarct core is a dynamic process which is dependent on the severity and duration of blood flow reduction, and is therefore heavily influenced by the presence and robustness of residual collateral blood flow [8,13,15]. While there is large interindividual variability in collateral supply, accounting for the variability in infarct progression, it is estimated that 1.9 million neurons per minute undergo irreversible damage in a typical stroke patient [16]. Patients with poor collateral blood flow can have up to 100mL per hour of infarct growth [17]. Acute ischemic stroke is therefore a time-critical emergency—captured by the mantra "time is brain."

Treatment of acute ischemic stroke aims to restore blood flow to the ischemic penumbra and prevent further infarct growth by recanalizing the occluded artery. While the first-line recanalization therapy is intravenous thrombolysis (IVT), it has a limited therapeutic window of just 4.5h [18]. Endovascular thrombectomy has been shown to be effective and safe for recanalizing intracranial anterior circulation large vessel occlusions (LVOs) [19–24]. A number of trials have shown that stroke patients who have LVOs that involve either the internal carotid artery (ICA) or the M1 segment of the middle cerebral artery (MCA) have improved functional outcomes and significantly less neurological disability when treated with thrombectomy rather than standard medical management [19–21,23–25]. Unlike IVT, thrombectomy has an extended therapeutic window, and can be performed safely in carefully selected patients up to 24h following stroke onset [18,19,23]. It has therefore revolutionized the management of acute ischemic stroke and is the standard-of-care treatment for stroke patients with ICA and M1 segment MCA occlusions within the 24-h window [18]. Thrombectomy can also be performed in selected patients with more distal occlusions [18,26,27].

15.2.1.2 Role of perfusion in acute stroke

The likelihood that a patient will benefit from thrombectomy (or any reperfusion therapy) is related to the presence of ischemic but salvageable brain tissue, while the risk of complication increases with the volume of infarcted brain tissue [28,29]. Therefore, in order to optimize outcomes, accurate identification of the infarct core and viable but critically hypoperfused tissue (the ischemic penumbra) is important.

While the majority of centers in North America use multimodal computed tomography (CT) with CT perfusion as the first-line imaging modality in acute ischemic stroke patients, many centers in Europe and most centers in Asia use MRI [30]. Perfusion is not required to identify the infarct core on MRI, since diffusion-weighted imaging allows direct interrogation of cytotoxic edema and is therefore the imaging gold standard for identification of the infarct core, with a reported sensitivity of up to 100% [31–34]. MR perfusion is used to identify salvageable at-risk tissue [14,35].

The initial evidence that reperfusion is associated with favorable outcomes in patients who have viable penumbral tissue came from MRI-based trials that used dynamic susceptibility contrast perfusion-weighted imaging (DSC-PWI) to identify and quantify viable tissue [14,35]. In the DEFUSE 2 trial, serial MRI scans were used to show that critically hypoperfused tissue progresses to infarction without timely reperfusion (Fig. 15.1). Mismatch analysis was performed to determine the absolute volume difference as well as the ratio between at-risk tissue and the infarct core. A "target mismatch" was defined as follows: the absolute volume of at-risk tissue exceeded the volume of the infarct core by more than 15mL; and the ratio of the volumes of at-risk and infarcted tissue exceeded 1.8. Early reperfusion was associated with more favorable clinical outcomes in patients who had a "target mismatch" but not in those who did not.

Following DEFUSE 2, a number of thrombectomy trials used mismatch analysis to identify patients who may benefit from thrombectomy [19,21,23,24]. These trials used either exclusively or predominantly CT perfusion, since CT is easier to access than MRI in the emergent setting. Patient selection criteria differed between these trials; however, the trials that used perfusion imaging-based selection to identify the presence of salvageable brain tissue and exclude large completed infarcts demonstrated better outcomes with both thrombectomy and standard medical management [19,20] than those that relied upon nonenhanced CT, CT angiography, and clinical criteria alone [18,21,22]. This indicates that the use of advanced imaging-based patient selection is associated with better outcomes. Therefore, while current guidelines do not mandate perfusion to identify at-risk tissue in the early time-window (within 6h of stroke onset) [18], many centers now use perfusion to determine whether patients are likely to benefit from thrombectomy. A study published in 2015 reported that approximately 40% of 223 centers in Europe, North America, and Asia that were surveyed used perfusion for penumbral assessment [30] and this figure is likely to be even higher now.

In the late window, one of the two key trials, DEFUSE 3, used perfusion to identify the presence and volume of ischemic penumbra in patients treated with endovascular thrombectomy up to 16h after stroke onset or "last seen well" [19,23]. Therefore, the American Heart Association guidelines

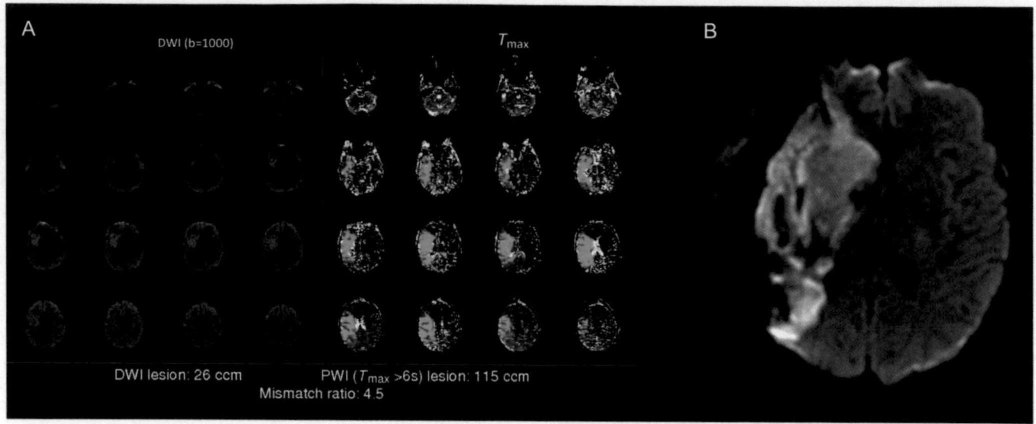

FIG. 15.1

Examples of infarct growth into the ischemic penumbra in the absence of reperfusion. (A) Mismatch analysis in a 59-year-old woman who presented with an acute ischemic stroke due to right middle cerebral artery occlusion. The diffusion-weighted imaging (DWI) lesion visible in the apparent diffusion coefficient (ADC) maps (*pink*, measured using an ADC threshold of $<620 \times 10^{-6}\,mm^2/s$) is the infarct core. The area with T_{max} >6s *(green)* represents the critically hypoperfused tissue. The difference in volume between the T_{max} lesion (115mL) and the DWI lesion (26mL) is the "ischemic penumbra" (89mL) of viable but critically hypoperfused tissue that can be salvaged with reperfusion. The ratio of the T_{max} lesion volume to the DWI lesion volume is the mismatch ratio. This patient has a target mismatch (volume > 15mL and ratio > 1.8). Unfortunately, reperfusion failed. (B) The follow-up study at day 5 showing a large area of signal abnormality on the diffusion trace images (representing a combination of restricted diffusion and T_2 shine-through at this stage) that corresponds to the T_{max} lesion on the initial study. This study illustrates how the T_{max} >6s lesion undergoes infarction in the absence of reperfusion.

recommend the use of perfusion to identify the amount and ratio of salvageable brain tissue to infarct core when the DEFUSE 3 criteria are applied in these late time window patients [18].

Penumbral imaging may also be used to guide IVT decisions [30,36]. Treatment with intravenous alteplase 4.5–9h following stroke onset or "last seen well" has been shown to be associated with less neurological deficit than placebo in patients who have salvageable brain tissue demonstrated on perfusion imaging [36]. This study, which has only just been published, is likely to alter practice guidelines and result in the recommendation of perfusion to identify salvageable brain tissue for late window IVT.

15.2.1.3 Quantitative parameters

The parameter that is most widely used for identifying tissue that is at risk of undergoing infarction without reperfusion is the time to maximum of the tissue residue function obtained by deconvolution (T_{max}). Theoretically, T_{max} is the arrival delay between the arterial input function (AIF) and tissue concentration-time curve [37] (see Chapter 13 for more details). However, other factors, such as the deconvolution process itself, do influence the T_{max} parameter. Bolus temporal dispersion due to proximal arterial occlusion or stenosis is also an important influence in the setting of acute ischemic stroke which may affect the accuracy of the T_{max} parameter [37].

T_{max} has been used in a number of thrombectomy and IVT trials to identify at-risk tissue [14,19,21,24,35,36]. The optimal T_{max} threshold for identifying critically hypoperfused tissue that is destined to undergo infarction without reperfusion has been shown to be greater than 6 s [38,39]. This threshold has since been validated through use in high profile thrombectomy trials to identify at-risk tissue [19,21,24].

The mismatch or difference between the volume of critically hypoperfused tissue and the infarct core, otherwise known as the ischemic penumbra, is a quantitative parameter describing the amount of salvageable tissue that will undergo infarction without timely reperfusion. Mismatch analysis involves calculation of the absolute volume of this mismatch (the mismatch volume) as well as the ratio (mismatch ratio) between the volume of critically hypoperfused tissue and infarcted tissue. Mismatch analysis has been used in a number of high-profile thrombectomy and IVT trials. Examples of mismatch analysis using DSC-PWI are shown in Figs. 15.1 and 15.2.

The "target mismatch," which was the minimum mismatch required for patient triage to the intervention arm, varied between the thrombectomy trials. For example, EXTENT-IA used a mismatch ratio of >1.2 and a mismatch volume of >10 mL while both DEFUSE 2 and 3 used >1.5 and >15 mL mismatch volume and ratio, respectively [14,19,21]. In the clinical setting, mismatch criteria are more loosely applied in the early window, while guidelines recommend the use of the DEFUSE 3 criteria (unless the DAWN criteria are instead followed) in the late window [18].

T_{max} can also be used to assess the status of leptomeningeal collaterals and predict the rate of infarct progression in acute ischemic stroke patients. The hypoperfusion intensity ratio (HIR) is defined as the volume of tissue with T_{max} >10 s delay to the volume of tissue with T_{max} >6 s delay. An HIR >0.4 has been shown to be associated with poor collateral status, with significantly higher infarct growth velocity and volume [40]. Identification of patients with poor collaterals is important since these patients can have rapid infarct growth. Infarct growth is very time-sensitive in these patients in whom rapid reperfusion is critical for tissue salvage and this has implications for triage and transfer decisions.

Apart from allowing quantification of the tissue at-risk, the T_{max} parameter can be used in the clinical setting to expedite identification of presence and site of an intracranial arterial occlusion. An example is shown in Fig. 15.3.

15.2.1.4 Hemorrhage prediction

The most feared complication of reperfusion therapy is symptomatic hemorrhagic transformation (SHT). Advanced imaging predictive markers of SHT have been the focus of some recent studies which have shown that marked reduction in blood volume and severely delayed arrival of blood in tissue are associated with a higher risk of SHT [41–43]. The mechanism underlying SHT is endothelial damage, with a breakdown of the tight junctions that form the blood-brain barrier (BBB) [44]. BBB breakdown allows administered intravascular nondiffusible contrast agent to leak into the extravascular space (interstitial compartment). The integrity of the BBB can be assessed using permeability imaging. Therefore, methods that assess tissue permeability enable more direct interrogation of the mechanism underlying SHT, providing a more accurate prediction of this dreaded complication [42,45,46].

DCE perfusion is used to map vascular permeability, usually measured by the endothelial transfer constant K^{trans}, i.e., the volume of blood plasma delivered to the interstitium per minute and per mL tissue. The extraction fraction (E)—the proportion of tracer that leaves the bloodstream and enters the tissue compartment—multiplied by the plasma flow yields K^{trans}. K^{trans} can also be measured using DSC perfusion, but this measurement can be degraded by T_1 and T_2^* contamination. Multiecho (e.g., combined spin and gradient echo) techniques can be used to overcome these confounding effects, allowing more accurate measurement of K^{trans} [47,48].

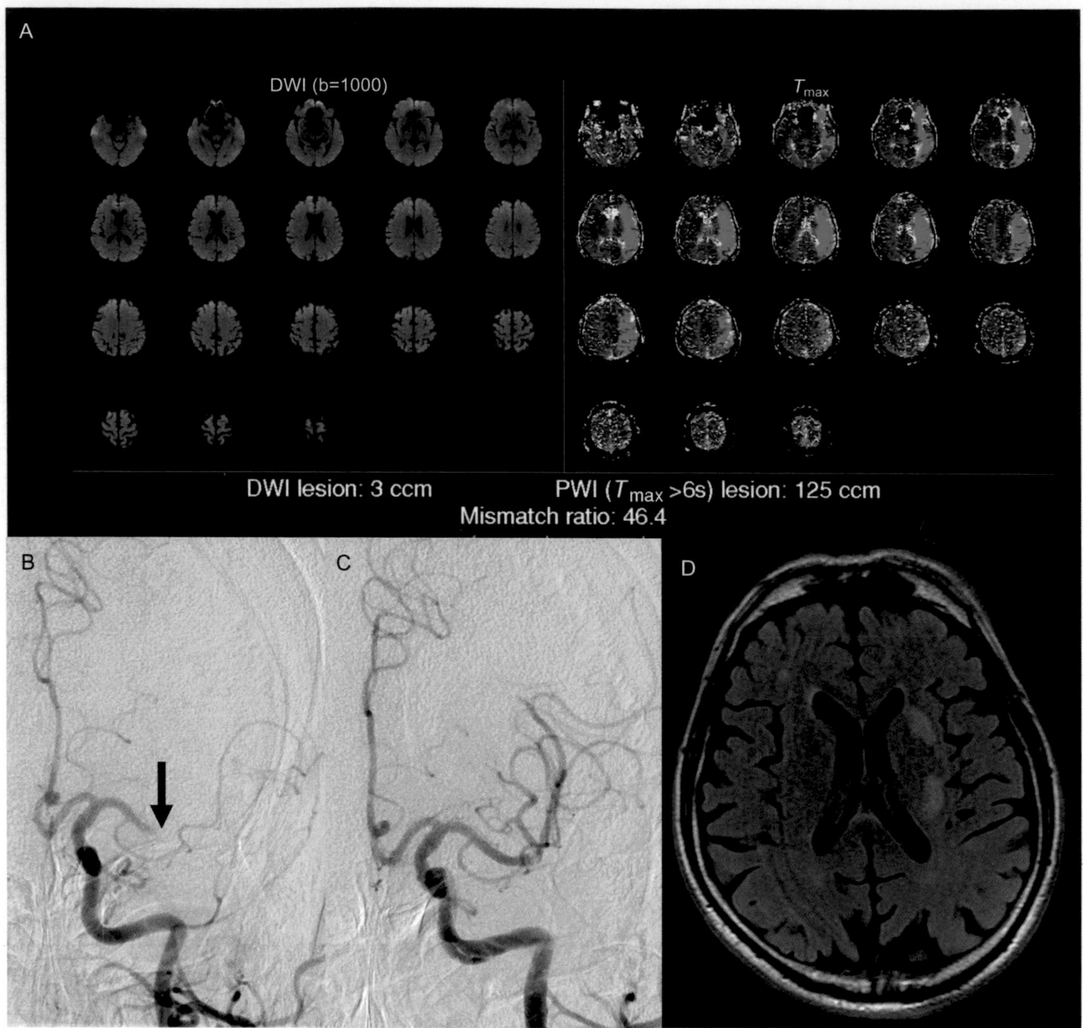

FIG. 15.2

A 75-year-old man who presented to the hospital approximately 3h following acute onset of right-sided weakness and dysphasia. (A) Mismatch analysis: the DWI lesion seen on ADC (*pink*, ADC $<620\times10^{-6}\,mm^2/s$) was small, confined to the left caudate nucleus and internal capsule. There was a much larger area of critical hypoperfusion in the perfusion maps *(green)*, indicated by T_{max} delay >6s, within the left middle cerebral artery territory. The mismatch volume (penumbral volume) was 122mL while the mismatch ratio (of T_{max} >6s lesion volume to DWI lesion volume) was 46.4, a target mismatch. The patient was therefore triaged to endovascular thrombectomy. (B) Anterior-to-posterior projection from the initial angiographic run with a selective injection of the left internal carotid artery shows occlusion of the mid M1 segment *(arrow)* of the left middle cerebral artery. (C) Post clot retrieval angiographic image shows the recanalization of the M1 segment. (D) Day 5 follow-up axial fluid-attenuated inversion recovery image shows a small area of completed infarction, while the remainder of the critically hypoperfused tissue (T_{max} >6s lesion) has been salvaged by the timely endovascular thrombectomy.

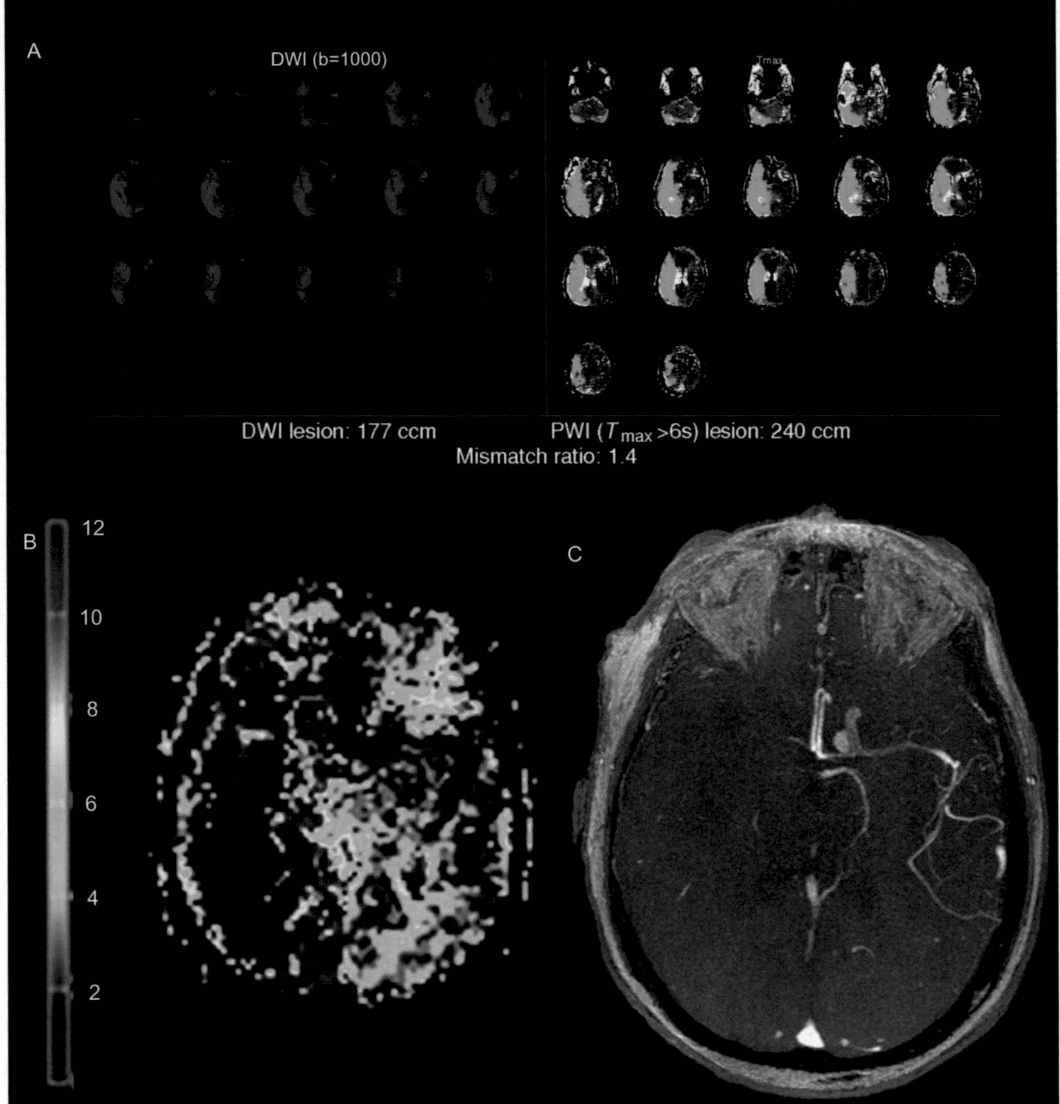

FIG. 15.3

A 79-year-old woman who presented with a terminal internal carotid artery (ICA) occlusion. (A) The mismatch analysis in this case shows a large infarct core (diffusion-weighted imaging (DWI) lesion shown on ADC maps, in *pink*) that has almost entirely grown into the area of critical hypoperfusion (T_{max} >6 s). This indicates an almost completed infarct in the right cerebral hemisphere. Reperfusion would be futile in this patient, who has an increased risk of symptomatic intracranial hemorrhage due to the large infarct size. (B) The T_{max} maps show that the area of perfusion delay involves not only the right middle cerebral artery territory but also the right posterior cerebral artery territory. This T_{max} pattern is seen with carotid terminus occlusions in patients with the fetal origin of the posterior cerebral artery (from the internal carotid artery via a posterior communicating segment) where the occlusion is at or proximal to the origin of the posterior communicating segment. The anterior cerebral artery territory is spared due to the presence of an anterior communicating segment that provides cross-flow from the contralateral internal carotid artery. Recognition of the T_{max} pattern helps the reader quickly identify the occlusion site and recognize the variants in the circle of Willis anatomy. (C) Time-of-flight Magnetic Resonance Angiogram (MRA) maximum intensity projection (MIP) confirming right internal carotid artery occlusion, absence of flow in the right posterior cerebral artery (indicating fetal origin), and cross-supply of the right anterior cerebral artery.

15.2.1.5 ASL in acute stroke

ASL is a completely noninvasive measurement of cerebral blood flow (CBF) [49,50]. Unlike DSC-MRI, which is a bolus perfusion technique, ASL does not require administration of an exogenous contrast agent. Instead, arterial blood water is magnetically labeled in a plane proximal to the brain (typically around the skull base) and acts as an endogenous and freely diffusible tracer [49,51] (see Chapter 12 for more details). This approach allows repeated measurements to be made, and can also be used in patients in whom gadolinium-based contrast agent is contraindicated. Another advantage of ASL is that it enables CBF quantification [50]. Advances in ASL techniques (such as development of pseudo-continuous labeling [52]), streamlining of post-processing, the availability of 3 T MRI scanners (which provide higher signal-to-noise ratio [SNR]), and the use of multichannel receive coils (enabling faster scanning using parallel imaging) have made ASL feasible in routine clinical practice.

A number of studies have evaluated the performance of ASL for the detection of the ischemic penumbra in acute stroke [53–55]. Agreement between DSC, which is well established for mismatch analysis, and ASL has been evaluated. ASL was found to overestimate the perfusion deficit [53,55]. This is likely related to the delayed arrival of blood in ischemic regions causing a reduced signal change as a result of T_1 relaxation rather than reduced perfusion. This limits the clinical utility of ASL since it can result in incorrect triage decisions. The optimal threshold for identifying critical hypoperfused tissue was found to be 40% of mean contralateral CBF in one of these studies [53]. Another study which used a quantitative CBF threshold of 20 mL/100 g per minute found 100% agreement between ASL and DSC for mismatch based on a mean transit time of ≥ 10 s (when delay-sensitive deconvolution techniques are used, the mean transit time can be used as a surrogate for T_{max}) [56].

Despite its advantages, ASL is not widely used in acute stroke imaging. This is due to a number of important limitations. ASL has a lower SNR compared to DSC. Also, the ASL signal is approximately proportional to CBF [50,57], which is markedly reduced in the infarct core and penumbra. Blood reaches the ischemic penumbra via collateral pathways, therefore is markedly delayed (as indicated by prolongation of T_{max}). Consequently, when a standard post label delay (PLD) of 1500–2000 ms is used, the labeled blood may not have yet traversed these collateral pathways and reached the capillary bed to exchange into the parenchymal tissue. Therefore, blood flow reduction in tissue is overestimated and may not necessarily reflect a true decrease in blood flow. An example is shown in Fig. 15.4.

Using a longer PLD to allow blood to reach the ischemic tissue is a potential solution [57]. In order to improve accuracy of quantification, measurements with a 3000 ms labeling time and 3000 ms PLD, or multidelay techniques, have been proposed [57,58]. However, a longer delay comes at a cost in terms of SNR since ASL signal decays with the T_1 relaxation time of blood (approximately 1.2 to 1.8 s at the magnetic field strengths used in clinical practice), resulting in reduced measurement precision [57].

It is noted that any slow transit of labeled blood in proximal arteries and collateral pathways can also result in high signal within these structures ("arterial transit artifact," Fig. 15.4). This high signal in ASL can be of value in identifying the presence of stenosis or occlusion [6].

15.2.2 **Chronic steno-occlusive disease**

15.2.2.1 Background

Chronic cerebral hypoperfusion occurs due to occlusion or high-grade stenosis of large arteries of the neck or within the circle of Willis. This is most commonly atherosclerotic in etiology but can also be due to other vasculopathies (e.g., Moyamoya disease). Brain ischemia occurs due to further compromise of blood flow due to:

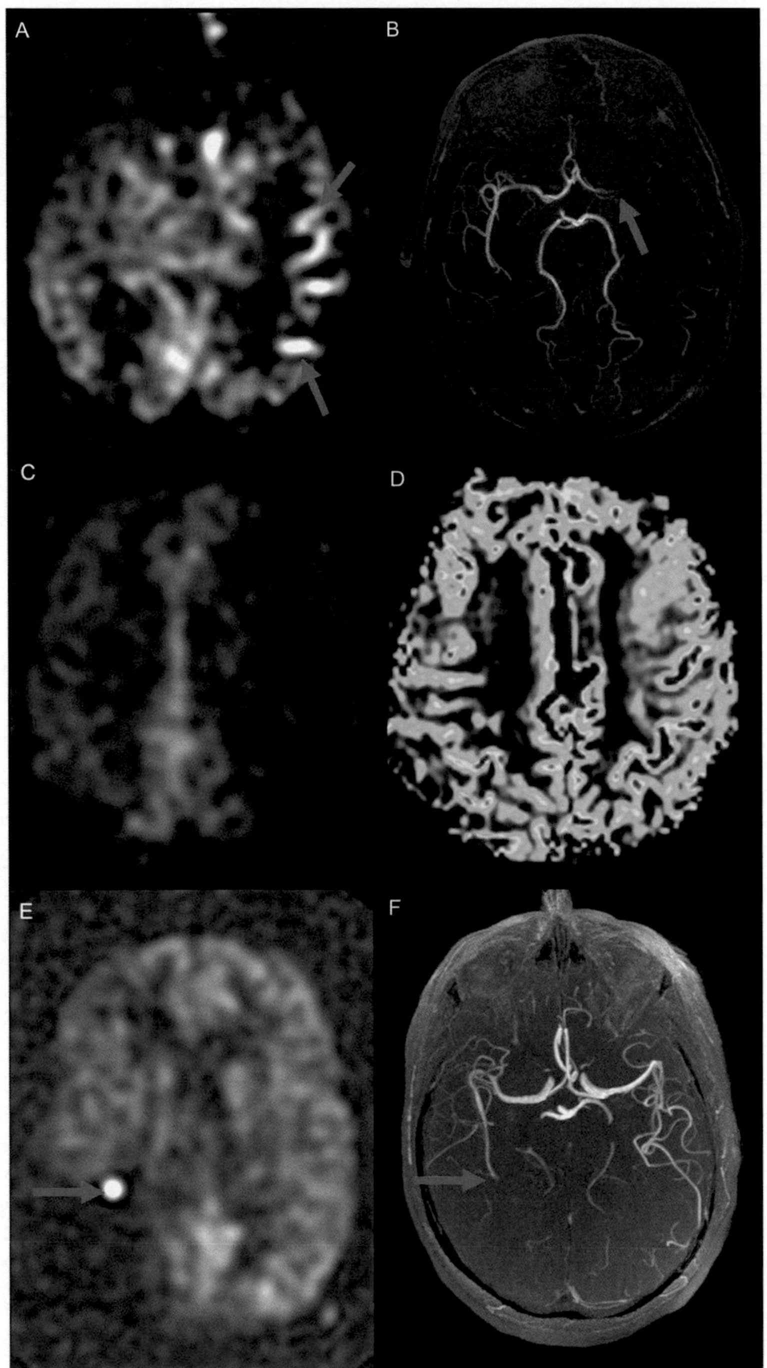

FIG. 15.4

See legend on next page.

1. In-situ thrombosis secondary to atherosclerotic plaque disruption;
2. Embolism from atherosclerotic plaque; and
3. Systemic hemodynamic changes that further reduce cerebral perfusion pressure [59].

A number of changes occur due to decrease in cerebral perfusion pressure (CPP) [60–63]. Powers proposed a 2-stage classification of hemodynamic impairment in chronic cerebrovascular disease which has since been adapted [62,63]. In stage I, compensatory autoregulatory vasodilatation of distal arterioles reduces cerebral vascular resistance. This results in increased cerebral blood volume (CBV) and mean transit time (MTT), maintaining CBF. Oxygen extraction fraction (OEF) has been shown to slightly increase during this stage [61]. Once the maximum autoregulatory capacity is reached, any further decrease in CPP results in a transition to stage II (autoregulatory failure), where CBF decreases. This in turn causes neurons to markedly increase extraction of oxygen from blood in order to maintain function. This compensatory stage where CBF is decreased and OEF is markedly increased is termed "misery perfusion." Once the OEF has reached its maximum, any further decrease in CPP results in blood flow being insufficient to maintain metabolic demand (ischemia).

Evaluation of these compensatory mechanisms is important for prognostication (i.e., to determine the risk of future ischemic events and the need for treatment) and for treatment planning. Cerebrovascular reserve (CVR) testing can be used to assess the stage of compensation [64].

15.2.2.2 Principles of cerebrovascular reserve (CVR) testing

Cerebrovascular reactivity refers to the ability of the cerebral vasculature to increase blood flow within a vascular territory through vasodilatation. In patients with chronic steno-occlusive disease who have maximal vasodilatation within the affected vascular territory, no further vasodilatation can occur in response to this challenge. Cerebrovascular reactivity can therefore be estimated by measuring CBF at baseline and following a vasodilatory stimulus such as acetazolamide (a carbonic anhydrase inhibitor which can penetrate the BBB) or carbon dioxide inhalation [64,65]. Acetazolamide, which is administered intravenously as a bolus, is more commonly used since it is less cumbersome. The peak CBF increase in response to acetazolamide typically occurs 10–15 min after administration.

The response to the acetazolamide challenge depends on the stage of hemodynamic impairment, and three types of responses within the affected vascular territory have been described [66]:

FIG. 15.4—CONT'D

Arterial transit artifact on arterial spin labeling (ASL) images. (A) Pseudocontinuous ASL with a standard post-label delay of 2000 ms in a 69-year-old man with chronic occlusion of the left middle cerebral artery proximal M1 segment. Due to the delayed transit time in the affected vascular territory, labeled blood is seen in M2 and M3 branches of the middle cerebral artery *(arrows)*. (B) Proximal M1 segment occlusion confirmed on time-of-flight MRA *(arrow)*. (C) An ASL difference image further shows an apparent reduction in cerebral blood flow throughout the left middle cerebral artery, which is an artifact due to the delayed arrival of blood rather than a true decrease in blood flow. (D) Relative cerebral blood flow map obtained using DSC perfusion shows preserved and elevated blood flow within the region. (E) Pseudocontinuous ASL obtained with a PLD of 2000 ms in a 81-year-old woman with acute stroke showing focal very high signal in the posterior right Sylvian fissure *(arrow)* due to hold up of labeled blood proximal to the occlusion site. (F) Time-of-flight MRA confirms occlusion of the inferior M2 segment of the right middle cerebral artery. The artifact helps locate the site of occlusion.

- Type I: normal CBF at baseline, with increase after acetazolamide administration
- Type II: decreased CBF at baseline, with increase after acetazolamide administration
- Type III: decreased CBF at baseline with reduced CBF following acetazolamide. In these patients, vasodilatation in unaffected territories results in "steal" of blood flow away from the maximally vasodilated, diseased territory resulting in paradoxical decrease in CBF.

Normal subjects (Type I) demonstrate 30%–60% increase in CBF following acetazolamide administration [67]. Increase in the absolute CBF by <10 mL/100 mg/min or < 10% is considered abnormal (Types II and III) [64]. Type III patients have a loss of cerebrovascular reserve and are most likely to benefit from revascularization surgery.

15.2.2.3 CBF measurement for CVR testing

Quantitative CBF measurement is required for CVR testing. Perfusion assessment with DSC is limited by the complex, nonlinear relationship between contrast agent concentration and signal, which is an obstacle to absolute quantification of CBF. ASL is therefore the mainstay of MR-based CVR testing. ASL has previously been shown to be equivalent to single-photon emission CT (SPECT) for noninvasive testing of CVR [68]. However, as in acute stroke, a major limitation of this technique is the delay in arterial transit times (ATTs) that occur with arterial steno-occlusive disease, where blood reaches brain parenchyma through collateral pathways. This prolonged transit results in delayed arrival of labeled blood in tissue as well as T_1-related signal decay in transit, causing underestimation of CBF.

One study compared three different ASL implementations (standard delay, multidelay, and long label-long delay [LL LD]) against the reference standard of simultaneous [15O]-positron emission tomography (PET) for measurement of relative CBF in patients with Moyamoya disease [69]. The PLD for standard-delay ASL was 2.025 s. The multidelay implementation used five different PLD times ranging from 0.7 to 3 s, which allowed measurement of, followed by correction for, the arterial transit time. The LL LD implementation used a PLD of 4.0 s, which allowed blood to reach tissue downstream from the chronic occlusion via collateral pathways, with a longer labeling time to improve the SNR. DSC was also performed in order to determine T_{max} within each vascular territory, as a measure of the degree of arterial transit delay. Standard-delay ASL underestimated relative CBF by 20% in areas of severe T_{max} delay, while the LL LD acquisition showed the strongest correlation with PET with no difference in mean relative CBF even in the areas of markedly prolonged T_{max}. LL LD ASL may therefore allow more accurate assessment of CBF for CVR testing in steno-occlusive disease such as Moyamoya, by allowing a distinction between nonperfused tissue from perfused tissue with extremely long T_{max}. An example with multidelay and LL LD ASL is shown in Fig. 15.5.

15.3 Applications of perfusion MRI in brain cancer

15.3.1 Introduction

The clinical standard of care for brain cancer diagnosis and monitoring is the acquisition of anatomical, contrast-enhanced MR images. From these scans, morphological features (e.g., location, size) are identified for tumor burden. A fundamental limitation to these anatomical MR images is that they rely on downstream manifestations of the tumor's pathophysiology. However, MR perfusion techniques have the ability to assess the tumor's underlying physiological and cellular properties more directly.

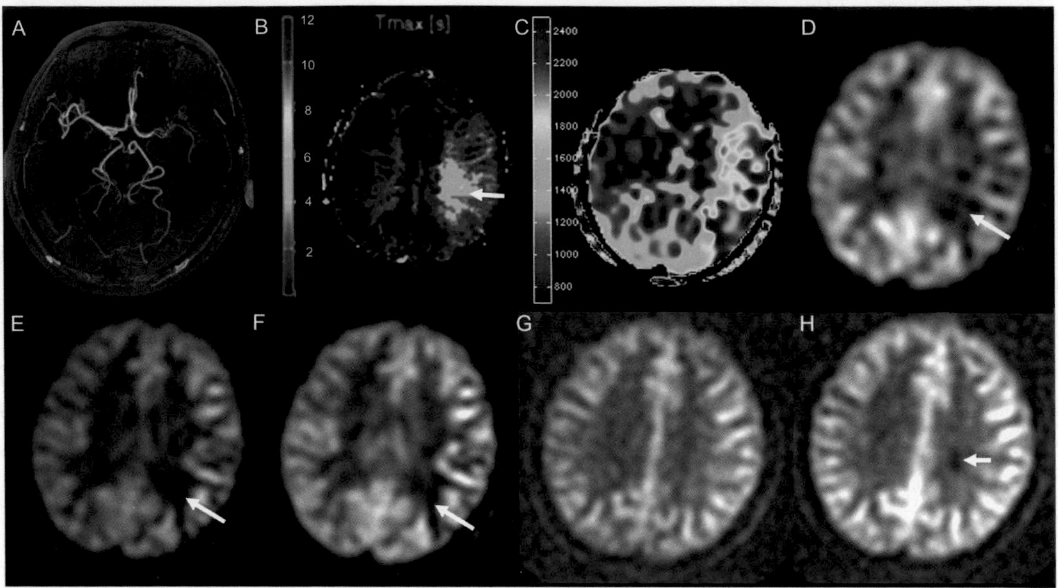

FIG. 15.5

Examples of standard delay, multi-delay and long-label long-delay arterial spin labeling (ASL) in a 49-year-old woman with chronic occlusion of the left middle cerebral artery. (A) Time-of-flight MRA shows chronic occlusion of the proximal M1 segment with prominent collaterals within the left Sylvian cistern. (B) T_{max} map obtained from dynamic susceptibility contrast (DSC) perfusion shows delayed arrival of blood, most marked in the left centrum semiovale *(arrow)*, the deep white matter watershed. (C) Multidelay ASL transit time map (in units of ms) also showing this delay. (D) Delay-corrected blood flow map obtained from multidelay ASL (five time points from 700 ms to 3000 ms). There is an apparent decrease in blood flow in the centrum semiovale and left parietal white matter *(arrow)*. (E) Baseline and (F) post-acetazolamide blood flow maps obtained using a standard post label delay of 2000 ms. There is an apparent decrease in blood flow in the left parietal white matter *(arrow)* that does not augment with the vasodilatory stimulus, while augmentation can be seen in the unaffected contralateral hemisphere and ipsilateral anterior and posterior cerebral artery territories. (G) Baseline and (H) post acetazolamide long-label long-delay ASL blood flow images. No left parietal blood flow reduction is seen, indicating that the apparent reduction on the standard and multidelay ASL was an artifact related to transit delay. There is a small area of steal, with blood flow reduction post acetazolamide in the posterior left centrum semiovale *(arrow)*. This area is at risk of infarction.

The most frequently used perfusion technique for brain cancer is DSC [70,71] and most studies focus on CBV rather than CBF. In general, absolute quantification of CBV is difficult in DSC and therefore most papers report *relative* CBV (rCBV) by normalizing CBV to normal-appearing white matter (NAWM). A second issue with applying DSC in brain cancer is the disruption of the BBB which causes contrast agent extravasation (leakage). This violates the standard DSC signal model, in particular the assumptions that changes in T_1 have a negligible effect on the signal and that T_2* relaxivity is a constant (Fig. 15.6). Both T_1 and T_2* leakage effects alter the relationship between signal change and concentration and potentially confound rCBV measurements [72]. Nevertheless, optimization of

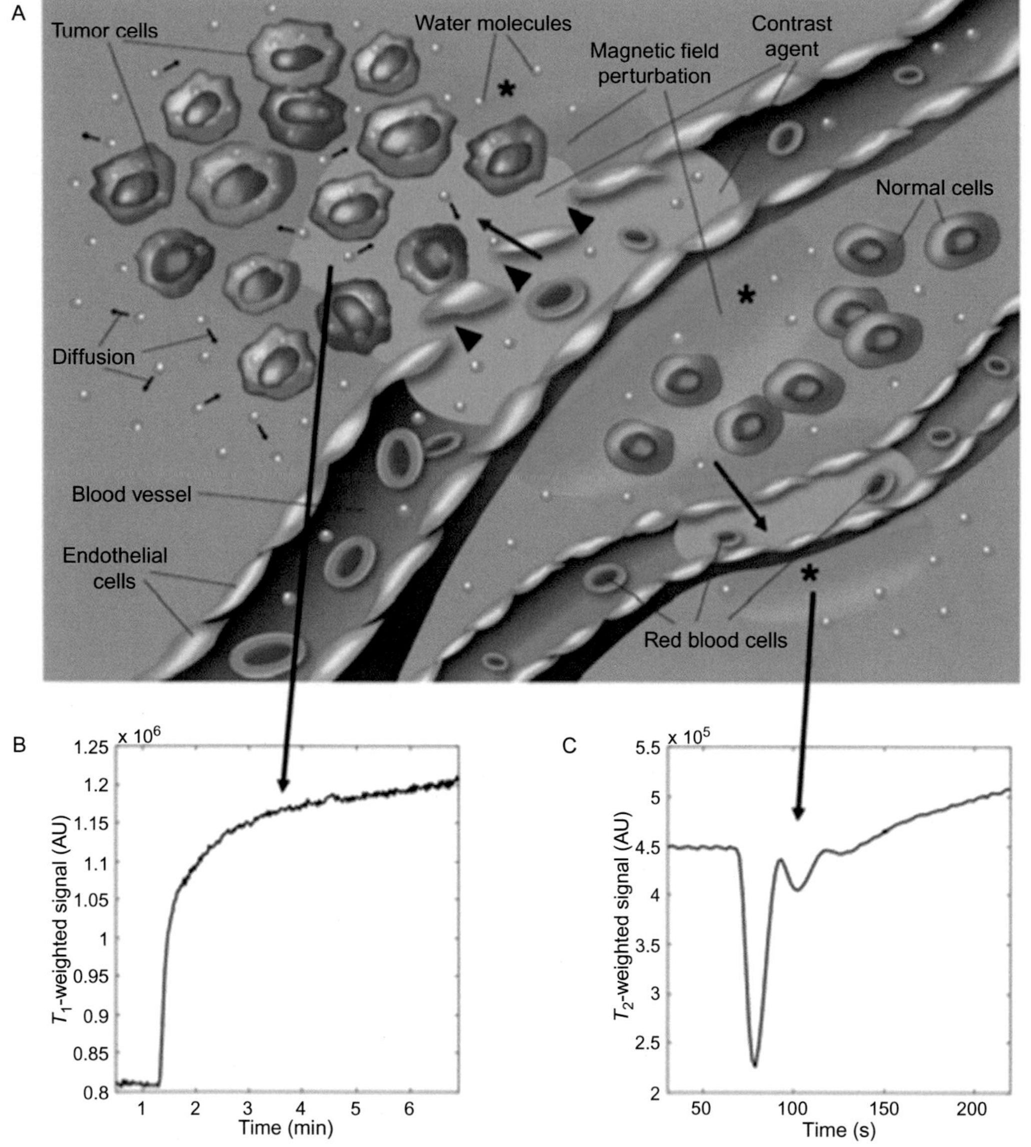

FIG. 15.6

Illustration of CA distribution within tissue, its interaction with water protons (A) and the induced T_1-weighted (B) or T_2-weighted (C) signal changes. When the blood brain barrier is intact, as illustrated in the lower blood vessel, the CA only has direct access to intravascular water *(red arrow)* so that the associated change in the effective tissue T_1 is small. However, if the blood brain barrier is disrupted (top blood vessel, *black triangles*) the CA distribution and microscopic interaction with water within the extravascular space *(red arrow)* substantially decreases tissue T_1 and increases a T_1-weighted signal (B), like that used for DCE-MRI. The compartmentalization of CA in blood (lower blood vessel) or in the extravascular extracellular space (top blood vessel) gives rise to mesoscopic magnetic field gradients surrounding these compartments (as denoted by the asterisks). The diffusion of water through those fields *(small black arrows)* leads to a T_2-weighted signal (C), like that used for DSC-MRI.

(From Quarles CC, Bell LC, Stokes AM: Imaging vascular and hemodynamic features of the brain using dynamic susceptibility contrast and dynamic contrast-enhanced MRI. Neuroimage 2019;187:32–55.)

acquisition protocol (e.g., prebolus injection "preload" and imaging parameters) and application of leakage correction methods can mitigate these confounding effects [72–79].

DCE-MRI can also be applied in brain tumors to measure perfusion (CBF and CBV), and when the contrast-agent crosses into the interstitium, it can also be used to assess capillary permeability (PS) and parameters such as K^{trans} (transfer rate), and v_e (fractional extracellular extravascular volume) [80]. Outside the brain tumor, low enhancement-to-noise in healthy brain tissue due to the intact BBB impacts the precision of CBF and CBV measurements, though this can be mitigated to some extent by using model-based deconvolution [81,82]. Within the tumor, DCE-MRI may be more suitable when absolute quantification is warranted or when DSC is known to fail (e.g., susceptibility artifacts due to shunts, resection cavities, air-tissue interfaces) [83].

Compared to contrast-based perfusion techniques, ASL has been used infrequently in brain tumors, and current studies are limited albeit promising [83,84]. Recent improvements in acquisitions (e.g., 3D imaging, improved SNR, background suppression, low imaging artifacts) and concerns regarding the use of gadolinium have increased clinical interest in using ASL for CBF mapping as it is unaffected by leakage. An additional benefit of ASL in brain tumors when compared to DSC is the suppression of large blood vessels, allowing areas of high CBF to be more noticeable.

In a 2018 survey of 220 institutions by the European Society of Neuroradiology, 85.5% (DSC specifically: 81.8%) responded that contrast-based MR perfusion is currently used for brain cancer imaging for initial grading and/or follow-up [70]. In the United States, 87% of those surveyed included perfusion imaging in their standard clinical imaging protocol [71]. Specifically, for the evaluation of tumor progression and treatment response, these values were 96% and 66% [70]. Despite extensive research, formal clinical adoption of DSC-MRI has been slow due to concerns about reproducibility [85–87].

Several recent initiatives (e.g., National Cancer Institute's Quantitative Imaging Network (QIN), Radiological Society of North America's Quantitative Imaging Biomarkers Alliance (QIBA), and the National Brain Tumor Society's Jumpstarting Brain Tumor Drug Development Coalition) have focused on DSC standardization as studies have shown strong reproducibility with standardized protocols [88–91]. As of 2020, for the first time, a standardized DSC perfusion protocol is included in the "ideal" protocol for brain tumor imaging (BTIP) for clinical trials [92]. This section will focus on how MR perfusion techniques can be applied to all aspects of brain cancer management from diagnosis and neurosurgery to evaluating treatment response and disease progression.

15.3.2 Diagnosis and neurosurgery

15.3.2.1 Background

Glioma types consist of astrocytomas (including GBMs), ependymomas, and oligodendrogliomas. The World Health Organization (WHO) grades these gliomas on a scale from I to IV based on histological features (e.g., cellularity, necrosis, microvascular proliferation, nuclear atypia, and mitotic activity) [93]. The histologic phenotype of grade I gliomas is fairly benign, and the treatment course straightforward (surgical resection only). On the other hand, grade II–IV gliomas demonstrate a heterogeneous histologic profile, and their standard clinical care consists of a combination of surgical resection followed by radiation therapy and/or chemotherapy [83,94]. Unlike low-grade gliomas (LGGs; grade I–II), high-grade gliomas (HGGs; grade III–IV) are characterized by a disrupted BBB leading to disorganized microvasculature, hypoxia-induced neovascularity, and angiogenesis. Angiogenesis is the hallmark characteristic of grade IV gliomas known as GBMs.

Updated WHO criteria include identifying molecular biomarkers such as IDH1/2 mutations and epidermal growth factor receptor (EGFR) in primary GBMs, and co-deletion of 1p and 19q in oligodendrogliomas to compliment the glioma grading [93]. Targeted drug therapies, currently the focus of brain cancer drug development, depend on the identification of these molecular biomarkers [95]. To aid in this, the National Cancer Institute (NCI) and The Cancer Genome Atlas (TCGA) are curating a database of genetically diverse HGG to help guide risk stratification for existing protocols and identify key driver genes as potential therapeutic targets [96]. However, only 35% of the image-guided (using anatomical MR images) biopsy samples contained adequate tumor content for genetic and molecular analysis [96]. With recent advances in the molecular understanding of gliomas, MR perfusion techniques may improve both tumor diagnosis and neurosurgery.

15.3.2.2 Role of DSC/DCE perfusion

Characterizing the tumor microvasculature is a primary feature in tumor grading. The most extensively researched DSC parameter, rCBV, has been positively correlated with tumor grade reflecting microvascular proliferation [83,97,98] (Fig. 15.7). Elevated rCBV values are observed in GBMs due to the highly vascular, angiogenic state of the glioma. Additionally, elevated rCBV values located within the edema regions may indicate the infiltration of tumor cells outside of the contrast-enhancing regions [99–101]. Identification of infiltrating tumor cells can better guide biopsy sampling as well as the extent of tumor resection, improving prognosis [101]. Percentage of signal intensity recovery (PSR), a semi-quantitative measure of capillary permeability that relies on extravasation of contrast agent due to BBB breakdown, has been shown to be negatively correlated with tumor grade [87,102–104]. Capillary transit heterogeneity (CTH), potentially an indicator of tumor hypoxia, has also been shown to differentiate tumor grade [100,105] (Fig. 15.8). Additionally, CTH was demonstrated to be a survival predictor as hypoxic tumors are more resistant to chemotherapy [100].

Kinetic model coefficients K^{trans}, v_p, and v_e derived from DCE have also been positively correlated with tumor grade, reflecting the increased capillary permeability, angiogenesis, and cellularity, respectively [83,91,106,107] (Fig. 15.9). However, likely due to differences in the models applied, these DCE parameters have shown conflicting results in the literature [83,91]. Anzalone et al. conducted a study comparing the clinical value of both DSC and DCE parameters for tumor grading and correlating molecular alterations [91]. High accuracy for tumor grading was found using DSC rCBV (86.4% sensitivity, 85.7% specificity). Combining DSC and DCE parameters for multiparametric analysis tumor grading did not improve accuracy compared to using DSC rCBV alone, but did perform better than DCE alone [91].

With recent improvements in multiecho acquisitions, more advanced perfusion parameters such as vessel size imaging (VSI) [108,109] and relaxivity contrast imaging (RCI) [110,111] are being investigated. These parameters probe tumor cytoarchitecture and may further improve tumor grading and image-guided biopsies.

Lastly, conventional contrast-based perfusion techniques have not proven to be prognostic markers for molecular markers, specifically isocitrate dehydrogenase (IDH) mutation 1p/19q codeletion, or ATRX expression [91,112,113]. Increases in DSC rCBV for GBMs with *EGFR* mutations have been demonstrated [113]. More advanced post-processing technique known as radiogenomics shows promise for distinguishing molecular characteristics, and this field is continuing to evolve [83,91,114–117].

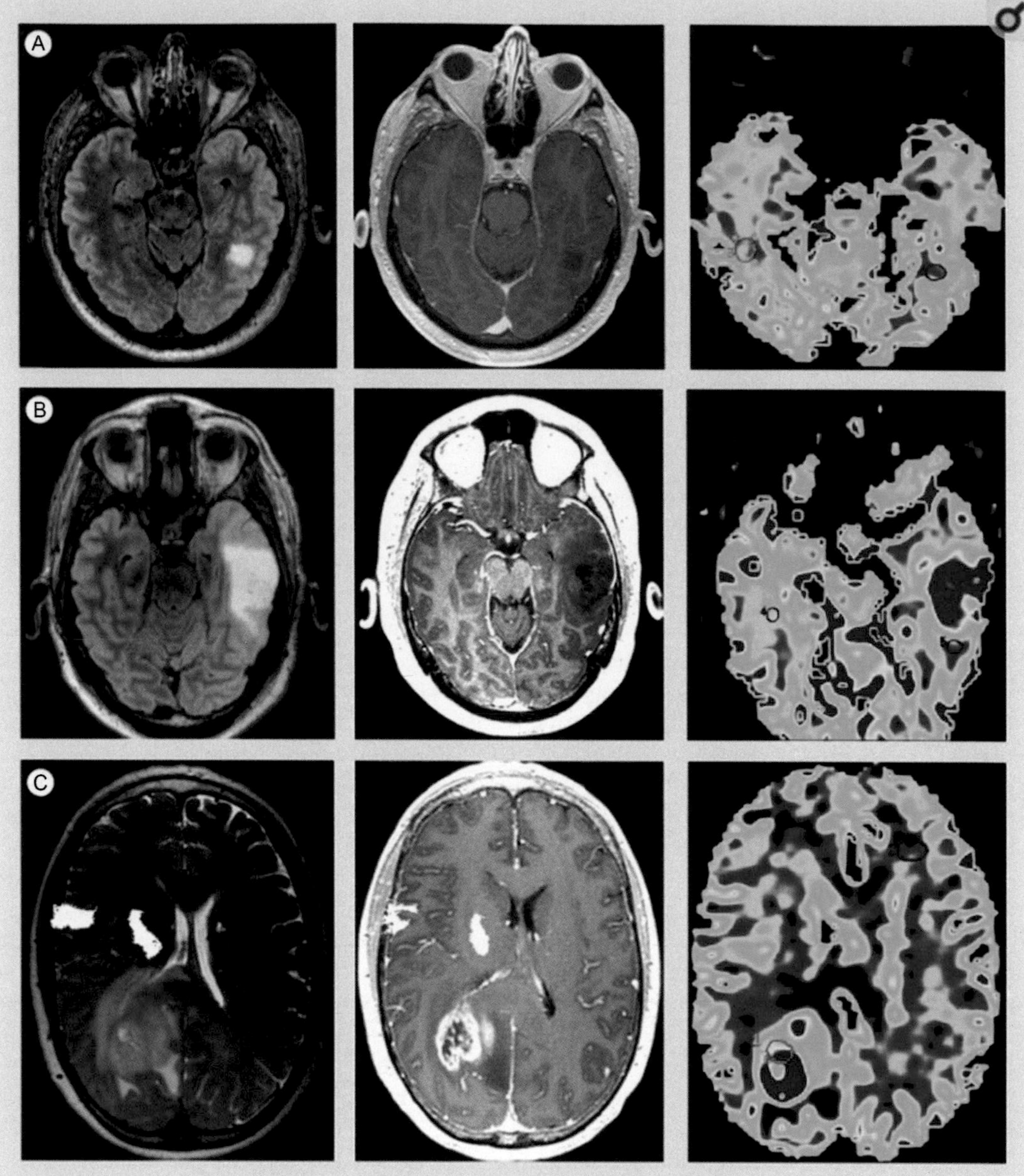

FIG. 15.7

Cerebral blood volume differentiates high from low-grade glioma. (A) Diffuse astrocytoma (WHO grade II) is morphologically manifested as a fluid-attenuated inversion recovery hyperintense (FLAIR; *left*) nonenhancing *(middle)* mass with cerebral blood volume *(right)* measurements similar to normal appearing white matter. (B) Anaplastic astrocytoma (WHO grade III) typically presents as a FLAIR hyperintense mass with minimal if any contrast enhancement; however, unlike low-grade glioma, demonstrates elevated cerebral blood volume. The presence of increased perfusion metrics within a nonenhancing glioma suggests the presence of aggressive biological features that portend a high-grade diagnosis. (C) Glioblastoma (WHO grade IV) can present as a rim-enhancing T_2/FLAIR hyperintense matt with markedly elevated cerebral blood volume.

(From https://www.ncbi.nlm.nih.gov/pmc/articles/PMC4277861/figure/F0004/.)

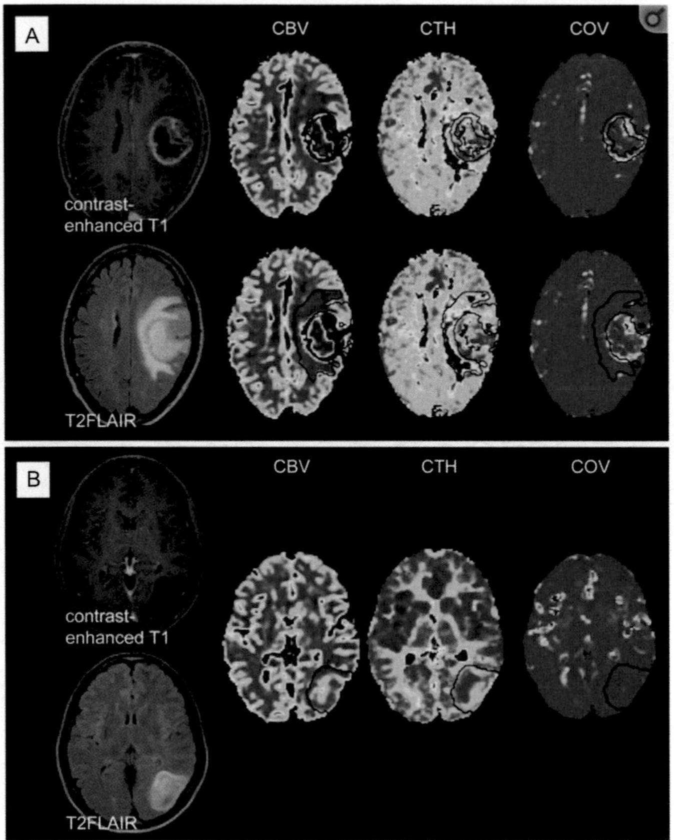

FIG. 15.8

Example of a high-grade and a low-grade glioma. Contrast-enhanced T_1, T_2FLAIR, cerebral blood volume (CBV), capillary transit time heterogeneity (CTH), and coefficient of variance (COV) maps in a patient with (A) a glioblastoma and (B) an astrocytoma grade II. The enhancing tumor and the peri-focal edema are outlined with black lines on the parameter maps. (A) The glioblastoma shows increased COV in the enhancing part and high CTH in the peri-tumoral edema, whereas (B) the astrocytoma grade II is characterized by low CBV, CTH, and COV.

(From https://www.ncbi.nlm.nih.gov/pmc/articles/PMC4395250/figure/pone.0123044.g002/?report=objectonly.)

15.3.2.3 Role of ASL

ASL is increasingly being studied as an alternative to contrast-based perfusion techniques because of its simplified acquisition demands (e.g., no setup of a power injector required) and minimal postprocessing [118]. CBF derived from ASL is reflective of angiogenesis and has shown diagnostic accuracy comparable with DSC for tumor grading [119,120]. Despite concerns about transit time effects, recent studies have indicated a correlation between ASL rCBF and DSC rCBV [121] (Fig. 15.10). Preliminary results from ASL studies indicate that there are mild to strong correlations between IDH1 genotypes [112], but no statistical difference was found between 1p/19q status [120,122]. The effectiveness of ASL in other indications shows promise for use in brain cancer imaging.

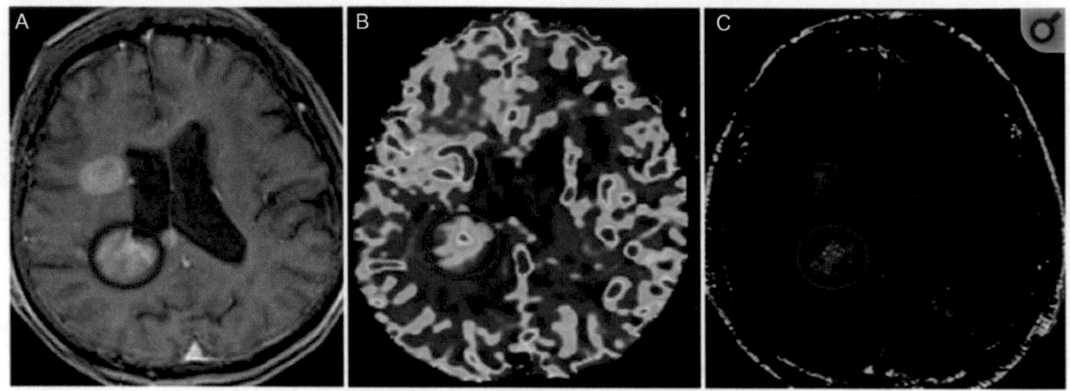

FIG. 15.9

Contrast-enhanced T_1-weighted images (T_1WI) (A), corrected cerebral blood volume (CBV) (B), and volume transfer coefficient (K^{trans}) (C) in patient with high grade glioma. Contrast-enhanced T_1WI shows an enhanced mass in the right frontal and parietal lobe. Axial corrected CBV shows increased vascularity in the peripheral lesion, and axial K^{trans} shows a small degree of increased vascular permeability.

(Reproduced with permission from Murayama K, Nishiyama Y, Hirose Y, Abe M, Ohyu S, Ninomiya A, et al. Differentiating between central nervous system lymphoma and high-grade glioma using dynamic susceptibility contrast and dynamic contrast-enhanced MR imaging with histogram analysis. Magnet Reson Med Sci 2017;17:42–9. © Japanese Society for Magnetic Resonance in Medicine.)

15.3.3 Evaluation of tumor progression and treatment response

15.3.3.1 Background

After diagnosis and neurosurgery for tumor resection, standard clinical care calls for a combination of radiation therapy, chemotherapy, and/or target therapy. If the disease progresses during the treatment, the treatment changes. For this reason, it is essential to distinguish treatment response from disease progression—one of the biggest challenges in brain cancer management [123,124].

Current response criteria rely on morphological changes in structural, contrast-enhanced MR images to determine treatment response and disease progression [125]. An increase in contrast-enhanced T_1-weighted and T_2-weighted/fluid-attenuated inversion recovery (FLAIR) region sizes typically indicate disease progression, whereas a decrease indicates a positive treatment response. However, tumors may display pseudoprogression and pseudoresponse characteristics during treatment, demanding serial imaging to accurately assess tumor size changes [83]. Pseudoprogression is an inflammatory response at the end of chemotherapy and is seen in 30% of HGG patients and even observed in LGG patients [83,94]. Pseudoresponse is a change in the vascular permeability due to BBB normalization and may be observed in the hours after introducing antiangiogenic agents (e.g., bevacizumab) [126,127]. It has been shown that the degree of decreased enhancement in T_1-weighted and T_2-weighted/FLAIR images correlates with overall survival suggesting pseudoresponse may be associated with a clinical benefit [126,127].

Currently, there are limited studies ($n = 2$) using ASL for assessing tumor progression and their results indicate the low diagnostic value, and no currently published clinical studies for assessing

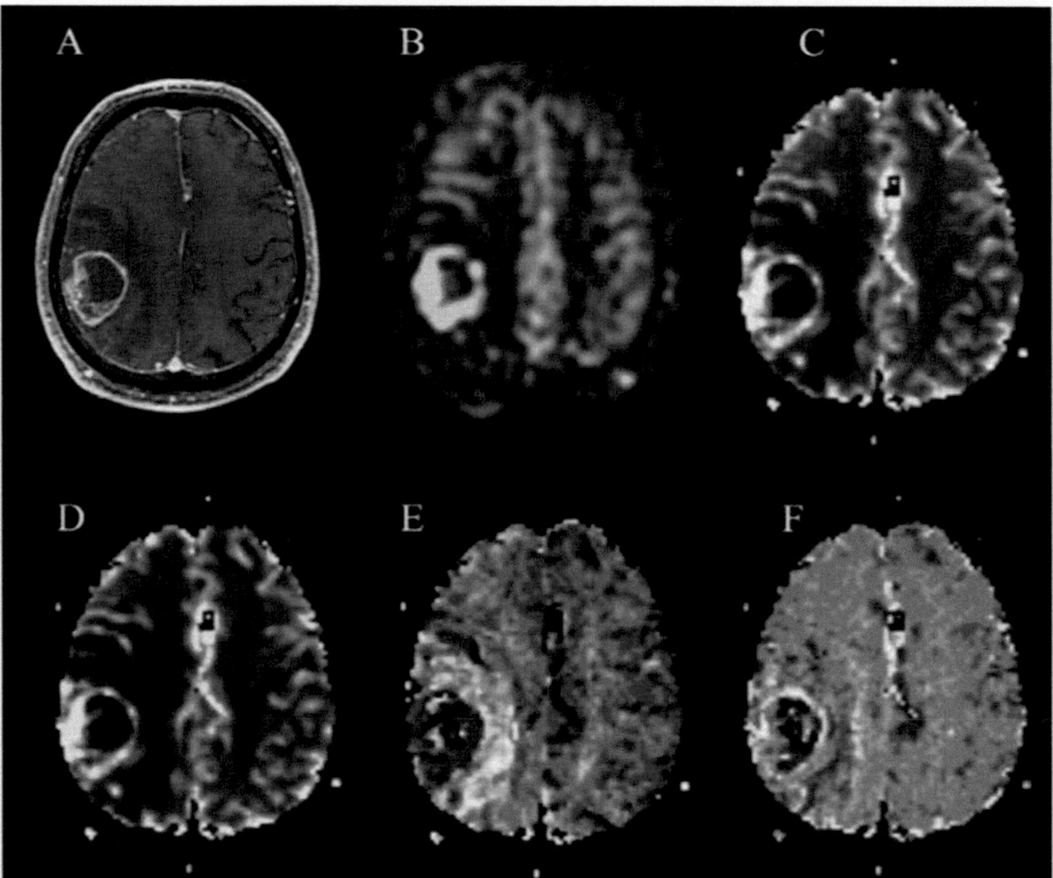

FIG. 15.10

MRI images of a patient with glioblastoma in the right temporal lobe with peritumoral edema. The tumor shows contrast rim-enhancement on (A) CE-T_1WI and hyperperfusion on the (B) ASL CBF map, (C) DSC rCBF map, and (D) DSC rCBV map. (E) T_{max} map demonstrates a corresponding perfusion defect in the tumor lesion that disappears on the (F) DSC MTT map. *ASL*, arterial spin labeling; *CBF*, cerebral blood flow; *CE-T_1WI*, contrast-enhanced T_1-weighted image; *DSC*, dynamic susceptibility contrast; *MTT*, mean transit time; *rCBF*, relative cerebral blood flow; *rCBV*, relative cerebral blood volume; T_{max}; time to maximum.

(From Khashbat, MD D, Abe, MD T, Ganbold, MD M, et al. Correlation of 3D arterial spin labeling and multi-parametric dynamic susceptibility contrast perfusion MRI in brain tumors. J Med Investig 2016;63(3.4):175–81.)

treatment response [98]. However, there is currently one ongoing clinical trial to evaluate ASL for evaluating treatment response [128]. At this time, most of the promising research for evaluation of treatment response and disease progression involves contrast-based MR perfusion techniques and will be the focus of the remaining section.

15.3.3.2 Role of DSC/DCE MR perfusion

Contrast-based MR perfusion techniques are beneficial for evaluating treatment progression. A meta-analysis of current studies demonstrated superior pooled sensitivity and specificity for treatment response evaluation for contrast-based MR perfusion techniques (DSC: 87% and 86%, respectively, over 18 studies; DCE: 92%, 85%, respectively, over five studies) compared to anatomical MRI (68%, 77%, respectively) [98].

Studies have demonstrated an increase in DSC, rCBV, and rCBF with tumor progression when compared to treatment effects [83,123,129–131]. Another promising DSC-derived marker of interest is fractional tumor burden (FTB), which is the percentage of tumor pixels above a certain rCBV threshold and has shown to differentiate treatment effects from tumor [132,133] (Fig. 15.11). The PSR in DSC was reported to be lower in recurrent GBM than in patients with radiation necrosis [134]; however, in a separate study, Prah et al. did not see a statistical difference using PSR [135]. Conflicting results are most likely due to differences in the imaging protocol, specifically the administration of a preloaded dose [136,137]. Lastly, DCE-based K^{trans} measurements have also been shown to be higher with tumor progression when compared to treatment effects and to be a similar prognostic marker as DSC rCBV [138,139].

Contrast-based MR perfusion may also be beneficial for determining treatment response [131]. Results from the ACRIN (American College of Radiology Imaging Network) 6677/RTOG 0625 multisite, phase II clinical trial demonstrated early decreases in DSC rCBV correlated with greater overall survival [130] (Fig. 15.12). In addition, results in a separate study indicated that standardized DSC rCBV pre- and post-treatment below a certain threshold predicted overall survival [140]. A separate study indicated that DSC absolute CBV was not prognostic marker of overall survival, however a different definition of CBV was used and the time between imaging points was much longer [129]. Although fewer studies have been done with DCE, K^{trans} shows great promise as an early marker for treatment response, where decreases in K^{trans} have been associated with overall survival [126]. Results from the multicenter ACRIN study showed strong agreement in DCE K^{trans} during pretreatment; however, agreement significantly decreased during the post-bevacizumab imaging timepoint [141]. The decreased agreement in K^{trans} was most likely due to poor interreader agreement on ascertaining tumor margins post-treatment. With recent improvements in multiecho acquisitions, advanced perfusion parameters from vessel architectural imaging (VAI) indicate promise to differentiate responders from nonresponders [142].

15.4 Applications of perfusion MRI in dementia

15.4.1 Background

One of the main characteristic pathological correlates of dementia is the accumulation of extracellular amyloid plaques and intraneuronal neurofibrillary tau tangles; formal diagnosis of AD requires postmortem confirmation of the presence of amyloid plaques in the brain. While the precise mechanisms of neurodegeneration caused by the accumulation of these neurotoxic proteins are not well understood, it is well known that these increases are accompanied by associated decreases in metabolism, which can be measured using ^{18}F-labeled fluorodeoxyglucose (FDG) PET (FDG PET). In the initial stages of the diseases, these changes occur in specific anatomical locations: for example, the posterior cingulate

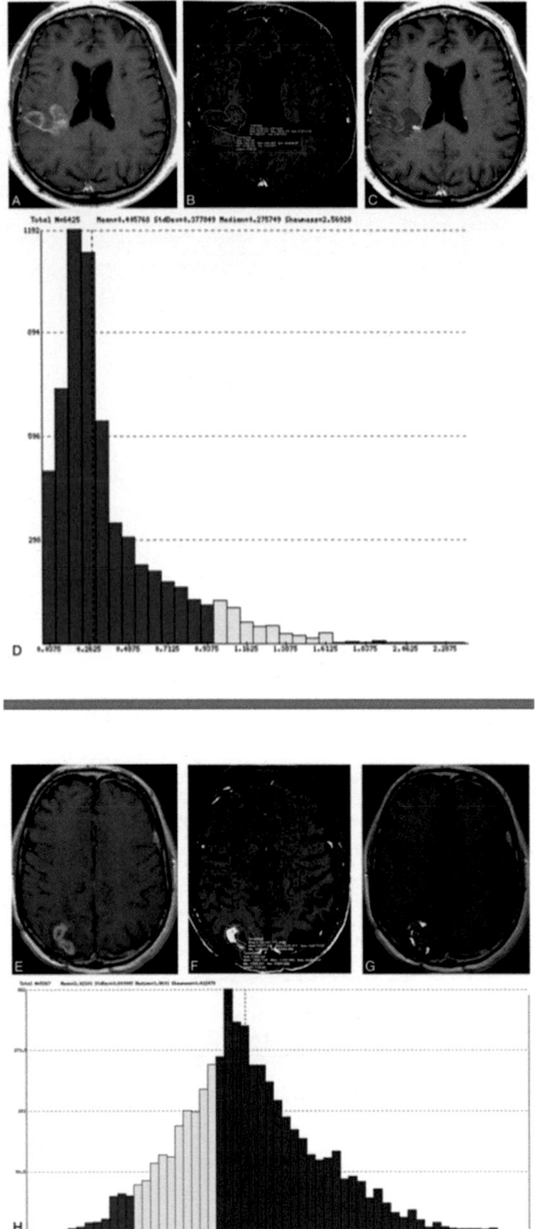

FIG. 15.11

Representative examples of treatment effect (A–D) and recurrent tumor (E–H) in two patients with previously resected and irradiated glioblastomas. Contrast-enhancing lesions on postcontrast T_1-weighted (A and E) and ΔT_1 (B and F) images. Output FTB maps superimposed on the contrast-enhanced T_1-weighted images (C and G). *Blue* represents areas of low-blood volume (FTB_{low}) and *red* represents areas of high-blood volume (FTB_{high}). Histograms (D and H) show all voxels of the contrast-enhancing volume classified into the respective FTB_{low} (blue), FTB_{med} (yellow), and FTB_{high} (red) classes, which is based on the rCBV thresholds of 10 and 175.

(From Iv M, Liu X, Lavezo J, Gentles AJ, Ghanem R, Lummus S, et al. Perfusion MRI-based fractional tumor burden differentiates between tumor and treatment effect in recurrent glioblastomas and informs clinical decision-making. AJNR Am J Neuroradiol 2019;40 (10):1649–57 doi:10.3174/ajnr.a6211.)

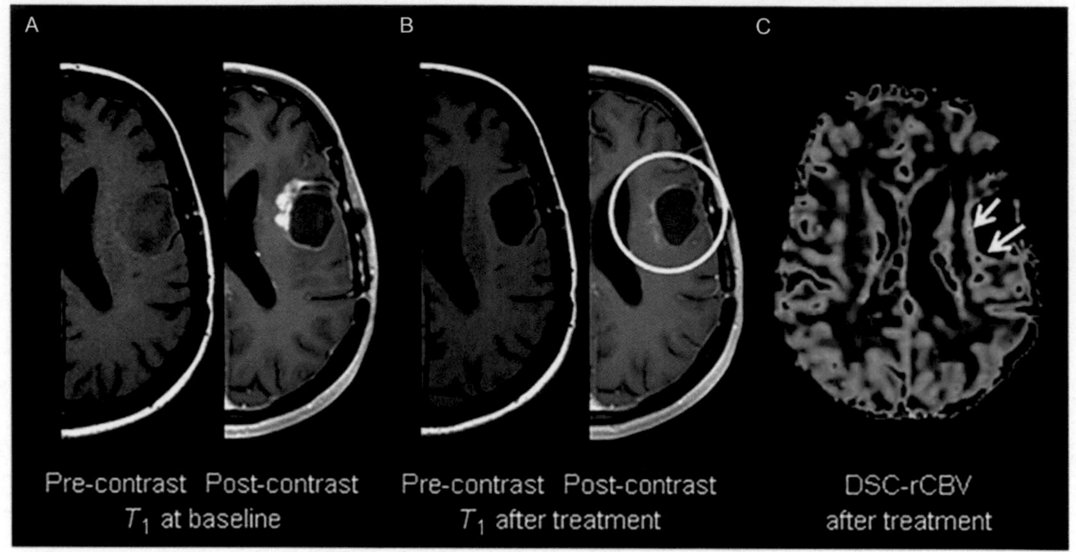

FIG. 15.12

Pseudoresponse identified by dynamic susceptibility contrast (DSC). Patient with a recurrent glioblastoma with new contrast enhancement on T_1-weighted MRI after completion of chemotherapy (A). The patient received second-line antiangiogenic treatment with bevacizumab. After the first course, follow-up MRI (B) showed a decrease in contrast-enhancing lesions *(white circle)*, suggestive of apparent response. However, DSC demonstrated persisting high perfusion values *(arrows)* confirming the changes were due to pseudoresponse (C). Subsequent follow-up scans demonstrated an increase in contrast enhancement and rCBV and the patient deteriorated. *DSC*, dynamic susceptibility contrast; *rCBV*, relative cerebral blood volume.

(From https://www.ncbi.nlm.nih.gov/pmc/articles/PMC6590309/figure/jmri26306-fig-0005/.)

cortex and medial temporal regions display clear hypometabolism in mild cognitive impairment (MCI, in which cognition is affected but not to the level required for a diagnosis of dementia) and AD [143].

These changes in metabolism are mirrored by local changes in cerebral perfusion, which can also be measured by PET [144] or by MRI methods such as DSC or ASL. The pattern of perfusion abnormality seen with ASL has been shown to match well with the hypometabolism identified by FDG PET [145]. Recent work has suggested that vascular dysregulation and perfusion changes may even precede metabolic abnormalities in the pathological cascade [146]. Given the limitations of PET in terms of cost [147] and general availability, and the equivalence of the information provided by PET and MR methods for perfusion estimation [148,149], the potential advantages of using MR are clear. In addition, significant recent progress in the development of disease-specific PET tracers of amyloid and tau has increased the requirement for alternative MR-based techniques that can be used to provide perfusion information. Due to its noninvasiveness and the lack of requirement of an injectable tracer, ASL is the most widely used MR perfusion method in dementia.

15.4.2 Diagnosis

Given that perfusion changes occur in the initial stages of disease progression, and significantly before tissue atrophy becomes apparent on structural imaging [150], MR perfusion imaging offers good potential for early diagnosis [151]. It is able to provide useful diagnostic information due to the characteristic perfusion patterns associated with different diseases. For example, while AD is typically associated with bilateral hypometabolism in the parietal and temporal areas, leaving the occipital lobe unaffected [152,153], DLB is associated with hypometabolism in the occipital cortex, with preservation of posterior cingulate [154], and FTD has been shown to present hypoperfusion in the right frontal lobe, but with perfusion in parietal regions and posterior cingulate being relatively well maintained compared to AD [155].

ASL can, therefore, be used in this context for differential diagnosis of AD and FTD [156] (Fig. 15.13). A current international multicenter study of genetic FTD (the GENetic FTD Initiative GENFI; genfi.org) has recently shown that perfusion deficits can be identified presymptomatically: in the C9orf72 genetic subgroup, CBF changes were seen in bilateral insulae/orbitofrontal cortices, anterior cingulate/paracingulate gyri, and inferior parietal cortices up to 12.5 years before the expected age of symptom onset [157]. The AD subtype of posterior cortical atrophy (PCA) affects different brain areas than typical AD, and the regions known to be affected by atrophy in this disease also show reductions in CBF [158] (Fig. 15.14). Patients with vascular dementia have impaired cerebral perfusion by definition, and display decreases in CBF across the whole brain, in particular in bilateral frontal and parietal areas [159,160].

15.4.3 Longitudinal monitoring of disease progression

The quantitative nature of perfusion methods such as ASL makes them particularly well suited to longitudinal studies, as the CBF measurements should be directly comparable across sessions and over arbitrarily long periods. Between-session consistency has been demonstrated in the context of using ASL for functional imaging over extended periods [161], though it is known that a large range of factors can act as "perfusion modifiers" and therefore affect global CBF values for reasons completely unrelated to disease [162] (Fig. 15.15). It is therefore important to standardize conditions for scanning as much as possible (e.g., keeping the scanning environment, such as light levels, ear protection, etc. constant) and to ensure a consistent physiological status of the subject across sessions e.g., by scanning them at the same time of day, with the same caffeine intake, and hunger/stress levels. If this is not possible, careful logging of differences in the known perfusion modifiers is recommended.

15.4.4 Limitations of ASL in neurodegenerative disease

As discussed earlier in this section, one of the primary limitations of ASL is its low SNR. This is exacerbated in elderly individuals, and inpatient populations with diseases affecting the cerebral vasculature. In general, ATTs increase with age [163,164], which means that longer TI or PLD (for PASL and pCASL, respectively) must be used to ensure accurate CBF quantification, leading to reduced SNR due to T_1 decay. The ASL "white paper" [165], which outlines general guideline parameter choices for brain perfusion measurements, recommends a TI/PLD value of 1800 ms for healthy subjects younger than 70 years, and 2000 ms for healthy subjects older than 70 or adult clinical patients when a single

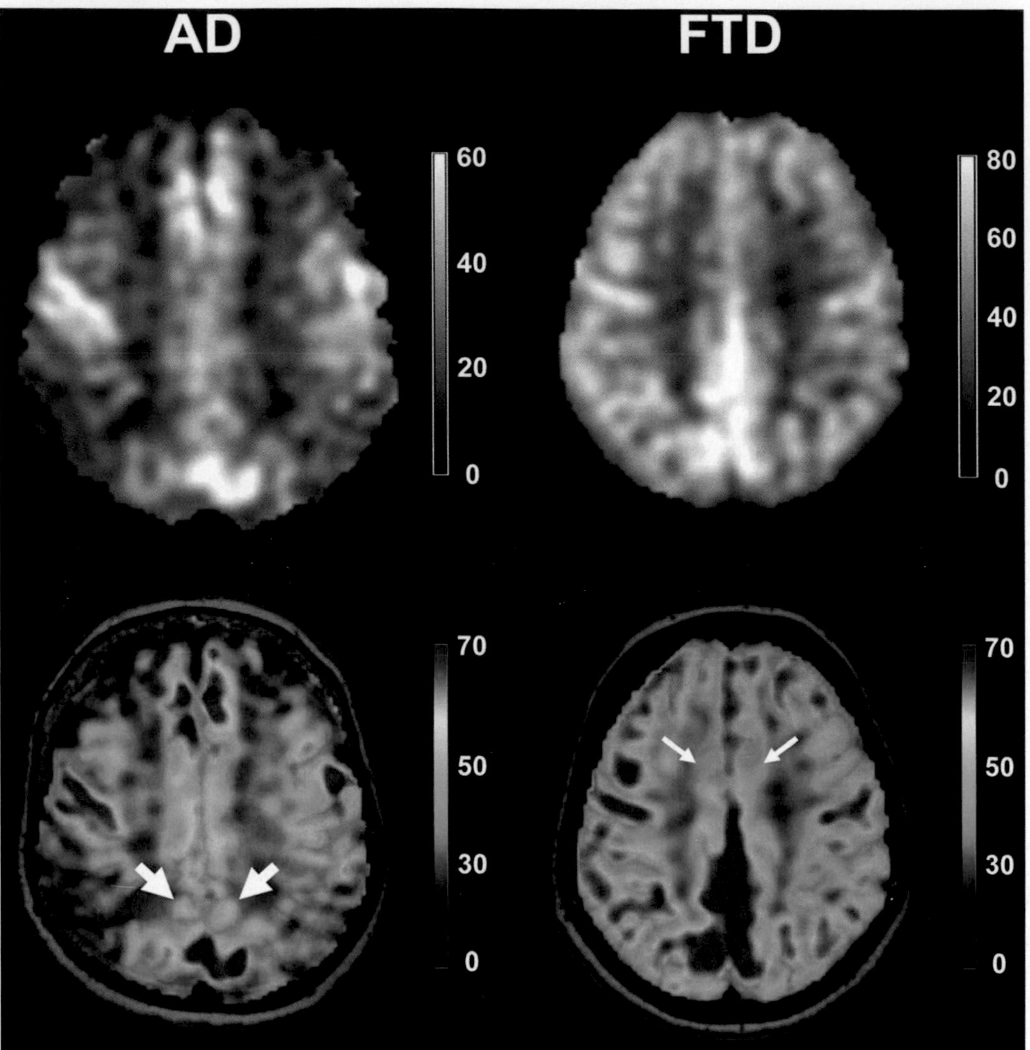

FIG. 15.13

Cerebral blood flow (CBF in mL/100g/min) maps for a representative AD *(left column)* and FTD patient *(right column)*. The *top row* shows the skull-stripped CBF maps, the *bottom row* shows the color-coded CBF maps overlaid on the structural T_1-weighted images. Hypoperfusion is prominent in the PCC *(thick arrows)* in AD compared to FTD. Also, note the global and more extensive hypoperfusion in AD compared to the focal hypoperfusion in the ACC in FTD *(thin arrows)*. *CBF*, cerebral blood flow; *AD*, Alzheimer's disease; *FTD*, frontotemporal dementia; *PCC*, posterior cingulate cortex; *ACC*, anterior cingulate cortex.

(From Steketee RM, et al. Eur Radiol 2016;26(1):244–53.)

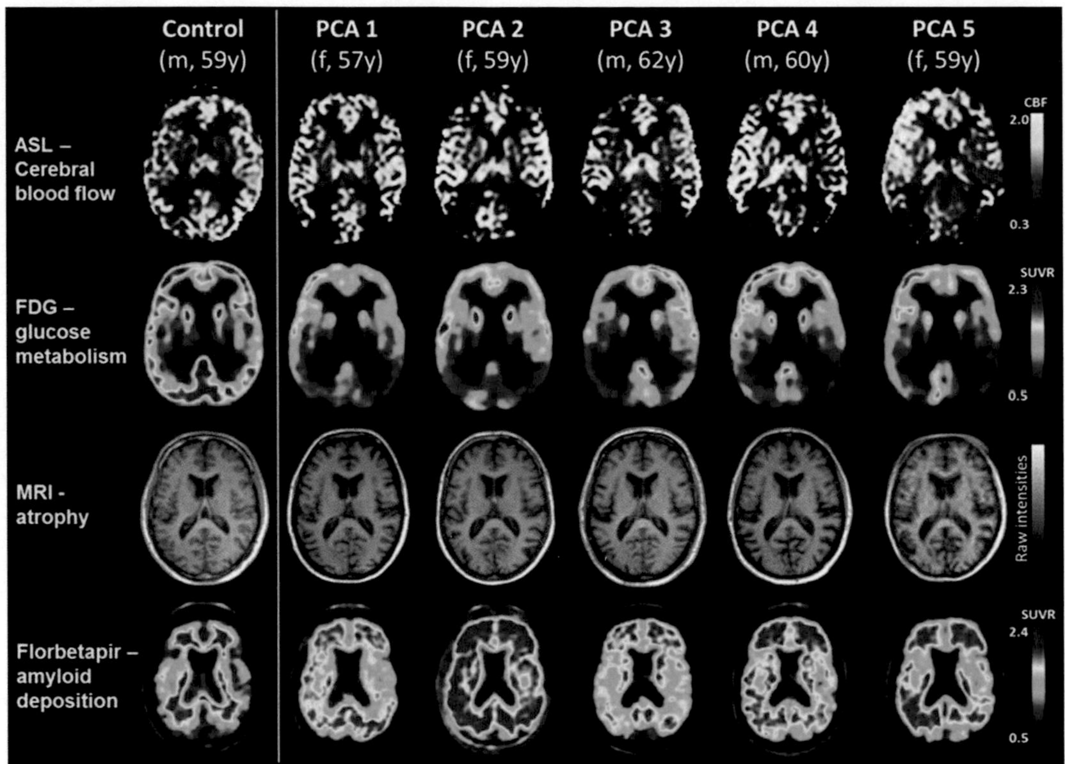

FIG. 15.14

Single-participant axial images for one control participant and five patients with PCA showing cerebral blood flow (ASL), glucose metabolism (FDG-PET), atrophy (structural MRI), and amyloid deposition (florbetapir-PET). For clinical purposes, 18F-florbetapir images should be read on a gray scale. *ASL*, arterial spin labeling; *CBF*, cerebral blood flow; *FDG-PET*, 18F-labeled fluorodeoxyglucose positron emission tomography; *PCA*, posterior cortical atrophy; *SUVR*, standard uptake value ratio.

(From Lehmann M, et al. J Neurol Neurosurg Psychiatry 2016;87(9):1032–34.)

TI/PLD acquisition scheme is used. If an insufficiently long TI/PLD is used, systematic biases in CBF values will result [166], which could lead to misinterpretation and/or misdiagnosis. On the other hand, too long a TI/PLD will result in substantial SNR loss and reduction of image quality, making the resulting CBF maps of little clinical value. An alternative approach is to acquire ASL images over multiple TI/PLDs and fit the data for both CBF and ATT; the relative pros and cons of this approach on CBF accuracy and precision are yet to be fully determined, though the use of optimization techniques to choose the best combination of TI/PLDs [167–170], or more advanced pCASL pulse trains, which alternate between labeling and control phases in a cycled manner [171–173], have improved the potential applicability of this type of approach. It is also important to note that ASL is still almost exclusively

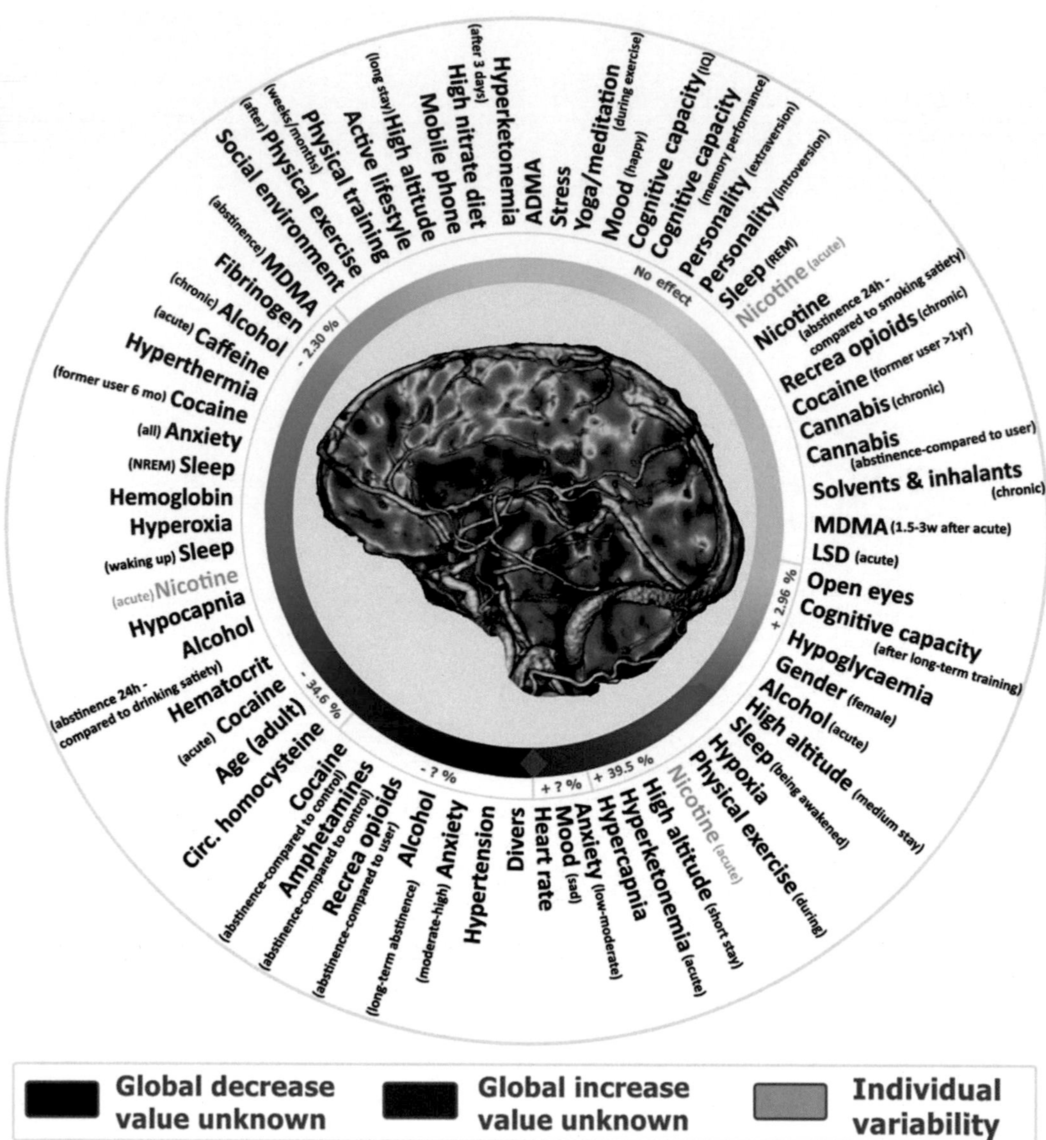

FIG. 15.15

Effects of modifiers on global brain perfusion summarized as a color gradient: factors in the *green area* induce no effect, the *blue* and *red areas* represent global decrease and increase respectively. All factors are classified both according to their effect and the corresponding magnitude on global perfusion changes. Other factors, whose value is still unknown, are grouped around the gray rectangle at the bottom of the circle.

(From Clement P, et al. J Cereb Blood Flow Metab 2018;38(9):1418–37.)

only able to measure perfusion in the gray matter; extended ATT and low CBF values in white matter mean that the signal is very close to the noise level at 1.5 T and 3 T. Therefore, although white matter perfusion changes are potentially of interest in dementia, ASL is not currently able to provide useful information relating to this physiological parameter.

In order to address the issue of low SNR, the ASL white paper recommends the use of multishot 3D acquisition methods (e.g., 3D GRASE or 3D stack-of-spirals) [165]. Single-shot 3D approaches are not appropriate due to the long acquisition window and associated widening of the point spread function [174]. However, the use of multishot acquisition schemes inherently introduces greater sensitivity to motion, given that the different shots are acquired over a period of several tens of seconds. As the ASL signal arises from the relatively small difference in signal between the labeled and control images, artifacts introduced by intershot motion are likely to have a noticeable effect on the ASL images and on the resulting quantitative CBF maps, even in the presence background suppression. In combination with the fact that patients with presymptomatic or early dementia are likely to have a greater tendency to move during scanning compared to cognitively healthy subjects, it is important to assess ASL images for evidence of motion and to be careful not to misinterpret artefactual signal differences as perfusion abnormalities in dementia patients.

15.5 Summary

This chapter has discussed the most common clinical application areas of perfusion MRI in the brain: cerebrovascular disease, brain cancer, and dementia.

In acute ischemic stroke, MR perfusion is used to identify salvageable at-risk tissue, i.e., critically hypoperfused tissue that progresses to infarction without timely reperfusion. This information can then be used to identify patients that may benefit from reperfusion treatment, and there is strong evidence to suggest that the use of advanced imaging-based patient selection is associated with better outcomes. In addition, permeability imaging with DCE-MRI enables more direct interrogation of the mechanism underlying SHT, allowing more accurate prediction of this dire complication. An important potential application for ASL in cerebrovascular disease is the measurement of the cerebrovascular reserve for prognostication and treatment planning on the chronic steno-occlusive disease.

In brain cancer, DSC/DCE has been used for the noninvasive assessment of tumor grade and malignancy, potentially allowing a reduction in the number of brain biopsies. Contrast-based MR perfusion techniques are also beneficial for evaluating treatment progression and demonstrate a superior sensitivity and specificity compared to anatomical imaging alone. Finally, they may also be beneficial for determining treatment response, supported by phase II trial evidence which demonstrated early decreases in DSC correlated with greater overall survival.

In dementia, given that perfusion changes occur in the initial stages of disease progression, and significantly before tissue atrophy becomes apparent on structural imaging, MR perfusion imaging offers good potential for early diagnosis and for differential diagnosis between AD and FTD. The quantitative nature of perfusion methods such as ASL makes them particularly well suited to longitudinal studies, as the CBF measurements should be directly comparable across sessions and over arbitrarily long periods.

References

[1] Bi WL, Beroukhim R. Beating the odds: extreme long-term survival with glioblastoma. Neuro Oncol 2014;16:1159–60.

[2] Jemal A, et al. Annual report to the nation on the status of cancer, 1975-2014, featuring survival. J Natl Cancer Inst 2017;109:djx030. https://doi.org/10.1093/jnci/djx030.

[3] Husain M, Schott J. Oxford textbook of cognitive neurology and dementia. Oxford University Press; 2016. https://doi.org/10.1093/med/9780199655946.001.0001.

[4] Grysiewicz RA, Thomas K, Pandey DK. Epidemiology of ischemic and hemorrhagic stroke: incidence, prevalence, mortality, and risk factors. Neurol Clin 2008;26:871–95.

[5] Sacco RL, et al. An updated definition of stroke for the 21st century: a statement for healthcare professionals from the American heart association/American stroke association. Stroke 2013;44(7):2064–89. https://doi.org/10.1161/STR.0b013e318296aeca.

[6] Amukotuwa SA, Yu C, Zaharchuk G. 3D pseudocontinuous arterial spin labeling in routine clinical practice: a review of clinically significant artifacts. J Magn Reson Imaging 2016;43:11–27.

[7] Rosamond W, et al. Heart disease and stroke statistics-2008 update: a report from the American heart association statistics committee and stroke statistics subcommittee. Circulation 2008;117(4): e25–146.

[8] Jones TH, et al. Thresholds of focal cerebral ischemia in awake monkeys. J Neurosurg 1981;54:773–82.

[9] Deb P, Sharma S, Hassan KM. Pathophysiologic mechanisms of acute ischemic stroke: an overview with emphasis on therapeutic significance beyond thrombolysis. Pathophysiology 2010;17:197–218.

[10] Astrup J, Symon L, Branston NM, Lassen NA. Cortical evoked potential and extracellular k+ and h+ at critical levels of brain ischemia. Stroke 1977;8:51–7.

[11] Symon L, Pasztor E, Branston NM. The distribution and density of reduced cerebral blood flow following acute middle cerebral artery occlusion: an experimental study by the technique of hydrogen clearance in baboons. Stroke 1974;5:355–64.

[12] Astrup J, Siesjö BK, Symon L. Thresholds in cerebral ischemia—the ischemic penumbra. Stroke 1981;12:723–5.

[13] Bardutzky J, et al. Characterizing tissue fate after transient cerebral ischemia of varying duration using quantitative diffusion and perfusion imaging. Stroke 2007;38:1336–44.

[14] Lansberg MG, et al. MRI profile and response to endovascular reperfusion after stroke (DEFUSE 2): a prospective cohort study. Lancet Neurol 2012;11:860–7.

[15] Rocha M, Jovin TG. Fast versus slow progressors of infarct growth in large vessel occlusion stroke: clinical and research implications. Stroke 2017;48:2621–7.

[16] Saver JL. Time is brain – quantified. Stroke 2006;37:263–6.

[17] Albers GW. Late window paradox. Stroke 2018;49:768–71.

[18] Powers WJ, et al. 2018 guidelines for the early management of patients with acute ischemic stroke: a guideline for healthcare professionals from the American heart association/American stroke association. Stroke 2018;49:e46–e110.

[19] Albers GW, et al. Thrombectomy for stroke at 6 to 16 hours with selection by perfusion imaging. N Engl J Med 2018;378:708–18.

[20] Berkhemer OA, et al. A randomized trial of intraarterial treatment for acute ischemic stroke. N Engl J Med 2015;372:11–20.

[21] Campbell BCV, et al. Endovascular therapy for ischemic stroke with perfusion-imaging selection. N Engl J Med 2015;372:1009–18.

[22] Goyal M, et al. Randomized assessment of rapid endovascular treatment of ischemic stroke. N Engl J Med 2015;372:1019–30.

[23] Nogueira RG, et al. Thrombectomy 6 to 24 hours after stroke with a mismatch between deficit and infarct. N Engl J Med 2018;378:11–21.

[24] Saver JL, et al. Stent-retriever thrombectomy after intravenous t-PA vs t-PA alone in stroke. N Engl J Med 2015;372:2285–95.
[25] Goyal M, et al. Endovascular thrombectomy after large-vessel ischaemic stroke: a meta-analysis of individual patient data from five randomised trials. Lancet 2016;387:1723–31.
[26] Grossberg JA, et al. Beyond large vessel occlusion strokes: distal occlusion thrombectomy. Stroke 2018;49:1662–8.
[27] Sarraj A, et al. Endovascular therapy for acute ischemic stroke with occlusion of the middle cerebral artery M2 segment. JAMA Neurol 2016;73:1291–6.
[28] Lansberg MG, et al. Risk factors of symptomatic intracerebral hemorrhage after tPA therapy for acute stroke. Stroke 2007;38:2275–8.
[29] Olivot JM, et al. Impact of diffusion-weighted imaging lesion volume on the success of endovascular reperfusion therapy. Stroke 2013;44:2205–11. https://doi.org/10.1161/STROKEAHA.113.000911.
[30] Wintermark M, et al. International survey of acute stroke imaging used to make revascularization treatment decisions. Int J Stroke 2015;10:759–62.
[31] Campbell BCV, et al. The infarct core is well represented by the acute diffusion lesion: sustained reversal is infrequent. J Cereb Blood Flow Metab 2012;32:50–6.
[32] Gill R, et al. A comparison of the early development of ischaemic damage following permanent middle cerebral artery occlusion in rats as assessed using magnetic resonance imaging and histology. J Cereb Blood Flow Metab 1995;15:1–11.
[33] González RG, et al. Diffusion-weighted MR imaging: diagnostic accuracy in patients imaged within 6 hours of stroke symptom onset. Radiology 1999;210:155–62.
[34] Wheeler HM, et al. Early diffusion-weighted imaging and perfusion-weighted imaging lesion volumes forecast final infarct size in DEFUSE 2. Stroke 2013;44:681–5.
[35] Davis SM, et al. Effects of alteplase beyond 3 h after stroke in the Echoplanar imaging thrombolytic evaluation trial (EPITHET): a placebo-controlled randomised trial. Lancet Neurol 2008;7:299–309.
[36] Ma H, et al. Thrombolysis guided by perfusion imaging up to 9 hours after onset of stroke. N Engl J Med 2019;380:1795–803.
[37] Calamante F, et al. The physiological significance of the time-to-maximum (Tmax) parameter in perfusion MRI. Stroke 2010;41:1169–74.
[38] Campbell BCV, et al. Comparison of computed tomography perfusion and magnetic resonance imaging perfusion-diffusion mismatch in ischemic stroke. Stroke 2012;43:2648–53.
[39] Olivot JM, et al. Optimal tmax threshold for predicting penumbral tissue in acute stroke. Stroke 2009;40:469–75.
[40] Olivot JM, et al. Hypoperfusion intensity ratio predicts infarct progression and functional outcome in the DEFUSE 2 cohort. Stroke 2014;45:1018–23.
[41] Campbell BCV, et al. Regional very low cerebral blood volume predicts hemorrhagic transformation better than diffusion-weighted imaging volume and thresholded apparent diffusion coefficient in acute ischemic stroke. Stroke 2010;41:82–8.
[42] Kassner A, Roberts T, Taylor K, Silver F, Mikulis D. Prediction of hemorrhage in acute ischemic stroke using permeability MR imaging. Am J Neuroradiol 2005;26:2213–7.
[43] Lansberg MG, Albers GW, Wijman CAC. Symptomatic intracerebral hemorrhage following thrombolytic therapy for acute ischemic stroke: a review of the risk factors. Cerebrovasc Dis 2007;24:1–10.
[44] Hamann GF, Okada Y, Del Zoppo GJ. Hemorrhagic transformation and microvascular integrity during focal cerebral ischemia/reperfusion. J Cereb Blood Flow Metab 1996;16:1373–8.
[45] Kassner A, Mandell DM, Mikulis DJ. Measuring permeability in acute ischemic stroke. Neuroimaging Clin N Am 2011;21:315–25.
[46] Thornhill RE, Chen S, Rammo W, Mikulis DJ, Kassner A. Contrast-enhanced MR imaging in acute ischemic stroke: T2* measures of blood-brain barrier permeability and their relationship to T1 estimates and hemorrhagic transformation. Am J Neuroradiol 2010;31:1015–22.

[47] Newbould RD, et al. Perfusion mapping with multiecho multishot parallel imaging EPI. Magn Reson Med 2007;58:70–81.
[48] Vonken EJPA, Van Osch MJP, Bakker CJG, Viergever MA. Simultaneous quantitative cerebral perfusion and Gd-DTPA extravasation measurement with dual-echo dynamic susceptibility contrast MRI. Magn Reson Med 2000;43:820–7.
[49] Williams DS, Detre JA, Leigh JS, Koretsky AP. Magnetic resonance imaging of perfusion using spin inversion of arterial water. Proc Natl Acad Sci U S A 1992;89:212–6.
[50] Zaharchuk G. Theoretical basis of hemodynamic MR imaging techniques to measure cerebral blood volume, cerebral blood flow, and permeability. Am J Neuroradiol 2007;28:1850–8.
[51] Detre JA, Leigh JS, Williams DS, Koretsky AP. Perfusion imaging. Magn Reson Med 1992;23:37–45.
[52] Dai W, Garcia D, De Bazelaire C, Alsop DC. Continuous flow-driven inversion for arterial spin labeling using pulsed radio frequency and gradient fields. Magn Reson Med 2008;60:1488–97.
[53] Bivard A, et al. Arterial spin labeling versus bolus-tracking perfusion in hyperacute stroke. Stroke 2014;45:127–33.
[54] Bokkers RPH, et al. Whole-brain arterial spin labeling perfusion MRI in patients with acute stroke. Stroke 2012;43:1290–4.
[55] Zaharchuk G, El Mogy IS, Fischbein NJ, Albers GW. Comparison of arterial spin labeling and bolus perfusion-weighted imaging for detecting mismatch in acute stroke. Stroke 2012;43:1843–8.
[56] Niibo T, et al. Arterial spin-labeled perfusion imaging to predict mismatch in acute ischemic stroke. Stroke 2013;44:2601–3.
[57] Zaharchuk G. Arterial spin-labeled perfusion imaging in acute ischemic stroke. Stroke 2014;45:1202–7.
[58] Hendrikse J, et al. Internal carotid artery occlusion assessed at pulsed arterial spin-labeling perfusion MR imaging at multiple delay times. Radiology 2004;233:899–904.
[59] Derdeyn CP. Cerebral hemodynamics in carotid occlusive disease. Am J Neuroradiol 2003;24:1497–9.
[60] Derdeyn CP, Powers WJ, Grubb RL. Hemodynamic effects of middle cerebral artery stenosis and occlusion. Riv Neuroradiol 1998;11:211–5.
[61] Derdeyn CP, et al. Variability of cerebral blood volume and oxygen extraction: stages of cerebral haemodynamic impairment revisited. Brain 2002;125:595–607.
[62] Nemoto EM, Yonas H, Chang Y. Stages and thresholds of hemodynamic failure [1]. Stroke 2003;34:2–3.
[63] Powers WJ. Cerebral hemodynamics in ischemic cerebrovascular disease. Ann Neurol 1991;29:231–40.
[64] Vagal AS, Leach JL, Fernandez-Ulloa M, Zuccarello M. The acetazolamide challenge: techniques and applications in the evaluation of chronic cerebral ischemia. Am J Neuroradiol 2009;30:876–84.
[65] Fisher JA. The CO2 stimulus for cerebrovascular reactivity: fixing inspired concentrations vs. targeting end-tidal partial pressures. J Cereb Blood Flow Metab 2016;36:1004–11.
[66] Rogg J, et al. The acetazolamide challenge: imaging techniques designed to evaluate cerebral blood flow reserve. Am J Neuroradiol 1989;10:803–10.
[67] Yonas H, Darby JM, Marks EC, Durham SR, Maxwell C. CBF measured by Xe-CT: approach to analysis and normal values. J Cereb Blood Flow Metab 1991;11:716–25.
[68] Noguchi T, et al. Noninvasive method for mapping CVR in moyamoya disease using ASL-MRI. Eur J Radiol 2015;84:1137–43.
[69] Fan AP, et al. Long-delay arterial spin labeling provides more accurate cerebral blood flow measurements in Moyamoya patients: a simultaneous positron emission tomography/MRI study. Stroke 2017;48:2441–9.
[70] Thust SC, et al. Glioma imaging in Europe: a survey of 220 centres and recommendations for best clinical practice. Eur Radiol 2018;28:3306–17.
[71] Dickerson E, Srinivasan A. Multicenter survey of current practice patterns in perfusion MRI in neuroradiology: why, when, and how is it performed? Am J Roentgenol 2016;207:406–10.
[72] Boxerman JL, Schmainda KM, Weisskoff RM. Relative cerebral blood volume maps corrected for contrast agent extravasation significantly correlate with glioma tumor grade, whereas uncorrected maps do not. AJNR Am J Neuroradiol 2006;27:859–67.

[73] Leu K, et al. Bidirectional contrast agent leakage correction of dynamic susceptibility contrast (DSC)-MRI improves cerebral blood volume estimation and survival prediction in recurrent glioblastoma treated with bevacizumab. J Magn Reson Imaging 2016;44:1229–37.

[74] Quarles CC, Gochberg DF, Gore JC, Yankeelov TE. A theoretical framework to model DSC-MRI data acquired in the presence of contrast agent extravasation. Phys Med Biol 2009;54:5749–66.

[75] Semmineh NB, et al. Optimization of acquisition and analysis methods for clinical dynamic susceptibility contrast MRI using a population-based digital reference object. Am J Neuroradiol 2018;39:1981–8.

[76] Schmainda KM, et al. Moving toward a consensus DSC-MRI protocol: validation of a low-flip angle single-dose option as a reference standard for brain tumors. Am J Neuroradiol 2019;40:626–33.

[77] Willats L, Calamante F. The 39 steps: evading error and deciphering the secrets for accurate dynamic susceptibility contrast MRI. NMR Biomed 2013;26:913–31.

[78] Leu K, Boxerman JL, Ellingson BM. Effects of MRI protocol parameters, preload injection dose, fractionation strategies, and leakage correction algorithms on the fidelity of dynamic-susceptibility contrast MRI estimates of relative cerebral blood volume in gliomas. Am J Neuroradiol 2017;38:478–84.

[79] Hu LS, et al. Optimized preload leakage-correction methods to improve the diagnostic accuracy of dynamic susceptibility-weighted contrast-enhanced perfusion MR imaging in posttreatment gliomas. Am J Neuroradiol 2010;31:40–8.

[80] Quarles CC, Bell LC, Stokes AM. Imaging vascular and hemodynamic features of the brain using dynamic susceptibility contrast and dynamic contrast enhanced MRI. Neuroimage 2019;187:32–55.

[81] Sourbron S, Ingrisch M, Siefert A, Reiser M, Herrmann K. Quantification of cerebral blood flow, cerebral blood volume, and blood-brain-barrier leakage with DCE-MRI. Magn Reson Med 2009;62:205–17.

[82] Larsson HBW, Courivaud F, Rostrup E, Hansen AE. Measurement of brain perfusion, blood volume, and blood-brain barrier permeability, using dynamic contrast-enhanced T_1-weighted MRI at 3 tesla. Magn Reson Med 2009;62:1270–81.

[83] Villanueva-Meyer JE, Mabray MC, Cha S. Current clinical brain tumor imaging. Neurosurgery 2017; 81:397–415.

[84] Haller S, et al. Arterial spin labeling perfusion of the brain: emerging clinical applications. Radiology 2016;281:337–56.

[85] Bell LC, et al. Evaluating multisite rCBV consistency from DSC-MRI imaging protocols and postprocessing software across the NCI quantitative imaging network sites using a digital reference object (DRO). Tomography 2019;5:110–7.

[86] Patel P, et al. MR perfusion-weighted imaging in the evaluation of high-grade gliomas after treatment: a systematic review and meta-analysis. Neuro Oncol 2017;19:118–27.

[87] Chakravorty A, Steel T, Chaganti J. Accuracy of percentage of signal intensity recovery and relative cerebral blood volume derived from dynamic susceptibility-weighted, contrast-enhanced MRI in the preoperative diagnosis of cerebral tumours. Neuroradiol J 2015;28:574–83.

[88] Welker K, et al. ASFNR recommendations for clinical performance of MR dynamic susceptibility contrast perfusion imaging of the brain. Am J Neuroradiol 2015;36:E41–51.

[89] Prah MA, et al. Repeatability of standardized and normalized relative CBV in patients with newly diagnosed glioblastoma. Am J Neuroradiol 2015;36:1654–61.

[90] Schmainda KM, et al. Multisite concordance of DSC-MRI analysis for brain tumors: results of a National Cancer Institute quantitative imaging network collaborative project. AJNR Am J Neuroradiol 2018; 39:1008–16.

[91] Anzalone N, et al. Brain gliomas: multicenter standardized assessment of dynamic contrast-enhanced and dynamic susceptibility contrast MR images. Radiology 2018;287:933–43.

[92] Kaufmann TJ, et al. Consensus recommendations for a standardized brain tumor imaging protocol for clinical trials in brain metastases. Neuro Oncol 2020;22:757–72.

[93] Louis DN, et al. The 2016 World Health Organization classification of tumors of the central nervous system: a summary. Acta Neuropathol 2016;131:803–20.

[94] Le Rhun E, Taillibert S, Chamberlain MC. Current management of adult diffuse infiltrative low grade gliomas. Curr Neurol Neurosci Rep 2016;16:15.
[95] Staedtke V, Dzaye ODA, Holdhoff M. Actionable molecular biomarkers in primary brain tumors. Trends Cancer 2016;2:338–49.
[96] Cancer Genome Atlas Research Network. Comprehensive genomic characterization defines human glioblastoma genes and core pathways. Nature 2008;455:1061–8.
[97] Schmainda KM, et al. Characterization of a first-pass gradient-echo spin-echo method to predict brain tumor grade and angiogenesis. AJNR Am J Neuroradiol 2004;25:1524–32.
[98] van Dijken BRJ, et al. Perfusion MRI in treatment evaluation of glioblastomas: clinical relevance of current and future techniques. J Magn Reson Imaging 2019;49:11–22.
[99] Hu LS, et al. Multi-parametric MRI and texture analysis to visualize spatial histologic heterogeneity and tumor extent in glioblastoma. PLoS One 2015;10:e0141506.
[100] Tietze A, Mouridsen K, Lassen-Ramshad Y, Østergaard L, Perfusion MRI. Derived indices of microvascular shunting and flow control correlate with tumor grade and outcome in patients with cerebral Glioma. PLoS One 2015;10:e0123044.
[101] Cha S, et al. Differentiation of glioblastoma multiforme and single brain metastasis by peak height and percentage of signal intensity recovery derived from dynamic susceptibility-weighted contrast-enhanced perfusion MR imaging. Am J Neuroradiol 2007;28:1078–84.
[102] Mangla R, et al. Percentage signal recovery derived from MR dynamic susceptibility contrast imaging is useful to differentiate common enhancing malignant lesions of the brain. Am J Neuroradiol 2011; 32:1004–10.
[103] Hatzoglou V, et al. Comparison of the effectiveness of MRI perfusion and fluorine-18 FDG PET-CT for differentiating radiation injury from viable brain tumor: a preliminary retrospective analysis with pathologic correlation in all patients. Clin Imaging 2013;37:451–7.
[104] Smitha KA, Gupta AK, Jayasree RS. Relative percentage signal intensity recovery of perfusion metrics—an efficient tool for differentiating grades of glioma. Br J Radiol 2015;88:20140784.
[105] Bell LC, Stokes AM, Quarles CC. Analysis of postprocessing steps for residue function dependent dynamic susceptibility contrast (DSC)-MRI biomarkers and their clinical impact on glioma grading for both 1.5 and 3T. J Magn Reson Imaging 2020;51:547–53.
[106] Jain R. Measurements of tumor vascular leakiness using DCE in brain tumors: clinical applications. NMR Biomed 2013;26:1042–9.
[107] Roberts HC, et al. Quantitative measurement of microvascular permeability in human brain tumors achieved using dynamic contrast-enhanced MR imaging: correlation with histologic grade. AJNR Am J Neuroradiol 2000;21:891–9.
[108] Chakhoyan A, et al. Validation of vessel size imaging (VSI) in high-grade human gliomas using magnetic resonance imaging, image-guided biopsies, and quantitative immunohistochemistry. Sci Rep 2019;9:2846.
[109] Troprès I, et al. Vessel size imaging. Magn Reson Med 2001;45:397–408.
[110] Sourbron S, et al. Bolus-tracking MRI with a simultaneous T1- and T2*-measurement. Magn Reson Med 2009;62:672–81.
[111] Semmineh NB, et al. Assessing tumor cytoarchitecture using multiecho DSC-MRI derived measures of the transverse relaxivity at tracer equilibrium (TRATE). Magn Reson Med 2015;74:772–84.
[112] Brendle C, et al. Glioma grading and determination of IDH mutation status and ATRX loss by DCE and ASL perfusion. Clin Neuroradiol 2018;28:421–8.
[113] Barajas RF, Cha S, Cha S. Benefits of dynamic susceptibility-weighted contrast-enhanced perfusion MRI for glioma diagnosis and therapy. CNS Oncol 2014;3:407–19.
[114] Wiestler B, et al. Multiparametric MRI-based differentiation of WHO grade II/III glioma and WHO grade IV glioblastoma. Sci Rep 2016;6:35142.

[115] Artzi M, et al. Differentiation between treatment-related changes and progressive disease in patients with high grade brain tumors using support vector machine classification based on DCE MRI. J Neurooncol 2016;127:515–24.
[116] Kaufmann TJ, Erickson BJ. Can my computer tell me if this tumor is IDH mutated? Neuro Oncol 2020;22:311–2.
[117] Hu LS, et al. Radiogenomics to characterize regional genetic heterogeneity in glioblastoma. Neuro Oncol 2017;19:128–37.
[118] Ohno Y, et al. Assessment of bolus injection protocol with appropriate concentration for quantitative assessment of pulmonary perfusion by dynamic contrast-enhanced MR imaging. J Magn Reson Imaging 2007;25:55–65.
[119] Kim MJ, Kim HS, Kim J-H, Cho K-G, Kim SY. Diagnostic accuracy and interobserver variability of pulsed arterial spin labeling for glioma grading. Acta Radiol 2008;49:450–7.
[120] Wang N, Xie S-Y, Liu H-M, Chen G-Q, Zhang W-D. Arterial spin labeling for glioma grade discrimination: correlations with IDH1 genotype and 1p/19q status. Transl Oncol 2019;12:749–56.
[121] Khashbat D, et al. Correlation of 3D arterial spin labeling and multi-parametric dynamic susceptibility contrast perfusion MRI in brain tumors. J Med Investig 2016;63:175–81.
[122] Yamashita K, et al. MR imaging-based analysis of glioblastoma multiforme: estimation of IDH1 mutation status. Am J Neuroradiol 2016;37:58–65.
[123] Huang RY, Neagu MR, Reardon DA, Wen PY. Pitfalls in the neuroimaging of glioblastoma in the era of antiangiogenic and immuno/targeted therapy – detecting illusive disease, defining response. Front Neurol 2015;6:33.
[124] Fink J, Born D, Chamberlain MC. Pseudoprogression: relevance with respect to treatment of high-grade Gliomas. Curr Treat Options Oncol 2011;12:240–52.
[125] Chukwueke UN, Wen PY. Use of the response assessment in neuro-oncology (RANO) criteria in clinical trials and clinical practice. CNS Oncol 2019;8:CNS28.
[126] Sorensen AG, et al. A “vascular normalization index” as potential mechanistic biomarker to predict survival after a single dose of cediranib in recurrent glioblastoma patients. Cancer Res 2009;69:5296–300.
[127] Hygino Da Cruz LC, Rodriguez I, Domingues RC, Gasparetto EL, Sorensen AG. Pseudoprogression and pseudoresponse: imaging challenges in the assessment of posttreatment glioma. Am J Neuroradiol 2011;32:1978–85.
[128] University of Texas Southwestern Medical Center. Non-contrast perfusion using arterial spin labeled MR imaging for assessment of therapy response in glioblastoma. ClinicalTrials.gov; 2019.
[129] Stadlbauer A, et al. Quantification of serial changes in cerebral blood volume and metabolism in patients with recurrent glioblastoma undergoing antiangiogenic therapy. Eur J Radiol 2015;84:1128–36.
[130] Schmainda KM, et al. Dynamic susceptibility contrast MRI measures of relative cerebral blood volume as a prognostic marker for overall survival in recurrent glioblastoma: results from the ACRIN 6677/RTOG 0625 multicenter trial. Neuro Oncol 2015;17:1148–56.
[131] Thust SC, van den Bent MJ, Smits M. Pseudoprogression of brain tumors. J Magn Reson Imaging 2018;48:571.
[132] Iv M, et al. Perfusion MRI-based fractional tumor burden differentiates between tumor and treatment effect in recurrent glioblastomas and informs clinical decision-making. Am J Neuroradiol 2019;40:1649–57.
[133] Hu LS, et al. Reevaluating the imaging definition of tumor progression: perfusion MRI quantifies recurrent glioblastoma tumor fraction, pseudoprogression, and radiation necrosis to predict survival. Neuro Oncol 2012;14:919–30.
[134] Barajas RF, et al. Differentiation of recurrent glioblastoma multiforme from radiation necrosis after external beam radiation therapy with dynamic susceptibility-weighted contrast-enhanced perfusion MR imaging. Radiology 2009;253:486–96.

[135] Prah MA, et al. Spatial discrimination of glioblastoma and treatment effect with histologically-validated perfusion and diffusion magnetic resonance imaging metrics. J Neurooncol 2018;136:13–21.
[136] Bell LC, et al. Characterizing the influence of preload dosing on percent signal recovery (PSR) and cerebral blood volume (CBV) measurements in a patient population with high-grade glioma using dynamic susceptibility contrast MRI. Tomography 2017;3:89–95.
[137] Lee MD, Baird GL, Bell LC, Quarles CC, Boxerman JL. Utility of percentage signal recovery and baseline signal in DSC-MRI optimized for relative CBV measurement for differentiating glioblastoma, lymphoma, metastasis, and meningioma. AJNR Am J Neuroradiol 2019;40:1445–50.
[138] van Dijken BRJ, van Laar PJ, Holtman GA, van der Hoorn A. Diagnostic accuracy of magnetic resonance imaging techniques for treatment response evaluation in patients with high-grade glioma, a systematic review and meta-analysis. Eur Radiol 2017;27:4129–44.
[139] Shin KE, et al. DCE and DSC MR perfusion imaging in the differentiation of recurrent tumour from treatment-related changes in patients with glioma. Clin Radiol 2014;69:e264–72.
[140] Schmainda KM, et al. Dynamic-susceptibility contrast agent MRI measures of relative cerebral blood volume predict response to bevacizumab in recurrent high-grade glioma. Neuro Oncol 2014;16:880–8.
[141] Barboriak DP, et al. Interreader variability of dynamic contrast-enhanced MRI of recurrent glioblastoma: the multicenter ACRIN 6677/RTOG 0625 study. Radiology 2019;290:467–76.
[142] Emblem KE, et al. Vessel architectural imaging identifies cancer patient responders to anti-angiogenic therapy. Nat Med 2013;19:1178–83.
[143] Mosconi L, et al. Multicenter standardized 18F-FDG PET diagnosis of mild cognitive impairment, Alzheimer's disease, and other dementias. J Nucl Med 2008;49:390–8.
[144] Frackowiak RSJ, Lenzi GL, Jones T, Heather JD. Quantitative measurement of regional cerebral blood flow and oxygen metabolism in man using 15O and positron emission tomography: theory, procedure, and normal values. J Comput Assist Tomogr 1980;4:727–36.
[145] Chen Y, et al. Voxel-level comparison of arterial spin-labeled perfusion MRI and FDG-PET in Alzheimer disease. Neurology 2011;77:1977–85.
[146] Iturria-Medina Y, et al. Early role of vascular dysregulation on late-onset Alzheimer's disease based on multifactorial data-driven analysis. Nat Commun 2016;7:11934.
[147] McMahon PM, Araki SS, Sandberg EA, Neumann PJ, Gazelle GS. Cost-effectiveness of PET in the diagnosis of Alzheimer disease. Radiology 2003;228:515–22.
[148] Donahue MJ, Lu H, Jones CK, Pekar JJ, van Zijl PCM. An account of the discrepancy between MRI and PET cerebral blood flow measures. A high-field MRI investigation. NMR Biomed 2006;19:1043–54.
[149] Xu G, et al. Reliability and precision of pseudo-continuous arterial spin labeling perfusion MRI on 3.0 T and comparison with 15O-water PET in elderly subjects at risk for Alzheimer's disease. NMR Biomed 2010;23:286–93.
[150] Jack CR, et al. Tracking pathophysiological processes in Alzheimer's disease: an updated hypothetical model of dynamic biomarkers. Lancet Neurol 2013;12:207–16.
[151] Dashjamts T, et al. Simultaneous arterial spin labeling cerebral blood flow and morphological assessments for detection of Alzheimer's disease. Acad Radiol 2011;18:1492–9.
[152] Yoshiura T, et al. Arterial spin labelling at 3-T MR imaging for detection of individuals with Alzheimer's disease. Eur Radiol 2009;19:2819–25.
[153] Dai W, et al. Mild cognitive impairment and Alzheimer disease: patterns of altered cerebral blood flow at MR imaging. Radiology 2009;250:856–66.
[154] Mak E, Su L, Williams GB, O'Brien JT. Neuroimaging characteristics of dementia with Lewy bodies. Alzheimer's Res Ther 2014;6(2):18. https://doi.org/10.1186/alzrt248.
[155] Du AT, et al. Hypoperfusion in frontotemporal dementia and Alzheimer disease by arterial spin labeling MRI. Neurology 2006;67:1215–20.

[156] Steketee RME, et al. Early-stage differentiation between presenile Alzheimer's disease and frontotemporal dementia using arterial spin labeling MRI. Eur Radiol 2016;26:244–53.
[157] Mutsaerts HJMM, et al. Cerebral perfusion changes in presymptomatic genetic frontotemporal dementia: a GENFI study. Brain 2019;142:1108–20.
[158] Lehmann M, et al. A novel use of arterial spin labelling MRI to demonstrate focal hypoperfusion in individuals with posterior cortical atrophy: a multimodal imaging study. J Neurol Neurosurg Psychiatry 2016;87:1032–4.
[159] Schuff N, et al. Cerebral blood flow in ischemic vascular dementia and Alzheimer's disease, measured by arterial spin-labeling magnetic resonance imaging. Alzheimers Dement 2009;5:454–62.
[160] Gao Y-Z, et al. Regional cerebral blood flow and cerebrovascular reactivity in Alzheimer's disease and vascular dementia assessed by arterial spinlabeling magnetic resonance imaging. Curr Neurovasc Res 2013;10:49–53.
[161] Wang J, et al. Arterial spin labeling perfusion fMRI with very low task frequency. Magn Reson Med 2003;49:796–802.
[162] Clement P, et al. Variability of physiological brain perfusion in healthy subjects – a systematic review of modifiers. Considerations for multi-center ASL studies. J Cereb Blood Flow Metab 2018;38:1418–37.
[163] Dai W, et al. Effects of arterial transit delay on cerebral blood flow quantification using arterial spin labeling in an elderly cohort. J Magn Reson Imaging 2017;45:472–81.
[164] Liu Y, et al. Arterial spin labeling MRI study of age and gender effects on brain perfusion hemodynamics. Magn Reson Med 2012;68:912–22.
[165] Alsop DC, et al. Recommended implementation of arterial spin-labeled perfusion MRI for clinical applications: a consensus of the ISMRM perfusion study group and the European consortium for ASL in dementia. Magn Reson Med 2015;73:102–16.
[166] Alsop DC, Detre JA. Reduced transit-time sensitivity in noninvasive magnetic resonance imaging of human cerebral blood flow. J Cereb Blood Flow Metab 1996;16:1236–49.
[167] Owen D, et al. Optimisation of arterial spin labelling using bayesian experimental design. Lect Notes Comput Sci 2016;9902:511–8.
[168] Woods JG, Chappell MA, Okell TW. A general framework for optimizing arterial spin labeling MRI experiments. Magn Reson Med 2019;81:2474–88.
[169] Kramme J, et al. Improving perfusion quantification in arterial spin labeling for delayed arrival times by using optimized acquisition schemes. Z Med Phys 2015;25:221–9.
[170] Xie J, Gallichan D, Gunn RN, Jezzard P. Optimal design of pulsed arterial spin labeling MRI experiments. Magn Reson Med 2008;59:826–34.
[171] Wells JA, Lythgoe MF, Gadian DG, Ordidge RJ, Thomas DL. In vivo Hadamard encoded continuous arterial spin labeling (H-CASL). Magn Reson Med 2010;63:1111–8.
[172] Teeuwisse WM, Schmid S, Ghariq E, Veer IM, Van Osch MJP. Time-encoded pseudocontinuous arterial spin labeling: basic properties and timing strategies for human applications. Magn Reson Med 2014;72:1712–22.
[173] von Samson-Himmelstjerna F, Madai VI, Sobesky J, Guenther M. Walsh-ordered hadamard time-encoded pseudocontinuous ASL (WH pCASL). Magn Reson Med 2016;76:1814–24.
[174] Vidorreta M, et al. Evaluation of segmented 3D acquisition schemes for whole-brain high-resolution arterial spin labeling at 3T. NMR Biomed 2014;27:1387–96.

CHAPTER

16 Applications of Quantitative Perfusion and Permeability in the Liver

Maxime Ronot[a,b,c], Florian Joly[c], and Bernard E. Van Beers[a,b,c]

[a]*Department of Radiology, APHP, University Hospitals Paris Nord Val de Seine, Beaujon, Clichy, France*
[b]*University of Paris, Paris, France* [c]*Laboratory of Imaging Biomarkers, INSERM U1149, Centre for Research on Inflammation, Paris, France*

16.1 Introduction

Perfusion quantification has been extensively deployed in various oncological and nononcological abdominal conditions. The purpose of this chapter is to describe the technical challenges and clinical applications of magnetic resonance (MR) perfusion quantification in the liver. The liver is a large, highly vascularized, solid organ that can be imaged with various imaging methods, including Magnetic Resonance Imaging (MRI). The liver has a dual blood supply and receives approximately 25% of its blood from the hepatic artery and the remaining 75% from the portal vein, which carries blood from the gastrointestinal tract, gallbladder, pancreas, and spleen to the liver. There is no hepatic capillary network per se. Instead, the liver is perfused through a system of fenestrated sinusoids. The two afferent vascular systems communicate through transsinusoidal and transversal connections as well as the peribiliary plexuses. One of the fundamental adaptive mechanisms involved in vascular abnormalities of the liver is the presence of an arterioportal balance called the "hepatic buffer response." It is characterized by a compensatory increase in arterial blood supply when portal supply decreases, although the reverse does not occur [1].

MR perfusion mapping of the liver is based on the same principles as those used in other organs, namely injection of a gadolinium-chelate contrast medium (used as a tracer) and data acquisition by a rapid temporal sampling of signal-time curves that provide information on variations in contrast agent concentrations over time. The physiological parameters are extracted from these curves by adjusting them to mathematical perfusion models. However, perfusion mapping in the liver has specific challenges due to its large size, strong deformations with breathing motion, dual blood supply, and high permeability of the sinusoids.

Perfusion quantification is indicated in the liver for two main conditions: (1) assessment of malignant liver tumors, in particular, hepatocellular carcinomas (HCCs), and liver metastases, and (2) investigation of chronic liver diseases. Imaging already plays an important role in these two fields because imaging methods (mainly computerized tomography (CT) and MRI) provide accurate qualitative data for the detection and characterization of liver lesions, treatment assessment, and patient follow-up. Perfusion mapping does not replace such qualitative imaging methods but can be used as a complementary tool to adapt patient management or provide earlier and more reproducible disease evaluation.

Advances in Magnetic Resonance Technology and Applications. Volume 1. ISSN 2666-9099. https://doi.org/10.1016/B978-0-12-817057-1.00018-4

16.2 The technical challenges of liver perfusion analysis

The required characteristics for optimal liver perfusion analysis have been reported previously [2] and include a need for accurate quantification both in the whole liver and hepatic focal areas to assess diffuse and focal abnormalities, high spatial resolution to examine small lesions, high temporal resolution to correctly resolve the rapid signal changes caused by the tracer, adequate modeling of the complex physiology of liver perfusion, and compatibility with morphological imaging methods for combined assessment of perfusion and conventional metrics.

16.2.1 Image acquisition

Time-resolved data collection approaches are needed to accurately sample tracer kinetics for quantitative perfusion assessment. High spatial resolution and extensive coverage are also important but both limit the speed of data collection. Classically, contrast-enhanced multiphase liver MRI is performed with a T_1-weighted fat-saturated three-dimensional (3D) sequence with Cartesian k-space sampling in a breath-hold. However, this method is sensitive to respiratory motion and can result in suboptimal images in patients who cannot adequately hold their breath.

Multiple methods have been developed to obtain time-resolved, free-breathing, motion-robust, perfusion MR imaging [3,4]. These methods combine non-Cartesian k-space sampling, typically radial or spiral trajectories, with spatial and temporal undersampling. Images can be reconstructed from this accelerated data by exploiting data redundancies using methods such as parallel imaging and/or compressed sensing [5]. Free-breathing 3D perfusion MRI of the liver with a time resolution of 2 s has been shown to be feasible with these advanced methods including golden-angle radial sparse parallel (GRASP) imaging [6] and undersampled spiral acquisition with 3D through-time generalized autocalibrating partially parallel acquisition (GRAPPA) [3].

16.2.2 Liver perfusion modeling

There are two main mathematical approaches to derive measures of liver perfusion: the semiquantitative approach based on the shape of the signal-time curve analysis (descriptive methods) and the quantitative approach based on perfusion models (pharmacokinetic approach).

16.2.2.1 Descriptive methods

Descriptive analysis of signal-time curves is not based on any underlying physiological model. Instead, parameters that describe the shape of the signal-time curves are extracted and used to produce semiquantitative parameter maps that enable detection of perfusion abnormalities (e.g., hyperenhanced areas). Several such descriptive or "heuristic" parameters are commonly used, such as the slope of enhancement (maximum slope), maximum enhancement (peak height), and the time-to-peak. Descriptive parameters may be affected by noise or signal fluctuations caused by liver and vessel displacement. The area under the curve (AUC), i.e., the integral under the enhancement curve, is less affected by this type of error and therefore commonly used [7].

Semiquantitative evaluation is confounded by the vascular kinetics of the contrast agent, which may differ significantly among patients depending on the injection protocol (volume, concentration, injection rate, etc.) and physiological conditions (respiration, cardiac output). These effects can be accounted for to some extent by normalizing descriptive parameters in the liver to those of a reference tissue such as the muscle or a nondiseased portion of the liver.

16.2.2.2 Compartmental pharmacokinetic models

Compartmental pharmacokinetic models use a top-down vision, i.e., these models aim to represent the liver as one or several functional well-mixed compartments in order to reproduce the MRI measurements. The models considered here incorporate specific characteristics of liver perfusion and the contribution of the arterial input (in tumors) or arterial and portal venous input (in diffuse liver disease), obtained from the signal enhancement curves of the afferent blood vessels.

The dual-input, single-compartmental model for liver perfusion (Fig. 16.1) has been validated with radiolabeled microspheres and is often used [8]. This model reflects the fact that the liver has dual blood supply from both the aorta (through the hepatic artery) and the portal vein, and therefore has two inflow rate constants. Moreover, the liver sinusoids and extravascular, extracellular space (called the space of Disse) are modeled as a single compartment because lateral diffusional equilibration of small-molecular-weight contrast agents (including conventional extracellular gadolinium-based contrast agents) occurs virtually instantaneously due to the presence of sinusoidal fenestrae with a diameter of 50–200 nm [9]. The mathematical equation for the dual-input, single-compartmental model is:

$$\frac{dC_L(t)}{dt} = k_{1a}C_a(t-\tau_a) + k_{1p}C_p(t-\tau_p) - k_2C_L(t)$$

where $C_L(t)$, $C_a(t)$, and $C_p(t)$ (μM) represent the contrast agent concentration in the liver tissue, aorta, and portal vein compartments, respectively; k_{1a} represents the aortic inflow rate constant, k_{1p} represents the portal venous inflow rate constant, and k_2 represents the outflow rate constant in mL min^{-1} 100 g^{-1}; and τ_a and τ_b (min) represent the transit time from the aorta and portal vein to the liver. Liver perfusion parameters, such as arterial fraction (*AF*, %, also called hepatic perfusion index (*HPI*)), total liver perfusion (*F*, mL min^{-1} 100 g^{-1}), distribution volume (*DV*), and mean transit time (*MTT*, min), can be further calculated using the following equations:

$$AF = HPI = \frac{k_{1a}}{k_{1a} + k_{1p}}$$

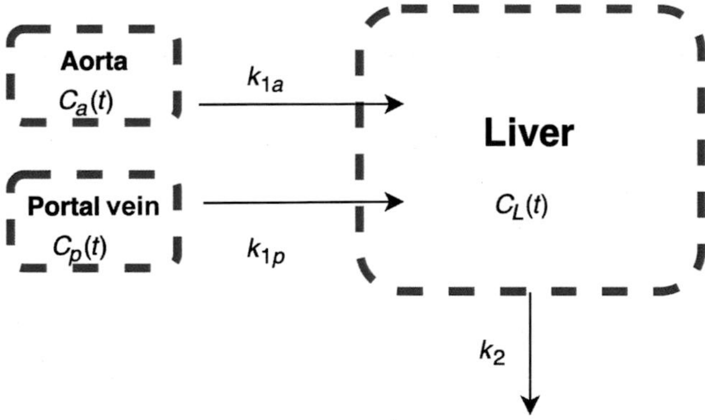

FIG. 16.1

Dual-input single-compartmental model for hepatic perfusion. In this model, k_{1a} and k_{1p} are the two inflow rate constants, k_2 is the outflow rate constant, and $C_a(t)$, $C_p(t)$, and $C_L(t)$ represent the concentration of the contrast agent from the aorta, the portal vein, and the liver compartments, respectively.

$$F = k_{1a} + k_{1p}$$

$$DV = \frac{k_{1a} + k_{1p}}{k_2}$$

$$MTT = \frac{1}{k_2}$$

The most common approach to extract the perfusion parameters is to fit the observed data to a model, i.e., solve a minimization problem to match measured and simulated liver signal intensities. First, the vascular inputs must be extracted from regions of interest (ROIs) placed in the portal vein and the abdominal aorta. Delays for both inputs are included in the model to take into account the temporal offset between actual input to the compartment and measured signals from upstream ROIs. The addition of these two fitting parameters in the model increases the degrees of freedom, creating the risk of overfitting or convergence to local minima. Alternatively, it has been proposed to fix the delays manually. While the arterial delay can be estimated from a curve analysis because of the sharp signal intensity increase, manual estimation of portal venous delay is more challenging. To address this issue, it has been assumed that portal venous and arterial delays are equal [8] or that the portal venous delay can be fixed to zero [10]. Another method is to include both delays in the model and use advanced optimization procedures such as multistart approaches [11]. The main limitation of these approaches is the increase in computing time due to the repetition of the fitting procedure.

In contrast to the liver parenchyma, primary and secondary tumors of the liver do not have a portal venous input, except at an early stage [12]. Therefore, the perfusion of hepatic tumors may be analyzed with single-input rather than dual-input models. Using goodness-of-fit as the model selection technique, it has been reported that single-input and dual-input models should be used in hepatic tumors and healthy liver tissue, respectively [13].

There are several single input models available to assess tumors. The most frequently used models include two compartments, such as the Kety or Tofts model. In these models, the transfer constant between plasma and extravascular extracellular space (K^{trans}, $\mathrm{mL\,min^{-1}\,100\,g^{-1}}$) and the extravascular extracellular fractional volume (v_e, %) are assessed. The extended Kety or Tofts model (which takes into account the contribution of the tracer in the vascular space) can also be used, in which K^{trans}, v_e, and fractional plasma volume (v_p, %) are assessed. The more complex St Lawrence and Lee model is a distributed-parameter model with four free parameters, namely plasma perfusion (F, $\mathrm{mL\,min^{-1}\,100\,g^{-1}}$), extraction fraction ($E$, %), extravascular volume (v_e, %), and capillary mean transit time (MTT, min). The capillary permeability-surface (PS, $\mathrm{mL\,min^{-1}\,100\,g^{-1}}$), and plasma fractional volume (v_p, %) can also be derived using this model [14].

There is still some debate about the best tumor perfusion model to use [15]. The distributed St Lawrence and Lee model is more physiological with separate perfusion and permeability parameters but is less precise than the compartmental models due to the interdependency of the free parameters and sensitivity to initial values. The extended Tofts model may be a good compromise to estimate perfusion parameters in tumors because neither data interpolation nor supervised fitting is required [15]. The transfer constant K^{trans} and v_e have been recommended as respectively primary and secondary endpoints of perfusion measurements [15]. Both variables should be obtained, as the reproducibility of v_e is better than that of K^{trans} in some studies, and v_e can be used as a surrogate for vascular permeability by determining the volume accessible to contrast agents with different molecular weights [14,16,17].

It has been suggested that the same model can be used for both liver parenchyma and tumors, instead of using the dual-input single-compartment "Materne—Van Beers" model in the liver parenchyma and the single-input two-compartment "extended Kety" model in liver tumors. For this purpose, both the dual-input single-compartment "Materne—Van Beers" model [3,18] and a dual-input two-compartment distributed model have been proposed [19–21]. With the dual input two-compartment model, the vascular and the extravascular—extracellular spaces in the liver and the tumors are considered to be two different compartments. This assumption may be particularly relevant in advanced fibrosis/cirrhosis and in hepatocellular carcinomas in which sinusoidal capillarization (meaning defenestration) occurs [22]. Overall, the diagnostic relevance of the various pharmacokinetic models must be assessed in context by comparing their goodness of fit, repeatability, and concordance with known perfusion parameters measurements [23].

16.2.3 Correcting for liver movement

Radiographic studies using fixed landmarks, radioscopy, and CT [24] have shown that the liver is an organ that moves considerably during breathing, shifting approximately 20 mm along its head-feet axis, 10 mm along its anteroposterior axis and 5 mm laterally. Because of long acquisition times for MRI-based perfusion quantification (at least 2–3 min), free-breathing acquisitions are highly recommended. Thus, to prevent pixel scale mismatches and to obtain diagnostic information from quantitative pharmacokinetic data analysis, correct registration of the acquired images is essential.

In a non-co-registered dataset of two-dimensional (2D) images collected over time, respiratory motion will introduce temporal noise and misregistrations in both inputs and tissue functions, reducing the robustness of perfusion modeling. This effect is especially marked in the portal venous input function because the portal venous trunk has an oblique orientation relative to the main head-feet direction motion. Coronal rather than transverse views may be acquired to limit this effect. Another possibility is to include a registration-based motion correction method in the postprocessing chain. A wide range of approaches exists to register images, from the simplest combination of rotation and translation to the use of deep learning [25]. Some methods use MRI specificities/selected ROIs to continuously register dynamic contrast-enhanced (DCE) images despite intensity variations [26].

Most registration methods require three steps: image deformation, computation of an objective function, and iterative minimization. While deformation and minimization are problems shared with many other fields, finding the best objective function remains challenging because the MRI signal may vary through time because of contrast agent transport and substantial liver displacement caused by respiratory motion. Image similarity (e.g., gradient, intensity, or entropy) is typically used, but modality independent neighborhood descriptors (MIND) [27] show low sensitivity to contrast agent-induced intensity variation.

Instead of registering one image onto another, some methods work with complete time series, i.e., time-resolved 2D images or time-resolved 3D volumes, at once. For example, principal component analysis-based group-wise registration [28] is robust to contrast changes in time-resolved 3D quantitative MRI datasets.

16.2.4 Reproducibility of liver perfusion measurements

The estimated values of the perfusion parameters derived with MRI may vary depending on the acquisition strategy, reconstruction methods, and software [29–31]. Therefore, acquisition protocols should be standardized in multicenter studies and central analysis is favored to ensure uniformity of approach [32].

Liver perfusion measurements should be performed in a fasted state, as the portal venous flow is known to increase after a meal, changing the arterial-portal venous balance [33]. Moreover, it has been recommended that the measurement repeatability should be assessed before beginning clinical trials involving perfusion MRI of the liver. This is especially important when perfusion MRI is used to assess response to treatment. In this case, the treatment effect on perfusion measurements (critical % change) should be higher than the repeatability index (%), which corresponds to $2.77 \times$ wCV, where wCV is the within-subject coefficient of variation. For instance, K^{trans} has a wCV of 15%–20% based on a review of the literature. This suggests that a change of approximately 40%–55% is required in a single subject to be confident that the detected change in the individual is not due to the repeatability error [34].

16.3 Clinical applications

The two main clinical applications of liver perfusion mapping are liver oncology and chronic liver diseases. Imaging is important in both cases for noninvasive detection, characterization, treatment evaluation, and patient follow-up. Because of the complexity of perfusion mapping and the steep learning curve associated with this method, the goal is not to compare perfusion mapping with conventional imaging methods such as ultrasound, computed tomography, MRI or positron emission tomography. It is more interesting to determine the potential benefits of adding perfusion mapping to conventional imaging, and how such measurements may influence the management of patients.

16.3.1 Liver oncology

A combination of conventional MRI sequences has been shown to be highly accurate in detecting and characterizing liver tumors. These conventional MR images include unenhanced T_2-weighted, T_1-weighted, and diffusion-weighted images, as well as multiphase dynamic contrast-enhanced T_1-weighted images (MDCE-MRI) obtained with breath-holding during the arterial phase (30–40 s after bolus injection of a nonspecific extracellular gadolinium chelate), portal venous phase (60–70 s postinjection) and delayed phase (3–5 min postinjection). In routine clinical practice, the signal intensity pattern of the tumors is assessed on the contrast-enhanced MR images, and quantitative signal intensity enhancement or perfusion measurements are not typically performed for tumor detection or characterization.

Imaging is also used to evaluate antitumoral locoregional or systemic treatments. In the vast majority of cases, morphological (i.e., nonperfusion) imaging criteria are used. The response evaluation criteria in solid tumors (RECIST) guidelines, based on the measurement of tumor diameter variation during treatment, are approved as the standard method to evaluate tumor response in patients in clinical trials and are considered to be a surrogate endpoint to predict survival in patients with solid tumors [35,36].

Other imaging criteria have been evaluated to assess the effects of treatment on tumor vascularization based on changes of contrast-enhanced images [37–39]. These morphological criteria include the mRECIST criteria [38], in which the diameter of tumor tissue showing signal enhancement during the arterial phase is measured, and the Choi criteria [39], in which tumor diameter and signal intensity enhancement are measured.

In patients with advanced HCC treated with sorafenib, the Choi criteria are more efficient than the RECIST and mRECIST criteria to identify patients with long survival [40]. These results suggest that perfusion parameters (in this case the signal intensity enhancement after contrast material injection included in the Choi criteria) are more sensitive markers than tumor morphological criteria (diameter measurement with RECIST or mRECIST criteria). These results have been confirmed in an MDCE-MRI study of patients with HCC treated with transcatheter arterial chemoembolization (TACE) [41]. In these patients, it was shown that overall survival was significantly higher in patients showing decreased tumor portal venous enhancement after TACE, whereas no significant differences in survival were observed in the patients who were good or poor responders according to RECIST or mRECIST criteria.

Moreover, volumetric changes as markers of tumor response to treatment are obtained several weeks after the initiation of treatment to identify responders and nonresponders. Thus, nonresponders who could benefit from early modification of their treatment pathway are assessed late, which could influence their outcome. Quantitative functional methods such as perfusion mapping could discriminate responders from nonresponders earlier because they record early vascularization changes that occur before systematic changes in tumor size [42] and might even predict patient response before treatment [43,44].

16.3.1.1 Detection and characterization of focal liver lesions

It is well known that MDCE-MRI can improve the detection of hyperenhanced tumors, especially HCC, which show transient enhancement during the arterial phase [45]. Some studies have shown that semiquantitative perfusion parameters obtained using MDCE-MRI images differ between benign and malignant tumors [46,47]. Using time-resolved perfusion MRI and either the dual-input single-compartment model or dual-input two-compartment model, it has been shown that liver metastases and HCC can be differentiated based on their perfusion and permeability parameters [18,21]. It has also been observed that hypovascular and hypervascular liver metastases from neuroendocrine tumors can be differentiated based on differences in perfusion and distribution volume using quantitative perfusion MRI [20].

Most studies in HCC have evaluated the value of MRI-based perfusion mapping in differentiating between dysplastic nodules and HCC. Arterial hepatic blood flow and the arterial fraction have been found to be higher, while the distribution volume and portal venous blood flow were significantly lower in HCC compared to the liver parenchyma [48]. Similar results have been found with perfusion CT [49,50], suggesting that perfusion methods can provide quantitative information about tumor-related angiogenesis in patients with cirrhosis and HCC. Perfusion parameters (evaluated with perfusion CT) were correlated with tumor differentiation; well-differentiated HCC had significantly higher perfusion values than other grades [51].

The presence of overt hepatic metastases results in hemodynamic changes in the liver parenchyma, including an increase in arterial perfusion and a decrease in portal venous perfusion. These liver hemodynamic changes were first shown with scintigraphy and CT [52–54] and have been confirmed with MRI [55]. However, these hepatic features are of limited value when the tumors can already be observed with morphological imaging techniques. Studies showing similar results in small animals with occult liver metastases (with either Doppler or perfusion-CT) [56–58] are more interesting, although the results have not yet been confirmed in humans.

16.3.1.2 Assessing response to treatment—Locoregional therapies

Assessing liver tumor response and recurrence after percutaneous ablation (using radiofrequency or microwave) is based on the depiction of complete destruction and reappearance of tumor tissue, respectively. These criteria are well described and robust with conventional cross-sectional imaging [59,60]. Therefore, perfusion mapping is usually not needed in this context. However, in a perfusion CT study, blood volume was shown to be useful for detecting recurrence in contact with ablation zones [61], but similar results were not reported with MRI.

The usefulness of perfusion measurements in TACE has been examined using perfusion CT and MRI. TACE treatment involves the selective intraarterial injection of different chemotherapy molecules, either mixed with iodized oil (the conventional approach) or with loaded drug delivery beads, which interrupt the arterial supply to the tumor. Significant changes in tumor and peri-tumor perfusion parameters can be expected following chemoembolization. Choi et al. prospectively evaluated the feasibility of perfusion CT to follow-up TACE in rabbits and showed early changes in perfusion (at 1 week) in treated compared to untreated areas. They concluded that perfusion CT could help assess the early response to treatment [62]. There are few clinical studies available. Ippolito et al. obtained semiquantitative perfusion parameters using MDCE-MRI in tumor residues after TACE and found differences between completely and incompletely treated tumors similar to those of Choi et al. in animals [63].

Results from a rabbit model have validated the use of DCE-MRI to quantify tumor perfusion after several sequences of embolization [64]. A group from Chicago has also reported significant changes in perfusion during embolization using a descriptive semiquantitative approach [65–67]. As expected, they found a significant decrease in the AUC of time-intensity curves of tumors following treatment. Similar results were reported by Taouli et al., who observed higher arterial fraction and lower portal venous hepatic blood flow in untreated HCCs than in those treated with TACE [48].

The use of perfusion imaging to show early changes related to tumor necrosis or to predict good or poor responders has been reported. Recently, Braren et al. showed that the extravascular extracellular volume fraction v_e assessed with perfusion MRI one day after the embolization procedure in a rodent model was promising for the prediction of tumor necrosis [68]. Michielsen et al. showed that perfusion parameters before TACE were predictive of progression-free survival, independent of tumor size and number of lesions [69].

Selective internal radiation therapy (SIRT) is a locoregional method that has been found to be of interest in malignant liver tumors [70]. Radioactive microspheres are injected into the arteries that feed the tumors. Like other intraarterial procedures, SIRT is usually performed in unresectable tumors and in patients with diffuse, infiltrating, and/or multifocal disease. Unlike what is observed after TACE, it is difficult to assess tumor response after SIRT because most changes occur 3–6 months after treatment. Morsbach et al. recently published preliminary results with perfusion CT in a series of patients with colorectal liver metastases treated with SIRT [71]. The authors showed that a significant difference in arterial perfusion was found in pretreatment CT perfusion between responders and nonresponders and that 1-year survival was significantly higher in patients with high pretreatment arterial perfusion.

16.3.1.3 Assessing response to treatment—Systemic chemotherapy and targeted therapies

Systemic treatment of liver metastases, especially those of colorectal origin, is based on cytotoxic agents that can be associated with targeted therapy. In contrast, the few systemic treatments that have been shown to improve overall survival in advanced HCC are targeted therapies. This explains the differences in imaging features for tumor response, because cytotoxic agents cause tumor fibrosis and shrinkage without necrosis [72], while targeted therapies are known to result in sustained tumor stabilization and reduce tumor vascularization provoking tumor necrosis. Thus, the determination of perfusion changes after targeted therapy could be of major interest (Fig. 16.2). Although quantitative perfusion MRI is rarely used in current oncologic trials, some studies have included this functional method in their study design together with conventional tumor evaluation criteria such as RECIST.

Hsu et al. performed MRI-based perfusion mapping before treatment and after 14 days of treatment in a phase II study evaluating sorafenib combined with metronomic tegafur/uracil as first-line therapy for advanced HCC [73]. They selected the region of the tumor with the highest signal enhancement and measured the volume transfer constant, K^{trans}. The baseline K^{trans} was significantly higher in patients in whom the disease was controlled than in those with progressive disease, and it significantly decreased after treatment. A vascular response, defined as $\geq$40% decrease in K^{trans} after treatment, was associated with improved progression-free and overall survival. These results were confirmed in more recent studies by the same research group showing that the semiquantitative perfusion parameter "HCC peak enhancement" before systemic therapy, as well as high peak reduction 1 week after systemic therapy, were markers of good overall survival [74,75]. Finally, another study evaluating sunitinib in the treatment of advanced HCC found a significant decrease in K^{trans} in all patients and a larger decrease in patients with the controlled disease than in those with progressive disease [76].

Most published studies evaluating liver metastases have focused on colorectal metastases treated with targeted therapies in combination with conventional cytotoxic agents, and similar results have been reported with K^{trans} and other perfusion parameters. Coenegrachts et al. showed that the baseline k_{ep} ($k_{ep}=K^{trans}/v_e$, i.e., the rate constant between extravascular extracellular space and blood plasma) was significantly higher in responders than in nonresponders, and that responders had a significant decrease in k_{ep} after 6 weeks of treatment [77]. De Bruyne et al. showed progression-free survival improvement in patients with >40% reduction in K^{trans} [78]. These results were supported by those of Hirashima et al. in lesions treated with bevacizumab and FOLFIRI chemotherapy, showing that a variation in both K^{trans} and k_{ep} as early as 1 week after treatment could help predict response to chemotherapy [79]. There are very few studies regarding other liver metastases, such as those from neuroendocrine tumors, but existing results are consistent with those observed in colorectal liver metastases [80].

16.3.2 Chronic liver disease

Fibrogenesis causes changes in hepatic architecture and function. Following chronic liver injury, inflammatory macrophages infiltrate the hepatic parenchyma, releasing fibrogenic mediators. The hepatic stellate cells undergo phenotypical activation into myofibroblasts, secreting large amounts of extracellular matrix proteins. This leads to extravascular fibrosis and loss of sinusoidal fenestrations, i.e., sinusoidal capillarization. The enlargement of the extravascular space, the capillarization of the sinusoids, and the tonic contraction of the activated stellate cells decrease the sinusoidal space and increase the intrahepatic vascular resistance leading to portal hypertension [81,82]. The increased vascular resistance decreases the portal venous perfusion. This is only partly compensated by increased arterial perfusion (buffer response) and leads to decreased global liver perfusion.

The first studies evaluating chronic liver diseases with perfusion CT were published in the 1990s. Miles et al. and Blomley et al. described the hepatic buffer response with a descriptive slope model [83,84]. Using a pharmacokinetic dual-input single-compartment model, a decrease of total liver

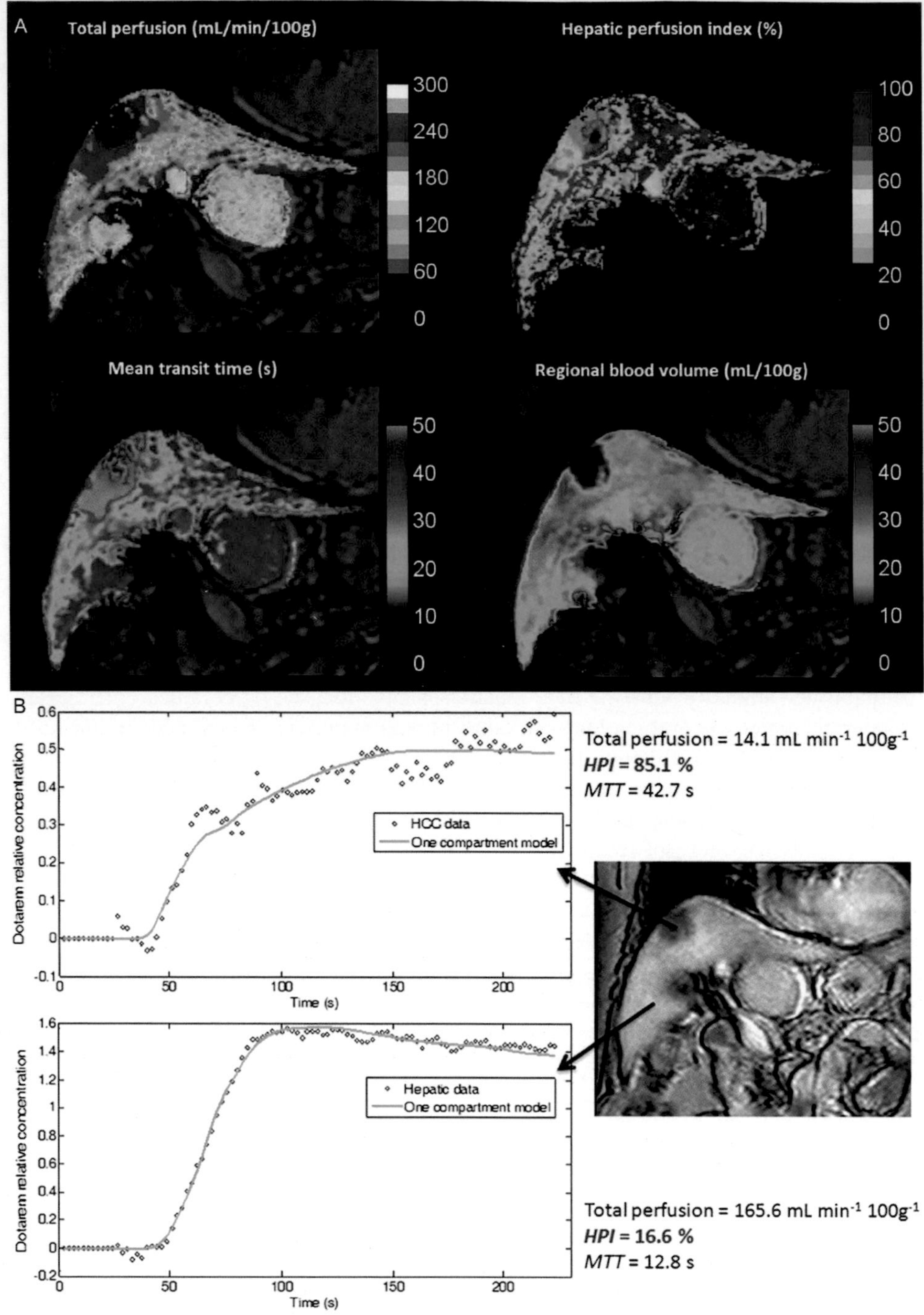

FIG. 16.2

(A) Perfusion maps (arterial, portal venous and total perfusion, hepatic perfusion index (HPI), mean transit time (MTT), and regional blood volume) obtained from a patient with hepatocellular carcinoma 7 days after the initiation of sorafenib treatment. These maps are computed from images acquired with a 3D FLASH acquisition with 2.0 s temporal resolution. Gd-DOTA is used as a tracer. Perfusion parameters are extracted using a nonlinear least square fit on the dual-input single-compartment model including two delays (arterial and portal venous). (B) The lesion is located in the dome of the liver. Comparison between the lesion *(upper part)* and the surrounding liver *(lower part)*. The lesion shows a significant decrease in the total perfusion, with significant increases in the HPI and MTT, consistent with tumor response to treatment.

perfusion and an increase in arterial fraction and mean transit time was observed in patients with cirrhosis compared to controls and patients with liver fibrosis [85]. More recently, it has been shown that quantitative perfusion CT could identify the early stages of liver fibrosis, although a large amount of overlap in the measured parameters limits the clinical utility of this test in minimal and intermediate fibrosis [86].

MRI perfusion studies in animal models of chronic liver diseases [8,22,87] have confirmed previous results. In patients with cirrhosis, a reduction in portal venous perfusion and an increase in both arterial perfusion and mean transit time have been described [88–90]. Perfusion changes were also observed at intermediate stages of liver fibrosis [88,90], but were more marked in cirrhosis, where it was shown that the perfusion changes were correlated with the degree of liver dysfunction and portal hypertension [88]. Although these results must be confirmed in larger studies, they suggest that perfusion mapping with MRI could be useful in assessing the severity of cirrhosis. Similar results were reported in a recent study using a dual-input two-compartmental model. In this study, a significantly lower total hepatic perfusion, lower fractional volume of the vascular space, higher fractional volume of the extravascular, extracellular space, and lower permeability-surface area product were noted in patients with liver cirrhosis than in normal volunteers [18,21].

16.4 Perfusion mapping with hepatobiliary contrast agents

When contrast-enhanced MRI is performed with a hepatobiliary contrast agent such as gadoxetic acid (Gd-EOB-DTPA, Primovist; Bayer, Berlin, Germany), the liver perfusion and the hepatocyte transport function can be assessed [10,91]. In humans, gadoxetic acid is partially taken up within hepatocytes via the organic anion transporting polypeptides OATP1 B1/B3, and then excreted into bile through the multidrug resistance protein MRP2 transporters, whereas sinusoidal backflow occurs through MRP3 and the bidirectional OATP1B1/B3 transporters [92]. In chronic liver diseases, expression and function of the hepatocyte transporters change, leading to changes of gadoxetic acid enhancement during the hepatobiliary phase. The transporter changes consist mainly of decreased OATP1 B1/B3 and MRP2 expression, variable MRP3 expression, and MRP2 internalization. As shown in animal models of chronic liver disease, these organic anion transporter changes cause a decrease in liver signal intensity in the static hepatobiliary phase, as well as changes in the pharmacokinetic rate constants (hepatocyte influx, efflux, and backflux rates) which can be assessed via dynamic MRI [93,94].

Thus, when using gadoxetic acid-enhanced MRI in clinical practice, in addition to the usual arterial, portal venous, and delayed phases, an additional imaging phase is performed 20 min after injection of gadoxetic acid. During this static hepatobiliary phase, the contrast agent is located mainly in the hepatocytes and the bile ducts.

Another more challenging approach is to acquire MRI data dynamically for up to 30–40 min after injection to assess liver perfusion and hepatocyte transport function with pluri-compartmental modeling of the signal intensity versus time curves [10,93,95]. A dual-input, three-compartment model can be used to assess the transport of gadoxetic acid in the liver (Fig. 16.3), where the compartments are the extracellular space (containing both the sinusoids and the space of Disse), the hepatocytes, and the intrahepatic bile ducts [96,97]. The model can be mathematically described by a set of ordinary differential equations:

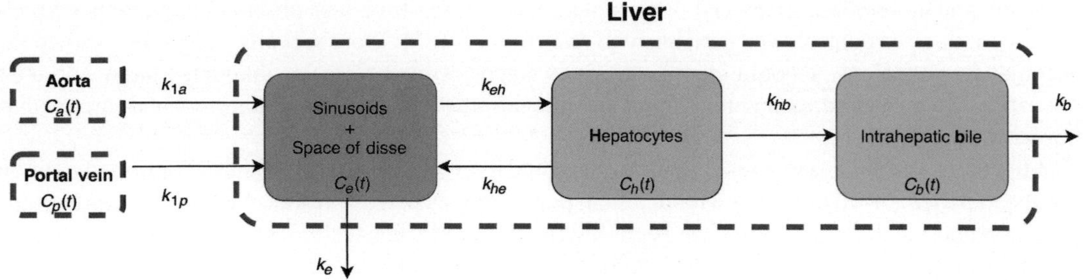

FIG. 16.3

Dual-input, three compartment hepatobiliary model. Gadoxetic acid enters into the extracellular compartment (including intravascular compartment and extravascular extracellular space of Disse) through arterial and portal venous inputs with rate constants k_{1a} and k_{1p}. A fraction of gadoxetic acid is taken up with rate constant k_{eh} into hepatocytes and excreted into the intrahepatic (k_{hb}) and extrahepatic (k_b) bile ducts or redistributed into extracellular compartment through sinusoidal backflux (k_{he}). The fraction of tracer not taken up by hepatocytes leaves the liver through hepatic veins (k_e).

$$\begin{cases} \dfrac{dC_e}{dt} = k_{1a}C_a(t-\tau_a) + k_{1p}C_p(t-\tau_p) - (k_e + k_{eh})C_e + k_{he}C_h \\ \dfrac{dC_h}{dt} = k_{eh}C_e - (k_{he} + k_{hb})C_h \\ \dfrac{dC_b}{dt} = k_{hb}C_h - k_bC_b \end{cases}$$

where C_a, C_p, C_e, C_h and C_b (μM) are the contrast agent concentration in the aortic blood plasma, portal vein blood plasma, and in the extracellular, hepatocyte and intrahepatic bile duct compartments (compartment concentrations are the product of the contrast agent concentration and compartment volume fraction); k_{1a} and k_{1p} are the inflow rate constants from the aorta and portal vein, in $\text{mL}\,\text{min}^{-1}\ 100\,\text{g}^{-1}$; τ_a and τ_b are the arterial and portal delays, typically in minutes; and t is time. For rate constants between compartments, the following convention is used: k_{ij} = constant rate from compartment i to j, in $\text{mL}\,\text{min}^{-1}\ 100\,\text{g}^{-1}$; thus k_{eh} is the influx rate constant between the extracellular space and the hepatocytes, k_{he} is the backflux rate constant between the hepatocyte and the extracellular space, k_{hb} is the efflux rate constant between hepatocytes and intrahepatic bile ducts, k_b is the rate constant between intra and extrahepatic bile ducts, and k_e is the hepatic venous outflow rate constant.

The observed concentration in the liver ROI is the sum of the three concentrations:

$$C_L = C_e + C_h + C_b$$

The hepatocyte uptake fraction (E, %) is defined as:

$$E = \frac{k_{eh}}{k_{eh} + k_e}$$

Both static and dynamic gadoxetic acid-enhanced MRI have been proposed to assess the severity of liver fibrosis, nonalcoholic steatohepatitis (NASH) and to evaluate liver function in chronic liver disease [96,98–101] (Figs. 16.4 and 16.5). Although dynamic gadoxetic acid-enhanced MRI with

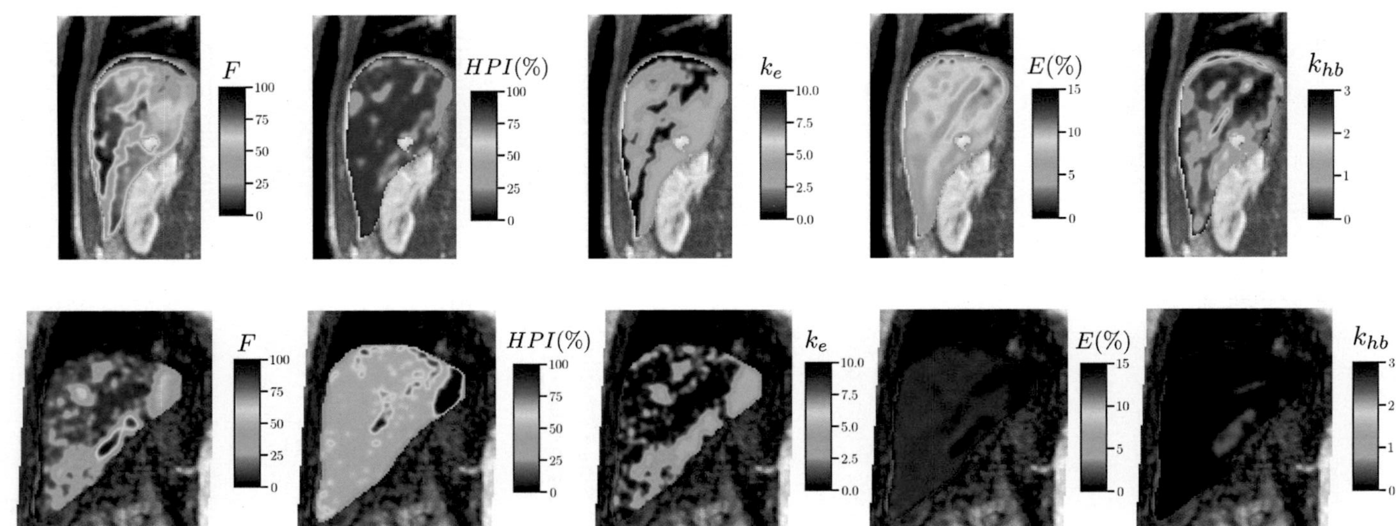

FIG. 16.4

Parametric maps obtained with the dual-input, three-compartment hepatobiliary model. Total hepatic perfusion (F in $mL\,min^{-1}\,100g^{-1}$), hepatic perfusion index (*HPI* in %), outflow rate (k_e in $mL\,min^{-1}\,100g^{-1}$), hepatocyte uptake fraction (E in %), and biliary efflux rate constant (k_{hb} in $mL\,min^{-1}\,100g^{-1}$) in patients without fibrosis *(first row)* and with cirrhosis *(second row)*. In the patient with liver cirrhosis, a decrease of hepatic perfusion, increase of arterial fraction, decrease of hepatocyte uptake fraction and biliary efflux rate are observed relative to the patient without fibrosis.

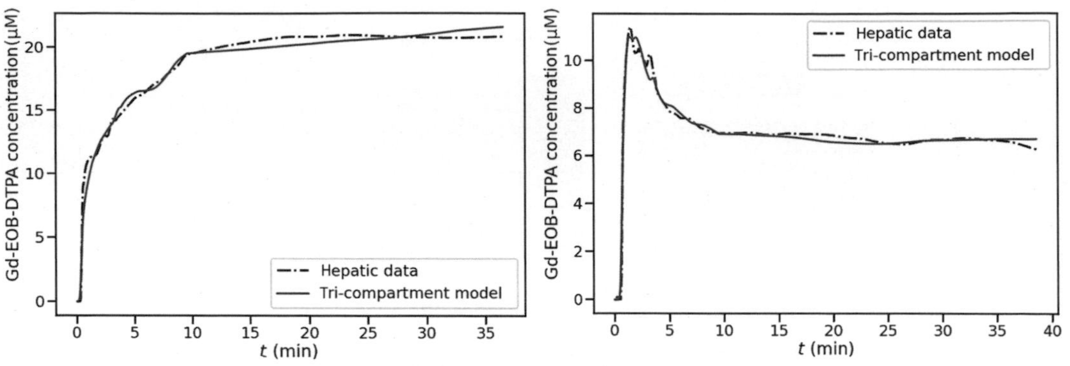

FIG. 16.5

Time course of hepatic gadoxetic acid (Gd-EOB-DTPA) concentration and fit of dual-input three-compartment model in a patient without liver fibrosis (F0, *left panel*) and in a patient with liver cirrhosis (F4, *right panel*). High gadoxetic acid concentration within the liver is observed for more than 30min in the patient without liver fibrosis. This may be explained by persistent hepatocyte uptake and biliary excretion of gadoxetic acid. In contrast, an early peak of hepatic gadoxetic acid concentration is observed in the patient with liver cirrhosis, a condition in which transporter mediated hepatobiliary transfer of gadoxetic acid is known to be decreased.

pharmacokinetic modeling has the potential to improve the assessment of liver transport function relative to the use of a static hepatic enhancement ratio during the hepatobiliary phase, the difficulty of performing dynamic MRI acquisition for up to 40min after contrast material injection, as well as the complexity of the required pharmacokinetic modeling, may limit its clinical use. Methods that are based on sparse data acquisition may prove to be useful in this context [102]. Besides dynamic imaging, texture analysis, and deep learning with convolutional neural networks might also be promising methods to improve the diagnostic performance of gadoxetic-acid-enhanced MRI but this should be studied further [103,104].

Finally, as the hepatocyte anion transporters that carry the hepatobiliary contrast agents during their hepatic transport are also used by various drugs, dynamic hepatobiliary enhanced imaging may be used in vitro and in vivo to assess transporter inhibition and drug-induced liver injury [105–107].

16.5 Alternative methods to assess liver perfusion

Another approach to evaluate liver perfusion is via diffusion MRI, with the intravoxel incoherent motion (IVIM) model. It has been shown that rats with liver fibrosis have reduced in vivo apparent diffusion coefficient (ADC) values compared to controls, although this difference disappeared ex vivo, underscoring the role of decreased perfusion in ADC decrease related to liver fibrosis [108]. Another IVIM study published by Luciani et al. in patients confirmed the decrease in ADC in patients with liver cirrhosis compared to controls and showed that the restriction in diffusion was largely caused by changes in microperfusion and to a lesser extent by a reduction in pure hepatic diffusion [109]. These results were confirmed by Yoon et al. in patients with chronic liver disease [110], and by Chow et al. and Zhang et al. in rodents [111,112].

More recently, several teams have investigated the IVIM model for the assessment of steatohepatitis with contradictory results. A study by Lee et al. did not show any significant correlation between the hepatic fat fraction and IVIM-assessed perfusion parameters [113] while Guiu et al. [114] found decreased parenchymal perfusion in liver steatosis with IVIM diffusion MRI. In a study in rabbits by Joo et al. the perfusion fraction was found to be significantly lower in rabbits with nonalcoholic fatty liver disease (NAFLD) than in controls with a progressive perfusion decrease as the severity of NAFLD increased [115].

Some results with IVIM have been reported in patients with liver tumors. Doblas et al. showed that compared with the ADC, the diffusion parameters derived from the IVIM model did not improve the determination of malignancy and characterization of hepatic tumor type [116]. The limited usefulness of IVIM to assess liver diseases and tumors might be partially explained by the poor reproducibility of the perfusion-related diffusion parameters [117].

Finally, liver perfusion assessment without contrast material injection can also be performed with arterial spin labeling [118]. With this method, acute changes in liver perfusion after a meal challenge have been observed, and differences in the response to the meal challenge between controls and patients with liver cirrhosis have been detected [119]. This method might thus be useful to assess liver hemodynamics after physiological challenges. Similarly, in a mouse model of liver metastases, arterial spin labeling has been used to assess the acute hemodynamic changes caused by a targeted vascular disrupting agent [120].

16.6 Summary

Quantitative perfusion mapping is not at this time part of the routine MRI protocol in the liver. Currently, quantitative perfusion measurements are mainly made in clinical and experimental research because data collection at relevant spatiotemporal resolution with 3D coverage is challenging. Results are encouraging, showing the potential use of perfusion imaging in liver tumors and chronic liver diseases.

In liver tumors, the main indication is the early assessment of tumor response to treatment. In this context, studies show higher diagnostic confidence when using perfusion parameters rather than classical tumor size assessment. Moreover, preliminary studies suggest that pharmacokinetic parameters (K^{trans}) are superior to semiquantitative parameters (AUC, enhancement ratios) for liver tumor assessment. However, the acquisition and processing of perfusion MR images should be improved and standardized to increase clinical reproducibility and use. The availability of fast, volumetric, motion-free imaging is the current bottleneck. Recent developments in time-resolved perfusion MRI methods using optimal data sampling and advanced reconstruction frameworks appear promising and will become more widely available in the clinics.

In patients with chronic liver diseases, perfusion MRI can be used to assess the severity of cirrhosis and portal hypertension. Perfusion changes can also be observed at earlier stages of chronic liver disease (fibrosis) but are usually inconsistent.

With hepatobiliary contrast-enhanced MRI, liver perfusion and hepatocyte transport can be assessed separately. Moreover, as hepatocyte transport is slower than perfusion, the constraints on MR image acquisition speed are much lower when assessing hepatobiliary transport than perfusion. This might facilitate the more widespread use of hepatobiliary contrast-enhanced MRI in chronic liver disease.

More clinical validation studies of liver perfusion mapping are needed. They include comparative studies between perfusion MRI and morphological MRI in the assessment of liver tumors, and between hepatobiliary contrast-enhanced MRI and MR elastography in the assessment of chronic liver disease. Large multicenter studies are needed before perfusion and hepatocyte transport parameters can be considered reliable biomarkers of liver disease and response to treatment.

Acknowledgment

This work was performed by a research team, member of France Life Imaging network (grant ANR-11-INBS-0006).

References

[1] Itai Y, Matsui O. Blood flow and liver imaging. Radiology 1997;202(2):306–14.

[2] Pandharipande PV, Krinsky GA, Rusinek H, Lee VS. Perfusion imaging of the liver: current challenges and future goals. Radiology 2005;234(3):661–73.

[3] Chen Y, Lee GR, Wright KL, et al. Free-breathing liver perfusion imaging using 3-dimensional through-time spiral generalized autocalibrating partially parallel acquisition acceleration. Investig Radiol 2015; 50(6):367–75.

[4] Chandarana H, Feng L, Block TK, et al. Free-breathing contrast-enhanced multiphase MRI of the liver using a combination of compressed sensing, parallel imaging, and golden-angle radial sampling. Investig Radiol 2013;48(1):10–6.

[5] Wright KL, Hamilton JI, Griswold MA, Gulani V, Seiberlich N. Non-Cartesian parallel imaging reconstruction. J Magn Reson Imaging 2014;40(5):1022–40.

[6] Feng L, Axel L, Chandarana H, Block KT, Sodickson DK, Otazo R. XD-GRASP: golden-angle radial MRI with reconstruction of extra motion-state dimensions using compressed sensing. Magn Reson Med 2016;75(2):775–88.

[7] Roberts C, Issa B, Stone A, Jackson A, Waterton JC, Parker GJ. Comparative study into the robustness of compartmental modeling and model-free analysis in DCE-MRI studies. J Magn Reson Imaging 2006;23(4):554–63.

[8] Materne R, Smith AM, Peeters F, et al. Assessment of hepatic perfusion parameters with dynamic MRI. Magn Reson Med 2002;47(1):135–42.

[9] Goresky CA, Rose CP. Blood-tissue exchange in liver and heart: the influence of heterogeneity of capillary transit times. Fed Proc 1977;36(12):2629–34.

[10] Sourbron S, Sommer WH, Reiser MF, Zech CJ. Combined quantification of liver perfusion and function with dynamic gadoxetic acid-enhanced MR imaging. Radiology 2012;263(3):874–83.

[11] Leporq B, Dumortier J, Pilleul F, Beuf O. 3D-liver perfusion MRI with the MS-325 blood pool agent: a noninvasive protocol to asses liver fibrosis. J Magn Reson Imaging 2012;35(6):1380–7.

[12] Liu Y, Matsui O. Changes of intratumoral microvessels and blood perfusion during establishment of hepatic metastases in mice. Radiology 2007;243(2):386–95.

[13] Banerji A, Naish JH, Watson Y, Jayson GC, Buonaccorsi GA, Parker GJ. DCE-MRI model selection for investigating disruption of microvascular function in livers with metastatic disease. J Magn Reson Imaging 2012;35(1):196–203.

[14] Michoux N, Huwart L, Abarca-Quinones J, et al. Transvascular and interstitial transport in rat hepatocellular carcinomas: dynamic contrast-enhanced MRI assessment with low- and high-molecular weight agents. J Magn Reson Imaging 2008;28(4):906–14.

[15] Leach MO, Brindle KM, Evelhoch JL, et al. Assessment of antiangiogenic and antivascular therapeutics using MRI: recommendations for appropriate methodology for clinical trials. Br J Radiol 2003;76: S87–91. Spec No 1.
[16] Galbraith SM, Lodge MA, Taylor NJ, et al. Reproducibility of dynamic contrast-enhanced MRI in human muscle and tumours: comparison of quantitative and semi-quantitative analysis. NMR Biomed 2002; 15(2):132–42.
[17] Padhani AR, Hayes C, Landau S, Leach MO. Reproducibility of quantitative dynamic MRI of normal human tissues. NMR Biomed 2002;15(2):143–53.
[18] Pahwa S, Liu H, Chen Y, et al. Quantitative perfusion imaging of neoplastic liver lesions: a multi-institution study. Sci Rep 2018;8(1):4990.
[19] Koh TS, Thng CH, Lee PS, et al. Hepatic metastases: in vivo assessment of perfusion parameters at dynamic contrast-enhanced MR imaging with dual-input two-compartment tracer kinetics model. Radiology 2008;249(1):307–20.
[20] Koh TS, Thng CH, Hartono S, et al. Dynamic contrast-enhanced MRI of neuroendocrine hepatic metastases: a feasibility study using a dual-input two-compartment model. Magn Reson Med 2011;65(1):250–60.
[21] Ghodasara S, Pahwa S, Dastmalchian S, Gulani V, Chen Y. Free-breathing 3D liver perfusion quantification using a dual-input two-compartment model. Sci Rep 2017;7(1):17502.
[22] Van Beers BE, Materne R, Annet L, et al. Capillarization of the sinusoids in liver fibrosis: noninvasive assessment with contrast-enhanced MRI in the rabbit. Magn Reson Med 2003;49(4):692–9.
[23] Shukla-Dave A, Obuchowski NA, Chenevert TL, et al. Quantitative imaging biomarkers alliance (QIBA) recommendations for improved precision of DWI and DCE-MRI derived biomarkers in multicenter oncology trials. J Magn Reson Imaging 2019;49(7):e101–21.
[24] Langen KM, Jones DT. Organ motion and its management. Int J Radiat Oncol Biol Phys 2001;50(1):265–78.
[25] Liu J, Pan Y, Li M, et al. Applications of deep learning to MRI images: a survey. Big Data Mining Anal 2018;1(1):1–18.
[26] Zhang T, Li Z, et al. Improved registration of DCE-MR images of the liver using a prior segmentation of the region of interest, In: Paper presented at: Medical imaging 2016: Image processing; 2020.
[27] Towards Realtime Multimodal Fusion for Image-Guided Interventions Using Self-similarities. SpringerLink; 2020.
[28] Huizinga W, Poot DH, Guyader JM, et al. PCA-based groupwise image registration for quantitative MRI. Med Image Anal 2016;29:65–78.
[29] Goh V, Halligan S, Bartram CI. Quantitative tumor perfusion assessment with multidetector CT: are measurements from two commercial software packages interchangeable? Radiology 2007;242(3):777–82.
[30] Heye T, Davenport MS, Horvath JJ, et al. Reproducibility of dynamic contrast-enhanced MR imaging. Part I. Perfusion characteristics in the female pelvis by using multiple computer-aided diagnosis perfusion analysis solutions. Radiology 2013;266(3):801–11.
[31] Heye T, Merkle EM, Reiner CS, et al. Reproducibility of dynamic contrast-enhanced MR imaging. Part II. Comparison of intra- and interobserver variability with manual region of interest placement versus semiautomatic lesion segmentation and histogram analysis. Radiology 2013;266(3):812–21.
[32] Leach MO, Morgan B, Tofts PS, et al. Imaging vascular function for early stage clinical trials using dynamic contrast-enhanced magnetic resonance imaging. Eur Radiol 2012;22(7):1451–64.
[33] Jajamovich GH, Dyvorne H, Donnerhack C, Taouli B. Quantitative liver MRI combining phase contrast imaging, elastography, and DWI: assessment of reproducibility and postprandial effect at 3.0 T. PLoS ONE 2014;9(5):e97355.
[34] https://qibawiki.rsna.org/images/1/12/DCE-MRI_Quantification_Profile_v1.0.pdf. Accessed 12 July 2019.
[35] Therasse P, Arbuck SG, Eisenhauer EA, et al. New guidelines to evaluate the response to treatment in solid tumors. European Organization for Research and Treatment of Cancer, National Cancer Institute of the United States, National Cancer Institute of Canada. J Natl Cancer Inst 2000;92(3):205–16.

[36] Eisenhauer EA, Therasse P, Bogaerts J, et al. New response evaluation criteria in solid tumours: revised RECIST guideline (version 1.1). Eur J Cancer 2009;45(2):228–47.

[37] Bruix J, Sherman M, Llovet JM, et al. Clinical management of hepatocellular carcinoma. Conclusions of the Barcelona-2000 EASL conference. European Association for the Study of the Liver. J Hepatol 2001;35(3):421–30.

[38] Lencioni R, Llovet JM. Modified RECIST (mRECIST) assessment for hepatocellular carcinoma. Semin Liver Dis 2010;30(1):52–60.

[39] Choi H, Charnsangavej C, Faria SC, et al. Correlation of computed tomography and positron emission tomography in patients with metastatic gastrointestinal stromal tumor treated at a single institution with imatinib mesylate: proposal of new computed tomography response criteria. J Clin Oncol 2007;25(13): 1753–9.

[40] Ronot M, Bouattour M, Wassermann J, et al. Alternative Response Criteria (Choi, European association for the study of the liver, and modified Response Evaluation Criteria in Solid Tumors [RECIST]) Versus RECIST 1.1 in patients with advanced hepatocellular carcinoma treated with sorafenib. Oncologist 2014;19(4):394–402.

[41] Bonekamp S, Jolepalem P, Lazo M, Gulsun MA, Kiraly AP, Kamel IR. Hepatocellular carcinoma: response to TACE assessed with semiautomated volumetric and functional analysis of diffusion-weighted and contrast-enhanced MR imaging data. Radiology 2011;260(3):752–61.

[42] Kamel IR, Liapi E, Reyes DK, Zahurak M, Bluemke DA, Geschwind JF. Unresectable hepatocellular carcinoma: serial early vascular and cellular changes after transarterial chemoembolization as detected with MR imaging. Radiology 2009;250(2):466–73.

[43] Nakamura Y, Kawaoka T, Higaki T, et al. Hepatocellular carcinoma treated with sorafenib: arterial tumor perfusion in dynamic contrast-enhanced CT as early imaging biomarkers for survival. Eur J Radiol 2018;98:41–9.

[44] Luo Y, Pandey A, Ghasabeh MA, et al. Prognostic value of baseline volumetric multiparametric MR imaging in neuroendocrine liver metastases treated with transarterial chemoembolization. Eur Radiol 2019; 29(10):5160–71.

[45] Takahashi N, Yoshioka H, Yamaguchi M, Saida Y, Itai Y. Accelerated dynamic MR imaging with a parallel imaging technique for hypervascular hepatocellular carcinomas: usefulness of a test bolus in examination and subtraction imaging. J Magn Reson Imaging 2003;18(1):80–9.

[46] Alicioglu B, Guler O, Bulakbasi N, Akpinar S, Tosun O, Comunoglu C. Utility of semiquantitative parameters to differentiate benign and malignant focal hepatic lesions. Clin Imaging 2013;37(4):692–6.

[47] Chen HJ, Roy TL, Wright GA. Perfusion measures for symptom severity and differential outcome of revascularization in limb ischemia: preliminary results with arterial spin labeling reactive hyperemia. J Magn Reson Imaging 2018;47(6):1578–88.

[48] Taouli B, Johnson RS, Hajdu CH, et al. Hepatocellular carcinoma: perfusion quantification with dynamic contrast-enhanced MRI. AJR Am J Roentgenol 2013;201(4):795–800.

[49] Ippolito D, Sironi S, Pozzi M, et al. Perfusion computed tomographic assessment of early hepatocellular carcinoma in cirrhotic liver disease: initial observations. J Comput Assist Tomogr 2008;32(6):855–8.

[50] Ippolito D, Sironi S, Pozzi M, et al. Hepatocellular carcinoma in cirrhotic liver disease: functional computed tomography with perfusion imaging in the assessment of tumor vascularization. Acad Radiol 2008; 15(7):919–27.

[51] Sahani DV, Holalkere N-S, Mueller PR, Zhu AX. Advanced hepatocellular carcinoma: CT perfusion of liver and tumor tissue—initial experience. Radiology 2007;243(3):736–43.

[52] Miles KA, Kelley BB. Altered perfusion adjacent to hepatic metastases. Clin Radiol 1997;52(2):162–3.

[53] Leggett DA, Kelley BB, Bunce IH, Miles KA. Colorectal cancer: diagnostic potential of CT measurements of hepatic perfusion and implications for contrast enhancement protocols. Radiology 1997;205(3):716–20.

[54] Meijerink MR, van Waesberghe JH, van der Weide L, van den Tol P, Meijer S, van Kuijk C. Total-liver-volume perfusion CT using 3-D image fusion to improve detection and characterization of liver metastases. Eur Radiol 2008;18(10):2345–54.

[55] Totman JJ, O'Gorman RL, Kane PA, Karani JB. Comparison of the hepatic perfusion index measured with gadolinium-enhanced volumetric MRI in controls and in patients with colorectal cancer. Br J Radiol 2005;78(926):105–9.

[56] Leen E, Angerson WG, Cooke TG, McArdle CS. Prognostic power of Doppler perfusion index in colorectal cancer. Correlation with survival. Ann Surg 1996;223(2):199–203.

[57] Tsushima Y, Blomley MJ, Yokoyama H, Kusano S, Endo K. Does the presence of distant and local malignancy alter parenchymal perfusion in apparently disease-free areas of the liver? Dig Dis Sci 2001;46(10):2113–9.

[58] Cuenod C, Leconte I, Siauve N, et al. Early changes in liver perfusion caused by occult metastases in rats: detection with quantitative CT. Radiology 2001;218(2):556–61.

[59] Chopra S, Dodd 3rd GD, Chintapalli KN, Leyendecker JR, Karahan OI, Rhim H. Tumor recurrence after radiofrequency thermal ablation of hepatic tumors: spectrum of findings on dual-phase contrast-enhanced CT. AJR Am J Roentgenol 2001;177(2):381–7.

[60] Forner A, Ayuso C, Varela M, et al. Evaluation of tumor response after locoregional therapies in hepatocellular carcinoma: are response evaluation criteria in solid tumors reliable? Cancer 2009;115(3):616–23.

[61] Meijerink MR, van Waesberghe JH, van der Weide L, et al. Early detection of local RFA site recurrence using total liver volume perfusion CT initial experience. Acad Radiol 2009;16(10):1215–22.

[62] Choi SH, Chung JW, Kim HC, et al. The role of perfusion CT as a follow-up modality after transcatheter arterial chemoembolization: an experimental study in a rabbit model. Investig Radiol 2010;45(7):427–36.

[63] Ippolito D, Trattenero C, Talei Franzesi C, et al. Dynamic contrast-enhanced magnetic resonance imaging with gadolinium ethoxybenzyl diethylenetriamine pentaacetic acid for quantitative assessment of vascular effects on hepatocellular-carcinoma lesions treated by transarterial chemoembolization or radiofrequency ablation. J Comput Assist Tomogr 2016;40(5):692–700.

[64] Wang D, Bangash AK, Rhee TK, et al. Liver tumors: monitoring embolization in rabbits with VX2 tumors—transcatheter intraarterial first-pass perfusion MR imaging. Radiology 2007;245(1):130–9.

[65] Larson AC, Wang D, Atassi B, et al. Transcatheter intraarterial perfusion: MR monitoring of chemoembolization for hepatocellular carcinoma—feasibility of initial clinical translation. Radiology 2008; 246(3):964–71.

[66] Gaba RC, Wang D, Lewandowski RJ, et al. Four-dimensional transcatheter intraarterial perfusion MR imaging for monitoring chemoembolization of hepatocellular carcinoma: preliminary results. J Vasc Interv Radiol 2008;19(11):1589–95.

[67] Wang D, Jin B, Lewandowski RJ, et al. Quantitative 4D transcatheter intraarterial perfusion MRI for monitoring chemoembolization of hepatocellular carcinoma. J Magn Reson Imaging 2010;31(5):1106–16.

[68] Braren R, Altomonte J, Settles M, et al. Validation of preclinical multiparametric imaging for prediction of necrosis in hepatocellular carcinoma after embolization. J Hepatol 2011;55(5):1034–40.

[69] Michielsen KDKF, Verslype C, Dymarkowski S, van Malenstein H, Oyen R, Maleux G, Vandecaveye V. Pretreatment DCE-MRI for prediction of PFS in patients with inoperable HCC treated with TACE. Cancer Imaging 2011;11:S114. Spec No A.

[70] Memon K, Lewandowski RJ, Kulik L, Riaz A, Mulcahy MF, Salem R. Radioembolization for primary and metastatic liver cancer. Semin Radiat Oncol 2011;21(4):294–302.

[71] Morsbach F, Pfammatter T, Reiner CS, et al. Computed tomographic perfusion imaging for the prediction of response and survival to transarterial radioembolization of liver metastases. Investig Radiol 2013; 48(11):787–94.

[72] Rubbia-Brandt L, Giostra E, Brezault C, et al. Importance of histological tumor response assessment in predicting the outcome in patients with colorectal liver metastases treated with neo-adjuvant chemotherapy followed by liver surgery. Ann Oncol 2007;18(2):299–304.

[73] Hsu C-Y, Shen Y-C, Yu C-W, et al. Dynamic contrast-enhanced magnetic resonance imaging biomarkers predict survival and response in hepatocellular carcinoma patients treated with sorafenib and metronomic tegafur/uracil. J Hepatol 2011;55(4):858–65.

[74] Chen BB, Hsu CY, Yu CW, et al. Dynamic contrast-enhanced MR imaging of advanced hepatocellular carcinoma: comparison with the liver parenchyma and correlation with the survival of patients receiving systemic therapy. Radiology 2016;281(2):454–64.
[75] Chen BB, Hsu CY, Yu CW, et al. Early perfusion changes within 1 week of systemic treatment measured by dynamic contrast-enhanced MRI may predict survival in patients with advanced hepatocellular carcinoma. Eur Radiol 2017;27(7):3069–79.
[76] Zhu AX, Sahani DV, Duda DG, et al. Efficacy, safety, and potential biomarkers of sunitinib monotherapy in advanced hepatocellular carcinoma: a phase II study. J Clin Oncol 2009;27(18):3027–35.
[77] Coenegrachts K, Bols A, Haspeslagh M, Rigauts H. Prediction and monitoring of treatment effect using T1-weighted dynamic contrast-enhanced magnetic resonance imaging in colorectal liver metastases: potential of whole tumour ROI and selective ROI analysis. Eur J Radiol 2012;81(12):3870–6.
[78] De Bruyne S, Van Damme N, Smeets P, et al. Value of DCE-MRI and FDG-PET/CT in the prediction of response to preoperative chemotherapy with bevacizumab for colorectal liver metastases. Br J Cancer 2012;106(12):1926–33.
[79] Hirashima Y, Yamada Y, Tateishi U, et al. Pharmacokinetic parameters from 3-tesla DCE-MRI as surrogate biomarkers of antitumor effects of bevacizumab plus FOLFIRI in colorectal cancer with liver metastasis. Int J Cancer 2012;130(10):2359–65.
[80] Miyazaki K, Orton MR, Davidson RL, et al. Neuroendocrine tumor liver metastases: use of dynamic contrast-enhanced MR imaging to monitor and predict radiolabeled octreotide therapy response. Radiology 2012;263(1):139–48.
[81] Friedman SL. Liver fibrosis—from bench to bedside. J Hepatol 2003;38(Suppl 1):S38–53.
[82] Tacke F. Targeting hepatic macrophages to treat liver diseases. J Hepatol 2017;66(6):1300–12.
[83] Miles KA, Hayball MP, Dixon AK. Functional images of hepatic perfusion obtained with dynamic CT. Radiology 1993;188(2):405–11.
[84] Blomley MJ, Coulden R, Dawson P, et al. Liver perfusion studied with ultrafast CT. J Comput Assist Tomogr 1995;19(3):424–33.
[85] Van Beers BE, Leconte I, Materne R, Smith AM, Jamart J, Horsmans Y. Hepatic perfusion parameters in chronic liver disease: dynamic CT measurements correlated with disease severity. AJR Am J Roentgenol 2001;176(3):667–73.
[86] Ronot M, Asselah T, Paradis V, et al. Liver fibrosis in chronic hepatitis C virus infection: differentiating minimal from intermediate fibrosis with perfusion CT. Radiology 2010;256(1):135–42.
[87] Zhou L, Chen TW, Zhang XM, et al. Liver dynamic contrast-enhanced MRI for staging liver fibrosis in a piglet model. J Magn Reson Imaging 2014;39(4):872–8.
[88] Annet L, Materne R, Danse E, Jamart J, Horsmans Y, Van Beers BE. Hepatic flow parameters measured with MR imaging and Doppler US: correlations with degree of cirrhosis and portal hypertension. Radiology 2003;229(2):409–14.
[89] Baxter S, Wang ZJ, Joe BN, Qayyum A, Taouli B, Yeh BM. Timing bolus dynamic contrast-enhanced (DCE) MRI assessment of hepatic perfusion: initial experience. J Magn Reson Imaging 2009;29(6):1317–22.
[90] Hagiwara M, Rusinek H, Lee VS, et al. Advanced liver fibrosis: diagnosis with 3D whole-liver perfusion MR imaging—initial experience. Radiology 2008;246(3):926–34.
[91] Van Beers BE, Garteiser P, Leporq B, Rautou PE, Valla D. Quantitative imaging in diffuse liver diseases. Semin Liver Dis 2017;37(3):243–58.
[92] Van Beers BE, Pastor CM, Hussain HK. Primovist, Eovist: what to expect? J Hepatol 2012;57(2):421–9.
[93] Giraudeau C, Leporq B, Doblas S, et al. Gadoxetate-enhanced MR imaging and compartmental modelling to assess hepatocyte bidirectional transport function in rats with advanced liver fibrosis. Eur Radiol 2017;27(5):1804–11.
[94] Lagadec M, Doblas S, Giraudeau C, et al. Advanced fibrosis: correlation between pharmacokinetic parameters at dynamic gadoxetate-enhanced MR imaging and hepatocyte organic anion transporter expression in rat liver. Radiology 2015;274(2):379–86.

[95] Forsgren MF, Dahlqvist Leinhard O, Dahlstrom N, Cedersund G, Lundberg P. Physiologically realistic and validated mathematical liver model reveals [corrected] hepatobiliary transfer rates for Gd-EOB-DTPA using human DCE-MRI data. PLoS ONE 2014;9(4):e95700.
[96] Leporq B, Daire JL, Pastor CM, et al. Quantification of hepatic perfusion and hepatocyte function with dynamic gadoxetic acid-enhanced MRI in patients with chronic liver disease. Clin Sci (Lond) 2018; 132(7):813–24.
[97] Hernandez Lozano I, Karch R, Bauer M, et al. Towards improved pharmacokinetic models for the analysis of transporter-mediated hepatic disposition of drug molecules with positron emission tomography. AAPS J 2019;21(4):61.
[98] Ba-Ssalamah A, Bastati N, Wibmer A, et al. Hepatic gadoxetic acid uptake as a measure of diffuse liver disease: where are we? J Magn Reson Imaging 2017;45(3):646–59.
[99] Feier D, Balassy C, Bastati N, Stift J, Badea R, Ba-Ssalamah A. Liver fibrosis: histopathologic and biochemical influences on diagnostic efficacy of hepatobiliary contrast-enhanced MR imaging in staging. Radiology 2013;269(2):460–8.
[100] Yoon JH, Lee JM, Kang HJ, et al. Quantitative assessment of liver function by using gadoxetic acid-enhanced MRI: hepatocyte uptake ratio. Radiology 2019;290(1):125–33.
[101] Forsgren MF, Karlsson M, Dahlqvist Leinhard O, et al. Model-inferred mechanisms of liver function from magnetic resonance imaging data: validation and variation across a clinically relevant cohort. PLoS Comput Biol 2019;15(6):e1007157.
[102] Noren B, Forsgren MF, Dahlqvist Leinhard O, et al. Separation of advanced from mild hepatic fibrosis by quantification of the hepatobiliary uptake of Gd-EOB-DTPA. Eur Radiol 2013;23(1):174–81.
[103] Kim H, Park SH, Kim EK, et al. Histogram analysis of gadoxetic acid-enhanced MRI for quantitative hepatic fibrosis measurement. PLoS ONE 2014;9(12):e114224.
[104] Yasaka K, Akai H, Kunimatsu A, Abe O, Kiryu S. Liver fibrosis: deep convolutional neural network for staging by using gadoxetic acid-enhanced hepatobiliary phase MR images. Radiology 2018; 287(1):146–55.
[105] Ulloa JL, Stahl S, Yates J, et al. Assessment of gadoxetate DCE-MRI as a biomarker of hepatobiliary transporter inhibition. NMR Biomed 2013;26(10):1258–70.
[106] Bonnaventure P, Cusin F, Pastor CM. Hepatocyte concentrations of imaging compounds associated with transporter inhibition: evidence in perfused rat livers. Drug Metab Dispos 2019;47(4):412–8.
[107] Karageorgis A, Lenhard SC, Yerby B, et al. A multi-center preclinical study of gadoxetate DCE-MRI in rats as a biomarker of drug induced inhibition of liver transporter function. PLoS ONE 2018;13(5):e0197213.
[108] Annet L, Peeters F, Abarca-Quinones J, Leclercq I, Moulin P, Van Beers BE. Assessment of diffusion-weighted MR imaging in liver fibrosis. J Magn Reson Imaging 2007;25(1):122–8.
[109] Luciani A, Vignaud A, Cavet M, et al. Liver cirrhosis: intravoxel incoherent motion MR imaging—pilot study. Radiology 2008;249(3):891–9.
[110] Yoon JH, Lee JM, Baek JH, et al. Evaluation of hepatic fibrosis using intravoxel incoherent motion in diffusion-weighted liver MRI. J Comput Assist Tomogr 2014;38(1):110–6.
[111] Chow AM, Gao DS, Fan SJ, et al. Liver fibrosis: an intravoxel incoherent motion (IVIM) study. J Magn Reson Imaging 2012;36(1):159–67.
[112] Zhang Y, Jin N, Deng J, et al. Intra-voxel incoherent motion MRI in rodent model of diethylnitrosamine-induced liver fibrosis. Magn Reson Imaging 2013;31(6):1017–21.
[113] Lee JT, Liau J, Murphy P, Schroeder ME, Sirlin CB, Bydder M. Cross-sectional investigation of correlation between hepatic steatosis and IVIM perfusion on MR imaging. Magn Reson Imaging 2012;30(4):572–8.
[114] Guiu B, Petit JM, Capitan V, et al. Intravoxel incoherent motion diffusion-weighted imaging in nonalcoholic fatty liver disease: a 3.0-T MR study. Radiology 2012;265(1):96–103.
[115] Joo I, Lee JM, Yoon JH, Jang JJ, Han JK, Choi BI. Nonalcoholic fatty liver disease: intravoxel incoherent motion diffusion-weighted MR imaging-an experimental study in a rabbit model. Radiology 2014; 270(1):131–40.

[116] Doblas S, Wagner M, Leitao HS, et al. Determination of malignancy and characterization of hepatic tumor type with diffusion-weighted magnetic resonance imaging: comparison of apparent diffusion coefficient and intravoxel incoherent motion-derived measurements. Investig Radiol 2013;48(10):722–8.
[117] Kakite S, Dyvorne H, Besa C, et al. Hepatocellular carcinoma: short-term reproducibility of apparent diffusion coefficient and intravoxel incoherent motion parameters at 3.0T. J Magn Reson Imaging 2015;41(1):149–56.
[118] Martirosian P, Pohmann R, Schraml C, et al. Spatial-temporal perfusion patterns of the human liver assessed by pseudo-continuous arterial spin labeling MRI. Z Med Phys 2019;29(2):173–83.
[119] Cox EF, Palaniyappan N, Aithal GP, Guha IN, Francis ST. Using MRI to study the alterations in liver blood flow, perfusion, and oxygenation in response to physiological stress challenges: meal, hyperoxia, and hypercapnia. J Magn Reson Imaging 2019;49(6):1577–86.
[120] Johnson SP, Ramasawmy R, Campbell-Washburn AE, et al. Acute changes in liver tumour perfusion measured non-invasively with arterial spin labelling. Br J Cancer 2016;114(8):897–904.

CHAPTER

Applications of Quantitative Perfusion and Permeability in the Body

17

Yong Chen[a], Muhummad Sohaib Nazir[b], Sebastian Kozerke[c], Sven Plein[d], and Shivani Pahwa[a,e]

[a]*Department of Radiology, Case Western Reserve University, Cleveland, OH, United States*

[b]*Biomedical Engineering and Imaging Sciences, Kings College London, London, United Kingdom*

[c]*Department of Information Technology and Electrical Engineering, ETH Zürich, Zurich, Switzerland*

[d]*Leeds Institute of Cardiovascular and Metabolic Medicine, University of Leeds, Leeds, United Kingdom*

[e]*Department of Radiology, University Hospitals Cleveland Medical Center, Cleveland, OH, United States*

17.1 Introduction

Tissue perfusion is a fundamental physiological phenomenon that allows the delivery of oxygen and nutrients to different organs in the body. Tissue perfusion is typically measured in units of milliliters per 100 g per minute (mL/min/100 g). Many studies have shown that accurate quantification of perfusion provides important information about the underlying tissue properties and pathologies [1,2]. This method was first applied for brain imaging and then gradually translated for perfusion quantification in other organs throughout the body. In this chapter, recent advances in body perfusion mapping using Magnetic Resonance Imaging (MRI) are reviewed. While similarities exist between different organs in the body in terms of acquisition methods and kinetic models, the application of these methods often faces special challenges that are organ/disease-specific. Therefore, this chapter is divided into several sections, with each section covering one organ of interest. Perfusion mapping in multiple organs in the body will be discussed, with the exception of the liver, which is covered separately in another chapter.

While many kinds of MR imaging techniques have been developed for the purpose of perfusion quantification, they mostly fall into two categories depending on whether an exogenous contrast agent is applied. Dynamic contrast-enhanced MRI (DCE-MRI) is one approach commonly applied in clinical-practice and can be used to provide tissue perfusion measurements. With the reduced T_1 relaxation times associated with contrast agents, DCE-MRI often provides better SNR as compared to other techniques, resulting in improved spatiotemporal resolution, volumetric coverage, and motion robustness. However, DCE-MRI has its own limitations such as potential contrast agent deposition in the brain and safety concerns for patients with kidney insufficiency. Therefore, perfusion quantification approaches that do not require contrast agents have also been developed. Arterial spin labeling (ASL) represents one major technique in this category, which uses magnetically labeled water as the tracer for perfusion quantification.

In this chapter, special attention will be paid to the development and application of fast MR imaging techniques, as they enable rapid data sampling in body MR, improving spatiotemporal resolutions of the acquisitions and making perfusion quantification feasible despite the various sources of motion in

Advances in Magnetic Resonance Technology and Applications. Volume 1. ISSN 2666-9099. https://doi.org/10.1016/B978-0-12-817057-1.00019-6

certain organs. Fast imaging methods including parallel imaging, compressed sensing, and view-sharing have been developed and deployed for perfusion quantification. Especially, parallel imaging techniques using non-Cartesian sampling patterns, such as conjugate gradient SENSE (CG-SENSE), iterative self-consistent parallel imaging reconstruction (SPIRiT), and non-Cartesian GRAPPA, have been applied to reduce acquisition time in body MRI [3–6]. This chapter will briefly describe these techniques and their application in body perfusion quantification.

17.2 Renal perfusion

17.2.1 Background

The kidneys are essential in maintaining homeostasis by filtering the blood and excreting body waste through urine. Glomerular filtration rate (GFR) measurement based on serum creatinine values is commonly used for the evaluation of kidney function, but this metric lacks specificity and cannot provide spatial information. As a result, imaging techniques have been developed to provide additional localized functional information to characterize the health of the kidney. Owing to its critical role in processing blood through filtration, quantitative perfusion MRI techniques for the kidney have emerged rapidly over the past two decades. Multiple methods with and without the need for exogenous contrast agents have been developed and applied in the assessment of renal function in various kidney diseases.

17.2.2 Technical developments

17.2.2.1 DCE-MRI for renal perfusion imaging

Quantitative DCE-MRI has been shown to provide valuable information for both renal perfusion and filtration quantification. However, development of DCE-MRI methods for renal imaging is not trivial, particularly as three-dimensional imaging with a high spatial resolution and whole kidney coverage is desired. To obtain accurate perfusion measurements, a high temporal resolution is also required to appropriately sample the arterial input function and the enhancement of renal parenchyma, especially in the arterial phase. Various fast imaging methods have thus been developed for this purpose. Multiple studies have used view-sharing approaches to achieve a high temporal resolution with three-dimensional (3D) coverage [7–9]. For example, Chandarana et al. demonstrated a high spatial resolution of $2.4 \times 1.7 \times 2.5\,\text{mm}^3$ (10 cm volume) with an effective temporal resolution of 1.2 s [9]. In this approach, only 20% of the central *k*-space area and 20% of the outer *k*-space lines are updated within each 1.2-s window, and the rest of the *k*-space data is "shared" from neighboring time frames. In this type of acquisition, the actual temporal resolution is much longer, leading to a broad temporal foot-print across the shared time frames which affects the accuracy of the pharmacokinetic analysis [7]. Compressed sensing has also been applied for renal perfusion imaging and a high acceleration factor was achieved by undersampling the *k*-space data along both phase-encoding and slice-encoding directions using a pseudorandom sampling pattern [10,11]. Chen et al. applied this method for renal perfusion quantification in rabbits, and 3D imaging with a spatial resolution of $1.4 \times 1.4 \times 3\,\text{mm}^3$ (5 cm volume) was achieved with a temporal resolution of 2.5 s. Advanced parallel imaging techniques for rapid body imaging, specifically 3D radial GRAPPA, have also been used to enable high-resolution renal perfusion imaging [12]. A stack-of-stars trajectory undersampled with an in-plane acceleration factor of 12.6 with respect to Nyquist sampling can be used to collect images with a spatial resolution of $2.2\,\text{mm}^3$ with full 3D coverage of both kidneys ($36 \times 36 \times 8\,\text{cm}^3$) in 2.1–2.9 s per volume, enabling a

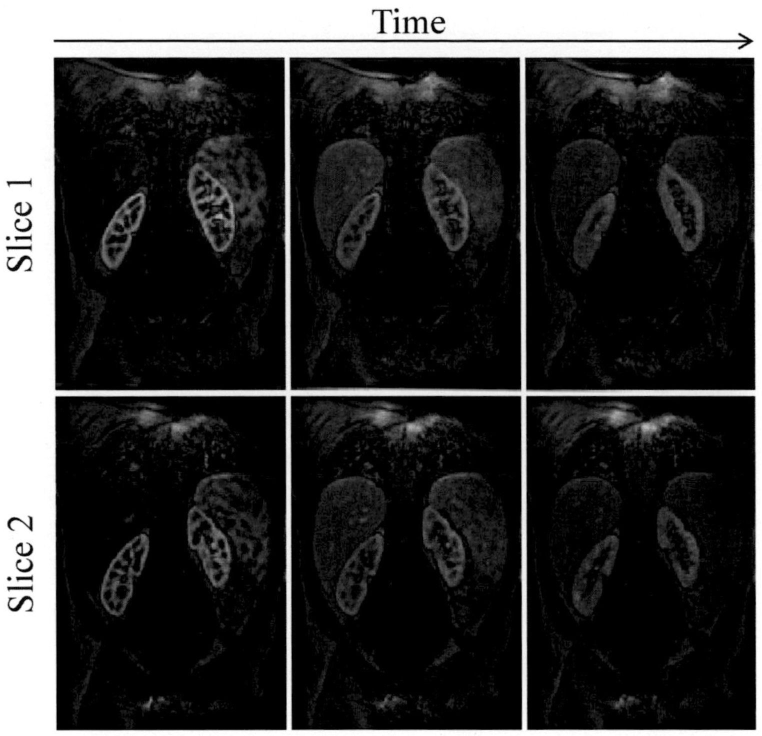

FIG. 17.1

DCE-MRI images of kidneys acquired from a healthy volunteer using a rapid 3D radial GRAPPA technique. Whole kidney coverage was achieved with a high temporal resolution of 2.1 s/volume and the acquisition was performed without breath-hold. Representative images from two slices across three different time points are presented.

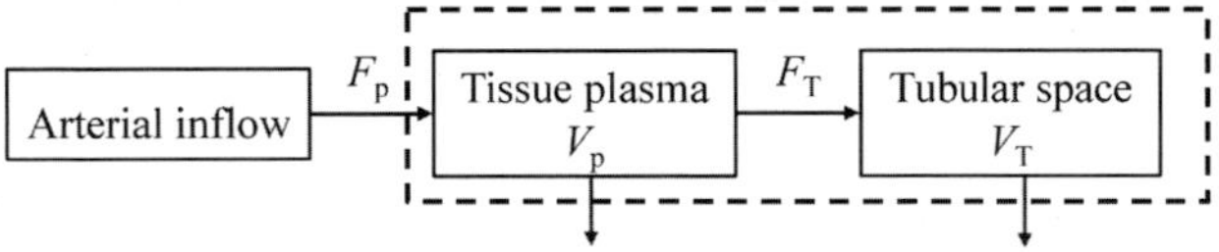

FIG. 17.2

A diagram illustrating the separable compartment model for kidney perfusion. The contrast agent is delivered from the arterial region to kidney tissues *(dotted region)*. The contrast agent is first delivered to the tissue plasma region (Volume, V_p) and then to the tubular space (Volume, V_T). F_p, renal perfusion; F_T, filtration rate.

completely free-breathing scan. Representative kidney DCE-MRI images reconstructed using this non-Cartesian parallel imaging approach are presented in Fig. 17.1.

A two-compartment filtration model is typically used for quantification of renal perfusion and filtration [13]. This model describes the perfusion of contrast agents from arteries to renal tissue plasma and then the filtration from tissue plasma into renal tubules (Fig. 17.2). Four perfusion parameters,

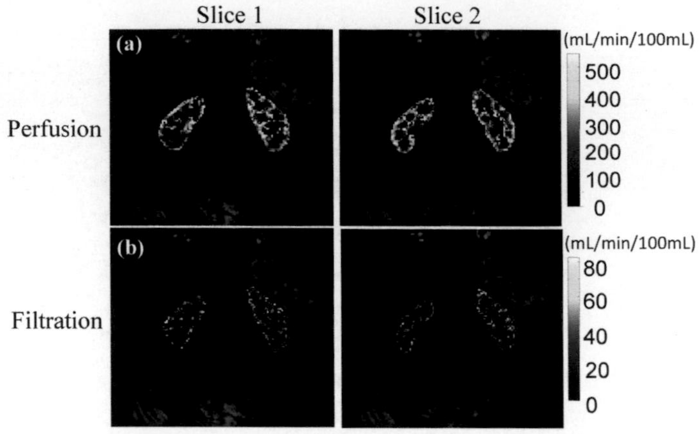

FIG. 17.3

Representative renal perfusion (A) and filtration (B) maps acquired from a healthy volunteer using a rapid 3D radial GRAPPA technique.

including F_p (perfusion rate), T_p (mean transit time in the tissue plasma), F_t (filtration rate), and T_t (mean transit time in the tubular compartment), are quantified with such a model. Fig. 17.3 shows representative perfusion maps acquired from a normal subject using images collected using the free-breathing 3D radial GRAPPA technique shown in Fig. 17.1.

17.2.2.2 ASL for renal perfusion imaging

Owing to the concern of nephrogenic systemic fibrosis caused by gadolinium-based contrast agents, non-contrast-enhanced MR perfusion imaging techniques such as ASL are of particular interest in the kidneys. ASL was first proposed for perfusion quantification in the brain [14–16] and then extended to other organs in the body. Similar to its application in neuroimaging, the method labels the endogenous blood water with RF pulses and measures this signal while the blood flows through the kidneys. To eliminate the signal from the stationary kidney tissues, an image without any labeled blood is also acquired. The subtraction of these two images provides the perfusion-weighted image, which can be utilized to calculate renal perfusion. A tracer kinetic model is often used to extract perfusion values from the ASL measurements [17]. Multiple parameters including tissue T_1 relaxation time and ASL labeling efficiency must be considered during the computation. A single-compartment model is typically used in these analyses, as the use of more complex multi-compartment models is precluded by the limited signal-to-noise ratio (SNR) and motion sensitivity in ASL measurements [18].

A number of factors lead to a low SNR in ASL measurements. As the perfusion signal is generated by inverting the magnetization in the blood water, the label lasts only a few seconds due to T_1 relaxation. While this effect limits the signal level, it also has the drawback that only blood perfusion, and not glomerular filtration, can be accessed from kidney ASL data. One advantage of ASL techniques is that multiple measurement averages can be performed back-to-back to increase the SNR. This capability also enables the monitoring of the temporal changes in perfusion using ASL [19]. While breath-holds can be applied to reduce motion artifacts, free-breathing ASL scans are more preferred by the community [20]. To promote wide application of this technique in renal perfusion quantification, advances in image acquisition, and post-processing methods, especially the design of novel labeling strategies are still needed to improve the SNR and image quality.

To date, multiple studies have been performed to compare the perfusion values obtained with ASL to those acquired using DCE-MRI. By scanning 16 healthy subjects, Cutajar et al. reported consistent cortical renal blood flow between ASL and DCE-MRI (263 ± 41 vs. 287 ± 70 mL/min/100 g) [21]. On the other hand, Wu et al. applied back-to-back ASL and DCE-MRI on 19 healthy subjects and found substantial differences between the two methods despite good correlation in renal perfusion values (ASL results, 227 ± 30 mL/min/100 g for the cortex and 101 ± 21 mL/min/100 g for the medulla; DCE-MRI results, 272 ± 60 mL/min/100 g for the cortex and 122 ± 30 mL/min/100 g for the medulla) [22]. Representative perfusion maps obtained from the same subject using DCE-MRI and ASL in the iBEAT study (prognostic imaging biomarkers for diabetic kidney disease) are shown in Fig. 17.4. Most of these studies were performed with the conventional ASL approach with two images (one labeled and one non-labeled) acquired for perfusion quantification. Recent studies using multiple perfusion-weighted images seem to provide better agreement between ASL and DCE-MRI methods [23–25]. Based on a study performed on 15 healthy subjects, a good correlation in quantitative renal blood flow between

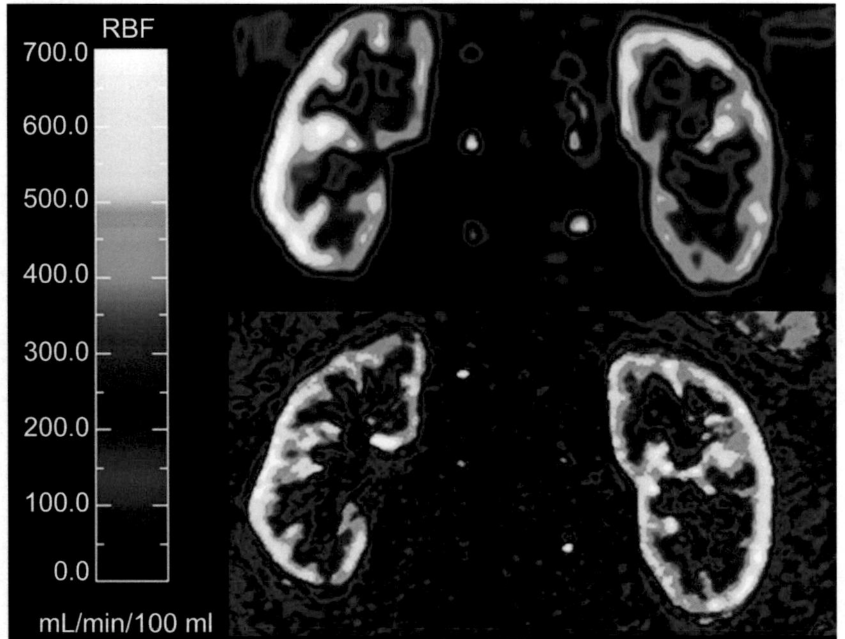

FIG. 17.4

Representative renal perfusion maps in units of mL/min/100 g acquired from a volunteer using ASL (top) and DCE-MRI (bottom) techniques.

ASL and DCE-MRI methods ($R = 0.92$) was reported when 16 perfusion-weighted images were acquired, and the mean difference was only 9 ± 30 mL/min. When only five perfusion-weighted images were used in the same study, the correlation coefficient dropped to 0.81 [24]. While improved correlation is achieved by collecting multiple ASL images, the improvement comes at the cost of longer acquisition times and potentially lower SNR in the quantitative maps as more perfusion-weighted images are acquired during one breath-hold.

17.2.3 Clinical applications

Quantitative perfusion MRI has been applied to various kidney diseases. In this section, we will review its application related to renal tumors, chronic and acute kidney diseases, and renal transplant.

17.2.3.1 Renal tumors

Quantitative renal perfusion MRI has been widely applied for the detection, diagnosis, and monitoring of renal tumors. Most of these studies related to cancer were performed using DCE-MRI. For example, Notohamiprodio et al. used a two-compartment exchange model together with DCE-MRI measurements to demonstrate significant differences in both renal plasma flow and plasma volume between tumor and normal kidney tissues [26]. In addition, the study also demonstrated the potential to detect tumor subtypes and features of vessel infiltration and necrosis. Chandarana et al. applied a view-sharing-based perfusion mapping approach on 24 patients with renal tumors. These results suggest that K^{trans} can be used to differentiate chromophobe renal tumors from other renal lesions [9]. In addition to differentiating tumor subtypes, Palmowski et al. computed perfusion levels from the entire tumor and most vascularized part of tumors, and the findings suggest that renal perfusion can be utilized for grading renal cell carcinoma [27].

Besides the detection and diagnosis of renal tumors, quantitative perfusion MRI has also been applied for monitoring the treatment response of renal cell carcinoma. For example, Flaherty et al. performed a DCE-MRI study on a small cohort of patients with renal cell carcinoma and showed that K^{trans} decreased significantly during treatment with sorafenib [28]. In addition, the baseline K^{trans} is also associated with progression-free survival. Hahn conducted a perfusion study on 44 patients treated with sorafenib and found that high baseline K^{trans} values are associated with a longer progression-free survival [29]. This finding is consistent with a recent study on 34 patients treated with sunitinib, showing that higher baseline and day 14 K^{trans} values are significantly associated with a longer progression-free survival [30].

17.2.3.2 Chronic kidney diseases

Chronic kidney disease (CKD) is a condition characterized by gradually impaired kidney function and affects ~37 million people in the United States [31–36]. Diabetes, hypertension, and heart disease are the main risk factors for CKD. With the capability to measure renal perfusion and filtration rate, perfusion MRI holds great potential for early diagnosis and monitoring of CKD. With increased concern of gadolinium deposition in brain tissues with repeated DCE-MRI scans, ASL presents a promising opportunity for monitoring the progression of this developing disorder [37]. Rossi et al. performed an ASL study on eight healthy subjects and nine patients with CKD (stage 1–3) and found a significant difference in the mean perfusion values in the renal parenchyma between the two groups of subjects [34]. The findings are consistent with a recent study performed on 30 healthy controls and 33 patients with stage 3 CKD [31]. Significantly reduced renal blood flow was reported in both the cortex (108 ± 36 vs. 207 ± 42 mL/min/100 g; $P < .001$) and medulla (23 ± 9 vs. 43 ± 16 mL/min/100 g; $P < .001$). The study also suggests a threshold value of 143 mL/min/100 g for cortical blood flow and 24 mL/min/100 g for medullary blood flow to differentiate the two groups of subjects.

17.2.3.3 Renal transplant

With the aim to improve the outcome of kidney transplant, imaging techniques, including quantitative perfusion MRI, have been increasingly applied in patients before and after the transplant procedure [38,39]. Owing to the concern of side effects related to gadolinium-based contrast agents, many of these studies were performed using ASL approaches [40–44]. Renal perfusion measurements in patients with early and delayed graft function demonstrate that quantitative perfusion values correlate well with allograft function [42,43]. In addition, renal perfusion impairment during the early stage of kidney transplants also has the potential to predict inferior renal outcomes [43]. In a study with a small cohort of eight kidney donors, Cutajar et al. used the ASL technique to show that renal perfusion could be potentially used as a non-invasive biomarker to assess loss of renal reserve in potential kidney donors [21].

17.3 Pancreatic perfusion

17.3.1 Background

Pancreatic perfusion quantification has value in the evaluation of a wide variety of pancreatic conditions, such as evaluation of chronic pancreatitis, assessment of the severity of acute pancreatitis, diagnosis, and staging of pancreatic cancers, and evaluation of pancreatic grafts after transplant [45–48]. Besides disease diagnosis and characterization, quantitative pancreatic perfusion mapping also holds potential in elucidating mechanisms for novel therapeutic approaches and evaluating efficacy of treatment in pancreatic cancer [49].

However, non-invasive and accurate estimation of pancreatic perfusion poses technical challenges, due to physiological motion and the requirement for both high spatial and temporal resolution. Computed tomography (CT) has been applied in many studies to investigate various pancreatic pathologies and can provide perfusion images with high spatiotemporal resolution [50,51]. However, this method is limited by the exposure to ionizing radiation and many patients with acute and chronic pancreatitis are young and require repeated imaging. Compared to CT, MRI has no radiation exposure and can provide excellent soft-tissue contrast. However, with standard Cartesian sampling methods, DCE-MRI can only provide limited spatial and temporal resolution [47,52]. In addition, to reduce motion artifacts due to respiration, multiple breath-holds are often used which is especially difficult for patients with pancreatic lesions, many of which cause debilitating pain [53]. Besides DCE-MRI, ASL has also been recently applied to pancreatic perfusion imaging [54,55].

17.3.2 Technical developments

17.3.2.1 DCE-MRI for pancreatic perfusion quantification

As in renal DCE-MRI, many advanced parallel imaging techniques using Cartesian and non-Cartesian sampling patterns have been developed for pancreatic perfusion quantification [3–6]. For example, Huh et al. applied CAIPIRINHA-VIBE with a high acceleration factor of 4 (2 along the phase-encoding direction and 2 along the partition-encoding direction) to evaluate pancreatic malignancies [56].

Kim et al. applied a three-dimensional radial acquisition combined with view sharing to acquire of a volumetric scan with 40 slices (20 cm volume) in 4.1 s [47]. Non-Cartesian spiral GRAPPA has also been used to accelerate perfusion imaging in the pancreas [57] (Fig. 17.5), achieving a high spatiotemporal resolution ($1.9 \times 1.9 \times 3\,\text{mm}^3$; ~2 s/vol) for whole pancreas and liver coverage. A single-input tracer kinetic model is often used for pancreatic perfusion quantification from DCE-MRI images [46]. Two perfusion parameters, the rate constant of contrast agent from arterial blood plasma to extracellular space (K^{trans}) and volume of distribution (v_e) in extracellular space (often reported as a fractional volume of distribution v_e, which ranges from 0 to 1) can be quantified.

17.3.2.2 ASL for pancreatic perfusion quantification

ASL has also been used in a few studies for pancreatic perfusion quantification [54,58,59]. For example, pilot studies have used pulsed-labeling methods such as flow-sensitive alternating inversion recovery (FAIR) for this purpose. More recently, Taso et al. applied a pseudo-continuous ASL (pCASL) labeling method, which is known to provide an increased sensitivity as compared to FAIR strategies [59]. However, compared to its application in renal perfusion quantification, ASL in pancreatic imaging faces more critical challenges due to lower SNR and higher motion sensitivity.

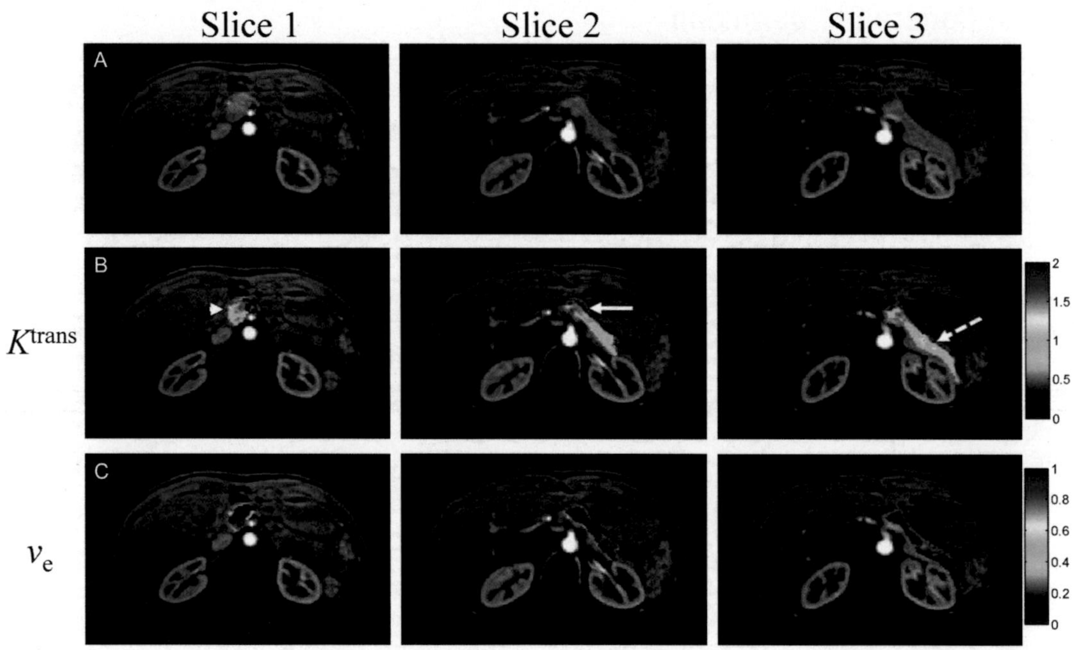

FIG. 17.5

Representative pancreatic perfusion maps acquired using 3D spiral GRAPPA. A 2 s temporal resolution was achieved with a spatial resolution of $1.9 \times 1.9 \times 3\,\text{mm}^3$ for whole pancreas and liver coverage. Results obtained at three different slices in one scan are presented. (A) T_1-weighted images acquired at the arterial phase. Corresponding maps for K^{trans} (B) and v_e (C). Spatial heterogeneities in K^{trans} values across pancreatic head, body, and tail can be observed. *Arrow head*, head; *arrow*, body; *dotted arrow*, tail.

Therefore, more advances in technical development are needed before the method can be evaluated for clinical use. Most of the findings in the following sections were obtained using DCE-MRI for perfusion quantification.

17.3.3 Clinical applications

In this section, perfusion measurements made in pancreatic parenchyma in healthy subjects are reviewed, followed by an examination of the variation in these values across different regions in the organ. Clinical applications of perfusion quantification in the pancreas are then introduced, specifically in pancreatic cancer and other pancreatic diseases.

17.3.3.1 Baseline values

Table 17.1 lists the perfusion values for normal pancreatic parenchyma obtained from several recent studies using the single-input tracer kinetic model. Substantial variation exists in the literature and multiple factors, including the acquisition methods, post-processing algorithms, and age of the subjects, could potentially contribute to these differences. Therefore, it is critical to pay attention to the baseline values when applying this technique in clinical studies.

Besides the variation across different studies, regional variations in perfusion values across the head, body, and tail of the pancreas have also been observed. For example, Bali et al. reported significant difference in all three regions, with the lowest perfusion values in the head and highest in the tail [52]. Kim et al. noticed a trend of higher K^{trans} in the head versus the tail ($0.43 \pm 0.22\,min^{-1}$ vs. $0.35 \pm 0.17\,min^{-1}$) and a similar finding was also reported by Naish et al. using a different perfusion model in healthy subjects (head, $0.4 \pm 0.2\,min^{-1}$; tail, $0.2 \pm 0.1\ min^{-1}$) [47,60]. In another study [57], Chen et al. reported that the mean K^{trans} for the head and tail of the pancreas was 1.92 ± 1.09 and $2.12 \pm 1.30\,min^{-1}$, respectively, both of which were significantly higher than that from the body of pancreas ($1.40 \pm 0.84\,min^{-1}$; $P < .05$). The exact mechanism contributing to the regional difference in pancreatic perfusion remains to be explored. It is known that the pancreatic head is supplied by both the celiac and superior mesenteric arteries, whereas the body and tail are mostly supplied by branches of

Table 17.1 Comparison of pancreatic perfusion values obtained in healthy subjects.

	n	Age range	Region	K^{trans} (min^{-1})	v_e
Chen et al. [57]	11	19–23	Head	1.92 ± 1.09	0.25 ± 0.11
			Body	1.40 ± 0.84	0.29 ± 0.16
			Tail	2.12 ± 1.30	0.26 ± 0.13
Bali et al. [52]	10	22–29	Head	1.69–2.00	0.15 ± 0.04
			Body	1.90–2.23	0.16 ± 0.03
			Tail	2.25–2.34	0.17 ± 0.04
Yao et al. [53]	40	30–65	Head	2.86 ± 1.23	0.90 ± 0.02
			Body	2.81 ± 1.08	0.82 ± 0.11
			Tail	2.79 ± 1.39	0.70 ± 0.19
Kim et al. [47]	10	24–79	Head	0.43 ± 0.22	0.072 ± 0.036
			Tail	0.35 ± 0.17	0.073 ± 0.569

the splenic artery [52]. Therefore, the heterogeneity of blood supply to the pancreas might cause significant difference in perfusion, but this hypothesis has not yet been validated. On the other hand, some studies have also reported similar perfusion values across the whole pancreas [53]. In theory, quantitative perfusion measurements should be consistent between studies using different imaging techniques. In practice, however, the accuracy of measurements collected using different imaging techniques could be influenced by many factors, including motion artifacts and partial volume effects due to limited spatial resolution. In addition, whether pancreatic perfusion is dependent on subject age is also an open question.

17.3.3.2 Pancreatic cancer detection and diagnosis

According to 2019 cancer statistics, pancreatic cancer is the fourth leading cause of cancer-related death in the United States and its 5-year survival rate is only 9%, the lowest among all major cancer types [61]. Multiple clinical studies using quantitative perfusion MRI have been performed for detection and diagnosis of pancreatic cancer [47,53,56,62]. A retrospective study showed that both K^{trans} and k_{ep} are significantly lower in patients with pancreatic cancer as compared to another group of patients with normal pancreas [47]. These results are consistent with a recent study comparing perfusion values obtained from pancreatic lesions versus normal-appearing pancreas parenchyma [56]. Maria et al. also compared the perfusion values obtained from malignant and benign solid pancreatic focal lesions and observed significant differences in K^{trans} [62]. All these results suggest that quantitative perfusion measurements can provide critical information for detection and diagnosis of pancreatic cancer.

17.3.3.3 Other clinical applications

Perfusion MRI has also been applied to investigate other pancreatic diseases, including pancreatitis [45,57,63] and pancreatic transplants [48]. Chronic pancreatitis is a progressive inflammatory disease that could lead to permanent damage to pancreatic structure and function. Using the spiral GRAPPA technique, perfusion values from a patient with chronic pancreatitis were assessed. Both K^{trans} and v_e values were reduced as compared to normal subjects (Fig. 17.6) [57]. A recent study also assessed the perfusion values in patients with acute pancreatitis [63]. Compared to normal pancreatic tissue, significant decreases in K^{trans} and v_p were observed. More interestingly, a trend of decreasing pancreatic perfusion values as the severity of acute pancreatitis increases was reported. All these pilot studies suggest that quantitative perfusion MRI can be used as an alternative non-invasive means for diagnosis and monitoring of these pancreatic diseases.

17.4 Prostate perfusion

17.4.1 Background

Prostate cancer is the most common solid tumor in males worldwide. Based on the 2019 cancer statistics in the United States, the number of estimated new cases was 174,650 and the number of estimated deaths was 31,620, representing the first and second leading cancer type among men in US, respectively [61]. Multi-parametric MRI plays a critical role in prostate imaging for cancer detection, staging, treatment planning, and follow-up. Among various clinical MRI protocols, DCE-MRI is an important component which offers information related to the level of tumor angiogenesis. Similar to tumors in other organs, prostate cancer shows rapid and intense contrast enhancement compared with normal surrounding tissue,

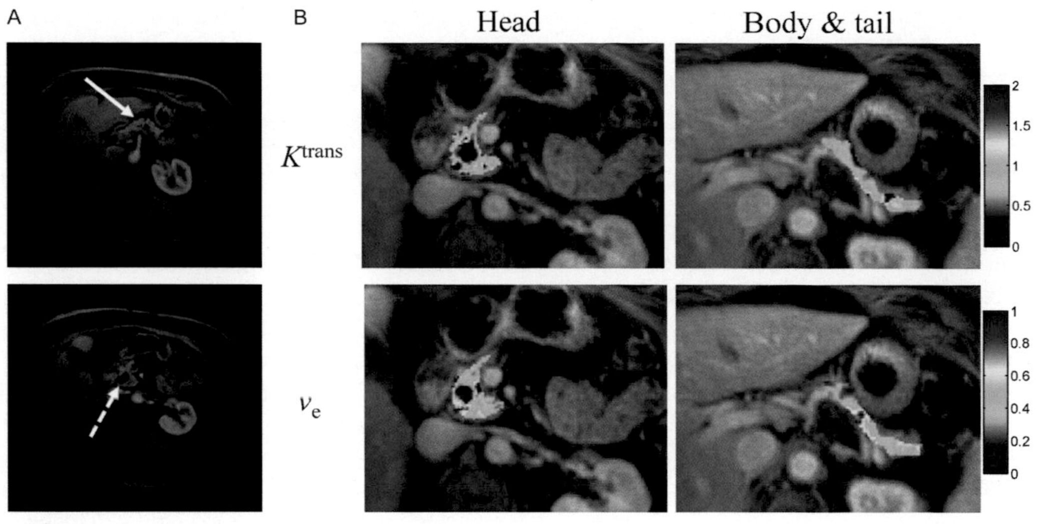

FIG. 17.6

Pancreatic perfusion maps acquired using 3D spiral GRAPPA in a 64-year-old patient with a proven branch duct intraductal papillary mucinous neoplasm. (A) Representative DCE-MRI images acquired at the arterial phase (~20 s after contrast injection). The pancreas showed diffuse fatty atrophy with lobulated outline *(arrow)* and a cystic lesion communicating with the pancreatic duct in the head of pancreas *(dotted arrow)*. (B) K^{trans} and v_e maps obtained at two different regions. Minimal contrast enhancement was noted for the cystic lesion in the head and therefore both K^{trans} and v_e were largely reduced as compared to values obtained from other regions in the pancreas.

and this enhancement also washes out quickly [64–66]. Coupled with tracer kinetic models, quantitative perfusion mapping techniques have been developed for better detection of prostate cancer and monitoring of treatment response.

17.4.2 Technical developments

While ASL has been used for perfusion quantification in prostate in a few studies [67,68], most of the studies are performed using DCE-MRI for this purpose. Compared to other organs in the body, respiratory motion is less of a concern for prostate imaging and therefore many techniques developed for brain imaging can be applied for prostate with an adjusted imaging field of view and spatial resolution. Fast imaging techniques have also been applied to achieve higher spatial and temporal resolutions for prostate imaging. Several studies have been performed to determine an optimal temporal resolution for accurate perfusion quantification in prostate. Ream et al. used a fast imaging technique called GRASP (Golden-angle RAdial Sparse Parallel) to evaluate the effect of temporal resolution on tumor detection using quantitative K^{trans} and v_e measurements [69]. The findings demonstrate that a temporal resolution of 10 s is sufficient and further improvement does not offer any benefit in diagnosis. However, when both perfusion and diffusion measurements are combined for the detection of prostate cancer, another study using the GRASP technique indicated that a higher temporal resolution of 2.5 s can significantly improve the diagnostic performance as compared to those obtained using a standard temporal resolution of 10s [70]. With these discrepancies between literature papers, more studies using fast imaging techniques are needed to determine the optimal temporal resolution for perfusion quantification and its application in prostate cancer.

17.4.3 Clinical applications

17.4.3.1 Diagnosis and staging of prostate cancer

Perfusion parameters, especially K^{trans} and k_{ep}, have been used for the detection and characterization of prostate tumors. For example, significant differences in perfusion values were found between normal prostate tissue and cancer, and between high-grade cancer and chronic prostatitis [64]. In addition, quantitative perfusion values can also be used to differentiate low-grade from high-grade prostate tumors [71]. However, using quantitative metrics from DCE-MRI alone results in a low overall diagnostic performance, and thus recent studies propose to combine perfusion metrics with other quantitative measures such as T_2 and diffusion to improve diagnostic performance. In a study of 50 patients, Tamada et al. demonstrated that combination of T_2-weighted, DCE-MRI, and diffusion-weighted imaging can significantly improve the sensitivity for detecting prostate tumor as compared to methods using each individual method alone [72]. These findings are consistent with a recent prospective trial performed on 45 patients [73].

17.4.3.2 Monitoring of treatment response

Perfusion measurements have also been used to assess the response to radiation therapy and aid in treatment planning [74,75]. In a study of 87 patients with prostate cancer treated with robotic stereotactic body radiation therapy, K^{trans} values were observed to gradually reduce from a baseline value of $1.79\,min^{-1}$ before treatment to $0.22\,min^{-1}$ measured 24months after the treatment [75]. The information obtained with DCE-MRI has also been used to aid the treatment planning of patients with local recurrent cancer after radiotherapy [76].

17.5 Breast perfusion

17.5.1 Background

Breast cancer is the most common cancer in women and is also the leading cause of cancer death in women worldwide [77,78]. Breast MRI is a valuable tool in screening and management of breast cancer, alongside mammography and ultrasound [79]. DCE-MRI allows evaluation of tissue characteristics by enabling both qualitative and quantitative assessments of perfusion. Neoplastic tissues often are supplied by leaky blood vessels that allow faster extravasation of the contrast material compared to the normal tissues. The rapid appearance and washout behavior of contrast agent in cancer tissues as compared to normal tissues has the potential to aid in detection of contralateral, multifocal, or multicentric breast cancer; diagnosis of cancer in women with dense breasts; detection of occult primary breast cancer in patients presenting with metastatic axillary lymphadenopathy; differentiating the more aggressive triple negative breast cancers from cancers which have a more favorable prognosis; and assessment of response to neoadjuvant chemotherapy [80]. Conventional MRI methods rely on semi-quantitative signal enhancement curves derived from high spatial resolution and low temporal resolution (90–120 s) images which are subjectively evaluated [81]. Quantitative analyses can provide objective parameters which reflect tissue properties such as vessel permeability, volume of extravascular/extracellular space, and tissue perfusion.

17.5.2 Technical developments

DCE-MRI is used to measure perfusion in the breast using MRI. To accurately evaluate lesion margins and architecture, a high spatial resolution is needed in a DCE-MRI study of the breast [82]. The American College of Radiology (ACR) recommends an in-plane pixel resolution of 1 mm or less, a slice of thickness of 3 mm or less, and acquisition of enhancement data at specified intervals separated by 4 min or less for qualitative analyses [83]. In clinical DCE-MRI acquisitions, the high spatial resolution ($1\,mm^3$) is achieved by collecting data with low temporal resolutions (90–120 s). In addition, uniform fat suppression is required over a large field of view that includes both breasts, which further prolongs the scan time and lowers the temporal resolution. However, quantitative models for derivation of tissue and tumor perfusion metrics require a temporal resolution of 10–15 s [84]. A number of acceleration approaches have been examined to address this spatiotemporal resolution tradeoff. While 2D keyhole-based approaches have been tested, increased ghosting artifacts and blurring were observed, which affected diagnostic accuracy [85]. Other data acquisition acceleration approaches have included undersampled radial imaging and k-t segmentation schemes. These techniques rely on view-sharing to reconstruct an image by combining the high spatial frequency *k*-space data from adjacent undersampled *k*-space intervals [81,86–88]. However, these methods run the risk of inaccurate depiction of lesions edges due to less frequent updates of the *k*-space periphery. To overcome this potential drawback, a technique using the differential subsampling with cartesian ordering (DISCO) sampling pattern in combination with view sharing, two-point Dixon fat-water separation, and parallel imaging has been recently described. This technique was able to achieve the same spatial resolution as a clinical DCE-MRI sequence while shortening the temporal resolution six-fold [89]. Similarly, ultrafast MRI breast perfusion methods have been developed for use at 3 T incorporating view sharing and compressed sensing techniques [90,91].

Blood flow parameters derived from dynamic susceptibility contrast-enhanced imaging (DSC) have also been evaluated to probe the molecular subtypes of breast [92]. Parameters such as relative blood flow (rBF), relative blood volume (rBV), and mean transit time (MTT) can be derived from DSC data by fitting a gamma variate model function to the changing tissue signal intensities from the first passage of a bolus of contrast agent in the vascular space [93]. Although the rBV and rBF values were higher in triple negative breast cancers, the results were not statistically significant.

17.5.3 Clinical applications

The following pharmacokinetic parameters derived from the quantitative DCE-MRI sequences have been explored in the evaluation of breast cancer: extravasation transfer constant (K^{trans}), the extravascular-extracellular space (EES) volume fraction (v_e), and the reverse volume transfer constant (k_{ep}). These parameters are most frequently extracted from the data using the extended Tofts model [94]. Biomarkers derived from histopathology such as neoangiogenesis, cytokines as estrogen receptor (ER), progesterone receptor (PR), human epidermal growth factor receptor-2 (HER-2), and Ki-67 help in prognostication, selecting the appropriate therapy, assessing the response assessment to chemotherapy, and are correlated with survival outcomes. For example, VEGF expression is correlated with microvascular density (MVD) in tumors, and a higher MVD is in turn correlated with greater neoangiogenesis and worse prognosis. The presence of ER expression reduces the expression of vascular endothelial growth factor (VEGF) and hence tumor neoangiogenesis. Therefore, tumors not manifesting ER receptors are expected to have greater vascularity, more aggressive behavior, and worse outcomes. On DCE-MRI, such tumors would be expected to have increased blood flow. v_e represents the volume of EES and therefore reflects tumor stroma. A high v_e value is an indicator of high tumor cellularity and poorer prognosis. Therefore, these imaging biomarkers have the potential to act as surrogates for histopathology derived biomarkers and could possibly decrease the need for biopsy.

Various studies have demonstrated a correlation between DCE-MRI derived quantitative parameters and histopathologically derived biomarkers. Liu et al. prospectively evaluated quantitative perfusion measurements in 151 patients with invasive ductal carcinoma with following surgery [95]. They found a significant positive correlation between K^{trans} values and tumor size, histological grade, axillary lymph node metastases, and HER2 and Ki67 expression ($P < .001$), and negative correlation between ER and PR expression ($P < .001$). k_{ep} values were also positively correlated to tumor size ($P < .001$) and negatively correlated to ER and PR expression ($P < .001$). v_e was negatively related to HER2 expression ($P = .004$). Larger tumor size was correlated with greater tumor vascularity, explaining the higher K^{trans} values found in these tumors. Similar findings were reported by Kim et al. [80], who found that higher K^{trans} values were associated with a larger tumor size (greater than 2 cm) and increased MVD, and Li et al. [96] who found that K^{trans} and k_{ep} values were significantly higher in invasive ductal carcinoma (IDC) and ductal carcinoma in situ (DCIS) than in mammary ductal dysplasia.

Cancer-associated fibroblasts are known to lay down stroma that promotes tumor progression, invasion, and metastases. It has been shown that collagen-dominant cancers have worse prognosis, whereas as cancers with lymphocytic infiltration have been associated with better overall survival. In a study of 61 patients with triple negative breast cancer, Park et al. found that a higher v_e value was associated with poorer disease specific survival [97], as higher v_e values indicate higher tumor cellularity and stromal components. Yim et al. evaluated 64 cancers in 64 patients and attempted to classify the perfusion characteristics of these cancers according to the dominant stroma type using quantitative perfusion parameters derived from DCE-MRI [98]. They found that median k_{ep} values were significantly higher in the lymphocyte-dominant group than in the collagen-dominant group ($P = .003$), with higher v_e values in patients.

Makkat et al. used pixel-wise deconvolution of the relative signal intensity changes from two separate contrast injections on a pre-operative DCE-MRI exam to calculate the total tumor blood flow (TBF) in tumors in 57 women [99]. They found that the tumors larger than 2 cm, PR-tumors, and tumors with amplified HER2 gene demonstrated significantly higher TBF values. Ki-67 is another histological identifier of aggressive breast cancer and is a prognostic marker for pathological complete response and overall survival [100]. In a retrospective study evaluating DCE-MRI-derived perfusion parameters in 88 patients with ER+ breast cancer, Shin et al. found that a high K^{trans} value independently predicted a high Ki-67 proliferation status in the patients [101].

de Bazelaire et al. evaluated K^{trans} and v_e values in 24 women before and after neoadjuvant chemotherapy using a high spatial resolution and low temporal resolution DCE-MRI sequence [102]. Using the measured arterial input function, they found that K^{trans} and v_e differed significantly between non-responders and responders ($P < .01$). The responders demonstrated a greater than 87% decrease in v_e (sensitivity 89%, specificity 83%) reflecting a decrease in the number of immature vessels.

It is well-known that cancers cells in the same patient can be highly variable due to the presence of mutations, epigenetic modulations, and chromosomal rearrangements. This heterogeneity has major implications in decision support for individual patients because response to neoadjuvant chemotherapy is poorer with a more heterogeneous tumor cell population. However, a full course of chemotherapy is necessary before response can be assessed by conventional imaging and pathological methods, thereby exposing the patient to harmful side effects due to the therapy itself without the guarantee of a beneficial effect. In their seminal work, Wu et al. aimed to characterize intratumor perfusion heterogeneity as seen on DCE-MRI and investigate this heterogeneity as a predictor of recurrence-free survival [103]. In this retrospective study, they used a cohort of 60 patients as a discovery set and a cohort of 186 patients as a validation set. MRI-based perfusion parameters were used to divide each tumor into phenotypically consistent sub-regions. Aggressive tumors were associated with a larger volume of poorly perfused sub-regions, and imaging-based markers were independently associated with risk-free survival beyond traditional risk predictors such as ER and PR status, HER2 status, tumor volume, and pathological complete response.

These studies demonstrate that DCE-MRI derived perfusion metrics could potentially serve as useful biomarkers for the non-invasive assessment of the aggressiveness of breast cancer, help in treatment planning, and also serve as prognostication factors. However, further studies in larger patient cohorts and clinical trials are needed to validate these findings for wider applicability. The availability of robustness tests of perfusion metrics in clinical trials would enable the addition of quantitative MRI measurements to the clinical armamentarium against breast cancer.

17.6 Cardiac perfusion

17.6.1 Background

The assessment of myocardial perfusion is of importance for the diagnosis of a range of cardiovascular disorders, among which myocardial ischemia is the most frequent. In general, myocardial ischemia occurs if the blood supply to myocardial tissue is insufficient to meet oxygen demand. If this imbalance persists, a cascade of cellular, inflammatory, and biochemical events is triggered, ultimately leading to the irreversible death of myocytes. In consequence, affected myocardial tissue becomes mechanically inactive, potentially compromising the overall pump performance of the heart.

In order to understand the relevance of perfusion assessment, it is important to review the underlying physiology of coronary blood flow and myocardial perfusion. In brief, the coronary circulation is divided into large epicardial arteries (diameter 1–6 mm), pre-arterioles, and a downstream network of arterioles and capillaries (diameter < 300–400 μm), which penetrate and supply cardiac muscle tissue. This microvascular network regulates myocardial blood flow over a wide range of perfusion pressures to balance myocardial oxygen supply and demand. Microvascular resistance is closely adjusted at rest via autoregulation to maintain blood supply commensurate with cardiac workload [104]. In case of increased oxygen demand, for example during exercise, myocardial perfusion increases as a result of an increase in heart rate and a release of vasoactive mediators (such as adenosine) that cause vasodilatation of the arterioles, which reduces vascular resistance and increases flow (and thus myocardial perfusion) to the myocardium [105]. It is important to note that coronary flow becomes primarily

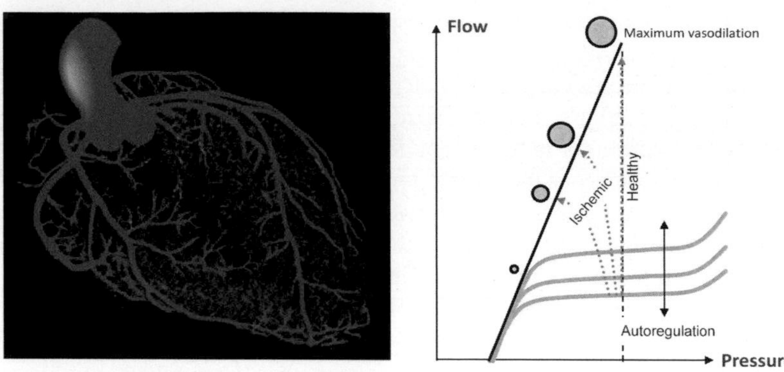

FIG. 17.7

Illustration of epicardial coronary arteries, arterioles and capillaries *(left)*. Coronary flow-pressure relationship *(right)*. At rest, autoregulation adapts flow to a wide range of demand across a wide range of pressures *(light grey solid curves)*. Without autoregulation *(solid black line)*, flow depends on coronary pressure up to a maximum at maximum vasodilation. In a healthy heart, coronary flow can be maximally increased through maximum vasodilation. However, increased pressure differences are required when increasing the flow is not possible, such as in the case of ischemia due to coronary stenosis, as shown in the dotted grey lines/curves which reflect reduced vasodilation and hence increasing microvascular resistance.

(Left: Adapted from DOI: https://doi.org/10.1016/j.jacc.2018.09.042.)

dependent on perfusion pressure during vasodilation as microvascular resistance is minimized (Fig. 17.7). Therefore, the assessment of myocardial perfusion under adenosine stress incurring maximum vasodilation is a key component of any cardiac perfusion imaging protocol.

Beyond these basic interplays, the microcirculation is further modulated by compressive forces exerted by the cardiac muscle itself, rendering the sub-endocardium particularly vulnerable to ischemia, especially at elevated heart rates or low perfusion pressure [106]. Accordingly, sufficient spatial resolution in the perfusion images and maps is required to resolve the transmural layers of the myocardium.

Image-based quantitative assessment of myocardial ischemia includes quantification of regional absolute myocardial blood flow (MBF; in units of mL/min/g) as well as relative parameters, such as the myocardial perfusion reserve (MPR), which is the ratio of "MBF under exercise-induced or pharmacologically induced stress" to "MBF at rest" [107]. If two- or multi-compartment modeling is used, secondary parameters including the permeability-surface area (PS) product are obtained in addition to MBF and MPR.

17.6.2 Technical developments

17.6.2.1 Perfusion acquisition

An overview of myocardial perfusion imaging and quantitative perfusion analysis is given in Fig. 17.8. The desire to detect regional and transmural differences of myocardial blood flow with sufficient sensitivity and specificity translates into specific imaging and protocol settings:

- Cardiac-triggered saturation recovery dynamic single-shot imaging.
- Three or more short-axis slices with in-plane resolution $\leq$2.5 mm and 8–10 mm slice thickness.
- Bolus injection of extravascular Gadolinium-based contrast agent (0.05–0.1 mmol/kg b.w. @ 4 mL/s).

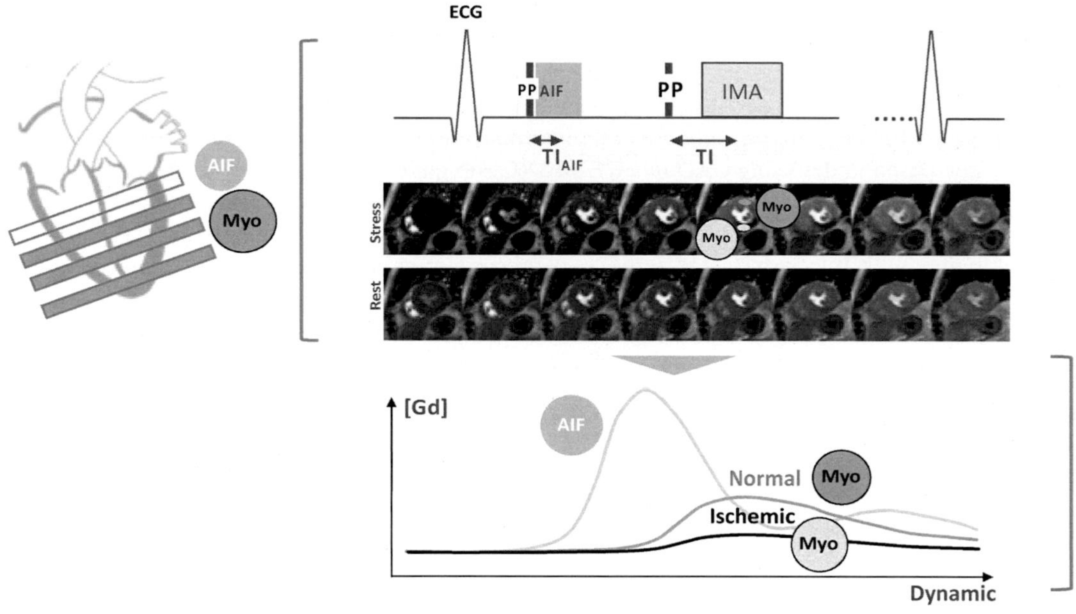

FIG. 17.8

Schematic overview of cardiac perfusion imaging and quantification. Typically, three short-axis slices are acquired to record dynamic myocardial tissue signal (Myo) along with the arterial input function (AIF). An ECG triggered, multi-slice, singe-shot imaging sequence (IMA) is employed which includes saturation pre-pulses (PP) with short delay (TI_{AIF}) to measure the AIF and long delay (TI) to record Myo signals. The MR signals are subsequently converted into dynamic contrast agent concentration curves [Gd] and processed to calculate myocardial blood flow (MBF) and potentially secondary parameters such as the permeability-surface area (PS) product, depending on the model complexity.

- Scan acceleration using parallel imaging, compressed sensing or constrained reconstruction for sufficient spatiotemporal resolution.
- Interleaved imaging to obtain the arterial input function (AIF), enabling conversion of the signal to contrast agent concentration.
- Motion compensation to align dynamic short-axis slices prior to quantitative perfusion analysis.
- Stress exam using Adenosine infusion (140 mg/kg b.w. over 3 min).
- Rest exam after wait time of ≥ 10 min to allow for sufficient contrast agent washout.
- Regional or pixel-wise calculation of MBF of stress and rest exams, MPR, and optional secondary parameters depending on model complexity (e.g., PS).
- Regional (AHA 17-segment model) or pixel-wise reporting of MBF and MPR (and secondary parameters).

17.6.2.2 Perfusion quantification

Two main strategies have been applied to quantify myocardial blood flow from pixel-based concentration-time data: model-free methods, parametric models, and physiological models [108]. Model-free analysis is based on the central volume principle [109], which does not assume any specifics about the structure of the perfused tissue territories; parametric models describe the tissue response function using mathematical models that have no direct physical meaning; and physiological models approximate tissue structure using compartments that exchange the tracer across permeable interfaces [110].

Among the parametric model-based approaches, Fermi deconvolution [111] is frequently applied in myocardial perfusion mapping due to its relative robustness [112]. For example, Fermi deconvolution has been used in detecting CAD in a CE-MARC sub-study [113] and to describe microvascular dysfunction in patients with dilated cardiomyopathies [114]. For model-based methods, the two-compartment exchange model is often used to represent the vascular and interstitial spaces as separate volumes with tracer exchange across a permeable membrane which is characterized by PS. Since capillary recruitment during vasodilation results in an increase in both MBF and PS, there is additional information available through PS to characterize microvascular function [115]. Beyond two-compartment modeling, distributed modeling approaches, including the blood tissue exchange model [116], which has been implemented as part of recent inline perfusion quantification pipelines [117,118], have attracted increasing attention.

17.6.3 Clinical applications

There are two main types of disease that may cause a reduction in myocardial blood flow. Coronary artery disease (CAD), the single most common cause of death worldwide [119], results from atherosclerosis, which leads to a reduction in the luminal diameter of the epicardial arteries and thus results in a reduction of perfusion pressure to the myocardium. Conversely, in microvascular disease, dysfunction of the small myocardial blood vessels impedes the vasodilatory response and leads to an impaired myocardial perfusion reserve. It is important to note that reduced distal pressure caused by stenosed epicardial arteries can also compromise regulation of the microcirculation.

17.6.3.1 Coronary artery disease

The diagnostic value of quantitative cardiac perfusion mapping in CAD has been demonstrated in numerous studies [120,121]. A recent meta-analysis summarizing many of these studies reported a sensitivity of 83% and specificity of 76% for various quantitative metrics to diagnose CAD [122]. Fully automated perfusion mapping has been proposed and applied as a diagnostic tool. In healthy volunteers, good intra-study, and inter-study repeatability of stress MBF values have been demonstrated [118]. In an observational study of 80 patients with known or suspected CAD, a sensitivity and specificity of 86% and 84% have been achieved compared with the reference standard of invasive coronary angiography with coronary stenosis greater than 70% [121]. In another study, which used hemodynamically significant CAD defined by invasive angiography and fractional flow reserve (FFR) as the reference standard, quantitative perfusion analysis had a sensitivity and specificity of 85% and 81%, respectively [123].

Moreover, it has been reported that MPR is an independent risk factor for the prognosis of patients with CAD, outperforming both a baseline clinical model (comprised of age, sex, and presence of late gadolinium enhancement) and visual assessment of ischemia [124]. In a randomized controlled cross-over trial in patients with refractory angina, quantitative perfusion analysis was utilized to assess the change in myocardial perfusion following a period of lipoprotein apheresis (in which certain cholesterols that are responsible for atherosclerosis are removed from human plasma). The authors demonstrated an increase in stress MBF and MPR in patients who underwent apheresis compared to sham treatment [125]. These changes were accompanied by improvement in symptoms, exercise capacity, and reduction in atherosclerotic burden in the carotid arteries. This is the first time that quantitative perfusion analysis was used as a primary endpoint to evaluate the efficacy of a medical intervention.

17.6.3.2 Microvascular disease

Causes for microvascular dysfunction include smoking, hyperlipidemia, diabetes, hypertension, aortic stenosis, and dilated and hypertrophic cardiomyopathy [126]. The diagnosis of microvascular disease can be challenging and patients typically present with anginal chest pain, abnormal functional tests but normal coronary arteries. Several established tests can be used to determine the presence of microvascular dysfunction including positron emission tomography and invasive coronary angiography, and there is emerging evidence for deploying MR-based quantitative perfusion measurement in this context (Fig. 17.9).

In hypertrophic cardiomyopathy (HCM), abnormal thickening of the myocardium can cause symptoms such as chest pain, breathlessness, and sudden loss of consciousness. Furthermore, HCM has been associated with sudden cardiac death, and therefore the accurate detection and risk stratification of these patients is important to guide medical therapy and device therapy. MR-based quantitative perfusion analysis has been applied to a cohort of patients with HCM; a higher resting MBF and lower stress MBF in the endocardial compared to the epicardial layers of the myocardium were reported [127]. In fact, stress MBF values were reduced below the rest MBF values in patients with severe microvascular ischemia. Hence, quantitative perfusion analysis may have a role in the diagnosis of microvascular disease with different disease conditions such as HCM and may aid in clinical decision making for medical therapy and risk stratification. In another study, MBF was measured in a cohort of patients with non-ischemic DCM. A higher resting MBF and lower stress MBF was measured compared to healthy volunteers [114]. This study provided new insights into the mechanisms of non-ischemic dilated cardiomyopathy, which was previously not thought to involve microvascular dysfunction.

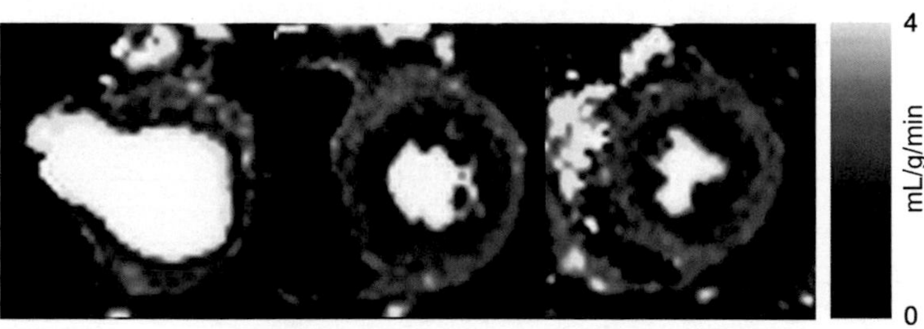

FIG. 17.9

Pixel-wise quantitative myocardial blood flow perfusion maps obtained in a patient with typical angina and unobstructed coronary arteries. *Left* to *right*: basal, mid ventricular and apical slices. There is a circumferential subendocardial perfusion defect at stress, corresponding to reduced myocardial blood flow *(blue)* in all slices. In the context of unobstructed coronary arteries, these findings may be indicative of microvascular disease.

In addition to MBF, the permeability-surface area is also a potential diagnostic parameter in patients with microvascular disease. Animal studies have demonstrated PS to be a sensitive indicator of functional vascular injury [128,129]. There are potential clinical applications of permeability indices as imaging biomarkers for diagnosis and disease progression in conditions that are associated with endothelial dysfunction, including hypertension and diabetes. Currently, however, only limited data are available in humans beyond reports of initial feasibility [115].

In conclusion, MR-based perfusion mapping has found application in assessing patients with coronary artery disease and/or microvascular disease. The method has shown good diagnostic accuracy relative to positron emission tomography and invasive readouts. As quantitative perfusion protocols become more widely available for different sites and vendors, myocardial perfusion mapping is poised to play an important role in diagnosis, prognosis, and guidance for patients with cardiac disease.

17.7 Summary

In this chapter, recent developments in quantitative perfusion MRI in the body were introduced. Owing to the limited space, this chapter only covers the kidney, pancreas, prostate, breast, and heart, although perfusion measurements have been made via MRI in other body organs, such as the lung [130–134] and bowel [135–137]. While many studies have been performed, further development is needed to make perfusion mapping via MRI more robust and feasible for routine clinical practice. First of all, technical developments with the aim to improve spatial resolution, temporal resolution, and motion robustness of perfusion measurements are needed. In addition, while fast imaging techniques have been developed to reduce potential motion during data collection, the combination of novel motion correction algorithms could help provide more reliable results in body perfusion mapping. Second, the developed perfusion metrics must be validated against gold-standard measurements. For perfusion, validation requires comparison with results obtained using other imaging modalities, such as CT, PET, or microsphere measurements. Finally, standardization of imaging sequences and analysis parameters is needed. This step requires efforts from the scientific community, radiology societies, and MRI vendors to ensure that consistent results can be acquired across scanners, sites, and vendor platforms. As each organ in the body has specific modeling and acquisition requirements, this implementation must be performed for each organ individually. Based on promising initial clinical studies, such technological advances are warranted, followed by large-scale clinical trials for applications of perfusion mapping in the body.

References

[1] Lacerda S, Law M. Magnetic resonance perfusion and permeability imaging in brain tumors. Neuroimaging Clin N Am 2009;9(4):527–57. https://doi.org/10.1016/j.nic.2009.08.007.

[2] Essig M, Anzalone N, Combs SE, Dörfler A, Lee SK, Picozzi P, et al. MR imaging of neoplastic central nervous system lesions: review and recommendations for current practice. Am J Neuroradiol 2012;33(5):803–17. https://doi.org/10.3174/ajnr.A2640.

[3] Pruessmann KP, Weiger M, Bornert P, Boesiger P. Advances in sensitivity encoding with arbitrary k-space trajectories. Magn Reson Med 2001;46:638–51.

[4] Lustig M, Pauly JM. SPIRiT: iterative self-consistent parallel imaging reconstruction from arbitrary k-space. Magn Reson Med 2010;64:457–71.

[5] Seiberlich N, Lee G, Ehses P, Duerk JL, Gilkeson R, Griswold M. Improved temporal resolution in cardiac imaging using through-time spiral GRAPPA. Magn Reson Med 2011;66:1682–8.

[6] Seiberlich N, Ehses P, Duerk J, Gilkeson R, Griswold M. Improved radial GRAPPA calibration for real-time free-breathing cardiac imaging. Magn Reson Med 2011;65:492–505.

[7] Song T, Laine AF, Chen Q, Rusinek H, Bokacheva L, Lim RP, et al. Optimal k-space sampling for dynamic contrast-enhanced MRI with an application to MR renography. Magn Reson Med 2009;61:1242–8. https://doi.org/10.1002/mrm.21901.

[8] Vakil P, Carr JC, Carroll TJ. Combined renal MRA and perfusion with a single dose of contrast. Magn Reson Imaging 2012;30:878–85. https://doi.org/10.1016/j.mri.2011.12.027.

[9] Chandarana H, Amarosa A, Huang WC, Kang SK, Taneja S, Melamed J, et al. High temporal resolution 3D gadolinium-enhanced dynamic MR imaging of renal tumors with pharmacokinetic modeling: preliminary observations. J Magn Reson Imaging 2013;38:802–8. https://doi.org/10.1002/jmri.24035.

[10] Chen B, Zhao K, Li B, Cai W, Wang X, Zhang J, et al. High temporal resolution dynamic contrast-enhanced MRI using compressed sensing-combined sequence in quantitative renal perfusion measurement. Magn Reson Imaging 2015;33:962–9. https://doi.org/10.1016/j.mri.2015.05.004.

[11] Parikh N, Ream JM, Zhang HC, Block KT, Chandarana H, Rosenkrantz AB. Performance of simultaneous high temporal resolution quantitative perfusion imaging of bladder tumors and conventional multi-phase urography using a novel free-breathing continuously acquired radial compressed-sensing MRI sequence. Magn Reson Imaging 2016;34:694–8. https://doi.org/10.1016/j.mri.2015.12.033.

[12] Wright KL, Chen Y, Saybasili H, Griswold MA, Seiberlich N, Gulani V. Quantitative high-resolution renal perfusion imaging using 3-dimensional through-time radial generalized autocalibrating partially parallel acquisition. Invest Radiol 2014;49:666–74. https://doi.org/10.1097/RLI.0000000000000070.

[13] Sourbron SP, Michaely HJ, Reiser MF, Schoenberg SO. MRI-measurement of perfusion and glomerular filtration in the human kidney with a separable compartment model. Invest Radiol 2008;43:40–8. https://doi.org/10.1097/RLI.0b013e31815597c5.

[14] Detre JA, Leigh JS, Williams DS, Koretsky AP. Perfusion imaging. Magn Reson Med 1992;23(1):37–45. https://doi.org/10.1002/mrm.1910230106.

[15] Williams DS, Detre JA, Leigh JS, Koretsky AP. Magnetic resonance imaging of perfusion using spin inversion of arterial water. Proc Natl Acad Sci U S A 1992;89(1):212–6. https://doi.org/10.1073/pnas.89.1.212.

[16] Roberts DA, Detre JA, Bolinger L, Insko EK, Leigh JS. Quantitative magnetic resonance imaging of human brain perfusion at 1.5 T using steady-state inversion of arterial water. Proc Natl Acad Sci U S A 1994;91(1):33–7. https://doi.org/10.1073/pnas.91.1.33.

[17] Buxton RB, Frank LR, Wong EC, Siewert B, Warach S, Edelman RR. A general kinetic model for quantitative perfusion imaging with arterial spin labeling. Magn Reson Med 1998;40:383–96. https://doi.org/10.1002/mrm.1910400308.

[18] Nery F, Gordon I, Thomas D. Non-invasive renal perfusion imaging using arterial spin labeling MRI: challenges and opportunities. Diagnostics 2018;8(1):2. https://doi.org/10.3390/diagnostics8010002.

[19] Buchanan C, Mohammed A, Cox E, Köhler K, Canaud B, Taal MW, et al. Intradialytic cardiac magnetic resonance imaging to assess cardiovascular responses in a short-term trial of hemodiafiltration and hemodialysis. J Am Soc Nephrol 2017;28:1269–77. https://doi.org/10.1681/ASN.2016060686.

[20] Nery F, Buchanan CE, Harteveld AA, Odudu A, Bane O, Cox EF, et al. Consensus-based technical recommendations for clinical translation of renal ASL MRI. Magn Reson Mater Phys Biol Med 2020;33:141–61. https://doi.org/10.1007/s10334-019-00800-z.

[21] Cutajar M, Thomas DL, Hales PW, Banks T, Clark CA, Gordon I. Comparison of ASL and DCE MRI for the non-invasive measurement of renal blood flow: quantification and reproducibility. Eur Radiol 2014;24:1300–8. https://doi.org/10.1007/s00330-014-3130-0.

[22] Wu WC, Su MY, Chang CC, Tseng WYI, Liu KL. Renal perfusion 3-T MR imaging: a comparative study of arterial spin labeling and dynamic contrast-enhanced techniques. Radiology 2011;261:845–53. https://doi.org/10.1148/radiol.11110668.

[23] Kim DW, Shim WH, Yoon SK, Oh JY, Kim JK, Jung H, et al. Measurement of arterial transit time and renal blood flow using pseudocontinuous ASL MRI with multiple post-labeling delays: feasibility, reproducibility, and variation. J Magn Reson Imaging 2017;46:813–9. https://doi.org/10.1002/jmri.25634.

[24] Conlin CC, Oesingmann N, Bolster B, Huang Y, Lee VS, Zhang JL. Renal plasma flow (RPF) measured with multiple-inversion-time arterial spin labeling (ASL) and tracer kinetic analysis: validation against a dynamic contrast-enhancement method. Magn Reson Imaging 2017;37:51–5. https://doi.org/10.1016/j.mri.2016.11.010.

[25] Shirvani S, Tokarczuk P, Statton B, Quinlan M, Berry A, Tomlinson J, et al. Motion-corrected multiparametric renal arterial spin labelling at 3 T: reproducibility and effect of vasodilator challenge. Eur Radiol 2019;29:232–40. https://doi.org/10.1007/s00330-018-5628-3.

[26] Notohamiprodjo M, Sourbron S, Staehler M, Michaely HJ, Attenberger UI, Schmidt GP, et al. Measuring perfusion and permeability in renal cell carcinoma with dynamic contrast-enhanced mri: a pilot study. J Magn Reson Imaging 2010;31:490–501. https://doi.org/10.1002/jmri.22028.

[27] Palmowski M, Schifferdecker I, Zwick S, Macher-Goeppinger S, Laue H, Haferkamp A, et al. Tumor perfusion assessed by dynamic contrast-enhanced MRI correlates to the grading of renal cell carcinoma: initial results. Eur J Radiol 2010;74:e176–80. https://doi.org/10.1016/j.ejrad.2009.05.042.

[28] Flaherty KT, Rosen MA, Heitjan DF, Gallagher ML, Schwartz B, Schnall MD, et al. Pilot study of DCE-MRI to predict progression-free survival with sorafenib therapy in renal cell carcinoma. Cancer Biol Ther 2008;7:496–501. https://doi.org/10.4161/cbt.7.4.5624.

[29] Hahn OM, Yang C, Medved M, Karczmar G, Kistner E, Karrison T, et al. Dynamic contrast-enhanced magnetic resonance imaging pharmacodynamic biomarker study of sorafenib in metastatic renal carcinoma. J Clin Oncol 2008;26:4572–8. https://doi.org/10.1200/JCO.2007.15.5655.

[30] Hudson JM, Bailey C, Atri M, Stanisz G, Milot L, Williams R, et al. The prognostic and predictive value of vascular response parameters measured by dynamic contrast-enhanced-ct, -mri and-us in patients with metastatic renal cell carcinoma receiving sunitinib. Eur Radiol 2018;28:2281–90. https://doi.org/10.1007/s00330-017-5220-2.

[31] Li LP, Tan H, Thacker JM, Li W, Zhou Y, Kohn O, et al. Evaluation of renal blood flow in chronic kidney disease using arterial spin labeling perfusion magnetic resonance imaging. Kidney Int Rep 2017;2:36–43. https://doi.org/10.1016/j.ekir.2016.09.003.

[32] Prasad PV, Li LP, Thacker JM, Li W, Hack B, Kohn O, et al. Cortical perfusion and tubular function as evaluated by magnetic resonance imaging correlates with annual loss in renal function in moderate chronic kidney disease. Am J Nephrol 2019;49:114–24. https://doi.org/10.1159/000496161.

[33] Tan H, Koktzoglou I, Prasad PV. Renal perfusion imaging with two-dimensional navigator gated arterial spin labeling. Magn Reson Med 2014;71:570–9. https://doi.org/10.1002/mrm.24692.

[34] Rossi C, Artunc F, Martirosian P, Schlemmer HP, Schick F, Boss A. Histogram analysis of renal arterial spin labeling perfusion data reveals differences between volunteers and patients with mild chronic kidney disease. Invest Radiol 2012;47:490–6. https://doi.org/10.1097/RLI.0b013e318257063a.

[35] Breidthardt T, Cox EF, Squire I, Odudu A, Omar NF, Eldehni MT, et al. The pathophysiology of the chronic cardiorenal syndrome: a magnetic resonance imaging study. Eur Radiol 2015;25:1684–91. https://doi.org/10.1007/s00330-014-3571-5.

[36] Gillis KA, McComb C, Patel RK, Stevens KK, Schneider MP, Radjenovic A, et al. Non-contrast renal magnetic resonance imaging to assess perfusion and corticomedullary differentiation in health and chronic kidney disease. Nephron 2016;133(3):183–92. https://doi.org/10.1159/000447601.

[37] Odudu A, Nery F, Harteveld AA, Evans RG, Pendse D, Buchanan CE, et al. Arterial spin labelling MRI to measure renal perfusion: a systematic review and statement paper. Nephrol Dial Transplant 2018;33(ii):15–21. https://doi.org/10.1093/ndt/gfy180.

[38] Hart A, Smith JM, Skeans MA, Gustafson SK, Stewart DE, Cherikh WS, et al. OPTN/SRTR 2015 annual data report: kidney. Am J Transplant 2017;17:21–116. https://doi.org/10.1111/ajt.14124.

[39] Benjamens S, Glaudemans AWJM, Berger SP, Slart RHJA, Pol RA. Have we forgotten imaging prior to and after kidney transplantation? Eur Radiol 2018;28:3263–7. https://doi.org/10.1007/s00330-018-5358-6.

[40] Artz NS, Sadowski EA, Wentland AL, Grist TM, Seo S, Djamali A, et al. Arterial spin labeling MRI for assessment of perfusion in native and transplanted kidneys. Magn Reson Imaging 2011;29:74–82. https://doi.org/10.1016/j.mri.2010.07.018.

[41] Niles DJ, Artz NS, Djamali A, Sadowski EA, Grist TM, Fain SB. Longitudinal assessment of renal perfusion and oxygenation in transplant donor-recipient pairs using arterial spin labeling and blood oxygen level-dependentmagnetic resonance imaging. Invest Radiol 2016;51:113–20. https://doi.org/10.1097/RLI.0000000000000210.

[42] Ren T, Wen CL, Chen LH, Xie SS, Cheng Y, Fu YX, et al. Evaluation of renal allografts function early after transplantation using intravoxel incoherent motion and arterial spin labeling MRI. Magn Reson Imaging 2016;34:908–14. https://doi.org/10.1016/j.mri.2016.04.022.

[43] Hueper K, Gueler F, Bräsen JH, Gutberlet M, Jang MS, Lehner F, et al. Functional MRI detects perfusion impairment in renal allografts with delayed graft function. Am J Physiol Renal Physiol 2015;308:F1444–51. https://doi.org/10.1152/ajprenal.00064.2015.

[44] van Eijs MJM, van Zuilen AD, de Boer A, Froeling M, Nguyen TQ, Joles JA, et al. Innovative perspective: gadolinium-free magnetic resonance imaging in long-term follow-up after kidney transplantation. Front Physiol 2017;8:1–12. https://doi.org/10.3389/fphys.2017.00296.

[45] Coenegrachts K, Van Steenbergen W, De Keyzer F, Vanbeckevoort D, Bielen D, Chen F, et al. Dynamic contrast-enhanced MRI of the pancreas: initial results in healthy volunteers and patients with chronic pancreatitis. J Magn Reson Imaging 2004;20:990–7.

[46] Akisik MF, Sandrasegaran K, Bu G, Lin C, Hutchins GD, Chiorean EG. Pancreatic cancer: utility of dynamic contrast-enhanced MR imaging in assessment of antiangiogenic therapy. Radiology 2010;256:441–9.

[47] Kim JH, Lee JM, Park JH, Kim SC, Joo I, Han JK, et al. Solid pancreatic lesions: characterization by using timing bolus dynamic contrast-enhanced MR imaging assessment—a preliminary study. Radiology 2013;266:185–96.

[48] Heverhagen JT, Wagner H, Ebel H, Levine AL, Klose KJ, Hellinger A. Pancreatic transplants: noninvasive evaluation with secretin-augmented mr pancreatography and MR perfusion measurements—preliminary results. Radiology 2004;233:273–80.

[49] Van Laethem JL, Verslype C, Iovanna JL, Michl P, Conroy T, Louvet C, et al. New strategies and designs in pancreatic cancer research: consensus guidelines report from a European expert panel. Ann Oncol 2012;23:570–6.

[50] Sheiman RG, Sitek A. Feasibility of measurement of pancreatic perfusion compartment kinetic model enhanced CT images. Radiology 2008;249(3):878–82.

[51] Bize PE, Platon A, Becker CD, Poletti PA. Perfusion measurement in acute pancreatitis using dynamic perfusion MDCT. Am J Roentgenol 2006;186:114–8.

[52] Bali MA, Devie J. Pancreatic perfusion: noninvasive quantitative assessment with dynamic contrast-enhanced MR imaging healthy volunteers—initial results. Radiology 2008;247:115–21.

[53] Yao X, Zeng M, Wang H, Sun F, Rao S, Ji Y. Evaluation of pancreatic cancer by multiple breath-hold dynamic contrast-enhanced magnetic resonance imaging at 3.0T. Eur J Radiol 2012;81:e917–22.

[54] Schraml C, Schwenzer NF, Martirosian P, Claussen CD, Schick F. Perfusion imaging of the pancreas using an arterial spin labeling technique. J Magn Reson Imaging 2008;28:1459–65.

[55] Cox EF, Smith JK, Chowdhury AH, Lobo DN, Francis ST, Simpson J. Temporal assessment of pancreatic blood flow and perfusion following secretin stimulation using noninvasive MRI. J Magn Reson Imaging 2015;42:1233–40.

[56] Huh J, Choi Y, Woo DC, Seo N, Kim B, Lee CK, et al. Feasibility of test-bolus DCE-MRI using CAIPIRINHA-VIBE for the evaluation of pancreatic malignancies. Eur Radiol 2016;26:3949–56.

[57] Chen Y, Pahwa S, Griswold M, Seiberlich N, Gulani V. 3D pancreatic perfusion MRI using through-time spiral GRAPPA acceleration. Proc Int Soc Magn Reson Med 2017;25:324.

[58] Schawkat K, Ith M, Christe A, Kühn W, Chittazhathu Y, Bains L, et al. Dynamic non-invasive asl perfusion imaging of a normal pancreas with secretin augmented mr imaging. Eur Radiol 2018;28:2389–96. https://doi.org/10.1007/s00330-017-5227-8.

[59] Taso M, Guidon A, Zhao L, Mortele KJ, Alsop DC. Pancreatic perfusion and arterial-transit-time quantification using pseudocontinuous arterial spin labeling at 3T. Magn Reson Med 2019;81:542–50. https://doi.org/10.1002/mrm.27435.

[60] Naish JH, Hutchinson CE, Caunce A, Roberts C, Waterton JC, Hockings PD, et al. Multiple-bolus dynamic contrast-enhanced MRI in the pancreas during a glucose challenge. J Magn Reson Imaging 2010;32:622–8.

[61] Siegel RL, Miller KD, Jemal A. Cancer statistics, 2019. CA Cancer J Clin 2019;69:7–34. https://doi.org/10.3322/caac.21551.

[62] Maria A, Bali M, Thierry Metens P, Vincent Denolin P, Myriam Delhaye P, Pieter Demetter P, Jean Closset M, et al. Tumoral and nontumoral pancreas: correlation between quantitative dynamic contrast- enhanced MR imaging and histopathologic parameters. Radiology 2011;261:456–66.

[63] Hu R, Yang H, Chen Y, Zhou T, Zhang J, Chen TW, et al. Dynamic contrast-enhanced MRI for measuring pancreatic perfusion in acute pancreatitis: a preliminary study. Acad Radiol 2019;26:1641–9. https://doi.org/10.1016/j.acra.2019.02.007.

[64] Franiel T, Lüdemann L, Rudolph B, Rehbein H, Staack A, Taupitz M, et al. Evaluation of normal prostate tissue, chronic prostatitis, and prostate cancer by quantitative perfusion analysis using a dynamic contrast-enhanced inversion-prepared dual-contrast gradient echo sequence. Invest Radiol 2008;43(7):481–7. https://doi.org/10.1097/RLI.0b013e31816b2f63.

[65] Barentsz JO, Engelbrecht M, Jager GJ, Witjes JA, De LaRosette J, Van Der Sanden BPJ, et al. Fast dynamic gadolinium-enhanced MR imaging of urinary bladder and prostate cancer. J Magn Reson Imaging 1999;10(3):295–304. https://doi.org/10.1002/(SICI)1522-2586(199909)10:3<295::AID-JMRI10>3.0.CO;2-Z.

[66] Engelbrecht MR, Huisman HJ, Laheij RJF, Jager GJ, Van Leenders GJLH, Hulsbergen-Van De Kaa CA, et al. Discrimination of prostate cancer from normal peripheral zone and central gland tissue by using dynamic contrast-enhanced MR imaging. Radiology 2003;229(1):248–54. https://doi.org/10.1148/radiol.2291020200.

[67] Li X, Metzger GJ. Feasibility of measuring prostate perfusion with arterial spin labeling. NMR Biomed 2013;26:51–7. https://doi.org/10.1002/nbm.2818.

[68] Cai W, Li F, Wang J, Du H, Wang X, Zhang J, et al. A comparison of arterial spin labeling perfusion MRI and DCE-MRI in human prostate cancer. NMR Biomed 2014;27:817–25. https://doi.org/10.1002/nbm.3124.

[69] Ream JM, Doshi AM, Dunst D, Parikh N, Kong MX, Babb JS, et al. Dynamic contrast-enhanced MRI of the prostate: an intraindividual assessment of the effect of temporal resolution on qualitative detection and quantitative analysis of histopathologically proven prostate cancer. J Magn Reson Imaging 2017;45:1464–75. https://doi.org/10.1002/jmri.25451.

[70] Winkel DJ, Heye TJ, Benz MR, Glessgen CG, Wetterauer C, Bubendorf L, et al. Compressed sensing radial sampling MRI of prostate perfusion: utility for detection of prostate cancer. Radiology 2019;290:702–8. https://doi.org/10.1148/radiol.2018180556.

[71] Schlemmer HP, Merkle J, Grobholz R, Jaeger T, Michel MS, Werner A, et al. Can pre-operative contrast-enhanced dynamic MR imaging for prostate cancer predict microvessel density in prostatectomy specimens? Eur Radiol 2004;14:309–17. https://doi.org/10.1007/s00330-003-2025-2.

[72] Tamada T, Sone T, Higashi H, Jo Y, Yamamoto A, Kanki A, et al. Prostate cancer detection in patients with total serum prostate-specific antigen levels of 4-10 ng/mL: diagnostic efficacy of diffusion-weighted imaging, dynamic contrast-enhanced MRI, and T2-weighted imaging. Am J Roentgenol 2011;197:664–70. https://doi.org/10.2214/AJR.10.5923.

[73] Turkbey B, Mani H, Shah V, Rastinehad AR, Bernardo M, Pohida T, et al. Multiparametric 3T prostate magnetic resonance imaging to detect cancer: histopathological correlation using prostatectomy specimens processed in customized magnetic resonance imaging based molds. J Urol 2011;186(5):1818–24. https://doi.org/10.1016/j.juro.2011.07.013.

[74] Franiel T, Lüdemann L, Taupitz M, Böhmer D, Beyersdorff D. MRI before and after external beam intensity-modulated radiotherapy of patients with prostate cancer: the feasibility of monitoring of radiation-induced tissue changes using a dynamic contrast-enhanced inversion-prepared dual-contrast gradient echo sequen. Radiother Oncol 2009;93:241–5. https://doi.org/10.1016/j.radonc.2009.08.016.
[75] Low RN, Fuller DB, Muradyan N. Dynamic gadolinium-enhanced perfusion MRI of prostate cancer: assessment of response to hypofractionated robotic stereotactic body radiation therapy. Am J Roentgenol 2011;197:907–15. https://doi.org/10.2214/AJR.10.6356.
[76] Moman MR, van den Berg CAT, Boeken Kruger AE, Battermann JJ, Moerland MA, van der Heide UA, et al. Focal salvage guided by T2-weighted and dynamic contrast-enhanced magnetic resonance imaging for prostate cancer recurrences. Int J Radiat Oncol Biol Phys 2010;76(3):741–6. https://doi.org/10.1016/j.ijrobp.2009.02.055.
[77] DeSantis CE, Ma J, Gaudet MM, Newman LA, Miller KD, Goding Sauer A, et al. Breast cancer statistics, 2019. CA Cancer J Clin 2019;69:438–51. https://doi.org/10.3322/caac.21583.
[78] Azamjah N, Soltan-Zadeh Y, Zayeri F. Global trend of breast cancer mortality rate: a 25-year study. Asian Pac J Cancer Prev 2019;20:2015–20. https://doi.org/10.31557/APJCP.2019.20.7.2015.
[79] Mann RM, Cho N, Moy L. Reviews and commentary: state of the art. Radiology 2019;292:520–36. https://doi.org/10.1148/radiol.2019182947.
[80] Kim SH, Lee HS, Kang BJ, Song BJ, Bin KH, Lee H, et al. Dynamic contrast-enhanced MRI perfusion parameters as imaging biomarkers of angiogenesis. PLoS One 2016;11:1–12. https://doi.org/10.1371/journal.pone.0168632.
[81] Saranathan M, Rettmann DW, Hargreaves BA, Lipson JA, Daniel BL. Variable spatiotemporal resolution three-dimensional dixon sequence for rapid dynamic contrast-enhanced breast MRI. J Magn Reson Imaging 2014;40:1392–9. https://doi.org/10.1002/jmri.24490.
[82] Kuhl CK, Schild HH, Morakkabati N. Dynamic bilateral contrast-enhanced MR imaging of the breast: trade-off between spatial and temporal resolution. Radiology 2005;236:789–800.
[83] The American College of Radiology. Practice parameter for the performance of contrast-enhanced magnetic resonance imaging (CE-MRI) of the breast. J Am Coll Radiol 2018;1076:1–11.
[84] Turnbull LW. Dynamic contrast-enhanced MRI in the diagnosis and management of breast cancer. NMR Biomed 2009;22:28–39. https://doi.org/10.1002/nbm.1273.
[85] Plewes DB, Bishop J, Soutar I, Cohen E. Errors in quantitative dynamic three-dimensional keyhole MR imaging of the breast. J Magn Reson Imaging 1995;5(3):361–4. https://doi.org/10.1002/jmri.1880050322.
[86] Saranathan M, Rettmann DW, Hargreaves BA, Clarke SE, Vasanawala SS. DIfferential subsampling with cartesian ordering (DISCO): a high spatio-temporal resolution Dixon imaging sequence for multiphasic contrast enhanced abdominal imaging. J Magn Reson Imaging 2012;35:1484–92. https://doi.org/10.1002/jmri.23602.
[87] Le Y, Kipfer H, Majidi S, Holz S, Dale B, Geppert C, et al. Application of time-resolved angiography with stochastic trajectories (twist)-dixon in dynamic contrast-enhanced (dce) breast mri. J Magn Reson Imaging 2013;38:1033–42. https://doi.org/10.1002/jmri.24062.
[88] Ramsay E, Causer P, Hill K, Plewes D. Adaptive bilateral breast MRI using projection reconstruction time-resolved imaging of contrast kinetics. J Magn Reson Imaging 2006;24:617–24. https://doi.org/10.1002/jmri.20685.
[89] Morrison CK, Henze Bancroft LC, DeMartini WB, Holmes JH, Wang K, Bosca RJ, et al. Novel high spatiotemporal resolution versus standard-of-care dynamic contrast-enhanced breast MRI: comparison of image quality. Invest Radiol 2017;52:198–205. https://doi.org/10.1097/RLI.0000000000000329.
[90] Heacock L, Gao Y, Heller SL, Melsaether AN, Babb JS, Block TK, et al. Comparison of conventional DCE-MRI and a novel golden-angle radial multicoil compressed sensing method for the evaluation of breast lesion conspicuity. J Magn Reson Imaging 2017;45:1746–52. https://doi.org/10.1002/jmri.25530.

[91] Vreemann S, Rodriguez-Ruiz A, Nickel D, Heacock L, Appelman L, Van Zelst J, et al. Compressed sensing for breast MRI: resolving the trade-off between spatial and temporal resolution. Invest Radiol 2017;52:574–82. https://doi.org/10.1097/RLI.0000000000000384.

[92] Li SP, Padhani AR, Taylor NJ, Beresford MJ, Ah-See MLW, Stirling JJ, et al. Vascular characterisation of triple negative breast carcinomas using dynamic MRI. Eur Radiol 2011;21:1364–73. https://doi.org/10.1007/s00330-011-2061-2.

[93] D'Arcy JA, Collins DJ, Padhani AR, Walker-Samuel S, Suckling J, Leach MO. Informatics in radiology (info RAD): magnetic resonance imaging work-bench: analysis and visualization of dynamic contrast-enhanced MR imaging data. Radiographics 2006;26:621–32. https://doi.org/10.1148/rg.262045187.

[94] Tofts PS, Brix G, Buckley DL, Evelhoch JL, Henderson E, Knopp MV, et al. Estimating kinetic parameters from dynamic contrast-enhanced T1-weighted MRI of a diffusable tracer: standardized quantities and symbols. J Magn Reson Imaging 1999;10:223–32. https://doi.org/10.1002/(SICI)1522-2586(199909)10:3<223::AID-JMRI2>3.0.CO;2-S.

[95] Liu F, Wang M, Li H. Role of perfusion parameters on DCE-MRI and ADC values on DWMRI for invasive ductal carcinoma at 3.0 tesla. World J Surg Oncol 2018;16:1–12. https://doi.org/10.1186/s12957-018-1538-8.

[96] Li L, Wang K, Sun X, Wang K, Sun Y, Zhang G, et al. Parameters of dynamic contrast-enhanced mri as imaging markers for angiogenesis and proliferation in human breast cancer. Med Sci Monit 2015;21:376–82. https://doi.org/10.12659/MSM.892534.

[97] Park VY, Kim EK, Kim MJ, Yoon JH, Moon HJ. Perfusion parameters on breast dynamic contrast-enhanced MRI are associated with disease-specific survival in patients with triple-negative breast cancer. Am J Roentgenol 2017;208:687–94. https://doi.org/10.2214/AJR.16.16476.

[98] Yim H, Kang DK, Jung YS, Jeon GS, Kim TH. Analysis of kinetic curve and model-based perfusion parameters on dynamic contrast enhanced MRI in breast cancer patients: correlations with dominant stroma type. Magn Reson Imaging 2016;34:60–5. https://doi.org/10.1016/j.mri.2015.07.010.

[99] Makkat S, Luypaert R, Stadnik T, Bourgain C, Sourbron S, Dujardin M, et al. Deconvolution-based dynamic contrast-enhanced MR imaging of breast tumors: correlation of tumor blood flow with human epidermal growth factor receptor 2 status and clinicopathologic findings-preliminary results. Radiology 2008;249:471–82. https://doi.org/10.1148/radiol.2492071147.

[100] Fasching PA, Heusinger K, Haeberle L, Niklos M, Hein A, Bayer CM, et al. Ki67, chemotherapy response, and prognosis in breast cancer patients receiving neoadjuvant treatment. BMC Cancer 2011;11:486. https://doi.org/10.1186/1471-2407-11-486.

[101] Shin JK, Kim JY. Dynamic contrast-enhanced and diffusion-weighted MRI of estrogen receptor-positive invasive breast cancers: associations between quantitative MR parameters and Ki-67 proliferation status. J Magn Reson Imaging 2017;45:94–102. https://doi.org/10.1002/jmri.25348.

[102] de Bazelaire C, Calmon R, Thomassin I, Brunon C, Hamy AS, Fournier L, et al. Accuracy of perfusion MRI with high spatial but low temporal resolution to assess invasive breast cancer response to neoadjuvant chemotherapy: a retrospective study. BMC Cancer 2011;11:361. https://doi.org/10.1186/1471-2407-11-361.

[103] Wu J, Cao G, Sun X, Lee J, Rubin DL, Napel S, et al. Intratumoral spatial heterogeneity at perfusion MR imaging predicts recurrence-free survival in locally advanced breast cancer treated with neoadjuvant chemotherapy. Radiology 2018;288:26–35. https://doi.org/10.1148/radiol.2018172462.

[104] Goodwill AG, Dick GM, Kiel AM, Tune JD. Regulation of coronary blood flow. Compr Physiol 2017;7(2):321–82. https://doi.org/10.1002/cphy.c160016.

[105] Hoffman JIE, Spaan JAE. Pressure-flow relations in coronary circulation. Physiol Rev 1990;70(2)):331–90. https://doi.org/10.1152/physrev.1990.70.2.331.

[106] Fokkema DS, Van Teeffelen JWGE, Dekker S, Vergroesen I, Reitsma JB, Spaan JAE. Diastolic time fraction as a determinant of subendocardial perfusion. Am J Physiol Heart Circ Physiol 2005;288(5):H2450–6. https://doi.org/10.1152/ajpheart.00790.2004.

[107] Kramer CM, Barkhausen J, Bucciarelli-Ducci C, Flamm SD, Kim RJ, Nagel E. Standardized cardiovascular magnetic resonance imaging (CMR) protocols: 2020 update. J Cardiovasc Magn Reson 2020;22:17. https://doi.org/10.1186/s12968-020-00607-1.

[108] Jerosch-Herold M. Quantification of myocardial perfusion by cardiovascular magnetic resonance. J Cardiovasc Magn Reson 2010;12:57. https://doi.org/10.1186/1532-429X-12-57.

[109] Zierler KL. Theoretical basis of indicator-dilution methods for measuring flow and volume. Circ Res 1962;10:393–407. https://doi.org/10.1161/01.res.10.3.393.

[110] Kroll K, Wilke N, Jerosch-Herold M, Wang Y, Zhang Y, Bache RJ, et al. Modeling regional myocardial flows from residue functions of an intravascular indicator. Am J Physiol Heart Circ Physiol 1996; 271(4 Pt 2):H1643–55. https://doi.org/10.1152/ajpheart.1996.271.4.h1643.

[111] Axel L. Tissue mean transit time from dynamic computed tomography by a simple deconvolution technique. Invest Radiol 1983;18(1):94–9. https://doi.org/10.1097/00004424-198301000-00018.

[112] Broadbent DA, Biglands JD, Larghat A, Sourbron SP, Radjenovic A, Greenwood JP, et al. Myocardial blood flow at rest and stress measured with dynamic contrast-enhanced MRI: comparison of a distributed parameter model with a fermi function model. Magn Reson Med 2013;70(6):1591–7. https://doi.org/10.1002/mrm.24611.

[113] Biglands JD, Ibraheem M, Magee DR, Radjenovic A, Plein S, Greenwood JP. Quantitative myocardial perfusion imaging versus visual analysis in diagnosing myocardial ischemia: a CE-MARC substudy. JACC Cardiovasc Imaging 2018;11(5):711–8. https://doi.org/10.1016/j.jcmg.2018.02.019.

[114] Gulati A, Ismail TF, Ali A, Hsu L-Y, Gonçalves C, Ismail NA, et al. Microvascular dysfunction in dilated cardiomyopathy. JACC Cardiovasc Imaging 2019;12(8 Pt 2):1699–708. https://doi.org/10.1016/j.jcmg.2018.10.032.

[115] Li X, Springer CS, Jerosch-Herold M. First-pass dynamic contrast-enhanced MRI with extravasating contrast reagent: evidence for human myocardial capillary recruitment in adenosine-induced hyperemia. NMR Biomed 2009;22(2):148–57. https://doi.org/10.1002/nbm.1293.

[116] Bassingthwaighte JB, Wang CY, Chan IS. Blood-tissue exchange via transport and transformation by capillary endothelial cells. Circ Res 1989;65(4):997–1020. https://doi.org/10.1161/01.RES.65.4.997.

[117] Kellman P, Hansen MS, Nielles-Vallespin S, Nickander J, Themudo R, Ugander M, et al. Myocardial perfusion cardiovascular magnetic resonance: optimized dual sequence and reconstruction for quantification. J Cardiovasc Magn Reson 2017;19:43. https://doi.org/10.1186/s12968-017-0355-5.

[118] Brown LAE, Onciul SC, Broadbent DA, Johnson K, Fent GJ, Foley JRJ, et al. Fully automated, inline quantification of myocardial blood flow with cardiovascular magnetic resonance: repeatability of measurements in healthy subjects. J Cardiovasc Magn Reson 2018;20(1):48. https://doi.org/10.1186/s12968-018-0462-y.

[119] Virani SS, Alonso A, Benjamin EJ, Bittencourt MS, Callaway CW, Carson AP, et al. Heart disease and stroke statistics-2020 update: a report from the American Heart Association. Circulation 2020;141: e139–596. https://doi.org/10.1161/CIR.0000000000000757.

[120] Mordini FE, Haddad T, Hsu LY, Kellman P, Lowrey TB, Aletras AH, et al. Diagnostic accuracy of stress perfusion CMR in comparison with quantitative coronary angiography: fully quantitative, semiquantitative, and qualitative assessment. JACC Cardiovasc Imaging 2014;7:14–22. https://doi.org/10.1016/j.jcmg.2013.08.014.

[121] Hsu LY, Jacobs M, Benovoy M, Ta AD, Conn HM, Winkler S, et al. Diagnostic performance of fully automated pixel-wise quantitative myocardial perfusion imaging by cardiovascular magnetic resonance. JACC Cardiovasc Imaging 2018;11(5):697–707. https://doi.org/10.1016/j.jcmg.2018.01.005.

[122] Van Dijk R, Van Assen M, Vliegenthart R, De Bock GH, Van Der Harst P, Oudkerk M. Diagnostic performance of semi-quantitative and quantitative stress CMR perfusion analysis: a meta-analysis. J Cardiovasc Magn Reson 2017;19(1):92. https://doi.org/10.1186/s12968-017-0393-z.

[123] Kotecha T, Martinez-Naharro A, Boldrini M, Knight D, Hawkins P, Kalra S, et al. Automated pixel-wise quantitative myocardial perfusion mapping by CMR to detect obstructive coronary artery disease and coronary microvascular dysfunction: validation against invasive coronary physiology. JACC Cardiovasc Imaging 2019;12(10):1958–69. https://doi.org/10.1016/j.jcmg.2018.12.022.

[124] Sammut EC, Villa ADM, Di Giovine G, Dancy L, Bosio F, Gibbs T, et al. Prognostic value of quantitative stress perfusion cardiac magnetic resonance. JACC Cardiovasc Imaging 2018;11(5):686–94. https://doi.org/10.1016/j.jcmg.2017.07.022.

[125] Khan TZ, Hsu LY, Arai AE, Rhodes S, Pottle A, Wage R, et al. Apheresis as novel treatment for refractory angina with raised lipoprotein(a): a randomized controlled cross-over trial. Eur Heart J 2017;38(20):1561–9. https://doi.org/10.1093/eurheartj/ehx178.

[126] Camici PG, Crea F. Coronary microvascular dysfunction. N Engl J Med 2007;356:830–40. https://doi.org/10.1056/NEJMra061889.

[127] Ismail TF, Hsu LY, Greve AM, Gonçalves C, Jabbour A, Gulati A, et al. Coronary microvascular ischemia in hypertrophic cardiomyopathy—a pixel-wise quantitative cardiovascular magnetic resonance perfusion study. J Cardiovasc Magn Reson 2014;16(1):49. https://doi.org/10.1186/s12968-014-0049-1.

[128] Dauber IM, Van Benthuysen KM, McMurtry IF, Wheeler GS, Lesnefsky EJ, Horwitz LD, et al. Functional coronary microvascular injury evident as increased permeability due to brief ischemia and reperfusion. Circ Res 1990;66(4):986–98. https://doi.org/10.1161/01.RES.66.4.986.

[129] Sunnergren KP, Rovetto MJ. Myocyte and endothelial injury with ischemia reperfusion in isolated rat hearts. Am J Physiol Heart Circ Physiol 1987;252(6 Pt 2):H1211–7. https://doi.org/10.1152/ajpheart.1987.252.6.h1211.

[130] Berthezène Y, Croisille P, Wiart M, Howarth N, Houzard C, Faure O, et al. Prospective comparison of MR lung perfusion and lung scintigraphy. J Magn Reson Imaging 1999;9:61–8. https://doi.org/10.1002/(SICI)1522-2586(199901)9:1<61::AID-JMRI8>3.0.CO;2-Z.

[131] Ohno Y, Hatabu H, Higashino T, Takenaka D, Watanabe H, Nishimura Y, et al. Dynamic perfusion MRI versus perfusion scintigraphy: prediction of postoperative lung function in patients with lung Cancer. Am J Roentgenol 2004;182:73–8. https://doi.org/10.2214/ajr.182.1.1820073.

[132] Henzler T, Schmid-Bindert G, Schoenberg SO, Fink C. Diffusion and perfusion MRI of the lung and mediastinum. Eur J Radiol 2010;76:329–36. https://doi.org/10.1016/j.ejrad.2010.05.005.

[133] Risse F, Eichinger M, Kauczor HU, Semmler W, Puderbach M. Improved visualization of delayed perfusion in lung MRI. Eur J Radiol 2011;77:105–10. https://doi.org/10.1016/j.ejrad.2009.07.025.

[134] Johns CS, Swift AJ, Rajaram S, Hughes PJC, Capener DJ, Kiely DG, et al. Lung perfusion: MRI vs. SPECT for screening in suspected chronic thromboembolic pulmonary hypertension. J Magn Reson Imaging 2017;46:1693–7. https://doi.org/10.1002/jmri.25714.

[135] Fidler JL, Guimaraes L, Einstein DM. MR imaging of the small bowel. Radiographics 2009;29:1811–25. https://doi.org/10.1148/rg.296095507.

[136] Fletcher JG, Fidler JL, Bruining DH, Huprich JE. New concepts in intestinal imaging for inflammatory bowel diseases. Gastroenterology 2011;140:1795–1806.e7. https://doi.org/10.1053/j.gastro. 2011.02.013.

[137] Ippolito D, Lombardi S, Talei Franzesi C, Drago SG, Querques G, Casiraghi A, et al. Dynamic contrast-enhanced mr with quantitative perfusion analysis of small bowel in vascular assessment between inflammatory and fibrotic lesions in crohns disease: a feasibility study. Contrast Media Mol Imaging 2019. https://doi.org/10.1155/2019/1767620.

SECTION

3

Diffusion

CHAPTER

Physical and Physiological Principles of Diffusion

18

Christopher D. Kroenke
Advanced Imaging Research Center, Oregon Health & Science University, Portland, OR, United States

18.1 Introduction

In most applications of Magnetic Resonance Imaging (MRI), images are comprised of volume elements (voxels) on the order of 1–3 mm^3 for typical human studies. This resolution is sufficient to resolve sub-structures in many organs, such as the gray matter (GM), white matter (WM), and cerebrospinal fluid (CSF) in the brain. However, this size-scale is far too large to measure cellular-scale anatomy, such as individual axon and dendritic processes in neural tissue. Nevertheless, this is not to say that MRI cannot be used to assess the structure of cellular processes. One desirable feature of MRI is that the image intensity can be manipulated to encode various properties of tissue through different endogenous "contrast mechanisms," such as the longitudinal and transverse spin relaxation time constants T_1 and T_2, respectively. This portion of the book concerns the use of molecular diffusion as a contrast mechanism in MRI. As introduced in this chapter, water diffusion is a physical phenomenon that can be harnessed in so-called "diffusion-weighted" MRI, or "diffusion MRI" experiments, to probe the 1–10 μm size-scale structural environment and physiological status within every voxel of a MRI. Diffusion MRI data, therefore, measure characteristics of tissue that typically require light microscopy to visualize; however, the information is provided as aggregate quantities in MRI, averaged over entire image voxels, and this characteristic of diffusion MRI interferes with the straightforward interpretation of experimental results.

One example of the exquisite sensitivity of diffusion MRI to cell biological structures in brain tissue is the ability to measure the orientations of white matter fiber tracts (Fig. 18.1). In the corpus callosum, large differences in image intensity are observed for diffusion-weighted images depending on whether the diffusion-sensitizing gradients are applied parallel or perpendicular to the axon fibers. The goal of this chapter is to define the process of molecular diffusion, introduce how it is measured in MRI experiments, and review general characteristics of cellular morphology and physiology that are thought to be most influential in determining diffusion-mediated image contrast. Subsequent chapters provide more in-depth reviews of these topics. The example applications reviewed in this chapter are drawn from biomedical applications focused on brain tissue, however, it should be noted that considerable work uses diffusion MRI techniques to characterize multiple other organs, and with few exceptions, the principles described here are also applicable "below the neck."

Advances in Magnetic Resonance Technology and Applications. Volume 1. ISSN 2666-9099. https://doi.org/10.1016/B978-0-12-817057-1.00020-2

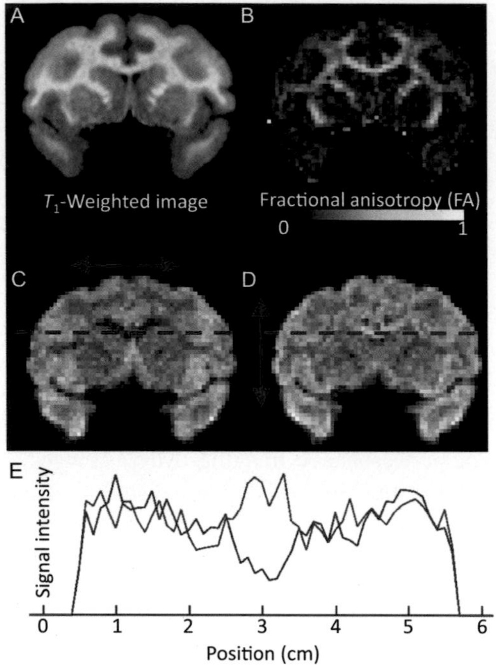

FIG. 18.1

Diffusion anisotropy in the brain. Coronal images of an adult rhesus macaque brain at a location that intersects the rostral corpus callosum (the genu). (A) A T_1-weighted "anatomical" image is shown, with relatively high resolution, consisting of isotropic 0.5-mm-sided voxels. (B) A map of fractional anisotropy (FA) of water diffusion for the same coronal image, with isotropic resolution of 1-mm-sided voxels. FA is defined in the text, and ranges from 0 (water diffusion does not depend on direction) to 1 (water diffusion depends very strongly on direction). High FA is observed within regions of white matter. (C) and (D) are two of the diffusion-weighted images used to calculate the FA image. In (C), the direction of diffusion sensitization is oriented left-to-right *(red arrow)*. Signal intensity is lowest in regions where water diffusion is least restricted in the left/right directions, such as the corpus callosum, where the red dashed line intersects the midline. In (D), the direction of diffusion sensitization is oriented dorsal-to-ventral *(blue arrow)*. Signal intensity is low in regions with vertically-oriented structures that do not restrict dorsal/ventral displacement. Notably, signal intensity is relatively high in the corpus callosum because myelinated axon fibers restrict displacement in the dorsal/ventral directions. Signal intensity is plotted as a function of left/right position in (E). The red trace is from (C) at the location of the *red dashed line*, and the blue trace is from (D) at the location of the *blue dashed line*. Signal intensity differs dramatically at the location of the corpus callosum ($\sim$3 cm).

(Data acquired in collaboration with Wang X, Weiss A, McBride J. Oregon National Primate Research Center.)

18.2 Diffusion

Many biological tissues can be viewed as compartments of aqueous solutions, with the different compartments being (1) membrane-bound cells and organelles and (2) the interstitial spaces between them. In a large single compartment of an aqueous solution, such as within a glass of water, many of the

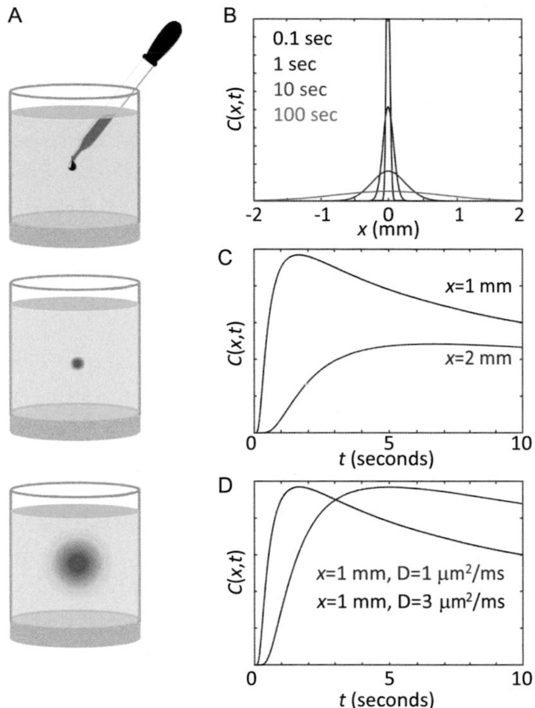

FIG. 18.2

Example of unrestricted diffusion in aqueous solution. (A) A small drop of red food coloring is introduced into the center of a glass of water. Over time (A, lower panels), diffusion will cause the food coloring to spread throughout the glass. (B) The concentration of food coloring as a function of position along the horizontal (*x*) axis at 0.1 *(black)*, 1 *(red)*, 10 *(blue)*, and 100 *(green)* seconds after the drop is introduced into the glass of water. As described in the text, the concentration profile is a Gaussian function of *x*, with a standard deviation that increases according to $\sqrt{2Dt}$. (C) The evolution of food coloring concentration 1 mm *(black)* and 2 mm *(red)* displaced from the center of the glass of water as a function of time. (D) The evolution of food coloring concentration at a location 1 mm displaced from the center, for a diffusion coefficient of 3 μm^2/ms *(black)* or 1 μm^2/ms *(red)*.

principles of molecular diffusion are highly intuitive. For example, a drop of food coloring placed in the middle of the glass at time $t=0$ will spread throughout the glass as time progresses (Fig. 18.2). Molecular self-diffusion is the process that underlies this redistribution of the concentration of the food coloring with time. A useful exercise for understanding how diffusion is measured with magnetic resonance techniques is to consider the concentration profile along a single direction, $C(x,t)$, which is a function of time t, and position along the direction axis, x. The evolution of $C(x,t)$ is governed by Fick's second law, which is also known as *the diffusion equation*, and it serves to define the diffusion coefficient, D [1]

$$\frac{\partial C(x,t)}{\partial t} = D\frac{\partial^2 C(x,t)}{\partial x^2} \tag{18.1}$$

Fig. 18.2 illustrates the implications of this 1-dimensional example. In a plot of the food coloring concentration as a function of position, the maximal value is at $x=0$, which is defined as the center of the drop. For any value of t, there is a region centered around the peak concentration that is concave-down, which means that the term $\partial^2 C/\partial x^2$ in the right-hand side of Eq. (18.1) is negative, and due to the requirement that D is positive, the concentration in this region decreases with time (i.e., $\partial C/\partial t$ on the left-hand side of Eq. (18.1) is negative). The remaining regions of the $C(x,t)$ curve are concave-up, and the concentration of food coloring increases with time as it spreads from the center of the glass outward throughout the liquid. As this occurs, the extent of the concave-down concentration profile expands, so that at any position $x \neq 0$, the concentration initially increases with time, and subsequently decreases (Fig. 18.2C). The diffusion coefficient influences the curves shown in Fig. 18.2D by determining the rate with which the food coloring spreads.

The diffusion equation can be used to determine the evolution of $C(x,t)$ provided a set of *initial conditions* and a set of *boundary conditions*. The initial conditions specify $C(x,t)$ at time $t=0$. In the example of food coloring being introduced at a point, it is assumed that $C(x,0)$ equals 0 for $|x| > 0$, and the total concentration equals 1. The boundary conditions define the spatial extent over which the food coloring can range. Food coloring cannot spread outside of the cup of water, and therefore a realistic boundary condition would be to impose that $C(x,t)=0$ for $|x| > r$, where r is the radius of the cup. However, for the sake of simplicity in this example, it will be assumed that the food coloring is not restricted by the boundary of the cup (i.e., r is very large relative to the spread over the time range of interest). Given these initial and boundary conditions, the Gaussian function of x, with a mean value, $\langle x \rangle = 0$, and a variance of $2Dt$, is a solution to the diffusion equation. Specifically,

$$C(x,t) = \frac{1}{\sqrt{4\pi Dt}} \exp\left(x^2/2Dt\right) \tag{18.2}$$

which can be verified by determining the derivative with respect to t (left-hand side of Eq. 18.1) and comparing it to the second derivative with respect to x multiplied by D. The variance in the position, x, of a food coloring molecule is $\langle x^2 \rangle - \langle x \rangle^2$. Owing to the fact that $\langle x \rangle = 0$, the standard deviation represents the root-mean-squared displacement $\langle x^2 \rangle^{\frac{1}{2}}$ for the food color molecules, and is given by

$$\langle x^2 \rangle^{\frac{1}{2}} = \sqrt{2Dt} \tag{18.3}$$

which is termed the Einstein relationship. The Einstein relationship extends the intuition that the dye will spread throughout the cup of water to the quantitative conclusion that the diffusion coefficient for a molecular species in a solution can be used to express the root-mean-squared displacement of the molecules at a given time t.

As will be reviewed here, diffusion MRI can provide measurements of D (or, more precisely, the "apparent diffusion coefficient," *ADC*) for molecules within living tissue, but in order to interpret these measurements, it is important to know the factors that can influence the value of D. The Stokes-Einstein expression

$$D = \frac{k_B T}{6\eta R} \tag{18.4}$$

is helpful in this regard. The diffusion coefficient is proportional to the absolute temperature T, and inversely proportional to the viscosity of the solution η, as well as the hydrodynamic radius of the molecule R. The remaining term in Eq. (18.4) is Boltzmann's constant k_B. The molecular species of interest in most diffusion MRI experiments performed on biological tissue is water. At a physiological temperature of 310K (37° C), the water diffusion coefficient is 3.0 μm^2/ms. At room temperature (293 K or 20° C), a value perhaps of relevance for diffusion MRI experiments performed on ex vivo tissue samples, the diffusion coefficient is 2.0 μm^2/ms. The viscosity of a dilute aqueous solution, such a cerebrospinal fluid, at 310 K (37° C) is ~0.7 cP, but at 293 K (20° C), it is ~1.0 cP. The reduced water diffusion coefficient at room temperature compared to physiological temperature thus reflects both a direct dependence on temperature given in Eq. (18.4), as well as an indirect effect through the temperature dependence on viscosity. As a comparison, corn syrup is characterized by a 100-fold higher viscosity than aqueous solution. Lastly, although diffusion-weighted MRI experiments nearly exclusively focus on water, in vivo MRI Spectroscopy methods have been employed to measure the diffusion coefficients of larger molecular species [2]. As predicted by Eq. (18.4), molecules with larger molecular weight (and hence, larger hydrodynamic radius) are characterized by smaller diffusion coefficients within a given solution. Given these factors, it is interesting that the water apparent diffusion coefficient (*ADC*, defined below) in most biological tissues is approximately 1 μm^2/ms, which is one third of the diffusion coefficient in temperature-matched dilute aqueous solution. Why is it this much lower? Although there is some ambiguity in its ultimate answer, this question will be discussed further in the following sections.

18.3 The Stejskal-Tanner pulse sequence: A magnetic resonance method for measuring diffusion

Diffusion MRI experiments do not directly measure cell morphology, but instead, they infer cellular structural properties by encoding properties of water diffusion in the intensity of the MRI signal. The techniques for doing this are described in detail in Chapter 19. Hahn [3] and Torrey [4,5] first introduced the mathematical framework for including diffusion in the description of magnetization dynamics in a MR experiment. Stejskal and Tanner [6] subsequently combined this theory with an experimental method, using pulsed magnetic field gradients, for measuring molecular diffusion. The Stejskal-Tanner method and its variants remains to be the most common method used for measuring diffusion with magnetic resonance techniques. The evolution of magnetization through the fundamental elements of a Stejskal-Tanner pulse sequence is diagrammed in Fig. 18.3. In this simplified example, the effects of spin relaxation are ignored.

The ^{1}H magnetization associated with a localized volume of tissue can be represented as a vector. In Fig. 18.3, the magnetization vector associated with one voxel within a 3D image is illustrated. For the purpose of describing the evolution of magnetization through the Stejskal-Tanner pulse sequence, the magnetization vector is conceptually decomposed into a series of magnetization vectors that would arise if the voxel were separated into a series adjacent sub-slices. The aggregate magnetization is the vector sum of the vectors associated with each sub-slice. Prior to the beginning of the pulse sequence, magnetization is aligned parallel to the static magnetic field of the MRI system. Following a radio frequency (RF) excitation pulse with a flip angle of 90°, magnetization is rotated into the transverse plane (time point A). At this point, magnetization could be described as "in-phase" due to the common phase of each sub-slice's magnetization vector in the *x-y* plane. The magnitude of the transverse magnetization vector at point A equals the magnitude of the longitudinal magnetization vector prior to the application of the 90° RF pulse. Between points A and B, a magnetic field gradient of

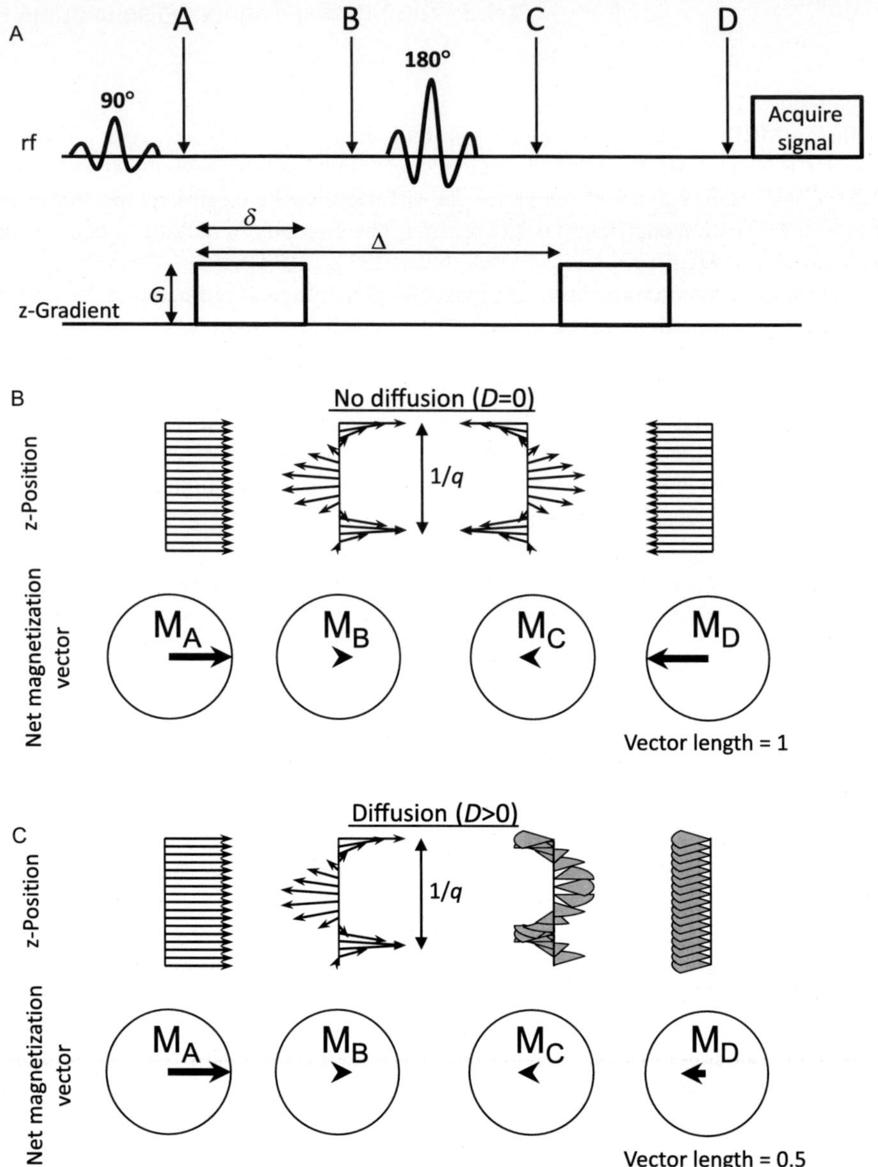

FIG. 18.3

A diagram of a Stejskal-Tanner pulse sequence for measuring molecular self-diffusion by MRI. (A) The timing of the primary elements of the pulse sequence. The *upper row* shows the radiofrequency (RF) excitation (90°) and refocusing (180°) pulses, followed by acquisition of the signal. The *lower row* shows the diffusion dephasing and refocusing gradient pulses, assumed to be aligned along the *z*-axis. The gradient pulses are characterized by amplitudes G, lengths δ, and interval between pulse onsets Δ (see text for details). The evolution of magnetization in the absence (B) and presence (C) of diffusion is considered for a set of sub-slices along the *z*-axis. In both cases, the dephasing gradient pulse converts the in-phase magnetization at time point A into a magnetization helix at time point B. The spatial frequency of the helix is q, as defined in the text, and the helix wavelength is $1/q$. In the presence of diffusion, the magnetization vector associated with each sub-slice is converted to a distribution of magnetization phases. Therefore, while magnetization is perfectly refocused in the absence of diffusion (B), magnetization is incompletely refocused in the presence of diffusion. The net magnetization vector in the transverse plane is thus of lesser magnitude in the presence of diffusion.

strength G, aligned along the z-axis, is applied. This gradient pulse has two effects. The first is to encode the phase of each sub-slice's magnetization vector to be the product of the gradient strength G, the duration of the gradient pulse δ, the position of the slice along the z-axis, and the gyromagnetic ratio for the nuclear spin of interest γ, which in this case is ^{1}H (the gyromagnetic ratio for ^{1}H is 267.5 $(\text{mT}\cdot\text{ms})^{-1}$). Thus, the expression for the magnetization phase for a sub-slice is $\varphi=\gamma G\delta z$, and as can be seen in Fig. 18.3, this organizes the set of magnetization vectors into a magnetization helix at time point B. The second effect of the applied magnetic field gradient pulse is to diminish the vector sum of the sub-slices, and hence the magnitude of the magnetization vector associated with the voxel, essentially to zero. Thus, the first magnetic field gradient pulse can be termed a "dephasing" pulse.

An important property of the magnetization helix produced by the dephasing gradient pulse is its spatial frequency, $q=\gamma G\delta/(2\pi)$. A standard clinical MRI instrument can produce a magnetic field gradient strength of 40 mT/m, and if it is applied during a 10 ms pulse, then the induced spatial frequency in ^{1}H magnetization phase is 267.5 $(\text{mT}\cdot\text{ms})^{-1} \times 40$ mT/m $\times$ 10 ms $\times 1/(2\pi)$ = 1.703×10^4 m^{-1}, or 0.017 μm^{-1}. The wavelength associated with this spatial frequency is the reciprocal of q (as indicated in Fig. 18.3), and is 59 μm.

Two scenarios will be considered for the evolution of magnetization beyond time point B in the Fig. 18.3 pulse sequence. The first scenario will consider the case where no diffusion occurs (e.g., $D=0$). Between time points B and C the refocusing RF pulse has the effect of reversing the polarity of the magnetization helix. Between time points C and D, a magnetic field gradient pulse of equal magnitude and duration to the dephasing pulse is applied, and due to the fact that the magnetization helix polarity was reversed by the refocusing RF pulse, the magnetization is "rephased" by this gradient pulse at time point D. The signal intensity for the voxel, which is proportional to the magnitude of the magnetization vector's projection onto the transverse plane, is ultimately not affected by the magnetic field gradient pulses.

In the second scenario, in the presence of diffusion, the magnetic field gradient pulses lead to an attenuation of the signal at time point D. For the water ^{1}H signal in an unrestricted dilute aqueous solution kept at 37°C, the diffusion coefficient equals 3.0 μm^2/ms. At time point B, the magnetization phase associated with sub-slice i, at position z_i, is $\gamma G\delta z_i$. Over the period between time points B and C, the concentrations of water molecules within sub-slice i will spread to neighboring sub-slices. According to Eq. (18.3), the root mean squared displacement will be $\sqrt{2Dt}$. In the terminology introduced by Stejakal and Tanner, the interval between the onsets of the two gradient pulses is labeled Δ. If Δ is 50 ms, the root-mean-squared displacement of spins originating at position z_i is $\sqrt{2Dt}=\sqrt{2\times 50\,\text{ms}\times 3\,\mu\text{m}^2/\text{ms}}=$ 17 μm. Thus, a water molecule that experiences a root-mean-squared displacement along the z axis by time point D will reside in a sub-slice associated with magnetization that possesses a phase difference of 360° × 17 μm/59 μm = 104° from the magnetization in sub-slice z_i. Owing to this shuffling of magnetization phases, the rephasing gradient pulse at point C produces a set of magnetization vectors that sum to a vector with magnitude less than the magnitude at time point B.

Stejeskal and Tanner [6] determined an analytical expression for the reduction in the magnetization vector magnitude due to diffusion, and defined the "b-value," $b=(\gamma\delta G)^2(\Delta-\delta/3)$. Under conditions of unrestricted diffusion, the signal intensity, S, depends on the b-value according to the relationship

$$S(b)/S(0)=\exp(-bD) \tag{18.5}$$

in which $S(0)$ is the signal intensity that would be observed in the absence of diffusion-sensitizing magnetic field gradient pulses. In the example gradient strengths and lengths described above,

$b = (267.5\ (\text{mT}\cdot\text{ms})^{-1} \times 40\ \text{mT/m} \times 10\ \text{ms})^2 \times 46.7\ \text{ms} = 0.53\ \text{ms}/\mu\text{m}^2$, and the signal remaining after the application of the diffusion-sensitization gradients is $S(b)/S(0) = exp(-0.53 \times 3) = 0.2$.

In practice, the diffusion coefficient of a molecular species can be determined by recording the signal intensity over a range of b-values, and performing a nonlinear fit for the parameters $S(0)$ and D (or to fit the logarithm of both sides of Eq. (18.5) to a line to determine $S(0)$ and D). There are three experimentally adjustable components intrinsic to the b-value. These are the diffusion-sensitizing gradient pulse amplitude G, length δ, and the inter-pulse interval Δ. The latter, or $(\Delta - \delta/3)$, which specifically appears in the definition of the b-value, is frequently referred to as the "diffusion time". There are practical, and in the case of restricted diffusion (i.e., diffusion restricted by the presence of boundaries) there are scientific reasons to motivate the specific choice of the three parameters to vary while performing diffusion measurements (e.g., see ref. [7]). By far the most common approach is to measure the signal intensity while varying the diffusion-sensitizing gradient amplitude G.

It is worthwhile to understand the similarities and differences between the Stejskal-Tanner method of measuring diffusion and the direct measurement of concentration changes illustrated in Fig. 18.2. The initial conditions for the Stejskal-Tanner experiment closely resemble the 1D initial condition shown in Fig. 18.2: the concentration of spins encoded with the phase $\gamma G \delta z_i$ is sharply peaked at position z_i immediately following the diffusion-encoding gradient pulse. The concentration of spins labeled with phase $\gamma G \delta z_i$ can therefore be approximated as a Gaussian function of distance from z_i, as given in Eq. (18.2). An important difference, however, is that all other sub-slices within the voxel also contribute to the signal intensity measured after the rephasing gradient pulse at time point D. In the case of water in an aqueous solution, the fact that the recorded signal is a weighted average of all sub-slices is of little consequence, as diffusion affects the signal intensities equally. However, if there are differences between sub-slices in either the diffusion coefficient, or in the boundary conditions restricting diffusion, the measured diffusion coefficient for the voxel will reflect an aggregate value. As will be explained below, such intra-voxel heterogeneity is present in virtually every diffusion measurement performed on biological tissue, and this presents a considerable challenge for interpreting diffusion MRI results in terms of the tissue's anatomical and physiological properties.

18.4 Diffusion in biological tissue

Heterogeneity in factors that influence molecular diffusion exists on several scales in biological tissue. On the size scale of an individual voxel (1–10 mm), there is heterogeneity in tissue subtype composition. This is also termed "partial volume averaging." On the size scale of the spatial wavelength for a standard Stejskal-Tanner experiment (1–10 μm), there is heterogeneity in the compartments of tissue.

For example, in diffusion MRI studies of the brain, it is common to classify voxels in terms of three main tissue subtypes, which are GM, WM, and CSF. For a voxel that contains more than one of these components, the measured signal intensity will be a weighted average: $S^{total}(b) = c_1 S^{CSF}(b) + c_2 S^{GM}(b) + c_3 S^{WM}(b)$. The weighting coefficients c_1, c_2, and c_3 depend on both the volume fractions and the spin relaxation characteristics of each tissue subtype. The effects of partial volume averaging have been addressed using various strategies, such as explicitly incorporating estimates of the weighting coefficients in the analysis, or excluding voxels that contain volume fractions above a threshold level for a certain tissue subcomponent.

Water diffusion differs dramatically between CSF and other components of brain tissue. The CSF is a dilute aqueous solution in which water diffusion is not impeded by biological membranes. Therefore, the water diffusion coefficient in CSF is 3.0 μm^2/ms. Water diffusion within cellular biological tissues such as GM and WM is quantified in terms of the *apparent* diffusion coefficient (*ADC*), rather than the diffusion coefficient *D*. The water *ADC* in GM and WM is $\sim$1 μm^2/ms. The qualification "apparent" is made for two reasons. First, the measured signal intensity results from an averaged diffusivity over all tissue microenvironments, including the extracellular space, and intracellular/intraorganellar spaces. If the diffusion coefficient of water is different within these different compartments, the average diffusivity could differ from the diffusivity within any of the individual compartments. Secondly, biological membranes impose restrictions on molecular displacement. As an example, the boundary conditions appropriate for diffusion within a cylinder with reflecting, or semi-permeable walls could be used to approximate diffusion within an axon. The *ADC* is therefore an operational definition of the diffusion coefficient that would be determined using Eq. (18.5) if diffusion within the voxel were uniform throughout, and unrestricted by boundaries. Although systematic differences exist between the data and the fitted mono-exponential expression (Eq. 18.5) have long been recognized [8,9], the standard practice in many applications is to use Eq. (18.5) in *ADC* determinations.

Additional differences exist between GM and WM. Most notably, in WM the *ADC* is highly *anisotropic*, whereas in most GM structures, the *ADC* is *isotropic* or only mildly anisotropic. In other words, in WM the *ADC* depends on the direction of the diffusion-sensitizing gradients, whereas in GM brain structures, the dependence on the direction of the diffusion-sensitizing gradient pair is subtle or completely absent. In the pulse sequence diagram shown in Fig. 18.3 pulse sequence diagram, the diffusion-sensitizing gradient pair was assumed to be along the *z*-axis. However, MRI systems are equipped with three magnetic field gradient coils, each orthogonal to the other two, that can produce gradients along the *x*, *y*, or *z*-axes. These gradient coils can also be combined to produce a magnetic field gradient along any arbitrary direction. In WM, if the diffusion sensitizing gradients are applied along a direction that is parallel to the underlying fiber axis, the measured *ADC* is larger than if the gradients are applied along a direction that is perpendicular to the fiber axis (Fig. 18.1) [10]. Interestingly, water diffusion is highly anisotropic in both myelinated and unmyelinated axon fascicles [11], which supports the interpretation that coherently oriented membranes, rather than myelin per se restrict diffusion in directions perpendicular to the fiber axis but not parallel to it. In GM, the organization of cells is in some sense more complex, and there is no preferential direction of unrestricted diffusion, or if there is, in most cases it only mildly differs with other directions. In analyses involving diffusion anisotropy, it is necessary to account for partial volume averaging effects between GM and WM, in a manner similar to that described for CSF, above.

18.5 Intravoxel incoherent motion

Blood is a fourth component of tissue that possesses unique characteristics in diffusion MRI experiments. Water molecules that are flowing within the vasculature will acquire a velocity-dependent phase throughout the course of the diffusion experiment of Fig. 18.3 (the effects of flow are described in detail in ref. [12]). However, the brain vasculature consists of a complex capillary network, and within a given voxel, velocity directions for blood in different vessels will contribute to an overall dephasing of the diffusion-weighted MRI signal. In recognition of the flow-based mechanism of dephasing rather than purely diffusion-based dephasing, measurements influenced by flow are sometimes said to be influenced by this intravoxel incoherent motion (IVIM). Complete dephasing of the flow-related mechanism is largely achieved at relatively small b-values compared to those used to measure diffusion [13]. Further, the blood volume fraction for most brain voxels is sufficiently small that the IVIM effect is small. However, early diffusion MRI measurements utilized instrumentation that could not generate high b-values [14], and therefore such studies were careful to utilize IVIM terminology [15]. Deliberate measurements of IVIM using low b-values are used to study organ systems that are more strongly affected by blood flow [16]. The standard approach in these studies is to replace Eq. (18.5) with a bi-exponential function in the analysis of the diffusion-weighted MRI signal intensity

$$S(b)/S(0) = f_{ivim}\exp(\text{-}bD^{*}) + (1 - f_{ivim})\exp(\text{-}bD) \tag{18.6}$$

in which f_{ivim} is the fraction of the MRI signal that arises from the blood, and D^{*} is a pseudo-diffusion coefficient that contains the contribution from incoherent flow, in addition to motion due to diffusion (see ref. [17] for a recent review).

18.6 Using anisotropy in water diffusion to characterize cellular anatomy

The observation of anisotropic water diffusion in axon fascicles using diffusion MRI was an extremely influential finding [10,11]. A second advance to occur shortly afterwards was the implementation of the diffusion tensor imaging (DTI) strategy for modeling diffusion in WM [18,19]. The DTI method of analysis provides a way to simultaneously estimate the direction of least (as well as the direction of the most) restricted diffusion, as well as the *ADC* values associated with these directions. From this information it is possible to infer the directions of white matter fascicles within each voxel in a 3D diffusion MRI dataset.

The DTI formalism characterizes diffusion within each image voxel with three different diffusion coefficients reflecting displacements along three orthogonal directions. To do this, the diffusion coefficient D is replaced by a 3×3 symmetric, positive definite matrix that represents a diffusion tensor. Both the direction and magnitude of the diffusion-sensitizing magnetic field gradient can be expressed by specifying the x, y, and z-components in a vector $\vec{G} = (G_x, G_y, G_z)$, and in so doing, the spatial direction and spatial frequency of the magnetization helix formed by the diffusion-sensitizing magnetic field gradient pulse are represented in the vector $\vec{q} = \gamma \vec{G}\,\delta/(2\pi)$. The Stejskal-Tanner expression (Eq. 18.5) in the presence of anisotropic diffusion, under the assumption that $\delta \ll \Delta$, becomes

$$S(\vec{q})/S(0) = \exp\left(\text{-}\Delta\,\vec{q}\,D\vec{q}^{T}\right) \tag{18.7}$$

and the matrix form for D is

$$D = \begin{pmatrix} D_{xx} & D_{xy} & D_{xz} \\ D_{xy} & D_{yy} & D_{yz} \\ D_{xz} & D_{yz} & D_{zz} \end{pmatrix} \tag{18.8}$$

Owing to the symmetry of the diffusion tensor ($D_{ij} = D_{ji}$), there are 6 distinct matrix elements of D. The three diagonal terms, D_{xx}, D_{yy}, and D_{zz} represent the diffusion coefficients, and, as shown in Eq. (18.3), are proportional to the variance in displacements (i.e., the mean squared displacement) parallel to the x, y, and z gradients, respectively. The three off-diagnoal terms D_{xy}, D_{xz}, and D_{yz}, represent covariance in

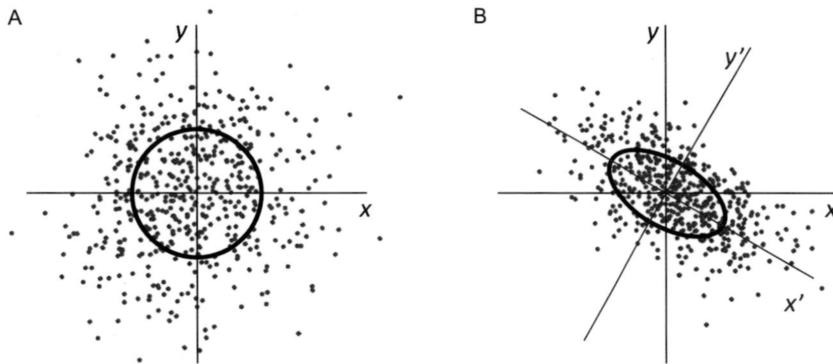

FIG. 18.4

Example molecular displacements in the *x-y* plane under conditions of (A) isotropic diffusion, as is encountered in brain cerebrospinal fluid, and (B) anisotropic diffusion, as is encountered in brain white matter. Each of the 250 *blue symbols* in each plot represents the displacement of one molecule from the origin over a 50 ms diffusion time. The standard deviation in displacements is indicated as a function of direction as a circle in (A) and an ellipse in (B). Under conditions of isotropic diffusion characterized by a diffusion coefficient of 3 μm²/ms, the standard deviation in the displacement distance is 17 μm. In (B), diffusion coefficients of 1 μm²/ms, and 0.25 μm²/ms, along the *x'* and *y'* axes *(red)* are simulated. The principal axis system for diffusion is represented by the *x'* and *y'* axes *(red)*, and these are rotated 30° from the *x* and *y* axes defined by the orientations of the magnetic field gradients *(black)*. As described in the text, the algebraic representation of the diffusion tensor differs between the principal reference frame and the frame of the diffusion gradients, such that it is diagonal in the principal axis frame.

molecular displacements along the subscripted directions. In order to illustrate the meaning of these terms, Fig. 18.4 compares isotropic displacements characterized by a diffusion coefficient of 3 μm²/ms, that might be anticipated for a voxel within CSF (Fig. 18.4A), with anisotropic displacements, that might be anticipated for a voxel within WM that courses through the *x-y* plane, oriented at a 30° angle to the *x*-axis. In the Fig. 18.4B example, diffusion parallel to the WM fiber axis is assumed to be characterized by a diffusion coefficient of 1 μm²/ms, and a value of 0.25 μm²/ms in directions perpendicular to the fiber axis. The dashed circle (Fig. 18.4A) and ellipse (Fig. 18.4B) represent the root mean squared displacement (which is proportional to the square root of the diffusion coefficient) as a function of orientation within the *x-y* plane. For isotropic diffusion, the root mean squared displacement is uniformly 17 μm for all orientations, consistent with a diffusion coefficient of 3 μm²/ms and assuming a 50 ms diffusion time. In contrast, for the example of anisotropic diffusion shown in Fig. 18.4B, the root mean squared displacement varies with orientation. It is 9.06 μm along the *x*-axis (D_{xx}=0.821 μm²/ms for a 50 ms diffusion time), it is 6.57 μm along the *y*-axis (D_{yy}=0.433 μm²/ms for a 50 ms diffusion time), and it achieves smaller values than 6.57 μm and larger values than 9.06 μm along directions not collinear with the *x* or *y*-axes. The covariance $\langle xy \rangle$ equals -32.6 μm², and correspondingly, D_{xy}=-0.326 μm²/ms for a 50 ms diffusion time. Along the *z* direction, the diffusion coefficient is 0.25 μm²/ms, and D_{xz} and D_{yz} are both zero because the fiber courses through the

x-y plane, and hence does not induce correlations between x or y displacements and displacements in the z direction. The diffusion tensor is therefore

$$D = \begin{pmatrix} 0.821 & -0.326 & 0 \\ -0.326 & 0.433 & 0 \\ 0 & 0 & 0.25 \end{pmatrix} \tag{18.9}$$

Notably, the off-diagonal terms of the diffusion tensor can attain negative values, but because the diagonal terms represent variances in displacement along specific directions, they are strictly positive. One could imagine that, if the orientation of the fiber bundle was oriented at a -30° angle to the x-axis, displacements in the x and y directions would be positively correlated, and a positive covariance $\langle xy \rangle$ of 32.6 μm^2 would be observed. In addition, if the fiber bundle was oriented parallel to the x-axis, displacement variance would be expected to be larger along the x direction, smaller along the y direction, and the covariance would be zero. The relative values of the diffusion tensor elements are influenced by both the size of the diffusion coefficient, and the orientation of the smallest and largest displacements.

It is possible to determine the direction and magnitude of smallest and largest displacements by diagonalizing the diffusion tensor. Specifically an eigenvalue decomposition of the diffusion tensor can be performed to express D in terms of a rotation matrix, R, and the diagonal matrix Λ

$$D = R\Lambda R^{-1} = R(\phi, \theta, \psi) \begin{pmatrix} \lambda_1 & 0 & 0 \\ 0 & \lambda_2 & 0 \\ 0 & 0 & \lambda_3 \end{pmatrix} R^{-1}(\phi, \theta, \psi) \tag{18.10}$$

The positive eigenvalues of the diffusion tensor (λ_1, λ_2, and λ_3) represent the diffusion coefficients that express molecular displacement within the principal axis system, in which the largest displacement variance is aligned along the x' direction, and the smallest is oriented along the z' direction of a local (voxel-specific) "principal" axis system. The Euler angles ϕ, θ, and ψ relate the orientation of the principal axis system to the directions of the x, y, and z gradients. The average of the three eigenvalues is the directionally-averaged apparent diffusion coefficient. This quantity is frequently termed the mean diffusivity (*MD*)

$$MD = (\lambda_1 + \lambda_2 + \lambda_3)/3 \tag{18.11}$$

The rows of the rotation matrix $R(\phi, \theta, \psi)$ are the eigenvectors of the diffusion tensor. In the example of Fig. 18.4B, diagonalization of the diffusion tensor expressed in Eq. (18.9) yields the three eigenvalues of 1.0, 0.25, and 0.25 $\mu m^2/ms$. A popular visualization method for representing the orientations of diffusion tensors in a 2D slice (Fig. 18.5A) is to show "whisker plots" reflecting the projection of the primary eigenvector (the eigenvector associated with the largest eigenvalue) onto the 2D slice.

The magnitude of diffusion anisotropy relates to the differences between the three eigenvalues of the diffusion tensor. If the eigenvalues are approximately equal, then diffusion is isotropic. In contrast, if there is a large difference between the largest and smallest eigenvalues, diffusion is highly anisotropic. Fractional anisotropy (FA) is a popular metric for expressing the magnitude of diffusion anisotropy [20]

$$FA = \sqrt{\frac{3}{2}} \sqrt{\frac{(\lambda_1 - MD)^2 + (\lambda_2 - MD)^2 + (\lambda_3 - MD)^2}{\lambda_1^2 + \lambda_2^2 + \lambda_3^2}} \tag{18.12}$$

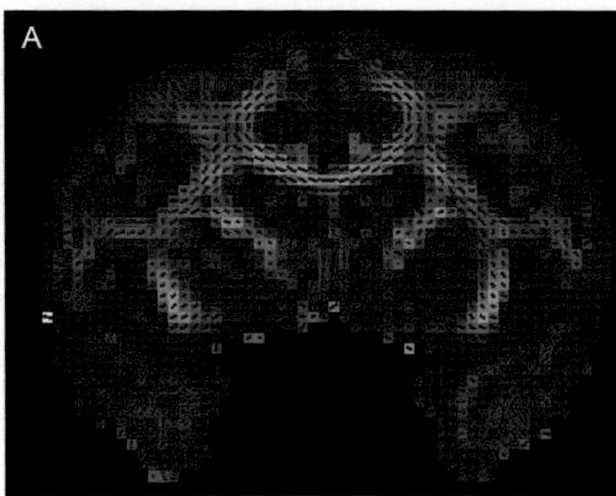

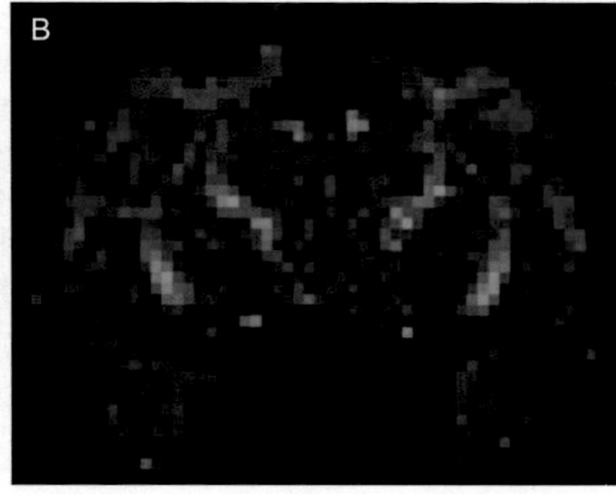

FIG. 18.5

Representation of diffusion tensor imaging analyses. (A) Maps of the diffusion tensor primary eigenvector for each voxel, projected onto the coronal plane, are overlaid in *red*. The underlay is an FA map. (B) A color-FA map, in which the direction of the primary eigenvector is encoded in the color, and the brightness of each voxel is proportional to FA. Colors are encoded such that *red* is proportional to the magnitude of the left/right primary eigenvector component, *green* is proportional to the through-plane (rostral/caudal) primary eigenvector component, and *blue* is proportional to the dorsal/ventral primary eigenvector component.

(Data acquired in collaboration with Wang X, Weiss A, McBride J. Oregon National Primate Research Center.)

This parameter ranges from 0 (equal eigenvalues) to 1 (extreme anisotropy, such that one of the eigenvalues equals zero). As an example, the value of FA for the displacements illustrated in Fig. 18.4B is 0.71. Diffusion anisotropy can be visualized in a grayscale *FA* map (Fig. 18.1B), or another popular method for simultaneously presenting direction and anisotropy information in a single image is to prepare a color *FA* map (Fig. 18.5B). In such a map, the image intensity is scaled by *FA*, and the color of a given voxel is determined by the x, y, and z components of the primary eigenvector, on a red/green/blue (rgb) scale. Specifically, the red, green, and blue color channels are rendered proportional to the x, y, and z components of the primary eigenvector, respectively.

18.7 Beyond FA and MD

Since the introduction of DTI, significant effort has been devoted to further extend the analysis of diffusion MRI data on the intra- and inter-voxel level. On the intra-voxel level, several alternates to the DTI modeling strategy have been proposed to facilitate more accurate and/or more detailed interpretations of diffusion MRI data and underlying cellular morphology. In recognition of the fact that axons are cylindrically symmetric structures, an approach has been proposed to analyze the diffusion tensor in terms of the diffusivity in the axial direction, parallel to the axon fiber bundle, which is equal to the largest eigenvalue $D_{ax} = \lambda_1$, and diffusivity in the radial direction, perpendicular to the axon bundle, which is the average of the two smaller eigenvalues $D_{rad} = (\lambda_2 + \lambda_3)/2$ [21]. In studies of WM pathology, it has been proposed that the former is sensitive to axon injury, while the latter is sensitive to myelin pathology. Many others have proposed mathematical models that are elaborations to the DTI analysis. Examples include the summation of multiple diffusion tensors, representing multiple WM fascicles of differing orientations intersecting the same voxel [22]; mathematical formulas to represent dispersion in fiber orientation [23,24], which is present in GM [25], as well as WM [26]; or explicit estimation of the average axon diameter [27], or distribution of diameters [28] of axons within a voxel. These modeling approaches are described in greater detail in other chapters of this volume (Chapters 20 and 22).

Inter-voxel analyses are another series of developments facilitated by DTI. As can be observed in the whisker plot of Fig. 18.5A, there is a tendency for adjacent WM voxels to have similar primary eigenvector orientations. This observation is not surprising, given that WM tracts are known to course through most neighboring voxels that have similar primary eigenvector orientations. Streamline tractography algorithms [29–31] were the first to utilize this observation to delineate WM fibers using the primary eigenvector field determined within an individual's brain. These algorithms are deterministic. They compute one fiber tract from a seed voxel by iteratively propagating to neighboring voxels by following the direction of the eigenvector until a stopping criterion is reached. Typical stopping criteria are that the tract encounters a voxel with lower than a threshold *FA* value, or that a turn of an angle exceeding a threshold value is necessary for further propagation of the tract. The second generation of tractography algorithms are termed probabilistic, rather than deterministic [32]. For these, a number of tracts are propagated from a given seed voxel, with the direction of each step of the tract being guided by a probability associated with the diffusion properties within the intersected voxel. From this procedure, the probability that a given pair of voxels, or the average probability within pairs of regions of voxels in the brain, can be estimated, in addition to the structure of the WM fiber system connecting the initiation and termination points. Further details of tractography procedures are described in Chapter 21 of this volume.

18.8 Sensitivity of diffusion to cellular physiology and metabolism

In addition to its high sensitivity to cellular structure, water diffusion revealed through MRI also strongly depends on dynamic tissue properties, such as physiological condition and perhaps metabolic rate. The most notable manifestation of this interrelationship is the striking, nearly immediate response of the water *ADC* to cerebral ischemia [10]. The water *ADC* acutely decreases by a factor of 30%–50% in the presence of an ischemic insult [33], and, as a consequence, regions of high signal intensity in a diffusion-weighted image can be used to delineate the affected tissue in clinical assessments of stroke [34,35]. An example diffusion-weighted image acquired on a rhesus macaque ~48 h following an experimentally induced ischemic event is shown, in comparison to T_1- and T_2-weighted images acquired at the same time, in Fig. 18.6.

In spite of three decades of scientific investigation, ambiguity remains regarding the mechanism by which cerebral ischemia leads to a rapid and significant *ADC* reduction. A number of cellular physiological changes are temporally coincident with the reduction in water *ADC*, including depletion of adenosine tri-phosphate (ATP), disruption of homeostatic ion gradient balance, and an increase in the intracellular volume fraction ("cell swelling") [36]. It has been challenging to establish causal relationships between any subset of such changes and a water *ADC* response because it is difficult to influence one of these factors without affecting the others.

Several specific mechanisms have been proposed for directly mediating the acute response in water *ADC* following ischemia [37]. The potential role of a shift in water from the extracellular to intracellular environment [38], and the ensuing intense investigations of this possibility, has had a strong influence on how diffusion MRI data are interpreted, both for applications to studies of brain physiology

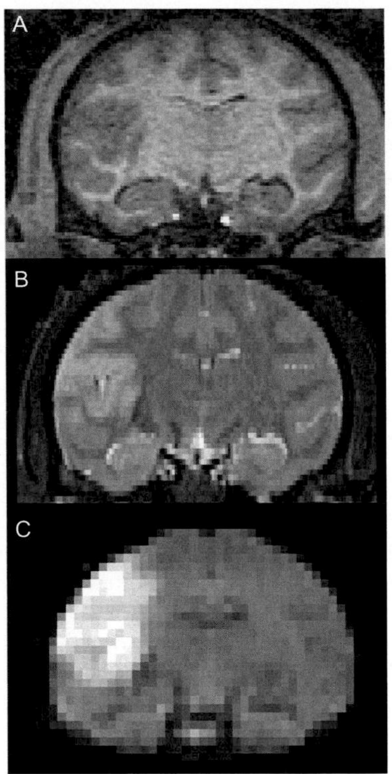

FIG. 18.6

The water ADC is reduced in ischemic brain tissue. Coronal (A) T_1-weighted, (B) T_2-weighted, and (C) diffusion-weighted images are shown of a rhesus macaque that suffered an ischemic event 48h prior to being imaged. The region of reduced diffusivity is obvious in the diffusion-weighted image, and can also be discerned in the T_2-weighted image.

(Data acquired in collaboration with Kohama S. Oregon National Primate Research Center.)

and structure. The analysis of tetramethylammonium ion (TMA+) diffusion, following its iontophoretic release in the brain extracellular space, is an established method for estimating the volume fraction of the extracellular space in brain tissue [39]. Under normal physiological conditions, the volume fraction of the extracellular space is 15%–20%, whereas under acute conditions of ischemia, the extracellular space is reduced to ~5% [36,40]. It has been proposed that the *ADC* associated with intracellular water is lower than that of extracellular water, and that the ischemia-induced reduction in overall (population-averaged) *ADC* arises from the redistribution of water from extracellular to intracellular spaces [38]. Such reasoning has also been extended to the analysis of the shape of the observed decay in signal intensity with increasing b-value magnitude. If the *ADC* values for the intracellular and extracellular spaces (ADC_{in} and ADC_{ex}, respectively) were uniform within those compartments, and if the permeability of boundaries separating the two compartments were sufficiently low to result in the slow exchange regime [41], then the signal decay with b-value would follow

$$S(b) = p_{in}\,exp(\text{-}bADC_{in}) + p_{ex}\,exp(\text{-}bADC_{ex}) \tag{18.13}$$

with p_{in} and p_{ex} reflecting the volume fractions of the intra- and extracellular compartments, and $p_{in}+p_{ex}=1$. Indeed, the "biexponential" Eq. 18.13 approximates experimental measurements much more closely than does a monoexponential equation such as Eq. (18.5) [8,9], however, such analyses associate the smaller *ADC* value with a volume fraction of ~0.2, which is inconsistent with the expected value of 0.8–0.85. Thus, regardless of whether cell swelling in the presence of differential intracellular and extracellular *ADC* values contribute to the ischemia-induced reduction in overall brain *ADC*, it is not straightforward to assign intracellular and extracellular water to rapidly and slowly exponentially decaying components of the MRI signal with increasing *b*-value.

Direct measurements of diffusion in brain intracellular and extracellular spaces have been performed as another strategy to test the proposal that cell swelling, in the presence of differential intracellular and extracellular *ADC* values, underlies the reduction in water *ADC* with ischemia. Duong and co-workers [42] introduced ^{19}fluoro-deoxyglucose (FDG) exclusively into the intracellular or extracellular brain compartments, and used ^{19}F Magnetic Resonance Spectroscopy methods to measure the *ADC* of this molecule in healthy and ischemic conditions. The findings that the intracellular and extracellular FDG *ADC* values were approximately equal, and both decrease under ischemic conditions, do not support the direct role of water redistribution due to cell swelling in the reduction of the water *ADC* with ischemia. An additional experiment utilizing a contrast reagent to selectively suppress the extracellular water [43] has provided further evidence that the intracellular and extracellular water *ADC* values are comparable.

Another method for directly characterizing intracellular and extracellular water diffusion has involved more nuanced modeling approaches than the biexponential formula in Eq. (18.13). Expressions have been derived for the case in which extracellular water is assumed to be hindered, but not restricted (i.e., diffusion in the presence of obstacles, such as permeable cell membranes), and intracellular water is restricted by cylindrical elements of varying degrees of orientation dispersion [23,24,44,45]. Within this framework, two combinations of solutions have been found that approximate diffusion MRI data equally well. In one case, the extracellular diffusivity is larger than the intracellular diffusivity, and in the other case, the extracellular diffusivity is smaller [46]. One strategy for removing this degeneracy has been to focus on endogenous molecules that are localized to the intracellular space. A study of *N*-acetylaspartate (NAA) showed that diffusion within neurons is approximately half the diffusion coefficient for NAA in temperature-matched free media [45], which is higher than would be expected if differential intra/extracellular diffusivity were to cause the reduction in water *ADC* following ischemic injury. Another way to remove the degeneracy in diffusion modeling is to perform diffusion measurements at multiple diffusion times, and this has also lead to findings consistent with intracellular diffusivity being large relative to extracellular diffusivity [47].

A third approach for directly measuring the intracellular water *ADC* is to utilize very small, and highly sensitive MRI signal reception and gradient instrumentation (the technique of "MRI microscopy") to resolve the intracellular compartments of large cells in diffusion-weighted images. This technique has demonstrated that the cytoplasmic water *ADC* is comparable to the temperature-corrected brain tissue water *ADC* in the giant axon of the squid [48], the *Aplysia* L7 neuron [49], and *Xenopus* oocyte [50]. As an interesting side note, although these efforts have not identified a difference between extracellular and cytoplasmic water *ADC* values, they have convincingly shown that the water *ADC* within the nucleus is markedly higher than the water *ADC* in cytoplasm. In fact, the water *ADC* in the nucleus more closely resembles free diffusion than diffusion within brain tissue [49,50].

This difference between nuclear and cytoplasmic diffusivity is also apparent in mammalian central nervous system cell types using highly specialized MRI microscopy instrumentation [51].

Given the experimental evidence against the large differences in water *ADC* values between the intracellular and extracellular environments necessary to support the cell swelling hypothesis, other possibilities have been proposed. One such proposal is that the neural shape changes associated with the increased intracellular volume fraction observed in ischemia causes the reduction in water *ADC* [52]. It has been demonstrated that axons form beaded structures, rather than cylinders, under stress. Extensive simulations support that, as dendrites and axons form beaded structures, the observed water *ADC* would decrease [52,53]. Thus beading could underlie the observed water diffusivity in ischemia.

Studies of the brain under normal conditions may provide additional insight into how cell physiological processes influence water diffusion. The water *ADC* has been reported to correlate with neural activity, and this phenomenon has been exploited in diffusion functional MRI (DfMRI) [54–56]. The biophysical mechanism linking the water *ADC* and neural activity is not completely understood, though cell swelling has been proposed to play a role [57]. In addition, the definitive assignment of neural-activity-related intensity fluctuations to changes in diffusion, rather than other potential factors related to IVIM, has also been scrutinized [58,59]. An alternative mechanism linking metabolic activity to the water *ADC* posits that intracellular/extracellular water exchange, mediated through coupling to sodium potassium pump activity, could regulate the water *ADC* by influencing the permeability of water to biological membranes [60]. Reduced permeability to cellular membranes has long been recognized as a potential mediator of the effect of ischemic conditions on the water *ADC* [61]. An attractive aspect of this proposed mechanism is that ATP hydrolysis is necessary to drive the sodium potassium pump, and therefore cellular energy failure in ischemia could be associated with a reduced permeability of water to biological membranes. Further evaluation of the role of this proposed mechanism would benefit from future experimental work to determine the water permeability to membrane systems of relevance to brain tissue, as well as theoretical work incorporating the effects of exchange between biological compartments.

18.9 Conclusions

Molecular diffusion is an endogenous contrast mechanism that allows researchers and clinicians to probe tissue on the cellular scale. Owing to the well-characterized physical principles and mathematics of factors that govern thermal molecular displacements, diffusion MRI is a very powerful method for characterizing cell morphology and physiological status. Further, water diffusion anisotropy in brain white matter and changes in the water *ADC* in cerebral ischemia serve as examples in which biological phenomena of great interest significantly influence the signal intensity of a diffusion-weighted image or diffusion map. The biggest challenge with the quantitative interpretation of diffusion MRI data acquired on biological tissue is associated with the complexity of the material being imaged. Heterogeneity on several size scales interferes with the straightforward analysis of image intensity in terms of cellular structural or physiological parameters of interest. Continual refinement of modeling strategies and experimental evaluation of the assumptions behind them has provided an increasingly nuanced understanding of the potential of diffusion MRI in characterizing biological processes on the cellular level. This refinement will undoubtedly continue, which will further improve the value of this tool in clinical and research settings.

References

[1] Crank J. The mathematics of diffusion. Oxford University Press; 1979.
[2] Sehy JV, Ackerman JJ, Neil JJ. Apparent diffusion of water, ions, and small molecules in the Xenopus oocyte is consistent with Brownian displacement. Magn Reson Med 2002;48(1):42–51.
[3] Hahn EL. Spin echoes. Phys Rev 1950;80:580–94.
[4] Torrey HC. Bloch equations with diffusion terms. Phys Rev 1956;104:563–5.
[5] Torrey HC. Nuclear spin relaxation by translational diffusion. Phys Rev 1953;92:962–9.
[6] Stejskal EO, Tanner JE. Spin diffusion measurements: spin echoes in the presence of time-dependent field gradients. J Chem Phys 1965;42:288–92.
[7] Meier C, Dreher W, Leibfritz D. Diffusion in compartmental systems. II. Diffusion-weighted measurements of rat brain tissue in vivo and postmortem at very large b-values. Magn Reson Med 2003;50(3):510–4.
[8] Mulkern RV, Gudbjartsson H, Westin CF, Zengingonul HP, Gartner W, Guttmann CR, et al. Multi-component apparent diffusion coefficients in human brain. NMR Biomed 1999;12(1):51–62.
[9] Niendorf T, Dijkhuizen RM, Norris DG, van Lookeren CM, Nicolay K. Biexponential diffusion attenuation in various states of brain tissue: implications for diffusion-weighted imaging. Magn Reson Med 1996; 36(6):847–57.
[10] Moseley ME, Cohen Y, Mintorovitch J, Chileuitt L, Shimizu H, Kucharczyk J, et al. Early detection of regional cerebral ischemia in cats: comparison of diffusion- and T2-weighted MRI and spectroscopy. Magn Reson Med 1990;14(2):330–46.
[11] Beaulieu C. The basis of anisotropic water diffusion in the nervous system—a technical review. NMR Biomed 2002;15(7–8):435–55.
[12] Callaghan PT. Translational dynamics and magnetic resonance. Principles of pulsed gradient spin echo NMR. Oxford: Oxford University Press; 2011.
[13] Conturo TE, McKinstry RC, Aronovitz JA, Neil JJ. Diffusion MRI: precision, accuracy and flow effects. NMR Biomed 1995;8(7–8):307–32.
[14] Le Bihan D. Diffusion, confusion and functional MRI. Neuroimage 2012;62(2):1131–6.
[15] Le Bihan D, Breton E, Lallemand D, Grenier P, Cabanis E, Laval-Jeantet M. MR imaging of intravoxel incoherent motions: application to diffusion and perfusion in neurologic disorders. Radiology 1986; 161(2):401–7.
[16] Koh DM, Collins DJ, Orton MR. Intravoxel incoherent motion in body diffusion-weighted MRI: reality and challenges. AJR Am J Roentgenol 2011;196(6):1351–61.
[17] Le Bihan D. What can we see with IVIM MRI? NeuroImage 2019;187:56–67.
[18] Basser PJ, Mattiello J, LeBihan D. Estimation of the effective self-diffusion tensor from the NMR spin echo. J Magn Reson B 1994;103(3):247–54.
[19] Basser PJ, Mattiello J, LeBihan D. MR diffusion tensor spectroscopy and imaging. Biophys J 1994;66(1):259–67.
[20] Basser PJ, Pierpaoli C. Microstructural and physiological features of tissues elucidated by quantitative-diffusion-tensor MRI. J Magn Reson B 1996;111(3):209–19.
[21] Song SK, Sun SW, Ramsbottom MJ, Chang C, Russell J, Cross AH. Dysmyelination revealed through MRI as increased radial (but unchanged axial) diffusion of water. Neuroimage 2002;17(3):1429–36.
[22] Behrens TE, Berg HJ, Jbabdi S, Rushworth MF, Woolrich MW. Probabilistic diffusion tractography with multiple fibre orientations: what can we gain? Neuroimage 2007;34(1):144–55.
[23] Zhang H, Schneider T, Wheeler-Kingshott CA, Alexander DC. NODDI: practical in vivo neurite orientation dispersion and density imaging of the human brain. Neuroimage 2012;61(4):1000–16.
[24] Jespersen SN, Kroenke CD, Ostergaard L, Ackerman JJ, Yablonskiy DA. Modeling dendrite density from magnetic resonance diffusion measurements. Neuroimage 2007;34(4):1473–86.

[25] Jespersen SN, Leigland LA, Cornea A, Kroenke CD. Determination of axonal and dendritic orientation distributions within the developing cerebral cortex by diffusion tensor imaging. IEEE Trans Med Imaging 2012;31(1):16–32.

[26] Budde MD, Annese J. Quantification of anisotropy and fiber orientation in human brain histological sections. Front Integr Neurosci 2013;7:3.

[27] Assaf Y, Freidlin RZ, Rohde GK, Basser PJ. New modeling and experimental framework to characterize hindered and restricted water diffusion in brain white matter. Magn Reson Med 2004;52(5):965–78.

[28] Assaf Y, Blumenfeld-Katzir T, Yovel Y, Basser PJ. AxCaliber: a method for measuring axon diameter distribution from diffusion MRI. Magn Reson Med 2008;59(6):1347–54.

[29] Conturo TE, Lori NF, Cull TS, Akbudak E, Snyder AZ, Shimony JS, et al. Tracking neuronal fiber pathways in the living human brain. Proc Natl Acad Sci U S A 1999;96(18):10422–7.

[30] Mori S, Crain BJ, Chacko VP, van Zijl PC. Three-dimensional tracking of axonal projections in the brain by magnetic resonance imaging. Ann Neurol 1999;45(2):265–9.

[31] Jones DK, Simmons A, Williams SC, Horsfield MA. Non invasive assessment of axonal fiber connectivity in the human brain via diffusion tensor MRI. Magn Reson Med 1999;42(1):37–41.

[32] Behrens TE, Woolrich MW, Jenkinson M, Johansen-Berg H, Nunes RG, Clare S, et al. Characterization and propagation of uncertainty in diffusion-weighted MR imaging. Magn Reson Med 2003;50(5):1077–88.

[33] Sotak CH. The role of diffusion tensor imaging in the evaluation of ischemic brain injury—a review. NMR Biomed 2002;15(7–8):561–9.

[34] Jauch EC, Saver JL, Adams Jr HP, Bruno A, Connors JJ, Demaerschalk BM, et al. Guidelines for the early management of patients with acute ischemic stroke: a guideline for healthcare professionals from the American Heart Association/American Stroke Association. Stroke 2013;44(3):870–947.

[35] Le Bihan D. Looking into the functional architecture of the brain with diffusion MRI. Nat Rev Neurosci 2003;4(6):469–80.

[36] van der Toorn A, Sykova E, Dijkhuizen RM, Vorisek I, Vargova L, Skobisova E, et al. Dynamic changes in water ADC, energy metabolism, extracellular space volume, and tortuosity in neonatal rat brain during global ischemia. Magn Reson Med 1996;36(1):52–60.

[37] Ackerman JJ, Neil JJ. The use of MR-detectable reporter molecules and ions to evaluate diffusion in normal and ischemic brain. NMR Biomed 2010;23(7):725–33.

[38] Benveniste H, Hedlund LW, Johnson GA. Mechanism of detection of acute cerebral ischemia in rats by diffusion-weighted magnetic resonance microscopy. Stroke 1992;23(5):746–54.

[39] Nicholson C, Sykova E. Extracellular space structure revealed by diffusion analysis. Trends Neurosci 1998;21(5):207–15.

[40] Vorisek I, Sykova E. Ischemia-induced changes in the extracellular space diffusion parameters, K+, and pH in the developing rat cortex and corpus callosum. J Cereb Blood Flow Metab 1997;17(2):191–203.

[41] Karger J, Pfeifer H, Heink W. Principles and application of self-diffusion measurements by nuclear magnetic resonance. Adv Magn Opt Reson 1988;12:1–89.

[42] Duong TQ, Ackerman JJ, Ying HS, Neil JJ. Evaluation of extra- and intracellular apparent diffusion in normal and globally ischemic rat brain via 19F NMR. Magn Reson Med 1998;40(1):1–13.

[43] Kunz N, da Silva AR, Jelescu IO. Intra- and extra-axonal axial diffusivities in the white matter: which one is faster? Neuroimage 2018;181:314–22.

[44] Jespersen SN, Bjarkam CR, Nyengaard JR, Chakravarty MM, Hansen B, Vosegaard T, et al. Neurite density from magnetic resonance diffusion measurements at ultrahigh field: comparison with light microscopy and electron microscopy. Neuroimage 2010;49(1):205–16.

[45] Kroenke CD, Ackerman JJ, Yablonskiy DA. On the nature of the NAA diffusion attenuated MR signal in the central nervous system. Magn Reson Med 2004;52(5):1052–9.

[46] Jelescu IO, Veraart J, Fieremans E, Novikov DS. Degeneracy in model parameter estimation for multi-compartmental diffusion in neuronal tissue. NMR Biomed 2016;29(1):33–47.

[47] Jespersen SN, Olesen JL, Hansen B, Shemesh N. Diffusion time dependence of microstructural parameters in fixed spinal cord. Neuroimage 2018;182:329–42.

[48] Beaulieu C, Allen PS. Water diffusion in the giant axon of the squid: implications for diffusion-weighted MRI of the nervous system. Magn Reson Med 1994;32(5):579–83.

[49] Grant SC, Buckley DL, Gibbs S, Webb AG, Blackband SJ. MR microscopy of multicomponent diffusion in single neurons. Magn Reson Med 2001;46(6):1107–12.

[50] Sehy JV, Ackerman JJ, Neil JJ. Evidence that both fast and slow water ADC components arise from intracellular space. Magn Reson Med 2002;48(5):765–70.

[51] Flint JJ, Hansen B, Fey M, Schmidig D, King MA, Vestergaard-Poulsen P, et al. Cellular-level diffusion tensor microscopy and fiber tracking in mammalian nervous tissue with direct histological correlation. Neuroimage 2010;52(2):556–61.

[52] Budde MD, Frank JA. Neurite beading is sufficient to decrease the apparent diffusion coefficient after ischemic stroke. Proc Natl Acad Sci U S A 2010;107(32):14472–7.

[53] Skinner NP, Kurpad SN, Schmit BD, Budde MD. Detection of acute nervous system injury with advanced diffusion-weighted MRI: a simulation and sensitivity analysis. NMR Biomed 2015;28(11):1489–506.

[54] Darquie A, Poline JB, Poupon C, Saint-Jalmes H, Le Bihan D. Transient decrease in water diffusion observed in human occipital cortex during visual stimulation. Proc Natl Acad Sci U S A 2001;98(16):9391–5.

[55] Le Bihan D, Urayama S, Aso T, Hanakawa T, Fukuyama H. Direct and fast detection of neuronal activation in the human brain with diffusion MRI. Proc Natl Acad Sci U S A 2006;103(21):8263–8.

[56] Song AW, Harshbarger T, Li T, Kim KH, Ugurbil K, Mori S, et al. Functional activation using apparent diffusion coefficient-dependent contrast allows better spatial localization to the neuronal activity: evidence using diffusion tensor imaging and fiber tracking. Neuroimage 2003;20(2):955–61.

[57] Abe Y, Tsurugizawa T, Le Bihan D. Water diffusion closely reveals neural activity status in rat brain loci affected by anesthesia. PLoS Biol 2017;15(4):e2001494.

[58] Bai R, Stewart CV, Plenz D, Basser PJ. Assessing the sensitivity of diffusion MRI to detect neuronal activity directly. Proc Natl Acad Sci U S A 2016;113(12):E1728–37.

[59] Miller KL, Bulte DP, Devlin H, Robson MD, Wise RG, Woolrich MW, et al. Evidence for a vascular contribution to diffusion FMRI at high b value. Proc Natl Acad Sci U S A 2007;104(52):20967–72.

[60] Springer Jr CS. Using (1)H2O MR to measure and map sodium pump activity in vivo. J Magn Reson 2018;291:110–26.

[61] Helpern JA, Ordidge RJ, Knight RA. The effect of cell membrane water permeability on the apparent diffusion coefficient of water, In: Proc SMRM, 11th annual meeting, Berlin; 1992. p. 1805.

CHAPTER

Acquisition of Diffusion MRI Data

19

Grant Yang and Jennifer A. McNab

Department of Radiology, Stanford University, Stanford, CA, United States

19.1 Introduction

Acquisition of diffusion MRI data requires a pulse sequence that is specifically sensitized to the microscopic diffusive motion of water molecules. This sensitivity is achieved using magnetic field gradients that dephase the transverse magnetization when diffusive motion occurs. The loss in MR signal through intravoxel dephasing is the basis of diffusion contrast [1,2]. By adjusting the orientation, strength, and timing of the diffusion-encoding gradients, the signal can be sensitized to various characteristics of the tissue microstructure and used for clinical diagnosis [3,4] as well as the study of brain connectivity [5], microstructure [6–10], and the etiology of neurodegenerative diseases [11,12]. Here the acquisition considerations for diffusion MRI are divided into three key sequence components: (I) diffusion encoding, (II) signal refocusing, and (III) image encoding.

19.2 Diffusion encoding strategies

Magnetic field gradients alter the strength of the magnetic field linearly with position resulting in a spatial dependence of the Larmor frequency:

$$\omega(\boldsymbol{r}) = \gamma(B_0 + \mathbf{g}\cdot\mathbf{r}) \tag{19.1}$$

where γ is the gyromagnetic ratio, B_0 is the main magnetic field, and $\mathbf{g}$ is the gradient field. The linear dependence of the Larmor frequency on the spin position, $\mathbf{r}$, is the basis of measurements of spin diffusion. In the presence of a magnetic field gradient, spins accumulate phase over time:

$$\phi(\mathbf{r}) = \gamma\int_0^\tau \mathbf{g}(t)\cdot\mathbf{r}(t)dt \tag{19.2}$$

Any spatial variation of the phase across the voxel causes a reduction in the net magnetization. The magnetization can be restored by rewinding the phase accumulation with a gradient waveform of equal area and opposite effective polarity. In the presence of spin diffusion, however, this gradient does not perfectly restore the original phase of the spin isochromats. The intravoxel dephasing caused by this incomplete rephasing results in a loss in magnetization, which can be used to measure the diffusive properties of the voxel. In the case of Gaussian diffusion resulting from Brownian motion [13], the

Advances in Magnetic Resonance Technology and Applications. Volume 1. ISSN 2666-9099. https://doi.org/10.1016/B978-0-12-817057-1.00021-4

resultant signal attenuation of the MR signal is exponentially related to the dimensionless product of D, the variance of the Gaussian distribution of the spin displacements, and b, the b-value, according to:

$$S = S_0 e^{-bD} \tag{19.3}$$

where S_0 is the signal magnitude without diffusion. The diffusion coefficient, D, is a property of the sample/tissue, while the b-value is determined by the gradient waveforms applied. In general, both b and D may be tensor valued, and the resulting signal attenuation is exponentially related to the matrix inner product between the b-tensor and the diffusion tensor [6,14].

The effect of molecular self-diffusion on the MR signal during the application of a spatially varying gradient can be described by modifying the Bloch equations, which govern the evolution of spin magnetization over time [15,16]. The Bloch-Torrey equation, describing the evolution of the complex transverse magnetization in the rotating frame, M_+, in the presence of a magnetic field gradient, $\mathbf{g}$, is:

$$\frac{\partial M_+}{\partial t} = -i\gamma M_+ \mathbf{g} \cdot \mathbf{r} - \frac{M_+}{T_2} + D\nabla^2 M_+ \tag{19.4}$$

The Bloch-Torrey equation has the following solution, which describes the evolution of the complex-valued MR signal in time and space:

$$M_+(\mathbf{r}, t) = E(t) \exp\left(-i\gamma \mathbf{r} \cdot \int_0^t \mathbf{g}^*(t')dt'\right) \exp\left(-\frac{t}{T_2}\right) \tag{19.5}$$

where $\mathbf{g}^*(t)$ is the effective gradient waveform after accounting for the phase-reversal effects of the applied 180° refocusing RF pulses. $E(t)$ is the echo attenuation caused by diffusive motion, which is exponential in the case of stochastic (Brownian) motion according to Eq. (19.3). An expression for $E(t)$ can be derived by substituting Eq. (19.5) back into Eq. (19.4):

$$E(t) = \exp\left(-D\gamma^2 \int_0^t \left[\int_0^{t'} \mathbf{g}^*(t'')dt''\right]^2 dt'\right) \tag{19.6}$$

From Eq. (19.6), an expression for the b-value in Eq. (19.3) follows:

$$b = \gamma^2 \int_0^t \left[\int_0^{t'} \mathbf{g}^*(t'')dt''\right]^2 dt' \tag{19.7}$$

The b-value in Eq. (19.7) can be tensor-valued when diffusion is encoded along multiple directions before the signal readout. This can be done intentionally to encode particular microstructural information into the diffusion signal [17], or can be the result of interactions between imaging gradients and the diffusion gradients [14]. Eqs. (19.6), (19.7) describe the echo attenuation for any arbitrary gradient waveform caused by Gaussian diffusion. However, for more complicated diffusion patterns such as restricted diffusion between boundaries [18] or time-dependent diffusion in disordered media [19], alternate methods are needed to calculate the signal attenuation [20–22].

19.2.1 Single-pulsed gradients

While any balanced gradient waveform, $\int_0^{TE} \mathbf{g}^*(t')dt' = 0$, can be used for diffusion encoding, by far the most widely used diffusion-encoding waveform is the single-pulsed field gradient encoding [23,24] originally introduced by Stejskal and Tanner shown in Fig. 19.1.

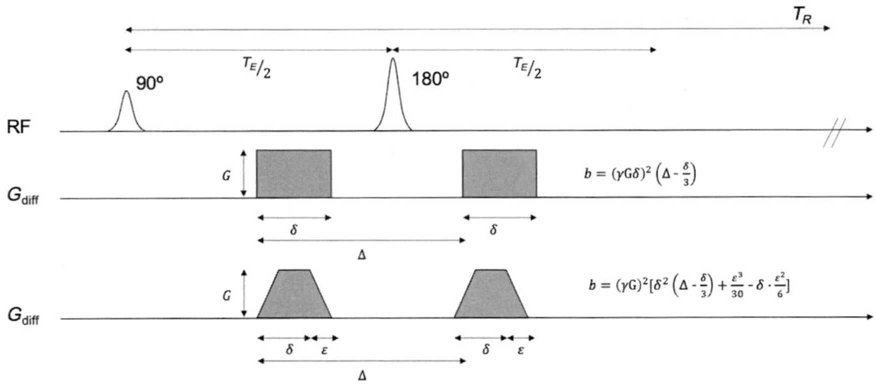

FIG. 19.1

Single-pulsed field gradient spin echo experiment. The derivations for the *b*-value also hold true for the same effective gradient waveform using a gradient echo or stimulated-echo sequence.

The intravoxel dephasing caused by a pair of pulsed gradients with duration δ, diffusion time Δ, and gradient amplitude G due to Gaussian diffusion attenuates the MR signal according to:

$$E(TE) = \exp\left(-(\gamma G\delta)^2(\Delta - \delta/3)D\right) \tag{19.8}$$

In practice, limitations on the gradient slew rates result in trapezoidal gradient waveforms. Taking the ramp times into account in Eq. (19.5) leads to the modified expression for the echo attenuation [14]:

$$E(TE) = \exp\left(-(\gamma G)^2\left[\delta^2\left(\Delta - \frac{\delta}{3}\right) + \frac{\epsilon^3}{30} - \delta\epsilon^2/6\right]D\right) \tag{19.9}$$

The single-pulsed field gradient experiment can be used to measure the diffusion rate along the direction of the gradient field. By acquiring measurements with different gradient orientations, the orientation dependence of the diffusion rate can be observed. The variation between diffusion rates measured along different orientations, known as the diffusion anisotropy, is of interest in many diffusion MRI applications including the analysis of structural connectivity in the brain [5,25], neurodegeneration [26–28], myocardial tissue [29] and musculoskeletal injury [30].

19.2.2 The diffusion propagator

The Bloch-Torrey equation is insufficient to describe the more complicated non-Gaussian diffusive motion caused by restricted spaces and/or heterogenous environments within tissues. For these more complicated diffusion patterns, the effects of diffusion can be described analytically in terms of a diffusion propagator [20], $P(\mathbf{r}'|\mathbf{r},\Delta)$ for a pulsed gradient experiment where diffusive motion during the gradient pulse is minimal. The diffusion propagator describes the probability that a spin diffuses from initial position $\mathbf{r}$ to $\mathbf{r}'$ during the diffusion time Δ. Consider a spin isochromat initially located at position $\mathbf{r}$ during the first diffusion pulse, which diffuses to $\mathbf{r}'$ by the second diffusion pulse. The diffusion-encoding gradients impart a phase $\phi(\mathbf{r}, \mathbf{r}') = \gamma \mathbf{g}\delta(\mathbf{r} - \mathbf{r}')$ on the spins. Given a diffusion propagator $P(\mathbf{r}'|\mathbf{r},\Delta)$, the dephasing of the MR signal can be calculated by integrating over all spin populations:

$$S(\mathbf{g},\delta) = S_0\int\rho(\mathbf{r})\int P(\mathbf{r}'|\,\mathbf{r},\Delta)\exp(-i\phi(\mathbf{r},\mathbf{r}'))d\mathbf{r}'d\mathbf{r} \tag{19.10}$$

where $\rho(\mathbf{r})$ is the spin density function and S_0 is the MR signal without diffusion weighting. For ease of analysis, a uniform spin density is assumed within each voxel: $\rho(\mathbf{r})=1/V$. The signal expression can then be simplified to:

$$S(\mathbf{g},\delta)=S_0\int P(\mathbf{R}|\,\Delta)\exp(-i\gamma\delta\mathbf{g}\cdot\mathbf{R})d\mathbf{R} \tag{19.11}$$

where $\mathbf{R}=\mathbf{r}-\mathbf{r}'$ is the displacement of the spin isochromat during the diffusion time. Note that the diffusion signal as a function of the wave-vector, $\mathbf{q}=\frac{\gamma}{2\pi}\mathbf{g}\delta$, is the Fourier Transform of the diffusion propagator:

$$S(\mathbf{q})=S_0\int P(\mathbf{R}|\,\Delta)\exp(-i2\pi\mathbf{q}\cdot\mathbf{R})d\mathbf{R} \tag{19.12}$$

Just as an image can be reconstructed by acquiring points in k-space, the ensemble average diffusion propagator can be reconstructed by acquiring points in q-space. The ensemble average diffusion propagator represents the 3D spin displacement probability density function during the experimental diffusion time. q-space spectrum imaging [31] aims to reconstruct [32] the ensemble average diffusion propagator from q-space measurements. Note that the diffusion propagator approach relies on the assumption that diffusion gradient pulse durations are sufficiently narrow such that motion is negligible during their duration. In practice diffusion gradient durations on clinical scanners can approach the diffusion time, resulting in nonnegligible effects on the propagator estimation [33].

19.2.3 Oscillating gradients and time-dependent diffusion

While the diffusion tensor and the diffusion propagator at a single diffusion time provide a wealth of information about the diffusive motion within a voxel, a more complete picture of the diffusive motion, and by extension the microstructural environment within a voxel, can be obtained by examining time-dependent diffusion. The apparent diffusion coefficient will decrease at longer diffusion times as the diffusing molecules encounter restrictions. This time dependence can be characterized by acquiring measurements of the apparent diffusion coefficient at different diffusion times, Δ, in a single-pulsed field gradient experiment. Unfortunately, at short diffusion times, the diffusion sensitivity is drastically reduced since the diffusion gradient duration is limited by the diffusion time. A potential remedy is to use a train of oscillating gradients [34] as shown in Fig. 19.2. Oscillating gradients repeat multiple diffusion encodings with a short effective diffusion time along a single direction to build up diffusion contrast. Measuring the diffusion characteristics at high gradient oscillation frequencies can be useful for separating the effects of restricted diffusion from heterogeneity in the tissue [35], and improving sensitivity to diffusion to shorter or more specific length scales [36–40], thereby providing complementary microstructural information compared to conventional single-pulsed gradient encoding [41–44]. The effect of oscillating gradient waveforms on the diffusion signal can be expressed in a frequency dependent form [36]:

$$\ln(S/S_0)=-\int\frac{1}{\pi}\mathbf{Q}(\omega)\mathbf{D}(\omega)\mathbf{Q}(-\omega)d\omega \tag{19.13}$$

where $\mathbf{Q}(\omega)$ describes the frequency content of the diffusion encoding, and is given by the Fourier transform of the q-space trajectory

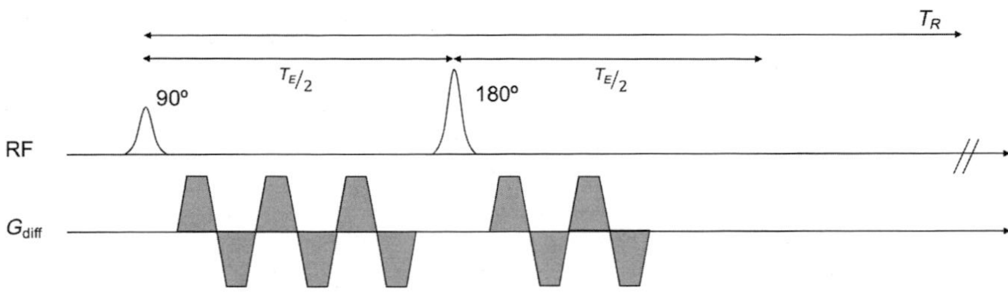

FIG. 19.2

Oscillating gradient diffusion encoding enables measurements of the diffusion coefficient at short diffusion times with improved diffusion sensitivity.

$$\mathbf{Q}(\omega) = \int_0^{\infty} \left(\int_0^t \gamma \mathbf{g}(\tau) d\tau \right) \exp(i\omega t) dt \tag{19.14}$$

To characterize $\mathbf{D}(\omega)$, measurements must be acquired using diffusion encodings with varying oscillation frequencies. Oscillating gradient waveforms can be designed for spectral selectivity and diffusion encoding efficiency [45,46].

At long diffusion times, acquisition of the MR signal is limited by the transverse relaxation of the magnetization. As discussed in the next section, a stimulated-echo sequence can be used to limit signal loss during the diffusion time by storing the magnetization along the longitudinal axis such that it decays according to T_1 relaxation rather than the faster T_2 relaxation rate in the transverse plane [47].

19.2.4 Multiple-pulsed gradients

While single-pulsed gradient experiments are broadly sensitive to the shapes, orientations, and sizes of diffusive compartments within tissues, they provide limited specificity when relating the diffusion signal to biophysical changes [48]. These effects can be separated experimentally using multiple-pulsed gradient experiments which encode diffusion along multiple orientations before the signal readout [17,49,49a]. By changing the orientation between subsequent diffusion encodings, the effect of orientation on the diffusion signal can be modulated, allowing separation of the effects of changes in orientation dispersion and local diffusion anisotropy. For time-independent diffusion, where diffusion can be adequately described as a sum of Gaussian displacement distributions (note the ensemble average diffusion propagator is not necessarily Gaussian), the effect of multiple-pulsed gradients can be examined using the b-tensor, $\mathbf{b}$, described in Eq. (19.7):

$$E(TE) = \int P(D) \exp(-\boldsymbol{b}D) dD \tag{19.15}$$

where $P(D)$ is a distribution of diffusion tensors representing diffusion within different subvoxel tissue components [50]. Altering the orientation between multiple diffusion encodings changes the rank or shape of the b-tensor, which can improve the specificity of the relationship between the diffusion-encoded signal and microstructural parameters.

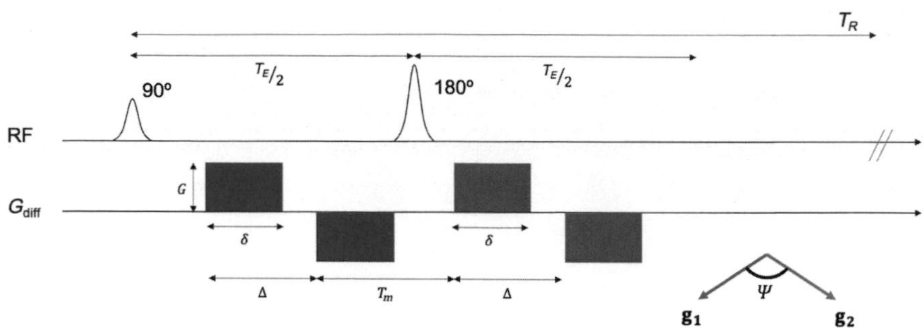

FIG. 19.3

Double diffusion encoding pulse sequence. Diffusion encoding is performed twice before the readout. By altering the timing (T_m) and orientation (Ψ) between the first diffusion-encoding gradient pair and the second diffusion-encoding gradient pair, additional information can be gathered compared to a conventional single encoding experiment.

Double diffusion encoding (DDE) [17,51–56] has recently been investigated as a potential method for realizing the benefits of multiple-pulsed gradient experiments on conventional MRI scanners [9,57–59]. DDE extends conventional diffusion imaging by adding a second set of diffusion-encoding gradients pairs before the signal readout as shown in Fig. 19.3.

The time between the application of the first diffusion-encoding gradient pair and the second diffusion-encoding gradient pair is referred to as the "mixing time." By varying the mixing time, the correlation of the diffusive motion between the two diffusion-encoding pairs can be controlled. Short mixing time experiments produce a signal modulation related to the size of the restricted compartments, for example, cell size [51]. Another key parameter for DDE is the relative orientation between the diffusion-encoding orientation of the first diffusion-encoding pair relative to the second diffusion-encoding pair (ψ). The microscopic anisotropy within the tissue can be observed as a signal modulation when plotting signal variation as a function of the angle between the two diffusion-encoding pairs. By acquiring multiple measurements with different angles between the diffusion-encoding pairs along with a specific mixing time, information about compartment size and shape can be inferred independent of the orientation distribution of those compartments. Notably, DDE imaging provides information on diffusion anisotropy at a microscopic scale even when the tissue appears macroscopically isotropic in a conventional single-pulsed field gradient experiment.

Diffusion-encoding waveforms have also been proposed with additional pulsed gradient pairs to produce an isotropic b-tensor encoding, which removes the effects of tissue orientation on the diffusion measurements [60]. Encoding diffusion equally along three orthogonal directions after the excitation and before the readout (as shown in Fig. 19.4A) produces an isotropic b-tensor according to Eq. (19.7). Isotropic diffusion encoding results in a signal that is weighted by the rotationally invariant trace of the diffusion tensor as shown in Fig. 19.5. This type of isotropic diffusion encoding can be used for rapid measurement of mean diffusivity and/or in the context of probing microscopic diffusion anisotropy.

19.2.5 Generalized diffusion waveforms

While multiple-pulsed diffusion waveforms can provide novel information [17], they are challenging to implement on whole-body MRI scanners with commercial gradient systems (e.g., 40–80 mT/m strength,

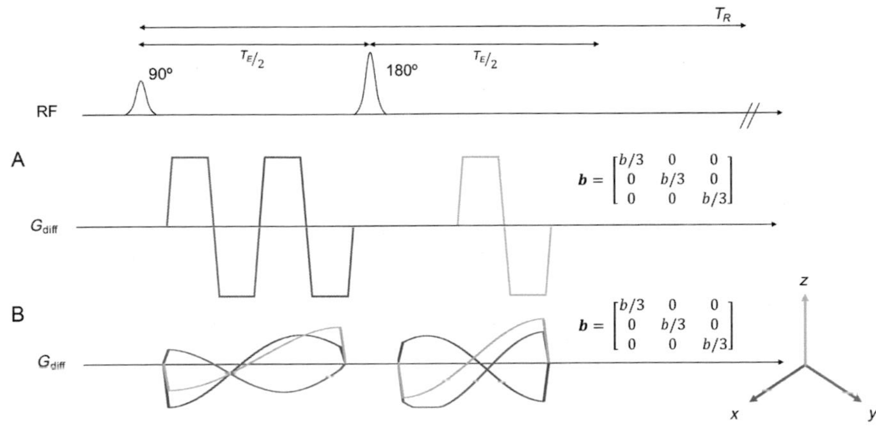

FIG. 19.4

(A) An isotropic *b*-tensor encoded using three consecutive pulsed gradient pairs. (B) Generalized diffusion gradients can be designed to achieve a desired *b*-tensor in a time efficient manner. The encoding scheme used in (A) is less efficient, requiring larger gradient amplitudes and increased gradient heating for the same sequence timing compared to the isotropic *b*-tensor encoded using a generalized diffusion gradient waveform (B). Numerical optimization can also be used to design diffusion-encoding waveforms with intrinsic compensation of gradient imperfections such as eddy currents, background fields, or concomitant fields.

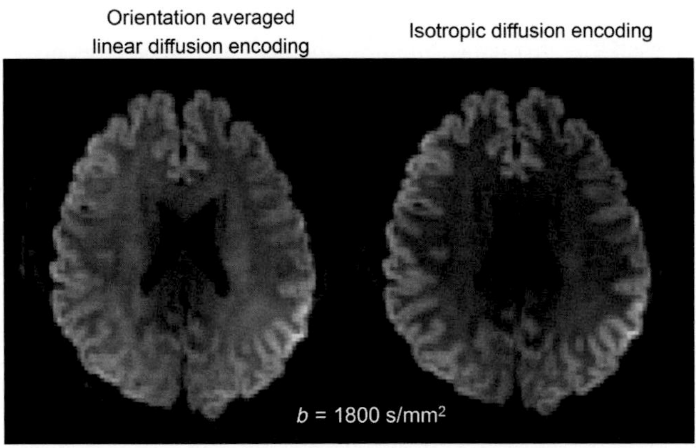

FIG. 19.5

The diffusion contrast in the image is dependent on the shape of the *b*-tensor. The image on the left is the result of averaging 60 single-pulsed diffusion encodings with orientations distributed uniformly on a half-sphere. The image on the right is acquired with isotropic diffusion encoding. The decreased signal within the white matter on the isotropic diffusion-encoded image reflects strong microscopic diffusion anisotropy.

100–200 T/m/s slew rate) due to the extended diffusion-encoding times and subsequent long echo times and low signal-to-noise ratio (SNR). One solution to this problem is the use of optimization frameworks [61–63] to design time-optimal diffusion encodings, such as those shown in Fig. 19.4B, which are not constrained to the pulsed-gradient encoding paradigm. For time-independent diffusion, the diffusion contrast resulting from a gradient waveform is characterized by the b-tensor from Eq. (19.7). Generalized diffusion encoding can encode a desired b-tensor shape more efficiently than multiple-pulsed gradient pairs and reduce the echo time needed to produce the desired diffusion contrast.

Another benefit of generalized diffusion waveforms is the ability to integrate intrinsic compensation of gradient imperfections such as eddy currents [64,65] and concomitant fields (Maxwell terms) [66,67] into the encoding waveform and to account for gradient heating [68]. While the b-tensor formalism is applicable only to time-independent diffusion, restriction effects from generalized encoding waveforms can be accounted for simple geometries using the matrix propagator method [69,70]. The matrix propagator formalism discretizes the gradient waveform into well-defined time intervals and assumes that all translational motion occurs at the boundary of those time intervals, allowing analysis using a diffusion propagator approach similar to the analysis for narrow-pulsed gradients. This approach has been used to optimize the sensitivity of gradient-encoding waveforms to specific features of the tissue microstructure such as axon diameter or microscopic diffusion anisotropy [40,71,72,72a].

19.3 Refocusing mechanisms

In theory, the diffusion-encoding gradients described in Section 19.2 may be incorporated into any MR pulse sequence. The motion-induced phase shifts are solely dependent on the effective gradient waveform (see Fig. 19.6). In practice, the attenuation of the MR signal due to relaxation effects is dependent on the refocusing mechanism. Therefore, the choice of refocusing strategy is driven by the need to maximize the MR signal and minimize the negative effects of gradient imperfections. Refocusing strategies used for diffusion imaging include: single spin echo [73], double spin echo [74], stimulated-echo [47], and steady-state free precession (SSFP) [75–77].

Limitations on the gradient amplitude and slew-rate can necessitate long diffusion-encoding times to achieve sufficient diffusion weighting. The loss of signal due to transverse relaxation during the diffusion encoding can be significant. The vast majority of diffusion pulse sequences employ spin-echoes (Fig. 19.6B) rather than gradient echoes (Fig. 19.6A) due to the reduced signal decay for a given echo time. Gradient echo signals are affected by T_2^* relaxation, which can lead to low signal at long diffusion times. Spin echoes are influenced by T_2 relaxation, as they restore the magnetization lost to the effects of static field inhomogeneities, which can significantly increase the MR signal for a given echo time. However, T_2 signal loss can still be prohibitive when long diffusion times are employed. The use of stimulated echoes avoids T_2 decay during the diffusion time by storing the magnetization of the desired echo pathway along the longitudinal axis using a second 90° RF pulse. Magnetization along the longitudinal axis decays with T_1, which is longer than T_2, and thus more signal can be preserved using this mechanism. Before the signal readout, the magnetization along the longitudinal axis is moved back to the transverse plane using a third 90° RF pulse as shown in Fig. 19.6C.

The stimulated-echo sequence requires crushers on either side of the second and third RF pulse to eliminate unwanted coherence pathways. The stimulated-echo pathway can be selected by using crushers of equal area for the first and last crusher which is different than the combined area of the

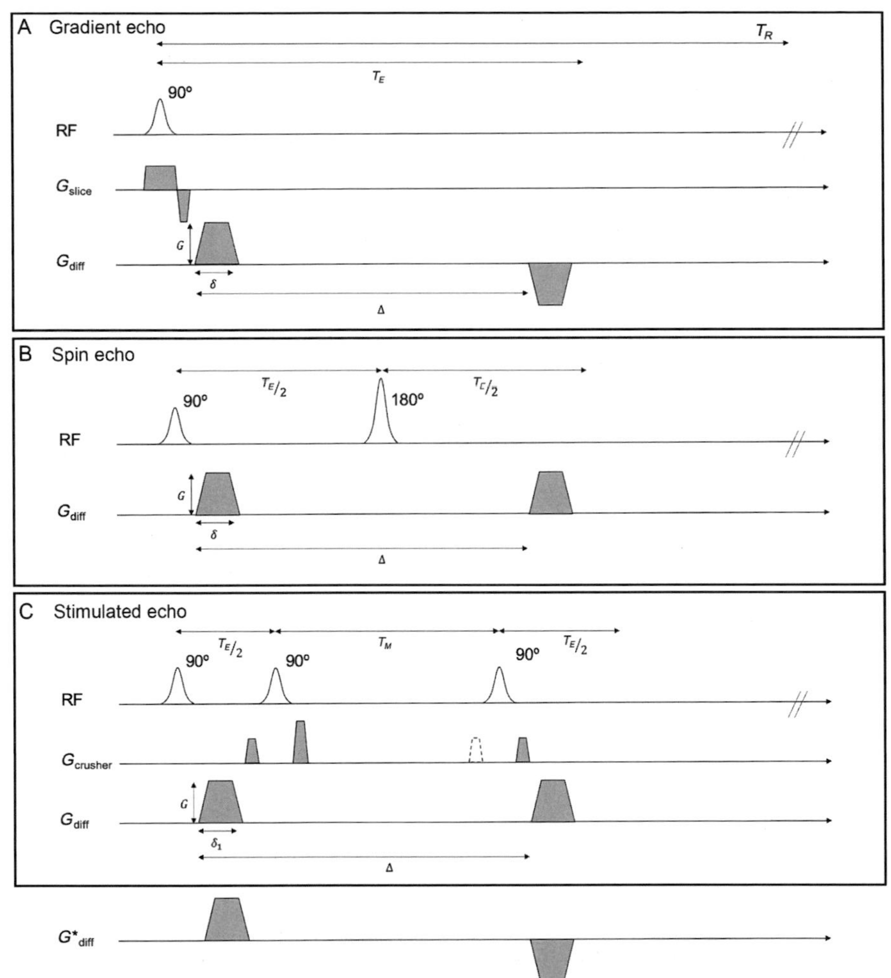

FIG. 19.6

Single-pulsed field gradient diffusion experiment using the (A) gradient echo, (B) spin echo and (C) stimulated-echo sequences. Although all three sequences can produce the same effective diffusion-encoding waveform (G^*), they will have different sensitivities to relaxation effects and thus different signal levels.

crushers in between the second and third RF pulse. The crusher shown with the dashed line in Fig. 19.6C is optional and can be combined with the crusher after the second RF pulse. As a consequence of eliminating the unwanted coherence pathways, stimulated echoes lose half of the original magnetization since the transverse component of the magnetization after the second RF pulse is never refocused. Stimulated-echo sequences are more common in preclinical settings with small-bore scanners where stronger gradient hardware allows relatively short diffusion pulse widths. Short diffusion pulse widths compared to the diffusion time result in significant improvements in SNR due to reduced transverse relaxation which overcomes the factor of two signal reduction of the stimulated-echo pathway. On clinical scanners, the diffusion pulse width is often close to the same duration as the diffusion time and the advantages of stimulated echoes are difficult to realize.

The refocusing scheme can also be selected to minimize the effect of gradient imperfections. Eddy-current induced magnetic fields are generated when the gradient fields are altered, leading to a different gradient moment than actually intended. Eddy-current fields can distort both the diffusion encoding and image encoding gradient waveforms as shown in Fig. 19.7.

The use of bipolar diffusion-encoding waveforms [78] can reduce the effect of eddy currents, as eddy-current fields generated by the positive and negative diffusion-encoding gradient pulses cancel each other out in this scheme. However, bipolar pulses reduce the achievable diffusion weighting when used with single spin echo sequences. A popular method for reducing eddy currents while maintaining diffusion encoding efficiency is to employ a double spin echo sequence [74] as shown in Fig. 19.7B. RF refocusing pulses change the effective polarity of diffusion encoding, but not the polarity of eddy-current-induced gradient fields. A double spin echo sequence allows the diffusion encoding and decoding pulses to be split into a set of bipolar gradients on either side of the first and second refocusing pulse, respectively. Since the effective diffusion polarity is unaltered, the double spin echo does not compromise the effective diffusion time and enables a higher diffusion encoding efficiency to be maintained than a single spin echo diffusion encoding sequence with two sets of bipolar diffusion-encoding gradients. Eddy current reduction has also been demonstrated by adding a stimulated echo after the diffusion preparation [79,80]. The stimulated-echo stores the diffusion

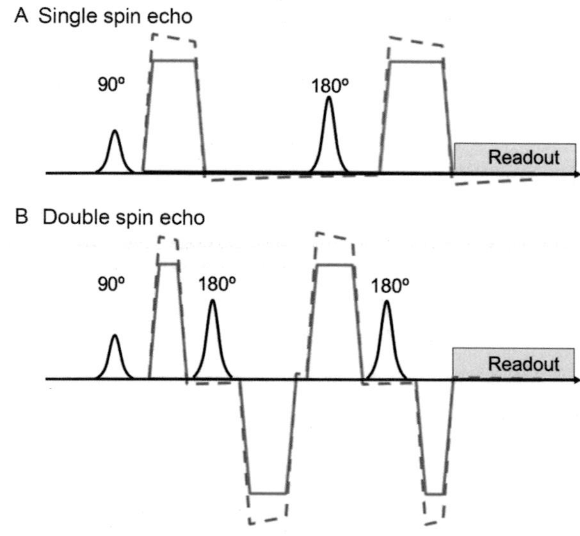

FIG. 19.7

Eddy currents result in a distortion of the applied gradient field (dashed lines). Eddy-current fields which (A) persist during the readout result in image distortions which cause misalignments between different diffusion-encoding directions. (B) Bipolar diffusion-encoding gradients often used with double spin echo pulse sequences can reduce the effects of the eddy-current fields.

prepared magnetization along the longitudinal axis while the eddy-current field decays. The magnetization is restored before the signal readout, thereby reducing eddy-current distortions while avoiding signal loss due to transverse relaxation.

The refocusing scheme used in a diffusion pulse sequence can also be designed to minimize the effects of internal or background gradients. Background gradients can be caused by imperfect B_0 shimming or differences in the magnetic susceptibility within or around an object. Cross-terms between the applied gradients and the background gradients can have a significant effect on the signal attenuation calculated using Eqs. (19.6), (19.7) [81]. These effects can be suppressed in both spin echo [82] and stimulated-echo [83,84] diffusion sequences by adding additional 180° refocusing pulses to minimize the accumulation of spin dephasing caused by background gradients.

While spin and stimulated echoes are used to refocus the signal of a single magnetization pathway, steady-state imaging diffusion imaging combines signal from magnetization pathways spanning multiple TRs, allowing more efficient diffusion encoding [85]. Diffusion-weighted steady-state sequences achieve their efficiency using a rapid train of pulse-acquisition cycles [75]. Steady-state imaging establishes an equilibrium longitudinal and transverse magnetization using a series of rapid RF pulses ($TR < T_2 < T_1$) as shown in Fig. 19.8. Following a transient period, the effect of the RF pulse is exactly balanced by T_1 and T_2 relaxation and precession during the TR. The short TR allows the magnetization to be sampled more frequently than spin- or stimulated-echo sequences. The additional time spent acquiring the signal improves the SNR efficiency of these steady-state imaging sequences [86]. Diffusion weighting can be added to a steady-state sequence by using a single diffusion sensitizing gradient pulse per TR as shown in Fig. 19.8. The effective diffusion weighting is a combination of the diffusion-weighted spin echo and stimulated-echo coherence pathways which comprise the steady-state magnetization. The proliferation of the signal across multiple pathways can potentially provide contrast from longer diffusion times than achievable using a conventional spin echo sequence. However, the analysis and quantification of the signal in diffusion-weighted steady-state imaging has a complicated dependence on T_1, T_2 and the flip angle [76]. In addition, the segmented readout used in steady-state imaging is more vulnerable to motion artifacts [87].

19.4 Image encoding

Image encoding strategies for diffusion MRI are driven by two key requirements. Firstly, there is a need to acquire multiple image slices/volumes within a reasonable scan time. Applications aimed at

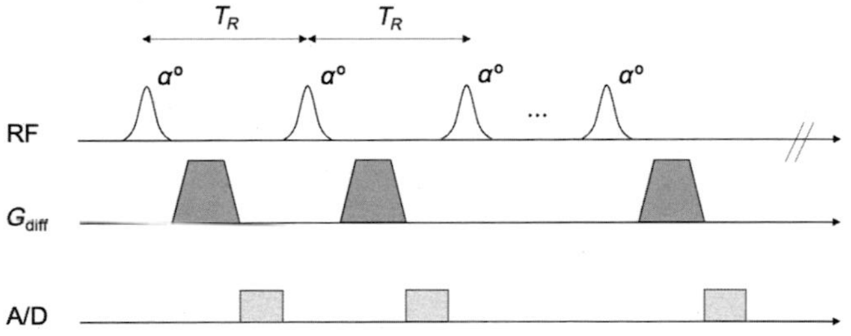

FIG. 19.8

Diffusion-weighted steady-state free precession pulse sequence.

mapping properties of the tissue microstructure, diffusion tensor imaging (DTI), and tractography typically require the acquisition of 30–500 image slices/volumes with different types of diffusion encodings [88,89]. Secondly, there is a need to mitigate the increased sensitivity to bulk and physiological motion induced by the diffusion-encoding gradients. Motion considerations for a diffusion-weighted pulse sequence are very different than for other pulse sequences. The diffusion-encoding gradients are sufficiently strong to encode diffusive motion on the order of microns and therefore highly sensitive to any bulk body motion or pulsation, which typically span greater length scales. Motion during the diffusion encoding results in a spatially varying image phase during the echo readout, and since the motion and subsequent phase offsets will be different across different excitations, signal dropouts and ghosting artifacts can arise if *k*-space data are combined across multiple excitations. For these reasons, single-shot imaging encoding strategies such as single-shot echo-planar imaging (EPI) [90], spiral [91], and fast spin echo sequences [92] are commonly used for diffusion imaging.

19.4.1 Single-shot 2D echo-planar imaging

Currently the most popular image encoding method for diffusion sequences is single-shot 2D EPI shown in Fig. 19.9. EPI samples *k*-space using a train of gradient echoes generated by a series of bipolar readout gradients accompanied by corresponding phase encode blips between readouts. By using more of the transverse magnetization lifetime for the readout, images can be acquired much faster compared to single-line readouts. EPI can sample a full 2D image after every excitation, and therefore provides the speed and robustness to motion necessary to perform diffusion imaging.

One of the downsides of the EPI approach is that low bandwidth (long echo spacing) along the phase encode direction renders the image encoding process particularly vulnerable to off-resonance effects, which can be caused by differences in magnetic susceptibility, chemical shift, eddy currents, and concomitant fields. Magnetic susceptibility differences near tissue-air interfaces and metallic implants cause off-resonance effects, which can result in severe image distortions in these regions as shown in Fig. 19.10A.

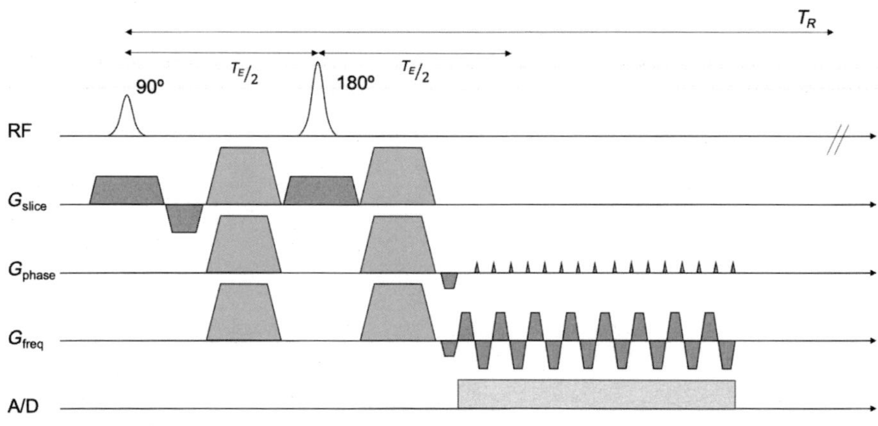

FIG. 19.9

Single spin echo diffusion-weighted pulse sequence with 2D echo-planar imaging readout. The blue gradients are the diffusion gradients.

A Susceptibility induced distortions

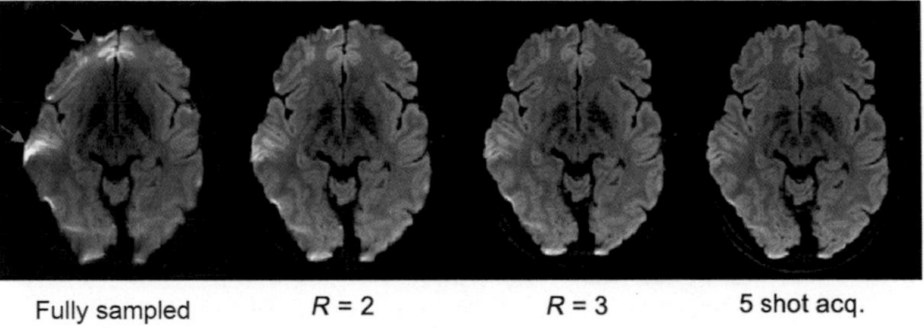

B Chemical shift

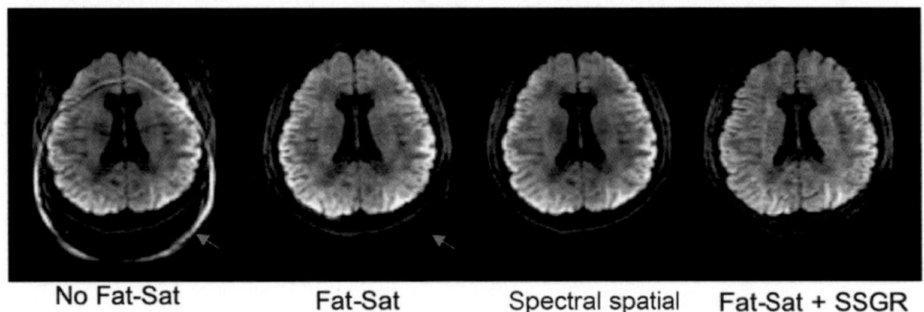

C Eddy-current induced image distortions

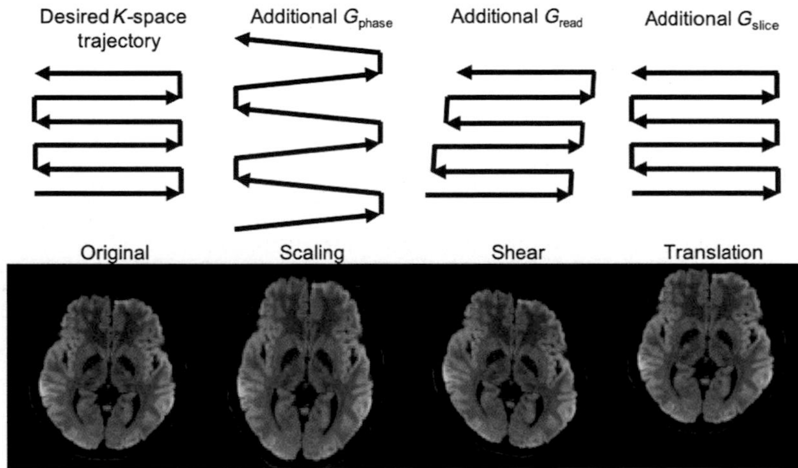

FIG. 19.10

(A) Susceptibility changes at air-tissue interfaces result in distortions in the magnetic field which result in image distortions. These distortions can be reduced by using acceleration techniques to reduce the effective bandwidth in the phase encode direction, including parallel imaging or multishot acquisitions. Reduced distortions can be appreciated near the sinuses (orange arrows) in brain images from left to right as the number of phase encode lines acquired within a single readout is reduced. (B) Chemical shift artifacts resulting from the displacement of fat signal (images courtesy of Matt Middione). The fat signal can be suppressed using a fat-saturation prepulse, spectral spatial excitation, or slice select gradient reversal (SSGR) [93]. (C) Eddy-current fields which persist during the read-out alter the *k*-space trajectory, resulting in image distortions which depend on the orientation of the diffusion encoding. Eddy-current-induced image distortions can cause a mismatch between different diffusion-encoded image volumes and lead to inaccurate model fitting.

One way to address these off-resonance effects is to acquire images with opposing phase encode polarities such that images with equal and opposite distortions are produced. Field maps can be estimated using the two sets of images and used to correct image distortions resulting from off-resonance [94].

Chemical shift artifacts in EPI can also be prominent due to the low bandwidth in the phase encode direction as shown in Fig. 19.10B. Conventional excitation pulses excite both fat and water. In the brain, the 3.5 ppm difference between the resonance frequencies of fat and water results in a shift along the phase encode direction in the location of subdural fat within the image. The number of voxels of fat-shift depends on the field strength and the echo spacing of the EPI readout. For example, at 3 T with an echo spacing of 1 ms and a 24 cm field of view (FOV), the fat will be shifted by 10.73 cm in the image, causing significant ghosting artifacts in the phase encoding direction. For this reason, a combination of spectral-spatial RF excitations [95], fat-saturation preparation pulses [96], and slice-select gradient reversal [97] are commonly used to suppress the fat signal for EPI acquisitions. Since these techniques are based on the spectral profile, they are sensitive to B_0 inhomogeneities. For body imaging, short T_1 inversion recovery [98] is often used for fat suppression, trading scan efficiency for robustness to field inhomogeneities.

Another source of artifacts are the eddy-current fields generated by diffusion-encoding gradients. Ramping the gradients induces currents in other conducting structures in the magnet, producing additional unwanted magnetic fields that are time-varying [99,100]. While eddy currents are generated by both imaging and diffusion gradients, the large gradient amplitudes and high slew rates of diffusion gradients make eddy currents especially problematic for diffusion imaging. Eddy-current fields from diffusion-encoding gradients that persist during the EPI readout result in image distortions along the phase encode direction that can cause a mismatch between different diffusion-encoded image volumes and inaccurate model fitting (see Fig. 19.10C). Hardware improvements including gradient shielding [101] and gradient preemphasis [102] can reduce the magnitude and effect of eddy-current fields. Diffusion-encoding gradient waveforms [64,78,103] and refocusing strategies [74,80,104] can also be designed to cancel out eddy currents as described in Sections 19.2 and 19.3. Finally, postprocessing techniques can be used to align different diffusion-encoded image volumes [105–112].

Yet another source of off-resonance is the read-out gradients in the EPI readout, which produce additional concomitant fields according to the Maxwell equations [113,114]. For a typical EPI readout, the concomitant fields can be sufficiently strong to cause an image shift in the phase-encode direction, which is quadratically related to the slice position. This shift can be corrected by adding a linear phase modulation across the echo train to introduce a slice-by-slice offset in the phase encode direction.

In addition to the challenges associated with the low bandwidth along the phase encoding direction, the use of a long single-shot EPI echo train constrains the achievable spatial resolution. This limitation arises due to the limited readout time before complete signal decay due to relaxation; additionally, significant T_2^* decay during the readout induces image blurring. Reduced-FOV or Zoomed EPI [115–118], which use inner-volume excitation or outer-volume suppression to reduce the size of the image volume, is one way to increase resolution capabilities.

19.4.2 Multishot EPI

Another strategy to overcome problems caused by the long readout time of single-shot EPI is to segment the *k*-space acquisition across several EPI readouts as shown in Fig. 19.11. The most common way to segment the acquisition is to acquire several interleaved acquisitions with reduced FOV. Multishot strategies have also been developed which retain the full FOV by segmenting in the readout

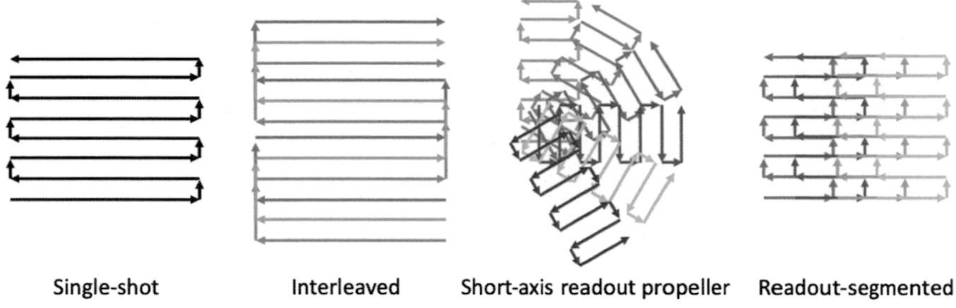

FIG. 19.11

Multishot EPI k-space trajectories. Segmented readouts can be used to reduce the echo-train length and/or improve the resolution over single-shot EPI.

direction rather than the phase-encode orientation. Read-out segmented EPI has been implemented with both Cartesian [119,120] and radial (PROPELLER) [121] k-space trajectories. Multishot EPI trades time-efficiency for a faster effective echo spacing resulting in reduced image blurring and distortions (Fig. 19.10B) and/or increased resolution capabilities. However, motion-induced phase errors must be corrected to avoid signal dropouts and ghosting artifacts in the reconstructed image. The motion-induced phase can be corrected by acquiring low-resolution navigators to estimate the slowly varying motion-induced phase [122–125]. More recently, navigatorless reconstruction methods for multishot EPI have been proposed, which leverage parallel imaging reconstruction methods to estimate and correct the phase-offsets associated with each k-space segment [126,127].

19.4.3 Alternatives to EPI

Instead of the train of gradient echoes used for EPI, rapid acquisition with relaxation enhancement (RARE) shown in Fig. 19.12 utilizes a train of spin echoes to rapidly collect data after the diffusion preparation [92]. Many k-space trajectories including Cartesian [128], radial [129], PROPELLER [130], and spiral [131] can be used with a RARE readout. Compared to EPI, RARE trades off slightly reduced encoding efficiency with improved robustness to off-resonance effects. The refocusing pulses reverse the phase accrual from B_0 field inhomogeneities, tissue susceptibility variations, and eddy currents, thereby reducing the resulting image blurring and distortions. However, the multiple refocusing pulses in the RARE echo train can increase the specific absorption rate (SAR) causing undesirable heating of the tissue. For this reason, SAR-limited refocusing pulses are often used in RARE imaging, resulting in nonideal refocusing profiles and/or flip angles lower than 180°, which can introduce stimulated echoes and other coherence pathways. As the echo train gets longer, these unwanted coherence pathways can interfere destructively with each other, resulting in a loss of signal. The additional coherence pathways are especially problematic for diffusion imaging, since motion-induced phase caused by the diffusion encoding makes it difficult to fulfill the CPMG condition [132]. This problem can be combated by using crushers to prevent the formation of unwanted spin echoes at the cost of SNR, or using a phase cycling scheme for the refocusing pulses [133,134]. The difficulties of implementing diffusion-weighted RARE are exacerbated at high field strengths due to increased SAR, B_1 inhomogeneities, and more pronounced magnetization transfer saturation of tissues [135].

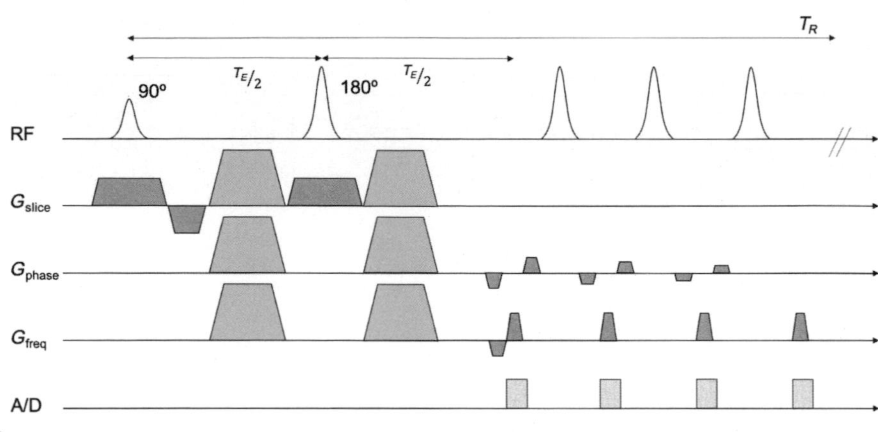

FIG. 19.12

Diffusion-weighted spin echo with a RARE readout using a Cartesian *k*-space trajectory.

Spiral readouts are an alternative to EPI. Since gradients slew smoothly in both the readout and phase encode axis, the spiral trajectory can be more efficient than a Cartesian trajectory. Furthermore, the image artifacts associated with EPI are reduced, the bandwidth of the spiral readout is equal along all directions. For spiral acquisitions, the *k*-space center can be acquired at the beginning of the acquisition, allowing a longer diffusion-encoding period and therefore shorter echo times for a given *b*-value compared to an equivalent EPI readout, in which *k*-space lines are collected before the echo. Artifacts in spiral imaging manifest as image blurring and incoherent aliasing, which appear more noise-like and at least qualitatively less intrusive than EPI artifacts. However, image reconstruction for spiral trajectories requires gridding or nonuniform FFT operations which can be computationally costlier than a Cartesian reconstruction. In addition, the availability of commercial implementations of spiral diffusion sequences is limited compared to EPI. Like EPI, spirals can be either single-shot or interleaved acquisitions. Variable density spirals trajectories have been used to perform self-navigated interleaved acquisitions for high-resolution DTI [136].

19.4.4 Acceleration methods

Diffusion images acquired with Cartesian readouts are often undersampled in the phase encode direction to reduce the effective echo spacing and the length of the echo train. Parallel imaging can be used to restore the unaliased images by using spatial information inherent in the coil sensitivity profiles of a multichannel receive coil [137,138]. Another common strategy to accelerate diffusion imaging is to acquire fewer frequency encode lines prior to the collecting *k*-space center, resulting in an asymmetric *k*-space [139]. In theory MR images are real-valued, and thus the missing information can be synthesized using the conjugate symmetry of the spatial frequency space. In practice, these types of reconstructions usually benefit from phase correction to account for phase variations from off-resonance effects, flow and motion [140,141]. These acceleration techniques can be employed to reduce the length of the EPI readout, allowing shorter echo times, improved image resolution, or reduced blurring and distortion artifacts (Fig. 19.10). Typically in diffusion MRI, the reduced echo time from accelerated imaging results in a net gain in SNR despite the loss of signal due to reduced acquisition time.

Compressed sensing is another way to accelerate diffusion imaging by using *a priori* information about sparsity patterns to reduce sampling requirements [142]. Compressed sensing can be used to reconstruct images from pseudo-randomly undersampled acquisitions. Such undersampling results in incoherent aliasing which has noise-like properties in the sparsifying transform domain. Because the image information is compressed into a few significant coefficients in the sparse domain, the noise and incoherent aliasing can be removed by thresholding smaller coefficients. In a typical compressed sensing reconstruction, an iterative method is used where the sparsity requirement in the transform domain is alternatively enforced with data fidelity in the acquisition domain until the solution converges. In practice, compressed sensing in the image domain is more often implemented with non-Cartesian sampling trajectories, which generate noise-like artifacts, rather than 2D Cartesian sampling schemes [143], which generate coherent artifacts. Sparsity constraints in the diffusion domains, which can be combined with constraints in the spatial domain [144], have been demonstrated to reduce the number of diffusion measurements needed for resolving crossing fibers [145] and q-space spectrum imaging [146], which require high angular resolution.

Accelerated acquisition methods have also been developed in the slice direction using simultaneous multislice imaging [147]. Simultaneous multislice imaging excites and encodes several slices at the same time, resulting in an aliased image with overlapping slices. Like in-plane parallel imaging, the slice information can then be separated using spatial information from coil sensitivity profiles in a multichannel receive coil [137,148]. Simultaneous multislice imaging can reduce the TR significantly while maintaining full coverage of the anatomy of interest and therefore improve the SNR efficiency of diffusion imaging. Since simultaneous multislice imaging reduces the number of excitations and diffusion encodings necessary to cover an image volume, it can also reduce gradient heating, which can limit the duty cycle and efficiency of diffusion imaging especially when using multiple-pulsed gradient acquisitions. However, simultaneous multislice RF excitations and refocusing pulses can be SAR intensive, and designing thin slice profiles for high-resolution imaging can be problematic. An alternative is to design a multislab excitation. The slices can then be resolved within each slab by phase encoding in the slice direction [149] or with a spatially varying phase profile in the slice direction [150]. Very thin slices with accurate slice profiles can be reconstructed from several acquisitions with alternating phase polarities. Multislab acquisitions retain some of the SNR benefits of volumetric imaging, while avoiding the prohibitively long echo trains necessary to encode a full 3D space, to generate high-resolution diffusion images as shown in Fig. 19.13.

19.5 Hardware considerations and system limitations

Diffusion imaging capabilities are primarily driven by gradient performance [151,152]. Strong gradients and high slew rates reduce the diffusion-encoding time, which improves the SNR by reducing the TE. High slew rates also enable faster image encoding, which can further reduce TE and help mitigate distortions by shortening the echo spacing. Efficient diffusion encoding is especially important for multipulsed diffusion encoding methods such as DDE. Oscillating gradient diffusion encoding as well as generalized diffusion encoding benefit from both increased gradient strength and slew rate.

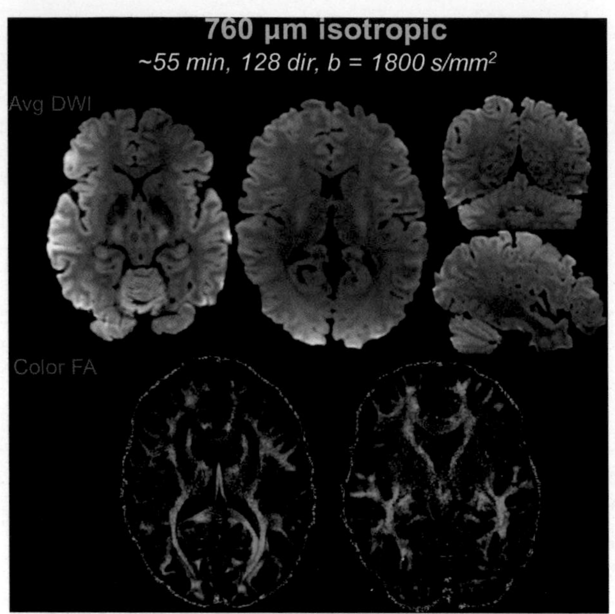

FIG. 19.13

Submillimeter resolution diffusion tensor imaging with generalized slice dithered enhanced resolution: simultaneous multislice acquisition [150].

Images courtesy of Kawin Setsompop.

Powerful gradient amplifiers are also necessary to keep up with the demands of diffusion sequences. Power drop due to insufficient amplifiers can be a significant problem, and heating of the gradient coils and amplifiers can also be a limiting factor for SNR-efficient diffusion imaging. Peripheral nerve stimulation is a fundamental limitation of gradient slew rates. Varying the applied magnetic field can interfere with the conduction of nerves within the body, causing mild to moderate discomfort and in extreme cases the potential to cause the subject to experience magnetophosphenes. One way to reduce peripheral nerve stimulation is to build compact magnets or gradient insert coils [153–156]. The reduced coverage of compact coil designs limits the gradient-induced electric field, which increases quadratically with distance from the gradient isocenter. This design can allow EPI imaging at much higher bandwidths and result in significant reductions in image distortion [157,158]. Compact or head-only gradients also reduce the power requirements [159] on the gradient amplifier to reach high gradient amplitudes, allowing shorter diffusion-encoding waveforms and higher image quality.

High-field diffusion has promise for providing higher SNR since the MR signal scales roughly with field strength [160]. Unfortunately, for diffusion imaging, it is potentially more difficult to realize this improvement in SNR compared to other types of MRI. At higher field strengths, T_1 increases and there is an apparent shortening of T_2. Therefore, the SNR advantage of higher field strength is not always retained for diffusion imaging because there is more T_2 decay and less T_1 recovery compared to equivalent TEs and TRs at lower field strength. Further, diffusion imaging depends primarily on spin echo refocusing mechanisms and it is more difficult, and more SAR intensive, to achieve an accurate refocusing pulse at high field. Increased B_0 inhomogeneities at high field can also increase artifacts and distortion levels for traditional EPI readouts. Despite the seemingly increased challenges associated with diffusion imaging at high-field, many groups have demonstrated exemplary data quality at 7 T [161–163] and many methods [164] already exist to help mitigate the challenges discussed above (e.g., navigated-segmented readouts, parallel receive and transmit [165,166], B_1 mapping, adiabatic pulses, field mapping, zoomed-EPI, etc.).

19.6 Diffusion mapping outside the brain

Diffusion mapping is most commonly deployed in the brain, and thus most of the considerations above are based on brain imaging. However, there are multiple applications of diffusion mapping outside the brain, including the study of myocardial tissue [29], musculoskeletal injury [30], breast imaging, spine and the peripheral nervous system. Each imaging target presents a unique set of challenges and therefore diffusion acquisitions should ideally be optimized for the competing demands relevant to each application. Modifications to the b-value should be made to account for differences in diffusion rates of the target tissue, and relaxation differences can dictate the choice of refocusing scheme. In addition, applications outside the brain often have additional challenges such as increased motion or off-resonance effects, which must be accounted for in the image encoding strategy or through post-processing corrections. Here, a brief summary of challenges related to the acquisition of diffusion-weighted MRI outside the brain are presented. Diffusion MRI applications outside the brain are discussed in more detail in Chapter 24.

19.6.1 Cardiac imaging

There is great interest in quantitative diffusion MRI of the heart because it offers a potential way to assess the structure and function of the myocardium. The key challenges in cardiac diffusion MRI are the relatively short T_2^* values of the heart ($\sim$25 ms at 3 T) [167] and the superposition of respiratory and cardiac motion. Respiratory motion is generally managed using breath holding, which inherently limits data acquisition to $<$20 s, or with navigator-based approaches [168], which can extend data acquisition windows to several minutes. Cardiac motion is managed first by cardiac (prospective) triggering to synchronize imaging to a patient's specific cardiac rhythm. This alone, however, is insufficient owing to the significant cardiac motion that occurs during the application of the diffusion-encoding gradients (20–80 ms). Hence, despite some existing reports, conventional SE-EPI diffusion MRI approaches with breath holding and cardiac triggering are not reliable for quantitative diffusion mapping of the heart. Two approaches are currently most widespread. The stimulated-echo acquisition mode (STEAM) EPI approach mitigates the cardiac motion problem with triggering and two short diffusion-encoding gradients separated by an entire cardiac cycle [169]. This approach has excellent motion robustness, but inherently low SNR-efficiency owing to the low amplitude of the stimulated echo and the limited image acquisition rate of one single-shot image for every two heartbeats. Alternately, the diffusion gradients can be designed to include nulling of the first and second gradient moments in the SE-EPI approach, thereby mitigating bulk motion sensitivity while retaining diffusion weighting [170]. This approach has inherently better SNR efficiency than the STEAM approach, as the TE can be lengthened without motion artifacts. To mitigate the signal loss that accompanies the longer TE (due to moment nulling, single-shot EPI, and a shorter T_2^* than the brain) newer approaches use optimization methods to define very short diffusion-encoding gradient waveforms [63] or single-shot spiral readouts [171]. Slice-following approaches can also improve SNR-efficiency [172].

19.6.2 Spinal cord

The assessment of microstructural properties of the spinal cord using diffusion MRI has great promise for improved patient diagnosis and care [173–175]. The key challenges for spinal cord diffusion MRI are the low SNR (due to poor coil coverage), physiological motion, susceptibility artifacts, and dynamic shifts in B_0 due to respiration [176]. Advanced coil designs [177], novel shim hardware [178], and reduced field-of-view pulse sequences [115,179] have been developed to address these challenges. In addition, software advancements have been developed to correct residual motion artifacts [180], as well as to register, analyze, and visualize spinal cord images [181].

19.6.3 Peripheral nervous system

Diffusion tensor MRI has shown promising results in detecting various disease conditions [182–186] and tracking degenerative/regenerative changes in the myelin sheaths and axonal membranes of peripheral nerves [187–189], which can offer more specific treatment guidance than the conventional T_2-weighted sequences. Unlike brain diffusion MRI, the need to resolve crossing neuronal fibers rarely occurs in peripheral nerve diffusion MRI. However, distortions can be more severe due to the larger FOVs, strong off-resonance effects (e.g., around the brachial plexus), and gradient nonlinearity effects due to targets being relatively far off-isocenter (e.g., shoulder and arm). The small size of peripheral nerves is another challenging factor, because feasible spatial resolutions (e.g., 2 mm × 2 mm × 3 mm) are often insufficient to separate the nerves from neighboring blood vessels and muscles. For these reasons, there is a great interest in segmented image read-outs and reduced FOV sequences.

19.6.4 Breast

Diffusion MRI in the breast has been extensively investigated for a range of applications including improvement of lesion characterization, distinguishing invasive from noninvasive disease, and assessing response to treatment [190]. However, challenges associated with off-resonance to which diffusion-weighted EPI are vulnerable are further magnified by the significant fat content in the breast, large air-tissue interfaces, and off-isocenter imaging. Additionally, single-shot diffusion MRI methods cannot achieve the 1 mm × 1 mm × 3 mm minimum resolution recommended for standard dynamic contrast-enhanced breast imaging [191] even with parallel imaging and breast receive coils with increasing number of channels. Advanced diffusion imaging methods have demonstrated promise to improve the resolution and hence the depiction of lesions morphology. Notably, exquisite depiction of lesion morphology has been demonstrated with a reduced FOV method [192,193]; however, the limited FOV is not acceptable for a screening protocol. Multishot and readout segmented methods have also shown promise for improved resolution but come with increased susceptibility to respiratory and cardiac motion [194,195].

19.6.5 Musculoskeletal

Diffusion MRI also has potential applications in the assessment of musculoskeletal injury and disease. Compared to brain tissue, muscles have shorter T_2 and a much higher percentage of fat. Sequences with relatively short TE are needed to maintain sufficient SNR. To achieve short TEs, lower b-values are typically used compared to neuroimaging. This is partially justified by the higher apparent diffusion coefficient of skeletal muscles compared to white and gray matter, which enables sufficient diffusion contrast at lower b-values. The EPI readout typically employed in diffusion imaging is susceptible to chemical shift artifacts from the fat in and around muscle. Overlapping fat and water signals result in image artifacts and bias the estimation of diffusion parameters [196] and fiber tracking [197]. Chemical shift-based fat suppression strategies can successfully suppress the aliphatic fat peak but do not affect the olefinic fat peak. Therefore, additional strategies to reduce the contribution from the olefinic fat peak are often employed [198,199].

Diffusion imaging is also used to characterize the microstructure of the proteoglycan and collagen architecture of knee cartilage based on differences in diffusion anisotropy [200]. This type of cartilage assessment is relevant to the study and early diagnosis of osteoarthritis. The key challenge for quantitative diffusion MRI of articular cartilage is the need for high spatial resolution (<1 mm) combined with the short T_2 relaxation time of cartilage (40ms at 3T). To address these issues, alternatives to conventional 2D single-shot EPI diffusion imaging have been proposed including segmented acquisitions, rapid k-space trajectories, line scan DTI [201], and steady-state sequences [202].

19.7 Summary

In summary, the development of new diffusion acquisition methods is an active area of research. As hardware capabilities continue to improve, new diffusion and image encoding methods are enabled that may not have been feasible previously. Improvements in available computing power also allow for more comprehensive numerical optimizations of sequence designs and novel image reconstruction and postprocessing techniques that in turn enable more complicated and/or highly undersampled diffusion acquisitions. As such, the future of quantitative diffusion MRI is rich with possibility in terms of the development of acquisition strategies that provide new types of image contrast and/or improvements in encoding efficiency.

Acknowledgments

The authors would like to thank Professor Julien Cohen-Adad, Professor Daniel Ennis, Professor Brian Hargreaves, DaeHyun Yoon Ph.D., Kitty Moran Ph.D., and Valentina Mazzoli Ph.D. for their contributions to the discussion on the applications of diffusion imaging outside the brain.

References

[1] Hahn EL. Spin echoes. Phys Rev 1950;80(4):580–94.

[2] Carr HY, Purcell EM. Effects of diffusion on free precession in nuclear magnetic resonance experiments. Phys Rev 1954;94(3):630–8.

[3] Moseley ME, Kucharczyk J, Mintorovitch J, Cohen Y, Kurhanewicz J, Derugin N, Asgari H, Norman D. Diffusion-weighted MR imaging of acute stroke: correlation with T_2-weighted and magnetic susceptibility-enhanced MR imaging in cats. AJNR Am J Neuroradiol 1990;11(3):423–9.

[4] Kucharczyk J, Mintorovitch J, Asgari HS, Moseley M. Diffusion/perfusion MR imaging of acute cerebral ischemia. Magn Reson Med 1991;19(2):311–5.

[5] Basser PJ, Pajevic S, Pierpaoli C, Duda J, Aldroubi A. In vivo fiber tractography using DT-MRI data. Magn Reson Med 2000;44(4):625–32.

[6] Basser PJ, Pierpaoli C. Microstructural and physiological features of tissues elucidated by quantitative-diffusion-tensor MRI. J Magn Reson B 1996;111(3):209–19.

[7] Klingberg T, Hedehus M, Temple E, Salz T, Gabrieli JD, Moseley ME, Poldrack RA. Microstructure of temporo-parietal white matter as a basis for reading ability: evidence from diffusion tensor magnetic resonance imaging. Neuron 2000;25(2):493–500.

[8] Zhang H, Alexander DC. Axon diameter mapping in the presence of orientation dispersion with diffusion MRI. Med Image Comput Comput Assist Interv 2010;13(Pt. 1):640–7.

[9] Lawrenz M, Finsterbusch J. Mapping measures of microscopic diffusion anisotropy in human brain white matter in vivo with double-wave-vector diffusion-weighted imaging. Magn Reson Med 2015;73(2): 773–83.

[10] Szczepankiewicz F, Lasic S, van Westen D, Sundgren PC, Englund E, Westin CF, Stahlberg F, Latt J, Topgaard D, Nilsson M. Quantification of microscopic diffusion anisotropy disentangles effects of orientation dispersion from microstructure: applications in healthy volunteers and in brain tumors. Neuroimage 2015;104:241–52.

[11] Rocca MA, Cercignani M, Iannucci G, Comi G, Filippi M. Weekly diffusion-weighted imaging of normal-appearing white matter in MS. Neurology 2000;55(6):882–4.

[12] Bozzali M, Cercignani M, Sormani MP, Comi G, Filippi M. Quantification of brain gray matter damage in different MS phenotypes by use of diffusion tensor MR imaging. AJNR Am J Neuroradiol 2002;23(6):985–8.

[13] Einstein A. Über die von der molekularkinetischen Theorie der Wärme geforderte Bewegung von in ruhenden Flüssigkeiten suspendierten Teilchen. Ann Phys 1905;322(8):549–60.

[14] Mattiello J, Basser PJ, Lebihan D. Analytical expressions for the b matrix in NMR diffusion imaging and spectroscopy. J Magn Reson A 1994;108(2):131–41.

[15] Torrey HC. Bloch equations with diffusion terms. Phys Rev 1956;104(3):563–5.

[16] Abragam PA, Abragam A. The principles of nuclear magnetism. Clarendon Press; 1961.

[17] Mitra PP. Multiple wave-vector extensions of the NMR pulsed-field-gradient spin-echo diffusion measurement. Phys Rev B Condens Matter 1995;51(21):15074–8.

[18] Callaghan PT, Coy A, MacGowan D, Packer KJ, Zelaya FO. Diffraction-like effects in NMR diffusion studies of fluids in porous solids. Nature 1991;351:467.

[19] Novikov DS, Kiselev VG. Effective medium theory of a diffusion-weighted signal. NMR Biomed 2010;23(7):682–97.

[20] Kärger J, Heink W. The propagator representation of molecular transport in microporous crystallites. J Magn Reson 1983;51(1):1–7.

[21] Pfeuffer J, Flogel U, Dreher W, Leibfritz D. Restricted diffusion and exchange of intracellular water: theoretical modelling and diffusion time dependence of 1H NMR measurements on perfused glial cells. NMR Biomed 1998;11(1):19–31.

[22] Assaf Y, Basser PJ. Composite hindered and restricted model of diffusion (CHARMED) MR imaging of the human brain. Neuroimage 2005;27(1):48–58.

[23] Stejskal EO. Use of spin echoes in a pulsed magnetic-field gradient to study anisotropic restricted diffusion and flow. J Chem Phys 1965;43(10):3597–603.

[24] Tanner JE, Stejskal EO. Restricted self-diffusion of protons in colloidal systems by the pulse-gradient, spin-echo method. J Chem Phys 1968;49:9.

[25] Kinosada Y, Ono M, Okuda Y, Seta H, Hada Y, Hattori T, Nomura Y, Sakuma H, Takeda K, Ishii Y, et al. MR tractography—visualization of structure of nerve fiber system from diffusion weighted images with maximum intensity projection method. Nihon Igaku Hoshasen Gakkai Zasshi 1993;53(2):171–9.
[26] Song S-K, Sun S-W, Ramsbottom MJ, Chang C, Russell J, Cross AH. Dysmyelination revealed through MRI as increased radial (but unchanged axial) diffusion of water. Neuroimage 2002;17(3):1429–36.
[27] Vaillancourt D, Spraker M, Prodoehl J, Abraham I, Corcos D, Zhou X, Comella C, Little D. High-resolution diffusion tensor imaging in the substantia nigra of de novo Parkinson disease. Neurology 2009;72(16): 1378–84.
[28] Rose SE, Chen F, Chalk JB, Zelaya FO, Strugnell WE, Benson M, Semple J, Doddrell DM. Loss of connectivity in Alzheimer's disease: an evaluation of white matter tract integrity with colour coded MR diffusion tensor imaging. J Neurol Neurosurg Psychiatry 2000;69(4):528–30.
[29] Reese TG, Weisskoff RM, Smith RN, Rosen BR, Dinsmore RE, Wedeen VJ. Imaging myocardial fiber architecture in vivo with magnetic resonance. Magn Reson Med 1995;34(6):786–91.
[30] Zaraiskaya T, Kumbhare D, Noseworthy MD. Diffusion tensor imaging in evaluation of human skeletal muscle injury. J Magn Reson Imaging 2006;24(2):402–8.
[31] Wedeen VJ, Hagmann P, Tseng WY, Reese TG, Weisskoff RM. Mapping complex tissue architecture with diffusion spectrum magnetic resonance imaging. Magn Reson Med 2005;54(6):1377–86.
[32] Tian Q, Rokem A, Folkerth RD, Nummenmaa A, Fan Q, Edlow BL, JA MN. *q*-Space truncation and sampling in diffusion spectrum imaging. Magn Reson Med 2016;76:1750–63.
[33] Bar-Shir A, Avram L, Özarslan E, Basser PJ, Cohen Y. The effect of the diffusion time and pulse gradient duration ratio on the diffraction pattern and the structural information estimated from *q*-space diffusion MR: experiments and simulations. J Magn Reson 2008;194(2):230–6.
[34] Gross B, Kosfeld R. Anwendung der spin-echo-methode der messung der selbstdiffusion. Messtechnik 1969;77:171–7.
[35] Parsons EC, Does MD, Gore JC. Modified oscillating gradient pulses for direct sampling of the diffusion spectrum suitable for imaging sequences. Magn Reson Imaging 2003;21(3–4):279–85.
[36] Callaghan PT, Stepišnik J. Frequency-domain analysis of spin motion using modulated-gradient NMR. Academic Press; 1995.
[37] Parsons Jr EC, Does MD, Gore JC. Temporal diffusion spectroscopy: theory and implementation in restricted systems using oscillating gradients. Magn Reson Med 2006;55(1):75–84.
[38] Kakkar LS, Bennett OF, Siow B, Richardson S, Ianus A, Quick T, Atkinson D, Phillips JB, Drobnjak I. Low frequency oscillating gradient spin-echo sequences improve sensitivity to axon diameter: an experimental study in viable nerve tissue. Neuroimage 2018;182:314–28.
[39] Mercredi M, Vincent TJ, Bidinosti CP, Martin M. Assessing the accuracy of using oscillating gradient spin echo sequences with AxCaliber to infer micron-sized axon diameters. MAGMA 2017;30(1):1–14.
[40] Drobnjak I, Zhang H, Ianus A, Kaden E, Alexander DC. PGSE, OGSE, and sensitivity to axon diameter in diffusion MRI: Insight from a simulation study. Magn Reson Med 2016;75(2):688–700.
[41] Wu D, Martin LJ, Northington FJ, Zhang J. Oscillating-gradient diffusion magnetic resonance imaging detects acute subcellular structural changes in the mouse forebrain after neonatal hypoxia-ischemia. J Cereb Blood Flow Metab 2019;39:1336–48. 271678X18759859.
[42] Reynaud O, Winters KV, Hoang DM, Wadghiri YZ, Novikov DS, Kim SG. Surface-to-volume ratio mapping of tumor microstructure using oscillating gradient diffusion weighted imaging. Magn Reson Med 2016;76(1):237–47.
[43] Wu D, Martin LJ, Northington FJ, Zhang J. Oscillating gradient diffusion MRI reveals unique microstructural information in normal and hypoxia-ischemia injured mouse brains. Magn Reson Med 2014;72(5):1366–74.
[44] Aggarwal M, Burnsed J, Martin LJ, Northington FJ, Zhang J. Imaging neurodegeneration in the mouse hippocampus after neonatal hypoxia-ischemia using oscillating gradient diffusion MRI. Magn Reson Med 2014;72(3):829–40.

[45] Baron CA, Beaulieu C. Oscillating gradient spin-echo (OGSE) diffusion tensor imaging of the human brain. Magn Reson Med 2014;72(3):726–36.
[46] Van AT, Holdsworth SJ, Bammer R. In vivo investigation of restricted diffusion in the human brain with optimized oscillating diffusion gradient encoding. Magn Reson Med 2014;71(1):83–94.
[47] Merboldt K-D, Hanicke W, Frahm J. Self-diffusion NMR imaging using stimulated echoes. J Magn Reson 1985;64(3):479–86.
[48] Jelescu IO, Veraart J, Fieremans E, Novikov DS. Degeneracy in model parameter estimation for multi-compartmental diffusion in neuronal tissue. NMR Biomed 2016;29(1):33–47.
[49] Cheng Y, Cory DG. Multiple scattering by NMR. J Am Chem Soc 1999;121(34):7935–6.
[49a] Topgaard D. Multidimensional diffusion MRI. J Magn Reson 1999;275:98–113.
[50] Jian B, Vemuri BC, Ozarslan E, Carney PR, Mareci TH. A novel tensor distribution model for the diffusion-weighted MR signal. Neuroimage 2007;37(1):164–76.
[51] Koch MA, Finsterbusch J. Compartment size estimation with double wave vector diffusion-weighted imaging. Magn Reson Med 2008;60(1):90–101.
[52] Komlosh ME, Ozarslan E, Lizak MJ, Horkay F, Schram V, Shemesh N, Cohen Y, Basser PJ. Pore diameter mapping using double pulsed-field gradient MRI and its validation using a novel glass capillary array phantom. J Magn Reson 2011;208(1):128–35.
[53] Ozarslan E, Basser PJ. Microscopic anisotropy revealed by NMR double pulsed field gradient experiments with arbitrary timing parameters. J Chem Phys 2008;128(15):154511.
[54] Lawrenz M, Koch MA, Finsterbusch J. A tensor model and measures of microscopic anisotropy for double-wave-vector diffusion-weighting experiments with long mixing times. J Magn Reson 2010;202(1):43–56.
[55] Shemesh N, Ozarslan E, Komlosh ME, Basser PJ, Cohen Y. From single-pulsed field gradient to double-pulsed field gradient MR: gleaning new microstructural information and developing new forms of contrast in MRI. NMR Biomed 2010;23(7):757–80.
[56] Jespersen SN, Lundell H, Sonderby CK, Dyrby TB. Orientationally invariant metrics of apparent compartment eccentricity from double pulsed field gradient diffusion experiments. NMR Biomed 2013;26(12):1647–62.
[57] Lawrenz M, Brassen S, Finsterbusch J. Microscopic diffusion anisotropy in the human brain: reproducibility, normal values, and comparison with the fractional anisotropy. Neuroimage 2015;109:283–97.
[58] Lawrenz M, Brassen S, Finsterbusch J. Microscopic diffusion anisotropy in the human brain: age-related changes. Neuroimage 2016;141:313–25.
[59] Yang G, Tian Q, Leuze C, Wintermark M, McNab JA. Double diffusion encoding MRI for the clinic. Magn Reson Med 2018;80(2):507–20.
[60] Mori S, van Zijl PC. Diffusion weighting by the trace of the diffusion tensor within a single scan. Magn Reson Med 1995;33(1):41–52.
[61] Wong EC, Cox RW, Song AW. Optimized isotropic diffusion weighting. Magn Reson Med 1995;34(2):139–43.
[62] Topgaard D. Isotropic diffusion weighting in PGSE NMR: Numerical optimization of the q-MAS PGSE sequence. Microporous Mesoporous Mater 2013;178:60–3.
[63] Aliotta E, Wu HH, Ennis DB. Convex optimized diffusion encoding (CODE) gradient waveforms for minimum echo time and bulk motion-compensated diffusion-weighted MRI. Magn Reson Med 2017;77(2):717–29.
[64] Aliotta E, Moulin K, Ennis DB. Eddy current-nulled convex optimized diffusion encoding (EN-CODE) for distortion-free diffusion tensor imaging with short echo times. Magn Reson Med 2018;79:663–72.
[65] Yang G, JA MN. Eddy current nulled constrained optimization of isotropic diffusion encoding gradient waveforms. Magn Reson Med 2018;81:1818–32.

[66] Szczepankiewicz F, Nilsson M. Maxwell-compensated waveform design for asymmetric diffusion encoding. Proc Intl Soc Magn Reson Med 2018;26:207, Paris, France.

[67] Baron CA, Lebel RM, Wilman AH, Beaulieu C. The effect of concomitant gradient fields on diffusion tensor imaging. Magn Reson Med 2012;68(4):1190–201.

[68] Sjolund J, Szczepankiewicz F, Nilsson M, Topgaard D, Westin CF, Knutsson H. Constrained optimization of gradient waveforms for generalized diffusion encoding. J Magn Reson 2015;261:157–68.

[69] Drobnjak I, Zhang H, Hall MG, Alexander DC. The matrix formalism for generalised gradients with time-varying orientation in diffusion NMR. J Magn Reson 2011;210(1):151–7.

[70] Callaghan PT. A simple matrix formalism for spin echo analysis of restricted diffusion under generalized gradient waveforms. J Magn Reson 1997;129(1):74–84.

[71] Ianus A, Drobnjak I, Alexander DC. Model-based estimation of microscopic anisotropy using diffusion MRI: a simulation study. NMR Biomed 2016;29(5):672–85.

[72] Ianus A, Shemesh N, Alexander DC, Drobnjak I. Double oscillating diffusion encoding and sensitivity to microscopic anisotropy. Magn Reson Med 2017;78(2):550–64.

[72a] Lampinen B, Szczepankiewicz F, Martensson J, van Westen D, Sundgren PC, Nilsson M. Neurite density imaging versus imaging of microscopic anisotropy in diffusion MRI: a model comparison using spherical tensor encoding. Neuroimage 2017;147:517–31.

[73] Stejskal EO, Tanner JE. Spin diffusion measurements: spin echoes in the presence of a time-dependent field gradient. J Chem Phys 1965;42(1):288–92.

[74] Reese TG, Heid O, Weisskoff RM, Wedeen VJ. Reduction of eddy-current-induced distortion in diffusion MRI using a twice-refocused spin echo. Magn Reson Med 2003;49(1):177–82.

[75] Kaiser R, Bartholdi E, Ernst R. Diffusion and field-gradient effects in NMR Fourier spectroscopy. J Chem Phys 1974;60(8):2966–79.

[76] Wu EX, Buxton RB. Effect of diffusion on the steady-state magnetization with pulsed field gradients. J Magn Reson 1990;90(2):243–53.

[77] Mcnab JA, Miller KL. Sensitivity of diffusion weighted steady state free precession to anisotropic diffusion. Magn Reson Med 2008;60(2):405–13.

[78] Alexander AL, Tsuruda JS, Parker DL. Elimination of eddy current artifacts in diffusion-weighted echo-planar images: the use of bipolar gradients. Magn Reson Med 1997;38(6):1016–21.

[79] Jerschow A, Müller N. Suppression of convection artifacts in stimulated-echo diffusion experiments. Double-stimulated-echo experiments. J Magn Reson 1997;125(2):372–5.

[80] Gibbs SJ, Johnson CS. A PFG NMR experiment for accurate diffusion and flow studies in the presence of eddy currents. J Magn Reson 1991;93(2):395–402.

[81] Price WS, Stilbs P, Jönsson B, Söderman O. Macroscopic background gradient and radiation damping effects on high-field PGSE NMR diffusion measurements. J Magn Reson 2001;150(1):49–56.

[82] Sorland GH, Aksnes D, Gjerdaker L. A pulsed field gradient spin-echo method for diffusion measurements in the presence of internal gradients. J Magn Reson 1999;137(2):397–401.

[83] Cotts R, Hoch M, Sun T, Markert J. Pulsed field gradient stimulated echo methods for improved NMR diffusion measurements in heterogeneous systems. Je Magn Reson 1989;83(2):252–66.

[84] Shemesh N, Cohen Y. Overcoming apparent susceptibility-induced anisotropy (aSIA) by bipolar double-pulsed-field-gradient NMR. J Magn Reson 2011;212(2):362–9.

[85] Mcnab JA, Miller KL. Steady-state diffusion-weighted imaging: theory, acquisition and analysis. NMR Biomed 2010;23(7):781–93.

[86] Bihan DL, Turner R, MacFall J. Effects of intravoxel incoherent motions (IVIM) in steady-state free precession (SSFP) imaging: application to molecular diffusion imaging. Magn Reson Med 1989;10(3):324–37.

[87] Merboldt KD, Hanicke W, Gyngell ML, Frahm J, Bruhn H. The influence of flow and motion in MRI of diffusion using a modified CE-FAST sequence. Magn Reson Med 1989;12(2):198–208.

[88] Jones DK. The effect of gradient sampling schemes on measures derived from diffusion tensor MRI: a Monte Carlo study. Magn Reson Med 2004;51(4):807–15.

[89] Wedeen VJ, Wang RP, Schmahmann JD, Benner T, Tseng WY, Dai G, Pandya DN, Hagmann P, D'Arceuil H, de Crespigny AJ. Diffusion spectrum magnetic resonance imaging (DSI) tractography of crossing fibers. Neuroimage 2008;41(4):1267–77.

[90] Turner R, Le Bihan D, Maier J, Vavrek R, Hedges LK, Pekar J. Echo-planar imaging of intravoxel incoherent motion. Radiology 1990;177(2):407–14.

[91] Li TQ, Takahashi AM, Hindmarsh T, Moseley ME. ADC mapping by means of a single-shot spiral MRI technique with application in acute cerebral ischemia. Magn Reson Med 1999;41(1):143–7.

[92] Beaulieu CF, Zhou X, Cofer GP, Johnson GA. Diffusion-weighted MR microscopy with fast spin-echo. Magn Reson Med 1993;30(2):201–6.

[93] Middione M, Wu H, Dougherty R, Zhu K, Kerr A, Pauly J. Single-spin echo multiband diffusion imaging with slice select gradient reversal. Toronto, CA: Proc Intl Soc Magn Reson Med; 2015.

[94] Andersson JL, Skare S, Ashburner J. How to correct susceptibility distortions in spin-echo echo-planar images: application to diffusion tensor imaging. Neuroimage 2003;20(2):870–88.

[95] Block W, Pauly J, Kerr A, Nishimura D. Consistent fat suppression with compensated spectral-spatial pulses. Magn Reson Med 1997;38(2):198–206.

[96] Keller PJ, Hunter Jr W, Schmalbrock P. Multisection fat-water imaging with chemical shift selective presaturation. Radiology 1987;164(2):539–41.

[97] Gomori J, Holland G, Grossman R, Gefter W, Lenkinski R. Fat suppression by section-select gradient reversal on spin-echo MR imaging. Work in progress. Radiology 1988;168(2):493–5.

[98] Takahara T, Imai Y, Yamashita T, Yasuda S, Nasu S, Van Cauteren M. Diffusion weighted whole body imaging with background body signal suppression (DWIBS): technical improvement using free breathing, STIR and high resolution 3D display. Matrix 2004;160(160):160.

[99] Van Vaals J, Bergman A. Optimization of eddy-current compensation. J Magn Reson 1990;90(1): 52–70.

[100] Price WS. Pulsed-field gradient nuclear magnetic resonance as a tool for studying translational diffusion: part II. Experimental aspects. Concepts Magn Reson 1998;10(4):197–237.

[101] Bowtell R, Mansfield P. Gradient coil design using active magnetic screening. Magn Reson Med 1991;17(1):15–9 discussion 19-21.

[102] Boesch C, Gruetter R, Martin E. Temporal and spatial analysis of fields generated by eddy currents in superconducting magnets: optimization of corrections and quantitative characterization of magnet/gradient systems. Magn Reson Med 1991;20(2):268–84.

[103] Finsterbusch J. Eddy-current compensated diffusion weighting with a single refocusing RF pulse. Magn Reson Med 2009;61(3):748–54.

[104] Mueller L, Wetscherek A, Kuder TA, Laun FB. Eddy current compensated double diffusion encoded (DDE) MRI. Magn Reson Med 2017;77(1):328–35.

[105] Truong TK, Chen B, Song AW. Integrated SENSE DTI with correction of susceptibility- and eddy current-induced geometric distortions. Neuroimage 2008;40(1):53–8.

[106] Mohammadi S, Moller HE, Kugel H, Muller DK, Deppe M. Correcting eddy current and motion effects by affine whole-brain registrations: evaluation of three-dimensional distortions and comparison with slicewise correction. Magn Reson Med 2010;64(4):1047–56.

[107] Embleton KV, Haroon HA, Morris DM, Ralph MA, Parker GJ. Distortion correction for diffusion-weighted MRI tractography and fMRI in the temporal lobes. Hum Brain Mapp 2010;31(10):1570–87.

[108] Zhuang J, Lu ZL, Vidal CB, Damasio H. Correction of eddy current distortions in high angular resolution diffusion imaging. J Magn Reson Imaging 2013;37(6):1460–7.

[109] Truong TK, Song AW, Chen NK. Correction for eddy current-induced echo-shifting effect in partial-fourier diffusion tensor imaging. Biomed Res Int 2015;2015:185026.

[110] Nilsson M, Szczepankiewicz F, van Westen D, Hansson O. Extrapolation-based references improve motion and eddy-current correction of high B-value DWI data: application in Parkinson's disease dementia. PLoS One 2015;10(11):e0141825.
[111] Andersson JLR, Sotiropoulos SN. An integrated approach to correction for off-resonance effects and subject movement in diffusion MR imaging. Neuroimage 2016;125:1063–78.
[112] Zahneisen B, Aksoy M, Maclaren J, Wuerslin C, Bammer R. Extended hybrid-space SENSE for EPI: off-resonance and eddy current corrected joint interleaved blip-up/down reconstruction. Neuroimage 2017;153:97–108.
[113] Norris DG, Hutchison JM. Concomitant magnetic field gradients and their effects on imaging at low magnetic field strengths. Magn Reson Imaging 1990;8(1):33–7.
[114] Bernstein MA, Zhou XJ, Polzin JA, King KF, Ganin A, Pelc NJ, Glover GH. Concomitant gradient terms in phase contrast MR: analysis and correction. Magn Reson Med 1998;39(2):300–8.
[115] Finsterbusch J. High-resolution diffusion tensor imaging with inner field-of-view EPI. J Magn Reson Imaging 2009;29(4):987–93.
[116] Feinberg DA, Turner R, Jakab PD, Kienlin MV. Echo-planar imaging with asymmetric gradient modulation and inner-volume excitation. Magn Reson Med 1990;13(1):162–9.
[117] Jeong E-K, Kim S-E, Guo J, Kholmovski EG, Parker DL. High-resolution DTI with 2D interleaved multislice reduced FOV single-shot diffusion-weighted EPI (2D ss-rFOV-DWEPI). Magn Reson Med 2005;54(6):1575–9.
[118] Wheeler-Kingshott CAM, Parker GJM, Symms MR, Hickman SJ, Tofts PS, Miller DH, Barker GJ. ADC mapping of the human optic nerve: Increased resolution, coverage, and reliability with CSF-suppressed ZOOM-EPI. Magn Reson Med 2002;47(1):24–31.
[119] Porter DA, Heidemann RM. High resolution diffusion-weighted imaging using readout-segmented echo-planar imaging, parallel imaging and a two-dimensional navigator-based reacquisition. Magn Reson Med 2009;62(2):468–75.
[120] Holdsworth SJ, Skare S, Newbould RD, Guzmann R, Blevins NH, Bammer R. Readout-segmented EPI for rapid high resolution diffusion imaging at 3T. Eur J Radiol 2008;65(1):36–46.
[121] Skare S, Newbould RD, Clayton DB, Bammer R. Propeller EPI in the other direction. Magn Reson Med 2006;55(6):1298–307.
[122] Bammer R, Stollberger R, Augustin M, Simbrunner J, Offenbacher H, Kooijman H, Ropele S, Kapeller P, Wach P, Ebner F. Diffusion-weighted imaging with navigated interleaved echo-planar imaging and a conventional gradient system. Radiology 1999;211(3):799–806.
[123] Butts K, Pauly J, de Crespigny A, Moseley M. Isotropic diffusion-weighted and spiral-navigated interleaved EPI for routine imaging of acute stroke. Magn Reson Med 1997;38(5):741–9.
[124] Butts K, de Crespigny A, Pauly JM, Moseley M. Diffusion-weighted interleaved echo-planar imaging with a pair of orthogonal navigator echoes. Magn Reson Med 1996;35(5):763–70.
[125] McNab JA, Gallichan D, Miller KL. 3D steady-state diffusion-weighted imaging with trajectory using radially batched internal navigator echoes (TURBINE). Magn Reson Med 2010;63(1):235–42.
[126] N-k C, Guidon A, Chang H-C, Song AW. A robust multi-shot scan strategy for high-resolution diffusion weighted MRI enabled by multiplexed sensitivity-encoding (MUSE). Neuroimage 2013;72:41–7.
[127] Hu Y, Levine EG, Tian Q, Moran CJ, Wang X, Taviani V, Vasanawala SS, McNab JA, Daniel BA, Hargreaves BL. Motion-robust reconstruction of multishot diffusion-weighted images without phase estimation through locally low-rank regularization. Magn Reson Med 2019;81(2):1181–90.
[128] Hennig J, Nauerth A, Friedburg H. RARE imaging: a fast imaging method for clinical MR. Magn Reson Med 1986;3(6):823–33.
[129] Hall LD, Sukumar S. Rapid data-acquisition technique for NMR imaging by the projection-reconstruction method. J Magn Reson 1984;56(1):179–82.
[130] Pipe JG. Motion correction with PROPELLER MRI: application to head motion and free-breathing cardiac imaging. Magn Reson Med 1999;42(5):963–9.

[131] Pauly J, Spielman D, Meyer C, Macovski A. A RARE-spiral pulse sequence. Kyoto, Japan: Proc Intl Soc Mag Reson Med 1993;1258:12.

[132] Meiboom S, Gill D. Modified spin-echo method for measuring nuclear relaxation times. Rev Sci Instrum 1958;29(8):688–91.

[133] Shaka A, Rucker S, Pines A. Iterative carr-purcell trains. J Magn Reson 1988;77(3):606–11.

[134] Le Roux P. Non-CPMG fast spin echo with full signal. J Magn Reson 2002;155(2):278–92.

[135] Wolff SD, Balaban RS. Magnetization transfer contrast (MTC) and tissue water proton relaxation in vivo. Magn Reson Med 1989;10(1):135–44.

[136] Liu C, Bammer R, Kim DH, Moseley ME. Self-navigated interleaved spiral (SNAILS): application to high-resolution diffusion tensor imaging. Magn Reson Med 2004;52(6):1388–96.

[137] Pruessmann KP, Weiger M, Scheidegger MB, Boesiger P. SENSE: sensitivity encoding for fast MRI. Magn Reson Med 1999;42(5):952–62.

[138] Griswold MA, Blaimer M, Breuer F, Heidemann RM, Mueller M, Jakob PM. Parallel magnetic resonance imaging using the GRAPPA operator formalism. Magn Reson Med 2005;54(6):1553–6.

[139] Cuppen J, van Est A. Reducing MR imaging time by one-sided reconstruction. Magn Reson Imaging 1987;5(6):526–7.

[140] Noll DC, Nishimura DG, Macovski A. Homodyne detection in magnetic resonance imaging. IEEE Trans Med Imaging 1991;10(2):154–63.

[141] McGibney G, Smith M, Nichols S, Crawley A. Quantitative evaluation of several partial Fourier reconstruction algorithms used in MRI. Magn Reson Med 1993;30(1):51–9.

[142] Lustig M, Donoho DL, Santos JM, Pauly JM. Compressed sensing MRI. IEEE Signal Process Mag 2008;25(2):72–82.

[143] Mani M, Jacob M, Guidon A, Magnotta V, Zhong J. Acceleration of high angular and spatial resolution diffusion imaging using compressed sensing with multichannel spiral data. Magn Reson Med 2015; 73(1):126–38.

[144] Michailovich O, Rathi Y, Dolui S. Spatially regularized compressed sensing for high angular resolution diffusion imaging. IEEE Trans Med Imaging 2011;30(5):1100–15.

[145] Landman BA, Bogovic JA, Wan H, ElShahaby FEZ, Bazin P-L, Prince JL. Resolution of crossing fibers with constrained compressed sensing using diffusion tensor MRI. Neuroimage 2012;59(3):2175–86.

[146] Menzel MI, Tan ET, Khare K, Sperl JI, King KF, Tao X, Hardy CJ, Marinelli L. Accelerated diffusion spectrum imaging in the human brain using compressed sensing. Magn Reson Med 2011;66(5):1226–33.

[147] Setsompop K, Cohen-Adad J, Gagoski BA, Raij T, Yendiki A, Keil B, Wedeen VJ, Wald LL. Improving diffusion MRI using simultaneous multi-slice echo planar imaging. Neuroimage 2012;63(1): 569–80.

[148] Griswold MA, Jakob PM, Heidemann RM, Nittka M, Jellus V, Wang JM, Kiefer B, Haase A. Generalized autocalibrating partially parallel acquisitions (GRAPPA). Magn Reson Med 2002;47(6):1202–10.

[149] Frost R, Miller KL, Tijssen RH, Porter DA, Jezzard P. 3D multi-slab diffusion-weighted readout-segmented EPI with real-time cardiac-reordered *k*-space acquisition. Magn Reson Med 2014;72(6):1565–79.

[150] Setsompop K, Fan Q, Stockmann J, Bilgic B, Huang S, Cauley SF, Nummenmaa A, Wang F, Rathi Y, Witzel T, et al. High-resolution in vivo diffusion imaging of the human brain with generalized slice dithered enhanced resolution: simultaneous multislice (gSlider-SMS). Magn Reson Med 2018;79(1):141–51.

[151] Duval T, McNab JA, Setsompop K, Witzel T, Schneider T, Huang SY, Keil B, Klawiter EC, Wald LL, Cohen-Adad J. In vivo mapping of human spinal cord microstructure at 300 mT/m. Neuroimage 2015; 118:494–507.

[152] Huang SY, Nummenmaa A, Witzel T, Duval T, Cohen-Adad J, Wald LL, McNab JA. The impact of gradient strength on in vivo diffusion MRI estimates of axon diameter. Neuroimage 2015;106:464–72.

[153] Lee SK, Mathieu JB, Graziani D, Piel J, Budesheim E, Fiveland E, Hardy CJ, Tan ET, Amm B, Foo TK. and others. Peripheral nerve stimulation characteristics of an asymmetric head-only gradient coil compatible with a high-channel-count receiver array. Magn Reson Med 2016;76(6):1939–50.

[154] Chronik BA, Rutt BK. Simple linear formulation for magnetostimulation specific to MRI gradient coils. Magn Reson Med 2001;45(5):916–9.
[155] Chronik BA, Rutt BK. A comparison between human magnetostimulation thresholds in whole-body and head/neck gradient coils. Magn Reson Med 2001;46(2):386–94.
[156] Zhang B, Yen YF, Chronik BA, McKinnon GC, Schaefer DJ, Rutt BK. Peripheral nerve stimulation properties of head and body gradient coils of various sizes. Magn Reson Med 2003;50(1):50–8.
[157] Tan ET, Lee SK, Weavers PT, Graziani D, Piel JE, Shu Y, Huston 3rd J, Bernstein MA, Foo TK. High slew-rate head-only gradient for improving distortion in echo planar imaging: preliminary experience. J Magn Reson Imaging 2016;44(3):653–64.
[158] Foo TKF, Laskaris E, Vermilyea M, Xu M, Thompson P, Conte G, Van Epps C, Immer C, Lee SK, Tan ET, et al. Lightweight, compact, and high-performance 3T MR system for imaging the brain and extremities. Magn Reson Med 2018;80:2232–45.
[159] Chu KC, Rutt BK. MR gradient coil heat dissipation. Magn Reson Med 1995;34(1):125–32.
[160] Gallichan D. Diffusion MRI of the human brain at ultra high field (UHF): a review. Neuroimage 2018;168:172–80.
[161] Heidemann RM, Porter DA, Anwander A, Feiweier T, Heberlein K, Knosche TR, Turner R. Diffusion imaging in humans at 7T using readout-segmented EPI and GRAPPA. Magn Reson Med 2010;64(1):9–14.
[162] Wen Q, Kelley DA, Banerjee S, Lupo JM, Chang SM, Xu D, Hess CP, Nelson SJ. Clinically feasible NODDI characterization of glioma using multiband EPI at 7 T. Neuroimage Clin 2015;9:291–9.
[163] Wu W, Poser BA, Douaud G, Frost R, In M-H, Speck O, Koopmans PJ, Miller KL. High-resolution diffusion MRI at 7T using a three-dimensional multi-slab acquisition. Neuroimage 2016;143:1–14.
[164] Winkler SA, Schmitt F, Landes H, DeBever J, Wade T, Alejski A, Rutt BK. Gradient and shim technologies for ultra high field MRI. Neuroimage 2018;168:59–70.
[165] Setsompop K, Alagappan V, Gagoski B, Witzel T, Polimeni J, Potthast A, Hebrank F, Fontius U, Schmitt F, Wald LL. and others. Slice-selective RF pulses for in vivo B1+ inhomogeneity mitigation at 7 tesla using parallel RF excitation with a 16-element coil. Magn Reson Med 2008;60(6):1422–32.
[166] Setsompop K, Wald LL, Alagappan V, Gagoski BA, Adalsteinsson E. Magnitude least squares optimization for parallel radio frequency excitation design demonstrated at 7 Tesla with eight channels. Magn Reson Med 2008;59(4):908–15.
[167] Roy C, Slimani A, de Meester C, Amzulescu M, Pasquet A, Vancraeynest D, Vanoverschelde J-L, Pouleur A-C, Gerber BL. Age and sex corrected normal reference values of T1, T2 T2* and ECV in healthy subjects at 3T CMR. J Cardiovasc Magn Reson 2017;19(1):72.
[168] Nielles-Vallespin S, Mekkaoui C, Gatehouse P, Reese TG, Keegan J, Ferreira PF, Collins S, Speier P, Feiweier T, de Silva R, et al. In vivo diffusion tensor MRI of the human heart: reproducibility of breath-hold and navigator-based approaches. Magn Reson Med 2013;70(2):454–65.
[169] von Deuster C, Stoeck CT, Genet M, Atkinson D, Kozerke S. Spin echo versus stimulated echo diffusion tensor imaging of the in vivo human heart. Magn Reson Med 2016;76(3):862–72.
[170] Welsh CL, DiBella EVR, Hsu EW. Higher-order motion-compensation for in vivo cardiac diffusion tensor imaging in rats. IEEE Trans Med Imaging 2015;34(9):1843–53.
[171] Gorodezky M, Scott AD, Ferreira PF, Nielles-Vallespin S, Pennell DJ, Firmin DN. Diffusion tensor cardiovascular magnetic resonance with a spiral trajectory: an in vivo comparison of echo planar and spiral stimulated echo sequences. Magn Reson Med 2017;80(2):648–54.
[172] Moulin K, Croisille P, Feiweier T, Delattre BMA, Wei H, Robert B, Beuf O, Viallon M. In vivo free-breathing DTI and IVIM of the whole human heart using a real-time slice-followed SE-EPI navigator-based sequence: a reproducibility study in healthy volunteers. Magn Reson Med 2015;76(1):70–82.
[173] Cohen-Adad J. Microstructural imaging in the spinal cord and validation strategies. Neuroimage 2018;182:169–83.

[174] Cadotte DW, Akbar MA, Fehlings MG, Stroman PW, Cohen-Adad J. What has been learned from magnetic resonance imaging examination of the injured human spinal cord: a canadian perspective. J Neurotrauma 2018;35(16):1942–57.

[175] Budde MD, Janes L, Gold E, Turtzo LC, Frank JA. The contribution of gliosis to diffusion tensor anisotropy and tractography following traumatic brain injury: validation in the rat using Fourier analysis of stained tissue sections. Brain 2011;134(Pt. 8):2248–60.

[176] Saritas EU, Holdsworth SJ, Bammer R. Chapter 2.3—susceptibility artifacts. In: Cohen-Adad J, CAM W-K, editors. Quantitative MRI of the spinal cord. San Diego: Academic Press; 2014. p. 91–105.

[177] Cohen-Adad J, Mareyam A, Keil B, Polimeni J, Wald L. 32-channel RF coil optimized for brain and cervical spinal cord at 3 T. Magn Reson Med 2011;66(4):1198–208.

[178] Topfer R, Starewicz P, Lo KM, Metzemaekers K, Jette D, Hetherington HP, Stikov N, Cohen-Adad J. A 24-channel shim array for the human spinal cord: design, evaluation, and application. Magn Reson Med 2016;76(5):1604–11.

[179] Saritas EU, Cunningham CH, Lee JH, Han ET, Nishimura DG. DWI of the spinal cord with reduced FOV single-shot EPI. Magn Reson Med 2008;60(2):468–73.

[180] Middleton DM, Mohamed FB, Barakat N, Hunter LN, Shellikeri S, Finsterbusch J, Faro SH, Shah P, Samdani AF, Mulcahey M. An investigation of motion correction algorithms for pediatric spinal cord DTI in healthy subjects and patients with spinal cord injury. Magn Reson Imaging 2014;32(5):433–9.

[181] De Leener B, Lévy S, Dupont SM, Fonov VS, Stikov N, Louis Collins D, Callot V, Cohen-Adad J. SCT: spinal cord toolbox, an open-source software for processing spinal cord MRI data. Neuroimage 2017;145:24–43.

[182] Guggenberger R, Markovic D, Eppenberger P, Chhabra A, Schiller A, Nanz D, Prüssmann K, Andreisek G. Assessment of median nerve with MR neurography by using diffusion-tensor imaging: normative and pathologic diffusion values. Radiology 2012;265(1):194–203.

[183] Lindberg PG, Feydy A, Le Viet D, Maier MA, Drapé J-L. Diffusion tensor imaging of the median nerve in recurrent carpal tunnel syndrome—initial experience. Eur Radiol 2013;23(11):3115–23.

[184] Breitenseher JB, Kranz G, Hold A, Berzaczy D, Nemec SF, Sycha T, Weber M, Prayer D, Kasprian G. MR neurography of ulnar nerve entrapment at the cubital tunnel: a diffusion tensor imaging study. Eur Radiol 2015;25(7):1911–8.

[185] Chhabra A, Thakkar RS, Andreisek G, Chalian M, Belzberg AJ, Blakeley J, Hoke A, Thawait GK, Eng J, Carrino JA. Anatomic MR imaging and functional diffusion tensor imaging of peripheral nerve tumors and tumorlike conditions. AJNR Am J Neuroradiol 2013;34(4):802–7.

[186] Meek MF, Stenekes MW, Hoogduin HM, Nicolai J-PA. In vivo three-dimensional reconstruction of human median nerves by diffusion tensor imaging. Exp Neurol 2006;198(2):479–82.

[187] Heckel A, Weiler M, Xia A, Ruetters M, Pham M, Bendszus M, Heiland S, Baeumer P. Peripheral nerve diffusion tensor imaging: assessment of axon and myelin sheath integrity. PLoS One 2015;10(6):e0130833.

[188] Simon NG, Kliot M. Diffusion weighted MRI and tractography for evaluating peripheral nerve degeneration and regeneration. Neural Regen Res 2014;9(24):2122–4.

[189] Boyer RB, Kelm ND, Riley DC, Sexton KW, Pollins AC, Shack RB, Dortch RD, Nanney LB, Does MD, Thayer WP. 4.7-T diffusion tensor imaging of acute traumatic peripheral nerve injury. Neurosurg Focus 2015;39(3):E9.

[190] Partridge SC, Nissan N, Rahbar H, Kitsch AE, Sigmund EE. Diffusion-weighted breast MRI: clinical applications and emerging techniques. J Magn Reson Imaging 2017;45(2):337–55.

[191] ACR. Practice paramater for the performance of contrast-enhanced magnetic resonance imaging (MRI) of the breast. Revised 2018;Resolution 34.

[192] Barentsz MW, Taviani V, Chang JM, Ikeda DM, Miyake KK, Banerjee S, van den Bosch MA, Hargreaves BA, Daniel BL. Assessment of tumor morphology on diffusion-weighted (DWI) breast MRI: diagnostic value of reduced field of view DWI. J Magn Reson Imaging 2015;42(6):1656–65.

[193] Singer L, Wilmes LJ, Saritas EU, Shankaranarayanan A, Proctor E, Wisner DJ, Chang B, Joe BN, Nishimura DG, Hylton NM. High-resolution diffusion-weighted magnetic resonance imaging in patients with locally advanced breast cancer. Acad Radiol 2012;19(5):526–34.

[194] Filli L, Ghafoor S, Kenkel D, Liu W, Weiland E, Andreisek G, Frauenfelder T, Runge VM, Boss A. Simultaneous multi-slice readout-segmented echo planar imaging for accelerated diffusion-weighted imaging of the breast. Eur J Radiol 2016;85(1):274–8.

[195] Kim YJ, Kim SH, Kang BJ, Park CS, Kim HS, Son YH, Porter DA, Song BJ. Readout-segmented echo-planar imaging in diffusion-weighted mr imaging in breast cancer: comparison with single-shot echo-planar imaging in image quality. Korean J Radiol 2014;15(4):403–10.

[196] Froeling M, Nederveen AJ, Heijtel DF, Lataster A, Bos C, Nicolay K, Maas M, Drost MR, Strijkers GJ. Diffusion-tensor MRI reveals the complex muscle architecture of the human forearm. J Magn Reson Imaging 2012;36(1):237–48.

[197] Damon BM. Effects of image noise in muscle diffusion tensor (DT)-MRI assessed using numerical simulations. Magn Reson Med 2008;60(4):934–44.

[198] Hernando D, Karampinos DC, King KF, Haldar JP, Majumdar S, Georgiadis JG, Liang ZP. Removal of olefinic fat chemical shift artifact in diffusion MRI. Magn Reson Med 2011;65(3):692–701.

[199] Burakiewicz J, Hooijmans MT, Webb AG, Verschuuren J, Niks EH, Kan HE. Improved olefinic fat suppression in skeletal muscle DTI using a magnitude-based dixon method. Magn Reson Med 2018;79(1):152–9.

[200] Raya JG. Techniques and applications of in vivo diffusion imaging of articular cartilage. J Magn Reson Imaging 2015;41(6):1487–504.

[201] Raya JG, Horng A, Dietrich O, Krasnokutsky S, Beltran LS, Storey P, Reiser MF, Recht MP, Sodickson DK, Glaser C. Articular cartilage: in vivo diffusion-tensor imaging. Radiology 2012;262(2):550–9.

[202] Staroswiecki E, Granlund KL, Alley MT, Gold GE, Hargreaves BA. Simultaneous estimation of T(2) and ADC in human articular cartilage in vivo with a modified 3D DESS sequence at 3 T. Magn Reson Med 2012;67(4):1086–96.

CHAPTER

Modeling Fiber Orientations Using Diffusion MRI

20

Daan Christiaens[a,b,c] and J. Donald Tournier[a,b]

[a]*Centre for the Developing Brain, School of Biomedical Engineering & Imaging Sciences, King's College London, London, United Kingdom* [b]*Department of Biomedical Engineering, School of Biomedical Engineering & Imaging Sciences, King's College London, London, United Kingdom* [c]*Department of Electrical Engineering, ESAT/PSI, KU Leuven, Leuven, Belgium*

20.1 Introduction

Diffusion MRI [1,2] is a noninvasive technique that can probe fiber orientations, albeit indirectly, through an in vivo measurement of water diffusion on a subvoxel scale. Indeed, an apparent diffusion coefficient (ADC) on the order of μm^2/ms effectively provides a length scale on the order of 3–10 μm for diffusion times around 10–100 ms measurable with modern MRI scanners—far below the imaging resolution and generally commensurate with cell dimensions [3]. In fibrous tissue, such as neural white matter or muscle tissue, cell membranes are expected to hinder diffusion in the direction perpendicular to the fiber orientation [4,5]. Diffusion MRI can be used to measure and exploit this directional dependence of diffusion in tissue to estimate the local fiber orientation.

The potential of diffusion MRI as a probe of fiber orientation was recognized early on. Thomsen et al. [6] observed large regional variations of the ADC in human white matter in vivo and attributed these differences to anisotropic diffusion in the underlying tissue structure, possibly related to the orientation of myelinated axons. Moseley et al. [7] subsequently studied diffusion anisotropy in cat brain and spinal cord and demonstrated that the ADC was indeed anisotropic in white matter and isotropic in gray matter. Similar observations were made in human spinal cord [8]. The idea of exploiting this anisotropy to model and estimate fiber orientations was launched soon after [9] and led to the development of diffusion tensor imaging (DTI) [10] and later to the first principles of streamline tractography [11–15].

As discussed in the previous chapters, the loss of phase coherence due to diffusion leads to attenuation of the MRI signal $S(b, \vec{g})$ that depends on the diffusion encoding gradient strength (b-value) and orientation (unit vector $\vec{g}$) [16,17]. Fig. 20.1 illustrates this radial and directional dependence of the diffusion MRI signal in human brain, showing first and foremost that the signal is larger in directions perpendicular to the main fiber orientation, where diffusion is hindered or even restricted. For example, the splenium (a structure consisting of left-right oriented fibers) is bright in diffusion-weighted MRI images with superior-inferior diffusion encoding. Second, the image contrast increases at higher b-values, albeit at the cost of reduced SNR. Therefore, a collection of diffusion-weighted images densely sampled at a high b-value *shell* produces the best angular contrast for discriminating fiber orientations.

Advances in Magnetic Resonance Technology and Applications. Volume 1. ISSN 2666-9099. https://doi.org/10.1016/B978-0-12-817057-1.00022-6

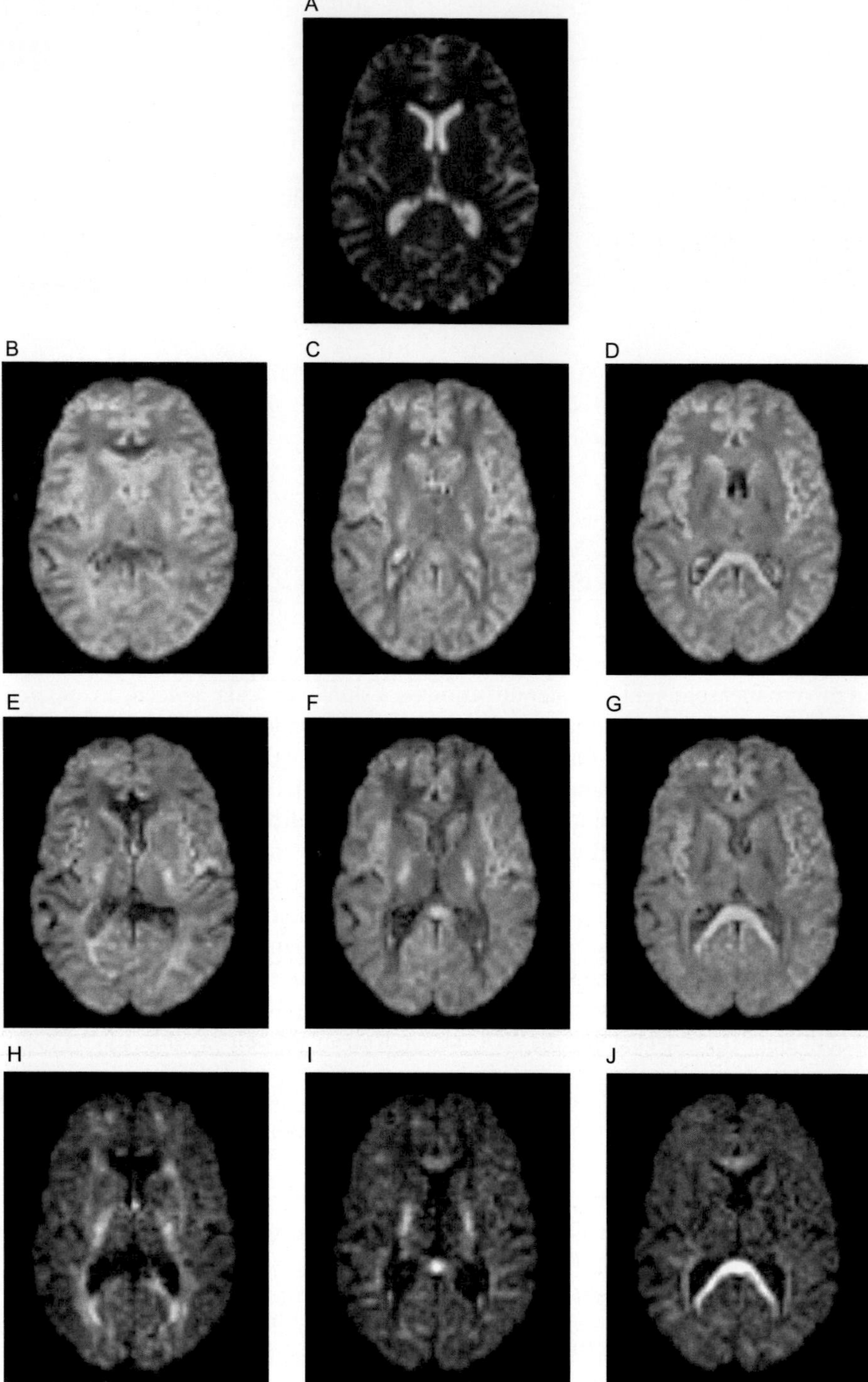

FIG. 20.1

Diffusion MRI contrast obtained when varying diffusion sensitizing gradient encoding $\vec{G}$. *Rows*: gradient strength (b-value). *Columns*: gradient direction along left-right (LR), anterior-posterior (AP), and superior-inferior (SI) axes. (A) $b = 0$ s/mm^2; (B) $b = 700$ s/mm^2, LR; (C) $b = 700$ s/mm^2, AP; (D) $b = 700$ s/mm^2, SI; (E) $b = 1000$ s/mm^2, LR; (F) $b = 1000$ s/mm^2, AP; (G) $b = 1000$ s/mm^2, SI; (H) $b = 2800$ s/mm^2, LR; (I) $b = 2800$ s/mm^2, AP; (J) $b = 2800$ s/mm^2, SI.

All methods discussed in this chapter exploit the directional dependence of the diffusion MRI signal to estimate the underlying fiber orientation distribution in the voxel. While the main focus will be on applications in brain white matter, the principles behind said methods generally translate to applications outside the brain too. The concept of q-space as the most complete characterization of the diffusion propagator will be reviewed. Subsequently, the main developments toward practical, scan-time-efficient fiber modeling will be discussed. The chapter starts with an introduction of DTI as the first proof of principle of mapping the predominant fiber orientation, before moving on to higher-order signal representations and their use for inferring complex fiber topologies. Spherical deconvolution (SD) will be described, as it is the most widely adopted approach to modeling fiber orientation distributions. Finally, a brief overview of efforts toward validation of these techniques will be provided, as well as a discussion of the differences and similarities between many of these methods.

20.2 *q*-Space imaging

For general linear diffusion encoding sequences, the fiber orientation information is encoded in the diffusion propagator $P(\vec{r}, \tau)$, which describes the probability density function (PDF) of a spin displacement $\vec{r}$ in diffusion time τ. As derived in the previous chapter, the measured diffusion MRI signal attenuation $S(q)/S_0$ as a function of q is related to the diffusion propagator via the Fourier transform:

$$\frac{S(q)}{S_0} = \int_{\vec{r} \in \mathbb{R}^3} P(\vec{r}, \tau)\, e^{-2\pi i q \cdot \vec{r}}\, d\vec{r} = \mathcal{F}\{P(\vec{r}, \tau)\} \tag{20.1}$$

In this equation, $q = \sqrt{\frac{b}{\tau}}\, \vec{g}$ describes the signal as a function of $\vec{g}$, the diffusion-sensitizing gradient strength and direction. By acquiring a large collection of images, sampled on a Cartesian grid in q-space, we can thus sample the frequency spectrum of the diffusion propagator in each voxel. The diffusion PDF can subsequently be computed as the inverse Fourier transform of the acquired data in each voxel. This is the principle of q-space imaging (QSI) [2], also known as diffusion spectrum imaging [18]. The q-space concept bears an elegant analogy with k-space, the spatial frequency spectrum of MRIs, and offers the richest characterization of local diffusion.

However, the dense q-space sampling required in QSI imposes long acquisition times, which limit its practical applicability. Most of the work discussed in the rest of this chapter is therefore focused on estimating fiber orientations in more realistic diffusion MRI acquisitions, either through parametric signal representations, selective acquisitions, or constrained tissue microstructure models. The rest of this chapter will outline the most prominent of these techniques.

20.3 Diffusion tensor imaging

Basser et al. [10] introduced the first model of anisotropic diffusion that became known as DTI. DTI models the diffusion propagator $P(\vec{r}, \tau)$ of the net diffusion displacement $\vec{r}$ in time τ as a three-dimensional (3D) Gaussian distribution, characterized by its covariance matrix

$$\mathbf{D} = \frac{1}{6\tau}\left\langle \vec{r}\, \vec{r}^{T} \right\rangle = \begin{pmatrix} D_{xx} & D_{xy} & D_{xz} \\ D_{xy} & D_{yy} & D_{yz} \\ D_{xz} & D_{yz} & D_{zz} \end{pmatrix} \tag{20.2}$$

This symmetric, positive-definite matrix, known as the *apparent diffusion tensor*, is fully determined by six parameters [10,19]. Under this Gaussian assumption, the Fourier relation in Eq. (20.1) can be solved analytically and reduces to a mono-exponential signal decay in b:

$$S(b, \vec{g}) = S_0 e^{-b\vec{g}^T \mathbf{D}\vec{g}} \tag{20.3}$$

The scalar $\vec{g}^T \mathbf{D}\, \vec{g}$ measures the ADC along gradient direction $\vec{g}$. From Eq. (20.3), it follows that the ADC is linearly proportional to the logarithm of the signal attenuation:

$$\ln\left(\frac{S(b, \vec{g})}{S_0}\right) = -b\,\vec{g}^T\, \mathbf{D}\, \vec{g} = -b\,\mathrm{ADC} \tag{20.4}$$

In DTI [10], the elements of the diffusion tensor D are estimated from ADC measurements along six or more gradient directions $\vec{g} = (g_{ix}, g_{iy}, g_{iz})$. This is most commonly achieved as the least-squares solution to a set of linear equations

$$\mathbf{B}\,\vec{\beta} = \vec{\sigma} \tag{20.5}$$

with vectors

$$\vec{\beta} = (\ \ln S_0, D_{xx}, D_{xy}, D_{xz}, D_{yy}, D_{yz}, D_{zz})$$
$$\vec{\sigma} = (\ \ln S(b, \vec{g}_1),\ \ln S(b, \vec{g}_2), \ldots,\ \ln S(b, \vec{g}_N))$$

and the system matrix [20]

$$\mathbf{B} = \begin{bmatrix} 1 & -bg_{1x}^2 & -2bg_{1x}g_{1y} & -2bg_{1x}g_{1z} & -bg_{1y}^2 & -2bg_{1y}g_{1z} & -bg_{1z}^2 \\ 1 & -bg_{2x}^2 & -2bg_{2x}g_{2y} & -2bg_{2x}g_{2z} & -bg_{2y}^2 & -2bg_{2y}g_{2z} & -bg_{2z}^2 \\ \vdots & \vdots & \vdots & \vdots & \vdots & \vdots & \vdots \\ 1 & -bg_{Nx}^2 & -2bg_{Nx}g_{Ny} & -2bg_{Nx}g_{Nz} & -bg_{Ny}^2 & -2bg_{Ny}g_{Nz} & -bg_{Nz}^2 \end{bmatrix}$$

The system matrix is of full rank and a unique solution can be computed if at least six diffusion-weighted images are acquired along noncollinear gradient directions, in addition to at least one image of different b-value, typically at $b = 0$ s/mm^2. With a larger number of diffusion encoding experiments with different gradients, the tensor estimation will be more robust to noise. Studies have shown that at least 30 unique gradient directions are needed to obtain a robust estimate of the tensor [21,22].

20.3.1 Geometric interpretation

The diffusion tensor $\mathbf{D}$ is the covariance matrix of a 3D Gaussian diffusion PDF. The iso-surface of this PDF is an ellipsoid described by $\vec{u}^T \mathbf{D}\, \vec{u}\ \ \forall \vec{u} \in \mathbb{S}_2$. Its principal axes and the diffusivity along those axes are defined with the eigenvalue decomposition of the diffusion tensor:

$$\mathbf{D} = \mathbf{E}\ \Lambda\ \mathbf{E}^T = (\vec{e}_1\ \ \vec{e}_2\ \ \vec{e}_3) \begin{pmatrix} \lambda_1 & 0 & 0 \\ 0 & \lambda_2 & 0 \\ 0 & 0 & \lambda_3 \end{pmatrix} (\vec{e}_1\ \ \vec{e}_2\ \ \vec{e}_3)^T \tag{20.6}$$

with $\lambda_1 \geq \lambda_2 \geq \lambda_3$ the eigenvalues of $\mathbf{D}$ and $\vec{e}_i$ the corresponding eigenvectors. As $\mathbf{D}$ is a real, symmetric matrix, its eigenvalues are real and its eigenvectors are orthonormal. The principal eigenvector $\vec{e}_1$ is directed along the axis of largest diffusion, conventionally expected to coincide with the main fiber orientation. The leading eigenvector $\vec{e}_1$ thus offered the first estimate of fiber orientation with diffusion MRI, laying the foundation for more advanced techniques discussed in the next sections. The corresponding eigenvalue λ_1 is the ADC along this axis.

20.3.2 DTI metrics and DEC-FA

In addition, a number of scalar measures have been defined from the eigenvalue decomposition. As these measures only depend on the eigenvalues, not the eigenvectors, they are invariant to rotation. The most frequently used are

- mean diffusivity (MD) is the average ADC across all directions:

$$\mathrm{MD} = \frac{\lambda_1 + \lambda_2 + \lambda_3}{3} = \overline{\lambda} \tag{20.7}$$

  which also equals the mean of the diagonal elements of the diffusion tensor, that is, the trace divided by 3. A typical MD map is shown in Fig. 20.2A.
- Fractional anisotropy (FA), illustrated in Fig. 20.2B, is defined as

$$\mathrm{FA} = \frac{\mathrm{std}(\lambda_i)}{\mathrm{rms}(\lambda_i)} = \sqrt{\frac{3}{2}}\frac{\sqrt{(\lambda_1 - \overline{\lambda})^2 + (\lambda_2 - \overline{\lambda})^2 + (\lambda_3 - \overline{\lambda})^2}}{\sqrt{\lambda_1^2 + \lambda_2^2 + \lambda_3^2}} \tag{20.8}$$

  The FA is scaled within the unit range and quantifies the amount of anisotropy. For isotropic diffusion, the FA equals 0. For cigar-shaped or pancake-shaped diffusion tensors, the FA approaches 1.

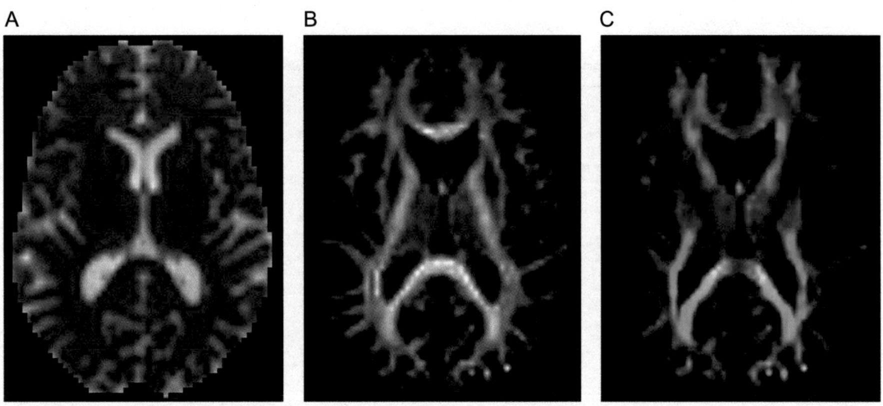

FIG. 20.2

Common metrics used in DTI in a healthy adult. All metrics are derived from a linear least-squares tensor fit in single-shell diffusion MRI data with $b = 1000\ \mathrm{s/mm^2}$. (A) Mean diffusivity; (B) fractional anisotropy; (C) color FA (DEC-FA).

The FA is often used to modulate the principal eigenvector $\vec{e}_1$ as a means of visualizing the local principal diffusion orientation in a directionally-encoded color FA map (DEC-FA) [23]. By convention, red indicates the left-right axis, green indicates the anterior-posterior axis, and blue indicates the inferior-superior axis. The DEC-FA is the RGB image obtained by projecting absolute values of $FA \cdot \vec{e}_1$ onto this reference frame, as shown in Fig. 20.2C.

20.4 Toward modeling crossing fibers: Higher-order signal representations

A major drawback of the diffusion tensor model is its inability to represent complex intravoxel topologies such as crossing fibers [24–26]. As illustrated in Fig. 20.3, the diffusion tensor is only capable of representing one principal fiber direction; when two or more fiber populations of approximately equal density are present in a single voxel, the leading eigenvector of the diffusion tensor is no longer well defined. The fraction of WM voxels containing crossing fibers has been estimated to be between 30% and 90% [27,28]. As such, this limitation has motivated the development of more advanced models capable of representing more complex intravoxel fiber topologies.

20.4.1 Diffusion kurtosis imaging

Complex fiber topologies, as well as signal contributions from restricted compartments, lead to non-Gaussian diffusion in neural tissue. Diffusion kurtosis imaging (DKI) [29,30] is a method to estimate

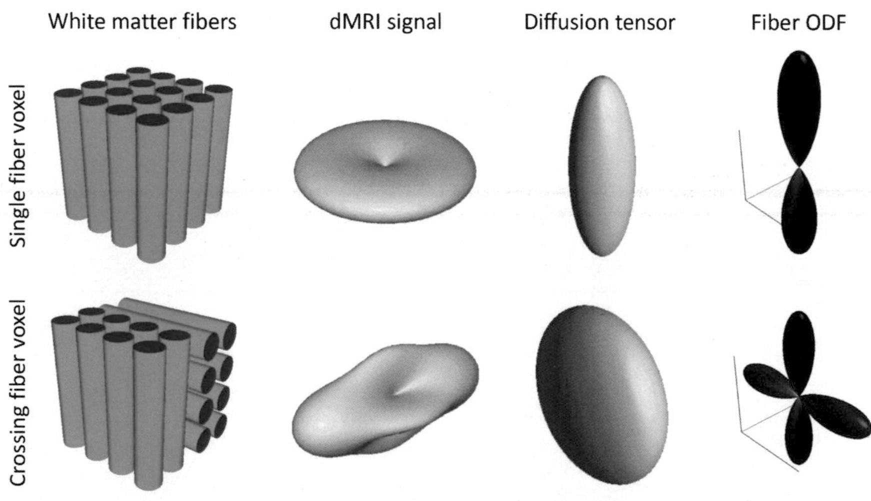

FIG. 20.3

Limitations of DTI for modeling fiber crossings. The *top row* illustrates a voxel with a single fiber population. The diffusion MRI signal is pancake-shaped and the diffusion tensor is cigar-shaped with principal direction along the fiber orientation. The *bottom row* illustrates a voxel with two orthogonal fiber populations. In this case, the diffusion tensor is no longer directed along the fiber orientation. The fiber orientation distribution function (ODF) in the last column is capable of representing these more complex fiber topologies.

excess kurtosis as a metric of non-Gaussianity of the diffusion PDF. For any gradient direction, Eq. (20.3) can be extended to

$$\ln\left(\frac{S(b,\vec{g})}{S_0}\right) = -bD + \frac{1}{6}b^2D^2K + \mathcal{O}(b^3) \tag{20.9}$$

where D is the ADC and K is the apparent diffusional kurtosis in that gradient direction [29]. Eq. (20.9) is essentially a Maclaurin series expansion of the log-attenuation in powers of b. This description was subsequently related to the cumulant expansion of the diffusion propagator [31,32]. The second-order cumulant is the variance of the diffusion PDF and thus related to the ADC. The fourth-order cumulant relates to kurtosis. All odd-order cumulants are zero due to the symmetry of the diffusion PDF.

DKI extends DTI to enable modeling of the full directionality of the signal with the use of the kurtosis tensor, a fully symmetric $3 \times 3 \times 3 \times 3$ tensor that contains 15 unique elements, resulting in 21 parameters in total. Estimating these parameters requires at least three distinct b-values and 15 unique gradient directions [29,33]. The kurtosis tensor contains information about the intravoxel fiber topology related to a fourth-order spherical harmonics (SH) decomposition, which can be used to represent fiber orientation and for tractography [34].

20.4.2 Multi-tensor models

Other work has extended the single-fiber diffusion tensor model to a population of n fiber bundles with distinct orientation, each modeled by a diffusion tensor [24]. As such, the diffusion MRI signal in crossing fiber voxels can be represented as the sum of n Gaussian distributions, each characterized by a unique diffusion tensor $\mathbf{D}_i$ and fraction f_i:

$$S(b,\vec{g}) = S_0 \sum_{i=1}^{n} f_i \, e^{-b\vec{g}^T\mathbf{D}_i\vec{g}} \tag{20.10}$$

Unlike the diffusion tensor model, the parameters of the multitensor model cannot be expressed as a linear function of the measurements, and thus this model requires more complicated nonlinear fitting strategies. Moreover, multi-tensor fitting can be unstable unless constrained to axial symmetry or fixed FA, particularly for single-shell data [35,36]. A further drawback of multitensor methods is the need to select the number of fascicles n for each voxel [37].

20.5 High-angular resolution diffusion imaging

The richest source of information about the fiber orientation is the full diffusion PDF, which can be reconstructed as the inverse Fourier transform of the q-space signal (cf. Section 20.2). However, doing so requires dense q-space sampling with long acquisition times and can thus be prohibitive for clinical use. Therefore, a class of methods has been introduced that aims to maximize angular resolution, sacrificing the radial component of the diffusion PDF. These methods are nowadays referred to as high-angular resolution diffusion imaging (HARDI) techniques. The commonality between then is that the q-space is sampled on a single *shell*, that is, with gradients of a fixed b-value in uniformly distributed directions [24]. The number of directions is as large as the scan time allows, typically around 60, and b-values over 2500 s/mm^2 are used to maximize angular contrast. In recent years, the radial component of the diffusion PDF has been reintroduced with multishell HARDI acquisition schemes.

However, the conceptual switch from Cartesian to spherical coordinates in q-space has introduced several important new signal representations, most notably the SH decomposition and q-ball imaging.

20.5.1 Spherical Harmonic decomposition

Spherical harmonics (SH) of order ℓ and degree m provide a convenient basis for representing complex functions on the unit sphere $\mathbb{S}_2$. They are defined as

$$Y_\ell^m(\theta,\phi) = \sqrt{\frac{(2\ell+1)}{4\pi}\frac{(\ell\text{-}m)!}{(\ell+m)!}}\,P_\ell^m(\cos\theta)\,e^{im\phi} \tag{20.11}$$

where $P_\ell^m(x)$ is the associated Legendre polynomial of order ℓ and degree $m \in [\text{-}\ell, \ell]$. The normalization is chosen such that the inner product

$$\langle Y_\ell^m(\theta,\phi), Y_{\ell'}^{m'}(\theta,\phi)\rangle = \delta_{\ell,\ell'}\,\delta_{m,m'} \tag{20.12}$$

where $\delta_{i,j}$ is the Kronecker delta. Any complex function of the unit sphere can be decomposed as a linear combination of these basis functions, akin to a Fourier series expansion of a periodic function in sines and cosines of increasing frequency. Here, SH of higher-order ℓ correspond to higher "frequency" components of the spherical function.

By its very nature, the HARDI signal is assumed to be real and antipodally symmetric. Therefore, for applications in diffusion MRI, the SH basis is also often restricted to real, symmetric functions [38–40]. Antipodal symmetry is enforced by selecting SH basis functions of even order only. Real functions are selected using the modified basis

$$Y_j(\theta,\phi) = \begin{cases} \sqrt{2}\,\mathrm{Re}(Y_\ell^m) & \text{if } \text{-}\ell \le m < 0 \\ Y_\ell^0 & \text{if } m = 0 \\ \sqrt{2}\,\mathrm{Im}(Y_\ell^m) & \text{if } 0 < m \le \ell \end{cases} \tag{20.13}$$

where $j = (\ell+1)(\ell+2)/2 \text{ - } \ell + m$ for $\ell = 0,2,4,\ldots,\ell_{\max}$ and $m = \text{-}\ell,\ldots,\ell$. These basis functions $Y_j(\theta, \phi)$ are depicted in Fig. 20.4. The measured HARDI signal $S(q)$ is then represented as a linear combination of these basis functions

$$S(\theta,\phi) \approx \sum_{j=1}^{n} s_j\,Y_j(\theta,\phi) \tag{20.14}$$

where $n = (\ell_{\max} + 1)(\ell_{\max} + 2)/2$. Assuming that the diffusion MRI signal is a smooth function of direction, the harmonic order can be band-limited to a maximum $\ell_{\max}$, typically chosen to be around 8. The coefficients s_j form a compact representation of the signal function as a vector of length n. They are estimated from a linear least squares fit of the measured signal.

The SH basis thus provides a natural, model-free representation of the HARDI signal. Many advanced operations in spherical coordinates, including rotation and convolution, become direct, linear operations when cast into the SH basis. Therefore, SH have become a mathematical framework of utmost importance for the HARDI techniques described here.

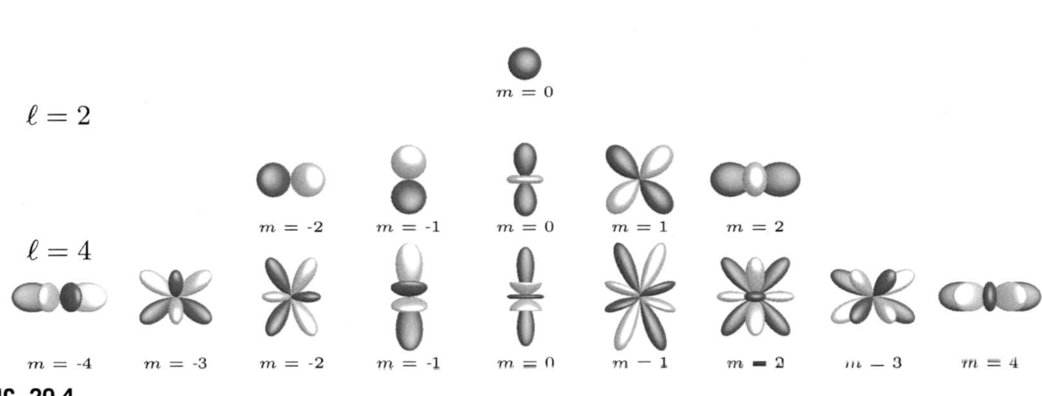

FIG. 20.4

The modified spherical harmonics basis functions (Eq. 20.13) for order ℓ (*rows*) and degree *m* (*columns*). *White lobes* denote negative amplitude.

20.5.2 *Q*-ball imaging

Reconstructing the full diffusion PDF requires dense q-space imaging, resulting in long acquisition times. Q-ball imaging (QBI) was introduced as a fast alternative to reconstruct the directional information only, namely, the diffusion orientation distribution function (dODF) [41]. The dODF is defined as the radial integral of the diffusion PDF:

$$\mathrm{dODF}(\vec{u}) = \int_0^\infty P(\hat{r}\ \vec{u}, \tau)\, \hat{r}^2\, \mathrm{d}\hat{r} \tag{20.15}$$

where $\mathbf{u} \in \mathbb{S}_2$ is a unit vector that encodes for the position (θ, ϕ) on the sphere. The factor $\hat{r}^2$ is the Jacobian of the spherical coordinate transformation that accounts for the solid angle consideration [42,43].

QBI estimates the dODF directly from single-shell HARDI data. Tuch [41] has shown that the dODF is closely approximated by the Funk-Radon transform (FRT) of $S(\mathbf{q})$, that is,

$$\mathrm{dODF}(\vec{u}) \approx \mathrm{FRT}\,\{S(q)\}(\vec{u}) = \int_{\mathbb{S}^2} \delta(q^T\,\vec{u})\, S(q)\, \mathrm{d}q \tag{20.16}$$

where $\delta(\,.\,)$ denotes the Dirac-delta function. For any point $\mathbf{u}$ on the unit sphere $\mathbb{S}^2$, the FRT is defined as the integral over the corresponding equator, that is, the set of points perpendicular to $\mathbf{u}$. Intuitively, this corresponds to calculating the total hindrance to diffusion in the plane perpendicular to any given orientation. Along the fibers, this *perpendicular hindrance* is large, whereas in other directions it will be smaller. As such, the dODF will have local maxima along the main fiber orientations in the voxel. To enhance the contrast, the dODF is usually rescaled between its minimum and maximum in every voxel. Fig. 20.5B shows these min-max normalized dODFs, illustrating that the dODF is capable of characterizing fiber crossings and other complex fiber topologies in the voxel.

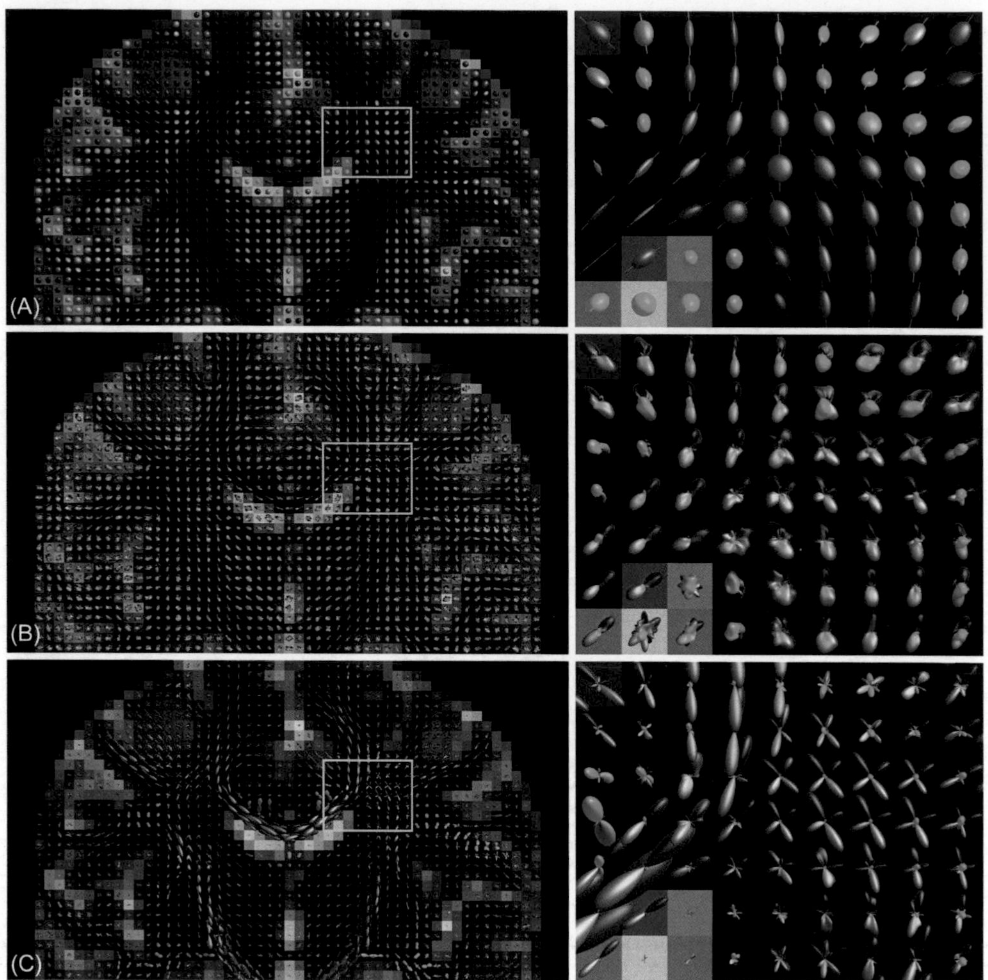

FIG. 20.5

(A) Rendering of the diffusion tensor (DTI) ellipsoids in a coronal slice of the brain, overlaid onto the mean $b = 0$ image. The highlighted region in the centrum semiovale is known to contain crossing fibers, but these are not adequately represented by the DTI model. (B) Corresponding diffusion orientation distribution functions (dODF) calculated with *Q*-ball imaging and min-max normalized. The dODF peaks can reveal multiple fiber directions within a single voxel. (C) Fiber orientation distribution functions (fODF) estimated with single-shell constrained spherical deconvolution (CSD). The fODF can also represent crossing fibers in the centrum semiovale. The *colors* indicate the direction of the principal DTI eigenvector (A) and of the ODF lobes (B and C) according to the standard convention, that is, *red* is L-R, *green* is A-P, and *blue* is I-S.

The dODF approximation via the FRT relies on ignoring the solid angle consideration, which leads to a smoothed estimate of the true dODF. This approximation was shown to improve for higher b-values [41]. Recent work has proposed an alternative formulation that allows the correct dODF to be estimated [42–44]. The FRT is a linear operation in the SH basis, facilitating fast computation of the dODF without the need for interpolation [40].

20.6 Multifascicle compartment models

In parallel with the development of higher-order signal representations, a broad range of biophysical models have been proposed that aim to relate the diffusion MRI signal to characteristics of the white matter microstructure. These models decompose the diffusion MRI signal into a small number of compartments, typically for intraaxonal and extraaxonal diffusion [45–47]. Readers are referred to Chapter 22 for a more detailed discussion of microstructure modeling. Here, only the concepts relevant to fiber orientation mapping are summarized, partly because of their historical importance and partly because they will help introduce spherical deconvolution in the next section.

Compartment models assume that every microstructure compartment in the voxel contributes linearly and independently to the measured diffusion MRI signal. Each compartment is then represented with a selected functional form that captures its expected properties. For instance, the intraaxonal compartment is often considered *restricted*, meaning that water molecules are trapped within the axonal membrane on the time-scale of the diffusion MRI experiment. In its simplest form, a restricted compartment can be modeled as a stick in direction $\vec{n}$ with axial diffusivity $d_{\|}$ and transverse diffusivity $d_{\perp} = 0$. The extra-axonal compartment is usually considered *hindered*, meaning that water molecules can diffuse throughout the extracellular space, typically modeled with a axially symmetric Gaussian or a fully isotropic ball. Combining different selected functional forms gives rise to a broad class of models, such as the ball-and-stick model [48] or the composite hindered and restricted model of diffusion (CHARMED) [49].

The axon orientation is an inherent part of these models and has to be estimated with nonlinear optimization, together with the compartment fractions and diffusivities. In their basic form, compartment models can therefore be regarded as extensions of the DTI model beyond the Gaussian form. Since then, studies have pointed at the importance of modeling axonal fiber crossings and dispersion [27,28,50,51]. Microstructure models have therefore been extended to incorporate fiber crossings as multiple discrete compartments each with their own distinct orientation [27,35,49,52]. Such approach is conceptually very similar to the multitensor signal representations discussed in Section 20.4.2.

20.7 Spherical deconvolution

The developments in microstructure modeling showed the potential of non-Gaussian models of white matter diffusion. Around the same time, the introduction of Q-ball imaging paved the way for recognizing the capability of diffusion MRI to represent complex fiber topologies with an ODF. The combination of these two insights inspired a broad class of methods that model fiber orientation not with one or multiple discrete sticks, but rather with a continuous *fiber* ODF (fODF) capable of also representing fanning and dispersing structures. While the dODF describes the orientation-dependence of the

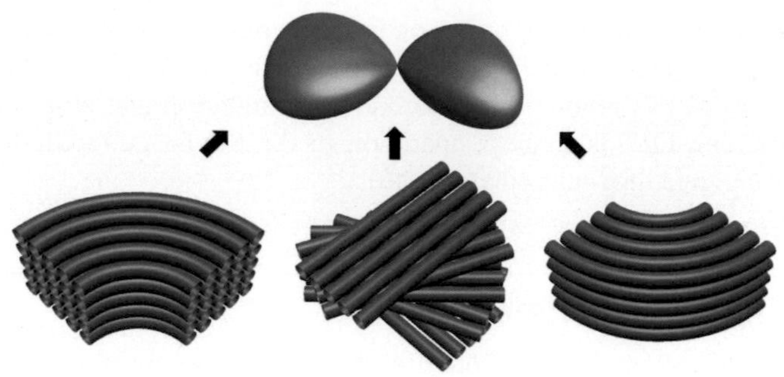

FIG. 20.6

Illustration of the inherent ambiguities in the fiber ODF representation. In all three configurations, the volume fraction taken up by fibers with any given orientation is comparable, yielding an identical fODF shown at the *top*.

local diffusion process, the fODF describes the orientation of the local tissue microstructure and is therefore a sharper characteristic better suited for fiber tractography. This paradigm is known as spherical (de)convolution and assumes that all fiber orientations in the voxel (and often in the image) share the same microstructural properties.

Note that the fODF representation, while more general, still does not resolve many of the inherent ambiguities in the underlying arrangement of axonal fibers, as illustrated in Fig. 20.6, where there is a spread of the orientations arising from a number of fundamentally quite distinct fiber configurations. In all these configurations, the volume fraction taken up by fibers with any given orientation is comparable, meaning that their fODF will be indistinguishable. This limitation is inherent to diffusion imaging and is essentially a consequence of the minimum achievable resolution. Inevitably, this will have distinct implications for tractography that can only be resolved by incorporating spatial neighborhood information.

20.7.1 The spherical convolution model

Spherical deconvolution (SD) [53–56] assumes that coherently aligned white matter fibers have a fixed and equal contribution to the diffusion MRI signal, also known as the *fiber response function* or *kernel* $H(\alpha)$. In single-shell HARDI data, for which this technique was originally developed, the response function is a function on a sphere, symmetric around an axis of low amplitude (large diffusion) and with high amplitude (low diffusion) in the radial plane. In addition, SD assumes that there is essentially no exchange (i.e., of water molecules) between white matter fibers on the time scale of the diffusion MRI acquisition. As such, the contribution of individual fiber populations in the voxel is considered independent, and their response functions are added linearly after reorientation along the fiber direction. Consider, for example, two discrete fiber populations of weights f_1 and f_2 along directions $\vec{n}_1$ and $\vec{n}_2$, respectively, as illustrated in Fig. 20.7. The predicted signal then can be written as

$$S(\theta,\phi) = f_1 H'_{\vec{n}_1}(\theta,\phi) + f_2 H'_{\vec{n}_2}(\theta,\phi) \tag{20.17}$$

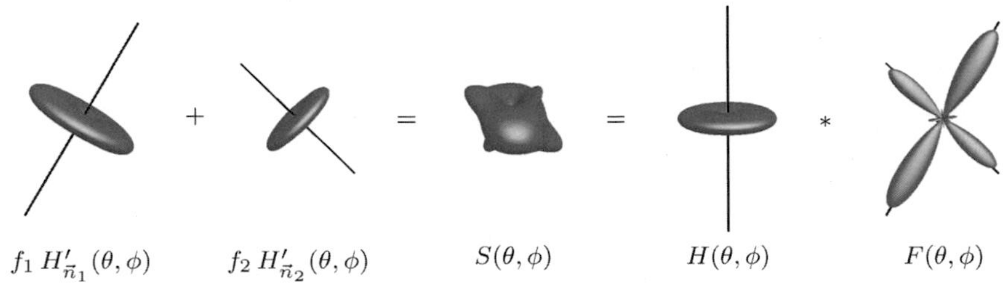

$f_1\, H'_{\vec{n}_1}(\theta,\phi)$ $f_2\, H'_{\vec{n}_2}(\theta,\phi)$ $S(\theta,\phi)$ $H(\theta,\phi)$ $F(\theta,\phi)$

FIG. 20.7

The spherical convolution model assumes a fixed, constant *fiber response function* $H(\alpha)$ of constant anisotropy. The diffusion MRI signal $S(\theta, \phi)$ is a linear combination of this response function rotated along the direction of each individual fiber population in the voxel. For arbitrary fiber geometry, this generalizes to a *spherical convolution* of $H(\alpha)$ with a fiber orientation distribution function $F(\theta, \phi)$.

where $H'_{\vec{n}}(\theta,\phi)$ denotes the kernel rotated along axis $\vec{n}$. In Cartesian coordinates $\vec{g}=(\cos\phi\,\sin\theta, \sin\phi\,\sin\theta, \cos\theta)\in\mathbb{S}_2$, the rotation becomes $H'_{\vec{n}}(\vec{g})=H(\cos^{-1}(\vec{n}\cdot\vec{g}))$. In general, one may consider an fODF $F(\theta, \phi)$, such that

$$S(\vec{g})=\int_{\mathbb{S}_2} H(\cos^{-1}(\vec{n}\cdot\vec{g}))\,F(\vec{n})\,\mathrm{d}\,\vec{n} \tag{20.18}$$

$$=(H*F)(\vec{g}) \tag{20.19}$$

where the operator $*$ denotes convolution on the unit sphere.

The response function H can either take the form of a particular biophysical compartment model as discussed in Chapter 22 [55,57,58], or, as is often done, assumed to be constant across the brain. In the latter case, all observed regional white matter differences are attributed to partial volume effects, in both space and orientation [53]. The required fiber response function is then either modeled explicitly [54,59] or estimated from the data at hand [53,56,60,61].

20.7.2 Deconvolution and constraints

In order to estimate the fiber ODF in each voxel, the HARDI data are deconvolved with the fiber response function. This is typically solved in the SH basis because the convolution operation then reduces to a matrix multiplication [53,59]. Let $s_{\ell,m}$ and $f_{\ell,m}$ denote the SH coefficients of order ℓ and degree m of the signal and the fODF, respectively. The fiber response function $H(\alpha)$ is represented in the same basis with coefficients $h_\ell = h_{\ell,m=0}$ of the zero-degree *zonal* harmonics: due to the symmetry around the z-axis, all nonzero degree coefficients $h_{\ell,m\neq 0} = 0$. Spherical convolution of H and F then corresponds to a multiplication of their SH coefficients of corresponding order:

$$s_{\ell,m}=\sqrt{\frac{4\pi}{2\ell+1}}\,h_\ell\cdot f_{\ell,m} \tag{20.20}$$

As such, the fODF could be computed directly from the signal SH coefficients as a simple division, or more commonly as a matrix inversion that incorporates the least-squares fit of the signal coefficients $s_{\ell,m}$ to the HARDI data samples.

However, deconvolution is a highly ill-conditioned operation that inevitably amplifies noise in the data. This typically leads to spurious side lobes, both positive and negative, that are not physically plausible. Initial approaches mediated this problem to some extent by including a low-pass filter in the estimation [53], but the real breakthrough came with the introduction of nonnegativity-constrained spherical deconvolution (CSD) [56,62,63]. CSD incorporates a nonnegativity constraint on the fODF amplitude, hence prohibiting negative side lobes. This results in a constrained quadratic programming (QP) problem:

$$\begin{aligned} \vec{f}^{\star} &= \arg\min_{\vec{f}} \| \vec{S}(\vec{g}) - \mathbf{Q}\mathbf{H}\vec{f} \|_F^2 \\ \text{s.t.} \quad & \mathbf{A}\vec{f} \geq 0 \end{aligned} \tag{20.21}$$

where $\vec{f}$ is the SH coefficient vector of the fODF, $\vec{S}(\vec{g})$ is a vector of diffusion MRI signal measurements at gradient directions $\vec{g}$, $\mathbf{Q}$ and $\mathbf{A}$ are matrices that evaluate the SH basis along the gradient directions $\vec{g}$ and across a dense set of directions, respectively, and $\mathbf{H}$ is a diagonal matrix implementing the convolution operation (Eq. 20.20).

Fig. 20.5 illustrates the result of CSD in comparison to DTI and Q-ball imaging. The fODF is capable of representing the crossing fibers of the corpus callosum and the corticospinal tract in the centrum semiovale, while producing a sharper orientation profile than the dODF. The angular resolution can be further increased with denser HARDI sampling schemes and higher SH basis order $\ell_{\max}$ [56,60].

Subsequent research has investigated the benefits of employing various regularization schemes, priors, and non-Gaussian noise models. One class of methods incorporates spatial regularization to improve robustness to noise in low angular resolution data [64–68]. A fiber continuity prior can furthermore augment the reconstruction to asymmetric fiber ODFs [69]. Other methods have imposed fODF sparsity [70–73], often in a context of compressed sensing [74–76].

20.7.3 Response function estimation

The response function, required to generate the fODF, can be modeled either at the voxel level or at the tissue level. We refer to Chapter 22 for voxel-level modeling, and in particular to recent work on rotation-invariant microstructure modeling [57,58]. For tissue-level modeling, a brain-wide fiber response function is typically estimated from the data using a mask of high-anisotropy voxels of coherent single-fiber structure. For example, Tournier et al. [56] selected the 300 voxels of highest FA within a white matter mask and reoriented the data in each of those voxels such that the principal eigenvector of the diffusion tensor is aligned with the z-axis. Zonal SH are subsequently fitted to each of those reoriented data samples and averaged to obtain the fiber response kernel. As such, this procedure is highly data-driven, calibrating the response function to the parameters of the acquisition sequence.

Nevertheless, some authors have highlighted the sensitivity of CSD to inaccurate response function calibration and isotropic partial volume effects [77,78]. These effects can result in spurious (false-positive) peaks of the fODF, reducing specificity and possibly hampering subsequent tractography. One study also found that an alternative deconvolution algorithm based on Richardson-Lucy damping [62,79] was less affected by perturbations of the response function [77]. Several recursive kernel estimation methods have therefore been introduced [60,61], which improve the selection and alignment of single-fiber voxels based on extracted fODF peaks from the previous iteration. Alternatively, some papers take a hybrid approach in which the response function is parameterized with one degree of freedom that encodes the optimized kernel anisotropy in each voxel [54,72].

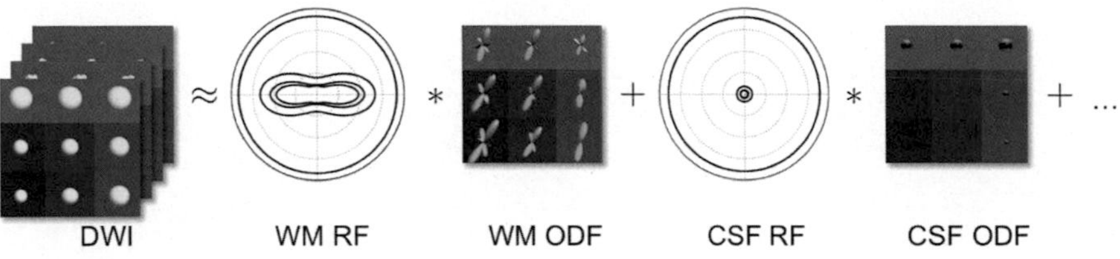

FIG. 20.8

Multi-tissue spherical deconvolution of multi-shell DWI data. Given response functions (RF) of white matter (WM), cerebrospinal fluid (CSF), and other tissues, orientation distribution functions (ODF) of those tissues can be reconstructed.

20.7.4 Multi-tissue spherical deconvolution

SD assumes a single fiber response function and attributes all regional signal variations to partial voluming of WM in different orientations. However, it ignores partial voluming with adjacent tissues such as GM and CSF, which are not adequately modeled with a WM fiber response function. Such non-WM partial volme effects were shown to affect the fODF reconstruction in 35%–50% of all WM voxels [78]. Jeurissen et al. [80] therefore extended CSD to multiple tissue classes, reconstructing *tissue* ODFs for WM, GM, and CSF, as illustrated in Fig. 20.8. In order to recover multiple tissue ODFs, multi-shell HARDI data are required with at least as many b-values as the number of tissues. The spherical convolution model (Eq. 20.19) is then generalized to a sum of N tissues

$$S_b(\vec{g}) = \sum_{t=1}^{N} (H_{t,b} * F_t)(\vec{g}) \tag{20.22}$$

with b-value dependent tissue response functions $H_{t,b}(\theta)$ and tissue ODFs $F_t(\theta,\phi)$. Akin to CSD, these tissue ODFs are the solution to a constrained QP problem [80]. The comparison between single-tissue and multi-tissue CSD in Fig. 20.9 illustrates that including GM and CSF response functions can substantially reduce partial volume contamination at tissue interfaces, suppressing spurious peaks in the fODF and improving subsequent tractography [80].

The tissue response functions can be estimated from the collected data in voxels with little to no partial volume effects. Alternatively, Eq. (20.22) can also be regarded as a blind source separation problem where both the kernels and the tissue ODFs are considered unknown. In this case, multidimensional nonnegative matrix factorization approaches have been used to recover the tissue responses and ODFs simultaneously, subject to minimal constraints [81–83]. A further advantage of these approaches is that no prior knowledge about the tissue types is used, facilitating a decomposition into an arbitrary number of tissue components potentially associated with other tissue types or pathology. The observation that, in healthy adult brain, a truly unsupervised method factorizes the data into components associated with WM, GM, and CSF [82] confirms the practical validity of the assumed three-tissue model in the initial work.

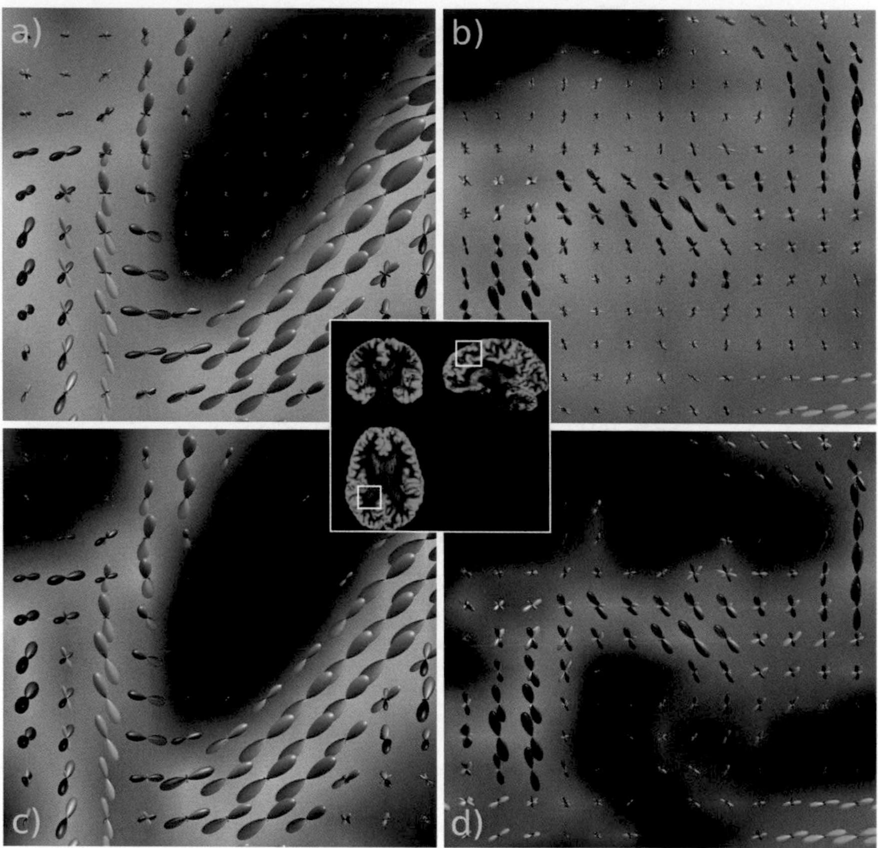

FIG. 20.9

Single-tissue (a and b) versus multi-tissue (c and d) constrained spherical deconvolution. (a) and (c) show an axial cross-section at the ventricular CSF-WM interface. (b) and (d) show a sagittal cross-section of the cortical GM-WM interface. The background contrast is the WM fODF density. These images illustrate how multi-tissue CSD reduces partial volume contamination from adjacent tissues on the fODF.

20.8 Validation of fiber orientation estimation

A reliable ground truth of in vivo neural tissue structure is unfortunately out of reach. This absence of a gold standard is a major impediment to the validation and comparison of microstructure models and fiber orientation estimation methods. Nevertheless, a number of *indirect* validation strategies can be used, in phantoms and ex vivo.

Phantom data are by far the most commonly used for validation of diffusion MRI techniques. These can either consist of simulated data (numerical phantoms) or of a physical object (hardware phantoms). Numerical phantoms offer exact ground truth and full control over the parameters. They are either simulated as a combination of basis functions with added noise [84,85], or using Monte Carlo simulations of water diffusion for a given microstructure geometry [86–90]. Hardware phantoms are constructed with microscopic capillaries or synthetic fibers in a known geometry [91–97]. While more challenging to build, hardware phantoms offer the advantage of replicating effects of noise propagation and image artifacts throughout the entire reconstruction pipeline.

In addition, advanced microscopy techniques can provide detailed information on the tissue microstructure in ex vivo samples [98]. In particular, diffusion MRI fiber ODFs have been compared to *histological* fODFs obtained from postmortem tissue sections [99–104], provided a good geometric alignment between them. Most recent techniques obtain these histological fODFs from 2D or 3D structure tensor analysis [101–103] in confocal microscopy [101,104].

Finally, in the absence of a reliable ground truth, assessment of fiber orientation estimates and tractography results is often necessarily limited to visual inspection based on high-level expert knowledge. In this perspective, comparison between methods is facilitated by the use of publicly available diffusion MRI data that are specifically acquired for research purposes using dedicated high-resolution imaging protocols, such as the Human Connectome Project (HCP) database [105].

20.9 Conclusions

Although, at first glance, the range of techniques for fiber orientation estimation can have seemingly very different motivations, a few broad patterns emerge on closer look. First, parametric and nonparametric models can be discriminated. Parametric models estimate, in each voxel, a discrete number of fiber populations and represent each with a vector or parametric distribution. Examples include multi-tensor models [24,35–37], the ball-and-sticks model [27] and certain other compartment models [49,50]. Nonparametric models avoid discretizing the fiber orientation, relying on a continuous orientation distribution instead. Techniques like Q-ball imaging [41], CSD [56], and other SD methods [55,62,63], therefore, have the capacity to represent complex fiber configurations and dispersion, while avoiding having to determine the number of fascicles [27,37]. However, ultimately almost all signal models reduce to a spherical convolution of a microstructure kernel with a discrete or continuous representation of the fODF. The difference resides in the fODF representation and in the assumptions made about the microstructure kernel.

A second distinction can be made between model-based and data-driven methods. Model-based techniques adopt a functional form for the microstructure kernel, often in the form of a microstructure compartment model [48–50, 54,55,57,58]. Data-driven techniques aim to avoid strong assumptions on the local microstructure, learning the kernel from the data instead [56,59,62,63]. Such techniques usually rely on the assumption of an invariant response function for each tissue type [80,83], which leads to a better conditioned problem at the expense of losing specificity about microstructural tissue changes. It should be noted, however, that deconvolution with an invariant response function can still retain sensitivity to microstructural changes thanks to the linearity of the convolution operation. Indeed, the fODF lobe integral in CSD, so-called *apparent fiber density*, was shown to be a useful biomarker of tissue alterations [106,107].

Since the first observation of anisotropic diffusion in cat spinal cord [7], the field has significantly advanced in its ability to model and estimate white matter fiber orientation in vivo. These developments in voxel-wise orientation mapping have led to major advances in fiber tractography [27,59,108–112], which is nowadays used for presurgical planning [113] and in structural connectomics [114]. Furthermore, orientation-resolved modeling is increasingly translated to non-brain applications such as for muscle tissue [5]. With continued advances in MRI technology, these advanced fiber orientation mapping methods will increasingly be used for routine clinical and neuroscientific investigations alike.

References

[1] Le Bihan D, Breton E, Lallemand D, Grenier P, Cabanis E, Laval-Jeantet M. MR imaging of intravoxel incoherent motions: application to diffusion and perfusion in neurologic disorders. Radiology 1986;161(2):401–7. https://doi.org/10.1148/radiology.161.2.3763909.

[2] Callaghan PT, Eccles CD, Xia Y. NMR microscopy of dynamic displacements: k-space and q-space imaging. J Phys E Sci Instrum 1988;21(8):820–2. https://doi.org/10.1088/0022-3735/21/8/017.

[3] Novikov DS, Fieremans E, Jespersen SN, Kiselev VG. Quantifying brain microstructure with diffusion MRI: theory and parameter estimation. NMR Biomed 2018;e3998. https://doi.org/10.1002/nbm.3998.

[4] Beaulieu C. The basis of anisotropic water diffusion in the nervous system—a technical review. NMR Biomed 2002;15(7–8):435–55. https://doi.org/10.1002/nbm.782.

[5] Oudeman J, Nederveen AJ, Strijkers GJ, Maas M, Luijten PR, Froeling M. Techniques and applications of skeletal muscle diffusion tensor imaging: a review. J Magn Reson Imaging 2015;43(4):773–88. https://doi.org/10.1002/jmri.25016.

[6] Thomsen C, Henriksen O, Ring P. In vivo measurement of water self diffusion in the human brain by magnetic resonance imaging. Acta Radiol 1987;28(3):353–61. https://doi.org/10.3109/02841858709177362.

[7] Moseley ME, Cohen Y, Kucharczyk J, Mintorovitch J, Asgari HS, Wendland MF, et al. Diffusion-weighted MR imaging of anisotropic water diffusion in cat central nervous system Radiology 1990;176(2):439–45. https://doi.org/10.1148/radiology.176.2.2367658.

[8] Hajnal JV, Doran M, Hall AS, Collins AG, Oatridge A, Pennock JM, et al. MR imaging of anisotropically restricted diffusion of water in the nervous system: technical, anatomic, and pathologic considerations. J Comput Assist Tomogr 1991;15(1):1–9218.

[9] Douek P, Turner R, Pekar J, Patronas N, Le Bihan D. MR color mapping of myelin fiber orientation. J Comput Assist Tomogr 1991;15(6):923–9.

[10] Basser PJ, Mattiello J, Le Bihan D. MR diffusion tensor spectroscopy and imaging. Biophys J 1994;66(1):259–67.

[11] Conturo TE, Lori NF, Cull TS, Akbudak E, Snyder AZ, Shimony JS, et al. Tracking neuronal fiber pathways in the living human brain. Proc Natl Acad Sci 1999;96(18):10422–7. https://doi.org/10.1073/pnas.96.18.10422.

[12] Mori S, Crain BJ, Chacko VP, Van Zijl PC. Three-dimensional tracking of axonal projections in the brain by magnetic resonance imaging. Ann Neurol 1999;45(2):265–9.

[13] Jones DK, Simmons A, Williams SC, Horsfield MA. Non-invasive assessment of axonal fiber connectivity in the human brain via diffusion tensor MRI. Magn Reson Med 1999;42(1):37–41.

[14] Basser PJ, Pajevic S, Pierpaoli C, Duda J, Aldroubi A. In vivo fiber tractography using DT-MRI data. Magn Reson Med 2000;44(4):625–32.

[15] Poupon C, Clark CA, Frouin V, Régis J, Bloch I, Le Bihan D, et al. Regularization of diffusion-based direction maps for the tracking of brain white matter fascicles. NeuroImage 2000;12(2):184–95. https://doi.org/10.1006/nimg.2000.0607.

[16] Bammer R. Basic principles of diffusion-weighted imaging. Eur J Radiol 2003;45(3):169–84. https://doi.org/10.1016/s0720-048x(02)00303-0.

[17] Luypaert R, Boujraf S, Sourbron S, Osteaux M. Diffusion and perfusion MRI: basic physics. Eur J Radiol 2001;38(1):19–27.

[18] Wedeen VJ, Hagmann P, Tseng WYI, Reese TG, Weisskoff RM. Mapping complex tissue architecture with diffusion spectrum magnetic resonance imaging. Magn Reson Med 2005;54(6):1377–86. https://doi.org/10.1002/mrm.20642.

[19] Crank J. The mathematics of diffusion. Oxford, United Kingdom: Oxford University Press; 13 Mar 1980, 2nd Revised edition, ISBN10 0198534116, ISBN13 9780198534112.

[20] Mattiello J, Basser PJ, Le Bihan D. The b matrix in diffusion tensor echo-planar imaging. Magn Reson Med 1997;37(2):292–300. https://doi.org/10.1002/mrm.1910370226.

[21] Papadakis NG, Murrills CD, Hall LD, Huang CL, Adrian Carpenter T. Minimal gradient encoding for robust estimation of diffusion anisotropy Magn Reson Imaging 2000;18(6):671–9.

[22] Jones DK. The effect of gradient sampling schemes on measures derived from diffusion tensor MRI: a Monte Carlo study. Magn Reson Med 2004;51(4):807–15.

[23] Pajevic S, Pierpaoli C. Color schemes to represent the orientation of anisotropic tissues from diffusion tensor data: application to white matter fiber tract mapping in the human brain. Magn Reson Med 1999;42(3):526–40.

[24] Tuch DS, Reese TG, Wiegell MR, Makris N, Belliveau JW, Wedeen VJ. High angular resolution diffusion imaging reveals intravoxel white matter fiber heterogeneity Magn Reson Med 2002;48(4):577–82. https://doi.org/10.1002/mrm.10268.

[25] Jansons KM, Alexander DC. Persistent angular structure: new insights from diffusion MRI data. Dummy version. In: Lecture Notes in Computer ScienceBerlin, Heidelberg: Springer; 2003. p. 672–83. https://doi.org/10.1007/978-3-540-45087-0_56.

[26] Özarslan E, Shepherd TM, Vemuri BC, Blackband SJ, Mareci TH. Resolution of complex tissue microarchitecture using the diffusion orientation transform (DOT). NeuroImage 2006;31(3):1086–103. https://doi.org/10.1016/j.neuroimage.2006.01.024.

[27] Behrens TEJ, Johansen-Berg H, Jbabdi S, Rushworth MFS, Woolrich MW. Probabilistic diffusion tractography with multiple fibre orientations: what can we gain? NeuroImage 2007;34(1):144–55.

[28] Jeurissen B, Leemans A, Tournier JD, Jones DK, Sijbers J. Investigating the prevalence of complex fiber configurations in white matter tissue with diffusion magnetic resonance imaging. Hum Brain Mapp 2013;34(11):2747–66. https://doi.org/10.1002/hbm.22099.

[29] Jensen JH, Helpern JA, Ramani A, Lu H, Kaczynski K. Diffusional kurtosis imaging: the quantification of non-Gaussian water diffusion by means of magnetic resonance imaging. Magn Reson Med 2005; 53(6):1432–40. https://doi.org/10.1002/mrm.20508.

[30] Lu H, Jensen JH, Ramani A, Helpern JA. Three-dimensional characterization of non-Gaussian water diffusion in humans using diffusion kurtosis imaging. NMR Biomed 2006;19(2):236–47. https://doi.org/10.1002/nbm.1020.

[31] Minati L, Aquino D, Rampoldi S, Papa S, Grisoli M, Bruzzone MG, et al. Biexponential and diffusional kurtosis imaging, and generalised diffusion-tensor imaging (GDTI) with rank-4 tensors: a study in a group of healthy subjects. Magn Reson Mater Phys Biol Med 2007;20(5–6):241–53. https://doi.org/10.1007/s10334-007-0091-1.

[32] Kiselev VG. The cumulant expansion: an overarching mathematical framework for understanding diffusion NMR. In: Jones DK, editor. Diffusion MRI, November. Oxford University Press; 2010. p. 152–68. https://doi.org/10.1093/med/9780195369779.003.0010.

[33] Poot DHJ, den Dekker AJ, Achten E, Verhoye M, Sijbers J. Optimal experimental design for diffusion kurtosis imaging. IEEE Trans Med Imaging 2010;29(3):819–29. https://doi.org/10.1109/TMI.2009.2037915.

[34] Lazar M, Jensen JH, Xuan L, Helpern JA. Estimation of the orientation distribution function from diffusional kurtosis imaging. Magn Reson Med 2008;60(4):774–81. https://doi.org/10.1002/mrm.21725.

[35] Hosey TP, Williams GB, Ansorge RE. Inference of multiple fiber orientations in high angular resolution diffusion imaging. Magn Reson Med 2005;54(6):1480–9.

[36] Scherrer B, Warfield S. Why multiple b-values are required for multi-tensor models. Evaluation with a constrained log-Euclidean model. In: IEEE international symposium on biomedical imaging: from nano to macro. p. 1389–92.

[37] Schultz T, Westin CF, Kindlmann G. Multi-diffusion-tensor fitting via spherical deconvolution: a unifying framework. In: Medical image computing and computer-assisted intervention—MICCAI 2010, Berlin, Heidelberg: Springer; 2010. p. 674–81. https://doi.org/10.1007/978-3-642-15705-9_82.

[38] Frank LR. Characterization of anisotropy in high angular resolution diffusion-weighted MRI. Magn Reson Med 2002;47(6):1083–99. https://doi.org/10.1002/mrm.10156.

[39] Descoteaux M, Angelino E, Fitzgibbons S, Deriche R. Apparent diffusion coefficients from high angular resolution diffusion imaging: estimation and applications. Magn Reson Med 2006;56(2):395–410. https://doi.org/10.1002/mrm.20948.

[40] Descoteaux M, Angelino E, Fitzgibbons S, Deriche R. Regularized, fast and robust analytical Q-ball imaging. Magn Reson Med 2007;58(3):497–510. https://doi.org/10.1002/mrm.21277.

[41] Tuch DS. Q-ball imaging. Magn Reson Med 2004;52(6):1358–72. https://doi.org/10.1002/mrm.20279.

[42] Tristán-Vega A, Westin CF, Aja-Fernández S. Estimation of fiber orientation probability density functions in high angular resolution diffusion imaging. NeuroImage 2009;47(2):638–50. https://doi.org/10.1016/j.neuroimage.2009.04.049.

[43] Aganj I, Lenglet C, Sapiro G, Yacoub E, Ugurbil K, Harel N. Reconstruction of the orientation distribution function in single- and multiple-shell Q-ball imaging within constant solid angle. Magn Reson Med 2010;64(2):554–66. https://doi.org/10.1002/mrm.22365.

[44] Tristán-Vega A, Westin CF, Aja-Fernández S. A new methodology for the estimation of fiber populations in the white matter of the brain with the Funk-Radon transform. NeuroImage 2010;49(2):1301–15. https://doi.org/10.1016/j.neuroimage.2009.09.070.

[45] Stanisz GJ, Wright GA, Henkelman RM, Szafer A. An analytical model of restricted diffusion in bovine optic nerve. Magn Reson Med 1997;37(1):103–11. https://doi.org/10.1002/mrm.1910370115.

[46] Panagiotaki E, Schneider T, Siow B, Hall MG, Lythgoe MF, Alexander DC. Compartment models of the diffusion MR signal in brain white matter: a taxonomy and comparison. NeuroImage 2012;59(3):2241–54. https://doi.org/10.1016/j.neuroimage.2011.09.081.

[47] Jelescu IO, Budde MD. Design and validation of diffusion MRI models of white matter. Front Phys 2017;5: https://doi.org/10.3389/fphy.2017.00061.

[48] Behrens TEJ, Woolrich MW, Jenkinson M, Johansen-Berg H, Nunes RG, Clare S, et al. Characterization and propagation of uncertainty in diffusion-weighted MR imaging. Magn Reson Med 2003;50(5):1077–88. https://doi.org/10.1002/mrm.10609.

[49] Assaf Y, Basser PJ. Composite hindered and restricted model of diffusion (CHARMED) MR imaging of the human brain. NeuroImage 2005;27(1):48–58. https://doi.org/10.1016/j.neuroimage.2005.03.042.

[50] Zhang H, Hubbard PL, Parker GJM, Alexander DC. Axon diameter mapping in the presence of orientation dispersion with diffusion MRI. NeuroImage 2011;56(3):1301–15. https://doi.org/10.1016/j.neuroimage.2011.01.084.

[51] Nilsson M, Lätt J, Ståhlberg F, Westen D, Hagslätt H. The importance of axonal undulation in diffusion MR measurements: a Monte Carlo simulation study. NMR Biomed 2012;25(5):795–805. https://doi.org/10.1002/nbm.1795.

[52] Scherrer B, Schwartzman A, Taquet M, Prabhu SP, Sahin M, Akhondi-Asl A, et al. Characterizing the distribution of anisotropic micro-structural environments with diffusion-weighted imaging (DIAMOND). In: Medical image computing and computer-assisted intervention—MICCAI 2013, vol. 16. Springer; 2013. p. 518–26. https://doi.org/10.1007/978-3-642-40760-4_65.

[53] Tournier JD, Calamante F, Gadian DG, Connelly A. Direct estimation of the fiber orientation density function from diffusion-weighted MRI data using spherical deconvolution. NeuroImage 2004;23(3):1176–85. https://doi.org/10.1016/j.neuroimage.2004.07.037.

[54] Anderson AW. Measurement of fiber orientation distributions using high angular resolution diffusion imaging. Magn Reson Med 2005;54(5):1194–206. https://doi.org/10.1002/mrm.20667.
[55] Jespersen SN, Kroenke CD, Østergaard L, Ackerman JJH, Yablonskiy DA. Modeling dendrite density from magnetic resonance diffusion measurements. NeuroImage 2007;34(4):1473–86. https://doi.org/10.1016/j.neuroimage.2006.10.037.
[56] Tournier JD, Calamante F, Connelly A. Robust determination of the fibre orientation distribution in diffusion MRI: non-negativity constrained super-resolved spherical deconvolution. NeuroImage 2007;35(4):1459–72. https://doi.org/10.1016/j.neuroimage.2007.02.016.
[57] Reisert M, Kellner E, Dhital B, Hennig J, Kiselev VG. Disentangling micro from mesostructure by diffusion MRI: a Bayesian approach. NeuroImage 2017;147:964–75. https://doi.org/10.1016/j.neuroimage.2016.09.058.
[58] Novikov DS, Veraart J, Jelescu IO, Fieremans E. Rotationally-invariant mapping of scalar and orientational metrics of neuronal microstructure with diffusion MRI. NeuroImage 2018;174:518–38. https://doi.org/10.1016/j.neuroimage.2018.03.006.
[59] Descoteaux M, Deriche R, Knosche TR, Anwander A. Deterministic and probabilistic tractography based on complex fibre orientation distributions. IEEE Trans Med Imaging 2009;28(2):269–86. https://doi.org/10.1109/TMI.2008.2004424.
[60] Tournier JD, Calamante F, Connelly A. Determination of the appropriate b value and number of gradient directions for high-angular-resolution diffusion-weighted imaging NMR Biomed 2013;26(12):1775–86. https://doi.org/10.1002/nbm.3017.
[61] Tax CMW, Jeurissen B, Vos SB, Viergever MA, Leemans A. Recursive calibration of the fiber response function for spherical deconvolution of diffusion MRI data. NeuroImage 2014;86:67–80. https://doi.org/10.1016/j.neuroimage.2013.07.067.
[62] Dell'Acqua F, Rizzo G, Scifo P, Clarke RA, Scotti G, Fazio F. A model-based deconvolution approach to solve fiber crossing in diffusion-weighted MR imaging. IEEE Trans Biomed Eng 2007;54(3):462–72. https://doi.org/10.1109/TBME.2006.888830.
[63] Jian B, Vemuri BC. A unified computational framework for deconvolution to reconstruct multiple fibers from diffusion weighted MRI. IEEE Trans Med Imaging 2007;26(11):1464–71.
[64] Goh A, Lenglet C, Thompson PM, Vidal R. Estimating orientation distribution functions with probability density constraints and spatial regularity. In: Yang GZ, Hawkes D, Rueckert D, Noble A, Taylor C, editors. Medical image computing and computer-assisted intervention—MICCAI 2009. Lecture Notes in Computer Science5761:Berlin, Heidelberg: Springer; 2009. p. 877–85. https://doi.org/10.1007/978-3-642-04268-3_108.
[65] Reisert M, Kiselev VG. Fiber continuity: an anisotropic prior for ODF estimation. IEEE Trans Med Imaging 2011;30(6):1274–83. https://doi.org/10.1109/TMI.2011.2112769.
[66] Tournier JD, Calamante F, Conelly A. A robust spherical deconvolution method for the analysis of low SNR or low angular resolution diffusion data. In: Proceedings of international society of magnetic resonance in medicine21:USA: Salt-Lake City; 2013. p. 772.
[67] Zhou Q, Michailovich OV, Rathi Y. Spatially regularized reconstruction of fibre orientation distributions in the presence of isotropic diffusion. Comput Res Repos 2014;abs/1401.6.
[68] Canales-Rodríguez EJ, Daducci A, Sotiropoulos SN, Caruyer E, Aja-Fernández S, Radua J, et al. Spherical deconvolution of multichannel diffusion MRI data with non-Gaussian noise models and spatial regularization. PLoS ONE 2015;10(10):e0138910. https://doi.org/10.1371/journal.pone.0138910.
[69] Reisert M, Kellner E, Kiselev VG. About the geometry of asymmetric fiber orientation distributions. IEEE Trans Med Imaging 2012;31(6):1240–9. https://doi.org/10.1109/TMI.2012.2187916.
[70] Tristán-Vega A, Westin CF. Probabilistic ODF estimation from reduced HARDI data with sparse regularization. In: Medical image computing and computer-assisted intervention—MICCAI 2011. LNCS6892: Springer; 2011. p. 182–90. https://doi.org/10.1007/978-3-642-23629-7_23.

[71] Daducci A, Van De Ville D, Thiran JP, Wiaux Y. Sparse regularization for fiber ODF reconstruction: from the suboptimality of L2 and L1 priors to L0. Med Image Anal 2014;18(6):820–33. https://doi.org/10.1016/j.media.2014.01.011.

[72] Schultz T, Groeschel S. Auto-calibrating spherical deconvolution based on ODF sparsity. In: Medical image computing and computer-assisted intervention—MICCAI 2013. LNCS16:Springer; 2013. p. 663–70. https://doi.org/10.1007/978-3-642-40811-3_83.

[73] Yeh FC, Tseng WYI. Sparse solution of fiber orientation distribution function by diffusion decomposition. PLoS ONE 2013;8(10):e75747. https://doi.org/10.1371/journal.pone.0075747.

[74] Michailovich O, Rathi Y, Dolui S. Spatially regularized compressed sensing for high angular resolution diffusion imaging IEEE Trans Med Imaging 2011;30(5):1100–15. https://doi.org/10.1109/TMI.2011.2142189.

[75] Landman BA, Bogovic JA, Wan H, ElShahaby FEZ, Bazin PL, Prince JL. Resolution of crossing fibers with constrained compressed sensing using diffusion tensor MRI. NeuroImage 2012;59(3):2175–86. https://doi.org/10.1016/j.neuroimage.2011.10.011.

[76] Mani M, Jacob M, Guidon A, Liu C, Song A, Magnotta V, et al. Acceleration of high angular and spatial resolution diffusion imaging using compressed sensing. In: 2012 9th IEEE international symposium on biomedical imaging (ISBI), MayIEEE; 2012. p. 326–9. https://doi.org/10.1109/ISBI.2012.6235550.

[77] Parker GD, Marshall AD, Rosin PL, Drage N, Richmond S, Jones DK. A pitfall in the reconstruction of fibre ODFs using spherical deconvolution of diffusion MRI data. NeuroImage 2013;65:433–48. https://doi.org/10.1016/j.neuroimage.2012.10.022.

[78] Roine T, Jeurissen B, Perrone D, Aelterman J, Leemans A, Philips W, et al. Isotropic non-white matter partial volume effects in constrained spherical deconvolution. Front Neuroinform 2014;8:28. https://doi.org/10.3389/fninf.2014.00028.

[79] Dell'acqua F, Scifo P, Rizzo G, Catani M, Simmons A, Scotti G, et al. A modified damped Richardson-Lucy algorithm to reduce isotropic background effects in spherical deconvolution. NeuroImage 2010;49(2): 1446–58. https://doi.org/10.1016/j.neuroimage.2009.09.033.

[80] Jeurissen B, Tournier JD, Dhollander T, Connelly A, Sijbers J. Multi-tissue constrained spherical deconvolution for improved analysis of multi-shell diffusion MRI data. NeuroImage 2014;103:411–26. https://doi.org/10.1016/j.neuroimage.2014.07.061.

[81] Reisert M, Mader I, Umarova R, Maier S, Tebartz van Elst L, Kiselev VG. Fiber density estimation from single Q-shell diffusion imaging by tensor divergence NeuroImage 2013;77:166–76. https://doi.org/10.1016/j.neuroimage.2013.03.032.

[82] Christiaens D, Maes F, Sunaert S, Suetens P. Convex non-negative spherical factorization of multi-shell diffusion-weighted images. In: Navab N, Hornegger J, Wells WM, Frangi AF, editors. Medical image computing and computer-assisted intervention—MICCAI 2015Munich, Germany: Springer; 2015. p. 166–73. https://doi.org/10.1007/978-3-319-24553-9_21.

[83] Christiaens D, Sunaert S, Suetens P, Maes F. Convexity-constrained and nonnegativity-constrained spherical factorization in diffusion-weighted imaging. NeuroImage 2017;146:507–17. https://doi.org/10.1016/j.neuroimage.2016.10.040.

[84] Close TG, Tournier JD, Calamante F, Johnston L, Mareels I, Connelly A. A software tool to generate simulated white matter structures for the assessment of fibre-tracking algorithms. NeuroImage 2009;47(4): 1288–300. https://doi.org/10.1016/j.neuroimage.2009.03.077.

[85] Neher PF, Laun FB, Stieltjes B, Maier-Hein KH. Fiberfox: facilitating the creation of realistic white matter software phantoms. Magn Reson Med 2013;72(5):1460–70. https://doi.org/10.1002/mrm.25045.

[86] Fieremans E, Deene YD, Delputte S, Özdemir MS, D'Asseler Y, Vlassenbroeck J, et al. Simulation and experimental verification of the diffusion in an anisotropic fiber phantom. J Magn Reson 2008;190(2):189–99. https://doi.org/10.1016/j.jmr.2007.10.014.

[87] Hall MG, Alexander DC. Convergence and parameter choice for Monte-Carlo simulations of diffusion MRI. IEEE Trans Med Imaging 2009;28(9):1354–64. https://doi.org/10.1109/tmi.2009.2015756.

[88] Alexander DC, Hubbard PL, Hall MG, Moore EA, Ptito M, Parker GJM, et al. Orientationally invariant indices of axon diameter and density from diffusion MRI NeuroImage 2010;52(4):1374–89. https://doi.org/10.1016/j.neuroimage.2010.05.043.

[89] Landman BA, Farrell JAD, Smith SA, Reich DS, Calabresi PA, van Zijl PCM. Complex geometric models of diffusion and relaxation in healthy and damaged white matter. NMR Biomed 2009;23(2):152–62. https://doi.org/10.1002/nbm.1437.

[90] Yeh CH, Schmitt B, Bihan DL, Li-Schlittgen JR, Lin CP, Poupon C. Diffusion microscopist simulator: a general Monte Carlo simulation system for diffusion magnetic resonance imaging. PLoS ONE 2013;8(10): e76626. https://doi.org/10.1371/journal.pone.0076626.

[91] Lin CP, Wedeen VJ, Chen JH, Yao C, Tseng WYI. Validation of diffusion spectrum magnetic resonance imaging with manganese-enhanced rat optic tracts and ex vivo phantoms. NeuroImage 2003;19(3): 482–95. https://doi.org/10.1016/s1053-8119(03)00154-x.

[92] Perrin M, Poupon C, Rieul B, Leroux P, Constantinesco A, Mangin JF, et al. Validation of Q-ball imaging with a diffusion fibre-crossing phantom on a clinical scanner. Philos Trans R Soc B Biol Sci 2005;360(1457):881–91. https://doi.org/10.1098/rstb.2005.1650.

[93] Yanasak N, Allison J. Use of capillaries in the construction of an MRI phantom for the assessment of diffusion tensor imaging: demonstration of performance. Magn Reson Imaging 2006;24(10):1349–61. https://doi.org/10.1016/j.mri.2006.08.001.

[94] Tournier JD, Yeh CH, Calamante F, Cho KH, Connelly A, Lin CP. Resolving crossing fibres using constrained spherical deconvolution: validation using diffusion-weighted imaging phantom data. NeuroImage 2008;42(2):617–25. https://doi.org/10.1016/j.neuroimage.2008.05.002.

[95] Fieremans E, Deene YD, Delputte S, Özdemir MS, Achten E, Lemahieu I. The design of anisotropic diffusion phantoms for the validation of diffusion weighted magnetic resonance imaging. Phys Med Biol 2008;53(19):5405–19. https://doi.org/10.1088/0031-9155/53/19/009.

[96] Fillard P, Descoteaux M, Goh A, Gouttard S, Jeurissen B, Malcolm J, et al. Quantitative evaluation of 10 tractography algorithms on a realistic diffusion MR phantom. NeuroImage 2011;56(1):220–34.

[97] Farrher E, Kaffanke J, Celik AA, Stöcker T, Grinberg F, Shah NJ. Novel multisection design of anisotropic diffusion phantoms. Magn Reson Imaging 2012;30(4):518–26. https://doi.org/10.1016/j.mri.2011.12.012.

[98] Helmstaedter M, Briggman KL, Turaga SC, Jain V, Seung HS, Denk W. Connectomic reconstruction of the inner plexiform layer in the mouse retina. Nature 2013;500(7461):168–74. https://doi.org/10.1038/nature12346.

[99] Leergaard TB, White NS, de Crespigny A, Bolstad I, D'Arceuil H, Bjaalie JG, et al. Quantitative histological validation of diffusion MRI fiber orientation distributions in the rat brain. PLoS ONE 2010;5(1):e8595. https://doi.org/10.1371/journal.pone.0008595.

[100] Choe AS, Stepniewska I, Colvin DC, Ding Z, Anderson AW. Validation of diffusion tensor MRI in the central nervous system using light microscopy: quantitative comparison of fiber properties. NMR Biomed 2012;25(7):900–8. https://doi.org/10.1002/nbm.1810.

[101] Khan AR, Cornea A, Leigland LA, Kohama SG, Jespersen SN, Kroenke CD. 3D structure tensor analysis of light microscopy data for validating diffusion MRI. NeuroImage 2015;111:192–203. https://doi.org/10.1016/j.neuroimage.2015.01.061.

[102] Seehaus A, Roebroeck A, Bastiani M, Fonseca L, Bratzke H, Lori N, et al. Histological validation of high-resolution DTI in human post mortem tissue. Front Neuroanat 2015;9. https://doi.org/10.3389/fnana.2015.00098.

[103] Wang H, Lenglet C, Akkin T. Structure tensor analysis of serial optical coherence scanner images for mapping fiber orientations and tractography in the brain. J Biomed Opt 2015;20(3):036003. https://doi.org/10.1117/1.jbo.20.3.036003.

[104] Schilling K, Janve V, Gao Y, Stepniewska I, Landman BA, Anderson AW. Comparison of 3D orientation distribution functions measured with confocal microscopy and diffusion MRI. NeuroImage 2016;129: 185–197. https://doi.org/10.1016/j.neuroimage.2016.01.022.

[105] Van Essen DC, Smith SM, Barch DM, Behrens TEJ, Yacoub E, Ugurbil K. The WU-Minn human connectome project: an overview. NeuroImage 2013;80:62–79. https://doi.org/10.1016/j.neuroimage.2013.05.041.

[106] Raffelt D, Tournier JD, Fripp J, Crozier S, Connelly A, Salvado O. Symmetric diffeomorphic registration of fibre orientation distributions. NeuroImage 2011;56(3):1171–80.

[107] Dell'Acqua F, Simmons A, Williams SCR, Catani M. Can spherical deconvolution provide more information than fiber orientations? Hindrance modulated orientational anisotropy, a true-tract specific index to characterize white matter diffusion. Human Brain Mapping 2013;34(10):2464–83. https://doi.org/10.1002/hbm.22080.

[108] Mori S, Van Zijl PCM. Fiber tracking: principles and strategies—a technical review. NMR Biomed 2002;15(7–8):468–80. https://doi.org/10.1002/nbm.781.

[109] Jeurissen B, Leemans A, Jones DK, Tournier JD, Sijbers J. Probabilistic fiber tracking using the residual bootstrap with constrained spherical deconvolution. Hum Brain Mapp 2011;32(3):461–79. https://doi.org/10.1002/hbm.21032.

[110] Reisert M, Mader I, Anastasopoulos C, Weigel M, Schnell S, Kiselev V. Global fiber reconstruction becomes practical. NeuroImage 2011;54(2):955–62. https://doi.org/10.1016/j.neuroimage.2010.09.016.

[111] Tournier JD, Calamante F, Connelly A. MRtrix: diffusion tractography in crossing fiber regions. Int J Imaging Syst Technol 2012;22(1):53–66. https://doi.org/10.1002/ima.22005.

[112] Christiaens D, Reisert M, Dhollander T, Sunaert S, Suetens P, Maes F. Global tractography of multi-shell diffusion-weighted imaging data using a multi-tissue model. NeuroImage 2015;123:89–8101. https://doi.org/10.1016/j.neuroimage.2015.08.008.

[113] Pujol S, Wells W, Pierpaoli C, Brun C, Gee J, Cheng G, et al. The DTI challenge: toward standardized evaluation of diffusion tensor imaging tractography for neurosurgery. J Neuroimaging 2015;25(6):875–82. https://doi.org/10.1111/jon.12283.

[114] Smith RE, Tournier JD, Calamante F, Connelly A. The effects of SIFT on the reproducibility and biological accuracy of the structural connectome. NeuroImage 2015;104:253–65. https://doi.org/10.1016/j.neuroimage.2014.10.004.

CHAPTER

Diffusion MRI Fiber Tractography 21

Robert Elton Smith[a,b], Alan Connelly[a,b,c], and Fernando Calamante[b,d,e]

[a]*Florey Institute of Neuroscience and Mental Health, Melbourne, VIC, Australia* [b]*Florey Department of Neuroscience and Mental Health, University of Melbourne, Melbourne, VIC, Australia* [c]*Department of Medicine, Austin Health and Northern Health, University of Melbourne, Melbourne, VIC, Australia* [d]*The University of Sydney, School of Biomedical Engineering, Sydney, NSW, Australia* [e]*The University of Sydney, Sydney Imaging, Sydney, NSW, Australia*

21.1 Introduction

In the presence of anisotropic diffusion sensitization gradients, diffusion Magnetic Resonance Imaging (MRI) yields a three-dimensional (3D) voxel grid where the image intensities encode information related to the anisotropic organization of the underlying microstructure within each grid element. If these voxels are sufficiently small relative to the length and curvature of these microscopic fibers, one intuitively expects that the anisotropic information encoded within the image data will demonstrate some form of coherence in orientation between adjacent voxels [1]. The question then is: Given the observation of this anisotropic signal upon a regular grid lattice, is it possible to reconstruct the complete spatial trajectories of the underlying fibers (Fig. 21.1)? Attempting to address this inverse problem is the fundamental premise of "tractography."

This goal of this chapter is a review of diffusion tractography [2–11] with a concise discussion of the most fundamental principles of the streamline tractography paradigm to which almost all algorithms used in the field conform. Alternative, nonstreamline tractography concepts are briefly described in order to contextualize streamline-based approaches. Finally, particular attention is paid to the experimental conditions in which tractography may be utilized to derive quantitative outcomes.

21.2 Streamline tractography

21.2.1 Method summary

The fundamental streamline paradigm is based on a simple observation (Fig. 21.2) [12–16]: If the fiber orientation at some point in space is known, one can take a small "step" in the direction of the underlying fibers, re-assess the fiber orientation at this new location, and take *another* small step in this new direction. By repeating this process many times, one can construct a continuous path through space, which is consistent with the underlying fiber orientations, and is therefore a reasonable estimate of the trajectory of the underlying fibers from which those local orientations were observed.

Advances in Magnetic Resonance Technology and Applications. Volume 1. ISSN 2666-9099. https://doi.org/10.1016/B978-0-12-817057-1.00023-8

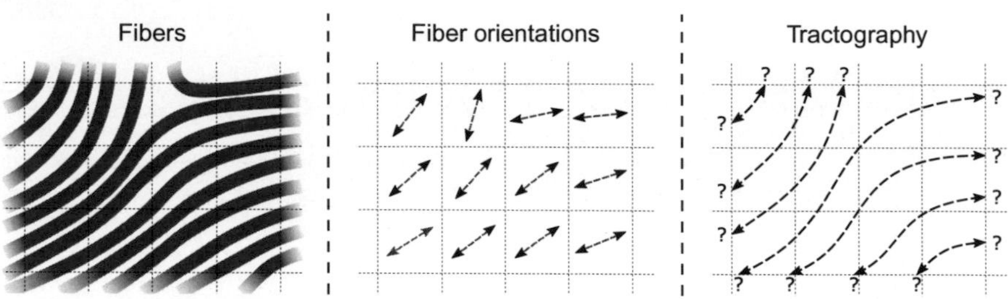

FIG. 21.1

The basic premise of diffusion MRI tractography. A system of fibers *(left panel)* leads to the observation of anisotropy upon an image grid, from which local fiber orientations can be estimated *(middle panel)*; the role of tractography is to attempt to reconstruct the underlying fiber trajectories from these observations *(right panel).*

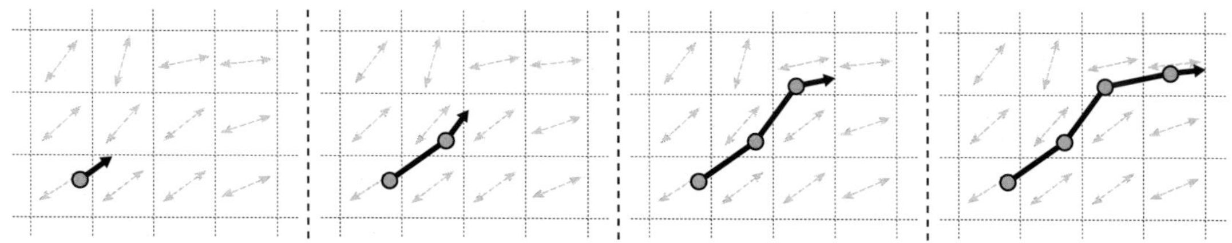

FIG. 21.2

Demonstration of basic streamline tractography paradigm. At each tracking "step" *(from leftmost to rightmost panel),* the streamline is extended along the direction of the local fiber orientation estimate.

This concept is the fundamental principle upon which almost all tractography algorithms that are used in scientific applications are based. These are referred to as "streamline tractography" algorithms, with each individual reconstructed continuous path referred to as a "streamline" or "track." These synthetic trajectories only provide *estimates* of pathways of the underlying fiber bundles and should not be conflated with either microscopic (e.g., "fiber"/"axon") or macroscopic (e.g., "tract"/"fascicle") biological entities [2].

In addition to the simple description above, there are many details regarding the nuances of how these algorithms operate. Decisions must be made with respect to algorithmic design/parameter selection, and the constraints that may apply when utilizing such an algorithm. Thus, details are included in this chapter for separating out the roles and influences of different aspects of performing a streamline tractography experiment.

The decisions to be made during the reconstruction component of a streamline tractography experiment can be broken into the four independent "Algorithm Components," which are listed and described in further detail below. While implementations or descriptions of streamline tractography may sometimes blur the lines between these components, for the purpose of comprehension, the building blocks of a streamline algorithm are best decomposed as follows (Fig. 21.3):

Four algorithm components of streamline tractography:

1. Where to *start* the streamline;
2. In what direction to propagate the streamline by a *step* at each iteration;

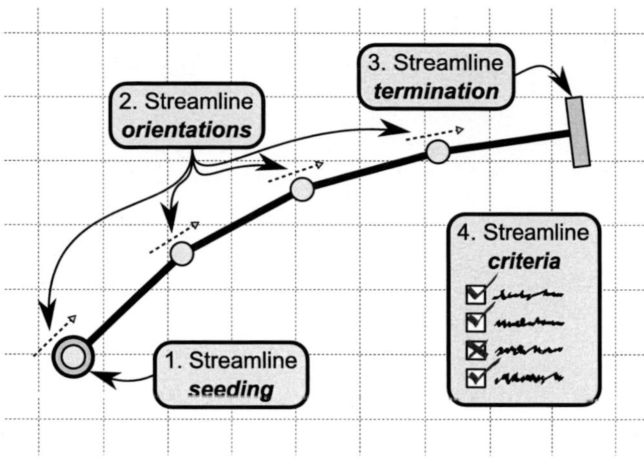

FIG. 21.3

The four fundamental algorithm components of streamline tractography.

3. Where to *stop* the streamline;
4. Whether or not the streamline is *satisfactory* given a set of criteria.

21.2.1.1 Component 1: Where to start: Seeding

In order for each individual streamline to be generated along a particular trajectory, it is necessary to define a starting location that will form the first streamline vertex from which propagation will commence; this is colloquially referred to as streamline *seeding*. Exactly how this seed point is determined, and how the locations of these seed points may vary for different streamlines, must be defined, depending on the application/end goal. A wide range of options is available for the selection of a seed point (Fig. 21.4). These include a precise predetermined coordinate in 3D space, a manually or automatically defined specific region of interest (volume or surface) of finite size corresponding to some anatomical structure for which the fiber connectivity is sought, or an entire organ or tissue of interest based on segmentation of either its volume or a surface-based representation of its extremities (e.g., the interface between gray and white matter in the brain) [17–20].

When streamline seeds are placed in the middle of fiber bundles, rather than at their start or endpoints, it is common to treat these as *bidirectional* seed points, and proceed to propagate the streamline in *antipodal directions*.

21.2.1.2 Component 2: Where to go: Stepping along fiber orientations

When propagating a streamline through 3D space, a decision must be made at each discrete streamline vertex as to the direction in which the streamline propagation should continue. This determination depends most vitally on some estimation of fiber orientation at the location of the streamline; it must also depend on the current tangent of the streamline, in order to preserve spatial smoothness. However, a large number of parameters are involved in this calculation, all of which may have a significant influence on the outcomes of the tractography experiment.

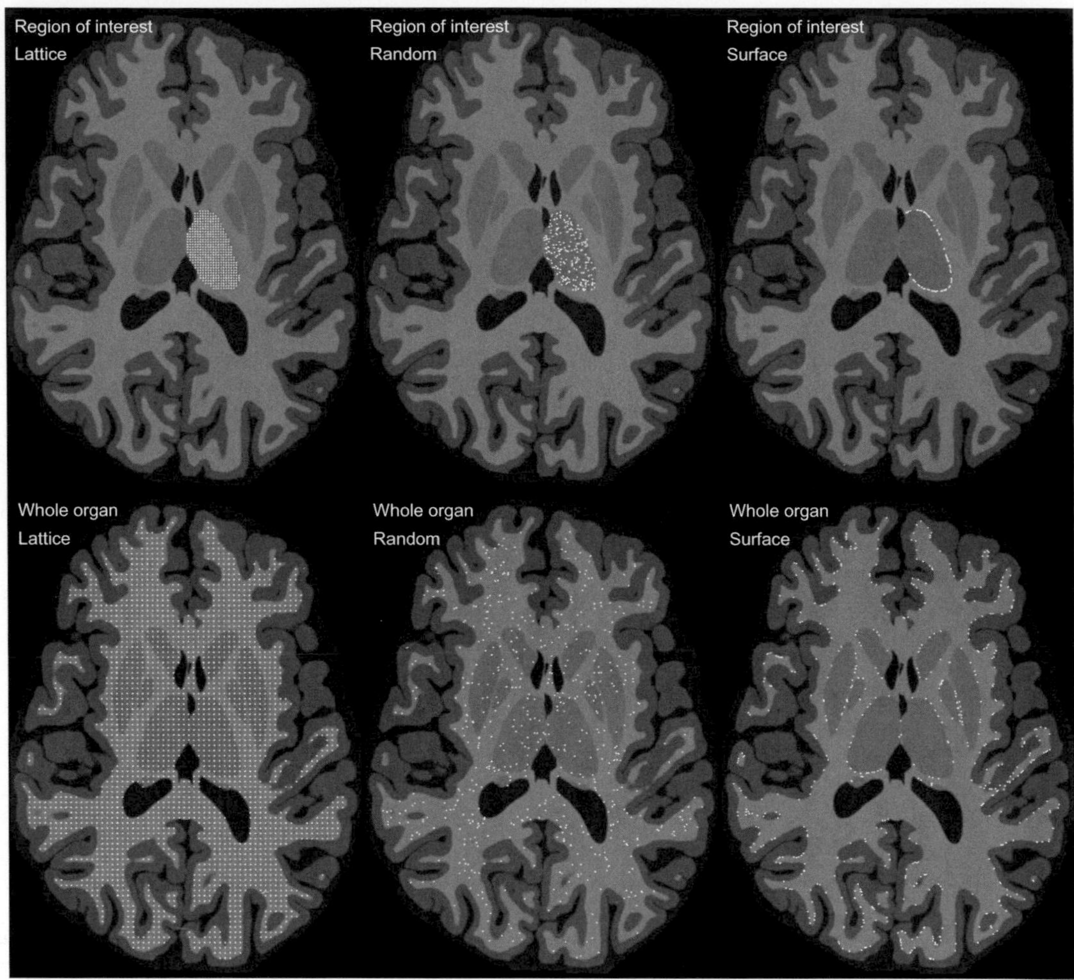

FIG. 21.4

Examples of common streamline seeding strategies for both a specific region of interest *(top)* and for reconstruction of whole-organ structural connectivity *(bottom)* in an axial human brain slice; the region of interest in the top row is the left thalamus. Each individual seed point appears as a white dot.

The most important consideration is the diffusion model to be used to provide the fiber orientation estimates in each image voxel. Different models provide different information regarding the underlying structure; important factors include whether or not *more than one* fiber orientation can be estimated in a single image voxel, and whether the estimated fiber orientations are *discrete* (i.e., represented as a single direction on the unit hemisphere for each fiber bundle) or *continuous* (i.e., a smooth function on the unit hemisphere). If orientation distribution functions are continuous, another important factor is whether they represent the *diffusion* orientation distribution function (ODF) or the *fiber* ODF, with the latter being preferable for the reconstruction of fiber trajectories.

For a given precise location in 3D space, another consideration is how a representative diffusion model is obtained from which to sample a fiber direction, given that the orientation estimates provided by the diffusion model are defined within image voxels on a regular 3D lattice. Exactly how this *interpolation* can be done depends on the particulars of the diffusion model (Fig. 21.5). If a model provides a *single fiber orientation* on the unit hemisphere in each voxel, then either a simple weighted average of these orientations or a weighted least-squares solution [21] can be taken. For the *diffusion tensor model*, such interpolation requires calculus that is tailored to the mathematical properties of the tensor [22,23]. If a model provides *multiple discrete fiber orientations* on the unit hemisphere in each voxel (which may be referred to as "*fixels*" [24]), such data in fact *cannot be interpolated* in a naïve fashion. There is no intrinsic correspondence between fixels in adjacent voxels, and the number of fixels may vary between adjacent voxels. Hence, streamline tractography using such models may use "nearest-neighbor interpolation," where the diffusion model for the voxel in which the streamline vertex resides is used regardless of the exact position of the vertex within the voxel (i.e., *no* interpolation). Alternatively, a "roulette wheel" sampling scheme may be used [25], where the surrounding voxel from which to sample the diffusion model is chosen stochastically. In both cases, the sampled fiber orientations do not vary smoothly through space, and reconstructed streamline trajectories are correspondingly nonsmooth. It is possible to instead *interpolate the diffusion data* themselves, and fit the diffusion model to the data at the location of the streamline vertex [26–28]; this can however be very computationally expensive for more complex diffusion models. If a model is defined using *coefficients in a continuous basis* (e.g., an ODF in the spherical harmonic basis), then direct interpolation of these coefficients at the location of the streamline vertex is possible [29,30].

From a given intermediate streamline vertex at any precise location in space, the streamline must be appropriately extended through the definition of a new streamline vertex. A number of decisions must be made, many of which are arbitrary yet highly consequential (Fig. 21.6). Due to the antipodal symmetry of diffusion models and the necessity for a smooth continuity of reconstructed streamlines, any chosen orientation must be *consistent with the prior tangent* of the streamline, and not result in a reversal of direction. If the chosen diffusion model provides multiple discrete fiber orientations on the unit hemisphere in each voxel, then it becomes necessary to either *select one particular fiber bundle* from which to sample the orientation (this would typically be the fiber bundle that is most collinear with the prior tangent of the streamline [30–33]) or to *split* the streamline such that multiple fiber orientations are followed [34,35]. The *permissible turning angle* from the prior streamline tangent would typically be constrained to some threshold less than 90° (alternatively expressed as the *minimal radius of curvature* [30]). While biological fibers may curve very sharply in reality, such trajectories cannot be properly represented using orientations on a coarse image grid. The *distance* from the current vertex where the new vertex should be defined frequently referred to as the "*step size*" of the streamline algorithm; while seemingly trivial, this parameter is well known to be highly consequential for tractography outcomes [36–38].

Mathematically, streamline tractography is a numerical procedure for solving a differential equation for a given initial value: the streamline seed is the initial value, the estimated fiber orientations are the local derivatives of the function, and the constructed streamline trajectory is the estimated solution. As such, knowledge and capabilities regarding such *integration* are applicable in the context of streamline tractography. Some streamline methods remain first-order ("Euler integration") due to the difficulties with interpolation issues described earlier; others are intrinsically second-order [39]; in some circumstances, the Runge-Kutta method may be used to perform a higher-order integration using an

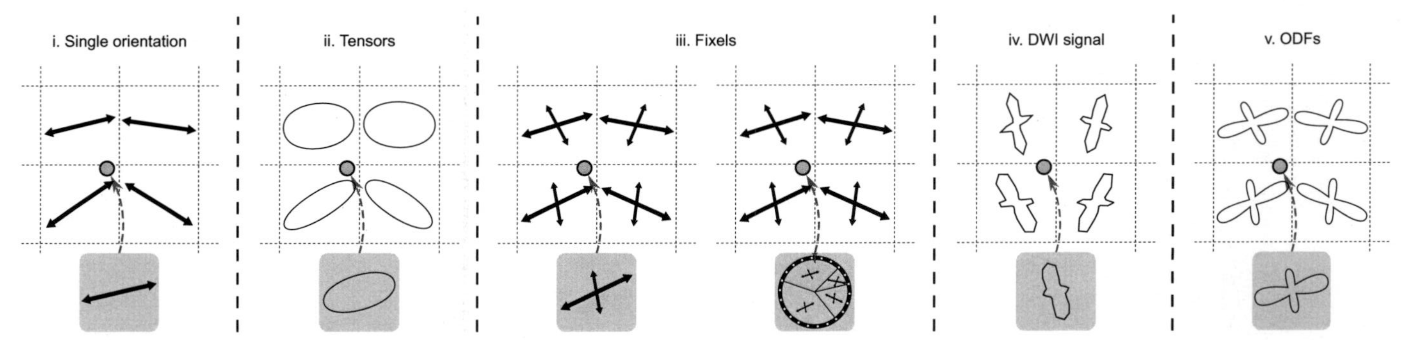

FIG. 21.5

Methods for interpolation/selection of diffusion models to obtain fiber orientations at a streamline vertex *(gray dot)* that does not reside precisely at the center of an image voxel. The orientations provided by the diffusion model for the four nearest voxels are shown at the top, and the resulting fiber direction for the streamline vertex in *gray* at the *bottom*. For "iii. Fixels," both deterministic *(left)* and stochastic *(right)* strategies are shown.

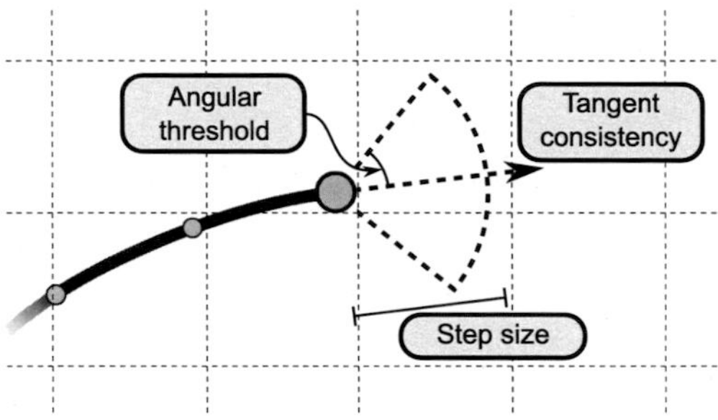

FIG. 21.6

Basic parameters for propagation within a streamline tractography algorithm.

underlying first-order method [15,40]. The most obvious effect of integration order is in a curved orientation field, where trajectories reconstructed using low-order methods notoriously underestimate the amount of curvature (Fig. 21.7) [36].

In some streamline tractography methods, it is possible for *data other than the local estimated fiber orientation* to influence the selected orientation in which to propagate a streamline. These additional factors include properties enforced by the local diffusion model over and above the dominant fiber direction(s) alone, such as the tensor/ODF shape [41–44] and the preservation of microstructural properties along the trajectory [45]. Note that if the magnitude with which a streamline is curved/"deflected" during propagation is modulated by the anisotropy of the underlying model, as is done in many such methods, this will exacerbate the effect of curvature overshoot demonstrated in Fig. 21.7. Additional factors include trajectory-based smoothness of diffusion model estimation [27,28,46–48], use of the structure tensor from gradient echo imaging [49], imposition of a model of fiber orientation near the cortical surface such that streamline trajectories better mimic the patterns observed in histology [50], and bundle-specific spatial orientation priors [51].

21.2.1.3 Component 3: Where to stop: Streamline termination

While diffusion models provide direct information regarding fiber orientations for streamline propagation, they only *indirectly* provide information about where the underlying fibers *end* (and hence where reconstructed streamlines should ideally also terminate). Appropriate determination of the position at which each streamline should cease propagation has thus historically been problematic, with various heuristic criteria employed. Some *explicit mask* may be derived, which streamlines are forbidden from exiting. A threshold may be applied to *streamline curvature*, as if estimated fiber orientations are no longer spatially consistent, the underlying trajectories cannot be reliably reconstructed. A threshold may additionally be applied to some measure of *anisotropy*, as a tendency toward isotropy/small fiber volume indicates that fiber trajectories should not be reconstructed; examples include fractional anisotropy (FA) from the diffusion tensor model [52], volume fractions of a discrete multi-fiber model, or the amplitude of the relevant ODF.

These criteria however typically do not empirically provide the kind of performance that would be desired from a streamline tractography algorithm: application of predefined masks can lead to "jagged"/"staircase" effects at the mask edges; other thresholds are neither sensitive nor specific,

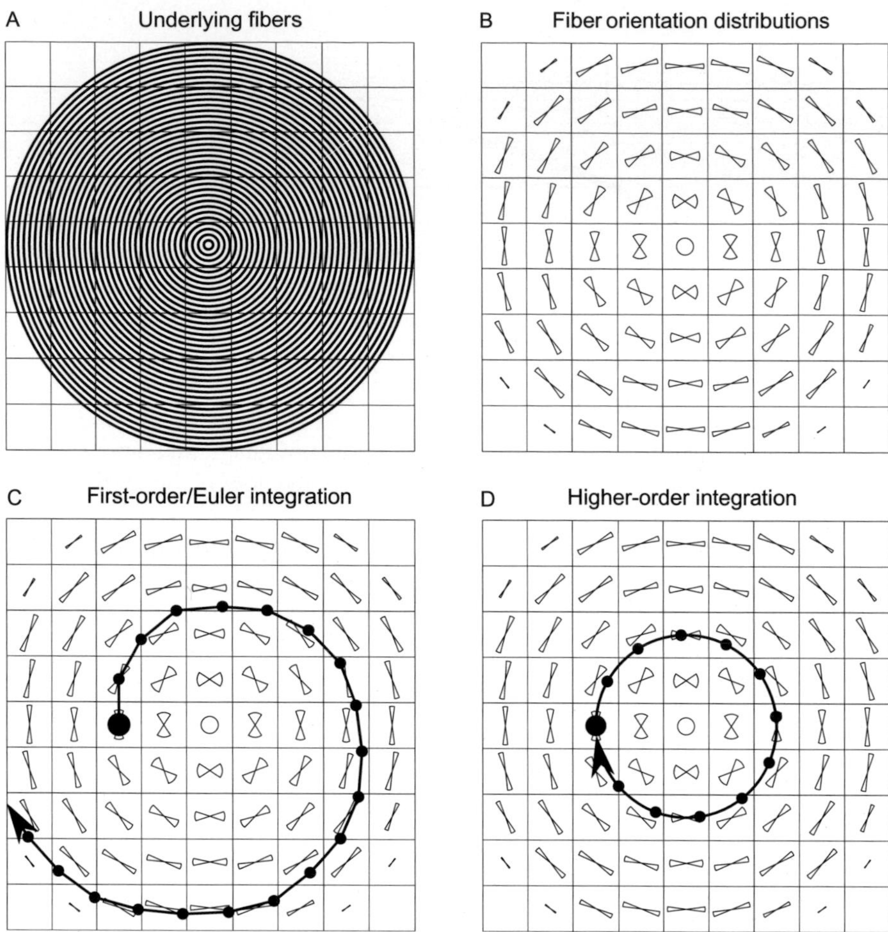

FIG. 21.7

Effects of integration order on streamline trajectories in a curved orientation field. (A) The underlying fibers, all following a circular trajectory. (B) The resulting fiber orientation distribution field; note that the angular spread of each fiber orientation distribution function reflects the amount of fiber curvature within that particular voxel, and that this effect is greater in magnitude near the center of the circle; moreover, the reduced overall amplitudes of these functions in the corners of the images reflect the reduced local fiber density within the relevant voxels. (C) When using only the fiber orientation at the current vertex location to determine the direction of propagation, the streamline moves further outward radially as it propagates, due to interrogating the local fiber orientation only, forming a spiral rather than a circle. (D) Use of higher-order integration techniques to account for the curvature of the orientation field can correct this issue (note how the path between each streamline vertex dot is represented as a curve rather than a straight line when using such an approach).

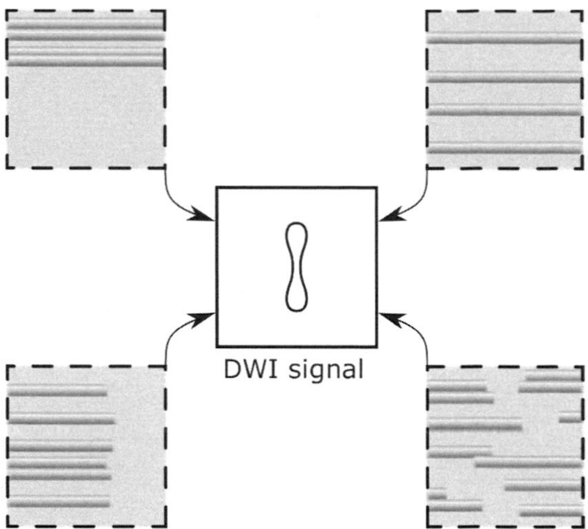

FIG. 21.8

Insensitivity of the diffusion-weighted signal to fiber terminations. In the two upper voxels, all fibers traverse the entire length of the voxel (and thus reconstructed streamlines should ideally pass all the way though), whereas in the two lower voxels this is not the case (and thus streamlines would ideally be terminated). However, all four exemplar voxels in the figure contain approximately the same volume of cylindrical restrictive compartments, which in turn leads to the observation of approximately the same diffusion-weighted signal in each.

resulting in premature streamline terminations due to reduced fiber bundle partial volumes and permitting propagation of streamlines through regions where they should be forbidden. Indeed the diffusion signal itself shows only limited sensitivity/specificity to fiber terminations (Fig. 21.8) (which is exacerbated at lower spatial resolutions), making termination of streamlines using only information from diffusion-weighted imaging highly ill-posed.

It is becoming increasingly common to enforce streamline terminations using *tissue segmentation* rather than anisotropy information from the diffusion model [19,53,54]. If the fibers to be reconstructed are known to be present in some tissues (e.g., the white matter of the brain), but are not present or should not be reconstructed in other tissues (e.g., within fluid-filled regions), then deriving a tissue decomposition from image data may be used to better inform the streamline algorithm as to where streamlines should be terminated (Fig. 21.9). This could be a spatial map of tissue partial volumes and/or a surface-based representation of interfaces between tissues, which must be accurately spatially aligned with the diffusion data (which may necessitate nonlinear geometric distortion correction depending on the imaging techniques used) [56,57].

21.2.1.4 Component 4: Whether or not to accept: Selection criteria

Finally, once a complete streamline trajectory has been generated, a decision must be made as to whether or not the streamline is deemed *satisfactory* according to all relevant criteria. The decision to *reject* a generated streamline can be made based on one or more of a wide range of criteria, with the most common being streamline length, a priori constraints, and anatomical plausibility.

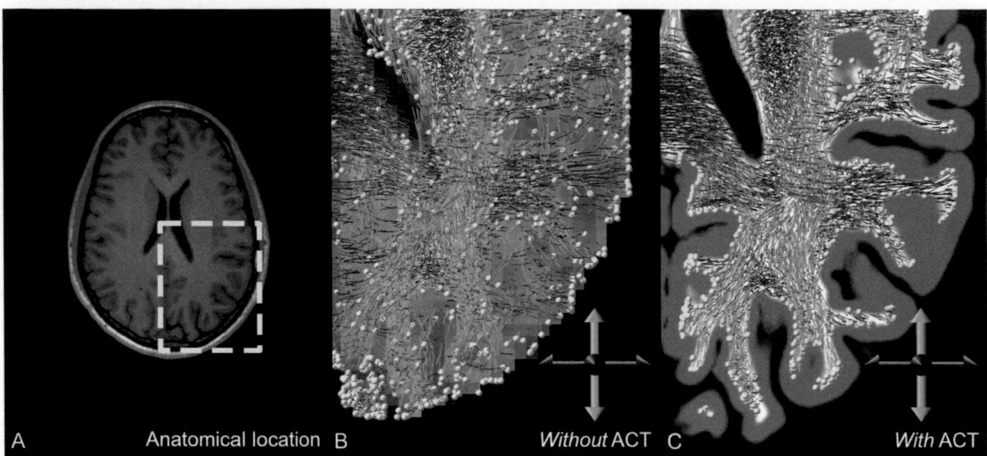

FIG. 21.9

The influence of anatomical constraints on streamline tractography (illustrated here specifically using the anatomically constrained tractography (ACT) framework [19]). (A) Axial human brain slice, showing the anatomical location of the zoomed region shown in (B) and (C), highlighted on a T_1-weighted image. (B) The outcomes of tractography when relying on information from diffusion imaging alone, where the background image is the mean amplitude of the fiber orientation distribution functions (fODFs) estimated by constrained spherical deconvolution (CSD) [55]; streamlines are colored according to their local orientation *(red= left-right; green= anterior-posterior; blue= inferior-superior)*, and streamline terminations are shown as *yellow spheres*. Note how streamline terminations occur throughout the brain volume. (C) The outcomes of tractography when incorporating anatomical tissue information, where the background image reflects the tissue segmentation of the subject's T_1-weighted image. Note how streamlines only terminate at the interfaces between *gray* and *white* matter.

Streamline tractography algorithms typically enforce some minimum streamline length, in order to preclude very short meaningless connections that arise due to noise and/or trajectories that are shorter than a known fiber bundle being reconstructed. A maximum length is typically also enforced to prevent reconstruction of "circular" trajectories within the tissue of interest.

In instances where streamline tractography is to be used to reconstruct only some subset of the organ, some constraints must be imposed in order to select the appropriate streamlines. These most typically take the form of so-called "include" or "waypoint" regions of interest (ROIs), and/or "exclude" ROIs (Fig. 21.10): streamlines must traverse or stop within *all* regions designated as the former, and must *not* traverse or stop within *any* regions designated as the latter, in order to satisfy the imposed selection conditions. Such regions may be defined manually by a researcher [58,59], or may be derived through some automated approach, such as transformation of a segmented structure/brain parcellation from some template space onto the subject's image data [60,61].

In addition to any tractography constraints that are specific to a particular hypothesis or fiber bundle of interest, in some instances, it is also possible to impose selection criteria on individual streamlines based on anatomical knowledge of the relevant tissues. These selection criteria can extend beyond a simple tractography "mask" (constraining where streamlines may/may not propagate) as mentioned in Component 3. For instance, in the case of the brain, neuronal axons are known to not synapse within the

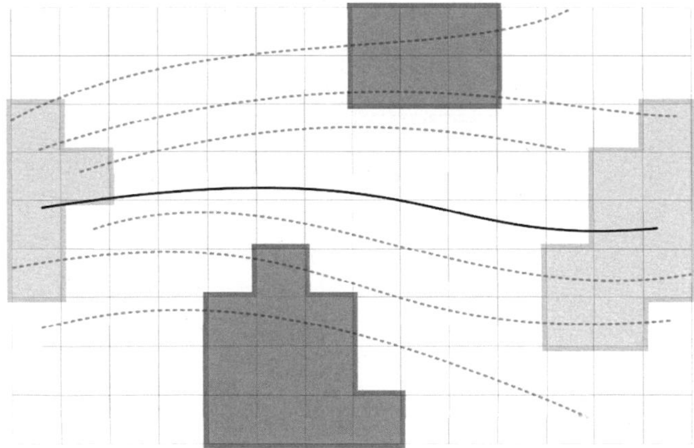

FIG. 21.10

The effects of the application of regions of interest (ROIs). Two "inclusion"/"waypoint" ROIs *(light, left, and right)*, and two "exclusion" ROIs *(dark, top, and bottom)* are defined here. The solid line is the only streamline for which these constraints are satisfied, as it intersects both inclusion regions and neither exclusion region; *dashed lines* are streamlines that fail at least one of these criteria and hence would be rejected.

white matter, instead traversing the entire white matter as a single cell before synapsing in the gray matter. This knowledge can be exploited in conjunction with a tissue segmentation derived from image data to reject streamlines whose terminations are incongruent with constraints imposed based on this prior knowledge [19,20,53,54] (e.g., note the absence of streamline terminations within brain white matter in Fig. 21.9C).

21.2.2 Deterministic vs probabilistic algorithms

When considering the attributes of particular streamline tractography algorithms, one of the most common classifications is whether the algorithm is "*deterministic*" or "*probabilistic*." While it is in fact possible for any of the four Components enumerated above to exhibit stochastic behavior [53], such a description is made almost exclusively in reference to component 2, which is the selection of an orientation in which to propagate the streamline based on the underlying diffusion image data.

The empirical difference between deterministic and probabilistic approaches can be described as follows: If multiple streamlines are generated from the same seed point using a deterministic algorithm, then all resulting streamlines will be *identical*; conversely, with a probabilistic algorithm, each streamline will almost certainly follow a *unique trajectory*, as each draws independent samples from distributions of plausible fiber orientations along its trajectory (Fig. 21.11).

Historically, deterministic streamline algorithms have been considered to be "specific but not sensitive": they may robustly reconstruct known major fiber bundle pathways, but may fail to reconstruct smaller pathways. On the other hand, probabilistic algorithms are considered "sensitive but not specific," in that a known pathway between two points of interest can almost always be reconstructed, but a large number of false-positive trajectories will also be produced as a consequence. While this simplistic description is somewhat consistent with experimental evidence [62,63], the reality is more

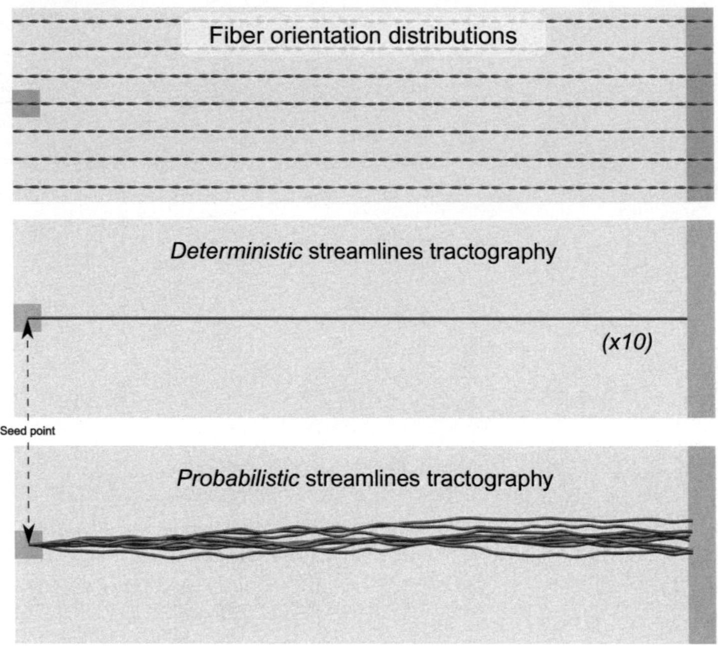

FIG. 21.11

The fundamental difference between streamline algorithms that work by selecting fiber orientations deterministically vs probabilistically. The *top image* shows the underlying fiber orientation distribution function (fODF) field from which streamline orientations are sampled. In the deterministic case, all 10 streamlines seeded from the singular location (seed voxel highlighted at *left edge*) follow precisely the same trajectory in reaching the target region of interest (highlighted voxels at *right edge*); in the probabilistic case, each of the 10 streamlines realizes a unique trajectory, as each streamline is influenced independently by the uncertainty in the underlying image data.

nuanced. In the presence of image noise, a deterministic algorithm may generate a very dense reconstruction of an entirely nonexistent fiber pathway, due to a single misleading fiber orientation at some point along the length of the bundle. Additionally, a deterministic algorithm may reliably reconstruct only a small portion of a known fiber pathway rather than its entire extent. Probabilistic algorithms, on the other hand, produce a larger amount of spatial dispersion between streamlines, which both reflect the uncertainty associated with noisy image data and attempts to capture the full spatial extent of fiber bundles.

These points are also relevant for the aesthetic appearance of streamlines; many "prefer" the appearance of deterministic streamlines, despite the fact that such trajectories may be misleading in a number of ways. Note that the classification of a streamline algorithm as "deterministic" or "probabilistic" is not strictly tied to the particular model used to estimate fiber orientations. Indeed it is conceptually possible to perform both deterministic and probabilistic streamline tractography for any diffusion model. The particular model utilized will also influence the "sensitivity" and "specificity" of any particular streamline tractography algorithm (as discussed earlier) over and above the presence or absence of stochastic behavior.

Within the range of probabilistic streamline algorithms, the various approaches differ in the *origin* of nondeterminism of fiber orientation samples, and in the *interpretation* of the way in which the algorithm handles and/or provides "probabilistic" information. Confusion has been known to ensue when two discussion participants fail to identify their disagreements on these points; hence they are being addressed explicitly here.

The stochastic behavior of fiber orientation selection for streamline tractography typically arises from one (or potentially multiple) of the following sources:

i. Sampling from a set of *plausible realizations of the diffusion model*. These realizations could be obtained from multiple repetitions of the imaging experiment itself [64] (typically prohibitive), or more commonly through data-driven bootstrap approaches, where residuals of the diffusion model fit drive the estimates of uncertainty [33,65–70].
ii. Sampling from a *measure of fiber orientation dispersion* that is parameterized for each discrete fiber bundle as part of the diffusion model [71–76].[a]
iii. Sampling from an estimated *continuous distribution* of fiber orientations, as parameterized by the diffusion model [26,29,30,35,39]; preferably a *fiber* orientation distribution function (since this more directly represents the target information required by a tractography algorithm than a *diffusion* ODF [35]). Directions in which the estimated fiber density is greater are more likely to be followed by any particular streamline.[a]
iv. As mentioned in Section 21.2.1.2 *interpolation* of the surrounding diffusion model data for a particular streamline vertex location in 3D space may also be stochastic [25].

The outcomes of a probabilistic streamline tractography experiment are commonly understood in one of the two following ways (Fig. 21.12):

i. Each generated streamline is *individually* a *plausible trajectory* given the uncertainty in the data. Typically there is not an actual "probability" ascribed to each streamline (though there is some effort to retrospectively quantify the likelihood of particular trajectories being false positives [28,47,77–79]); instead, the accumulation of multiple streamline trajectories generated within the criteria of a particular streamline tractography experiment are thought to represent the "possible extent of coverage" of fiber pathways that satisfy those criteria. This is the requisite interpretation for Section 21.4.1 below.
ii. The streamlines indicate a "*probability of connectivity*" from a specific point in space to one or more targets, based on the *fraction of streamlines* generated from that seed point that intersect the target(s) [25,80] (targets can be anything from individual image voxels or surface facets to macroscopic structures of interest).

Note, however, that this "probability of connectivity" interpretation technically only holds if two conditions are met. First, all streamlines must be generated from *precisely* the same starting point. If a seed region is of finite size, then each infinitesimally small point within that region has its own "probability of connectivity" to any particular target, and hence aggregating these values throughout the seed volume intrinsically involves computing the *mean* "probability

[a]Note however that both points ii and iii are technically erroneous interpretations of such information. Such fiber orientation dispersion is not the set of *fiber* orientations that should be *sampled from* during streamline tractography, but is rather the set of *streamline* orientations that should be present in the *outcome* of a tractography experiment (taking into account within-voxel curvature) if it is to be unbiased with respect to the underlying fiber orientation structure.

FIG. 21.12

Two different presentations of the outcomes of a probabilistic tractography experiment using a fixed seed point location, for which the interpretations may differ. In this 3D view of a human brain, the seed point is located at the interface between gray and white matter in the middle of the right motor strip *(white arrows)*. *Left*: Individual streamlines propagating from the seed point are shown; each individual streamline is interpreted as a plausible fiber trajectory; in some instances, the density of streamlines may have a physical interpretation (see Section 21.4.1). *Right*: color/intensity of each voxel reflects the proportion of generated streamlines intersecting that voxel; these may be interpreted as the "probability of connectivity" of each voxel to the seed location.

of connectivity" from seed to target throughout the seed (i.e., *not* the probability of connectivity from seed region to target, as one may desire).

To explain this effect, consider a seed region *A* where 50% of the volume of that region is connected with 100% certainty to some target region *B*, but the other 50% of region *A* connects to other regions. Within this framework, region *A* may (somewhat misleadingly) be considered to be "connected to region *B* with 50% probability." It would be more accurate to instead state that "the mean probability of connectivity to region *B* throughout the volume of region *A* is 50%" (which is an entirely valid metric to derive, but nevertheless notably differs from the intended interpretation). Second, the seed point is strictly *considered* to be either "connected to" or "not connected to" the target, and the tractography experiment is intended to assess the *likelihood of the presence* of such a connection. Any notion of "density" of fiber connectivity (e.g., Region *A* being connected to both regions *B* and *C*, but *more strongly connected* to region *B* than region *C*) is *inconsistent* with this "probability of connectivity" interpretation.

Both of these interpretations are susceptible to the fact that distant targets are likely to be intersected less frequently than nearby targets [81,82], due to the spatial dispersion of probabilistic streamlines [37]. In the case of interpretation ii above, it is in principle possible to statistically correct for this effect [83].

21.2.3 Targeted tracking/virtual dissection vs whole-brain fiber tracking

The phrases "targeted tracking," "virtual dissection," and "whole-brain fiber tracking" are frequently used both in publication and informal discussion around the use of tractography specifically in neuroscience. They are best understood as holistic terms that integrate multiple components of the streamline tractography algorithm components enumerated earlier (Fig. 21.13). "*Targeted tracking*"

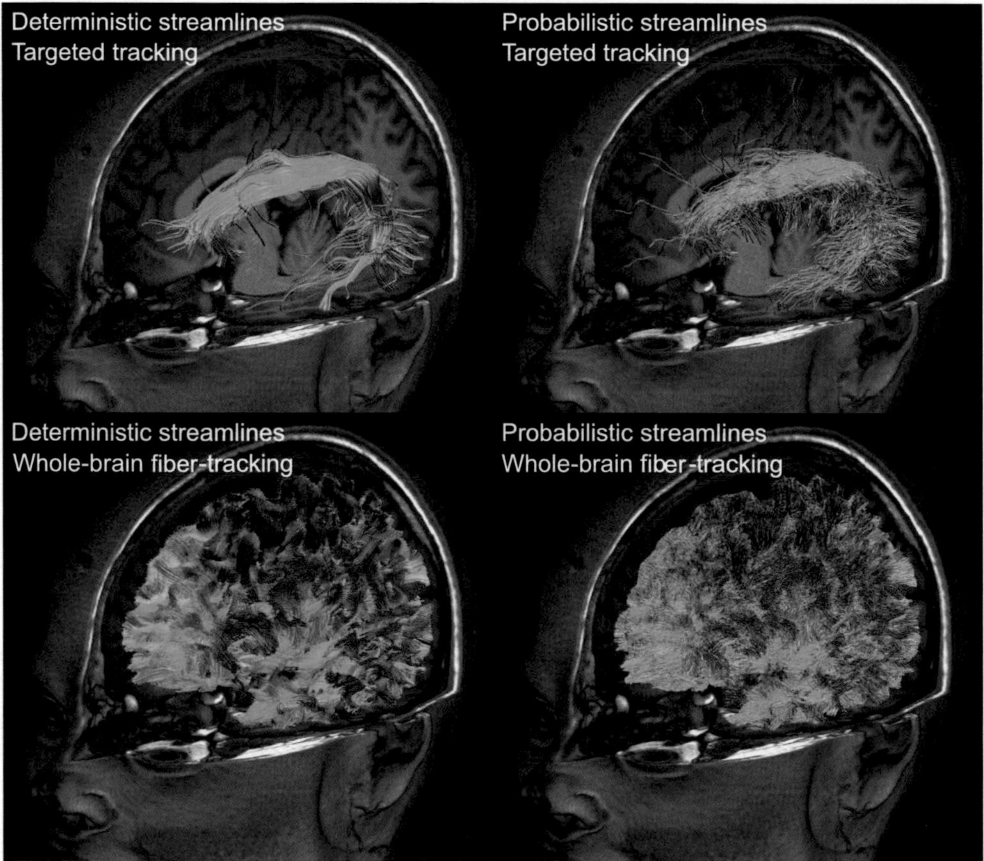

FIG. 21.13

Differences between targeted tracking for reconstructing a particular fiber pathway of interest *(top row)*, and whole-brain fiber tracking for reconstructing the entire brain white matter structural connectivity *(bottom row)*. The reconstructed bundle in the *top row* is the arcuate fasciculus between frontal and temporal lobes in the *left* hemisphere of the human brain. Images are shown for both deterministic *(left column)* and probabilistic *(right column)* streamline tractography algorithms. Streamlines are colored according to their local orientation *(red: left-right; green: anterior-posterior (front-back); blue: inferior-superior (top-to-bottom))*.

typically involves both a restricted streamline seeding region (for Component 1), and one or more inclusion ("waypoint")/exclusion regions defining where the streamlines must/must not traverse/stop as additional constraints for whether or not a streamline satisfies criteria for selection (as per Component 4). "*Whole-brain fiber tracking*" refers to both the use of some mechanism for streamline seeding that covers the entire brain (for Component 1), and does not involve any criteria for streamline selection (Component 4) that are specific to a particular fiber bundle or hypothesis.

As an alternative to "targeted tracking," it is possible to perform whole-brain fiber tracking, and then *retrospectively* apply criteria in order to select a subset of streamlines from the whole-brain tractogram that correspond to a particular pathway of interest [12,59,61,84,85]. While this approach (sometimes referred to as "track editing") may typically yield fewer reconstructed streamlines corresponding to the pathway of interest compared to an approach involving targeted seeding, such an approach may be requisite for particular quantitative interpretations of the data (more on this in Section 21.4 below). The application of either targeted tracking or retrospective selection of streamlines corresponding to pathways of interest may be referred to in more application-based contexts as "*virtual dissection*" [86–89].

21.3 Nonstreamline tractography

While streamline tractography is by far the most frequently used paradigm in diffusion MRI tractography, there are a small number of alternative approaches that warrant mention (Fig. 21.14). The following common classifications are demonstrated to give some insight into the wide range of tractography methods available, though note that some methods possess attributes from more than one of these classes.

21.3.1 Front evolution tractography

In this class of methods (which may alternatively be referred to as "fast marching" or "level set" methods [90]), rather than propagating individual streamline trajectories from a given seed point, a *surface* is propagated outward from the seed point, with the speed of expansion of that surface influenced by the underlying diffusion model fit [91–93]. The "arrival time" of this front is often interpreted as some measure of likelihood of connectivity to the seed location. It is typically also possible to determine, once the front reaches some location of interest, some optimal trajectory ("geodesic") from that location through the image back to the seed point, which may represent an underlying fiber trajectory.

21.3.2 Geodesic tractography

The term "geodesic" refers to the shortest possible path between two points. In the context of diffusion MRI, geodesic tractography refers to any algorithm where the presence of a connection between two points in space is *assumed*, and the role of the tractography algorithm is to determine the spatial trajectory or probability of that connection [77,94–98]. While the data resulting from such an approach may somewhat mimic that of a streamline algorithm (i.e., a trajectory through space), the intrinsic and explicit constraint of *both* trajectory endpoints means that both the operation of such algorithms, and the reasonable interpretation of what they provide, differ substantially from a streamline tractography experiment. Derivation and utilization of such algorithms have become increasingly rare over time.

21.3.3 Global tractography

In a whole-brain fiber-tracking experiment, one hopes that by generating a large number of streamlines independently and using a wide range of seeding locations, a reconstruction of all fiber connections within the organ of interest will be obtained. However, because each streamline is generated

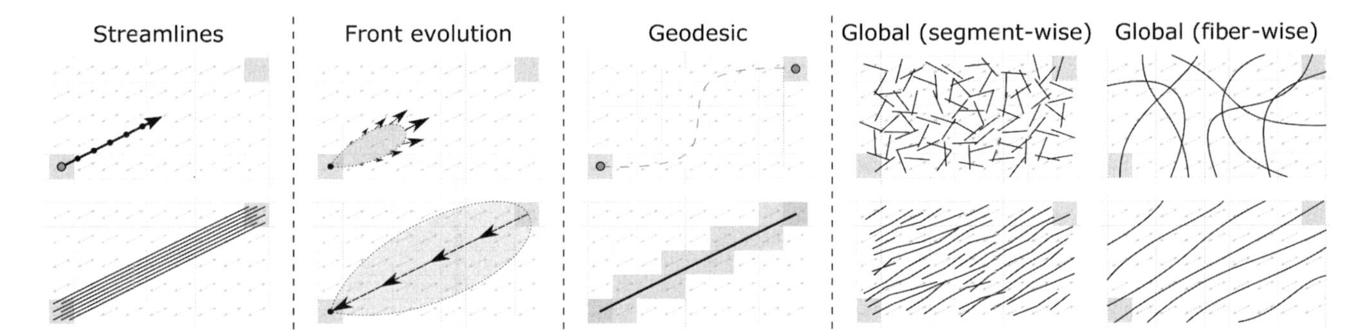

FIG. 21.14

Comparison between streamline-based tractography and other classes of tractography algorithms. For each class of algorithm, the *top panel* demonstrates some aspect of how the algorithm is initialized, while the *bottom panel* presents a typical final outcome of such an algorithm. Connectivity between the *bottom-left* and *top-right* voxels (highlighted) is expected given the underlying fiber orientation field.

independently, there is no feedback mechanism by which to ensure that all regions of the organ are adequately reconstructed. Similarly, there is no guarantee regarding the *density* of reconstructed streamlines within different pathways (this is addressed in greater detail in Section 21.4 below).

"Global tractography" algorithms approach this inverse problem in a different way. An optimal tractogram configuration is sought such that, when an appropriate forward model is invoked (i.e., generating predicted diffusion-weighted images from the tractogram), it is concordant with the empirical image data. Achieving this property has important implications for the interpretation of the resulting data, which is described in greater detail in Section 21.4 below. Such methods can be classified into two groups:

i. "Segment-wise" [99–105]: The tractogram reconstruction is initialized as consisting of many short fiber "segments," each with a length comparable to that of an image voxel, and these are distributed throughout the image volume. This reconstruction is then optimized by repeatedly perturbing the data through operations such as creating new fiber segments, deleting segments, moving segments, changing segment orientations, or "linking" adjacent segments to form longer fiber trajectories.

A significant barrier to the utilization of such methods is their failure to guarantee that each resulting fiber connection terminates in an anatomically appropriate location. Just as these methods commence their optimization using very short fiber segments that do not represent macroscopic bundle connectivity, there is no mechanism precluding such very short connections from existing within the finalized tractogram, fitting the empirical image data very well but not actually providing any tractable macroscale connectivity information.

ii. "Fiber-wise" [106–108]: The tractogram reconstruction is initialized with a set of candidate pathways of complete length. The inclusion or exclusion of each candidate pathway from the final reconstruction, as well as their trajectories, are iteratively optimized according to the correspondence of the reconstruction with the empirical image data.

Since each individual perturbation is a small modification to the reconstruction, a large number of such operations must be applied, which typically results in significantly greater computational expense than streamline tractography algorithms (for a given number of reconstructed connections). Additionally, a large number of parameters (even more than those of streamline tractography algorithms) must be defined to adequately condition the optimization.

21.3.4 Voxel-constrained tractography algorithms

In addition to the algorithm classifications described above, there is an additional dimension along which tractography algorithms may vary; namely, whether the processing/outcomes occur in continuous 3D space, or if they are *intrinsically constrained to the voxel grid.*

Many of the tractography classifications presented above are amenable to calculations on the voxel grid. In "particle jumping"/"random walk" algorithms, trajectories are constructed by iteratively linking adjacent voxels [34,109–111], which is akin to streamline propagation where streamline vertices are forced to reside on the image voxel grid. Front evolution methods are more naturally computed on the voxel grid [112–121]. Geodesic tractography can also be performed on the voxel grid [78,122].

In addition, some tractography algorithms are *only* applicable if calculations are performed on the voxel grid. By precomputing a *graph*, where each image voxel is a node, and the set of edges denotes some measure of transition between adjacent voxels based on the diffusion model, various trajectories (e.g., the geodesic path between two points) and measures of connectivity throughout the image volume

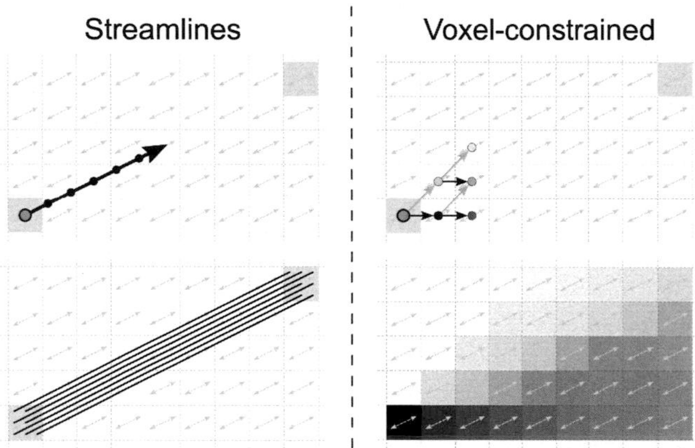

FIG. 21.15

Difference between a streamline algorithm *(left)*, where the streamline vertices may exist at any subvoxel location, and a comparable tractography algorithm that is computed directly on the diffusion-weighted imaging voxel grid *(right)*. When the propagation of connectivity is constrained to the voxel grid *(top right image)*, but the fiber orientations are not well-aligned with adjacent voxel neighbors on the image grid, errors in spatial localization of connectivity from a source accumulate as the connectivity estimate is propagated, potentially resulting in erroneous connectivity inferences *(darkness of voxels in bottom-left image)*.

can be derived [97,111,123–126]. Such methods can be considered as being loosely related to the "segment-wise" global tractography algorithms described above, as a large number of finite local connectivity estimates are used to project long-distance pathways.

Voxel-constrained approaches are appealing from a computational perspective, as reconstructing the connectivity between any pair of regions would typically require substantially fewer calculations than the generation of an adequate number of streamlines between them. However, methods that operate within this domain suffer from an issue resulting from the discretization of fiber orientations into connectivities/transition probabilities between adjacent voxels on a regular 3D lattice. Whenever a fiber orientation does not perfectly align with the image axes, the resulting connectivity from that voxel is measured as being somehow "divided" between adjacent voxels; while this scenario may be realistic between immediately adjacent voxels, subvoxel position information is lost when extending that connectivity across multiple image voxels, accumulating errors in fiber location information along the length of a bundle (Fig. 21.15). This effect may be only somewhat mitigated by considering a wider voxel adjacency neighborhood [120,125].

21.4 Quantification

Given the focus of this book on *quantitative* MRI, this section will describe some of the experimental techniques in which tractography may be used over and above its historical limitations as a qualitative tool. This section is broken into two parts. The direct inference of connection densities of fiber bundles is first described, where quantification is based principally on the outcomes of tractography. A shortlist of other contexts in which tractography plays only a partial role in the realization of quantitative experiments follows.

21.4.1 Streamline-based connection densities

This section refers to a specific type of experiment in which a quantitative estimate of "fiber connectivity" is sought. This can be either the assessment of a particular anatomically labeled fiber bundle of interest, or of the magnitude of "connectivity" between two spatially distant endpoints (between which tractography provides a reconstruction of the fiber pathway).

In order for such an experiment to be robust, anatomically meaningful, and quantitative, the following four requirements are imposed:

1. The *trajectories* of the reconstructed connection pathways must be consistent with the orientations of the underlying fiber bundles. This requirement has been addressed through the development of diffusion models for estimating fiber orientations, and the validation of these models and tractography algorithms based on phantoms (both digitally simulated [54,63,123,127–134] and physically synthetic [135–138]) and anatomical references [139,140] including tract-tracing [62,84,141–145]. As described above in Section 21.2, the actual generation of fiber trajectories based on these orientations has remained relatively unchanged for the last 20 years.
2. The *attribution* of streamlines to the fiber pathway of interest must be mechanistically robust and reflective of the underlying biology. Among features such as position and shape, the segmentation of any particular fiber bundle of interest is almost always influenced by the identification of those anatomical elements connected at the two endpoints of the pathway. For instance, many brain white matter pathways are intrinsically defined based on the gray matter areas for which they are responsible for providing structural connectivity [146]. As such, the mechanism by which streamlines are selected as being a part of the fiber bundle of interest (as well as *not* being a part of that bundle) should not be sensitive to esoteric details of the tractography experiment or handling of the resulting data. An important step in providing such is ensuring that streamline terminations (see Section 21.2.1.3 above) are consistent with the anatomical information used to drive the bundle classification process [19,52,147–149].
3. The *number of streamlines* generated for reconstruction of a particular pathway/whole-brain structural connectivity must be sufficiently large to capture the extent of both the complexity of the underlying structure, and the stochastic nature of the tractography experiment. If too few streamlines are generated, then there may be trajectories that are possible to generate from the image data and yet are absent from the tractogram data. Similarly, any quantities derived from the experiment may demonstrate undesirable variability under repetition of the tractography reconstruction [150–152].
4. The manner in which "*connectivity*" of a fiber bundle is *quantified* must have some biological relevance, and not be strongly biased by the mechanisms of the reconstruction process. The notion of "connectivity" in the context of tractography has historically remained ambiguous, particularly due to the well-recognized issue that the number of streamlines reconstructed for a bundle is not necessarily reflective of the underlying fiber connection density of that bundle (Fig. 21.16) [82,153–155]. While some researchers have investigated the use of heuristic corrections [17,156] or alternative metrics of "connectivity" [157], others have instead resorted to the use of experimental designs where quantitative values are only *partly* dependent on the tractography experiment (explored in more detail in the Section 21.4.2 below).

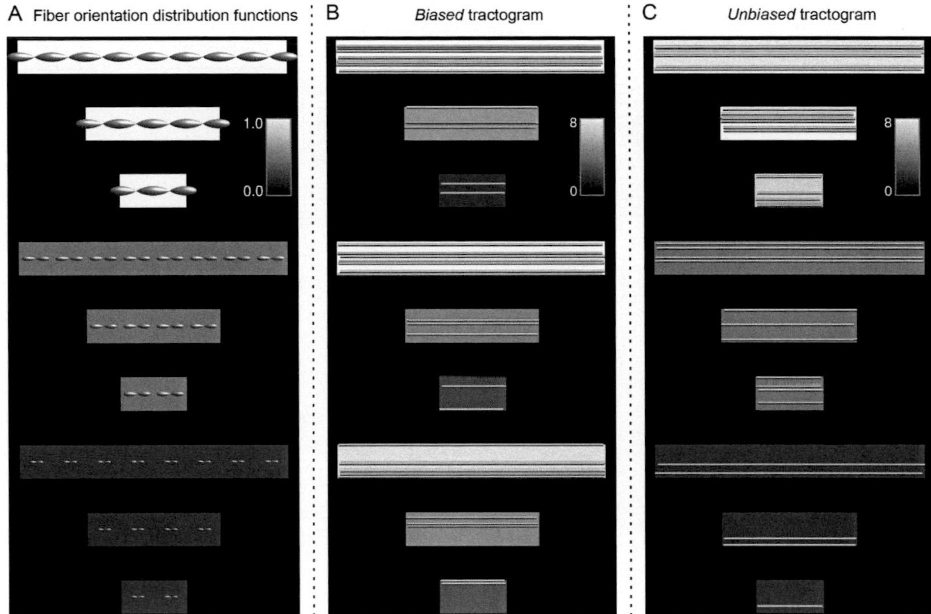

FIG. 21.16

Synthetic diffusion data and reconstructed tractograms demonstrating the requirements for streamline count to be interpreted in a quantitative manner. (A) Fiber orientation distribution functions (fODFs) of nine synthetic bundles, with variations between them in both bundle length (horizontal widths) and underlying fiber density (as reflected in both the sizes of the fODF glyphs drawn from the center of each voxel, and the intensities of the background image voxels). (B) A biased tractogram, such as that generated by seeding one streamline in each image voxel. Background image intensities reflect the streamline count in each voxel; note that the longer the bundle, the brighter the intensity, due to the increased volumes of these bundles leading to a greater number of streamlines being seeded there. Consequently, streamline densities do not match the underlying fiber densities (column A). (C) An aspirational unbiased tractogram, where the number of streamlines within different bundles is determined not by bundle length, but is instead modulated by the underlying fODF amplitudes. The larger the underlying fODFs in a bundle, the greater the number of streamlines reconstructed, and the brighter the background image voxels, leading to the concordance of these relative background voxel intensities with column A.

Here, the capabilities made possible through use of a new class of methods that aim to "imbue" a streamline tractogram with quantitative properties based on a particular physical model are explored.

In the context of tractography, it is assumed that "connectivity" refers to some notion of *density of fibers*. This definition is not entirely specific however, as it could conceivably refer to a fiber *count*, *volume*, *cross-sectional area*, or any other feature that would reasonably reflect the capability of fibers to *transfer information*. The specific metric of interest investigated here is that depicted in (Fig. 21.17): we seek the *total intracellular cross-sectional area* of those fibers belonging to any specific bundle of interest [148,154,158–163]. While other biological features of fiber bundles may affect some

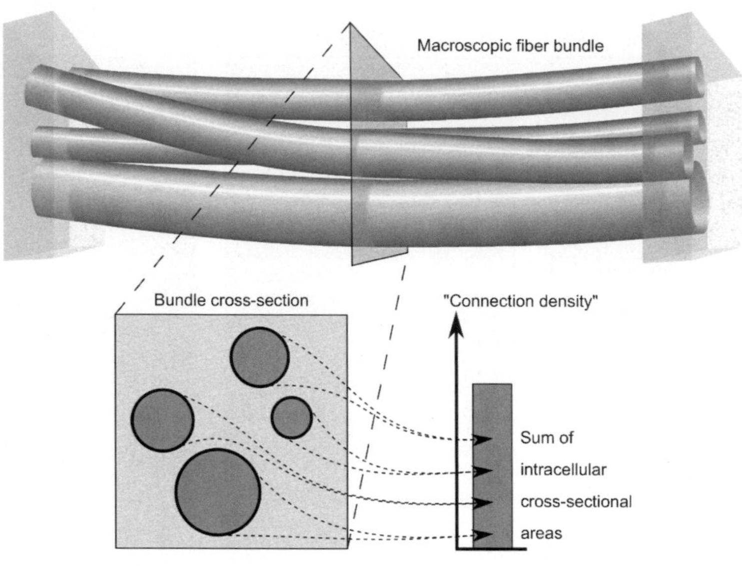

FIG. 21.17

Quantification of "connectivity" in a tractography experiment. Between two regions of interest *(rectangular prisms)*, structural connections are represented as a set of cylinders, each possessing some radius; the sum of the cross-sectional areas of these cylinders provides an estimate of "connection density" between the two regions.

subjective notion of "connectivity" between areas (including cellular diameters, presence of myelin sheath in the case of brain white matter fascicles, total distance between fiber endpoints, conduction velocity), this discussion is restricted to the intracellular cross-sectional area metric, due to both the dominance of this feature on capacity of fiber bundle information transfer, and its accessibility using existing imaging techniques and computational methods.

Estimation of this connectivity metric can be conceptualized as follows. The diffusion MRI signal at high *b*-values is proportional to the *intracellular fiber volume* in any particular image voxel [25,31,55,71,74,164–170]. Such data may be further processed using a diffusion model to provide direct estimates of intracellular fiber volumes for one or more fiber bundles within each image voxel [154,167,171,172]. Each streamline in a tractogram can be thought of as a *cylinder* of fibers, each of which possesses some *intracellular cross-sectional area*. The *product* of this cross-sectional area with the *intersection length* of the streamline with any particular voxel yields the *intra-cellular volume* of fibers represented by that particular streamline within that particular voxel. Ideally, if a streamline tractogram is wholly consistent with the underlying fiber pathways, in both *trajectories* and *densities* of reconstructed streamlines, then in each image voxel, the total fiber intracellular volume predicted from the streamlines in the tractogram should be consistent with the total fiber intracellular volume predicted by the empirical image data (e.g., the diffusion MRI signal at high *b*-values). *If this consistency can be achieved*, then the total intracellular cross-sectional area ascribed to any particular fiber pathway can be extracted as the *sum* of the intracellular cross-sectional areas ascribed to those individual streamlines attributed to that fiber pathway.

The role of the aforementioned new class of quantitative tractography methods, sometimes referred to as "semi-global," "top-down," or "tractogram filtering" methods, is to *determine the appropriate*

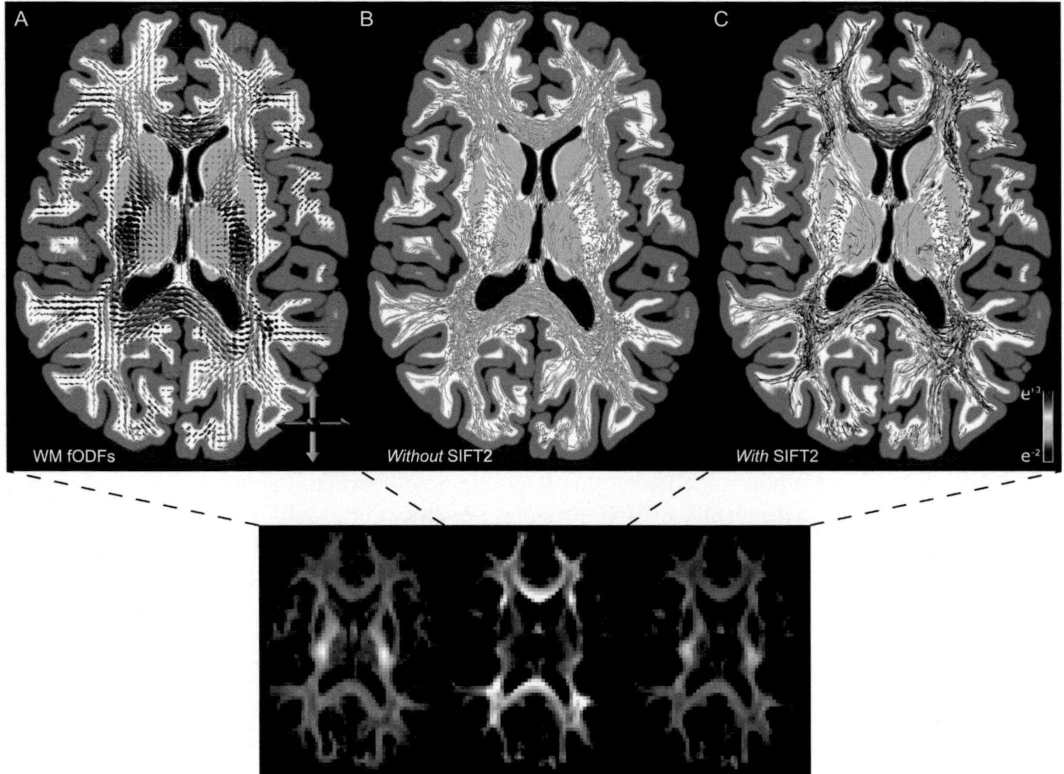

FIG. 21.18

Quantitative properties of a whole-brain tractogram; demonstrated here using the SIFT2 algorithm [162]. (A) *(top)* The white matter fiber orientation distribution functions (fODFs) as estimated by multishell multitissue (MSMT) constrained spherical deconvolution (CSD) [173]; *(bottom)* the orientation-averaged white matter fiber density estimated in each image voxel. (B) *(top)* Streamlines generated through whole-brain fiber-tracking; *(bottom)* the spatial distribution of streamline density within this tractogram. (C) *(top)* Streamlines colored according to the cross-sectional areas ascribed to them by the SIFT2 algorithm; *(bottom)* the spatial distribution of streamline density when the contribution from each streamline is modulated by its ascribed fiber cross-sectional area. Note how the distribution of streamline density following SIFT2 is much more similar to the distribution of white matter fiber density estimated by MSMT CSD than that of the unmodulated tractogram.

fiber cross-sectional area to ascribe to each individual reconstructed streamline, in order to achieve this concordance between tractogram and image data (Figs. 21.16C and 21.18) [160–162,174]. Importantly, by utilizing such a method prior to the extraction of the connectivity measure of interest, this connectivity measure is informed by both the physical constraints imposed on the biological system, and the underlying fiber intracellular volumes inferred from the image data, providing biological relevance to the experimental outcomes [148]. It has historically been the *absence* of such concordance that precluded the interpretation of streamline count in a quantitative manner.

The “fiber-wise” global tractography algorithms described in the earlier Section 21.3 bear some relation to the quantitative tractography algorithms described in this section. The key difference is that the former optimizes *all aspects* of the tractogram reconstruction—including *positions* and *orientations* of connections—based on persistent utilization of all diffusion image information, whereas the latter relies on the initial production of a whole-brain tractogram using a simpler streamline-based algorithm, utilizing global image information only for subsequent modulation of streamline cross-sectional areas. This approach significantly improves the computational tractability of the problem, enabling reconstructions sufficiently dense for robust quantification, i.e., satisfaction of quantitative tractography requirement 3 described above.

Some members of this class of methods involve the selection of a *subset of streamlines from a larger set* of candidate trajectories, which when combined together adequately correlate with the empirical image data [154,158,159,175]. These methods still obey the description above: they simply consider all selected streamlines as having some fixed cross-sectional area, and those streamlines not selected as having zero cross-sectional area.

The methods discussed in this section for providing tractograms with quantitative properties can only provide such quantification within the limitations imposed by the other requirements for quantitative streamline tractography. Specifically, the connection density between regions can only be made quantitative by such a method if the underlying tractogram with which it is provided contains trajectories that are accurate anatomically [62,63], the subset of streamlines within the tractogram that represent the macroscopic fiber bundle of interest can be robustly attributed as such, and the tractogram is sufficiently densely reconstructed.

While the above text describes the quantification of fiber connectivity of some specific fiber bundle of interest, an increasingly common quantitative application of tractography is the estimation of the (macroscopic) brain *structural connectome* [17,123,176–180], which encapsulates a measure of connectivity between *all possible pairs* of brain gray matter regions (based on some parcellation of these regions [181–187]) as a *connectivity matrix* (Fig. 21.19). There is an intuitive way of conceptualizing this representation: every element in the connectome matrix corresponds to a fiber connectivity quantification experiment such as that described above, where the specific fiber bundle of interest happens to be the set of white matter fibers that connect two specific brain gray matter areas corresponding to the row/column location of the element within the matrix (Fig. 21.19).

The popularity of connectome estimation experiments is due in part to the possibility for calculating and assessing various higher-order emergent features of the network based on the mathematical field of graph theory [188–191]. These include so-called "global metrics," which reduce the connectivity matrix down to a small number of scalar values, encapsulating attributes such as network "communicability," "efficiency," and "modularity" [192]. While some of these measures may be considered quantitative, skepticism of such interpretation is recommended. For instance, many such metrics are not invariant with respect to the density of the reconstructed tractogram, and thus may not be specific to the feature that they purport to quantify.

21.4.2 Other quantitative methods involving tractography

There exists within the field of diffusion MRI analysis a wide range of methods that can be considered "quantitative," which also utilize tractography in some manner, but are distinct from the methods and metric described in Section 21.4.1.

The shapes of streamline trajectories may be used to derive various quantitative parameters, such as geometric invariants [193], measures of bundle dispersion [194] or group-wise deformation

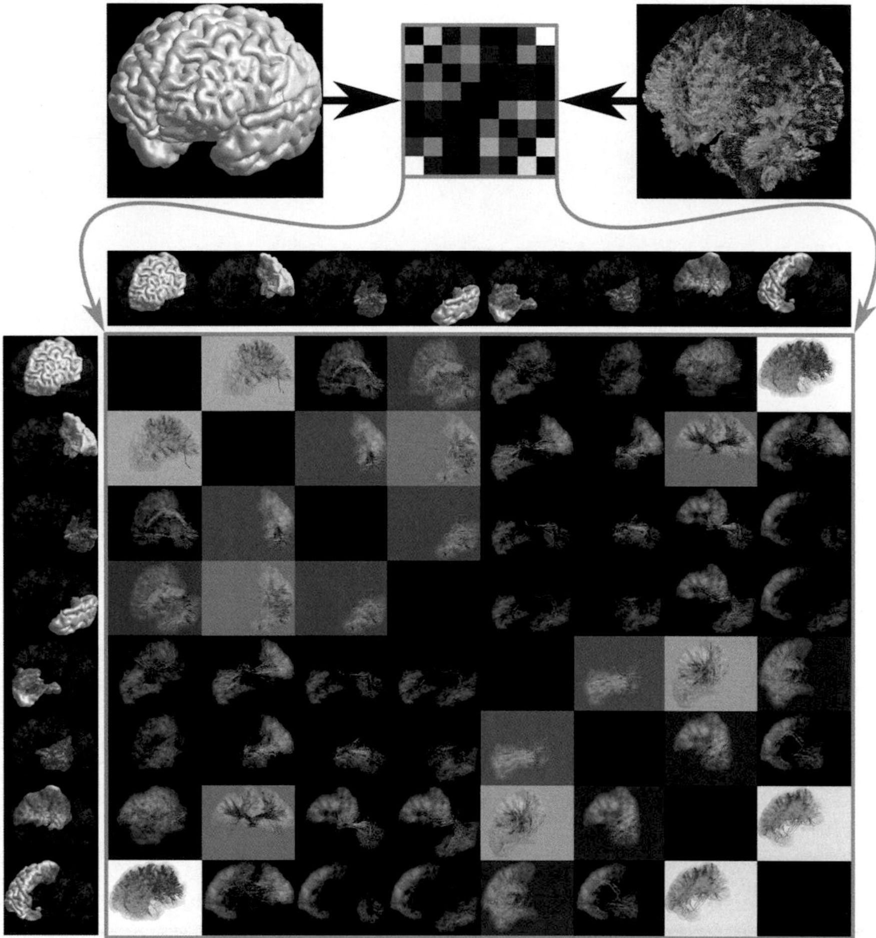

FIG. 21.19

Visualization of the various white matter pathways contributing to structural connectome construction. Brain *gray* matter is parcellated into eight regions (frontal, parietal, occipital and temporal lobes bilaterally, as shown at the *top left*); streamlines from a whole-brain tractogram (shown at the *top right*) are assigned to pairs of *gray* matter regions based on the locations of their terminations. The intensity in the connectome matrix *(top, center)* reflects the number of streamlines connecting the two relevant regions. The main window shows, for each connectome edge, the two *gray matter regions* involved in the connection, and all streamlines connecting those regions, with the background intensity indicating the number of streamlines.

[195], curvature [196,197], length [54,196,198–201], or coefficients in an alternative mathematical basis (e.g., Fourier) [193,202].

When the value of a quantitative parameter from a diffusion model is sought for a particular fiber bundle of interest, it is commonplace to use tractography to delineate that bundle in order to select those regions of the image from which that quantitative value will be drawn (Fig. 21.20). It is, however,

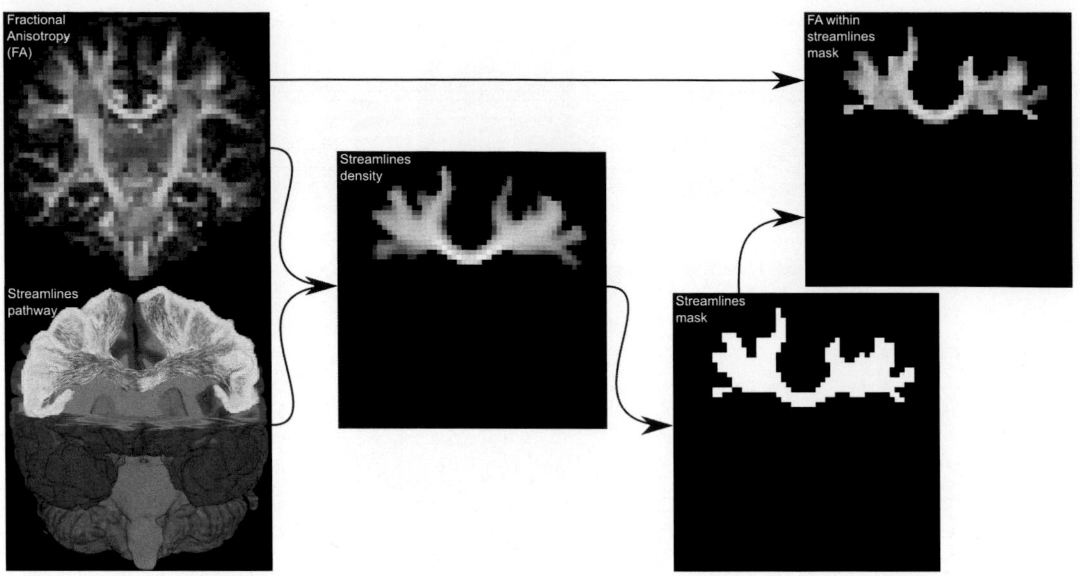

FIG. 21.20

Demonstration of using streamline tractography to define a spatial mask corresponding to a specific pathway of interest, from which values of some quantitative metric may be drawn. In this example, the fractional anisotropy (FA) is the quantitative metric of interest *(top left)*. A particular white matter bundle (connections between precentral gyri bilaterally in this example) is reconstructed using tractography *(bottom left)*. Those streamlines are then mapped to the voxel grid of the FA image *(middle)*, and a threshold applied in order to derive a voxel mask *(bottom right)*; this mask provides a direct estimate of pathway volume. The mask can also be used to obtain some statistics (e.g., mean) of the quantitative image within those voxels corresponding to the mask *(top right)*.

important to clearly distinguish the roles of the different mechanisms being used. In this case, tractography is simply used to derive a *mask* from within which quantitative values are to be sampled; tractography itself does not directly *provide* quantitative measures in this context. Such experiments also inherit any detrimental attributes of the underlying quantitative metric. For example, extracting the FA of the tensor model within a voxel mask defined within a bundle delineated using tractography [203] may avoid the quantification issues associated with streamline count but inherits all of the issues intrinsic to the FA metric.

Similarly, in the process of deriving a spatial mask corresponding to a fiber bundle of interest, another quantitative property that can be extracted directly from such a representation is the *volume* of the fiber bundle [85,200,204,205] (Fig. 21.20). This analysis does, however, have a number of limitations, including sensitivity to outlier streamlines, partial volume effects at the outer extremities of the bundle, and sensitivity to bundle length, with which the bundle volume scales directly despite being of lesser interest (as described in Section 21.4.1).

Instead of reducing the values of some quantitative metric within a tractography-derived mask to a single scalar mean, it is possible to instead consider the values of that metric *along the length* of the bundle [98,206–211]. In the track-weighted imaging (TWI) framework, quantitative values ascribed to streamlines are subsequently mapped to an underlying image [196,212]. Such images may possess quantitative properties that depend on the nature of those values associated with each streamline, and on the appropriateness of the statistic by which the values from multiple streamlines traversing a single image element are collapsed to a single scalar value per voxel. Some examples of quantitative properties that could be used in such a way include streamline count [213,214] (though such utility is discouraged in the absence of methods such as those described in Section 21.4.1 [155]), streamline curvature [197,215,216], streamline length [198], and values from some underlying image (that is itself quantitative) that have been sampled along the trajectory of each streamline [217].

In some methods in which statistical inference of quantitative metrics in the brain white matter is performed, tractography in template space is used to encapsulate the expected statistical correlations in the data and enhance statistical power, on the presumption that any genuine biological effects are likely to manifest *along the lengths of fiber bundles*. This is the case for the connectivity-based fixel enhancement (CFE) method [218], which is responsible for the statistical inference portion of the fixel-based analysis (FBA) framework [24]. The numbers of streamlines traversing pairs of fixels within a template image are used for statistical enhancement in a manner akin to the threshold-free cluster enhancement (TFCE) method [219]. A related example is the connectometry method [220], which uses deterministic streamline tractography on a template brain to perform statistical inference where the lengths of streamlines generated after masking form the quantities used to generate or compare against the null distribution.

21.5 Conclusions

A thorough appreciation of the utility and limitations of tractography in the field of diffusion MRI requires a comprehensive understanding of all underlying fundamental mechanisms. This is becoming even more pertinent as more quantitative methods and applications are introduced into the field. Here, we have disambiguated the various aspects of tractography into their most primitive forms, with the hope of encouraging improved understanding and communication of these techniques.

References

[1] Basser PJ, Mattiello J, Lebihan D. MR diffusion tensor spectroscopy and imaging. Biophys J 1994;66:259–67.

[2] Mori S, van Zijl PCM. Fiber tracking: principles and strategies—a technical review. NMR Biomed 2002;15(7–8):468–80.

[3] Johansen-Berg H, Behrens TEJ. Just pretty pictures? What diffusion tractography can add in clinical neuroscience. Curr Opin Neurol 2006;19(4):379–85.

[4] Mori S, Zhang J. Principles of diffusion tensor imaging and its applications to basic neuroscience research. Neuron 2006;51(5):527–39.

[5] Hagmann P, Cammoun L, Gigandet X, et al. MR connectomics: principles and challenges. In: Proceedings of the workshop "Neuroanatomical tracing and systems neuroscience: The state of the art", vol. 194(1):2010, p. 34–45.

[6] Jbabdi S, Johansen-Berg H. Tractography: where do we go from here? Brain Connect 2011;1(3):169–83.

[7] Tournier J-D, Mori S, Leemans A. Diffusion tensor imaging and beyond. Magn Reson Med 2011; 65(6):1532–56.

[8] Dell'acqua F, Catani M. Structural human brain networks: hot topics in diffusion tractography. Curr Opin Neurol 2012;25(4):375–83.

[9] Le Bihan D, Johansen-Berg H. Diffusion MRI at 25: exploring brain tissue structure and function. NeuroImage 2012;61(2):324–41.

[10] Daducci A, Dal Palú A, Descoteaux M, Thiran J-P. Microstructure informed tractography: pitfalls and open challenges. Front Neurosci 2016;10:247.

[11] Jeurissen B, Descoteaux M, Mori S, Leemans A. Diffusion MRI fiber tractography of the brain. NMR Biomed 2017;32:e3785.

[12] Conturo TE, Lori NF, Cull TS, et al. Tracking neuronal fiber pathways in the living human brain. Proc Natl Acad Sci U S A 1999;96(18):10422–7.

[13] Jones DK, Simmons A, Williams SCR, Horsfield MA. Non-invasive assessment of axonal fiber connectivity in the human brain via diffusion tensor MRI. Magn Reson Med 1999;42(1):37–41.

[14] Mori S, Crain BJ, Chacko VP, van Zijl PCM. Three-dimensional tracking of axonal projections in the brain by magnetic resonance imaging. Ann Neurol 1999;45(2):265–9.

[15] Basser PJ, Pajevic S, Pierpaoli C, Duda J, Aldroubi A. In vivo fiber tractography using DT-MRI data. Magn Reson Med 2000;44(4):625–32.

[16] Poupon C, Clark CA, Frouin V, et al. Regularization of diffusion-based direction maps for the tracking of brain white matter fascicles. NeuroImage 2000;12(2):184–95.

[17] Hagmann P, Cammoun L, Gigandet X, et al. Mapping the structural core of human cerebral cortex. PLoS Biol 2008;6(7):e159.

[18] Li L, Rilling JK, Preuss TM, Glasser MF, Hu X. The effects of connection reconstruction method on the interregional connectivity of brain networks via diffusion tractography. Hum Brain Mapp 2012;33(8):1894–913.

[19] Smith RE, Tournier J-D, Calamante F, Connelly A. Anatomically-constrained tractography: improved diffusion MRI streamlines tractography through effective use of anatomical information. NeuroImage 2012;62(3):1924–38.

[20] Yeh C-H, Smith RE, Dhollander T, Connelly A. Mesh-based anatomically-constrained tractography for effective tracking termination and structural connectome construction, In: Proceedings of the ISMRM; 2017, p. 0058.

[21] Buss SR, Fillmore JP. Spherical averages and applications to spherical splines and interpolation. ACM Trans Graph 2001;20(2):95–126.

[22] Batchelor PG, Moakher M, Atkinson D, Calamante F, Connelly A. A rigorous framework for diffusion tensor calculus. Magn Reson Med 2005;53(1):221–5.

[23] Arsigny V, Fillard P, Pennec X, Ayache N. Log-Euclidean metrics for fast and simple calculus on diffusion tensors. Magn Reson Med 2006;56(2):411–21.

[24] Raffelt DA, Tournier J-D, Smith RE, et al. Investigating white matter fibre density and morphology using fixel-based analysis. NeuroImage 2016;144:58–73.

[25] Behrens TEJ, Woolrich MW, Jenkinson M, et al. Characterization and propagation of uncertainty in diffusion-weighted MR imaging. Magn Reson Med 2003;50(5):1077–88.

[26] Tournier JD, Calamante F, Gadian DG, Connelly A. Probabilistic fibre tracking through regions containing crossing fibres. In: Proceedings of the international society for magnetic resonance in medicine; 2005, p. 1343.

[27] Malcolm JG, Shenton ME, Rathi Y. Neural tractography using an unscented Kalman filter. In: Information processing in medical imaging. 2009, p. 126–38.

[28] Malcolm JG, Michailovich O, Bouix S, Westin C-F, Shenton ME, Rathi Y. A filtered approach to neural tractography using the Watson directional function. Med Image Anal 2010;14(1):58–69.

[29] Ramirez-Manzanares A, Rivera M. Basis tensor decomposition for restoring intra-voxel structure and stochastic walks for inferring brain connectivity in DT-MRI. Int J Comput Vis 2006;69(1):77–92.
[30] Tournier J-D, Calamante F, Connelly A. MRtrix: diffusion tractography in crossing fiber regions. Int J Imaging Syst Technol 2012;22(1):53–66.
[31] Behrens TEJ, Johansen-Berg H, Jbabdi S, Rushworth MFS, Woolrich MW. Probabilistic diffusion tractography with multiple fibre orientations: what can we gain? NeuroImage 2007;34(1):144–55.
[32] Wedeen VJ, Wang RP, Schmahmann JD, et al. Diffusion spectrum magnetic resonance imaging (DSI) tractography of crossing fibers. NeuroImage 2008;41(4):1267–77.
[33] Jeurissen B, Leemans A, Jones DK, Tournier J-D, Sijbers J. Probabilistic fiber tracking using the residual bootstrap with constrained spherical deconvolution. Hum Brain Mapp 2011;32(3):461–79.
[34] Kreher BW, Schneider JF, Mader I, Martin E, Hennig J, Il'yasov KA. Multitensor approach for analysis and tracking of complex fiber configurations. Magn Reson Med 2005;54(5):1216–25.
[35] Descoteaux M, Deriche R, Knosche T, Anwander A. Deterministic and probabilistic tractography based on complex fibre orientation distributions. IEEE Trans Med Imaging 2009;28(2):269–86.
[36] Tournier J-D, Calamante F, King MD, Gadian DG, Connelly A. Limitations and requirements of diffusion tensor fiber tracking: an assessment using simulations. Magn Reson Med 2002;47(4):701–8.
[37] Tournier J-D, Calamante F, Connelly A. Effect of step size on probabilistic streamlines: implications for the interpretation of connectivity analyses. In: Proceedings of the international society for magnetic resonance in medicine; 2011, p. 2019.
[38] Moldrich RX, Pannek K, Hoch R, Rubenstein JL, Kurniawan ND, Richards LJ. Comparative mouse brain tractography of diffusion magnetic resonance imaging. NeuroImage 2010;51(3):1027–36.
[39] Tournier J-D, Calamante F, Connelly A. Improved probabilistic streamlines tractography by 2nd order integration over fibre orientation distributions, In: Proceedings of the international society for magnetic resonance in medicine; 2010, p. 1670.
[40] Cherifi D, Boudjada M, Morsli A, Girard G, Deriche R. Combining improved Euler and Runge-Kutta 4th order for Tractography in diffusion-weighted MRI. Biomed Signal Process Control 2018;41:90–9.
[41] Lazar M, Weinstein D, Tsuruda J, et al. White matter tractography using diffusion tensor deflection. Hum Brain Mapp 2003;18(4):306–21.
[42] Perrin M, Poupon C, Cointepas Y, et al. Fiber tracking in q-ball fields using regularized particle trajectories. In: Information processing in medical imaging. 2005, p. 52–63.
[43] Chou M-C, Wu M-L, Chen C-Y, et al. Tensor deflection (TEND) tractography with adaptive subvoxel stepping. J Magn Reson Imaging 2006;24(2):451–8.
[44] Guo W, Zeng Q, Chen Y, Liu Y. Using multiple tensor deflection to reconstruct white matter fiber traces with branching, In: 3rd IEEE international symposium on biomedical imaging: Nano to macro; 2006, p. 69–72.
[45] Girard G, Daducci A, Petit L, et al. AxTract: toward microstructure informed tractography. Hum Brain Mapp 2017;38(11):5485–500.
[46] Lienhard S, Malcolm JG, Westin C-F, Rathi Y. A full bi-tensor neural tractography algorithm using the unscented Kalman filter. EURASIP J Adv Signal Process 2011;2011(1):77.
[47] Cetingul HE, Dumont L, Nadar M, Thompson P, Sapiro G, Lenglet C. Simultaneous ODF estimation and robust probabilistic tractography from HARDI, In: Computational diffusion MRI (CDMRI'12) workshop; 2012.
[48] Reddy P, Rathi Y. Joint multi-fiber NODDI parameter estimation and tractography using the unscented information filter. Front Neurosci 2016;10:166.
[49] Kleinnijenhuis M, Barth M, Alexander DC, van Cappellen van Walsum A-M, Norris DG. Structure tensor informed fiber tractography (STIFT) by combining gradient echo MRI and diffusion weighted imaging. NeuroImage 2012;59(4):3941–54.
[50] St-Onge E, Daducci A, Girard G, Descoteaux M. Surface-enhanced tractography (SET). NeuroImage 2018;169:524–39.

[51] Rheault F, St-Onge E, Sidhu J, et al. Bundle-specific tractography with incorporated anatomical and orientational priors. NeuroImage 2019;186:382–98.

[52] Basser PJ, Pierpaoli C. Microstructural and physiological features of tissues elucidated by quantitative-diffusion-tensor MRI. J Magn Reson 1996;111(3):209–19.

[53] Girard G, Descoteaux M. Anatomical tissue probability priors for tractography. In: CDMRI. 2012, p. 174–85.

[54] Girard G, Whittingstall K, Deriche R, Descoteaux M. Towards quantitative connectivity analysis: reducing tractography biases. NeuroImage 2014;98:266–78.

[55] Tournier J-D, Calamante F, Connelly A. Robust determination of the fibre orientation distribution in diffusion MRI: non-negativity constrained super-resolved spherical deconvolution. NeuroImage 2007;35(4):1459–72.

[56] Andersson JLR, Skare S, Ashburner J. How to correct susceptibility distortions in spin-echo echo-planar images: application to diffusion tensor imaging. NeuroImage 2003;20(2):870–88.

[57] Andersson JLR, Sotiropoulos SN. An integrated approach to correction for off-resonance effects and subject movement in diffusion MR imaging. NeuroImage 2016;125:1063–78.

[58] Stieltjes B, Kaufmann WE, van Zijl PCM, et al. Diffusion tensor imaging and axonal tracking in the human brainstem. NeuroImage 2001;14(3):723–35.

[59] Wakana S, Jiang H, Nagae-Poetscher LM, van Zijl PC, ter MS. Fiber tract-based atlas of human white matter anatomy. Radiology 2004;230(1):77–87.

[60] Hagler Jr DJ, Ahmadi ME, Kuperman J, et al. Automated white-matter tractography using a probabilistic diffusion tensor atlas: application to temporal lobe epilepsy. Hum Brain Mapp 2008;30(5):1535–47.

[61] Zhang Y, Zhang J, Oishi K, et al. Atlas-guided tract reconstruction for automated and comprehensive examination of the white matter anatomy. NeuroImage 2010;52(4):1289–301.

[62] Thomas C, Ye FQ, Irfanoglu MO, et al. Anatomical accuracy of brain connections derived from diffusion MRI tractography is inherently limited. Proc Natl Acad Sci 2014;111(46):16574–9.

[63] Maier-Hein KH, Neher PF, Houde J-C, et al. The challenge of mapping the human connectome based on diffusion tractography. Nat Commun 2017;8(1):1349.

[64] Jones DK, Pierpaoli C. Confidence mapping in diffusion tensor magnetic resonance imaging tractography using a bootstrap approach. Magn Reson Med 2005;53(5):1143–9.

[65] Lazar M, Alexander A. Bootstrap white matter tractography (BOOT-TRAC). NeuroImage 2005;24(2):524–32.

[66] Friman O, Farneback G, Westin C-F. A Bayesian approach for stochastic white matter tractography. IEEE Trans Med Imaging 2006;25(8):965–78.

[67] Berman JI, Chung S, Mukherjee P, Hess CP, Han ET, Henry RG. Probabilistic streamline q-ball tractography using the residual bootstrap. NeuroImage 2008;39(1):215–22.

[68] Jones DK. Tractography gone wild: probabilistic fibre tracking using the wild bootstrap with diffusion tensor MRI. IEEE Trans Med Imaging 2008;27(9):1268–74.

[69] Haroon HA, Morris DM, Embleton KV, Alexander DC, Parker G. Using the model-based residual bootstrap to quantify uncertainty in fiber orientations from Q-ball analysis. IEEE Trans Med Imaging 2009;28(4):535–50.

[70] Campbell JSW, MomayyezSiahkal P, Savadjiev P, Siddqi K, Leppert IR, Pike GB. Beyond crossing fibers: bootstrap probabilistic tractography using complex subvoxel fiber geometries. Front Neurol 2014;5:216.

[71] Kaden E, Knösche TR, Anwander A. Parametric spherical deconvolution: inferring anatomical connectivity using diffusion MR imaging. NeuroImage 2007;37(2):474–88.

[72] Seunarine KK, Cook PA, Hall MG, Embleton KV, Parker GJM, Alexander DC. Exploiting peak anisotropy for tracking through complex structures, In: ICCV'07; 2007, p. 1–8.

[73] Sotiropoulos SN, Behrens TEJ, Jbabdi S. Ball and rackets: inferring fiber fanning from diffusion-weighted MRI. NeuroImage 2012;60(2):1412–25.

[74] Zhang H, Schneider T, Wheeler-Kingshott CA, Alexander DC. NODDI: practical \em in vivo neurite orientation dispersion and density imaging of the human brain. NeuroImage 2012;61(4):1000–16.

[75] Rowe M, Zhang H, Oxtoby N, DanielC A. Beyond crossing fibers: tractography exploiting sub-voxel fibre dispersion and neighbourhood structure. In: Lecture notes in computer science. vol. 7917. Springer Berlin Heidelberg; 2013, p. 402–13.

[76] Tariq M, Schneider T, Alexander DC, Gandini Wheeler-Kingshott CA, Zhang H. Bingham-NODDI: mapping anisotropic orientation dispersion of neurites using diffusion MRI. NeuroImage 2016;133:207–23.
[77] Sherbondy AJ, Dougherty RF, Ben-Shachar M, Napel S, Wandell BA. ConTrack: finding the most likely pathways between brain regions using diffusion tractography. J Vis 2008;8(9):1–16.
[78] Zalesky A. DT-MRI fiber tracking: a shortest paths approach. IEEE Trans Med Imaging 2008; 27(10):1458–71.
[79] Aydogan DB, Shi Y. Track filtering via iterative correction of TDI topology. In: Medical image computing and computer-assisted intervention. Cham: Springer International Publishing; 2015, p. 20–7.
[80] Parker GJM, Haroon HA, Wheeler-Kingshott CAM. A framework for a streamline-based probabilistic index of connectivity (PICo) using a structural interpretation of MRI diffusion measurements. J Magn Reson Imaging 2003;18(2):242–54.
[81] Lazar M, Alexander AL. An error analysis of white matter tractography methods: synthetic diffusion tensor field simulations. NeuroImage 2003;20(2):1140–53.
[82] Jones DK. Challenges and limitations of quantifying brain connectivity in vivo with diffusion MRI. Quant Imaging Med Surg 2010;2:341–55.
[83] Morris DM, Embleton KV, Parker GJM. Probabilistic fibre tracking: differentiation of connections from chance events. NeuroImage 2008;42(4):1329–39.
[84] Schmahmann JD, Pandya DN, Wang R, et al. Association fibre pathways of the brain: parallel observations from diffusion spectrum imaging and autoradiography. Brain 2007;130(3):630–53.
[85] Wakana S, Caprihan A, Panzenboeck MM, et al. Reproducibility of quantitative tractography methods applied to cerebral white matter. NeuroImage 2007;36(3):630–44.
[86] Catani M, Howard RJ, Pajevic S, Jones DK. Virtual in vivo interactive dissection of white matter fasciculi in the human brain. NeuroImage 2002;17(1):77–94.
[87] Hagmann P, Thiran J-P, Jonasson L, et al. DTI mapping of human brain connectivity: statistical fibre tracking and virtual dissection. NeuroImage 2003;19(3):545–54.
[88] Catani M, Jones DK, ffytche DH. Perisylvian language networks of the human brain. Ann Neurol 2005;57(1):8–16.
[89] Catani M, de Schotten MT. A diffusion tensor imaging tractography atlas for virtual in vivo dissections. Cortex 2008;44(8):1105–32. Special Issue on "Brain Hodology—Revisiting disconnection approaches to disorders of cognitive function".
[90] Osher S, Sethian JA. Fronts propagating with curvature-dependent speed: algorithms based on Hamilton-Jacobi formulations. J Comput Phys 1988;79(1):12–49.
[91] Tournier J-D, Calamante F, Gadian DG, Connelly A. Diffusion-weighted magnetic resonance imaging fibre tracking using a front evolution algorithm. NeuroImage 2003;20(1):276–88.
[92] Pichon E, Westin C-F, Tannenbaum AR. A Hamilton-Jacobi-Bellman approach to high angular resolution diffusion tractography. Med Image Comput Comput Assist Interv 2005;8(Pt 1):180–7.
[93] Sepasian N, ten Thije Boonkkamp J, Ter Haar Romeny B, Vilanova Bartroli A. Multivalued geodesic ray-tracing for computing brain connections using diffusion tensor imaging. SIAM J Imag Sci 2012;5(2): 483–504.
[94] Jbabdi S, Woolrich MW, Andersson JLR, Behrens TEJ. A Bayesian framework for global tractography. NeuroImage 2007;37(1):116–29.
[95] Jbabdi S, Bellec P, Toro R, Daunizeau J, Pelegrini-Issac M, Benali H. Accurate anisotropic fast marching for diffusion-based geodesic tractography. Int J Biomed Imaging 2008;2008:1–12.
[96] Wu X, Xu Q, Xu L, Zhou J, Anderson AW, Ding Z. Genetic white matter fiber tractography with global optimization. J Neurosci Methods 2009;184(2):375–9.
[97] Li M, Ratnanather JT, Miller MI, Mori S. Knowledge-based automated reconstruction of human brain white matter tracts using a path-finding approach with dynamic programming. NeuroImage 2014;88:271–81.
[98] Schreiber J, Riffert T, Anwander A, Knösche TR. Plausibility tracking: a method to evaluate anatomical connectivity and microstructural properties along fiber pathways. NeuroImage 2014;90:163–78.

[99] Mangin J-F, Poupon C, Cointepas Y, et al. A framework based on spin glass models for the inference of anatomical connectivity from diffusion-weighted MR data—a technical review. NMR Biomed 2002;15(7–8):481–92.

[100] Kreher BW, Mader I, Kiselev VG. Gibbs tracking: a novel approach for the reconstruction of neuronal pathways. Magn Reson Med 2008;60(4):953–63.

[101] Fillard P, Poupon C, Mangin J-FA. Novel global tractography algorithm based on an adaptive spin glass model. In: Medical image computing and computer-assisted intervention. Lecture notes in computer science, vol. 5761. Springer; 2009, p. 927–34.

[102] Reisert M, Mader I, Anastasopoulos C, Weigel M, Schnell S, Kiselev V. Global fiber reconstruction becomes practical. NeuroImage 2011;54(2):955–62.

[103] Mangin J-F, Fillard P, Cointepas Y, Le Bihan D, Frouin V, Poupon C. Toward global tractography. NeuroImage 2013;80:290–6. Mapping the Connectome.

[104] Christiaens D, Reisert M, Dhollander T, Sunaert S, Suetens P, Maes F. Global tractography of multi-shell diffusion-weighted imaging data using a multi-tissue model. NeuroImage 2015;123:89–101.

[105] Teillac A, Beaujoin J, Poupon F, Mangin J-F, Poupon C. A novel anatomically-constrained global tractography approach to monitor sharp turns in gyri. In: Medical image computing and computer assisted intervention—MICCAI 2017. Cham: Springer International Publishing; 2017, p. 532–9.

[106] Wu X, Xie M, Zhou J, Anderson AW, Gore JC, Ding Z. Globally optimized fiber tracking and hierarchical clustering—a unified framework. Magn Reson Imaging 2012;30(4):485–95.

[107] Lemkaddem A, Skiöldebrand D, Dal Palú A, Thiran J-P, Daducci A. Global tractography with embedded anatomical priors for quantitative connectivity analysis. Front Neurol 2014;5:232.

[108] Close TG, Tournier J-D, Johnston LA, Calamante F, Mareels I, Connelly A. Fourier tract sampling (FouTS): a framework for improved inference of white matter tracts from diffusion MRI by explicitly modelling tract volume. NeuroImage 2015;120:412–27.

[109] Koch MA, Norris DG, Hund-Georgiadis M. An investigation of functional and anatomical connectivity using magnetic resonance imaging. NeuroImage 2002;16(1):241–50.

[110] Anwander A, Tittgemeyer M, von Cramon D, Friederici A, Knösche T. Connectivity-based parcellation of Broca's area. Cereb Cortex 2007;17(4):816–25.

[111] Lifshits S, Tamir A, Assaf Y. Combinatorial fiber-tracking of the human brain. NeuroImage 2009; 48(3):532–40.

[112] Batchelor PG, Hill DLG, Atkinson D, Calamante F. Study of connectivity in the brain using the full diffusion tensor from MRI. In: Information processing in medical imaging. Berlin, Heidelberg: Springer Berlin Heidelberg; 2001, p. 121–33.

[113] O'Donnell L, Haker S, Westin C-F. New approaches to estimation of white matter connectivity in diffusion tensor MRI: elliptic PDEs and geodesics in a tensor-warped space. In: Lecture notes in computer science. vol. 2488. Berlin Heidelberg: Springer; 2002, p. 459–66.

[114] Parker GJM, Wheeler-Kingshott CAM, Barker GJ. Estimating distributed anatomical connectivity using fast marching methods and diffusion tensor imaging. IEEE Trans Med Imaging 2002;21(5):505–12.

[115] Lenglet C, Deriche R, Faugeras O. Inferring white matter geometry from diffusion tensor MRI: application to connectivity mapping. In: Pajdla T, Matas J, editors. Lecture notes in computer science. vol. 3024. Berlin Heidelberg: Springer; 2004, p. 127–40.

[116] Campbell JSW, Siddiqi K, Rymar VV, Sadikot AF, Pike GB. Flow-based fiber tracking with diffusion tensor and q-ball data: validation and comparison to principal diffusion direction techniques. NeuroImage 2005;27(4):725–36.

[117] Jackowski M, Kao CY, Qiu M, Constable RT, Staib LH. White matter tractography by anisotropic wavefront evolution and diffusion tensor imaging. Med Image Comput Comput Assist Interv 2005; 9(5):427–40.

[118] Kang N, Zhang J, Carlson E, Gembris D. White matter fiber tractography via anisotropic diffusion simulation in the human brain. IEEE Trans Med Imaging 2005;24(9):1127–37.

[119] Prados E, Soatto S, Lenglet C, et al. Control theory and fast marching techniques for brain connectivity mapping, In: IEEE computer society conference on computer vision and pattern recognition (CVPR'06), vol. 1; 2006, p. 1076–83.

[120] Staempfli P, Jaermann T, Crelier GR, Kollias S, Valavanis A, Boesiger P. Resolving fiber crossing using advanced fast marching tractography based on diffusion tensor imaging. NeuroImage 2006;30(1):110–20.

[121] Hageman NS, Toga AW, Narr KL, Shattuck DW. A diffusion tensor imaging Tractography algorithm based on Navier-stokes fluid mechanics. IEEE Trans Med Imaging 2008;28(3):348–60.

[122] Fletcher PT, Tao R, Jeong W-K, Whitaker RT. A volumetric approach to quantifying region-to-region white matter connectivity in diffusion tensor MRI. In: Information processing in medical imaging. Berlin, Heidelberg: Springer Berlin Heidelberg; 2007, p. 346–58.

[123] Iturria-Medina Y, Canales-Rodríguez EJ, Melie-García L, et al. Characterizing brain anatomical connections using diffusion weighted MRI and graph theory. NeuroImage 2007;36(3):645–60.

[124] Zalesky A, Fornito A. A DTI-derived measure of cortico-cortical connectivity. IEEE Trans Med Imaging 2009;28(7):1023–36.

[125] Sotiropoulos SN, Bai L, Morgan PS, Constantinescu CS, Tench CR. Brain tractography using Q-ball imaging and graph theory: improved connectivities through fibre crossings via a model-based approach. NeuroImage 2010;49(3):2444–56.

[126] Vorburger RS, Reischauer C, Boesiger P. BootGraph: probabilistic fiber tractography using bootstrap algorithms and graph theory. NeuroImage 2013;66:426–35.

[127] Leemans A, Sijbers J, Verhoye M, Van der Linden A, Van Dyck D. Mathematical framework for simulating diffusion tensor MR neural fiber bundles. Magn Reson Med 2005;53(4):944–53.

[128] Cheng P, Magnotta VA, Wu D, et al. Evaluation of the GTRACT diffusion tensor tractography algorithm: a validation and reliability study. NeuroImage 2006;31(3):1075–85.

[129] Close TG, Tournier J-D, Calamante F, Johnston LA, Mareels I, Connelly A. A software tool to generate simulated white matter structures for the assessment of fibre-tracking algorithms. NeuroImage 2009;47(4):1288–300.

[130] Côté M-A, Girard G, Boré A, Garyfallidis E, Houde J-C, Descoteaux M. Tractometer: towards validation of tractography pipelines. Med Image Anal 2013;17(7):844–57. Special Issue on the 2012 Conference on Medical Image Computing and Computer Assisted Intervention.

[131] Caruyer E, Daducci A, Descoteaux M, Houde J-C, Thiran J-P, Verma R. Phantomas: a flexible software library to simulate diffusion MR phantoms. In: Proceedings of the ISMRM. 2014.

[132] Neher PF, Laun FB, Stieltjes B, Maier-Hein KH. Fiberfox: facilitating the creation of realistic white matter software phantoms. Magn Reson Med 2014;72(5):1460–70. https://doi.org/10.1002/mrm.25045.

[133] Neher PF, Descoteaux M, Houde J-C, Stieltjes B, Maier-Hein KH. Strengths and weaknesses of state of the art fiber tractography pipelines: a comprehensive in-vivo and phantom evaluation study using tractometer. Med Image Anal 2015;26(1):287–305.

[134] Perrone D, Jeurissen B, Aelterman J, et al. D-BRAIN: anatomically accurate simulated diffusion MRI BRAIN data. PLoS ONE 2016;11(3):e0149778.

[135] Perrin M, Poupon C, Rieul B, et al. Validation of q-ball imaging with a diffusion fibre-crossing phantom on a clinical scanner. Philos Trans R Soc B 2005;360(1457):881–91.

[136] Poupon C, Rieul B, Kezele I, Perrin M, Poupon F, Mangin J-F. New diffusion phantoms dedicated to the study and validation of high-angular-resolution diffusion imaging (HARDI) models. Magn Reson Med 2008;60(6):1276–83.

[137] Fillard P, Descoteaux M, Goh A, et al. Quantitative evaluation of 10 tractography algorithms on a realistic diffusion MR phantom. NeuroImage 2011;56(1):220–34.

[138] Li L, Rilling JK, Preuss TM, Glasser MF, Damen FW, Hu X. Quantitative assessment of a framework for creating anatomical brain networks via global tractography. NeuroImage 2012;61(4):1017–30.

[139] Lin C-P, Tseng W-YI, Cheng H-C, Chen J-H. Validation of diffusion tensor magnetic resonance axonal fiber imaging with registered manganese-enhanced optic tracts. NeuroImage 2001;14(5):1035–47.

[140] Khan AR, Cornea A, Leigland LA, Kohama SG, Jespersen SN, Kroenke CD. 3D structure tensor analysis of light microscopy data for validating diffusion MRI. NeuroImage 2015;111:192–203.
[141] Dauguet J, Peled S, Berezovskii V, et al. Comparison of fiber tracts derived from in-vivo DTI tractography with 3D histological neural tract tracer reconstruction on a macaque brain. NeuroImage 2007;37(2):530–8.
[142] Dyrby TB, Søgaard LV, Parker GJ, et al. Validation of in vitro probabilistic tractography. NeuroImage 2007;37(4):1267–77.
[143] Seehaus AK, Roebroeck A, Chiry O, et al. Histological validation of DW-MRI tractography in human postmortem tissue. Cereb Cortex 2013;23(2):442–50.
[144] Knösche TR, Anwander A, Liptrot M, Dyrby TB. Validation of tractography: comparison with manganese tracing. Hum Brain Mapp 2015;36(10):4116–34.
[145] Donahue CJ, Sotiropoulos SN, Jbabdi S, et al. Using diffusion tractography to predict cortical connection strength and distance: a quantitative comparison with tracers in the monkey. J Neurosci 2016;36(25):6758–70.
[146] Wassermann D, Makris N, Rathi Y, et al. The white matter query language: a novel approach for describing human white matter anatomy. Brain Struct Funct 2016;1–17.
[147] Tozer DJ, Chard DT, Bodini B, et al. Linking white matter tracts to associated cortical grey matter: a tract extension methodology. NeuroImage 2012;59(4):3094–102.
[148] Smith RE, Tournier J-D, Calamante F, Connelly A. The effects of SIFT on the reproducibility and biological accuracy of the structural connectome. NeuroImage 2015;104:253–65.
[149] Yeh C-H, Smith RE, Dhollander T, Calamante F, Connelly A. The influence of node assignment strategies and track termination criteria on diffusion MRI-based structural connectomics, In: Proceedings of the ISMRM; 2016, p. 0118.
[150] Cheng H, Wang Y, Sheng J, et al. Optimization of seed density in DTI tractography for structural networks. J Neurosci Methods 2012;203(1):264–72.
[151] Gauvin A, Petit L, Descoteaux MSATA. Achieving volume saturation of streamline bundles in tractography, In: Proceedings of the ISMRM diffusion workshop; 2016.
[152] Yeh C-H, Smith R, Liang X, Calamante F, Connelly A. Investigating the streamline count required for reproducible structural connectome construction across a range of brain parcellation resolutions. In: Proceedings of the ISMRM, 2018.
[153] Jones DK, Knösche TR, Turner R. White matter integrity, fiber count, and other fallacies: the do's and don'ts of diffusion MRI. NeuroImage 2013;73:239–54.
[154] Smith RE, Tournier J-D, Calamante F, Connelly A. SIFT: spherical-deconvolution informed filtering of tractograms. NeuroImage 2013;67:298–312.
[155] Calamante F, Smith RE, Tournier J-D, Raffelt D, Connelly A. Quantification of voxel-wise total fibre density: investigating the problems associated with track-count mapping. NeuroImage 2015;117:284–93.
[156] Yeh C-H, Smith RE, Liang X, Calamante F, Connelly A. Correction for diffusion MRI fibre tracking biases: the consequences for structural connectomic metrics. NeuroImage 2016;142:150–62.
[157] Colon-Perez LM, Spindler C, Goicochea S, et al. Dimensionless, scale invariant, edge weight metric for the study of complex structural networks. PLoS ONE 2015;10(7):e0131493.
[158] Sherbondy AJ, Dougherty RF, Ananthanarayanan R, Modha DS, Wandell BA. Think global, act local; projectome estimation with BlueMatter. In: Medical image computing and computer-assisted intervention. London, UK: Springer-Verlag; 2009, p. 861–8.
[159] Sherbondy A, Rowe M, Alexander D. MicroTrack: an algorithm for concurrent projectome and microstructure estimation. In: Jiang T, Navab N, Pluim J, Viergever M, editors. Medical image computing and computer-assisted intervention. vol. 6361. Berlin/Heidelberg: Springer; 2010, p. 183–90.
[160] Daducci A, Dal Palú A, Lemkaddem A, Thiran J. COMMIT: convex optimization modeling for microstructure informed Tractography, In: IEEE transactions on medical imaging, vol. 34: 2014, p. 246–57.
[161] Pestilli F, Yeatman JD, Rokem A, Kay KN, Wandell BA. Evaluation and statistical inference for human connectomes. Nat Methods 2014;11(10):1058–63.

[162] Smith RE, Tournier J-D, Calamante F, Connelly A. SIFT2: enabling dense quantitative assessment of brain white matter connectivity using streamlines tractography. NeuroImage 2015;119:338–51.
[163] Sommer S, Kozerke S, Seifritz E, Staempfli P. Uniformity and deviation of intra-axonal cross-sectional area coverage of the gray-to-white matter interface. Front Neurosci 2017;11:729.
[164] Assaf Y, Basser PJ. Composite hindered and restricted model of diffusion (CHARMED) MR imaging of the human brain. NeuroImage 2005;27(1):48–58.
[165] Assaf Y, Blumenfeld-Katzir T, Yovel Y, Basser PJ. AxCaliber: a method for measuring axon diameter distribution from diffusion MRI. Magn Reson Med 2008;59(6):1347–54.
[166] Alexander DC, Hubbard PL, Hall MG, et al. Orientationally invariant indices of axon diameter and density from diffusion MRI. NeuroImage 2010;52(4):1374–89.
[167] Raffelt D, Tournier J-D, Rose S, et al. Apparent fibre density: a novel measure for the analysis of diffusion-weighted magnetic resonance images. NeuroImage 2012;59(4):3976–94.
[168] Zhang H, Hubbard PL, Parker GJM, Alexander DC. Axon diameter mapping in the presence of orientation dispersion with diffusion MRI. NeuroImage 2011;56(3):1301–15.
[169] Kaden E, Kelm ND, Carson RP, Does MD, Alexander DC. Multi-compartment microscopic diffusion imaging. NeuroImage 2016;139:346–59.
[170] Reisert M, Kellner E, Dhital B, Hennig J, Kiselev VG. Disentangling micro from mesostructure by diffusion MRI: a Bayesian approach. NeuroImage 2017;147:964–75.
[171] Dell'Acqua F, Simmons A, Williams SCR, Catani M. Can spherical deconvolution provide more information than fiber orientations? Hindrance modulated orientational anisotropy, a true-tract specific index to characterize white matter diffusion. Hum Brain Mapp 2012;34:2464–83.
[172] Riffert TW, Schreiber J, Anwander A, Knösche TR. Beyond fractional anisotropy: extraction of bundle-specific structural metrics from crossing fiber models. NeuroImage 2014;100:176–91.
[173] Jeurissen B, Tournier J-D, Dhollander T, Connelly A, Sijbers J. Multi-tissue constrained spherical deconvolution for improved analysis of multi-shell diffusion MRI data. NeuroImage 2014;103:411–26.
[174] Sommer S, Kozerke S, Seifritz E, Staempfli P. Fiber up-sampling and quality assessment of tractograms—towards quantitative brain connectivity. Brain Behav 2017;7(1):e00588.
[175] Aganj I, Lenglet C, Jahanshad N, et al. A Hough transform global probabilistic approach to multiple-subject diffusion MRI tractography. Med Image Anal 2011;15(4):414–25. Special section on IPMI 2009.
[176] Hagmann P. From diffusion MRI to brain connectomics. https://doi.org/10.5075/epfl-thesis-3230.
[177] Sporns O, Tononi G, Kötter R. The human connectome: a structural description of the human brain. PLoS Comput Biol 2005;1(4):e42.
[178] Fornito A, Zalesky A, Breakspear M. Graph analysis of the human connectome: promise, progress, and pitfalls. NeuroImage 2013;80:426–44. Mapping the Connectome.
[179] Sporns O. The human connectome: origins and challenges. NeuroImage 2013;80:53–61. Mapping the Connectome.
[180] Sotiropoulos SN, Zalesky A. Building connectomes using diffusion MRI: why, how and but. NMR Biomed 2017;32:e3752.
[181] Fischl B, van der Kouwe A, Destrieux C, et al. Automatically parcellating the human cerebral cortex. Cereb Cortex 2004;14(1):11–22.
[182] Cohen AL, Fair DA, Dosenbach NUF, et al. Defining functional areas in individual human brains using resting functional connectivity MRI. NeuroImage 2008;41(1):45–57.
[183] Zalesky A, Fornito A, Harding IH, et al. Whole-brain anatomical networks: does the choice of nodes matter? NeuroImage 2010;50(3):970–83.
[184] Cammoun L, Gigandet X, Meskaldji D, et al. Mapping the human connectome at multiple scales with diffusion spectrum MRI. J Neurosci Methods 2012;203(2):386–97.
[185] de Reus Marcel A, van den Heuvel MP. The parcellation-based connectome: limitations and extensions. NeuroImage 2013;80:397–404. Mapping the Connectome.

[186] Glasser MF, Coalson TS, Robinson EC, et al. A multi-modal parcellation of human cerebral cortex. Nature 2016;536:171.

[187] Arslan S, Ktena SI, Makropoulos A, Robinson EC, Rueckert D, Parisot S. Human brain mapping: a systematic comparison of parcellation methods for the human cerebral cortex. NeuroImage 2018;170:5–30. Segmenting the Brain.

[188] van den Heuvel MP, Sporns O. Rich-club organization of the human connectome. J Neurosci 2011;31(44):15775–86.

[189] Clayden JD, Dayan M, Clark CA. Principal networks. PLoS ONE 2013;8(4):e60997.

[190] Griffa A, Baumann PS, Thiran J-P, Hagmann P. Structural connectomics in brain diseases. NeuroImage 2013;80:515–26. Mapping the Connectome.

[191] Sporns O. Network attributes for segregation and integration in the human brain. Curr Opin Neurobiol 2013;23(2):162–71. Macrocircuits.

[192] Rubinov M, Sporns O. Complex network measures of brain connectivity: uses and interpretations. NeuroImage 2010;52(3):1059–69. Computational Models of the Brain.

[193] Batchelor PG, Calamante F, Tournier J-D, Atkinson D, Hill DLG, Connelly A. Quantification of the shape of fiber tracts. Magn Reson Med 2006;55(4):894–903.

[194] Ratnarajah N, Simmons A, Davydov O, Hojjatoleslami A. A novel approach for improved tractography and quantitative analysis of probabilistic fibre tracking curves. Med Image Anal 2012;16(1):227–38.

[195] Glozman T, Bruckert L, Pestilli F, Yecies DW, Guibas LJ, Yeom KW. Framework for shape analysis of white matter fiber bundles. NeuroImage 2018;167:466–77.

[196] Calamante F, Tournier J-D, Smith RE, Connelly A. A generalised framework for super-resolution track-weighted imaging. NeuroImage 2012;59(3):2494–503.

[197] O'Halloran R, Feldman R, Marcuse L, et al. A method for u-fiber quantification from 7T diffusion-weighted MRI data tested in patients with nonlesional focal epilepsy. Neuroreport 2017;28:457–61.

[198] Pannek K, Mathias JL, Bigler ED, Brown G, Taylor JD, Rose SE. The average pathlength map: a diffusion MRI tractography-derived index for studying brain pathology. NeuroImage 2011;55(1):133–41.

[199] Reijmer YD, Leemans A, Heringa SM, et al. Improved sensitivity to cerebral white matter abnormalities in Alzheimer's disease with spherical deconvolution based tractography. PLoS ONE 2012;7(8):e44074.

[200] Wang JY, Abdi H, Bakhadirov K, Diaz-Arrastia R, Devous S Michael D. A comprehensive reliability assessment of quantitative diffusion tensor tractography. NeuroImage 2012;60(2):1127–38.

[201] Bajada CJ, Schreiber J, Caspers S. Fiber length profiling: a novel approach to structural brain organization. NeuroImage 2019;186:164–73.

[202] Liang X, Zhuang Q, Cao N, Zhang J. Shape modeling and clustering of white matter fiber tracts using Fourier descriptors, In: Computational intelligence in bioinformatics and computational biology 6: 2009, p. 292–7.

[203] Rose S, Pannek K, Salvado O, Raniga P, Baumann F, Henderson R. The FA connectome: a quantitative strategy for studying neurological disease processes, In: Proceedings of the international society for magnetic resonance in medicine; 2010. p. 579.

[204] Ciccarelli O, Parker GJM, Toosy AT, et al. From diffusion tractography to quantitative white matter tract measures: a reproducibility study. NeuroImage 2003;18(2):348–59.

[205] Besseling RMH, Jansen JFA, Overvliet GM, et al. Tract specific reproducibility of tractography based morphology and diffusion metrics. PLoS ONE 2012;7(4):e34125.

[206] Jones D, Travis A, Eden G, Pierpaoli C, Basser P. PASTA: pointwise assessment of streamline tractography attributes. Magn Reson Med 2005;53(6):1462–7.

[207] Goodlett CB, Fletcher PT, Gilmore JH, Gerig G. Group analysis of DTI fiber tract statistics with application to neurodevelopment. NeuroImage 2009;45(1, Supplement 1):S133–42. Mathematics in Brain Imaging.

[208] O'Donnell LJ, Westin C-F, Golby AJ. Tract-based morphometry for white matter group analysis. NeuroImage 2009;45(3):832–44.

[209] Colby JB, Soderberg L, Lebel C, Dinov ID, Thompson PM, Sowell ER. Along-tract statistics allow for enhanced tractography analysis. NeuroImage 2012;59(4):3227–42.

[210] Yeatman JD, Dougherty RF, Myall NJ, Wandell BA, Feldman HM. Tract profiles of white matter properties: automating fiber-tract quantification. PLoS ONE 2012;7(11):e49790.

[211] Wang D, Luo Y, Mok VCT, Chu WCW, Shi L. Tractography atlas-based spatial statistics: statistical analysis of diffusion tensor image along fiber pathways. NeuroImage 2016;125:301–10.

[212] Pannek K, Mathias JL, Rose SE. MRI diffusion indices sampled along streamline trajectories: quantitative tractography mapping. Brain Connect 2011;1(4):331–8.

[213] Calamante F, Tournier J-D, Jackson GD, Connelly A. Track-density imaging (TDI): super-resolution white matter imaging using whole-brain track-density mapping. NeuroImage 2010;53(4):1233–43.

[214] Bozzali M, Parker GJM, Serra L, et al. Anatomical connectivity mapping: a new tool to assess brain disconnection in Alzheimer's disease. NeuroImage 2011;54(3):2045–51.

[215] Wright DK, Trezise J, Kamnaksh A, et al. Behavioral, blood, and magnetic resonance imaging biomarkers of experimental mild traumatic brain injury. Sci Rep 2016;6:28713.

[216] Wright DK, Johnston LA, Kershaw J, Ordidge R, O'Brien TJ, Shultz SR. Changes in apparent fiber density and track-weighted imaging metrics in white matter following experimental traumatic brain injury. J Neurotrauma 2017;34(13):2109–18.

[217] Willats L, Raffelt D, Smith RE, Tournier J-D, Connelly A, Calamante F. Quantification of track-weighted imaging (TWI): characterisation of within-subject reproducibility and between-subject variability. NeuroImage 2014;87:18–31.

[218] Raffelt DA, Smith RE, Ridgway GR, et al. Connectivity-based fixel enhancement: whole-brain statistical analysis of diffusion MRI measures in the presence of crossing fibres. NeuroImage 2015;117:40–55.

[219] Smith SM, Nichols TE. Threshold-free cluster enhancement: addressing problems of smoothing, threshold dependence and localisation in cluster inference. NeuroImage 2009;44(1):83–98.

[220] Yeh F-C, Badre D, Verstynen T. Connectometry: a statistical approach harnessing the analytical potential of the local connectome. NeuroImage 2016;125:162–71.

CHAPTER

22 Measuring Microstructural Features Using Diffusion MRI

Noam Shemesh
Champalimaud Research, Champalimaud Centre for the Unknown, Lisbon, Portugal

22.1 Introduction

22.1.1 What is the motivation for measuring microstructure using diffusion MRI?

Biological systems often require hierarchical organization to endow functionality: a single cell requires membranes and organelles to fulfill its purpose; a tissue is comprised of a collection of cell populations that serve to execute specific functions, such as neural computation or muscle contraction; and whole organisms require numerous functional systems to survive. Correspondingly, numerous spatial scales govern the various hierarchical units in living systems. Roughly speaking, cellular and subcellular scales typically span ~1 nm to ~tens of microns; clusters of cells, forming functional units within tissues (e.g., cortical columns), typically span ~100–1000 μm; and a collection of systems can span much larger scales, depending on the organism under investigation.

Contemporary MRI provides excellent anatomical resolution (~1 mm^3 in humans or ~200 μm^3 in rodents) and is thus capable of contrasting macroscopic anatomical features very well [1]. However, the cellular and subcellular scales—which elude the currently attainable spatial resolution of MRI—can be highly relevant in both normal and disease contexts. To name but a few examples: cellular size distributions are highly regulated in many biological systems [2], and their disruption may cause significant functionality loss [3]; in the central nervous system, cell density and distribution changes are associated with early stages of dementia [4]; microscopic beading occurs upon ischemic events [5]; axon density and diameter distribution, along with myelin thickness, are highly conserved to optimize conduction velocity [6,7], and their disruption can cause significant impairments [8,9]. Although current (typical) MRI scanner resolution exceeds such small dimensions by orders of magnitude, water diffusion can play a role as a surrogate reporter for microscopic length scales [10]. Fortuitously, the diffusion coefficient of bulk water at physiological temperature is ~3 μm^2/ms. In the practical observation times associated with MR (typically ~1–100 ms) the effective length scale (root mean squared displacement (rmsd)) traversed by freely diffusing water molecules is roughly on the order of ~1–100 μm [11]. When molecules diffuse in media containing microscopic boundaries (e.g., cell membranes or subcellular organelles) the rmsd can become smaller (as compared to free diffusion) if the molecules encounter these boundaries [12,13]. Hence, information about the enclosing geometry becomes imprinted on the diffusion-weighted signal, facilitating the derivation of microstructural quantities [14–18].

The motivation for measuring microstructure is thus that features on microscopic scales govern the functionality of crucial hierarchical units, and noninvasive characterization of these units could provide

Advances in Magnetic Resonance Technology and Applications. Volume 1. ISSN 2666-9099. https://doi.org/10.1016/B978-0-12-817057-1.00024-X

much insight into normal tissue function as well as potentially offer means for detecting aberrations. Since direct imaging of the microstructure is impractical, we turn to diffusion MRI to report in a voxel-wise manner on microscopic features.

22.1.2 What is "microstructure"?

Before diving into the cornucopia of methods that have been developed over the years for measuring tissue microstructure, it is worth considering what "microstructure" encompasses in the context of MR measurements. In the following discussion, we shall not limit ourselves to biological systems, since the following principles pertain to most porous media—from those found in biology [15,19], through petrochemistry [20], material science [21], and other fields. For the remainder of this chapter, flow effects [22] are ignored.

First, it is worth differentiating between *intrinsic* properties of the microstructure, and *measured quantities* obtained from a particular set of experiments. Consider an arbitrarily shaped pore filled with Nuclear Magnetic Resonance (NMR)-observable nuclei such that signal arises only from the intrapore domain (Fig. 22.1A). The pore space contains several "intrinsic" features that can be considered independent of any measurement. The pore density function, $\rho(\boldsymbol{r})$, is perhaps the most detailed of these intrinsic features: it reflects the pore geometry in its entirety; it is an "image" of the pore itself. Another intrinsic feature of the pore is its diffusion spectrum, $D(\omega)$, which is defined as the Fourier transform (FT) of the pore velocity autocorrelation function associated with reflections at the pore boundaries [23]. Other intrinsic properties are surface-to-volume (S/V) ratio [24] tortuosity [25], and the (ideal) averaged propagator and its associated power spectrum [26]. At least in principle, an "ideal" characterization of the pore microstructure would entail fully resolving $\rho(\boldsymbol{r})$, either by brute-force high-resolution MRI imaging, or by using more sophisticated methods.

In contrast to these intrinsic properties, a set of derived quantities, or otherwise indirect measures of pore microstructure, can be used for microstructural characterization. We could, for example, forego knowledge of all the detailed, high-resolution information described above, and rather settle on a

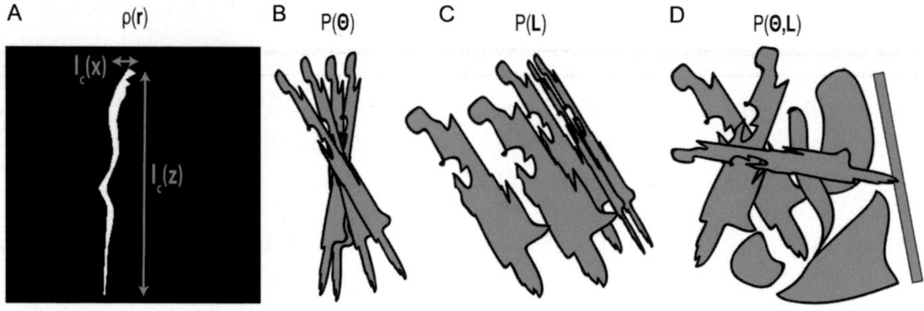

FIG. 22.1

Microstructural information and configuration. (A) An arbitrarily shaped pore corresponding to a pore density function $\rho(\boldsymbol{r})$, which would be returned if the space could be directly imaged. $l_c(z)$ and $l_c(x)$ represent approximate characteristic length scales along two orthogonal dimensions, which is sufficient to describe the pore anisotropy. (B) A different arbitrarily shaped pore with an orientation distribution; (C) size distribution; (D) both orientation and size distributions. In (B)–(D), it is of interest to measure properties of the ensemble as well as of the constituents.

sparser determination of a few characteristic features. These quantities and their correspondence with the intrinsic pore properties will often depend on how they were measured. The apparent diffusion coefficient (ADC) is a good example of a "derived" property [10,14]; though it tells us little about the pore itself, it gives us a notion of the effective length scales traversed in a given direction under the particular conditions of the measurement (Fig. 22.1A) and on the pore anisotropy. ADC values can also reveal the relationship between the pore and its environment, e.g., the pore's absolute orientation in some coordinate system of interest.

Still, further characterization can be sought on the *ensemble* level. For example, a collection of identically-shaped pores may be characterized by polydispersity in orientation (Fig. 22.1B) or size (Fig. 22.1C), or a combination thereof (Fig. 22.1D). In this case, it may be more feasible or convenient to characterize properties of the associated distributions, such as their moments or number of peaks. Additionally, *volume fractions* associated with different microscopic constituents are typically of much interest: for example, the volume of intra- and extracellular spaces. Finally, although perhaps not a microstructural property per se, exchange between different constituents may also be an important feature of the microstructure since it defines the "leakiness" of the barriers.

Thus, we can disentangle the somewhat obscure word "microstructure" into four main categories:

- intrinsic features, such as $\rho(\boldsymbol{r})$, $D(\omega)$, S/V, tortuosity or membrane permeability;
- derived properties, such as characteristic length scales in a given direction, ADCs, anisotropy, and absolute orientation;
- ensemble properties, such as the underlying polydispersity (e.g., moments of size-, shape-, or diffusivity-distributions);
- volumetric properties (volume fractions) associated with different putative distinct populations.

Below, we shall describe how to gain access to some of these properties using diffusion MR.

22.2 Directly imaging intrinsic microstructural features

22.2.1 The pore density function

The pore density function $\rho(\boldsymbol{r})$ contains all the relevant information on the spatial features of the pore morphology. At least in principle, high-resolution traditional MRI imaging can be used to resolve $\rho(\boldsymbol{r})$ (Fig. 22.1A). Unconventionally, Patterson patterns can report higher-resolution features from lower resolution k-space (Patterson functions estimate relative distances in $\rho(\boldsymbol{r})$ from k-space [27]). However, given the microscopic dimensions of the pore, we shall assume that direct k-space imaging is impractical. In the early 1990s, Cory, Garroway, and Miller [28] and in parallel Callaghan et al. [29] made a leap towards measuring a quantity connected to $\rho(\boldsymbol{r})$—its power spectrum—using the Stejskal-Tanner diffusion NMR experiment [30] (also known as the pulsed-gradient spin echo (PGSE) experiment), later rebranded single diffusion encoding (SDE) [31] for MRI. The SDE signal decay, when measured by varying the q-value, can be written quite generally as [10,28,29]:

$$E(\boldsymbol{q},\Delta)_{SDE}=\frac{S(\boldsymbol{q},\Delta)}{S_0}=\iint d\boldsymbol{r}_0 d\boldsymbol{r}_1 \rho(\boldsymbol{r}_0)\widetilde{P}(\boldsymbol{r}_0,\boldsymbol{r}_1,\Delta)e^{i2\pi\boldsymbol{q}(\boldsymbol{r}_1-\boldsymbol{r}_0)} \tag{22.1}$$

where $E(\boldsymbol{q},\Delta)$ is the normalized diffusion-driven signal decay, $S(\boldsymbol{q},\Delta)$ is the diffusion attenuated signal at diffusion time Δ, S_0 is the signal in the absence of diffusion weighting, $\boldsymbol{q}$ is the wavevector given by $\frac{1}{2\pi}\gamma\delta \boldsymbol{G}$, γ is the gyromagnetic ratio, δ is the gradient duration, $\boldsymbol{G}$ is the gradient wavevector, $\boldsymbol{r_0}$ and $\boldsymbol{r_1}$ are initial and final positions of a spin, $\widetilde{P}(\boldsymbol{r_0}, \boldsymbol{r_1}, \Delta)$ is the probability of moving the spin from $\boldsymbol{r_0}$ to $\boldsymbol{r_1}$ given a diffusion time Δ, and $e^{i2\pi \boldsymbol{q}(\boldsymbol{r_1}-\boldsymbol{r_0})}$ is the phase factor accrued by diffusion from $\boldsymbol{r_0}$ to $\boldsymbol{r_1}$ while under the influence of a wavevector $\boldsymbol{q}$. Callaghan realized that for a collection of identical pores with MR-observable nuclei resonating only in the (impermeable) intrapore domain characterized by a pore density function $\rho(\boldsymbol{r})$, in the limits of $\delta \rightarrow 0$ (the short gradient pulse (SGP) approximation) and $\Delta \rightarrow \infty$ (long diffusion limit), the diffusing spins lose "memory" of their starting point, and so $\widetilde{P}(\boldsymbol{r_0}, \boldsymbol{r_1}, \infty)$ simply reduces to $\rho(\boldsymbol{r_1})$ [29]. This was a profound insight indeed, since it suggested that

$$E(\boldsymbol{q}, \Delta \rightarrow \infty)_{SDE} = \int d\boldsymbol{r_0}\rho(\boldsymbol{r_0})e^{-i2\pi \boldsymbol{q}\boldsymbol{r_0}} \int d\boldsymbol{r_1}\rho(\boldsymbol{r_1})e^{2\pi \boldsymbol{q}\boldsymbol{r_1}} = \widetilde{\rho}^*(\boldsymbol{q})\,\widetilde{\rho}(\boldsymbol{q}) = \left|\widetilde{\rho}(\boldsymbol{q})\right|^2 \tag{22.2}$$

where $\widetilde{\rho}(\boldsymbol{q})$ is the pore structure function given by the FT of the pore density function $\widetilde{\rho}(\boldsymbol{q}) = \int \rho(\boldsymbol{r})e^{i\boldsymbol{q}\boldsymbol{r}}d\boldsymbol{r}$. The quantity $\left|\widetilde{\rho}(\boldsymbol{q})\right|^2$ is the (phaseless) power spectrum of the pore density function. Eq. (22.2) thus provides a very elegant way of accessing a salient intrinsic feature of the microstructure—its power spectrum—by simply measuring the SDE signal attenuation. In addition, the power spectrum bears an important Fourier relationship with the averaged propagator, $\widetilde{P}(\boldsymbol{R}, \Delta)$, which describes the possible displacements $\boldsymbol{R}$ in the system given a diffusion time Δ (described in more detail in Section 22.2).

Fig. 22.2 illustrates this idea for two idealized pore shapes with rectangular and cylindrical geometries, respectively (Fig. 22.2A). The pore density functions in the direction perpendicular to the main axes are shown for both geometries in Fig. 22.2B, while the respective structure functions $\widetilde{\rho}(\boldsymbol{q})$ are shown in Fig. 22.2C. Note that the pore density functions contain all the information about the pore, including its exact size and shape, and the associated structure functions exhibit phase. The corresponding averaged propagators shown in Fig. 22.2D are similar in shape for both geometries due to the loss of phase information. Finally, Fig. 22.2E shows the pore power spectra, which will be obtained directly from the SDE signal decay, $\left|\widetilde{\rho}(\boldsymbol{q})\right|^2$, and will display positive nonmonotonic coherence features, termed "diffusion diffractions." These coherence phenomena can be used to obtain compartment sizes very accurately since the characteristic size will be proportional to the inverse of the diffraction "dip" [10,29] (the first diffraction dip occurs around $q \sim 250\,\text{cm}^{-1}$ in Fig. 22.2E), suggesting the maximum displacement is proportional to $1/q_{\text{dip}} = \sim 40\,\mu\text{m}$).

Such diffusion diffraction patterns have been empirically observed in many porous systems including packed beads [29], emulsions [32] and (water-filled) microfibers [33], and pore sizes can indeed be obtained very accurately. Kuchel et al. showed diffusion diffraction patterns in red blood cells (RBCs) suspensions [34] that could be used to dynamically monitor transitions from echinocytes to discocytes [35]. Note, however, that differently shaped pores (of the same dimension) give rise to very similar SDE power spectra (Fig. 22.2E) [36].

Laun et al. introduced an elegant approach for recovering the phase information inherently lost in single diffusion encoding, by breaking the symmetry of the gradient waveform [37]. Rather than applying the commonly used identically shaped SDE gradient lobes for a time δ and amplitude $|\boldsymbol{G}|$, Laun et al. proposed applying a gradient which completely violates the SGD approximation, $|\boldsymbol{G_1}|$, for a duration δ_1, followed by an opposite-sense gradient $|\boldsymbol{G_2}|$ applied for a duration δ_2 that fulfills the SGP approximation, such that $G_1\delta_1 = G_2\delta_2$ (assuming for simplicity that the gradients are rectangular). This symmetry-breaking SDE pulse sequence (sb-SDE) leads to an attenuation factor of the following form [38]:

$$E(\boldsymbol{q}, \Delta \rightarrow \infty)_{sb\text{-}SDE} = e^{i2\pi \boldsymbol{q}\boldsymbol{r}_{cm}} \int d\boldsymbol{r_1}\rho(\boldsymbol{r_1})e^{i2\pi \boldsymbol{q}\boldsymbol{r_1}} \tag{22.3}$$

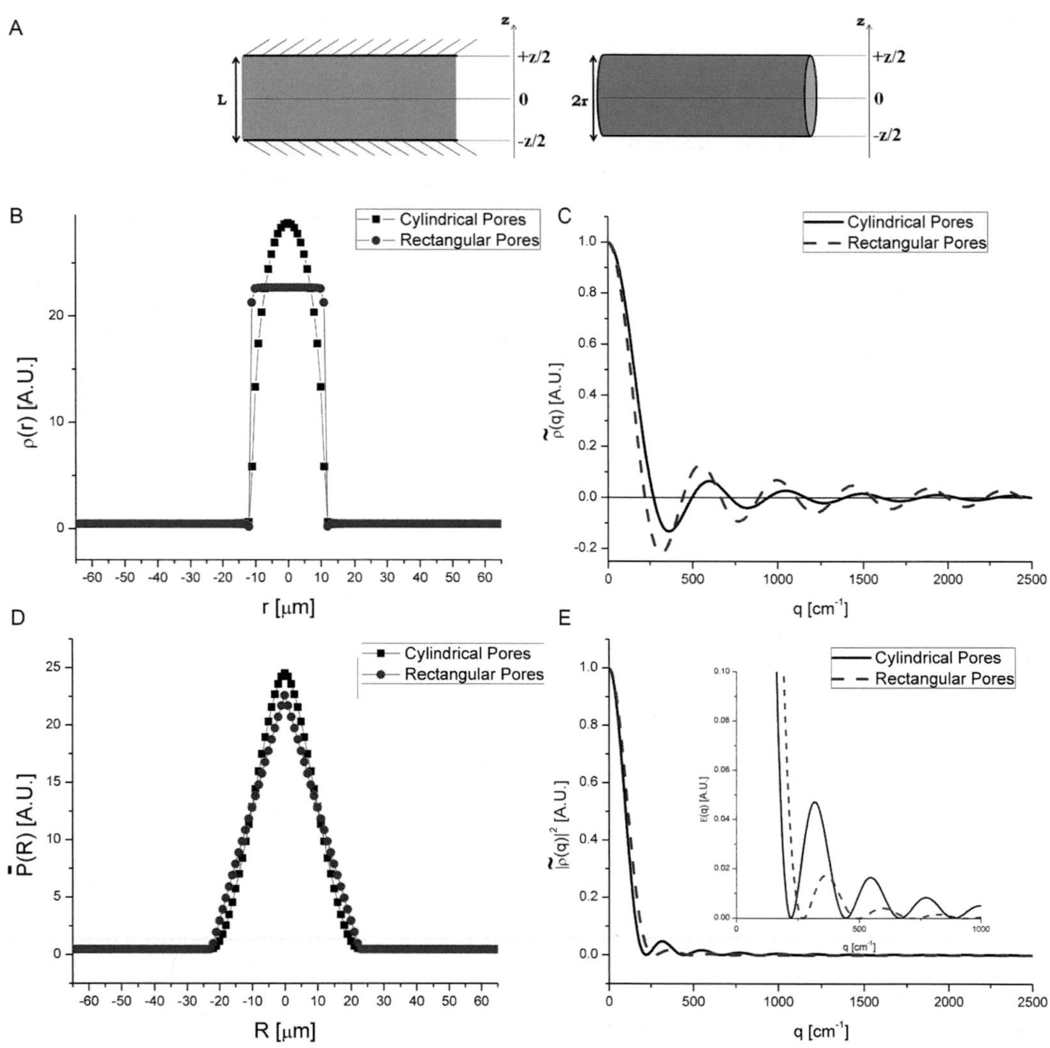

FIG. 22.2

Pore density functions, their Fourier pairs and power spectra. (A) Examples of rectangular and cylindrical pores (assumed to be infinite along their long dimension and perfectly impermeable in the perpendicular dimension. (B) The respective pore density functions and (C) their Fourier transforms. (D) The corresponding averaged propagators and (E) power spectra. Note the loss of shape information in (D) due to the loss of phase information in (E).

(Reproduced from Shemesh N, Westin CF, Cohen Y. Magnetic resonance imaging by synergistic diffusion-diffraction patterns. Phys Rev Lett 2012;108(5):058103. doi:10.1103/PhysRevLett.108.058103.)

where $\boldsymbol{r}_{cm}$ is the pore center of mass. In the long diffusion-time limit, the sb-SDE signal decay reduces to $E(\boldsymbol{q},\infty)_{sb\text{-}SDE} = e^{i2\pi \boldsymbol{q}\boldsymbol{r}_{cm}}\tilde{\rho}(\boldsymbol{q})$; the first term in Eq. (22.3) reflects a perhaps uninteresting phase of the pore center of mass, but the latter term is exactly the desired quantity—the pore structure function. Thus, $\rho(\boldsymbol{r})$—the quantity which is an effective "image" of the pore space, which contains all the detailed microstructural information on its size and shape—can be obtained immediately by an inverse Fourier transformation of $E(\boldsymbol{q},\infty)_{sb\text{-}SDE}$. Importantly, Laun et al. beautifully demonstrated how a triangular pore—a shape not easily inferred from SDE power spectra—could be directly reconstructed using sb-SDE [37,38] (Fig. 22.3). The first experimental validation of the sb-SDE methodology for imaging a microscopic domain [39] revealed the potential of the approach for characterizing porous media [40,41], and the triangular domain reconstruction was first realized experimentally using millimetric pores probed by hyperpolarized gas diffusion [42].

At the same time, Shemesh et al. targeted the same problem of reconstructing $\rho(\boldsymbol{r})$, but using synergistic diffusion diffraction patterns arising from a pulse sequence termed double diffusion encoding (DDE), and those arising from SDE [36] (the reader is referred to Chapter 19 and Section 22.3.1.1 for more information on DDE). The DDE signal decay at short mixing times had been previously shown to follow [43]:

$$E(\boldsymbol{q},\Delta\to\infty)_{DDE} = \tilde{\rho}(\boldsymbol{q})^2\tilde{\rho}^*(2\boldsymbol{q}) \tag{22.4}$$

where in this notation $\boldsymbol{q}=\boldsymbol{q}_1=\boldsymbol{q}_2$ for the two wavevectors of DDE. Shemesh et al. suggested that it would be possible to combine Eq. (22.4) and Eq. (22.2) to provide a synergistic signal attenuation $N(\boldsymbol{q})$ that retains phase information—and thereby information on the pore density function itself, via [36]:

$$N(\boldsymbol{q}) = \frac{E(\boldsymbol{q},\Delta\to\infty)_{DDE}}{E(\boldsymbol{q},\Delta\to\infty)_{SDE}} = \tilde{\rho}^*(2\boldsymbol{q})e^{2i\varphi(\boldsymbol{q})} \tag{22.5}$$

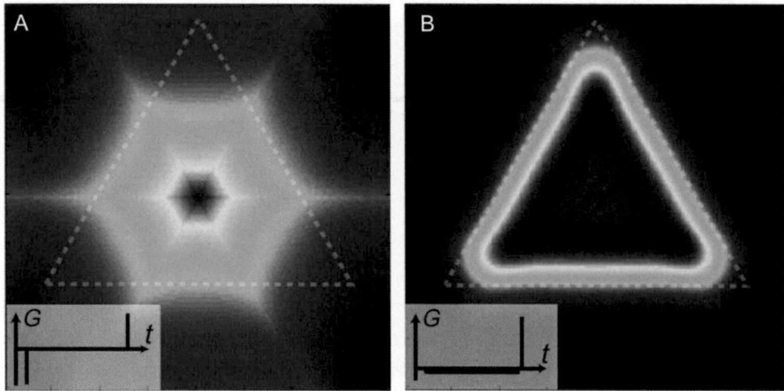

FIG. 22.3

Imaging the pore density function. Laun et al. showed how the loss of phase information which leads to a distortion of shape in SDE-derived pore imaging (A) can be fully addressed using the symmetry-breaking approach (B).

(Reproduced from Laun FB, Kuder TA, Wetscherek A, Stieltjes B, Semmler W. NMR-based diffusion pore imaging. Phys Rev E Stat Nonlin Soft Matter Phys 2012;86(2):021906. doi:10.1103/PhysRevE.86.021906.)

where the latter phase term, $e^{2i\varphi(\boldsymbol{q})} = \frac{\tilde{\rho}(\boldsymbol{q})}{\tilde{\rho}^*(\boldsymbol{q})}$, first pointed out by Kiselev and Novikov [44], is necessary for structures without point-symmetry (roughly speaking, point-symmetry refers to geometries invariant towards reflection about the center in any direction). In [36], the pore density functions of micron-scale (point-symmetric) cylinders was measured experimentally using this synergistic diffusion diffraction approach. Kuder and Laun then optimized the method [45] to image $\rho(\boldsymbol{r})$ directly from DDE signals (Eq. 22.4) [39,42,45].

Despite the potential of these approaches for directly imaging micron-scale pores, they also suffer from several practical drawbacks. (1) Densely sampled q-space measurements are required for Fourier inversions [46], rendering the measurements very long by design. (2) The measurements require exceptionally high signal-to-noise (SNR) to practically detect diffusion diffraction patterns or zero-crossings, whose signals are attenuated to orders of magnitude lower than the nondiffusion-weighted signal. (3) High maximum q-values must be reached to resolve small pores, necessitating very powerful gradient hardware to fulfill the SGP and long-time limit approximations invoked above. Finally, (4) the pores were assumed to be identical and nonexchanging; an averaged image [47,48] would be obtained in polydisperse systems [38].

22.2.2 The averaged propagator

Since realistic systems typically contain distributions, Cory, Garroway, and Miller generalized Eq. (22.1) to [28]:

$$E(\boldsymbol{q},\Delta)_{SDE} = \int d\boldsymbol{R}\,\tilde{P}(\boldsymbol{R},\Delta)e^{i2\pi\boldsymbol{qR}} \tag{22.6}$$

where $\boldsymbol{R}$ is the displacement vector $\boldsymbol{R}=\boldsymbol{r_1}-\boldsymbol{r_0}$ and $\tilde{P}(\boldsymbol{R},\Delta)$ is the averaged propagator describing the probability for displacement $\boldsymbol{R}$ during a time Δ. Interestingly, this formulation suggests that the SDE signal decay (as function of the q-value) is always the FT of the averaged displacement propagator $\tilde{P}(\boldsymbol{R},\Delta)$, which can provide interesting microstructural features; its full width at half maximum (FWHM), for example, describes a characteristic length-scale traversed by the diffusing spins. The ensuing q-space imaging (QSI) methodology entails voxel-wise mapping of $\tilde{P}(\boldsymbol{R},\Delta)$ properties. Ong and Wehrli [49] provided a striking example of the usefulness of QSI in characterizing neural tissues. Using a custom-made gradient system capable of reaching extremely high q-values, $\tilde{P}(\boldsymbol{R},\Delta)$ was determined in spinal cords with high accuracy and resolution in displacement space (Fig. 22.4). Remarkably, the FWHM in the different tracts accurately approximated axonal sizes as validated histologically [49]. $\tilde{P}(\boldsymbol{R},\Delta)$ can additionally provide rich orientational information as shown by diffusion spectrum imaging (DSI) approaches [50]. We note in passing that QSI typically shares the drawbacks described in the previous section, although the sensitivity penalty is somewhat reduced since the signal decays smoothly [51], which assists with the initial SNR requirement.

22.2.3 The diffusion spectrum

Self-diffusion can also be described by considering the instantaneous velocity of molecules; if diffusion is free, these velocities will be randomly distributed, and will have very little autocorrelation on the

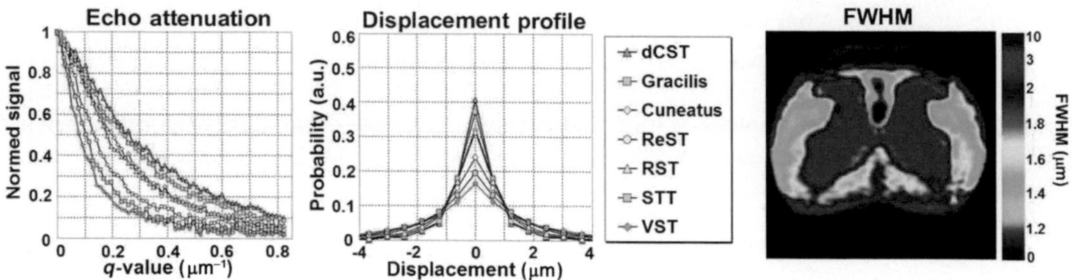

FIG. 22.4

q-space imaging (QSI) in an ex vivo mouse spinal cord reveals distinct attenuation behavior for each tract *(left)*, as well as different displacement profiles *(middle)*, leading to a FWHM-contrasted map *(right)*, which reveals the different tracts. Unusually, the short gradient pulse (SGP) approximation was approximately fulfilled in this experiment. *dCST*, dorsal cerebrospinal tract; *ReST*, reticulospinal tract; *RST*, rubrospinal tract; *STT*, spinothalamic tract; *VST*, vestibulospinal tract.

(Adapted from Ong HH, Wehrli FW. Quantifying axon diameter and intra-cellular volume fraction in excised mouse spinal cord with q-space imaging. Neuroimage 2010;51(4):1360–6. doi:10.1016/j.neuroimage.2010.03.063.)

timescale of NMR or MRI experiments. However, when a boundary is introduced to the system, a molecule that had a velocity v just before colliding with the boundary will bounce back with the same velocity in the opposite direction (assuming ideal conditions), and hence, autocorrelations are introduced into the system. The diffusion spectrum tensor $D_{ij}(\omega)$ is the velocity autocorrelation spectrum given by [52,53].

$$D_{ij}(\omega) = \int_0^{\infty} dt e^{i\omega t} < v_i(t) v_j(0) > \tag{22.7}$$

where <> represents an ensemble average, v is the instantaneous velocity, i and j are the Cartesian coordinates (c.f. [53,54]). For free, Gaussian diffusion, $D(\omega)$ is constant (Fig. 22.5), since the instantaneous velocity is random and frequency independent. For restricted diffusion, $D(\omega)$ will depart from this flat behavior, and its shape will reflect microstructural characteristics; in well-defined geometries, the diffusion spectrum is a sum of Lorentzians, typically only one of which is dominant. For example, for a simple geometry (e.g., an ideal sphere, cylinder, slab...), $D(\omega) = D_0 \sum_{k \neq 0} b_k \frac{\tau_k^2 \omega^2}{1+\tau_k^2 \omega^2}$ where D_0 is the intrinsic free diffusion coefficient, b_k are factors depending on the specific geometry, and τ_k are the characteristic times of the kth diffusion mode [23,52]. The microstructural information can be obtained, for example, by fitting b_k or by examining how the curves approach infinite or zero frequency.

Probing $D(\omega)$ with MRI requires tailored gradient waveforms that have well-defined and band-limited gradient dephasing spectra (Fig. 22.5, red trace). These specialized waveforms appear in oscillating gradient spin echo (OGSE) pulse sequences, where the oscillating nature of the gradient defines the frequency with which $D(\omega)$ is probed. While $D(\omega)$ is frequently used to characterize porous media microstructure [23,52,55], such measurements are somewhat less common in MRI of biological systems. Still, $D(\omega)$ has been measured in cells [53,56], tumors [57], and normal tissues [58]. In addition, mean axon diameters in ex vivo spinal cord were mapped based on $D(\omega)$ (Fig. 22.6), and investigated against simulated extra- and intraaxonal contributions [59]. Robust tract-specific contrasts can be obtained from this axon diameter mapping (Fig. 22.6B), and very good correlations (though with some

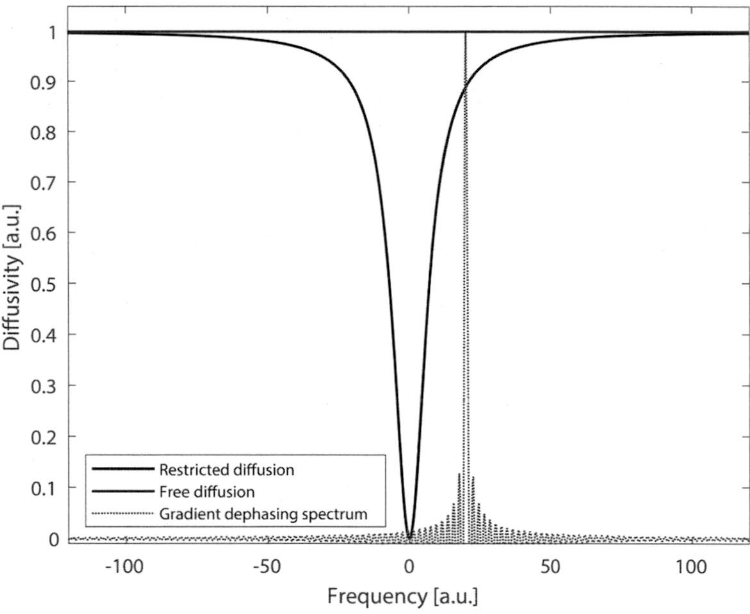

FIG. 22.5

Representative diffusion spectra for restricted *(black)* and free *(blue)* diffusion. Free diffusion is independent of the probing frequency, while restricted diffusion tends to 0 at 0 frequency and to free diffusivity at very high frequencies. A typical gradient dephasing spectrum is shown in red, probing at a particular frequency. This dephasing spectrum is shifted to probe more frequencies in $D(\omega)$.

bias) were observed with histology. Aggarwal et al. have shown strong contrast enhancements with increasing oscillation frequency (Fig. 22.6C) [60,61], while others have shown that $D(\omega)$ is less sensitive than PGSE-driven ADC contrast for delineating stroke [62].

22.3 Strategies for indirect quantification of microstructure

In the face of insufficient experimental time, low SNR, or lack of specialized hardware for direct characterization of the metrics defined above, we may endeavor to consider alternative approaches for quantifying microstructure. Novikov et al. [63] have recently roughly categorized these approaches into:

- signal representations;
- tissue models;
- biophysical models.

Signal representations describe diffusion-driven signal attenuation in certain regimes irrespective of specific underlying microstructural features; for example, the signal decay at low b-values is quite featureless and can nearly always be well-characterized by diffusivity and kurtosis terms. While the former approach makes no assumption of underlying features, **tissue models** explicitly assume a priori

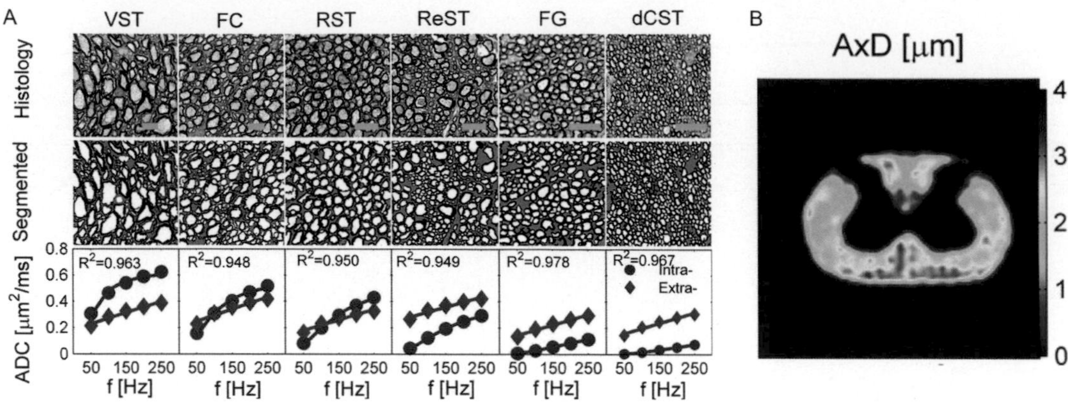

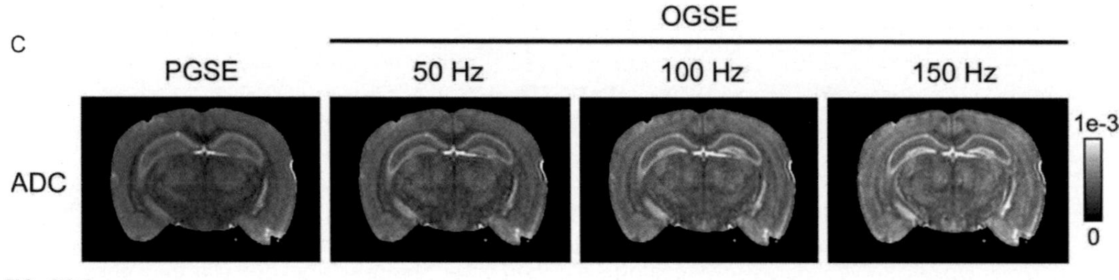

FIG. 22.6

(A) Histology of the different spinal cord tracts, along with simulations for the diffusion spectrum inside and outside of the pores. (B) An axon diameter map derived from oscillating gradient spin echo (OGSE) data in the rat spinal cord. (C) Contrast enhancements using OGSE with increasing frequency. *dCST*, dorsal cerebrospinal tract; *FG*, fasiculus gracilis; *FC*, fasiculus cuneatis; *ReST*, reticulospinal tract; *RST*, rubrospinal tract; *STT*, spinothalamic tract; *VST*, vestibulospinal tract.

(Adapted from Xu J, Li H, Harkins KD, Jiang X, Xie J, Kang H, Does MD, Gore JC. Mapping mean axon diameter and axonal volume fraction by MRI using temporal diffusion spectroscopy. Neuroimage 2014;103:10–9. doi:10.1016/j.neuroimage.2014.09.006. Aggarwal M, Jones MV, Calabresi PA, Mori S, Zhang J. Probing mouse brain microstructure using oscillating gradient diffusion magnetic resonance imaging. Magn Reson Med 2012;67(1):98–109. doi:10.1002/mrm.22981.)

knowledge of the components making up the tissue, their respective geometry, and the associated diffusion modes; the signal is then represented by the combination of the diffusion-driven attenuations for each component. The measured signal is then fit to what the researcher believes is the most appropriate combination of diffusion modes and geometries in the tissue under investigation. **Biophysical models** are different from tissue models in that they attempt to construct a more generalized view of tissue microstructure, without idealizing it to perfect geometric models (a cylinder, a sphere, etc.), and then formulate functional forms of the signal decay that could empirically verify the model assumptions (e.g., power laws). Below, these approaches are briefly described to familiarize the reader with the concepts, and then recent innovations are highlighted.

22.3.1 Single diffusion encoding signal representations

Signal representations provide exact expressions to characterize features of the diffusion-driven signal decay, without attempting to assign these features to underlying tissue components within the voxel. For example, at low b-values, nearly irrespective of the substrate, the SDE signal decay will follow the cumulant expansion [63]:

$$\ln\left(E(n,b)_{SDE}\right) = \ln\left(\frac{S(nb)_{SDE}}{S_{0SDE}}\right) = -bD(n) + \frac{1}{6}b^2 D_{app}(n)^2 K_{app}(n) + O\left(b^3\right) \tag{22.8}$$

where $b = \int_0^{TE} dt(\gamma \int_0^t dt' G(t'))^2$ is the b-value ($b = (\gamma\delta G)^2\left(\Delta\text{-}\frac{\delta}{3}\right)$) for a simple SDE experiment with gradient duration δ, gradient separation Δ, and gradient amplitude G), n is the direction of the applied diffusion gradient wavevector, $D_{app}(n)$ is the ADC obtained in direction n, and $K_{app}(n)$ is the apparent kurtosis measured in direction n (where both can be time-dependent). The apparent quantities bear the following relationships with the full diffusion and kurtosis tensors [64]: $D_{app}(n) - \sum_{i,j=1}^{3} D_{ij} n_i n_j$ and $K_{app}(n) = \sum_{i,j,k,l=1}^{3} \frac{MD^2}{D_{app}^2(n)} W_{ijkl} n_i n_j n_k n_l$, where MD is the mean diffusivity and W_{ijkl} is the full excess kurtosis tensor.

Eq. (22.8) describes a somewhat featureless nonmonoexponential decay. The parameters D and K thus only indirectly, and nonspecifically, reflect the influence of the underlying microstructural features on the signal decay. Still, numerous quantitative metrics and invariants can be derived from each tensor, such as the mean diffusivity, fractional anisotropy (FA), or the axial and radial kurtosis, just to name a few examples. While these metrics typically offer high sensitivity, the generic nature of the signal decay entails a loss of *specificity*. Kurtosis, for example, will arise from any of the following: multiple Gaussian tensors with different magnitude, identical tensors with orientation dispersion, restricted diffusion in one or more compartment, and any combination of the above [65]. As such, the interpretation of these metrics to reveal the underlying microstructure is likely to be ambiguous. Contrasts emerging from D and K are typically used to characterize white matter tissues [66,67], better highlight aberrations in disease [68–71], and enable resolution of crossing fibers [72,73]. The cumulant expansion is a convenient yet certainly not the only representation for diffusion-driven decays, and other signal bases exist [74].

22.3.1.1 Disentangling orientation dispersion from microscopic anisotropy without model assumptions from double diffusion encoding signal representations

The above SDE representation (Eq. 22.8) conflates intravoxel microstructural and orientational metrics. For example, an ensemble of spheres and an ensemble of randomly oriented anisotropic pores (Fig. 22.7A) will both produce isotropic signal decays (FA = 0) with similar values of D and K, from which it is difficult to infer on the underlying morphology.

DDE (Fig. 22.7B) was proposed as a model-free methodology for quantifying microstructure even when significant orientation dispersion exists [28,75]. The DDE pulse sequences have been described in a previous chapter (Chapter 19); briefly, DDE entails the application of two diffusion encoding epochs Δ_1 and Δ_2 spanned by diffusion gradients of duration δ_1 and δ_2 and gradient vectors $\boldsymbol{G_1}$ and $\boldsymbol{G_2}$, respectively, separated by a variable mixing time τ_m (Fig. 22.7B). Since the gradient wavevectors can be varied independently, DDE can probe correlations along different directions, which provides insights into microscopic anisotropy [28,76].

In 1995, Mitra formulated the "angular" DDE experiment (Fig. 22.7C), where the orientation of the second gradient is systematically varied while the first gradient is kept constant [77]. Mitra proposed

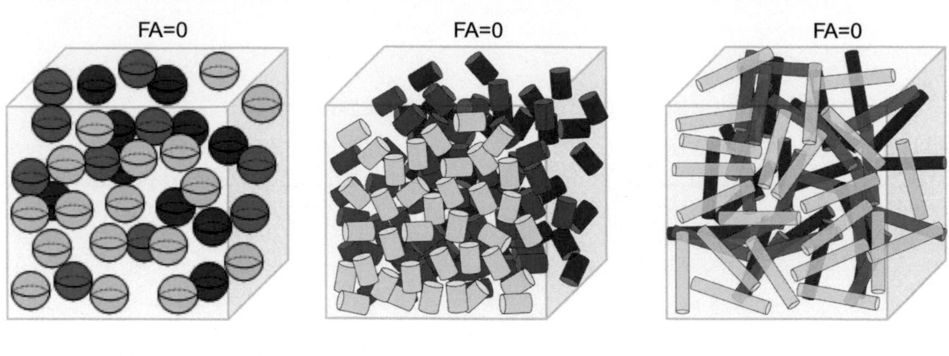

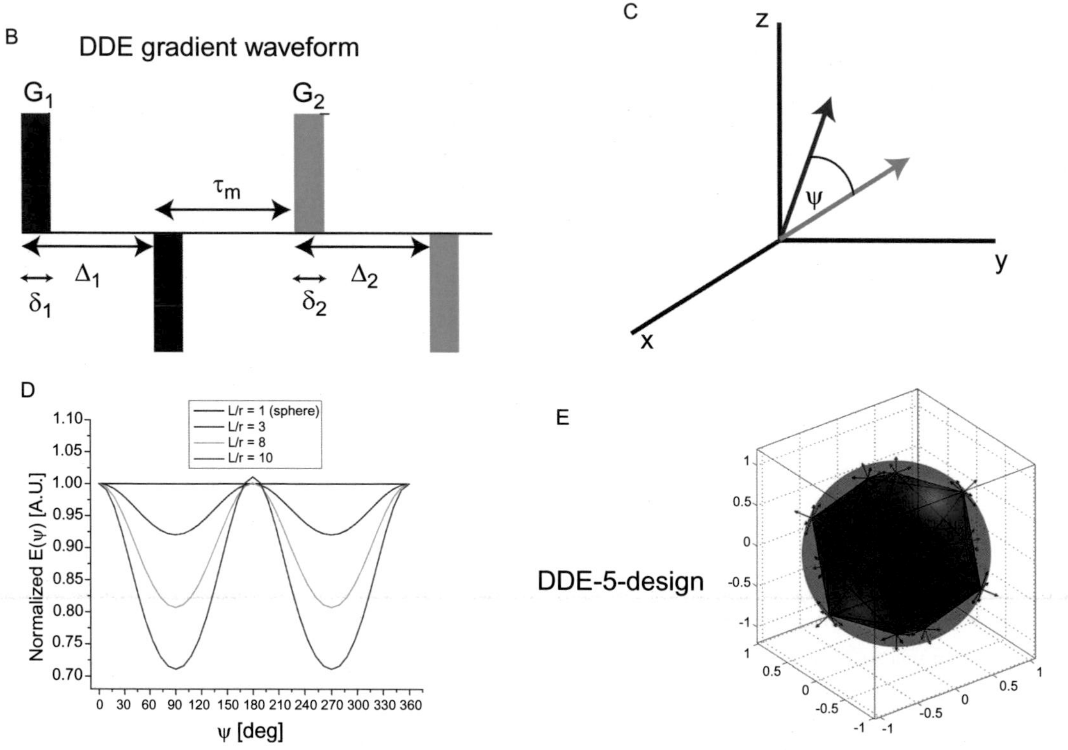

FIG. 22.7

(A) Macroscopically isotropic systems with increasing microscopic anisotropy. Even when the local pore eccentricity is increased, the overall randomly oriented fractional anisotropy (FA) remains zero. (B) The DDE gradient waveform. If the mixing time is zero, the second and third gradient lobes are superimposed. (C) A schematic of the "angular" DDE experiment, whereby the second gradient orientation is systematically rotated about the axis spanned by the first wavevector through an angle ψ. (D) The result of such a long mixing time angular DDE experiment simulated for different levels of eccentricity (the L/r ratio where L is the length of an eccentric pore and r its radius) for powder-averaged systems; note that spheres exhibit a flat behavior, while increasing eccentricities are reflected as increasing signal modulations. (E) A schematic of Jespersen's 5-design, which allows for efficient powder-averaging of DDE signals up to order 5 in q-values. The units of the axes are unit vectors.

(Panel (E): Adapted from Jespersen SN, Lundell H, Sønderby CK, Dyrby TB. Orientationally invariant metrics of apparent compartment eccentricity from double pulsed field gradient diffusion experiments. NMR Biomed 2013;26(12): 1647–62. doi:10.1002/nbm.2999.)

that this methodology could decipher the origins of kurtosis observed in SDE. In systems characterized by multiple, freely diffusing moieties making up a distribution of isotropic tensor magnitudes, angular DDE experiment would yield a constant signal as orientational correlations are irrelevant. However, Mitra [77] ingeniously predicted that, if kurtosis arises from restricted diffusion, the angular DDE signal at short mixing time and at low q-values would exhibit a unique amplitude modulation that could be considered a "signature" for the correlations introduced by restricting boundaries. In particular, Mitra showed that in the long diffusion time limit and short mixing time regime, for restricted diffusion [77]:

$$E_{DDE}(q,\Delta\rightarrow\infty,\tau_m\rightarrow 0)=\frac{S_{DDE}(q,\Delta\rightarrow\infty,\tau_m\rightarrow 0)}{S(q=0,\Delta\rightarrow\infty,\tau_m\rightarrow 0)}=1-\frac{1}{3}q^2<R_g^2>\left(1+2\cos^2\left(\frac{\theta}{2}\right)\right)+O(q^4) \tag{22.9}$$

where $q=|\mathbf{q}|=|\mathbf{q_1}|=|\mathbf{q_2}|$, where $\mathbf{q_1}$ and $\mathbf{q_2}$ are two diffusion wavevectors used in the DDE experiment, $\Delta=\Delta_1=\Delta_2$ is the diffusion time associated with the each of the diffusion-weighting epochs, $<R_g^2>$ is the pore radius of gyration, and the angle between the DDE gradients is given by $\theta=\mathbf{n_1}\ \mathbf{n_2}$, where $\mathbf{n_1}$ and $\mathbf{n_2}$ are unit vectors pointing along $\mathbf{q_1}$ and $\mathbf{q_2}$, respectively. Eq. 22.9 is remarkable since it predicts that a microstructural metric—the pore radius of gyration, which can be related for simple geometries with the pore size—can be inferred from low q-value angular DDE experiments.

This DDE amplitude modulation at short mixing time was first experimentally demonstrated by Koch and Finsterbusch in spinal cord tissues and packed beads [78], while Shemesh et al. measured the same signal modulation in a controlled system comprising microcapillaries where validation was perhaps somewhat more straightforward [79]. Indeed, compartment sizes could be readily obtained from angular DDE, demonstrating its potential as a microstructural reporter.

The angular DDE signal up to 4th order in q was derived in [80] for powder-averaged ideal pores (namely, spheres, ellipsoids, and cylinders):

$$E_{DDE}(q,\Delta\rightarrow\infty,\tau_m\rightarrow 0)=1-c_0q^2(2+\cos(\theta))+c_1q^4(c_2+c_3\cos(\theta)+c_4\cos(2\theta))+O(q^6) \tag{22.10}$$

where c_i represent geometry-specific coefficients (n.b., the $2+\cos(\theta)$ oscillation in the second order term is equivalent to the $1+2\cos^2\left(\frac{\theta}{2}\right)$ in Eq. (22.9) through elementary trigonometric identities). Interestingly, Eq. (22.10) suggests that the higher-order contribution can introduce further oscillations in DDE signals, both with $\cos(\theta)$ and with $\cos(2\theta)$, which can be confounding for estimating compartment sizes if neglected. However, Mitra had already predicted that, at longer mixing times, the higher order $\cos(2\theta)$ oscillation could yield unique information in the "local" anisotropy. The expressions were later explicitly derived for the long mixing time regime in powder-averaged systems [80]:

$$E_{DDE}(q,\Delta\rightarrow\infty,\tau_m\rightarrow\infty)=1-c_0'q^2+c_1'q^4\left(c_2'+c_3'\cos(2\theta)\right)+O(q^6) \tag{22.11}$$

where $c'_i\neq c_i$ are again geometry-specific coefficients and, importantly, $c_3'(\text{spheres})=0$. Eq. (22.11) clearly shows how the $\cos(\theta)$ oscillation in Eqs. (22.9) and (22.10) is effectively decoupled at longer mixing times, both in the 2nd and the 4th order in q-value, leaving only a 4th order $\cos(2\theta)$ oscillation.

The c_3' coefficients depend on the "local" anisotropy of the randomly oriented pores [80]. For example, for randomly oriented cylinders of radius R and length L, $c_3'\propto(3R^2-L^2)^2$ [80]. Therefore, higher the "local" anisotropy ($L>R$), the stronger the amplitude modulation in the fourth order term. This $\cos(2\theta)$ signature was verified experimentally in numerous systems [48,81,82] and has been shown to provide rich information on the underlying microstructure in heterogeneous systems. Fig. 22.7D shows how the angular DDE experiment distinguishes between equivalent FA=0 scenarios, by the depth of the signal amplitude modulation at long mixing times.

In a series of insightful papers, Jespersen and colleagues derived a general DDE signal representation using the cumulant expansion [83–85] (n.b. Lawrenz and Finsterbusch expanded the DDE signals using a Taylor expansion earlier [86]). In particular, it was shown that (assuming for simplicity, but without loss of generality, $q=|\mathbf{q}|=|\mathbf{q_1}|=|\mathbf{q_2}|$ and $\Delta=\Delta_1=\Delta_2$) the DDE signal decay follows the following expression [86]:

$$\ln\left(\frac{S_{DDE}(q,\Delta,\tau_m)}{S_0}\right) = -q^2\left(2D_{ij}\Delta - Q_{ij}\right) + q^4\left(\frac{1}{12}K_{ijkl} + \frac{1}{4}Z_{ijkl} - \frac{1}{3}S_{ijkl}\right) + O\left(q^6\right) \tag{22.12}$$

where D_{ij} is the diffusion tensor, Q_{ij} is the displacement correlation tensor, K_{ijkl} is the usual rank four kurtosis tensor, and Z_{ijkl} and S_{ijkl} are rank four displacement correlation tensors that cannot be obtained from SDE. Jespersen also showed that [85].

$$Q_{ij}(\Delta,\tau_m) = D_{ij}(2\Delta+\tau_m)\times(2\Delta+\tau_m) + D_{ij}(\tau_m)\times\tau_m - 2D_{ij}(\Delta+\tau_m)\times(\Delta+\tau_m) \tag{22.13}$$

where the notation $D_{ij}(t)\times(t)$ refers to the value of the diffusion tensor at time t, multiplied by that particular time t. Thus, the displacement tensor Q *simply reflects the time-dependence of the diffusion tensor*, and hence Mitra's short τ_m angular DDE experiment is equivalent to a time-dependent SDE experiment.

Recall that we were aiming to obtain information on the pore anisotropy irrespective of the orientation distribution function. It is thus instructive to consider the DDE signal from an ensemble of identical, locally anisotropic, yet randomly oriented pores. At the short mixing time regime ($\tau_m \ll l_c^2/2D_0$, where l_c is the characteristic length scale), Jespersen showed [83,84] that Eq. (22.12) in such a "powder-averaged" system reduces to:

$$\begin{aligned}\ln\left(\frac{S_{DDE}(q,\Delta,\tau_m)}{S(q=0,\Delta,\tau_m)}\right)^{p.a.} &= -q^2(2D\Delta - \cos\theta Q)\\ &+\frac{1}{12}q^4K_{zzzz} + \frac{1}{4}q^4\left(\cos^2\theta(Z_{zzzz}-Z_{zzxx})+Z_{zzxx}\right)\\ &-\frac{1}{3}q^4\cos\theta\, S_{zzzz}\end{aligned} \tag{22.14}$$

where θ is the angle between the DDE wavevectors, $D=\frac{Tr(\mathbf{D})}{3}$ is and $Q=\frac{Tr(\mathbf{Q})}{3}$. Eq. (22.14) beautifully reveals the origin of the oscillations described above, from the DDE signal representation perspective. At low q-values, where higher-order terms are much less important (typically, when $2\pi q l_c \ll 1$), a $\cos\theta$ dependence emerges from the Q tensor. Since the Q tensor itself reflects diffusion time-dependence (arising from restricted diffusion), this modulation can be considered a signature of restriction. At the long diffusion time regime and zero mixing time limits, the size of the compartment can be extracted from $\langle R_g^2\rangle = -3Q$, where $\langle R_g^2\rangle$is the pore radius of gyration [77]. Note however that Eq. (22.14) also shows explicitly the coupling between the $\cos\theta$ arising from the second order Q term and oscillations arising from the higher order contributions, namely, from a $\cos\theta$ coupled to the S tensor and a $\cos^2\theta$ arising from the Z tensor. These are perfectly analogous to the oscillations described above (Eqs. (22.10), (22.11), with some trigonometric conversions), but with an explicit connection to underlying tensor representations. Remarkably, Jespersen showed that at long τ_m, the tensors

Q and S approach zero since the spins "lose memory" between encodings [83]. By contrast, at long τ_m, the Z tensor does not vanish; rather, it reflects the variance of the mean squared displacement tensor over all pores (or tensors). Thus the Z tensor extracted from DDE contains information that cannot be derived from SDE.

It is useful at this point to define a new quantity, termed "microscopic anisotropy", denoted μA. Although different authors used the same term to define different quantities, we here adopt the notation provided in a recent consensus paper [31]. The μA (or more conveniently, its square μA^2) is proportional to the anisotropy in the pore (or tensor) eigenframe irrespective of orientation distribution. For an ensemble of identical pores (or tensors) with diffusion tensor D, and with arbitrary orientation distribution [31]:

$$\mu A^2 = \frac{3}{5} V_\lambda(D) = \frac{3}{5}\left((\lambda_1 - MD)^2 + (\lambda_2 - MD)^2 + (\lambda_3 - MD)^2\right) \tag{22.15}$$

where $V_\lambda(D)$ is the variance of the "individual" diffusion tensor eigenvalues and $MD = \frac{1}{3}(\lambda_1 + \lambda_2 + \lambda_3)$ is the mean diffusivity. To show how μA can provide insight into the microstructure, consider an ensemble of tensors (or pores represented by tensors) with different diffusion tensors D_i, where "i" denotes the ith component. The diffusion coefficient of the entire ensemble is then $D = <D_i>$ where $<>$ denotes an ensemble average. The total fractional anisotropy of the system, as obtained by, for example, SDE measurements, will be defined as [10]:

$$FA = \sqrt{\frac{3}{2}\frac{V_\lambda(<D_i>)}{V_\lambda(<D_i>) + (Tr(<D_i>)/3)^2}} = \sqrt{\frac{3}{2}\frac{V_\lambda(D)}{V_\lambda(D) + (Tr(D)/3)^2}} \tag{22.16}$$

Eq. (22.16) shows that the FA depends on the variance of the ensemble average over all tensors, $V_\lambda(<D_i>) = V_\lambda(D)$. If the tensors are completely randomly oriented, the ensemble averaging produces FA = 0, in contrast with the microscopic anisotropy which will still reflect the anisotropy present in the system.

Like FA, μA can be scaled such that its values range between zero and one. The microscopic FA (μFA) is then defined, for an individual pore, as [31]:

$$\mu FA_i = \sqrt{\frac{3}{2}\frac{V_\lambda(D_i)}{V_\lambda(D_i) + (Tr(D_i)/3)^2}} \tag{22.17}$$

while for the entire ensemble of pores [87]:

$$\mu FA = \sqrt{\frac{3}{2}\frac{\langle V_\lambda(D_i)\rangle}{\langle V_\lambda(D_i)\rangle + (\langle Tr(D_i)\rangle/3)^2}} \tag{22.18}$$

where brackets again indicate averaging. As can be appreciated from Eq. (22.18), the variance of the individual tensors D_i is averaged, thereby providing an accurate measure of the (average) microscopic anisotropy in the ensemble.

With this result, the real usefulness of DDE, especially in powder-averaged systems, becomes apparent. By varying the angle between the gradients at long mixing times, the Q and S oscillations are suppressed (Eq. 22.14), and an oscillation proportional to the displacement tensor's (Z_{zzzz} - Z_{zzxx}) elements—which directly reflect the microscopic anisotropy (Eq. 22.19)—emerges. Once (Z_{zzzz} - Z_{zzxx}) is estimated from the oscillation amplitude, at long mixing times, the microscopic anisotropy can be estimated by [83,84]:

$$\mu A^2 = \frac{(Z_{zzzz} - Z_{zzxx})}{4\Delta^2} \tag{22.19}$$

where $\Delta \equiv \Delta_1 = \Delta_2$. $\langle V_\lambda(D_i)\rangle$, i.e., the variance of the "individual" diffusion tensor eigenvalues, then follows immediately. The mean diffusivity can be estimated from the parallel, $\theta = 0$ experiments, and together with $\langle V_\lambda(D_i)\rangle$, can be used in Eq. (22.19) to compute the μFA. Therefore, a simple DDE measurement facilitates the assessment of microscopic anisotropy.

A major assumption of the calculations above is that the microstructure is "powder-averaged," that is, that pores are completely randomly oriented. In real-life systems, this is certainly not guaranteed. Jespersen et al. resolved this potentially confounding factor by proposing a spherical sampling scheme that powder-averages *signals measured in different orientations*, thereby mimicking powder-averaged systems [83] (Fig. 22.7E). The so-called 5-design (Fig. 22.7E) produces sufficient powder averaging up to 5th order in q, and the μA can be easily obtained from [83]:

$$\log \overline{E_{||}} / \overline{E_{\perp}} = \mu A^2 b^2 + O(b^3) \tag{22.20}$$

where $\overline{E_{||}}$ and $\overline{E_{\perp}}$ are the normalized powder-averaged parallel and perpendicular ($\theta = \frac{\pi}{2}$) signals, respectively, from the DDE 5-design [83].

μFA has been measured using DDE in many different systems ranging from ex vivo tissues [87,88] to in vivo human brains [89–92]. As expected, μFA is typically higher than its FA counterpart, especially in areas of crossing fibers where orientation dispersion effects tend to make FA appear low (Fig. 22.8). Thus, μFA is a potentially powerful metric for quantifying microstructure in disordered systems, including in vivo on clinical scanners [89–91]. The only assumption for μFA quantification is that experiments are in long τ_m limit [83], which can be tested empirically by comparing signals at

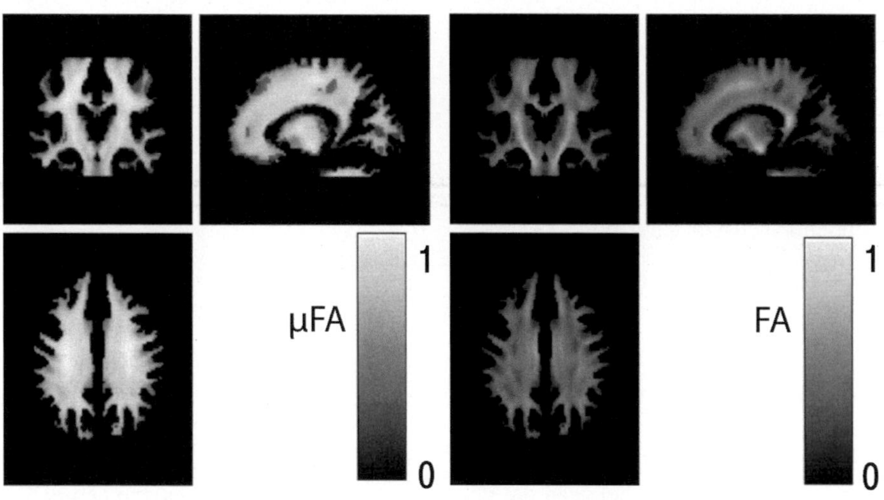

FIG. 22.8

A comparison of μFA and FA in human white matter in vivo. μFA exhibits much higher values in white matter, suggesting that it is robust towards orientation dispersion effects.

(Adapted from Lawrenz M, Brassen S, Finsterbusch J. Microscopic diffusion anisotropy in the human brain: reproducibility, normal values, and comparison with the fractional anisotropy. Neuroimage 2015;109:283–297. doi:10.1016/j.neuroimage.2015.01.025.)

$\theta = 0$ and $\theta = \pi$. At long τ_m, the signals should be identical (up to noise), since the Q and S terms in Eq. (22.14) will vanish. Time or frequency dependencies can provide additional information on the underlying microstructure [93].

Some practical issues with DDE, however, include potentially long echo times due to long mixing and diffusion times [94]. In addition, the 5-design requires many distinct measurements, making the acquisition quite long. The McNab group recently suggested a simplified orientation sampling scheme that still produces powder-averaged signals from only 12 acquisitions (compared to 72 in the 5-design) under the explicit assumption that diffusion is approximately Gaussian [95]. This acceleration is promising for future DDE application—along with other variants [95,96] facilitating the characterization of smaller dimensions [88,97]—in clinical settings. Another potential source of error in microscopic anisotropy quantification arises from higher-order terms, which may bias the extracted metrics [88,93]. Several correction schemes have been recently proposed, increasing accuracy though compromising precision to some extent, and in any case requiring several "shells" of the 5-design to be acquired [88,93], which can increase scan time.

22.3.1.2 Spherical mean representations

Generalizing the powder-averaging concepts mentioned above, the diffusion-driven signal decay with a gradient waveform $\boldsymbol{G}$ can be considered to be a convolution between an arbitrary microstructural kernel $\mathcal{K}$ and an orientation distribution function $\mathcal{P}(\boldsymbol{n})$, explicitly [63,98,99]:

$$S_{G}(b) = S_0 \int_{|\boldsymbol{n}|=1} d\boldsymbol{n}\, \mathcal{P}(\boldsymbol{n}) \mathcal{K}(b, \boldsymbol{G} \cdot \boldsymbol{n}) \tag{22.21}$$

where $\boldsymbol{n}$ is an orientation vector, $\boldsymbol{G}$ is the diffusion gradient, and b is the b-value associated with the measurement. Note how microstructural information and orientational information can be conflated in a single measurement (Eq. 22.21). In 1979, Callaghan et al. showed that the kernel can be estimated in some cases irrespective of the orientation distribution function by performing a spherical mean (referred to above as "powder averaging") of the signal [98]. The orientation distribution can then be factorized out of Eq. (22.21), facilitating the estimation of the microstructural kernel alone. For example, in a system characterized by a single anisotropic tensor with parallel and perpendicular diffusivities, $D_{\parallel}$ and $D_{\perp}$, respectively (arbitrary orientation dispersion), Callaghan [98], Kroenke et al. [99], and later Kaden et al. [100] showed that the powder-averaged SDE signal attenuation will follow:

$$\overline{S}(b)_{SDE} = S_0 e^{-(bD_{\perp})} \frac{\sqrt{\pi}}{2} \frac{\mathrm{erf}\left(\sqrt{b(D_{\parallel} - D_{\perp})}\right)}{\sqrt{b(D_{\parallel} - D_{\perp})}} \tag{22.22}$$

where $\overline{S}$ represents a powder average of diffusion-weighted signals measured with gradient orientations distributed on a sphere, and erf(x) is the error function. Here, the kernel parameters ($D_{\parallel}$ and $D_{\perp}$) can be estimated by fitting $\overline{S}$ (measured with at least two b-values) to Eq. (22.22). Such rotationally invariant schemes [101] have recently (re)gained popularity and extended to different kernels; however, the fitting landscapes are typically very flat [87,101,102], and it can be difficult to map the kernel parameters accurately, especially with a small number of b-values. To stabilize the fit, different constraints are typically imposed: e.g., assuming that the tissue is characterized by a single, time-independent diffusion tensor [100], which the tortuosity assumption [103] holds, or trying to estimate the orientation distribution directly, without spherical averaging, while assuming fixed diffusivity [104]. However, some of these constraints are unrealistic in living tissues [87]. Other methods for estimating $\mathcal{K}$ with better accuracy have been put forward but they also typically require the acquisition of more b-values [105].

22.3.1.3 b-tensor representations

Powder-averaging approaches inherently require multiple acquisitions in different orientations for every b-value shell, which can sometimes prove to be prohibitively time-consuming. However, the diffusion tensor trace is rotationally invariant; therefore, a single measurement encompassing three successive diffusion encodings (termed here "isotropic triple diffusion encoding, ITDE, because it is designed to measure the isotropic part of the diffusion tensor—its trace) along three orthogonal axes can provide a signal decay weighted by the tensor trace $\frac{S(b)_{ITDE}}{S_0} = e^{-3bTr(\boldsymbol{D})}$ (assuming that the three diffusion weightings are all identical in magnitude and that the system comprises a single diffusion tensor with an arbitrary orientation distribution function) [106]. IDTE thus introduces a rapid means for measuring the magnitude of the diffusion tensor from just a single measurement. However, performing three successive diffusion encodings renders the IDTE echo time inherently long, thereby reducing sensitivity.

A renewed surge of interest in isotropic diffusion encoding (IDE) techniques emerged from the development of "magic angle spinning of the q-vector" (qMAS) approach in 2013 (Fig. 22.9) [107]. Eriksson et al. [107] realized that the diffusion weighting q-vector could be rotated in space, averaging the diffusion tensor's anisotropic components to zero (much like MAS does to chemical shift anisotropy in solid-state NMR). The trace of the diffusion tensor then governs the diffusion-driven signal decay—just like in an ITDE experiment [108] (under the assumption that kurtosis arising from restricted diffusion is negligible [109]).

This concept was later generalized by decomposing the diffusion tensor into isotropic, anisotropic, and asymmetric components. Given that the diffusion tensor is defined as the symmetric 3×3 matrix $D = \begin{pmatrix} D_{xx} & D_{xy} & D_{xz} \\ D_{yx} & D_{yy} & D_{yz} \\ D_{zx} & D_{zy} & D_{zz} \end{pmatrix}$, it can be shown that [108]

$$D = D_{iso}\left\{\begin{pmatrix} 1 & 0 & 0 \\ 0 & 1 & 0 \\ 0 & 0 & 1 \end{pmatrix} + D_\Delta\left[\begin{pmatrix} -1 & 0 & 0 \\ 0 & -1 & 0 \\ 0 & 0 & 2 \end{pmatrix} + D_\eta\begin{pmatrix} -1 & 0 & 0 \\ 0 & 1 & 0 \\ 0 & 0 & 0 \end{pmatrix}\right]\right\} \tag{22.23}$$

where D_{iso} is the isotropic diffusivity, D_Δ represents the normalized anisotropy ($D_\Delta = \frac{(D_{\|} - D_{\perp})}{3D_{iso}}$), and D_η is the diffusion tensor asymmetry, which is typically assumed to be zero.

Assuming again time-independent diffusion (and for now, also just a single tensor), the signal decay can be generally written as $\frac{S(\boldsymbol{b})}{S_0} = e^{-\boldsymbol{b}:\boldsymbol{D}}$, where $\boldsymbol{b}:\boldsymbol{D} = \sum_i \sum_j b_{ij} D_{ij}$, and b is the weighting tensor $\boldsymbol{b} = \int_0^{TE} dt q(t)^2 \boldsymbol{n}(t)^T \boldsymbol{n}(t)$ where $q(t) = \gamma \int_0^t dt' \boldsymbol{G}(t')$. The tensor nature of the b-matrix is key here since the ensuing b-tensor can be parameterized by [108]:

$$\boldsymbol{b} = \frac{b}{3}\left\{\begin{pmatrix} 1 & 0 & 0 \\ 0 & 1 & 0 \\ 0 & 0 & 1 \end{pmatrix} + b_\Delta\left[\begin{pmatrix} -1 & 0 & 0 \\ 0 & -1 & 0 \\ 0 & 0 & 2 \end{pmatrix} + b_\eta\begin{pmatrix} -1 & 0 & 0 \\ 0 & 1 & 0 \\ 0 & 0 & 0 \end{pmatrix}\right]\right\} \tag{22.24}$$

where b, b_Δ and b_η are the isotropic, anisotropic, and asymmetric representations of the b-matrix (Fig. 22.10A). Following Topgaard's notation [108], assuming that $D_\eta = 0$, the product is now solely a function of the orientation of the diffusion tensor within the b-tensor frame of reference. That is, $\boldsymbol{b}:\boldsymbol{D} = bD(\alpha, \beta)$ where

$$D(\alpha, \beta) = D_1 \sin^2\beta \sin^2\alpha + D_2 \sin^2\beta \cos^2\alpha + D_3 \cos^2\beta \tag{22.25}$$

and

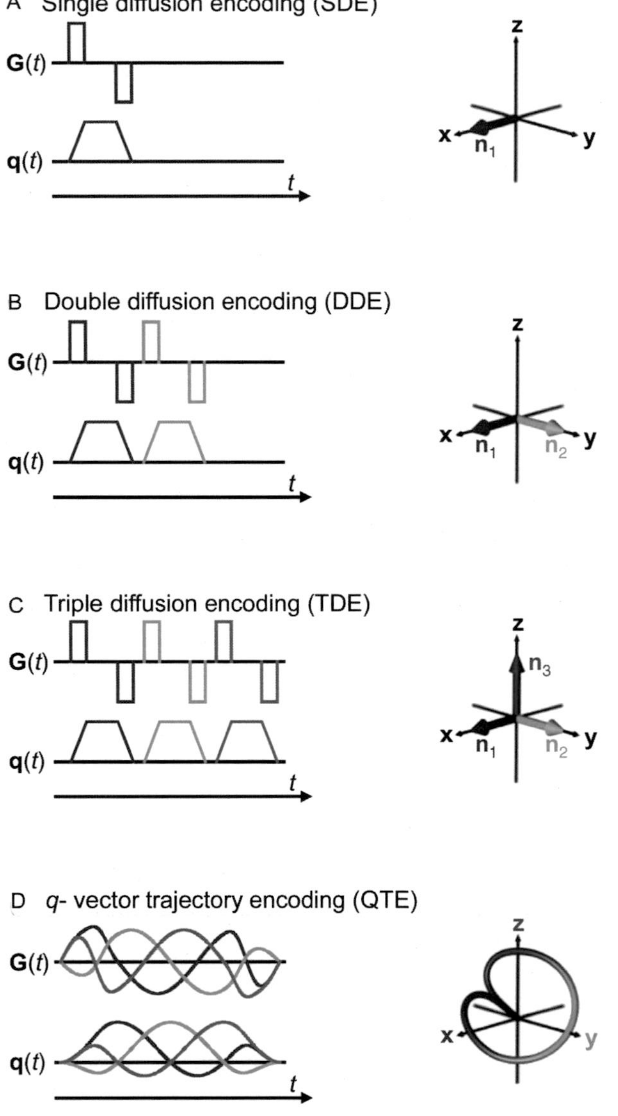

FIG. 22.9

Generalized encoding schemes and their orientational encoding. (A) Single diffusion encoding (SDE) corresponds to a single direction vector. (B) DDE spans a plane from its two wavevectors. (C) (Isotropic) triple diffusion encoding spans a magic angle that encodes the trace of the diffusion tensor. (D) QTE oscillates the gradient orientation, producing spherical tensor encoding when the oscillation is about the magic angle. Note that the vectors on the right reflect the trajectories of the *q*-vector.

(Adapted from Topgaard D. Multidimensional diffusion MRI. J Magn Reson 2017;275:98–113. doi:10.1016/j.jmr.2016.12.007.)

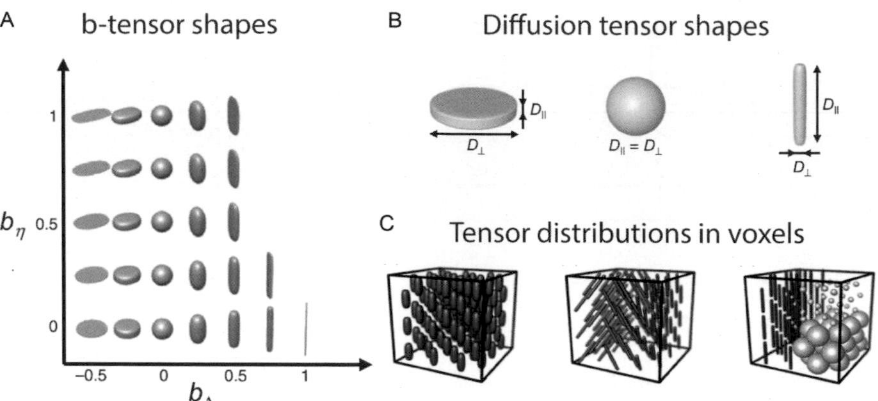

FIG. 22.10

Concepts of *q*-trajectory encoding. (A) *b*-tensor shapes encoded through different waveforms, that serve as the filter for the diffusion tensor. (B) Diffusion tensor shapes that are "filtered" by a particular *b*-tensor shape. For example, if a spherical *b*-tensor shape is used, only the isotropic parts of the diffusion tensor "pass" that filter and are encoded in the signal decay, which is then proportional to the trace of the diffusion tensor. (C) A conceptual scheme considering the voxel as a sum of different types of tensors.

(Adapted from Topgaard D. Multidimensional diffusion MRI. J Magn Reson 2017;275:98–113. doi:10.1016/j.jmr.2016.12.007.)

$$\begin{aligned} D_1 &= D_{iso}\left(1 - D_\Delta b_\Delta\left(1 + b_\eta\right)\right) \\ D_2 &= D_{iso}\left(1 - D_\Delta b_\Delta\left(1 - b_\eta\right)\right) \\ D_3 &= D_{iso}\left(1 + 2D_\Delta b_\Delta\right) \end{aligned} \tag{22.26}$$

(cf. Fig. 22.10B), and (α, β) are the angles between the diffusion tensor and the *b*-tensor frame. Importantly, Eqs. (22.25), (22.26) suggest a new conceptual framework for imparting diffusion encoding using the *b*-tensor shape, which will govern how different diffusion tensor elements contribute to the signal decay. For example, waveforms nullifying b_Δ, such as qMAS or IDTE, can be constructed; the diffusivities in Eq. (22.26) then become identical to D_{iso}.

Eq. (22.24) can also be rewritten to explicitly represent a *b*-tensor geometry in terms of spherical, planar, and linear components [108]:

$$\boldsymbol{b} = \frac{b_s}{3}\left\{\begin{pmatrix} 1 & 0 & 0 \\ 0 & 1 & 0 \\ 0 & 0 & 1 \end{pmatrix} + \frac{b_p}{2}\begin{pmatrix} 0 & 0 & 0 \\ 0 & 1 & 0 \\ 0 & 0 & 1 \end{pmatrix} + b_L\begin{pmatrix} 0 & 0 & 0 \\ 0 & 0 & 0 \\ 0 & 0 & 1 \end{pmatrix}\right\} \tag{22.27}$$

where b_s represents the spherical encoding part of the tensor, b_p represents a planar encoding, and b_L represents a linear encoding. Assuming that $b_\eta = 0$ [108]:

$$\boldsymbol{b} : \boldsymbol{D} = b_s D_{iso} + b_L D_{iso}\left(1 + 2D_\Delta P_2(\cos\beta)\right) \tag{22.28}$$

where $P_2(\cos\beta) = \frac{1}{2}(3\cos^2\beta\text{-}1)$. Therefore, by choosing different wavevector encoding "geometries", different parts of the diffusion tensor can be probed. For a more detailed discussion on waveform design, the reader is referred to [110–112].

When the tissue is described by a distribution of diffusion tensors *P*(*D*), with varying shapes and magnitudes, varying the *b*-tensor magnitude and shape in a multidimensional fashion can provide information on the underlying distribution [113–116]. While a detailed exposition of such experiments is beyond the scope of this book chapter, it is worth noting that quantities such as the second moment of the D_{iso} distribution, the volume fraction of D_{iso}, and the microscopic anisotropy can be resolved [113–116]. For example, the cumulant expansion for b-tensor encoding can be written as $\frac{S(b)}{S_0} = e^{-b<D> + \frac{1}{2}b^2\mu_2 + \frac{1}{6}b^3\mu_3 + O(b^4)}$, where, $<D> = \int_0^\infty dDP(D)D$, and $\mu_n = \int_0^\infty dD(D - <D>)^n P(D)$, are the moments of the distribution (Fig. 22.10C) [113]. The moments can be related to metrics obtainable from b-tensor encoding, in particular, $<D> = <D_{iso}>$, $\mu_2 = \frac{4}{5} < D^2_{aniso} > f_2 + V(D_{iso})$ where $<D^2_{aniso}>$ is the mean squared anisotropic diffusivity, $f_2 = b^2_\Delta \frac{b^2_\eta + 3}{3}$ and $V(D_{iso})$ is the variance of the isotropic diffusivity in the sample.

22.3.2 Tissue models

The signal representation approaches above may be extremely useful and informative, but they lack specificity to underlying biological components such as, e.g., cell bodies, neurites, astrocytic branches, synapse, extracellular matrix, etc. The tissue model approach assigns putative signal decays to each of underlying the components assumed in the model and fits the unknown model parameters (compartment size, density, etc.) to the experimental data [117,118]. The tissue model can be constructed generally as:

$$E(b)_{SDE} = \sum_{n=1}^{N} f_n S_n \tag{22.29}$$

where n is the component index, f_n is the volume fraction, and S_n is a signal associated with component "n," whether it is free diffusion or restricted diffusion in a cylinder of radius R, for example. It is then tempting to try to assign specific biological components to the extracted fractions. For example, early on, diffusion in neural tissue was thought to comprise of exactly two distinct Gaussian components associated with the intra- and extracellular spaces, leading to $E(b)_{SDE} = f_{intra} e^{-bD_{intra}} + (1 - f_{intra}) e^{-bD_{extra}}$, where f_{intra} is the intracellular volume fraction, and D_{intra} and D_{extra} are the intracellular and extracellular ADCs, respectively [119], and the signal fractions sum to unity. The implicit assumption would be that $N = 2$, $S_n = e^{-bD_n}$, and the extracted fractions and diffusivities could be assigned to intra/extracellular spaces. Note that another implicit assumption is that diffusion kurtosis for both intra- and extracellular components is zero as only the first term is included in the cumulant expansion. Another early suggestion involved spheres and sticks representing diffusion in cell bodies and diffusion in neurites, respectively [120]. Such approaches have evolved very rapidly, with ever-increasing model complexity (based on solutions to diffusion in different geometries [13,121]) attempting to extract increasingly more specific microstructural features. AxCaliber [122,123] for example, assumes that the diffusion signal can be represented by two components: a hindered Gaussian diffusion mode, typically associated with extraaxonal and cerebrospinal fluid water pools, and a component undergoing restricted diffusion in infinite cylinders with a predefined (radial) size distribution. AxCaliber's radius distribution has been tentatively ascribed to intra-axonal water [122,123].

Tissue models can indeed provide useful contrast between tissues if applied consistently [117,124]. However, the association of the extracted metrics to a specific biological component is often debatable. For example, the simple intra/extracellular model described above yields volume fractions that are inconsistent with the actual intracellular or extracellular fractions known from biology [125,126]. The fitting landscape of such models is very flat and, in some cases, also ill-posed [87,101,105].

For example, assuming that the system is comprised of a distribution of diffusion tensors $P(D)$, the SDE signal decay can be written as: $E(b)_{SDE} = \int dDP(D)e^{-bD}$, an ill-posed inverse Laplace transform of $P(D)$. The issue is unfortunately similar for axon diameter mapping: the metrics extracted from AxCaliber overestimate the histologically measured average axon diameter by a factor of more than three and in some cases more than five [127]. This underscores the importance of validation when choosing a model, and how difficult model selection can be in practice [63].

We conclude that that tissue models can be used to contrast differences between groups [128,129], but assignments to specific biological components should be exercised with great care.

22.3.3 Biophysical models

Quite complementarily to tissue models, the rapidly evolving field of biophysical modeling in the context of microstructural diffusion MRI seeks to derive functional forms of the signal decay which can *inform* on underlying features in the system. This is best illustrated by an example. Suppose we believe that white matter tissue consists of small axons (sticks) and extraaxonal space. The diffusion-driven signal attenuation from the former is then negligible in the radial direction ($D_{\perp} \rightarrow 0$); the extraaxonal water is assumed to diffuse with a simple tensor. Given Eqs. (22.21), (22.22), the normalized powder-averaged SDE signal can then be written as $E_{SDE}^{WM}(b) = f_a E_a(b) + f_e E_e(b), f_a + f_e = 1, f_a$ and f_e represent the intra-axonal and extraaxonal water fractions, respectively, and E_a and E_e represents the respective signal attenuations, where $E_a = \frac{\mathrm{erf}\left(\sqrt{b(D_{a\|})}\right)}{\sqrt{b(D_{a\|})}}$ and $E_e = e^{-bD_{e\perp}} \frac{\sqrt{\pi}}{2} \frac{\mathrm{erf}\left(\sqrt{b(D_{e\|} - D_{e\perp})}\right)}{\sqrt{b(D_{e\|} - D_{e\perp})}}$ and subscripts reflect each component. The term associated with extraaxonal space will vanish at high b-values (larger than $b_{\min}$ for which $E_e << E_a$) leaving $E_{SDE}^{WM}(b > b_{min}) = \frac{f_a}{\sqrt{b(D_{a\|})}}$. Notice the "peculiar" $b^{-\frac{1}{2}}$ scaling, which is predictive of the model's functional accuracy—"stick-like" diffusion will always provide this form of attenuation. This $b^{-\frac{1}{2}}$ scaling has been observed for N-acetyl aspartate (NAA) diffusing in neurons [99] and more recently for water diffusion in white matter [130] (Fig. 22.11). Effective axonal diameters can even be derived from a regime in which the power law breaks, thereby supplying ample microstructural parameters for imaging [130].

Other scaling laws involving diffusion time dependence [131] were recently proposed by Novikov et al. to reveal different "disorder regimes" [132]. In the short time regime [24], given a free diffusivity D_0 and spatial degrees of freedom d, the SDE and (cosine modulated) OGSE waveforms follow [133]:

$$D_{SDE}(t) = D_0\left(1 - \frac{4}{3d\sqrt{\pi}} \frac{S}{V} \sqrt{D_0 t}\right) + O(D_0 t) \tag{22.30}$$

$$D_{OGSE}(\omega) = D_0\left(1 - \frac{c(N)}{d\sqrt{2}} \frac{S}{V} \sqrt{\frac{D_0}{\omega}}\right) + O\left(\frac{D_0}{\omega}\right)$$

where $C(N)$ is a correction factor depending on the number of oscillations in the OGSE, and S/V is the surface-to-volume ratio. At very short diffusion times, the S/V ratio and free diffusivities can be obtained from plotting the diffusivity as a function of $\sqrt{t}$ or $\frac{1}{\sqrt{\omega}}$ (Fig. 22.12).

At the very long-time regime, diffusion coefficients approach a tortuosity-limited diffusivity $D_{SDE\infty} \rightarrow \frac{D_0}{\alpha}$ where α is the tortuosity of the medium [25,134]. A new treatment for the long-time

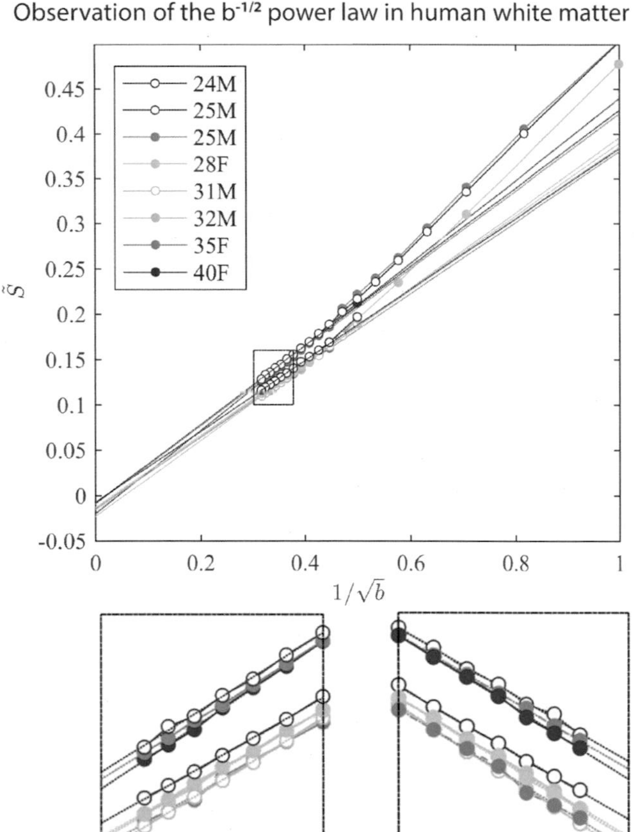

FIG. 22.11

The $1/\sqrt{b}$ power law was observed for the predicted range of *b*-values (box in the *top panel*), suggesting that a fraction of sticks is present in human white matter in vivo. The assignment to intra-axonal space is made based on other considerations, and remains to be proven and validated.

(Adapted from Veraart J, Fieremans E, Novikov DS. On the scaling behavior of water diffusion in human brain white matter. Neuroimage 2019;15:379–387. doi:10.1016/j.neuroimage.2018.09.075.)

regime by Novikov et al. revealed that the manner with which the diffusivity approaches the tortuosity limit reflects degrees of structural disorder [132] via:

$$D_{inst}(t) \approx D_{\infty} + c \cdot t^{-\theta} \tag{22.31}$$

where D_{inst} is the instantaneous diffusion coefficient given by the time derivative of the root mean squared displacement, c is a constant, and $\theta = \frac{p+d}{2}$, where p is the structural exponent representing coarse-grained spatial correlations and d is the spatial dimension. Novikov et al. classified the

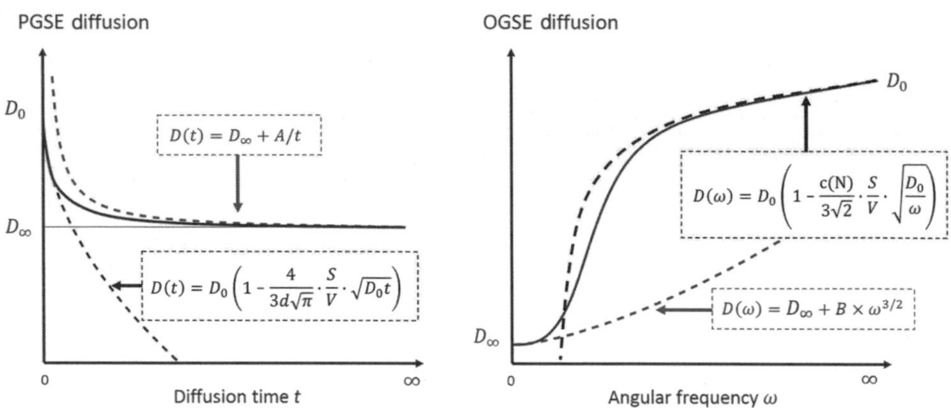

FIG. 22.12

Decay curves in porous systems as function of diffusion time *(left)* or frequency of the oscillating gradient spin echo (OGSE) oscillation *(right)* along with the expressions for the asymptotic tendencies.

(Adapted from Reynaud O. Time-dependent diffusion MRI in cancer: tissue modeling and applications. Front Physiol 2017; 5(58):1–16. doi:10.3389/fphy.2017.00058.)

coarse-grained landscape to three main classes: ordered ($p = \infty$), short-range disorder ($p = 0, \theta = \frac{d}{2}$), and extended disorder ($p = -(d-1), \theta = \frac{1}{2}$ or $p = -(d-2)$, $\theta = 1$), (c.f. Fig. 22.13). The $t^{-\theta}$ scaling thus allows contrasting between these disorder "universality classes".

Finally, we note in passing the neurite density model, one of the most widely used biophysical models in neural tissues, which can reveal the neurite density with relatively few assumptions [135–139].

22.4 Frontiers of microstructural MRI

A major challenge in microstructural imaging involves enhancing the specificity of MRI signals without compromising sensitivity. We can identify several avenues that could assist in this:

(1) Magnetic Resonance Spectroscopy (MRS). Especially at ultrahigh fields, MRS can reduce the complexity of diffusion experiments due to the specific compartmentalization of observable metabolites, such as NAA (concentrated nearly only in neurons [140]) or myo-inositol (predominantly astrocytic [141]). Applying advanced diffusion MRS acquisitions [142–144] can provide cell-specific morphologies, which may advance our understanding of the diffusion physics in tissues [99,143,145–149] as well as enhance diagnostic capacities.

(2) Tissue-inspired modeling. Rather than making the simplifying assumptions of simple geometric shapes for particular microstructural features, a new branch of modeling reconstructs the tissue from real 3D microscopy, thereby enabling a more specific simulation of the relative contribution of specific tissue elements such as cell bodies, axons, branches, etc., and providing a better framework for modeling [143,147,150]. With the ever-increasing microscopy capacity, such modeling is expected to prevail in the future over the over-simplified geometric models.

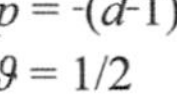

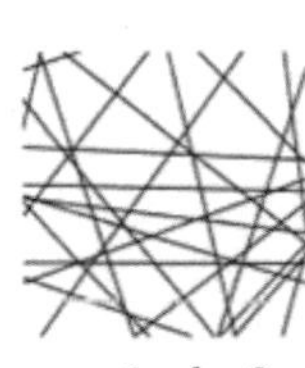

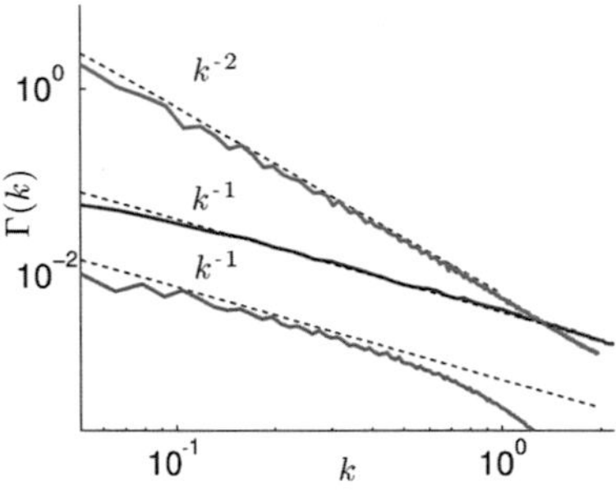

FIG. 22.13

Structural disorder classes. (A) Uncorrelated structure. (B) Periodic structure. (C) Extended disorder, where permeable random membranes are present in the voxel. (D) Extended disorder for impermeable random rods. (E) The corresponding *k*-space density correlation functions reveal the very different nature of the examples given in C and D, which underlies their differentiation through the power-law time dependencies.

(Adapted from Novikov DS, Jensen JH, Helpern JA, Fieremans E. Revealing mesoscopic structural universality with diffusion. Proc Natl Acad Sci U S A 2014;111(14):5088–93. doi:10.1073/pnas.1316944111.)

(3) Multidimensional acquisitions. Just as multidimensional acquisitions transformed NMR and enabled it to deliver very specific information in overlapping spectra using additional dimensions [151], we expect that diffusion MRI can be coupled to other quantification techniques such as relaxometry [152,153] or alternatively, as in porous media [22,154,155], be performed in multiple dimensions within a single experiment to resolve exchange. With increasingly more accurate axon diameter mapping [156], such methods will perhaps aid in resolving additional parameters, such as the g-ratio [157,158], whose mapping can be important in neuroscience and biomedical applications.

22.5 Summary

This chapter introduced several different concepts for mapping tissue microstructure, from imaging the pore density function to mapping coarse-grained parameters reflecting the microscopic correlations in the sample. The different approaches vary in specificity, sensitivity, and underlying assumptions and entail varying levels of accuracy and precision. With the increasing level of sophistication in methods and hardware, more specific microstructural quantification is expected to move into use for the improved characterization of disease and healthy processes.

Acknowledgments

The author is indebted to his many collaborators and friends for countless hours of discussions, exchanges, and debates on diffusion MR over the years. In particular, the author would like to especially thank the following: Prof. Yoram Cohen, Prof. Lucio Frydman, Prof. Sune Jespersen, Prof. Daniel Alexander, Prof. Yaniv Assaf, Dr. Gonzalo Augustin Alvarez, Prof. Mark Does, Prof. Ivana Drobnjak, Prof. Els Fieremans, Prof. Jurgen Finsterbusch, Prof. Samuel Grant, Dr. Rafael Neto Henriques, Dr. Andrada Ianus, Prof. Derek Jones, Prof. Valerij Kiselev, Prof. Denis Le Bihan, Prof. Jennifer McNab, Prof. Karla Miller, Prof. Markus Nilsson, Prof. Dmitry Novikov, Mr. Jonas Lynge Olesen, Dr. Evren Ozarlsan, Dr. Marco Palombo, Prof. Itamar Ronen, Prof. Julien Valette, and Prof. Jelle Veraart. In addition, thanks go to Ms. Francisca Fernandes for editorial assistance with this Book Chapter and the Shemesh Lab in Champalimaud Center for the Unknown.

References

[1] Johansen-Berg H, TEJ B. Diffusion MRI: from quantitative measurement to in vivo neuroanatomy. Elsevier/Academic Press; 2009. https://doi.org/10.1016/B978-0-12-374709-9.X0001-6.

[2] Tzur A, Kafri R, LeBleu VS, Lahav G, Kirschner MW. Cell growth and size homeostasis in proliferating animal cells. Science 2009;325(5937):167–71. https://doi.org/10.1126/science.1174294.

[3] Lai WS, Xu B, Westphal KGC, Paterlini M, Olivier B, Pavlidis P, Karayiorgou M, Gogos JA. Akt1 deficiency affects neuronal morphology and predisposes to abnormalities in prefrontal cortex functioning. Proc Natl Acad Sci U S A 2006;103(45):16906–11. https://doi.org/10.1073/pnas.0604994103.

[4] Hardy J, Selkoe DJ. The amyloid hypothesis of Alzheimer's disease: progress and problems on the road to therapeutics. Science 2002;297(5580):353–6. https://doi.org/10.1126/science.1072994.

[5] Budde MD, Frank JA. Neurite beading is sufficient to decrease the apparent diffusion coefficient after ischemic stroke. Proc Natl Acad Sci U S A 2010;107(32):14472–7. https://doi.org/10.1073/pnas.1004841107.

[6] Caminiti R, Carducci F, Piervincenzi C, Battaglia-Mayer A, Confalone G, Visco-Comandini F, Pantano P, Innocenti GM. Diameter, length, speed, and conduction delay of callosal axons in macaque monkeys and humans: comparing data from histology and magnetic resonance imaging diffusion tractography. J Neurosci 2013;33(36):14501–11. https://doi.org/10.1523/JNEUROSCI.0761-13.2013.

[7] Caminiti R, Ghaziri H, Galuske R, Hof PR, Innocenti GM. Evolution amplified processing with temporally dispersed slow neuronal connectivity in primates. Proc Natl Acad Sci U S A 2009;106(46):19551–6. https://doi.org/10.1073/pnas.0907655106.

[8] Stahon KE, Bastian C, Griffith S, Kidd GJ, Brunet S, Baltan S. Age-related changes in axonal and mitochondrial ultrastructure and function in white matter. J Neurosci 2016;36(39):9990–10001. https://doi.org/10.1523/jneurosci.1316-16.2016.

[9] Nikić I, Merkler D, Sorbara C, Brinkoetter M, Kreutzfeldt M, Bareyre FM, Brück W, Bishop D, Misgeld T, Kerschensteiner M. A reversible form of axon damage in experimental autoimmune encephalomyelitis and multiple sclerosis. Nat Med 2011;17(4):495–9. https://doi.org/10.1038/nm.2324.

[10] Price WS. Pulsed-field gradient nuclear magnetic resonance as a tool for studying translational diffusion: part II. Experimental aspects. Concepts Magn Reson 1998;10(4):197–237. https://doi.org/10.1002/(SICI)1099-0534(1998)10:4<197::AID-CMR1>3.0.CO;2-S.

[11] Cohen Y, Avram L, Evan-Salem T, Slovak S, Shemesh N, Frish L. Diffusion NMR in supramolecular chemistry and complexed systems. In: Schalley CA, (Ed.), Analytical methods in supramolecular chemistry. 2012. p. 197–285. https://doi.org/10.1002/9783527644131.ch6.

[12] Metzler R, Klafter J. The random walk's guide to anomalous diffusion: a fractional dynamics approach. Phys Rep 2000;339(1):1–77. https://doi.org/10.1016/s0370-15730000070-3.

[13] Neuman CH. Spin echo of spins diffusing in a bounded medium. J Chem Phys 1974;60(11):4508–11. https://doi.org/10.1063/1.1680931.

[14] Grebenkov DS. NMR survey of reflected Brownian motion. Rev Mod Phys 2007;79(3):1077–137. https://doi.org/10.1103/RevModPhys.79.1077.

[15] Le Bihan D. Looking into the functional architecture of the brain with diffusion MRI. Nat Rev Neurosci 2003;4(6):469–80. https://doi.org/10.1038/nrn1119.

[16] Jespersen SN. White matter biomarkers from diffusion MRI. J Magn Reson 2018;291:127–40. https://doi.org/10.1016/j.jmr.2018.03.001.

[17] Beaulieu C. The basis of anisotropic water diffusion in the nervous system—a technical review. NMR Biomed 2002;15(7–8):435–55. https://doi.org/10.1002/nbm.782.

[18] Sen PN. Diffusion and tissue microstructure. J Phys Condens Matter 2004;16(44):5213–20. https://doi.org/10.1088/0953-8984/16/44/018.

[19] Zatorre RJ, Fields RD, Johansen-Berg H. Plasticity in gray and white: neuroimaging changes in brain structure during learning. Nat Neurosci 2012;15(4):528–36. https://doi.org/10.1038/nn.3045.

[20] Song Y, Ryu S, Sen PN. Determining multiple length scales in rocks. Nature 2000;406(6792):178–81. https://doi.org/10.1038/35018057.

[21] Ambrosone L, Ceglie A, Colafemmina G, Palazzo G. A novel approach for determining the droplet size distribution in emulsion systems by generating function. J Chem Phys 1997;107(24):10756–63. https://doi.org/10.1063/1.474191.

[22] Stapf S, Han S, Heine C, Blu B. Spatiotemporal correlations in transport processes determined by multiple pulsed field gradient experiments. Concepts Magn Reson 2002;14(3):172–211. https://doi.org/10.1002/cmr.10021.

[23] Stepišnik J, Lasič S, Mohorič A, Serša I, Sepe A. Spectral characterization of diffusion in porous media by the modulated gradient spin echo with CPMG sequence. J Magn Reson 2006;182(2):195–9. https://doi.org/10.1016/j.jmr.2006.06.023.

[24] Mitra PP, Sen PN, Schwartz LM. Short-time behavior of the diffusion coefficient as a geometrical probe of porous media. Phys Rev B Condens Matter 1993;47(14):8565–74. https://doi.org/10.1103/PhysRevB.47.8565.

[25] Sen PN. Time-dependent diffusion coefficient as a probe of geometry. Concepts Magn Reson 2004;23A(1):1–21. https://doi.org/10.1002/cmr.a.20017.

[26] Mitra PP, Sen PN, Schwartz LM, Le Doussal P. Diffusion propagator as a probe of the structure of porous media. Phys Rev Lett 1992;68(24):3555–8. https://doi.org/10.1103/PhysRevLett.68.3555.

[27] Barral GA, Frydman L, Chingas GC. NMR diffraction and spatial statistics of stationary systems. Science 1992;255(5045):714–7. https://doi.org/10.1126/science.255.5045.714.

[28] Cory DG, Garroway AN, Miller JB. Applications of spin transport as a probe of local geometry. Polym Prepr 1990;31:149–50.

[29] Callaghan PT, Coy A, MacGowan D, Packer KJ, Zelaya FO. Diffraction-like effects in NMR diffusion studies of fluids in porous solids. Nature 1991;351(6326):467–9. https://doi.org/10.1038/351467a0.

[30] Stejskal EO, Tanner JE. Spin diffusion measurements: spin echoes in the presence of a time-dependent field gradient. J Chem Phys 1965;42(1):288–92. https://doi.org/10.1063/1.1695690.

[31] Shemesh N, Jespersen SN, Alexander DC, Cohen Y, Drobnjak I, Dyrby TB, Finsterbusch J, Koch MA, Kuder T, Laun F, Lawrenz M, Lundell H, Mitra PP, Nilsson M, Özarslan E, Topgaard D, Westin CF. Conventions and nomenclature for double diffusion encoding NMR and MRI. Magn Reson Med 2016;75(1):82–87. https://doi.org/10.1002/mrm.25901.

[32] Håkansson B, Pons R, Söderman O. Structure determination of a highly concentrated W/O emulsion using pulsed-field-gradient spin-echo nuclear magnetic resonance “diffusion diffractograms”, Langmuir 1999;15(4): 988–991. https://doi.org/10.1021/la9803631.

[33] Avram L, Özarslan E, Assaf Y, Bar-Shir A, Cohen Y, Basser PJ. Three-dimensional water diffusion in impermeable cylindrical tubes: theory versus experiments. NMR Biomed 2008;21(8):888–98. https://doi.org/10.1002/nbm.1277.

[34] Pagès G, Szekely D, Kuchel PW. Erythrocyte-shape evolution recorded with fast-measurement NMR diffusion-diffraction. J Magn Reson Imaging 2008;28(6):1409–16. https://doi.org/10.1002/jmri.21588.

[35] Pagès G, Yau TW, Kuchel PW. Erythrocyte shape reversion from echinocytes to discocytes: kinetics via fast-measurement NMR diffusion-diffraction. Magn Reson Med 2010;64(3):645–52. https://doi.org/10.1002/mrm.22457.

[36] Shemesh N, Westin CF, Cohen Y. Magnetic resonance imaging by synergistic diffusion-diffraction patterns. Phys Rev Lett 2012;108(5):058103. https://doi.org/10.1103/PhysRevLett.108.058103.

[37] Laun FB, Kuder TA, Semmler W, Stieltjes B. Determination of the defining boundary in nuclear magnetic resonance diffusion experiments. Phys Rev Lett 2011;107(4):048102. https://doi.org/10.1103/PhysRevLett.107.048102.

[38] Laun FB, Kuder TA, Wetscherek A, Stieltjes B, Semmler W. NMR-based diffusion pore imaging. Phys Rev E Stat Nonlin Soft Matter Phys 2012;86(2):021906. https://doi.org/10.1103/PhysRevE.86.021906.

[39] Hertel S, Hunter M, Galvosas P. Magnetic resonance pore imaging, a tool for porous media research. Phys Rev E Stat Phys Plasmas Fluids Relat Interdiscip Topics 2013;87(3):030802. https://doi.org/10.1103/PhysRevE.87.030802.

[40] Hertel SA, Wang X, Hosking P, Simpson MC, Hunter M, Galvosas P. Magnetic-resonance pore imaging of nonsymmetric microscopic pore shapes. Phys Rev E 2015;92(1):012808. https://doi.org/10.1103/PhysRevE.92.012808.

[41] Demberg K, Laun FB, Windschuh J, Umathum R, Bachert P, Kuder TA. Nuclear magnetic resonance diffusion pore imaging: experimental phase detection by double diffusion encoding. Phys Rev E 2017; 95(2):022404. https://doi.org/10.1103/PhysRevE.95.022404.

[42] Kuder TA, Bachert P, Windschuh J, Laun FB. Diffusion pore imaging by hyperpolarized xenon-129 nuclear magnetic resonance. Phys Rev Lett 2013;112(3):028101. https://doi.org/10.1103/PhysRevLett.111.028101.

[43] Özarslan E, Basser PJ. MR diffusion-“diffraction” phenomenon in multi-pulse-field-gradient experiments. J Magn Reson 2007;188(2):285–94. https://doi.org/10.1016/j.jmr.2007.08.002.

[44] Kiselev VG, Novikov DS. Comment on “magnetic resonance imaging by synergistic diffusion diffraction patterns”, Phys Rev Lett 2013;110(10):109801. https://doi.org/10.1103/PhysRevLett.110.109801.

[45] Kuder TA, Laun FB. NMR-based diffusion pore imaging by double wave vector measurements. Magn Reson Med 2013;70(3):836–41. https://doi.org/10.1002/mrm.24515.

[46] Callaghan PT, Codd SL, Seymour JD. Spatial coherence phenomena arising from translational spin motion in gradient spin echo experiments. Concepts Magn Reson 1999;11(4):181–202. https://doi.org/10.1002/(SICI)1099-0534(1999)11:4<181::AID-CMR1>3.0.CO;2-T.

[47] Shemesh N, Özarslan E, Basser PJ, Cohen Y. Detecting diffusion-diffraction patterns in size distribution phantoms using double-pulsed field gradient NMR: theory and experiments. J Chem Phys 2010; 132(3):034703. https://doi.org/10.1063/1.3285299.

[48] Shemesh N, Özarslan E, Adiri T, Basser PJ, Cohen Y. Noninvasive bipolar double-pulsed-field-gradient NMR reveals signatures for pore size and shape in polydisperse, randomly oriented, inhomogeneous porous media. J Chem Phys 2010;133(4):044705. https://doi.org/10.1063/1.3454131.

[49] Ong HH, Wehrli FW. Quantifying axon diameter and intra-cellular volume fraction in excised mouse spinal cord with q-space imaging. Neuroimage 2010;51(4):1360–6. https://doi.org/10.1016/j.neuroimage.2010.03.063.

[50] Wedeen VJ, Hagmann P, Tseng WY, Reese TG, Weisskoff RM. Mapping complex tissue architecture with diffusion spectrum magnetic resonance imaging. Magn Reson Med 2005;54(6):1377–86. https://doi.org/10.1002/mrm.20642.

[51] Cohen Y, Assaf Y. High b-value q-space analyzed diffusion-weighted MRS and MRI in neuronal tissues—a technical review. NMR Biomed 2002;15(7–8):516–42. https://doi.org/10.1002/nbm.778.

[52] Stepišnik J. Time-dependent self-diffusion by NMR spin-echo. Phys B Condens Matter 1993;183(4):343–50. https://doi.org/10.1016/0921-4526(93)90124-O.

[53] Gore JC, Xu J, Colvin DC, Yankeelov TE, Parsons EC, Does MD. Characterization of tissue structure at varying length scales using temporal diffusion spectroscopy. NMR Biomed 2010;23(7):745–56. https://doi.org/10.1002/nbm.1531.

[54] Sukstanskii AL, Ackerman JJH. Concise derivation of oscillating-gradient-derived ADC. J Magn Reson 2018;296:165–8. https://doi.org/10.1016/j.jmr.2018.09.010.

[55] Lasič S, Stepišnik J, Mohorič A. Displacement power spectrum measurement by CPMG in constant gradient. J Magn Reson 2006;182(2):208–14. https://doi.org/10.1016/j.jmr.2006.06.030.

[56] Jiang X, Li H, Xie J, Zhao P, Gore JC, Xu J. Quantification of cell size using temporal diffusion spectroscopy. Magn Reson Med 2016;75(3):1076–85. https://doi.org/10.1002/mrm.25684.

[57] Xu J, Li K, Smith RA, Waterton JC, Zhao P, Chen H, Does MD, Manning HC, Gore JC. Characterizing tumor response to chemotherapy at various length scales using temporal diffusion spectroscopy. PLoS One 2012;7(7):e41714. https://doi.org/10.1371/journal.pone.0041714.

[58] Xu J, Does MD, Gore JC. Quantitative characterization of tissue microstructure with temporal diffusion spectroscopy. J Magn Reson 2009;200(2):189–97. https://doi.org/10.1016/j.jmr.2009.06.022.

[59] Xu J, Li H, Harkins KD, Jiang X, Xie J, Kang H, Does MD, Gore JC. Mapping mean axon diameter and axonal volume fraction by MRI using temporal diffusion spectroscopy. Neuroimage 2014;103:10–9. https://doi.org/10.1016/j.neuroimage.2014.09.006.

[60] Aggarwal M, Mori S, Shimogori T, Blackshaw S, Zhang J. Three-dimensional diffusion tensor microimaging for anatomical characterization of the mouse brain. Magn Reson Med 2010;64(1):249–61. https://doi.org/10.1002/mrm.22426.

[61] Aggarwal M, Jones MV, Calabresi PA, Mori S, Zhang J. Probing mouse brain microstructure using oscillating gradient diffusion magnetic resonance imaging. Magn Reson Med 2012;67(1):98–109. https://doi.org/10.1002/mrm.22981.

[62] Baron CA, Kate M, Gioia L, Butcher K, Emery D, Budde M, Beaulieu C. Reduction of diffusion-weighted imaging contrast of acute ischemic stroke at short diffusion times. Stroke 2015;46(8):2136–42. https://doi.org/10.1161/STROKEAHA.115.008815.

[63] Novikov DS, Kiselev VG, Jespersen SN. On modeling. Magn Reson Med 2018;79(6):3172–93. https://doi.org/10.1002/mrm.27101.

[64] Jensen JH, Helpern JA. MRI quantification of non-Gaussian water diffusion by kurtosis analysis. NMR Biomed 2010;23(7):698–710. https://doi.org/10.1002/nbm.1518.

[65] Jensen JH, Helpern JA, Ramani A, Lu H, Kaczynski K. Diffusional kurtosis imaging: the quantification of non-Gaussian water diffusion by means of magnetic resonance imaging. Magn Reson Med 2005;53(6):1432–40. https://doi.org/10.1002/mrm.20508.

[66] Fieremans E, Jensen JH, Helpern JA. White matter characterization with diffusional kurtosis imaging. Neuroimage 2011;58(1):177–88. https://doi.org/10.1016/j.neuroimage.2011.06.006.

[67] Hansen B, Shemesh N, Jespersen SN. Fast imaging of mean, axial and radial diffusion kurtosis. Neuroimage 2016;142:381–93. https://doi.org/10.1016/j.neuroimage.2016.08.022.

[68] Raz E, Bester M, Sigmund EE, Tabesh A, Babb JS, Jaggi H, Helpern J, Mitnick RJ, Inglese M. A better characterization of spinal cord damage in multiple sclerosis: a diffusional kurtosis imaging study. AJNR Am J Neuroradiol 2013;34(9):1846–52. https://doi.org/10.3174/ajnr.A3512.

[69] Hui ES, Cheung MM, Qi L, Wu EX. Towards better MR characterization of neural tissues using directional diffusion kurtosis analysis. Neuroimage 2008;42(1):122–34. https://doi.org/10.1016/j.neuroimage.2008.04.237.

[70] Van Cauter S, Veraart J, Sijbers J, Peeters RR, Himmelreich U, De Keyzer F, Van Gool SW, Van Calenbergh F, De Vleeschouwer S, Van Hecke W, Sunaert S. Gliomas: diffusion kurtosis MR imaging in grading. Radiology 2012;263(2):492–501. https://doi.org/10.1148/radiol.12110927.

[71] Wang JJ, Lin WY, Lu CS, Weng YH, Ng SH, Wang CH, Liu HL, Hsieh RH, Wan YL, Wai YY. Parkinson disease: diagnostic utility of diffusion kurtosis imaging. Radiology 2011;261(1):210–7. https://doi.org/10.1148/radiol.11102277.

[72] Henriques RN, Correia MM, Nunes RG, Ferreira HA. Exploring the 3D geometry of the diffusion kurtosis tensor—impact on the development of robust tractography procedures and novel biomarkers. Neuroimage 2015;111:85–99. https://doi.org/10.1016/j.neuroimage.2015.02.004.

[73] Qi L, Han D, Wu EX. Principal invariants and inherent parameters of diffusion kurtosis tensors. J Math Anal Appl 2009;349(1):165–80. https://doi.org/10.1016/j.jmaa.2008.08.049.

[74] Özarslan E, Koay CG, Shepherd TM, Komlosh ME, İrfanoğlu MO, Pierpaoli C, Basser PJ. Mean apparent propagator (MAP) MRI: a novel diffusion imaging method for mapping tissue microstructure. Neuroimage 2013;78:16–32. https://doi.org/10.1016/j.neuroimage.2013.04.016.

[75] Callaghan PT, Komlosh ME. Locally anisotropic motion in a macroscopically isotropic system: displacement correlations measured using double pulsed gradient spin-echo NMR. Magn Reson Chem 2002;40(13):15–9. https://doi.org/10.1002/mrc.1122.

[76] Cheng Y, Cory DG. Multiple scattering by NMR. J Am Chem Soc 1999;121(34):7935–6. https://doi.org/10.1021/ja9843324.

[77] Mitra PP. Multiple wave-vector extensions of the NMR pulsed-field-gradient spin-echo diffusion measurement. Phys Rev B Condens Matter 1995;51(21):15074–8. https://doi.org/10.1103/PhysRevB.51.15074.

[78] Koch MA, Finsterbusch J. Compartment size estimation with double wave vector diffusion-weighted imaging. Magn Reson Med 2008;60(1):90–101. https://doi.org/10.1002/mrm.21514.

[79] Shemesh N, Özarslan E, Basser PJ, Cohen Y. Measuring small compartmental dimensions with low-q angular double-PGSE NMR: the effect of experimental parameters on signal decay. J Magn Reson 2009;198(1):15–23. https://doi.org/10.1016/j.jmr.2009.01.004.

[80] Özarslan E. Compartment shape anisotropy (CSA) revealed by double pulsed field gradient MR. J Magn Reson 2009;199(1):56–67. https://doi.org/10.1016/j.jmr.2009.04.002.

[81] Shemesh N, Adiri T, Cohen Y. Probing microscopic architecture of opaque heterogeneous systems using double-pulsed-field-gradient NMR. J Am Chem Soc 2011;133(15):6028–35. https://doi.org/10.1021/ja200303h.

[82] Lawrenz M, Brassen S, Finsterbusch J. Microscopic diffusion anisotropy in the human brain: age-related changes. Neuroimage 2016;141:313–25. https://doi.org/10.1016/j.neuroimage.2016.07.031.

[83] Jespersen SN, Lundell H, Sønderby CK, Dyrby TB. Orientationally invariant metrics of apparent compartment eccentricity from double pulsed field gradient diffusion experiments. NMR Biomed 2013;26(12):1647–62. https://doi.org/10.1002/nbm.2999.

[84] Jespersen SN. Equivalence of double and single wave vector diffusion contrast at low diffusion weighting. NMR Biomed 2012;25(6):813–8. https://doi.org/10.1002/nbm.1808.

[85] Jespersen SN, Buhl N. The displacement correlation tensor: microstructure, ensemble anisotropy and curving fibers. J Magn Reson 2011;208(1):34–43. https://doi.org/10.1016/j.jmr.2010.10.003.

[86] Lawrenz M, Koch MA, Finsterbusch J. A tensor model and measures of microscopic anisotropy for double-wave-vector diffusion-weighting experiments with long mixing times. J Magn Reson 2010;202(1):43–56. https://doi.org/10.1016/j.jmr.2009.09.015.

[87] Henriques RN, Jespersen SN, Shemesh N. Microscopic anisotropy misestimation in spherical-mean single diffusion encoding MRI. Magn Reson Med 2019;81(5):3245–61. https://doi.org/10.1002/mrm.27606.

[88] Shemesh N. Axon diameters and myelin content modulate microscopic fractional anisotropy at short diffusion times in fixed rat spinal cord. Front Physiol 2018;6(49):1–15. https://doi.org/10.3389/fphy.2018.00049.
[89] Lawrenz M, Finsterbusch J. Mapping measures of microscopic diffusion anisotropy in human brain white matter in vivo with double-wave-vector diffusion-weighted imaging. Magn Reson Med 2015;73(2): 773–783. https://doi.org/10.1002/mrm.25140.
[90] Lawrenz M, Finsterbusch J. Detection of microscopic diffusion anisotropy in human cortical gray matter in vivo with double diffusion encoding. Magn Reson Med 2019;81(2):1296–306. https://doi.org/10.1002/mrm.27451.
[91] Avram AV, Özarslan E, Sarlls JE, Basser PJ. In vivo detection of microscopic anisotropy using quadruple pulsed-field gradient (qPFG) diffusion MRI on a clinical scanner. Neuroimage 2013;64:229–39. https://doi.org/10.1016/j.neuroimage.2012.08.048.
[92] Lawrenz M, Brassen S, Finsterbusch J. Microscopic diffusion anisotropy in the human brain: reproducibility, normal values, and comparison with the fractional anisotropy. Neuroimage 2015;109:283–97. https://doi.org/10.1016/j.neuroimage.2015.01.025.
[93] Ianuş A, Jespersen SN, Serradas Duarte T, Alexander DC, Drobnjak I, Shemesh N. Accurate estimation of microscopic diffusion anisotropy and its time dependence in the mouse brain. Neuroimage 2018; 183:934–49. https://doi.org/10.1016/j.neuroimage.2018.08.034.
[94] Shemesh N, Cohen Y. Overcoming apparent susceptibility-induced anisotropy (aSIA) by bipolar double-pulsed-field-gradient NMR. J Magn Reson 2011;212(2):362–9. https://doi.org/10.1016/j.jmr.2011.07.015.
[95] Yang G, Tian Q, Leuze C, Wintermark M, McNab JA. Double diffusion encoding MRI for the clinic. Magn Reson Med 2018;80(2):507–20. https://doi.org/10.1002/mrm.27043.
[96] Ianuş A, Shemesh N, Alexander DC, Drobnjak I. Double oscillating diffusion encoding and sensitivity to microscopic anisotropy. Magn Reson Med 2017;78(2):550–64. https://doi.org/10.1002/mrm.26393.
[97] Drobnjak I, Zhang H, Ianuş A, Kaden E, Alexander DC. PGSE, OGSE, and sensitivity to axon diameter in diffusion MRI: insight from a simulation study. Magn Reson Med 2016;75(2):688–700. https://doi.org/10.1002/mrm.25631.
[98] Callaghan PT, Jolley KW, Lelievre J. Diffusion of water in the endosperm tissue of wheat grains as studied by pulsed field gradient nuclear magnetic resonance. Biophys J 1979;28(1):133–41. https://doi.org/10.1016/S0006-3495(79)85164-4.
[99] Kroenke CD, Ackerman JJH, Yablonskiy DA. On the nature of the NAA diffusion attenuated MR signal in the central nervous system. Magn Reson Med 2004;52(5):1052–9. https://doi.org/10.1002/mrm.20260.
[100] Kaden E, Kruggel F, Alexander DC. Quantitative mapping of the per-axon diffusion coefficients in brain white matter. Magn Reson Med 2016;75(4):1752–63. https://doi.org/10.1002/mrm.25734.
[101] Novikov DS, Veraart J, Jelescu IO, Fieremans E. Rotationally-invariant mapping of scalar and orientational metrics of neuronal microstructure with diffusion MRI. Neuroimage 2018;174:518–38. https://doi.org/10.1016/j.neuroimage.2018.03.006.
[102] Jelescu IO, Veraart J, Fieremans E, Novikov DS. Degeneracy in model parameter estimation for multi-compartmental diffusion in neuronal tissue. NMR Biomed 2016;29(1):33–47. https://doi.org/10.1002/nbm.3450.
[103] Kaden E, Kelm ND, Carson RP, Does MD, Alexander DC. Multi-compartment microscopic diffusion imaging. Neuroimage 2016;139:346–59. https://doi.org/10.1016/j.neuroimage.2016.06.002.
[104] Zhang H, Schneider T, Wheeler-Kingshott CA, Alexander DC. NODDI: practical in vivo neurite orientation dispersion and density imaging of the human brain. Neuroimage 2012;61(4):1000–16. https://doi.org/10.1016/j.neuroimage.2012.03.072.
[105] Jelescu I, Budde M. Design and validation of diffusion MRI models of white matter. Front Physiol 2017;5(61):1–18. https://doi.org/10.3389/fphy.2017.00061.
[106] Tang X, Sigmund EE, Song Y. Simultaneous measurement of diffusion along multiple directions. J Am Chem Soc 2004;126(50):16336–7. https://doi.org/10.1021/ja0447457.

[107] Topgaard D. Isotropic diffusion weighting in PGSE NMR: numerical optimization of the q-MAS PGSE sequence. Microporous Mesoporous Mater 2013;178:60–3. https://doi.org/10.1016/j.micromeso.2013.03.009.

[108] Topgaard D. Multidimensional diffusion MRI. J Magn Reson 2017;275:98–113. https://doi.org/10.1016/j.jmr.2016.12.007.

[109] Jespersen SN, Olesen JL, Ianuş A, Shemesh N. Effects of nonGaussian diffusion on "isotropic diffusion" measurements: an ex-vivo microimaging and simulation study. J Magn Reson 2019;300:84–94. https://doi.org/10.1016/j.jmr.2019.01.007.

[110] Sjölund J, Szczepankiewicz F, Nilsson M, Topgaard D, Westin CF, Knutsson H. Constrained optimization of gradient waveforms for generalized diffusion encoding. J Magn Reson 2015;261:157–68. https://doi.org/10.1016/j.jmr.2015.10.012.

[111] Wong EC, Cox RW, Song AW. Optimized isotropic diffusion weighting. Magn Reson Med 1995;34(2): 139–143. https://doi.org/10.1002/mrm.1910340202.

[112] Vellmer S, Stirnberg R, Edelhoff D, Suter D, Stöcker T, Maximov II. Comparative analysis of isotropic diffusion weighted imaging sequences. J Magn Reson 2017;275:137–47. https://doi.org/10.1016/j.jmr.2016.12.011.

[113] De Almeida Martins JP, Topgaard D. Two-dimensional correlation of isotropic and directional diffusion using NMR. Phys Rev Lett 2016;116(8), 087601. https://doi.org/10.1103/PhysRevLett.116.087601.

[114] Szczepankiewicz F, Lasič S, Van Westen D, Sundgren PC, Englund E, Westin CF, Ståhlberg F, Lätt J, Topgaard D, Nilsson M. Quantification of microscopic diffusion anisotropy disentangles effects of orientation dispersion from microstructure: applications in healthy volunteers and in brain tumors. Neuroimage 2015;104:241–52. https://doi.org/10.1016/j.neuroimage.2014.09.057.

[115] Lampinen B, Szczepankiewicz F, Mårtensson J, Van Westen D, Sundgren PC, Nilsson M. Neurite density imaging versus imaging of microscopic anisotropy in diffusion MRI: a model comparison using spherical tensor encoding. Neuroimage 2017;147:517–31. https://doi.org/10.1016/j.neuroimage.2016.11.053.

[116] Westin CF, Knutsson H, Pasternak O, Szczepankiewicz F, Özarslan E, Van Westen D, Mattisson C, Bogren M, O'Donnell LJ, Kubicki M, Topgaard D, Nilsson M. Q-space trajectory imaging for multidimensional diffusion MRI of the human brain. Neuroimage 2016;135:345–62. https://doi.org/10.1016/j.neuroimage.2016.02.039.

[117] Panagiotaki E, Schneider T, Siow B, Hall MG, Lythgoe MF, Alexander DC. Compartment models of the diffusion MR signal in brain white matter: a taxonomy and comparison. Neuroimage 2012;59(3):2241–54. https://doi.org/10.1016/j.neuroimage.2011.09.081.

[118] Stanisz GJ, Szafer A, Wright GA, Henkelman RM. An analytical model of restricted diffusion in bovine optic nerve. Magn Reson Med 1997;37(1):103–11. https://doi.org/10.1002/mrm.1910370115.

[119] Niendorf T, Dijkhuizen RM, Norris DG, Van Lookeren CM, Nicolay K. Biexponential diffusion attenuation in various states of brain tissue: implications for diffusion-weighted imaging. Magn Reson Med 1996;36(6):847–57. https://doi.org/10.1002/mrm.1910360607.

[120] Behrens TEJ, Woolrich MW, Jenkinson M, Nunes RG, Clare S, Matthews PM, Brady JM, Smith SM. Characterization and propagation of uncertainty in diffusion-weighted MR imaging. Magn Reson Med 2003;50(5):1077–88. https://doi.org/10.1002/mrm.10609.

[121] Ryland BN, Callaghan PT. Spin echo analysis of restricted diffusion under generalized gradient waveforms for spherical pores with relaxivity and interconnections. Isr J Chem 2003;43(1–2):1–7. https://doi.org/10.1560/JF3Q-URL3-5U20-WHLY.

[122] Barazany D, Basser PJ, Assaf Y. In vivo measurement of axon diameter distribution in the corpus callosum of rat brain. Brain 2009;132(5):1210–20. https://doi.org/10.1093/brain/awp042.

[123] Assaf Y, Blumenfeld-Katzir T, Yovel Y, Basser PJ. AxCaliber: a method for measuring axon diameter distribution from diffusion MRI. Magn Reson Med 2008;59(6):1347–54. https://doi.org/10.1002/mrm.21577.

[124] Panagiotaki E, Walker-Samuel S, Siow B, Johnson SP, Rajkumar V, Pedley RB, Lythgoe MF, Alexander DC. Noninvasive quantification of solid tumor microstructure using VERDICT MRI. Cancer Res 2014;74(7):1902–12. https://doi.org/10.1158/0008-5472.CAN-13-2511.

[125] Duong TQ, Sehy JV, Yablonskiy DA, Snider BJ, Ackerman JJH, Neil JJ. Extracellular apparent diffusion in rat brain. Magn Reson Med 2001;45(5):801–10. https://doi.org/10.1002/mrm.1108.

[126] Sehy JV, Ackerman JJH, Neil JJ. Evidence that both fast and slow water ADC components arise from intracellular space. Magn Reson Med 2002;48(5):765–70. https://doi.org/10.1002/mrm.10301.

[127] Innocenti GM, Caminiti R, Aboitiz F. Comments on the paper by Horowitz et al. (2014). Brain Struct Funct 2015;220(3):1789–90. https://doi.org/10.1007/s00429-014-0974-7.

[128] Colgan N, Siow B, O'Callaghan JM, Harrison IF, Wells JA, Holmes HE, Ismail O, Richardson S, Alexander DC, Collins EC, Fisher EM, Johnson R, Schwarz AJ, Ahmed Z, O'Neill MJ, Murray TK, Zhang H, Lythgoe MF. Application of neurite orientation dispersion and density imaging (NODDI) to a tau pathology model of Alzheimer's disease. Neuroimage 2016;125:739–44. https://doi.org/10.1016/j.neuroimage.2015.10.043.

[129] Churchill NW, Caverzasi E, Graham SJ, Hutchison MG, Schweizer TA. White matter microstructure in athletes with a history of concussion: comparing diffusion tensor imaging (DTI) and neurite orientation dispersion and density imaging (NODDI). Hum Brain Mapp 2017;38(8):4201–11. https://doi.org/10.1002/hbm.23658.

[130] Veraart J, Fieremans E, Novikov DS. On the scaling behavior of water diffusion in human brain white matter. Neuroimage 2019;15:379–87. https://doi.org/10.1016/j.neuroimage.2018.09.075.

[131] Novikov DS, Fieremans E, Jensen JH, Helpern JA. Random walks with barriers. Nat Phys 2011;7(6): 508–514. https://doi.org/10.1038/nphys1936.

[132] Novikov DS, Jensen JH, Helpern JA, Fieremans E. Revealing mesoscopic structural universality with diffusion. Proc Natl Acad Sci U S A 2014;111(14):5088–93. https://doi.org/10.1073/pnas.1316944111.

[133] Reynaud O. Time-dependent diffusion MRI in cancer: tissue modeling and applications. Front Physiol 2017;5(58):1–16. https://doi.org/10.3389/fphy.2017.00058.

[134] De Swiet TM, Sen PN. Time dependent diffusion coefficient in a disordered medium. J Chem Phys 2006;104(1):206–9. https://doi.org/10.1063/1.470890.

[135] Jespersen SN, Bjarkam CR, Nyengaard JR, Chakravarty MM, Hansen B, Vosegaard T, Østergaard L, Yablonskiy D, Nielsen NC, Vestergaard-Poulsen P. Neurite density from magnetic resonance diffusion measurements at ultrahigh field: comparison with light microscopy and electron microscopy. Neuroimage 2010;49(1):205–16. https://doi.org/10.1016/j.neuroimage.2009.08.053.

[136] Jespersen SN, Leigland LA, Cornea A, Kroenke CD. Determination of axonal and dendritic orientation distributions within the developing cerebral cortex by diffusion tensor imaging. IEEE Trans Med Imaging 2012;31(1):16–32. https://doi.org/10.1109/TMI.2011.2162099.

[137] Jespersen SN, Kroenke CD, Østergaard L, Ackerman JJH, Yablonskiy DA. Modeling dendrite density from magnetic resonance diffusion measurements. Neuroimage 2007;34(4):1473–86. https://doi.org/10.1016/j.neuroimage.2006.10.037.

[138] Lampinen B, Szczepankiewicz F, Novén M, van Westen D, Hansson O, Englund E, Mårtensson J, Westin CF, Nilsson M. Searching for the neurite density with diffusion MRI: challenges for biophysical modeling. Hum Brain Mapp 2019;40:2529–45. https://doi.org/10.1002/hbm.24542.

[139] Jelescu IO, Veraart J, Adisetiyo V, Milla SS, Novikov DS, Fieremans E. One diffusion acquisition and different white matter models: how does microstructure change in human early development based on WMTI and NODDI? Neuroimage 2015;107:242–56. https://doi.org/10.1016/j.neuroimage.2014.12.009.

[140] Moffett JR, Ross B, Arun P, Madhavarao CN, Namboodiri AM. N-Acetylaspartate in the CNS: from neurodiagnostics to neurobiology. Prog Neurobiol 2007;81(2):89–131. https://doi.org/10.1016/j.pneurobio.2006.12.003.

[141] Fisher SK, Novak JE, Agranoff BW. Inositol and higher inositol phosphates in neural tissues: homeostasis, metabolism and functional significance. J Neurochem 2002;82(4):736–54. https://doi.org/10.1046/j.1471-4159.2002.01041.x.

[142] Govindaraju V, Young K, Maudsley AA. Proton NMR chemical shifts and coupling constants for brain metabolites. NMR Biomed 2000;13(3):129–53. https://doi.org/10.1002/1099-1492(200005)13:3<129::AID-NBM619>3.0.CO;2-V.

[143] Palombo M, Ligneul C, Najac C, Le Douce J, Flament J, Escartin C, Hantraye P, Brouillet E, Bonvento G, Valette J. New paradigm to assess brain cell morphology by diffusion-weighted MR spectroscopy in vivo. Proc Natl Acad Sci U S A 2016;113(24):6671–6. https://doi.org/10.1073/pnas.1504327113.

[144] Palombo M, Shemesh N, Ronen I, Valette J. Insights into brain microstructure from in vivo DW-MRS. Neuroimage 2019;182:329–42.

[145] Shemesh N, Rosenberg JT, Dumez JN, Grant SC, Frydman L. Distinguishing neuronal from astrocytic subcellular microstructures using in vivo Double Diffusion Encoded ^{1}H MRS at 21.1 T. PLoS One 2017;12(10): e0185232. https://doi.org/10.1371/journal.pone.0185232.

[146] Palombo M, Shemesh N, Ronen I, Valette J. Insights into brain microstructure from in vivo DW-MRS. Neuroimage 2018;182:97–116. https://doi.org/10.1016/j.neuroimage.2017.11.028.

[147] Valette J, Ligneul C, Marchadour C, Najac C, Palombo M. Brain metabolite diffusion from ultra-short to ultra-long time scales: what do we learn, where should we go? Front Neurosci 2018;12(2):1–6. https://doi.org/10.3389/fnins.2018.00002.

[148] Ronen I, Ercan E, Webb A. Axonal and glial microstructural information obtained with diffusion-weighted magnetic resonance spectroscopy at 7T. Front Integr Neurosci 2013;7(13):1–10. https://doi.org/10.3389/fnint.2013.00013.

[149] Palombo M, Ligneul C, Valette J. Modeling diffusion of intracellular metabolites in the mouse brain up to very high diffusion-weighting: diffusion in long fibers (almost) accounts for non-monoexponential attenuation. Magn Reson Med 2017;77(1):343–50. https://doi.org/10.1002/mrm.26548.

[150] Palombo M, Ligneul C, Hernandez-Garzon E, Valette J. Can we detect the effect of spines and leaflets on the diffusion of brain intracellular metabolites? Neuroimage 2018;182:283–93. https://doi.org/10.1016/j.neuroimage.2017.05.003.

[151] Sattler M, Schleucher J, Griesinger C. Heteronuclear multidimensional NMR experiments for the structure determination of proteins in solution employing pulsed field gradients. Prog Nucl Mag Res Sp 1999;34(2):93–158. https://doi.org/10.1016/S0079-6565(98)00025-9.

[152] Veraart J, Novikov DS, Fieremans E. TE dependent diffusion imaging (TEdDI) distinguishes between compartmental T_2 relaxation times. Neuroimage 2018;15:360–9. https://doi.org/10.1016/j.neuroimage.2017.09.030.

[153] Silva MD, Helmer KG, Lee JH, Han SS, Springer Jr CS, Sotak CH. Deconvolution of compartmental water diffusion coefficients in yeast-cell suspensions using combined T(1) and diffusion measurements. J Magn Reson 2002;156(1):52–63. https://doi.org/10.1006/jmre.2002.2527.

[154] Stapf S, Packer KJ, Graham RG, Thovert J-F, Adler PM. Spatial correlations and dispersion for fluid transport through packed glass beads studied by pulsed field-gradient NMR. Phys Rev E 1998;58(5):6206–21. https://doi.org/10.1103/PhysRevE.58.6206.

[155] Seland JG. Dynamic correlations between inhomogeneous magnetic fields, internal gradients, diffusion and transverse relaxation, as a probe for pore geometry and heterogeneity. Diffus Fundam 2014;22(10):1–5.

[156] Veraart J, Nunes D, Rudrapatna U, Fieremans E, Jones DK, Novikov DS, Shemesh N. Noninvasive quantification of axon radii using diffusion MRI. Elife 2020;9(e49855):1–27.

[157] Guy J, Ellis EA, Kelley K, Hope GM. Spectra of G ratio, myelin sheath thickness, and axon and fiber diameter in the Guinea pig optic nerve. J Comp Neurol 1989;287(4):446–54. https://doi.org/10.1002/cne.902870404.

[158] Campbell JSW, Leppert IR, Narayanan S, Boudreau M, Duval T, Cohen-Adad J, Pike GB, Stikov N. Promise and pitfalls of g-ratio estimation with MRI. Neuroimage 2018;182:80–96. https://doi.org/10.1016/j.neuroimage.2017.08.038.

CHAPTER

Diffusion MRI: Applications in the Brain

23

Marco Bozzali[a,b,c], Andrew W. Barritt[c,d], and Laura Serra[b]

[a]*Department of Neuroscience, Brighton and Sussex Medical School, University of Sussex, Brighton, United Kingdom* [b]*Neuroimaging Laboratory, Santa Lucia Foundation IRCCS, Rome, Italy* [c]*Hurstwood Park Neurosciences Centre, Haywards Heath, West Sussex, United Kingdom* [d]*Clinical Imaging Sciences Centre, Brighton and Sussex Medical School, Brighton, United Kingdom*

23.1 Introduction

This chapter focuses on a selection of brain disorders in which diffusion Magnetic Resonance Imaging (MRI) is instrumental in clinical diagnosis or a useful tool for understanding the underlying pathophysiology. The section first provides an overview of routine clinical applications of diffusion imaging followed by research applications in neurology and psychiatry.

23.2 Clinical applications of quantitative diffusion mapping

MRI of the nervous system has become one of the primary modalities used in the diagnosis and management of a range of disorders in clinical neurology. The ever-evolving constellation of available MRI sequences provides subtly different information about anatomical structures. Clinical brain imaging protocols consist of at least T_1-weighted, T_2-weighted, and fluid-attenuated inversion recovery (FLAIR) images, with diffusion-weighted sequences and T_2*- or susceptibility-weighted imaging commonly collected as well. Diffusion MRI can refer to either the diffusion-weighted images (typically with isotropic diffusion weighting, and colloquially referred to as diffusion-weighted imaging [DWI]) or apparent diffusion coefficient (ADC) maps; the former are the raw images collected after the application of diffusion weighting gradients, and the latter is in the quantitative diffusion maps that describe the ADC in units of square millimeter per second. These diffusion imaging studies are widely performed to aid the characterization of vascular, neoplastic, traumatic, neuroinflammatory, infective, and neurodegenerative lesions affecting the brain and spinal cord in the acute and chronic phases of the disease. The DWI and ADC maps must always be reviewed together as the DWI is sensitive to transverse relaxation signals whereas the mathematical construction of the ADC removes T_2 shine-through effects [1]. More advanced diffusion techniques, such as diffusion tensor imaging (DTI), remain largely confined to research settings but do have the potential not only to reveal a greater insight into the neural basis of disease but also assist clinical decision making and prognostication for patients.

Perhaps the most widely appreciated primary application of diffusion imaging in the brain among physicians is acute stroke, in which perfusion is suddenly reduced after blood vessel occlusion or

Advances in Magnetic Resonance Technology and Applications. Volume 1. ISSN 2666-9099. https://doi.org/10.1016/B978-0-12-817057-1.00025-1

hemorrhage in a certain vascular territory. Although the DWI and ADC maps are considered superior or equivalent to computed tomography (CT) for detecting acute ischemia and hemorrhage, respectively [2], non-contrast CT and CT angiography remain the cornerstone of the initial assessment to guide eligibility for early thrombolytic reperfusion therapies within most hyperacute stroke services owing to their availability in emergency departments, patient tolerability, and device compatibility [3,4]. Nevertheless, access to emergent and rapid MRI is increasing, particularly at extended time windows beyond the onset of symptoms. Diffusion, perfusion, and susceptibility-weighted imaging can identify stroke patients with large vessel occlusions who may still benefit from interventional thrombolysis [5] or endovascular treatment [6–8] within the first 24 h. Increased restriction of water diffusion, denoted by largely uniform hyperintensity on DWI and hypointensity on the ADC map, is detectable within 60 min of vessel obstruction as an ischemic "core," [9], well before any lesion becomes visible on conventional T_2 and FLAIR sequences. This reduction in ADC is believed to be caused by cellular (cytotoxic) edema from the failure of the heavily ATP-dependent sodium/potassium exchange membrane transporters and other conformational changes within the hypoxic tissue [10–12]. The ADC usually remains abnormally reduced for up to several weeks before a pseudonormalization and later chronic elevation occurs (Fig. 23.1A–D) [14,15]. These dynamic changes may enable approximate ages to be conferred upon different crops of ischemic lesions in complex and progressive vasculopathies associated with infective, vasculitic, or vasoconstrictive syndromes, for instance. Besides, metrics derived from DTI within the corticospinal tracts (CSTs) and other motor tracts during the subacute stage of stroke may be used to predict performance outcomes and to serially monitor the remodeling of neural pathways underlying functional recovery, although more extensive longitudinal imaging data are required from larger clinical trials in neurorehabilitation [16–18].

Large abscesses also typically demonstrate homogeneous hyperintensity on DWI and hypointensity on the ADC maps (Fig. 23.2) due to the water restriction imposed by cellular and macromolecular constituents within pus [19,20]. This information can be extremely useful in helping to distinguish between infective processes and cystic components of higher grade neoplastic lesions, as both may display suspicious "ring enhancement" on a CT or T_1-weighted MRI scan with paramagnetic contrast media, denoting the breakdown of the blood-brain-barrier (BBB) [20,21]. However, a small proportion of abscesses, including perhaps less sizeable ones, may demonstrate a reversed pattern on DWI and ADC, or instead exhibit an outer hypointense margin or hyperintense center on the ADC in the shape of a ring [22–25] (not to be confused with contrast ring-enhancement). This characteristic ring morphology on diffusion imaging is also reported in some cases of acute ischemia in addition to a diverse list of alternative pathologies including bacterial and fungal infections, malignant brain tumors, and neuroinflammatory lesions, with those in association with multiple sclerosis more of an incomplete ring resembling a horseshoe [23]. The clinical history, demographics, and examination of the patient in these cases will help determine the most likely diagnosis, including lesion location and appearances on other conventional MRI sequences (Table 23.1), as exemplified by conditions such as infective endocarditis in which areas of abnormally restricted diffusion in the brain may potentially represent either acute infarct or abscess formation [27].

Intracranial tumors display a range of ADC values usually above, but occasionally extending to slightly less than, normal white and gray matter (Table 23.2) [21]. Areas containing a high-cellular density, and thus membrane and organelle barriers to water diffusion, tend to lower the ADC value, whereas cystic or necrotic regions tend to raise the ADC (Fig. 23.3) [20,34]. A negative correlation has been demonstrated between ADC and World Health Organization grade in neuroepithelial tumors, with malignant grade IV averaging almost half the ADC value compared to grade I lesions [35],

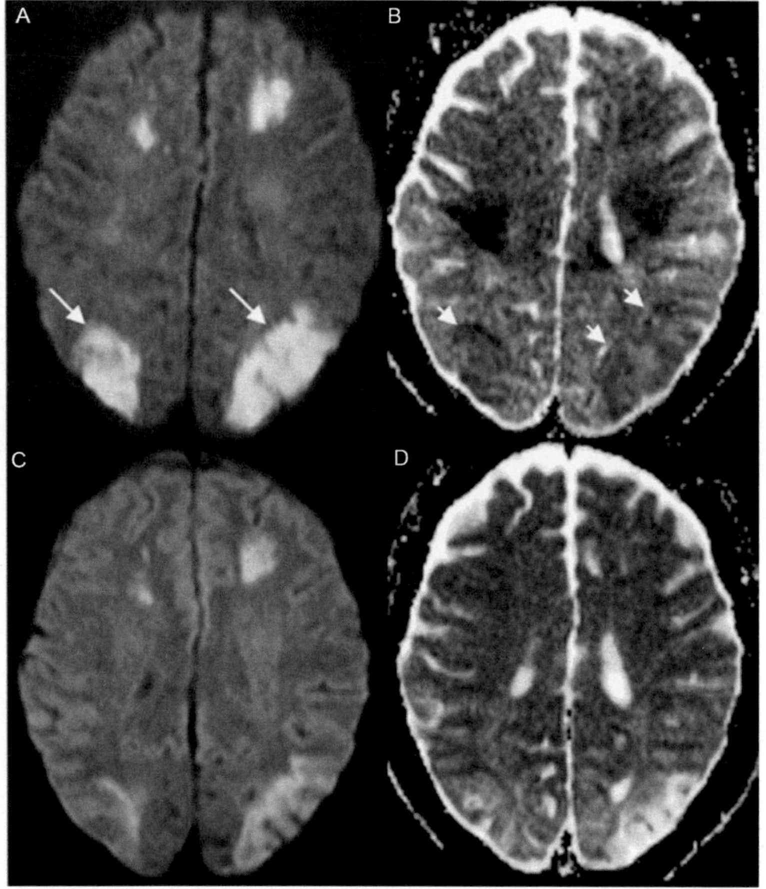

FIG. 23.1

Evolution of diffusion MR changes after stroke in a patient suffering from an occlusive *Varicella zoster* virus vasculopathy [13]. (A) At 1 week, hyperintensity on DWI is visible within the parieto-occipital infarcts bilaterally (*long arrows*) although the lesions tend towards isointensity on the ADC map (B; *short arrowheads*). (C) After 3 weeks, the hyperintensity on DWI is far less marked, and (D) the lesions exhibit a heterogeneous mixture of iso- and hyperintensity on the ADC map.

although the heterogeneous content within some higher-grade lesions does complicate matters [36]. Indeed, other factors such as vascularity, edema, and macromolecular content between different histological types of neoplasm influence the diffusion properties, and thus direct comparison of absolute values is not necessarily representative of the same underlying mechanism [21,37]. Dynamic changes in the ADC maps over time, such as increases post cytotoxic chemotherapy and radiotherapy treatment might also enable prognostication based on inferred changes in cellularity [37,38]. Furthermore, DTI with tractography analysis is being explored preoperatively and intraoperatively to estimate the distortion, penetration and destruction of white matter tracts by invasive tumors to help guide the optimal margins for surgical resection or radiotherapy to achieve better functional preservation

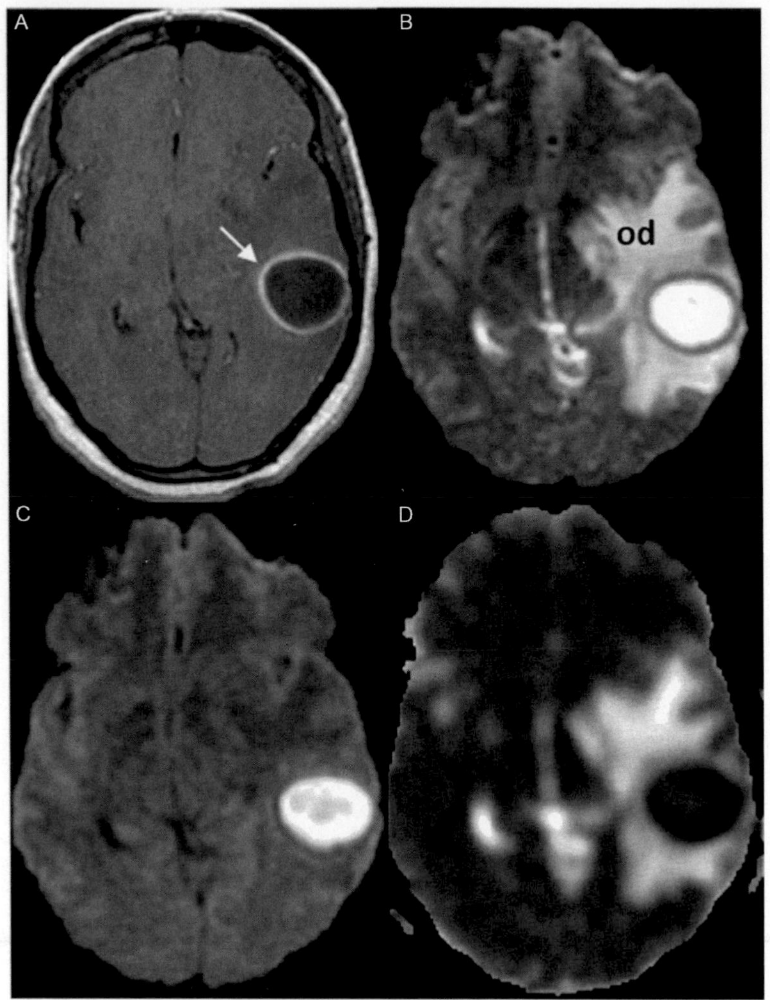

FIG. 23.2

MR appearances of a bacterial brain abscess. (A) Ring enhancement following gadolinium administration is apparent in the T_1-weighted image (*arrow*) with midline shift and surrounding vasogenic edema observed on the T_2-weighted images (B; od). (C) The center of the abscess shows a hyperintensity on the DWI and (D) homogeneous hypointensity on the ADC map, confirming the restricted diffusion expected of pus.

(Reprinted with minor modification from Reddy JS, et al. The role of diffusion-weighted imaging in the differential diagnosis of intracranial cystic mass lesions: a report of 147 lesions. Surg Neurol 2006;66:246–50; discussion 250–241. Copyright (2006) with permission from Elsevier.)

and long-term outcomes for patients [39,40]. Although it can be informative for management of selected patients, use of DTI in this context has yet to become standard practice. The measure of fractional anisotropy (FA) is often confounded by peritumoral edema and areas of multidirectional fiber intersections, and so alternative imaging methods sensitive to multiple diffusion vectors within each

Table 23.1 Radiological appearances of selected clinical conditions affecting the brain.

	MRI contrast and signal						
Clinical entity	***T_1w***	***T_2w***	***FLAIR***	***DWI***	***ADC***	***Enh***	**Comments**
Vascular							
Acute stroke	↔	↔	↔	↑	↓	Yes*	*DWI/ADC pattern of cytotoxic edema*
Chronic stroke	↓	↑	↑	↓	↑	No	*Enhancement with Gd. may develop over the subacute phase* [26]
Infective							
Abscess	↓↔	↑	↑	↑	↓	Ring	*Chronic abscesses often show a hypointense capsule on T_2*
sCJD	↔	↑	↑	↑	↓	No	*Chronic HSV shows increasing ADC in line with more necrosis*
Acute HSV encephalitis	↓	↑	↑↔	↑	↓	Yes	
Neoplastic tumor							
Cystic/necrotic	↓	↑	↓	↓	↑	Ring	*Lesions with very high cellularity often demonstrate reduced diffusion coefficients*
Highly cellular	↓↔	↑	↑	↑↔	↓	Ring	
Cystic lesions							
Epidermoid	↓	↑	↑	↑	↓	Rare	
Arachnoid	↓	↑	↑	↔	↑	No	
Colloid	↑	↓↔	↑	↔	↑	Rare	
Inflammatory							
Acute MS lesion	↓	↑	↑	↑	↑↓	Yes	*Periventricular and perpendicular to the ependymal surface*
Chronic MS lesion	↓	↑	↑	↑	↑	No	
Metabolic							
Acute Mitochondrial Disorders (MELAS)	↓	↑	↑	↑	↔↑	Yes	*Restricted diffusion extends between vascular territories with DWI/ADC pattern of vasogenic edema*

sCJD, *sporadic Creutzfeldt-Jakob disease;* HSV, *herpes simplex virus encephalitis;* MS, *multiple sclerosis;* MELAS, *mitochondrial encephalomyopathy with lactic acidosis and stroke-like episodes;* T_1w, *T_1-weighted image;* T_2w, *T_2-weighted image;* ADC, *apparent diffusion coefficient map;* DWI, *diffusion-weighted image;* Enh, *enhancement with gadolinium contrast;* FLAIR, *fluid-attenuated inversion recovery.*

voxel are in development. Standardization of post-processing methods, shorter scan times, and further validation in the context of established procedures for minimizing damage to eloquent pathways (such as intraoperative electrical stimulation) might assist more extensive application of sophisticated perioperative diffusion MRI [21,39,41].

Aside from the value of distinguishing the blend of appearances of tumors from other semisolid pathologies including non-neoplastic intracranial cysts [20,42], serial DWI and ADC maps collected

Table 23.2 ADC values of selected brain tumors and other pathologies.

Normal brain tissue	ADC μm²/ms
Normal white matter [28]	0.705±0.014
Deep gray matter [29]	0.75±0.03
Neuroepithelial tumors	
WHO grade I. Dysembryoplastic neuroepithelial tumor	2.546±0.135
WHO grade I. Pilocytic astrocytoma [19]	1.659±0.260
WHO grade II. Diffuse astrocytoma [19]	1.530±0.148
WHO grade II. Oligodendroglioma [19]	1.455
WHO grade II. Ependymoma [19]	1.230±0.119
WHO grade III. Anaplastic astrocytoma [19]	1.245±0.153
WHO grade III. Anaplastic oligodendroglioma [19]	1.222±0.093
WHO grade III. Anaplastic ependymoma [19]	1.103±0.101
WHO grade IV. Glioblastoma [19]	1.079±0.154
WHO grade IV, PNET [19]	0.835±0.122
WHO grade IV. Medulloblastoma [24]	0.66±0.15
Other brain tumors	
Chraniopharyngioma [19]	1.572±0.210
Schwannoma [19]	1.384±0.140
Epidermoid [19]	1.263±0.174
Germ cell tumor [19]	1.189±0.175
Metastatic tumor [19]	1.149±0.192
Pituitary adenoma	1.121±0.202
Typical meningeoma [30]	1.17±0.21
Atypical malignant meningioma [30]	0.75±0.21
Malignant lymphoma [19]	0.725±0.192
Secondary changes and other pathologies	
Vasogenic (peritumoral) edema [20]	1.30±0.11
Peritumoral edema (high-grade glial tumors) [18]	1.825±0.115
Cytotoxic (ischemic) edema [20]	1.04±0.05
Cystic/necrotic tumor areas [31]	2.70±0.31
Abscess [32]	0.65±0.16
Acute stroke [33]	0.401±0.143

Reproduced from Maier SE, Sun Y, Mulkern RV. Diffusion imaging of brain tumors. NMR Biomed 2010;23:849–64 with permission from John Wiley & Sons. References can be found in the original paper.

at multiple time points are particularly useful for informing the differential diagnoses of other parenchymal infective processes such as encephalitis and prion disorders. Hyperintensity on DWI and corresponding hypointensity on ADC maps is observed in the acute and subacute phases of Herpes simplex virus (HSV) encephalitis (Fig. 23.4) following early cytotoxic edema within mesial temporal and limbic systems, and reveals a greater extent of the lesion burden than conventional T_2 or FLAIR contrasts with

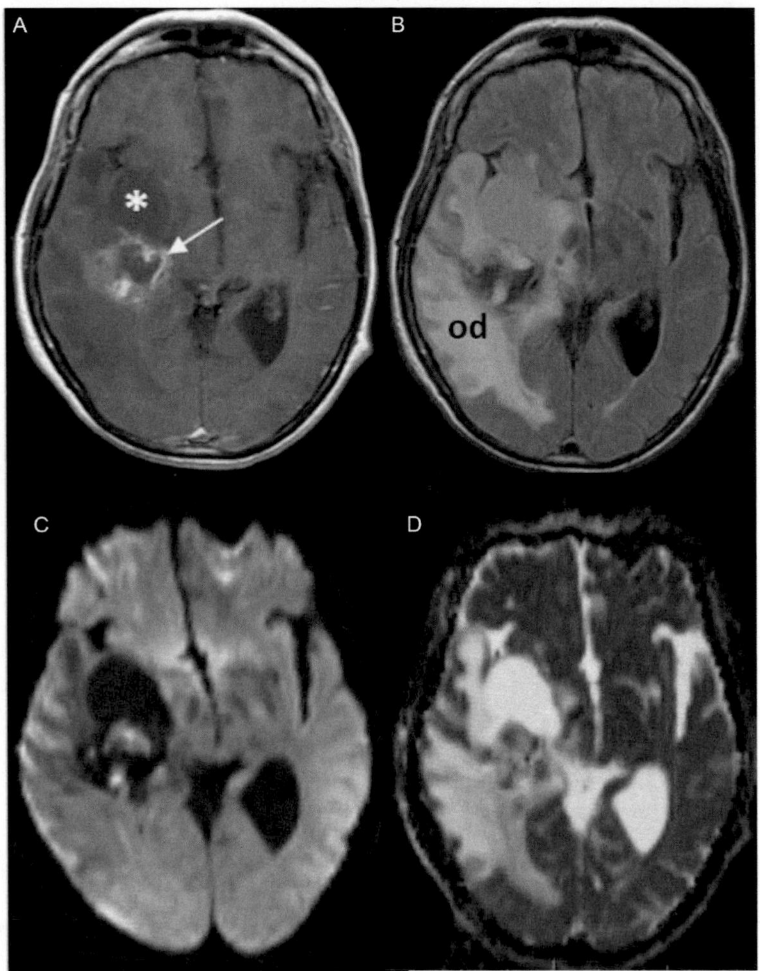

FIG. 23.3

MR brain imaging showing mass effect, midline shift, and obstructive hydrocephalus from enlargement of a histologically benign, right temporal papillary endothelial hyperplasia mass lesion comprising fibrin-rich blood clot along with a close network of thin-walled blood vessels and necrotic material [13]. (A) A ring of enhancement with gadolinium is demonstrated within the semi-solid aspect of the lesion in the T_1-weighted image (*arrow*), which also shows patchy hypointensity on the DWI (C; b1000 image) and hyperintensity on the ADC map (D), reflecting areas of necrosis. A much more cystic component is seen (*) separately from the surrounding vasogenic edema (od) demonstrated on FLAIR (B).

cortical areas of involvement [43,44]. However, for deep gray matter structures and more established encephalitic processes, FLAIR is considered superior. Furthermore, the evolution of ADC through an initial reduction to an increased level after several weeks is believed to reflect the ensuing necrosis characteristic of HSV encephalitis, and this information can contribute to the radiological likelihood of this

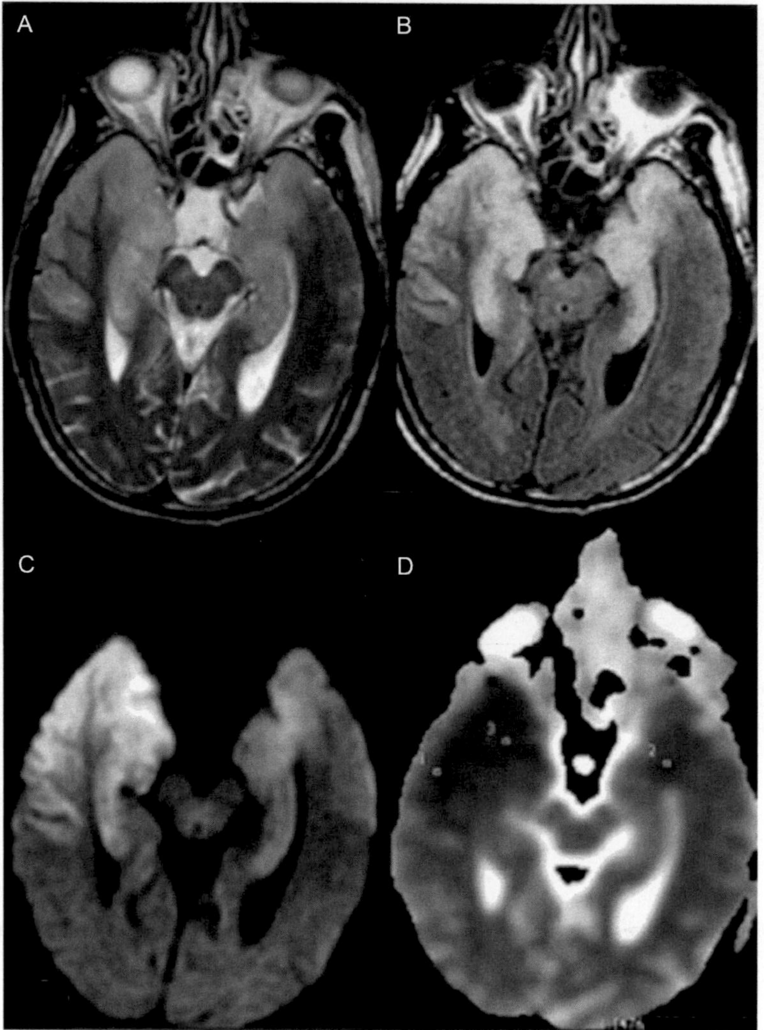

FIG. 23.4

MR brain imaging of Herpes simplex virus encephalitis within 1 week of symptom onset. Bilateral involvement of the temporal lobes is demonstrated with prominent mesial gyral swelling secondary to cytotoxic edema on the axial T_2-weighted (A) and FLAIR (B) images, with hyperintensity on DWI (C) and hypointensity on the ADC map (D) especially about the cortex.

(Reprinted from Sawlani V. Diffusion-weighted imaging and apparent diffusion coefficient evaluation of herpes simplex encephalitis and Japanese encephalitis. J Neurol Sci 2009;287:221–26. Copyright (2009), with permission from Elsevier.)

diagnosis alongside features of gyral swelling, hemorrhage, and enhancement demonstrated on standard sequences [43–45]. A specific role for diffusion imaging in the autoimmune encephalitides is less clear [32], although the insidious tempo of symptoms, corroborative clinical signs, and temporo-limbic signal abnormalities on T_2-weighted and FLAIR images may be more suggestive.

Encephalitis driven by autoimmunity or infection is, nevertheless, a differential diagnosis for the spongiform encephalopathies in which diffusion imaging constitutes part of the diagnostic criteria [46]. Patients with the most common manifestation, sporadic Creutzfeldt-Jakob disease (sCJD), typically demonstrate signal hyperintensity within the deep gray matter of the basal ganglia, notably the striatum and caudate, on T_2-weighted, FLAIR and proton density contrasts. However, changes in these areas and certainly within the cortex are more readily detectable on DWI and ADC maps [45,47]. The cortical DWI hyperintensity and ADC hypointensity follow the gyral undulations, usually within the cingulate and neocortex, appearing as a distinctive "ribbon" (Fig. 23.5), where the exact basis for

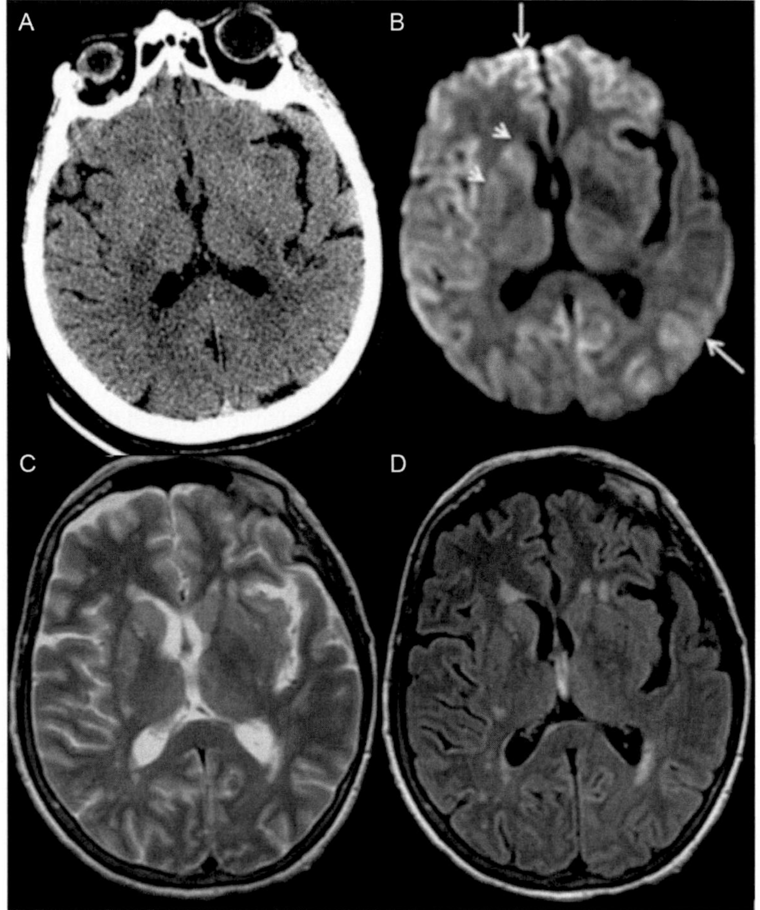

FIG. 23.5

Brain imaging of sporadic Creutzfeldt-Jakob disease (sCJD). (A) The unenhanced CT is unrevealing whereas (B) the DWI demonstrates bilateral hyperintensity in the frontal and occipital cortices *(long arrows)* in addition to the right caudate and anterior putamen *(arrowheads)*. The abnormalities are far less evident on the (C) T_2-weighted and (D) FLAIR images.

(Reproduced from Gaudino S, et al. Neuroradiology of human prion diseases, diagnosis and differential diagnosis. Radiol Med 2017;122:369–85 with permission from Springer Nature.)

the abnormally restricted diffusion unknown. As time passes MRI findings become more extensive, given that mitochondriopathies such as MELAS (mitochondrial encephalomyopathy with lactic acidosis and stroke-like episodes) can precipitate similar cortical ribboning appearances on DWI, but corresponding contrast enhancement or swelling is not seen in sCJD [45,48].

23.3 Research applications of diffusion imaging

In addition to the standard diffusion imaging currently employed for clinical investigation, more advanced forms of diffusion imaging in the brain are increasingly being used to study patients with neuroinflammatory, neurodegenerative, neoplastic, vascular, and psychiatric conditions to understand the neural correlates of these disorders and also establish MRI as a noninvasive and objective biological marker ("biomarker") of disease activity in vivo. The use of diffusion may enable more accurate prognostication and treatment planning or monitoring of individual patients' responses, particularly in the setting of clinical trials for potential new therapies.

23.3.1 Multiple sclerosis (MS)

MS is an autoimmune disease of the central nervous system (CNS) that typically affects both the brain and the spinal cord. It is the greatest cause of nontraumatic disability in young adults in Western world populations. The most common clinical phenotype of the disease is the so-called relapsing-remitting (RR) MS, which is characterized by recurrent events of inflammation and demyelination ("relapses") that, according to the anatomical distribution of tissue damage, affect various neurological systems and produce a wide range of symptoms including visual loss, deficits of other cranial nerves, motor and sensory impairments, coordination loss, and cognitive impairment. These episodes are typically followed by a spontaneous recovery that may be complete (especially at the beginning of the disease) or partial, in the latter case resulting in permanent disabilities. In a proportion of patients, MS relapses tend to overlap over time with a less clear-cut recovery, such that there is a progressive accumulation of disability. This change of clinical course is known as conversion or transition from RR-MS to the secondary progressive (SP) MS. About 10%–15% of patients present with a progressive clinical course from the very beginning, and are classified as suffering from primary progressive (PP) MS.

The pathological hallmark of MS is the presence of demyelinated lesions within the white matter (WM) and gray matter (GM) of the brain and spinal cord, and optic nerves. Immune-cell infiltration across the BBB causes inflammation and demyelination that are followed by subsequent gliosis and axonal/neuronal degeneration. Inflammation, demyelination, and axonal loss, although linked to each other, can also occur independently in MS brains [49]. Some repair mechanisms may also occur, although histological evidence of remyelination reveals that the myelin sheaths do not recover their original properties [50]. In clinical practice T_2- and T_1-weighted images are used to detect and monitor the accumulation of MS lesions. Gadolinium-enhanced T_1-weighted images are used to demonstrate the presence of BBB disruption. Despite the usefulness of this information for the clinical management of MS patients, the correlation between lesion volumes and clinical disability is moderate in RRMS and modest in SPMS and PPMS [51,52]. This is due to the complexity of MS pathophysiology and the widespread distribution of microscopic tissue damage outside of visible lesions, in the so-called normal-appearing WM (NAWM) and GM (NAGM) [53]. This diffuse damage causes a disconnection between areas of the CNS and ultimately accounts for the disability accumulated by MS patients, particularly those with progressive MS. [54]

MS has been widely investigated using diffusion MRI with over 300 published papers. DTI parameters have been reported to be altered within the macroscopic MS lesions compared to the NAWM, with an increase in diffusivity (mean, radial, and axial diffusivity) and reduced FA. Although nonspecific, these changes reflect the loss of myelin and axons, and the presence of gliosis, whose combination is extremely heterogeneous across lesions [55]. Remarkably, DTI abnormalities are detectable also in the NAWM of patients with MS, indicating the presence of widespread, subtle microscopic brain tissue damage from the early stages of the disease [53]. The NAGM is also characterized by abnormal diffusion parameters that reflect the presence of invisible lesions in addition to neuronal loss due to Wallerian degeneration secondary to remote WM lesions. This range of diffuse abnormalities across large portions of WM and GM may help to explain the moderate correlations found between macroscopic tissue damage (such as visible lesions on T_2-weighted imaging) and disability in MS. Interestingly, a paradoxical mismatch between DTI parameters has been found in the basal ganglia of patients with MS, with an increase of FA alongside a reduction of mean diffusivity (MD) [56]. This result was interpreted as a selective degeneration of fibers due to remote WM lesions [56], and reported to correlate with disability in patients with RR- and SPMS [57–60]. The principle contribution of these early DTI studies in MS was to highlight the importance of the diffuse anatomical distribution of invisible damage that may be quantified via diffusion and correlated with patients' disability. Their main limitation lies in the inability to distinguish between pathophysiological mechanisms that coexist in various combinations in the CNS of MS patients at different clinical stages.

More recently, diffusion imaging methods such as "q-space imaging" (QSI) and "diffusion kurtosis imaging" (DKI) have been introduced and may have the ability to assess more detailed biophysical properties of the pathological substrates occurring in MS. A comparison between QSI and DTI demonstrated a higher sensitivity of the former technique in detecting subtle pathological abnormalities within the NAWM of patients with mild to severe MS. [61] QSI has been shown to have a high sensitivity in detecting biophysical abnormalities in the spinal cord of patients with MS, again accompanied by associations with clinical symptoms [62,63].

Similarly, DKI has proven sensitive to microscopic damage of both NAWM and NAGM in patients with MS [31,64,65]. Besides, when applied to specific WM tracts, interesting associations were reported between DKI-derived metrics, neuropsychological measures, and neurophysiological parameters from evoked potentials [66]. This association with neurophysiological data (i.e., evoked potential latencies reflect the degree of myelination) indicates that DKI is particularly sensitive to the underlying phenomena of demyelination [67], as supported by animal model studies [68,69]. Despite a higher sensitivity to pathological damage, QSI and DKI still lack specificity on the nature of different pathological substrates. A novel technique with the ability to model water diffusion in different tissue compartments is called Neurite Orientation and Density Imaging (NODDI), which has been shown to provide accurate microstructural information in postmortem samples [70]. This approach is expected to capture the morphology of dendrites and axons and, for this reason, is particularly suitable for GM investigations. A study in a group of 35 patients with either RRMS and SPMS performed on a clinical scanner has identified orientation dispersion computed by NODDI within the thalamus as a possible biomarker of disease progression [71]. Interestingly, this finding supports the theory that selective degeneration of fibers within the basal ganglia occurs in MS, as was previously proposed to explain DTI results [56]. Fig. 23.6 shows the association between the principal NODDI-derived metrics and measures of disability in RR- and SPMS patients.

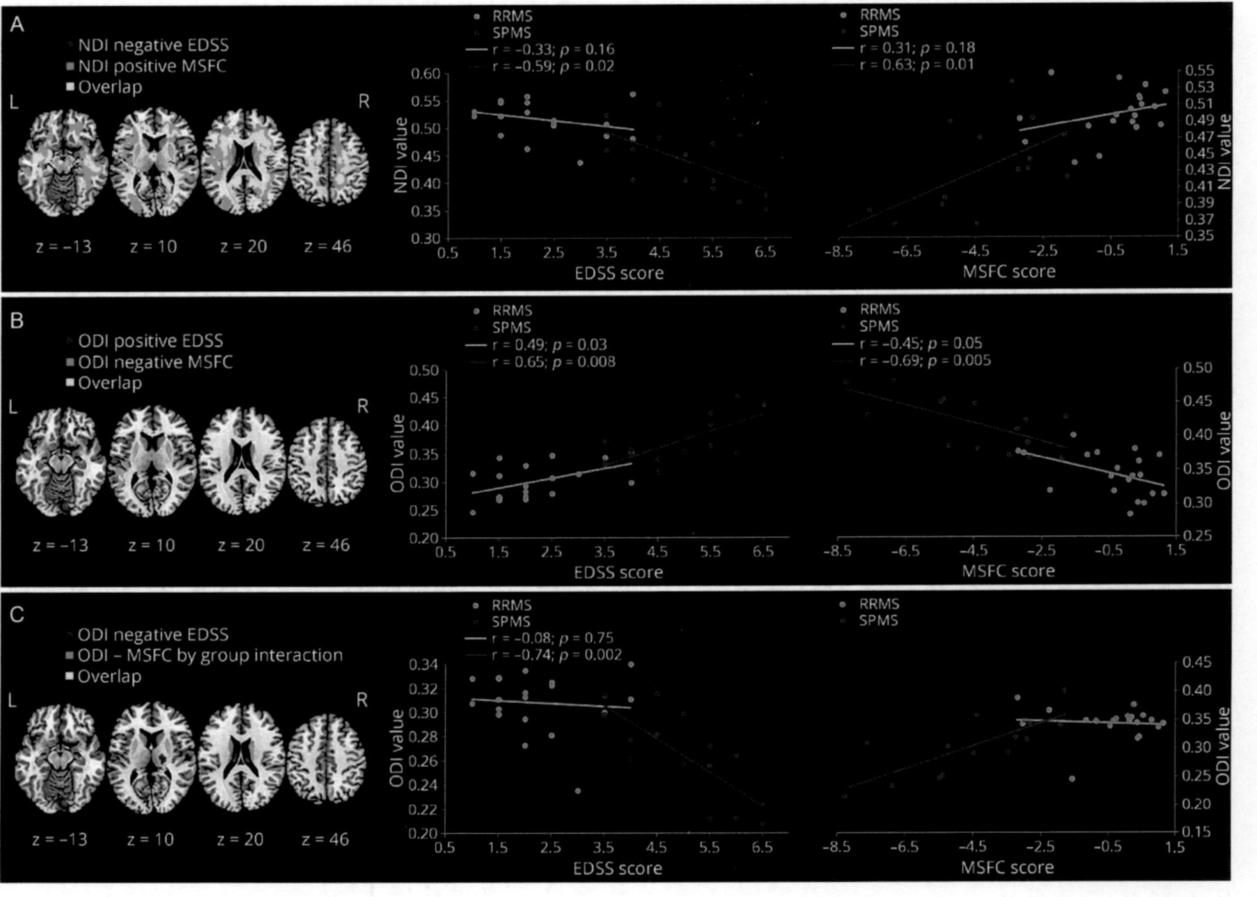

FIG. 23.6

Areas of a significant association between NODDI metrics and EDSS *(in red)* and MSFC *(in green)*. The overlap is shown in *yellow*. (A) Areas of a significant association between NDI and EDSS/MSFC. (B) Areas of a significant association between ODI and EDSS (positive) and MSFC (negative). (C) Areas of significant correlation between ODI and EDSS (negative) and MSFC (positive). For each panel, the scatterplot shows the trends for RRMS and SPMS separately. In all scatterplots NDI, ODI, and FA are averaged across all significant voxels, ranging from 0 to 1, and are dimensionless. Significant clusters are shown at *P*-value $<.05$ (FWE corrected) overlaid onto a template in Montreal Neurological Institute space. Abbreviations: *EDSS*, Expanded Disability Status Scale; *FA*, fractional anisotropy; *FWE*, family-wise error; *MSFC*, MS functional composite; *NDI*, neurite density; *NODDI*, neurite orientation dispersion and density imaging; *ODI*, orientation dispersion; *RRMS*, relapsing-remitting MS; *SPMS*, secondary progressive MS.

(Reproduced from Spano B, et al. Disruption of neurite morphology parallels MS progression. Neurol Neuroimmunol Neuroinflamm 2018;5(6):e502 with permission from Wolters Kluwer Health Inc.)

Diffusion MRI can be used not only to examine the histopathological features (e.g., demyelination, axonal loss, gliosis, etc.) occurring within the CNS of patients with MS but also to clarify the impact of local damage within neurological systems. Indeed, DTI-based tractography allows reconstruction and segmentation of the main WM tracts in vivo, as well as an assessment of macro- (tract volume) and microscopic measures of tissue integrity. This approach offers the unique opportunity to target pathways associated with specific functional impairments, and to focus on clinically eloquent areas. Within the corticospinal tract, mean diffusivity (MD), axial diffusivity (AD), and radial diffusivity (RD) were consistently found to be increased in patients with MS, and associated with measures of functional impairment, such as the timed-walk test or the pyramidal functional system of the expanded disability status scale (EDSS) [72,73]. A diffusion tractography based approach, called anatomical connectivity mapping (ACM), was introduced to assess the structural brain connectivity in a data-driven fashion, by running tractography from every voxel of the brain and counting how many streamlines pass through each voxel [74]. When applied to patients with RRMS, this method showed reduced ACM in the thalamus and the head of the caudate nucleus, and strict associations with the patients' level of cognitive impairment [75].

Another approach to look into functional systems by diffusion imaging is based on the use of the graph-theory [76]. Relevant GM areas are modeled as "nodes" that are connected through "edges." Edges represent WM connections and are characterized by topological properties expressing measures of integration/segregation and efficiency of the network. Using this approach, a motor network efficiency score based on FA, tissue volume, and magnetization transfer ratio (MTR, proportional to myelin content), was found to account for 58% of the variation in EDSS in a group of MS patients [77].

23.3.2 Amyotrophic lateral sclerosis (ALS)

ALS is a rapidly progressive, multisystem neurodegenerative syndrome primarily involving the loss of pyramidal and spinal motor neurons, leading to progressive weakness and death. Extramotor involvement including frontal dysexecutive impairments is common [78,79] along with a smaller percentage of patients who fulfill the criteria for overt frontotemporal dementia [78–80] with which there is a recognized neuropathological overlap [81]. The clinical presentation comprises a phenotypic spectrum ranging from limb, bulbar, respiratory, or cognitive symptom onset [80,82–84] followed by, usually, contiguous propagation of symptoms to adjacent body regions [82,85,86], but the disease remains heterogeneous with varying rates of progression between individuals and only very modest benefit from medication. More effective disease-modifying treatment is desperately needed and, consequently, neuroimaging biomarkers sensitive to the mechanisms and patterns of tissue damage over time are highly sought. Although hyperintensity of the corticospinal tract [87–89] or hypointensity of the precentral gray matter [89,90] on T_2-weighted imaging or FLAIR is sometimes observed, this appearance is inconsistent, and DWI and ADC maps have no added value [91,92]. Therefore, conventional MRI contrasts are used only to rule out disease mimics ALS, rather than confirm the diagnosis or enlighten mechanisms of degeneration [93]. However, DTI has yielded a wealth of information on structural alterations primarily in white matter tracts and constitutes the most widely researched MRI diffusion modality in patients with ALS.

FA is consistently reduced in ALS patients, often alongside increased MD or RD, within the CSTs [94–107] and body of the corpus callosum, through which interconnecting fibers from each hemisphere's motor cortices pass [95,97–100,102,104,108,109]. Indeed, DTI changes are perhaps most reliably encountered within the posterior limb of the internal capsule [110,111] which forms a common conduit for several descending motor pathways including the CST and corticorubral connections [112]. Additional areas within the frontal and temporal lobes, including cingulum/cingulate gyrus and insula [28,29,103], and parietal areas [30,103], have shown reduced FA, which is consistent with known regions of neuropathological damage postmortem [33,113,114] and altered metabolism and function were seen on single-photon emission computed tomography (SPECT) [115], positron emission tomography (PET) [116–119], and functional MRI [120,121]. Although these are often referred to as "extramotor" areas, pyramidal neurons from the cingulate cortex project to the red nucleus and spinal cord, and are thought to be heavily integrated into motor functioning [29,122]. Furthermore, pyramidal cells within the somatosensory cortex and parietal lobe contribute directly to the CST [123] and a DTI fiber tracking technique have been used to demonstrate that loss of fibers from the postcentral gyrus in ALS underlies a small proportion of the reduced FA within the CST [103]. The relationship between changes in DTI metrics within the brain and clinical severity on ALS symptom rating scales is also highly variable [97,108], perhaps in part, because clinical motor deficits are more reflective of spinal motor neuron loss in the anterior horn [124]. The ability to link DTI metrics with ALS symptoms may be improved with developments in diffusion MRI of the spinal cord, which is a small number of studies, has demonstrated reduced FA [125–128], increased RD [126,128], and reduced cord cross-sectional area [125,127], and significant associations with clinical scores.

Longitudinal DTI scans of the CSTs have indicated both the presence [129–133] and absence [94,125] of demonstrable change over intervals of between 6–9 months. Those patients who present with signs representative of more CST damage appear to show the least difference over time [132], which suggests detectable damage is already "saturated" from the outset and echo the longitudinal studies of cortical thickness change in ALS [134,135]. Meta-analyses to determine the capabilities of averaged brain CST FA to diagnose the condition has suggested modest overall sensitivity and specificity of up to 0.68 and 0.73, respectively [136,137]. Discriminative power may be enhanced by applying DTI of the spinal cord [136,138,139] or a mixture of modalities, although further work is required. Nevertheless, as diffusion MRI techniques evolve they may become clinically applicable for diagnosis and indicate early response to disease-modifying treatments.

Indeed, it is widely accepted that the DTI model loses consistency when fibers bend or where aligned tracts cross each other [97], and thus a reduction in FA cannot be used as a surrogate marker for "loss of integrity." [140] The alternative three-compartment diffusion MRI technique known as NODDI (neurite orientation dispersion and density imaging) may be able to provide a more meaningful interpretation of these areas. NODDI parameters include ISO (isotropic volume fraction), NDI (neurite density index), and ODI (orientation dispersion index; a marker of the geometric complexity of neurites) with the latter two considered to provide a more structurally useful breakdown of single FA values. Although the use of NODDI in ALS is in its infancy, whole-brain analysis has recently shown a significant reduction in NDI throughout the CSTs and across the corpus callosum, with less extensive changes seen in FA at the same statistical threshold (Fig. 23.7) [141]. Indeed, combined NODDI and DTI have also been performed in a cohort of pre-manifest carriers of the *C9orf72* gene mutation for familial ALS, alongside noncarrier relatives. The degree of reduction in NDI values within more than 60% of white matter tracts studies, including the CSTs, was more marked than changes observed for DTI metrics (represented by increased AD, RD, and MD rather than decreased FA in this instance),

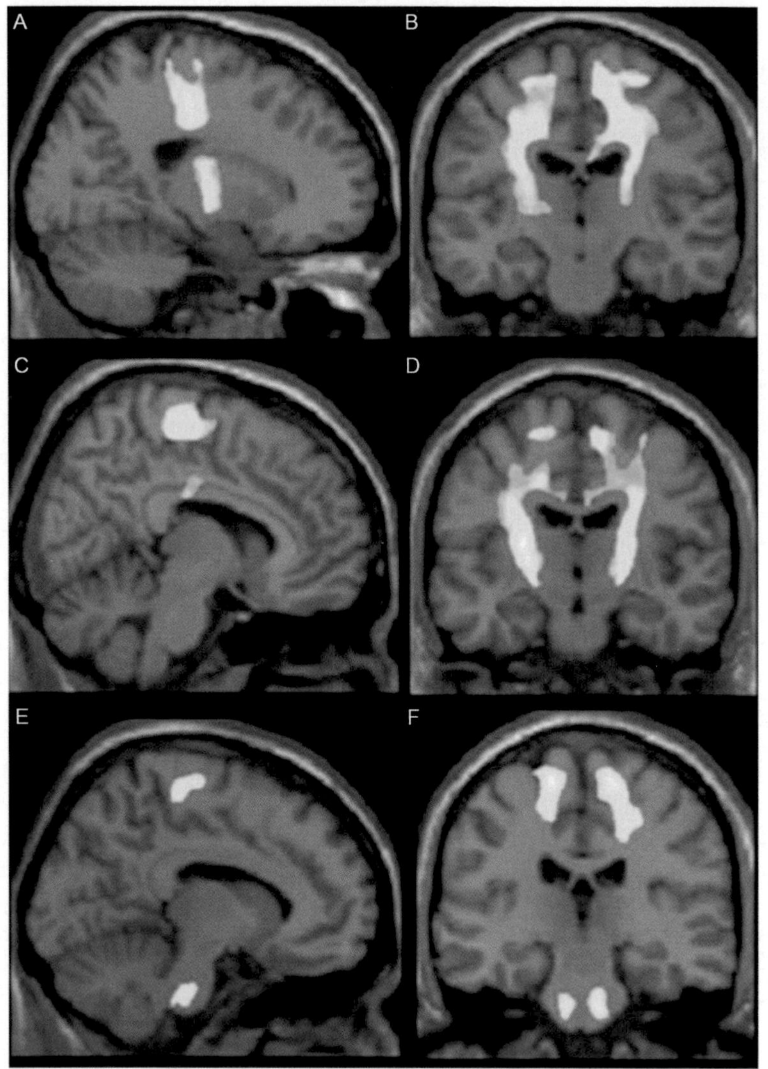

FIG. 23.7

NODDI brain imaging in amyotrophic lateral sclerosis (ALS). (A)–(D) show areas of significant difference in neurite density index (NDI) within the corticospinal tracts and corpus callosum between patients and controls, whereas the changes measured by FA from DTI (in E and F) are less marked.

(Reproduced from Broad RJ, et al. Neurite orientation and dispersion density imaging (NODDI) detects cortical and corticospinal tract degeneration in ALS. J Neurol Neurosurg Psychiatry 2018;90(4):404–11 with permission from BMJ Publishing Group Ltd.)

although statistical significance was reached in only two tracts [142]. Nevertheless, the results imply that NODDI may be more sensitive than DTI and able to corroborate the implication that reduced FA (or increased diffusivity) in the CSTs and corpus callosum results from the loss of axon fibers rather than their increased complexity or dispersion. As imaging methods evolve and data are analyzed with evermore sophisticated techniques, further insights into the degenerative process in ALS are anticipated [143].

23.3.3 Dementia

The diagnosis of different forms of neurodegenerative dementias is currently based on their clinical and neuropsychological characterization along with neuroimaging biomarkers. Neurodegenerative dementias, such as Alzheimer's disease (AD) [144,145], dementia with Lewy Bodies (DLB) [146,147], and frontotemporal dementia (FTD) [148–151] are typically characterized by an insidious clinical onset which is followed by a gradual progression of cognitive and behavioral symptoms. Especially at early clinical stages, the underlying neurodegenerative processes produce selective cognitive dysfunctions that may correspond to both a focal distribution of brain damage and disconnection mechanisms.

23.3.3.1 Alzheimer's disease (AD)

From a neuropathological viewpoint, AD is characterized by an accumulation of neurofibrillary tangles and β-Amyloid plaques that cause a progressive neuronal loss in the cerebral cortex [152]. These tangles and plaques typically arise in the entorhinal cortex and limbic system and eventually spread to the associative neocortices. The cognitive symptoms parallel the distribution of brain damage: first limited to temporo-limbic dysfunctions (isolated episodic memory, language, and emotional dysfunctions) and then engulfing other cognitive domains in the framework of progressive cognitive deterioration.

AD has been traditionally considered a neurodegenerative disorder involving mainly the GM tissue [153]. However, several studies in the last decades using DWI and regional assessment of measures of WM integrity (such as MD and FA) have shown widespread WM damage in AD brains [153]. On this basis, a disconnection hypothesis was put forward to explain some of the clinical symptoms observed in AD [154]. Early DWI studies [155–159] revealed the presence of microstructural abnormalities in several associative WM areas, including the splenium of the corpus callosum, the superior longitudinal fasciculus, and the cingulum, with relative sparing of the motor pathways and the occipital lobes [155,159]. Importantly, DWI-derived measures reflective of reduced WM integrity correlated with the severity of patients' cognitive decline [155,159]. When using a histogram analysis to assess global measures of DTI changes (FA and MD) in the GM and WM of patients with AD, the temporal lobes emerged as the most affected areas [156]. This simple approach to DTI analysis has been recently applied to large cohorts of patients with AD and mild cognitive impairment (MCI) [160] (the prodromal stage of AD) to assess the most prominent WM changes over the disease evolution [161]. Axial diffusivity in the WM was suggested as an early marker of microstructural brain tissue damage that might be useful for assessing disease progression [161]. Further studies based on voxel-wise image analysis methods confirmed a prominent disruption of associative WM tracts in AD. In particular, investigations based on the Tract Based Spatial Statistics (TBSS) method [162] revealed that WM damage is at least partially independent from GM atrophy and, again, associated with cognitive symptoms [163–165]. Fig. 23.8 shows the pattern of FA reductions in the WM tissue across disease evolution when comparing normal aging to the prodromal condition of amnestic MCI and then fully-developed AD [165].

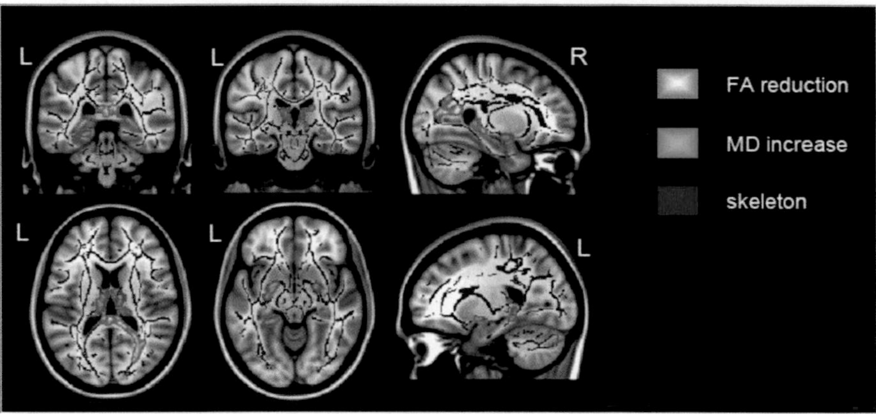

FIG. 23.8

Regional patterns of a progressive decrease in WM FA (*in pink, in blue* the TBSS skeleton) and increase in MD *(in green)* passing from healthy controls through amnestic MCI to AD patients. Decrease of FA has been found mainly in the splenium of the corpus callosum, right fornix, right cingulum, bilateral anterior thalamic radiations, and right posterior thalamic radiation. The images are overlaid on top of the MNI T_1-weighted template provided with FSL. Abbreviations: *FA*, fractional anisotropy; *MD*, mean diffusivity; *MCI*, mild cognitive impairment; *R*, right; *TBSS*, tract-based spatial statistics; *WM*, white matter.

(Reprinted from Serra L, et al. Grey and white matter changes at different stages of Alzheimer's disease. J Alzheimers Dis 2010;19:147–59 with permission from IOS Press.)

Recently TBSS was used to assess WM microstructural differences between patients with AD and those with vascular dementia (VD) [166]. AD and VD patients share the presence of macroscopic WM lesions, and distinguishing between these two clinical conditions may be difficult. Specific microstructural abnormalities were identified in the parahippocampal tract of AD patients and in the thalamic radiation of VD patients, respectively, alongside a different distribution of WM abnormalities along the corpus callosum and prominent involvement of the splenium in AD and genu in VD [166]. The disruption of some specific WM tracts seems to play an important role in the pathophysiological mechanisms of AD.

Diffusion-based tractography (a technique that allows reconstruction of WM tracts and bundles) has been successfully used to investigate AD brains at different clinical stages. For instance, microstructural deterioration of the cingulum (a structure connecting the medial temporal lobes with the rest of the brain) is associated with the transition from MCI to fully-developed AD (Fig. 23.9) [167]. Moreover, the uncinate bundle that connects the temporal pole with the orbitofrontal lobe, was found to be damaged in patients with AD [168–170]. Interestingly, damage to this tract was associated with patients' memory and executive performances [168], which are cognitive abilities mediated by the temporal and frontal lobes. This same tract was found to be equally damaged in patients with AD and DLB (the second most common form of neurodegenerative dementia) [146,147] but not in those with MCI [168]. This is consistent with the clinical observation that behavioral symptoms are particularly early and common in patients with DLB whilst, with AD pathology, they typically occur at advanced disease stages. Within the framework of diffusion-based tractography, the anatomical connectivity

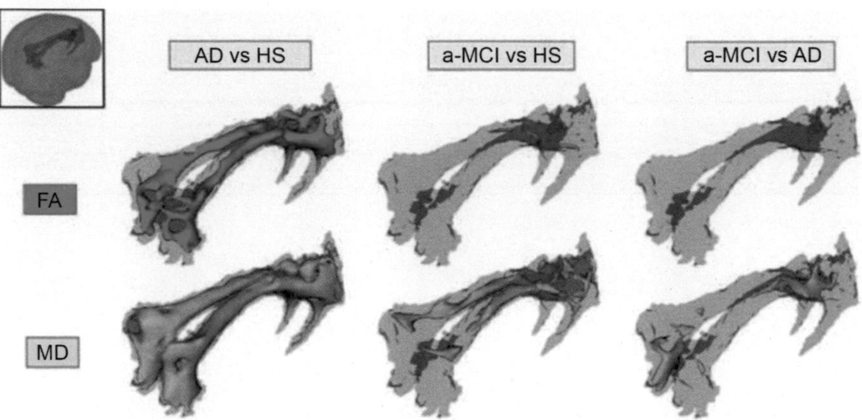

FIG. 23.9

Results of between-group voxel-wise comparisons of FA *(in green)* and MD *(in yellow)* measured in the Cingulum bundle. Patients with a-MCI compared to HS showed a few regions of reduced FA and a diffuse increase of MD along the Cingulum. Conversely, patients with AD showed widespread areas of reduced FA and increased MD compared to HS. Abbreviations: *AD*, Alzheimer's disease; *a-MCI*, amnestic mild cognitive impairment; *FA*, fractional anisotropy; *HS*, healthy subjects; *MD*, mean diffusivity.

(Reproduced from Bozzali M, et al. Damage to the cingulum contributes to Alzheimer's disease pathophysiology by deafferentation mechanism. Hum Brain Mapp 2012;33:1295–1308 by permission of John Wiley and Sons.)

mapping [74] method has been used to investigate the changes in structural brain connectivity in a voxel-wise fashion across the transitional stage between normal aging and fully-developed AD [171]. Expected areas of reduced connectivity were identified in the supramarginal gyrus of AD patients [171]. Besides, unexpected areas of increased connectivity were found in the anterior thalamic radiation of AD patients when compared to both patients with MCI and healthy controls [171]. These findings were replicated in a larger study [172], and interpreted as reflecting mechanisms of plasticity due to pharmacological intervention (Fig. 23.10). This indicates a potential capability of diffusion imaging to be used as a tool for monitoring clinical trials for AD patients.

It has been recognized that alongside the typical form of AD (usually the amnestic variant) there are the so-called "atypical" presentations of AD, which include language deficits (logopenic variant of primary progressive aphasia; lv-PPA), visuospatial deficits (posterior cortical atrophy; PCA), and executive dysfunction (behavioral variant) [144]. A recent study using DTI data in a whole-brain voxel-based analysis (DTI-VBA) showed that different AD phenotypes, including typical AD, lv-PPA, and PCA, present with degeneration of both common and specific structural networks [173]. Alterations of the fornix, the corpus callosum, the posterior thalamic radiation, the superior and inferior longitudinal fasciculi were observed in all AD variants [173]. Conversely, degeneration of the cingulum was associated specifically with the typical amnestic variant form of AD [173]. Abnormalities of the fronto-occipital and uncinate fasciculi were associated with lv-PPA, and changes in the posterior part of the cingulum and the splenium of the corpus callosum were associated with the PCA variant [173]. More recently, VBA was used to assess DTI differences in different subtypes of MCI patients, showing that FA and MD abnormalities are present in the hippocampal part of the

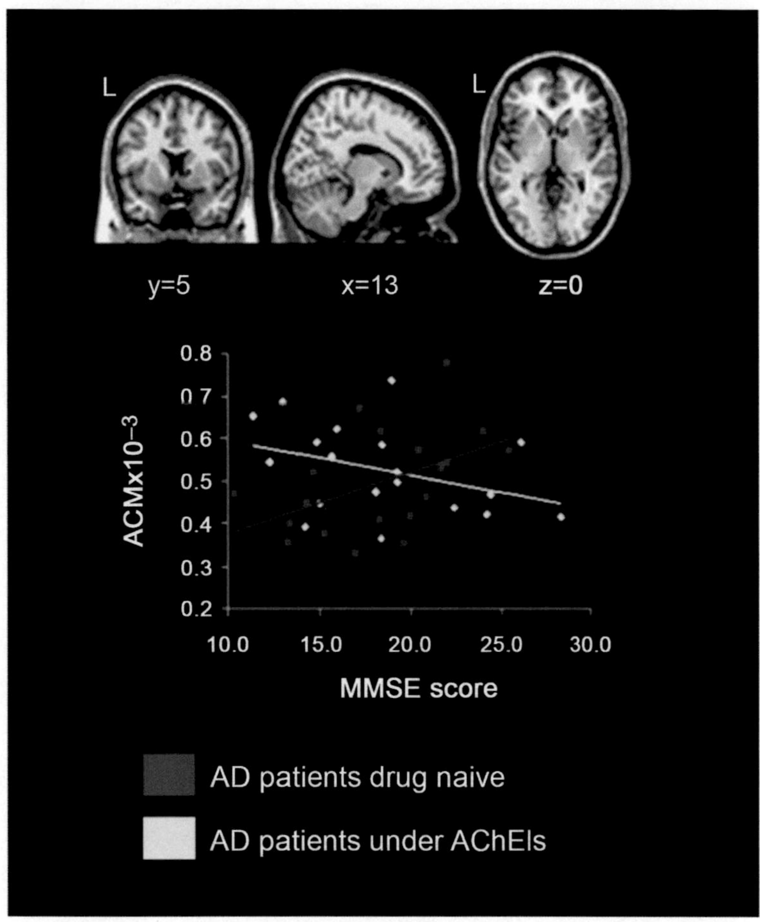

FIG. 23.10

The relationship between the administration of Acetylcholinesterase inhibitors (AChEIs; yes or no) and the global level of cognition (as measured by MMSE) on ACM of patients with AD. The *red area* largely overlaps with the one found to be directly associated with exposure to AChEIs. In the graph, there is a reported an association between individual MMSE scores and ACM values derived from the brain area of interaction for the two groups of patients, drug-naive *(in violet)*, and under medication *(in yellow)*. This direct correlation is present in the former group of patients and it is lost in the latter one. Abbreviations: *AChEIs*, acetylcholinesterase inhibitors; *ACM*, anatomical connectivity mapping; *AD*, Alzheimer's disease; *MMSE*, mini-mental state examination.

(Reproduced from Bozzali M, et al. Brain tissue modifications induced by cholinergic therapy in Alzheimer's disease. Hum Brain Mapp 2013;34:3158–67 by permission of John Wiley and Sons.)

cingulum of amnestic MCI patients when compared to both healthy controls and non-amnestic MCI patients [174]. Nir and colleagues, using the DTI maximum density path (MDP) analysis, a novel DTI approach based on graph theory, identified different patterns of WM abnormalities across different transitional stages of AD [175]. Specifically, AD patients showed significantly lower FA and higher

MD throughout the commissural and long associative fibers compared to normal controls [175]. Patients at a later stage of MCI showed higher MD in the temporal lobe tracts compared to controls, whereas no differences were observed with patients at earlier MCI stages [175]. These DTI features extracted using the MDP method were entered into a machine learning model to identify MRI biomarkers useful for detecting early features of AD progression. MD was found to be associated with higher accuracy, sensitivity, and specificity than FA to correctly identify patients at different stages of AD progression [175].

DTI measures have also been combined with histopathological markers of neurodegeneration to investigate their relationship with measures of clinical disease severity ex vivo [176]. A group of clinically-diagnosed AD patients with antemortem DTI data and postmortem neuropathological confirmation were considered in the study. Patients with a high neurofibrillary tangle load had significantly increased MD values in the crus of the fornix and the ventral cingulum, precuneus, and entorhinal WM [176]. This pattern of abnormalities was strongly associated with patients' clinical-stage but, interestingly, no significant association was observed between MD or FA metrics and β-amyloid plaques [176].

23.3.3.2 Non-AD forms of neurodegenerative dementia

WM microstructural abnormalities have been identified also in non-AD types of neurodegenerative dementia. Similar to AD, peculiar patterns of diffusion-related changes seem to account for the clinical characteristics observed in patients with non-AD types of dementia.

As mentioned earlier, DLB is regarded as the second most common form of dementia in terms of prevalence and incidence in the population [146,147], and it shares some clinical symptoms with AD. In patients with DLB, a seminal DTI-based study identified WM abnormalities expressed in terms of FA reductions and MD increases, involving mainly the corpus callosum, the frontoparietal and occipital areas, and the putamen, with a less remarkable involvement of the temporal lobes, compared to controls [177]. This pattern of abnormalities fits well with the core clinical features of DLB [146,147], which include cognitive decline dominated by visuospatial deficits, parkinsonism, and visual hallucinations. Besides, DTI metrics correlated with patients' visuo-perceptive deficits, the cognitive hallmark of DLB. The relative sparing of memory impairment characteristic of DLB is supported by neuroimaging data, with evidence of higher FA values in the parahippocampal regions compared to AD patients [178]. A TBSS study investigated the integrity of WM in AD and DLB patients and revealed a peculiar pattern of FA reduction in visuo-perceptive regions, along with the pons and in the thalamus, of DLB patients compared to those with AD [179]. A longitudinal TBSS investigation demonstrated that WM abnormalities arise relatively early but remain stable over time in DLB patients [180]. After 1-year follow-up, MD increases were greater in AD patients compared normal controls, while no longitudinal differences were observed between patients with DLB and controls [180].

Several studies have highlighted the occurrence of specific WM damages among different clinical phenotypes of FTD. For instance, a study based on a voxel-wise assessment of GM and WM compared the different variants of FTD patients against healthy controls [181]. In patients with the non-fluent/agrammatic variant of a primary progressive aphasia (PPA), GM, and WM abnormalities were identified in the frontal and temporal language areas, with selective microscopic damage in the left superior longitudinal/arcuate fasciculus [181]. Conversely, in patients with the semantic variant of PPA (SD), the damage was restricted to the uncinate fasciculus bilaterally and to the left inferior longitudinal fasciculus [181] TBSS has been used to identify the longitudinal progression of WM abnormalities in

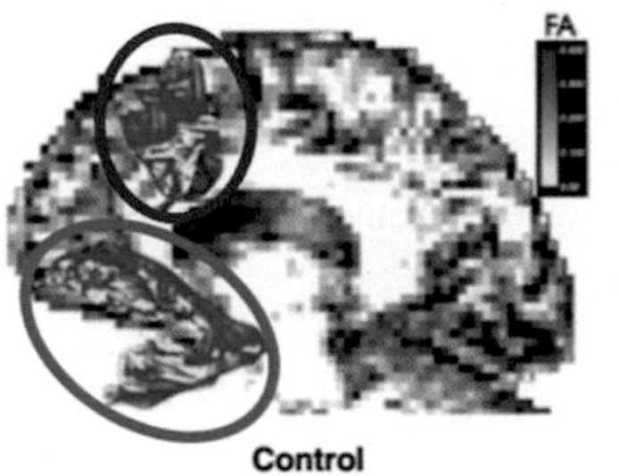

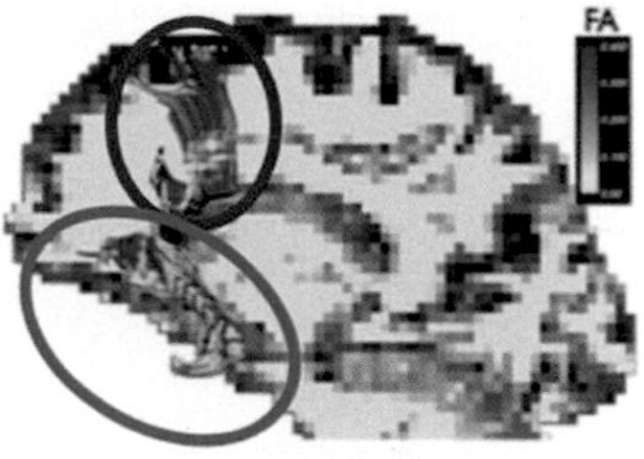

FIG. 23.11

The figure illustrates the differences of FA in the frontal aslant tract *(circled in red)* and uncinate fasciculus *(circled in blue)* between healthy controls, patients with non-fluent/agrammatic variant of Primary Progressive Aphasia (PPA), and semantic variant of PPA. Compared to controls, non-fluent/agrammatic variant of PPA patients showed significantly reduced FA in the FAT, while semantic variant of PPA patients showed significantly reduced FA in the UNC. Abbreviations: *FA*, fractional anisotropy; *FAT*, frontal aslant tract; *UNC*, uncinated fasciculus.

(Reproduced from Catani M, et al. A novel frontal pathway underlies verbal fluency in primary progressive aphasia. Brain 2013;136:2619–28 by permission of Oxford University Press.)

patients with PPA [182]. Over a 1-year timeframe, the left inferior longitudinal fasciculus was highly disrupted in the logopenic variant of PPA, while patients with SD showed a more prominent disruption of the uncinate fasciculus [182]. Interestingly, a DTI tractography study revealed that microscopic abnormalities in the frontal aslant tract, which connects the supplementary and pre-supplementary motor areas with Broca's area (the motor language area), are associated with the speech disorder observed in patients with the logopenic variant of PPA, while damage in the uncinate fasciculus correlates with the semantic deficits observed in patients with SD (Fig. 23.11) [183].

23.3.4 Psychiatric disorders

Diffusion imaging has improved the pathophysiological understanding of various psychiatric disorders. This section describes how diffusion imaging has informed three distinct diagnostic categories in current psychiatric nosology, namely, schizophrenia, bipolar disorder, and major depressive disorder, for which common as well as differential patterns of GM and WM abnormalities have been identified [184]. Fig. 23.12 shows the significant differences in FA observed among groups of patients with schizophrenia, bipolar disorder, and major depressive disorder.

23.3.4.1 Schizophrenia

Insufficient or inefficient communication between brain networks has been considered as a critical pathophysiological substrate for the symptoms observed in patients with schizophrenia. Several DTI-based studies have shown alterations in the WM of the uncinate fasciculus, corpus callosum, cingulum, and arcuate fasciculus of patients with schizophrenia [185]. In the view of brain disconnection, a TBSS study revealed that patients with chronic and severe schizophrenia present with reduced FA along the corpus callosum that, especially in the splenium segment, correlates with the disease duration [186]. A more recent study investigating structural networks identified by DTI tractography showed an

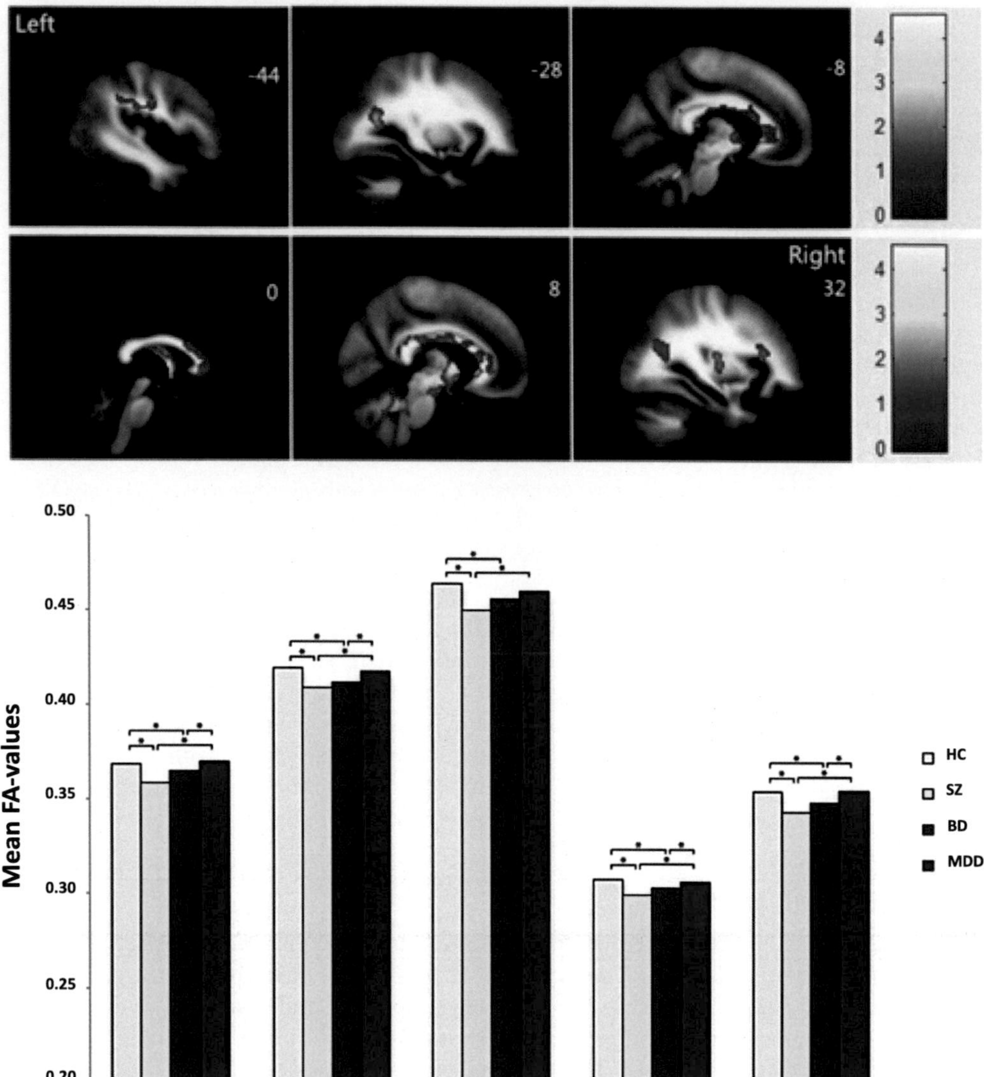

FIG. 23.12

The *top panel* shows significant differences in FA values *(in red-yellow)* between patients with schizophrenia, bipolar disorder, major depressive disorder, and healthy controls. The color scale represents t-values overlaid onto an FA template. The *bottom panel* shows FA values in WM tracts, demonstrating significant differences among the three groups. Abbreviations: *FA*, fractional anisotropy; *CC*, corpus callosum; *PTCR*, posterior thalamic radiations; *EC-R*, right external capsule; *SLF-L*, left superior longitudinal fasciculus.

(Reproduced from Chang M, et al. Neurobiological commonalities and distinctions among three major psychiatric diagnostic categories: a structural MRI study. Schizophr Bull 2018;44:65–74 by permission of Oxford University Press.)

association between brain topological measures (indicating the brain efficiency in information processing) and a higher genetic risk for schizophrenia [187]. An increased risk for schizophrenia was indeed found to be associated with increased MD values in the splenium of the corpus callosum, in the arcuate fasciculus, and the anterior thalamic radiations [187].

23.3.4.2 Bipolar disorder

Bipolar disorder is a psychiatric condition that is characterized by intermittent episodes of depression and mania or hypomania [188]. During the mania or hypomanic episodes, the mood becomes euphoric and labile, while in the depression states, patients experience a reduction in the pleasure-seeking and consider their actions as poorly rewarding. Patients with bipolar disorder share some psychotic features with those suffering from schizophrenia [188], and there is a lack of a clear-cut distinction between the two syndromes. Consistent with these clinical considerations, common patterns of abnormal frontal connectivity have been identified in both schizophrenia and bipolar disorder [189]. Conversely, disconnection in frontotemporal WM was found most likely associated with schizophrenia, while interhemispheric and limbic microstructural abnormalities were more strictly observed in bipolar disorder [189]. Further, abnormalities have been observed in the corpus callosum of patients with bipolar disorder. A recent study investigating the different portions of corpus callosum reported an abnormal increase of ADC in the right anterior body and the right splenium of patients with bipolar disorder. This study suggests a specific role played by the right hemisphere in the manifestation of the clinical symptoms in patients with bipolar disorder [190].

Bipolar disorder is currently regarded as a more complex syndrome, which can be divided into two different subtypes, namely, bipolar disorder type-I and type-II. The distinction between them depends on the intensity, duration, and presence of psychotic symptoms during the episodes of mania [191]. In terms of clinical severity, bipolar disorder type-II is regarded as a milder form of bipolar disorder type-I. Inefficient connectivity between prefrontal areas and subcortical regions, which are involved in cognitive and emotional processing, has been postulated for both conditions [191]. A recent DTI-based tractography study reported a bilateral reduction of FA in the uncinate fasciculus of patients with bipolar disorder type-I as compared to both healthy controls and patients with bipolar disorder type-II [191]. Interestingly, patients suffering from the less severe type-II form of bipolar disorder did not differ from controls. Overall, these findings suggest the existence of different pathophysiology underlying the two types of bipolar disorders.

23.3.4.3 Major depressive disorder

This is a psychiatric condition characterized by a prominent low mood accompanied by pain with no clear cause, low energy, low self-esteem, anhedonia, loss of motivation, and apathetic behavior. Several DTI studies have revealed reduced FA in several WM tracts of patients with major depressive disorder. In particular, a meta-analysis on 188 patients revealed diffusion abnormalities in the left superior longitudinal fasciculus [192], which is believed to play a significant role in depressive symptoms. More recent studies show WM abnormalities also in the genu of corpus the callosum [193], and the frontal lobes, right fusiform, and occipital lobes of patients with major depressive disorder [194] However, it remains unclear whether these WM abnormalities are present before the onset of clinical symptoms or are associated with disease severity and duration. In an attempt to disentangle this issue, Ganzola and coworkers have recently investigated the presence of WM abnormalities in a cohort of 106 young individuals (age range 16–25 years) with a high familial risk for developing a major depressive disorder

[195]. After a 2-year follow-up, 78 patients remained asymptomatic while 28 developed a major depressive disorder. DTI data collected at baseline revealed widespread reductions of FA in all major associative tracts in both groups (those who remained asymptomatic and those who developed major depressive disorder) compared to controls. Conversely, no longitudinal differences were observed between the two groups. This study suggests that the baseline FA abnormalities are most likely associated with familial risk for major depressive disorder in the absence of any predictive value for a subsequent diagnosis.

23.4 Summary

Diffusion MRI of the brain has an important role in the diagnosis and management of patients with a range of acute and chronic neurological conditions. More advanced techniques may potentially enable indirect assessments of tissue architecture before destructive neurosurgery and provide an understanding of the patterns of neural involvement within a range of pathophysiologies (only a selection of which have been presented here) evolving in vivo. With the refinement of analysis methods and shorter acquisition times, diffusion MRI will continue to exert a major influence on clinical practice and become an invaluable biomarker for use in investigative trials of new medicinal products.

Conflict of interest

There are none declared.

Funding

This article received no specific grant from any funding agency in the public, commercial, or not-for-profit sectors.

References

[1] Le Bihan D, et al. MR imaging of intravoxel incoherent motions: application to diffusion and perfusion in neurologic disorders. Radiology 1986;161:401–7.

[2] Chalela JA, et al. Magnetic resonance imaging and computed tomography in emergency assessment of patients with suspected acute stroke: a prospective comparison. Lancet 2007;369:293–8.

[3] Rastogi R, et al. Recent advances in magnetic resonance imaging for stroke diagnosis. Brain Circ 2015;1:26–37.

[4] Bang OY, et al. Multimodal MRI-based triage for acute stroke therapy: challenges and progress. Front Neurol 2018;9:586.

[5] Thomalla G, et al. MRI-guided thrombolysis for stroke with unknown time of onset. N Engl J Med 2018;379:611–22.

[6] Albers GW, et al. Thrombectomy for stroke at 6 to 16 hours with selection by perfusion imaging. N Engl J Med 2018;378:708–18.

[7] Nogueira RG, et al. Thrombectomy 6 to 24 hours after stroke with a mismatch between deficit and infarct. N Engl J Med 2018;378:11–21.

[8] Longo M, et al. MRI patient selection for endovascular thrombectomy in acute ischemic stroke: correlation between pretreatment diffusion weighted imaging and outcome scores. Radiol Med 2018;123:609–17.
[9] Moseley ME, et al. Diffusion-weighted MR imaging of acute stroke: correlation with T2-weighted and magnetic susceptibility-enhanced MR imaging in cats. AJNR Am J Neuroradiol 1990;11:423–9.
[10] Le Bihan D. Apparent diffusion coefficient and beyond: what diffusion MR imaging can tell us about tissue structure. Radiology 2013;268:318–22.
[11] Macintosh BJ, Graham SJ. Magnetic resonance imaging to visualize stroke and characterize stroke recovery: a review. Front Neurol 2013;4:60.
[12] Budde MD, Skinner NP. Diffusion MRI in acute nervous system injury. J Magn Reson 2018;292:137–48.
[13] Barritt AW, Vundavalli S, Hughes PJ. Varicella vasculopathy presenting with thunderclap headache. JRSM Open 2017;8(4):2054270416675081. https://doi.org/10.1177/2054270416675081.
[14] Copen WA, et al. Ischemic stroke: effects of etiology and patient age on the time course of the core apparent diffusion coefficient. Radiology 2001;221:27–34.
[15] Schulz UG, Briley D, Meagher T, Molyneux A, Rothwell PM. Diffusion-weighted MRI in 300 patients presenting late with subacute transient ischemic attack or minor stroke. Stroke 2004;35:2459–65.
[16] Kumar P, Kathuria P, Nair P, Prasad K. Prediction of upper limb motor recovery after subacute ischemic stroke using diffusion tensor imaging: a systematic review and meta-analysis. J Stroke 2016;18:50–9.
[17] Puig J, et al. Diffusion tensor imaging as a prognostic biomarker for motor recovery and rehabilitation after stroke. Neuroradiology 2017;59:343–51.
[18] Stinear CM, Ward NS. How useful is imaging in predicting outcomes in stroke rehabilitation? Int J Stroke 2013;8:33–7.
[19] Mishra AM, et al. Biological correlates of diffusivity in brain abscess. Magn Reson Med 2005;54:878–85.
[20] Reddy JS, et al. The role of diffusion-weighted imaging in the differential diagnosis of intracranial cystic mass lesions: a report of 147 lesions. Surg Neurol 2006;66:246–50. discussion 250–241.
[21] Maier SE, Sun Y, Mulkern RV. Diffusion imaging of brain tumors. NMR Biomed 2010;23:849–64.
[22] Morris SA, Esquenazi Y, Tandon N. Pyogenic cerebral abscesses demonstrating facilitated diffusion. Clin Neurol Neurosurg 2016;144:77–81.
[23] Finelli PF, Foxman EB. The etiology of ring lesions on diffusion-weighted imaging. Neuroradiol J 2014;27:280–7.
[24] Guo AC, Provenzale JM, Cruz Jr LC, Petrella JR. Cerebral abscesses: investigation using apparent diffusion coefficient maps. Neuroradiology 2001;43:370–4.
[25] Cartes-Zumelzu FW, et al. Diffusion-weighted imaging in the assessment of brain abscesses therapy. AJNR Am J Neuroradiol 2004;25:1310–7.
[26] Karonen JO, Partanen PL, Vanninen RL, Vainio PA, Aronen HJ. Evolution of MR contrast enhancement patterns during the first week after acute ischemic stroke. AJNR Am J Neuroradiol 2001;22:103–11.
[27] Pruitt AA. Neurologic complications of infective endocarditis. Curr Treat Options Neurol 2013;15:465–76.
[28] Sage CA, et al. Quantitative diffusion tensor imaging in amyotrophic lateral sclerosis: revisited. Hum Brain Mapp 2009;30:3657–75.
[29] Agosta F, et al. Structural brain correlates of cognitive and behavioral impairment in MND. Hum Brain Mapp 2016;37:1614–26.
[30] Senda J, et al. Progressive and widespread brain damage in ALS: MRI voxel-based morphometry and diffusion tensor imaging study. Amyotroph Lateral Scler 2011;12:59–69.
[31] Qian W, et al. Application of diffusional kurtosis imaging to detect occult brain damage in multiple sclerosis and neuromyelitis optica. NMR Biomed 2016;29:1536–45.
[32] Bacchi S, et al. Magnetic resonance imaging and positron emission tomography in anti-NMDA receptor encephalitis: a systematic review. J Clin Neurosci 2018;52:54–9.
[33] Brownell B, Oppenheimer DR, Hughes JT. The central nervous system in motor neurone disease. J Neurol Neurosurg Psychiatry 1970;33:338–57.

[34] Sugahara T, et al. Usefulness of diffusion-weighted MRI with echo-planar technique in the evaluation of cellularity in gliomas. J Magn Reson Imaging 1999;9:53–60.
[35] Yamasaki F, et al. Apparent diffusion coefficient of human brain tumors at MR imaging. Radiology 2005;235:985–91.
[36] Kono K, et al. The role of diffusion-weighted imaging in patients with brain tumors. AJNR Am J Neuroradiol 2001;22:1081–8.
[37] Ellingson BM, Bendszus M, Sorensen AG, Pope WB. Emerging techniques and technologies in brain tumor imaging. Neuro Oncol 2014;16(Suppl 7):vii12–23.
[38] Chakhoyan A, et al. Mono-exponential, diffusion kurtosis and stretched exponential diffusion MR imaging response to chemoradiation in newly diagnosed glioblastoma. J Neurooncol 2018;139(3):651–9.
[39] Panesar SS, et al. Tractography for surgical neuro-oncology planning: towards a gold standard. Neurotherapeutics 2018;16(1):36–51.
[40] Potgieser AR, et al. The role of diffusion tensor imaging in brain tumor surgery: a review of the literature. Clin Neurol Neurosurg 2014;124:51–8.
[41] Voets NL, Bartsch A, Plaha P. Brain white matter fibre tracts: a review of functional neuro-oncological relevance. J Neurol Neurosurg Psychiatry 2017;88:1017–25.
[42] Taillibert S, Le Rhun E, Chamberlain MC. Intracranial cystic lesions: a review. Curr Neurol Neurosci Rep 2014;14:481.
[43] Renard D, Nerrant E, Lechiche C. DWI and FLAIR imaging in herpes simplex encephalitis: a comparative and topographical analysis. J Neurol 2015;262:2101–5.
[44] Sawlani V. Diffusion-weighted imaging and apparent diffusion coefficient evaluation of herpes simplex encephalitis and Japanese encephalitis. J Neurol Sci 2009;287:221–6.
[45] Gaudino S, et al. Neuroradiology of human prion diseases, diagnosis and differential diagnosis. Radiol Med 2017;122:369–85.
[46] Vitali P, et al. Diffusion-weighted MRI hyperintensity patterns differentiate CJD from other rapid dementias. Neurology 2011;76:1711–9.
[47] Macfarlane RG, Wroe SJ, Collinge J, Yousry TA, Jager HR. Neuroimaging findings in human prion disease. J Neurol Neurosurg Psychiatry 2007;78:664–70.
[48] Ito H, Mori K, Kagami S. Neuroimaging of stroke-like episodes in MELAS. Brain Dev 2011;33:283–8.
[49] Bodini B, et al. Exploring the relationship between white matter and gray matter damage in early primary progressive multiple sclerosis: an in vivo study with TBSS and VBM. Hum Brain Mapp 2009;30:2852–61.
[50] Stadelmann C, Bruck W. Interplay between mechanisms of damage and repair in multiple sclerosis. J Neurol 2008;255(Suppl 1):12–8.
[51] Dutta R, Trapp BD. Mechanisms of neuronal dysfunction and degeneration in multiple sclerosis. Prog Neurobiol 2011;93:1–12.
[52] Mahad DH, Trapp BD, Lassmann H. Pathological mechanisms in progressive multiple sclerosis. Lancet Neurol 2015;14:183–93.
[53] Kutzelnigg A, et al. Cortical demyelination and diffuse white matter injury in multiple sclerosis. Brain 2005;128:2705–12.
[54] Vrenken H, et al. Diffusely abnormal white matter in progressive multiple sclerosis: in vivo quantitative MR imaging characterization and comparison between disease types. AJNR Am J Neuroradiol 2010;31:541–8.
[55] Filippi M, Cercignani M, Inglese M, Horsfield MA, Comi G. Diffusion tensor magnetic resonance imaging in multiple sclerosis. Neurology 2001;56:304–11.
[56] Ciccarelli O, et al. Investigation of MS normal-appearing brain using diffusion tensor MRI with clinical correlations. Neurology 2001;56:926–33.
[57] Calabrese M, et al. Cortical diffusion-tensor imaging abnormalities in multiple sclerosis: a 3-year longitudinal study. Radiology 2011;261:891–8.

[58] Cavallari M, et al. Microstructural changes in the striatum and their impact on motor and neuropsychological performance in patients with multiple sclerosis. PLoS One 2014;9:e101199.
[59] Haider L, et al. Multiple sclerosis deep grey matter: the relation between demyelination, neurodegeneration, inflammation and iron. J Neurol Neurosurg Psychiatry 2014;85:1386–95.
[60] Hannoun S, et al. Diffusion tensor-MRI evidence for extra-axonal neuronal degeneration in caudate and thalamic nuclei of patients with multiple sclerosis. AJNR Am J Neuroradiol 2012;33:1363–8.
[61] Assaf Y, et al. High b-value q-space analyzed diffusion-weighted MRI: application to multiple sclerosis. Magn Reson Med 2002;47:115–26.
[62] Abdel-Aziz K, et al. Evidence for early neurodegeneration in the cervical cord of patients with primary progressive multiple sclerosis. Brain 2015;138:1568–82.
[63] Farrell JA, et al. High b-value q-space diffusion-weighted MRI of the human cervical spinal cord in vivo: feasibility and application to multiple sclerosis. Magn Reson Med 2008;59:1079–89.
[64] de Kouchkovsky I, et al. Quantification of normal-appearing white matter tract integrity in multiple sclerosis: a diffusion kurtosis imaging study. J Neurol 2016;263:1146–55.
[65] Yoshida M, et al. Diffusional kurtosis imaging of normal-appearing white matter in multiple sclerosis: preliminary clinical experience. Jpn J Radiol 2013;31:50–5.
[66] Takemura MY, et al. Alterations of the optic pathway between unilateral and bilateral optic nerve damage in multiple sclerosis as revealed by the combined use of advanced diffusion kurtosis imaging and visual evoked potentials. Magn Reson Imaging 2017;39:24–30.
[67] Nossin-Manor R, Duvdevani R, Cohen Y. q-Space high b value diffusion MRI of hemi-crush in rat spinal cord: evidence for spontaneous regeneration. Magn Reson Imaging 2002;20:231–41.
[68] Fujiyoshi K, et al. Application of q-space diffusion MRI for the visualization of white matter. J Neurosci 2016;36:2796–808.
[69] Tanikawa M, et al. Q-space myelin map imaging for longitudinal analysis of demyelination and remyelination in multiple sclerosis patients treated with fingolimod: a preliminary study. J Neurol Sci 2017;373:352–7.
[70] Zhang H, Schneider T, Wheeler-Kingshott CA, Alexander DC. NODDI: practical in vivo neurite orientation dispersion and density imaging of the human brain. Neuroimage 2012;61:1000–16.
[71] Spano B, et al. Disruption of neurite morphology parallels MS progression. Neurol Neuroimmunol Neuroinflamm 2018;5(6):e502.
[72] Hubbard EA, Wetter NC, Sutton BP, Pilutti LA, Motl RW. Diffusion tensor imaging of the corticospinal tract and walking performance in multiple sclerosis. J Neurol Sci 2016;363:225–31.
[73] Lin X, Tench CR, Morgan PS, Niepel G, Constantinescu CS. 'Importance sampling' in MS: use of diffusion tensor tractography to quantify pathology related to specific impairment. J Neurol Sci 2005;237:13–9.
[74] Cercignani M, Embleton K, Parker GJ, Bozzali M. Group-averaged anatomical connectivity mapping for improved human white matter pathway visualisation. NMR Biomed 2012;25:1224–33.
[75] Bozzali M, et al. Anatomical brain connectivity can assess cognitive dysfunction in multiple sclerosis. Mult Scler 2013;19:1161–8.
[76] Sporns O. Structure and function of complex brain networks. Dialogues Clin Neurosci 2013;15:247–62.
[77] Pardini M, et al. Motor network efficiency and disability in multiple sclerosis. Neurology 2015;85:1115–22.
[78] Phukan J, et al. The syndrome of cognitive impairment in amyotrophic lateral sclerosis: a population-based study. J Neurol Neurosurg Psychiatry 2012;83:102–8.
[79] Ringholz GM, et al. Prevalence and patterns of cognitive impairment in sporadic ALS. Neurology 2005;65:586–90.
[80] Coan G, Mitchell CS. An assessment of possible neuropathology and clinical relationships in 46 sporadic amyotrophic lateral sclerosis patient autopsies. Neurodegener Dis 2015;15:301–12.
[81] Neumann M, et al. Ubiquitinated TDP-43 in frontotemporal lobar degeneration and amyotrophic lateral sclerosis. Science 2006;314:130–3.

[82] Ravits J, et al. Deciphering amyotrophic lateral sclerosis: what phenotype, neuropathology and genetics are telling us about pathogenesis. Amyotroph Lateral Scler Frontotemporal Degener 2013;14(Suppl 1):5–18.
[83] Wijesekera LC, et al. Natural history and clinical features of the flail arm and flail leg ALS variants. Neurology 2009;72:1087–94.
[84] Gautier G, et al. ALS with respiratory onset: clinical features and effects of non-invasive ventilation on the prognosis. Amyotroph Lateral Scler 2010;11:379–82.
[85] Ravits J, Paul P, Jorg C. Focality of upper and lower motor neuron degeneration at the clinical onset of ALS. Neurology 2007;68:1571–5.
[86] Gargiulo-Monachelli GM, et al. Regional spread pattern predicts survival in patients with sporadic amyotrophic lateral sclerosis. Eur J Neurol 2012;19:834–41.
[87] Peretti-Viton P, et al. MRI of the intracranial corticospinal tracts in amyotrophic and primary lateral sclerosis. Neuroradiology 1999;41:744–9.
[88] Hecht MJ, et al. MRI-FLAIR images of the head show corticospinal tract alterations in ALS patients more frequently than T2-, T1- and proton-density-weighted images. J Neurol Sci 2001;186:37–44.
[89] Waragai M. MRI and clinical features in amyotrophic lateral sclerosis. Neuroradiology 1997;39:847–51.
[90] Cheung G, et al. Amyotrophic lateral sclerosis: correlation of clinical and MR imaging findings. Radiology 1995;194:263–70.
[91] Hofmann E, Ochs G, Pelzl A, Warmuth-Metz M. The corticospinal tract in amyotrophic lateral sclerosis: an MRI study. Neuroradiology 1998;40:71–5.
[92] Rocha AJ, Maia Junior AC. Is magnetic resonance imaging a plausible biomarker for upper motor neuron degeneration in amyotrophic lateral sclerosis/primary lateral sclerosis or merely a useful paraclinical tool to exclude mimic syndromes? A critical review of imaging applicability in clinical routine. Arq Neuropsiquiatr 2012;70:532–9.
[93] Turner MR, Talbot K. Mimics and chameleons in motor neurone disease. Pract Neurol 2013;13:153–64.
[94] Blain CR, et al. A longitudinal study of diffusion tensor MRI in ALS. Amyotroph Lateral Scler 2007;8:348–55.
[95] Douaud G, Filippini N, Knight S, Talbot K, Turner MR. Integration of structural and functional magnetic resonance imaging in amyotrophic lateral sclerosis. Brain 2011;134:3470–9.
[96] Huynh W, et al. Assessment of the upper motor neuron in amyotrophic lateral sclerosis. Clin Neurophysiol 2016;127:2643–60.
[97] Menke RAL, Agosta F, Grosskreutz J, Filippi M, Turner MR. Neuroimaging endpoints in amyotrophic lateral sclerosis. Neurotherapeutics 2016;1–13.
[98] Simon NG, et al. Quantifying disease progression in amyotrophic lateral sclerosis. Ann Neurol 2014;76:643–57.
[99] Turner MR, Verstraete E. What does imaging reveal about the pathology of amyotrophic lateral sclerosis? Curr Neurol Neurosci Rep 2015;15:45.
[100] Verstraete E, Foerster BR. Neuroimaging as a new diagnostic modality in amyotrophic lateral sclerosis. Neurotherapeutics 2015;12:403–16.
[101] Grolez G, et al. The value of magnetic resonance imaging as a biomarker for amyotrophic lateral sclerosis: a systematic review. BMC Neurol 2016;16:155.
[102] Muller HP, et al. A large-scale multicentre cerebral diffusion tensor imaging study in amyotrophic lateral sclerosis. J Neurol Neurosurg Psychiatry 2016;87:570–9.
[103] Sage CA, Peeters RR, Gorner A, Robberecht W, Sunaert S. Quantitative diffusion tensor imaging in amyotrophic lateral sclerosis. Neuroimage 2007;34:486–99.
[104] Iwata NK, et al. White matter alterations differ in primary lateral sclerosis and amyotrophic lateral sclerosis. Brain 2011;134:2642–55.
[105] Iwata NK, et al. Evaluation of corticospinal tracts in ALS with diffusion tensor MRI and brainstem stimulation. Neurology 2008;70:528–32.

[106] Stagg CJ, et al. Whole-brain magnetic resonance spectroscopic imaging measures are related to disability in ALS. Neurology 2013;80:610–5.
[107] Sarica A, et al. The corticospinal tract profile in amyotrophic lateral sclerosis. Hum Brain Mapp 2017;38:727–39.
[108] Kollewe K, Korner S, Dengler R, Petri S, Mohammadi B. Magnetic resonance imaging in amyotrophic lateral sclerosis. Neurol Res Int 2012;2012:608501.
[109] Agosta F, et al. Voxel-based morphometry study of brain volumetry and diffusivity in amyotrophic lateral sclerosis patients with mild disability. Hum Brain Mapp 2007;28:1430–8.
[110] Turner MR, et al. Neuroimaging in amyotrophic lateral sclerosis. Biomark Med 2012;6:319–37.
[111] Li J, et al. A meta-analysis of diffusion tensor imaging studies in amyotrophic lateral sclerosis. Neurobiol Aging 2012;33:1833–8.
[112] Lindenberg R, et al. Structural integrity of corticospinal motor fibers predicts motor impairment in chronic stroke. Neurology 2010;74:280–7.
[113] Martin JE, Swash M. The pathology of motor neuron disease. In: Leigh PN, Swash M, editors. Motor neuron disease: biology and management. London: Springer-Verlag; 1995. p. 93–118.
[114] Smith MC. Nerve fibre degeneration in the brain in amyotrophic lateral sclerosis. J Neurol Neurosurg Psychiatry 1960;23:269–82.
[115] Habert MO, et al. Brain perfusion imaging in amyotrophic lateral sclerosis: extent of cortical changes according to the severity and topography of motor impairment. Amyotroph Lateral Scler 2007;8:9–15.
[116] Turner MR, et al. [11C]-WAY100635 PET demonstrates marked 5-HT1A receptor changes in sporadic ALS. Brain 2005;128:896–905.
[117] Cistaro A, et al. Brain hypermetabolism in amyotrophic lateral sclerosis: a FDG PET study in ALS of spinal and bulbar onset. Eur J Nucl Med Mol Imaging 2012;39:251–9.
[118] Kew JJ, et al. The relationship between abnormalities of cognitive function and cerebral activation in amyotrophic lateral sclerosis. A neuropsychological and positron emission tomography study. Brain 1993;116(Pt 6):1399–423.
[119] Kew JJ, et al. Cortical function in amyotrophic lateral sclerosis. A positron emission tomography study. Brain 1993;116(Pt 3):655–80.
[120] Abrahams S, et al. Word retrieval in amyotrophic lateral sclerosis: a functional magnetic resonance imaging study. Brain 2004;127:1507–17.
[121] Tessitore A, et al. Subcortical motor plasticity in patients with sporadic ALS: an fMRI study. Brain Res Bull 2006;69:489–94.
[122] Devinsky O, Morrell MJ, Vogt BA. Contributions of anterior cingulate cortex to behaviour. Brain 1995;118(Pt 1):279–306.
[123] Lemon RN. Descending pathways in motor control. Annu Rev Neurosci 2008;31:195–218.
[124] Toosy AT, et al. Diffusion tensor imaging detects corticospinal tract involvement at multiple levels in amyotrophic lateral sclerosis. J Neurol Neurosurg Psychiatry 2003;74:1250–7.
[125] Agosta F, et al. A longitudinal diffusion tensor MRI study of the cervical cord and brain in amyotrophic lateral sclerosis patients. J Neurol Neurosurg Psychiatry 2009;80:53–5.
[126] Cohen-Adad J, et al. Involvement of spinal sensory pathway in ALS and specificity of cord atrophy to lower motor neuron degeneration. Amyotroph Lateral Scler Frontotemporal Degener 2013;14:30–8.
[127] Valsasina P, et al. Diffusion anisotropy of the cervical cord is strictly associated with disability in amyotrophic lateral sclerosis. J Neurol Neurosurg Psychiatry 2007;78:480–4.
[128] Nair G, et al. Diffusion tensor imaging reveals regional differences in the cervical spinal cord in amyotrophic lateral sclerosis. Neuroimage 2010;53:576–83.
[129] Abhinav K, et al. Use of diffusion spectrum imaging in preliminary longitudinal evaluation of amyotrophic lateral sclerosis: development of an imaging biomarker. Front Hum Neurosci 2014;8:270.
[130] Keil C, et al. Longitudinal diffusion tensor imaging in amyotrophic lateral sclerosis. BMC Neurosci 2012;13:141.

[131] Nickerson JP, et al. Linear longitudinal decline in fractional anisotropy in patients with amyotrophic lateral sclerosis: preliminary results. Klin Neuroradiol 2009;19:129–34.

[132] van der Graaff MM, et al. Upper and extra-motoneuron involvement in early motoneuron disease: a diffusion tensor imaging study. Brain 2011;134:1211–28.

[133] Zhang Y, et al. Progression of white matter degeneration in amyotrophic lateral sclerosis: a diffusion tensor imaging study. Amyotroph Lateral Scler 2011;12:421–9.

[134] Kwan JY, Meoded A, Danielian LE, Wu T, Floeter MK. Structural imaging differences and longitudinal changes in primary lateral sclerosis and amyotrophic lateral sclerosis. Neuroimage Clin 2013;2:151–60.

[135] Schuster C, et al. Longitudinal course of cortical thickness decline in amyotrophic lateral sclerosis. J Neurol 2014;261:1871–80.

[136] Foerster BR, et al. Diagnostic accuracy of diffusion tensor imaging in amyotrophic lateral sclerosis: a systematic review and individual patient data meta-analysis. Acad Radiol 2013;20:1099–106.

[137] Foerster BR, et al. Diagnostic accuracy using diffusion tensor imaging in the diagnosis of ALS: a meta-analysis. Acad Radiol 2012;19:1075–86.

[138] Foerster BR, et al. Multimodal MRI as a diagnostic biomarker for amyotrophic lateral sclerosis. Ann Clin Transl Neurol 2014;1:107–14.

[139] Querin G, et al. Multimodal spinal cord MRI offers accurate diagnostic classification in ALS. J Neurol Neurosurg Psychiatry 2018;89(11):1220–1.

[140] Jones DK, Knosche TR, Turner R. White matter integrity, fiber count, and other fallacies: the do's and don'ts of diffusion MRI. Neuroimage 2013;73:239–54.

[141] Broad RJ, et al. Neurite orientation and dispersion density imaging (NODDI) detects cortical and corticospinal tract degeneration in ALS. J Neurol Neurosurg Psychiatry 2018;90(4):404–11.

[142] Wen J, et al. Neurite density is reduced in the presymptomatic phase of C9orf72 disease. J Neurol Neurosurg Psychiatry 2018;90(4):387–94.

[143] Barritt AW, Gabel MC, Cercignani M, Leigh PN. Emerging magnetic resonance imaging techniques and analysis methods in amyotrophic lateral sclerosis. Front Neurol 2018;9:1065.

[144] McKhann GM, et al. The diagnosis of dementia due to Alzheimer's disease: recommendations from the National Institute on Aging-Alzheimer's Association workgroups on diagnostic guidelines for Alzheimer's disease. Alzheimers Dement 2011;7:263–9.

[145] Jack Jr CR, et al. NIA-AA research framework: toward a biological definition of Alzheimer's disease. Alzheimers Dement 2018;14:535–62.

[146] McKeith IG, et al. Diagnosis and management of dementia with Lewy bodies: fourth consensus report of the DLB consortium. Neurology 2017;89:88–100.

[147] McKeith IG, et al. Diagnosis and management of dementia with Lewy bodies: third report of the DLB consortium. Neurology 2005;65:1863–72.

[148] Gorno-Tempini ML, et al. Classification of primary progressive aphasia and its variants. Neurology 2011;76:1006–14.

[149] Mackenzie IR, et al. Nomenclature and nosology for neuropathologic subtypes of frontotemporal lobar degeneration: an update. Acta Neuropathol 2010;119:1–4.

[150] Rascovsky K, et al. Sensitivity of revised diagnostic criteria for the behavioural variant of frontotemporal dementia. Brain 2011;134:2456–77.

[151] Whitwell JL, et al. Altered functional connectivity in asymptomatic MAPT subjects: a comparison to bvFTD. Neurology 2011;77:866–74.

[152] Braak H, Braak E. Staging of Alzheimer's disease-related neurofibrillary changes. Neurobiol Aging 1995; 16:271–8. discussion 278–284.

[153] Bozzali M, Padovani A, Caltagirone C, Borroni B. Regional grey matter loss and brain disconnection across Alzheimer disease evolution. Curr Med Chem 2011;18:2452–8.

[154] Bozzali M, Serra L, Cercignani M. Quantitative MRI to understand Alzheimer's disease pathophysiology. Curr Opin Neurol 2016;29:437–44.

[155] Bozzali M, et al. White matter damage in Alzheimer's disease assessed in vivo using diffusion tensor magnetic resonance imaging. J Neurol Neurosurg Psychiatry 2002;72:742–6.

[156] Bozzali M, et al. Quantification of tissue damage in AD using diffusion tensor and magnetization transfer MRI. Neurology 2001;57:1135–7.

[157] Hanyu H, et al. Diffusion-weighted and magnetization transfer imaging of the corpus callosum in Alzheimer's disease. J Neurol Sci 1999;167:37–44.

[158] Hanyu H, et al. Diffusion-weighted MR imaging of the hippocampus and temporal white matter in Alzheimer's disease. J Neurol Sci 1998;156:195–200.

[159] Rose SE, et al. Loss of connectivity in Alzheimer's disease: an evaluation of white matter tract integrity with colour coded MR diffusion tensor imaging. J Neurol Neurosurg Psychiatry 2000;69:528–30.

[160] Albert MS, et al. The diagnosis of mild cognitive impairment due to Alzheimer's disease: recommendations from the National Institute on Aging-Alzheimer's Association workgroups on diagnostic guidelines for Alzheimer's disease. Alzheimers Dement 2011;7:270–9.

[161] Giulietti G, et al. Whole brain white matter histogram analysis of diffusion tensor imaging data detects microstructural damage in mild cognitive impairment and Alzheimer's disease patients. J Magn Reson Imaging 2018. https://doi.org/10.1002/jmri.25947.

[162] Smith SM, et al. Tract-based spatial statistics: voxelwise analysis of multi-subject diffusion data. Neuroimage 2006;31:1487–505.

[163] Agosta F, et al. White matter damage in Alzheimer disease and its relationship to gray matter atrophy. Radiology 2011;258:853–63.

[164] Salat DH, et al. White matter pathology isolates the hippocampal formation in Alzheimer's disease. Neurobiol Aging 2010;31:244–56.

[165] Serra L, et al. Grey and white matter changes at different stages of Alzheimer's disease. J Alzheimers Dis 2010;19:147–59.

[166] Palesi F, et al. Specific patterns of white matter alterations help distinguishing Alzheimer's and vascular dementia. Front Neurosci 2018;12:274.

[167] Bozzali M, et al. Damage to the cingulum contributes to Alzheimer's disease pathophysiology by deafferentation mechanism. Hum Brain Mapp 2012;33:1295–308.

[168] Serra L, et al. White matter damage along the uncinate fasciculus contributes to cognitive decline in AD and DLB. Curr Alzheimer Res 2012;9:326–33.

[169] Taoka T, et al. Fractional anisotropy—threshold dependence in tract-based diffusion tensor analysis: evaluation of the uncinate fasciculus in Alzheimer disease. AJNR Am J Neuroradiol 2009;30:1700–3.

[170] Yasmin H, et al. Diffusion abnormalities of the uncinate fasciculus in Alzheimer's disease: diffusion tensor tract-specific analysis using a new method to measure the core of the tract. Neuroradiology 2008; 50:293–9.

[171] Bozzali M, et al. Anatomical connectivity mapping: a new tool to assess brain disconnection in Alzheimer's disease. Neuroimage 2011;54:2045–51.

[172] Bozzali M, et al. Brain tissue modifications induced by cholinergic therapy in Alzheimer's disease. Hum Brain Mapp 2013;34:3158–67.

[173] Madhavan A, et al. Characterizing white matter tract degeneration in Syndromic variants of Alzheimer's disease: a diffusion tensor imaging study. J Alzheimers Dis 2016;49:633–43.

[174] Gyebnar G, et al. What can DTI tell about early cognitive impairment? Differentiation between MCI subtypes and healthy controls by diffusion tensor imaging. Psychiatry Res Neuroimaging 2018;272:46–57.

[175] Nir TM, et al. Diffusion weighted imaging-based maximum density path analysis and classification of Alzheimer's disease. Neurobiol Aging 2015;36(Suppl 1):S132–40.

[176] Kantarci K, et al. White-matter integrity on DTI and the pathologic staging of Alzheimer's disease. Neurobiol Aging 2017;56:172–9.

[177] Bozzali M, et al. Brain tissue damage in dementia with Lewy bodies: an in vivo diffusion tensor MRI study. Brain 2005;128:1595–604.

[178] Nedelska Z, et al. White matter integrity in dementia with Lewy bodies: a voxel-based analysis of diffusion tensor imaging. Neurobiol Aging 2015;36:2010–7.

[179] Watson R, et al. Characterizing dementia with Lewy bodies by means of diffusion tensor imaging. Neurology 2012;79:906–14.

[180] Firbank MJ, et al. Longitudinal diffusion tensor imaging in dementia with Lewy bodies and Alzheimer's disease. Parkinsonism Relat Disord 2016;24:76–80.

[181] Zhang Y, et al. MRI signatures of brain macrostructural atrophy and microstructural degradation in frontotemporal lobar degeneration subtypes. J Alzheimers Dis 2013;33:431–44.

[182] Tu S, Leyton CE, Hodges JR, Piguet O, Hornberger M. Divergent longitudinal propagation of white matter degradation in logopenic and semantic variants of primary progressive aphasia. J Alzheimers Dis 2016;49:853–61.

[183] Catani M, et al. A novel frontal pathway underlies verbal fluency in primary progressive aphasia. Brain 2013;136:2619–28.

[184] Chang M, et al. Neurobiological commonalities and distinctions among three major psychiatric diagnostic categories: a structural MRI study. Schizophr Bull 2018;44:65–74.

[185] Burns J, et al. Structural disconnectivity in schizophrenia: a diffusion tensor magnetic resonance imaging study. Br J Psychiatry 2003;182:439–43.

[186] Holleran L, et al. Altered interhemispheric and temporal lobe white matter microstructural organization in severe chronic schizophrenia. Neuropsychopharmacology 2014;39:944–54.

[187] Alloza C, et al. Polygenic risk score for schizophrenia and structural brain connectivity in older age: a longitudinal connectome and tractography study. Neuroimage 2018;183:884–96.

[188] Belmaker RH, Bersudsky Y. Bipolar disorder: mania and depression. Discov Med 2004;4:239–45.

[189] O'Donoghue S, Holleran L, Cannon DM, McDonald C. Anatomical dysconnectivity in bipolar disorder compared with schizophrenia: a selective review of structural network analyses using diffusion MRI. J Affect Disord 2017;209:217–28.

[190] Foley SF, et al. Fractional anisotropy of the uncinate fasciculus and cingulum in bipolar disorder type I, type II, unaffected siblings and healthy controls. Br J Psychiatry 2018;213:548–54.

[191] Prunas C, et al. Diffusion imaging study of the corpus callosum in bipolar disorder. Psychiatry Res Neuroimaging 2018;271:75–81.

[192] Murphy ML, Frodl T. Meta-analysis of diffusion tensor imaging studies shows altered fractional anisotropy occurring in distinct brain areas in association with depression. Biol Mood Anxiety Disord 2011;1:3.

[193] Wise T, et al. Voxel-based meta-analytical evidence of structural disconnectivity in major depression and bipolar disorder. Biol Psychiatry 2016;79:293–302.

[194] Liao Y, et al. Is depression a disconnection syndrome? Meta-analysis of diffusion tensor imaging studies in patients with MDD. J Psychiatry Neurosci 2013;38:49–56.

[195] Ganzola R, et al. Diffusion tensor imaging correlates of early markers of depression in youth at high-familial risk for bipolar disorder. J Child Psychol Psychiatry 2018;59:917–27.

CHAPTER

Diffusion MRI: Applications Outside the Brain

24

Ricardo Donners[a], Mihaela Rata[b], Neil Peter Jerome[c], Matthew Orton[d], Matthew Blackledge[d], Christina Messiou[b], and Dow-Mu Koh[b]

[a]Department of Imaging, University Hospital of Basel, Basel, Switzerland [b]Department of Radiology, Royal Marsden Hospital, Sutton, United Kingdom [c]Department of Circulation and Medical Imaging, Norwegian University of Science and Technology, Trondheim, Norway [d]Division of Radiotherapy and Imaging, Institute of Cancer Research, Sutton, United Kingdom

24.1 Introduction

Diffusion imaging is a noninvasive technique that yields information on tissue structure without the need for exogenous contrast administration or the use of ionizing radiation. The technique can be used to visualize and quantify differences in water mobility in human tissues, which are composed of approximately 70% water. In the body, water mobility (diffusion) is impeded in regions with increased tissue cellularity, cellular membrane integrity, fluid viscosity, and extracellular space tortuosity, which lead to a higher observed signal intensity on diffusion-weighted imaging (DWI) compared to tissues where water can move freely. Although the first clinical use of DWI was in the brain, advances in hardware and scanning sequences have largely overcome the challenges of implementing the technique in extracranial applications, both at 1.5 and 3 T. DWI has become a core element of many standard body MRI protocols for disease detection, characterization, and response assessment. Quantification of water mobility using the apparent diffusion coefficient (ADC) with a simple monoexponential model, or via more complex measurements using bi-exponential or non-Gaussian models, are still being refined. In this chapter, we provide readers with a perspective of the technical development of body diffusion imaging, its implementation on current Magnetic Resonance Imaging (MRI) platforms, approaches to the quantification of diffusion, applications of DWI and diffusion mapping, evolving developments.

24.2 Principles of diffusion imaging as applied in the body

24.2.1 General considerations

The dependency of the MRI signal on molecular water diffusion was described as early as 1950 [1]. The principle of adding diffusion-sensitizing magnetic field gradients, known as "diffusion gradients," to a T_2-weighted pulse sequence to impart diffusion-weighted contrast into an MR image was described in 1965, and still forms the basis for many diffusion measurements today [2]. The most basic diffusion sequence involves the addition of two diffusion gradients. The first gradient dephases the magnetic

Advances in Magnetic Resonance Technology and Applications. Volume 1. ISSN 2666-9099. https://doi.org/10.1016/B978-0-12-817057-1.00026-3

spins of the protons in water molecules by adding a spatially dependent phase shift. The second gradient is of the same magnitude and duration, but with the opposite direction to the first gradient, thus reversing the phase shift. Since there is molecular motion in the time between the application of the two diffusion gradients, spins moving during this period experienced a different magnetic field during the rephasing and rephasing gradients, leading to an overall dephasing and signal loss. Increased molecular motion (diffusion) leads to a larger signal decrease, which results in the diffusion-weighted image contrast. By contrast, impeded or restricted water diffusion leads to less signal attenuation and relatively preserved high signal. It should be noted that, in the clinical context, the term "restricted" diffusion is commonly used to refer to decreased diffusivity from any cause. However, diffusion restriction technically only refers to molecules encountering physical boundaries such as cell membranes leading to the tapering of diffusion-related signal loss with increasing diffusion time. This phenomenon would not be encountered if there was simply decreased (but unrestricted) diffusivity as it would occur in highly viscous fluids. This distinction is presently not made in clinical interpretation.

The amount of signal attenuation at a particular location within a diffusion-weighted image depends on two quantitative parameters: (1) the "b-value," which summarizes the gradient amplitude, duration, and the time interval between the paired diffusion sensitizing gradients, and (2) the "ADC," which is an empirical parameter that describes the mobility of water at that location. For systems where the distribution of proton displacements in a given time is Gaussian, the signal decay as a function of b-value is a monoexponential curve, and the rate constant of this decay is the diffusion coefficient. In biological systems the diffusion environment is more complex, so to indicate this complexity the rate constant of a monoexponential fit to the signal decay curve is known as the "ADC." Given a particular b-value and ADC, signal (S) within a diffusion-weighted image is attenuated according to a monoexponential decay model, with an exponent equal to the negative product of these parameters. If S_0 is the MRI signal at baseline, the DWI signal is equal to

$$S = S_0\, e^{-b\,\mathrm{ADC}}$$

Typical b-values for body imaging range from 0 to 1000 s/mm^2, although higher b-values up to 4000 s/mm^2 have been applied in specific disease contexts. Using higher b-values is desirable to enhance diffusivity-based tissue contrasts but decreases the image signal to noise ratio (SNR). Typical ADCs encountered in the human body range from $0.5–3.0 \times 10^{-3}$ mm^2/s. Although the relationship between ADC value and tissue cellularity is complex and varies between disease settings and low diffusivity can also be seen in viscous fluids, a lesion with low ADC value (e.g., between $0.5–1.0 \times 10^{-3}$ mm^2/s) is often more cellular compared with adjacent tissues (Fig. 24.1).

24.2.2 Technical considerations

24.2.2.1 Echo-planar imaging technique

One of the key considerations of performing diffusion imaging in the body is the need to overcome the effects of motion arising from the heart, bowel, blood flow, respiration, and gross patient movement. In this regard, the acquisition of diffusion images needs to be fast to be motion-robust. Single-shot echo-planar imaging (SS-EPI) is now the most widely used diffusion imaging technique, as physiological effects of motion are small within the rapid readout of the sequence (typically less than 100 ms per image). This image readout technique is commonly used as part of a spin echo pulse sequence, and the long echo time (T_E) required to obtain the diffusion sensitization gives the overall image a T_2-weighted

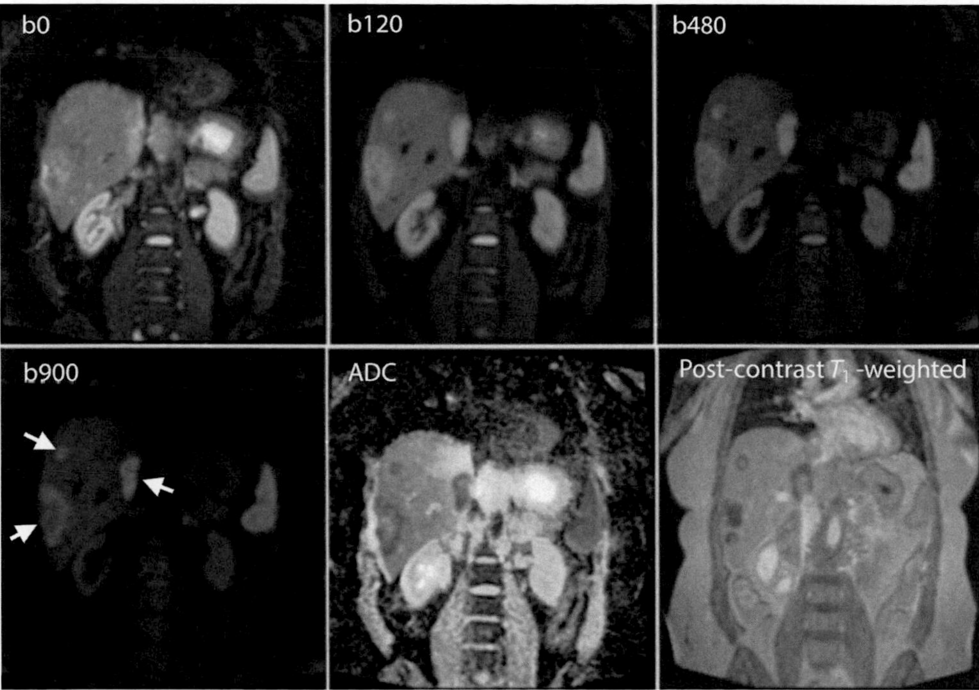

FIG. 24.1

Abdominal diffusion imaging of a 48-year-old female patient with hepatic metastasis of colorectal cancer. Coronal EPI DW images of the abdomen with different *b*-values acquired during free breathing (b0, b120, b480, b900), and the corresponding ADC map calculated using all the *b*-values. Three discrete metastases can be seen *(arrows)*. The T_1-weighted post-gadolinium image shows partial enhancement of the metastases. The mean ADC value for the nonnecrotic areas of liver metastases is 0.8–0.9 $\times$ 10^{-3} mm^2/s, while the ADC of normal liver is 1.2 $\times$ 10^{-3} mm^2/s.

contrast as well. SS-EPI diffusion imaging is highly sensitive to magnetic field inhomogeneities, susceptibility effects caused by tissue interfaces, and eddy-currents induced in the coils by fast switching imaging gradients, sometimes leading to severe geometric distortions. A major technical breakthrough, making diffusion imaging outside the brain practicable, was the development of parallel imaging and partial Fourier reconstruction for faster readout of undersampled data using shorter echo-trains [3]. Despite these advances in image acquisition, however, the SS-EPI diffusion imaging technique is still prone to image distortion, which must be accounted for in the radiological interpretation of diffusion-weighted images. SS-EPI diffusion imaging is most frequently performed in free-breathing, although motion-controlled acquisitions (breath-hold or respiratory triggered) can be considered in selected areas [4].

Fat suppression is required at image acquisition for robust diffusion imaging. This is commonly achieved using a spectral adiabatic inversion recovery (SPAIR) technique for smaller field of view (FoV) imaging [5], and using short-tau inversion recovery (STIR) technique over larger imaging FoVs. Diffusion imaging sequences should be optimized by an expert physicist or technologist to maximize image SNR and to minimize image artifacts, to ensure reliable and consistent performance.

24.2.2.2 Non-EPI diffusion imaging

With improvements in imaging hardware and image acquisition acceleration techniques, there has been interesting in using non-EPI diffusion techniques in the body. Diffusion-sensitizing gradients may be added to turbo spin echo (TSE) or fast spin echo (FSE) sequences. The 180° refocusing pulse of these sequences reduces phase shifts, reducing the sensitivity to susceptibility effects in tissues, hence reducing image distortion, which can be advantageous at anatomical areas with gas-tissue interfaces. The acquisition times remain short but are longer than for SS-EPI (approximately 300 ms per image). Potential issues related to the associated longer overall image acquisition times, lower image SNR, and motion blurring have reduced the wider adoption of these non-EPI techniques. Segmented, parallel and non-Cartesian readout models have been used to increase image SNR and motion robustness, such as periodically overlapping parallel lines read-out (PROPELLER), split-echo PROPELLER (SPLICE), and self-navigated interleaved spirals (SNAILS) acquisitions [6, 7].

24.2.2.3 Reduced FoV diffusion imaging

One of the strengths of MRI is the ability to interrogate specific organs and structures using reduced FoV imaging to improve image spatial resolution within the same scan time. This is frequently employed when using conventional morphological imaging to improve disease visualization.

For diffusion imaging, a limited FoV can be achieved by inner volume imaging (IVI), where two or three perpendicularly oriented gradients excite only the intersecting voxels; or outer volume suppression (OVS), where the signal of outer tissues is nulled [8, 9]. Variants of IVI have been developed by the major vendors: FOCUS (General Electric), ZOOMit (Siemens), and iZOOM (Philips). Reduced FoV imaging has been shown to improve image quality compared with larger FoV diffusion imaging in the spinal cord, prostate, pancreas, breast, head and neck, and cervical cancer [9–13]. As an alternative to reduced FoV diffusion imaging, segmented multishot-EPI can also be applied to decrease image distortion and increase acquisition matrix size [14] (Fig. 24.2). Such techniques are increasingly applied to improve the quality of targeted diffusion imaging across the body. Early studies suggested some discrepancies in quantitative ADC values using limited FoV compared with conventional larger FoV imaging, but more recently equivalent ADC measurements were reported in larger studies [11, 13].

24.2.2.4 Computed DWI

The use of higher *b*-values (i.e., higher diffusion weighting) results in greater suppression of the MR signal from normal tissues and can, therefore, increase lesion conspicuity on DWI. However, using higher *b*-values increases the sensitivity to susceptibility artifacts and image distortion, and decreases

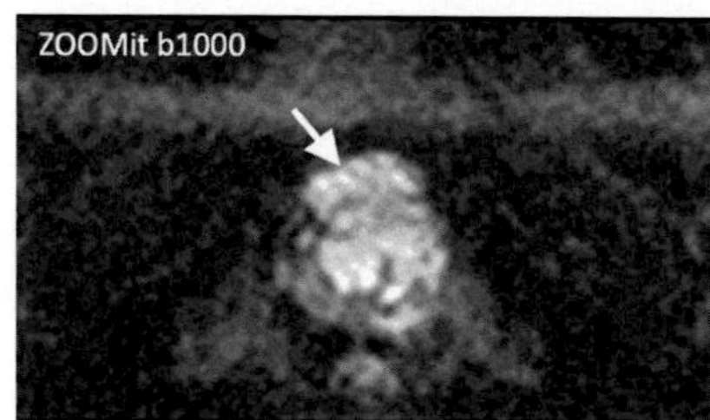

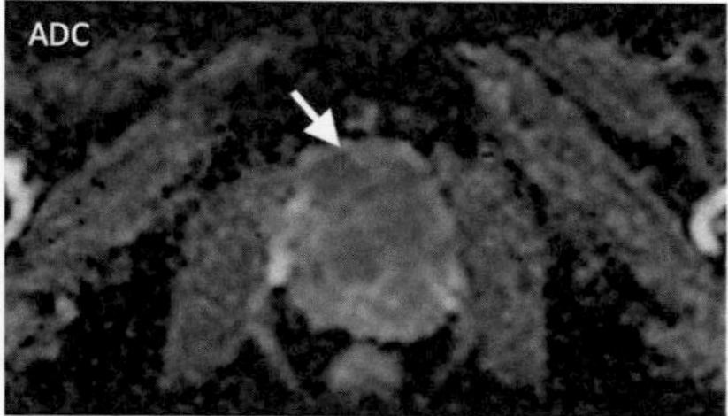

FIG. 24.2

Limited field-of-view imaging. Using an inner volume excitation technique (ZOOMit) at a *b*-value of 1000 s/mm^2, the prostate gland is well seen showing a tumor *(arrows)* in the transitional zone, with a high signal intensity due to reduced diffusion, and low ADC values.

SNR and image quality. Computed DWI is an image postprocessing technique that can be applied to generate a synthetic image simulating any higher b-value image from the quantitative ADC map obtained using images with lower diffusion weightings, a strategy that can overcome the aforementioned drawbacks. In a phantom study, computed DWI of a higher b-value yielded higher SNR than images acquired using an equal b-value, especially with b greater than 840 s/mm^2 [15]. Computed DWI at a b-value of 2000 s/mm^2 resulted in higher diagnostic accuracy than acquired $b = 900$ s/mm^2 images for metastatic bone disease detection using whole-body diffusion (WB-DWI) while maintaining good image quality [15, 16] (Fig. 24.3).

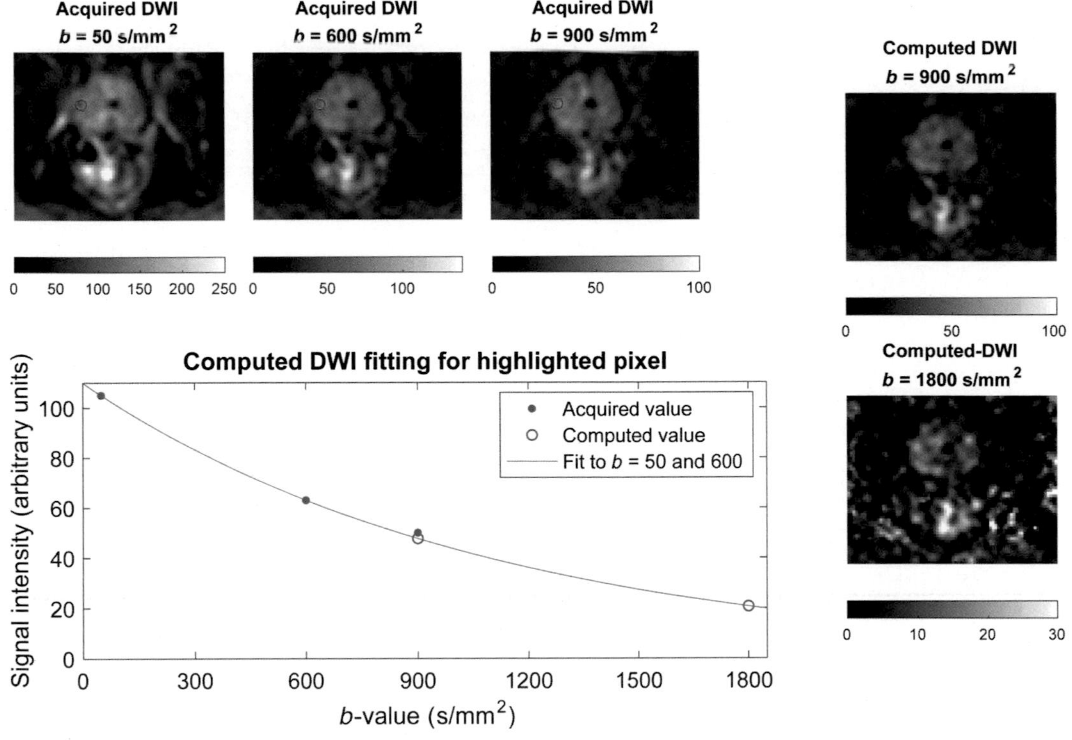

FIG. 24.3

Example showing the computed DWI technique applied to generate high b-value diffusion-weighted images in a 68-year-old man with prostate cancer. The three top left images are diffusion-weighted images acquired at $b = 50$, 600, and 900 s/mm^2. The plot shows values for the pixel highlighted in *red*. The *curve* in this plot is derived by fitting a mono-exponential function to the first two b-values (50 and 600 s/mm^2, *filled circles*), which is used to generate computed values at two higher b-values (900 and 1800 s/mm^2, *open circles*). The unfitted value at $b = 900$ s/mm^2 is also shown for reference. Application of this fitting process to every pixel can be used to synthesize an image at any b-value, and the images in the right-hand panels show images computed at $b = 900$ and 1800 s/mm^2. Comparison of the acquired and computed images at $b = 900$ s/mm^2 indicates a good agreement, while the computed image at $b = 1800$ s/mm^2 demonstrates extrapolation to a diffusion weighting that may be difficult to acquire in practice.

24.2.2.5 Diffusion imaging at 1.5 T versus 3 T

Imaging at 3 T has the potential to increase image SNR over 1.5 T diffusion imaging, though quantitative measurements should remain constant as the field strength does not affect molecular mobility. However, general considerations for 1.5 versus 3 T imaging and issues associated with higher field strength also apply to diffusion imaging [17]. Particular challenges of diffusion imaging at 3 T have increased eddy currents from the rapidly switching gradients used in EPI, and higher impact of magnetic susceptibility variations of neighboring tissues causing image distortion, misregistration, and overall degradation of image quality [5]. Furthermore, uniform fat suppression can be more difficult to achieve due to increased B_1 field inhomogeneities at 3 T, which leads to chemical shift and ghosting artifacts [5]. The decreased image quality of 3 T versus 1.5 T diffusion imaging has been reported in phantom studies [18, 19], although increased lesion conspicuity was also observed at 3 T [20, 21]. One of the recent implementations at 3 T to improve B_1 field inhomogeneity is the use of image-based shimming techniques, which can significantly improve the quality of extracranial diffusion studies, especially over large FoVs in the body [22].

24.3 Quantitative diffusion mapping

Qualitative visual assessment of signal intensities is currently the mainstay for the interpretation of diffusion imaging in clinical practice. The radiologist utilizes all available MRI sequences and arrives at a diagnostic conclusion by a cognitive appraisal of signal contrasts and tissue morphology. The qualitative approach is commonly used in most clinical settings, but is subjective and has several limitations including interoperator and interscanner variability of disease assessment, SNR floors, and interpretation errors due to confounders from competing brightness effects from different contrast mechanisms (e.g., "T_2 shine-through") [23]. These limitations can be mitigated by quantitative analyses of water mobility, improve the characterization of lesion heterogeneity, confirm diffusivity changes occult to the naked eye, and increase overall objectivity.

24.3.1 Quantitative measurements using the monoexponential model

The most widely used quantitative parameter, derived by using a monoexponential model for the measured DWI signal with two or more *b*-values, is the ADC. Most MRI systems provide an in-line calculation of an ADC map. By drawing regions of interest (ROIs) on this map, the ADC value of tissues can be recorded. In clinical practice, it is the mean ADC across an ROI that is most frequently reported, although other ADC histogram parameters are also being used; the relative strengths and weaknesses of these are discussed in the following section (Fig. 24.4).

24.3.1.1 Mean ADC

Studies have provided biological validation showing an inverse correlation between the ROI-derived mean ADC value and the tissue cellularity and tumor grade [24–26]. In clinical studies, an excellent interreader agreement was reported for the mean ADC [27]. The mean ADC value has approximately 3%–6% interstudy variation, increasing with smaller volume measurements. Besides, intervendor measurement variability of a similar magnitude can also contribute to the measurement variations [28–31]. Overall, changes of mean ADC value greater than 15%–30% from comparable ROIs may be considered as confidently detectable.

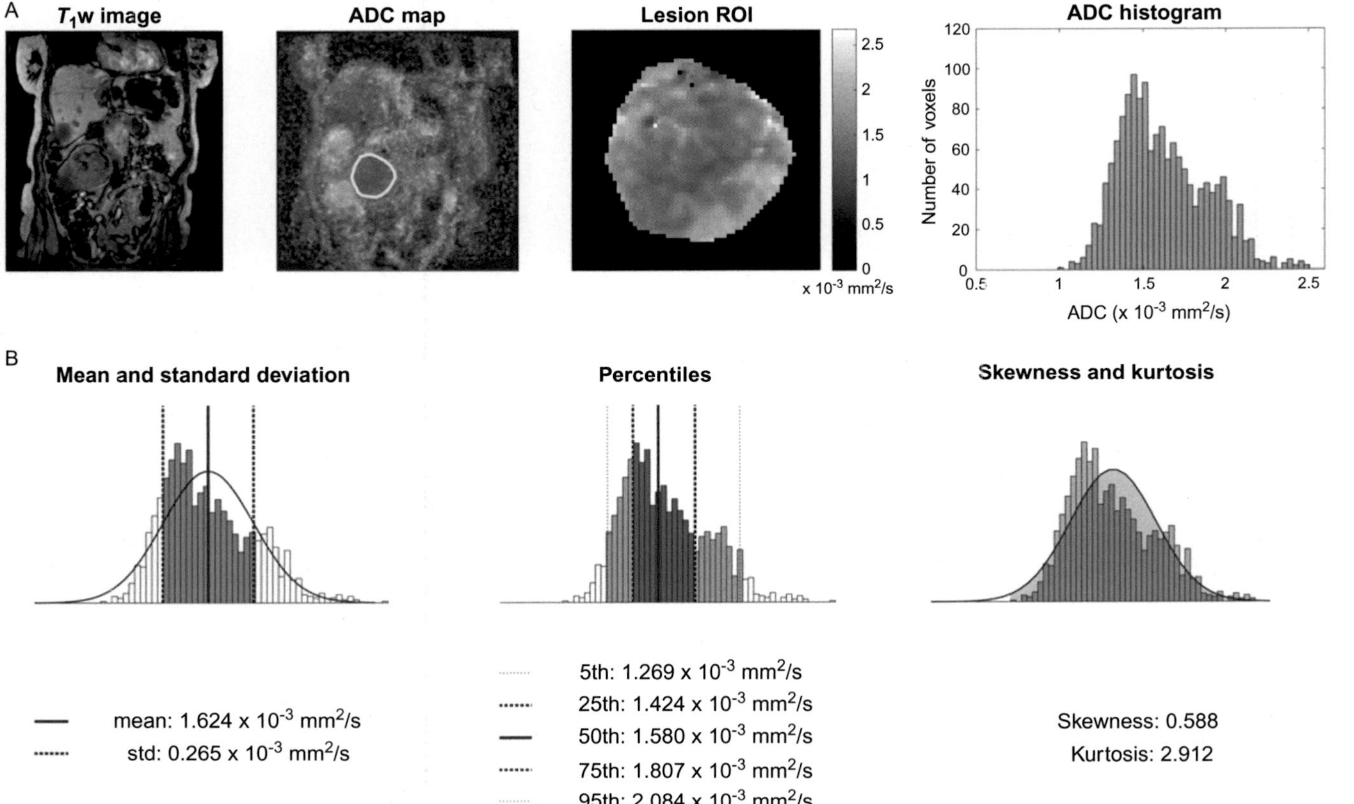

FIG. 24.4

Renal cell carcinoma in a 72-year-old man. (A) (left to right) T_1-weighted image, and ADC map from diffusion-weighted images (10 *b*-values, 0–1000 s/mm^2). The tumor appears dark on the ADC map due to impeded water diffusion (ROI shown in outline). The individual voxel ADC values from the tumor are extracted to give the ADC histogram. (B) Histogram analysis is performed to generate: (Left) The mean and standard deviation (assuming normal distribution) as summary parameters, but which can be affected by outliers. (Center) The median (50th percentile) is less sensitive to outliers and may be a better summary parameter. Using other percentiles values, such as interquartile range, gives a measure of spread. The lower percentiles, down to 5th percentile, may be informative in oncological diffusion imaging, since these correspond to more impeded water diffusion which is linked to higher cell density. Minima (and maxima) of the histogram have large statistical variability and should be avoided. (Right) Higher moments of the histogram can be calculated, such as skewness (3rd moment) and kurtosis (4th moment). Positive skewness indicates a longer right-side tail, with negative skewness vice versa (symmetrical distributions have zero skewness). Kurtosis values above 3 indicate both tails are heavier than a normal distribution, and values below 3 indicate lighter tails than a normal distribution.

24.3.1.2 Minimum and maximum ADC values, and ADC percentile values

By hypothesis, the area with minimum ADC value should correspond to the area of highest cellularity, thus indicating the most viable or most aggressive tumor. In contrast, the maximum ADC should indicate the least cellular areas, thus may help identify early response to therapy associated with cell death and decreased cellularity. However, both the minimum and maximum ADC are samples arising from the tails of the ADC histogram, which are subject to larger sampling variability than other statistical properties (e.g., the mean), and thus show poor measurement repeatability. For these reasons, it may be more robust to report on the 5th and 95th percentiles to reflect changes in the lower and upper ranges of ADC [32]. Measures of location and spread from assessing percentiles use the median (50th percentile), and interquartile range (75th–25th percentile).

24.3.1.3 Skewness and kurtosis

The skewness and kurtosis of diffusion measurements are related to the shape of the histogram of ADC values. Skewness reflects the asymmetry of the ADC distribution; a positive skewness indicates a long right-hand tail of the ADC distribution. Kurtosis is related to the prevalence of extreme values in the ADC distribution, and kurtosis values greater than three are associated with longer histogram tails than a Gaussian distribution. Both parameters usually behave in a coherent pattern in cancers: a large skewness and kurtosis of the ADC distribution are often present in untreated, highly cellular, and viable tumor. A decrease of skewness and kurtosis throughout treatment is associated with therapy response [33]. However, similar to a minimum and maximum ADC, skewness, and kurtosis show poor measurement repeatability with high interobserver and intraobserver variance [34]. For these reasons, the visual appraisal of the histogram distribution may be more practical than the absolute quantification of the skewness and kurtosis values.

24.3.2 Nonmonoexponential quantitative measurements

The observed signal decay of the diffusion signal in tissues is in practice nonmonoexponential to a varying degree, reflecting the complexity of tissue organization. Hence, although the simple ADC measurement is robust in summarizing complex tissue diffusion properties [35], there is a significant interest in deploying more sophisticated diffusion models to derive additional parameters that may improve disease characterization. These nonmonoexponential diffusion models make different assumptions about the tissue microstructure and the three most widely used models of this sort—the IVIM model, the stretched-exponential model, and the diffusion-kurtosis model—are briefly reviewed in the following section.

24.3.2.1 IVIM modeling of diffusion signals: D, D*, and f

The intravoxel incoherent motion (IVIM) model is a description of the diffusion signal that accounts for two distinct compartments of water molecules within a voxel during imaging, with separate signal attenuation characteristics. With diffusion sensitizing gradients over a certain threshold value, changes in signal intensity with *b*-value are mostly related to "true" (random) diffusion, labeled by the coefficient D, and are modeled as an exponential decay similar to the ADC model. The second component describes signals arising from water molecules undergoing convective transport in the capillaries. Under the assumption of the random orientation of vessels within each voxel, this motion also leads to signal dephasing and, therefore, signal loss, which manifests as a fast pseudodiffusion process. This can also be modeled with an exponential decay, whose rate constant is the pseudodiffusion coefficient D^*.

The diffusion signal attenuation at low b-values, commonly less than 200 s/mm^2, reflects both compartments. Consequently, low b-value signal attenuation is greater than expected when considering only "true" diffusion effects. Thus, using the ADC model in the presence of pseudodiffusion would lead to values higher than expected for the random diffusion component alone [36, 37]. Under the assumptions of the IVIM model, the diffusion signal is the sum of true diffusion (D) and pseudodiffusion components (D^*) and their relative contribution is quantified by the pseudodiffusion fraction (f) which is reflective of a perfusion contribution [37, 38]. The bi-exponential IVIM signal function can be expressed as follows:

$$S = S_0\left(f\mathrm{e}^{-b(D+D^*)} + (1-f)\mathrm{e}^{-bD}\right)$$

To apply this model effectively, measurements at multiple b-values are necessary. Although the ideal number and location depend on the organ and pathology, between 5 and 16 b-values are commonly used. Acceptable repeatability and variability have been reported for D, but f and D^* have much larger variations [39, 40]. IVIM diffusion imaging has shown promising results on a cohort basis for imaging of tumors of the kidney, head and neck, pancreas, breast, bladder, and liver as well as functional imaging of the kidneys [41–46], but its applicability on a per-patient basis requires further investigation.

24.3.2.2 Stretched exponential model: α, DDC

In tissues, multiple processes contribute to water diffusion within a voxel, leading to nonmonoexponential signal attenuation by considering these processes as relating to microscopic heterogeneity. The signal can be modeled as a sum of many Gaussian diffusion-related signals decays at different rates. The stretched exponential can be used to model the overall signal decay as arising from a continuous distribution of decay rates [47]. This is achieved by including a dimensionless stretching term α in the diffusion attenuation model, which accounts for deviations from monoexponential behavior, and is constrained to values between 0 and 1:

$$S = S_0 \exp\left[-(b \times DDC)^{\alpha}\right]$$

where DDC is the distributed diffusion coefficient. A α value of 1 indicates a Gaussian diffusion process with homogenous diffusion coefficients within the voxel. Values of α which are less than 1 indicate increasing heterogeneity. The DDC is a metric of the tissue diffusivity derived from the stretched-exponential function [47]. Stretched exponential parameters have been reported to aid the characterization and staging of diffuse liver disease, bladder, ovarian, and breast cancers [46, 48–51].

24.3.2.3 Diffusion kurtosis imaging: K, D

Another approach to model diffusion signal attenuation to reflect non-Gaussian diffusion caused by microscopic heterogeneity is diffusion kurtosis imaging (DKI), which uses ultrahigh b-values (greater than 1500 s/mm^2), to sensitize the signal to a greater range of tissue properties. In tissues, the increased mobility of extracellular water compared to intracellular water implies that at very high b-values the extracellular water signal is attenuated more than the intracellular water, and the DKI approach is designed to sensitize the measurement to such microstructural properties [50]. Using the DKI model, the parameters derived include ADC (D_{app}) and the apparent diffusion kurtosis, K_{app}. The DKI signal function is expressed as follows:

$$S = S_0\left(\mathrm{e}^{-bD + b^2D^2K/6}\right)$$

K_{app} characterizes the degree of non-Gaussian diffusion. A value close to 0 reflects Gaussian diffusion; values greater than zero are indicative of a signal decay that is less attenuated at high b-values than monoexponential tissues with the same D_{app} [50]. For example, K_{app} is significantly larger in prostate cancer than normal parenchyma [51], which is indicative of altered tissue structure in carcinoma.

24.3.3 Whole-body quantitative diffusion measurements: Diffusion volume, global ADC

Whole-body diffusion-weighted imaging, WB-DWI, was introduced in 2004 and has evolved to become a powerful diagnostic tool for disease detection and staging. It is especially advantageous for evaluating systemic bone diseases such as metastatic breast and prostate cancer, as well as multiple myeloma [52]. WB-DWI is typically performed by the sequential acquisition of 4–6 axial image stacks, each providing a field-of-view of approximately 20 cm in the head-foot direction. These images are combined into a total-body diffusion study in postprocessing and can be viewed using volumetric displays such as a maximum intensity projection (MIP). As with anatomically-specific diffusion examinations, the highly cellular tumor is highlighted while healthy background tissue is suppressed, creating high lesion-to-background contrast. This contrast may be further increased by utilizing calculated ultrahigh b-values, facilitating lesion segmentation [15, 53]. Disease segmentation based on the disease signal intensity allows estimation of the total disease burden, termed the total diffusion volume (tDV), which is a promising marker for disease prognosis and response assessment. For example, in metastatic castration-resistant prostate carcinoma (mCRPC) patients, the tDV showed an inverse correlation with overall survival [54]. A 40%–50% tDV decrease during oncological therapy may indicate therapy response [53, 55]. In addition, the ADC values associated with entire segmented disease volume (global ADC) can also inform on disease cellularity (Fig. 24.5). A mean gADC increase of 30% or more may be indicative of therapy response. tDV and global ADC (gADC) have also been shown to have good measurement reproducibility and interreader agreement [33, 34, 54, 56].

24.4 Clinical applications

Diffusion imaging has become a standard MR sequence regardless of body region and even in a whole-body setting. It is currently employed in many nononcological and oncological applications. The reader should bear in mind the strengths and limitations of the technique, as well as the need to combine diffusion imaging with anatomical MRI sequences for optimal interpretation. In the following sections, we survey the established deployment of extracranial diffusion imaging in clinical practice, focusing on indications where there is significant evidence for its added value.

24.4.1 Breast cancer

24.4.1.1 Disease detection

Malignant breast lesions show impeded diffusion compared with normal fibro-glandular tissue [57]. A metaanalysis evaluating 964 breast lesions, 615 malignant and 349 benign, demonstrated a combined sensitivity of 84% and specificity of 79% for discriminating between malignant and benign lesions based on DWI [58]. Diffusion imaging increases the diagnostic accuracy of breast MRI complementary

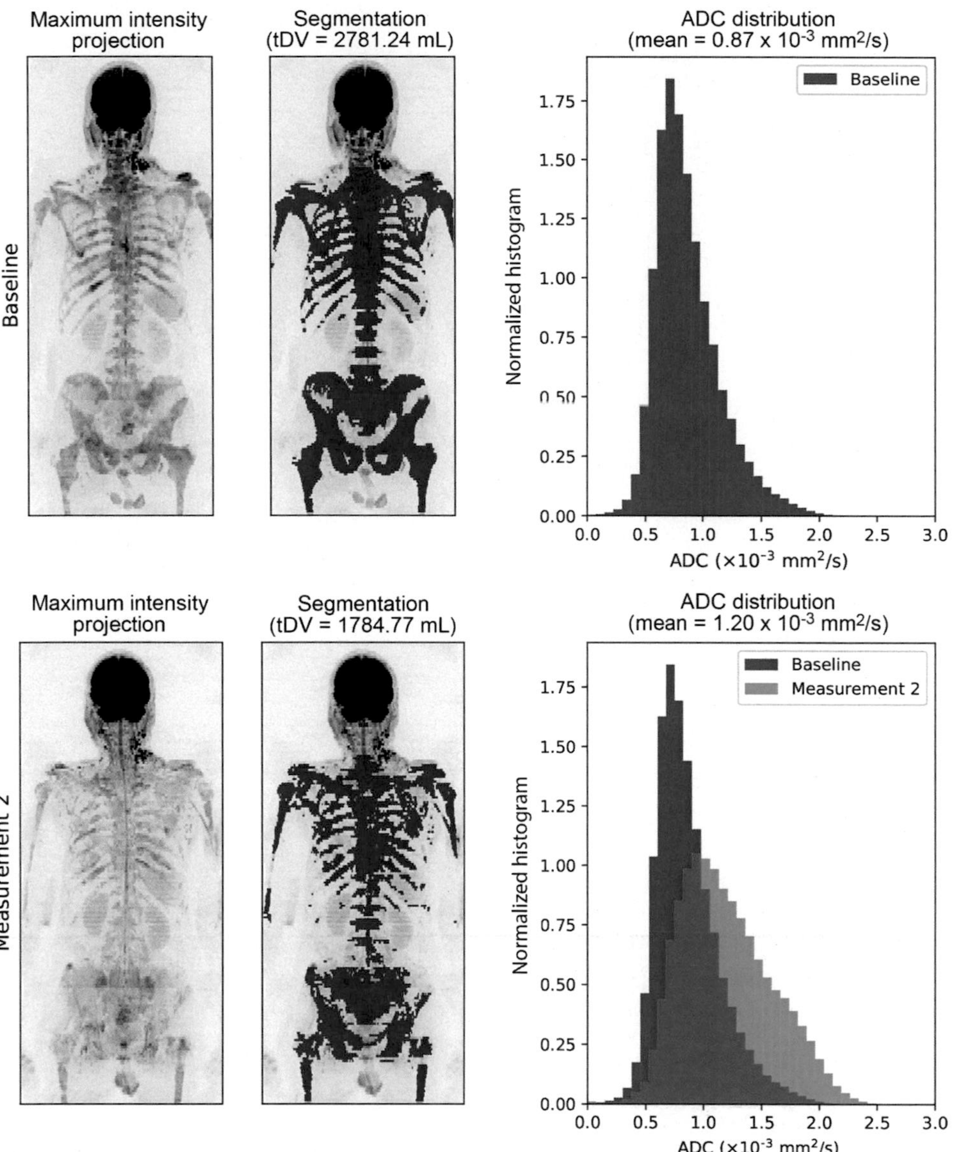

FIG. 24.5

An elderly male with prostate carcinoma with diffuse bone metastases. Inverted maximum intensity projections (MIP) and corresponding segmentation of the total diffusion volume (tDV in *red*) of the metastatic bone disease derived from whole-body diffusion imaging. Measurement 2 was performed after chemotherapy. When comparing the ADC histogram derived from the tDV at baseline and after chemotherapy, an increase in ADC as well as a reduction of skewness and kurtosis is observed, consistent with response to therapy.

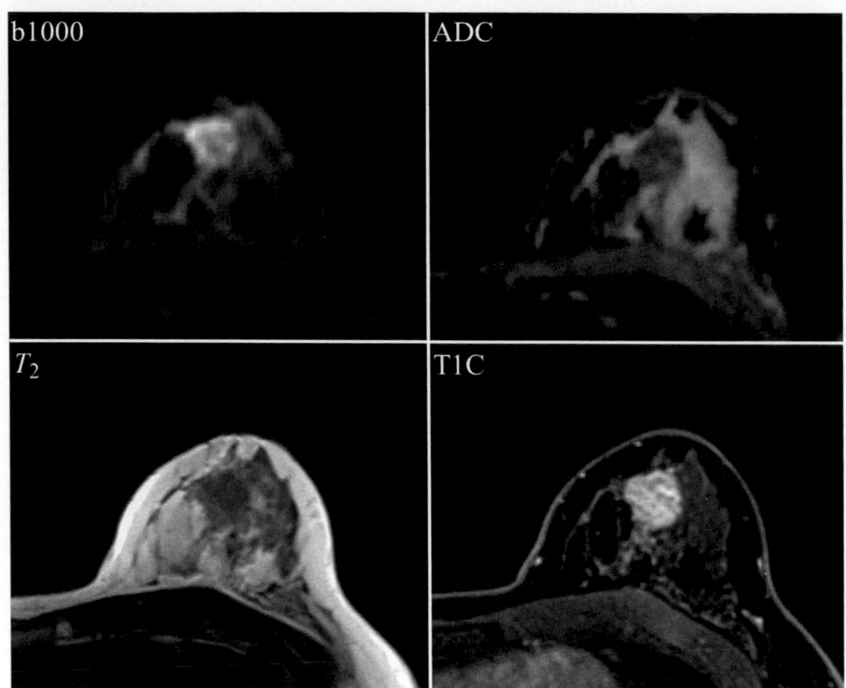

FIG. 24.6

A 38-year-old woman with breast cancer. A 2 cm tumor is visible in the left breast showing impeded diffusion (b1000 diffusion-weighted image), low ADC value (ADC image), low T_2 signal intensity (T_2 image) and avid contrast enhancement (T1C image) typical of a breast carcinoma.

to contrast-enhanced imaging [59] (Fig. 24.6) and may reduce unnecessary biopsies for mammogram screen-detected lesions [60]. Quantitative ADC cut-off values to discriminate malignant from benign lesions are not consistent, due to ADC dependence on chosen *b*-values and the lack of a universally accepted imaging standard. However, the sensitivity and specificity for the detection of malignancy do not appear affected by different *b*-values in clinical use [61] or prior intravenous contrast administration [62].

24.4.1.2 Disease characterization

The menstrual cycle does not significantly affect the ADC values of glandular tissue [63]. However, the ADC value is reduced in lactating breasts [64]. ADC correlates with breast density, thus breast tissue ADC values are lower in postmenopausal than premenopausal women [55]. In either case, the normal range of glandular tissue remains higher than in malignancies, thus the diagnostic performance of ADC is not compromised. Ductal carcinoma in situ (DCIS) lesions are associated with higher ADC values than invasive cancer, and lesions that become invasive cancers showed lower ADC values than those that remained as DCIS [65–67]. Lower ADC values in breast cancer are correlated with higher proliferation and cellularity. Although a strong negative correlation between ADC value and tumor grade was reported [63, 65], the ADC correlations with other known prognostic factors remain inconsistent [64].

24.4.2 Head and neck cancers

24.4.2.1 Disease detection

Malignancy is associated with impeded diffusion, leading to high signal on DWI and low ADC. Proposed ADC cut-offs discriminating malignant from benign lesions range between $1.15–1.3 \times 10^{-3}$ mm^2/s with reportedly high diagnostic accuracy (86% to 96%) using SS-EPI DWI and *b*-values of 0 and 1000 s/mm^2 [68–70].

24.4.2.2 Response assessment

Complete therapy response was associated with significant ADC increase, while therapy failure was correlated with ADC decrease throughout chemoradiation of squamous cell cancer [71, 72]. One study observed that a lower ADC increase at 2 and 4 weeks after treatment was associated with higher recurrence rates [73]. Diffusion imaging can help to distinguish between posttherapeutic tissue changes and disease recurrence, the latter being more likely to show impeded diffusion against the reactive, inflammatory tissue changes due to an increase in cellularity [74]. Low pretreatment ADC values were associated with better therapy response and longer overall survival than high ADC values [72–74]. High pretreatment IVIM D and *f* values were also associated with the poor response of squamous cell cancer [75]. However, the predictive and prognostic value of ADC in this disease setting requires further validation.

24.4.3 Focal liver lesions

24.4.3.1 Disease detection and characterization

Diffusion imaging using *b*-values greater than 50–100 s/mm^2 suppresses the intrahepatic vascular signal, improving the detection of small focal liver lesions compared with T_2 or contrast-enhanced images, and also improves the reader confidence [75–77]. However, the combination of diffusion images with contrast-enhanced images is superior to either sequence by itself for the detection of colorectal liver metastases [75, 76] (Fig. 24.7). Diffusion imaging is deemed the most sensitive contrast for the detection of neuroendocrine liver metastases [78]. In the noncirrhotic liver, an ADC value greater than 1.7×10^{-3} mm^2/s has good diagnostic sensitivity and specificity for discrimination between benign and malignant focal lesions but should be combined with all morphological imaging findings and not used as a stand-alone criterion due to the considerable overlap of ADC values between benign and malignant lesions.

In the cirrhotic liver, lesion detection for hepatocellular carcinoma (HCC) is reduced as fibrosis leads to impeded diffusion of the parenchyma, thus reducing the lesion to parenchyma contrast [79]. An inverse correlation between ADC and tumor grade in HCC was shown in multiple studies. More recently, IVIM diffusion parameters performed better than conventional DWI for assessing tumor grade [80].

24.4.3.2 Response assessment

Diffusion imaging has shown promising results for assessing tumor response to interventional procedures and systemic therapies. ADC increase is associated with the degree of necrosis after transarterial chemoembolization (TACE) [81, 82]; observable blood flow reduction after transarterial radioembolization (TARE) may be assessed by IVIM *f* measurements [83], and high ADC values after radiation therapy are associated with a recurrence-free survival of HCC patients [84]. An increase in the ADC values of metastases was observed in response to systemic chemotherapy with responders

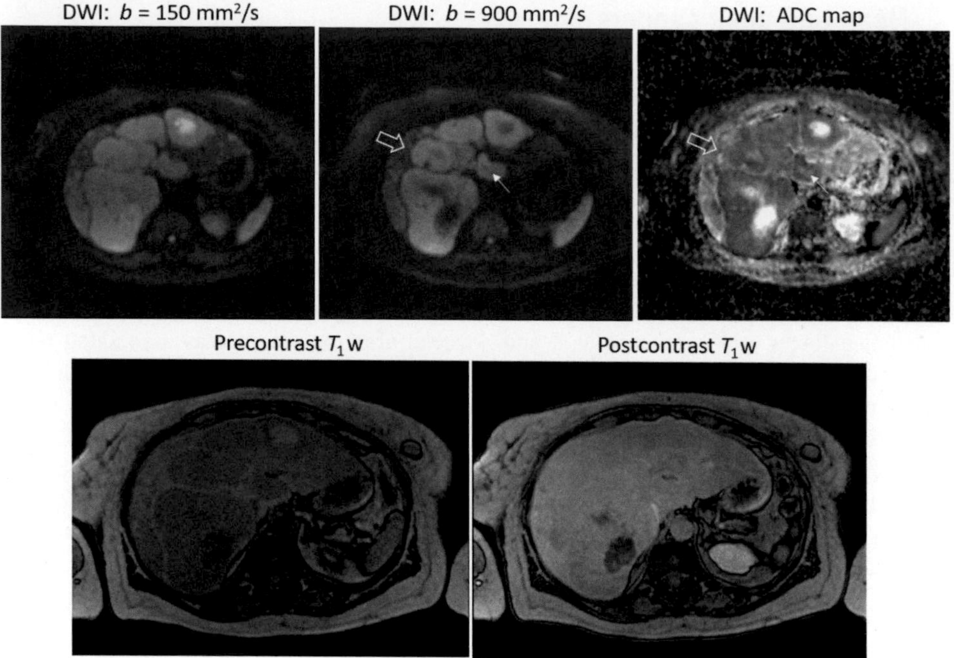

FIG. 24.7

Liver metastasis of 66-year-old woman with known colorectal cancer. Intrahepatic cellular lesions, such as metastases, are easily identified on diffusion-weighted imaging *(arrows)*. Diffusion-weighted images (top row) showing the lower (b150) and higher (b900) *b*-value images, as well as the corresponding ADC map. The smaller lesion at the hepatic hilum *(thin arrow)* returned an ADC value of 0.9×10^{-3} mm^2/s, while normal liver ADC (right lobe) was 1.1×10^{-3} mm^2/s. Pre/postcontrast T_1-weighted images are also shown (bottom row) demonstrating lower lesion conspicuity compared with the diffusion-weighted images.

showing 26% ADC increase 7 days after treatment [25]. Moreover, ADC changes precede a reduction in the size of responding hepatic metastases [85]. However, the percentage of ADC increase that is associated with longer-term improved treatment outcomes requires validation.

24.4.4 Focal pancreatic lesions

24.4.4.1 Disease detection

The pancreas appears largely homogenous on diffusion images [86]. An inhomogeneous diffusion signal of the parenchyma should raise suspicion for disease. Using diffusion imaging can improve tumor detection compared with conventional T_2-weighted images [87]. Very high detection rates and diagnostic accuracy of 96% have been reported for ductal adenocarcinomas, using a pooled mean ADC of less than 1.332×10^{-3} mm^2/s as a threshold for a suspicious focal abnormality [87, 88]. Besides, the pseudodiffusion fraction (f) measured in IVIM is decreased in adenocarcinomas and has shown superior diagnostic performance over ADC or D values [89, 90]. Diffusion imaging is even more sensitive and accurate for the detection of pancreatic neuroendocrine tumors (NETs) [88] (Fig. 24.8).

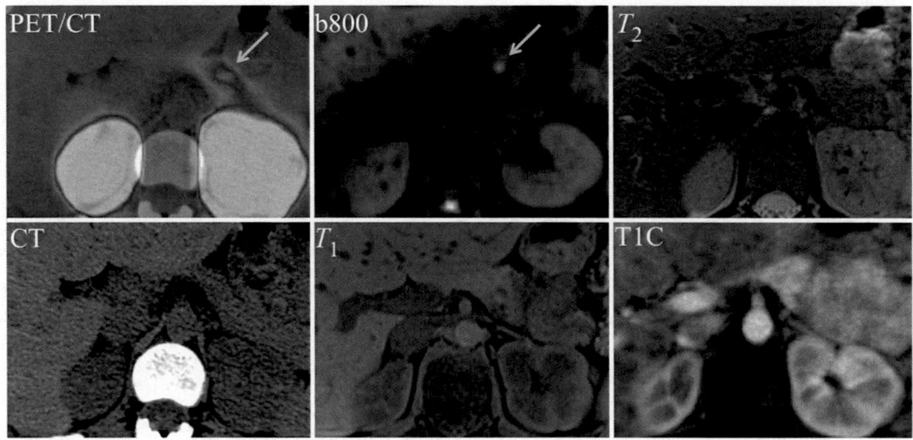

FIG. 24.8

Insulinoma in a 40-year-old patient. The *yellow arrows* point to a 0.5 cm tumor in the body of the pancreas with increased metabolic activity on the DOTATOC PET/CT, which is also easily seen on the b800 diffusion-weighted image. The lesion is however not visible on the CT, T_2-weighted (T_2), T_1-weighted (T_1) or post-contrast T_1-weighted (T1C) images.

24.4.4.2 Characterization of malignancy

The mean ADC value of normal parenchyma ranges from $1.270–0.611 \times 10^{-3}$ mm^2/s [86]. However, conflicting results have been published resulting in overlapping ADC ranges for mass-forming pancreatitis and adenocarcinoma [88]. The ADC value is inversely correlated with tumor grade in neuroendocrine tumors [91]. IVIM diffusion imaging is useful for characterizing pancreatic masses: f and D^* were significantly higher in neuroendocrine tumors than in adenocarcinoma (but lower than normal parenchyma), and showed superior diagnostic accuracy over other diffusion parameters for discrimination between the two malignant entities with the excellent interreader agreement [92–94].

24.4.5 Renal masses and renal function

24.4.5.1 Lesion detection and characterization

Diffusion imaging is routinely utilized in renal cancer imaging. A metaanalysis including 764 patients across 17 studies concluded that DWI can be used to discriminate between malignant and benign focal renal lesions [95]. Mean ADC values were significantly lower in renal cell carcinoma (1.61×10^{-3} mm^2/s) and uroepithelial malignancies (1.30×10^{-3} mm^2/s) than in normal parenchyma (2.10×10^{-3} mm^2/s) and oncocytomas (2.00×10^{-3} mm^2/s). In a further metaanalysis including 397 renal cell carcinomas (RCC), DWI showed moderate diagnostic performance for differentiating between high- and low-grade RCC [96]. However, it is again important to note that lesion characterization of renal tumors should not be entirely reliant on ADC due to the overlap of the ADC values between different pathologies, and should be interpreted alongside all other imaging findings.

24.4.5.2 Renal function

Early-stage kidney disease was found to be associated with lower ADC values than normal parenchyma, making diffusion mapping a potentially useful tool to monitor the function of the native or transplanted kidney (Fig. 24.9). ADC values showed a negative linear correlation with increasing grade of kidney disease [97]. The kidneys receive about 25% of the cardiac output volume. Conversely, this translates into strong cortical perfusion and medullary tubular flow, which affects ADC measurements. Thus, using IVIM diffusion imaging, the cortical IVIM parameters f, D, and D^* were significantly lower in patients with chronic kidney disease than in healthy individuals [98]. Besides, a negative correlation has been reported between f and D with 24-h urinary protein, serum creatine levels, and histopathological glomerular injury and fibrosis score. The f and D values showed a positive correlation with eGFR [98, 99].

24.4.6 Gynecological tumors

24.4.6.1 Endometrial cancer

The use of diffusion imaging increases the detection rate of endometrial cancer when added to T_2-weighted images versus T_2-weighted images alone, and is especially helpful where leiomyomas or adenomyosis cause altered anatomy [100]. Besides, diffusion imaging can aid disease staging by accurately assessing myometrial invasion. Diffusion measurements can help the physician to avoid the pitfall of including peri-tumoral inflammation, which has similar contrast enhancement compared to malignancy but which does not show impeded diffusion [101].

24.4.6.2 Cervical cancer

Diffusion imaging is as accurate as contrast-enhanced MRI for detecting cervical cancer (diagnostic accuracy = 0.95) [102]. ADC values were shown to inversely correlate with tumor grade [103, 104]. Diffusion measurements can help to delineate small tumors for surgical planning [105]. Diffusion imaging is useful for following up chemoradiation treatment and can detect disease recurrence and monitor tumor response—a significant increase in ADC values has been reported in responders as early as 2 weeks after initiating therapy [106].

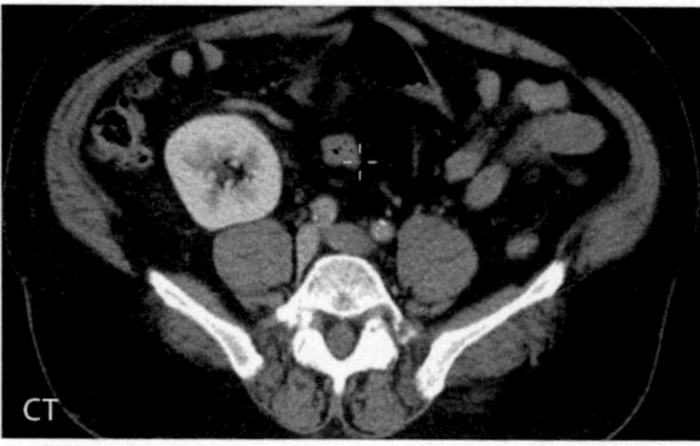

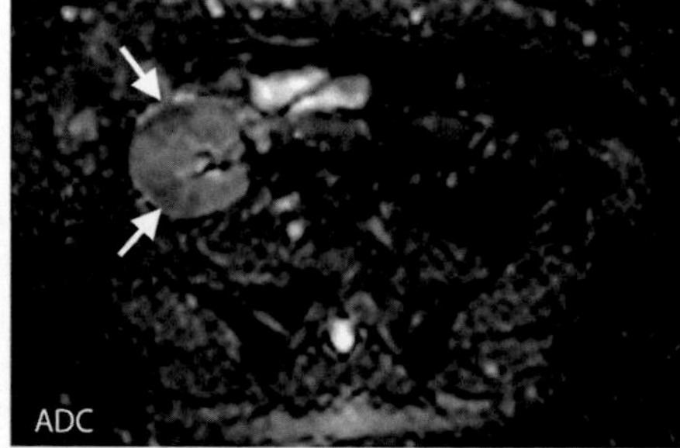

FIG. 24.9

A 54-year-old man with a transplant kidney in the right iliac fossa presenting with slight impairment of renal function. Axial contrast-enhanced CT in the portovenous phase shows differential enhancement of the cortex and medulla but no focal abnormality is detected. The MRI-derived ADC map shows focal areas of low ADC values in the renal parenchyma in keeping with focal nephritis.

24.4.6.3 Adnexal masses

Diffusion imaging has recently been included as a standard contrast for assessing sonographically indeterminate adnexal masses by the European Society of Urogenital Radiology [107]. Diffusion is included in the adnexal masses MRI scoring system and is deemed especially helpful when assessing nonlipomatous, nonhemorrhagic solid, or complex lesions [108]. Such adnexal masses with ADC values lower than 1.00×10^{-3} mm^2/s should be viewed with suspicion. Conversely, a low T_2-signal mass associated with low signal intensity on DWI is highly predictive of benignity [103]. Diffusion imaging can also improve disease staging and surveillance by reliably identifying peritoneal deposits and recurrent disease [103].

24.4.7 Prostate cancer

The prostate is one of the most active areas of extracranial diffusion imaging research. In combination with T_2-weighted MRI, DWI (together with the ADC map) has become one of the key sequences for tumor detection and staging. This approach is encapsulated in the Prostate Imaging Reporting and Data System (PIRADS). In the most recent version 2.1, DWI is termed the dominant sequence for assessing tumors of the peripheral zone [109]. For ADC calculation, a low b-value between 0–100 s/mm^2 and a high b-value less than 1000 s/mm^2 are recommended. The ADC value has been shown to inversely correlate with the Gleason score [110] and may indicate tumor progression on serial measurements [111] or tumor relapse following treatment [112]. PIRADS also recommends separate acquisition of an ultrahigh b-value (greater than 1400 s/mm^2) [109], which may help with lesion detection and also discrimination between glandular hyperplasia and transition zone tumors [113]. In a metaanalysis of 789 patients across 11 studies, measurements with high b-values greater than 1000 s/mm^2 showed better diagnostic accuracy than standard high b-values between 800–1000 s/mm^2 for detecting prostate cancer (pooled sensitivity 80% versus 78% and specificity 92% versus 87%) [114]. A promising application for diffusion imaging in this context is computed high b-values. Computed b1500 and b2000 images showed higher diagnostic accuracy than acquired b1000 images and comparable performance to acquired ultrahigh b-value images [115, 116].

24.4.8 Bone marrow disease: Myeloma, bone metastases

Adult bone marrow represents a unique environment for diffusion imaging because of its high-fat content. The large fat cells paired with complex trabecular bone structure lead to a signal suppression on DWI and very low ADC values in healthy bone (vertebral bone ADC $0.2–0.5 \times 10^{-3}$ mm^2/s). The presence of bone marrow disease results in high signal on DWI but paradoxically higher ADC values (typically greater than 0.5×10^{-3} mm^2/s). WB-DWI is superior to radionuclide bone scans, and at least equivalent if not superior to ^{18}F-choline PET for the detection of bone metastases from prostate cancer [117]. WB-DWI has also been shown to be better than ^{18}F-FDG PET for the detection of focal disease and diffuse disease in myeloma in all body parts except the skull [58]. DWI is also of value in discriminating between malignant and benign lesions such as hemangiomas [118]. Besides, tDV and gADC can be monitored during treatment and have shown promising results as biomarkers for therapy response and failure [53–56, 119]. Reporting and data systems for whole-body DWI, aiming to achieve standardization for imaging of advanced prostate cancer and multiple myeloma have been developed and published recently by multidisciplinary expert panels of radiologists, medical physicists, and clinicians [120, 121].

24.5 Future developments

Further developments in hardware and software will undoubtedly consolidate the role of extracranial diffusion imaging in clinical care. One of the disadvantages of MRI as a technique is the comparative long acquisition time compared with CT, especially for WB-DWI studies. Techniques that can improve acquisition efficiency, such as simultaneous multislice acquisitions (Fig. 24.10), or improve image reconstruction from sparse sampling will help to make the technique even more accessible within the radiological community.

Further developments of quantitative diffusion values as biomarkers will continue to evolve. Larger multicenter studies are underway to investigate and validate quantitative ADC values as a diagnostic, response, and prognostic biomarkers. Recent trials using WB-MRI including diffusion imaging in

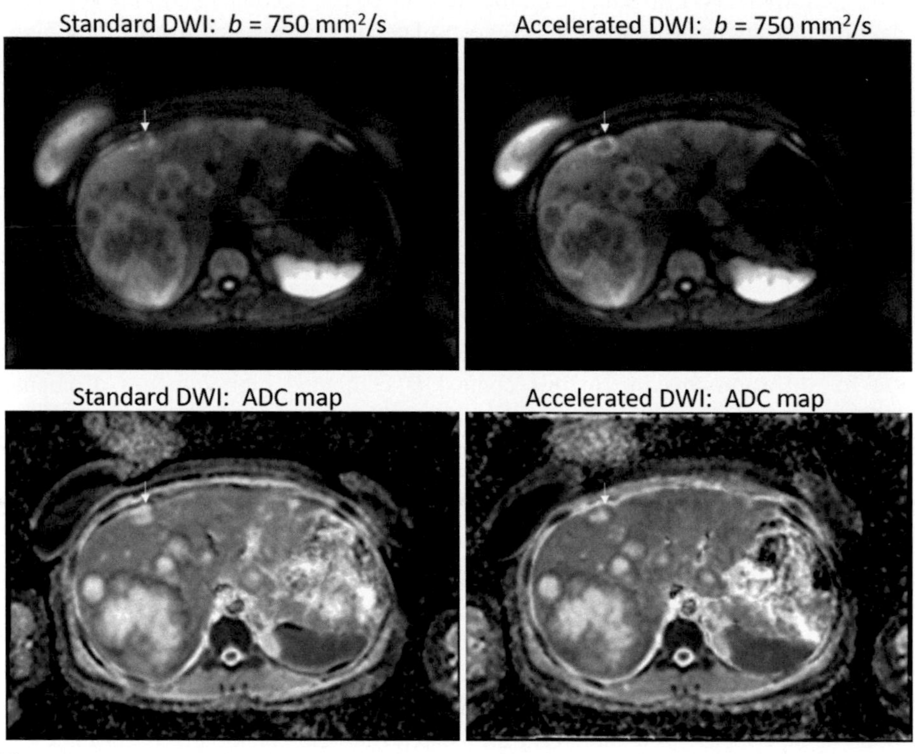

FIG. 24.10

A 53-year-old woman with colorectal liver metastases. Standard (left) versus accelerated (right) DWI demonstrating faster acquisition (3:37 versus 2:46 min) and improved quality *(white arrows)* using the accelerated protocol. Both DWIs were acquired under free-breathing using a monopolar scheme with 3 b-values (0, 100, 750), four signal averages per b-value, TE/TR = 53/7000 ms and a resolution of $1.5 \times 1.5 \times 6\,mm^3$. The accelerated DWI used a prototype sequence that allowed a slice acceleration factor of 2 and a reduced TR of 5000 ms while keeping the other parameters similar. The prototype sequence also employed a motion correction algorithm.

patients with newly diagnosed lung and colorectal cancer [122] have shown that diffusion imaging can potentially replace the conventional imaging pathways of using CT and PET-CT for disease staging. However, real-world implementation of the technique may be challenging and better radiological education and training in these areas are imperative. Last but not least, artificial intelligence and machine learning are major disruptors in radiology, which are advancing at a rapid pace. There is potential to harness these technologies across the whole spectrum from image acquisition, data modeling, and image interpretation to drive innovations in body diffusion imaging.

References

[1] Hahn E. Spin echoes. Phys Rev 1950;80:580.

[2] Stejskal E, Tanner J. Spin diffusion measurements: spin echoes in the presence of a time-dependent field gradient. J Chem Phys 1965;1(42):288–92.

[3] Jaermann T, Pruessmann KP, Valavanis A, Kollias S, Boesiger P. Influence of SENSE on image properties in high-resolution single-shot echo-planar DTI. Magn Reson Med 2006;55(2):335–42. https://doi.org/10.1002/mrm.20769.

[4] Jerome NP, Orton MR, d'Arcy JA, Collins DJ, Koh DM, Leach MO. Comparison of free-breathing with navigator-controlled acquisition regimes in abdominal diffusion-weighted magnetic resonance images: effect on ADC and IVIM statistics. J Magn Reson Imaging 2014;39(1):235–40. https://doi.org/10.1002/jmri.24140.

[5] Koh DM, Blackledge M, Padhani AR, Takahara T, Kwee TC, Leach MO, Collins DJ. Whole-body diffusion-weighted MRI: tips, tricks, and pitfalls. AJR Am J Roentgenol 2012;199(2):252–62. https://doi.org/10.2214/AJR.11.7866.

[6] Dietrich O, Biffar A, Baur-Melnyk A, Reiser MF. Technical aspects of MR diffusion imaging of the body. Eur J Radiol 2010;76(3):314–22. https://doi.org/10.1016/j.ejrad.2010.02.018.

[7] Deng J, Omary RA, Larson AC. Multishot diffusion-weighted SPLICE PROPELLER MRI of the abdomen. Magn Reson Med 2008;59(5):947–53. https://doi.org/10.1002/mrm.21525.

[8] Feinberg DA, Hoenninger JC, Crooks LE, Kaufman L, Watts JC, Arakawa M. Inner volume MR imaging: technical concepts and their application. Radiology 1985;156(3):743–7. https://doi.org/10.1148/radiology.156.3.4023236.

[9] Wilm BJ, Svensson J, Henning A, Pruessmann KP, Boesiger P, Kollias SS. Reduced field-of-view MRI using outer volume suppression for spinal cord diffusion imaging. Magn Reson Med 2007;57(3):625–30. https://doi.org/10.1002/mrm.21167.

[10] Kim H, Lee JM, Yoon JH, Jang JY, Kim SW, Ryu JK, Kannengiesser S, Han JK, Choi BI. Reduced field-of-view diffusion-weighted magnetic resonance imaging of the pancreas: comparison with conventional single-shot echo-planar imaging. Korean J Radiol 2015;16(6):1216–25. https://doi.org/10.3348/kjr.2015.16.6.1216.

[11] Hwang J, Hong SS, Kim HJ, Chang YW, Nam BD, Oh E, Lee E, Cha H. Reduced field-of-view diffusion-weighted MRI in patients with cervical cancer. Br J Radiol 2018;91(1087):20170864. https://doi.org/10.1259/bjr.20170864.

[12] Vidiri A, Minosse S, Piludu F, Curione D, Pichi B, Spriano G, Marzi S. Feasibility study of reduced field of view diffusion-weighted magnetic resonance imaging in head and neck tumors. Acta Radiol 2017;58(3):292–300. https://doi.org/10.1177/0284185116652014.

[13] Warndahl BA, Borisch EA, Kawashima A, Riederer SJ, Froemming AT. Conventional vs. reduced field of view diffusion weighted imaging of the prostate: comparison of image quality, correlation with histology, and inter-reader agreement. Magn Reson Imaging 2018;47:67–76. https://doi.org/10.1016/j.mri.2017.10.011.

[14] Porter DA, Heidemann RM. High resolution diffusion-weighted imaging using readout-segmented echo-planar imaging, parallel imaging and a two-dimensional navigator-based reacquisition. Magn Reson Med 2009;62(2):468–75. https://doi.org/10.1002/mrm.22024.

[15] Blackledge MD, Leach MO, Collins DJ, Koh DM. Computed diffusion-weighted MR imaging may improve tumor detection. Radiology 2011;261(2):573–81. https://doi.org/10.1148/radiol.11101919.

[16] O'Flynn EA, Blackledge M, Collins D, Downey K, Doran S, Patel H, Dumonteil S, Mok W, Leach MO, Koh DM. Evaluating the diagnostic sensitivity of computed diffusion-weighted MR imaging in the detection of breast cancer. J Magn Reson Imaging 2016;44(1):130–7. https://doi.org/10.1002/jmri.25131.

[17] Soher BJ, Dale BM, Merkle EM. A review of MR physics: 3T versus 1.5T, Magn Reson Imaging Clin N Am 2007;15(3):277–90. https://doi.org/10.1016/j.mric.2007.06.002.

[18] Lavdas I, Miquel ME, McRobbie DW, Aboagye EO. Comparison between diffusion-weighted MRI (DW-MRI) at 1.5 and 3 tesla: a phantom study. J Magn Reson Imaging 2014;40(3):682–90. https://doi.org/10.1002/jmri.24397.

[19] Rosenkrantz AB, Oei M, Babb JS, Niver BE, Taouli B. Diffusion-weighted imaging of the abdomen at 3.0 tesla: image quality and apparent diffusion coefficient reproducibility compared with 1.5 tesla. J Magn Reson Imaging 2011;33(1):128–35. https://doi.org/10.1002/jmri.22395.

[20] Beyersdorff D, Taymoorian K, Knösel T, Schnorr D, Felix R, Hamm B, Bruhn H. MRI of prostate cancer at 1.5 and 3.0 T: comparison of image quality in tumor detection and staging. AJR Am J Roentgenol 2005;185(5):1214–20. https://doi.org/10.2214/AJR.04.1584.

[21] Matsuoka A, Minato M, Harada M, Kubo H, Bandou Y, Tangoku A, Nakano K, Nishitani H. Comparison of 3.0- and 1.5-tesla diffusion-weighted imaging in the visibility of breast cancer. Radiat Med 2008;26(1):15–20. https://doi.org/10.1007/s11604-007-0187-6.

[22] Zhang H, Xue H, Alto S, Hui L, Kannengiesser S, Berthold K, Jin Z. Integrated shimming improves lesion detection in whole-body diffusion-weighted examinations of patients with plasma disorder at 3 T. Investig Radiol 2016;51(5):297–305. https://doi.org/10.1097/RLI.0000000000000238.

[23] Donners R, Blackledge M, Tunariu N, Messiou C, Merkle EM, Koh DM. Quantitative whole-body diffusion-weighted MR imaging. Magn Reson Imaging Clin N Am 2018;26(4):479–94. https://doi.org/10.1016/j.mric.2018.06.002.

[24] Sun Y, Tong T, Cai S, Bi R, Xin C, Gu Y. Apparent diffusion coefficient (ADC) value: a potential imaging biomarker that reflects the biological features of rectal cancer. PLoS One 2014;9(10):e109371. https://doi.org/10.1371/journal.pone.0109371.

[25] Cui Y, Zhang XP, Sun YS, Tang L, Shen L. Apparent diffusion coefficient: potential imaging biomarker for prediction and early detection of response to chemotherapy in hepatic metastases. Radiology 2008;248(3):894–900. https://doi.org/10.1148/radiol.2483071407.

[26] Lambrecht M, Van Calster B, Vandecaveye V, De Keyzer F, Roebben I, Hermans R, Nuyts S. Integrating pretreatment diffusion weighted MRI into a multivariable prognostic model for head and neck squamous cell carcinoma. Radiother Oncol 2014;110(3):429–34. https://doi.org/10.1016/j.radonc.2014.01.004.

[27] Donati OF, Chong D, Nanz D, Boss A, Froehlich JM, Andres E, Seifert B, Thoeny HC. Diffusion-weighted MR imaging of upper abdominal organs: field strength and intervendor variability of apparent diffusion coefficients. Radiology 2014;270(2):454–63. https://doi.org/10.1148/radiol.13130819.

[28] Moreau B, Iannessi A, Hoog C, Beaumont H. How reliable are ADC measurements? A phantom and clinical study of cervical lymph nodes. Eur Radiol 2018. https://doi.org/10.1007/s00330-017-5265-2.

[29] Sadinski M, Medved M, Karademir I, Wang S, Peng Y, Jiang Y, Sammet S, Karczmar G, Oto A. Short-term reproducibility of apparent diffusion coefficient estimated from diffusion-weighted MRI of the prostate. Abdom Imaging 2015;40(7):2523–8. https://doi.org/10.1007/s00261-015-0396-x.

[30] Braithwaite AC, Dale BM, Boll DT, Merkle EM. Short- and midterm reproducibility of apparent diffusion coefficient measurements at 3.0-T diffusion-weighted imaging of the abdomen. Radiology 2009;250(2):459–65. https://doi.org/10.1148/radiol.2502080849.

[31] Sasaki M, Yamada K, Watanabe Y, Matsui M, Ida M, Fujiwara S, Shibata E, Investigators ASISG-JA-J. Variability in absolute apparent diffusion coefficient values across different platforms may be substantial: a multivendor, multi-institutional comparison study. Radiology 2008;249(2):624–30. https://doi.org/10.1148/radiol.2492071681.

[32] Jerome NP, Miyazaki K, Collins DJ, Orton MR, d'Arcy JA, Wallace T, Moreno L, Pearson AD, Marshall LV, Carceller F, Leach MO, Zacharoulis S, Koh DM. Repeatability of derived parameters from histograms following non-Gaussian diffusion modelling of diffusion-weighted imaging in a paediatric oncological cohort. Eur Radiol 2017;27(1):345–53. https://doi.org/10.1007/s00330-016-4318-2.

[33] De Paepe KN, De Keyzer F, Wolter P, Bechter O, Dierickx D, Janssens A, Verhoef G, Oyen R, Vandecaveye V. Improving lymph node characterization in staging malignant lymphoma using first-order ADC texture analysis from whole-body diffusion-weighted MRI. J Magn Reson Imaging 2018. https://doi.org/10.1002/jmri.26034.

[34] Blackledge MD, Tunariu N, Orton MR, Padhani AR, Collins DJ, Leach MO, Koh DM. Inter- and intra-observer repeatability of quantitative whole-body, diffusion-weighted imaging (WBDWI) in metastatic bone disease. PLoS One 2016;11(4):e0153840. https://doi.org/10.1371/journal.pone.0153840.

[35] Winfield JM, Tunariu N, Rata M, Miyazaki K, Jerome NP, Germuska M, Blackledge MD, Collins DJ, de Bono JS, Yap TA, de Souza NM, Doran SJ, Koh DM, Leach MO, Messiou C, Orton MR. Extracranial soft-tissue tumors: repeatability of apparent diffusion coefficient estimates from diffusion-weighted MR imaging. Radiology 2017;284(1):88–99. https://doi.org/10.1148/radiol.2017161965.

[36] Le Bihan D, Breton E, Lallemand D, Grenier P, Cabanis E, Laval-Jeantet M. MR imaging of intravoxel incoherent motions: application to diffusion and perfusion in neurologic disorders. Radiology 1986;161(2): 401–7. https://doi.org/10.1148/radiology.161.2.3763909.

[37] Koh DM, Collins DJ, Orton MR. Intravoxel incoherent motion in body diffusion-weighted MRI: reality and challenges. AJR Am J Roentgenol 2011;196(6):1351–61. https://doi.org/10.2214/AJR.10.5515.

[38] Jerome NP, d'Arcy JA, Feiweier T, Koh DM, Leach MO, Collins DJ, Orton MR. Extended T2-IVIM model for correction of TE dependence of pseudo-diffusion volume fraction in clinical diffusion-weighted magnetic resonance imaging. Phys Med Biol 2016;61(24):N667–80. https://doi.org/10.1088/1361-6560/61/24/N667.

[39] Andreou A, Koh DM, Collins DJ, Blackledge M, Wallace T, Leach MO, Orton MR. Measurement reproducibility of perfusion fraction and pseudodiffusion coefficient derived by intravoxel incoherent motion diffusion-weighted MR imaging in normal liver and metastases. Eur Radiol 2013;23(2):428–34. https://doi.org/10.1007/s00330-012-2604-1.

[40] Dyvorne H, Jajamovich G, Kakite S, Kuehn B, Taouli B. Intravoxel incoherent motion diffusion imaging of the liver: optimal b-value subsampling and impact on parameter precision and reproducibility. Eur J Radiol 2014;83(12):2109–13. https://doi.org/10.1016/j.ejrad.2014.09.003.

[41] Klauss M, Lemke A, Grünberg K, Simon D, Re TJ, Wente MN, Laun FB, Kauczor HU, Delorme S, Grenacher L, Stieltjes B. Intravoxel incoherent motion MRI for the differentiation between mass forming chronic pancreatitis and pancreatic carcinoma. Investig Radiol 2011;46(1):57–63. https://doi.org/10.1097/RLI.0b013e3181fb3bf2.

[42] Chandarana H, Kang SK, Wong S, Rusinek H, Zhang JL, Arizono S, Huang WC, Melamed J, Babb JS, Suan EF, Lee VS, Sigmund EE. Diffusion-weighted intravoxel incoherent motion imaging of renal tumors with histopathologic correlation. Investig Radiol 2012;47(12):688–96. https://doi.org/10.1097/RLI.0b013e31826a0a49.

[43] Fujima N, Yoshida D, Sakashita T, Homma A, Tsukahara A, Tha KK, Kudo K, Shirato H. Intravoxel incoherent motion diffusion-weighted imaging in head and neck squamous cell carcinoma: assessment of perfusion-related parameters compared to dynamic contrast-enhanced MRI. Magn Reson Imaging 2014;32(10):1206–13. https://doi.org/10.1016/j.mri.2014.08.009.

[44] Suo S, Lin N, Wang H, Zhang L, Wang R, Zhang S, Hua J, Xu J. Intravoxel incoherent motion diffusion-weighted MR imaging of breast cancer at 3.0 tesla: comparison of different curve-fitting methods. J Magn Reson Imaging 2015;42(2):362–70. https://doi.org/10.1002/jmri.24799.

[45] Iima M, Le Bihan D. Clinical intravoxel incoherent motion and diffusion MR imaging: past, present, and future. Radiology 2016;278(1):13–32. https://doi.org/10.1148/radiol.2015150244.

[46] Wang Y, Hu D, Yu H, Shen Y, Tang H, Kamel IR, Li Z. Comparison of the diagnostic value of monoexponential, biexponential, and stretched exponential diffusion-weighted MRI in differentiating tumor stage and histological grade of bladder cancer. Acad Radiol 2019;26(2):239–46. https://doi.org/10.1016/j.acra.2018.04.016.
[47] Bennett KM, Schmainda KM, Bennett RT, Rowe DB, Lu H, Hyde JS. Characterization of continuously distributed cortical water diffusion rates with a stretched-exponential model. Magn Reson Med 2003; 50(4):727–34. https://doi.org/10.1002/mrm.10581.
[48] Anderson SW, Barry B, Soto J, Ozonoff A, O'Brien M, Jara H. Characterizing non-Gaussian, high b-value diffusion in liver fibrosis: stretched exponential and diffusional kurtosis modeling. J Magn Reson Imaging 2014;39(4):827–34. https://doi.org/10.1002/jmri.24234.
[49] Jin YN, Zhang Y, Cheng JL, Zheng DD, Hu Y. Monoexponential, biexponential, and stretched-exponential models using diffusion-weighted imaging: a quantitative differentiation of breast lesions at 3T. J Magn Reson Imaging 2019. https://doi.org/10.1002/jmri.26729.
[50] Fujima N, Yoshida D, Sakashita T, Homma A, Kudo K, Shirato H. Residual tumour detection in post-treatment granulation tissue by using advanced diffusion models in head and neck squamous cell carcinoma patients. Eur J Radiol 2017;90:14–9. https://doi.org/10.1016/j.ejrad.2017.02.025.
[51] Winfield JM, de Souza NM, Priest AN, Wakefield JC, Hodgkin C, Freeman S, Orton MR, Collins DJ. Modelling DW-MRI data from primary and metastatic ovarian tumours. Eur Radiol 2015;25(7):2033–40. https://doi.org/10.1007/s00330-014-3573-3.
[52] Takahara T, Imai Y, Yamashita T, Yasuda S, Nasu S, Van Cauteren M. Diffusion weighted whole body imaging with background body signal suppression (DWIBS): technical improvement using free breathing, STIR and high resolution 3D display. Radiat Med 2004;22(4):275–82.
[53] Blackledge MD, Collins DJ, Tunariu N, Orton MR, Padhani AR, Leach MO, Koh DM. Assessment of treatment response by total tumor volume and global apparent diffusion coefficient using diffusion-weighted MRI in patients with metastatic bone disease: a feasibility study. PLoS One 2014;9(4):e91779. https://doi.org/10.1371/journal.pone.0091779.
[54] Perez-Lopez R, Lorente D, Blackledge MD, Collins DJ, Mateo J, Bianchini D, Omlin A, Zivi A, Leach MO, de Bono JS, Koh DM, Tunariu N. Volume of bone metastasis assessed with whole-body diffusion-weighted imaging is associated with overall survival in metastatic castration-resistant prostate cancer. Radiology 2016;280(1):151–60. https://doi.org/10.1148/radiol.2015150799.
[55] Perez-Lopez R, Mateo J, Mossop H, Blackledge MD, Collins DJ, Rata M, Morgan VA, Macdonald A, Sandhu S, Lorente D, Rescigno P, Zafeiriou Z, Bianchini D, Porta N, Hall E, Leach MO, de Bono JS, Koh DM, Tunariu N. Diffusion-weighted imaging as a treatment response biomarker for evaluating bone metastases in prostate cancer: a pilot study. Radiology 2017;283(1):168–77. https://doi.org/10.1148/radiol.2016160646.
[56] Giles SL, Messiou C, Collins DJ, Morgan VA, Simpkin CJ, West S, Davies FE, Morgan GJ, de Souza NM. Whole-body diffusion-weighted MR imaging for assessment of treatment response in myeloma. Radiology 2014;271(3):785–94. https://doi.org/10.1148/radiol.13131529.
[57] Sinha S, Lucas-Quesada FA, Sinha U, DeBruhl N, Bassett LW. In vivo diffusion-weighted MRI of the breast: potential for lesion characterization. J Magn Reson Imaging 2002;15(6):693–704. https://doi.org/10.1002/jmri.10116.
[58] Chen X, Li WL, Zhang YL, Wu Q, Guo YM, Bai ZL. Meta-analysis of quantitative diffusion-weighted MR imaging in the differential diagnosis of breast lesions. BMC Cancer 2010;10:693. https://doi.org/10.1186/1471-2407-10-693.
[59] Zhang L, Tang M, Min Z, Lu J, Lei X, Zhang X. Accuracy of combined dynamic contrast-enhanced magnetic resonance imaging and diffusion-weighted imaging for breast cancer detection: a meta-analysis. Acta Radiol 2016;57(6):651–60. https://doi.org/10.1177/0284185115597265.
[60] Bickelhaupt S, Laun FB, Tesdorff J, Lederer W, Daniel H, Stieber A, Delorme S, Schlemmer HP. Fast and noninvasive characterization of suspicious lesions detected at breast cancer X-ray screening: capability of diffusion-weighted MR imaging with MIPs. Radiology 2016;278(3):689–97. https://doi.org/10.1148/radiol.2015150425.

[61] Peters NH, Vincken KL, van den Bosch MA, Luijten PR, Mali WP, Bartels LW. Quantitative diffusion weighted imaging for differentiation of benign and malignant breast lesions: the influence of the choice of b-values. J Magn Reson Imaging 2010;31(5):1100–5. https://doi.org/10.1002/jmri.22152.

[62] Dorrius MD, Dijkstra H, Oudkerk M, Sijens PE. Effect of b value and pre-admission of contrast on diagnostic accuracy of 1.5-T breast DWI: a systematic review and meta-analysis. Eur Radiol 2014;24(11):2835–47. https://doi.org/10.1007/s00330-014-3338-z.

[63] Costantini M, Belli P, Rinaldi P, Bufi E, Giardina G, Franceschini G, Petrone G, Bonomo L. Diffusion-weighted imaging in breast cancer: relationship between apparent diffusion coefficient and tumour aggressiveness. Clin Radiol 2010;65(12):1005–12. https://doi.org/10.1016/j.crad.2010.07.008.

[64] Partridge SC, Nissan N, Rahbar H, Kitsch AE, Sigmund EE. Diffusion-weighted breast MRI: clinical applications and emerging techniques. J Magn Reson Imaging 2017;45(2):337–55. https://doi.org/10.1002/jmri.25479.

[65] Choi SY, Chang YW, Park HJ, Kim HJ, Hong SS, Seo DY. Correlation of the apparent diffusion coefficiency values on diffusion-weighted imaging with prognostic factors for breast cancer. Br J Radiol 2012;85(1016): e474–9. https://doi.org/10.1259/bjr/79381464.

[66] Mori N, Ota H, Mugikura S, Takasawa C, Ishida T, Watanabe G, Tada H, Watanabe M, Takase K, Takahashi S. Luminal-type breast cancer: correlation of apparent diffusion coefficients with the Ki-67 labeling index. Radiology 2015;274(1):66–73. https://doi.org/10.1148/radiol.14140283.

[67] Bickel H, Pinker-Domenig K, Bogner W, Spick C, Bagó-Horváth Z, Weber M, Helbich T, Baltzer P. Quantitative apparent diffusion coefficient as a noninvasive imaging biomarker for the differentiation of invasive breast cancer and ductal carcinoma in situ. Investig Radiol 2015;50(2):95–100. https://doi.org/10.1097/RLI.0000000000000104.

[68] Wang J, Takashima S, Takayama F, Kawakami S, Saito A, Matsushita T, Momose M, Ishiyama T. Head and neck lesions: characterization with diffusion-weighted echo-planar MR imaging. Radiology 2001;220(3): 621–30. https://doi.org/10.1148/radiol.2202010063.

[69] Razek AA, Elkhamary S, Mousa A. Differentiation between benign and malignant orbital tumors at 3-T diffusion MR-imaging. Neuroradiology 2011;53(7):517–22. https://doi.org/10.1007/s00234-011-0838-2.

[70] Srinivasan A, Dvorak R, Perni K, Rohrer S, Mukherji SK. Differentiation of benign and malignant pathology in the head and neck using 3T apparent diffusion coefficient values: early experience. AJNR Am J Neuroradiol 2008;29(1):40–4. https://doi.org/10.3174/ajnr.A0743.

[71] King AD, Mo FK, Yu KH, Yeung DK, Zhou H, Bhatia KS, Tse GM, Vlantis AC, Wong JK, Ahuja AT. Squamous cell carcinoma of the head and neck: diffusion-weighted MR imaging for prediction and monitoring of treatment response. Eur Radiol 2010;20(9):2213–20. https://doi.org/10.1007/s00330-010-1769-8.

[72] Kim S, Loevner L, Quon H, Sherman E, Weinstein G, Kilger A, Poptani H. Diffusion-weighted magnetic resonance imaging for predicting and detecting early response to chemoradiation therapy of squamous cell carcinomas of the head and neck. Clin Cancer Res 2009;15(3):986–94. https://doi.org/10.1158/1078-0432.CCR-08-1287.

[73] Vandecaveye V, Dirix P, de Keyzer F, de Beeck KO, Vander Poorten V, Roebben I, Nuyts S, Hermans R. Predictive value of diffusion-weighted magnetic resonance imaging during chemoradiotherapy for head and neck squamous cell carcinoma. Eur Radiol 2010;20(7):1703–14. https://doi.org/10.1007/s00330-010-1734-6.

[74] Vaid S, Chandorkar A, Atre A, Shah D, Vaid N. Differentiating recurrent tumours from post-treatment changes in head and neck cancers: does diffusion-weighted MRI solve the eternal dilemma? Clin Radiol 2017;72(1):74–83. https://doi.org/10.1016/j.crad.2016.09.019.

[75] Koh DM, Brown G, Riddell AM, Scurr E, Collins DJ, Allen SD, Chau I, Cunningham D, de Souza NM, Leach MO, Husband JE. Detection of colorectal hepatic metastases using MnDPDP MR imaging and diffusion-weighted imaging (DWI) alone and in combination. Eur Radiol 2008;18(5):903–10. https://doi.org/10.1007/s00330-007-0847-z.

[76] Donati OF, Fischer MA, Chuck N, Hunziker R, Weishaupt D, Reiner CS. Accuracy and confidence of Gd-EOB-DTPA enhanced MRI and diffusion-weighted imaging alone and in combination for the diagnosis of liver metastases. Eur J Radiol 2013;82(5):822–8. https://doi.org/10.1016/j.ejrad.2012.12.005.

[77] Vilgrain V, Esvan M, Ronot M, Caumont-Prim A, Aubé C, Chatellier G. A meta-analysis of diffusion-weighted and gadoxetic acid-enhanced MR imaging for the detection of liver metastases. Eur Radiol 2016;26(12):4595–615. https://doi.org/10.1007/s00330-016-4250-5.

[78] d'Assignies G, Fina P, Bruno O, Vullierme MP, Tubach F, Paradis V, Sauvanet A, Ruszniewski P, Vilgrain V. High sensitivity of diffusion-weighted MR imaging for the detection of liver metastases from neuroendocrine tumors: comparison with T2-weighted and dynamic gadolinium-enhanced MR imaging. Radiology 2013;268(2):390–9. https://doi.org/10.1148/radiol.13121628.

[79] Taouli B, Koh DM. Diffusion-weighted MR imaging of the liver. Radiology 2010;254(1):47–66. https://doi.org/10.1148/radiol.09090021.

[80] Zhu SC, Liu YH, Wei Y, Li LL, Dou SW, Sun TY, Shi DP. Intravoxel incoherent motion diffusion-weighted magnetic resonance imaging for predicting histological grade of hepatocellular carcinoma: comparison with conventional diffusion-weighted imaging. World J Gastroenterol 2018;24(8):929–40. https://doi.org/10.3748/wjg.v24.i8.929.

[81] Kamel IR, Bluemke DA, Eng J, Liapi E, Messersmith W, Reyes DK, Geschwind JF. The role of functional MR imaging in the assessment of tumor response after chemoembolization in patients with hepatocellular carcinoma. J Vasc Interv Radiol 2006;17(3):505–12. https://doi.org/10.1097/01.RVI.0000200052.02183.92.

[82] Kamel IR, Liapi E, Reyes DK, Zahurak M, Bluemke DA, Geschwind JF. Unresectable hepatocellular carcinoma: serial early vascular and cellular changes after transarterial chemoembolization as detected with MR imaging. Radiology 2009;250(2):466–73. https://doi.org/10.1148/radiol.2502072222.

[83] Pieper CC, Willinek WA, Meyer C, Ahmadzadehfar H, Kukuk GM, Sprinkart AM, Block W, Schild HH, Mürtz P. Intravoxel incoherent motion diffusion-weighted MR imaging for prediction of early arterial blood flow stasis in radioembolization of breast cancer liver metastases. J Vasc Interv Radiol 2016;27(9):1320–8. https://doi.org/10.1016/j.jvir.2016.04.018.

[84] Yu JI, Park HC, Lim DH, Choi Y, Jung SH, Paik SW, Kim SH, Jeong WK, Kim YK. The role of diffusion-weighted magnetic resonance imaging in the treatment response evaluation of hepatocellular carcinoma patients treated with radiation therapy. Int J Radiat Oncol Biol Phys 2014;89(4):814–21. https://doi.org/10.1016/j.ijrobp.2014.03.020.

[85] Koh DM, Scurr E, Collins D, Kanber B, Norman A, Leach MO, Husband JE. Predicting response of colorectal hepatic metastasis: value of pretreatment apparent diffusion coefficients. AJR Am J Roentgenol 2007;188(4):1001–8. https://doi.org/10.2214/AJR.06.0601.

[86] Dale BM, Braithwaite AC, Boll DT, Merkle EM. Field strength and diffusion encoding technique affect the apparent diffusion coefficient measurements in diffusion-weighted imaging of the abdomen. Investig Radiol 2010;45(2):104–8. https://doi.org/10.1097/RLI.0b013e3181c8ceac.

[87] Kartalis N, Lindholm TL, Aspelin P, Permert J, Albiin N. Diffusion-weighted magnetic resonance imaging of pancreas tumours. Eur Radiol 2009;19(8):1981–90. https://doi.org/10.1007/s00330-009-1384-8.

[88] Barral M, Taouli B, Guiu B, Koh DM, Luciani A, Manfredi R, Vilgrain V, Hoeffel C, Kanematsu M, Soyer P. Diffusion-weighted MR imaging of the pancreas: current status and recommendations. Radiology 2015;274(1):45–63. https://doi.org/10.1148/radiol.14130778.

[89] Concia M, Sprinkart AM, Penner AH, Brossart P, Gieseke J, Schild HH, Willinek WA, Mürtz P. Diffusion-weighted magnetic resonance imaging of the pancreas: diagnostic benefit from an intravoxel incoherent motion model-based 3 b-value analysis. Investig Radiol 2014;49(2):93–100. https://doi.org/10.1097/RLI.0b013e3182a71cc3.

[90] Re TJ, Lemke A, Klauss M, Laun FB, Simon D, Grünberg K, Delorme S, Grenacher L, Manfredi R, Mucelli RP, Stieltjes B. Enhancing pancreatic adenocarcinoma delineation in diffusion derived intravoxel incoherent motion f-maps through automatic vessel and duct segmentation. Magn Reson Med 2011;66(5):1327–32. https://doi.org/10.1002/mrm.22931.

[91] Wang Y, Chen ZE, Yaghmai V, Nikolaidis P, McCarthy RJ, Merrick L, Miller FH. Diffusion-weighted MR imaging in pancreatic endocrine tumors correlated with histopathologic characteristics. J Magn Reson Imaging 2011;33(5):1071–9. https://doi.org/10.1002/jmri.22541.

[92] Kang KM, Lee JM, Yoon JH, Kiefer B, Han JK, Choi BI. Intravoxel incoherent motion diffusion-weighted MR imaging for characterization of focal pancreatic lesions. Radiology 2014;270(2):444–53. https://doi.org/10.1148/radiol.13122712.

[93] De Robertis R, Cardobi N, Ortolani S, Tinazzi Martini P, Stemmer A, Grimm R, Gobbo S, Butturini G, D'Onofrio M. Intravoxel incoherent motion diffusion-weighted MR imaging of solid pancreatic masses: reliability and usefulness for characterization. Abdom Radiol (NY) 2019;44(1):131–9. https://doi.org/10.1007/s00261-018-1684-z.

[94] Kim B, Lee SS, Sung YS, Cheong H, Byun JH, Kim HJ, Kim JH. Intravoxel incoherent motion diffusion-weighted imaging of the pancreas: characterization of benign and malignant pancreatic pathologies. J Magn Reson Imaging 2017;45(1):260–9. https://doi.org/10.1002/jmri.25334.

[95] Lassel EA, Rao R, Schwenke C, Schoenberg SO, Michaely HJ. Diffusion-weighted imaging of focal renal lesions: a meta-analysis. Eur Radiol 2014;24(1):241–9. https://doi.org/10.1007/s00330-013-3004-x.

[96] Woo S, Suh CH, Kim SY, Cho JY, Kim SH. Diagnostic performance of DWI for differentiating high-from low-grade clear cell renal cell carcinoma: a systematic review and meta-analysis. AJR Am J Roentgenol 2017;209(6):W374–81. https://doi.org/10.2214/AJR.17.18283.

[97] Liu H, Zhou Z, Li X, Li C, Wang R, Zhang Y, Niu G. Diffusion-weighted imaging for staging chronic kidney disease: a meta-analysis. Br J Radiol 2018;91(1091):20170952. https://doi.org/10.1259/bjr.20170952.

[98] Mao W, Zhou J, Zeng M, Ding Y, Qu L, Chen C, Ding X, Wang Y, Fu C. Chronic kidney disease: pathological and functional evaluation with intravoxel incoherent motion diffusion-weighted imaging. J Magn Reson Imaging 2018;47(5):1251–9. https://doi.org/10.1002/jmri.25861.

[99] Mao W, Zhou J, Zeng M, Ding Y, Qu L, Chen C, Ding X, Wang Y, Fu C, Gu F. Intravoxel incoherent motion diffusion-weighted imaging for the assessment of renal fibrosis of chronic kidney disease: a preliminary study. Magn Reson Imaging 2018;47:118–24. https://doi.org/10.1016/j.mri.2017.12.010.

[100] Inada Y, Matsuki M, Nakai G, Tatsugami F, Tanikake M, Narabayashi I, Yamada T, Tsuji M. Body diffusion-weighted MR imaging of uterine endometrial cancer: is it helpful in the detection of cancer in nonenhanced MR imaging? Eur J Radiol 2009;70(1):122–7. https://doi.org/10.1016/j.ejrad.2007.11.042.

[101] Sala E, Rockall A, Rangarajan D, Kubik-Huch RA. The role of dynamic contrast-enhanced and diffusion weighted magnetic resonance imaging in the female pelvis. Eur J Radiol 2010;76(3):367–85. https://doi.org/10.1016/j.ejrad.2010.01.026.

[102] Kuang F, Yan Z, Li H, Feng H. Diagnostic accuracy of diffusion-weighted MRI for differentiation of cervical cancer and benign cervical lesions at 3T: comparison with routine MRI and dynamic contrast-enhanced MRI. J Magn Reson Imaging 2015;42(4):1094–9. https://doi.org/10.1002/jmri.24894.

[103] Addley H, Moyle P, Freeman S. Diffusion-weighted imaging in gynaecological malignancy. Clin Radiol 2017;72(11):981–90. https://doi.org/10.1016/j.crad.2017.07.014.

[104] Xue H, Ren C, Yang J, Sun Z, Li S, Jin Z, Shen K, Zhou W. Histogram analysis of apparent diffusion coefficient for the assessment of local aggressiveness of cervical cancer. Arch Gynecol Obstet 2014;290(2):341–8. https://doi.org/10.1007/s00404-014-3221-9.

[105] Nougaret S, Tirumani SH, Addley H, Pandey H, Sala E, Reinhold C. Pearls and pitfalls in MRI of gynecologic malignancy with diffusion-weighted technique. AJR Am J Roentgenol 2013;200(2):261–76. https://doi.org/10.2214/AJR.12.9713.

[106] Harry VN, Semple SI, Gilbert FJ, Parkin DE. Diffusion-weighted magnetic resonance imaging in the early detection of response to chemoradiation in cervical cancer. Gynecol Oncol 2008;111(2):213–20. https://doi.org/10.1016/j.ygyno.2008.07.048.

[107] Forstner R, Thomassin-Naggara I, Cunha TM, Kinkel K, Masselli G, Kubik-Huch R, Spencer JA, Rockall A. ESUR recommendations for MR imaging of the sonographically indeterminate adnexal mass: an update. Eur Radiol 2017;27(6):2248–57. https://doi.org/10.1007/s00330-016-4600-3.

[108] Thomassin-Naggara I, Aubert E, Rockall A, Jalaguier-Coudray A, Rouzier R, Daraï E, Bazot M. Adnexal masses: development and preliminary validation of an MR imaging scoring system. Radiology 2013; 267(2):432–43. https://doi.org/10.1148/radiol.13121161.

[109] Turkbey B, Rosenkrantz AB, Haider MA, Padhani AR, Villeirs G, Macura KJ, Tempany CM, Choyke PL, Cornud F, Margolis DJ, Thoeny HC, Verma S, Barentsz J, Weinreb JC. Prostate imaging reporting and data system version 2.1: 2019 update of prostate imaging reporting and data system version 2. Eur Urol 2019. https://doi.org/10.1016/j.eururo.2019.02.033.

[110] Gibbs P, Liney GP, Pickles MD, Zelhof B, Rodrigues G, Turnbull LW. Correlation of ADC and T2 measurements with cell density in prostate cancer at 3.0 tesla. Investig Radiol 2009;44(9):572–6. https://doi.org/10.1097/RLI.0b013e3181b4c10e.

[111] van As NJ, de Souza NM, Riches SF, Morgan VA, Sohaib SA, Dearnaley DP, Parker CC. A study of diffusion-weighted magnetic resonance imaging in men with untreated localised prostate cancer on active surveillance. Eur Urol 2009;56(6):981–7. https://doi.org/10.1016/j.eururo.2008.11.051.

[112] Park YM, Park JS, Yoon HK, Yang WT. Imaging-pathologic correlation of diseases in the axilla. AJR Am J Roentgenol 2013;200(2):W130–42. https://doi.org/10.2214/AJR.12.9259.

[113] Katahira K, Takahara T, Kwee TC, Oda S, Suzuki Y, Morishita S, Kitani K, Hamada Y, Kitaoka M, Yamashita Y. Ultra-high-b-value diffusion-weighted MR imaging for the detection of prostate cancer: evaluation in 201 cases with histopathological correlation. Eur Radiol 2011;21(1):188–96. https://doi.org/10.1007/s00330-010-1883-7.

[114] Woo S, Suh CH, Kim SY, Cho JY, Kim SH. Head-to-head comparison between high- and standard-b-value DWI for detecting prostate cancer: a systematic review and meta-analysis. AJR Am J Roentgenol 2018;210(1):91–100. https://doi.org/10.2214/AJR.17.18480.

[115] Yoshida R, Yoshizako T, Katsube T, Tamaki Y, Ishikawa N, Kitagaki H. Computed diffusion-weighted imaging using 1.5-T magnetic resonance imaging for prostate cancer diagnosis. Clin Imaging 2017;41: 78–82. https://doi.org/10.1016/j.clinimag.2016.10.005.

[116] Rosenkrantz AB, Chandarana H, Hindman N, Deng FM, Babb JS, Taneja SS, Geppert C. Computed diffusion-weighted imaging of the prostate at 3 T: impact on image quality and tumour detection. Eur Radiol 2013;23(11):3170–7. https://doi.org/10.1007/s00330-013-2917-8.

[117] Shen G, Deng H, Hu S, Jia Z. Comparison of choline-PET/CT, MRI, SPECT, and bone scintigraphy in the diagnosis of bone metastases in patients with prostate cancer: a meta-analysis. Skelet Radiol 2014;43(11): 1503–13. https://doi.org/10.1007/s00256-014-1903-9.

[118] Winfield JM, Poillucci G, Blackledge MD, Collins DJ, Shah V, Tunariu N, Kaiser MF, Messiou C. Apparent diffusion coefficient of vertebral haemangiomas allows differentiation from malignant focal deposits in whole-body diffusion-weighted MRI. Eur Radiol 2017. https://doi.org/10.1007/s00330-017-5079-2.

[119] Latifoltojar A, Hall-Craggs M, Bainbridge A, Rabin N, Popat R, Rismani A, D'Sa S, Dikaios N, Sokolska M, Antonelli M, Ourselin S, Yong K, Taylor SA, Halligan S, Punwani S. Whole-body MRI quantitative biomarkers are associated significantly with treatment response in patients with newly diagnosed symptomatic multiple myeloma following bortezomib induction. Eur Radiol 2017;27(12):5325–36. https://doi.org/10.1007/s00330-017-4907-8.

[120] Padhani AR, Lecouvet FE, Tunariu N, Koh DM, De Keyzer F, Collins DJ, Sala E, Schlemmer HP, Petralia G, Vargas HA, Fanti S, Tombal HB, de Bono J. METastasis reporting and data system for prostate cancer: practical guidelines for acquisition, interpretation, and reporting of whole-body magnetic resonance imaging-based evaluations of multiorgan involvement in advanced prostate cancer. Eur Urol 2017;71(1):81–92. https://doi.org/10.1016/j.eururo.2016.05.033.

[121] Messiou C, Hillengass J, Delorme S, Lecouvet FE, Moulopoulos LA, Collins DJ, Blackledge MD, Abildgaard N, Østergaard B, Schlemmer HP, Landgren O, Asmussen JT, Kaiser MF, Padhani A. Guidelines for acquisition, interpretation, and reporting of whole-body MRI in myeloma: myeloma response assessment and diagnosis system (MY-RADS). Radiology 2019;291(1):5–13. https://doi.org/10.1148/radiol.2019181949.

[122] Taylor SA, Mallett S, Ball S, Beare S, Bhatnagar G, Bhowmik A, Boavida P, Bridgewater J, Clarke CS, Duggan M, Ellis S, Glynne-Jones R, Goh V, Groves AM, Hameeduddin A, Janes SM, Johnston EW, Koh DM, Lock S, Miles A, Morris S, Morton A, Navani N, Oliver A, O'Shaughnessy T, Padhani AR, Prezzi D, Punwani S, Quinn L, Rafiee H, Reczko K, Rockall AG, Russell P, Sidhu HS, Strickland N, Tarver K, Teague J, Halligan S, Investigators S. Diagnostic accuracy of whole-body MRI versus standard imaging pathways for metastatic disease in newly diagnosed non-small-cell lung cancer: the prospective streamline L trial. Lancet Respir Med 2019;7(6):523–32. https://doi.org/10.1016/S2213-2600(19)30090-6.

SECTION

4

Fat and Iron Quantification

CHAPTER

25 Physical and Physiological Properties of Fat

Shigeki Sugii[a,b] and S. Sendhil Velan[c]

[a]Institute of Bioengineering and Nanotechnology (IBN), A*STAR, Singapore, Singapore [b]Cardiovascular and Metabolic Disorders Program, Duke-NUS Medical School, Singapore, Singapore [c]Metabolic Imaging Group (MIG), Singapore Bioimaging Consortium (SBIC) & Singapore Institute for Clinical Sciences (SICS), A*STAR, Singapore, Singapore

25.1 Introduction

In general, the term "fat" may refer to either of two different entities—lipids (such as triglyceride molecules) or adipose tissue (which are mainly comprised of adipocytes). Adipocytes are specialized cells which store fat, and are characterized by a high abundance of lipid droplets, which are subcellular compartments in which intracellular lipids are stored. While most lipid accumulates in the adipocytes, other cells such as liver and muscle cells may also be induced to accumulate lipid droplets. Thus, when MRI detects fat-rich regions, these are typically adipocytes and adipose tissue that can harbor a large amount of lipids, but may sometimes be other cells or areas accumulating a high amount of intracellular lipids. In this chapter, the content will focus more on fundamental aspects of adipose tissue and adipocytes, as they are commonly characterized entities by MRI. While adipocytes specialize in storing lipids (predominantly triglycerides), they are increasingly recognized as endocrine cells that secrete diverse bioactive cytokines (adipokines), respond to insulin for metabolic activities, regulate inflammation, influence vascular function, and exert nonshivering thermogenesis, in addition to other specific functions. For instance, in contrast to the energy storage function of white adipocytes, brown, and beige adipocytes can expend excessive calories by increasing uncoupled respiration using oxidized fatty acids as fuel in mitochondria. Since adipocytes impact whole-body metabolism, their dysfunctions are often associated with pathophysiological conditions including insulin resistance, diabetes, obesity, lipodystrophy, and others.

25.2 Molecular and cellular characteristics of adipose tissue

Adipose tissue (or fat tissue) is a connective tissue, in which the predominant cell type is the adipocyte (fat cell). There are several different types of adipose tissue, including white adipose tissue (WAT) and brown adipose tissue (BAT). WAT is considered one of the most plastic organs in the body [1]. WAT content depends on an individual's metabolic homeostasis and varies widely, ranging from 0% of body mass in lipodystrophy to ~60% of body mass in morbid obesity. WAT starts to develop in the second trimester of pregnancy and depots of both subcutaneous and visceral adipose tissue are present at birth in humans [2]. Adipocytes, the major constituent cell type of WAT, perform

Advances in Magnetic Resonance Technology and Applications. Volume 1. ISSN 2666-9099. https://doi.org/10.1016/B978-0-12-817057-1.00027-5

a number of physiological functions affecting whole-body metabolism, which are summarized in Fig. 25.1. White adipocytes typically possess lipid droplets as the dominant intracellular organelles, which specialize in storing excess calories mainly in the form of triglycerides. The formation of lipid droplets is highly dynamic and tightly regulated by a specific cellular pathway during the process of adipocyte differentiation in order to accommodate excess neutral lipids [3]. The size of lipid droplets can range from 20–40 nm to 100 μm, and their numbers in adipocytes can also vary from one large droplet (called "unilocular" lipid droplets) to a number of small droplets (called "multilocular" lipid droplets) in each cell. The structure of lipid droplets includes a boundary with a monolayer of phospholipids and droplet-specific proteins and a central core containing neutral lipids (mainly triglycerides and sterol esters).

Besides mature adipocytes, WAT consists of diverse cell types that include adipose-derived stem cells, preadipocytes, smooth muscle cells, endothelial cells, and immune cells such as macrophages [4]. While adipocytes occupy more than 90% of WAT in volume, other cell types can account for as many as 50% in cell numbers depending on the physiological status of the tissue. It is believed that adipose-derived stem cells are the origin of mature adipocytes by way of commitment to preadipocytes. The process of adipocyte differentiation is relatively well-studied, mainly by using in vitro cell culture systems with preadipocyte cell lines. Interested readers should refer to several published reviews for detail [5–9].

In addition to lipid storage functions, adipocytes influence whole-body metabolism by secreting various adipokines. Among the most extensively studied adipokine is adiponectin, which is almost exclusively secreted by adipocytes. Adiponectin possesses insulin-sensitizing and anti-inflammatory functions and generally induces positive effects on other metabolic organs [10]. Leptin is another specific adipocyte-secreted hormone that acts on the hypothalamus and controls appetite and energy homeostasis [10, 11]. Genetic mutations in leptin result in severe obesity and associated metabolic complications in mice and humans. Many other adipokines are secreted by adipocytes; interested readers can refer to some of the recent comprehensive reviews for further detail [12–15]. A significant number of these adipokines exhibit pro-inflammatory functions and their secretion is

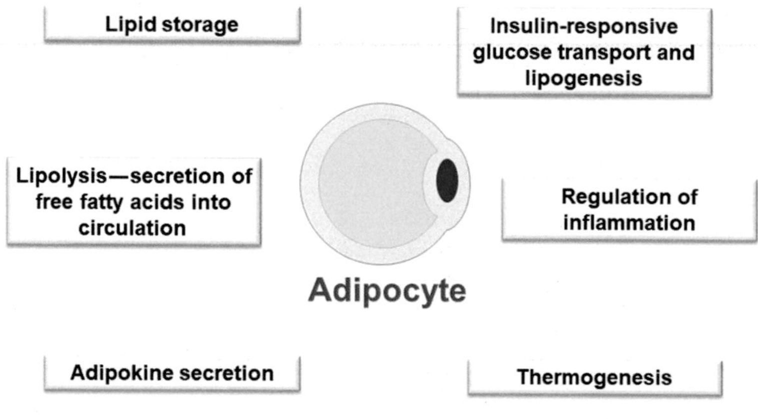

FIG. 25.1

Main biological properties of adipocytes.

often influenced by the pathophysiological status of WAT (e.g., onset of obesity, infiltration of immune cells) [16]. Physiological functions of adipocytes are also regulated by hormones and cytokines secreted by other tissues and cells. Adipogenic functions dynamically change during the cycle of feeding and fasting. Insulin is likely among the most important hormone in modulating these processes. After feeding, insulin is secreted by pancreatic beta cells and exerts "lipogenic" effects on adipocytes. That is, insulin promotes the uptake of glucose via its specific receptor GLUT4 on the cell surface, activates the synthesis of de novo fatty acids, and enhances uptake of exogenous lipids and production of triglycerides for storage in lipid droplets [17].

Besides WAT, another type of adipose tissue, BAT, has increasingly attracted attention due to the therapeutic potential of BAT to reverse obesity and its associated complications [18]. In contrast to the unilocular morphology of white adipocytes, brown adipocytes typically exhibit multilocular lipid droplets and abundant mitochondria, reflecting active lipid catabolism. Brown adipocytes specialize in expending energy and generating heat, thereby facilitating the metabolism of glucose and fatty acids and improving systemic glucose and lipid metabolism [19, 20]. Cold exposure, exercise, and adrenergic activation are three major physiological stimuli known to activate thermogenesis in brown adipocytes. It was previously thought that classical BAT is present in specific locations, particularly the interscapular region, only in human infants and some animals including rodents. Interest in BAT increased when it was discovered that even adult humans possess BAT-like activity, especially after cold exposure [21–25]. Recent studies have identified the presence of thermogenic adipocytes within WAT, named "beige" fat [26]. Beige adipocytes are found interspersed within subcutaneous WAT upon "browning," that is, the induction of activation with cold or adrenergic stimulation. Similar to classical brown adipocytes, beige adipocytes also exhibit multilocular lipid droplets. It was reported that in terms of molecular characteristics, the BAT-corresponding interscapular region in adult humans has more similarity to beige fat than classical BAT in rodents or human infants [26, 27]. Advancement in imaging methods is expected to further clarify the structural and functional difference between BAT and beige fat [28, 29]. In addition, BAT exhibits distinct characteristics of abundant vascularization and oxygenation. Major differences among white, beige, and brown fat are summarized in Fig. 25.2.

25.3 Adipocyte functions

In WAT, intracellular levels of free fatty acids are dynamically regulated and determined by the balance between triglyceride biosynthesis (lipogenesis) and hydrolysis (lipolysis; releasing free fatty acid moieties from triglycerides). The majority of free fatty acids can be synthesized by humans, with the exception of α-linolenic acid (omega-3 fatty acid) and linoleic acid (omega-6 fatty acid), which are thus called essential fatty acids and need to be ingested from dietary sources. Long-chain omega-3 fatty acids, docosahexaenoic acid (DHA), and eicosapentaenoic acid (EPA) can be synthesized from α-linolenic acid, but their efficiencies in the enzymatic reaction are low and therefore dietary supplementation is also beneficial for optimal human health. Lipogenesis is the process by which fatty acids are synthesized and esterified with glycerol to become triglycerides, and is activated mainly by insulin. Lipogenesis also occurs in the liver, where synthesized triglycerides are mostly destined for packaging into lipoproteins and exported into circulation. In contrast, in adipocytes, most of newly synthesized

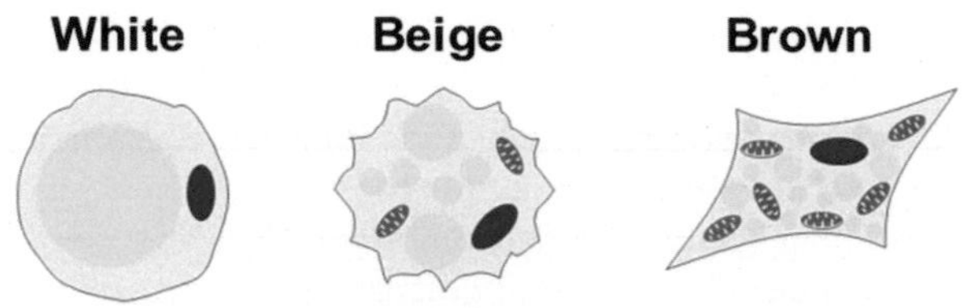

	White	Beige	Brown
Lipid droplets	Unilocular	Multilocular	Multilocular
Mitochondria	Not abundant	Relatively abundant	Abundant
Thermogenesis	Low	High by induction	Constitutively high
Lipid storage	High	Relatively low	Low
Lipolysis	Low	Relatively high	High
Location/depot	Subcutaneous, visceral or other	Mainly subcutaneous	Mainly inter/sub-scapular
Major activators	TZDs, high caloric diet	Adrenergic agonists, cold exposure, exercise	Adrenergic agonists, cold exposure, exercise

FIG. 25.2

Comparison of biological characteristics of white, beige, and brown adipocytes. TZDs: thiazolidinediones.

triglycerides are stored in lipid droplets. Lipolysis is the process by which triglycerides are broken down into fatty acids and glycerol. Lipolysis mainly occurs in adipocytes and is activated by various hormones, including glucagon and epinephrine, and inhibited by insulin. Fatty acids generated by lipolysis are either secreted into circulation or enter the fatty acid oxidation pathway in mitochondria. The overall schematic of lipogenesis and lipolysis is shown in Fig. 25.3.

The mitochondria in the adipocytes of WAT and BAT exhibit different and distinct characteristics. Mitochondria play a critical role in cellular bioenergetics and metabolism, generating a large amount of ATP. Mitochondria are also involved in other processes such as reactive oxygen species production, autophagy, apoptosis, and calcium regulation [30]. WAT have few mitochondria, whereas brown adipocytes possess a large number of mitochondria, ensuring proper functions of energy storage and dissipation in WAT versus BAT. Mitochondria are also partially involved in lipogenesis and lipolysis in WAT [31]. Free fatty acids generated by lipolysis are transported into the mitochondria by carnitine shuttle system, where they are broken into acetyl-CoA by beta-oxidation. Acetyl-CoA is used to generate ATP through the tricarboxylic acid (TCA) cycle and oxidative phosphorylation by electron transport chain. While lipogenesis mainly occurs in the cytosol, its two important intermediate metabolites, acetyl-CoA, and glycerol-3-phosphate, are generated in mitochondria. Mitochondria in brown adipocytes are essential for nonshivering thermogenesis, which is mediated by BAT-specific uncoupling protein-1 (UCP1) localized in the inner mitochondrial membrane. Upon stimulation by cold exposure or beta-adrenergic activation, UCP1 dissipates the proton gradient and uncouples ATP synthesis in the electron transport chain. As a result, the energy of oxidized substrates in BAT is converted into heat rather than being used for ATP production.

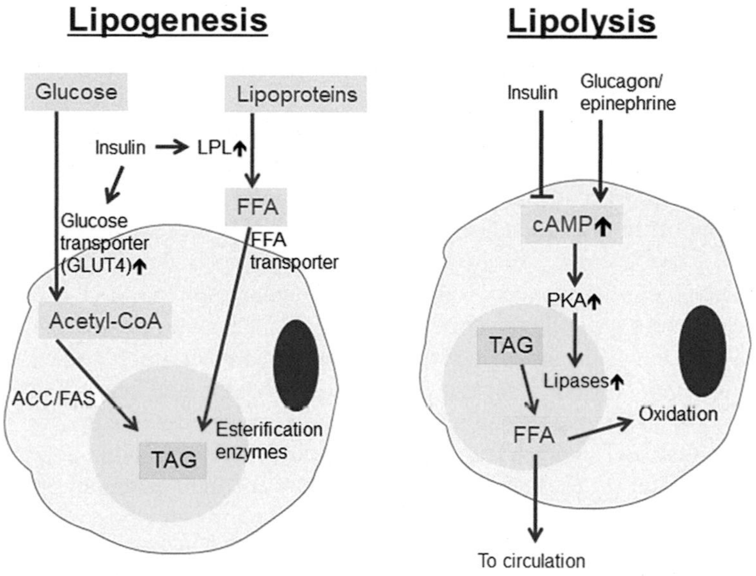

FIG. 25.3

Diagram depicting pathways of lipogenesis and lipolysis. Insulin enhances glucose transport through GLUT4 and catabolism of triacylglycerol (TAG) components of lipoproteins into free fatty acids (FFA) through lipoprotein lipase (LPL). Insulin also facilitates glycolysis that converts glucose into acetyl-CoA, and synthesis of fatty acids from acetyl-CoA through two enzymes, acetyl-CoA carboxylase (ACC) and fatty acid synthase (FAS). Glucagon and epinephrine enhances and insulin suppresses lipolysis through changes in cyclic AMP (cAMP) levels, which in turn regulate activities of lipases through protein kinase A (PKA).

25.4 Fat distribution in humans

MRI and MRS methods permit quantitative measurement of fat volumes and fat composition from various parts of the body. In humans, WAT is distributed throughout the body, which includes predominantly two major depots, subcutaneous and visceral (a.k.a. intra-abdominal). Subcutaneous WAT (SAT) is located beneath the skin layer and often around the regions of buttocks, thighs, and hips, while visceral WAT (VAT) is located in the abdominal cavity that surrounds internal organs (e.g., stomach, intestines, kidney, and liver) [2, 32]. Additional smaller adipose tissue depots do exist around the heart and skeletal muscles, but are not discussed here in detail. The abdominal SAT is divided by fascia superficialis into superficial and deep layers. These layers perform different functions and contribute differently to metabolic complications of obesity [33, 34].

In addition, WAT or adipocytes are found in other locations including bone marrow, facial, cranial, intermuscular, intramuscular, and retro-orbital space. It is evident that the accumulation of VAT (also called central obesity) increases the risk for metabolic complications such as insulin resistance, type 2 diabetes, and inflammatory and cardiovascular diseases [35, 36]. In contrast, expansion of SAT (also called peripheral obesity) is considered to have a protective effect against developing these conditions. In general, decreases in SAT and increases in VAT are observed during aging. This pathophysiological difference between the two depots is likely derived from various biological differences between the tissues. Adipocytes found in VAT exhibit higher basal lipolysis rates, greater resistance to insulin, poor browning activity, and increased inflammatory responses due to infiltration of pro-inflammatory macrophages and other immune cells in this tissue. Cells in SAT, in contrast, show higher lipogenic capacity, are more sensitive to insulin, have a greater tendency to browning into beige fat, and exhibit anti-inflammatory activities. Therefore, an inability to expand SAT and the subsequent excessive accumulation of VAT is believed to contribute to metabolic derangement because SAT is capable of storing excess energy in response to insulin (and burning it in some cases). VAT, on the other hand, is not highly responsive to insulin and excretes excessive free fatty acids into circulation. In addition, the insulin-sensitizing hormone adiponectin is secreted by SAT at a higher rate than VAT [37]. In contrast, VAT is believed to secrete more pro-inflammatory adipokines. Thus, popular liposuction procedures, which remove only SAT, may cause metabolic problems by inducing compensatory VAT expansion rather than leading to metabolic improvement. Drugs such as thiazolidinedione preferentially expand and activate SAT, thereby improving systemic insulin resistance despite an increase in adiposity [38, 39].

Studies indicate that SAT and VAT are developmentally distinct and that genetic differences, especially in developmental genes, at least partially account for their pathophysiological differences [40–42]. The depot-specific difference is also recapitulated in vitro, in which progenitor or stem cells isolated from VAT exhibit distinct molecular characteristics and poorly differentiated into mature functional adipocytes compared to those from SAT [1, 41, 43].

SAT and VAT also differ in plasticity during the onset of obesity. Fat mass expansion occurs either through hypertrophy (existing adipocytes growing larger in size to accommodate excess lipids) or hyperplasia (differentiation of new adipocytes from progenitor or stem cells, leading to an increased number of adipocytes). The widely believed view was that VAT expands mainly through hypertrophy and that SAT expands through hyperplasia, although this view has been challenged based on rodent studies [44, 45]. In fact, hypertrophy occurs irrespective of fat depots during diet-induced obesity. Hypertrophic adipocytes are larger in size with large unilocular lipid droplets, whereas hyperplastic adipocytes are smaller in size and typically contain multilocular lipid droplets. It is reported that hypertrophic adipocytes secrete a lower level of the active form of adiponectin and more pro-inflammatory adipokines [46, 47]. Assessment of lipid droplet size in adipose tissues is thus important in understanding health and assessing the presence of disease. Measuring lipid droplet size, however, has been technically challenging; analyzing histological images of WAT (typically H&E staining images) is still the only commonly accepted standard method. Techniques based on diffusion-weighted MRS and MRI are currently being developed to noninvasively measure adipocyte cell size and lipid droplet size [48, 49], which may potentially provide further insight into obesity and related diseases.

Expansion of VAT is also correlated with ectopic fat deposition, indicating that the measurement of VAT volume may be a marker for dysfunction of systemic metabolism. For example, excess VAT is highly associated with incidence of nonalcoholic fatty liver disease, which increases the risk of cardiovascular disease [50]. Drugs such as thiazolidinedione reduce fatty liver by channeling excessive lipids into SAT for proper storage.

BAT is distributed in various locations including cervical, supraclavicular, axillary, mediastinal, paraspinal, and abdominal depots in children and adults [51, 52]. A number of groups are currently exploring BAT as a target for the treatment of obesity and diabetes.

High amounts of lipids, especially triglycerides, can also be stored outside adipocytes as ectopic fat, often observed during development of insulin resistance and type 2 diabetes. Ectopic fat may accumulate in the liver [53], pancreas [54, 55], heart [56, 57], and muscle [58], which often results in disruption of their normal metabolic functions. In most cases, ectopic lipids accumulate in lipid droplets formed within cells of these tissues, with the exception of skeletal muscle, where new adipocytes may develop to accommodate lipids within the tissue.

In skeletal muscle, lipids are mainly accumulated either as intramyocellular lipid, which is located in lipid droplets of muscle cells, or as extramyocellular lipid, which is found in interstitial adipocytes. Intramyocellular lipids form droplet-like structures, mostly situated in the close neighborhood of mitochondria, and have been shown to be a metabolically active lipid pool used as a substrate during endurance exercise. Intramyocellular lipid content increases during the course of weight gain and aerobic exercise training [58]. In addition, intramyocellular lipid is a major component of regional fat accumulation and has been associated with obesity, insulin resistance, and type 2 diabetes. In these subjects, intramyocellular lipid content seems to be inversely related to the whole body insulin sensitivity [59, 60]. On the other hand, extramyocellular lipid content has been reported to be high in obese and overweight subjects, but not in exercise trained athletes.

While bone marrow is an important tissue which houses hematopoietic stem cells for blood cell production, it also contains mesenchymal stem cells, which are responsible for the production of adipocytes and bone cells. Ectopic accumulation of adipocytes in bone marrow is observed during the onset of obesity and aging, which appears to disrupt functions of hematopoiesis and bone remodeling [61]. The amount of bone marrow fat is inversely associated with bone mineral density [62]. In order to further study the clinical consequence of bone marrow fat accumulation, quantitative imaging of bone marrow physiology can be performed with MRI to understand water-fat composition, fatty acid composition, perfusion, and diffusion [63].

25.5 Pathophysiological association

During the onset of obesity and diabetes, lipid storage activity of adipocytes becomes dysfunctional due to resistance to the lipogenic insulin response upon feeding [64]. The inability of adipocytes and WAT to properly store excess energy leads to a "spillover" of lipids into other organs such as the liver, skeletal muscle, pancreas, and heart, disrupting their normal metabolic functions through "lipotoxicity" [65]. As body weight gain continues, adipocytes start to secrete chemokines, attracting immune cells, especially pro-inflammatory macrophages, into the WAT. This immune cell infiltration worsens insulin resistance and disrupts functions of adipocytes, eventually leading to WAT atrophy and dysfunction.

Besides too much fat, too little fat can also negatively influence whole body metabolism. This is exemplified by another extreme condition, namely lipodystrophy, where patients typically exhibit conditions of metabolic syndrome, including type 2 diabetes and cardiovascular diseases. Lipodystrophy is often caused by inherited genetic mutations, and entails a partial or total lack of adipose tissue. One severe form, congenital generalized lipodystrophy (a.k.a. Berardinelli-Seip syndrome), is characterized by near total loss of adipose tissue and build-up of ectopic lipid accumulation in the liver (i.e., hepatic steatosis) and other organs, leading to severe glucose intolerance and diabetes [66]. Some patients develop other conditions such as hypertriglyceridemia, hepatomegaly, muscular hypertrophy, splenomegaly, acanthosis nigricans, pancreatitis, polycystic ovary syndrome, muscular dystrophy, and hypertrophic cardiomyopathy, which often result in early death. The pathology of lipodystrophy supports the hypothesis that WAT is a "sink" for safely storing lipids, and that its absence results in negative metabolic consequence due to excessive lipid spillover. In addition, the inability to secrete some adipokines, particularly adiponectin and leptin, exacerbates impairment of the systemic metabolism.

Various genetic, environmental, and dietary factors differentially affect the development of adipose tissue. These include age, race, and gender (through sex hormones) influences, which result in different fat distributions and functions. These determinants significantly impact the metabolic consequences of excessive food consumption, which varies widely among individuals.

25.6 Magnetic resonance of adipose tissues

MRI can be used to obtain structural and functional images which can aid in the understanding of the physiology of adipose tissues, and MRS enables the assessment of the biochemical tissue composition. Fat and water protons exhibit slightly different resonance frequencies due to differences in their chemical structure and molecular electron configurations, which can be exploited to differentiate the two species. In addition, fat and water signals differ due to differences in their proton density, T_1 values, T_2/T_2^* values, and diffusion characteristics. There is a wide range of imaging methods that are available to quantitatively assess these MR properties from fat and water signals from both white and brown adipose tissues [48, 49, 63, 67]. Table 25.1 summarizes some of the recent articles describing quantification of fat in various organs.

The morphological differences between WAT and BAT also alter the relaxation properties of the water and lipid protons in MRI. These properties can be exploited to generate contrast within MR images and permit quantitative assessment of WAT and BAT. More recently, improvement in imaging methods of BAT and beige fat have facilitated the exploration of its anatomical distribution and novel functions. Specifically, MRI techniques including fat fraction imaging, fat diffusion measurements, water diffusion measurements, excitation of intermolecular multiple quantum coherences, and hyperpolarized imaging have been utilized to image WAT and BAT [67]. In addition, recent MR-based diffusion measurements have demonstrated the feasibility of measuring the lipid droplet size in adipose tissues [48, 49] and skeletal muscle [71, 72]. These measurements can help in understanding the remodeling of the tissue due to specific pathology.

MRS techniques have emerged as a powerful tool to investigate tissue samples for various biomedical applications, including the biochemical composition of healthy and abnormal tissues. In order to

Table 25.1 Imaging references for various fat depots.

Organ	References
Abdominal fat	[68]
BAT	[67]
Bone marrow	[63]
Ectopic fat	[60] [59] [69] [53]
Pancreatic fat	[70]

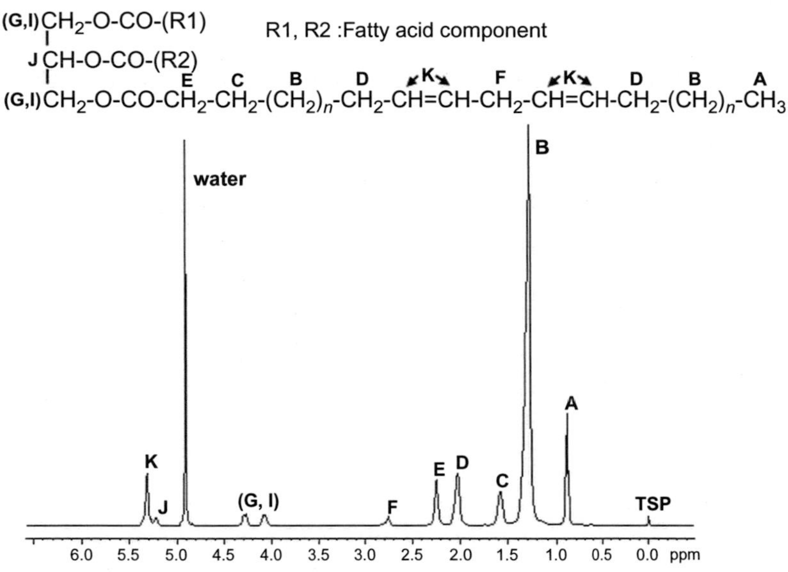

FIG. 25.4

^{1}H High resolution magic angle spinning spectroscopy (HR-MAS) spectrum obtained from human subcutaneous adipose tissue using a 9.4T NMR system with a spinning speed of 4kHz.

understand disease mechanisms and develop diagnostic biomarkers and therapeutic targets, it is important to profile the metabolite changes that may indicate alterations in biochemical pathways in pathological conditions. Lipid composition may provide important information concerning the nutritional status and metabolic disorders in humans [73]. The family of solution NMR techniques and High Resolution Magic Angle Spinning (HRMAS) spectroscopic approaches permits detailed characterization of fat composition. Even though specific fatty acid chains cannot be assessed, quantitative measurements of major classes of saturated and unsaturated lipids can be performed. Solution NMR studies are usually performed with Folch extraction of tissues [74], in which lipids are extracted from tissues using chemicals like chloroform and methanol. HRMAS avoids the restrictions of solution NMR caused by the relative immobility of intra- and intercellular molecules, and thus provides highly resolved spectra containing resonances from numerous metabolites [75]. This approach provides spectra similar to solution state NMR without the need for tissue extractions with chemicals. Fig. 25.4 shows a representative HRMAS spectrum obtained from the human SAT using a 9.4T NMR system with a spinning speed of 4kHz. Various resonances of triglyceride are labeled with reference to trimethylsilylpropionic acid (TMS) in the spectrum.

25.7 Summary

WAT is found throughout the body and often detected as fat-rich regions by MRI. Adipocytes are the major cell type in WAT and store lipids, mainly in the form of triglycerides, in lipid droplets. Other cell types such as liver and muscle cells may accumulate ectopic lipids in lipid droplets if adipose tissue is unable to accommodate them. Distribution of WAT is an important factor in assessing the metabolic health of individuals. Expansion of visceral WAT is highly correlated with metabolic complications, while the presence of subcutaneous WAT may have a protective effect. BAT is another type of adipose tissue that specializes in thermogenesis by oxidizing lipids in mitochondria and is believed to be beneficial in fighting against obesity and associated conditions. The fat and water signals arising from BAT exhibit distinct MR characteristics compared to WAT. Development of novel methods that distinguish WAT and BAT may contribute to better pathophysiological understanding of adipose tissue roles in metabolic diseases.

References

[1] Cawthorn WP, Scheller EL, MacDougald OA. Adipose tissue stem cells meet preadipocyte commitment: going back to the future. J Lipid Res 2012;53(2):227–46.

[2] Gesta S, Tseng YH, Kahn CR. Developmental origin of fat: tracking obesity to its source. Cell 2007;131(2):242–56.

[3] Guo Y, et al. Lipid droplets at a glance. J Cell Sci 2009;122(Pt 6):749–52.

[4] Ong WK, Sugii S. Adipose-derived stem cells: fatty potentials for therapy. Int J Biochem Cell Biol 2013;45(6):1083–6.

[5] Lowe CE, O'Rahilly S, Rochford JJ. Adipogenesis at a glance. J Cell Sci 2011;124(Pt 16):2681–6.

[6] Rosen ED, MacDougald OA. Adipocyte differentiation from the inside out. Nat Rev Mol Cell Biol 2006;7(12):885–96.

[7] Sarjeant K, Stephens JM. Adipogenesis. Cold Spring Harb Perspect Biol 2012;4(9): a008417.

[8] Tang QQ, Lane MD. Adipogenesis: from stem cell to adipocyte. Annu Rev Biochem 2012;81(1):715–36.

[9] Sugii S, Evans RM. Epigenetic codes of PPARγ in metabolic disease. FEBS Lett 2011;585(13):2121–8.

[10] Stern JH, Rutkowski JM, Scherer PE. Adiponectin, leptin, and fatty acids in the maintenance of metabolic homeostasis through adipose tissue crosstalk. Cell Metab 2016;23(5):770–84.

[11] Friedman J. The long road to leptin. J Clin Invest 2016;126(12):4727–34.

[12] Bluher M. Adipokines—removing road blocks to obesity and diabetes therapy. Mol Metab 2014;3(3): 230–240.

[13] Fasshauer M, Bluher M. Adipokines in health and disease. Trends Pharmacol Sci 2015;36(7):461–70.

[14] Francisco V, et al. Adipokines: linking metabolic syndrome, the immune system, and arthritic diseases. Biochem Pharmacol 2019;65:196–206.

[15] Nakamura K, Fuster JJ, Walsh K. Adipokines: a link between obesity and cardiovascular disease. J Cardiol 2014;63(4):250–9.

[16] Ouchi N, et al. Adipokines in inflammation and metabolic disease. Nat Rev Immunol 2011;11(2):85–97.

[17] Czech MP, et al. Insulin signalling mechanisms for triacylglycerol storage. Diabetologia 2013;56(5):949–64.

[18] Kajimura S, Saito M. A new era in brown adipose tissue biology: molecular control of brown fat development and energy homeostasis. Annu Rev Physiol 2014;76:225–49.

[19] Bartelt A, et al. Brown adipose tissue activity controls triglyceride clearance. Nat Med 2011;17(2):200–5.

[20] Gunawardana SC, Piston DW. Reversal of type 1 diabetes in mice by brown adipose tissue transplant. Diabetes 2012;61(3):674–82.

[21] Cypess AM, et al. Identification and importance of brown adipose tissue in adult humans. N Engl J Med 2009;360(15):1509–17.

[22] Nedergaard J, Bengtsson T, Cannon B. Unexpected evidence for active brown adipose tissue in adult humans. Am J Physiol Endocrinol Metab 2007;293(2):E444–52.

[23] Saito M, et al. High incidence of metabolically active brown adipose tissue in healthy adult humans: effects of cold exposure and adiposity. Diabetes 2009;58(7):1526–31.
[24] van Marken Lichtenbelt WD, et al. Cold-activated brown adipose tissue in healthy men. N Engl J Med 2009;360(15):1500–8.
[25] Virtanen KA, et al. Functional brown adipose tissue in healthy adults. N Engl J Med 2009;360(15):1518–25.
[26] Wu J, et al. Beige adipocytes are a distinct type of thermogenic fat cell in mouse and human. Cell 2012;150(2):366–76.
[27] Pfeifer A, Hoffmann LS. Brown, beige, and white: the new color code of fat and its pharmacological implications. Annu Rev Pharmacol Toxicol 2015;55:207–27.
[28] Hu HH. Magnetic resonance of brown adipose tissue: a review of current techniques. Crit Rev Biomed Eng 2015;43(2–3):161–81.
[29] Ong FJ, et al. Recent advances in the detection of brown adipose tissue in adult humans: a review. Clin Sci (Lond) 2018;132(10):1039–54.
[30] Boengler K, et al. Mitochondria and ageing: role in heart, skeletal muscle and adipose tissue. J Cachexia Sarcopenia Muscle 2017;8(3):349–69.
[31] Onder Y, Green CB. Rhythms of metabolism in adipose tissue and mitochondria. Neurobiol Sleep Circadian Rhythms 2018;4:57–63.
[32] Tran TT, Kahn CR. Transplantation of adipose tissue and stem cells: role in metabolism and disease. Nat Rev Endocrinol 2010;6(4):195–213.
[33] Sadananthan SA, et al. Automated segmentation of visceral and subcutaneous (deep and superficial) adipose tissues in normal and overweight men. J Magn Reson Imaging 2015;41(4):924–34.
[34] Smith SR, et al. Contributions of total body fat, abdominal subcutaneous adipose tissue compartments, and visceral adipose tissue to the metabolic complications of obesity. Metabolism 2001;50(4):425–35.
[35] Despres JP. Body fat distribution and risk of cardiovascular disease: an update. Circulation 2012; 126(10):1301–13.
[36] Despres JP, Lemieux I. Abdominal obesity and metabolic syndrome. Nature 2006;444(7121):881–7.
[37] Frederiksen L, et al. Subcutaneous rather than visceral adipose tissue is associated with adiponectin levels and insulin resistance in young men. J Clin Endocrinol Metab 2009;94(10):4010–5.
[38] Fonseca V. Effect of thiazolidinediones on body weight in patients with diabetes mellitus. Am J Med 2003; 115(Suppl. 8A):42S–48S.
[39] Yang X, Smith U. Adipose tissue distribution and risk of metabolic disease: does thiazolidinedione-induced adipose tissue redistribution provide a clue to the answer? Diabetologia 2007;50(6):1127–39.
[40] Chau YY, Hastie N. Wt1, the mesothelium and the origins and heterogeneity of visceral fat progenitors. Adipocytes 2015;4(3):217–21.
[41] Takeda K, et al. Retinoic acid mediates visceral-specific adipogenic defects of human adipose-derived stem cells. Diabetes 2016;65(5):1164–78.
[42] Gesta S, et al. Evidence for a role of developmental genes in the origin of obesity and body fat distribution. Proc Natl Acad Sci USA 2006;103(17):6676–81.
[43] Ong WK, et al. Identification of specific cell-surface markers of adipose-derived stem cells from subcutaneous and visceral fat depots. Stem Cell Rep 2014;2(2):171–9.
[44] Kim SM, et al. Loss of white adipose hyperplastic potential is associated with enhanced susceptibility to insulin resistance. Cell Metab 2014;20(6):1049–58.
[45] Wang QA, et al. Tracking adipogenesis during white adipose tissue development, expansion and regeneration. Nat Med 2013;19(10):1338–44.
[46] Mancuso P. The role of adipokines in chronic inflammation. Immunotargets Ther 2016;5:47–56.
[47] Meyer LK, et al. Adipose tissue depot and cell size dependency of adiponectin synthesis and secretion in human obesity. Adipocytes 2013;2(4):217–26.

[48] Verma SK, et al. Differentiating brown and white adipose tissues by high-resolution diffusion NMR spectroscopy. J Lipid Res 2017;58(1):289–98.
[49] Weidlich D, et al. Measuring large lipid droplet sizes by probing restricted lipid diffusion effects with diffusion-weighted MRS at 3T. Magn Reson Med 2019;81(6):3427–39.
[50] Kotronen A, Yki-Jarvinen H. Fatty liver: a novel component of the metabolic syndrome. Arterioscler Thromb Vasc Biol 2008;28(1):27–38.
[51] Leitner BP, et al. Mapping of human brown adipose tissue in lean and obese young men. Proc Natl Acad Sci USA 2017;114(32):8649–54.
[52] Sacks H, Symonds ME. Anatomical locations of human brown adipose tissue: functional relevance and implications in obesity and type 2 diabetes. Diabetes 2013;62(6):1783–90.
[53] Caussy C, et al. Noninvasive, quantitative assessment of liver fat by MRI-PDFF as an endpoint in NASH trials. Hepatology 2018;68(2):763–72.
[54] Kuhn JP, et al. Pancreatic steatosis demonstrated at MR imaging in the general population: clinical relevance. Radiology 2015;276(1):129–36.
[55] Smits MM, van Geenen EJ. The clinical significance of pancreatic steatosis. Nat Rev Gastroenterol Hepatol 2011;8(3):169–77.
[56] Homsi R, et al. 3D-Dixon MRI based volumetry of peri- and epicardial fat. Int J Cardiovasc Imaging 2016;32(2):291–9.
[57] Lahera V. Epicardial fat and cardiovascular disease. Clin Investig Arterioscler 2018;30(3):118–9.
[58] Hasegawa N, et al. Intramyocellular and extramyocellular lipids are associated with arterial stiffness. Am J Hypertens 2015;28(12):1473–9.
[59] Boesch C. Musculoskeletal spectroscopy. J Magn Reson Imaging 2007;25(2):321–38.
[60] Loher H, et al. The flexibility of ectopic lipids. Int J Mol Sci 2016;17(9):1554.
[61] Ambrosi TH, et al. Adipocyte accumulation in the bone marrow during obesity and aging impairs stem cell-based hematopoietic and bone regeneration. Cell Stem Cell 2017;20(6)771–784 e6.
[62] Paccou J, et al. The role of bone marrow fat in skeletal health: usefulness and perspectives for clinicians. J Clin Endocrinol Metab 2015;100(10):3613–21.
[63] Karampinos DC, et al. Quantitative MRI and spectroscopy of bone marrow. J Magn Reson Imaging 2018;47(2):332–53.
[64] Guilherme A, et al. Adipocyte dysfunctions linking obesity to insulin resistance and type 2 diabetes. Nat Rev Mol Cell Biol 2008;9(5):367–77.
[65] Kusminski CM, Bickel PE, Scherer PE. Targeting adipose tissue in the treatment of obesity-associated diabetes. Nat Rev Drug Discov 2016;15(9):639–60.
[66] Garg A. Clinical review#: lipodystrophies: genetic and acquired body fat disorders. J Clin Endocrinol Metab 2011;96(11):3313–25.
[67] Karampinos DC, et al. Techniques and applications of magnetic resonance imaging for studying brown adipose tissue morphometry and function. Handb Exp Pharmacol 2018;251:299–324.
[68] Hong CW, et al. Fat quantification in the abdomen. Top Magn Reson Imaging 2017;26(6):221–7.
[69] Machann J, Stefan N, Schick F. (1)H MR spectroscopy of skeletal muscle, liver and bone marrow. Eur J Radiol 2008;67(2):275–84.
[70] Chouhan MD, et al. Quantitative pancreatic MRI: a pathology-based review. Br J Radiol 2019;92(1099): 20180941.
[71] Brandejsky V, Boesch C, Kreis R. Proton diffusion tensor spectroscopy of metabolites in human muscle in vivo. Magn Reson Med 2015;73(2):481–7.
[72] Cao P, et al. Diffusion magnetic resonance monitors intramyocellular lipid droplet size in vivo. Magn Reson Med 2015;73(1):59–69.

[73] Bondia-Pons I, et al. Nutri-metabolomics: subtle serum metabolic differences in healthy subjects by NMR-based metabolomics after a short-term nutritional intervention with two tomato sauces. OMICS 2013;17(12):611–8.

[74] Folch J, Lees M, Sloane Stanley GH. A simple method for the isolation and purification of total lipides from animal tissues. J Biol Chem 1957;226(1):497–509.

[75] Dietz C, et al. Applications of high-resolution magic angle spinning MRS in biomedical studies II-human diseases. NMR Biomed 2017;30(11), e3784.

CHAPTER

Physical and Physiological Properties of Iron

26

Suraj D. Serai[a,c], Hansel J. Otero[a,c], and Janet L. Kwiatkowski[b,c]

[a]Department of Radiology, The Children's Hospital of Philadelphia, Philadelphia, PA, United States [b]Division of Hematology, The Children's Hospital of Philadelphia, Philadelphia, PA, United States [c]Department of Pediatrics, Perelman School of Medicine of the University of Pennsylvania, Philadelphia, PA, United States

26.1 Introduction

Iron is an important bioelement and an essential dietary mineral for most forms of life. In humans, iron is present throughout the body in different tissues and cells and plays an essential role in transporting oxygen [1]. Iron also plays a role in cell signaling, gene expression, and regulation of cell growth and differentiation [2]. Normally, total body iron remains within a relatively narrow range of normal values, about 5 g in adults, with approximately 65%–70% present in the red blood cells as hemoglobin. Iron homeostasis is highly regulated through tightly controlled iron absorption. Most of the iron in the body is contained as part of the heme group, which is part of several proteins responsible for oxygen binding and transport; the rest is stored as ferritin, a mainly intracellular protein circulating in small quantities in the plasma. Iron is regulated and mineralized within the ferritin core via oxidation. Any conditions that disturb this equilibrium result in deficiency or overload. In this chapter, the form and function or iron, impacts of iron balance, iron deficiency, and iron balance will be discussed.

26.2 The form and function of iron in the body

Iron is essential for energy metabolism, cell signaling, gene expression, and the regulation of cell growth and differentiation. With minor exceptions, almost all human cells employ iron as a cofactor for fundamental biochemical activities such as oxygen transport and energy metabolism. In particular, iron is contained within the functional heme group, found in proteins. Heme, which gives proteins the ability to bind oxygen, is a component in the electron transport chain, and participates in ATP production [2–5]. Each heme group contains an iron atom that is able to bind to one oxygen molecule. Iron that is not in use is stored in the body as ferritin and hemosiderin. The regulation of iron is controlled by the hormone hepcidin, which is responsible for recycling iron stored in macrophages (20–25 mg per day) and absorbing a small amount of iron (1–2 mg per day) in the intestine [1].

Advances in Magnetic Resonance Technology and Applications. Volume 1. ISSN 2666-9099. https://doi.org/10.1016/B978-0-12-817057-1.00028-7

Most of the iron in the body is present in the globins, the family of proteins containing heme, which share a common structure including eight alpha helical segments and are responsible for oxygen binding and transport. In fact, two-thirds of the body's iron is contained in hemoglobin, which transports oxygen from the lungs to the peripheral tissues. Another 5% of iron is bound to myoglobin, which regulates the release of oxygen to muscles. The remaining 25%–30% of the iron in the body is stored as ferritin, found in cells and in smaller quantities in circulation in the blood. When ferritin's iron storage capacity is exceeded, iron accumulates in the tissues as hemosiderin. Hemosiderin forms when macrophages phagocytose hemoglobin in the tissues and can accumulate in the liver, spleen, bone marrow, or myocardium.

The average adult male has 9.9 mg/kg of stored iron, whereas women on average have only about 5.5 mg/kg [6]. When iron intake is chronically low, stores can become depleted, resulting in anemia. When iron stores are exhausted, the condition is called iron depletion. Further decreases lead to iron-deficient erythropoiesis and still further decreases produce iron deficiency anemia. Blood loss is the most common cause of iron deficiency. In men and postmenopausal women, iron deficiency is almost always the result of gastrointestinal blood loss. In women in their child-bearing years, menstrual blood loss often accounts for increased iron requirements. Other causes including genitourinary bleeding and respiratory tract bleeding also increase iron requirements.

As described above, iron in the tissues is bound to proteins and does not exist as a free cation. In aqueous media, such as blood or plasma, iron can transition between to two oxidation states, reduced Fe^{2+} (ferrous), and oxide form Fe^{3+} (ferric). Factors that influence the redox equilibrium of iron in aqueous solution include pH, oxygen tension, and ionic composition. Transferrin is the protein in the blood which keeps iron soluble and serves as a mediator between the cellular and systemic deposits. Once intracellular, iron can be stored as hemosiderin, ferritin or in iron-containing intracellular proteins. A fasting blood serum iron test allows the clinician to estimate the amount of circulating iron that is bound to transferrin and serum ferritin. Normal iron levels are defined and vary based on age and gender (Table 26.1).

26.3 Iron balance

Iron deficiency, typically due to malnutrition or chronic blood loss, causes anemia, and leads to systemic abnormalities such as blue sclerae, impaired exercise capacity, fatigue, and increased propensity to infection [7]. Conversely, when there is overload, free iron behaves as a free radical and attacks cell

Table 26.1 Summary of clinically accepted normal to elevated levels of iron biomarkers [43–48].

	Typical normal levels	Mild to moderately elevated (at risk for liver fibrosis)	Severely elevated (at risk of cardiac and liver failure)
Liver iron content	0.1–1.8 mg Fe/g	1.8–15 mg Fe/g	>15 mg Fe/g
Serum ferritin	10–300 ng/mL	300–1500 ng/mL	>1500 ng/mL
Liver iron R_2^* MRI	<50 s^{-1}	50–200 s^{-1}	>200 s^{-1}
Cardiac T_2^* MRI	>20 msec	6–20 msec	<6 msec
Pancreas R_2^* MRI	<40 s^{-1}	40–100 s^{-1}	>100 s^{-1}

membranes and proteins, leading to cell injury and fibrosis depending on the affected organ and level of accumulation [8]. Conditions that increase intestinal iron absorption (e.g., hereditary hemochromatosis) cause iron overload which generally manifests in adulthood. Conditions that are treated with recurrent blood transfusions (e.g., sickle cell anemia or thalassemia) also cause iron overload in children and adults [9].

Maintaining the optimal levels of iron in the circulation is critical for the functioning of cells and tissues (Fig. 26.1). Iron levels that are too high or too low may indicate various different health issues. Too little iron leads to iron-restricted erythropoiesis and consequent anemia, whereas too much can lead to tissue iron overload and related chronic liver diseases including hepatitis, liver cirrhosis and liver failure, congestive heart failure and arrhythmias, and endocrinopathies including diabetes mellitus, hypogonadotropic hypogonadism, and hypothyroidism. Regulating iron levels during infections is also important in the innate immune response to pathogens. However, the body lacks the means to actively excrete excess iron, and in order to maintain homeostasis it must maintain an optimal balance between adequate dietary iron absorption and iron loss [10]. Iron is lost mainly by desquamation of cells of the gastrointestinal and genitourinary tracts. A very small amount (22.5 μg/L) of iron is also lost in sweat. Finally, recycling also plays an important role in iron homeostasis. These mechanisms respond to many exogenous stimuli including hypoxia, erythropoietic signals, inflammation and infection either to decrease or increase iron availability. Patients with low levels of iron may need to make changes to diet or take iron supplements. A patient with iron overload may need to undergo phlebotomy to remove blood from the body or under iron chelation therapy.

A number of diagnostic tests to assess iron loading such as serum ferritin and liver biopsy are clinically available, but these may be unreliable, limiting clinical acceptance. Serum ferritin

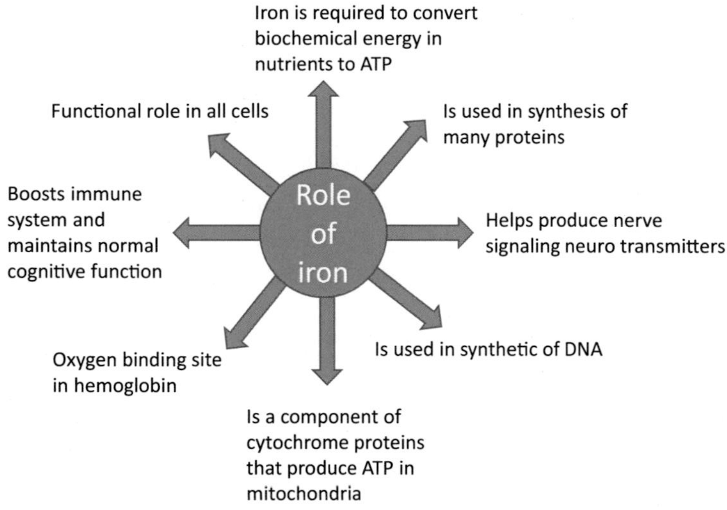

FIG. 26.1

Some of the many biological roles of iron in the body.

concentration is correlated with tissue iron stores, but has a low sensitivity and specificity because its levels are affected by many factors that can be concomitant with iron overload [11]. For instance, serum ferritin is an acute-phase protein, and can become elevated due to acute inflammation, infection, or malignancies. Due to the high variability of serum ferritin, clinicians anecdotally use a trending pattern over three or more sequential serum ferritin measurements to assess a change in iron load. Liver iron assay from a needle biopsy under ultrasound guidance has been considered the gold standard reference technique for LIC, also commonly referred to as hepatic iron content (HIC). However, liver biopsy is an invasive procedure with risks including bleeding, bile leak, and pain, which limits acceptance by providers and patients and their families. In addition, the combination of small biopsy tissue samples and heterogeneity of iron distribution yields significant sampling error. In patients with iron overload that can potentially result in liver fibrosis, obtaining a successful biopsy may be challenging, as the fibrotic tissue does not store iron [12]. The variability of results can present a significant problem when using biopsy for serial measurements of patients undergoing therapy. Due to these limitations, the estimation of LIC using noninvasive and radiation-free imaging methods that also encompass the entire liver such as MRI have an important role to play in patients with iron overload [13–15].

26.3.1 Absorption

The average adult diet contains between 10 mg and 30 mg of iron in a day with an average absorption of 5%–10%, which is enough to replace daily losses. However, inadequately low iron intake has been documented among multiple different populations including those individuals that follow a vegetarian diet [16–20]. Most people absorb around 10% of the iron they consume. When there are sufficient stores of iron, the body reduces iron intestinal absorption to prevent levels from rising too high. Iron is absorbed across the apical membrane of intestinal epithelial cells as free iron (Fe^{2+}) or as heme iron (i.e., iron bound to hemoglobin or myoglobin) [21]. The rate of iron absorption is regulated by hepcidin [22]. The production of hepcidin in the liver often increases to limit absorption in cases of iron overload and inflammation. Although hepcidin levels should increase in response to iron overload, many iron overload disorders are also triggered by inappropriately low hepcidin levels [23].

Iron absorption occurs in the proximal small bowel for both iron in ferrous form and bound to heme. Dietary iron from animal sources (meat, seafood, poultry) is in the heme form and is directly absorbed through the intestinal mucosa. Heme is the most easily absorbable form (15%–35%) and contributes 10% or more of the total absorbed iron.

Conditions that degrade the mucosa of the duodenum decrease absorption of iron (e.g., Celiac disease, Tropical sprue, Crohn's disease, Duodenal ulcers). When proton-pump inhibiting drugs such as omeprazole are used, iron absorption is also greatly reduced. Additionally, the duodenal pH-dependent process of iron absorption is inhibited or enhanced by certain dietary compounds. Phytates, which are found in whole grains, legumes, nuts, and seeds inhibit iron absorption. Enhancers of iron absorption include ascorbic acid (vitamin C) which can overcome the effects of other dietary inhibitors. Ascorbic acid forms a chelate with ferric (Fe^{3+}) iron in the low pH environment of the stomach, which persists and remains soluble in the alkaline environment of the duodenum.

26.3.2 Excretion

Unlike other minerals, the human body does not have a physiological regulatory mechanism for iron excretion, and thus iron levels are controlled primarily by absorption. The mechanism of iron excretion is an unregulated process that includes losses in the sweat, menstruation, shedding of hair and skin cells, and rapid turnover and excretion of enterocytes [24]. On average, approximately 1 mg of iron is lost each day. Disorders of iron overload are seen in those who cannot regulate iron absorption when the amount of iron overwhelms the body's ability to bind and store it [5,16].

26.3.3 Deposition

Ferritin is the main form of iron storage in the body. This protein has a capacity to store about 4500 iron ions per protein molecule. If the capacity for storage of iron in ferritin is exceeded, an extravascular complex of iron with phosphate and hydroxide, called hemosiderin, forms. Hemosiderin is only found within the cells after macrophages phagocytose the hemoglobin to degrade it. As the level of iron overload increases, excess hemosiderin is deposited in the liver and heart. The iron overload can reach the point that the function of these organs is impaired, and, if untreated, leads to death. People with hereditary hemochromatosis may absorb up to 30% of the iron they consume [25]. At this rate, the body cannot expel the extra iron fast enough, so it builds up. The body stores the excess in the tissues of major organs, primarily in the liver, but also in the heart and the pancreas. People with hemochromatosis may eventually build up between 5 and 20 times the normal amount of iron. Over time this excess iron can damage organs, resulting in organ failure and chronic diseases, such as cirrhosis, heart disease, and diabetes. Multiple blood transfusions, used in the treatment of beta-thalassemia and other anemias, also lead to an excess body burden of iron [26].

26.4 Iron deficiency

Iron deficiency is the most common micronutrient deficiency worldwide, accounting for about one-half of all cases with nutrient deficiency, and has a high incidence in developing countries driven by poor nutrition and parasitic infections. The World Health Organization defines iron deficiency as a health-related condition in which iron availability is insufficient to meet the body's needs and which can be present with or without anemia. The risk for iron deficiency is highest in young children and adolescents due to rapid growth and expanding erythropoiesis, women in child-bearing years, and the elderly [27–29].

Iron deficiency results from insufficient iron intake, either from inadequate dietary sources or malabsorption, from abnormal iron metabolism, or due to blood loss. Iron availability can be impaired by functional iron deficiency or absolute iron deficiency. In functional iron deficiency, body iron is present but sequestered into inaccessible iron stores; this condition can be identified by measuring low serum iron, serum transferrin, and serum transferrin saturation with a normal or elevated serum ferritin.

Iron deficiency causes anemia and leads to systemic abnormalities such as blue sclerae, koilonychia, impaired exercise capacity, fatigue, increased lead absorption, and an increased susceptibility to infection [7]. Iron deficiency without anemia implies that hemoglobin synthesis is impaired, but the hemoglobin concentration has not fallen sufficiently to meet the definition of anemia. Iron deficiency is typically treated with dietary supplements but intravenous forms of iron also may be necessary. Challenges in the treatment of iron deficiency include finding and addressing the underlying cause and the selection of an iron replacement product that meets the needs of the patient [30].

26.5 Iron overload

Healthy men and women of average weight in the USA have a total storage of iron of approximately 750mg (9.9mg/kg) and 300mg (5.5mg/kg), respectively [6,31]. Under normal circumstances, about one-third of stored iron (ferritin and hemosiderin) in the body is found in the liver. Approximately 98% of hepatic iron is found in hepatocytes, which make up 80% of total liver mass. The liver is frequently the first organ affected by overload because it is the principal site for iron storage. Iron that enters the cells in excess of that required accumulates in the major storage forms of iron, ferritin and hemosiderin. Progressive accumulation of stored iron is associated with cellular toxicity. Excess iron can only be removed by phlebotomy and/or specific chelation therapies. Untreated individuals may develop life-threatening organ toxicity. Thus, it is important to identify and treat iron overload before organ damage occurs.

26.5.1 Causes

Primary iron overload results entirely from increased transfer of dietary iron. Primary hemochromatosis, a slow process (intakes of up to 0.6mg/kg/day), is caused by a defect in the genes that control how much iron is absorbed. People with hereditary hemochromatosis absorb up to 30% of the iron they consume, which is triple the rate of most normal individuals. This excess iron can damage organs, resulting in organ failure and chronic diseases, such as cirrhosis, heart disease, diabetes, and eventually death.

Secondary hemochromatosis is an iatrogenic condition, typically the result of another disease or condition that causes iron overload due to red blood cell transfusion or by intake of iron supplements over substantial periods. Thalassemia, a genetic blood disorder, is the major cause of secondary hemochromatosis. There are two primary types of thalassemia: alpha thalassemia, which is typically caused by deletions of the alpha globin gene, and beta thalassemia, usually caused by mutations in the beta globin gene. These mutations or deletions lead to reduced production of beta globin (beta thalassemia) or alpha globin (alpha thalassemia), which results in an abnormal globin ratio. This abnormal ratio leads to ineffective production of hemoglobin with resulting anemia. Regular transfusions provide thalassemia patients with the red blood cells they need to survive. Transfusion therapy also is used in the management of other inherited anemias including sickle cell anemia, to prevent or treat complications, other hemolytic anemias, myelodysplastic syndrome, and bone marrow failure syndromes. However, once the transfused red blood cells are broken down, the body is left with an excess of iron. Thus, a consequence of chronic transfusion therapy is secondary iron overload, which adversely affects the function of the heart, the liver, and other organs. If hemochromatosis is left untreated, the accumulation of iron can lead to severe complications. Life expectancy is expected to be normal if hemochromatosis is diagnosed and treated early, before additional iron accumulation and organ toxicity is evident. Chemical chelating agents that bind the iron to an extractable molecule are thus used to treat to these patients to reduce iron accumulation.

26.5.2 Iron toxicity

Like most transition metal ions, iron in excess is toxic. Excess iron promotes Fenton chemistry to produce hydroxyl radicals and other reactive oxygen species (ROS), which damage lipids, DNA, and other cellular constituents. Because of the intimate relation between iron and oxygen metabolism, tissues and organs that have high oxidative metabolism are very susceptible to ROS damage and even more sensitive to adverse consequences of iron loading and its related toxicities.

Although the exact mechanism by which iron causes tissue damage is not completely known, it is proposed that free-radical intermediates, including the superoxide radical anion, underlie the biologically noxious effects of iron. Iron is known to initiate lipid peroxidation with mitochondrial membranes particularly vulnerable to injury, perhaps because of the variety of biological oxidations taking place near them [32]. It similarly explains the increased susceptibility of membrane lipids to peroxidation observed in thalassemic red cells [33], which may be a function of the excessive iron seen in thalassemic erythrocytes by light and electron microscopy [34]. Evidence of lasting liver damage may start to occur after approximately four years of transfusions with symptoms appearing as early as after two years [35]. The onset of cardiac dysfunction is more complex and less well understood, but seems to occur only after liver iron loading has occurred [36].

26.6 Iron accumulation in the liver

The liver is the primary organ involved in iron regulation in the body. Iron stored within ferritin is bioavailable; thus, hepatocytes have a crucial role in the mobilization of iron to satisfy metabolic requirements. The liver produces the majority of proteins involved in iron metabolism, including hepcidin and transferrin. The main characteristic of transferrin is its ability to reversibly bind iron, which allows it to be a cellular iron donor or iron acceptor. The liver is also the dominant iron storage organ in the body and hence LIC represents the best single surrogate of changes in total body iron. When excess iron deposits in the body, the liver is one of the first organs to demonstrate iron overload (Fig. 26.2).

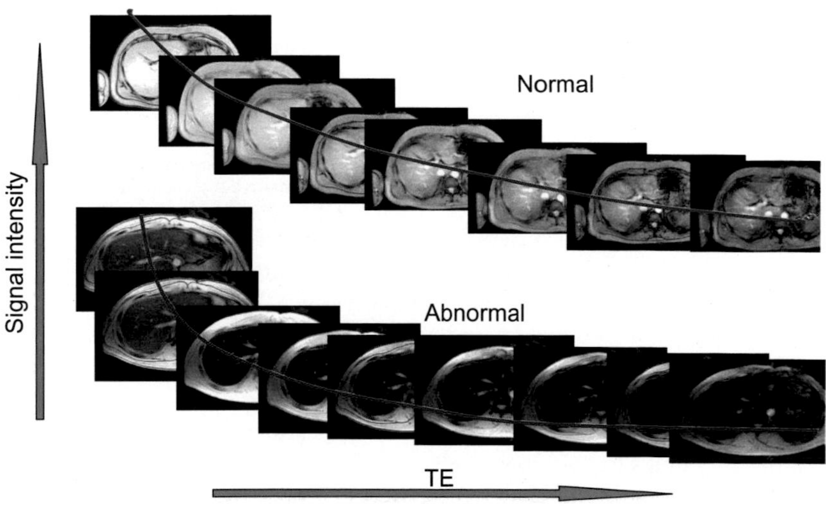

FIG. 26.2

MR images with increasing TE in a normal liver (*top, blue curve*) vs. a liver with iron overload (*bottom, red curve*). Note that with elevated LIC, the signal intensity at each TE is lower and the rate of signal intensity loss is higher than in normal liver.

Measurement of LIC can be used to infer total body iron stores and the risk of organ damage and clinical complications, thereby guiding therapy [15]. In addition, considering the critical role played by the liver in iron metabolism, it follows that liver diseases affect iron homeostasis. The clinical consequences of hepatic iron overload include liver fibrosis, cirrhosis, and increased risk for hepatocellular carcinoma (HCC) [15].

Assessment of iron stores in the liver is critical; it enables determination of the timing of treatment initiation and appropriate chelator dosing as well as monitoring for treatment efficacy. Iron overload therapy can be lifelong, expensive, and demanding on the patient and their family. When iron overload is effectively managed, patients can expect good survival without significant co-morbidities. A central requirement of therapy is accurate and precise measurements of iron levels in the liver, as this provides the most reliable marker of total iron burden. Prior to the availability of MRI, quantitative liver iron measurements were determined by liver biopsy. This method, although limited and inadequate, continues to remain acceptable. However, noninvasive, quantitative liver iron assessment by MRI performed at an experienced center is as accurate and less prone to measurement error, and thus this approach has gained clinical acceptance and is recommended to be used in place of biopsy whenever possible [15]. The behavior of ferritin in the magnetic field has been extensively studied. Measuring liver iron levels is critical to the diagnosis and therapy of patients with iron overload. Iron overload therapy can be lifelong, demanding on the patient and expensive. When iron loading is effectively managed patients can expect good survival without significant comorbidities. A central requirement of therapy is accurate precise measurement of iron levels in the liver as this provides the most reliable marker of total iron burden. In vitro and in vivo studies have shown that the transverse relaxation rates R_2 and R_2^* (the reciprocal of the relaxation time constants T_2 and T_2^*) increase linearly with the loading factor of ferritin, provided that the protein concentration remains constant [37]. Relaxivity is defined as transverse relaxation rate enhancement caused by an increase of 1 mg (Fe)/g in the iron concentration, indicated in s^{-1}/(mg (Fe)/g). Thus, the contribution to relaxation rate per iron atom is constant, regardless of low or high ferritin loading, and R_2 or R_2^* may be used as a measure of tissue iron concentration [13,14,37].

26.7 Iron accumulation in the heart

In addition to the liver, the heart also suffers from iron accumulation. Cardiomyopathy is the most life threatening of the iron-related complications [36]. The heart often remains iron-free for many years. Once cardiac iron loading starts, it progresses very rapidly, since the presence of iron in the heart further increases the rate of influx of iron due to oxidative stress. Removal of iron from the heart is a slow process, with a removal decay constant of approximately 17 months. Iron overload related cardiomyopathy is the leading cause of death in patients receiving chronic blood transfusion therapy [36,38]. Even though there is no linear correlation between LIC and cardiac iron, the heart often does not begin to unload until the LIC drops to very low levels.

The cornerstone of effective treatment of iron cardiomyopathy is continuous chelation therapy. This treatment can reduce cardiac arrhythmias and dysfunction even before the heart begins to unload iron. The actual dose of chelator depends primarily on the LIC and must be reduced as the LIC approaches normal in order to avoid symptoms of over-chelation. However, in the presence of cardiac iron, and especially if there is cardiac dysfunction such as arrhythmia or decreased left ventricular ejection fraction, chelation cannot be stopped. This treatment is considered to be emergent and multiple drug therapy, in particular, involving deferiprone and/or continuous deferoxamine infusions, is typically considered in this circumstance. Clinicians look for a reproducible index of iron loading in the heart in order to modulate and personalize therapy. Consultation with an iron chelation specialist and cardiologist is strongly recommended in the management of all patients with an abnormal cardiac MRI. Since patients may have low body iron but high cardiac iron, iron chelation therapy decisions may be complex. As in the liver, R_2^* (assessed clinically by its reciprocal T_2^*) measured in the ventricular septum is commonly used to assess cardiac iron [14,39].

26.8 Iron accumulation in other organs

Iron overload leads to deposition in a range of tissues including the liver, heart, pancreas, and pituitary gland. Typically liver iron and cardiac iron are assessed annually in regularly transfused patients, and the results help predict prognosis and direct therapy. However, less is known in clinical practice about iron accumulation in hormone-producing organs such as the pancreas (which produces insulin), pituitary gland, and thyroid.

While cardiac T_2^* is an early biomarker for risk of cardiac dysfunction, it is a relatively late indicator of endocrine risk. Although the heart and pancreas accumulate nontransferrin bound iron (NTBI), the pancreas appears to do so earlier, serving as an "early warning system" for inadequate suppression of NTBI [40].

26.8.1 Effect of iron overload in hormone-producing endocrine glands

The two most frequent endocrine complications of hemochromatosis are diabetes mellitus and hypogonadotrophic hypogonadism [41]. Pancreatic iron monitoring is likely to be the next addition to clinical practice. We can expect this work to continue where MR has established a role in iron management. Loss of insulin secretory capacity and insulin resistance is secondary to liver damage. The presence of obesity and/or genetic predisposition may be an additive risk factor for the development of metabolic disease. Further research is needed to establish if the addition of pancreatic iron monitoring will substantially alter patient outcomes in acquired or genetic iron overload conditions.

26.8.2 Effect of iron overload in the brain

Ferritin (a major iron storage molecule) levels in the basal ganglia and the cortex closely match the distribution of iron in the body. Excessive iron deposition has also been observed in specific regions of the brain in neurodegenerative diseases such as Parkinson's disease, Alzheimer's disease, Amytrophic lateral sclerosis, Huntington's disease, Friedreich's ataxia, and multiple sclerosis. The presence of higher than normal iron in specific areas of the brain can cause oxidative stress, which in turn causes damage to proteins. Although it is unclear if excessive iron is a cause of neurodegeneration, the damaged, misfolded protein structures accumulate within intracellular inclusion bodies as in Alzheimer's, Parkinson's, Huntington diseases, and multiple sclerosis. Because there is no known cure for neurodegeneration due to brain iron accumulation, treatment is primarily symptomatic and supportive. The use of deferiprone, an iron chelator which crosses the blood-brain barrier, is being explored. Medications may be used to target to the underlying cause of iron accumulation in the brain.

26.9 Management of patients with iron overload

The only treatment options for removing excess iron are phlebotomy and chelation. Phlebotomy is the treatment of choice for patients with hereditary hemochromatosis. However, phlebotomy is not appropriate for patients with thalassemia except after bone marrow transplantation. Patients with thalassemia who are not transfusion dependent cannot maintain an adequate hemoglobin level and become symptomatic after phlebotomy. Outpatient exchange transfusion is very effective in reducing or eliminating iron overload in patients with sickle cell disease where the transfusion goal often is to lower the sickle cell hemoglobin level. Exchange transfusion can be used in selected regularly transfused patients with thalassemia and other anemias to decrease iron intake, but it is not effective by itself in rapidly reducing heavy iron loads and would not be appropriate by itself in the face of cardiac iron loading. The primary treatment for iron overload in thalassemia is chelation, which is described below.

There are two goals of iron chelation therapy: the binding of toxic nontransferrin bound iron in the plasma and the removal of iron from the body. Detoxification of excess iron is the most important function of chelation therapy. It is clear that certain symptoms of iron overload, such as cardiac arrhythmia and heart failure, can be improved well before local tissue levels of iron have decreased by the continual presence of a chelator in the plasma. It is useful to think about the toxicity of iron according to the following relation:

$$\text{Toxicity} = [\text{tissue iron}] \times [\text{patient and tissue specific factors}] \times [\text{time}]$$

It takes somewhere between three to ten years of chronic exposure to high levels of iron before measurable organ dysfunction occurs. Fortunately, this means that there is time to implement treatment strategies to reduce iron loading before the organs are damaged. However, depending upon the organ, it can take a long time to significantly reduce iron, so the best strategy is to act early and, in fact, try to prevent significant iron loading from the start.

In general, chelation is started as soon as the patient becomes iron loaded, typically after 10 to 20 transfusions (a serum ferritin of approximately 1000 ng/mL). In infants, chelation therapy is usually delayed until 2 years of age because of concern for toxicity of chelators in young children. Since removal of iron from normal tissues can result in toxicity from over-chelation, the start of chelation is delayed until the patient has excess iron stores. Because iron loading occurs much faster than toxicity develops, this delay does not put the patient in danger. Starting a daily regimen of chelation therapy, whether oral or parenteral, represents a significant commitment and disruption of lifestyle. Before commencement of chelation, the patient and family should be taught about the reasons for the treatment, as well as how to prepare and take the medication. A continued education and support program involving the physician, nurse, a child life specialist, and social workers can enhance acceptance and compliance with this kind of chronic therapy.

Chelation guidelines are based on total amount of blood transfused, ferritin levels, and degree of iron loading based on LIC and cardiac T_2^* MRI [14]. LIC is the best measure of total iron loading. Typically, chelation is initiated after the LIC has reached 3000–5000 μg/g dry weight. The guidelines for iron chelation are gradually changing. While general recommendations have been to maintain a ferritin level between 500 and 1500 ng/mL, several programs are aiming to maintain serum ferritin in the normal range in adult patients [42].

It was once thought that liver iron correlated with heart iron, but it is now clearly understood that iron transport into and removal from various organs occurs at different rates. Ferritin levels can be misleading and periodic direct measurement of iron in both organs can be of great benefit in monitoring patients. New iron measurement techniques have had a direct impact on management of iron overload [13,14]. For example, it is now known that a patient can almost completely empty the liver of iron and reduce ferritin to very low levels even though significant amounts of iron may remain in the heart. This means that patients with such iron levels must cautiously proceed with chelation to empty the heart iron, when they might otherwise have considered stopping or reducing chelation treatment.

26.10 Summary

In summary, iron is a key element needed for oxygen transport and other essential functions with a highly regulated metabolism. As a potent free radical creator, excess iron generates hydroxyl radicals leading to significant oxidative stress. This chapter outlines the physiological principles of iron, its function, and mechanisms to maintain its balance as well as the consequences of deficiency and overload conditions. Additionally, the reduction of iron overload through chelation was briefly introduced and described.

References

[1] Aisen P, Enns C, Wessling-Resnick M. Chemistry and biology of eukaryotic iron metabolism. Int J Biochem Cell Biol 2001; 33(10):940–59.
[2] Furuyama K, Kaneko K, Vargas PD. Heme as a magnificent molecule with multiple missions: heme determines its own fate and governs cellular homeostasis. Tohoku J Exp Med 2007; 213(1):1–16.
[3] Aisen P, Wessling-Resnick M, Leibold EA. Iron metabolism. Curr Opin Chem Biol 1999; 3(2):200–6.
[4] Ponka P. Cell biology of heme. Am J Med Sci 1999; 318(4):241–56.
[5] Wessling-Resnick M. Excess iron: considerations related to development and early growth. Am J Clin Nutr 2017; 106(Suppl 6):1600s–1605s.
[6] Cook JD, Flowers CH, Skikne BS. The quantitative assessment of body iron. Blood 2003; 101(9):3359–64.
[7] Booth IW, Aukett MA. Iron deficiency anaemia in infancy and early childhood. Arch Dis Child 1997; 76(6):549–53. [discussion 553–4].
[8] Lambing A, Kachalsky E, Mueller ML. The dangers of iron overload: bring in the iron police. J Am Acad Nurse Pract 2012; 24(4):175–83.
[9] Coates TD, Wood JC. How we manage iron overload in sickle cell patients. Br J Haematol 2017; 177(5):703–16.
[10] Hentze MW, et al. Two to tango: regulation of mammalian iron metabolism. Cell 2010; 142(1):24–38.
[11] Karam LB, et al. Liver biopsy results in patients with sickle cell disease on chronic transfusions: poor correlation with ferritin levels. Pediatr Blood Cancer 2008; 50(1):62–5.
[12] Serai SD, Trout AT. Can MR elastography be used to measure liver stiffness in patients with iron overload? Abdom Radiol (NY) 2018; 44(1):104–9.
[13] Barrera CA, et al. Biexponential R2* relaxometry for estimation of liver iron concentration in children: a better fit for high liver iron states. J Magn Reson Imaging 2019; 50(4):1191–8.
[14] Barrera CA, et al. Protocol optimization for cardiac and liver iron content assessment using MRI: what sequence should I use? Clin Imaging 2019; 56:52–7.
[15] Towbin AJ, Serai SD, Podberesky DJ. Magnetic resonance imaging of the pediatric liver: imaging of steatosis, iron deposition, and fibrosis. Magn Reson Imaging Clin N Am 2013; 21(4):669–80.
[16] Zhang C, Rawal S. Dietary iron intake, iron status, and gestational diabetes. Am J Clin Nutr 2017; 106(Suppl 6):1672s–1680s.

[17] Kehoe L, et al. Dietary strategies for achieving adequate vitamin D and iron intakes in young children in Ireland. J Hum Nutr Diet 2017; 30(4):405–16.

[18] Gorczyca D, et al. Iron status and dietary iron intake of vegetarian children from Poland. Ann Nutr Metab 2013; 62(4):291–7.

[19] Denney L, et al. Nutrient intakes and food sources of filipino infants, toddlers and young children are inadequate: findings from the National Nutrition Survey 2013. Nutrients 2018; 10(11).

[20] Meng L, et al. Dietary diversity and food variety in chinese children aged 3(–)17 years: are they negatively associated with dietary micronutrient inadequacy? Nutrients 2018; 10(11).

[21] Costanzo LS. Physiology. Elsevier; 2018.

[22] Nemeth E, Ganz T. The role of hepcidin in iron metabolism. Acta Haematol 2009; 122(2–3):78–86.

[23] Papanikolaou G, et al. Hepcidin in iron overload disorders. Blood 2005; 105(10):4103–5.

[24] Ems T, Huecker MR. Biochemistry, iron absorption. In: StatPearls. Treasure Island, FL: StatPearls Publishing LLC; 2018.

[25] Kowdley KV, et al. ACG clinical guideline: hereditary hemochromatosis. Am J Gastroenterol 2019; 114(8):1202–18.

[26] Shah FT, et al. Challenges of blood transfusions in beta-thalassemia. Blood Rev 2019; 37:100588.

[27] Peyrin-Biroulet L, Williet N, Cacoub P. Guidelines on the diagnosis and treatment of iron deficiency across indications: a systematic review. Am J Clin Nutr 2015; 102(6):1585–94.

[28] Guralnik JM, et al. Prevalence of anemia in persons 65 years and older in the United States: evidence for a high rate of unexplained anemia. Blood 2004; 104(8):2263–8.

[29] Musallam KM, Taher AT. Iron deficiency beyond erythropoiesis: should we be concerned? Curr Med Res Opin 2018; 34(1):81–93.

[30] Munoz M, et al. Current misconceptions in diagnosis and management of iron deficiency. Blood Transfus 2017; 15(5):422–37.

[31] Andrews NC. Disorders of iron metabolism. N Engl J Med 1999; 341(26):1986–95.

[32] Hunter Jr FE, et al. Swelling and lysis of rat liver mitochondria induced by ferrous ions. J Biol Chem 1963; 238:828–35.

[33] Stocks J, et al. The susceptibility to autoxidation of human red cell lipids in health and disease. Br J Haematol 1972; 23(6):713–24.

[34] Bessis MC, Breton-Gorius J. Iron metabolism in the bone marrow as seen by electron microscopy: a critical review. Blood 1962; 19:635–63.

[35] Li CK, et al. Liver disease in transfusion dependent thalassaemia major. Arch Dis Child 2002; 86(5):344–7.

[36] Gujja P, et al. Iron overload cardiomyopathy: better understanding of an increasing disorder. J Am Coll Cardiol 2010; 56(13):1001–12.

[37] Serai SD, et al. Retrospective comparison of gradient recalled echo R2* and spin-echo R2 magnetic resonance analysis methods for estimating liver iron content in children and adolescents. Pediatr Radiol 2015; 45(11):1629–34.

[38] Olivieri NF, et al. Survival in medically treated patients with homozygous beta-thalassemia. N Engl J Med 1994; 331(9):574–8.

[39] Serai SD, et al. Measuring liver T2* and cardiac T2* in a single acquisition. Abdom Radiol (NY) 2018; 43(9):2303–8.

[40] Pfeifer CD, et al. Pancreatic iron and fat assessment by MRI-R2* in patients with iron overload diseases. J Magn Reson Imaging 2015; 42(1):196–203.

[41] Pelusi C, et al. Endocrine dysfunction in hereditary hemochromatosis. J Endocrinol Invest 2016; 39(8):837–47.

[42] Farmaki K, et al. Normalisation of total body iron load with very intensive combined chelation reverses cardiac and endocrine complications of thalassaemia major. Br J Haematol 2010; 148(3):466–75.

[43] Wood JC. Estimating tissue iron burden: current status and future prospects. Br J Haematol 2015; 170(1):15–28.
[44] Bassett ML, Halliday JW, Powell LW. Value of hepatic iron measurements in early hemochromatosis and determination of the critical iron level associated with fibrosis. Hepatology 1986; 6(1):24–9.
[45] Cartwright GE, et al. Hereditary hemochromatosis. Phenotypic expression of the disease. N Engl J Med 1979; 301(4):175–9.
[46] Modell B. Total management of thalassaemia major. Arch Dis Child 1977; 52(6):489–500.
[47] Loreal O, et al. Liver fibrosis in genetic hemochromatosis. Respective roles of iron and non-iron-related factors in 127 homozygous patients. J Hepatol 1992; 16(1–2):122–7.
[48] Angelucci E, et al. Effects of iron overload and hepatitis C virus positivity in determining progression of liver fibrosis in thalassemia following bone marrow transplantation. Blood 2002; 100(1):17–21.

CHAPTER

Fat Quantification Techniques

27

Tess Armstrong and Holden H. Wu

Department of Radiological Sciences, David Geffen School of Medicine, University of California Los Angeles, Los Angeles, CA, United States

27.1 MR properties of fat

The different MR properties of fat (i.e., adipose tissue and tissue fat content) compared to water-based tissues [1–5], including longitudinal relaxation T_1, transverse relaxation T_2, chemical shift, and diffusion, give rise to its distinct appearance and behavior on MR images. These MR properties of fat, specifically triglycerides, (Table 27.1) provide opportunities to suppress, identify, and quantify fat in vivo in the human body.

27.1.1 T_1 and T_2 of fat

At 1.5 T, the T_1 of fat is around 300–350 ms and T_2 is around 50–60 ms [6,7]. These values are slightly longer at 3 T, with T_1 of fat being in the range of 350–400 ms and T_2 around 50–70 ms [6,7]. Owing to its shorter T_1, fat has a brighter signal intensity than other tissues on T_1-weighted images. Fat has an intermediate T_2 compared to other tissues, but can still appear brighter than tissues such as muscle. On T_2-weighted turbo spin echo MRI, fat becomes even brighter, as there is less attenuation due to the presence of J-coupling when there is short spacing between multiple RF pulses [8]. Examples are shown in Fig. 27.1. The bright signal from fat on T_1-weighted images, T_2-weighted images, and balanced steady-state free precession images (T_2/T_1 contrast) can affect the dynamic range (window/level) for image display and in some cases may obscure structures and pathologies of interest, such as edema, inflammation, or contrast-enhancing tissues. On the other hand, the differences in signal intensity between fat and other water-based tissues on T_1-weighted or T_2-weighted images, and even quantitative T_1 and T_2 maps, can be leveraged to delineate and segment fat distribution in the area of interest (see Chapter **28**).

The difference between the T_1 values of fat and other tissues can be exploited to suppress signal from fat. A common approach is short tau inversion recovery (STIR) imaging [9–11], where a preparatory 180° RF pulse is used to invert the magnetization, and data acquisition is timed to occur at the point when T_1 recovery causes the fat magnetization to cross through the nulling point. For acquisitions using TR values much longer than T_1, we can approximate the inversion time (TI) for nulling a certain T_1 species as $TI_{null} = T_1 \times \ln(2)$, where ln represents the natural logarithm (base e). For fat, with a T_1 value of 300 ms, TI_{null} is ~208 ms. Adiabatic RF pulses can be designed to achieve uniform inversion across a range of resonance frequencies and RF transmit field variations for robust STIR imaging.

Advances in Magnetic Resonance Technology and Applications. Volume 1. ISSN 2666-9099. https://doi.org/10.1016/B978-0-12-817057-1.00029-9

Table 27.1 Summary of key MR properties of fat (adipose tissue and tissue fat content).

MR property	Values at 1.5 T	Values at 3 T
T_1	300–350 ms	350–400 ms
T_2	50–60 ms	50–70 ms
Chemical shift[a]	-210 Hz	-420 Hz

[a]*Chemical shift for the dominant peak due to methylene (—CH_2—). See Table 27.2 for more details.*

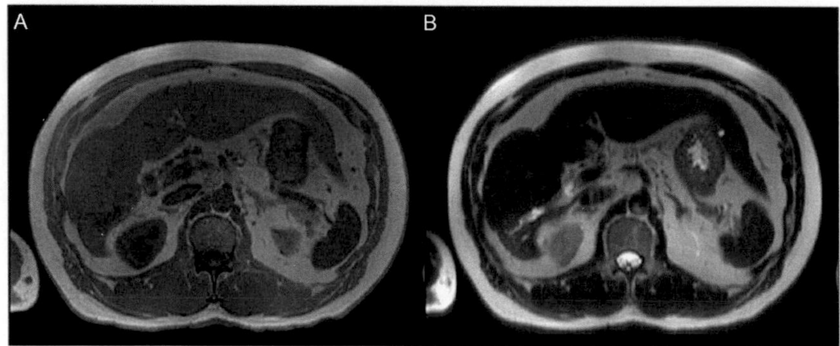

FIG. 27.1

Example axial abdominal MR images acquired at 3 T using (A) T_1-weighted 3D gradient echo imaging and (B) T_2-weighted 2D single-shot turbo spin echo imaging. Note the brighter signals from fat compared to other tissues on both T_1-weighted and T_2-weighted images.

However, STIR for fat suppression has some disadvantages, such as inadvertently nulling other tissues with T_1 values similar to fat, altering T_1 weighting in other tissues, and suppressing the contrast enhancement in blood and tissues due to T_1-shortening contrast agents.

27.1.2 Chemical shift of fat

Fat has a multipeak spectrum due to its complex molecular structure (see Section 27.2 for more details). The dominant peak due to methylene (—CH_2—) is located approximately -3.5 ppm from the water peak at a body temperature of 37°C [12,13]. At 1.5 T and 3 T, the chemical shift (δ) of -3.5 ppm translates to fat having a main off-resonance frequency Δf of -210 and -420 Hz, respectively (Eq. 27.1):

$$\Delta f\,[\text{in Hz}] = \frac{\gamma}{2\pi} B_0 \cdot 10^{-6} \cdot \delta\,[\text{in ppm}] \tag{27.1}$$

where γ is the gyromagnetic ratio of ^{1}H. Although the resonance frequency of fat does not change with temperature, the resonance frequency of water does vary with temperature [14–16]; therefore, the observed chemical shift of fat relative to water changes with temperature [17]. The chemical shift of fat, when unaccounted for, can lead to several common MRI artifacts including dark lines at fat/water interfaces on gradient echo MRI and balanced steady-state free precession MRI [18], as well as pixel

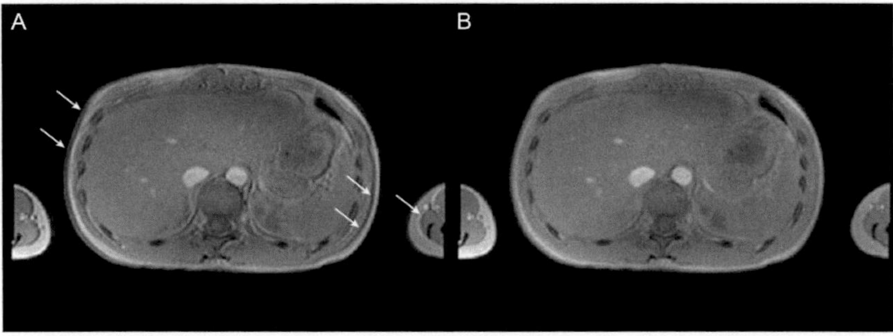

FIG. 27.2

Examples of fat-water pixel shifts in axial abdominal MR images acquired at 3 T using (A) a low readout bandwidth of 400 Hz/pixel and (B) high readout bandwidth of 1170 Hz/pixel. The pixel shift artifact is evident for low-bandwidth acquisitions (shift of fat by ~1 pixel in the left-right readout direction; arrows in A) and suppressed (reduced to subpixel shifts) using high readout bandwidths.

shifts of fat-containing structures [18]. High readout bandwidths are typically utilized to suppress pixel shift artifacts (Fig. 27.2). For fast scanning sequences that utilize echo-planar imaging and other non-Cartesian trajectories, the signal from fat can cause strong image artifacts and must be suppressed or resolved to maintain high image quality.

The chemical shift of fat can actually be leveraged to either suppress fat signal and reduce chemical shift image artifacts, or to isolate and quantify fat (see Sections 27.2 and 27.3). A commonly employed method, known as chemical-shift selective (CHESS) imaging [19], uses a preparatory module with a 90° RF excitation pulse tuned to the resonance frequency of fat followed by gradients to de-phase the signal from fat. Data are acquired right after the CHESS module is played out to obtain images that do not contain fat signal, thus suppressing fat and creating "water-only" images. CHESS imaging can also be performed with the RF pulse tuned to the resonance frequency of water to obtain "fat-only" images. CHESS water and fat imaging provides a practical approach for fat suppression, as well as characterization of fat content. While CHESS imaging works well in theory, it fails when increased variations in the main field B_0 shift the effects of the CHESS RF pulse away from the intended resonance frequency [2]. In severe situations, CHESS may even inadvertently suppress water signal when it was intended for fat suppression. In addition, CHESS is also sensitive to variations in the transmit RF field (B_1^+). When the intended chemical shift species is not fully excited into the transverse plane (i.e., by a 90° excitation pulse) and dephased by gradients, residual signal will be present during image acquisition [2]. These undesirable effects of CHESS become more pronounced at 3 T compared to 1.5 T, due to the increased B_0 and B_1^+ inhomogeneity at 3 T.

An alternative to signal suppression using CHESS is spatial-spectral excitation. Multidimensional RF pulses can be designed to selectively excite a slice and a specific chemical shift species at the same time [20,21]. In this way, it is possible to perform "water-only" excitation to avoid generating signals from fat altogether and obtain water-only images. This approach is more robust to B_1^+ inhomogeneity than CHESS, since imperfectly excited signals can still be used to create images. However, spatial-spectral excitation is still sensitive to B_0 inhomogeneity, as it relies on precisely aligning the excitation bandwidth with the resonance frequency of the desired chemical shift species.

When B_0 or B_1^+ inhomogeneity reduces the effectiveness of CHESS or spatial-spectral excitation, STIR imaging (see Section 27.1.1) may be used instead if its limitations are acceptable. In addition, modern MRI scanners offer improved fat suppression methods that combine CHESS or spatial-spectral RF pulses with STIR principles. For example, the CHESS module may employ a fat-selective 180° inversion pulse in place of a typical 90° excitation pulse (known as SPECtral Inversion At Lipid, or SPECIAL) and data acquisition would be timed to the nulling of the fat signal during the course of T_1 recovery. The fat-selective inversion pulse may also be $<180°$ (known as spectral presaturation with inversion recovery, SPIR). To improve robustness to B_1^+ inhomogeneity, the fat-selective 180° inversion pulse may be an adiabatic pulse (known as spectral attenuated inversion recovery, SPAIR). Examples are shown in Fig. 27.3.

The suppression of fat based on chemical shift differences, as described in this subsection, has a long history in qualitative MRI and is routinely used in clinical protocols. At the same time, magnetic resonance spectroscopy (MRS) methods have exploited the unique resonance frequencies of fat peaks to study the amount and composition of fat in vivo (see Section 27.2). These two developments are joined together in chemical-shift-encoded MRI to improve fat suppression in the presence of B_0 and B_1^+ variations, and to further provide spatially resolved quantitative measurements of fat in vivo (see Section 27.3).

27.1.3 Diffusion of fat

Compared to the diffusion of water protons, the protons in fat molecules exhibit much lower apparent diffusion coefficients (ADC) due to the larger macromolecular weight and the increased restriction in its environment [22–24]. In order to characterize the diffusion characteristics of fat protons, substantially higher diffusion weighting (i.e., *b*-values) is required. For example, *b*-values on the order of 10^6 s/mm^2 may be needed to measure the ADC of fat protons, which could be on the order of 10^{-6} mm^2/s [22–24]. This is in contrast to the measurement of the ADC of water protons in aqueous tissues, where *b*-values on the order of 10^3 s/mm^2 are typically used to measure ADC values around 10^{-3} mm^2/s. The required high *b*-values for measuring the ADC of fat protons are challenging to achieve on standard clinical whole-body MRI systems due to limitations in gradient performance.

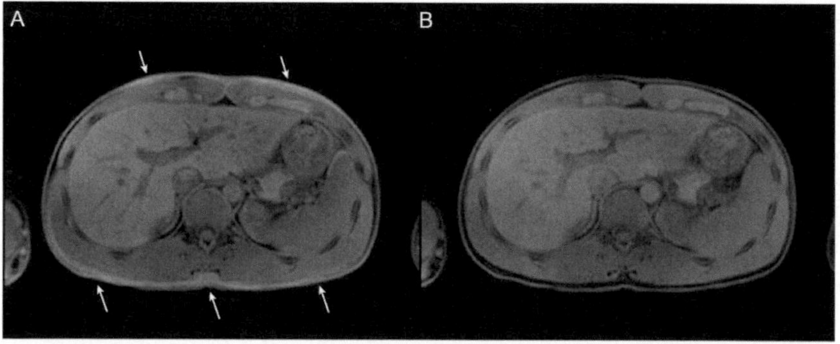

FIG. 27.3

Examples of fat suppression at 3T using (A) chemical-shift selective (CHESS) fat saturation and (B) spectral attenuated inversion recovery (SPAIR). In this example, there was incomplete fat suppression using CHESS due to B_0 field variations (arrows in A).

Preclinical systems with high gradient performance (high amplitude and slew rate) have been used to study tissue samples and animal models [22–24]. Signals from intramyocellular lipid (IMCL) and extramyocellular lipid (EMCL) can be distinguished based on the differences in restricted diffusion observed at different diffusion times [22,23]. In addition, brown adipose tissue (BAT) exhibits a reduced ADC compared to white adipose tissue (WAT) [24].

27.2 Quantifying fat using MR spectroscopy

Single-voxel proton (^1H) MRS is widely accepted as the gold standard for noninvasive quantification of fat content [3,4,25]. MRS takes advantage of the differences in the chemical shift of fat, including the multiple distinct peaks in its spectrum, to quantify the amount of fat versus water, the chain length of triglycerides, and degree of triglyceride saturation in tissues. MRS has been shown to be practical, accurate, and reproducible in quantifying fat in vivo and is often used as the endpoint in clinical trials for fat-reducing procedures and medication [26–30]. The information gained from MRS are further used as a reference to develop efficient chemical-shift-encoded MRI techniques for spatially resolved fat quantification (see Section 27.3).

27.2.1 Signal model

Fat has a complex molecular structure with multiple distinct ^1H moieties. The chemical shift of each peak is reported in ppm (see Section 27.1). The proton peak of tetramethylsilane (TMS) is used to define the reference point of 0 ppm and water (H_2O) is at 4.7 ppm at a temperature of 37°C. The human liver fat spectrum has nine distinct proton moieties and six peaks are usually reliably observed in vivo at 3 T [12,13,31] (Table 27.2). Two of the peaks in the fat spectrum (peaks 1 and 2 in Table 27.2) are close to the water peak and contribute to around 8–9% of the total fat signal. If these peaks are not accounted for, the quantification of fat content would be underestimated.

The fat spectrum varies in different tissue types, such as liver, bone marrow, subcutaneous adipose tissue, and visceral adipose tissue [12,13,31–33]. A priori knowledge of the multipeak fat spectrum is an important factor for achieving accurate chemical-shift-encoded MRI-based fat quantification (see Section 27.3).

Table 27.2 Peaks in the in vivo liver proton spectrum measured at 3 T [12].

Peak	Chemical environment	Chemical shift (ppm)	Percent of total fat signal
1	**—CH=CH—** **—CH—**O—CO—	5.3	4.7%
Water	**H_2O**	4.7	N/A
2	**—CH_2—**O—CO—	4.2	3.9%
3	—CH=CH—**CH_2**—CH=CH—	2.75	0.6%
4	—CO—**CH_2**—CH$_2$— —**CH_2**—CH=CH—**CH_2**—	2.1	12.0%
5	—CO—CH$_2$—**CH_2**— —**$(CH_2)_n$**—	1.3	70.0%
6	—$(CH_2)_n$—**CH_3**	0.9	8.8%

27.2.2 MRS pulse sequences

The two most commonly used sequences for single-voxel MR spectroscopy are point resolved spectroscopy (PRESS) [34] (Fig. 27.4) and stimulated echo acquisition mode (STEAM) [35] (Fig. 27.5). PRESS has a longer TE and is more sensitive to J-coupling effects; STEAM achieves a shorter TE, but has lower signal-to-noise ratios compared to PRESS. STEAM is typically preferred over PRESS, since it is less sensitive to J-coupling effects that can lead to inconsistency in fat quantification [36].

Typical STEAM sequence parameters for a breath-held liver acquisition [31] include: single voxel with dimensions of $10–30 \times 10–30 \times 10–30\,\text{mm}^3$; five echoes with TE = 12, 24, 36, 48, and 72 ms; TR = 3000 ms; mixing time = 10 ms; temporal vector size = 1024 points; readout bandwidth = 1200 Hz/pixel; and a total acquisition time of 15 s. This choice of TR minimizes bias caused by incomplete T_1 relaxation. In addition, the acquisition of data with multiple TEs allows the characterization and compensation of T_2 relaxation to ensure the accuracy of fat quantification. A representative example is shown in Fig. 27.6.

Prior to the MRS acquisition, B_0 shimming should be performed to achieve a uniform background field in the organ and tissue of interest. In regions of anatomy with potentially rapid field variations (e.g., due to air/tissue interfaces), the shim volume may be manually prescribed to be localized to the tissue of interest. For fat quantification, contributions of the water peak need to be measured as well, thus water saturation (commonly used for MRS) should be disabled [12]. Spatial saturation pulses should also be avoided, as they may have nonuniform effects on water and fat spectral signals [12].

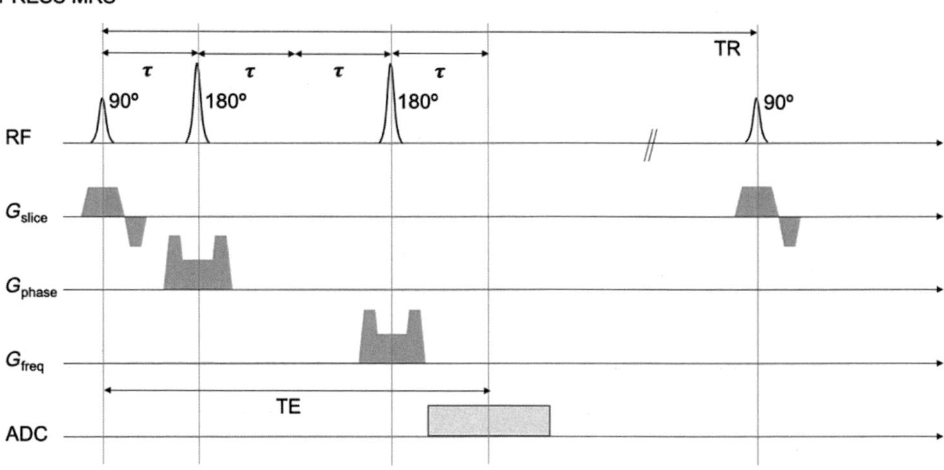

FIG. 27.4

Pulse sequence diagram for single-voxel point-resolved MR spectroscopy (PRESS). A single voxel is localized in three dimensions by a combination of a slice-selective 90° RF excitation pulse, a phase-encoding selective 180° RF refocusing pulse, and a frequency-encoding selective 180° RF refocusing pulse. τ denotes the separation between the 90° excitation pulse and the initial 180° refocusing pulse. RF, radiofrequency; G_{slice}, slice select gradient; G_{phase}, phase encoding gradient; G_{freq}, frequency encoding gradient; ADC, analog to digital converter; TE, echo time; TR, repetition time.

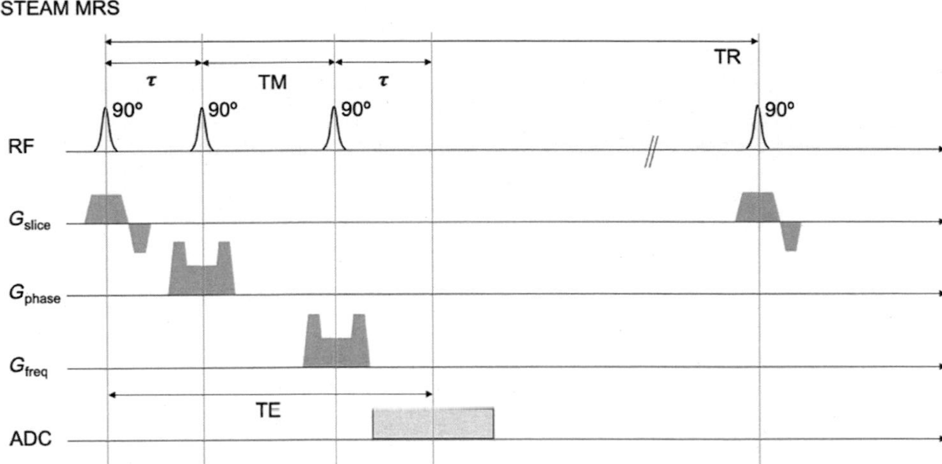

FIG. 27.5

Pulse sequence diagram for single-voxel stimulated echo acquisition mode (STEAM) MR spectroscopy (MRS). A single voxel is localized in three dimensions by a combination of a slice-selective 90° RF excitation pulse, a phase-encoding selective 90° RF pulse, and a frequency-encoding selective 90° RF pulse. τ denotes the separation between the 90° excitation pulse and the second 90° RF pulse. As a result of the second 90° RF pulse, a portion of the magnetization is returned to the longitudinal axis and experiences T_1 relaxation during the mixing time (TM). The third 90° RF pulse re-excites a portion of the magnetization into the transverse plane, which then forms a stimulated echo after τ. A short TM can be used to achieve a short echo time (TE). RF, radiofrequency; G_{slice}, slice select gradient; G_{phase}, phase encoding gradient; G_{freq}, frequency encoding gradient; ADC, analog to digital converter; TR, repetition time.

Since MRS measures signal from a single voxel, the voxel position should be carefully prescribed in a representative homogenous region of the tissue of interest to avoid partial volume effects. For example, the placement of a voxel for liver MRS should avoid structures such as liver edges, blood vessels, bile ducts, and adjacent visceral adipose tissue.

Multivoxel MR spectroscopy, also known as MR spectroscopic imaging (MRSI) [37,38], uses 2D or 3D phase encoding to extend single-voxel MRS. The acquisition of multiple voxels allows characterization of spatial variations in fat content, thereby reducing partial volume effects, sampling bias, and the demand for operator specification of the voxel location. Typical MRSI 2D matrix sizes are in the range of 16×16 to 32×32 for a field-of-view encompassing the tissue of interest (e.g., $300 \times 300\,\text{mm}^2$ for the abdomen in the axial orientation). However, MRSI voxel shapes are less ideal than MRS, there is more signal leakage from neighboring voxels and regions, the shimming is less uniform for a larger volume, and the prolonged acquisition time is not amenable to breath-holding acquisitions in abdominal organs. MRSI may be improved by exploiting acceleration methods, such as echo-planar spectroscopic imaging [39], to achieve clinically acceptable acquisition times for fat quantification. While MRSI has demonstrated promise for several clinical and research applications, its use for fat quantification has been limited thus far. New advances in MRSI technology [37–39] may benefit fat quantification.

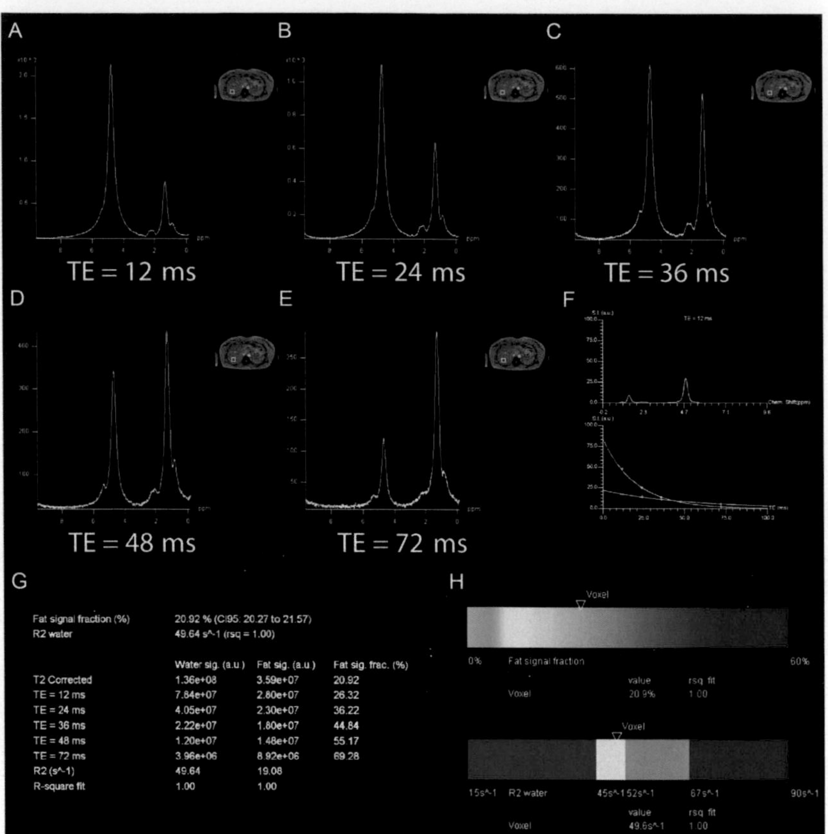

FIG. 27.6

Example liver fat and water spectra measured in a patient with nonalcoholic fatty liver disease using a commercially available stimulated echo acquisition mode (STEAM) MR spectroscopy sequence at 3T. (A–E) Five acquisitions with different echo times (TE) were obtained within a single breath-hold to correct for T_2 effects and quantify proton-density fat fraction. The inset images indicate the placement of the STEAM voxel in the right lobe of the liver. (F) The T_2-corrected fat and water spectrum and T_2 decay curves. (G) Quantitative measurements. (H) Visual report of the measured fat fraction and R_2 ($1/T_2$) values.

For both single-voxel MRS and multivoxel MRSI, motion needs to be managed in mobile organs affected by physiological motion. Common strategies include breath-holding or navigator triggering to limit artifacts due to respiratory motion, and cardiac triggering to reduce artifacts due to cardiac motion and vascular pulsation. For example, sequence parameters are judiciously selected to allow breath-hold acquisitions (typically 10–20 s) for liver fat quantification in a clinical setting [31].

27.2.3 Signal fitting

After acquiring the time-domain signals, the frequency spectrum is obtained by performing a Fourier transform. Mild filtering is usually also applied to suppress noise. To extract the spectral information, each peak can be modeled as a Gaussian distribution or set of Gaussian functions [12,13,31].

Peak modeling can be performed using software packages on the scanner, which is often automated for vendor-supplied commercial sequences, or carried out offline with dedicated software packages [12,13,31]. Offline processing involves more manual input from an expert, but also allows for fine tuning to improve the spectral analysis for each specific case. Following the extraction of each spectral peak, the area of each fat peak is calculated. The fat signal is then obtained by summing the areas of all fat peaks.

27.2.4 Quantitative measurements

Based on the information from spectral analysis, several quantitative measurements can be calculated to characterize fat content. Currently, the accepted quantitative MR biomarker for fat content is the proton-density fat fraction (PDFF) in percent [40], defined as the ratio between MR-observable fat protons and all MR-observable fat and water protons (i.e., fat/[water + fat]) [41] (also see Section 27.3). To accurately measure PDFF, factors that affect the fat and water signals to a different degree, such as T_1 and T_2 effects (see Section 27.1), need to be addressed. T_1 effects must be reduced, for example, by using a sufficiently long TR (e.g., 3000 ms or longer) [12,31]. T_2 effects can be accounted for by acquiring multiple signals at different TEs, estimating T_2, and then correcting for T_2 signal decay [12,31]. By accounting for all of these potentially confounding factors, the measured PDFF should ideally be independent of field strength, sequence type, and sequence parameters. The accuracy of MRS PDFF has been validated in rat models of hepatic steatosis [41], demonstrating a significant positive linear correlation with respect to histopathological measurements of macrovesicular steatosis.

The diagnostic performance of MRS PDFF has been confirmed in several patient studies and achieves high accuracy for detecting hepatic steatosis compared to liver biopsy [25,42]. In addition, MRS PDFF has been shown to have high intra-exam and inter-exam repeatability for quantifying hepatic fat content, with standard deviations $<0.5\%$ [43] and coefficients of repeatability $<1.5\%$ [44] (Table 27.3). The reproducibility of MRS PDFF in the liver across 1.5 T and 3 T has also been shown to be excellent [45]. Based on the consistent findings across multiple studies, the PDFF measured by MRS is now accepted as an accurate and reproducible biomarker that can be used for diagnosis of disorders involving fat metabolism and monitoring of interventions [26–30] (see Chapter 28 for more details regarding applications).

In addition to quantifying the fat content in tissue, MRS also has the capability to model and quantify molecular characteristics of fatty acid composition [12,13,32,33,47–49]. The chemical structure of triglycerides is comprised of three fatty acid chains connected to a glycerol backbone. Each chain has distinct properties with respect to length and the number of unsaturated bonds. Based on differences in chemical structure, triglyceride saturation can be characterized as saturated, monounsaturated, or polyunsaturated. The degree of triglyceride saturation or unsaturation in a tissue of interest can be characterized by MR methods (see Section 27.4.3) and provides important information regarding metabolic disorders, cancer, osteoporosis, and other conditions.

27.3 Quantifying fat using chemical-shift-encoded MRI

The suppression or separation of bright fat signal from water-based tissue signals on MR images has been an important ongoing topic in MRI research and applications for over three decades. While MRS is able to exploit the fundamental chemical-shift differences between fat and water to precisely measure

Table 27.3 Examples of repeatability and reproducibility studies of MRS PDFF in the liver.

Technique	Subjects	Type of assessment	Metric	Reference
STEAM; 3T	$n=29$	Intra-exam (three acquisitions)	Mean SD=0.49%	[43]
		Inter-exam (three scans, same day)	Mean SD=0.46%	[43]
PRESS; 3T	$n=24$	Inter-exam (two scans, same day)	RC=0.4%	[44]
		Inter-exam (two scans, 4 weeks apart)	RC= 1.3%	[44]
STEAM; 1.5 T and 3T	$n=25$	1.5 T vs. 3T (same day)	$m=0.98$, $R^2=0.90$	[45]
STEAM; 3T	$n=23$	Inter-exam (two scans, median 30 days apart)	$m=1.0$, ICC=0.95	[46]

SD, *standard deviation;* RC, *repeatability coefficient;* m, *slope of linear regression;* R^2, *coefficient of determination;* ICC, *intra-class correlation coefficient.*

their individual contributions (see Section 27.2), MRS (or MRSI) has insufficient spatial resolution compared to what is required for MRI. Therefore, MRI techniques have been developed to encode the chemical-shift differences between fat and water signals and reconstruct separate fat and water images with the desired spatial resolution. These chemical-shift-encoded (CSE) MRI techniques assume that the spectral peak(s) of fat are known (e.g., calibrated by MRS experiments) and use simplified signal models, which allow the acquisition of substantially reduced amounts of spectrally encoded information compared to MRS. The earliest forms of CSE-MRI were developed by W. T. Dixon [50] and extended by others, hence the term "Dixon" is often used to describe MRI methods for fat-water separation. Recent work has extended and generalized CSE-MRI acquisitions and analysis methods beyond the early Dixon methods to achieve flexible and accurate fat quantification.[a]

27.3.1 Fat-water separation using CSE-MRI

27.3.1.1 Original two-point Dixon method

The first CSE-MRI technique for fat-water imaging was developed by Dixon [50] and will be referred to as the "original two-point Dixon" method in this section. The term "point" is used to refer to the number of echo times. The MRI signal (S) at an echo time (TE), or point, due to protons in fat and water can be represented by a vector $S(\text{TE})=S_0e^{i\psi}$, which has a magnitude S_0 and phase ψ (Fig. 27.7A).

When fat and water are both present in a voxel, the MRI signal can be approximated as:

$$S=\left(W+Fe^{i\alpha}\right)e^{i\phi_{off}}e^{i\phi_0} \quad (27.2)$$

where ϕ_{off} is the phase accrued from off-resonance effects due to B_0 main field inhomogeneity (often referred to as the field map) and ϕ_0 is the bulk phase offset due to other sources; $\alpha=2\pi\Delta f TE$ is a linear function of echo time TE and Δf, the chemical shift frequency difference between fat and water in Hz

[a]This chapter uses the term CSE-MRI in general and uses "Dixon" for specific types of CSE-MRI methods.

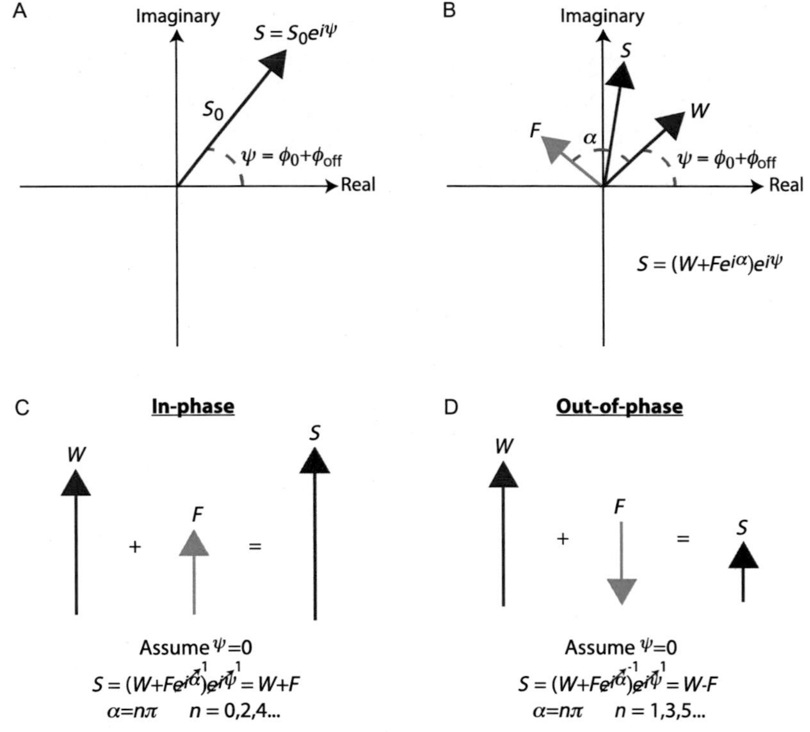

FIG. 27.7

(A) Vector notation of the MRI signal in the transverse plane. (B) The vector notation of the MRI signal with two chemical shift species, water (*W*) and fat (*F*) with a chemical shift induced phase difference (α). (C) The signal at an in-phase echo time ($\alpha = 0, 2\pi, 4\pi, \ldots$) can be represented as a sum of the individual fat and water signals. (D) The signal at an out-of-phase echo time ($\alpha = \pi, 3\pi, 5\pi, \ldots$) can be represented as the difference between the individual fat and water signals.

(Fig. 27.7B) [1,50]; and W and F are the magnitudes of the MR signal for water and fat protons, respectively [1,50]. The original two-point Dixon method assumes ϕ_{off} and ϕ_0 to be zero and this approximation reduces Eq. (27.2) to:

$$S = W + Fe^{i\alpha} \tag{27.3}$$

To solve for W and F in Eq. (27.3), MRI signals (images) are acquired at echo times when the fat and water signals are in-phase ($\alpha = n\pi$, where $n = 0, 2, 4, \ldots$) (Fig. 27.7C) and out-of-phase ($\alpha = n\pi$, where $n = 1, 3, 5, \ldots$) (Fig. 27.7D). At in-phase echo times, $S(in\text{-}phase) = W + F$, and at out-of-phase echo times, $S(out\text{-}of\text{-}phase) = W - F$ [1,50]. Therefore, W and F can be determined by adding and subtracting the in-phase and out-of-phase MR images. $S(in\text{-}phase)$ and $S(out\text{-}of\text{-}phase)$ are the magnitudes of the source images at the in-phase and out-of-phase echo times, respectively:

$$W = \frac{|S(in\text{-}phase) + S(out\text{-}of\text{-}phase)|}{2} \tag{27.4}$$

$$F = \frac{|S(in\text{-}phase) - S(out\text{-}of\text{-}phase)|}{2} \tag{27.5}$$

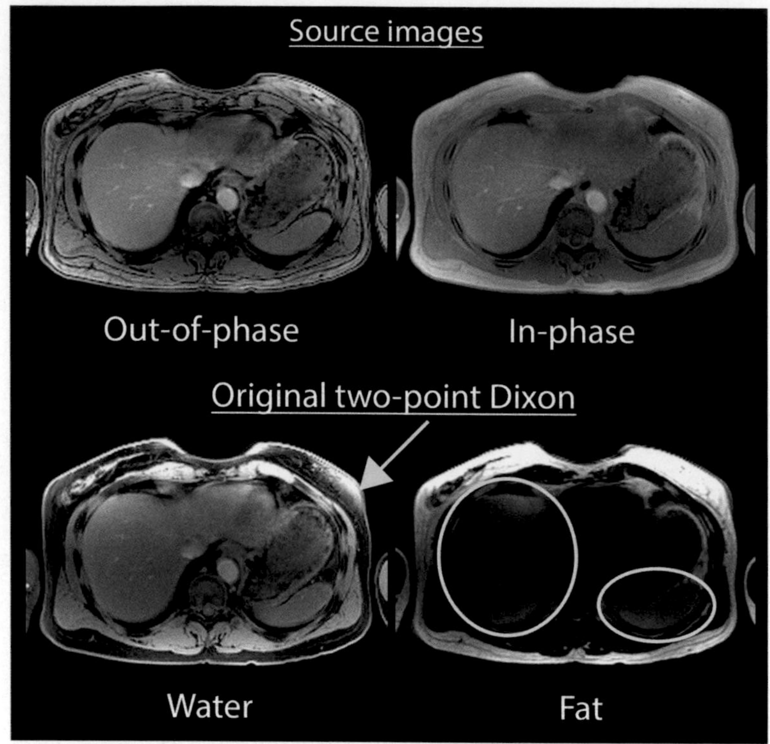

FIG. 27.8

Original two-point Dixon fat-water separation resulting in water and fat images using simple addition and subtraction. Images were acquired in the axial orientation using a breath-held 3D multiecho gradient echo sequence at 3T in a healthy adult. The yellow arrows and yellow ellipses indicate errors in the original two-point Dixon fat-water separation results due to B_0 field inhomogeneities that cause leakage of the water signal.

An example of in-phase and out-of-phase images and the resultant fat (F) and water (W) images determined using this calculation are shown in Fig. 27.8.

The original two-point Dixon method has advantages and limitations. Due to the simplicity in the calculation, fat-water separation can be obtained easily from the in-phase and out-of-phase MR images. Furthermore, a two-point Dixon technique has shown improved agreement with MRS compared to other Dixon techniques for intramuscular fat quantification at 3 T [51]. However, the original two-point Dixon method assumes that ϕ_{off} is 0; therefore, in regions with large B_0 field inhomogeneity, the original two-point Dixon method fails (Fig. 27.8). In addition, fat has a multipeak spectrum (see Section 27.2). The original two-point Dixon method assumes a single fat peak, which only accounts for ~70% of the fat signal and leads to underestimation of the fat content. Another limitation of this method is that it does not correct for additional confounding factors, such as T_1 or T_2^* bias. All confounding factors in the signal model must be addressed to ensure accurate PDFF measurements (see Section 27.3.3) [3,40]. For these reasons, there are limited studies investigating the repeatability and reproducibility of fat quantification using the original two-point Dixon technique.

27.3.1.2 Three-point Dixon method

The three-point Dixon technique was introduced to account for B_0 field variations (ϕ_{off}) [1,52]. In this method, three images are acquired at in-phase and out-of-phase echo times, and the off-resonance induced phase map ϕ_{off} is estimated and used to calculate water-only and fat-only images. Assuming ϕ_0 is zero and ϕ_{off} is nonzero, and that the signals at the first echo time ($S_1 = S(TE_1)$) and third echo time ($S_3 = S(TE_3)$) are in-phase and the second echo time ($S_2 = S(TE_2)$) is out-of-phase, (i.e., $TE_2 = 2 \cdot TE_1$ and $TE_3 = 3 \cdot TE_1$), the complex MRI signals can be approximated as:

$$S_1 = W + F \tag{27.6}$$

$$S_2 = (W - F)e^{i\phi_{off}} \tag{27.7}$$

$$S_3 = (W + F)e^{i2\phi_{off}} \tag{27.8}$$

For the three-point Dixon technique, S_1, S_2, and S_3 are complex images containing both magnitude and phase information used to calculate ϕ_{off}. Using these equations, ϕ_{off} can be calculated as:

$$\phi_{off} = \frac{1}{2} \cdot \arg\left(S_3 \cdot S_1^*\right) \tag{27.9}$$

where S_1^* is the complex conjugate of S_1. ϕ_{off} can be removed from the signals S_2 and S_3, yielding the equations used for the original two-point Dixon technique:

$$S_2' = S_2 e^{-i\phi_{off}} = W - F \tag{27.10}$$

$$S_3' = S_3 e^{-i2\phi_{off}} = W + F \tag{27.11}$$

The water and fat images can be calculated as:

$$W = \frac{|S_3' + S_2'|}{2} \tag{27.12}$$

$$F = \frac{|S_3' - S_2'|}{2} \tag{27.13}$$

By accounting for ϕ_{off}, the three-point Dixon method can improve the accuracy, repeatability, and reproducibility of fat-water separation (Fig. 27.9) [53,54]. Another advantage is that the three-point Dixon method is still a relatively simple calculation. A limitation of the three-point Dixon technique is that it requires the acquisition of images at three echo times, which may increase the scan time. Similar to the original two-point Dixon method, the three-point Dixon method assumes a single fat peak and does not correct for additional confounding factors, such as T_1 or T_2^* bias. Although the fat-water separation image quality is improved using the three-point Dixon method, fat-water swaps may still occur due to phase wrapping (Fig. 27.9). Phase unwrapping techniques have been developed and used to improve fat-water separation (See Section 27.3.1.3).

27.3.1.3 Extended two-point Dixon method

Similar to the strategy for the three-point Dixon technique, the two-point Dixon technique can be extended to estimate and account for B_0 field inhomogeneities [1,66]. Using the equations for S_1 and S_2 stated above and assuming S_1 and S_2 are complex images:

$$S_1 = W + F \tag{27.14}$$

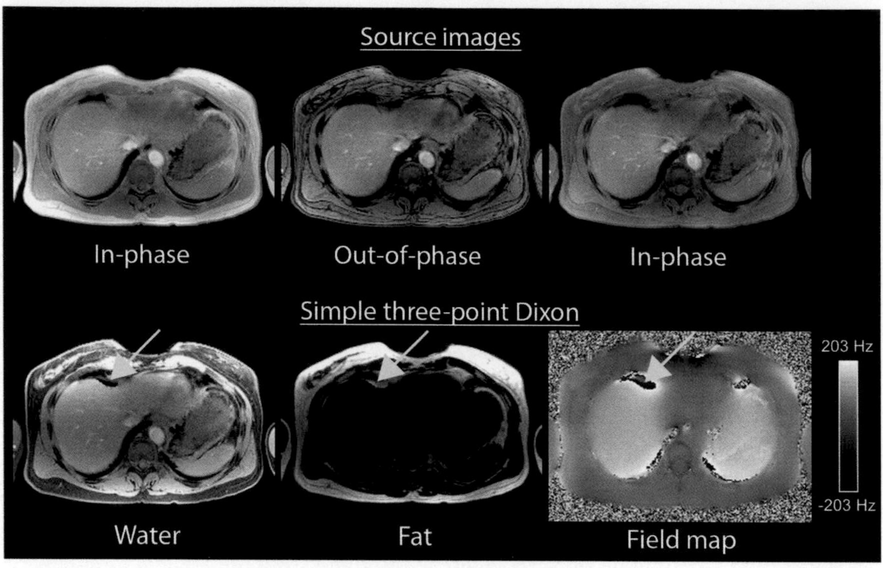

FIG. 27.9

Three-point Dixon fat-water separation resulting in water and fat images. Images were acquired in the axial orientation using a breath-held 3D multiecho gradient echo sequence at 3 T in the same healthy adult shown in Fig. 27.8. The leakage of the fat signal into the water images was removed by resolving the field map. However, there are residual fat-water swaps due to phase wrapping (yellow arrows).

$$S_2 = (W - F)e^{i\phi_{off}} \tag{27.15}$$

ϕ_{off} can be calculated as:

$$\phi_{off} = \frac{1}{2} \cdot \arg\left(\left(S_2 \cdot S_1{}^*\right)^2\right) \tag{27.16}$$

After ϕ_{off} is estimated, it can be removed from the signal S_2 and leads to the equations used for the original two-point Dixon method. Both the extended two-point Dixon and the three-point Dixon techniques rely on phase processing, which is challenged by phase wraps that occur because the argument function has a solution range $[0, 2\pi]$. In areas of large phase variations due to B_0 field inhomogeneity, a fat-water swap will occur. Compared to the original two-point Dixon technique, the extended two-point Dixon technique improves fat-water separation by accounting for the field map. However, compared to three-point Dixon, extended two-point Dixon is more susceptible to phase wrapping and fat-water swaps because of the extra factor of two used to solve for the phase map in Eq. (27.16) [66]. Current clinical protocols using Dixon techniques typically implement a version of the extended two-point Dixon approach with phase unwrapping (Fig. 27.10).

Commonly-used phase unwrapping techniques such as region growing [55,56], polynomial fitting [52,57,58], or solving Poisson's equations [59] have been combined with extended two-point Dixon and three-point Dixon techniques. These methods are based on the assumption that the B_0 field varies smoothly across the image [1]. Region-growing methods begin by defining a seed point, or starting voxel, then extending out from this point to calculate the unwrapped phase map. For example, if

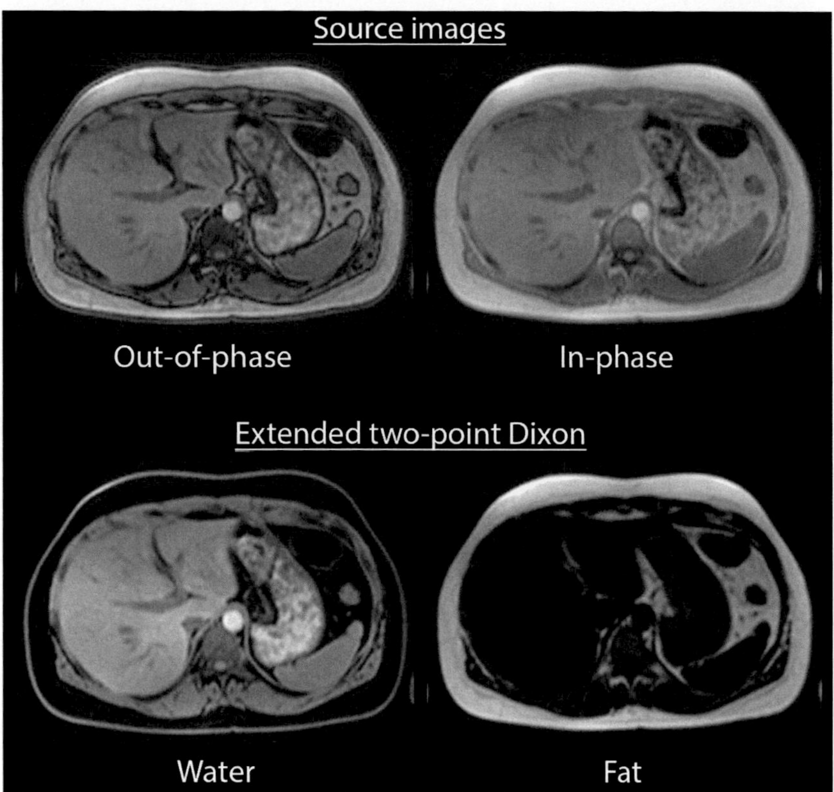

FIG. 27.10

Extended two-point Dixon fat-water separation with phase unwrapping, resulting in water-only and fat-only images. Images were acquired in the axial orientation using a breath-held 3D multiecho gradient echo sequence at 3 T in a patient.

the phase difference between two adjacent voxels is approximately 2π, a phase wrap has occurred and the true phase can be recovered by adding or subtracting 2π from one of the voxels. Minimum-norm methods form an optimization problem to enforce smoothness of the phase map. The most commonly used minimum-norm method is to formulate a least-squares problem (i.e., using the L^2-norm). Although there are many proposed methods for phase map or field map estimation, phase processing remains an important area of research to improve fat-water separation [1,60–65].

27.3.1.4 Single-point Dixon method

In the single-point Dixon method [1,67], data are acquired such that fat is in the imaginary channel and water is in the real channel by choosing an echo time when $\alpha = \pi/2$. Assuming that the B_0 field inhomogeneity induced phase (ϕ_{off}) and the bulk phase offset (ϕ_0) are zero, the signal model is:

$$S = W + Fe^{i\alpha} \tag{27.17}$$

By extracting the real and imaginary parts of S, the water and fat images can be obtained, respectively. In practice, however, the assumption of a homogeneous B_0 field map is not valid and a precalibration of the field map (e.g., using three-point Dixon) would be required. Single-point Dixon has potential advantages for dynamic imaging, where the overhead for acquiring multiple echo times is eliminated to achieve high frame rates. This technique is insufficient for fat quantification because of the simplified assumptions of the fat-water signal model and is not used clinically for fat quantification.

27.3.1.5 Advanced methods for fat-water separation

Limitations of the original two-point Dixon, extended two-point Dixon, three-point Dixon, single-point Dixon, and multipoint Dixon methods are that they require in-phase and out-of-phase TEs, do not allow for flexible echo spacing and selection of TEs, and face challenges when unwrapping large phase errors (greater than 2π) [1]. Allowing for flexible choices of echo times can improve the effective number of signals averaged (NSA) for fitting the signal model to calculate fat and water images [68]. For example, with three echoes, the optimal choice of echo times would be such that the fat-water phase difference accrued between echoes is $2\pi/3$ [68]. This can improve the SNR for signal model fitting and reduce fat-water swaps.

A method known as direct phase encoding was developed to support more flexible choices of echo times, but is still limited to equal echo spacing [1,69]. Many tissues in the body contain either fat-dominant or water-dominant tissues. For pixels with negligible contributions of either fat or water, region growing is utilized in the reconstruction steps of direct phase encoding to decipher the pixels containing only fat from the pixels containing only water [69]. Note that including region growing in the fat/water separation complicates the reconstruction and increases the reconstruction time [1].

The Iterative Decomposition of water and fat with Echo Asymmetry and Least squares estimation (IDEAL) method is a complex fitting method developed to combat phase wrapping challenges [70,72]. The IDEAL method iteratively linearizes a nonlinear problem to solve for fat and water images. This is advantageous as it allows for arbitrary echo times and thus more flexible acquisitions which may improve SNR for signal model fitting. The IDEAL method can also be extended to consider confounding factors, such as the multipeak spectrum of fat and T_2^* bias, for fat quantification [72,73]. However, there are also limitations of this method. The IDEAL method tries to linearize a nonlinear problem, where there are multiple local minima or solutions to the equation. The solution for the field map is dependent on the initial guess [1]. Thus, region growing algorithms are often used to refine the initial guess of the field map [74]. System imperfections can lead to additional phase errors that are not considered in the signal model and can lead to fat/water swaps or quantification errors. In addition, applying a stringent constraint on B_0 field map variations by enforcing smoothness of the field map in regions with large spatial variations can lead to errors [70,71].

Since the development of IDEAL, advanced complex fitting algorithms using graph cut approaches to improve the field map estimation [62–65] have been developed for fat-water separation and quantification. Graph-cut algorithms have a less stringent requirement on field map smoothness to allow for more rapid field variations [63–65]. Advanced magnitude-based fitting methods [75] have also been developed and are more robust to phase errors and can avoid the field map challenges of complex fitting. However, magnitude-based fitting has lower SNR for solving for fat and water due to the removal of phase information [76]. When they are carefully implemented, both complex and magnitude-based algorithms can achieve high accuracy for fat-water separation and fat quantification.

27.3.2 CSE-MRI pulse sequences

Spin echo [71] and gradient echo (GRE) [73,76,78–80] based CSE-MRI sequences have been used to acquire data at multiple TEs for fat-water separation and fat quantification (see Section 27.3.3). However, spin echo sequences are not commonly used clinically for fat quantification because this type of acquisition can be time consuming and the desired echo spacing for quantification may not be achievable. Either single echo acquisitions repeated multiple times at different TEs or multiecho acquisitions (multiple TEs in each TR) can be used to acquire data for CSE-MRI. Single echo acquisitions are more robust to system imperfections, such as phase errors due to gradient delays, eddy currents, and other effects; however, they require significantly longer acquisition times due to the need for multiple single echo scans, and are challenging to perform for scans that require breath-holding.

Multiecho techniques have a shorter acquisition time for the same imaging parameters and can be further categorized into monopolar (unipolar) and bipolar readouts (Fig. 27.11). Compared to bipolar readouts, monopolar readouts are more robust to system imperfections but require additional fly-back gradients and thereby increase echo spacing (ΔTE) and repetition time (TR) [81–83]. Bipolar readouts are more efficient than monopolar readouts because they allow for shorter echo spacing per TR [81–83], which can improve the signal-to-noise ratio efficiency for fitting to the signal model. However, bipolar readouts are more sensitive to phase errors due to system imperfections and require phase correction techniques [81–83] or fitting algorithms that are robust to phase errors.

27.3.3 Fat quantification using CSE-MRI

To quantify fat and water content based on CSE-MRI, it is necessary to consider and address the various factors that influence the acquired MRI signals. After addressing confounding factors, quantitative PDFF [3,40] can be calculated.

27.3.3.1 Signal model

The simplified fat-water model in Eq. (27.2) only considers the apparent water (W) and fat (F) signals. It is possible to calculate the signal fat fraction (SFF) $= F/(W + F)$ in each voxel as a first step towards quantification. However, W and F are actually influenced by numerous factors and the measured SFF would vary when the sequence type or parameters change.

The most commonly used sequence for fat-water imaging and quantification is the RF-spoiled GRE sequence, and its steady-state signal (S) is:

$$S(TE) = \left(\sum_{j=1}^{N} \frac{\rho_j e^{i\alpha_j} e^{-\frac{TE}{T_{2,j}^*}} \left(1 - e^{-\frac{TR}{T_{1,j}}}\right) \sin(\theta)}{1 - e^{-\frac{TR}{T_{1,j}}} \cos(\theta)} \right) e^{i\phi_{off}} e^{i\phi_0} \quad (27.18)$$

where ϕ_{off} describes the off-resonance phase due to main field B_0 inhomogeneity, ϕ_0 is the bulk phase offset due to other sources, ρ_j is the proton density for a chemical species j (total number of chemical species N), $T_{1,j}$ and $T_{2,j}^*$ are relaxation parameters of the chemical shift species j, α_j is the phase difference due to the chemical shift for the species j relative to water protons, θ is the flip angle used to acquire the data, TE is the echo time, and TR is the repetition time.

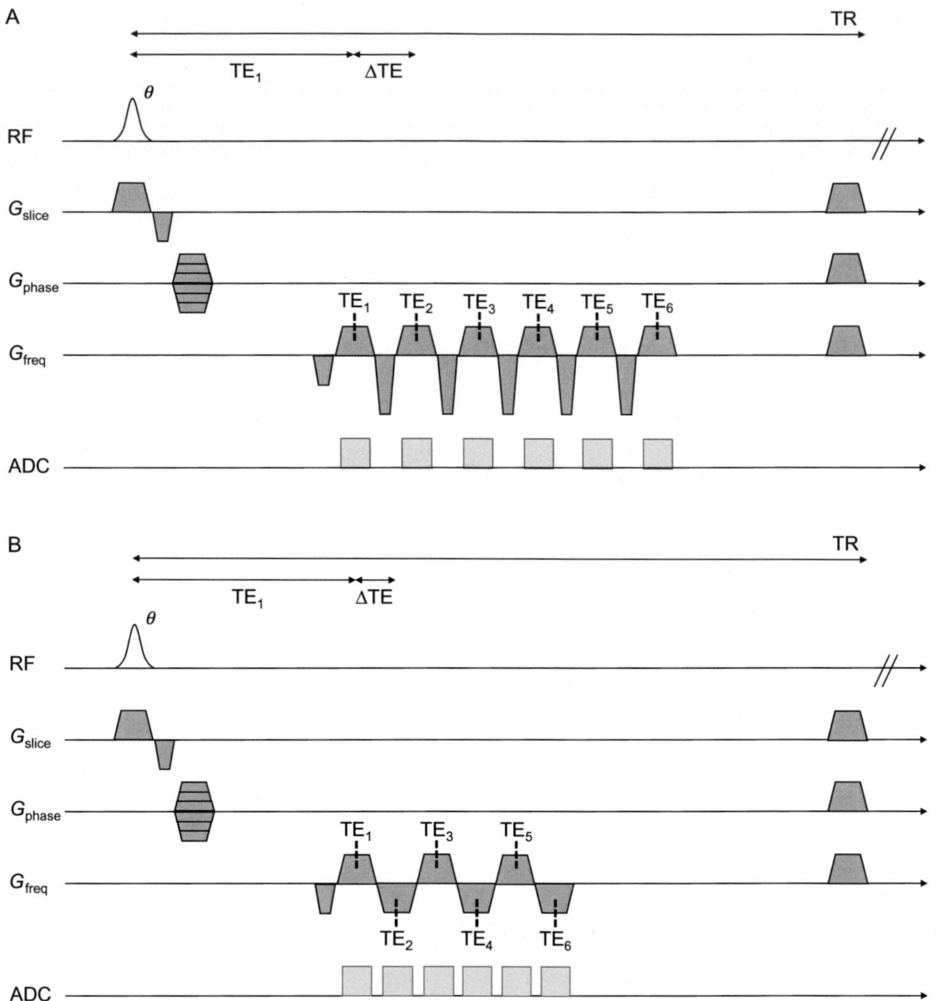

FIG. 27.11

Multiecho gradient echo (GRE) MRI sequence diagram using (A) monopolar (unipolar) and (B) bipolar readout gradients. RF, radiofrequency; θ, flip angle; G_{slice}, slice select gradient; G_{phase}, phase encoding gradient; G_{freq}, frequency encoding gradient; ADC, analog to digital converter; TE, echo time; ΔTE, echo time spacing; TR, repetition time.

When the effects of $T_{1,j}$ are removed or accounted for, and a single effective $T_2{}^*$ is assumed, the signal model for a GRE sequence in a single voxel r with water proton density ρ_W and fat proton density ρ_F becomes:

$$S_r(TE) = \left(\rho_{W,r} + \rho_{F,r} c_F\right) e^{-\frac{TE}{T_{2,r}{}^*}} e^{i\phi_{off,r}} \tag{27.19}$$

where $c_F = \sum_{j=1}^{N_f} A_j e^{i2\pi f_j \mathrm{TE}}$, N_f indicates the number of peaks in the fat spectrum, and A_j and f_j are the relative amplitudes and chemical shift frequencies of components j in the fat spectrum (typically calibrated a priori).

By accounting for confounding factors, fat-water separation would yield maps of ρ_W and ρ_F, which are used to compute PDFF $= \rho_F/(\rho_W + \rho_F)$ [40]. Eq. (27.19) is the signal model used for computing PDFF in clinical CSE-MRI applications using GRE sequences, and is used in all the examples in the remainder of this section. Many fat-water signal fitting methods can be used to solve for ρ_W, ρ_F, and ϕ_{off} (see Section 27.3.1). An example of a PDFF map calculated by fitting signals collected at six echo times to the signal model and addressing confounding factors in a patient is shown in Fig. 27.12. Specific considerations for each factor are discussed in the following subsections.

27.3.3.2 Multipeak fat spectrum

A single peak fat model assumes a single spectral peak at 3.5 ppm relative to water, which is the largest peak in the multipeak fat spectrum (see Section 27.2). In the Dixon methods, echo times are chosen to achieve in-phase and out-of-phase signals based on this single fat peak [1,50]. However, all of the peaks in the fat spectrum (see Section 27.2) need to be considered to accurately quantify the PDFF. Recall from Section 27.2, a single fat peak at 3.5 ppm relative to water only accounts for approximately 70% of the total fat signal. An a priori multipeak fat spectrum can be calibrated by MRS and used in the CSE-MRI signal model to achieve accurate fat quantification. Commonly used fat spectral models for liver fat quantification include a 7-peak model [13] and a 6-peak model [12]. As long as a reasonable multipeak fat model is used for quantification, the choice of specific multipeak fat model will not have a significant impact on the PDFF results [83]. Several fitting algorithms (see Section 27.3.1) can be adapted to support either a multipeak or a single peak fat spectral model.

27.3.3.3 T_2 or T_2^* bias

Fat and water have different inherent T_2 and T_2^* relaxation properties (see Section 27.1). Without accounting for $T_2 = 1/R_2$ or $T_2^* = 1/R_2^*$, the calculation of PDFF will be inaccurate [73,76,86–88]. By using the signal models in Eqs. (27.18), (27.19), the T_2^* decay affecting GRE signals can be accounted for by assuming either a single effective R_2^* or dual R_2^* (fat R_2^* and water R_2^*) model per voxel [85,76]. Although a dual R_2^* model better represents the underlying physics, dual R_2^* methods are more sensitive to noise and the fitting can become unstable, which negatively impacts the ability of this model to quantify fat and R_2^* accurately [73,76,86–88]. Because of these considerations, the majority of models used for PDFF quantification currently specify a single effective R_2^* for each voxel (Eq. 27.19).

27.3.3.4 T_1 bias

Fat and water have different inherent T_1 values (see Section 27.1). Therefore, the PDFF determined by the separation of water and fat using a signal equation that does not account for T_1 will be overestimated [75,84] due to the shorter inherent T_1 values for fat compared to water [75,84,86–88]. For GRE sequences, bias in PDFF due to fat and water T_1 differences can be addressed by using a low flip angle [75,84,86–88], long TR, or by incorporating T_1 mapping [84,86,88,89]. Fig. 27.13 shows the effect of T_1 bias on liver PDFF maps calculated from RF-spoiled GRE images acquired at various flip angles.

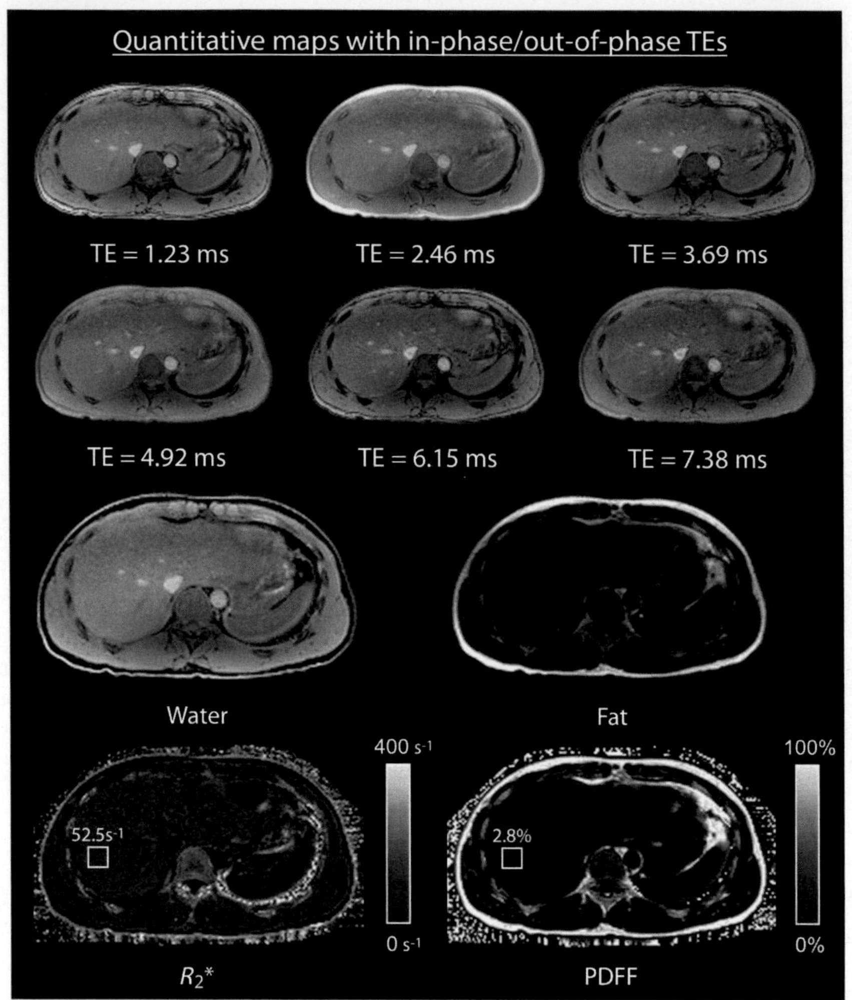

FIG. 27.12

Water images, fat images, and R_2* and proton-density fat fraction (PDFF) [0%–100%] maps calculated using a breath-held axial RF-spoiled 3D gradient echo sequence at 3T with six echo times in a healthy subject reconstructed on the MRI scanner using mixed complex and magnitude-based fitting.

27.3.3.5 Noise bias

Noise bias can lead to an overestimation of PDFF in areas with low fat content [84,88]. Noise bias can be minimized by using magnitude discrimination to calculate the PDFF as $[1 - \rho_W/(\rho_W + \rho_F)]$ in areas of low fat content [84,88].

27.3.3.6 Signal fitting considerations

Six echoes (or more) are typically acquired to ensure reliable fitting of the fat signal model (e.g., Eq. 27.19). Both complex-based and magnitude-based methods for fat-water signal fitting (see Section 27.3.1) can be used to calculate the fat and water content in each voxel for fat quantification.

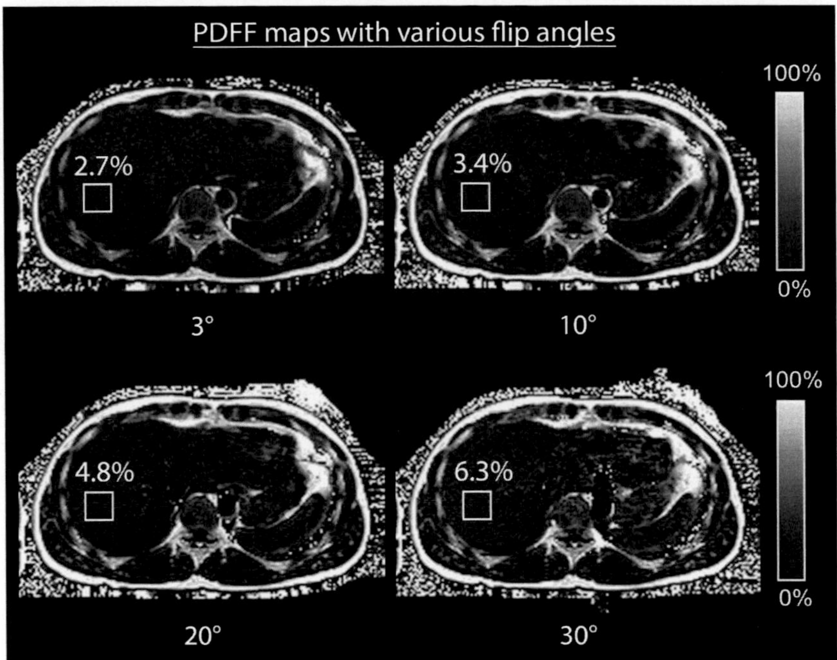

FIG. 27.13

Proton-density fat fraction (PDFF) [0%–100%] maps calculated using a breath-held axial RF-spoiled 3D gradient-echo sequence acquired at 3T in a healthy volunteer with various flip angles (3°, 10°, 20°, and 30°). In this example, using a 30° flip angle resulted in an overestimation in PDFF compared to using a 3° flip angle due to the effect of T_1.

Because the phase information is removed, magnitude-based fitting can only resolve the difference between fat and water for PDFF $\leq$50% [84,76]. In contrast, complex-based fitting algorithms have higher SNR for solving for fat and water and can solve for the entire range of PDFF [0, 100%]; however, they are more sensitive to phase errors due to system imperfections and are sensitive to noise bias that can hinder quantification [84,76].

To overcome the respective limitations and combine the advantages of complex-based and magnitude-based methods, mixed (or hybrid) magnitude-complex-based [60,77,90] fitting algorithms have been proposed. Mixed fitting is more robust to phase errors due to system imperfections, noise bias, and can solve for the entire range of fat fraction [0%, 100%] [60,77,90] and are now used clinically (Figs. 27.12–27.14).

27.3.3.7 Quantitative fat measurements

By accounting for the key confounding factors [4,40,84], the separated fat and water images represent ρ_W and ρ_F and can be used to quantify PDFF [40,91,92]. A multivendor, multisite and multiple field strength study in a quantitative fat fraction phantom concluded that CSE-MRI PDFF is accurate and reproducible across sites, vendors, field strengths and protocols [93]. Moreover, a meta-analysis concluded that CSE-MRI PDFF demonstrated excellent linearity, bias, and precision across vendors, field strengths, and reconstruction methods [92]. PDFF can be used for many applications that require fat quantification, such as evaluating fatty liver disease [3,84] and analyzing body composition [94–97].

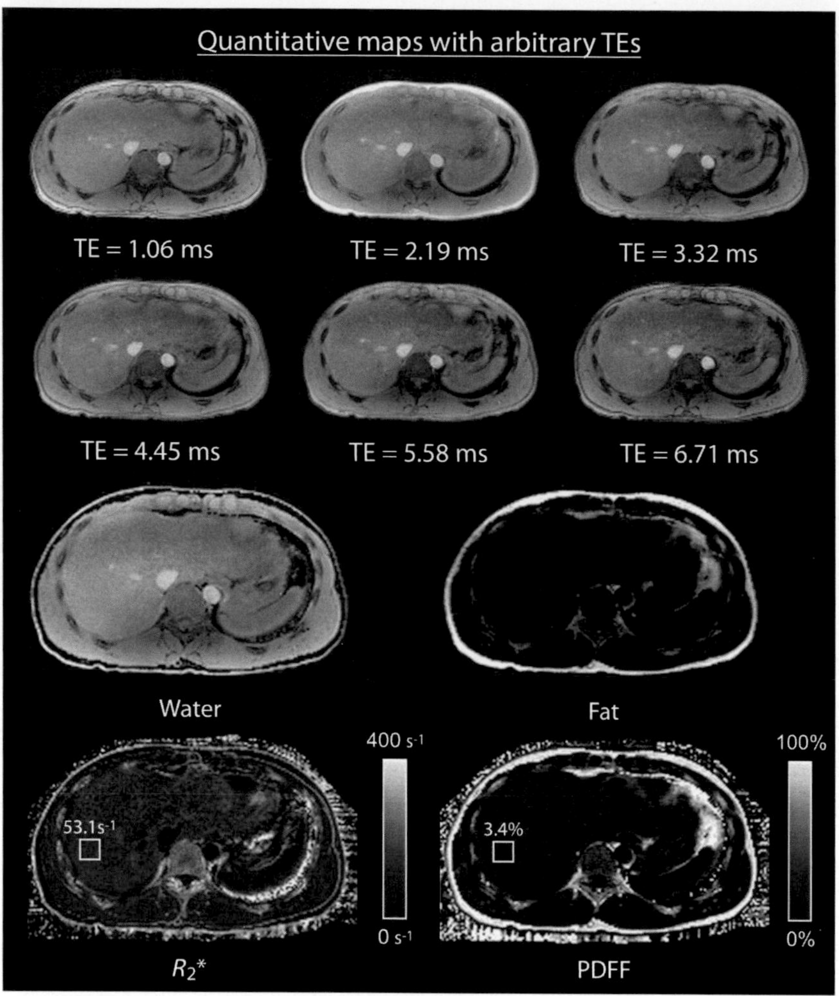

FIG. 27.14

Individual echo time images from a breath-held axial 3D MRI of the liver acquired at 3T. PDFF and $R_2{}^*$ are subsequently calculated from the data using a mixed complex and magnitude-based fitting algorithm for the same subject in Fig. 27.12. TE, echo time; PDFF, proton-density fat fraction.

MRS is also used to quantify liver PDFF and is accurate compared to the gold standard, histopathology [25,42,46]. However, MRS is limited by spatial sampling bias [25,42,46]. CSE-MRI PDFF has been shown to achieve accurate quantification compared to the noninvasive reference MRS [43,45,98–100] and the gold standard histopathology in patients with fatty liver disease [99,101] and in ex vivo livers [99]. Using histopathology as a reference, CSE-MRI PDFF and MRS PDFF have higher sensitivity and specificity for diagnosing fatty liver disease compared to computed tomography and ultrasound [25]. CSE-MRI PDFF has also demonstrated strong repeatability and reproducibility for liver fat quantification in many studies [43,92,93,99,102]. Moreover, CSE-MRI PDFF showed stronger repeatability, intra-reader, and inter-reader agreement compared to histologic steatosis grading [99]. Table 27.4 summarizes recent studies evaluating the accuracy, repeatability, reproducibility, intra-reader, and inter-reader agreement of CSE-MRI PDFF.

27.3.4 Standardized phantoms

Phantoms containing compartments of known PDFF values are needed to develop, evaluate, and calibrate fat quantification techniques. Many types of oil, such as peanut oil, safflower oil, soya oil, and vegetable oil, can be used to design and construct PDFF phantoms. Of these several types of oils, peanut oil may be a desirable choice as its fat spectrum is similar to what has been observed in the subcutaneous fat of the human knee [72]. The simplest PDFF phantom design uses partial volume effects to achieve a range of PDFF values [104–107]. These phantoms are relatively easy to design and construct because they do not require creating a fat-water emulsion. However, because these phantoms are not emulsified, flow artifacts can affect quantification. To design a phantom with specific T_1, T_2, and T_2^* properties, gadolinium-based and iron-based contrast agents can be added to water. However, many of these agents are not soluble in oil and because of partial volume effects, designing a specific T_1, T_2, and T_2^* in a partial volume phantom is challenging. Emulsion phantoms have been designed to create fat and water emulsions with various PDFF, T_1, T_2, and T_2^* values. A popular design was first developed by Bernard et al. [107] and modified by Hines et al. [73] and includes deionized water, oil to represent fat, gadolinium-based and/or iron-based contrast agents, a surfactant to emulsify the oil and water solution, agar or carrageenan to gelatinize the emulsion, and/or a preservative to extend the life of the phantom [73,107].

Standardized PDFF phantoms have recently been developed by institutions and companies. For example, phantoms from Calimetrix (Fig. 27.15) [93] and the National Institute of Standards and Technology (NIST) (Fig. 27.16) [108], are constructed to validate fat quantification techniques. Using PDFF phantoms, multisite and multivendor studies have concluded that CSE-MRI PDFF quantification is accurate and reproducible across sites, vendors, 1.5 T and 3 T scanners, and protocols [93].

27.4 Emerging CSE-MRI techniques for fat quantification

A better understanding of the fat-water signal model and adoption of PDFF as a quantitative biomarker (see Section 27.3) over the past few years has launched CSE-MRI into the mainstream for clinical inquiry and research of fat in the human body. Nevertheless, the requirements of acquiring additional data (multiple TEs) with volumetric coverage and robustly fitting the fat-water signal model places constraints on the achievable imaging parameters and the applications in different patient populations. New CSE-MRI acquisition and reconstruction techniques are being developed to improve robustness to motion, reduce scan time, and enable further quantification of fatty acid composition.

27.4.1 Free-breathing Cartesian CSE-MRI fat quantification techniques

Conventional CSE-MRI fat quantification techniques [1–5] typically employ Cartesian trajectories [2–5, 73, 79, 80, 110–117] because of their reduced sensitivity to phase errors caused by system imperfections and straightforward Fourier-transform image reconstruction. In the presence of motion, however, Cartesian methods can exhibit motion-induced coherent aliasing artifacts, which degrade

Table 27.4 Summary of linearity, precision, repeatability, reproducibility, intra-reader and inter-reader agreement results from studies evaluating chemical-shift-encoded MRI for quantification of PDFF.

Paper	Number of sites	Vendor	Field strength	Number of subjects	Readout gradient	Number of echoes	Delta TE	Linearity	Bias	Repeatability	Reproducibility	Intra-reader agreement	Inter-reader agreement
Hernando 2017 [93]	6	GE Healthcare, Siemens, Phillips	1.5 T and 3 T	Phantom	Monopolar and bipolar	3–6	~2 ms (1.5 T) ~1 ms (3 T)	$R^2 > 0.995$ (true PDFF with Calimetrix phantom)	MD = 0.22% [0.7%–0.38%] (True PDFF with Calimetrix Phantom)		ICC = 0.999 (vendors, sites, field strength, and protocols)		
Kim 2018 [100]	1	GE Healthcare	1.5 T and 3 T	$N = 20$ adults with NAFLD and a phantom	Not specified	6	1.3 ms (1.5 T) 0.8 ms (3 T)	$R^2 \geq 0.985$ (MRS), $R^2 \geq$ 0.996 (3 T vs. 1.5 T)	MD = -3.4% [-8.9%, 2.1%] (MRS)	RC ≤ 1.5% (1.5 T) RC < 2.0% (3 T)	RC ≤ 2.5% (1.5 T and 3 T) RC < 3.0% (across field strengths)	ICC = 0.998–0.999	ICC = 0.999
Tyagi 2015 [43]	1	GE Healthcare	3 T	$N = 20$ pediatric, $N = 9$ adults (overweight and obese)	Not specified	6	0.8 and 1.15 ms	$R^2 \geq 0.986$ (MRS)	MD = 1.61% (magnitude fitting) (MRS) MD = 0.40% (complex fitting) (MRS)	ICC ≥ 0.997	ICC ≥ 0.992		
Kramer 2017 [98]	1	GE Healthcare	1.5 T	$N = 19$ healthy, $N = 17$ overweight, $N = 14$ obese	Monopolar	6	1.98 ms	$R^2 \geq 0.992$ (MRS)					
Middleton 2017 [101]	7	GE Healthcare, Siemens	1.5 T and 3 T	$N = 113$ adults with NASH	Not Specified	6	2.3 ms (1.5 T) 1.15 ms (3 T)	$R^2 = 0.64$ (histopathology)					
Bannas 2015 [99]	1	GE Healthcare	1.5 T	$N = 13$ ex vivo liver (9 segments)	Monopolar	6	1.98 ms	$R^2 = 0.968$ (MRS) $R^2 = 0.723$ (histopathology) $R^2 = 0.759$ (biochemical triglyceride extraction)		MD = 1.0%		MD = 0.9%	MD = -0.7%
Artz 2015 [45]	1	GE Healthcare	1.5 T and 3 T	$N = 24$ obese	Not specified (2D) Monopolar (3D)	6	2.3 ms (1.5 T, 2D) 1.15ms (3 T, 2D) 2 ms (1.5 T, 3D) 1 ms (3 T, 3D)	$R^2 \geq 0.94$ (MRS)	MD ≤ 2.9% (MRS)				
Sofue 2015 [102]	1	Siemens	3 T	$N = 150$ patients	Bipolar	6	1.23 ms			|MD| = 0.03%	| MD | < 0.84%, ICC > 0.979 (for R_2^* and PDFF)		ICC2 ≥ 0.9
Yokoo 2018 [92]	28 studies	GE Healthcare, Siemens, Phillips	1.5 T and 3 T	$N = 1909$	Monopolar and Bipolar	6		$R^2 = 0.96$ (MRS)	MD = -0.13 [3.95%, 3.40%] (MRS)	RC = 2.99%	RC = 4.12%		

R^2, coefficient of determination; MD, mean difference; MRS, magnetic resonance spectroscopy; ICC, intra-class correlation coefficient; RC, repeatability coefficient; NAFLD, non-alcoholic fatty liver disease; NASH, non-alcoholic steatohepatitis

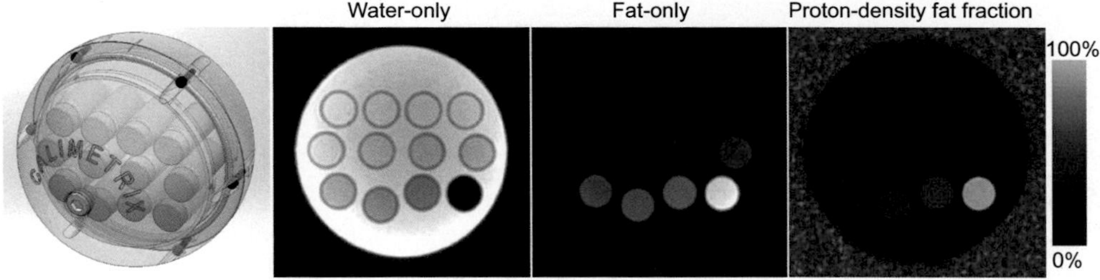

FIG. 27.15

Quantitative complex chemical-shift-encoded MRI of a commercial spherical fat fraction phantom (Calimetrix, Madison WI, left), with separate water and fat images, and the proton-density fat fraction (PDFF) maps. The 12-vial phantom includes PDFF values of 0, 2.5%, 5%, 7.5%, 10%, 15%, 20%, 25%, 30%, 40%, 50%, and 100%.

Figure courtesy of Diego Hernando, PhD, Jean Brittain, PhD, and Scott Reeder, MD, PhD, University of Wisconsin.

image quality and negatively impact fat quantification accuracy. Therefore, Cartesian MRI acquisitions in the abdomen are performed during a 10–20 s breath-hold to mitigate motion artifacts. By limiting the scan time to fit within a breath-hold, the spatial coverage, resolution and/or SNR may be reduced. Many populations such as children, infants, elderly patients, patients with chronic diseases, or patients with disabilities may have limited or no breath-hold ability. In particular, infants and children often have more voluntary and involuntary motion than adults, and children may not be able to comply with scan instructions [118–120].

Free-breathing MRI techniques using Cartesian trajectories have been developed to mitigate motion artifacts in the abdomen. These techniques include respiratory gating using bellows [120,121], MRI-based navigators [120], and MRI-based self-navigation [122,123]. Respiratory gating with bellows involves fastening a belt-like apparatus around the chest or abdomen. This device can detect breathing motion by the mechanical stretching of the device. Repiratory gating using bellows requires proper placement of the bellows device and its effectiveness may be limited in patients with irregular respiratory cycles [120]. MRI-based navigators detect breathing motion by acquiring signals along the direction where motion is expected (typically along the superior-inferior direction for breathing motion). Respiratory gating and navigators can be applied prospectively to determine when to acquire MRI data, or retrospectively to remove data corrupted by motion or bin data into different motion states during reconstruction. A limitation of performing these techniques prospectively is that the acquisition times may vary and may be lengthy when the respiratory pattern has variations [121]. Navigation also requires additional scan time to acquire the navigator signals. MRI-based self-navigation utilizes the data acquired for imaging as a tool for navigation and additional acquisition of navigator data is not required. Due to the potential for reduced scan time compared to navigators or respiratory gating, self-navigation may be beneficial for many applications.

Motion detection and compensation using free-breathing navigator and self-navigation techniques with Cartesian trajectories have been investigated for fat quantification [120,122]. One study using navigators and one study using self-navigation for motion compensation demonstrated accurate hepatic fat quantification compared to breath-held techniques [120,122]. However, respiratory gating or self-navigation can be technically challenging and may fail in cases when breathing is heavy or irregular [118,120]. Due to these limitations, these techniques may not perform well in all patient populations. In particular, children may have anxiety during the MRI procedure, resulting in heavy or irregular breathing, or even noncompliance with operator instructions [118,120].

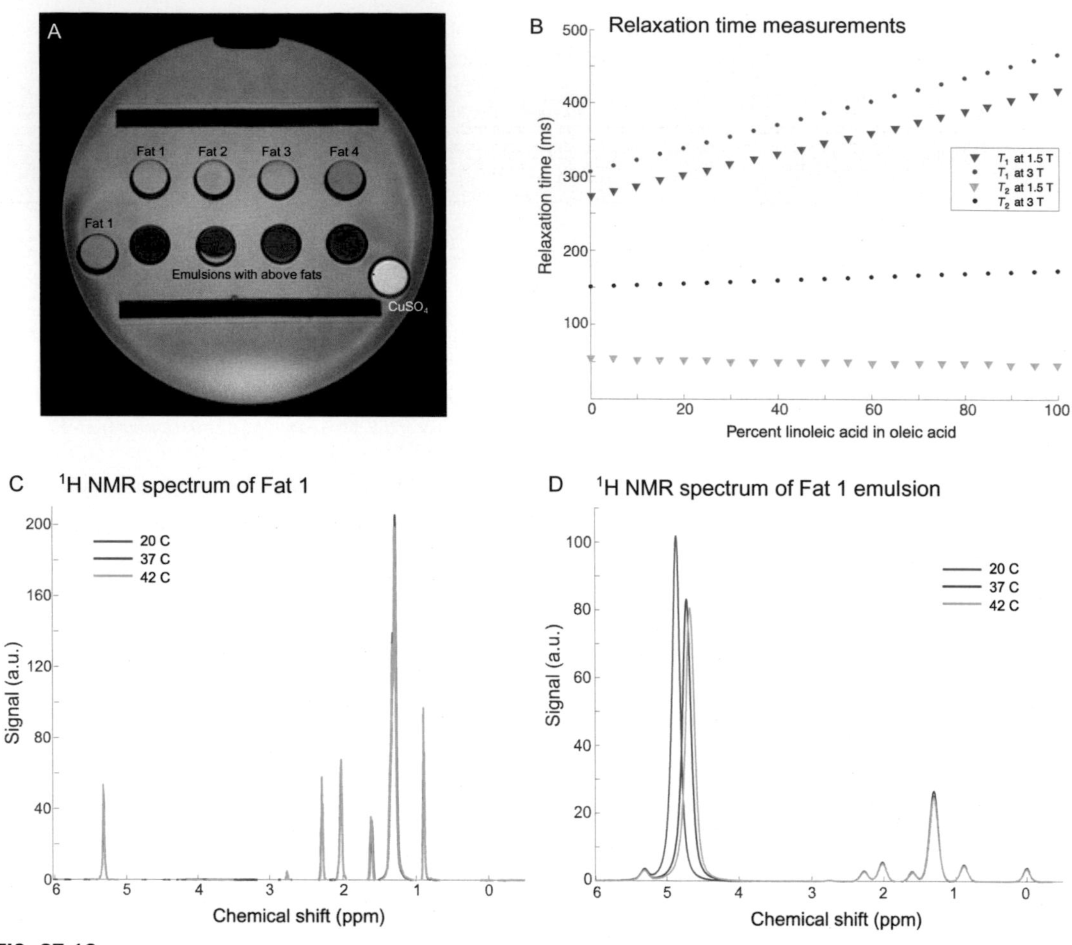

FIG. 27.16

Quantitative fat fraction phantom developed at the National Institute of Standards and Technology (NIST). Gradient echo MR image of oleic and linoleic acid fat mimics and water-fat emulsions created with 30% of the corresponding fat mimic and 70% water (A). The fat mimics shown here include a range of oleic/linoleic acid ratios: Fat 1 is 72.9% oleic, 27.1% linoleic; Fat 2 is 21.9% oleic, 78.1% linoleic; Fat 3 is 20.3% oleic, 79.7% linoleic; and Fat 4 is 45.0% oleic, 55.0% linoleic. The T_1 relaxation time increases with increasing linoleic acid content (B), measured at 20°C. Finally, the ^{1}H NMR spectra of the fat mimics, acquired at 14 T, are invariant with temperature, as expected (C) and the emulsions demonstrate the expected shift from the water peak (D). The observed peak at 0 ppm is 4,4-dimethyl-4-silapentane-1-sulfonic acid, which serves as a frequency reference. Of note, the water peak shifts with temperature, as expected.

Figure courtesy of NIST.

Recently, a motion-robust 2D sequential CSE-MRI technique has been investigated for free-breathing hepatic fat quantification in adults [124]. Compared to 2D interleaved CSE-MRI, 3D CSE-MRI, and MRS, the 2D sequential CSE-MRI technique accurately quantified hepatic fat during free-breathing in a patient population [124]. Further work must be done to investigate these techniques in other populations with limited breath-hold ability.

27.4.2 Free-breathing non-Cartesian CSE-MRI fat quantification techniques

For populations that have limited breath-hold ability, non-Cartesian trajectories offer a desirable alternative to Cartesian trajectories. Non-Cartesian trajectories (examples in Fig. 27.17) have a greater inherent robustness to motion compared to Cartesian trajectories due to their dispersed distribution of motion artifacts (examples in Figs. 27.18 and 27.19) [107,126–128]. These trajectories have considerably less obtrusive motion artifacts that do not obscure the anatomy of interest even while data is acquired during free-breathing and all the data is used for reconstruction [107,126–128]. Therefore, non-Cartesian MRI can be performed during free-breathing to achieve higher spatial resolutions, larger volumetric coverage, and/or higher SNR. Non-Cartesian trajectories such as radial [107,129–131], spiral [132–134], PROPELLER [134,135], and concentric rings [136] have been investigated for fat-water separation, but thus far only the 3D stack-of-radial (also called stack-of-stars) trajectory has been investigated for fat quantification [106,126].

In order to utilize non-Cartesian trajectories for fat quantification, system imperfections [106,137] such as gradient delays, eddy current effects, and phase errors, must be addressed. Non-Cartesian trajectories are also susceptible to B_0 off-resonance and chemical shift artifacts [129], which can impact fat-water separation and quantification. Unlike in Cartesian trajectories where chemical shift causes a shift of the fat signal in image space, in non-Cartesian trajectories, chemical shift causes blurring of the fat signal [129]. Off-resonance and chemical shift artifacts can be corrected using k-space

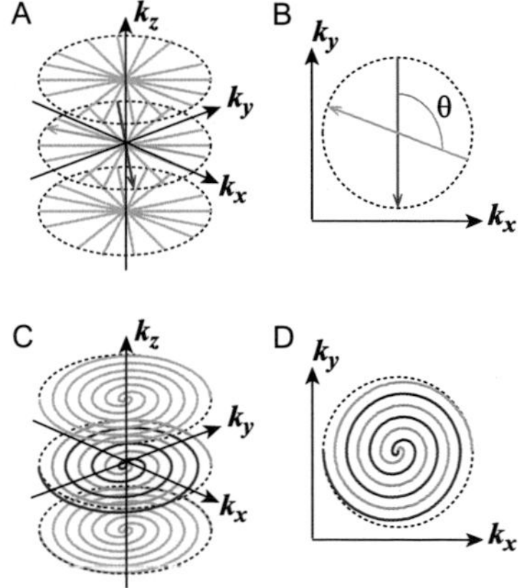

FIG. 27.17

(A and B) 3D stack-of-radial or stack-of-stars trajectories. (A) Radial spokes are acquired along the partition encoded direction k_z prior to (B) rotation by the azimuthal angle (θ). (C and D) 3D stack-of-spiral trajectory.

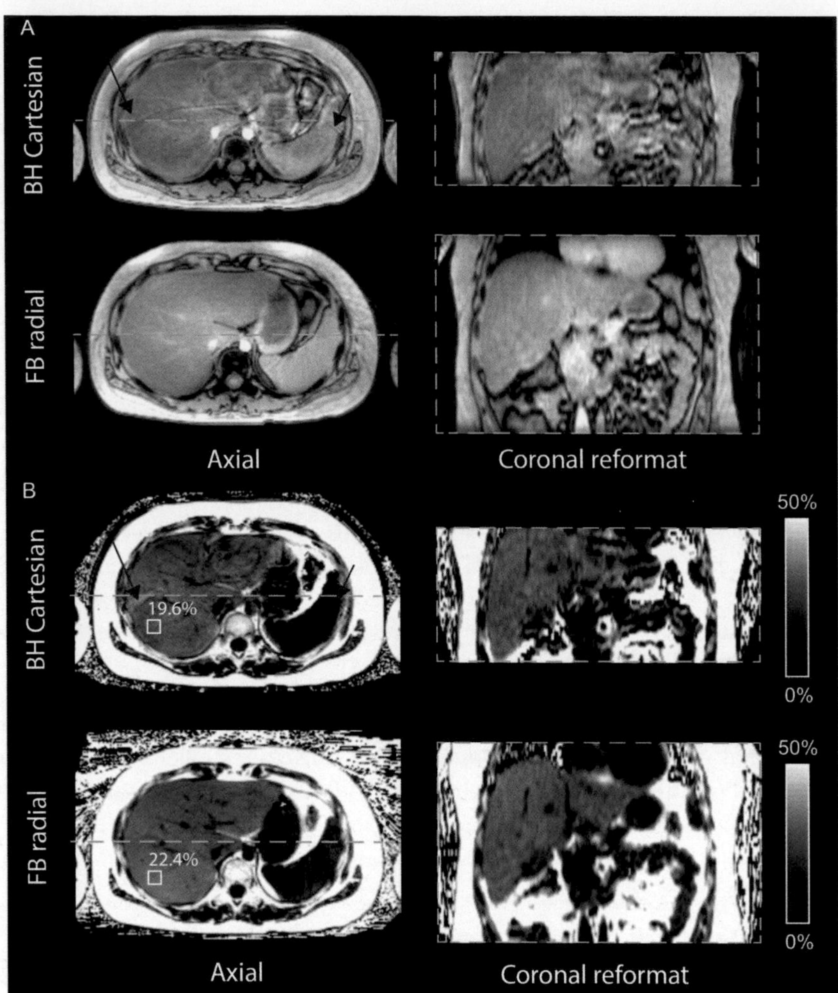

FIG. 27.18

Examples of breath-held (BH) 3D Cartesian and free-breathing (FB) 3D stack-of-radial chemical-shift-encoded MRI at 3T from a pediatric subject (15years old, female, body mass index=35.2kg/m^2) with nonalcoholic fatty liver disease. (A) Source images with echo time of 1.23ms. (B) Proton-density fat fraction (PDFF) maps. Axial and coronal reformats are shown. Arrows point to motion-induced coherent aliasing artifacts in the images and PDFF maps for the BH Cartesian scan.

decomposition of the signal model [129] and/or by using a large readout bandwidth such that off-resonance and chemical shift blurring is confined within a voxel.

The free-breathing 3D stack-of-radial trajectory (FB radial) has shown promising results for CSE-MRI PDFF quantification in adults and children [106,126]. To ensure accurate quantification of PDFF, this technique incorporates gradient error calibration and correction for the bipolar multiecho radial data. In a study of healthy adults, a 3–4min FB radial scan achieved accurate PDFF quantification compared to conventional breath-held 3D Cartesian CSE-MRI and breath-held MRS techniques [106].

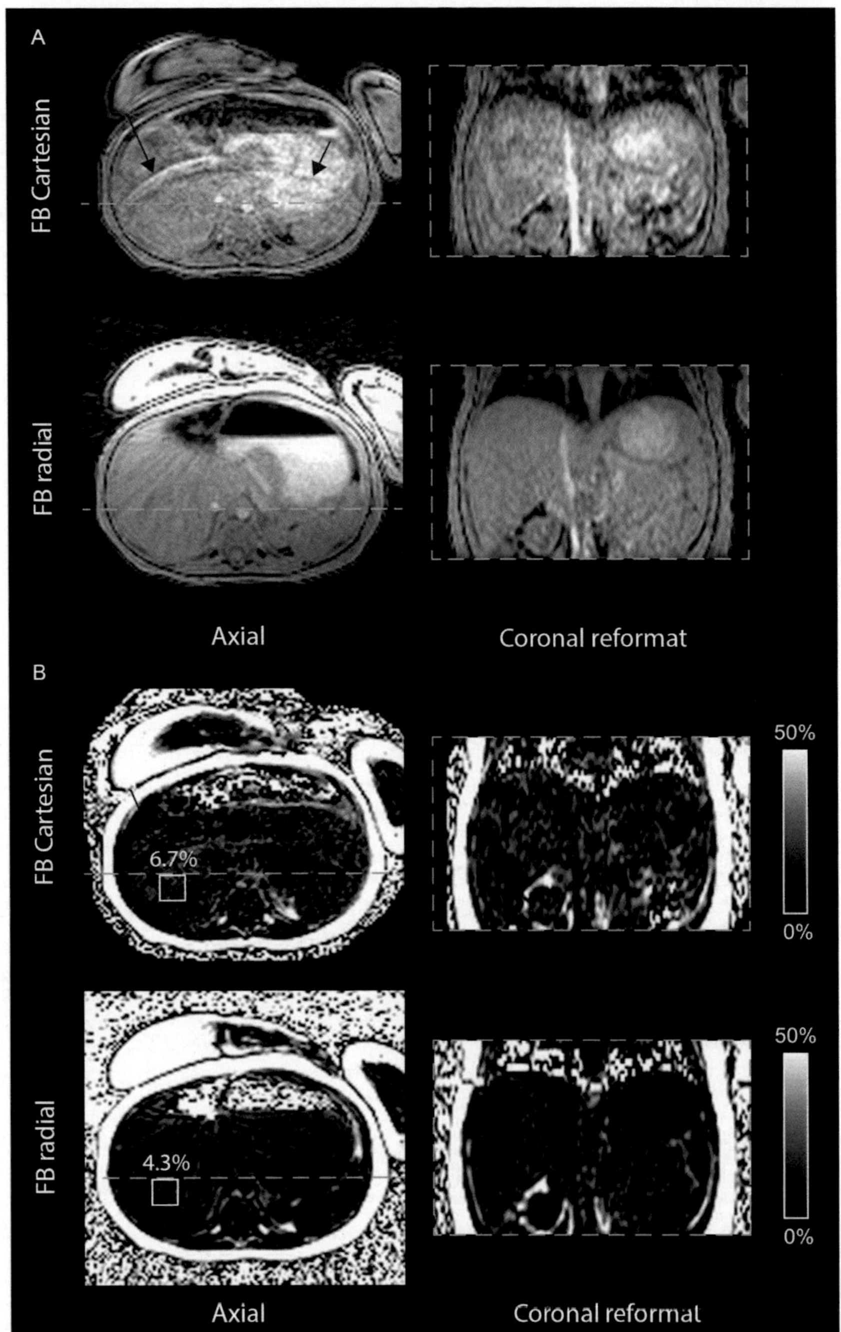

FIG. 27.19

Examples of free-breathing (FB) 3D Cartesian and FB 3D stack-of-radial chemical-shift-encoded MRI at 3T from an infant (2.3 months, male, 7.1 kg). (A) Source images with echo time of 1.23 ms. (B) Proton-density fat fraction (PDFF) maps. Axial and coronal reformats are shown. Arrows point to motion-induced coherent aliasing artifacts in the images and PDFF maps for the Cartesian scan.

By using golden-angle ordering, the 3D stack-of-radial trajectory allows for flexible reconstruction of an arbitrary number of radial views and improves the undersampling characteristics of the FB radial acquisition to reduce scan time. In a recent study [106], twofold and threefold accelerated FB radial scans with a reduced scan time of approximately 2 and 1.5 min, respectively, achieved accurate PDFF quantification in healthy adults compared to breath-held 3D Cartesian CSE-MRI techniques: Lin's concordance correlation coefficient and Pearson's correlation coefficient were significant and >0.98 and the absolute mean difference between radial and Cartesian PDFF was approximately 1%.

The accuracy and repeatability of the FB radial technique for liver PDFF quantification was also evaluated in healthy children and children with nonalcoholic fatty liver disease (NAFLD). FB radial was shown to be accurate, with Lin's concordance correlation coefficient and Pearson's correlation coefficient >0.99 with respect to conventional breath-held 3D Cartesian CSE-MRI and breath-held MRS [126]. FB radial achieved repeatable PDFF quantification with a coefficient of repeatability of <2% [126]. Along with fat quantification accuracy and repeatability, this promising FB radial CSE-MRI technique has shown improved image quality compared to breath-held 3D Cartesian CSE-MRI in children with NAFLD [126]. An example of breath-held Cartesian and free-breathing radial images collected at a TE of 1.23 ms and PDFF maps in a child with NAFLD is shown in Fig. 27.18. Breath-held Cartesian images can have coherent aliasing artifacts even while a breath-hold is performed; in contrast, FB radial imaging shows improved image quality with no coherent aliasing artifacts (Fig. 27.18).

Recently, the FB radial method has also been evaluated for PDFF quantification in infants, a population that cannot perform breath-holding [96]. In infants without sedation, FB radial images demonstrated improved image quality compared to free-breathing 3D Cartesian images and showed a coefficient of repeatability of <2% for liver PDFF quantification. Free-breathing Cartesian and free-breathing radial images and PDFF maps in an infant are shown in Fig. 27.19. In this study, all free-breathing Cartesian scans were scored as nondiagnostic by an experienced pediatric radiologist. FB radial improved the image quality in children with NAFLD and infants who have limited or no breath-hold ability, and may be extended to other populations that cannot perform a breath-hold.

The 3D stack-of-radial trajectory samples the center of *k*-space during the acquisition of each radial view or spoke (Fig. 27.17). Data from the center of *k*-space ($k_x = k_y = k_z = 0$), or a set of points along the k_z axis ($k_x = k_y = 0$), can be used to generate a self-navigation signal for motion detection and compensation [131,140–142]. Motion compensation techniques can be used to further improve free-breathing image quality by reducing blurring and radial streaking artifacts [107,131,140–142]. These advantages make FB radial a desirable technique for quantifying fat in organs with motion and in difficult populations with limited breath-hold ability or are unable to breath-hold.

27.4.3 Advanced CSE-MRI reconstruction and signal modeling

The additional time required to collect images at multiple TEs in CSE-MRI prolongs the clinical protocol time and increases the potential sensitivity to motion artifacts. Scan acceleration methods aim to reduce the acquisition time to achieve shorter breath-hold durations and minimize motion sensitivity. After acquiring undersampled *k*-space data, advanced reconstruction techniques, such as parallel imaging, can be used to fill in missing *k*-space data. Due to the breath-hold scan time limitation, fully sampled clinical abdominal scans are typically performed using 2D single or multislice Cartesian acquisitions. In order to enable 3D Cartesian CSE-MRI scans, twofold or fourfold acceleration is needed and these acquisitions are reconstructed using parallel imaging techniques such as generalized auto calibrating partially parallel acquisitions (GRAPPA) [141] or controlled aliasing in parallel imaging results in higher acceleration (CAIPIRINHA) [142]. A fourfold accelerated 3D Cartesian scan with CAIPIRHINIA reconstruction has shown good accuracy and high repeatability for quantifying liver PDFF and R_2^* [102,110]. The limitations of these acceleration techniques are that they can result in reconstruction errors due to inadequate coil sensitivity coverage (e.g., tissues in the center of the imaging volume, which are farther away from the coils).

Compressed sensing is another advanced reconstruction technique that can be used to accelerate CSE-MRI scans for PDFF quantification. Compressed sensing approaches acquire undersampled k-space data with incoherent undersampling artifacts and then exploit underlying data sparsity in a nonlinear reconstruction approach. Compressed sensing techniques have been applied to fat-water separation [143–145], but have not been well studied for fat quantification. Recently, new techniques have been developed to combine parallel imaging and compressed sensing, using both Cartesian and radial trajectories [130,140,146–150]. Although promising, only preliminary studies of quantitative performance have been performed [147,148]. Limitations of these techniques are that they are technically challenging and can also require longer reconstruction times. Other novel advanced MRI techniques, such as MR fingerprinting, can produce quantitative maps of multiple parameters from a single scan [151], and a recent technique combining MR Fingerprinting with dictionary-based fat-water separation showed accurate fat quantification compared to IDEAL [152,153]. However, these techniques are still in preliminary stages and require further investigation.

Extensions of the fat signal model are also being explored to enable the quantification of fatty acid composition in tissues. Advanced fat spectral signal modeling can be used to characterize the chemical structure of triglycerides by measuring carbon chain length, number of double bonds, and number of methylene-interrupted double bonds [33,47–49]. The MRI signal in voxel r can be described using the signal model:

$$S_r(t) = \left(\alpha_W \rho_{W,r} + c_F \rho_{F,r}\right) e^{-R_{2,r}^* t} e^{i\phi_{off,r}} \tag{27.20}$$

where

$$\alpha_W = \beta_W e^{i2\pi f_W t} \tag{27.21}$$

and

$$c_F = \sum_{j=1}^{n} \beta_j e^{i2\pi f_j t} \tag{27.22}$$

where $\beta_W = 2, f_W = 0$ Hz, $n = 9$ is the number of characterized fat hydrogen bonds, f_j is the chemical shift of each fat hydrogen bond in Hertz, and β_j represents the proton characteristics of each hydrogen bond in fat. See Eq. (27.19) for previously defined variables. The values for f_j and β_j have been characterized a priori and are shown in Table 27.5 and chain length and number of methylene-interrupted double bonds can be written as a function of the number of double bonds as shown in Eqs. (27.23), (27.24).

$$CL = 16.8 + 0.25 \times ndb \tag{27.23}$$

$$nmidb = 0.093 \times ndb^2 \tag{27.24}$$

During the disease progression of NAFLD, simple steatosis can progress to non-alcoholic steatohepatitis, which is characterized by fibrosis, cirhosis, and liver failure [154,155]. To distinguish between NAFLD and nonalcoholic steatohepatitis, a liver tissue biopsy is typically needed [156–159]. However, biopsies are invasive, can cause complications, and are limited by spatial sampling bias [156–159].

Table 27.5 The frequencies (f_j) at 3 T, and proton characteristics (β_j) for fat hydrogen bonds characterized in terms of the number of double bonds (ndb), number of methylene-interrupted double bonds (nmidb), and chain length (CL).

j	f_j (Hz)	β_j
1	-75.3	$2 \times$ ndb
2	-62.6	1
3	63.9	4
4	249	$2 \times$ nmidb
5	314	6
6	342	$4 \times$ (ndb - nmidb)
7	396	6
8	434	$(6 \times (\text{CL} - 4)) - (8 \times \text{ndb}) + (2 \times \text{nmidb})$
9	485	9

Quantifying the saturation of triglycerides by CSE-MRI may help to distinguish simple steatosis from nonalcoholic steatohepatitis noninvasively [33,48,49]. Moreover, other conditions, such as cancer, cardiovascular disease, type 2 diabetes, and osteoporosis may also be associated with the degree of triglyceride saturation [47,48]. Characterizing the chemical structure of triglycerides may provide insight to investigating body composition and conditions associated with metabolic syndrome. These novel techniques have the potential to improve the management of diseases associated with metabolic syndrome and cancer.

27.5 Summary and outlook

MRI and MRS are noninvasive technologies that enable accurate, repeatable, and reproducible quantification of the distribution, content, and composition of fat in the human body. MR signals from fat and water spins have distinctly different MR relaxation and chemical shift properties, which are leveraged by MRI and MRS to separate, identify, and quantify the contributions from fat. In particular, MRS and CSE-MRI take advantage of one of the most fundamental properties of MR—resonance frequency—to accurately quantify fat content; these techniques are used to calculate the quantitative PDFF metric and are now widely adopted for research and clinical use. New fat quantification techniques using free-breathing MRI acquisition and/or advanced MRI reconstruction have demonstrated promising performance and are now being further evaluated for clinical translation. In addition, advanced models of triglyceride chemical structure and saturation can enable in-depth characterization of not just fat content, but also composition. CSE-MRI and MRS techniques have already become the reference standard for quantifying fat and studying metabolic disorders, and will no doubt see further advances and applications in the coming years.

References

[1] Ma J. Dixon techniques for water and fat imaging. J Magn Reson Imaging 2008;28(3):543–58.

[2] Bley TA, Wieben O, Francois CJ, Brittain JH, Reeder SB. Fat and water magnetic resonance imaging. J Magn Reson Imaging 2010;31(1):4–18.

[3] Reeder SB, Cruite I, Hamilton G, Sirlin CB. Quantitative assessment of liver fat with magnetic resonance imaging and spectroscopy. J Magn Reson Imaging 2011;34(4):729–49.
[4] Hu HH, Kan HE. Quantitative proton MR techniques for measuring fat. NMR Biomed 2013;26(12):1609–29.
[5] Eggers H, Bornert P. Chemical shift encoding-based water-fat separation methods. J Magn Reson Imaging 2014;40(2):251–68.
[6] de Bazelaire CM, Duhamel GD, Rofsky NM, Alsop DC. MR imaging relaxation times of abdominal and pelvic tissues measured in vivo at 3.0 T: preliminary results. Radiology 2004;230(3):652–9.
[7] Rakow-Penner R, Daniel B, Yu H, Sawyer-Glover A, Glover GH. Relaxation times of breast tissue at 1.5 T and 3 T measured using IDEAL. J Magn Reson Imaging 2006;23(1):87–91.
[8] Henkelman RM, Hardy PA, Bishop JE, Poon CS, Plewes DB. Why fat is bright in RARE and fast spin-echo imaging. J Magn Reson Imaging 1992;2(5):533–40.
[9] Bydder GM, Pennock JM, Steiner RE, Khenia S, Payne JA, Young IR. The short TI inversion recovery sequence—an approach to MR imaging of the abdomen. Magn Reson Imaging 1985;3(3):251–4.
[10] Bydder GM, Steiner RE, Blumgart LH, Khenia S, Young IR. MR imaging of the liver using short TI inversion recovery sequences. J Comput Assist Tomogr 1985;9(6):1084–9.
[11] Dousset M, Weissleder R, Hendrick RE, Stark DD, Fretz CJ, Elizondo G, et al. Short TI inversion-recovery imaging of the liver: pulse-sequence optimization and comparison with spin-echo imaging. Radiology 1989;171(2):327–33.
[12] Hamilton G, Yokoo T, Bydder M, Cruite I, Schroeder ME, Sirlin CB, et al. In vivo characterization of the liver fat (1)H MR spectrum. NMR Biomed 2011;24(7):784–90.
[13] Ren J, Dimitrov I, Sherry AD, Malloy CR. Composition of adipose tissue and marrow fat in humans by ^{1}H NMR at 7 Tesla. J Lipid Res 2008;49(9):2055–62.
[14] Hindman JC. Proton resonance shift of water in the gas and liquid states. J Chem Phys 1966;44(12):4582–92.
[15] Ishihara Y, Calderon A, Watanabe H, Okamoto K, Suzuki Y, Kuroda K, et al. A precise and fast temperature mapping using water proton chemical shift. Magn Reson Med 1995;34(6):814–23.
[16] Rieke V, Butts PK. MR thermometry. J Magn Reson Imaging 2008;27(2):376–90.
[17] Hernando D, Sharma SD, Kramer H, Reeder SB. On the confounding effect of temperature on chemical shift-encoded fat quantification. Magn Reson Med 2014;72(2):464–70.
[18] Bernstein M, King K, Zhou X. Handbook of MRI pulse sequences. 1st ed. Academic Press; 2004, 1040 pp.
[19] Haase A, Frahm J, Hanicke W, Matthaei D. ^{1}H NMR chemical shift selective (CHESS) imaging. Phys Med Biol 1985;30(4):341–4.
[20] Meyer CH, Pauly JM, Macovski A, Nishimura DG. Simultaneous spatial and spectral selective excitation. Magn Reson Med 1990;15(2):287–304.
[21] Schick F. Simultaneous highly selective MR water and fat imaging using a simple new type of spectral-spatial excitation. Magn Reson Med 1998;40(2):194–202.
[22] Cao P, Fan SJ, Wang AM, Xie VB, Qiao Z, Brittenham GM, et al. Diffusion magnetic resonance monitors intramyocellular lipid droplet size in vivo. Magn Reson Med 2015;73(1):59–69.
[23] Cao P, Wu EX. In vivo diffusion MRS investigation of non-water molecules in biological tissues. NMR Biomed 2017;30(3).
[24] Verma SK, Nagashima K, Yaligar J, Michael N, Lee SS, Xianfeng T, et al. Differentiating brown and white adipose tissues by high-resolution diffusion NMR spectroscopy. J Lipid Res 2017;58(1):289–98.
[25] Bohte AE, van Werven JR, Bipat S, Stoker J. The diagnostic accuracy of US, CT, MRI and ^{1}H-MRS for the evaluation of hepatic steatosis compared with liver biopsy: a meta-analysis. Eur Radiol 2011; 21(1):87–97.
[26] Dulai PS, Sirlin CB, Loomba R. MRI and MRE for non-invasive quantitative assessment of hepatic steatosis and fibrosis in NAFLD and NASH: clinical trials to clinical practice. J Hepatol 2016;65(5):1006–16.
[27] Hallsworth K, Thoma C, Hollingsworth KG, Cassidy S, Anstee QM, Day CP, et al. Modified high-intensity interval training reduces liver fat and improves cardiac function in non-alcoholic fatty liver disease: a randomized controlled trial. Clin Sci (Lond) 2015;129(12):1097–105.

[28] Jeong JY, Sohn JH, Baek YH, Cho YK, Kim Y, Kim H. New botanical drug, HL tablet, reduces hepatic fat as measured by magnetic resonance spectroscopy in patients with nonalcoholic fatty liver disease: a placebo-controlled, randomized, phase II trial. World J Gastroenterol 2017;23(32):5977–85.

[29] Kim W, Kim BG, Lee JS, Lee CK, Yeon JE, Chang MS, et al. Randomised clinical trial: the efficacy and safety of oltipraz, a liver X receptor alpha-inhibitory dithiolethione in patients with non-alcoholic fatty liver disease. Aliment Pharmacol Ther 2017;45(8):1073–83.

[30] Le TA, Chen J, Changchien C, Peterson MR, Kono Y, Patton H, et al. Effect of colesevelam on liver fat quantified by magnetic resonance in nonalcoholic steatohepatitis: a randomized controlled trial. Hepatology 2012;56(3):922–32.

[31] Pineda N, Sharma P, Xu Q, Hu X, Vos M, Martin DR. Measurement of hepatic lipid: high-speed T_2-corrected multiecho acquisition at ^{1}H MR spectroscopy—a rapid and accurate technique. Radiology 2009; 252(2):568–76.

[32] Hamilton G, Schlein AN, Middleton MS, Hooker CA, Wolfson T, Gamst AC, et al. In vivo triglyceride composition of abdominal adipose tissue measured by (1) H MRS at 3 T. J Magn Reson Imaging 2017; 45(5):1455–63.

[33] Leporq B, Lambert SA, Ronot M, Vilgrain V, Van Beers BE. Quantification of the triglyceride fatty acid composition with 3.0 T MRI. NMR Biomed 2014;27(10):1211–21.

[34] Bottomley PA. Spatial localization in NMR spectroscopy in vivo. Ann N Y Acad Sci 1987;508:333–48.

[35] Frahm J, Merboldt K-D, Hänicke W. Localized proton spectroscopy using stimulated echoes. J Mag Reson (1969) 1987;72(3):502–8.

[36] Hamilton G, Middleton MS, Bydder M, Yokoo T, Schwimmer JB, Kono Y, et al. Effect of PRESS and STEAM sequences on magnetic resonance spectroscopic liver fat quantification. J Magn Reson Imaging 2009;30(1):145–52.

[37] Posse S, Otazo R, Dager SR, Alger J. MR spectroscopic imaging: principles and recent advances. J Magn Reson Imaging 2013;37(6):1301–25.

[38] Vidya Shankar R, Chang JC, Hu HH, Kodibagkar VD. Fast data acquisition techniques in magnetic resonance spectroscopic imaging. NMR Biomed 2019, e4046.

[39] Lin YR, Chiu JJ, Tsai SY. Feasibility and reproducibility of echo planar spectroscopic imaging on the quantification of hepatic fat. PLoS One 2014;9(12), e114436.

[40] Reeder SB, Hu HH, Sirlin CB. Proton density fat-fraction: a standardized MR-based biomarker of tissue fat concentration. J Magn Reson Imaging 2012;36(5):1011–4.

[41] Heger M, Marsman HA, Bezemer R, Cloos MA, van Golen RF, van Gulik TM. Non-invasive quantification of triglyceride content in steatotic rat livers by (1)H-MRS: when water meets (too much) fat. Acad Radiol 2011;18(12):1582–92.

[42] Georgoff P, Thomasson D, Louie A, Fleischman E, Dutcher L, Mani H, et al. Hydrogen-1 MR spectroscopy for measurement and diagnosis of hepatic steatosis. AJR Am J Roentgenol 2012;199(1):2–7.

[43] Tyagi A, Yeganeh O, Levin Y, Hooker JC, Hamilton GC, Wolfson T, et al. Intra- and inter-examination repeatability of magnetic resonance spectroscopy, magnitude-based MRI, and complex-based MRI for estimation of hepatic proton density fat fraction in overweight and obese children and adults. Abdom Imaging 2015;40(8):3070–7.

[44] van Werven JR, Hoogduin JM, Nederveen AJ, van Vliet AA, Wajs E, Vandenberk P, et al. Reproducibility of 3.0 Tesla magnetic resonance spectroscopy for measuring hepatic fat content. J Magn Reson Imaging 2009;30(2):444–8.

[45] Artz NS, Haufe WM, Hooker CA, Hamilton G, Wolfson T, Campos GM, et al. Reproducibility of MR-based liver fat quantification across field strength: same-day comparison between 1.5 T and 3 T in obese subjects. J Magn Reson Imaging 2015;42(3):811–7.

[46] Runge JH, Smits LP, Verheij J, Depla A, Kuiken SD, Baak BC, et al. MR spectroscopy-derived proton density fat fraction is superior to controlled attenuation parameter for detecting and grading hepatic Steatosis. Radiology 2018;286(2):547–56.
[47] Berglund J, Ahlstrom H, Kullberg J. Model-based mapping of fat unsaturation and chain length by chemical shift imaging—phantom validation and in vivo feasibility. Magn Reson Med 2012;68(6):1815–27.
[48] Bydder M, Girard O, Hamilton G. Mapping the double bonds in triglycerides. Magn Reson Imaging 2011;29(8):1041–6.
[49] Peterson P, Mansson S. Simultaneous quantification of fat content and fatty acid composition using MR imaging. Magn Reson Med 2013;69(3):688–97.
[50] Dixon WT. Simple proton spectroscopic imaging. Radiology 1984;153(1):189–94.
[51] Noble JJ, Keevil SF, Totman J, Charles-Edwards GD. In vitro and in vivo comparison of two-, three- and four-point Dixon techniques for clinical intramuscular fat quantification at 3 T. Br J Radiol 2014; 87(1036): 20130761.
[52] Glover GH, Schneider E. Three-point Dixon technique for true water/fat decomposition with B_0 inhomogeneity correction. Magn Reson Med 1991;18(2):371–83.
[53] Kovanlikaya A, Guclu C, Desai C, Becerra R, Gilsanz V. Fat quantification using three-point Dixon technique: in vitro validation. Acad Radiol 2005;12(5):636–9.
[54] Sinclair CD, Morrow JM, Yousry TA, Golay X, Thornton JS, editors. Test-retest reproducibility of MTR, T_2 and 3-point Dixon fat quantification methods in muscle MRI. International Society of Magnetic Resonance in Medicine 18th Annual Scientific Meeting, Stockholm, Sweden; 2010.
[55] Szumowski J, Coshow WR, Li F, Quinn SF. Phase unwrapping in the three-point Dixon method for fat suppression MR imaging. Radiology 1994;192(2):555–61.
[56] Coombs BD, Szumowski J, Coshow W. Two-point Dixon technique for water-fat signal decomposition with B_0 inhomogeneity correction. Magn Reson Med 1997;38(6):884–9.
[57] Schneider E, Glover G. Rapid in vivo proton shimming. Magn Reson Med 1991;18(2):335–47.
[58] Liang ZP. A model-based method for phase unwrapping. IEEE Trans Med Imaging 1996;15(6):893–7.
[59] Moon-Ho Song S, Napel S, Pelc NJ, Glover GH. Phase unwrapping of MR phase images using Poisson equation. In: IEEE Transactions on Image Processing. vol. 4. May 1995. p. 667–76. https://doi.org/10.1109/83.382500no. 5.
[60] Hernando D, Hines CDG, Yu H, Reeder SB. Addressing phase errors in fat-water imaging using a mixed magnitude/complex fitting method. Magn Reson Med 2012;67(3):638–44.
[61] Cheng JY, Mei YJ, Liu BS, Guan JJ, Liu XY, Wu EX, et al. A novel phase-unwrapping method based on pixel clustering and local surface fitting with application to Dixon water-fat MRI. Magn Reson Med 2018; 79(1):515–28.
[62] Baselice F, Ferraioli G. Modified Dixon technique for MRI water-fat separation using jointly amplitude and phase. Biomed Res-India 2017;28(10):4324–8.
[63] Cui C, Wu X, Newell JD, Jacob M. Fat water decomposition using globally optimal surface estimation (GOOSE) algorithm. Magn Reson Med 2015;73(3):1289–99.
[64] Cui C, Shah A, Wu XD, Jacob M. A rapid 3D fat-water decomposition method using globally optimal surface estimation (R-GOOSE). Magn Reson Med 2018;79(4):2401–7.
[65] Hernando D, Kellman P, Haldar JP, Liang ZP. Robust water/fat separation in the presence of large field Inhomogeneities using a graph cut algorithm. Magn Reson Med 2010;63(1):79–90.
[66] Skinner TE, Glover GH. An extended two-point Dixon algorithm for calculating separate water, fat, and B_0 images. Magn Reson Med 1997;37(4):628–30.
[67] Yu H, Reeder SB, McKenzie CA, Brau AC, Shimakawa A, Brittain JH, et al. Single acquisition water-fat separation: feasibility study for dynamic imaging. Magn Reson Med 2006;55(2):413–22.

[68] Pineda AR, Reeder SB, Wen Z, Pelc NJ. Cramer-Rao bounds for three-point decomposition of water and fat. Magn Reson Med 2005;54(3):625–35.

[69] Xiang QS, An L. Water-fat imaging with direct phase encoding. J Magn Reson Imaging 1997;7(6):1002–15.

[70] Reeder SB, Wen Z, Yu H, Pineda AR, Gold GE, Markl M, et al. Multicoil Dixon chemical species separation with an iterative least-squares estimation method. Magn Reson Med 2004;51(1):35–45.

[71] Reeder SB, Pineda AR, Wen Z, Shimakawa A, Yu H, Brittain JH, et al. Iterative decomposition of water and fat with echo asymmetry and least-squares estimation (IDEAL): application with fast spin-echo imaging. Magn Reson Med 2005;54(3):636–44.

[72] Yu H, Shimakawa A, McKenzie CA, Brodsky E, Brittain JH, Reeder SB. Multiecho water-fat separation and simultaneous R_2* estimation with multifrequency fat spectrum modeling. Magn Reson Med 2008; 60(5):1122–34.

[73] Hines CD, Yu H, Shimakawa A, McKenzie CA, Brittain JH, Reeder SB. T_1 independent, T_2* corrected MRI with accurate spectral modeling for quantification of fat: validation in a fat-water-SPIO phantom. J Magn Reson Imaging 2009;30(5):1215–22.

[74] Yu H, Reeder SB, Shimakawa A, Brittain JH, Pelc NJ. Field map estimation with a region growing scheme for iterative 3-point water-fat decomposition. Magn Reson Med 2005;54(4):1032–9.

[75] Bydder M, Yokoo T, Hamilton G, Middleton MS, Chavez AD, Schwimmer JB, et al. Relaxation effects in the quantification of fat using gradient echo imaging. Magn Reson Imaging 2008;26(3):347–59.

[76] Hernando D, Liang ZP, Kellman P. Chemical shift-based water/fat separation: a comparison of signal models. Magn Reson Med 2010;64(3):811–22.

[77] Zhong XD, Nickel MD, Kannengiesser SAR, Dale BM, Kiefer B, Bashir MR. Liver fat quantification using a multi-step adaptive fitting approach with multi-Echo GRE imaging. Magn Reson Med 2014; 72(5):1353–65.

[78] Yokoo T, Shiehmorteza M, Hamilton G, Wolfson T, Schroeder ME, Middleton MS, et al. Estimation of hepatic proton-density fat fraction by using MR imaging at 3.0 T. Radiology 2011;258(3):749–59.

[79] Yokoo T, Bydder M, Hamilton G, Middleton MS, Gamst AC, Wolfson T, et al. Nonalcoholic fatty liver disease: diagnostic and fat-grading accuracy of low-flip-angle multiecho gradient-recalled-Echo MR imaging at 1.5 T. Radiology 2009;251(1):67–76.

[80] Yu H, Shimakawa A, McKenzie CA, Lu W, Reeder SB, Hinks RS, et al. Phase and amplitude correction for multi-echo water-fat separation with bipolar acquisitions. J Magn Reson Imaging 2010;31(5): 1264–71.

[81] Peterson P, Mansson S. Fat quantification using multiecho sequences with bipolar gradients: investigation of accuracy and noise performance. Magn Reson Med 2014;71(1):219–29.

[82] Lu W, Yu H, Shimakawa A, Alley M, Reeder SB, Hargreaves BA. Water-fat separation with bipolar multiecho sequences. Magn Reson Med 2008;60(1):198–209.

[83] Wang XK, Hernando D, Reeder SB. Sensitivity of chemical shift-encoded fat quantification to calibration of fat MR spectrum. Magn Reson Med 2016;75(2):845–51.

[84] Reeder SB, Sirlin CB. Quantification of liver fat with magnetic resonance imaging. Magn Reson Imaging Clin N Am 2010;18(3):337–57 [ix].

[85] Horng DE, Hernando D, Hines CD, Reeder SB. Comparison of R_2* correction methods for accurate fat quantification in fatty liver. J Magn Reson Imaging 2013;37(2):414–22.

[86] Yang IY, Cui Y, Wiens CN, Wade TP, Friesen-Waldner LJ, McKenzie CA. Fat fraction bias correction using T_1 estimates and flip angle mapping. J Magn Reson Imaging 2014;39(1):217–23.

[87] Kuhn JP, Jahn C, Hernando D, Siegmund W, Hadlich S, Mayerle J, et al. T_1 bias in chemical shift-encoded liver fat-fraction: role of the flip angle. J Magn Reson Imaging 2014;40(4):875–83.

[88] Liu CY, McKenzie CA, Yu H, Brittain JH, Reeder SB. Fat quantification with IDEAL gradient echo imaging: correction of bias from T_1 and noise. Magn Reson Med 2007;58(2):354–64.

[89] Deoni SCL, Rutt BK, Peters TM. Rapid combined T-1 and T-2 mapping using gradient recalled acquisition in the steady state. Magn Reson Med 2003;49(3):515–26.

[90] Yu HZ, Shimakawa A, Hines CDG, McKenzie CA, Hamilton G, Sirlin CB, et al. Combination of complex-based and magnitude-based multiecho water-fat separation for accurate quantification of fat-fraction. Magn Reson Med 2011;66(1):199–206.

[91] Idilman IS, Aniktar H, Idilman R, Kabacam G, Savas B, Elhan A, et al. Hepatic steatosis: quantification by proton density fat fraction with MR imaging versus liver biopsy. Radiology 2013;267(3):767–75.

[92] Yokoo T, Serai SD, Pirasteh A, Bashir MR, Hamilton G, Hernando D, et al. Linearity, bias, and precision of hepatic proton density fat fraction measurements by using MR imaging: a meta-analysis. Radiology 2018;286(2):486–98.

[93] Hernando D, Sharma SD, Aliyari Ghasabeh M, Alvis BD, Arora SS, Hamilton G, et al. Multisite, multivendor validation of the accuracy and reproducibility of proton-density fat-fraction quantification at 1.5 T and 3 T using a fat-water phantom. Magn Reson Med 2017;77(4):1516–24.

[94] Hu HH, Yin L, Aggabao PC, Perkins TG, Chia JM, Gilsanz V. Comparison of brown and white adipose tissues in infants and children with chemical-shift-encoded water-fat MRI. J Magn Reson Imaging 2013;38(4):885–96.

[95] Hu HH, Perkins TG, Chia JM, Gilsanz V. Characterization of human brown adipose tissue by chemical-shift water-fat MRI. AJR Am J Roentgenol 2013;200(1):177–83.

[96] Armstrong T, Ly KV, Ghahremani S, Calkins KL, Wu HH. Free-breathing 3-D quantification of infant body composition and hepatic fat using a stack-of-radial magnetic resonance imaging technique. Pediatr Radiol 2019;49(7):876–88.

[97] Ly KV, Armstrong T, Yeh J, et al. Free-breathing magnetic resonance imaging assessment of body composition in healthy and overweight children: an observational study. J Pediatr Gastroenterol Nutr. 2019; 68(6):782–7. https://doi.org/10.1097/MPG.0000000000002309.

[98] Kramer H, Pickhardt PJ, Kliewer MA, Hernando D, Chen GH, Zagzebski JA, et al. Accuracy of liver fat quantification with advanced CT, MRI, and ultrasound techniques: prospective comparison with MR spectroscopy. AJR Am J Roentgenol 2017;208(1):92–100.

[99] Bannas P, Kramer H, Hernando D, Agni R, Cunningham AM, Mandal R, et al. Quantitative magnetic resonance imaging of hepatic steatosis: validation in ex vivo human livers. Hepatology 2015;62(5):1444–55.

[100] Kim HJ, Cho HJ, Kim B, You MW, Lee JH, Huh J, et al. Accuracy and precision of proton density fat fraction measurement across field strengths and scan intervals: a phantom and human study. J Magn Reson Imaging 2018.

[101] Middleton MS, Heba ER, Hooker CA, Bashir MR, Fowler KJ, Sandrasegaran K, et al. Agreement between magnetic resonance imaging proton density fat fraction measurements and pathologist-assigned steatosis grades of liver biopsies from adults with nonalcoholic steatohepatitis. Gastroenterology 2017;153(3): 753–761.

[102] Sofue K, Mileto A, Dale BM, Zhong X, Bashir MR. Interexamination repeatability and spatial heterogeneity of liver iron and fat quantification using MRI-based multistep adaptive fitting algorithm. J Magn Reson Imaging 2015;42(5):1281–90.

[103] Namimoto T, Yamashita Y, Mitsuzaki K, Nakayama Y, Makita O, Kadota M, et al. Adrenal masses: quantification of fat content with double-echo chemical shift in-phase and opposed-phase FLASH MR images for differentiation of adrenal adenomas. Radiology 2001;218(3):642–6.

[104] Hussain HK, Chenevert TL, Londy FJ, Gulani V, Swanson SD, McKenna BJ, et al. Hepatic fat fraction: MR imaging for quantitative measurement and display—early experience. Radiology 2005;237(3):1048–55.

[105] Hayashi N, Miyati T, Minami T, Takeshita Y, Ryu Y, Matsuda T, et al. Quantitative analysis of hepatic fat fraction by single-breath-holding MR spectroscopy with T(2) correction: phantom and clinical study with histologic assessment. Radiol Phys Technol 2013;6(1):219–25.

[106] Armstrong T, Dregely I, Stemmer A, Han F, Natsuaki Y, Sung K, et al. Free-breathing liver fat quantification using a multiecho 3D stack-of-radial technique. Magn Reson Med 2018;79(1):370–82.
[107] Bernard CP, Liney GP, Manton DJ, Turnbull LW, Langton CM. Comparison of fat quantification methods: a phantom study at 3.0T. J Magn Reson Imaging 2008;27(1):192–7.
[108] Carnicka SC, Keenan K, Mirowski E, Brown M, Suiter C, Fortin T, ... Russek SE, editors. Fat tissue mimics for validation of magnetic resonance thermometry. International Society of Magnetic Resonance in Medicine 25th Scientific Meeting; HonoluluUnited States: Hawaii; 2017.
[109] Middleton MS, Van Natta ML, Heba ER, Alazraki A, Trout AT, Masand P, et al. Diagnostic accuracy of magnetic resonance imaging hepatic proton density fat fraction in pediatric nonalcoholic fatty liver disease. Hepatology 2018;67(3):858–72.
[110] Zhong X, Nickel MD, Kannengiesser SA, Dale BM, Kiefer B, Bashir MR. Liver fat quantification using a multi-step adaptive fitting approach with multi-echo GRE imaging. Magn Reson Med 2014; 72(5):1353–65.
[111] Koh H, Kim S, Kim MJ, Kim HG, Shin HJ, Lee MJ. Hepatic fat quantification magnetic resonance for monitoring treatment response in pediatric nonalcoholic steatohepatitis. World J Gastroenterol 2015; 21(33):9741–8.
[112] Joshi M, Dillman JR, Singh K, Serai SD, Towbin AJ, Xanthakos S, et al. Quantitative MRI of fatty liver disease in a large pediatric cohort: correlation between liver fat fraction, stiffness, volume, and patient-specific factors. Abdom Radiol 2018;43(5):1168–79.
[113] Meisamy S, Hines CDG, Hamilton G, Sirlin CB, McKenzie CA, Yu HZ, et al. Quantification of hepatic steatosis with T_1-independent, T_2*-corrected MR imaging with spectral modeling of fat: blinded comparison with MR spectroscopy. Radiology 2011;258(3):767–75.
[114] Achmad E, Yokoo T, Hamilton G, Heba ER, Hooker JC, Changchien C, et al. Feasibility of and agreement between MR imaging and spectroscopic estimation of hepatic proton density fat fraction in children with known or suspected nonalcoholic fatty liver disease. Abdom Imaging 2015;40(8):3084–90.
[115] Bashir MR, Zhong X, Nickel MD, Fananapazir G, Kannengiesser SA, Kiefer B, et al. Quantification of hepatic steatosis with a multistep adaptive fitting MRI approach: prospective validation against MR spectroscopy. AJR Am J Roentgenol 2015;204(2):297–306.
[116] Schwimmer JB, Middleton MS, Behling C, Newton KP, Awai HI, Paiz MN, et al. Magnetic resonance imaging and liver histology as biomarkers of hepatic steatosis in children with nonalcoholic fatty liver disease. Hepatology (Baltimore, MD) 2015;61(6):1887–95.
[117] Courtier J, Rao AG, Anupindi SA. Advanced imaging techniques in pediatric body MRI. Pediatr Radiol 2017;47(5):522–33.
[118] Chavhan GB, Babyn PS, Vasanawala SS. Abdominal MR imaging in children: motion compensation, sequence optimization, and protocol organization. Radiographics 2013;33(3):703–19.
[119] Jaimes C, Gee MS. Strategies to minimize sedation in pediatric body magnetic resonance imaging. Pediatr Radiol 2016;46(6):916–27.
[120] Motosugi U, Hernando D, Bannas P, Holmes JH, Wang K, Shimakawa A, et al. Quantification of liver fat with respiratory-gated quantitative chemical shift encoded MRI. J Magn Reson Imaging 2015; 42(5):1241–8.
[121] Ehman RL, McNamara MT, Pallack M, Hricak H, Higgins CB. Magnetic resonance imaging with respiratory gating: techniques and advantages. AJR Am J Roentgenol 1984;143(6):1175–82.
[122] Arboleda C, Aguirre-Reyes D, Garcia MP, Tejos C, Munoz L, Miquel JF, et al. Total liver fat quantification using three-dimensional respiratory self-navigated MRI sequence. Magn Reson Med 2016; 76(5):1400–9.
[123] Mendes J, Kholmovski E, Parker DL. Rigid-body motion correction with self-navigation MRI. Magn Reson Med 2009;61(3):739–47.

[124] Pooler BD, Hernando D, Ruby JA, Ishii H, Shimakawa A, Reeder SB. Validation of a motion-robust 2D sequential technique for quantification of hepatic proton density fat fraction during free breathing. J Magn Reson Imaging 2018;48(6):1578–85.

[125] Chandarana H, Block TK, Rosenkrantz AB, Lim RP, Kim D, Mossa DJ, et al. Free-breathing radial 3D fat-suppressed T_1-weighted gradient echo sequence a viable alternative for contrast-enhanced liver imaging in patients unable to suspend respiration. Invest Radiol 2011;46(10):648–53.

[126] Armstrong T, Ly KV, Murthy S, Ghahremani S, Kim GHJ, Calkins KL, et al. Free-breathing quantification of hepatic fat in healthy children and children with nonalcoholic fatty liver disease using a multi-echo 3-D stack-of-radial MRI technique. Pediatr Radiol 2018;48(7):941–53.

[127] Block TK, Chandarana H, Milla S. Towards routine clinical use of radial stack-of-stars 3D gradient-echo sequences for reducing motion sensitivity. J Korean Soc Magn Reson Med 2014;87–106.

[128] Moran CJ, Brodsky EK, Bancroft LH, Reeder SB, Yu H, Kijowski R, et al. High-resolution 3D radial bSSFP with IDEAL. Magn Reson Med 2014;71(1):95–104.

[129] Brodsky EK, Holmes JH, Yu H, Reeder SB. Generalized k-space decomposition with chemical shift correction for non-Cartesian water-fat imaging. Magn Reson Med 2008;59(5):1151–64.

[130] Benkert T, Feng L, Sodickson DK, Chandarana H, Block KT. Free-breathing volumetric fat/water separation by combining radial sampling, compressed sensing, and parallel imaging. Magn Reson Med 2017;78(2):565–76.

[131] Bornert P, Koken P, Eggers H. Spiral water-fat imaging with integrated off-resonance correction on a clinical scanner. J Magn Reson Imaging 2010;32(5):1262–7.

[132] Moriguchi H, Lewin JS, Duerk JL. Dixon techniques in spiral trajectories with off-resonance correction: a new approach for fat signal suppression without spatial-spectral RF pulses. Magn Reson Med 2003;50(5): 915–924.

[133] Wang D, Zwart NR, Li Z, Schar M, Pipe JG. Analytical three-point Dixon method: with applications for spiral water-fat imaging. Magn Reson Med 2016;75(2):627–38.

[134] Weng D, Pan Y, Zhong X, Zhuo Y. Water-fat separation with parallel imaging based on BLADE. Magn Reson Imaging 2013;31(5):656–63.

[135] Huo D, Li Z, Aboussouan E, Karis JP, Pipe JG. Turboprop IDEAL: a motion-resistant fat-water separation technique. Magn Reson Med 2009;61(1):188–95.

[136] Wu HH, Lee JH, Nishimura DG. Fat/water separation using a concentric rings trajectory. Magn Reson Med 2009;61(3):639–49.

[137] Peters DC, Derbyshire JA, McVeigh ER. Centering the projection reconstruction trajectory: reducing gradient delay errors. Magn Reson Med 2003;50(1):1–6.

[138] Armstrong T, Martin T, Stemmer A, Li X, Natsuaki Y, Sung K, Wu HH, editors. Free-breathing fat quantification in the liver using a multiecho 3D stack-of-radial technique: investigation of motion compensation and quantification accuracy. Proceedings of the International Society for Magnetic Resonance in Medicine 25th Annual Scientific Meeting, Honolulu, Hawaii, United States; 2017.

[139] Armstrong T, Martin T, Ghahremani S, Sung K, Calkins KL, Wu HH, editors. Free-breathing hepatic fat quantification in children and infants using a 3D stack-of-radial technique: assessment of accuracy and repeatability. Proceedings of the International Society for Magnetic Resonance in Medicine 26th Annual Scientific Meeting; Paris, France; 2018.

[140] Feng L, Axel L, Chandarana H, Block KT, Sodickson DK, Otazo R. XD-GRASP: golden-angle radial MRI with reconstruction of extra motion-state dimensions using compressed sensing. Magn Reson Med 2016;75(2):775–88.

[141] Griswold MA, Jakob PM, Heidemann RM, Nittka M, Jellus V, Wang J, et al. Generalized autocalibrating partially parallel acquisitions (GRAPPA). Magn Reson Med 2002;47(6):1202–10.

[142] Breuer FA, Blaimer M, Heidemann RM, Mueller MF, Griswold MA, Jakob PM. Controlled aliasing in parallel imaging results in higher acceleration (CAIPIRINHA) for multi-slice imaging. Magn Reson Med 2005;53(3):684–91.
[143] Doneva M, Bornert P, Eggers H, Mertins A, Pauly J, Lustig M. Compressed sensing for chemical shift-based water-fat separation. Magn Reson Med 2010;64(6):1749–59.
[144] Sharma SD, Hu HH, Nayak KS. Accelerated water-fat imaging using restricted subspace field map estimation and compressed sensing. Magn Reson Med 2012;67(3):650–9.
[145] Lugauer F, Nickel D, Wetzl J, Kiefer B, Hornegger J, Maier A. Accelerating multi-echo water-fat MRI with a joint locally low-rank and spatial sparsity-promoting reconstruction. MAGMA 2017;30(2):189–202.
[146] Sharma SD, Hu HH, Nayak KS. Chemical shift encoded water-fat separation using parallel imaging and compressed sensing. Magn Reson Med 2013;69(2):456–66.
[147] Hollingsworth KG, Higgins DM, McCallum M, Ward L, Coombs A, Straub V. Investigating the quantitative fidelity of prospectively undersampled chemical shift imaging in muscular dystrophy with compressed sensing and parallel imaging reconstruction. Magn Reson Med 2014;72(6):1610–9.
[148] Mann LW, Higgins DM, Peters CN, Cassidy S, Hodson KK, Coombs A, et al. Accelerating MR imaging liver steatosis measurement using combined compressed sensing and parallel imaging: a quantitative evaluation. Radiology 2016;278(1):247–56.
[149] Wiens CN, McCurdy CM, Willig-Onwuachi JD, McKenzie CA. R_2*-corrected water-fat imaging using compressed sensing and parallel imaging. Magn Reson Med 2014;71(2):608–16.
[150] Tamada D, Wakayama T, Onishi H, Motosugi U. Multiparameter estimation using multi-echo spoiled gradient echo with variable flip angles and multicontrast compressed sensing. Magn Reson Med 2018; 80(4):1546–55.
[151] Ma D, Gulani V, Seiberlich N, Liu KC, Sunshine JL, Duerk JL, et al. Magnetic resonance fingerprinting. Nature 2013;495(7440):187–92.
[152] Liu D, Steingoetter A, Parker HL, Curcic J, Kozerke S. Accelerating MRI fat quantification using a signal model-based dictionary to assess gastric fat volume and distribution of fat fraction. Magn Reson Imaging 2017;37:81–9.
[153] Cencini M, Biagi L, Kaggie JD, Schulte RF, Tosetti M, Buonincontri G. Magnetic resonance fingerprinting with dictionary-based fat and water separation (DBFW MRF): a multi-component approach. Magn Reson Med 2018.
[154] Than NN, Newsome PN. A concise review of non-alcoholic fatty liver disease. Atherosclerosis 2015; 239(1):192–202.
[155] Rinella ME. Nonalcoholic fatty liver disease: a systematic review. JAMA 2015;313(22):2263–73.
[156] Sumida Y, Nakajima A, Itoh Y. Limitations of liver biopsy and non-invasive diagnostic tests for the diagnosis of nonalcoholic fatty liver disease/nonalcoholic steatohepatitis. World J Gastroenterol 2014; 20(2):475–85.
[157] Ratziu V, Charlotte F, Heurtier A, Gombert S, Giral P, Bruckert E, et al. Sampling variability of liver biopsy in nonalcoholic fatty liver disease. Gastroenterology 2005;128(7):1898–906.

CHAPTER

Applications of Fat Mapping 28

Hermien E. Kan[a], Dimitrios C. Karampinos[b], and Jürgen Machann[c,d,e]

[a]*C.J. Gorter Center for High Field MRI, Department of Radiology, Leiden University Medical Center, Leiden, The Netherlands* [b]*Department of Diagnostic and Interventional Radiology, School of Medicine, Technical University of Munich, Munich, Germany* [c]*Institute for Diabetes Research and Metabolic Diseases, Helmholtz Center Munich at the University of Tübingen, Tübingen, Germany* [d]*German Center for Diabetes Research, Tübingen, Germany* [e]*Section on Experimental Radiology, Department of Diagnostic and Interventional Radiology, University Hospital Tübingen, Tübingen, Germany*

28.1 Introduction

Quantitative fat measurements by Magnetic Resonance Imaging (MRI) and magnetic resonance spectroscopy (MRS) are primarily used to study diseases and conditions related to musculoskeletal disorders, the pathophysiology of obesity, and abnormalities and comorbidities related to the metabolic syndrome [1–4]. (See Table 28.1.) Fat quantification can assist clinicians with diagnosis and prognosis, health risk assessment, and disease stratification. In current practice, fat quantification can be divided into three categories. First is the measurement of adipose tissue volume, which is performed with imaging and typically involves the counting of the number of voxels that represent adipose tissue. Second is the measurement of organ or tissue fat content, which is performed with imaging or spectroscopy, and is typically reported as a fat fraction within a voxel or group of voxels. Third is the characterization of triglyceride (TG) properties, which is performed mostly with spectroscopy, to measure the relative amounts of mono- and polyunsaturated fatty acids as well as the average TG chain length.

In clinical and translational research, quantitative fat imaging is commonly used to assess differences in body adiposity between groups of people (i.e., gender, race/ethnicity) [50] and to monitor changes in adipose tissue volume longitudinally over time due to natural progression, lifestyle intervention (i.e., diet/exercise), or medical intervention (i.e., bariatric surgery) [51]. Typically, the volume of subcutaneous adipose tissue (SAT) and visceral adipose tissue (VAT) are of interest. Additionally, ectopic organ fat content, namely in the liver and pancreas [52–57], heart [58], skeletal muscles [59], kidneys [60,61], brown adipose tissue (BAT) [62], and bone marrow [63], are also assessed. Over the past two decades, there has been a significant increase in publications on MRI and MRS applications in adipose tissue volume and organ fat fraction quantification.

In this chapter, fat quantification in terms of adipose tissue volume (i.e., number of voxels representing adipose tissue) and organ/tissue fat fraction (i.e., the percent fat content within a voxel or group of voxels) are described in detail. Both metrics have been rigorously developed and refined over the past decade, and exhibit strong accuracy against reference measurements and precision (i.e., reproducibility and repeatability) [64,65]. Both, adipose tissue volume and fat fraction measurements, can be

Advances in Magnetic Resonance Technology and Applications. Volume 1. ISSN 2666-9099. https://doi.org/10.1016/B978-0-12-817057-1.00030-5

Table 28.1 Complications and health risk factors associated with central obesity and excess subcutaneous, visceral and ectopic organ fat.

Endocrine system	Cancers	Cardiovascular system	Muskuloskeletal	Gastrointestinal	Hepatic	Pulmonary system	Skin disorders	Genitourinary system	Neurological
Insulin resistance [5]	Breast [6]	Myocardial infarction [7]	Dorsal pain [8]	Diaphragmatic hernia [9]	NAFLD [40]	Sleep apnea [41]	Psoriasis [42]	Infertility [43]	Cognitive health [44]
Type 2 diabetes mellitus [10]	Prostate [11]	Aneurysm [12]	Osteoarthritis [13]	Inguinal hernia	NASH [45]	Ventilatory dysfunction [46]		Polycystic Ovarian Syndrome [47]	Dementia [47a]
Dyslipidemia [14]	Colorectal [15]	Atherosclerosis [16]	Bone fractures [17]	Gallbladder disease [18]		COPD [48]		Incontinence [49]	
Thyroid hypofunction [19]	Pancreas [20]	Cardiomyopathy [21]	Inflammation [22]	Pancreatitis [23]					
Cushing's syndrome [24]	Kidney [25]	Hypertension [26]							
Endothelial dysfunction [27]	Endometrial [28]	Ischemic heart disease [29]							
	Gastroesophageal [30]	Cerebrovascular disease [31]							
	Lung [32]	Thrombosis [33]							
	Liver [34]	Peripheral vascular disease [35]							
	Ovarian [36]	Coronary artery disease [37]							
	Oesophageal [38]	Left ventricular dysfunction [39]							

performed at 1.5 T and 3 T, across multiple system vendors, and are stable within reasonable variations in image acquisition parameters (i.e., sequence timings, spatial resolution, slice thickness, etc.). They are at present commonly adopted in multi-site clinical trials and longitudinal studies. The chapter provides abundant literature references and in vivo examples of how adipose tissue volume and fat fraction measurements have been employed, and review the specific MRI and MRS methods and approaches to obtain them. The chapter concludes with an outlook on future directions and unmet needs.

28.2 Quantification of abdominal adipose tissue

Determination of distribution and quantity of adipose tissue in the human body has gained increasing interest during the last decades due to the increasing prevalence of obesity and metabolic disorders. Herein, emphasis is placed on abdominal adipose tissue including subcutaneous (SAT) and—probably most important—intraabdominal or visceral adipose tissue (VAT), which has been shown to be metabolically active. These compartments cannot be differentiated by simple anthropometric measures but require volumetric imaging approaches for assessment of the respective volumes. This chapter focuses on MR-based strategies for abdominal adipose tissue quantification. Representative examples highlighting age- and gender-related differences in abdominal adipose tissue distribution are shown. Additionally, cross-sectional data in normal-weight and obese subjects are shown, along with volumetric changes in abdominal adipose tissue after lifestyle intervention. The ability to accurately assess abdominal adipose tissue distribution is important in phenotyping of subjects and adds important information on the metabolic/clinical outcome of the individual.

28.2.1 Subcutaneous and visceral adipose tissue

The determination of adipose tissue volume distributions within the body has been a longstanding application in quantitative fat MRI [66]. In recent literature, several studies have been undertaken to evaluate the robustness of adipose tissue segmentation. Newman, et al. demonstrated in 30 normal and obese subjects that test-retest variations in SAT volumes had a coefficient of variation of less than 3%. For VAT volumes, the coefficient of variation was 6.3% when the segmentation was performed manually by an image analyst, versus 1.8% when performed by a semiautomated segmentation algorithm [67]. Similarly, Addeman et al. proposed an automated segmentation approach and demonstrated coefficients of variation around 1.2% for SAT and 2.7% for intra-abdominal VAT [68]. A recent work by Middleton et al. also reported coefficients of variation in the range of 1.5%–3.6% for adipose tissue volume quantification [69]. West et al. specifically focused on a study in postmenopausal women, and coefficients of variation between 1.1% and 1.5% were reported [70].

SAT can be further divided into superficial (SSAT) and deep (DSAT) compartments by the fascia superficialis. The volume of the DSAT compartment has been suggested to have greater correlations with metabolic and health risks than SSAT [71]. DSAT is thought to be associated with increased inflammation and oxidative stress as it shows stronger associations with multiple metabolic risk factors than SSAT and might therefore be seen as an important determinant for the metabolic syndrome.

VAT, often also referred to as intraabdominal adipose tissue (IAAT) in the literature, is located inside the cavity of the abdomen surrounding the organs and the digestive system [72]. Its primary function is the mechanical protection of the organs and it has a higher lipolytic capacity compared to SAT [73,74]. Fig. 28.1 shows examples of cross-sectional T_1-weighted images at the umbilical level

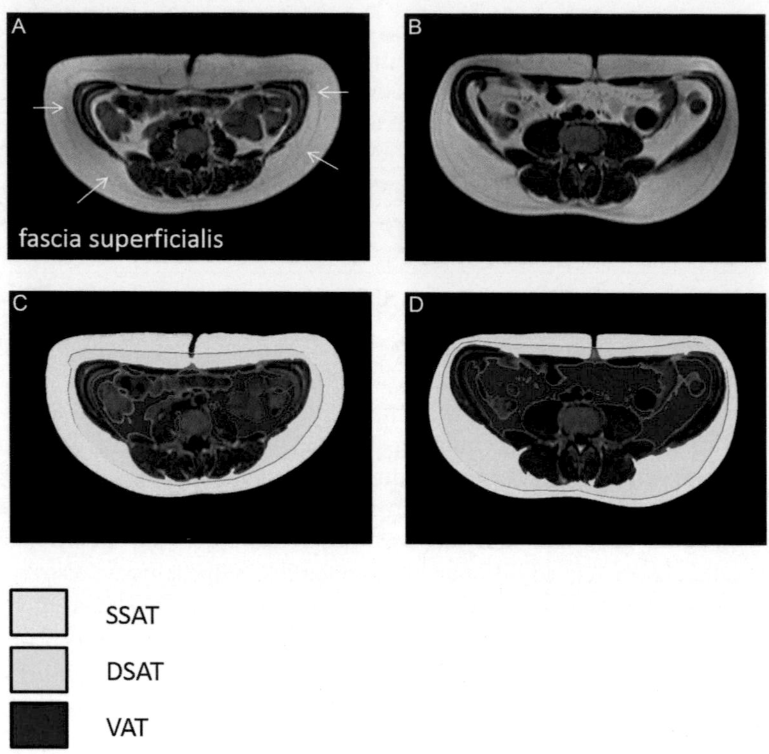

FIG. 28.1

Axial cross-sections at the umbilical level assessed by T_1-weighted fast spin echo imaging of (A) a 43-year-old female subject with a body mass index (BMI) of 28.9 kg/m^2 and (B) a 44-year-old male subject with a similar BMI of 28.8 kg/m^2 (B). Segmented superficial subcutaneous adipose (SSAT), deep subcutaneous adipose tissue (DSAT) and visceral adipose tissue (VAT) are indicated in the overlays (C and D). Typically, multiple axial slices across the abdomen are quantified, resulting in volume measurements of the three depots.

of a female and male subject of similar age and body-mass index (BMI), highlighting differences in SAT and VAT distributions in gender.

VAT is considered the most important adipose tissue compartment in the human body. Clinical interest for VAT quantification has increased due to its special role in the pathogenesis of insulin resistance and type 2 diabetes mellitus (T2D), regulation during lifestyle intervention, use in identification of described phenotypes, and also its predictive power concerning treatment strategies in various pathologies. The accumulation of VAT and organ fat is very strongly correlated to insulin resistance, which is a primary precursor of T2D [75–77], and incidence of T2D [78,79]. Abdominal adiposity is also a key factor in determining metabolic syndrome and its comorbidities. [80]. Table 28.1 summarizes primary complications and health risk factors associated with excessive fat accumulation in the body.

Table 28.2 summarizes a few comparison studies between MRI and other modalities in adipose tissue quantification. It is difficult to accurately estimate SAT and VAT from anthropometric parameters such as height, weight, BMI, and waist circumference measures. There are several more technical approaches for quantitative assessment of abdominal fat with inherent advantages and drawbacks. For

Table 28.2 Quantification of fat mass and volume by MRI compared to other modalities—exemplary studies and correlation coefficients are provided (if available).

Modality	Description	References
ADP	Tool of choice to predict VAT volume in boys ($r^2 = 0.81$) but not in girls, no surrogate for MRI if precision is needed	Winsley et al. [81]
	Limited to gross body composition analysis	Borga et al. [82]
	High accuracy and reproducibility for whole-body adipose tissue analysis ($r = 0.97–0.98$)	Ludwig et al. [83]
BIA	Requires different model parameters to be used (e.g., anthropometrics, physical activity, and ethnicity)	Borga et al. [82]
	Better correlations in the extremities than in the trunk	Kyle et al. [84]
	Good correlation to total abdominal fat ($r = 0.92–0.94$), not advised for measuring VAT ($r = 0.64–0.65$)	Browning et al. [85]
US	VAT: depth from the peritoneum to the lumbar spine	Rolfe et al. [85a]
	($r = 0.82/0.80$ for males/females)	
	SAT: depth from the skin to the abdominal muscles	
	($r = 0.63/0.68$ for males/females)	
DXA	Underestimation of total fat mass and VAT, ($r = 0.86–0.88$ for SAT, $r = 0.35–0.37$ for VAT)	Karlsson et al. [85b]
	Good correlation but systematic underestimation of VAT ($r = 0.90$)	Cheung et al. [86]
	Strong correlation ($r = 0.96$) with underestimation for lower VAT volumes, overestimation for higher VAT	Reinhardt et al. [87]
	Very strong correlation ($r = 0.99$) for body fat and VAT ($r = 0.97$) as predicted from DXA	Borga et al. [82]
CT	Strong correlation ($r = 0.89/0.92/0.95$ for VAT/SAT/TAT)	Klopfenstein et al. [88]
	Strong correlation: total abdominal fat $r = 0.90$, subcutaneous abdominal $r = 0.85$, VAT $r = 0.88$	Waduud et al. [89]
MR	VAT: 2D TSE vs 3D 2-pt Dixon and 3D SPGR, $r > 0.99$ for all	Fallah et al. [90]

ADP, air displacement plethysmography; BIA, bioelectrical impedance analysis; US, ultrasound; DXA, dual-energy X-ray absorptiometry, CT, computed tomography, SPGR, spoiled gradient recalled echo.

instance, bioelectrical impedance analysis correlates well with total abdominal fat but is not reliable for VAT quantification [85,91]. As another example, quantitative computed tomography can be used to measure SAT and VAT, but involves some radiation exposure for the subject. MRI offers several different approaches for SAT and VAT quantification and in particular is especially applicable in children as it is safe, does not use ionizing radiation, and can facilitate free-breathing scans [92]. Standard T_1-weighted techniques enable segmentation of adipose and lean tissue due to the inherent short longitudinal relaxation time (T_1) of fat in comparison to all other (lean) tissues in the body [93,94]. Additionally, fat can be separated from water-containing tissue by chemical-shift-encoding MRI techniques. This enables the reconstruction of complementary water-only and fat-only image pairs, the latter of which can be used to quantify VAT [69,95] (see Figs. 28.2 and 28.3, for example).

For segmentation of both SAT and VAT compartments, different strategies from manual to automated procedures have been developed. In brief, threshold-based segmentation with manual demarcation of VAT [94], automated fuzzy C-means, separation of VAT by orthonormal snakes [96,97],

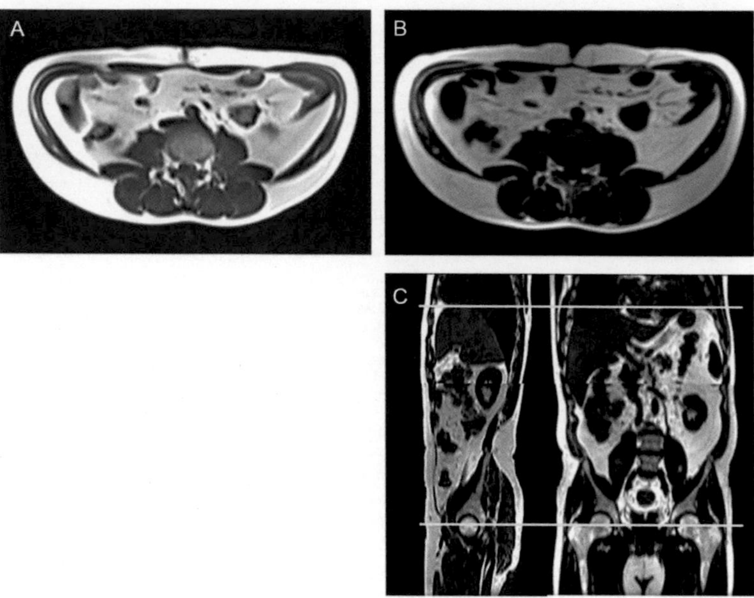

FIG. 28.2

Axial cross-sections at the umbilical level assessed by (A) T_1-weighted fast spin echo and (B) fat selective image from a 2-point Dixon acquisition in a 51-year-old male subject (BMI 24.7 kg/m^2). Note that non-adipose tissue appears almost black in (B). In (C), the images from (B) are reformatted in the sagittal and coronal cross-sections indicated by anatomical landmarks demarcating the typical extent analyzed by studies quantifying subcutaneous and visceral adipose tissue. Volumetric quantification of subcutaneous and visceral adipose tissue depots is typically performed in the space from the femoral head to the thoracic diaphragm.

histogram-based region growing [98,99], hybrid algorithms incorporating anatomical knowledge with segmentation algorithms [100] or atlas-based nonrigid image registration [82] have all been employed for this purpose. Semiautomated techniques require a few minutes with little human intervention for analysis of the entire abdomen, whereas manual segmentation is time-consuming and user-dependent. Table 28.3 shows a brief list of some commercial segmentation software. Deep learning and artificial intelligence-assisted strategies are emerging and will potentially accelerate the segmentation process to a few seconds in the near future [106–109].

In lieu of whole-abdomen measurements of SAT and VAT, the use of a representative single slice at the umbilicus or a small stack of slices (i.e., from the lumbar vertebrae L1–L5) has been suggested as a possible surrogate measure of total body SAT and VAT. These approaches have been implemented to reduce acquisition time, breath-holding requirements, and subsequent postprocessing efforts. There are various anatomical landmarks that can be considered: different lumbar vertebral bodies (or intervertebral disks) or the umbilical level. Schwenzer et al. showed strong significant correlations at the umbilical level ($r = 0.87/0.93$ for males/females) [110]. Maislin et al. revealed that measurements at the L2/L3 lead to a better prediction of VAT volume ($r = 0.96$) than those at the L4/L5 level ($r = 0.83$) [111]. The most reliable estimates of VAT volume are measurements at L2 for males ($r = 0.97$) and L3 for females ($r = 0.98$), as reported by Schweitzer et al. [112]. However, due to many confounding factors, a consensus on standardized anatomical landmark remains challenging [66].

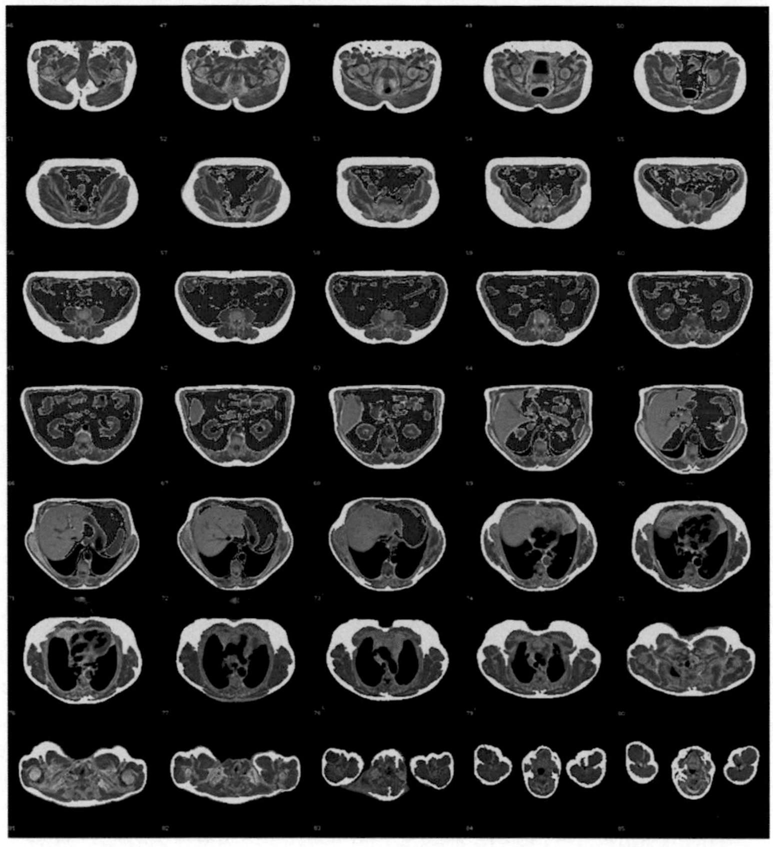

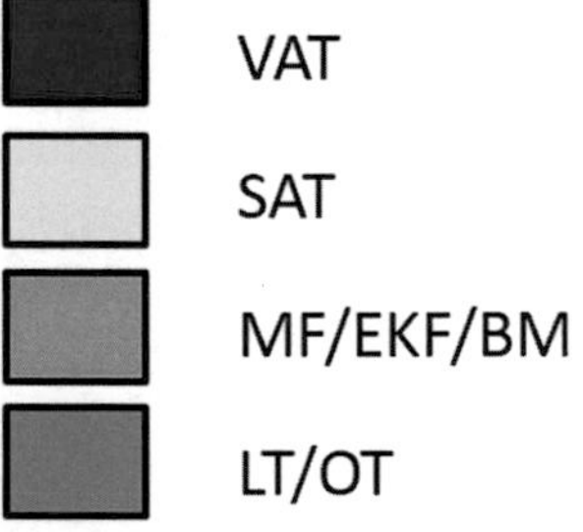

FIG. 28.3

Abdominal segmentation of subcutaneous adipose tissue (SAT), visceral adipose tissue (VAT), muscular/epicardial/bone marrow fat (MF/EKF/BM) and lean tissue/organ tissue (LT/OT) by an automated algorithm based on fuzzy-clustering methods, requiring a postprocessing time of 70s for the 35 axial slices shown.

Table 28.3 Examples of software available for quantification of body adipose tissue.

Software	Technique	Coverage	Principle	Variability SAT/VAT (%)	References
GE + in-house	T_1W-SE	Multi-slice	Histogram	3/<1	[101]
SliceOmatic™	T_1W-SE	Multi-slice	Threshold	1.8/5.2	[102]
Adobe Photoshop	T_1W-SE	Multi-slice	Manual	0.2/10.8	[103]
HippoFat™	T_1W-GRE	Multi-slice	Fuzzy C-mean	0.9/13.4	[96]
Analyze	T_1W	Multi-slice	Manual	1.5/8.1	[104]
ATsegment	T_1W-SE	Multi-slice	Fuzzy C-mean	1.5/1.1	[97]
ImageJ	2 pt-Dixon	3D	Fuzzy C-mean	0.5/6.2	[105]
AMRA-Profiler	2 pt-Dixon	3D	Atlas-based	1.1/1.6	[82]

SE, spin echo; GRE, gradient recalled echo.

MRI-based quantification of SAT and VAT volume has been applied in many cross-sectional studies [94,113–116]. Large-scale epidemiological studies using standardized MR protocols aim to assess relations of VAT to medical complications in further life [113,115,117]. Different questions can be answered using these data. For instance, gender-related differences have been elucidated, with males having a nearly doubled VAT but lower SAT volume at identical BMI as compared with females [77,115]. Moreover, males have higher portions of DSAT and less SSAT compared to females, and these compartments differ morphologically and physiologically and display unique endocrine and metabolic characteristics [118]. Additionally, VAT increases with increasing age [116], and there is a significant negative connection between the amount of VAT and insulin sensitivity [77,115]. See Fig. 28.4 for example.

For VAT quantification, it is worth noting that a more detailed classification of the compartment can be performed to differentiate the fat depot into sub-compartments including mesenteric, gonadal, epicardial, retroperitoneal, omental and peri-renal portions. However, at this point it remains unclear whether such stratification adds significantly important additional information regarding the metabolic status of a subject. For example, it has been shown that adipose tissue in the renal hilum or periaortic fat is involved in altered organ function (e.g., renal dysfunction or atherosclerosis) [5,119]. Furthermore, subjects with different body habitus and yet similar VAT may exhibit different metabolic risk profiles. Recently it has been proposed to correct absolute measurements of VAT volume by normalizing the values by subject height. The VAT-index ($VATi = VAT[l]/height[m]^2$) has been suggested as an improved parameter for reliable classification across populations [115,120,121].

28.2.2 Applications and trends

Different phenotypes of adipose tissue distribution, especially regarding VAT, have been described in recent years. It has been shown that there is a large variability in VAT volume for subjects with the same BMI. In obese subjects with a BMI >30 kg/m^2, VAT measurements ranged between 1 and 8.6 l in females and between 2 and 10.5 l in males. Thus, there are obese subjects which have low VAT volumes and concomitant good insulin sensitivity. The phenotype of this beneficial phenomenon is called metabolically healthy obesity (MHO) [122,123]. Fig. 28.5 shows exemplary cross-sections of a metabolically

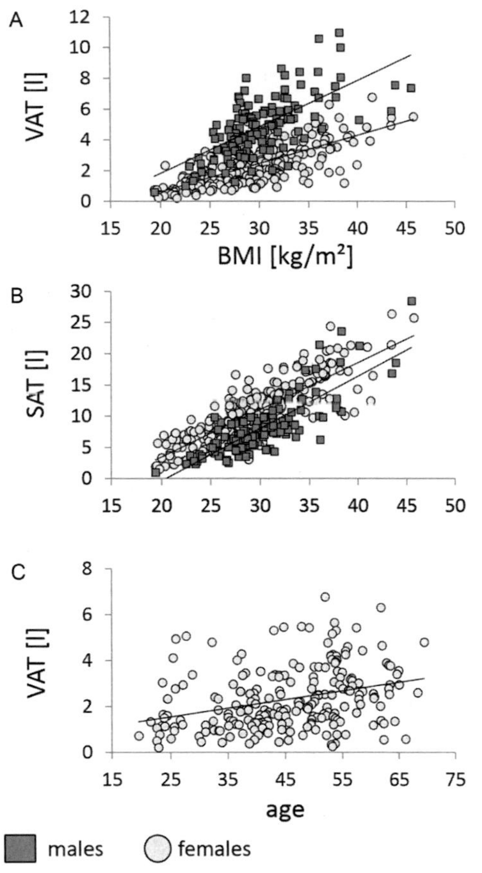

FIG. 28.4

(A) Linear correlation between VAT volume and BMI, (B) SAT volume and BMI, (C and D) VAT volume and age, and (E and F) VAT volume and insulin sensitivity in a cohort of 360 Caucasian subjects (130 males, 230 females) at increased risk for type 2 diabetes. Males have almost twice the VAT volume compared to females with identical BMI, whereas SAT volume measurements between the two genders are similar. For both genders, note that VAT increases with age and that there is a negative correlation between VAT and insulin sensitivity (ISI Matsuda determined by oral glucose tolerance test).

healthy obese female subject (A) and a metabolically unhealthy obese female subject (B) with identical BMIs of 31 kg/m^2 and clearly different amounts of VAT (1.2l vs 6.8l VAT). As the total amount of body fat is comparable, it has been suggested that metabolically healthy subjects have a larger amount of fat in the lower extremities and unhealthy subjects accumulate fat in the abdomen, reflecting the android (apple-shaped) and gynoid (pear-shaped) fat distribution. Additionally, there are lean subjects with normal BMI (<25 kg/m^2) showing a surprisingly large VAT volume and reduced insulin sensitivity. This phenotype is called TOFI (thin outside, fat inside) [124] and an example is depicted in Fig. 28.5 C and D for two male subjects with BMIs of 23.5 kg/m^2. For both phenotypes, MHO and TOFI, fat quantification with MRI is a helpful technique for reliable identification.

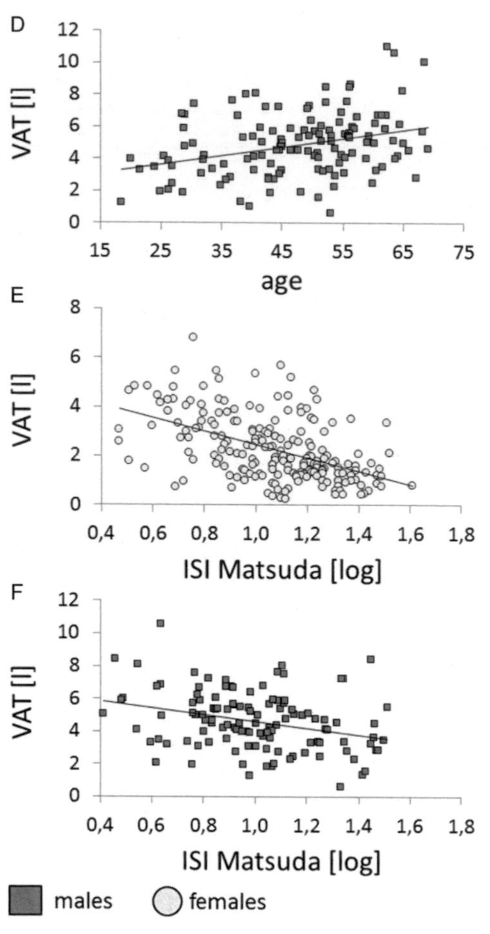

FIG. 28.4—Cont'd

Lifestyle intervention programs for prevention of T2D in subjects at increased risk for metabolic diseases, including dietary changes and/or increased physical exercise, have proven to be beneficial in modifying the metabolic status of unhealthy individuals. Various studies including the Diabetes Prevention Program [125], the Diabetes Prevention Study [126] and others [127,128] have shown that a reduction of the incidence of diabetes can be achieved through lifestyle changes. A weight reduction of >5% of the initial weight is the primary goal of mostlifestyle intervention studies. With such a reduction in weight, the VAT is disproportionally reduced [129], as it is more metabolically active than SAT [73] due to its higher lipolytic capacity, higher density, and stronger supply from blood vessels and nerves [129,130]. In a recentlifestyle intervention study combining dietary changes and exercise performed in a cohort of 243 subjects at increased risk for T2D, a reduction in VAT of approximately 15% from the initial value was observed in conjunction with a weight reduction of only 3% [77]. Gepner et al. report a 22% reduction of VAT after an 18-month randomized controlled dietary trial in 278 sedentary subjects with abdominal

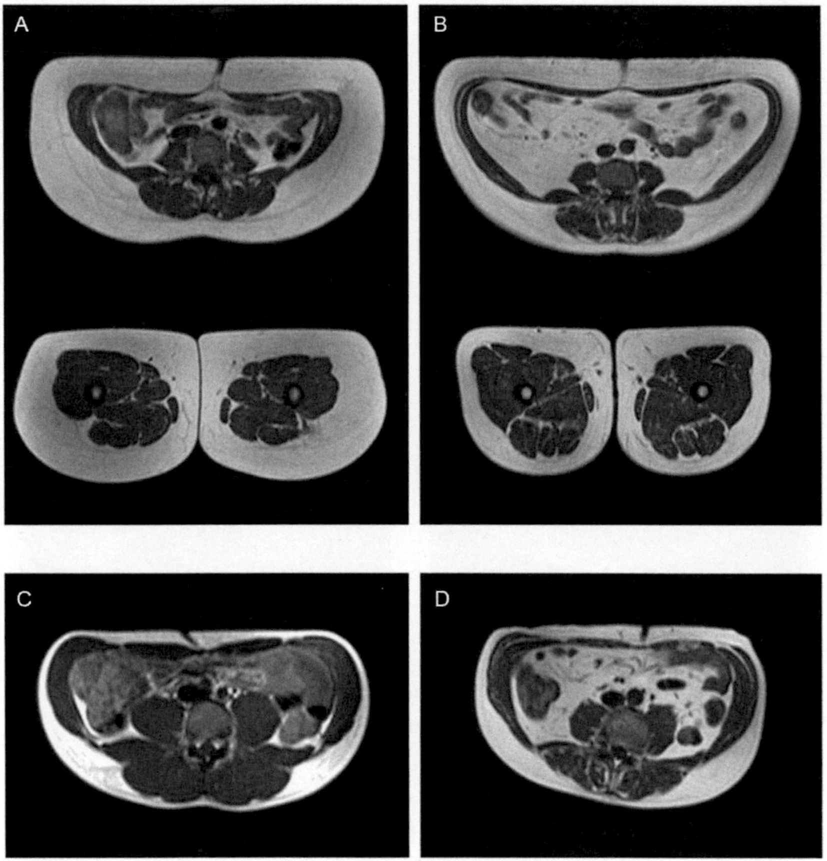

FIG. 28.5

Representative examples of different phenotypes of adipose tissue distribution: The subject in (A) is a metabolically healthy, insulin-sensitive obese female with a low amount of VAT but high SAT in the abdomen and the lower extremities. In contrast, the subject in (B) is an insulin-resistant female with an identical BMI of 31 kg/m^2, who exhibits high VAT and a thinner layer of SAT in the lower extremities. (C) A normal weight (BMI 23.5 kg/m^2) insulin-sensitive male, with minimal SAT and VAT, in contrast to (D) a subject with the same BMI but with the TOFI-phenotype (thin outside, fat inside). Note the significant VAT volume of the subject in (D).

obesity [131] with a corresponding weight reduction of only 3.2%. However, there are subjects who are not able to benefit from a change in their lifestyle, the phenotype of so-called "nonresponders." It has been shown that insulin-resistant subjects with high amounts of VAT and high intrahepatic lipids (IHLs) prior to lifestyle intervention cannot reduce their VAT and weight and are prone to even worsen their metabolic status during (although not due to) lifestyle intervention [77]. Exemplary images prior to and after participation in a lifestyle intervention program of 9 months are shown in Fig. 28.6. For those subjects, in order to avoid a metabolic deterioration, early pharmacological treatment, for example, by metformin, is advised.

With increasing prevalence of childhood obesity worldwide [132], body composition assessment by MRI is becoming popular for children, especially as there is no radiation exposure. Since children may

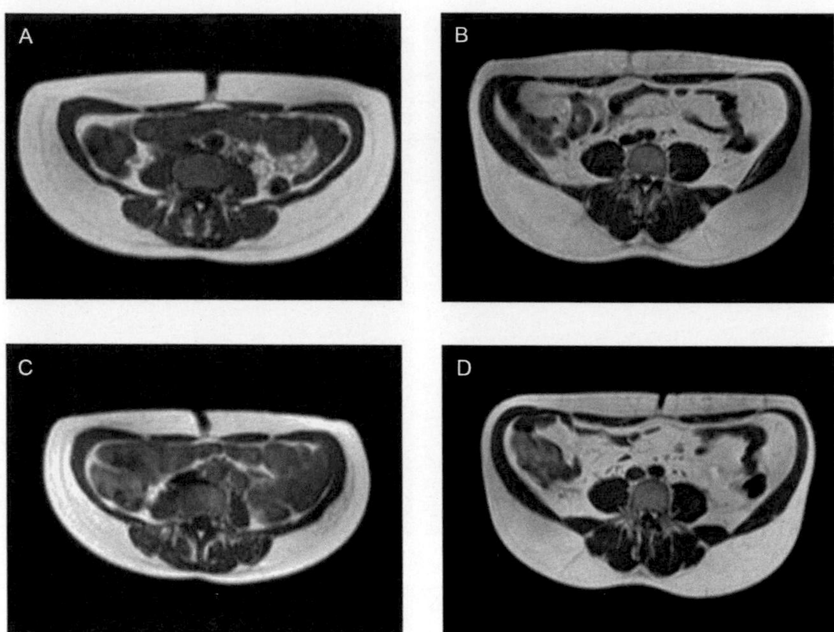

FIG. 28.6

Representative examples of individuals undergoing lifestyle intervention to reduce SAT and VAT. (A and C) Longitudinal images show significant reduction in SAT and VAT over time, while the images of the subject shown in (B and D) show no major changes in adipose tissue volumes due to intervention.

have impaired breath-hold capabilities, radial read-out techniques enable reliable artifact-free acquisition during free breathing [92,133–135]. In children and adolescents there are gender-related differences, and VAT volume is smaller compared to BMI-matched adults, not reflecting the effects of insulin sensitivity which is even worse in obese children [136]. Shen et al. highlight the sexual dimorphism of adipose tissue distribution across the lifespan, showing increasing VAT and SAT volumes with greater age. The proportion of VAT to total adipose tissue increases with age, whereas the proportion of SAT to total adipose tissue decreases with age [137]. This is confirmed by Hübers et al. who describe the age-related development of VAT in a cohort of children, adolescents, young adults, and adults [138], additionally showing that VAT volume in males and females is very similar at comparable BMIs until the age of 30.

Finally, MR-based quantification of adipose tissue volume and differentiation of SAT and VAT is of increasing interest for prospective clinical studies, epidemiological observations in population-based surveys, and also in clinical routine as it has been shown that an increased VAT volume bears severe health risk factors as shown in Table 28.1. Being aware of the age- and gender-related differences of adipose tissue distribution in the body (i.e., more VAT in older subjects, more fat in males compared to females at identical BMI) and the knowledge about different phenotypes including MHO and TOFI will help to identify subjects or patients at increased health risk, which is not possible by simple anthropometrics or visual assessment.

28.3 Current applications of fat quantification in organs

28.3.1 Liver

Hepatic steatosis, also called nonalcoholic fatty liver disease (NAFLD), is a liver disease with increasing prevalence worldwide [139]. NAFLD can progress to the advanced form called nonalcoholic steatohepatitis (NASH), which is accompanied by inflammation and eventually fibrosis, finally resulting in liver cirrhosis [140,141].

Historically, invasive needle biopsy of the liver and microscopic evaluation of the extracted tissue by pathologists has been considered the gold-standard for quantification of hepatic steatosis [142]. This type of analysis enables reliable detection of macrovesicular steatosis but in most instances underestimates microvesicular fat inclusions [143]. It must be noted that biopsy-based quantification of steatosis is derived from a small tissue sample and may, therefore, be misleading in cases of uneven fat distribution in the liver. Thus, noninvasive techniques for quantification of the degree of fatty infiltration and assessment of the pattern of hepatic fat distribution are preferable.

The first measurements of IHLs were performed with single-voxel proton magnetic resonance spectroscopy (^{1}H-MRS). The main challenge to obtain spectra of reliable quality from the liver is the movement of the organ due to breathing. Thus, data collection has to be performed in a defined respiratory state: data acquisition in exhalation or automated gating (more time-consuming) is recommended. Fatty liver is defined as a spectroscopic IHL-content of >5.56%, derived from the general population in the framework of the Dallas Heart Study [144]. It is important to note that ^{1}H-MRS can neither distinguish between nonalcoholic (NAFLD) or alcoholic fatty liver disease nor between NAFLD and NASH (nonalcoholic steatohepatitis).

Fig. 28.7 shows spectra recorded from a 49-year-old female and a 51-year-old male subject with NAFLD and very similar IHL (about 9%–10%). Water and fat resonances are well resolved; however, it is difficult to distinguish all fat metabolites [120] from liver spectra. The spectral pattern is influenced by the microscopic magnetic field inhomogeneities in liver tissue. Younger males and females generally differ in linewidth of the metabolites, which is broader in males compared to fertile women, as women are capable of washing-out iron during menstruation.

For quantification of low amounts of IHL, a single breath-hold might not be sufficient as just four to five averages can be taken and the SNR will not be sufficient to detect IHL <3% of the water signal. To avoid signal bias from T_1 and T_2 relaxation, the repetition time (TR) has to be set to at least 4 s (to reduce the effects of T_1 relaxation) and the echo time (TE) as short as possible (to reduce the effects of T_2 relaxation, standard minimum TE: 10 ms for STEAM, 30 ms for PRESS). However, these measurements do not accurately reflect proton density fat fraction (PDFF) which is a fundamental tissue property independent of the employed MR parameters and can be considered to be an objective MR-based metric of liver TG concentration [145], Therefore, relaxation correction using the T_2 times of fat and water is still required for this purpose. A spectroscopic technique in which five echoes are acquired with different echo times in a single acquisition and corrected for the T_2 decay of water and fat for the calculation of PDFF has been introduced and validated against single-voxel spectroscopy [145] and imaging approaches [146], and will be described later on. An exemplary dataset of this approach using the HISTO-MRS (HIgh-Speed T_2-corrected multiechO) technique is shown in Fig. 28.8.

As TGs are composed of several different chemical groups (methyl, methylene, β-methylene, allylic, α-methylene, diallylic, olefinic) which can theoretically be separated in ^{1}H-MRS, each of these resonances should be included in the fitting model. However, it is challenging to distinguish metabolites with low concentrations in the liver due to microscopic magnetic field inhomogeneities (e.g., iron deposition), resulting in broad linewidths and insufficient SNR for PDFF measurement. Fitting of the methyl proton signal (at 0.9 ppm) and the dominant methylene signal (at 1.3 ppm) has been proposed as a compromise for reliable quantification of IHL, resulting in fat fraction values which are lower than measured PDFF values. Implementation of a fat signal model with fixed amplitudes for the remaining metabolites has been also suggested to estimate the PDFF more accurately [147].

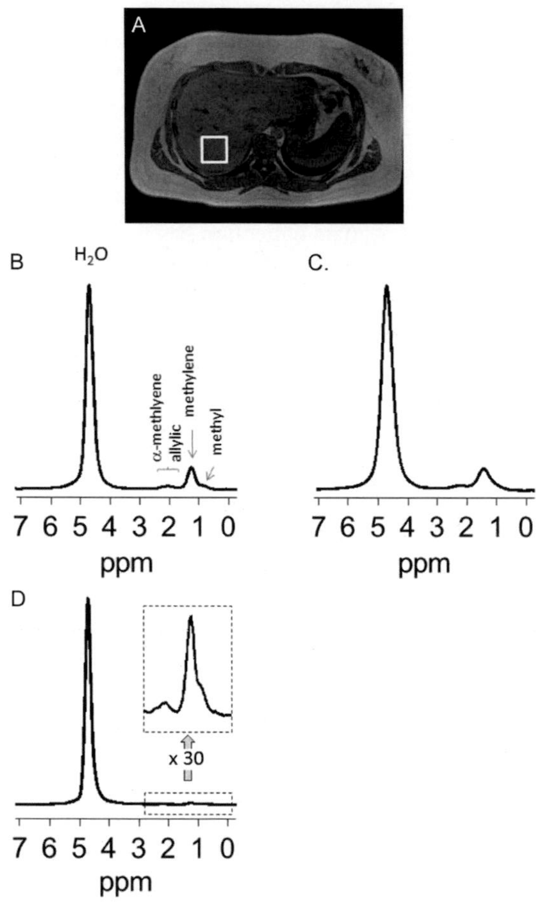

FIG. 28.7

Representative spectra from the liver acquired at 1.5 T (sample voxel position indicated in (A) for quantification of intrahepatic lipids (IHL). (B) MRS data from a female subject with 9.8% IHL. (C) A male subject with 9.6% IHL. Note identification of major resonance peaks including water and triglyceride protons. (D) demonstrates that single-voxel MRS can be used to reliably quantify IHL content of less than 1%, as shown in a representative lean subject.

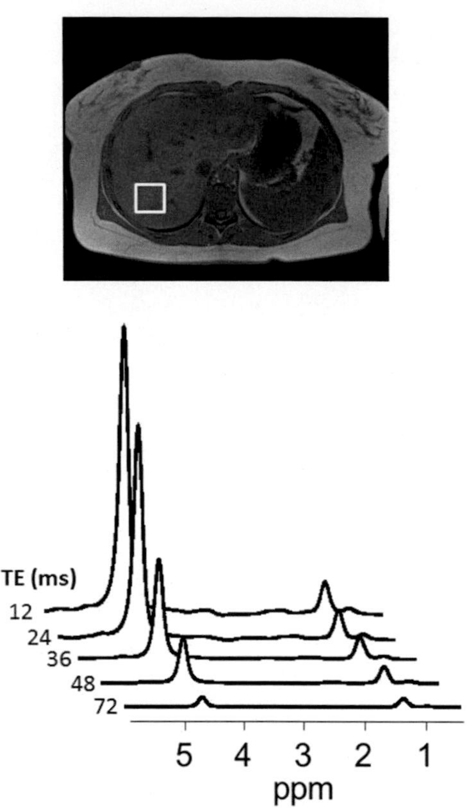

FIG. 28.8

HISTO-MRS (HIgh-Speed T_2-corrected multiechO) from the liver of a female subject. These spectra were collected at five different and increasing echo times, recorded in a single breath-hold for automated correction of T_2 signal decay of water and fat peaks.

As shown in Fig. 28.9, chemical-shift-encoding-based water-fat separation techniques have been applied for measuring a spatially resolved fat fraction map. Special attention has been paid to removing effects confounding liver fat quantification and extracting the PDFF [148].

Multiple studies have also reported on the spatial heterogeneity of liver PDFF, with the highest values measured in liver segment VII and the lowest values in liver segment II [149]. An excellent agreement has been shown between region of interest (ROI)-based and parametric map-based PDFF estimation over a wide range of imaging and analysis conditions [150]. However, it has been recommended that for improved reproducibility and repeatability of liver PDFF as much area of the liver should be sampled using multiple large ROIs [151,152]. In addition to the extensive cross-sectional results on liver PDFF reported in the literature, liver PDFF mapping has been also recently applied in longitudinal studies involving overfeeding of healthy volunteers [153] and the pharmacological treatment of patients with nonalcoholic steatohepatitis [154,155]. Overall, assessments of liver PDFF using MRI has enabled multiple insights into liver pathophysiology [156].

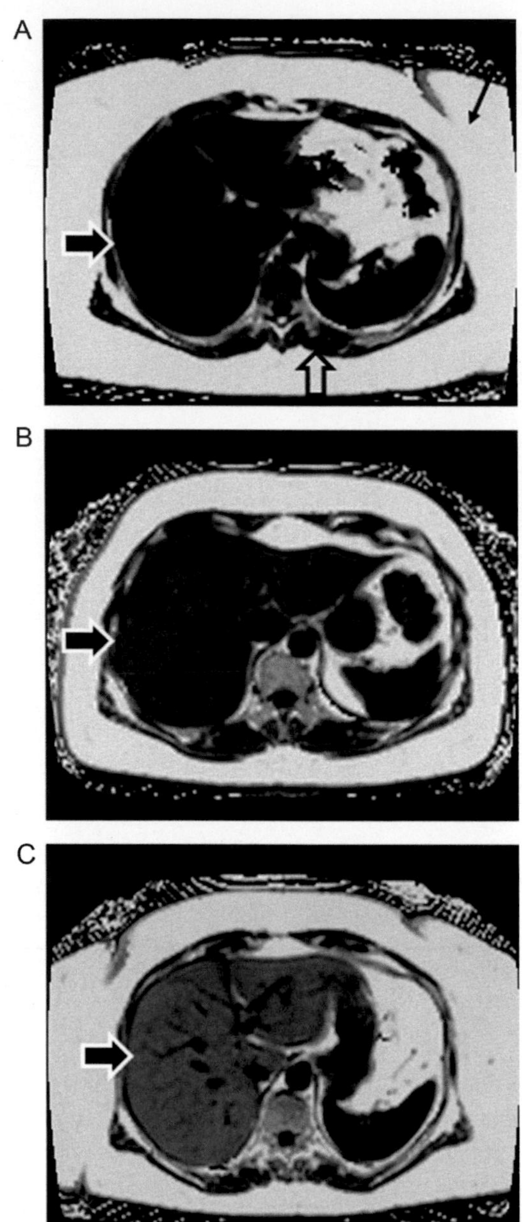

FIG. 28.9

Representative T_2*-corrected proton density fat fraction (PDFF) maps from axial multiecho chemical-shift-encoded MRI data of the liver acquired at 3T in three female subjects. The maps are displayed on a 0% (black) to 100% (white) scale. Note that SAT (thin black arrow) appears white, and muscle appears black (white arrow with black border). Note the different shades of grey within the liver between the three subjects (black arrows with white borders), indicating different fat fractions. Subject in (A) has an IHL of 1.1%; Subject in (B) has an IHL of 9.8%, and subject in (C) has an IHL of 25.3%.

There are multiple applications for quantification of IHL. In clinical routine, fat selective MRI is commonly added to the standard protocol for identification and diagnosis of hepatic steatosis, with dedicated additional imaging sequences for a detailed rating of further liver pathologies. For this purpose, frequency-selective techniques as DIXON [157,158] or IDEAL [159,160] imaging are chosen. It has to be mentioned that is not necessarily essential to determine the exact fat fraction (i.e., PDFF) but in many cases sufficient to get an impression of whether or not hepatic steatosis is present— information that can be derived by visual inspection of weighted images by an experienced radiologist. MRS is usually not applied in daily routine as most clinicians are not familiar with the spectral information, the acquisition and postprocessing of spectra are time-consuming, and most clinical scanners are not equipped with the MRS option.

For prospective cross-sectional and/or longitudinal research studies it is important to exactly assess IHL by MRI or MRS as this information is needed, for instance, to select individuals for an intervention (NAFLD as an inclusion criterion), to predict NAFLD [161] or to determine changes of IHL during specific lifestyle intervention programs, including change in dietary habits and increased exercise [77,162] or pharmacological intervention [163–165].

28.3.2 Heart, pancreas, kidneys, and brown adipose tissue

In addition to the liver, there are other abdominal organs and ectopic fat depots which are of clinical interest in fat quantification. The following subsection describes the application of quantitative fat MRS and MRI in the heart, pancreas and kidney, and discusses some organ-specific shortcomings and limitations.

28.3.2.1 Heart

Quantification of myocardial triglyceride content (MTGC) [166–168] (Table 28.4) is of special interest in patients with metabolic syndrome or T2D, as higher MTGC levels are correlated to myocardial dysfunction and therefore a higher risk for heart failure [170,174]. Furthermore, this measurement is essential for characterization of myocardial dysfunction [175,176].

To quantify MTCG, a ^{1}H-MRS spectrum is usually collected in the ventricular septum. Such an acquisition is challenging as it requires an initial cine scan for reliable planning of the spectroscopic measurement, respiratory gating due to the breathing-dependent movement of the heart, and cardiac

Table 28.4 Variability/reproducibility of MTGC.

Citation	Field strength (T)	*n*	Fitting routine	Reference	Intrasession CV (%)	Intersession CV (%)
[169]	1.5	12	Versatile frequency domain	Water	13	
[170]	1.5	6	NUTS software (Acorn NMR, Inc.)	Water	17	
[171]	3	9	jMRUI/AMARES	Water		6.3
[172]	3	8	jMRUI/AMARES	Water	5	6.5
[173]	1.5	19	jMRUI/AMARES	Water	5.2	

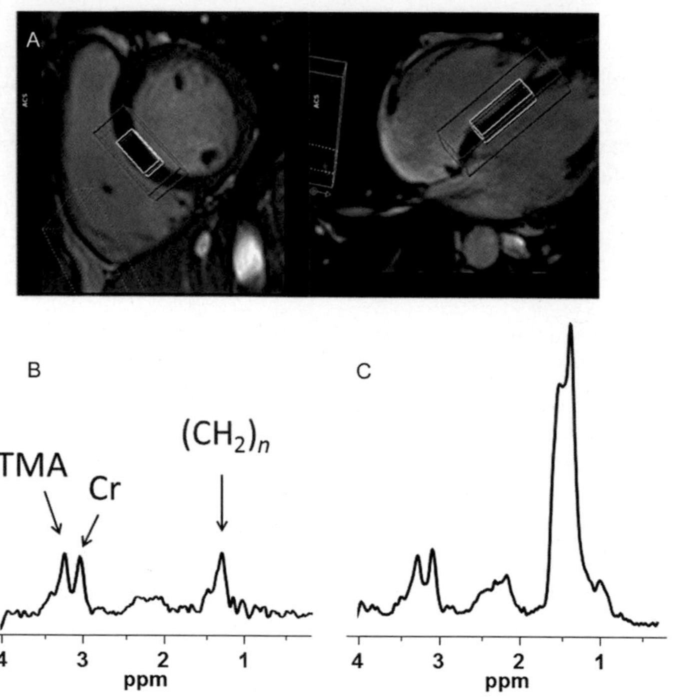

FIG. 28.10

Examples of myocardial fat quantification by single-voxel MRS at 3T. (A) The measurement voxel (white box) is placed along the ventricular septum in short-axis and two-chamber views. The bounding green box is the B_0 magnetic field shim box. Representative spectra are shown in (B) for a normal-weight male and in (C) for an obese male. Note the similar amplitudes of (trimethylamine N-oxide) TMA and (creatine) Cr metabolites and marked differences in the CH_2 methyl peak of triglycerides.

gating to perform the examination in the end-systolic phase. After careful shimming, single-voxel spectra of good quality can be obtained within a few minutes. Reproducibility measurements have resulted in test-retest-variabilities between 5% and 17% (see Table 28.4). Fig. 28.10 depicts the typical position of the volume of interest (VOI) in the ventricular septum and resulting spectra recorded from a healthy male subject with a low MTGC (BMI 21 kg/m^2) and in a subject with a high MTGC (BMI 30 kg/m^2). Fitting of spectra can be performed using common postprocessing tools (see the section on intramyocellular lipids, IMCL) and for quantification of MTGC, internal references are used (water from unsuppressed spectra or methylene resonance of creatine). Comparable to IMCL, MRS-based MTGC measurements show diurnal changes with a depletion of >30% in the evening compared to the early morning after overnight fasting [171]. Endurance athletes have been shown to be characterized by lower MTGC compared to untrained healthy controls [177]. Patients with hypertensive heart disease have higher MTGC levels than patients with hypertrophic cardiomyopathy [178].

Imaging-based quantification of MTGC remains technically challenging due to the high accuracy and precision needed to measure MTGC, with typical values around 1%. Liu et al. showed a moderate agreement in the fat fraction between a 2-point Dixon imaging technique and MRS in the heart of healthy subjects [179]. The mean myocardial fat fraction as assessed with 2-point Dixon imaging was 1.04% ± 0.4% (range: 0.32%–2.44%). Water-fat separation methods have also been recently successfully applied for measuring pericardial and epicardial fat volume with good inter-reader agreement [180]. Data from chemical-shift-encoded MRI have been used to quantify left atrial epicardial fat volume, which has been shown to be associated with atrial fibrillation [181].

28.3.2.2 Pancreas

The role of pancreatic steatosis in the pathogenesis of T2D is not yet clear; similarly, the relevant factors in the accumulation of fat in this wedge-shaped gland are unknown [182–184]. Fat accumulation is associated with reduced insulin secretion in glucose-intolerant humans [185–190] but it is yet unknown whether and how adipocyte infiltration affects islet function.

Due to its inhomogeneous composition and narrow width, spectroscopic examinations are challenging. Even small movements of the subject or minor organ movement/displacement between morphologic imaging and spectroscopic data acquisition, for example, after coughing, may lead to inclusion of signal from nearby VAT. Thus, MRS of the pancreas is highly prone to errors and not advised for scientific or diagnostic purposes. Imaging-based measurements of pancreatic fat content are more practical and thus more extensively employed. Spectral-spatial fat selective techniques [191] have been used to show different amounts of fat in the pancreas caput, corpus, and cauda [185,191] (see Figs. 28.11 and 28.12).

Pancreatic PDFF mapping has been performed in both healthy subjects and patients with obesity, diabetes and NAFLD [192,193], and studies have used PDFF from MRI to characterize the fat content in separate compartments of the pancreas (i.e., head, body, tail) [186,192]. Due to the irregular shape of the pancreas, a higher spatial resolution should be employed for PDFF mapping in the pancreas compared to the liver. Dedicated ROI analysis methods have been proposed for improving the interobserver agreement for quantifying intrapancreatic fat [186]. At higher levels of pancreatic fat measurements, dedicated ROI analysis methods have been shown to yield interobserver agreement with a coefficient of 4.3%. However, there is in general a lack of studies validating PDFF mapping with reference methods in the pancreas [194,195]. Similar to PDFF quantification in the liver, pancreatic PDFF quantification has been shown to benefit from T_1 and $T_2{}^*$ correction [196].

28.3.2.3 Kidney

Renal steatosis (or fatty kidney) is characterized by an accumulation of fat in tubular/glomerular cells of the kidney [197]. There have been a few studies applying ^{1}H-MRS in the renal cortex of humans, including [198], which use a respiratory-gated technique to improve spectral quality and reproducibility. According to Hammer et al. who performed a study in a cohort of subjects without a history of renal or cardiovascular disease there is almost no fat in the kidney (<1% with water serving as an internal reference) [198]. Dekkers et al. report on good intra- and inter-examination reproducibility and a higher renal TG content in patients with T2D compared to matched healthy controls [199]. Fig. 28.13 shows spectra recorded from the left kidney in a healthy volunteer without renal fat and in another volunteer with approximately 1% renal fat (Fig. 28.12C). Like the pancreas, small movements of the organ from respiratory and physiological motion can lead to signal contamination from nearby VAT.

Imaging-based methods for renal PDFF mapping have been also applied in a small number of studies [61,200]. There is in general limited knowledge of the renal fat fraction in the healthy kidney. However, renal fat fraction has been shown to increase in patients with type 2 diabetes [200] and in patients with early-stage diabetic nephropathy [61].

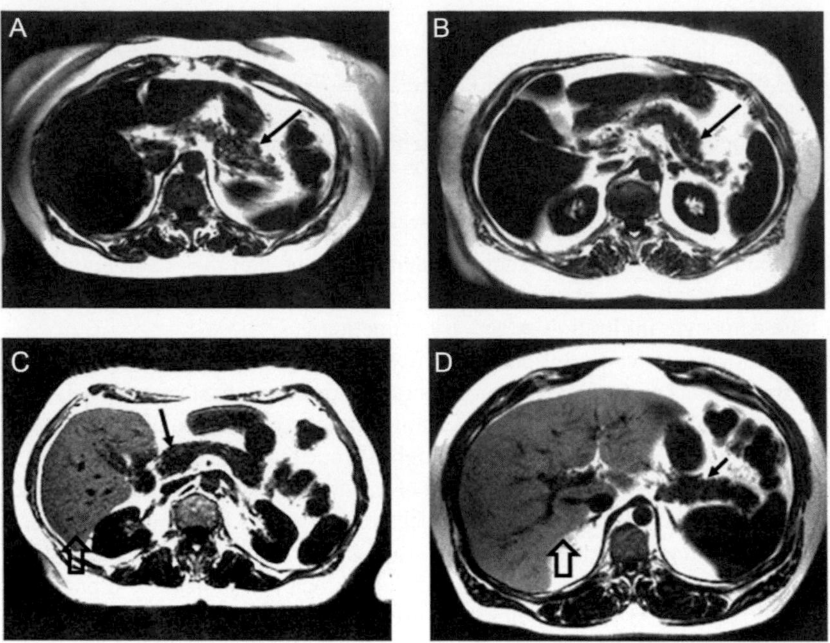

FIG. 28.11

Spectral-spatial fat-selective images of the pancreas in four subjects acquired at 1.5T. (A and B) Note that the pancreas has a *light grey* speckled appearance within the organ (*arrows*), indicating inhomogeneous levels of fat within the organ. (C and D) The pancreas is darker and more homogeneous (*arrows*), while the liver (*open arrows*) has a *light grey* appearance, indicative of fat within the organ.

28.3.2.4 **Brown adipose tissue**

There has been an increased recent research interest in the noninvasive imaging of BAT, due to the potential value of BAT as a therapeutic target in obesity. It has been shown that activated BAT can be observed in a significant percentage of the adult population using positron emission tomography (PET) [201,202], with the largest volume found in the supraclavicular fat depot. BAT is known to have a reduced fat fraction compared to white adipose tissue, due to the higher concentration of intracellular and extracellular water in BAT.

The human supraclavicular fat fraction has been measured in infants [203], adolescents [204] and adults [205–208] using primarily chemical-shift-encoding-based water-fat imaging techniques. It should be noted that differentiating between a cluster of brown adipocytes and a mixed cluster of white and brown adipocytes is not possible using fat fraction measurements. Although the fat fraction does not reflect mass or volume of BAT, supraclavicular MR fat fraction mapping is currently a popular noninvasive technique for detecting the presence of BAT in humans due to its excellent reproducibility [209] and repeatability independent of BAT activation status [210]. Supraclavicular fat fraction reliability has been reported to be 0.97 for test-retest, 0.95 for intra-observer, and 0.56 for inter-observer

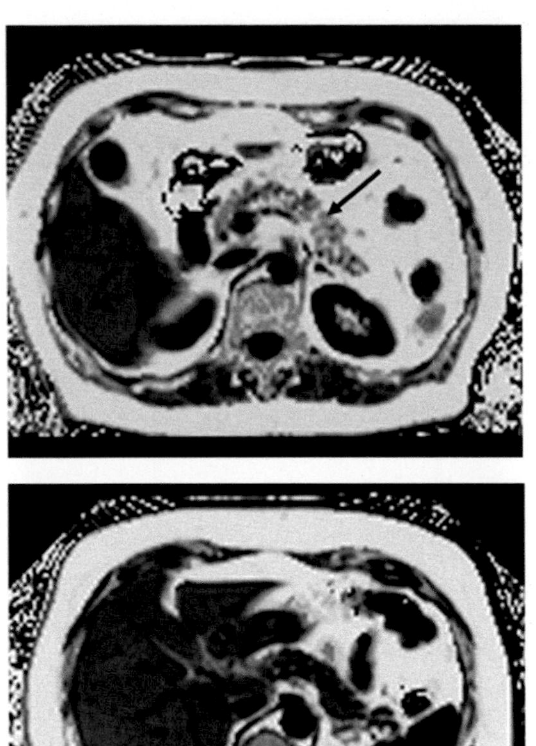

FIG. 28.12

Representative T_2*-corrected proton density fat fraction (PDFF) maps from axial multiecho chemical-shift-encoded MRI data of the pancreas acquired at 3 T in two male subjects. The data are displayed on a 0% (*black*) to 100% (*white*) scale. The map in (A) was collected in a subject with high pancreatic fat (*arrow*).

measurements [209]. Supraclavicular fat fraction agreement displayed mean differences of 0.5% for test-retest, -0.5% for intra-observer and 5.6% for inter-observer measurements [209]. To improve the inter-observer variability of manual segmentations, techniques for automated segmentation of the human cervical-supraclavicular adipose have been developed showing an excellent agreement to reference manual segmentations (Dice coefficient of 0.93) [211].

Supraclavicular MR fat fraction mapping has been also recently applied in a limited number of studies in patients. In adult patients with a clinical manifestation of cardiovascular disease, BAT presence based on supraclavicular MR fat fraction has been associated with obesity and metabolic dysfunction [205]. MRS-based supraclavicular fat fraction has been also shown to be higher in patients with high insulin resistance compared to subjects with normal and lower insulin resistance [212].

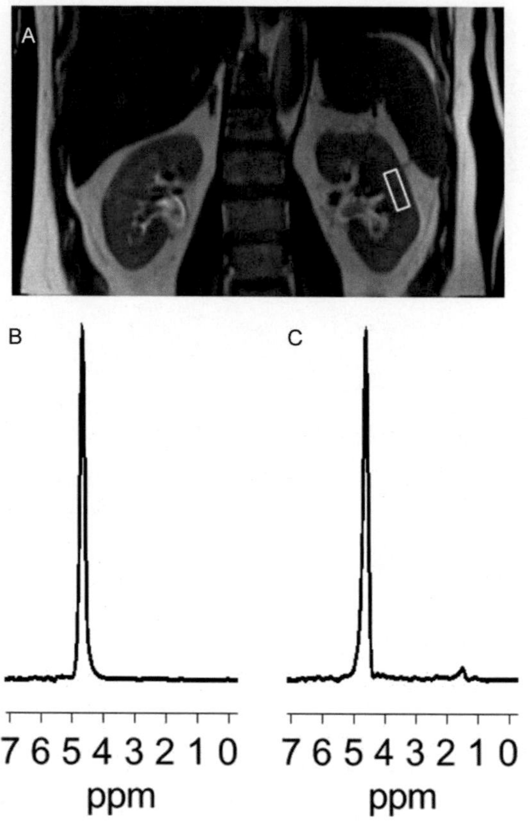

FIG. 28.13

Representative MR spectra of the kidneys in two subjects, acquired at 3T. (A) Representative voxel placement. (B) and (C) Spectra showing very low 0.05% fat content and higher 1.1% fat content in the renal cortex, respectively. Note in (C) the small triglyceride peak near 1.3 ppm.

28.4 Current applications of fat quantification in skeletal muscle and bone marrow

28.4.1 IMCL and EMCL in skeletal muscle

The assessment of lipids and TGs in skeletal muscle can be divided into two areas: localization and characterization of fat and assessment of lipid metabolism. Lipids exist in two different compartments in skeletal muscle, namely in myocytes in the form of lipid droplets within the cytoplasm of muscle cells (intramyocellular lipids, IMCL), and outside myocytes as fatty septa around the muscle fiber bundles (extramyocellular lipids, EMCL). While EMCL are metabolically rather inert and primarily serve as a storage site for TG, IMCL can be metabolized to provide an energy source for muscle activity. The assessment of IMCL can be performed using ^{1}H MRS spectroscopy, but the low concentration of IMCL and the proximity in resonance frequency to EMCL precludes the use of chemical-shift-encoded quantification. IMCL levels can either be quantified by expressing the area under the peak as ratio to an internal reference standard, such as water, creatine or bone marrow, or by using an external reference. Fig. 28.14 shows spectra recorded from tibialis anterior and soleus at 1.5 T and 3 T showing how the separation of the spectral peaks of IMCL and EMCL is improved at higher field strength.

Since IMCL are metabolically active, most applications in the assessment of IMCL concern diurnal or physiological changes, or diseases where metabolism is affected [213]. Baseline IMCL levels have been shown to vary significantly within a subject in the course of a day under defined dietary conditions

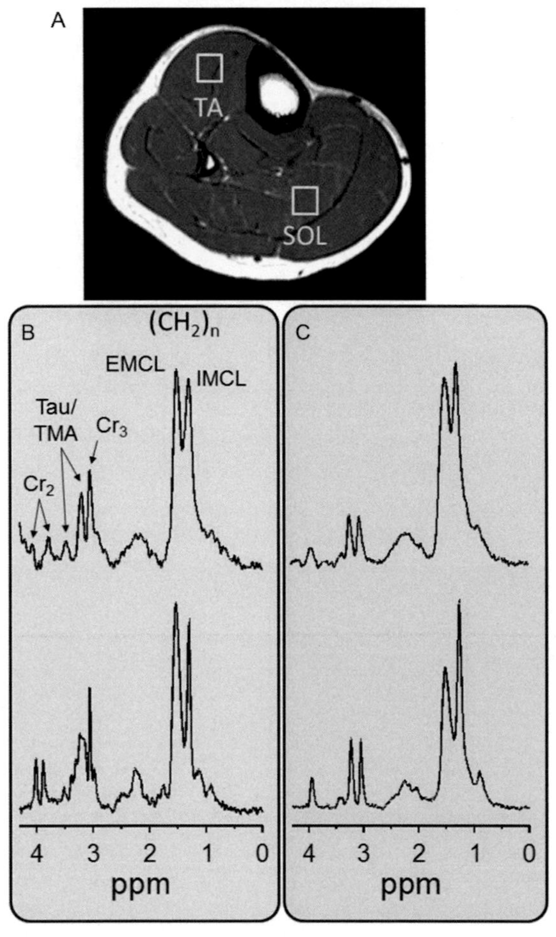

FIG. 28.14

Single-voxel MRS spectra acquired from the tibialis anterior (TA in (A)) muscle and soleus muscle (SOL in (A)). TA spectra are shown in (B) and SOL spectra are shown in (C). In (B) and (C), the top spectra were acquired at 1.5 T, and the bottom spectra were acquired at 3 T. Note the improved spectral dispersion at the higher field strength which enables improved separation of intramyocellular (IMCL) and extramyocellular lipids (EMCL).

and exercise [214]. Furthermore, IMCL levels vary considerably between subjects due to a number of factors including gender [215], training and physical activity [216], diet and fasting state [213,217–219] and body composition [220]. An overview of all effects on IMCL levels can be found in the review article by Popadic Gacesa et al. [221] and in Fig. 28.15. Ith et al. have proposed a standardized protocol to measure IMCL depletion for future study designs to provide more stable measurements and thus better insight into IMCL depot dynamics in physiological and pathological conditions [222]. Reproducibility and repeatability have been assessed in several studies at field strengths between 1.5 T and 3 T, and coefficients of variation of IMCL levels ranged between 4% and 24.4%.

Higher IMCL levels and lower insulin sensitivity are typical characteristics of obese, sedentary, and diabetic patients [220,223]. In trained athletes, however, a paradox exists where both high IMCL and high insulin sensitivity have been observed [224,225]. This is exemplarily depicted in Fig. 28.16, which shows

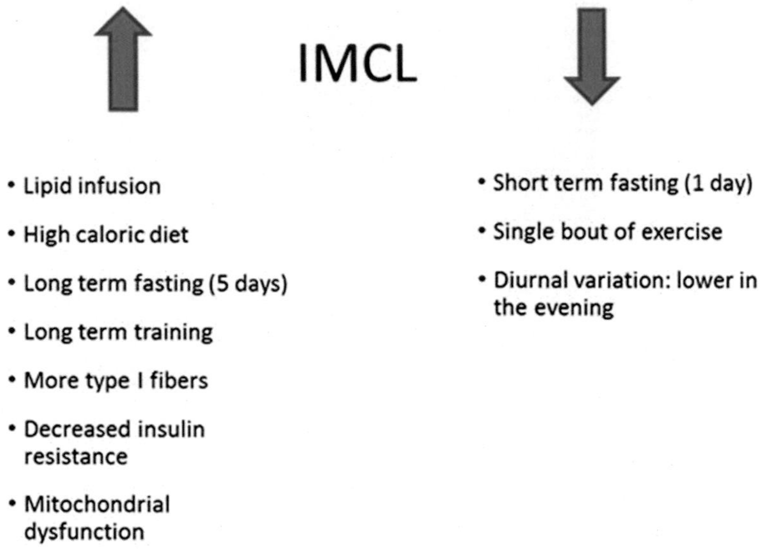

IMCL

- Lipid infusion
- High caloric diet
- Long term fasting (5 days)
- Long term training
- More type I fibers
- Decreased insulin resistance
- Mitochondrial dysfunction

- Short term fasting (1 day)
- Single bout of exercise
- Diurnal variation: lower in the evening

FIG. 28.15

An overview of influences on IMCL levels [221].

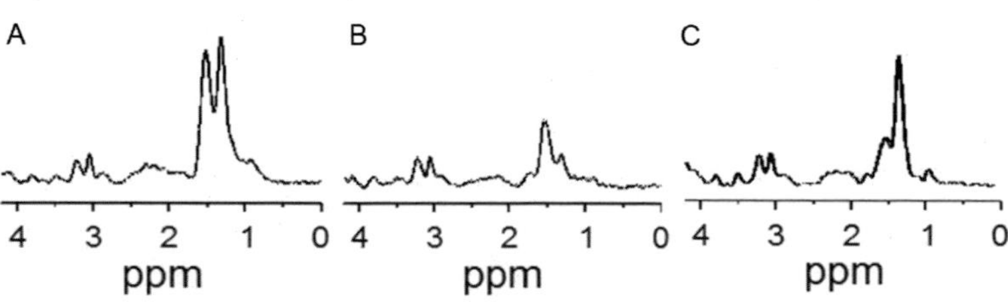

FIG. 28.16

The U-shaped phenomenon showing increased IMCL levels in tibialis anterior muscle for an insulin-resistant untrained subject (A), decreased IMCL levels in an insulin-sensitive untrained subject (B), and again high IMCL levels in a well-trained insulin-sensitive athlete (C).

spectra from the tibialis anterior muscle of a sedentary insulin-resistant subject, a sedentary insulin-sensitive subject, and a well-trained insulin-sensitive athlete. From left to right, a U-shaped progression of IMCL levels can be observed. Schrauwen-Hinderling et al. showed that increase of IMCL is a very early response to training [226]—an observation that aggravates interpretation of IMCL content after lifestyle intervention for prevention of metabolic disease. On the one hand, there is an expected decrease of IMCL due to improving insulin sensitivity, but on the other hand there should be an increase due to improving training status (e.g., VO2 max). Perhaps due to these competing effects, IMCL levels showed only minor changes (reduction of 12%–13%) in a longitudinal observation of Machann et al. [77] after 9 months, compared to short-term variations of up to 60% after exercise or >600% after 72 h of fasting [227]. Lower IMCL levels have also been observed in healthy adults who are predisposed to longevity due to their family history, in comparison to environmentally matched controls [228]. Furthermore, IMCLs are depleted by exercise and are subsequently replenished [229]. Additional studies have shown that the rate of IMCL depletion strongly depends on the type and duration of exercise performed, the fiber type of the muscle involved, and the level of baseline IMCL prior to the onset of exercise [230,231]. Moreover, following exercise, the rate of IMCL replenishment is similarly influenced by factors such as the percent fat content in the consumed diet and insulin levels. Taken combined, interpretation of IMCL content in relation to metabolic parameters is complex and standardized preparation of the subjects regarding food intake and exercise prior to MRS is mandatory. A novel application is the use of diffusion-weighted MRS, where it was shown that the apparent diffusion coefficient of IMCL is an order of magnitude lower compared to that of EMCL [232]. Due to the strong similarity in the chemical properties of both lipid pools, the authors concluded that this difference could only be attributed to restricted or severely hindered diffusion in IMCL.

The characterization of TG and fatty acids is another area of research in skeletal muscle. Measurements of TG composition using MRI and MRS have been performed to estimate saturated, mono-, and polyunsaturated lipids. Ren, et al. have used long echo time MRS to separate saturated and unsaturated lipids [233], whereas a recent article by Lindeboom and de Graaf showed that a spectral editing approach can be used to separate all three lipid species [234]. It has been hypothesized that these different fat species play unique roles in insulin sensitivity [234].

28.4.2 Fat infiltration in skeletal muscle

The measurement of skeletal muscle fat infiltration due to the increased presence of EMCL has a wide range of applications both in the context of diseases affecting directly the skeletal muscles and in the context of injuries and disorders affecting the musculoskeletal system.

In neuromuscular disease (NMD) and especially in muscular dystrophies, fat quantification using MRI plays an increasingly important role [59,235]. Muscular dystrophies are often characterized by progressive replacement of muscle tissue by fat and fibrosis, particularly at the chronic stage. The loss of muscle tissue results in increasing loss of muscle function and as a result, chronic disability. There has been a rapid increase in therapy development for these NMDs in recent years [236]. The availability of potential therapies coupled with the lack of sensitive qualitative assessments for detecting fat changes in muscle [237–240] has prompted an urgent need to develop objective, noninvasive outcome measures to monitor disease progression and treatment effect [241]. Fat measurements using MRI have shown promise as an outcome measure in clinical trials [242,243], as the technique is noninvasive, has the possibility to be repeated often, is objective, can sample a large volume and is largely independent of the motivation of the subjects. As such, it is not plagued by the disadvantages of other commonly used outcome measures including muscle biopsies and physical and functional testing.

Like liver applications, there are several techniques being used to assess fat replacement in NMDs, including single-voxel ^{1}H MRS, and 2D and 3D fat-water imaging. These different MR fat quantification methods have been assessed and benchmarked against each other and other methods for fat quantification [82,238,239,244,245]. Muscle PDFF measurements have been shown to be highly reproducible day-to-day and across centers, with coefficient of variation values ranging between 1.8% and 14% [244,246–249]. However, in situations where muscles inevitably change in between measurements, for instance in a maturing study population like in Duchenne muscular dystrophy or spinal muscular atrophy, repositioning according to internal muscle references and bony landmarks becomes more challenging and could affect the reproducibility. In addition, in several muscular dystrophies, the level of fat replacement varies along the length of the muscle [235], highlighting the importance of planning the measurement carefully to avoid sample bias. Quantitative assessment of fat replacement using MR has been related to strength and function, the rate of disease progression, response to therapy in clinical trials, and differences between and within individual muscles [59]. All these findings together show that muscle fat replacement differs between muscles and diseases, that the fat fraction is highly associated with disease progression, and that functional and strength measures are correlated to the fat fraction in NMD (Fig. 28.17). Unfortunately, a clear-cut relation to muscle function is still lacking, despite cross-sectional correlations of fat fraction and function [59]. Correlations between muscle fat fraction, functional endpoints, and sentinel events range from 0.59 to 0.78, depending on the muscle studied [250]. However, as in any progressive disease, any

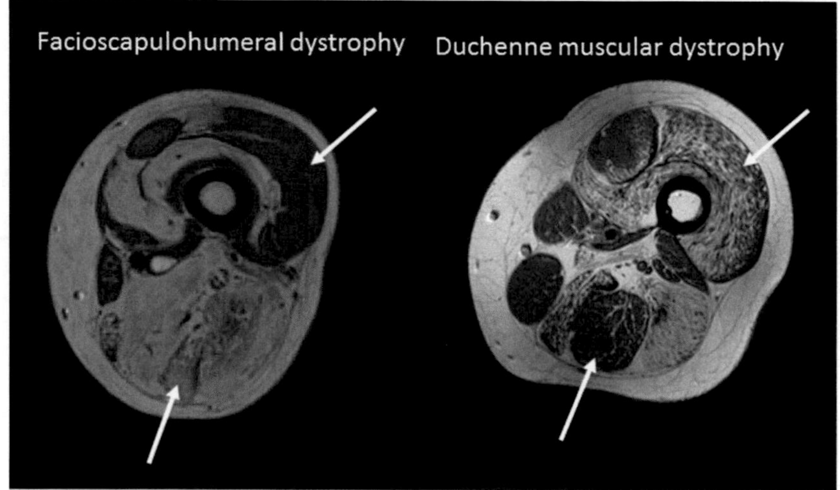

FIG. 28.17

T_1-weighted images of a typical muscle involvement pattern in facioscapulohumeral dystrophy (*left*) and Duchenne muscular dystrophy (*right*). *Arrows* denote the vastus lateralis muscle at the anterior side of the leg, and the semimembranosus muscles at the posterior side of the leg. The vastus lateralis muscle is involved earlier in the Duchenne disease process compared to facioscapulohumeral dystrophy, while the semimembranosus is involved earlier in facioscapulohumeral dystrophy.

parameter that correlates with age will also show a correlation to functional loss, and thus a predictive relation between fat fraction and function still needs to be determined.

Skeletal muscle fat infiltration is also a common imaging finding in orthopedics and a wide range of musculoskeletal diseases. In orthopedics, skeletal muscle fat infiltration has been traditionally assessed based on the qualitative grading of T_1-weighted images [251]. The quantification of skeletal muscle fat infiltration via imaging-based fat fraction has been recently adopted as an objective metric that can be used to relate muscle fat to muscle strength, biomechanical behavior and other clinical parameters and symptoms in orthopedic research.

Skeletal muscle PDFF measurements have been shown to be a reproducible metric across body locations. In the healthy spinal musculature, the intra-reader reproducibility error of PDFF (expressed as root mean square absolute precision error in absolute units) was reported to be 0.72% in erector spinae muscles and 0.05% in psoas muscles, whereas the inter-reader reproducibility was 0.64% in erector spinae muscles and 0.46% in psoas muscles [252]. The long-term reproducibility error of the PDFF measurements by a single reader after a 4-week period was 0.38% in erector spinae muscles and 0.70% in psoas muscles [252]. In the shoulder musculature, the absolute precision errors for inter-reader reproducibility of intramuscular fat quantification based on ROIs generated by manual segmentation of the rotator cuff muscles ranged between fat fractions of 0.6% and 1.0% with 0.60%, 0.65%, 0.87%, and 1.0% for supraspinatus, infraspinatus, subscapularis, and teres minor, respectively, considering all muscles separately [253]. In the thigh musculature, the intraclass correlation coefficient for intra-rater reproducibility was 0.97 (95% confidence intervals of 0.92, 0.99) for quadriceps intramuscular PDFF [254].

Recent studies applying imaging-based PDFF in the musculature of healthy subjects have shown an association between muscle fat fraction and biomechanical strength in the thigh muscles [255] and in the paraspinal muscles [252] (Fig. 28.18). A few studies have also reported on the application of quantitative skeletal muscle PDFF measurements to characterize muscle alternations in patients with knee osteoarthritis, low back pain and rotator cuff tendon injuries. In the clinical context of knee osteoarthritis, Kumar et al. showed that quadriceps intramuscular fat fraction is higher in people with knee osteoarthritis and is related to symptomatic and structural severity of knee osteoarthritis, whereas the quadriceps cross-sectional area is not [254]. In the clinical context of back pain, measurements of paraspinal muscle fat fraction have been reported using both single-voxel MRS and imaging techniques in patients with low back pain [256]. However, little is known about the exact relationship between muscle fat fraction and low back pain [257]. In the clinical context of rotator cuff tendon injuries,

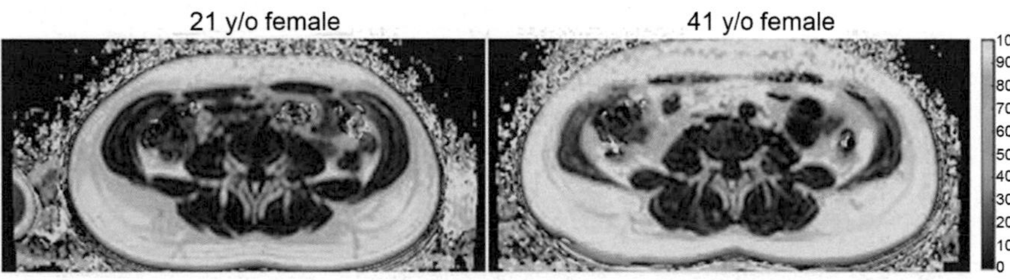

FIG. 28.18

Paraspinal musculature PDFF maps at the L5 level of a 21-year-old (y/o) female and a 41-year-old female, respectively. Note the increasing intramuscular PDFF with age in the erector spinae and the psoas muscles.

Images by courtesy of Michael Dieckmeyer (Technical University of Munich).

rotator cuff muscle intramuscular fat fraction has been associated with shoulder pain and range of motion [253]. In addition, cuff muscle fat fraction has been associated with isometric strength independent of muscle atrophy and tendon rupture in shoulders with early and advanced degenerative changes [258], and has been proposed for predicting postoperative recurrence of tears and injury [259].

Despite the above studies, the application of skeletal muscle fat fraction measurements in orthopedics remains limited primarily to the research setting and not used in the clinical diagnostic orthopedic imaging setting, where fat infiltration is typically assessed via qualitatively methods using a Likert-rating scale. Quantitative fat measurements however do provide a continuous variable as an objective measure of muscle fat infiltration and may therefore have the potential to replace the commonly used qualitative assessment of fatty infiltration based on a nominal-graded scale, especially in the longitudinal assessment of muscle degenerative changes.

28.4.3 Bone marrow adipose tissue

Bone marrow is the main hematopoietic organ and one of the largest body organs, typically accounting for up to 4%–5% of the human body weight, and often the organ of interest in aging, osteoporosis, fractures, and radiation therapy. Its primary components are hematopoietic tissue islands and adipocytes, dispersed within trabecular bone matrix. Bone marrow is therefore a tissue target for different diseases affecting body fat, red blood cells and bone matrix. There are two main types of bone marrow, namely yellow and red bone marrow. Yellow bone marrow is primarily composed of fat cells and is sparsely vascularized, whereas red bone marrow contains hematopoietic cells and rich vasculature.

Bone marrow is one of the few tissues in the human body where both water and fat can be present in equal amounts. The bone marrow water–fat composition has been extensively characterized using both single-voxel MRS and MRI techniques. MRS-based fat fraction measurements were reported in vertebral bone marrow as early as 1992 [260]. Compared to other tissues containing fat, bone marrow can include trabecular bone matrix, which results in poor magnetic field homogeneity. This inhomogeneity can lead to significantly broadened linewidths, confounding quantitative measurements of the fat content. Significant progress has been made to remove such confounding effects when measuring the bone marrow fat fraction [63]. The broad spectral linewidth of bone marrow water–fat components requires appropriate consideration in the peak fitting analysis of bone marrow MR spectra [261] and the inclusion of T_2* decay effects in the analysis of bone marrow chemical-shift encoding-based water–fat imaging data [262,263]. Exemplary vertebral bone marrow PDFF maps in the lumbar spine are shown in Fig. 28.19.

The intraclass correlation coefficient of MRS-based fat fraction measurements in repeated examinations of the proximal femur has been reported to range between 0.90 and 0.98. Li et al. reported a good reproducibility of MRS-based lumbar vertebral bone marrow fat fraction measurements with a coefficient of variation of 1.7% averaged across four vertebral bodies [264]. Baum et al. reported an absolute precision error of imaging-based vertebral PDFF measurements of 1.7% (PDFF absolute units) averaged over the entire spine C3–L5 with the worse absolute precision error in the cervical spine (3.3% in C7) [265].

The anatomic, age, and gender variation of bone marrow fat fraction has been extensively investigated using both single-voxel proton MRS and chemical-shift-encoding-based water–fat imaging [266–272]. There is an increase of the bone marrow fat fraction with age in children [273] and in adults [269] throughout the lifespan due to the gradual conversion of red marrow to yellow marrow. Males tend to have greater vertebral bone marrow fat fraction compared to females, although there is a reversal of this gender difference over the age of 60 years [268].

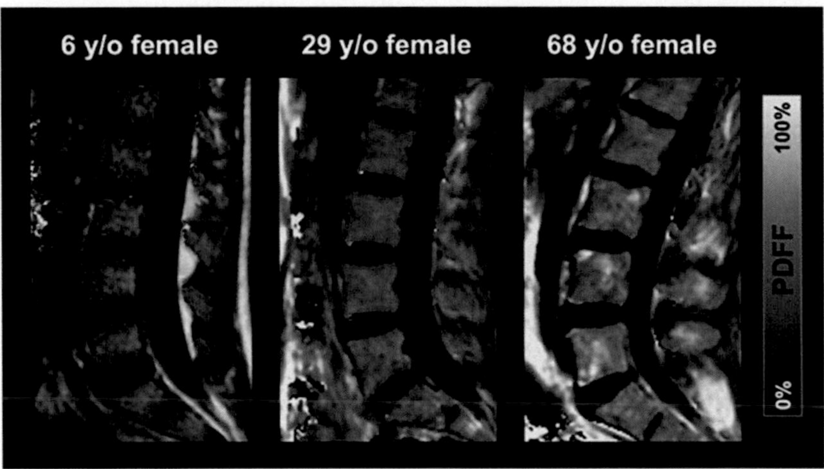

FIG. 28.19

Vertebral bone marrow PDFF maps in the lumbar spine of a 6-year-old female, a 29-year-old female and a 68-year-old female, respectively. Note the increasing PDFF with age and from L2 to L5, respectively.

Images by courtesy of Stefan Ruschke (Technical University of Munich).

The study of bone marrow fat has recently drawn interest with regards to increasing the understanding in the pathophysiology of osteoporosis. Mesenchymal stem cells can differentiate to either osteoblastic or adipocytic cell lines [274]. The composition of the bone marrow therefore shifts towards the presence of adipocytes not only with increasing age but also with osteoporosis. Griffith et al. reported in two seminal publications the results of MRS-based vertebral bone marrow fat fraction in older men and women with varying bone mineral density (BMD) assessed by dual-energy X-ray absorptiometry (DXA) [275,276]. L3 vertebral bone marrow fat fraction was significantly increased in male subjects with osteoporosis (58.2% ± 7.8%) and osteopenia (55.7% ± 10.2%) compared to that of male subjects with normal BMD (50.4% ± 8.7%), and also increased in postmenopausal women with osteoporosis (67.8% ± 8.5%) compared to that in postmenopausal women with normal BMD (59.2% ± 10.0%) [276].

It has also recently been reported that imaging-based bone marrow fat fraction can be used to differentiate malignant from benign vertebral fractures [277,278] and characterize the effects of chemotherapy and radiation therapy on bone marrow composition [279,280]. MR-based quantification of bone marrow water–fat composition is expected to find additional applications given the increased interest in understanding bone marrow physiology and the limited biological and clinical knowledge on the role of bone marrow adipocytes in health and disease [281].

28.5 Future directions and unmet needs

Both adipose tissue volume and PDFF have become well-established biomarkers over the past decade. In obesity and metabolic syndrome research, the complete automation of postprocessing steps, from image segmentation of adipose tissue depots to organ fat quantification in critical areas such as the liver or pancreas, must be pursued. Additional work is also needed to specifically evaluate reproducibility and repeatability in skeletal muscle segmentation and ectopic fat quantification, particularly focusing on standardization in selecting ROIs, in large multi-center trials across multiple system platforms [150,151,282].

Beyond historical and widespread uses in body composition [1,70,283] and organ fat analysis in the liver, skeletal muscles [59,248], pancreas [51,60,284–289], heart, kidneys, and bone marrow, new applications continue of fat quantification continue to emerge. Recent explorations of PDFF quantification in the thymus [290], in differentiating pathology [277,278,291,292], in the orbital adipose tissues of the eye [293,294], and in salivary glands [295] continue to test the accuracy and precision of the biomarker. The added benefits, tradeoffs need to be assessed for these applications [296,297].

In addition to tissue-level characterization, there is increasing interest to quantitatively assess adipocyte properties with MRI and MRS at the molecular and cellular levels. One example is the measurement of adipocyte cell size using diffusion-weighted techniques [298]. Larger adipocytes are commonly associated with greater body adiposity, especially in visceral and ectopic depots, and greater metabolic risk. Additionally, as advanced water-fat signal models continue to evolve and become more viable for estimating TG unsaturation and chain length properties in addition to PDFF, studies that evaluate the reproducibility and repeatability of these new and novel quantitative parameters across longitudinal studies within a subject and between multiple system platforms and sites are needed [299–301]. Their reliability and robustness as a function of imaging parameters also need to be evaluated. Joint efforts between industry partners, academic sites, and professional societies such as the National Institute of Standards and Technology and the Quantitative Imaging Biomarker Alliance of the Radiological Society of North America can further facilitate these comparisons with standardized high-quality phantoms [302].

Lastly, as summarized in other chapters of this book, techniques that accelerate the data acquisition speed of quantitative chemical-shift-encoded pulse sequences for PDFF computation continue to be developed, including non-Cartesian (i.e., radial) trajectories that facilitate free-breathing scans [92,303–306], compressed sensing [307–310], simultaneous multi-slice imaging, and MR fingerprinting [311]. While these are innovative and notable efforts in of themselves from a methodological development perspective, one existing challenge remains their widespread commercial availability. Similar pathways to establish their accuracy and precision against conventional approaches and reference standards are needed prior to their broad adoption in clinical and research trial settings.

References

[1] Franz D, et al. Magnetic resonance imaging of adipose tissue in metabolic dysfunction. Rofo 2018;190(12):1121–30.

[2] Baum T, et al. MR-based assessment of body fat distribution and characteristics. Eur J Radiol 2016;85(8):1512–8.

[3] Gruzdeva O, et al. Localization of fat depots and cardiovascular risk. Lipids Health Dis 2018;17(1), 218.

[4] Ding C, Chan Z, Magkos F. Lean, but not healthy: the 'metabolically obese, normal-weight' phenotype. Curr Opin Clin Nutr Metab Care 2016;19(6):408–17.

[5] Stefan N, et al. Obesity and renal disease: not all fat is created equal and not all obesity is harmful to the kidneys. Nephrol Dial Transplant 2016;31(5):726–30.

[6] Guo W, Key TJ, Reeves GK. Adiposity and breast cancer risk in postmenopausal women: results from the UK Biobank prospective cohort. Int J Cancer 2018;143(5):1037–46.

[7] Wiklund P, et al. Abdominal and gynoid adipose distribution and incident myocardial infarction in women and men. Int J Obes (Lond) 2010;34(12):1752–8.

[8] Frilander H, et al. Role of overweight and obesity in low back disorders among men: a longitudinal study with a life course approach. BMJ Open 2015;5(8), e007805.
[9] Feakins RM. Obesity and metabolic syndrome: pathological effects on the gastrointestinal tract. Histopathology 2016;68(5):630–40.
[10] Huang T, et al. Genetic predisposition to central obesity and risk of type 2 diabetes: two independent cohort studies. Diabetes Care 2015;38(7):1306–11.
[11] Lavalette C, et al. Abdominal obesity and prostate cancer risk: epidemiological evidence from the EPICAP study. Oncotarget 2018;9(77):34485–94.
[12] Wang L, et al. Associations of diabetes and obesity with risk of abdominal aortic aneurysm in men. J Obes 2017;2017:3521649.
[13] Lee R, Kean WF. Obesity and knee osteoarthritis. Inflammopharmacology 2012;20(2):53–8.
[14] Klop B, Elte JW, Cabezas MC. Dyslipidemia in obesity: mechanisms and potential targets. Nutrients 2013;5(4):1218–40.
[15] Jung IS, et al. Association of visceral adiposity and insulin resistance with colorectal adenoma and colorectal cancer. Intest Res 2019;17(3):404–12.
[16] Alexopoulos N, Katritsis D, Raggi P. Visceral adipose tissue as a source of inflammation and promoter of atherosclerosis. Atherosclerosis 2014;233(1):104–12.
[17] Sadeghi O, et al. Abdominal obesity and risk of hip fracture: a systematic review and meta-analysis of prospective studies. Adv Nutr 2017;8(5):728–38.
[18] Aune D, Norat T, Vatten LJ. Body mass index, abdominal fatness and the risk of gallbladder disease. Eur J Epidemiol 2015;30(9):1009–19.
[19] Marzullo P, et al. The impact of the metabolic phenotype on thyroid function in obesity. Diabetol Metab Syndr 2016;8(1):59.
[20] Michaud DS. Obesity and pancreatic cancer. Recent Results Cancer Res 2016;208:95–105.
[21] Mandavia CH, et al. Over-nutrition and metabolic cardiomyopathy. Metabolism 2012;61(9):1205–10.
[22] Wu H, Ballantyne CM. Skeletal muscle inflammation and insulin resistance in obesity. J Clin Invest 2017;127(1):43–54.
[23] Yoon SB, et al. Impact of body fat and muscle distribution on severity of acute pancreatitis. Pancreatology 2017;17(2):188–93.
[24] Drey M, et al. Cushing's syndrome: a model for sarcopenic obesity. Endocrine 2017;57(3):481–5.
[25] Corgna E, et al. Renal cancer. Crit Rev Oncol Hematol 2007;64(3):247–62.
[26] Niskanen L, et al. Inflammation, abdominal obesity, and smoking as predictors of hypertension. Hypertension 2004;44(6):859–65.
[27] Virdis A. Endothelial dysfunction in obesity: role of inflammation. High Blood Press Cardiovasc Prev 2016;23(2):83–5.
[28] Shaw E, et al. Obesity and endometrial cancer. Recent Results Cancer Res 2016;208:107–36.
[29] Freedman DS, et al. Relation of body fat distribution to ischemic heart disease. The national health and nutrition examination survey I (NHANES I) epidemiologic follow-up study. Am J Epidemiol 1995;142(1): 53–63.
[30] Du X, Hidayat K, Shi BM. Abdominal obesity and gastroesophageal cancer risk: systematic review and meta-analysis of prospective studies. Biosci Rep 2017;37(3), BSR20160474.
[31] Isozumi K. Obesity as a risk factor for cerebrovascular disease. Keio J Med 2004;53(1):7–11.
[32] Hidayat K, et al. Abdominal obesity and lung cancer risk: systematic review and meta-analysis of prospective studies. Nutrients 2016;8(12):810.
[33] Bureau C, et al. Central obesity is associated with non-cirrhotic portal vein thrombosis. J Hepatol 2016;64(2):427–32.
[34] Zhao J, Lawless MW. Stop feeding cancer: pro-inflammatory role of visceral adiposity in liver cancer. Cytokine 2013;64(3):626–37.

[35] Lu B, et al. Abdominal obesity and peripheral vascular disease in men and women: a comparison of waist-to-thigh ratio and waist circumference as measures of abdominal obesity. Atherosclerosis 2010;208(1):253–7.
[36] Delort L, et al. Central adiposity as a major risk factor of ovarian cancer. Anticancer Res 2009;29(12):5229–34.
[37] Sundell J. Obesity and diabetes as risk factors for coronary artery disease: from the epidemiological aspect to the initial vascular mechanisms. Diabetes Obes Metab 2005;7(1):9–20.
[38] Long E, Beales IL. The role of obesity in oesophageal cancer development. Therap Adv Gastroenterol 2014;7(6):247–68.
[39] Ammar KA, et al. Central obesity: association with left ventricular dysfunction and mortality in the community. Am Heart J 2008;156(5):975–81.
[40] Jakobsen MU, et al. Abdominal obesity and fatty liver. Epidemiol Rev 2007;29:77–87.
[41] Drager LF, et al. Obstructive sleep apnea: a cardiometabolic risk in obesity and the metabolic syndrome. J Am Coll Cardiol 2013;62(7):569–76.
[42] Gisondi P, et al. Psoriasis and the metabolic syndrome. Clin Dermatol 2018;36(1):21–8.
[43] Silvestris E, et al. Obesity as disruptor of the female fertility. Reprod Biol Endocrinol 2018;16(1), 22.
[44] Dye L, et al. The relationship between obesity and cognitive health and decline. Proc Nutr Soc 2017;76(4):443–54.
[45] Kapuria D, et al. Association of hepatic steatosis with subclinical atherosclerosis: systematic review and meta-analysis. Hepatol Commun 2018;2(8):873–83.
[46] Manuel AR, Hart N, Stradling JR. Correlates of obesity-related chronic ventilatory failure. BMJ Open Respir Res 2016;3(1), e000110.
[47] Zheng SH, Li XL. Visceral adiposity index as a predictor of clinical severity and therapeutic outcome of PCOS. Gynecol Endocrinol 2016;32(3):177–83.
[47a] Cereda E, Sansone V, Meola G, Malavazos AE. Increased visceral adipose tissue rather than BMI as a risk factor for dementia. Age Ageing 2007;36(5):488–91.
[48] Cebron Lipovec N, et al. The prevalence of metabolic syndrome in chronic obstructive pulmonary disease: a systematic review. COPD 2016;13(3):399–406.
[49] Dursun M, et al. Stress urinary incontinence and visceral adipose index: a new risk parameter. Int Urol Nephrol 2014;46(12):2297–300.
[50] Misra A, Jayawardena R, Anoop S. Obesity in South Asia: phenotype, morbidities, and mitigation. Curr Obes Rep 2019;8(1):43–52.
[51] Hui SCN, et al. Observed changes in brown, white, hepatic and pancreatic fat after bariatric surgery: evaluation with MRI. Eur Radiol 2019;29(2):849–56.
[52] Middleton MS, et al. Diagnostic accuracy of magnetic resonance imaging hepatic proton density fat fraction in pediatric nonalcoholic fatty liver disease. Hepatology 2018;67(3):858–72.
[53] Pourhassan M, et al. Impact of weight loss-associated changes in detailed body composition as assessed by whole-body MRI on plasma insulin levels and homeostatis model assessment index. Eur J Clin Nutr 2017;71(2):212–8.
[54] Otto M, et al. Postoperative changes in body composition—comparison of bioelectrical impedance analysis and magnetic resonance imaging in bariatric patients. Obes Surg 2015;25(2):302–9.
[55] Herring LY, et al. The effects of supervised exercise training 12-24 months after bariatric surgery on physical function and body composition: a randomised controlled trial. Int J Obes (Lond) 2017;41(6): 909–916.
[56] Watson ED, et al. The effect of lifestyle interventions on maternal body composition during pregnancy in developing countries: a systematic review. Cardiovasc J Afr 2017;28(6):397–403.
[57] Wadolowska L, et al. Changes in sedentary and active lifestyle, diet quality and body composition nine months after an education program in polish students aged 11(-)12 years: report from the ABC of Healthy Eating Study. Nutrients 2019;11(2):331.
[58] Ortega-Loubon C, et al. Obesity and its cardiovascular effects. Diabetes Metab Res Rev 2019;35(4):e3135.

[59] Burakiewicz J, et al. Quantifying fat replacement of muscle by quantitative MRI in muscular dystrophy. J Neurol 2017;264(10):2053–67.

[60] Idilman IS, et al. Quantification of liver, pancreas, kidney, and vertebral body MRI-PDFF in non-alcoholic fatty liver disease. Abdom Imaging 2015;40(6):1512–9.

[61] Wang YC, et al. Renal fat fraction and diffusion tensor imaging in patients with early-stage diabetic nephropathy. Eur Radiol 2018;28(8):3326–34.

[62] Karampinos DC, et al. Techniques and applications of magnetic resonance imaging for studying brown adipose tissue morphometry and function. Handb Exp Pharmacol 2019;251:299–324.

[63] Karampinos DC, et al. Quantitative MRI and spectroscopy of bone marrow. J Magn Reson Imaging 2018;47(2):332–53.

[64] Szczepaniak LS, et al. Measurement of intracellular triglyceride stores by H spectroscopy: validation in vivo. Am J Physiol 1999;276(5):E977–89.

[65] Thomas EL, et al. Whole body fat: content and distribution. Prog Nucl Magn Reson Spectrosc 2013;73: 56–80.

[66] Hu HH, Chen J, Shen W. Segmentation and quantification of adipose tissue by magnetic resonance imaging. MAGMA 2016;29(2):259–76.

[67] Newman D, et al. Test-retest reliability of rapid whole body and compartmental fat volume quantification on a widebore 3T MR system in normal-weight, overweight, and obese subjects. J Magn Reson Imaging 2016;44(6):1464–73.

[68] Addeman BT, et al. Validation of volumetric and single-slice MRI adipose analysis using a novel fully automated segmentation method. J Magn Reson Imaging 2015;41(1):233–41.

[69] Middleton MS, et al. Quantifying abdominal adipose tissue and thigh muscle volume and hepatic proton density fat fraction: repeatability and accuracy of an MR imaging-based, semiautomated analysis method. Radiology 2017;283(2):438–49.

[70] West J, et al. Precision of MRI-based body composition measurements of postmenopausal women. PLoS One 2018;13(2), e0192495.

[71] Kim SH, et al. Relationship between deep subcutaneous abdominal adipose tissue and metabolic syndrome: a case control study. Diabetol Metab Syndr 2016;8:, 10.

[72] Powell K. Obesity: the two faces of fat. Nature 2007;447(7144):525–7.

[73] Wajchenberg BL. Subcutaneous and visceral adipose tissue: their relation to the metabolic syndrome. Endocr Rev 2000;21(6):697–738.

[74] Ibrahim MM. Subcutaneous and visceral adipose tissue: structural and functional differences. Obes Rev 2010;11(1):11–8.

[75] Neeland IJ, et al. Associations of visceral and abdominal subcutaneous adipose tissue with markers of cardiac and metabolic risk in obese adults. Obesity (Silver Spring) 2013;21(9):E439–47.

[76] Kantartzis K, et al. The impact of liver fat vs visceral fat in determining categories of prediabetes. Diabetologia 2010;53(5):882–9.

[77] Machann J, et al. Follow-up whole-body assessment of adipose tissue compartments during a lifestyle intervention in a large cohort at increased risk for type 2 diabetes. Radiology 2010;257(2):353–63.

[78] Ohlson LO, et al. The influence of body fat distribution on the incidence of diabetes mellitus. 13.5 years of follow-up of the participants in the study of men born in 1913. Diabetes 1985;34(10):1055–8.

[79] Rothney MP, et al. Abdominal visceral fat measurement using dual-energy X-ray: association with cardiometabolic risk factors. Obesity (Silver Spring) 2013;21(9):1798–802.

[80] O'Neill S, O'Driscoll L. Metabolic syndrome: a closer look at the growing epidemic and its associated pathologies. Obes Rev 2015;16(1):1–12.

[81] Winsley RJ, et al. Prediction of visceral adipose tissue using air displacement plethysmography in children. Obes Res 2005;13(12):2048–51.

[82] Borga M, et al. Advanced body composition assessment: from body mass index to body composition profiling. J Invest Med 2018;66(5):1–9.

[83] Ludwig UA, et al. Whole-body MRI-based fat quantification: a comparison to air displacement plethysmography. J Magn Reson Imaging 2014;40(6):1437–44.
[84] Kyle UG, et al. Aging, physical activity and height-normalized body composition parameters. Clin Nutr 2004;23(1):79–88.
[85] Browning LM, et al. Validity of a new abdominal bioelectrical impedance device to measure abdominal and visceral fat: comparison with MRI. Obesity (Silver Spring) 2010;18(12):2385–91.
[85a] Rolfe EDL, Sleigh A, Finucane FM, Brage S, Stolk RP, Cooper C, Sharp SJ, Wareham NJ, Ong KK. Ultrasound measurements of visceral and subcutaneous abdominal thickness to predict abdominal adiposity among older men and women. Obesity 2010;18:625–31. https://doi.org/10.1038/oby.2009.309.
[85b] Karlsson A-K, Kullberg J, Stokland E, Allvin K, Gronowitz E, Svensson PA, Dahlgren J. Measurements of total and regional body composition in preschool children: a comparison of MRI, DXA, and anthropometric data. Obesity 2013;21:1018–24. https://doi.org/10.1002/oby.20205.
[86] Cheung AS, et al. Correlation of visceral adipose tissue measured by Lunar Prodigy dual X-ray absorptiometry with MRI and CT in older men. Int J Obes (Lond) 2016;40(8):1325–8.
[87] Reinhardt M, et al. Cross calibration of two dual-energy X-ray densitometers and comparison of visceral adipose tissue measurements by iDXA and MRI. Obesity (Silver Spring) 2017;25(2):332–7.
[88] Klopfenstein BJ, et al. Comparison of 3 T MRI and CT for the measurement of visceral and subcutaneous adipose tissue in humans. Br J Radiol 2012;85(1018):e826–30.
[89] Waduud MA, et al. Validation of a semi-automated technique to accurately measure abdominal fat distribution using CT and MRI for clinical risk stratification. Br J Radiol 2017;90(1071), 20160662.
[90] Fallah F, et al. Comparison of T1-weighted 2D TSE, 3D SPGR, and two-point 3D Dixon MRI for automated segmentation of visceral adipose tissue at 3 Tesla. MAGMA 2017;30(2):139–51.
[91] Fang H, et al. How to best assess abdominal obesity. Curr Opin Clin Nutr Metab Care 2018;21(5):360–5.
[92] Armstrong T, et al. Free-breathing 3-D quantification of infant body composition and hepatic fat using a stack-of-radial magnetic resonance imaging technique. Pediatr Radiol 2019;49(7):876–88.
[93] Thomas EL, et al. Magnetic resonance imaging of total body fat. J Appl Physiol (1985) 1998;85(5): 1778–1785.
[94] Machann J, et al. Standardized assessment of whole body adipose tissue topography by MRI. J Magn Reson Imaging 2005;21(4):455–62.
[95] Kullberg J, et al. Automated assessment of whole-body adipose tissue depots from continuously moving bed MRI: a feasibility study. J Magn Reson Imaging 2009;30(1):185–93.
[96] Positano V, et al. An accurate and robust method for unsupervised assessment of abdominal fat by MRI. J Magn Reson Imaging 2004;20(4):684–9.
[97] Wurslin C, et al. Topography mapping of whole body adipose tissue using A fully automated and standardized procedure. J Magn Reson Imaging 2010;31(2):430–9.
[98] Elbers JM, et al. Reproducibility of fat area measurements in young, non-obese subjects by computerized analysis of magnetic resonance images. Int J Obes Relat Metab Disord 1997;21(12):1121–9.
[99] Brennan DD, et al. Rapid automated measurement of body fat distribution from whole-body MRI. AJR Am J Roentgenol 2005;185(2):418–23.
[100] Shen W, et al. Reproducibility of single- and multi-voxel 1H MRS measurements of intramyocellular lipid in overweight and lean subjects under conditions of controlled dietary calorie and fat intake. NMR Biomed 2008;21(5):498–506.
[101] Lancaster JL, et al. Measurement of abdominal fat with T1-weighted MR images. J Magn Reson Imaging 1991;1(3):363–9.
[102] Ross R, et al. Quantification of adipose tissue by MRI: relationship with anthropometric variables. J Appl Physiol 1985;72(2):787–95.
[103] Gronemeyer SA, et al. Fast adipose tissue (FAT) assessment by MRI. Magn Reson Imaging 2000;18(7): 815–818.

[104] Bonekamp S, et al. Quantitative comparison and evaluation of software packages for assessment of abdominal adipose tissue distribution by magnetic resonance imaging. Int J Obes (Lond) 2008;32(1): 100–111.

[105] Maddalo M, et al. Validation of a free software for unsupervised assessment of abdominal fat in MRI. Phys Med 2017;37:24–31.

[106] Lee H, et al. Pixel-level deep segmentation: artificial intelligence quantifies muscle on computed tomography for body morphometric analysis. J Digit Imaging 2017;30(4):487–98.

[107] Küstner T, et al. Automated whole-body adipose tissue segmentation in T1-weighted fast spin echo imaging in a cohort of subjects at increased risk for type 2 diabetes. In: ISMRM's 27th annual meeting and exhibition. 2019. Montreal, Canada.

[108] Yang YX, et al. Automated assessment of thigh composition using machine learning for Dixon magnetic resonance images. MAGMA 2016;29(5):723–31.

[109] Grainger AT, et al. Deep learning-based quantification of abdominal fat on magnetic resonance images. PLoS One 2018;13(9):e0204071.

[110] Schwenzer NF, et al. Quantitative analysis of adipose tissue in single transverse slices for estimation of volumes of relevant fat tissue compartments: a study in a large cohort of subjects at risk for type 2 diabetes by MRI with comparison to anthropometric data. Invest Radiol 2010;45(12):788–94.

[111] Maislin G, et al. Single slice vs. volumetric MR assessment of visceral adipose tissue: reliability and validity among the overweight and obese. Obesity (Silver Spring) 2012;20(10):2124–32.

[112] Schweitzer L, et al. What is the best reference site for a single MRI slice to assess whole-body skeletal muscle and adipose tissue volumes in healthy adults? Am J Clin Nutr 2015;102(1):58–65.

[113] Bamberg F, et al. Subclinical disease burden as assessed by whole-body MRI in subjects with prediabetes, subjects with diabetes, and normal control subjects from the general population: the KORA-MRI study. Diabetes 2017;66(1):158–69.

[114] Bamberg F, et al. Whole-body MR imaging in the german national cohort: rationale, design, and technical background. Radiology 2015;277(1):206–20.

[115] Linge J, et al. Body composition profiling in the UK biobank imaging study. Obesity (Silver Spring) 2018;26(11):1785–95.

[116] Machann J, et al. Age and gender related effects on adipose tissue compartments of subjects with increased risk for type 2 diabetes: a whole body MRI/MRS study. MAGMA 2005;18(3):128–37.

[117] Diabetes Prevention Program Research Group, et al. 10-year follow-up of diabetes incidence and weight loss in the Diabetes Prevention Program Outcomes Study. Lancet 2009;374(9702):1677–86.

[118] Yaskolka Meir A, et al. Intrahepatic fat, abdominal adipose tissues, and metabolic state: magnetic resonance imaging study. Diabetes Metab Res Rev 2017;33(5). https://doi.org/10.1002/dmrr.2888.

[119] Randrianarisoa E, et al. Periaortic adipose tissue compared with peribrachial adipose tissue mass as markers and possible modulators of cardiometabolic risk. Angiology 2018;69(10):854–60.

[120] Machann J, et al. Intra- and interindividual variability of fatty acid unsaturation in six different human adipose tissue compartments assessed by (1) H-MRS in vivo at 3 T. NMR Biomed 2017;30(9). https://doi.org/10.1002/nbm.3744.

[121] Storz C, et al. Phenotypic multiorgan involvement of subclinical disease as quantified by magnetic resonance imaging in subjects with prediabetes, diabetes, and normal glucose tolerance. Invest Radiol 2018;53(6):357–64.

[122] Stefan N, et al. Identification and characterization of metabolically benign obesity in humans. Arch Intern Med 2008;168(15):1609–16.

[123] Stefan N, Haring HU, Schulze MB. Metabolically healthy obesity: the low-hanging fruit in obesity treatment? Lancet Diabetes Endocrinol 2018;6(3):249–58.

[124] Thomas EL, et al. The missing risk: MRI and MRS phenotyping of abdominal adiposity and ectopic fat. Obesity (Silver Spring) 2012;20(1):76–87.

[125] Knowler WC, et al. Reduction in the incidence of type 2 diabetes with lifestyle intervention or metformin. N Engl J Med 2002;346(6):393–403.
[126] Tuomilehto J, et al. Prevention of type 2 diabetes mellitus by changes in lifestyle among subjects with impaired glucose tolerance. N Engl J Med 2001;344(18):1343–50.
[127] Ramachandran A, et al. The Indian Diabetes Prevention Programme shows that lifestyle modification and metformin prevent type 2 diabetes in Asian Indian subjects with impaired glucose tolerance (IDPP-1). Diabetologia 2006;49(2):289–97.
[128] Li G, et al. The long-term effect of lifestyle interventions to prevent diabetes in the China Da Qing Diabetes Prevention Study: a 20-year follow-up study. Lancet 2008;371(9626):1783–9.
[129] Kloting N, Stumvoll M, Bluher M. The biology of visceral fat. Internist (Berl) 2007;48(2):126–33.
[130] Tchernof A, Despres JP. Pathophysiology of human visceral obesity: an update. Physiol Rev 2013;93(1): 359–404.
[131] Gepner Y, et al. Effect of distinct lifestyle interventions on mobilization of fat storage pools: CENTRAL magnetic resonance imaging randomized controlled trial. Circulation 2018;137(11):1143–57.
[132] Sahoo K, et al. Childhood obesity: causes and consequences. J Family Med Prim Care 2015;4(2):187–92.
[133] Shin HJ, et al. Comparison of image quality between conventional VIBE and radial VIBE in free-breathing paediatric abdominal MRI. Clin Radiol 2016;71(10):1044–9.
[134] Benkert T, et al. Free-breathing volumetric fat/water separation by combining radial sampling, compressed sensing, and parallel imaging. Magn Reson Med 2017;78(2):565–76.
[135] Springer F, et al. Changes in whole-body fat distribution, intrahepatic lipids, and insulin resistance of obese adolescents during a low-level lifestyle intervention. Eur J Pediatr 2015;174(12):1603–12.
[136] Linder K, et al. Relationships of body composition and liver fat content with insulin resistance in obesity-matched adolescents and adults. Obesity (Silver Spring) 2014;22(5):1325–31.
[137] Shen W, et al. Sexual dimorphism of adipose tissue distribution across the lifespan: a cross-sectional whole-body magnetic resonance imaging study. Nutr Metab (Lond) 2009;6:, 17.
[138] Hubers M, et al. Definition of new cut-offs of BMI and waist circumference based on body composition and insulin resistance: differences between children, adolescents and adults. Obes Sci Pract 2017;3(3):272–81.
[139] Younossi Z, et al. Global burden of NAFLD and NASH: trends, predictions, risk factors and prevention. Nat Rev Gastroenterol Hepatol 2018;15(1):11–20.
[140] Akazawa Y, Nakao K. To die or not to die: death signaling in nonalcoholic fatty liver disease. J Gastroenterol 2018;53(8):893–906.
[141] Michelotti GA, Machado MV, Diehl AM. NAFLD, NASH and liver cancer. Nat Rev Gastroenterol Hepatol 2013;10(11):656–65.
[142] Selzner M, Clavien PA. Fatty liver in liver transplantation and surgery. Semin Liver Dis 2001;21(1):105–13.
[143] Fishbein TM, et al. Use of livers with microvesicular fat safely expands the donor pool. Transplantation 1997;64(2):248–51.
[144] Szczepaniak LS, et al. Magnetic resonance spectroscopy to measure hepatic triglyceride content: prevalence of hepatic steatosis in the general population. Am J Physiol Endocrinol Metab 2005;288(2):E462–8.
[145] Pineda N, et al. Measurement of hepatic lipid: high-speed T2-corrected multiecho acquisition at 1H MR spectroscopy—a rapid and accurate technique. Radiology 2009;252(2):568–76.
[146] Hetterich H, et al. Feasibility of a three-step magnetic resonance imaging approach for the assessment of hepatic steatosis in an asymptomatic study population. Eur Radiol 2016;26(6):1895–904.
[147] Hamilton G, et al. In vivo characterization of the liver fat (1)H MR spectrum. NMR Biomed 2011;24(7):784–90.
[148] Reeder SB, et al. Quantitative assessment of liver fat with magnetic resonance imaging and spectroscopy. J Magn Reson Imaging 2011;34(4):729–49.
[149] Bonekamp S, et al. Spatial distribution of MRI-determined hepatic proton density fat fraction in adults with nonalcoholic fatty liver disease. J Magn Reson Imaging 2014;39(6):1525–32.

[150] Manning PM, et al. Agreement between region-of-interest- and parametric map-based hepatic proton density fat fraction estimation in adults with chronic liver disease. Abdom Radiol (NY) 2017;42(3):833–41.

[151] Campo CA, et al. Standardized approach for ROI-based measurements of proton density fat fraction and R2* in the liver. AJR Am J Roentgenol 2017;209(3):592–603.

[152] Hong CW, et al. Optimization of region-of-interest sampling strategies for hepatic MRI proton density fat fraction quantification. J Magn Reson Imaging 2018;47(4):988–94.

[153] Nemeth A, et al. 3D chemical shift-encoded MRI for volume and composition quantification of abdominal adipose tissue during an overfeeding protocol in healthy volunteers. J Magn Reson Imaging 2019;49(6):1587–99.

[154] Jayakumar S, et al. Longitudinal correlations between MRE, MRI-PDFF, and liver histology in patients with non-alcoholic steatohepatitis: analysis of data from a phase II trial of selonsertib. J Hepatol 2019;70(1): 133–141.

[155] Loomba R, et al. Ezetimibe for the treatment of nonalcoholic steatohepatitis: assessment by novel magnetic resonance imaging and magnetic resonance elastography in a randomized trial (MOZART trial). Hepatology 2015;61(4):1239–50.

[156] Bray TJ, et al. Fat fraction mapping using magnetic resonance imaging: insight into pathophysiology. Br J Radiol 2018;91(1089):20170344.

[157] Bashir MR, et al. Quantification of hepatic steatosis with a multistep adaptive fitting MRI approach: prospective validation against MR spectroscopy. AJR Am J Roentgenol 2015;204(2):297–306.

[158] Henninger B, et al. 3D multiecho dixon for the evaluation of hepatic iron and fat in a clinical setting. J Magn Reson Imaging 2017;46(3):793–800.

[159] Chiang HJ, et al. Magnetic resonance fat quantification in living donor liver transplantation. Transplant Proc 2014;46(3):666–8.

[160] Eskreis-Winkler S, et al. IDEAL-IQ in an oncologic population: meeting the challenge of concomitant liver fat and liver iron. Cancer Imaging 2018;18(1), 51.

[161] Kantartzis K, et al. An extended fatty liver index to predict non-alcoholic fatty liver disease. Diabetes Metab 2017;43(3):229–39.

[162] Stefan N, et al. A high-risk phenotype associates with reduced improvement in glycaemia during a lifestyle intervention in prediabetes. Diabetologia 2015;58(12):2877–84.

[163] Bergholm R, et al. CB(1) blockade-induced weight loss over 48 weeks decreases liver fat in proportion to weight loss in humans. Int J Obes (Lond) 2013;37(5):699–703.

[164] Kantartzis K, et al. Effects of resveratrol supplementation on liver fat content in overweight and insulin-resistant subjects: a randomized, double-blind, placebo-controlled clinical trial. Diabetes Obes Metab 2018;20(7):1793–7.

[165] Phielix E, et al. Effects of pioglitazone versus glimepiride exposure on hepatocellular fat content in type 2 diabetes. Diabetes Obes Metab 2013;15(10):915–22.

[166] Venkatesh BA, et al. MR proton spectroscopy for myocardial lipid deposition quantification: a quantitative comparison between 1.5T and 3T. J Magn Reson Imaging 2012;36(5):1222–30.

[167] Kellman P, Hernando D, Arai AE. Myocardial fat imaging. Curr Cardiovasc Imaging Rep 2010;3(2):83–91.

[168] Kimura F, et al. Myocardial fat at cardiac imaging: how can we differentiate pathologic from physiologic fatty infiltration? Radiographics 2010;30(6):1587–602.

[169] Felblinger J, et al. Methods and reproducibility of cardiac/respiratory double-triggered (1)H-MR spectroscopy of the human heart. Magn Reson Med 1999;42(5):903–10.

[170] Szczepaniak LS, et al. Myocardial triglycerides and systolic function in humans: in vivo evaluation by localized proton spectroscopy and cardiac imaging. Magn Reson Med 2003;49(3):417–23.

[171] Ith M, et al. Cardiac lipid levels show diurnal changes and long-term variations in healthy human subjects. NMR Biomed 2014;27(11):1285–92.

[172] de Heer P, et al. Parameter optimization for reproducible cardiac (1) H-MR spectroscopy at 3 Tesla. J Magn Reson Imaging 2016;44(5):1151–8.

[173] Gastl M, et al. Cardiac- versus diaphragm-based respiratory navigation for proton spectroscopy of the heart. MAGMA 2019;32(2):259–68.

[174] Bizino MB, Hammer S, Lamb HJ. Metabolic imaging of the human heart: clinical application of magnetic resonance spectroscopy. Heart 2014;100(11):881–90.

[175] van der Meer RW, et al. The ageing male heart: myocardial triglyceride content as independent predictor of diastolic function. Eur Heart J 2008;29(12):1516–22.

[176] Wei J, et al. Myocardial steatosis as a possible mechanistic link between diastolic dysfunction and coronary microvascular dysfunction in women. Am J Physiol Heart Circ Physiol 2016;310(1):H14–9.

[177] Sai E, et al. Association between myocardial triglyceride content and cardiac function in healthy subjects and endurance athletes. PLoS One 2013;8(4):e61604.

[178] Sai E, et al. Myocardial triglyceride content in patients with left ventricular hypertrophy: comparison between hypertensive heart disease and hypertrophic cardiomyopathy. Heart Vessels 2017;32(2):166–74.

[179] Liu CY, et al. Myocardial fat quantification in humans: evaluation by two-point water-fat imaging and localized proton spectroscopy. Magn Reson Med 2010;63(4):892–901.

[180] Homsi R, et al. 3D-dixon MRI based volumetry of peri- and epicardial fat. Int J Cardiovasc Imaging 2016;32(2):291–9.

[181] Nakamori S, et al. Left atrial epicardial fat volume is associated with atrial fibrillation: a prospective cardiovascular magnetic resonance 3D Dixon study. J Am Heart Assoc 2018;7(6):e008232.

[182] Hollingsworth KG, et al. Pancreatic triacylglycerol distribution in type 2 diabetes. Diabetologia 2015;58(11):2676–8.

[183] Lingvay I, et al. Noninvasive quantification of pancreatic fat in humans. J Clin Endocrinol Metab 2009;94(10):4070–6.

[184] Yamazaki H, et al. Lack of independent association between fatty pancreas and incidence of type 2 diabetes: 5-year Japanese cohort study. Diabetes Care 2016;39(10):1677–83.

[185] Heni M, et al. Pancreatic fat is negatively associated with insulin secretion in individuals with impaired fasting glucose and/or impaired glucose tolerance: a nuclear magnetic resonance study. Diabetes Metab Res Rev 2010;26(3):200–5.

[186] Al-Mrabeh A, et al. Quantification of intrapancreatic fat in type 2 diabetes by MRI. PLoS One 2017;12(4), e0174660.

[187] Dong Z, et al. Noninvasive fat quantification of the liver and pancreas may provide potential biomarkers of impaired glucose tolerance and type 2 diabetes. Medicine (Baltimore) 2016;95(23), e3858.

[188] Chai J, et al. MRI chemical shift imaging of the fat content of the pancreas and liver of patients with type 2 diabetes mellitus. Exp Ther Med 2016;11(2):476–80.

[189] Patel NS, et al. Association between novel MRI-estimated pancreatic fat and liver histology-determined steatosis and fibrosis in non-alcoholic fatty liver disease. Aliment Pharmacol Ther 2013;37(6):630–9.

[190] Honka H, et al. The effects of bariatric surgery on pancreatic lipid metabolism and blood flow. J Clin Endocrinol Metab 2015;100(5):2015–23.

[191] Schwenzer NF, et al. Quantification of pancreatic lipomatosis and liver steatosis by MRI: comparison of in/opposed-phase and spectral-spatial excitation techniques. Invest Radiol 2008;43(5):330–7.

[192] Kuhn JP, et al. Pancreatic steatosis demonstrated at MR imaging in the general population: clinical relevance. Radiology 2015;276(1):129–36.

[193] Li J, et al. Noninvasive quantification of pancreatic fat in healthy male population using chemical shift magnetic resonance imaging: effect of aging on pancreatic fat content. Pancreas 2011;40(2):295–9.

[194] Hu HH, et al. Comparison of fat-water MRI and single-voxel MRS in the assessment of hepatic and pancreatic fat fractions in humans. Obesity (Silver Spring) 2010;18(4):841–7.

[195] Schawkat K, et al. Preoperative evaluation of pancreatic fibrosis and lipomatosis: correlation of magnetic resonance findings with histology using magnetization transfer imaging and multigradient echo magnetic resonance imaging. Invest Radiol 2018;53(12):720–7.

[196] Yuan F, et al. Quantification of pancreatic fat with dual-echo imaging at 3.0-T MR in clinical application: how do the corrections for T1 and T2* relaxation effect work and simplified correction strategy. Acta Radiol 2018;59(9):1021–8.

[197] de Vries AP, et al. Fatty kidney: emerging role of ectopic lipid in obesity-related renal disease. Lancet Diabetes Endocrinol 2014;2(5):417–26.

[198] Hammer S, et al. Metabolic imaging of human kidney triglyceride content: reproducibility of proton magnetic resonance spectroscopy. PLoS One 2013;8(4):e62209.

[199] Dekkers IA, et al. 1 H-MRS for the assessment of renal triglyceride content in humans at 3T: a primer and reproducibility study. J Magn Reson Imaging 2018;48(2):507–13.

[200] Yokoo T, et al. Quantification of renal steatosis in type II diabetes mellitus using dixon-based MRI. J Magn Reson Imaging 2016;44(5):1312–9.

[201] Cypess AM, et al. Identification and importance of brown adipose tissue in adult humans. N Engl J Med 2009;360(15):1509–17.

[202] Virtanen KA, et al. Functional brown adipose tissue in healthy adults. N Engl J Med 2009;360(15):1518–25.

[203] Hu HH, et al. MRI detection of brown adipose tissue with low fat content in newborns with hypothermia. Magn Reson Imaging 2014;32(2):107–17.

[204] Kim MS, et al. Presence of brown adipose tissue in an adolescent with severe primary hypothyroidism. J Clin Endocrinol Metab 2014;99(9):E1686–90.

[205] Franssens BT, et al. Relation between brown adipose tissue and measures of obesity and metabolic dysfunction in patients with cardiovascular disease. J Magn Reson Imaging 2017;46(2):497–504.

[206] Franz D, et al. Association of proton density fat fraction in adipose tissue with imaging-based and anthropometric obesity markers in adults. Int J Obes (Lond) 2018;42(2):175–82.

[207] Gifford A, et al. Characterizing active and inactive brown adipose tissue in adult humans using PET-CT and MR imaging. Am J Physiol Endocrinol Metab 2016;311(1):E95–E104.

[208] McCallister A, et al. A pilot study on the correlation between fat fraction values and glucose uptake values in supraclavicular fat by simultaneous PET/MRI. Magn Reson Med 2017;78(5):1922–32.

[209] Franssens BT, et al. Reliability and agreement of adipose tissue fat fraction measurements with water-fat MRI in patients with manifest cardiovascular disease. NMR Biomed 2016;29(1):48–56.

[210] Franz D, et al. Discrimination between brown and white adipose tissue using a 2-point Dixon water-fat separation method in simultaneous PET/MRI. J Nucl Med 2015;56(11):1742–7.

[211] Lundstrom E, et al. Automated segmentation of human cervical-supraclavicular adipose tissue in magnetic resonance images. Sci Rep 2017;7(1), 3064.

[212] Koksharova E, et al. The relationship between brown adipose tissue content in supraclavicular fat depots and insulin sensitivity in patients with type 2 diabetes mellitus and prediabetes. Diabetes Technol Ther 2017;19(2):96–102.

[213] Boesch C, et al. Role of proton MR for the study of muscle lipid metabolism. NMR Biomed 2006;19(7):968–88.

[214] Machann J, et al. Morning to evening changes of intramyocellular lipid content in dependence on nutrition and physical activity during one single day: a volume selective 1H-MRS study. MAGMA 2011;24(1):29–33.

[215] Ortiz-Nieto F, et al. Quantification of lipids in human lower limbs using yellow bone marrow as the internal reference: gender-related effects. Magn Reson Imaging 2010;28(5):676–82.

[216] Schrauwen-Hinderling VB, et al. Intramyocellular lipid content is increased after exercise in nonexercising human skeletal muscle. J Appl Physiol (1985) 2003;95(6):2328–32.

[217] Bachmann OP, et al. Effects of intravenous and dietary lipid challenge on intramyocellular lipid content and the relation with insulin sensitivity in humans. Diabetes 2001;50(11):2579–84.

[218] Zehnder M, et al. Intramyocellular lipid stores increase markedly in athletes after 1.5 days lipid supplementation and are utilized during exercise in proportion to their content. Eur J Appl Physiol 2006;98(4):341–54.

[219] Jonkers RA, et al. Multitissue assessment of in vivo postprandial intracellular lipid partitioning in rats using localized 1H-[13C] magnetic resonance spectroscopy. Magn Reson Med 2012;68(4):997–1006.
[220] Krssak M, et al. Intramyocellular lipid concentrations are correlated with insulin sensitivity in humans: a 1H NMR spectroscopy study. Diabetologia 1999;42(1):113–6.
[221] Popadic Gacesa J, et al. Intramyocellular lipids and their dynamics assessed by (1) H magnetic resonance spectroscopy. Clin Physiol Funct Imaging 2017;37(6):558–66.
[222] Ith M, et al. Standardized protocol for a depletion of intramyocellular lipids (IMCL). NMR Biomed 2010;23(5):532–8.
[223] Jacob S, et al. Association of increased intramyocellular lipid content with insulin resistance in lean nondiabetic offspring of type 2 diabetic subjects. Diabetes 1999;48(5):1113–9.
[224] Goodpaster BH, et al. Skeletal muscle lipid content and insulin resistance: evidence for a paradox in endurance-trained athletes. J Clin Endocrinol Metab 2001;86(12):5755–61.
[225] Thamer C, et al. Intramyocellular lipids: anthropometric determinants and relationships with maximal aerobic capacity and insulin sensitivity. J Clin Endocrinol Metab 2003;88(4):1785–91.
[226] Schrauwen-Hinderling VB, et al. The increase in intramyocellular lipid content is a very early response to training. J Clin Endocrinol Metab 2003;88(4):1610–6.
[227] Wietek BM, et al. Muscle type dependent increase in intramyocellular lipids during prolonged fasting of human subjects: a proton MRS study. Horm Metab Res 2004;36(9):639–44.
[228] Wijsman CA, et al. Proton magnetic resonance spectroscopy shows lower intramyocellular lipid accumulation in middle-aged subjects predisposed to familial longevity. Am J Physiol Endocrinol Metab 2012;302(3):E344–8.
[229] Decombaz J, et al. Postexercise fat intake repletes intramyocellular lipids but no faster in trained than in sedentary subjects. Am J Physiol Regul Integr Comp Physiol 2001;281(3):R760–9.
[230] Vermathen P, et al. Skeletal muscle (1)H MRSI before and after prolonged exercise. I. Muscle specific depletion of intramyocellular lipids. Magn Reson Med 2012;68(5):1357–67.
[231] Brechtel K, et al. Utilisation of intramyocellular lipids (IMCLs) during exercise as assessed by proton magnetic resonance spectroscopy (1H-MRS). Horm Metab Res 2001;33(2):63–6.
[232] Brandejsky V, Kreis R, Boesch C. Restricted or severely hindered diffusion of intramyocellular lipids in human skeletal muscle shown by in vivo proton MR spectroscopy. Magn Reson Med 2012;67(2):310–6.
[233] Ren J, Sherry AD, Malloy CR. 1H MRS of intramyocellular lipids in soleus muscle at 7 T: spectral simplification by using long echo times without water suppression. Magn Reson Med 2010;64(3):662–71.
[234] Lindeboom L, de Graaf RA. Measurement of lipid composition in human skeletal muscle and adipose tissue with (1) H-MRS homonuclear spectral editing. Magn Reson Med 2018;79(2):619–27.
[235] Strijkers GJ, et al. Exploration of new contrasts, targets, and MR imaging and spectroscopy techniques for neuromuscular disease—a workshop report of working group 3 of the biomedicine and molecular biosciences COST action BM1304 MYO-MRI. J Neuromuscul Dis 2019;6(1):1–30.
[236] www.treat-nmd.eu.
[237] Fischmann A, et al. Quantitative MRI can detect subclinical disease progression in muscular dystrophy. J Neurol 2012;259(8):1648–54.
[238] Willis TA, et al. Quantitative magnetic resonance imaging in limb-girdle muscular dystrophy 2I: a multinational cross-sectional study. PLoS One 2014;9(2):e90377.
[239] Wokke BH, et al. Comparison of dixon and T1-weighted MR methods to assess the degree of fat infiltration in duchenne muscular dystrophy patients. J Magn Reson Imaging 2013;38(3):619–24.
[240] Gloor M, et al. Quantification of fat infiltration in oculopharyngeal muscular dystrophy: comparison of three MR imaging methods. J Magn Reson Imaging 2011;33(1):203–10.
[241] Straub V, et al. Stakeholder cooperation to overcome challenges in orphan medicine development: the example of Duchenne muscular dystrophy. Lancet Neurol 2016;15(8):882–90.
[242] Carlier PG, et al. Skeletal muscle quantitative nuclear magnetic resonance imaging and spectroscopy as an outcome measure for clinical trials. J Neuromuscul Dis 2016;3(1):1–28.

[243] Hollingsworth KG, et al. Towards harmonization of protocols for MRI outcome measures in skeletal muscle studies: consensus recommendations from two TREAT-NMD NMR workshops, 2 May 2010, Stockholm, Sweden, 1-2 October 2009, Paris, France. Neuromuscul Disord 2012;22(Suppl. 2):S54–67.
[244] Triplett WT, et al. Chemical shift-based MRI to measure fat fractions in dystrophic skeletal muscle. Magn Reson Med 2014;72(1):8–19.
[245] Smith AC, et al. Muscle-fat MRI: 1.5 Tesla and 3.0 Tesla versus histology. Muscle Nerve 2014;50(2):170–6.
[246] Morrow JM, et al. Reproducibility, and age, body-weight and gender dependency of candidate skeletal muscle MRI outcome measures in healthy volunteers. Eur Radiol 2014;24(7):1610–20.
[247] Forbes SC, et al. Skeletal muscles of ambulant children with Duchenne muscular dystrophy: validation of multicenter study of evaluation with MR imaging and MR spectroscopy. Radiology 2013;269(1): 198–207.
[248] Grimm A, et al. Repeatability of Dixon magnetic resonance imaging and magnetic resonance spectroscopy for quantitative muscle fat assessments in the thigh. J Cachexia Sarcopenia Muscle 2018;9(6): 1093–1100.
[249] Ponrartana S, et al. Repeatability of chemical-shift-encoded water-fat MRI and diffusion-tensor imaging in lower extremity muscles in children. AJR Am J Roentgenol 2014;202(6):W567–73.
[250] Barnard AM, et al. Skeletal muscle magnetic resonance biomarkers correlate with function and sentinel events in Duchenne muscular dystrophy. PLoS One 2018;13(3):e0194283.
[251] Fuchs B, et al. Fatty degeneration of the muscles of the rotator cuff: assessment by computed tomography versus magnetic resonance imaging. J Shoulder Elbow Surg 1999;8(6):599–605.
[252] Schlaeger S, et al. Association of paraspinal muscle water-fat MRI-based measurements with isometric strength measurements. Eur Radiol 2019;29(2):599–608.
[253] Nardo L, et al. Quantitative assessment of fat infiltration in the rotator cuff muscles using water-fat MRI. J Magn Reson Imaging 2014;39(5):1178–85.
[254] Kumar D, et al. Quadriceps intramuscular fat fraction rather than muscle size is associated with knee osteoarthritis. Osteoarthr Cartil 2014;22(2):226–34.
[255] Baum T, et al. Association of quadriceps muscle fat with isometric strength measurements in healthy males using chemical shift encoding-based water-fat magnetic resonance imaging. J Comput Assist Tomogr 2016;40(3):447–51.
[256] Fischer MA, et al. Quantification of muscle fat in patients with low back pain: comparison of multi-echo MR imaging with single-voxel MR spectroscopy. Radiology 2013;266(2):555–63.
[257] Ranger TA, et al. Are the size and composition of the paraspinal muscles associated with low back pain? A systematic review. Spine J 2017;17(11):1729–48.
[258] Karampinos DC, et al. Proton density fat-fraction of rotator cuff muscles is associated with isometric strength 10 years after rotator cuff repair: a quantitative magnetic resonance imaging study of the shoulder. Am J Sports Med 2017;45(9):1990–9.
[259] Nozaki T, et al. Predicting retear after repair of full-thickness rotator cuff tear: two-point Dixon MR imaging quantification of fatty muscle degeneration-initial experience with 1-year follow-up. Radiology 2016;280(2): 500–509.
[260] Schick F, et al. Volume-selective proton MRS in vertebral bodies. Magn Reson Med 1992;26(2):207–17.
[261] Dieckmeyer M, et al. The need for T(2) correction on MRS-based vertebral bone marrow fat quantification: implications for bone marrow fat fraction age dependence. NMR Biomed 2015;28(4):432–9.
[262] Karampinos DC, et al. Bone marrow fat quantification in the presence of trabecular bone: initial comparison between water-fat imaging and single-voxel MRS. Magn Reson Med 2014;71(3):1158–65.
[263] Karampinos DC, et al. Modeling of T2* decay in vertebral bone marrow fat quantification. NMR Biomed 2015;28(11):1535–42.
[264] Li X, et al. Quantification of vertebral bone marrow fat content using 3 Tesla MR spectroscopy: reproducibility, vertebral variation, and applications in osteoporosis. J Magn Reson Imaging 2011;33(4):974–9.
[265] Baum T, et al. Assessment of whole spine vertebral bone marrow fat using chemical shift-encoding based water-fat MRI. J Magn Reson Imaging 2015;42(4):1018–23.

[266] Aoki T, et al. Quantification of bone marrow fat content using iterative decomposition of water and fat with echo asymmetry and least-squares estimation (IDEAL): reproducibility, site variation and correlation with age and menopause. Br J Radiol 2016;89(1065):20150538.

[267] Baum T, et al. Assessment of whole spine vertebral bone marrow fat using chemical shift-encoding based water-fat MRI. J Magn Reson Imaging 2015;42(4):1018–23.

[268] Griffith JF, et al. Bone marrow fat content in the elderly: a reversal of sex difference seen in younger subjects. J Magn Reson Imaging 2012;36(1):225–30.

[269] Kugel H, et al. Age- and sex-specific differences in the 1H-spectrum of vertebral bone marrow. J Magn Reson Imaging 2001;13(2):263–8.

[270] Liney GP, et al. Age, gender, and skeletal variation in bone marrow composition: a preliminary study at 3.0 Tesla. J Magn Reson Imaging 2007;26(3):787–93.

[271] Roldan-Valadez E, et al. Gender and age groups interactions in the quantification of bone marrow fat content in lumbar spine using 3T MR spectroscopy: a multivariate analysis of covariance (Mancova). Eur J Radiol 2013;82(11):e697–702.

[272] Schellinger D, et al. Normal lumbar vertebrae: anatomic, age, and sex variance in subjects at proton MR spectroscopy—initial experience. Radiology 2000;215(3):910–6.

[273] Ruschke S, et al. Measurement of vertebral bone marrow proton density fat fraction in children using quantitative water-fat MRI. MAGMA 2017;30(5):449–60.

[274] Rosen CJ, Bouxsein ML. Mechanisms of disease: is osteoporosis the obesity of bone? Nat Clin Pract Rheumatol 2006;2(1):35–43.

[275] Griffith JF, et al. Vertebral bone mineral density, marrow perfusion, and fat content in healthy men and men with osteoporosis: dynamic contrast-enhanced MR imaging and MR spectroscopy. Radiology 2005;236(3): >945–951.

[276] Griffith JF, et al. Vertebral marrow fat content and diffusion and perfusion indexes in women with varying bone density: MR evaluation. Radiology 2006;241(3):831–8.

[277] Schmeel FC, et al. Proton density fat fraction (PDFF) MR imaging for differentiation of acute benign and neoplastic compression fractures of the spine. Eur Radiol 2018;28(12):5001–9.

[278] Schmeel FC, et al. Proton density fat fraction (PDFF) MRI for differentiation of benign and malignant vertebral lesions. Eur Radiol 2018;28(6):2397–405.

[279] Bolan PJ, et al. Water-fat MRI for assessing changes in bone marrow composition due to radiation and chemotherapy in gynecologic cancer patients. J Magn Reson Imaging 2013;38(6):1578–84.

[280] Carmona R, et al. Fat composition changes in bone marrow during chemotherapy and radiation therapy. Int J Radiat Oncol Biol Phys 2014;90(1):155–63.

[281] Devlin MJ, Rosen CJ. The bone-fat interface: basic and clinical implications of marrow adiposity. Lancet Diabetes Endocrinol 2015;3(2):141–7.

[282] Hooker JC, et al. Inter-reader agreement of magnetic resonance imaging proton density fat fraction and its longitudinal change in a clinical trial of adults with nonalcoholic steatohepatitis. Abdom Radiol (NY) 2019;44(2):482–92.

[283] Hong CW, et al. Fat quantification in the abdomen. Top Magn Reson Imaging 2017;26(6):221–7.

[284] Coe PO, et al. Development of MR quantified pancreatic fat deposition as a cancer risk biomarker. Pancreatology 2018;18(4):429–37.

[285] Staaf J, et al. Pancreatic fat is associated with metabolic syndrome and visceral fat but not beta-cell function or body mass index in pediatric obesity. Pancreas 2017;46(3):358–65.

[286] Regnell SE, et al. Pancreas volume and fat fraction in children with Type 1 diabetes. Diabet Med 2016;33(10):1374–9.

[287] Sakai NS, Taylor SA, Chouhan MD. Obesity, metabolic disease and the pancreas—quantitative imaging of pancreatic fat. Br J Radiol 2018;91(1089):20180267.

[288] Covarrubias Y, et al. Pilot study on longitudinal change in pancreatic proton density fat fraction during a weight-loss surgery program in adults with obesity. J Magn Reson Imaging 2019;50(4):1092–102.

[289] Idilman IS, et al. The feasibility of magnetic resonance imaging for quantification of liver, pancreas, spleen, vertebral bone marrow, and renal cortex R2* and proton density fat fraction in transfusion-related iron overload. Turk J Haematol 2016;33(1):21–7.
[290] Fishbein KW, et al. Measurement of fat fraction in the human thymus by localized NMR and three-point Dixon MRI techniques. Magn Reson Imaging 2018;50:110–8.
[291] Skorpil M, et al. The effect of radiotherapy on fat content and fatty acids in myxoid liposarcomas quantified by MRI. Magn Reson Imaging 2017;43:37–41.
[292] Meng X, et al. Proton-density fat fraction measurement: a viable quantitative biomarker for differentiating adrenal adenomas from nonadenomas. Eur J Radiol 2017;86:112–8.
[293] Kaichi Y, et al. Orbital fat volumetry and water fraction measurements using T2-weighted FSE-IDEAL imaging in patients with thyroid-associated orbitopathy. AJNR Am J Neuroradiol 2016;37(11):2123–8.
[294] Das T, et al. T2-relaxation mapping and fat fraction assessment to objectively quantify clinical activity in thyroid eye disease: an initial feasibility study. Eye (Lond) 2019;33(2):235–43.
[295] Chikui T, et al. Estimation of proton density fat fraction of the salivary gland. 91(1085):20170671.
[296] Franz D, et al. Differentiating supraclavicular from gluteal adipose tissue based on simultaneous PDFF and T2 * mapping using a 20-echo gradient-echo acquisition. J Magn Reson Imaging 2019;50(2):424–34.
[297] Bydder M, et al. Sources of systematic error in proton density fat fraction (PDFF) quantification in the liver evaluated from magnitude images with different numbers of echoes. NMR Biomed 2018;31(1). https://doi.org/10.1002/nbm.3843.
[298] Weidlich D, et al. Measuring large lipid droplet sizes by probing restricted lipid diffusion effects with diffusion-weighted MRS at 3T. Magn Reson Med 2019;81(6):3427–39.
[299] Nemeth A, et al. Comparison of MRI-derived vs. traditional estimations of fatty acid composition from MR spectroscopy signals. NMR Biomed 2018;31(9):e3991.
[300] Schlaeger S, et al. Thigh muscle segmentation of chemical shift encoding-based water-fat magnetic resonance images: the reference database MyoSegmenTUM. PLoS One 2018;13(6):e0198200.
[301] Simchick G, et al. Fat spectral modeling on triglyceride composition quantification using chemical shift encoded magnetic resonance imaging. Magn Reson Imaging 2018;52:84–93.
[302] Keenan KE, et al. Quantitative magnetic resonance imaging phantoms: a review and the need for a system phantom. Magn Reson Med 2018;79(1):48–61.
[303] Armstrong T, et al. Free-breathing liver fat quantification using a multiecho 3D stack-of-radial technique. Magn Reson Med 2018;79(1):370–82.
[304] Armstrong T, et al. 3D R 2 * mapping of the placenta during early gestation using free-breathing multiecho stack-of-radial MRI at 3T. J Magn Reson Imaging 2019;49(1):291–303.
[305] Armstrong T, et al. Free-breathing quantification of hepatic fat in healthy children and children with nonalcoholic fatty liver disease using a multi-echo 3-D stack-of-radial MRI technique. Pediatr Radiol 2018;48(7):941–53.
[306] Ly KV, et al. Free-breathing magnetic resonance imaging assessment of body composition in healthy and overweight children: an observational study. J Pediatr Gastroenterol Nutr 2019;68(6):782–7.
[307] Liu D, et al. Accelerating MRI fat quantification using a signal model-based dictionary to assess gastric fat volume and distribution of fat fraction. Magn Reson Imaging 2017;37:81–9.
[308] Lugauer F, et al. Accelerating multi-echo water-fat MRI with a joint locally low-rank and spatial sparsity-promoting reconstruction. MAGMA 2017;30(2):189–202.
[309] Mann LW, et al. Accelerating MR imaging liver steatosis measurement using combined compressed sensing and parallel imaging: a quantitative evaluation. Radiology 2016;278(1):247–56.
[310] Tamada D, et al. Multiparameter estimation using multi-echo spoiled gradient echo with variable flip angles and multicontrast compressed sensing. Magn Reson Med 2018;80(4):1546–55.
[311] Cencini M, et al. Magnetic resonance fingerprinting with dictionary-based fat and water separation (DBFW MRF): a multi-component approach. Magn Reson Med 2019;81(5):3032–45.

CHAPTER

Iron Mapping Techniques and Applications

29

Ralf B. Loeffler[a], Samir D. Sharma[b], and Claudia M. Hillenbrand[a]

[a]Research Imaging NSW, University of New South Wales, Sydney, NSW, Australia [b]Canon Medical Research USA, Inc., Mayfield, Village, OH, United States

29.1 Introduction

Various tools have been defined for the assessment of iron overload using Magnetic Resonance Imaging (MRI). This chapter provides an overview of the quantitative MRI techniques used to map iron. These methods include basic measurements of iron content, such as R_2 and $R_2{}^*$ relaxometry, as well as advanced approaches, specifically quantitative susceptibility mapping (QSM) techniques [1]. Examples in the liver are given, although many of these techniques are further generalizable to quantify iron in other organs, such as the brain, heart, pancreas, and kidneys. In particular, the pulse sequences, acquisition strategies, and signal models for iron quantification will be presented, and confounding factors impacting R_2 ($1/T_2$) and $R_2{}^*$ ($1/T_2{}^*$) relaxometry measurements and QSM will be discussed.

29.1.1 Liver

Iron overload is a severe complication in patients with increased gastrointestinal absorption of dietary iron or receiving chronic blood transfusions [2–6]. In particular, hepatic iron content (HIC) correlates significantly with total body iron stores and is considered to be a reliable marker for assessment of iron overload (see Chapter 26) [7, 8]. Normal HIC values are up to 1.8 mg Fe/g dry weight. Levels up to 7 mg/g dry weight (mild iron overload) are seen in some patient populations without apparent adverse effects [5, 9]. HIC levels $>$7 mg Fe/g (moderate iron overload) are associated with increased risk of hepatic fibrosis and diabetes mellitus [2, 10–12]. Patients with HIC $>$15 mg Fe/g (severe iron overload) have greatly increased risk for cirrhosis, cardiac disease, and death [13–15].

Monitoring of body iron loading and unloading is essential in the management of iron-overloaded patients, specifically for initiating and assessing the response to chelation therapy, as well as adjusting dose and intensity of the regimen to effectively maintain or reduce iron levels and to avoid side effects associated with excess chelation [16–18]. The chelation regimen and dosage are primarily governed by HIC levels and total transfusion intake. HIC values of $<$3 mg Fe/g are considered to be the optimal maintenance level and chelation will be stopped once this level has been reached [19].

Advances in Magnetic Resonance Technology and Applications. Volume 1. ISSN 2666-9099. https://doi.org/10.1016/B978-0-12-817057-1.00031-7

29.1.2 Other organs

In addition to the liver, several other organs in the body, such as the brain, heart, pancreas, spleen, and kidneys, can also suffer from excessive iron accumulation. For an extensive review of iron physiology and pathophysiology in these organs, please see Chapter 26. In the brain, iron deposition has been reported in several neurodegenerative diseases and the measurement of iron in the brain by MRI is used to monitor disease progression [20–37]. Cardiac iron quantification is clinically relevant [38–41]. It is established that cardiac siderosis is an important marker for cardiac failure, especially in patients with thalassemia [42, 43].

Other organs where iron quantification have been demonstrated include the pancreas, spleen, and kidneys [44–53]. Pancreatic iron overload has been assumed to be a surrogate marker for cardiac iron overload in thalassemia [41, 52, 54]. However, the correlation between cardiac and pancreatic overload may be more complicated in patients treated for iron overload [55]. Pancreatic iron overload is also suspected in the genesis of diabetes mellitus in thalassemia patients [56].

In general, whether or not the iron accumulation in different organs is correlated seems to be dependent on the underlying disease [46, 56], and most likely depends on the pathways that are involved or interrupted in the particular process [57]. Therefore, it is advisable to quantify iron in the specific organ of interest if clinically warranted for a certain indication.

29.2 R_2^*-based iron quantification

Iron quantification based on R_2^* ($=1/T_2^*$) is mainly performed in the liver. Cardiac applications are the second most important use case; other organs are less often assessed for iron [58] and existing studies are mainly proof of concepts or exploratory investigations. The following sections will examine these different applications.

29.2.1 Liver

Most published work on liver iron quantification focusses on two major families of methods: the signal intensity ratio (SIR) technique, and R_2^* quantification-based approaches. The SIR technique relies on the fact that the signal intensity in the liver changes with hepatic iron overload at a given echo time, but the signal intensity in muscle, particularly the paraspinal muscle, is not affected; therefore, the SIR can be used as a surrogate to estimate HIC [59–62]. To assess iron using this approach, images are collected with a gradient echo sequence at several different echo times. Typically, two to five echo measurements are employed. The sequence can be implemented either as a multiecho sequence in a single breath-hold or as a single echo sequence in several breaths holds. The SIR between paraspinal muscle (which is visible in transverse slices depicting the liver) and liver parenchyma is then measured for each of the T_2^*-weighted images in several regions of interest [63]. Fig. 29.1 shows T_2^*-weighted images from three patients, with mild, moderate, and severe iron overload (top to bottom). The varying signal intensities of liver parenchyma observed in the T_2^*-weighted images are recorded from three ROIs placed in liver parenchyma avoiding blood vessels (see red circles); another two ROIs are placed in each paraspinal muscle (yellow circles). From these ROIs, five liver-to-muscle SIRs are calculated which can be analyzed with algorithms provided by Gandon et al. [60] to obtain an estimate of the liver iron content. Note that in these images, ROIs are shown for illustration only, as the SIR method requires data from volume coils.

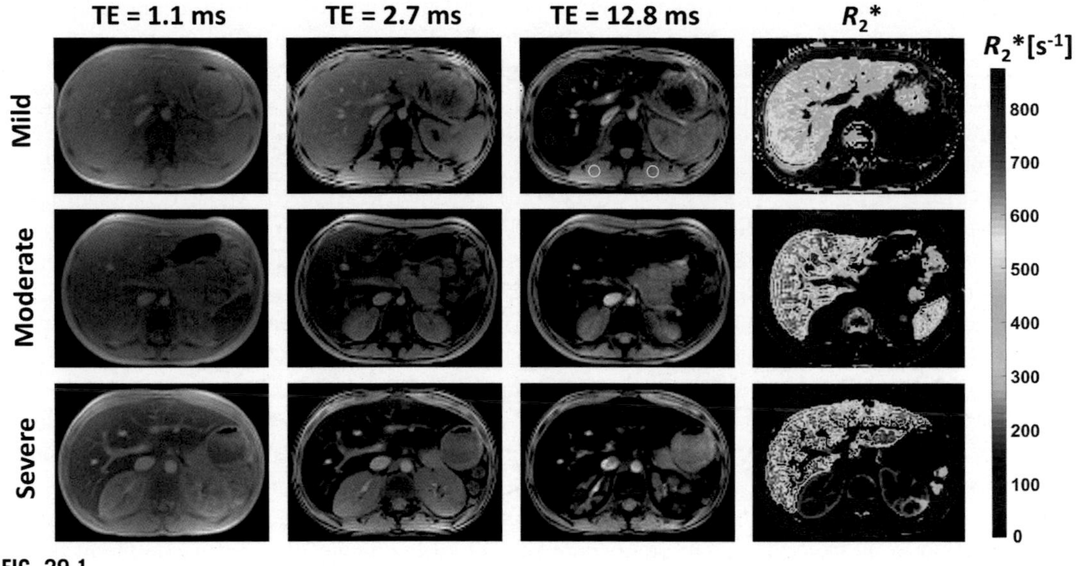

FIG. 29.1

Representative axial T_2*-weighted GRE images and corresponding R_2* maps of three patients with mild (M, 19 years old, estimated HIC: 4.1 mg Fe/g dry weight, top), moderate (F, 12 years old, est. HIC: 10.1 mg Fe/g dw, middle), and severe transfusional iron overload (M, 13 years old, est. HIC: 17.3 mg Fe/g dw, bottom).

A calibration formula can then be used to determine HIC content from these ratios. Several web-based tools are available for iron quantification based on SIR. However, for the signal intensity to be meaningful, the signal must be homogeneous across the slice. For this reason, the images must be acquired with the built-in body volume coil and not surface coils, limiting the SNR of the images, and precluding the use of parallel imaging. This is one of the main limitations of this technique.

R_2* relaxometry is the most researched iron quantification technique [57, 64–66]; T_2* mapping approaches are discussed in detail in Chapter 3. In most implementations, a multiecho gradient echo sequence is used to measure R_2* (see Fig. 29.1) [67–69]. Once measured, the R_2* value can be converted into iron concentration using a calibration curve, which maps the R_2* value to the iron concentration. In the literature, a variety of acquisition parameters, noise adjustments, and ROI selection methods have been reported. The most pertinent ones are reviewed in the following section. Besides, several calibration curves directly relating R_2* to HIC have been reported, and there is currently no consensus on the preferred or most optimal approach at 1.5 T or 3 T [70].

The first step in R_2*-based iron quantification is measuring the R_2* values via a gradient-echo-type sequence. Typically, R_2* measurement sequences are optimized to have the shortest possible first echo time [71], and the shortest possible inter-echo time [72]. The collection of data at short echo times allows the initial descent of the R_2* decay curve to be sampled with high precision [73]. These short echo and inter-echo times can be ensured by using a high pixel bandwidth. Both monopolar and bipolar multiecho acquisitions can be used [74]. Monopolar (i.e., with flyback gradients) acquisition has the advantage that there are no phase errors introduced by gradient offsets or similar, whereas bipolar acquisition is more efficient and can achieve shorter inter-echo times [75–77]. The number of echoes collected also varies with different implementations. As a general rule, it is most advantageous to acquire as many echoes as possible, up to an echo time of about 20 ms, to be able to accurately quantify low iron content (see Fig. 29.2) [72]. Moderate flip angles [70] are typically employed to avoid saturation effects. Typical sequence parameters are given in Table 29.1.

As an example, representative axial T_2*-weighted gradient recalled echo (GRE) images and corresponding R_2* maps from three patients with mild (M, 19 years old, estimated HIC: 4.1 mg Fe/g dry weight, top), moderate (F, 12 yo, est. HIC: 10.1 mg Fe/g dw, middle), and severe transfusional iron overload (M, 13 yo, est. HIC: 17.3 mg Fe/g dw, bottom) are shown in Fig. 29.1. Signal decay at different rates can be appreciated in the liver: for the mild case, the signal from hepatic parenchyma vanishes at the latest echo time; for moderate iron overload, the signal from liver tissue is noticeably attenuated at an echo time of 2.7 ms; and for the severely overloaded case, the liver already appears dark at the first echo time of 1.1 ms and the signal is almost vanished at TE = 2.7 ms. The last column shows R_2* maps calculated from multi-gradient echo datasets consisting of 20 echoes ($TE_1 = 1.1$ ms, $TE_{max} = 17.3$ ms) using a mono-exponential fitting model for Rician noise bias [69, 78].

Several different methods can be used to select an appropriate and replicable region-of-interest (ROI) for analysis. For instance, the ROI can be defined in a single 2D transversal slice at the height of the portal vein [67–69, 71, 79]; the portal vein serves as a landmark to ensure reproducible placement of the ROI, such that sufficient liver parenchyma is in the field-of-view, and that the ROI is located away from the diaphragm, where susceptibility changes may influence the measured R_2* values. Some methods rely on a single or multiple small ROIs which are drawn in areas with no visible vessels to avoid blood contamination [44, 80]. Other methods circumscribe the whole liver [81] and use different methods for blood contamination, mostly by excluding voxels containing mainly blood contributions [80, 82–85]. Fig. 29.3 shows how the use of different ROI selection methods for liver iron assessment can lead to different results in a 25-year-old male patient with sickle cell disease and biopsy confirmed severe transfusional iron overload of 29.6 mg Fe/g dry weight. In the top left panel, a small ROI is placed in the liver parenchyma to avoid blood vessels. The middle left panel shows a large ROI outlining the entire liver which is used to calculate the mean LIC value; signal contributions from blood vessels and potential ghosting artifacts from imperfect breath-holding lead to higher T_2* values which can be removed via thresholding based on the T_2* histogram (right). Note that this method requires user input and a visual overlay tool to confirm that the excluded pixels are indeed those containing blood and artifacts. An alternative method to remove R_2* signal contributions from blood is based on using a Frangi Vesselness Filter (bottom left panel) [80]. Other than tracing the contour of the liver, no user input is needed, which renders this method the most objective among these three. Only marginal differences in R_2* values are observed between ROI selection methods when using the same fitting algorithm (see bottom row of Fig. 29.3). However, when using different algorithms, for example, nonlinear least square (NLS) [67], squared NLS [86], and analytical computation [87, 88], the calculated R_2* maps and mean R_2* values in the ROI as well as the cut-off values for thresholding are different, as can be seen in the right panel. Therefore, attention needs to be paid to how R_2* values are derived and calculated before entering numbers into published biopsy calibration equations. When R_2*-derived HIC measurements are desired, the current recommendation is, therefore, to match data acquisition, ROI selection, and R_2* analysis methods with the approach used to derive published biopsy calibration equations [70].

Currently, there is no clear advantage of one method over the others. To ensure accurate quantification results, the ROI selection method for the measurement and calibration model must be the same [70], since calibration parameters can depend on the ROI selection method (e.g., blood contamination or border effects can lead to slightly different correlation parameters). For example, if one employs a

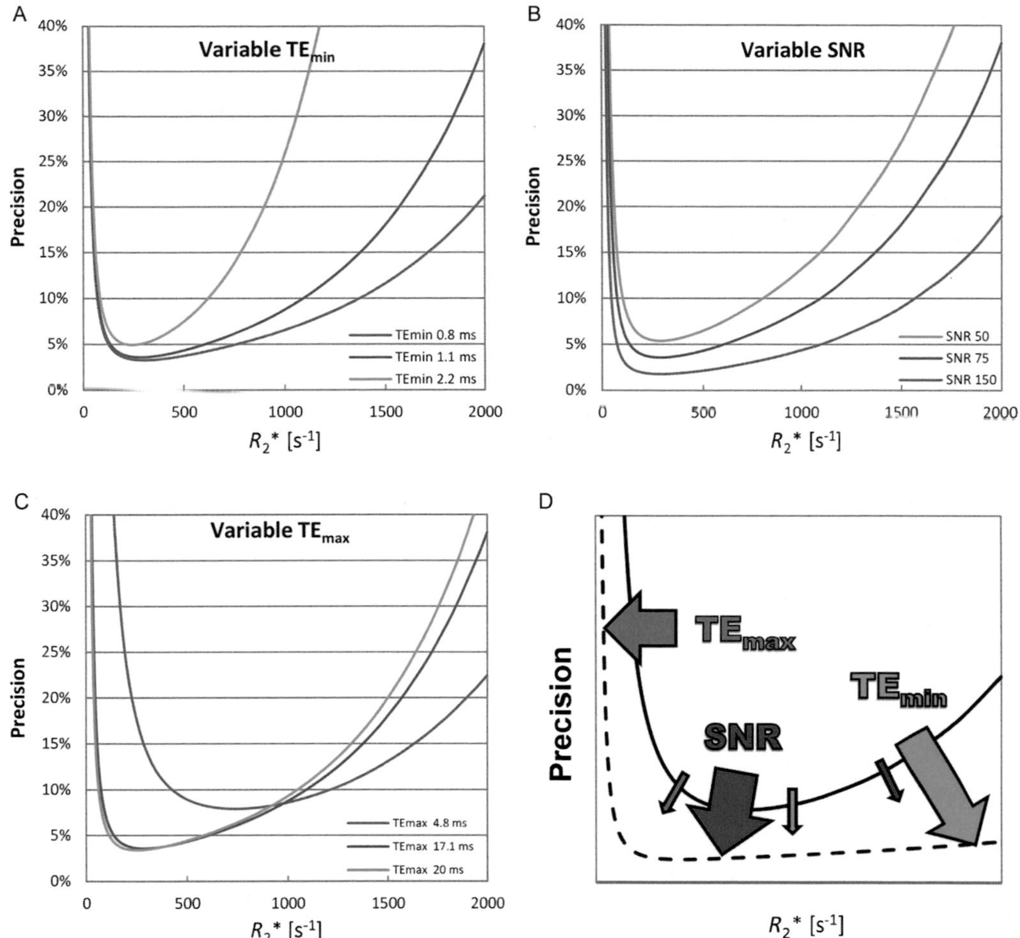

FIG. 29.2

Influence of key MR parameters on the precision (expressed as coefficient of variation) of R_2* measurements. (A) With TE_{min} as the variable, a shorter TE_{min} extends the range of measurable R_2* values with high precision to higher R_2* values. (B) With SNR as the variable, there is a direct relationship between SNR and precision, implying that even experiments with relatively long TE_{min} can provide precise R_2* measurements in the upper limit if SNR is sufficiently high. (C) With TE_{max} as the variable, the position and shape of the sharp increase of the error at very low R_2* values are mainly determined by TE_{max}, and longer TE_{max} generate higher precision in the low R_2* range (0–300 Hz (s^{-1})); this lower range is important for therapeutic decisions, e.g., when to start and stop chelation therapy. (D) A schematic diagram indicating the interplay among the three parameters and the R_2* range in which TE_{min}, TE_{max}, and SNR variations exert the largest influence on measurement precision. TE_{max} impacts the precision for low R_2*, TE_{min} for high R_2* values, and SNR enhances the overall precision. The R_2* MRI model parameters used here are $n = 20$ images, $TE_{min} = 1.1$ ms, $TE_n = TE_{min} + (n - 1) \cdot 0.8$ ms (TE_{min}, TE_{max} and estimated SNR from [67–69]). The analytical model for the precision analysis is described in [72].

Table 29.1 Typical sequence parameters for iron quantification via R_2^* measurement in the liver.

Parameter	Value
Initial echo time	~1.0 ms (as short as possible)
Echo spacing	~1.0 ms (as small as possible)
Number of echoes	12–20 (16 is common)
TR	120–200 ms
Flip angle	20–40° (dependent on TR)
Readout bandwidth	~1800 Hz/pixel

calibration curve that was established based on using four small ROIs across the liver, one cannot use a larger ROI to make a subsequent measurement and apply the calibration. Methods for liver volume segmentation using deep learning have recently been proposed [89, 90], and it can be expected that ROI selection will be fully automated shortly [91].

The R_2^* fitting method used may also affect the iron measurements, and thus care should be taken to obtain valid iron quantification results. Over time, several fitting methods have been introduced and tested. The main reason for the existence of these different fitting algorithms is the need to correct the fact that magnitude images are generally used for quantification, which introduces a noise bias on the later echoes in low SNR scenarios that may affect quantification [86]. Most published work uses non-linear fitting to obtain the R_2^* measurement, since the linear fitting of the logarithmic data, which often is used to simplify the fitting of exponential data, can yield large errors due to this noise bias [92]. Different ways of reducing the noise bias are currently used, including (a) echo truncation, i.e., only using echoes above the noise floor for fitting [71, 79]; (b) fitting the noise as an additional free parameter [67]; (c) noise subtraction, either by directly subtracting the value of the estimated noise from the signal [68] or by using a more realistic, quadratic signal model [69, 78, 93]; (d) fitting the square of the measured magnitude signal to the second moment of the expected signal [86]. The latter two methods have been suggested to be the most accurate [93].

The use of complex images instead of magnitude images to avoid this noise bias problem has not been as successful as hoped. The additional degree of freedom introduced by the use of complex images increases the complexity of the model and has led to no significant improvement over the superior methods discussed earlier [70]. Complex fitting is generally more successfully used in fat quantification or combined iron and fat quantification [94, 95]. Methods that do not rely on fitting have been recently presented, where the R_2^* value is obtained analytically without a fitting step [87, 88], which dramatically speeds up the computation process.

Concern has been voiced about the ability of R_2^* methods to accurately quantify iron concentration [96], but these fears have largely subsided, as expressed in recent publications [97] and review articles [70, 71, 79, 98]. Part of this original concern was due to the fact that some of the first published calibration studies [68, 99, 100] used suboptimal parameters, especially long first echo times [71], which led to imprecise quantification of high iron values and a subsequently skewed calibration line (see Fig. 29.4) [79, 95]. Later studies were able to use shorter echo times due to improved scanner technology, leading to more consistent calibration parameters [63, 71].

Using the acquisition and processing parameters described in [69, 81], mixed-effects modeling based on multireviewer analysis revealed a strong association between biopsy-confirmed HIC and

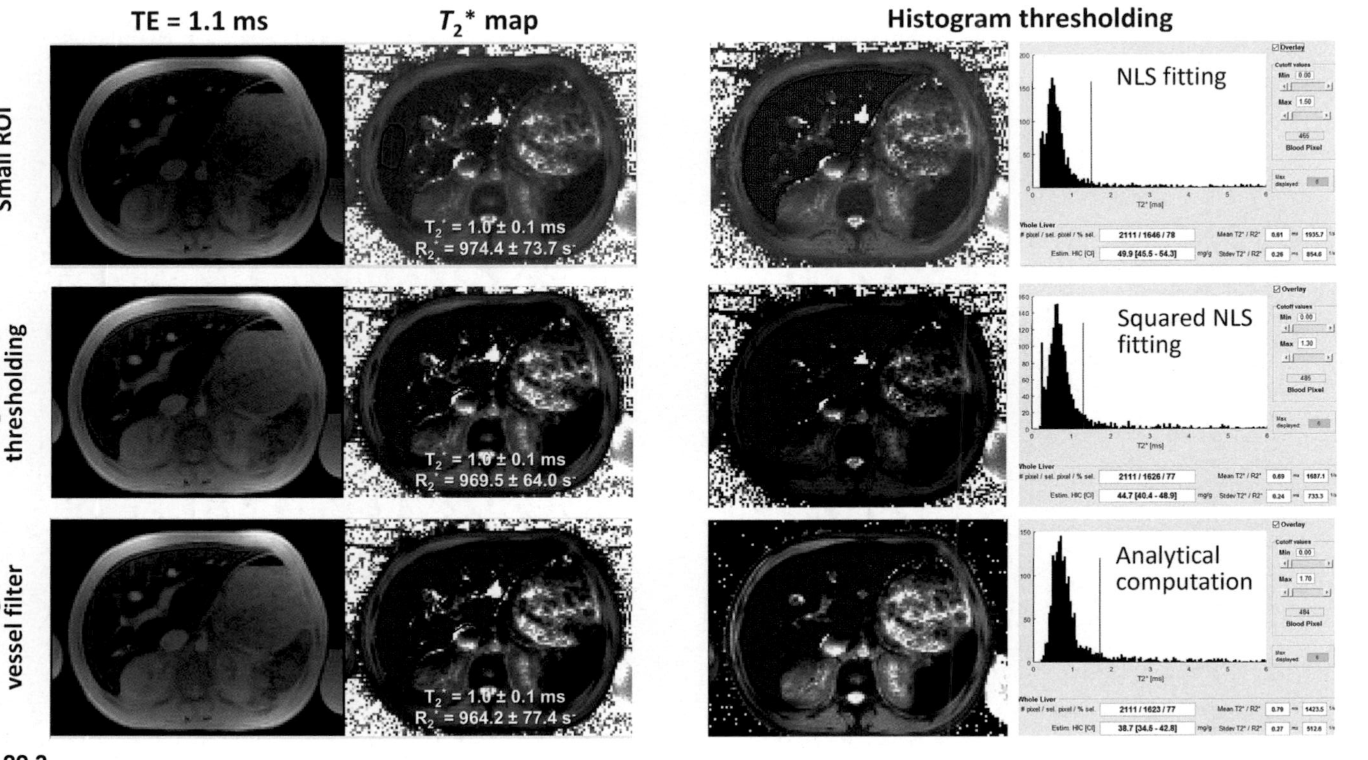

FIG. 29.3

Demonstration of three ROI selection methods for liver iron assessment in a 25-year-old male patient with sickle cell disease and biopsy confirmed severe transfusional iron overload of 29.6 mg Fe/g dry weight (left panel). The results of different curve fitting methods can be seen on the right panel.

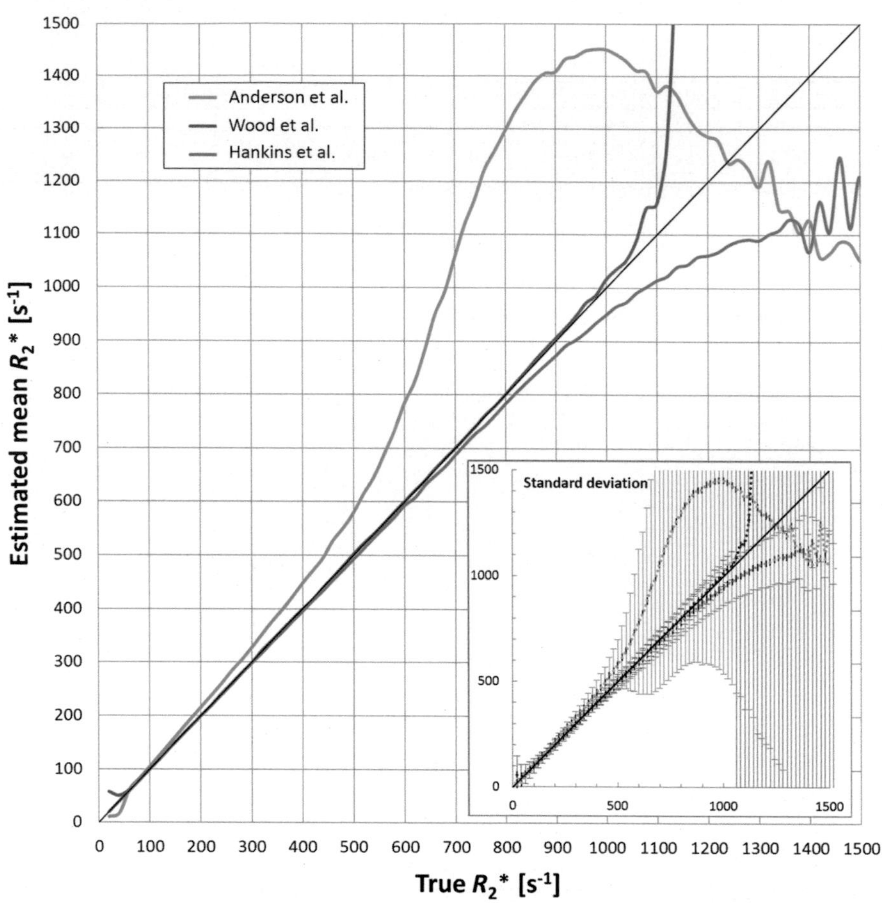

FIG. 29.4

R_2* fit accuracy resulting from the three different experimental approaches and curve fitting algorithms used to derive the first-generation R_2* biopsy calibration equations [67–69] as determined by Monte-Carlo simulations. For each simulated R_2* value, 10,000 independent samples were calculated. Experimental MR parameters (TE_{min}, TE_{max}, number of echoes), and SNR (50, 75, 150) were applied as in the three published methods. The Wood et al. model algorithm [67] (under the assumed best SNR conditions of 150) and Hankins et al. model [69] (SNR = 75) provide relatively accurate R_2* estimates (deviation <10% of true R_2*) over the range of 0–1000 s^{-1}, whereas the Anderson et al. model [68] with an estimated SNR of 50 starts to deviate from the line of unity at about 400 s^{-1} and overestimates the true R_2* value. As the SNR deteriorates, overestimations of the Anderson et al. model become more severe, and a true R_2* of 600 s^{-1} may be overestimated by 64% (33%) and calculated as 984 s^{-1} (800 s^{-1}) at a typical measurement SNR of 50. The inset shows the standard deviation of the simulated data points which is a measure of precision. The method of Wood et al. is imprecise at relatively low R_2* values most likely because of the relatively short TE_{max}. The model of Hankins et al. tends to underestimate R_2* for severe iron overload. For high R_2* values, the Anderson et al. method does overestimate R_2* and becomes increasingly imprecise as seen by the steep increase of the standard deviation.

R_2* measurements for a single, small ROI, and an ROI circumscribing the whole liver at 1.5 and 3T (R^2 0.83–0.92). For small ROI analyses at 1.5 and 3T, prediction curves had slopes of 0.027 s^{-1}/(mg Fe/g dry weight) and 0.015 s^{-1}/(mg Fe/g dry weight), respectively, and intercepts of -0.1288 and -0.027 s^{-1}, and for the large ROI the slopes were 0.031 s^{-1}/(mg Fe/g dry weight) and 0.016 s^{-1}/(mg Fe/g dry weight), respectively, and intercepts -0.58 and -0.087 s^{-1} [101].

In the meantime, a multitude of centers use R_2*-based HIC quantification as an alternative to biopsies or commercial R_2-based iron quantification (see the following section). Many of these centers rely on homegrown solutions or non-FDA approved web-based tools to obtain quantitative iron values, but efforts are underway to standardize acquisition and processing [70, 102]. Besides, several commercial tools for R_2* quantification are available, and their performance has been compared for agreement with R_2-based iron quantification [103]. Although there is currently no consensus for a single acquisition and processing method, there is a general understanding that accurate quantitative results can be obtained if the appropriate acquisition and processing methods are used in conjunction with the appropriate calibration curve [70, 103, 104].

Moreover, fat is a confounding factor when quantifying liver iron via R_2* (and vice versa, see also Chapter 27) [70]. Crucially, the use of a fat suppression pulse in the sequence—even in the absence of fat—affects the measured signal and can lead to inaccurate iron values if not corrected [93, 105, 106]. Therefore, fat suppression should not necessarily be applied unconditionally. Whether the fat is present in the liver partly depends on the patient's primary medical condition; for example, patients with sickle cell disease, seldom have significant hepatic steatosis [107], whereas transfusion-dependent oncology patients often receive steroids during treatment which can lead to steatosis [95]. Thus, a knowledge of the specific pathology under investigation may influence the interpretation of the iron concentration measurement.

29.2.2 Other organs

The fundamental steps of R_2*-based relaxometry and iron quantification employed in the liver can be applied to other organs, including the brain, heart, pancreas, spleen, and kidneys. Cardiac iron quantification is almost exclusively performed using R_2* quantification [64]; R_2 methods cannot be reliably used [108]. The most used technique is multiecho gradient echo acquisition similar to liver R_2*, however, fewer echoes are acquired (most often eight) to avoid artifacts due to cardiac motion. Respiratory motion artifacts are mitigated using breath holds. To evaluate myocardial iron content, an ROI is drawn in the midventricular wall of the left heart, preferably in the septum since this area is least prone to susceptibility artifacts [109, 110]. Bright blood and dark blood acquisition techniques have been used [111], with dark blood being preferred since it allows for better delineation of the ventricle and there are no potential artifacts from bright blood [111, 112]. Cardiac iron burden usually is assessed using the T_2* value (the inverse of R_2*), since there is no biopsy calibration data available due to the high risk of cardiac biopsies. T_2* values of higher than 20 ms generally are considered healthy [113, 114], T_2* values between 10 and 20 ms are considered indicative of mild to moderate iron overload, and T_2* values lower than 10 ms are considered as severe iron overload [115]. Compared to liver iron quantification, there seems to be a broader consensus about the preferred acquisition and postprocessing methods, as the published methods have less variation in sequence parameters and described postprocessing steps [39, 115].

Pancreatic iron quantification may be performed without any additional measurement time if a patient is undergoing hepatic iron concentration evaluation, as the abdominal coverage typically includes the pancreas in addition to the liver [116]. Several studies have been published quantifying the iron content of the spleen [44–46, 58, 117]. Similar to the pancreas, the spleen is also generally in the field of view when performing hepatic iron quantification, so that results can be easily obtained without an additional scan [116]. The clinical value of iron overload in the spleen has not been determined [57]. Several studies of renal iron load have found that renal iron is related to hemolysis [118, 119]. Established clinical markers for kidney dysfunction may, however, be sufficient for diagnosis of renal hemosiderosis without reliance on MRI-based iron quantification [120].

29.3 R_2-based iron quantification

R_2-based iron quantification is almost exclusively used in the liver and is dominated by an FDA approved commercial solution (Ferriscan). Five (T_2-weighted) spin echoes are acquired at increasing echo times during free breathing [121, 122]. A Ferriscan acquisition lasts about 20 min [70], which is rather long compared to other techniques mentioned in this chapter. For quantification, the data must be sent to a central location for evaluation. Due to the commercial nature of this approach, the exact steps taken during quantification are not completely publicly known, and only the basic workflow is described in publications that presented the calibration [96, 121–123]. However, it is known that postprocessing steps do include filters to remove motion and other artifacts [124] before curve fitting for quantification is performed [122]. This quantification technique has several advantages, specifically that the technique has regulatory approval in several countries, scanners are calibrated before they are permitted/licensed for patient evaluation, and the evaluation is done in one central location which ensures consistency. The latter point, however, is also one of the practical drawbacks of this method. Central processing, requiring the transfer of data back and forth, does not permit ad-hoc availability of results, as the turnaround time typically is one business day [125]. After the initial setup, customers are charged on a case-by-case basis. Other than the St. Pierre workgroup, which developed the Ferriscan product based on their research, only a few researchers actively working on R_2-based iron quantification [126, 127].

29.4 Quantitative susceptibility mapping

29.4.1 Introduction

Magnetic susceptibility (often denoted by the Greek symbol χ) is a dimensionless, quantitative property of all materials including human tissue. The magnetic susceptibility of an object describes the degree to which it becomes magnetized in response to an externally applied magnetic field. The object will interact with an externally applied magnetic field based on both the magnitude and polarity of its magnetic susceptibility. A diamagnetic material, such as human tissue, induces a magnetic field that is in the opposite direction of the externally applied magnetic field. Paramagnetic materials, such as ferritin and hemosiderin, induce a magnetic field that is in the same direction as the externally applied field [128]. For both diamagnetic and paramagnetic materials, the susceptibility represents the scale factor that relates the externally applied field (H) to the magnetization (M), as shown in Eq. (29.1). Materials may also be classified as superparamagnetic and ferromagnetic. For these materials, the relationship between M and H is nonlinear and potentially time-dependent. Materials that exhibit nonlinear or time-dependent behavior are not relevant in this discussion and will not be further discussed.

$$M = \chi H \tag{29.1}$$

The magnetic susceptibility of many common materials is known. In particular, the magnetic susceptibility of normal tissue without iron can be well approximated by the susceptibility of water (-9.05 ppm). The presence of iron in the tissue alters the magnetic susceptibility of the tissue by an amount that is proportional to the iron concentration. This is demonstrated by way of Eqs. 29.2a–29.2c.

$$\chi_{tissue,normal} = -9.05 \cdot 10^{-6} \tag{29.2a}$$

$$\chi_{Fe} = 0.266 \cdot 10^{-6}\ (\text{g dry tissue})/(\text{mg Fe}) \tag{29.2b}$$

$$\chi_{tissue,Fe} = \chi_{tissue,normal} + [Fe] \cdot \chi_{Fe} \tag{29.2c}$$

Therefore, with knowledge of the susceptibility of normal tissue and human iron stores (Eqs. 29.2a, 29.2b, respectively), one can measure the susceptibility of an iron-loaded tissue and calculate the iron concentration of iron [Fe] (mg Fe/g dry tissue) via Eq. (29.2c).

The magnetic susceptibility of tissue is not directly measurable by MRI. Instead, as discussed in Chapter 31, the magnetic susceptibility distorts the externally applied B_0 magnetic field by an amount that is proportional to the magnetic susceptibility, and thus the iron concentration. Eqs. (29.3a), (29.3b) show the mathematical relationship between the magnetic susceptibility and the susceptibility-induced B_0 field, $B_\chi(r)$ [129–131],

$$B_\chi(r) = d(r) \star \chi(r) \tag{29.3a}$$

$$d(r) = \frac{3\cos^2(\theta) - 1}{4\pi|r|^3} \tag{29.3b}$$

where the function $d(r)$ represents the spatial response of a magnetic dipole moment, r is the position, θ is the angle between the position r with respect to the main magnetic field, and $\star$ is the linear convolution operator. It is important to note that this function exists in 3D space; therefore, to properly estimate the magnetic susceptibility at a position r, one must have information about $B_\chi(r)$ in 3D space.

In addition to the susceptibility-induced field, there are additional contributions to the B_0 field in MRI, including contributions from magnet system imperfections as well as contributions from shim fields. These contributions are collectively known as the background field $B_B(r)$. Combined with the susceptibility-induced field, the total B_0 field at a spatial position r is written as

$$B_0(r) = B_\chi(r) + B_B(r) \tag{29.4}$$

The B_0 information is encoded into the phase of the acquired MR signal. Unlike relaxation information, which resides in the MR signal decay, the magnetic susceptibility information resides in the MR signal phase.

Quantitative Susceptibility Mapping (QSM) is a technique that can be used to measure the magnetic susceptibility of tissue. Since the relationship between magnetic susceptibility and iron concentration is direct and well-understood, QSM offers an attractive alternative to relaxation-based techniques, which have an indirect relationship to iron concentration and require the empirical derivation of a calibration curve to relate the relaxation parameter to the iron concentration.

The following sections discuss data acquisition and reconstruction steps for QSM, followed by clinical applications of QSM for mapping iron.

29.4.2 Data acquisition

Information about the magnetic susceptibility of the object of interest resides in the B_0 field of the MR system. Therefore, to recover the magnetic susceptibility distribution using QSM, the MR data acquisition must be sensitive to the B_0 field.

For QSM, a 3D multiecho gradient echo acquisition is the most used sequence. The acquisition must be 3D, rather than 2D, as mandated by the physical relationship of the magnetic susceptibility distribution and the B_0 field. Other sequences, such as an asymmetrically sampled multiecho spin echo sequence, may be used; however, the gradient echo acquisition is often the sequence of choice because data can be acquired in a relatively short time. This time consideration is important for applications including body imaging, where the patient is often required to maintain a breath-hold to minimize respiratory-induced image artifacts.

Data acquisition must occur at multiple different echo times to perform QSM. At any one echo time, information about the B_0 field map is indeed encoded into the phase of the acquired signal. However, contributions from other sources are also encoded into the phase of the acquired signal. With only one measurement, it is generally not possible to differentiate the phase contributions from the B_0 field (which is of interest) from the phase contributions of other sources (which can be considered as nuisance parameters in this case). Therefore, data must be acquired at multiple different echo times to separate the phase contributions. At a minimum, data at two echo times (containing complex-valued measurements) must be acquired to estimate a water signal and the B_0 field map term. In body applications, additional echo times are required to distinguish the phase contributions from the chemical shift of fat. In practice in body applications, it is common to acquire data at six different echo times, which also permits reliable estimation of $R_2{}^*$ in addition to the water, fat, and B_0 field map terms.

The requirement of a 3D acquisition at multiple different echo times contributes to a lengthened scan time. Therefore, to acquire 3D, multiecho data in the prescribed scan time, accelerated imaging techniques are often used. Most commonly, parallel imaging is used [132, 133]. Other techniques, like compressed sensing, can also be incorporated to reduce scan time [134]. Regardless of the acceleration technique used, the technique must maintain the phase evolution across the echo times so that the B_0 field can be accurately estimated from the acquired data.

In the brain, iron accumulation is on the order of tenths of milligrams of iron per gram of dry tissue. These relatively low concentrations introduce subtle changes to the magnetic field. Therefore, for mapping brain iron using QSM, long echo times are often used to resolve the small magnetic field distortions. In contrast, iron concentration in the liver can be on the order of tens of milligrams of iron per gram of dry tissue. These high concentrations cause rapid signal decay. To capture the transverse signal at multiple different echo times, short initial echo time and echo spacing must be used. Table 29.2 lists some relevant acquisition parameters that have been used for QSM of the brain and body. The optimal sequence parameter combination for QSM remains an open question currently.

29.4.3 Magnetic susceptibility reconstruction

As previously discussed, information about the magnetic susceptibility distribution is encoded in the acquired multiecho images. In particular, the B_0 field map contains magnetic susceptibility information. The general QSM reconstruction consists of three steps: (1) estimating the B_0 field map, corrected for confounding phase contributions, (2) background field removal, and (3) dipole inversion (see Fig. 29.5).

Table 29.2 Typical acquisition parameters used in QSM of the body.

Parameter	Brain QSM	Body QSM
Initial echo time	Minimum allowable	
Echo spacing	3–5 ms	2 ms (1.5 T) I 1 ms (3 T)
Number of echoes	≥2, preferably 8–12	≥3, preferably 6
TR	Minimum allowable after setting the echo times	
Flip angle	20	5[a] (1.5 T) I 3[a] (3 T)
Readout bandwidth	300 Hz/pixel	1100 Hz/pixel

[a]*Small flip angles have been used to avoid T_1 bias for concurrent estimation of the proton-density fat fraction (PDFF). However, if PDFF is not a parameter of interest, then a higher flip angle (e.g., Ernst angle) may be used to increase the SNR.*

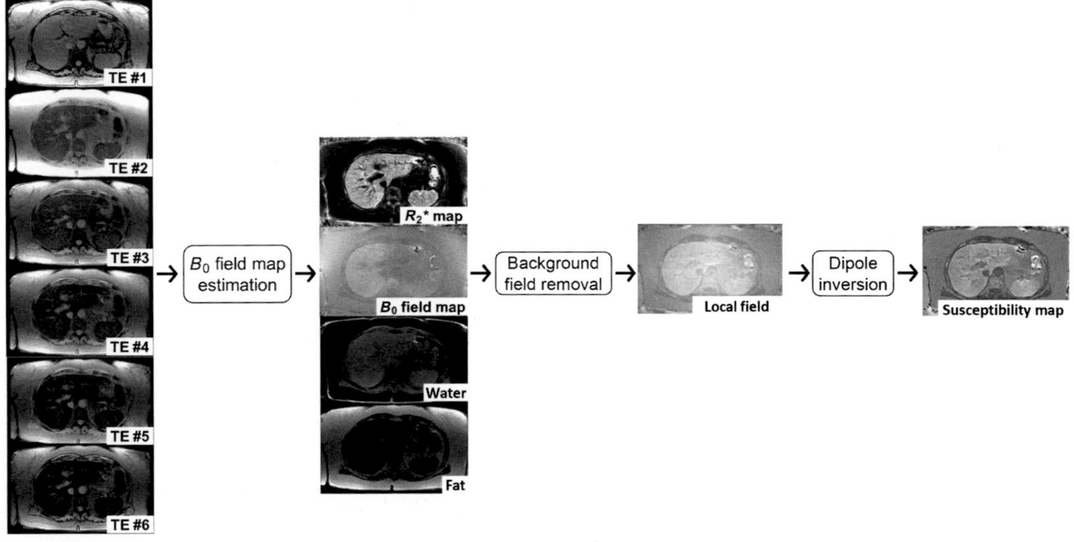

FIG. 29.5

The QSM reconstruction can be separated into three steps. The first step estimates the B_0 field map from the multiecho acquisition. When fat in present, such as in liver imaging, it must also be estimated so that the B_0 field map is accurately estimated. The second step removes the background field, resulting in only the local field, which is the field of interest. Finally, a dipole inversion step is performed to recover the susceptibility map.

Step 1: Estimation of the B_0 field map

The first step of a QSM reconstruction is an estimation of the B_0 field map. The B_0 field map can be estimated using a chemical shift encoded reconstruction, which corrects for the presence of fat [135, 136]. When fat is not present, such as in the brain, a linear fit to the measured phase is sufficient. The reconstruction must process the complex-valued acquired data to recover the B_0 field map, as the B_0 field map resides in the phase of the acquired signal and a magnitude value-based reconstruction removes this phase information. For those acquisitions that are at least three echoes (and more commonly at least six echoes), the relaxation rate R_2^* is often also estimated. In this way, both R_2^* and magnetic susceptibility parameters are estimated from the same acquisition.

Step 2: Background field removal

The B_0 field map contains components of both the susceptibility-induced field B_χ and the background field B_B. In QSM, only B_χ is of interest since it alone results from the presence of iron of the tissues of interest. Therefore, the background field component must be removed from the B_0 field map.

Several different background field removal techniques have been reported. The projection onto the dipole fields method [137] exploits the approximate orthogonality between the susceptibility-induced field and the background field. By projecting the B_0 field onto the space of functions that span the susceptibility-induced field, the background field can be mostly removed. The sophisticated harmonic artifact reduction for phase data (SHARP) method [138] exploits the observation that the background field (B_B) is a harmonic function within the tissues of interest while the susceptibility-induced field (B_χ) is assumed not to be harmonic within the tissues. Using the mean value property of harmonic functions, the background field can be removed by solving the following expression for B_χ:

$$WLB_0 = WLB_\chi \tag{29.5}$$

where L represents a discrete Laplace operator and W is a weighting mask that defines the reliability of the estimate at each voxel. The matrix WL is singular, therefore regularization must be incorporated into the estimation. Truncated singular value decomposition [138] and Tikhonov regularization [139] techniques have been proposed to solve this problem. Due to its high performance and computational efficiency, SHARP and its variants such as RESHARP and V-SHARP [139, 140] are commonly used for background field removal in QSM.

Step 3: Dipole inversion

Having isolated the susceptibility-induced field B_χ, the final step in the QSM reconstruction is dipole inversion. The Fourier-space representation of Eq. (29.3a) is shown below in Eq. (29.6a). Dipole inversion consists of solving the following expression for the tissue magnetic susceptibility (χ):

$$B_\chi(k) = d(k) \cdot \chi(k) \tag{29.6a}$$

$$d(k) = \frac{1}{3} - \frac{k_z^2}{|k|^2} \tag{29.6b}$$

where the expression $\cdot$ represents elementwise multiplication. Dipole inversion cannot occur via simple inversion of the operator *d*(*k*). This is because the dipole response function contains values that are equal to or close to zero (in the Fourier domain) at or near the magic angle of 54.74° [141]. Therefore, regularization must be incorporated into dipole inversion. Fourier domain methods modify the Fourier representation of the dipole kernel to improve the conditioning of the inversion [142, 143]. However, Fourier domain methods have been shown to introduce bias into the magnetic susceptibility estimate [144]. Image domain methods impose spatial constraints on the magnetic susceptibility map. By constraining the location of edges in the magnetic susceptibility map, image domain methods have demonstrated accurate susceptibility estimation [141, 145].

Some recent works have demonstrated the feasibility of performing joint background field removal and dipole inversion [146–148]. Potential benefits of this approach include the need for only one form of regularization (as opposed to separate regularization for background field removal and dipole inversion) as well as the mitigation of errors from the background field removal step to the dipole inversion step.

29.4.4 Postprocessing

In QSM, the relative susceptibility values are reconstructed, and not the absolute susceptibility values. This is perhaps most clearly understood by reviewing the Fourier domain representation of the dipole response function. At the origin ($\mathbf{k} = 0$), the value of the function is undefined and, therefore, often set to zero, resulting in ambiguity. Thus, the susceptibility values in a QSM reconstruction are correct relative to one another, but there is a global shift of the values. The relative susceptibility values can be converted to absolute susceptibility values by anchoring the relative map to a region of the image with a known absolute susceptibility value. An anchor via the susceptibility CSF is often used in the brain, whereas anchors via the susceptibility of muscle [149] and subcutaneous fat [150] are used to recover absolute susceptibility values in body QSM.

29.4.5 Applications of QSM for iron mapping

29.4.5.1 Liver

The primary application to date of QSM of the body has been for HIC quantification. Recent works have demonstrated that $R_2{}^*$ is sensitive to factors other than iron concentration, including fibrosis, edema, and fat [151–153]. These factors can confound the $R_2{}^*$-based estimate of HIC. Magnetic susceptibility is less sensitive to fibrosis and edema and can be corrected to account for the phase induced by fat. In this way, there is the potential for QSM-based estimates of HIC that are accurate even the presence of fibrosis, edema, and fat.

Early attempts at the susceptibility-based estimation of HIC made simplifying approximations [154, 155]. In these works, it was assumed that the difference in the B_0 field map between two adjacent tissues is directly proportional to the magnetic susceptibility difference between the tissues. By measuring the B_0 difference between two adjacent regions, a simple mathematical operation can be performed to derive the susceptibility difference between the two tissues. Assuming that the susceptibility of one of the tissues is known, then the susceptibility of tissue of interest can be calculated based on the susceptibility of the reference tissue and the calculated susceptibility change.

The feasibility of this technique has been demonstrated in several works. However, this technique has some important limitations. First, the technique assumes that the orientation of the tissues relative to the B_0 field is known or can be measured. This assumption is needed to simplify data collection and processing. Further, this technique is limited to a small region of tissue that is near an adjacent tissue with known susceptibility value. These restrictions have limited the applicability of this technique for routine clinical practice.

QSM-based techniques have been developed for the quantification of HIC [147, 156], with fundamental principles based on QSM applications in the brain [138, 141, 145]. These techniques have addressed the general technical challenges of QSM (which have been described in Section 29.4.3) as well as the additional challenges of QSM of the body, which include respiratory motion during the acquisition, the presence of fat, and the potential for rapid signal decay in cases of severe iron overload.

In a study of 43 subjects, a strong correlation was reported between QSM to the Ferriscan R_2-based estimate of HIC ($r^2 = 0.76$ for QSM at 1.5 T vs. Ferriscan at 1.5 T and $r^2 = 0.83$ for QSM at 3 T vs. Ferriscan at 1.5 T) [147]. The QSM estimates also showed a strong correlation to $R_2{}^*$ measurements, which were estimated from the same multiecho, gradient echo acquisition ($R^2 = 0.94$ for QSM vs. $R_2{}^*$ at 3 T and $R^2 = 0.93$ for QSM vs. $R_2{}^*$ at 3 T). Further, the QSM estimates at 1.5 and 3 T showed close agreement (slope = 0.96, y-intercept = -0.05, r^2 = 0.96), demonstrating the reproducibility of magnetic susceptibility across field strength, and reinforcing the field strength independence of magnetic susceptibility.

Biomagnetic liver susceptometry (BLS) using a superconducting quantum interference device (SQUID) has been used to provide magnetic susceptibility based HIC quantification. Despite the advantage of this technique to measure a quantitative property of tissue (i.e., magnetic susceptibility), there are only four such devices worldwide for BLS. This limited accessibility has severely limited the widespread use of this technique. However, SQUID offers the opportunity to provide an in vivo reference for magnetic susceptibility estimates. In a study of 22 patients undergoing routine monitoring for iron overload, MRI-based QSM measurements were compared to susceptibility estimates from SQUID [147]. A strong correlation was found between the two susceptibility estimates (r^2 = 0.88). However, the slope and y-intercept of the linear regression indicate a discrepancy between the susceptibility estimates (slope = 0.49, y-intercept = -0.22). Since both techniques are supposed to measure magnetic susceptibility, a slope and y-intercept of 1.0 and 0.0, respectively, would be expected in the ideal situation. Currently, the source of the discrepancy remains an open question.

29.4.5.2 Other organs

QSM in the brain has been applied to establish normative values in young adults [157] in deep gray matter structures and to assess differences between gender. Besides, the technique has been used to compare iron levels cross-sectionally and longitudinally in adolescence with growth and aging [158]. More recently, the feasibility of performing QSM in neonates and newborns has been demonstrated for studying myelination patterns in the brain [159]. Furthermore, the robustness of QSM as an imaging biomarker in iron quantification is being established. Feng et al. have performed intra-scanner repeatability of QSM and R_2* in the human brain at 3 T [160] across four scans, with promising intraclass correlation coefficients between 0.8 and 0.9. Lancione et al. has performed QSM reproducibility studies in the brain at different magnetic field strengths, including 3 T and 7 T, and emphasized that the proper choice of TE times between different field strengths is critical [161]. Similar works by Santin et al. on intra-scanner reproducibility [162] and by Ippoliti et al. [163] comparing QSM results between 1.5 T and 3 T continue to demonstrate QSM as a promising technique for the quantification of iron. More recently, QSM applications for iron quantification in the heart, spleen, and kidneys have been investigated [164–167].

29.5 Future directions

Several groups are currently working on standardizing iron quantification methods in multicenter studies across vendors. These efforts currently focus on R_2*-based quantification methods [65]. Standardization and calibration are achieved by measuring standardized or identical phantoms and volunteers or patients at different scanners, and by harmonizing acquisition parameters [65, 168]. At the same time, scanner vendors are also working on commercial solutions for quantitative iron analysis; work toward developing FDA submissions is currently underway.

There is also work ongoing to create comprehensive quantification solutions ("one-stop shops") where fat and iron quantification can be performed with a single acquisition in conjunction with a comprehensive postprocessing solution that outputs combined quantitative iron and fat values.

Yokoo et al. provided a comprehensive review of the relevant literature [169]. An additional focus of research groups and vendors is to automate acquisition and postprocessing as much as possible. On the acquisition side, this includes advanced user interfaces that aid in the selection of acquisition slices; for postprocessing, automated region selection/segmentation with additional features like automated vessel exclusion can be performed (see Fig. 29.3)[80]. These efforts will certainly be aided by the current surge of AI solutions in medical imaging, and developments that remove the burden of segmenting can be expected soon.

Further, the use of ultrashort echo time imaging [73, 170] will advance iron quantification in patients with very high iron overload, especially at higher field strengths. It is important to be able to accurately quantify iron in these patients to be able to fine-tune chelation therapy, monitor medication adherence, and verify therapeutic success. Fig. 29.6 shows two different approaches for R_2^*-based assessment for iron assessment at 3 T in a 27-year-old male subject with sickle cell anemia, >150 transfusions of packed red blood cells in his lifetime, and a biopsy confirmed HIC of 30 mg Fe/g dry wt. In the conventional breath-hold GRE image acquired at the first echo time ($TE_1 = 1.1$ ms) the liver signal has already significantly decayed (inlay), and overlaid liver T_2^* map, where the inhomogeneous T_2^* distribution in the map indicates that fit results are not reliable. This poor quality map can be attributed to the very short T_2^* relaxation time associated with severe siderosis and the higher field strength at 3 T. In the middle, images collected using a free-breathing interleaved multiecho ultrashort echo time (UTE) imaging approach are shown, in which a dramatically shorter echo time can be used ($TE_1 = 0.1$ ms). The first UTE image still exhibits liver signal, and the interleaved echo acquisition with $\Delta TE = 0.25$ m the fast signal decay to be sampled with additional data points at submillisecond TEs. As a result, a homogenous T_2^* distribution in the liver region can be observed, and the fit quality is much better, i.e., the map is smoother and exhibits anatomical features. The histogram plots on the right show the recorded T_2^* values in the liver parenchyma when using the GRE and UTE approaches. For the breath-hold GRE sequence, the histogram distribution does not display a clear maximum, hampering mean R_2^* quantitation, whereas the free-breathing UTE data exhibits a well-defined maximum allowing for a meaningful assessment of mean hepatic R_2^*. As an added benefit, the free-breathing interleaved multiecho UTE approach is intrinsically motion-corrected and, therefore, less prone to

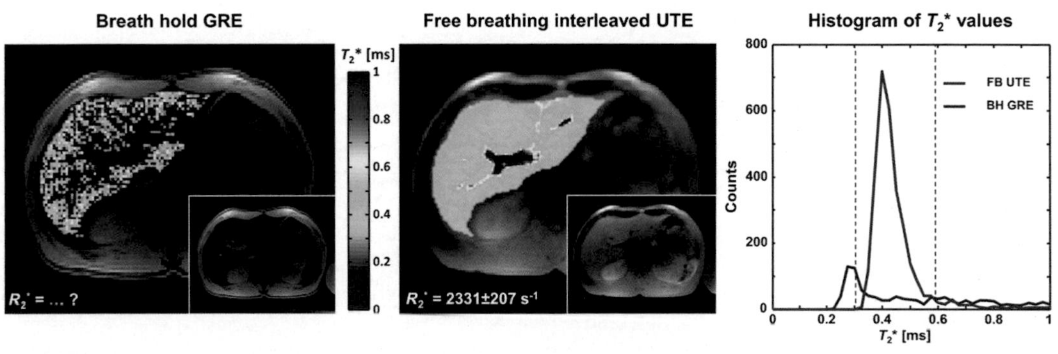

FIG. 29.6

R_2^*-based massive iron assessment at 3 T in a 27-year-old male subject with sickle cell anemia, >150 transfusions of packed red blood cells in his lifetime, and a biopsy confirmed HIC of 30 mg Fe/g dry wt.

breathing artifacts. UTE is therefore not only suited for assessment of severe iron overload, but also for screening subjects who are unable to hold their breath, e.g., children and sedated patients [171], and could be used to improve iron quantification in several clinical scenarios.

29.6 Summary

MRI provides noninvasive, accurate, and reproducible quantification of the distribution of iron in the human body. During the past decade, MRI has replaced needle biopsy as a reference standard for the assessment of body iron burden and monitoring excess iron removal therapy. MR signals from iron-loaded tissues have distinctly different MR relaxation and susceptibility properties, which are leveraged by MRI to separate, identify, and quantify the contributions from iron. In particular, R_2- and R_2^*-based iron quantification techniques have been widely adopted for clinical and research use in the body, while QSM is the main technique used in the brain [1]. New techniques for iron quantification in massively iron overloaded patients, free-breathing imaging, and advanced reconstruction have demonstrated promising performance and are now being further evaluated for clinical translation. Besides, advanced signal modeling can now also correct for confounding factors of iron quantification, specifically fat; indeed, recent work has shown that iron and fat can be calculated from a single scan.

References

[1] Yan F, et al. Iron deposition quantification: applications in the brain and liver. J Magn Reson Imaging 2018;48(2):301–17.
[2] Nottage K, et al. Trends in transfusion burden among long-term survivors of childhood hematological malignancies. Leuk Lymphoma 2013;54(8):1719–23.
[3] Eng J, Fish JD. Insidious iron burden in pediatric patients with acute lymphoblastic leukemia. Pediatr Blood Cancer 2011;56(3):368–71.
[4] Prati D, et al. Clinical and histological characterization of liver disease in patients with transfusion-dependent beta-thalassemia. A multicenter study of 117 cases. Haematologica 2004;89(10):1179–86.
[5] Olivieri NF. Progression of iron overload in sickle cell disease. Semin Hematol 2001;38(1 Suppl. 1):57–62.
[6] Olynyk JK, et al. Duration of hepatic iron exposure increases the risk of significant fibrosis in hereditary hemochromatosis: a new role for magnetic resonance imaging. Am J Gastroenterol 2005;100(4):837–41.
[7] Pippard MJ. Measurement of iron status. Prog Clin Biol Res 1989;309:85–92.
[8] Angelucci E, et al. Hepatic iron concentration and total body iron stores in thalassemia major. N Engl J Med 2000;343(5):327–31.
[9] Cartwright GE, et al. Hereditary hemochromatosis. Phenotypic expression of the disease. N Engl J Med 1979;301(4):175–9.
[10] Risdon RA, Barry M, Flynn DM. Transfusional iron overload: the relationship between tissue iron concentration and hepatic fibrosis in thalassaemia. J Pathol 1975;116(2):83–95.
[11] Merkel PA, et al. Insulin resistance and hyperinsulinemia in patients with thalassemia major treated by hypertransfusion. N Engl J Med 1988;318(13):809–14.
[12] Haap M, et al. Insulin sensitivity and liver fat: role of iron load. J Clin Endocrinol Metab 2011;96(6): E958–61.
[13] Adams PC, Speechley M, Kertesz AE. Long-term survival analysis in hereditary hemochromatosis. Gastroenterology 1991;101(2):368–72.

[14] Adams PC, et al. The relationship between iron overload, clinical symptoms, and age in 410 patients with genetic hemochromatosis. Hepatology 1997;25(1):162–6.

[15] Crownover BK, Covey CJ. Hereditary hemochromatosis. Am Fam Physician 2013;87(3):183–90.

[16] Majhail NS, Lazarus HM, Burns LJ. A prospective study of iron overload management in allogeneic hematopoietic cell transplantation survivors. Biol Blood Marrow Transplant 2010;16(6):832–7.

[17] Christoforidis A, et al. Four-year evaluation of myocardial and liver iron assessed prospectively with serial MRI scans in young patients with beta-thalassaemia major: comparison between different chelation regimens. Eur J Haematol 2007;78(1):52–7.

[18] Chan PC, et al. The use of nuclear magnetic resonance imaging in monitoring total body iron in hemodialysis patients with hemosiderosis treated with erythropoietin and phlebotomy. Am J Kidney Dis 1992; 19(5):484–9.

[19] Brittenham GM. Iron-chelating therapy for transfusional iron overload. N Engl J Med 2011;364(2):146–56.

[20] Bilgic B, et al. MRI estimates of brain iron concentration in normal aging using quantitative susceptibility mapping. Neuroimage 2012;59(3):2625–35.

[21] Lim IA, et al. Human brain atlas for automated region of interest selection in quantitative susceptibility mapping: application to determine iron content in deep gray matter structures. Neuroimage 2013; 82:449–69.

[22] Acosta-Cabronero J, et al. In vivo quantitative susceptibility mapping (QSM) in Alzheimer's disease. PLoS One 2013;8(11):e81093.

[23] Wisnieff C, et al. Quantitative susceptibility mapping (QSM) of white matter multiple sclerosis lesions: interpreting positive susceptibility and the presence of iron. Magn Reson Med 2015;74(2):564–70.

[24] Yang Q, et al. Brain iron deposition in type 2 diabetes mellitus with and without mild cognitive impairment—an in vivo susceptibility mapping study. Brain Imaging Behav 2018;12(5):1479–87.

[25] Du L, et al. Increased iron deposition on brain quantitative susceptibility mapping correlates with decreased cognitive function in Alzheimer's disease. ACS Chem Nerosci 2018;9(7):1849–57.

[26] Zivadinov R, et al. Brain iron at quantitative MRI is associated with disability in multiple sclerosis. Radiology 2018;289(2):487–96.

[27] Dimov AV, et al. High-resolution QSM for functional and structural depiction of subthalamic nuclei in DBS presurgical mapping. J Neurosurg 2018;131(2):360–7.

[28] Sethi SK, et al. Iron quantification in Parkinson's disease using an age-based threshold on susceptibility maps: the advantage of local versus entire structure iron content measurements. Magn Reson Imaging 2019;55:145–52.

[29] Chen L, et al. Altered brain iron content and deposition rate in Huntington's disease as indicated by quantitative susceptibility MRI. J Neurosci Res 2019;97(4):467–79.

[30] Shahmaei V, et al. Evaluation of iron deposition in brain basal ganglia of patients with Parkinson's disease using quantitative susceptibility mapping. Eur J Radiol Open 2019;6:169–74.

[31] Ghassaban K, et al. Regional high iron in the substantia Nigra differentiates Parkinson's disease patients from healthy controls. Front Aging Neurosci 2019;11:106.

[32] De A, et al. Rapid quantitative susceptibility mapping of intracerebral hemorrhage. J Magn Reson Imaging 2020;51(3):712–8.

[33] Fujiwara T, et al. Quantitative susceptibility mapping (QSM) evaluation of infantile neuroaxonal dystrophy. BJR Case Rep 2019;5(2):20180078.

[34] Mazzucchi S, et al. Quantitative susceptibility mapping in atypical Parkinsonisms. Neuroimage Clin 2019;24:101999.

[35] He N, et al. Visualizing the lateral habenula using susceptibility weighted imaging and quantitative susceptibility mapping. Magn Reson Imaging 2020;65:55–61.

[36] Manara R, et al. Brain iron content in systemic iron overload: a beta-thalassemia quantitative MRI study. Neuroimage Clin 2019;24:102058.

[37] Oshima S, et al. Brain MRI with quantitative susceptibility mapping: relationship to CT attenuation values. Radiology 2020;294(3):600–9.
[38] Akcay A, et al. Cardiac T_2* MRI assessment in patients with thalassaemia major and its effect on the preference of chelation therapy. Int J Hematol 2014;99(6):706–13.
[39] Baksi AJ, Pennell DJ. T_2* imaging of the heart: methods, applications, and outcomes. Top Magn Reson Imaging 2014;23(1):13–20.
[40] Reitman AJ, Coates TD, Freyer DR. Early cardiac iron overload in a child on treatment of acute lymphoblastic Leukemia. Pediatrics 2015;136(3):e697–700.
[41] Meloni A, et al. Cardiac iron overload in sickle-cell disease. Am J Hematol 2014;89(7):678–83.
[42] Wood JC, Noetzli L. Cardiovascular MRI in thalassemia major. Ann N Y Acad Sci 2010;1202:173–9.
[43] Wood JC. Cardiac iron across different transfusion-dependent diseases. Blood Rev 2008;22(Suppl. 2): S14–21.
[44] Schwenzer NF, et al. T_2* relaxometry in liver, pancreas, and spleen in a healthy cohort of one hundred twenty-nine subjects-correlation with age, gender, and serum ferritin. Invest Radiol 2008;43(12):854–60.
[45] Kolnagou A, et al. Liver iron and serum ferritin levels are misleading for estimating cardiac, pancreatic, splenic and total body iron load in thalassemia patients: factors influencing the heterogenic distribution of excess storage iron in organs as identified by MRI T_2*. Toxicol Mech Methods 2013;23(1):48–56.
[46] Gutierrez L, et al. Tissue iron distribution assessed by MRI in patients with iron loading anemias. PLoS One 2015;10(9):e0139220.
[47] Papakonstantinou O, et al. Assessment of iron distribution between liver, spleen, pancreas, bone marrow, and myocardium by means of R_2 relaxometry with MRI in patients with beta-thalassemia major. J Magn Reson Imaging 2009;29(4):853–9.
[48] Noetzli LJ, et al. Pancreatic iron and glucose dysregulation in thalassemia major. Am J Hematol 2012;87(2):155–60.
[49] Au WY, et al. A T_2* magnetic resonance imaging study of pancreatic iron overload in thalassemia major. Haematologica 2008;93(1):116–9.
[50] Brewer CJ, Coates TD, Wood JC. Spleen R_2 and R_2* in iron-overloaded patients with sickle cell disease and thalassemia major. J Magn Reson Imaging 2009;29(2):357–64.
[51] de Assis RA, et al. Pancreatic iron stores assessed by magnetic resonance imaging (MRI) in beta thalassemic patients. Eur J Radiol 2012;81(7):1465–70.
[52] Meloni A, et al. Pancreatic iron overload by T_2* MRI in a large cohort of well treated thalassemia major patients: can it tell us heart iron distribution and function? Am J Hematol 2015;90(9):E189–90.
[53] Pfeifer CD, et al. Pancreatic iron and fat assessment by MRI-R_2* in patients with iron overload diseases. J Magn Reson Imaging 2015;42(1):196–203.
[54] Mokhtar GM, et al. Pancreatic functions in adolescents with beta thalassemia major could predict cardiac and hepatic iron loading: relation to T_2-star (T_2*) magnetic resonance imaging. J Invest Med 2016;64(3):771–81.
[55] Pinto VM, et al. Lack of correlation between heart, liver and pancreas MRI-R_2*: results from long-term follow-up in a cohort of adult beta-thalassemia major patients. Am J Hematol 2018;93(3):E79–82.
[56] Azarkeivan A, et al. Correlation between heart, liver and pancreas hemosiderosis measured by MRI T_2* among thalassemia major patients from Iran. Arch Iran Med 2016;19(2):96–100.
[57] Wood JC. Use of magnetic resonance imaging to monitor iron overload. Hematol Oncol Clin North Am 2014;28(4):747–64, vii.
[58] Maximova N, et al. MRI-based evaluation of multiorgan iron overload is a predictor of adverse outcomes in pediatric patients undergoing allogeneic hematopoietic stem cell transplantation. Oncotarget 2017; 8(45):79650–61.
[59] Hernandez RJ, et al. MR evaluation of liver iron overload. J Comput Assist Tomogr 1988;12(1):91–4.
[60] Gandon Y, et al. Non-invasive assessment of hepatic iron stores by MRI. Lancet 2004;363(9406):357–62.
[61] Gandon Y, et al. Hemochromatosis: diagnosis and quantification of liver iron with gradient-echo MR imaging. Radiology 1994;193(2):533–8.

[62] d'Assignies G, et al. Non-invasive measurement of liver iron concentration using 3-Tesla magnetic resonance imaging: validation against biopsy. Eur Radiol 2018;28(5):2022–30.
[63] Paisant A, et al. MRI for the measurement of liver iron content, and for the diagnosis and follow-up of iron overload disorders. Presse Med 2017;46(12 Pt. 2):e279–87.
[64] Menacho K, et al. T_2* mapping techniques: iron overload assessment and other potential clinical applications. Magn Reson Imaging Clin N Am 2019;27(3):439–51.
[65] Meloni A, et al. Multicenter validation of the magnetic resonance T_2* technique for quantification of pancreatic iron. Eur Radiol 2019;29(5):2246–52.
[66] Henninger B. Demystifying liver iron concentration measurements with MRI. Eur Radiol 2018; 28(6):2535–6.
[67] Wood JC, et al. MRI R_2 and R_2* mapping accurately estimates hepatic iron concentration in transfusion-dependent thalassemia and sickle cell disease patients. Blood 2005;106(4):1460–5.
[68] Anderson LJ, et al. Cardiovascular T_2-star (T_2*) magnetic resonance for the early diagnosis of myocardial iron overload. Eur Heart J 2001;22(23):2171–9.
[69] Hankins JS, et al. R_2* magnetic resonance imaging of the liver in patients with iron overload. Blood 2009;113(20):4853–5.
[70] Henninger B, et al. Practical guide to quantification of hepatic iron with MRI. Eur Radiol 2019; 30(1):383–93.
[71] Henninger B, et al. R_2* relaxometry for the quantification of hepatic iron overload: biopsy-based calibration and comparison with the literature. Rofo 2015;187(6):472–9.
[72] Tipirneni-Sajja A, et al. Ultrashort echo time imaging for quantification of hepatic iron overload: comparison of acquisition and fitting methods via simulations, phantoms, and in vivo data. J Magn Reson Imaging 2019;49(5):1475–88.
[73] Krafft AJ, et al. Quantitative ultrashort echo time imaging for assessment of massive iron overload at 1.5 and 3 Tesla. Magn Reson Med 2017;78(5):1839–51.
[74] Zhong X, et al. Liver fat quantification using a multi-step adaptive fitting approach with multi-echo GRE imaging. Magn Reson Med 2014;72(5):1353–65.
[75] Alecci M, Jezzard P. Characterization and reduction of gradient-induced eddy currents in the RF shield of a TEM resonator. Magn Reson Med 2002;48(2):404–7.
[76] Yu H, et al. Phase and amplitude correction for multi-echo water-fat separation with bipolar acquisitions. J Magn Reson Imaging 2010;31(5):1264–71.
[77] Hutton C, et al. Validation of a standardized MRI method for liver fat and T_2* quantification. PLoS One 2018;13(9):e0204175.
[78] Loeffler RB, et al. Can multi-slice or navigator-gated R_2* MRI replace single-slice breath-hold acquisition for hepatic iron quantification? Pediatr Radiol 2017;47(1):46–54.
[79] Garbowski MW, et al. Biopsy-based calibration of T_2* magnetic resonance for estimation of liver iron concentration and comparison with R_2 Ferriscan. J Cardiovasc Magn Reson 2014;16:40.
[80] Tipirneni-Sajja A, et al. Automated vessel exclusion technique for quantitative assessment of hepatic iron overload by R_2*-MRI. J Magn Reson Imaging 2018;47(6):1542–51.
[81] McCarville MB, et al. Comparison of whole liver and small region-of-interest measurements of MRI liver R_2* in children with iron overload. Pediatr Radiol 2010;40(8):1360–7.
[82] Feng Y, et al. A novel semiautomatic parenchyma extraction method for improved MRI R_2* relaxometry of iron loaded liver. J Magn Reson Imaging 2014;40(1):67–78.
[83] Saiviroonporn P, Viprakasit V, Krittayaphong R. Improved R_2* liver iron concentration assessment using a novel fuzzy c-mean clustering scheme. BMC Med Imaging 2015;15:52.
[84] Positano V, et al. Improved T_2* assessment in liver iron overload by magnetic resonance imaging. Magn Reson Imaging 2009;27(2):188–97.
[85] Deng J, et al. A semiautomatic postprocessing of liver R_2* measurement for assessment of liver iron overload. Magn Reson Imaging 2012;30(6):799–806.

[86] Feng Y, et al. Improved MRI R2 * relaxometry of iron-loaded liver with noise correction. Magn Reson Med 2013;70(6):1765–74.
[87] Song R, et al. Fast quantitative parameter maps without fitting: integration yields accurate mono-exponential signal decay rates. Magn Reson Med 2018;79(6):2978–85.
[88] Song R, et al. Erratum to: Fast quantitative parameter maps without fitting: integration yields accurate mono-exponential signal decay rates (Magn Reson Med 2018;79:2978-2985). Magn Reson Med 2019;81(2):1470.
[89] Fu Y, et al. A novel MRI segmentation method using CNN-based correction network for MRI-guided adaptive radiotherapy. Med Phys 2018;45(11):5129–37.
[90] van Gastel MDA, et al. Automatic measurement of kidney and liver volumes from MR images of patients affected by autosomal dominant polycystic kidney disease. J Am Soc Nephrol 2019;30(8):1514–22.
[91] Loeffler RB, et al. Automated MR HIC determination using deep learning and Frangi filters. In: Proceedings of the 28th annual meeting of ISMRM. 2020.
[92] Otto R, et al. Limitations of using logarithmic transformation and linear fitting to estimate relaxation rates in iron-loaded liver. Pediatr Radiol 2011;41(10):1259–65.
[93] Krafft AJ, et al. Does fat suppression via chemically selective saturation affect R_2*-MRI for transfusional iron overload assessment? A clinical evaluation at 1.5T and 3T. Magn Reson Med 2016;76(2):591–601.
[94] Hernando D, Kramer JH, Reeder SB. Multipeak fat-corrected complex R_2* relaxometry: theory, optimization, and clinical validation. Magn Reson Med 2013;70(5):1319–31.
[95] Tipirneni-Sajja A, et al. Autoregressive moving average modeling for hepatic iron quantification in the presence of fat. J Magn Reson Imaging 2019;50(5):1620–32.
[96] St Pierre TG, et al. Multicenter validation of spin-density projection-assisted R2-MRI for the noninvasive measurement of liver iron concentration. Magn Reson Med 2014;71(6):2215–23.
[97] Jhaveri KS, et al. Prospective evaluation of an R_2* method for assessing liver iron concentration (LIC) against FerriScan: derivation of the calibration curve and characterization of the nature and source of uncertainty in the relationship. J Magn Reson Imaging 2019;49(5):1467–74.
[98] Wood JC, et al. Liver MRI is more precise than liver biopsy for assessing total body iron balance: a comparison of MRI relaxometry with simulated liver biopsy results. Magn Reson Imaging 2015;33(6):761–7.
[99] Christoforidis A, et al. MRI assessment of liver iron content in thalassamic patients with three different protocols: comparisons and correlations. Eur J Haematol 2009;82(5):388–92.
[100] Virtanen JM, Komu ME, Parkkola RK. Quantitative liver iron measurement by magnetic resonance imaging: in vitro and in vivo assessment of the liver to muscle signal intensity and the R_2* methods. Magn Reson Imaging 2008;26(8):1175–82.
[101] Hillenbrand CM, et al. A global prediction model for hepatic iron concentration measurements using R_2*-MRI. In: 3rd annual sickle cell research and educational symposium, Fort Lauderdale, FL, USA. 2009.
[102] Pooler BD, Hernando D, Reeder SB. Clinical implementation of a focused MRI protocol for hepatic fat and iron quantification. AJR Am J Roentgenol 2019;1–6.
[103] Bacigalupo L, et al. Comparison between different software programs and post-processing techniques for the MRI quantification of liver iron concentration in thalassemia patients. Radiol Med 2016;121(10):751–62.
[104] Meloni A, et al. The use of appropriate calibration curves corrects for systematic differences in liver R_2* values measured using different software packages. Br J Haematol 2013;161(6):888–91.
[105] Meloni A, et al. Effect of inversion recovery fat suppression on hepatic R_2* quantitation in transfusional siderosis. AJR Am J Roentgenol 2015;204(3):625–9.
[106] Sanches-Rocha L, et al. Comparison between multi-echo T_2* with and without fat saturation pulse for quantification of liver iron overload. Magn Reson Imaging 2013;31(10):1704–8.
[107] Oguntoye OO, et al. Hepatobiliary ultrasonographic abnormalities in adult patients with sickle cell anaemia in steady state in Ile-Ife, Nigeria. Pol J Radiol 2017;82:1–8.
[108] Mavrogeni SI, et al. T2 relaxation time study of iron overload in b-thalassemia. MAGMA 1998;6(1):7–12.

[109] Ghugre NR, et al. Improved R_2* measurements in myocardial iron overload. J Magn Reson Imaging 2006;23(1):9–16.
[110] Wood JC, et al. Onset of cardiac iron loading in pediatric patients with thalassemia major. Haematologica 2008;93(6):917–20.
[111] Barrera CA, et al. Protocol optimization for cardiac and liver iron content assessment using MRI: what sequence should I use? Clin Imaging 2019;56:52–7.
[112] He T. Cardiovascular magnetic resonance T_2* for tissue iron assessment in the heart. Quant Imaging Med Surg 2014;4(5):407–12.
[113] Anderson LJ, et al. Myocardial iron clearance during reversal of siderotic cardiomyopathy with intravenous desferrioxamine: a prospective study using T_2* cardiovascular magnetic resonance. Br J Haematol 2004;127(3):348–55.
[114] Ghugre NR, et al. MRI detects myocardial iron in the human heart. Magn Reson Med 2006;56(3):681–6.
[115] Chu WC, Au WY, Lam WW. MRI of cardiac iron overload. J Magn Reson Imaging 2012;36(5):1052–9.
[116] Franca M, et al. Tissue iron quantification in chronic liver diseases using MRI shows a relationship between iron accumulation in liver, spleen, and bone marrow. Clin Radiol 2018;73(2):215.e1–9.
[117] Wood JC, et al. Organ iron accumulation in chronically transfused children with sickle cell anaemia: baseline results from the TWiTCH trial. Br J Haematol 2016;172(1):122–30.
[118] ElAlfy MS, et al. Renal iron deposition by magnetic resonance imaging in pediatric beta-thalassemia major patients: relation to renal biomarkers, total body iron and chelation therapy. Eur J Radiol 2018;103:65–70.
[119] Hashemieh M, et al. T_2-star (T_2*) magnetic resonance imaging for assessment of kidney iron overload in thalassemic patients. Arch Iran Med 2012;15(2):91–4.
[120] Hashemieh M, et al. Renal hemosiderosis among Iranian transfusion dependent beta-thalassemia major patients. Int J Hematol Oncol Stem Cell Res 2017;11(2):133–8.
[121] St Pierre TG, et al. Noninvasive measurement and imaging of liver iron concentrations using proton magnetic resonance. Blood 2005;105(2):855–61.
[122] St Pierre TG, Clark PR, Chua-Anusorn W. Single spin-echo proton transverse relaxometry of iron-loaded liver. NMR Biomed 2004;17(7):446–58.
[123] St Pierre TG, Clark PR, Chua-Anusorn W. Measurement and mapping of liver iron concentrations using magnetic resonance imaging. Ann N Y Acad Sci 2005;1054:379–85.
[124] Clark PR, Chua-anusorn W, St Pierre TG. Reduction of respiratory motion artifacts in transverse relaxation rate (R_2) images of the liver. Comput Med Imaging Graph 2004;28(1–2):69–76.
[125] Wunderlich AP, et al. Noninvasive MRI-based liver iron quantification: methodic approaches, practical applicability and significance. Rofo 2016;188(11):1031–6.
[126] Pirasteh A, et al. Inter-method reproducibility of biexponential R_2 MR relaxometry for estimation of liver iron concentration. Magn Reson Med 2018;80(6):2691–701.
[127] Calle-Toro JS, et al. R_2 relaxometry based MR imaging for estimation of liver iron content: a comparison between two methods. Abdom Radiol (NY) 2019;44(9):3058–68.
[128] Schenck JF. The role of magnetic susceptibility in magnetic resonance imaging: MRI magnetic compatibility of the first and second kinds. Med Phys 1996;23(6):815–50.
[129] Salomir R, De Senneville BD, Moonen CTW. A fast calculation method for magnetic field inhomogeneity due to an arbitrary distribution of bulk susceptibility. Concepts Magn. Reson. Part B: Magn. Reson. Eng. 2003;19b(1):26–34.
[130] Koch KM, et al. Rapid calculations of susceptibility-induced magnetostatic field perturbations for in vivo magnetic resonance. Phys Med Biol 2006;51(24):6381–402.
[131] Marques JP, Bowtell R. Application of a Fourier-based method for rapid calculation of field inhomogeneity due to spatial variation of magnetic susceptibility. Concepts Magn. Reson. Part B: Magn. Reson. Eng. 2005;25b(1):65–78.
[132] Pruessmann KP, et al. SENSE: sensitivity encoding for fast MRI. Magn Reson Med 1999;42(5):952–62.

[133] Griswold MA, et al. Generalized autocalibrating partially parallel acquisitions (GRAPPA). Magn Reson Med 2002;47(6):1202–10.
[134] Lustig M, Donoho D, Pauly JM. Sparse MRI: the application of compressed sensing for rapid MR imaging. Magn Reson Med 2007;58(6):1182–95.
[135] Reeder SB, et al. Multicoil Dixon chemical species separation with an iterative least-squares estimation method. Magn Reson Med 2004;51(1):35–45.
[136] Yu H, et al. Multiecho water-fat separation and simultaneous R_2* estimation with multifrequency fat spectrum modeling. Magn Reson Med 2008;60(5):1122–34.
[137] Liu T, et al. A novel background field removal method for MRI using projection onto dipole fields (PDF). NMR Biomed 2011;24(9):1129–36.
[138] Schweser F, et al. Quantitative imaging of intrinsic magnetic tissue properties using MRI signal phase: an approach to in vivo brain iron metabolism? Neuroimage 2011;54(4):2789–807.
[139] Sun HF, Wilman AH. Background field removal using spherical mean value filtering and Tikhonov regularization. Magn Reson Med 2014;71(3):1151–7.
[140] Wu B, et al. Whole brain susceptibility mapping using compressed sensing. Magn Reson Med 2012;67(1):137–47.
[141] de Rochefort L, et al. Quantitative susceptibility map reconstruction from MR phase data using Bayesian regularization: validation and application to brain imaging. Magn Reson Med 2010;63(1):194–206.
[142] Shmueli K, et al. Magnetic susceptibility mapping of brain tissue in vivo using MRI phase data. Magn Reson Med 2009;62(6):1510–22.
[143] Wharton S, Schafer A, Bowtell R. Susceptibility mapping in the human brain using threshold-based *k*-space division. Magn Reson Med 2010;63(5):1292–304.
[144] Wang Y, Liu T. Quantitative susceptibility mapping (QSM): decoding MRI data for a tissue magnetic biomarker. Magn Reson Med 2015;73(1):82–101.
[145] Liu T, et al. Morphology enabled dipole inversion (MEDI) from a single-angle acquisition: comparison with COSMOS in human brain imaging. Magn Reson Med 2011;66(3):777–83.
[146] Liu T, et al. Differential approach to quantitative susceptibility mapping without background field removal. In: Proceedings of the 22nd annual meeting of ISMRM, Milan, Italy. 2014.
[147] Sharma SD, et al. MRI-based quantitative susceptibility mapping (QSM) and R_2* mapping of liver iron overload: comparison with SQUID-based biomagnetic liver susceptometry. Magn Reson Med 2017; 78(1):264–70.
[148] Liu Z, et al. Preconditioned total field inversion (TFI) method for quantitative susceptibility mapping. Magn Reson Med 2017;78(1):303–15.
[149] Taylor BA, et al. Simultaneous field and *R*-2* mapping to quantify liver iron content using autoregressive moving average modeling. J Magn Reson Imaging 2012;35(5):1125–32.
[150] Hernando D, et al. Magnetic susceptibility as a B_0 field strength independent MRI biomarker of liver iron overload. Magn Reson Med 2013;70(3):648–56.
[151] Bashir MR, et al. Quantification of hepatic steatosis with a multistep adaptive fitting MRI approach: prospective validation against MR spectroscopy. AJR Am J Roentgenol 2015;204(2):297–306.
[152] Mamidipalli A, et al. Cross-sectional correlation between hepatic R_2* and proton density fat fraction (PDFF) in children with hepatic steatosis. J Magn Reson Imaging 2018;47(2):418–24.
[153] Li J, et al. Quantitative susceptibility mapping (QSM) minimizes interference from cellular pathology in R_2* estimation of liver iron concentration. J Magn Reson Imaging 2018;48(4):1069–79.
[154] Wang ZJ, Li S, Haselgrove JC. Magnetic resonance imaging measurement of volume magnetic susceptibility using a boundary condition. J Magn Reson 1999;140(2):477–81.
[155] Chu Z, et al. MRI measurement of hepatic magnetic susceptibility-phantom validation and normal subject studies. Magn Reson Med 2004;52(6):1318–27.

[156] Dong J, et al. Simultaneous phase unwrapping and removal of chemical shift (SPURS) using graph cuts: application in quantitative susceptibility mapping. IEEE Trans Med Imaging 2015;34(2):531–40.
[157] Zhao Y, et al. Magnetic susceptibility in normal brains of young adults based on quantitative susceptibility mapping. J Craniofac Surg 2019;30(6):1836–9.
[158] Peterson ET, et al. Distribution of brain iron accrual in adolescence: evidence from cross-sectional and longitudinal analysis. Hum Brain Mapp 2019;40(5):1480–95.
[159] Zhang Y, et al. Neonate and infant brain development from birth to 2 years assessed using MRI-based quantitative susceptibility mapping. Neuroimage 2019;185:349–60.
[160] Feng X, Deistung A, Reichenbach JR. Quantitative susceptibility mapping (QSM) and $R_2(*)$ in the human brain at 3T: evaluation of intra-scanner repeatability. Z Med Phys 2018;28(1):36–48.
[161] Lancione M, et al. Echo-time dependency of quantitative susceptibility mapping reproducibility at different magnetic field strengths. Neuroimage 2019;197:557–64.
[162] Santin MD, et al. Reproducibility of R_2* and quantitative susceptibility mapping (QSM) reconstruction methods in the basal ganglia of healthy subjects. NMR Biomed 2017;30(4):e3491.
[163] Ippoliti M, et al. Quantitative susceptibility mapping across two clinical field strengths: contrast-to-noise ratio enhancement at 1.5T. J Magn Reson Imaging 2018;48(5):1410–20.
[164] Dibb R, et al. Magnetic susceptibility anisotropy outside the central nervous system. NMR Biomed 2017;30(4).
[165] Wen Y, et al. Cardiac quantitative susceptibility mapping (QSM) for heart chamber oxygenation. Magn Reson Med 2018;79(3):1545–52.
[166] Wong R, et al. Visualizing and quantifying acute inflammation using ICAM-1 specific nanoparticles and MRI quantitative susceptibility mapping. Ann Biomed Eng 2012;40(6):1328–38.
[167] Xie L, et al. Quantitative susceptibility mapping of kidney inflammation and fibrosis in type 1 angiotensin receptor-deficient mice. NMR Biomed 2013;26(12):1853–63.
[168] Pepe A, et al. MRI multicentre prospective survey in thalassaemia major patients treated with deferasirox versus deferiprone and desferrioxamine. Br J Haematol 2018;183(5):783–95.
[169] Yokoo T, Browning JD. Fat and iron quantification in the liver: past, present, and future. Top Magn Reson Imaging 2014;23(2):73–94.
[170] Doyle EK, et al. Ultra-short echo time images quantify high liver iron. Magn Reson Med 2018; 79(3):1579–85.
[171] Tipirneni-Sajja A, et al. Radial ultrashort TE imaging removes the need for breath-holding in hepatic iron overload quantification by R_2* MRI. AJR Am J Roentgenol 2017;209(1):187–94.

SECTION 5

Quantification of Other MRI-Accessible Tissue Properties

CHAPTER

Electrical Properties Mapping

30

Ulrich Katscher

Philips Research Hamburg, Hamburg, Germany

30.1 Electrical properties: Physical and physiological background

Electrical properties are intrinsic features of all substances, organic as well as nonorganic. The term "electrical properties" describes two specific properties, permittivity and electric conductivity. Permittivity is the ability of a substance to reduce the strength of an applied electric field. Electric conductivity is the ability of a substance to conduct an applied electric current.[a] Both electrical properties depend on the type of substance, and thus also on the type of biologic tissue or the state of this tissue, which makes electrical properties relevant in the framework of medical diagnostics. Moreover, electrical properties depend on a number of additional general parameters, for instance, the temperature of the substance and the frequency of the applied electric field or electric current. While temperature has a more or less straight-forward linear impact on electrical properties ([1], Fig. 30.1), the frequency has a highly complex influence on these properties. In principle, electrical properties are determined by the concentration and mobility of ions. Ion concentration of course does not depend on the applied frequency, but mobility depends dramatically on the applied frequency, as illustrated in Fig. 30.2 for the example of conductivity. The applied frequency determines the time, and thus distance, an ion travels through the tissue until polarization is switched, at which point the ion starts to travel in the opposite direction. The higher the frequency, the shorter the distance an ion is able to travel during a switching period. The traveling distance corresponds to the spatial scale probed by the conductivity; it can be as large as cell size at low frequencies, or much smaller for high frequencies like the radio frequencies (RF) applied during MR. Thus investigating conductivity at low frequencies yields information on cellular membranes, fibers, and other "macroscopic" structures limiting the mobility of ions (and thus limiting conductivity). When working at RF, it is unlikely that ions encounter a cell membrane due to short traveling distance, and as such conductivity measurements at high frequencies are mostly influenced by ion concentration and not ion mobility.

[a]Since there are other types of conductivities known, e.g., thermal or hydraulic conductivity, this chapter is officially about "electrical conductivity". However, since this chapter does not touch other types of conductivities, it is sufficient to talk just about "conductivity" for the sake of brevity. On the other hand, since there is only one type of permittivity known (the "electrical permittivity"), it is common to talk just about "permittivity" anyway.

Advances in Magnetic Resonance Technology and Applications. Volume 1. ISSN 2666-9099. https://doi.org/10.1016/B978-0-12-817057-1.00032-9

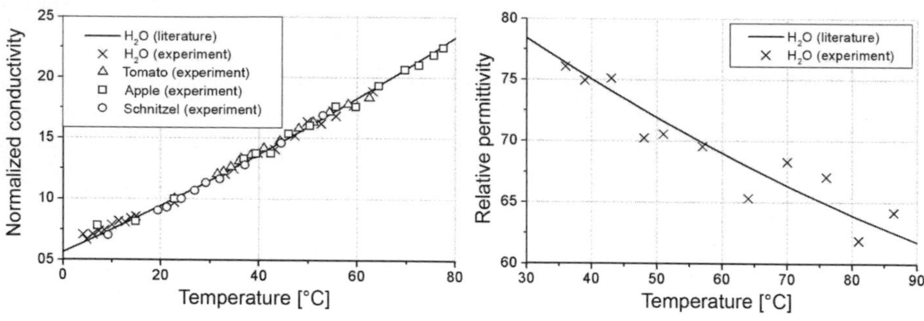

FIG. 30.1

Temperature dependence of electrical properties measured with EPT for different biologic substances [1]. The temperature dependence of conductivity is roughly +2%/°C for all substances investigated, and -0.3%/°C for the permittivity of water.

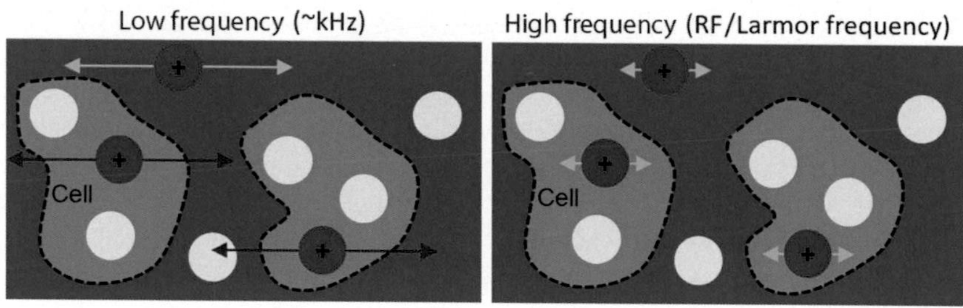

FIG. 30.2

Schematic illustration of the frequency dependence of conductivity. The higher the frequency, the shorter the distance an ion is able to travel during a switching period (*arrows*), and vice versa. Investigating conductivity at low frequencies (*left*) yields information on cellular membranes limiting the mobility of ions (*red arrows*), thus limiting conductivity. When applying radio frequencies (*right*), it is unlikely that ions encounter a cell membrane due to short distance that they travel. Thus ion *mobility* has only a minor impact on the measurement, but ion *concentration* has a large impact on resulting conductivity at radio frequency.

30.2 Development of EPT

MR is an electromagnetic imaging modality, and it might be surprising that imaging electromagnetic tissue properties is a rather new development in the history of MR. The idea of electrical properties tomography (EPT) was born 1991 in an article from Prof. Mark Haacke [2], although he did not call it EPT. The concept was further developed in 2003 by [3], outlining all its central aspects, and the term EPT was introduced in 2006 by [4]. Following an EPT article from 2009 [5], roughly 100 journal articles and hundreds of conference abstracts from all over the world have been published on EPT in the following decade.

Two families of MR-based conductivity measurements have been reported: specifically MR Electrical Impedance Tomography (MR-EIT, for a review see, for example, [6]) at low frequencies (around kHz) and MR Electrical Properties Tomography (MR-EPT, for a review see, for example, [7]) at the Larmor frequency (RF). Although cellular information cannot be extracted using MR-EPT (as described earlier) this chapter focuses on MR-EPT as it can be performed on any standard MR system with standard MR sequences. In contrast, MR-EIT requires the application of externally applied currents via electrodes mounted on the patient's skin, with the risk of sensation of pain and interaction with physiology, thus hampering approvals and clinical applications.

With MR-EIT or MR-EPT, it is not possible to identify the type of ions contributing to the observed conductivity. The observed conductivity is determined by adding the contributions from all types of ions present in the investigated tissue. It is expected that among multiple types of ions typically occurring in tissue, sodium has the highest concentration, and thus has the highest impact on the observed conductivity. Sodium can be measured independently with MRI [8], and a comparison between MR sodium imaging and MR-EPT showed a correlation in healthy tissue [9]. This correlation confirms the minor impact of ion mobility on conductivity at RF, since MR sodium imaging shows exclusively sodium concentration. It should be furthermore noted that the impact of active electrical physiological processes, like cellular ion pumps or action potentials, on MR-EIT or MR-EPT measurements is negligible.

While MR-EIT is able to measure only conductivity, MR-EPT is able to measure both electrical properties, conductivity and permittivity. However, this is not an overwhelming advantage of MR-EPT, since—for reasons discussed later—permittivity is much harder to measure accurately, and most MR-EPT studies concentrate on conductivity. The noise figures seen in Fig. 30.1 might serve as an illustration for the different accuracy obtainable for conductivity and permittivity imaging with MR-EPT.

30.3 Physical/mathematical background of EPT

The shape of the RF excitation field B_1 is impacted ("distorted") by the electrical properties of the human tissue. By measuring and processing this distorted B_1 field, it is possible to reveal the underlying electrical properties responsible for the observed distortions. The distortions are caused by eddy currents induced by B_1, which in turn interfere with B_1 in a nontrivial way; in fact, the B_1 phase, or φ^+, takes on a 3D parabolic shape (like a "vortex" in 3D) due to the eddy currents induced by the rotating field. The most simplified equation describing the relationship between the conductivity and this induced phase reads:

$$\sigma = \Delta\varphi^+ / (\omega\mu_0) \tag{30.1}$$

In other words, conductivity σ is proportional to the curvature of the B_1 phase φ^+, where φ^+ can be obtained via MRI and the curvature calculated numerically in a post-processing step. Mathematically, the curvature is given by the Laplacian $\Delta = \nabla^2$, which is the second derivative in all three spatial dimensions. The Larmor frequency ω and vacuum permeability μ_0 (both constant) are required to convert phase curvature to quantitative conductivity values with the standard conductivity unit S/m. Thus, in this simplest version, no iteration, matrix inversion, or other "advanced" numerical action is required for EPT, as conductivity can be calculated locally in a straight-forward manner. The idea of Eq. (30.1) is sketched in Fig. 30.3, and more detailed descriptions can be found in EPT review articles (see, e.g., [7,10]).

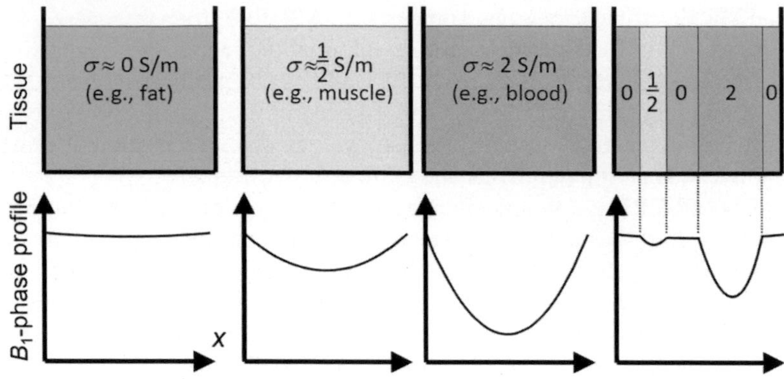

FIG. 30.3

Schematic illustration of the EPT principle. Electrical properties of the patient's tissue distort the B_1 applied during RF spin excitation. In particular, nonzero tissue conductivity causes an approximately parabolic shape of the B_1 phase, according to Maxwell's equations. The higher the local tissue conductivity, the higher the local B_1 phase curvature. Thus numerically calculating the B_1 phase curvature yields an estimation of tissue conductivity.

If not only conductivity but also permittivity is of interest, Eq. (30.1) has to be rewritten in a complex manner by substituting the Laplacian of the B_1 phase φ^+ with the Laplacian of the complex B_1 field, $B_1 = |B_1| \exp(i\varphi^+)$ via

$$\kappa \equiv \omega\epsilon\text{-}i\sigma = \text{-}\Delta B_1/(\omega\mu_0 B_1) \tag{30.2}$$

The real part of Eq. (30.2) is the permittivity, and the imaginary part the conductivity. The measurement of the complex B_1 field is discussed later. Eq. (30.2) is accurate if it can be assumed that electrical properties κ are locally constant, that is, $\nabla\kappa = 0$ (the so-called Local Homogeneity Assumption, LHA). If LHA cannot be considered valid, for instance at boundaries between tissues, an additional term is required:

$$\kappa\mathbf{B} = \text{-}\Delta\mathbf{B}/(\omega\mu_0) - (\nabla\kappa/\kappa) \times (\nabla \times \mathbf{B})/(\omega\mu_0) \tag{30.3}$$

This modification requires furthermore the transition to a vector equation, that is, it requires knowledge of the vector **B** (describing the RF transmit coil's full magnetic field) instead of the previously used scalar B_1 (the positive circularly polarized component of **B**). Eq. (30.3) is a combination of Faraday's and Ampere's laws for time-harmonic fields assuming constant permeability, which is sufficiently fulfilled throughout the body. A phase-only version of Eq. (30.3) has been presented by [11]:

$$\sigma = \Delta\varphi^+/(\omega\mu_0) - (\nabla\sigma/\sigma) \cdot (\nabla\varphi^+)/(\omega\mu_0) \tag{30.4}$$

which is in the form of a convection-reaction equation. For locally constant σ, Eq. (30.4) is equivalent to Eq. (30.1).

30.4 EPT measurement methods

MR measurements of **B**, B_1, or even φ^+ are challenging. The longitudinal component of the RF excitation field B_z is generally not measurable, but for conventional RF quadrature volume coils this component is much smaller than B_x and B_y and thus frequently neglected. The transverse components B_x

and B_y could be derived from the positive and negative circularly polarized components, related to the transmit and receive field of an RF coil. However, MR physics allow only the magnitude of B_1 to be measured exactly, but not the B_1 phase φ^+, as it is only possible to measure the so-called transceive phase $\varphi^{\pm} = \varphi^+ + \varphi^-$, that is, the superposition of φ^+ with its counterpart from RF reception φ^-. The "Transceive Phase Assumption" (TPA) is often applied to extract the B_1 phase φ^+:

$$\varphi^+ \approx \varphi^{\pm}/2 \tag{30.5}$$

This expression is exactly valid for Eqs. (30.1) and (30.4), and approximately valid for Eqs. (30.2) and (30.3), as long as quadrature volume coils are used for RF transmission and reception.

Although $|B_1|$ can be determined exactly (see, e.g., [12–14]) and φ^+ only approximately via Eq. (30.5), it is much more common to determine φ^+ instead of $|B_1|$. The measurement of $|B_1|$ typically requires the comparison of two distinct data sets in a post-processing step, and is thus burdened with some error propagation specific for the chosen type of $|B_1|$ mapping. This error propagation has been investigated without [15] and with reference to EPT [16]. In practice, $|B_1|$ mapping is cumbersome; suffers from low spatial resolution, low SNR, and/or high SAR; and usually requires an additional scan, thereby increasing total examination time. In contrast, measuring the transceive phase $\varphi^{\pm}$ to determine φ^+ can be performed quickly and very accurately, and in some examinations without additional scan time. The main requirement for measuring $\varphi^{\pm}$ is the absence of off-resonance effects, which produce additional non-RF-related phase; this requirement is fulfilled for spin-echo (SE)-based sequences or sequences with balanced gradients, like steady-state free precession (SSFP) [17]. In these cases, the image phase can be used directly as the transceive phase. Typically, SSFP sequences provide higher SNR efficiency than SE-based sequences, and thus, are the optimal choice for the measurement of $\varphi^{\pm}$ (as long as the banding artefacts, which occasionally occur in SSFP, can be neglected). For instance, SSFP sequences for the whole brain can be performed with an isotropic voxel size of $1 \times 1 \times 1\,\text{mm}^3$, repetition time $TR = 3.5\,\text{ms}$, echo time $TE = 1.7\,\text{ms}$, and flip angle $\alpha = 25°$ within 2 min. Last but not least, significant curvature of φ^+ is observed at main field strengths of $B_0 = 3\,\text{T}$ or below, but significant curvature of $|B_1|$ only at $B_0 = 7\,\text{T}$ or above [18]. After measuring the transceive phase $\varphi^{\pm}$ with the sequence chosen, this phase must only be divided by two (Eq. 30.5) before using it to calculate maps of conductivity via Eq. (30.1).

A flow chart showing the process from data collection to maps is depicted in Fig. 30.4.

30.5 Reconstruction algorithms

The term "EPT" acts as an umbrella for a large variety of reconstruction algorithms, too many for a detailed discussion in this chapter. Instead, a general classification of main algorithm types is proposed, as illustrated in Fig. 30.5. Two aspects are used for general classification: *which* EPT equation is solved, and *how* it is solved. On the one hand, the EPT equation to be solved can include phase only (Eqs. 30.1 and 30.4), or phase and magnitude (Eqs. 30.2 and 30.3).[b] On the other hand, the equation can be solved by applying the Local Homogeneity Assumption using Eqs. 30.1 and 30.2, or without invoking LHA using Eqs. 30.3 and 30.4.

[b]Also equations based on magnitude only can be applied, particularly for determination of permittivity at high main field strengths, but is not among the main algorithm types yet.

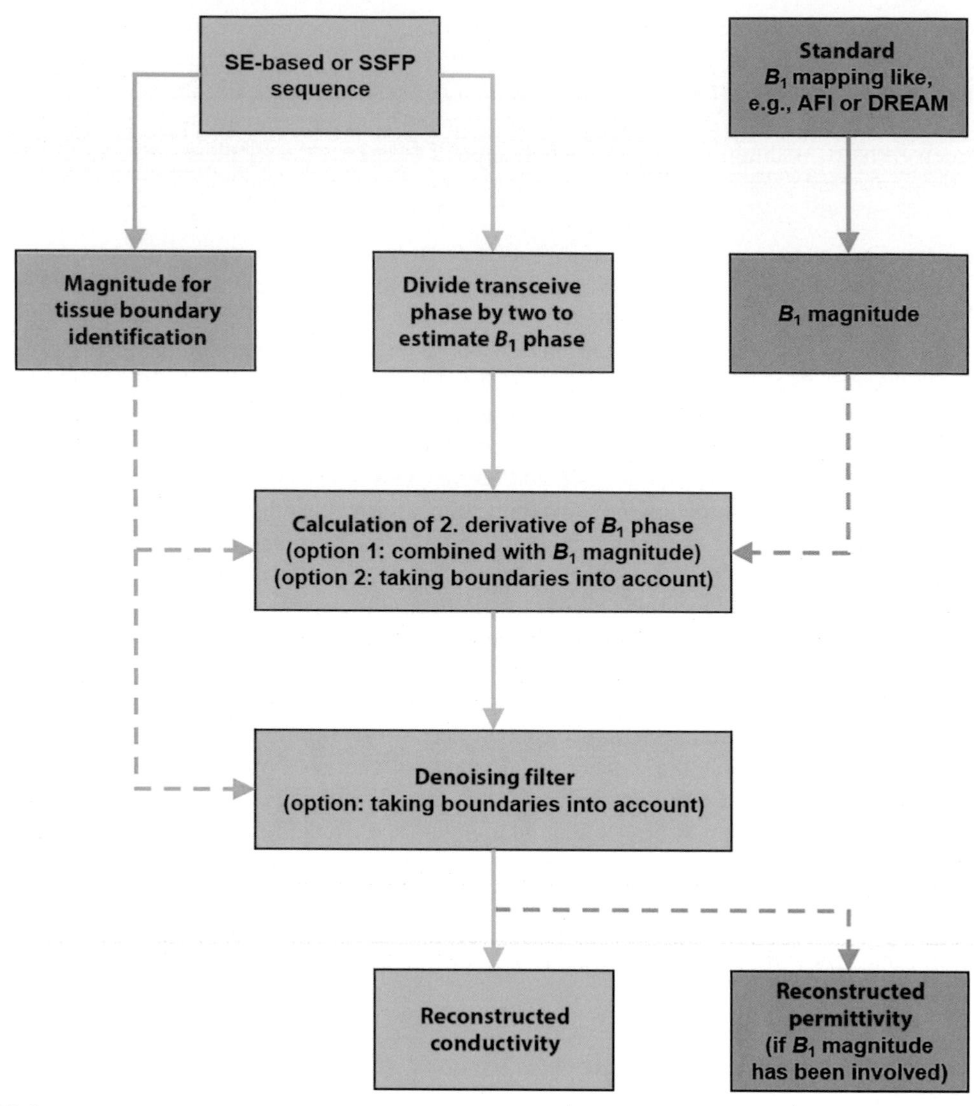

FIG. 30.4

Flow chart showing the EPT process, from data collection to maps. The basic version of EPT only processes the B_1 phase measured by spin-echo-based or SSFP sequences, yielding a conductivity map (*blue boxes*). Two optional extensions are added by *pink boxes* (taking B_1 magnitude into account, yielding additionally a permittivity map) and the *orange box* (taking tissue boundaries into account to avoid tissue boundary artefacts).

Apart from the specific equation to be solved, either a single or multi-channel RF transmit system can be used to collect data. Since tissue electrical properties of course do not depend on the RF transmit coil, multiple measurements with different transmit coils yield a surplus of information, which can be used to compensate for incomplete knowledge of **B**. For both single or multi-channel systems, and for

Which equation is solved	With local homogeneity assumption	Without local homogeneity assumption
Phase only	Eq.(30.1), up to now preferred equation for clinical studies performed	Eq.(30.4), proposed by Gurler [11]
Phase and magnitude	Eq.(30.2), "standard" EPT	Eq.(30.3), most general solution

How is equation solved	Backward / local solution (B_1 → electric properties)	Forward / global solution (electric properties → B_1)
Single RF TX channel	"Standard" EPT	Proposed by e.g. [19]
Multiple RF TX channels	Proposed by e.g. [21]	Proposed by e.g. [20]

FIG. 30.5

Overview of main EPT reconstruction types, which can be classified by examining "*which* EPT equation is solved" (top) and "*how* the EPT equation is solved" (bottom) [11, 19–21].

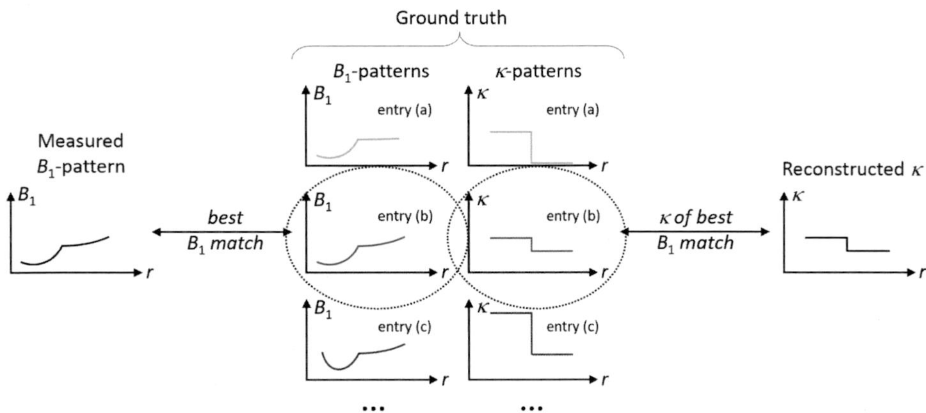

FIG. 30.6

Sketch of machine learning EPT. Machine learning can be used to match the ground truth B_1 pattern (obtained via, for example, electromagnetic simulations) and measured B_1 pattern, yielding the desired κ map without explicit numerical differentiation. For the sake of illustration, 1D patterns are sketched, although studies with 2D patterns [23] and 3D patterns [22] have been conducted.

all underlying EPT equations, backward/local or forward/global algorithms can be applied. Backward/local algorithms calculate the electrical properties κ locally from the measured part of **B**. Forward/global algorithms start from a spatial κ distribution and minimize the difference between **B** as resulting from this κ distribution, and the measured (part of) **B**.

The differences between the presented types of algorithms may be resolved with the onset of machine learning in EPT [22,23]. The ground truth for this approach can be obtained, for example, by generating B_1 patterns in 2D [23] or 3D [22] which correspond to κ patterns as derived via electromagnetic simulations. Machine learning algorithms can be trained to match the ground truth B_1 and measured B_1, yielding the desired maps of electrical tissue properties κ without explicit numerical differentiation (Fig. 30.6).

30.6 Limitations and challenges of EPT

From a theoretical point of view, the need for the Transceive Phase Assumption (to separate the required transmit phase from the inevitable receive phase) and Local Homogeneity Assumption (the approximation that the electrical properties are constant to avoid reconstruction artefacts along tissue boundaries) are unsolved problems of EPT. In practice, however, these challenges are not the main roadblocks toward clinical use of EPT, since simple tricks are able to circumvent these approximations sufficiently. The main challenge for in vivo EPT is the presence of "spurious phase effects unrelated to RF penetration", as stated in the very first EPT publication [2]. Spurious phase effects include any phase arising from sources other than RF penetration, including off-resonance due to poor shimming or T_2* effects. Even when theoretically ideal sequences are deployed for EPT, additional phase errors might arise from patient and physiological motion or system/scanning imperfections not taken into account. These phase effects have a much higher impact on reconstruction reliability than the assumptions described earlier. Thus, to move EPT to routine clinical application, the origins of spurious phase effects and suitable countermeasures to reduce their effects must be undertaken, requiring extensive phantom, volunteer, and patient studies.

30.7 Clinical applications

While EPT is emerging as a quantitative technique and research is ongoing to tackle the technical challenges described earlier, small clinical studies have been performed with MR-EPT [24–26] to evaluate the potential diagnostic value of the approach. All these studies are in the framework of oncology, for several reasons: a modified tumor conductivity is expected from prior work (particularly ex vivo, see, for example [27]), an increased sodium level in tumors has been reported [8], and size and shape of tumors coincide with the core abilities of MR-EPT. All studies observe not only systematically elevated tumor conductivity measurements in comparison to surrounding healthy tissue conductivity (Fig. 30.7), but also specific correlations between tumor conductivity versus malignancy or prognostic factors. It has been found in invasive animal studies that permittivity might have an even higher diagnostic value than conductivity [28]. However, due to the much higher noise figure of permittivity as reasoned earlier, it has not yet been included in any clinical EPT study.

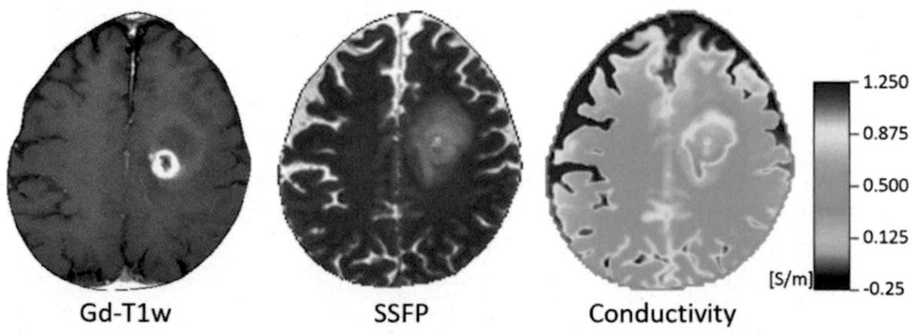

FIG. 30.7

Brain tumor example from a glioblastoma patient [26]. From *left to right*: Contrast-enhanced T_1-weighted image, Steady-State Free Precession (SSFP) image, and conductivity map measured with EPT.

A couple of single case studies report the investigation of stroke with MR-EPT, particularly in the framework of animal models, however without allowing definite conclusions yet [29,30].

Another potential application area is in therapy planning and therapy monitoring. The knowledge of patient-specific conductivity values might improve the planning and outcome of hyperthermia treatment [31]. Measurement of conductivity might reflect direct tissue response to RF ablation, thus enabling monitoring of the ablation procedure without use of contrast agent [32,33]. Conductivity measurements have also been reported for monitoring radiation therapy [34].

Yet another area where MR-EPT might play a role is RF safety management for patient-specific SAR estimation [35,36]. Local SAR depends on local conductivity (at RF, as obtainable via MR-EPT) as well as on local electric fields, which are a by-product in several MR-EPT algorithms. Unfortunately, EPT-based estimation of local SAR requires additional model assumptions, which might counterbalance the advantages of patient-specific measurements.

30.8 Summary

Conductivity and permittivity can be determined quantitatively in vivo using standard MR systems and sequences. In contrast to earlier approaches, the measurements are possible without the need to apply external currents or to mount electrodes on the patient. Instead, the complex B_1 map (containing B_1 magnitude and B_1 phase) is measured and processed to calculate conductivity and permittivity according to Maxwell's equations, in an approach called "Electrical Properties Tomography" (EPT). A simplified version of EPT requires the measurement of only the B_1 phase to derive the conductivity. Using this simplified version, first clinical studies have been successfully performed, particularly in the framework of tumor characterization.

Acknowledgments

The author would like to thank Khin Khin Tha, Nils Hampe, and Philipp Karkowski for their help in writing this chapter.

References

[1] Leussler C, Karkowski P, Katscher U. Temperature dependent conductivity change using MR based electrical properties tomography. In: Proceedings of the 20th annual meeting ISMRM, Melbourne, Australia. 2012. p. 3451.

[2] Haacke EM, Pepropoulos LS, Nilges EW, Wu DH. Extraction of conductivity and permittivity using magnetic resonance imaging. Phys Med Biol 1991;36:723–34.

[3] Wen H. Non-invasive quantitative mapping of conductivity and dielectric distributions using the RF wave propagation effects in high field MRI. Proc SPIE Int Soc Opt Eng 2003;5030:471–7.

[4] Katscher U, Hanft M, Vernickel P, Findeklee C. Electrical properties tomography (EPT) via MRI. ISMRM 2006;14:3037.

[5] Katscher U, Voigt T, Findeklee C, Vernickel P, Nehrke K, Dössel O. Determination of electrical conductivity and local SAR via B1 mapping. IEEE Trans Med Imaging 2009;28:1365–74.

[6] Seo JK, Woo EJ. Electrical tissue property imaging at low frequency using MREIT. IEEE Trans Biomed Eng 2014 May;61(5):1390–9. https://doi.org/10.1109/TBME.2014.2298859.
[7] Katscher U, van den Berg CAT. Electrical properties tomography: biochemical, physical and technical background, evaluation and clinical applications. NMR Biomed 2017;30(8). https://doi.org/10.1002/nbm.3729.
[8] Ouwerkerk R, Bleich KB, Gillen JS, Pomper MG, Bottomley PA. Tissue sodium concentration in human brain tumors as measured with 23Na MR imaging. Radiology 2003;227:529–37.
[9] van Lier ALH, de Bruin PW, Aussenhofer SA, et al. 23Na-MRI and EPT: are sodium concentration and electrical conductivity at 298 MHz (7T) related?, In: Proceedings of the 21st annual meeting ISMRM, Salt Lake City, UT, USA; 2013. p. 115.
[10] Liu J, Wang Y, Katscher U, He B. Electrical properties tomography based on B1 maps in MRI: principles, applications, and challenges. IEEE Trans Biomed Eng 2017;64(11):2515–30. https://doi.org/10.1109/TBME.2017.2725140.
[11] Gurler N, Ider YZ. Gradient-based electrical conductivity imaging using MR phase. Magn Reson Med 2017;77:137–50.
[12] Nehrke K, Börnert P. DREAM-A novel approach for robust, ultrafast, multislice B1 mapping. Magn Reson Med 2012;68:1517–26.
[13] Sacolick LI, Wiesinger F, Hancu I, Vogel MW. B1 mapping by Bloch-Siegert shift. Magn Reson Med 2010;63:1315–22.
[14] Yarnykh VL. Actual flip-angle imaging in the pulsed steady state: a method for rapid three-dimensional mapping of the transmitted radiofrequency field. Magn Reson Med 2007;57:192–200.
[15] Pohmann R, Scheffler K. A theoretical and experimental comparison of different techniques for B_1 mapping at very high fields. NMR Biomed 2013;26:265–75.
[16] Gavazzi S, van den Berg CAT, Sbrizzi A, Kok HP, Stalpers LJA, Lagendijk JJW, Crezee H, van Lier ALHMW. Accuracy and precision of electrical permittivity mapping at 3T: the impact of three B1 mapping techniques. Magn Reson Med 2019;81:3628–42.
[17] Stehning C, Voigt TR, Katscher U. Real-time conductivity mapping using balanced SSFP and phase-based reconstruction, In: Proceedings of the 19th annual meeting ISMRM, Montreal, QC, Canada; 2011. p. 128.
[18] van Lier ALH, Raaijmakers A, Voigt T, Lagendijk JJ, Katscher U, van den Berg CAT. Electrical properties tomography in the human brain at 1.5, 3, and 7 T: a comparison study. Magn Reson Med 2014;71:354–63.
[19] Balidemaj E, van den Berg CA, Trinks J, van Lier AL, Nederveen AJ, Stalpers LJ, Crezee H, Remis RF. CSI-EPT: a contrast source inversion approach for improved MRI-based electrical properties tomography. IEEE Trans Med Imaging 2015;34(9):1788–96. https://doi.org/10.1109/TMI.2015.2404944.
[20] Serralles JEC, Polymeridis AG, Vaidya M, Haemer G, White JK, Sodickson DK, Daniel L, Lattanzi R. Global Maxwell tomography: a novel technique for electrical properties mapping without symmetry assumptions or edge artifacts, In: 24th scientific meeting of the international society for magnetic resonance in medicine (ISMRM). Singapore, 7–13 May; 2016. p. 2993.
[21] Zhang X, Zhu S, He B. Imaging electrical properties of biological tissues by RF field mapping in MRI. IEEE Trans Med Imaging 2010;29:474–81.
[22] Hampe N, Herrmann M, Amthor T, Findeklee C, Doneva M, Katscher U. Dictionary-based electrical properties tomography. Magn Reson Med 2019;81:342–9.
[23] Mandija S, Meliadò EF, Huttinga NRF, Luijten PR, van den Berg CAT. Opening a new window on MR-based electrical properties tomography with deep learning Sci Rep 2019;9:8895. https://doi.org/10.1038/s41598-019-45382-x.
[24] Kim SY, Shin J, Kim DH, et al. Correlation between conductivity and prognostic factors in invasive breast cancer using magnetic resonance electrical properties tomography (MREPT). Eur Radiol 2016;26:2317–26.
[25] Shin JW, Kim MJ, Lee JS, et al. Initial study on in vivo conductivity mapping of breast cancer using MRI. J Magn Reson Imaging 2015;42:371–8.

[26] Tha KK, Katscher U, Yamaguchi S, Stehning C, Terasaka S, Fujima N, Kudo K, Kazumata K, Yamamoto T, Van Cauteren M, Shirato H. Noninvasive electrical conductivity measurement by MRI: a test of its validity and the electrical conductivity characteristics of glioma. Eur Radiol 2018;28(1):348–55. https://doi.org/10.1007/s00330-017-4942-5.

[27] Joines WT, Zhang Y, Li C, Jirtle RL. The measured electrical properties of normal and malignant human tissues from 50 to 900 MHz. Med Phys 1994;21:547–50.

[28] Hancu I, Roberts JC, Bulumulla S, Lee SK. On conductivity, permittivity, apparent diffusion coefficient, and their usefulness as cancer markers at MRI frequencies. Magn Reson Med 2015;73:2025.

[29] Amouzandeh G, Mentink-Vigier F, Helsper S, Bagdasarian FA, Rosenberg JT, Grant S. Magnetic resonance electrical property mapping at 21.1 T: a study of conductivity and permittivity in phantoms, ex vivo tissue and in vivo ischemia. Phys Med Biol 2019;15. https://doi.org/10.1088/1361-6560/ab3259.

[30] Jensen-Kondering U, Shu L, Böhm R, Katscher U, Jansen O. In-vivo pilot study at 3 Tesla: feasibility of electrical properties tomography in a rat model of stroke. Phys Med 2020;9:100024.

[31] Balidemaj E, Kok HP, Schooneveldt G, van Lier AL, Remis RF, Stalpers LJ, Westerveld H, Nederveen AJ, van den Berg CA, Crezee J. Hyperthermia treatment planning for cervical cancer patients based on electrical conductivity tissue properties acquired in vivo with EPT at 3 T MRI. Int J Hyperthermia 2016;32(5):558–68. https://doi.org/10.3109/02656736.2015.1129440.

[32] Kwon OI, Chauhan M, Kim HJ, Jeong WC, Wi H, Oh TI, Woo EJ. Fast conductivity imaging in magnetic resonance electrical impedance tomography (MREIT) for RF ablation monitoring. Int J Hyperthermia 2014;30(7):447–55. https://doi.org/10.3109/02656736.2014.966337.

[33] Yeo S-Y, Katscher U, Kim Y-S, Gruell H. Conductivity imaging for assessing the treatment outcome of MR-HIFU ablation of uterine fibroids. ISMRM 2017;25:2102.

[34] Park JA, Kang KJ, Ko IO, Lee KC, Choi BK, Katoch N, Kim JW, Kim HJ, Kwon OI, Woo EJ. In Vivo Measurement of Brain Tissue Response After Irradiation: Comparison of T2 Relaxation, Apparent Diffusion Coefficient, and Electrical Conductivity. IEEE Trans Med Imaging 2019;38(12):2779–84. https://doi.org/10.1109/TMI.2019.2913766.

[35] Voigt T, Homann H, Katscher U, Doessel O. Patient-individual local SAR determination: in vivo measurements and numerical validation. Magn Reson Med 2012;68(4):1117–26. https://doi.org/10.1002/mrm.23322.

[36] Zhang X, Schmitter S, Van de Moortele PF, Liu J, He B. From complex B1 mapping to local SAR estimation for human brain MR imaging using multi-channel transceiver coil at 7T. IEEE Trans Med Imaging 2013;32(6):1058–67. https://doi.org/10.1109/TMI.2013.2251653.

CHAPTER

Quantitative Susceptibility Mapping

31

Karin Shmueli

Department of Medical Physics and Biomedical Engineering, University College London, London, United Kingdom

31.1 Physical principles of susceptibility and MRI phase

31.1.1 Susceptibility: What and why?

Magnetic susceptibility is an intrinsic bulk material or tissue property that determines how a material or tissue will interact with and behave in an applied magnetic field. Tissues with positive susceptibility values are paramagnetic (i.e., their macroscopic magnetization increases in proportion with the applied magnetic field strength) and those with negative susceptibility values are diamagnetic (i.e., their bulk magnetization decreases with increasing field strength). Most biological tissue is weakly diamagnetic with susceptibility values close to that of water ($\sim$-9 ppm) [1]. Although it is beyond the scope of this chapter to explain the physical origins of paramagnetism or diamagnetism, a tissue's magnetic susceptibility is mostly determined by the electronic configuration (spins and orbital motions) within its constituent molecules [2–4] and is directly related to the tissue composition and microstructure. Susceptibility maps, therefore, have the potential to yield useful information about pathophysiology-related changes in tissue composition and microstructure.

A simple way to understand how different tissue constituents contribute to the overall bulk magnetic susceptibility of the tissue is through Wiedemann's additivity law [5]. This law states that the overall susceptibility of a mixture of components is the sum of the susceptibility of each component weighted by its mass fraction or relative volume of occupation, depending on whether we are calculating mass or dimensionless (volume) susceptibilities, respectively. There are, of course, complications to this law (such as chemical bonding or conformational changes in macromolecules) but it is a useful conceptual aid nonetheless.

31.1.2 The relationship between magnetic susceptibility and MRI phase

The Magnetic Resonance Imaging (MRI) signal is complex, with a magnitude and a phase component. For many years, air-tissue susceptibility differences were thought of primarily as a source of artifacts such as geometric distortion and signal dropout [6]. However, it is not these effects on the magnitude images that are exploited when measuring magnetic susceptibility. Rather, the key to MRI measurement of susceptibility is that the phase in T_2*-weighted gradient echo MRI sequences is affected by the subtle underlying tissue susceptibility distribution [7, 8]. It is useful to picture a small spherical point "source," with a different susceptibility than its surroundings, in a magnetic field (B_0 along the z-direction). The source will produce small magnetic field perturbations that have a dipolar distribution ($d(\mathbf{r})$)

Advances in Magnetic Resonance Technology and Applications. Volume 1. ISSN 2666-9099. https://doi.org/10.1016/B978-0-12-817057-1.00033-0

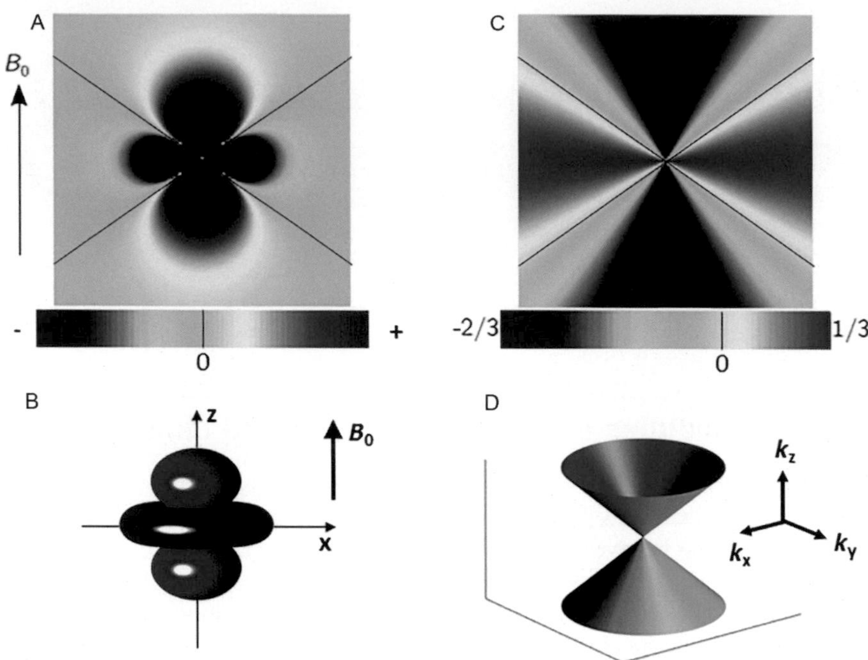

FIG. 31.1

Magnetic dipole. A coronal slice through the unit dipole $d(\mathbf{r})$ in real or image space (A) has field perturbations $\Delta B_z(\mathbf{r})$ associated with a point source with a susceptibility greater than that of the surrounding material when placed in a magnetic field B_0. A three-dimensional (3D) rendering of $d(\mathbf{r})$ (surfaces of constant field) is shown in (B). Note that the dipole field pattern is oriented along B_0. This is the basis for the orientation dependence of the MRI phase. A slice through the Fourier transform of $d(\mathbf{r})$, $d(\mathbf{k})$, is shown in (C). A 3D rendering of the location of zeroes in k-space (conical surfaces at $d(\mathbf{k})=0$) oriented at the magic angle to k_z ($=54.7°$, *black lines* in (A) and (C)) is shown in (D). These zeroes cause the inverse problem in QSM (Eq. 31.3) to be ill-conditioned.

(Fig. 31.1A and B). A more complicated spatial susceptibility distribution $\chi(\mathbf{r})$ generates a more complicated field distribution $\Delta B_z(\mathbf{r})$, which can be understood as the superposition of many dipole fields from many small point sources of susceptibility:

$$\Delta B_z(\mathbf{r}) = B_0 \cdot d(\mathbf{r}) \otimes \chi(\mathbf{r}) \tag{31.1}$$

Thus, if we knew the susceptibility distribution inside an area of tissue ($\chi(\mathbf{r})$) it would be possible to calculate the field distribution $\Delta B_z(\mathbf{r})$ by convolving ($\otimes$) $\chi(\mathbf{r})$ with the unit dipole field kernel $d(\mathbf{r})$ which is known as the "forward problem." However, $\chi(\mathbf{r})$ is typically unknown, but we can measure the susceptibility-induced field perturbations $\Delta B_z(\mathbf{r})$ because they are linearly related to the phase ϕ of the MRI signal according to

$$\phi(\mathbf{r}, \mathrm{TE}) = \gamma \Delta B_z(\mathbf{r}) \cdot \mathrm{TE} + \phi_0(\mathbf{r}) \tag{31.2}$$

where γ is the gyromagnetic ratio, TE is the echo time, and $\phi_0(\mathbf{r})$ is the phase at TE=0 (Fig. 31.2). There are some exceptions to this linear relationship, particularly in white matter where the

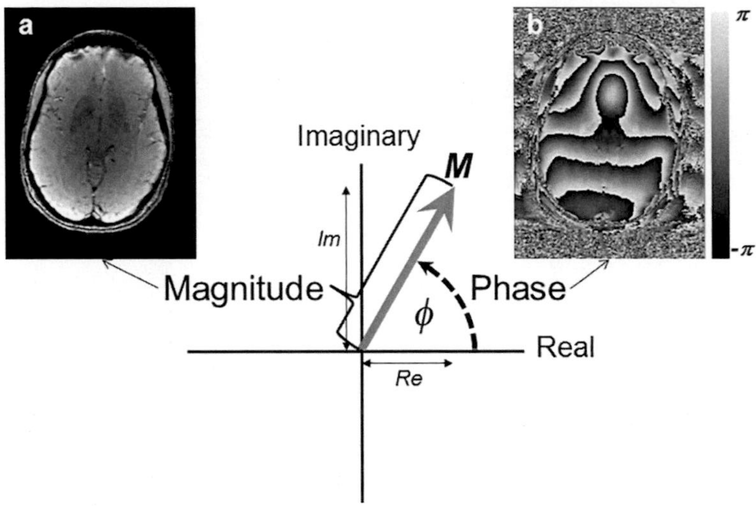

FIG. 31.2

Phase in MRI. The MRI signal (S) is complex, consisting of a magnitude M and a phase ϕ, i.e., $S = Me^{i\phi}$. The length (M) of the magnetization vector is used in conventional T_2*-weighted MRI to form the magnitude image (a). The angle that the magnetization vector makes *(dashed curve)* is the phase (ϕ) and can be used to form a phase image (b). The magnetization vector precesses in the transverse x–y plane, also understood to be the complex (real-imaginary) plane, at an angular velocity $\omega = \gamma \Delta B_z(\mathbf{r})$, which helps to explain Eq. (31.2). Note the wraps in the phase image (ϕ jumps from π to $-\pi$) wherever the magnetization vector crosses the negative real axis.

microstructure leads to nonlinear phase evolution due to the presence of multiple frequency components in each voxel [9–12]. Nevertheless, based on these relationships (Eqs. 31.1 and 31.2), the rich contrast available in phase images [13], which were often discarded in the past, can be used to calculate maps of the underlying tissue magnetic susceptibility distribution.

One might think that it is unnecessary to calculate χ from ϕ (and solve the "inverse problem") if the phase images are immediately available. However, there are several disadvantages to using phase images directly. For example, the phase-contrast is nonlocal, extending beyond the structures of interest, and also depends on the orientation of these structures with respect to the main magnetic field B_0. Quantitative susceptibility mapping (QSM) overcomes these disadvantages [14].

31.2 Imaging methodology and image processing pipeline

The process of mapping the tissue magnetic susceptibility, which has come to be known as QSM, has developed rapidly since its inception in 2009 and has been described in several review papers [3, 15–21]. Here, the conceptual stages in QSM are summarized, as illustrated in Fig. 31.3. This framework is useful for understanding fundamental QSM processing concepts as well as the historical development of QSM, although some more recent algorithms diverge substantially from this template

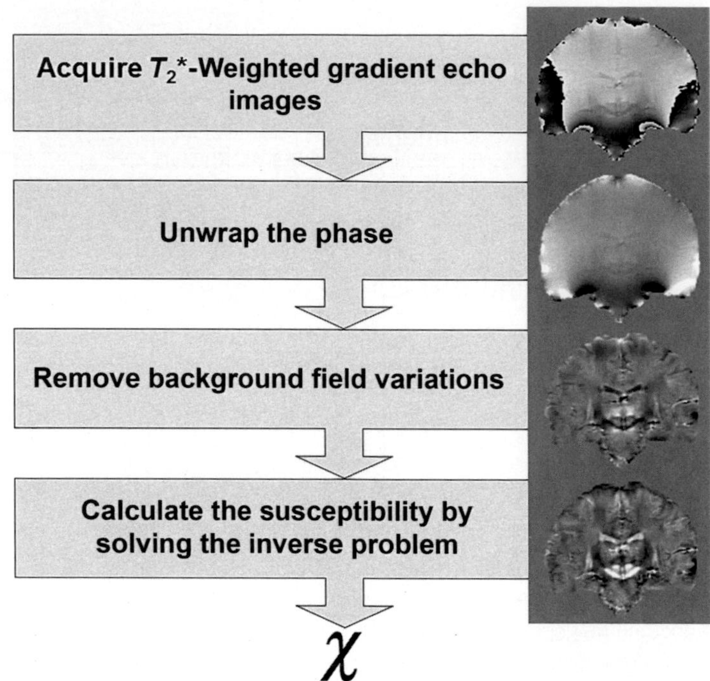

FIG. 31.3

Conceptual stages in quantitative susceptibility mapping. The stages of QSM processing illustrated with coronal brain images of a healthy human volunteer acquired at 3T. The first step is to acquire the complex signal and make sure that the raw phase (top row image) is saved and not discarded. If multiple echoes are acquired, the phase should be fitted over echo time to provide a total field map. The next stage is to perform phase unwrapping to remove jumps of $\sim 2\pi$ (wraps) that appear in the raw phase image or fitted field map (unwrapped image, 2nd row). Background field perturbations must be removed to reveal the field perturbations induced by subtle tissue magnetic susceptibility differences (background-field-free field map, 3rd row). Finally, regularization methods can be applied to solve the inverse problem and provide a tissue magnetic susceptibility map (bottom row).

in their implementation [22–26]. The first step is the acquisition of T_2*-weighted gradient echo images, taking care to save the complex (magnitude and phase) images. Any signal-to-noise-ratio (SNR)-efficient T_2*-weighted sequence can be used: three-dimensional gradient echo (3D GRE) is the most widely used although echo-planar imaging (EPI) is also efficient for QSM [23, 27]. One example of 3D GRE parameters for collecting images suitable for whole-brain QSM in 5 min and 18 s at 3 T is to acquire $1 \times 1 \times 1$ mm voxels at five TEs starting at and spaced by 4.92 ms with TR = 30 ms, flip angle = 15°, pixel bandwidth = 280 Hz, FoV = $256 \times 192 \times 176$ mm, transverse slices, phase encoding right to left, $2 \times$ GRAPPA (or SENSE) acceleration in the PE (R-L) direction, monopolar readout gradients, 75% partial Fourier acquisition in both PE directions, and no flow compensation. Further practical implementation details and potential pitfalls are discussed later.

To obtain the most accurate estimate of $\Delta B_z(\mathbf{r})$ it is often useful to fit phase $\phi(\mathbf{r},\mathrm{TE})$ (or complex) images measured at multiple TEs [28, 29] to Eq. (31.2) to guarantee removal of $\phi_0(\mathbf{r})$ and maximize contrast-to-noise [30, 31]. Phase images suffer from phase wrapping (as the phase is an angle defined only between $\pm\pi$, Fig. 31.2) and there is a large variety of unwrapping algorithms available, e.g., [32–36], each with their own advantages and drawbacks. Phase unwrapping is the second conceptual stage in the QSM pipeline (Fig. 31.3).

The next step in calculating susceptibility maps is to remove large scale background field variations caused primarily by the relatively large susceptibility difference between tissue and air in cavities and outside the body. These background fields are often much larger than the susceptibility-induced fields of interest and there are now several techniques for removing them, e.g., [31, 37–40]. Many of these rely on the assumption that the fields generated from susceptibility sources outside the region of interest are harmonic inside this region. Projection onto dipole fields (PDF) [37, 41] is a popular and robust background field removal technique which can be understood as finding an arrangement of susceptibility sources outside the region of interest (that generate dipole fields) which best models the fields inside the region of interest.

Masking out noisy phase in areas where there is no MRI signal (e.g., in air spaces or outside the body) is often a prerequisite for applying unwrapping and background field removal, and the performance of many background field removal methods depends strongly on the mask used [40]. It is important to note that, mainly as a result of removing background fields, the contrast observed in susceptibility maps is relative rather than absolute [42]. There is, therefore, an ongoing debate regarding the use of reference tissues in QSM [43–45], although susceptibility referencing may be less important in group comparisons where global susceptibility offsets are unlikely.

The final step in the pipeline is to solve the inverse problem, i.e., to calculate the tissue susceptibility distribution $\chi(\mathbf{r})$ from the measured tissue-susceptibility-induced field distribution $\Delta B_z(\mathbf{r})$ free from background fields. Formulated in real space, $\mathbf{r}$, this is the inverse of Eq. (31.1), i.e., a computationally intensive deconvolution of the unit dipole function $d(\mathbf{r})$ from $\Delta B_z(\mathbf{r})$. However, this problem becomes much simpler in the Fourier domain (k-space) [7, 8] as we can exploit the Fourier convolution theorem so that the inverse problem can be written as a simple division:

$$\chi(\mathbf{k}) = \Delta B_z(\mathbf{k}) / (\mathrm{B}_0 \cdot d(\mathbf{k})) \tag{31.3}$$

where $\chi(\mathbf{k})$ is the Fourier transform (FT) of $\chi(\mathbf{r})$, $\Delta B_z(\mathbf{k}) = \mathrm{FT}(\Delta B_z(\mathbf{r}))$ and $d(\mathbf{k}) = \mathrm{FT}(d(\mathbf{r}))$. Problems occur where the denominator $d(\mathbf{k})$ tends to zero, as the result will then tend to infinity: $d(\mathbf{k})$ tends to zero in "ill-conditioned" regions on and near two conical surfaces in k-space (see Fig. 31.1C and D). The inverse problem is thus both ill-posed (having no uniqueness or stability of solutions) and ill-conditioned (where a small change in the inputs gives a large change in the solution).

Several methods have been developed to overcome this ill-posed or ill-conditioned nature of the inverse problem or regularize it. k-space-based algorithms do this by removing, substituting, or correcting the data inside the ill-conditioned regions in k-space. A subset of these methods based on thresholding the denominator $d(\mathbf{k})$ (so-called Truncated or Thresholded k-space Division or TKD methods [41, 46]) may be affected by streaking artifacts, but these artifacts can be minimized by an appropriate choice of the threshold and a corresponding scaling of the resulting susceptibility map to avoid underestimation of susceptibility values [47]. k-space-based approaches [48] are straightforward and computationally efficient relative to image-space-based methods and scored highly in the 2016

QSM challenge [49] where they did not suffer from the oversmoothing that affected many of the more computationally intensive image-space-based regularization methods. The image-space-based approaches (e.g., [48, 50–60]), which are often iterative, usually involve solving an equation of the following form:

$$\chi(r) = \operatorname{argmin} \chi\, w(\Delta B_z - d \otimes \chi)_2^2 + \lambda R(\chi) \tag{31.4}$$

where w is a noise weighting for the data fidelity term and the second term is the regularization term containing the regularization parameter λ and $R(\chi)$, a function of the susceptibility map which can have many different forms. The regularization term often incorporates spatial prior information on the susceptibility map, e.g., piece-wise constant or smooth susceptibility, or morphological consistency with the magnitude image. Therefore, the use of high levels of regularization may result in a smoothed or inaccurate susceptibility map, strongly affected by the spatial prior information introduced. For example, if edges from the magnitude image are used to enforce morphological consistency, structures in the susceptibility map are calculated such that they have edges at the same locations, even if these are inaccurate [61].

Some hybrid methods exploit the advantages of both formulating the problem in k-space and solving it using image-space information [54, 62]. Although several separate conceptual steps in QSM have been described here, these can be combined, practically or computationally, into fewer steps [22, 47] or even a single step [23, 24]. There are now a plethora of QSM algorithms available, each with its own relative merits and disadvantages, many of which were highlighted by the first QSM challenge [49] organized by the QSM community to systematically compare several susceptibility calculation (inversion) algorithms and quantitatively assess their ability to faithfully recover the underlying brain susceptibility distribution from phase images of a healthy volunteer. Deep learning using convolutional neural networks is also beginning to be applied to the background field removal and the final, dipole inversion steps of the QSM pipeline [25, 26, 63–65]. A challenge for clinical applications is to reach consensus on "the best" QSM reconstruction algorithm [49, 66]. However, it is difficult to create a "gold standard" and anatomically realistic susceptibility phantom [67] and different algorithms may be best suited for different applications so convergence on a single "one size fits all" algorithm may never be achieved.

The tissue magnetic susceptibility maps produced using QSM methods have important advantages over the phase images from which they were calculated (Fig. 31.4); specifically, they overcome the nonlocal and orientation-dependent nature of the contrast in phase images [14], improving the visualization of tissue structure and composition. These properties make QSM more reproducible and comparable, across different subjects and field strengths, than phase imaging. These advantages also stand against the earlier and clinically more widespread precursor to QSM known as susceptibility-weighted imaging (SWI). In SWI, phase images are unwrapped, filtered, and multiplied with the corresponding magnitude images to emphasize susceptibility-induced phase changes [69, 70]. Although SWI images combine magnitude image contrast familiar to radiologists with phase-contrast to emphasize primarily vascular susceptibility-induced changes such as microbleeds, they still suffer from nonlocal contrast artifacts [68]. These effects can be mitigated while preserving the advantage of combined contrast by multiplying (inverted) susceptibility maps with magnitude images [71–74] (Fig. 31.4) although, unlike the original susceptibility maps, these so-called "true SWI" images are no longer quantitative.

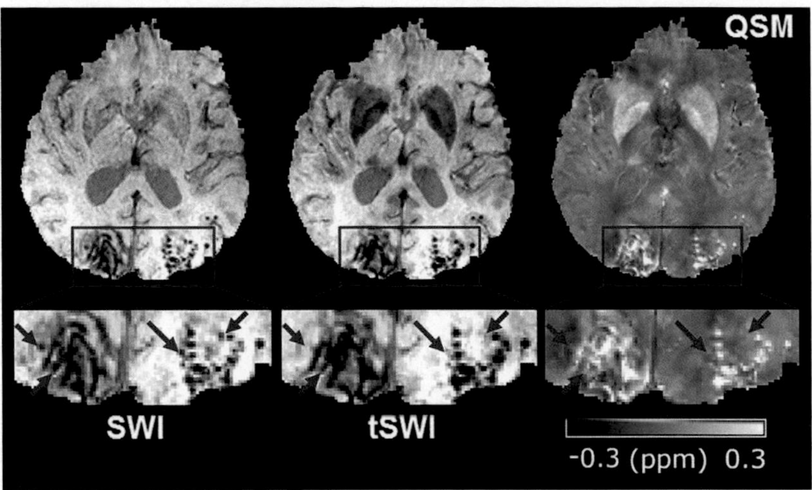

FIG. 31.4

Advantages of QSM illustrated in a patient with cerebral amyloid angiopathy (CAA) [68]. The *arrows* show what appear to be four cerebral microbleeds in the SWI but are probably duplicates as they are not visible in the QSM and true SWI images (tSWI, created by scaling the QSM and multiplying it with the magnitude image). The broadening or duplication of the microbleeds in the SWI is due to the dipolar phase around them (see Fig. 31.1A and B). This nonlocal contrast is overcome by QSM so the duplicates are not visible in the QSM and the tSWI image derived from it. This patient has a heavy microbleed burden as well as a lobar intracerebral hemorrhage.

31.3 Practical considerations and limitations of QSM techniques

Several practical issues to consider for successful QSM as well as the limitations that arise as consequences of the assumptions behind this technique are discussed in this section. As with many other quantitative MRI techniques, QSM benefits from high magnetic field strengths largely because of the increased contrast-to-noise ratio (CNR) in the phase images (Eq. 31.1) and increased resolution [75].

Different QSM methods can be classified according to whether they require acquisitions with the region or organ of interest tilted at multiple angles with respect to the main magnetic field (B_0) [43, 61, 76, 77] or at a single orientation. The majority of current QSM methods rely on single-orientation acquisitions because of the additional time and discomfort involved in acquiring images with the subject or area of interest at several orientations (not to mention the impossibility of positioning for some human body applications). Note that acquisitions at multiple orientations are required for susceptibility tensor imaging (STI, [78–80]) which moves beyond the implicit assumption of QSM that tissue susceptibility has a single scalar value in each voxel and calculates a susceptibility tensor in each voxel. As discussed later, susceptibility anisotropy is especially prominent in highly ordered white matter where local microstructural effects can lead to artifacts in QSM [81].

For single-orientation acquisitions, axial or coronal slices are ideal for QSM as $d(\mathbf{k})$ can then be accurately constructed and applied for inversion. If slices are acquired tilted at an angle to B_0, it is important to account for this in the QSM pipeline to avoid artifacts or inaccurate susceptibility values. For k-space-based susceptibility calculation methods, it has been found [82] that the most accurate approach is to rotate the image volume to align it with $d(\mathbf{k})$ before background field removal using the PDF algorithm [37] and then inversion.

A common practical pitfall in QSM is the acquisition of images with insufficient resolution and/or coverage [15, 83–85] for accurate susceptibility calculation. It is important to ensure that the field perturbations $\Delta B_z(\mathbf{r})$ induced by susceptibility sources $\chi(\mathbf{r})$ are sufficiently sampled so that they can be accurately inverted. Guidelines for achieving this include using high, isotropic resolution with a field-of-view large enough to cover the nonlocal dipolar fields generated by the structures of interest [85].

Furthermore, when using multiple channel radiofrequency coils, it is crucial to ensure that the phase images from each of the coil channels are combined correctly to reconstruct an accurate phase image [35, 86–90]. If the phase images are not combined correctly, local noise enhancement and, in the worst case, intractable artifacts known as open-ended fringe lines or phase singularities can propagate into susceptibility maps [91].

The measured phase also depends upon imaging parameters such as the TE (Eq. 31.2) and the voxel aspect ratio [92, 93] so these should be chosen carefully. In general, the maximum CNR in a $T_2{}^*$-weighted phase image is achieved at a TE close to the $T_2{}^*$ value [31]. As tissues of interest often cover a range of $T_2{}^*$ values, acquiring multiple echoes helps to maximize the contrast across several tissues as well as allowing more accurate estimation of $\Delta B_z(\mathbf{r})$ for QSM as explained earlier [30, 94]. For QSM of fatty tissues together with water-based tissues (e.g., in the pelvis, breast, or head-and-neck region [95–97]), choosing TEs at which the fat protons are in-phase with the water protons is effective in reducing chemical-shift-induced phase errors that result in QSM artifacts [36].

Other imaging parameters such as image acceleration, gradient warp correction, and the use of monopolar versus bipolar readout gradients have been investigated and found to have a negligible effect on QSM susceptibility measurements [98]. If vascular susceptibility measurements are needed, for example for venous oxygenation imaging [99, 100], flow compensation of multiple echoes is advisable [101].

A final note of caution: it is important to be aware that the phase will also be affected by hardware differences in vendor systems such that there are two-phase sign conventions [102]. Despite confusing historical differences in SWI and QSM display, it is intuitive and has become conventional to show paramagnetic (relatively positive) tissue susceptibilities as bright in susceptibility maps.

31.4 Sources of susceptibility contrast and clinical applications of QSM

Several clinical applications of QSM are emerging based on its sensitivity to tissue composition. Although according to Wiedemann's additivity law, tissue susceptibility is the weighted sum of all constituent susceptibilities, the dominant sources of contrast in susceptibility maps are widely accepted to be iron (primarily in ferritin [103–105]) and myelin [106, 107] as well as deoxyhemoglobin in blood vessels [99, 108] and calcifications [109–111]. Of course, different susceptibility sources will dominate in different tissue structures and pathologies [4]. A comprehensive review [112–114] is beyond the scope of this chapter but some key applications are included here.

31.4.1 Tissue iron—Deep-brain structures and dementia

Tissues rich in ferritin (stored iron) are relatively paramagnetic and show strong contrast in susceptibility maps. Several studies have found strong correlations between the susceptibility measured in deep brain regions such as the red nucleus, substantia nigra, and putamen (Fig. 31.5) and their iron content, often estimated from postmortem studies [38, 43, 46, 61, 115]. These correlations have been verified using independent methods such as X-ray fluorescence imaging and inductively coupled plasma mass spectrometry [104, 105]. In vivo, the observed monotonic increase in susceptibility values measured in these structures with age should be taken into account [58, 116–125] (Fig. 31.5).

The observed dependence of susceptibility image contrast on tissue iron content has been exploited for several clinical applications, for example, to improve targeting of structures for deep-brain stimulation [126–128] and as a marker of increased iron content in the substantia nigra in patients with Parkinson's disease (PD) [129–138]. QSM has also been applied in Alzheimer's disease (AD) in which the characteristic amyloid beta protein plaques have been found to colocalize with iron [139, 140]. Initial QSM studies in patients with early-stage AD [139–142] found susceptibility differences relative to healthy controls in both deep gray matter and cortical regions. QSM studies in animal models of AD

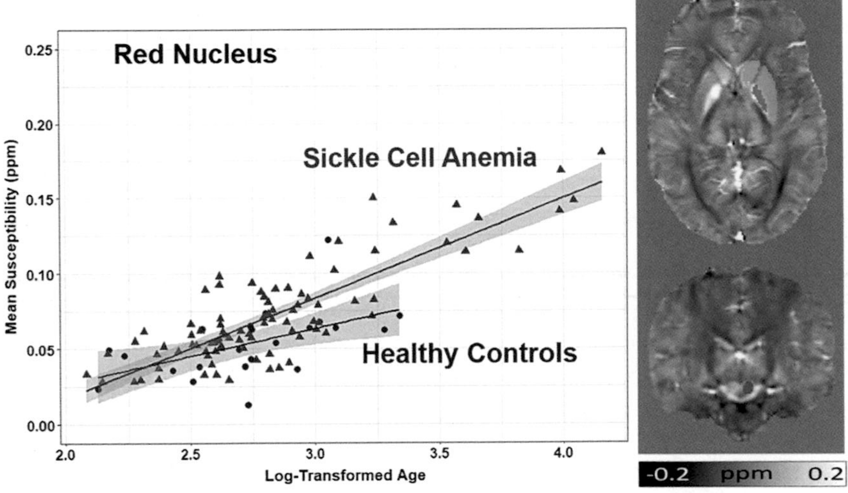

FIG. 31.5

QSM shows a faster increase in the susceptibility of the red nucleus in patients with sickle cell anemia with age. The graph shows the mean susceptibility in the red nucleus, which increases faster with age in nontransfused sickle cell anemia patients than in healthy controls. This finding suggests an accumulation of paramagnetic iron in this region in sickle cell anemia. The regions of interest are shown on the right superimposed on a susceptibility map (axial and coronal slices) from a representative healthy volunteer. Deep-brain regions investigated include the caudate *(green)*, putamen *(orange)*, globus pallidus *(pale blue)*, and the red nucleus *(red)*.

have also shown susceptibility increases associated with increased microbleed load [143] and demyelination [144]. Therefore, QSM shows exciting potential to provide imaging biomarkers to facilitate early diagnosis of PD and AD.

31.4.2 Deoxyhemoglobin and blood iron—Brain oxygenation and microvascular disease

Deoxyhemoglobin is paramagnetic; therefore, susceptibility maps highlight the deoxyhemoglobin-containing venous vasculature. Moreover, because the venous susceptibility depends linearly on the deoxyhemoglobin concentration [108], QSM allows quantification of venous oxygenation [99, 101, 145–149]. An emerging application is the use of endogenous oxygenation-dependent susceptibility contrast for functional susceptibility mapping (fQSM) [150–155] which shows the potential for improved spatial localization of BOLD functional activity.

The high paramagnetic susceptibility of deoxyhemoglobin and other blood products (e.g., hemosiderin) has also enabled QSM to reveal and assess hemorrhages and microbleeds [68, 143, 156–158] (Fig. 31.4), for example in traumatic brain injury [159, 160]. A further advantage of susceptibility mapping over phase imaging or SWI is that these strongly paramagnetic hemorrhagic features can be easily distinguished from calcifications in susceptibility maps [109, 110, 161, 162] as calcium compounds are strongly diamagnetic.

31.4.3 Myelin—Demyelination and microstructure

Myelin is thought to be slightly more diamagnetic compared with other tissues due to its high lipid content [13, 107]. Demyelination, induced by a cuprizone diet [107] or in shiverer mice [106], has been shown to almost completely remove the susceptibility-induced contrast between gray and white matter. QSM has also been used to reveal demyelination in a model of tau pathology [144]. Changes in the susceptibility contrast in and around multiple sclerosis (MS) lesions have been attributed to changes in both myelination and iron content, possibly associated with microglia or macrophages involved in inflammation [86, 163–172].

White matter susceptibility is anisotropic [78–80] and is also affected locally by tissue microstructure and compartmentalization, and investigation of white matter susceptibility is an active, and occasionally controversial, area of research [75, 81, 173–180]. Note that QSM implicitly assumes a single isotropic susceptibility value in each voxel, but the MRI phase is also affected by anisotropic susceptibility, microstructure, and compartmentalization [10–12, 81] as well as chemical-exchange-induced frequency shifts [181–183] and chemical shift effects [95, 97]. Including these effects in a more sophisticated tissue susceptibility model or combining QSM measurements with other MRI measurements such as magnetization transfer [184], R_2^*[185], and diffusion-weighted measures of fiber orientation [186] may allow the contributions of myelin, iron, and microstructure to be disentangled.

31.4.4 Other applications

Applications of QSM have moved out of the brain and into the rest of the body (Fig. 31.6) from heart to liver, pelvis, and cartilage in the knee joint [42, 74, 97, 187–192]. Due to its ability to reveal multiple pathophysiologically important tissue components, QSM is likely to be increasingly used to assess tissue composition and microstructure in a variety of diseases.

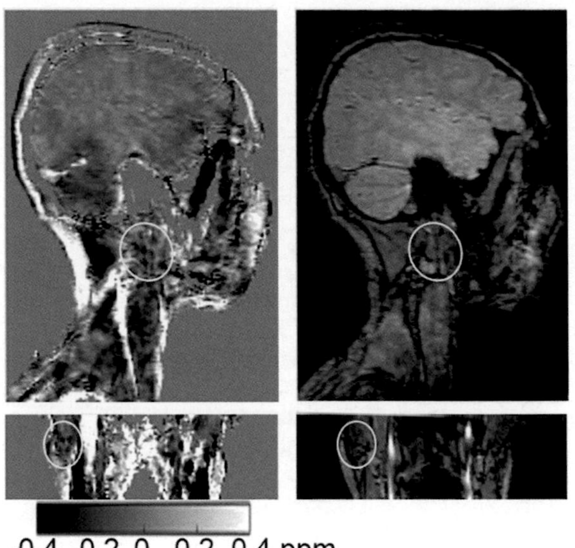

FIG. 31.6

QSM in the head and neck region. A sagittal slice (top) and a section of the coronal slice (bottom) of a susceptibility map (left) and a magnitude image (right) (TE = 24.6 ms). The *yellow ellipses* highlight the parotid glands, which are visible as a cluster of dark spots in the susceptibility map. This internal structure is not clear in the magnitude image.

Acknowledgment

I would like to thank Anita Karsa, Barbara Dymerska, Emma Biondetti, and Russell Murdoch for their contributions to the figures and helpful feedback.

References

[1] Schenck JF. The role of magnetic susceptibility in magnetic resonance imaging: MRI magnetic compatibility of the first and second kinds. Med Phys 1996;23(6):815–50.

[2] Duyn J. MR susceptibility imaging. J Magn Reson 2013;229:198–207.

[3] Wang Y, Liu T. Quantitative susceptibility mapping (QSM): decoding MRI data for a tissue magnetic biomarker. Magn Reson Med 2015;73(1):82–101.

[4] Duyn JH, Schenck J. Contributions to magnetic susceptibility of brain tissue. NMR Biomed 2017;30(4): e3546.

[5] Kuchel PW, Chapman BE, Bubb WA, Hansen PE, Durrant CJ, Hertzberg MP. Magnetic susceptibility: solutions, emulsions, and cells. Concepts Magn Reson A Br Educ Res J 2003;18(1):56–71.

[6] Reichenbach JR, Venkatesan R, Yablonskiy DA, Thompson MR, Lai S, Haacke EM. Theory and application of static field inhomogeneity effects in gradient-echo imaging. J Magn Reson Imag 1997;7(2):266.

[7] Salomir R, De Senneville BD, Moonen CTW. A fast calculation method for magnetic field inhomogeneity due to an arbitrary distribution of bulk susceptibility. Concepts Magn Reson B Magn Reson Eng 2003;(1):26–34, 19B.

[8] Marques JP, Bowtell R. Application of a Fourier-based method for rapid calculation of field inhomogeneity due to spatial variation of magnetic susceptibility. Concepts Magn Reson B Magn Reson Eng 2005; 25B(1):65–78.

[9] Wharton S, Bowtell R. Fiber orientation-dependent white matter contrast in gradient echo MRI. Proc Natl Acad Sci 2012;109(45):18559–64.

[10] Cronin MJ, Wang N, Decker KS, Wei H, Zhu W-Z, Liu C. Exploring the origins of echo-time-dependent quantitative susceptibility mapping (QSM) measurements in healthy tissue and cerebral microbleeds. NeuroImage 2017;149:98–113.

[11] Sood S, Urriola J, Reutens D, O'Brien K, Bollmann S, Barth M, Vegh V. Echo time-dependent quantitative susceptibility mapping contains information on tissue properties. Magn Reson Med 2017;77(5):1946–58.

[12] Tendler BC, Bowtell R. Frequency difference mapping applied to the corpus callosum at 7T. Magn Reson Med 2019;81(5):3017–31.

[13] Duyn JH, van Gelderen P, Li TQ, de Zwart JA, Koretsky AP, Fukunaga M. High-field MRI of brain cortical substructure based on signal phase. Proc Natl Acad Sci U S A 2007;104(28):11796–801.

[14] Shmueli K, Van Gelderen P, Yao B, De Zwart J, Fukunaga M, Duyn J. The dependence of tissue phase contrast on orientation can be overcome by quantitative susceptibility mapping, In: Proc ISMRM, Honolulu, Hawai'i, USA, vol. 17; 2009, p. 466.

[15] Haacke EM, Liu S, Buch S, Zheng W, Wu D, Ye Y. Quantitative susceptibility mapping: current status and future directions. Magn Reson Imaging 2015;33(1):1–25.

[16] Liu C, Li W, Tong KA, Yeom KW, Kuzminski S. Susceptibility-weighted imaging and quantitative susceptibility mapping in the brain. J Magn Reson Imaging 2015;42(1):23–41.

[17] Liu C, Wei H, Gong NJ, Cronin M, Dibb R, Decker K. Quantitative susceptibility mapping: contrast mechanisms and clinical applications. Tomography 2015;1(1):3–17.

[18] Reichenbach JR, Schweser F, Serres B, Deistung A. Quantitative susceptibility mapping: concepts and applications. Clin Neuroradiol 2015;25:225–30.

[19] Schweser F, Deistung A, Reichenbach JR. Foundations of MRI phase imaging and processing for quantitative susceptibility mapping (QSM). Z Med Phys 2016;26(1):6–34.

[20] Deistung A, Schweser F, Reichenbach JR. Overview of quantitative susceptibility mapping. NMR Biomed 2017;30(4):e3569.

[21] Kee Y, Liu Z, Zhou L, Dimov A, Cho J, de Rochefort L, et al. Quantitative Susceptibility Mapping (QSM) algorithms: mathematical rationale and computational implementations. IEEE Trans Biomed Eng 2017;64(11):2531–45.

[22] Li W, Avram AV, Wu B, Xiao X, Liu C. Integrated Laplacian-based phase unwrapping and background phase removal for quantitative susceptibility mapping. NMR Biomed 2014;27(2):219–27.

[23] Langkammer C, Bredies K, Poser BA, Barth M, Reishofer G, Fan AP, et al. Fast quantitative susceptibility mapping using 3D EPI and total generalized variation. NeuroImage 2015;111:622–30.

[24] Chatnuntawech I, McDaniel P, Cauley SF, Gagoski BA, Langkammer C, Martin A, et al. Single-step quantitative susceptibility mapping with variational penalties. NMR Biomed 2017;30(4). https://doi.org/10.1002/nbm.3570.

[25] Yoon J, Gong E, Chatnuntawech I, Bilgic B, Lee J, Jung W, et al. Quantitative susceptibility mapping using deep neural network: QSMnet. NeuroImage 2018;179:199–206.

[26] Bollmann S, Rasmussen KGB, Kristensen M, Blendal RG, Ostergaard LR, Plocharski M, et al. DeepQSM – using deep learning to solve the dipole inversion for quantitative susceptibility mapping. NeuroImage 2019;195:373–83.

[27] Sun H, Wilman AH. Quantitative susceptibility mapping using single-shot echo-planar imaging. Magn Reson Med 2015;73(5):1932–8.

[28] Liu T, Wisnieff C, Lou M, Chen W, Spincemaille P, Wang Y. Nonlinear formulation of the magnetic field to source relationship for robust quantitative susceptibility mapping. Magn Reson Med 2013;69:467–76.

[29] Biondetti E, Thomas DL, Shmueli K. Application of laplacian-based methods to multi-echo phase data for accurate susceptibility mapping, In: Proc ISMRM, Singapore, vol. 24; 2016, p. 1547.

[30] Gilbert G, Savard G, Bard C, Beaudoin G. Quantitative comparison between a multiecho sequence and a single-echo sequence for susceptibility-weighted phase imaging. Magn Reson Imaging 2012; 30(5):722–30.

[31] Wu B, Li W, Avram AV, Gho SM, Liu CL. Fast and tissue-optimized mapping of magnetic susceptibility and T2*with multi-echo and multi-shot spirals. NeuroImage 2012;59(1):297–305.

[32] Jenkinson M. Fast, automated, N-dimensional phase-unwrapping algorithm. Magn Reson Med 2003;49(1):193.

[33] Schofield MA, Zhu YM. Fast phase unwrapping algorithm for interferometric applications. Opt Lett 2003;28(14):1194–6.

[34] Witoszynskyj S, Rauscher A, Reichenbach JR, Barth M. Phase unwrapping of MR images using Phi UN – a fast and robust region growing algorithm. Med Image Anal 2009;13(2):257–68.

[35] Robinson SD, Bredies K, Khabipova D, Dymerska B, Marques JP, Schweser F. An illustrated comparison of processing methods for MR phase imaging and QSM: combining array coil signals and phase unwrapping. NMR Biomed 2017;30(4):e3601.

[36] Karsa A, Shmueli K. SEGUE: a speedy region-growing algorithm for unwrapping estimated phase. IEEE Trans Med Imaging 2019;38(6):1347–57.

[37] Liu T, Khalidov I, de Rochefort L, Spincemaille P, Liu J, Tsiouris AJ, Wang Y. A novel background field removal method for MRI using projection onto dipole fields (PDF). NMR Biomed 2011;24(9):1129–36.

[38] Schweser F, Deistung A, Lehr BW, Reichenbach JR. Quantitative imaging of intrinsic magnetic tissue properties using MRI signal phase: an approach to in vivo brain iron metabolism? NeuroImage 2011;54(4): 2789–2807.

[39] Zhou D, Liu T, Spincemaille P, Wang Y. Background field removal by solving the Laplacian boundary value problem. NMR Biomed 2014;27(3):312–9.

[40] Schweser F, Robinson SD, de Rochefort L, Li W, Bredies K. An illustrated comparison of processing methods for phase MRI and QSM: removal of background field contributions from sources outside the region of interest. NMR Biomed 2017;30(4):e3604.

[41] Wharton S, Schafer A, Bowtell R. Susceptibility mapping in the human brain using threshold-based k-space division. Magn Reson Med 2010;63(5):1292–304.

[42] Sharma SD, Fischer R, Schoennagel BP, Nielsen P, Kooijman H, Yamamura J, et al. MRI-based quantitative susceptibility mapping (QSM) and R2* mapping of liver iron overload: comparison with SQUID-based biomagnetic liver susceptometry. Magn Reson Med 2017;78(1):264–70.

[43] Lim IAL, Faria AV, Li X, Hsu JTC, Airan RD, Mori S, van Ziji PCM. Human brain atlas for automated region of interest selection in quantitative susceptibility mapping: application to determine iron content in deep gray matter structures. NeuroImage 2013;82:449–69.

[44] Straub S, Schneider TM, Emmerich J, Freitag MT, Ziener CH, Schlemmer HP, et al. Suitable reference tissues for quantitative susceptibility mapping of the brain. Magn Reson Med 2017;78(1):204–14.

[45] Liu Z, Spincemaille P, Yao Y, Zhang Y, Wang Y. MEDI+0: morphology enabled dipole inversion with automatic uniform cerebrospinal fluid zero reference for quantitative susceptibility mapping. Magn Reson Med 2018;79(5):2795–803.

[46] Shmueli K, de Zwart JA, van Gelderen P, Li TQ, Dodd SJ, Duyn JH. Magnetic susceptibility mapping of brain tissue in vivo using MRI phase data. Magn Reson Med 2009;62(6):1510–22.

[47] Schweser F, Deistung A, Sommer K, Reichenbach JR. Toward online reconstruction of quantitative susceptibility maps: superfast dipole inversion. Magn Reson Med 2013;69(6):1582–94.

[48] Kressler B, de Rochefort L, Liu T, Spincemaille P, Jiang Q, Wang Y. Nonlinear regularization for per voxel estimation of magnetic susceptibility distributions from MRI field maps. IEEE Trans Med Imaging 2010;29(2):273–81.

[49] Langkammer C, Schweser F, Shmueli K, Kames C, Li X, Guo L, et al. Quantitative susceptibility mapping: report from the 2016 reconstruction challenge. Magn Reson Med 2018;79(3):1661–73.

[50] de Rochefort L, Brown R, Prince MR, Wang Y. Quantitative MR susceptibility mapping using piece-wise constant regularized inversion of the magnetic field. Magn Reson Med 2008;60(4):1003–9.

[51] de Rochefort L, Liu T, Kressler B, Liu J, Spincemaille P, Lebon V, et al. Quantitative susceptibility map reconstruction from MR phase data using bayesian regularization: validation and application to brain imaging. Magn Reson Med 2010;63(1):194–206.

[52] Liu T, Liu J, de Rochefort L, Spincemaille P, Khalidov I, Ledoux JR, Wang Y. Morphology enabled dipole inversion (MEDI) from a single-angle acquisition: comparison with COSMOS in human brain imaging. Magn Reson Med 2011;66(3):777–83.

[53] Liu J, Liu T, de Rochefort L, Ledoux J, Khalidov I, Chen W, et al. Morphology enabled dipole inversion for quantitative susceptibility mapping using structural consistency between the magnitude image and the susceptibility map. NeuroImage 2012;59(3):2560–8.

[54] Schweser F, Sommer K, Deistung A, Reichenbach JR. Quantitative susceptibility mapping for investigating subtle susceptibility variations in the human brain. NeuroImage 2012;62(3):2083–100.

[55] Wu B, Li W, Guidon A, Liu CL. Whole brain susceptibility mapping using compressed sensing. Magn Reson Med 2012;67(1):137–47.

[56] Bilgic B, Fan AP, Polimeni JR, Cauley SF, Bianciardi M, Adalsteinsson E, et al. Fast quantitative susceptibility mapping with L1-regularization and automatic parameter selection. Magn Reson Med 2014;72(5):1444–59.

[57] Li W, Wang N, Yu F, Han H, Cao W, Romero R, et al. A method for estimating and removing streaking artifacts in quantitative susceptibility mapping. NeuroImage 2015;108:111–22.

[58] Poynton CB, Jenkinson M, Adalsteinsson E, Sullivan EV, Pfefferbaum A, Wells 3rd W. Quantitative susceptibility mapping by inversion of a perturbation field model: correlation with brain iron in normal aging. IEEE Trans Med Imaging 2015;34(1):339–53.

[59] Liu Z, Kee Y, Zhou D, Wang Y, Spincemaille P. Preconditioned total field inversion (TFI) method for quantitative susceptibility mapping. Magn Reson Med 2017;78(1):303–15.

[60] Acosta-Cabronero J, Milovic C, Mattern H, Tejos C, Speck O, Callaghan MF. A robust multi-scale approach to quantitative susceptibility mapping. NeuroImage 2018;183:7–24.

[61] Wharton S, Bowtell R. Whole-brain susceptibility mapping at high field: a comparison of multiple- and single-orientation methods. NeuroImage 2010;53(2):515–25.

[62] Tang J, Liu S, Neelavalli J, Cheng YC, Buch S, Haacke EM. Improving susceptibility mapping using a threshold-based K-space/image domain iterative reconstruction approach. Magn Reson Med 2013;69(5):1396–407.

[63] Bollmann S, Kristensen MH, Larsen MS, Olsen MV, Pedersen MJ, Ostergaard LR, et al. SHARQnet – sophisticated harmonic artifact reduction in quantitative susceptibility mapping using a deep convolutional neural network. Z Med Phys 2019;29(2):139–49.

[64] Liu J, Koch KM. Deep gated convolutional neural network for QSM background field removal. In: Medical image computing and computer assisted intervention – MICCAI. 2019. p. 83–91.

[65] Wei H, Cao S, Zhang Y, Guan X, Yan F, Yeom KW, Liu C. Learning-based single-step quantitative susceptibility mapping reconstruction without brain extraction. NeuroImage 2019;202:116064.

[66] QSM Reconstruction Challenge 2.0. Available from: http://www.listsnu.org/qsm-challenge/; 2019.

[67] Marques JP, Bilgic B, Meineke J, Milovic C, Chan K-s, Zwaag Wvd, et al. Towards QSM challenge 2.0: creation and evaluation of a realistic magnetic susceptibility phantom, In: Proceedings of the International Society for Magnetic Resonance in Medicine, Montreal, Canada, vol. 27; 2019, p. 1122.

[68] Dymerska B, Banerjee G, Dixon E, Biondetti E, Barnes A, Schott JM, et al. Inaccurate visualisation of haemorrhagic markers in cerebral amyloid angiopathy in susceptibility weighted imaging can be overcome using susceptibility mapping, In: Proceedings of the International Society for Magnetic Resonance in Medicine, Montreal, Canada, vol. 27; 2019, p. 2933.

[69] Reichenbach JR, Venkatesan R, Schillinger DJ, Kido DK, Haacke EM. Small vessels in the human brain: MR venography with deoxyhemoglobin as an intrinsic contrast agent. Radiology 1997;204(1):272–7.

[70] Haacke EM, Xu Y, Cheng YC, Reichenbach JR. Susceptibility weighted imaging (SWI). Magn Reson Med 2004;52(3):612–8.

[71] Gho SM, Liu C, Li W, Jang U, Kim EY, Hwang D, Kim DH. Susceptibility map-weighted imaging (SMWI) for neuroimaging. Magn Reson Med 2014;72(2):337–46.

[72] Liu S, Mok K, Neelavalli J, Cheng YC, Tang J, Ye Y, Haacke EM. Improved MR venography using quantitative susceptibility-weighted imaging. J Magn Reson Imaging 2014;40(3):698–708.

[73] Nissi MJ, Tóth F, Wang L, Carlson CS, Ellermann JM. Improved visualization of cartilage canals using quantitative susceptibility mapping. PLoS One 2015;10(7):e0132167.

[74] Dymerska B, Bohndorf K, Schennach P, Rauscher A, Trattnig S, Robinson SD. In vivo phase imaging of human epiphyseal cartilage at 7 T. Magn Reson Med 2018;79(4):2149–55.

[75] Duyn JH. Studying brain microstructure with magnetic susceptibility contrast at high-field. NeuroImage 2018;168:152–61.

[76] Liu T, Spincemaille P, de Rochefort L, Kressler B, Wang Y. Calculation of susceptibility through multiple orientation sampling (COSMOS): a method for conditioning the inverse problem from measured magnetic field map to susceptibility source image in MRI. Magn Reson Med 2009;61(1):196–204.

[77] Bilgic B, Xie L, Dibb R, Langkammer C, Mutluay A, Ye H, et al. Rapid multi-orientation quantitative susceptibility mapping. NeuroImage 2016;125:1131–41.

[78] Lee J, Shmueli K, Fukunaga M, van Gelderen P, Merkle H, Silva AC, Duyn JH. Sensitivity of MRI resonance frequency to the orientation of brain tissue microstructure. Proc Natl Acad Sci U S A 2010; 107(11):5130–5.

[79] Li W, Wu B, Avram AV, Liu C. Magnetic susceptibility anisotropy of human brain in vivo and its molecular underpinnings. NeuroImage 2012;59(3):2088–97.

[80] Li W, Liu C, Duong TQ, van Zijl PC, Li X. Susceptibility tensor imaging (STI) of the brain. NMR Biomed 2017;30(4):e3540.

[81] Wharton S, Bowtell R. Effects of white matter microstructure on phase and susceptibility maps. Magn Reson Med 2015;73(3):1258–69.

[82] Dixon E. Applications of MRI magnetic susceptibility mapping in PET-MRI brain studies. Doctor of philosophy, London: University College London; 2018.

[83] Elkady AM, Sun H, Wilman AH. Importance of extended spatial coverage for quantitative susceptibility mapping of iron-rich deep gray matter. Magn Reson Imaging 2016;34(4):574–8.

[84] Zhou D, Cho J, Zhang J, Spincemaille P, Wang Y. Susceptibility underestimation in a high-susceptibility phantom: dependence on imaging resolution, magnitude contrast, and other parameters. Magn Reson Med 2017;78(3):1080–6.

[85] Karsa A, Punwani S, Shmueli K. The effect of low resolution and coverage on the accuracy of susceptibility mapping. Magn Reson Med 2019;81(3):1833–48.

[86] Hammond KE, Lupo JM, Xu D, Metcalf M, Kelley DA, Pelletier D, et al. Development of a robust method for generating 7.0 T multichannel phase images of the brain with application to normal volunteers and patients with neurological diseases. NeuroImage 2008;39(4):1682–92.

[87] Robinson S, Grabner G, Witoszynskyj S, Trattnig S. Combining phase images from multi-channel RF coils using 3D phase offset maps derived from a dual-echo scan. Magn Reson Med 2011;65(6):1638–48.

[88] Parker DL, Payne A, Todd N, Hadley JR. Phase reconstruction from multiple coil data using a virtual reference coil. Magn Reson Med 2014;72(2):563–9.

[89] Robinson SD, Dymerska B, Bogner W, Barth M, Zaric O, Goluch S, et al. Combining phase images from array coils using a short echo time reference scan (COMPOSER). Magn Reson Med 2017;77(1):318–27.

[90] Eckstein K, Dymerska B, Bachrata B, Bogner W, Poljanc K, Trattnig S, Robinson SD. Computationally efficient combination of multi-channel phase data from multi-echo acquisitions (ASPIRE). Magn Reson Med 2018;79(6):2996–3006.

[91] Metere R, Kober T, Möller HE, Schäfer A. Simultaneous quantitative MRI mapping of T1, T2* and magnetic susceptibility with multi-echo MP2RAGE. PLoS One 2017;12(1):e0169265.
[92] Xu YB, Haacke EM. The role of voxel aspect ratio in determining apparent vascular phase behavior in susceptibility weighted imaging. Magn Reson Imaging 2006;24(2):155–60.
[93] Deistung A, Rauscher A, Sedlacik J, Stadler J, Witoszynskyj S, Reichenbach JR. Susceptibility weighted imaging at ultra high magnetic field strengths: theoretical considerations and experimental results. Magn Reson Med 2008;60(5):1155–68.
[94] Biondetti E, Karsa A, Thomas DL, Shmueli K. Evaluating the accuracy of susceptibility maps calculated from single-echo versus multi-echo gradient-echo acquisitions, In: Proceedings of the International Society for Magnetic Resonance in Medicine, Honolulu, Hawaii, USA, 25; 2017, p. 1955.
[95] Dimov AV, Liu T, Spincemaille P, Ecanow JS, Tan H, Edelman RR, Wang Y. Joint estimation of chemical shift and quantitative susceptibility mapping (chemical QSM). Magn Reson Med 2015;73(6):2100–10.
[96] Karsa A, Punwani S, Shmueli K. Fat correction of MRI phase images for accurate susceptibility mapping in the head and neck, In: Proceedings of the International Society for Magnetic Resonance in Medicine, Paris, France, vol. 26; 2018, p. 4988.
[97] Bray TJP, Karsa A, Bainbridge A, Sakai N, Punwani S, Hall-Craggs MA, Shmueli K. Association of bone mineral density and fat fraction with magnetic susceptibility in inflamed trabecular bone. Magn Reson Med 2019;81(5):3094–107.
[98] Lauzon ML, McCreary CR, McLean DA, Salluzzi M, Frayne R. Quantitative susceptibility mapping at 3 T: comparison of acquisition methodologies. NMR Biomed 2017;30(4):e3492.
[99] Fan AP, Bilgic B, Gagnon L, Witzel T, Bhat H, Rosen BR, Adalsteinsson E. Quantitative oxygenation venography from MRI phase. Magn Reson Med 2014;72(1):149–59.
[100] Biondetti E, Rojas-Villabona A, Sokolska M, Pizzini FB, Jager HR, Thomas DL, Shmueli K. Investigating the oxygenation of brain arteriovenous malformations using quantitative susceptibility mapping. NeuroImage 2019;199:440–53.
[101] Xu B, Liu T, Spincemaille P, Prince M, Wang Y. Flow compensated quantitative susceptibility mapping for venous oxygenation imaging. Magn Reson Med 2014;72(2):438–45.
[102] Hagberg GE, Welch EB, Greiser A. The sign convention for phase values on different vendor systems: definition and implications for susceptibility-weighted imaging. Magn Reson Imaging 2010;28(2):297–300.
[103] Fukunaga M, Li TQ, van Gelderen P, de Zwart JA, Shmueli K, Yao B, et al. Layer-specific variation of iron content in cerebral cortex as a source of MRI contrast. Proc Natl Acad Sci U S A 2010;107(8):3834–9.
[104] Langkammer C, Schweser F, Krebs N, Deistung A, Goessler W, Scheurer E, et al. Quantitative susceptibility mapping (QSM) as a means to measure brain iron? A post mortem validation study. NeuroImage 2012;62(3):1593–9.
[105] Zheng WL, Nichol H, Liu SF, Cheng YCN, Haacke EM. Measuring iron in the brain using quantitative susceptibility mapping and X-ray fluorescence imaging. NeuroImage 2013;78:68–74.
[106] Liu CL, Li W, Johnson GA, Wu B. High-field (9.4 T) MRI of brain dysmyelination by quantitative mapping of magnetic susceptibility. NeuroImage 2011;56(3):930–8.
[107] Lee J, Shmueli K, Kang BT, Yao B, Fukunaga M, van Gelderen P, et al. The contribution of myelin to magnetic susceptibility-weighted contrasts in high-field MRI of the brain. NeuroImage 2012;59(4):3967–75.
[108] Jain V, Abdulmalik O, Propert KJ, Wehrli FW. Investigating the magnetic susceptibility properties of fresh human blood for noninvasive oxygen saturation quantification. Magn Reson Med 2012;68(3):863–7.
[109] Schweser F, Deistung A, Lehr BW, Reichenbach JR. Differentiation between diamagnetic and paramagnetic cerebral lesions based on magnetic susceptibility mapping. Med Phys 2010;37(10):5165–78.
[110] Chen W, Zhu W, Kovanlikaya I, Kovanlikaya A, Liu T, Wang S, et al. Intracranial calcifications and hemorrhages: characterization with quantitative susceptibility mapping. Radiology 2014;270(2):496–505.
[111] Straub S, Laun FB, Emmerich J, Jobke B, Hauswald H, Katayama S, et al. Potential of quantitative susceptibility mapping for detection of prostatic calcifications. J Magn Reson Imaging 2017;45(3):889–98.

[112] Eskreis-Winkler S, Zhang Y, Zhang J, Liu Z, Dimov A, Gupta A, Wang Y. The clinical utility of QSM: disease diagnosis, medical management, and surgical planning. NMR Biomed 2017;30(4):e3668.

[113] Soman S, Bregni JA, Bilgic B, Nemec U, Fan A, Liu Z, et al. Susceptibility-based neuroimaging: standard methods, clinical applications, and future directions. Curr Radiol Rep 2017;5(3). Article number: 11.

[114] Wang Y, Spincemaille P, Liu Z, Dimov A, Deh K, Li J, et al. Clinical quantitative susceptibility mapping (QSM): biometal imaging and its emerging roles in patient care. J Magn Reson Imaging 2017;46(4):951–71.

[115] Schweser F, Deistung A, Lehr BW, Sommer K, Reichenbach JR. SEMI-TWInS: simultaneous extraction of myelin and iron using a T2*-weighted imaging sequence, In: Proceedings 19th Scientific Meeting, International Society for Magnetic Resonance in Medicine; 2011. p. 120.

[116] Bilgic B, Pfefferbaum A, Rohlfing T, Sullivan EV, Adalsteinsson E. MRI estimates of brain iron concentration in normal aging using quantitative susceptibility mapping. NeuroImage 2012;59(3):2625–35.

[117] Li W, Wu B, Batrachenko A, Bancroft-Wu V, Morey RA, Shashi V, et al. Differential developmental trajectories of magnetic susceptibility in human brain gray and white matter over the lifespan. Hum Brain Mapp 2014;35(6):2698–713.

[118] Persson N, Wu J, Zhang Q, Liu T, Shen J, Bao R, et al. Age and sex related differences in subcortical brain iron concentrations among healthy adults. NeuroImage 2015;122:385–98.

[119] Acosta-Cabronero J, Betts MJ, Cardenas-Blanco A, Yang S, Nestor PJ. In vivo MRI mapping of brain iron deposition across the adult lifespan. J Neurosci 2016;36(2):364–74.

[120] Betts MJ, Acosta-Cabronero J, Cardenas-Blanco A, Nestor PJ, Duzel E. High-resolution characterisation of the aging brain using simultaneous quantitative susceptibility mapping (QSM) and R2* measurements at 7T. NeuroImage 2016;138:43–63.

[121] Darki F, Nemmi F, Moller A, Sitnikov R, Klingberg T. Quantitative susceptibility mapping of striatum in children and adults, and its association with working memory performance. NeuroImage 2016;136:208–14.

[122] Keuken MC, Bazin PL, Backhouse K, Beekhuizen S, Himmer L, Kandola A, et al. Effects of aging on T(1), T(2)*, and QSM MRI values in the subcortex. Brain Struct Funct 2017;222(6):2487–505.

[123] Peterson ET, Kwon D, Luna B, Larsen B, Prouty D, De Bellis MD, et al. Distribution of brain iron accrual in adolescence: evidence from cross-sectional and longitudinal analysis. Hum Brain Mapp 2019;40(5):1480–95.

[124] Zhang Y, Wei H, Cronin MJ, He N, Yan F, Liu C. Longitudinal data for magnetic susceptibility of normative human brain development and aging over the lifespan. Data Brief 2018;20:623–31.

[125] Zhang Y, Wei H, Cronin MJ, He N, Yan F, Liu C. Longitudinal atlas for normative human brain development and aging over the lifespan using quantitative susceptibility mapping. NeuroImage 2018; 171:176–89.

[126] O'Gorman RL, Shmueli K, Ashkan K, Samuel M, Lythgoe DJ, Shahidiani A, et al. Optimal MRI methods for direct stereotactic targeting of the subthalamic nucleus and globus pallidus. Eur Radiol 2011; 21(1):130–6.

[127] Liu T, Eskreis-Winkler S, Schweitzer AD, Chen WW, Kaplitt MG, Tsiouris AJ, Wang Y. Improved Subthalamic nucleus depiction with quantitative susceptibility mapping. Radiology 2013;269(1):216–23.

[128] Chandran AS, Bynevelt M, Lind CRP. Magnetic resonance imaging of the subthalamic nucleus for deep brain stimulation. J Neurosurg 2016;124(1):96–105.

[129] Lotfipour AK, Wharton S, Schwarz ST, Gontu V, Schafer A, Peters AM, et al. High resolution magnetic susceptibility mapping of the substantia nigra in Parkinson's disease. J Magn Reson Imaging 2012;35(1):48–55.

[130] Ide S, Kakeda S, Ueda I, Watanabe K, Murakami Y, Moriya J, et al. Internal structures of the globus pallidus in patients with Parkinson's disease: evaluation with quantitative susceptibility mapping (QSM). Eur Radiol 2014;25(3):710–8.

[131] Barbosa JHO, Santos AC, Tumas V, Liu MJ, Zheng WL, Haacke EM, Salmon CEG. Quantifying brain iron deposition in patients with Parkinson's disease using quantitative susceptibility mapping, R2 and R2. Magn Reson Imaging 2015;33(5):559–65.

[132] He NY, Ling HW, Ding B, Huang J, Zhang Y, Zhang ZP, et al. Region-specific disturbed iron distribution in early idiopathic Parkinson's disease measured by quantitative susceptibility mapping. Hum Brain Mapp 2015;36(11):4407–20.

[133] Murakami Y, Kakeda S, Watanabe K, Ueda I, Ogasawara A, Moriya J, et al. Usefulness of quantitative susceptibility mapping for the diagnosis of Parkinson disease. AJNR Am J Neuroradiol 2015;36(6):1102–8.

[134] Acosta-Cabronero J, Cardenas-Blanco A, Betts MJ, Butryn M, Valdes-Herrera JP, Galazky I, Nestor PJ. The whole-brain pattern of magnetic susceptibility perturbations in Parkinson's disease. Brain 2017; 140(1):118–31.

[135] Azuma M, Hirai T, Yamada K, Yamashita S, Ando Y, Tateishi M, et al. Lateral asymmetry and spatial difference of iron deposition in the substantia nigra of patients with Parkinson disease measured with quantitative susceptibility mapping. Am J Neuroradiol 2016;37(5):782–8.

[136] Du GW, Liu T, Lewis MM, Kong L, Wang Y, Connor J, et al. Quantitative susceptibility mapping of the midbrain in Parkinson's disease. Mov Disord 2016;31(3):317–24.

[137] Langkammer C, Pirpamer L, Seiler S, Deistung A, Schweser F, Franthal S, et al. Quantitative susceptibility mapping in Parkinson's disease. PLos One 2016;11(9):e0162460.

[138] Guan X, Xuan M, Gu Q, Huang P, Liu C, Wang N, et al. Regionally progressive accumulation of iron in Parkinson's disease as measured by quantitative susceptibility mapping. NMR Biomed 2017;30(4): e3489.

[139] van Bergen JM, Li X, Hua J, Schreiner SJ, Steininger SC, Quevenco FC, et al. Colocalization of cerebral iron with amyloid beta in mild cognitive impairment. Sci Rep 2016;6:35514.

[140] Ayton S, Fazlollahi A, Bourgeat P, Raniga P, Ng A, Lim YY, et al. Cerebral quantitative susceptibility mapping predicts amyloid-beta-related cognitive decline. Brain 2017;140(8):2112–9.

[141] Acosta-Cabronero J, Williams GB, Cardenas-Blanco A, Arnold RJ, Lupson V, Nestor PJ. In vivo quantitative susceptibility mapping (QSM) in Alzheimer's disease. PLos One 2013;8(11):e81093.

[142] Moon Y, Han SH, Moon WJ. Patterns of brain iron accumulation in vascular dementia and Alzheimer's dementia using quantitative susceptibility mapping imaging. J Alzheimers Dis 2016;51(3):737–45.

[143] Klohs J, Deistung A, Schweser F, Grandjean J, Dominietto M, Waschkies C, et al. Detection of cerebral microbleeds with quantitative susceptibility mapping in the ArcAbeta mouse model of cerebral amyloidosis. J Cereb Blood Flow Metab 2011;31(12):2282–92.

[144] O'Callaghan J, Holmes H, Powell N, Wells JA, Ismail O, Harrison IF, et al. Tissue magnetic susceptibility mapping as a marker of tau pathology in Alzheimer's disease. NeuroImage 2017;159:334–45.

[145] Fan AP, Govindarajan ST, Kinkel RP, Madigan NK, Nielsen AS, Benner T, et al. Quantitative oxygen extraction fraction from 7-Tesla MRI phase: reproducibility and application in multiple sclerosis. J Cereb Blood Flow Metab 2015;35(1):131–9.

[146] Ozbay PS, Rossi C, Kocian R, Redle M, Boss A, Pruessmann KP, Nanz D. Effect of respiratory hyperoxic challenge on magnetic susceptibility in human brain assessed by quantitative susceptibility mapping (QSM). NMR Biomed 2015;28(12):1688–96.

[147] Hsieh MC, Kuo LW, Huang YA, Chen JH. Investigating hyperoxic effects in the rat brain using quantitative susceptibility mapping based on MRI phase. Magn Reson Med 2017;77(2):592–602.

[148] Hsieh MC, Tsai CY, Liao MC, Yang JL, Su CH, Chen JH. Quantitative susceptibility mapping-based microscopy of magnetic resonance venography (QSM-mMRV) for in vivo morphologically and functionally assessing cerebromicrovasculature in rat stroke model. PLoS One 2016;11(3):e0149602.

[149] Wehrli FW, Fan AP, Rodgers ZB, Englund EK, Langham MC. Susceptibility-based time-resolved whole-organ and regional tissue oximetry. NMR Biomed 2017;30(4):e3495.

[150] Reichenbach JR. The future of susceptibility contrast for assessment of anatomy and function. NeuroImage 2012;62(2):1311–5.

[151] Balla DZ, Sanchez-Panchuelo RM, Wharton SJ, Hagberg GE, Scheffler K, Francis ST, Bowtell R. Functional quantitative susceptibility mapping (fQSM). NeuroImage 2014;100:112–24.

[152] Bianciardi M, van Gelderen P, Duyn JH. Investigation of BOLD fMRI resonance frequency shifts and quantitative susceptibility changes at 7 T. Hum Brain Mapp 2014;35(5):2191–205.
[153] Chen Z, Calhoun VD. Task-evoked brain functional magnetic susceptibility mapping by independent component analysis (chiICA). J Neurosci Methods 2016;261:161–71.
[154] Ozbay PS, Warnock G, Rossi C, Kuhn F, Akin B, Pruessmann KP, Nanz D. Probing neuronal activation by functional quantitative susceptibility mapping under a visual paradigm: a group level comparison with BOLD fMRI and PET. NeuroImage 2016;137:52–60.
[155] Sun H, Seres P, Wilman AH. Structural and functional quantitative susceptibility mapping from standard fMRI studies. NMR Biomed 2017;30(4):e3619.
[156] Liu T, Surapaneni K, Lou M, Ch eng LQ, Spincemaille P, Wang Y. Cerebral microbleeds: burden assessment by using quantitative susceptibility mapping. Radiology 2012;262(1):269–78.
[157] Klohs J, Politano IW, Deistung A, Grandjean J, Drewek A, Dominietto M, et al. Longitudinal assessment of amyloid pathology in transgenic ArcA beta mice using multi-parametric magnetic resonance imaging. PLoS One 2013;8(6):e66097.
[158] Tan H, Liu T, Wu Y, Thacker J, Shenkar R, Mikati AG, et al. Evaluation of iron content in human cerebral cavernous malformation using quantitative susceptibility mapping. Investig Radiol 2014;49(7):498–504.
[159] Chary K, Nissi MJ, Rey RI, Manninen E, Shmueli K, Sierra A, Grohn O. Quantitative susceptibility mapping of the rat brain after traumatic brain injury, In: Proceedings of the 24th Annual Meeting of the International Society for Magnetic Resonance in Medicine, Singapore, vol. 24; 2016, p. 34.
[160] Liu W, Soderlund K, Senseney JS, Joy D, Yeh PH, Ollinger J, et al. Imaging cerebral microhemorrhages in military service members with chronic traumatic brain injury. Radiology 2016;278(2):536–45.
[161] Schweser F, Herrmann K-H, Deistung A, Atterbury M, Baltzer PA, Burmeister HP, et al. Quantitative magnetic susceptibility mapping (QSM) in breast disease reveals additional information for MR-based characterization of carcinoma and calcification, In: Proceedings 19th Scientific Meeting, International Society for Magnetic Resonance in Medicine; 2011. p. 1014.
[162] Deistung A, Schweser F, Wiestler B, Abello M, Roethke M, Sahm F, et al. Quantitative susceptibility mapping differentiates between blood depositions and calcifications in patients with glioblastoma. PLoS One 2013;8(3):e57924.
[163] Yablonskiy DA, Luo J, Sukstanskii AL, Iyer A, Cross AH. Biophysical mechanisms of MRI signal frequency contrast in multiple sclerosis. Proc Natl Acad Sci U S A 2012;109(35):14212–7.
[164] Yao B, Bagnato F, Matsuura E, Merkle H, van Gelderen P, Cantor FK, Duyn JH. Chronic multiple sclerosis lesions: characterization with high-field-strength MR imaging. Radiology 2012;262(1):206–15.
[165] Langkammer C, Liu T, Khalil M, Enzinger C, Jehna M, Fuchs S, et al. Quantitative susceptibility mapping in multiple sclerosis. Radiology 2013;267(2):551–9.
[166] Chen W, Gauthier SA, Gupta A, Comunale J, Liu T, Wang S, et al. Quantitative susceptibility mapping of multiple sclerosis lesions at various ages. Radiology 2014;271(1):183–92.
[167] Eskreis-Winkler S, Deh K, Gupta A, Liu T, Wisnieff C, Jin M, et al. Multiple sclerosis lesion geometry in quantitative susceptibility mapping (QSM) and phase imaging. J Magn Reson Imaging 2015;42(1):224–9.
[168] Wisnieff C, Ramanan S, Olesik J, Gauthier S, Wang Y, Pitt D. Quantitative susceptibility mapping (QSM) of white matter multiple sclerosis lesions: interpreting positive susceptibility and the presence of iron. Magn Reson Med 2015;74(2):564–70.
[169] Cronin MJ, Wharton S, Al-Radaideh A, Constantinescu C, Evangelou N, Bowtell R, Gowland PA. A comparison of phase imaging and quantitative susceptibility mapping in the imaging of multiple sclerosis lesions at ultrahigh field. MAGMA 2016;29(3):543–57.
[170] Li X, Harrison DM, Liu H, Jones CK, Oh J, Calabresi PA, van Zijl PC. Magnetic susceptibility contrast variations in multiple sclerosis lesions. J Magn Reson Imaging 2016;43(2):463–73.
[171] Stuber C, Pitt D, Wang Y. Iron in multiple sclerosis and its noninvasive imaging with quantitative susceptibility mapping. Int J Mol Sci 2016;17(1):e100.

[172] Zhang Y, Gauthier SA, Gupta A, Comunale J, Chia-Yi Chiang G, Zhou D, et al. Longitudinal change in magnetic susceptibility of new enhanced multiple sclerosis (MS) lesions measured on serial quantitative susceptibility mapping (QSM). J Magn Reson Imaging 2016;44(2):426–32.
[173] Duyn JH. Frequency shifts in the myelin water compartment. Magn Reson Med 2014;71(6):1953–5.
[174] Duyn JH, Barbara TM. Sphere of lorentz and demagnetization factors in white matter. Magn Reson Med 2014;72(1):1–3.
[175] Sukstanskii AL, Yablonskiy DA. On the role of neuronal magnetic susceptibility and structure symmetry on gradient Echo MR signal formation. Magn Reson Med 2014;71(1):345–53.
[176] Yablonskiy DA, He X, Luo J, Sukstanskii AL. Lorentz sphere versus generalized lorentzian approach: what would lorentz say about it? Magn Reson Med 2014;72(1):4–7.
[177] Yablonskiy DA, Sukstanskii AL. Biophysical mechanisms of myelin-induced water frequency shifts. Magn Reson Med 2014;71(6):1956–8.
[178] Yablonskiy DA, Sukstanskii AL. Generalized Lorentzian Tensor Approach (GLTA) as a biophysical background for quantitative susceptibility mapping. Magn Reson Med 2015;73(2):757–64.
[179] Yablonskiy DA, Sukstanskii AL. Effects of biological tissue structural anisotropy and anisotropy of magnetic susceptibility on the gradient echo MRI signal phase: theoretical background. NMR Biomed 2017;30(4):e3655.
[180] Yablonskiy DA, Sukstanskii AL. Lorentzian effects in magnetic susceptibility mapping of anisotropic biological tissues. J Magn Reson 2018;292:129–36.
[181] Shmueli K, Dodd SJ, Li TQ, Duyn JH. The contribution of chemical exchange to MRI frequency shifts in brain tissue. Magn Reson Med 2011;65(1):35–43.
[182] Shmueli K, Dodd SJ, van Gelderen P, Duyn JH. Investigating lipids as a source of chemical exchange-induced MRI frequency shifts. NMR Biomed 2017;30(4):e3525.
[183] Schweser F, Zivadinov R. Quantitative susceptibility mapping (QSM) with an extended physical model for MRI frequency contrast in the brain: a proof-of-concept of quantitative susceptibility and residual (QUASAR) mapping. NMR Biomed 2018;31(12):e3999.
[184] van Gelderen P, Jiang X, Duyn JH. Rapid measurement of brain macromolecular proton fraction with transient saturation transfer MRI. Magn Reson Med 2017;77(6):2174–85.
[185] Lee J, Shin HG, Jung W, Nam Y, Oh SH, Lee J. An R2* model of white matter for fiber orientation and myelin concentration. NeuroImage 2017;162:269–75.
[186] Kaden E, Rudrapatna U, Barskaya IY, Does MD, Jones DK, Alexander DC. Microscopic susceptibility anisotropy imaging: a clinically viable gradient-echo MRI technique, In: Proceedings of the International Society for Magnetic Resonance in Medicine, Paris, France, vol. 26; 2018, p. 192.
[187] Dibb R, Xie L, Wei H, Liu C. Magnetic susceptibility anisotropy outside the central nervous system. NMR Biomed 2017;30(4):e3544.
[188] Wei H, Dibb R, Decker K, Wang N, Zhang Y, Zong X, et al. Investigating magnetic susceptibility of human knee joint at 7 Tesla. Magn Reson Med 2017;78(5):1933–43.
[189] Finnerty E, Ramasawmy R, O'Callaghan J, Connell JJ, Lythgoe M, Shmueli K, et al. Noninvasive quantification of oxygen saturation in the portal and hepatic veins in healthy mice and those with colorectal liver metastases using QSM MRI. Magn Reson Med 2019;81(4):2666–75.
[190] Lin H, Wei H, He N, Fu C, Cheng S, Shen J, et al. Quantitative susceptibility mapping in combination with water-fat separation for simultaneous liver iron and fat fraction quantification. Eur Radiol 2018;28(8):3494–504.
[191] Nykanen O, Rieppo L, Toyras J, Kolehmainen V, Saarakkala S, Shmueli K, Nissi MJ. Quantitative susceptibility mapping of articular cartilage: ex vivo findings at multiple orientations and following different degradation treatments. Magn Reson Med 2018;80(6):2702–16.
[192] Wen Y, Nguyen TD, Liu Z, Spincemaille P, Zhou D, Dimov A, et al. Cardiac quantitative susceptibility mapping (QSM) for heart chamber oxygenation. Magn Reson Med 2018;79(3):1545–52.

CHAPTER

Magnetization Transfer

32

Tobias C. Wood[a] and Shaihan J. Malik[b]

[a]*Department of Neuroimaging, King's College London, London, United Kingdom* [b]*School of Imaging Sciences and Biomedical Engineering, King's College London, London, United Kingdom*

32.1 Introduction

The typical resolution of an MR image (on the order of millimeters) is several orders of magnitude larger than typical biological structures in tissue (on the order of micrometers). These structures, including cell membranes, myelin, intracellular and extracellular spaces, each encompass a different physical environment with distinct characteristics. Hence, it is incorrect to treat the MR signal from biological tissue as arising from protons with a single longitudinal and transverse relaxation time. A more accurate approach is to model the signal as arising from multiple components, or pools, of magnetization with their own relaxation characteristics. A particular class of these models considers water (aqueous) protons interacting with protons from different molecules entirely. Within the MRI literature these effects are typically referred to under the term "magnetization transfer" (MT).

Tissues such as the brain and cartilage incorporate long-chain hydrocarbons in the form of various lipids and proteins. These molecules contain large quantities of nonaqueous hydrogen protons, which results in increased spin-lattice interactions and shortened longitudinal relaxation times. The nonaqueous protons have very short transverse relaxation times, which also results in broad excitation spectra. The protons bound to these molecules can hence interact with radiofrequency (RF) pulses applied at a frequency distant from the aqueous proton resonance frequency. If an off-resonance saturation pulse is applied, the nonaqueous proton longitudinal magnetization is reduced, although the aqueous proton magnetization is undisturbed.

If the aqueous and nonaqueous protons can exchange with each other after the application of this off-resonance saturation pulse, then after a short time of mixing the aqueous magnetization will be reduced by inflow from the nonaqueous pool. The reduced aqueous longitudinal magnetization can then be excited by an on-resonance RF pulse and read-out. In tissues with large amounts of nonaqueous protons, this process can lead to a large reduction in signal intensity. This gives rise to the so-called MT contrast first demonstrated by Wolff and Balaban [1]. A simple method for visualizing the MT effect is to compare images obtained with S_{sat} and without a saturation pulse S_{ref}, as shown in Fig. 32.1. The MT ratio ($MTR = 1\text{-}\frac{S_{sat}}{S_{ref}}$) can be calculated and used to directly visualize the tissues in which the MT effect is significant. Although such a ratio is semiquantitative, the observed value depends critically on the imaging sequence as well as the tissue parameters, so it is not a truly quantitative measurement [2]. MTRs can, however, be used to compare tissues acquired using the same pulse sequence.

Advances in Magnetic Resonance Technology and Applications. Volume 1. ISSN 2666-9099. https://doi.org/10.1016/B978-0-12-817057-1.00035-4

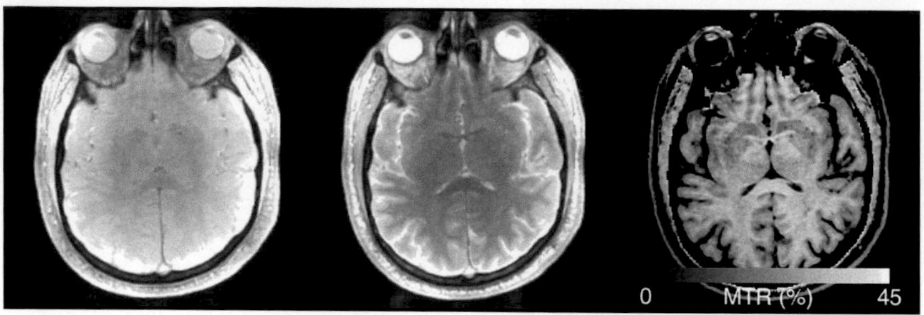

FIG. 32.1

An example of magnetization transfer contrast. *Left*: a proton density-weighted (long TR, low flip angle) gradient echo image. *Center*: adding an off-resonance (2 kHz) saturation pulse to the sequence reduces the signal intensity in white matter, leading to a large increase in contrast between white and gray matter. The windowing of both images is the same. *Right*: the magnetization transfer ratio is the fraction of signal reduction caused by the saturation pulse.

There are multiple mechanisms by which magnetization can be exchanged between aqueous and nonaqueous protons in close proximity. The dominant mechanism is thought to be simple dipole-dipole interactions, in which only magnetization is "exchanged." In certain circumstances, it is possible for the protons themselves to exchange between a water molecule and the nonaqueous molecule. A distinction is often drawn in the literature between MT, which involves water and long-chain semisolid molecules, and chemical exchange saturation transfer (CEST), which involves water and shorter chain labile molecules. These shorter molecules have an intermediate transverse relaxation rate and hence require slightly different measurement approaches when compared to MT.

Although most biological structures are relatively unordered on the microscopic scale, myelin in particular is highly ordered and semicrystalline in nature. This property allows it to sustain dipolar-order effects, which can lead to an enhanced rate of MT at specific frequency offsets [3,4] and different behavior under single and dual frequency saturation. Such "inhomogeneous" magnetization transfer (ihMT) is thought to be highly specific to myelin, although other ordered tissues such as muscle can also produce a weak ihMT effect [5–7]. An example of the difference between MT and ihMT is shown in Fig. 32.2.

Because almost all tissues in the body contain nonnegligible amounts of hydrocarbons, MT effects are common and have been widely exploited to generate informative contrast. However, an underappreciated issue is how MT affects imaging sequences more generally, and hence influences other quantitative imaging techniques. This is a particular concern in measurements of relaxation times, where it is common to assume that only a single pool of water protons exists in a voxel. In this chapter, we will describe how MT can be modeled and then demonstrate how it can affect various common quantitative methods.

32.2 Modeling MT effects

Systems of exchanging magnetic pools are usually modeled with the Bloch-McConnell equations [8]. While these equations are appropriate for modeling general multicompartment systems, including CEST where the exchanging protons are mobile [9] (see Chapter 33), MT can be better modeled by the phenomenological binary spin bath model [10]. This model assumes two pools of magnetization,

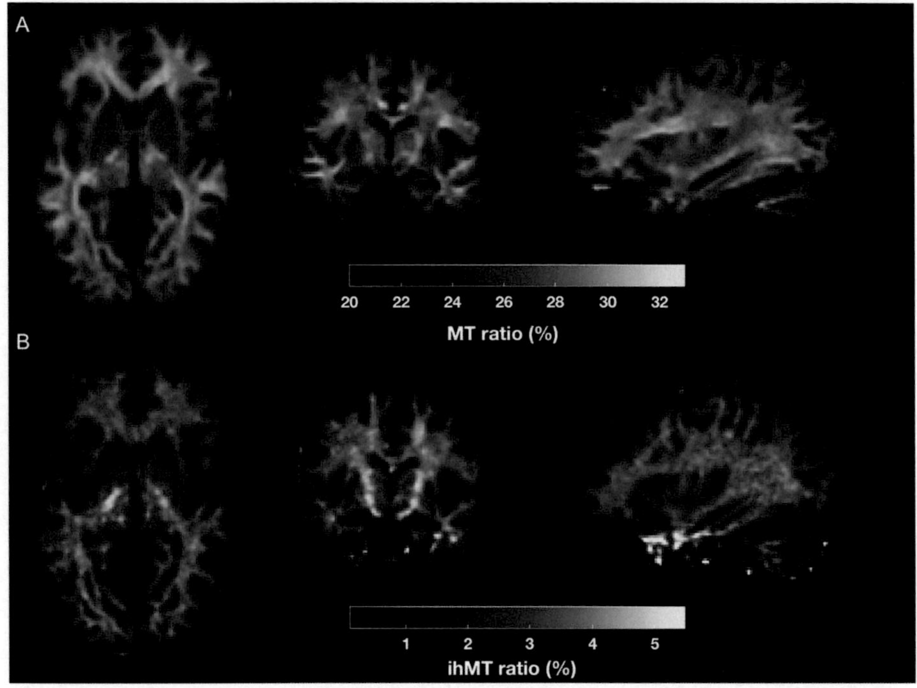

FIG. 32.2

Maps showing the magnetization transfer ratio (MTR; A) and inhomogenous magnetization transfer ratio (ihMTR; B) in the same subject. The latter typically shows more white-matter-specific contrast.

Image reproduced from Malik SJ, Teixeira RPAG, West DJ, Wood TC, Hajnal JV. Steady-state imaging with inhomogeneous magnetization transfer contrast using multiband radiofrequency pulses. Magn Reson Med 2019. https://doi.org/10.1002/mrm.27984.

one of which represents aqueous protons or "free" water, and the other represents nonaqueous protons. Different names are used throughout the literature for this pool, including the "bound," "restricted," "macromolecular," or "semisolid" pool; in this chapter, the latter will be used. The important distinction between this model and the Bloch-McConnell equations is that the transverse magnetization of the semisolid pool is not modeled, and hence only the longitudinal magnetization is permitted to exchange between pools. Under this assumption, the state vector for the system becomes

$$\mathbf{m} = \left[m_{xf} \;\; m_{yf} \;\; m_{zf} \;\; m_{zs}\right]^T \tag{32.1}$$

where the subscripts f and s refer to the free and semisolid pools, and x, y, z refer to the magnetization components. We define the proton density in the two pools as M_{0f} and M_{0s}. In a real experiment, the apparent proton densities will also be influenced by receive coil (B_1^-) inhomogeneity and arbitrary scanner scaling factors. It is hence useful to express instead the relative amount of nonaqueous protons. Two conventions exist; one is the pool-size ratio (PSR) defined as $F = M_{0s}/M_{0f}$, and the other is the semisolid fraction defined as $f_s = M_{0s}/(M_{0f} + M_{0s})$ (note in several papers the semisolid fraction is denoted as f_b as the authors refer to the semisolid pool as the bound pool). It is also useful to define the free-water fraction $f_f = 1 - f_s$, and to note that $F = f_s/(1 - f_s)$.

The system dynamics can then be expressed as:

$$\dot{\mathbf{m}} = \mathbf{A}\mathbf{m} + \mathbf{C} \tag{32.2}$$

from which **A** can be decomposed as $\mathbf{A} = \Lambda + \Omega$ where

$$\Lambda = \begin{bmatrix} -R_{2f} & \delta\omega & 0 & 0 \\ -\delta\omega & -R_{2f} & 0 & 0 \\ 0 & 0 & -R_{1f}\text{-}kf_s & kf_f \\ 0 & 0 & kf_s & -R_{1s}\text{-}kf_f \end{bmatrix} \quad \Omega = \begin{bmatrix} 0 & 0 & -\gamma B_{1,y} & 0 \\ 0 & 0 & \gamma B_{1,x} & 0 \\ \gamma B_{1,y} & -\gamma B_{1,x} & 0 & 0 \\ 0 & 0 & 0 & -W \end{bmatrix} \quad \mathbf{C} = \begin{bmatrix} 0 \\ 0 \\ R_{1f}M_{0f} \\ R_{1s}M_{0s} \end{bmatrix} \tag{32.3}$$

The matrix Λ contains relaxation effects also included in the Bloch equation, where the relaxation times are described here as rates $R_1 = 1/T_1$ and $R_2 = 1/T_2$, and $\delta\omega$ represents any frequency offset between the free compartment and the scanner center frequency, as with the standard Bloch equations approach. Note that the free and semisolid compartments each have distinct longitudinal relaxation rates. The vector **C** describes recovery to thermal equilibrium. In addition, Λ describes exchange between the free and semisolid compartments with an intrinsic rate k. The forward (free to semisolid) and backward (semisolid to free) exchange rates are obtained by multiplying k by the relative proton density (f_s and f_f) in the opposite pool [11]. This is true assuming that mass equilibrium is maintained, that is, the relative fraction of protons in each pool is constant and only magnetization exchanges back and forth.

The matrix Ω describes the effect of RF pulses with rotating frame transverse magnetic field $\mathbf{B_1} = [B_{1,x} B_{1,y}]$ applied at an offset frequency Δ. The upper left 3×3 part of Ω describes the effect of RF pulses on the free water compartment, and is identical to the treatment in the regular Bloch equation, where a Lorentzian lineshape intrinsically arises from the interaction of transverse relaxation and RF excitation. In contrast, the lineshape G of the semisolid pool must be modeled explicitly and enters the equations via the saturation rate $W = \pi\gamma^2|B_1|^2 G(\Delta;T_{2s})$. In general, $\mathbf{B_1}$ is time-varying, particularly for sequences involving short RF pulses, as opposed to continuous wave saturation. It is common practice in this scenario to replace the instantaneous saturation rate W with $\langle W \rangle$, which is the root-mean-square saturation over the duration of the RF pulse [12,13]. Note that $W(\Delta = 0)$ is not necessarily negligible—that is, on-resonance RF pulses can also affect the magnetization of the semisolid protons.

The lineshape is a function of both the offset frequency and the relaxation time of the semisolid pool (T_{2s}). In simple substances such as agar gel, a Gaussian is an appropriate lineshape [10]. The prevailing best model for more complex substances, such as myelin, is the super-Lorentzian [14]. Although in a normal MR experiment the transverse magnetization of the semisolid pool decays before it can be observed, it can be measured in an NMR spectrum or using specialized MR hardware, and the super-Lorentzian and its Fourier transform (the super exponential) have been, respectively, shown to fit the spectrum and free induction decay of myelin [15,16]. A significant problem with the super-Lorentzian is that the mathematical description diverges at the resonance frequency, which is unrealistic. Practical approaches to dealing with this are either to only acquire data where the super-Lorentzian fits the data well (i.e., above 1 kHz offsets) or to interpolate the lineshape values below a similar threshold [17]. Examples of different lineshapes are shown in Fig. 32.3. The lineshape in white matter has been measured to be offset from water by approximately 2.5 ppm [18], illustrated by the offset in the diagram. This is a combination of the chemical shift of the protons in the semisolid (thought to be dominated by methylene protons in myelin, for example) and structural susceptibility shifts due to microstructure [19].

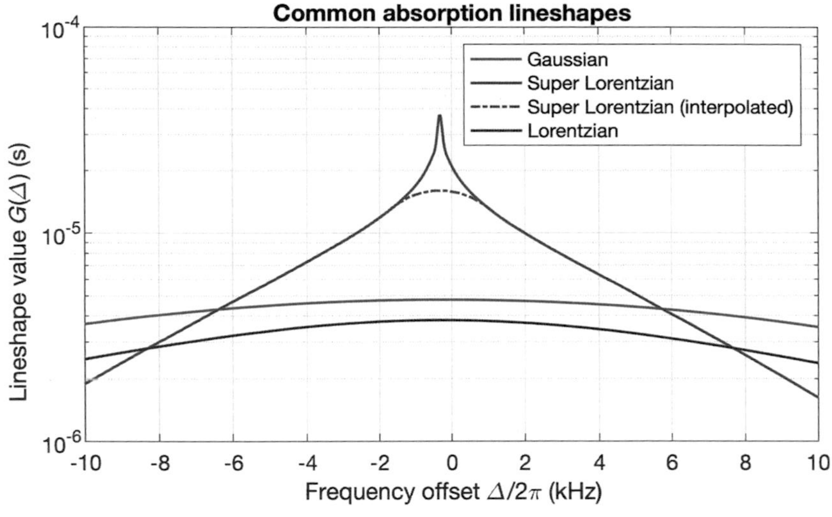

FIG. 32.3

Some common lineshapes—the super-Lorentzian may be the most commonly used function for modeling signals in biological tissue. $G(\Delta; T_{2s})$ is a function of T_{2s}; in these examples T_{2s} was fixed at 12 μs.

The so-called "inhomogeneous" MT effect occurs when saturation using dual frequency irradiation at $\pm\Delta$ produces different results when compared with saturation at these frequencies separately. This effect was shown *not* to be due to an asymmetry in the absorption lineshape; indeed, the effect cannot be explained by the mathematical model for MT described so far. The name "inhomogeneous" was motivated by the initial interpretation that this effect was due to inhomogeneous broadening of the semisolid absorption line. Subsequent work has, however, shown that the ihMT effect can actually be understood by the inclusion of dipolar-order effects into the mathematical model [3,4,20]. The semisolid pool is further subdivided into "Zeeman" and "dipolar"-order subcompartments that exchange with one another [6,20,21]. Crucially this exchange only occurs under *off-resonance* RF irradiation, and the effect is linear in frequency offset such that a dual frequency irradiation at $\pm\Delta$ cancels the coupling, yielding the observed difference between single and dual frequency saturation. For a full mathematical description, see Malik et al. [22]. Dipolar-order effects were discussed at length in Morrison et al. [23] and appear in other work on quantitative MT [24] but were subsequently neglected until the work of Varma et al. [6] and Girard et al. [5] who proposed the use of dual frequency saturation to probe the effect more directly.

32.3 Effects of MT on relaxometry

Relaxation measurement approaches are often designed under the assumption that the MR signal from a tissue is well described by the Bloch equations (see Section 32.1). The presence of strong MT effects can therefore be seriously disruptive to relaxometry, and the effect will differ depending on the sequences used and how the data are analyzed.

32.3.1 Inversion recovery measurement of R_1

Inversion recovery is perhaps the "gold standard" method for measuring longitudinal relaxation times, as described in Chapter 2. Typically measurements are obtained by collecting images at different delay times t after an inversion pulse, then fitting the expected signal relationship to obtain R_1:

$$S(t) = 1 - 2e^{-R_1 t} \tag{32.4}$$

However, Eq. (32.2) suggests that recovery follows a different dynamic when MT effects are present. Rather than being governed by a single relaxation rate R_1, the longitudinal magnetizations from the free and semisolid compartments evolve as a coupled system governed by the following equation:

$$\frac{d}{dt}\begin{bmatrix} m_{zf} \\ m_{zs} \end{bmatrix} = \begin{bmatrix} -R_{1f}\text{-}kf_s & kf_f \\ kf_s & -R_{1s}\text{-}kf_f \end{bmatrix}\begin{bmatrix} m_{zf} \\ m_{zs} \end{bmatrix} + \begin{bmatrix} R_{1f}M_{0f} \\ R_{1s}M_{0s} \end{bmatrix} \tag{32.5}$$

$$\dot{\mathbf{m}}_{\mathbf{z}} = \Lambda_{\mathbf{L}}\mathbf{m}_{\mathbf{z}} + \mathbf{C}_{\mathbf{L}} \tag{32.6}$$

where RF effects have been excluded. Hence, after inversion the system exhibits biexponential recovery with two relaxation rates that are the eigenvalues of the matrix Λ_L [10], as illustrated in Fig. 32.4. Typically there is one fast rate and one slower rate; the latter dominates recovery at most delay times longer than a few tens or hundreds of milliseconds. This slower rate is usually referred to as the "observed" relaxation rate R_1^{obs} and can be related to the underlying model parameters in the following way:

$$R_1^{obs} = \frac{1}{2}\left\{R_{1f} + R_{1s} + k - \sqrt{(R_{1f} + R_{1s} + k)^2 - 4(R_{1f}R_{1s} + R_{1f}kf_f + R_{1s}kf_s)}\right\} \tag{32.7}$$

It should therefore be kept in mind that for a tissue that can be described by this two compartment model, the classic inversion recovery measurement does not yield the free water relaxation rate.

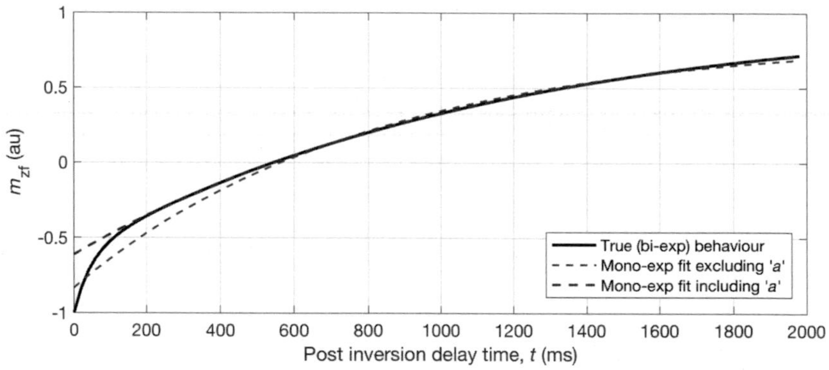

FIG. 32.4

Inversion recovery behavior when MT effects are present. The *black curve* is a plot of the biexponential behavior that is observed. The *dotted lines* show the result of fitting these data (excluding times below 400 ms) with a monoexponential function as is usually done. The longer relaxation time constant R_1^{obs} can be more reliably estimated if fitting to a function of the form shown in Eq. (32.8). When a is allowed to vary, a good fit can be obtained, where the estimated R_1 is equal to R_1^{obs}.

Rather it measures R_1^{obs}, which is in fact a composite of the relaxation rates from both compartments, and the exchange rate. Another important consideration is that if fitting a mono-exponential relationship to observed data, the observed signal curve does not follow the form in Eq. (32.4). More stable results can be obtained by fitting a function of the form

$$S(t) = 1 - 2ae^{-R_1 t} \tag{32.8}$$

where a is a parameter to be estimated. The standard use of $a < 1$ accounts for the reduced "inversion efficiency" of the RF inversion pulse, that is, an inversion flip angle of less than 180° which may result from nonuniform B_1 for example. In practice, for a coupled system, this parameter can also be used to account for the presence of early biexponential recovery, and including it will lead to improved stability in the estimation of R_1^{obs}, as shown in Fig. 32.4. Hence, the actual value of a depends on multiple factors, including B_1, the relative pool sizes, and how much the inversion pulse also saturates the semisolid magnetization [18].

32.3.2 Spin echo measurement of R_2

Eq. (32.3) implies that while the presence of semisolid protons has a significant effect on longitudinal relaxation, it does not affect transverse relaxation. Hence, it may be expected that measurements of R_2 would not be affected by MT. R_2 is often measured using spin echo or multi-spin echo pulse sequences (see Chapter 3 for more information), and it is commonplace to use multislice versions of the former to make image acquisition more efficient. Multislice acquisitions are strongly MT-weighted because the excitation and refocusing pulses applied to neighboring slices are seen by the semisolid protons in a given location as off-resonance saturation. Hence, though the aqueous protons within a given slice are not affected by the acquisition of neighboring slices, the nonaqueous protons are [25]. Though the main impact of this effect is on longitudinal magnetization, small differences between single and multislice R_2 measurements have been observed in brain tissue [26]. This can be explained by the fact that myelin sheaths are arranged in layers, with water in between alternating layers of lipids and protons [27]. This "trapped" water has a much shorter T_2 than free water in the intraaxonal and extraaxonal spaces, and also exchanges faster with the semisolids due to the close proximity [28]. Hence, depending on the exact MT properties of a particular sequence (pulse power and spacing), the signal from pools with different T_2 values can be attenuated differently, leading to bias in the measurement of a single T_2 value [28].

32.3.3 Steady-state measurements of R_1 and R_2

There are a number of relaxometry methods that measure signals in the steady-state and go by a wide variety of names. Perhaps the most familiar of these is the variable flip angle (VFA) or driven equilibrium single pulse observation of T_1 (DESPOT) sequence, which uses multiple fully spoiled gradient echo images acquired at different flip angles to estimate T_1 [29,30]. Similar methods incorporate balanced steady-state free-precession images to estimate T_2 [31,32] or use images acquired at different phase increments instead of flip angles [33,34].

As well as exciting the free-water magnetization for image formation, each RF pulse also acts to saturate the semisolid pool, as indicated by the parameter W in Eq. (32.3). For rapid gradient echo sequences in which the repetition time is short compared to the exchange times, we may treat the saturation from each individual RF pulse as a continuous wave irradiation with average power $\bar{W}$. The steady-state reached during imaging will then depend on $\bar{W}$. It can be demonstrated that under this condition, the system will respond with an apparent longitudinal relaxation rate [35]:

$$R_1^{app} = R_{1f} + kf_f\left(1 - \frac{kf_s}{R_{1s} + kf_s + \bar{W}}\right) \tag{32.9}$$

Hence, as $\bar{W} \to 0$, $R_1^{app} \to R_{1f} + \frac{kf_f R_{1s}}{R_{1s} + kf_s}$ while as $\bar{W} \to \infty$, $R_1^{app} \to R_{1f} + kf_f$, giving rise to a large range of possible measured R_1 values in brain tissues. This effect can be seen in Fig. 32.5 which shows brain T_1 maps acquired using different $\bar{W}$ (here given in terms of B_1^{rms}) [35]. Note that according to this analysis the transverse relaxation rate is unaffected.

A major challenge for relaxometry methods is that in general $\bar{W}$ is not held constant across all measurements. Indeed, in order to achieve the different flip angles required of some techniques, the excitation pulses are usually scaled either in amplitude or duration (or both) which directly changes $\bar{W}$. The effect of doing so is that individual measurements made in a VFA acquisition are effectively made for systems with different relaxation rates. Combining these measurements into the estimation of a single parameter therefore results in biases, where the measured values depend on the pulse sequences used. It should be stressed that here it is the *on-resonance* excitation pulses that are causing saturation of the semisolid magnetization. It is a common misconception that only off-resonance pulses lead to MT effects. In fact, saturation can be stronger on-resonance, as seen by examining the lineshape function. Off-resonance saturation is classically used to create MT contrast because these pulses can be used to affect the semisolid without affecting the free water; however, the effect of on-resonance saturation cannot be ignored. This effect has been observed by many authors; for example, Ou and Gochberg [36] go so far as to state that "T_1 quantification is inaccurate if MT is ignored." Teixeira et al. [37] showed that this effect causes major differences in measured relaxation times across

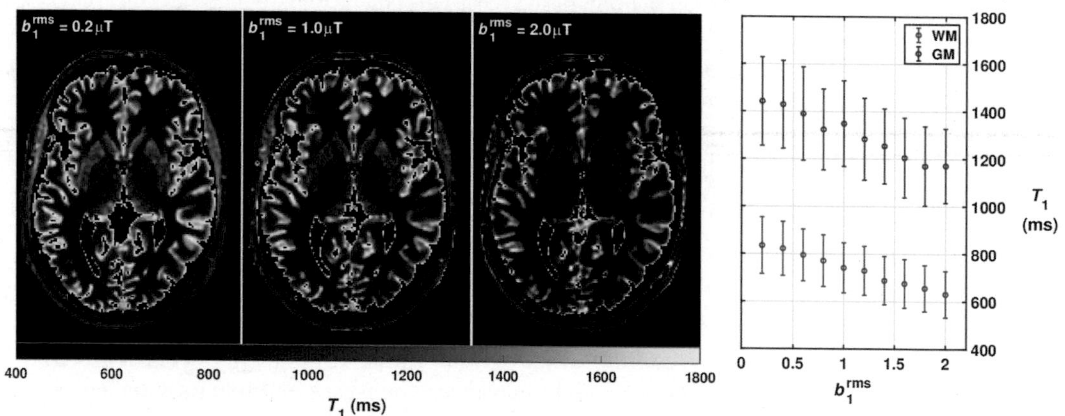

FIG. 32.5

T_1 estimated using VFA methods with different levels of RF power $\bar{W}$, here quantified by B_1^{rms} (in this figure denoted as b_1^{rms}). The estimated T_1 is a function of $\bar{W}$ as implied by Eq. (32.9). GM, gray matter; WM, white matter.

Reproduced from Teixeira RP, Malik SJ, Hajnal JV. Fast quantitative MRI using controlled saturation magnetization transfer. Magn Reson Med 2019; 81(2):907–920. https://doi.org/10.1002/mrm.27442.

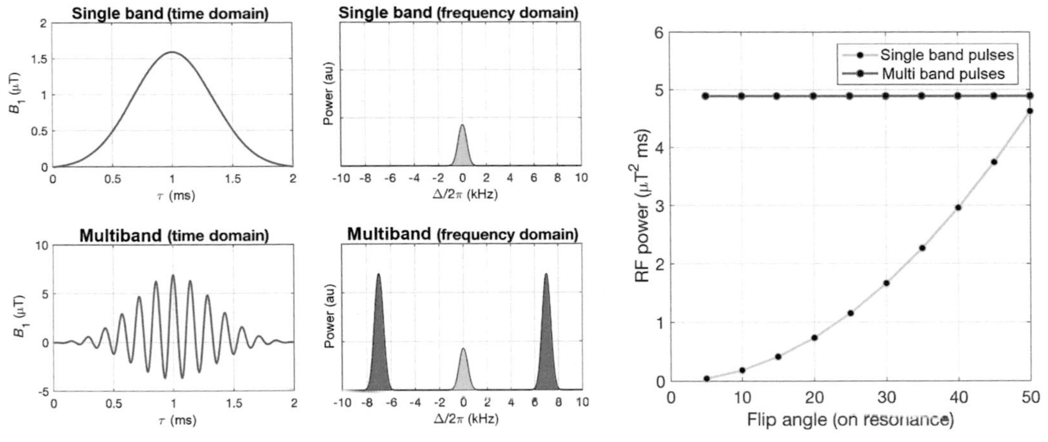

FIG. 32.6

Standard single band excitation pulse (*top, left*) compared with a multiband excitation (*bottom, left*). Their respective power spectra are shown in the central column. The pulses both have a flip angle of 20°, such that their on-resonance frequency component (*shaded green*) is the same. However, the multiband pulse also has additional off-resonance bands at ±7 kHz (*shaded red*). Semisolid saturation depends on the *total* RF power, that is, summed across all bands of the multiband pulses (weighted by the lineshape at each frequency). For the single band pulse, changing the flip angle means also changing the applied power, leading to variable saturation of semisolid magnetization. For the multiband case, the total RF power can be held constant by adding or taking away power from the off-resonance bands (*red*) as the power in the on-resonance band (*green*) changes with changing flip angle. The plot on the right illustrates how the RF power varies as a function of flip angle in the two cases; it has been shown that use of constant RF power across flip angles stabilizes VFA relaxometry methods [35,37].

vendor platforms and across protocols when using the same hardware, and that these differences can lead to biased estimates of R_2 as well as systematic errors in R_1 measurement.

Teixeira et al. [35] proposed a solution to this problem, which involves replacing regular excitation pulses with multiband pulses. Instead of using the multiple frequency bands to excite multiple slices simultaneously, they are used to simultaneously excite on-resonance spins and saturate off-resonance spins at some frequency offset Δ, as illustrated in Fig. 32.6. The offset Δ is set to be large enough that there is no direct excitation of the free water due to the off-resonant bands. A key property is that the saturation of the semisolid protons depends on the RF power applied at all frequencies—for a multiband pulse the saturation rate W is determined by the sum of RF power weighted by the lineshape at each frequency. Hence, as the on-resonance power changes with flip angle (shaded green area on Fig. 32.6), the power in the off-resonance bands (shaded red) can be adjusted such that the total power is constant. Neglecting variation in the lineshape, doing so results in a constant saturation rate W independent of flip angle. This method, referred to as "controlled saturation of magnetization transfer" (CSMT), has been shown to stabilize T_1 and T_2 estimation from rapid gradient-echo-based sequences. A subsequent cross-vendor study [37] showed that CMST could reduce cross-protocol variability from 18.3% to 4.0% and cross-vendor variability (with the same protocol) from 19% to 4.5%.

A study of the same human subject at multiple sites using scanners from different vendors showed that CSMT would lead to similar variability in relaxation time measurements for test-retest on the same scanner as between different scanners.

32.3.4 Outlook: Relaxometry in the presence of MT effects

The CSMT approach is an attempt to stabilize quantitative relaxation time measurements but lays bare an often overlooked fact—longitudinal relaxation and cross-saturation with semisolid magnetization form a coupled system (Eq. 32.6). As a result, it is not possible to quantify one independently of the other. This basic fact is true for inversion recovery experiments, where the *observed* relaxation rate R_1^{obs} is a function of the full set of model parameters, and it is also true for rapid gradient-echo-based measurements. The CSMT method works by holding the RF power $\bar{W}$ constant, but as implied by Eq. (32.9), the apparent relaxation rate is a function of $\bar{W}$ and other model parameters. The implication is that stable and reproducible measurements are possible but they depend on $\bar{W}$, as can be seen in Fig. 32.5. As a result, the RF power level used to measure relaxation values is an important parameter that should be quoted alongside the measured values. A possible alternative to equalizing measurements at a relatively high $\bar{W}$ using multiband pulses as Teixeira et al. have done would be to use only very low $\bar{W}$ measurements, for instance, by incorporating long repetition times and low-energy RF pulses. Both approaches could yield stable measurements, but the measurements themselves would be *different*. Likewise, any of the gradient echo approaches discussed would not yield the same R_1 as an inversion recovery experiment (R_1^{obs}), since the effects of the underlying model parameters described in Eqs. (32.7), (32.9) are not equivalent.

32.4 Quantitative MT approaches

The nonaqueous protons that are responsible for MT effects are a key constituent of biological tissue, and there is a significant body of literature describing how to quantify the properties in the model detailed earlier. These approaches are known as quantitative magnetization transfer (qMT). This section will not give an exhaustive description of all methods but will instead summarize important results from several categories of measurements. A fuller treatment of many of these methods can be found in [38].

Quantitative MT methods may attempt to measure any of the additional parameters included in the binary spin bath model. These often include the semisolid fraction f_s, semisolid transverse relaxation rate T_{2s}, and exchange rate k. Maps of these properties are illustrated in Fig. 32.7. Not all qMT methods can measure all parameters, due to the specifics of the sequence used or simplifications in their exact model. R_{1f} is sometimes also referred to as an "MT" parameter since this is not equivalent to the observed single pool model R_1. Other parameters such as R_{1s} are often excluded from fitting since qMT methods can struggle to measure them with useful precision.

The semisolid fraction represents the proportion of protons that are bound to macromolecules in a voxel, which in the brain is often used as a proxy for myelination [39]. In preference to the fundamental exchange rate k, the literature often shows the forward exchange rate k_{fs}. There is some evidence that this metric is associated with inflammatory processes [40].

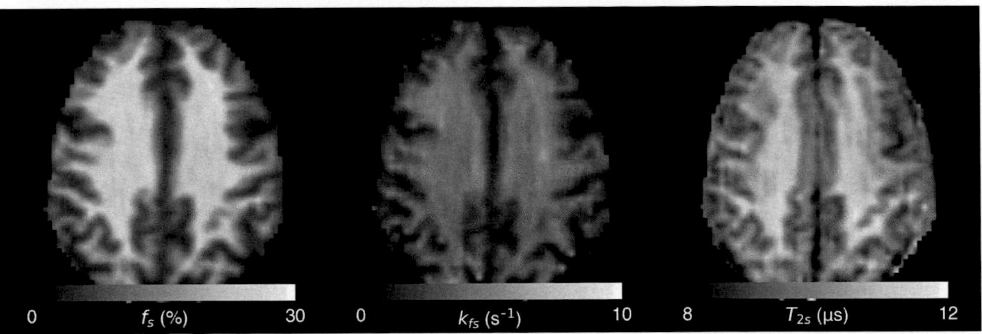

FIG. 32.7

Example qMT parameter maps from a pulsed MT experiment.

This work was performed as part of the NIMA Consortium which was funded by a strategic award from the Wellcome Trust (104025) in partnership with Janssen, GlaxoSmithKline, Lundbeck, and Pfizer.

There is also evidence that the MT effect in white matter depends on the orientation of the myelin sheath with respect to the main magnetic field. In a qMT experiment, this appears to manifest as a slight variation in the semisolid relaxation rate across white matter tracts [41].

32.4.1 Continuous wave Z-spectrum measurements

A direct method for examining MT is to apply a long off-resonant saturation pulse, followed quickly by an excitation pulse to image the free water [42]. The saturation pulse is applied for a long enough duration that a steady-state is reached, that is, the conditions are equivalent to continuous wave irradiation. The measurement is repeated multiple times by applying the saturation pulse at different frequencies, such that a range of saturation images is obtained—the signal as a function of frequency offset is known as the "Z-spectrum" [10]. Fig. 32.8 illustrates some simulated Z-spectra, showing the rather different shapes observed when MT is present. These curves deviate from the lineshape functions shown in Fig. 32.3 because of exchange and direct saturation effects, as they are a steady-state solution to Eq. (32.2) that depends on all of the model parameters. A measurement of the Z-spectrum may thus be used to fit for the model parameters and derive tissue properties such as R_{1s}, R_{1f}, k, f_s, and T_{2s}.

32.4.2 Pulsed measurements

Instead of using a long saturation pulse to generate a well-defined state to then read out, pulsed qMT methods examine effects arising over whole pulse sequences, including both saturation and excitation pulses. Sled and Pike used a spoiled gradient echo sequence with an off-resonance saturation pulse applied before each excitation pulse to generate MT-weighted images with variable saturation powers and frequency offsets [43]. Model parameters are estimated by fitting experimental measurements to a signal model, determined by numerical integration of the binary spin bath model. Mathematically, modeling the pulsed saturation sequence is more complex than continuous wave irradiation where the saturation rate W is constant, and the frequency offset Δ is well defined. For pulsed sequences, these parameters are variable during and between each pulse. The common mathematical treatment

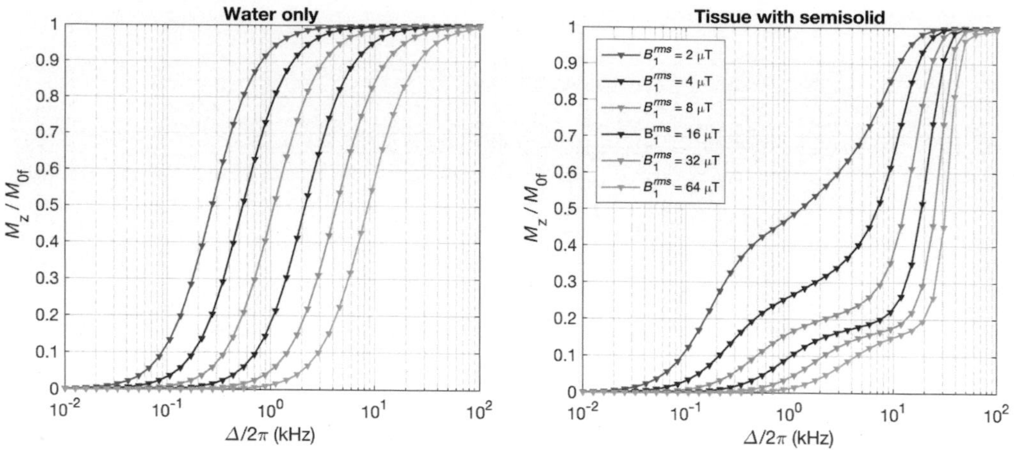

FIG. 32.8

Simulated Z-spectra for water only (*left*) and a tissue with semisolid pool (*right*) with semisolid fraction of 10%. In both examples $R_{1f} = 1\ \text{s}^{-1}$ and $R_{2f} = 10\ \text{s}^{-1}$. For the example including the semisolid, $R_{1s} = 1\ \text{s}^{-1}$, $k = 50\ \text{s}^{-1}$, and $T_{2s} = 12\ \mu\text{s}$ with super-Lorentzian lineshape. The semisolid has an attenuating effect on the Z-spectrum that is a function of the lineshape, but at first glance does not resemble it (cf. Fig. 32.3). The saturation also depends nonlinearly on the amount of RF power applied (determined by B_1^{rms}).

is to consider the effective saturation rate defined by the root-mean-square $\mathbf{B_1}$ of each pulse $\langle W \rangle$ acting instantaneously, and at a single well-defined frequency [12]. Extensions using numerical integration to consider evolution during long RF pulses have also been proposed [44]. Other methods aim to acquire data in specific regions of the Z-spectrum to simplify the model and fitting [13,45].

Because exchange acts both ways between the aqueous and nonaqueous protons, it is also possible to probe some aspects of the MT model without using off-resonance pulses. For example, balanced steady-state free precession (bSSFP) measurements using only on-resonance saturation from the excitation pulses themselves have been proposed for qMT [17,46,47]. bSSFP can have a higher intrinsic SNR than spoiled imaging, but the exclusive use of on-resonance excitation pulses means that the ability to probe spectral properties of the semisolid protons is limited. bSSFP sequences are often used as part of combined R_1 and R_2 VFA measurement schemes. These have been extended to multicompartment models consisting of multiple compartments of aqueous protons (which are beyond the scope of this chapter); more complex models that combine compartments with aqueous and nonaqueous (i.e., semisolid) protons have also been proposed [48].

The use of multiband pulses within both spoiled and balanced rapid gradient echo sequences has also been demonstrated to enable quantitative parameter estimation [22]. The additional frequency bands allow the spectral response of the semisolid to be probed without the need to include separate saturation pulses. This approach has also been demonstrated to enable parameter estimation in more complex models including inhomogeneous MT effects.

Pulsed qMT measurements require the acquisition of many images with different saturation powers or frequency offsets to provide enough data points for an accurate model fit. To keep the resulting scan time reasonable, the resolution is often reduced to around 2 mm isotropic. A compromise method is to estimate a semiquantitative surrogate measurement that summarizes the MT properties. The MT ratio (MTR) is one such example, though this metric is highly sequence dependent. A "more quantitative" alternative is MT_{SAT}, in which an effective saturation value is computed by combining three scans: one PD-weighted, one T_1-weighted, and one MT-weighted [49]. The use of two images without saturation allows for longitudinal relaxation and influence of the excitation flip angle to be accounted for in the estimation of MT_{SAT}, yielding a measure that represents only the saturation effect of a single MT pulse. Such an image can be acquired at higher resolution than full qMT methods but cannot separately resolve the effects of semisolid fraction, exchange rate, and lineshape. The trade-off between resolution and model complexity is a choice to be made for each experiment.

32.4.3 Inversion or saturation recovery methods

Inversion recovery is classically used to measure R_1 and so it is a natural choice to also characterize MT effects that are inherently tied to longitudinal relaxation processes [50], illustrated in Fig. 32.4. Recent developments at high-field have allowed full-brain mapping of a subset of MT parameters including PSR and exchange rate in a reasonable time [51,52].

While the relaxation rate at longer inversion delay times is governed by R_1^{obs}, the early behavior of the signal is governed by a faster decay rate, and the mixture between these two behaviors depends on the state of the magnetization immediately after inversion. Van Gelderen et al. used this feature to probe the system properties by studying the recovery after a range of different initial inversion pulses implemented with different amounts of RF power (hence resulting in different saturation of the semisolid protons) or indeed replacing the inversion pulse with only an off-resonance saturation [53].

The same group subsequently used a saturation recovery method to quickly estimate the semisolid proton fraction [18], though to do so efficiently they made the unusual assumption that longitudinal relaxation rates R_{1f} and R_{1s} are actually uniform across the brain; doing so resulted in higher semisolid proton fraction estimates than other methods. Quantitative MT methods in general need to estimate multiple parameters from a rather complex model with as few measurements as is feasible. Depending on the approach taken, the measurement may be rather insensitive to some model parameters—for example, R_{1s} is typically very hard to estimate and in many cases it is either fixed to a "plausible" value of 1 s^{-1} or to the free water value ($R_{1s} = R_{1f}$). Neither of these assumptions is particularly well motivated from the biophysical model. Indeed, another study used measurements at multiple B_0 field strengths [54] (0.55, 1.5, 3, and 7 T) to show that plausible results can be obtained by assuming that $R_{1f} = 0.4$ s^{-1} across all tissues *and independent of field strength*. In this case, it was shown that the semisolid longitudinal relaxation rate R_{1s} depends strongly on field strength, undermining other commonly made assumptions about this parameter. The authors hypothesized that variations in R_{1s} are actually the driver for the field-dependence of T_1 contrast.

32.5 CEST

As mentioned earlier, in real tissue, small-chain hydrocarbons are present alongside the long-chain macromolecules. These molecules exist as low concentration solutes within the water pool and exchange magnetization with water through various processes including direct proton exchange, molecular exchange, and the nuclear overhauser effect (NOE) [55]. In addition, the solute molecules tumble and experience motional narrowing, and hence have an appreciable transverse magnetization, such that the dynamics must be described using the full Bloch-McConnell equations. CEST is covered in detail in Chapter 33.

CEST experiments often aim to recover information about multiple molecules at different resonant frequencies, which usually necessitates the collection of a highly sampled Z-spectrum with tens of offset frequencies. Analytical solutions to the resulting Bloch-McConnell equations are challenging to derive [56], and so current best practices are semiquantitative methods such as Lorentzian difference fitting, which recovers the relative contribution of different molecules to the Z-spectrum [57]. However, this method cannot separate the effects of concentration and the exchange rate, both of which contribute to CEST [58]. If only one molecular species is of interest, very simple approaches similar to MTR exist that require a minimal number of images to be collected [59].

There exist both continuous-wave [55] and pulsed versions of CEST [60]. However, modern RF amplifiers are not designed to support a continuous-wave pulse of the duration required to reach the CEST steady-state (typically around 5 s). Thus, a hybrid version is common, where a long train of short pulses is used to equilibrate the magnetization before a rapid readout module is applied [57]. The degrees of freedom offered by variations in the pulse widths and spacing in such a sequence allow different aspects of CEST to be probed [61,62].

32.6 Concluding remarks

MT effects are an important part of the magnetization dynamics of tissue in MRI. They are a strong confound for relaxometry methods that are designed by considering the Bloch equations alone—indeed, it may be more accurate to view MT as a major driver of the observed relaxation properties of tissue. Measurement of MT properties—so-called quantitative MT—is a field of quantitative MRI distinct from relaxation measurements alone, though typically these methods struggle as large numbers of parameters must be estimated using a complex model. Simplified measurements that aim to estimate only a subset of these tissue properties [63] are a possible means for including some of the rich additional microstructural information provided by MT into clinically feasible quantitative MRI sequences.

References

[1] Wolff SD, Balaban RS. Magnetization transfer contrast (MTC) and tissue water proton relaxation in vivo. Magn Reson Med 1989;10(1):135–44. https://doi.org/10.1002/mrm.1910100113.

[2] Cercignani M, Symms MR, Ron M, Barker GJ. 3D MTR measurement: from 1.5 T to 3.0 T. NeuroImage 2006;31(1):181–6.

[3] Swanson SD, Malyarenko DI, Fabiilli ML, Welsh RC, Nielsen JF, Srinivasan A. Molecular, dynamic, and structural origin of inhomogeneous magnetization transfer in lipid membranes. Magn Reson Med 2017. https://doi.org/10.1002/mrm.26210.

[4] Manning AP, Chang KL, MacKay AL, Michal CA. The physical mechanism of "inhomogeneous" magnetization transfer MRI. J Magn Reson 2017;274(Suppl C):125–36. https://doi.org/10.1016/j.jmr.2016.11.013.

[5] Girard OM, Prevost VH, Varma G, Cozzone PJ, Alsop DC, Duhamel G. Magnetization transfer from inhomogeneously broadened lines (ihMT): experimental optimization of saturation parameters for human brain imaging at 1.5 Tesla: optimizing saturation parameters for ihMT brain imaging at 1.5 T. Magn Reson Med 2015;73(6):2111–21. https://doi.org/10.1002/mrm.25330.

[6] Varma G, Duhamel G, de Bazelaire C, Alsop DC. Magnetization transfer from inhomogeneously broadened lines: a potential marker for myelin. Magn Reson Med 2015;73(2):614–22. https://doi.org/10.1002/mrm.25174.

[7] Prevost VH, Girard OM, Mchinda S, Varma G, Alsop DC, Duhamel G. Optimization of inhomogeneous magnetization transfer (ihMT) MRI contrast for preclinical studies using dipolar relaxation time (T1D) filtering. NMR Biomed 2017;30(6):e3706.

[8] McConnell HM. Reaction rates by nuclear magnetic resonance. J Chem Phys 1958;28(3):430–1.

[9] Zaiss M, Bachert P. Chemical exchange saturation transfer (CEST) and MR Z-spectroscopy in vivo: a review of theoretical approaches and methods. Phys Med Biol 2013;58(22):R221.

[10] Henkelman RM, Huang X, Xiang QS, Stanisz GJ, Swanson SD, Bronskill MJ. Quantitative interpretation of magnetization transfer. Magn Reson Med 1993;29(6):759–66.

[11] Pike GB. Pulsed magnetization transfer contrast in gradient echo imaging: a two-pool analytic description of signal response. Magn Reson Med 1996;36(1):95–103. https://doi.org/10.1002/mrm.1910360117.

[12] Graham SJ, Henkelman RM. Understanding pulsed magnetization transfer. J Magn Reson Imaging 1997;7(5):903–12. https://doi.org/10.1002/jmri.1880070520.

[13] Ramani A, Dalton C, Miller DH, Tofts PS, Barker GJ. Precise estimate of fundamental in-vivo MT parameters in human brain in clinically feasible times. Magn Reson Imaging 2002;20(10):721–31. https://doi.org/10.1016/S0730-725X(02)00598-2.

[14] Morrison C, Mark Henkelman R. A model for magnetization transfer in tissues. Magn Reson Med 1995;33(4):475–82. https://doi.org/10.1002/mrm.1910330404.

[15] Weiger M, Froidevaux R, Baadsvik EL, Brunner DO, Rösler MB, Pruessmann KP. Advances in MRI of the myelin bilayer. NeuroImage 2020;217:116888. https://doi.org/10.1016/j.neuroimage.2020.116888.

[16] Seifert AC, Li C, Wilhelm MJ, Wehrli SL, Wehrli FW. Towards quantification of myelin by solid-state MRI of the lipid matrix protons. NeuroImage 2017;163:358–67. https://doi.org/10.1016/j.neuroimage.2017.09.054.

[17] Gloor M, Scheffler K, Bieri O. Quantitative magnetization transfer imaging using balanced SSFP. Magn Reson Med 2008;60(3):691–700. https://doi.org/10.1002/mrm.21705.

[18] Gelderen PV, Jiang X, Duyn JH. Rapid measurement of brain macromolecular proton fraction with transient saturation transfer MRI. Magn Reson Med 2017;77(6):2174–85. https://doi.org/10.1002/mrm.26304.

[19] Chen WC, Foxley S, Miller KL. Detecting microstructural properties of white matter based on compartmentalization of magnetic susceptibility. NeuroImage 2013;70:1–9.

[20] Varma G, Girard OM, Prevost VH, Grant AK, Duhamel G, Alsop DC. Interpretation of magnetization transfer from inhomogeneously broadened lines (ihMT) in tissues as a dipolar order effect within motion restricted molecules. J Magn Reson 2015;260:67–76. https://doi.org/10.1016/j.jmr.2015.08.024.

[21] Goldman M. Spin temperature and nuclear magnetic resonance in solids. Oxford: Clarendon Press; 1970.

[22] Malik SJ, Teixeira RPAG, West DJ, Wood TC, Hajnal JV. Steady-state imaging with inhomogeneous magnetization transfer contrast using multiband radiofrequency pulses. Magn Reson Med 2019. https://doi.org/10.1002/mrm.27984.

[23] Morrison C, Stanisz G, Henkelman RM. Modeling magnetization transfer for biological-like systems using a semi-solid pool with a super-Lorentzian lineshape and dipolar reservoir. J Magn Reson B 1995;108(2):103–13.

[24] Sled JG, Pike G. Quantitative interpretation of magnetization transfer in spoiled gradient echo MRI sequences. J Magn Reson 2000;145(1):24–36. https://doi.org/10.1006/jmre.2000.2059.

[25] Melki PS, Mulkern RV. Magnetization transfer effects in multislice RARE sequences. Magn Reson Med 1992;195:189–95.

[26] Radunsky D, Blumenfeld-Katzir T, Volovyk O, Tal A, Barazany D, Tsarfaty G, et al. Analysis of magnetization transfer (MT) influence on quantitative mapping of T2 relaxation time. Magn Reson Med 2019;82(1):145–58. https://doi.org/10.1002/mrm.27704.

[27] Mackay A, Whittall K, Adler J, Li D, Paty D, Graeb D. In vivo visualization of myelin water in brain by magnetic resonance. Magn Reson Med 1994;31(6):673–7. https://doi.org/10.1002/mrm.1910310614.

[28] Vavasour IM, Whittall KP, Li DKB, MacKay AL. Different magnetization transfer effects exhibited by the short and longT2 components in human brain. Magn Reson Med 2000;44(6):860–6. https://doi.org/10.1002/1522-2594(200012)44:6¡860::AID-MRM6¿3.0.CO;2-C.

[29] Gupta RK. A new look at the method of variable nutation angle for the measurement of spin-lattice relaxation times using Fourier transform {NMR}. J Magn Reson (1969) 1977;25(1):231–5. https://doi.org/10.1016/0022-2364(77)90138-X.

[30] Fram EK, Herfkens RJ, Johnson GA, Glover GH, Karis JP, Shimakawa A, et al. Rapid calculation of {T1} using variable flip angle gradient refocused imaging. Magn Reson Imaging 1987;5(3):201–8.

[31] Deoni SCLL, Rutt BK, Peters TM. Rapid combined {T1} and {T2} mapping using gradient recalled acquisition in the steady state. Magn Reson Med 2003;49(3):515–26. https://doi.org/10.1002/mrm.10407.

[32] Teixeira RPAG, Malik SJ, Hajnal JV. Joint system relaxometry (JSR) and Crámer-Rao lower bound optimization of sequence parameters: a framework for enhanced precision of DESPOT T_1 and T_2 estimation: JSR and CRLB optimization of sequence parameters. Magn Reson Med 2018;79(1):234–45. https://doi.org/10.1002/mrm.26670.

[33] Shcherbakova Y, van den Berg CAT, Moonen CTW, Bartels LW. PLANET: an ellipse fitting approach for simultaneous T1 and T2 mapping using phase-cycled balanced steady-state free precession. Magn Reson Med 2018;79(2):711–22. https://doi.org/10.1002/mrm.26717.

[34] Leroi L, Coste A, de Rochefort L, Santin MD, Valabregue R, Mauconduit F, et al. Simultaneous multiparametric mapping of total sodium concentration, T1, T2 and ADC at 7 T using a multi-contrast unbalanced SSFP. Magn Reson Imaging 2018;53:156–63. https://doi.org/10.1016/j.mri.2018.07.012.

[35] Teixeira RP, Malik SJ, Hajnal JV. Fast quantitative MRI using controlled saturation magnetization transfer. Magn Reson Med 2019;81(2):907–20. https://doi.org/10.1002/mrm.27442.

[36] Ou X, Gochberg DF. MT effects and T1 quantification in single-slice spoiled gradient echo imaging. Magn Reson Med 2008;59(4):835–45. https://doi.org/10.1002/mrm.21550.

[37] Teixeira RP, Neji R, Wood TC, Baburamani AA, Malik SJ, Hajnal JV. Controlled saturation magnetization transfer for reproducible multivendor variable flip angle T1 and T2 mapping. Magn Reson Med 2020;84(1):221–36. https://doi.org/10.1002/mrm.28109.

[38] Battiston M, Cercignani M. MT: magnetization transfer (chapter 10). In: Cercignani M, Dowell NG, Tofts PS, editors. Quantitative MRI of the Brain Principles of Physical Measurement. 2nd ed. CRC Press; 2018.

[39] Schmierer K, Wheeler-Kingshott CAM, Tozer DJ, Boulby PA, Parkes HG, Yousry TA, et al. Quantitative magnetic resonance of postmortem multiple sclerosis brain before and after fixation. Magn Reson Med 2008;59(2):268–77.

[40] Harrison NA, Cooper E, Dowell NG, Keramida G, Voon V, Critchley HD, et al. Quantitative magnetization transfer imaging as a biomarker for effects of systemic inflammation on the brain. Biol Psychiatry 2015;78(1):49–57. https://doi.org/10.1016/j.biopsych.2014.09.023.

[41] Pampel A, Müller DK, Anwander A, Marschner H, Möller HE. Orientation dependence of magnetization transfer parameters in human white matter. NeuroImage 2015;114:136–46. https://doi.org/10.1016/j.neuroimage.2015.03.068.

[42] Grad J, Bryant RG. Nuclear magnetic cross-relaxation spectroscopy. J Magn (1969) 1990;90(1):1–8. https://doi.org/10.1016/0022-2364(90)90361-C.

[43] Sled JG, Pike GB. Quantitative imaging of magnetization transfer exchange and relaxation properties in vivo using MRI. Magn Reson Med 2001;46(5):923–31.

[44] Portnoy S, Stanisz GJ. Modeling pulsed magnetization transfer. Magn Reson Med 2007;58(1):144–55. https://doi.org/10.1002/mrm.21244.

[45] Yarnykh VL. Pulsed Z-spectroscopic imaging of cross-relaxation parameters in tissues for human MRI: theory and clinical applications. Magn Reson Med 2002;47(5):929–39. https://doi.org/10.1002/mrm.10120.

[46] Bieri O, Scheffler K. On the origin of apparent low tissue signals in balanced SSFP. Magn Reson Med 2006;56(5):1067–74. https://doi.org/10.1002/mrm.21056.

[47] Wood TC, Teixeira RPAG, Malik SJ. Magnetization transfer and frequency distribution effects in the SSFP ellipse. Magn Reson Med 2019. https://doi.org/10.1002/mrm.28149.

[48] Liu F, Block WF, Kijowski R, Samsonov A. Rapid multicomponent relaxometry in steady state with correction of magnetization transfer effects. Magn Reson Med 2016;75(4):1423–33. https://doi.org/10.1002/mrm.25672.

[49] Helms G, Dathe H, Kallenberg K, Dechent P. High-resolution maps of magnetization transfer with inherent correction for RF inhomogeneity and T_1 relaxation obtained from 3D FLASH MRI. Magn Reson Med 2008;60(6):1396–407. https://doi.org/10.1002/mrm.21732.

[50] Gochberg DF, Kennan RP, Gore JC. Quantitative studies of magnetization transfer by selective excitation and T1 recovery. Magn Reson Med 1997;38(2):224–31. https://doi.org/10.1002/mrm.1910380210.

[51] Dortch RD, Bagnato F, Gochberg DF, Gore JC, Smith SA. Optimization of selective inversion recovery magnetization transfer imaging for macromolecular content mapping in the human brain. Magn Reson Med 2018;80(5):1824–35. https://doi.org/10.1002/mrm.27174.

[52] Cronin MJ, Xu J, Bagnato F, Gochberg DF, Gore JC, Dortch RD. Rapid whole-brain quantitative magnetization transfer imaging using 3D selective inversion recovery sequences. Magn Reson Imaging 2020;68:66–74. https://doi.org/10.1016/j.mri.2020.01.014.

[53] van Gelderen P, Jiang X, Duyn JH. Effects of magnetization transfer on {T1} contrast in human brain white matter. NeuroImage 2016;128:85–95.

[54] Wang Y, van Gelderen P, de Zwart JA, Duyn JH. B0-field dependence of MRI T1 relaxation in human brain. NeuroImage 2020;213:116700. https://doi.org/10.1016/j.neuroimage.2020.116700.

[55] Ward KM, Aletras AH, Balaban RS. A new class of contrast agents for MRI based on proton chemical exchange dependent saturation transfer (CEST). J Magn Reson 2000;143(1):79–87. https://doi.org/10.1006/jmre.1999.1956.

[56] Gochberg DF, Does MD, Zu Z, Lankford CL. Towards an analytic solution for pulsed CEST. NMR Biomed 2018;31(5):e3903. https://doi.org/10.1002/nbm.3903.

[57] Deshmane A, Zaiss M, Lindig T, Herz K, Schuppert M, Gandhi C, et al. 3D gradient echo snapshot CEST MRI with low power saturation for human studies at 3 T. Magn Reson Med 2018. https://doi.org/10.1002/mrm.27569.

[58] Chen L, Xu X, Zeng H, Chan KWY, Yadav N, Cai S, et al. Separating fast and slow exchange transfer and magnetization transfer using off-resonance variable-delay multiple-pulse (VDMP) MRI. Magn Reson Med 2018;80(4):1568–76. https://doi.org/10.1002/mrm.27111.

[59] Zaiss M, Xu J, Goerke S, Khan IS, Singer RJ, Gore JC, et al. Inverse Z-spectrum analysis for spillover-, MT-, and T1-corrected steady-state pulsed CEST-MRI—application to pH-weighted MRI of acute stroke. NMR Biomed 2014;27(3):240–52. https://doi.org/10.1002/nbm.3054.

[60] Zu Z, Li K, Janve VA, Does MD, Gochberg DF. Optimizing pulsed-chemical exchange saturation transfer imaging sequences. Magn Reson Med 2011;66(4):1100–8. https://doi.org/10.1002/mrm.22884.

[61] Lin EC, Li H, Zu Z, Louie EA, Lankford CL, Dortch RD, et al. Chemical exchange rotation transfer (CERT) on human brain at 3 Tesla. Magn Reson Med 2018;80(6):2609–17. https://doi.org/10.1002/mrm.27365.

[62] Xu J, Yadav NN, Bar-Shir A, Jones CK, Chan KWY, Zhang J, et al. Variable delay multi-pulse train for fast chemical exchange saturation transfer and relayed-nuclear overhauser enhancement MRI. Magn Reson Med 2014;71(5):1798–812. https://doi.org/10.1002/mrm.24850.

[63] Yarnykh VL. Fast macromolecular proton fraction mapping from a single off-resonance magnetization transfer measurement. Magn Reson Med 2012;68(1):166–78. https://doi.org/10.1002/mrm.23224.

CHAPTER

Chemical Exchange Mapping

33

Zhongliang Zu[a,b], Moriel Vandsburger[c], and Phillip Zhe Sun[d,e]

[a]Institute of Imaging Science, Vanderbilt University Medical Center, Nashville, TN, United States [b]Department of Radiology, Vanderbilt University Medical Center, Nashville, TN, United States [c]Department of Bioengineering, University of California, Berkeley, CA, United States [d]Yerkes Imaging Center, Yerkes National Primate Research Center, Emory University, Atlanta, GA, United States [e]Department of Radiology and Imaging Sciences, Emory University School of Medicine, Atlanta, GA, United States

33.1 Principles of chemical exchange saturation transfer

Magnetization transfer (MT) imaging describes MRI experiments that probe the exchange of magnetization between dilute labile protons and bulk water protons [1,2]. To observe the effects of magnetization exchange, an MT experiment requires the acquisition of at least two measurements where acquisition parameters are kept constant, but the influence of MT is toggled. An MT measurement typically involves measuring the bulk water signal after saturating the labile protons, and allowing cross-relaxation/exchange between the saturated protons and bulk water signal. The exchange effect is then assessed by comparing the bulk water signal with and without saturation. There are generally two types of MT experiments: semisolid macromolecular MT imaging and chemical exchange saturation transfer (CEST) imaging. Macromolecular MT investigates the exchange of magnetization between protons associated with macromolecules, which have very short T_2 relaxation times (tens of μs) and surrounding bulk water protons. The resonant frequencies of these macromolecules cover a large range, and thus the saturation pulses can take a variety of forms. In contrast, CEST imaging typically probes mobile exchangeable protons, such as those from intracellular metabolites, proteins and peptides, whose T_2 times are on the order of tens of ms [3]. These metabolites have narrow resonant frequencies different from that of bulk water. In both cases, the contrast generated via labeling and exchange is a function of the underlying concentration of labile protons, their exchange rates with surrounding bulk water protons, the sequence parameters, the spatial uniformity of B_0 and B_1, and the background tissue relaxation properties. MT imaging is described in detail in Chapter 32. This chapter focuses on CEST MRI, but the described mathematical modeling applies to semisolid MT experiments with some minor modifications.

Advances in Magnetic Resonance Technology and Applications. Volume 1. ISSN 2666-9099. https://doi.org/10.1016/B978-0-12-817057-1.00034-2

33.1.1 Bloch-McConnell equations

The saturation transfer effect can generally be described via modification of the Bloch McConnell equations [4,5]. For a representative two-pool system (one labile proton pool and one bulk water proton pool) (Fig. 33.1A), the modified Bloch-McConnell equations can be expressed as:

$$\frac{dM_{xs}}{dt} = -\Delta\omega_s M_{ys} - R_{2s}M_{xs} - k_{sw}M_{xs} + k_{ws}M_{xw} \tag{33.1.a}$$

$$\frac{dM_{ys}}{dt} = \Delta\omega_s M_{xs} + \omega_1 M_{zs} - R_{2s}M_{ys} - k_{sw}M_{ys} + k_{ws}M_{yw} \tag{33.1.b}$$

$$\frac{dM_{zs}}{dt} = -\omega_1 M_{ys} - R_{1s}(M_{zs} - M_{0s}) - k_{sw}M_{zs} + k_{ws}M_{zw} \tag{33.1.c}$$

$$\frac{dM_{xw}}{dt} = -\Delta\omega_w M_{yw} - R_{2w}M_{xw} + k_{sw}M_{xs} - k_{ws}M_{xw} \tag{33.1.d}$$

$$\frac{dM_{yw}}{dt} = \Delta\omega_w M_{xw} + \omega_1 M_{zw} - R_{2w}M_{yw} + k_{sw}M_{ys} - k_{ws}M_{yw} \tag{33.1.e}$$

$$\frac{dM_{zw}}{dt} = -\omega_1 M_{yw} - R_{1w}(M_{zw} - M_{0w}) + k_{sw}M_{zs} - k_{ws}M_{zw} \tag{33.1.f}$$

where subscripts s and w represent the solute and water pools, respectively; R_1 and R_2 are their longitudinal and transverse relaxation rates; k_{sw} and k_{ws} are the exchange rates from the solute protons to the bulk water pool (k_{sw}) and vice versa (k_{ws}); ω_1 is the RF saturation power used during spin labeling, and $\Delta\omega$ is the frequency offset from the spin labeling to the solute ($\Delta\omega_s$) and water resonance ($\Delta\omega_w$) frequency. The inclusion of exchange terms in the Bloch-McConnell equations links two

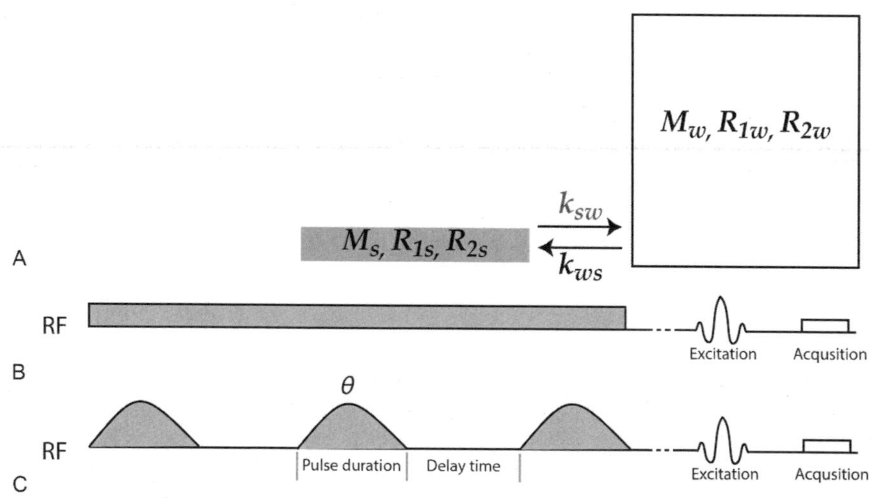

FIG. 33.1

(A) Illustration of the two-pool exchange model. CEST-MRI pulse sequences with (B) CW- and (C) pulsed-RF irradiation, respectively.

otherwise independent sets of Bloch equations. While this example is intended to provide the framework for a simple two-pool system, the Bloch-McConnell equations can easily be extended to describe multipool CEST effects through a logical expansion of Eq. (33.1). It is also worth noting that the Bloch-McConnell equations commonly only consider the exchange between labile and bulk water protons without modeling the exchange among dilute pools because of their relatively weak interactions [5]. Finally, these equations ignore more complex but lower amplitude exchange processes such as the relayed nuclear overhauser enhancement effect (rNOE). Readers can find a detailed explanation of these exchange processes in Ref. [3].

33.1.2 Spinlock theory

Although the Bloch-McConnell equations are straightforward in describing the saturation transfer phenomenon by directly including the exchange terms (k_{sw} and k_{ws} in Eqs. 33.1.a–33.1.f), the matrix form is not compact in describing multipool CEST processes. It has been shown that the magnetization exchange in MRI can be described by the spinlock (SL) theorem, which combines relaxation and exchange effects into an apparent relaxation rate along a fictitious field [6,7]. The spinlock solution in the context of CEST MRI is similar to the well-known longitudinal relaxation phenomenon, except that it contains a modified SL relaxation rate ($R_{1\rho}$) and an equilibrium state ($S_0 \cdot \frac{R_{1w}}{R_{1\rho}} \cdot \cos^2\theta$). In this representation, the signal at offset frequency $\Delta\omega$ can be expressed as:

$$S(\Delta\omega) = S_0 \cdot e^{-R_{1\rho} \cdot t_{sat}} + S_0 \cdot \frac{R_{1w}}{R_{1\rho}} \cdot \cos^2\theta \cdot \left(1 - e^{-R_{1\rho} \cdot t_{sat}}\right) \tag{33.2}$$

where $R_{1\rho}$ is the longitudinal relaxation rate in the rotating frame, in which $R_{1\rho} = R_{1w} \cdot \cos^2\theta + R_{2w} \cdot \sin^2\theta + R_{ex}^{CEST}$, $\theta = \text{atan}(\omega_1/\Delta\omega)$, $R_{ex}^{CEST} = f_s \cdot k_{sw} \cdot \alpha(B_1)$, $\alpha(B_1) = \frac{(2\pi\gamma B_1)^2}{(2\pi\gamma B_1)^2 + p \cdot q}$ is the labeling efficiency (where $p = (R_{2s} + k_{sw}) - \frac{k_{sw} \cdot k_{ws}}{R_{2w} + k_{ws}}$, $q = (R_{1s} + k_{sw}) - \frac{k_{sw} \cdot k_{ws}}{R_{1w} + k_{ws}}$, and k_{ws} is the reverse exchange rate from the bulk water to labile protons), R_{1s} and R_{2s} are the labile proton longitudinal and transverse relaxation rates, respectively, and f_s is the ratio of the concentration of labile proton to that of bulk water (also known as the labile proton ratio). Note that Eq. (33.2) can be extended to describe complex multipool CEST processes by simply adding more terms with the distinct parameters for each additional pool to the equation for R_{ex}^{CEST}.

33.1.3 Exchange metrics and parameters

In the simplest systems, such as a two-pool CEST phantom, the equilibrium CEST contrast is a function only of the parameters detailed in Eq. (33.2): the concentration of the CEST target molecule expressed by the term for the labile proton ratio (f_s), the exchange rate (k_{sw}) between pools, the saturation efficiency of the target protons (α), the bulk water R_{1w}, and the bulk water spin-lock relaxation rate ($R_{1w} \cdot \cos^2\theta + R_{2w} \cdot \sin^2\theta$) that via the inclusion of the θ and α terms account for the impact of B_1 power used to generate CEST contrast. Note that in this chapter, the term "CEST contrast" is used as a shorthand to describe the effect of chemical exchange after saturation of the labile protons on the bulk water signal. In some CEST publications, the same contrast is referred to as the "CEST-effect." For well-controlled two-pool systems, individual parameters for saturation of labile protons can be systematically varied to quantify both the labile proton ratio and exchange rate. However, different tissues are characterized by unique intracellular concentrations of multiple metabolites, each with distinct resonant frequencies and exchange rates that may overlap at specific RF saturation schemes. Additionally, for RF saturation within 10–20 ppm of water, MT and CEST contrasts are concomitantly stimulated.

Although it is feasible to determine f_s and k_{sw} simultaneously, it is often tedious to map them in vivo due to the presence of multipool exchange. Subsequently, the acquisition of CEST MRI data relies on sophisticated sequence design (described in Section 33.2) that limits the impact of the aforementioned confounding processes. R_{ex}^{CEST} can be estimated and used as a simplistic approximation of CEST processes (i.e., $R_{ex}^{CEST} = f_s \cdot k_{sw} \cdot \alpha$). Changes observed in R_{ex}^{CEST} are assumed to be dominated by changes in f_s and/or k_{sw} based on a priori knowledge of the underlying pathophysiology or complementary experiments.

Over the last two decades, several indices have emerged as common methods to quantify the experimental CEST contrast, including MT ratio asymmetry (MTR_{asym}, Section 33.3.1), multipool Lorentzian fitting of Z-spectra (Section 33.3.2), apparent exchange-dependent relaxation (AREX, Section 33.3.3), etc. Each method attempts to either control or compensate for confounding processes to quantify the underlying target labile proton ratio and exchange rate.

33.2 CEST MRI pulse sequences and data collection

33.2.1 Basic CEST MRI sequence design

In a CEST MRI acquisition (shown in Fig. 33.1), the target labile protons are saturated using either a single long continuous wave (CW) saturation pulse or a train of short discrete RF pulses with a defined inter-pulse delay time (pulsed-CEST) tuned to the appropriate frequency offset. In CW-CEST, a long (i.e., a few seconds) rectangular RF pulse is followed by a fast image readout. The saturation pulse is described by the amplitude and duration of the irradiation pulse (Fig. 33.1B). The use of CW preparation is advantageous due to the simplicity of the saturation scheme and more straightforward signal modeling using the spinlock theorem. CW saturation has been commonly deployed on preclinical scanners but limited by tightly restricted maximal RF durations on previous generations of clinical scanners. However, the combination of more relaxed RF duration restrictions and parallel transmit technology for pseudo-CW saturation has led to increased use of CW-CEST on more modern scanners. Given early restrictions on RF pulse duration and amplifier performance, the pulsed-CEST MRI sequence emerged as an alternative to CW-CEST MRI. The pulsed-CEST saturation scheme is described by the pulse duration and flip angle/average RF power of constituent RF pulses, the inter-pulse delay time, and the total number of pulses (Fig. 33.1C). Due to the use of inter-pulse delays, pulsed-CEST MRI is not limited by hardware restrictions on pulse duration but may be limited by duty cycle.

For both CW and pulsed CEST MRI, saturation is followed by a fast imaging readout (e.g., EPI, FSE, and FISP) or, in cases where physiological constraints restrict the acquisition window, a segmented gradient echo. Importantly, the greater number of free parameters in pulsed-CEST MRI can be exploited to probe the exchange and exchange-rate specific effects [8]. For example, more advanced CEST preparation schemes that are derived from pulsed-CEST principles such as variable delay multipulse (VDMP) [9], frequency labeled exchange transfer (FLEX) [10], chemical exchange rotation transfer (CERT) [11], frequency alternating RF irradiation (SAFARI) [12], and length and offset varied saturation (LOVARS) [13] all use variations in the timing and design of saturation schemes to capture differences in relaxation, chemical shift, and exchange/cross-relaxation rates for improved specificity over basic methods for CEST MRI. However, basic CW and pulsed-CEST methods remain the most widely used CEST MRI approaches to date.

33.2.2 Collection of CEST MRI data

In principle, CEST contrast can be derived from two CEST-weighted images of opposite saturation offset frequencies relative to the resonant frequency of water. However, just the presence of spatial B_0 inhomogeneity across an imaging plane will result in different relative saturation offset frequencies. The impact of such inhomogeneity is limited in cases where the saturation offset frequencies are significantly afield from the resonant frequency of water, and a broader bandwidth saturation pulse can be used, as is the case with paramagnetic CEST MRI (see Section 33.5.2). However, for CEST MRI of endogenous metabolites, whose labile protons resonate at a frequency which is relatively close to that of water, CEST contrast derived from such images could be contaminated by even small changes in B_0. Subsequently, most CEST MRI experiments involve the acquisition of a series of images in which the frequency offset of the saturation module is varied across a predetermined range. For a given voxel, the signal intensity at each frequency offset is normalized to the corresponding signal intensity from a control image (identical acquisition parameters without saturation). The subsequent array of normalized signal intensity values are plotted as a function of the saturation offset frequency and presented as a "Z-spectrum," as shown in Fig. 33.2. Representation of CEST data via the Z-spectrum highlights the unique contrasts generated by each population of labile protons. Several of the more quantitative analysis methods described in the next section are based on an analysis of the Z-spectrum.

33.3 CEST data analysis

33.3.1 MTR asymmetry analysis

The earliest method used to quantify CEST contrast was the calculation of MTR asymmetry (MTR_{asym}), as shown in Eq. (33.3). For a given voxel, the CEST contrast at a solute's labile target frequency ($+\Delta\omega$) is calculated by normalizing the difference in signal intensity between images acquired following CEST preparation at the labile target resonant frequency ($+\Delta\omega$) and the corresponding conjugate offset frequency ($-\Delta\omega$) relative to water, to that from a reference image (S_0).

$$MTR_{asym} = \frac{S(-\Delta\omega) - S(+\Delta\omega)}{S_0} \tag{33.3}$$

The use of MTR_{asym} as a metric for quantifying CEST contrast compensates for the direct saturation of water, which is presumed to be identical at offsets that are equidistant from the resonant frequency

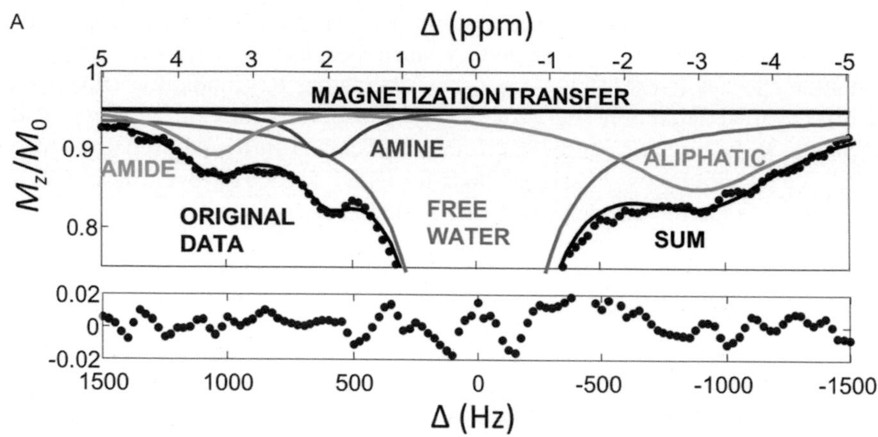

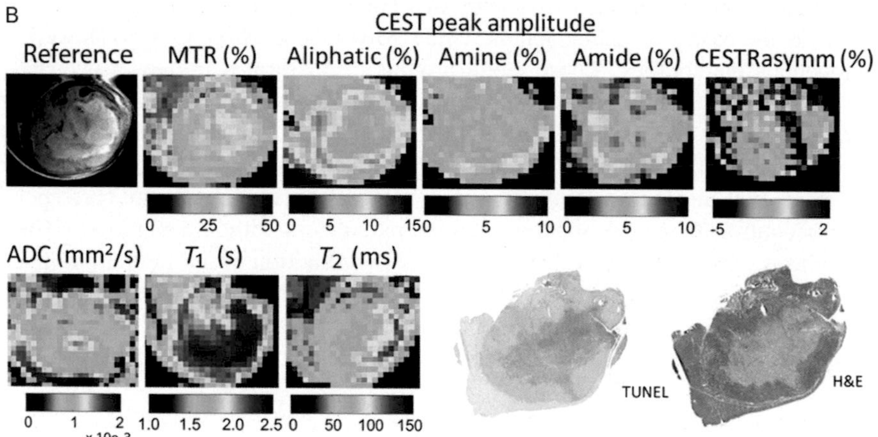

FIG. 33.2

(A) An example of multiple-pool Lorentzian decomposition of the Z-spectrum from an MDA animal model. The composite CEST peak amplitude reflects mixed contributions from labile proton ratio, exchange rate, and saturation efficiency. (B) Images showing the peak amplitude of the multiple-pool Lorentzian fits for each of the CEST signals; ADC, T_1, and T_2 maps; and the terminal deoxynucleotidyl transferase dUTP nick end labeling (TUNEL) and hematoxylin and eosin (H&E) histology of the corresponding slice. H&E staining shows the tumor morphological identification and the TUNEL highlights regions of apoptosis and necrosis.

of water, but opposite in field directions. The CEST contrasts generated when RF irradiation is applied at the resonant frequency of the labile proton ($+\Delta\omega$), and the conjugate offset frequency ($-\Delta\omega$) will be different (there will be a CEST effect in the former but not the latter). By subtracting the two measurements with saturation, the disruptive influence of the direct saturation of water on the CEST effect can be reduced.

This simple approach is useful under a strict set of conditions. First, the identification of points along a Z-spectrum that correspond to the correct offset pairs ($\pm\Delta\omega$) requires the accurate identification of the resonance frequency of water. In cases where low RF powers ($<1\ \mu$T) are used to generate CEST contrast, this can be accomplished by finding the minimum value along a Z-spectrum. However, in cases where higher RF power is used to generate CEST contrast, the impact of direct saturation is often sufficient to cause multiple points near the resonant frequency of water to demonstrate similar signal intensities. In such cases, B_0 correction methods such as water saturation shift reference (WASSR) must be employed prospectively to ensure that the assumption of equal direct saturation of water between image pairs remains accurate. Second, the conjugate frequency offset ($-\Delta\omega$) preferably falls outside the range of nuclear overhauser enhancement (NOE, roughly - 1 to - 5 ppm). As this is not the case for most endogenous targets (e.g., amine, amide), the measurement of MTR_{asym} is contaminated by additional NOE contrast. Importantly, NOE contrast varies between different tissues (e.g., brain and muscle) and even within tissues depending on pathology (e.g., tumor vs. healthy). Third, recent studies have demonstrated that MT contrast within a Z-spectrum is not uniformly distributed within the range of relevant offset frequencies (- 10 to +10 ppm relative to water). Specifically, this contrast is caused by the saturation and subsequent exchange of magnetization from an array of semisolid molecules (for example, the family of matricellular proteins that make up the extracellular matrix), each with unique center frequencies but overlapping bandwidths. Subsequently, the presence of macromolecules will bias MTR_{asym} measurements [14]. The appropriate choice of saturation parameters (power, duty cycle, and offset spacing) can help mitigate the confounding impacts of the factors mentioned earlier upon the quantification of MTR_{asym} for endogenous metabolites. In contrast, for paramagnetic and hyperpolarization-based CEST contrast agents with resonant frequencies far afield from water, the use of MTR_{asym} is straightforward.

Measurement of MTR_{asym} is a form of quantification of the CEST contrast within an image, but this is not equivalent to direct quantitation of the underlying exchange properties. However, the magnitude of MTR_{asym} in a given experiment is a function of the labile proton ratio, exchange rate, and experimental conditions [15]. For a simplistic two-pool CEST system, MTR_{asym} can be reasonably described as:

$$\text{MTR}_{\text{asym}} = \frac{f_s \cdot k_{sw}}{R_{1w}} \alpha(B_1) \cdot (1 - \alpha) \tag{33.4}$$

where α is the labeling coefficient that quantifies the labile proton saturation efficiency, and σ is the spillover effect that describes the concomitant direct RF saturation of the bulk water protons. In specific experimental cases where the bias of MTR_{asym} measurement by NOE and MT mechanisms is either absent or mitigated, measurement of MTR_{asym} can be used to derive either f_s or k_{sw} if the parameters R_{1w}, α, and σ are known a priori. As a result of studies performed over the last 20 years, the exchange rates for most CEST targets have been well-characterized as a function of field strength and microenvironmental conditions such as pH. Subsequently, if either f_s or k_{sw} is known or can be directly controlled or measured, the unknown parameter can be experimentally determined. Importantly, both the saturation efficiency and spillover effects are functions of B_1, and each can change with field strength. For example, Fig. 33.3A shows that while the labeling coefficient increases with B_1, the RF spillover effect worsens in parallel. Thus, for each labile proton, there exists an optimal experimental set-up to balance these two competing processes. Fig. 33.3B shows that for a given B_1 field, the simulated CEST contrast does not persistently increase with the exchange rate but instead peaks at an intermediate exchange rate.

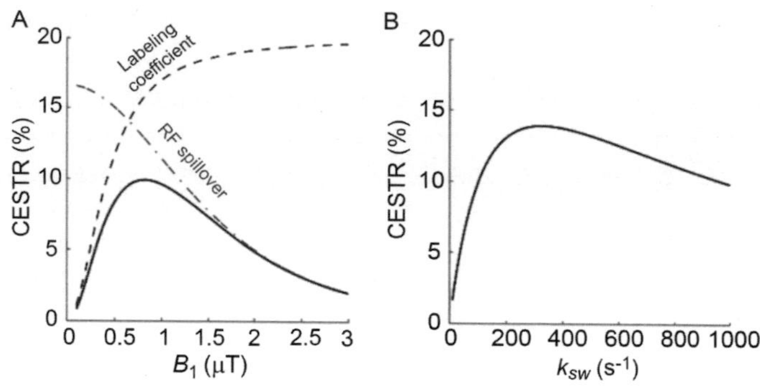

FIG. 33.3

(A) The measurable CEST signal as a function of RF irradiation power, which can be described by a labeling coefficient and spillover factor. Simulation parameters: $f_s = 0.1\%$, $k_{sw} = 100\,s^{-1}$, and B_1 from 0 to 3, chemical shift of 2 ppm. The plot shows that there is an intermediate RF power level that maximizes the experimentally measurable CEST effect, due to the competing labeling coefficient and spillover factor. (B) The maximal achievable CEST effect as a function of the exchange rate $k_{sw} = 0$ to $1000\,s^{-1}\mu T$. This plot shows that due to experimental factors, the CEST effect does not simply scale with the exchange rate, but peaks at an intermediate exchange rate.

33.3.2 Lorentzian fitting

Although asymmetry analysis can be used to characterize CEST contrast at a predetermined off-resonance saturation frequency, Z-spectra are required to assess complex multipool exchange. To resolve multiple and partially overlapping CEST effects, Lorentzian decoupling can be performed on a Z-spectrum. Here it is assumed that the bulk water signal decrease caused by each labile pool can be described as a Lorentzian lineshape; the Lorentzian fitting can be written as:

$$S(\omega) = 1 - \sum_{i=1}^{N} A_i \left(1 + \left(\frac{\Delta\omega - \Delta\omega_{0i}}{0.5 \cdot W_i}\right)^2\right)^{-1} \tag{33.5}$$

where N is the number of exchanging pools and A_i, $\Delta\omega_{0i}$ and W_i are the amplitude, labile proton resonance frequency, and full width at half maximum of the ith pool, respectively. With this technique, it is crucial to sample a Z-spectrum with adequate density to resolve target pools.

The Lorentzian fitting has been deployed to quantify the magnitude of CEST contrast in vivo in the setting of three-pool [16], four-pool [17], and five-pool [18,19] exchange systems. A representative example in Fig. 33.2A shows a composite and decomposed CEST spectrum from an MDA animal tumor model. Fig. 33.2B shows the fitted amplitudes for each pool (e.g., amine, amide, MT) in comparison to histology. In Fig. 33.4, the impact of pool number upon quantification of CEST contrast via Lorentzian fitting is shown using in vivo data from a mouse kidney. A notable limitation to multipool Lorentzian fitting is that most optimization methods used to fit the Z-spectrum allow the water and MT pools to dominate due to the bandwidth of these line-shapes. Subsequently, advanced fitting algorithms such as Lorentzian difference (LD) analysis [20] and extrapolated semisolid MT line as the reference (EMR) [21] have been established to refine the widely used multipool Lorentzian decomposition. Such analyses derive the reference signal by fitting a portion of the Z-spectrum against a model of the direct RF saturation and semisolid MT contribution. The residual difference between the

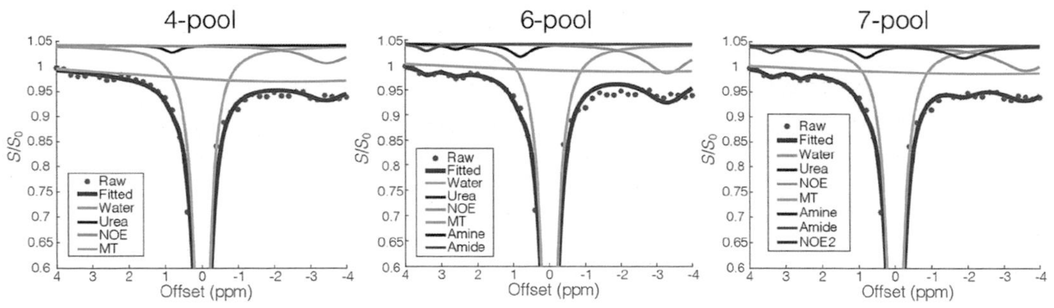

FIG. 33.4

Representative Z-spectra acquired in the mouse kidney inner medulla and papilla under resting conditions at 7 T using a pulsed CEST sequence (peak B_1 of 0.6 μT) following by a single shot GRE readout. Fitting of such spectra using a Lorentzian combination approach reveals the influence of the number of assumed pools upon the accuracy of the fitting. When using a 4-pool model (water, urea, MT, and single NOE pool), the linewidth of the Lorentzian function representing urea is increased, and the amplitude diminished by additional contrasts originating from amine (2 ppm) and amide (3.6 ppm) groups within the inner medulla. Similarly, the magnitude of MT is fit to a larger value to compensate for the absence of pools at those resonances. Increasing the number of pools to 6 by adding the amine and amide groups leads to an increase in measured urea contrast and a reduction in measured MT. However, fitting of the conjugate side of the spectrum with only one NOE pool leads to improper fitting along with the negative offset frequencies. The inclusion of a second NOE pool with a center frequency of -1.6 ppm improves the overall quality of fit.

Data shown in this graph is unpublished and provided courtesy of Mr. Soo Hyun Shin at U.C. Berkeley.

measured and reference signals, as shown in Fig. 33.2B can then be used to quantify CEST contrast either as the amplitude of a spectrally constrained Lorentzian function or simply by measurement of the amplitude at a designated offset frequency. In both cases, this amplitude can be substituted for MTR_{asym} and used to calculate either exchange or pool size as previously described.

Importantly, while this approach does not require the absence of exchangeable protons at the conjugate offset frequency, there are limitations to consider. First, the acquisition of a complete Z-spectrum to adequately sample each line-shape, in particular those of water and MT, can be time-consuming. While accelerated approaches exist to model direct saturation of water and MT using only three offset frequencies [22,23], these approaches are generally only valid at high field strengths ($\geq$7T) [24]. However, a direct RF saturation effect-corrected CEST (DISC-CEST) approach has been developed to calculate the RF spillover effect using spinlock theory [25]. Second, the amplitude of CEST contrast generated in a given microenvironment (e.g., intracellular, extracellular, intravascular) is strongly influenced by R_{1w}. In pathologies where R_{1w} is either nonuniform or changes as a function of disease stage, the derivation of exchange parameters from measured CEST contrast requires R_{1w} correction.

33.3.3 R_{1w}-scaled inverse analysis

To account for the influence of R_{1w} upon the measured CEST contrast, the previously described MTR_{asym} measurement is inversely normalized to R_{1w} using the following formula, and termed the apparent relaxation exchange (AREX) [26] contrast:

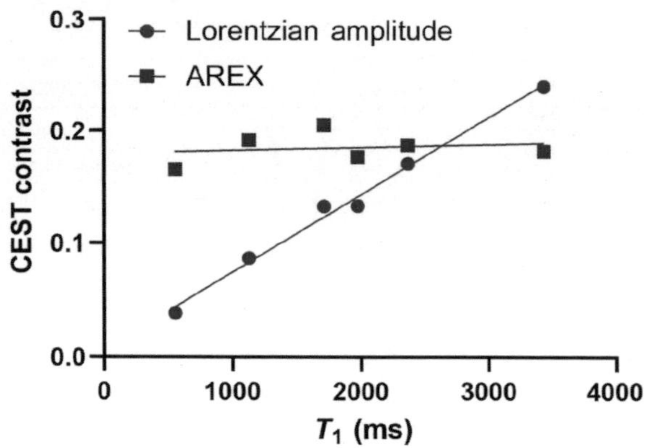

FIG. 33.5

Representative data from a phantom containing identical concentrations of urea (50 mM) but doped with gadolinium at varying concentrations to generate a range of T_{1w} values. Measurement of Lorentzian amplitude demonstrates a clear dependence upon the T_{1w} times of the bulk water pool. In juxtaposition, AREX contrast, which compensates for the R_{1w} of the bulk water pool, remains constant.

Data shown in this graph is unpublished and provided courtesy of Mr. Soo Hyun Shin at U.C. Berkeley.

$$\text{AREX} = R_{1w} \cdot \left(\frac{S_0}{S(+\Delta\omega)} - \frac{S_0}{S(-\Delta\omega)} \right) \tag{33.6}$$

The calculation and presentation of AREX values can be performed for every voxel in an image as long as both CEST-weighted images and R_{1w} maps are acquired with identical resolution. A useful example to consider is the impact of R_{1w} upon quantification of CEST contrast from urea, as shown in Fig. 33.5.

33.4 Exchange rate mapping

The contrast generated in a CEST MRI experiment not only depends on the labile proton ratio but also varies with the labile proton exchange rate. Enormous information can be obtained by making the transition from CEST-weighted imaging to quantitative CEST (qCEST) mapping [27,28]. Concurrent determination of labile proton exchange rate and solute concentration provides additional physiologically relevant information about the underlying system [28]. It is worth noting that although the confounding effects of RF irradiation power and duration on the CEST MRI signal were originally considered detrimental for CEST imaging, they have proven to be versatile variables for characterization and quantification of exchange rates and solute concentrations from CEST data.

33.4.1 qCEST with saturation time and power dependency

Because the experimental CEST measurement depends on both the saturation efficiency and saturation time, the underlying system can be assessed by varying the RF saturation, via quantification of exchange rate using varying saturation power (QUESP) or RF saturation time (QUEST) [29]

$$\text{CESTR} = \frac{f_s \cdot k_{sw}}{R_{1w}} \cdot \alpha(B_1) \cdot e^{-(R_{1w} + f_s \cdot k_{sw}) \cdot t_{sat}} \quad (33.7)$$

where the t_{sat} is the total saturation time. In such experiments, the CEST scan is repeated at multiple B_1 levels using a fixed saturation time or at multiple saturation times using a fixed B_1 level, and the product of the exchange rate and solute concentration (i.e., $k_{ws} \cdot f_s$) is determined by least-squares nonlinear fitting of the RF power- or saturation time-dependent CEST effect. In reciprocal linear QUEST (RL-QUEST), the natural log of CESTR is calculated so the exponential fitting becomes a linear function [30]. Moreover, it is possible to take advantage of the dependency of the CEST effect on both saturation power and time using QUESPT, which has the advantage of being less susceptible to fitting bias [31]

It has also been recognized that the apparent relaxation rate in QUEST analyses is governed not by the intrinsic R_{1w}, but by $R_{1\rho}$ [32]. The QUEST approach has been modified to include ratiometric analysis (QUESTRA) by normalizing the label image signal with that of the reference image [33]. In this experiment, the label and reference scans are repeated for two saturation durations, including one long saturation time (∞) that reaches the steady-state and another finite saturation time (t_{sat}).

$$k_{ws} = -\frac{1}{f_s \cdot t_{sat}} \ln \left(\left. 1 - \frac{MTR_{label}(t_{sat})}{MTR_{label}(\infty)} \right/ 1 - \frac{MTR_{ref}(t_{sat})}{MTR_{ref}(\infty)} \right) \quad (33.8)$$

Because the same $R_{1\rho}$ is experienced by both label and reference scans, the spinlock effect can be normalized without an explicit $R_{1\rho}$ measurement, enabling a more accurate calculation of the exchange rate.

33.4.2 Omega plot and generalized omega plot analysis

While the measurement of the product of the exchange rate and solute concentration may be useful, it is more valuable to tease these parameters apart for an improved understanding of the system. It has been shown that the optimal RF power, at which the measurable CEST effect is maximized, varies with the exchange rate but not the labile proton ratio [23]. By using multiple RF irradiation levels to generate CEST signals, both the labile proton exchange rate and concentration ratio can be determined [27]. Although it is not straightforward to accurately determine the optimal RF power level, this approach demonstrates that experiments of this type can be used to quantify both the exchange rate and solute concentration. For instance, it has been shown that an "omega plot," where the CEST signal is plotted against the inverse of the square of the RF power, can be used to determine the concentration-independent exchange rate. The initial demonstration of this analysis used a paramagnetic CEST (paraCEST) MRI agent (with a negligible direct RF saturation effect, which simplifies the mathematical description) [34]. In this case, the following relationship can be written:

$$\frac{M_{ss}^w}{M_0^w - M_{ss}^w} = \left(\frac{k_{sw} \cdot R_{1w}}{f_s} \right) \cdot \left(\frac{1}{\omega_1^2} + \frac{1}{k_{sw}^2} \right) \quad (33.9)$$

where M_{ss}^w is the steady-state signal of bulk water when the saturation pulse is applied at the labile proton frequency, and ω_1 is the RF irradiation power ($\omega_1 = 2\pi\gamma B_1$). The exchange rate can be determined from the slope and intercept (i.e. $\frac{1}{k_{sw}^2}$) when plotting $\frac{M_{ss}^w}{M_0^w - M_{ss}^w}$ as a function of $\frac{1}{\omega_1^2}$ (i.e., $k_{sw} = \sqrt{\frac{C_1}{C_0}}$, where c_0 and c_1 are the intercept and slope of the omega plot, respectively).

The simplistic omega plot analysis has been extended for diamagnetic CEST (diaCEST) MRI. The modified solution accounts for direct RF saturation with RF spillover effect (1 - σ) correction using Eq. (33.4) [35]

$$\frac{1}{\mathrm{CESTR}_{\sigma}}=\left(1+\frac{R_{1w}}{f_s\cdot k_{sw}}\right)+\frac{k_{sw}\cdot r_{2s}}{\omega_1^2}\left(1-\frac{f_s\cdot k_{sw}}{R_{1w}+f_s\cdot k_{sw}}\right)\left(1+\frac{R_{1w}}{f_s\cdot k_{sw}}\right) \tag{33.10}$$

where CESTR_{σ} is the RF spillover-corrected CEST effect. The modified omega plot analysis (based on Eq. 33.10) involves plotting the inverse measured CEST signal (CESTR_{σ}) as a function of $\frac{1}{\omega_1^2}$. Both the labile proton exchange rate and the labile proton ratio can be determined from the intercept and slope of this modified omega plot:

$$k_{sw}=\left(\sqrt{R_{2s}^2+\frac{4C_1}{C_0\text{-}1}}-R_{2s}\right)/2 \tag{33.11a}$$

$$f_s=R_{1w}/(k_{sw}\cdot(C_0-1)) \tag{33.11b}$$

in which C_0 and C_1 are the intercept and slope of the modified omega plot, respectively. Note that the RF spillover effect can also be corrected using the inversed normalization approach (i.e., $\frac{S_0}{S(+\Delta\omega)}$-$\frac{S_0}{S(-\Delta\omega)}$) [36]. Fig. 33.6 demonstrates the concurrent determination of the labile proton ratio and the exchange rate in a creatine phantom. Fig. 33.6A shows the chemical exchange rate map calculated using Eq. (33.11a), following a dominantly base-catalyzed exchange rate relationship. The labile proton ratio map can also be derived from Eq. (33.11b). Notably, the concentration map in Fig. 33.6C shows similar values for vials with the same creatine concentrations, despite their pH differences, as expected. The labile proton ratio scales linearly with creatine concentration (Fig. 33.6D).

33.4.3 Ratiometric analysis

Ratiometric CEST MRI analyses have been developed to remove the labile proton ratio dependence, thus making the ratiometric map more specific to the exchange rate [2,37,38]. Chemical shift-based ratiometric CEST analyses, such as acidoCEST [39] and amine/amide concentration-independent detection (AACID) [40], examine the ratio of CEST effects at different chemical shifts, which are caused by different distinguishable labile proton groups. Ratiometric CEST MRI has also been generalized to account for CEST MRI effects obtained under different RF power levels [41,42]. A general description of ratiometric CEST MRI (*r*CESTR) is given by:

$$r\mathrm{CESTR}(k_{sw})=\frac{\mathrm{CESTR}\,(\delta_1,\omega_{1a})}{\mathrm{CESTR}\,(\delta_2,\omega_{1b})} \tag{33.12}$$

where either the chemical shift (δ) or RF power level (ω) can serve the ratio dimension [43]. This generalization makes ratiometric CEST MRI versatile, such that the appropriate metrics can be selected for different applications. For example, the exchange rate can be derived from the ratiometric analysis of CEST effects obtained under two RF power levels (ω_{1a} *and* ω_{1b}):

$$k_{sw}=\frac{\sqrt{R_{2s}^2+4\omega_{1a}^2\omega_{1b}^2\frac{1-r\mathrm{CESTR}}{\omega_{1b}^2 r\mathrm{CESTR}-\omega_{1a}^2}}-R_{2s}}{2} \tag{33.13}$$

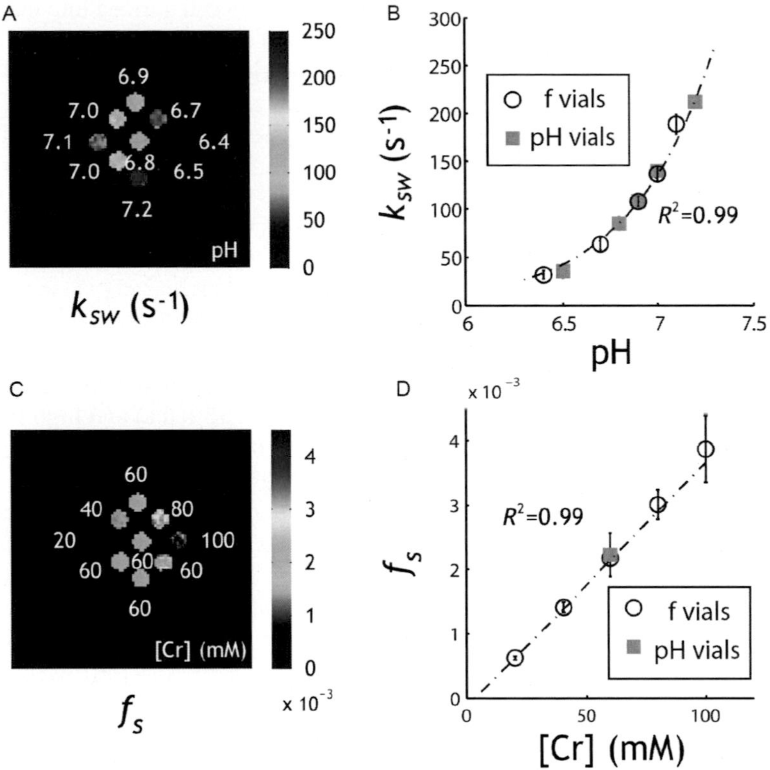

FIG. 33.6

Quantitative analysis of pH-sensitive CEST imaging in a multivial CEST phantom with mixed creatine concentration and pH. (A) Chemical exchange rate map as a function of pH from 6.5 to 7.2. (B) Dominantly base-catalyzed relationship between the derived chemical exchange rate and pH. The "*f*" vials refer to those with the different concentrations of creatine, and the "pH" vials to those with different pH values at the same creatine concentration (see C). (C) Labile proton ratio map (f_S) along with ground-truth creatine concentrations. (D) Linear regression between the derived labile proton ratio and creatine concentration (mM); note that the "pH" vials which have the same creatine concentration fall together on this plot, as expected.

33.5 CEST contrast agents

CEST MRI uses a well-designed frequency-selective RF saturation to induce an exchange-dependent CEST contrast. This set-up is advantageous because the CEST contrast can be turned on and off at will. Moreover, CEST MRI has a higher sensitivity than direct MR spectroscopy (MRS) measurements because the saturation transfer mechanism amplifies the signal from the low-concentration labile CEST protons by a factor which is on the order of the chemical exchange rate. Additionally, the development of exogenous CEST agents, as well as labeling approaches, has immensely improved the detection sensitivity of CEST imaging. Overall, CEST agents are generally categorized into diamagnetic CEST (diaCEST) and paramagnetic CEST (paraCEST) agents based on the characteristics of the compound responsible for the chemical shift of the labile protons.

33.5.1 Diamagnetic CEST agents

Diamagnetic CEST agents are labile protons with resonant frequencies that are often relatively close to that of bulk water (within 5–6 ppm). The frequency offset relative to water, typical cellular concentration, and range of exchange rates within the brain for the most commonly studied endogenous diaCEST contrast sources are summarized in Table 33.1. Despite relatively closely spaced resonant frequencies, the design of the saturation module used to generate CEST contrast within a CEST MRI experiment can be fine-tuned so that the desired CEST contrast is selectively enhanced to dominate the contrast. For example, studies have shown that glutamate can be detected via CEST MRI experiments at 3 ppm (GluCEST) using a moderate RF power level (>3.6 μT) and high field (>7 T) [44]. Under such conditions, the endogenous amide CEST MRI effect at 3.5 ppm is significantly smaller [45]. Similarly, CEST derivative sequences such as the VDMP method use power and duty cycle settings to create exchange rate filters to restrict the measured contrast to desired endogenous pools with specific exchange rates, despite surrounding labile pools. Further, the infusion of diamagnetic CEST agents, including glucose [46–48] and urea [49] have been used to selectively enhance CEST contrast. Besides, chemical modifications and derivatives of endogenous diaCEST agents, such as aspirin, have been utilized to shift the resonant frequencies of the labile protons substantially further afield from water and beyond the range of endogenous pools [50]. Genetically encoded reporter gene and viral gene transfer methods have also been used to stimulate the expression of artificial polypeptides that generate diamagnetic CEST contrast [51–54]. Furthermore, cellular delivery and enzymatic restriction of diaCEST agents have been used to identify populations of implanted cells [52]. Finally, the Lorentzian decomposition approach can be used to quantify CEST contrast and, with sufficient knowledge of pool size, can be used to map changes in the chemical exchange rate.

Table 33.1 A brief list of commonly used diamagnetic CEST groups, their resonance frequency offsets, typical labile proton concentrations, and exchange rates under physiological conditions. Please note that glucose is often used as an exogenous agent in CEST imaging.

	$\Delta\omega_0$(ppm)	Concentration (mM)	k_{sw} (s^{-1})
Proteins/peptides [55]	3.5	~72	~30–100
Glutamate [44, 56]	3	~10	~2000–5000
Creatine [44, 57–62]	1.9	~6	~500–1000
Myo-inositol (MI) [63]	0.6	~10	~600
Glucose [64]	1.2	–	~5000

33.5.2 paraCEST MRI

As stated earlier, the resonance frequencies of diaCEST agents are close to that of bulk water. Thus, although diaCEST agents are readily available and have been widely used, it may be advantageous to design CEST agents with large chemical shifts to probe exchange in the intermediate and fast exchange regimes [3]. Paramagnetic lanthanide chelates have been used to induce large chemical shifts for use as CEST contrast agents. Here the labile protons are those from the macrocyclic structure or the co-ordinated water molecule(s) [65]. Table 33.2 lists several of the most widely studied paramagnetic CEST (paraCEST) agents with their chemical shifts and exchange rate. In murine models, these agents have been used for vascular imaging to track the distribution and fates of exogenously delivered cells [66,67], and to track microenvironmental changes in disease [68,69]

Besides, for some contrast agents, the chemical-physical properties of the solution (e.g., pH and temperature) impact either the lanthanide-induced chemical shift (e.g., Eu-HPDO3A has a chemical shift of 20 ppm at room temperature but 15 ppm at physiological core body temperature) or the pool sizes at different offset frequencies (e.g., the sizes of the two pools associated with Yb-HPDO3A are a function of solution pH). Subsequently, CEST contrast following injection of paraCEST agents has been demonstrated as a novel method to image in vivo metal ion concentration, pH, and temperature [70]. Similar approaches have been used with computed tomography iodinated contrast agents [71,72]. In each case, either the magnitude of CEST contrast or direct measurement of the underlying exchange rate can be mapped. While most studies have used either MTR_{asym} or Lorentzian amplitude, the qCEST-based optimization and quantification can be used to fine-tune the measurement of the chemical exchange rate of these systems, and thus their responsiveness and sensitivity.

Table 33.2 A brief table of representative paraCEST agents with their chemical shifts and exchange rates.

	$\Delta\omega_0$ (ppm)	k_{sw} (s^{-1})
Pr-DOTA-4AmCE [73]	-60	~50,000
Nd-DOTA-4AmCE [73]	-32	~12,500
Eu-DOTA-4AmCE [73]	50	~2500
Yb-DOTA-4AmCE [73]	200	~300,000
Eu-DOTAM-Gly [74]	-4	–
Dy-DOTAM-Gly [74]	77	–
Ho-DOTAM-Gly [74]	39	~3000
Er-DOTAM-Gly [74]	-22	~3000
Tm-DOTAM-Gly [74]	-51	~2500
Yb-DOTAM-Gly [74]	-16	~2500
Yb-HPDO3A [75]	71/99	~10,000
Eu-DO3A-tris(amide) [76]	50:54	~15,000

33.6 Applications

A large variety of CEST MRI techniques have been developed and primarily applied in research settings since 2010. Among these methods, CEST MRI of amide proton transfer (APT) and glucose (GlucoCEST) have been most widely used in humans. APT MRI probes the chemical exchange of the endogenous amide protons on the backbones of mobile proteins/peptides with bulk water protons. Applications of APT imaging include acute stroke [55,77–79] and cancer [80,81], where the physiological balance of pH and mobile peptides changes. More recently, GlucoCEST MRI has been investigated as a means to detect intravenously delivered glucose and its analogs for tumor imaging [82–84,85], similar to positron emission tomography of radiolabeled glucose. In this section, the application of CEST in acute stroke and cancer will be discussed.

33.6.1 pH-sensitive APT imaging of acute stroke

Intact cerebral tissue is characterized by tightly-regulated intracellular and extracellular pH. Following acute ischemia, impaired aerobic metabolism of glucose causes pH to decrease considerably [86]. As noted by Hossmann, tissue acidosis becomes pronounced after the decline of the cerebral metabolic rate of glucose (CMRG) and buildup of lactate [87]. The amide proton exchange rate is dominantly base-catalyzed in the brain, and APT MRI can be used as a sensitive pH measurement technique within the physiologically relevant pH range of tissues [55,77,88–91]. Derivation of tissue pH from APT MRI has been used to study ischemic acidosis in acute stroke patients [92] both for diagnosis/confirmation of ischemic stroke, as well as to refine the perfusion/diffusion lesion mismatch into perfusion/pH (benign oligemia) and the pH/diffusion mismatches (metabolic penumbra) [93]. It has been shown that a moderate RF power provides the highest contrast-to-noise ratio (CNR) between the ischemic and contralateral normal regions. Under such conditions, simple measurement of in vivo $\mathrm{MTR_{asym}}$ is confounded by semisolid MT and NOE effects. Further, changes in the tissue relaxation times and MT can occur following ischemic stroke. Together, these effects limit the pH specificity of simple $\mathrm{MTR_{asym}}$ measurements [94]. However, two methods to correct for these changes have been introduced. First, the $\mathrm{MTR_{asym}}$ metric can be corrected to assess pH by applying baseline MT and relaxation normalization [93]

$$\Delta\mathrm{MRAPTR} = R_{1w} \cdot \mathrm{MTR_{asym}} - f(R_{1w}, \mathrm{MMTR}) \tag{33.14}$$

where the non-pH dependent image heterogeneity in the intact tissue (i.e., $R_{1w} \cdot \mathrm{MTR_{asym}}$) can be generally described by a regression function $\mathrm{F}(R_{1w}, \mathrm{MMTR})$ based on the relaxation and MT contrast. With the correction of the baseline heterogeneity, ΔMRAPTR is more conspicuous to pH-induced amide proton exchange rate change, and we have

$$\Delta\mathrm{MRAPTR} \propto \mathrm{C}_0 \cdot 10^{\mathrm{C}_1 \cdot \mathrm{pH_{norm}}} \cdot \left(10^{\mathrm{C}_1 \cdot (\mathrm{pH} - \mathrm{pH_{norm}})} - 1\right) \tag{33.15}$$

in which $\mathrm{pH_{norm}}$ is the normal tissue pH, and Cs are coefficients from the pH-ΔMRAPTR calibration. Tissue pH can be derived from ΔMRAPTR as $\mathrm{pH} = \mathrm{pH_{norm}} + \log 10\left(1 + \frac{\Delta\mathrm{MRAPTR}}{C_0 \cdot 10^{C_1 \cdot \mathrm{pH_{norm}}}}\right)/C_1$. Fig. 33.7 shows a pH-specific MRAPTR image in a representative acute stroke rat. The $\mathrm{MTR_{asym}}$ (Fig. 33.7A) heterogeneity in the contralateral normal brain can be corrected by regression with R_{1w} and mean MT ratio at ±3.5 ppm (MMTR), which yields a pH-specific ΔMRAPTR image

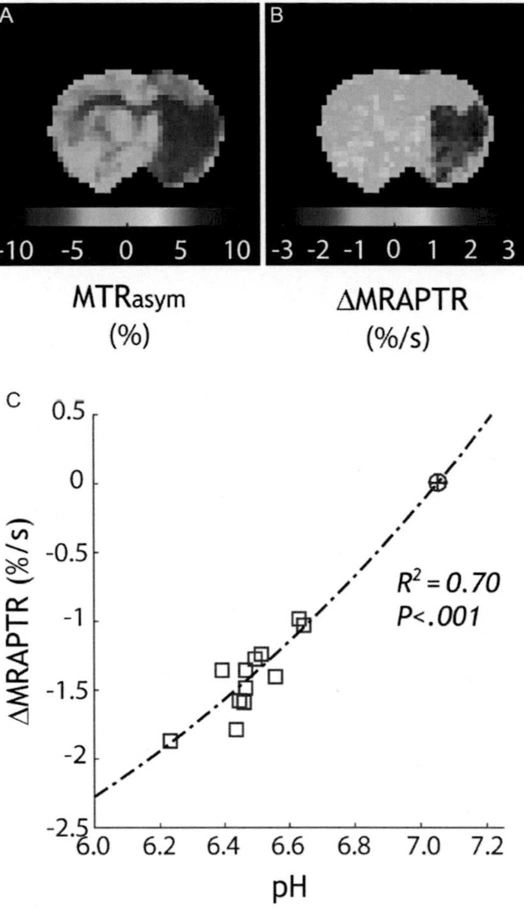

FIG. 33.7

pH-specific MRAPT MRI from a representative acute stroke rat. (A) pH-weighted MTR_{asym} image. (B) pH-specific ΔMRAPTR MRI. (C) Correlation between voxel pH determined from MRS and pH-specific ΔMRAPTR MRI. The blue squares are ipsilateral ischemic ROIs from stroke animals, and the red circle represents the mean pH and ΔMRAPTR from the contralateral normal ROI.

(Fig. 33.7B). The lower-pH lesion seen in the pH-specific ΔMRAPTR image confirms graded tissue acidification. Fig. 33.7C shows that ΔMRAPTR is highly correlated with pH, and can thus be used to map absolute tissue pH. Second, Lorentzian-based decomposition (as described in Section 33.3) has been applied to resolve ischemic lesions in patients [95]. Fig. 33.8 presents images from multi-parametric stroke MRI, showing that both asymmetric APT and Lorentzian APT effects complement time to peak (TTP) and diffusion MRI, aiding in the prediction of stroke outcomes [96]. The multipool fitting approach has been reported to be superior over model-free techniques for acute stroke imaging [97]

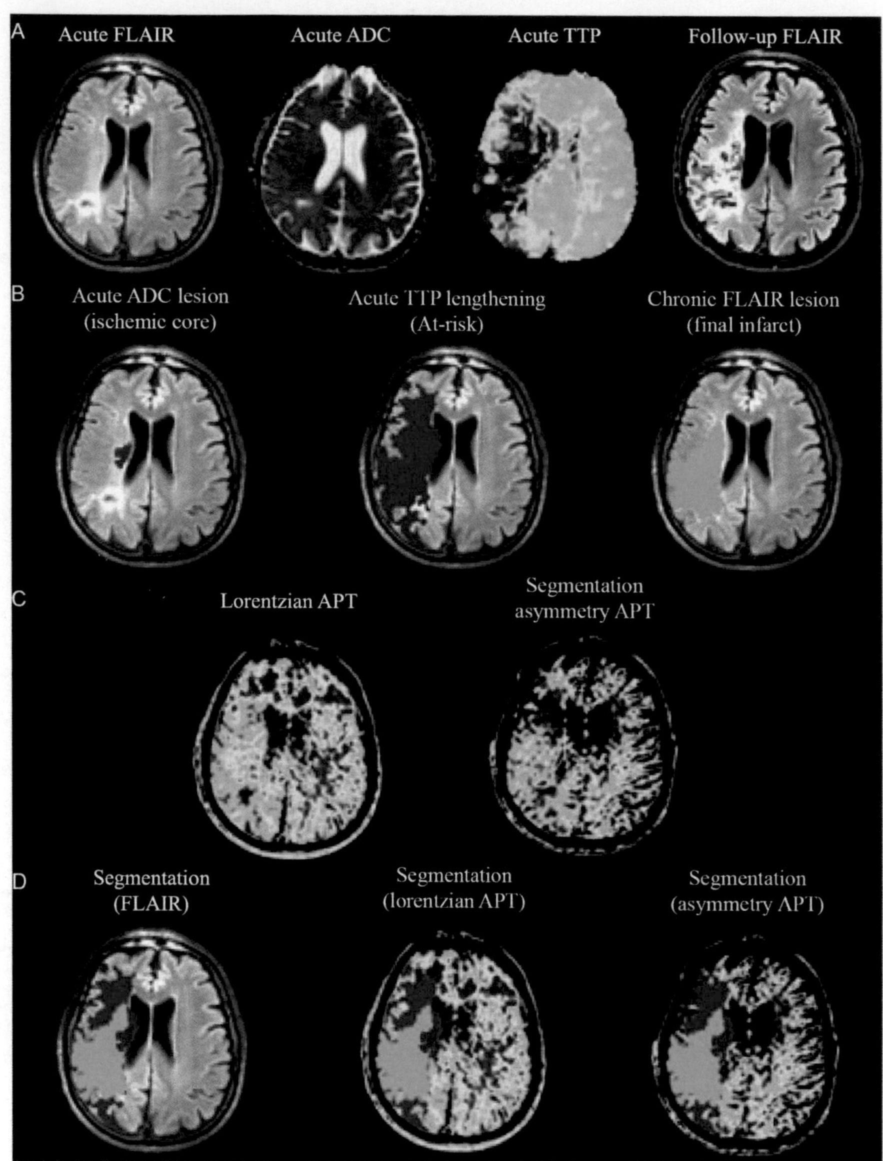

FIG. 33.8

(A) Example of acute T_{2w} FLuid Attenuated Inversion Recovery (T_{2w} FLAIR), apparent diffusion coefficient (ADC), time-to-peak (TTP), and follow-up (>1 month) T_{2w} FLAIR images in a stroke patient. (B) Semiautomated segmentation is used to define the ischemic core (hypointensity in the acute ADC map), the at-risk tissue (lengthening on the TTP map), and the final infarct volume (hyperintensity on the follow-up T_{2w} FLAIR). (C) The APT maps, calculated according to the Lorentzian and asymmetry approaches. (D) Each region is overlaid on the coregistered acute images (acute T_{2w} FLAIR and amide proton transfer, APT, maps shown).

33.6.2 CEST imaging of tumor

Among the hallmarks of cancer, high proliferation rate, extracellular acidification [98], and high glucose uptake (Warburg effect) [99] are physiological characteristics that can be detected by CEST MRI. In tumor cells that undergo rapid proliferation, higher cellular protein content than normal cells [100] results in changes in the contrast generated by the endogenous APT process. Early studies that utilized APT-weighted MRI have demonstrated the detection of malignant brain tumors [101] and the capacity to differentiate tumor recurrence from radiation necrosis [80]. In parallel, the tumor extracellular pH (6.7–7.1) is uniquely lower than the intracellular pH (7.1–7.3) mainly due to glycolysis in anaerobic conditions in cancer. pH-sensitive CEST contrast agents such as iopromide [39,69], and iopamidol [37] remain extracellular and can provide measurements of the pH of the extracellular and extravascular space. In response to treatment, intracellular pH has been shown to change in specific cell types, and the CEST technique known as AACID has been used to map the intracellular pH changes induced by anticancer drugs [40,102–104]. Fig. 33.9 shows AACID images before and after injection of antiepileptic drug topiramate (TPM), which induces acute intracellular acidification in a murine model of the brain tumor [102]. Finally, due to a higher glycolytic rate of glucose than normal tissue, CEST imaging of glucose and its analogs (e.g., 2-deoxy-D-glucose (2DG), 2-deoxy-fluoro-D-glucose (FDG), 3-o-methyl-D-glucose (3oMG), glucosamine, sucrose, etc.) has been examined as a method for assessing tumor metabolism [85,105–110]. Finally, sugar-based polymers (e.g., dextran) can also be used as contrast agents to characterize permeability [111] in tumors.

33.7 Practical limitations

Significant progress has been achieved in the field of CEST MRI with promising in vivo applications. Nevertheless, CEST MRI has limitations and pitfalls, which need to be considered to guide the future development of CEST MRI.

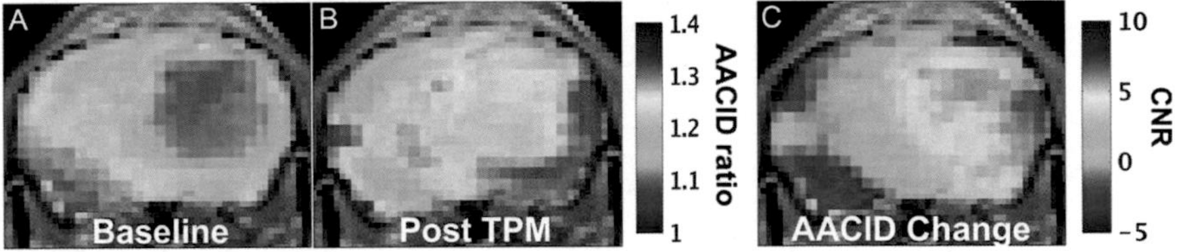

FIG. 33.9

Amine/Amide Concentration-Independent detection (AACID) ratio maps from a representative NU-NU mouse brain with a tumor. CEST images were acquired immediately before (A) and ~75 min after (B) i.p. injection of 120 mg/kg TPM. The AACID contrast map (C) was calculated as the change in AACID divided by the background noise in the contralateral region before TPM treatment , representing the change in AACID value induced by a single dose of TPM and showing tumor-selective acidification.

33.7.1 SNR efficiency

For endogenous metabolites, CEST contrast is only a few percent due to the low metabolite concentration and exchange rates [112,113]. Therefore, it is necessary to optimize the signal-to-noise ratio (SNR) per unit time (i.e., SNR efficiency) to achieve the highest sensitivity for given total scan time. To this end, a general form of the CNR in CEST MRI has been derived. The CNR depends on experimental parameters such as repetition time, saturation time, and imaging flip angle, and all of which need to be considered to optimize SNR efficiency [114,115]:

$$\mathrm{SNR_{efficiency}} = \frac{\mathrm{CESTR}}{\sqrt{2+\mathrm{CESTR}^2}\cdot\sqrt{\mathrm{TR}}}\cdot \mathrm{SNR}_{S_0} \tag{33.16}$$

where SNR_{S_0} is the SNR of the control image without saturation. Fig. 33.10A shows that the SNR efficiency-based optimization strategy identifies the peak SNR efficiency, and results in a substantially higher SNR than when using the assumption of a thermal equilibrium state (i.e., $\mathrm{TR}=5 \times T_{1w}$). Besides, the optimal B_1 level determined from the exhaustive optimization strategy is noticeably higher than that of the routine prediction based on a long *TR* solution (Fig. 33.10B). This shows the importance of using the SNR efficiency to guide optimization. It is worth mentioning that the CEST MRI sensitivity can be enhanced by using segmented RF saturation interleaved with either a multislice image readout [113] or a multiecho readout [116]

33.7.2 Field inhomogeneity correction

Measurement of CEST contrast and derivation of subsequent exchange, concentration, or pH parameters is highly susceptible to magnetic field inhomogeneities. Correction for B_0 inhomogeneities is routinely performed following the acquisition of either a B_0 field map or a WASSR map. However, such an approach requires densely sampled Z-spectral images, at a minimum around the label and

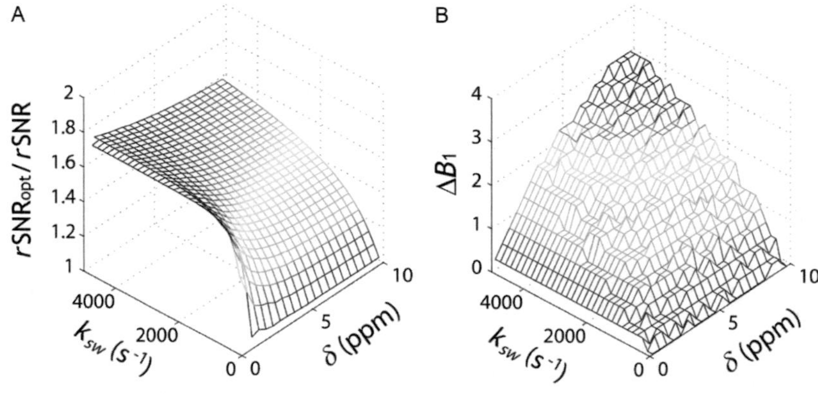

FIG. 33.10

Demonstration of the advantage of the exhaustive CEST MRI optimization strategy. (A) The ratio of peak SNR efficiency from the exhaustive optimization strategy (TR, FA, and B_1 optimization) over that assuming a long TR. (B) The optimal B_1 difference between the exhaustive optimization strategy and routine optimization approach assuming a long TR.

reference offsets, which prolongs the scan time [117,118]. More recently, correction for spatial B_1 inhomogeneity has become more commonplace in CEST MRI. The saturation efficiency for CEST labeling is dependent on both the irradiation frequency and power. Besides, the MT asymmetry analysis assumes an identical RF spillover effect for the reference and label saturated scans, which is no longer valid in the presence of such field inhomogeneities. For a simplistic two-pool CEST system, fast field inhomogeneity correction has been developed by accounting for the spillover effects and saturation efficiency [119]. Recently, fast field inhomogeneity correction has been extended to pH-specific in vivo MRAPT analysis, without requiring the collection of time-consuming Z-spectra [120].

33.7.3 The specificity of CEST measurement

Tissue relaxation plays a pivotal role in understanding and quantifying CEST contrast. Simulations indicate that MTR_{asym} has a complex dependence on T_{1w}: MTR_{asym} is proportional to T_{1w} at the high field or low power, while it becomes roughly insensitive to T_{1w} at the low field or very high power [121,122]. In vivo relaxation effects become even more complex in chronic stroke and tumor due to concurrent changes in water content, partial volume, and concomitant NOE and MT effects. Although APT has been studied the most, there may be additional nonnegligible effects from exchangeable guanidyl and hydroxyl protons. These exchanging pools, along with the semisolid MT and NOE effects, need to be modeled to fully characterize and quantify complex in vivo CEST parameters. While the Lorentzian decomposition algorithm has been adopted to resolve multipool CEST effects, it may not perform well at relatively high power levels or low magnetic fields due to the coalescence of the fast exchanging pool and water pool [123]. A systematic study to decouple these contributions is necessary to measure the in vivo CEST MRI effect accurately. Most importantly for quantitative exchange rate and labile proton concentration measurements, the development of approaches for collecting in vivo omega plots is critical to determine the labile proton ratio and exchange rate independently, a leap from the current simplistic modeling of the CEST effect (where the product of these desired quantities, $f_s \times k_{sw}$, is gathered).

33.8 Summary

CEST MRI provides a sensitive means to detect dilute labile protons via their chemical exchange with the bulk tissue water. Although the CEST experimental measurement depends on not only labile proton ratio and exchange rate, but also relaxation constant and experimental conditions, substantial progress has been achieved towards exchange rate-specific measurements, which lays the foundation of quantitative CEST (qCEST) analysis. Further development is needed to extend qCEST MRI to a multipool exchange phenomenon and ultimately establish fast and quantitative in vivo CEST imaging.

References

[1] Henkelman RM, Stanisz GJ, Graham SJ. Magnetization transfer in MRI: a review. NMR Biomed 2001;14:57–64.

[2] Ward KM, Balaban RS. Determination of pH using water protons and chemical exchange dependent saturation transfer (CEST). Magn Reson Med 2000;44:799–802.

[3] van Zijl PCM, Lam WW, Xu JD, Knutsson L, Stanisz GJ. Magnetization transfer contrast and chemical exchange saturation transfer MRI. Features and analysis of the field-dependent saturation spectrum. Neuroimage 2018;168:222–41.

[4] Woessner DE, Zhang SR, Merritt ME, Sherry AD. Numerical solution of the bloch equations provides insights into the optimum design of paracest agents for MRI. Magn Reson Med 2005;53:790–9.

[5] Zhou J, Wilson DA, Sun PZ, Klaus JA, Van Zijl PC. Quantitative description of proton exchange processes between water and endogenous and exogenous agents for WEX, CEST, and APT experiments. Magn Reson Med 2004;51:945–52.

[6] Jin T, Kim SG. Advantages of chemical exchange-sensitive spin-lock (CESL) over chemical exchange saturation transfer (CEST) for hydroxyl- and amine-water proton exchange studies. NMR Biomed 2014;27: 1313–1324.

[7] Trott O, Palmer 3rd AG. R1 rho relaxation outside of the fast-exchange limit. J Magn Reson 2002;154:157–60.

[8] Zu Z, Li K, Janve VA, Does MD, Gochberg DF. Optimizing pulsed-chemical exchange saturation transfer imaging sequences. Magn Reson Med 2011;66:1100–8.

[9] Xu JD, Yadav NN, Bar-Shir A, Jones CK, Chan KWY, Zhang JY, et al. Variable delay multi-pulse train for fast chemical exchange saturation transfer and relayed-nuclear overhauser enhancement MRI. Magn Reson Med 2014;71:1798–812.

[10] Friedman JI, McMahon MT, Stivers JT, Van Zijl PC. Indirect detection of labile solute proton spectra via the water signal using frequency-labeled exchange (FLEX) transfer. J Am Chem Soc 2010;132:1813–5.

[11] Zu Z, Janve VA, Xu J, Does MD, Gore JC, Gochberg DF. A new method for detecting exchanging amide protons using chemical exchange rotation transfer. Magn Reson Med 2013;69:637–47.

[12] Scheidegger R, Vinogradov E, Alsop DC. Amide proton transfer imaging with improved robustness to magnetic field inhomogeneity and magnetization transfer asymmetry using saturation with frequency alternating RF irradiation. Magn Reson Med 2011;66:1275–85.

[13] Song X, Gilad AA, Joel S, Liu G, Bar-Shir A, Liang Y, et al. Cest phase mapping using a length and offset varied saturation (LOVARS) scheme. Magn Reson Med 2012;68:1074–86.

[14] Hua J, Jones CK, Blakeley J, Smith SA, van Zijl PCM, Zhou JY. Quantitative description of the asymmetry in magnetization transfer effects around the water resonance in the human brain. Magn Reson Med 2007; 58:786–93.

[15] Sun PZ, van Zijl PC, Zhou J. Optimization of the irradiation power in chemical exchange dependent saturation transfer experiments. J Magn Reson 2005;175:193–200.

[16] Zaiss M, Schmitt B, Bachert P. Quantitative separation of cest effect from magnetization transfer and spillover effects by lorentzian-line-fit analysis of *z*-spectra. J Magn Reson 2011;211:149–55.

[17] Desmond KL, Moosvi F, Stanisz GJ. Mapping of amide, amine, and aliphatic peaks in the CEST spectra of murine xenografts at 7 T. Magn Reson Med 2014;71:1841–53.

[18] Zhou IY, Lu D, Ji Y, Wu L, Wang E, Cheung JS, et al. Determination of multipool contributions to endogenous amide proton transfer effects in global ischemia with high spectral resolution in vivo chemical exchange saturation transfer MRI. Magn Reson Med 2019;81(1):645–52. https://doi.org/10.1002/mrm.27385.

[19] Zhang XY, Wang F, Jin T, Xu JZ, Xie JP, Gochberg DF, et al. MR imaging of a novel NOE-mediated magnetization transfer with water in rat brain at 9.4 T. Magn Reson Med 2017;78:588–97.

[20] Jones CK, Huang A, Xu JD, Edden RAE, Schar M, Hua J, et al. Nuclear overhauser enhancement (NOE) imaging in the human brain at 7 T. Neuroimage 2013;77:114–24.

[21] Heo HY, Zhang Y, Jiang S, Lee DH, Zhou J. Quantitative assessment of amide proton transfer (APT) and nuclear overhauser enhancement (NOE) imaging with extrapolated semisolid magnetization transfer reference (EMR) signals. II. Comparison of three emr models and application to human brain glioma at 3 tesla. Magn Reson Med 2016;75:1630–9.

[22] Jin T, Wang P, Zong XP, Kim SG. Mr imaging of the amide-proton transfer effect and the ph-insensitive nuclear overhauser effect at 9.4 T. Magn Reson Med 2013;69:760–70.

[23] Sun PZ. Simultaneous determination of labile proton concentration and exchange rate utilizing optimal RF power: radio frequency power (RFP) dependence of chemical exchange saturation transfer (CEST) MRI. J Magn Reson 2010;202:155–61.

[24] Zhang XY, Wang F, Li H, Xu JZ, Gochberg DF, Gore JC, et al. Accuracy in the quantification of chemical exchange saturation transfer (CEST) and relayed nuclear overhauser enhancement (RNOE) saturation transfer effects. NMR Biomed 2017;30.

[25] Yuwen Zhou I, Wang E, Cheung JS, Lu D, Ji Y, Zhang X, et al. Direct saturation-corrected chemical exchange saturation transfer MRI of glioma: simplified decoupling of amide proton transfer and nuclear overhauser effect contrasts. Magn Reson Med 2017;78:2307–14.

[26] Zaiss M, Bachert P. Exchange-dependent relaxation in the rotating frame for slow and intermediate exchange—modeling off-resonant spin-lock and chemical exchange saturation transfer. NMR Biomed 2013;26:507–18.

[27] Sun PZ, Wang Y, Xiao G, Wu R. Simultaneous experimental determination of labile proton fraction ratio and exchange rate with irradiation radio frequency power-dependent quantitative CEST MRI analysis. Contrast Media Mol Imaging 2013;8:246–51.

[28] Kim J, Wu Y, Guo Y, Zheng H, Sun PZ. A review of optimization and quantification techniques for chemical exchange saturation transfer MRI toward sensitive in vivo imaging. Contrast Media Mol Imaging 2015;10:163–78.

[29] McMahon MT, Gilad AA, Zhou J, Sun PZ, Bulte JW, van Zijl PC. Quantifying exchange rates in chemical exchange saturation transfer agents using the saturation time and saturation power dependencies of the magnetization transfer effect on the magnetic resonance imaging signal (QUEST and QUESP): pH calibration for poly-L-lysine and a starburst dendrimer. Magn Reson Med 2006;55:836–47.

[30] Randtke EA, Chen LQ, Pagel MD. The reciprocal linear QUEST analysis method facilitates the measurements of chemical exchange rates with CEST MRI. Contrast Media Mol Imaging 2014;9:252–8.

[31] Randtke EA, Chen LQ, Corrales LR, Pagel MD. The Hanes-Woolf linear QUESP method improves the measurements of fast chemical exchange rates with CEST MRI. Magn Reson Med 2014;71:1603–12.

[32] Jin T, Autio J, Obata T, Kim S-G. Spin-locking versus chemical exchange saturation transfer MRI for investigating chemical exchange process between water and labile metabolite protons. Magn Reson Med 2011;65:1448–60.

[33] Sun PZ. Simplified quantification of labile proton concentration-weighted chemical exchange rate (k_{ws}) with RF saturation time dependent ratiometric analysis (QUESTRA): normalization of relaxation and RF irradiation spillover effects for improved quantitative chemical exchange saturation transfer (CEST) MRI. Magn Reson Med 2012;67:936–42.

[34] Dixon WT, Ren J, Lubag AJ, Ratnakar J, Vinogradov E, Hancu I, et al. A concentration-independent method to measure exchange rates in paracest agents. Magn Reson Med 2010;63:625–32.

[35] Sun PZ, Wang Y, Dai Z, Xiao G, Wu R. Quantitative chemical exchange saturation transfer (qCEST) MRI-RF spillover effect-corrected omega plot for simultaneous determination of labile proton fraction ratio and exchange rate. Contrast Media Mol Imaging 2014;9:268–75.

[36] Wu R, Xiao G, Zhou IY, Ran C, Sun PZ. Quantitative chemical exchange saturation transfer (qCEST) MRI-omega plot analysis of RF-spillover-corrected inverse cest ratio asymmetry for simultaneous determination of labile proton ratio and exchange rate. NMR Biomed 2015;28:376–83.

[37] Moon BF, Jones KM, Chen LQ, Liu PL, Randtke EA, Howison CM, et al. A comparison of iopromide and iopamidol, two acidocest MRI contrast media that measure tumor extracellular ph. Contrast Media Mol Imaging 2015;10:446–55.

[38] Longo DL, Dastru W, Digilio G, Keupp J, Langereis S, Lanzardo S, et al. Iopamidol as a responsive mri-chemical exchange saturation transfer contrast agent for pH mapping of kidneys: in vivo studies in mice at 7 T. Magn Reson Med 2011;65:202–11.

[39] Chen LQ, Howison CM, Jeffery JJ, Robey IF, Kuo PH, Pagel MD. Evaluations of extracellular pH within in vivo tumors using acidocest MRI. Magn Reson Med 2014;72:1408–17.

[40] McVicar N, Li AX, Meakin SO, Bartha R. Imaging chemical exchange saturation transfer (CEST) effects following tumor-selective acidification using lonidamine. NMR Biomed 2015;28:566–75.

[41] Longo DL, Sun PZ, Consolino L, Michelotti FC, Uggeri F, Aime S. A general mri-cest ratiometric approach for pH imaging: demonstration of in vivo pH mapping with iobitridol. J Am Chem Soc 2014;136:14333–6.

[42] Wu R, Longo DL, Aime S, Sun PZ. Quantitative description of radiofrequency (RF) power-based ratiometric chemical exchange saturation transfer (CEST) pH imaging. NMR Biomed 2015;28:555–65.

[43] Wu Y, Zhou IY, Igarashi T, Longo DL, Aime S, Sun PZ. A generalized ratiometric chemical exchange saturation transfer (CEST) MRI approach for mapping renal pH using iopamidol. Magn Reson Med 2018;79:1553–8.

[44] Cai K, Haris M, Singh A, Kogan F, Greenberg JH, Hariharan H, et al. Magnetic resonance imaging of glutamate. Nat Med 2012;18:302–6.

[45] Sun PZ, Zhou J, Huang J, van Zijl P. Simplified quantitative description of amide proton transfer (APT) imaging during acute ischemia. Magn Reson Med 2007;57:405–10.

[46] Kim M, Torrealdea F, Adeleke S, Rega M, Evans V, Beeston T, et al. Challenges in glucocest mr body imaging at 3 tesla. Quant Imag Med Surg 2019;9:1628.

[47] Zaiss M, Anemone A, Goerke S, Longo DL, Herz K, Pohmann R, et al. Quantification of hydroxyl exchange of D-glucose at physiological conditions for optimization of glucocest MRI at 3, 7 and 9.4 tesla. NMR Biomed 2019;32.

[48] Xu X, Sehgal AA, Yadav NN, Laterra J, Blair L, Blakeley J, et al. D-glucose weighted chemical exchange saturation transfer (glucocest)-based dynamic glucose enhanced (DGE) MRI at 3 T: early experience in healthy volunteers and brain tumor patients. Magn Reson Med 2019.

[49] Shin SH, Wendland MF, Zhang B, Tran A, Tang A, Vandsburger MH. Noninvasive imaging of renal urea handling by CEST-MRI. Magn Reson Med 2020;83:1034–44.

[50] Yang X, Song XL, Li YG, Liu GS, Banerjee SR, Pomper MG, et al. Salicylic acid and analogues as diacest MRI contrast agents with highly shifted exchangeable proton frequencies. Angew Chem Int Ed 2013;52:8116–9.

[51] Meier S, Gilad AA, Brandon JA, Qian CH, Gao E, Abisambra JF, et al. Non-invasive detection of adeno-associated viral gene transfer using a genetically encoded CEST-MRI reporter gene in the murine heart. Sci Rep 2018;8.

[52] Minn I, Bar-Shir A, Yarlagadda K, Bulte JWM, Fisher PB, Wang H, et al. Tumor-specific expression and detection of a CEST reporter gene. Magn Reson Med 2015;74:544–9.

[53] Farrar CT, Buhrman JS, Liu GS, Kleijn A, Lamfers MLM, McMahon MT, et al. Establishing the lysine-rich protein cest reporter gene as a CEST MR imaging detector for oncolytic virotherapy. Radiology 2015;275:746–54.

[54] Gilad AA, McMahon MT, Walczak P, Winnard PT, Raman V, van Laarhoven HWM, et al. Artificial reporter gene providing MRI contrast based on proton exchange. Nat Biotechnol 2007;25:217–9.

[55] Zhou J, Payen JF, Wilson DA, Traystman RJ, van Zijl PC. Using the amide proton signals of intracellular proteins and peptides to detect pH effects in MRI. Nat Med 2003;9:1085–90.

[56] Jin T, Wang P, Zong XP, Kim SG. Magnetic resonance imaging of the amine-proton exchange (APEX) dependent contrast. Neuroimage 2012;59:1218–27.

[57] Zhang XY, Xie JP, Wang F, Lin EC, Xu JZ, Gochberg DF, et al. Assignment of the molecular origins of CEST signals at 2 ppm in rat brain. Magn Reson Med 2017;78:881–7.

[58] Chen L, Zeng H, Xu X, et al. Investigation of the contribution of total creatine to the CEST Z-spectrum of brain using a knockout mouse model. NMR Biomed 2017;30(12). https//doi.org/10.1002/nbm.3834.

[59] Cai K, Singh A, Poptani H, Li W, Yang S, Lu Y, et al. Cest signal at 2 ppm (cest@2 ppm) from *z*-spectral fitting correlates with creatine distribution in brain tumor. NMR Biomed 2015;28:1–8.

[60] Goerke S, Zaiss M, Bachert P. Characterization of creatine guanidinium proton exchange by water-exchange (WEX) spectroscopy for absolute-ph CEST imaging in vitro. NMR Biomed 2014;27:507–18.

[61] Haris M, Nanga RPR, Singh A, Cai K, Kogan F, Hariharan H, et al. Exchange rates of creatine kinase metabolites: feasibility of imaging creatine by chemical exchange saturation transfer MRI. NMR Biomed 2012;25:1305–9.

[62] Sun PZ, Sorensen AG. Imaging pH using the chemical exchange saturation transfer (CEST) MRI: correction of concomitant RF irradiation effects to quantify CEST MRI for chemical exchange rate and pH. Magn Reson Med 2008;60:390–7.

[63] Haris M, Cai KJ, Singh A, Hariharan H, Reddy R. In vivo mapping of brain myo-inositol. Neuroimage 2011;54:2079–85.

[64] Jin T, Mehrens H, Hendrich KS, Kim SG. Mapping brain glucose uptake with chemical exchange-sensitive spin-lock magnetic resonance imaging. J Cerebr Blood F Met 2014;34:1402–10.

[65] Woods M, Woessner DE, Sherry AD. Paramagnetic lanthanide complexes as paracest agents for medical imaging. Chem Soc Rev 2006;35:500–11.

[66] Ferrauto G, Di Gregorio E, Delli Castelli D, Aime S. CEST-MRI studies of cells loaded with lanthanide shift reagents. Magn Reson Med 2018;80:1626–37.

[67] Pumphrey AL, Ye SJ, Yang ZS, Simkin J, Gensel JC, Abdel-Latif A, et al. Cardiac chemical exchange saturation transfer MR imaging tracking of cell survival or rejection in mouse models of cell therapy. Radiology 2017;282:131–8.

[68] Longo DL, Cutrin JC, Michelotti F, Irrera P, Aime S. Noninvasive evaluation of renal pH homeostasis after ischemia reperfusion injury by CEST-MRI. NMR Biomed 2017;30.

[69] Jones KM, Randtke EA, Yoshimaru ES, Howison CM, Chalasani P, Klein RR, et al. Clinical translation of tumor acidosis measurements with acidocest MRI. Mol Imaging Biol 2017;19:617–25.

[70] Sheth VR, Li Y, Chen LQ, Howison CM, Flask CA, Pagel MD. Measuring in vivo tumor phe with CEST-FISP MRI. Magn Reson Med 2012;67:760–8.

[71] Anemone A, Consolino L, Arena F, Capozza M, Longo DL. Imaging tumor acidosis: a survey of the available techniques for mapping in vivo tumor pH. Cancer Metastasis Rev 2019;38:25–49.

[72] Anemone A, Consolino L, Longo DL. Mri-cest assessment of tumour perfusion using X-ray iodinated agents: comparison with a conventional GD-based agent. Eur Radiol 2017;27:2170–9.

[73] Zhang SR, Sherry AD. Physical characteristics of lanthanide complexes that act as magnetization transfer (MT) contrast agents. J Solid State Chem 2003;171:38–43.

[74] Aime S, Barge A, Delli Castelli D, Fedeli F, Mortillaro A, Nielsen FU, et al. Paramagnetic lanthanide(iii) complexes as ph-sensitive chemical exchange saturation transfer (CEST) contrast agents for MRI applications. Magn Reson Med 2002;47:639–48.

[75] Delli Castelli D, Terreno E, Aime S. Yb-iii-hpdo3a: a dual pH- and temperature-responsive CEST agent. Angew Chem Int Ed 2011;50:1798–800.

[76] Wu YK, Soesbe TC, Kiefer GE, Zhao PY, Sherry AD. A responsive Europium(III) chelate that provides a direct readout of pH by MRI. J Am Chem Soc 2010;132:14002–3.

[77] Sun PZ, Zhou J, Sun W, Huang J, van Zijl PC. Detection of the ischemic penumbra using pH-weighted MRI. J Cereb Blood Flow Metab 2007;27:1129–36.

[78] Harston GW, Tee YK, Blockley N, Okell TW, Thandeswaran S, Shaya G, et al. Identifying the ischaemic penumbra using pH-weighted magnetic resonance imaging. Brain J Neurol 2015;138:36–42.

[79] Wang EF, Wu Y, Cheung JS, Zhou IY, Igarashi T, Zhang XA, et al. pH imaging reveals worsened tissue acidification in diffusion kurtosis lesion than the kurtosis/diffusion lesion mismatch in an animal model of acute stroke. J Cerebr Blood F Met 2017;37:3325–33.

[80] Zhou JY, Tryggestad E, Wen ZB, Lal B, Zhou TT, Grossman R, et al. Differentiation between glioma and radiation necrosis using molecular magnetic resonance imaging of endogenous proteins and peptides. Nat Med 2011;17:130–U308.

[81] Jones CK, Schlosser MJ, van Zijl PCM, Pomper MG, Golay X, Zhou JY. Amide proton transfer imaging of human brain tumors at 3 t. Magn Reson Med 2006;56:585–92.

[82] Walker-Samuel S, Ramasawmy R, Torrealdea F, Rega M, Rajkumar V, Johnson SP, et al. In vivo imaging of glucose uptake and metabolism in tumors. Nat Med 2013;19:1067–72.

[83] Chan KWY, McMahon MT, Kato Y, Liu GS, Bulte JWM, Bhujwalla ZM, et al. Natural D-glucose as a biodegradable mri contrast agent for detecting cancer. Magn Reson Med 2012;68:1764–73.

[84] Rivlin M, Tsarfaty I, Navon G. Functional molecular imaging of tumors by chemical exchange saturation transfer mri of 3-o-methyl-D-glucose. Magn Reson Med 2014;72:1375–80.

[85] Xu X, Chan KWY, Knutsson L, Artemov D, Xu JD, Liu G, et al. Dynamic glucose enhanced (DGE) MRI for combined imaging of blood-brain barrier break down and increased blood volume in brain cancer. Magn Reson Med 2015;74:1556–63.

[86] Astrup J, Siesjo BK, Symon L. Thresholds in cerebral ischemia—the ischemic penumbra. Stroke 1981;12:723–5.

[87] Hossmann KA. Viability thresholds and the penumbra of focal ischemia. Ann Neurol 1994;36:557–65.

[88] Sun PZ, Cheung JS, Wang E, Lo EH. Association between pH-weighted endogenous amide proton chemical exchange saturation transfer MRI and tissue lactic acidosis during acute ischemic stroke. J Cereb Blood Flow Metab 2011;31:1743–50.

[89] Sun PZ, Wang E, Cheung JS. Imaging acute ischemic tissue acidosis with pH-sensitive endogenous amide proton transfer (APT) MRI—correction of tissue relaxation and concomitant RF irradiation effects toward mapping quantitative cerebral tissue pH. Neuroimage 2012;60:1–6.

[90] McVicar N, Li AX, Goncalves DF, Bellyou M, Meakin SO, Prado MA, et al. Quantitative tissue pH measurement during cerebral ischemia using amine and amide concentration-independent detection (AACID) with MRI. J Cereb Blood Flow Metab 2014;34:690–8.

[91] Jokivarsi KT, Grohn HI, Grohn OH, Kauppinen RA. Proton transfer ratio, lactate, and intracellular pH in acute cerebral ischemia. Magn Reson Med 2007;57:647–53.

[92] Lin GS, Zhuang CY, Shen ZW, Xiao G, Chen YZ, Shen YY, et al. Apt weighted mri as an effective imaging protocol to predict clinical outcome after acute ischemic stroke. Front Neurol 2018;9:901.

[93] Guo Y, Zhou IY, Chan ST, Wang Y, Mandeville ET, Igarashi T, et al. Ph-sensitive MRI demarcates graded tissue acidification during acute stroke—pH specificity enhancement with magnetization transfer and relaxation-normalized amide proton transfer (APT) MRI. Neuroimage 2016;141:242–9.

[94] Wu Y, Zhou IY, Lu D, Manderville E, Lo EH, Zheng H, et al. pH-sensitive amide proton transfer effect dominates the magnetization transfer asymmetry contrast during acute ischemia-quantification of multipool contribution to in vivo CEST MRI. Magn Reson Med 2018;79:1602–8.

[95] Tee YK, Harston GWJ, Blockley N, Okell TW, Levman J, Sheerin F, et al. Comparing different analysis methods for quantifying the MRI amide proton transfer (APT) effect in hyperacute stroke patients. NMR Biomed 2014;27:1019–29.

[96] Tietze A, Blicher J, Mikkelsen IK, Ostergaard L, Strother MK, Smith SA, et al. Assessment of ischemic penumbra in patients with hyperacute stroke using amide proton transfer (APT) chemical exchange saturation transfer (CEST) MRI. NMR Biomed 2014;27:163–74.

[97] Msayib Y, Harston GWJ, Tee YK, Sheerin F, Blockley NP, Okell TW, et al. Quantitative cest imaging of amide proton transfer in acute ischaemic stroke. NeuroImage Clin 2019;23:101833.

[98] Gillies RJ, Gatenby RA. Hypoxia and adaptive landscapes in the evolution of carcinogenesis. Cancer Metastasis Rev 2007;26:311–7.

[99] Warburg O. On the origin of cancer cells. Science 1956;123:309–14.

[100] Hobbs SK, Shi GY, Homer R, Harsh G, Atlas SW, Bednarski MD. Magnetic resonance image-guided proteomics of human glioblastoma multiforme. J Magn Reson Imaging 2003;18:530–6.

[101] Wen ZB, Hu SG, Huang FH, Wang XL, Guo LL, Quan XY, et al. MR imaging of high-grade brain tumors using endogenous protein and peptide-based contrast. Neuroimage 2010;51:616–22.

[102] Marathe K, McVicar N, Li A, Bellyou M, Meakin S, Bartha R. Topiramate induces acute intracellular acidification in glioblastoma. J Neurooncol 2016;130:465–72.

[103] Desmond KL, Mehrabian H, Chavez S, Sahgal A, Soliman H, Rola R, et al. Chemical exchange saturation transfer for predicting response to stereotactic radiosurgery in human brain metastasis. Magn Reson Med 2017;78:1110–20.

[104] Albatany M, Li A, Meakin S, Bartha R. Dichloroacetate induced intracellular acidification in glioblastoma: in vivo detection using aacid-CEST MRI at 9.4 tesla. J Neurooncol 2018;136:255–62.

[105] Rivlin M, Navon G. Molecular imaging of tumors by chemical exchange saturation transfer MRI of glucose analogs. Quant Imaging Med Surg 2019;9:1731–46.

[106] Sehgal AA, Li YG, Lal B, Yadav NN, Xu X, Xu JD, et al. CEST MRI of 3-o-methyl-D-glucose uptake and accumulation in brain tumors. Magn Reson Med 2019;81:1993–2000.

[107] Bagga P, Haris M, D'Aquilla K, Wilson NE, Marincola FM, Schnall MD, et al. Non-caloric sweetener provides magnetic resonance imaging contrast for cancer detection. J Transl Med 2017;15(1):119.

[108] Wang JH, Weygand J, Hwang KP, Mohamed ASR, Ding Y, Fuller CD, et al. Magnetic resonance imaging of glucose uptake and metabolism in patients with head and neck cancer. Sci Rep 2016;6:30618. https://doi.org/10.1038/srep30618.

[109] Bagga P, Wilson N, Rich L, Marincola FM, Schnall MD, Hariharan H, et al. Sugar alcohol provides imaging contrast in cancer detection. Sci Rep 2019;9(1):11092.

[110] Rivlin M, Navon G. CEST MRI of 3-o-methyl-D-glucose on different breast cancer models. Magn Reson Med 2018;79:1061–9.

[111] Li YG, Qiao Y, Chen HW, Bai RY, Staedtke V, Han Z, et al. Characterization of tumor vascular permeability using natural dextrans and CEST MRI. Magn Reson Med 2018;79:1001–9.

[112] Zaiss M, Bachert P. Chemical exchange saturation transfer (CEST) and MR *z*-spectroscopy in vivo: a review of theoretical approaches and methods. Phys Med Biol 2013;58:R221–69.

[113] Sun PZ, Cheung JS, Wang E, Benner T, Sorensen AG. Fast multislice pH-weighted chemical exchange saturation transfer (CEST) MRI with unevenly segmented RF irradiation. Magn Reson Med 2011;65: 588–594.

[114] Jiang W, Zhou IY, Wen L, Zhou X, Sun PZ. A theoretical analysis of chemical exchange saturation transfer echo planar imaging (CEST-EPI) steady state solution and the cest sensitivity efficiency-based optimization approach. Contrast Media Mol Imaging 2016;11:415–23.

[115] Sun PZ, Lu J, Wu Y, Xiao G, Wu R. Evaluation of the dependence of CEST-EPI measurement on repetition time, RF irradiation duty cycle and imaging flip angle for enhanced pH sensitivity. Phys Med Biol 2013;58: N229–40.

[116] Sun PZ, Wang Y, Lu J. Sensitivity-enhanced chemical exchange saturation transfer (CEST) MRI with least squares optimization of carr Purcell meiboom gill multi-echo echo planar imaging. Contrast Media Mol Imaging 2014;9:177–81.

[117] Kim M, Gillen J, Landman BA, Zhou J, van Zijl PC. Water saturation shift referencing (WASSR) for chemical exchange saturation transfer (CEST) experiments. Magn Reson Med 2009;61:1441–50.

[118] Schuenke P, Windschuh J, Roeloffs V, Ladd ME, Bachert P, Zaiss M. Simultaneous mapping of water shift and b-1(WASAbi) application to field-inhomogeneity correction of CEST MRI data. Magn Reson Med 2017;77:571–80.

[119] Sun PZ, Farrar CT, Sorensen AG. Correction for artifacts induced by b(0) and b(1) field inhomogeneities in ph-sensitive chemical exchange saturation transfer (CEST) imaging. Magn Reson Med 2007;58: 1207–1215.

[120] Sun PZ. Fast correction of b0 field inhomogeneity for pH-specific magnetization transfer and relaxation normalized amide proton transfer imaging of acute ischemic stroke without *z*-spectrum. Magn Reson Med 2020;83:1688–97.

[121] Heo HY, Lee DH, Zhang Y, Zhao XN, Jiang SS, Chen M, et al. Insight into the quantitative metrics of chemical exchange saturation transfer (CEST) imaging. Magn Reson Med 2017;77:1853–65.

[122] Zu ZL. Towards the complex dependence of mtrasym on t-1w in amide proton transfer (APT) imaging. NMR Biomed 2018;31:e3934.

[123] Zhang XY, Wang F, Li H, Xu JZ, Gochberg DF, Gore JC, et al. CEST imaging of fast exchanging amine pools with corrections for competing effects at 9.4 t. NMR Biomed 2017;30:e3715.

CHAPTER

MR Thermometry

34

Bruno Madore

Brigham and Women's Hospital, Harvard Medical School, Advanced Lab for MRI and Acoustics (ALMA), Boston, MA, United States

34.1 Introduction

MR thermometry is the measurement of absolute temperature or temperature changes using MRI. One of the primary applications of MR thermometry is the guidance of ablation therapies, which typically involve inserting one or more needle-like device(s) into benign or malignant lesions to deliver a treating agent. While this treating agent may take the form of chemicals such as alcohol, or electric fields such as in electroporation, more typically it consists of changes in temperature large enough to kill tissues. In cryotherapy tissues are cooled well below 0°C and cell death occurs between -20°C and -50°C [1]. Alternately, tissues can be ablated through heat, as temperatures above 60°C cause almost immediate coagulation and irreversible damage [2]. Heat can be delivered in a number of different ways, such as laser, microwave, and radiofrequency (RF) energy. High-intensity focused ultrasound (HIFU) can also deliver heat for ablation purposes, and HIFU has the added advantage that all related hardware can remain outside of the body, without any need to break the skin. In general, tumor ablation therapies can help reduce trauma, recovery time and overall costs compared to surgical resection.

In this application, MR thermometry can help answer key questions such as "Is the heat/cold delivered at the right location and in the expected amount?," "Has a sufficient temperature dose been delivered already so that the treatment can stop?," or "Are there healthy tissues of special importance that are inadvertently being exposed to heat/cold and at risk of being damaged?" Answers to these questions can be used to make real-time decisions that may greatly enhance the effectiveness and safety of ablation therapies, and MR thermometry provides the data to inform these decisions.

34.2 MR thermometry: Theory

The MR signal depends mostly on just a handful of physical parameters such as the bulk magnetization M_0, the longitudinal relaxation time T_1, the transverse relaxation times T_2 and T_2*, the Larmor frequency f_0, and the apparent diffusion coefficient (ADC) of the imaged tissues. These parameters all have a dependency on temperature [3–6] and these dependencies can be exploited toward actually measuring temperature.

Advances in Magnetic Resonance Technology and Applications. Volume 1. ISSN 2666-9099. https://doi.org/10.1016/B978-0-12-817057-1.00036-6

More generally, if p represents a given MR parameter (e.g., M_0, T_1 or T_2) and $f_{tt}(\cdot)$ is a function specific to a given "tissue type" (e.g., muscle, brain, or fat), a change in temperature could be detected through:

$$\Delta T = f_{tt}(p_1, p_2) \tag{34.1}$$

where p_1 and p_2 are the values of the MR parameter p at a first time point t_1 and a second time point t_2, respectively, while ΔT is the change in temperature that occurred between t_1 and t_2. Relationships of the type shown in Eq. (34.1) can be found for just about every MR parameter, for example M_0 [7], T_1 [8–13], T_2 [12,14,15], f_0 [16–19], and ADC [20–22]. An excellent review of these various MR thermometry approaches can be found in Rieke and Pauly [23]. Among all of these options, most currently-employed MR thermometry methods are based on the temperature dependence of f_0, for reasons explained below.

34.3 Proton resonance frequency (PRF) thermometry

Water has many unusual properties which can be attributed to the hydrogen bond, whereby water molecules can make links with their neighbors. As water warms, water molecules move faster and these bonds are less likely to form and to last. Conversely, as water cools, more of these bonds are formed and they tend to be more stable. Hydrogen bonds are mediated by the interaction between the electrons of an oxygen atom in a given water molecule and the electron of a hydrogen atom from a different water molecule. Water and biological tissues are diamagnetic, meaning that in the presence of an external magnetic field they become weakly magnetized and this magnetization points in the direction opposite to that of the external field. In contrast, the hydrogen nuclei, the source of MRI signals, are paramagnetic and as such their magnetization aligns with the field, in a direction that opposes the magnetization from electrons and that of the overall biological tissue they belong to. By affecting the mean position and behavior of electrons, hydrogen bonds alter the field that these electrons generate. As hydrogen bonds are more likely to stretch and break with increasing temperature, the field felt by the nuclei changes with temperature [24–26], which in turns changes the Larmor frequency of MR signals.

Thus, when the temperature changes, the Larmor frequency also changes and it does so in a manner that is almost entirely independent of tissue type (with fat being a notable exception) [27]. As a result, the *tt* subscript in Eq. (34.1) can be dropped and a single function $f(\cdot)$ can be employed. Furthermore, $f(\cdot)$ can be approximated by a linear function over a wide range of temperature values [28]; as such, only the difference in frequency, Δf_0, actually matters, as opposed to frequency values at both t_1 and t_2. As a result, Eq. (34.1) becomes a simple equation that applies to nearly all biological tissues; this equation relates the change in frequency in Hz, Δf_0, and the temperature change in °C, ΔT:

$$\Delta T = -\frac{\Delta f_0}{0.426 \times B_0} \tag{34.2}$$

where B_0 is the scanner's field strength expressed in T and the 0.426 constant is equal to 0.01 times the gyromagnetic ratio for hydrogen (i.e., $0.01 \times 42.6\,\text{MHz/T}$), as further explained later in the text. For example, from Eq. (34.2), a change in Larmor frequency of 1.28 Hz at 3 T corresponds to a change

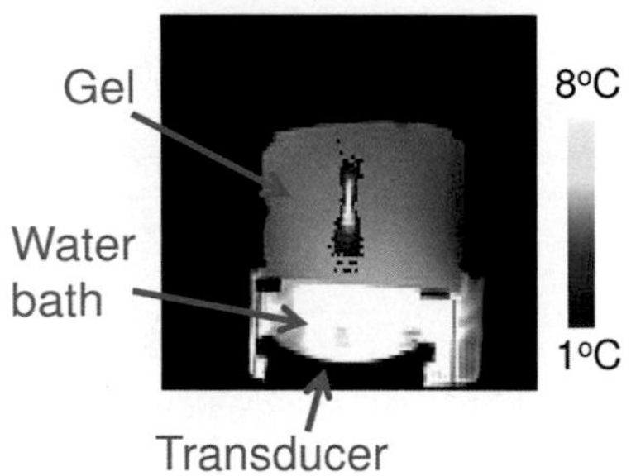

FIG. 34.1

A hot spot was created in a gel phantom using ultrasound energy. A water bath ensured proper acoustic coupling between transducer and gel. The heating process was imaged using PRF thermometry.

in temperature by 1°C. The main point here is that Eq. (34.2) is linear, simple, and for the most part tissue independent. For these reasons, detecting changes in f_0 has become the widely-accepted manner in which temperature changes are measured using MRI, an approach referred to as proton resonance frequency (PRF) shift imaging, or PRF thermometry. An example is shown in Fig. 34.1 where ultrasound energy was used to produce a hot spot within a gel phantom, and the heating process was captured using PRF thermometry.

34.4 Anatomy of traditional PRF thermometry pulse sequences

Fig. 34.2 represents magnetization vectors in the transverse plane, the source of MRI signals. Gradient echo imaging is used most commonly for PRF, but other pulse sequences are possible (as detailed in Section 34.5). The signal evolution for a water-containing material at baseline (i.e., before heating) and after heating is indicated using blue and red arrows, respectively. Magnetization flipped into the transverse plane at a time $TE_0 = 0$ proceeds to rotate in the transverse plane. The blue and red arrows represent the same experiment, performed at two different moments in time: before heating (blue) and after heating (red). One can observe from Fig. 34.2 that the magnetization rotates at a lower frequency in the heating case (red) than in the baseline case (blue), which is consistent with the minus sign in Eq. (34.2). The rotation frequency for baseline and heating cases can be measured, and the difference Δf_0 can be used to calculate ΔT from Eq. (34.2).

Fig. 34.2A–C shows the evolution of the magnetization vectors from $TE_0 = 0$ to a later time $TE_1 > TE_0$ and then $TE_2 > TE_1$ in a multi-TE acquisition. As TE increases, the phase difference between baseline and heating cases grows, as highlighted in green in Fig. 34.3B and C. Furthermore, as TE grows, the length of the magnetization vectors shrinks according to $T_2{}^*$. The angle between the magnetization vectors becomes more difficult to measure precisely as signals get weaker, suggesting that signals should be measured early in the TR interval, before they decay away. On the other hand, sampling as late as possible in the TR interval would give more time for the temperature-related frequency difference Δf_0 to generate larger phase differences $\Delta\theta$, which are easier to detect and measure. As described below, the ideal TE setting is a compromise between these two conflicting demands: keeping

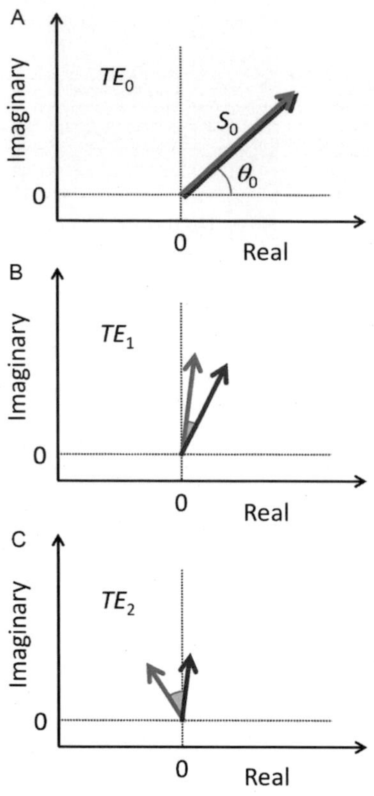

FIG. 34.2

(A) Magnetization vectors before and after heating are shown in blue and red, respectively. At $TE=0$, they start at the same angular position θ_0. (B) At $TE_1 > 0$, a phase difference has grown between the two, shown in green. (C) At $TE_2 > TE_1$ the phase difference has grown further. All along, the size of the signals shrinks with TE according to T_2*.

TE short to obtain stronger signals and making TE long so that larger $\Delta\theta$ values might be measured. To optimize this tradeoff between signal strength S and phase difference $\Delta\theta$, an equation is sought that describes the SNR of temperature measurements, called "temperature-to-noise ratio" (TNR).

Fig. 34.3A shows a magnetization vector with a "fuzzy ball" at the end of it, which represents the probability density function of measurement noise. The normal-distributed noise has a standard deviation equal to σ along both real and imaginary dimensions. Fig. 34.3B shows in red one possible example value for the effect of noise on the signal, and this noise causes an error on the angle θ being measured, n_θ. The noise on S was separated into two components, $n_\parallel$ and $n_\perp$, which are parallel and perpendicular to S, respectively. Assuming $S \gg n_\parallel$, then $n_\parallel$ has negligible effect on n_θ and is not considered here. Because $S \gg n_\perp$ as well, one can assume the error on θ to be a small angle, such that:

$$n_\theta \approx \tan(n_\theta) \approx n_\perp / S \tag{34.3}$$

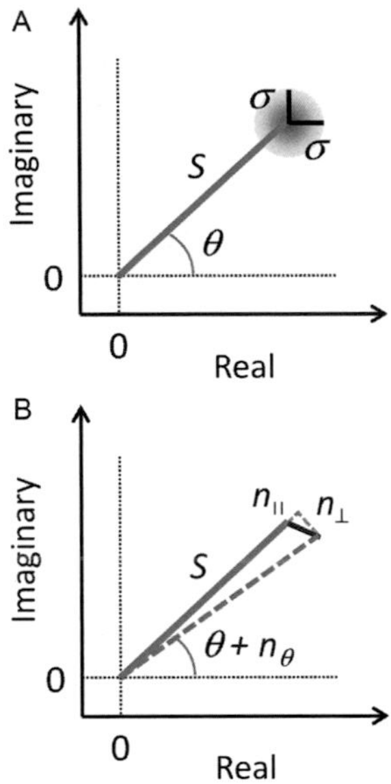

FIG. 34.3

(A) A magnetization vector is shown in the transverse plane. The measurement noise is depicted with a "fuzzy" region at the tip of the vector, with standard deviation σ along both real and imaginary axes. (B) An example showing the effect of noise on the measured phase; this example helps illustrate the steps from Eq. (34.3) to Eq. (34.9), for the SNR of Δf_0.

Because $n_{\perp}$ is in fact a random variable with standard deviation σ (see Fig. 34.3A), it follows from Eq. (34.3) that n_{θ} is also a random variable and that its standard deviation must be scaled by $1/S$ compared to σ [29]:

$$\sigma_{\theta} \approx \frac{\sigma}{S} \tag{34.4}$$

with S and σ as defined above and in Fig. 34.3.

The variables $\theta_p(TE)$ and $\theta_h(TE)$ are defined here as the TE-dependent phase value for the preheating and heating cases, respectively. For the time being, the same starting value θ_0 is assumed for both cases (Fig. 34.2A). Frequencies are defined as f_p and f_h for preheating and heating cases, respectively (f_p and f_h actually represent offset values from the nominal Larmor frequency, to avoid handling needlessly-large frequency numbers). Phase and frequency values are related through:

$$\theta_p(TE) = \theta_0 + 2\pi TE \times f_p \tag{34.5a}$$

$$\theta_h(TE) = \theta_0 + 2\pi TE \times f_h \tag{34.5b}$$

From Eqs. (34.5a), (34.5b), the measured phase difference is:

$$\Delta\theta = \theta_h\text{-}\theta_p = 2\pi TE \times \left(f_h - f_p\right) \tag{34.6}$$

Note that when using a phased-array coil to receive MRI signals, a phase-sensitive multicoil combination may be required [30] to obtain values for $\Delta\theta$ that include information from all coil elements.

The PRF-related change in frequency as described in Eq. (34.2) is given by $\Delta f_0 = (f_h - f_p)$, and Eq. (34.6) can be rephrased as:

$$\Delta f_0 = \frac{\Delta\theta}{2\pi TE}. \tag{34.7}$$

Both θ_h and θ_p in Eq. (34.6) are associated with a noise σ_θ; because standard deviations of normal-distributed random variables add in quadrature, the noise on $\Delta\theta$ is thus $\sqrt{2}\sigma_\theta$. Further involving the factors $1/2\pi TE$ and $1/S$ from Eqs. (34.7), (34.4), respectively, one obtains an expression for the noise on Δf_0 as a function of the noise in the original MR images, σ:

$$\sigma_{\Delta f_0} = \frac{\sqrt{2}\sigma}{2\pi TE \times S} \tag{34.8}$$

Dividing Δf_0 from Eq. (34.7) by its noise level in Eq. (34.8), one obtains a relation for SNR:

$$\mathrm{SNR}_{\Delta f_0} = \frac{\Delta\theta \times S}{\sqrt{2}\sigma} \tag{34.9}$$

TNR is directly related to the SNR on Δf_0 (see Eq. 34.2), and Eq. (34.9) shows that TNR depends on $\Delta\theta$, S, and σ. Eq. (34.9) can be used to explain the main features of a PRF thermometry sequence, below.

To optimize TE, Eq. (34.9) is first converted into a function of TE. The phase difference $\Delta\theta$ is proportional to TE (see Eq. 34.6) and the signal S is proportional to exp($-TE/T_2^*$) due to T_2^* decay. The relationship between noise, σ, and readout duration, τ, is well known [31], as noise is inversely proportional to the square-root of τ. As depicted in Fig. 34.4A–C, the readout duration may be expressed as $\tau \approx 2 \times (TR - TE)$, with extreme cases $\tau \to TR$ and $\tau \to 0$ depicted in Fig. 34.4A and B, respectively. Putting together all TE dependencies for all terms on the right-hand side of Eq. (34.9), one obtains:

$$\mathrm{SNR}_{\Delta f_0} \propto \left(TE \times \sqrt{2 \times (TR\text{-}TE)} \times \exp(\text{-}TE/T_2^*) \right) \tag{34.10}$$

Intuitively, using all of the available time for sampling data, as depicted in Fig. 34.4A, should lead to optimum TNR. This case is associated with $TR \approx 2 \times TE$ (Fig. 34.4A); by replacing TR with this expression in Eq. (34.10) and dropping the factor $\sqrt{2}$ one obtains:

$$\mathrm{SNR}_{\Delta f_0} \propto \left(TE^{3/2} \times \exp(\text{-}TE/T_2^*) \right) \tag{34.11}$$

By taking the derivative of Eq. (34.11) with respect to TE to find a maximum, one obtains:

$$\frac{3TE^{1/2}}{2} \exp(\text{-}TE/T_2^*) - \frac{TE^{3/2}}{T_2^*} \times \exp(\text{-}TE/T_2^*) = 0 \tag{34.12}$$

which leads to $TE = 3 \times T_2^*/2$. As a consequence, the following settings should be employed to optimize TNR:

$$TE \approx 3 \times T_2^*/2 \quad TR \approx 2 \times TE \quad \tau \approx TR \tag{34.13}$$

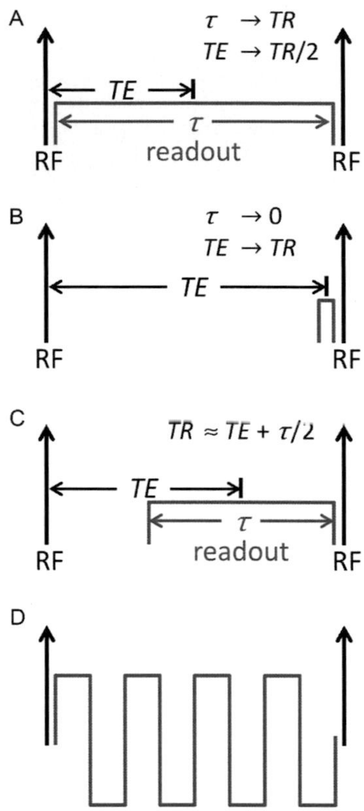

FIG. 34.4

(A) Making the readout duration, τ, as long as possible allows noise to be minimized. (B) Making *TE* as long as possible allows the phase difference, $\Delta\theta$, to be maximized. (C) Optimizing SNR leads to a compromise whereby τ is about 2/3 of *TR*. (D) To combine long readout duration and high bandwidth, modern PRF sequences may often fill the *TR* interval with readout windows whose nature may vary, see text for details.

The expression from Eq. (34.10) is plotted in Fig. 34.5, showing the maxima on *TE* and *TR* as expressed in Eq. (34.13). However, there may be limits on how large τ should be, irrespective of TNR considerations. A long τ leads to a low acquisition bandwidth, which in turn leads to vulnerability to chemical shift artifacts. In Eq. (34.13), $\tau \approx 3 \times T_2{}^*$, which in many situations might correspond to an unrealistically long setting. If we assume for a moment that τ is fixed for reasons unrelated to TNR, the resulting pulse sequence may look like that depicted in Fig. 34.4C. Removing τ from the optimization process, Eq. (34.10) becomes:

$$SNR_{\Delta f_0} \propto (TE \times \exp(\text{-}TE/T_2{}^*)) \tag{34.14}$$

By taking the derivative of Eq. (34.14) with respect to *TE*, one obtains:

$$\exp(\text{-}TE/T_2{}^*) - \frac{TE}{T_2{}^*} \times \exp(\text{-}TE/T_2{}^*) = 0 \tag{34.15}$$

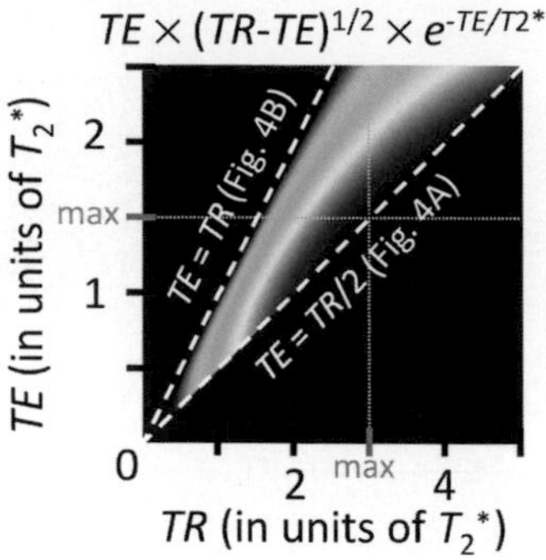

FIG. 34.5

The expression $TE \times (TR\text{-}TE)^{1/2} \times \exp(-TE/T_2^*)$, which is linearly proportional to TNR, is plotted as a function of TE and TR. The limit cases $TE = TR/2$ and $TE = TR$, as depicted in Fig. 34.4A and B, are indicated with dashed white lines. A maximum is obtained for $TE = 3\,T_2^*/2$, $TR = 3T_2^*$ and $\tau = TR$, see dashed gray lines.

which leads to:

$$TE \approx T_2^* \tag{34.16}$$

Further optimization would require taking the steady-state signal into account, which in turn would involve further parameters such as T_1 and the flip angle. Because signal levels are optimized when recovery time is maximized, that is, at a very impractical setting of $TR \rightarrow \infty$, one should optimize the TNR per unit of time, also known as TNR efficiency, instead of the TNR itself; this process typically involves tissue-specific simulations which go beyond the scope of the present text. But TNR-related rules of thumb as expressed in Eqs. (34.13), (34.16), for shorter-T_2^* and longer-T_2^* ranges, respectively, can prove helpful.

34.5 Improving upon the traditional design

Traditional PRF sequences, such as depicted in Fig. 34.4A and C may have serious drawbacks: relatively-long readout durations may lead to vulnerability to chemical shifts, and relatively-long *TR* settings may lead to long scan times and vulnerability to motion. For these reasons, a variety of alternative approaches have been proposed.

Modern PRF sequences may often resemble the drawing in Fig. 34.4D, in the sense that many different readout windows may be found throughout the *TR* interval. The nature of these readout windows may vary: they might represent different *k*-space lines in one given *k*-space matrix as in echo-planar imaging (EPI) [32], or the same *k*-space locations in many separate *k*-space matrices as in multi-*TE* imaging, or different types of signals altogether as in multipathway imaging, or some hybrid combination of these various cases. Traditionally, spoiled gradient echo sequences have been used most often for MR thermometry, but several other types of gradient echo sequences (GRE) exist, as explained in Fig. 34.6. Some of these other GRE sequences offer advantages over spoiled GRE in various situations, as further described below.

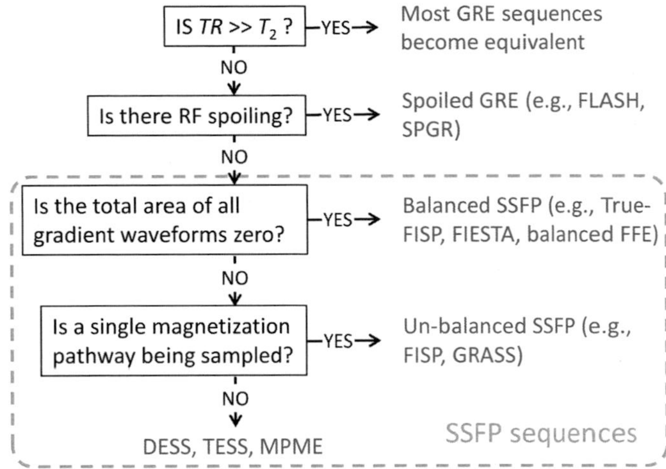

FIG. 34.6

A "family tree" of gradient echo (GRE) pulse sequences is shown, see text for more details.

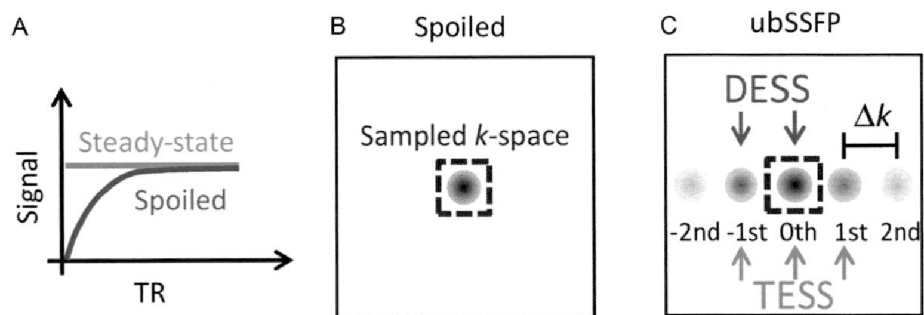

FIG. 34.7

Spoiled and steady-state GRE sequences behave differently in a few key aspects. (A) As TR tends toward zero, the signal level of spoiled GRE sequences also tends to zero while that of steady-state sequences does not. (B, and C) Furthermore, SSFP sequences create many different k-space replicas separated by an increment $\Delta\vec{k}$, unlike RF-spoiled sequences.

RF spoiling was developed to help ensure that magnetization excited in a given TR interval would contribute only to that TR interval and no other [33,34]. As seen in Fig. 34.6, GRE sequences that are not RF-spoiled are referred to as "steady-state free precession" (SSFP) sequences. Fig. 34.7 illustrates some key differences between RF-spoiled and SSFP GRE sequences. As TR tends to zero, the signal from RF-spoiled sequences also tends to zero but that of SSFP sequences does not (Fig. 34.7A). While the SSFP signal level is a function of many parameters and may change with TR in complicated ways [35,36], the simple point conveyed by Fig. 34.7A is that it does not tend toward zero as TR is shortened. Another key difference between RF-spoiled and SSFP sequences is illustrated in Fig. 34.7B and C, where the red square depicts the typically-sampled k-space area. SSFP sequences create replicas of k-space signals that can be pushed far away in k-space [37,38], and the distance $\Delta\vec{k}$ that separates adjacent replicas is related to the zeroth moment of the gradient waveforms:

$$\Delta\vec{k} = -\gamma\int_{t=0}^{TR}\vec{G}(t)dt \tag{34.17}$$

where γ is the gyromagnetic ratio for hydrogen (42.6 MHz/T). As shown in Fig. 34.7C, different SSFP sequences differ in terms of the size of $\Delta\vec{k}$, and the size of the sampled k-space region. In the special case where all gradients are balanced, that is, if their zeroth moment and $\Delta\vec{k}$ is zero (Eq. 34.17), then all replicas overlap at the k-space center. This special case corresponds to the well-known balanced SSFP (bSSFP) sequence, sometimes called True-FISP, FIESTA, or balanced-FFE. The overlap of all pathways leads to a high SNR for on-resonance signals, but also to dark band artifacts wherever/whenever pathways interact destructively, a well-known limitation of bSSFP. Otherwise, whenever $|\Delta\vec{k}| > 0$, one obtains an unbalanced SSFP (ubSSFP) sequence. In such case, adjacent pathways are separated in k-space and only the 0th pathway, the one nearest k-space center, is typically sampled (see red square in Fig. 34.7C). However, sequences do exist that sample a larger k-space area and in the process capture two or more pathways: the "dual-echo in the steady-state" (DESS) sequence [39] captures both the -1st and 0th pathways, the "triple-echo in the steady-state" (TESS) sequence [40] goes one step further and captures the 1st pathway as well, and the multipathway multiecho (MPME) sequence may capture three or more pathways at two or more different TE values [41,42] (Fig. 34.7C). The main rationale for sampling more than one pathway typically comes from the vast differences in tissue contrast that often exist among pathway signals, for example see Fig. 34.8.

PRF thermometry can, in principle at least, be performed with any of the sequences mentioned in Fig. 34.6. In the equations below, subscripts p and j will be included to discriminate between pathways and/or echo times, respectively. Signals from any pathway and/or echo time could lead to temperature measurements, through:

$$\Delta T_{p,j} = \Delta\theta_{p,j}/\Lambda_{p,j} \tag{34.18}$$

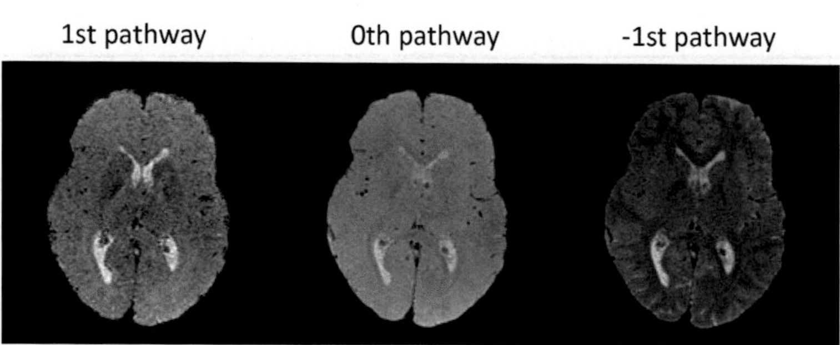

FIG. 34.8

Different signal pathways may vastly differ in terms of image contrast. ubSSFP sequences generate signals from multiple pathways and distribute them through k-space (see Fig. 34.7). Typically, only the most intense 0th pathway signal may actually be sampled, although a number of sequences exist that capture two or more pathways. In the context of PRF thermometry, different pathway signals are characterized by interestingly different sensitivities to temperature changes, see the effect of p in Eq. (34.20).

where $\Lambda_{p,j}$ is the sensitivity of a given pathway/echo to temperature changes. For example, replacing Eq. (34.7) into Eq. (34.2), one obtains a special case of Eq. (34.18) for the 0th pathway; in such case, the temperature sensitivity would be:

$$\Lambda_{p=0} = 2\pi \times \gamma\alpha B_0 TE \tag{34.19}$$

where α is the PRF change coefficient (-0.01 ppm/°C); the parameters γ and α have been replaced by their numerical values in Eq. (34.2) to obtain a simpler relation. More generally, the temperature sensitivity can be expressed as [43]:

$$\Lambda_{p,j} = (2\pi \times \gamma\alpha B_0) \times \left(pTR + TE_{p,j}\right) \tag{34.20}$$

As seen from Eq. (34.20), the temperature sensitivity depends both on the pathway number p and the echo time $TE_{p,j}$. For a given temperature change, a larger/smaller temperature sensitivity means that a larger/smaller phase difference, $\Delta\theta_{p,j}$, is generated, which impacts SNR and TNR (Eq. 34.9). Whether $|p| > 0$ pathways can improve TNR depends on the type of tissue being imaged [44].

Figs. 34.4–34.7, along with Eqs. (34.18)–(34.20), explain why many different pulse sequences can be, and are, employed in PRF thermometry. To improve imaging speed compared to a "traditional" sequence such as that depicted in Fig. 34.4C, one may sample many different k-space lines every TR as in EPI, and/or shorten TR. As TR becomes shorter, differences between RF-spoiled and SSFP sequence become more noticeable, and SSFP sequences may be preferred based on SNR considerations (Fig. 34.7A). The ultimate short-TR high-SNR SSFP sequence, bSSFP, has been successfully employed for PRF thermometry [45,46], but by examining Eq. (34.20) some of the challenges associated with this sequence can be understood. Because bSSFP is characterized by overlapping pathway signals ($\Delta\vec{k}=0$), and that different pathways may have different temperature sensitivities (Eq. 34.20) and decay rates, the bSSFP sequence may lead to more complicated, nonlinear temperature dependencies. An interesting consequence of Eq. (34.20) is that negative pathways, with $p<0$, have a temperature sensitivity $|\Lambda_{p,j}|$ that is largest at $TE=0$ and that decreases with increasing TE. This is in sharp contrast with the usual 0th pathway, whose sensitivity increases with TE (Eq. 34.19). For this reason, it may be advantageous to sample $p<0$ and $p\geq 0$ pathways in the early and late parts of the TR interval, respectively, while their respective temperature sensitivities are large [44,47].

The simple PRF sequence depicted in Fig. 34.4C acquired a single type of signal, presumably either an RF-spoiled or a 0th pathway GRE signal, with near-optimum TNR. In contrast, Fig. 34.4D represents a sequence that samples many different types of signals every TR. Regardless of whether these signals represent different echo times [48] or different magnetization pathways [43], they should be combined in a manner that optimizes TNR, as described in the next section. There is also considerable variation in the manner these signals may be employed to cover k-space. Cartesian schemes (whereby a single k-space line is sampled per TR), EPI-like schemes (whereby many k-space lines are sampled every TR [49,50]) or spiral k-space trajectories [48,51,52] all have characteristic strengths and weaknesses. The choice of signal type (e.g., RF-spoiled vs. SSFP, single-TE vs. multi-TE, single-pathway vs. multipathway) is mostly independent of the choice of k-space trajectory (e.g., Cartesian vs. spiral, single-shot vs. multishot). While this text focused primarily on the former, that is, the signal type, the choice of k-space trajectory may also of course affect performance and tradeoffs.

34.6 TNR-optimum combination of multiple signals

Whenever signals are obtained from different pathways p and/or echo times j, each signal could in principle lead to its own thermometry measurement, see Eq. (34.18). As shown in Fig. 34.9, these measurements can be combined into a single TNR-optimum estimate. For example, assuming that data at several echo times TE_j were obtained for a single (0th, or RF-spoiled) pathway, one could estimate ΔT through a linear least-square fit by first expressing the problem in vector form:

$$\mathbf{\Delta\theta} = \mathbf{\Lambda} \times (2\pi\Delta f_0) \tag{34.21a}$$

$$\mathbf{\Delta\theta} = [\Delta\theta_1 \ \cdots \ \Delta\theta_{N_{TE}}]^{\mathrm{T}} \tag{34.21b}$$

$$\mathbf{\Lambda} = [TE_1 \ \cdots \ TE_{N_{TE}}]^{\mathrm{T}} \tag{34.21c}$$

where the superscript "T" represents a transpose operation, N_{TE} is the total number of echo times TE_j at which data are available for fitting, and the elements of Λ correspond to the second term of $\Lambda_{p,j}$ in Eq. (34.20) for the case $p=0$. By replacing Eq. (34.21b) and Eq. (34.21c) into Eq. (34.21a), an equation is obtained that can be solved for the frequency offset; however, such solution would not be TNR-optimized. Matrices **A** and **W** can be introduced on both sides of Eq. (34.21a) to take into accounts variations in signal strength and in noise level that might be expected from one echo TE_j to the next:

$$\mathbf{A} \times \mathbf{W} \times \mathbf{\Delta\theta} = \mathbf{A} \times \mathbf{W} \times \mathbf{\Lambda} \times (2\pi\Delta f_0) \tag{34.22a}$$

$$\mathrm{diag}(\mathbf{A}) = [A_1 \ \cdots \ A_{N_{TE}}]^{\mathrm{T}} \tag{34.22b}$$

$$\mathrm{diag}(\mathbf{W}) = [W_1 \ \cdots \ W_{N_{TE}}]^{\mathrm{T}} \tag{34.22c}$$

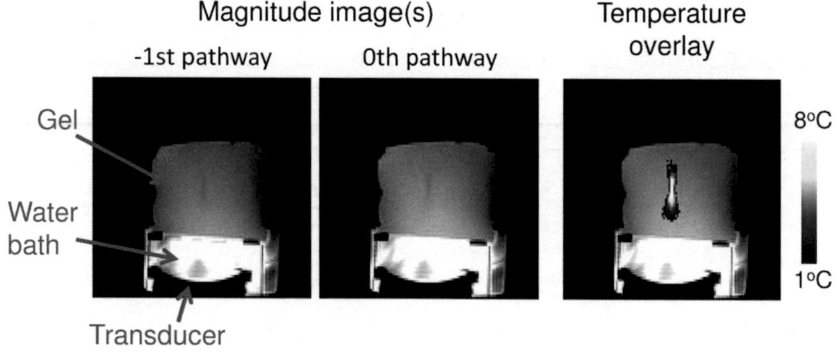

FIG. 34.9

Signals from different magnetization pathways can be combined into temperature measurements with improved TNR. Because a negative pathway has optimum temperature sensitivity early in TR and positive pathways late in TR, they can be readily combined. How much of an improvement is obtained depends on the relative strength of these signals, which in turns depends on a variety of parameters such as T_1, T_2, TR and flip angle. In materials with both long T_1 and long T_2, such as the phantom imaged here, improvements can be substantial (~35% improvement in TNR compared to using the 0th pathway alone). The time frame with maximal heating is shown here, using the same phantom and experimental set-up as in Fig. 34.1.

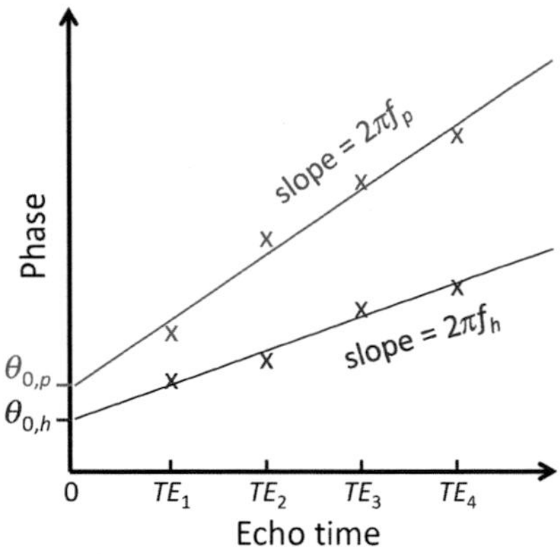

FIG. 34.10

Measurements can be obtained for preheating f_p (blue line and markers) and heating f_h (red line and markers) frequencies, through linear least-square fits of phase vs. *TE* measurements. For optimum-TNR results, proper weights should be included in the fit, see Eqs. (34.23a)–(34.23c).

More specifically, A_j could be estimated through a sum-of-square combination of images obtained from all coil elements at $TE = TE_j$, while $W_j = 1/\sigma_j$ could represent variations in noise level due, for example, to changes in sampling bandwidth from one echo to the next.

As illustrated in Fig. 34.10, instead of solving for Δf_0 based on $\Delta\theta$ values as in Eqs. (34.22a)–(34.22c), one could instead solve for the preheating and heating cases separately, finding f_p and f_h values from θ_p and θ_h measurements, respectively, and calculating Δf_0 as $(f_h - f_p)$. A fit similar to that of Eqs. (34.22a)–(34.22c) would still be employed, for example:

$$\mathbf{A} \times \mathbf{W} \times \boldsymbol{\theta}_p = \mathbf{A} \times \mathbf{W} \times \boldsymbol{\Lambda} \times \begin{bmatrix} 2\pi f_p \\ \theta_{0,p} \end{bmatrix} \tag{34.23a}$$

$$\boldsymbol{\theta}_p = [\theta_{1,p} \quad \cdots \quad \theta_{N_{TE},p}]^{\mathrm{T}} \tag{34.23b}$$

$$\boldsymbol{\Lambda} = \begin{bmatrix} TE_1 & \cdots & TE_{N_{TE}} \\ 1 & \cdots & 1 \end{bmatrix}^{\mathrm{T}} \tag{34.23c}$$

for the preheating case. The advantage of Eqs. (34.23a)–(34.23c) is that θ_0 is not assumed to be the same in preheating and heating cases, as seen in Fig. 34.10. But because two degrees of freedom are introduced as $\theta_{0,p}$ and $\theta_{0,h}$ instead of a single θ_0 value, using Eqs. (34.23a)–(34.23c) solves for an extra degree of freedom and achieves lower TNR than Eqs. (34.22a)–(34.22c). On the other hand, using Eqs. (34.23a)–(34.23c) can be advantageous in cases, as depicted in Fig. 34.10, where θ_0 may indeed drift between preheating and heating acquisitions.

34.7 Dealing with motion and other confounders

PRF thermometry encodes temperature changes into signal phase, but phase can be influenced by many other physical properties besides temperature. For example, the B_1 sensitivity at the transmit and/or receive stages, the presence/absence of artifacts, motion, magnetic susceptibility, and field inhomogeneity can all very much affect MRI phase values. For this reason, PRF thermometry typically requires a reference measurement to have been performed before any heating occurred. Assuming everything but temperature remained unchanged, then changes in phase can be attributed to temperature alone. But motion, in particular, can wreak havoc with this assumption. As tissues of interest may move from one voxel location to another, through B_1 sensitivity profiles and changing B_0 fields, possibly generating motion artifacts that overlap with legitimate signals, phase errors due to motion can readily overcome the underlying and often-subtle temperature-related phase changes that are sought.

Two main strategies have been proposed for PRF thermometry in the presence of motion. One, called multibaseline thermometry, replaces the preheating reference scan by a whole family of preheating scans that capture the anatomy of interest at various stages of motion [53–56]. While the reconstruction process still assumes that only the temperature changed between preheating reference and the heating data, the preheating reference image that best matches the current state of motion can be selected from the many different potential candidates. In a different approach, called referenceless thermometry, preheating time frames are replaced by nonheated tissue regions outside the area of interest as a source of reliable phase reference to compare signals against [57–61]. Because the processing does not compare different time frames, the method is intrinsically robust to motion, but it must make assumptions about the way heat-related and nonheat-related phase components may vary spatially to discriminate these effects. Hybrid algorithms that aim to combine strengths and mitigate weaknesses from both the multibaseline and the referenceless thermometry approaches have also been proposed [62,63].

Another, somewhat insidious difficulty in PRF thermometry comes from the fact that the susceptibility of tissues can change during the course of treatment [64,65]. In other words, the lesion itself, as it becomes "cooked," can become a source of field changes affecting surrounding tissues and masquerading as temperature changes. However, challenges can sometimes lead to opportunity, and such phase changes might possibly help detect the formation of treated regions, as susceptibility-induced changes are associated with spatial patterns based on the magnetic dipole, while legitimate temperature changes would be expected to respect the Pennes heat equation [66,67].

Furthermore, although more subtle an effect, it may be worth noting that TE in Eqs. (34.5a), (34.5b) and subsequent equations may not be as constant as it may seem at first sight. The echo time TE is defined as the time interval between RF excitation and the sampling of k-space center, which is where the main bulk of the MRI signal is assumed to be. However, in the presence of spatial gradients in the B_0 field, signal can be displaced away from k-space center. In such cases, TE should be replaced by one's best estimate of the time available for phase evolution, that is, the interval between RF excitation and the sampling of the main bulk of the MRI signals. Required changes to the nominal TE value will be greatest wherever/whenever the B_0 spatial gradients are highest, for example near the edges of an ablative hotspot, where accurate PRF thermometry may be most critical. The solution involves employing the phase spatial gradients, in addition to the phase values themselves, as part of the PRF reconstruction [65,68].

34.8 Limits of PRF thermometry

Because PRF thermometry exploits special properties that H_2O molecules exhibit while in their liquid form, PRF thermometry is limited to water-containing nonfrozen tissues. Most notably, PRF thermometry cannot be expected to work in cryotherapy, where the tissues of interest may be frozen, or in fatty tissues where much of the MRI signal come from fat molecules rather than water molecules. Fat molecules are larger and more complicated than water molecules and their hydrogen atoms do not engage in hydrogen bonding. Because the frequency of the fat signal is mostly temperature independent, it can be used as a reference, a stable temperature-independent signal against which the temperature-dependent water signals can be compared. More specifically, the frequency difference between fat and water signals allows the absolute temperature, as opposed to temperature change, to be measured [69–74]. However, such spectroscopic approaches to absolute temperature mapping tend to be slow and often require significant quantities of both fat and water to be present at the same location. For these reasons PRF thermometry is most often employed in its simpler and more limited form, to measure changes in temperature rather than to make absolute temperature measurements. Typically, in PRF thermometry, fat signals need to be suppressed or resolved so that water-only signals might be obtained [72,75–81], to enable accurate measurements free of corruption from fat signals.

T_1-based [8–13] and T_2-based [12,14,15] MR thermometry methods can prove helpful in situations where PRF thermometry is not applicable. For example, during the thermal ablation of breast lesions [82], it would be advisable to monitor the temperature elevation of adipose tissues near the target, for safety purposes. While PRF thermometry cannot detect the temperature elevation in fat, relationships between T_1, T_2 and temperature can be obtained for breast adipose tissues. For example, at 1.5 T, a 0.9 ms/°C temperature dependence was found for T_2, and a nonlinear relationship with a slope of about 5 ms/°C at 25°C and about 10 ms/°C at 65°C was found for T_1 [83]. The fact that α in Eqs. (34.19), (34.20) is mostly independent of tissue type is a great strength of PRF thermometry, one that is not shared by T_1-based and T_2-based methods, as the relation between T_1, T_2 and temperature is very much tissue dependent. Nevertheless, in specific tissues where PRF cannot provide the needed temperature monitoring, T_1- and T_2-based methods can provide a valuable alternative. Hybrid methods have been developed that combine PRF and T_1-based thermometry, to monitor both water-based and adipose tissues simultaneously [84].

34.9 Applications and future directions

MR thermometry is employed primarily for the guidance of thermal ablations. However, the equipment involved in such procedures, for example in microwave or RF ablation, is not readily MR-compatible. Furthermore, such ablations are often performed in mobile organs such as the liver and kidneys, where motion can limit the accuracy and precision of PRF thermometry. For these reasons, historically, the field of MR thermometry has not benefited from many "low hanging fruits" or easy entries into the clinical realm. However, technical advances, along with the continued rise of image-guided minimally invasive interventions as a means to reduce cost and patient trauma compared to surgical resection, suggest a bright future for MR thermometry methods. For example, PRF-thermometry has become a necessary component of successful procedures such as the treatment of essential tremor [85], see Fig. 34.11.

Demands for temporal resolution are typically dictated by the need to capture the heating curve and resolve the underlying motion. Ten to twenty frames per second may be needed to resolve breathing motion, for applications in the torso, and for the foreseeable future motion compensation is likely to remain a focus of development and research. Multidimensional reconstruction methods, with low-rank

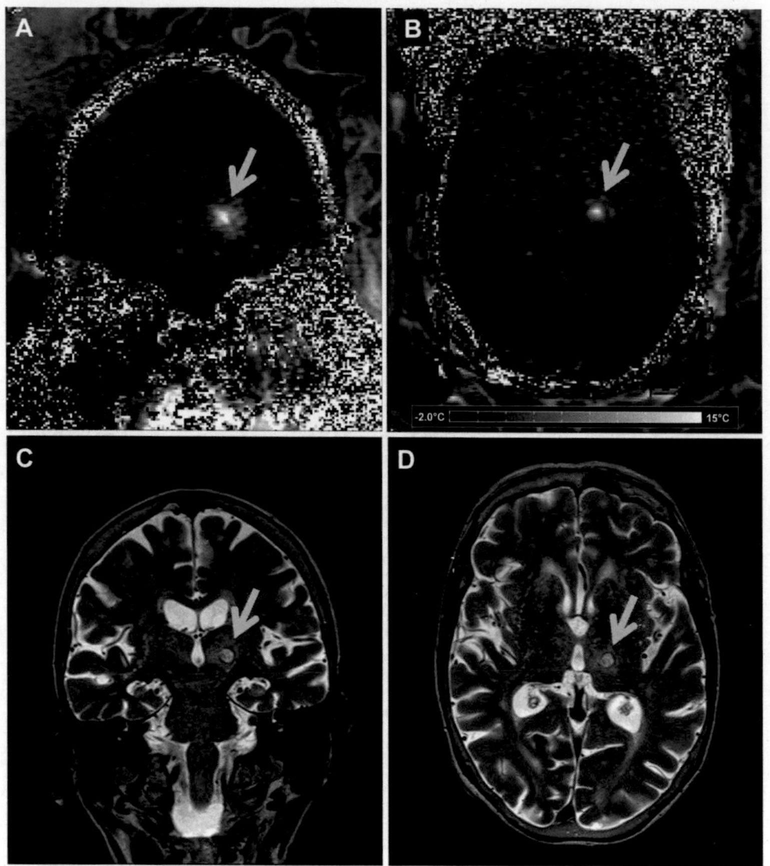

FIG. 34.11

(A and B) Coronal and axial temperature maps obtained during treatment for essential tremor show the lesion being created in the brain, see arrows. (C and D) T_2-weighted images obtained the day after treatment confirm the presence and location of the lesion.

Courtesy of Dr. Nathan McDannold, Harvard Medical School, Brigham and Women's Hospital, Boston, MA, USA.

constraints and/or sophisticated regularization schemes [86,87], have proved capable of simultaneously resolving temporal and spatial dimensions based on vastly-undersampled datasets; similar approaches could, in principle at least, help resolve motion in PRF thermometry as well. The ability to resolve many parameters with relatively little sampled data might even make absolute temperature mapping [69–74] more practical, by helping resolve the chemical-shift dimension while avoiding prohibitive increases in scan time. However, such computing-heavy methodologies may, to a large degree, remain incompatible with real-time guidance for the foreseeable future. Alternately, machine learning has been taking many fields by storm both within and beyond the realm of healthcare, and PRF thermometry may prove to be no exception. For example, heated locations do not appear in isolation;

they form patterns. While these patterns may be modeled using a heat equation [88], they might alternately be learned through experience and the accumulation of clinically relevant datasets, with yet-unknown benefits to the accuracy and precision of PRF thermometry.

At the pulse sequence level, sequences that sample many different signal types with high bandwidths, high slew rates, and low spatial distortions may become the norm in PRF thermometry. The more diversified these signals may be in terms of echo time and/or magnetization pathway, for example, the more likely it is that useful information might be gleaned from them beyond temperature measurements. For example, tissue damage is linked with changes in relaxation parameters [64] and simultaneous measurements of temperature along with T_1 or T_2 might prove more informative than measurements of temperature alone [47,84]. More generally, quantitative multiparametric imaging [40,42,89,90] represents a possible future for the MR guidance of thermal ablations, with MR thermometry only one important parameter among several, for better discrimination of normal, targeted and treated tissues.

34.10 Conclusion

The fact that MRI signals are sensitive to so many different physical properties can be both a blessing and a curse: a blessing because many different properties can be probed and a curse because they may need to be untangled from each other. Much about PRF thermometry sequences is geared toward isolating temperature-related effects so as to minimize confounding factors. This often involves comparing identically acquired images from different time points, before and after heating, and motion in-between these time points becomes a natural nemesis that tends to limit applicability and to drive upward the complexity of PRF methods. Despite these challenges, PRF thermometry has grown into a powerful tool, especially for the guidance of thermal ablation procedures.

Acknowledgments

Many thanks to Drs. Viola Rieke, Cheng-Chieh Cheng and Nicholas Todd who helped proofread and correct the text.

References

[1] Baust J, Gage AA, Ma H, Zhang CM. Minimally invasive cryosurgery—technological advances. Cryobiology 1997;34(4):373–84.

[2] Goldberg SN, Gazelle GS, Mueller PR. Thermal ablation therapy for focal malignancy: a unified approach to underlying principles, techniques, and diagnostic imaging guidance. AJR Am J Roentgenol 2000;174(2): 323–331.

[3] Graham SJ, Bronskill MJ, Henkelman RM. Time and temperature dependence of MR parameters during thermal coagulation of ex vivo rabbit muscle. Magn Reson Med 1998;39(2):198–203.

[4] Bottomley PA, Foster TH, Argersinger RE, Pfeifer LM. A review of normal tissue hydrogen NMR relaxation times and relaxation mechanisms from 1–100 MHz: dependence on tissue type, NMR frequency, temperature, species, excision, and age. Med Phys 1984;11(4):425–48.

[5] Parker DL. Applications of NMR imaging in hyperthermia: an evaluation of the potential for localized tissue heating and noninvasive temperature monitoring. IEEE Trans Biomed Eng 1984;31(1):161–7.

[6] Jolesz FA, Bleier AR, Jakab P, Ruenzel PW, Huttl K, Jako GJ. MR imaging of laser-tissue interactions. Radiology 1988;168(1):249–53.
[7] Chen J, Daniel BL, Butts PK. Investigation of proton density for measuring tissue temperature. J Magn Reson Imaging 2006;23(3):430–4.
[8] Dickinson RJ, Hall AS, Hind AJ, Young IR. Measurement of changes in tissue temperature using MR imaging. J Comput Assist Tomogr 1986;10(3):468–72.
[9] Parker DL, Smith V, Sheldon P, Crooks LE, Fussell L. Temperature distribution measurements in two-dimensional NMR imaging. Med Phys 1983;10(3):321–5.
[10] Castro DJ, Saxton RE, Layfield LJ, Fetterman HR, Tartell PB, Robinson JD, To SY, Nishimura E, Lufkin RB, et al. Interstitial laser phototherapy assisted by magnetic resonance imaging: a new technique for monitoring laser-tissue interaction. Laryngoscope 1990;100(5):541–7.
[11] Cline HE, Hynynen K, Hardy CJ, Watkins RD, Schenck JF, Jolesz FA. MR temperature mapping of focused ultrasound surgery. Magn Reson Med 1994;31(6):628–36.
[12] Young IR, Hand JW, Oatridge A, Prior MV. Modeling and observation of temperature changes in vivo using MRI. Magn Reson Med 1994;32(3):358–69.
[13] Lewa CJ, Majewska Z. Temperature relationships of proton spin-lattice relaxation time T1 in biological tissues. Bull Cancer 1980;67(5):525–30.
[14] Gultekin DH, Gore JC. Temperature dependence of nuclear magnetization and relaxation. J Magn Reson 2005;172(1):133–41.
[15] Cline HE, Hynynen K, Schneider E, Hardy CJ, Maier SE, Watkins RD, Jolesz FA. Simultaneous magnetic resonance phase and magnitude temperature maps in muscle. Magn Reson Med 1996;35(3):309–15.
[16] De Poorter J, De Wagter C, De Deene Y, Thomsen C, Stahlberg F, Achten E. Noninvasive MRI thermometry with the proton resonance frequency (PRF) method: in vivo results in human muscle. Magn Reson Med 1995;33(1):74–81.
[17] De Poorter J. Noninvasive MRI thermometry with the proton resonance frequency method: study of susceptibility effects. Magn Reson Med 1995;34(3):359–67.
[18] Ishihara Y, Calderon A, Watanabe H, Okamoto K, Suzuki Y, Kuroda K. A precise and fast temperature mapping using water proton chemical shift. Magn Reson Med 1995;34(6):814–23.
[19] MacFall JR, Prescott DM, Charles HC, Samulski TV. ^{1}H MRI phase thermometry in vivo in canine brain, muscle, and tumor tissue. Med Phys 1996;23(10):1775–82.
[20] Le Bihan D, Delannoy J, Levin RL. Temperature mapping with MR imaging of molecular diffusion: application to hyperthermia. Radiology 1989;171(3):853–7.
[21] Bleier AR, Jolesz FA, Cohen MS, Weisskoff RM, Dalcanton JJ, Higuchi N, Feinberg DA, Rosen BR, McKinstry RC, Hushek SG. Real-time magnetic resonance imaging of laser heat deposition in tissue. Magn Reson Med 1991;21(1):132–7.
[22] Zhang Y, Samulski TV, Joines WT, Mattiello J, Levin RL, LeBihan D. On the accuracy of noninvasive thermometry using molecular diffusion magnetic resonance imaging. Int J Hyperthermia 1992;8(2):263–74.
[23] Rieke V, Butts Pauly K. MR thermometry. J Magn Reson Imaging 2008;27(2):376–90.
[24] Schneider WG, Bernstein HJ, Pople JA. Proton magnetic resonance shift of free (gaseous) and associated (liquid) hydride molecules. J Chem Phys 1958;28:601–7.
[25] Hindman JC. Proton resonance shift of water in gas and liquid states. J Chem Phys 1966;44:4582–92.
[26] Némethy G, Scheraga H. Structure of water and hydrophobic bonding in proteins. I. A model for the thermodynamic properties of liquid water. J Chem Phys 1962;36(12):3382–400.
[27] Peters RD, Hinks RS, Henkelman RM. Ex vivo tissue-type independence in proton-resonance frequency shift MR thermometry. Magn Reson Med 1998;40(3):454–9.
[28] McDannold N. Quantitative MRI-based temperature mapping based on the proton resonant frequency shift: review of validation studies. Int J Hyperthermia 2005;21(6):533–46.

[29] Gudbjartsson H, Patz S. The Rician distribution of noisy MRI data. Magn Reson Med 1995;34(6):910–4. PMCID: PMC2254141.

[30] Bernstein MA, Grgic M, Brosnan TJ, Pelc NJ. Reconstructions of phase contrast, phased array multicoil data. Magn Reson Med 1994;32(3):330–4.

[31] Macovski A. Noise in MRI. Magn Reson Med 1996;36:494–7.

[32] Mansfield P. Multi-planar image formation using NMR spin echoes. J Phys C 1977;10:L55–8.

[33] Zur Y, Wood ML, Neuringer LJ. Spoiling of transverse magnetization in steady-state sequences. Magn Reson Med 1991;21(2):251–63.

[34] Zur Y, Stokar S, Bendel P. An analysis of fast imaging sequences with steady-state transverse magnetization refocusing. Magn Reson Med 1988;6(2):175–93.

[35] Gyngell ML. The steady-state signals in short-repetition-time sequences. J Magn Reson 1989;81:474–83.

[36] Hanicke W, Vogel HU. An analytical solution for the SSFP signal in MRI. Magn Reson Med 2003;49(4): 771–775.

[37] Hennig J. Echoes - how to generate, recognize, use or avoid them in MR-imaging sequences. Part I. Fundamental and not so fundamental properties of spin echoes. Concepts MR 1991;3:125–43.

[38] Hennig J. Echoes—how to generate, recognize, use or avoid them in MR-imaging sequences. Part II. Echoes in imaging sequences. Concepts MR 1991;3:179–92.

[39] Bruder H, Fischer H, Graumann R, Deimling M. A new steady-state imaging sequence for simultaneous acquisition of two MR images with clearly different contrasts. Magn Reson Med 1988;7(1):35–42.

[40] Heule R, Ganter C, Bieri O. Triple echo steady-state (TESS) relaxometry. Magn Reson Med 2014;71(1): 230–237.

[41] Cheng CC, Preiswerk F, Hoge WS, Kuo TH, Madore B. Multipathway multi-echo (MPME) imaging: all main MR parameters mapped based on a single 3D scan. Magn Reson Med 2019;81(3):1699–1713. PMCID: PMC6347518.

[42] Cheng CC, Preiswerk F, Madore B. Multi-pathway multi-echo acquisition and neural contrast translation to generate a variety of quantitative and qualitative image contrasts. Magn Reson Med 2020;83(6):2310–21.

[43] Madore B, Panych LP, Mei CS, Yuan J, Chu R. Multipathway sequences for MR thermometry. Magn Reson Med 2011;66(3):658–68. PMCID: PMC3134596.

[44] Ciris PA, Cheng CC, Mei CS, Panych LP, Madore B. Dual-Pathway sequences for MR thermometry: when and where to use them. Magn Reson Med 2017;77(3):1193–1200. PMCID:PMC5018245.

[45] Paliwal V, El-Sharkawy AM, Du X, Yang X, Atalar E. SSFP-based MR thermometry. Magn Reson Med 2004;52(4):704–8.

[46] Scheffler K. Fast frequency mapping with balanced SSFP: theory and application to proton-resonance frequency shift thermometry. Magn Reson Med 2004;51(6):1205–11.

[47] Cheng CC, Mei CS, Duryea J, Chung HW, Chao TC, Panych LP, Madore B. Dual-pathway multi-echo sequence for simultaneous frequency and T2 mapping. J Magn Reson 2016;265:177–187. PMCID: PMC4818735.

[48] Marx M, Butts Pauly K. Improved MRI thermometry with multiple-echo spirals. Magn Reson Med 2016;76 (3):747–756. PMCID:PMC4772149.

[49] Cernicanu A, Lepetit-Coiffe M, Roland J, Becker CD, Terraz S. Validation of fast MR thermometry at 1.5 T with gradient-echo echo planar imaging sequences: phantom and clinical feasibility studies. NMR Biomed 2008;21(8):849–58.

[50] Stafford RJ, Price RE, Diederich CJ, Kangasniemi M, Olsson LE, Hazle JD. Interleaved echo-planar imaging for fast multiplanar magnetic resonance temperature imaging of ultrasound thermal ablation therapy. J Magn Reson Imaging 2004;20(4):706–14.

[51] Stafford RJ, Hazle JD, Glover GH. Monitoring of high-intensity focused ultrasound-induced temperature changes in vitro using an interleaved spiral acquisition. Magn Reson Med 2000;43(6):909–12.

[52] Fielden SW, Feng X, Zhao L, Miller GW, Geeslin M, Dallapiazza RF, Elias WJ, Wintermark M, Butts Pauly K, Meyer CH. A spiral-based volumetric acquisition for MR temperature imaging. Magn Reson Med 2018;79(6):3122–7.

[53] Vigen KK, Daniel BL, Pauly JM, Butts K. Triggered, navigated, multi-baseline method for proton resonance frequency temperature mapping with respiratory motion. Magn Reson Med 2003;50(5):1003–10.

[54] de Senneville BD, Mougenot C, Moonen CT. Real-time adaptive methods for treatment of mobile organs by MRI-controlled high-intensity focused ultrasound. Magn Reson Med 2007;57(2):319–30.

[55] Ries M, de Senneville BD, Roujol S, Berber Y, Quesson B, Moonen C. Real-time 3D target tracking in MRI guided focused ultrasound ablations in moving tissues. Magn Reson Med 2010;64(6):1704–12.

[56] Kohler MO, Denis de Senneville B, Quesson B, Moonen CT, Ries M. Spectrally selective pencil-beam navigator for motion compensation of MR-guided high-intensity focused ultrasound therapy of abdominal organs. Magn Reson Med 2011;66(1):102–11.

[57] Rieke V, Vigen KK, Sommer G, Daniel BL, Pauly JM, Butts K. Referenceless PRF shift thermometry. Magn Reson Med 2004;51(6):1223–31.

[58] Kuroda K, Kokuryo D, Kumamoto E, Suzuki K, Matsuoka Y, Keserci B. Optimization of self-reference thermometry using complex field estimation. Magn Reson Med 2006;56(4):835–43.

[59] Rieke V, Kinsey AM, Ross AB, Nau WH, Diederich CJ, Sommer G, Pauly KB. Referenceless MR thermometry for monitoring thermal ablation in the prostate. IEEE Trans Med Imaging 2007;26(6):813–21.

[60] McDannold N, Tempany C, Jolesz F, Hynynen K. Evaluation of referenceless thermometry in MRI-guided focused ultrasound surgery of uterine fibroids. J Magn Reson Imaging 2008;28(4):1026–32.

[61] Grissom WA, Lustig M, Holbrook AB, Rieke V, Pauly JM, Butts-Pauly K. Reweighted l1 referenceless PRF shift thermometry. Magn Reson Med 2010;64(4):1068–77. PMCID: PMC3155729.

[62] Grissom WA, Rieke V, Holbrook AB, Medan Y, Lustig M, Santos J, McConnell MV, Pauly KB. Hybrid referenceless and multibaseline subtraction MR thermometry for monitoring thermal therapies in moving organs. Med Phys 2010;37(9):5014–26. PMCID: PMC2945742.

[63] Rieke V, Werner B, McDannold NJ, Grissom W, Martin E, Butts PK. Hybrid referenceless and multi-baseline thermometry for MRgFUS brain applications. Montréal, Canada: ISMRM; 2011521.

[64] Graham SJ, Stanisz GJ, Kecojevic A, Bronskill MJ, Henkelman RM. Analysis of changes in MR properties of tissues after heat treatment. Magn Reson Med 1999;42(6):1061–71.

[65] Sprinkhuizen SM, Konings MK, van der Bom MJ, Viergever MA, Bakker CJ, Bartels LW. Temperature-induced tissue susceptibility changes lead to significant temperature errors in PRFS-based MR thermometry during thermal interventions. Magn Reson Med 2010;64(5):1360–72.

[66] Pennes HH. Analysis of tissue and arterial blood temperatures in the resting human forearm. 1948. J Appl Physiol (1985) 1998;85(1):5–34.

[67] Todd N, Payne A, Parker DL. Model predictive filtering for improved temporal resolution in MRI temperature imaging. Magn Reson Med 2010;63(5):1269–79. PMCID:PMC5450947.

[68] Mei CS, Chu R, Hoge WS, Panych LP, Madore B. Accurate field mapping in the presence of B0 inhomogeneities, applied to MR thermometry. Magn Reson Med 2015;73(6):2142–51. PMCID: PMC4277742.

[69] Hall L, Talagala S. Mapping of pH and temperature distribution using chemical-shift-resolved tomography. J Magn Reson 1985;65:501–5.

[70] Kuroda K, Abe K, Tsutsumi S, Ishihara Y, Suzuki Y, Satoh K. Water proton magnetic resonance spectroscopic imaging. Biomed Thermol 1993;13:43–62.

[71] Lutz NW, Kuesel AC, Hull WE. A ^{1}H-NMR method for determining temperature in cell culture perfusion systems. Magn Reson Med 1993;29(1):113–8.

[72] Kuroda K, Oshio K, Chung AH, Hynynen K, Jolesz FA. Temperature mapping using the water proton chemical shift: a chemical shift selective phase mapping method. Magn Reson Med 1997;38(5):845–51.

[73] Kuroda K, Mulkern RV, Oshio K, Panych LP, Nakai T, Moriya T, Okuda S, Hynynen K, Jolesz FA. Temperature mapping using the water proton chemical shift: self-referenced method with echo-planar spectroscopic imaging. Magn Reson Med 2000;43(2):220–5.

[74] Soher BJ, Wyatt C, Reeder SB, MacFall JR. Noninvasive temperature mapping with MRI using chemical shift water-fat separation. Magn Reson Med 2010;63(5):1238–1246. PMCID:PMC2980328.

[75] Glover GH, Schneider E. Three-point Dixon technique for true water/fat decomposition with B0 inhomogeneity correction. Magn Reson Med 1991;18(2):371–83.

[76] de Zwart JA, Vimeux FC, Delalande C, Canioni P, Moonen CT. Fast lipid-suppressed MR temperature mapping with echo-shifted gradient-echo imaging and spectral-spatial excitation. Magn Reson Med 1999;42(1):53–9.

[77] Mulkern RV, Panych LP, McDannold NJ, Jolesz FA, Hynynen K. Tissue temperature monitoring with multiple gradient-echo imaging sequences. J Magn Reson Imaging 1998;8(2):493–502.

[78] Leupold J, Wieben O, Mansson S, Speck O, Scheffler K, Petersson JS, Hennig J. Fast chemical shift mapping with multiecho balanced SSFP. MAGMA 2006;19(5):267–73.

[79] Grissom WA, Kerr AB, Holbrook AB, Pauly JM, Butts-Pauly K. Maximum linear-phase spectral-spatial radiofrequency pulses for fat-suppressed proton resonance frequency-shift MR thermometry. Magn Reson Med 2009;62(5):1242–50.

[80] Mei CS, Panych LP, Yuan J, McDannold NJ, Treat LH, Jing Y, Madore B. Combining two-dimensional spatially selective RF excitation, parallel imaging, and UNFOLD for accelerated MR thermometry imaging. Magn Reson Med 2011;66(1):112–22.

[81] Yuan J, Mei CS, Madore B, McDannold NJ, Panych LP. Fast fat-suppressed reduced field-of-view temperature mapping using 2DRF excitation pulses. J Magn Reson 2011;210(1):38–43.

[82] Merckel LG, Bartels LW, Kohler MO, van den Bongard HJ, Deckers R, Mali WP, Binkert CA, Moonen CT, Gilhuijs KG, van den Bosch MA. MR-guided high-intensity focused ultrasound ablation of breast cancer with a dedicated breast platform. Cardiovasc Intervent Radiol 2013;36(2):292–301.

[83] Baron P, Deckers R, Knuttel FM, Bartels LW. T1 and T2 temperature dependence of female human breast adipose tissue at 1.5 T: groundwork for monitoring thermal therapies in the breast. NMR Biomed 2015;28(11):1463–70.

[84] Todd N, Diakite M, Payne A, Parker DL. A hybrid PRF/T1 technique for simultaneous temperature monitoring in adipose and aqueous tissues. Magn Reson Med 2013;69(1):62–70.

[85] Elias WJ, Lipsman N, Ondo WG, Ghanouni P, Kim YG, Lee W, Schwartz M, Hynynen K, Lozano AM, Shah BB, Huss D, Dallapiazza RF, Gwinn R, Witt J, Ro S, Eisenberg HM, Fishman PS, Gandhi D, Halpern CH, Chuang R, Butts Pauly K, Tierney TS, Hayes MT, Cosgrove GR, Yamaguchi T, Abe K, Taira T, Chang JW. A randomized trial of focused ultrasound Thalamotomy for essential tremor. N Engl J Med 2016;375(8):730–9.

[86] Ong F, Lustig M. Beyond low rank + sparse: multi-scale low rank matrix decomposition. IEEE J Sel Top Signal Process 2016;10(4):672–687. PMCID:PMC5403160.

[87] Feng L, Axel L, Chandarana H, Block KT, Sodickson DK, Otazo R. XD-GRASP: Golden-angle radial MRI with reconstruction of extra motion-state dimensions using compressed sensing. Magn Reson Med 2016;75 (2):775–788. PMCID:PMC4583338.

[88] Todd N, Adluru G, Payne A, DiBella EV, Parker D. Temporally constrained reconstruction applied to MRI temperature data. Magn Reson Med 2009;62(2):406–19.

[89] Ma D, Gulani V, Seiberlich N, Liu K, Sunshine JL, Duerk JL, Griswold MA. Magnetic resonance fingerprinting. Nature 2013;495(7440):187–192. PMCID:PMC3602925.

[90] Deoni SC, Rutt BK, Arun T, Pierpaoli C, Jones DK. Gleaning multicomponent T1 and T2 information from steady-state imaging data. Magn Reson Med 2008;60(6):1372–87.

CHAPTER

Motion Encoded MRI and Elastography

35

Prashant P. Nair[a,b] and Yogesh K. Mariappan[b]

[a]*Manipal Academy of Higher Education, Manipal, India* [b]*Philips Healthcare, Bangalore, India*

35.1 O Motion! Where art thou?

Physiological motions, including respiration, motion of the beating heart, and intestinal peristalsis, are essential for life. Disturbance to these physiological motions can be related to disease processes, for example hypertension, shortness of breath, gastric ulcer, or infarcts. Thus, the measurement of motion is clinically relevant and has significant diagnostic utility. Three major types of intrinsic physiological motion exist within the body: blood flow, rigid body motion, and nonrigid body motion. Measurement of the blood flow with MR is a vast field and is covered in the next chapter. In this chapter, we will first briefly describe quantitative MR imaging techniques that are useful for the measuring intrinsic physiological motion.Then, we will describe MR Elastography, a quantitative tissue stiffness mapping technique based on measurement of displacement where the motion is typically extrinsically induced.

35.2 Motion encoding

Typically, motion during MR imaging is associated with motion-induced artifacts, for example, respiratory ghosts [1]. However, quantification of the displacement of specific spins embedded in tissue can be useful in a variety of applications. A multitude of approaches have been developed for imaging tissue motion, including spatial magnetization modification [2,3] (SPAMM), phase-contrast MRI [4] (PCMRI), displacement encoding with stimulated echoes [5] (DENSE), strain encoding [6] (SENC), etc. We will briefly review some of these techniques assuming a basic understanding of the MR physics on part of the reader. A few motion encoding strategies will be highlighted as examples; more details on these and other motion imaging techniques can be found in the literature [7].

35.2.1 Phase-contrast MRI

Phase-contrast MRI was one of the earliest MR techniques used for motion quantification. A velocity-sensitizing bipolar gradient [4,8] is applied after the excitation pulse. Both the stationary and the moving spins experience phase accumulation due to these additional gradients. However, for the stationary spins the net phase accumulated is zero, as the second lobe of the gradient completely cancels the phase

Advances in Magnetic Resonance Technology and Applications. Volume 1. ISSN 2666-9099. https://doi.org/10.1016/B978-0-12-817057-1.00037-8

accumulated due to the first lobe. For the spins moving with a certain velocity, the net phase accumulated is proportional to the velocity with which the spins move:

$$v = \left(\frac{\Delta\Phi}{\text{VENC}}\right) \cdot \pi \tag{35.1}$$

where v is the velocity, $\Delta\Phi$ is the phase accumulated by the spins and the velocity encoding parameter (VENC) is the highest velocity that can be observed without aliasing. While this formulation is more widely used for the measurement of blood flow [9], it has found use in applications such as myocardial motion mapping at a high spatial coverage [10,11]. This technique is covered in more detail in Chapter 36.

35.2.2 Spatial modulation of magnetization

Spatial modulation of magnetization (SPAMM) is a commonly used MR-based motion measurement technique. As the name indicates, the key step in SPAMM is spatial modulation of the longitudinal magnetization, which is achieved by applying preparatory RF pulses, resulting in alternating dark and bright bands [3] in the image.

The preparatory pulse consists of two RF pulses (θ_1 and θ_2) with gradient G between them, as shown in Fig. 35.1. The longitudinal signal as a function of position, $M_z(r)$, can be calculated as:

$$M_z(r) = -M_0 \cdot [\sin\theta_1 \sin\theta_2 \cos\Phi(r) - \cos\theta_1 \cos\theta_2] \tag{35.2}$$

where M_0 is the initial magnetization and $\Phi(r)$ is the accumulated phase of the spins due to the gradient G. Note that the signal is spatially modulated as a cosine function in the direction of the

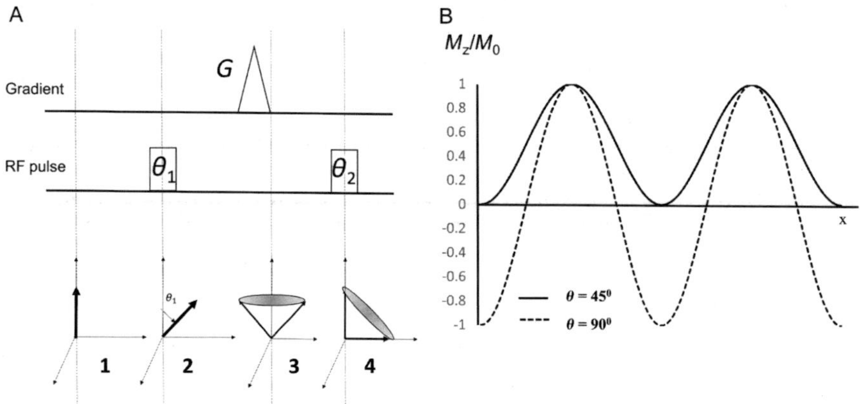

FIG. 35.1

(A) SPAMM tagging preparation module. This module contains two RF pulses θ_1 and θ_2 interspaced by the tagging gradient G. (B) Spatial variation of the magnetization vector following SPAMM preparation. (1) Magnetization vector just prior to the first RF pulse θ_1. (2) Magnetization just after the first pulse. (3) Magnetization after the dephasing under the influence of the gradient, just prior to the second RF pulse θ_2. (4) Magnetization after the second RF pulse for tag preparation θ_2. At the end of the preparation, the M_z, which is the projection of the transverse magnetization along the z-axis, is proportional to the location of the spin. Different flip angles of the RF pulses can be deployed to create different amounts of tagging depth.

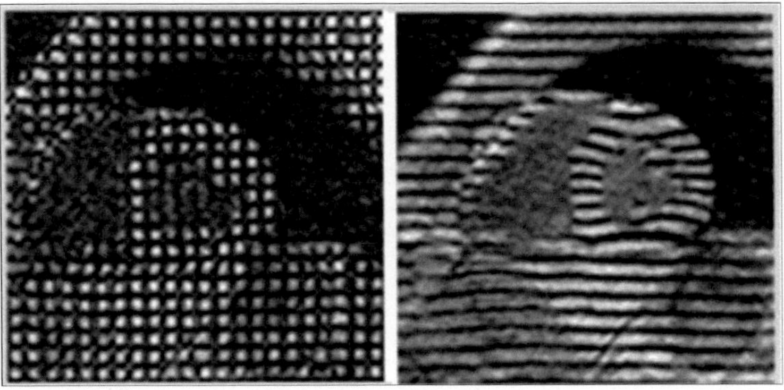

FIG. 35.2

Example SPAMM tagged cardiac images, where a grid is shown on the left, and stripes on the right. The tags are tracked using these images and the displacement can be calculated.

applied gradient (mm^{-1}). The combination of pulses and gradients creates periodic areas of bright and dark signal in one or two dimensions that appear as stripes or grids, respectively, as seen in Fig. 35.2. Note that the depth of the tagging can be controlled by adjusting the flip angles of the RF pulses, as can be seen in Fig. 35.1B.

The amount by which these spatial markers deform indicates the local motion of the different regions of the tissue, and this deformation can be quantified using techniques like Harmonic phase technique (HARP) [12]. In practical implementation, the basic 1 - 1 tagging pulse sequence (where $\theta_2 = \theta_1$) as shown in Fig. 35.1A is seldom used. A series of binomial pulses, where the flip angle ratios are set to be the coefficients of a binomial series (1 - 3 - 3 - 1), are typically used to address the problem of 'tag blur' where the tags do not have a definite edge.

One of the practical challenges of SPAMM tagging is the signal bias due to T_1 relaxation. The time required for tag preparation must be short compared to the T_1 relaxation time of the tissue of interest to ensure sufficient tag contrast. Another issue is the reduced availability of magnetization after multiple RF pulses. Both of these issues can be addressed with the use of complementary RF pulse pairs in subsequent tagging steps [13], followed by an appropriate combination of these signals. In this modified preparation sequence, in one acquisition the RF flip angle combination is +90°/+90° and in the subsequent acquisition is +90°/-90°. By combining these two signals, the tag contrast can be improved, and the bias can be removed.

35.2.3 Displacement encoding with stimulated echoes

Another widely investigated technique for motion quantification is DENSE, which is based on the stimulated echo acquisition mode (STEAM) [14]. DENSE combines the advantages of both tagging and phase velocity mapping techniques [5]. Similar to SPAMM, DENSE uses a bipolar gradient, but the gradients are split into two lobes (G_1 and G_2) with a mixing time, T_M, between them, as shown in Fig. 35.3.

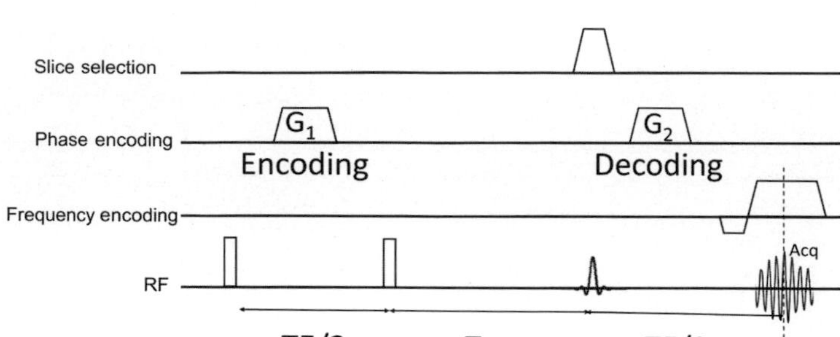

FIG. 35.3

Displacement encoding using a stimulated echo (DENSE) sequence. The first nonselective RF pulse tips the magnetization into the transverse plane, and the gradient G_1 dephases the spins. The second nonselective RF pulse returns the dephased magnetization back to the longitudinal axis. After a mixing time T_M, a third slice selective RF pulse then brings the magnetization back to the transverse plane, and a rephasing gradient, G_2, unwinds the phase induced by the gradient G_1. At the end of this sequence, there is a displacement-dependent phase accumulation for moving spins, but no net phase accumulation for static spins.

The spins that are displaced in the direction of the gradient during the period T_M will accumulate an additional phase that is proportional to the displacement [5]. The final transverse magnetization of a spin which has a simple displacement in the x-direction can be written as

$$M_{xy}(x,t) = \left[M_0 + \left(\frac{M_0}{2}\cdot(\exp(\text{-}jklx)) + (\exp(+jklx)) - M_0\right)\right]\exp\left(-\frac{t}{T_1}\right)\cdot\exp(\text{-}jkl(x+\Delta x))\cdot\sin\theta \qquad (35.3)$$

where kl is the spatial frequency during the displacement encoding gradient module. The signal acquired with DENSE is comprised of three echoes: a stimulated echo, a conjugate echo, and a T_1-weighted echo; the stimulated echo (STE) contains the displacement encoded information. Various schemes have been investigated to extract the STE signal from the DENSE echo, details of which can be found in [15–17]. Techniques like DENSE and SENC (discussed below) are preferred over the basic tagging schemes as they can provide highly robust quantitative information for tissue viability.

35.2.4 Strain encoding

Strain is defined as the deformation (compared to a reference) in the direction of applied force, and can potentially be used as a quantitative biomarker. One of the MRI-based techniques that is used to measure strain is known as SENC. SENC produces an image in which the intensity is proportional to the strain. The strain is directly encoded by playing out gradients in two parallel planes; the effect of these gradients together is to "tag" the tissue that moves from one plane into the other [6,17a]. While static tissues will not be tagged, tissue undergoing "compressions" or "expansion" will be tagged, with tissue compression resulting in increased frequencies and tissues expansion resulting in decreased frequencies in the frequency spectra. The vector sum of the tag pattern can be used to calculate the "strain map" in the slice direction.

The pulse sequence used for SENC is typically based on STEAM, where the tagging is similar to SPAMM (Fig. 35.1A), with one important difference: SENC tagging is applied in the slice direction, which produces a cosine modulation of the longitudinal M_z magnetization. The user typically inputs a strain range ($[\epsilon_{min}, \epsilon_{max}]$), that determines the number of modulations to be performed on a single slice. The strain of the moving tissue can be measured in this range; outside of this range values measured may no longer a true reflection of the actual strain.

In addition to the tagging preparation, the key step in SENC is the acquisition of images at two different tuning frequencies (low-tuning and high-tuning frequencies, ω_L and ω_H) using additional gradients (known as tuning gradients) in the slice selection direction (Fig. 35.4A). These tuning frequencies are calculated based on the input strain values, the tagging frequency (ω_0), and the slice thickness (S) as shown below:

$$\omega_0 = \frac{\left(\frac{1}{S}\right)(1+\epsilon_{max})(1+\epsilon_{min})}{\epsilon_{max} - \epsilon_{min}}; \ \omega_L = \frac{\omega_0}{1+\epsilon_{max}}; \ \omega_H = \frac{\omega_0}{1+\epsilon_{min}} \tag{35.4}$$

The images acquired at $\omega_L(I_L)$ and at $\omega_H(I_H)$ are called the low-tuned and the high-tuned images respectively. From these low-tuned and high-tuned images, the strain $\epsilon'(y,t)$ can be calculated as

$$\epsilon'(y,t) = \pm\left(1 - \frac{\omega_0}{\omega'(y,t)}\right) \tag{35.5}$$

where the sign is determined based on whether the deformation is caused by compression or expansion. Here ω' indicates the shifted tagging frequency estimated from ω_L and ω_H by the center of mass method as detailed in Ref. [6].

For cardiac imaging, several anatomical images—typical three short-axis slices (base, mid-section, and apical) along with the two-chamber, three-chamber, and four-chamber images—are also acquired along with the SENC image acquisition. Using these reference images and the SENC images, pixelwise strain calculation can be performed with the help of postprocessing software like *MYOSTRAIN* [18–20].

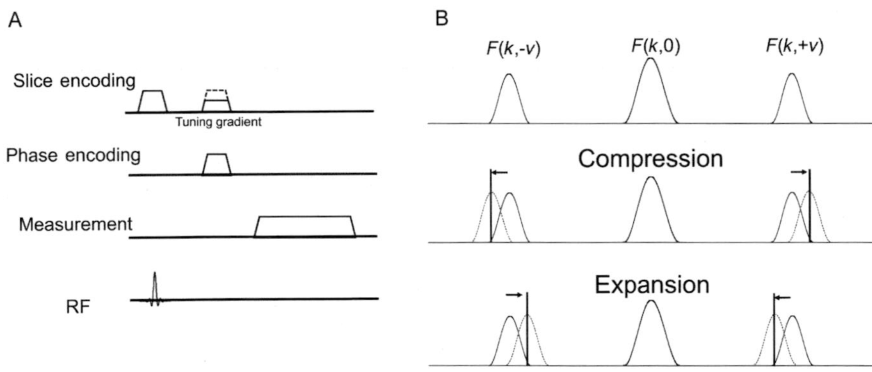

FIG. 35.4

(A) An example of a SENC-tuned imaging sequence. The imaging RF pulse and the slice selection gradients, including the low *(solid line)* and high *(dotted line)* tuning gradients. (B) The frequency spectrum of a voxel for a static tissue (top) and for tissue undergoing compression (center) or expansion (bottom) in the slice direction. With compression and expansion, the frequency content increases and decreases, respectively, compared to the tag freqeuncy.

Example SENC-based strain maps obtained from a healthy heart are shown in Fig. 35.5. The strain report provides global results as well as the regional results, which are represented as the longitudinal and circumferential strains.

Note that it may be possible to improve upon SENC by using composite SENC [21], where strain information is extracted from the high-tuned images while the no-tuned images (which have T_1 contrast) provide information on structural damage such as infarct.

35.2.5 Applications

The majority of the applications of MR-based motion mapping are aimed at measuring the regional motion of the heart. MR tagging techniques have been employed to study the effects of infarct on the shape of the myocardium and the decrease in strain at various locations with respect to the infarct, adjacent and remote [22–25]. Infarcts lead to wall thickening and affect contractile function. Conventional methods of wall thickening analysis are prone to physiological factors and may lead to incorrect values, whereas the measurement of in-plane strain through tagging is more accurate [26]. Myocardial contraction can be quantified through tagging, providing clinically useful information about cardiac health [27]. In cardiac dyssynchrony, contraction of various segments of the heart wall is out of synchronization and DENSE has been useful in the quantification of the degree of dyssynchrony [28–30].

As motion is ubiquitous within the body, the abovementioned techniques have also been investigated to measure motion in organs including the brain, liver, and lungs. SPAMM grid tagging has been used to tag hyperpolarized ^{3}He images to obtain displacement fields and principal strains during a breath cycle for various lung regions [31]; SPAMM has also been used for radiation therapy planning to address the issue of respiration through the calculation of instantaneous motion fields [32]. Conventional tagging and PC MRI have been used to assess anatomical deformation in various parts of the brain [33] with respect to the cardiac motion and the pulsatile blood flow. SENC has also been used in the assessment of liver function, where the peak strain in the left lobe of the liver and the velocity of shear wave due to the cardiac motion can be measured [34]. The strains thus measured are found to be correlated with fibrosis, and hence are being investigated as qualitative diagnostic and prognostic tool for the assessment of fibrosis.

35.3 Magnetic Resonance Elastography

As discussed above, motion and strain measured by MRI are key elements in physiology that can shed light on normal function and on various disease processes. However, these measurements do not have a direct one-to-one correspondence with any intrinsic tissue property. To calculate the mechanical properties of a tissue, knowledge of the absolute stimulus that resulted in the observed motion is necessary. To this end, MR elastography (MRE, [35]) was developed. MRE is a relatively new technique which introduces known vibrations into the tissue of interest, measures the resultant displacement, and calculates the mechanical properties of tissue, specifically the shear modulus. Shear modulus is known to vary widely across normal physiological and pathological conditions, and MRE has shown increased utility as a sensitive diagnostic technique [36–38] (Fig. 35.6).

MRE is essentially a modern way of performing manual palpation to "feel" the difference in mechanical properties, a procedure that many clinicians employ routinely even today. It belongs to a group

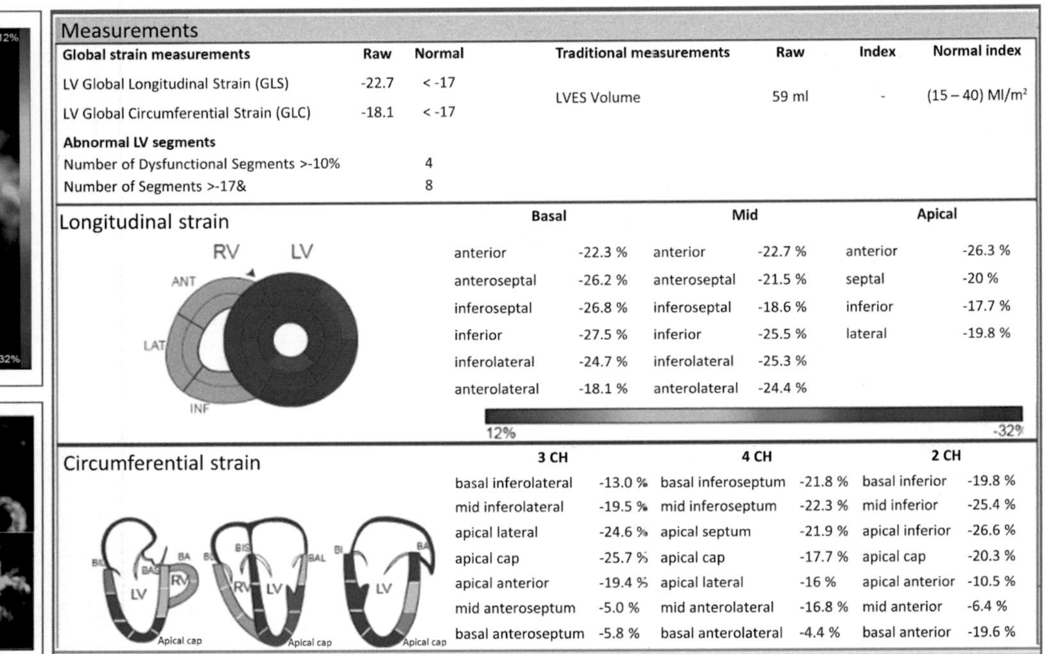

LA 2Ch
12%
10/24
-32%
Measurements
Global strain measurements
Raw
Normal
LV Global Longitudinal Strain (GLS)
-22.7
< -17
LV Global Circumferential Strain (GLC)
-18.1
< -17
Abnormal LV segments
Number of Dysfunctional Segments >-10%
4
Number of Segments >-17&
8
Traditional measurements
Raw
Index
Normal index
LVES Volume
59 ml
-
(15 – 40) Ml/m²
Longitudinal strain
RV
LV
ANT
LAT
INF
Basal
anterior -22.3 %
anteroseptal -26.2 %
inferoseptal -26.8 %
inferior -27.5 %
inferolateral -24.7 %
anterolateral -18.1 %
Mid
anterior -22.7 %
anteroseptal -21.5 %
inferoseptal -18.6 %
inferior -25.5 %
inferolateral -25.3 %
anterolateral -24.4 %
Apical
anterior -26.3 %
septal -20 %
inferior -17.7 %
lateral -19.8 %
12%
-32%
Circumferential strain
3 CH
basal inferolateral -13.0 %
mid inferolateral -19.5 %
apical lateral -24.6 %
apical cap -25.7 %
apical anterior -19.4 %
mid anteroseptum -5.0 %
basal anteroseptum -5.8 %
4 CH
basal inferoseptum -21.8 %
mid inferoseptum -22.3 %
apical septum -21.9 %
apical cap -17.7 %
apical lateral -16 %
mid anterolateral -16.8 %
basal anterolateral -4.4 %
2 CH
basal inferior -19.8 %
mid inferior -25.4 %
apical inferior -26.6 %
apical cap -20.3 %
apical anterior -10.5 %
mid anterior -6.4 %
basal anterior -19.6 %
LV
RV
Apical cap

FIG. 35.5

The strain report contains global and regional longitudinal and circumferential strain values. Example data from the left ventricle is shown here.

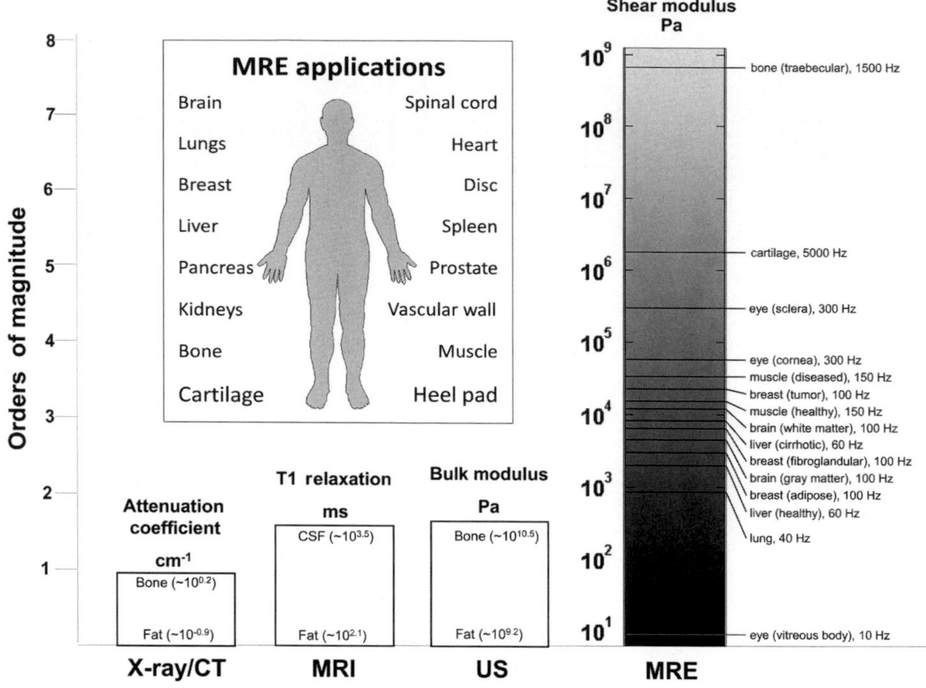

FIG. 35.6

Imaging modalities and dynamic range of the corresponding contrast parameters. Shear modulus that can be measured with MRE has the highest dynamic range among human tissues. Indicative shear stiffness values obtained with MRE for different anatomies are also indicated.

Adapted from Litwiller et al. (2012).

of techniques collectively termed as "Elasticity Imaging," detailed discussions of which can be found in previous publications [36,39,40]. MRE measurements are typically comprised of three steps which are detailed in the following sections.

35.3.1 MRE Step 1: introduce shear vibrations into the tissue of interest

The first step in MRE is to induce shear vibrations in the tissue. Various approaches with different sources and temporal characteristics of the vibrations have been investigated. Current standard MRE techniques induce continuous vibration of a particular frequency using a pneumatic driver. The displacement/position vector $\vec{r}\,(t)$ as a function of time can be expressed as:

$$\vec{r}\,(t) = \vec{r}_0 + \vec{\xi}_0 e^{\left(j\left(\vec{k}\cdot\vec{r}-\omega t+\theta\right)\right)} \tag{35.6}$$

where $\vec{r}_0$ is the mean position of the isochromats, $\vec{\xi}_0$ is the peak amplitude of the displacement, $\vec{k}$ is the wave number, ω is the angular frequency ($2\pi f$) of the harmonic wave, f is the frequency of the motion, and θ is an initial phase offset [35]. Pneumatic driver systems are suited only for continuous vibration of a small range of frequencies; details of driver systems suited for other applications can be found in Refs. [41,42]. The typical vibrations applied across different anatomies and frequencies are quite safe and are well below the vibration acceleration limits set by the European Union directive occupational exposure to whole-body and extremity vibration (EU 2002/4/EC) [43,44]

35.3.2 MRE Step 2: imaging of shear wave propagation

Shear waves propagating within the tissue of interest are imaged using the phase-contrast MR technique [45] using motion encoding (or motion sensitizing) gradient pairs (MEG) inserted into normal MR imaging pulse sequences. The displacement of the tissue is mapped onto the phase ($\varphi(t)$) of an MR image as follows:

$$\varphi(t) = \gamma \int_0^t \vec{G}_r(t') \cdot \vec{r}\,(t')dt' \tag{35.7}$$

where γ is the gyromagnetic ratio, $\vec{G}_r(t)$ is the motion-sensitizing gradient vector, and $\vec{r}\,(t)$ is the position vector (as indicated in Eq. 35.6) of the moving spin [8]. As can be seen from Eqs. (35.6), (35.7), the phase of a harmonically vibrating isochromat φ is directly proportional to its displacement, the gradient strength $\vec{G}$ and the duration (T) for which the gradient is active, and is given as

$$\varphi\left(\vec{r}, \theta\right) = \frac{2\gamma NT\left(\vec{G} \cdot \xi_0\right)}{\pi} \cos\left(\vec{k} \cdot \vec{r} + \theta\right) \tag{35.8}$$

where N is the number of MEG gradient pairs used to sensitize the motion, and θ is the phase offset between the MEG gradient and the motion. Note that the phase varies pixelwise throughout the entire slice/volume. Once the motion encoding has been performed, the data are collected using a standard MRI readout. Over the years, many different flavors of MRE pulse sequences based on fast field echo (FFE) or spin echo (SE) with multiple optimizations like fractional encoding, broadband sensitivity, etc. have been developed, details of which can be found in the following references: [35,46–48].

The propagation of the wave is captured at typically 4–8 temporal samples (phase offset images) equidistant within the period of the motion by manipulating the phase offset between the motion and the MEG (θ). Acquisition of the wave at multiple time points allows the downstream wave inversion algorithms to be used to calculate the temporal first harmonics, removing residual static and higher harmonic phase information [49].

Typically, two images with opposing MEG polarities are obtained and are combined to obtain a phase difference image which depicts only the motion-dependent phase and also has the added advantage of having twice the motion sensitivity. In the presence of MEG, there is no additional phase accrual for the static spins, as the displacement is 0. However, there is a net phase accrual for moving spins as given by Eq. (35.8) where the key determinants are the MEG strength and the displacement amplitude. The signal of a moving spin can be indicated as below:

$$S_1 = M_1 e^{i\varphi_1} \tag{35.9}$$

where M is the magnitude of the signal and φ_1 is the corresponding phase. The phase φ_1 is equal to $\varphi_s + \varphi_m$, where φ_s is the phase of the static spin and φ_m is the phase due to motion. The phase of the static spin will be dependent on multiple pulse sequence and experimental parameters. This background phase can be removed using an acquisition with opposite MEG polarity:

$$S_2 = M_2 e^{i\varphi_2} \tag{35.10}$$

where the phase φ_2 is equal to φ_s-φ_m, due to the opposite polarity of the MEG. From these two signals, the motion-dependent phase can then be extracted as

$$\angle S_1 S_2 = \angle M_1 M_2 e^{i(\varphi_1 - \varphi_2)} = \angle M_1 M_2 e^{i(2\varphi_m)} \tag{35.11}$$

It can be noted that the phase due to the motion is separated out from the phase of the static spin (background phase) with twice the sensitivity as well. With the removal of this background phase, practical issues which can be confounders in other quantitative measurements, including B_0/B_1 inhomogeneities, can be mitigated.

Motion in any arbitrary direction [50–52] can be imaged with MRE by placing the MEGs on different axes. This capability is becoming significant as the field of MRE is moving from 2D to 3D, as the propagation of shear waves is 3D in nature. In cases where the wave propagation can be approximated to a planar wave, for example, in the liver, 2D representation of shear wave propagation is sufficient. However, in other cases where the propagation of waves is complex, for example, in small organs like the prostate, in organs with complicated geometries like pancreas, in moving tissues like cardiac tissue, or in organs where the wave propagation is predominantly anisotropic, 3D imaging, where the propagation of the shear wave is captured in the three orthogonal directions, is essential. While 3D MRE is more accurate in capturing the wave propagation, the need for more acquisition time, and expensive postprocessing makes the 2D MRE the preferred approach where possible.

35.3.3 MRE Step 3: Quantification of mechanical parameters

Quantitative shear modulus values, μ, are calculated from the displacement information obtained in Step 2 using constitutive wave equation [35,53] based inversion algorithms with many simplifying assumptions like isotropy, local homogeneity, negligible attenuation, and incompressibility, etc. as follows:

$$\mu = \rho V_s^2 \tag{35.12}$$

where ρ is the density (assumed to be 1000 kg/m^3) and V_s is the wave speed of the propagating shear wave.

Fig. 35.7 shows a simple flow diagram of the calculation of shear stiffness maps, which are referred to as elastograms. Since the displacement in each direction satisfies the wave equation separately, theoretically it is possible to calculate the stiffness map from a single direction of motion. There are multiple approaches including manual estimation, Local Frequency Estimation, the phase gradient technique, and finite element-based techniques for the calculation of shear stiffness maps; interested readers should refer to [49,54–57].

Fig. 35.8 shows an example dataset obtained in a phantom with known regions of softness and hardness. A shear wave of 100 Hz was introduced into the phantom and the propagation of this wave was imaged with four phase offsets. A wave image obtained after first harmonic filtering of the four phase offsets is shown in Fig. 35.8B. The elastogram calculated from this data is shown in Fig. 35.8C. The difference in shear wavelength and the shear stiffness between the soft and hard regions is readily apparent in the wave image and the elastogram, respectively.

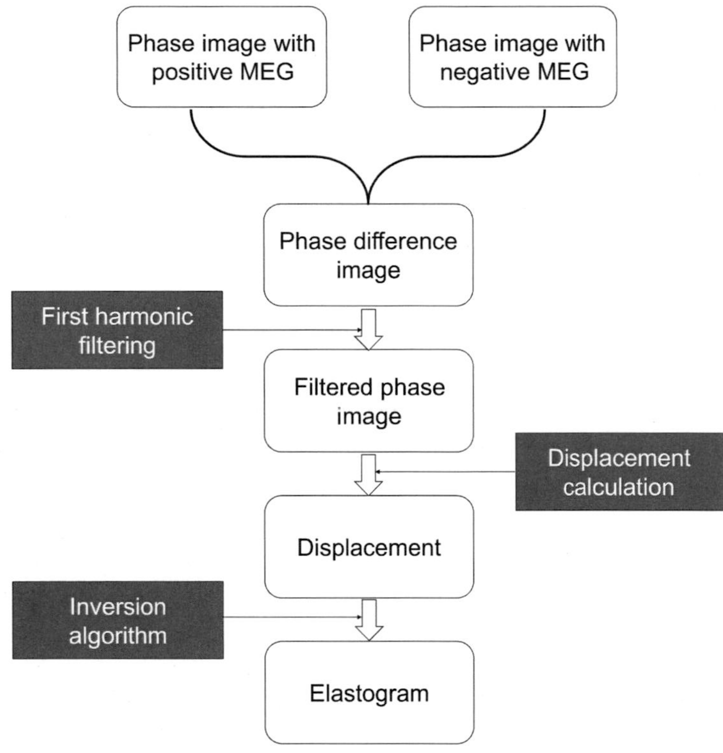

FIG. 35.7

Schematic diagram illustrating the workflow, imaging, and processing steps used to generate MRE measurements.

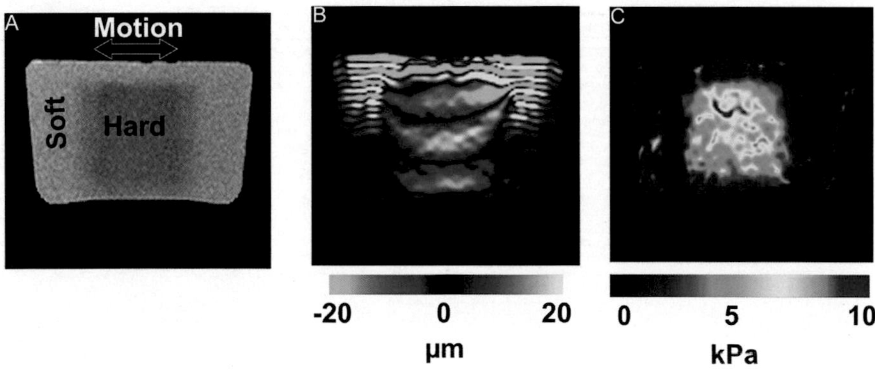

FIG. 35.8

MRE on a phantom with a hard inclusion within a soft background. (A) Conventional MR magnitude image of the phantom with the soft and hard regions as indicated. (B) A single wave image from the MRE data, where the longer shear wavelength within the harder region is visible. (C) An elastogram obtained from this data showing the stiff and soft regions.

Adapted from Mariappan et al. (2009).

35.3.4 Applications of MR elastography

The field of MRE has been expanding rapidly and some of the applications being investigated with MRE are discussed briefly below.

35.3.4.1 Hepatic MRE

MRE is currently clinically available for the measurement of liver stiffness to assess fibrosis/cirrhosis. A clinical hepatic MRE exam has the three following steps, as described in the previous sections:

1. Shear waves of 60 Hz frequency are induced into the liver using a pressure-activated acoustic driver system.

Fig. 35.9 shows a clinical mechanical actuator system (Resoundant Inc., Rochester, MN) consisting of an active driver located in the technical room, a passive drum driver to be placed on the anatomy of interest, and a long connecting tube through which the vibrations are pneumatically transferred as longitudinal pressure waves. Typically, an elastic belt is used to keep the passive driver taut for efficient coupling of vibrations. Please note that while the motion is transferred as longitudinal waves, what is actually imaged with MRE are shear waves created by mode conversion at organ boundaries [58].

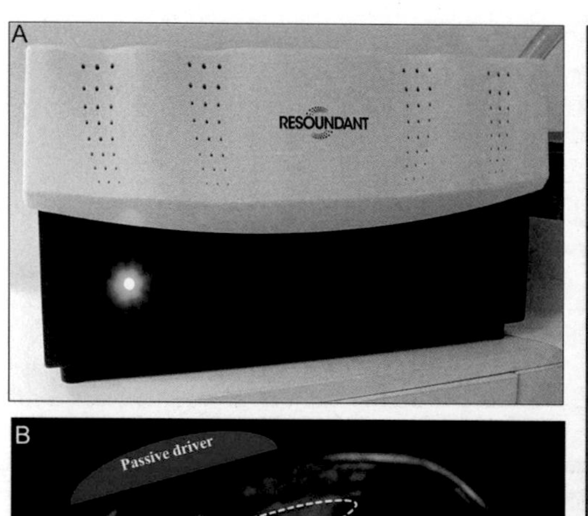

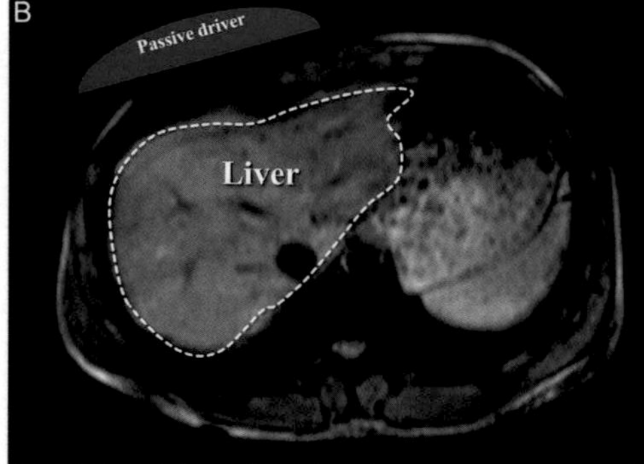

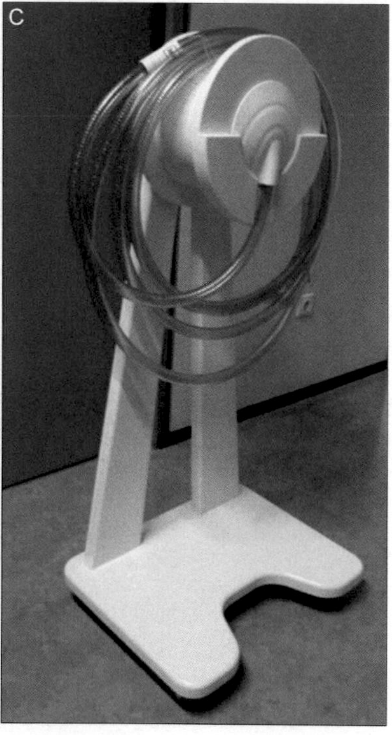

FIG. 35.9

Pneumatic based pressure-activated driver system (Resoundant Inc., Rochester, MN, USA). (A) Active driver kept in the technical room. (B) Positioning of the passive driver on the human subject for hepatic MRE application. (C) Passive driver and the connecting tube in its housing (Philips Healthcare, Best, the Netherlands).

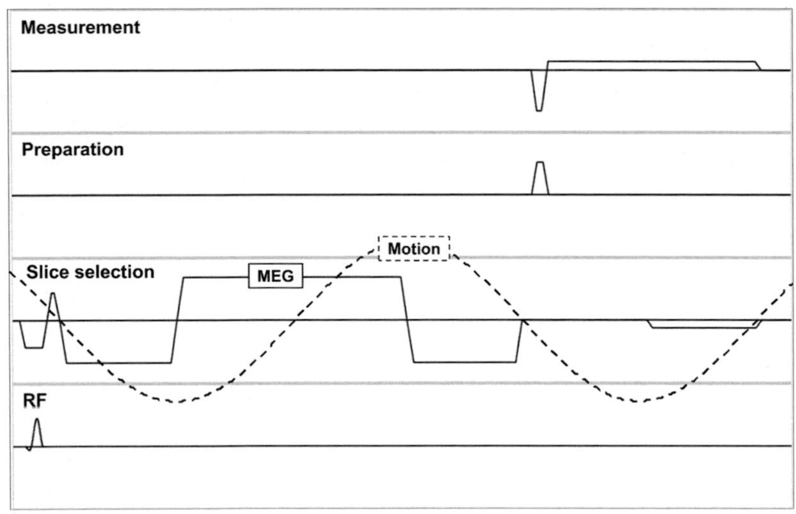

FIG. 35.10

FFE MRE pulse sequence. A typical flow-compensated motion-encoding gradient and a schematic of the motion waveform is shown for a motion of frequency 60 Hz. Please note that the duration of the MEG is equal to the period of the motion.

2. The propagation of these waves is imaged using a protocol in which four slices are acquired at four phase offsets.

Fig. 35.10 shows an example fast field echo (FFE, i.e., Gradient Refocused Echo, GRE) based MRE pulse sequence, where the MEG is shown in the slice selection axis. The induced motion is indicated as the dotted line. Typically the MEGs are flow compensated (1-2-1 type gradient to provide gradient moment nulling) thus reducing the artifacts due to blood flow [8,59].

3. The shear stiffness map is calculated, typically using the multimodel direct inversion (MMDI) algorithm, using the direct inversion of the Helmholtz equation [49,55,57,60]; the shear modulus μ is calculated as follows:

$$\mu = -\rho\omega^2 \frac{u}{\nabla^2 u} \tag{35.13}$$

where ω ($2\pi f$, where f is the frequency of the motion) is the angular frequency, u is the displacement of the particle, and ∇^2 is the Laplace operator. As seen earlier from Eq. (35.8), the phase measured in MRE is directly proportional to the spin position vector $\vec{r}\,(t)$, and therefore is also proportional to the displacement. Thus, the measured phase can be used for the calculation of the shear modulus. Various preprocessing steps including phase unwrapping and directional filtering are typically applied to the data before calculating the sheer stiffness map [49,61].

Example data and elastograms obtained from a clinical MRE exam using the MREView package (Philips, Eindhoven, the Netherlands) are shown in Fig. 35.11. The magnitude image, a single offset wave image, and the corresponding shear stiffness map obtained from a healthy liver are shown in their

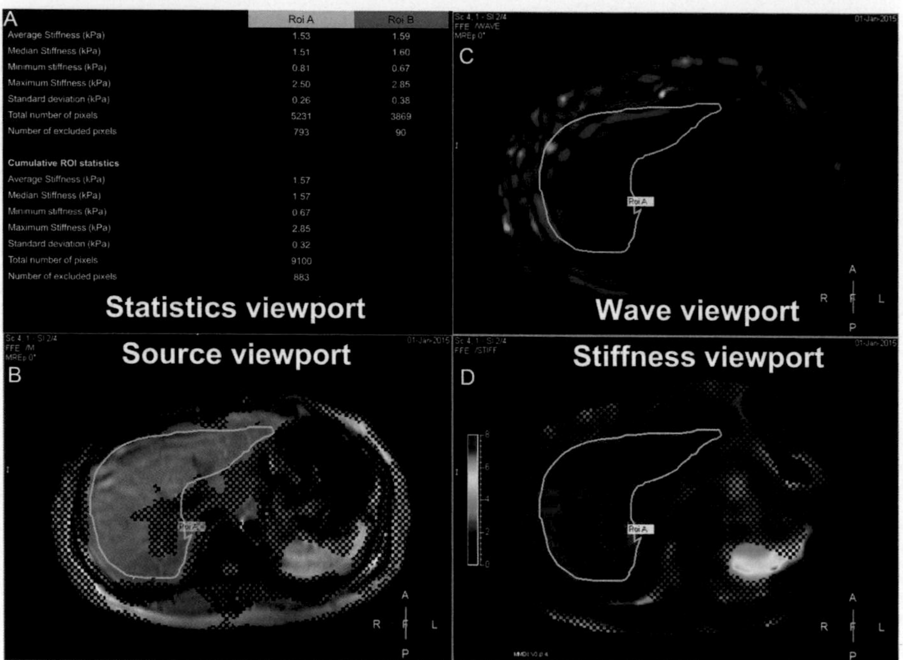

FIG. 35.11

Example hepatic MRE exam in a healthy subject. (A) Statistics viewport with the stiffness measurements for individual ROIs and the cumulative values. (B) A magnitude image of one of the imaging slices is shown in the source viewport. (C) A filtered wave image is shown in the wave viewport and (D) the corresponding elastogram (stiffness map) of the slice is shown in the stiffness viewport. The "mmdi" inversion algorithm version that was used for the stiffness calculation is shown in the stiffness viewer. A checkerboard pattern indicating the reliability of the stiffness inversion is shown overlaid on the source and stiffness images. A manually drawn ROI (ROI A) is also shown and the corresponding stiffness value is reported in the statistics viewer.

respective viewports. The checkerboard pattern on these images indicates regions of unreliable stiffness in the stiffness maps, (typically < 0.95 goodness of fit). Once the stiffness maps are calculated, regions-of-interest (ROIs) are drawn and various ROI statistics including mean, median, standard deviation are reported as shown in Fig. 35.11A. Care should be taken while drawing the regions of interest so as not to include regions of unreliable stiffness. Within the MREView package, even if the ROI includes regions of unreliable stiffness, these regions are excluded from the calculation of the ROI statistics, as can be seen from the field "# of excluded pixels" in the statistics viewer.

Fig. 35.12 shows a graph adapted from [62] indicating the direct relationship of the stiffness with biopsy-determined fibrosis stages, as well as example liver stiffness maps obtained from a healthy liver and liver with high-grade fibrosis. The stiffness of the hepatic tissue is significantly higher in livers with fibrosis. Based on a recent metaanalysis, the pooled sensitivity and specificity of MRE (from a total of 9 studies with 1470 patients) for the diagnosis of significant fibrosis, advanced fibrosis, and cirrhosis were 92.8% and 93.7%, 89.6% and 93.2%, 89.5% and 92.0%, respectively [63]. MRE outperformed noninvasive detection of fibrosis compared to other MR-based features including liver

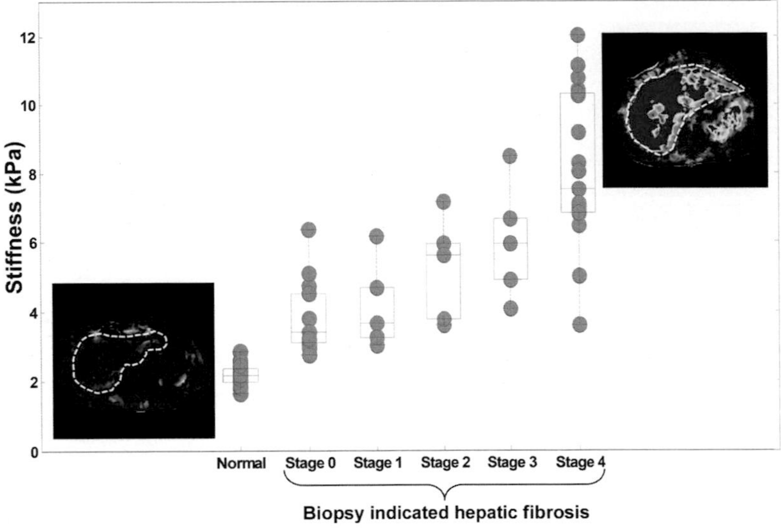

FIG. 35.12

MRE-derived shear stiffness obtained at 60 Hz of livers without and with different levels of fibrosis. The stiffness increases gradually with the progression of the disease.

Data courtesy of Dr. Meng Yin, Mayo clinic.

parenchyma texture, surface nodularity, volumetric changes, and portal hypertension [64], or Fibroscan [63]. This high diagnostic capability, combined with the noninvasiveness of MRE and the robustness in the presence of fat deposition, ascites, etc., has resulted in expedited clinical acceptance of this technique, especially considering the need for additional hardware.

While FFE-based MRE is typically robust with a high technical success rate (94.4%), [65], this approach can fail when the T_2* of the liver is significantly decreased [66], especially at high fields. Spin-echo-based MRE pulse sequences can result in improve mapping in these scenarios.

Example images and maps obtained from a patient with excess iron deposition within the liver obtained with FFE- and SE-based MRE are shown in Fig. 35.13; with an SE-based sequence, since there is sufficient signal in the liver, the MRE exam was successful [67]. A recent study indicates that the technical success rate can be significantly improved when using SE-based sequences [68]

When performing MRE of the liver, the following practical considerations should be noted:

1. The passive driver should be placed in the upper abdomen at the level of the xiphisternum, which ensures that a large portion of liver will exhibit high shear wave displacement. The passive driver should be placed with tight coupling using the elastic belt. It is recommended to place the imaging surface coil array over the passive driver and the elastic belt.
2. The positioning of the imaging slices is critical, especially in scenarios where only 2D imaging is performed. While the slices are prescribed near the dome to have a largest cross-sectional area, prescribing on the dome itself should be avoided to reduce breathhold artifacts [69].

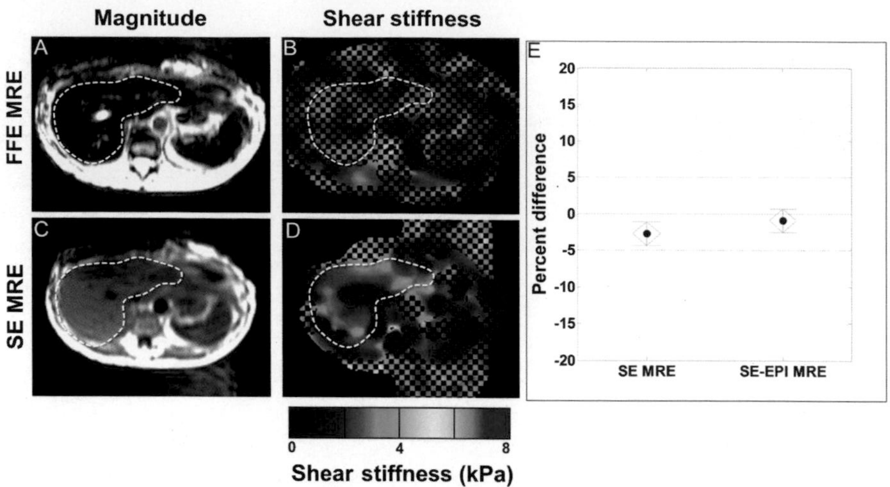

FIG. 35.13

Hepatic MRE data obtained from a patient with liver iron overload using FFE MRE (top row) and SE MRE (bottom row) with the liver indicated. The low signal (A) within the liver using FFE resulted in (B) a nonreliable stiffness map. (C) Data obtained with a SE-based MRE technique yielded a successful scan with sufficient signal (C) and (D) reliable liver stiffness values. (E) Graph showing the equivalence of the shear stiffness values obtained with the SE-based techniques compared to the FFE-based technique (Mariappan et al., Radiology, 2016).

3. To improve the reproducibility of the liver position due to respiration, it is recommended to perform the MRE scan at end expiration. As with any breathhold scan, MRE scans will benefit from coaching the patient before the actual scan is performed.
4. Similarly, it is important to coach the patient about what to expect during the MRE scan, specifically with respect to the vibrations to be applied. The data from the first imaging slice may be affected by patient motion, attributed to the patient's sudden experience of the applied vibration. Artifacts can be reduced by either having the motion to ramp up to the maximum applicable motion amplitude or by allowing the patient to gain experience with the vibration prior to imaging.
5. While the stiffness values of liver are the same irrespective of the field strength (1.5 T vs. 3 T, [66,68]), the technical success rate is higher at lower field strengths. It is thus recommended that MRE be performed at 1.5 T if possible, especially if the pulse sequence is FFE-based.

35.3.4.2 MR Elastography in other abdominal organs

In addition to hepatic fibrosis assessment, MRE is also being investigated for the assessment of hepatic tumors [70] and for other abdominal organs including the spleen, pancreas, kidneys, prostate, abdominal aorta, etc. [69]. In most cases, the data is acquired during hepatic MRE , and thus no additional scan time is required.

Spleen: Shear waves can be seen propagating into the spleen during MRE of the liver. Splenic stiffness is found to be well-correlated with liver stiffness, spleen size, platelet count and the presence of esophageal varices [71].

Pancreas: Due to the complex anatomy of the pancreas and the complexity of the shear wave propagation, 3D MRE with wave propagation measured in the three orthogonal directions is required. MRE-derived stiffness is directly proportional to the subject's age [72], is higher in patients with chronic/acute pancreatitis [73,74] and has been found to be potentially useful for noninvasive differentiation of pancreatic ductal adenocarcinoma and mass forming pancreatitis [51,73].

Kidneys: The smaller size of the kidneys necessitates the use of higher frequencies and 3D MRE. A driving frequency of 90 Hz has been used with imaging typically in coronal imaging plane where both the kidneys are visible. Recent evidence suggests that MRE can be applicable for fibrosis monitoring in renal transplant patients [75] and for the assessment of renal tumors [76].

Prostate: The location and the size of the prostate hinders efficient propagation of the waves into the organ. Using a shear vibration of 100 Hz frequency, recent results indicate MRE-derived stiffness was significantly higher in prostate cancer lesions compared to regions with benign prostatitis or healthy peripheral zone [77]. To improve the wave penetration, transperineal and transurethral actuation methods are being developed and show clinical promise [78, 79].

35.3.4.3 Brain MRE

MR Elastography of the brain holds significant clinical potential, as the stiffness of the brain changes significantly during healthy aging and in different disease processes such as Alzheimers, multiple sclerosis, hydrocephalus, cancer etc. [80–83]. An example anatomical reference image and the corresponding stiffness image of a brain are shown in Fig. 35.14A and E, and the relationship is easily visible.

35.3.4.4 Breast MRE

As breast cancer is one of the most common cancers in women, and breast tumors are stiffer than the normal tissue, there is significant interest in measuring the breast stiffness with MRE [84,85]. Fig. 35.14B and F show an example anatomical image and the corresponding stiffness map of a patient with adenocarcinoma, where the higher stiffness of the tumor is clearly visible. Recent evidence indicates that the addition of MRE information to other clinical biomarkers improves the diagnostic accuracy [84].

35.3.4.5 Cardiac MRE

Despite challenges including cardiac motion and the deeper location within the ribcage, multiple groups have successfully shown that MRE can be used to quantitatively measure stiffness changes within the cardiac muscle [86,87]. Example images and maps using 3D MRE obtained from a healthy volunteer with a vibration of 80 Hz are shown in Fig. 35.14C and G. Myocardial stiffness is higher at systole compared to that at diastole. Similarly, stiffness variations have been found in patients with cardiac amyloidosis, hypertension, and myocardial infarcts [88,89], suggesting clinical diagnostic potential.

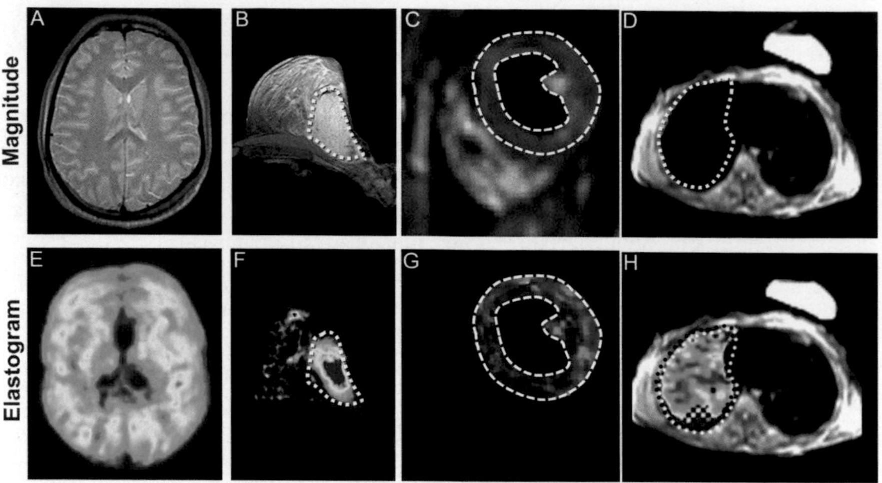

FIG. 35.14

Example images and elastograms obtained in the brain (A, E), breast (B, F), heart (C, G), and lungs (D, H). The correlation of magnitude images (top row) and the stiffness maps (bottom row) are readily apparent in the brain data. Within the breast, the higher stiffness of the adenocarcinoma is apparent. In the heart and lungs, despite the obvious challenges, shear stiffness maps could be successfully measured.

35.3.4.6 Pulmonary MRE

Key challenges for pulmonary MRE include low tissue density and ultra-short T_2* of lung parenchyma. Recent advances in specialized spin-echo-based pulse sequences with very short TE values have shown promise in providing sufficient signal and motion sensitivity to measure the shear stiffness [48,90,91]. Example images and maps are shown in Fig. 35.14D and H. Recent studies have shown that MRE-derived shear stiffness is higher in patients with interstitial lung disease compared to their normal counterparts, at both residual volume (RV) and total lung capacity (TLC).

35.3.4.7 Specialized applications of MR elastography

In addition to the MRE applications where the main contrast is the shear stiffness of the anatomy, there are other related techniques being developed for certain specific applications. For example, shearline or slip interface imaging is a technique related to MRE which can successfully predict the degree of adhesion between tissue interfaces in patients. Used in patients with meningioma and vestibular schwannoma, this technique has been shown to be clinically helpful in assessing the surgical risk and tumor resectability [92–94]. With a technique referred to as high-frequency mode conversion MRE, the presence of stiff areas can be quickly qualitatively detected in the wave image itself without the need for any inversion algorithm [95]. The higher frequency also allows more accurate lesion characterization. Another related technique is Wav-MRE (Wave Amplitude Variation with MRE) where the amplitude of the vibrations measured in heart muscle can qualitatively indicate the stiffness [96]. In addition to the clinical applications discussed in this chapter, there is also considerable interest in using MRE-derived mechanical parameters for the assessment of small tissue samples such as tissue engineering constructs [97,98]. MRE techniques have also been adapted for bench-top devices which use permanent magnets with a low MR field strength to provide rapid measurements of mechanical parameters in laboratory settings [99].

35.4 Conclusion

In this chapter, various MR methods for motion quantitation have been discussed, including imaging of both intrinsic physiological motion and extrinsically induced known motion. Both motion quantification and Magnetic Resonance Elastography hold significant clinical potential in a variety of applications.

References

[1] Zaitsev M, Maclaren J, Herbst M. Motion artifacts in MRI: a complex problem with many partial solutions: motion artifacts and correction. J Magn Reson Imaging 2015;42(4):887–901.

[2] Zerhouni EA, Parish DM, Rogers WJ, Yang A, Shapiro EP. Human heart: tagging with MR imaging—a method for noninvasive assessment of myocardial motion. Radiology 1988;169(1):59–63.

[3] Axel L, Dougherty L. MR imaging of motion with spatial modulation of magnetization. Radiology 1989;171(3):841–5.

[4] Pelc NJ, Sommer FG, Li KC, Brosnan TJ, Herfkens RJ, Enzmann DR. Quantitative magnetic resonance flow imaging. Magn Reson Q 1994;10(3):125–47.

[5] Aletras AH, Ding S, Balaban RS, Wen H. DENSE: displacement encoding with stimulated echoes in cardiac functional MRI. J Magn Reson 1999;137(1):247–52.

[6] Osman NF, Sampath S, Atalar E, Prince JL. Imaging longitudinal cardiac strain on short-axis images using strain-encoded MRI. Magn Reson Med 2001;46(2):324–34.

[7] Wang H, Amini AA. Cardiac motion and deformation recovery from MRI: a review. IEEE Trans Med Imaging 2012;31(2):487–503.

[8] Moran PR. A flow velocity zeugmatographic interlace for NMR imaging in humans. Magn Reson Imaging 1982;1(4):197–203.

[9] Isoda H, Ohkura Y, Kosugi T, Hirano M, Takeda H, Hiramatsu H, et al. In vivo hemodynamic analysis of intracranial aneurysms obtained by magnetic resonance fluid dynamics (MRFD) based on time-resolved three-dimensional phase-contrast MRI. Neuroradiology 2010;52(10):921–8.

[10] Jung B, Markl M, Föll D, Hennig J. Investigating myocardial motion by MRI using tissue phase mapping. Eur J Cardio-Thorac Surg Off J Eur Assoc Cardio-Thorac Surg 2006;29(Suppl 1):S150–7.

[11] Arai AE, Gaither CC, Epstein FH, Balaban RS, Wolff SD. Myocardial velocity gradient imaging by phase contrast MRI with application to regional function in myocardial ischemia. Magn Reson Med 1999;42(1):98–109.

[12] Osman NF, Kerwin WS, McVeigh ER, Prince JL. Cardiac motion tracking using CINE harmonic phase (HARP) magnetic resonance imaging. Magn Reson Med 1999;42(6):1048–60.

[13] Fischer SE, McKinnon GC, Maier SE, Boesiger P. Improved myocardial tagging contrast. Magn Reson Med 1993;30(2):191–200.

[14] Frahm J, Merboldt KD, Hänicke W, Haase A. Stimulated echo imaging. J Magn Reson 1985;64(1):81–93.

[15] Kim D, Epstein FH, Gilson WD, Axel L. Increasing the signal-to-noise ratio in DENSE MRI by combining displacement-encoded echoes. Magn Reson Med 2004;52(1):188–92.

[16] Gilson WD, Yang Z, French BA, Epstein FH. Measurement of myocardial mechanics in mice before and after infarction using multislice displacement-encoded MRI with 3D motion encoding. Am J Physiol Heart Circ Physiol 2005;288(3):H1491–7.

[17] Aletras AH, Wen H. Mixed echo train acquisition displacement encoding with stimulated echoes: an optimized DENSE method for in vivo functional imaging of the human heart. Magn Reson Med 2001;46(3):523–34.

[17a] Osman NF. Detecting stiff masses using strain-encoded (SENC) imaging. Magn Reson Med 2003 49(3):605–8.

[18] Neizel M, Lossnitzer D, Korosoglou G, Schäufele T, Peykarjou H, Steen H, et al. Strain-encoded MRI for evaluation of left ventricular function and transmurality in acute myocardial infarction. Circ Cardiovasc Imaging 2009;2(2):116–22.

[19] Oyama-Manabe N, Ishimori N, Sugimori H, Van Cauteren M, Kudo K, Manabe O, et al. Identification and further differentiation of subendocardial and transmural myocardial infarction by fast strain-encoded (SENC) magnetic resonance imaging at 3.0 Tesla. Eur Radiol 2011;21(11):2362–8.

[20] Choi E-Y, Rosen BD, Fernandes VRS, Yan RT, Yoneyama K, Donekal S, et al. Prognostic value of myocardial circumferential strain for incident heart failure and cardiovascular events in asymptomatic individuals: the Multi-Ethnic Study of Atherosclerosis. Eur Heart J 2013;34(30):2354–61.

[21] Ibrahim E-SH, Stuber M, Kraitchman DL, Weiss RG, Osman NF. Combined functional and viability cardiac MR imaging in a single breathhold. Magn Reson Med 2007;58(4):843–9.

[22] Bogaert J, Bosmans H, Maes A, Suetens P, Marchal G, Rademakers FE. Remote myocardial dysfunction after acute anterior myocardial infarction: impact of left ventricular shape on regional function: a magnetic resonance myocardial tagging study. J Am Coll Cardiol 2000;35(6):1525–34.

[23] Carlsson M, Osman NF, Ursell PC, Martin AJ, Saeed M. Quantitative MR measurements of regional and global left ventricular function and strain after intramyocardial transfer of VM202 into infarcted swine myocardium. Am J Physiol Heart Circ Physiol 2008;295(2):H522–32.

[24] Rademakers F, Van de Werf F, Mortelmans L, Marchal G, Bogaert J. Evolution of regional performance after an acute anterior myocardial infarction in humans using magnetic resonance tagging. J Physiol 2003; 546(Pt 3):777–87.

[25] Young AA, French BA, Yang Z, Cowan BR, Gilson WD, Berr SS, et al. Reperfused myocardial infarction in mice: 3D mapping of late gadolinium enhancement and strain. J Cardiovasc Magn Reson Off J Soc Cardiovasc Magn Reson 2006;8(5):685–92.

[26] Götte MJ, van Rossum AC, Twisk JWR, JPA K, Marcus JT, Visser CA. Quantification of regional contractile function after infarction: strain analysis superior to wall thickening analysis in discriminating infarct from remote myocardium. J Am Coll Cardiol 2001;37(3):808–17.

[27] de Roos A, van der Wall EE, Bruschke AV, van Voorthuisen AE. Magnetic resonance imaging in the diagnosis and evaluation of myocardial infarction. Magn Reson Q 1991;7(3):191–207.

[28] Budge LP, Helms AS, Salerno M, Kramer CM, Epstein FH, Bilchick KC. MR cine DENSE dyssynchrony parameters for the evaluation of heart failure: comparison with myocardial tissue tagging. JACC Cardiovasc Imaging 2012;5(8):789–97.

[29] Chang S-A, Chang H-J, Choi SI, Chun EJ, Yoon YE, Kim H-K, et al. Usefulness of left ventricular dyssynchrony after acute myocardial infarction, assessed by a tagging magnetic resonance image derived metric, as a determinant of ventricular remodeling. Am J Cardiol 2009;104(1):19–23.

[30] El Ghannudi S, Germain P, Jeung M-Y, Breton E, Croisille P, Durand E, et al. Quantification of left ventricular dyssynchrony in patients with systolic dysfunction: a comparison of circumferential strain MR-tagging metrics. J Magn Reson Imaging JMRI 2014;40(5):1238–46.

[31] Cai J, Altes TA, Miller GW, Sheng K, Read PW, Mata JF, et al. MR grid-tagging using hyperpolarized helium-3 for regional quantitative assessment of pulmonary biomechanics and ventilation. Magn Reson Med 2007;58(2):373–80.

[32] von Siebenthal M, Székely G, Gamper U, Boesiger P, Lomax A, Cattin P. 4D MR imaging of respiratory organ motion and its variability. Phys Med Biol 2007;52(6):1547–64.

[33] Soellinger M, Ryf S, Boesiger P, Kozerke S. Assessment of human brain motion using CSPAMM. J Magn Reson Imaging JMRI 2007;25(4):709–14.

[34] Harouni AA, Gharib AM, Osman NF, Morse C, Heller T, Abd-Elmoniem KZ. Assessment of liver fibrosis using fast strain-encoded MRI driven by inherent cardiac motion: assessment of liver stiffness using FSENC MRI. Magn Reson Med 2015;74(1):106–14.

[35] Muthupillai R, Lomas DJ, Rossman PJ, Greenleaf JF, Manduca A, Ehman RL. Magnetic resonance elastography by direct visualization of propagating acoustic strain waves. Science 1995;269(5232): 1854–7.

[36] Hirsch S, Sack I, Braun J. Magnetic resonance elastography: physical background and medical applications. John Wiley & Sons; 2017. 452 pp.

[37] Mariappan Y, McGee K, Ehman R. Imaging tissue elasticity using magnetic resonance elastography, In: Muftuler L, editor. Quantifying morphology and physiology of the human body using MRI. Taylor & Francis; 2013. p. 381–430. [cited 2018 Sep 3]. Available from: http://www.crcnetbase.com/doi/abs/10.1201/b14814-15.

[38] Venkatesh SK, Ehman RL, editors. Magnetic resonance elastography. New York: Springer-Verlag; 2014 [cited 2018 Sep 3]. Available from:www.springer.com/gp/book/9781493915743.

[39] Jones JP, editor. Acoustical imaging. Springer US; 1995[cited 2018 Sep 3]. (Acoustical Imaging). Available from:www.springer.com/us/book/9781461357971.

[40] Wilson LS, Robinson DE, Dadd MJ. Elastography—the movement begins. Phys Med Biol 2000;45(6):1409–21.

[41] Uffmann K, Ladd ME. Actuation systems for MR elastography: design and applications. IEEE Eng Med Biol Mag Q Mag Eng Med Biol Soc 2008;27(3):28–34.

[42] Mariappan YK, Glaser KJ, Ehman RL. Magnetic resonance elastography: a review. Clin Anat N Y N 2010;23(5):497–511.

[43] Directive 2002/44/EC—vibration—safety and health at work—EU-OSHA, [cited 2018 Sep 5]. Available from:https://osha.europa.eu/en/legislation/directives/19; 2002.

[44] Ehman EC, Rossman PJ, Kruse SA, Sahakian AV, Glaser KJ. Vibration safety limits for magnetic resonance elastography. Phys Med Biol 2008;53(4):925.

[45] Dumoulin CL, Hart JH. Magnetic resonance angiography in the head and neck. Acta Radiol Suppl 1986;369:17–20.

[46] Bieri O, Maderwald S, Ladd ME, Scheffler K. Balanced alternating steady-state elastography. Magn Reson Med Off J Int Soc Magn Reson Med 2006;55(2):233–41.

[47] Guenthner C, Kozerke S. Encoding and readout strategies in magnetic resonance elastography. NMR Biomed 2018;31(10), e3919.

[48] Mariappan YK, Glaser KJ, Levin DL, Vassallo R, Hubmayr RD, Mottram C, et al. Estimation of the absolute shear stiffness of human lung parenchyma using ^{1}H spin echo, echo planar MR elastography. J Magn Reson Imaging 2014;40(5):1230–7.

[49] Manduca A, Oliphant TE, Dresner MA, Mahowald JL, Kruse SA, Amromin E, et al. Magnetic resonance elastography: non-invasive mapping of tissue elasticity. Med Image Anal 2001;5(4):237–54.

[50] Arunachalam SP, Arani A, Baffour F, Rysavy JA, Rossman PJ, Glaser KJ, et al. Regional assessment of in vivo myocardial stiffness using 3D magnetic resonance elastography in a porcine model of myocardial infarction. Magn Reson Med 2018;79(1):361–9.

[51] Shi Y, Glaser KJ, Venkatesh SK, Ben-Abraham EI, Ehman RL. Feasibility of using 3D MR elastography to determine pancreatic stiffness in healthy volunteers. J Magn Reson Imaging 2015;41(2):369–75.

[52] Wang K, Manning P, Szeverenyi N, Wolfson T, Hamilton G, Middleton MS, et al. Repeatability and reproducibility of 2D and 3D hepatic MR elastography with rigid and flexible drivers at end-expiration and end-inspiration in healthy volunteers. Abdom Radiol N Y 2017;42(12):2843–54.

[53] Auld BA. Acoustic fields and waves in solids. Рипол Классик, 1973.

[54] Barnhill E, Davies PJ, Ariyurek C, Fehlner A, Braun J, Sack I. Heterogeneous multifrequency direct inversion (HMDI) for magnetic resonance elastography with application to a clinical brain exam. Med Image Anal 2018;46:180–8.

[55] Doyley MM. Model-based elastography: a survey of approaches to the inverse elasticity problem. Phys Med Biol 2012;57(3):R35.

[56] McGarry MDJ, Van Houten EEW, Johnson CL, Georgiadis JG, Sutton BP, Weaver JB, et al. Multiresolution MR elastography using nonlinear inversion. Med Phys 2012;39(10):6388–96.

[57] Papazoglou S, Hamhaber U, Braun J, Sack I. Algebraic Helmholtz inversion in planar magnetic resonance elastography. Phys Med Biol 2008;53(12):3147–58.
[58] Yin M, Rouvière O, Glaser KJ, Ehman RL. Diffraction-biased shear wave fields generated with longitudinal magnetic resonance elastography drivers. Magn Reson Imaging 2008;26:770–80.
[59] Grimm RC, Yin M, Ehman RL. Gradient moment nulling in MR elastography of the liver, In: Proceedings of the 15th annual meeting of ISMRM, Berlin, Germany; 2007. p. 961.
[60] Silva AM, Grimm RC, Glaser KJ, Fu Y, Wu T, Ehman RL, et al. Magnetic resonance elastography: evaluation of new inversion algorithm and quantitative analysis method. Abdom Imaging 2015;40(4): 810–7.
[61] Manduca A, Lake DS, Kruse SA, Ehman RL. Spatio-temporal directional filtering for improved inversion of MR elastography images. Med Image Anal 2003;7(4):465–73.
[62] Yin M, Talwalkar JA, Glaser KJ, Manduca A, Grimm RC, Rossman PJ, et al. Assessment of hepatic fibrosis with magnetic resonance elastography. Clin Gastroenterol Hepatol Off Clin Pract J Am Gastroenterol Assoc 2007;5(10). 1207–1213.e2.
[63] Xiao H, Shi M, Xie Y, Chi X. Comparison of diagnostic accuracy of magnetic resonance elastography and Fibroscan for detecting liver fibrosis in chronic hepatitis B patients: a systematic review and meta-analysis. PLoS One 2017;12(11):e0186660.
[64] Venkatesh SK, Yin M, Takahashi N, Glockner JF, Talwalkar JA, Ehman RL. Non-invasive detection of liver fibrosis: MR imaging features vs. MR elastography. Abdom Imaging 2015;40(4):766–75.
[65] Yin M, Glaser KJ, Talwalkar JA, Chen J, Manduca A, Ehman RL. Hepatic MR elastography: clinical performance in a series of 1377 consecutive examinations. Radiology 2016 Jan;278(1):114–24.
[66] Wagner M, Corcuera-Solano I, Lo G, Esses S, Liao J, Besa C, et al. Technical failure of MR elastography examinations of the liver: experience from a large single-center study. Radiology 2017;284(2):401–12.
[67] Mariappan YK, Dzyubak B, Glaser KJ, Venkatesh SK, Sirlin CB, Hooker J, et al. Application of modified spin-echo-based sequences for hepatic MR elastography: evaluation, comparison with the conventional gradient-echo sequence, and preliminary clinical experience. Radiology 2016;282(2):390–8.
[68] Kim DW, Kim SY, Yoon HM, Kim KW, Byun JH. Comparison of technical failure of MR elastography for measuring liver stiffness between gradient-recalled echo and spin-echo echo-planar imaging: a systematic review and meta-analysis. J Magn Reson Imaging 2020;51(4):1086–102.
[69] Venkatesh SK, Ehman RL. Magnetic resonance elastography of abdomen. Abdom Imaging 2015;40(4): 745–59.
[70] Venkatesh SK, Yin M, Glockner JF, Takahashi N, Araoz PA, Talwalkar JA, et al. MR elastography of liver tumors: preliminary results. Am J Roentgenol 2008;190(6):1534–40.
[71] Talwalkar JA, Yin M, Venkatesh S, Rossman PJ, Grimm RC, Manduca A, et al. Feasibility and significance of in vivo mean spleen stiffness measurement by magnetic resonance elastography for assessing portal hypertension. AJR Am J Roentgenol 2009;193(1):122–7.
[72] Kolipaka A, Schroeder S, Mo X, Shah Z, Hart PA, Conwell DL. Magnetic resonance elastography of the pancreas: Measurement reproducibility and relationship with age. Magn Reson Imaging 2017;42:1–7.
[73] Mariappan Y, Glaser KJ, Takahashi N, Young P, Ehman R. Assessment of chronic pancreatitis with MR elastography, In: 19th annual ISMRM scientific meeting and exhibition 2011. Curran Associates, Montral, Quebec, Canada; 2011.
[74] Shi Y, Liu Y, Liu Y, Gao F, Li J, Li Q, et al. Early diagnosis and severity assessment of acute pancreatitis (AP) using MR elastography (MRE) with spin-echo echo-planar imaging. J Magn Reson Imaging 2017;46(5): 1311–9.
[75] Kirpalani A, Hashim E, Leung G, Kim JK, Krizova A, Jothy S, et al. Magnetic resonance elastography to assess fibrosis in kidney allografts. Clin J Am Soc Nephrol 2017. CJN.01830217.

[76] Prezzi D, Neji R, Stirling J, Jeljeli S, Verma H, O'Brien T, et al. Characterisation of solid renal tumours with magnetic resonance elastography (MRE) at 3T: integrating biomechanical, morphological and functional assessment. Eur Urol Suppl 2017;16(3). e1343-4.

[77] Li S, Chen M, Wang W, Zhao W, Wang J, Zhao X, et al. A feasibility study of MR elastography in the diagnosis of prostate cancer at 3.0T. Acta Radiol 2011;52(3):354–8.

[78] Sahebjavaher RS, Baghani A, Honarvar M, Sinkus R, Salcudean SE. Transperineal prostate MR elastography: initial in vivo results. Magn Reson Med 2013;69(2):411–20.

[79] Thörmer G, Reiss-Zimmermann M, Otto J, Hoffmann K-T, Moche M, Garnov N, et al. Novel technique for MR elastography of the prostate using a modified standard endorectal coil as actuator. J Magn Reson Imaging 2013;37(6):1480–5.

[80] Freimann FB, Streitberger K-J, Klatt D, Lin K, McLaughlin J, Braun J, et al. Alteration of brain viscoelasticity after shunt treatment in normal pressure hydrocephalus. Neuroradiology 2012;54(3):189–96.

[81] Murphy MC, Huston J, Jack CR, Glaser KJ, Manduca A, Felmlee JP, et al. Decreased brain stiffness in Alzheimer's disease determined by magnetic resonance elastography. J Magn Reson Imaging 2011;34(3):494–8.

[82] Sack I, Streitberger K-J, Krefting D, Paul F, Braun J. The influence of physiological aging and atrophy on brain viscoelastic properties in humans. PLoS One 2011;6(9), e23451.

[83] Wuerfel J, Paul F, Beierbach B, Hamhaber U, Klatt D, Papazoglou S, et al. MR-elastography reveals degradation of tissue integrity in multiple sclerosis. NeuroImage 2010;49(3):2520–5.

[84] Balleyguier C, Lakhdar AB, Dunant A, Mathieu M-C, Delaloge S, Sinkus R. Value of whole breast magnetic resonance elastography added to MRI for lesion characterization. NMR Biomed 2018;31(1), e3795.

[85] McKnight AL, Kugel JL, Rossman PJ, Manduca A, Hartmann LC, Ehman RL. MR elastography of breast cancer: preliminary results. Am J Roentgenol 2002;178(6):1411–7.

[86] Arani A, Glaser KL, Arunachalam SP, Rossman PJ, Lake DS, Trzasko JD, et al. In vivo, high-frequency three-dimensional cardiac MR elastography: feasibility in normal volunteers. Magn Reson Med 2017;77(1): 351–60.

[87] Kolipaka A. Cardiac magnetic resonance elastography, In: Constantinides C, editor. Protocols and methodologies in basic science and clinical cardiac MRI. Cham: Springer International Publishing; 2018. p. 237–59. [cited 2018 Sep 5]. Available from: https://doi.org/10.1007/978-3-319-53001-7_7.

[88] Arani A, Arunachalam SP, Chang ICY, Baffour F, Rossman PJ, Glaser KJ, et al. Cardiac MR elastography for quantitative assessment of elevated myocardial stiffness in cardiac amyloidosis. J Magn Reson Imaging 2017;46(5):1361–7.

[89] Mazumder R, Schroeder S, Mo X, Clymer BD, White RD, Kolipaka A. In vivo quantification of myocardial stiffness in hypertensive porcine hearts using MR elastography. J Magn Reson Imaging 2017;45(3): 813–20.

[90] Mariappan YK, Glaser KJ, Hubmayr RD, Manduca A, Ehman RL, McGee KP. MR elastography of human lung parenchyma: technical development, theoretical modeling and in vivo validation. J Magn Reson Imaging 2011;33(6):1351–61.

[91] Fakhouri F, Dong H, Kolipaka A. Magnetic resonance elastography of the lungs: a repeatability and reproducibility study. NMR Biomed 2019;e4102.

[92] Mariappan YK, Glaser KJ, Manduca A, Ehman RL. Cyclic motion encoding for enhanced MR visualization of slip interfaces. J Magn Reson Imaging 2009;30(4):855–63.

[93] Yin Z, Hughes JD, Glaser KJ, Manduca A, Gompel JV, Link MJ, et al. Slip interface imaging based on MR-elastography preoperatively predicts meningioma-brain adhesion. J Magn Reson Imaging 2017;46(4):1007–16.

[94] Yin Z, Glaser KJ, Manduca A, Van Gompel JJ, Link MJ, Hughes JD, et al. Slip interface imaging predicts tumor-brain adhesion in vestibular Schwannomas. Radiology 2015;277(2):507–17.

[95] Mariappan YK, Glaser KJ, Manduca A, Romano AJ, Venkatesh SK, Yin M, et al. High-frequency mode conversion technique for stiff lesion detection with magnetic resonance elastography (MRE). Magn Reson Med 2009;62(6):1457–65.

[96] Elgeti T, Tzschätzsch H, Hirsch S, Krefting D, Klatt D, Niendorf T, et al. Vibration-synchronized magnetic resonance imaging for the detection of myocardial elasticity changes. Magn Reson Med 2012;67(4):919–24.

[97] Kotecha M, Klatt D, Magin RL. Monitoring cartilage tissue engineering using magnetic resonance spectroscopy, imaging, and elastography. Tissue Eng Part B Rev 2013;19(6):470–84.

[98] Othman SF, Xu H, Mao JJ. Future role of MR elastography in tissue engineering and regenerative medicine. J Tissue Eng Regen Med 2015;9(5):481–7.

[99] Ipek-Ugay S, Drießle T, Ledwig M, Guo J, Hirsch S, Sack I, et al. Tabletop magnetic resonance elastography for the measurement of viscoelastic parameters of small tissue samples. J Magn Reson 2015;251:13–8.

CHAPTER

Flow Quantification with MRI

36

Jacob A. Macdonald[a] and Oliver Wieben[b]

[a]*Department of Radiology, University of Michigan, Ann Arbor, MI, United States* [b]*Departments of Medical Physics and Radiology, University of Wisconsin-Madison, Madison, WI, United States*

36.1 Introduction

The assessment of blood flow was one of the first clinically adopted quantitative measures in Magnetic Resonance Imaging (MRI). This measurement is based on phase-contrast (PC) MRI, which can be used to visualize flow dynamics in vivo and derive additional hemodynamic parameters. In this chapter, the physical principles of encoding motion into the phase of the MR signal, methodology for implementation of PC sequences, confounding factors, artifacts, and their remedies, as well as clinical applications of PC MRI are reviewed.

36.2 Principles of flow encoding

The underlying principle of encoding information about flow into the MR signal was first described by Carr and Purcell in 1954 [1], and subsequently proposed to measure sea water motion by Hahn in 1960 [2]. The first in vivo flow imaging was reported in 1982 [3] and 2D cine phase-contrast imaging was one of the first methods introduced for clinical scanning [4]. With this approach, motion encoding is accomplished through the application of bipolar magnetic field gradients that sensitize the acquisition to the motion of spins along the direction of the spatial gradient. This phenomenon is somewhat similar to that encountered in diffusion MRI, except that the bipolar gradients in diffusion imaging are much greater in the area to encode microscopic motion rather than the macroscopic motion captured with PC MRI. In this section, the physical principles of the PC encoding strategy are described for one-directional encoding and then extended to describe how the second and third directional components of the velocity vector can also be captured using this approach.

36.2.1 One-directional flow encoding

The MR signal originates from the net magnetization vector of magnetic spins. As shown in Fig. 36.1, this signal is typically represented by the length of the net magnetization vector in the transverse plane, and is measured by means of the voltage that this rotating magnetization induces in an RF coil. The magnitude of this signal is used to generate the commonly used magnitude image in MRI. In addition to its magnitude, another important property of the MR signal is its phase, which corresponds to the alignment of the transverse magnetization vector with the chosen coordinate system defined by the receiver coil.

Advances in Magnetic Resonance Technology and Applications. Volume 1. ISSN 2666-9099. https://doi.org/10.1016/B978-0-12-817057-1.00038-X

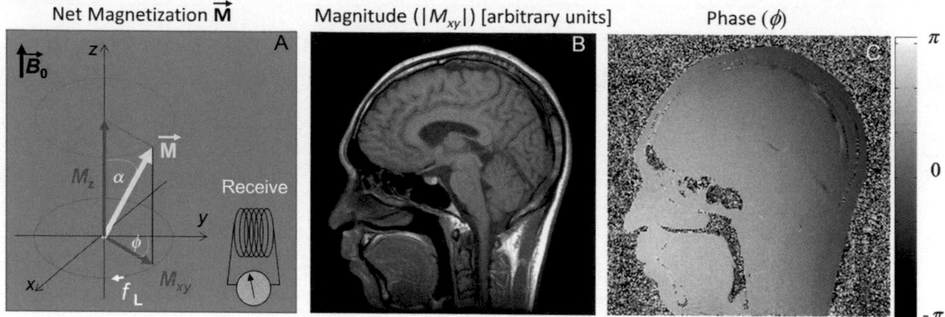

FIG. 36.1

(A) The net magnetization $\vec{\mathbf{M}}$ in an imaging voxel precesses at its Larmor frequency f_L around the direction of the main magnetic field $\vec{\mathbf{B}}_0$, which is aligned with the *z*-axis in this example. The magnetization can be described as a longitudinal component M_z and a transversal component M_{xy}. The transverse component can be measured as an induced voltage with an RF coil tuned to the Larmor frequency. This MRI signal is typically used to generate the so-called magnitude image (B), which represents the length of M_{xy}. In addition, a phase image can be generated that represents the offset between the transverse magnetization vector and a coordinate system established by the RF coil (C). Note that phase is a cyclic entity and therefore the phase map has a limited dynamic range from $-\pi$ to π.

In PC MRI, motion is encoded into the phase of the MR signal. When a magnetic spin isochromat is placed in a spatially varying gradient field, its resonance frequency offset is described by:

$$\Delta f(r,t) = \gamma(\Delta B_0 + r(\mathrm{t})G(t)) \tag{36.1}$$

where $\Delta f(r,t)$ is the frequency offset with respect to the Larmor frequency, γ is the gyromagnetic ratio, ΔB_0 describes local inhomogeneity in the main magnetic field $\vec{\mathbf{B}}_0$, and $r(t)$ is the spin's position along the axis of the magnetic field gradient $G(t)$. In a rotating reference frame at the Larmor frequency, the total phase accumulation, $\phi(r,t')$ at a time point t' is expressed as the time integral of the offset frequency:

$$\phi(r,t') = \int_0^{t'} \Delta f(r,t)dt = \gamma \int_0^{t'} \Delta B_0\, dt + \gamma \int_0^{t'} r(t)G(t)dt \tag{36.2}$$

A Taylor series expansion of $r(t)$ yields:

$$\phi(r,t') = \phi_0 + \gamma r_0 \int_0^{t'} G(t)\, dt + \gamma v \int_0^{t'} G(t)t\, dt + \gamma a \int_0^{t'} G(t)t^2 dt \tag{36.3}$$

which can alternatively be expressed as:

$$\phi(r,t') = \phi_0 + \gamma r_0 m_0 + \gamma v m_1 + \gamma a m_2 + \cdots \tag{36.4}$$

where ϕ_0 is an unpredictable initial background phase resulting from numerous factors including magnetic field inhomogeneity, magnetic susceptibility, hardware imperfections such as gradient delays, and uncompensated eddy currents, r_0 is the initial position of the spin isochromat along the gradient axis, v and a are the velocity and acceleration of the spin moving along the gradient axis, and m_n is the nth gradient moment:

$$m_n = \int t^n G(t)dt \tag{36.5}$$

In Eq. (36.4), the second term represents phase accrual for stationary spins, the third term represents the additional phase accumulation by the spin isochromat moving with a constant velocity, and higher order terms represent contributions from higher orders of motion (acceleration, jerk, etc.). In essence, the phase of a spin isochromat is determined by its motion history and the local magnetic field strength it was exposed to. This enables the design of temporally varying magnetic field gradients that sensitize MRI acquisitions to motion. The same principle can also be used to suppress motion effects and intravoxel dephasing by effectively nulling gradient moments at the echo time, a concept known as gradient moment nulling or flow compensation [5,6].

In standard PC MRI, the motion across an individual voxel is considered to be of constant velocity and higher order terms are neglected, leaving three unknown terms that contribute to the net phase of the magnetization in a voxel:

$$\phi(r, t') = \phi_0 + \gamma r_0 m_0 + \gamma v m_1 \tag{36.6}$$

In this equation, m_0 and m_1 are determined by the known gradient waveform design in the pulse sequence and ϕ_0 is an unknown background phase that needs to be taken into account. In order to use the phase measurement for the assessment of the velocity v, the background phase ϕ_0 needs to be assessed and the zeroth order and first order motion contributions need to be separated. This can be achieved by applying a bipolar gradient with successive lobes of equal strength but opposite polarity along a gradient axis. Such a bipolar gradient pair is characterized by a zeroth moment $m_0 = 0$ and a first moment $m_1 \neq 0$. Fig. 36.2 demonstrates the effects of bipolar gradients on phase accrual in both stationary (red) and moving (blue) spins.

A single MR acquisition with bipolar gradients for motion encoding is insufficient for quantitative velocity measurements as the spatially varying unknown background phase ϕ_0 needs to be accounted for (Eq. 36.6). Hence, a minimum of two measurements is required. A commonly used approach acquires (1) a flow-compensated scan, $m_0 = m_1 = 0$, without velocity-encoding gradients, followed by (2) the same sequence with added bipolar gradients [7]. A simple subtraction of the two phase measurements provides a phase difference $\Delta\phi$ map where the pixel value is directly proportional to the velocity in the direction of the magnetic field gradient:

$$v = \frac{\Delta\phi}{\gamma \Delta m_1} = \frac{\Delta\phi}{\pi}\text{venc} \tag{36.7}$$

where Δm_1 is the difference in the first gradient moments, and $venc = \pi/(\gamma\Delta m_1)$ is the velocity encoding setting, dictated by the chosen gradient waveform. The resulting phase difference map can be displayed as a grayscale image, as shown in Fig. 36.3 where each voxel intensity represents the velocity in the encoding direction of the bipolar gradient. It should be noted that the directionality of the velocity is captured but that there is no general convention on which motion direction is displayed in black or in white for each of the three body axes (superior/inferior, left/right, and anterior/posterior), and the implementation varies among vendors.

The velocity encoding parameter, or *venc*, is a critical parameter in the PC MRI acquisition as it defines the maximum velocity that can be measured without ambiguity. The *venc* is chosen prior to the acquisition by adjusting the area under the bipolar gradient pair accordingly. The dynamic range

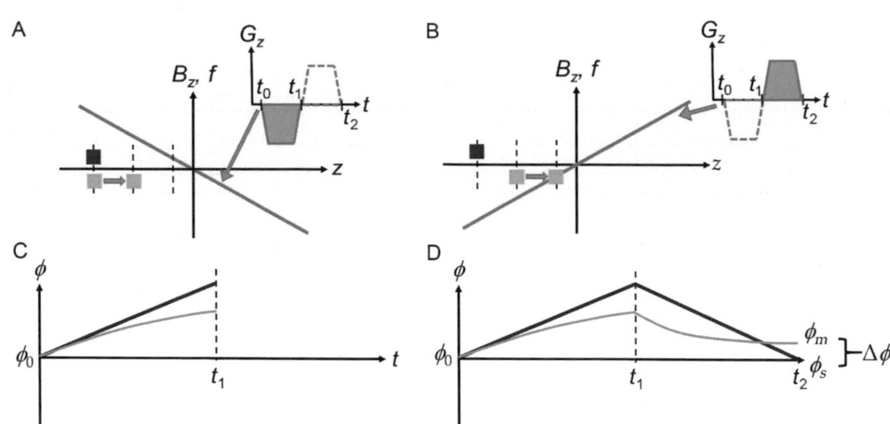

FIG. 36.2

Use of bipolar gradients (A and B) for encoding velocity information into the phase difference of the MR signal (C and D). Here, a stationary spin (red) and a spin moving with constant velocity (blue) in the direction of the bipolar gradient (z) are assumed to have the same background phase ϕ_0. The effects of bipolar gradients on the phase of these spins can be appreciated by following their phase evolution over time. (A) When the first lobe of the bipolar gradient is played, the magnetic field, and consequently the Larmor frequency, linearly decreases along the z-axis. (C) Due to their exposure to continually weaker gradient field magnitudes (green), moving spins (blue, ϕ_m) accumulate less total phase than stationary spins (red, ϕ_s) for the duration of the first lobe of the bipolar gradient. (B) When the gradient lobe of reverse polarity is played, (D) stationary spins are exposed to an equal-but-opposite gradient field magnitude, resulting in a zero net phase accumulation. In contrast, moving spins, which continue to see weaker field strengths, accumulate a net phase ($\Delta\phi$) that is directly related to their velocity along the axis of the bipolar gradient.

of the quantitative velocity map is inherently limited to [-*venc*,*venc*] as a consequence of the cyclic nature of the underlying phase map [$-\pi,\pi$], the basis for the velocity map (see Fig. 36.3D). The smaller the chosen *venc* is, the higher the required gradient moment becomes and, hence, a larger area under the gradients is required, which typically necessitates longer TE and TR times.

One approach to shorten the TE and the TR is the use of an alternate scheme for motion encoding. Instead of acquiring (1) flow compensated and (2) velocity encoded data, one can acquire (1) a scan with bipolar gradients for motion encoding and then (2) a second velocity-encoded gradient with reversed polarity of the bipolar gradient pair with respect to the first acquisition [7,8]. Using paired bipolar gradients allows for faster encoding relative to the first method, as encoding is spread across two acquisition with only half the moment and half the area under the gradient waveform needed for velocity encoding. Thus, shorter gradient waveforms can be used, resulting in a shorter TE and TR, which reduces overall scan time and intravoxel dephasing.

36.2.2 Two-directional & three-directional flow encoding

The velocity of moving spin isochromats in a voxel can be characterized as a time-varying three-dimensional vector. In some applications, it might be sufficient to acquire only a single, one-directional

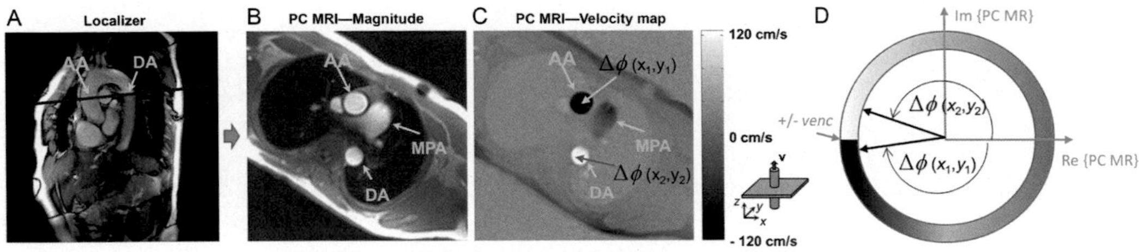

FIG. 36.3

Velocity mapping with PC MRI: A localizer image (A) is used to prescribe a 2D PC MRI scan (B and C) with through-plane velocity encoding perpendicular to the ascending aorta (AA), as indicated by the red line. The PC magnitude image (B) does not reflect velocity, but provides additional anatomical information that is inherently co-registered to the PC velocity map (C). The quantitative velocity map (C) is generated by simple phase difference processing and proper scaling according to Eq. (36.7) and shown here for peak systolic flow. The grayscale intensity in each voxel corresponds to the through-plane velocity v as displayed in the colorbar. Dark voxels (e.g., ascending aorta AA) represent flow in the foot to head direction, bright voxels (e.g., descending aorta DA) represent flow in the opposing direction, head to foot, and medium grey represents no motion. The main pulmonary artery (MPA) is also in the field of view, but has little velocity contributions in the *z*-direction. The dynamic range of the acquisition is limited to $\pm$*venc* because phase is a cyclic measure as shown in the unit circle (D). The *venc* (velocity encoding setting) is determined by the gradient waveform and chosen to be 120cm/s here to capture peak aortic velocities in this subject. The locations of representative voxels in the AA and DA are shown in (C) with corresponding phase measures on the unit circle in (D).

component of this vector, e.g., when measuring blood flow in the ascending aorta, as shown in Fig. 36.3. However, in other applications it might be prudent to also capture a second or all three components of the velocity vector, as shown in Fig. 36.4. This can be accomplished by additional measurements with bipolar gradients played out successively on the corresponding axes. In its simplest form, pairs of measurements are conducted for each velocity encoding direction, thus requiring a total of four measurements for two-directional and six measurements for three-directional velocity encoding [9]. With the exception of the velocity-encoding gradients, the scan parameters should be identical between all required acquisitions, including the TE and TR, for consistency of the background phase.

To reduce total scan time for two-directional and three-directional flow encoding, a common reference acquisition—often with simultaneous flow compensation in all encoding directions—can be shared between all velocity-encoded steps [10]. This corresponds to 25% and 33% reductions in scan time for two-directional and three-directional encoding schemes, respectively. This technique is referred to as 3 point (2 encoding steps + 1 reference step) or 4 point (3 encoding steps + 1 reference step) referenced encoding. Alternative techniques for three-directional velocity encoding include 4 point balanced (or Hadamard) encoding [7] and 5 point balanced encoding [11], the latter improving the signal-to-noise ratio (SNR) and the velocity-to-noise ratio (VNR) at the expense of slightly longer scan times. The ideal encoding method depends on the application. When two or three components of the velocity vector are captured, it is possible to calculate a "speed image", where velocities are represented as their vector lengths, that is, as a square root of the sum of squares of the individual lengths.

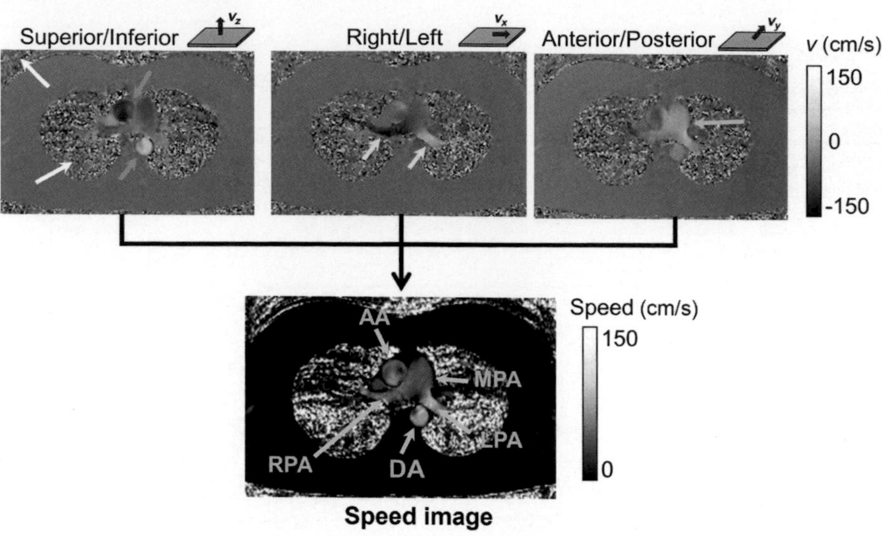

FIG. 36.4

Three-directional velocity encoding in the chest. Velocity maps for blood flow in three directions are acquired (top), and show high velocities in the superior/inferior direction for the ascending aorta (AA) and descending aorta (DA—blue arrows); right/left direction in the left and right branches of the pulmonary artery (LPA and RPA—yellow arrows); and flow in the anterior/posterior direction in the main pulmonary artery (MPA—green arrow). A speed image can be generated by calculating the length of the velocity vector from these three components at each voxel. Also note that the velocity and speeds maps erroneously assign high velocities to random voxels in air in the lungs and outside the body (white arrows). These voxels contain no signal and hence random noise, which can have high phase values. In comparison, signal from air was suppressed in Fig. 36.3.

36.2.3 4D flow MRI

While the term is somewhat ambiguous, 4D flow MRI commonly describes time-resolved, three-directional velocity-encoded PC acquisitions with volumetric coverage [12,13]. It is the only imaging technique to capture dynamic changes in the vascular velocity field in vivo and provides comprehensive insight of the hemodynamics, as each voxel in the acquired imaging volume contains velocity vectors along the three principle spatial directions. Such an acquisition allows for more advanced quantification and visualization of more complex flow dynamics than is possible with traditional planar imaging (see Fig. 36.5). The feasibility of retrospective analysis in arbitrary scan planes within the acquired volume is an added advantage of 4D flow MRI. This enables a "point and shoot" approach without the need for a clinical expert to be present during scanning. In addition, there is reduced likelihood of a missed vessel segment of importance in complicated cases such as congenital heart disease. However, the scan time for 4D flow MRI can be prohibitively long, the data volumes are large, and user-intuitive visualization and the compression of the rich information into robust and clinically useful measures can be challenging. 4D flow MRI is becoming more widespread now that accelerated imaging approaches involving parallel imaging or undersampling have reduced scan times for many applications to 10 min or less [14] and several commercial software solutions for clinical analysis have been recently introduced.

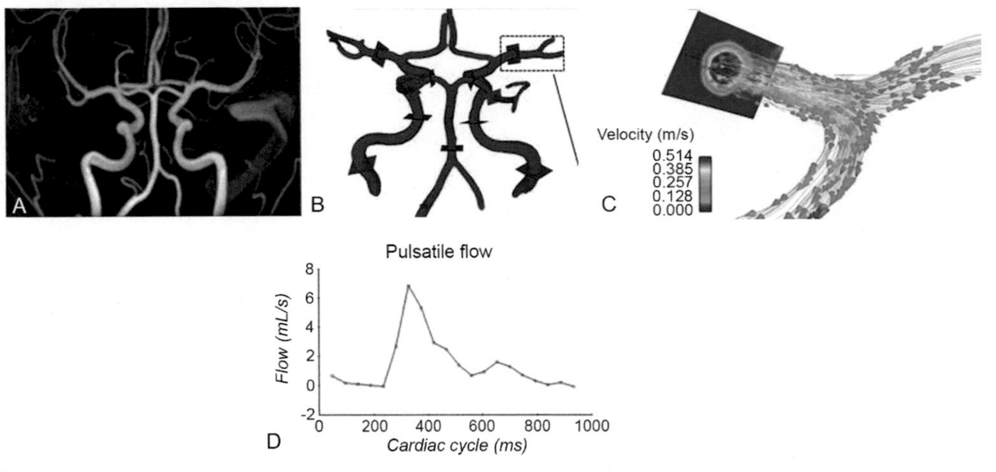

FIG. 36.5

4D flow MRI of the circle of Willis. (A) The volumetric acquisition can capture large volumes as shown in the coronal maximum intensity projection (MIP) image of the angiogram generated from the 4D flow data. (B) Analysis planes can be interactively defined and analyzed outside the scan session as shown in this segmented and volume rendered display of the circle of Willis. (C) The velocity vectors are displayed in direction and speed (color) for a single time frame and can be analyzed throughout the cardiac cycle as in (D), e.g., for analysis of peak velocity and flow, mean velocity and flow, and pulsatility in all vessel segments of interest.

36.3 Phase contrast methodology

36.3.1 Acquisition

36.3.1.1 Sequence design

Phase-contrast acquisitions are commonly conducted by adding bipolar velocity-encoding gradients to a spoiled gradient echo (SPGR) sequence. The reduced TR and TE offered by gradient echo sequences relative to spin echo sequences results in reduced intra-voxel dephasing during imaging. SPGR sequences also feature strong inflow signal enhancement, allowing for improved SNR in the vasculature. Gradient and RF spoiling are used to enforce a steady-state by preventing signal build-up of leftover transversal magnetization across multiple TRs. The bipolar gradients are applied along the axis for which velocity encoding is desired following RF excitation but prior to data readout. With the exception of the velocity-encoding gradients, the RF pulse, gradients, and sequence parameters should be identical between the encoding and reference acquisitions to allow for proper correction of the background phase. A common application is the use of one-directional velocity encoding in the through-plane direction by adding bipolar gradients on the same axis as the slice selection gradient in a 2D SPGR sequence, as shown in Fig. 36.6.

For velocity encoding in other directions, the bipolar gradient is simply moved to the corresponding axis. Sequences with three-directional flow encoding utilizing balanced flow encoding methods may include bipolar gradients on multiple imaging axes simultaneously and detangle the individual contributions by a linear combination of the measurements. In practice, bipolar gradients are often superimposed onto other sections of the gradient waveforms [8] to reduce the TE, and subsequently the TR, for reduced intravoxel dephasing and scan time.

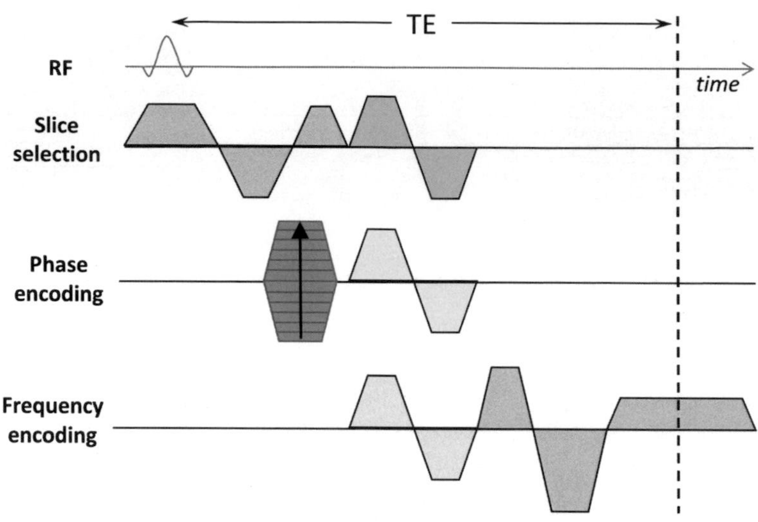

FIG. 36.6

Pulse sequence diagram for velocity encoded acquisitions with PC MRI. In this example, flow compensated gradients (grey gradient lobes) are used in the slice and frequency direction to acquire a reference scan for assessing the unknown background phase. Phase encoding gradients are displayed in dark blue. One-directional flow encoding is achieved by adding a bipolar gradient pair to the flow encoding direction of choice (orange for slice selection, yellow for phase encoding, or light blue for frequency encoding). If desired, the second and third component of the velocity vector can be captured by additional acquisitions with bipolar gradients on the respective encoding directions.

36.3.1.2 Imaging considerations

As shown in Fig. 36.2 and Eqs. (36.2)–(36.7), the bipolar gradient design will influence the sequence sensitivity to motion, characterized by the *venc*. Proper *venc* selection is critical for optimal image quality in PC MRI. It can be shown that the *VNR* is related to the *venc* by the following expression [4]:

$$\mathrm{VNR} = \frac{\pi v}{\sqrt{2}venc}\mathrm{SNR} \tag{36.8}$$

where SNR is the corresponding signal-to-noise ratio in a voxel. Thus, VNR decreases with increasing *venc*. If the *venc* is too low, however, velocity aliasing (discussed in more detail later) may occur. The suggested approach to achieve optimal *VNR* with PC MRI is to set the *venc* as low as possible while still exceeding the maximum expected velocity in the vessels of interest.

Scan planes for 2D PC MRI with through-plane velocity encoding should be prescribed to be orthogonal to the vessel-of-interest. Small angles of misalignment ($<15°$) will not significantly affect flow measurements, as the reduction in measured velocity will be offset by the increase in measured vessel cross-section. Imaging volumes for 4D flow MRI should encompass all vessels of interest.

36.3.1.3 Physiologic gating

PC MRI is typically performed as a *cine* acquisition [15], where the data acquisition is synchronized to the cardiac cycle via a gating signal, typically from an ECG or pulsoximeter. Data are acquired over multiple heart beats using the segmented *k*-space paradigm [15], ultimately generating a single time loop composed of signal contributions from numerous individual cycles. This extends the total acquisition time, but the availability of multiple measurement points across an average cardiac cycle allows for the analysis of dynamic velocity and flow features such as peak and mean velocity and flow and pulsatility as shown in Fig. 36.5.

The collection of data at least 20 cardiac phases are recommended to accurately characterize the flow waveform. Many PC sequences from vendors utilize prospective cardiac gating, where data collection begins following the detection of an R-wave and ceases near the end of the predicted heart beat length until the detection of the next R-wave. This approach is robust in the presence of arrhythmias but data is not collected at end-diastole. An alternative approach is retrospective cardiac gating, where data is collected continuously across the entire imaging session and assigned to cardiac phases postimaging. This method is more time-efficient but may require additional postprocessing to account for irregular heartbeats.

Most 2D PC sequences rely on end-expiratory breath holds to minimize respiratory motion during imaging. This is not feasible in some patient populations or for 4D flow sequences which require longer scan times. Instead, respiratory gating can be used to reject data corresponding to certain respiratory positions, mitigating motion artifacts. Respiratory motion can be characterized through flexible abdominal bellows, which produces a trace corresponding to bellows' flex as the subject breathes. Alternatively, an interleaved navigator acquisition can be used to measure displacement of the diaphragm during data acquisition. A common threshold for data inclusion is 50% of the data closest to the end-expiratory position, although more aggressive thresholds can be used to reduce blurring from respiratory motion.

36.3.1.4 Accelerated imaging

Similar to other cardiovascular imaging applications, PC MRI greatly benefits from accelerated imaging. Faster imaging permits shorter breath-holds for cine acquisitions, higher spatial or temporal resolution, or increased coverage in a given scan time. In addition, shorter echo times will reduce intravoxel dephasing and displacement artifacts that are caused by the different encoding times for space and motion in the PC sequence [16]. Hence, PC MRI has greatly benefitted from recent hardware advances, particularly improved gradient performance and the use of high receiver count RF coils for parallel imaging.

View-sharing [17] is a common method to reduce the scan time for cine PC acquisitions [18] by sharing acquired data for adjacent time frames. Partial Fourier acquisitions are used for more efficient scans [19], particularly with fractional echo readouts to minimize the TE and intravoxel dephasing. However, limitations are noted for applications such as turbulent kinetic energy (TKE) mapping [20].

Further accelerations have been demonstrated by the use of parallel imaging methods such as SENSE and GRAPPA. Combinations of parallel imaging with constrained reconstructions such as k-t BLAST and k-t SENSE [21]; k-t principal component analysis [22]; and compressed sensing [23] with high acceleration factors have been demonstrated in research applications.

36.3.1.5 Non-Cartesian trajectories

Cartesian trajectories have been the mainstay of MRI vendors' product sequences used for clinical scanning. They are efficiently reconstructed on commercial hardware and clinicians are familiar with associated artifacts. Non-Cartesian trajectories can offer advantages in scan efficiency, robustness to artifacts, and suitability to undersampling for accelerated acquisitions. In particular, radial and spiral trajectories have been employed in a variety of research applications. Spiral trajectories are well suited for continuous, real-time PC acquisitions given their highly efficient sampling of k-space with long readouts and robustness to flow artifacts [14]. One such application is the implementation of a real-time color flow display [24], which is similar to Doppler ultrasound and thus familiar to clinicians.

Radial trajectories have several benefits for 2D and 4D flow MRI. They can be used to acquire data with extremely short echo times when run as a center-out trajectory where every readout starts in the center of k-space in a star-like pattern [25]. High undersampling factors can be achieved with radial in-plane [26] and truly 3D radial PC implementations [27,28]. Golden-angle spacing [29] between projections (and similar trajectories) support reconstructions with flexible retrospective gating schemes for cardiac and respiratory motion [30], as well as robust variable view sharing for improved SNR. Further, radial sampling is well-suited for compressed sensing as the views can be better randomized than in Cartesian acquisitions, and high-temporal resolution acquisitions are thereby enabled [31,32].

While offering many advantages, non-Cartesian trajectories require more precise gradient waveforms, and thus measurements of the actual gradients applied because of their increased sensitivity to differences between the nominal and the actual k-space trajectory. In addition, the reconstruction is computationally more demanding than the simple 2D or 3D Fourier transform for Cartesian sampling which is efficiently implemented in hardware.

36.3.2 Reconstruction & visualization

36.3.2.1 Phase difference reconstruction

The standard reconstruction for quantitative flow analysis with PC MRI is the phase difference reconstruction. In its simplest form, all velocity-encoded and reference acquisitions are reconstructed independently. Magnitude and phase images are generated by applying the Fourier transform to the raw data and using absolute value and two-argument arc tangent functions, respectively. For a scan with one-directional velocity encoding, a phase difference image is then generated by subtracting the reference phase image from the velocity-encoded phase image. The phase in the resulting image can be converted to measures of velocity using Eq. (36.7). For multidirectional encoding schemes including 4D flow MRI, each velocity-encoded phase image is subtracted from the reference phase image and separate velocity images for each encoding direction are produced. Speed images can then be produced by adding the velocity images for each direction in quadrature and subsequently taking the square root. The presented magnitude image for PC MRI is typically the magnitude image from the reference acquisition or an average of the magnitude of all acquired images to improve SNR characteristics. Fig. 36.3 shows examples of typical magnitude and phase images as produced from a phase difference reconstruction. The phase difference reconstruction produces images that show both velocity magnitude and direction. Black and white coloring correspond to flow in different directions while gray corresponds to zero flow.

36.3.2.2 Flow visualization

The availability of 4D flow MRI has brought a new tool to the clinical observer that can be powerful in visualizing and analyzing complex in vivo flow patterns in an unprecedented way. In some instances, visual feedback on the vascular anatomy, collateral vessels, and directionality of the flows can provide important insights into normal and pathological conditions as a precursor or in addition to quantitative analysis. However, the proper display can be challenging as it typically involves the display of a

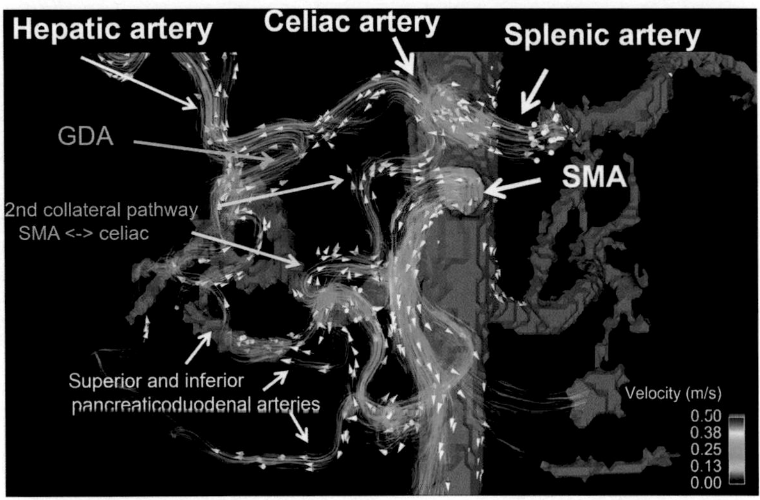

FIG. 36.7

4D flow visualization of the abdomen in a 53-year-old male patient. This display superimposes the flow direction onto streamlines color-coded with velocity, showing that the flow through both the gastroduodenal artery (GDA) and a second collateral pathway through the superior and inferior pancreaticoduodenal arteries is reversed. Hence, all blood entering the celiac artery is really supplied from the superior mesenteric artery (SMA). These findings demonstrate that the celiac artery stenosis is hemodynamically significant.

volumetric dynamic velocity vector field onto a 2D screen. Streamlines and pathlines are commonly used techniques to visualize complex 3D flow from 4D flow scans [33]. Streamlines are curves that are tangent to the velocity vector in each voxel for any given time frame. These images show the direction in which a massless particle would move if it was placed at any point in the velocity field for a specific time frame. Fig. 36.7 shows a visualization of streamlines in the abdomen and Fig. 36.5C shows streamlines with superimposed velocity vectors in a segment of the Circle of Willis. Pathlines represent the trajectory of massless particles through the changing velocity fields over time. These are representative of typical blood motion. Pathline visualizations are often presented as animations. Streamlines and pathlines are equivalent when velocity fields are constant in time.

36.3.2.3 Vascular anatomy visualization

3D and 4D PC MRI acquisitions can be useful for the display of vessel luminography in form of a volumetric angiogram. This is advantageous for inherently co-registered vessel segmentation and as a method for noncontrast-enhanced MRA in light of concerns over the safety of gadolinium-based contrast-enhanced MRA, particularly for patients with compromised kidney function. With proper complex difference processing and high resolution acquisitions, high quality phase-contrast MR angiograms (PC MRAs) can be generated that have good agreement for vessel assessment with contrast-enhanced MRA [34].

Examples of a cranial PC MRAs are shown in Figs. 36.5A and 36.8A.

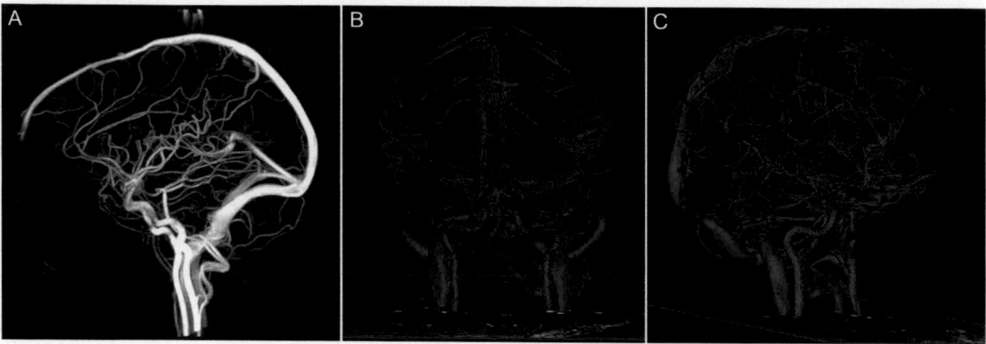

FIG. 36.8

Cranial PC MR angiogram acquired with a 4D flow MRI scan with high spatial resolution (0.67 mm isotropic). The sagittal maximum intensity projection (MIP) image (A) shows great detail of both arteries and veins. With proper semiautomated segmentation, a volume rendered display (B and C) can be generated with colorcoding for arteries (red) and veins (blue).

36.3.3 Hemodynamic analysis

PC MRI is used to generate quantitative velocity maps, which are frequently analyzed to extract measures of instantaneous and net flow. With appropriate postprocessing tools, more advanced hemodynamic parameters such as pressure gradients, wall shear stress (WSS), kinetic energy, and others can be derived.

36.3.3.1 Basic hemodynamic analysis

The most common hemodynamic measurements of clinical interest from PC scans are derived from the analysis of time-resolved flow waveforms. To quantify such flow waveforms in 2D PC acquisitions, the reconstructed phase and magnitude images are imported into specialized software. A region-of-interest (ROI) can be drawn delineating the boundaries of the vessel-of-interest throughout the cardiac cycle, as shown in Fig. 36.9. Owing to cardiac pulsatility and the associated changes in vessel lumen and position, this ROI often has to be adjusted throughout the cardiac cycle. Depending on the body region and flow rate, the ROI is drawn using the magnitude image, the phase image, the complex difference image, or a combination thereof. The flow rate through a voxel i is given by the product of its measured velocity v_i and its area A. The instantaneous flow rate $Q_{\mathrm{ROI}}(t)$ through an ROI at a given cardiac phase p in the cardiac cycle is determined by summing the flow contributions from all voxel across the ROI:

$$Q_{\mathrm{ROI}}(p) = \sum_{i=1}^{N_{\mathrm{pixel}}} A v_i \tag{36.9}$$

where N_{pixel} is the number of pixels in the segmented ROI, A is the area of the pixels, and v_i is the measured velocity in the ith pixel. The net flow through the ROI, Q_{net}, is the time integral (or sum) of the instantaneous flow across the cardiac cycle and typically reported in units of [ml/cardiac cycle] or [L/min]:

$$Q_{\mathrm{net}} = \sum_{p=1}^{N_{\mathrm{cardiac\ phases}}} Q_{\mathrm{ROI}}(p)\Delta T \tag{36.10}$$

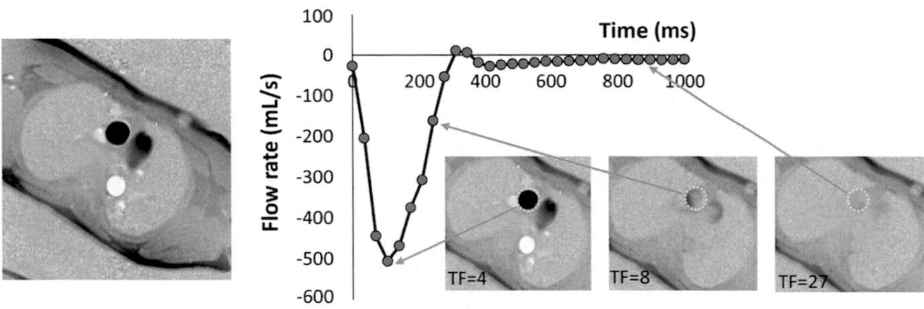

FIG. 36.9

Time-resolved flow waveform in the ascending aorta obtained with 2D PC MRI. The instantaneous flow rate at a given time in the cardiac cycle is obtained by the multiplication of the velocities and the voxel area over a user-drawn ROI (yellow circles), here shown for three distinct time points and plotted as a function of time for all 30 measurements within the cardiac cycle. The net flow is represented by the area under curve and closely related to the subject's cardiac output except for flow contributions to the coronary arteries not captured at this imaging slice location.

where $N_{\text{cardiac phases}}$ represents the total number of phases covering the cardiac cycle and ΔT is the length of each cardiac phase.

A similar approach is used for flow quantification with 4D flow MRI. Using dedicated commercial, open source, or custom-made software packages, 3D angiograms, typically generated from a complex difference reconstruction (Figs. 36.5A and 36.8A) are visualized and 2D measurement planes are interactively or semiautomatically aligned orthogonal to vessels of interest as shown in Fig. 36.5B. 2D maps of the anatomy and through-plane velocities are generated and then the task of flow quantification is identical to that of 2D PC processing. ROIs are drawn around vessel boundaries in the 2D measurement planes and Eq. (36.10) is used to calculate the volumetric flow rate. The ability to position and align measurement planes after scan completion with volumetric 4D flow acquisitions is a notable advantage of this approach, as it allows for more accurate plane positioning when trying to measure flow in tortuous or moving vessels.

Common hemodynamic parameters of interest derived from PC MRI include peak systolic velocity, mean velocity, peak flow, mean flow, and net flow across a single cardiac cycle (often referred to as stroke volume in cardiac applications). Vessel geometry can also be assessed through measurements of vessel diameter and cross-sectional area.

36.3.3.2 Advanced hemodynamic analysis

Beyond straightforward flow and velocity measurements, PC MRI can be used to quantify a variety of more complex hemodynamic parameters. Pulsatility index (*PI*), a common parameter quantified with Doppler ultrasound, can be used to quantify flow variance across the cardiac cycle with the following expression:

$$PI = \frac{v_{\text{sys}} - v_{\text{dia}}}{\overline{v}} \tag{36.11}$$

where v_{sys} is the peak systolic velocity, v_{dia} is the end-diastolic velocity, and $\overline{v}$ is the mean velocity across the cardiac cycle.

Similar to Doppler ultrasound, the pressure gradient (Δp) across a vessel narrowing or valve can be approximated with a modified Bernoulli's equation:

$$\Delta p = 4\left(v_2^2 - v_1^2\right) \tag{36.12}$$

where v_1 and v_2 are the measured velocities proximal and distal to the valve or the vessel narrowing. More advanced methods seek to calculate pressure difference maps in a vascular territory by applying Navier-Stokes equations to the time resolved velocity vector field measured with 2D PC with three-directional velocity encoding [35] or 4D flow MRI [36,37].

A parameter of interest in many research applications is the pulse wave velocity (PWV), which is the rate at which the systolic blood bolus moves through a vessel [38]. PWV is a surrogate for vessel wall stiffness, as more elastic vessels are characterized by a decreased PWV, and similar to the concept of tonometry. PWV is potentially a very strong early biomarker of atherosclerosis, given that arterial stiffness first increases without changes in vascular geometry—via the Glagov phenomenon [39]. The MRI-based measurement of PWV requires the acquisition of flow waveforms at two or more locations along the vessel path as shown in Fig. 36.10. The distance Δd between the flow planes is measured from an accompanying MR angiogram or a PC MR angiogram from a 4D flow MRI, often based on a centerline calculation. The time shift Δt of the arrival of the wavefront is obtained as the difference in characteristic points in the pulsatile waveforms at the two locations, for example, the time to foot (TTF) of the waveform prior to flow increase in systole between those positions [40] (Fig. 36.10B). The PWV is simply calculated as the ratio of Δd and Δt:

$$PWV = \frac{\Delta d}{\Delta t} \tag{36.13}$$

Typically, calculation of this parameter is performed by acquiring multiple 2D PC acquisitions along the vessel of interest [40] or placing multiple measurement planes in a single 4D flow acquisition [38]. PC MRI based PWV measurements are challenging for short vessel paths and very stiff vessels as a high temporal resolution is required.

WSS is also of clinical interest as a biomarker for vascular remodeling. This parameter characterizes the drag of the blood flow on the vessel wall and is often represented as a vector with a main and a circumferential component. As such, WSS is typically measured using 4D flow MRI, predominantly in the aorta [41]. It should be noted that MRI-based WSS estimates likely underestimate the true WSS because limitations in spatial and temporal resolution make it challenging to properly capture a velocity derivate at the vessel wall, an area prone to errors from partial volume effects, low velocities, and motion of the vessel wall itself [42].

Additional hemodynamic parameters of interest which can be extracted from PC MRI data include kinetic energy (KE) and turbulent kinetic energy (TKE). KE in the ventricles is a surrogate for external work performed by the heart [43]. Turbulence calculated from the distribution of velocities in voxel-wise TKE measurements reflects irreversible energy loss as a result of disturbed flow, for instance in poststenotic regions [44], and requires the collection of data with multiple *vencs*.

36.3.4 Confounding factors and artifacts

36.3.4.1 Phase errors

Phase errors from a variety of sources can influence the accuracy and precision of quantitative phase-contrast measurements. Whenever gradient waveforms are played out on one axis, concomitant gradient fields are inevitably generated along the other axes as dictated by Maxwell's equations.

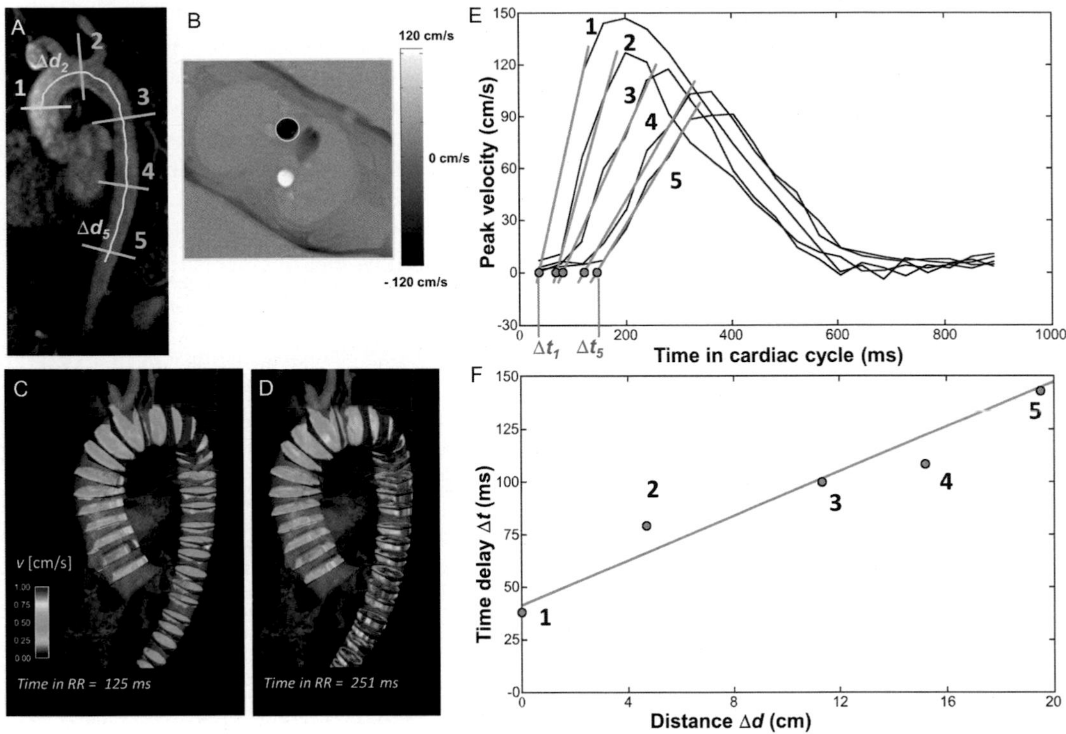

FIG. 36.10

Pulse wave velocity (PWV) analysis requires two or more analysis planes to assess the progression of the systolic blood bolus through the arterial system, here shown for five planes in the aorta (A). 2D cine PC acquisitions at prospectively selected planes (B shows plane location 1) or a 4D flow MRI (C and D) scan analyzed at selected planes are used to measure velocities throughout the cardiac cycle (E). Here, the time delay Δt between the arrival of the systolic bolus at the analysis plane and the reference plane 1 is measured by a time to foot (TTF) measurement (gray circles). The distances Δd between the analysis planes and the reference plane are typically established by a centerline processing from a 3D angiogram (A). In this subject, the PWV is fairly constant along the aorta as indicated by the slope of the plot of the time delay vs distance for all planes (F).

Fortunately, these additional gradients are deterministic and can be properly accounted for during image reconstruction [45]. Similarly, phase errors from gradient nonlinearities can be effectively compensated by taking them into account [46]. In contrast, eddy current effects require additional correction in postprocessing. Effects from uncompensated eddy current typically manifest as a smoothly varying phase across the image. There are two primary methods for correcting for this phase error. In a common approach, the background phase is approximated as a low-order polynomial using regions identified as static tissue by either manual selection or semiautomated processing based on signal fluctuations [47]. That background phase estimate is then subtracted from the velocity map. Alternatively, eddy current phase effects can be accurately reproduced with a separate acquisition in a homogenous phantom using identical scan parameters [48]. This method is more accurate than the polynomial fitting but requires additional scan time which is impractical in clinical practice.

A variety of artifacts can occur when the assumption that all spins in a voxel are moving at the same constant velocity is invalid. When a voxel contains phase contributions from both static and moving spins, there is the potential for partial volume artifacts. If the static and moving spins have similar signal contributions, partial volume effects are minimal, as decreases to measured phase accrual are closely related to the relative signal contribution from moving spins. When moving spins have a much higher signal, which can be expected due to in-flow enhancement, the measured phase contribution will be artificially high, resulting in inaccurate phase and velocity measurements. Partial volume artifacts can be mitigated by improving spatial resolution. It is generally recommended at least 10 voxels should be fully contained within the diameter of vessels for accurate flow measurements.

36.3.4.2 Intravoxel dephasing

The signal model is also violated if a spatial or temporal spread of velocities is present in a voxel. In areas of accelerated flow such as a poststenotic region, the phase of individual spins differs, resulting in a signal decrease and inaccuracies in the velocity measurement [49]. This effect is called intravoxel dephasing and can be partially overcome with ultrashort TE sequences based on radial center-out trajectories [25]. Intravoxel dephasing can be mitigated through the reduction of sequence TE and nulling of higher order motion terms.

36.3.4.3 Displacement artifacts

Displacement artifacts describe an artifact where measured velocities are misplaced downstream from where they actually occur. This can happen as a result of the nonzero time interval between spatial encoding and velocity encoding [50]. These artifacts are shown by the yellow arrows in Fig. 36.11. These effects can be reduced by reducing the sequence TE.

36.3.4.4 Phase aliasing

Another type of artifact that occurs in PC MRI is velocity aliasing, also referred to as phase wrapping. This artifact occurs when a velocity in the image exceeds the user-selected *venc* setting (Eq. 36.7) on either end of the spectrum. The dynamic range of a phase measurement is a cyclic entity that is limited to a range of $\pm\pi$ or $\pm venc$, respectively, as shown in Fig. 36.3D. If the velocity exceeds this range, the phase will "wrap-around" the unit circle, causing the large velocity to appear as a velocity in

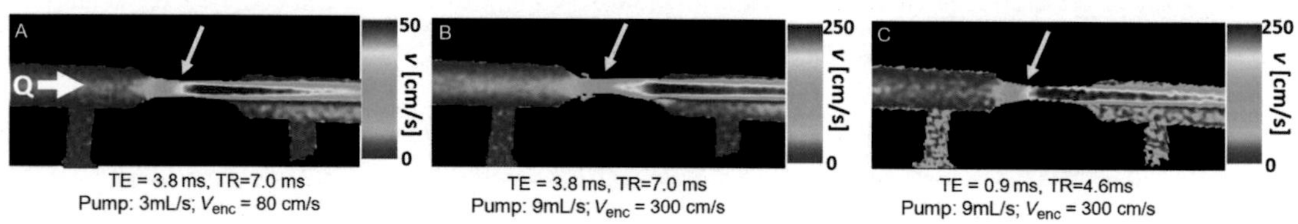

FIG. 36.11

Displacement artifact from acceleration. This stenosis phantom was connected to a pump that generated constant slow flow of $Q = 3$ mL/s (A) and fast flow of 9 mL/s (B and C). When using a standard TE of 3.8 ms, the accelerated poststenotic flow causes a substantial displacement in the velocity map because of the delay between the velocity encoding and the spatial encoding (yellow arrow in A and B). When using a very short TE of 0.9 ms with a radial center-out trajectory, the displacement is negligible (C).

Images courtesy of Kevin Johnson, PhD, University of Wisconsin-Madison.

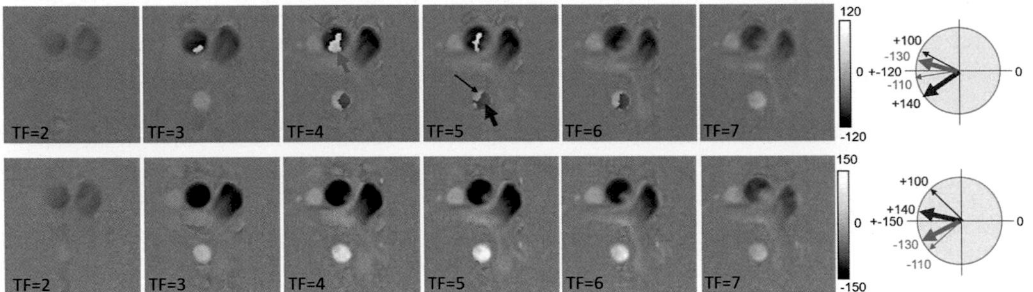

FIG. 36.12

Example of velocity aliasing. The upper row shows six time frames around peak systole acquired in the chest with a *venc* = 120 cm/s. Velocity aliasing is present in three of the time frames (TF = 3, 4, and 5) in the ascending aorta (blue arrows) and in three time frames (TF = 4, 5, and 6) in the descending aorta (red arrows). With a higher *venc* setting of 150 cm/s, all velocities are properly captured without aliasing (bottom row). The position of the velocity measurements as a phase on the unit circle is displayed in the right column, showing proper separation for the higher *venc* scan.

the opposite direction. An example of this effect is shown in Fig. 36.12, where it appears that the flow in the ascending aorta is upward in most of the vessel but downward during peak systolic time frames 3, 4, and 5. The actual phase measurement assigns these fast upward velocities to the same point on the unit circle as a slower downward velocity, making them indistinguishable based on a single point measure alone. Phase unwrapping is a notoriously difficult problem that has been explored in applications outside of MRI [51]. Automated algorithms can help to remove certain levels of aliasing by imposing constraints based on the temporal evolution or neighborhood of phase measures. However, these algorithms have failure modes in the presence of noise and perform poorly when multiple phase wraps exist [52].

36.4 Applications

Flow imaging with PC MRI has shown great utility in clinical and research applications, aiding diagnosis, and prognosis for a variety of cardiovascular diseases [12,53–55].

36.4.1 Cardiac

PC MRI is used very commonly in clinical cardiac MRI. Measurements of stroke volume and cardiac output, measured as systemic flow Q_s in the ascending aorta, are standard when assessing basic cardiac function (see Fig. 36.9). Similarly, the pulmonary flow Q_p from the right ventricle to the lung scan be measured from a single 2D PC acquisition perpendicular to the main pulmonary artery. An abnormal ratio of Q_p/Q_s is indicative of ventricular or septal defects that can be otherwise missed if either the Q_p or Q_s measurement alone looks normal. In patients with aortic coarctation or vascular stenosis, as well as valvular insufficiencies, PC MRI is used to quantify peak blood velocities and estimate the pressure drop across the vessel narrowing or valve, as described above [56]. PC MRI is also deployed in the diagnosis of aortic dissection and identification of false lumens [57]. In addition to these applications, PC MRI acquisitions are routinely used to quantify shunt flows, regurgitant flows, and collateral flows [56]. 4D Flow MRI has been used effectively to visualize abnormal cardiac flow dynamics in patients with congenital heart disease and assess the efficacy of surgical repair [58].

36.4.2 Cranial

While 2D PC techniques can be challenging to use in cranial applications given the small, tortuous vessels, 4D flow techniques have shown promise in this region towards clinical use [59]. In patients with atherosclerotic disease, PC angiograms can be used to evaluate the degree of vascular stenosis and impact on blood flow [60]. 4D flow MRI has also shown utility in monitoring aneurysm growth through the evaluation of flow dynamics in the region [61]. Similar techniques have been employed to characterize the implications of arteriovenous malformations on cerebrovascular flow [62].

36.4.3 Abdominal

4D Flow MRI has shown value in a variety of abdominal conditions in research studies [63]. Hepatic applications include evaluation of collateral flow, shunt fraction, and the effects of meal challenges in patients with liver cirrhosis, and assistance in surgical planning for living donor transplants. In the kidneys, PC MRI has been used to grade the hemodynamic significance or renal artery stenosis [64].

36.5 Summary

In summary, PC MRI is an efficient and established method for quantitative in vivo velocity measurements of blood flow. It has found widespread clinical use in cardiovascular applications, particularly in a compact 2D PC MRI acquisition with one-directional velocity encoding. Additional hemodynamic parameters of clinical interest can be derived from knowledge of the velocity field, particularly with 4D flow MRI. The motion encoding principles shown here can be used in a similar fashion for the characterization of cerebrospinal flow [65] (CSF, low *venc*), diffusion MRI [66] (very large gradient moments), and MR Elastography [67] (motion encoding synchronized with an accentuator for shear waves).

References

[1] Carr HY, Purcell EM. Effects of Diffusion on free precession in nuclear magnetic resonance experiments. Phys Rev 1954;94(3):630–8.

[2] Hahn EL. Detection of sea-water motion by nuclear precession. J Geophys Res 1960;65(2):776–7.

[3] Moran P. A flow velocity zeugmatographic interlace for NMR imaging in humans. Mag Reson Imaging 1982;197–203.

[4] Pelc NJ, Herfkens RJ, Shimakawa A, Enzmann DR. Phase contrast cine magnetic resonance imaging. Magn Reson Q 1991;7(4):229–54.

[5] Haacke EM, Lenz GW. Improving MR image quality in the presence of motion by using rephasing gradients. AJR Am J Roentgenol 1987;148(6):1251–8.

[6] Pattany PM, Phillips JJ, Chiu LC, Lipcamon JD, Duerk JL, McNally JM, Mohapatra SN. Motion artifact suppression technique (MAST) for MR imaging. J Comput Assist Tomogr 1987;11(3):369–77.

[7] Pelc NJ, Bernstein MA, Shimakawa A, Glover GH. Encoding strategies for three-direction phase-contrast MR imaging of flow. J Magn Reson Imaging 1991;1(4):405–13.
[8] Bernstein MA, Shimakawa A, Pelc NJ. Minimizing TE in moment-nulled or flow-encoded two- and three-dimensional gradient-echo imaging. J Magn Reson Imaging 1992;2(5):583–8.
[9] Dumoulin CL, Souza SP, Walker MF, Wagle W. Three-dimensional phase contrast angiography. Magn Reson Med 1989;9(1):139–49.
[10] Hausmann R, Lewin JS, Laub G. Phase-contrast MR angiography with reduced acquisition time: new concepts in sequence design. J Magn Reson Imaging 1991;1(4):415–22.
[11] Johnson KM, Markl M. Improved SNR in phase contrast velocimetry with five-point balanced flow encoding. Magn Reson Med 2010;63(2):349–55.
[12] Markl M, Frydrychowicz A, Kozerke S, Hope M, Wieben O. 4D flow MRI. J Magn Reson Imaging 2012;36(5):1015–36.
[13] Dyverfeldt P, Bissell M, Barker AJ, Bolger AF, Carlhall CJ, Ebbers T, Francios CJ, Frydrychowicz A, Geiger J, Giese D, Hope MD, Kilner PJ, Kozerke S, Myerson S, Neubauer S, Wieben O, Markl M. 4D flow cardiovascular magnetic resonance consensus statement. J Cardiovasc Magn Reson 2015;17:72.
[14] Nayak KS, Nielsen JF, Bernstein MA, Markl M, Gatehouse PD, Botnar RM, Saloner D, Lorenz C, Wen H, Hu BS, Epstein FH, Oshinski JN, Raman SV. Cardiovascular magnetic resonance phase contrast imaging. J Cardiovasc Magn Reson 2015;17:71.
[15] Atkinson DJ, Edelman RR. Cineangiography of the heart in a single breath hold with a segmented turbo-FLASH sequence. Radiology 1991;178(2):357–60.
[16] Thunberg P, Wigstrom L, Ebbers T, Karlsson M. Correction for displacement artifacts in 3D phase contrast imaging. J Magn Reson Imaging 2002;16(5):591–7.
[17] Riederer SJ, Tasciyan T, Farzaneh F, Lee JN, Wright RC, Herfkens RJ. MR fluoroscopy: technical feasibility. Magn Reson Med 1988;8(1):1–15.
[18] Markl M, Hennig J. Phase contrast MRI with improved temporal resolution by view sharing: *k*-space related velocity mapping properties. Magn Reson Imaging 2001;19(5):669–76.
[19] Szarf G, Dori Y, Rettmann D, Tekes A, Nasir K, Amado L, Foo TK, Bluemke DA. Zero filled partial fourier phase contrast MR imaging: in vitro and in vivo assessment. J Magn Reson Imaging 2006;23(1):42–9.
[20] Walheim J, Gotschy A, Kozerke S. On the limitations of partial Fourier acquisition in phase-contrast MRI of turbulent kinetic energy. Magn Reson Med 2019;81(1):514–23.
[21] Baltes C, Kozerke S, Hansen MS, Pruessmann KP, Tsao J, Boesiger P. Accelerating cine phase-contrast flow measurements using k-t BLAST and k-t SENSE. Magn Reson Med 2005;54(6):1430–8.
[22] Giese D, Schaeffter T, Kozerke S. Highly undersampled phase-contrast flow measurements using compartment-based k-t principal component analysis. Magn Reson Med 2013;69(2):434–43.
[23] Tariq U, Hsiao A, Alley M, Zhang T, Lustig M, Vasanawala SS. Venous and arterial flow quantification are equally accurate and precise with parallel imaging compressed sensing 4D phase contrast MRI. J Magn Reson Imaging 2013;37(6):1419–26.
[24] Nayak KS, Pauly JM, Kerr AB, Hu BS, Nishimura DG. Real-time color flow MRI. Magn Reson Med 2000;43(2):251–8.
[25] O'Brien KR, Myerson SG, Cowan BR, Young AA, Robson MD. Phase contrast ultrashort TE: a more reliable technique for measurement of high-velocity turbulent stenotic jets. Magn Reson Med 2009;62(3):626–36.
[26] Barger AV, Peters DC, Block WF, Vigen KK, Korosec FR, Grist TM, Mistretta CA. Phase-contrast with interleaved undersampled projections. Magn Reson Med 2000;43(4):503–9.
[27] Gu T, Korosec FR, Block WF, Fain SB, Turk Q, Lum D, Zhou Y, Grist TM, Haughton V, Mistretta CA. PC VIPR: a high-speed 3D phase-contrast method for flow quantification and high-resolution angiography. AJNR Am J Neuroradiol 2005;26(4):743–9.
[28] Johnson KM, Lum DP, Turski PA, Block WF, Mistretta CA, Wieben O. Improved 3D phase contrast MRI with off-resonance corrected dual echo VIPR. Magn Reson Med 2008;60(6):1329–36.

[29] Winkelmann S, Schaeffter T, Koehler T, Eggers H, Doessel O. An optimal radial profile order based on the Golden Ratio for time-resolved MRI. IEEE Trans Med Imaging 2007;26(1):68–76.

[30] Schrauben EM, Anderson AG, Johnson KM, Wieben O. Respiratory-induced venous blood flow effects using flexible retrospective double-gating. J Magn Reson Imaging 2015;42(1):211–6.

[31] Feng L, Grimm R, Block KT, Chandarana H, Kim S, Xu J, Axel L, Sodickson DK, Otazo R. Golden-angle radial sparse parallel MRI: combination of compressed sensing, parallel imaging, and golden-angle radial sampling for fast and flexible dynamic volumetric MRI. Magn Reson Med 2014;72(3):707–17.

[32] Joseph A, Kowallick JT, Merboldt KD, Voit D, Schaetz S, Zhang S, Sohns JM, Lotz J, Frahm J. Real-time flow MRI of the aorta at a resolution of 40 msec. J Magn Reson Imaging 2014;40(1):206–13.

[33] Buonocore MH. Visualizing blood flow patterns using streamlines, arrows, and particle paths. Magn Reson Med 1998;40(2):210–26.

[34] Francois CJ, Lum DP, Johnson KM, Landgraf BR, Bley TA, Reeder SB, Schiebler ML, Grist TM, Wieben O. Renal arteries: isotropic, high-spatial-resolution, unenhanced MR angiography with three-dimensional radial phase contrast. Radiology 2011;258(1):254–60.

[35] Thompson RB, McVeigh ER. Fast measurement of intracardiac pressure differences with 2D breath-hold phase-contrast MRI. Magn Reson Med 2003;49(6):1056–66.

[36] Lum DP, Johnson KM, Paul RK, Turk AS, Consigny DW, Grinde JR, Mistretta CA, Grist TM. Transstenotic pressure gradients: measurement in swine—retrospectively ECG-gated 3D phase-contrast MR angiography versus endovascular pressure-sensing guidewires. Radiology 2007;245(3):751–60.

[37] Tyszka JM, Laidlaw DH, Asa JW, Silverman JM. Three-dimensional, time-resolved (4D) relative pressure mapping using magnetic resonance imaging. J Magn Reson Imaging 2000;12(2):321–9.

[38] Wentland AL, Grist TM, Wieben O. Review of MRI-based measurements of pulse wave velocity: a biomarker of arterial stiffness. Cardiovasc Diagn Ther 2014;4(2):193–206.

[39] Glagov S, Weisenberg E, Zarins CK, Stankunavicius R, Kolettis GJ. Compensatory enlargement of human atherosclerotic coronary arteries. N Engl J Med 1987;316(22):1371–5.

[40] el Ibrahim SH, Johnson KR, Miller AB, Shaffer JM, White RD. Measuring aortic pulse wave velocity using high-field cardiovascular magnetic resonance: comparison of techniques. J Cardiovasc Magn Reson 2010;12:26.

[41] van Ooij P, Markl M, Collins JD, Carr JC, Rigsby C, Bonow RO, Malaisrie SC, McCarthy PM, Fedak PWM, Barker AJ. Aortic valve stenosis alters expression of regional aortic wall shear stress: new insights from a 4-dimensional flow magnetic resonance imaging study of 571 subjects. J Am Heart Assoc 2017;6(9).

[42] Petersson S, Dyverfeldt P, Ebbers T. Assessment of the accuracy of MRI wall shear stress estimation using numerical simulations. J Magn Reson Imaging 2012;36(1):128–38.

[43] Jeong D, Anagnostopoulos PV, Roldan-Alzate A, Srinivasan S, Schiebler ML, Wieben O, Francois CJ. Ventricular kinetic energy may provide a novel noninvasive way to assess ventricular performance in patients with repaired tetralogy of Fallot. J Thorac Cardiovasc Surg 2015;149(5):1339–47.

[44] Dyverfeldt P, Hope MD, Tseng EE, Saloner D. Magnetic resonance measurement of turbulent kinetic energy for the estimation of irreversible pressure loss in aortic stenosis. JACC Cardiovasc Imaging 2013;6(1):64–71.

[45] Bernstein MA, Zhou XJ, Polzin JA, King KF, Ganin A, Pelc NJ, Glover GH. Concomitant gradient terms in phase contrast MR: analysis and correction. Magn Reson Med 1998;39(2):300–8.

[46] Markl M, Bammer R, Alley MT, Elkins CJ, Draney MT, Barnett A, Moseley ME, Glover GH, Pelc NJ. Generalized reconstruction of phase contrast MRI: analysis and correction of the effect of gradient field distortions. Magn Reson Med 2003;50(4):791–801.

[47] Walker PG, Cranney GB, Scheidegger MB, Waseleski G, Pohost GM, Yoganathan AP. Semiautomated method for noise reduction and background phase error correction in MR phase velocity data. J Magn Reson Imaging 1993;3(3):521–30.

[48] Chernobelsky A, Shubayev O, Comeau CR, Wolff SD. Baseline correction of phase contrast images improves quantification of blood flow in the great vessels. J Cardiovasc Magn Reson 2007;9(4):681–5.

[49] Stahlberg F, Sondergaard L, Thomsen C, Henriksen O. Quantification of complex flow using MR phase imaging—a study of parameters influencing the phase/velocity relation. Magn Reson Imaging 1992;10(1):13–23.

[50] Frayne R, Rutt BK. Understanding acceleration-induced displacement artifacts in phase-contrast MR velocity measurements. J Magn Reson Imaging 1995;5(2):207–15.

[51] Ghiglia DC, Pritt MD. Two-Dimensional Phase Unwrapping: Theory, Algorithms, and Software. Wiley; 1998.

[52] Loecher M, Schrauben E, Johnson KM, Wieben O. Phase unwrapping in 4D MR flow with a 4D single-step laplacian algorithm. J Magn Reson Imaging 2016;43(4):833–42.

[53] Gatehouse PD, Keegan J, Crowe LA, Masood S, Mohiaddin RH, Kreitner KF, Firmin DN. Applications of phase-contrast flow and velocity imaging in cardiovascular MRI. Eur Radiol 2005;15(10):2172–84.

[54] Varaprasathan GA, Araoz PA, Higgins CB, Reddy GP. Quantification of flow dynamics in congenital heart disease: applications of velocity-encoded cine MR imaging. Radiographics 2002;22(4):895–905. discussion 905-896.

[55] Markl M, Schnell S, Wu C, Bollache E, Jarvis K, Barker AJ, Robinson JD, Rigsby CK. Advanced flow MRI: emerging techniques and applications. Clin Radiol 2016;71(8):779–95.

[56] Srichai MB, Lim RP, Wong S, Lee VS. Cardiovascular applications of phase-contrast MRI. AJR Am J Roentgenol 2009;192(3):662–75.

[57] Silverman JM, Raissi S, Tyszka JM, Trento A, Herfkens RJ. Phase-contrast cine MR angiography detection of thoracic aortic dissection. Int J Card Imaging 2000;16(6):461–70.

[58] Francois CJ, Srinivasan S, Schiebler ML, Reeder SB, Niespodzany E, Landgraf BR, Wieben O, Frydrychowicz A. 4D cardiovascular magnetic resonance velocity mapping of alterations of right heart flow patterns and main pulmonary artery hemodynamics in tetralogy of Fallot. J Cardiovasc Magn Reson 2012;14:16.

[59] Schnell S, Wu C, Ansari SA. Four-dimensional MRI flow examinations in cerebral and extracerebral vessels—ready for clinical routine? Curr Opin Neurol 2016;29(4):419–28.

[60] Hope TA, Hope MD, Purcell DD, von Morze C, Vigneron DB, Alley MT, Dillon WP. Evaluation of intracranial stenoses and aneurysms with accelerated 4D flow. Magn Reson Imaging 2010;28(1):41–6.

[61] Boussel L, Rayz V, Martin A, Acevedo-Bolton G, Lawton MT, Higashida R, Smith WS, Young WL, Saloner D. Phase-contrast magnetic resonance imaging measurements in intracranial aneurysms in vivo of flow patterns, velocity fields, and wall shear stress: comparison with computational fluid dynamics. Magn Reson Med 2009;61(2):409–17.

[62] Ansari SA, Schnell S, Carroll T, Vakil P, Hurley MC, Wu C, Carr J, Bendok BR, Batjer H, Markl M. Intracranial 4D flow MRI: toward individualized assessment of arteriovenous malformation hemodynamics and treatment-induced changes. AJNR Am J Neuroradiol 2013;34(10):1922–8.

[63] Roldan-Alzate A, Francois CJ, Wieben O, Reeder SB. Emerging applications of abdominal 4D flow MRI. AJR Am J Roentgenol 2016;207(1):58–66.

[64] Schoenberg SO, Knopp MV, Bock M, Kallinowski F, Just A, Essig M, Hawighorst H, Schad L, van Kaick G. Renal artery stenosis: grading of hemodynamic changes with cine phase-contrast MR blood flow measurements. Radiology 1997;203(1):45–53.

[65] Battal B, Kocaoglu M, Bulakbasi N, Husmen G, Tuba Sanal H, Tayfun C. Cerebrospinal fluid flow imaging by using phase-contrast MR technique. Br J Radiol 2011;84(1004):758–65.

[66] Wu W, Miller KL. Image formation in diffusion MRI: a review of recent technical developments. J Magn Reson Imaging 2017;46(3):646–62.

[67] Venkatesh SK, Yin M, Ehman RL. Magnetic resonance elastography of liver: technique, analysis, and clinical applications. J Magn Reson Imaging 2013;37(3):544–55.

CHAPTER

37 Hyperpolarized Magnetic Resonance Spectroscopy and Imaging

Thomas R. Eykyn

School of Biomedical Engineering and Imaging Sciences, King's College London, St Thomas' Hospital, London, United Kingdom

37.1 Introduction

Magnetic Resonance Spectroscopy (MRS) is a powerful technique that can provide chemically specific measurement of metabolite concentrations. Both Nuclear Magnetic Resonance (NMR) and its spatially resolved version, Magnetic Resonance Spectroscopic Imaging (MRSI), are quantitative techniques in the sense that the area under a spectral peak in a fully relaxed spectrum is proportional to equilibrium magnetization and therefore also to nuclide concentration. Peak areas can be used to quantify metabolite concentration (when normalized to a known reference standard [1]), to calculate metabolite peak ratios [2] and to probe the dynamics of exchange between metabolites. In biological systems, NMR and MRS yield a wealth of information relating to enzyme function and dysregulated metabolism in disease, as well as offering prognostic biomarkers of response to therapeutics [3, 4]. Historically NMR has been hampered by low signal strength due to low thermal spin polarization and much lower metabolite concentrations compared to endogenous H_2O in the body. NMR spectroscopy and MRSI techniques are therefore subject to constraints in both their detection sensitivity, as well as their spatial and temporal resolution, especially for nuclei other than ^{1}H. Nonetheless, biological applications of NMR in cells or in vivo were already being developed during the 1970s, concurrent with the developments that lead to MRI. The first observations exploited simple surface coils for localization, largely restricted to ^{1}H acquisition due to sensitivity. However, seminal papers also showed that the acquisition of ^{31}P NMR spectra was possible in skeletal muscle and in the heart, yielding key insights into cellular physiology and function [5–7]. Importantly, it was recognized that chemical shift information could be encoded spatially, and over the years a number of sequences have been proposed to localize the NMR signal within a defined voxel, including PRESS, STEAM, ISIS, and 2D/3D spectral localization using chemical shift imaging (CSI) [8]. Despite the intrinsic chemical and biochemical information afforded by these techniques, their clinical adoption has been significantly hampered by a lack of sensitivity, leading to long scan times and poor spatial resolution. Hyperpolarization can be viewed as a disruptive technology that addresses the fundamental sensitivity limitations of both NMR and in vivo MRI.

Advances in Magnetic Resonance Technology and Applications. Volume 1. ISSN 2666-9099. https://doi.org/10.1016/B978-0-12-817057-1.00039-1

37.2 Principles of hyperpolarization—Basic concepts and sensitivity

NMR spectroscopy and magnetic resonance imaging (MRI) exploit an intrinsic property of certain nuclei known as spin. When placed in an external magnetic field B_0, nuclei with spin $I = ½$ become quantized in either the $|\alpha\rangle$ or $|\beta\rangle$ spin-state. The expectation value of the z-component of the angular momentum operator I_z is quantized along the direction of the external field. The eigenvalues of this operator correspond to an alignment either parallel (lower energy) or antiparallel (higher energy) to the magnetic field, and the ensemble average over the sample yields a net magnetic moment proportional to the population difference between the two spin-states, depicted in Fig. 37.1A and B. Since the $|\alpha\rangle$ and $|\beta\rangle$ spin-states contribute $+½\hbar\gamma$ and $-½\hbar\gamma$ to the magnetization, respectively, the net sum over the sample gives rise to a bulk z-magnetization M_z given by

$$M_z = \frac{1}{2}\hbar\gamma\left(n_\alpha - n_\beta\right) \tag{37.1}$$

where n_α and n_β are the populations of the $|\alpha\rangle$ and $|\beta\rangle$ spin-states, respectively, γ is the gyromagnetic ratio of a given nucleus, and $\hbar$ is the reduced Planck's constant $h/2\pi$.

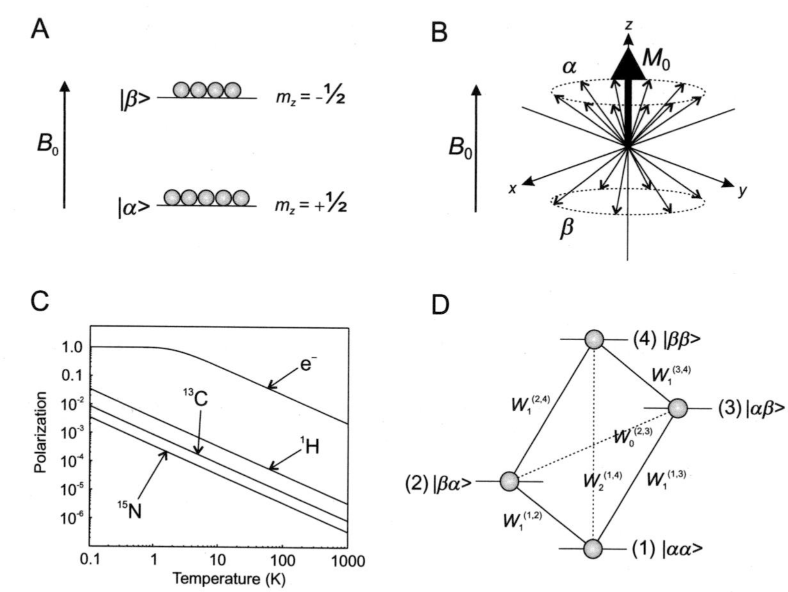

FIG. 37.1

(A) Schematic energy level diagram for an isolated spin ½ system where α and β represent the configuration of spin-up and spin-down states, parallel or antiparallel to B_0, with relative populations given by the Boltzmann distribution. (B) The ensemble average of the spin-states yields a net magnetization vector in the direction of the external magnetic field B_0. (C) Temperature dependence of the thermal polarization, given by Eq. (37.3), which increases as temperature is lowered, and for unpaired electrons reaches unity at temperatures approaching ~1 K. (D) Schematic energy level diagram for a coupled two-spin system consisting of spins I and S, where rate constants for the different transitions are denoted $W^{(i,j)}$ between levels i and j.

The population of spin-states is given by the Boltzmann distribution

$$n_\alpha = \frac{1}{2}\mathrm{N}\exp(-E_\alpha/k_BT)$$
$$n_\beta = \frac{1}{2}\mathrm{N}\exp(-E_\beta/k_BT) \tag{37.2}$$

where k_B is the Boltzmann constant, T is the temperature, $E_{\alpha\beta} = \pm\frac{1}{2}\hbar\gamma B_0$ are the energies of the two levels E_α and E_β, and the factor one half arises due to the partition function across the two available energy levels. For a spin system consisting of N spin ½ nuclei, the polarization P can be defined as the difference in populations normalized to the total number of spins

$$P = \frac{(n_\alpha - n_\beta)}{(n_\alpha + n_\beta)} = \tanh\left(\frac{\hbar\gamma B_0}{2k_BT}\right) \tag{37.3}$$

Combining Eqs. (37.1)–(37.3), the bulk z-magnetization of a sample is given by

$$M_z = \frac{1}{2}\hbar\gamma NP = \frac{1}{2}\hbar\gamma N\tanh\left(\frac{\hbar\gamma B_0}{2k_BT}\right) \tag{37.4}$$

which in the high temperature limit can be approximated by

$$M_z^0 = \frac{\hbar^2\gamma^2 NB_0}{4k_BT} \tag{37.5}$$

The net thermal equilibrium magnetization M_z^0 is therefore proportional to the number of spins N (or concentration per unit volume in the active region of the coil), the square of the gyromagnetic ratio, the strength of the applied magnetic field, and inversely proportional to temperature. The current induced in the receiver coil is proportional to the bulk magnetization and to the detection frequency, and therefore it follows that the equilibrium signal is proportional to $\gamma^3 B_0^2$, while the degree of noise induced in the receiver coil (which also depends on the receiver bandwidth) is proportional to the square root of the detection frequency $(\gamma B_0)^{1/2}$, yielding an overall sensitivity proportional to $\gamma^{5/2}B_0^{3/2}$ (although other relationships exist for example in resistive or conducting samples).

At room temperature, the thermal nuclear polarization (defined in Eq. (37.3)) within magnetic fields employed for NMR or MRI is very small, on the order 10^{-6}, and only reaches appreciable levels when the temperature is decreased, as shown in Fig. 37.1C. MR is therefore an insensitive method when compared to techniques such as electron paramagnetic resonance (EPR) or optical spectroscopies, which have an intrinsically greater Boltzmann factor. Both NMR and MRI are restricted by this lack of sensitivity, since this places limits on the concentration of a given substrate that can be detected, which in turn limits the spatial and/or temporal resolution that can be achieved. The drive to achieve greater sensitivity has been one of the primary motives for pushing technological advances in MR over the years. Increasing magnetic field strength, with advances in cryogenic and superconducting technologies (e.g., from 3 T to 7 T for clinical MRI systems or up to 23.5 T for high-field NMR), leads to an increase in the Boltzmann polarization, and therefore sensitivity, as well as an increase in detection frequency and spectral resolution. Alternatively, reducing detection noise in the RF circuit is achievable through low noise preamplifiers and receivers, and cryogenically cooled coils are now routinely used in high-field NMR, as well as some preclinical MRI systems. Sensitivity enhancement can also be achieved by exploiting intrinsic properties of nuclear spin systems, such as dipolar or scalar couplings.

Low gyromagnetic ratio nuclei can be enhanced by transferring polarization from nuclei with high gyromagnetic ratios, for example, using RF pulse sequences such as INEPT [9] or cross-polarization [10] in solids or liquids [11, 12]. Alternatively polarization can be transferred through the nuclear Overhauser effect (NOE) [13].

Despite significant technological advances, MRI and NMR remain insensitive techniques at thermal equilibrium compared to the theoretical maximum that could be achieved for a fully polarized spin-system ($P=1$). For example, the polarization of ^{1}H at room temperature in a 23.5 T NMR magnet is $P=8\times10^{-5}$, a factor of 12,400 times below that which could theoretically be achieved. The goal of hyperpolarization is to increase this polarization far above the thermal value and therefore enhance the magnetization to a highly nonequilibrium state, leading to a transient increase in the sensitivity by many orders of magnitude.

To understand possible mechanisms of polarization enhancement one can consider the case of a dipolar coupled pair of nuclear spins which may be homonuclear, for example, ^{1}H-^{1}H, heteronuclear, for example, ^{1}H-^{15}N, ^{1}H-^{13}C, a nuclear spin and an unpaired electron spin (for example a free radical), or nuclear spins coupled to unpaired conduction band electrons in a metallic lattice, as originally proposed by Overhauser [13]. The energy level diagram for a coupled two-spin system consisting of spins I and S is shown schematically in Fig. 37.1D. Relaxation is described in terms of rate constants for the different transitions [14], denoted $W^{(i,j)}$ between levels i and j, with allowed transitions $W_1^{(1,2)}$ and $W_1^{(3,4)}$ for spin I, $W_1^{(1,3)}$ and $W_1^{(2,4)}$ for spin S, as well as zero and double quantum transitions, $W_0^{(2,3)}$ and $W_2^{(1,4)}$, which are formally forbidden in the sense that they cannot be directly observed but are relaxation-allowed. Differential equations can be derived for the rate of change of spin populations given by the Solomon equations [15, 16]. For example, the rate of change of the population of level 1 is given by

$$\frac{dn_1}{dt}=-W_1^{(1,2)}n_1-W_1^{(1,3)}n_1-W_2^{(1,4)}n_1+W_1^{(1,2)}n_2+W_1^{(1,3)}n_3+W_2^{(1,4)}n_4\ldots\text{etc.} \tag{37.6}$$

Recognizing that the longitudinal magnetizations I_z and S_z are given by the difference in populations $I_z=n_1-n_3+n_2-n_4$ and $S_z=n_1-n_2+n_3-n_4$, Eq. (37.6) can be recast in a more familiar form [16].

$$\begin{aligned}\frac{d\left(I_z-I_z^0\right)}{dt}&=-R_I\left(I_z-I_z^0\right)-\sigma_{IS}\left(S_z-S_z^0\right)-\Delta_I 2I_zS_z\\ \frac{d\left(S_z-S_z^0\right)}{dt}&=-R_S\left(S_z-S_z^0\right)-\sigma_{IS}\left(I_z-I_z^0\right)-\Delta_S 2I_zS_z\\ \frac{d(2I_zS_z)}{dt}&=-\Delta_I\left(I_z-I_z^0\right)-\Delta_S\left(S_z-S_z^0\right)-R_{IS}2I_zS_z\end{aligned} \tag{37.7}$$

where R_I and R_S are the longitudinal self-relaxation rates ($R_1=1/T_1$) of spins I and S given by $R_I=W_1^{(1,3)}+W_1^{(2,4)}+W_0^{(2,3)}+W_2^{(1,4)}$ and $R_S=W_1^{(1,2)}+W_1^{(3,4)}+W_0^{(2,3)}+W_2^{(1,4)}$, σ_{IS} is the cross-relaxation rate $\sigma_{IS}=W_2^{(1,4)}-W_0^{(2,3)}$ between single-spin orders I_z and S_z, Δ_I and Δ_S are cross-correlation rates between single-spin order I_z or S_z and two-spin order $2I_zS_z$, and R_{IS} is the self-relaxation rate of the two-spin order $2I_zS_z$ given by $R_{IS}=W_1^{(1,2)}+W_1^{(3,4)}+W_1^{(1,3)}+W_1^{(2,4)}$.

These equations have a number of consequences. For a dipolar coupled system, the longitudinal relaxation will only be monoexponential in the absence of cross-relaxation and cross-correlation effects. A second important consequence is the nuclear Overhauser effect (NOE), where cross-relaxation can cause a transient perturbation of one of the spins due to cross-talk with the other.

For example, under conditions where one of the spins S is saturated (populations equalized), there will be a transient steady-state enhancement of the I spin given by

$$\eta_{SS} = \frac{\sigma_{IS} S_z^0}{R_I I_z^0} \tag{37.8}$$

Signal enhancements can be achieved by exploiting the NOE, particularly when the irradiated nucleus has a greater gyromagnetic ratio.

37.3 Hyperpolarization technologies

Over the years a number of different strategies have been proposed for achieving hyperpolarization. Dynamic nuclear polarization (DNP) is a microwave driven process that involves a transfer of polarization from an unpaired electron (in the form of a stable free radical) to MR-active nuclei (such as ^{13}C) in the solid-state mediated via the dipolar coupling [17]. The energy level diagram for a dipolar coupled two-spin system can be adapted to represent a two-spin electron-^{13}C system, shown schematically in Fig. 37.2A [17]. At low temperatures and high magnetic field strength, the unpaired radical electron centers are polarized to near unity owing to their much larger gyromagnetic ratio (see Fig. 37.1C and Eq. (37.3)). In the presence of microwave irradiation at frequencies $\omega_0 = \omega_e - \omega_C$ (zero-quantum transition, Fig. 37.2B), or $\omega_0 = \omega_e + \omega_C$ (double quantum transition, not shown), the electron-nuclear dipolar interaction permits flip-flop or flip-flip transitions of electron and nuclear spins [17]. Continuous wave irradiation equalizes the populations of the connected $|\alpha\beta>$ and $|\beta\alpha>$ spin-states or $|\alpha\alpha>$ and $|\beta\beta>$ spin-states, respectively. At low temperature, electron relaxation occurs faster than nuclear spin relaxation, leading to an overpopulation of the lower or upper ^{13}C nuclear spin-states (Fig. 37.2C) giving rise to positive or negative polarization, respectively. Several mechanisms contribute to the polarization transfer process including the solid effect and NOE described above, as well as cross effect and thermal mixing [18] depending on factors such as field strength, temperature, electron mobility, nature of the radical, and concentration [19–21].

DNP techniques were originally proposed for enhancing solid state NMR experiments, and early successes demonstrated polarization enhancements of up to a factor 100 for arginine and the protein T4 lysozyme in frozen 4-amino-TEMPO glycerol-water solutions [22]. Alternatively, methods employing Overhauser-enhanced MRI were being explored for in vivo applications with the development of classes of stable triarylmethyl free radicals (trityl) [23]. It was subsequently demonstrated that ^{13}C and ^{15}N hyperpolarization generated by DNP using trityl radicals in the solid-state at low temperature was conserved if the sample was rapidly melted and dissolved using an aqueous buffer, leading to enhancements in excess of 10,000-fold that of the corresponding thermal signal [24, 25]. These key discoveries opened the door to many new applications for dissolution DNP, notably in biological systems.

Other methods that can be employed for hyperpolarization include brute force methods, where reducing the temperature below 1 K (to near absolute zero) within a strong magnetic field [26–30] leads to an increase in polarization (see Eq. (37.4), Fig. 37.1C). These methods have a number of limitations, including very slow polarization build-up rates limited by extremely long T_1 spin-lattice relaxation times, which can be days or months long owing to the near absence of molecular motion at very

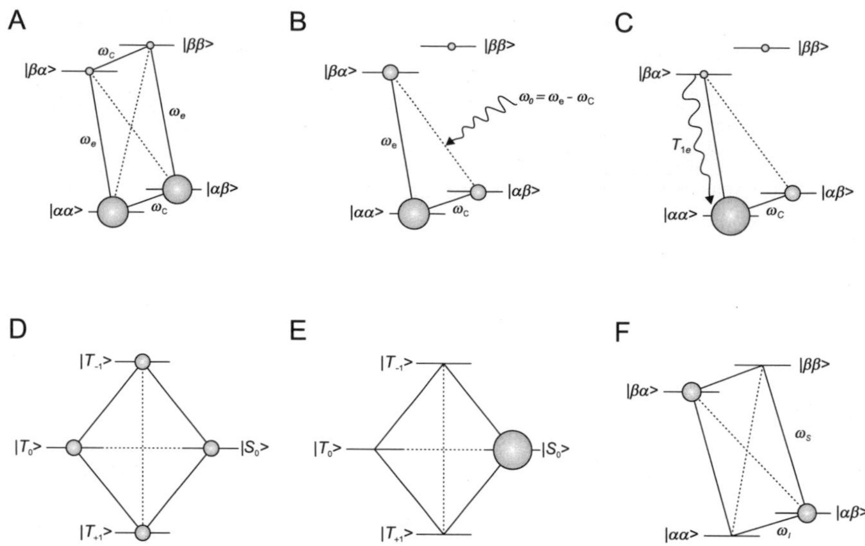

FIG. 37.2

(A) Energy level diagram representing a coupled two-spin electron-^{13}C system showing a large polarization (population difference) across the electron transitions and a much smaller population difference across the ^{13}C transitions. (B) Microwave irradiation at frequency $\omega_0 = \omega_e - \omega_C$ equalizes the populations of the connected $|\alpha\beta>$ and $|\beta\alpha>$ spin-states. (C) At low temperatures, electron relaxation occurs faster than nuclear spin relaxation, leading to an overpopulation of the lower ^{13}C nuclear spin-state. (D) Energy level diagram representing the H_2 molecule. The populations are almost equally populated at room temperature; however, conversion between the singlet and triplet spin-states are symmetry forbidden and therefore very slow. (E) In the presence of a paramagnetic catalyst such as Fe_2O_3 at low temperatures, the parahydrogen spin-state becomes overpopulated. (F) If the bond symmetry of the H_2 molecule is broken by chemical reaction, for example via hydrogenation reactions, then the spin polarization becomes visible.

low temperatures. Polarization efficiency can be improved by transferring polarization between a more rapidly relaxing ^1H spin reservoir and more slowly relaxing ^{13}C or ^{31}P nuclei [31], or by introduction of paramagnetic lanthanide ions such as holmium and dysprosium in the form of their DTPA complexes to act as relaxation agents [32].

Hyperpolarized nuclei can also be generated with parahydrogen induced polarization (PHIP) through catalyst-mediated chemical reactions with para-H_2 gas [33, 34]. The hydrogen molecule H_2 exists as two different spin isomers; 75% orthohydrogen, a triplet state ($S=1$) with symmetric wave functions $|T_{+1}>=|\alpha\alpha>$, $|T_0>=|\alpha\beta+\beta\alpha>/\sqrt{2}$ and $|T_{-1}>=|\beta\beta>$, and 25% parahydrogen, a singlet state ($S=0$) with an antisymmetric wave function $|S_0>=|\alpha\beta\text{-}\beta\alpha>/\sqrt{2}$. The energy level diagram is shown schematically in Fig. 37.2D, where the two protons are equivalent. The populations are almost equally populated at thermal equilibrium, but conversion between the singlet and triplet spin-states is symmetry forbidden and therefore very slow. Owing to the requirement that the overall wavefunction ($\varphi_{total}=\varphi_{el}+\varphi_{vib}+\varphi_{rot}+\varphi_{ns}$) of the H_2 molecule is antisymmetric with respect to interchange of the nuclei, there is a coupling between the nuclear and rotational states such that parahydrogen exists only in J_{even} rotational quantum states while ortho hydrogen exists only in J_{odd} rotational quantum states, with the two isomers exhibiting different thermodynamic properties. As a consequence, at low temperatures in the presence of a paramagnetic catalyst such as Fe_2O_3, the parahydrogen spin-state becomes overpopulated (50% p-H_2 at liquid nitrogen temperature of 77 K or up to 100% when cryo-cooled to <20 K, as shown in Fig. 37.2E). Parahydrogen is a pure spin-state that has zero total spin angular momentum and is therefore MR invisible. However, if the bond symmetry of the H_2 molecule is broken by chemical reaction (Fig. 37.2F) then the spin polarization becomes visible, for example via hydrogenation reactions, with an antiphase enhancement of the resulting NMR signals [33]. Generating hyperpolarized hydrogen via PHIP is relatively inexpensive, portable, and easy to maintain, as the hyperpolarization can take place in low field magnets (~mT). PHIP also has the advantage that polarization can be re-generated by introducing a constant flow of parahydrogen to achieve a steady-state rather than being limited by T_1 relaxation [35].

Hyperpolarization of nobel gases can be achieved with laser optical pumping techniques, including alkali-metal spin exchange optical pumping (SEOP) and metastability exchange [36]. Spin-exchange techniques employ circularly polarized light resonant with the D1 electronic transition of rubidium (Rb) vapor contained in an optical cell located in a low magnetic field to generate a large electron-spin polarization. Collisional spin-exchange leads to transfer of polarization from Rb to gas atoms such as ^{3}He, ^{129}Xe, and ^{83}Kr [37–39].

The net result of such signal enhancement techniques is that magnetic polarization can be increased, enabling the acquisition of spectroscopic images with much higher signal intensity.

37.4 System set-up for hyperpolarized ^{13}C

A key driver for the development of hyperpolarization techniques has been their translation into the clinic [40, 41]. Specialized imaging sequences as well as hardware are required for hyperpolarized experiments. For DNP, preclinical work has been facilitated by the development of the experimental Hyersense system (Oxford Instruments, United Kingdom). A dedicated clinical hyperpolarizer, the SPINlab (GE Healthcare, United States), has also been developed, enabling multisample polarization, liquid helium recycling, automated dissolution, and quality assurance [42]. The concurrent development of experimental polarizers is also ongoing, with important developments in cryogen-free magnets which significantly reduce helium usage, as well as reducing the cost of such experiments [43, 44]. Significant efforts have been made to carry out this process under sterile GMP conditions [42].

As a first step in the DNP hyperpolarization process, a metabolite of interest is isotopically enriched with ^{13}C, either synthetically or commercially available, and prepared at a high concentration using a glassing solvent such as glycerol/water or DMSO/water. Some compounds like [1-^{13}C] pyruvic acid are self-glassing without addition of a co-solvent. The solution is doped with a low concentration of a free radical such as tris{8-carboxyl-2,2,6,6-benzo(1,2-*d*,4,5-*d*)-bis(1,3)dithiole-4-yl} methyl sodium salt (trityl OX063, 15 mM), 4-oxo-2,2,6,6-tetramethyl-1-piperidinyloxy (4-oxo-TEMPO 30–50 mM), 1,3-bisdiphenylene-2-phenylallyl (BDPA), or bi-radicals such as TOTAPOL. Alternatively, it has been shown that endogenous stable free radicals can be generated by UV irradiation of frozen pyruvic acid with subsequent quenching of the photo-excited triplet state on dissolution, thus removing the need to add an exogenous radical [45]. At this point, the sample contains a source of unpaired electrons, and is inserted into the cryostat of the superconducting magnet of a polarizer, located within a microwave cavity. The field strength originally proposed for this purpose was 3.35 T, although higher polarization levels can be achieved at higher field strengths [46]. The system is then cooled to nearly 1 K by reducing the pressure, at which point the unpaired electron becomes almost fully polarized, and the sample is irradiated close to the EPR frequency ($\omega_0 = \omega_e \pm \omega_C$) [47]. In addition to the direct microwave-driven electron-^{13}C polarization transfer, magnetization propagates between ^{13}C-^{13}C by spin-diffusion, such that the bulk ^{13}C lattice reaches a common spin temperature with a characteristic solid-state build-up time T_{SS}. Hyperpolarization of substrates such as [1-^{13}C] pyruvic acid typically take less than an hour to reach a steady-state polarization level of about 20% or greater. Addition of an optional 1–2 mM Gd-DOTA, or other lanthanide chelates such as holmium, enhances the polarization by decreasing the free radical electron T_1 [48–50].

Once in a hyperpolarized state, the substrate is dissolved in an aqueous physiological buffer such as phosphate-buffered saline or Tris buffer, heated under high pressure (10 bar) and injected into the cryostat of the polarizer. Dissolution yields a hyperpolarized solution with a temperature of about 40°C, and pH adjusted to pH$\sim$7 for biological use. Preclinical in vivo experiments typically employ pyruvate concentrations of 40–80 mM, which can be reduced for in vitro and ex vivo cell or perfused organ experiments, while higher concentrations and greater volumes are required for clinical studies.

The main practical limitation imposed by hyperpolarized ^{13}C MR is that once in solution state, the spin-states relax back to their nonpolarized thermal equilibrium populations with characteristic spin-lattice relaxation times T_1. Transfer of the sample between the polarizer and the scanner, therefore, needs to occur as quickly as possible to minimize relaxation losses. In addition, during this transit, hyperpolarized samples can also be subject to significant magnetic field gradients when moving between fields. To minimize loss of polarization, the hyperpolarized magnetization vector in Fig. 37.1B should follow the direction of the field adiabatically to become aligned in the same direction as the field of the scanner. Polarization losses can be minimized by keeping the sample in a magnetic field using a portable electromagnet or magnetic glove to avoid zero-field crossing points.

Substrates used for dissolution DNP must have long T_1 relaxation times to give a sufficient time-window for transport of the sample and subsequent imaging or spectroscopy. This characteristic is generally associated with low gyromagnetic ratio spin ½ nuclei such as ^{13}C, ^{15}N, ^{29}Si, ^{89}Y among others, within small molecules that are shielded from their dipolar environment, that is, lacking directly bound ^{1}H, or substituting ^{1}H with ^{2}H. For example, ^{13}C carbonyl-containing substrates have relatively long T_1 relaxation times (in the range 20–60 s) arising from remote dipole-dipole interactions (no directly bound proton), and thus are good candidates for DNP.

37.5 Imaging hyperpolarized substrates

The true power of hyperpolarization technologies is their utility in quantifiying the spatial distribution of low concentrations of injected metabolites. This spectroscopic information can be used to localize and quantify the rates of metabolic interconversion in vivo. In order to assess metabolic processes, one must be able to distinguish the hyperpolarized MR signal of the parent metabolite from its metabolic product and to measure the signal intensity of both (corresponding to the spectral peak integrals) as a function of time. These peaks and their temporal behavior can then be fit to kinetic models to derive rate constants for the chemical reaction.

First, for any heteronuclear MRI applications (not just limited to hyperpolarization experiments) there are additional hardware requirements. The first requirement is a broad-band transmitter amplifier for the X-nucleus excitation and X-nucleus coils, which are standard in most high-resolution NMR probes but not typically provided as standard hardware in MRI scanners. The lower X-nucleus gyromagnetic ratios also impose greater requirements for gradient amplifiers. For example, the gyromagnetic ratio of ^{13}C is four times lower than that of ^{1}H, and thus a quadrupled gradient strength is required when imaging ^{13}C species to cover a given field-of-view or slice thickness.

For X-nucleus MRI, a number of possible coil configurations have been explored, including simple transmit-receive surface coils which are challenged by spatially dependent B_1 fields and receiver sensitivity, birdcage transmit/receive volume coils which yield more uniform B_1 and receiver profiles over a given field-of-view but at the expense of reduced sensitivity, combinations of the two with birdcage transmit volume coils (yielding uniform B_1) and surface receive coils (yielding high sensitivity), or combination birdcage volume coils with multireceiver arrays for parallel imaging. A challenge encountered in nonproton MRI is that the transmitter gain and frequency are not known a priori, as they are dependant on coil loading and B_1 and B_0 inhomogeneity. Transmitter and frequency adjustments are readily performed for ^{1}H MR by calibrating the sinusoidal response to an RF pulse with varying flip angles. This procedure can also be performed for X-nuclei by incorporating a high concentration reference phantom within the imaging field-of-view. For hyperpolarized gas imaging, transmitter adjustment can be performed by administering a small inhalation of gas, and measuring the depletion of the polarization using a series of spoiled small flip angle pulses to calculate B_1. Alternative methods have been explored based on the Bloch-Siegert shift, where the phase shift arising due to an off-resonance pulse can be used to calculate B_1 [51].

Prior to performing hyperpolarized imaging, conventional ^{1}H images are acquired to provide anatomical reference images, perform localized shimming over a region of interest, plan the geometry of the subsequently acquired hyperpolarized images, and enable co-registration of the resulting images. Following intravenous injection or inhalation, dynamic imaging studies are typically performed by applying multiple small flip angle excitation pulses to allow efficient sampling of the temporal evolution of the magnetization while minimizing losses due to the application of RF pulses [52]. Since the magnetization relaxes to its thermal equilibrium state, the hyperpolarized magnetization is lost after the application of a pulse and not normally re-generated. Application of a series of RF pulses causes additional loss of the signal, with an effective relaxation rate constant $r_1 = T_1^{-1} - \mathrm{TR}^{-1}\ln(\cos\theta)$, where TR is the repetition time between pulses [53].

A number of strategies for hyperpolarized imaging have been investigated, and these are typically optimized by exploring the trade-off between SNR, temporal resolution, spatial resolution, and RF flip angle to yield 2D or 3D spatial localization with a large field-of-view. Given the sparsity of the metabolite spectra, which may contain only three or four metabolites of interest when working with ^{13}C or ^{129}Xe (or only a single resonance in the case of ^{3}He), an approach for imaging hyperpolarized substrates is to borrow imaging techniques adapted from normal ^{1}H MRI but incorporating small flip angle excitation. This approach has been motivated by challenging applications such as pulmonary imaging of hyperpolarized gases and cardiac ^{13}C imaging, where both the cardiac cycle and respiratory motion must be considered. In the case of hyperpolarized gas imaging, radial spoiled gradient echo sequences have shown utility. Balanced steady-state free precession methods (bSSFP) have also been explored. These approaches have many advantages, including the ability to selectively excite a single metabolite and thus make efficient use of the magnetization, greater SNR and/or increased temporal resolution, and the potential for full 3D isotropic resolution [54]. These methods were employed for the first demonstration of real-time in vivo imaging of hyperpolarized ^{13}C substrates, including their temporal dynamics, by performing angiography [52] (as shown in Fig. 37.3A).

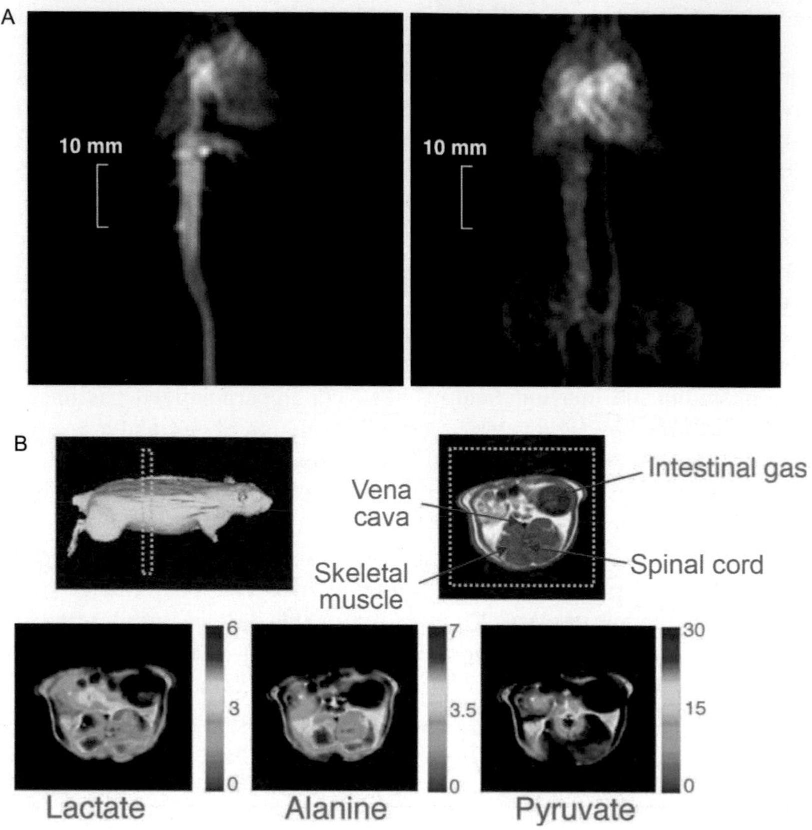

FIG. 37.3

(A) ^{13}C angiography performed in the rat following tail vein injection of 2 mL of 100 mM hyperpolarized [^{13}C] urea solution (injection rate, 0.5 mL/s). Imaging was performed on a 2.35 T Bruker Biospec with a 72 mm diameter dual tuned birdcage coil using fully balanced steady-state precession imaging sequence, a field of view of 7 × 7 cm^2, a 64 × 64 matrix (interpolated to 128 × 128), and scan time of 240 ms. Images correspond to a coronal projection, that is, without slice selection. (B) In vivo transverse ^{13}C CSI images acquired 30 s after the start of injection of 3 mL of ~80 mM hyperpolarized [1-^{13}C] pyruvate acquired with a matrix size of 16 × 16, a field of view of 80 × 80 × 10 mm, a 10° flip angle, and total scan time of 13.9 s. Images were reconstructed by zero filling to a 32 × 32 matrix size. Metabolite maps were calculated from the peak amplitudes of the respective metabolites normalized to the maximum signal in each image and scaled relative to the pyruvate signal.

(A) Golman K, et al. Molecular imaging with endogenous substances. Proc Natl Acad Sci U S A 2003;100(18):10435–10439. Copyright (2003) National Academy of Sciences. (B) Golman K, in't Zandt R, Thaning M, Real-time metabolic imaging. Proc Natl Acad Sci U S A 2006;103 (30):11270–11275. Copyright (2006) National Academy of Sciences.

The other major challenge for hyperpolarized ^{13}C spectroscopy has been to quantify the rates of metabolic interconversion of a parent substrate to its downstream metabolic products in vivo, so-called metabolic imaging. This measurement relies on the ability to distinguish different metabolites based on their chemical shift difference, for example, pyruvate and lactate. In the simplest case, some spatial localization of the hyperpolarized signal can be achieved using a surface coil and a pulse-acquire sequence comprised of small flip angle pulses or slice-selective spectroscopy. These techniques yield high sensitivity and high temporal resolution but only limited spatial localization. Alternatively, the first demonstrations that the metabolic conversion of an injected substrate, in this case, pyruvate to lactate and alanine, could be monitored using spectroscopic imaging techniques [55, 56] (see Fig. 37.3B) employed standard slice-selective 2D chemical shift imaging (CSI) with small flip angle pulses. This type of experiment yields spatially resolved spectroscopic data with relatively low spatial resolution. From these data, a map of each metabolite can be constructed by measuring the areas under the metabolite peak, which is assumed to be a surrogate measure of the concentration of the metabolite; these maps can be co-registered with a reference proton image acquired with the same field-of-view to provide anatomical context. However, since a single FID is acquired per spatial k-space point, CSI techniques using Cartesian sampling are not the most efficient way to sample k-space data and have relatively low temporal resolution. Alternative imaging strategies have been explored for accelerating both hyperpolarized gas and ^{13}C imaging; for example, echo-planar spectroscopic imaging (EPSI) can be used to collect all lines in k-space in a single readout, allowing rapid and full 3D spatial coverage. Alternatively, single slice time-resolved 2D EPSI allows rapid sampling of the temporal kinetics. Non-Cartesian schemes such as spiral CSI are able to encode k-space within a single spiral readout trajectory, but may suffer from artifacts such as spectral aliasing. Additional acceleration can be achieved using data undersampling and parallel imaging or compressed sensing reconstruction strategies that can be used to achieve greater spatial resolution with fewer RF pulses [57–59].

Alternatively single and multiband spectral-spatial pulses can be used to selectively excite different metabolites with different flip angles followed by a single-shot EPI or spiral readout, conserving the magnetization of the injected metabolite (low flip angle excitation), while maximizing signal from generated metabolites (high flip angle excitation) [60–63]. To collect images of each metabolite, the imaging acquisitions can be interleaved. This scheme has shown particular utility for accelerating hyperpolarized cardiac imaging [64]. Variable flip angle schemes can also be employed to compensate for the decay of the polarization as a function of time. More recent work has exploited the Dixon/IDEAL methods, similar to those used for water-fat separation in conventional ^{1}H MRI. Based on a single shot spiral encoding, images can be acquired at a number of different echo times (TE) to provide chemical shift encoding of the different metabolite signals. Given prior knowledge of the peak positions, images of the different metabolites can be recovered [65]. A recent example depicting pyruvate metabolism imaging in the normal human brain using this approach is shown in Fig. 37.4. The regional metabolite distributions of pyruvate, lactate, and bicarbonate can be imaged. Provided an injected metabolite and its downstream metabolic product can be imaged separately with sufficient temporal resolution, then their time courses can be fit to pharmacokinetic models and parameterized to derive maps of the conversion rate constant. In this case, both the location of the metabolites and the temporal dynamics of the conversion of pyruvate to lactate can be measured, yielding a map of the rate constant k_{PL} for the conversion of pyruvate to lactate, an important step toward understanding normal brain metabolism [66].

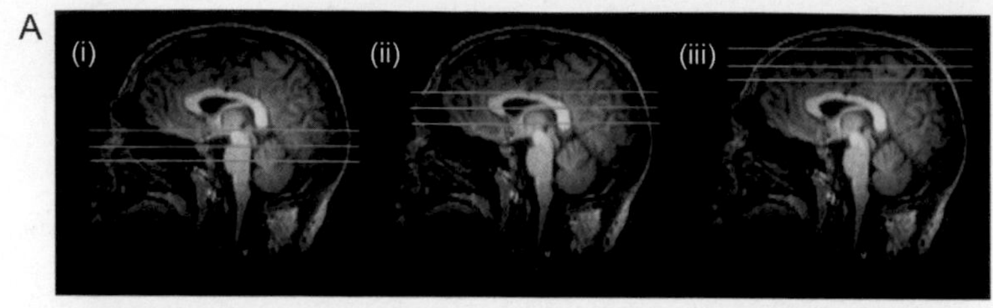

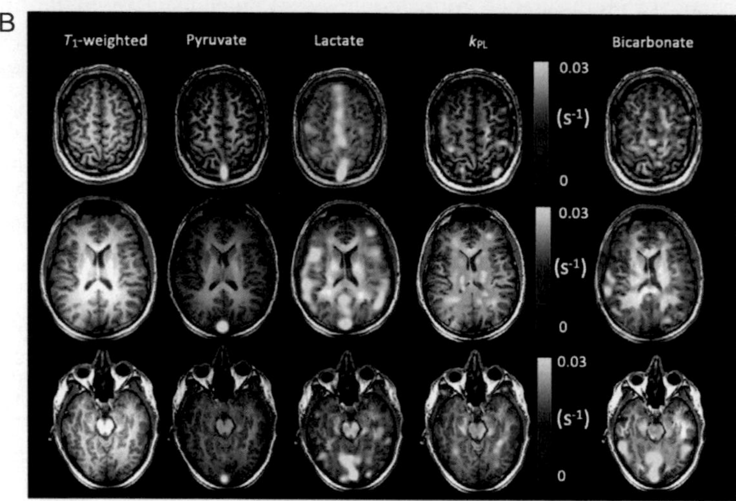

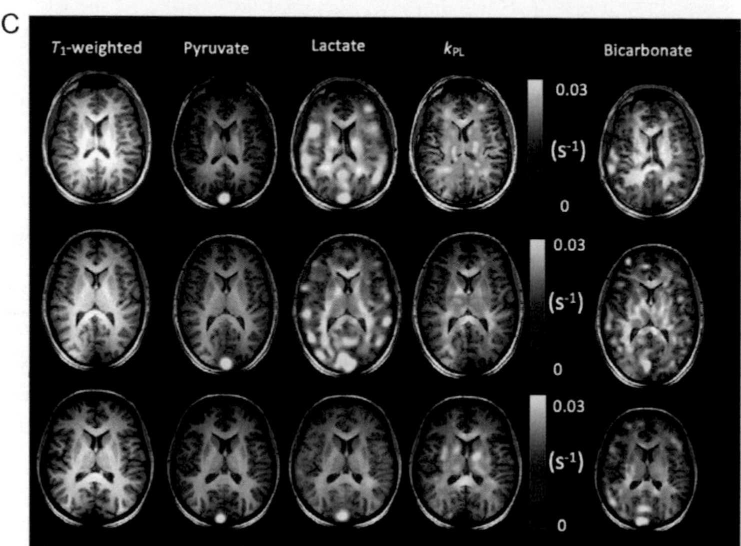

FIG. 37.4

IDEAL spiral ^{13}C CSI in the normal human brain acquired on a 3T MR system (MR750, GE Healthcare, Waukesha WI), using a dual-tuned ^{1}H/^{13}C quadrature head coil (Rapid Biomedical, Rimpar Germany) with a pulse bandwidth of 2500 Hz, TR = 0.5 s, time resolution = 4 s, flip angle = 15° degrees, FOV = 240 mm, spatial resolution = 12 × 12 mm^2, reconstructed resolution = 5 × 5 mm^2, slice thickness = 30 mm, acquired voxel volume = 4.32 cm^3, total imaging time = 60 s. (A) Position of three separate 3 cm imaging slices, inferior (i), central (ii) and superior (iii). (B) ^{13}C maps from a single volunteer co-registered with standard T_1-weighted images showing metabolite distribution and calculated rate constant k_{PL} from the three slices shown in (A). (C) Images, concentration maps, and rate constant maps from the central slice in three different volunteers [66] https://doi.org/10.1016/j.neuroimage.2019.01.027.

37.6 Quantifying temporal kinetics

In biological systems, hyperpolarized ^{13}C substrates are introduced into the extracellular interstitial space by blood delivery and perfusion, where they are quickly transported into the cell through membrane transporters, and subject to fast enzyme-mediated reactions. Different metabolites, or the same metabolite located in different environments, can be distinguished by virtue of differences in chemical shifts, for example, between the parent substrate and its metabolic products.

By way of example, Fig. 37.5A shows a typical time series of hyperpolarized ^{13}C spectra for hyperpolarized [1-^{13}C] pyruvate added to a suspension of cancer cells [53, 67–69]. In this experiment, hyperpolarized pyruvate was generated ex situ in a commercial Hypersense polarizer and 100 µL of a 50 mM solution of pyruvate was added to a 500 µL suspension of 94×10^6 cells contained within a 5 mm NMR tube. The sample was instantaneously mixed and inserted into an 11.7 T Bruker 500 MHz NMR magnet. Dynamic data were acquired as a time series, corresponding to a series of 1D spectra with a small flip angle (5°) pulse. Each FID was acquired with a single acquisition, 16,000 data points, and a spectral width of 150 ppm (18,796 Hz). With an acquisition time of 0.436 s and a prescan delay of 0.564 s, a temporal resolution of 1 s per scan was achieved. By collecting a total of 256 time points, the total experiment duration was 4.2 min. The experiment commenced during the dissolution, i.e., before the sample is inserted into the spectrometer, and hence the first few spectra are blank. In this case, the primary metabolic fate of hyperpolarized [1-^{13}C] pyruvate is reduction to form [1-^{13}C] lactate and reaction with water to form the [1-^{13}C] pyruvate hydrate. The peak integrals of the pyruvate and lactate signals are measured as a function of time to give two vectors $P(t)$ and $L(t)$ (data points in Fig. 37.5B).

To quantify the temporal kinetics and derive rate constants, compartmental models representing the biological system are employed. Fitting the hyperpolarized temporal data to mathematical models [70, 71] gives estimates of "apparent" rate constants for the reactions. Assuming first order kinetics, the observable magnetization for the conversion of a hyperpolarized substrate to downstream metabolites can be modeled as a multicompartment system described by the modified Bloch-McConnell equations. This set of coupled equations includes both the rates of chemical reaction, and the effective relaxation of the hyperpolarized signal due to longitudinal relaxation and the influence of RF pulses [72].

$$\frac{d\mathbf{M}(t)}{dt} = (\mathbf{K} - \mathbf{R})\mathbf{M}(t) \tag{37.9}$$

where $\mathbf{M}(t)$ is a time-dependent vector of the longitudinal magnetizations $M_z(t)$ of each metabolite, proportional to their peak area, $\mathbf{K}$ is a $\mathrm{N} \times \mathrm{N}$ matrix with elements k_{ij} that are the characteristic rate constants of the reaction, and $\mathbf{R}$ is a diagonal relaxation matrix containing the relaxation rate constants of the hyperpolarized signal decay $r_1 = T_1^{-1} - \mathrm{TR}^{-1}\ln(\cos\theta)$. The dimension of the system N is dependent on the number of metabolites which are included in the system, but also by biological compartmentation (such as intracellular and extracellular substrate pools) and transport between compartments.

The general solution to the system of differential equations in Eq. (37.9) is given by a discrete set of exponentials

$$\begin{gathered}\mathbf{M}(t) = \exp(\mathbf{L}t)\mathbf{M}(0) \\ \mathbf{M}(t) = \mathbf{U}^{-1}\exp(\mathbf{D}t)\mathbf{U}\mathbf{M}(0)\end{gathered} \tag{37.10}$$

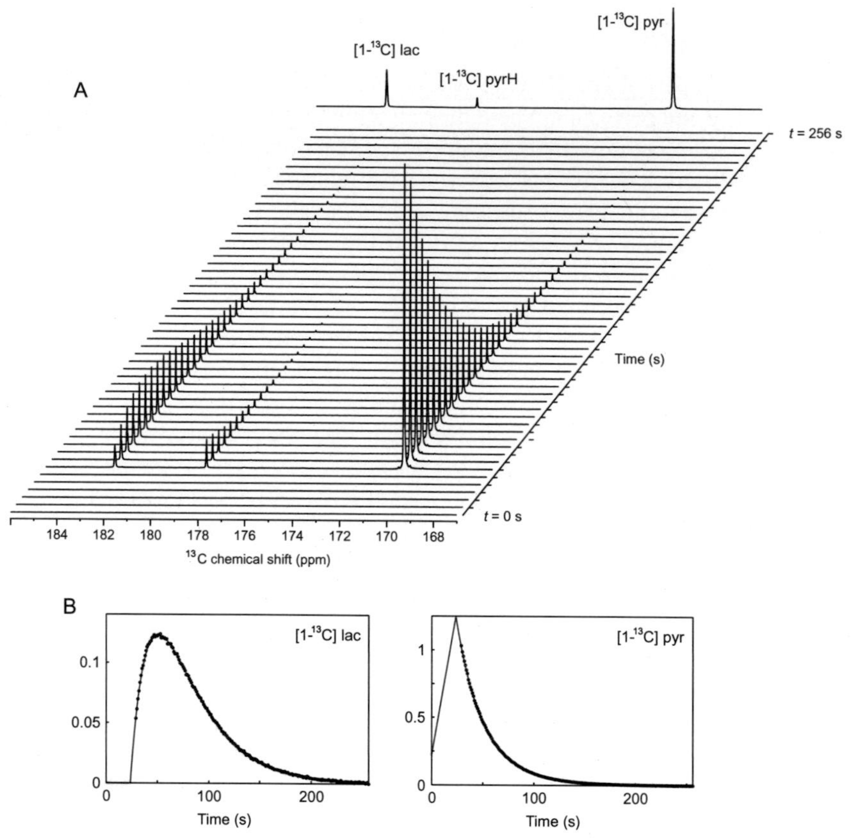

FIG. 37.5

(A) A typical time series of spectra when 8 mM hyperpolarized [1-^{13}C] pyruvate is added to a suspension of 100×10^6 cancer cells. For clarity every fifth spectrum is displayed. All 256 spectra can be summed along the time dimension to yield a single sum spectrum, shown above at the end of the time series. (B) Time course of the peak integrals of the lactate signal *L(t)* *(left)* and the pyruvate signal *P(t)* *(right)* and a nonlinear least squares fit to Eq. (37.12).

Each element of the vector $\mathbf{M}(t)$ describes the evolution in time of the longitudinal magnetization of one component, where $\mathbf{L} = \mathbf{K} - \mathbf{R}$ is a matrix comprising both exchange and relaxation processes, $\mathbf{U}$ is a unitary matrix defined by $\mathbf{D} = \mathbf{ULU}^{-1}$ and $\mathbf{D}$ is a diagonal matrix with rates λ_i corresponding to the eigenvalues of the matrix $(\mathbf{K}-\mathbf{R})$ in Eq. (37.9). The eigenvalues λ_i are linear combinations of the rates of exchange between compartments, either transport or enzyme mediated, and the effective relaxation rates.

The simplest model of differential equations that describes first-order one-way reaction kinetics of an exchange reaction of hyperpolarized substrate $A^* \leftrightarrow B^*$ can be written as:

$$\frac{d}{dt}\begin{bmatrix} A^*(t) \\ B^*(t) \end{bmatrix} = \begin{bmatrix} -k_{AB} - r_{1A} & k_{BA} \\ k_{AB} & -k_{BA} - r_{1B} \end{bmatrix} \begin{bmatrix} A^*(t) \\ B^*(t) \end{bmatrix} \tag{37.11}$$

where * denotes hyperpolarized substrate pools, k_{AB} and k_{BA} are first-order exchange rate constants, and r_{1A} and r_{1B} represent effective longitudinal relaxation rate constants of A^* and B^* given by $r_{1A,B} = T_{1A,B}^{-1} - \mathrm{TR}^{-1}\ln(\cos\theta)$ [53].

Assuming an instantaneous delivery of hyperpolarized substrate A^* at time $t=0$ and the boundary conditions $A^*(0)=A_0^*$ and $B^*(0)=0$, then the solution to this type of compartmental model is given by

$$\begin{aligned} A^*(t) &= \frac{A_0^*[(k_{AB}+r_{1A}-\lambda_2)\exp(-\lambda_1 t)+((k_{BA}+r_{1B}-\lambda_2))\exp(-\lambda_2 t)]}{\lambda_1 - \lambda_2} \\ B^*(t) &= \frac{A_0^* k_{AB}[\exp(-\lambda_2 t)-\exp(-\lambda_1 t)]}{\lambda_1 - \lambda_2} \\ \lambda_{1,2} &= -\frac{1}{2}\left[(k_{AB}+k_{BA}+r_{1A}+r_{1B}) \pm \sqrt{((r_{1A}+k_{AB})-(r_{1B}+k_{BA}))^2+4k_{AB}k_{BA}}\right] \end{aligned} \quad (37.12)$$

The problem of finding the exchange rates and relaxation rates can be formulated as an optimization problem. For example, pyruvate and lactate temporal data can be fit simultaneously using nonlinear least squares fitting to the differential equations in Eq. (37.11) using an ODE solver, or by fitting to the solution given in Eq. (37.12) [73–75]. Fig. 37.5B (solid lines) shows a simultaneous fit of the lactate and pyruvate peak integrals $L(t)$ and $P(t)$, respectively, to Eq. (37.12). The first few points of the data are missing due to mixing of the sample outside the spectrometer and an additional variable $t+\delta t$ was introduced to account for the variable start time in the data. Normalization of the data is a key consideration, as the initial concentration of substrate must be known to derive an accurate reaction rate, while the rate constant is independent of concentration. Rate constants are critically dependent on the total amount of enzyme present, which will depend on the number of metabolically active cells in the active region of the coil.

As alternatives to compartmental modeling, a number of semiquantitative methods have also been proposed, such as area under the curve (AUC) [53] or time-to-peak [76]. These methods have the advantage of reducing the temporal dynamics to metrics that are model independent. An example of this approach is shown at the end of the time course in Fig. 37.5A, displaying a single spectrum corresponding to the sum of all 256 spectra, annotated with the relevant metabolites. The peak integrals of the lactate and pyruvate signals in this sum spectrum corresponds to the areas under the curves of $L(t)$ and $P(t)$ in Fig. 37.5B. For an exchanging system such as pyruvate and lactate, the ratio of the area under the lactate curve to the area under the pyruvate curve derived from Eq. (37.11) can be shown to be proportional to the rate constants for the exchange reaction:

$$\frac{\sum L(t)}{\sum P(t)} = \frac{\mathrm{AUC}(L)}{\mathrm{AUC}(P)} = \frac{k_{PL}}{k_{LP}+r_{1L}} \quad (37.13)$$

Under the conditions that $k_{LP} << r_{IL}$, or for one-way reaction kinetics (i.e., $k_{LP}=0$), the ratio of lactate AUC to pyruvate AUC is proportional to k_{PL}. Under conditions that $k_{LP} >> r_{IL}$, the ratio of lactate AUC to pyruvate AUC is proportional to the equilibrium constant k_{PL}/k_{LP}. An estimate of the AUC ratio is readily calculated from experimental data by measuring the ratio of the lactate and pyruvate peak integrals in the sum spectrum. A good correlation has been shown between the semiquantitative AUC ratio and k_{PL} derived from the fully quantitative two-site model across a range of cancer cell lines both in vitro as well as in vivo [53]. Important features of this AUC metric are that it is independent of the pyruvate input function and the pyruvate relaxation rate, as well as being independent of rate constants associated with conversion of pyruvate to other metabolites.

37.7 Conservation of mass

A challenge to the interpretation of data from ^{13}C hyperpolarization experiments is that it is only possible to measure the time dependence of the hyperpolarized ^{13}C pools of metabolites; ^{12}C metabolites and cofactors are MR-invisible [67] but are still able to participate in the reaction kinetics. The Bloch-McConnell equations describe the evolution of the observable magnetization, which decays to thermal equilibrium (in this case zero in Eqs. (37.11), (37.12) since the thermal signal is usually below the detection limit) rather than describing molecular concentrations. Therefore, these equations do not agree with the principles of conservation of mass [77], a problem recently discussed in the literature [77–79]. This is potentially important since enzyme kinetics are described by Michaelis-Menten kinetics $V = V_{max}[A]/(K_m + [A])$ (or modified versions thereof) and hence V_{max} and K_m of an enzyme are described in terms of substrate concentration [A]. However, the Bloch-McConnell equations describe the evolution of hyperpolarized magnetization A^*. This discrepancy can be addressed phenomenologically by extending the above differential equations such that the hyperpolarized pool of substrates A^* and B^* relax to an unpolarized "MR invisible" pool of substrates A and B, as depicted in Fig. 37.5A [77, 78].

$$\frac{d}{dt}\begin{bmatrix} A^*(t) \\ B^*(t) \\ A(t) \\ B(t) \end{bmatrix} = \begin{bmatrix} -k_{AB} - r_{1A} & k_{BA} & 0 & 0 \\ k_{AB} & -k_{BA} - r_{1B} & 0 & 0 \\ r_{1A} & 0 & -k_{AB} & k_{BA} \\ 0 & r_{1B} & k_{AB} & -k_{BA} \end{bmatrix} \begin{bmatrix} A^*(t) \\ B^*(t) \\ A(t) \\ B(t) \end{bmatrix} \tag{37.14}$$

When formulated in this way, Eq. (37.14) agrees with the principle of conservation of mass, since the rate of change $d[A^*(t) + A(t) + B^*(t) + B(t)]/dt$ is equal to zero and $A^*(t) + A(t)$ and $B^*(t) + B(t)$ are proportional to $[A]$ and $[B]$, respectively. Eq. (37.14) can be rewritten as

$$\frac{d}{dt}\begin{bmatrix} A^*(t) + A(t) \\ B^*(t) + B(t) \end{bmatrix} = \begin{bmatrix} -k_{AB} & k_{BA} \\ k_{AB} & -k_{BA} \end{bmatrix} \begin{bmatrix} A^*(t) + A(t) \\ B^*(t) + B(t) \end{bmatrix} \tag{37.15}$$

thereby recapitulating the conventional form of chemical reaction kinetics, as shown in Fig. 37.6B and C. An advantage of formulating the system in this way is that it can be extended for reaction kinetics involving enzyme cofactors which are nonhyperpolarized [78].

37.8 Applications of hyperpolarized ^{13}C MRI

The ability to probe flux or exchange kinetics between different enzymes in real-time in living cells or in vivo is a unique feature of hyperpolarized MR. Substrates that are amenable to hyperpolarization by DNP are those that achieve a 10^4–10^5 increase in polarization, can be prepared in biologically

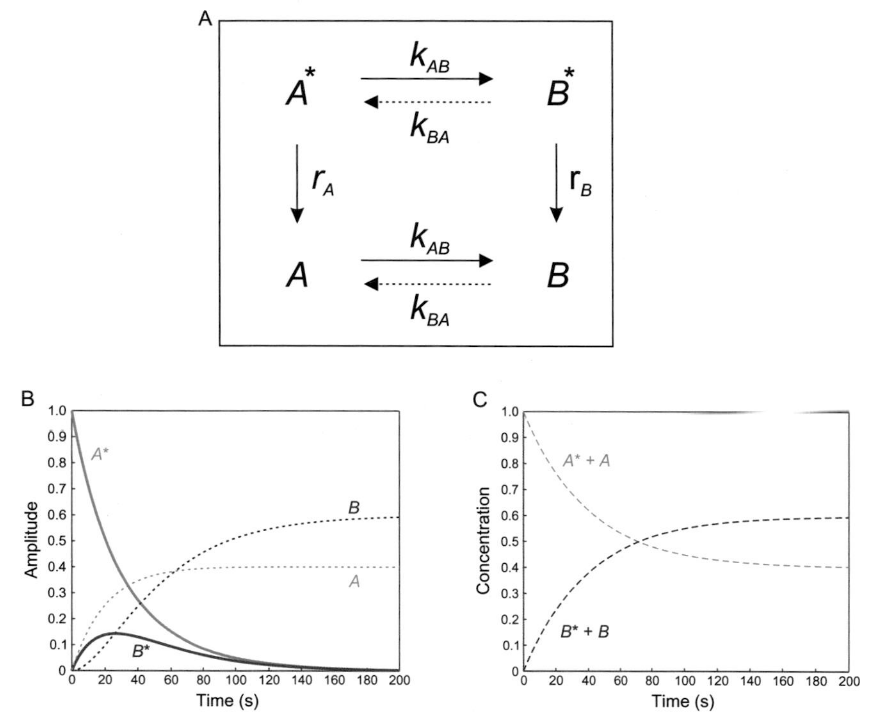

FIG. 37.6

(A) Compartmental model agreeing with the principle of conservation of mass for the reaction of a hyperpolarized substrate A^* subject to an enzyme mediated exchange reaction to give a hyperpolarized product B^*. The two substrates interconvert with rate constants k_{AB} and k_{BA} for the forwards and reverse reactions, respectively. In this phenomenological model, the hyperpolarized signals relax to unpolarized pools of the same substrate with rate constants given by r_A and r_B. (B) Simulated plots for the temporal evolution of the hyperpolarized signals A^* and B^* and their unpolarized counterparts A and B where only A^* is present at time $t=0$; that is, $A^*(0)=1$, $A(0)=0$, $B^*(0)=0$, $B(0)=0$. Simulated parameters were $k_{AB}=0.015\,s^{-1}$, $k_{BA}=0.01\,s^{-1}$, $r_A=1/50\,s^{-1}$, $r_B=1/30\,s^{-1}$. (C) The model recapitulates standard chemical kinetics where the total pools of A^*+A and B^*+B reach their equilibrium values at the end of the reaction given by the equilibrium constant for the reaction $K=k_{AB}/k_{BA}=[B]/[A^*]$. Only the hyperpolarized pools A^* and B^* are visible by MR.

compatible solutions, exhibit T_1 values that are sufficiently long to probe metabolic processes, and are involved in or directly influenced by central metabolism. These include [1-^{13}C] pyruvate [80–82], [2-^{13}C] pyruvate [83], [1-^{13}C] lactate [84], [1-^{13}C] alanine [85], [1-^{13}C] glycine [85], [1,4-^{13}C] fumarate [86], [1-^{13}C] glutamate [87], [1-^{13}C] glutamine [88, 89], [U-^{13}C,U-^{2}H] glucose [90], [2-^{13}C] fructose [91], [1-^{13}C] dehydroascorbate [92, 93], [1-^{13}C] acetate [94], [1-^{13}C] butyrate [95], ^{13}C bicarbonate [96], [1-^{13}C] ketoisocaproate [97], [1-^{13}C] aspartate [85], [1-^{13}C] ethyl pyruvate [98], ^{13}C urea [99–101], ethyl acetoacetate [102], among others. The possibility of ^{13}C labeling of multiple carbon positions on a molecule has been explored to simultaneously investigate multiple metabolic pathways, for example [1,2-^{13}C] pyruvate [103].

Pyruvate is the most widely studied substrate, due to its favorable polarization and relaxation characteristics of both the C1 and C2 carbonyl groups. It has been used in a number of applications including the assessment of cancer [104], cardiac metabolism [105], liver metabolism [106], renal metabolism [107] as well as in the brain, where penetration across the blood-brain barrier can be enhanced via esterification in the form of [1-^{13}C] ethyl pyruvate [108]. Pyruvate is a simple α-keto acid situated at a key metabolic crossroads at the end of glycolysis and at the entry point to the TCA cycle, and plays a key role in central carbon metabolism. Depending on cell type, different enzymatic fates of [1-^{13}C] pyruvate include [1-^{13}C] lactate by the enzyme lactate dehydrogenase (LDH), [1-^{13}C] alanine by the enzyme alanine transaminase (ALT), decarboxylation by the pyruvate dehydrogenase complex (PDH) to form [^{13}C] CO_2 (which is in rapid pH-dependent equilibrium with [^{13}C] bicarbonate), or carboxylation via pyruvate carboxylase (PC), with entry into the TCA cycle via anaplerosis and conversion to [1-^{13}C] and [4-^{13}C] aspartate.

In cancer cells or in vivo in tumors, the primary metabolic fate of hyperpolarized [1-^{13}C] pyruvate is the reduction to form lactate. Apparent rates of the exchange reaction are influenced by factors such as LDH activity and expression levels [109, 110], the level of LDH cofactors (NAD/NADH) and their relative redox balance [90], the activity and expression of the monocarboxylate (MCT) family of transporters [111, 112] (which mediate cellular pyruvate (MCT1) influx and lactate efflux (MCT4) [113, 114]), and substrate supply due to flow or perfusion. Alterations in exchange rates or metabolic flux, as measured by a change in apparent rate constant, may be a potential biomarker for disease progression or response to therapy [73]. For example, anticancer therapies have almost universally been shown to lead to a reduction in the ^{13}C pyruvate-lactate exchange rates (although there are a few published exceptions) and indicate a drop in metabolic activity and/or modulation of transport into the cell. This result has been previously correlated with cell death by apoptosis [73] and used as an early marker of treatment response to targeted cancer therapeutics [55, 68, 69, 80, 109, 115–117].

The metabolic fate of hyperpolarized [1-^{13}C] pyruvate has also been extensively investigated in the heart [105] and is of particular relevance since most cardiomyopathies, including hypertrophy, ischemic heart disease, diabetic cardiomyopathy, and the progression to heart failure, all exhibit switches in substrate preference. The decarboxylation of hyperpolarized [1-^{13}C] pyruvate and subsequent CO_2 and bicarbonate formation (mediated by carbonic anhydrase) allows the rate of PDH flux to be measured either ex vivo in the perfused heart [81, 118] or in vivo under pathophysiological conditions such as diabetic cardiomyopathy and hypertrophy [82, 119, 120]. Labeling of pyruvate at the keto [2-^{13}C] carbonyl position allows measurement of the flux of pyruvate into the TCA cycle leading to formation of TCA cycle intermediates, such as ^{13}C citrate and ^{13}C glutamate, which have been shown to decrease in response to myocardial ischemia [121]. Fatty acid metabolism can be investigated through the buffering of hyperpolarized [1-^{13}C] acetate with [1-^{13}C] acetylcarnitine in response to reperfusion after ischemia [122], or through the addition of water-soluble fatty acids such as octanoate [81].

In 2011 a phase I clinical trial of hyperpolarized [1-^{13}C] pyruvate was carried out as a dose escalation study in 31 men with biopsy-proven prostate cancer [123]. In humans, intravenous injection reaches the right atrium and lungs in ~4 s, the left atrium in ~10 s, and the other major organs in 15–40 s [124]. The time from dissolution of hyperpolarized [1-^{13}C] pyruvate to injection was ~67 s, including quality assurance (QA) steps to filter the free radical and check solution temperature and pH. Three [1-^{13}C] pyruvate dose levels (0.14, 0.28, and 0.43 mL/kg body weight of 230 mM solution) were explored and a number of different image acquisition schemes were used to compare the spatial distribution of the downstream metabolite lactate in tumor to that found in normal prostate. The study showed no dose-limiting toxicity. Slice selective ^{13}C spectra acquired in a patient with biopsy proven prostate cancer showed low lactate in a region of benign tissue and significant conversion to lactate in a region containing tumor. MRSI data obtained from 15 patients was used to assess regional variability of metabolism, co-registered with T_2-weighted and diffusion-weighted imaging. Regions with high rates of conversion to lactate, as indicated by voxels with a [1-^{13}C] lactate/[1-^{13}C] pyruvate ratio >0.6, were indicative of pathology, with normal prostate tissue displaying low rates of conversion.

37.9 Application of hyperpolarized gases

Hyperpolarized gases have found important clinical applications in pulmonary imaging. The human lung is a challenging area for conventional ^1H MRI because normal lung parenchyma has low ^1H density, suffers from high magnetic susceptibility due to tissue-air interfaces, and is subject to artifacts caused by respiratory and cardiovascular motion [125]. The first hyperpolarized ^3He and ^{129}Xe images were reported in the ex vivo rat lung [126], in vivo in guinea pig lungs [127], and shortly after in the human lung in vivo [128, 129]. Hyperpolarized ^3He gas imaging has found a range of medical imaging applications particularly in lung physiology for visualizing normal lung ventilation and ventilation defects arising from conditions such as asthma, cystic fibrosis, chronic obstructive pulmonary disease, and lung cancer. Multiple important physiological parameters can be assessed using ^3He gas imaging, including real-time visualization of perfusion, mapping of the apparent diffusion coefficient, and imaging lung pO_2, as the T_1 of ^3He is linearly dependent on O_2 concentration [130]. In contrast, ^{129}Xe is relatively lipophilic, and thus it is able to cross the cell membrane, enabling characterization of gas transport and exchange, while its solubility in red blood cells facilitates imaging of distal organs such as the brain [131, 132].

37.10 Summary

Hyperpolarized magnetic resonance spectroscopy and imaging has shown significant development in both the basic sciences and in their biological and clinical application. Development of techniques to improve image quality as well as the ability to derive and quantify kinetic parameters are ongoing. The techniques have the potential to give important insights into dysregulated metabolism in health and disease, as well as in the assessment of therapeutics. Many further clinical studies are underway including the use of hyperpolarization approaches to quantify physiological parameters of interest in cardiovascular disease, hypertension, hypertrophy, brain cancers, breast cancer, prostate cancer, traumatic brain injury, and fatty liver disease, among others.

Acknowledgments

I would like to acknowledge the importance of interdisciplinary Team Science. Special thanks to Martin Leach, Philip Kuchel and Geoffrey Bodenhausen for their kindness, guidance, and inspiration over the years. This work is supported by the NIHR Biomedical Research Centre at Guy's and St Thomas' NHS Foundation Trust and KCL; the Centre of Excellence in Medical Engineering funded by the Wellcome Trust and Engineering and Physical Sciences Research Council (EPSRC) (WT 088641/Z/09/Z); KCL Comprehensive Cancer Imaging Centre funded by the Cancer Research UK (CRUK) and EPSRC in association with the Medical Research Council (MRC) and the Department of health (DoH). The views expressed are those of the author and not necessarily those of the NHS, the NIHR or DoH.

References

[1] Keevil SF, et al. Absolute metabolite quantification by in vivo NMR spectroscopy: II. A multicentre trial of protocols for in vivo localised proton studies of human brain. Magn Reson Imaging 1998;16(9):1093–106.

[2] Neubauer S, et al. Myocardial phosphocreatine-to-ATP ratio is a predictor of mortality in patients with dilated cardiomyopathy. Circulation 1997;96(7):2190–6.

[3] Beloueche-Babari M, et al. Metabolic assessment of the action of targeted cancer therapeutics using magnetic resonance spectroscopy. Br J Cancer 2010;102(1):1–7.

[4] Beloueche-Babari M, Workman P, Leach MO. Exploiting tumor metabolism for non-invasive imaging of the therapeutic activity of molecularly targeted anticancer agents. Cell Cycle 2011;10(17):2883–93.

[5] Hoult DI, et al. Observation of tissue metabolites using P-31 nuclear magnetic-resonance. Nature 1974;252(5481):285–7.

[6] Gadian DG, et al. Phosphorus nuclear magnetic-resonance studies on normoxic and ischemic cardiac tissue. Proc Natl Acad Sci U S A 1976;73(12):4446–8.

[7] Garlick PB, Radda GK, Seeley PJ. Phosphorus Nmr-studies on perfused heart. Biochem Biophys Res Commun 1977;74(3):1256–62.

[8] Keevil SF. Spatial localization in nuclear magnetic resonance spectroscopy. Phys Med Biol 2006;51(16): R579–636.

[9] Morris GA, Freeman R. Enhancement of nuclear magnetic-resonance signals by polarization transfer. J Am Chem Soc 1979;101(3):760–2.

[10] Hartmann SR, Hahn EL. Nuclear double resonance in rotating frame. Phys Rev 1962;128(5):2042.

[11] Muller L, Ernst RR. Coherence transfer in the rotating frame—application to heteronuclear cross-correlation spectroscopy. Mol Phys 1979;38(3):963–92.

[12] Chiarparin E, Pelupessy P, Bodenhausen G. Selective cross-polarization in solution state NMR. Mol Phys 1998;95(5):759–67.

[13] Overhauser AW. Polarization of nuclei in metals. Phys Rev 1953;92(2):411–5.

[14] Bloembergen N, Purcell EM, Pound RV. Nuclear magnetic relaxation. Nature 1947;160(4066):475.

[15] Solomon I. Relaxation processes in a system of 2 spins. Phys Rev 1955;99(2):559–65.

[16] Keeler J. Understanding NMR spectroscopy. 2nd ed. John Wiley & Sons, Ltd; 2010.

[17] Abragam A, Goldman M. Principles of dynamic nuclear-polarization. Rep Prog Phys 1978;41(3):395–467.

[18] Borghini M, Deboer W, Morimoto K. Nuclear dynamic polarization by resolved solid-state effect and thermal mixing with an electron spin-spin interaction reservoir. Phys Lett A 1974;A 48(4):244–6.

[19] Maly T, et al. Dynamic nuclear polarization at high magnetic fields. J Chem Phys 2008;128(5), 052211.

[20] Banerjee D, et al. The interplay between the solid effect and the cross effect mechanisms in solid state (1)(3)C DNP at 95 GHz using trityl radicals. J Magn Reson 2013;230:212–9.

[21] Lumata L, et al. DNP by thermal mixing under optimized conditions yields >60,000-fold enhancement of 89Y NMR signal. J Am Chem Soc 2011;133(22):8673–80.

[22] Hall DA, et al. Polarization-enhanced NMR spectroscopy of biomolecules in frozen solution. Science 1997;276(5314):930–2.

[23] Ardenkjaer-Larsen JH, et al. EPR and DNP properties of certain novel single electron contrast agents intended for oximetric imaging. J Magn Reson 1998;133(1):1–12.

[24] Ardenkjaer-Larsen JH, et al. Increase in signal-to-noise ratio of > 10,000 times in liquid-state NMR. Proc Natl Acad Sci U S A 2003;100(18):10158–63.

[25] Wolber J, et al. Generating highly polarized nuclear spins in solution using dynamic nuclear polarization. Nucl Instrum Methods Phys Res, Sect A 2004;526(1–2):173–81.

[26] Johnson RT, et al. Bulk nuclear polarization of solid H-3. J Low Temp Phys 1973;10(1–2):35–58.

[27] Terhaar E, Frossati G, Clark WG. Brute force nuclear-polarization of D(2). J Low Temp Phys 1994;94(3–4):361–71.

[28] Krjukov EV, O'Neill JD, Owers-Bradley JR. Brute force polarization of Xe-129. J Low Temp Phys 2005;140(5–6):397–408.
[29] Honig A, et al. High equilibrium spin polarizations in solid Xe-129. Physica B 2000;284:2049–50.
[30] Biskup N, Kalechofsky N, Candela D. Spin polarization of xenon films at low-temperature induced by He-3. Phys B Condens Matter 2003;329:437–8.
[31] Gadian DG, et al. Preparation of highly polarized nuclear spin systems using brute-force and low-field thermal mixing. Phys Chem Chem Phys 2012;14(16):5397–402.
[32] Peat DT, et al. Achievement of high nuclear spin polarization using lanthanides as low-temperature NMR relaxation agents. Phys Chem Chem Phys 2013;15(20):7586–91.
[33] Duckett SB, Sleigh CJ. Applications of the parahydrogen phenomenon: a chemical perspective. Prog Nucl Magn Reson Spectrosc 1999;34(1):71–92.
[34] Green RA, et al. The theory and practice of hyperpolarization in magnetic resonance using parahydrogen. Prog Nucl Magn Reson Spectrosc 2012;67:1–48.
[35] Hovener JB, et al. A hyperpolarized equilibrium for magnetic resonance. Nat Commun 2013;4:2946.
[36] Walker TG, Happer W. Spin-exchange optical pumping of noble-gas nuclei. Rev Mod Phys 1997;69(2): 629–642.
[37] Kauczor HU, et al. Normal and abnormal pulmonary ventilation: visualization at hyperpolarized He-3 MR imaging. Radiology 1996;201(2):564–8.
[38] Appelt S, et al. Theory of spin-exchange optical pumping of He-3 and Xe-129. Phys Rev A 1998;58(2): 1412–1439.
[39] Pavlovskaya GE, et al. Hyperpolarized krypton-83 as a contrast agent for magnetic resonance imaging. Proc Natl Acad Sci U S A 2005;102(51):18275–9.
[40] Kurhanewicz J, et al. Analysis of cancer metabolism by imaging hyperpolarized nuclei: prospects for translation to clinical research. Neoplasia 2011;13(2):81–97.
[41] Kurhanewicz J, et al. Hyperpolarized (13)C MRI: path to clinical translation in oncology. Neoplasia 2019;21(1):1–16.
[42] Ardenkjaer-Larsen JH, et al. Dynamic nuclear polarization polarizer for sterile use intent. NMR Biomed 2011;24(8):927–32.
[43] Baudin M, et al. A cryogen-consumption-free system for dynamic nuclear polarization at 9.4 T. J Magn Reson 2018;294:115–21.
[44] Ardenkjaer-Larsen JH, et al. Cryogen-free dissolution dynamic nuclear polarization polarizer operating at 3.35 T, 6.70 T, and 10.1 T. Magn Reson Med 2019;81(3):2184–94.
[45] Eichhorn TR, et al. Hyperpolarization without persistent radicals for in vivo real-time metabolic imaging. Proc Natl Acad Sci U S A 2013;110(45):18064–9.
[46] Johannesson H, Macholl S, Ardenkjaer-Larsen JH. Dynamic nuclear polarization of [1-13C]pyruvic acid at 4.6 tesla. J Magn Reson 2009;197(2):167–75.
[47] Boer WD, et al. Dynamic polarization of protons, deuterons, and C-13 nuclei—thermal contact between nuclear spins and an electron spin-spin interaction reservoir. J Low Temp Phys 1974;15(3–4):249–67.
[48] Ardenkjaer-Larsen JH, Macholl S, Johannesson H. Dynamic nuclear polarization with trityls at 1.2 K. Appl Magn Reson 2008;34(3–4):509–22.
[49] Gordon JW, Fain SB, Rowland IJ. Effect of lanthanide ions on dynamic nuclear polarization enhancement and liquid-state T1 relaxation. Magn Reson Med 2012;68(6):1949–54.
[50] Lumata L, et al. Impact of Gd3+ on DNP of [1-C-13]pyruvate doped with trityl OX063, BDPA, or 4-oxo-TEMPO. J Phys Chem A 2012;116(21):5129–38.
[51] Schulte RF, et al. Transmit gain calibration for nonproton MR using the Bloch-Siegert shift. NMR Biomed 2011;24(9):1068–72.
[52] Golman K, et al. Molecular imaging with endogenous substances. Proc Natl Acad Sci U S A 2003; 100(18):10435–9.

[53] Hill DK, et al. Model free approach to kinetic analysis of real-time hyperpolarized 13C magnetic resonance spectroscopy data. PLoS ONE 2013;8(9):e71996.
[54] Shang H, et al. Spectrally selective three-dimensional dynamic balanced steady-state free precession for hyperpolarized C-13 metabolic imaging with spectrally selective radiofrequency pulses. Magn Reson Med 2017;78(3):963–75.
[55] Golman K, in't Zandt R, Thaning M. Real-time metabolic imaging. Proc Natl Acad Sci U S A 2006;103(30):11270–5.
[56] Golman K, et al. Metabolic imaging by hyperpolarized C-13 magnetic resonance imaging for in vivo tumor diagnosis. Cancer Res 2006;66(22):10855–60.
[57] Larson PEZ, et al. Fast dynamic 3D MR spectroscopic imaging with compressed sensing and multiband excitation pulses for hyperpolarized C-13 studies. Magn Reson Med 2011;65(3):610–9.
[58] Hu S, et al. 3D compressed sensing for highly accelerated hyperpolarized C-13 MRSI with in vivo applications to transgenic mouse models of cancer. Magn Reson Med 2010;63(2):312–21.
[59] Hu S, et al. Compressed sensing for resolution enhancement of hyperpolarized C-13 flyback 3D-MRSI. J Magn Reson 2008;192(2):258–64.
[60] Cunningham CH, et al. Sequence design for magnetic resonance spectroscopic imaging of prostate cancer at 3T. Magn Reson Med 2005;53(5):1033–9.
[61] Larson PE, et al. Multiband excitation pulses for hyperpolarized 13C dynamic chemical-shift imaging. J Magn Reson 2008;194(1):121–7.
[62] Levin YS, et al. Optimization of fast spiral chemical shift imaging using least squares reconstruction: application for hyperpolarized C-13 metabolic imaging. Magn Reson Med 2007;58(2):245–52.
[63] Schricker AA, et al. Dualband spectral-spatial RF pulses for prostate MR spectroscopic imaging. Magn Reson Med 2001;46(6):1079–87.
[64] Cunningham CH, et al. Hyperpolarized C-13 metabolic MRI of the human heart initial experience. Circ Res 2016;119(11):1177–82.
[65] Wiesinger F, et al. IDEAL spiral CSI for dynamic metabolic MR imaging of hyperpolarized [1-13C]pyruvate. Magn Reson Med 2012;68(1):8–16.
[66] Grist JT, et al. Quantifying normal human brain metabolism using hyperpolarized [1-(13)C]pyruvate and magnetic resonance imaging. NeuroImage 2019;189:171–9.
[67] Hill DK, et al. H-1 NMR and hyperpolarized C-13 NMR assays of pyruvate-lactate: a comparative study. NMR Biomed 2013;26(10):1321–5.
[68] Lin G, et al. Dichloroacetate induces autophagy in colorectal cancer cells and tumours. Br J Cancer 2014;111(2):375–85.
[69] Lin GG, et al. Reduced warburg effect in cancer cells undergoing autophagy: steady-state H-1-MRS and real-time hyperpolarized c-13-MRS studies. PLoS ONE 2014;9(3):e92645.
[70] Atherton HJ, et al. Validation of the in vivo assessment of pyruvate dehydrogenase activity using hyperpolarised 13C MRS. NMR Biomed 2011;24(2):201–8.
[71] Menichetti L, et al. Assessment of real-time myocardial uptake and enzymatic conversion of hyperpolarized [1-C-13] pyruvate in pigs using slice selective magnetic resonance spectroscopy. Contrast Media Mol Imaging 2012;7(1):85–94.
[72] Ernst RR, Bodenhausen G, Wokaun A. Principles of nuclear magnetic resonance in one and two dimensions. Oxford: Clarendon Press; 1987.
[73] Day SE, et al. Detecting tumor response to treatment using hyperpolarized C-13 magnetic resonance imaging and spectroscopy. Nat Med 2007;13(11):1382–7.
[74] Zierhut ML, et al. Kinetic modeling of hyperpolarized 13C1-pyruvate metabolism in normal rats and TRAMP mice. J Magn Reson 2010;202(1):85–92.
[75] Spielman DM, et al. In vivo measurement of ethanol metabolism in the rat liver using magnetic resonance spectroscopy of hyperpolarized [1-C-13]pyruvate. Magn Reson Med 2009;62(2):307–13.

[76] Daniels CJ, et al. A comparison of quantitative methods for clinical imaging with hyperpolarized (13) C-pyruvate. NMR Biomed 2016;29(4):387–99.
[77] Pages G, Tan YL, Kuchel PW. Hyperpolarized [1,C-13] pyruvate in lysed human erythrocytes: effects of co-substrate supply on reaction time courses. NMR Biomed 2014;27(10):1203–10.
[78] Mariotti E, et al. Modeling non-linear kinetics of hyperpolarized [1-C-13] pyruvate in the crystalloid-perfused rat heart. NMR Biomed 2016;29(4):377–86.
[79] Shishmarev D, et al. Sub-minute kinetics of human red cell fumarase: H-1 spin-echo NMR spectroscopy and C-13 rapid-dissolution dynamic nuclear polarization. NMR Biomed 2018;31(3):e3870.
[80] Golman K, et al. Metabolic imaging by hyperpolarized 13C magnetic resonance imaging for in vivo tumor diagnosis. Cancer Res 2006;66(22):10855–60.
[81] Merritt ME, et al. Hyperpolarized C-13 allows a direct measure of flux through a single enzyme-catalyzed step by NMR. Proc Natl Acad Sci U S A 2007;104(50):19773–7.
[82] Schroeder MA, et al. In vivo assessment of pyruvate dehydrogenase flux in the heart using hyperpolarized carbon-13 magnetic resonance. Proc Natl Acad Sci U S A 2008;105(33):12051–6.
[83] Schroeder MA, et al. Real-time assessment of Krebs cycle metabolism using hyperpolarized 13C magnetic resonance spectroscopy. FASEB J 2009;23(8):2529–38.
[84] Chen AP, et al. Feasibility of using hyperpolarized [1-C-13]lactate as a substrate for in vivo metabolic C-13 MRSI studies. Magn Reson Imaging 2008;26(6):721–6.
[85] Jensen PR, et al. Hyperpolarized amino acids for in vivo assays of transaminase activity. Chemistry 2009;15(39):10010–2.
[86] Gallagher FA, et al. Production of hyperpolarized [1,4-13C2]malate from [1,4-13C2]fumarate is a marker of cell necrosis and treatment response in tumors. Proc Natl Acad Sci U S A 2009;106(47):19801–6.
[87] Gallagher FA, et al. Detection of tumor glutamate metabolism in vivo using (13)C magnetic resonance spectroscopy and hyperpolarized [1-(13)C]glutamate. Magn Reson Med 2011;66(1):18–23.
[88] Gallagher FA, et al. C-13 MR spectroscopy measurements of glutaminase activity in human hepatocellular carcinoma cells using hyperpolarized C-13-labeled glutamine. Magn Reson Med 2008;60(2):253–7.
[89] Canape C, et al. Probing treatment response of glutaminolytic prostate cancer cells to natural drugs with hyperpolarized [5-C]glutamine. Magn Reson Med 2015;73:2296–305.
[90] Christensen CE, et al. Non-invasive in-cell determination of free cytosolic [NAD+]/[NADH] ratios using hyperpolarized glucose show large variations in metabolic phenotypes. J Biol Chem 2014;289(4):2344–52.
[91] Keshari KR, et al. Hyperpolarized [2-C-13]-fructose: a hemiketal DNP substrate for in vivo metabolic imaging. J Am Chem Soc 2009;131(48):17591–6.
[92] Bohndiek SE, et al. Hyperpolarized [1-C-13]-ascorbic and dehydroascorbic acid: vitamin C as a probe for imaging redox status in vivo. J Am Chem Soc 2011;133(30):11795–801.
[93] Keshari KR, et al. Hyperpolarized C-13 dehydroascorbate as an endogenous redox sensor for in vivo metabolic imaging. Proc Natl Acad Sci U S A 2011;108(46):18606–11.
[94] Menichetti L, et al. Cardiovascular molecular imaging with hyperpolarized [1-13C] acetate and [1-13C] pyruvate in middle size animal model. Eur J Nucl Med Mol Imaging 2012;39:S272.
[95] Ball DR, et al. Hyperpolarized butyrate: a metabolic probe of short chain fatty acid metabolism in the heart. Magn Reson Med 2014;71(5):1663–9.
[96] Gallagher FA, et al. Magnetic resonance imaging of pH in vivo using hyperpolarized 13C-labelled bicarbonate. Nature 2008;453(7197):940–3.
[97] Karlsson M, et al. Imaging of branched chain amino acid metabolism in tumors with hyperpolarized 13C ketoisocaproate. Int J Cancer 2010;127(3):729–36.
[98] Hurd RE, et al. Metabolic imaging in the anesthetized rat brain using hyperpolarized [1-13C] pyruvate and [1-13C] ethyl pyruvate. Magn Reson Med 2010;63(5):1137–43.
[99] von Morze C, et al. Imaging of blood flow using hyperpolarized [C-13] urea in preclinical cancer models. J Magn Reson Imaging 2011;33(3):692–7.

[100] von Morze C, et al. Investigating tumor perfusion and metabolism using multiple hyperpolarized C-13 compounds: HP001, pyruvate and urea. Magn Reson Imaging 2012;20(3):305–11.

[101] Pages G, et al. Transmembrane exchange of hyperpolarized C-13-urea in human erythrocytes: subminute timescale kinetic analysis. Biophys J 2013;105(9):1956–66.

[102] Jensen PR, et al. Hyperpolarized [1,3-(13) C2]ethyl acetoacetate is a novel diagnostic metabolic marker of liver cancer. Int J Cancer 2015;136(4):E117–26.

[103] Chen AP, et al. Simultaneous investigation of cardiac pyruvate dehydrogenase flux, Krebs cycle metabolism and pH, using hyperpolarized [1,2-(13) C(2)]pyruvate in vivo. NMR Biomed 2012;25(2):305–11.

[104] Brindle KM, et al. Tumor imaging using hyperpolarized 13C magnetic resonance spectroscopy. Magn Reson Med 2011;66(2):505–19.

[105] Schroeder MA, et al. Hyperpolarized magnetic resonance a novel technique for the in vivo assessment of cardiovascular disease. Circulation 2011;124(14):1580–94.

[106] Merritt ME, et al. Flux through hepatic pyruvate carboxylase and phosphoenolpyruvate carboxykinase detected by hyperpolarized C-13 magnetic resonance. Proc Natl Acad Sci U S A 2011;108(47):19084–9.

[107] Clatworthy MR, et al. Magnetic resonance imaging with hyperpolarized [1,4-C-13(2)]fumarate allows detection of early renal acute tubular necrosis. Proc Natl Acad Sci U S A 2012;109(33):13374–9.

[108] Hurd RE, et al. Metabolic imaging in the anesthetized rat brain using hyperpolarized [1-C-13] pyruvate and [1-C-13] ethyl pyruvate. Magn Reson Med 2010;63(5):1137–43.

[109] Albers MJ, et al. Hyperpolarized C-13 lactate, pyruvate, and alanine: noninvasive biomarkers for prostate cancer detection and grading. Cancer Res 2008;68(20):8607–15.

[110] Ward CS, et al. Noninvasive detection of target modulation following phosphatidylinositol 3-kinase inhibition using hyperpolarized (13)C magnetic resonance spectroscopy. Cancer Res 2010;70(4):1296–305.

[111] Witney TH, Kettunen MI, Brindle KM. Kinetic modeling of hyperpolarized C-13 label exchange between pyruvate and lactate in tumor cells. J Biol Chem 2011;286(28):24572–80.

[112] Harris T, et al. Kinetics of hyperpolarized C-13(1)-pyruvate transport and metabolism in living human breast cancer cells. Proc Natl Acad Sci U S A 2009;106(43):18131–6.

[113] Keshari KR, et al. Hyperpolarized C-13-pyruvate magnetic resonance reveals rapid lactate export in metastatic renal cell carcinomas. Cancer Res 2013;73(2):529–38.

[114] Beloueche-Babari M, et al. MCT1 inhibitor AZD3965 increases mitochondrial metabolism, facilitating combination therapy and noninvasive magnetic resonance spectroscopy. Cancer Res 2017;77(21):5913–24.

[115] Golman K, Petersson JS. Metabolic imaging and other applications of hyperpolarized C-13. Acad Radiol 2006;13(8):932–42.

[116] Park I, et al. Hyperpolarized 13C magnetic resonance metabolic imaging: application to brain tumors. Neuro-Oncology 2010;12(2):133–44.

[117] Ward CS, et al. Noninvasive detection of target modulation following phosphatidylinositol 3-kinase inhibition using hyperpolarized 13C magnetic resonance spectroscopy. Cancer Res 2010;70(4):1296–305.

[118] Merritt ME, et al. Inhibition of carbohydrate oxidation during the first minute of reperfusion after brief ischemia: NMR detection of hyperpolarized (CO2)-C-13 and (HCO3-)-C-13. Magn Reson Med 2008;60(5):1029–36.

[119] Atherton HJ, et al. Investigating metabolic flux in the hyperthyroid heart using hyperpolarised magnetic resonance. Circulation 2008;118(18):S996.

[120] Atherton HJ, et al. Hyperpolarized magnetic resonance spectroscopy study in the hyperthyroid rat heart: a combined magnetic resonance imaging and role of pyruvate dehydrogenase inhibition in the development of hypertrophy. Circulation 2011;123:2552–61.

[121] Schroeder MA, et al. Real-time assessment of Krebs cycle metabolism using hyperpolarized C-13 magnetic resonance spectroscopy. FASEB J 2009;23(8):2529–38.

[122] Jensen PR, et al. Tissue-specific short chain fatty acid metabolism and slow metabolic recovery after ischemia from hyperpolarized NMR in vivo. J Biol Chem 2009;284(52):36077–82.

[123] Nelson SJ, et al. Metabolic imaging of patients with prostate cancer using hyperpolarized [1-C-13]pyruvate. Sci Transl Med 2013;5(198):198ra108.

[124] Mansson S, et al. C-13 imaging—a new diagnostic platform. Eur Radiol 2006;16(1):57–67.

[125] van Beek EJR, et al. Functional MRI of the lung using hyperpolarized 3-helium gas. J Magn Reson Imaging 2004;20(4):540–54.

[126] Albert MS, et al. Biological magnetic resonance imaging using laser-polarized 129Xe. Nature 1994;370(6486):199–201.

[127] Black RD, et al. In vivo He-3 MR images of guinea pig lungs. Radiology 1996;199(3):867–70.

[128] Mugler 3rd JP, et al. MR imaging and spectroscopy using hyperpolarized 129Xe gas: preliminary human results. Magn Reson Med 1997;37(6):809–15.

[129] MacFall JR, et al. Human lung air spaces: potential for MR imaging with hyperpolarized He-3. Radiology 1996;200(2):553–8.

[130] Albert MS, Hane FT. Hyperpolarized and inert gas MRI from technology to application in research and medicine. Academic Press; 2017.

[131] Rao M, et al. High resolution spectroscopy and chemical shift imaging of hyperpolarized Xe-129 dissolved in the human brain in vivo at 1.5 Tesla. Magn Reson Med 2016;75(6):2227–34.

[132] Rao MR, et al. Imaging human brain perfusion with inhaled hyperpolarized Xe-129 MR imaging. Radiology 2018;286(2):659–65.

Index

Note: Page numbers followed by "*f*" indicate figures and "*t*" indicate tables.

B

C

D

E

F

G

H

J

K

L

M

N

Q

R

S

T

U

V

Printed in the United States
By Bookmasters